COMPREHENSIVE TEXTBOOK
OF AIDS PSYCHIATRY

COMPREHENSIVE TEXTBOOK OF AIDS PSYCHIATRY

A PARADIGM FOR INTEGRATED CARE

SECOND EDITION

EDITED BY

Mary Ann Cohen, MD,

Jack M. Gorman, MD,

Jeffrey M. Jacobson, MD,

Paul Volberding, MD,

and

Scott L. Letendre, MD

OXFORD
UNIVERSITY PRESS

OXFORD
UNIVERSITY PRESS

Oxford University Press is a department of the University of Oxford. It furthers the University's objective of excellence in research, scholarship, and education by publishing worldwide. Oxford is a registered trade mark of Oxford University Press in the UK and certain other countries.

Published in the United States of America by Oxford University Press
198 Madison Avenue, New York, NY 10016, United States of America.

© Oxford University Press 2017
First edition published in 2008
Second edition published in 2017

CIP data is on file at the Library of Congress
ISBN 978–0–19–939274–2

9 8 7 6 5 4 3 2 1
Printed by Sheridan Books, Inc., United States of America

This book is dedicated to the courageous men, women, and children with HIV and to their families and loved ones. It is dedicated to the orphans left behind by AIDS and to the HIV advocates who continue to work to diminish stigma and improve care for persons with HIV throughout the world. It is also dedicated to the devoted teams of HIV clinicians and researchers who work tirelessly to provide care and support for persons with HIV. We thank our families and friends for their support.

M.A.C., J.M.G., J.M.J., P.V., S.L.L.

TABLE OF CONTENTS

Foreword   xi

List of Contributors   xiii

In Memoriam   xxi

PART I
RELEVANCE AND IMPLICATIONS OF HIV PSYCHIATRY AS A PARADIGM FOR INTEGRATED CARE

1. HIV Psychiatry—A Paradigm for Integrated Care   3
   Mary Ann Cohen, Michael J. Mugavero, and Elise Hall

2. HIV/AIDS in the Fourth Decade: Origins, Epidemiology,
   Clinical Manifestations, and Treatment   19
   Michael J. Mugavero and J. Michael Kilby

3. Epidemiology of Psychiatric Disorders Associated
   with HIV and AIDS   29
   *Francine Cournos, Karen McKinnon,
   and Milton Wainberg*

4. Global Aspects of the HIV Pandemic   46
   HIV AIDS in Africa   48
   Emilio Letang and Francine Cournos
   HIV and AIDS in the Asia-Pacific Region   52
   *Dimitri Prybylski, Donn Colby, E. Kainne Dokubo,
   and Chuan-Mei Lee*
   HIV and AIDS in Europe   55
   Julia del Amo, Jordi Blanch, and Esteban Martínez
   HIV and AIDS in the Americas   57
   *Gaddy Noy, Farah Ahmad-Stout,
   and Marshall Forstein*

5. AIDS Orphans and Other Children Affected by HIV   66
   Getrude Makurumidze, Anna Gamell, and Emilio Letang

6. HIV Discrimination, Stigma, and
   Gender-Based Violence   73
   *Antoine Douaihy, Neeta Shenai, Kimberly Clinebell,
   and Mary Ann Cohen*

PART II
INTEGRATED CARE AND ADVOCACY FOR PERSONS WITH HIV

7. Models of Care for Persons with HIV   83
   *James Bourgeois, Mary Ann Cohen, John A. R. Grimaldi,
   Jon A. Levenson, Yavar Moghimi, Weston Scott Fisher,
   and David Tran*

8. How to Establish an Integrated Ambulatory Care
   Program Co-located in an HIV Clinic   97
   *Mary Ann Cohen, James Bourgeois, Weston Scott Fisher,
   and David Tran*

9. Sociocultural Factors Influencing the Transmission
   of HIV/AIDS in the United States: AIDS and the
   Nation's Prisons   103
   Robert E. Fullilove

10. HIV Advocacy   108
    *Simon Collins, Tim Horn, Loon Gangte, Emmanuel
    Trenado, and Vuyiseka Dubula*

PART III
COMPREHENSIVE HIV PSYCHIATRIC ASSESSMENT, EDUCATION, AND TRAINING

11. A Biopsychosocial Approach to Psychiatric
    Consultation in Persons with HIV and AIDS   121
    Kenneth Ashley, Daniel Safin, and Mary Ann Cohen

12. Neuropsychological Evaluation for Persons with
    HIV and AIDS   135
    Bibilola D. Oladeji and Kevin R. Robertson

13. Training in HIV Psychiatry   143
    *David M. Stoff, Mary Ann Cohen, Marshall Forstein,
    Anna L. Dickerman, and Daena L. Petersen*

PART IV
PSYCHIATRIC DISORDERS AND HIV INFECTION

14. Substance-Related and Addictive Disorder? The Special
    Role in HIV Transmission   157
    Philip A. Bialer, Kenneth Ashley, and John A. R. Grimaldi

15. Depressive and Bipolar Disorders   168
   Antoine Douaihy, Matthew Conlon, and Maria Ferrara

16. HIV-Associated Neurocognitive Disorders   175
   *Scott L. Letendre, Jennifer Iudicello, Beau Ances,
   Thomas D. Marcotte, Serena Spudich,
   and Mary Ann Cohen*

17. Trauma and Posttraumatic Stress Disorder—
   The Special Role in HIV Transmission   204
   *Antoine Douaihy, Melanie Grubisha, Maureen E. Lyon,
   and Mary Ann Cohen*

18. Anxiety Disorders   210
   *Antoine Douaihy, Meredith Spada, Nicole Bates, Julia
   Macedo, and Jack M. Gorman*

19. Psychotic Disorders and Serious Mental Illness   222
   *Alexander Thompson, Daniel Williams,
   Oliver Freudenreich, Andrew Angelino,
   and Glenn J. Treisman*

20. The Role of Personality in HIV Risk Behaviors:
   Implications for Treatment   231
   Heidi E. Hutton and Glenn J. Treisman

PART V

UNIQUE PSYCHIATRIC MANIFESTATIONS
OF HIV INFECTION

21. Psychoneuroimmunology and HIV   241
   Adam W. Carrico and Michael H. Antoni

22. Distress in Persons with HIV and AIDS   255
   *Mary Ann Cohen, Anna L. Dickerman,
   and Harold W. Goforth*

23. Insomnia and HIV: A Biopsychosocial Approach   262
   Mary Alice O'Dowd and Maria Fernanda Gomez

24. Fatigue and HIV   271
   Anna L. Dickerman and William Breitbart

25. Suicide and HIV   285
   *César A. Alfonso, Eva Stern-Rodríguez,
   and Mary Ann Cohen*

PART VI

NEUROPATHOLOGICAL MANIFESTATIONS
OF HIV INFECTION

26. Neurological Complications of HIV in the Central
   Nervous System   295
   *Christopher Woldstad, Michael Boska,
   and Howard E. Gendelman*

27. Neurological Complications of HIV in the Peripheral
   Nervous System   317
   John R. Keltner, Cherine Akkari, and Ronald J. Ellis

PART VII

PSYCHIATRIC ASPECTS OF RISK
BEHAVIORS, PREVENTION OF HIV
TRANSMISSION, AND ADHERENCE
TO MEDICAL CARE

28. The Role of Psychiatric Disorders in HIV
   Transmission and Prevention   325
   *Andréa L. Hobkirk, Seth C. Kalichman,
   David M. Stoff, and Christina S. Meade*

29. Psychiatric Aspects of Care Engagement
   and Medication Adherence in Antiretroviral-Based
   HIV Treatment and Prevention   334
   Jeffrey J. Weiss and Michael J. Stirratt

30. Homelessness and HIV Transmission   346
   *Kimberly Livingstone, Daniel B. Herman,
   Naomi Adler, and Ezra S. Susser*

31. Routine Testing for HIV Infection and
   Pre-Exposure and Post-Exposure Prophylaxis   353
   Bisrat K. Abraham, Inti Flores, and Roy M. Gulick

32. Vaccines for the Prevention and Treatment of
   HIV Infection   366
   *Josephine H. Cox, Stuart Z. Shapiro, Liza Dawson,
   Cynthia Geppert, Andrew M. Siegel,
   and M. Patricia D'Souza*

PART VIII

HIV PSYCHIATRY THROUGH THE
LIFE CYCLE

33. Childhood and Adolescence   383
   *Suad Kapetanovic, Lori Wiener, Lisa K. Tuchman,
   and Maryland Pao*

34. Young Adulthood and Serodiscordant Couples   405
   Marshall Forstein, Farah Ahmad-Stout, and Gaddy Noy

35. Women's Issues   419
   *Sara Gorman, Judith Currier, Elise Hall,
   and Julia del Amo*

36. Older Age and HIV   429
   *Karl Goodkin, David M. Stoff, Dilip V. Jeste,
   and Maria J. Marquine*

PART IX

HIV PSYCHIATRIC TREATMENT AND
PSYCHOTHERAPEUTIC MODALITIES

37. Psychotherapeutic Interventions   451
   *Jocelyn Soffer, César A. Alfonso, John A. R. Grimaldi,
   and Jack M. Gorman*

38. Integrative Treatments 465
Cheryl Gore-Felton, Lawrence McGlynn,
Andrei Kreutzberg, and David Spiegel

39. Social Service Interventions 475
Mary Ann Malone

40. Nursing Support 483
Carl Kirton

41. Palliative Care and Spiritual Care of Persons with
HIV and AIDS 494
Anna L. Dickerman, Yesne Alici, William Breitbart,
and Harvey Max Chochinov

42. Psychopharmacological Treatment Issues in
HIV/AIDS Psychiatry 514
Kelly L. Cozza, Gary H. Wynn, Glenn W. Wortmann,
Scott G. Williams, and Rita Rein

PART X

HIV PSYCHIATRY AND MULTIMORBID
MEDICAL CONDITIONS

43. Hepatitis C and HIV Co-infection 571
Jennifer Cohen Price, Priyanka Amin,
and Antoine Douaihy

44. HIV-Associated Nephropathy, End-Stage Renal
Disease, Dialysis, and Kidney Transplant 579
Jonathan Winston, Etti Zeldis, John A. R. Grimaldi,
and Esteban Martínez

45. Endocrine Comorbidities in Persons with HIV 589
Jocelyn Soffer and Harold W. Goforth

46. Cardiovascular Disease, Metabolic Complications
and Lipodystrophy in Persons with HIV 602
Luis F. Pereira, Harold W. Goforth,
Esteban Martínez, Joseph Z. Lux, Maria Ferrara,
and Michael P. Mullen

47. Overview of HIV-Associated Multimorbidities 611
Luis F. Pereira, Mark Bradley, Harold W. Goforth,
César A. Alfonso, Joseph Z. Lux, Esteban Martínez,
and Michael P. Mullen

PART XI

ETHICAL AND HEALTH POLICY ASPECTS
OF AIDS PSYCHIATRY

48. Clinician Burnout in HIV/AIDS Healthcare 629
Asher D. Aladjem and Mary Ann Cohen

49. End-of-Life Issues, Ethical Issues, Advance
Directives, and Surrogate Decision-Making
in the Care of Persons with HIV 638
Cynthia Geppert, Mary Ann Cohen, and
Rebecca Weintraub Brendel

50. Health Services and Policy Issues in
AIDS Psychiatry 647
James T. Walkup and Stephen Crystal

Resource Appendix for Persons with HIV/AIDS,
Their Families, Caregivers, Clinicians, Educators,
and Researchers 657
Getrude Makurumidze

Index 671

FOREWORD

There have been tremendous strides in the prevention and treatment of HIV in the decade since the last edition was published. Most people living with HIV in resource rich countries are now living longer in better health. However, there remains great need for mental health and supportive services throughout the world. While there may be an overall sense that the stigma surrounding HIV has diminished, stigma continues to be a barrier to getting tested and engaged in HIV care. The stress and stigma associated with living with HIV may create feelings of hopelessness and despair. Also, individuals who are addicted to drugs or misusing prescription drugs and alcohol as well as persons with other underlying psychiatric disorders may not achieve the same benefits from the available HIV therapies, given the risk for suboptimal adherence to care and medication, or because of potential drug interactions between medically needed therapies to control multiple conditions. Dr. Cohen and colleagues have once again mastered the subject matter and offer us guidance on how to address the most challenging of issues confronting this delicate and at risk population. The authors have included new chapters in this edition,

including a chapter on orphans, written by an AIDS orphan, a chapter on advocacy, written by HIV advocates, and new chapters on global aspects of HIV, women and HIV, stigma and gender-based violence, HIV vaccines, routine testing for HIV, and pre- and post-exposure prophylaxis. The authors provide useful and practical information on how to create integrated services to best identify, diagnose and offer appropriate medical and mental health care. Furthermore, the chapters are written to appeal to those who practice HIV primary care as well as those who are experts in neurology, psychology and psychiatry. HIV affects the person as a whole and its management cannot be delivered in silos. Cohen's textbook provides us with the insight and guidance to help us all communicate and understand the challenges and conditions that often create barriers to achieving wellness. Once again, I congratulate all for providing us with a wonderful resource.

Judith A. Aberg, MD, FIDSA, FACP
Dr. George Baehr Professor of Medicine
Chief, Division of Infectious Diseases
Icahn School of Medicine at Mount Sinai

LIST OF CONTRIBUTORS

Judith A. Aberg, MD, FIDSA, FACP
Dr. George Baehr Professor of Medicine
Chief, Division of Infectious Diseases
School of Medicine at Mount Sinai
New York, New York

Bisrat K. Abraham, MD, MPH
Clinical Assistant Professor of Medicine
Division of Infectious Diseases
Weill Medical College of Cornell University
Assistant Attending Physician
New York Presbyterian Hospital
New York, New York

Naomi Adler, MD
Emergency Physician
Kaiser Permanente
Oakland, California

Farah Ahmad-Stout, MD
Cambridge Health Alliance
Cambridge, Massachusetts

Cherine Akkari, MD
Yale University School of Medicine
New Haven, Connecticut

Asher D. Aladjem, MD
Clinical Associate Professor
Department of Psychiatry
Department of Population Health
Director, Ethics Committee for BHC
NYU School of Medicine
New York, New York

César A. Alfonso, MD
Associate Clinical Professor of Psychiatry
Columbia University Medical Center
New York, New York

Yesne Alici, MD
Assistant Attending Psychiatrist
Memorial Sloan Kettering Cancer Center
New York, New York

Priyanka Amin, MD
Department of Psychiatry
University of Pittsburgh
Pittsburgh, Pennsylvania

Beau Ances, MD
Associate Professor of Neurology
Department of Neurology
Washington University School of Medicine
St. Louis, Missouri

Andrew Angelino, MD
Director of Psychiatry
Howard County General Hospital
Associate Professor of Psychiatry and Behavioral Sciences
Johns Hopkins University School of Medicine
Columbia, Maryland

Michael H. Antoni, PhD
Professor
Director, Center for Psycho-Oncology Research
University of Miami
Miami, Florida

Kenneth Ashley, MD
Assistant Professor of Clinical Psychiatry
Icahn School of Medicine
Mount Sinai
New York, New York

Nicole Bates, MD
Department of Psychiatry
University of Pittsburgh
Pittsburgh, Pennsylvania

Philip A. Bialer, MD
Attending Psychiatrist
Memorial Sloan Kettering Cancer Center
Associate Professor of Clinical Psychiatry
Weill Cornell Medical College
New York, New York

Jordi Blanch, MD, PhD
Psychiatry Service
Hospital Clinic
Barcelona, Spain

Michael Boska, PhD
Professor and Vice Chairman for Research
Department of Radiology
University of Nebraska Medical Center
Omaha, Nebraska

James Bourgeois, OD, MD
Clinical Professor and Vice Chair, Clinical Affairs
Department of Psychiatry/Langley Porter
    Psychiatric Institute
UCSF School of Medicine
University of California, San Francisco
UCSF Weill Institute for Neurosciences
San Francisco, California

Mark Bradley, MD
Clinical Assistant Professor, Department of Psychiatry
Director, Psychiatry Psychosomatic Fellowship Program
NYU School of Medicine
New York, New York

William Breitbart, MD
Chair, Department of Psychiatry and Behavioral Sciences
Jimmie C. Holland Chair in Psychiatric Oncology
Memorial Sloan Kettering Cancer Center
New York, New York

Rebecca Weintraub Brendel, MD, JD
Medical Director, The One Fund Center
Director of Ethics, Center for Law, Brain, and Behavior
Associate Psychiatrist
Massachusetts General Hospital
Director of the Master of Bioethics Program
Assistant Professor of Psychiatry
Center for Bioethics
Harvard University
Boston, Massachusetts

Adam W. Carrico, MS, PhD
Associate Professor of Public Health Sciences
    and Psychiatry
University of Miami School of Medicine
Miami, Florida

Harvey Max Chochinov, MD, PhD
Distinguished Professor of Psychiatry
Director, Manitoba Palliative Care Research Unit
University of Manitoba
Winnipeg, Manitoba, Canada

Kimberly Clinebell, MD
Department of Psychiatry
University of Pittsburgh
Pittsburgh, Pennsylvania

Mary Ann Cohen, MD
Clinical Professor of Psychiatry
Icahn School of Medicine at Mount Sinai
Founder, Academy of Psychosomatic Medicine
HIV/AIDS Psychiatry Special Interest Group
New York, New York

Donn Colby, MD, MPH
Clinical Research Physician
Thai Red Cross Research Center
Bangkok, Thailand

Simon Collins
HIV i-Base
London, United Kingdom

Matthew Conlon, MD
Department of Psychiatry
University of Pittsburgh
Pittsburgh, Pennsylvania

Francine Cournos, MD
Professor of Clinical Psychiatry
Columbia University
New York, New York

Josephine H. Cox, PhD
Clinical Laboratory Coordinator
Clinical Trials Program
VRC/NIAID/National Institute of Health
Bethesda, Maryland

Kelly L. Cozza, MD, DFAPA, FAPM
Associate Professor
Psychiatry Clinical Clerkship Director
Department of Psychiatry
Scientist, Center for the Study of Traumatic Stress
Uniformed Services University of the Health Sciences
Bethesda, Maryland

Stephen Crystal, PhD
Research Professor
Associate Director for Health Services Research
Chair, Division on Aging and AIDS
Rutgers, the State University of New Jersey
New Brunswick, New Jersey

Judith Currier, MD
Professor of Medicine
UCLA Division of Infectious Diseases
Department of Medicine Division Chief
University of California, Los Angeles
Los Angeles, California

Liza Dawson, PhD
Team Leader, Research Ethics Team
Basic Sciences Program
Division of AIDS
National Institute of Allergy and Infectious Diseases
    National Institutes of Health
Bethesda, Maryland

Julia del Amo, MD, PhD
Professor of Research in Biomedical Sciences
National Center for Epidemiology
Institute of Health Carlos III
Madrid, Spain

Anna L. Dickerman, MD
Assistant Professor of Clinical Psychiatry
Weill Cornell Medical College
Assistant Attending Psychiatrist
Consultation-Liaison Service
New York–Presbyterian Hospital/Weill Cornell
New York, New York

E. Kainne Dokubo, MD, MPH
Medical Officer
Centers for Disease Control and Prevention
Atlanta, Georgia

Antoine Douaihy, MD
Professor of Psychiatry and Medicine
Department of Psychiatry
University of Pittsburgh
Pittsburgh, Pennsylvania

M. Patricia D'Souza, PhD
Team Lead, Clinical Laboratory Program
Vaccine Clinical Research Branch
Division of AIDS
National Institute of Allergy and Infectious Diseases, NIH
Bethesda, Maryland

Vuyiseka Dubula
Treatment Action Campaign
Cape Town, South Africa

Ronald J. Ellis, MD
Professor
Department of Neurosciences
University of California San Diego School of Medicine
San Diego, California

Maria Ferrara, MD
Specialist in Psychiatry
Department of Mental Health and Substance Abuse
AUSL Modena
Modena, Italy

Weston Scott Fisher, MD
Assistant Clinical Professor
Department of Psychiatry
University of California, San Francisco
Weill Institute for Neurosciences
San Francisco, California

Inti Flores, MD
Psychiatrist
UCSF Medical Center
San Francisco, California

Marshall Forstein, MD
Department of Psychiatry
Cambridge Health Alliance
Associate Professor of Psychiatry
Harvard Medical School
Cambridge, Massachusetts

Oliver Freudenreich, MD
Associate Professor of Psychiatry
Director, First Episode and Early Psychosis Program
Director, Schizophrenia Program
Harvard Medical School
Boston, Massachusetts

Robert E. Fullilove, EdD
Associate Dean for Community and Minority Affairs
Professor of Clinical Sociomedical Sciences
Columbia University Mailman School of Public Health
New York, New York

Anna Gamell, MD
Pediatrician, Coordinator of the One Stop Clinic
   of Ifakara, Tanzania
Swiss Tropical & Public Health Institute
Basel, Switzerland

Loon Gangte
Delhi Network of Positive People (DNP+)
New Delhi, India

Howard E. Gendelman, MD
Margaret R. Larson Professor of Internal Medicine
   and Infectious Diseases
Professor and Chair, Department of Pharmacology
   and Experimental Neuroscience
Director, Center for Neurodegenerative Disorders
University of Nebraska Medical Center
Omaha, Nebraska

Cynthia Geppert, MD, MA, MPH, MSB, DPS
Professor
Chief, Consultation Psychiatry and Ethics
New Mexico Veteran Affairs Health Care System
Director of Ethics Education
Attending Psychiatrist
Veterans Administration Medical Center
Albuquerque, New Mexico

Harold W. Goforth, MD
Assistant Clinical Professor of Medicine
Cleveland Clinic Foundation
Neurological Institute
Section of Headache Medicine
Cleveland, Ohio

María Fernanda Gómez, MD
Associate Professor of Clinical Psychiatry and
   Behavioral Sciences
Albert Einstein College of Medicine
Associate Director
Psychosomatic Medicine
Montefiore Medical Center
Bronx, New York

Karl Goodkin, MD, PhD
Professor and Chair
Department of Psychiatry and Behavioral Sciences
James H. Quillen College of Medicine
East Tennessee State University
Johnson City, Tennessee

Cheryl Gore-Felton, PhD
Associate Dean, Academic Affairs
Professor and Associate Chairman
   Department of Psychiatry and Behavioral Sciences
Stanford University School of Medicine
Stanford, California

Jack M. Gorman, MD
Behavioral Health Consultant
Franklin Behavioral Health Consultants
New York, New York

Sara Gorman, PhD, MPH
Project Manager
Johnson & Johnson Global Public Health
New York, New York

John A. R. Grimaldi, MD
Associate Director
Brigham Psychiatric Specialties
Brigham and Women's Hospital
Harvard Medical School
Boston, Massachusetts

Melanie Grubisha MD
Department of Psychiatry
University of Pittsburgh
Pittsburgh, Pennsylvania

Roy M. Gulick, MD, MPH
Professor of Medicine
Chief, Division of Infectious Diseases
Weill Medical College of Cornell University
Attending Physician
New York Presbyterian Hospital
New York, New York

Elise Hall, MD
Psychiatrist
San Francisco, California

Daniel B. Herman, MSW, PhD
Professor
Hunter College Silberman School of Social Work
City University of New York
New York, New York

Andréa L. Hobkirk, PhD
Duke University Medical Center
Durham, North Carolina

Tim Horn
Treatment Action Group
New York, New York

Heidi E. Hutton, PhD
Johns Hopkins University School of Medicine
Baltimore, Maryland

Jennifer Iudicello, PhD
University of California, San Diego
San Diego, California

Jeffrey M. Jacobson, MD
Professor, Medicine
Professor, Neuroscience
Co-Director, Center for Translational AIDS Research
Lewis Katz School of Medicine Temple University
Philadelphia, Pennsylvania

Dilip V. Jeste, MD
Senior Associate Dean, Healthy Aging and Senior Care
Estelle and Edgar Levi Chair in Aging
Distinguished Professor of Psychiatry and Neurosciences
Director, Sam and Rose Stein Institute for Research
    on Aging
University of California, San Diego
San Diego, California

Seth C. Kalichman, PhD
Professor of Psychology (Principal Investigator)
Institute for Collaboration on Health, Intervention,
    and Policy
University of Connecticut
Storrs, Connecticut

Suad Kapetanovic, MD
Assistant Professor of Clinical Psychiatry
Behavioral Sciences Medical Director
Keck School of Medicine of USC
University of Southern California
Los Angeles, California

John R. Keltner, MD, PhD
Mental/Behavioral Health
VA San Diego Healthcare System
San Diego, California

J. Michael Kilby, MD (deceased)
Medical University of South Carolina
Charleston, South Carolina

Carl Kirton, DNP, RN, MBA
Chief Nursing Officer
University Hospital
Newark University
Newark, New Jersey

Andrei Kreutzberg, MD
Psychiatrist
University of California, San Francisco
San Francisco, California

Chuan-Mei Lee, MD
Psychiatrist
University of California, San Francisco
San Francisco, California

Emilio Letang, MD, MPH, PhD
Assistant Research Professor
IS Global
Barcelona Institute for Global Health–Campus Clinic
Hospital Clinic
University of Barcelona
Barcelona, Spain
Swiss Tropical and Public Health Institute
University of Basel
Basel, Switzerland

Scott L. Letendre, MD
Professor of Medicine and Psychiatry
Division of Infectious Diseases
University of California, San Diego
San Diego, California

Jon A. Levenson, MD
Associate Professor of Psychiatry
Columbia University Medical Center
Attending Psychiatrist, Division of Consultation-Liaison
    Psychiatry
Director, Undergraduate Medical Education in
    Consultation-Liaison Psychiatry
New York, New York

Kimberly Livingstone, MSW
Adjunct Lecturer
The Graduate Center &
Silberman School of Social Work
Hunter College
New York, New York

Joseph Z. Lux, MD
Clinical Associate Professor
Department of Psychiatry
NYU School of Medicine/Bellevue Hospital Center
New York, New York

Maureen E. Lyon, PhD, ABPP
Research Professor in Pediatrics
Children's National Health System
Center for Translational Science/Children's
    Research Institute
Division of Adolescent and Young Adult Medicine
George Washington School of Medicine
    and Health Sciences
Washington, DC

Julia Macedo, MD
Department of Psychiatry
University of Pittsburgh
Pittsburgh, Pennsylvania

Getrude Makurumidze, BA
Program Assistant
New York State Department of Health
AIDS Institute
New York, New York

Mary Ann Malone, LCSW
Clinical Social Worker
New York, New York

Thomas D. Marcotte, PhD
Associate Professor of Psychiatry
HIV Neurobehavioral Research Program
Center for Medicinal Cannabis Research
University of California, San Diego
San Diego, California

Maria J. Marquine, PhD
Assistant Professor
Department of Psychiatry
University of California, San Diego
San Diego, California

Esteban Martínez, MD, PhD
Virology Education
Utrecht, The Netherlands

Lawrence McGlynn, MD
Clinical Professor of Psychiatry and Behavioral Sciences
Stanford University School of Medicine
Stanford, California

Karen McKinnon, MA
Research Scientist
New York State Psychiatry Institute
Department of Psychiatry
Columbia University College of Physicians and Surgeons
New York, New York

Christina S. Meade, PhD
Associate Professor of Psychiatry and Behavioral Sciences
Duke Global Health Institute
Duke University School of Medicine
Durham, North Carolina

Yavar Moghimi, MD
Whitman-Walker Health
The George Washington University
Washington, DC

Michael J. Mugavero, MD, MHSC
Associate Professor
Department of Health Behavior
School of Public Health
The University of Alabama at Birmingham
Birmingham, Alabama

Michael P. Mullen, MD
Professor, Medicine, Infectious Diseases
Mount Sinai Beth Israel
The Mount Sinai Hospital
Mount Sinai St. Luke's
Mount Sinai West
New York, New York

Gaddy Noy, DO
Cambridge Health Alliance
Harvard Medical School
Boston, Massachusetts

Mary Alice O'Dowd, MD
Director of Psychosomatic Medicine
Professor of Clinical Psychiatry
Albert Einstein College of Medicine
New York, New York

Bibilola D. Oladeji, MD
Senior Lecturer
Department of Psychiatry
College of Medicine
University of Ibadan
Ibadan, Nigeria

Maryland Pao, MD
Clinical Director
National Institute of Mental Health
Bethesda, Maryland

Luis F. Pereira, MD
Department of Psychiatry
Mount Sinai Beth Israel
New York, New York

Daena L. Petersen, MD, MPH, MA
Assistant Professor
Community and Public Safety Psychiatry Division
Medical University of South Carolina
Charleston, South Carolina

Jennifer Cohen Price, MD, PhD
Assistant Clinical Professor of Medicine
Division of Gastroenterology/Liver
Transplant
University of California, San Francisco
San Francisco, California

Dimitri Prybylski, PhD, MPH
Associate Director for Science
Centers for Disease Control and Prevention
Atlanta, Georgia

Rita Rein, MD, CPT, USA, MC
National Capital Consortium Combined Internal Medicine
    and Psychiatry Resident
Teaching Fellow, Departments of Psychiatry and Medicine
Uniformed Services University of the Health Sciences
    School of Medicine
Bethesda, Maryland

Kevin R. Robertson, PhD
Department of Neurology
UNC School of Medicine
University of North Carolina, Chapel Hill
Chapel Hill, North Carolina

Daniel Safin, MD
Division of Consultation-Liaison Psychiatry and
    Psychosomatic Medicine
Mount Sinai Beth Israel
New York, New York

Stuart Z. Shapiro, MD, PhD
Vaccine Discovery Team Leader
Preclinical Research & Development Branch
Vaccine Research Program
Division of AIDS
National Institute of Allergy and Infectious Diseases
Rockville, Maryland

Neeta Shenai, MD
Department of Psychiatry
University of Pittsburgh
Pittsburgh, Pennsylvania

Andrew M. Siegel, MD, MA
Assistant Professor of Clinical Psychiatry
Perelman School of Medicine
Hospital of the University of Pennsylvania
Philadelphia, Pennsylvania

Jocelyn Soffer, MD
Psychiatrist
Clinical Assistant Professor
Department of Child and Adolescent Psychiatry
NYU School of Medicine, Child Study Center
New York, New York

Meredith Spada, MD
Department of Psychiatry
University of Pittsburgh
Pittsburgh, Pennsylvania

David Spiegel, MD
Jack, Samuel & Lulu Wilson Professor in Medicine
Psychiatry and Behavioral Sciences
Stanford University School of Medicine
Stanford, California

Serena Spudich, MD
Professor of Neurology
Division Chief, Neurological Infections & Global Neurology
Yale University School of Medicine
New Haven, Connecticut

Eva Stern-Rodríguez
Wellesley College
Class of 2017
Wellesley, Massachusetts

Michael J. Stirratt, PhD
Division of AIDS Research
National Institute of Mental Health
Bethesda, Maryland

David M. Stoff, PhD
Division of AIDS Research
National Institute of Mental Health
Bethesda, Maryland

Ezra S. Susser, MD, DrPH
Director, Psychiatric Epidemiology Training Program
Columbia University Mailman School of Public Health
Columbia University Medical Center
New York, New York

Alexander W. Thompson, MD, MBA, MPH
Director of Integrated Care
Clinical Associate Professor
University of Iowa
Carver College of Medicine
Iowa City, Iowa

David Tran, MD, MPP
Medical Director
South Van Ness Behavioral Health Services
HIV and Gender Services
San Francisco Department of Public Health
San Francisco, California

Glenn J. Treisman, MD, PhD
Director, AIDS Psychiatry Service
Professor of Psychiatry and Behavioral Sciences
Johns Hopkins School of Medicine
Baltimore, Maryland

Emmanuel Trenado
AIDES
Paris, France

Lisa K. Tuchman, MD, MPH
Associate Professor of Pediatrics
Chief, Division of Adolescent and Young Adult Medicine
Children's National Health System
Washington, DC

Milton Wainberg, MD
Associate Clinical Professor of Psychiatry
Columbia University Medical Center
New York, New York

James T. Walkup, PhD
Professor
Chair, Clinical Psychology Department
Director of Clinical Training
Graduate School of Applied and Professional Psychology
Rutgers University
New Brunswick, New Jersey

Jeffrey J. Weiss, PhD, MS
Associate Professor
Icahn School of Medicine at Mount Sinai
New York, New York

Lori Wiener, PhD
Co-Director, Behavioral Health Core
Director, Psychosocial Support and Research Program
Pediatric Oncology Branch
Center for Cancer Research, National Cancer Institute
National Institutes of Health
Bethesda, Maryland

Daniel Williams, MD
Attending Psychiatrist
Tyler, Texas

Scott G. Williams, MD
Assistant Professor of Medicine
Uniformed Services University of the Health Sciences
Bethesda, Maryland

Jonathan Winston, MD
Nephrology & Internal Medicine
The Mount Sinai Hospital
New York, New York

Christopher Woldstad, BS
Graduate Student
Department of Pharmacology and Experimental
 Neuroscience
Boska Laboratory
University of Nebraska Medical Center
Omaha, Nebraska

Glenn W. Wortmann, MD, FIDSA, FACP
Section Chief, Infectious Diseases
MedStar Washington Hospital Center
Washington, DC
Professor of Medicine
Uniformed Services University of the Health Sciences
Bethesda, Maryland

Gary H. Wynn, MD
Associate Professor of Psychiatry and Neuroscience
Assistant Chair
Department of Psychiatry
Uniformed Services University of the Health Sciences
Bethesda, Maryland

Etti Zeldis, MD
Nephrology & Internal Medicine
Mount Sinai Health System
New York, New York

IN MEMORIAM

The editors and authors of our second edition acknowledge with gratitude the remarkable contributions of co-author Dr. Michael Kilby, internationally known and respected for his contributions to the care of persons with HIV and for his prodigious research and academic work in the field of infectious disease and HIV care.

The editors and authors of our first edition acknowledge with gratitude the outstanding contribution of co-author Dr. Alan Berkman, a tireless advocate for people with HIV/AIDS and mental illness across the globe. Based on his work on the chapter in the first edition, Dr. Berkman has contributed to Chapter 30 of our textbook. We appreciate the outstanding indirect contributions to HIV researchers and authors by Dr. Scott C. Armstrong and Dr. Robert Malow. We acknowledge Dr. Armstrong for his work in HIV psychiatry and psychopharmacology and Dr. Malow for his work at maintaining an online updated HIV psychiatry bibliography.

PART I

RELEVANCE AND IMPLICATIONS OF HIV PSYCHIATRY AS A PARADIGM FOR INTEGRATED CARE

1.

HIV PSYCHIATRY—A PARADIGM FOR INTEGRATED CARE

Mary Ann Cohen, Michael J. Mugavero, and Elise Hall

We shall assume that everyone is much more simply human than otherwise. . . . [M]an, . . . as long as he is entitled to the term human personality, will be very much more like every other instance of human personality than he is like anything else in the world. —H.S. Sullivan (1953)

Psychiatric factors take on new relevance and meaning in the fourth decade of the human immunodeficiency virus (HIV) pandemic. Persons with HIV are living longer and healthier lives as a result of medical care as well as advances in research and antiretroviral therapy (ART). Some of the medical advances and concomitant changes in society have catalyzed research and led to vast improvements in care. Many of these changes evolved as a result of the advocacy and activism of gay men and their clinicians from the outset of the epidemic. In some areas of the world advocates' voices have been heard and have led to diminution of HIV stigma and discrimination. However, HIV stigma, discrimination, and criminalization still exist throughout the world.

Much work is still needed, with a greater emphasis on sexual health (Satcher et al., 2015), harm reduction, and competent and compassionate care for persons with HIV and for persons with psychiatric disorders that may serve as vectors for HIV transmission (Cohen, 2016; Cohen et al., 2016). Much work is still needed to diminish stigma and discrimination against persons with psychiatric disorders (Corrigan, 2016), including substance use disorders (Beyrer and Strathdee, 2015; Choopanya et al., 2013). Despite advances in medical care and advocacy for persons with HIV, in the United States and throughout the world, some men, women, and children with HIV and acquired immune deficiency syndrome (AIDS) are unable to benefit from medical progress. Inadequate access to HIV care is multifactorial and multidimensional and includes economic, social, cultural, political, societal, and psychiatric obstacles. Psychiatric disorders and distress play a significant role in the exposure to and transmission of HIV (Blank et al., 2002; Cohen and Alfonso, 1994, 1998; Cohen et al., 2002, 2016). They are relevant to prevention, clinical care, and adherence throughout every aspect of illness, from the initial risk behavior to death. They result in considerable suffering from diagnosis to end-stage illness (Cohen and Alfonso, 2004). The prevalence of HIV in persons with untreated psychiatric illness may be 10 to 20 times that of the general population (Blank et al., 2002). Furthermore, many of the changes in the prevention and treatment of HIV have significant psychological implications.

This chapter presents a list of facts, changes, and advances in the prevention of HIV and in the care of persons with HIV that have salience to HIV psychiatry. These are of particular significance in substantiating the need for an integrated approach to the care of persons with HIV and AIDS. Integrated care can improve retention in care, decrease the incidence of missed clinic visits, and decrease morbidity and mortality in persons with HIV (Flickinger et al., 2013; Levison and Alegria, 2016; Michael et al., 2014; Mugavero et al., 2014). Stigma, discrimination, and fear, in conjunction with denial, omnipotence, and lack of awareness, complicate and perpetuate the HIV pandemic. The creation of a supportive, nurturing, nonjudgmental healthcare environment can help to diminish the stigma of HIV and mental illness and can provide comprehensive and compassionate care for persons with HIV. In this chapter we also review the history of HIV psychiatry, explore HIV psychiatry as paradox and paradigm, delineate HIV health care disparities, and address issues of adherence to treatment. We outline a biopsychosocial approach to sexual health and mental health, which, along with diminution of stigma, is essential to HIV prevention and HIV care. In this chapter and throughout this textbook, we make an effort to eliminate words that stigmatize and dehumanize both medical illness and medical care and present an evidence-based approach to the prevention of HIV transmission and the care of persons with HIV and AIDS.

HIV/AIDS—THE GREAT MAGNIFIER OF MALADIES—IS ENTIRELY PREVENTABLE

If lupus, multiple sclerosis, malaria, Lyme disease, and syphilis are the "great masqueraders" because many of their symptoms are similar to those of other illnesses, HIV/AIDS can be thought of as the "great magnifier of maladies"—of symptoms, illnesses, and aspects of healthcare. HIV magnifies disparities, stigma, and discrimination in healthcare, and it leads to transmission of HIV, lack of access to diagnosis and care, and nonadherence to treatment (Cohen, 2016). As long as HIV is stigmatized, persons who have risk behaviors or suspect that they have HIV will fear discrimination or ostracism and may delay or avoid getting tested, being diagnosed, disclosing HIV to potential partners, or accessing care. Hence, there are extremely negative aspects of HIV as the great magnifier of maladies.

The negative aspects of HIV as magnifier are as follows:

- Health care disparities
- Stigma and discrimination
  - Ageism
  - Misogyny
  - Racism
  - Addictophobia
  - Homophobia
  - Mental illness stigma
  - AIDSism
- Avoidance of getting tested
- Avoidance of access to care
- Treatment refusal
- Nonadherence to care
- Many medical and psychiatric illnesses occur in persons with HIV
- HIV occurs with much higher frequency in persons with psychiatric illness
- Non-disclosure of HIV infection for fear of rejection or ostracism
- Criminalization of HIV, of risk behaviors, and of persons at potential risk

Ironically, as a consequence of the concerted efforts of advocacy and activism on the part of gay men with HIV and AIDS and by some of their clinicians, there are positive aspects of HIV as the great magnifier of maladies. The HIV pandemic and its advocates forced topics of sexuality, gender identity, and death to "come out of the closet," which led to the need for integration of medical and mental health care and contributed to the development and application of bioethical principles such as patient self-determination, advance directives, and care planning.

Positive aspects of HIV as magnifier are as follows:

- Need for a biopsychosociocultural approach to care in order to
  - Prevent transmission
  - Ensure comprehensive assessment and diagnosis
  - Access treatment
  - Improve and enhance doctor patient communication and care
  - Improve doctor and patient satisfaction

- Need for integration of mental health care into HIV medical care
- Need for compassionate empathic care
- Need for routine HIV testing as part of health care and prevention of HIV
- Involvement of every system and organ in the body, including the brain
- Need for the skills of every discipline and subspecialty
- Need for awareness of bioethical issues
- Entirely preventable through risk reduction, behavior change, and integrated medical and psychiatric care and antiretroviral medication

FACTS, CHANGES, AND ADVANCES IN HIV PREVENTION AND CARE

1. Worldwide, an estimated 36.7 million people are living with HIV, and 2.1 new infections occur each year (UNAIDS, 2016; World Health Organization [WHO], 2016a).

2. In the United States an estimated 1.2 million persons are living with HIV, including 156,300 (1 in 8 persons or 12.8%) who are unaware of their infection (Centers for Disease Control and Prevention [CDC], 2015), thus emphasizing that routine testing is critically important for HIV prevention and early intervention and treatment.

3. The estimated incidence of new HIV infections in the United States has remained stable over the last decade, at about 50,000 new HIV infections per year (CDC, 2015).

4. In the United States, fewer than 50% of persons diagnosed with HIV are engaged in care, and an estimated 30% of all persons living with HIV attain viral suppression (Bradley et al., 2014).

5. HIV continues to magnify healthcare disparities in the United States and throughout the world. The global pandemic is characterized by a compilation of distinct regional epidemics, with varying geographic impact across age groups, among men, women, men who have sex with men, and persons who inject drugs. There has been a new onset of HIV transmission throughout the United States in rural areas as well as in urban settings as a result of an increase in the epidemic of heroin use. Addressing the opioid epidemic would be a crucial aspect of preventing this new incidence of HIV. Beyrer and Strathdee (2015) have documented ways to address the recent outbreak of HIV in rural Indiana catalyzed by the heroin epidemic.

6. While there are now far fewer perinatal transmissions in areas of the world with access to perinatal care and

ART, there are many more problems for children with perinatally acquired HIV transitioning to adolescence and adulthood. These include the attendant problems of nonadherence and early demise or the issues surrounding pregnancy, labor, and delivery for newborn girls who were infected perinatally and are now emerging into womanhood and motherhood.

7. Severe multimorbid medical illnesses are prevalent in persons with access to appropriate HIV medical care; these include severe illnesses requiring complex treatments, such as hepatitis C, cancers related and unrelated to HIV, renal disease, diabetes mellitus, as well as cardiovascular illness, including coronary artery disease.

8. There is evidence that early intervention can prevent the central nervous system (CNS) from becoming an independent reservoir for HIV and ultimately prevent HIV-associated neurocognitive disorders, such as HIV-associated dementia. Starting treatment as soon as HIV is diagnosed can prevent the development of independent HIV reservoirs in the brain and thus protect against HIV-associated dementia.

9. At present, one of the leading causes of death for persons with HIV is hepatitis C virus (HCV)-related liver disease. Thus, the treatment of persons with HIV/HCV co-infection has become a major concern. This of course involves understanding how to motivate people with HIV infection to get tested for HCV and to accept treatment. Issues of depression and cognitive impairment are magnified by the affinity of both viruses for the brain. Adherence to two regimens is even harder than to one. The need for integrated medical and psychiatric care is intensified in co-infected individuals.

10. One of the most salient advances in the United States has been the recommendation for routine HIV screening of all adolescents, adults, and pregnant women. The recommendation is for routine HIV testing in medical settings available to everyone from age 13 to 64 and to all persons at substantial risk at even younger or older ages.

11. Biomedical advances in prevention include pre-exposure prophylaxis (PrEP) and post-exposure prophylaxis (PEP) in combination with other prevention measures. PrEP and PEP can prevent HIV transmission from an HIV-positive to an HIV-negative individual. In 2012, the U.S. Food and Drug Agency (FDA) approved the first drug treatment for PrEP. Occupational exposure is no longer the only indication for PEP, and PEP can be used for sexual exposures such as coerced sexual encounters, unprotected sexual encounters, or parenteral exposures such as intravenous drug injection with contaminated paraphernalia.

12. Treatment as prevention (TasP) is a proven approach to prevent new infections by suppression of viral load among persons living with HIV such that they become virtually "noninfectious." In contrast to primary prevention among persons who are HIV-uninfected, via condoms, microbicides, PrEP, and PEP, secondary prevention among persons living with HIV infection via TasP is a complementary approach. Widespread scale-up of ART allowing for population-level reductions in circulating HIV is largely responsible for the 35% reduction in annual new global HIV cases since 2000 (UNAIDS, 2015; WHO 2015).

13. Simple, rapid HIV testing is widely available around the world.

14. Aging with HIV has become more complex, and research is underway to explore aspects of successful aging with HIV.

15. The *Diagnostic and Statistical Manual for Mental Disorders*, 5th edition (DSM-5), in 2013, introduced alternative categorizations and definitions of diagnoses frequently used in HIV psychiatry. These alternative categorizations include the reclassification of neurocognitive disorders and bereavement.

16. The area of adherence research continues to advance, with new evidence regarding expanding adherence beyond ART to also include adherence to clinical care (Flickinger et al., 2013; Levison and Alegria, 2016; Michael et al., 2014; Mugavero et al., 2014).

17. AIDSism (Cohen, 1989), stigma, and discrimination (Blendon and Donelan, 1988; Crowley et al., 2015; Fullilove, 1989; Kelly et al., 1987; Mahajan et al., 2008), as well as criminalization of drugs of abuse, sex work, and behaviors that may unintentionally expose individuals to HIV all serve to complicate and perpetuate the HIV pandemic (Center for HIV Law and Policy, 2010; Lehman et al., 2014).

18. Following an unanticipated, unplanned, or forced unsafe sexual encounter, any person can be encouraged to take tenofovir and emtricitabine for PEP after unsafe sex. One of the authors (MAC) had a patient who was HIV negative and unable to access PEP after unsafe sex until 74 hours after his exposure to HIV and developed an acute antiretroviral syndrome within 10 days after exposure.

19. The syndemic of substance abuse (and other mental illness), violence, and AIDS (SAVA) (Eisenberg and Blank, 2014) complicates and perpetuates the HIV pandemic.

20. There is evidence that an integrated approach to care can improve adherence to medical treatment.

HIV AND PSYCHIATRIC ILLNESS

Understanding the interplay between HIV and psychiatric illness leads to improved insight into how integration of care allows persons with HIV and AIDS to better cope with their illness, live their lives to the fullest extent, and minimize pain and suffering for them and their loved ones. The personal and societal costs to health, productivity, fitness, careers, partners, spouses, parents, and children take an enormous toll in suffering. Related to this is the suffering of the loved ones and orphans left behind by AIDS. The tragedy of preventable death in young and productive individuals is heightened by the multiplicity of infections, severity of illness, and the multisystem and multiorgan involvement of this devastating illness. The illness is complicated by the psychological reactions to and psychiatric manifestations of HIV infection. Psychiatric disorders can accelerate the spread of the virus by creating barriers to risk reduction, including risky sexual behaviors and sharing of needles in persons who inject drugs.

Some persons with HIV may have no psychiatric disorder, while others may have one or more of the psychiatric disorders described in the *DSM-5* (American Psychiatric Association, 2013). The diagnosis of psychiatric disorders is covered extensively in Chapters 11 and 12 and the most prevalent psychiatric disorders are explored in detail in Chapters 14 through 20 of this textbook. A brief overview here of the psychiatric disorders that have most relevance to transmission of HIV and adherence to care will serve to clarify the need for the integration of psychiatric and medical care for persons with HIV. The relevant diagnoses include addictive disorders, trauma-related disorders, depressive disorders, psychotic disorders, and neurocognitive disorders.

Substance-related and addictive disorders, including alcohol and other drug use, result in multidimensional obstacles to risk reduction and adherence to care. These include obvious barriers to prevention of transmission, such as sharing of drug paraphernalia, and more subtle barriers, such as the inability to adhere to perinatal ART because of intoxication, withdrawal, and drug-seeking behaviors. Furthermore, intoxication and disinhibition associated with alcohol and drug use and exchange of sex for drugs result in risky sexual behaviors and difficulty with adherence to complex medical regimens. Cognitive disorders associated with alcohol and other drugs can also impair judgment and ability to adhere to care. Active substance use may interfere with adherence to prevention strategies, to medical care, and to the care of children infected with or affected by the virus. Mortality trends indicate an increase in death from end-stage liver disease as a result of comorbid infection with HIV and HCV in persons who inject drugs.

A trauma-related disorder, posttraumatic stress disorder (PTSD), is highly prevalent in persons with HIV infection and increases morbidity risk (Boarts et al., 2006; Cohen et al., 2001; Samuels et al., 2011; Sikkema et al., 2007). It is often overlooked in persons with HIV/AIDS because it may be overshadowed by other psychiatric diagnoses (Samuels et al., 2011). The effect is bidirectional. For example, intimate partner violence or a history of childhood trauma or childhood sexual trauma are all risk factors for HIV infection as well as for PTSD. The severity of HIV-related PTSD symptoms is associated with a greater number of HIV-related physical symptoms, extensive history of pre-HIV trauma, decreased social support, increased perception of stigma, and negative

life events. Moreover, PTSD is often multimorbid with other psychiatric and medical disorders, pain, and depressive symptoms. PTSD can lead to risky behaviors and decrease harm avoidance as a result of both dissociative phenomena and a sense of a foreshortened future. Persons with PTSD as a result of early childhood trauma may have difficulty protecting themselves from harm or may unconsciously seek to re-enact their early trauma in later life.

PTSD is associated with nonadherence to risk reduction and medical care (Boarts et al., 2006; Cohen et al., 2001). The diagnosis of PTSD is further complicated by repression or retrograde amnesia for traumatic events and difficulties in forming trusting relationships and disclosing trauma if it is recalled (Samuels et al., 2011). In persons with HIV infection, there is a high incidence of early childhood and other trauma with consequent PTSD, substance use disorders, and other psychiatric disorders (Cohen et al., 2001; Samuels et al., 2011). Violence may include perpetuation of early trauma in persons with PTSD who may unconsciously seek to master early childhood trauma in adult relationships. Synergistic epidemics, or syndemics, were first described by Singer (1994) and subsequently associated with nonadherence to HIV care and poorer outcomes (Boarts et al., 2006; Eisenberg and Blank, 2014). Syndemics of triple diagnoses include co-occurring substance use disorder, other psychiatric disorder, and HIV (Meyer et al., 2011). The association of nonadherence with the syndemic of substance abuse, violence, and AIDS (the SAVA syndemic) has been documented (Eisenberg and Blank, 2014; Sullivan et al., 2015).

Other psychiatric disorders such as psychotic disorders, depressive disorders, and neurocognitive disorders may be associated with HIV transmission and nonadherence to care. Risky behavior and nonadherence may result from poor judgment with regard to sexual partner choice, lack of attention to barrier contraception, and, at times hypersexuality, disinhibition, and having multiple sexual partners. When persons are psychotic, they may seek sexual contact or may become victims of sexual predators as a result of efforts to obtain love, affection, and attention or in attempting to relieve the anguish of psychosis. Depressive disorders can lead to apathy and a negative self-image that can lead to vulnerability, self-neglect, and unsafe sex practices. Mania, due either to bipolar disorder, HIV-related infections, or use of prescribed or illicit drugs, can result in hypersexuality, poor impulse control, and impaired judgment. A further complication is the occurrence of HIV-associated neurocognitive disorders (HAND), including HIV-associated dementia (HAD). Cognitive impairment can lead to poor judgment in sexual partner choice, unsafe sex, and disinhibition. Lastly, HIV infection and AIDS also are risk factors for suicide; the rate of suicide has been shown to be higher in persons with HIV.

The high prevalence of psychiatric conditions in persons with HIV infection has resulted in closer clinical collaboration among primary care physicians, infectious disease specialists, and psychiatrists. While there are psychiatric disorders linked directly and indirectly to risk behaviors, HIV infection, or AIDS, people with HIV may have no psychiatric disorder or they may have any disorder described in the *DSM-5*.

Alternatively, psychiatric disorders may be the first and, at times, the only manifestation of HIV infection. Early diagnosis of HIV can lead to the timely introduction of treatment with appropriate HIV medical care and ART and prevent the establishment of independent CNS reservoirs for HIV. The immediate introduction of ART within 72 hours after HIV exposure may entirely prevent HIV infection as well as the establishment of independent CNS reservoirs for HIV. Early neuropsychiatric disorders can be a reaction to awareness of a diagnosis of HIV infection. Alternatively, psychopathology can be related to intrinsic involvement of the brain with HIV or opportunistic infections such as toxoplasmosis or cryptococcosis in persons who lack access to care or are nonadherent to care. In addition, antiretroviral therapies, treatments for opportunistic infections, and treatment for multimorbid illnesses, such as with chemotherapy for cancer, can have CNS side effects, including psychiatric symptoms.

In addition to the role of psychiatric disorders in the transmission of HIV, psychiatric factors also play a major role in the suffering endured by patients, their partners, families, and caregivers. If psychiatric disorders go untreated, persons with HIV may have difficulty attending appointments and adhering to the complex medical treatments involved with care. Physicians and clinicians in every specialty may find themselves frustrated that patients are not adhering to appointments and are getting ill in the same ways they did in the beginning of the pandemic, when few or no treatments were available and mortality was high. Now that perinatal HIV transmission can be prevented by antiretroviral protocols, even obstetricians may find themselves stymied when pregnant women do not adhere to prenatal care and to antiretroviral treatment. There is an ample body of evidence that psychiatric treatment can decrease transmission, diminish suffering, improve adherence, and decrease morbidity and mortality.

Persons with HIV have a high prevalence of multimorbid complex and severe medical and psychiatric illnesses with psychosocial and public health implications and consequences. Despite remarkable advances in the care of persons with HIV that has transformed AIDS from a fatal infectious disease to a chronic manageable illness, the incidence of HIV in the United States has remained stable at about 50,000 new cases annually. Missed HIV clinic visits are independently associated with all-cause mortality in persons with HIV (Mugavero et al., 2014). Thus, communication, integration, and coordination of care are of special significance in order to improve adherence to risk reduction as well as medical care. Since HIV is associated with discrimination and stigma and also disproportionately affects vulnerable populations and magnifies health care disparities, providing compassionate, comprehensive, and coordinated care becomes even more significant.

THE HISTORY OF HIV/AIDS PSYCHIATRY

In 1981, previously healthy young men and women were being admitted with pneumonia and severe respiratory distress to the intensive care unit of our municipal academic medical center in New York City. They were dying of respiratory failure, and the reason for these deaths was not clear. At about the same time, Michael Gottlieb, an immunologist in an academic medical center in Los Angeles, California, began to investigate the reasons for the occurrence of *Pneumocystis carinii* pneumonia (PCP) in five previously healthy young men. On June 5, 1981, his report of these cases was published in the *Morbidity and Mortality Weekly Report* (CDC, 1981a). Gottlieb's first patients were also described as having cytomegalovirus and candida infections. As a result of the publication of this report, specialists in pulmonary medicine, internal medicine, and infectious disease in high-endemic area hospitals recognized that the young men and women were severely ill with this new disease and that, in addition to intensive medical treatment, some would benefit from psychiatric consultations to help them cope with this devastating illness.

In a more detailed article, published on December 10, 1981, in the *New England Journal of Medicine*, Gottlieb and colleagues (1981) linked an immune deficiency with this new cluster of infections. They presented evidence for an association of the illnesses PCP, candidiasis, and multiple viral infections and "a new acquired cellular immunodeficiency" with a decrease in CD4 T cells as a hallmark. Another article (Masur et al., 1981) described this "outbreak of community-acquired *Pneumocystis carinii* pneumonia" as a manifestation of an "immune deficiency." Over the next year, several other articles described the opportunistic infections and cancers that characterized this new syndrome of immune deficiency, including not only *Pneumocystis carinii* (subsequently designated as *Pneumocystis jeroveci*) pneumonia but also cytomegalovirus retinitis, CNS toxoplasmosis and lymphoma, progressive multifocal leukoencephalopathy, and disseminated Kaposi's sarcoma. Initially, the immune deficiency was thought to occur only in gay men (CDC, 1981b), but later in 1981 and in 1982 it became clear that this acquired immune deficiency syndrome, or AIDS, as it came to be called in 1982 (CDC, 1982a), was transmitted by exchange of blood or body fluids through sexual contact, including heterosexual contact (CDC, 1983), by sharing of needles or drug paraphernalia in intravenous drug use (CDC, 1982a), through transfusions of contaminated blood and blood products (CDC, 1982b), and through perinatal transmission (CDC, 1982c). When it became evident that this immune deficiency might itself have an infectious etiology and that it led to rapidly fatal complications, many staff members became fearful of the possibility of contagion. An "epidemic of fear" (Hunter, 1990) began to develop along with the AIDS epidemic. As a result, some persons with AIDS who were admitted to hospitals for medical care experienced difficulty getting their rooms cleaned, obtaining water or food, or even getting adequate medical attention.

At a municipal hospital in New York City in 1981, initial psychiatric consultations for persons with AIDS were requested for depression, withdrawal, confusion, and treatment refusal. One of the authors of this chapter (MAC) was the psychiatrist responding to these initial consultations. It was clear that the uncertainty about the etiology of the immune deficiency had resulted in palpable fear of contagion in staff. This fear was leading to distress and an increase in frequency of absences and requests for transfers away from the floors with the most AIDS admissions. These reactions in staff members seemed to heighten the sense of isolation and depression in patients.

In the early years of the epidemic, Many persons with AIDS were treated as lepers. Some found that they were shunned and ostracized. In some areas of the world, persons with AIDS were quarantined because of the irrational fears, discrimination, and stigma associated with this pandemic. Persons with AIDS were subjected to the agony of being rejected by family, friends, and communities. Some persons with AIDS lost their homes, some lost their jobs, and some children and adolescents were excluded from classrooms. In the early 1980s, a diagnosis of AIDS led to rejection by shelters for the homeless and by nursing homes, long-term care facilities, and facilities for the terminally ill. The attitudes of families, houses of worship, prison guards, employers, teachers, hospital staff, and funeral directors led to catastrophic stigma and discrimination. Persons with AIDS had difficulty finding support, obtaining healthcare, keeping a job, finding a home, and finding a chronic-care facility or even a place to die.

Although the AIDS epidemic was first described in the medical literature in 1981, it was not until 1983 that the first articles were published about the psychosocial or psychiatric aspects of AIDS. The first article, written by Holtz and colleagues (1983), was essentially a plea for attention to the psychosocial aspects of AIDS. They stated that "noticeably absent in the flurry of publications about the current epidemic of acquired immune deficiency syndrome (AIDS) is reference to the psychosocial impact of this devastating new syndrome." The authors deplored ostracism of persons with AIDS by both their families and their medical systems of care, and were the first to describe the profound withdrawal from human contact as the "sheet sign" observed when persons with AIDS hid under their sheet and completely covered their faces. The first psychiatrist to address these issues was Stuart E. Nichols (1983). In his article in *Psychosomatics*, Nichols described the need for compassion, support, and understanding to address the fear, depression, and alienation experienced by patients. He also made recommendations for use of psychotherapy and group therapy as well as antidepressant medications to help persons with AIDS cope with intense feelings about this new illness that was still of undetermined etiology. Nichols stated: "Since AIDS apparently is a new disease, there is no specific psychiatric literature to which one can refer for guidance. One must be willing to attempt to provide competent and compassionate care in an area with more questions than answers." The earliest articles published in the first decade of AIDS psychiatry, from 1983 to 1993, were primarily descriptive observations, case reports, case series, and documentation of prevalence of psychiatric diagnoses associated with AIDS. They were written by sensitive and compassionate clinicians, some of whom openly expressed their outrage at ostracism and rejection of persons with HIV and AIDS by not only the community at large but also the medical community. These clinicians also emphasized the need for compassion and for competent medical and psychiatric care. These early articles are summarized in Table 1.1.

In the 33 years (1983–2016) since HIV/AIDS psychiatry references first appeared in the medical literature, there have been many thousands of articles written, in addition to four textbooks (Cohen and Gorman, 2008; Cohen et al., 2010; Fernandez and Ruiz, 2006; Joska et al., 2014), other books (Treisman and Angelino, 2004), and chapters. Most of the articles reflect a growing body of research in the area as well as an evidence base for the practice of HIV psychiatry. Some of these articles provide evidence for the need for a comprehensive integrated biopsychosocial approach to the care of persons with HIV and AIDS.

HIV PSYCHIATRY: PARADOX AND PARADIGM

PARADOX

The HIV pandemic presents us with many paradoxes. One of the most tragic paradoxes of HIV is the disparity in access to care resulting from racial, political, and economic factors throughout the world. Another tragic paradox is the disparity in access to care among persons with psychiatric illness. Age, intelligence, and level of education do not necessarily correlate with ability to adhere to risk reduction, safe sexual and drug use behaviors, and medical care (Cochran and Mays, 1990; De Buono et al., 1990; MacDonald et al., 1990; Reinisch and Beasley, 1990). At every age, from adolescents, who say "I can use a condom, I just don't" (Mustanski et al., 2006), to the elderly (Goodkin et al., 2003; Karpiak et al., 2006; Stoff, 2004), who may not feel a need for barrier contraception to prevent pregnancy and whose physicians may be uncomfortable discussing sexual health and activities, there are high rates of HIV infection.

Discrimination against persons with AIDS has been described as a new form of discrimination called "AIDSism" (Cohen, 1989). AIDSism results from a multiplicity of prejudicial and discriminatory factors. It is built on a foundation of racism, homophobia, ageism, misogyny, and discomfort with mental and medical illness, poverty, sexuality, infection, and fear of contagion and death in many communities throughout the world, as well as in the United States. Discrimination and stigma were recognized early in the HIV/AIDS psychiatry literature as contributing to psychological distress (Blendon and Donelan, 1988; Chesney and Smith, 1992; Cohen, 1989; Cohen et al., 2002; Cohen and Weisman, 1986; Deuchar, 1984; Fullilove, 1989; Holland and Tross, 1985; Holtz et al., 1983; Nichols, 1983, 1984) and have been explored subsequently following the introduction of efficacious ART (Brown et al., 2003; Crowley et al., 2015; Herek et al., 2002; Kaplan et al., 2005; Mahajan et al., 2008; Parker and Aggleton, 2003).

Early in the epidemic, many physicians surveyed had negative attitudes toward persons with HIV and AIDS (Kelly et al., 1987; Thompson, 1987; Wormser and Joline, 1989). Although the medical profession has made great strides against discrimination and stigma and most physicians are "accustomed to caring for HIV-infected patients with

Table 1.1. EARLY LITERATURE OF AIDS PSYCHIATRY*

YEAR	ISSUES ADDRESSED, COMMENTS
1983	Psychosocial impact of AIDS—ostracism, the "sheet sign," and the need for psychiatric literature about AIDS (Holtz et al.)
1983	Psychiatric aspects of AIDS—need for psychiatric consultations and for group therapy; first article by a psychiatrist about AIDS psychiatry (Nichols)
1984	Psychiatric implications of AIDS—the first book about AIDS psychiatry (Nichols and Ostrow)
1984	Psychosocial aspects of AIDS—the first description of the biopsychosocial approach applied in the general care setting by Cohen (Deuchar)
1984a	AIDS anxiety in the "worried well" (Forstein)
1984b	Psychosocial impact of AIDS (Forstein)
1984	Case reports and treatment recommendations for persons with AIDS seen in psychiatric consultation (Barbuto)
1984	Psychiatric complications of AIDS (Nurnberg et al.)
1984	Neuropsychiatric complications of AIDS (Hoffman)
1984	Cryptococcal meningitis presenting as mania in AIDS (Thienhaus and Khosla)
1984	Description of a support group for persons with AIDS (Nichols)
1984	Psychiatric problems in patients with AIDS at New York Hospital (Perry and Tross)
1985	Findings in 13 of 40 persons with AIDS seen in psychiatric consultation (Dilley et al.)
1985	Description of psychiatric and psychosocial aspects of AIDS (Holland and Tross)
1986	A biopsychosocial approach to AIDS (Cohen and Weisman)
1986	Neuropsychiatric aspects of AIDS (Price and Forejt)
1987	Psychiatric aspects of AIDS (Faulstich)
1987	Dementia as the presenting or sole manifestation of HIV infection (Navia and Price)
1987	Psychiatric aspects of AIDS: a biopsychosocial approach—comprehensive chapter (Cohen)
1987	Stigmatization of AIDS patients by physicians (Kelly et al.)
1988	Discrimination against people with AIDS (Blendon and Donelan)
1988	First article on high prevalence of suicide among persons with AIDS (Marzuk et al.)
1989	AIDSism, a new form of discrimination (Cohen)
1989	Anxiety and stigmatizing aspects of HIV infection (Fullilove)
1990	Firesetting and HIV-associated dementia (Cohen et al.)
1990	Suicidality and HIV testing (Perry et al.)
1992	A biopsychosocial approach to the HIV epidemic (Cohen)
1992	Suicidality and HIV status (McKegney and O'Dowd)
1993	Manic syndrome early and late in the course of HIV (Lyketsos et al.)

*Listed here are descriptions of psychosocial and psychiatric aspects of AIDS with emphasis on discrimination. This table contains a sample of articles, chapters, and books published in the first decade of AIDS psychiatry (1983–1993).

concern and compassion" (Gottlieb, 2001), society as a whole has not kept up. In June 2006, a full quarter-century since the epidemic was first described, a child with AIDS was excluded from attending a New York sleep-away camp until his parents threatened legal action. In April 2012, a plastic surgeon refused to remove a facial lesion from a woman with HIV, citing his fear of infection. In May 2014, an allergist refused to test or treat a man with HIV. AIDS stigma and AIDSism have implications not only for the health and well-being of individuals who experience them but also for public health.

Stigma and AIDSism present a barrier to getting tested for HIV, obtaining test results, disclosing serostatus to intimate partners, obtaining optimal medical care in a timely manner, and engaging in safer sex practices and safer injection drug use. Despite availability of HIV prevention by means of barrier contraception as well as PrEP and PEP, many persons continue to engage in risky sexual behaviors.

Despite availability of competent medical care and ART, the majority of persons in treatment for HIV do not attain viral suppression; in the United States, only 30% of persons living with HIV have attained viral suppression, given those not diagnosed and those not engaged in care. While throughout the world the incidence of HIV has dropped dramatically, attributable to the scale-up of ART since 2000, in the United States the rate of new infections has remained relatively stable, at about 50,000 per year.

The process of care for persons with AIDS at the end of life is also paradoxical, in that there is a clear need for provision of care along a continuum that includes both palliative and curative care. This concept has been proposed but appears hard to implement. The need to overcome the "false dichotomy of curative vs. palliative care for late-stage AIDS" has been suggested (Selwyn and Forstein, 2003). From risk behavior to exposure, from infection to course of illness, and from progression of illness to end of life, we need to recognize, clarify, and make the changes necessary to close the gaps in care and address the treatment cascade, to maintain viral suppression and improve the lives of persons living with HIV and AIDS.

PARADIGM

Psychosomatic medicine psychiatrists who specialize in HIV psychiatry, as well as general psychiatrists and other mental health clinicians, are in a unique position to work with primary HIV clinicians, infectious disease specialists, cardiologists, neurologists, surgeons, and other physicians and health professionals to combat HIV stigma and AIDSism. For psychiatrists who subspecialize in psychosomatic medicine, AIDS and other manifestations of HIV infection may be thought of as a paradigm of a medical illness. AIDS is an illness similar to the other complex and severe medical illnesses that define the subspecialty. Psychosomatic medicine (formerly consultation-liaison psychiatry), the psychiatric care of persons with complex and severe medical illness, was designated a subspecialty of psychiatry in 2003. AIDS is a paradigm of psychosomatic medicine because it has elements of nearly every illness described in the *American Psychiatric Publishing Textbook of Psychosomatic Medicine* (Levenson, 2011). Persons with HIV and AIDS are also vulnerable to other multimorbid complex and severe medical illnesses, including those related and unrelated to HIV infection. The concept of AIDS as a paradigm of the psychiatric care of persons with medical illness (psychosomatic medicine) is illustrated in Figure 1.1.

Lipowski (1967) provided a classification of commonly encountered problems in psychosomatic medicine. Querques and Stern (2004) suggested a modification of Lipowski's original classification. With minor modifications, Lipowski's

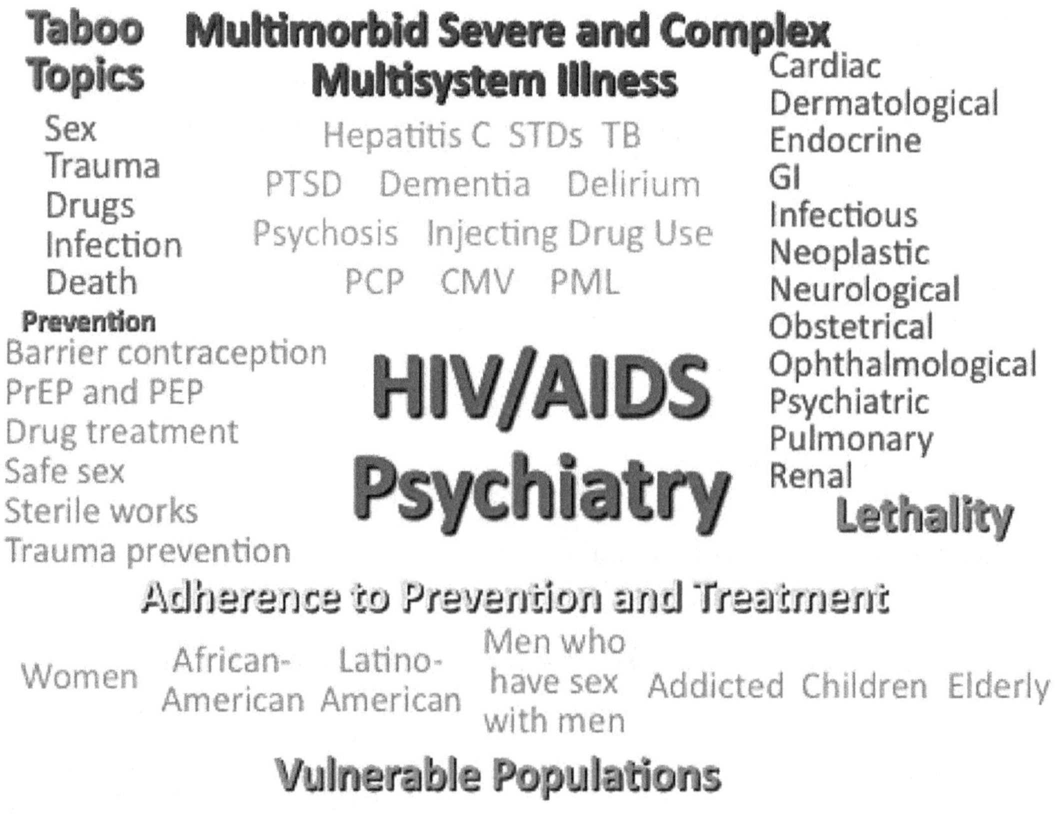

Figure 1.1 HIV/AIDS psychiatry: a paradigm of psychosomatic medicine. CMV, cytomegalovirus; GI, gastrointestinal; PCP, phencyclidine; PEP, post-exposure prophylaxis; PML, progressive multifocal leukoencephalopathy; PrEP, pre-exposure prophylaxis; PTSD, posttraumatic stress disorder; STDs, sexually transmitted diseases; TB, tuberculosis.

classification remains relevant to HIV/AIDS psychiatric care. The five commonly encountered problems in HIV psychiatry include psychiatric presentation of medical illness, psychiatric complications of medical illnesses or treatments, psychological response to medical illness or treatments, medical presentation of psychiatric illness or treatments, and comorbid medical and psychiatric illness. These are illustrated in the following vignettes.

ILLUSTRATIVE CASE VIGNETTES

Case Vignette 1.1: Inpatient Medical Unit Psychiatric Consultation: Psychiatric Presentation of Medical Illness

Ms. A is a 62-year-old retired librarian, single and living alone, admitted with fever, abnormal chest x-ray, and late-stage AIDS (diagnosed only 1 month earlier), who was referred for psychiatric consultation during her second admission when she reported new-onset visual hallucinations. One month earlier, Ms. A had been admitted for evaluation of pain on swallowing (odynophagia), weakness, wasting, and weight loss. She was found to have esophageal candidiasis, a CD4 of 2, and a viral load of >750,000. Ms. A was treated for candida and started on antiretrovirals shortly after her discharge. On her second admission she reported seeing frightening faces. Her fever and abnormal chest x-ray were due to *Mycobacterium avium* pneumonia.

Ms. A had a psychiatric presentation of a medical illness, visual hallucinations due to cytomegalovirus retinitis, and encephalitis. Her visual hallucinations resolved when she was treated with gancyclovir.

Case Vignette 1.2: Outpatient HIV Clinic Psychiatric Consultation: Psychiatric Complication of Medical Illness or Treatment

Ms. B is a 52-year-old unemployed former administrative assistant with HIV and a CD4 of 317. She also had ulcerative colitis, osteoarthritis, and hypertension. She presented with depression and suicidal ideation after being started on efavirenz, a non-nucleoside reverse transcriptase inhibitor. Ms. B was found to have PTSD due to early childhood trauma, and major depressive disorder, recurrent. She responded well to psychotherapy, antidepressants, and discontinuation of efavirenz as well as her other antiretroviral medications. She has been adherent to psychiatric and medical care and understands that she may need to resume ART.

Ms. B had a psychiatric complication of her medical treatment, developing neuropsychiatric side effects secondary to efavirenz, with an improvement of symptomatology when efavirenz was discontinued and depression and PTSD were treated.

Case Vignette 1.3: Outpatient HIV Clinic Psychiatric Consultation: Psychological Response to Medical Illness

Ms. C is a 31-year-old unemployed teacher's assistant with HIV and a CD4 of 1,024 who presented with depression and anxiety. Ms. C felt isolated and alone because she was unable to disclose her diagnosis. She withdrew from friends, did not tell family members, and feared being seen attending the HIV clinic. Ms. C felt that she would never again be able to date anyone because she feared rejection if she disclosed her HIV serostatus. In psychotherapy, she was able to work through her fears of rejection and to some extent was able to come to terms with the embarrassment about her diagnosis in psychotherapy. Ms. C returned to work and responded to suggestions to join an HIV-positive social group.

Ms. C had a psychological response to medical illness related to the stigma of HIV infection.

Case Vignette 1.4: Inpatient General Care Psychiatric Consultation: Medical Presentation of Psychiatric Illness

Mr. D is a 29-year-old unemployed actor and former Walt Disney World Donald Duck character who was admitted to medicine unit of a general hospital with weight loss, cough, night sweats, and fever and gave a history of PCP and AIDS. A psychiatric consultation was requested when his history of PCP and AIDS could not be verified and he refused HIV testing. He was living in New York City–supported housing for persons with AIDS and had fabricated his history to pursue his acting career in New York and obtain both housing and entitlements.

Mr. D was malingering with AIDS in order to obtain entitlements and housing to further his acting career by establishing a home and support in New York City (Cohen, 1992).

Case Vignette 1.5: Outpatient HIV Clinic Psychiatric Consultation: Multimorbid Medical and Psychiatric Illness

Mr. E is a 58-year-old disabled lawyer with chronic obstructive pulmonary disease (oxygen-dependent), rheumatic heart disease, HCV, and HIV (CD4 count of 1,384 and undetectable viral load) who was referred for depression with suicidal ideation since his diagnosis of HIV infection. Mr. E was found to have major depressive disorder, recurrent, and a history of opioid dependence in full, sustained remission on agonist therapy for 30 years. He responded well to long-term psychodynamic psychotherapy and antidepressants but became intermittently depressed and suicidal until specific goals were established and family members were involved in his care.

Mr. E had multimorbid medical and psychiatric illness that responded to psychiatric care including psychodynamic and meaning-centered psychotherapy, family therapy, and antidepressants.

THE MULTIPLE DISPARITIES OF HIV AND AIDS

RACIAL, ETHNIC, AND SOCIOECONOMIC DISPARITIES

Racial, ethnic, and socioeconomic disparities have been observed and documented in all aspects of the United States healthcare system (Agency for Healthcare Research and Quality, 2005a). The overall HIV death rate of African Americans was found to be 10.95 times higher than that of whites (Agency for Healthcare Research and Quality, 2005b), and racial disparities have been shown to contribute to increased HIV incidence and inadequate access to medical and psychiatric care (CDC, 2006a). U.S. correctional facilities and urban drug epicenters may be seen as microcosms of discrimination. Correctional facilities may also be instrumental in perpetuating the HIV epidemic both inside and outside of prison walls (Blankenship et al., 2005; CDC, 2006b; Fullilove, 2011; Golembeski and Fullilove, 2005; Hammett et al., 2002).

It would be difficult to calculate the true impact of these disparities on persons with HIV. In addition to the incalculable distress, suffering, and anguish (Cohen et al., 2002), persons with HIV/AIDS have multimorbid medical and psychiatric illnesses, all of which are also found among those who experience disparities in care (Cohen, 1996; Cohen et al., 1991; Kolb et al., 2006).

PSYCHIATRIC DISPARITIES

Psychiatric factors take on new relevance and meaning as we near the end of the fourth decade of the HIV pandemic. In a multisite study ($n = 1,061$), Blank and colleagues (2014) sought to highlight the HIV prevalence and associated risk factors among persons receiving care in various psychiatric treatment settings. After administering rapid HIV testing to this patient population, their results showed that the rate of HIV infection was four times the base rate for the general public in Baltimore and Philadelphia. Although the majority of patients (76%) were already aware of their HIV diagnosis, the new diagnoses discovered through screening patients in a mental health setting likely reflect a failure in the public and mental health care system. This study showed that patients with more severe symptoms of mental illness were at higher risk for being HIV-infected, and also that issues such as homelessness were linked to a higher prevalence of HIV.

Risk factors for infection in patients with severe mental illness are similar to risk factors in the general population (Blank et al., 2014). Untreated psychiatric disorders can be exacerbated by HIV stigma to make persons with HIV and AIDS especially vulnerable to suicide (Alfonso and Cohen, 1997; Marzuk et al., 1988; McKegney and O'Dowd, 1992; Perry et al., 1990). Psychiatric treatment with individual (Cohen, 1987; Cohen and Alfonso, 1998, 2004; Cohen and Weisman, 1986), group (Alfonso and Cohen, 1997), and family therapy can alleviate suffering, improve adherence (Gwadz et al., 2015; Pyne et al., 2011), and prevent suicide.

ISSUES OF PREVENTION AND ADHERENCE

Since the development of effective ART, the life expectancy of persons with HIV has increased, and for persons with access and adherence to care, the incidence of the opportunistic infections and cancers previously associated with AIDS has decreased (Huang et al., 2006). However, persons with untreated psychiatric disorders may lack access to care because severe mental illness is associated with nonadherence to care. Persons with severe mental illness may have difficulty getting to medical appointments, taking medications regularly, or obtaining laboratory tests and follow-up care. As a result, persons with HIV and untreated psychiatric disorders may present with AIDS-related illnesses not usually encountered in countries with access to care since the introduction of effective ART in 1996.

Harm reduction is an innovative and significant approach to care that has become an increasingly popular treatment paradigm to target patient populations at risk for HIV infection. Harm reduction is rooted in the goal of decreasing harm to the individual and self without requiring abstinence from the unwanted behavior. Although this multidisciplinary approach originated in prevention of addiction, the harm reduction model has been applied to various high-risk or unwanted behaviors over time. The harm reduction approach to HIV care gained momentum in the early to mid-1980s in response to the crisis of HIV and AIDS, the main focus being on decreasing transmission that occurred through intravenous drug use. When considering sexual transmission, the number one factor in sexual risk reduction is the knowledge of HIV status (Marlatt et al., 2012). Worldwide, 54% of persons with HIV (19 million of the 36.7 million persons with HIV) are unaware of their serostatus (UNAIDS, 2016). Therefore, harm reduction programs that encourage behavioral changes to reduce risk of sexual transmission are crucial, particularly when a large proportion of the population may not be aware of their HIV status. Behavioral change achieved over the past 10 years accounts for a very significant increase in awareness worldwide, with the number of persons HIV unaware of their serostatus decreasing from 90% (Kamya et al., 2007) to 54% (UNAIDS, 2014).

Prevention strategies that have shown promise include those that target specific sexual acts (e.g., decreasing sex acts that involve an exchange of bodily fluids), address sexual partner concerns (e.g., negotiating condom use or decreasing number of overall partners), and address intrapersonal and situational antecedents of risky sexual behaviors (e.g., intimate partner violence) (Marlatt et al., 2012). Although some critics state that harm reduction enables high-risk behavior, research has shown that harm reduction programs do not undermine treatment efforts or exacerbate high-risk behavior such as drug use. In fact, the World Health Organization (WHO) and the United Nations (UNAIDS) support harm reduction as best practice and crucial for decreasing HIV infection, particularly for persons who inject drugs (WHO, UNODC, UNAIDS, 2013). The use of PrEP and PEP represent a very important harm reduction approach when used in conjunction with counseling and barrier contraception.

BIOMEDICAL PREVENTION WITH PRE- AND POST-EXPOSURE PROPHYLAXIS

Strategies have been developed for communication to best address prevention of HIV transmission, improvement of adherence to risk reduction and medical care, addressing healthcare disparities, and amelioration of stigma. These strategies include the National HIV/AIDS Strategy: Updated to 2020 (White House Office of National AIDS Policy, 2015), the 2015 Blueprint to Eliminate AIDS in New York State (New York State Department of Health, 2015), and the World Health Organization Guidelines (WHO, 2016b). Key prevention strategies for all patients are presented in Table 1.2.

Persons who are thought to be the most substantially vulnerable to HIV infection include HIV-negative members of serodiscordant couples and HIV-negative persons who inject drugs. An HIV-negative member of a serodiscordant couple may take PrEP to prevent infection. PrEP and PEP with antiretroviral medications such as tenofovir together with emtricitabine in combination with safe sex, barrier contraception, and safe injecting drug practices can prevent HIV transmission in serodiscordant couples. The evidence for the effective use of PrEP and PEP in serodiscordant couples is strong (Beaten et al., 2012; Cohen et al., 2011; Grant et al., 2010; White House Office of National AIDS Strategy, 2015; Thigpen et al., 2012).

PrEP may also be an effective measure in persons with HIV who inject drugs. In 2014 and 2015, both the Centers for Disease Control and Prevention and WHO included persons who inject drugs in their endorsement of PrEP as an HIV prevention method. Much of the evidence for the efficacy of PrEP in injecting drug users was derived from the Bangkok Tenofovir Study, which showed a 48.9% reduction in HIV infections (Choopanya et al., 2013). Ongoing PrEP demonstration projects have included persons who inject drugs in their participant pool, but data concerning overall awareness, uptake, and engagement in persons who inject drugs are

Table 1.2. KEY HIV PREVENTION STRATEGIES FOR ALL PSYCHIATRIC PATIENTS

- Routine HIV testing is now recommended for all persons from 13 to 64 years of age and for persons of any age with risk behaviors (CDC, 2015)
- Consider encouraging and offering routine HIV testing as part of initial comprehensive psychiatric assessment (Smith et al., 2014)
- Provide education for HIV prevention and make condoms available in psychiatric inpatient and outpatient facilities
- Assess for risk behaviors and encourage barrier contraception, treatment for substance use disorders, and safe injecting drug use
- Prevention or diminution of HIV risk behaviors can prevent transmission
- Treatment of substance use and other psychiatric disorders can prevent HIV transmission
- Early treatment with antiretrovirals, within the first 72 hours after exposure to HIV, can prevent both HIV infection and development of independent reservoirs for HIV in the brain (Heaton et al., 2011)
- Initiation of antiretroviral therapy in early asymptomatic HIV infection, regardless of CD4 count, improves outcomes and can prevent development of independent CNS reservoirs for HIV (CDC, 2016; Heaton et al., 2011)

Table 1.3 SUMMARY OF RECOMMENDATIONS FOR PREVENTION AND PRE- AND POST-EXPOSURE PROPHYLAXIS

- Persons with risk behaviors for sexual transmission can be encouraged to take PrEP alone or in combination with barrier contraception.
- Persons with HIV who inject drugs can take PrEP in combination with barrier contraception and safe injecting practices
- Following an unanticipated, unplanned or forced unsafe sexual encounter, any person can be encouraged to take tenofovir and emtricitabine for PEP after unsafe sex (Smith et al., 2014)
- PEP is no longer for occupational exposure to HIV only

PEP, post-exposure prophylaxis; PrEP, pre-exposure prophylaxis.

limited. A summary of recommendations for prevention and pre- and post-exposure prophylaxis is provided in Table 1.3. With adequate support, empowerment, and education, people are more likely to make more positive health choices. See Chapter 31 for a more detailed discussion of PrEP and PEP.

In addition, among persons who are adherent to care, there has been an increase in the prevalence of endocrine, pulmonary, cardiac, gastrointestinal, renal, and metabolic disorders, some of which may be multimorbid and unrelated to HIV, while others may be related to HIV or to its treatments. Persons with HIV who are adherent to care and are virally suppressed are living longer, and aging accounts, in part, for the high prevalence of medical multimorbidities. The life expectancy of persons with HIV who have access to care and are treated with ART is similar to that of the general population (Manfredi, 2004a, 2004b).

Morbidity and mortality due to non-AIDS-related events has surpassed that due to AIDS-related events among HIV-infected persons in developed countries (Marin et al., 2009; May et al., 2014; Samji et al., 2013). The majority of non-AIDS-defining deaths are due to liver disease, non-AIDS-defining malignancies, cardiovascular disease, and non-AIDS defining infections (Antiretroviral Therapy Cohort Collaboration, 2010; Data Collection on Adverse Events of Anti-HIV Drugs [D:A:D] Study Group, 2010; Marin et al., 2009; Neuhaus et al., 2010; Samji et al., 2013). Other non-AIDS-related causes of death include renal disease, respiratory disease, suicide, homicide, drug overdose, and accidents. A number of non-AIDS-related multimorbidities are more common among HIV-infected persons and occur at a younger age than in the general population, including cardiovascular disease, diabetes mellitus, renal disease, and bone fractures, and multimorbidity is more common (Guaraldi et al., 2011).

Sackoff and colleagues (2006) and Aberg (2006) have recommended a paradigm shift in the care of persons with AIDS from a primary focus on HIV prevention and care to a more comprehensive approach to medical and mental health. The complexity and severity of the multiple medical and psychiatric illnesses prevalent in persons with HIV and AIDS are important in the psychiatric assessment and substantiate the need for a comprehensive and compassionate biopsychosocial approach that takes into account the full range of medical, psychiatric, social, and cultural factors and their synergistic implications relevant to patient care (Cohen, 1987, 1992; Cohen et al., 2010; Cohen and Gorman, 2008; Cohen and Weisman, 1986, 1988; Deuchar, 1984).

AN INTEGRATED BIOPSYCHOSOCIAL APPROACH TO HIV AND AIDS

In the summer of 1981, one of the authors of this chapter (MAC) began to respond to her first psychiatric consultations requested for persons with AIDS. She described finding her AIDS patients' rooms inadequately cleaned, often with very sticky floors that made her shoes stick to them when entering (Cohen, 2008; Cohen and Gorman, 2008). Many patients were young, severely cachectic, and withdrawn, and some had their sheets drawn over their heads.

The "sticky-floor syndrome" joined the "sheet sign" as one of the early unique responses to the AIDS pandemic, with frequent spills as a result. It was clear that only a hospital-wide, multidisciplinary program and education for every level of staff on all shifts would improve the care of persons with AIDS, diminish stigma and discrimination, and help to alleviate fear, anxiety, and stigma in caregivers. In 1983, the infectious disease director, a social worker, and Dr. Mary Ann Cohen developed a multidisciplinary AIDS program at the hospital to provide coordinated, integrated, and comprehensive care for persons with AIDS and to provide education for hospital staff as well as medical students and their faculty. This program was the first of its kind to be described in the literature as a response to the epidemic (Cohen and Weisman, 1986; Deuchar, 1984). Deuchar, a British medical student on an elective in HIV psychiatry on the consultation-liaison psychiatry service in 1983, wrote an article about the psychosocial aspects of AIDS in New York City. He described this multidisciplinary program as a means of providing coordination of care and communication among the multiple subspecialties and disciplines involved in the care of persons with AIDS (Deuchar, 1984). He characterized the program as a "comprehensive program" with a "bio-psycho-social approach" that "maintains a view that each individual is a member of a family and community and deserves a coordinated approach to medical care and treatment with dignity." He wrote: "The programme includes maintenance of a multidisciplinary treatment team, provision of ongoing psychological support for patients and families, and education and support for hospital staff. As such, it is clearly a good example of consultation-liaison psychiatry." Since Deucher's description, an integrated biopsychosocial approach to the care of persons with HIV and AIDS has proved to improve treatment entry, engagement, retention, and adherence (Gwadz et al., 2015; Pyne et al. 2011; Thompson et al., 2012) and decrease morbidity and mortality (Mugavero et al., 2014).

Psychiatrists make ideal HIV educators. General psychiatrists who work in the areas of inpatient and outpatient psychiatry settings, private offices, addiction psychiatry, geriatric psychiatry, child and adolescent psychiatry, correctional facilities, and long-term care facilities are all in a prime position to provide education, help prevent transmission of HIV, suggest or provide condoms and information about safe sex, and suggest or offer HIV testing to lead toward early diagnosis and treatment. Psychiatrists take detailed sexual and drug histories and work with patients to help them change behaviors. The significance of taking a detailed sexual history was especially evident in a population-based study of men in New York City. This study revealed discordance between sexual behavior and self-reported sexual identity; nearly 10% of straight-identified men reported at least one sexual encounter with another man in the previous year (Pathela et al., 2006). Most psychiatrists form long-term, ongoing relationships with their patients and work with patients toward achieving gratification in long-term, intimate-partner relationships. All of these characteristics can be of major importance in primary prevention as well as early diagnosis and treatment of HIV infection.

There are some overlapping skill sets that mental health professionals and other HIV clinicians share, and there are therapeutic modalities that integrated psychiatrists can both utilize and teach to other clinicians in HIV clinics. Motivational interviewing (MI) was developed in the early 1980s as a counseling strategy to promote behavioral change in patients abusing alcohol or substances. It is a patient-centered approach with the goal of promoting intrinsic motivation for change and exploring ambivalence. While an estimated 50–70% of HIV patients take their antiretroviral medications as prescribed (Krummenacher et al., 2011), MI has been explored as a possible tool to further increase adherence as well as decrease high-risk HIV behaviors. HIV care professionals have been found to unknowingly utilize MI skills more often than not when counseling patients with high-risk behaviors for HIV transmission (Flickinger et al., 2013). Therefore, it is a reasonable and promising intervention for psychiatrists and other HIV clinicians to consider using that has shown efficacy in reducing risky sex and substance-using behaviors (Parsons et al., 2013), but it requires further study in its utility as a strategy to increase antiretroviral medication adherence (Hill and Kavookjian, 2012).

Psychosomatic medicine psychiatrists and HIV psychiatrists are in a unique position to provide psychiatric care for persons with HIV, from the time of infection to the time of death and its aftermath, with provision of support for partners and families. Most HIV psychiatrists rarely have the chance to take care of their patients until they are they are diagnosed with HIV. However, Ruiz (2000) provided a detailed description of his care of a patient that begins prior to the diagnosis of HIV and continues throughout the course of illness and progression to end-stage AIDS and the end of his life. In his article, Ruiz also described his attendance at the memorial service and his support of the patient's family during their time of loss and grief. HIV psychiatrists can provide colocated psychiatric services, education and support for trainees, and support and leadership for the multidisciplinary teams of physicians, nurses, social workers, other health professionals, and staff. It is especially gratifying to work as part of a dedicated and compassionate team of clinicians who are providing comprehensive care for persons with HIV and AIDS. There is growing evidence that integrating HIV and mental health services leads to fewer emotional and psychological difficulties, a decrease in alcohol and substance use, and an increased likelihood of receiving antiretrovirals and adequate psychotropics, when needed (Whetten et al., 2006; Winiarski et al., 2005). When persons with HIV have delayed, declined, or discontinued ART, behavioral interventions can improve medical outcomes (Gwadz et al., 2015) and decrease morbidity and mortality (Mugavero et al., 2014). Furthermore, advances such as rapid HIV testing hold great promise for integrating routine HIV testing into mental health services in a variety of different clinical settings (Blank et al., 2014).

CONCLUSIONS

Comprehensive, coordinated care by a multidisciplinary team including HIV psychiatrists can provide an integrated approach that is supportive to patients, families, and clinicians. Integrated care can lead to full viral suppression and diminishes both suffering and discrimination (Crowley et al., 2015; Gwadz et al., 2015; Mugavero et al., 2014; Pyne et al., 2011; Thompson et al., 2012). Integrated care has public health implications and diminishes HIV transmission (Satcher et al., 2015). Psychiatric interventions are valuable in every phase of infection, from identification of risk behaviors to anticipation about HIV testing; from exposure and initial infection to confirmation with a positive HIV antibody test; from entry into systems of care engagement and retention in care and adherence to an antiretroviral regimen; from being healthy and seropositive to the onset of first HIV-related or unrelated illness; from severe illness to late stage and death. AIDSism, stigma, discrimination, criminalization, and fear, in conjunction with denial and lack of awareness, complicate and perpetuate the HIV pandemic. The creation of supportive, nurturing, nonjudgmental, integrated healthcare environments can help combat AIDSism and provide comprehensive and compassionate care (Cohen, 1996). HIV psychiatrists and other mental health professionals need to be integrated closely into clinical, academic, and research aspects of HIV prevention and treatment. In order for persons with HIV to live more comfortable lives, with preservation of independence and dignity, it is important to establish special nurturing, supportive, and loving healthcare environments. Such environments can enable persons with HIV, their loved ones, and caregivers to meet the challenges of HIV with optimism and dignity (Cohen and Alfonso, 2004). Such environments may also result in the concept of HIV/AIDS as the "great magnifier of maladies" receding into history.

REFERENCES

Aberg JA (2006). The changing face of HIV care: common things really are common. *Ann Intern Med* 145:463–465.

Agency for Healthcare Research and Quality (2015). National Healthcare Quality and Disparities Report and 5th anniversary update on the National Quality Strategy, 2015. http://www.ahrq.gov/research/findings/nhqrdr/nhqdr15/index.html. Accessed December 16, 2016.

Alfonso CA, Cohen MA (1997). The role of group psychotherapy in the care of persons with AIDS. *J Am Acad Psychoanal* 25:623–638.

American Psychiatric Association (2013). *Diagnostic and Statistical Manual of Mental Disorders*. 5th ed. (DSM-5). Washington, DC: American Psychiatric Association.

Antiretroviral Therapy Cohort Collaboration (2010). Causes of death in HIV-1-infected patients treated with antiretroviral therapy 1996–2006: collaborative analysis of 13 HIV cohort studies. *Clin Infect Dis* 50:1387–1396.

Baeten JM, Donnell D, Ndase P, et al. (2012). Antiretroviral prophylaxis for HIV prevention in heterosexual men and women. *N Engl J Med* 367:399–410.

Barbuto J (1984). Psychiatric care of seriously ill patients with acquired immune deficiency syndrome. In SE Nichols, DG Ostrow (eds.), *Psychiatric Implications of Acquired Immune Deficiency Syndrome*. Washington, DC: American Psychiatric Press.

Bétené A, Dooko C, De Wit S, et al.; INSIGHT SMART; ESPRIT Study Groups (2014). Interleukin-6, high-sensitivity C-reactive protein, and the development of type 2 diabetes among HIV-positive patients taking antiretroviral therapy. *J Acquir Immune Defic Syndr* 67:538–546.

Beyrer C, Strathdee SA (2015). Threading the needle how to stop the HIV outbreak in rural Indiana. *N Engl J Med* 373:397–399.

Blank MB, Himelhoch SS, Balaji AB, et al. (2014). A multisite study of the prevalence of HIV with rapid testing in mental health settings. *Am J Public Health* 104:2377–2384.

Blank MB, Mandell DS, Aiken L, Hadley TR. (2002). Co-occurrence of HIV and serious mental illness among Medicaid recipients. *Psychiatr Serv* 53:868–873.

Blankenship KM, Smoyer AB, Bray SJ, Mattocks K (2005). Black–white disparities in HIV/AIDS: the role of drug policy in the corrections system. *J Health Care Poor Underserved* 16:140–156.

Blendon RJ, Donelan K (1988). Discrimination against people with AIDS: the public's perspective. *N Engl J Med* 319:1022–1026.

Boarts M, Sledjeski M, Bogart L, Delahanty D (2006). The differential impact of PTSD and depression on HIV disease markers and adherence to HAART among people living with HIV. *AIDS Behav* 10:253–261.

Bradley H, Hall HI, Wolitski RJ, et al. (2014). Vital signs: HIV diagnosis, care, and treatment among persons living with HIV—United States, 2011. *MMWR Morb Mortal Wkly Rep* 63:1113–1117.

Brown L, Macintyre K, Trujillo L (2003). Interventions to reduce HIV/AIDS stigma: what have we learned? *AIDS Educ Prev* 15:49–69.

Center for HIV Law and Policy (2010). *Ending and Defending Against HIV Criminalization: State and Federal Laws and Prosecutions*, Vol.1, 2nd ed. (updated May 2015). http://www.hivlawandpolicy.org/resources/ending-and-defending-against-hiv-criminalization-state-and-federal-laws-and-prosecutions Accessed June 11, 2016.

Centers for Disease Control and Prevention (CDC) (1981a). *Pneumocystis* pneumonia—Los Angeles. *MMWR Morb Mortal Wkly Rep* 30:250–252.

Centers for Disease Control and Prevention (CDC) (1981b). Kaposi's sarcoma and *Pneumocystis* pneumonia among homosexual men—New York City and California. *MMWR Morb Mortal Wkly Rep* 30:305–308.

Centers for Disease Control and Prevention (CDC) (1982a). Current trends on acquired immune deficiency syndrome (AIDS)—United States. *MMWR Morb Mortal Wkly Rep* 31:507–508, 513–514.

Centers for Disease Control and Prevention (CDC) (1982b). Possible transfusion-associated acquired immune deficiency syndrome (AIDS)—California. *MMWR Morb Mortal Wkly Rep* 31:652–654.

Centers for Disease Control and Prevention (CDC) (1982c). Unexplained immunodeficiency and opportunistic infections in infants—New York, New Jersey, California. *MMWR Morb Mortal Wkly Rep* 31:665–667.

Centers for Disease Control and Prevention (CDC) (1983). Immunodeficiency in female partners of males with acquired immune deficiency syndrome (AIDS)—New York. *MMWR Morb Mortal Wkly Rep* 31:697–698

Centers for Disease Control and Prevention (CDC) (2006a). Racial/ethnic disparities in diagnoses of HIV/AIDS—33 states, 2001–2004. *MMWR Morb Mortal Wkly Rep* 2006; 55:121–125.

Centers for Disease Control and Prevention (CDC) (2006b). HIV transmission among male inmates in a state prison system—Georgia, 1992–2005. *MMWR Morb Mortal Wkly Rep* 55:421–426.

Centers for Disease Control and Prevention (CDC) (2015). *HIV Surveillance Report, 2014*; vol. 26. https://www.cdc.gov/hiv/pdf/library/reports/surveillance/cdc-hiv-surveillance-report-2014-vol-26.pdf/. Accessed December 12, 2016.

Centers for Disease Control and Prevention (CDC) (2016). HIV in the United States: at a glance. http://www.cdc.gov/hiv/statistics/overview/ataglance.html. Accessed May 29, 2016.

Chesney MA, Smith AW (1992). Critical delays in HIV testing and care: the potential role of stigma. *Am Behav Sci* 42:1162–1174.

Choopanya K, Martin M, Suntharasamai P, et al. (2013). Antiretriviral prophylaxis for HIV infection in injecting drug users in Bangkok, Thailand (The Bangkok Tenofovir Study Group): a randomized, double-blind, placebo-controlled phase 3 trial. *Lancet* 381:2083–2090.

Cochran SD, Mays VM (1990). Sex, lies and HIV. *N Engl J Med* 22:774–775.

Cohen MA (1987). Psychiatric aspects of AIDS: A biopsychosocial approach. In GP Wormser, RE Stahl, EJ Bottone (eds.), *AIDS, Acquired Immune Deficiency Syndrome and Other Manifestations of HIV Infection*. Park Ridge, NJ: Noyes Publishers.

Cohen MA (1989). AIDSism, a new form of discrimination. *Am Med News,* January 20, 32:43.

Cohen MA (1992). Biopsychosocial aspects of the HIV epidemic. In GP Wormser (ed.), *AIDS and Other Manifestations of HIV Infection,* 2nd ed. (pp. 349–371). New York: Raven Press.

Cohen MA (1996). Creating health care environments to meet patients' needs. *Curr Issues Public Health* 2:232–240.

Cohen MA (2008). History of AIDS psychiatry—a biopsychosocial approach: paradigm and paradox. In MA Cohen, JM Gorman (eds.), *Comprehensive Textbook of AIDS Psychiatry* (pp. 3–14). New York: Oxford University Press.

Cohen MA (2016). HIV/AIDS—The great magnifier of maladies—is entirely preventable. *India Empire Magazine,* November. http://indiaempire.com/article/1195/hivaids__the_great_magnifier_of_maladies__is_entirely_preventable. Accessed on December 17, 2016.

Cohen MA, Aladjem AD, Brenin D, Ghazi M (1990). Firesetting by patients with the acquired immunodeficiency syndrome (AIDS). *Ann Intern Med* 112:386–387.

Cohen MA, Aladjem AD, Horton A, Lima J, Palacios A, Hernandez L, Mehta P (1991). How can we combat excess mortality in Harlem? A one-day survey of adult general care. *Int J Psychiatry Med* 21:369–378.

Cohen MA, Alfonso CA (1994). Dissemination of HIV: how serious is it for women, medically and psychologically? *Ann N Y Acad Sci* 736:114–121.

Cohen MA, Alfonso CA (1998). Psychiatric care and pain management in persons with HIV infection. In GP Wormser (ed.), *AIDS and Other Manifestations of HIV Infection,* 3rd ed. Philadelphia: Lippincott-Raven.

Cohen MA, Alfonso CA (2004). AIDS psychiatry: psychiatric and palliative care, and pain management. In GP Wormser (ed.), *AIDS and Other Manifestations of HIV Infection,* 4th ed. (pp. 537–576). San Diego: Elsevier Academic Press.

Cohen MA, Cozza KL, Bourgeois JA, Moghimi Y, Douaihy A (2016). The role of psychiatrists in HIV prevention. *Psychiatric Times,* 30–32.

Cohen MA, Goforth HW, Lux JZ, Batista SM, Khalife S, Cozza KL, Soffer J (2010). *Handbook of AIDS Psychiatry.* New York: Oxford University Press.

Cohen MA, Gorman JM (2008). *Comprehensive Textbook of AIDS Psychiatry.* New York: Oxford University Press.

Cohen MA, Hoffman RG, Cromwell C, et al. (2002). The prevalence of distress in persons with human immunodeficiency virus infection. *Psychosomatics* 43:10–15.

Cohen MA, Weisman H (1986). A biopsychosocial approach to AIDS. *Psychosomatics* 27:245–249.

Cohen MA, Weisman HW (1988). A biopsychosocial approach to AIDS. In RP Galea, BF Lewis, LA Baker (eds.), *AIDS and IV Drug Abusers.* Owings Mills, MD: National Health Publishing.

Cohen MS, Chen YQ, McCauley M, et al. (2011). Prevention of HIV-1 infection with early antiretroviral therapy. *N Engl J Med* 365:493–505.

Corrigan PW (2016). Lessons learned from unintended consequences about erasing the stigma of mental illness. *World Psychiatry* 15:67–73.

Crowley JS, Nevins GR, Thompson M (2015). The Americans with Disabilities Act and HIV/AIDS discrimination: unfinished business. *JAMA* 314:227–228.

Data Collection on Adverse Events of Anti-HIV Drugs (D:A:D) Study Group (2010). Factors associated with specific causes of death amongst HIV-positive individuals in the D:A:D study. *AIDS* 24:1537–1548.

De Buono BA, Zinner SH, Daamen M, McCormack WM (1990). Sexual behavior of college women in 1975, 1986 and 1989. *N Engl J Med* 322:821–825.

Deuchar N (1984). AIDS in New York City with particular reference to the psychosocial aspects. *Br J Psychiatry* 145:612–619.

Dilley JW, Ochitill HN, Perl M, Volberding PA (1985). Findings in psychiatric consultation with patients with acquired immune deficiency syndrome. *Am J Psychiatry* 142:82–86.

Eisenberg MM, Blank MB (2014). The syndemic of the triply diagnosed: HIV positives with mental illness and substance abuse or dependence. *Clin Res HIV/AIDS* 1:1006.

Faulstich ME (1987). Psychiatric aspects of AIDS. *Am J Psychiatry* 144:551–556.

Fernandez F, Ruiz P (2006). *Psychiatric Aspects of HIV/AIDS* (pp. 39–47). Philadelphia: Lippincott Williams & Wilkins.

Flickinger TE, Saha S, Moore RD, Beach MC (2013). Higher quality communication and relationships are associated with improved patient engagement in HIV care. *J Acquir Immune Defic Syndr* 63(3):362–366.

Forstein M (1984a). AIDS anxiety in the worried well. In SE Nichols, DG Ostrow (eds.), *Psychiatric Implications of Acquired Immune Deficiency Syndrome* (pp. 77–82). Washington, DC: American Psychiatric Press.

Forstein M (1984b). The psychosocial impact of the acquired immunodeficiency syndrome. *Semin Oncol* 11:77–82.

Fullilove MT (1989). Anxiety and stigmatizing aspects of HIV infection. *J Clin Psychiatry* 50(Suppl.):5–8.

Fullilove RE (2011). Mass incarceration in the United States and HIV/AIDS: cause and effect? *Ohio State J Criminal Law* 9:353–361.

Golembeski C, Fullilove RE (2005). Criminal (in)justice in the city and its associated health consequences. *Am J Public Health* 95:1701–1706.

Goodkin K, Heckman T, Siegel K, et al. (2003). "Putting a face" on HIV infection/AIDS in older adults: a psychosocial context. *J Aquir Immune Defic Syndr* 33(Suppl. 2):S171–S184.

Gottlieb MS (2001). AIDS—past and future. *N Engl J Med* 344:1788–1791.

Gottlieb MS, Schroff R, Schanker HM, Weisman JD, Fan PT, Wolf RA, Saxon A (1981). *Pneumocystis carinii* pneumonia and mucosal candidiasis in previously healthy homosexual men: evidence of a new acquired cellular immunodeficiency. *N Engl J Med* 305:1425–1431.

Grant RM, Lama JR, Anderson PL, et al. (2010). Pre-exposure chemoprophylaxis for HIV prevention in men who have sex with men. *N Engl J Med* 363:2587–2599.

Guaraldi G, Orlando G, Zona S, et al. (2011). Premature age-related comorbidities among HIV-infected persons compared with the general population. *Clin Infect Dis* 53:1120–1126.

Gwadz M, Cleland CM, Applegate E, et al. (2015). Behavioral intervention improves treatment outcomes among HIV-infected individuals who have delayed, declined, or discontinued antiretroviral therapy: a randomized controlled trial of a novel intervention. *AIDS Behav* 19:1801–1817.

Hammett TM, Harmon MP, Rhodes W (2002). The burden of infectious disease among inmates of and releasees from US correctional facilities 1997. *Am J Public Health* 92:1789–1794.

Heaton RK, Franklin DR, Ellis RJ, et al. (2011) HIV-associated neurocognitive disorders before and during the era of combination antiretroviral therapy: differences in rates, nature, and predictors. *J Neurovirol* 17:3–16.

Herek GM, Capitanio JP, Widaman KF (2002). HIV-related stigma and knowledge in the United States: prevalence and trends, 1991–1999. *Am J Public Health* 92:371–377.

Hill S, Kavookjian J (2012). Motivational interviewing as a behavioral intervention to increase HAART adherence in patients who are HIV-positive: a systematic review of the literature. *AIDS Care* 24(5):583–592.

Hoffman RS (1984). Neuropsychiatric complications of AIDS. *Psychosomatics* 25:393–340.

Holland JC, Tross S (1985). Psychosocial and neuropsychiatric sequelae of the acquired immunodeficiency syndrome and related disorders. *Ann Intern Med* 103:760–764.

Holtz H, Dobro J, Kapila R, Palinkas R, Oleske J (1983). Psychosocial impact of acquired immunodeficiency syndrome. *JAMA* 250:167.

Huang L, Quartin A, Jones D, Havlir DV (2006). Intensive care of patients with HIV infection. *N Engl J Med* 355:173–181.

Hunter ND (1990). Epidemic of fear: a survey of AIDS discrimination in the 1980s and policy recommendations for the 1990s. American Civil Liberties Union AIDS Project 1990. New York: ACLU.

Joska JA, Stein DJ, Grant I (2014). *HIV/AIDS and Psychiatry*. Hoboken, NJ: Wiley Blackwell.

Kamya MR, Wanyenze R, Namale AS (2007). Routine HIV testing: the right not to know versus the rights to care, treatment and prevention. *Bull World Health Organ* 85(5):B.

Kaplan AH, Scheyett A, Golin CE (2005). HIV and stigma: analysis and research program. *Curr HIV/AIDS Rep* 2:184–188.

Karpiak SE, Shippy RA, Cantor MH (2006). *Research on Older Adults with HIV*. New York: AIDS Community Research Initiative of America.

Kelly JA, St. Lawrence JS, Smith S Jr, Hood HV, Cook DJ (1987). Stigmatization of AIDS patients by physicians. *Am J Public Health* 77:789–791.

Kolb B, Wallace AM, Hill D, Royce M (2006). Disparities in cancer care among racial and ethnic minorities. *Oncology* 20:1256–1261.

Krummenacher I, Cavassini M, Bugnon O, Schenider MP (2011). An interdisciplinary HIV-adherence program combining motivational interviewing and electronic antiretroviral drug monitoring. *AIDS Care* 23(5):550–561.

Lehman JS, Carr MH, Nichol AJ, et al. (2014). Prevalence and public health implications of state laws that criminalize potential HIV exposure in the United States. *AIDS Behav* 18:997–1006.

Levenson JL (2005). *American Psychiatric Publishing Textbook of Psychosomatic Medicine* (pp. 3–14). Washington, DC: American Psychiatric Publishing.

Levenson JL (2011). *American Psychiatric Publishing Textbook of Psychosomatic Medicine: Psychiatric Care of the Medically Ill* (pp. 3–14). Washington, DC: American Psychiatric Publishing.

Levison JH, Alegria M (2016). Shifting the HIV training and research paradigm to address disparities in HIV outcomes. *AIDS Behav* 20(Suppl 2):265–272.

Lipowski ZJ (1967). Review of consultation psychiatry and psychosomatic medicine: II. Clinical aspects. *Psychosom Med* 29:201–224.

Lyketsos CG, Hanson AL, Fishman M, Rosenblatt A, McHugh PR, Treisman GJ (1993). Manic syndrome early and late in the course of HIV. *Am J Psychiatry* 150(2):326–327.

MacDonald NE, Wells GA, Fisher WA, Warren WK, King MA, Doherty JA, Bowie WR (1990). High-risk STD/HIV behavior among college students. *JAMA* 263:3155–3159.

Mahajan AP, Sayles JN, Patel VA, Remien RH, Ortiz D, Szekeres G, Coates TJ (2008). Stigma in the HIV/AIDS epidemic: a review of the literature and recommendations for the way forward. *AIDS* 22(Suppl 2):S67–S79.

Manfredi R (2004a). HIV infection and advanced age: emerging epidemiological, clinical and management issues. *Ageing Res Rev* 3:31–54.

Manfredi R (2004b). Impact of HIV infection and antiretroviral therapy in the older patient. *Expert Rev Anti Infect Ther* 2:821–824.

Marin B, Thiébault R, Buchar HC, et al. (2009). Non-AIDS defining deaths and immunodeficiency in the era of combination antiretroviral therapy. *AIDS* 23:1743–1753.

Marlatt GA, Larimer ME, Witkiewitz K (2012). *Harm Reduction: Pragmatic Strategies for Managing High Risk Behaviors*, 2nd ed. New York: Guilford Press.

Marzuk PM, Tierney H, Tardiff K, Gross EM, Morgan EB, Hsu MA, Mann JJ (1988). Increased risk of suicide in persons with AIDS. *JAMA* 259:1333–1337.

Masur H, Michelis MA, Greene JB, et al. (1981). An outbreak of community-acquired *Pneumocystis carinii* pneumonia: initial manifestation of cellular immune dysfunction. *N Engl J Med* 305:1431–1438.

May MT, Gompels M, Delpech V, et al.; UK Collaborative HIV Cohort (UK CHIC) Study (2014). Impact on life expectancy of HIV-1 positive individuals of CD4+ cell count and viral load response to antiretroviral therapy. *AIDS* 28:1193–1202.

McKegney FP, O'Dowd MA (1992). Suicidality and HIV status. *Am J Psychiatry* 149:396–398.

Meyer JP, Springer SA, Altice FL (2011). Substance abuse, violence, and HIV in women: a literature review of the syndemic. *J Womens Health* 20(7):991–1006.

Michael MJ, Westfall AO, Cole SR, et al., on behalf of CFAR Network of Integrated Clinical Systems (CNICS) (2014). Beyond core indicators of retention in HIV care: missed clinic visits are independently associated with all-cause mortality. *Clin Infect Dis* 59:1471–1479.

Mugavero MJ, Westfall AO, Cole SR, et al. (2014). Beyond core indicators of retention in HIV care: missed clinic visits are independently associated with all-cause mortality. *Clin Infect Dis* 59:1471–1419.

Mustanski B, Donenberg G, Emerson E (2006). I can use a condom, I just don't: the importance of motivation to prevent HIV in adolescent seeking psychiatric care. *AIDS Behav* 10:753–762.

National HIV/AIDS Strategy for the United States: Updated to 2020 (2015). https://www.aids.gov/federal-resources/national-hiv-aids-strategy/nhas-update.pdf. Accessed January 2, 2017.

Navia BA, Price RW (1987). The acquired immunodeficiency syndrome dementia as the presenting or sole manifestation of human immunodeficiency virus infection. *Arch Neurol* 44:65–69.

Neuhaus J, Angus B, Kowalska JD, et al. (2010). Risk of all-cause mortality associated with non-fatal AIDS and serious non-AIDS events among adults infected with HIV. *AIDS* 24: 697–706.

New York State Department of Health (2015). *End AIDS 2015 Blueprint*. https://www.health.ny.gov/diseases/aids/ending_the_epidemic/docs/blueprint.pdf. Accessed January 3, 2017.

Nichols SE (1983). Psychiatric aspects of AIDS. *Psychosomatics* 24:1083–1089.

Nichols SE (1984). Social and support groups for patients with acquired immune deficiency syndrome. In SE Nichols, DG Ostrow (eds.), *Psychiatric Implications of Acquired Immune Deficiency Syndrome* (pp. 77–82). Washington, DC: American Psychiatric Press.

Nichols SE, Ostrow DG (eds.) (1984). *Psychiatric Implications of Acquired Immune Deficiency Syndrome*. Washington, DC: American Psychiatric Press.

Nurnberg HG, Prudic J, Fiori M, Freedman EP (1984). Psychopathology complicating acquired immune deficiency syndrome. *Am J Psychiatry* 141:95–96.

Parker R, Aggleton P (2003). HIV and AIDS-related stigma and discrimination: a conceptual framework and implications for action. *Soc Sci Med* 57:13–24.

Parsons JT, Lelutit-Weinberger C, Botsko M, Golub SA (2013). A randomized controlled trial utilizing motivational interviewing to reduce HIV risk and drug use in young gay and bisexual men. *J Consult Clin Psych* 82(1):9–18.

Pathela P, Hajat A, Schillinger J, Blank S, Sell R, Mostashari F (2006). Discordance between sexual behavior and self-reported sexual identity: a population-based survey of New York City men. *Ann Intern Med* 145:416–425.

Perry S, Jacobsberg L, Fishman B (1990). Suicidal ideation and HIV testing. *JAMA* 263:679–682.

Perry SW, Tross S (1984). Psychiatric problems of AIDS inpatients at the New York Hospital: preliminary report. *Public Health Rep* 99:200–205.

Price WA, Forejt J (1986). Neuropsychiatric aspects of AIDS: a case report. *Gen Hosp Psychiatry* 8:7–10.

Pyne JM, Fortney JC, Curran GM, et al. (2011) Effectiveness of collaborative care for depression in HIV clinics. *Arch Intern Med* 17:23–31.

Querques J, Stern TA (2004). Approach to consultation psychiatry: assessment strategies. In TA Stern, GL Fricchione, NH Cassem, MS Jellinek MS, JF Rosenbaum (eds.), *Massachusetts General Hospital Handbook of General Hospital Psychiatry,* 5th ed. (pp. 9–19). Philadelphia: Mosby.

Reinisch JM, Beasley R (1990). America fails sex information test. In *The Kinsey Institute New Report on Sex: What You Must Know to Be Sexually Literate* (pp. 1–26). New York: St. Martin's Press.

Ruiz P (2000). Living and dying with HIV/AIDS: a psychosocial perspective. *Am J Psychiatry* 157:110–113.

Sackoff JE, Hanna DB, Pfeiffer MR, Torian LV (2006). Causes of death among persons with AIDS in the era of highly active antiretroviral therapy: New York City. *Ann Intern Med* 145:397–406.

Samji H, Cescon A, Hogg RS, et al., for the North American AIDS Cohort Collaboration on Research and Design (NA-ACCORD) of IeDEA (2013). Closing the gap: increases in life expectancy among treated HIV-positive individuals in the United States and Canada. *PLoS One* 8:e81355.

Samuels E, Khalife S, Alfonso C, Alvarez R, Cohen MA (2011). Early childhood trauma, posttraumatic stress disorder, and non-adherence in persons with AIDS: a psychodynamic perspective. *J Am Acad Psychoanal Dyn Psychiatry* 39:633–650.

Satcher D, Hook EW, Coleman E (2015). Sexual health in America—improving patient care and public health. *JAMA* 314:765–766.

Selwyn PA, Forstein M (2003). Overcoming the false dichotomy of curative vs. palliative care for late-stage AIDS. "Let me live the way I want to live until I can't." *JAMA* 290:806–814.

Sikkema KJ, Hansen NB, Kochman A, Tarakeshwar N, Neufeld S, Meade CS, Fox AM (2007). Outcomes from a group intervention for coping with HIV/AIDS and childhood sexual abuse: reductions in traumatic stress. *AIDS Behav* 11(1):49–60.

Singer M (1994). AIDS and the health crisis of the U.S. urban poor; the perspective of critical medical anthropology. *Soc Sci Med* 39:931–948.

Smith DK, Koenig LJ, Martin M, et al. (2014) *Preexposure Prophylaxis for the Prevention of HIV Infection in the United States—2014. Clinical Practice Guideline.* http://www.cdc.gov/hiv/pdf/prepguidelines2014.pdf. Accessed May 29, 2016.

Stoff DM (2004). Mental health research in HIV/AIDS and aging: problems and prospects. *AIDS* 18(Suppl. 1): S3–S10.

Sullivan HS (1953). *The Interpersonal Theory of Psychiatry* (pp. 32–33). New York: W.W. Norton and Company.

Sullivan KA, Messer LC, Quinlivan EB. (2015). Substance abuse, violence, and HIV/AIDS (SAVA) syndemic effects on viral suppression among HIV positive women of color. *AIDS Patient Care STDs* 29(Suppl 1):S42–S48.

Thienhaus OJ, Khosla N (1984). Meningeal cryptococcosis misdiagnosed as a manic episode. *Am J Psychiatry* 141:1459–1460.

Thigpen MC, Kebaabetswe PM, Paxton LA, et al. (2012). Antiretroviral pre-exposure prophylaxis for heterosexual HIV transmission in Botswana. *N Engl J Med* 367:423–434.

Thompson LM (1987). Dealing with AIDS and fear: would you accept cookies from an AIDS patient? *South Med J* 80:228–232.

Thompson MA, Mugavero MJ, Amico KR, et al. (2012). Guidelines for improving entry into and retention in care and antiretroviral adherence for persons with HIV: evidence-based recommendations from an International Association of Physicians in AIDS Care panel. *Ann Intern Med* 156:817–833.

Treisman GJ, Angelino AF (2004). *The Psychiatry of AIDS: A Guide to Diagnosis and Treatment.* Baltimore: Johns Hopkins University Press.

UNAIDS (2014). *The Gap Report.* http://www.unaids.org/sites/default/files/media_asset/UNAIDS_Gap_report_en.pdf. Accessed December 17, 2016.

UNAIDS (2016). Global AIDS update 2016. http://www.unaids.org/sites/default/files/media_asset/global-AIDS-update-2016_en.pdf. Accessed December 17, 2016.

Whetten K, Leserman J, Lowe K, et al. (2006). Prevalence of childhood sexual abuse and physical trauma in an HIV-positive sample from the Deep South. *Am J Public Health* 96(6):1028–1030.

White House Office of National AIDS Policy (2015). *National HIV/AIDS Strategy for the United States: Updated to 2020.* https://www.aids.gov/federal-resources/national-hiv-aids-strategy/nhas-update.pdf. Accessed January 2, 2017.

World Health Organization (WHO) (2016a). Global Health Observatory (GHO) data: HIV/AIDS. http://www.who.int/gho/hiv/en/. Accessed December 17, 2016.

World Health Organization (WHO) (2016b). World Health Organization Global Sector strategy on HIV 2016–2021: toward ending AIDS. http://apps.who.int/iris/bitstream/10665/246178/1/WHO-HIV-2016.05-eng.pdf?ua=1. Accessed January 4, 2017.

WHO, UNODC, UNAIDS (2013). *WHO, UNODC, UNAIDS Technical Guide for Countries to Set Targets for Universal Access to HIV Prevention, Treatment and Care for Injecting Drug Users.* Geneva: World Health Organization.

Winiarski MG, Beckett E, Salcedo J (2005). Outcomes of an inner-city HIV mental health programme integrated with primary care and emphasizing cultural responsiveness. *AIDS Care* 6:747–756.

Wormser GP, Joline C (1989). Would you eat cookies prepared by an AIDS patient? Survey reveals harmful attitudes among professionals. *Postgrad Med* 86:174–184.

2.

HIV/AIDS IN THE FOURTH DECADE

ORIGINS, EPIDEMIOLOGY, CLINICAL MANIFESTATIONS, AND TREATMENT

*Michael J. Mugavero and J. Michael Kilby**

Acquired immunodeficiency syndrome (AIDS) appeared nearly four decades ago and mystified doctors and scientists alike as it became one of the worst plagues in human history. Currently, an estimated 36.7 million people are living worldwide with human immunodeficiency virus (HIV) infection (UNAIDS, 2016; WHO, 2016b). The last decade has witnessed dramatic scientific advances in HIV prevention and treatment and the intersection of the two. Moreover, there has been a sizeable scale-up of combination antiretroviral therapy (ART), with an estimated 17 million people on treatment as of June 2016. New infections decreased by 35% from 2000 to 2010 but have not declined in adults since then, while AIDS-related deaths have declined by 45% after peaking in 2005 (UNAIDS, 2016; WHO, 2016e). Despite these considerable advances, formidable challenges remain. The HIV "treatment cascade," also referred to as the "care continuum," depicts steps following HIV acquisition including diagnosis, linkage to care, retention in care, and ART receipt and adherence to achieve viral suppression (Bradley et al., 2014; Gardner et al., 2011; White House Office of National AIDS Policy, 2015; WHO, 2016c). Globally, a minority of persons living with HIV have achieved viral suppression, largely attributable to undiagnosed infection, failure to engage in sustained longitudinal medical treatment, and/or failure to consistently access ART, with varying contributions of these steps across geographic regions. While effective prevention and treatment options have expanded substantially, a cure or protective vaccine remains elusive. Accordingly, global efforts to further thwart the HIV pandemic have focused on enhanced and more efficient implementation of proven behavioral and biomedical prevention and treatment modalities. Achieving ambitious targets for serostatus awareness via HIV testing, widespread ART treatment, and near universal viral suppression to maximize individual and population health outcomes will essentially require integrated care responsive to the complex comorbid medical and psychiatric illnesses often seen among persons living with HIV.

ORIGINS AND PATHOBIOLOGY

A BRIEF HISTORY OF HIV

Human immunodeficiency virus type 1 (HIV-1), the agent causing AIDS, is a lentivirus genetically closely related to SIVcpz, found in chimpanzees (Keele et al., 2006). HIV-2 is less pathogenic than HIV-1 and likely originated from macaques and sooty mangabeys. Analysis of the phylogenetic relationships between circulating human and simian immunodeficiency viruses (SIV) suggests that multiple, independent cross-species transmission events occurred between nonhuman primates and humans, resulting in the present circulating HIV-1 strains. The HIV strains that spread around the world belong predominantly to HIV-1 group M, whereas HIV-1 group N, HIV-1 group O, and HIV-2 have a more restricted geographic distribution (e.g., Western and Central Africa). HIV-1 group M comprises nine major clades that differ in frequency and global distribution: 50–55% of all infections are due to subtype C (Thomson and Najera, 2005). In this text, use of the acronym *HIV* refers to HIV-1 unless otherwise specified.

Estimates suggest that HIV-1 was introduced into humans in the first decades of the past century but remained rare and unrecognized for several decades (Korber et al., 2000). The earliest time point that HIV infection could be documented retrospectively in humans is 1959 (Zhu et al., 1998). Case reports of opportunistic infections in people without clear reason for immune suppression indicate sporadic occurrence throughout the 1950–1970s, with HIV-specific genetic materials being detected in retrospect in some of the preserved tissues (Zhu et al., 1998).

It was not until 1981 that HIV/AIDS first emerged as a public health issue, after a clustering of unusual opportunistic infections and cancers were reported in men who have sex with men, in New York and San Francisco (Centers for Disease Control and Prevention, 1981). It was hypothesized that the men were suffering from a common syndrome; a report from the Centers for Disease Control and Prevention

---

* Posthumously; in honor of a brilliant scientist and physician, and a dedicated and loving husband and father.

(CDC) suggested that the disease might be caused by a sexually transmitted infectious agent (CDC, 1982a). The disease was initially associated with men who have sex with men, despite the fact that similar clinical cases had been reported in injecting drug users, hemophiliacs, and newborns and infants receiving blood transfusions (CDC, 1982b). In 1982, the acronym *AIDS* was coined to describe this syndrome of unknown origin, which was associated with a variety of opportunistic infections and unusual tumors, in persons with the risk behaviors described here as well as in persons with hemophilia and in newborns who had received blood transfusions (CDC, 1982b). HIV, initially designated HTLV-III (human T-lymphotropic virus III), was isolated from AIDS patients in subsequent years by several research groups (Barre-Sinoussi, 1996; Barre-Sinoussi et al., 1983; Popovic et al., 1983). Soon after, an HIV-1 antibody screening test was developed, which allowed for the diagnosis of HIV prior to the development of clinically apparent end-stage immunodeficiency (Popovic et al., 1984; Sarngadharan et al., 1984). This was pivotal not only for gaining a better understanding of the extent of the epidemic and the course of infection, but, most importantly, for allowing screening of blood and blood products.

THE VIRUS AND THE CELL

The manipulation and hijacking of cellular processes is an essential viral survival strategy, since viruses rely on the cell machinery of the infected host for their replication. An impressive 8% of the human genome is composed of sequences of viral origin, suggesting that humans and viruses share a lengthy common history (Lander et al., 2001). Humans have evolved sophisticated defenses in the form of innate and acquired immunity (Stevenson, 2003). The HIV pandemic illustrates that the virus has found efficient ways to evade innate and adapted immunity and to silence essential components of the intrinsic immune system (Simon et al., 2006).

Lentiviruses, which include HIV, are small, enveloped retroviruses that package their genome in the form of two RNA copies. The name is due to the slow and chronic nature of diseases associated with these viruses. Like all retroviruses, they encode for a unique enzyme that allows the virus to reverse transcribe their (RNA) genome into DNA with subsequent insertion into the host chromosomes, thereby becoming an integral part of the cell's chromosomal DNA. Reverse transcription generates a swarm of related but distinct viral variants (known as viral quasi-species), since the viral enzyme reverse transcriptase (RT) is prone to error (Coffin, 1995). Every transcribed viral genome, therefore, differs from one another on average by one nucleotide. HIV replication in vivo is very dynamic, with more than 10 billion viruses being produced per day in an untreated, chronically infected patient (Coffin, 1996; Simon and Ho, 2003). The high replication rate, together with the high error rate of reverse transcription, is at the root of the extensive HIV sequence diversification that complicates treatment interventions and vaccine development.

The HIV life cycle can be divided into early and late phases, with integration indicating the mid-point of infection and irreversibly rendering the cell infected. The virus enters the target cell through binding with a high-affinity interaction between its envelope gp120 protein and the CD4 receptor on the T cells, followed by gp120 interaction with a co-receptor, usually the chemokine receptors CCR5 or CXCR4. Once internalized, the viral core disassembles as proviral DNA is generated by the viral reverse transcriptase incorporated into the incoming core. The double-stranded proviral DNA ultimately integrates into the host genome. Host and viral factors drive transcription of viral proteins, which are assembled into new virions adjacent to the cell membrane. Immature viral particles are released from the infected cells in a noncytolytic manner. Lastly, infectious HIV-1 is generated when the viral Gag protein is cleaved by the viral enzyme protease (PR). Essential viral proteins, including the viral envelope, reverse transcriptase, protease, and integrase, have been major targets for the development of antiretroviral drugs.

EPIDEMIOLOGY

GLOBAL BURDEN OF DISEASE

The most recent estimates (2016) suggest that 71% of the 36.7 (34.0–39.8) million people living with HIV/AIDS worldwide live in sub-Saharan Africa (UNAIDS, 2016). Globally, women account for 17.4 (16.1–20.0) million HIV infections, with children (<15 years old) representing 2.6 (2.4–2.8) million infections. The first decade of the pandemic was characterized by a restricted distribution of HIV infection in (a) industrialized countries where risk behaviors included unprotected sexual contact among men who have sex with men (MSM) and sharing of contaminated needles and drug paraphernalia by injecting drug users, and (b) central, east, and West Africa and the Caribbean where the virus spread in the general population through heterosexual transmission. The second decade witnessed the rapid spread of HIV to almost every part of the world, along with increasing viral subtype diversity. There was an explosive increase of HIV in sub-Saharan Africa. In the third and fourth decades, sub-Saharan Africa remains the epicenter of the pandemic and accounts for 71% of all new HIV infections worldwide (UNAIDS, 2016). Heterosexual transmission continues to be the dominant route of transmission worldwide, while injection drug use accounts for almost one-third of all new infections outside of sub-Saharan Africa. This is particularly notable in the Eastern Europe and Central Asia region, which has witnessed a 30% increase in new HIV infections between 2000 and 2014, a time period during which most other global regions witnessed sizeable declines in new infections (UNAIDS, 2015).

Please see Chapter 3 of this textbook for a more detailed discussion of global HIV and AIDS.

THE EPIDEMIC IN THE UNITED STATES

In the United States there have been long-standing disparities in HIV infection, with higher rates observed among African Americans and Latinos; in 2013 the rates were (per 100,00

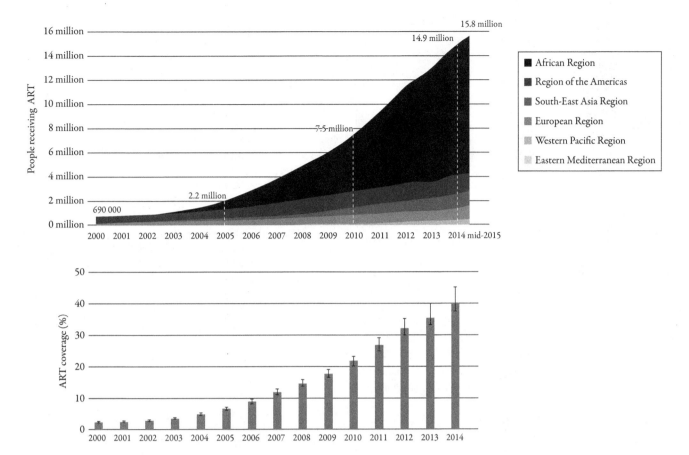

Figure 2.1 Estimated number of persons receiving antiretroviral therapy (ART) globally and by World Health Organization (WHO) region, and percentage of HIV-infected persons covered globally, 2000–2015 (WHO, 2015).

population) 55.9 for African Americans and 18.7 for Latinos, compared to 6.6 for whites; these disparities are particularly magnified among women (CDC, 2015). Moreover, similar racial/ethnic disparities are observed for mortality, even among persons living with HIV with access to ART (Lesko et al., 2015). In the United States, the majority of infections are observed among men who have sex with men (68%), with recent epidemiological trends demonstrating young men who have sex with men of color being particularly impacted (CDC, 2015). Indeed, a sobering report from the CDC suggests that the lifetime risk of acquiring HIV is 1 in 2 for African American men who have sex with men and 1 in 4 for Latino men who have sex with men at current infection rates (Hess et al., 2016).

THE TREATMENT CASCADE

The depiction of the treatment cascade united and galvanized providers, researchers, advocates, and policymakers (Gardner et al., 2011; White House Office of National AIDS Policy, 2015; WHO, 2016c). A simple bar graph showing the steps following acquisition of HIV infection, including diagnosis (via HIV testing), linkage to care, retention in care, receipt of ART, and adherence to ART to achieve viral suppression, provided a foundation on which to evaluate where the greatest challenges exist, at a population level, to achieving universal viral suppression. Globally, an estimated 17.1 million persons living with

HIV do not know they have the virus and need to be reached by HIV testing services (UNAIDS, 2015). Moreover, late diagnosis remains a challenge throughout the world, with a high proportion of persons with HIV having severely depleted CD4 counts at the time they become aware of their status (Lesko et al., 2013; Siedner et al., 2015). Taken together, these data indicate the importance of more widespread HIV testing to allow for enhanced serostatus awareness and more timely diagnosis of HIV infection, with implications for improved individual and population health outcomes.

Despite dramatic scale-up of ART since 2000, worldwide, a minority of HIV-infected persons in need of treatment are receiving therapy (Figure 2.1). Whereas 41% (38–46%) of adults living with HIV were accessing ART in 2014, only 32% (30–34%) of children were accessing treatment, a notable treatment gap.

In response to these sobering global statistics and HIV diagnosis and treatment, UNAIDS has developed a fast-track approach to achieve ambitious 90-90-90 goals by 2020: 90% serostatus awareness among persons living with HIV through testing services, 90% ART access among persons diagnosed with HIV, and 90% viral suppression among those on ART.

In the United States, the greatest challenge on the treatment cascade is the step of engagement in care, with over 50% of persons diagnosed with HIV not receiving regular medical care (Figure 2.2). Beyond the deleterious impact on individual health, persons with HIV not receiving regular

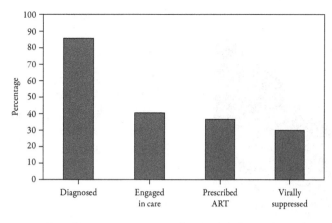

Figure 2.2 United States treatment cascade, 2011 (Bradley et al., 2014).

medical care account for an estimated 61% of new HIV cases, with an additional 30% attributable to those living with HIV who are undiagnosed, estimated to represent 14% of persons living with HIV in the United States (Bradley et al., 2014; Skarbinski et al., 2015). Taken together, these data suggest that less than 10% of new infections in the United States are attributable to persons diagnosed with HIV and engaged in care, a majority of whom are on ART and virally suppressed.

BEYOND THE TREATMENT CASCADE: THE IMPACT OF MISSED CLINIC VISITS

While the treatment cascade has provided a powerful tool to measure and monitor success in achieving universal viral suppression, it represents a static image at the population level and does not capture the dynamic and often bidirectional journey individuals living with HIV face when navigating these steps over time. At an individual level, missed clinic visits are common and easily measured in real time. Moreover, missed clinic visits have been associated with a threefold increased mortality risk—a magnitude equivalent to having a CD4 count <200, indicative of immunological AIDS (Mugavero et al., 2009). Similar findings have been observed across the globe, with dramatic implications for morbidity, mortality, and prevention of new infections (Brennan et al., 2010; Zhang et al., 2012). As psychological and psychiatric factors have been linked with missed HIV clinic visits, integrated programs to screen for and treat such comorbidities are essential to reducing the likelihood and untoward consequences of missed visits. Moreover, effective interventions amenable to implementation in a wide range of settings are available and may be proactively implemented to prevent missed visits rather than reactively attempting to identify and re-engage those who are lost to medical care, which has proven time and resource intensive (Gardner et al., 2014; Thompson et al., 2012).

CLINICAL MANIFESTATIONS

THE VIRUS AND THE INFECTED PATIENT

The hallmark of HIV infection is the slow depletion of naïve and memory CD4+ T lymphocytes, cell populations that are crucial for effective humoral and cellular immune responses. Expansion in CD8+ T-cell numbers and dysregulation of CD8+ T-cell functions are also seen throughout most of the disease.

Upon sexual transmission, HIV first replicates in the epithelium and the local lymphoid organs such as the draining lymph nodes. T lymphocytes, macrophages, and dendritic cells located in the lamina propria of the vaginal, cervical, and rectal epithelium are probably among the first infected target cells (Shattock and Moore, 2003). Local amplification and migration of infected cells and/or virions throughout the body via the bloodstream lead to the very high levels of circulating virus in the plasma compartment associated with acute HIV-1 infection. According to experimental infections of rhesus macaques with SIV, viral dissemination occurs within days following exposure (Haase, 2005). Most infected humans develop HIV-specific CD8+ cytotoxic T lymphocytes (CTL) within 6 weeks of infection, whereas seroconversion with HIV-specific antibodies is generally observed after 1–3 months (see Figure 2.3).

The mounting of an HIV-specific immune response (e.g., CTL) is temporally correlated with a reduction in the peak of viremia, as determined by the quantity of viral RNA copies per milliliter of plasma, to a level that is maintained over years in the untreated individual. This association suggests that cell-mediated immunity plays a role in controlling replication, although this control is incomplete. The established level of viral RNA in the plasma, termed the *viral set point*, differs between patients and predicts disease progression (Mellors et al., 1997). Thus, CD8+-mediated cellular immune responses initially reduce viral replication, but the rapid selection of viral CTL escape mutants limits the long-term efficacy during chronic infection (Lichterfeld et al., 2005).

It is important to note that although symptoms may be mild in the first years of disease (so-called latent/dormant phase), HIV continuously replicates in the vast majority of those infected until the replacement of CD4+ cells cannot keep pace with the loss of these cells. The time from infection to the point when CD4+ T cells fall below a critical circulating level needed to prevent opportunistic infections varies among individuals (e.g., 10 to 15 years). Genetic factors have been identified to account for some of the observed variation, including HLA haplotypes, and mutations in CCR5 co-receptor gene/promoter or co-receptor ligands (O'Brien and Nelson, 2004).

DIAGNOSIS

Many commercially available kits enable the detection of HIV-specific antibodies. The availability of simple and rapid antibody detection systems have allowed for broader screening and earlier identification of infected individuals (Branson et al., 2006). More recently, fourth-generation antigen/antibody testing technology that detects p24 antigen as well as HIV-specific antibodies has enabled better detection of early infections. These serological tests fail to provide a reliable diagnosis in newborns and infants born to HIV-infected mothers who bear maternal antibodies and in the setting of acute infection

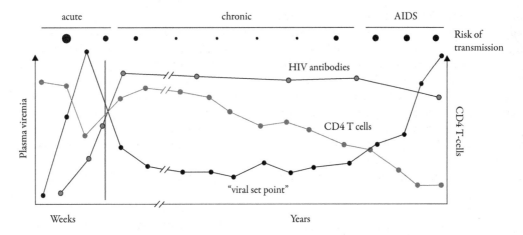

Figure 2.3 The natural course of HIV infection as depicted by the surrogate markers plasma viremia and CD4+ T-cell counts. Primary infection can be associated with clinical symptoms. During the first weeks of infection the risk of transmission is high, while HIV antibodies are still absent. Viremia stabilizes after the first month of infection, reaching an individual viral set point. Opportunistic diseases and certain HIV-associated malignancies define the stage of clinically apparent immunodeficiency (AIDS). Reproduced with permission from *Nature Reviews Microbiology*, Simon V, and Ho DD (2003). HIV-1 dynamics in vivo: implications for therapy. 1(3):181–190, copyright 2003, Macmillan Magazines Ltd.

when antibodies are still absent. In these clinical scenarios, only the direct detection of viral nucleic acids establishes a diagnosis, via quantification of the plasma HIV viral load.

SIGNS AND SYMPTOMS

The natural course of HIV infection can be divided into three phases: acute, chronic, and immunodeficiency stages (see Figure 2.1). During primary infection, flu-like symptoms with rash and fever may occur (acute retroviral syndrome). The probability of transmission has been linked to the level of viral replication (Quinn et al., 2000). Since the plasma viral loads are highest during acute infection, in the late stages of HIV disease and during concurrent sexually transmitted infections, these are considered high-risk periods for transmission. Therefore, the risk of transmission may be high during relatively asymptomatic periods of infection. Newly infected individuals are often unaware of their serostatus and thus inadvertently may expose others to a very high risk of HIV acquisition.

In the chronic phase of infection, the number of absolute and relative CD4 T cells is maintained and eventually gradually decreases. However, patients are generally free of major symptoms until CD4+ T-cell depletion reaches a certain level (e.g., <200/mm³) and the immunodeficiency becomes clinically apparent. A variety of pathogens, such as viruses, bacteria, fungi, or protozoa, may cause opportunistic diseases (Benson et al., 2005). Infections with *Pneumocystis carinii* (e.g., pneumonia), *Toxoplasma gondii* (e.g., cerebral manifestation), cytomegalovirus (CMV) (e.g., generalized CMV, encephalitis), and *Mycobacterium avium* complex, and neoplastic diseases such as Kaposi sarcoma and non-Hodgkin lymphoma were common AIDS-defining events in patients in North America and Europe during the pre-ART era. In other geographic settings (e.g., sub-Saharan Africa) mycobacterium tuberculosis or wasting syndrome takes a more prominent role as an AIDS-defining disease.

STAGING SYSTEMS

In the first decade of the pandemic, classifications systems (Walter Reed, CDC classification) served as important tools in predicting disease progression and initiating clinical interventions such as preemptive prophylactic treatments (e.g., *Pneumocystis carinii* prophylaxis). In the era of ART, HIV/AIDS disease is staged on the basis of CDC classification from 1993, which combines CD4+ cell counts (categories 1–3) and clinical manifestation of certain opportunistic infections or tumors (CDC, 1993). Its relevance for daily management of the disease is somewhat reduced, since the single most important determinant of disease progression, the level of virus replication as measured in the plasma, is not part of the classification. Additionally, ART increases CD4+ T cells to near-normal levels, drastically reducing the risk of opportunistic infections. But backstaging from a more advanced CDC category is not a part of current staging. In resource-limited regions, infrastructure may not allow sophisticated laboratory testing, and clinical symptoms are the only available criteria on which to base treatment decisions. The World Health Organization (WHO) has therefore developed a classification system based solely on clinical presentations (clinical stages 1–4) (WHO, 2006).

BASIC PRINCIPLES OF TREATMENT AND PREVENTION

ANTIRETROVIRAL MEDICATIONS

Since 1996, combination antiretroviral therapy has been the mainstay of treatment for HIV infection. Heralded as one of the greatest biomedical and population health advances, combination ART transformed a uniformly fatal illness into a manageable chronic disease for persons with consistent access and adherence to treatment. Over the two decades following the advent of combination ART, pharmacological advances in medications have allowed for treatment regimens with fewer pills, daily dosing, better tolerability, and lower toxicity, which have translated to improved adherence and higher rates of viral suppression among persons on treatment (Althoff et al., 2012; Nachega et al., 2014). As of 2016, numerous antiretroviral medications, including fixed-dose combination and single-tablet regimens, belonging to a wide range of classes acting on varying drug targets were approved for the treatment of HIV infection (Table 2.1) (WHO, 2016a, 2016d). Ongoing research is evaluating injectable, long-acting antiretroviral medications, which may become a potential alternative to daily oral medications.

ANTIRETROVIRAL TREATMENT PRINCIPLES

While there is considerable global variability in recommendations of what medications to start as recommended therapy, consensus has been achieved on when to start. Past guidance on starting therapy when the CD4+ count falls below a specified threshold has been abandoned, with global treatment guidelines now recommending ART treatment for all persons after HIV diagnosis, regardless of CD4 count (WHO, 2016a, 2016d). This shift in treatment paradigm is largely attributable to a large cohort study and subsequent clinical trial demonstrating the treatment benefits of immediate versus delayed initiation of ART, with reduction in morbidity and mortality when ART is initiated at higher CD4+ counts (INSIGHT START Study Group, 2015; Kitahata et al., 2009). Once antiretroviral treatment is initiated, uninterrupted therapy is recommended. The Strategies for Management of Antiretroviral Therapy (SMART) randomized trial demonstrated an elevated risk of opportunistic infections and mortality among participants treated with episodic ART guided by CD4+ count compared to risk for those on continuous treatment with a goal of achieving sustained viral suppression (SMART Study Group, 2006). Moreover, once continuous treatment was instituted in the episodic ART arm, attenuated, but persistent risk for clinical events was observed, suggesting propagated deleterious effects of the prior intermittent treatment strategy, despite the institution of continuous ART to achieve sustained viral suppression (SMART Study Group, 2008).

LIMITATIONS OF ANTIRETROVIRAL TREATMENT

The success of ART is limited by virological, biological, and behavioral factors. The selection of viral variants with reduced drug susceptibility, the limited penetration of drugs in biological compartments (e.g., brain), the presence of long-lived cells that harbor the virus, and short- and long-term toxicities are some of the obstacles that need to be overcome before a long-lasting cure becomes available. Furthermore, successful response to combination ART requires rigorous individual adherence to a daily regimen indefinitely. Emergence of drug resistance in the setting of nonadherence limits the efficacy of antiretroviral medications. Different classes of antiretroviral medications have varying genetic barriers to resistance, such

that some agents are more forgiving in terms of the emergence of resistance in the setting of nonadherence.

On a cellular level, there are reservoirs in the body where the virus is integrated in the genome but the cell does not produce viral proteins or infectious virus. These reservoirs, however, can be induced to produce virus. These latent reservoirs may be quite longed-lived and remain a challenge for an ultimate cure (Blankson et al., 2002). Viral reservoirs comprise anatomical sanctuaries such as the central nervous system, the testis, and the kidney, as well as a small pool of circulating latently infected, long-lived memory T lymphocytes (Blankson et al., 2002; Finzi et al., 1999). These quiescent cell populations are inaccessible to current combination antiretroviral treatments that only work on active virus replication. Furthermore, they are not recognized by the immune system and therefore elude the goal of total eradication. A number of strategies are under active investigation to eradicate these latent pools and allow for potential cure.

PROPHYLACTIC INTERVENTIONS AGAINST OPPORTUNISTIC INFECTIONS

Chemotherapeutic prophylaxis for *Pneumocystis carinii*, *Mycobacterium avium* complex, and *Toxoplasma gondii* (for antibody-positive patients) is recommended once CD4+ cell counts drop below a certain level (e.g., 200/mm^3 for *Pneumocystis carinii*). Secondary prophylaxis may prevent recurrence of an opportunistic manifestation such as *Cryptococcus neoformans* encephalitis or cerebral toxoplasmosis (Panel on Antiretroviral Guidelines for Adults and Adolescents, 2016; U.S. Department of Health and Human Services, 2006). These interventions depend on an assessment of an individual's immune status, which currently is based largely on the stable measurement of CD4+ helper T cells. Most of the primary and secondary prophylaxis for opportunistic infections can be stopped in patients who have had sustained recovery of CD4+ cells in response to ART (Benson et al., 2005).

PRIMARY HIV PREVENTION

Dramatic scientific advances have changed the landscape of primary HIV prevention, the prevention of HIV infection among HIV-uninfected persons. Pre-exposure prophylaxis (PrEP), the daily ingestion of certain antiretroviral medications among high-risk HIV-negative persons has proven efficacious in reducing the risk of acquiring HIV infection (Grant et al., 2010). The biomedical prevention toolkit has also been bolstered by studies demonstrating the efficacy of topical microbicides in reducing the risk of new HIV infections. The CAPRISA004 study documented a 50% reduction in HIV acquisition among women randomized to an intravaginal antiretroviral microbicide (vs. placebo) applied within 12 hours before and 12 hours after sex (Abdool Karim et al., 2010). Studies evaluating these biomedical prevention tools have consistently observed that efficacy is associated with adherence, with one trial comparing PrEP and a topical microbicide observing no prevention benefit to

Table 2.1 APPROVED ANTIRETROVIRAL MEDICATIONS FOR TREATMENT
OF HIV INFECTION, 2016

ANTIRETROVIRAL DRUG CLASS (ABBREVIATION)	GENERIC NAME (ABBREVIATION)	U.S. FDA APPROVAL DATE
Nucleoside reverse transcriptase inhibitor (NRTI)	Abacavir (ABC)	December 17, 1998
NRTI	Didanosine (ddI)	October 9, 1991
NRTI	Emtricitabine (FTC)	July 2, 2003
NRTI	Lamivudine (3TC)	November 17, 1995
NRTI	Stavudine (d4T)	June 24, 1994
NRTI	Tenofovir disoproxil fumarate (TDF)	October 26, 2001
NRTI	Zidovudine (AZT, ZDV)	March 19, 1987
Non-nucleoside reverse transcriptase inhibitor (NNRTI)	Efavirenz (EFV)	September 17, 1998
NNRTI	Etravirine (ETR)	January 18, 2008
NNRTI	Nevirapine (NVP)	June 21, 1996
NNRTI	Rilpivirine (RPV)	May 20, 2011
Protease inhibitor (PI)	Atazanavir (ATV)	June 20, 2003
PI	Darunavir (DRV)	June 23, 2006
PI	Fosamprenavir (FPV)	October 20, 2003
PI	Indinavir (IDV)	March 13, 1996
PI	Nelfinavir (NFV)	March 14, 1997
PI	Ritonavir (RTV)	March 1, 1996
PI	Saquinavir (SQV)	December 6, 1995
PI	Tipranavir (TPV)	June 22, 2005
Fusion inhibitor	Enfuvirtide (T-20)	March 13, 2003
Entry inhibitor	Maraviroc (MVC)	August 6, 2007
Integrase inhibitors		
Integrase inhibitor	Dolutegravir (DTG)	August 13, 2013
Integrase inhibitor	Elvitegravir (EVG)	September 24, 2014
Integrase inhibitor	Raltegravir (RAL)	October 12, 2007
Pharmacokinetic enhancer	Cobicistat (COBI)	September 24, 2014
Fixed-dose combination antiretroviral medications	Abacavir and lamivudine (ABC/3TC)	August 2, 2004
	Abacavir, lamivudine, and dolutegravir (ABC/3TC/DTG)	August 22, 2014
	Abacavir, lamivudine, and zidovudine (ABC/3TC/ZDV)	November 14, 2000
	Atazanavir and cobicistat (ATV/COBI)	January 29, 2015
	Darunavir and cobicistat (DRV/COBI)	January 29, 2015
	Emtricitabine, tenofovir disoproxil fumarate, and efavirenz (FTC/TDF/EFV)	July 12, 2006

(continued)

Table 2.1 CONTINUED

ANTIRETROVIRAL DRUG CLASS (ABBREVIATION)	GENERIC NAME (ABBREVIATION)	U.S. FDA APPROVAL DATE
	Emtricitabine, tenofovir alafenamide fumarate, elvitegravir, and cobicistat (FTC/TAF/EVG/COBI)	November 5, 2015
	Emtricitabine, tenofovir disoproxil fumarate, elvitegravir, and cobicistat (FTC/TDF/EVG/COBI)	August 27, 2012
	Emtricitabine, tenofovir alafenamide fumarate, and rilpivirine (FTC/TAF/RPV)	March 1, 2016
	Emtricitabine, tenofovir disoproxil fumarate, and rilpivirine (FTC/TDF/RPV)	August 10, 2011
	Emtricitabine and tenofovir alafenamide fumarate (FTC/TAF)	April 4, 2016
	Emtricitabine and tenofovir disoproxil fumarate (FTC/TDF)	August 2, 2004
	Lamivudine and zidovudine (3TC/ZDV)	September 27, 1997
	Lopinavir and ritonavir (LPV/r)	September 15, 2000

either approach, attributable to low adherence to study drugs (Marrazzo et al., 2015). Indeed, as with HIV treatment, the efficacy of biomedical prevention of HIV is directly linked to adherence—behavior fuels biology in both realms.

ANTIRETROVIRAL TREATMENT AS PREVENTION

A dose–response relationship between plasma viral load and risk for sexual HIV transmission among serodiscordant couples was identified in a landmark study conducted prior to the availability of combination ART in a cohort in Rakai, Uganda (Quinn et al., 2000). This observational study provided a scientific foundation for the principle of HIV treatment as prevention, positing that suppression of plasma viral load via combination ART could render a person living with HIV virtually noninfectious. Ecological studies at a population level provided further evidence suggesting that expansion of ART uptake in a geographic region could lead to a decrease in newly diagnosed HIV cases via decreased community viral load, suggesting a population health benefit to treatment as prevention (Montaner et al., 2010). The HIV Prevention Trials Network 052 randomized clinical trial provided definitive scientific evidence of the efficacy of HIV treatment as prevention. A 96% reduction in paired HIV transmission among serodiscordant couples was observed when the HIV-positive partner was randomized to immediate versus deferred ART based on CD4+ thresholds for treatment initiation aligned with treatment guidelines in place at the time of the study (Cohen et al., 2011). Beyond benefits to the individual, the population health and prevention benefits of ART are part of the rationale for global treatment guidelines now recommending ART initiation and treatment for all persons following HIV diagnosis, regardless of CD4+

count. Please see Chapters 29 and 31 of this textbook for a more detailed discussion of prevention measures and treatment as prevention.

CONCLUSIONS

In the fourth decade of the global HIV pandemic, it remains as dynamic as ever. However, scientific breakthroughs in treatment and prevention, and substantial investment in global ART scale-up have resulted in some degree of stabilization of a maturing epidemic in many regions of the world, many of which have witnessed dramatic declines in the number of new cases annually since 2000 (UNAIDS, 2015; WHO, 2016c). Indeed, while a preventative vaccine and long-lasting cure do not appear to be on the horizon, the expansion of the treatment and prevention armamentarium, and the intersection of the two, provide a scientific foundation and basis on which to further hasten and halt the scourge of HIV/AIDS on society. Considerable work lies ahead to address the large gaps on the treatment cascade, most notably, serostatus awareness via HIV testing and engagement in care to allow for uninterrupted ART access and adherence, to sustain viral suppression at an individual and population level. Moreover, as behavior fuels biology, beyond financial resources, the collective global success of HIV treatment and prevention will ultimately be dictated by adherence to testing, prevention, and treatment guidelines, biomedical, and behavioral tools. Achieving success in this realm will essentially require integrated care that is responsive to the complex comorbid psychiatric illnesses often seen among persons living with HIV, as these are among the most critical determinants of adherence, which ultimately will be a critical determinant in our global effectiveness.

REFERENCES

Abdool Karim Q, Abdool Karim SS, Frohlich JA, et al. (2010). Effectiveness and safety of tenofovir gel, an antiretroviral microbicide, for the prevention of HIV infection in women. *Science* 329:1168.

Althoff KN, Buchacz K, Hall HI, et al. (2012). HIV RNA plasma viral loads and CD4 T-lymphocyte counts among human immunodeficiency virus (HIV)-infected persons in care in the United States, 2000–2008. *Ann Intern Med.* 157:325–335

Barre-Sinoussi F (1996). HIV as the cause of AIDS. *Lancet* 348(9019):31–35.

Barre-Sinoussi F, Chermann JC, Rey F, et al. (1983). Isolation of a T-lymphotropic retrovirus from a patient at risk for acquired immune deficiency syndrome (AIDS). *Science* 220(4599):868–871.

Benson CA, Kaplan JE, Masur H, Pau A, Holmes KK (2005). Treating opportunistic infections among HIV-infected adults and adolescents: recommendations from CDC, the National Institutes of Health, and the HIV Medicine Association/Infectious Diseases Society of America. *Clin Infect Dis* 40(Suppl. 3), 131–235.

Blankson JN, Persaud D, Siliciano RF (2002). The challenge of viral reservoirs in HIV-1 infection. *Annu Rev Med* 53:557–593.

Bradley H, Hall HI, Wolitski RJ, et al. (2014). Vital Signs: HIV diagnosis, care, and treatment among persons living with HIV—United States, 2011. *MMWR Morb Mortal Wkly Rep* 63(47):1113–1117.

Branson BM, Handsfield HH, Lampe MA, Janssen RS, Taylor AW, Lyss SB, Clark JE (2006). Revised recommendations for HIV testing of adults, adolescents, and pregnant women in health-care settings. *MMWR Morb Mortal Wkly Rep* 55(RR–14):1–17.

Brennan AT, Maskew M, Sanne I, Fox MP. (2010) The importance of clinic attendance in the first six months on antiretroviral treatment: a retrospective analysis at a large public sector HIV clinic in South Africa. *J Int AIDS Soc* 13:49

Centers for Disease Control and Prevention (CDC) (1981). *Pneumocystis* pneumonia—Los Angeles. *MMWR Morb Mortal Wkly Rep* 30(21):1–3.

Centers for Disease Control and Prevention (CDC) (1982a). A cluster of Kaposi's sarcoma and *Pneumocystis carinii* pneumonia among homosexual male residents of Los Angeles and Orange Counties, California. *MMWR Morb Mortal Wkly Rep* 31:305–307.

Centers for Disease Control and Prevention (CDC) (1982b). Update on acquired immune deficiency syndrome (AIDS)—United States. *MMWR Morb Mortal Wkly Rep* 31(37):507–508, 513–514.

Centers for Disease Control and Prevention (CDC) (1993). 1993 revised classification system for HIV infection and expanded surveillance case definition for AIDS among adolescents and adults. *JAMA* 269(6):729–730.

Centers for Disease Control and Prevention (CDC) (2015). *HIV Surveillance Report, 2013*; Vol. 25. http://www.cdc.gov/hiv/library/reports/surveillance/. Accessed May 23, 2016.

Coffin JM (1995). HIV population dynamics in vivo: implications for genetic variation, pathogenesis, and therapy. *Science* 267(5197):483–489.

Coffin JM (1996). HIV viral dynamics. *AIDS* 10(Suppl. 3):S75–S84.

Cohen MS, Chen YQ, McCauley M, Gamble T, Hosseinipour MC, Kumarasamy N, et al. (2011). Prevention of HIV-1 infection with early antiretroviral therapy. *N Engl J Med*; 365: 493–505.

Finzi D, Blankson J, Siliciano JD, et al. (1999). Latent infection of CD4+ T cells provides a mechanism for lifelong persistence of HIV-1, even in patients on effective combination therapy. *Nat Med* 5(5):512–517.

Gardner EM, McLees MP, Steiner JF, Del Rio C, Burman WJ (2011). The spectrum of engagement in HIV care and its relevance to test-and-treat strategies for prevention of HIV infection. *Clin Infect Dis* 52(6):793–800.

Gardner LI, Giordano TP, Marks G, et al. (2014) Enhanced personal contact with HIV patients improves retention in primary care: a randomized trial in six U.S. HIV clinics. *Clin Infect Dis* 59:725–734.

Grant RM, Lama JR, Anderson PL, et al. (2010). Preexposure chemoprophylaxis for HIV prevention in men who have sex with men. *N Engl J Med* 363(27):2587–2599.

Haase AT (2005). Perils at mucosal front lines for HIV and SIV and their hosts. *Nat Rev Immunol* 5(10):783–792.

Hess K, Hu X, Lansky A, Mermin J, Hall HI (2016). Estimating the lifetime risk of a diagnosis of HIV infection in the United States. Conference on Retroviruses and Opportunistic Infections (CROI), February 22–25, 2016, Boston. Abstract 52.

INSIGHT START Study Group (2015). Initiation of antiretroviral therapy in early asymptomatic HIV infection. *N Engl J Med* 373:795–807.

Keele BF, Van Heuverswyn F, Li Y, et al. (2006). Chimpanzee reservoirs of pandemic and nonpandemic HIV-1. *Science* 313(5786):523–526.

Kitahata MM, Gange SJ, Abraham AG, et al. (2009) Effect of early versus deferred antiretroviral therapy for HIV on survival. *N Engl J Med* 2009;360:1815–1826.

Korber B, Muldoon M, Theiler J, et al. (2000). Timing the ancestor of the HIV-1 pandemic strains. *Science* 288(5472):1789–1796.

Lander ES, Linton LM, Birren B, et al. (2001). Initial sequencing and analysis of the human genome. *Nature* 409(6822):860–921.

Lesko CR, Cole SR, Miller WC, et al. (2015). Ten-year survival by race/ethnicity and sex among treated, HIV-infected adults in the United States. *Clin Infect Dis* 60(11):1700–1707.

Lesko CR, Cole SR, Poole C, Zinski A, Mugavero MJ (2013). A systematic review and meta-regression of temporal trends in adult CD4+ cell count at presentation to HIV care, 1992–2011. *Clin Infect Dis* 57:1027–1037.

Lichterfeld M, Yu XG, Le Gall S, Altfeld M (2005). Immunodominance of HIV-1-specific CD8+ T-cell responses in acute HIV-1 infection: at the crossroads of viral and host genetics. *Trends Immunol* 26(3):166–171.

Marrazzo JM, Ramjee G, Richardson BA, et al. (2015). Tenofovir-based pre-exposure prophylaxis for HIV infection among African women. *N Engl J Med* 372:509–518.

Mellors JW, Munoz A, Giorgi JV, et al. (1997). Plasma viral load and CD4+ lymphocytes as prognostic markers of HIV-1 infection. *Ann Intern Med* 126(12):946–954.

Montaner JSG, Lima VD, Barrios R, et al. (2010). Association of highly active antiretroviral therapy coverage, polulation viral load, and yearly new HIV diagnoses in British Columbia, Canada: a population-based study. *Lancet* 376:532–539.

Mugavero MJ, Lin HY, Willig JW, et al. (2009). Missed visits and mortality in patients establishing initial outpatient HIV treatment. *Clin Infect Dis* 48:248–256.

Nachega JB, Parienti JJ, Uthman OA, et al. (2014). Lower pill burden and once-daily antiretroviral treatment regimens for HIV infection: a meta-analysis of randomized controlled trials. *Clin Infect Dis* 58:1297–1307.

New York State Department of Health (2015). End AIDS 2015 blueprint. https://www.health.ny.gov/diseases/aids/ending_the_epidemic/docs/blueprint.pdf. Accessed January 3, 2017.

O'Brien SJ, Nelson GW (2004). Human genes that limit AIDS. *Nat Genet* 36(6):565–574.

Panel on Antiretroviral Guidelines for Adults and Adolescents (2016). Guidelines for the use of antiretroviral agents in HIV-1-infected adults and adolescents. Department of Health and Human Services. https://aidsinfo.nih.gov/contentfiles/lvguidelines/adultandadolescentgl.pdf. Accessed December 18, 2016.

Popovic M, Sarin PS, Robert-Gurroff M, Kalyanaraman VS, Mann D, Minowada J, Gallo RC (1983). Isolation and transmission of human retrovirus (human T-cell leukemia virus). *Science* 219(4586):856–859.

Popovic M, Sarngadharan MG, Read E, Gallo RC (1984). Detection, isolation, and continuous production of cytopathic retroviruses (HTLV-III) from patients with AIDS and pre-AIDS. *Science* 224(4648):497–500.

Quinn TC, Wawer MJ, Sewankambo N, et al. (2000). Viral load and heterosexual transmission of human immunodeficiency virus type 1. Rakai Project Study Group. *N Engl J Med* 342(13):921–929.

Sarngadharan MG, Popovic M, Bruch L, Schupbach J, Gallo RC (1984). Antibodies reactive with human T-lymphotropic retroviruses (HTLV-III) in the serum of patients with AIDS. *Science* 224(4648):506–508.

Shattock RJ, Moore JP (2003). Inhibiting sexual transmission of HIV-1 infection. *Nat Rev Microbiol* 1(1):25–34.

Siedner MJ, Ng CK, Bassett IV, Katz IT, Bangsberg DR, Tsai AC (2015). Trends in CD4 count at presentation to care and treatment initiation in sub-Saharan Africa, 2002–2013: a meta-analysis. *Clin Infect Dis* 60(7):1120–1127.

Simon V, Ho DD (2003). HIV-1 dynamics in vivo: implications for therapy. *Nat Rev Microbiol* 1(3):181–190.

Simon V, Ho DD, Abdool Karim Q (2006). HIV/AIDS epidemiology, pathogenesis, prevention, and treatment. *Lancet* 368(9534):489–504.

Skarbinski J, Rosenberg E, Paz-Bailey G, et al. (2015). Human immunodeficiency virus transmission at each step of the care continuum in the United States. *JAMA Intern Med* 175(4):588–596.

Stevenson M (2003). HIV-1 pathogenesis. *Nat Med* 9(7):853–860.

Strategies for Management of Antiretroviral Therapy (SMART) Study Group (2006). CD4+ count–guided interruption of antiretroviral treatment. *N Engl J Med* 355:2283–2296.

Strategies for Management of Antiretroviral Therapy (SMART) Study Group (2008). Risk for opportunistic disease and death after reinitiating continuous antiretroviral therapy in patients with HIV previously receiving episodic therapy: a randomized trial. *Ann Intern Med* 149(5):289–299.

Thomson MM, Najera R (2005). Molecular epidemiology of HIV-1 variants in the global AIDS pandemic: an update. *AIDS Rev* 7(4):210–224.

Thompson MA, Mugavero MJ, Amico KR, et al. (2012). Guidelines for improving entry into and retention in care and antiretroviral adherence for persons with HIV: evidence-based recommendations from an IAPAC Expert Panel. *Ann Intern Med* 156:817–833.

UNAIDS (2015). AIDS by the numbers 2015. http://www.unaids.org/sites/default/files/media_asset/AIDS_by_the_numbers_2015_en.pdf. Accessed December 18, 2016.

UNAIDS (2016). UNAIDS fact sheet, November 2016. http://www.unaids.org/en/resources/fact-sheet. Accessed December 18, 2016.

U.S. Department of Health and Human Services (2006). U.S. Department of Health and Human Services, Panel on Clinical Practices for Treatment of HIV Infection. Guidelines for the use of antiretroviral agents in HIV-1-infected adults and adolescents. http://

www.aidsinfo.nih.gov/ContentFiles/AdultandAdolescentGL.pdf. Accessed March 16, 2007.

White House Office of National AIDS Policy (2015). *National HIV/AIDS Strategy: Updated to 2020*. https://www.aids.gov/federal-resources/national-hiv-aids-strategy/nhas-update.pdf. Accessed January 3, 2017.

World Health Organization (WHO) (2006). WHO case definitions of HIV for surveillance and revised clinical staging and immunological classification of HIV-related disease in adults and children. http://www.who.int/hiv/pub/guidelines/hivstaging/en/index.html. Accessed December 18, 2016.

World Health Organization (WHO) (2015). Guideline on when to start antiretroviral therapy and on pre-exposure prophylaxis for HIV. http://www.who.int/hiv/pub/guidelines/earlyrelease-arv/en/. Accessed January 2, 2017.

World Health Organization (WHO) (2016a). *Consolidated Guidelines on the Use of Antiretroviral Drugs for Treating and Preventing HIV Infection: Recommendations for a Public Health Approach*, 2nd ed. http://apps.who.int/iris/bitstream/10665/208825/1/9789241549684_eng.pdf?ua=1. Accessed January 2, 2017.

World Health Organization (WHO) (2016b). Global Health Observatory (GHO) data. http://www.who.int/gho/hiv/en/. Accessed December 18, 2016.

World Health Organization (WHO) (2016c). Global health sector strategy on HIV 2016–2021. Towards ending AIDS. http://apps.who.int/iris/bitstream/10665/246178/1/WHO-HIV-2016.05-eng.pdf?ua=1. Accessed January 2, 2017.

World Health Organization (WHO) (2016d). Guidelines: HIV. http://www.who.int/hiv/pub/guidelines/en/. Accessed January 1, 2017.

World Health Organization (WHO) (2016e). Media centre: HIV/AIDS fact sheet. http://www.who.int/mediacentre/factsheets/fs360/en/. Accessed December 22, 2016.

Zhang Y, Dou Z, Sun K, et al. (2012) Association between missed early visits and mortality among patients of china national free antiretroviral treatment cohort. *J Acquir Immune Defic Syndr* 60(1):59–67.

Zhu T, Korber BT, Nahmias AJ, Hooper E, Sharp PM, Ho DD (1998). An African HIV-1 sequence from 1959 and implications for the origin of the epidemic. *Nature* 391(6667):594–597.

3.

EPIDEMIOLOGY OF PSYCHIATRIC DISORDERS ASSOCIATED WITH HIV AND AIDS

Francine Cournos, Karen McKinnon, and Milton Wainberg

For persons with HIV, mental health problems can occur as risk factors for HIV infection, coincidentally with HIV infection, or as a result of HIV infection and its complications. Psychiatric disorders are associated with HIV transmission, poor prognosis, and inadequate adherence to antiretroviral regimens (Cournos et al., 2005). The majority of individuals with HIV will experience a diagnosable psychiatric disorder (Stoff et al., 2004), as the prevalence of these disorders among those living with HIV is many times greater than in the general population (Blank et al., 2002, 2014; Lyketsos et al., 1996). Further, HIV infects the brain, and a variety of central nervous system (CNS) complications can result. These complications are detailed in Chapter 26. Psychiatric and neurocognitive aspects of HIV disease are expected to become more prominent and important for addressing the continuum of care in the coming years (Wainberg et al., 2014). Despite the move toward preexposure prophylaxis, and until a widely available and highly effective vaccination to prevent HIV infection or a cure for HIV is developed—neither of which is anticipated in the near future—the HIV epidemic will not be adequately controlled without greater attention to co-occurring psychiatric disorders along the entire continuum of care.

Given the high rates of psychiatric disorders among people with HIV, psychiatrists and other mental health care clinicians are squarely in charge of treatment decisions that affect the course of patients' illness, the quality of their lives, and, ultimately, containment of the epidemic. Most psychiatric disorders comorbid with HIV are highly treatable, but they offer a challenge to clinicians in terms of differential diagnosis and management. An understanding of the epidemiology of comorbid psychiatric disorders can help clinicians conduct a differential diagnosis and intervene in ways that minimize further spread of the virus and its devastating effects on the brain and body. *Epidemiology* refers to the incidence, distribution, and control of disease in a population. With respect to HIV, incidence studies of psychiatric disorders are rare, so for our purposes we will focus on the distribution of psychiatric conditions (i.e., their prevalence) across the populations in which they have been studied.

This chapter focuses on rates of psychiatric disorders among adults with HIV infection. All prevalences cited in this chapter were derived from U.S. studies unless otherwise stated. We discuss commonly seen psychiatric disorders among people with HIV infection in the United States. We begin with HIV-associated neurocognitive disorders resulting from the direct effects of HIV on the central nervous system (CNS) and then follow with a discussion of alcohol and other substance use disorders; depressive disorders; anxiety disorders; posttraumatic stress disorder (PTSD); mania; psychosis; and personality disorders. We also describe what is known about rates of HIV infection among people with psychiatric disorders. We briefly mention how psychiatrists and other healthcare professionals can help to contain the epidemic and to improve care to their patients.

Consistent with the diagnostic approaches of both the *Diagnostic and Statistical Manual of Mental Disorders*, fifth edition (DSM-5) and the World Health Organization's *International Classification of Diseases* (ICD), we use the terms *mental disorders* and *psychiatric disorders* to include alcohol/substance-related diagnoses, other mental illnesses, and HIV-related neurocognitive impairment. Almost all of the U.S. studies we cite here used DSM-IV nomenclature. However, we have organized the chapter so that it is consistent with how disorders are now classified in the DSM-5. Most relevant to this chapter, in the DSM-5 the term *mood disorders* has been eliminated and depressive and bipolar disorders are in separate categories; PTSD has been separated from anxiety disorders and is now classified as part of the new category of stress disorders; and disorders of alcohol and other drug (AOD) use are differentiated on a continuum of intensity and duration of use, and the terms *abuse* and *dependence* have been eliminated.

In this discussion we have moved away from the concept of risk groups, because anyone who engages in risky sexual and drug use behaviors can potentially acquire or transmit HIV. Use of the concept of risk groups has been stigmatizing and falsely reassuring to persons who may not be members of the groups or countries affected early in the epidemic (Cohen, 1988). Nonetheless, it remains true that most countries currently have epidemics that are concentrated in vulnerable populations. Vulnerable populations include the economically disadvantaged, racial and ethnic minorities, the uninsured, adolescents and younger adults and the elderly, homeless people, and those with other chronic health conditions, including severe mental illness. It may also include rural residents, who often encounter barriers to accessing healthcare services. In vulnerable populations, health and

Table 3.1. SUBSTANCE USE AND OTHER MENTAL HEALTH DISORDERS IN CONCENTRATED HIV EPIDEMICS

- Injection drug users: high rates of addictive and other psychiatric disorders
- Men who have sex with men: elevated rates of alcohol/substance use disorders and depression
- Sex workers: high rates of childhood sexual abuse; elevated rates of addictive disorders and post-traumatic stress disorder

healthcare problems intersect with social determinants of health, including substandard and unstable housing, food insecurity, and low education (*American Journal of Managed Care*, 2006). Among the most vulnerable to HIV infection are men who have sex with men (MSM), people who inject drugs (PWID), and sex workers (SWs), all three of whom have elevated rates of specific psychiatric disorders (see Table 3.1) that may in part be related to their disenfranchisement from the dominant culture, to the corresponding stigma and legal and other sanctions, and to inadequate access to prevention services. Each of these factors is associated with increased risk behaviors (Acuff et al., 1999; Cournos et al., 2005).

Underlying the daunting task of preventing the spread of HIV within and beyond vulnerable populations are numerous structural factors, including social discrimination, political indifference or oppression, poverty, and violence. Fundamental changes in behavior within entire populations need to occur, and mental health must become part of the fabric of public health initiatives to accomplish this task. Models of behavior change need to be incorporated into prevention initiatives to understand what motivates people to engage in risky behavior, what incentives are available to change such behavior, and what skills are needed to implement and maintain safer practices. In addition, detecting, understanding, and treating behavioral and psychiatric problems that interfere with safer practices or even promote unsafe practices must be a priority. It is our hope that the information presented in this chapter will contribute to these efforts.

RATES OF PSYCHIATRIC DISORDERS AMONG PEOPLE LIVING WITH HIV INFECTION

Accuracy of available prevalence estimates is unclear because most studies of psychiatric disorders among people with HIV infection used convenience samples, often of the historic risk groups, had small sample sizes, or were confined to specific geographic areas.

OVERVIEW: POPULATION-BASED STUDIES

Population-based estimates of psychiatric disorders among HIV-positive people are scarce, and the occasional study that had a larger and more representative sample may not represent current trends. Most notably, the landmark HIV Cost and Services Utilization Study (HCSUS) administered a brief, structured psychiatric instrument that screened for major depression, dysthymia, generalized anxiety disorder, panic disorder, heavy drinking, and drug dependence in a large, nationally representative probability sample of adults receiving medical care for HIV in the United States in early 1996 (N = 2,864: 2,017 men, 847 women) (Bing et al., 2001). Elevated rates of probable mental disorders were found, which are discussed in this chapter under specific diagnoses. However, the baseline study was not set up to make definitive psychiatric diagnoses. Subsequently, a follow-up study using the original screen, followed shortly thereafter by a full diagnostic interview, in a subsample of patients estimated lower rates of psychiatric disorders. For many psychiatric disorders these rates nonetheless remained higher than general population estimates (Orlando et al., 2002). It is also of note that 1996 marked the year that more effective treatments for HIV infection became available in the United States, significantly modifying the outcomes of HIV infection and potentially changing the pattern of psychiatric comorbidities. In addition, HCSUS did not obtain rates of PTSD, psychosis, bipolar disorder, and most alcohol and substance use disorders as they were then defined in DSM-IV. Another important aspect of the HCSUS study to note is that people with HIV infection who are receiving medical care may be different from those not receiving medical care in terms of underlying comorbidities and their impact on illness progression.

Hospital admissions for AIDS-related illnesses decreased soon after the introduction of effective antiretroviral therapy (ART), but a study of hospitalizations of 8376 patients in six U.S. HIV care sites showed that among patients hospitalized at least once, the third most common admission diagnosis after AIDS-defining illnesses (21%) and gastrointestinal disorders (9.5%) was a mental illness (9%) (Betz et al., 2005). This study also found that, compared with Caucasians, African Americans had higher admission rates for mental illnesses but not for AIDS-defining illnesses. The relatively large number of mental illness admissions highlights the need for co-management of substance use disorders and other psychiatric illnesses among people with HIV Infection.

One probability sample study was conducted using South Carolina hospital discharge data from all of the state's 68 hospitals: among 378,710 adult cases of discharge from all hospitalizations and emergency room visits during 1995, 422 had a diagnosis of HIV/AIDS and mental illness (using ICD-9 criteria), 1,353 had a diagnosis of HIV/AIDS alone, and 67,092 had a diagnosis of mental illness alone. People with a mental illness, regardless of race, gender, or age, were 1.44 times as likely to have HIV/AIDS as people without a mental illness (Stoskopf et al., 2001). In this study, two categories of mental illness—alcohol/drug abuse and depressive disorders—were found to have relative risks significantly associated with HIV infection.

A population sample of all persons who resided in Stockholm County, Sweden, as of December, 31, 2012 (N = 2,212,435; with HIV N = 3,031) found that HIV-positive men had a 3- to 4-fold higher age-adjusted odds of being diagnosed with depression and a 3-fold higher odds of anxiety disorders. HIV-positive women had a 1.6- to 2-fold higher age-adjusted odds of depression and anxiety disorders than males and females in the general population, respectively (Jallow et al., 2015).

The 2004–2005 National Epidemiologic Survey on Alcohol and Related Conditions (NESARC) Wave 2, a large nationally representative sample of U.S. adults ($N = 34,653$), also reported on how HIV status was associated with 12-month prevalence of psychiatric disorders (Lopes et al., 2012), but the HIV sample size was quite small ($N = 149$ HIV-positive people: 79 women, 70 men). Consistent with previous reports (Bing et al., 2001; Galvan et al., 2002; McDaniel et al., 1995), psychiatric disorders were common among HIV-positive adults: 64% of the men and 38% of the women had a psychiatric disorder, respectively. Rates of psychiatric disorders were significantly higher in HIV-positive men than in their HIV-negative counterparts. By contrast, HIV-positive women were not significantly more likely than HIV-negative women to have psychiatric disorders.

Many studies of psychiatric disorders among people with HIV infection do not include data on neurocognitive disorders. However, such data have been collected in a number of large clinical trials focused on HIV treatment. Most of the psychiatric disorders that we discuss here are explored in greater detail in other sections of this textbook.

HIV-ASSOCIATED NEUROCOGNITIVE DISORDERS

HIV is a neurotropic virus that enters the CNS at the time of initial infection and persists there, causing neurocognitive syndromes that can vary from subtle impairments to profoundly disabling dementia (Ho et al., 1985, Navia et al., 1986). HIV-associated dementia (HAD) confers an increased risk for early mortality, independent of other medical predictors, and is more frequently seen in advanced stages of HIV disease but can occur even in individuals with otherwise medically asymptomatic HIV infection (Cournos et al., 2005, Heaton et al., 2011). In untreated HIV infection, symptoms are predominantly subcortical and include decreased attention and concentration, psychomotor slowing, reduced speed of information processing, executive dysfunction, and, in more advanced cases, verbal memory impairment. However, this pattern of brain injury and the nomenclature used to describe it has evolved with earlier detection of HIV infection and treatment advances. The use of effective ART has seen the neuropsychiatric complications of HIV evolve from a predominantly subcortical disorder to one that now prominently includes the cortex, with volumetric loss and ventricular enlargement (Cohen et al., 2010). Finally, increased life expectancy of HIV patients may add cerebrovascular or degenerative CNS diseases to the clinical presentation of HIV neurocognitive disorders (Cournos et al., 2005). Although early neurocognitive complications are usually mild and survival is not compromised (Sevigny et al., 2007, Tozzi et al., 2007), they may over time negatively affect quality of life (Tozzi et al., 2007), employment, independence in daily activities, including driving, and adherence to treatment and safer sex practices (Heaton et al., 2004).

Since 2007, the term *HIV-associated neurocognitive disorder* (HAND) has been established to capture the wide spectrum of HIV-related neurocognitive deficits and encompasses three conditions: asymptomatic neurocognitive impairment (ANI) without significant impact on day-to-day functioning, mild neurocognitive disorder (MND) with mild to moderate impairment, and debilitating HAD (Antinori et al., 2007). The research diagnostic criteria of HAND require comprehensive neuropsychological evaluation to detect ANI and MND. Such testing is seldom available in clinical settings, even in high-income countries (Butters et al., 1990, Cherner et al., 2007). Clinical assessment or brief screening tools are the norm, although their validity is still being evaluated (Simioni et al., 2010).

The introduction of effective ART in the mid-1990s and the widespread use of primary prophylaxis against opportunistic infections have dramatically decreased the incidence of the most common HIV-related opportunistic diseases affecting the brain (Kaplan et al., 2000; Sacktor et al., 2001; Sonneville et al., 2011). However, neurological complications of HIV infection still cause considerable morbidity and mortality, and more than 50% of patients develop neurological disorders, even in the ART era (d'Arminio at al., 2000; Power, et al., 2009; Sonneville et al., 2011). Conservative estimates from resource-rich countries suggest that the number of individuals of all ages living with HIV neurocognitive disorders will increase 5- to 10- fold by 2030 (Cysique et al., 2011).

Prior to effective ART, HAD prevalence estimates were approximately 15–20% in persons with AIDS (McArthur et al., 1993; Simpson, 1999), whereas more recent estimates are less than 5–10% (Dore et al., 1999; Heaton et al., 2010; Sacktor et al., 1999). Among HIV-positive patients who received ART, the proportion of HAD as a percentage of all AIDS-defining illnesses rose from 4.4% to 6.5% between 1995 and 1997, a time period that marked the introduction of more effective HIV treatment (Dore et al., 1999). This shift was thought to reflect the decrease in rates of other AIDS-defining conditions, thereby leading to the relative rise in HAD cases. Even though some initial studies reported a decrease in incidence of HAD from 21.1/1,000 person years in 1990–1992 to 14.7/1,000 person years in 1995–1997 (Dore et al., 1999; Sacktor et al., 1999), others reported HAD incidence irrespective of the use of ART (McArthur, 2004)

While the prevalence of HAD decreased considerably in the era of ART, HAND continues to occur, with a high prevalence of 28–50%, although mostly in mild forms (Ances and Ellis, 2007; Dore et al., 2003; Heaton et al., 2011; Letendre et al., 2009; Levine et al., 2012; Sacktor et al., 2002). Longitudinal studies among ART-treated patients have documented high persisting rates of mild-to-moderate neurocognitive impairment (Heaton et al., 2011; McArthur and Brew, 2010; Tozzi et al., 2007) even with undetectable HIV RNA in plasma (Sacktor et al., 2016; Simioni et al., 2010). However, the majority of HAND-diagnosed ART-treated patients with systemic virological suppression do not experience HAND progression over 3 to 4 years of follow-up (Brouillette et al., 2016; Sacktor et al., 2016).

Possible explanations for the lack of response of HAND to ART include incomplete viral suppression in the CNS due to poor antiretroviral (ARV) CNS penetration, presence of drug-resistant viral strains, neurotoxicity of ARV drugs, metabolic abnormalities, neurovascular pathology, or the neurocognitive effects of comorbid conditions such as syphilis or chronic hepatitis (Cournos et al., 2005; Heaton et al., 2011; Letendre et al., 2009). Hepatitis C virus (HCV) is highly comorbid with HIV, and HCV can create its own neuropsychiatric problems as well as exacerbate those caused by HIV. Screening for HCV is simple, and treatment advances have revolutionized the tolerability and cure rates associated with HCV treatment, including among those with HIV infection (Bichoupan et al., 2014). Approximately 100 million people worldwide are infected with HCV, yet it has been estimated in resource-rich countries that less than 30% of people with HCV know they are infected (National Institutes of Health, 1997). HCV is an important diagnosis of exclusion in the evaluation and treatment of the neuropsychiatric complications of HIV. A full discussion of HCV in persons with HIV can be found in Chapter 43 of this textbook.

Asymptomatic neurocognitive impairment may be found in 22–30% of otherwise asymptomatic patients with HIV infection (White et al., 1995). Before effective ART, the prevalence of MND (which was classified as minor cognitive motor disorder prior to 2007) was estimated at 20–30% for HIV-asymptomatic patients and 60–90% for HIV late-stage patients (Goodkin et al., 1997). Following effective ART, these rates have remained fairly constant for patients with late-stage disease, but fortunately earlier use of ART has meant that fewer patients reach this stage. At the same time, following the introduction of ART, the prevalence of HAND increased for HIV asymptomatic patients by about 20% in most studies (Gisslén et al., 2011) up to a total of 52% in this population (Neuenburg et al., 2002; Simioni et al., 2010). Testing for ANI raises important ethical issues as well as diagnostic and therapeutic implications by categorizing patients who don't have any symptoms as neurocognitively impaired (Gisslén et al., 2011). This research definition should not be used to establish a clinical diagnosis, especially in patients with ongoing effective ARV treatment, as there is currently no evidence that patients with ANI are at increased risk to develop more severe impairment or need any specific intervention (Gisslén et al., 2011).

Please see Chapters 16 and 26 for more comprehensive and detailed discussions of HIV-associated neurocognitive disorders.

ALCOHOL-RELATED, DRUG-RELATED, AND ADDICTIVE DISORDERS

Among HIV-infected individuals with or without hepatitis B or C, heavy drinking predicts HIV end-stage disease and mortality (DeLorenze et al., 2011; Joshi et al., 2011; Rosenthal et al., 2009). Prior to ART, the Multicenter AIDS Cohort Study found no association between alcohol use and HIV disease progression (Kaslow et al., 1989). However, post-ART

availability, in one study of people living with HIV infection who had current or past alcohol problems and were prospectively assessed for up to 7 years, among individuals who were not on ART, heavy alcohol consumption was associated with a lower CD4 cell count but not with higher HIV viral load (Samet et al., 2007). In another study, among women who were on ART, heavy alcohol consumption was not associated with a lower CD4 cell count or higher HIV viral load (Ghebremichael et al., 2009). A patient's visit time, high viral load, and drug use were found to be predictors of alcohol use in women with HIV, which in turn was associated with depression and then HIV disease progression (Ghebremichael et al., 2009). Bing et al. (2001) found that patients in medical care for HIV had a rate of heavy drinking of 8%, almost twice that found in the general population.

The prevalence of current alcohol-related disorders among people with HIV infection has been estimated to range from 3% to 12% (Brown et al., 1992; Burnam et al., 2001; Dew et al., 1997; Ferrando et al., 1998; Galvan et al., 2002; Lopes et al., 2012; Rabkin et al., 1997; Sullivan et al., 2008), which is similar to the estimated 5–10% prevalence of current alcohol use disorders in the general population (Kessler et al., 1994; Regier et al., 1990).

Recreational drug use was found among 50% of people in medical care for HIV in the HCSUS study (Bing et al., 2001). Turning to the prevalence of current drug use disorders among HIV-infected individuals, the estimates vary from 2% to 19% (Bing et al., 2001; Brown et al., 1992; Dew et al., 1997; Ferrando et al., 1998; Lopes et al., 2012; Rabkin et al., 1997). The prevalence rate of current drug use disorder in the general population is about 2–3.6% (Kessler et al., 1994; Regier et al., 1990).

The HCSUS study also screened participants for the most severe form of drug use disorder: drug dependence. Here the rate was 2.6% in the previous 12 months. Specific drugs for which dependence had developed were not reported.

On the basis of these studies, it appears that the prevalence of current alcohol and other drug-related disorders is not different for people living with HIV compared with general-population estimates; however, lifetime prevalence for both alcohol- and other drug-related disorders does appear to be higher. Across studies, the lifetime prevalence of alcohol-related disorders for people with HIV was 22% to 64% (Dew et al., 1997; Ferrando et al., 1998; Rabkin, 1996) compared with a general-population prevalence of 14% (Regier et al., 1990) to 24% (Kessler et al., 1994). Similarly, the lifetime prevalence of drug-related disorders for people with HIV was 23% to 56% (Dew et al., 1997; Ferrando et al., 1998; Rabkin, 1996), whereas for the general population it was 6% (Regier et al., 1990) to 12% (Kessler et al., 1994). In a study of adults aged 50 and older, HIV was associated with a 20% rate of drug-related disorders in the past year (Beatie et al., 2015), which is consistent with previous reports of older adults with HIV infection (Justice et al., 2004).

Please see Chapter 14 for a more comprehensive and detailed discussion of addictive disorders in persons with HIV.

DEPRESSION, ANXIETY, AND STRESS DISORDERS

Depression, anxiety, and stress disorders are seen throughout the course of HIV infection with considerable comorbidity among them (McDaniel and Blalock, 2000). There is an increased likelihood of the emergence of symptoms during pivotal disease points (such as HIV antibody testing, declines in immune status, and occurrence of opportunistic infections). These common mental disorders are much more prevalent in people living with HIV infection than in the U.S. general population (Kessler et al., 1994). There may also be gender differences. Among the 70 men and 79 women with HIV infection in the NESARC study (Lopes et al., 2012), HIV-positive men had significantly greater odds of having any mood disorder (7.17) and any anxiety disorder (3.45) than HIV-positive women. Comparing prevalence of psychiatric disorders among those HIV infected with that of their HIV-negative counterparts, HIV-positive men had significantly greater odds of having any mood disorder (6.10), major depressive disorder/dysthymia (3.77), and any anxiety disorder (4.02). By contrast, HIV-positive women were not significantly more likely than HIV-negative women to have psychiatric disorders. As noted previously, however, this study had a very small sample size.

DEPRESSION

Depression, and more specifically major depression and persistent depressive disorder (dysthymia), is the most common reason for psychiatric referral among people with HIV infection (Strober et al., 1997) and the most common mental disorder among patients with HIV infection, with estimates of its current prevalence ranging from 7% to 67% (Bing et al., 2001; Ickovics et al., 2001; Kacanek et al., 2010; Lopes et al., 2012; McDaniel and Blalock, 2000; Morrison et al., 2002; Pence et al., 2006, 2012). Its prevalence is always greater than the general-population rate of 6–10% (Kessler, et al., 1994; Regier et al., 1990). Up to 85% of HIV-seropositive individuals report some depression symptoms (Stolar et al., 2005).

In the HCSUS study the baseline rate for a 12-month diagnosis of probable major depression using a brief screening instrument (the Composite International Diagnostic Interview-Short Form [CIDI-SF]) was 36%. At the first follow-up interview, using the same screening instrument, conducted approximately 8 months later the 12-month rate of probable major depression in the sample had dropped to 27% (Orlando et al., 2002). Full diagnostic interviews (CIDI) conducted shortly after the first follow-up on a subsample of patients, however, showed a 12-month rate of major depression of 19%, suggesting that the screen overestimated major depression rates. For dysthymia the rates were 27% on the baseline screen, 21% on the follow-up screen, but only 4% with a full diagnostic interview (Orlando et al., 2002). This study makes clear that some brief screening tools give much higher estimated rates of depressive disorders than those established by using more thorough diagnostic interviews.

A recent study examined the excess burden of depression among a nationally representative sample of more than 4,000 HIV-infected people receiving medical care in the United States and compared these rates to those for the general U.S. population (Do et al., 2014). Among people with HIV infection 12.4% had current major depression and 13.2% had other depression diagnoses, yielding 25.6% with any current depression. This was almost three times greater than rates in the general population, where 4.1% had major depression and 5.1% had other depression diagnoses for a 9.1% rate of any current depression (Do et al., 2014). This finding was replicated in data collected about active members of the U.S. Armed Services from 2001–2011 (Mirza et al., 2012). This study compared 1906 active service members with HIV and/or HSV2 infection to 19,060 service members who had neither of these infections (the referent group). Active service members with HIV infection were 2.9 times more likely to have a depression diagnosis than veterans who had neither HIV nor HSV2 infection (Mirza et al., 2012).

Risk factors that have been cited for depression among persons with HIV include female gender, prior history of depression, comorbid psychiatric disorders/problems (e.g., substance abuse, PTSD, generalized anxiety disorder, and lifetime attempted suicide), family history of psychiatric disorder, psychosocial impairment, unemployment, food insecurity, use of avoidance coping strategies, lack of social support, increasing negative life events, multiple losses, and HIV-related physical symptoms (Bradley et al., 2008; Cournos et al., 2005; Goodkin, 1996). Depression rates tend to be lower among community-based HIV-positive samples and are highest among people who inject drugs and among women.

But as already noted, and in striking departure from patterns of depression seen in the general population and in some of the other studies of HIV-positive populations, the NERSAC Wave 2 study found that HIV-positive men had significantly greater odds of having any mood disorder compared to HIV-positive women (7.17) or HIV-negative men (6.10) (Lopes et al., 2012).

Rates of depression may be higher among patients with more advanced HIV disease, particularly those hospitalized for medical illness. Thus clinicians working with patients with HIV/AIDS must consider underlying medical causes for depression, such as medication side effects, opportunistic disorders of the CNS, and endocrine disorders. A 2-year prospective study comparing men living with HIV infection to uninfected same risk-group controls found that the 2-year cumulative rate of a major depressive episode was about 40% in persons with symptomatic advanced illness compared to about 20% for asymptomatic individuals and for same risk-group controls (Atkinson et al., 2008), which was also higher than in the epidemiological community surveys, in which 6- to 12-month rates ranged from 6% to 10% (Kessler et al., 1994; Regier et al., 1990). In this same study neither HIV disease progression during 2-year follow-up nor the baseline presence of neurocognitive impairment, clinical brain imaging abnormality, or marked life adversity predicted a later major depressive episode (Atkinson et al., 2008). Rather, prior psychiatric history was the strongest predictor of future vulnerability.

The authors concluded that symptomatic HIV disease, but not HIV infection itself, increases intermediate-term risk of major depression. However, in other studies, while people with HIV infection were almost twice as likely as those who were HIV negative to be diagnosed with major depression, depression was equally prevalent in people with symptomatic and asymptomatic HIV infection (Chander et al., 2006; Ciesla and Roberts, 2001; Treisman et al., 1998, 2001).

Studies have shown that untreated depressive disorders increase HIV transmission risk behaviors (Bradley et al., 2008; Kelly et al., 1993), decrease immune status (Ickovics et al., 2001; Leserman et al., 2007), and decrease adherence to ART (Chesney, 2003; Horberg et al., 2008; Kacanek et al., 2010), which may result in decreased clinical effectiveness of ART and potential development of drug resistance (Bangsberg, 2008; Kozal et al., 2005). Thus, depression poses challenging barriers to effective medical care at multiple points along the continuum of care engagement and treatment (i.e., "HIV treatment cascade") (Pence et al., 2012). Untreated depression has been associated with a lower likelihood of receiving antiretrovirals (Nilsson Schönnesson et al., 2007; Wagner, 2002), with poor adherence (Ammassari et al., 2004; Kelly et al., 1993), and with increased morbidity (Bouhnik et al., 2005; Cook et al., 2004; Hartzell et al., 2008; Ironson et al., 2005) and mortality (Ickovics et al., 2001). Depression is a predictor of clinical progression independent of nonadherence behaviors (Bouhnik et al., 2005). Depression is frequently underdiagnosed and even when recognized is often poorly treated, particularly in primary medical settings where HIV/AIDS patients receive care (Asch et al., 2003; Cournos et al., 2005). Mounting evidence suggests that effectively treating depression in patients with HIV may reap benefits for their HIV treatment retention, ART adherence, and virological suppression and, therefore, for community viral load (Pence et al., 2012).

Please see Chapter 15 for a detailed discussion of depression in persons with HIV.

ANXIETY

Estimates of the prevalence of anxiety disorders in patients with HIV/AIDS range from almost negligible to as high as 40% (Blalock et al., 2005; Dew et al., 1997; Rabkin et al., 1997). In a study of adults aged 50 and older, HIV was associated with a 32% rate of anxiety disorders (Beatie et al., 2015), which is consistent with previous reports for older adults with HIV infection (Justice et al., 2004).

The rates vary for numerous reasons, including a host of psychosocial correlates and because anxiety frequently coexists with depression and substance use problems. Higher rates generally are seen as HIV illness progresses, and the presence of anxiety symptoms may increase HIV fatigue and physical functional limitations (Barroso et al., 2010).

Despite the wide range of prevalence estimates, a pattern emerged in the late 1990s: several studies showed a point prevalence of anxiety disorders in HIV-seropositive patients not significantly different from that of HIV-seronegative clinical comparison groups, even though lifetime rates are higher in

the HIV clinical population than in the general population (Dew et al., 1997; Rabkin et al., 1997; Sewell, et al., 2000).

Using a brief screen (CIDI-SF), the HCSUS estimated the 12-month rate of generalized anxiety disorder (GAD) at 16%, a follow-up rate approximately 8 months later of 11%, and the rate using a full diagnostic interview (CIDI) shortly after the first follow-up of 4%. For panic disorder these rates were 13% at baseline, 11% at first follow-up, and 9% for the full diagnostic interview. The authors note that the brief screening instrument overestimated GAD but did well in providing an accurate 12-month rate for panic disorder (Orlando et al., 2002).

The NERSAC Wave 2 study found that HIV-positive men had a 12-month prevalence of 33% for any anxiety disorder, compared to 24% among HIV-positive women; HIV-negative men and women had 11% and 21% 12-month prevalence for any anxiety disorder, respectively (Lopes et al., 2012). The rate of panic disorder did not appear to be elevated above community norms. Mirza et al.'s study (2012) found that active service members of the U.S. Armed Forces who had HIV infection were twice as likely to have an anxiety disorder than active service members with neither HIV nor HSV2 infection.

Please see Chapter 18 for a detailed discussion of anxiety in persons with HIV.

POSTTRAUMATIC STRESS DISORDER

PTSD is a stress disorder that has received substantial attention from HIV researchers. The rate of PTSD among individuals infected with HIV varies across studies for reasons similar to those for other mental disorders (e.g., varying assessments, diagnostic criteria, symptomatology, sample size and characteristics) (Delahanty et al., 2004; Kelly et al., 1998; Safren et al., 2003). Diverse definitions of qualifying traumatic events or trauma indices (Breslau and Kessler, 2001), the traumatic histories of many of the most vulnerable groups affected by HIV, and the variability of traumatic events that surround those infected with HIV make establishing PTSD prevalence and comparison rates to the general populations a complex determination.

PTSD may precede an HIV diagnosis because of previously experienced traumatic events, or it may emerge post-HIV diagnosis as a result of the stress of being diagnosed with a life-threatening illness (Breslau and Kessler, 2001; Martin and Kagee, 2011) or subsequent challenges over the course of the HIV disease trajectory. Stresses include fears and worries about access to appropriate treatment, the welfare of dependents, stigma, discrimination, possible isolation, dying, traumatic events, loss of employment, and physical decline and disability (Carr and Gramling 2004; Kagee, 2008; Poindexter, 1997; Safren et al., 2003). As with HIV-negative populations, the level of PTSD among people living with HIV infection also has been found to be positively correlated with the total number of traumatic life events experienced (Katz and Nevid, 2005; Martinez et al., 2002). Further, PTSD comorbid with other mental disorders such as schizophrenia, schizoaffective disorder, and bipolar disorder can be an important predictor of HIV infection (Essock et al., 2003). Among people living with HIV infection, greater psychological trauma and PTSD have been associated with several adverse health outcomes, including AIDS-defining illnesses or mortality, substance use, high-risk behaviors, and decreased medication adherence (Kalichman et al., 2002; Mugavero et al., 2007; Whetten et al., 2006).

Available studies suggest that the lifetime prevalence of PTSD among people living with HIV infection ranges from 30% to 64% (Brief et al., 2004; Cohen et al., 2002; Kelly et al., 1998; Kimerling et al., 1999; Martinez et al., 2002; Safren et al., 2003) and is higher than in the general population, 7.8% (5–6% in males and 10–11% in females), in the United States (Breslau et al., 1991; Kessler et al., 1995).

Please see Chapter 17 for a detailed discussion of PTSD in persons with HIV.

BIPOLAR DISORDER

Cases of mania were reported in the context of severe HIV-associated neurocognitive impairment early in the HIV epidemic in the United States, and such cases are still being documented in sub-Saharan Africa (Nakimuli-Mpungu et al., 2009). This has often been referred to as *secondary mania* (Nakimuli-Mpungu et al., 2009). Such cases are less common in the United States now that earlier and more effective treatment for HIV is available.

There are few studies documenting rates of bipolar disorder among people living with HIV infection in the United States. In one study conducted with data collected about active service members in the U.S. Armed Forces from 2001 to 2011, those with HIV infection were 3.27 times as likely to have bipolar disorder as service members who were not HIV infected (Mirza et al., 2012). In the handful of other studies, the prevalence of bipolar disorder among HIV-infected persons ranged from 2.6% to 9.1% (Atkinson et al., 2005; Druss et al., 2007; Robins et al., 1988).

Bipolar disorder affects approximately 2% of the general population [Merikangas et al., 2007). Therefore, bipolar disorder and HIV infection co-occur at higher rates than would be expected in the general population. The prevalence of HIV is particularly elevated among persons with bipolar disorder, perhaps approaching 10% Beyer et al., 2005, 2007; Cournos and McKinnon, 1997; Evans and Charney, 2003; Walkup et al., 1999).

Please see Chapter 15 for a detailed discussion of bipolar disorder in persons with HIV.

PSYCHOSIS

An overview of the literature suggests that the pathophysiology of psychosis in HIV infection is complex, and a multifactorial etiology of psychotic symptoms is likely in many cases. Psychotic symptoms may be part of a major depressive disorder, schizophrenia, mania, obsessive-compulsive disorder (OCD), or medication side effects or may be secondary to drug or alcohol use, CNS complications, medications, or a wide array of systemic physical illnesses. There are many reports of psychotic symptoms in HIV-infected persons in the absence of concurrent harmful substance use, iatrogenic causes, evidence of opportunistic infection or neoplasm, or detectable cognitive impairment. A common clinical feature of new-onset psychosis in HIV-infected patients is the acute onset of symptoms. Estimates of the prevalence of new-onset psychosis in HIV-infected patients vary widely, from less than 0.5% to 15% (Boccellari and Dilley, 1992; Halstead et al., 1988; Harris et al., 1991; Navia et al., 1986; Prier et al., 1991); post-ART studies indicate a prevalence closer to 3% for new-onset psychosis (Alciati et al., 2001; de Ronchi et al., 2000). New-onset psychotic disorder is found most often in late stages of the disease, particularly in subjects with neurocognitive disorders (Gallego et al., 2011; Sewell, 1996; Walkup et al., 1999). The NERSAC Wave 2 study found that HIV-positive men had a 12-month prevalence of 9.2% compared to 3.4% among HIV-positive women for any psychotic disorder in the last 12 months; HIV-negative men and women had a 0.6% 12-month prevalence for any psychotic disorder (Lopes et al., 2012). In one study, HIV/AIDS was the leading cause of death among young semirural New York patients experiencing their first hospitalization for a psychotic episode (Susser et al., 1997). Among active service members in the U.S. Armed Forces from 2001–2011, those with HIV infection were 6.22 times as likely to have schizophrenia or another psychotic disorder as service members who were not infected with HIV or HSV2 (Mirza et al., 2012).

Please see Chapter 19 for a detailed discussion of psychosis in persons with HIV.

PERSONALITY DISORDERS

Personality disorders can be detected in up to 30% of HIV-positive persons (Perkins et al., 1993). Borderline, antisocial, dependent, histrionic, and disorders not otherwise specified are, in this order, the most frequent personality disorders among HIV-positive individuals (Gallego et al., 2011; Jacobsberg et al., 1995; Johnson et al., 1995; Perkins et al., 1993). Evidence suggests that the presence of pathological personality traits or disorders may potentiate risk of HIV infection and transmission, adversely affect adherence to HIV treatments, and contribute to disease progression (Disney et al., 2006; Hansen et al., 2009). The NERSAC Wave 2 study found that, among a small sample of HIV-positive people, HIV-positive men had significantly greater odds of having any personality disorder (2.66) than HIV-positive women: a 43% 12-month prevalence among men compared to 19% for women. Comparing prevalence among those HIV infected with their HIV-negative counterparts, HIV-positive men had significantly greater odds of having any personality disorder (2.50), whereas an increased prevalence was not found among HIV-positive women; HIV-negative men and women had 23% and 20% 12-month prevalence for any personality disorder, respectively (Lopes et al., 2012). With regard to specific diagnoses, HIV-positive men and women had the following 12-month prevalence rates: schizotypal (16% vs. 8%), schizoid (14% vs. 7%), paranoid (15% vs. 6%), borderline (19% vs. 9.8%), narcissistic (15% vs. 7%), and avoidant (13% vs. 11%) (Lopes et al., 2012).

Please see Chapter 20 for a detailed discussion of personality disorders in persons with HIV.

RATES OF HIV INFECTION AMONG PEOPLE LIVING WITH PSYCHIATRIC DISORDERS

RATES OF HIV INFECTION AMONG PEOPLE WITH ALCOHOL AND OTHER SUBSTANCE USE DISORDERS

The extent to which addiction fuels injection drug use is the most obvious link between psychiatric disorders and HIV transmission. Kral et al. (1998) estimated an overall HIV infection rate among American who inject drugs of 13%, with wide geographic variability between cities in the East (where rates exceeded 40%) and in the Midwest and West (where rates generally were under 5%). Yet many studies of this population did not obtain alcohol and other drug (AOD) use disorder diagnoses, so summarizing across studies to generalize rates of HIV infection for specific diagnostic groups is methodologically problematic. People discharged from general hospitals who had documented AOD use disorders were twice as likely to be HIV infected as those without AOD use disorders (Stoskopf et al., 2001). Studies of people admitted to treatment for primary alcohol abuse or dependence reported HIV infection rates of 5% to 10.3% (Avins et al., 1994; Mahler et al., 1994; Woods et al., 2000), and these rates are 10 to 20 times higher than those among the general population (McQuillan et al., 1997).

More recent studies of AOD use disorders among people with HIV are scarce, although DeLorenze et al. (2011) investigated mortality after diagnosis of psychiatric disorders and co-occurring substance use disorders among HIV-infected patients in the Kaiser Permanente Northern California (KPNC) health plan over a 12-year period. Among the 9,757 HIV-infected patients in the study sample, 25.4% ($n = 2,472$) had received a psychiatric diagnosis, and 25.5% ($n = 2,489$) had been diagnosed with substance use disorder; 1,180 (12.1%) patients had received both psychiatric and substance use problem diagnoses. The prevalence of specific psychiatric disorders among the 2,472 patients who received a psychiatric diagnosis was major depression (81.1%), panic disorder (17.1%), bipolar disorder (14.2%), and anorexia/bulimia (8.1%). Multiple drug dependence/abuse (41.0%) and alcohol alone (32.7%) were the most prevalent substance use diagnoses in the subpopulation with substance use disorders. Other single substance use diagnoses included cannabis (8.5%), amphetamines (7.7%), cocaine (3.9%), opioids (1.9%), alcohol or drug psychoses (1.8%), and unspecified (18.8%); 47.6% had a single substance use diagnosis. In contrast, a study of the KPNC general health plan membership found that 10.8% were diagnosed with depression and 2.1% were diagnosed with a substance use disorder, based on medical records (Satre et al., 2010).

Please see Chapter 14 for a detailed discussion of addictive disorders in persons with HIV.

RATES OF HIV INFECTION AMONG PEOPLE WITH SEVERE MENTAL ILLNESS

Most studies of rates of HIV infection in psychiatric populations focus on people with severe mental illness (SMI). *Severe mental illness* is a term used to describe a heterogeneous group of psychiatric conditions, most commonly including schizophrenia, bipolar disorder, and major depression with psychotic features (Lagios and Deane, 2007) that are characterized by acute or persistent duration, functional disability, and, typically, a significant history of hospitalization and/or maintenance medication (McKinnon and Rosner, 2000).

Among adults in treatment for such conditions in the United States, infection with HIV has been documented in seroprevalence studies at rates of 0% to 29% (Table 3.2). Rates found in seroprevalence studies where blood was drawn for HIV antibody testing generally are more reliable than those found in prevalence studies that relied on patient knowledge of their HIV status or on what had been recorded in the medical record; still, generalizability of seroprevalence to other patient populations is limited.

Another study documented a 1.2% HIV infection rate among adult patients attending a system of psychiatric outpatient clinics ($N = 11,284$ individuals), approximately four times the occurrence of HIV infection in the general adult population of the United States at the time (Beyer et al., 2007). The major psychiatric diagnostic categories with a high prevalence of HIV infection were substance abuse disorders (5%), personality disorders (3.1%), bipolar disorders (2.6%), and PTSD (2.1%) (Beyer et al., 2007). Patients with unipolar depressive disorders had a HIV prevalence of 1.4%. The authors estimated that those with personality disorders ($p < 0.001$), bipolar disorder ($p < 0.001$), PTSD ($p < 0.05$), or depressive disorders ($p < 0.05$) had significantly higher risk of HIV infection than the general psychiatric population (and even greater risk than the general adult U.S. population). One assumption is that HIV rates in personality and bipolar disorders would be elevated because of the impulse-control problems involved in the diseases, whereas depression and PTSD rates may be elevated because of factors involved in HIV exposure or the disease itself. Alternatively, it is possible that these diseases may "self-select" for comorbid infections, since the risk of substance abuse has long been noted to be high in these disorders and substance use is in turn associated with increased risk for a variety of infections, including HIV. However, the impact of substance abuse was different in each of these categories. Patients with bipolar disorder, PTSD, and personality disorders had a much lower substance abuse/HIV risk ratio (1.7, 2.6, and 3.1, respectively) compared with the full sample. This suggests that comorbid substance abuse, though still a significant risk factor, was less important in these conditions than in other psychiatric diagnoses. The highest risk ratio (6.4) was for depressive disorders, which suggests that, in this group, substance abuse comorbidity played a much more significant role in HIV risk.

Taken together, available studies provide an evidence base regarding differences in HIV infection among those with SMI

Table 3.2. HIV SEROPREVALENCE AMONG PSYCHIATRIC PATIENTS IN THE UNITED STATES

STUDY	TESTING METHOD	U.S. REGION	SAMPLE	N	RATE OF HIV INFECTION
Clair et al., 1989	Blood	South Carolina	Psychiatric facility inpatients	1,228	0.3%
Hatem et al., 1990	Blood	Massachusetts	Psychiatric facility inpatients	163	1.8%
Cournos et al., 1991	Blood	New York City	Acute-care inpatient	451	5.5%
Volavka et al., 1991	Blood	New York City	Psychiatric hospital inpatients	515	8.9%
Lee et al., 1992	Blood	New York City	Psychiatric inpatient unit of hospital	135	16.3%
Sacks et al., 1992	Blood	New York City	Inpatient	350	7.1%
Empfield et al., 1993	Blood	New York City	Inpatients homeless psychiatric unit	203	6.4%
Meyer et al., 1993	Blood	New York City	Long-stay psychiatric inpatient unit	199	4.0%
Susser et al., 1993	Blood	New York City	Homeless men's shelter psychiatric program	62	19.4%
Cournos et al., 1994	Blood	New York City	Psychiatric facility inpatients	971	5.2%
Silberstein et al., 1994	Blood	New York City	Municipal hospital dual-diagnosis inpatients	118	22.9%
Stewart et al., 1994	Blood	Baltimore, Maryland	Psychiatric hospital inpatient/outpatient new admissions	533	5.8%
Meyer et al., 1995	Blood	New York City	Inpatients homeless psychiatric unit	87	5.8%
Schwartz-Watts et al., 1995	Chart	Columbia, South Carolina	Forensic inpatient unit for pretrial detainees	220	5.5%
Doyle and Labbate, 1997	Chart	National	Military hospital new-onset psychosis	246	0
Susser et al., 1997	Chart	Suffolk County, New York	First-admission psychiatric inpatients referred from 12 hospitals	320	3.8%
Krakow et al., 1998	Blood	New York City	Municipal hospital dual-diagnosis unit inpatients	113	19.0%
Rosenberg et al., 2001	Blood	Connecticut, Maryland, New Hampshire, North Carolina	Inpatient/outpatient treatment recipients in public mental health systems or VA	931 CT = 158 MD = 133 NH = 288 NC (VA) = 185	3.1%
Blank et al., 2002	Chart	Philadelphia, Pennsylvania	Medicaid and welfare recipients with schizophrenia spectrum disorder or major affective disorder	391,454	1.8%

Table 3.2 CONTINUED

STUDY	TESTING METHOD	U.S. REGION	SAMPLE	N	RATE OF HIV INFECTION
Klinkenberg et al., 2003	Blood	St. Louis, Missouri	Homeless outpatient with SMI+SUD	172	6.2%
Beyer et al., 2005	chart	Durham, North Carolina	Outpatient psychiatric clinic patients with bipolar disorder	1,379	2.8%
Pirl et al., 2005	Chart	Boston, Massachusetts	Psychiatric hospital inpatients	62	29.0%
Beyer et al., 2007	Chart	Durham, North Carolina	General hospital psychiatric outpatients	11,284	1.2%
Himelhoch et al., 2007	Chart	National	Inpatient/outpatient veterans with versus without SMI	SMI: 191,625 No SMI: 67,965	SMI: 1.0% No SMI: 0.5%
Rothbard et al., 2009	Chart and blood	Philadelphia, Pennsylvania	Inpatient psychiatric units	588	10.0%
Walkup et al., 2010	Chart	California, Florida, Georgia, Illinois, New Jersey, New York, Ohio, Texas	Medicaid and Medicare claims from recipients with schizophrenia	1,000,000+	1.8%
Himelhoch et al., 2011	Blood	Baltimore metro area, Maryland	Outpatients in public mental health treatment settings with SMI+SUD	153	6.1%
Jackson-Malik et al., 2011	Saliva	Philadelphia, Pennsylvania	Veterans with a history of mental health and substance abuse diagnoses, residing in assisted living facilities	64	3.1%
Walkup et al., 2011	Chart	California, Florida, Georgia, Illinois, New Jersey, New York, Ohio, Texas	Medicaid beneficiaries with schizophrenia treated for HIV	Not reported	1.6%
Prince et al., 2012	Chart	California, Florida, Georgia, Illinois, New Jersey, New York, Ohio, Texas	Medicaid beneficiaries who were without HIV in 2001 but diagnosed with HIV 2002–2004	6,417,676 SMI: 443,994 SMI+SUD: 72,752 MDD: 130,788 BPD: 55,582 SCH: 184,872	SMI: 0.7% SMI+SUD: 2.0% MDD: 0.6% BPD: 0.6% SCH: 0.5%
Blank et al., 2014	Saliva	Philadelphia, Pennsylvania and Baltimore, Maryland	University-based inpatient psychiatric units (287), intensive case-management programs (273), community mental health centers (501)	1,061	4.8% Inpatient = 5.9% ICM = 5.1% CMHC = 4.0% Baltimore = 5.9% Philadelphia = 3.9%

BPD, bipolar disorder; CMHC, community mental health center, ICM, intensive case management; MDD, major depressive disorder; SCH, schizophrenia; SMI, severe mental illness; SUD, substance use disorder; VA, Veterans Affairs.

that are based on geographic location, subpopulation characteristics, and risk behaviors. For instance, HIV rates generally are lower among veterans than among homeless populations and those who have injection-drug use histories. A summary of rates among different subpopulations, some of which are overlapping, is presented next.

Geographic location. One study directly compared HIV infection rates among those with SMI in urban versus other locations, with rates varying from 1.7% in rural areas to 5% in metropolitan areas (Brunette et al., 1999; Rosenberg et al., 2001). Many environmental factors associated with a greater prevalence of HIV/AIDS risk behaviors and infection, including poverty, unstable housing, and injection drug use, are more common in some urban neighborhoods (Carey et al., 1997; McKinnon et al., 2002; McKinnon and Rosner, 2000).

Treatment setting. Psychiatric inpatients and outpatients compared in one study showed different HIV infection rates, with inpatients infected at higher rates than those in intensive case-management programs or community mental health centers (Blank et al., 2014).

Forensic. One study among pretrial detainees showed a 5.5% rate of HIV infection (Schwartz-Watts et al., 1995).

Homeless. In one study homeless people with concurrent SMI and substance use disorders had a 6.2% HIV rate (Klinkenberg et al., 2003). Among homeless people with severe mental illness who may or may not have also had a secondary substance use disorder, rates of HIV have ranged from 5.8% to 19.4% (Empfield et al., 1993; Meyer et al., 1993; Susser et al., 1993).

Veterans. HIV prevalence among American veterans with SMI is 1% (compared to veterans without SMI whose infection rate is 0.5%) (Himelhoch et al., 2007). In a study of veterans with a history of mental health and substance abuse diagnoses who are residing in assisted living facilities, the rate of HIV infection was 3.1% (Jackson-Malik et al., 2011).

Men who have sex with men. Approximately one in four of those with a history of male–male sex were HIV positive (Cournos and McKinnon, 1997).

Dual diagnosis. The highest rates of infection are among those dually diagnosed with SMI and substance-related disorders, with rates ranging from 6.1% to 22.9% (Himelhoch et al., 2011; Krakow et al., 1998; Prince et al., 2012; Silberstein et al., 1994).

First-episode/onset psychosis. Two studies examined rates of HIV infection among people having their first episode of psychosis or first psychiatric hospitalization, with rates of 0 to 3.8% (Doyle and Labbate, 1997; Susser et al., 1997).

These studies provide dramatic evidence that a main driver of the HIV epidemic among people with SMI is substance use, even for sexual transmission, so prevention of HIV infection among people with SMI, half of whom are likely to develop substance use disorders, should start with the onset of the first disorder (Table 3.3) by ensuring adequate treatment and appropriate prevention of the secondary disorder.

Table 3.3. SUBSTANCE USE AND OTHER MENTAL DISORDER COMORBIDITY ESTIMATES FROM THE U.S. NATIONAL COMORBIDITY STUDY

- 51% of people with lifetime alcohol or other drug (AOD) use disorders met criteria for at least one other lifetime mental disorder, and vice versa.
- 15% of people with a mental disorder in the past year also met criteria for an AOD disorder in the past year.
- 43% of people with an AOD in the past year also met criteria for another mental disorder in the past year.

RESPONDING TO COMORBIDITIES AMONG PEOPLE AFFECTED BY HIV

More often than not, HIV is syndemic with additional medical conditions such as hepatitis C and other parenterally or sexually transmitted infections. These medical conditions can be associated with neuropsychiatric complications. Other psychiatric comorbidities are also common and multiple psychiatric disorders may be present.

The National Comorbidity Study (Kessler et al., 1996) showed that substance use disorders are highly comorbid with other psychiatric disorders (e.g., bipolar disorder, depression, psychotic disorders, anxiety disorders, and antisocial and borderline personality disorders). Possible explanations for this have been propounded, including that one disorder is a marker for the other disorder, that mental illness leads to self-medication with alcohol and other drugs, and that substance use or withdrawal leads to symptoms of mental illness. Often it is impossible to know which disorder came first or is primary, although onset of non–substance use mental disorders appears to occur at a younger age than that for addictive disorders (Kessler et al., 1996). In clinical settings of any kind it is prudent to screen patients with one type of disorder for the other type of disorder.

Those individuals with dual psychiatric and alcohol/substance use disorders may be at higher risk for HIV infection than those with either disorder alone (Ferrando and Batki, 2000), and these disorders are likely to be found together across populations of HIV-infected people. The HCSUS study established estimates of the prevalence of co-occurring psychiatric symptoms and either or both drug dependence symptoms or heavy drinking: 13% of their sample had co-occurring psychiatric symptoms and either or both drug dependence symptoms or heavy drinking (Galvan et al., 2003). Sixty-nine percent of those with a substance-related condition also had psychiatric symptoms; 27% of those with psychiatric symptoms also had a substance-related condition.

In the United States, as in most other places in the world, psychiatric disorders are common and undertreated in HIV patients and health disparities are common. For instance, in the HCSUS sample significant disparities were found between African Americans and others in the prescription of medication for depression (Table 3.4).

The rates of mental disorders encountered by HIV/AIDS care clinicians warrant our attention if we are to strengthen both the evidence base from which treatment and prevention

Table 3.4. HIV COST AND SERVICES UTILIZATION STUDY: PSYCHOTROPIC MEDICATIONS AMONG 1,489 HIV-POSITIVE MEDICAL PATIENTS

- 27% took psychotropic medication:
  - 21% antidepressants
  - 17% anxiolytics
  - 5% antipsychotics
  - 3% psychostimulants
- About half of patients with depressive disorders did not receive antidepressants; African Americans were overrepresented.

planning can be sustainably implemented and the quality of care individuals receive for their comorbid conditions. Addressing mental disorders as part of HIV care and treatment must be seen in the larger context of the mental health treatment gap—the proportion of persons who need but do not receive care. This gap is large for both severe and common mental disorders worldwide (Lopez et al., 2006; Prince et al., 2007). The diagnosis and treatment of mental disorders has been largely absent despite the fact that the World Health Organization has issued numerous reports documenting that mental illnesses are among the world's most disabling illnesses and account for 13% of the total global burden of disease (Chander et al., 2006; Demyttenaere et al., 2004). In the United States and other high-income countries there is a 35–50% treatment gap for mental disorders.

Historically, service delivery systems (medical care, mental health care, alcohol and other substance use treatment) were structured to work separately (due to different funding streams), and efforts to navigate multiple systems failed (Messeri et al., 2002; Satriano et al., 2007; Staab and Evans, 2001). In our rapidly changing healthcare environment, the current focus on integrated care, including under the U.S. Affordable Care Act, is now shifting more toward integrating both mental health care and HIV care into larger primary care systems. Time will tell how effective these changes will be for people living with HIV infection.

CONCLUSIONS

Although the rates vary, the bulk of the available evidence shows that people living with HIV infection in the United States have rates of mental disorders that are considerably higher than for the general population, and that mental disorders are associated with a multitude of negative outcomes. Despite incredible scientific advances, the absence of a strong focus on mental disorders remains a glaring omission in our progress on HIV prevention, care, and treatment, especially for the special populations that most need these services. Attention to mental disorders has always been a struggle to achieve in healthcare, but advocacy efforts have led to some improvements in this domain, and further progress is both necessary and achievable. Taking the lead from the subspecialty of psychosomatic medicine (previously consultation-liaison psychiatry), the field of HIV medicine is more advanced than many other branches of medicine in integrating mental health care into healthcare, but mental health professionals have valuable insights, expertise, and experiences to contribute to larger efforts to integrate mental health care into primary care for people living with HIV.

REFERENCES

Acuff C, Archambeault J, Greenberg B, et al. (1999). *Mental Health Care for People Living with or Affected by HIV/AIDS: Practical Guide.* Substance Abuse and Mental Health Services Administration Monograph (project no. 6031). Rockville, MD: Research Triangle Institute.

Alciati A, Fusi A, D'Arminio Monforte A, Coen M, Ferri A, Mellado C (2001). New-onset delusions and hallucinations in patients infected with HIV. *J Psychiatr Neurosci* 26:229–324.

American Journal of Managed Care (2006). Vulnerable populations: who are they? http://www.ajmc.com/journals/supplement/2006/2006-11-vol12-n13suppl/nov06-2390ps348-s352. Retrieved December 20, 2016.

Ammassari A, Antinori A, Aloisi MS, et al. (2004). Depressive symptoms, neurocognitive impairment, and adherence to highly active antiretroviral therapy among HIV-infected persons. *Psychosomatics* 45(5):394–402.

Ances BM, Ellis RJ (2007). Dementia and neurocognitive disorders due to HIV-1 infection. *Semin Neurol* 27(1):86–92.

Antinori A, Arendt G, Becker JT, et al. (2007). Updated research nosology for HIV-associated neurocognitive disorders. *Neurology* 69:1789–1799.

Asch SM, Kilbourne AM, Gifford AL, et al. (2003). Underdiagnosis of depression in HIV: who are we missing? *J Gen Intern Med* 18(6): 450–460.

Atkinson JH, Heaton RK, Patterson TL, et al. (2008). Two-year prospective study of major depressive disorder in HIV-infected men. *Journal of Affective Disorders* 108(3): 225–234.

Atkinson JH, Young C, Pham T, et al. (eds.) (2005). Prioritizing adherence intervention based on self-assessment. Enhancing Adherence: A State of the Science Meeting on Intervention Research to Improve Anti-Retroviral Adherence, New Haven, CT.

Avins AL, Woods WJ, Lindan CP, Hudes ES, Clark W, Hulley SB (1994). HIV infection and risk behaviors among heterosexuals in alcohol treatment programs. *JAMA* 271:515–518.

Bangsberg DR (2008). Preventing HIV antiretroviral resistance through better monitoring of treatment adherence. *J Infect Dis* 197(Suppl 3): S272–278.

Barroso J, Hammill BG, Leserman J, Salahuddin N, Harmon JL, Pence BW (2010). Physiological and psychosocial factors that predict HIV-related fatigue. *AIDS Behav* 14(6):1415–1427.

Beatie BE, Mackenzie CS, Chou KL (2015). Prevalence of psychiatric and medical comorbidities in HIV-positive middle-aged and older adults: findings from a nationally representative survey. *J Ther Manage HIV Infect* 3(1):7–16.

Betz ME, Gebo KA, Barber E, et al.; HIV Research Network (2005). Patterns of diagnoses in hospital admissions in a multistate cohort of HIV-positive adults in 2001. *Med Care* 43:3–14.

Beyer J, Kuchibhatla M, Gersing K, Krishnan KR (2005). Medical comorbidity in a bipolar outpatient clinical population. *Neuropsychopharmacology* 30:401–404.

Beyer J, Taylor L, Gersing KR, Krishnan KR (2007). Prevalence of HIV infection in a general psychiatric outpatient population. *Psychosomatics* 48:31–37.

Bichoupan K, Dieterich DT, Martel-Laferrière V (2014). HIV-hepatitis C virus co-infection in the era of direct-acting antivirals. *Curr HIV/AIDS Rep* 11(3):241–249.

Bing EG, Burnam A, Longshore D, et al. (2001). Psychiatric disorders and drug use among human immunodeficiency virus–infected adults in the United States. *Arch Gen Psychiatry* 58 (8): 721–728.

Blalock AC, Sharma SM, McDaniel JS (2005). Anxiety disorders and HIV disease. In K Citron, M-J Brouillette, A Beckett (eds.), *HIV and Psychiatry: A Training and Resource Manual*, 2nd ed. (pp. 120–127). Cambridge, UK: Cambridge University Press.

Blank MB, Himelhoch SS, Balaji AB, et al. (2014). A multisite study of the prevalence of HIV with rapid testing in mental health settings. *Am J Public Health* 104(12): 2377–2384.

Blank MB, Mandell DS, Aiken L, Hadley TR (2002). Co-occurrence of HIV and serious mental illness among Medicaid recipients. *Psychiatr Serv* 53(7):868–873.

Boccellari AA, Dilley JW (1992). Management and residential placement problems of patients with HIV-related cognitive impairment. *Hosp Community Psychiatry* 43:32–37.

Bouhnik AD, Préau M, Vincent E, et al.; MANIF 2000 Study Group (2005). Depression and clinical progression in HIV-infected drug users treated with highly active antiretroviral therapy. *Antivir Ther* 10(1): 53–61.

Bradley MV, Remien RH, Dolezal C (2008). Depression symptoms and sexual HIV risk behavior among serodiscordant couples. *Psychosom Med* 70(2):186–191.

Breslau N, Davis GC, Andreski P, Peterson E (1991). Traumatic events and posttraumatic stress disorder in an urban population of young adults. *Arch Gen Psychiatry* 48(3):216–222.

Breslau N, Kessler RC (2001). The stressor criterion in DSM-IV post-traumatic stress disorder: an empirical investigation. *Biol Psychiatry* 50(9):699–704.

Brief DJ, Bollinger AR, Vielhauer MJ, et al.; HIV/AIDS Treatment Adherence, Health Outcomes and Cost Study Group (2004). Understanding the interface of HIV, trauma, post-traumatic stress disorder, and substance use and its implications for health outcomes. *AIDS Care* 16(Suppl 1):S97–S120.

Brouillette M-J, Yuen T, Fellows LK, Cysique LA, Heaton RK, Mayo NE (2016) Identifying neurocognitive decline at 36 months among HIV-positive participants in the CHARTER cohort using group-based trajectory analysis. *PLoS ONE* 11(5):e0155766. doi:10.1371/journal.pone.0155766

Brown GR, Rundell JR, McManis SE, Kendall SN, Zachary R, Temoshok L (1992). Prevalence of psychiatric disorders in early stages of HIV infection. *Psychosom Med* 54:588–601.

Brunette MF, Rosenberg SD, Goodman LA, et al. (1999). HIV risk factors among people with severe mental illness in urban and rural areas. *Psychiatr Serv* 50:556–558.

Burnam MA, Bing EG, Morton SC, et al. (2001). Use of mental health and substance abuse treatment services among adults with HIV in the United States. *Arch Gen Psychiatry* 58(8):729–736.

Butters N, Grant I, Haxby J, et al. (1990). Assessment of AIDS-related cognitive changes: recommendations of the NIMH Workshop on Neuropsychological Assessment Approaches. *J Clin Exp Neuropsychol* 12:963–978.

Carey MP, Carey KB, Kalichman SC (1997). Risk for human immunodeficiency virus (HIV) infection among persons with severe mental illness. *Clin Psychol Rev* 17:271–291.

Carr RL, Gramling LF (2004). Stigma: a health barrier for women with HIV/AIDS. *J Assoc Nurses AIDS Care* 15(5):30–39.

Chander G, Himelhoch S, Moore RD (2006). Substance abuse and psychiatric disorders in HIV-positive patients: epidemiology and impact on antiretroviral therapy, *Drugs* 66(6):769–789.

Cherner M, Cysique L, Heaton RK, et al., HNRC Group (2007). Neuropathologic confirmation of definitional criteria for human immunodeficiency virus-associated neurocognitive disorders. *J Neurovirol* 13:23–28.

Chesney M (2003). Adherence to HAART regimens. *AIDS Patient Care STDs* 17(4):169–177.

Ciesla JA, Roberts JS (2001). Meta-analysis of the relationship between HIV-1 infection and risk for depressive disorders. *Am J Psychiatry* 158:725–730.

Clair WK, Eleazer GP, Hazlett LJ, Morales BA, Sercy JM, Woodbury LV. (1989). Seroprevalence of human immunodeficiency virus in mental health patients. *J S C Med Assoc* 85(3):103–106.

Cohen M, Hoffman RG, Cromwell C, et al. (2002). The prevalence of distress in persons with human immunodeficiency virus infection. *Psychosomatics* 43(1):10–15.

Cohen RA, Harezlak J, Schifitto G, et al.; HIV Neuroimaging Consortium (2010). Effects of nadir CD4 count and duration of human immunodeficiency virus infection on brain volumes in the highly active antiretroviral therapy era. *J Neurovirolog* 16:25–32.

Cook JA, Grey D, Burke J, et al. (2004). Depressive symptoms and AIDS-related mortality among a multisite cohort of HIV-positive women. *Am J Public Health* 94(7):1133–1140.

Cournos F, Empfield M, Horwath E, et al. (1991). HIV seroprevalence among patients admitted to two psychiatric hospitals. *Am J Psychiatry* 148:1225–1230.

Cournos F, Guido J, Coomaraswamy S, Meyer- Bahlburg H, Sugden R, Horwath W (1994). Sexual activity and risk of HIV infection among patients with schizophrenia. *Am J Psychiatry* 151:228–232.

Cournos F, McKinnon K (1997). HIV seroprevalence among people with severe mental illness in the United States: a critical review. *Clin Psychol Rev* 17:259–269.

Cournos F, McKinnon K, Wainberg M (2005). What can mental health interventions contribute to the global struggle against HIV/AIDS? *World Psychiatry* 4:135–141.

Cysique LA, Bain MP, Brew BJ, Murray JM (2011). The burden of HIV-associated neurocognitive impairment in Australia and its estimates for the future. *Sexual Health* 8(4):541–550.

d'Arminio Monforte A, Duca PG, Vago L, Grassi MP, Moroni M (2000). Decreasing incidence of CNS AIDS-defining events associated with antiretroviral therapy. *Neurology* 54:1856–1859

Delahanty DL, LM Bogart, Figler JL. (2004). Posttraumatic stress disorder symptoms, salivary cortisol, medication adherence, and CD4 levels in HIV-positive individuals. *AIDS Care* 16(2):247–260.

DeLorenze GN, Weisner C, Tsai AL, Satre DD, Quesenberry CP Jr, (2011). Excess mortality among HIV-infected patients diagnosed with substance use dependence or abuse receiving care in a fully integrated medical care program. *Alcohol Clin Exp Res* 35(2):203–210.

Demyttenaere K, Bruffaerts R, Posada-Villa J, et al. (2004). Prevalence, severity, and unmet need for treatment of mental disorders in the World Health Organization World Mental Health Surveys *JAMA* 291(21):2581–2590.

de Ronchi D, Faranca I, Forti P, Ravaglia G, Borderi M, Manfredi R, Volterra V (2000). Development of acute psychotic disorders and HIV-1 infection. *Int J Psychiatry Med* 30:173–183.

Dew MA, Becker JT, Sanchez J, et al. (1997). Prevalence and predictors of depressive, anxiety and substance use disorders in HIV-infected and uninfected men: a longitudinal evaluation. *Psychol Med* 27:395–409.

Disney E, Kidorf M, Kolodner K, King V, Peirce J, Beilenson P, Brooner RK (2006). Psychiatric comorbidity is associated with drug use and HIV risk in syringe exchange participants. *J Nerv Ment Dis* 194(8):577–583.

Do AN, Rosenberg ES, Sullivan PS, et al. (2014). Excess burden of depression among HIV-infected persons receiving medical care in the United States: data from the medical monitoring project and the behavioral risk factor surveillance system. *PLoS One* 9(3):e92842.

Dore GJ, Correll PK, Li Y, Kaldor JM, Cooper DA, Brew BJ (1999). Changes to AIDS dementia complex in the era of highly active anti-retroviral therapy. *AIDS* 13(10):1249–1253.

Dore GJ, McDonald A, Li Y, Kaldor J, Brew B, for the National HIV Surveillance Committee (2003). Marked improvement in survival following AIDS dementia complex in the era of highly active antiretroviral therapy. *AIDS* 17(10):1539–1545.

Doyle ME, Labbate LA (1997). Incidence of HIV infection among patients with new-onset psychosis. *Psychiatr Serv* 48(2): 237–238.

Druss BG, Wang PS, Sampson NA, et al. (2007). Understanding mental health treatment in persons without mental diagnoses: results from the National Comorbidity Survey Replication. *Arch Gen Psychiatry* 64:1196–1203.

Empfield M, Cournos F, Meyer I, et al. (1993). HIV seroprevalence among street homeless patients admitted to a psychiatric inpatient unit. *Am J Psychiatry* 150:47–52.

Essock SM Dowden S, Constantine NT, et al. (2003). Risk factors for HIV, hepatitis B, and hepatitis C among persons with severe mental illness. *Psychiatr Serv* 54(6):836–841.

Evans DL, Charney DS (2003). Mood disorders and medical illness: a major public health problem. *Biol Psychiatry* 54:177–180.

Ferrando SJ, Batki SL (2000). Substance abuse and HIV infection. *New Dir Ment Health Serv* 87:57–67.

Ferrando S, Goggin K, Sewell M, Evans S, Fishman B, Rabkin J (1998). Substance use disorders in gay/bisexual men with HIV and AIDS. *Am J Addict* 7(1):51–60.

Gallego L, Barreiro P, López-Ibor JJ (2011). Diagnosis and clinical features of major neuropsychiatric disorders in HIV infection. *AIDS Rev* 13(3):171–179.

Galvan FH, Bing EG, Fleishman JA, et al. (2002). The prevalence of alcohol consumption and heavy drinking among people with HIV in the United States: results from the HIV Cost and Services Utilization Study. *J Stud Alcohol* 63(2):179–186.

Galvan FH, Burnam MA, Bing EG (2003). Co-occurring psychiatric symptoms and drug dependence or heavy drinking among HIV-positive people. *J Psychoactive Drugs* 35(SARC Suppl. 1):153–160.

Ghebremichael M, Paintsil E, Ickovics JR, et al. (2009). Longitudinal association of alcohol use with HIV disease progression and psychological health of women with HIV. *AIDS Care* 21(7):834–841.

Gisslen M, Price RW, Nilsson S (2011). The definition of HIV-associated neurocognitive disorders: are we overestimating the real prevalence? *BMC Infect Dis* 11:356.

Goodkin K (1996). HIV-related neuropsychiatric complications and treatments. In *AIDS and HIV Disease: A Mental Health Perspective*. Washington DC: AIDS Program Office, American Psychiatric Association.

Goodkin K, Wilkie FL, Concha J, et al. (1997). Subtle neuropsychological impairment and minor cognitive-motor disorder in HIV-1 infection. Neuroradiological, neurophysiological, neuroimmunological, and virological correlates. *Neuroimaging Clin N Am* 3:561–579.

Halstead S, Riccio M, Harlow P, Oretti R, Thompson C (1988). Psychosis associated with HIV infection. *Br J Psychiatry* 153:618–623.

Hansen NB, Vaughan EL, Cavanaugh CE, Connell CM, Sikkema KJ (2009). Health-related quality of life in bereaved HIV-positive adults: relationships between HIV symptoms, grief, social support, and Axis II indication. *Health Psychol* 28(2):249–257.

Harris MJ, Jeste DV, Gleghorn A, Sewell DD (1991). New-onset psychosis in HIV-infected patients. *J Clin Psychiatry* 52:369–376.

Hartzell JD, Janke IE, Weintrob AC (2008). Impact of depression on HIV outcomes in the HAART era. *J Antimicrob Chemother* 62(2):246–255.

Hatem DS, Hurowitz JC, Greene HL, Sullivan JL (1990). Seroprevalence of human immunodeficiency virus in a state psychiatric institution. *Arch Intern Med* 50(10):2209.

Heaton RK, Cysique LA, Jin H, et al.; HNRC Group (2010). Neurobehavioral effects of human immunodeficiency virus infection among former plasma donors in rural China. *J Neurovirol* 16(2):185–188.

Heaton RK, Franklin DR, Ellis RJ, et al. (2011). HIV-associated neurocognitive disorders before and during the era of combination antiretroviral therapy: differences in rates, nature, and predictors. *J Neurovirol* 17:3–16.

Heaton RK, Marcotte TD, Rivera-Mindt M, Sadek J, Moore DJ (2004). The impact of HIV-associated neuropsychological impairment on everyday functioning. *J Int Neuropsychol Soc JINS* 10:317–331.

Himelhoch S, Goldberg R, Calmes C, et al. (2011). Screening for and prevalence of HIV and hepatitis C among an outpatient urban sample of people with serious mental illness and co-occurring substance abuse. *J Commun Psychol* 39(2):231–239.

Himelhoch S, McCarthy JF, Ganoczy D, Medoff D, Dixon LB, Blow FC (2007). Understanding associations between serious mental illness and HIV among patients in the VA health system. *Psychiatr Serv* 58:1165–1172.

Ho DD, Rota TR, Schooley RT, et al. (1985). Isolation of HTLV-III from cerebrospinal fluid and neural tissues of patients with neurologic syndromes related to the acquired immunodeficiency syndrome. *N Engl J Med* 313:1493–1497.

Horberg MA, Silverberg MJ, Hurley LB, et al. (2008). Effects of depression and selective serotonin reuptake inhibitor use on adherence to highly active antiretroviral therapy and on clinical outcomes in HIV-infected patients. *J Aquir Imunne Defic Syndr* 47(3):384–390.

Ickovics JR, Hamburger ME, Vlahov D, et al., for the HIV Epidemiology Research Study Group (2001). Mortality, CD4 cell count decline, and depressive symptoms among HIV-seropositive women: longitudinal analysis from the HIV Epidemiology Research Study. *JAMA* 285(11):1466–1474.

Ironson G, O'Cleirigh C, Fletcher MA, et al. (2005). Psychosocial factors predict CD4 and viral load change in men and women with human immunodeficiency virus in the era of highly active antiretroviral treatment. *Psychosom Med* 67(6):1013–1021.

Jackson-Malik P, McLaughlin MJ, O'Hara KT, Buxbaum LU (2011). Rapid oral fluid testing for HIV in veterans with mental health diagnoses and residing in community-assisted living facilities. *J Assoc Nurses AIDS Care* 22(2):81–89.

Jacobsberg L, Frances A, Perry S (1995). Axis II diagnoses among volunteers for HIV testing and counseling. *Am J Psychiatry* 152(8):1222–1224.

Jallow A, Ljunggren G, Wändell P, Carlsson AC (2015). Prevalence, incidence, mortality and co-morbidities amongst human immunodeficiency virus (HIV) patients in Stockholm County, Sweden–The Greater Stockholm HIV Cohort Study. *AIDS Care* 27(2):142–149.

Johnson JG, Williams JB, Rabkin JG, Goetz RR, Remien RH (1995) Axis I psychiatric symptoms associated with HIV infection and personality disorder. *Am J Psychiatry* 152(4):551–554.

Joshi D, O'Grady J, Dieterich D, Gazzard B, Agarwal K (2011). Increasing burden of liver disease in patients with HIV infection. *Lancet* 377(9772):1198–1209.

Justice AC, McGinnis KA, Atkinson JH, et al. (2004). Psychiatric and neurocognitive disorders among HIV-positive and negative veterans in care: Veterans Aging Cohort Five-Site Study. *AIDS* 18(Suppl1):S49–S59.

Kacanek D, Jacobson DL, Spiegelman D, Wanke C, Isaac R, Wilson IB (2010). Incident depression symptoms are associated with poorer HAART adherence: a longitudinal analysis from the Nutrition for Healthy Living study. *J Acquir Imuune Defic Syndr* 53(2):266–272.

Kagee A (2008). Application of the DSM-IV criteria to the experience of living with AIDS: some concerns. *J Health Psychol* 13(8):1008–1011.

Kalichman SC, Sikkema KJ, DiFonzo K, Luke W, Austin J (2002). Emotional adjustment in survivors of sexual assault living with HIV-AIDS. *J Trauma Stress* 15(4):289–296.

Kaplan JE, Hanson D, Dworking MS, et al. (2000). Epidemiology of human immunodeficiency virus-associated opportunistic infections in the United States in the era of highly active antiretroviral therapy. *Clin Infect Dis* 30S1:S5–S14.

Kaslow RA, Blackwelder, WC, Ostrow DG, Yerg D, Palenicek J, Coulson AH, Valdiserri RO (1989). No evidence for a role of alcohol or other psychoactive drugs in accelerating immunodeficiency in HIV-1-positive individuals. A report from the Multicenter AIDS Cohort Study. *JAMA* 261(23):3424–3429.

Katz S, Nevid JS (2005). Risk factors associated with posttraumatic stress disorder symptomatology in HIV-infected women. *AIDS Patient Care STDs* 19(2):110–120.

Kelly B, Raphael B, Judd F, et al. (1998). Posttraumatic stress disorder in response to HIV infection. *Gen Hosp Psychiatry* 20(6):345–352.

Kelly JA, Murphy DA, Bahr GR, et al. (1993). Factors associated with severity of depression and high-risk sexual behavior among persons diagnosed with human immunodeficiency virus (HIV) infection. *Health Psychol* 12(3):215–219.

Kessler RC, McGonagle KA, Zhao S, et al. (1994). Lifetime and 12-month prevalence of DSM III-R psychiatric disorders in the United States: results from the National Comorbidity Survey. *Arch Gen Psychiatry* 51(1):8–19.

Kessler RC, Nelson CB, McGonagle KA, Edlund MJ, Frank RG, Leaf PJ (1996). The epidemiology of co-occurring addictive and mental disorders: implications for prevention and service utilization. *Am J Orthopsychiatry* 66:17–31.

Kessler RC, Sonnega A, Bromet E, Hughes M, Nelson CB (1995). Posttraumatic stress disorder in the National Comorbidity Survey. *Arch Gen Psychiatry* 52(12):1048–1060.

Kimerling R, Calhoun KS, Forehand R, et al. (1999). Traumatic stress in HIV-infected women. *AIDS Educ Prev* 11(4):321–330.

Klinkenberg W, Caslyn R, Morse G, et al. (2003). Prevalence of human immunodeficiency virus, hepatitis B and hepatitis C among homeless persons with co-occurring severe mental illness and substance use disorders. *Compr Psychiatry* 44:293–302.

Kozal MJ, Amico KR, Chiarella J, Cornman D, Fisher W, Fisher J, Friedland G (2005). HIV drug resistance and HIV transmission risk behaviors among active injection drug users. *J Acquir Immune Defic Syndr* 40(1):106–109.

Krakow DS, Galanter M, Dermatis H, Westreich LM (1998). HIV risk factors in dually diagnosed patients. *Am J Addict* 7:74–80.

Kral AH, Bluthenthal RN, Booth RE, Watters JK (1998). HIV seroprevalence among street-recruited injection drug and crack cocaine users in 16 US municipalities. *Am J Public Health* 88:108–113.

Lagios K, Deane FP (2007). Severe mental illness is a new risk marker for blood-borne viruses and sexually transmitted infections. *Aust N Z J Public Health* 31:562–566.

Lee HK, Travin S, Bluestone H (1992). HIV-1 in inpatients. *Hosp Community Psychiatry* 43:181–182.

Leserman J, Pence BW, Whetten K, Mugavero MJ, Thielman NM, Swartz MS, Stangl D (2007). Relation of lifetime trauma and depressive symptoms to mortality in HIV. *Am J Psychiatry* 164(11):1707–1713.

Letendre S, Ellis RJ, Everall I, Ances B, Bharti A, McCutchan JA (2009). Neurologic complications of HIV disease and their treatment. *Top HIV Med* 17(2):46–56.

Levine AJ, Service S, Miller EN, et al. (2012). Genome-wide association study of neurocognitive impairment and dementia in HIV-infected adults. *Am J Med Genet B Neuropsychiatr Genet* 159B(6):669–683.

Lopes M, Olfson M, Rabkin J, et al. (2012). Gender, HIV status, and psychiatric disorders: results from the National Epidemiologic Survey on Alcohol and Related Conditions. *J Clin Psychiatry* 73(3):384–391.

Lopez AD, Mathers CD, Ezzati M, Jamison DT, Murray CJL (2006). Measuring the global burden of disease and risk factors, 1990–2001. In AD Lopez, Mathers CD, Ezzati M, Jamison DT, Murray CL (eds.), *Global Burden of Disease and Risk Factors*. New York: Oxford University Press.

Lyketsos CG, Hoover DR, Guccione M (1996). Depression and survival among HIV-infected persons. *JAMA* 275(1):35–36..

Mahler J, Yi D, Sacks M, Dermatis H, Stebinger A, Card C, Perry S (1994). Undetected HIV infection among patients admitted to an alcohol rehabilitation unit. *Am J Psychiatry* 151:439–440.

Martin L, Kagee A (2011). Lifetime and HIV-related PTSD among persons recently diagnosed with HIV. *AIDS Behav* 15(1):125–131.

Martinez A, Israelski D, Walker C, Koopman C (2002). Posttraumatic stress disorder in women attending human immunodeficiency virus outpatient clinics. *AIDS Patient Care STDs* 16(6):283–291.

McArthur JC (2004). HIV dementia: an evolving disease. *J Neuroimmunol* 157(1–2):3–10.

McArthur JC, Brew BJ (2010). HIV-associated neurocognitive disorders: is there a hidden epidemic? *AIDS* 24(9):1367–1370.

McArthur JC, Hoover DR, Bacellar H, et al. (1993). Dementia in AIDS patients: incidence and risk factors. Multicenter AIDS Cohort Study. *Neurology* 43(11):2245–2252.

McDaniel JS, Blalock AC (2000). Mood and anxiety disorders. *New Dir Ment Health Serv* 87:51–56.

McDaniel JS, Fowlie E, Summerville MB, Farber EW, Cohen-Cole SA (1995). An assessment of rates of psychiatric morbidity and functioning in HIV disease. *Gen Hosp Psychiatry* 17(5):346–352.

McKinnon K, Cournos F (1998). HIV infection linked to substance use among hospitalized patients with severe mental illness. *Psychiatr Serv* 49:1269.

McKinnon K, Cournos F, Herman R (2002). HIV among people with chronic mental illness. *Psychiatr Q* 73:17–31.

McKinnon K, Rosner J (2000). Severe mental illness and HIV-AIDS. *New Dir Ment Health Serv* 87:69–76.

McQuillan GM, Khare M, Karon JM, Schable CA, Vlahov D (1997). Update on the seroepidemiology of human immunodeficiency virus in the United States household population: NHANES III, 1988–1994. *J Aquir Immune Defic Syndr Hum Retrovirol* 14:355–360.

Merikangas KR, Akiskal HS, Angst J, Greenberg PE, Hirschfeld RMA, Petukhova M, Kessler RC (2007). Lifetime and 12-month prevalence of bipolar spectrum disorder in the National Comorbidity Survey replication. *Arch Gen Psychiatry* 64(5):543–552.

Messeri PA, Abramson DM, Aidala AA, Lee F, Lee G (2002). The impact of ancillary HIV services on engagement in medical care in New York City. *AIDS Care* 14(Suppl 1):S15–S29.

Meyer I, Empfield M, Engel D, Cournos F (1995). Characteristics of HIV-positive chronically mentally ill inpatients. *Psychiatr Q* 66(3):201–207.

Meyer I, McKinnon K, Cournos F, Empfield M, Bavli S, Engel D, Weinstock A (1993). HIV seroprevalence among long-stay patients in a state psychiatric hospital. *Hosp Community Psychiatry* 44:282–284.

Mirza RA, Eick-Cost A, Otto JL (2012). The risk of mental health disorders among U.S. military personnel infected with human immunodeficiency virus, active component, U.S. Armed Forces, 2000–2011. *MSMR* 19(5):10–13.

Morrison MF, Petitto JM, Ten Have T, et al. (2002). Depressive and anxiety disorders in women with HIV infection. *Am J Psychiatry* 159:789–796.

Mugavero MJ, Pence BW, Whetten K, et al. (2007). Predictors of AIDS-related morbidity and mortality in a southern U.S. Cohort. *AIDS Patient Care STDs* 21(9): 681–690.

Nakimuli-Mpungu E, Musisi S, Mpungu SK, Katabira (2009). Clinical presentation of bipolar mania in HIV-positive patients in Uganda. *Psychosomatics* 50:325–330.

National Institutes of Health Consensus Development Conference Panel (1997). Management of hepatitis C. *Hepatology* 26:2S–10S.

Navia BA, Jordan BD, Price RW (1986). The AIDS dementia complex: I. Clinical features. *Ann Neurol* 19:517–524.

Neuenburg JK, Brodt HR, Herndier BG, et al. (2002). HIV-related neuropathology, 1985 to 1999: rising prevalence of HIV encephalopathy in the era of highly active antiretroviral therapy. *J Acquir Immune Defic Syndr* 31:171–177.

Nilsson Schönnesson L, Williams ML, Ross MW, Bratt G, Keel B (2007). Factors associated with suboptimal antiretroviral therapy adherence to dose, schedule, and dietary instructions. *AIDS Behav* 11(2):175–183.

Orlando M, Burnam MA, Beckman R, Morton SC, London AS, Bing EG, Fleishman JA (2002). Re-estimating the prevalence of psychiatric disorders in a nationally representative sample of persons receiving care for HIV: results from the HIV Cost and Services Utilization Study. *Int J Methods Psychiatr Res* 11(2):75–82.

Pence BW, Miller WC, Whetten K, Eron JJ, Gaynes BN (2006). Prevalence of DSM-IV-defined mood, anxiety, and substance use disorders in an HIV clinic in the Southeastern United States. *J Acquir Immune Defic Syndr* 42(3):298–306.

Pence BW, O'Donnell JK, Gaynes BN (2012). Falling through the cracks: the gaps between depression prevalence, diagnosis, treatment, and response in HIV care. *AIDS* 26(5):656–658.

Perkins DO, Davidson EJ, Leserman J, Liao D, Evans DL (1993). Personality disorder in patients infected with HIV: a controlled study with implications for clinical care. *Am J Psychiatry* 150(2):309–315.

Pirl WF, Greer JA, Weissgarber C, Liverant G, Safren SA (2005). Screening for infectious diseases among patients in a state psychiatric hospital. *Psychiatr Serv* 56:1614–1616.

Poindexter CC (1997). In the aftermath: serial crisis intervention for people with HIV. *Health Soc Work* 22(2):125–132.

Power C, Boissé L, Rourke S, Gill MJ (2009). NeuroAIDS: an evolving epidemic. *Can J Neurol Sci* 36:285–295.

Prier RE, McNeil JG, Burge JR (1991). Inpatient psychiatric morbidity of HIV-infected soldiers. *Hosp Community Psychiatry* 42:619–623.

Prince JD, Walkup J, Akincigil A, Amin S, Crystal S (2012). Serious mental illness and risk of new HIV/AIDS diagnoses: an analysis of Medicaid beneficiaries in eight states. *Psychiatr Serv* 63(10):1032–1038.

Prince M, Patel V, Saxena S, Maj M, Maselko J, Phillips MR, Rahman A (2007). No health without mental health. *Lancet* 370:859–877.

Rabkin JG (1996). Prevalence of psychiatric disorders in HIV illness. *Int Rev Psychiatry* 8:157–166.

Rabkin JG, Ferrando SJ, Jacobsberg LB, Fishman B (1997). Prevalence of axis I disorders in an AIDS cohort: a cross-sectional, controlled study. *Compr Psychiatry* 38(3):146–154.

Regier DA, Farmer ME, Rae S, Locke BZ, Keith SJ, Judd LL, Goodwin FK (1990). Comorbidity of mental disorders with alcohol and other drug abuse. *JAMA* 264(19):2511–2518.

Robins LN, Wing J, Wittchen HU, et al. (1988) The Composite International Diagnostic Interview. An epidemiologic instrument suitable for use in conjunction with different diagnostic systems and in different cultures. *Arch Gen Psychiatry* 45(12):1069–1077.

Rosenberg SD, Goodman LA, Osher FC, et al. (2001). Prevalence of HIV, hepatitis B, and hepatitis C in people with severe mental illness. *Am J Public Health* 91:31–37.

Rosenberg SD, Trumbetta SL, Meuser LA, Goodman LA, Osher FC, Vidaver RM, Metzger DS (2001). Determinants of risk behavior for human immunodeficiency virus/acquired immunodeficiency syndrome in people with severe mental illness. *Compr Psychiatry* 42(4):263–271.

Rosenthal E, Salmon-Ceron D, Lewden C, et al. (2009). Liver-related deaths in HIV-infected patients between 1995 and 2005 in the French GERMIVIC Joint Study Group Network (Mortavic 2005 study in collaboration with the Mortalite 2005 survey, ANRS EN19). *HIV Med* 10(5):282–289.

Rothbard AB, Blank MB, Staab JP, TenHave T, Young DS, Berry SD, Eachus S (2009). Previously undetected metabolic syndromes and infectious diseases among psychiatric inpatients. *Psychiatr Serv* 60(4): 534–537.

Sacks M, Dermatis H, Looser-Ott S, Perry S (1992). Seroprevalence of HIV and risk factors for AIDS in psychiatric inpatients. *Hosp Community Psychiatry* 43:736–737.

Sacktor NC, Lyles RH, Skolasky RL, et al. (1999). Combination antiretroviral therapy improves psychomotor speed performance in HIV-seropositive homosexual men: Multicenter AIDS Cohort Study (MACS). *Neurology* 52(8):1640–1647.

Sacktor N, Lyles RH, Skolasky R, et al. (2001). HIV-associated neurologic disease incidence changes: Multicenter AIDS Cohort Study, 1990–1998. *Neurology* 56:257–260.

Sacktor N, McDermott MP, Marder K, et al. (2002). HIV-associated cognitive impairment before and after the advent of combination therapy. *J Neurovirol* 8(2):136–142.

Sacktor N, Skolasky RL, Seaberg E, et al. (2016). Prevalence of HIV-associated neurocognitive disorders in the Multicenter AIDS Cohort Study. *Neurology* 86:1–7.

Safren SA, BS Gershuny, Hendriksen E (2003). Symptoms of posttraumatic stress and death anxiety in persons with HIV and medication adherence difficulties. *AIDS Patient Care STDs* 17(12):657–664.

Samet JH, Cheng DM, Libman H, Nunes DP, Alperen JK, Saitz R (2007). Alcohol consumption and HIV disease progression. *J Acquir Immune Defic Syndr* 46(2):194–199.

Satre DD, Campbell CI, Gordon NS, Weisner C (2010). Ethnic disparities in accessing treatment for depression and substance use disorders in an integrated health plan. *Int J Psychiatry Med* 40:57–76.

Satriano J, McKinnon K, Adoff S (2007). HIV service provision for people with severe mental illness in outpatient mental health care settings in New York. *J Prev Interv Community* 33:95–108.

Schwartz-Watts D, Montgomery LD, Morgan DW (1995). Seroprevalence of human immunodeficiency virus among inpatient pretrial detainees. *Bull Am Acad Psychiatry Law* 23:285–288.

Sevigny JJ, Albert SM, McDermott MP, et al (2007). An evaluation of neurocognitive status and markers of immune activation as predictors of time to death in advanced HIV infection. *Arch Neurol* 64:97–102.

Sewell DD (1996). Schizophrenia and HIV. *Schizophrenia Bulletin* 22(3): 465–473.

Sewell MC, Goggin KJ, Rabkin JG, Ferrando SJ, McElhiney MC, Evans S (2000). Anxiety syndromes and symptoms among men with AIDS: a longitudinal controlled study. *Psychosomatics* 41:294–300.

Silberstein C, Galanter M, Marmor M, Lifshutz H, Krasinski K (1994). HIV-1 among inner city dually diagnosed inpatients. *Am J Drug Alcohol Abuse* 20:101–131.

Simioni S, Cavassini M, Annoni J-M, et al. (2010). Cognitive dysfunction in HIV patients despite long-standing suppression of viremia. *AIDS* 24:1243–1250.

Simpson DM (1999). Human immunodeficiency virus–associated dementia: review of pathogenesis, prophylaxis, and treatment studies of zidovudine therapy. *Clin Infect Dis* 29(1):19–34.

Sonneville R, Ferrand H, Tubach F, et al. (2011). Neurological complications of HIV infection in critically ill patients: clinical features and outcomes. *J Infect* 62:301–308.

Staab JP, Evans DL (2001). A streamlined method for diagnosing common psychiatric disorders in primary care. *Clin Cornerstone* 3:1–9.

Stewart DL, Zuckerman CJ, Ingle JM (1994). HIV seroprevalence in a chronic mentally ill population. *J Natl Med Assoc* 86:519–523.

Stoff DM, Mitnick L, Kalichman S (2004). Research issues in the multiple diagnoses of HIV/AIDS, mental illness and substance abuse. *AIDS Care* 16(Suppl. 1):S1–S5.

Stolar A, Catalano G, Hakala S, Bright RP, Fernandez F (2005). Mood disorders and psychosis in HIV. In K Citron, M-J Brouillette, A Beckett (eds.), *HIV and Psychiatry: A Training and Resource Manual*, 2nd ed. (pp. 88–109). Cambridge, UK: Cambridge University Press.

Stoskopf CH, Kim YK, Glover SH (2001). Dual diagnosis: HIV and mental illness, a population-based study. *Community Ment Health J* 37:469–479.

Strober DR, Schwartz JAJ, McDaniel JS, Abrams RF (1997). Depression and HIV disease: prevalence, correlates and treatment. *Psychiatr Ann* 27:372–377.

Sullivan LE, Saitz R, Cheng DM, Libman H, Nunes D, Samet JH (2008). The impact of alcohol use on depressive symptoms in human immunodeficiency virus–infected patients. *Addiction* 103(9):1461–1467.

Susser E, Colson P, Jandorf L, et al. (1997). HIV infection among young adults with psychotic disorders. *Am J Psychiatry* 154:864–866.

Susser E, Valencia E, Conover S (1993). Prevalence of HIV infection among psychiatric patients in a New York City men's shelter. *Am J Public Health* 83:568–570.

Tozzi V, Balestra P, Bellagamba R, et al. (2007). Persistence of neuropsychologic deficits despite long-term highly active antiretroviral therapy in patients with HIV-related neurocognitive impairment: prevalence and risk factors. *J Acquir Immune Defic Syndr* 45:174–182.

Treisman GJ, Angelino AF, Hutton HE (2001). Psychiatric issues in the management of patients with HIV infection. *JAMA* 286:2857–2864.

Treisman G, Fishman M, Schwartz J, Hutton H, Lyketsos C (1998). Mood disorders in HIV infection. *Depress Anxiety* 7:178–187.

Volavka J, Convit A, Czobor P, Dwyer R, O'Donnell J, Ventura A (1991). HIV seroprevalence and risk behaviors in psychiatric inpatients. *Psychiatr Res* 39:109–114.

Wagner GJ (2002). Predictors of antiretroviral adherence as measured by self-report, electronic monitoring, and medication diaries. *AIDS Patient Care STDs* 16(12):599–608.

Wainberg ML, McKinnon K, Cournos F. (2014) Epidemiology of psychopathology in HIV. In JA Joska, DJ Stein, I Grant (eds.), *HIV/AIDS and Psychiatry* (pp. 1–33). West Essex, UK: John Wiley and Sons.

Walkup JT, Akincigil A, Amin S, Hoover D, Siegel M, Crystal S (2010). Prevalence of diagnosed HIV disease among medicaid beneficiaries with schizophrenia in U.S. metropolitan areas. *J Nerv Ment Dis* 198(9):682–686.

Walkup J, Akincigil A, Hoover DR, Siegel MJ, Amin S, Crystal S (2011). Use of Medicaid data to explore community characteristics associated with HIV prevalence among beneficiaries with schizophrenia. *Public Health Rep* 126(Suppl 3):89–101.

Walkup J, Crystal S, Sambamoorthi U (1999). Schizophrenia and major affective disorder among Medicaid recipients with HIV/AIDS in New Jersey. *Am J Public Health* 89:1101–1103.

Whetten K, Leserman J, Lowe K, et al. (2006). Prevalence of childhood sexual abuse and physical trauma in an HIV-positive sample from the deep south. *Am J Public Health* 96(6):1028–1030.

White JL, Darko DF, Brown SJ, Miller JC, Hayduk R, Kelly T, Mitler MM (1995). Early central nervous system response to HIV infection: sleep distortion and cognitive-motor decrements. *AIDS* 9:1043–1050.

Woods WJ, Lindan CP, Hudes ES, Boscarino JA, Clark W, Avins AL (2000). HIV infection and risk behaviors in two cross-sectional surveys of heterosexuals in alcoholism treatment. *J Stud Alcohol* 61:262–266.

4.

GLOBAL ASPECTS OF THE HIV PANDEMIC

Emilio Letang, Francine Cournos, Dimitri Prybylski, Donn Colby, E. Kainne Dokubo,

Chuan-Mei Lee, Julia del Amo, Jordi Blanch, Esteban Martínez, Gaddy Noy,

Farah Ahmad-Stout, Marshall Forstein, and Sara Gorman

While HIV/AIDS is a global epidemic, the nature of the illness and its effects on the people living with it varies across regions and is deeply affected by the stigma of HIV and its associated risk behaviors, socioeconomic and gender inequalities, the reach and capacity of local health systems, and cultural factors, among other influences. This chapter explores the current state of the epidemic in four regions: sub-Saharan Africa, Asia-Pacific, Europe, and the Americas.

The chapter begins with an exploration of HIV/AIDS in the hardest-hit region of the world, sub-Saharan Africa, which bears a disproportionate share of the global burden with more than two-thirds of all people living with HIV globally (Figure 4.1). Even within sub-Saharan Africa, the disease burden and epidemiological characteristics differ across countries, heavily concentrating in southern and eastern Africa. Encouragingly, much progress has been made in recent years, with the rate of new HIV infections decreasing in 25 sub-Saharan African countries by 50% between 2001 and 2011. However, HIV has still continued to spread faster than its treatment in this part of the world, and despite the achievements in the past decade, many challenges remain.

At the same time, there have been tremendous advances in access to antiretroviral treatment (ART) in sub-Saharan Africa, especially in the past decade, with more than 12 million people having received life-saving ART in Africa. In general, scale-up of ART has resulted in improved life expectancy in HIV-positive individuals in sub-Saharan Africa, as well as reduced secondary sexual transmission and reduced HIV incidence. Moreover, scale-up of prevention of mother-to-child transmission (PMTCT) has resulted in a dramatic decrease in vertical transmission. Besides ART scale-up, efforts to focus on prevention, including male circumcision, pre-exposure prophylaxis (PrEP), and vaginal microbicides, are also on the rise in sub-Saharan Africa, although these efforts have shown slower progress than increasing access to ART. The authors of this section stress the need for ART rollout and HIV prevention programs to be critically scaled up among key populations in Africa, in particular men who have sex with men (MSM), sex workers, vulnerable youth, and people who inject drugs (PWID).

The remaining challenges in Africa are strongly related to more general systemic problems in this part of the world, namely poverty and inequity, including transportation barriers, health worker shortages, and lack of access to viral load testing. Also, new challenges for African clinicians and health systems result from the changing face of the epidemic due to increasing survival on ART and aging of the HIV population, with its associated multimorbidities. Finally, the burden of HIV is not limited to the effects of the illness itself. Mental illness and comorbid chronic diseases are as much a concern in the African epidemic as in other parts of the world. With the many advances in controlling the HIV epidemic in Africa come many challenges, some old and some new. Political will, sufficient funding, health system improvements, and more effective ways of overcoming stigma will be needed to cope with the current and emerging challenges associated with the HIV epidemic in this region of the world.

In contrast, the epidemic in the Asia-Pacific region seems to be in a dynamic equilibrium that is rapidly evolving, with increases in numbers of people living with HIV in the region and decreases in newly infected individuals. However, these aggregate statistics obscure the considerable variation that exists subregionally. A more accurate perspective is gained from dividing the region into five subregions, one with a declining epidemic, one with a maturing epidemic, one with an expanding epidemic, one with a latent epidemic, and one a low-prevalence area. In this area, the epidemic is most concentrated in particular groups, including transgender individuals, MSM, female sex workers, and PWID. To further complicate things, large countries in the region, including China, India, and Indonesia, show considerable variations in the nature and prevalence of the epidemic even within their own borders.

Stigma is the major barrier to HIV prevention and treatment, as is lack of proper linkages to care and community-based HIV treatment. Many countries in this region still depend heavily on international donors to fund HIV treatment programs, although rapid economic development in places such as China has altered this profile slightly. More work is needed not only to understand the nuanced barriers

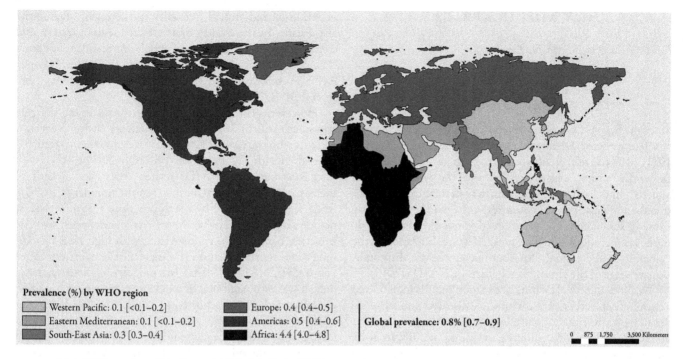

Figure 4.1. Adult HIV prevalence (15–49 years) 2015, globally, by WHO region.
SOURCE: http://www.who.int/gho/hiv/hiv_013.jpg?ua=1. Accessed January 3, 2017.

Prevalence (%) by WHO region

Western Pacific: 0.1 [<0.1–0.2]
Eastern Mediterranean: 0.1 [<0.1–0.2]
South-East Asia: 0.3 [0.3–0.4]
Europe: 0.4 [0.4–0.5]
Americas: 0.5 [0.4–0.6]
Africa: 4.4 [4.0–4.8]

Global prevalence: 0.8% [0.7–0.9]

0   875   1,750   3,500 Kilometers

and challenges in different subpopulations within the very large and diverse Asia-Pacific region but also to strengthen health systems and reduce stigma and discrimination to ensure that at-risk individuals are receiving the prevention and treatment services they need.

In Europe, the epidemic is as diverse as the population with a clear division between Eastern and Western European countries. Although ART has led to great advances in health in this region, late identification of illness is a ubiquitous problem across all the countries of the European Union, particularly in the East. Stigma and discrimination makes it difficult for MSM to seek treatment, especially in Eastern Europe. Of particular relevance, migrant populations from high–HIV endemic countries are a significant part of the European epidemic, and migrants face inequity, stigma, and increasing barriers to access health care. The authors of this section note the considerable mental health challenges for vertically infected HIV-positive adolescents in Europe, who represent a small, albeit significant, group.

The epidemic in the United States has changed a lot over time, and the country is faced with a situation in which rates of new HIV infection have dropped among certain groups but continue to rise among others. In particular, African Americans and, to some extent, other minority groups as well as MSM, are key vulnerable populations. Given the increasing availability and efficacy of treatment for HIV, the number of people living with HIV in the United States continues to grow, and is now estimated at 1.2 million. The high prevalence of the infection creates an increased opportunity for transmission, making prevention and testing key strategies to reduce incidence. Addressing disparities in access to healthcare, increased attention to targeted prevention, and attending to the social determinants of health remain vital strategies in controlling the epidemic in the United States.

In Canada, the number of PLHIV has increased over the last few years, as advances in treatment have led to longer lifespans for PLHIV. Overall, the incidence of new HIV infections has decreased over the last 30 years, although some vulnerable populations, particularly the Aboriginal population, experience higher rates of HIV infection.

The epidemic is also extremely varied across Latin American, South American, and Central American countries. Some countries, such as Mexico, have experienced significant declines in rates of new infections in recent years, while others, such as Brazil, have seen increases. Once again, in these regions, the impact of the epidemic varies across demographic groups, with MSM, sex workers, and transgender people showing the highest rates of new infection.

While the HIV epidemic and its accompanying mental health issues are incredibly diverse across and within regions examined in this chapter, it is also important to recognize some striking similarities that cross cultural and geographic lines. Almost universally, HIV-positive individuals face serious stigma and discrimination that can make access to treatment difficult. In addition, while ART has been the most significant factor in the reduction of HIV-related deaths, too little attention is paid to preventive efforts as well as to the social circumstances associated with the illness across the globe. A global effort that simultaneously recognizes the common, underlying problems still facing HIV-positive individuals worldwide and takes into account the nuances in the different manifestations of the epidemic in different regions and populations around the world is absolutely essential to make progress against this disease.

HIV AIDS IN AFRICA

Emilio Letang and Francine Cournos

THE BURDEN OF HIV/AIDS IN SUB-SAHARAN AFRICA

Since the first AIDS cases were reported in California 36 years ago (Centers for Disease Control and Prevention [CDC], 1981), HIV has relentlessly spread, to become one of the worst epidemics in human history. All areas of the globe have been affected, but the burden of disease has dramatically concentrated among the poorest countries in the world, particularly those in sub-Saharan Africa (SSA). Despite the efforts made in the last decade, which have resulted in a stabilization of the epidemic in the region, SSA continues to bear a disproportionate share of the global HIV burden (UNAIDS, 2016).

Declines in new HIV infections among adults have slowed alarmingly in recent years, with the estimated annual number of new infections among adults remaining nearly static at about 2.1 million [1.8 million–2.4 million] in 2015. In 2015, an estimated 36.7 million (34.0 million–39.8 million) people were living with HIV (PLHIV) worldwide, with more than half—51.2%, or 19.0 million (17.7 million–20.5 million)—in sub-Saharan Africa (UNAIDS 2016). HIV prevalence in SSA in 2015 was higher than in any other area of the world, including the Caribbean, Asia, Eastern Europe, Western and Central Europe, and North America (UNAIDS, 2016). New infections and AIDS-related deaths were also disproportionately concentrated in SSA in 2012, accounting for 69% (1.8 million) of the 2.3 million new infections and 70% (1.2 million) of the 1.7 million AIDS-related deaths (UNAIDS, 2013a).

The epidemics in SSA differ greatly among countries, with southern Africa most heavily affected. Thirty-four percent of all people living with HIV worldwide reside in 10 southern African countries: Angola, Botswana, Lesotho, Malawi, Mozambique, Namibia, South Africa, Swaziland, Zambia, and Zimbabwe (UNAIDS, 2013a). South Africa has experienced one of the fastest growing epidemics globally, and in 2012 it was home to 6.4 million PLHIV in a population of approximately 52 million, up from an estimated 4 million in 2002 (Shisana, 2013; Stats-SA, 2010, 2013; UNAIDS, 2010, 2013a; United Nations, Population Division, 2015). In turn, Nigeria had 3.4 million PLHIV, Kenya 1.6 million, Tanzania 1.5 million, Uganda and Mozambique 1.4 million each, Zimbabwe 1.2 million, and Zambia and Malawi 1 million each, whereas Ethiopia (790,000), Ghana (230,000), and Lesotho (320,000) had considerably smaller numbers of PLHIV (UNAIDS, 2013a).

Encouragingly, the overall growth of the epidemic appears to have stabilized worldwide as well as in most of the countries in southern and eastern Africa. The rate of new HIV infections decreased in 25 sub-Saharan African countries by 50% between 2001 and 2011, with further declines in 2012, including all countries mentioned except for Lesotho and Angola, where the epidemic remains stable (UNAIDS, 2013b). In addition, the remarkable scale-up of ART in resource-limited settings (RLS) has resulted in a reduction of AIDS-related annual mortality in the region during the last decade. In the world's most affected region, eastern and southern Africa, the number of people on treatment has more than doubled since 2010, reaching nearly 10.3 million people. AIDS-related deaths in the region have decreased by 36% since 2010 (UNAIDS, 2016).

However, HIV has continued to spread faster than its treatment, and in 2010 it was estimated that for every two patients who started ART, five to six new infections occurred (World Health Organization [WHO], 2010a). Also, new infections outnumber AIDS-related deaths as a result of increased life expectancy on ART, so the number of PLHIV in Africa has increased by nearly one third (31%) in the last decade (UNAIDS, 2013a). Many challenges persist as HIV infection continues to be associated with high rates of morbidity and mortality, and HIV incidence remains unacceptably high (UNAIDS, 2013a). In a model using South African data, it was estimated that, if incidence rates were maintained constant at the rates reported in 2008, 40–50% of 15-year-olds would become HIV infected by age 60 (Johnson et al., 2012). Importantly, the consequences of this epidemic extend beyond the individual level and include impacts on education, industry, agriculture, transport, human resources, and the economy in general, with decades of economic development having been rolled back (Dixon et al., 2002; Urassa et al., 2001).

ART SCALE-UP PROGRAMS IN SUB-SAHARAN AFRICA AND IMPACT

The HIV epidemic has mobilized a tremendous political, financial, and human response, both globally and in SSA. Important initiatives include the World Bank Multi-Country AIDS program (1999); the United Nations Millennium Declaration (United Nations [UN], 2000) in 2000 and corresponding goals report in 2010 (UN, 2010; UNAIDS, 2016); the UN General Assembly Special Session on AIDS in 2001; the creation of the Global Fund to Fight AIDS, Tuberculosis, and Malaria (GFATM) in 2002; the adoption by the U.S. government of the President's Emergency Plan for AIDS Relief (PEPFAR) in 2003; and the 3 by 5 initiative launched in 2003 by the World Health Organization (WHO) and the Joint United Nations Program on HIV/AIDS (UNAIDS; WHO, 2003). Global expenditures for the HIV epidemic increased from 3.8 billion U.S. dollars in 2001 to 18.9 billion U.S. dollars in 2012 (UNAIDS, 2013a). Between 2000 and 2011, 51.6 billion U.S. dollars from development assistance for health (DAH) resources have been spent in HIV programs in low- and middle-income countries (Institute for Health Metrics and Evaluation, 2014).

Before ART became available in SSA, HIV infection resulted in premature death for most infected people (Morgan and Whitworth, 2001). Increased international funding, coupled with a dramatic reduction in ART prices about a decade ago (Badri et al., 2006), has resulted in previously unimaginable access to ART, prevention services, and evidence-based care interventions for PLHIV in Africa (Reynolds and Quinn, 2010). At the end of 2015, more than 15 million people were receiving HIV treatment worldwide, including an estimated 10.7 million in SSA, remarkably having met the AIDS target of Millennium Development Goal (MDG)-6 nine months ahead of schedule (UNAIDS, 2015). This figure compares to only 2% of individuals in need receiving ART 10 years earlier, and overall, the number of people receiving therapy has tripled since 2007 (UNAIDS, 2013b).

ART rollout in RLS has had a dramatic impact on the dynamics of the HIV epidemic and constitutes one of the great achievements of global health in the last decade. Today, HIV-infected people on ART in SSA can expect to have an overall life expectancy similar to that of HIV-negative individuals, and population-level benefits include declining mortality rates in adults and children and increasing life expectancy (Bor et al., 2012, 2013; Tanser et al., 2013). Scale-up of prevention of mother-to-child transmission (PMTCT) programs makes the elimination of MTCT seem within reach (Kerber et al., 2013), and ART has been shown to be effective in reducing heterosexual transmission and HIV incidence at individual (Cohen et al., 2011) and population levels (Johnson et al., 2012; Tanser et al., 2013). Based on a recent estimate by the Global Burden of Disease collaboration, PMTCT and ART rollout have resulted in a gain of 19 million extra years of life globally (Murray et al., 2014). The evidence of the impact of ART on sexual transmission of HIV has led to the concept of treatment as prevention (TasP), reinforcing the prominent role of ART in HIV prevention. Indeed, a recent population study in South Africa showed a direct relationship between ART coverage and reduced incidence of HIV infection, estimating reductions of about 20% with 20–30% ART coverage and 40% with ART coverage above 30% (Tanser et al., 2013). Four large population-based randomized trials are currently ongoing in South Africa, Botswana, Zambia, Kenya, and Uganda, to further evaluate the impact of TasP at a population level by assessing the effectiveness of immediate initiation of ART in reducing HIV incidence (Iwuji et al., 2013).

As evidence emerged that earlier initiation of ART further delayed HIV disease progression (De Cock and El-Sadr, 2013; Le et al., 2013; Severe et al., 2010; When to Start Consortium, 2009), the WHO launched several revisions to its guidelines, recommending initiation at progressively higher CD4 counts. The latest revision, in September 2015, recommends initiating ART in all HIV-positive individuals with any CD4 cell count (WHO, 2015). This recommendation markedly contrasts with using CD4 cell count cutoffs of <200 cells/μl in the 2006 guidelines, <350 cells/μl in the 2010 guidelines, and <500 cells/μl in the 2013 guidelines, among other criteria. Additional recent evidence shows a delayed time to AIDS events, including tuberculosis (TB), and decreased morbidity when ART is started as soon as possible (Grinsztejn et al., 2014; WHO, 2015). This concurs with previous evidence showing an average 65% decrease in TB incidence associated with ART, consistent across different CD4 strata (Suthar et al., 2012), and is particularly relevant in SSA, where TB is the main cause of death among PLHIV. However, acknowledging the limitations in feasibility of implementing these guidelines in some SSA countries, a stepwise approach to implementation was recommended, determined by each country's capabilities.

Progress toward universal access to ART remains mixed. Botswana and Namibia achieved greater than 80% ART coverage by the end of 2009, whereas Mozambique and South Africa barely surpassed 30% coverage (UNAIDS, 2013b). The AIDS targets of MDG-6 were achieved ahead of schedule (UNAIDS, 2015), and new goals have been set beyond MDG 6, aiming to identify 90% of PLHIV, providing ART to 90% of individuals testing positive for HIV, and achieving virological suppression in 90% of those treated by 2020 (UNAIDS, 2014). These ambitious goals should be pursued in parallel with the urgent strengthening of HIV prevention programs.

BEYOND ART ROLLOUT: HIV PREVENTION IN SUB-SAHARAN AFRICA

The field of HIV prevention has evolved dramatically, and today, together with the progressive expansion of ART, a comprehensive toolbox of preventive strategies lays the groundwork to end the AIDS epidemic. While increased condom use in South Africa between 2000 and 2008 appeared to play a major role in decreasing HIV incidence (Johnson et al., 2012), behavioral interventions are generally less effective than biomedical strategies. As described earlier, today we know that ART is key in reducing both vertical and sexual transmission and, therefore, HIV incidence. Other biomedical interventions that have shown varying degrees of efficacy include pre-exposure prophylaxis (PrEP), vaginal microbicides, and voluntary male medical circumcision (VMMC). PrEP was shown to be 44% effective in reducing HIV transmission among MSM, with a strong correlation with drug blood levels (Grant, 2010). Another study conducted among serodiscordant couples in Kenya and Uganda showed a reduction of HIV transmission by 67% and 75% for men and women, respectively (Baeten et al., 2012). Overall, efficacy trials targeting different populations show that PrEP works. Antiretroviral-based vaginal microbicides appeared promising after a trial conducted in South Africa in 2010 (Karim et al., 2010), but a further trial conducted to confirm these results was stopped early due to futility (Van Damme et al., 2012; Vaginal and Oral Interventions to Control the Epidemic [VOICE], 2013). Recently, two placebo-controlled clinical trials of use of a monthly vaginal ring containing dapivirine, involving a total of 4588 women in SSA, showed an overall 30% protection in the acquisition of HIV (Baeten et al., 2016; Nel et al., 2016). However, both PrEP and topical microbicides are strongly influenced by the problem of nonadherence and may not always represent feasible prevention strategies in SSA. Further research is ongoing to develop culturally tailored programs to improve acceptance of PrEP among diverse populations.

In contrast, expanding VMMC appears to be a promising strategy and is being scaled up with the target of circumcising 80% of all African males aged 15 to 49 years. VMMC was shown to reduce female-to-male transmission by 60% in three trials conducted in South Africa, Kenya, and Uganda (Auvert et al., 2005; Bailey et al., 2007; Gray et al., 2007). Although VMMC does not prevent male-to-female transmission, sufficient coverage would indirectly benefit females by reducing HIV prevalence and sexually transmitted infections among their male partners. Despite this considerable efficacy, provision and uptake of VMMC in Africa has been slow and heterogeneous in Africa, with Kenya having achieved 63% of the coverage target, Ethiopia 57%, South Africa 10.2%, and Lesotho, Zimbabwe, Namibia, Malawi, and Rwanda each below 10% (UNAIDS, 2013b). Financial constraints, stock-outs of equipment, and shortage of staff in part explain this low uptake (UNAIDS, 2013b). New strategies are being devised to increase uptake, including several delivery modes, innovative service structures, and on-demand immediate interventions. Of note, VMMC is more cost-effective than ART in averting new infections, making the scale-up of medical circumcision followed by the scale-up of ART the most cost-effective strategies for HIV prevention in SSA (Barnighausen et al., 2012).

AN EPIDEMIC IN TRANSITION: OLD AND NEW CHALLENGES

Although the success in scaling up ART and stabilization of the epidemic needs to be widely acknowledged, challenges remain in SSA, including logistical factors undermining the success of ART scale-up programs, the neglected epidemic among key populations, and aging of the HIV-infected population complicating HIV management with associated comorbidities. In the long-term fight ahead, optimization of local health systems will be key to overcoming these challenges and providing ongoing, sustainable, and comprehensive HIV care (Barker et al., 2007; Mutevedzi and Newell, 2014).

OBSTACLES TO SUCCESSFUL ART SCALE-UP IN AFRICA

ART scale-up programs in Africa are hindered by low linkage into care, late presentation, lack of virological monitoring, obstacles in treatment delivery, and low long-term retention in care. The majority of individuals in SSA are not aware of their HIV status and do not seek early medical attention, limiting their entry into care and thus posing serious challenges to national scale-up plans (Bunnell et al., 2008). Despite recommendations of immediate ART initiation (WHO, 2015), an important proportion of individuals in SSA still present late and start ART with CD4 cell counts around 100 cells/μl (Nash et al., 2008). Late presentation is associated with a higher rate of opportunistic infections and much greater mortality during the first year of treatment (Keiser et al., 2008). Once treatment is initiated, response to ART should be monitored both immunologically and virologically, but only limited treatment sites have access to viral load testing.

The high cost of virological monitoring led to the development of the WHO public health approach to following patients on ART (WHO, 2006). This strategy, now widely implemented in RLS, uses clinical and, if available, CD4 cell count results to identify treatment failure and guide the switch to second-line regimens. However, clinical and immunological monitoring lacks sensitivity to identify true virological failure and can result in late switching to second-line regimens and in significant accumulation of genotypic resistance to ART (Hosseinipour et al., 2009). In addition, this approach can result in misclassification of therapeutic response, thereby leading to unnecessary switching (Moore et al., 2006). Also, sustained viremia in the presence of drug pressure increases the risk of secondary transmission of drug-resistant virus (Vekemans et al., 2007). These concerns prompted revision of the WHO guidelines, which now recommend switching to second-line ART regimens when the HIV viral load is higher than 1,000 copies/mL in settings where HIV RNA assessment is available (WHO, 2013). Ultimately, emergence of transmitted HIV resistance in Africa might roll back the tremendous benefits of ART observed during the first decade of ART scale-up. A South African study in 2013 showed a 6% prevalence of at least one drug-resistant mutation, with 15% having a significantly compromised regimen, implying a reduced efficacy of second-line regimens (Manasa et al., 2013). At present there are limited choices of antiretroviral options to treat patients with treatment failure in Africa, and third-line antiretroviral drugs such as integrate inhibitors are urgently needed.

Treatment delivery is also hindered by transportation barriers, difficult communication with healthcare workers in rural settings, and lack of human resources. Many ART programs in RLS have suffered from inequitable distribution of care, with rural areas being the most disadvantaged because of such barriers as higher costs and time loss incurred from traveling long distances to the health center (Egger et al., 2005). There is a large research gap on how best to deliver ART and sustain care in remote areas. Strategies of decentralization such as home-based delivery of ART (MacPherson et al., 2014; Weidle et al., 2006), task shifting from more to less skilled health professionals (Brentlinger et al., 2010; Kredo et al., 2014), and mobile phone technology (Chang et al., 2008; Gentry et al., 2013; Kunutsor et al., 2010) have emerged as possible strategies for making ART more accessible in these settings.

After patients have initiated treatment, long-term retention in care represents an enormous challenge in sub-Saharan Africa. A recent systematic review shows that, overall, ART programs in SSA have retained about 80% of their patients after 6 months and 60% at the end of the second year of treatment. Most patient attrition occurs during the first year of treatment and is mainly due to loss to follow-up and early death. Encouragingly, some programs appear to have been highly successful in retaining patients (up to 76.5% at 2 years of treatment in Botswana or even higher in Rwanda) and may provide examples that others can follow (Nsanzimana et al., 2015; Rosen and Fox, 2011). Better patient tracing, better understanding of loss to follow-up, and earlier initiation of ART to reduce mortality are needed.

Finally, ART initiation at higher CD4 counts and the resulting increased survival is increasing demand for ART in RLS. With stagnation of international funding for HIV programs, the focus of the major donors is on further reducing the cost per year of ART. This should be pursued in parallel with improvement in quality of ART programs. Program quality is heterogeneous in SSA; a globally standardized evaluation of costs and outcomes at regular intervals, including viral load suppression and patient transfers, is urgently needed in order to maximize efficiency and quality (Murray, 2015).

NEGLECTED HIV EPIDEMICS AMONG KEY POPULATIONS IN AFRICA

As mentioned earlier, HIV epidemics are in decline among the general population worldwide. However, both globally and in SSA, epidemics among key populations are far from being controlled. These include the previously neglected epidemics among MSM, sex workers, vulnerable youth, and PWID. The epidemics in these key populations in Africa are often fuelled by lack of access to healthcare resulting from stigma and discrimination (Beyrer et al., 2013). In 2009, in some African countries, substantial numbers of new infections were estimated to occur among sex workers and their clients, PWID, MSM, and prisoners, contributing jointly to about 33% of new infections in Kenya and 26% in South Africa. Sex work contributed to between 7% and 11% of new infections in Uganda, Swaziland, and Zambia and to up to a third of new infections in West Africa (Gouws and Cuchi, 2012).

Median HIV prevalence among MSM exceeds 1% in all regions of the world; it has been reported to be highest in Western and Central Africa (19%) and eastern and southern Africa (15%) (UNAIDS, 2013a). In Africa and across the African diaspora, pooled estimates show that black MSM are 15 times more likely to be HIV positive compared with the general population and 8.5 times more likely compared with black non-MSM populations (Millet et al., 2012). Homophobia, stigma, secrecy, discrimination, violence, and punitive laws regarding same-sex relations impede HIV surveillance and prevention and create a climate of fear and intolerance that limits the access of MSM to HIV treatment and care. Disparities in the prevalence of HIV infection are greater in countries that criminalize sexual behavior between men than those that do not (Millet et al., 2012). In addition, domestic and international funding invested in HIV programs for MSM in SSA is virtually nonexistent.

Sex workers also harbor a disproportionately high HIV prevalence. It is estimated that globally, female sex workers are 13.5 times more likely to be HIV infected than other women (Baral et al., 2012), the highest rates of infection being in SSA, ranging from 22% in eastern and southern Africa and 17% in Western and Central Africa to less than 5% in all other regions (UNAIDS, 2013a). However, these figures likely underestimate the true prevalence. An analysis by the World Bank found a pooled HIV prevalence among female sex workers of 37% in SSA, compared to 11% in Eastern Europe and 6% in Latin America (Kerrigan et al., 2010). These disparities speak to the lack of reliable data, which in turn reflects the scant attention that this vulnerable group has received. Similar to MSM, sex workers in

Africa face social and legal disadvantages that increase their vulnerability and deter individuals from obtaining the services they need. An exception to this rule is southern Africa, where domestic spending on prevention services for sex workers outweighs international contributions (UNAIDS, 2013b).

Women aged 15–24 years are another key population in Africa affected by HIV. Prevalence in this group remains more than twice as high as among young men (UNAIDS, 2013a), and the reasons for this are multifactorial (Cournos et al., 2014). Women may be partnered with men who are included in high-risk sexual networks, including MSM, with the highest risk occurring in countries where being openly gay is highly stigmatized and/or illegal. Sexual and gender-based violence and a lack of economic opportunities may make it difficult for women to be assertive and break free from abusive relationships. The pattern of adolescent girls having sex with older male partners is another frequently observed risk; the vaginal mucosa is more vulnerable to HIV infection in adolescents than in adult women.

Knowledge of HIV among adolescents remains low. Sexual violence, inadequate access to youth-friendly HIV and sexual reproductive health services and to comprehensive sex education, and limited protection for confidentiality challenge effective HIV prevention among this group (Binagwaho et al., 2012; Jewkes et al., 2010; UNESCO, 2013). Cash transfers incentivizing safer behaviors have emerged as an effective strategy to reduce young people's vulnerability to HIV (Baird et al., 2012; Björkman-Nyqvist et al., 2013; UNESCO, 2013).

HIV-infected women of reproductive age who become pregnant are at risk of passing HIV infection to their babies through perinatal transmission. The majority of children who have lost one or both parents to HIV infection reside in SSA, and their protection and care represent considerable challenges. While programs have been developed to help these children, largely through providing school fees, shelter, nutrition, healthcare, and psychosocial support, these programs are often spread thin and their impact has not been well studied (Cournos et al., 2014).

The epidemic among PWID is comparatively less prevalent in Africa, with regional prevalence estimated at 0.2%, 10 times lower than in Eastern Europe and Central Asia (UNAIDS, 2013a). However, there is a paucity of data—again because criminalization, stigma, and discrimination make uptake of voluntary HIV testing and counseling extremely low among PWID. Moreover, Africa has had an increasing role in global drug trafficking, leading to increasing transmission of HIV through drug injection in some regions, especially in Nigeria, Kenya, Tanzania, South Africa, and Mauritius (Strathdee and Stockman, 2010). In 2008, 7% of Kenya's new HIV infections were attributable to drug injection, and 42% of Kenya's population of PWID are HIV infected (Strathdee and Stockman, 2010).

ART rollout and HIV prevention programs need to be critically scaled up among key populations in Africa. Research to optimize and operationalize prevention strategies among these vulnerable populations is needed.

THE DOUBLE BURDEN OF COMMUNICABLE AND NONCOMMUNICABLE DISEASES

The aging of persons with HIV complicates HIV management and threatens to roll back the initial benefits of ART programs in Africa. In addition to HIV-related morbidity, older adults are at increased risk of noncommunicable diseases (Gebo, 2008; Gebo and Justice, 2009; Grabar et al., 2006; Haregu et al., 2014; Nylor et al., 2005). Studies have shown that older people with HIV infection have more rapid HIV disease progression (Babiker et al., 2001; Collaborative Group on AIDS Incubation and HIV Surveillance, 2000; Todd et al., 2007), higher mortality, and suboptimal immune reconstitution (Greig et al., 2012; Mutevedzi et al., 2011; Nguyen and Holodniy 2008; Sabin et al., 2009). Arterial hypertension, diabetes mellitus, obesity, dyslipidemia, heart disease, and non-AIDS malignancies are emerging problems among PLHIV in SSA. This poses challenges not only for already overburdened African clinicians but also to African health systems, calling for the transition from vertical models to comprehensive horizontal chronic-diseases programs. Multisectoral responses and national coordination mechanisms will be needed to face this emerging challenge.

HIV/AIDS AND MENTAL HEALTH IN AFRICA

HIV infection travels with an enormous burden of mental illness, which is the primary topic of this textbook and will not be further elaborated upon here. This is as true in African countries as it is in other parts of the world, but responding to this burden is hampered by the fact that low- and middle-income countries spend a very small percentage of their healthcare budgets on addressing mental illnesses (Cournos et al., 2014).

The WHO has created guidelines for treating mental illness in RLS. These include the mental health components of the initiative known as the Integrated Management of Adult and Adolescent Illnesses (IMAI; WHO, 2011) and modules for treating mental health, substance use, and neurological problems, known as mhGAP (WHO, 2010b). Fledgling efforts are being made to roll out these guidelines in Africa, but this is a slow process with many barriers.

CONCLUSIONS

In summary, although much has been achieved in tackling the HIV epidemic in sub-Saharan Africa, much remains to be done and new challenges are emerging. Improving early detection of HIV infection, linkage to care, and access to ART remain key to preventing new infections and avoiding late presentations with their associated poor prognoses. Overcoming the logistical obstacles to ART scale-up is of paramount importance, and dedicated programs are needed to improve lifelong retention in care. HIV viral load monitoring, now recommended by the WHO, needs to be rapidly adopted by national programs and scaled up to detect treatment failure as soon as possible and maximize the limited therapeutic arsenal available. New classes of ART need to be made available to allow for the effective replacement of failing regimens among patients. Managing HIV as a chronic condition is posing new challenges for African clinicians and health systems and new strategies are needed to respond to this emerging double burden of communicable and noncommunicable diseases. Prevention programs need to be strengthened, with special attention given to key populations such as MSM, PWID, sex workers, and vulnerable youth. The changing face of the HIV epidemic in Africa challenges African health systems to provide sustainable, quality programs with appropriate support. Ultimately, political will, effective approaches to overcoming stigma, availability of sustained funding, and efficient spending will determine the long-term success or failure of HIV programs in Africa.

HIV AND AIDS IN THE ASIA-PACIFIC REGION

Dimitri Prybylski, Donn Colby, E. Kainne Dokubo, and Chuan-Mei Lee

HIV EPIDEMIOLOGY

Almost five million (4.9 million) people were estimated to be living with HIV in the Asia-Pacific region in 2012, a 20% increase from 4.1 million in 2001 (UNAIDS, 2013). Of this total, about one-third (1.7 million) were women. The estimated number of annual AIDS deaths increased slightly in the region, from 250,000 in 2001 to 270,000 in 2012. On the other hand, the estimated number of people newly infected with HIV has decreased by 26% since 2001 to 350,000 in 2012. In addition, there were 210,000 children living with HIV in the region in 2012. New infections among children have declined by 28% to 23,000 since 2001. Taken together, these data indicate that the epidemic is stabilizing in the region, but these aggregated summary trends mask important subregional variations in epidemic transmission dynamics. UNAIDS has grouped Asia-Pacific countries into at least five different categories according to variations in trends of new infections, the number of PLHIV, and the number of AIDS-related deaths (Table 4.1).

As the UNAIDS profiles reflect, the Asia-Pacific region is home to striking differences in current and new HIV infection rates both within and across countries. Of the 38 countries in the region, 12 are home to 96% of persons living with HIV, 90% of all new HIV infections, and 97% of all AIDS deaths (Table 4.2) (UNAIDS, 2013). In addition, infections are focused in select urban settings in almost every country. For example, more than half of the new infections in India are concentrated in 16% of India's 655 districts (UNAIDS Regional Support Team for Asia and the Pacific, 2013).

Historically, commercial sex work and injection drug use were recognized drivers of the epidemic in the region (UNAIDS, 2011; Lazarus et al., 2010). Now, after early neglect, it is recognized in almost every country that there is evidence of significant and often increasing infection rates among MSM and transgender individuals (Beyrer et al., 2012;

Table 4.1. FIVE COUNTRY EPIDEMIC PROFILES IN THE ASIA-PACIFIC REGION

	NUMBER OF NEW HIV INFECTIONS	NUMBER OF PERSONS LIVING WITH HIV	NUMBER OF AIDS-RELATED DEATHS	COUNTRY EXAMPLES
Profile 1: Declining epidemic	Declining	Declining	Stable	Cambodia, India, Nepal, Myanmar, Thailand
Profile 2: Maturing epidemic	Declining	Increasing or stable	Varies	China, Malaysia, Papua New Guinea, Vietnam
Profile 3: Expanding epidemic	Increasing	Increasing	Increasing	Indonesia, Pakistan, Philippines
Profile 4: Latent epidemic	Increasing or stable	Increasing but <10,000	Low (<500)	Afghanistan, Bangladesh, Lao PDR, Sri Lanka
Profile 5: Low prevalence	Low (<500)	Low (1000)	Low	Bhutan, Fiji, Maldives, Mongolia, Pacific Island Countries and Territories, Timor Leste

SOURCE: Adapted from UNAIDS (2012).

van Griensven et al., 2013). The majority of incident infections can be attributed to the behavioral risks faced by key populations such as female sex workers (FSW), their clients, PWID, MSM, and transgender people (Cassell et al., 2014). The substantial variations *across* countries in the concentration of new infections in different populations also mask substantial variations in incidence patterns in different settings and populations *within* countries. Large countries, such as China, India, and Indonesia, are characterized by distinct regional patterns in primary drivers of epidemic transmission (UNAIDS, 2013).

The concentration of HIV in key populations in the region suggests strategic opportunities to concentrate resources toward maximizing intervention impact (Cassell et al., 2014). However, the marginalization and stigmatization experienced by these populations are major challenges to scaling up effective prevention programs. While some countries have made progress in reaching key populations, there remain large gaps in access to HIV prevention and treatment services among FSW, MSM, transgender people, and PWID. Reports conducted by countries in the region show that median coverage of MSM and male and female sex workers by HIV prevention programs in the region (i.e., those who knew where to get an HIV test and received condoms in the previous year) is less than 60% (UNAIDS, 2013). The proportion of PWID reporting safe injection practices decreased slightly, from 83% in 2010 to 80% in 2013 (in 11 countries reporting consistently over those years) (UNAIDS, 2013). Between 2011 and 2012, the number of eligible people accessing ART increased by 150,000. However, only half (51%) of the eligible HIV-infected individuals were receiving ART under the 2010 WHO treatment guidelines (UNAIDS, 2013). Substantial challenges exist in reaching, testing, treating, and retaining individuals in the continuum cascade of prevention, care, and treatment services. These challenges also vary across the region: in China, the major gaps involve low rates of HIV testing and diagnosis, whereas in Vietnam the critical challenge is low registration and retention in ART clinics (WHO, 2013).

MENTAL HEALTH ISSUES AMONG PERSONS LIVING WITH HIV

There is a strong association between HIV and mental health, with a high prevalence of substance use and mental disorders among PLHIV (Maj et al., 1994). PLHIV are subject to societal challenges, including lack of social support and HIV-related stigma, which can adversely impact their mental health. Mental disorders are also associated with HIV-related risk behaviors, acquisition of HIV infection, and poor HIV clinical outcomes among PLHIV. In the Asia-Pacific region, approximately one in three (36.4%) PLHIV have evidence of depression, and 12% of patients have moderate to severe HIV-related neurocognitive impairment (Wright et al., 2008).

Mental health disorders are prevalent among the key populations at high risk for HIV infection—FSW, MSM, and PWID. These often stigmatized populations are vulnerable to psychosocial stressors and demonstrate high rates of alcohol, stimulant, and other substance use disorders, which are associated with HIV-related risk behaviors and result in higher HIV incidence. Studies indicate increased suicidal behaviors among FSW; high rates of suicidal ideation, depression, and anxiety among MSM; and a higher prevalence of depression, anxiety, and suicidal ideation among PWID in Asia-Pacific countries.

Mental health disorders present challenges to PLHIV in accessing HIV care and treatment services, affect adherence to ART, and are associated with more rapid disease progression and increased mortality (Mayston et al., 2012). Identifying and treating mental disorders has a positive impact on clinical outcomes, as studies have shown that antidepressant treatment improves ART adherence among PLHIV with depression (Springer et al., 2012).

The relationship between HIV and mental health underscores the importance of routine screening for depression and substance use disorders and provision of mental health services for PLHIV. Because persons with mental disorders are also at increased risk for HIV, there is benefit to incorporating HIV

Table 4.2. SUBREGIONAL CONCENTRATION OF HIV IN THE ASIA-PACIFIC REGION

COUNTRY	NUMBER OF PERSONS LIVING WITH HIV (% of Regional Total)	NUMBER OF NEW HIV INFECTIONS (% of Regional Total)	ANNUAL AIDS-RELATED DEATHS (% of Regional Total)
India	2,100,000 (43%)	130,000 (37%)	147,000 (54%)
China	780,000 (16%)	48,000 (14.0%)	28,000 (10%)
Indonesia	610,000 (12%)	76,000 (22%)	27,000 (10%)
Thailand	450,000 (9%)	8,800 (3%)	19,000 (7%)
Vietnam	260,000 (5%)	13,000 (4%)	12,500 (5%)
Myanmar	200,000 (4%)	7,100 (2%)	12,000 (4%)
Pakistan	87,000 (3%)	19,000 (5%)	3,500 (1%)
Malaysia	82,000 (2%)	7,400 (2%)	5,200 (2%)
Cambodia	76,000 (2%)	1,400 (<1%)	2,700 (1%)
Nepal	49,000 (1%)	1,200 (<1%)	4,100 (1%)
Papua New Guinea	25,000 (<1%)	<1,000 (<1%)	<1,000 (<1%)
Philippines	15,000 (<1%)	1,800 (<1%)	<500 (<1%)
Total	4,734,000 (96%)	314,700 (90%)	262,500 (97%)

SOURCE: Adapted from UNAIDS (2013).

prevention services in mental health programs. Addressing mental health issues and integrating HIV and mental health services will contribute significantly to the overall health and outcomes among PLHIV in the Asia-Pacific region.

STIGMA AND DISCRIMINATION AMONG PERSONS LIVING WITH HIV

One of the major barriers to accessing HIV testing and treatment services is HIV-related stigma, which can be understood as a complex social process that takes shape within specific contexts of culture and power and is inextricably linked to social inequality (Parker and Aggelton, 2003). One framework describes several stigma mechanisms that impact PLHIV, including internalized stigma (i.e., negative self-beliefs and attitudes), anticipated stigma (i.e., expected discrimination from others), and experienced stigma (i.e., actual discrimination against PLHIV) (Earnshaw et al., 2013). Results from the AIDS Treatment for Life Survey (ATLIS), a multi-country, cross-sectional survey of PLHIV conducted in 2010, showed that living in the Asia-Pacific region was associated with greater anticipated stigma, particularly the perception that other people believe PLHIV engage in risky behavior, such as drug use or prostitution. Furthermore, PLHIV respondents from Asia-Pacific countries were more likely to be very concerned about disclosure of their HIV status, citing social discrimination and concerns about future relationships as the most common fears (Nachega et al., 2012).

Although the HIV/AIDS epidemic in the Asia-Pacific region is spreading increasingly to the general population, the epidemic is still largely driven by populations of persons who carry out risky behaviors (Cassell et al., 2014). In East Asia, there is an emerging epidemic among MSM, while other routes of infection have largely remained stable, and there is an urgent need to address discrimination against homosexuality and the LGBT population and to provide outreach to MSM (Suguimoto et al., 2014). In other regions of Asia, the epidemic is largely among PWID and FSW, and more outreach efforts are required to tackle the epidemic in these groups. Throughout the continent, criminalization of high-risk behavior, including sex between men, drug use, and sex work, creates barriers to providing HIV prevention services to those with the greatest need (UNAIDS, 2013).

Discrimination based on gender, including gender-based violence and gender inequalities, hinder the effectiveness of HIV and AIDS responses and have been shown to make women, girls, MSM, and transgender people more vulnerable to HIV infection (UNAIDS, 2013). There are multiple reasons for this, ranging from physical trauma that increases the risk of HIV infection, to vulnerable populations being less capable of negotiating safer sex.

HIV CARE AND MENTAL HEALTH SERVICES

ART for HIV infection has expanded rapidly in the Asia-Pacific region; by 2013 an estimated 51% of eligible PLHIV were receiving antiretroviral medications. However, this rate is less than the 61% global coverage for ART—even though 80% of the generic antiretroviral drugs used worldwide are produced in the region (UNAIDS, 2013). Lack of financial resources and failure to prioritize existing health resources are barriers to broader ART access; Asia-Pacific countries rely on international donors for 41% of HIV program funding, only slightly less than the global average of 47% for developing countries. Rapid economic development has allowed many Asian countries, such as China, India, Malaysia, and Thailand, to fund 80–100% of their national AIDS responses.

Delays in HIV testing and linkage to care result in late HIV treatment, with one in four PLHIV starting ART with CD4 counts below 100 cells/mm^3 in developing countries. Delayed treatment increases the risk for mortality and morbidity related to HIV infection. Tuberculosis, the most common opportunistic infection diagnosed among PLWH in countries in the region, disproportionately affects the Asia-Pacific; half of the world's 22 high-burden countries are located in Asia. With 15% of global cases, Southeast Asia has the highest TB burden in the world.

Strict adherence to ART is the key to health and long-term survival for PLHIV. Asian countries have very high adherence rates for those on ART, with a median of 87%. However, significant barriers remain to identifying all eligible PLHIV in the region and providing the necessary linkages and support to successfully initiate and maintain ART. The foremost barrier is stigma and discrimination, including criminalization in many Asian countries, against high-risk populations such as MSM, PWID and FSW, which leads to poor provision of and access to health services, including HIV testing. UNAIDS (2016) reports that fewer than half of these high-risk individuals in the Asia-Pacific know their HIV status and that there is a "lack of clear commitment to scaling up HIV testing, counseling and treatment coverage" for these populations. Expansion of community-based HIV testing and counseling is one method that can increase access to HIV services for high-risk populations while relieving the burden on overextended public services.

Mental health services in the Asia-Pacific region are poorly developed, with limited availability and accessibility. For example, India has only 1 psychiatrist per 350,000 people (Das and Leibowitz, 2011). PLHIV in the region suffer from higher burdens of depression, suicide, anxiety disorders, and substance abuse than other populations. Integration of mental health services with HIV clinical care has been shown to improve retention in HIV care and to benefit overall health status among PLHIV in diverse settings such as Thailand, Japan, and India (Das and Leibowitz, 2011; Li et al., 2010; Tominari et al., 2013). Methadone maintenance treatment has been shown to reduce injection drug use, improve mental health, decrease mortality, increase retention in care, and improve ART adherence in settings where IDU is a major factor in HIV transmission, including China, Vietnam, and Malaysia (Tran et al., 2012; Wickersham et al., 2013; Zhao et al., 2013).

CONCLUSIONS

The Asia-Pacific region has produced some of the greatest successes in the worldwide AIDS response, from the production of low-cost generic antiretroviral drugs to increases in domestic funding and the rapid scale-up of ART. However, almost half of PWID eligible for ART still lack access, and stigma, discrimination, and injustice against people affected by HIV remain the major barriers to HIV prevention and service provision. Continued success in reducing HIV infections and deaths will require prioritization of domestic resources toward national AIDS responses and active engagement in policy reform to eliminate stigma and discrimination and uphold human rights for all.

HIV AND AIDS IN EUROPE

Julia del Amo, Jordi Blanch, and Esteban Martínez

MAGNITUDE, TRENDS, AND OUTCOMES OF HIV INFECTION AND AIDS IN EUROPE 2008–2012

The HIV epidemic continues to be a significant public health issue in Europe (European Centre for Disease Prevention and Control [ECDC]/WHO, 2015; Nakagawa et al., 2014). The epidemic has distinct regional traits regarding its magnitude and evolution, the age and sex distribution of HIV diagnoses, the mechanisms of transmission, and affected individuals' socioeconomic background and country of birth. The burden of late HIV diagnoses and the disparities in access to testing and care also vary greatly across Europe (ECDC/WHO, 2015). Ultimately, all of these aspects, together with the various countries' respective healthcare structures and economic and social development, will shape the physical and mental health of people living with HIV in Europe.

There are a number of administrative definitions of the WHO European Region (53 countries),[1] the European Union (EU) (30 EU countries), and the European Economic Area (EEA) (28 EU countries/ 2 EEA countries)[2] which will be clarified in this section. Of the 131,202 HIV diagnoses reported in 2012 in the 53 countries of the WHO European Region, 75,708 (58%) were reported by the Russian Federation and

---

1. *WHO/European Region countries*—**Western Europe:** Andorra, Austria,* Belgium,* Denmark,* Finland,* France,* Germany,* Greece,* Iceland, Ireland,* Israel, Italy,* Luxembourg,* Malta,* Monaco, the Netherlands,* Norway, Portugal,* San Marino, Spain,* Sweden,* Switzerland, United Kingdom.* **Central Europe:** Albania, Bosnia and Herzegovina, Bulgaria,* Croatia, Cyprus,* Czech Republic,* Hungary,* Macedonia, Montenegro, Poland,* Romania,* Serbia, Slovakia,* Slovenia,* Turkey. **Eastern Europe:** Armenia, Azerbaijan, Belarus, Estonia,* Georgia, Kazakhstan, Kyrgyzstan, Latvia,* Lithuania,* Republic of Moldova, Russian Federation, Tajikistan, Turkmenistan, Ukraine, Uzbekistan. (*Countries that constituted the EU as of January 1, 2007.)

2. *EU/EEA countries as of 2012:* Austria, Belgium, Bulgaria, Croatia, Cyprus, Czech Republic, Denmark, Estonia, Finland, France, Germany, Greece, Hungary, Ireland, Iceland, Italy, Lithuania, Luxemburg, Latvia, Malta, the Netherlands, Norway, Poland, Portugal, Romania, Slovenia, Slovakia, Spain, Sweden, United Kingdom.

29,381 (22%) by EU/EEA countries (ECDC/WHO, 2015). The rate of HIV diagnoses for 2012 in the WHO European Region was 7.8 per 100,000 population and 5.8 per 100,000 in the EU/EEA countries (ECDC/WHO, 2015). Eastern Europe has experienced a continued increase of HIV incidence (DeHovitz et al., 2014; ECDC/WHO, 2015; Nakagawa et al., 2014).

The overall rate of HIV diagnoses in the EU/EEA has remained constant from 2008 until 2012: 6.4 per 100,000 in 2006 (28,318 cases) and 6.2 per 100,000 (30,900 cases) in 2012 (ECDC/WHO, 2015), but there is variation within countries. The highest HIV incidence rates are in two eastern countries in the EU/EEA—Estonia (23.5 per 100,000) and Latvia (16.6 per 100,000)—where the initial driver of the epidemic was unsafe injecting drug use. The next highest rates are in Belgium (11.1 per 100,000) and the United Kingdom (10.3 per 100.000), where sex between men is the most common route of transmission, along with high rates of HIV diagnoses among migrants from sub-Saharan Africa (Del Amo et al., 2011; ECDC/WHO, 2015, Nakagawa et al., 2014).

The use of ART has led to important reductions in the rates of AIDS and HIV-related deaths in the EU/EEA (ECDC/WHO, 2015; Nakagawa et al., 2014). Except for countries in Eastern Europe, the number of AIDS cases has decreased continuously since the mid-1990s. In 2012, 4,313 AIDS cases were reported by 29 EU/EEA countries, for a rate of 0.8 cases per 100,000 population. The highest rates within the EU/EEA were reported by Latvia (6.8 per 100,000 population), Estonia (2.7 per 100,000 population), Portugal (2.4 per 100,000 population), and Spain (1.7 per 100,000 population), all of which were affected by explosive epidemics among PWIDs during the 1980s and early 1990s in the southern European countries and the late 1990s and 2000s in the Eastern European countries (ECDC/WHO, 2015).

Late HIV diagnosis is a major problem in the EU/EEA. Close to half (49%) of new HIV cases reported in 2012 within the 30 EU/EEA countries were late presenters, with a CD4 cell count <350/mm³ at the time of HIV diagnosis (ECDC/WHO, 2015). Among these, up to 30% of cases had advanced HIV infection; their CD4 cell counts at presentation were below 200/mm³. Delayed HIV presentation was more common in migrants from sub-Saharan Africa—particularly among the men—and was lowest among MSM, indicating different HIV testing patterns, disease awareness, and barriers to access services.

The Collaboration of Observational HIV Epidemiological Research Europe (COHERE) has published data from 35 European countries, showing that, between 2000 and 2011, late HIV presentation was associated with a 13-fold increased incidence of AIDS/death in southern Europe and a 6-fold increase in Eastern Europe (COHERE, 2013). Also, in the COHERE Collaboration, HIV-positive persons who did not become infected through intravenous drug use and maintained high CD4 counts while on ART had similar mortality rates to those of people in the general population (COHERE, 2012).

THE MOST AFFECTED POPULATIONS AND MAIN ROUTES OF HIV INFECTION IN EUROPE: IMPLICATIONS FOR MENTAL HEALTH

Heterosexual sex is the most frequent means of HIV transmission in the WHO/Europe Region, accounting for 46% of cases (ECDC/WHO, 2015). However, underreporting of HIV infection in MSM is likely in countries such as Russia and the Ukraine where sex between men is subject to political prosecution and high levels of social discrimination and stigma (ECDC, 2013c). Evidence shows that stigma and discrimination in healthcare settings keep people from accessing HIV prevention, care, and treatment services and from adopting prevention behaviors (Nyblade et al., 2009). Unsafe injection drug use was the initial and most potent driver of the epidemic in this part of the world and remains an important factor. Moreover, while most Western European countries have implemented opioid substitution therapy programs, the scale of such programs in many Eastern European countries remains very limited. Similarly, coverage of needle and syringe programs across the region is variable (DeHovitz et al., 2014).

Sex between men is the most common mode of HIV transmission in EU/EEA countries, with 40.4% of new infections reported in 2012, followed by 33.8% due to heterosexual sex and 6.1% to injection drug use (ECDC/WHO, 2015). The role of non-injection drug use among MSM has been identified as one of the main factors in HIV seroconversion in the last decade (Nakagawa et al., 2014); use of crystal methamphetamine ("meth") is associated with HIV spread among MSM. HIV-infected MSM who used crystal meth were more likely to report high-risk sexual behaviors, incident sexually transmitted infections, and serodiscordant unprotected anal intercourse than were HIV-infected MSM who did not use crystal meth. Meth users also had worse HIV-related health outcomes (Rajasingham et al., 2012).

The trends in numbers of HIV diagnoses by transmission category in the EU/EEA have varied over time. Whereas from 2008 to 2012 there was evidence for ongoing transmission of HIV in MSM, decreasing numbers of HIV infection secondary to heterosexually acquired infections were also seen; a significant proportion of these are thought to have taken place in sub-Saharan Africa (ECDC/WHO, 2015). The decline in heterosexually transmitted cases is particularly significant among females from sub-Saharan Africa (ECDC/WHO, 2015, Hernando et al., 2013). Regarding PWID, after years of witnessing decreases in the numbers of HIV diagnoses as a result of harm reduction programs, increases in HIV infection among PWID were observed in 2011 and 2012 with outbreaks in Greece and Romania, which were associated with fewer such programs due to budgetary cuts and austerity measures (ECDC/WHO, 2015, Karanikolos et al., 2013).

A distinct feature of the HIV epidemics in Western Europe is the contribution of migrants to national epidemics. Migrants are a heterogeneous group with different and non-mutually exclusive reasons for migration—poverty, job-seeking, political prosecution, and homophobia (Del Amo et al., 2011; Hernando et al., 2013). They comprise people with various and often accumulating types of social disadvantage, all of which make them especially vulnerable to physical and mental health problems. Moreover, several studies have shown that migrants are less likely than a country's natives to use general practitioner or emergency primary care services for mental health problems (Straiton et al., 2014). The majority of migrants are from sub-Saharan Africa, and the epidemics in Europe mimic those in origin—predominantly heterosexually transmitted, with more women infected than men (Del Amo et al., 2011; Hernando et al., 2013). As well as possibly reflecting selective HIV testing of women during antenatal care, the data suggest that women from sub-Saharan Africa suffer the greater burden of HIV in both their countries of origin and their countries of immigration. Growing numbers of migrants from Latin America and the Caribbean are being reported among HIV-positive MSM in Europe (Del Amo et al., 2011; Hernando et al., 2013). MSM from these parts of the world feel less exposed to discrimination and stigma when they arrive in some countries of Western Europe. However, in these more open-minded societies, migrants sometimes increase their engagement in unsafe sex and/or substance use (ECDC, 2013b).

Since HIV-related discrimination is still persistent across Europe, clear and active anti-discrimination policies that are in place in many European countries are not enough to combat HIV-related stigma and discrimination. A high proportion of European countries have programs in place and mechanisms for documenting and addressing cases of discrimination, but few mechanisms exist to uniformly assess the extent to which individuals experience stigma and discrimination and the actual impact this has on uptake of services. While the reduction of stigma and discrimination should remain central to national HIV programs to safeguard sexual and reproductive health and rights, targeted interventions are needed to promote both destigmatization and communication skills of service providers (Nöstlinger et al., 2014).

Finally, it's important to mention the mental health challenges faced by vertically HIV-infected adolescents who, despite being low in number, are a distinct group with specific needs. There are only a few studies in Europe about the mental health of children and young people living with HIV. A high percentage of HIV perinatally infected Spanish adolescents show difficulties in several areas (disease knowledge, peer relationships, school performance) that can impact their adult lives (García-Navarro et al., 2014). An Italian study observed worse scores on overall quality of life, school functioning, and psychosocial health, as well as withdrawal, anxiety, and delinquency behavior in children who were infected with HIV perinatally (Bomba et al., 2010).

ACCESS TO HIV TESTING AND CARE IN EUROPE, 2008–2012

In 2010, the European Centre for Disease Prevention and Control (ECDC) published their guidelines on HIV testing (ECDC, 2010), highlighting the strong evidence supporting the finding that earlier diagnosis and treatment reduces morbidity and mortality for the individual as well as the likelihood of HIV transmission (Cohen et al., 2011; Rodger et al., 2014). This document calls for HIV testing to be politically endorsed by countries within broader policies. Also, it reminds readers that HIV testing in Europe has been traditionally based on respect for basic individual rights, such as voluntary consent and confidentiality. ECDC guidelines thus emphasize that strategies should overcome stigma as well as legal and financial disincentives to testing. They particularly emphasize that HIV testing must be linked to care, even for special populations such as migrant populations of uncertain status, including undocumented people. Following HIV testing, it is essential to ensure access to treatment, care, and prevention (ECDC, 2010). The 2004 Dublin Declaration on Partnership to Fight HIV/AIDS in Europe and Central Asia was set up to provide universal access to comprehensive HIV prevention, treatment, care, and support for people living with HIV/AIDS (ECDC 2013a).

ART eligibility in Europe in terms of CD4 count has changed since the introduction of potent combination therapy in the mid-1990s. Most recent European guidelines advocate initiation of treatment in patients irrespective of their CD4 counts, if the patient is willing and/or in situations where the risk of HIV transmission is high, which applies particularly to serodiscordant couples (European AIDS Clinical Society [EACS] Guidelines, 2016). The European AIDS Clinical Society (EACS) has regularly released guidelines for treatment of HIV-infected adults in Europe since 2003 (EACS Guidelines, 2016). Initially focused on ART only, these guidelines now cover almost every aspect of the clinical management of HIV-infected adults, including assessment of HIV-positive persons at initial and subsequent visits, ART of HIV-positive persons, prevention and management of comorbidities in HIV-positive persons, clinical management and treatment of chronic hepatitis B and C co-infection in HIV-positive persons, and treatment of opportunistic infections and mental health issues. For example, the British HIV Association recommends that individuals testing HIV positive should have prompt access to specialist care, preferably within 48 hours and certainly within 2 weeks of receiving the result, to meet psychological needs (Asboe et al., 2012).

HIV AND AIDS IN THE AMERICAS

Gaddy Noy, Farah Ahmad-Stout, and Marshall Forstein

UNITED STATES

The spread of HIV in the United States began as an epidemic within West and East Coast cities among young, white, middle-class men who have sex with men but now affects a more diverse population in terms of age, sex, race, income, transmission route, and geography (Moore, 2011). The epidemiology of HIV and its evolution within the United States over time is presented in greater detail in Chapter 2 and Chapter 3 of this text but is summarized here.

According to the Centers for Disease Control and Prevention (CDC), approximately 50,000 people in the United States are newly infected with HIV each year. In the United States, from the start of the epidemic to 2013, 673,538 people with an AIDS diagnosis have died. Among the 44,073 new HIV diagnoses in the United States in 2014, about 80% were among adult and adolescent males (CDC, 2015e). Overall, an estimated 1.2 million people in the United States are currently living with HIV, and approximately 14% are unaware of their infection (CDC, 2015d).

Although rates of HIV infection have decreased in some communities (children of HIV-positive mothers), they continue to rise in others (MSM, especially African American MSM). Race, gender, sexual practices, income, geographic location, employment status, substance abuse, and other social determinants of health continue to play important roles in the spread of HIV infection. Addressing these disparities via prevention methods, surveillance, and increased access to care can help lead to a future in which HIV transmission is rare (CDC, 2015a).

Geography

While the highest number of individuals living with AIDS in 2009 was in the South, the rate of new infections was highest in the Northeast, followed by the South, the West, and the Midwest. In 2014, the South accounted for a majority of new AIDS diagnoses (CDC, 2016c). Urban centers tend to have higher rates of individuals either newly infected or living with HIV.

Race and Ethnicity

Blacks represent approximately 12% of the U.S. population but accounted for an estimated 44% of new HIV infections in 2014 and 41% of people living with HIV by the end of 2012 (CDC, 2016a). The rate of new HIV infections among blacks/African Americans was 7.9 times the rate in whites in 2014. Hispanics/Latinos are also disproportionately affected, as they represent 17% of the U.S. population but accounted for 23% of new HIV infections in 2010. The rate of new HIV infections for Latino males was 2.9 times that for white males, and the rate of new infections for Latinas was 4.2 times that for white females (CDC, 2015d). Data from 2012 and 2013 in African Americans and Hispanics/Latinos indicate that only about half of those diagnosed with HIV are retained in care. Overall, the rate of new HIV infections (~1%) among American Indians and Alaska Natives is proportional to their U.S. population size. However, of all races and ethnicities, American Indians and Alaska Natives had the highest percentage of diagnosed HIV infections due to injection drug use (CDC, 2016b).

Gender and Age

Among U.S. females, the estimated number of new HIV infections decreased from 12,000 in 2008 to 9,500 in 2010.

In 2010, the rate of new HIV infection among U.S. males was 4.2 times that of females, and the estimated number of new HIV infections was highest among younger individuals (31% among 25- to 34-year-olds and 26% in 13- to 24-year-olds). Among 13- to 24-year-olds, young gay and bisexual men accounted for 92% of all new HIV diagnoses in 2014.

Transmission Route

In 2014, 67% of new HIV infections in the United States were among MSM. Comparing data from 2008 to 2010, the number of new HIV infections among MSM increased 12%, from 26,700 in 2008 to 29,800 in 2010. There was also a 22% increase among MSM aged 13–24 during this time period (CDC, 2012). In 2014, the majority of new HIV infections occurred in MSM, followed by heterosexuals (~25% of new infections) and then PWID (6% of new infections). In 2011, among MSM who were aware of their diagnosis, 80.6% were linked to care but only 57.5% stayed in care, 52.9% were prescribed ART, and 44.6% achieved viral suppression (CDC, 2015b).

Pregnant Women and Perinatal Transmission

According to the CDC, the number of women with HIV giving birth in the United States increased by about 30%, from 6,000–7,000 in the year 2000 to 8,700 in 2006. At the same time, perinatal transmission has declined by more than 90% since the early 1990s, with the current risk of HIV transmission being 1% or less if a woman takes HIV medication as prescribed throughout pregnancy and provides HIV medicines to the baby for 4–6 weeks after birth (CDC, 2015c).

Access to Care

First enacted in 1990, the Ryan White CARE Act was passed by the Senate with overwhelming bipartisan support and had the goal of significantly increasing funding for HIV prevention and treatment services. Since the first year of the Ryan White program, when $220.6 million was allocated for such services, the budget has grown to $2.32 billion in 2016 (Health Resources & Services Administration [HRSA], 2016). The Affordable Care Act (ACA), passed in 2010, includes provisions to prevent health insurers from denying coverage to children living with HIV or AIDS, bring an end to exclusions based on pre-existing conditions, prohibit lifetime caps on insurance benefits, and require coverage of certain preventative services, including HIV testing (CDC, 2015f). Expanded insurance options may also decrease barriers among PLHIV to accessing medications and clinical care (U.S. Department of Health and Human Services, 2016).

CANADA

In Canada, the number of PLHIV at the end of 2014 was estimated at 75,500, with a rise of about 9.7% since 2011, as advances in treatment have led to longer lifespans for PLHIV. The incidence of new HIV infections has decreased over the last 30 years, with the number of new infections in 2014 estimated to be about 2,570 (Public Health Agency of Canada [PHAC], 2015).

Geographic Variability

There is great geographic variation between different provinces in HIV prevalence, incidence, and the predominant modes of HIV transmission (Canadian AIDS Treatment Information Exchange [CATIE], 2011a). For example, the PWID transmission category accounts for about 70% of HIV prevalence in Saskatchewan, whereas heterosexual transmission accounts for about half of prevalent infections in Alberta and Manitoba. The MSM category accounts for about half of people living with HIV in Ontario, Quebec, British Columbia, and the Atlantic Provinces (Prince Edward Island, New Brunswick, Nova Scotia, Newfoundland, and Labrador) (PHAC, 2014a).

Transmission Category

MSM, PWID, Aboriginal people, people in prisons, women, at-risk youth, and immigrants from HIV-endemic countries represent the greatest proportion of new infections (PHAC, 2013a). The overall decrease in HIV incidence is greater in some risk groups than in others. For example, while MSM remain the group with the highest proportion of people living with HIV/AIDS, the proportion of new positive HIV test reports among adults that are accounted for by MSM has decreased drastically, from 80% in 1985 to 42% in the years between 2002 and 2011. Encouraging as this is, the significant risk to this particular group should not be underestimated: MSM have HIV incidence rates that are 71 times higher than those for other men. Between 2002 and 2011, heterosexual transmission accounted for 30.8% of new positive HIV tests, with injection drug use following at 20.7%. PWID have incidence rates 46 times higher than those of people who do not inject drugs (CATIE, 2011b).

Gender

The HIV incidence rate for men is 3.3 times higher than for females, with the relative proportions of new male and female cases remaining relatively stable over the last 10 years. However, women, accounted for a greater percentage of new positive HIV tests reports in 2011 than they did in 1985 (23.3% vs. 5%). Increased HIV testing and high rates of ART treatment for HIV-positive pregnant women (93% in 2011) are thought to have contributed to the decrease in perinatal transmission of HIV, which was 1.3% in 2011, down from 8.8% in 2005. This reduction occurred despite the fact that the number of infants who were perinatally exposed to HIV rose between 2004 and 2010 (PHAC, 2013b).

Race and Ethnicity

Understanding racial and ethnic disparities related to the HIV epidemic presents a challenge, as data collection is variable between provinces, often incomplete, and limited in terms of categories. In 2012, only two-thirds of positive HIV test reports included information on race and ethnicity (PHAC, 2013a). The available data point to racial disparities in vertical transmission from mother to child. Black and Aboriginal infants make up 2.5% and 3.7% of the Canadian population, respectively, but accounted for 48.3% and 16.8% of all reported infants who were perinatally exposed to HIV between 1984 and 2011 (PHAC, 2013b). Among adults within these minority groups, Aboriginal populations have incidence rates about 3.5 times higher than those for people of other ethnicities (PHAC, 2014b). About 60% of positive HIV test reports due to injection of drugs are reported to be among Aboriginal people. Almost 90% of positive HIV test reports via heterosexual transmission are among people who self-identify as black (PHAC, 2013b). For some immigrant groups, access to necessary HIV treatment may not be possible, as foreign students and immigrants (not including refugees) are generally not eligible for the Interim Federal Health program or provincial healthcare coverage and would need to pay for services out of pocket or through private insurance (PHAC, n.d.).

In considering health status, certain social determinants of health have been identified that impact the overall well-being of people, including race, employment/job security, gender, disability, Aboriginal status, housing, income, education, social exclusion, and early life adversities (Mikkonen and Raphael, 2010). It is vital to address and reduce these disparities in prevention, testing, and treatment of HIV between different subpopulations in Canada.

LATIN AMERICA

In comparison to the hundreds of reports about the HIV epidemic in North America, data specific to South America and Central America are more limited. HIV prevalence and incidence rates have included widely ranging estimates for many reasons, including differences in surveillance, considerable missing data, different ways of organizing reports by region, and wide variations between and within countries. There are still fewer reports examining the similarities and differences in access to care and HIV policies between countries.

The epidemic in Latin America is considered to be relatively stable with an estimated prevalence of 1.6 million people living with HIV and about 83,000 new infections in 2011. As seen in other countries in the Americas, specific subpopulations bear a higher burden of the virus. Almost 75% of the people in Latin America living with HIV are concentrated in four countries: Brazil, Colombia, Mexico, and Venezuela. While there has been a general decline in new infections (of about 3%) in Latin America between 2005 and 2013, this has greatly varied between countries. For example, new infections have declined in Mexico by 39% but increased in Brazil by

11%. Young people between the ages of 15 and 24 account for one-third of new infections (UNAIDS, 2014).

Transmission Route

High-risk groups include MSM, PWID, sex workers, and transgender people. MSM are the largest transmission group for new infections in Latin America. Data from the UNAIDS global report in 2013 indicate that HIV infection rates among MSM range from 33% in the Dominican Republic to 56% in Peru (UNAIDS, 2013). Condom use in this group has been estimated to be almost 70%, but access to HIV testing and treatment is as low as 6% in countries such as Peru. Transgender women are a vulnerable group with HIV prevalence rates that are about 49 times higher than the general population (UNAIDS, 2014).

In terms of providing harm reduction to reduce HIV transmission through injection drug use, more Latin American countries (Brazil, Argentina, Paraguay, Uruguay) have needle exchange services than those (Mexico and Colombia) with opioid substitution therapy. Mexico and Colombia are the only countries with both types of treatment (Stone, 2014).

Treatment Coverage

Compared with rates of treatment coverage in other low- and middle-income countries, between December 2003 and June 2006, Latin America boasts the highest level of coverage at 75%, compared with 23% in sub-Saharan Africa and 16% in East, South, and Southeast Asia (WHO, 2006). In Cuba, the Dominican Republic, Mexico, and Guyana, coverage rates were greater than 80%. Greater than 60% coverage was reached in Argentina, Brazil, Chile, Ecuador, El Salvador, Jamaica, Nicaragua, Paraguay, Peru, and Venezuela. The lowest percentage of ART treatment coverage was in Bolivia, at less than 20% (UNAIDS, 2014). In 2004, the Minister of Health in Belize declared the government was committed to providing universal access to ART free of charge (WHO, 2005a). In Costa Rica, the government currently covers ART under national health insurance and has been absorbing the costs through the national health budget and World Bank loans (WHO, 2005b). In general, successful price negotiations have led to a significantly reduced cost of ART in Central America. Through the Accelerated Access Initiative in Central America and the Caribbean, six Central American countries reached a historic agreement with five pharmaceutical companies, in early 2003, to decrease the cost of ART by an average of 55% from current prices (WHO, 2005d).

Treatment coverage to prevent perinatal transmission from HIV-positive mothers varies greatly, from 70% (or greater) coverage in Ecuador, Mexico, Nicaragua, Panama, and Peru to less than 30% in Guatemala and Venezuela (UNAIDS, 2014).

SOUTH AMERICA

South America includes the following countries: Argentina, Bolivia, Brazil, Chile, Colombia, Ecuador, Guyana, Paraguay, Peru, Suriname, Uruguay, and Venezuela.

Brazil and Ecuador are examples of countries that have tried to limit the high cost of medication as a barrier to treatment with methods such as issuing a compulsory license for antiretrovirals for funded pharmaceutical programs. Other countries have, unfortunately, faced limitations related to patent laws, making medications prohibitive (UNAIDS, 2014).

Case Study: Brazil

Brazil is an interesting case study when considering the AIDS epidemic in South America. As early as 1983, the Sao Paulo State Secretariat of Health created the first governmental AIDS program in Brazil, and the first non-governmental agency providing AIDS services was also developed that year. In Brazil, health is considered a human right and, in accordance with this, several AIDS advocacy groups fought class action suits for access to free HIV testing and a greater number of antiretrovirals. The government has also funded a number of organizations that represent minority groups, including sex workers, LGBT people, people living with HIV, and drug users. Brazil also refused to bend to World Bank attempts to tie loans to agreements that Brazil would not provide universal access to certain HIV medications (Berkmann et al., 2005). More recently, Brazil has taken a leading role as the first developing country to adopt treatment as prevention. Since December 2013, treatment can be started after confirming an HIV diagnosis, irrespective of CD4 count (Brazil Ministry of Health, 2014).

CENTRAL AMERICA

The six countries of Central America are Belize, Costa Rica, El Salvador, Guatemala, Honduras, Nicaragua, and Panama. Although these countries are in close proximity to one another, there are vast differences in HIV infection rates, groups vulnerable to infection, government support for HIV/AIDS medications, policies on prevention services, and the history of the epidemic itself. The highest HIV prevalence rates in Latin America are in Belize, Guatemala, and Honduras, with approximately 1% of all adults infected with HIV at the end of 2003 (WHO, 2006).

In Costa Rica, more than half of AIDS cases between 1998 and 2002 were among MSM, and a significant proportion of those men also had sex with women, which may provide a significant route for HIV transmission into the wider population (WHO, 2005b). In contrast to Costa Rica, HIV is largely transmitted through heterosexual contact in Belize. Among those tested, women were infected at a younger age than men, which has serious implications for women in their reproductive years (WHO, 2005a). In Guatemala, approximately 75% of HIV infections in the country are attributed to heterosexual transmission, along with a high prevalence of HIV infection among people with tuberculosis. The most vulnerable populations include sex workers, MSM, prison populations, youth with social risks, street children, and people with tuberculosis (WHO, 2005d). In El Salvador, the major vulnerable groups include sex workers, MSM, and mobile population groups. The epidemic is largely concentrated in urban areas, with about 60% of cases being found in the metropolitan area of San Salvador (WHO, 2005c).

Within Central America there seems to be an understanding that countries have to work together to combat the HIV epidemic, and they have banded together with pharmaceutical companies to reduce the cost of life-saving therapies. Some, countries, such as Belize, have committed to universal access of antiretroviral therapy, while others are heavily subsidizing treatment costs.

REFERENCES FOR HIV/AIDS IN AFRICA

Auvert B, Taljaard D, Lagarde E, Sobngwi-Tambekou J, Sitta R, Puren A (2005). Randomized, controlled intervention trial of male circumcision for reduction of HIV infection risk: the ANRS 1265 trial. *PLoS Med* 2:e298.

Babiker AG, Peto T, Porter K, Walker AS, Darbyshire JH (2001). Age as a determinant of survival in HIV infection. *J Clin Epidemiol* 54:S16–S21.

Badri M, Maartens G, Mandalia S, et al. (2006). Cost-effectiveness of highly active antiretroviral therapy in South Africa. *PLoS Med* 3(1):e4.

Bailey RC, Moses S, Parker CB, et al. (2007). Male circumcision for HIV prevention in young men in Kisumu, Kenya: a randomised controlled trial. *Lancet* 369:643–656.

Baird S, McIntosh C, Özler B. (2012). Effect of a cash transfer programme for schooling on prevalence of HIV and herpes simplex type 2 in Malawi: a cluster randomised trial. *Lancet* 379(9823):1320–1329.

Baral S, Beyrer C, Muessig K, et al. (2012). Burden of HIV among female sex workers in low-income and middle-income countries: a systematic review and meta-analysis. *Lancet Infect Dis* 380:367–377.

Barker PM, McCannon CJ, Mehta N, et al. (2007). Strategies for the scale-up of antiretroviral therapy in South Africa through health system optimization. *J Infect Dis* 196(Suppl 3):S457–S463.

Barnighausen T, Bloom DE, Humair S (2012). Economics of antiretroviral treatment vs. circumcision for HIV prevention. *Proc Natl Acad Sci U S A* 109:21271–21276.

Baeten JM, Donnell D, Ndase P, et al. (2012) Antiretroviral prophylaxis for HIV prevention in heterosexual men and women. *N Engl J Med* 367:399–410.

Baeten JM, Palanee-Phillips T, Brown ER, et al.; MTN-020–ASPIRE Study Team (2016). Use of a vaginal ring containing dapivirine for HIV-1 prevention in women. *N Engl J Med* 375(22):2121–2132.

Beyrer C, Sullivan P, Sanchez J, et al. (2013). The increase in global HIV epidemics in MSM. *AIDS* 27(17):2665–2678.

Binagwaho A, Fuller A, Kerry V, et al. (2012). Adolescents and the right to health: eliminating age-relatedbarriers to HIV/AIDS services in Rwanda. *AIDS Care* 24(7):936–942.

Björkman-Nyqvist M, Corno L, de Walque D, Svensson J (2013). Evaluating the impact of short-term financial incentives on HIV and STI incidence among youth in Lesotho: a randomized trial. TUPDC0106–Poster Discussion Session, IAS 7th International AIDS Conference on HIV Pathogenesis, Treatment and Prevention, Kuala Lumpur, July.

Bor J, Tanser F, Newell ML, Barnighausen T (2012). In a study of a population cohort in South Africa, HIV patients on antiretrovirals had nearly full recovery of employment. *Health Affairs* 31:1459–1469.

Bor J, Herbst AJ, Newell M-L, Bärnighausen T (2013). Increases in adult life expectancy in rural South Africa: valuing the scale-up of HIV treatment. *Science* 339(6122):961–965.

Brentlinger PE, Assan A, Mudender F, et al. (2010). Task shifting in Mozambique: cross-sectional evaluation of non-physician clinicians' performance in HIV/AIDS care. *Hum Resource Health* 8:23.

Bunnell R, Opio A, Musinguzi J, et al. (2008). HIV transmission risk behavior among HIV-infected adults in Uganda: results of a nationally representative survey. *AIDS* 22(5):617–624.

Centers for Disease Control and Prevention (1981). Pneumocystis pneumonia--Los Angeles. *MMWR Morb Mortal Wkly Rep* 30(21):250–252.

Chang LW, Kagaayi J, Nakigozi G, et al. (2008). Responding to the human resource crisis: peer health workers, mobile phones, and HIV care in Rakai, Uganda. *AIDS Patient Care STDS* 22(3):173–174.

Cohen MS, Chen YQ, McCauley M, et al. (2011). Prevention of HIV-1 infection with early antiretroviral therapy. *N Engl J Med* 365:493–505.

Collaborative Group on AIDS Incubation and HIV Surveillance (2000). Time from HIV-1 seroconversion to AIDS and death before widespread use of highly active antiretroviral therapy: a collaborative re-analysis. *Lancet* 355:1131–1137.

De Cock KM, El-Sadr WM (2013). When to start ART in Africa—an urgent research priority. *N Engl J Med* 368:886–889.

Cournos F, Mckinnon K, Pinho V, Wainberg ML (2014). Special populations and public health aspects. In JA Joska, DJ Stein, I Grant (eds.), *HIV/AIDS and Psychiatry* (pp. 211–234). West Essex, UK: John Wiley and Sons.

Dixon S, McDonald S, Roberts J (2002). The impact of HIV and AIDS on Africa's economic development. *BMJ* 324(7331):232–234.

Egger M, Hirschel B, Francioli P, et al. (2005). Antiretroviral therapy in resource-poor settings: scaling up inequalities? *Int J Epidemiol* 34(3):509–512.

Gebo KA (2008). Epidemiology of HIV and response to antiretroviral therapy in the middle-aged and elderly. *Aging Health* 4:615–627.

Gebo KA, Justice A (2009). HIV infection in the elderly. *Curr Infect Dis Rep* 11:246–254.

Gentry S, van-Velthoven MH, Tudor Car L, Car J. (2013). Telephone delivered interventions for reducing morbidity and mortality in people with HIV infection. *Cochrane Database Syst Rev* 5:CD009189.

Gouws E, Cuchi P (2012). International collaboration on estimating HIV incidence by modes of transmission. Focusing the HIV response through estimating the major modes of HIV transmission: a multi-country analysis. *Sex Transm Infect.* 88(Suppl 2):i76–i85.

Grabar S, Weiss L, Costagliola D (2006). HIV infection in older patients in the HAART era. *J Antimicrob Chemother* 57:4–7.

Grant RM (2010). Antiretroviral agents used by HIV-uninfected persons for prevention: pre- and postexposure prophylaxis. *Clin Infect Dis* 50:S96–S101.

Gray RH, Kigozi G, Serwadda D, et al. (2007). Male circumcision for HIV prevention in men in Rakai, Uganda: a randomised control trial. *Lancet* 369:657–666.

Greig J, Carrillo CE, O'Brian D, Mills EJ, Ford N (2012). Association between older age and adverse outcomes on antiretroviral therapy: a cohort analysis of programme data from nine countries in sub-Saharan Africa. *AIDS* 26(Suppl 1):S31–S37.

Grinsztejn B, Hosseinipour MC, Ribaudo HJ, et al. (2014). Effects of early versus delayed initiation of antiretroviral treatment on clinical outcomes of HIV-1 infection: results from the phase 3 HPTN 052 randomised controlled trial. *Lancet Infect Dis.* 14(4):281–290.

Haregu TN, Setswe G, Elliott J, Oldenburg B (2014). National responses to HIV/AIDS and non-communicable diseases in developing countries: analysis of strategic parallels and differences. *J Public Health Res* 3(1):99.

Hosseinipour MC, van Oosterhout JJ, Weigel R, et al. (2009). The public health approach to identify antiretroviral therapy failure: high-level nucleoside reverse transcriptase inhibitor resistance among Malawians failing first-line antiretroviral therapy. *AIDS* 23(9):1127–1134.

Institute for Health Metrics and Evaluation (IHME) (2014). *Financing Global Health 2013: Transition in an Age of Austerity.* Seattle, WA: IHME.

Iwuji C, Orne-Gliemann J, Tanser F, et al. (2013). Evaluation of the impact of immediate versus WHO recommendations-guided ART initiation on HIV incidence: the ANRS 12249 TasP (Treatment as Prevention) trial in Hlabisa sub-district, Kwazulu-Natal, South Africa: study protocol for a randomised controlled trial. *Trials* 14:230.

Jewkes RK, Dunkle K, Nduna M, Shai N (2010). Intimate partner violence, relationship power inequity, and incidence of HIV infection in young women in South Africa: a cohort study. *Lancet* 376(9734):41–48.

Johnson LF, Hallett TB, Rehle T, Dorrington RE (2012). The effect of changes in condom usage and antiretroviral treatment coverage on human immunodeficiency virus incidence in South Africa: a model-based analysis. *J Roy Soc Interface* 9(72):1544–1554.

Karim Q, Karim SS, Frohlich JA, Grobler AC, Baxter C, Mansoor LE (2010). Effectiveness and safety of tenofovir gel, an antiretroviral microbicide, for the prevention of HIV infection in women. *Science* 329:1168–1174.

Keiser O, Anastos K, Schechter M, et al. (2008). Antiretroviral therapy in resource-limited settings 1996 to 2006: patient characteristics, treatment regimens and monitoring in sub-Saharan Africa, Asia and Latin America. *Trop Med Int Health* 13:870–879.

Kerber KJ, Lawn JE, Johnson LF, et al. (2013). South African child deaths 1990–2011: have HIV services reversed the trend enough to meet Millennium Development Goal 4? *AIDS* 27:2637–2648.

Kerrigan D, Wirtz A, Baral S, et al. (2010). *The Global HIV Epidemics among Sex Workers*. Washington, DC: World Bank.

Kredo T, Adeniyi FB, Bateganya M, Pienaar ED (2014). Task shifting from doctors to non-doctors for initiation and maintenance of antiretroviral therapy. *Cochrane Database Syst Rev* 7:CD007331.

Kunutsor S, Walley J, Katabira E, et al. (2010). Using mobile phones to improve clinic attendance amongst an antiretroviral treatment cohort in rural Uganda: a cross-sectional and prospective study. *AIDS Behav* 14(6):1347–1352.

Le T, Wright EJ, Smith DM, et al. (2013). Enhanced CD4+ T-cell recovery with earlier HIV-1 antiretroviral therapy. *N Engl J Med* 368:218–230.

MacPherson P, Lalloo DG, Webb EL, et al. (2014). Effect of optional home initiation of HIV care following HIV self-testing on antiretroviral therapy initiation among adults in Malawi: a randomized clinical trial. *JAMA* 312(4):372–379.

Manasa J, McGrath N, Lessells R, Skingsley A, Newell ML, De Oliveira T (2013). High levels of drug resistance after failure of first-line antiretroviral therapy in rural South Africa: impact on standardised second-line regimens. *PLoS ONE* 8:e72152.

Millett GA, Jeffries WL 4th, Peterson JL, et al. (2012). Common roots: a contextual review of HIV epidemics in black men who have sex with men across the African diaspora. *Lancet* 380(9839):411–423.

Moore DM, Mermin J, Awor A, Yip B, Hogg RS, Montaner JS (2006). Performance of immunologic responses in predicting viral load suppression: implications for monitoring patients in resource-limited settings. *J Acquir Immune Defic Syndr* 43(4):436–439.

Morgan D, Whitworth J (2001). The natural history of HIV-1 infection in Africa. *Nat Med* 7(2):143–145.

Murray CJL, Ortblad KF, Guinovart C, et al. (2014), Global, regional, and national incidence and mortality for HIV, tuberculosis, and malaria during 1990–2013: a systematic analysis for the Global Burden of Disease Study 2013. *Lancet* 384(9947):1005–1070.

Murray CJL (2015). Maximizing antiretroviral therapy in developing countries. The dual challenge of efficiency and quality. *JAMA* 313:359–360.

Mutevedzi PC, Lessells RJ, Rodger AJ, Newell ML (2011). Association of age with mortality and virological and immunological response to antiretroviral therapy in rural South Africa. *PLOS ONE* 6:e21795.

Mutevedzi PC, Newell ML (2014). The changing face of the HIV epidemic in sub-Saharan Africa. *Trop Med Int Health* 19(9):1015–1028.

Nash D, Katyal M, Brinkhof MWG, et al. (2008). Long-term immunologic response to antiretroviral therapy in low-income countries: a collaborative analysis of prospective studies. *AIDS* 22(17):2291–2302.

Nel, A, Kapiga S, Bekker L, et al. (2016). Safety and efficacy of dapivirine vaginal ring for HIV-1 prevention in African women. Abstract 110 LB. Conference on Retroviruses and Opportunistic Infections, Boston, MA.

Nguyen H, Holodniy M (2008). HIV infection if the elderly. *Clin Interv Aging* 3:453–472.

Nsanzimana S, Kanters S, Remera E, et al. (2015). HIV care continuum in Rwanda: a cross-sectional analysis of the national programme. *Lancet HIV* 2(5):e208–e215.

Nylor K, Li G, Vallejo AN (2005). The influence of age on T cell generation and TCR diversity. *J Immunol* 174:7446–7452.

Reynolds SJ, Quinn TC (2010). Setting the stage: current state of affairs and major challenges. *Clin Infect Dis* 50(Suppl 3):S71–S76.

Rosen S, Fox MP (2011). Retention in HIV care between testing and treatment in sub-Saharan Africa: a systematic review. *PLOS Med* 8:e1001056.

Sabin CA, Smith CJ, Delpech V, et al. (2009). The associations between age and the development of laboratory abnormalities and treatment discontinuation for reasons other than virological failure in the first year of highly active antiretroviral therapy. *HIV Med* 10:35–43.

Severe P, Juste MAJ, Ambroise A, et al. (2010) Early versus standard antiretroviral therapy for HIV-infected adults in Haiti. *N Engl J Med* 363:257–265.

Shisana O (2013). HIV/AIDS in South Africa: at last the glass is half full. 6th South African AIDS Conference. Durban, South Africa.

Stats-SA (2010). Mid-Year Population Estimates. Statistics South Africa, Pretoria.

Stats-SA (2013). Mid-Year Population Estimates. Statistics South Africa, Pretoria.

Strathdee SA, Stockman JK (2010). Epidemiology of HIV among injecting and non-injecting drug users: current trends and implications for interventions. *Curr HIV/AIDS Rep* 7(2):99–106.

Suthar AB, Lawn SD, del Amo J, et al. (2012). Antiretroviral therapy for prevention of tuberculosis in adults with HIV: a systematic review and meta-analysis. *PLoS Med* 9(7):e1001270.

Tanser F, Barnighausen T, Graspar E, Zaidi J, Newell ML (2013). High coverage of ART associated with decline in risk of HIV acquisition in rural KwaZulu-Natal, South Africa. *Science* 339:966–971.

Todd J, Glynn JR, Marston M, et al. (2007) Time from HIV seroconversion to death: a collaborative analysis of eight studies in six low and middle-income countries before highly active antiretroviral therapy. *AIDS* 21(Suppl. 6):S55–S63.

UNAIDS (2010). UNAIDS report on the global AIDS epidemic: HIV prevalence map. http://www.unaids.org/globalreport/HIV_prevalence_map.htm. Accessed January 2, 2017.

UNAIDS (2013a). *Global Report: UNAIDS Report on the Global AIDS Epidemic 2013*. http://files.unaids.org/en/media/unaids/contentassets/documents/epidemiology/2013/gr2013/UNAIDS_Global_Report_2013_en.pdf. Accessed December 26, 2016.

UNAIDS (2013b). UNAIDS special report update: how Africa turned AIDS around. http://www.unaids.org/sites/default/files/media_asset/20130521_Update_Africa_1.pdf. Accessed December 26, 2016.

UNAIDS (2014). Fast-Track—ending the AIDS epidemic by 2030. http://www.unaids.org/en/resources/documents/2014/JC2686_WAD2014report. Accessed January 27, 2015.

UNAIDS (2015). How AIDS changed everything—MDG6: 15 years, 15 lessons of hope from the AIDS response. http://www.unaids.org/sites/default/files/media_asset/MDG6Report_en.pdf Accessed April 20, 2016.

UNAIDS (2016). *Global AIDS Update 2016*. http://www.unaids.org/sites/default/files/media_asset/global-AIDS-update-2016_en.pdf. Accessed December 31, 2016.

UNESCO (2013). International technical guidance on sexuality education: an evidence-informed approach for schools, teachers and health educators. http://unesdoc.unesco.org/images/0018/001832/183281e.pdf. Accessed December 31, 2016.

United Nations (2000). United Nations Millenium Declaration. New York: United Nations.

United Nations (2010). *The Millennium Development Goals Report*. New York: United Nations.

United Nations, Population Division (2015). World population prospects, the 2015 revision. https://esa.un.org/unpd/wpp/. Accessed December 26, 2016.

Urassa M, Boerma JT, Isingo R, et al. (2001). The impact of HIV/AIDS on mortality and household mobility in rural Tanzania. *AIDS* 15(15):2017–2023.

Vaginal and Oral Interventions to Control the Epidemic (VOICE) (2013). Pre-exposure prophylaxis for HIV in women: daily oral tenofovir, oral tenofovir/emtricitabine, or vaginal tenofovir gel in the VOICE study (MTN 003). Presented at the 20th Conference on Retroviruses and Opportunistic Infections. Atlanta, GA.

Van Damme L, Corneli A, Ahmed K, et al. (2012) Pre-exposure prophylaxis for HIV infection among African women. *N Engl J Med* 367:411–422.

Vekemans M, John L, Colebunders R (2007). When to switch for antiretroviral treatment failure in resource-limited settings? *AIDS* 21(9):1205–1206.

Weidle PJ, Wamai N, Solberg P, et al. (2006). Adherence to antiretroviral therapy in a home-based AIDS care programme in rural Uganda. *Lancet* 368(9547):1587–1594.

When to Start Consortium (2009). Timing of initiation of antiretroviral therapy in AIDS-free HIV-1-infected patients: a collaborative analysis of 18 HIV cohort studies. *Lancet* 373:1352–1363.

World Health Organization (WHO) (2003). Treating 3 million by 2005. Making it happen. The WHO strategy. http://www.who.int/3by5/publications/documents/isbn9241591129/en/. Accessed December 26, 2016.

World Health Organization (WHO) (2006). Antiretroviral therapy for HIV infection in adults and adolescents: recommendations for a public health approach. Geneva: World Health Organization.

World Health Organization (WHO) (2010a). Antiretroviral therapy for HIV infection in adults and adolescence: recommendations for a public health approach, 2010 revision. http://www.who.int/hiv/pub/arv/adult2010/en/. Accessed January 3, 2017.

World Health Organization (WHO) (2010b). mhGAP Intervention guide for mental, neurological and substance use disorders nonspecialized health settings. http://www.who.int/mental_health/mhgap/. Accessed December 26, 2016.

World Health Organization (WHO) (2011). Approach to patients with mental health problems. In *IMAI District Clinician Manual: Hospital Care for Adolescents and Adults: Guidelines for the Management of Common Illnesses with Limited Resources* (Vol. 2, pp. 209–253) Geneva: World Health Organization.

World Health Organization (WHO) (2013). Consolidated guidelines on the use of antiretroviral drugs for treating and preventing HIV infection: recommendations for a public health approach. http://www.who.int/hiv/pub/guidelines/arv2013/en/. Accessed December 26, 2016.

World Health Organization (WHO) (2015). Guideline on when to start antiretroviral therapy and on pre-exposure prophylaxis for HIV. http://www.who.int/hiv/pub/guidelines/earlyrelease-arv/en/. Accessed Dember 26, 2016.

REFERENCES FOR HIV/AIDS IN THE ASIA-PACIFIC REGION

Beyrer C, Baral SD, van Griensven F, et al. (2012). Global epidemiology of HIV infection in men who have sex with men. *Lancet* 380(9839):367–377.

Cassell MM, Holtz TH, Wolfe MI, Hahn H, Prybylski D (2014). 'Getting to zero' in Asia and the Pacific through more strategic use of antiretrovirals for HIV prevention. *Sexual Health* 11(2):107–118.

Das S, Leibowitz GS (2011). Mental health needs of people living with HIV/AIDS in India: a literature review. *AIDS Care* 23(4):417–425.

Earnshaw VA, Smith LR, Chaudoir SR, Amico KR, Copenhaver MM (2013). HIV stigma mechanisms and well-being among PLWH: a test of the HIV stigma framework. *AIDS Behav* 17(5):1785–1795.

Lazarus JV, Curth N, Bridge J, Atun R (2010). Know your epidemic, know your response: targeting HIV in Asia. *AIDS* 24:S95–S99.

Li L, Lee SJ, Jiraphongsa C, et al. (2010). Improving the health and mental health of people living with HIV/AIDS: 12-month assessment of a behavioral intervention in Thailand. *Am J Public Health* 100(12):2418–2425.

Maj M, Satz P, Janssen R, et al. (1994). WHO neuropsychiatric AIDS study, cross-sectional phase II. Neuropsychological and neurological findings. *Arch Gen Psychiatry* 51(1):51–61.

Mayston R, Kinyanda E, Chishinga N, Prince M, Patel V (2012). Mental disorder and the outcome of HIV/AIDS in low-income and middle-income countries: a systematic review. *AIDS.* 26(Suppl 2):S117–S135.

Nachega JB, Morroni C, Zuniga JM, et al. (2012). HIV-related stigma, isolation, discrimination, and serostatus disclosure: a global survey of 2035 HIV-infected adults. *J Int Assoc Physicians AIDS Care (Chic).* 11(3):172–178.

Parker R, Aggelton P (2003). HIV and AIDS-related stigma and discrimination: a conceptual framework and implications for action. *Soc Sci Med* 57(1):13–24

Springer SA, Dushaj A, Azar MM (2012). The impact of DSM-IV mental disorders on adherence to combination antiretroviral therapy among adult persons living with HIV/AIDS: a systematic review. *AIDS Behav.* 16(8):2119–2143.

Suguimoto SP, Techasrivichien T, Musumari PM, et al. (2014). Changing patterns of HIV epidemic in 30 years in East Asia. *Curr HIV/AIDS Rep.* 11(2):134–145.

Tominari S, Nakakura T, Yasuo T, et al. (2013). Implementation of mental health service has an impact on retention in HIV care: a nested case-control study in a Japanese HIV care facility. PLOS ONE 8(7):e69603.

Tran BX, Ohinmaa A, Duong AT, et al. (2012). Changes in drug use are associated with health-related quality of life improvements among methadone maintenance patients with HIV/AIDS. *Qual Life Res.* 21(4):613–623.

UNAIDS (2011). *HIV in Asia and the Pacific: Getting to Zero.* Geneva: UNAIDS.

UNAIDS (2012). *Global Report: UNAIDS Report on the Global AIDS Epidemic 2012.* Geneva: UNAIDS.

UNAIDS (2013). *HIV in Asia and the Pacific: UNAIDS Report 2013.* Geneva: UNAIDS.

UNAIDS Regional Support Team for Asia and the Pacific (2013). HIV and AIDS data hub. Bangkok: HIV/AIDS Data Hub Office.

van Griensven F, Thienkrua W, McNicholl J, et al. (2013). Evidence of an explosive epidemic of HIV infection among men who have sex with men in Bangkok, Thailand. *AIDS* 27(5):825–832.

Wickersham JA, Zahari MM, Azar MM, Kamarulzaman A, Altice FL (2013). Methadone dose at the time of release from prison significantly influences retention in treatment: implications from a pilot study of HIV-infected prisoners transitioning to the community in Malaysia. *Drug Alcohol Depend* 132(1–2):378–382.

World Health Organization (WHO) (2013). Report of the national HIV/AIDS and STI programme managers' meeting for Asia and the Western Pacific region, 21 October 2013. Kunming, China. Manila: WHO Regional Office for the Western Pacific.

Wright E, Brew B, Arayawichanont A, et al. (2008). Neurologic disorders are prevalent in HIV-positive outpatients in the Asia-Pacific region. *Neurology.* 71(1):50–56.

Zhao Y, Shi CX, McGoogan JM, Rou K, Zhang F, Wu Z (2013). Methadone maintenance treatment and mortality in HIV-positive people who inject opioids in China. *Bull World Health Organ* 91(2):93–101.

REFERENCES FOR HIV AND AIDS IN EUROPE

Asboe D, Aitken C, Boffito M, et al. (2012). British HIV Association guidelines for the routine investigation and monitoring of adult HIV-1-infected individuals 2011. *HIV Med* 13(1):1–44.

Bomba M, Nacinovich R, Oggiano S, et al. (2010). Poor health-related quality of life and abnormal psychosocial adjustment in Italian children with perinatal HIV infection receiving highly active antiretroviral treatment. *AIDS Care* 22(7):858–865

Cohen MS, Chen YQ, McCauley M, et al. (2011). Prevention of HIV-1 infection with early antiretroviral therapy. *N Engl J Med* 365(6):493–505.

Collaboration of Observational HIV Epidemiological Research Europe (COHERE) in EuroCoord (2012). All-cause mortality in treated HIV-infected adults with CD4 ≥500/mm³ compared with the general population: evidence from a large European observational cohort collaboration. *Int J Epidemiol* 41(2):433–445.

Collaboration of Observational HIV Epidemiological Research Europe (COHERE) study in EuroCoord (2013). Risk factors and outcomes for late presentation for HIV-positive persons in Europe: results from the Collaboration of Observational HIV Epidemiological Research Europe Study (COHERE). *PLOS Med* 10:e1001510.

DeHovitz J, Uuskula A, El-Bassel N (2014). The HIV epidemic in Eastern Europe and Central Asia. *Curr HIV/AIDS Rep* 11(2):168–176.

Del Amo J, Likatavičius G, Pérez-Cachafeiro S, et al. (2011). The epidemiology of HIV and AIDS reports in migrants in the 27 European Union countries, Norway and Iceland: 1999–2006. *Eur J Public Health* 21(5):620–626

European AIDS Clinical Society (EACS). (2016, October). Guidelines. Version 8.1. http://www.eacsociety.org/guidelines/eacs-guidelines/eacs-guidelines.html. Accessed December 26, 2016.

European Centre for Disease Prevention and Control (2010). HIV testing: increasing uptake and effectiveness in the European Union. Stockholm: ECDC.

European Centre for Disease Prevention and Control (ECDC) (2013a). Thematic report: combined reporting. Monitoring implementation of the Dublin Declaration on Partnership to Fight HIV/AIDS in Europe and Central Asia: 2012 progress report. Stockholm: ECDC.

European Centre for Disease Prevention and Control (ECDC) (2013b). Thematic report: men who have sex with men. Monitoring implementation of the Dublin Declaration on Partnership to Fight HIV/AIDS in Europe and Central Asia: 2012 progress report. Stockholm: ECDC.

European Centre for Disease Prevention and Control (ECDC) (2013c). Thematic report: stigma and discrimination. Monitoring implementation of the Dublin Declaration on Partnership to Fight HIV/AIDS in Europe and Central Asia: 2012 progress report. Stockholm: ECDC.

European Centre for Disease Prevention and Control (ECDC)/WHO Regional Office for Europe (2015). *HIV/AIDS Surveillance in Europe 2014*. Stockholm: ECDC.

García-Navarro C, García I, Medín G, et al. (2014). Aspectos psicosociales en una cohorte de adolescentes con infección por el virus de la inmunodeficiencia humana por transmisión vertical. NeuroCoRISpeS. *Enferm Infecc Microbiol Clin*. pii:S0213-005X(13)00388-1.

Hernando V, Pharris A, Alvarez D, et al. (2013). Changes in the epidemiology of HIV infection in migrants in the EU/EEA, 2007–2011. Poster presentation at the 14th European Conference, European AIDS Clinical Society (EACS). Brusels, Belgium, October, 16–19, 2013.

Karanikolos M, Mladovsky P, Cylus J, et al. (2013). Financial crisis, austerity, and health in Europe. *Lancet* 381:1323–1331.

Nakagawa F, Phillips AN, Lundgren JD (2014). Update on HIV in Western Europe. *Curr HIV/AIDS Rep* 11:177–185.

Nöstlinger C, Rojas Castro D, Platteau T, Dias S, Le Gall J (2014). HIV-related discrimination in European health care settings. *AIDS Patient Care STDS* 28(3):155–161.

Nyblade L, Stangl A, Weiss E, Asburn K (2009). Combating stigma in health care settings: what works. *J Intl AIDS Soc* 12:15.

Rajasingham R, Mimiaga MJ, White JM, Pinkston MM, Baden RP, Mitty JA (2012). Systematic review of behavioral and treatment outcome studies among HIV-infected men who have sex with men who abuse crystal methamphetamine. *AIDS Patient Care STDs* 26(1):36–52.

Rodger A, Cambiano V, Bruun T, et al. (2014). HIV transmission risk through condomless sex if the HIV positive partner is on suppressive ART: PARTNER study. Abstract 153LB, CROI 2014, Boston, MA, March 3–6, 2014.

Straiton M, Reneflot A, Diaz E (2014). Immigrants' use of primary health care services for mental health problems. *BMC Health Serv Res* 14:341.

REFERENCES FOR HIV IN THE AMERICAS—UNITED STATES

Centers for Disease Control and Prevention (CDC). (2012). New HIV infections in the United States. http://www.cdc.gov/nchhstp/newsroom/docs/2012/hiv-infections-2007-2010.pdf. Accessed December 26, 2016.

Centers for Disease Control and Prevention (CDC). (2015a). High-impact HIV prevention: CDC's approach to reducing HIV infections in the United States. http://www.cdc.gov/hiv/policies/hip.html. Accessed November 29, 2015.

Centers for Disease Control and Prevention (CDC). (2015b). HIV among gay and bisexual men. http://www.cdc.gov/hiv/group/msm/index.html. Accessed May 1, 2016.

Centers for Disease Control and Prevention (CDC). (2015c). HIV among pregnant women, infants, and children. http://www.cdc.gov/hiv/group/gender/pregnantwomen/index.html. Accessed December 12, 2015.

Centers for Disease Control and Prevention (CDC). (2015d). HIV in the United States: at a glance. http://www.cdc.gov/hiv/statistics/overview/ataglance.html. Accessed December 10, 2015.

Centers for Disease Control and Prevention (CDC). (2015e). *HIV Surveillance Report, 2014*, vol. 26. http://www.cdc.gov/hiv/library/reports/surveillance/. Accessed October 18, 2015.

Centers for Disease Control and Prevention (CDC). (2015f). The Affordable Care Act helps people living with HIV/AIDS. http://www.cdc.gov/hiv/policies/aca.html. Accessed December 26, 2015.

Centers for Disease Control and Prevention (CDC). (2016a). HIV among African Americans. http://www.cdc.gov/hiv/group/racial-ethnic/africanamericans/index.html. Accessed May 1, 2016.

Centers for Disease Control and Prevention (CDC). (2016b). HIV among American Indians and Alaska Natives. http://www.cdc.gov/hiv/group/racialethnic/aian/index.html. Accessed May 22, 2016.

Centers for Disease Control and Prevention (CDC). (2016c). HIV and AIDS in the United States by geographic distribution. http://www.cdc.gov/hiv/statistics/overview/geographicdistribution.html. Accessed May 22, 2016.

Health Resources and Services Administration (HRSA) (2016). Global HIV/AIDS programs. http://hab.hrsa.gov/index.html. Accessed May 22, 2016.

Moore RD (2011). Epidemiology of HIV infection in the United States: implications for linkage to care. *Clin Infect Dis* 52(Suppl 2):S208–S213.

U.S. Department of Health and Human Services (2016). The Affordable Care Act and HIV/AIDS. https://www.aids.gov/federal-resources/policies/health-care-reform/. Accessed June 1, 2016,.

REFERENCES FOR HIV IN THE AMERICAS—CANADA

Canadian AIDS Treatment Information Exchange (CATIE). (2011a). People living with HIV in Canada. http://librarypdf.catie.ca/pdf/ATI-40000s/40239_B.pdf. Accessed October 4, 2015.

Canadian AIDS Treatment Information Exchange (CATIE). (2011b). Where is HIV hitting the hardest? http://librarypdf.catie.ca/pdf/ATI-40000s/40239_C.pdf. Accessed October 4, 2015.

Mikkonen J, Raphael D (2010). Social determinants of health: the Canadian facts. Toronto: York University School of Health Policy and Management. http://www.thecanadianfacts.org/The_Canadian_Facts.pdf.

Public Health Agency of Canada. (n.d.). Managing your health: A guide for people living with HIV. http://www.catie.ca/en/practical-guides/managing-your-health/17. Accessed October 29, 2015.

Public Health Agency of Canada (2013a). At a glance—HIV and AIDS in Canada: surveillance report to December 31st, 2012. http://www.phac-aspc.gc.ca/aids-sida/publication/survreport/2012/dec/index-eng.php. Accessed September 1, 2015.

Public Health Agency of Canada (2013b). Population-specific HIV/AIDS status report: people living with HIV/AIDS. Retrieved from http://www.catie.ca/sites/default/files/SR-People-Living-with-HIV.pdf. Accessed September 9, 2015.

Public Health Agency of Canada (2014a). HIV/AIDS Epi updates: national HIV prevalence and incidence estimates for 2011. http://www.phac-aspc.gc.ca/aids-sida/publication/epi/2010/1-eng.php. Accessed December 26, 2016.

Public Health Agency of Canada (2014b). HIV/AIDS Epi update: HIV/AIDS among Aboriginal people in Canada. http://www.phac-aspc.gc.ca/aids-sida/publication/epi/2010/pdf/ch8-eng.pdf. Accessed September 1, 2015.

Public Health Agency of Canada (2015). Summary: estimates of HIV incidence, prevalence and proportion undiagnosed in Canada, 2014. http://www.catie.ca/sites/default/files/2014-HIV-Estimates-in-Canada-EN.pdf. Accessed December 26, 2016.

REFERENCES FOR HIV IN THE AMERICAS—LATIN AMERICA

Berkman A, Garcia J, Muñoz-Laboy M, Paiva V, Parker R (2005). A critical analysis of the Brazilian response to HIV/AIDS: lessons learned for controlling and mitigating the epidemic in developing countries. *Am J Public Health* 95(7):1162–1172.

Brazil Ministry of Health (2014). Global AIDS response. Progress reporting (2014). Narrative reporting. http://www.unaids.org/sites/default/files/country/documents//file%2C94421%2Ces.pdf. Accessed October 12, 2016.

Stone K. (2014). The global state of harm reduction 2008: mapping the response to drug-related HIV and hepatitis C epidemics (4th ed., pp. 1–130) London: Harm Reduction International. http://www.ihra.net/files/2015/02/16/GSHR2014.pdf.

UNAIDS (2013). *Global Report: UNAIDS Report on the Global AIDS Epidemic, 2013*. Geneva: UNAIDS. Available from http://www.unaids.org/sites/default/files/media_asset/UNAIDS_Global_Report_2013_en_1.pdf.

UNAIDS (2014). *The Gap Report*. http://www.unaids.org/sites/default/files/media_asset/UNAIDS_Gap_report_en.pdf. Accessed May 31, 2016.

World Health Organization (2005b). Costa Rica (WHO Costa Rica). http://www.who.int/hiv/HIVCP_CRI.pdf. Accessed September 26, 2015.

World Health Organization (2005a). Belize (WHO Belize). http://www.who.int/hiv/HIVCP_BLZ.pdf. Accessed September 20, 2015.

World Health Organization (2005c). El Salvador (WHO El Salvador). http://www.who.int/hiv/HIVCP_SLV.pdf. Accessed September 24, 2015.

World Health Organization (2005d). Guatemala (WHO Guatemala). http://www.who.int/hiv/HIVCP_GTM.pdf. Accessed September 26, 2015.

World Health Organization (2006). HIV/AIDS Program—towards universal access by 2010—how WHO is working with countries to scale-up HIV prevention, treatment, care and support. http://www.who.int/hiv/toronto2006/towardsuniversalaccess.pdf. Accessed April 15, 2016.

5.

AIDS ORPHANS AND OTHER CHILDREN AFFECTED BY HIV

Getrude Makurumidze, Anna Gamell, and Emilio Letang

THE STORY OF ONE AIDS ORPHAN

A little girl is born in Zimbabwe in what she considers a rosy cradle, but it is not long before her fortunes plummet. Episodes of pain and misery begin to unfold during her childhood. Her life is punctuated by incidents of sorrow and joy, fear and comfort, despair and hope. The AIDS pandemic rocked the rosy cradle and pitched its tent within her home, wiping out her entire immediate family in brutal episodes, leaving her a solo remnant by the age of 9. She is faced with the loss of her mother, father, and baby sister all in less than a year. At 8 years of age she is uprooted from her home and family and sent from one family to the other, from one guardian to the next. The little girl is one of the 17.8 million AIDS orphans in the world today.

What happens to each of these little girls and boys as they grow up? This chapter explores the psychological, social, and cultural aspects of HIV/AIDS orphanhood. For a comprehensive description of the psychiatric aspects of HIV/AIIDS in children and adolescents please see Chapter 33 of this textbook. We begin this chapter with the story of one AIDS orphan, who is also one of the authors of this chapter (GM).

I am Getty, the little girl just described. Although my story may not be typical, it provides a personal account of trauma, loss, mourning, and recovery that are part of being an AIDS orphan. I have very little access to memories of my early childhood, and the little I have been told or remember of my childhood has survived in the memories of my uncles and aunts. My story is fragmented and has many gaps, as it was pieced together from my own memories as well as those of my remaining relatives.

My parents were both civil servants, my mother a nurse and my father a teacher. We could afford all necessities without difficulty, with a little surplus to give me something special whenever I was first in my class. I can recall blissful moments with my mother, when she taught me how to knit and when we spent time knitting together. I made scarves for my doll and teddy bear while she knitted more complicated sweaters and other clothing. From my early childhood I was full of energy and seemed much older than my chronological age. Unbeknownst to me, my father insisted on wanting another child. After two prior spontaneous abortions, my mother was able to maintain a third pregnancy by the time I was 8 years of age.

Shortly before that pregnancy, my mother began complaining of general body weakness and abdominal pain but had not sought medical help. As the pregnancy progressed, she got weaker and weaker—bringing pain, sadness, and anxiety to our family. My father was also suffering from abdominal pain and other symptoms of illness, but he seemed to tolerate them better than my mother. My mother sustained serious complications during pregnancy, which almost cost her life during delivery. She survived the delivery and gave birth to a sickly baby girl—my sister Natasha—who died when she was about 6 months old.

Natasha was born prematurely. She had an intestinal anomaly and spent most of her life in the hospital. My mother, who was also very sick, was not able to take care of both Natasha and me, so I was sent to stay with my great aunt. Natasha died while I was away and I never attended her funeral. There are not even any photographs of her. My parents' decision to protect me from the turbulence in the family left me feeling uprooted and without the ability to process either attachment to Natasha or mourning for her.

After the death of Natasha, I was sent back to live with my parents. My mother's health continued to deteriorate. My parents never told me what was wrong, concealing a secret and also a time bomb that was eventually going to explode. It was not until 8 years later that I found out how and when my mother was diagnosed with AIDS. After Natasha died, my mother decided to get tested for HIV and learned that she was HIV positive. The diagnosis came as a surprise to my father, but my mother had been suspecting it since the pregnancy. My father was in denial for a while and both my parents were very discreet and did not disclose my mother's HIV status to anyone. It is unclear when my father decided to get tested for HIV and learned that he had AIDS. It is also unclear whether he accepted responsibility for having infected my mother. During the next few months, my mother continued battling for her life, spending more days and hours in the hospital than at work. Medical bills, travel expenses, and stress all weighed heavily on my parents, giving rise to vicious tensions and violent fights within the family. At one point my mother took me away from our home and the fighting. She never explained why we had to leave. We stayed together for a short time in a room in an area of the hospital where she worked. I recall not knowing how to explain to my school friends why I was taking a different route home or why I could no longer walk with them on my way home. I was left during this period without any children my age that I could play with. My mother was all I had. My parents subsequently resolved some of their conflicts and we were once again reunited and back at home.

The fighting did not end when we returned home, however. Not long afterward, my mother was diagnosed with tuberculosis and lost a lot of weight. My father essentially rejected her by deciding not to pay for any of my mother's medical care. My mother got so weak that she could barely stand or walk. Ultimately, she lost control of her bowels and bladder and was unable to care for herself. My Aunt Auxilia came to stay with us and became my mother's caregiver. My mother's brother, Uncle Francis, lived 4 hours away. He drove to see my mother every week—bringing some food, settling some bills, and buying her medication. My mother was receiving symptomatic treatment and medication for tuberculosis, but at that time antiretroviral drugs were not available in Zimbabwe. Aunt Auxilia monitored my mother's health for a while until her condition worsened and she was admitted to the hospital. It was during the time that she stayed with us that my aunt learned about my mother's HIV status. Although some of my relatives had their suspicions, my mother did not disclose her status. Since she was the eldest in her family, my mother may have thought that informing her siblings would burden them or that there was so much stigma she could not risk letting even her immediate family know.

Uncle Francis made arrangements with his doctor to transfer my mother to a hospital that was closer to where he lived. This was when he learned that his sister was HIV positive. Three days after the transfer, my mother died in the tender and loving care of her brother. My mother had suffered from this highly stigmatized disease for at least 3 years and then had to grapple with the final blow—rejection by her husband.

A conspiracy of silence prevailed. As a result of the stigma related to HIV/AIDS, I never knew the cause of my mother's illness and ultimate death at the time of her illness and for many years thereafter. On the bus ride to the funeral home I still did not know that she had died, but I started to surmise that something terrible had happened when people were giving my aunt and uncle condolences. It was not until we reached the funeral home that my father told me of my mother's death. I was devastated. My mother had promised that we would celebrate my ninth birthday when she got well, which she never did. I never had a chance to say goodbye to her or to know what it was that had caused her death. Immediately after my mother's death, my father's health deteriorated, and he passed away 2 months later. At the time of his death, I was staying with my Aunt Rhonia, my father's elder sister. Although I suspected that something was wrong when my aunt, uncle, and I drove to my rural home, once again, it was only when we got to where the burial would take place that I was told that my father had died. Many months after my sister, mother, and father died, I received my mother's Bible, which contained a letter to me. The letter provided me with a memory of her love and faith in me. It conveyed to me the sense of her conviction that I would be able to do well despite my losses.

At the death of my parents, Uncle Francis became my guardian. I did not stay with him, since his work required travel. Instead, I continued living with my Aunt Rhonia and her family. This was a challenging phase in my life; I was trying to come to terms with the death of my family while learning to fit into a new family. Nevertheless, as a young and outgoing girl, I quickly made friends with my aunt's five children and she treated me as one of her children. I attended school with two of my aunt's children, who were about my age. I stayed with her family for a year but had to leave after the death of my uncle, who was the breadwinner. My aunt could not afford my upkeep. Once again, I had to relocate, this time to live with my mother's younger brother and his wife, Aunt Auxilia. In most families in Zimbabwe, children are not consulted about decision-making and have no say or control of what happens to them. Because I was not aware of the planning that was taking place, the decision was sudden and unexpected. I was very sad, because I had just adjusted to being part of this family and it had become home for me. Moving meant that I had to readjust to a new family, new place, new school, and new teachers. I had to make new friends all over again.

I stayed with my uncle, my Aunt Auxilia, and their three children at a rural village school where my uncle was a teacher. Theirs was a lovely home, one that reminded me of my earliest years when my parents were alive and together. My aunt was as gentle and loving as my mother. She taught me to be responsible. When she was away, I would take care of the children— bathing and dressing them before I went to school and helping them with their homework after school. Regardless of the limited resources and facilities at the school, I had the best grades, which qualified me for entrance into many secondary schools in the country. However, in spite of my good grades, my uncle could not afford to send me to a reputable school for my secondary education. I knew that sooner or later I would have to relocate, so I had emotionally prepared myself. In a way, I had also become an experienced mover. On the bright side, I learned quite a lot by living with different families and I was even more grateful that my relatives were willing to take care of me.

Another enormous loss occurred when Uncle Francis left his job to join a seminary, in response to his call to the Catholic priesthood. This decision had far-reaching implications for the entire family and for me in particular. Two years before entering the seminary, Uncle Francis had liquidated his assets, creating some investments meant to see me through my entire education. However, within a few months of creating the investments, there was a serious collapse in the Zimbabwean financial sector, which led to the closure of many banks. In the process of this disaster, most of my uncle's investments were lost. The amount he recovered was only enough to cover the first year of my secondary education in any one of the leading mission boarding schools. As a result, when I eventually completed my primary education, fierce battles arose among my uncles, with the majority insisting that I should go to a cheaper, rural government school, while Uncle Francis avowed that he was prepared to do anything in his capacity to see that I got the best education possible.

Amidst these vicious family fights, Uncle Francis convinced me to apply to any school of my choice.

Uncle Francis used his persuasion and pleading to convince his friend, "Uncle" Sydney, to take responsibility for my upkeep and educational expenses. Hence, I was adopted into Uncle Sydney's family. I was not aware of the planning that was taking place and the decision that had been made for me to move to my new home. I recall being sent off alone on a bus to Harare, a city that was 5 hours away, and, at my destination, being met by the people who were to become my new family. I started living with my new family and their four children in the capital city. During the 6 years that I stayed with Uncle Sydney and his family I attained my secondary education and attended high school.

It was only when I turned 16 that my Uncle Francis explained to me the causes and events leading to my parents' and sister's death. I was baffled. I just listened and cried as he told the story. Over the years, I had been told a number of stories to explain their deaths, most of which had to do with food poisoning. I had accepted these stories as the truth. I felt I had been lied to and betrayed. Everyone else around me had known the truth. I had heard stories of people dying from AIDS, but never for one moment or in my wildest imagination had I thought that my own parents had died from this deadly virus. I was not prepared to share this new revelation with my friends, and it took a while before I accepted it as part of my life. Since the death of my parents, I had always wanted to be a doctor, but once I learned about how AIDS destroyed my family, I developed a keen interest in specializing in the field of HIV/AIDS research.

In my final year in high school, I was accepted into the United States Achievers Program (USAP). USAP is a program that helps a selected number of talented but economically disadvantaged students to apply to colleges and universities in the United States. With the help and support from our education adviser, Amai Rebecca Zeigler Mano, I was accepted into Bryn Mawr College on a full scholarship. During the 6 months leading to my first semester at Bryn Mawr, I volunteered at Chiedza, a local childcare center where I taught math and English to primary school and high school children. Whenever I had the chance, I visited the Mother of Peace orphanage for HIV/AIDS orphans and spent time with the children. It was during these visits that I realized how fortunate I was to have had relatives who cared for me. Had I been born in a different family, I would have ended up at an orphanage too. I saw them as my little brothers and sisters. Most of the orphans were found outside the orphanage, left by their parents or relatives who could not or did not want to take responsibility for them. Some orphans may have had relatives who were willing to care for them but, given limited financial resources, could not afford to take care of them. Others, having experienced the harshness of society, detested the world so much that they rebelled against anyone who tried to lend a hand.

Through Amai Mano, I was introduced to Jillian Bonnardeaux and the U.S. Embassy Public Affairs Section team. They suggested that I work with Carol Wogrin as a motivational speaker for Women's History Month. The goal of these talks was to motivate elementary, middle school, and high school students to stay in school, work hard, and focus on learning despite adversity that may challenge them along the way. Using my own personal story of losing my immediate family to AIDS while I was a child of 8 to 9 years of age, I was able to inspire and relate to other children and adolescents and provide a role model for them. Together, Carol and I went to schools in Zimbabwe and addressed groups of young people.

While working with Carol, she became less and less of a colleague and more of a mother to me. She suggested that I visit all the places and relatives I had lived with before I left for college. Carol, Uncle Francis, and I traveled throughout the country for me to say farewell and thank the wonderful people who had made it possible for me to be where I was. Jillian introduced me to David and Lainie Wolovitz, whom she thought of as her adopted parents and who live close to Bryn Mawr College.

With no knowledge of when I would see my relatives and friends again, I bid them farewell and embarked on the journey that marked the beginning of the second chapter of my life. Upon my arrival in the United States, my host parents, David and Lainie, met me and welcomed me to their home. I stayed with them for a week before I settled in my college dorm. They made my transition into the United States very smooth and have been there for me ever since. Prior to my coming to the United States, Dr. Mary Ann Cohen, a Bryn Mawr alumna, read about my story in an alumnae newsletter. Mary Ann is also a psychiatrist who is passionate about prevention and care of persons with HIV and AIDS and offered to become my mentor. I got in contact with her and soon afterward arranged to meet with her. Mary Ann has not only assisted me in securing internships for summer projects but also warmly opened her home and family to me. With her help, I was introduced to Dr. Jeffrey Jacobson and Dr. Michele Kutzler, at Drexel University College of Medicine, who are passionate about their work in infectious diseases. I worked with Dr. Kutzler and her team in a research program that was designed to develop an HIV-1 DNA vaccine. We published a supplement on the research in the *Journal of Immunology* (Kutzler et al., 2014). For my second summer internship, I wanted to work in oncology, and through the Summer Clinical Oncology Research Experience (SCORE) program at the Memorial Sloan-Kettering Cancer Center, led by Dr. Laura Liberman, I interned in integrative medicine.

Having been denied the opportunity to bid farewell to my mother, father, and sister, I felt a strong urge to provide care for persons with end-stage illness and to be there for them at the end of their lives. My own past experience motivated me to do volunteer work at a local hospice throughout my sophomore year. My work in the hospice helped me realize that, although death is a painful moment for those left behind, it is even more scary and painful for persons at the end of life. I observed how patients who are dying have to acknowledge the impending losses of their goals, possessions, abilities, and loved ones and yet still look ahead, with no certainty, to what comes after death. I realized for the first time how it may have felt for my mother when she wrote her last letter to me on her death bed, knowing that she was about to die and being uncertain of how long my father would live and whether or not he would be able to care for me.

After my experience at Memorial Sloan Kettering Cancer Center and through volunteering in hospice care, I recognized the importance of collaborative care with an emphasis on addressing mental health needs. I then joined Dr. David C. Henderson and the Global Psychiatry team at Massachusetts General Hospital, where I learned the importance of integrating mental health services into clinical settings, the structure of clinical trials, and building capacity in areas lacking mental health services. I managed to reflect on my experiences and learn more about the mental health needs of AIDS orphans, who face discrimination and whose mental health needs are neglected worldwide.

In my senior year in college, I was selected as a Rhodes Scholarship finalist by the Zimbabwe Rhodes Scholarship Committee. Following completion of my undergraduate studies in May 2016, I accepted a full-time 1- to 2-year position as Program Assistant at the New York State Department of Health AIDS Institute. There, working with Dr. Bruce Agins, Medical Director, we are developing and implementing a collaborative project between HealthQual International and the Zimbabwe Ministry of Health and Child Care to evaluate quality improvement programs for HIV care in Zimbabwe. Subsequently, my goals are to attain a medical degree and work toward developing a global-oriented practice that would allow me to conduct HIV research and maintain a clinical practice in mental health. My goals include the development of institutions in Zimbabwe and abroad that provide comprehensive care for children affected by and infected with HIV.

FROM ONE AIDS ORPHAN TO 17.8 MILLION

As inspiring as Getty's heart-wrenching story is, she is the exception rather than the rule among AIDS orphans. It is extremely rare for an AIDS orphan to get to be a college student, and Getty is well aware of this and has made this clear in her story. This is why, despite not being easy for her, she has shared her story in high schools, in lectures, in college applications, and in an interview published in the *Philadelphia Inquirer*. This is the way Getty has chosen to fight against HIV/AIDS stigma, the first steps she has taken to improve the lives of millions of AIDS orphans in the world.

With generations of orphans left behind as a result of the HIV/AIDS pandemic, the overall effect is devastating, and no region has felt this devastation more than sub-Saharan Africa. We decided to start this chapter with a very successful, yet uncommon, AIDS orphan's life story. However, the life of most of the AIDS orphans is far different from Getty's experience. The rights and well-being of AIDS orphans are at tremendous risk, as are the development prospects of their countries, as a consequence of the morally unacceptable burden of AIDS orphans globally and, more specifically, in sub-Saharan Africa.

EPIDEMIOLOGY

According to the United Nations, in 2012, there were 17.8 million (16.1 million–21.6 million) children under the age of 18 orphaned by AIDS. As adults continue to die from AIDS-related illnesses over the next years, an increasing number of children will grow up without parental care. Eighty-five percent of the AIDS orphans (around 15 million) live in sub-Saharan Africa. In some African countries a large percentage of all orphaned children are AIDS orphans (74% in Zimbabwe, 63% in South Africa, and 59% in Malawi), and in some cases the number of AIDS orphans exceeds two million (2.5 million in South Africa, and 2.2 million in Nigeria) (UNICEF, 2013).

Moreover, the impact of the HIV epidemic on children extends well beyond the impact on the 17.8 million AIDS-orphaned and 1.8 million HIV-infected children (UNAIDS, 2016), as precise estimates of the real burden of children affected directly or indirectly by HIV globally are lacking. This burden includes a loss of workforce, a less educated population, and increased healthcare and economic costs—only a few aspects of the impact of orphanhood that we define and describe here.

DEFINING HIV/AIDS ORPHANS AND VULNERABLE CHILDREN

AIDS orphans are those children that have lost either or both parents due to HIV/AIDS and can be classified as follows:

- *Maternal orphan:* a child under the age of 18 years whose mother, and perhaps father, has died

- *Paternal orphan:* a child under the age of 18 years whose father, and perhaps mother, has died

- *Double orphan:* a child under the age of 18 years whose mother and father have both died

However, orphaning is not the only way children are affected by HIV/AIDS. Many children are made vulnerable by (1) having an ill parent; (2) being at risk of getting infected with HIV; (3) being forced to drop out of school; (4) experiencing developmental problems on account of food scarcity; (5) living in a poor household that has taken in AIDS orphans; (6) having social problems from not being cared for; and (7) being discriminated against because their parents or they themselves are HIV infected. In order to capture all children affected by HIV/AIDS in efforts to address their plight, the term *orphaned and vulnerable children* (OVC) was adopted.

The definition of vulnerability is extremely challenging, since many variables need to be considered. There is a disparity in definitions between communities and external agencies. Skinner et al. (2004) developed a common definition of orphaned and vulnerable children, focusing on three core areas of dependence:

- *Material problems:* access to money, food, clothing, shelter, healthcare, and education

- *Emotional problems:* containment of emotions and lack of experience of caring and love, support, and space to grieve
- *Social problems:* lack of a supportive peer group, of role models to follow, or of guidance in difficult situations, and risks in the immediate environment

Importantly, the definition of AIDS orphaned and vulnerable children needs to be adapted to various geographical and cultural circumstances in order to ensure that all affected children can benefit from policies and projects focused on this key population.

AREAS OF VULNERABILITY

The problems of children and families affected by HIV/AIDS are many and interrelated, making it very challenging for orphans and vulnerable children to avoid the circuit of poverty and the higher risk of HIV infection. Williamson illustrates the complexity of these problems in Figure 5.1.

HIV/AIDS orphans suffer from emotional neglect in many ways. Long before the death of one or both parents, it is not uncommon that children, of all ages, assume the role of caregivers, becoming responsible for feeding, bathing, toileting, and giving medication to their sick parents and younger siblings (Foster and Williamson, 2000). Eventually, they may suffer the death of their parent(s) and the emotional trauma that results, as well as the consequences of being moved from rural to urban areas, or vice versa, when taken care of by extended family members. AIDS orphans are also at risk of exploitation, some being recruited to work in farms, mines, or quarries, and others used for domestic and sex work (Andrews et al., 2006; UNICEF, 2004; UNICEF, UNAIDS, PEPFAR, 2006).

Also, at the death of their parent(s), AIDS orphans are faced with a shortage of material resources. They face a reduction in their quality of life, with basics like food, clothes, education, shelter, and healthcare becoming scarce (Andrews et al., 2006; UNICEF, 2004; UNICEF, UNAIDS, PEPFAR, 2006). Orphans are more likely than non-orphans to live in large, female-headed households where more people are dependent on fewer income earners, leading some children to work at very early ages. In addition, orphans are sometimes deprived of property and money left for them by their parents, as some relatives take advantage of them and access to their inheritance (UNICEF, 2004).

As a result of their situation, orphaned and vulnerable children may not be enrolled in school, be forced to drop out, or perform poorly because of their own illness or having to care for other family members. Moreover, children orphaned by AIDS will not have the opportunity to receive valuable life-skills and practical knowledge that would have been passed on by their parents. Lacking this knowledge and a basic primary school education, children are at higher risk to face social, economic, and health problems as they grow up.

While it is difficult for any child to lose a parent, loss due to HIV further magnifies the fear of abandonment. Stigma and discrimination surrounding HIV is still prevalent, especially in sub-Saharan Africa, where it is associated with shame, guilt, a curse, weakness, unfaithfulness, and isolation (Kalichman and Simbayi, 2003). AIDS orphans have a high chance of being rejected by their relatives (UNICEF, 2004). Stigma and its psychological consequences harm AIDS orphans' sense of self-worth and belonging, which are essential for learning, developing life skills, participating in society, and having faith in the future.

In sub-Saharan Africa, generally, members of the extended family take care of orphans, regardless of their economic

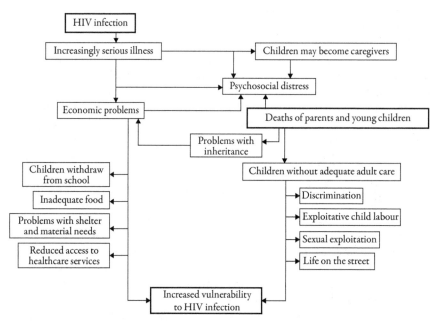

Figure 5.1 Problems among children and families affected by HIV/AIDS. From Williamson (2000).

status (UNICEF, 2003). In many cases surviving grandmothers feel compelled to take care of their grandchildren (Foster and Williamson, 2000). The demand of care and support is overwhelming in many areas, highlighting the need to give greater financial and emotional support to the extended families. In the absence of family support, some children are institutionalized or abandoned in the streets, thus increasing their vulnerability and their risk of being exploited.

Finally, all of these problems increase children's vulnerability to HIV infection and the vicissitudes of the vicious circle of poverty and AIDS illness (Operario et al., 2011).

SUPPORTING AIDS ORPHANS AND VULNERABLE CHILDREN

Addressing the material, social, and psychological impact that HIV has on millions of children requires complex multidimensional and multisectoral interventions. These interventions need to be customized to each country's reality and integrated within the existing prevention, care, and treatment programs.

Since the beginning of the pandemic, more than 35 years ago, the responsibility of taking care of children affected by HIV/AIDS and providing support for them has largely been left to families and communities. To strengthen these community initiatives, some non-governmental organizations and national aid programs have dedicated part of their funds to support orphaned and vulnerable children. The President's Emergency Plan for AIDS Relief (PEPFAR) from the U.S. government is the major donor globally, dedicating 10% of its budget to such children since 2003 (AVERT, 2017; UNICEF, UNAIDS, PEPFAR, 2006; USAID, 2016).

In order to address the multiple deleterious effects that HIV can have on children, PEPFAR OVC programs are designed to cover eight different sectors, each one with a specific aim (PEPFAR, 2012):

1. *Education:* reducing educational disparities and barriers to schooling

2. *Psychosocial care and support:* maintaining children in stable and affectionate environments

3. *Household economic strengthening:* empowering families to be able to provide for the needs of children in their care

4. *Social protection:* breaking the transmission of poverty from generation to generation by promoting human capital development

5. *Health and nutrition:* improving access to health and nutritional services for children and their families

6. *Child protection:* protecting children from abuse, exploitation, and violence and having strategies in place to respond to mistreatment

7. *Legal protection:* offering basic legal rights, birth registration, and inheritance rights to ensure children's access to essential services and opportunities

8. *Capacity building:* guaranteeing capacity-building and systems-strengthening interventions in the country where the program is implemented

These strategies to protect, support, and empower orphaned and vulnerable children have shown to be effective. Since 2003, many AIDS-orphaned children have been kept in school (Bryant et al., 2011), the psychosocial outcomes of HIV-affected children have been improved (Nyangara et al., 2009), and many children and their families have benefitted from better access to health and nutritional services (Adato and Bassett, 2009).

Despite the considerable progress achieved, multiple challenges still prevent many AIDS orphans and vulnerable children from receiving effective care and support. These challenges include the complexity of implementing multisectoral interventions properly integrated within the existing prevention, care, and treatment activities; inadequate program evaluation; and difficulty in monitoring children's outcomes. These aspects need to be strengthened in order to build evidence-based programs, be able to respond to the needs of all AIDS-affected children, and achieve the dream of an AIDS-free generation.

CONCLUSIONS

There is global enthusiasm for the possibility of achieving an AIDS-free generation and eliminating pediatric HIV. However, millions of children have already lost at least one parent, and millions more are likely to over the next few years. Creating a viable future for children orphaned and made vulnerable by HIV/AIDS is a task that must not be left aside. Individual needs of AIDS orphans should be met, including emotional, social, material, and financial requirements. There is an urgent need to help, care for, and protect the children of the HIV/AIDS pandemic. Moreover, HIV prevention programs need to be strengthened to decrease HIV incidence and minimize the number of orphans in the future. Programs like PEPFAR OVC need to be scaled up globally and widely and comprehensively implemented in order to reliably address the multiple challenges orphaned and vulnerable children face. Political will and increased and sustained funding will be required to keep up with the increasing number of children requiring support over the next years.

We must aim to ensure that children's rights are protected, respected, and fulfilled, so that AIDS orphans and vulnerable children grow into a strong generation, one able to contribute to repairing the profound social and personal damage caused by HIV/AIDS and to preventing the further spread of HIV, thus reducing the number of future orphans.

ACKNOWLEDGMENTS

The authors are very grateful to Dr. Kim Dean Mwamelo for her critical reading of the chapter.

REFERENCES

Adato M, Bassett L. (2009). Social protection to support vulnerable children and families: the potential of cash transfers to protect education, health and nutrition. *AIDS Care* 21(Suppl 1):60–75.

Andrews G, Skinner D, Zuma K (2006). Epidemiology of health and vulnerability among children orphaned and made vulnerable by HIV/AIDS in sub-Saharan Africa. *AIDS Care* 18:269–276.

AVERT (2017). Children and HIV/AIDS. http://www.avert.org/professionals/hiv-social-issues/key-affected-populations/children. Accessed January 18, 2017.

Bryant M, Shann M, Brooks B, Bukuluki P, Muhangi D, Lugalla J, Kwesigabo G (2011). Evaluating the effectiveness of educational block grants to orphans and vulnerable children. USAID Project SEARCH Research Report: Boston University OVC-CARE Project.

Foster G, Williamson J (2000). A review of current literature of the impact of HIV/AIDS on children in sub-Saharan Africa. *AIDS* 14(Suppl 3):S275–S284.

Kalichman SC, Simbayi LC (2003). HIV testing attitudes, AIDS stigma, and voluntary HIV counselling and testing in a black township in Cape Town, South Africa. *Sex Transm Infect* 79:442–447.

Kutzler M, Kathuria N, Curatola A, Makurumidze G, et al. (2014). CCR10 expression is required for immunogenicity of a HIV-1 env DNA vaccine encoding CCL28 to enhance HIV-1env-specific IgG and IgA at relevant mucosal sites. *J Immunol* 192(1 Suppl):141.31.

Nyangara F, Obiero W, Kalungwa Z, Thurman T (2009). Community-based psychosocial intervention for HIV-affected children and their caregivers: evaluation of the Salvation Army. USAID MEASURE Evaluation Project.

Operario D, Underhill K, Chuong C, Cluver L (2011). HIV infection and sexual risk behavior among youth who have experienced orphanhood: systematic review and meta-analysis. *J Intl AIDS Soc* 14:25.

President's Emergency Plan for AIDS Relief (PEPFAR) (2012). Guidance for orphans and vulnerable children programming, July 2012. Washington, DC: PEPFAR.

Skinner D, Tsheko N, Mtero-Munyati S, et al. (2004). *Defining Orphaned and Vulnerable Children*. Pretoria, South Africa: HSRC Press.

UNAIDS (2016). AIDS by the numbers. http://www.unaids.org/sites/default/files/media_asset/AIDS-by-the-numbers-2016_en.pdf. Retrieved January 19, 2017.

UNICEF (2003). *Africa's Orphaned Generations*. https://www.unicef.org/sowc06/pdfs/africas_orphans.pdf. Accessed January 10, 2017.

UNICEF (2004). The framework for the protection, care and support of orphans and vulnerable children living in a world with HIV and AIDS. https://www.unicef.org/ceecis/Framework_English.pdf. Accessed January 10, 2017.

UNICEF (2013). *Towards an AIDS-Free Generation—Children and AIDS: Sixth Stocktaking Report, 2013*. https://www.unicef.org/publications/files/Children_and_AIDS_Sixth_Stocktaking_Report_EN.pdf. Accessed Janaury 10, 2017.

UNICEF, UNAIDS, PEPFAR (2006). *Africa's Orphaned and Vulnerable Generations Children Affected by AIDS*. https://www.unicef.org/publications/files/Africas_Orphaned_and_Vulnerable_Generations_Children_Affected_by_AIDS.pdf. Accessed January 8, 2017.

USAID (2016). Orphans and vulnerable children affected by HIV. https://www.usaid.gov/what-we-do/global-health/hiv-and-aids/technical-areas/orphans-and-vulnerable-children-affected-hiv. Accessed January 8, 2017.

Williamson J. (2000). What can we do to make a difference? Situation analysis concerning children and families affected by AIDS. http://www.crin.org/en/docs/WhatCanWeDo.pdf. Accessed Janaury 8, 2017.

6.

HIV DISCRIMINATION, STIGMA, AND GENDER-BASED VIOLENCE

Antoine Douaihy, Neeta Shenai, Kimberly Clinebell, and Mary Ann Cohen

tigma and discrimination have haunted persons infected with and affected by HIV and AIDS throughout the pandemic, throughout the world, throughout the life cycle, and throughout the course of care from engagement in care to death (Cohen, 2008). In 1981 and in the initial phase of the pandemic, the cause of the new illness had not been identified. And the fact that AIDS was associated with infection, severe and inexorable devastation of the immune system, severe and profound wasting and a skeletal appearance, and inevitable death in young and previously healthy individuals contributed to development of both fear and stigma. The results of stigma have led to discrimination, beginning early in the pandemic with discrimination occurring in schools, acute and long-term-care medical facilities, the workplace, places of worship, and funeral homes. Some of the words used in the pandemic may have contributed to the stigma. The concept of "risk groups" led to stigmatization of populations of persons who belonged to the groups and falsely reassured members of the rest of the population that they were invulnerable to HIV and therefore did not need to use universal precautions or protect themselves from transmission of HIV. The stigma of HIV and AIDS was magnified by the various types of the stigma and discrimination associated with vulnerability to HIV: mental illness–based stigma and especially "addictophobia"; homophobia; poverty-based stigma; and gender-based stigma. These were some of the contributors that led to the term *AIDSism*, first introduced in 1989 (Cohen, 1989).

Although the prognosis for people with HIV infection has improved dramatically in recent years, attitudes about people with HIV infection have not improved nearly as much. As noted by Crowley and colleagues (2015):

> Twenty-five years ago . . . HIV and AIDS were significant sources of anxiety and public concern. . . . There was only one transiently effective treatment, and HIV was the third leading cause of death in the United States among adults aged 25 to 44 years and the leading cause of death among black men and Hispanic men in this age group. . . . Today, people with HIV who are diagnosed early, engaged in care, and able to continue treatment may live a normal lifespan. A broad array of effective, simple, and well-tolerated antiretroviral therapies (ART) are now available for treatment. Effective ART also has changed the

prevention landscape as data have shown that viral suppression substantially decreases the risk of HIV transmission. Additionally, tenofovir/emtricitabine has been proven effective in preventing infection as preexposure prophylaxis. Despite remarkable progress in both treatment and prevention, however, stigma and discrimination are still pervasive.

In this chapter, we present the current and tragic role that stigma, discrimination, and gender-based violence play in the HIV pandemic, as well as ways to apply the advances in medicine and society to ameliorate and eventually eliminate these negative conditions.

DEFINITIONS AND PREVALENCE

Since HIV was first described in 1981, despite vast improvements in the medical care of persons with access to HIV treatment, overall improvement in civil rights and patient rights, and, in many countries, amelioration of discrimination, the stigma and discrimination associated with HIV persist in the United States and throughout the world (Cohen, 2008; Crowley et al., 2015; Khalife and Cohen, 2010; Smita et al., 2012). Universally, *stigma* has been defined as any characteristic—real or perceived—that conveys a negative social identity (Goffman, 1963). HIV stigma and discrimination have been described as AIDSism (Cohen, 1989). The Joint United Nations Programme on HIV/AIDS (UNAIDS) developed a definition of stigma specific to HIV/AIDS infection: "a process of devaluation of people either living with or associated with, HIV and AIDS" (2003). Discrimination is often a product of stigma and is characterized by UNAIDS as the "unfair and unjust treatment of an individual based on his or her real or perceived AIDS status" (UNAIDS, 2003). Discrimination and stigma both prevail despite increasing knowledge about HIV and AIDS (Crowley et al., 2015).

Multiple studies have looked at the prevalence of HIV and AIDS stigma. One study in the 1990s showed a decline in support for punitive policies (quarantine and public identification) and in negative feelings toward those with HIV and AIDS. The authors concluded, however, that stigma still lingered, as a significant percentage of people surveyed expressed fear and disgust or supported public naming of those with

HIV (Herek et al., 2002). A study from Botswana, which previously had the highest prevalence of HIV in the world (National AIDS Coordinating Agency, 2002), showed high levels of stigma toward teachers and shopkeepers with HIV and AIDS (60%); however, stigma was drastically reduced with regard to caring for ill family members—only 11% of respondents reported they would be unwilling to care for them (Letamo, 2003). In this same study, women had fewer discriminatory beliefs, whereas younger people and those who believe HIV can be transmitted by sharing a meal with an infected person had more discriminatory beliefs. In another study, conducted by the Centers for Disease Control and Prevention (CDC), men and those who are white, are 55 years or older, have a high school education, have an income less than $30,000/year, and have poor health were more likely to have stigmatizing responses (Lentine et al., 2000). In summary, while prevalence of stigma and discrimination has decreased overall, it still remains a significant public health concern.

IMPACT OF STIGMA AND DISCRIMINATION

Stigma is a vital obstacle hindering prevention and treatment of HIV and AIDS. It can have profound effects on the patient, not only with regard to prevention and treatment but also in its psychological effects, including negative perceptions of the self. People may not get tested for HIV in a timely manner for fear of a positive result and the stigma that comes along with this, which, in turn, results in delay of treatment. Additionally, a person tested for HIV may not wish to receive the results, which can also prevent and delay treatment and may result in a poorer prognosis by the time the individual wishes to start treatment. This avoidance of testing or knowing test results can also have an unwanted impact on HIV transmission rates, as people may not be diligent in preventing transmission of HIV if they are unaware of their HIV status. Physical impairments linked with HIV, ranging from profound wasting and cognitive impairment to Kaposi's sarcoma, can play a psychological role, leading to negative self-perceptions. By internalizing negative social judgments, rates of depression and anxiety can increase (Skinner and Mfecane, 2004). In addition, other stigma-related obstacles to care include having to attend an HIV clinic or an infectious disease physician's office, picking up prescriptions or having them mailed to another address, and, in the past, having the telltale markers of lipoatrophy, lipodystrophy, or "protease paunch," resulting in disparaging and distressing "hunchback of Notre Dame" comments. Depression may play a role in compromising immune system functioning, leading to poorer outcomes (Leonard, 2000).

Unfortunately, HIV stigma exists among healthcare providers as well. This is a bidirectional relationship; people with HIV are less likely to access treatment if they perceive HIV stigma coming from their healthcare provider (Kinsler et al., 2007); one study from 2012 found that medical students have a diminished commitment to treating HIV patients (Hoffart et al., 2012). In the 1980s, HIV/AIDS stigma led to rejection

of persons with HIV/AIDS from homeless shelters, nursing homes, and long-term care facilities (Cohen, 1989). In a Brazilian study, higher rates of stigma and discrimination were correlated with poorer overall health (Kerrigan et al., 2015). Little has been done to address issues related to healthcare-related HIV stigma, in part because of uncertainty among healthcare managers on how to best address this problem (Nyblade et al., 2009), and in part owing to the common mistake that stigma is too large a problem to tackle (Piot, 2006). HIV stigma needs to be addressed with patients by clinicians, to aid in cultivating the physician–patient relationship.

Attitudes of the media and general public also play a role in HIV stigma. There is significant variation in stigma and discrimination across cultures; while stigma is declining in the United States (Herek et al., 2002), it remains present and persistent in other countries. In India, for example, there are reports that people have experienced prejudicial behaviors, ranging from job loss to eviction to denial of medical care (AIDS Alert, 2002; Bharat et al., 2001; U.S. National Intelligence Council, 2002). In Africa, there are reports that HIV-infected women have been beaten or abandoned by their husbands (Rankin et al., 2005). Even in the United States, in 1999, approximately 20% of people expressed fear regarding people with AIDS and approximately 16% expressed disgust regarding this population or backed public naming of persons with HIV infection (Herek et al., 2002). A year later, an Internet study regarding HIV stigma was conducted and roughly one in five people agreed with the statement, "People who got AIDS through sex or drug use have gotten what they deserve" (Centers for Disease Control and Prevention [CDC], 2000). While stigma has lessened with time and education, it is still present and needs to be addressed on an ongoing basis in order to be eradicated.

VULNERABLE POPULATIONS

Men who have sex with men (MSM) are disproportionately affected by the HIV/AIDS epidemic. In the United States, the prevalence of HIV infection in men who have sex with men is estimated by the CDC to be 28% for black MSM, 18% for Hispanic MSM, and 16% for white MSM (CDC, 2010). White MSM account for 46% of new HIV infections within the MSM population (CDC, 2008). Self-directed stigma plays a role in this population, in addition to perceived stigma by others. The late Oliver Sachs, who was born in Great Britain and suffered the consequences of homosexual stigma and criminalization, writes poignantly about his experience in his memoir, *On the Move* (Sacks, 2015). He states: "When, in 1951, my mother learned of my homosexuality and said 'I wish you had never been born,' she was speaking as a mother, though I am not sure I realized this at the time, out of anguish as much as accusation" (Sacks, 2015, p. 61). Although this example is more than half a century old, one of our authors (MAC) hears comments such as this from persons with HIV who are currently in her care. One study of MSM showed that internalization of negative beliefs about homosexuality ("internalized homophobia") may play a role in carrying out risky HIV behaviors, including decreased likelihood of practicing safe sex and increased likelihood of multiple sexual encounters or use of drugs and alcohol (Stokes and Peterson, 1998). Internalized homophobia can also decrease the likelihood of getting HIV testing, which can lead to lower rates of counseling about safe sex and knowledge about transmission. As a result, a person with HIV may not know that he has HIV or not want to disclose this to his partner and will thus transmit HIV. Interventions to reduce stigma in men who have sex with men would be particularly helpful given the disproportionate amount of men with HIV and AIDS.

It is well documented that women sex workers suffer from a disproportionate burden of HIV (Decker et al., 2013). Kerrigan and colleagues (2015) have described a community empowerment HIV response among these women, in which sex workers take ownership of HIV services, in turn reducing roadblocks to upholding their rights and improving HIV outcomes. However, such empowerment programs are rare, and efforts need to be made to increase the number and availability of programs for sex workers. Such interventions have been found to increase condom use and to decrease rates of HIV and sexually transmitted infections (STIs). Unfortunately, many barriers exist to implementing these programs. Such barriers are active on many levels (global, state, community) and include the illegality of sex work in many countries, stigma related to sex work, violence against sex workers, and poor access to appropriate medical care, among others (Kerrigan et al., 2015). Laws are in place in 116 countries that allow sex workers to be charged with a crime (Ahmed et al., 2011; Crowley et al., 2015). By decriminalizing sex work, barriers to prevention and treatment for sex workers would be decreased, allowing them to better protect themselves and facilitate community empowerment. Case reports of community empowerment programs show a decrease in police harassment, recognition of sex work as an occupation, assembly of an organization for sex workers, and access to free healthcare (Kerrigan et al., 2015). In a Ukrainian study reduction in both physical and sexual violence was shown to decrease rates of HIV among sex workers (Decker et al., 2013). Women sex workers are a particularly vulnerable group with regard to HIV infection and violence; taking steps to diminish violence has a positive impact on rates of HIV infection.

INTERVENTIONS TO REDUCE STIGMA

Reducing stigma plays an integral role in improving medical outcomes in persons with HIV (Barroso et al., 2014; Crowley et al., 2015). Multiple interventions to reduce HIV-related stigma have been implemented. One article that reviewed 22 studies intending to reduce AIDS stigma found that some interventions were effective in small groups and for a short period of time but that there are many gaps in the impact of these interventions (Brown et al., 2003). Authors of a newer article reviewed 48 studies from 2002 to 2013 that used strategies to reduce HIV stigma and discrimination. They found that while significant advances have been made in reducing stigma, gaps persist in national implementation of stigma reduction programs (Stangl et al., 2013). Because stigma reduction programs vary so much in their content, it is difficult to

make comparisons of programs. Moving forward, Grossman and Stangl (2013) call for linkage between interventions and specific stigma domains, assessment of these stigma domains in a homogenous manner, and linkage between stigma reduction programs and improved outcomes in HIV care.

HIV GENDER-BASED VIOLENCE

INTRODUCTION AND DEFINITION

Gender-based violence is a multidimensional term and has been described in numerous contexts, ranging from physical to emotional aspects. Traditionally, it has referred to the physical aspect of the definition, which includes forced, coerced, or attempted forced sex (Andersson et al., 2008). A more expanded definition by the United Nations cites gender-based violence as "any act that results in or is likely to result in physical, sexual, or psychological harm or suffering to women, including threats or such acts as coercion, or arbitrary deprivation of liberty, whether occurring in public or private life" (United Nations, 1993). This scope includes a wide range of circumstances, including female infanticide, female genital mutilation, sexual slavery, torture, rape, intimate partner violence (IPV), emotional violence, and neglect, to name a few.

Extensive evidence indicates that gender-based violence leads to higher rates of morbidity and mortality, including poorer outcomes in psychiatric illnesses, along with gynecological complications, pregnancy, chronic pain syndromes, and increased likelihood of acquiring an STI (Ellsberg et al., 2008). A multinational observational study by the World Health Organization found an association between lifetime experience of IPV and physical and mental health problems in all of the 10 study countries (Ellsberg et al., 2008). Given the high impact and burden on health factors, gender-based violence has been identified as a human rights issue and a global public health predicament (Shannon et al., 2009).

UNDERSTANDING GENDER-BASED VIOLENCE: EPIDEMIOLOGY AND PATHWAYS

Between 30% and 60% of women worldwide have experienced gender-based violence. International data show an elevated risk of sexually transmitted diseases in this population (Dunkle and Decker, 2013). Gender inequality and violence has been established as a twin epidemic alongside HIV, with women comprising 57% of the population in sub-Saharan Africa afflicted with HIV (Watts and Seeley, 2014). In 2002, worldwide statistics showed that sub-Saharan Africa represented 70% of HIV-infected adults, with African women being the most severely affected group (Dunkle et al., 2004). Further, an age differential between men and women exists, with women acquiring HIV 5 to 7 years earlier than men and peak prevalence occurring in women 20 to 24 years old (Karim et al., 2010). As women account for 90% of new HIV infections worldwide, this association has significant implications in HIV prevention, transmission pathways, and treatment (Li et al., 2014; Small et al., 2013).

Evaluation of the complex relationship between gender-based violence and HIV in women exposes several modes of transmission. Of these, the most conspicuous is sexual assault. Unwanted, unanticipated violent sexual encounters such as rape lead to an increased likelihood of HIV transmission because of the breakdown of epithelium and degree of trauma, tears, and abrasions that follow from forced sex. Notably, higher rates of HIV are reported in survivors of violence without co-occurring sexual assault. This points to an alternate pathway: long-term exposure to male perpetrators of violence increases vulnerability to HIV. Growing evidence suggests that men who are perpetrators of violence are more likely to be HIV positive through involvement in risky behaviors such as substance use, decreased condom use, and multiple sexual partners, with subsequent risk of infection with other sexually transmitted diseases. Revictimization can magnify transmission risk because survivors of gender-based violence are more likely to experience additional violent acts (Dunkle and Decker, 2013).

Sequelae of violence exposure among women can raise their susceptibility to HIV transmission through indirect means. A meta-analysis in the United States reported a prevalence rate of posttraumatic stress disorder (PTSD) of 30% in HIV-positive women, a rate of that is five times that for women in the general population (Machtinger et al., 2012). The same study suggested an estimated rate of IPV of 55.3%, which is more than twice the national rate.

A history of trauma in women may result in a repetition compulsion to master a sense of control by turning the passive into the active and unconsciously seeking a partner who is likely to be violent (Samuels et al., 2011; Tavakkoli et al., 2014). Mastery through repetition is frequently associated with high-risk behaviors as well as PTSD. In addition, PTSD is associated with both a sense of a foreshortened future and dissociative symptoms along with comorbid substance use disorder to further numb the painful memories and flashbacks to trauma. More specifically, childhood sexual trauma has been linked to higher-risk sexual behaviors, greater rates of future revictimization, and poorer adherence to antiretroviral medications (Tavakkoli et al., 2014). The interrelationship between violence and HIV acquisition identifies women as a particularly vulnerable population to HIV transmission (Draughon, 2012). A growing framework, described as the substance abuse, violence, AIDS, or SAVA, syndemic, is being used to analyze the relationship between substance use, violence, and HIV/AIDS. *Syndemic* is a term to describe synergistic epidemics. The SAVA syndemic describes the intricate relationship between health disparities and HIV outcomes in marginalized populations (Meyer et al., 2011). Authors of a study in the United States used this conceptualization to examine the level of viral suppression in HIV-positive women of color in relation to substance use, binge drinking, IPV, mental illness, and sexual risk-taking. The findings strengthened the concept of the SAVA syndemic, as women with substance abuse and violence were more likely to have HIV and high viral loads. This effect points to the importance of more comprehensive approaches focusing on health disparities to address prevention and HIV outcomes (Sullivan et al., 2015).

Other factors of gender inequality may contribute to increased HIV transmission, such as varying cultural and social norms related to relationship dynamics and control. For example, one study in South Africa found that women who were unsatisfied in their relationship were less likely to ask their partners for condom use (Dunkle et al., 2004). Although women have the highest burden of HIV infection in sub-Saharan Africa, few studies on gender inequality have been conducted in women, and there is a dearth of research on potential targets for prevention.

QUANTITATIVE ASSESSMENTS

Exposure to violence not only leads to disproportionate rates of HIV transmission but is also linked with poorer outcomes of the disease, including medical and psychiatric comorbidities. It is hypothesized that violence can negatively affect a woman's immune system; small studies have shown elevated cortisol and reduced T-cell function (Jewkes et al, 2015). One small longitudinal study of antiretroviral-naïve HIV-positive women found a more rapid decline in CD4+ and CD8+ T cells in those who experienced emotional abuse, highlighting the possible detrimental effect of advancing disease progression (Jewkes et al., 2015).

Women who experience violence are at risk for multiple mental health disorders, including PTSD, depression, and anxiety. Women who suffer concurrent diagnoses of HIV and major depression have poorer adherence to antiviral medications, resulting in increased viral load (Gonzalez et al., 2011). Interestingly, even with consistent adherence, lower rates of viral suppression are found in persons with a history of sexual trauma, possibly secondary to the negative impact of stress on the immune system (Brezing et al., 2015; Pence, 2009). In addition to worsening health outcomes, a multinational study by the World Health Organization found that the presence of violence was linked to higher frequencies of suicidal thoughts and attempts (Devries and Watts, 2011). HIV infection and AIDS have been found to be an independent risk factor for suicide despite the introduction of antiretroviral medications. In contrast to general suicide rates, HIV-positive women are at a higher risk for attempting and completing suicide compared to men. Drug overdose is the most commonly used means, which further illustrates the enmeshed relationship between psychosocial factors and health burden (Alfonso and Cohen, 2008).

INTERVENTIONS TO REDUCE GENDER-BASED VIOLENCE

Emerging research has been accumulating on the relationship between HIV and gender-based violence. Interventions in healthcare settings that address both HIV and IPV are needed. More interventions are found in community-based settings. This section will focus on interventions and programs that have been empirically evaluated and validated and whose methodology has been clearly defined. The interventions are divided into two kinds: primary and secondary. Primary interventions target the prevention of violence before it has begun, by focusing on societal and situational factors and using educational approaches. Secondary interventions address violence often at the situational or individual level. Many interventions combine both primary and secondary components.

Reviews examining the impact of interventions addressing HIV and IPV globally and in sub-Saharan Africa have highlighted the potential efficacy of multifaceted community-based interventions in reducing IPV; however, until recently, none have resulted in a decrease in HIV infection (Anderson et al., 2013; WHO, 2010). A recent review by Small et al. (2013) investigated gender-informed intervention studies that were conducted in sub-Saharan Africa and measured an outcome related to HIV. Their findings demonstrated wide variations in the types of interventions, from low-intensity educational content to multicomponent interventions. Study outcomes were categorized into biological outcomes and HIV, and reduction in risk of violence. Most interventions showed positive effects.

The first study of behavioral interventions (SHARE) to show significant decreases in both IPV and HIV incidence incorporated a multifaceted IPV and HIV prevention intervention and was in Rakai, Uganda (Wagman et al., 2015). SHARE used two main approaches: community-based mobilization to change attitudes and social norms that contribute to IPV and HIV risk, and a screening and brief intervention to reduce HIV disclosure–related violence and sexual risk in women seeking HIV counseling and testing. The SHARE intervention model could potentially inform other programs targeting both IPV and HIV and could be implemented in other programs in sub-Saharan Africa (Wagman et al., 2015). More research is needed to explore the effectiveness of gender-based programs in reducing HIV infections in sub-Saharan Africa.

South Africa has been in the midst of one of the world's most devastating HIV/AIDS epidemics with a well-documented association between violence against women and HIV transmission. Thus interventions integrating gender-based violence (GBV) and HIV risk reduction for South African men have been hypothesized to have synergistic effects. A recent study compared a five-session integrated intervention designed to simultaneously reduce GBV and HIV risk behaviors to a single 3-hour session on alcohol and HIV risk reduction (Kalichman et al., 2009). The five-session intervention was focused on behavior change self-efficacy and altering risk-related outcome expectancies. Men in the GBV/HIV intervention increased their talking with sex partners about condoms and were more likely to have been tested for HIV at follow-ups (1, 3, and 6 months post-intervention) compared to the comparison group. Furthermore, the GBV/HIV intervention reduced negative attitudes toward women as well as violence against women. The GBV/HIV intervention did not, however, reduce unprotected sex or increase condom use. The alcohol/HIV prevention intervention showed greater potential for reducing sexual risk. More research

incorporating an alcohol reduction approach, gender violence prevention, and HIV risk reduction for South African men may prove promising.

More studies have focused on health interventions shifting norms of masculinity to be more gender equitable, defined under the term *gender-transformative*. A recent systematic review of gender-transformative HIV and violence prevention programs with heterosexually active men assessed the efficacy of these programs (Dworkin et al., 2013). The evidence suggests that gender-transformative interventions can increase protective sexual behaviors, prevent partner violence, modify inequitable attitudes, and reduce STI/HIV infection risk. The authors concluded that further trials are warranted, particularly in establishing the impact on STI/HIV.

Gender-based violence constitutes a major structural barrier to effective HIV programming. A recent systematic review looked at the evidence on the costs and cost-effectiveness of effective gender-responsive HIV interventions (Remme et al., 2014). The effectiveness search identified 36 publications reporting on the effectiveness of 22 HIV interventions with a gender focus. Of these, 11 types of interventions had a corresponding/comparable-cost or cost-effectiveness study. The findings suggest that couple counseling for the prevention of vertical transmission; gender empowerment, community mobilization, and female condom promotion for female sex workers; expanded female condom distribution for the general population; and post-exposure HIV prophylaxis for rape survivors are cost-effective HIV interventions. Most interventions, however, had no economic analyses, making it difficult to assess their costs or monetary value in comparison to other potential areas of investment. The authors concluded that these cost-effective interventions should be considered as critical enablers in HIV investment approaches and that broader gender and development interventions can have positive HIV-related impacts.

More research is needed to build evidence on the effectiveness and costs of different interventions and programs addressing gender inequality and violence as part of an integrated HIV response. As important is the investment in broader social development and interventions that directly address gender inequalities (Watts and Seeley, 2014). Remme and colleagues (2014) have identified a broad range of options that relate to the HIV investment framework (Schwartlander et al., 2011).

CONCLUSION

HIV stigma and discrimination as well as gender-based violence contribute to the syndemics of substance abuse, violence, and HIV. The consequences of HIV stigma and discrimination magnify the suffering endured by persons with HIV and their loved ones. Stigma and discrimination also lead to criminalization of addiction, sex work, and HIV, which complicates and perpetuates the HIV pandemic. Reducing stigma decreases HIV transmission and plays an integral role in improving medical outcomes in persons with HIV (Barroso et al., 2014; Crowley et al., 2015).

REFERENCES

Ahmed A, Kaplan M, Symington A, Kismodi E (2011). Criminalising consensual sexual behaviour in the context of HIV: consequences, evidence, and leadership. *Glob Public Health* 6(Suppl 3):S357–S369.

AIDS Alert (2002). AIDS stigma forms an insidious barrier to prevention/care. HIV experts describe problem in India. 12(9):111–113.

Alfonso CA, Cohen MA (2008). Suicide. In MA Cohen, JM Gorman (eds.), *Comprehensive Textbook of AIDS Psychiatry* (pp. 195–203). New York: Oxford University Press.

Anderson JC, Campbell JC, Farley JE (2013). Interventions to address HIV prevention and intimate partner violence in sub-Saharan Africa: a review of the literature. *J Assoc Nurses AIDS Care* 24:383–390.

Andersson, N, Cockcroft, A, Shea B (2008). Gender based violence and HIV: relevance for HIV prevention in hyperendemic countries of Southern Africa. *AIDS* 22:73–86.

Barroso J, Relf MV, Williams MS, Arscott J, Moore ED, Caiola C, Silva SG (2014). *AIDS Patient Care STDs* 28(9):489–498.

Bharat S, Aggleton P, Tyrer P (2001). *India: HIV and AIDS-Related Discrimination, Stigma and Denial*. Geneva: UNAIDS.

Brezing C, Ferrera M, Freudenreich O (2015). The syndemic illness of HIV and trauma: implications for a trauma-informed model of care. *Psychosomatics* 56(2):107–118.

Brown L, Macintyre K, Trujillo L (2003). Interventions to reduce HIV/AIDS stigma: what have we learned? *AIDS Educ Prev* 15:49–69.

Centers for Disease Control and Prevention (CDC) (2000). HIV-related knowledge and stigma—United States, 2000. *MMWR Morb Mortal Wkly Rep* 49:1062–1064.

Centers for Disease Control and Prevention (CDC) (2008). Subpopulation estimates from the HIV incidence surveillance system—United States, 2006. *MMWR Morb Mortal Wkly Rep* 57(36):985–989.

Centers for Disease Control and Prevention (CDC) (2010). Prevalence and awareness of HIV infection among men who have sex with men—21 cities, United States, 2008. *MMWR Morb Mortal Wkly Rep* 59(37):1201–1207.

Cohen MA (1989). AIDSism, a new form of discrimination. *Am Med News* 32:43.

Cohen MA (2008). History of AIDS psychiatry: a biopsychosocial approach—paradigm and paradox. In MA Cohen, JM Gorman (eds.), *Comprehensive Textbook of AIDS Psychiatry* (pp. 3–14). New York: Oxford University Press.

Crowley JS, Nevins GR, Thompson M (2015). The Americans with Disabilities Act and HIV/AIDS discrimination: unfinished business. *JAMA* 314:227–228.

Decker MR, Wirtz AL, Pretorius C, et al. (2013). Estimating the impact of reducing violence against female sex workers on HIV epidemics in Kenya and Ukraine: a policy modeling exercise. *Am J Reprod Immunol* 69(Supp. 1):122–132.

Devries K, Watts C (2011). Violence against women is strongly associated with suicide attempts: evidence from the WHO multi-country study on women's health and domestic violence against women. *Soc Sci Med* 73(1):79–86.

Draughon JE (2012). Sexual assault injuries and increased risk of HIV transmission. *Adv Emerg Nurs J* 34:82–87.

Dunkle K, Decker M (2013). Gender based violence and HIV: reviewing the evidence for links and causal pathways in the general population and high risk groups. *Am J Reprod Immunol* 69(Suppl 1):20–26.

Dunkle KL, Jewkes RL, Brown HC, Gray GE, McIntyre JA, Harlow SD (2004). Gender based violence, relationship power, and risk of HIV infection in women attending antenatal clinics in South Africa. *Lancet* 363:1415–1421.

Dworkin SL, Treves-Kagan S, Lippman SA (2013). Gender-transformative interventions to reduce HIV risks and violence with heterosexually active men: a review of the global evidence. *AIDS Behav* 17(9):2845–2863.

Ellsberg M, Jansen HAFM, Heise L, Watts CH, Garcia-Moreno C. (2008). Intimate partner violence and women's physical and mental health in the WHO multi-country study on women's health and domestic violence: an observational study. *Lancet* 371:1165–1172.

Goffman E (1963). *Stigma: Notes on the Management of Spoiled Identity*. Englewood Cliffs, NJ: Prentice–Hall.

Gonzalez JS, Batchelder AW, Psaros C, Safren SA (2011). Depression and HIV/AIDS treatment nonadherence: a review and meta-analysis. *J Acquir Immune Defic Syndr* 58:18(2):181–187.

Grossman CI, Stangl AL (2013). Editorial: global action to reduce HIV stigma and discrimination. *J Intl AIDS Soc* 16(3 Suppl 2):18881.

Herek GM, Capitanio JP, Widaman KF (2002). HIV-related stigma and knowledge in the United States: prevalence and trends, 1991–1999. *Am J Public Health* 92(3):371–377.

Hoffart S, Ibrahim GM, Lam RA, Minty EP, Theam M, Schaefer JP (2012). Medical students' attitudes towards treating patients with HIV: a 12-year follow-up study. *Med Teach* 34(3):254.

Jewkes R, Dunkle K, Jama-Shai N, Gray G (2015). Impact of exposure to intimate partner violence on CD4+ and CD8+ T cell decay in HIV infected women: a longitudinal study. *PLoS One* 10(3):e0122001.

Kalichman SC, Simbayi LC, Cloete A, et al. (2009). Integrated gender-based violence and HIV risk reduction intervention for South African men: results of a quasi-experimental field trial. *Pre Sci* 10(3):260–269.

Karim Q, Siebko S, Baxter C. (2010). Preventing HIV infection in women: a global health imperative. *Clin Infect Dis* 50(3):122–129.

Kerrigan D, Vazzano A, Bertoni N, Malta M, Bastos FI (2015). Stigma, discrimination and HIV outcomes among people living with HIV in Rio de Janeiro, Brazil: the intersection of multiple social inequalities. *Glob Public Health* 10:1–15.

Khalife S, Cohen MA (2010). Stigma of HIV and AIDS—psychiatric aspects. In MA Cohen, HW Goforth, JZ Lux, SM Batista, S Khalife, KL Cozza, J Soffer (eds.), *Handbook of AIDS Psychiatry*. New York: Oxford University Press.

Kinsler JJ, Wong MD, Sayles JN, Davis C, Cunningham WE (2007). The effect of perceived stigma from a health care provider on access to care among a low-income HIV-positive population. *AIDS Patient Care STDs* 21(8):584–592.

Lentine DA, Iannacchione VG, Laird GH, McClamroch K, Thalji L (2000). HIV-related knowledge and stigma: United States 2000. *MMWR Morb Mortal Wkly Rep* 49(47):1062–1064.

Leonard B (2000). Stress, depression and the activation of the immune system. *World J Biol Psychiatry* 1(1):17–25.

Letamo G (2003). Prevalence of, and factors associated with, HIV/AIDS-related stigma and discriminatory attitudes in Botswana. *J Health Popul Nutr* 21(4):347–357.

Li Y, Marshall CM, Rees HC, Nunex A, Ezeanolue EE, Ehiri JE. (2014). Intimate partner violence and HIV infection among women: a systematic review and meta-analysis. *J Int AIDS Soc* 17:18845.

Machtinger EL, Wilson TC, Haberer JE, Weiss DS (2012). Psychological trauma and PTSD in HIV-positive women: a meta-analysis. *AIDS Behav* 16:2091–2100.

Meyer JP, Springer SA, Altice FL (2011). Substance abuse, violence, and HIV in women: a literature review of the syndemic. *J Womens Health* 20:991–1006.

National AIDS Co-ordinating Agency (2002). Botswana 2002 second generation HIV/AIDS surveillance: a technical report. Gaborone: National AIDS Coordinating Agency.

Nyblade L, Stangl A, Weiss E, Ashburn K (2009). Combating HIV stigma in health care settings: what works? *J Int AIDS Soc* 12:15.

Pence BW (2009). The impact of mental health and traumatic life experiences on antiretroviral treatment outcomes for people living with HIV/AIDS. *J Antimicrob Chemother* 63:636–640.

Piot P (2006). How to reduce the stigma of AIDS, Keynote address. Symposium at the XVI International AIDS Conference, Toronto.

Rankin WW, Brennan S, Schell E, Laviwa J, Rankin SH (2005). The stigma of being HIV-positive in Africa. *PLoS Med* 2(8):e247.

Remme M, Siapka M, Vassall A, et al. (2014). The cost and cost-effectiveness of gender-responsive interventions for HIV: a systematic review. *J Int AIDS Soc* 17(1):19228.

Sacks O (2015). *On the Move: A Life* (p. 61). New York: Alfred A. Knopf.

Samuels E, Khalife S, Alfonso C, Alvarez R, Cohen MA (2011). Early childhood trauma, posttraumatic stress disorder, and non-adherence in persons with AIDS: a psychodynamic perspective. *J Am Acad Psychoanal Dynam Psychiatry* 39:633–650.

Schwartlander B, Stover J, Hallett T, Atun R, Avila C, Gouws E (2011). Towards an improved investment approach for an effective response to HIV/AIDS. *Lancet* 377:2031–2041.

Shannon K, Kerr T, Strathdee SA, Shovellar J. (2009). Prevalence and structural correlates of gender based violence among a prospective cohort of female sex workers. *BMJ* 339:b2939.

Skinner D, Mfecane S (2004). Stigma, discrimination and the implications for people living with HIV/AIDS in South Africa. *SAHARA J* 1(3):157–164.

Small E, Nikolova SP, Narendorf SC. (2013). Synthesizing gender based HIV interventions in sub-Sahara Africa: a systematic review of the evidence. *AIDS Behav* 17(9):2831–2844.

Smita P, Brady M, Carter M, et al. (2012). HIV-related stigma within communities of gay men: a literature review. *AIDS Care* 24(4):405–412.

Stangl AL, Lloyd JK, Brady LM, Holland CE, Baral S (2013). A systematic review of interventions to reduce HIV-related stigma and discrimination from 2002 to 2013: how far have we come? *J Int AIDS Soc* 16(3 Suppl 2):18734.

Stokes JP, Peterson JL (1998). Homophobia, self-esteem, and risk for HIV among African American men who have sex with men. *AIDS Educ Prev* 10:278–292.

Sullivan KA, Messer LC, Quinlivan EB (2015). Substance abuse, violence, HIV/AIDS (SAVA) syndemic effects on viral suppression among HIV positive women of color. *AIDS Patient Care STDs* 29(S1):S42–S48.

Tavakkoli M, Cohen MA, Alfonso CA, Batista SM, Tiamson-Kassab MLA, Meyer P (2014). Caring for persons with early childhood trauma, PTSD, and HIV: a curriculum for clinicians. *Acad Psychiatry* 38:696–700.

UNAIDS (2003). UNAIDS fact sheet: stigma and discrimination. http://data.unaids.org/publications/Fact-Sheets03/fs_stigma_discrimination_en.pdf. Accessed December 27, 2016.

United Nations (1993). Declaration on the elimination of violence against women. New York: United Nations General Assembly.

U.S. National Intelligence Council (2002). The next wave of HIV/AIDS: Nigeria, Ethiopia, Russia, India, and China. https://fas.org/irp/nic/hiv-aids.html. Accessed January 10, 2017.

Wagman JA, Gray RH, Campbell JC, et al. (2015). Effectiveness of an integrated intimate partner violence and HIV prevention intervention in Rakai, Uganda: analysis of an intervention in an existing cluster randomized trial. *Lancet Glob Health* 3:e23–e33.

Watts C, Seeley J (2014). Addressing gender inequality and intimate partner violence as critical barriers to an effective HIV response in sub-Saharan Africa. *J Int AIDS Soc* 17(1):19849.

World Health Organization (WHO) (2010). *Addressing Violence Against Women and HIV/AIDS: What Works?* Geneva: World Health Organization.

PART II

INTEGRATED CARE AND ADVOCACY
FOR PERSONS WITH HIV

7.

MODELS OF CARE FOR PATIENTS WITH HIV

James Bourgeois, Mary Ann Cohen, John A. R. Grimaldi, Jon A. Levenson, Yavar Moghimi,

Weston Scott Fisher, and David Tran

INTRODUCTION

Persons with HIV deserve a nonjudgmental, nurturing healthcare environment throughout the course of their lives. Their families, loved ones, and caregivers can also benefit from a special kind of understanding, gentle support, and availability. Persons with HIV are more vulnerable because of the epidemics of fear, discrimination, and ignorance that lead to stigma and can magnify healthcare disparities. Creation of a healthcare environment to meet the needs of persons with HIV and AIDS (Cohen, 1996) can be accomplished with integrated models of care that includes psychiatric services.

Persons with HIV have a high prevalence of "multimorbid" complex and often severe systemic medical and psychiatric illnesses with psychosocial and public health implications and consequences. Communication and coordination of care are particularly important in order to improve adherence to risk reduction through behavioral interventions as well as medical management. Furthermore, missed HIV clinic visits are independently associated with all-cause mortality in persons with HIV (Mugavero et al., 2014). Since HIV is associated with discrimination and stigma, disproportionately affects vulnerable populations, and magnifies health care disparities, providing compassionate, comprehensive, and coordinated care becomes even more significant.

In this chapter, we describe various models of integrated psychiatric care for HIV patients at different institutions. We hope that the experience presented here in operating these models of care will be helpful to clinicians and administrators contemplating the adoption of similar models of care. In this context, we will review contemporary descriptive terms for the integration of psychiatric services into HIV care. This discussion parallels a greater trend toward integration of psychiatric services into general medical care.

BIOPSYCHOSOCIAL APPROACH

A unifying principle in the comprehensive clinical care of HIV patients is the *biopsychosocial approach*. This is a comprehensive model that includes systemic medical, psychiatric, social, cultural, community, spiritual, and supportive aspects of care. The term first introduced by George Engel in 1961 (Engel, 1961) to describe this approach was bio-psycho-social-cultural and was later shortened to biopsychosocial (Engel, 1977, 1980). The term and concept were later applied to HIV and AIDS (Cohen, 1987, 1992, 1996, 2013; Cohen and Alfonso, 2004; Cohen and Gorman; 2008; Cohen and Weisman, 1986; Cohen et al., 2010; Deuchar, 1984).

HIV PSYCHIATRY AS A MODEL OF PSYCHOSOMATIC MEDICINE

Consultation-liaison psychiatry (synonymous with psychosomatic medicine [PSM]) is psychiatric care focused on persons with complex and severe medical and surgical illness. As such, psychosomatic medicine is the model most closely identified with integrated psychiatric and systemic medical care for HIV patients (Bauer et al., 2010). Using the principles of psychosomatic medicine in integrated care models is especially applicable to HIV care. Models of psychiatric care for HIV patients have evolved as HIV psychiatry has become a subspecialty of psychosomatic medicine, analogous to transplant psychiatry, psycho-oncology, and psychonephrology.

For maximum efficiency in the deployment of clinical resources, the psychosomatic medicine psychiatrist's role is optimized when used for various functions beyond direct clinical service provision. Indeed, primary care/HIV physicians and non-physician HIV mental health clinicians will typically see and manage more common and uncomplicated psychiatric illness in HIV patients. It is critical for care models to have psychiatric consultants available to support such an empowered primary care model through educational interventions and clinical consultation to other groups of health care professionals. This saves the necessarily limited direct clinical time of the HIV psychiatrist to be responsible for only the most complex patients (e.g., those with multimorbid psychiatric illnesses and/or failure to respond well to first-line primary care psychiatric interventions).

It is understood that not all care delivery systems will have ready access to HIV psychiatry (or even outpatient psychosomatic medicine services). In this case, HIV psychiatry may need to be provided by general psychiatrists (perhaps one with a defined interest in HIV). A psychiatrist working in a private office, outpatient psychiatry clinic, or community mental health center may provide this valuable service in models where care is not truly integrated.

MODELS OF INTEGRATED CARE: A CONTEMPORARY SPECTRUM

Clinical models of comprehensive, multispecialty systems of care for patients with HIV are designed for the management of severe and complex multimorbid medical and psychiatric illness. In this chapter we define and describe models of varying degrees of integrated care as they apply to the care of persons with HIV and AIDS.

Throughout this textbook we will be using concepts to describe clinical models of care that are similar and at times overlapping but have been used in different contexts and settings. As care delivery systems have evolved, so too has the language used to concisely describe them. Current models of HIV psychiatry care delivery may thus span many of these.

Integrated care models of care for HIV psychiatry refers to various organizational designs wherein the HIV psychiatrist works closely with the patient's other physicians to provide coordinated systemic medical and psychiatric care for complex patients with multimorbid illnesses. The various models have evolved over the past 36 years; the development of these care models must take into account the local availability of HIV psychiatric expertise and experience, financial issues, and other important externalities.

We recognize that models of closely integrated systemic medical and psychiatric services may not be available at all institutions offering HIV care. Nonetheless, acknowledgement that HIV illness is often a psychologically stressful experience with a high prevalence of psychiatric comorbidity should inform efforts to optimize psychiatric care for HIV patients.

CONSULTATIVE PSYCHIATRIC CARE

Consultative psychiatric care is the simplest, least integrated care model. An example of "minimally integrated" psychiatric and HIV care is that of the HIV psychiatrist who maintains an office in a psychiatry clinic or individual office who makes him- or herself available for the psychiatric care of HIV patients. Such a psychiatrist may establish relationships with HIV physicians so as to facilitate the process of referral between the HIV physicians and the psychiatrist. HIV patients benefit from having a psychiatrist specialized in and/or dedicated to HIV psychiatry; however, there is limited or often no communication between psychiatric and primary care/HIV medicine providers. This model may be the simplest to arrange administratively but does not represent "integration" in the contemporary sense. Nonetheless, it may be the best way to arrange for HIV-specific psychiatric care at many institutions not offering this service. When such an arrangement features separate clinical charting and no physical co-location of physicians, the other benefits of co-location and care integration models (informal "curbsiding" discussions, integrated care team meetings, integration of other mental health professionals, common record-keeping) are not likely possible.

TELEMEDICINE

Another model of service delivery to consider is telemedicine, where an HIV psychiatrist sees patients via secure electronic media in the HIV clinic and offers specific psychiatric care plans for management to be operated by the HIV physicians with some availability of psychiatric follow-up by the same medium. Such models can be designed to allow for informal consultation with the psychiatrist (without the patient necessarily present) and common record-keeping (the distantly located psychiatrist and local clinic both need to maintain charting of the electronic encounters). This model requires clarity of the licensing and billing details of the clinical encounters.

CO-LOCATED CARE

Co-located care "transports" the psychiatrist to a location within the HIV clinic. However, the psychiatrist may have a caseload somewhat distinct from the other physicians and there are less intimately developed methods of integration of care. Co-located HIV psychiatrists may see patients in the HIV medical clinic, but this model does not necessarily provide common charting in a single medical record and may not necessarily allow for the HIV psychiatrist to participate in non-billable but important integrative activities, such as clinical team meetings, informal curbsiding discussions about patients, and clinical case review by the psychiatrist. This model may facilitate appointment making and attendance, in that the patient does not have to go to a separately located clinic for psychiatric care. In such an arrangement, the psychiatrist may bill the patient's insurer for the psychiatric services rendered separately.

INTEGRATED CARE

Integrated care involves more regular use of the psychiatrist seeing patients directly in the host clinic (there may be a multidisciplinary mental health team assigned to a medical clinic in some models). General medical and mental health clinicians regularly interface and chart in a common chart for integration of services

The practical advantages of integrating psychiatric care into the outpatient general medical setting are numerous. The patient can receive psychiatric care in the general medical clinic where care is already established. This avoids the perceived stigma of seeking care in a psychiatric clinic and having to interact with a different set of clinical administrative personnel, and it allows for common charting of all clinical interactions. The psychiatrist and other physicians can readily address medication interactions and side effects and toxicities, arrange for laboratory monitoring, and discuss case co-management. The psychiatrist is available to answer focused questions on psychiatric illness management for the other physicians (curbsiding).

Adoption of models of integrated care requires certain administrative and business arrangements. The psychiatrist may see patients in an HIV clinic and bill directly for services provided. An alternative model is where the internal medicine/HIV clinic pays for a fixed portion of the psychiatrist's time and then bills for services, with the medical clinic keeping the billings when paid. This arrangement can allow for negotiated coverage of non-billable time (e.g., team meetings, informal supervision, structured case reviews) in addition to direct service provision.

When the psychiatrist is placed in an HIV clinic, arrangements for administrative support, scheduling, and communication with patients need to be negotiated. These services are best provided by the host department on the same administrative platform used by the clinic's other physicians. Coverage models for the psychiatrist's absence and management of psychiatric emergencies also need to be arranged for.

COLLABORATIVE CARE

Collaborative care (Katon and Seeling, 2008) is a fully integrated model wherein psychiatric (and other mental health) clinical services are located in the primary care medical clinic. Collaborative care features several elements: routine screening instruments for psychiatric illness, and non-physician care managers (often RNs) who operate standardized psychiatric treatment protocols under psychiatric supervision; the psychiatrist does not directly see most patients but sees the more complex patients and/or those not responding to the standardized treatment model. The psychiatrist may provide more global supervision and caseload management assistance for the care manager(s).

In a collaborative care model, the primary relationship is between the primary care provider (PCP) and the patient. Once established in care with a PCP, mental health care is actively worked into the primary care model. There is routine administration of psychometric screening instruments (e.g., BDI, Zung, PHQ-9, HADS) for asymptomatic patients or use of similar instruments for initial evaluation of psychiatric symptoms diagnosed by the PCP.

Once psychiatric illness is discovered in a primary care patient in a collaborative care model, several options exist for effective treatment. Since psychiatric consultation (either for direct care of the patient or for advice to the PCP on his or her own management of the patient) is readily available when clinically indicated, PCPs are empowered to undertake first-line treatment of most common psychiatric disorders (often with collaboration with care managers). If patients are nonresponsive to initial treatment by PCP and/or if additional care is needed in the form of various psychotherapy models, non-MD mental health professionals can see the patient and co-manage with the PCP.

For patients nonresponsive to primary care management or patients with more complex psychiatric illness at presentation, early and direct consultation with the embedded psychiatrist is indicated. The psychiatrist's caseload in such a clinical model is thus composed primarily of the more complex psychiatric patients, who are more in need of the psychiatrist's focused attention.

One strength of collaborative care models is the multidisciplinary nature of the treatment teams. Typically, a collaborative care model includes PCPs, primary care nurse practitioners, a psychiatrist, other mental health professionals, RNs, and administrative staff. For clinical care models serving patient groups with high degrees of social problems and/or substance abuse, case managers and substance abuse counselors and addiction psychiatrists are beneficial additions. Ideally, treatment team members should meet regularly to discuss patients in an interdisciplinary forum.

The collaborative care model has been shown in 37 randomized trials to improve depression care in primary care (as compared to usual primary care) as well as patient and clinician satisfaction (Katon and Seeling, 2008). The overall benefit of greater patient functional improvement offsets the slightly increased costs in providing enhanced clinical services by this model. Collaborative care models also have been shown to simultaneously improve patient outcomes with systemic illness and comorbid psychiatric illness, as reflected by specific improvements in illness-specific outcome measures and patient function for collaborative care–managed depression with comorbid diabetes mellitus or coronary heart disease (Katon et al., 2012). It has also been shown to improve depression care and HIV symptom outcomes in HIV specialty clinics (Pyne et al., 2011).

ILLNESS MANAGEMENT/MANAGEMENT OF CHRONIC ILLNESS (IM/MCI)

Illness management/management of chronic illness (IM/MCI; also referred to in some literature as disease management) is a model designed for the management of relatively common illnesses that tend to be chronic. A major theme of IM/MCI programs is active engagement of patients in their own care, including the encouragement of patient involvement in medication dose adjustments, monitoring paradigms, and clinician-staffed telephone patient advice lines. A key concept in illness management is the patient "becoming his or her own agent" with the guidance and collaboration of medical professionals. While IM/MCI models do not typically prioritize management of psychiatric illness per se (other than in illnesses such as HIV, where psychiatric comorbidity is an important part of care), they do use behavioral medicine principles. Since chronic illness management is a major aspect of HIV care, this model is applicable.

IM/MCI models have been developed for many chronic illnesses (e.g., reactive airway disease, diabetes mellitus). The concept of illness management is that care cannot be completely curative, in that the underlying (and thus defining) illness by definition is chronic and in many cases, as in HIV, lifelong once established. An important aspect of illness management is patient education and empowerment. Patients are provided with patient educational materials in many media. Patients are advised and guided by professionals to learn as much as they need to be active self-advocates and more aware of their own care needs. Inasmuch as the remarkable advances in HIV care have transformed a once inherently grim and fatal illness into a chronic and, in most cases, largely manageable one, an illness management model is desirable. Therefore, modern and comprehensive HIV models of care, when fully developed and refined, are integrated and collaborative as well as focused on illness management.

PATIENT-CENTERED MEDICAL HOME

Patient-centered medical home (PCMH) is a contemporary term describing a model of care in which the various clinical services needed by a particular patient are coordinated around the patient. Whatever specialty services the patient requires are provided on an individualized basis. *Patient-centeredness* refers to all clinical activities being tailored to the specific needs of the patient. The initial application of this concept to medical patients, including patients with HIV, was described in the article "Creating Health Care Environments to Meet Patients' Needs" (Cohen, 1996). Ideally, all clinical interventions are thus calibrated to the patient's needs, as opposed to standardizing care excessively. When implemented optimally, the patient-centered medical home provides convenient and readily available primary care access, ongoing care with continuity, access (within a robustly resourced primary care model) to comprehensive care, and modern decision support and early adoption of innovative coordination of care, with new approaches to healthcare delivery (including office practice innovative healthcare delivery models) in a financial context of reimbursement reform (Arend et al., 2012). The inclusion of specific needs for psychiatric care is a recognizable, but far from exclusive, example of patient-centeredness.

Stange et al. (2010) defined the PCMH as providing prompt access, comprehensiveness, integration and coordination, and ongoing partnership relationships with patients, combined with organizational features of adoption of new clinical practices, optimization of clinical practices' internal capabilities, and, at a more macro level, healthcare system and financing/reimbursement changes. Analysis of the effectiveness of the PCMH model in delivering on its potential for providing more highly cost-effective care at a population level will require quantification of the core of primary care in the PCMH, outcome study of the process and system changes in practice, and analysis of PCMH relationship with other healthcare system and community resources. The emphasis of the PCMH on optimization of primary care models in delivering personalized care can then generalize to more robust population health.

Katon and Unutzer (2011) describe the PCMH as being the model well positioned to achieve the currently imperative "triple aim" in health care delivery: improved access, improved quality and outcomes, and overall medical cost reduction. The role of a consultation psychiatrist in this model functions in a multispecialty and multidisciplinary team model. The psychiatrist provides consultation for psychiatric illness managed by other specialists and disciplines and advice to primary care clinicians on the management of psychiatric illness. The psychiatrist also personally manages the more complex psychiatric patients who require ongoing specialty care.

Ferrante et al. (2010) have demonstrated that primary care models operating with PCMH principles (personal physician, physician-directed team, whole-person orientation, coordination of care, quality and safety, and enhanced access) were associated with enhanced delivery of preventive medical services (e.g., cancer screening, lipid screening, influenza vaccination, and behavioral counseling). The effect of the PCMH principles (in part emphasizing the role of the personal physician's relationship with the patient) was more robust than the effects of information technology per se. Scholle et al. (2011) studied various institutions that had achieved recognition of the National Committee for Quality Assurance as a "patient-centered medical home" and found that larger practice organizations were more able to achieve this recognition status.

COMPLEX PATIENT MODELS

Complex patient models are models emphasizing proper utilization of medical services, avoidance of excessive use of emergency department and inpatient hospitalization, and focus on a primary care–centered care model with judicious use of consultants. This is a new model, and it may be driven by large health plans seeking to decrease inappropriate utilization by a particularly troubled group of patients with systemic and psychiatric comorbidity.

The role of the psychiatrist in management of "medically complex patients" was detailed by Kathol et al. (2009). The essence of this argument is that certain medical patients are often characterized by "tri-morbidity" or "multimorbidity" leading to their overall complexity: significant systemic medical illness, psychiatric illness, and substance abuse. By having psychiatric care (and other mental health services, including substance abuse services) offered in a common location and with an integrated team approach, and by funding services by means of a common funding model (i.e., no mental health carve-outs), greater coordination of integrated care, enhanced patient outcomes, and overall cost-effectiveness are optimized. The HIV clinic model illustrates the tri-morbidity of clinical illness and thus the desirability of integrated care delivery exquisitely; indeed, a well-run integrated clinical model for HIV care can serve as a model of care integration that can then be exported to other clinics at a given institution.

In summary, contemporary models for the delivery of integrated general medical and psychiatric care include elements of collaborative care, disease management, patient-centered medical home, and the key role for psychiatry in the team-based management of complex patients. Given the complexity of HIV illness and frequent occurrence of other medical and psychiatric multimorbidities, clinical models for HIV psychiatric care need to be designed using elements of integrated care models. There are several illness-specific aspects to HIV psychiatric care, which will be summarized in the next section.

INTEGRATED CARE FOR HIV PSYCHIATRY: ILLNESS-SPECIFIC CONSIDERATIONS

The need to integrate psychiatric and other models of mental health care for patients with HIV is illustrated by the centrality of psychiatric multimorbidity in many persons affected by HIV. This relationship is strongly bidirectional, in that premorbid psychiatric illness is a major risk factor in exposure to and subsequent development of HIV illness, and HIV itself is associated with its own specific psychiatric complications. Often commingled with the bidirectional associations of multimorbid psychiatric illness(es) and HIV illness are complex social problems, again and in parallel, both antedating the development of HIV and as later complications of HIV infection after the fact.

As described by Freeman et al. (2005), the psychiatric comorbidity in HIV illness may be roughly classified along five dimensions, illustrating the need for readily available psychiatric care for HIV patients. These dimensions are as follows:

1. Neurocognitive disorders specifically caused by neurotropic infection of HIV itself (often complicated by subsequent opportunistic infections and neoplasms)

2. Anxiety and depressive disorders, common as comorbid psychiatric illness in HIV, which subsequently lead to a more complicated clinical course in adapting to HIV care models and other challenges of life with HIV

3. Comorbid substance use disorders common in this population, which often serve as an independent risk factor for HIV exposure

4. Psychiatric side effects of antiretroviral agents (and other medications used for common, comorbid illnesses; e.g., interferon for hepatitis C virus [HCV])

5. A wide range of social problems, including those experienced as a result of HIV-associated stigma and social discrimination

Clinical interventions for comorbid psychiatric illness may facilitate greater adherence to often complex medication regimens. For maximal effectiveness for patients, and for more widespread adoption by healthcare systems, HIV-associated psychiatric services need to be timely, cost-effective, closely integrated with primary HIV systemic medical care, and be subject to rigorous outcome studies. Such cost-effectiveness considerations are especially critical in the development of HIV care systems in the developing world.

Integrated psychiatric care plus social interventions may lead to greater medical adherence and improved clinical outcomes in HIV illness. Ashman et al. (2002) reported that HIV patients' utilization of ancillary services (including psychiatric services, substance use counseling, and social services) was associated with greater utilization of primary care medical services for HIV.

HIV-specific mental health services integrated with primary care medical services have been developed for the psychiatric and other mental health and social services needs in this population. Feingold and Slammon (1993) described the NOAH (No One Alone with HIV) program, a hospital-based program featuring family-focused HIV mental health services. The NOAH model makes use of is "family health facilitators" to assist patients receiving the appropriate intensity of mental health services when the patient's needs cannot be met by the primary care clinician alone.

Baldwin et al. (1998) addressed the importance of a community-specific needs assessment in the planning stages of the development of multispecialty and interdisciplinary HIV treatment models. Their survey assessment included HIV-positive individuals with AIDS, physicians, and other community stakeholders, as well as the application of health statistics. Their analysis found that the following areas of service were the greatest need: primary care access, patient self-care education, mental health services, family support services, case management, financial assistance, community education, and home health services. Given the needs of this community in the systemic medical, psychiatric/mental health, and social services, clinical models that can address all of these needs in one institution are highly desirable. Dodds et al. (2000) describe a program specifically tailored to the mental health service needs of HIV-positive pregnant and non-pregnant women in a clinic serving primarily cultural minority patients. Particularly common among HIV patients are comorbid psychiatric illness and substance use disorders, a condition referred to as "triple diagnosis" or sometimes "trimorbidity" (discussed earlier). Douaihy et al. (2003) reviewed this topic as it pertains to antiretroviral therapy acceptance, medication adherence, and ultimate medical treatment outcomes. Given the common occurrence of triple diagnosis in the HIV population, clinical care models are advised to have robust mental health and substance abuse services as routine clinical offerings.

Zaller et al. (2007) developed a model of multidisciplinary integrated mental health and substance use treatment within a primary care HIV care setting. Social service needs were also addressed. This population also had a high rate of HCV infection. The majority of participants were on antiretroviral therapy. Specific clinical interventions included intensive outpatient services, methadone, buprenorphine, residential treatment, and individual and group psychotherapy.

Budin et al. (2004) studied utilization of psychiatric services offered in an integrated model with primary HIV care and found that approximately 25% of the referred patients used 67% of the mental health services, qualifying as "high utilizers." Psychiatric services in HIV integrated clinics are advised to monitor utilization patterns and develop a broader range of psychiatric services for these patients.

Supporting the assumption that the provision of multidisciplinary support services improves care engagement and medication adherence in patients with HIV, Sherer et al. (2002) described an outcomes-based study that demonstrated a positive effect on care engagement and medical adherence of four support services: case management, transportation, mental health, and chemical dependency. The presence of a mental health provider in an HIV clinic has been shown to increase the likelihood of prompt initiation of depression treatment for HIV-affected patients, supporting the model of integrated HIV and psychiatric care (Sueoka et al., 2010).

An important issue in clinical care of HIV-infected patients is that of social stigma. Beyond the stigma associated with identification with variously marginalized social groups at higher risk for HIV exposure are the additive stigmata often associated with HIV infection itself and comorbid psychiatric illness (including substance use disorders). Farber et al. (2014) reported that the integration of HIV-specific mental health services in a primary care HIV clinic was associated with a decrease in patients' experience of various dimensions of HIV-associated stigma. Well-organized models of psychiatric care delivery within integrated models of medical care for HIV facilitate the development of a literature specific to the esoteric clinical phenomena in HIV psychiatry. Due to structural and methodological challenges, large numbers of randomized controlled clinical trials are unlikely to be completed to guide clinical interventions in HIV psychiatry. As such, expert panel opinion on the management of common clinical illnesses such as depression, psychotic disorders, and anxiety disorders is more practical and may facilitate some standardization in care for HIV psychiatric patients (Freudenreich et al., 2010).

Comorbid depression is common in HIV patients, and prompt initiation of treatment is highly desirable. Komiti et al. (2003) reported a prevalence of major depression in 22% of a primary care population. Hooshyar et al. (2010) reported that in a primary care HIV clinic, only one-third of outpatients identified as having depression on the basis of screening received treatment, with the remainder either not receiving treatment or being treated only after a long delay. This finding supports the provision of mental health care in the primary care HIV clinic to screen for and then initiate treatment for a larger percentage of patients.

Commonly associated with chronic HIV infection (even in patients without separately diagnosed mood and/or substance use disorders) is chronic pain. Given the medical complexity of HIV care, the use of opioids and other psychopharmacology can be problematic. To address this, Trafton et al. (2012) initiated a cognitive-behavioral therapy (CBT) treatment model focused on pain management provided in HIV primary clinics. The authors described improvements in clinical outcomes for pain intensity, pain-associated function, anxiety, acceptance, and mental health following a 12-week intervention.

With the common comorbidity of psychiatric illness and substance abuse in HIV patients, secondary prevention of HIV complications via behavioral interventions and medical care adherence are common concerns. Integrated models of care wherein comorbid psychiatric illness and substance use disorders are treated along with HIV are desirable in order to integrate these three areas of clinical concern (Brown and Di Clemente, 2011; Gonzalez et al., 2011).

An increasingly important and common clinical intervention for opioid dependence, which is of particular interest in

the HIV population, is buprenorphine treatment. Cheever at al. (2011) reported on an innovative multisite project to integrate buprenorphine treatment as a component of substance abuse treatment into HIV primary care. Khalsa et al. (2006) describe various models for integrating HIV primary care and substance use treatment, including buprenorphine treatment.

EXAMPLES OF INTEGRATED HIV CARE MODELS WITH EMBEDDED PSYCHIATRY SERVICES

BOSTON: BRIGHAM AND WOMEN'S HOSPITAL

The HIV Medical Service at Brigham and Women's Hospital (BWH) in Boston, Massachusetts, a branch of the Division of Infectious Disease, was established in 1990 in response to increasing HIV-associated morbidity and mortality and the growing need for specialized medical care and psychosocial support for people living with HIV/AIDS. The original goals included reducing inpatient length of stay and hospital readmissions and avoiding emergency department visits in addition to improving coordination of outpatient care, access to clinical trials, and education of the BWH community about HIV/AIDS. The patient population is composed of a large proportion of women with no history of drug use, many of whom were born in the Caribbean or Central America. Roughly two-thirds of all patients are non-white and the two most common non-English spoken languages are Spanish and Haitian Creole.

In 2009 the HIV Mental Health Program integrated an embedded psychiatrist with office space located in the BWH HIV Medical Clinic. Patients are scheduled for psychiatric consultation during one fixed 4-hour patient care session weekly, as well as during flexible hours the remaining days of the week on an as-needed basis.

The current integrated HIV Mental Health Program has been shaped by several influences. From its inception, the core BWH HIV Medical Service has had a strong social work presence that recognized an unfulfilled mental health need for their patient population. The addition in 2009 of an HIV-designated psychiatrist was a response to limited access to appropriate behavioral health services and the growing number of patients with psychiatric and substance-related comorbidity. Expansion of services has been guided by local patient- and staff-centered exigencies and aligned with institutional priorities, goals and resources.

The BWH HIV Mental Health Program shares features common to many integrated models of care. All patients newly enrolled in the outpatient clinic receive a comprehensive HIV-specific psychosocial evaluation by clinic LICSW-level social workers. The evaluation incorporates validated mental health screening tools such as the Patient Health Questionnaire-9 (PHQ-9), Generalized Anxiety Disorder 7-item (GAD-7) scale, and questions about drug and alcohol use. Patients who screen positive for a psychiatric or substance-related disorder are discussed with their HIV primary care provider. Mental health interventions may then proceed along one or more pathways depending on the nature of the problem being addressed:

- The HIV physician may initiate treatment with psychiatric medication.

- The social worker may provide psychological support while addressing housing-related, social, or financial barriers to treatment.

- The social worker may refer patients to either community-based mental health treatment or to psychiatric or substance-related therapies at BWH.

- The HIV psychiatrist may provide "curbside" consultation, conjoint consultation with the social worker and HIV physician, or a separate evaluation either in the HIV Clinic or in the BWH Adult Outpatient Psychiatry Clinic.

Patient and HIV provider need and preference determine behavioral health level, intensity, and location of care. For example, patients with low motivation and other significant barriers to access are seen in the HIV clinic with the options of same-day appointments or even conjoint appointments with the HIV primary care provider and psychiatrist. With patients for whom face-to-face assessment with a psychiatrist is warranted but not clinically advisable, the psychiatrist may serve as a coach to the primary care provider. Established patients who develop new-onset or recurrent psychiatric symptoms are triaged by the social worker along the same pathways described for new clinic patients.

Other features of the model include the following: (1) a shared electronic medical record with a capacity for electronic clinical messaging and scheduling visible to all clinicians and administrative staff; (2) a secure email system; (3) both ad hoc and regular team and staff clinical meetings during which specific patients are discussed and treatment strategies developed; a portion of the embedded psychiatrist's fixed time in the HIV clinic is devoted to meeting with HIV clinical staff both with and apart from patients; 4) the embedded psychiatrist serves as the primary mental health clinician for patients with the most severe symptomatology. This includes patients diagnosed with comorbid psychiatric and substance-related disorders and patients who are at high risk for self-injury, violence, or poor treatment adherence.

A fellow from the BWH Psychosomatic Medicine Fellowship Program rotates through the HIV Clinic on days that the embedded psychiatrist is present. The fellow is responsible for performing initial evaluations and providing ongoing treatment for the duration of his or her involvement in the clinic. The fellow may consult on HIV-infected clinic as well as non-clinic patients admitted to the inpatient medical or surgical services. Thus continuity of care is maintained across the full continuum of care.

The integration of HIV medical services and behavioral health is bidirectional. The program has also leveraged clinical resources from the Department of Psychiatry and other integrated mental health services to enhance educational and treatment-related functions.

A psychologist with clinical and research expertise in hepatitis C is a member of the multidisciplinary team. She is available for both consultation as well as ongoing cognitive-behavioral psychotherapy targeting engagement in care and adherence to HIV and HCV medication regimens. She has flexibility similar to that of the psychiatrist and is able to maximize access by seeing patients either in the clinic or in the BWH Outpatient Psychiatry Clinic. She has also been central to both research as well as education of HIV medical staff. A LICSW-level social worker with expertise in alcohol and drug addictions whose principal placement is in the outpatient psychiatry clinic is also able to see patients in both locations. She provides individual counseling and may lead recovery-oriented groups as need arises.

The potential adverse impact on staff of caring for patients with complex medical and psychosocial needs is well documented. The integrated program is designed to address these needs by providing ongoing education and support for clinic staff. The director of Addiction Services for the BWH Psychiatry Department provided training required for certification to prescribe suboxone to interested infectious disease physicians. The ability to assist previously unreachable opiate-dependent patients has improved both patient care and provider satisfaction by permitting patient access to pharmacological management of opioid addiction.

The integrated program leadership together with the BWH director of Addiction Services developed a curriculum to train infectious disease staff in motivational interviewing (MI) principles and techniques. The didactic component consisted of a half-day workshop during which the usual clinic activities were suspended. A 2-hour "booster" session was held 12 months after the initial training. Additionally, one of the clinic social workers with advanced MI training provided ongoing supervision and education to staff. The initial didactic experience was part of an IRB-approved protocol designed to study the feasibility and effectiveness of an abbreviated MI training curriculum for busy HIV clinicians. The study demonstrated that brief training in MI may lead to modest changes in clinician attitudes about behavior change counseling, improvement in MI skills, and reduction of clinician burnout.

Approximately 10–15% of clinic patients are nonadherent to their antiretroviral medication regimens, with nonadherence defined as having a non-suppressed viral load during a predefined period. A multidisciplinary team composed of the clinic social workers, an HIV physician, and psychiatrist have developed an MI-based intervention aimed at improving medication adherence. A novel feature of the intervention is the inclusion of a family member or other person designated by the patient. Research suggests that family members may "undo" the benefit of provider MI-informed communication through MI-inconsistent behavior. Thus a primary goal of the intervention is to teach family members to use MI-consistent behavior during interactions related to medication adherence. This intervention is being studied as part of an IRB-approved protocol designed to improve adherence and identify factors associated with poor antiretroviral adherence.

MULTIPLE LOCATIONS: HIV/LGBT COMMUNITY HEALTH CENTERS

Prior to the HIV epidemic, the gay rights movement in many large cities had identified a need for affirmative, nondiscriminatory gay men's health services, especially as it related to sexually transmitted diseases (STDs). Many gay men's STD clinics became the foundation for what would become the HIV/LGBT community health centers of today (Table 7.1).

Many of the HIV/LBGT community health centers were volunteer-run, free clinics at the time that the HIV epidemic began in gay men in major metropolitan areas. Because of the broad psychosocial impact of HIV, these clinics were forced to adopt a holistic approach to patient care at a time when integration was not common in healthcare, called "the San Francisco Model." In addition to medical services, many of these clinics incorporated other forms of care, including housing assistance, legal aid, public benefits, behavioral health, dental care, case management, day treatment programs, and community health, to meet the complex needs of HIV patients under one umbrella of care. The clinics were often the locations for some of the important early research that identified the cause and transmission of HIV, along with treatment trials. There was a clear recognition that any system of HIV care had to recognize the social context of the disease.

As local, state, and federal governments began to realize the important role that community-based clinics provided in diagnosing and treating those affected by the HIV epidemic, they began providing additional funds for their services. The Ryan White HIV/AIDS Program (RWP), established in 1990, became the main source of federal funding for HIV specialty or primary care. This funding helped the development of these clinics into health centers that now seem unrecognizable compared to their early predecessors. Integration of generalists providing primary care into a practice of HIV specialists helped broaden the scope of care. Many of them have become federally qualified health centers that serve the needs of anyone who enters, with a specialization in HIV/LGBT health needs.

Although initially developed independently of the medical home model, existing data indirectly support that, with emphasis on primary, comprehensive, and patient-centered care, HIV/LGBT community health centers operate as exemplars of medical homes (Beane et al., 2014). As HIV/AIDS evolved from a terminal to a chronic condition that required months and years of therapeutic interventions, including comprehensive medical, mental health, substance abuse, and social services to ensure adherence to HIV treatment and access to care, HIV/LGBT community health centers naturally evolved into "medical homes" that exceed traditional definitions of the model. A large component of this specialty care has been a focus on mental health and addiction treatment, including psychiatric care.

The behavioral health departments of HIV/LGBT health centers tend to provide a wide range of individual, group, and peer-led services. Many of the groups that are provided in the health centers are unique to the populations they serve, focusing on coming out, newly diagnosed or long-term survivors of HIV, HIV-associated neurocognitive disorders, transgender people, and dual-diagnosis patients. There remains a strong commitment to volunteerism in the health centers that can often be seen in the peer counselors who volunteer their time to meet with clients individually or in groups. The addiction services tend to be low-barrier with intensive outpatient or harm reduction–based programs. Many of the health centers are specialized in treating gay men who abuse methamphetamines, often fused with sex. Another substance abuse service that is integrated into medical care is buprenorphine maintenance treatment, which will also help facilitate the expanded treatment of co-infected and mono-infected HCV patients as newer treatments become available.

Depending on the health center and resources available, psychiatrists' integration in HIV/LGBT community health centers can range from co-located care to a more integrated part of medical team. While psychiatrists have been well integrated into the behavioral health or addictions department, integration with HIV providers has been slower and more inconsistent. With the introduction of collaborative care

Table 7.1 CONTEMPORARY HIV/LGBT COMMUNITY HEALTH CENTERS IN MAJOR U.S. CITIES

CITY	HEALTH CENTER	DATE INAUGURATED
Baltimore	Chase Brexton	1978
Boston	Fenway Health	1971
Chicago	Howard-Brown	1974
Los Angeles	Los Angeles LGBT Center	1969
New York	Callen-Lorde	1983
Philadelphia	Mazzoni Center	1979
Washington D.C.	Whitman-Walker Health	1978
Multiple Locations	AIDS Healthcare Foundation-AHF	1987

models and the expanded need for care with the Affordable Care Act, there has been more of an attempt to use psychiatrists in a consultative role working with mental health liaisons that are embedded in the medical clinics. Psychiatrists also have been involved in providing ongoing education for the HIV providers on mental health and addiction topics or case consultations on complicated patients.

NEW YORK: COLUMBIA UNIVERSITY MEDICAL CENTER

The HIV Liaison Psychiatry Program at Columbia University Medical Center in New York City started in 1990 at the end of the first decade of the AIDS crisis. In those early years before the widespread use of effective antiretroviral therapy, a half-time embedded HIV psychiatrist, a faculty member within the Psychosomatic Medicine Division, worked exclusively on the dedicated medical/infectious disease AIDS inpatient unit. Outpatient models of HIV medical and psychiatric care were limited or nonexistent at the outset of the HIV pandemic prior to development of HIV specialty care and effective antiretroviral therapy. Advancing, unchecked immunosuppression was the rule, with widespread consequences including florid neurological and neuropsychiatric conditions such as severe HIV dementia, myelopathy, and neuropathy as well as opportunistic central nervous system infections and malignancies.

In the AIDS program, from 1990 to 1994, the embedded psychosomatic medicine psychiatrist consulted on medical inpatients with acute neuropsychiatric complications: mood disorders (both depression and mania, as well as mixed mood states), apathy states, and psychotic presentations including delirium. Liaison involvement within the AIDS service included working closely on a daily basis with internal medicine residents, infectious disease fellows and attending physicians, and nursing and social work staff. Liaison activities included a weekly interdisciplinary team meeting in which all admitted and recently discharged HIV patients were discussed, with a focus on psychiatric diagnosis, psychosocial issues such as housing, insurance status, social support, and substance abuse, as well as psychiatric management and aftercare planning. Importantly, the work of this embedded psychiatrist also included the emerging subspecialty of palliative care psychiatry, with an emphasis on helping patients and their loved ones cope with the challenge of impending death, treating psychiatric complications at the end of life, and working closely with medical housestaff and nurses who were typically the same age as their patients.

Other issues that were confronted at that time included the stigma of "coming out twice," a descriptor meant for patients who had not shared their sexual orientation with their family of origin until overtly ill with far advanced AIDS-related medical complications. After the development and introduction of HIV testing in 1985, acute psychiatric complications associated with HIV testing and counseling were also a core part of the responsibilities of this embedded psychiatrist. The psychiatrist also supervised medical students and other staff who were learning a new skill set related to communicating and providing pre- and post-test counseling for persons with risk behaviors, including evaluation for and prevention of suicide.

With the introduction of effective antiretroviral therapy, in 1995, the scope of the responsibilities evolved with a significant psychiatric presence in the growing HIV medical clinic located in the Harkness Pavilion at Columbia-Presbyterian Medical Center. Thirty percent of the patients are women and a majority of patients are persons of color, including persons from the Dominican Republic. Substance use disorders and hepatitis C co-infection are prevalent. A second embedded psychiatrist was added to specifically address the psychosocial and psychiatric burden in the clinic population. Currently, there is a total of 0.7 FTE (two part-time psychiatrists who are embedded in the AIDS clinic and the medical inpatient AIDS service). Psychosomatic medicine psychiatry fellows rotate in the AIDS clinic, and fourth-year medical students also rotate in this setting. For the past 15 years, the HIV liaison program has participated in an American Psychiatric Association (APA) medical student elective for minority medical students who are interested in learning about the specialty of HIV psychiatry. The APA minority medical students spend a month elective in their senior year devoted to learning about HIV psychiatry by working in clinic settings.

Liaison activities include a monthly HIV psychiatry chief of service rounds for the medical housestaff rotating on the inpatient AIDS service, as well as a monthly psychosocial rounds for HIV clinic navigators, whose task is to connect and engage with high-risk, nonadherent HIV patients who have many psychiatric comorbidities and who have not been able to access HIV medical care in an enduring way. The medical HIV clinic has both infectious disease attending physicians and fellows as well as several general internal medicine AIDS specialists. Other core staff members include nurse practitioners, social workers, health educators, a dietician, medical case management staff, and peer educators.

The HIV Liaison Psychiatry Service at Columbia University Medical Center works closely with two other outpatient psychiatry clinics at Columbia. The Lucy Wicks Clinic is located within adult outpatient psychiatry, and its mission is to treat HIV-infected and/or HIV-affected persons who are psychiatrically symptomatic. This clinic focuses on providing psychotherapy and is staffed primarily with psychiatric social workers and psychologists. Two senior psychiatrists provide as-needed psychopharmacological assessment and management on a referral basis. The Special Needs Clinic is a pediatric psychiatry clinic which provides family-centered psychiatric and psychosocial care for HIV-infected children and adolescents. All family members receive a therapist and there is a family therapist available as well. With perinatally infected children now living on into their third decade, a special focus is made to assist perinatally infected young adults with the transition from medical care in a specialized pediatric AIDS setting to medical care in the adult AIDS clinic, as many young adults fail to engage in care and drop out of care once faced with this transition.

SAN FRANCISCO

San Francisco, one of the early epicenters of the HIV epidemic in the United States, beginning in the 1980s, has long been a city of clinical, academic, and social innovation. The University of California, San Francisco School of Medicine, one of the leading U.S. medical schools, has been among the national leaders in the development of models of HIV care. The School of Medicine clinical operations focus on its three main academic medical centers: San Francisco General Hospital (SFGH), San Francisco Veterans' Affair Medical Center (SFVAMC), and University of California, San Francisco (UCSF) Medical Center. Since these academic medical centers operate separately and in parallel with each other, San Francisco has the benefit of three distinct models of integrated care for HIV affected patients. Psychiatric services are prominently central in all three of these care systems.

SAN FRANCISCO GENERAL HOSPITAL

Started in the early 1980s at San Francisco General Hospital (SFGH), Ward 86 was the first HIV/AIDS specialized clinic that offered patients comprehensive care. Ward 86 is a primary care clinic that works in collaboration with the San Francisco Department of Public Health and the University of California, San Francisco (Departments of Medicine and Psychiatry). Ward 86 is also a part of the Positive Health Program at SFGH, a comprehensive effort devoted to HIV/AIDS primary care, research, and education.

Clinical administrative leadership includes a medical director (an internist who is also appointed to the Department of Internal Medicine at UCSF Medical Center) and an administrative director (a licensed clinical social worker). Other professional staff members include primary care physicians, psychiatrists, nurse practitioners, registered nurses and licensed vocational nurses, clinical pharmacists, clinical social workers, and counselors.

The clinic encourages and fosters an educational environment through grand rounds to discuss patient care, cases, and other diverse topics, and structured and supervised clinical rotations for health professional trainees, including psychiatry and internal medicine residents and infectious disease fellows. The clinic provides comprehensive care in a medical home–type model. Patients have access to multiple clinic professionals for appointments on the same day.

On Ward 86, two faculty psychiatrists offer psychiatric services on a daily basis. In addition, a women's clinic is offered on a drop-by once-a-week basis to integrate primary and psychiatric care. Funding is provided through various HIV-specific streams of funding, include Ryan White funds, the Department of Public Health, UCSF Alliance Health Project, and the Chronic Care HIV/AIDS Multidisciplinary Program (CCHAMP).

To be registered at the clinic, patients need to be HIV positive and are referred by health professionals or self-referred. Clinical social workers assess each referred individual before enrollment into the clinic. Initial evaluations with psychiatrists are booked for 1 hour and follow-up visits are 30 minutes. The HIV psychiatrist determines scheduling and timing of follow-up appointments. The drop-in clinic offers flexibility for patients if they need to be seen earlier.

Clinical documentation for all patient encounters is recorded on Harrison Electronic Record and Orders (HERO), an electronic medical record. Laboratory and radiology data, pharmacy data, e-prescribing medications to community pharmacies, and other reports are all available on HERO. Since 2000, all clinical documentation is uploaded onto SFGH's EMR (electronic medical records) Invision/LCR (Lifetime Clinical Record) and is made available to clinical providers and staff at SFGH and the Department of Public Health.

Patients' psychiatric disorders are primarily mood and substance use disorders. When needed, psychotropic medications are prescribed by the psychiatrist. There is limited psychotherapy at the clinic. Patients in need of psychotherapy are usually referred to outpatient settings, such as Alliance Health Project, a mental health organization providing comprehensive psychiatric care to the community.

Patients do not need to be San Francisco residents and are 18 years of age or older. Patient age ranges between 18 and 87. All patients have some form of insurance, including Medi-Cal, Medicare, Healthy San Francisco (a city initiative), and private insurance.

SAN FRANCISCO VETERANS AFFAIRS MEDICAL CENTER

The Infectious Disease Clinic at the San Francisco Veteran's Administration (VA) Medical Center is a multidisciplinary clinic for patients living with HIV and other infectious illnesses. The main clinic operates two half-days per week with full staffing, although a medical nurse practitioner sees drop-ins three additional half-days per week. A gradual process of integration of mental health providers has been under way since 2008.

Originally, persons with HIV at the VA saw both HIV medicine and mental health providers; however, clinicians had few opportunities to collaborate with one another and discuss management of shared patients. This situation has evolved to become an integrated and co-located team of a social worker, pharmacist, psychologist, and dietician, along with a full nursing staff to include a licensed vocational nurse (LVN), charge nurse (RN), and nurse practitioner, as well as a complement of many rotating internal medicine and psychiatry residents, infectious disease and psychology fellows, and infectious disease and psychiatry attending physicians.

Mental health integration began when a psychology fellow was introduced into the medical clinic as a way to begin a more collaborative-care experience. A staff psychologist was then added. Psychologists are located in the shared precepting room so that they are readily accessible for medical clinicians. In addition to clinician consultation, the psychologist conducts support groups, therapy groups, and provides triage and brief assessment.

A psychiatrist was integrated into the clinic part-time in 2013. This psychiatrist had been working with an overlapping panel of patients in a separately located building. Since the migration this psychiatrist is now located in the integrated clinic one half-day per week. During this half-day, the psychiatrist sees a pre-existing panel of patients for follow-up. Increasingly, patients no longer require follow-up with the psychiatrist directly and can be managed by the medical team with curbside consultation from the psychiatrist (now co-located) and psychologist. As a result, the psychiatrist is able to set aside time each day for curbside consultations and triage, expanding access to psychiatric assessment. Meanwhile, the psychiatry resident sees patients throughout the half-day under the attending's supervision.

To be seen by mental health clinicians in the Infectious Disease Clinic, patients can either have HIV or be at high risk of contracting HIV. Patients must be approved to receive medical services through the Veterans Health Administration. Mental health clinicians primarily see patients experiencing depression, PTSD, substance abuse and high-risk sexual behaviors, and anxiety disorders and patients who could benefit from behavioral interventions for their chronic medical conditions. Given that the VA population is older on average than with most outpatient HIV clinics, neuropsychological testing is provided by psychologists in the clinic. Patients receiving individual psychotherapy are treated with evidence-based acceptance and commitment therapy, cognitive-behavioral therapy, motivational interviewing, and interpersonal psychotherapy. These regularly scheduled individual therapy sessions are conducted outside of normal clinic hours and in a separate building where mental health providers have additional office space, but with the same therapists who originally saw them in the Infectious Disease Clinic.

As part of the educational experience, trainees are encouraged to interact and discuss cases with one another, especially across disciplines. Plans are to increase this activity through shared educational experiences such as case conferences. In addition to the many residents and fellows, medical students also spend time rotating though the clinic.

The clinic operates under the leadership of an infectious disease specialist who serves as chief of the Department of Infectious Disease at the VA and as chief for the Infectious Disease Clinic. All physicians working in the clinic have academic affiliation with the University of California, San Francisco. Trainees, under supervision of infectious disease faculty, provide care for the majority of patients. About 20% of the patients are seen by the faculty directly. Overall, there are roughly 600 patients followed at the clinic on an ongoing basis.

The clinic is set up as a medical home, providing HIV specialty and primary care. The social worker assists in case management and resource needs. The pharmacist reviews charts at the start of each day to review labs and look for drug interactions, handles most medication refills, and meets with patients when any new antiretroviral medications are started. For patients who need assistance, the pharmacist prepares pill boxes. Nurses in the clinic assist in population management and health maintenance and are able to help provide continuity of care on non-clinic days.

Documentation is completed using the VA CPRS EMR system that is shared by all VA providers. All relevant clinical data are accessible via the EMR. This system also enables providers to communicate securely with one another regarding shared patients and helps to prevent splitting between providers. Medications are ordered through this system and monitored by the clinic's pharmacist for drug–drug interactions.

UNIVERSITY OF CALIFORNIA, SAN FRANCISCO MEDICAL CENTER

The 360 Positive Care Center at UCSF is a multispecialty and multidisciplinary clinic devoted to the care of HIV patients. The clinic operates in a medical clinic building on the Parnassus Avenue campus of UCSF, across the street from UCSF Medical Center. The clinic began operations in 1984 with the goal of offering a range of high-quality services in a single location for people living with HIV. The clinic has had an embedded psychiatrist since 2010. Most patients are Bay Area residents; some come from other states and other countries. Patients must be 18 years or older and have a payer source (commercial insurance, Medicare, or Medicaid). Patient age range includes 18 to geriatric.

The clinic is operated under the Department of Medicine, Division of Infectious Diseases. Clinical administrative leadership includes a medical director (an infectious diseases physician who is also appointed to the Department of Internal Medicine at UCSF) and practice manager. Other professional staff includes 10 primary care clinicians specializing in infectious diseases, a primary care nurse practitioner, a clinical pharmacist, a licensed clinical social worker, clinic RN, and a registered dietitian. Psychiatric services are provided by faculty psychiatrist(s) from the consultation-liaison psychiatry service, Department of Psychiatry, UCSF. Paraprofessional and administrative staff includes a case manager and a peer advocate, four medical assistants, and reception and administrative staff members.

Patients need to be HIV positive and have active insurance to be registered. The clinic provides comprehensive HIV care in a collaborative care, chronic illness management, patient-centered medical home–type model. The social service team (clinical social worker, case manager, and peer advocate) directly addresses the psychosocial needs of patients. Patients frequently have several clinic appointments with various clinic professionals on the same day, coordinated for patient convenience. The social service team provides active and ongoing outreach to community agencies and other institutions, as well as home and community visits to support patients.

Psychiatric services are provided one day per week; currently, two faculty psychiatrists each conduct a 4-hour clinic once per week. The weekly 8 hours of clinical service is directly supported by a funding stream from the Department of Medicine as a 0.2 FTE agreement between the Departments of Medicine and Psychiatry. This arrangement is reviewed annually. The Internal Medicine Department then keeps any clinical revenue generated and paid on the basis of patient care activities of the faculty psychiatrists.

Patients are seen on a consult basis, in that patients need physician referrals to see the HIV psychiatrist. Initial evaluations are booked for 1 hour, follow-up visits are 30 minutes. The HIV psychiatrist determines the frequency and number of psychiatric visits; many patients are seen for a single session and thereafter managed by the patient's primary physician or nurse practitioner. Patients needing psychotropic medications following their psychiatric evaluation have such prescriptions written by the psychiatrist.

Patients who are seen by psychiatry faculty members are frequently found to have mood, substance use, and anxiety disorders, with relatively infrequent psychotic, cognitive, or other psychiatric illnesses. Supportive psychotherapy, typically along an illness acceptance/management and supportive focus, is the main psychotherapy model used. Limited psychodynamic psychotherapy is also offered for selected patients. Neuroimaging to evaluate psychiatric illness is readily available when needed.

The educational mission of the clinic includes providing structured and supervised clinical experiences for psychiatry residents, infectious disease fellows, internal medicine residents, pharmacy students, and dietician students. Senior psychiatry residents (PGY-3 and PGY-4) rotate through the clinic on the same half-days as faculty psychiatrists, interviewing new patients, providing ongoing evaluation and management, and referring for ancillary services. Residents discuss cases with their supervising faculty on an ongoing basis, and faculty psychiatrists have the opportunity to meet the patients before they leave. For many residents this serves as their first opportunity to work in a multidisciplinary setting outside of mental health, and there are many opportunities to coordinate face-to-face with social workers, nurses, medical providers, and other staff.

Residents are also invited to join clinic multispecialty and multidisciplinary team meetings. Residents with a specific interest in HIV may further choose a PG4 elective in advanced HIV psychiatry, wherein the residents are also invited to actively participate in projects on clinical service delivery, telemedicine, and other systems initiatives to provide care to HIV patients. Clinical research volunteers are also supported in the clinic; these personnel often work for a discrete amount of time on a specific clinical research project.

Additional clinical services include a weekly geriatric case conference, where primary care MDs and nurse practitioners present cases to a geriatric medicine specialist and one of the HIV clinic faculty psychiatrists. This conference is part of a clinic-based project targeting the clinical needs of patients with HIV who are older than 50 years of age. A comprehensive assessment, including social and housing status, mood and anxiety symptom rating scales, Mini Mental State Examination (MMSE) and Montreal Cognitive Assessment (MoCA), and various functional assessments are integrated with comprehensive medical and surgical history, medication review and reconciliation, and laboratory studies. Persons with cognitive impairment and/or mood or anxiety symptoms above a screening threshold are referred for psychiatric and/or geriatric assessment. Individuals with polypharmacy, especially patients receiving medications with high delirium risk, are regularly identified and medication modification and consolidation strategies shared with the primary care providers.

All professionals in the clinic accomplish clinical documentation using the Epic APeX EMR system, which was adopted system-side by UCSF Medical Center in 2012. All relevant clinical data (e.g., clinical provider notes, radiology studies, laboratory data, pharmacy, diagnostic imaging) are accessible via the EMR. This system also allows for direct patient-to-clinician and clinician-to-clinician secure electronic communication, e-prescribing of medication with direct link to pharmacies, and integration of medical information sent from other institutions and scanned into the EMR. All clinical providers have full access to each other's notes to provide fully integrated and collaborative care, as the psychiatry notes are considered "consultation" notes and are not classified as "psychotherapy notes," which would be inaccessible to other clinicians.

This model illustrates the value of having embedded psychiatric services in a highly specialized medical clinic to care for a HIV patient population with a high degree of psychiatric comorbidity. The roles of the psychiatrist include direct patient care (both single consultations and limited ongoing care), informal informational consultation to colleagues without direct patient contact (curbsiding), weekly geriatric/psychiatric case conference, regular interface with clinical pharmacy for drug–drug interactions, laboratory monitoring and other medication-specific matters, education of trainees, and involvement in clinical research.

CONCLUSIONS

Integrated care models for psychiatric care in general medical clinics are increasingly seen as desirable models for comprehensive care of medical and psychiatric multimorbid illness. HIV care is among the most illustrative models of this concept. The care models described here were all developed in accordance with local clinical needs, medical personnel resources, and administrative opportunities. Future designs in integrated care may include more elaborated use of evolving decisional support technology, outcome measures, protocols for standardized treatment, and evidence-based psychiatric care. HIV is an excellent model for an illness that is compatible with integrated care; its example may be followed when developing integrated psychiatric care models for other systemic illnesses with significant psychiatric comorbidity.

While a comprehensive model of HIV psychiatry care being offered by psychosomatic medicine psychiatrists is a highly elaborated model associated with and/or located at an academic medical center, not all clinical models of caring for HIV patients will have access to this range of clinical resources. It may not be practical to co-locate and integrate psychiatric care within the general medical clinic/HIV clinic.

At institutions that do not have psychosomatic medicine psychiatrists, it may be best to facilitate access to general psychiatrists (either working privately or within community mental health centers or clinics) for HIV patients. Some psychiatrists may have a particular interest in HIV and related illnesses and may save a fraction of their clinical time for providing care for psychiatric illness in HIV patients. In this situation, administrative procedures (including patients signing release of information documents to facilitate to-and-fro communication between the psychiatrist and HIV clinician) should be in place to enhance professional coordination and collaboration. Other mental health professionals working in the same clinic as the psychiatrist who themselves have an interest in HIV psychiatry can make themselves available to HIV clinicians in a similar fashion. Collaboration among HIV psychiatrists and the other mental health professionals is critically important in coordination of psychiatric aspects of care.

REFERENCES

Arend J, Tsang-Quinn J, Levine C, Thomas D (2012). The patient-centered medical home: history, components, and review of the evidence. *Mt Sinai J Med* 79(4):433–450.

Ashman JJ, Conviser R, Pounds MB (2002). Associations between HIV-positive individuals' receipt of ancillary services and medical care receipt and retention. *AIDS Care* 14(Suppl 1):S109–S118.

Baldwin KA, Marvin CL, Rodine MK (1998). The development of a comprehensive interdisciplinary HIV/AIDS center: a community needs assessment. *J Public Health Manag Pract* 4(4):87–96.

Bauer AM, Fielke K, Brayley J, Araya M, Alem A, Frankel BL, Fricchione GL (2010). Tackling the global mental health challenge: a psychosomatic medicine/consultation-liaison psychiatry perspective. *Psychosomatics* 51:185–193.

Beane SN, Culyba R, DeMayo M, Armstrong W (2014). Exploring the medical home in Ryan White HIV care settings: a pilot study. *J Assoc Nurses AIDS Care* 25(3):191–202.

Brown JL, DiClemente RJ (2011). Secondary HIV prevention: novel intervention approaches to impact populations most at risk. *Curr HIV/AIDS Rep* 8(4):269–276.

Budin J, Boslaugh S, Beckett E, Winiarski MG (2004). Utilization of psychiatric services integrated with primary care by persons of color with HIV in the inner city. *Community Ment Health J* 40(4):365–378.

Cheever LW, Kresina TF, Cajina A, Lubran R (2011). A model federal collaborative to increase patient access to buprenorphine treatment in HIV primary care. *J Acquir Immune Defic Syndr* 56(Suppl 1):S3–S6.

Cohen MA (1987). Psychiatric aspects of AIDS: A biopsychosocial approach. In GP Wormser, RE Stahl, EJ Bottone (eds.), *AIDS Acquired Immune Deficiency Syndrome and Other Manifestations of HIV Infection.* Park Ridge, NJ: Noyes Publishers.

Cohen MA (1992). Biopsychosocial aspects of the HIV epidemic. In GP Wormser (ed.), *AIDS and Other Manifestations of HIV Infection,* 2nd ed. (pp. 349–371). New York: Raven Press.

Cohen MAA (1996). Creating health care environments to meet patients' needs. *Curr Issues Public Health* 2:232–240.

Cohen, MA (2013). HIV: how to provide compassionate care. *Curr Psychiatry* 12:19–23.

Cohen MA, Alfonso CA (2004). AIDS psychiatry: psychiatric and palliative care, and pain management. In GP Wormser (ed.), *AIDS and Other Manifestations of HIV Infection,* 4th ed. (pp. 537–576). San Diego: Elsevier Academic Press.

Cohen MA, Goforth HW, Lux JZ, Batista SM, Khalife S, Cozza KL, Soffer J (2010). *Handbook of AIDS Psychiatry.* New York: Oxford University Press.

Cohen MA, Gorman JM (2008). *Comprehensive Textbook of AIDS Psychiatry.* New York: Oxford University Press.

Cohen MA, Weisman H (1986). A biopsychosocial approach to AIDS. *Psychosomatics* 27:245–249.

Deuchar N (1984). AIDS in New York City with particular reference to the psychosocial aspects. *Br J Psychiatry* 145:612–619.

Dodds S, Blaney NT, Nuehring EM, Blakley T, Lizzotte JM, Potter JE, O'Sullivan MJ (2000). Integrating mental health services into primary care for HIV-infected pregnant and non-pregnant women: Whole Life—a theoretically derived model for clinical care and outcomes assessment. *Gen Hosp Psychiatry* 22(4):251–260.

Douaihy AB, Jou RJ, Gorske T, Salloum IM (2003). Triple diagnosis: dual diagnosis and HIV disease, part 1. *AIDS Read.* 13(7):331–332, 339–341.

Engel GL (1961). To the editor. *Psychosom Med* 23:426–429.

Engel GL (1977). The need for a new medical model: a challenge for biomedicine. *Science* 196:129–136.

Engel GL (1980). The clinical application of the biopsychosocial model. *Am J Psychiatry* 137:535–544.

Farber EW, Shahane AA, Brown JL, Campos PE (2014). Perceived stigma reductions following participation in mental health services integrated within community-based HIV primary care. *AIDS Care* 26(6):750–753.

Feingold A, Slammon WR (1993). A model integrating mental health and primary care services for families with HIV. *Gen Hosp Psychiatry* 15(5):290–300.

Ferrante JM, Balasubramanian BA, Hudson SV, Crabtree BF (2010). Principles of the patient-centered medical home and preventive services delivery. *Ann Fam Med* 8(2):108–116.

Freeman MC, Patel V, Collins PY, Bertolote JM (2005). Integrating mental health in global initiatives for HIV/AIDS. *Br J Psychiatry* 187:1–3.

Freudenreich O, Goforth HW, Cozza KL, Mimiaga MJ, Safren SA, Bachmann G, Cohen MA (2010). Psychiatric treatment of persons with HIV/AIDS: an HIV-psychiatry consensus survey of current practices. *Psychosomatics* 51:480–488.

Gonzalez A, Barinas J, O'Cleirigh C (2011). Substance use: impact on adherence and HIV medical treatment. *Curr HIV/AIDS Rep* 8(4):223–234.

Hooshyar D, Goulet J, Chwastiak L, et al., for the VACS Project Team. (2010). Time to depression treatment in primary care among HIV-infected and uninfected veterans. *J Gen Intern Med* 25(7), 656–662.

Kathol RG, Kunkel EJS, Weiner JS, et al. (2009): Psychiatrists for medically complex patients: bringing value at the physical health/substance use disorder interface. *Psychosomatics* 50:93–107.

Katon W, Russo J, Lin EHB, et al. (2012). Cost-effectiveness of a multicondition collaborative care intervention: a randomized controlled trial. *Arch Gen Psychiatry* 69(5):506–514.

Katon W, Seeling M (2008). Population-based care of depression: team care approaches to improving outcomes. *J Occup Environ Med* 50:459–467.

Katon W, Unutzer J (2011). Consultation psychiatry in the medical home and accountable care organizations: achieving the triple aim. *Gen Hosp Psychiatry* 33:305–310.

Khalsa J, Vocci F, Altice F, Fiellin D, Miller V (2006). Buprenorphine and HIV primary care: new opportunities for integrated treatment. *Clin Infect Dis* 43(Suppl 4):S169–S172.

Komiti A, Judd F, Grech P, et al. (2003). Depression in people living with HIV/AIDS attending primary care and outpatient clinics. *Aust N Z J Psychiatry* 37(1):70–77.

Mugavero MJ, Westfall AO, Cole SR, et al.; for the Centers for AIDS Research Network of Integrated Clinical Systems (CNICS) (2014). Beyond core indicators of retention in HIV care: missed clinic visits are independently associated with all-cause mortality. *Clin Infect Dis* 59(10):1471–1479.

Pyne JM, Fortney JC, Curran GM, et al. (2011). Effectiveness of collaborative care for depression in human immunodeficiency virus clinics. *Arch Intern Med* 171(1):23–31.

Scholle SH, Saunders RC, Tirodkar MA, Torda P, Pawlson LG (2011). Patient-centered medical homes in the United States. *J Ambul Care Manage.* 34(1):20–32.

Sherer R, Stieglitz K, Narra J, et al. (2002). HIV multidisciplinary teams work: support services improve access to and retention in HIV primary care. *AIDS Care* 14(Suppl 1):S31–S44.

Stange KC, Nutting PA, Miller WL, Jaén CR, Crabtree BF, Flocke SA, Gill JM (2010). Defining and measuring the patient-centered medical home. *J Gen Intern Med* 25(6):601–612.

Sueoka K, Goulet JL, Fiellin DA, et al. (2010). Depression symptoms and treatment among HIV infected and uninfected veterans. *AIDS Behav* 14(2):272–279.

Trafton JA, Sorrell JT, Holodniy M, Pierson H, Link P, Combs A, Israelski D (2012). Outcomes associated with a cognitive-behavioral chronic pain management program implemented in three public HIV primary care clinics. *J Behav Health Serv Res* 39(2):158–173.

Zaller N, Gillani FS, Rich JD (2007). A model of integrated primary care for HIV-positive patients with underlying substance use and mental illness. *AIDS Care* 19(9):1128–1133.

8.

HOW TO ESTABLISH AN INTEGRATED AMBULATORY CARE PROGRAM CO-LOCATED IN AN HIV CLINIC

Mary Ann Cohen, James Bourgeois, Weston Scott Fisher, and David Tran

INTRODUCTION

Persons with HIV have a high prevalence of multimorbid psychiatric illness. Increasingly, creative departments of psychiatry and their corresponding departments of internal medicine/infectious diseases are willing to develop embedded psychiatric services to provide for integrated psychiatric and internal medicine care at a single location. The benefits to patients in terms of care coordination and clarity of communication among physicians are clear (Adams et al., 2011; Bottonari and Stepleman 2010; Coleman et al., 2012), and the improvements in engagement, retention, adherence, and survival are significant (Grimes et al., 2016; Mugavero et al., 2014).

This chapter is written from the perspective of the HIV psychiatrist who seeks to establish an HIV psychiatric embedded clinic. It focuses on the various administrative and logistical challenges involved. We hope that these reflected collective experiences are helpful to others in developing embedded psychiatric services in HIV clinics at various institutions.

The establishment of an integrated HIV psychiatry clinic service is an important area of clinical outreach. Like other clinic settings that lend themselves readily to embedded psychiatry services, such as psychooncology, psychonephrology, geriatrics, and palliative care, the placement of psychiatric services within a medical specialty clinic can facilitate patients being seen for psychiatric illness in a clinic that is familiar and comfortable to them. Such arrangements help patients accept psychiatric referrals and follow-up with psychiatric consultation as there is one less "barrier to cross" in the receipt of services.

Both mental illness and HIV are stigmatized, and attending two different clinical settings may lead to nonadherence; psychiatric services embedded in the HIV clinic diminishes one level of stigma. The collegiality among physician colleagues in caring for persons with multimorbid medical and psychiatric illness can be intrinsically rewarding and can provide educational opportunities. The collaborative, collegial, and comprehensive approach is also one that is ideal for trainees, including psychiatry residents, psychosomatic medicine fellows, internal medicine residents, and medical students. Finally, embedded models represent a model for clinic service delivery that, when operated efficiently, may prove to be a cost-effective model for outpatient care (Pyne et al., 2011; Sloan, 2014; Soto et al., 2004).

INITIAL DISCUSSIONS

When contemplating the establishment of an embedded psychiatry service in an HIV clinic, it may be helpful to have a preliminary discussion with the medical center leadership, in addition to discussions at the department level. Broad institutional support may be beneficial in a number of ways. The medical center may have a nascent interest in integrated care models and thus may be in a position to administratively and financially support such endeavors, thus minimizing the financial risk to the respective departments.

A medical center that has adopted a population-based care model, such as an accountable care organization (ACO), may be more inclined to support integrated models of service delivery for overall system efficiencies. For example, a medical center where there is an intolerably long waiting list for access to psychiatric services in the psychiatry department may see value in placing and supporting an embedded model to help alleviate the problem of access to services. In addition, an ACO may offer administrative incentives for better reimbursement for integrated services, as opposed to organizations that operate on a more traditional fee-for-service model.

CLINICAL MODEL DEVELOPMENT

Once an institution has made the commitment to establish an embedded psychiatry service within an HIV clinic, it may take several administrative steps by both the psychiatry and the internal medicine departments to facilitate the development of a highly functioning integrated care model. Several of the following steps will require official oversight by the two departments (the "macro" level), while other steps are the province of the clinical personnel themselves (the "micro" level). Both macro- and micro-level collaboration, collegiality, and cooperation are essential for the operation of a multispecialty and/or multidisciplinary clinic model.

From the point of view of the psychiatrist who anticipates being embedded in the HIV clinic, it is often best to first discuss the idea with the director of psychosomatic medicine, division chief, chair, and/or the vice chair for clinical services (depending on the department's complexity and organizational structure). Some departments, especially smaller ones, may have a relatively nonhierarchical or "flat" organizational structure, wherein the chair accomplishes direct oversight of individual clinical operations directly. The idea of having an embedded psychiatry service within the HIV clinic should be presented within the psychiatry department first. There are now a number of embedded clinics in operation to emulate and/or adapt for local needs for clinical structure and function. The idea can be presented as one of many contemporary models that progressive departments are likely to be interested in pursuing. An embedded psychiatry service within an HIV clinic model might be the first (or among few) embedded psychiatry models for a given psychiatry department to develop; if so, many administrative improvisations may be necessary to establish a functional clinical service.

BUSINESS CASE PLANNING

Assuming the department clinical leadership is receptive to the idea, it may be best to then have the department administrator model a business plan on how to integrate and be paid for services. In one model the host department pays a negotiated percentage of time (often expressed as a fraction of full-time equivalents (FTE). By this rubric, 0.2 FTE would be one full day of effort per week. In return, the host department bills for services provided by the psychiatry consultant. In the case of a full schedule, efficient clinic administration, prompt posting of charges for professional fees, and efficient billing through an electronic medical record and receipts, the host department may experience a net financial gain for psychiatric services rendered.

The business plan development could include the projected revenues and costs of various % of FTE effort for the consultant. It is unrealistic to expect that an HIV psychiatry consultant service could be 50% or more FTE in the first year, unless there is significant "outside" funding support (e.g., research grants, philanthropy). Such sources, when locally available, can be specifically earmarked for such a clinical venture. It may be more pragmatic initially to propose a "substantial enough part-time" presence (e.g., 20–40% FTE), to be followed by an ongoing utilization management analysis to examine the demand, services provided, waiting times, and other metrics. In the event of using grant money as a "seed," this may be transitionally acceptable, but this needs to be followed by a billing model that allows the embedded service eventually to be independently sustainable.

The business case exercise may be stronger if there is access to demographics and other utilization data for the HIV clinic. Examination of recent clinical demand for services, literature estimates of the rate of psychiatric illness in HIV patients, and examination of frequency of psychiatric illness coded by HIV clinicians in patients' charts all may be useful variables

in an initial estimate of % FTE effort for the consultant. It is a reasonable assumption that once the psychiatrist is in place, internal medicine physicians will make increasing use of the service over time, so that organic growth of the embedded service is likely.

IMPLEMENTATION OF THE CLINICAL MODEL

Once the department completes its business plan exercise, the host department needs to be approached to negotiate an agreement for clinical services, based on the initial analysis and business plan and the internal medicine department's response to it. Such interdepartmental agreements may be initiated for an academic or fiscal year and then be reviewed annually to assure mutual benefit and/or renegotiate the % effort provided by the consultant.

As the HIV psychiatrist seeking to establish an embedded psychiatry service, you and/or other members of the psychosomatic medicine department should start by contacting the medical director of the HIV clinic and setting up a meeting to discuss their needs and your suggestions for a plan for setting up the embedded service. It may be advantageous to include the HIV clinic administrative supervisor (if this is a different person from the medical director) in the initial meeting. Depending on the background and experience of the HIV clinic medical director and administrative supervisor, you may need to present some of the literature illustrating the embedded psychiatry clinic model. Be prepared to discuss the functional operations of the embedded model as they pertain to psychiatry services in primary care medicine in general and HIV services in particular.

In this meeting, endeavor to find out what their most pressing concerns and needs are and how they feel you can be of help. It is not unusual for primary care physicians to appreciate the need for psychiatric services but be unsure of exactly what psychiatric services are needed. Be prepared to cite the relevant HIV psychiatry literature on prevalence and as well as on the care of persons with HIV and psychiatric illness (Freudenreich et al., 2010; Hoang et al., 2009; Olagunju et al., 2013; Primeau et al., 2013).

Find out what the HIV clinic director's interests are. The HIV clinic will most likely welcome you with open arms. Many primary care physicians readily appreciate the ubiquity of psychiatric illness in their patients, although they may conflate psychiatric illness and social problems, and they may use nonspecific terms such as "mental health issues." However, beyond first-line psychopharmacology interventions for mood and anxiety disorders, they may feel that they have limited interventions to offer patients with HIV and concomitant psychiatric disorders.

ASSESSMENT OF THE CURRENT STATE

As with any new service proposal, it may be instructive to query how the HIV physicians are presently managing psychiatric comorbidity when they feel the need for a psychiatric consultation. Are they referring patients to the university psychiatry clinic, private practice psychiatrists, and/or community mental health centers? What has been their experience with the critical areas of patient access, usefulness/promptness of communication, opportunities for co-management, and sharing of clinical data? Often, these areas are rated as suboptimal if not frankly deficient. Be clear in communicating to primary HIV physicians how an embedded service will address these concerns.

The first thing to do is to ask them what they find most difficult in the care of their patients and how they feel you can be of help to them. Show them your own mastery of the HIV psychiatry literature, including comorbid psychiatric illness manifestations common in this population (e.g., neurocognitive disorders, mood disorders, substance use disorders) as well as the effects of these psychiatric illness on other aspects of medical care (e.g., nonadherence, suboptimal clinical attendance, more complicated clinical course following untreated psychiatric illness, more secondary complications of HIV due to continued high-risk behavior). Patients cared for with an integrated approach benefit from a clinician who is current in the evolving state of the art of psychiatric care for HIV patients (Freudenreich et al., 2010).

ESTABLISHING EXPECTATIONS AND ROLES

Explain how you envision yourself working in an HIV clinic. Many other physicians have common misconceptions of how psychiatrists work with other physicians. Emphasize the operations of the psychiatry consultant model, including common charting (i.e., no "secret psychiatry notes"), regular discussions with the other physicians, access to "curb-siding" for informal case-specific consultation, discussions regarding psychiatric medication issues, and other informal interactions. Show how you are willing to discuss cases and how psychiatric treatment may help patients be more adherent to their clinical appointments and care of their HIV illness. A compelling study (Mugavero et al., 2014) found that nonadherence to HIV clinic appointments is an independent predictor of all-cause mortality in persons with HIV. It may be useful for the HIV psychiatrist, in addition to maintaining currency in psychosomatic medicine continuing medical education (CME), to complete CME in the medical management of HIV and hepatitis C (HCV)-co-infected persons so as to have more knowledge of these treatments.

Once you have initial interest from your own department and the HIV clinical leadership, it may be best to next meet with the whole cohort of HIV physicians, nurse practitioners, and other clinicians. Set up the meeting at a time that is regularly scheduled for meetings with HIV clinic faculty and subsequently plan future meetings with full staff. At the first meeting, introduce yourself and get to know each HIV clinician by name. Explain what you are trying to set up and how you see this collaboration as making their jobs easier. Many HIV clinicians are facing many administrative and clinical care burdens and may feel like they are "in over their heads" managing psychiatric illness in a primary care model. Many have had the experience of having psychiatric services either completely unavailable or difficult to access. It is often noted that many HIV physicians have had the experience of having scant (if any) direct communication from consultant psychiatrists when their patients are in fact seen for consults. Explain how the embedded model directly addresses several of these access and boundary issues.

PLANNING OPERATIONAL DETAILS

In detail, discuss the following operational details. Emphasize how a daily or weekly ongoing psychiatric presence in their clinic results in regular availability for ambulatory consultations—an integrated co-located model of care. To ensure adequate access, a minimum schedule of at least one morning or afternoon each week is needed, with increased time allotments if supported by clinical demand. Depending on local scheduling procedures, you may ask the clinicians to call you to schedule patients with you; in the process of referral, encourage face-to-face discussion of the exact clinical concern of the referring physician. Establish an expectation of the "clear consult question" so as to focus your inquiries.

Early on in the interdepartmental negotiations on the clinic structure, be sure that some insurance and billing matters that are specific to psychiatric services delivery are settled. The usual billing model, wherein the "host" clinic bills insurers for services provided by the embedded psychiatrist, needs to be agreed upon. To make this work smoothly, the HIV clinic billers and coders may need help in mastering specific psychiatry procedure codes and psychiatric illness (usually DSM-5 or ICD-10-CM) diagnosis codes. The psychiatry department billing personnel may need to prepare a tutorial to assist the HIV clinic billers in adequately mastering psychiatric billing. If there is a problem with "mental health carve-outs" to pay for psychiatric services, it is best to handle this challenge preemptively. The clinic coders will need to ascertain the insurance status of all patients and to bill accordingly.

Once the clinical business model has been agreed to by both departments, a schedule template needs to be discussed. If practical within the business plan, leave time for doing a minimum of 90-minute first evaluations and 30- to 45-minute follow-ups. The need for time with patients has been of concern to primary care physicians (Baron, 1985; Byyny, 2016) as well as HIV clinicians and has been encroached on by technological advances. Electronic medical records (EMR) and e-prescribing have made great improvements in care coordination and teaching, but their implementation has not always addressed clinical needs and concerns and at times interferes with doctor–patient communication and can lead to both patient and physician dissatisfaction (Byyny, 2016; Linzer et al., 2009). While pressures of time and productivity may be of concern, developing a consensus around the minimum time needed for the use of a biopsychosocial approach to psychiatric consultation is essential for providing adequate care for persons with complex multimorbid medical and psychiatric disorders. Having adequate time for establishment of rapport, clinical history-taking, and full engagement in a collaborative approach to care can make the difference between attaining viral suppression and preventing illness progression, and mortality (Grimes et al., 2016; Mugavero et al., 2014).

PATIENT URGENCY AND ACUITY

Be clear from the beginning that the embedded clinic model is not designed primarily for crisis management and emergency drop-ins. At most, a very limited amount of short-notice drop-in cases should be allowed. A well-run clinic will not have much "extra time" built into the schedule for crisis management, which by nature is disruptive and time consuming. The message needs to be clear that suicidal, homicidal, and disorganized patients must go to the emergency department (ED) and not be expedited into the embedded clinic service. Depending on your clinical duties (e.g., if you also work on the psychosomatic medicine service at your medical center) you may see the crisis patient there anyway. Have a clear system in place for this, including methods of contacting law enforcement to contain a patient, procedures for obtaining or writing a psychiatric commitment order, security personnel to escort the crisis patient to the ED, and a direct communication to the psychiatry ED/psychosomatic medicine service (depending on your institution's organization), and a method by which the HIV clinic can monitor crisis/ED patients for details regarding emergency disposition and eventual re-engagement in the clinic model.

It is advisable to have an arrangement with the clinic social worker, who may need to periodically interface with external sources of psychiatric care for HIV psychiatric patients. The social worker needs to clearly understand that there are some patients whose psychiatric illness is sufficiently complex that they cannot be safely managed in an embedded psychiatry clinic service. Some individuals may be in need of psychiatric hospitalization, partial hospitalization, intensive case management, and/or assertive community treatment interventions. Be able to discuss this matter and have the HIV clinic social worker empowered to interface with community mental health agencies in order to arrange for comprehensive services that provide patients with the level of psychiatric and other mental health care that they need.

UTILIZATION MANAGMENT

Once you are seeing patients in the HIV clinic, develop a panel of patients and follow their clinic utilization pattern to ensure that you are always promptly available to see new consultations. This will require clinic administration assistance and analysis. Your office needs to be located in the HIV clinic, close to the other physicians, so that patients see you functioning as a consultant to the other physicians. This physical proximity also facilitates communication with your physician colleagues.

It is highly desirable for the embedded psychiatrist to also follow his or her established patients on the medical/surgical floors if they are admitted to the medical center. This allows for continuity of care and some greater ease and for scheduling follow-up visits after discharge. This continuity model is facilitated if the embedded HIV psychiatrist is also a faculty member on the inpatient consultation service; otherwise, a systematic interface with the inpatient consultation-liaison team is needed. An administrative mechanism should be developed by which you are either alerted to admissions of your patients or can yourself quickly learn of admissions (some of these functions can be somewhat automated with sophisticated EMR systems by using "in-basket" functions).

RANGE OF CLINICAL SERVICES

In establishing an integrated service, it is valuable to discuss with HIV clinicians the range of clinical services you wish to provide. In addition to initial patient consultations, brief psychotherapy, couple therapy, family therapy, and psychotropic medication management, consider adding other clinical interventions, such as an HIV support group. A support group can provide a way for you to provide psychoeducation as well as support for patients. The model usually works well, and is accepted readily by patients and clinicians alike. You will need a private space for seeing from 8 to 20 persons on a once-a-week basis. You can ask a social worker or psychologist to co-lead the group with you. This is a good way to develop a working relationship with the other mental health clinicians on the treatment team. Depending on the insurer, there may be specific administrative matters pertinent to billing for group therapy in this type of model.

Once the clinic is up and running, it is desirable to continue to have ongoing meetings with the HIV clinicians. Meet at least once a week with the HIV clinicians in their own professional staff meeting. Discuss mutual patients and their management from your various perspectives. Develop interdisciplinary treatment plans for especially complex patients. See if there is any interest in having clinical case conferences together; one useful model is the primary clinician and the psychiatrist presenting the same case from different points of view.

Depending on the level of development of the specialty services of the clinic, the clinic may have established an HIV prenatal program (such a program may in some institutions be part of a high-risk obstetrics clinic). See if you can be a part of that program for management of pregnancy/peripartum/postpartum psychiatric illness in HIV patients. A biopsychosocial approach to care in women who are pregnant can prevent perinatal HIV transmission and improve adherence to HIV and obstetrical care.

If there are adequate local clinical resources, consider having substance abuse counselors incorporated into the clinic structure. In clinics with access to addiction psychiatry, an expansion of clinical services to include therapy with buprenorphine and other psychopharmacological management of substance abuse (perhaps for only selected patients) may be worth developing (Weiss et al., 2011; Willenbring, 2005).

Establish a good working relationship with the clinical pharmacist and engage in regular discussions on medication profiling, drug–drug interactions, drug side effect monitoring/surveillance, and laboratory monitoring (e.g., serum drug levels, metabolic parameters, renal and hepatic monitoring) for patients treated with psychopharmacological treatments, especially those patients with complex systemic medication regimens.

ACADEMIC PRODUCTIVITY OPPORTUNITIES

Once you are established in the clinical operation of the HIV clinic, try to branch out into clinical research specific to HIV psychiatry. Consider working with the HIV clinicians on research projects such as prevalence of psychological distress, anxiety, and/or depression in HIV patients. Formal research protocols will require local IRB approval.

Development of joint meetings with HIV clinicians can be highly productive and lead to not only better communication but also improvement in patient care and collaborative research. Development of a regular case conference format can lead to increased collegiality and morale as well as better patient care.

Consider other research ideas if you and your colleagues are interested. Examples to consider include outcomes research on medication adherence, CD4 counts and viral load, and HIV neurocognitive disorder screening and management. Consider research projects of specific interest to other clinicians, such as pharmacists, who may have an interest in drug–drug interactions, medication side effects, and therapeutic monitoring.

Once established in the HIV clinic, consider developing an interface with the dementia clinical and research group at your medical center. In addition, consider branching out to interface with the pain medicine service. An important area of clinical overlap is between the HIV clinic and the hepatology clinic, in that many HIV patients have comorbid HCV, which needs specific psychiatric symptom monitoring (often with depression rating instruments) throughout treatment. Persons with HIV/HCV co-infection can be monitored closely throughout the period of HCV treatment with surveillance for medication-associated psychiatric side effects. Such surveillance can lead to low threshold intervention with antidepressants and/or evidence-based psychotherapy, consistent with the emerging literature (Sarkar and Schaefer, 2014).

Modern models of care routinely utilize standardized psychometric instruments for both screening and post-intervention symptoms quantification. There are many examples of these, but consider routine use of illness distress indices, the Hospital and Anxiety Depression Score (HADS), Distress Thermometer, Beck Depression Inventory, Zung Depression Inventory, Hamilton Rating Scale for Depression, Hamilton Depression Scale for Anxiety, and Montreal Cognitive Assessment (MoCA). Once you are accustomed to using these routinely, incorporate these numerical values in your EMR note in a searchable area on the EMR.

EDUCATIONAL, TRAINING, AND TECHNOLOGY OPPORTUNITIES

An integrated care model provides an ideal setting for HIV education for medical students, residents in internal medicine and psychiatry, fellows in psychosomatic medicine and infectious disease, and other trainees. With a biopsychosocial approach that provides a model for compassionate and multidimensional care, the program can provide superb training for many clinician disciplines. A 4-year curriculum for HIV/AIDS psychiatry residency training has been described and uses a biopsychosocial approach and can be integrated into an ambulatory setting (Cohen and Forstein, 2012).

Once your clinic is operating efficiently with a predictable clinic census, have a low threshold for including psychiatry residents/fellows, medical students, and psychology students/interns and postdoctoral fellows in your clinic and consider creating an elective or rotation in HIV psychiatry. The trainees can have some independent time with patients, with faculty oversight and supervision. Consider offering clinical experience to other health professional student groups needing to know psychiatric illness management as part of their own training experience. See Chapter 13 of this textbook for a detailed discussion of training in HIV psychiatry.

Depending on institutional priorities, HIV psychiatry can be a good area for exploration of information technology (IT) initiatives. Telemedicine consultation for psychiatry in primary care has been well established for several years, and is generally well accepted by patients and referring clinicians. Expertise in HIV psychiatry could be exported to other clinics via the telepsychiatry model, particularly to rural primary care clinics without local access to psychosomatic medicine psychiatry. Commitment to this model would require separate contractual and administrative arrangements with the external clinics receiving services.

In clinics with a sophisticated EMR system with advanced decisional support technology, HIV psychiatry is a good example of a clinical service where some clinical demand for services can be adequately met by electronic consultations ("e-consults"): the referring physician composes a case vignette of the patient and that patient's clinical database, and then poses a consult question for the psychiatrist to answer, based on the available data, without the psychiatrist actually seeing or engaging the patient directly. Modern EMR systems can capture the clinical activity in e-consults and offer some amount of compensation for each e-consult seen and responded to. The business aspects of the e-consult model may need separate negotiation; the medical center may be interested in promoting e-consults in general and thus may offer to subsidize this activity separately.

Be willing to interface with other areas of the medical center and medical school that have clinical relationships with your HIV clinic. At many institutions, the HIV clinic may be one of only a few (perhaps the only one) where an embedded psychiatry service is operating. In the current environment, there is a trend toward developing embedded psychiatry services within other medical specialty areas as well in general primary care clinics. A successful navigation of the development of an HIV psychiatric clinical model may therefore be generalized to other departments with similarly complex patients in need of interdisciplinary or multispecialty care.

Offer to present at department grand rounds on the basis of your work in HIV psychiatry. The clinical specifics of HIV psychiatry are sufficiently esoteric and relevant to be regarded as a "sub-subspecialty" of psychosomatic medicine, so that a summary of the current clinical activity and research developments in the field of HIV psychiatry should be of interest to both psychiatry and internal medicine departments.

Once your clinic has established a clinical routine, be sure to closely track important administrative variables. Depending on the sophistication of your institution's EMR system, there may be ready access to data on number of new versus follow-up visits, no-show rates, waiting list time for appointments, case mix/diagnosis data, and the like. Especially if clinical utilization is robust and wait times for service are considerable, it may be necessary to periodically renegotiate the percent weekly effort by the psychiatry consultant in the clinic in order to provide more clinical coverage for consultation. Such modifications of the time commitment must be mutually agreeable between departments.

CONCLUSION

The operation of an embedded psychiatry service in an HIV clinic offers an opportunity for creative, comprehensive ongoing care. Such models need to be operated in such a manner that they continuously meet the clinical service and fiscal needs and expectations of participating departments. These models facilitate the development of collaborative opportunities in clinical care, training, and clinically focused research. From the beginning, thoughtful planning of clinical collaborations is recommended to make a complex system work in the best interests of patients and clinicians.

REFERENCES

Adams J, Pollard R, Sikkena K (2011). Feasibility of integrated depression care in an HIV clinic. *Psychiatr Serv* 62:804.

Baron RJ (1985). An introduction to medical phenomenology: I can't hear you while I'm listening. *Ann Intern Med* 103:606–611.

Bottonari K, Stepleman L (2010). Improving access to mental health services via a clinic-wide mental health intervention in a Southeastern US infectious disease clinic. *AIDS Care* 22:133–136.

Byyny RL (2016). Time matters in caring for patients—twenty minutes isn't enough. *Pharos* 79:2–8.

Cohen MA, Forstein M (2012). A biopsychosocial approach to HIV/AIDS education for psychiatry residents. *Acad Psychiatry* 364:479–486.

Coleman S, Blashill A, Gandhi R, Safren S, Freudenreich O (2012). Impact of integrated and measurement-based depression care: clinical experience in an HIV clinic. *Psychosomatics* 53:51–57.

Freudenreich O, Goforth H, Cozza K, Mimiaga M, Safren S, Bachmann G, Cohen M (2010). Psychiatric treatment of persons with HIV/AIDS: an HIV-psychiatry consensus survey of current practices. *Psychosomatics* 51:480–488.

Grimes RM, Hallmark CJ, Watkins KL, Agarwal S, McNeese ML (2016). Re-engagement in HIV care: a clinical and public health priority. *J AIDS Clin Res* 7(2):543.

Hoang T, Goetz M, Yano E, et al. (2009). The impact of integrated HIV care on patient health outcomes. *Med Care* 47;560–567.

Linzer M, Baier Manwell L, et al.; for the MEMO (Minimizing Error, Maximizing Outcome) Investigators (2009). Working conditions in primary care: physician reactions and care quality. *Ann Intern Med* 151:28–36.

Mugavero MJ, Westfall AO, Cole SR, et al. (2014). Beyond core indicators of retention in HIV care: missed clinic visits are independently associated with all-cause mortality. *Clin Infect Dis* 59:1471–1479.

Olagunju A, Ogundipe O, Erinfolami A, Akinbode A, Adeyemi J (2013). Toward the integration of comprehensive mental health service in HIV care: an assessment of psychiatric morbidity among HIV-positive individuals in sub-Saharan Africa. *AIDS Care* 25:1193–1198.

Primeau M, Avelleneda V, Musselman D, St. Jean G, Illa L (2013). Treatment of depression in individuals living with HIV/AIDS. *Psychosomatics* 54:336–344.

Pyne J, Fortney J, Curran G, et al. (2011). Effectiveness of collaborative care for depression in human immunodeficiency virus clinics. *Arch Intern Med* 171:23–31.

Sarkar S, Schaefer M (2014). Antidepressant pretreatment for the prevention of interferon alfa-associated depression: a systematic review and meta-analysis. *Psychosomatics* 55:221–234.

Sloan E (2014). Retention in psychiatric treatment in a Canadian sample of HIV-positive women. *AIDS Care* 26:927–930.

Soto T, Bell J, Pillen M, for the HIV/AIDS Treatment Adherence, Health Outcomes, and Cost Study Group (2004). Literature on integrated HIV care: a review. *AIDS Care* 16:S43–S55.

Weiss L, Netherland J, Egan J, Flanagan T, Fiellin D, Finkelstein R, Altice F, for the BHIVES Collaborative (2011). Integration of buprenorphine/naloxone treatment into HIV clinical care: lessons from the BHIVES Collaborative. *J Acquir Defic Syndr* 56:S68–S75.

Willenbring M (2005). Integrating care for patients with infectious, psychiatric, and substance use disorders: concepts and approaches. *AIDS* 19:S227–S237.

9.

SOCIOCULTURAL FACTORS INFLUENCING THE TRANSMISSION OF HIV/AIDS IN THE UNITED STATES

AIDS AND THE NATION'S PRISONS

Robert E. Fullilove

This chapter examines the sociocultural factors that influence the transmission of HIV as well as the risk factors that create enduring risk of exposure to HIV in poor communities in the United States. A guiding assumption in this analysis is that persons at elevated risk for HIV infection are members of marginalized groups. Specifically, persons at substantial risk for HIV are part of marginalized social networks who reside in communities that are marginalized by poverty, racism, residential segregation, and high rates of engagement with the criminal justice system (Golembeski and Fullilove, 2005; Pellowski et al., 2013; Wilson et al., 2014).

The U.S. Public Health Service has, since the 1980s, placed specific emphasis on understanding and eliminating such "health disparities" as HIV/AIDS. *Health disparities* are defined as "preventable differences in the burden of disease, injury, violence, or opportunities to achieve optimal health that are experienced by socially disadvantaged populations" (Centers for Disease Control and Prevention [CDC], 2013a, p. 9). The identification of HIV/AIDS as a significant health disparity in the United States reflects the substantial overrepresentation of Hispanics/Latinos and blacks/African Americans among persons infected with HIV as well as their underrepresentation among persons benefitting from HIV treatments. Specifically, in comparison with whites, whose 2008 rate of HIV infection was 9.2 per 100,000, the infection rates among and Hispanic/Latinos (31.1/100,000) and black/African Americans (86/100,000) were, respectively, three times and nine times the rates observed among whites (CDC, 2013a). As stated in a CDC report:

Although the relative difference in HIV infection diagnoses between whites and blacks/African Americans decreased from 2008 to 2010, all racial/ethnic minorities, except Asians, continue to experience higher rates of HIV diagnoses than whites. These differences might reflect HIV incidence, testing patterns, or both. Compared with whites, lower percentages of blacks/African Americans were prescribed ART and lower percentages of both blacks/African Americans and Hispanics/ Latinos had suppressed viral loads. (CDC, 2013b, p. 116)

The focus on health disparities as an explanatory framework for conducting HIV/AIDS research also stems from the recognition that *social determinants*—specifically social, economic, political, and cultural influences—are major, predominant factors influencing patterns of health and disease. As confirmed by the CDC, "the socioeconomic conditions of the places where persons live and work have an even more substantial influence on health than personal socioeconomic position" (CDC, 2013a, p. 9). An exploration of these influences on the risk for HIV infection requires examining both individual risk factors as well as key elements of the social and physical environment. Accordingly, in the sections that follow, particular attention will be paid to the unique impact that social disadvantage in general and that the criminal justice systems in the United States in particular have on the conditions that drive the HIV/AIDS epidemic in this country.

SOCIAL DISADVANTAGE, CORRECTIONAL FACILITIES, AND HIV

Poverty and social disadvantage are well recognized contributors to HIV seroprevalence in the United States and worldwide. As Pellowski and colleagues state:

The greatest overall illness burden across all diseases occurs at the lowest levels of SES [socioeconomic status]. These health disparities are exaggerated in people living with HIV who are primarily concentrated in the lowest SES strata, among whom, racial and ethnic minorities are overrepresented. . . . HIV infection is so closely enmeshed in conditions of poverty that it is indeed a pandemic of the poor. (Pellowski et al., 2013, p. 205)

Of all the scourges of poverty in the United States, the risk of incarceration is perhaps the most impactful in terms of its influence on health and general well-being (Wacquant, 2000; Western and Pettit, 2010). The United States represents 5% of the world's population but incarcerates 25% of all the persons in the world who are imprisoned in a correctional facility. Residents of poor minority communities are overrepresented in these settings. More than two-thirds of those in state and federal prison facilities are black or Hispanic/Latino. In 2013, 2.2 million people were in U.S. prisons and jails, a 500% increase in in the incarcerated population in the nation during the 1970s. More than half of those serving sentences in federal prisons are there for drug-related convictions, and there has been a 10-fold increase in the number of persons imprisoned in state facilities for drug-related convictions since the 1970s, the majority being black or Hispanic/Latino (Justice Reinvestment Initiative, 2013; The Sentencing Project, 2016).

The large number of persons in prison for drug-related offenses, particularly persons from poor communities of color, contributes significantly to the fact that U.S. prisons have rates of HIV infection that are, historically, significantly higher than those reported for the U.S. general population. In 1999, for example, confirmed AIDS cases in prison were 4.8 times the rates observed in the U.S. general population that year, with the highest rates reported among black/African American incarcerated persons (Maruschak, 2015). The War on Drugs is largely responsible for these trends because, from its outset, it targeted one of the groups at highest risk for HIV infection: injection drug users (Fullilove, 2006, 2011).

Although often overlooked in discussions of the impact of prisons on both individuals and their communities, jails—places where individuals who have been arrested are housed before arraignment, trial, or being set free or sent to prison—are a very significant segment of the criminal justice system as well as a major setting for persons living with HIV/AIDS. Jails merit attention because of the sheer number of individuals who are involved. More than 731,000 persons were in jails on any given day in 2013 in the United States, and annually, jails held almost 12 million persons per year for much of the period between 2005 and 2013 (Subramanian et al., 2015). Although the majority of those who are arrested will not go to prison—approximately 62% of those in jail will not be convicted—the lasting impact of an arrest can be significant. Subramanian and colleagues note:

> Being detained (in jail) is often the beginning of a journey through the criminal justice system that can take many wrong turns. Just a few days in jail can increase the likelihood of a sentence of incarceration and the harshness of that sentence, reduce economic viability, promote future criminal behavior, and worsen the health of those who enter—making jail a gateway to deeper and more lasting involvement in the criminal justice system at considerable costs to the people involved and to society at large. (Subramanian et al., 2015, p. 5)

Jails have particular significance because of the large numbers of individuals they house who are living with an HIV infection (Begier et al., 2010; Brewer et al., 2014; Meyer et al., 2014; Spaulding et al., 2009; Vagenas et al., 2016). Estimates published in 2009 reported that one out of every seven persons living with HIV in the United States passed through a correctional facility in 2006, with the majority of those doing time in a local jail (Spaulding et al., 2009). The authors concluded that, although HIV-infected persons in such facilities are a declining share of the epidemic each year,

> the number of persons with HIV/AIDS leaving correctional facilities remains virtually identical. Jails and prisons continue to be potent targets for public health interventions. The fluid nature of incarcerated populations ensures that effective interventions will be felt not only in correctional facilities but also in the communities to which releases will return. (Spaulding et al., 2009, p. 1).

This cycle—community, correctional facility, community again—had a dramatic impact on injecting drug users. Significantly, the practice of sharing injection drug equipment, a major risk factor for HIV infection, became popular as a tactic to avoid arrest for the felony possession of syringes without a prescription during the 1970s (Bluthenthal et al., 1999). This fact suggests that, long before 1981, the year that is commonly recognized as the beginning of the AIDS pandemic, mass incarceration was contributing to seeding the epidemic in the communities from which many drug users were arrested and to which many returned upon release. Specifically, the cycle—arrest, incarceration, release from prison, return to the community, and then the return to prison as a recidivist—describes an effective mechanism for both seeding and maintaining pools of HIV infection in both correctional facilities and the communities to which individuals have returned since the 1970s, when HIV was unrecognized but was being transmitted by infected, asymptomatic individuals (Fullilove, 2006, 2011).

A history of incarceration produces significant barriers for those living with HIV that include risk for homelessness, chronic unemployment, and a general lack of access to healthcare re-entry to the community (Iroh et al., 2015; Kulkarni et al., 2010; Springer et al., 2004; Vagenas et al., 2016; Widman et al., 2014; Zelenev et al., 2013). Of particular concern is the health of HIV-infected men and women who start a regime of medication while incarcerated but who may struggle to enter and/or remain in care when released to the community. In the 5-year period right after the introduction of antiretroviral therapy (ART) in 1996, approximately two-thirds of HIV-infected persons in prison were diagnosed and introduced to treatment for the first time during the course of their incarceration. A critical component of their care was and continues to be engagement in treatment upon release. But, as Springer and colleagues note, "despite existing prison-release programs that are predicated on making appointments for patients and providing for their short-term needs, important biological outcomes associated with morbidity and mortality are not attained for those who are reincarcerated" (Springer et al., 2004, p. 1759).

A systematic literature review, conducted by Iroh and colleagues (2015), examining the diagnosis, treatment, and care cascade of incarcerated persons—in which particular attention was paid to the number of HIV-infected, formerly incarcerated persons who are either not in care or who drop out of HIV care—revealed that blacks and Hispanics were less likely to fill a first post-incarceration prescription for HIV medications within 10 to 30 days than were non-Hispanic whites. The authors conclude, "We have summarized HIV testing, engagement in care, and treatment at 3 stages—before, during, and after incarceration—and have found that the care cascade is dynamic, with large increases during and even larger declines after incarceration" (Iroh et al., 2015, p. e14). Failure to maintain appropriate levels of adherence to a medication regimen poses substantial risk for the transmission of drug-resistant strains of HIV to others in the community. Failure to utilize the potential that correctional facilities have to diagnose, treat, and maintain appropriate levels of adherence among those incarcerated persons who are living with HIV represents a major failure of HIV prevention and treatment policies in the United States, particularly given the extensive traffic back and forth between correctional facilities and the community (Iroh et al., 2015; Kulkarni et al., 2010; Springer et al., 2004; Vagenas et al., 2016; Widman et al., 2014; Zelenev et al., 2013).

Failure to more effectively prevent and treat HIV/AIDS in prison is particularly compelling, given the high rates of recidivism that exist in the United States. According to a 2014 study of recidivism among those released from state prisons, approximately 77% of those released were arrested within 5 years of their return to the community (Durose et al., 2014). The significance of this finding cannot be overemphasized. Many individuals currently in prison, as well as those who report a history of incarceration, may have had multiple stays in a correctional facility (Subramaniam et al., 2015), and each additional encounter with the criminal justice system may add to the challenge of providing sustained and effective HIV care both in correctional facilities as well as the in the community.

There is ample reason to suspect that persons who are sent back to prison with poorly controlled HIV disease may have had difficulty connecting to care specifically as a result of their status as formerly incarcerated persons (Frank et al., 2014; Marlow et al., 2010; Meyer et al., 2014; Springer et al., 2004; Vagenas et al., 2016). Findings from this series of research studies suggest that inadequate healthcare access for those who return to the community contributes to poor HIV healthcare outcomes. Such outcomes are experienced by those who have been released from prison for the first time as well as by those with a history of multiple incarcerations. Many persons who have a history of incarceration also report a lack of health insurance pre- and post-incarceration, failure to have an HIV healthcare provider, and a history of homelessness, factors that account in part for a failure to transition successfully to healthcare post-release (Vagenas et al., 2016). Additional complicating factors include a history of drug use, being a black man who has sex with men (Vagenas et al., 2016), or being a woman of color with a history of drug use (Meyer et al., 2014). Common to all the research cited here is the finding that currently and formerly incarcerated persons are a greatest risk for poor treatment outcomes for HIV disease, because they represent one of the most marginalized populations in the United States and they are often confronting comorbid conditions that significantly complicate their healthcare.

Managing the HIV/AIDS epidemic requires more than a focus on the problems and challenges associated with individual members of marginalized communities (previously further stigmatized with the use of the descriptor "risk groups"). Mass incarceration in the United States is also a community burden that has a dramatic, negative impact on the neighborhoods whose residents comprise a significant proportion of the incarcerated population (Abramovitz and Albrecht, 2013; Fullilove, 2011). As Abramovitz and Albrecht note, "prisoners and their families experience a tremendous resource loss (Hairston, 2001). Incarceration removes people from family, work, and community roles (Clear and Rose, 1999); creates emotional and financial voids in households that others must fill; and disrupts individual functioning, family solidarity, and overall community efficacy or effectiveness" (Abramovitz and Albrecht, 2013, p. 690). The removal of significant numbers of males from community life is associated with elevated levels of youth assault rates (Kruger et al., 2013). High levels of incarceration are also associated with increased risk of psychiatric morbidity among non-incarcerated residents of neighborhoods with high rates of incarceration (Hatzenbuehler et al., 2015).

Such community-level losses and negative impacts have been hypothesized to have a direct and significant impact on rates of HIV infection in the community (Fullilove, 2006, 2011; Johnson and Raphael, 2009). The loss of adult men to prison may change the manner in which sexual partnerships and mating rituals are conducted, increasing the risk of sexual transmission of HIV because exclusive, monogamous sexual relationships are unlikely to be sustained. Concurrent sexual partnerships in which, for example, the incarceration of one partner leads to the formation of a sexual relationship with another partner during the period incarceration have been associated with increased risk for HIV (Adimora et al., 2004). The inability of a formerly incarcerated person to find employment or stable housing may expose residents of the communities to which they are returned to a relapse in criminal behavior (Fagan et al., 2003) as well as relapses in drug use and unprotected sexual behavior (Knudsen et al., 2014; Widman et al., 2014).

Perhaps the most significant impact of this loss of adults to the community is in the weakening of the ability of community members to organize and sustain effective interventions to prevent disease and promote health. In essence, the "glue" that holds community life together is weakened with the loss of so many adults to prison, and the capacity to mount effective HIV prevention campaigns is likely to have been significantly weakened as well (Fullilove, 2011).

The presence of individuals in the community who are objects of stigma also poses a significant challenge to efforts at organizing communities to manage the risk of HIV/AIDS. Those most affected by HIV/AIDS—black and Hispanic/Latino men who have sex with men, individuals engaging in drug use, persons who are homeless, persons who live with mental illness, and individuals who were incarcerated—are often shunned or ignored. The social disadvantage of being formerly incarcerated only adds to the burdens created by being a member of a highly stigmatized group and serves to increase the risks of poor treatment outcomes for HIV disease (Knudsen et al., 2014; Meyer et al., 2014; Springer et al., 2004; Vagenas et al., 2016; Widman et al., 2013). Organizing community-wide efforts to support their struggles is, at best, a daunting task with a poor history of success in the United States.

HIV/AIDS is also just one of many social, political, and public health challenges facing poor, disadvantages communities. Accordingly, Wallace (1988) has described HIV/AIDS as a "synergy of plagues," to underscore how much HIV/AIDS is a unique product of those accumulated disadvantages. In recent years, the term *syndemic* has increasingly been used as a theoretical framework for explaining high rates of HIV/AIDS in marginalized populations, particularly among black and Latino men. The term is appropriate because, by definition, "syndemics include epidemics both of disease and the social conditions that contribute to the proliferation of disease" (Wilson et al., 2014, p. 985). Common to both of these formulations is the notion that HIV/AIDS interacts with social, behavioral, and structural factors to create a pattern of sustained devastation that has been visited upon marginalized persons and marginalized communities (Wilson et al., 2014). The implication is that, with a syndemic (or with a synergy of plagues), a varied set of policies, programs, interventions, and research strategies must be employed to confront the challenge of an epidemic that has endured worldwide for decades.

THE IMPORTANCE OF ADDRESSING MASS INCARCERATION AS AN EFFECTIVE RESPONSE TO HIV/AIDS

Perhaps the most promising element in confronting the myriad problems associated with mass incarceration is that changes in the social, economic, and political status of currently and formerly incarcerated persons can be improved with changes in the policies and regulations that contribute so significantly to their marginalization. Reforming the regulatory and political status of this group can dramatically improve the condition of both individuals as well as the communities that are significantly impacted by mass incarceration. The second-class status of currently and formerly incarcerated persons was created by policies that restrict them from exercising the right to vote and from having access to housing, educational opportunities, a full range of social services (e.g., access to healthcare) and, most importantly, employment (Alexander, 2010). Policy changes and the redrafting of key regulations that drive second-class status are more easily accomplished within the framework of U.S. democracy than, for example, through efforts to change condom use and safe sex behaviors of all sexually active persons. The long duration of the HIV/AIDS pandemic makes it clear that interventions designed to eliminate individual HIV risk behavior have not been successful in halting the spread of the virus. Working to alter regulatory policies and practices that marginalize formerly incarcerated individuals holds great promise for improving efforts to combat the scourge of HIV/AIDS.

Such changes would work synergistically with other recent policy initiatives. The Affordable Care Act, passed in 2010, for example, has extensive provisions to improve access to healthcare for formerly incarcerated persons as well as for a significant portion of the U.S. population who have historically been without health insurance (Kaiser Family Foundation, 2015). National levels of concern about the economic costs of incarceration have led to the reduction of prison populations in states such as New York (Carson, 2015), and alternatives to incarceration have been proposed that would dramatically ease the burdens on communities that have large numbers of incarcerated residents (Justice Reinvestment Initiative, 2013; Pew Center on the States, 2009). The removal of legislative barriers that limit the rights of incarcerated persons and their access to healthcare and employment will likely have benefits that go far beyond the potential impact such changes will have on HIV/AIDS. According to the Justice Reinvestment Initiative, "in nearly every state of the country, a political premium has developed in favor of containing correctional costs, scrutinizing proposals for further growth, and considering strategies to downsize correctional populations and budgets that were out of the question years ago" (Justice Reinvestment Initiative, 2013, p. 3). The voices of AIDS activists, scientists, healthcare workers, and HIV/AIDS researchers have the potential to add substantial weight to the drafting of proposals and initiatives to reduce the impact of mass incarceration. In the face of an epidemic that continues to wreak significant havoc in communities worldwide, joining this struggle against mass incarceration is both strategic, full of promise, and an idea whose time has come.

REFERENCES

Abramovitz M, Albrecht J (2013). The Community Loss Index: a new social indicator. *Soc Serv Rev* 37(4):677–724. www.hunter.cuny.edu/socwork/faculty/community_loss_paper_ssr.pdf. Accessed May 14, 2016.

Adimora AA, Schoenbach VJ, Martinson F, Donaldson KH, Stancil TR, Fullilove RE. (2004). Concurrent sexual partnerships among African Americans in the rural south. *Ann Epidemiol* 14:155–160.

Alexander M (2010). *The New Jim Crow: Mass Incarceration in the Age of Colorblindness*. New York: The New Press

Begier EM, Bennani Y, Forgione L, et al. (2010). Undiagnosed HIV infection among New York City jail entrants, 2006: results of a blinded serosurvey. *J Acquir Immune Defic Syndr* 54:93–101.

Bluthenthal RN, Lorvick J, Kral AH, Erringer EA, Kahn JG (1999). Collateral damage in the war on drugs: HIV risk behaviors among injection drug users. *Int J Drug Policy* 10:25–38.

Brewer RA, Magnus M, Kuo I, Wang L, Liu TY, Mayer KH (2014). The high prevalence of incarceration history among black men who have sex with men in the United States: associations and implications. *Am J Public Health* 104:448–454.

Carson EA (2015). *Prisoners in 2014*. U.S. Department of Justice, Bureau of Justice Statistics. http://www.bjs.gov/index.cfm?ty=pbdetail&iid=5387. Accessed May 17, 2016.

Centers for Disease Control and Prevention (CDC) (2013a). CDC Health disparities and inequalities report- United States, 2013. *MMWR Morb Mortal Wkly Rep* 62:3–5.

Centers for Diseases Control and Prevention (CDC) (2013b). HIV infection—United States, 2008 and 2010. *MMWR Morb Mortal Wkly Rep* 62:112–119.

Clear TR, Rose DR (1999). When neighbors go to jail: impact on attitudes about formal and informal social control. National Institute of Justice. https://www.ncjrs.gov/.../fs000243.pdf. Accessed May 18, 2016.

Durose MR, Cooper AD, Snyder HN (2014). Recidivism of prisoners releases in 30 states in 2005: patterns from 2005–2010. U.S. Department of Justice, Bureau of Justice Statistics. www.bjs.gov/content/pub/pdf/rprts05p0510.pdf. Accessed May 17, 2016.

Fagan J, West V, Holland J (2003). Reciprocal effects of crime and incarceration in New York City neighborhoods. *Fordham Urban Law Journal* 30:1551–1602. http://papers.ssrn.com/sol3/papers.cfm?abstract_id=392120. Accessed May 15, 2016.

Frank JW, Wang EA, Nunez-Smith M, Lee H, Comfort M (2014) Discrimination based on criminal record and healthcare utilization among men recently released from prison: a descriptive study. *Health and Justice* 2 e1–e8

Fullilove RE (2006). African Americans, health disparities and HIV/AIDS. National Minority AIDS Council. https://www.prisonlegalnews.org/news/publications/nmac-report-on-hiv-among-minorities-condoms-in-prison-2006/. Accessed May 13, 2016.

Fullilove RE (2011). Mass incarceration in the United States and HIV/AIDS: cause and effect? *Ohio State Journal of Criminal Law* 9:353–361.

Golembeski C, Fullilove RE (2005). Criminal (in)justice in the city and its associated health consequences. *Am J Public Health* 95:1701–1706.

Hairston CF (2001). Prisoner and families: parenting issues during incarceration. Paper presented at the Prison to Home Conference, U.S. Department of Health and Human Services, Washington, DC, January 30–31.

Hatzenbuehler ML, Keyes K, Hamilton A, Uddin M, Galea S (2015). The collateral damage of mass incarceration: risk of psychiatric morbidity among nonincarcerated residents of high-incarceration neighborhoods. *Am J Public Health* 105:138–143.

Iroh P, Mayo H, Nijhawan AE (2015). The HIV care cascade before, during, and after incarceration: a systematic review and data synthesis. *Am J Public Health* 105:e5–e16.

Johnson RC, Raphael S (2009). The effects of male incarceration dynamics on acquired immune deficiency syndrome infection rates among African American women and men. *J Law Econ* 52:251–293.

Justice Reinvestment Initiative (2013). Ending mass incarceration: charting a new justice reinvestment. Bureau of Justice Assistance. https://www.aclu.org/ending-mass-incarceration-charting-new-justice-reinvestment. Accessed May 17, 2016.

Kaiser Family Foundation (2015) Explaining the 2015 open enrollment period. Fact sheet. http://kff.org/health-reform/issue-brief/explaining-the-2015-open-enrollment-period/. Accessed May 18, 2016.

Knudsen HK, Staton-Tindall M, Oser CB, Havens JR, Leukefeld CG (2014). Reducing risky relationships: a multisite randomized trial of a prison-based intervention for reducing HIV sexual risk behaviors among women with a history of drug use. *AIDS Care Psychol Sociomed Aspects AIDS/HIV* 26(9):1071–1079.

Kruger DJ, Aiyer SM, Caldwell CH, Zimmerman MA (2013). Local scarcity of adult men predicts youth assault rates. *J Community Psychol* 42:119–125.

Kulkarni SP, Baldwin S, Lightstone AS, Gelberg L, Diamant AL (2010). Is incarceration a contributor to health disparities? Access to care of formerly incarcerated adults. *J Community Health* 35:268–274.

Marlow E, White MC, Cheslea CA (2010). Barriers and facilitators: parolees' perceptions of community health care. *J Correctional Health Care* 16:17–26.

Maruschak LM (2015). HIV in prisons, 2001–2010. U.S. Department of Justice, Bureau of Justice Statistics. www.bjs.gov/content/pub/pdf/hivp10.pdf. Accessed May 16, 2016.

Meyer JP, Zelenev A, Wickersham JA, Williams CT, Teixeira PA, Altice FL (2014). Gender disparities in HIV treatment outcomes following release from jail: results from a multicenter study. *Am J Public Health* 104(3):434–441.

Pellowski JA, Kalichman SC, Matthews KA, Adler (2013). A pandemic of the poor: social disadvantage and the U.S. HIV epidemic. *Am Psychologist* 78:197–209.

Pew Center on the States (2009). One in 31: the long reach of American corrections. Washington, DC: The Pew Charitable Trusts. http://www.pewtrusts.org/en/research-and-analysis/reports/2009/03/02/one-in-31-the-long-reach-of-american-corrections. Accessed May 20, 2016.

Spaulding AC, Seals RM, Page MJ, Brzozowski AK, Rhodes W, Hammett TM (2009). HIV/AIDS among inmates of and releases from US correctional facilities, 2006: declining share of epidemic but persistent public health opportunity. *PLoS ONE* 4:e7558.

Springer SA, Pesanti E, Hodges J, Macura T, Doros G, Altice FL (2004). Effectiveness of antiretroviral therapy among HIV-infected prisoners: reincarceration and the lack of sustained benefit after release to the community. *Clin Infect Dis* 38:1754–1760.

Subramanian R, Delaney R, Roberts S, Fishman N, McGarry (2015). Incarceration's front door: the misuse of jails in America. Vera Institute of Justice. http://www.vera.org/pubs/special/incarcerations-front-door-misuse-jails-america. Accessed May 14, 2016.

The Sentencing Project (2016). Fact sheet: trends in US corrections. http://www.sentencingproject.org/issues/incarceration/. Accessed May 17, 2016.

Vagenas P, Zelenev A, Altice FL, et al. (2016). HIV-infected men who have sex with men before and after release from jail: the impact of age and race, results from a multi-site study. *AIDS Care Psychol Sociomed Aspects AIDS/HIV* 28(1):22–31.

Wacquant L (2000). Deadly symbiosis: when ghetto and prison meet and mesh. *Punishment and Society* 3:95–134.

Wallace R (1988). A synergism of plagues: "planned shrinkage," contagious housing destruction, and AIDS in the Bronx. *Environ Res* 47:1–33.

Western B, Pettit B (2010), Incarceration & social inequality. *Daedalus* 139:95–133.

Widman L, Noar SM, Golin CE, Willoughby JF, Crosby R (2014). Incarceration and unstable housing interact to predict sexual risk behaviours among African American STD clinic patients. *Int J STD AIDS* 25:348–354.

Wilson PA, Nanin J, Amesty S, Wallace S, Cherenack EM, Fullilove R (2014). Using syndemic theory to understand vulnerability to HIV infection among black and Latino men in New York City. *J Urban Health* 91:983–998.

Zelenev A, Marcus R, Kopelev A, et al. (2013). Patterns of homelessness and implications for HIV health after release from jail. *AIDS Behav* 17:S181–S194.

ADDITIONAL RESOURCES

Sites for Learning about Prison Reform

The Vera Institute of Justice http://www.vera.org/
The Sentencing Project http://www.sentencingproject.org/

Minorities and HIV/AIDS

The National Minority AIDS Council (NMAC) http://nmac.org/

Data on Prisons and Jails

U.S. Department of Justice, Bureau of Justice Statistics http://www.bjs.gov/

Information on Health Disparities

U.S. Department of Health and Human Services (HHS) http://minorityhealth.hhs.gov/npa/
National Institute on Minority Health and Health Disparities http://www.nimhd.nih.gov/

10.

HIV ADVOCACY

Simon Collins, Tim Horn, Loon Gangte, Emmanuel Trenado, and Vuyiseka Dubula

Seeing people get better on antiretroviral treatment is without a doubt the most extraordinary thing I have ever seen. It made me become an activist.　POLLY CLAYDEN, *HIV i-Base, London*

I don't know why I am an activist but I have to do it. I remember that HIV used to mean going to the cemetery four or five times a month. Now this is once every four or five years.　LOON GANGTE, *Delhi Network of HIV+ People*

Getting the science of HIV treatment to where it is today has been only half the battle. Ensuring all people living with HIV have equitable access to the information, care, and ancillary support they need to benefit from this science is the other half—and the activist work that keeps me going.　TIM HORN, *Treatment Action Group, New York City*

INTRODUCTION

It is important for this book on HIV psychiatry to include a chapter written by HIV activists. The chapter brings perspectives that are rooted in community responses to HIV, with a focus on peer support and treatment advocacy, to complement and inform the medical perspectives explored in the rest of the book. The year 2016 is critical for establishing the goal of universal access to antiretroviral therapy (ART). In 2015, the randomized START (Strategic Timing of Antiretroviral Treatment) and TEMPRANO studies, in line with World Health Organization (WHO) guidelines, provided the best evidence that ART is sufficiently safe and effective to provide clinical benefits for all people living with HIV, regardless of CD4 count (World Health Organization, 2015).

Community responses to the AIDS crisis have challenged traditional responses to medical systems and research. Through collective mobilization on local, national, and global levels, community HIV programs rooted in personal experiences have been strengthened. These responses include the involvement of persons with HIV at all levels of care, outlined in the Denver and Greater Involvement of People living with AIDS (GIPA) principles (Denver Principles, 1983; UNAIDS, 2007). Throughout this chapter, the role of advocacy in several countries is illustrated from the perspective of personal advocacy and political activism, a dual approach that was developed by activists working in the same organizations. In addition, persons with HIV and HIV advocates remain a central part of every level of care and treatment and of all facets of research and policy that affect their lives.

Examples include the following:

- Support (one to one, in groups, through print and online media) to help persons with HIV come to terms with new diagnoses and decisions relating to starting and changing treatment. This also involves navigating and utilizing systems of care and support.

- Involvement in designing and providing health services and community support in both rich and poor countries

- Involvement in networks to represent the broader HIV community, including community advisory boards for research studies and treatment guidelines, healthcare systems, and community-based organizations

- Advocacy to change policy on a local, national, and/or international level

COMMON ROOTS OF COMMUNITY RESPONSES: FROM THE 1980S TO TODAY

Each country has its own history of HIV responses that, if recorded, is often found in community rather than academic accounts. Documenting social and advocacy responses is essential not just to record the history but also to help inform future services.

Although the history of HIV responses is different in Taiwan, Thailand, Australia, Uganda, and other countries, there are direct and indirect links to early activism in the United States, where most of the important innovative approaches were first developed. The U.S. response not only led the way but changed community involvement in medicine, through actively challenging the existing structures for research, drug development, and regulatory approval of new drugs.

The first cases of AIDS were barely reported by mainstream media, largely because the people affected were socially marginalized. This indifference rapidly developed into fear-driven and reactionary reporting by mainstream newspapers, television, and radio that led to high levels of stigma and discrimination. Instead of reporting HIV/AIDS as a health condition, mainstream newspaper and television coverage was largely responsible for creating an environment of social alienation and blame. The negative responses were alarming for their level of discrimination against persons showing symptoms of HIV infection.

In 2016, it is difficult to imagine how a similar response could happen in a Western country without generating a reaction that was anything other than evidence based, although some responses to Ebola in 2014 had close similarities. In the early 1980s, AIDS was seen not just as a new medical condition but as one with rapid progression and high mortality. This was as a result of information based on findings in persons with AIDS with very late–stage infection. It took many years before science showed that, for most people, HIV is a slowly progressive infection. Persons with HIV were primarily in marginalized populations—initially gay men, people who inject drugs, sex workers, Haitians and immigrants from Haiti, and people with hemophilia. Media coverage was vitriolic and homophobic. Gay men were a particularly vulnerable social group and an easy target. This response was often followed in other countries, even where the epidemic affected primarily heterosexual populations. In the 1980s, right wing and extremist religious organizations singled out HIV as an issue that could be used to support their political and moral views, ignoring the growing scientific consensus that the likely cause was a virus (Watney, 1987).

Since HIV was treated differently from every other serious medical condition, the results are still affecting care today. HIV-positive children, people who inject drugs, immigrants, HIV-positive health workers (BBC, 2014a) or health workers who do not have HIV (Kovac and Khandjiev, 2001) commonly suffer similar discrimination that gay men initially faced.

ACTIVISM, ADVOCACY, COMMUNITY ADVOCACY, PEER ADVOCACY, AND TREATMENT LITERACY

Activism is driven by the need to overcome present problems with better solutions. The biggest drive in activism is channeling anger into productivity. The authors of this chapter, from five countries with different HIV epidemics, have each been treatment advocates and activists for 15–20 years and from before the development of effective treatment in each of their countries.

Advocacy as a term broadly involves helping someone negotiate an aspect of life. It often involves professional services (health, legal, housing, etc.), and effective community advocacy can be provided by anyone with the skills and training to help negotiate these structures.

Peer advocacy in the context of HIV is carried out by people with a positive HIV diagnosis to provide advice and support. In this case, the shared experience of having HIV includes understanding the nature, determinants, and consequences of stigma and developing ways to help overcome it. It is an empowering experience to move forward with life.

While HIV status is not a criterion for becoming involved in providing HIV services, peer support can often overcome particular barriers that are still associated with discrimination. With peer support, individuals who have overcome complex issues related to an HIV diagnosis have the opportunity to provide help to other persons with HIV at a time when problems can seem insurmountable. Peer advocacy services enable people living with HIV to contribute their experiences through a personal and community response. Often, people work as volunteers providing services that help with not only new diagnoses but also the treatment pathway, including treatment literacy, adherence support, and access to other support services.

Treatment literacy is the empowerment of people living with HIV to understand more about HIV and treatment, including the natural history of HIV, laboratory testing and other cornerstones of comprehensive care, adherence, treatment choice, affordability and access, drug resistance, and pipeline research for better drugs in the future. The outcome is that persons with HIV who wish to do so are empowered to take an active role in their health. In some countries, peer advocacy has been central to the rollout of HIV treatment, including testing, counseling, and adherence support services, and to tackling legislative changes (or lack thereof) that underpin discrimination against marginalized groups.

PERSONAL RESPONSES TO AN HIV DIAGNOSIS AND THE ROLE OF PEER ADVOCACY

Getting an HIV diagnosis has always been far more complex than the medical management of a viral infection (Remien and Rabkin, 2001). Panic, anxiety, anger, guilt, shame, depression, and isolation are still commonly reported among persons with HIV. Few other single illnesses are associated with such fears about disclosure and openness. Stigma and discrimination are still widely prevalent in all countries (People Living with HIV Stigma Index, 2013; Sidibé and Goosby, 2013).

Even after availability of effective treatment for almost 20 years in Western countries, and for more than 10 years in many resource-limited countries, the personal response to an HIV diagnosis in 2016 can be as traumatic as it was in 1986. On an individual level, HIV is still seen as a fatal, stigmatizing infection that must be kept secret. It is only with support and information that HIV can become a routine aspect of someone's life.

Although HIV is now frequently compared to diabetes (as a chronic manageable condition), no one diagnosed with diabetes is told that it is just like having HIV. This perhaps helps illustrate the psychological impact of HIV. Reports of discrimination against persons with HIV that restricts their access to medical care, including denial of treatment, are still being documented (Human Rights Watch, 2014). An example of this irrational response to HIV in 2014 is that of an 8-year-old boy who was expelled from a Chinese village because he was HIV positive. The villagers that signed the petition included his grandparents and legal guardians (BBC, 2014b). Although access to treatment was soon arranged, this was perhaps only due to the media focus that the incident generated.

The criminalization of HIV exposure, even in the absence of transmission or with consent, also highlights the degree to which discrimination is sanctioned by law. This is true also in cases where HIV transmission would not be possible (Bernard, 2010; Bernard and Cameron, 2013; UNAIDS, 2008).

All of these factors combined contribute to a social environment in which much support is needed in order to prevent a diagnosis from inflicting lasting social and psychological damage that is out of proportion with the medical concerns for HIV. Part of the fear of HIV and the hostility toward persons with HIV is likely driven by a combination of inaccurate knowledge about HIV transmission risks (linked to personal fear) together with a lack of confidence in use of condoms and other strategies that have been proven to prevent transmission. For example, the risk of HIV transmission is commonly believed to be inevitable when having sex without a condom. In reality, although HIV is transmitted from a single exposure, the risk from each exposure is less than 1 in 200 in many situations and less than 1 in 10,000 for someone on effective treatment. Recent research into the impact of effective treatment on dramatically reducing the chance of HIV transmission has the potential to help normalize HIV (Rodger et al., 2016).

Newspapers publish hateful HIV-related stories in all countries, but the history of media responses to HIV still affects people who are living with HIV today, even after the availability of effective treatment should have normalized HIV. The sense of alienation following an HIV diagnosis makes peer advocacy from other persons with HIV particularly important in reducing one's sense of isolation. This connection with other people who have already worked through many of the same problems, including how to move on with life, navigate HIV care and treatment, and negotiate current and future relationship issues, can dramatically reduce the time needed to return to a sense of normalcy and the likelihood of a full life.

EARLY RESPONSES IN THE UNITED STATES: FIRST MODELS FOR COMMUNITY ADVOCACY

The United States was the first country to have severe morbidity and mortality rates of AIDS. As a high-income country with the largest budget for medical research, the United States was well poised to tackle a new and emerging medical crisis. However, the reality of limited political will meant that

it took years before AIDS was recognized as a national emergency, during which time many thousands of people died. When the first cases were reported in 1981, HIV was already endemic in the United States. The early crisis was driven by rapidly progressing late-stage infections in people, many of whom were excluded from healthcare. Tens of thousands of people likely had become HIV positive over the previous decade.

From 1981 to 1987, the response to HIV was almost entirely community based rather than institutionally generated, thus most affected individuals' records are either not available or lost. The response focused on managing opportunistic infections, counseling, and peer and grassroots community services, including complementary and alternative medicine, buyer's clubs, buddy programs, home meals, housing support, and palliative care. HIV advocacy also established models that were taken up internationally; funding (AIDS walks for life and benefits), remembrances (such as candlelight vigils, memorial quilts) and (in the U.S.) community research—including the Community Research Initiative (CRI) and the Community Based Clinical Trials (CBCT) Network of the American Foundation for AIDS Research (amfAR).

Patient-centered healthcare advocacy that was part of the rapid early community responses was possible because the United States had a vibrant lesbian and gay rights movement, which was closely linked to other movements for social change, such as the civil rights, women's rights, and anti-war movements. This level of community-based political activism was especially strong in the United States.

Hospitals in cities that were most affected developed new models of specialist care, launched and developed, in part, by doctors and health workers who were lesbian or gay. These new models involved medical care, sensitivity and expertise in medical management for fatal illness (choice of treatment, involvement in research, alternative treatment), and the structure of care (partner rights, end-of-life rights, visiting hours, hospital facilities including patient kitchens and even HIV smoking rooms). Many new services or facilities were community funded.

Some of the early U.S. history from 1981 of community response is well established (AIDS.gov, 2016; Centers for Disease Control and Prevention [CDC], 1981; Gottlieb et al., 1981; Graham, 2006; Mass, 1981, 1997). HIV cases were quickly reported in other capital cities, such as Paris and London. It was a year before the collective symptoms were termed *AIDS* (CDC, 1982) and another year before a virus was first identified as a likely cause (Barré-Sinoussi et al., 1983).

By early 1982, community organizations, established by small groups of gay men, were already providing some of the first support and information services. Both Gay Men's Health Crisis (GMHC) in New York City and San Francisco AIDS Foundation (SFAF) became models for hundreds of smaller organizations that were gradually established as cases were reported in increasing numbers in other U.S. cities. It was common for groups to first develop peer support networks and later expand to offer broader services. Both groups were initially volunteer based and were run from either homes or single-room offices before developing into organizations with multi-million dollar annual budgets (GMHC records, 1975–1978, 1982–1999; SFAF, n.d.).

In early 1983, the Denver Principles (see later discussion) were launched as a founding document for a new movement of people with AIDS (PWAs). This document demanded that people directly affected should be central to the organizations set up to support them and that services should be "by" rather than "for" an affected group. Persons with HIV set the stage, and HIV became the model of a medical illness in which peer involvement by persons most directly affected are empowered to have a leading role.

By the time the direct action activist group AIDS Coalition To Unleash Power (ACT-UP) was founded, in 1987, AIDS had become the leading cause of death of young men and women aged 25 to 44 years in New York City. As a large grassroots organization that was especially inclusive of people who were living with HIV, it quickly became the most important U.S. community HIV movement, with chapters formed in numerous cities in the United States and internationally. ACT-UP used mainstream media to change the government response to AIDS, mobilizing with key slogans: "Knowledge=Power," "Silence=Death," "Action=Life," and "Act up! Fight back! Fight AIDS." The group criticized, engaged with, and changed established medical structures of drug development. This included funding and design for research studies, programs for early access to experimental drugs, and regulatory approval. For example, the U.S. Food and Drug Administration (FDA) overturned its previous decision not to approve ganciclovir as a treatment for cytomegalovirus (CMV) because of pressure from ACT-UP (ACT-UP, n.d.; Gonsalves and Harrington, 1992, Harrington, 2012a, 2012b; Kramer, 2007). ACT-UP New York has an extensive online oral history archive and two recent documentary films, *How to Survive a Plague* and *United in Anger*, both released in 2012, showing different aspects of this history. The films include the development of the Treatment Action Group (TAG) in 1992, which helped lead much of the critical community activism for expedited, adequately funded, and scientifically sound research. A third documentary, *We Were Here*, documents personal responses from the first responses to AIDS in San Francisco.

DENVER PRINCIPLES AND GIPA AS A MODEL FOR PEER ADVOCACY

In spring 1983, the Denver Principles were launched as a community statement of rights and responsibilities (Callen and Turner, 1988; Strub, 2014). In retrospect, this remarkable document set out principles for interacting with medical care that, more than 30 years later, continue to be inspirational for other health settings.

Eleven people who had been publicly open about their diagnoses produced the document (including Michael Callen and Richard Berkowitz, from New York City, and Bobbi Campbell and Dan Turner, from San Francisco). Some of the

first doctors to lead the response to HIV, including Joseph Sonnabend in New York City and Marcus Conant in San Francisco, played an active role in developing and supporting a network of patients.

The Denver Principles covered four key areas.

(1) A demand for people to be called "people with AIDS" (PWA) rather than "victims" or even "patients," which both imply passive and often negative roles

(2) That recommendations, including employment and housing rights, be based on evidence supporting the lack of transmission from casual contact. This included not blaming or scapegoating people on the basis of their lifestyle.

(3) Recommendations for people with AIDS to be involved at all levels that affected care, including in provider organizations, in choosing community representatives, and at AIDS forums. This section also included ethical responsibilities of disclosure to sexual partners and limiting the risk of further transmission.

(4) Rights for people with AIDS to full and satisfying sexual and emotional lives, to access treatment and social support without discrimination, to be actively informed about and involved in all aspects of medical care, to privacy and confidentiality, to be able to self-nominate who else would be involved, and to live and die with dignity

Six years later, activists from the United States and Canada launched a Declaration of the Universal Rights and Needs of People Living with HIV Disease, at the 5th International AIDS Conference, outlining and developing updated demands (AIDS Action Now, 1989). These were further developed into the Greater Involvement of People living with AIDS (GIPA) principles, which were endorsed as the Paris Declaration in 1994, at the United Nations in 2001, and at high-level meetings on AIDS in 2006 and 2007 (UNAIDS, 2007).

GIPA sets forth principles that advocate for the meaningful involvement of people living with HIV in the development, implementation, and evaluation of all HIV-related policies and programs. It acknowledges the right of self-determination and participation in decisions that affect the lives of people with AIDS. The GIPA principles are just as important today in the context of HIV service delivery. Persons with HIV and their representatives want and demand to be formally included in the planning and delivery of services that affect their care.

MAJOR ISSUES ADDRESSED IN HIV ADVOCACY

THE DIFFICULTIES OF BEING A PATIENT

The Denver Principles emphasized the negative aspects of the traditional passivity implied in being a patient. As an HIV patient, one's life becomes dependent on another person, the physician. In addition to a doctor's skills and experience this can also include a doctor's vagaries, moods, workload, and, sometimes, his or her opinions or assumptions about the patient as a person. Doctors can also have very different approaches to openness about involving their patients in medical decisions and choices. Differences in language, class, income, education, race, gender, and sexuality can contribute to a patient having a very positive, negative, or indifferent experience (Malebranche et al., 2004; McCoy, 2005). In many cases, people with HIV are patients because of their diagnosis and symptoms. Additionally, since HIV is commonly contracted sexually or from drug use, patients are faced with revealing aspects of life that many people find difficult to discuss or that they prefer to remain private. Nevertheless, persons with HIV entrust their lives to the professionals involved in their care and follow their recommendations based on trust.

HIV advocacy has commonly stressed the importance of developing good relationships with doctors and other primary health workers, who are usually the gatekeepers to information, treatment, and other services. This engenders a power imbalance that can be intimidating. Many persons with HIV are not comfortable asking questions or challenging their doctors, for fear of being perceived as "difficult." Some doctors use overly technical medical terms, have limited time for discussion, or use language that can be construed as patronizing, judgmental, and/or stigmatizing. Advocacy can help to equalize this imbalance.

To help address these imbalances, HIV organizations produce treatment resources to enable HIV-positive persons to have access to information that is independent from, but can be used in discussions with, their doctor. Sometimes it is important that the patient has information that is different from the doctors' advice; this is where advocacy becomes interesting. Given the fast-changing pace of HIV research, an informed patient may be more up-to-date on current treatments than an uninformed doctor. Being informed is also critical in developing treatment readiness, since lifelong, daily HIV treatment must be started before symptoms appear, and patients must be willing to commit to strict adherence to avoid developing drug resistance—sometimes despite debilitating side effects from drug toxicities. Additionally, as we

learn more about HIV and treatment and as the evidence base increases, some medical decisions may simply be wrong for patients. With HIV advocacy shared decision-making can have a positive impact on physician–patient relationships.

Peer support advocates can help explain choices, including treatment choices, especially when an affected person is faced with language or cultural differences. Advocates may also work with providers within health systems or in partnership with medical societies to ensure that clinicians are trained to provide culturally competent, motivational, and nonjudgmental care for persons with HIV.

COMMUNITY PUBLICATIONS AND REDUCING THE MEDICAL TIMELINE FOR INFORMATION

HIV advocacy produced a demand for information that was up-to-date, reliable, and in appropriate formats. The traditional timeline for medical advances based on peer-reviewed publications mirrored the slow pace of research itself. Just as HIV activists challenged the timeline for drug development, for example, by demanding the validation and use of surrogate markers rather than clinical endpoints and earlier access to promising compounds, new publications produced treatment news, sometimes on a bi-weekly publication cycle (see Box 10.1).

With these advances activists became experts in reporting both traditional and experimental medical research. Reporters often came from a nonmedical background and acquired new skills in order to understand and interpret scientific studies. Some HIV-positive persons had to learn new languages in order to improve their health literacy. Community resources explained the growing understanding of the range of opportunistic infections and diverse ways to manage the infections; as the immune system becomes increasingly damaged during advanced HIV infection, incidence of bacterial, fungal, parasitic and viral infections, along with some cancers, wasting syndrome, and significant neurological deficits, increases.

Since most medical research is published in English, it is easier for English-speaking activists to report and develop resources. However, globally, many HIV organizations are closely connected through formal and informal networks, thus translations and adaptation of resources are encouraged without regard to copyright. As an example, some of the

---

Box 10.1 KEY COMMUNITY PUBLICATIONS

While most organizations produced newsletters, several U.S. publications (see advocacy resources in the Resource Appendix of this textbook) focused on experimental treatment, including *AIDS Treatment News* (ATN), produced every 2 weeks by John S. James from 1986, and bulletins from Gay Men's Health Crisis (GMHC), San Francisco AIDS Foundation (SFAF), and Project Inform.

HIV activists were quick to see the potential for Internet communication, and *scimedaids* was one of the first community medical bulletin boards. The Critical Path Project (founded by Kiyoshi Kuromiya in 1989) and AIDS Education Global Information System (AEGiS) (founded by Sister Mary Elizabeth Clark in 1990) quickly became sources of daily news, archiving discussions and publications. Similar publications provided similar information in other countries. Community publishing has been driven by the belief that people have a right to the latest information about their care. Publications are usually free to access and copyright-free. As part of the rights of patients to have free access to medical information, Jules Levin, at National AIDS Treatment Advocacy Project (NATAP), published conference slides and peer-reviewed journals to email lists and online. It is a great loss that an archive of this huge volume of community history is not currently available online.

nontechnical patient guides produced by i-Base in the United Kingdom have been translated into more than 35 languages by sister organizations in other countries. The arrival of these translated patient guides often represents the first time that persons with HIV in the recipients' countries have had comprehensive treatment information (HIV i-Base, 2017). Similarly, the leading Spanish activist group gTt has a long history of providing source material for resources in Spanish-speaking countries in Latin America.

IMPACT OF EFFECTIVE ANTIRETROVIRAL THERAPY

Effective antiretroviral treatment (ART) for HIV has changed the face of the epidemic in the United States and most Western countries since 1996. Durable responses to treatment were demonstrated for the first time by sustained viral suppression. Medical advances also meant that the impact of treatment could be measured in individuals in real time (within days or weeks in a typical clinical setting) compared to previous dependence on slow and indirect markers of immunological recovery (CD4 count) or by monitoring disease signs and symptoms. Using three antiretroviral drugs in combination, including a new drug class (protease inhibitors), not only reduced viral load but also kept it suppressed. In order for ART to be effective, high levels of adherence to complex dosing schedules were required, and with ART came a broad range side effects, which drove a new focus on treatment education (both advocacy and literacy). In low-income countries, community advocates played key roles in securing treatment access and in developing treatment literacy (Geffen, 2010; Heywood, 2009; Treatment Action Campaign, 2010).

For the first time in the epidemic, treatment not only extended life but also allowed the immune system to repair itself, reversing opportunistic infections that were previously untreatable and often fatal. For many people HIV became a chronic, manageable illness. Continued advances in drug development led to life expectancy that either matched or possibly exceeded that of the general population, especially for patients diagnosed early who had access to antiretroviral treatment, no comorbidities, and no key risk factors (e.g., smoking) (Samji et al., 2013; Wada et al., 2014).

As the focus on research led to more effective and tolerable treatment in Western countries, the demand for universal access resulted in new models of global healthcare. According to Dr. Peter Mugyenyi, a Kenyan HIV doctor, in lectures at international conferences on HIV it was not good enough for "the drugs to be where the disease [was] not" (Mugyenyi, 2000). Community advocates joined other healthcare activists to become involved in global funding, policy, guidelines, research, and access, a process that continues today. By 2015, more than 17 million people were accessing treatment (UNAIDS, 2016) that was developed originally for people in Western countries. It is remarkable that approaches by ACT-UP New York led to new U.S. groups like the Health Global Access Project (Health GAP), which challenged issues of patent law and international health funding, and the Treatment Action Group (TAG), which drove new foci on treating and preventing tuberculosis and hepatitis C virus (HCV) (Harrington, 2010; Smith and Simplon, 2006).

SOUTH AFRICA: OVERCOMING LEGAL AND POLITICAL CHALLENGES

Many of the community responses to HIV in the United States, including early examples of patient advocacy, were inspired by social movements for change. Similarly, HIV activism in many different countries (including the U.S., U.K., India, Namibia, and South Africa) included non-governmental organizations (NGOs) with legal expertise, establishing a human rights platform for access to care and treatment. Just as early U.S. advocacy provided a leading role for Western activists, the community responses in South Africa played a crucial role in promoting advocacy in the global South.

Advocates in South Africa brought the HIV crisis to the international stage when they formed a grassroots movement for treatment access that tackled discrimination across the board: They made HIV an issue that affected everyone, irrespective of HIV status, with education programs centered on treatment literacy. The Treatment Action Campaign (TAC) was founded in South Africa, in December 1998, to draw attention to the unnecessary suffering and HIV-related deaths of thousands of people in Africa. For example, when the epidemic developed in South Africa during the late 1990s, the South African political leadership backed HIV denialists and promoted a diet of lemon, garlic, and African potatoes, rather than ART, to combat HIV. The delay that this denial and pseudoscience caused is responsible for at least 330,000 unnecessary deaths (Chigwedere et al., 2008; Geffen and Cameron, 2009). TAC believed that, because health was a human right, people in developing countries were equally entitled to have access to the medicines that, by the late 1990s, had turned HIV into a life-threatening but no longer fatal cause of illness in the West. Conveniently and coincidentally, TAC's creation in the late 1990s meant that they could pick up on this medical development on the other side of the Atlantic. TAC could use the U.S.-initiated campaign for ART coverage to help its own mobilization and draw attention to its demands for access to medicines for people in Africa who were living with HIV.

TAC successfully used formal and informal strategies to fight for access to effective treatment. These strategies included the following:

- Negotiation with the South African government

- Direct actions such as public protests and demonstrations, often attended by thousands of people with HIV, their families, and ordinary people of South Africa, wearing T-shirts stating "HIV positive"

- Peaceful civil disobedience, such as illegally importing generic fluconazole from Thailand to challenge the patent abuse by Pfizer

- Working with AIDS Law Project on legal challenges to the government, to provide ART

The "HIV positive" T-shirts were closely linked to the movement's identity. They enabled those wearing the T-shirts to be identifiable and visible, to generate understanding and empathy about persons with HIV and to dispel myths. The T-shirts were also meant to generate a reaction and provide an opportunity for engagement and education for observers. This was critical in the early days of the AIDS epidemic, to challenge related stigma.

Treatment literacy programs trained community advocates, many of whom had positive HIV diagnoses, to lead education and adherence training when treatment eventually became available. Following is testimony from one advocate:

> As one of the advocates, I remember the day I tested HIV positive and being told that there was no medication. I became depressed, knowing that I was going to die from a disease that could be treated, especially as my government and the pharmaceutical companies had the power to decide who lives and who dies. I decided to die fighting for access to ART even if I would not have the opportunity to get the drugs myself. Our organization was rooted in experiences and struggles of the Anti-Apartheid Movement. Most of us came from poor and disadvantaged communities, so we were a grassroots organization. At the peak of our campaign, we had a regional network with close to 20,000 volunteers nationally. *Vuyiseka Dubula,*
> *Treatment Action Campaign*

Treatment literacy in South Africa involves literacy in maternal health, sexual health, HIV, and tuberculosis. The TAC program includes learning about the science of HIV and treatment, with workshops, posters, leaflets, the *HIV in Our Lives* series of booklets, and *Equal Treatment* magazine.

TAC also collaborated with Community Media Trust to produce a weekly mainstream HIV television series, broadcast on the leading South African network (from 1999 and still running), called *Siyayinqoba Beat it!*, in which many TAC advocates give a public face to everyday HIV issues. Since 1999, the program has provided a platform for people living with HIV to share their challenges and victories, and has enabled people living in isolation with HIV to feel connected to a growing community (Geffen, 2010; Heywood, 2009; Siyayinqoba Beat it!, 2014; Treatment Action Campaign, 2010). TAC has empowered many HIV-positive people to be open about their HIV status in a country where stigma and discrimination have remained high and that has one of the highest HIV prevalence rates. This magnification of the disparity between a common private experience and extreme public stigma is unique to HIV.

TAC successfully used strategic media advocacy through use of print and non-print media and their own media allies with NGOs. They also successfully used the law and the constitution to challenge the government, in the constitutional court, to provide ART to pregnant women. TAC further challenged pharmaceutical companies on their profiteering in developing countries. As stated earlier, TAC challenged

patent abuse by Pfizer by importing the generic drug, fluconazole, from Thailand, and worked with AIDS Law Project on legal challenges to the government to provide ART.

By 2015, 1 in 10 South African adults were living with HIV. This is the highest number of HIV-positive people in the world—approximately 6.9 million out of an estimated population of 54 million. By 2015, an estimated three million people were accessing treatment, the biggest ART program in the world, and numbers continue to increase. The prices of antiretroviral drugs have dropped significantly through competition for public contracts among companies producing generic antiretroviral drugs, allowing the South African government to negotiate for the cheapest price in order to treat more people. This remarkable achievement was directly due to community advocacy.

INDIA: HIV-POSITIVE ACTIVISM AND GENERIC ANTIRETROVIRALS

In India, the grassroots HIV community has worked with legal advocates at the Lawyers Collective to ensure access to treatment in a human-rights context. More than two million people are HIV positive in a country where adult prevalence is only 0.3%. Access to ART for most people began in 2004, nearly a quarter of a century after the epidemic began, and currently 800,000 people are receiving treatment.

Indian generic drugs are treating the majority of persons with HIV globally. HIV-positive activists in India have also been closely involved in the fight against restrictive trade patent laws. For example, the Delhi Network of HIV Positive People (DNP+) has a long history of leading community support publicly when patent cases are being challenged in court, often with hundreds of supporters demonstrating in the streets (Lawyers Collective, 2013).

In the 1970s, the Indian patent laws recognized patents during the research and development phase of drug discovery rather than with the final drug. This enabled generic manufacturers based in India to produce high-quality medicines at prices that were affordable for people in low- and middle-income countries. Cipla, under the direction of CEO Dr. Yusef Hamied, was the first generic manufacturer to formulate HIV medicines. Not only did Cipla formulate three antiretrovirals from different Western companies into a single tablet combination, but the company also reduced the cost of annual treatment, from US$10,000 to US$350, less than $1 a day.

The most important factor in global drug access has been drug pricing, which has consistently been reduced by competition. Patent barriers, prices, and availability of antiretroviral drugs have been carefully documented for HIV medicines in the annual Médecins Sans Frontières (MSF) "Untangling the Web" reports (Médecins Sans Frontières, 2016). Generic manufacturers are commercial companies that expand the market for medicines to countries that Western companies have never seen as profitable. Quality-assured generic antiretrovirals match the quality and safety of originator-produced formulations.

Although HIV medicines are one of the highest-profile groups of medicines, the challenges to patents also cover drugs to treat other major health problems, including cancer and hepatitis C, that would otherwise never be available to people in poor countries. In addition to HIV-positive activists in India advocating for their own treatment—for example, fighting against government recommendations supporting continued use of d4T (stavudine) after its difficult side effect profile had become clear—they provided grassroots support by fighting changes in patent laws that affected access to treatment for more than 90% of HIV-positive persons globally (Collins, 2012). The influence of the United States and European Union on further tightening and extending patent restrictions continues to jeopardize the long-term future of access to existing and new medicines globally.

HEALTH WORKERS AS ACTIVISTS

Notably, and importantly, within health services, some doctors, nurses, and other health workers provided care and services that later became models of care in other areas. This includes patient-centered care with similar approaches to the statements in the Denver Principles.

Many of the first activists were doctors and health professionals who encouraged persons with HIV to find their own voices with health systems that traditionally did not welcome active patient involvement. Doctors who were starting their professional careers in the early years of the HIV epidemic were faced with managing patients in resource-limited settings. The doctors developed strong and lasting relationships with community models of healthcare that were unlikely to have been included in their formal training. Without the support from doctors, many of the advances in patient-centered care may never have been developed. In addition to providing personal care, doctors played a major role in promoting active involvement of patients. Persons with HIV started participating on panels for national and international treatment guidelines, planning HIV medical conferences, and designing and running medical trials.

POSITIVE OUTCOMES: FROM SCIENCE AND GLOBAL ACCESS

This short and selected overview of some of the community responses to HIV includes the following:

- A key role in the development of new drugs (unparalleled, with over 25 antiretroviral drugs approved within 30 years), including new regulatory pathways for developing and approving drugs
- Models to involve people directly affected at all levels of care, including research; formal community representation on research groups and a network of local, national, and international community advisory boards

- Global access to generic drugs even when they are still covered by Western patents
- Elevating global health to new political levels, such as new funding for treatment (the Global Fund for HIV, TB and Malaria; at the World Health Organization; and on international guidelines panels)
- Archives, oral history projects, organizational history, films and documentaries. The first 20 years of the HIV epidemic took place before email, internet and digital technology. Some activist groups recorded films and videos but even photographs from this period are less common. Fortunately, several individuals and organizations have added their histories in library archives, but few of these have been digitized. Many of the community publications that could possibly be archived are not available online. Early research and medical history have become harder to access thus it is important to collect and archive the records electronically. Notably, important conference archives from the Conference on Retroviruses and Opportunistic Infections (CROI) and International AIDS Society (IAS) are no longer available online.
- The development of patient-centered care through HIV activism has provided a platform for patients to be at the center of their own medical care. This includes choosing when to use treatment, which treatment to use, rights for end-of-life care and living wills.
- The advocacy response to HIV has, in many cases, helped redefine the role of, and the relationship between, health care provider and patient. This has made it easier for patients to ask for information and options that will enable them to take an active role in their own care.
- HIV has also raised the importance of lay perspectives within medicine and of activism within healthcare professions. Some of the most effective activists have been doctors, nurses, scientists, researchers and drug companies.

CONCLUSIONS AND THE FUTURE

Remarkable HIV advocacy outcomes illustrate that change is possible, and the model used in the HIV response can be applied in other health areas. However, while some of the medical and scientific challenges have been overcome, there remains a need for continued HIV advocacy.

What continues to make us angry in 2016, after so many victories?

- Lack of funding for good-quality research
- Limited access to life-saving drugs
- High levels of discrimination and stigma toward key populations

- Criminalization
- Limited access to properly tailored combination-based prevention programs
- Escalating drug prices charged by pharmaceutical industries that limit access to the new drugs to treat HIV, hepatitis C, and tuberculosis

From a global perspective, many persons with positive HIV diagnoses are still unable to access care and treatment with antiretroviral medication. This shortage is further magnified by the move to begin treatment upon HIV diagnosis. Additionally, most people in low- and middle-income countries have limited access to treatment, especially for second- and third-line combination antiretroviral therapies. New goals for advocacy include improving access to better and more effective treatment for tuberculosis and hepatitis C, especially in countries with a high prevalence of these co-infections. Access in poor countries is dependent on sustaining international funding, for example, for the Global Fund to Fight AIDS, Tuberculosis and Malaria, perhaps through new models such as the proposed financial transaction tax to provide sufficient healthcare programs and drugs to all in need.

REFERENCES

ACT-UP (n.d.). AIDS Coalition to Unleash Power! (ACT-UP) Oral history project. http://www.actuporalhistory.org Accessed December 1, 2014.

AIDS ACTION NOW! (1989). Le Manifeste de Montréal: Declaration of the Universal Rights and Needs of People Living with HIV Disease. Opening of the Vth International AIDS Conference, June 4, 1989, Montreal, Canada.

AIDS.gov (2016). HIV timeline: 30 years of AIDS. http://www.aids.gov/hiv-aids-basics/hiv-aids-101/aids-timeline Accessed December 1, 2014.

Barré-Sinoussi F, Chermann JC, Rey F, et al. (1983). Isolation of a T-lymphotropic retrovirus from a patient at risk for acquired immune deficiency syndrome (AIDS). *Science* 220(4599):868–871.

BBC (2014a). Uganda HIV nurse Rosemary Namubiru jailed by Kampala court; May 19, 2014. http://www.bbc.co.uk/news/world-africa-27468741. Accessed January 10, 2017.

BBC (2014b). China village petitions to 'isolate' HIV positive boy. December 19, 2014. http://www.bbc.co.uk/news/world-asia-china-30527652. Accessed January 10, 2017.

Bernard EJ (ed.) (2010). *HIV and the Criminal Law.* London: NAM Publications.

Bernard EJ, Cameron S (2013). Advancing HIV justice: a progress report on achievement and challenges in global advocacy against HIV criminalization. Global Network of People Living with HIV (GNP+) and HIV Justice Network. http://www.hivjustice.net/wp-content/uploads/2013/05/Advancing-HIV-Justice-June-2013.pdf

Callen M, Turner D (1988). A history of the PWA self-empowerment movement. In M Callen (ed.), *Surviving and Thriving with AIDS: Collected Wisdom,* Vol. 2. New York: PWA Collection. http://michaelcallen.com/mikes-writing/a-history-of-the-pwa-self-empowerment-movement

Centers for Disease Control and Prevention (CDC) (1981). Pneumocystis pneumonia—Los Angeles. *Morb Mortal Wkly Rep MMWR* 31(21):1–3.

Centers for Disease Control and Prevention (CDC) (1982). Update on acquired immune deficiency syndrome (AIDS), United States. *Morb Mortal Wkly Rep MMWR* 31(37):507–508, 513–514.

Chigwedere P, Seage GR III, Gruskin S, Lee T-H, Essex M (2008). Estimating the lost benefits of antiretroviral drug use in South Africa. *J Acquir Immune Defic Syndr* 49(4):410–415.

Collins S (2012, June). Stavudine (d4T) phase-out festival in Delhi. HIV Treatment Bulletin, iBase (UK). http://i-base.info/htb/16625. Accessed January 10, 2017.

Denver Principles (1983). Statement from the People with AIDS advisory committee. Second National Forum on AIDS. http://www.actupny.org/documents/denver_principles.pdf

Gay Men's Health Crisis (GHMC) records. 1975–1978, 1982–1999. New York Public Library Archives & Manuscripts. http://archives.nypl.org/mss/1126#detailed

Geffen N (2010). *Debunking Delusions: The Inside Story of the Treatment Action Campaign.* Johannesburg: Jacana Media.

Geffen N, Cameron E (2009, July). The deadly hand of denial: governance and politically instigated AIDS denialism in South Africa. Centre for Social Science Research, Aids and Society Research Unit, Working Paper No. 257.

Gonsalves G, Harrington M (1992). AIDS research at the NIH: a critical review. Treatment Action Group. http://www.treatmentactiongroup.org/publications/1992

Gottlieb MS, Schroff R, Schanker HS, et al. (1981). *Pneumocystis carinii* pneumonia and mucosal candidiasis in previously healthy homosexual men. *N Engl J Med* 305:1425–1431.

Graham J (2006). 25 years of AIDS and HIV: a look back. 1981–1986: In the beginning. AIDS Survival Project, January/February. http://www.thebody.com/content/art32414.html

Harrington M (2010). From HIV to tuberculosis and back again: a tale of activism in 2 pandemics. *Clin Infect Dis.* 50(Suppl 3):S260–S266.

Harrington M (2012a). TAG at 20: Part I. Early campaigns. Reforming NIH AIDS research, boosting the budget, and revitalizing the basic science of HIV infection. *TAGline*, Spring. http://www.treatmentactiongroup.org/tagline/2012/spring/tag-20-early-campaigns

Harrington M (2012b). TAG at 20: Part II. On a darkling plain—the years of despair. *TAGline*, Fall. http://www.treatmentactiongroup.org/tagline/2012/fall/tag-20-darkling-plain

Heywood M (2009). South Africa's treatment action campaign: combining law and social mobilization to realize the right to health. *J Hum Rights Practice* 1(1):14–36.

HIV i-Base (2017). Translations of iBase treatment guides for HIV positive people. http://i-base.info/category/translations/

Human Rights Watch (2014). Yemen: HIV patients denied health care. http://www.hrw.org/news/2014/11/03/yemen-hiv-patients-denied-health-care

Kovac C, Khandjiev R. (2001). Doctors face murder charges in Libya. *BMJ* 322(260):7281.

Kramer L (2007). We are not crumbs; we must not accept crumbs. Remarks on the occasion of the 20th Anniversary of ACT UP, NY Lesbian and Gay Community Center, March 13, 2007. http://queer-justice-league.blogspot.co.uk/2007/03/full-text-of-larry-kramers-march-13.html

Lawyers Collective (2013). Attack on affordable medicines continues in EU-India trade negotiations: health groups rally in Delhi as protests spread across the developing world. April 10, 2013. http://www.lawyerscollective.org/updates/attack-affordable-medicines-continues-eu-india-trade-negotiations.html

Malebranche DJ, Peterson JL, Fullilove RE, Stackhouse RW (2004). Race and sexual identity: perceptions about medical culture and healthcare among black men who have sex with men. *J Natl Med Assoc* 96(1):97–107.

Mass L (1981). *New York Native*, May 18.

Mass LD (1997). *We Must Love One Another or Die: The Life and Legacies of Larry Kramer.* New York: St. Martin's Griffin.

McCoy L (2005). HIV-positive patients and the doctor–patient relationship: perspectives from the margins. *Qual Health Res* 15:791.

Médecins Sans Frontières (MSF) (2016, July). *Untangling the Web of Antiretroviral Price Reductions,* 18th edition. https://www.msfaccess.org/content/report-untangling-web-antiretroviral-price-reductions-18th-ed-july-2016

Mugyenyi P (2000). Improved access to HIV/AIDS drugs in developing countries, TAC/MSF symposium. XIII International AIDS Conference, July 9–14, 2000, Durban.

People Living with HIV Stigma Index (2016). About the Index. http://www.stigmaindex.org/about-index

Remien RH, Rabkin JG (2001). Psychological aspects of living with HIV disease: a primary care perspective. *West J Med* 175(5):332–335.

Rodger A, Bruun T, Cambiano V, et al., for the PARTNER Study Group (2014). HIV transmission risk through condomless sex if HIV+ partner on suppressive ART: PARTNER Study. Program and abstracts of the 21st Conference on Retroviruses and Opportunistic Infections, 3-6 March 3–6, 2014, Boston, MA. Oral late breaker abstract 153LB. http://www.croiconference.org/sites/default/files/abstracts/153LB.pdf

Rodger AJ, Cambiano V, Bruun T, et al., for the PARTNER Study Group (2016). Sexual activity without condoms and risk of HIV transmission in serodifferent couples when the HIV-positive partner is using suppressive antiretroviral therapy. *JAMA* 316:171–181.

Samji H, Cescon A, Hogg RS, et al., for the North American AIDS Cohort Collaboration on Research and Design (NA-ACCORD) (2013). Closing the gap: increases in life expectancy among treated HIV-positive individuals in the United States and Canada. *PLoS One* 8(12):e81355.

San Francisco AIDS Foundation (SFAF) (n.d.). Records. Online Archive of California (OAC). University of San Francisco California Library. Collection number MSS 94-60. http://www.oac.cdlib.org/findaid/ark:/13030/kt509nd35m

Sidibé M, Goosby EP (Eds.) (2013). Global action to reduce HIV stigma and discrimination. *J Int AIDS Soc* 16(Suppl. 2):18893.

Siyayinqoba Beat it! (2014). SABC Channel 1. http://www.cmt.org.za/siyayinqoba Accessed December 1, 2014.

Smith RA, Simplon PD (2006). Drugs into bodies! A history of AIDS treatment activism. Exerpt reprinted in *Body Positive* 19(2); archived at TheBody.com. http://www.thebody.com/content/art31153.html

Strub S (2014). *Body Counts: A Memoir of Politics, Sex, AIDS and Survival.* New York: Scribner, pp. 141–144.

Treatment Action Campaign (2010). *Fighting for Our Lives: The History of the Treatment Action Campaign 1998–2010.* Capetown: Treatment Action Campaign http://www.tac.org.za/files/10yearbook/files/tac%2010%20year%20draft5.pdf. Accessed January 11, 2017.

UNAIDS (2007). Policy brief: greater involvement of people living with HIV. http://www.unplus.org/downloads/jc1299_policy_brief_gipa.pdf

UNAIDS (2008). Policy brief: criminalization of HIV transmission. http://data.unaids.org/pub/basedocument/2008/20080731_jc1513_policy_criminalization_en.pdf

UNAIDS (2104). Executive Director's report—down to the details: fast-tracking the response to end the AIDS epidemic by 2030. http://www.unaids.org/en/resources/presscentre/unaidsspeeches/2014/20141209_SP_EXD_PCB-35

UNAIDS (2016). UNAIDS announces 2 million more people living with HIV on treatment in 2015, bringing new total to 17 million.

http://www.unaids.org/sites/default/files/20160531_PR_Global_AIDS_Update_en.pdf. Accessed January 19, 2017.

Wada N, Jacobson L, Cohen M, French A, Phair J, Muñoz A (2014). Cause-specific mortality among HIV-infected individuals, by CD4+ cell count at HAART initiation, compared with HIV-uninfected individuals. *AIDS* 28:257–265.

Watney S (1987). AIDS and the press. In *Policing Desire: Pornography, AIDS and the Media.* London: Cassell.

World Health Organization. (2015). Policy brief: Consolidated guidelines on the use of antiretroviral drugs for treating and preventing HIV infection: what's new. November 2015. http://apps.who.int/iris/bitstream/10665/198064/1/9789241509893_eng.pdf

FURTHER READING AND VIEWING

Film and Video Documentaries

How to Survive a Plague (2012). Director: David France. 110 minutes. http://www.imdb.com/title/tt2124803

United in Anger (2012). Director: Jim Hubbard. 90 minutes. http://www.imdb.com/title/tt2085974

We Were Here (2011). Directors: David Weissman, Bill Weber. 90 minutes. http://www.imdb.com/title/tt1787837

Community Publications

AIDS Treatment News (aidsnews.org). Produced from 1986. Only partial archive from 1998 on thebody.com. http://www.aids.org/sources/about-aidsnews-org

Diseased Pariah News (DPN) (archived 1990–1999). httpːwww.diseasedpariahnews.com San Francisco newsletter that led the field for talent, humor, and originality (including centerfold pin-ups whose vital statistics included their CD4 count).

Doctor Fax (Dr. Fax) (full archive 1996–2000). http://i-base.info/doctor-fax-archive/

Equal Treatment (South Africa) (archive only from 2005). http://www.tac.org.za/equal-treatment

HIV Treatment Bulletin (full archive 2000–current). http://i-base.info/htb/months

Positively Aware, from TPAN; *POZ* magazine; and aidsmed.com (1994 to current, also archived online) are other notable U.S. publications.

POZ magazine (full archive 1994–current). http://www.poz.com

Project Inform and the New Mexico AIDS Infonet (later AIDSinfonet). Produced extensive nontechnical and up-to-date fact sheets.

Remaides (France) (only partial archive from 2007). http://www.aides.org/tous-les-remaides

TAGline (full archive 1992–current). http://www.treatmentactiongroup.org/tagline/1994

PART III

COMPREHENSIVE HIV PSYCHIATRIC ASSESSMENT, EDUCATION, AND TRAINING

11.

A BIOPSYCHOSOCIAL APPROACH TO PSYCHIATRIC CONSULTATION IN PERSONS WITH HIV AND AIDS

Kenneth Ashley, Daniel Safin, and Mary Ann Cohen

All severe and complex medical illnesses have psychosocial and psychological aspects and meanings and may have associated psychiatric diagnoses and are the purview of psychosomatic medicine psychiatry. Every patient with a severe and complex medical illness referred for psychiatric evaluation deserves a thorough and comprehensive biopsychosocial assessment (Levenson, 2011). For persons with HIV and AIDS, such an assessment has far-reaching implications for competent, compassionate, and coordinated care; adherence to medical treatment; risk reduction; and public health. Psychiatric disorders are associated with inadequate adherence to risk reduction, medical care, and antiretroviral therapy (ART). Many persons with HIV and AIDS have psychiatric disorders (Stoff et al., 2004) and can benefit from psychiatric consultation and care.

In 1967, Lipowski provided a classification of commonly encountered problems at the medical–psychiatric interface that is still relevant to HIV psychiatry today. These problems (with a modification of the fifth item, discussed in Chapter 1 of this book) include psychiatric presentation of medical illness, psychiatric complications of medical illnesses or treatments, psychological response to medical illness or treatments, medical presentation of psychiatric illness or treatments, and comorbid medical and psychiatric illness. These five problems have been illustrated with case vignettes in Chapter 1. Some persons with HIV and AIDS have no psychiatric illness, while others have a multiplicity of complex psychiatric disorders. Persons with HIV and AIDS may have multimorbid psychiatric disorders that are co-occurring and may be unrelated to HIV (such as schizophrenia or bipolar disorder). Patients may also develop psychiatric symptoms in response to HIV/AIDS, its treatments, or associated conditions (such as HIV-associated dementia). Multimorbid related or co-occurring medical illnesses and treatments (such as hepatitis C, cirrhosis, or HIV nephropathy and end-stage renal disease) can also result in psychiatric symptoms. Persons with HIV may also have multimorbid unrelated medical illnesses and treatments (such as coronary artery disease, cancer, and endocrine disorders). The complexity of AIDS psychiatric consultation is illustrated in an article by Freedman et al. (1994), with the title "Depression, HIV Dementia, Delirium, Posttraumatic Stress Disorder (or All of the Above)."

Comprehensive psychiatric evaluations can provide diagnoses, inform treatment, and mitigate anguish, distress, depression, anxiety, and substance use in persons with HIV and AIDS. Furthermore, thorough and comprehensive assessment is crucial because HIV has an affinity for brain and neural tissue and can cause central nervous system (CNS) complications even in healthy seropositive individuals. These complications are discussed in Chapters 16 (on HIV-associated neurocognitive disorders) and 26 (on CNS neuropathology) of this textbook. In this chapter, we provide a basic approach to persons with HIV and AIDS who are referred to a psychosomatic medicine psychiatrist or an HIV psychiatrist as well as a template for a comprehensive psychiatric evaluation. Neuropsychological evaluation can be a valuable adjunct in some persons with HIV and AIDS; this is covered in Chapter 12.

SETTINGS FOR PSYCHIATRIC CONSULTATIONS FOR PERSONS WITH HIV/AIDS

Psychiatry consultations are requested across a wide variety of settings, requiring the psychiatric consultant to be adept at understanding the needs and resources of each setting. While consults continue to present in traditional settings, such as the inpatient and ambulatory settings of acute care facilities and long-term care facilities, since HIV/AIDS is increasingly regarded as a manageable chronic severe illness, most persons with HIV and AIDS are seen in outpatient settings, clinics, private offices, medical homes, and other ambulatory care facilities. These settings have become a critical juncture for psychiatric assessment of patients, with a particular eye to chronic management and prevention of additional complications. Psychiatric consultations have become an important component to enhance the survival and quality of life for persons living with HIV/AIDS. Additional unique settings include home care, the settings of marginal housing (such as shelters, single room occupancy, and transitional housing), correctional facilities, and in homeless outreach contexts. The complexities of the many special settings in which persons with HIV may be evaluated are covered in Chapter 7, as well as in Chapter 9, where correctional facility settings are addressed in further detail.

As the medical care of persons with HIV and AIDS has shifted to the ambulatory setting, various models of integrated care are used in the multidisciplinary ambulatory care setting:

1. The co-located psychiatrist who works in a comprehensive HIV program: A co-located psychiatrist can provide evaluations, crisis intervention, psychotherapy, follow-up care, support groups, consultations to patients admitted in the inpatient setting, curbside consultations, teaching, and supervision.

2. The mental health team leader model: A clinician directs a diverse group of mental health providers in delivering care to patients through a particular site or program.

3. The triage model: A clinician participates in the screening of patients, then provides guidance about the appropriate referral to make for a particular patient.

In these various models, the lead clinician can be a psychiatrist or another mental health clinician, with a psychiatrist available for consultation. For a more detailed description of integrated models of care please see Chapter 7 of this textbook. It is critical to keep abreast of resources locally available for patients, with an eye to providing personalized care. It is important to recognize the need for setting aside an adequate amount of time for a comprehensive psychiatric consultation of any individual with complex severe medical illness, and HIV considerably magnifies this need. Follow-up care with individual, psychotherapy, couple therapy, or family therapy also requires an adequate amount of time.

Both inpatient and ambulatory evaluations will be presented in this chapter, with the hope that a clinician can develop the tools needed for a comprehensive assessment in any setting.

COMPREHENSIVE PSYCHIATRIC CONSULTATIONS

OUTPATIENT CONSULTATIONS

An outpatient consultation is an opportunity for a thorough psychiatric evaluation. By creating a safe and supportive environment, the psychiatrist attempts to engage the patient in this process and sets the groundwork, if necessary, to become an integral part of the patient's care team. This is more easily done in a co-located HIV psychiatry team model, as a psychiatrist can provide on-site psychiatric evaluations and consultations as well as follow-up psychiatric care. In the setting of the HIV clinic, a consultation may be requested by the primary HIV clinician directly through personal contact, by telephone contact, or by written request. The HIV clinician may indirectly request a consultation through another member of the team. Providing support for the patient through the process of referral for psychiatric assessment can take time and may require

discussion at more than one appointment. Clinicians need to be aware that attending both a psychiatric clinic and an HIV clinic may be perceived by some patients as doubly stigmatizing; some patients with HIV and AIDS are relieved to learn that psychiatric care is also available in their HIV care setting, finding it more acceptable than having to be seen for psychiatric care outside of the HIV care setting.

Process of Psychiatric Outpatient Consultation

The consultation begins with a discussion between the clinician and the psychiatrist to determine the reason for the psychiatric referral, the expectations of the consultee, the urgency of the referral, and some of the feelings that the patient has engendered in the consultee. During this discussion, the clinician can provide a summary of the patient's medical history. The clinician should discuss his or her concerns and the reasons for the psychiatric consultation with the patient. This open discussion by a sensitive and caring clinician can serve to diminish anxiety in the patient. It may also serve to dispel, or at least mitigate, frightening myths about psychiatrists and mental health care.

If there is a co-located HIV psychiatrist, ideally, the patient can be introduced to the psychiatrist during a scheduled visit with the HIV clinician. This introduction by the HIV clinician may prove invaluable and demonstrate the level of coordination of care being offered to the patient. The HIV psychiatrist can be presented as an integral member of the multidisciplinary team providing ongoing patient care. This may lead to better acceptance of the referral and set the stage for a continued collaborative relationship.

If the HIV psychiatrist is not in the HIV care setting, the HIV clinician should inform the patient of their ongoing collaboration with the HIV psychiatrist. Once the patient accepts the referral, the consultation is scheduled. If the consulting HIV psychiatrist has access to the medical record, he or she can review it, otherwise the consultee can provide additional clinical history.

INPATIENT CONSULTATIONS

The inpatient consultation for HIV and AIDS patients can be as varied as the reasons for admission. As HIV and AIDS care has become more focused on care of chronic illness in persons with access to HIV care, most inpatient admissions are not specifically related to AIDS, whereas some may be directly related to AIDS. As a result, inpatients can range from fully alert and engaged in the consult process to severely cognitively impaired. It is important for the psychiatrist to first gather as much information as possible from other members of the team requesting the consult. The psychiatric consultant may help the consultee clarify or explain the reasons for consultation in order to appropriately focus the consultation. The medical record, including laboratory data, ancillary tests, and medications, should be reviewed prior to seeing the patient.

Prior to entering and beginning the consultation, the psychiatrist needs to ascertain the correct name and

Table 11.1 SECTIONS OF A COMPREHENSIVE
PSYCHIATRIC CONSULTATION

1. Chief Complaint
2. History of Present Illness
3. Past Psychiatric History
   a. Suicide History
   b. Psychiatric Hospitalizations
   c. Psychiatric Outpatient Care
   d. Treatment with Psychotropic Medications, if any
4. Family Psychiatric History
5. Past Medical History
6. Psychosocial History
   a. Early Childhood, Developmental, and Family History
   b. Spiritual History
   c. Educational and Occupational History
   d. Trauma History and Response to Trauma History
   e. Sexual History
   f. Substance Use History
7. Mental Status Examination
8. Assessment
9. Diagnosis
10. Recommendations

identification of the patient. While this goes without saying for all patient contacts, it is even more crucial when providing care for persons with HIV because of AIDSism, stigma, and discrimination associated with HIV. Privacy can be a challenge in inpatient settings, depending on the type of unit or room where a patient is located. If the patient has visitors at the bedside, they should be asked to leave the room, allowing more privacy for the interview. If the patient requests that visitors remain present for the evaluation, it should be ascertained as to whether they want to discuss all aspects of their general health and hospitalization with the visitor present. It should not be presumed by the clinician that every person visiting the patient knows of the patient's serostatus or that the patient wants them to know.

During the assessment, the psychiatrist needs to request permission from the patient to gather additional data from clinicians in the outpatient setting, as well as from family and friends. The psychiatrist has to use his or her clinical skill to determine how detailed to be in certain parts of the comprehensive psychiatric consultation. All sections of the interview, outlined in Table 11.1, may be addressed, but the depth can vary. The initial inpatient consultation might not require the psychiatrist to gather every detail of the psychosocial history, as the patient may be too medically ill to tolerate such a long interview, or the privacy concerns may be too great. The psychiatrist has to determine how much depth to go into during each interview, obtaining at least basic information and deciding which components can be gathered either in subsequent visits during the inpatient admission or later on during follow-up in the outpatient setting. It is important for the psychiatrist conducting an inpatient consultation to realize that patients often meet many new clinical staff and often have repeated their history multiple times prior to the psychiatrist's arrival. Being sensitive to this situation and addressing it with the patient often serves as source of building rapport over the course of an impatient admission.

COMPREHENSIVE PSYCHIATRIC CONSULTATION

When the patient is first encountered, the HIV psychiatrist can set the tone for a nonjudgmental evaluation by starting with an introduction that is sensitive to the patient's potential anxiety surrounding the consultation. Suggestions for such an introduction include greeting and shaking hands. Shaking hands is especially important for persons with HIV and AIDS. Persons with HIV are exquisitely sensitive to others' fears of contagion and may be reassured by a warm handshake. The introduction includes the psychiatrist addressing the patient by his or her title and last name (Mr. A) and stating his or her title and last name (Dr. P). After establishing privacy and providing for appropriate seating and/or comfort, the psychiatrist should ask the patient, "How are you feeling today?" After listening to the response and following leads, if applicable, the psychiatrist can then describe the reason for the consultation. "Dr. M asked me to evaluate you for depression. Did she tell you that she was asking me to see you? How do you feel about seeing a psychiatrist?" This may provide an opportunity to ask Mr. A if he has ever seen a psychiatrist or had contact with the mental health system in the past.

During the process of the introduction, the psychiatrist can begin to assess the patient through careful observation. While specific observations are described in detail later in the chapter, under the section General Appearance, Manner, and Attitude, observation should begin at the first moment of the encounter. Each of the following sections presents the ideal amount of information that one would want to collect with an alert and comfortable patient. The specific amount of information collected in each initial consultation will vary depending on the nature of the consultation request, the current setting (inpatient or outpatient), and the ability of the patient to physically and mentally sustain the interview. Some sections may not be as urgent to address on the initial interview; it may be appropriate to collect various components over a few visits.

Although there is no special set order, the history-taking process should follow leads, if possible, and proceed from less anxiety-provoking to more anxiety-provoking issues. The demographic information and current life situation may be easy for some individuals to start with. It may enable the patient to become comfortable and start to develop a connection with the psychiatrist while discussing these somewhat less charged issues. It is especially important to learn early on about the patient's occupational and family history. Expression of interest in these aspects of the patient's life can help establish rapport and allow the patient to feel that the psychiatrist is thinking about him or her as not just a patient, symptom, or illness but as a person in the context of family, society, and community. Specific recommendations for history-taking in the inpatient general care setting are summarized in Table 11.2.

Chief Complaint

A *chief complaint* is the patient's statement of his or her problem and how that may relate to being referred for psychiatric

Table 11.2 RECOMMENDATIONS FOR HISTORY-TAKING IN INPATIENT SETTINGS

1. Knock on the door of the room even if it is open, and await a response.
2. Ascertain the patient's identity verbally and also with identification bracelet while beginning introductions.
3. Introduce yourself by name and title: "Good morning, Ms. B, I am Dr. P and I am a psychiatrist" (said while shaking hands).
4. Establish privacy by using the privacy curtains or door of the room.
5. Sit down near the bedside, preferably at the same level as the patient, if possible.
6. Attend to distractions with the patient's permission.
7. If the television is on at high volume, ask to turn it down or off.
8. If visitors are present, determine whether to proceed with the interview, request time alone, or reschedule after the visitors leave. Visits by partners, family members, or friends are especially important to persons with HIV and AIDS who, in addition to feeling isolated and alone, as with any severe illness, are extremely sensitive to rejection and discrimination and may place a higher value on the presence of visitors.
9. Attend to comfort and address pain or other urgent issues.
10. Obstacles to communication
    a. The sleeping patient
       Since sleep disturbances are prevalent in persons with HIV and AIDS, consider allowing the patient to rest, and come back later. Attempt to arouse the patient and obtain permission to proceed with the introduction and interview with appropriate apology for disturbing his or her sleep.
    b. Pain
       Address pain issues with the primary nurse or physician.
    c. Nausea or vomiting
       Provide an emesis basin and report to primary nurse.
    d. Need for bedpan or assistance to the bedside commode
       Provide bedpan if available or contact nursing assistant.
    e. Sensory deficits
       i. Visual impairment
          Describe what you are doing and what is happening and be certain not to touch the patient before fully explaining that you would like to shake hands in greeting and who and where you are.
       ii. Hearing impairment
          Ascertain that hearing aids are in place or obtain amplifiers.
          Use lip reading if possible.
          Speak slowly, loudly, and clearly and on the side of the ear with the better hearing.
          Obtain a sign language interpreter if necessary.
    f. Obtain interpreters if there is a language barrier.
    g. Communication barriers: endotracheal tube, tracheostomy, or ventilator
       Use a clipboard, paper, and pen to enable the patient to write responses to simple questions, if possible.
       Make use of a communication board if writing is not feasible because of paralysis or paresis.
       If these measures are not possible, use closed-ended questions with a code, such as head-nodding, blinking (one blink designates "yes" and two blinks designates "no"), or finger squeezing (one squeeze means "yes" and two squeezes means "no").

consultation. This statement should be recorded in the patient's own words.

History of Present Illness

The *history of the present illness* includes the onset, course, and progression of the illness, medications, if any, along with the current medical and psychiatric symptoms. It is important for establishment of rapport to allow the patient to tell the story of the illness in his or her words, with minimal interruption or intrusion except for occasional redirection. Although the psychiatrist may wish to have a thorough review of the history in chronological order, it is better to allow the patient to provide the story and for the psychiatrist to reconstruct the chronology by asking questions if the history is unclear. Allowing the patient to tell his or her story enables the psychiatrist to observe for cognitive impairment and to determine whether the patient is an accurate historian. Hearing the history of present illness recounted as a story often provides more information about remote and recent memory than does routine questioning.

Past Psychiatric History

Persons with HIV and AIDS have a high prevalence of psychiatric disorders. While some persons with HIV and AIDS have no psychiatric disorders, others may have a multiplicity of serious and often incapacitating psychiatric illnesses. Persons with HIV and AIDS are at especially high risk for cognitive disorders, affective disorders, substance use disorders, and posttraumatic stress disorder. The prevalence of psychiatric disorders in persons with HIV and AIDS is discussed in depth in Chapter 3, and a comprehensive approach to each of the most prevalent psychiatric disorders is presented in Chapters 14 through 20 of this book.

A comprehensive assessment should include a history of psychiatric treatment, types of treatment, response or responses to treatments, a history of psychiatric diagnoses, course of illness, and current involvement in psychiatric care. It is important to determine whether the patient is still in the care of other mental health clinicians and to obtain permission to contact the treating mental health clinician. A full review of both current psychotropic medications and those previously prescribed is important.

Suicide History

An important part of the overall history-taking is the assessment of suicidality. There is no treatment for suicide, only prevention and education. To evaluate for suicide risk in vulnerable persons with HIV and AIDS, HIV psychiatrists and other mental health clinicians need to be able to take a suicide history, recognize and ensure that depression and other psychiatric disorders are treated, determine risk factors and etiologies, and, ultimately, help to resolve the suicidal crisis, if present. Psychiatrists need to feel comfortable with taking a suicide history and discussing suicide in depth with a person with HIV and AIDS. No suicidal patient ever gets the idea for suicide from talking openly about suicide. Some persons who are suicidal are able to admit to suicidal ideation and even to plans for suicide. Far from being harmful, some persons who are suicidal may feel relieved to be able to talk about their suicidality. Patients are also able to discuss prior attempts as well as precipitants. From these discussions, risk factors for the patient can be determined and crisis intervention initiated. This discussion entails the establishment of a trusting relationship, discussion of suicide and death in relation to both the illness and the individual's philosophies and religious beliefs, and awareness of the value of continuity of care and reassurance that the patient will not be abandoned (Cohen, 1992).

Sharing suicidal feelings with an empathic listener is not only relieving but may also provide the patient with a new perspective. Being able to speak openly about suicidal thoughts and feelings is highly cathartic for some patients. Thoughts of suicide may provide some measure of consolation and control, but these thoughts can also be frightening, distressing, and painful. To resolve a suicidal crisis, it is important to re-establish bonds; provide the patient with a supportive network of family, loved ones, friends, and caregivers; and identify and treat psychiatric disorders. Crisis intervention, networking, and ongoing psychiatric care may help prevent suicide. Suicide is explored in depth in in Chapter 25.

Family Psychiatric History

The clinician should gather information about family members who have known psychiatric illness as well as a history of psychiatric hospitalization, psychiatric treatment, suicide, and substance use. This is important, as there may be genetic risk factors that may be useful in terms of diagnosis.

Past Medical History and Understanding of Illness

The medical history should include information about medical illnesses and symptoms, hospitalizations, surgery, traumatic injuries, as well as medications and other treatments. It is also helpful to determine whether the patient is consulting clinicians other than the primary HIV referring clinician and, if so, whether other medications are being prescribed. Integrative healing modalities should be explored in a nonjudgmental manner. Additionally, information about nutrition and exercise can be addressed.

A comprehensive psychiatric assessment of a person with HIV or AIDS would not be complete without a determination of the patient's understanding of his or her illness and its treatments (Cohen and Alfonso 2004). It is helpful to ask the patient, "What do you understand about your illness?" While medical advances have made HIV a manageable chronic illness that is not likely to cause death in persons with access to HIV care and antiretroviral medications and full viral suppression, not all patients have integrated this concept into their understanding of the illness, nor do they see their illness as controllable or manageable. It is also important to ask the patient if he or she has told any family members or friends about the illness. Because of HIV-related stigma and discrimination, some patients may have a difficult time telling anyone about their illness and may even take the labels off their medicine bottles or hide them from family members. One patient asked to come to the HIV clinic via the back door, to avoid being seen by anyone in the waiting area who might know her. It is important to ask the patient if he or she has told anyone of the diagnosis, what the response was, and whether he or she has experienced direct or indirect HIV discrimination from family or friends.

Specifics about HIV medical history include how and when the patient first learned about his or her serostatus, when antiretrovirals were started, current and nadir CD4 counts, if known, viral load, course and responses to illness, which antiretrovirals the person has been and is currently on, as well as responses to treatments. If the patient is known to have hepatitis C, history of course, treatments, and results are also relevant. Review of laboratory data, X-rays and other imaging studies, and other ancillary data, through discussion with the primary physician and/or by a review of the medical record, is a necessary part of the psychiatric consultation.

Psychosocial History

Early Childhood, Developmental, and Family History

Once again, it is helpful to begin with less affect-laden material, such as age, date of birth, and place of birth. Open-ended questions, such as "What was it like for you growing up?" and "Who was in your family when you were growing up?" may be useful for beginning this part of the history. Exploration of relationships with parents, siblings, and other family members, as well as discussions about parental drug and alcohol use can follow. History and chronology of early childhood losses and trauma are highly significant and deserve careful interest and documentation.

A thorough housing history includes questions about where the patient lives, whether the patient lives alone or with others, and whether the patient is homeless or marginally housed. Specific information should be obtained regarding whether the patient is comfortable and has space, privacy, an elevator if mobility is compromised, heat, and hot water and if the home is free of rodents or other pests. Persons who live in marginal housing, in shelters, or on the street may feel embarrassed to discuss these issues and may not disclose this information as a result.

Family history includes information about family of origin as well as relational history with partners. Since it is hard to suffer an illness in silence, it is important to ask if a patient has a support network and who is in that network—family, friends, and partners. The psychiatrist may determine whether the patient has disclosed his or her serostatus and, if so, to whom. Disclosure may be easier for some patients and, as mentioned previously, difficult to near impossible for others. The multidimensional determinants in considerations of disclosure include relational, psychological, social, cultural, spiritual, and political factors. Fear of disclosure to aged parents or children is often used as a reason for not telling any family member about serostatus.

Ages and health status of parents, or dates and causes of death, along with number, ages, and health of siblings are all relevant. History of medical illnesses and their impact on the patient are also significant. Relational history includes information about past and current partners and whether the patient is in a relationship. Allowing the patient to discuss the relationship is important. Such discussions should include questions about disclosure of serostatus to his or her intimate partner. It is important to ask for the number, names, ages, health, and whereabouts of children, if any, along with the status of the parent–child relationship. The complex issues of whether and when to disclose to children are relevant here. A comprehensive discussion of disclosure to children can be found in Chapter 33 of this textbook. Dialogue about disclosure to family, friends, and partners can begin during history-taking.

Cultural Identity and Cultural Formulation

Given the demographics of the HIV epidemic and the role that culture plays in health-seeking attitudes, risk behaviors, and expressions of distress, it is important to understand an individual's cultural identity. *Cultural identity* is a group of various identities that come together to determine how individuals understand themselves in relation to their environment. Some aspects of cultural identity include race, ethnicity, gender, age, sexual orientation, country of origin/migration history, religious affiliation/spirituality, socioeconomic status, and any other means by which someone may self-identify. It should be noted that the significance of the various identities are fluid and will vary depending on the context. Awareness of a patient's cultural identity will promote development of rapport and therapeutic alliance and allows the psychiatrist to develop a culturally appropriate care plan. While a comprehensive psychosocial history would include a cultural formulation, the process of this is beyond the scope of this chapter. Please refer to the Cultural Formulation Interview (CFI) in the Appendix Section of the Diagnostic and Statistical Manual, 5th edition (American Psychiatric Association, 2013).

Spiritual History

Exploration of spiritual beliefs and practices allows the psychiatrist to have an enhanced understanding of the patient's world view. The patient's belief system can impact the patient in myriad ways on a continuum from being a source of strength and resilience to being a source guilt, stigma, and shame. Depending on the patient's beliefs, spirituality may be an area that the psychiatrist needs to focus on, as a way to provide support for the patient or helping to alleviate guilt. There are occasions in which the engagement of a spiritual leader may be beneficial to the patient. For further discussion of spirituality assessment see Chapter 41 of this textbook.

Two spiritual screening tools that may be used are as follows:

FICA (Borneman et al., 2010)

F (Faith)—Is religious faith an important part of your day-to-day life? This question could be followed by associated questions about formal religious identity and level of spirituality

I (influenced)—How has faith influenced your life, past and present?

C (Community)—Are you currently a part of a religious community? This question helps clarify the role a spiritual community might play in treatment interventions.

A (Address)—What are the spiritual needs that you would like me to address? This question allows the clinician to identify spiritual areas that may be part of a treatment plan.

SPIRIT (Ambuel, 2000)

Spiritual beliefs

Personal spirituality

Integration with a spiritual community

Rituals

Implications for medical care

Terminal events planning (e.g., advance directives)

Educational and Occupational History

Educational history includes the following questions and is relevant in determination of current level of intellectual and occupational function: (1) "How far did you go in school?" (2) "How did you do in school?" (3) "What was school like for you?" (4) "Were there any problems with learning?" (5) "Were you in special education classes?"

Occupational history is an important determinant of level of function. For individuals who have worked and who took pride in their career, the inability to work can be devastating and may be a significant contributor to a sense of loss or distress. It is important to ask questions about occupation in a way that is sensitive to the individual's current condition. If someone is bed-bound and near the end of life, it is helpful for the psychiatrist to acknowledge clearly that the patient is no longer able to work but may have worked in the past.

Similarly, in the ambulatory setting it is best not to make assumptions and instead to elicit information about occupation in a sensitive and compassionate manner. For some individuals who are still able to work, their work may be a source of validation and meaning, for others it may be a source of stress and fatigue. It is also important to be able to use the information in subsequent visits and to record it clearly in the medical record so that the information is available to other members of the team.

Trauma History and Response to Trauma History

History of early childhood and other trauma is not easy to obtain. Some patients may refuse to talk about painful experiences whether distant or recent, particularly on a first encounter with the psychiatrist. If there is a history of trauma and this trauma was perpetrated by a parent or other close relative, this absolute violation and betrayal may lead to a loss of the most significant paradigm and basis for future development of trusting relationships. Hence, the patient may find it difficult to trust physicians and other health professionals, who may represent those very figures of parental authority. A brief, supportive statement validating the difficulty of talking about early trauma may serve to mitigate discomfort. Additional reassurance that it is normal for persons who have experienced early childhood abuse or neglect to have problems with trust can also be comforting.

If the patient is willing to discuss the painful experiences, it is helpful to ask direct and closed-ended questions, unless the patient proceeds to tell the story in his or her own words. Questions may include those about physical and emotional abuse as well as neglect. The psychiatrist may also ask about exposure to an environment in which physical or threatened violence was frequent, such as in the home or the neighborhood. Discussion of these topics may be relieving to the patient who has not been able to tell anyone about it because of threats or fear of reprisals. Specific questions about sexual abuse should elicit information about unwanted touching, molesting, or fondling, as well as penetration, intercourse, and rape. Later trauma, such as rape, life-threatening robbery, kidnapping, or the witnessing of trauma, including combat-related trauma, can be explored in detail as well. It is important to determine the dates of the traumatic events wherever possible.

Awareness of a history of trauma is important because it can be associated with dissociative phenomena, hyperarousal, depression, eating disorders, substance use disorders, intimate partner violence, and sex work. Specific questions about posttraumatic stress disorder should be covered, including those about dissociation, intrusive thoughts, nightmares, easy startle, hypervigilance, insomnia, and a sense of a foreshortened future. Consult Chapter 17 of this textbook for a detailed discussion of trauma assessment and assessment for posttraumatic stress disorder.

Sexual History

Assessing an individual's sexual health is an important part of evaluating their overall health. Sexual health encompasses a patient's physical, emotional, mental, spiritual, and social well-being related to sexuality and sexual activities, as well as an integration of sexuality into one's life while avoiding and reducing harmful consequences for the individual and the community (see *Public Health Reports*, 2013). Persons with HIV and AIDS have sexual needs as well as needs for companionship, tenderness, love, and romance. The HIV psychiatrist can provide a nonjudgmental space that is open-minded and normalizes a sexual health discussion. Many individuals are extremely uncomfortable discussing sexual feelings and may suffer in silence with problems of arousal, pain, or excitement. Some persons find it difficult to ask a partner to use a condom. Men and women with HIV and AIDS have a high prevalence of alcohol and other drug use, and some may continue substance use and associated HIV risk behaviors, such as sharing of needles and exchange of sex for drugs or money. Suggestions for taking a sexual history are summarized in Table 11.3; the questions are organized by topic, but discussion should cover these areas in a more conversational manner.

TALKING ABOUT SEXUALITY   Sexuality is so much more than sex; it is integral to a person's identity, encompassing more than a person's sexual behaviors. Sexuality is also an area where lesbian, gay, bisexual, transgender, and queer (LGBTQ) individuals may identify anxieties, trauma, or, alternatively, a rich developmental history and concept of self. LGBTQ patients deserve, desire, and benefit from understanding and supportive clinicians. Being clear and open-minded regarding issues related to sexual orientation and gender identity will open up space for the patient to discuss these issues. It can also help in gaining a patient's confidence and trust and in demonstrating the clinician's respect. The questions asked and language used will determine whether patients perceive clinicians as nonjudgmental, accepting, and open or as judgmental, discriminatory, or biased. Additionally, clinicians need to understand that some men who engage in same-sex behavior (men who have sex with men [MSM]) do not identify as gay or bisexual.

A common frustration on the part of clinicians and LGBTQ persons alike is the "misreading" of sexuality—namely, making assumptions about gender identity, sexual orientation, and sexual behaviors (Greenfield, 2007) based on cultural stereotypes. One way to avoid reflexively resorting to stereotypes is to be respectful of the terminology that patients use in reference to themselves or to describe their experiences and to mirror that terminology. The clinician should never hesitate to ask patients for further elaboration regarding what they mean to describe—it may even be gratifying to them that a clinician is paying attention to their sexuality, as this aspect of a person's intimate life is often overlooked by clinicians. Gaining an understanding of the patient's experiences and perspective regarding their sexuality is beneficial for the clinician beyond as a means of establishing rapport with the patient—it also enhances the psychosocial formulation.

While some of these questions may seem irrelevant, they can open the door to taking a full sexual history, which is essential to assessment for behavior-specific risks of infection or transmission.

Table 11.3 SEXUAL-HISTORY-TAKING—AN EGO-SUPPORTIVE APPROACH

Setting the Tone
1. I would like to gather some information on your sexual history. Have you discussed your sexual history with a clinician in the past?
2. How comfortable are you with talking about your sexual history?
3. If previous discussions have been uncomfortable, how can I make this a better experience for you?

Sexual Experience
1. When was your first sexual experience? What feelings did you have about the experience?
2. How sexually active are you with others and yourself?
3. Who are you sexually active with?
4. What types of sex do you engage in?
5. Do you engage in any form of sexual behavior that worries you or your partner?
6. Have you noticed a change in the frequency of your sexual activity?
7. Have you been in significant love or romantic relationships in your life?

Sexual Orientation and Gender Identity (SOGI)
1. When did you first begin to understand your sexual orientation? How would you describe your sexual orientation?
2. When did you first begin to understand your gender identity? How would you describe your current gender identity?
3. What are the genders of your sexual partners?
4. What is the sex on your original birth certificate?
5. How do you self-identify? What words do you prefer?
6. Have you been able to express your sexual orientation? Your gender identity?
7. Do feelings about your sexual identity play a role in your current level of distress?
8. Who have you shared your sexual orientation and gender identity with? How did people respond when you shared this information?
9. Do you experience any conflicts in your daily life regarding your sexual orientation or gender identity?
10. What impact does your religion or spirituality have on your sexual orientation or gender identity?
11. Have you ever been a victim of a hate crime?

Sexual Functioning
1. How satisfied are you with your sexual functioning?
2. People with chronic medical illness may experience problems with their sexual function.
3. What was your sexual function like prior to your medical illness? What is your sexual function like since you have been ill?
4. Often people with psychiatric illness experience problems with their sexual function. What is your sexual function like when you experience (illness) symptoms?
5. Often people who need to take medications experience problems with their sexual function. How is your sexual function since you have been on (the medication) compared with that before starting on (the medication)?
6. When did you have your first period? What was the experience of having your first period like for you? How has your period changed over the years?
7. When did you have your first ejaculation/orgasm? What was the experience of having your first ejaculation/orgasm like for you? How has your ejaculation/orgasm changed over the years?
8. How have the changes in your hormones affected your sexual function?

Sexual Pleasure
1. What do you find sexually pleasurable?
2. How satisfied are you with your sexual pleasure?
3. How enjoyable is sex for you?
4. How enjoyable is masturbation for you?
5. How do your religious beliefs affect your sexuality?
6. How do your cultural beliefs affect your sexuality?
7. Which of your sexual practices do you associate with feelings of shame?
8. Which of your sexual practices do you associate with feelings of anxiety?
9. Which of your sexual practices do you associate with feelings of unhappiness?

Sexual Health Promotion
1. How confident are you about maintaining your sexual health?
2. How many sexual partners have you had?
3. How has your number of sexual partners changed over time?
4. Have you ever had a sexually transmitted disease?
5. What methods are you using to prevent yourself from getting sexually transmitted infections (herpes, gonorrhea, syphilis) or HIV infection? How many sexual partners have you had in the last month?
6. What forms of birth control do you use?
7. What kind of barrier contraception are you using?
8. What kind of spermicidal preparation are you using?
9. What lubricants do you use during sexual intercourse?
10. Are you aware that petroleum-based lubricants (Vaseline and others) can cause leakage of condoms?
11. How do you put a condom on?
12. At what point during intercourse do you put on a condom?
13. How do you ensure that there is no air bubble trapped inside the condom?
14. While wearing a condom, how do you ensure that there is no leakage during intercourse?
15. How do you ensure that there is no leakage upon condom removal?

Characteristics to assess when talking about sexuality (Levounis et al., 2012) include the following:

1. Sex: The biological and anatomical attributes of male and female. Compare with *gender*.

2. Gender: A cultural concept including the combination of social, psychological, and emotional traits associated with masculinity or femininity.

3. Gender identity: A person's self-identification as male or female or other gender (e.g., gender-queer). Compare with *gender role*.

4. Gender role: Refers to the behaviors and dress that distinguish a person as male or female. Compare with *gender identity*.

5. Sexual orientation: Whether someone is attracted to same-sex partners, other-sex partners, both, or neither.

Substance Use History

It is important to be able to take a complete history of substance use for each individual who is referred for psychiatric consultation. The comprehensive history-taking of substance use can provide information of significance to all members of the treatment team. The role of substance use disorders in HIV transmission is covered in Chapter 14. It is important to be aware of interactions between prescribed medication and substances of misuse or abuse, as well as the impact of substance use on diagnosis and treatment adherence. Patients can be reluctant to discuss substance use and may see it as so much a part of their everyday lives that it is not even given a second thought. This can be as true for a business executive who has a three-martini lunch and continues to drink during and after dinner on a daily basis as it is for a chronic heroin-, cocaine-, or sedative-hypnotic-addicted individual. Furthermore, defensiveness and denial may need to be understood as concomitants of substance use disorders. For each individual, a history of the chronology of the substance use, from the first use to the last. is essential. A nonjudgmental approach is needed to help diminish defensiveness. Substance use may be used to console or self-medicate at times of crisis, loss, or trauma. Using "how," "when," and "what" questions is generally useful and can facilitate history-taking and help to avoid the potential blaming aspects of "why" questions.

Specific questions for substance use history-taking are summarized in Table 11.4.

MENTAL STATUS EXAMINATION/ PSYCHIATRIC EXAMINATION

The psychiatric examination records the emotional and cognitive presentation of the patient at the time of the evaluation. As with history-taking, there is no set order for the mental status examination. The least challenging and affect-laden areas should be addressed first, and the more complex and difficult ones last. Many of the functions being evaluated will have been observed during the process of meeting the patient and taking other portions of the history.

GENERAL APPEARANCE, MANNER, AND ATTITUDE

The psychiatrist can observe for signs of medical or psychiatric illnesses: mobility, gait, weakness, abnormal movements, general appearance, grooming, appropriateness and neatness of attire, responsiveness, cooperation, and ability to maintain eye contact. Observation for psychomotor retardation (slowing) or agitation can be helpful. The psychiatrist should listen carefully for rate, clarity, quality, tone, volume, modulation, and form of speech, including evidence of prosody, aprosody, dysprosody, aphasias, or dysphasias. Additionally, observation of skin for icterus, pallor, cyanosis, edema, rashes, or other lesions can be helpful. The psychiatrist should also evaluate whether the patient appears healthy or ill, robust or cachectic, with signs of wasting. Obvious signs of specific medical illness or organ impairment include involuntary movements, tremors, paresis, paralysis, facial droop or asymmetry, exophthalmos, neck fullness, spider angiomata, ascites, anasarca, dyspnea, tachypnea, cyanosis, clubbing, and pedal edema. The psychiatrist can look for signs of delirium such as fluctuating levels of consciousness and changes in attention, awareness, and cognition during the evaluation. Similarly, delirium related to intoxication or withdrawal may be observed with signs of slurred speech, "nodding out," tremulousness, pinpoint pupils (from use of opioids), dilated pupils (from opioid withdrawal or PCP), tracks and abscesses from injection drug use, and skin lesions indicative of subcutaneous drug use. Finally, the psychiatrist can look for signs of side effects of medications, such as lipodystrophy from antiretroviral medications or orobuccolingual movements (tardive dyskinesia) from psychotropic medications.

It is also important to determine whether the patient appears his or her stated age and, if the patient is working, whether he or she is appropriately attired for the occupation. Observing for relational ability, eye contact, handshake, and ability to engage is also significant. The patient's willingness to cooperate and his or her hostility, depression, anxiety, and fear should be noted.

AFFECTIVITY AND MOOD

Observation of affect includes attention to euthymia, dyphoria, euphoria, anxiety, irritability, hostility, expansiveness, and constriction or fullness of range. Affectivity is a somewhat objective assessment by the clinician, while mood is more subjective and reflects the patient's assessment of how he or she feels and is documented in the patient's words. Moods can include happy, calm, depressed, sad, tearful, anxious, angry, or suspicious.

THOUGHT PROCESS

Flight of ideas, looseness of associations, thought blocking, circumstantiality, tangentiality, word salad, neologisms, punning, and clang associations are ways in which the patient

Table 11.4 SUBSTANCE USE HISTORY-TAKING—AN EGO-SUPPORTIVE APPROACH

1. I want to know more about how you use substances. Can you tell me about how substances are a part of your life?
   Many people may use drugs or alcohol to get through difficult times. What have you used to get through these times?
2. Specifically ask about all drugs by name and street name (reference sites for further information: www.drugabuse.gov and www.erowid.com):
   Alcohol
   Opioids:
   Heroin—dope, smack, horse
   Methadone
   Opioid pain medications
   Cocaine—crack, freebase
   Cannabis—marijuana, weed, dope, pot, joints
   Sedative-hypnotics:
   Benzodiazepines
   Barbiturates
   Non-benzodiazepine sleep medications
   Hallucinogens:
   Lysergic acid dethylamide, LSD, or acid
   Psilocybin or mushrooms
   Phencyclidine—angel dust
   Stimulants:
   Methamphetamine or speed, ice, crystal meth, crank
   Dimethoxymethylamphetamine or DOM, STP
   "Party drugs:"
   3,4-methylenedioxy-methamphetamine (MDMA), ecstasy, Molly, X, XTC
   Ketamine or K, special K, Ket, super K, vitamin K
   Gamma-hydroxybutyric acid or GHB, liquid E, Georgia Home Boy
   "Synthetics:"
   Bath salts (synthetic cathinones)
   K2/Spice ("synthetic marijuana")
   Steroids
   Inhalants
   Tobacco
3. Precipitants
   a. What led to your first trying (the specific substance or substances) _____?
   b. What was your reaction to it?
   c. How were you able to obtain it?
   d. What effect did it have if the use was in response to a problem, crisis, or trauma in your life?
4. Chronology
   a. When did you first use _____?
   b. What is your frequency and pattern of use following that first use?
   c. What other drugs or alcohol did you use?
   d. How did using _____ affect your school, work, and relationships?
   e. Has the substance use caused any disruptions in your life?
   f. When did you last use?
5. Amounts, routes, and access
   a. What is your heaviest use? Average use?
   b. What is the route of administration?
      Injection—with or without sharing of needles or works:
      IntravenousSubcutaneous or skin-poppingInsufflation or snortingSmokingOral
   c. What means did you use to get the substance?
      Income/employment
      Exchange of sex for drugs
      Selling drugs
      Selling belongings
      Selling family belongings
      Robbery, violent crime
6. Course, stage of change, and treatments
   Have you had treatment for your substance use?
   Has treatment been suggested to you in the past for your substance use?
   Have you had any periods of non-use?
   When was your last period of non-use? How was it achieved?
   What was your longest period of non-use? How was it achieved?
   How have psychiatric symptoms impacted your substance use?
   How did you cope with distressing emotions during periods of non-use?

may connect thoughts and indicates the process of his or her thinking.

THOUGHT CONTENT

Preoccupations, obsessions, delusions, ideas of reference, thought insertion/broadcasting/withdrawal, and danger to others are important to assess. Specific well-formed and systematic delusions (paranoid and/or grandiose) as well as general suspiciousness and guarding are indicative of underlying psychotic processes. Suicidal ideas or intentions as well as plans or thoughts should be explored (Table 11.5). Thoughts of no longer wanting to live, without any intent of self-harm or actions to hasten their own demise, should be distinguished from thoughts of suicide. Protective factors for suicidality should be assessed, such as involvement with family and friends, coping skills, child-related concerns, and cultural and religious beliefs against suicide. Violent or homicidal ideas or plans need to be discussed. Suicide and HIV is covered in more detail in Chapter 25 of this textbook.

PERCEPTION

The patient should be asked about perceptions in a supportive manner that does not create defensiveness. Asking whether the patient "ever sees shadows" or feels that his or her "mind may be playing tricks" may be helpful. Specific questions to determine the presence of auditory, visual, olfactory, or tactile hallucinations are necessary. Observation for signs that the patient is responding to internal stimuli should be documented.

COGNITION

This is a crucial part of the evaluation and needs to be done in a systematic, comprehensive, and non-threatening manner. The initial aspects have to do with observation as described earlier, in the section on general appearance, manner, and

Table 11.5 SUICIDE HISTORY-TAKING

1. Have you ever thought about killing yourself?
2. What specifically made you think of suicide?
3. Have you ever tried to commit suicide?
4. What precipitated your previous attempt or attempts? Were you intoxicated at the time of the attempts?
5. How did you try to kill yourself?
6. When did you try to kill yourself?
7. Was anyone present at the time you tried to kill yourself?
8. What happened following your suicide attempt/attempts?
9. Do you know anyone in your family or outside your family who committed suicide?
10. Do you feel like killing yourself now?
11. What would you accomplish this?
12. Do you plan to rejoin someone you lost?
13. Who would miss you?
14. Who and what would you miss?
15. Do you have any specific plans?
16. What are they?

attitude, observing for level of alertness, consciousness, confusion, fluctuation, somnolence, or stupor. Careful observation may reveal perseveration on words, numbers, or actions. Every patient deserves a full baseline cognitive assessment, since early cognitive changes may be very subtle. A patient may have no evidence of disorientation to person, place, or time, may be able to register and recall, and may not have a subjective awareness of any cognitive difficulty. However, executive dysfunction may appear in a clock drawing or may be indicated in constructional apraxia on copying a three-dimensional cube as well as following a three-step series of simple instructions or replication of hand movements. Executive function pertains to the ability to organize, plan, strategize, and modulate behavior and thought. This assessment of cognition will help inform decisions regarding the patient's ability to adhere to care. See Chapter 16 of this textbook for a full discussion of neurocognitive assessment in persons with HIV and for a full discussion of HIV-associated neurocognitive disorders (HAND) and HIV-associated dementia (HAD). The gold standard for the assessment of HAND is neuropsychological testing (see Chapter 12).

Assessment for Delirium

Delirium is a clinical syndrome of global impairment of cognition, especially orientation and attention, including abnormal sleep–wake cycle, thinking, perception, language, and affect, with acute onset and fluctuating course. While delirium is most commonly seen in the inpatient general care unit and intensive care unit, it is also seen at times in the outpatient setting.

The terms used to describe delirium include acute brain failure (probably most accurate), acute cerebral insufficiency, acute confusional state, encephalopathy, intensive care unit (ICU) psychosis, and reversible toxic psychosis. Delirium subtypes include hyperactive, hypoactive, and mixed, and any subtype may be superimposed on dementia. Hyperactive delirium is often misdiagnosed as psychosis or mania and is characterized by confusion, illusions, hallucinations (especially visual), restlessness, loud speech, anger, irritability, combativeness, impatience, uncooperativeness, wandering, and distractibility. Hypoactive delirium is often misdiagnosed as depression and is characterized by staring, apathy, paucity of speech, slow speech, decreased alertness, lethargy, and decreased motor activity.

Assessment for HIV-Associated Neurocognitive Disorders, HIV-Associated Dementia, and Other Forms of Dementia

Persons with HIV may present with HAND at any age or stage of illness regardless viral load or CD4 count. Since persons with HIV are now living to older ages, they can also have other forms of dementia or both HAND and HAD and other dementias. Since 18% of persons over 50 years of age may also have cognitive changes related to normal aging, these may be encountered as well (see Chapter 16 for further details). The changes seen in aging are summarized in Table 11.6

Table 11.6 SIGNS AND SYMPTOMS OF NORMAL AGING VERSUS DEMENTIA

NORMAL AGING AND COGNITION	ALZHEIMER'S DEMENTIA
• New onset beginning at age 50 • Lack of progression • Subjective memory complaints • Annoying but not disabling • Frequent problems with name retrieval • Minor difficulties in recalling detailed events • Problems related to overloaded neuronal systems • Not associated with any other signs or symptoms • May be intermittent • Prevalence is estimated at 18%	• Insidious onset • Unrelentingly progressive impairment • Prominent memory impairment • Leading cause of dementia and functional disability in the elderly • 50% to 75% of all dementia is Alzheimer's • The four As of Alzheimer's dementia: Amnesia, Aphasia, Apraxia, Agnosia • Prevalence is 6.5%

HIV-associated neurocognitive disorders are differentiated primarily in terms of severity of functional impairment and are classified in three categories:

Asymptomatic neurocognitive impairment (ANI): mild to moderate impairment in at least two domains without obvious impairment in daily functioning

Mild cognitive impairment (MCI): mild to moderate impairment in at least two domains with at least mild interference with daily functioning

HIV-associated dementia (HAD): a subcortical and cortical dementia that is severe enough to cause functional impairment and is characterized by slowed information processing, deficits in attention and memory, and impairments in abstraction and fine motor skills

A brief assessment for HAND was developed by Simioni and colleagues (2010) and is a helpful tool. The Simioni questions are adapted with additions:

1. Do you experience frequent memory loss—do you forget the occurrence of special events, even the more recent ones?

2. Do you feel that you are slower when reasoning, planning activities, or solving problems?

3. Do you find it more difficult to perform activities that used to be automatic for you (paying bills, making plans)?

4. Do you have difficulties paying attention (to a conversation, a book, or a movie)?

5. Do you have difficulty doing things that used to be easy for you (playing the piano, speaking a second language, knitting a sweater)?

See Tables 11.7 and 11.8 for a summary of signs and symptoms of HAND, HAD, cortical and subcortical dementia, and dementia of the Alzheimer's type.

Since no screening tools have been identified as reliable and valid for assessment of HAND (Zipursky et al., 2013), we recommend a full cognitive assessment for delirium and dementia as well as the Simioni questions and the Mental Alternation test. For further clarification, the patient should be referred for neuropsychological testing.

The full cognitive assessment includes evaluation of memory, orientation, abstraction, executive function, similarities testing, proverb interpretation, as well as clock and Bender drawings. A compassionate and sensitive cognitive assessment includes efforts to reassure patients as well as following leads rather than a rapid-fire series of questions to answer and tasks to complete.

If a patient spontaneously reveals that memory is a problem, this lead can be followed with a statement such as "Let's see how your memory is working now." This can provide a smooth transition into a formal assessment of cognitive abilities. A specific introduction may include a sentence such as "Some of the questions that I ask may be too easy and others too hard, but this is the only way we have to understand what the problem is that you are having with your memory."

Specific questions as to orientation can be approached in an ego-supportive manner. Memory can be tested by observing the patient's ability to provide his or her detailed medical history when compared with information from collaterals. Memory is tested with evaluation of remote, recent, registration, and recall memory. Drawings can help in the assessment of visuospatial function as well as for perseveration and fine hand tremor. The copying of a three-dimensional cube assesses for constructional apraxia, as does a clock drawing (Lyketsos et al., 2004). Additionally, clock drawing is helpful in assessing executive function and planning as well as hemineglect. The patient should be asked to draw the face of a clock, starting with a circle and placing the numbers on the face. The patient should then be asked to draw the hands to represent a time of 10 after 11 on the clock drawing to assess ability to change mental sets. Repetition of numbers indicates perseveration. Irregular spacing of clock numbers with some too close together or too far apart is indicative of executive dysfunction with difficulty in planning. Left hemineglect may be associated with a lesion in the right parietal lobe.

Executive function—the ability to abstract, plan, organize, and initiate—is further tested with verbal fluency (listing the names of as many animals, repeating the phrase "no ifs, ands or buts," and tests of abstraction). Testing for abstract thinking is performed in several ways. The first and easiest is by asking the patient for similarities between two

Table 11.7 CORTICAL VERSUS SUBCORTICAL DEMENTIA

CORTICAL DEMENTIA—4 AS	SUBCORTICAL DEMENTIA—4 DS
• Amnesia—not helped by cues • Aphasia • Agnosia • Apraxia • Alexia • Affective disorders—not frequent • Loss of initiative • Psychomotor retardation • Gait—normal until late • Extrapyramidal signs—late • Pathological reflexes— grasp, snout, suck, Babinski—late	• Dysmnesia—helped by cues • Dysexecutive—difficulty with planning and decision-making • Delay—slow thinking and moving • Depletion—reduced complexity of thought • Affective disorders—severe • Apathy and inertia • Absence of the 4 As • Slow diminution of cognitive functions • Psychomotor retardation • Abnormal gait • Loss of initiative, vitality, physical energy, and emotional drive • Extrapyramidal signs

items that are in the same category; for example, "How are an apple and an orange similar to each other?" or, more difficult, "What do a fly and a tree have in common?" The second test for abstraction is proverb interpretation; for example, one can ask, "What does it mean when people say 'Don't cry over spilled milk?'" or another proverb can be used that is appropriate for the patient's country of origin or culture. The third means of testing for abstract thinking is interpretation of current events. Intellectual function should be assessed in relation to educational and occupational levels and can be tested by observing vocabulary usage, comprehension level, and reasoning. To assess for concentration, calculation, and spelling, the patient can be asked to subtract serial 7's or 3's and spell the word *world* both forward and backward. Asking the patient about their understanding of their illness can provide an assessment of insight and judgment as well as abstract thinking.

RECOMMENDATIONS

Following the completion of either an outpatient or inpatient comprehensive psychiatric evaluation, it is critical that the psychiatrist discuss his or her findings with both the patient and the consultee. As patients often move quickly between various types of care environments such as outreach, ambulatory care, emergency departments, substance and physical rehabilitation facilities, inpatient medical and psychiatric settings over the course of their illness, it is important to ensure that all useful data are accessible to clinicians. During the course of the psychiatric evaluation, much information has been gained about the patient's potential psychiatric illness, how they understand and cope with their illness, and the strengths and barriers that exist in understanding their illness and maintaining their care plan. Each of these components is invaluable in addressing the needs of the patient in these

Table 11.8 ALZHEIMER'S DEMENTIA (AD) VERSUS HIV-ASSOCIATED DEMENTIA (HAD)—NOTE OVERLAP

AD	HAD
• Age over 65 years • Insidious onset • Unrelentingly progressive impairment • Prominent memory impairment • Amnesia • Aphasia • Apraxia • Agnosia • Impaired semantic fluency and naming • Impaired visuospatial analysis and praxis • Rapid forgetting of new information after brief delays • May have incontinence • May have cortical release signs	• Can occur at any age over 18 • Can be prevented • Can be reversed with antiretrovirals • Cognitive slowing • Psychomotor slowing • Impaired attention and concentration • Impaired impulse control • Impaired executive function • Apathy • Regression • Psychosis • Mood disorders • Dropping things • Impaired balance • Ataxia, tremor • Incontinence can occur late

various care settings. While providing useful information one should also consider the patient's privacy and who has access to his or her information in each setting. Working closely with these clinicians will ensure that they have the appropriate history they need while maintaining the patient's privacy in certain areas.

CONCLUSIONS

A biopsychosocial approach to psychiatric consultation can provide a sensitive and compassionate way to get to know the patient in the context of family, society, and community. This approach is a valuable asset to the comprehensive care of a person with HIV and AIDS.

REFERENCES

Ambuel B (2000). Fast Fact and Concept #019: Taking a spiritual history. End-of-Life Physician Resource Center.

Borneman T, Ferrell B, Pulchaski CM (2010). Evaluation of the FICA tool for spiritual assessment. *J Pain Symptom Manage* 40:163–173.

Cohen MA (1992). Biopsychosocial aspects of the HIV epidemic. In GP Wormser (ed.), *AIDS and Other Manifestations of HIV Infection*, 2nd ed. (pp. 349–371). New York: Raven Press.

Cohen MA, Alfonso CA (2004). AIDS psychiatry: psychiatric and palliative care, and pain management. In GP Wormser (ed.), *AIDS and Other Manifestations of HIV Infection*, 4h ed. (pp. 537–576). San Diego: Elsevier Academic Press.

Freedman JB, O'Dowd MA, Wyszynsk B, Torres JR, McKegney FP (1994). Depression, HIV dementia, delirium, posttraumatic stress disorder (or all of the above). *Gen Hosp Psychiatry* 16:426–434.

Greenfield J (2007). Coming out: the process of forming a positive identity. In HJ Makadon, KH Mayer, J Potter, H Goldhammer (eds.), *The Fenway Guide to Lesbian, Gay, Bisexual, and Transgender Health*. Philadelphia: American College of Physicians.

Levenson LL (2011). *American Psychiatric Publishing Textbook of Psychosomatic Medicine* (pp. 3–17). Washington, DC: American Psychiatric Publishing.

Levounis P, Drescher J, Barber ME (eds.) (2012). *The LGBT Casebook*. Washington, DC: American Psychiatric Publishing.

Lipowski ZJ (1967). Review of consultation psychiatry and psychosomatic medicine: II. Clinical aspects. *Psychosom Med* 29:201–224.

Lyketsos CG, Rosenblatt A, Rabins P (2004). Forgotten frontal lobe syndrome or "executive dysfunction syndrome." *Psychosomatics* 43(3):345–355.

Public Health Reports (2013). Understanding Sexual Health. Volume 128, Supplement 1.

Simioni S, Cavassini M, Annoni J-M, et al. (2010). Cognitive dysfunction in HIV patients despite long-standing suppression of viremia. *AIDS* 24(9):1243–1250.

Stoff DM, Mitnick L, Kalichman S (2004). Research issues in the multiple diagnoses of HIV/AIDS, mental illness and substance abuse. *AIDS Care* 16(Suppl. 1):S1–S5

Zipursky AR, Gogolishvili D, Rueda S, et al. (2013). Evaluation of brief screening tools for neurocognitive impairment in HIV/AIDS: a systematic review of the literature. *AIDS* 27:2385–2401.

ADDITIONAL RESOURCES

Erowid: http://www.erowid.com
Montreal Cognitive Assessment: http://www.mocatest.org
National Institute on Drug Abuse: http://www.drugabuse.gov

12.

NEUROPSYCHOLOGICAL EVALUATION FOR PERSONS WITH HIV AND AIDS

Bibilola D. Oladeji and Kevin R. Robertson

PATTERN OF NEUROCOGNITIVE IMPAIRMENTS IN HIV-ASSOCIATED NEUROCOGNITIVE DISORDER

HIV enters the central nervous system (CNS) early in the course of infection and can produce neurological complications at any stage during disease evolution, from seroconversion to late-stage AIDS (Heaton et al., 2011; Robertson and Hall, 1992). These neurological complications are usually characterized by cognitive, behavioral, and motor symptoms. In the pre–antiretroviral treatment (ART) era, HIV-associated neurocognitive disorder (HAND) manifested as a progressive subcortical dementia; cortical deficits were not observed until very late in the disease as the brain became globally affected (Brew and Chan, 2014). Early symptoms included inattention, forgetfulness, slowed thinking, reduced verbal fluency, gait unsteadiness, impaired handwriting, and social withdrawal, sometimes with irritability (Navia et al., 1986). These symptoms later progressed to flattening of affect and inability to understand written materials, marked slowing of cognitive and motor responses, and inability to maintain conversation. Gradually, as cognitive impairment progressed, symptoms worsened, and many individuals were incapable of activities of daily living (ADL) and living independently.

In the post-ART era, the rates of severe forms of neurocognitive disorders have markedly decreased, and there is increased heterogeneity of the neuropsychological profile of HAND (Schouten et al., 2011). However, HAND, even in its mildest forms, is associated with reduced medication adherence, impaired functioning in everyday activities, lower quality of life, and increased mortality (Farinpour et al., 2003; The Mind Exchange Working Group, 2013). The neurocognitive deficits most commonly observed are mental slowness, attention/memory deficits, and impaired executive functioning (Woods et al., 2009). This pattern of neurocognitive impairment is consistent with underlying pathology in the subcortical and frontostriatal systems.

In recent times, with greater longevity of adults living with HIV, additional cortical features such as impairments in learning ability and deficits in prospective memory are increasingly being observed in the neuropsychological profile (Brew and Chan, 2014; Heaton et al., 2011). Furthermore, there is evidence that HAND is beginning to have more extrapyramidal features (Brew and Chan, 2014). Apart from aging, other factors that may be contributing to this changing pattern of neurocognitive impairment in the post-ART era are co-infection with hepatitis C virus (HCV), substance abuse, and genetic factors (Foley et al., 2008). Even with advances in the diagnosis and treatment of HIV infection, cognitive impairment tends to correlate with disease severity.

It should be noted that the pattern of neurocognitive dysfunction is not consistent across individuals, and there is no single prototypical pattern of neuropsychological impairment associated with HIV infection (Dawes et al., 2008). However, the most commonly affected cognitive domains in HAND still fit the subcortical profile, with core deficits being mental slowness, attention/memory deficits, and impaired executive functioning (Schouten et al., 2011). This pattern of deficit has influenced the development of test batteries used in the assessment of neurocognitive impairments in HIV (Valcour et al., 2011).

Although the vast majority of persons with HIV/AIDS reside in sub-Saharan Africa, little research to date has documented the cognitive consequences of HIV infection in this and other resource-limited settings (RLS). The problem in these settings is particularly compounded by the co-occurrence of other HIV and non-HIV conditions, including opportunistic infections and malnutrition, as well as by a lack of normative data (Robertson et al., 2009). The few available studies suggest that HIV similarly affects the CNS and that existing neuropsychological instruments can be used detect neurocognitive deficits. For example, a study evaluating the pattern of neuropsychological performance in Uganda showed reduced processing speed, attention, executive functioning, and verbal learning/memory among HIV-positive individuals relative to controls (Robertson et al., 2007). Similarly, studies done on Asian populations have reported deficits in abstraction/executive function, speed of information processing, verbal fluency, working memory, and learning (Cysique et al., 2007; Gupta et al., 2007). These findings demonstrate that the pattern of neurocognitive impairment in sub-Saharan Africa and in other RLS is similar to that in developed countries, despite differences in culture and the predominant HIV clades (Robertson et al., 2009).

BRIEF HISTORY OF CURRENT NOMENCLATURE

Nervous system complications associated with HIV infections were recognized early in the epidemic, and a dementing syndrome was recognized soon after the definition of AIDS. Price and colleagues were the first to attempt a clinical and pathological characterization of this "progressive dementia," which they labeled the "AIDS dementia complex" (ADC) (Navia et al., 1986). ADC was characterized by progressive cognitive impairment in the absence of impaired consciousness usually evolving over weeks to months, with accompanying motor and behavioral disturbances. In an attempt to quantitate the degree of severity of dementia and to allow further research and characterization of this syndrome, they proposed the "Memorial Sloan-Kettering Scale," or the ADC staging. The ADC staging consisted of six levels of increasing severity: 0 = normal cognition, 0.5 = equivocal/minimal finding, 1 = mild dementia, 2 = moderate, 3 = severe, and 4 = end stage (Price and Sidtis, 1990).

Subsequently, the American Academy of Neurology (AAN) constituted a task force to develop for research purposes consensus nomenclature and case definitions for HIV-1-associated neurological conditions. The AAN proposed two levels of neurological manifestation of HIV infection: HIV-associated dementia (HAD) and minor cognitive motor disorder (MCMD) (AAN, 1991). Diagnosis of HAD required the presence of an acquired abnormality in at least two cognitive domains causing impairment in work or ADL and either an abnormality of motor function or specified neuropsychiatric or psychosocial functions. The AAN criteria recognized three subtypes of HAD: HAD with motor symptoms, HAD with behavioral or psychosocial symptoms, and HAD with both motor and behavioral/psychosocial symptoms. The less severe MCMD was characterized by impairment of cognitive/behavioral function in two areas, accompanied by mild impairment in work or ADL.

To better describe and classify the spectrum of cognitive and neurological impairments observed in HIV-infected people since the introduction of effective ART, a working group supported by the U.S. National Institutes of Health published a classification scheme in 2007 (Antinori et al., 2007). The term *HIV-associated neurocognitive disorders (HAND)* was suggested as a more comprehensive label for this group of disorders. The updated definitional criteria for the diagnosis of HAND, known as the Frascati criteria, give greater priority to the recognition of the presence of cognitive impairments over motor, personality, or emotional difficulties and emphasize performance on comprehensive neuropsychological testing batteries (Antinori et al., 2007). The Frascati criteria recognize three degrees of severity of neurocognitive disorders, ranging from the milder asymptomatic neurocognitive impairment (ANI), to mild neurocognitive disorder (MND), to the more severe HIV-associated dementia (HAD).

DIAGNOSTIC CRITERIA FOR HAND

The current diagnosis and classification of HAND is based on (1) the severity of neuropsychological impairment as determined by performance on neuropsychological evaluations, (2) the impact of the neuropsychological impairment on functioning, and (3) the absence of confounding factors or other causes for the observed impairment. A simple mnemonic for HAND diagnosis is the Rule of 3. There are three spheres of assessment, and three levels of severity within each sphere. The three spheres of assessment are (1) neurocognitive impairment, (2) functional impact, and (3) confounding factors. Within the neurocognitive sphere there are three levels of severity: (1) normal, (2) mild, and (3) moderate/severe impairment. Within the functional sphere there are three levels of impact: (1) no impact on adaptive daily living skills, (2) mild functional impact, and (3) marked functional impact. Within the confounding factors sphere there are three levels: (1) none or minimal, (2) contributing, and (3) confounded.

Neuropsychological impairment is defined by performance below appropriate normative comparative group means on formal neuropsychological tests (see Table 12.1). *ANI* is

Table 12.1 CATEGORIES OF HAND IN THE FRASCATI CRITERIA[*]

	CRITERIA[†] (NEUROPSYCHOLOGICAL TESTING AVAILABLE)	CRITERIA[‡] (NEUROPSYCHOLOGICAL TESTING NOT AVAILABLE)	FUNCTIONAL STATUS
Asymptomatic neurocognitive impairment (ANI)	1 SD below mean in at least two cognitive domains	Mild impairment in at least two cognitive domains	No impairment in ADL
Mild neurocognitive disorder (MND)	1 SD below mean in at least two cognitive domains	Mild impairment in at least two cognitive domains	Impairment in ADL
HIV-associated dementia (HAD)	2 SD below mean in at least two cognitive domains	Moderate impairment in at least two cognitive domains	Notable impairment in ADL

Abbreviations: ADL, activities of daily living; SD, standard deviation.

[*]Adapted from Antinori et al. (2007).

[†]At least five cognitive areas must be assessed.

[‡]Assessed on mental status examination (use of standard MSE tests such as Folstein MMSE [Folstein et al., 1975], HIV Dementia Scale, International HIV Dementia Scale).

defined as performance of 1 standard deviation (SD) below the mean of demographically adjusted normative scores in at least two cognitive areas (or domains) without any apparent changes in ADL.

As an important note of clinical relevance to the reader, we believe that asymptomatic neurocognitive impairment is a misnomer, since any level of discernable cognitive dysfunction is of concern and should be recognized and addressed as early as possible. We prefer the term *preclinical neurocognitive impairment (PNI)*, which is more appropriate given that we now know many individuals in this category progress to MND (Grant et al., 2014). However, in keeping with the current common nomenclature we will continue to refer to PNI as ANI.

MND is defined by the same test performance as ANI but with mild impairment in ADL. HAD diagnosis requires a test performance of at least 2 SD below demographically corrected means in at least two different cognitive areas, accompanied by marked difficulties in the activities of daily living.

ASSESSMENTS OF NEUROPSYCHOLOGICAL IMPAIRMENTS IN HAND

Cognitive domains of functioning are typically assessed using a variety of neuropsychological tests (see Table 12.2). Cognitive areas usually tested include the following: attention and working memory, speed of information processing, language/fluency, executive functioning, verbal and visual learning, verbal and visual memory, and motor skills. To provide an adequate and appropriate assessment of cognitive functioning for HAND diagnosis, at least five cognitive areas must be assessed and at least two test measures per domain are preferred to assess each domain (Antinori et al., 2007).

In routine clinical practice and in RLS where the instruments, time, and expertise to carry out formal psychological assessments may not be readily available, the current diagnostic algorithm makes provisions for the use of standardized mental status examinations to detect the presence of cognitive impairment (see Table 12.1). It is similarly required that at least two different areas of cognitive functioning be affected. At present, the reliability of HAND diagnosis made using the mental status examination is still uncertain.

ASSESSMENTS OF FUNCTIONAL CAPACITY

An assessment of functional capacity is necessary in the diagnosis of HAND. Functional capacity is usually measured as everyday functioning or ADL. It usually includes evaluations of areas such as mental acuity, employment, social functioning, shopping, cooking, driving, public transportation, laundry, household keeping, financial management, medication management, understanding media events, and childcare (Robertson and Yosief, 2014). Functional decline can be assessed by self-report (either individual or report from a knowledgeable informant) and objectively using performance-based measures. Self-report and performance-based measures should be assessed using standardized instruments. The level of functional impairment increases with the severity of cognitive impairment. This increased severity is included in the categorization of patients into different levels of HAND. In assessing level of functioning, it is important to rule out comorbid conditions that could be responsible for the functional decline or those that might bias a patient's reporting of symptoms such as depression.

Patients with ANI have no functional limitations. MND diagnosis requires mild impairment in functioning characterized by reduced work productivity or efficiency, difficulty in at least two areas of ADL, and a performance less than 1 SD on normative guidelines for the patient's country and demographic peer group on standardized instruments. Mild impairment may manifest as reduced mental acuity and inefficiency in work, home-making, or social functioning. HAD, by contrast, is characterized as a moderate-to-severe impairment in functioning. This is defined as dependence in two areas of functioning, inability to work, and a performance below 2 SD on normative guidelines for the patient's country and demographic peer group on standardized instruments. Patients present with an inability to function at work and require help with functions such as dressing, eating, maintenance of personal hygiene, handling money, and shopping, but their ability to communicate needs may remain intact (Antinori et al., 2007; Robertson and Yosief, 2014).

Commonly used self-report instruments for ADLs in HIV populations include Patient's Assessment of Own Functioning (PAOFI) (Chelune et al., 1986) and a modified version of the Lawton and Brody ADL scale (Lawton and Brody, 1969). Objective assessments of functional status involve the use of laboratory measures of shopping, cooking, driving an automobile, financial management, medication management, and vocational abilities. Medication management ability can be assessed using a revised version of the Medication Management Test (MMT-R) (Heaton et al., 2004), and financial skills can be assessed using the San Diego Finances tests (Gandhi et al., 2011). Even though objective measures of functioning provide improved assessment over subjective measures, their use is time consuming and requires specialized test materials or equipment and thus are often not practical for most clinical or research settings (Heaton et al., 2004).

Both the self-report and performance-based tests are influenced by educational, cultural, and societal biases and cannot predict who will develop progressive impairment (Clifford and Ances, 2013). Assessment of everyday functioning is affected by the complexity of everyday activities in different settings. For example, neurocognitive deficits that typically impact everyday life in a Western, developed society may be less likely to impact daily functioning in a rural, agrarian population to the same degree. Similarly, a patient with the same degree of neuropsychological impairment might have no problem in functioning in a rural area but might be significantly handicapped if the person has to live in the city. In addition, self-report measures are subjective and could be influenced by factors such as depression and degree of insight.

Table 12.2 EXAMPLES OF TESTS THAT CAN BE USED TO
EVALUATE IMPAIRMENTS IN ABILITY DOMAINS

DOMAIN		TESTS
Language/fluency	Language	• Wide Range Achievement Test (WRAT-4) • National Adult Reading Test (NART) • WAIS (III or IV) Vocabulary subtest
	Fluency	• Controlled Oral Word Association Test (FAS) • Category Fluency • Action Fluency
Executive functioning		• Stroop Color and Word Test • Trail Making Test–Part B • Color Trails-II • Wisconsin Card Sorting Test • Tower Test
Speed of information processing		• WAIS Symbol Search Subtest • WAIS Digit Symbol Subtest • Symbol Digit Modalities • Trail Making Test–Part A • Color Trails-I • Stroop Color Naming
Attention and working memory		• WAIS Digit Span • Letter Number Sequencing • Paced Auditory Serial Addition Test (PASAT)
Verbal and visual learning	Verbal learning	• California Verbal Learning Test • Rey Auditory Verbal Learning Test • Story Memory Test • Hopkins Verbal Learning Test (HVLT-R) • WMS-III Paired Associates Subtest • WMS-III Logical Memory Subtest
	Visual learning	• WMS-III Visual Reproduction Test • Brief Visuospatial Memory Test (BVMT-R) • Rey-Osterreith Complex Figure Test
Verbal and visual memory		• Delayed recall test of the verbal and visual learning tests listed above
Motor skills		• Grooved Pegboard Test • Timed Gait • Finger Tapping Test

Abbreviations: WAIS, Wechsler Adult Intelligence Scale; WMS, Wechsler Memory Scales.

As with neuropsychological tests mentioned earlier, most of the questionnaires and performance-based tests have been developed and standardized in Western countries, hence cannot be assumed to be valid across all populations. In order to be valid in a particular setting, ADL tests need to be appropriately adapted to reflect the everyday lives of the population in which it is to be applied.

CONFOUNDING/COMPOUNDING DISORDERS

Making a diagnosis of any of the subtypes of HAND requires a determination that the neurocognitive impairment and functional decline detected on evaluation are directly attributable to HIV infection rather than to other comorbid conditions. The

presence of comorbid conditions is very common in patients with HIV, and this presents a major problem in properly identifying and classifying HAND, especially in clinical settings. A study conducted in the United States found that up to 15% of patients had severe comorbid conditions that precluded HAND diagnoses and less severe comorbid conditions were identified in the rest of the sample (Heaton et al., 2011). The determination of whether the neurocognitive and functional impairments are caused by the comorbid conditions require detailed information about the condition and a clinician's judgment of the severity and impact of these conditions on neurocognitive and everyday functioning. Clinical judgment needs to take into account the time of onset and the course of the condition in relationship to the HIV infection and observed deficits.

Proper identification of comorbid conditions and making a judgment about their contribution to observed neurocognitive impairment require additional assessment. This includes a thorough medical and neurological history, developmental history (to ascertain premorbid level of neurocognitive functioning), alcohol and substance use history, and a thorough neurological examination. Laboratory tests may be important in excluding comorbid infections and metabolic or endocrine disorders. Brain imaging studies can be used to detect opportunistic infections, cerebrovascular disease, and other cerebral lesions.

The Frascati criteria provide guidelines for classifying confounding comorbid conditions into three levels: incidental, contributing, and confounding. Incidental conditions are of minimal severity and do not contribute to the cognitive or functional impairment observed on assessment. With incidental level of confounding, there is no difficulty in attributing the cause of neurocognitive impairment to HIV and no clouding of the diagnostic picture.

Contributing conditions, by contrast, can have a substantive impact on the level of observed impairment, but their presence is not sufficient to account for the totality of the impairment. HIV infection is also considered to contribute significantly to the cognitive impairment and functional decline observed. Developmental disorders, past history of traumatic brain injuries, and systemic diseases such as stroke are examples of conditions that could potentially contribute to impairment. HAND diagnosis can still be made in the presence of contributing conditions; however, the severity of the component of the neurocognitive impairment or functional limitation attributable to HIV is difficult to ascertain. In cases where it is unclear if the comorbid conditions preceded the observed impairments, continued follow-up will be required. If the comorbid condition improves or remains stable with follow-up but there is continued decline in the functional and cognitive impairment, a diagnosis of HAND can be made.

Confounding conditions are severe enough to account for the neurocognitive impairment and functional decline observed in the patient. HAND diagnosis cannot be made in the presence of confounding conditions. The patient will need to be reassessed after recovering from such conditions. For example, an initial diagnosis of HAND cannot be made in the presence of delirium. However, delirium may be seen superimposed on a patient with a previously established diagnosis of HIV-associated dementia or other HAND diagnosis. Conditions that can act as confounds include CNS opportunistic infections, medications, or developmental or acquired conditions that are not related to HIV (Antinori et al., 2007).

PURPOSE OF NEUROPSYCHOLOGICAL TESTING

The main aims of neuropsychological evaluations in HIV-infected populations include but are not limited to:

1. The identification of neurocognitive impairment directly attributable to HIV.

2. Assessing whether or not neurocognitive impairment is a result of other comorbid factors, such as co-infections

(e.g., with HCV) or psychiatric conditions (mood or substance use disorders).

3. Understanding the associations between neurocognitive impairment and HIV disease variables, such as viral load, current and nadir CD4 count, and neuropathological biomarkers.

4. Exploring the impact HAND has on typical activities of daily living, which can have very different cognitive requirements for different populations.

5. Determining optimal treatment parameters, including time of treatment initiation, ART regimen CNS penetration, and factors that facilitate medication adherence.

6. Offering feedback reports on illness progression and treatment response to patients and clinicians.

NEUROPSYCHOLOGICAL EVALUATION IN CLINICAL SETTINGS

Currently, there are no consensus guidelines on neuropsychological evaluations of patients with HIV in clinical settings. There is little evidence available to inform which subpopulations should be screened—for example, those who are symptomatic, or those with certain risk factors, or all patients—and, equally, how often to screen patients. Hence instituting widespread routine repeated neurocognitive screening in clinic patients cannot currently be recommended. However, neuropsychological testing continues to play a valuable role in longitudinal assessments for research (Barber et al., 2013; Clifford and Ances, 2013; Valcour et al., 2011). A baseline neuropsychological evaluation will allow documentation of where the patient started cognitively. If there are questions of decline later in the course of the disease, a baseline evaluation can always be referenced to put in context any changes.

The accepted standard for the diagnosis of HAND (especially the milder forms that have become more prevalent in the ART era) requires the use of neuropsychological test batteries assessing multiple cognitive domains. There is no agreement regarding the combination of tests in such batteries, and different studies have used different batteries comprising a variable number of tests (Robertson et al., 2009). The Frascati HAND study (Gandhi et al., 2010; Grant et al., 2014; Heaton et al., 2011) provides guidelines and details on possible tests with appropriate normative data in the supplemental tables. Tests and test batteries should be chosen bearing in mind the background and current life situation of the people with whom they will be used. Most test batteries for HAND take 1 to 4 hours to complete and require experts to administer them and interpret the results using appropriate norms; therefore, they are not feasible in most clinical settings and research settings in resource-limited countries.

This situation has led to the development and introduction of various rapid screening instruments for the assessment of neurocognitive impairment. While these screening tools

Table 12.3 COMMONLY USED SCREENING TOOLS

SCREENING TOOL	COGNITIVE DOMAIN ASSESSED	ESTIMATED TIME TO COMPLETE	COMMENTS
HIV Dementia Scale (HDS)	• Attention/working memory • Verbal memory • Spatial skills • Speed of information processing	10 minutes	Require training to use. Subject to education/cultural bias and not sensitive to milder forms of HAND. A score of 10 of the total score of 16 is considered impaired.
International HIV Dementia Scale (IHDS)	• Verbal memory • Speed of information processing • Motor	5 minutes	Less influenced by education and cultural bias. Can only identify severe forms of HAND. Cut-offs for some international settings are available.
NEU screen	• Attention and working memory • Executive functioning • Verbal fluency	10 minutes	Easy to administer. Ability to detect mild cognitive impairment. Normative data are available for the component tests (TMT-A, TMT-B, and COWAT)
Montreal Cognitive Assessment (MOCA)	• Visuospatial • Executive functions • Language • Memory • Attention and working memory	10 minutes	Readily available. May be influenced by education. Could detect impairment related to both cortical and subcortical dementia. Score of 26 and below of the total of 30 is rated as impaired.
Cogstate	• Psychomotor speed • Attention • Decision-making • Working memory • New learning	10–15 minutes	Requires training. Can be completed by patient with little supervision; time saving. Requires that patient be able to use a computer. Best for following participants over time, appropriate normative data are not available.

are not able to generate diagnoses, these tools are useful in identifying the presence or absence of cognitive impairment, selecting patients that may require more formal neuropsychological assessments, and monitoring the progression of HAND. Interpretations of scores on these screening instruments require that appropriate normative data are available for the setting. Most of the currently available screening tools are generally not ideal because they are neither sensitive nor specific for the milder forms of HAND (Kamminga et al., 2013; Valcour et al., 2011).

Available screening tools include standardized self-report questionnaires such as the Cognitive Functioning Subscale of the Medical Outcomes Study HIV Health Survey (MOS-HIV) (Revicki et al., 1998). Paper-based tools, such as the ACTG Brief Neurocognitive Screen (BNCS) (Ellis et al., 2005), HIV Dementia Scale (HDS) (Power et al., 1995), International HIV Dementia Scale (IHDS) (Sacktor et al., 2005), Montreal Cognitive Assessment (Nasreddine et al., 2005; Overton et al., 2013), and NEU Screen (Muñoz-Moreno et al., 2013), and computer-based tests, such as the Cogstate (Cysique et al., 2006) and Cambridge Neuropsychological Test Automated Battery (CANTAB) (Gibbie et al., 2006), are also available. Table 12.3 provides a description of the commonly used screening tools.

NORMATIVE DATA AND INTERPRETATION OF TEST SCORES

Appropriate demographically adjusted normative data are needed to accurately ascertain the presence of impairment and to interpret the scores from neuropsychological tests (Robertson et al., 2016). Test scores can be affected by the individual's, gender, age, education, literacy, race, geographic region of residence, primary language, and cultural background, among other factors. Hence, normative data which most closely approximate the individual's demographic characteristics are most appropriate to use in making a determination of impairment. Most of the commonly used cognitive measures have been validated for use in the United States and other Western countries, and their psychometric properties in these settings are well established.

Repeated assessments within the same individual allow a clear view of longitudinal change in test performance, and deficits emerging over time are evident (Robertson and Yosief, 2014).

Other important considerations in interpreting test scores include the concepts of test-wiseness and practice effects. *Practice effects* can be defined as an improvement in performance on a test due to repeated administration of the test.

Practice effects can vary between tests and also over time (Barber et al., 2013). To counter this effect, some tests have alternative forms, and it is suggested that there be an adequate length of time between repeat test administrations. *Test-wiseness* can be defined as test-taking skills that are acquired in formal educational environments. Such skills include the ability to sit still and be quiet, pay attention, use pen and pencil, take notes on verbal instruction, copy designs, solve problems, and work quickly and accurately. In developed countries, a high school education (10–12 years) usually provides enough experience for well-practiced test-taking skills, but the same may not be true for developing countries (Robertson et al., 2009). Performance on neuropsychological tests depends on these skills.

TESTING IN INTERNATIONAL SETTINGS

There are many challenges involved in conducting and interpreting neuropsychological assessments in international settings. These include the lack of neuropsychological expertise; differences in language, education, and culture; and unavailability of appropriate normative data for the interpretation of test results (Robertson et al., 2009, 2016). Existing neuropsychological tests have demonstrated sensitivity to HIV-associated neurocognitive effects in international studies and are therefore useful. However, the tests will need to be translated into target languages using standard procedures of back-translation. In addition, the tests need to be culturally adapted to ensure validity and reliability. Where there are no published normative data, an appropriate control group should be recruited and used for comparison purposes.

SUMMARY

Neuropsychological testing is important in the evaluation of persons with HIV and is central to the diagnosis of HIV-associated neurocognitive disorders. The diagnosis and classification of HAND require the use of comprehensive test batteries assessing multiple cognitive domains, which is generally not feasible in most clinical settings, such as the infectious disease or HIV clinic. Better screening tools and normative data need to be developed in order to be useful in identifying the presence of cognitive impairment, selecting patients that may require more formal neuropsychological assessments, and monitoring the progression of HAND. Currently available screening tools are limited by their lack of sensitivity to milder forms of HAND. While further studies are needed to establish the validity and usefulness of the currently available screening tools for HAND in everyday clinical practice, clinicians are encouraged to include screening for neurocognitive impairment in patient assessments. Where possible, neurocognitive assessments should be conducted early, prior to commencement of ART, to provide a baseline profile with which to monitor improvements or deterioration in the patient's status.

REFERENCES

American Academy of Neurology (AAN). (1991). Nomenclature and research case definitions for neurologic manifestations of human immunodeficiency virus-type 1 (HIV-1) infection. Report of a Working Group of the American Academy of Neurology AIDS Task Force. *Neurology* 41(6):778–785.

Antinori A, Arendt G, Becker JT, et al. (2007). Updated research nosology for HIV-associated neurocognitive disorders. *Neurology* 30:1789–1799.

Barber TJ, Bradshaw D, Hughes D, et al. (2013). Screening for HIV-related neurocognitive impairment in clinical practice: Challenges and opportunities. *AIDS Care* 26(2):160–168.

Brew BJ, Chan P. (2014). Update on HIV dementia and HIV-associated neurocognitive disorders. *Curr Neurol Neurosci Rep* 14(8):1–7.

Chelune GJ, Heaton RK, Lehman RAW. (1986). Neuropsychological and personality correlates of patients' complaints of disability. *Adv Clin Neuropsychol* 3:95–126.

Clifford DB, Ances BM. (2013). HIV-associated neurocognitive disorder. *Lancet Infect Dis* 13(11):976–986.

Cysique LA, Jin H, Franklin DR, et al. (2007). Neurobehavioral effects of HIV-1 infection in China and the United States: a pilot study. *J Int Neuropsychol Soc* 13(05):781–790.

Cysique LAJ, Maruff P, Darby D, Brew BJ. (2006). The assessment of cognitive function in advanced HIV-1 infection and AIDS dementia complex using a new computerised cognitive test battery. *Arch Clin Neuropsychol* 21(2):185–194.

Dawes S, Suarez P, Casey CY, et al. (2008). Variable patterns of neuropsychological performance in HIV-1 infection. *J Clin Exp Neuropsychol* 30(6):613–626.

Ellis RJ, Evans SR, Clifford DB, et al. 2005. Clinical validation of the NeuroScreen. *J Neurovirol* 11:503–511.

Farinpour R, Miller EN, Satz P, et al. (2003). Psychosocial risk factors of HIV morbidity and mortality: findings from the Multicenter AIDS Cohort Study (MACS). *J Clin Exp Neuropsychol* 25(5):654–670.

Foley J, Ettenhofer M, Wright M, Hinkin CH. (2008). Emerging issues in the neuropsychology of HIV infection. *Curr HIV/AIDS Rep* 5:204–211.

Folstein MF, Folstein SE, McHugh PR. (1975). "Mini-mental state". *J Psychiatr Res* 12(3):189–198.

Gandhi NS, Moxley RT, Creighton J, et al. (2010). Comparison of scales to evaluate the progression of HIV-associated neurocognitive disorder. *HIV Ther* 4(3):371–379.

Gandhi NS, Skolasky RL, Peters KB, et al. (2011). A comparison of performance-based measures of function in HIV-associated neurocognitive disorders. *J Neurovirol* 17(2):159–165.

Gibbie T, Mijch A, Ellen S, et al. (2006). Depression and neurocognitive performance in individuals with HIV/AIDS: 2-year follow-up. *HIV Med* 7:112–121.

Gupta JD, Satishchandra P, Gopukumar K, et al. (2007). Neuropsychological deficits in human immunodeficiency virus type 1 clade C-seropositive adults from South India. *J Neurovirol* 13(3):195–202.

Grant I, Franklin DR Jr, Deutsch R, et al.; CHARTER Group (2014). Asymptomatic HIV-associated neurocognitive impairment increases risk for symptomatic decline. *Neurology* 82(23):2055–2062.

Heaton RK, Franklin DR, Ellis RJ, et al. (2011). HIV-associated neurocognitive disorders before and during the era of combination antiretroviral therapy: differences in rates, nature, and predictors. *J Neurovirol* 17(1):3–16.

Heaton RK, Marcotte TD, Mindt MR, et al. (2004). The impact of HIV-associated neuropsychological impairment on everyday functioning. *J Int Neuropsychol Soc* 10(3):317–331.

Kamminga J, Cysique LA, Lu G, Batchelor J, Brew BJ. (2013). Validity of cognitive screens for HIV-associated neurocognitive disorder: a systematic review and an informed screen selection guide. *Curr HIV/AIDS Rep* 10(4):342–355.

Lawton MP, Brody EM. (1969). Assessment of older people: self-maintaining and instrumental activities of daily living. *Gerontologist* 9(3):179–186.

Muñoz-Moreno JA, Prats A, Pérez-Álvarez N, et al.; NEU Study Group. (2013). A brief and feasible paper-based method to screen for neurocognitive impairment in HIV-infected patients: the NEU Screen. *J Acquir Immune Defic Syndr* 63(5):585–592.

Nasreddine ZS, Phillips NA, Bédirian V, et al. (2005). The Montreal Cognitive Assessment, MoCA: a brief screening tool for mild cognitive impairment. *J Am Geriatr Soc* 53(4):695–699.

Navia BA, Jordan BD, Price RW. (1986). The AIDS dementia complex: I. Clinical features. *Ann Neurol* 19(6):517–524.

Overton ET, Azad TD, Parker N, et al. (2013). The Alzheimer's Disease-8 and Montreal Cognitive Assessment as screening tools for neurocognitive impairment in HIV-infected persons. *J Neurovirol* 19(1):109–116.

Power C, Selnes OA, Grim JA, McArthur JC. (1995). HIV Dementia Scale: a rapid screening test. *J Acquir Immune Defic Syndr Hum Retrovirol* 8:273–278.

Price RW, Sidtis JJ. (1990). Evaluation of the AIDS dementia complex in clinical trials. *J Acquir Immune Defic Syndr* 3(Suppl 2):S51–S60.

Revicki DA, Chan K, Gevirtz F. 1998. Discriminant validity of the Medical Outcomes Study cognitive function scale in HIV disease patients. *Qual Life Res* 7:551–559.

Robertson K, Liner J, Heaton RK. (2009). Neuropsychological assessment of HIV-infected populations in international settings. *Neuropsychol Rev* 19(2):232–249.

Robertson K, Yosief S. (2014). Neurocognitive assessment in the diagnosis of HIV-associated neurocognitive disorders. *Semin Neurol* 34(1):21–26.

Robertson KR, Hall CD. (1992). Human immunodeficiency virus-related cognitive impairment and the acquired immunodeficiency syndrome dementia complex. *Semin Neurol* 12:18–27.

Robertson K, Jiang H, Evans SR, et al.; AIDS Clinical Trials Group (2016). International neurocognitive normative study: neurocognitive comparison data in diverse resource-limited settings: AIDS Clinical Trials Group A5271. *J Neurovirol* 22(4):472–478.

Robertson KR, Nakasujja N, Wong M, et al. (2007). Pattern of neuropsychological performance among HIV positive patients in Uganda. *BMC Neurol* 7:8.

Sacktor NC, Wong M, Nakasujja N, et al. (2005). The International HIV Dementia Scale: a new rapid screening test for HIV dementia. *AIDS* 19(13):1367–1374.

Schouten J, Cinque P, Gisslen M, Reiss P, Portegies P. (2011). HIV-1 infection and cognitive impairment in the cART era: a review. *AIDS* 25(5):561–575.

The Mind Exchange Working Group. (2013). Assessment, diagnosis, and treatment of HIV-associated neurocognitive disorder: a consensus report of the Mind Exchange Program. *Clin Infect Dis* 56(7):1004–1017.

Valcour V, Paul R, Chiao S, Wendelken LA, Miller B. (2011). Screening for cognitive impairment in human immunodeficiency virus. *Clin Infect Dis* 53(8):836–842.

Woods SP, Moore DJ, Weber E, Grant I. (2009). Cognitive neuropsychology of HIV-associated neurocognitive disorders. *Neuropsychol Rev* 19(2):152–168.

13.

TRAINING IN HIV PSYCHIATRY

David M. Stoff, Mary Ann Cohen, Marshall Forstein, Anna L. Dickerman,

and Daena L. Petersen

INTRODUCTION

This chapter addresses HIV education and research training aimed at improving HIV treatment and prevention services by educating mental health clinicians and trainees about effective and ethical ways to deliver psychiatric services to people with HIV/AIDS. With the material presented here our goal is to improve HIV-related education for students and trainees in related mental health professions and to increase the number of practitioners and investigators who work with persons at risk for and living with HIV/AIDS. Effective education and research training programs in HIV embrace a model relevant to trends in the epidemic and the needs of persons infected and affected by HIV.

The development of effective antiretroviral therapy (ART) (initially designated as highly active antiretroviral therapy, or HAART) has transformed HIV/AIDS from an acute, infectious specialty illness to a chronic, complex primary care illness. Although the annual incidence of HIV in the United States has dropped precipitously from its peak of 130,000 in the 1980s to about 40,000 from 2010 to 2015 (Centers for Disease Control and Prevention [CDC], 2016c), the prevalence continues to rise, as more people with HIV infection are living for many years. With the longer lifespans that competent HIV clinical care and ART have made possible, HIV infection along with other noncommunicable multimorbid illnesses is occurring because of a combination of such factors as chronic immune activation, medication side effects, and the aging process itself. The emerging reality of HIV as a long-term illness makes integrated care approaches—also referred to as *shared care*—all the more relevant. Such models have been shown to be effective for improving health outcomes and reducing morbidity from HIV/AIDS in low- and middle-income countries (Nigatu, 2012) and from co-occurring mental and chronic medical illnesses in high-income countries (Smith et al., 2007). The concept of integrated care brings together delivery, management, and organization of services related to diagnosis, treatment, care, rehabilitation, and health promotion. Integrated care is based on the concept of a biopsychosocial model that maintains a view of each individual as a member of a family and community who deserves competent, compassionate,

and comprehensive care and treatment, provided with dignity. Ideally, integrated care provides more comprehensive management of complex and multiple health needs and is thus ideal for managing HIV, multimorbid medical, and psychiatric illnesses. Please refer to Chapters 1 and 11 for a detailed explanation of the biopsychosocial model, to Chapter 7 for further discussion of models of integrated care, and to Chapter 8 for a description of an approach to establishing an HIV psychiatry co-located program.

HIV curriculum and training programs need to focus on HIV as a chronic illness and concomitantly address prevention, integrated care, and treatment management. Some of the emerging behavioral and mental health issues that need to be addressed within the chronic/integrated model include (1) multimorbidity, (2) coping/quality of life/functionality, and (3) aging-related processes.

For patients who are motivated to adhere to therapy and who have access to lifelong treatment, AIDS-related illnesses are no longer the primary threat; instead, a new set of HIV-associated multimorbidities, complications, and co-infections have emerged, resulting in a novel chronic illness that for many will span several decades of life. Concerns are growing that the multimorbidity associated with HIV disease could affect healthy aging and overwhelm some healthcare systems, particularly those in resource-limited regions that have yet to fully develop a chronic care model. With persons living with HIV re-entering the workforce, a priority focus for outcomes should be redirected to real-world consequences of neurocognitive impairment—namely, the development, validation, and clinical implementation of cognitive neurorehabilitation interventions tailored to the needs of persons living with HIV infection. Finally, older people living with HIV are perhaps the most emergent population of relevance because the number of older individuals living with HIV/AIDS has risen dramatically over the last decade. In 2013, 26% of all HIV-infected Americans were over the age of 50 (CDC, 2016a) and that percentage is projected to double to 50% over the next years. Aging-related diseases and aging-related processes regarding HIV are of foremost importance. These issues may not necessarily be the focus of every HIV curriculum and training program, and some programs may emphasize them more than others. However, the issues are presented here as a reminder that HIV education and training programs will be most effective when curriculum and didactics are presented within the context of the nature and evolution of the HIV epidemic and tailored to the needs of infected and affected populations of interest.

We now turn our attention in this chapter to more detailed guidelines for curricula, education, and training in HIV psychiatry and introduce them within the comprehensive approach of the biopsychosocial model.

RELEVANCE OF HIV/AIDS EDUCATION FOR PSYCHIATRY TRAINEES

In recent years, there has been greater recognition in the literature of both the significance of and greater need for education of trainees in the field of HIV/AIDS psychiatry (Cohen and Forstein, 2012; Gitlin et al., 2004; Novack et al., 2007; Polan et al., 1990; Wright 2009). HIV psychiatry is an important area of training for several reasons. HIV psychiatry is a paradigm for teaching the biopsychosocial model (see Chapter 11), which has become standard in psychiatric training (Cohen, 2008, Cohen and Forstein, 2012; Cohen and Gorman, 2008; Cohen et al., 2010; Gitlin et al., 2004; Novack et al., 2007; Polan et al., 1990; Wright, 2009). Compassionate, comprehensive, and competent psychiatric care of persons with HIV/AIDS requires a nuanced understanding of the role of biological factors, such as acute and chronic medical illness; prevention and management of medical problems; and consideration of pharmacological issues, such as drug–drug and drug–illness interactions. Psychosocial factors, such as substance use, sexual practices and behavior, treatment adherence, and psychological reactions to illness, are all critical components of assessment and management in this patient population. End-of-life and palliative care issues require careful consideration throughout the course of treatment, not just as death approaches. Thus, in many ways, HIV psychiatry exemplifies the ideal integrative model and approach for working with the medically ill patient to improve adherence, reduce suffering, and decrease morbidity and mortality (Cohen and Forstein, 2012).

Psychiatric care of persons with HIV/AIDS also carries its own unique set of challenges and requires a distinctive skill set that necessitates a similarly specialized training. Some of these illness-specific concerns include prevention and risk reduction, associated public health implications, as well as "AIDSism," stigma, and discrimination (Cohen, 1989; Cohen and Forstein, 2012). Despite the apparent significance of these issues, however, there are numerous challenges and barriers to comprehensive training in HIV/AIDS psychiatry. These include, but are not limited to, a rapidly evolving landscape of epidemiology and treatment (see Chapters 2 and 3), pressures related to time and productivity in the setting of increasingly rigorous guidelines for accreditation in graduate medical education, and complacency or even denial about HIV and AIDS (see Chapter 6; Cohen and Forstein, 2012).

NEED FOR AND PRACTICE OF DIVERSITY TRAINING

With national headlines spotlighting the lives of rich and famous lesbian, gay, bisexual, and transgender (LGBT) people, youth and adults across the United States are seeking medical and psychiatric services for identity exploration, including gender transition (DeAngelis, 2002; Lambe, 2015; Out.com editors, 2016). Individuals and families are requesting counseling and mental health services with questions regarding gender identity, gender expression, sexual orientation, and sexual identity. Young people and adults, previously unable to openly question their sexual and gender identities, are appreciating a cultural change. Though not without experiences of stigma and bullying, individuals identifying as lesbian, gay, bisexual, transgender, questioning, and intersex (LGBTQI) are finding more support for identity confusion, including gender dysphoria. At the same time, in the context of LGBT national visibility, children and adolescents, as they pursue developmentally appropriate tasks, now have adults in their lives who reflect a diversity of lesbian, gay, bisexual, and transgender individuals. In addition, in popular culture, graphic-novel anime characters represent individuals whose sexual orientation and gender identity are represented on separate continua, which young people today understand as normal versus previously traditional male and female, masculine versus feminine, and homosexual versus heterosexual (DeAngelis, 2002).

In the sections that follow, one institution's initiative, in Charleston, SC, to provide medical and psychiatric services for identity exploration and gender transition is described.

MEDICAL UNIVERSITY OF SOUTH CAROLINA GENDER AND SEXUAL ORIENTATION EXPRESSIONS CLINIC

Within the state of South Carolina there are only a handful of psychiatrists with demonstrated experience working with individuals questioning their gender identity and sexual orientation. At Medical University of South Carolina (MUSC), family members started asking pediatric endocrinology clinical staff about potential mental health and psychiatry clinicians considered to be skilled clinicians who support the development of healthy and mature LGBT individuals. Thus, in response to the rising numbers of individuals requesting services through MUSC Department of Pediatric and Adult Endocrinology clinics and increased referrals from a local organization serving LGBTQI youth, and with direct patient and family access of services through MUSC Department of Psychiatry and Behavioral Sciences, Child and Adolescent, and General Psychiatry clinics, a special clinic focusing on sexuality, sexual orientation, and gender variance was started. The MUSC Gender and Sexual Orientation Expressions Clinic for identity exploration was developed to provide a safe and accepting place for patient self-exploration. The clinic was founded and implemented by a psychiatric resident with significant experience working within the LGBT community as well as in HIV and mental health. The objective of this special clinic is to prevent increased rates of suicide, alcohol and drug abuse, homelessness, and HIV and hepatis C infection (Stieglitz, 2010).

Children, adolescents, and their parents, as well as adult patients, receive support from a psychiatrist or psychotherapist during their exploration and, ideally, acceptance of their sexual orientation and gender identity.

The clinic provides psychiatric evaluation, individual and family psychotherapy for gender and sexual orientation exploration, as well as assessment regarding the need for psychotropic medications. Patients presenting to this clinic receive primarily psychotherapy, instead of psychotropic medication management independent of or in combination with psychotherapy.

Overall, through clinical evaluation, this patient population has shown that significant multiple life stressors related to revealing their personal conflicts about their sexual orientation or gender identity result in increased levels of anxiety and dysphoria. In addition, individuals seen in the clinic describe being bullied within educational systems, by teachers, guidance counselors, and peers. Many individuals and their families have already accessed mental health services through other psychiatric or mental health clinicians and have had mixed experiences with clinicians' attitudes about lesbian, gay, bisexual, transgender, intersex, and questioning individuals. Thus the established goals for the Gender and Sexual Orientation Expressions Clinic project include increasing patient access to quality care, providing resident education and training through didactic and clinical experience—which leads to the development of highly skilled and competent psychiatric clinicians—and increasing the level of collaborative care between endocrinology and psychiatry services for these patients and their families.

Initially, an experienced psychiatry resident physician started a one-half-day clinic project on Wednesday afternoons through the Child and Adolescent Psychiatry Clinic. The clinic time was chosen so that direct in-clinic supervision would be available with Dr. A. Lee Lewis, Child and Adolescent Psychiatry Clinic Medical Director (Levin, 2016). In addition, as part of the General Psychiatry Resident Clinic, time was made available for one experienced psychiatry resident physician to provide psychiatric services to children, youth, and adults. The resident was supervised by Dr. Frampton Gwynette, whose subspecialty area is autism spectrum disorder (ASD). Through his clinical services with children, youth, and families, Dr. Gwynette has provided individual, group, and family services as well as medication management for a disproportionate number of individuals with ASD presenting with co-occurring gender dysphoria (DeVries et al., 2010).

After 1 year of providing these collaborative clinical services, the clinic time has been increased to 2 half-days to address the increasing number of patients accessing these clinic services at MUSC. In addition to resident physician time in this clinic, two social workers, Sue King, MSW, and Meredith Lyons Crews, LISW, provide individual and family therapy for children, adolescents, and their families through the Child and Adolescent Psychiatry Clinic. Ms. King and Ms. Lyons Crews have provided services to this population as a part of the general child and adolescent clinic for many years, though without formalizing psychiatry resident involvement, as well as collaborative clinical coordination between the psychiatry and endocrinology departments in place.

OPPORTUNITIES FOR RESIDENT AND FELLOW TRAINING WITHIN THE LGBTQI POPULATION

Few psychiatry residency training programs in the United States provide education and training about sexual orientation and gender identity development and self-acceptance (Hausman, 2002; Johnson, 2015). Furthermore, as noted in the Institute of Medicine (IOM) 2011 report, *The Health of Lesbian, Gay, Bisexual, and Transgender People*, medical providers often feel discomfort in providing medical and psychiatric services to LGBT individuals. A study by Rutherford and colleagues (2012) examined the impact of provider stigma on LGBT patients in mental health care and raised the question of whether this stigma increases health disparities experienced by patients when presenting for psychiatric care. In addition, despite an increase in coverage of LGBT health and mental health topics within residency training, the IOM report indicates that deans of U.S. medical schools continue to express dissatisfaction with the education curriculum for teaching LGBT health– and mental health–related areas. The report further noted medical students' lack understanding of key health concepts that are critical for effective patient education. They continue to demonstrate significant challenges when attempting to differentiate between patient sexual behaviors and sexual identity, which leaves student doctors poorly prepared to discuss sexual health–related concerns when providing clinical services (IOM, 2011; Obedin-Maliver et al., 2011).

Formal psychiatry residency training within the Gender and Sexual Orientation Expressions Clinic is thus a unique experience, as it stands in stark contrast to the majority of psychiatry residency training programs across the United States. Clinicians working with LGBTQI persons provide a nonjudgmental clinical environment while providing developmentally appropriate mental health clinical services to ensure maturation of healthy individuals. To be effective clinicians, these young professionals must be able to create a positive developmentally appropriate space for individuals to explore the meaning of their questioning their sexual orientation or gender identity.

It is important for psychiatric trainees to have experience with LGBTQI individuals, children, young people, and adults. The LGBTQI population is a tremendously complex and vulnerable one with multiple risk factors and a high prevalence of HIV (Kates and Ranji, 2014). Residents and social workers support young people as they struggle with questions of identity often in ways most adults have not had to struggle to understand. Peer allies may also be an important resource for young persons and are now more available than ever before.

Members of the younger generation now have the opportunity to address these issues at a developmentally appropriate time. It is crucial that the therapeutic environment be established as a place where individuals may try on identities in order to determine which identities fit and those that do not fit. Some individuals may struggle with internal conflict regarding identity to such a degree that depression and other mental health problems develop or are exacerbated.

The Gender and Sexual Orientation Expressions Clinic is an extremely dynamic clinic. With LGBT individuals visible on local and national levels, adolescents who are struggling to fit into their peer groups are presenting to the clinic proclaiming their transgender and/or lesbian, gay, and bisexual identities. The majority of adolescents presenting with gender dysphoria will resolve and find acceptance of their cis-gender identities, or they will come to realize that they have actually been conflicted about their sexual orientation rather than their gender identity as initially believed.

CASE VIGNETTE

An adolescent female presented as transgender after verbalizing suicidal ideation and threats to a school counselor. The child grew up significantly sheltered by parents in a rural community of South Carolina. A parent and older sibling, who were worried about the patient threat of self-harm in school, accompanied the teen to her first appointment. During one-on-one psychiatric assessment, the teen stated that she was convinced she was transgender because "it is easiest to be transgender" in contrast to being cis-gender or lesbian, gay, or bisexual, or heterosexual. Young people seeing high-profile individuals experience these public figures as having significant power and influence. They wish to emulate them; this is particularly true for individuals or young people who, on evaluation, do not have a clear sense of self.

CURRICULUM AND CONTENT AREAS OF HIV/AIDS EDUCATION FOR PSYCHIATRY TRAINEES

Specialized teaching in HIV/AIDS psychiatry can be incorporated into numerous stages and various treatment settings throughout psychiatric training, including emergency room, inpatient, and outpatient locations. We propose here such a curriculum that can be implemented in specific care settings. In this model, comprehensive HIV/AIDS teaching can—and should—occur within the greater context of the more general psychiatric rotations, with curricula implemented via a variety of means and formats relevant to the particular clinical setting. For high-endemic areas, case-based teaching with opportunities for faculty development in supervision and education is ideal. Other areas with lower prevalence of HIV/AIDS may need to rely more on teaching via seminars, lecture didactics, journal clubs, or grand rounds. In such cases, telepsychiatry is another potentially rich resource for direct clinical experience.

Table 13.1 outlines the recommended curriculum content to be included in every program for psychiatric residents and fellows. One significant resource is the American Psychiatric Association (APA) Office of HIV Psychiatry, which provides speakers, a curriculum, and PowerPoint slide sets, at: www.psych.org/Resources/OfficeofHIVPsychiatry.aspx

Table 13.1. OUTLINE OF CONTENT AREAS OF HIV/AIDS EDUCATION FOR PSYCHIATRY RESIDENTS

1. Basic medical aspects of HIV
   a. Epidemiology
   b. Virology—CD4, viral load
   c. Transmission
   d. Immunology
   e. Medical and psychiatric illnesses related to HIV infection
   f. Multimorbid medical and psychiatric illnesses unrelated to HIV infection but associated with and prevalent in persons with HIV and AIDS
2. Education about prevention of HIV transmission and risk reduction in psychiatric settings
3. Psychiatric Assessment
   a. Establish rapport and set a non-judgmental tone
   b. Comprehensive assessment with special focus on sexual history, drug history, and suicidality
   c. Comprehensive psychiatric examination for symptoms and signs of
      (1) Mood disorders
      (2) Anxiety disorders—especially PTSD
      (3) Substance use disorders
      (4) Cognitive disorders
4. Differential Diagnosis
   a. Psychiatric
   b. Medical
      (1) HIV-related infections, cancers, neuropathies, myopathies, endocrinopathies, nephropathy, pancreatitis, hematologic illness
      (2) Non-HIV-related cardiovascular illness, cancers, endocrinopathies
      (3) ARV and other medication-related illnesses such as IRIS, lipodystrophy, lactic acidosis and metabolic disorders
   c. Psychosocial issues
5. Treatment of HIVAIDS
   a. Role of the psychiatrist as collaborator and member of a multidisciplinary team
   b. HIV psychopharmacology, ARVs, and drug-drug interactions
   c. Psychotherapeutic approaches to care
   d. Psychosocial aspects of care
   e. Palliative care
   f. End-of-life care

*Adapted from Cohen and Forstein (2012).

Other resources can be found in the Resource Appendix of this text.

BASIC MEDICAL ASPECTS OF HIV AND AIDS

Education about basic medical aspects of HIV and AIDS is an essential foundation for training in HIV psychiatry. Teaching in this area should include information about epidemiology, taking into consideration the inherently approximate and dynamic nature of prevalence and incidence rates. Thus, this information should be updated annually when teaching trainees. Competent psychiatric care of persons with HIV and AIDS also necessitates understanding of essential aspects of virology, immunology, transmission, and knowledge about the numerous medical and psychiatric illnesses—including both those that are directly related to HIV infection (e.g., HIV-associated neurocognitive disorders) and those associated conditions not directly caused by HIV infection but that are nonetheless prevalent in the HIV-infected population (e.g., substance use disorders).

PSYCHIATRIC ASPECTS OF HIV AND AIDS

In addition to psychiatric disorders directly related to or associated with HIV infection, there are numerous psychiatric issues highly relevant to treatment of persons with HIV and AIDS. Many of these are, in fact, routine components of psychiatric evaluation taught in training, such as assessment of substance use, sexual history and behaviors, and cognition. Other, more nuanced, aspects of HIV psychiatry include skills that all psychiatrists should ideally possess but that may require more specific training within the broader scope of residency education. These include clarification of psychodynamic issues and resolution of conflicts around risk-taking behaviors and nonadherence, such as assessment of readiness for change and timing of encouragement of behavior change. In this sense, training in HIV psychiatry provides a unique opportunity to teach specific psychotherapeutic concepts such as motivational interviewing.

Clinical experience in HIV/AIDS psychiatry also allows the trainee to develop confidence and proficiency in working with patients throughout the life cycle. This includes crucial skills relevant to certain developmental stages, such as sensitivity to issues of confidentiality and disclosure in childhood and adolescence, challenges and complexities of partnerships in the adult years (e.g., serodiscordant couples), and themes related to family planning and pregnancy.

Finally, psychiatric disorders (see Table 13.2) place patients at higher risk of both HIV transmission and suboptimal adherence to risk reduction and care (Blank et al., 2002; see Chapter 28 for further information about the role of psychiatric disorders in HIV transmission and prevention).

EDUCATION ABOUT HIV PREVENTION

Psychiatrists, by means of their frequently long-term relationships with patients, are in a unique position to incorporate education around HIV prevention into the therapeutic process. Though it may seem challenging, crisis or emergency settings offer a special opportunity for such counseling in an efficient, timely, and cost-effective manner. Trainees should be taught to routinely ask about risk behaviors and offer HIV testing to patients at risk for infection or who may be unaware of infection, thereby facilitating early intervention and treatment. This is important for both the patient and other potentially exposed

Table 13.2. PSYCHIATRIC DISORDERS AS VECTORS FOR HIV TRANSMISSION*

Posttraumatic stress disorder (PTSD)

- Sense of foreshortened future, problems with caring for self and body
- Unsafe sex

Mania
- Disinhibition and hypersexuality

Psychosis
- Disinhibition and regression

Depression

- Feelings of low self-esteem and self-worth, problems caring for self and body

Cognitive Disorders—Delirium and Dementia

- Disinhibition and regression

Substance Use Disorders

- Exchange of sex for drugs, sharing of needles and drug paraphernalia
- Intoxication or withdrawal from alcohol or other drugs
- Unsafe sexual behaviors

*Adapted from Cohen and Forstein (2012).

individuals. Important interventions that should be taught in this setting include education about risk behavior and risk reduction, including education about condom use and availability; referral for alcohol or other drug detoxification or treatment; and early recognition of HIV infection for early intervention (Cohen et al., 2011). Most importantly, referring a person who has been a victim of sexual violence or date rape for post-exposure prophylaxis may mean the difference between health and infection, life or death from HIV/AIDS, and prevention of potential suicide and, if past the 72-hour window, may be a chance to prevent development of independent central nervous system (CNS) reservoirs for HIV and thus prevent HIV-associated neurocognitive disorders. Please see Chapter 31 of this textbook for a detailed discussion of post-exposure prophylaxis.

PSYCHIATRIC ASSESSMENT IN HIV/AIDS

Recognition and treatment of psychiatric disorders in persons at risk for or diagnosed with HIV or AIDS can alleviate suffering and distress as well as improve medical adherence and prevent HIV transmission (Cohen and Forstein, 2012). Chapter 11 outlines a comprehensive, compassionate, and nonjudgmental approach to psychiatric evaluation of persons infected with or at risk for HIV that has been previously described in the literature (Cohen et al., 2010). In brief, this complete psychiatric consultation has been developed for both HIV prevention and those already affected by HIV/AIDS. Its model encapsulates the type of sensitive and

Table 13.3 PSYCHIATRIC ASSESSMENT IN HIV/AIDS*

1) Introduction, chief complaint, history of present illness
   a. Demonstration of compassion and respect by shaking the patient's hand
   b. Asking about the patient's understanding of his or her diagnosis or illness and its impact
2) Sexual history
3) Trauma history
4) Substance use history
   a. Benevolent and nonjudgmental approach
   b. Use of "how," "when," and "what" questions rather than the more potentially blaming "why"
   c. Awareness of street slang names for substances of abuse
5) Suicide history
6) Mental status examination
   a. Cognitive assessment
   b. Assessment of mood and affect

*Adapted from Cohen and Forstein (2012).

supportive evaluation involving invaluable skills for the psychiatric trainee to develop and that can help guide other nonpsychiatric clinicians in providing care.

Psychiatric assessment of persons with HIV and AIDS is complex (Freedman et al., 1994). Multimorbid psychiatric illness such as major mood and psychotic disorders (see Chapters 15–19 of this text) often co-occur and may be unrelated to HIV. Table 13.3 summarizes the crucial elements of a diagnostic approach that allow the trainee to provide diagnosis, inform treatment, and mitigate anguish, distress, depression, anxiety, and substance use in persons with HIV and AIDS. Suicide assessment in particular is an important focus of the assessment, as the rate of suicide remains high in persons with HIV and AIDS (Carrico, 2010; Carrico et al., 2007; Cohen et al., 2002; Kelser et al., 2010). Chapter 25 of this book is dedicated to a thorough review of suicide and HIV.

Obtaining a thorough trauma history is also crucial, as a history of trauma and posttraumatic stress disorder (PTSD) has been associated with suboptimal adherence to both medical care and risk reduction (Cohen and Forstein, 2012). See Chapter 17 in this text for more comprehensive information related to the role of trauma and PTSD in HIV transmission, as well as a curriculum specifically developed for clinicians treating the traumatized patient with HIV (Tavakkoli et al., 2014).

Tables 13.4 and 13.5 provide guides to empathic history-taking related to sexual history and substance use, respectively. Chapter 14 in this text also explores in-depth the role of substance use disorders in HIV transmission.

Thorough assessment of mood, affect, and cognition in particular is imperative for psychiatric assessment in HIV/AIDS. Cognitive evaluation is necessary in order to differentiate between delirium and dementia, as well as to recognize HIV-associated neurocognitive disorders (HAND) and other forms of cognitive impairment seen in immune reconstitution inflammatory syndrome (IRIS) when patients are started on ART. Most available standard screening tools are insufficiently

Table 13.4 SEXUAL-HISTORY-TAKING*

Setting the Tone

1. Often people with HIV/AIDS experience problems with their sexual function. How has HIV affected your sexual function?
2. How does your sexual function since you were diagnosed compare with that when you were HIV-negative?
3. Often people with psychiatric illness such as depression experience problems with their sexual function. What is your sexual function like since you have been ill?
4. How is your sexual function since you have been depressed (or had another psychiatric illness) compared with that when you were healthy?
5. Often people who need to take medications experience problems with their sexual function. What is your sexual function like since you have been on (the medication)?
6. How does your sexual function since you have been on (the medication) compare with that before starting on (the medication)?

Sexual Experience

7. How have the changes in your hormones affected your sexual function?
8. How enjoyable is sex for you?
9. How enjoyable is masturbation for you?
10. Do you have (a) sexual partner(s)?
11. Are you sexually active?
12. What is the frequency of your sexual activity?
13. Have you noticed a change in the frequency of your sexual activity?
14. How do your religious beliefs affect your sexuality?
15. How do your cultural beliefs affect your sexuality?
16. Which of your sexual practices do you associate with feelings of shame?
17. Which of your sexual practices do you associate with feelings of anxiety?
18. Which of your sexual practices do you associate with feelings of unhappiness?
19. Do you feel that you are addicted to sex?

Safe and Unsafe Sex

20. What methods are you using to prevent yourself from getting sexually transmitted infections (herpes, gonorrhea, chlamydia, syphilis, HPV) or HIV infection? How many sexual partners do you have?
21. How many sexual partners have you had?
22. How has your number of sexual partners changed over time?
23. What kind of barrier contraception are you using?
24. What kind of spermicidal preparation are you using?
25. What lubricants do you use during sexual intercourse?
26. Are you aware that petroleum-based lubricants (Vaseline and others) can cause leakage of condoms?
27. How do you put on a condom?
28. At what point during intercourse do you put on a condom?
29. How do you ensure that there is no air bubble trapped inside the condom?

(continued)

Table 13.4 CONTINUED

30. While wearing a condom, how do you ensure that there is no leakage during intercourse?

31. How do you ensure that there is no leakage upon condom removal?

32. Do you find it difficult to maintain an erection while using a condom?

33. Have you considered female condom use?

Questions to Assist in Sexuality History-Taking for LGBTQ Persons

34. What is your sexual orientation?

35. With which gender do you identify?

36. When and how did you discover your gender identity?

37. What words do you prefer to use to describe your sexual identity?

38. Do feelings about your sexual identity play a role in your current level of distress?

39. Have you come out as LGBT to your family? To your friends? To your coworkers or classmates?

40. Do you currently experience any conflicts regarding religion or spirituality and your sexuality?

41. Do you experience any conflicts in your daily life regarding your sexuality?

42. Have you been in significant love or romantic relationships in your life?

43. Have you ever been a victim of a hate crime?

44. Have you experienced bullying in school, camp, or in the workplace?

Follow-up Questions to Assist in Assessment of Sexual Orientation and Behavior

45. What is your sexual orientation?

46. What is your sexual activity like?

47. What types of sex do you engage in?

48. Do you engage in any form of sexual behavior that worries you or your partner?

49. Have you ever had a sexually transmitted disease?

*Adapted from Cohen and Forstein (2012).

Table 13.5 SUBSTANCE USE HISTORY-TAKING*

1. Many people who are ill may use drugs or alcohol to get through difficult times. What have you used to get through these times?

2. Specifically ask about all drugs by name and street name:
   - Alcohol
   - Heroin—dope, smack, horse, chieva, chiva, China white
   - Cocaine—coke, candy, nose candy, blow
   - Crack cocaine—crack, freebase, rock
   - Cannabis—marijuana, weed, dope, pot, joints
   - Sedative-hypnotics—primarily benzodiazepines such as alprazolam, Xanax, or "sticks"
   - Inhalants—printer cartridges, rubber cement and other glues, aerosolized chemicals
   - Hallucinogens
   - Lysergic acid dethylamide—LSD, acid, blotter, microdot
   - Psilocybin—mushrooms, 'shrooms
   - Methamphetamine—speed, ice, crystal meth, crank, Christina, Tina
   - Dimethoxymethylamphetamine—DOM, STP
   - Methylenedioxymethamphetamine—MDMA, Ecstasy, X, XTC, E, Thizz
   - Ketamine—K, special K, Ket, super K, vitamin K
   - Gamma-hydroxybutyric acid or GHB, liquid E, Georgia Home Boy
   - Phencyclidine—angel dust

3. Precipitants
   a. What led to your first trying (the specific substance or substances) _____?
   b. What was your reaction to it?
   c. How were you able to get it?
   d. What effect did it have on the problem, crisis, or trauma in your life?

4. Chronology
   a. When did you first use _____?
   b. What happened after that?
   c. What other drugs or alcohol did you use?
   d. How did using _____ affect your school, work, and relationships?
   e. What kind of trouble did you get into?
   f. When did you last use?

5. Amounts, routes, and access
   a. What is the most you can hold or use in a day?
   b. How do you take it?
      - Intravenous—with or without sharing of needles or works
      - Insufflation or snorting
      - Smoking
      - Subcutaneous or skin-popping
      - Oral
   c. What illegal means did you resort to in order to get it?
      - Exchange of sex for drugs
      - Shoplifting
      - Identity theft
      - Selling belongings
      - Selling family belongings
      - Robbery, violent crime

6. Course, stage of change, and treatments
   a. Have you been in substance abuse treatment programs?
   b. Have you ever wanted to or tried to stop using? If so, when?
   c. Does substance use pose a risk or harm to you at this time?

7. Have you considered 12-step programs such as Alcoholics Anonymous, Cocaine Anonymous, or Narcotics Anonymous?

8. Would you consider use of specific treatments (agonist therapy) such as methadone or buprenorphine for heroin addiction or naltrexone for alcohol addiction?

*Adapted from Cohen and Forstein (2012).

sensitive for detection of HAND, and some specific screening tools have been developed for this purpose (Berguis et al., 1999; Davis et al., 2002; Jones et al., 1993; Power et al., 1995). However, there is no current consensus on the validity, sensitivity, and specificity of a screening tool for HIV (Zipursky et al., 2013). Neuropsychological testing (not readily available in most clinical settings) along with the full cognitive assessment is the gold standard for diagnosing HAND. Chapter 16 of this text provides a comprehensive overview of HAND.

TEACHING TREATMENT APPROACHES TO AIDS PSYCHIATRY

As outlined in Chapters 37 to 42 of this text, psychiatric treatment approaches for persons with HIV/AIDS are diverse and

Table 13.6 ONLINE RESOURCES FOR TEACHING TREATMENT APPROACHES IN HIV PSYCHIATRY*

Johns Hopkins Point of Care Information Technology Site

http://www.hopkins-hivguide.org

University of Liverpool HIV Drug Interactions List

http://www.hiv-druginteractions.org

Medscape HIV/AIDS

http://www.medscape.com/hiv?src=pdown%2520and%2520

http://hivinsite.ucsf.edu

www.hiv-pharmacogenomics.org

New York Department of Health HIV Guidelines

http://www.hivguidelines.org

http://www.tthhivclinic.com/interact_tables.html

*Adapted from Cohen and Forstein (2012).

best approached in an integrated fashion. We recommend a case-based approach to teaching HIV/AIDS psychiatry. Chapter 1 of this text contains such vignettes as a model for training. This approach illustrates the complexities and nuances of differential diagnosis in persons with HIV and AIDS.

Trainees should be exposed to psychotherapeutic treatment modalities including crisis intervention, individual and couples psychotherapy, family psychotherapy, and group psychotherapy. Other complementary treatment approaches are also highly relevant in this patient population, including social services and outreach, relaxation response, yoga, meditation, exercise, and palliative and spiritual care. When teaching HIV psychopharmacology, it is important to include the particular vulnerability to adverse drug effects in this patient population, particularly extrapyramidal and anticholinergic side effects. Awareness of drug–drug interactions and hepatic metabolism is essential. Concepts of initiating dosage slowly and titrating cautiously are important to review with trainees.

Helpful online resources for teaching treatment approaches to HIV psychiatry are listed in Table 13.6 (see also the Resource Appendix of this text).

IMPLEMENTATION OF TRAINING CURRICULA

The curriculum outlined in this chapter is best taught through direct clinical experience. However, this may be challenging to implement depending on the geographic location and the type of treatment setting. Ideally, all clinical rotations can provide opportunities for specialized HIV/AIDS teaching. These may include inpatient psychiatry, forensic psychiatry, child and adolescent psychiatry, addiction, and geriatric psychiatry. Co-located care settings in particular—for example, HIV clinics with dedicated psychiatric staff—provide excellent learning experiences, if available. In such cases, trainees can subsequently follow patients during general care or psychiatric admissions for continuity.

In low-endemic areas, HIV psychiatrists may be consulted through the literature or the APA Office of HIV Psychiatry. Visiting electives in high-endemic areas can also offer valuable training experience. Regardless of the setting, case-based

learning and tutorials can and should be incorporated into both clinical and classroom or didactic teaching. Use of education "modules" linked with assigned reading of relevant chapters from textbooks such as this one are already being implemented in formal training programs around the country and are a useful means of helping trainees synthesize a large body of complex material. Finally, faculty development is necessary in order to deliver an inclusive, seamless approach to HIV psychiatry. In this way, trainees are offered role models and the ability to engage in a reciprocal teaching–learning experience.

RESEARCH TRAINING AND CAREER DEVELOPMENT OPPORTUNITIES

NIH RESEARCH TRAINING OPPORTUNITIES

Through separate pieces of legislation, different institutes and centers of the National Institutes of Health (NIH) have exhibited a long-standing commitment to fostering a highly capable biomedical and behavioral research workforce. Over the years, as science and the conduct of research have continued to evolve, as have workforce needs, there have been fluctuations in the NIH budget devoted to research training. Currently, the NIH funds extramural research training, career development, and diversity and capacity-building activities through a variety of programs at the undergraduate, graduate, postdoctoral, faculty, and institutional levels (see http://grants.nih.gov/training/extramural.htm).

Many of these programs are specific to a particular NIH institute and center. We illustrate this here with the most mission-relevant institute for our purposes, the National Institute of Mental Health (NIMH). There are three ways that an applicant can receive research training support from the NIMH (in all cases, one must be affiliated with an institution and have a mentor): (1) directly from the NIMH (Individual Awards—F, K, R36); (2) from an academic institution with an NIMH-supported training program (Institutional Awards—T32, R25); and (3) from an administrative supplement to an existing NIMH grant awarded to one's mentor (Diversity & Reentry Supplements). Recommended trajectories for research training, based on whether one is on a Ph.D. or M.D. track, should be consulted and used as guidelines and not fixed paths (see https://www.niaid.nih.gov/grants-contracts/training-career-grant-programs; http://www.niaid.nih.gov/researchfunding/traincareer/pages/careerphd.aspx; http://www.niaid.nih.gov/researchfunding/traincareer/pages/careermd.aspx).

The different kinds of NIH research training opportunities have varying goals, target different career levels, and are tailored to applicants and backgrounds and research needs. National Research Service Award (NRSA) programs have provided more than 160,000 training slots in the biomedical, behavioral, and clinical scientists to students and young investigators through a combination of individual fellowship awards and institutional training grants. NRSA awards are valuable and well regarded because they attract highly qualified people into biomedical research, direct training into specific research areas, and establish innovative training standards not only for NRSA awardees but also for all trainees, regardless of their mechanisms of support (National Research Council, 2011). Career Development Programs have two main goals: (1) to provide Ph.D. scientists with the advanced research training and additional experiences needed to become independent investigators, and (2) to provide holders of clinical degrees with the research training needed to conduct patient-oriented research. They can "jumpstart" a career in research and validate that a program participant is a viable clinician-scientist and transform an awardee from a neophyte clinician-scientist to a full-fledged researcher.

Since more researchers are needed to meet today's critical health needs, Loan Repayment Programs (LRPs) were initiated to encourage promising researchers and scientists to pursue research careers by repaying up to $35,000 of their qualified student loan debt each year through both extramural and intramural LRPs. Extramural LRPs for researchers outside the NIH may be in research areas related to clinical research, pediatric research, health disparities research, contraception and infertility research, and clinical research for individuals from disadvantaged backgrounds; intramural LRPs for NIH employee researchers are in areas of AIDS research, clinical research for individuals from disadvantaged backgrounds, and general research areas.

Because of the need for investigators who are well trained in both basic science and clinical research, the NIH established the Medical Scientist Training Program (MSTP) to support outstanding students who are motivated to undertake careers in biomedical research and academic medicine. This dual-degree program offers training in a diverse set of fields, including not only the behavioral and social sciences and the closely allied fields of public health, epidemiology, biostatistics, and bioethics but also the biological sciences and the chemical and physical sciences. Currently efforts are underway to expand the MSTP and to diversify it to include degrees in non-bench-oriented disciplines.

The NIH Research Education Program (R25) supports research educational activities that complement other formal training programs in the mission areas of the NIH institutes and centers. The overarching goals of the NIH R25 Program are to (a) complement and/or enhance the training of a workforce to meet the nation's biomedical, behavioral, and clinical research needs; (b) help recruit individuals with specific specialty or disciplinary backgrounds into research careers in biomedical, behavioral, and clinical sciences; (c) foster a better understanding of biomedical, behavioral, and clinical research and its implications; and (d) enhance the diversity of the biomedical, behavioral, and clinical research workforce. We address this diversity training goal in more detail in the following section.

DIVERSITY ISSUES IN HIV PSYCHIATRY

TRAINING A DIVERSE WORKFORCE

The Need for and Benefit of HIV Mentoring Programs

The demographics of the HIV epidemic indicate that there is a disproportionate impact of HIV infection and transmission among individuals according to race, sexual orientation, and gender. Yet investigators from the key populations most affected remain significantly underrepresented among HIV investigators in the NIH research grant portfolio. Compared to the general population of HIV-infected individuals, underrepresented minority group members infected with HIV have not benefited equally from the unprecedented scientific advances in the diagnosis, pathogenesis and pathophysiology, prevention, and treatment of HIV infection.

Mentorship is arguably the most intense and critical form of leadership associated with training in any field. It is one of the most frequently cited components of a successful research career. The absence of mentoring and research collaboration have been identified as critical barriers to research participation by investigators from communities disproportionately affected by HIV/AIDS. Over the years, the NIH has taken a number of steps to increase the representation of investigators from communities disproportionately affected by HIV/AIDS. Despite these efforts, the number of underrepresented racial and ethnic researchers who have obtained investigator-initiated research grants has remained low. Investigators from underrepresented racial and ethnic groups have unique qualifications for doing research with their respective communities, yet they often face obstacles (at the individual, institutional, and systemic levels) to obtaining funding for research and must overcome particular challenges to conducting research with populations of individuals from various racial and ethnic groups (Shavers et al., 2005). Creating opportunities for mentorship and collaboration may reduce the barriers to successful competition for research funding by investigators from underrepresented racial and ethnic groups.

Perhaps one of the most compelling arguments for racial and ethnic diversity at the research level is based not only on philosophical principles, ideals of fairness and equity, and our commitment to social justice but also on the practical benefits of ensuring full societal participation by our citizenry. The moral argument, linked to affirmative action, further ensures the practical benefit of full societal participation by all our citizens. Indeed, it has been argued that health disparity is a moral wrong that needs to be addressed as another step in the moral evolution toward fairness, commitment to social justice, and equality of opportunity in our society (Jones, 2010). Recognizing that health disparities are a moral wrong is a first step in developing the appropriate workforce to correct this wrong. Some more practical benefits, as summarized by others with respect to medical school admissions (Cohen, 2003), may be applied to HIV/AIDS research. They include the following:

(1) Diversity addresses the needs and concerns of underrepresented groups. Diversity in the research workforce promotes research on disparity-related factors that is more sensitive to and inclusive of the needs and concerns of underrepresented racial and ethnic groups.

(2) Diversity broadens the research agenda. Increasing the diversity of the research workforce can accelerate and strengthen advances in public health and biomedical

research on HIV/AIDS through harnessing a broad set of outlooks and experiences to bear upon the complex problems of HIV/AIDS.

(3) Diversity provides culturally appropriate healthcare. Increasing the proportion of scientists from underrepresented racial and ethnic populations will aid in preparing a culturally appropriate healthcare workforce.

(4) Diversity improves access to healthcare. Current evidence supports the notion that greater workforce diversity may lead to improved public health and a potentially positive impact on patient outcomes, primarily through greater access to care for underserved populations and better interactions between patients and health professionals.

(5) Diversity overcomes some of the challenges we face for improved mentoring by increasing the number of mentors, creating a culture of mentoring, and enriching our research grant portfolios.

NIH DIVERSITY-ENHANCING PROGRAMS

NIH diversity programs fall into two broad categories, based on eligibility for funding. (1) Institution-funding programs target regular or minority-serving institutions and are based on enrollment statistics. For institutional programs, the grant is awarded to a principal investigator who selects trainees for participation on the basis of his or her own criteria. (2) Individual-funding programs target meritorious individuals who come from a group that has been shown to be underrepresented in the sciences, including racial and ethnic minorities, individuals with disabilities, and people from economically disadvantaged backgrounds. For individual programs, the grant is awarded to the individual undergoing training through peer-review process.

Tables 1A and 1B in the Resources Appendix to this volume list NIH-supported HIV mentoring programs, awarded on an institutional or individual basis, for minorities alone and for both minorities and non-minorities. From the programs listed there the following is evident: (1) Research education programs (R25), which usually include mentoring, research and didactics/skills components, and a specialized, in-depth training experience (often during the summer), are perhaps the most common mechanism to be used. (2) There are a considerable number of programs targeted specifically for diverse populations, and these minority-targeted programs are primarily institution based rather than directly awarded to meritorious individuals. (3) Programs are relatively well balanced at the various levels among undergraduates, predoctoral, postdoctoral, and early career levels, with far fewer at the high school level.

CONCLUSIONS

In this chapter we have reviewed key issues in education and research training for HIV disease with the goal of guiding program development to best reflect our current understanding of HIV and to treat patients with comprehensive and compassionate care. We have also highlighted the importance of training in diverse populations (Health Resources and Services Administration, 2012). With an estimated 1.2 million people in the United States living with HIV in 2016, a 50% increase from 1996 (CDC, 2016b; Hall et al., 2008), the HIV clinical care workforce in the United States may be insufficient to meet our future needs. Moreover, our current models for HIV care, which are rooted in HIV education and training, may need to be expanded and revamped to better reflect and accommodate the transformation of HIV into a chronic, manageable illness. Persons with HIV still have a complex illness with medical and psychiatric multimorbidities and increasingly comprise an aging population.

Interdisciplinary models of HIV care have been proposed in the United States (Gallant et al., 2011) to better manage these complexities, and some policy changes have encouraged the adoption of interdisciplinary approaches to HIV care. The United States National HIV/AIDS Strategy, for example, has emphasized the need for interdisciplinary HIV care (White House Office of National AIDS Policy, 2010). To address physician and caregiver shortages, national HIV physician organizations have issued joint recommendations (Carmichael et al., 2009). Similarly, the U.S. National AIDS Strategy includes an objective to increase physician training and reimbursement by expanding the AIDS Education and Training Centers (White House Office of National AIDS Policy, 2010). Health care reform in the United States, initiated by the Patient Protection and Affordable Care Act, has promoted the expansion of community health centers to provide comprehensive, interdisciplinary, primary care for underserved populations.

At the same time, recent trends in HIV epidemiology, pathogenesis, and care services have reinforced the need for multidisciplinary teams with strong community linkages. Comprehensive multidisciplinary HIV care is needed now more than ever. Multidisciplinary teams for the care of people living with HIV have arisen out of necessity due to the broad range of clinical and psychosocial needs of patients, the diversity of affected individuals and families, and the great value of community support in the early days of the epidemic. As discussed in the Introduction of this chapter, we propose a biopsychosocial model for education and curriculum as a clear paradigm for such a comprehensive and multidisciplinary approach. It is incumbent upon the educational and training community to keep step with these developments and to offer the most cutting edge cross-disciplinary curriculum and opportunities to the next generation of HIV clinicians and researchers.

To further prime the pipeline and ultimately improve the capacity for HIV care, undergraduate education in HIV/AIDS is an appropriate place to begin. The most common model includes lectures in both the basic sciences and clinical aspects of HIV/AIDS (years 1 and 2), supplemented by seminars, forums, and various amounts of patient contact. Undergraduate curriculum should integrate training in basic sciences with clinical experience to reinforce links between

HIV pathophysiology and patient care, including experiential learning combined with conventional didactic approaches. An additional concept gaining interest in curricular reform is the increasingly interdisciplinary nature of modern medical practice, suggesting the need for interdisciplinary clerkships. Given their emerging multimorbidities and increasing longevity, HIV patients often rely on many physicians across a variety of specialties for the integrated management of HIV as a chronic illness. Thus, an important feature of medical student training is clinical exposure to integrated comprehensive management with opportunities to participate in the multidisciplinary and longitudinal care of an individual HIV patient. Early exposure to this kind of patient-centered care model will enhance clinical experiences as medical students move forward to their graduate medical education training, when it can be further developed and applied.

Graduate medical education should further emphasize parallel components of successful models of interdisciplinary HIV care. Such paradigms of care have been identified by Ojikutu et al. (2014) as (1) patient-centered, one-stop-shop approaches with integrated or co-located services; (2) diverse teams of clinical and nonclinical providers; (3) a site culture that promotes a stigma-reducing environment for clients; (4) the availability of a comprehensive array of medical, behavioral, health, and psychosocial services; (5) effective communication strategies, including electronic health records; and (6) a focus on quality. Because residency is a pivotal time to encourage a possible patient-oriented research career, such an approach is especially appropriate during graduate medical education.

Strengthening of a diverse HIV research workforce necessitates conceptualization within the context of research approaches for a broadened agenda such as a transdisciplinary model. A transdisciplinary model for health disparities calls for a multi-mentor training experience from a variety of fields and perspectives. The best transdisciplinary research training programs for the analysis of population health and health disparities and for broad-scale sustainable changes integrate proximal downstream factors (biologic/genetic pathways, individual risk factors), intermediate factors (social relationships, social/physical context), and distal upstream factors (institutions, social conditions and policies). The transdisciplinary trainee is thus faced with many challenges, including learning the languages and cultures of different disciplines as well as how to best navigate within and between disciplines.

HIV global health education and training, although of unquestionable importance, is beyond the scope of this chapter. Many HIV residency programs have already developed global health curricula including traditional forums such as seminar series involving global health topics, global health journal clubs, outreach activities, and elective didactics, as well as additional hands-on experience in international clinical rotations at foreign institutions. The newly trained HIV global health component physicians will not only have improved clinical skills and knowledge but will also be better equipped to serve the populations of our country and of the world.

A final point to make is that missed clinic appointments have been found to be an independent predictor of all-cause mortality in persons with HIV (Mugavero et al., 2014). Thus, strengthening undergraduate and graduate education and curricula in the theory and practice of behavioral prevention of HIV, when combined with the promising developments of treatment, can ultimately allow a powerful form of biological-behavioral prevention. These educational concepts have broad implications for prevention of suffering, morbidity, and mortality in persons with HIV and AIDS.

REFERENCES

Berguis JP, Uldall KK, Lalonde B (1999). Validity of two scales in identifying HIV-associated dementia. *J Acquir Immune Defic Syndr* 21:134–140.

Blank MB, Mandell DS, Aiken L, Hadley TR (2002). Co-occurrence of HIV and serious mental illness among Medicaid recipients. *Psychiatr Serv* 53:868–873.

Carmichael JK, Deckard DT, Feinberg J, et al.; for AAHIVM and HIVMA Medical Workforce Working Group. (2009). Averting a crisis in HIV care: A joint statement of the American Academy of HIV Medicine and the HIV Medicine Association on the HIV Medical Workforce. https://www.idsociety.org/uploadedFiles/IDSA/Policy_and_Advocacy/Current_Topics_and_Issues/Workforce_and_Training/Statements/AAHIVM%20HIVMA%20Workforce%20Statement%20062509.pdf. Accessed January 16, 2017.

Carrico AW (2010). Elevated suicide rate among HIV-positive persons despite benefits of antiretroviral therapy: implications for a stress and coping model of suicide. *Am J Psychiatry* 167:117–119.

Carrico AW, Johnson MO, Morin SF, Remien RH, Charlebois ED, Stewart WT, Chesney MA (2007). Correlates of suicide ideation among HIV-positive persons. *AIDS* 21:1199–1203

Centers for Disease Control and Prevention (CDC) (2016a). CDC fact sheet: HIV/AIDS among persons aged 50 and older. https://www.cdc.gov/hiv/group/age/olderamericans/. Accessed January 16, 2017.

Centers for Disease Control and Prevention (CDC) (2016b). HIV in the United States: at a glance, 2016. https://www.cdc.gov/hiv/statistics/overview/ataglance.html. Accessed January 17, 2017.

Centers for Disease Control and Prevention (CDC) (2016c). *HIV Surveillance Report*, 2015; vol. 27. https://www.cdc.gov/hiv/pdf/library/reports/surveillance/cdc-hiv-surveillance-report-2015-vol-27.pdf. Accessed January 25, 2017.

Cohen JJ (2003). The consequences of premature abandonment of affirmative action in medical school admissions. *JAMA* 289(9):1143–1149.

Cohen MA (1989). AIDSism, a new form of discrimination. *AMA News*, January 20, 1989; 32:43.

Cohen MA (2008). History of AIDS psychiatry—a biopsychosocial approach: paradigm and paradox. In MA Cohen, JM Gorman (eds.), *Comprehensive Textbook of AIDS Psychiatry* (pp. 3–14). New York: Oxford University Press.

Cohen MA, Forstein M (2012). A biopsychosocial approach to HIV/AIDS education for psychiatry residents. *Acad Psychiatry* 36:479–486.

Cohen MA, Goforth HW, Lux JZ, Batista SM, Khalife S, Cozza KL, Soffer J (2010). *Handbook of AIDS Psychiatry*. New York: Oxford University Press.

Cohen MA, Gorman JM (2008). *Comprehensive Textbook of AIDS Psychiatry*. New York: Oxford University Press.

Cohen MA, Hoffman RG, Cromwell C, et al. (2002). The prevalence of distress in persons with human immunodeficiency virus infection. *Psychosomatics* 43:10–15.

Cohen MS, Shaw GM, McMichael AJ, Haynes BF (2011). Acute HIV-1 infection. *N Engl J Med* 364:1943–1954.

Davis HF, Skolasky RL Jr, Selnes OA, Burgess DM, McArthur JC (2002). Assessing HIV-associated dementia: modified HIV Dementia Scale versus the grooved pegboard. *AIDS Read* 12:29–38.

DeAngelis T (2002). A new generation of issues for LGBT clients. *Monitor on Psychology* 33:42.

DeVries ALC, Noens ILJ, Cohen-Kettenis PT, Van Berckelaer-Onnes IA, Doreleijers TA (2010). Autism spectrum disorders in gender dysphoric children and adolescents. *J Autism Dev Disord* 40:930–936.

Freedman JB, O'Dowd MA, Wyszynski B, Torres JR, McKegney FP (1994). Depression, HIV dementia, delirium, posttraumatic stress disorder (or all of the above). *Gen Hosp Psychiatry* 16:426–434.

Gallant J, Adimora A, Carmichael J, Horberg M, Kitahata M, Quinlivan E, Williams S (2011). Essential components of effective HIV care: a policy paper of the HIV Medicine Association of the Infectious Diseases Society of America and the Ryan White Medical Providers Coalition. *Clin Infect Dis* 53:1043–1050.

Gitlin DF, Levenson JL, Lyketsos CG (2004). Psychosomatic medicine: a new psychiatric subspecialty. *Acad Psychiatry* 28:4–11.

Hall HI, Song R, Rhodes P, et al. (2008). Estimation of HIV incidence in the United States. *JAMA* 300:520–529.

Hausman K (2002). Gay residents grapple with unique training issues. *Psychiatric News*, 37.

Health Resources and Services Administration (2012). The Affordable Care Act and health centers. https://www.hrsa.gov/about/news/2012tables/healthcentersacafactsheet.pdf. Accessed Janaury 16, 2017.

Institute of Medicine (IOM) (2011). *The Health of Lesbian, Gay, Bisexual, and Transgender People: Building a Foundation for Better Understanding* (pp. 61–67). Washington, DC: National Academies Press.

Johnson SR (2015). Learning to be LGBT-friendly: systems train providers to consider sexual, gender orientation in all treatment decisions. *Modern Healthcare*. Detroit, MI: Crain Communications.

Jones BN, Teng EL, Folstein MF, Harrison KS (1993). A new bedside test of cognition for patients with HIV infection. *Ann Intern Med* 119:1001–1004.

Jones CM (2010). The moral problem of health disparities. *Am J Public Health* 100(S1):S47–S51.

Kates J, Ranji U (2014). Health care access and coverage for the lesbian, gay, bisexual, and transgender (LGBT) community in the United States: opportunities and challenges in a new era. http://kff.org/disparities-policy/perspective/health-care-access-and-coverage-for-the-lesbian-gay-bisexual-and-transgender-lgbt-community-in-the-united-states-opportunities-and-challenges-in-a-new-era/. Retrieved April 16, 2016.

Kelser O, Spoerri A, Brinkof MW, et al., for the Swiss HIV Cohort Study and the Swiss National Cohort (2010). Suicide in HIV-infected indiviuals and the general population in Switzerland, 1988–2088. *Am J Psychiatry* 167:143–150.

Lambe S. (2015). An oral history of transgender representation on scripted TV. *Out Magazine*. Los Angeles, CA: Here Media.

Levin A. (2016) Resident helps young people in gender transition find their way. *Psychiatric News,* 51. http://psychnews.psychiatryonline.org/doi/full/10.1176%2Fappi.pn.2016.3a13. Accessed Janaury 16, 2017.

Mugavero MJ, Westfall AO, Cole SR, et al. (2014). Beyond core indicators of retention in HIV care: missed clinic visits are independently associated with all-cause mortality. *Clin Infect Dis* 59:1471–1479.

National Research Council (2011). *Research Training in Biomedical, Behavioral and Clinical Research Sciences.* Washington, DC: National Academies Press.

Nigatu T (2012). Integration of HIV and noncommunicable diseases in health care delivery in low- and middle-income countries. *Prev Chronic Dis* 9:110331.

Novack DH, Cameron O, Epel E, et al. (2007). Psychosomatic medicine: the scientific foundation of the biopsychosocial model. *Acad Psychiatry* 31:388–401.

Obedin-Maliver J, Goldsmith ES, Stewart L, et al. (2011). Lesbian, gay, bisexual, and transgender-related content in undergraduate medical education. *JAMA* 306(9):971–977.

Ojikutu B, Holman J, Kunches L, et al. (2014). Interdisciplinary HIV care in a changing healthcare environment in the USA. *AIDS Care* 26:731–735.

Out.com editors (April, 14, 2016). OUT exclusives: Power 50. *Out Magazine*. Los Angeles, CA: Here Media.

Polan HJ, Auerbach MI, Viederman M (1990). AIDS as a paradigm of human behavior in disease. Impact and implications of a course. *Acad Psychiatry* 14:197–203.

Power C, Selnes OA, Grim JA, McArthur JC (1995). HIV Dementia Scale; a rapid screening test. *J Acquir Immune Defic Syndr Hum Retrovirol* 8:273–278.

Rutherford K, McIntyre J, Daley A, Ross LE (2012). Development of expertise in mental health service provision for lesbian, gay, bisexual, and transgender communities. *Med Ed* 46:903–913.

Shavers VL, Fagan P, Lawrence D, et al. (2005). Barriers to racial/ethnic minority application and competition for NIH research funding. *J Natl Med Assoc* 97(8):1063–1077.

Smith SM, Allwright S, O'Dowd T (2007). Effectiveness of shared care across the interface between primary and specialty care in chronic disease management. *Cochrane Database Syst Rev* (3):CD004910.

Stieglitz KA (2010). Development, risk, and resilience of transgender youth. *J Assoc Nurses AIDS Care* 21(3):192–206.

Tavakkoli M, Cohen MA, Alfonso CA, Batista SM, Tiamson-Kassab MLA, Meyer P (2014). Caring for persons with early childhood trauma, PTSD, and HIV: a curriculum for clinicians. *Acad Psychiatry* 38(6):696–700.

White House Office of National AIDS Policy (2010). *National HIV/AIDS Strategy (NAS) for the United States*. http://www.whitehouse.gov/sites/default/files/uploads/NHAS.pdf. Accessed Janaury 16, 2017.

Wright MT (2009). Training psychiatrists in nonpsychiatric medicine: what do our patients and our profession need? *Acad Psychiatry* 33:181–186.

Zipursky AR, Gogolishvili D, Rueda S, et al. (2013). Evaluation of brief screening tools for neurocognitive impairment in HIV/AIDS: a systematic review of the literature. *AIDS* 27:2385–2401.

PART IV

PSYCHIATRIC DISORDERS
AND HIV INFECTION

14.

SUBSTANCE-RELATED AND ADDICTIVE DISORDER? THE SPECIAL ROLE IN HIV TRANSMISSION

Philip A. Bialer, Kenneth Ashley, and John A. R. Grimaldi

Substance use disorder (SUD) in its many forms has been linked to HIV since the beginning of the epidemic. While injecting drug use (IDU) remains a highly prevalent mode of transmission of HIV (UNAIDS, 2016b), other substances such as alcohol, cocaine, and methamphetamine are associated with high-risk behaviors that contribute to transmission. Untreated SUD may be an obstacle to testing and optimal medical treatment, contributing to medical comorbidity and increased suffering for patients and their families. Women, young men who have sex with men, people of color, persons who have suffered trauma, and persons of low socioeconomic status are vulnerable and at high risk. These intersecting and synergistic epidemics have been characterized as a syndemic requiring higher levels of recognition and treatment (Brezing et al., 2015; Singer and Clair, 2003). Rapid assessment, identification, and treatment of SUD are essential for persons at risk for and those already diagnosed with HIV/AIDS.

Global population size estimates indicate that 13 million people inject drugs and 1.7 million are living with HIV (United Nations Office of Drugs and Crime [UNODC], 2016). Although people who inject drugs account for an estimated 0.2–0.5% of the world's population, they make up approximately 10% of all people living with HIV and 30% of people living with HIV outside of sub-Saharan Africa (UNODC, 2016). On average, 1 in 10 new HIV infections are caused by the sharing of needles.

While sexual transmission of HIV predominates in endemic areas such as sub-Saharan Africa, IDU and commercial sex are the major transmission modes in South and Southeast Asia (UNAIDS, 2014). IDU is also the main risk behavior in Latin America (HIV prevalence 1.8 million), and IDU accounted for 51% of HIV infections in Eastern Europe and Central Asia and 13% of HIV infections in the Asia-Pacific region in 2014 (UNAIDS, 2016a).

Approximately 18.5% of the cumulative adult cases of HIV/AIDS in the United States are due to IDU (Centers for Disease Control and Prevention [CDC], 2011). Heterosexual exposure to HIV in the United States most often involves sexual contact with persons who inject drugs. When taking this into account along with the category of men who have sex with men and are exposed to persons who inject drugs, the proportion of HIV/AIDS associated with injecting drug use approaches 50%. In addition, there is a high prevalence of non-injecting drug use among gay and bisexual men (Ferrando et al., 1998) that is associated with high-risk sex behavior and seroconversion (Chesney et al., 1998; Venable et al., 2004; Woody et al., 1999). Finally, the potential impact of substance use on HIV progression and neuropsychological functioning gives the subject of SUDs very special prominence in HIV/AIDS psychiatry.

Alcohol is consumed by more than half the American population, and binge drinking occurs at an alarmingly high rate among young adults aged 18–25, which can lead to risky behavior in a particularly vulnerable population (Substance Abuse and Mental Health Services Administration [SAMHSA], 2013). Among patients with HIV, surveys reveal that 66% reported drinking alcohol, 41% reported binge drinking, and 28% reported heavy alcohol use in the past 30 days (Broz et al., 2014). Alcohol use is associated with the use of other illicit drugs, sharing of needles, sex in exchange for drugs, and unprotected intercourse, probably because of the disinhibition caused by alcohol intoxication. In addition, heavy alcohol use may lead to blackouts and unprotected sex as well as poor adherence to medical treatment and progression of disease in patients with comorbid hepatitis C infection.

Hepatitis C virus (HCV) infects 185 million people worldwide and 3.4–4.4 million people in the United States. Co-infection has also become a major problem among persons with HIV (Kohli et al., 2014). Nearly 75% of people with HIV who inject drugs also are infected with HCV. HIV/HCV co-infection more than triples the risk for liver disease, liver failure, and liver-related death (CDC, 2016a, 2016c). See Chapter 43 of this textbook for further discussion of HCV and HIV. The sharing of contaminated needles can lead to multiple other medical problems including skin infections, endocarditis, septicemia, and pulmonary emboli.

This chapter will present in detail the substances of abuse most commonly associated with HIV, the biopsychosocial consequences of SUD, and recommendations for the care and treatment of persons with HIV and SUDs. The potential for drug–drug interactions will be described. The reader is referred to Chapter 42 of this textbook for an extensive discussion of psychopharmacology. The treatment of pain in patients with SUD will also be addressed (the reader is referred to Chapter 41 for further coverage of this topic).

TERMINOLOGY AND DEFINITIONS

Clinicians treating patients with HIV/AIDS must have a good working knowledge of SUDs, since many of their patients will have a current or lifetime history of at least one such disorder. Using *Diagnostic and Statistical Manual of Mental Disorders,* fifth edition (DSM-5; American Psychiatric Association, 2013) terminology, SUDs can be divided into two basic categories: substance use disorders and substance-induced disorders. The criteria for substance use disorders are listed in Table 14.1. Note that in DSM-5 the differentiation between abuse and dependence was eliminated, replaced with a single category of substance use disorders with the addition of specifiers for severity. *Tolerance* refers to an acquired decrease in the effect of a substance usually manifested by a need for increased amounts of the substance to achieve the desired effect. *Withdrawal* is a substance-specific group of signs and symptoms that follows the abrupt discontinuation, reduction, or antagonistic blockage of a substance. Additionally, the specifiers for course and descriptive features have been maintained, although the descriptive feature "on agonist therapy" in DSM-IV is now "on maintenance therapy" in DSM-5. The substance-induced disorders are listed in Table 14.2.

INITIAL EVALUATION OF THE PATIENT WITH SUBSTANCE USE DISORDERS

Obtaining a substance use history is essential when evaluating all patients with HIV/AIDS. Some clinicians may have negative feelings about working with persons who exhibit self-destructive behaviors such as substance abuse and dependence. It is important for clinicians to be aware of their feelings and realize that patients respond better when a working alliance

Table 14.1 SUBSTANCE USE DISORDERS: DSM-5 CRITERIA

A problematic pattern of substance use leading to clinically significant impairment or distress as manifested by two (or more) of the following occurring within a 12-month period:

- Larger amounts or over greater period than intended
- Continued use despite recurrent social or interpersonal problems
- Most time spent in addiction (i.e., activities needed to obtain, use, or recover from the substance)
- Important social, occupational, or recreational acitivties given up
- Use despite knowledge of persistent or recurrent physical or psychological problems
- Craving or strong desire to use
- Unsuccessful efforts to cut down
- Failure to meet obligations at work, school, or home
- Recurrent use in hazardous situations
- Tolerance
- Withdrawal

Table 14.2 DSM-5 SUBSTANCE-INDUCED DISORDERS

Intoxication
Withdrawal
Depressive disorder
Bipolar disorder
Psychotic disorder
Anxiety disorder
Sleep disorders
Sexual dysfunction
Delirium
Major or mild neurocognitive dysfunction

can be established by utilizing a nonthreatening and nonjudgmental manner. It is also important to reassure patients that the information they provide will be kept confidential to those outside of the treatment team and be used to develop the safest possible treatment plan. The clinician should ask about specific illicit substances such as heroin, cocaine, marijuana, and the club drugs. For taking a history of alcohol use, some clinicians have suggested the use of the CAGE questionnaire (Ewing, 1984):

1. **C**an you cut down on your drinking?
2. Are you **A**nnoyed when asked to stop?
3. Do you feel **G**uilty about your drinking?
4. Do you need an **E**ye-opener when you wake up in the morning?

One should also ask about sedative or stimulant use, whether prescribed or non-prescribed, and any dietary supplements or herbs the patient may be taking. A substance abuse review of systems, focusing on renal, cardiac, gastrointestinal, and, for HIV patients especially, neurological symptoms, is essential. Other points of inquiry are the date the substance was first used; patterns, amount, and frequency of use; and routes of administration and reactions to the use. The time of last use is important to know in order to determine if the patient is suffering from a substance-induced disorder or is at risk for withdrawal. If the patient has had past substance use treatment it is useful to know the response to this treatment. With the patient's permission, a urine toxicology screen should be obtained, in addition to routine blood tests. Finally, whenever possible, the clinician should try to obtain collateral information about the patient's substance use, since many people may wish to hide their substance use from clinicians and denial is a common defense mechanism.

SUBSTANCES OF ABUSE

OPIOIDS

Injection of heroin may be the most common, though not the only, source of HIV transmission associated with SUD.

Opium is one of the oldest medications known, especially for its use in the relief of pain and diarrhea. Morphine and codeine were isolated in the early 1800s, and heroin was developed as a semisynthetic opium derivative and introduced into medical practice in 1898. The mu-opioid receptor is the main one responsible for analgesia, respiratory depression, decreased gastric motility, miosis, euphoria, and dependence. These receptors appear to stimulate release of dopamine from the ventral tegmental area into the nucleus accumbens, the primary reward pathway of the brain. Heroin reaches peak serum concentration within 1 minute when taken intravenously but actually begins crossing the blood–brain barrier within 15–20 seconds. Physical signs of acute opiate intoxication include euphoria and tranquility, sedation, slurred speech, problems with memory and attention, and miosis. Signs and symptoms of opioid withdrawal can be both objective (rhinorrhea and lacrimation, nausea and vomiting, diarrhea, piloerection, mydriasis, yawning, and muscle spasms) and subjective (body aches, insomnia, craving, dysphoria, anxiety, hot and cold flashes, and anorexia). Heroin withdrawal usually begins within 4 to 8 hours after last use, whereas with methadone, with its longer elimination half-life, withdrawal may not begin until 24 to 48 hours after last use.

Early in the epidemic, heroin addiction led to a rapid spread of HIV and HCV among persons who inject drugs in the United States, since there was very limited access to clean needles and syringes. The increase in the purity and availability of heroin along with a decrease in its street price has led to a resurgence in its use. Also, there is evidence to suggest a relationship between increased nonmedical use of opioid analgesics and heroin abuse in the United States (Muhuri et al., 2013; U.S. Department of Health and Human Services, Office of the Surgeon General, 2016). According to the National Survey on Drug Use and Health (NSDUH), in 2012 about 669,000 Americans reported using heroin in the past year (SAMHSA, 2013).

The prevalence of HIV appears to be much higher among long-term heroin users who inject, compared with those who have short-term use or other methods of use. Chitwood and colleagues (2003) found an HIV seroprevalence rate of 25% among persons who inject drugs long-term and a rate of 13% among persons who are new to injection of heroin and to persons who use heroin by insufflation.

COCAINE AND OTHER STIMULANTS

Cocaine is an alkaloid extracted from the leaf of the Erythroxylon coca bush. The hydrochloride salt is water soluble and can be administered orally, intravenously, or intranasally (by insufflation). The intravenous route of administration has an onset of action of 10–60 seconds, with a peak effect achieved in minutes and duration of effect that lasts up to 1 hour. Administration of the drug by the intranasal route has an onset of action of up to 5 minutes, with a peak effect achieved in approximately 20 minutes. The total duration of action by the intranasal route is 1 hour. The free-base form, known as crack cocaine, can be heated and smoked. This form has the quickest onset of action, of 3–5 seconds, reaching its

peak effect in 1 minute (Lange and Hillis, 2001). The quick and intense effects of crack cocaine may make it the most addictive form of the drug.

The effects of cocaine are mediated by blocking the synaptic reuptake of norepinephrine and dopamine, resulting in an excess of these neurotransmitters at the postsynaptic receptor. It is by this mechanism and the alteration of synaptic transmission that cocaine acts as a powerful sympathomimetic agent. Metabolism of cocaine occurs in the liver and its metabolites are detectable in blood or urine for up to 36 hours after administration. Cardiovascular complications of cocaine use include cerebrovascular accident (CVA), myocardial ischemia and infarct (MI), arrhythmia, and sudden death (McCann and Ricuarte, 2000). Intravenous administration of any substance of abuse increases the risk of developing bacterial endocarditis. In contrast to endocarditis in relation to other drugs, endocarditis secondary to intravenous cocaine use more often affects the left-sided valves of the heart (Chambers et al., 1987).

Amphetamines produce many of the same effects as cocaine with similar routes of administration. In contrast to cocaine, amphetamines both stimulate the presynaptic release of dopamine and norepinephrine and then block their reuptake. High doses of amphetamine release 5-hydroxytryptamine (5-HT) and may affect serotonergic receptors. Metabolism occurs in the liver, mediated predominantly by the cytochrome P450 (CYP) 2D6 enzyme. As with cocaine, amphetamines are potent sympathomimetics and can cause MI, seizures, and CVA (Urbina and Jones, 2004).

Both injection and non-injection cocaine and stimulant use are well-known cofactors in HIV infection. The most widely studied forms of these drugs include powder cocaine, its free-base form crack cocaine, and methamphetamine, which like cocaine can be snorted, smoked, or injected. The prevalence of use of each substance varies in different cultures and geographic locations and according to demographic characteristics such as race/ethnicity, gender, and age (Mimiaga et al., 2013). Understanding current trends in distinct substance use behaviors and their associated clinical and demographic features may be especially important given recent attention to HIV prevention strategies "test and treat" and pre-exposure prophylaxis (Mimiaga et al., 2013). The success of these strategies may hinge on health-related behaviors such as medication adherence and virological suppression, both of which have been shown to be affected by substance use.

Crack cocaine has persisted as an important driver of HIV transmission since early in the epidemic (Wechsberg et al., 2012). Certain behaviors associated with its use may explain the enduring connection between crack cocaine and HIV. Perhaps more so than with other drugs, crack cocaine is often traded for sex involving high-risk practices. Mimiaga et al. (2013) found an association between unprotected vaginal sex and polydrug and crack cocaine use. Additionally, users were disproportionately black, less likely to report adherence to antiretroviral medications, and more likely to have a detectable viral load independent of medication adherence (Mimiaga et al., 2013). In another study, women crack cocaine users who traded sex for drugs and/or money were more often sexually active with higher numbers of partners, were more likely to use drugs before and after sex, and were more likely to have a history of sexually transmitted disease (STD) than women crack cocaine users who did not trade sex for drugs and/or money (Logan and Leukefeld, 2000). These and other studies stand in contrast to our relatively limited understanding of patterns of long-term drug use. However, existing studies suggest that a majority of affected individuals may use crack cocaine uninterrupted for a decade or longer (Falck et al., 2007). Further complicating the situation, evidence-based interventions that target this population with an aim of reducing sexual and healthrelated risk behaviors are scarce (Wechsberg et al., 2012).

Methamphetamine (MA) use has affected men who have sex with men and heterosexual individuals in both metropolitan and rural area across most regions of the United States (CDC, 2006). In studies of both populations MA users were shown to have more sexual partners and be less likely to use condoms and more likely to have a history of an STD including HIV (MMWR, 2006; Buchacz et al., 2005; Molitor et al., 1998; Shoptaw et al., 2002).

Methamphetamine use has been more extensively studied among men who have sex with men than among heterosexual men. In one San Francisco study, 9.7% of men who have sex with men had used MA in the past year (Yeon and Albrecht, 2007, 2008). Possible explanations for this high rate include MA use in the "circuit party culture" that some men who have sex with men take part in (Yeon and Albrecht, 2007, 2008) as well as its association with more intense sexual excitement. When amphetamines are taken along with sildenafil (Viagra), referred to as "sextasy," this combination allows for longer and rougher intercourse, which may result in tears in anal mucosa (Halkitis et al., 2001) and thus enable HIV transmission. In another study done in Los Angeles County, the authors surveyed men who have sex with men in high-risk locations, from 2008 to 2012, regarding substance use in the previous 30 days. Rates of MA use ranged from 23% to 27% and followed alcohol and marijuana as the most common substances reported (Reback et al., 2013). Although there was a slight but significant rise in MA use over the sampling period, the overall rates were lower than those reported in a similar study done from 1999 to 2007 (Reback et al., 2013).

Those few studies that have investigated HIV seroincidence demonstrated a positive association between MA use and seroconversion even after adjusting for use of other non-injectable drugs, including alcohol and marijuana (Buchacz et al., 2005; Plankey et al., 2007; Yeon and Albrecht, 2007). MA may be associated with adverse health consequences both indirectly, through poor adherence to antiretroviral medications and medical care, and directly. Chronic use leads to reduced dopamine transporter levels and neuropsychological impairment. Some investigators have suggested that MA use can enhance neurotoxicity in persons with HIV and accelerate the development of HIV-associated dementia (Urbina and Jones, 2004). Animal studies suggest that MA has a deleterious effect on the immune system (Yeon and Albrecht, 2007). It may also promote HIV replication (Phillips et al., 2000; Yeon and Albrecht, 2007).

ALCOHOL

In 2012, in the United States, 87.6% of people ages 18 or older reported that they had drunk alcohol at some point in their lifetime; 71% reported that they drank in the past year; 56.3% reported that they drank in the past month, 24.6% of people ages 18 or older reported that they engaged in binge drinking in the past month; and 7.1% reported that they engaged in heavy drinking in the past month (SAMHSA, 2013). Even higher rates are seen among men identifying as gay, regardless of their serostatus (McCabe et al., 2009).

Alcohol is rapidly absorbed from the duodenum with blood alcohol concentrations of 100–200mg%, causing impaired motor function and judgment; concentrations of 200–400mg% lead to stupor and coma. Alcohol activates GABA receptors, inhibits NMDA receptors, and has additional effects on 5-HT3, nicotinic, and opioid receptors. It is metabolized by alcohol dehydrogenase at a constant rate of 100 mg/kg/hour. Medical complications associated with heavy alcohol use are listed in Table 14.3. Problems such as anemia, peripheral neuropathy, and dementia are of particular concern in persons with HIV, who are already predisposed to these complications. More importantly, alcohol-induced liver disease may be worse in individusls co-infected with HCV, as alcoholism doubles the risk of cirrhosis (Maillard and Sorrell, 2005).

Among HIV-positive persons, alcohol use leads to additional medical complications because of reduced adherence to treatment (Neuman et al., 2012). Studies among veterans recieving care for HIV showed that binge drinkers missed many more doses of medications on drinking days compared with non-binge drinkers. The study demonstrated that this trend was especially strong for HIV-positive individuals as compared with HIV-negative individuals. The investigators concluded that HIV-positive persons may be particularly sensitive to the negative effects of alcohol consumption (Braithwaite et al., 2005).

Additionally, alcohol use is associated with risky sexual behaviors and often serves as a gateway to intravenous and other drug use, both of which are linked to higher rates of HIV transmission (Petry, 1999; Szerlip et al., 2005). Studies have repeatedly shown a strong association between alcohol use and the incidence of HIV infection (Shuper et al., 2010); there is an 87% increased risk of infection when alcohol is consumed prior to or at the time of sexual relations,

Table 14.3 MEDICAL COMPLICATIONS OF HEAVY ALCOHOL USE

Gastritis/peptic ulcer	Pancreatitis
Cirrhosis/hepatic failure	Anemia
Pneumonia	Malnutrition
Trauma	Peripheral neuropathy
Subdural hematoma	Dementia
Cardiomyopathy	Wernicke-Korsakoff syndrome

probably owing to the disinhibition associated with intoxication (Baliunas et al., 2010).

Binge drinking along with risky sexual behavior has been shown in one large-scale study to be a problem among men who have sex with men (Hess et al., 2015). The study showed a 59% prevalence of binge drinking, and the prevalence of risk behaviors was significantly higher among bingers than non-bingers. Binge drinkers were 30% more likely to participate in condomless anal receptive intercourse with a discordant partner and 20% more likely to participate in insertive unprotected intercourse. Other large surveys have demonstrated additional risk behaviors, including comorbid injecting drug use, sex exchange for money or drugs, and more casual sex partners; risk behaviors increased with a higher frequency of binge drinking (Wen et al., 2012).

Alcohol also plays a prominent role among women in the syndemic of substance abuse, violence, and AIDS (Meyer et al., 2011). Women using alcohol and other substances are more likely to experience physical violence and engage in higher-risk sexual activities. Women who have been victims of previous trauma are also more likely to become substance abusers. Disclosure of HIV status itself may expose women to intimate partner violence.

Alcohol use and violence among young men who have sex with men are also the strongest predictors of HIV risk behaviors (Mustanski et al., 2007).

TOBACCO/NICOTINE

Tobacco use is the leading preventable cause of disease, disability, and death in the United States. The Centers for Disease Control and Prevention (CDC) has reported that cigarette smoking results in greater than 480,000 premature deaths in the United States each year—about 20% of U.S. deaths. Additionally, 16 million people suffer with a serious illness caused by smoking (CDC, 2016b). While the prevalence of cigarette smoking in U.S. adults has declined to approximately 20%, studies have consistently reported prevalence rates of smoking two to three times higher for people living with HIV than for the general population (Rahmanian et al., 2011).

Cigarettes (and other forms of tobacco) contain nicotine, which is an addictive drug. Nicotine is quickly absorbed into the bloodstream and immediately the adrenal glands are stimulated to produce epinephrine, which increases blood pressure, respiration, and heart rate. Nicotine also increases levels of dopamine, which stimulates the reward and pleasure pathways in the brain.

With the current antiretroviral treatments for HIV, mortality from HIV-related causes has decreased. Instead, cardiovascular disease and non-HIV-related malignancies are major causes of morbidity and mortality in HIV-infected individuals, with cigarette smoking being a major contributor and decreasing quality of life. Studies have found that HIV-infected individuals with effective antiretroviral therapy lose more life-years to smoking than to HIV (Helleberg et al., 2015; Rahmanian et al., 2011).

Given these findings, identification of current cigarette smokers along with implementation of smoking cessation interventions is imperative. There are a variety of barriers to these efferots that must be overcome. Clinicians may be focused on managing other issues and lack confidence in their ability to influence smoking behaviors; HIV-infected individuals may not prioritize smoking cessation if they believe they will die from HIV; co-occurring addictions can perpetuate smoking; and comorbid psychiatric disorders have been associated with lower rates of successful smoking cessation (Rahmanian et al., 2011).

A host of smoking cessation interventions are available, which may involve counseling or pharmacological treatment. The pharmacological treatments include nicotine replacement therapy (NRT) via various routes, buproprion, and varenicline.

CLUB DRUGS

In addition to the more commonly thought of substances of abuse such as heroin, cocaine, and alcohol, substances used in the context of parties or clubs have taken on new significance in the HIV epidemic. These drugs are often used at raves, which are all-night parties in large spaces attended by hundreds to thousands of teenagers and young adults dancing to loud, repetitive electronic music (Weir, 2000). Stimulants and hallucinogens such as LSD and 3,4-methylenedioxymethamphetamine (MDMA), also known as Ecstasy or Molly, are the drugs most commonly used. Circuit parties are another venue where club drugs are used. These are attended mostly by young to middle-aged gay men and may be particularly problematic in terms of HIV transmission, as the parties and affiliated events often go on for several days, with drug use and sexual activity being significant components. Although some of these parties originally began as fundraisers for HIV service organizations, most of these organizations have since distanced themselves from such functions, which have taken on independent lives of their own through magazines and Websites. Drugs commonly used at circuit parties include MDMA, ketamine, gamma-hydroxybutyric acid (GHB), methamphetamine, cocaine, marijuana, and alcohol (Bialer, 2002). The club drugs of the most concern in relation to HIV/AIDS are MDMA, GHB, and methamphetamine.

Although MDMA was first synthesized in 1912, its use among youth and gay men has increased greatly only in recent years. One study from Seattle indicated that 41% of gay men aged 20 to 29 years surveyed used Ecstasy at some time in their lives (Community Epidemiologic Work Group, 2000). MDMA seems to achieve its effects by flooding the brain with serotonin. Similar to methamphetamine, it both stimulates the release of serotonin and then inhibits its uptake. MDMA may also be taken along with sildenafil to overcome side effects of sexual dysfunction (to promote "sextasy"). This combination can lead to unsafe sexual activity and thus an increased risk of HIV transmission. Although MDMA is considered a benign drug by many, there are now numerous reports of severe toxic, sometimes fatal, reactions (McCann et al., 1996, 1998, 2000, 2005; Pilgrim et al., 2011). In 2010, there was report of 18 Ecstasy overdoses, including one death, at a New Years Eve rave in Los Angeles (CDC, 2010). Chronic use may lead to mood instability and cognitive impairment, which are particular problems for people with HIV (Bolla et al., 1998; Kalant, 2001, Parrott, 2013).

GHB was initially developed as an anesthetic but was found to have too many side effects to be used regularly. In the club scene, GHB is taken for its sedating and euphoric effects. It has also been used as a date-rape drug; individuals given GHB may be exposed to HIV through unprotected sexual intercourse. Because of its amnestic effects, the they may not even know that they have been exposed to HIV. GHB has a relatively narrow therapeutic range; its toxic effects include seizures, coma, and death. In addition, a severe withdrawal syndrome among chronic users has been reported (Bialer, 2002). Gamma-butyrolactone (GBL) and 1,4-butanediol (1,4-BD) are precursors that can be converted to GHB after ingestion. They are available in a variety of dietary supplements for purported but unproven anabolic effects. Camacho et al. (2004) showed that 52% of their sample of HIV-positive patients reported using GHB or a substance containing GHB, but only 24% of these individuals were aware of the toxicities and addictive potential of this drug. GHB has been approved by the U.S. Food and Drug Administration (FDA) for the treatment of cataplexy associated with narcolepsy and excessive daytime sleepiness associated with narcolepsy, although its distribution is highly restricted.

COMORBIDITY

The triple diagnosis of HIV/AIDS, SUD, and other psychiatric disorder has long been recognized by those who work with persons with HIV. In the general population, approximately 50% of people with a psychiatric disorder will meet criteria for SUD in their lifetime; 21% of people with acohol dependence have a concurrent affective disorder (Pettinati et al., 2013). The lifetime prevalence of SUD is even higher, in the range of 70%, among schizophrenics and those with bipolar disease.

Rates of mental disorders including SUD tend to be higher among persons with HIV than in the general population. A large national study of HIV-infected patients demonstrated a strong association between SUD and being diagnosed with another mental disorder; screening positive for another psychiatric disorder was also associated with SUD (Bing et al., 2001). Depressive disorders have been found in 33% to 40% of HIV-seropositive persons who inject drugs (Klinkenberg and Sacks, 2004). In some studies, the rate of depressive disorders was higher among men with HIV who inject drugs than in a matching seronegative sample, but the rates of depression were similar among women studied (Lipsitz et al., 1994; Rabkin et al., 1997). However, in general, women with SUD tend to have a higher rate of comorbidity, particularly post-traumatic stress disorder.

Two major concerns for persons with HIV who also have comorbid SUD and a mental disorder are increased risk-taking behavior and the disorders' effects on treatment adherence. Among opiate users, a current and lifetime history of any mental disorder has been associated with a higher frequency of sharing injection equipment and less condom use (Klinkenberg and Sacks, 2004). Compared to other persons with SUD, schizophrenic individuals have been found to be more likely to trade sex for money and drugs. Persons with comorbid disorders are also less likely to receive medical treatment or to adhere to antiretroviral therapy (Klinkenberg and Sacks, 2004).

TREATMENT AND MANAGEMENT OF SUBSTANCE USE DISORDERS

To address the unique needs of the HIV person who is addicted to substances, it is necessary to find the balance between addiction treatment and harm reduction. A greater level of tolerance and flexibility is required than might otherwise be expected in a formalized addiction treatment program that stresses abstinence and the use of 12-step groups. This includes tolerance of ongoing substance use during the course of treatment.

The initial phase of addiction treatment is usually concerned with providing safe and humane detoxification from the substance of abuse. Benzodiazepines are recommended as the treatment of choice in management of alcohol or sedative/hypnotic withdrawal (Schuckit, 2014), although some clinicians have also advocated the use of anticonvulsants (Barrons and Roberts, 2010; Lum et al., 2006). Dexmetatomadine has been used in the intensive care setting for severe alcohol withdrawal (Rayner et al., 2012). Detoxification can generally be done at the same dosages as those for seronegative patients until the later stages of HIV illness, when lower doses may be necessary.

Methadone detoxification is the preferred method of managing opioid withdrawal. Schedules using buprenorphine and/or clonidine for opioid detoxification are also available (NIH Consensus Development Conference, 1998). Detoxification from cocaine and stimulants is not done pharmacologically.

After medical stabilization and detoxification, the goals of treatment should include maintenance of abstinence, when possible, and rapid treatment of relapse. Substance abuse treatment is usually provided on an outpatient basis, though treatment communities afford a higher level of care for those with a more severe and refractory SUD. Adjunctive anticraving agents may be used by HIV-positive individuals with severe addictive disorders to aid in abstinence. Disulfuram, acamprosate, and naltrexone have all been used to curb alcohol craving. Methadone maintenance therapy has been shown to be effective in managing abstinence from opiates (Mattick et al., 2009). Although buprenorphine is approved for the office management of opiate dependence and may work well in an integrated care system, there may be drug interactions with some antiretrovirals, which limit its use in this population (Li et al., 2014).

Harm reduction is a strategy that is particularly applicable to HIV-positive individuals with addiction (Ferrando and Batki, 2000). In harm reduction, many individuals in recovery will not maintain abstinence, and treatment strategies should therefore focus on reducing behavior that has potentially harmful consequences, such as the sharing of needles or illicit activities to pay for substance use. Sterile needle–exchange programs have not only been effective in decreasing risk-taking behaviors, but some studies and meta-analyses indicate that they may have contributed to a significant decrease in HIV seroconversion among the IDU population (Cochrane Collaborative Review Group, 2004; Des Jarlais et al., 2005).

Motivational interviewing (MI) is a useful method for assisting individuals with SUD (Miller and Rollnick, 1991). In this process, the practitioner assesses a patient's readiness to change and facilitates movement along a continuum of change (Prochaska and DiClemente, 1986). One goal is to engage the person in a manner that creates a disparity in wants expressed by the person and his or her current reality. In this process, the clinician should try to avoid eliciting the patient's defense mechanisms through the expression of empathy, avoid argumentation, create discrepancy, roll with the resistance, and support and reframe the patient's desires, all of which will effectively serve to create an environment that facilitates behavioral change. MI has been shown to decrease substance use and increase adherence among HIV-seropositive persons (Darvasula and Miller, 2014).

Network therapy is an office-based treatment of SUD advocated by Galanter and colleagues (Galanter and Brook, 2001) that employs both psychodynamic and cognitive-behavioral approaches. The treatment includes a therapeutic network of non-abusing family members, significant others, and peers who actively participate with the therapist to provide cohesiveness and support, undermine denial, and promote compliance with treatment. Studies have demonstrated significantly less illicit substance use among patients receiving this treatment for cocaine and opiate abuse (Galanter et al., 1997, 2004). Social support may be a protective factor, and increasing social networks, including recommendations for 12-step programs, should be a part of the overall treatment (Darvasula and Miller, 2014).

Two meta-analyses looking at the impact of psychosocial interventions on risk-taking behavior among injection drug users showed that simply undergoing a screening to enroll in the studies seemed to have a beneficial effect of reducing risky behavior in both experimental and comparison groups; there were no significant differences based on the length of time of the interventions (Gibson et al., 1998; Semann et al., 2002). These studies stress the importance of including information about HIV infection and HIV risk reduction and access to condoms and HIV testing along with other components of any drug intervention program. For individuals with comorbid SUD and mental disorder, successful treatment approaches stress the integration of mental health care and substance abuse treatment along with medical care. Individuals receiving ancillary services are more likely to link up with medical care (Klinkenberg and Sacks, 2004).

DRUG–DRUG INTERACTIONS

Potential drug–drug interactions between psychotropics and HIV medications are addressed in Chapter 42 of this volume.

A growing body of evidence exists for clinically significant interactions between HIV medications and medications used to treat substance use disorders. Less is known about interactions between HIV medications and substances of abuse, although some studies and case reports suggest this combination may result in serious adverse events.

Drug–drug interactions may occur with drugs when similar effects interact to produce a heightened response (pharmacodynamic), or when drugs share a common metabolic pathway that is altered by one or more compounds (pharmacokinetic). Most clinically significant interactions between HIV medications and other drugs involve hepatic metabolism via cytochrome P450 enzymes (CYP 450) or glucuronidation. Commonly prescribed HIV medication regimens consist of two nucleoside/nucleotide reverse transcriptase inhibitors (NRTI) combined with one or more drugs from the protease inhibitor (PI), non-nucleoside reverse transcriptase inhibitor (NNRTI), or integrase inhibitor classes. Among these agents only PIs and NNRIs make extensive use of CYP 450 enzymes. Most of the other drugs discussed in this chapter also undergo hepatic metabolism mainly through the CYP 450 system. Therefore, this section will focus primarily on drug interactions involving PIs and NNRTIs.

METHADONE, BUPRCNORPHINE, DISULFURAM, AND NALTREXONE

Methadone is frequently used to treat opioid addiction and chronic pain in HIV-infected individuals. Pharmacokinetic studies and case series have shown that interactions between antiretroviral medications (ARVs) and methadone commonly occur in the direction of altered metabolism of methadone. Consequently, the initiation of ARV therapy in a patient maintained on methadone risks precipitation of opioid withdrawal, while changing or stopping ARVs may result in methadone toxicity with oversedation, respiratory depression, and cardiac arrhythmias.

In studies examining NNRTIs, when efavirenz (EFV) or nevirapine (NVP) was started in injection drug users on stable methadone therapy, methadone AUC was significantly decreased. Individuals consequently experienced opioid withdrawal symptoms and required increased methadone doses (Arroyo et al., 2007; Grubner and McCance-Katz, 2010; McCance et al., 2002; Scholler-Gyure et al., 2008). The NNRTI etravirine does not appear to require methadone dose adjustment even though it induces CYP 3A4 (Scholler-Gyure et al., 2008).

Coadministration of PIs may also result in reduced methadone plasma concentrations and associated opioid withdrawal symptoms. Decreased methadone levels have been reported for the PIs darunavir (DRY), amprenavir (APV), tipranavir/ritonavir (TPV/r), and nelfinavir (NFV), although interactions did not always result in withdrawal and need for increased doses of methadone (HIVguidlines. org). Atazanavir (ATV) and fosamprenavir/ritonavir (FAV/r) appear not to affect methadone concentrations (Grubner and McCance-Katz, 2010).

In contrast to methadone, buprenorphine is not associated with opioid withdrawal or toxicity when combined with either NNRTs or PIs, even though buprenorphine concentrations may be altered. The exception is ATV, which may increase buprenorphine area under the curve (AUC) and result in drowsiness or cognitive impairment (Bruce and Altice, 2006; Grubner and McCance-Katz, 2010; McCance-Katz et al., 2007). Interactions in the opposite direction are uncommon. However, methadone has been shown to increase zidovudine levels through inhibition of glucuronidation and may potentially be associated with zidovudine toxicity (Grubner and McCance-Katz, 2010). Interactions between ARVs and naltrexone are not expected since naltrexone does not undergo metabolism primarily by the liver. Disulfuram, when coadministered with ARV regimens containing TPV, may result in an adverse reaction similar to that of alcohol (HIVguidelines.org).

ALCOHOL AND DRUGS OF ABUSE

Alcohol consumption has been shown to significantly increase the blood serum of abacavir (ABV) by competing for alcohol dehydrogenase (McDowell et al., 2000); however, with chronic use alcohol can induce CYP 3A4 and may decrease levels of some ARVs (Caballeri, 2003).

Certain benzodiazepines, including alprazolam, triazolam, midazolam, clonazepam, and flunitrazepam ("roofies"), rely on CYP 3A4 for metabolism. ARVs that inhibit CYP 3A4, such as ritonavir (RTV) and other PIs, can decrease clearance and lead to oversedation and respiratory depression if these drugs are abused (Antoniou and Lin-in Tseng, 2002; Wynn et al., 2005).

THC (tetrahydrocannabinol), the active ingredient of marijuana, is metabolized via CYP 3A4 and, to a lesser extent, via CYP 2C9 (Wynn et al., 2005). Therefore, strong CYP 3A4 inhibitors may be associated with marijuana toxicity (Antoniou and Lin-in Tseng, 2002). The limited pharmacokinetic studies done on the effects of cannabinoids on ARVs suggest that dose adjustment of ARVs is unnecessary (Wynn et al., 2005).

Cocaine is metabolized via several mechanisms, with CYP 3A4 being a minor pathway (Antoniou and Lin-in Tseng, 2002). However, metabolism of norcocaine, an active metabolite of cocaine, occurs via 3A4 and is hepatotoxic. Cocaine users whose ARV therapies induce CYP 3A4 may be at heightened risk for liver damage. There is limited human research on the impact of cocaine or ARV metabolism, although in rodents cocaine use is associated with 3A4 induction (Grubner and McCance-Katz, 2010).

Clinically significant interactions between ARVs and heroin, morphine, and codeine are unlikely because of their metabolism via glucuronidation and other non-CYP 450 pathways. Oxycodone and hydrocodone are widely available on the street and are metabolized via CYP 2D6. Because hydrocodone's metabolite, hydromorphone, is a potent analgesic, ARVs that induce CYP 2D6 may increase the risk of hydrocodone toxicity (Wynn et al., 2005).

MDMA ("Ecstasy"), methamphetamine, and GHB are primarily metabolized by CYP 2D6. Deaths have been reported among people who took methamphetamine while being treated with RTV, which is an inhibitor of CYP 2D6 (Hales et al., 2000). Ketamine (Hijazi and Boulieu, 2002; Wynn et al., 2005) and PCP (phencyclidine (Laurenzana and Owens, 1997) appear to be primarily metabolized by CYP 2B6 and CYP 3A4, respectively. Patients should be made aware of potential interactions with ARVs and other medications that inhibit these enzymes.

Stribild is a one-pill once-daily ARV regimen that contains cobicistat, a potent pharmacokinetic enhancer that has no activity against HIV. Cobicistat inhibits CYP 3A4 and 2D6. There is limited pharmacokinetic research on interactions between drugs of abuse and this newer medication. For more up-to-date information about drug interactions between this and other new HIV medications the reader is referred to the following websites: http://www.hivguidelines.org, http://www.aidsinfo.nih.gov, http://www.hiv-druginteractions.org, and http://hivinsite.ucsf.edu.

PAIN

Pain is highly prevalent among persons with HIV/AIDS, with reports varying from 28% to 97% of individuals experiencing pain, depending on the study population and setting. The pain can have many different causes (Cohen and Alfonso, 2004). Studies indicate that there is no difference in the prevalence of pain between persons with HIV with a history of IDU and non-drug users; in general, pain is undertreated in all persons with AIDS (Breitbart et al., 1996; Larue et al., 1997; McCormack et al., 1993). However, the treatment of pain in persons with HIV who have a history of SUD, particularly IDU, may be even more problematic. Breitbart et al. (1997) found that among persons with AIDS who have a history of SUD, only 8% received adequate analgesia compared to 20% of individuals without SUD. Former drug users arc often negatively stereotyped, and clinicians are hesitant to give opioid analgesics to former drug users for fear of being manipulated or fear of promoting substance abuse. The person may be resistant to taking analgesic medications for fear of causing a relapse. Finally, many practitioners do not feel comfortable treating pain because of their lack of knowledge about pain treatment and inadequate knowledge of the differences between substance dependence, tolerance, and addiction. When pain is undertreated, individuals may increase the use of their pain medications or ask for more medication. This behavior has been characterized as "pseudoaddiction" (Weissman and Haddox, 1980) and usually abates once pain is adequately treated.

The assessment and treatment of pain in persons with HIV, regardless of history of SUD, should not differ from the treatment of pain in persons with cancer and should follow the World Health Organization's analgesic pain ladder (Jacox et al., 1994). Two relatively small open-label studies indicate that opioid analgesics can be used safely and effectively in treating pain in persons with HIV with a history of SUD, although higher doses of analgesic may be required (Kaplan et al., 2000; Newshan and Lefkowitz, 2001). When developing a treatment plan for persons with HIV, SUD, and chronic pain, treatment goals should be overtly addressed, limits set with a treatment contract if necessary, and a single clinician should write all pain medication prescriptions (Swica and Breitbart, 2002). Some clinicians have suggested the use of methadone for opioid analgesia (Cruciani and Coggins, 2002). Patients in methadone maintenance should be given their usual dose in the morning and then receive additional methadone for analgesia in three or four divided doses. Opioid analgesics should be given around the clock. Maintaining an open line of communication with the patient's counselor in the methadone maintenance program is essential. We recommend including adjuvant medications and nonpharmacological modalities in the plan and using a multidisciplinary approach to address the psychosocial problems. The need for high doses of medication to control pain is not in and of itself a sign of misuse. More useful indicators of misuse are noncompliance with the treatment plan, any indications of loss of control with the medications, or indications of alcohol abuse or use of street drugs. Individuals on agonist therapy will require higher analgesic doses due to cross-tolerance with the maintenance medication and probable increased pain sensitivity (Alford et al., 2006).

CONCLUSION

Substance use disorder continues to play a major role in HIV in numerous ways. It may lead to direct transmission through IDU, but it also can lead to additional risk behaviors. Non-injecting drug use, particularly alcohol use, is highly associated with HIV transmission and co-infection with HCV. Untreated SUD may lead to suboptimal medical and mental health care for our patients. The syndemic of SUD, violence, low socioeconomic status, and HIV/AIDS is a profound problem that requires continued research and coordinated medical and governmental efforts.

REFERENCES

Alford DP, Compton P, Samet JH (2006). Acute pain management for patients receiving maintenance methadone or buprenorphine therapy. *Ann Intern Med* 144:127–134.

American Psychiatric Association (2013). *Diagnostic and Statistical Manual of Mental Disorders*, fifth edition. Washington, DC: American Psychiatric Association.

Antoniou T, Lin-in Tseng A (2002). Interactions between recreational drugs and antiretroviral agents. *Ann Pharmacother* 36:1598–1613.

Arroyo E, Valenzuela B, Portilla J, et al. (2007). Pharmacokinetics of methadone in human immunodeficiency virus–infected patients receiving nevirapine once daily. *Eur J Clin Pharmacol* 63:669–675.

Baliunas D, Rehm J, Irving H, Shuper P (2010). Alcohol consumption and risk of incident human immunodeficiency virus infections: a meta-analysis. *Int J Public Health* 55:159–166.

Barrons R, Roberts N (2010). The role of carbamazapine and oxcarbazepine in alcohol withdrawal syndrome. *J Clin Pharm Ther* 35:153–167.

Bialer PA (2002). Designer drugs in the general hospital. *Psychiatr Clin North Am* 25:231–243.

Bing EO, Burnam AM, Longshore D, et al. (2001). Psychiatric disorders and drug-use among human immunodeficiency virus–infected adults in the United States. *Arch Gen Psychiatry* 58:721–728.

Bolla KI, McCmm UD, Ricuarte GA (1998). Memory impairment in abstinent MDMA ("Ecstasy") users. *Neurology* 51:1532–1537.

Braithwaite RS, McGinnis KA, Conigliaro J, et al. (2005). A temporal and dose-response association between alcohol consumption and medication adherence among veterans in care. *Alcohol Clin Exp Res* 29:1190–1197.

Breitbart W, Rosenfeld BD, Passik SD, et al. (1996). The undertreatment of pain in ambulatory AIDS patients. *Pain* 65:243–249.

Breitbart W, Rosenfeld B, Passik S, et al. (1997). A comparison of pain report and adequacy of analgesic therapy in ambulatory AIDS patients with and without a history of substance abuse. *Pain* 72:235–243.

Brezing C, Ferrara M, Freudenreich O. (2015). The syndemic of HIV and trauma: implications for a trauma-informed model of care. *Psychosomatics* 56:107–118.

Broz D, Wejnart C, Pham HT, et al. (2014). HIV infection and risk, prevention, and testing behaviors among injecting drug users—National HIV Behavioral Surveillance System, 20 US cities, 2009. *MMWR Morb Mortal Wkly Rep* 63:1–51.

Bruce RD, Altice FL. (2006). Three case reports of a clinical pharmaco-kinetic interaction with buprenorphine and atazanavir plus ritonavir. *AIDS* 20:783–784.

Buchacz K, McFarland W, Kellog TA, et al. (2005). Amphetamine use is associated with increased HIV incidence among men who have sex with men in San Francisco. *AIDS* 19:1423–1438.

Caballeria J (2003). Current concepts in alcohol metabolism. *Ann Hepatol* 2:60–68.

Camacho A, Matthews SC, Dimsdale JE (2004). Use of GHB compounds by HIV-positive individuals. *Am J Addict* 13:120–127.

Centers for Disease Control and Prevention (CDC) (2006). Methamphetamine use and HIV risk behaviors among heterosexual men—preliminary results from five Northern California counties, December 2001–November 2003. *MMWR Morb Mortal Wkly Rep* 55:273–277.

Centers for Disease Control and Prevention (CDC) (2010). Ecstacy overdoses at a New Year's Eve rave – Los Angeles, California, 2010. *MMWR Morb Mortal Wkly Rep* 59(22):677–681.

Centers for Disease Control and Prevention (CDC) (2011). *HIV-AIDS Surveillance Report. Diagnoses of HIV Infection and AIDS in the United States and Dependent Areas*. Vol. 23, pp. 1–46. Atlanta: U.S. Department of Health and Human Services, Centers for Disease Control and Prevention.

Centers for Disease Control and Prevention (CDC) (2016a). HIV and viral hepatitis. https://www.cdc.gov/hiv/pdf/library/factsheets/hiv-viral-hepatitis.pdf. Accessed January 26, 2017.

Centers for Disease Control and Prevention (CDC) (2016b). Smoking and tobacco use: health effects of cigarette smoking. https://www.cdc.gov/tobacco/data_statistics/fact_sheets/health_effects/effects_cig_smoking/. Accessed January 16, 2017.

Centers for Disease Control and Prevention (CDC) (2016c). Viral hepatitis and injection drug users (IDU/HIV prevention fact sheet). http://www.cdc.gov/idu/hepatitis/viral_hep_drug_use.pdf. Accessed January 26, 2016.

Chambers HF, Morris DL, Tauber MG, Moclin G (1987). Cocaine use and the risk for endocarditis in intravenous drug users. *Ann Intern Med* 106:833–836.

Chesney MA, Barrett DC, Stall R (1998). Histories of substance use and risk behavior: precursors to HIV seroconversion in homosexual men. *Am J Public Health* 88:113–116.

Chitwood DO, Comerford M, Sanchez J (2003). Prevalence and risk factors for HIV among sniffers, short-term injectors, and long-term injectors of heroin. *J Psychoactive Drugs* 35:445–453.

Cochrane Collaborative Review Group on HIV Infection and AIDS (2004). Evidence assessment strategies for HIVIAIDS prevention treatment and care. University of California, San Francisco, Institute for Global Health.

Cohen MA, Alfonso CA (2004). AIDS psychiatry: psychiatric and palliative care, and pain management. In GP Wormser (eds.), *AIDS and Other Manifestations of HIV Infection*, 4th ed. San Diego: Elsevier Academic Press.

Community Epidemiologic Work Group (2000). *Epidemiologic Trends in Drug Abuse*. Vol. 1: Highlights and Executive Summmy (pp. 81–84). NIH publication No.00-4739A. Bethesda, MD: National Institutes of Health.

Cruciani R, Coggins C (2002). Current perspectives on pain in AIDS. *Oncology* 16:980–982.

Darvasula R, Miller TR (2014). Substance use treatment in persons with HIV/AIDS: challenges in managing triple diagnosis. *Behav Med* 40:43–52.

DesJarlais DC, Perlis T, Arasteh K, et al. (2005). HIV incidence among injection drug users in New York City, 1990 to 2002: use of serologic test algorithm to assess expansion of HIV prevention services. *Am J Public Health* 95:1439–1444.

Ewing J (1984). The CAGE questionnaire. *JAMA* 252:1903–1907.

Falck RS, Wang J, Carlson RG (2007). Crack cocaine trajectory among users in a midwestern American city. *Addiction* 102:1421–1431.

Ferrando S, Goggin K, Sewell M, Evans S, Fishman B, Rabkin J (1998). Substance use disorders in gay/bisexual men with HIV and AIDS. *Am J Addict* 7:51–60.

Ferrando SJ, Batki SL (2000). Substance abuse and HIV infection. *New Dir Ment Health Serv* 87:57–67.

Galanter M, Brook D (2001). Network therapy for addiction: bringing family and peer support into office practice. *Int J Group Psychother* 51:101–122.

Galanter M, Dermatis H, Glickman L, et al. (2004). Network therapy: decreased secondary opiate use during buprenorphine maintenance. *J Subst Abuse Treat* 26:313–318.

Galanter M, Keller DS, Dermatis H (1997). Network therapy for addiction: assessment of the clinical outcome of training. *Am J Drug Alcohol Abuse* 23:355–367.

Gibson DR, McCusker J, Chesney M (1998). Effectiveness of psychosocial interventions in preventing HIV risk behavior in injecting drug users. *AIDS* 12:919–929.

Grubner VA, McCance-Katz EF. (2010). Methadone, buprenorphine, and street drug interactions with antiretroviral medications. *Curr HIV/AIDS Rep* 7:152–160.

Hales G, Roth N, Smith D (2000). Possible fatal interaction between protease inhibitors and methamphetamine. *Antivir Ther* 5:19.

Halkitis PN, Parsons JT, Stirratt MJ (2001). A double epidemic: crystal methamphetamine drug use in relation to HIV transmission among gay men. *J Homosex* 41:17–35.

Helleberg M, May MT, Ingle SM, et al. (2015). Smoking and life expectancy among HIV-infected individuals on antiretroviral therapy in Europe and North America. *AIDS* 29:221–229

Hess KL, Pollyanna RC, Kanny D, DiNenno E, Lansky A, Paz-Bailey G. (2015) Binge drinking and risky behavior among HIV-negative and unknown HIV status men who have sex with men, 20 US cities. *Drug Alcohol Depend* 147:46–52.

Hijazi Y, Boulieu R (2002). Contribution of CYP3A4, CYP2B6, and CYP2C9 isoforms to Ndemethylation of ketamine in human liver microsomes. *Drug Metab Dispos* 30:853–858.

Jacox A, Carr D, Payne R, et al. (1994). *Clinical Practice Guideline Number 9: Management of Cancer Pain*. AHCPR Publ. No. 94-0592. Washington, DC: Agency for Health Care Policy and Research, U.S. Dept of Health and Human Services.

Kalant H (2001). The pharmacology and toxicology of "ecstasy" (MDMA) and related drugs. *CMAJ* 165:917–928.

Kaplan R, Slywka J, Slagle S, Ries K (2000). A titrated morphine analgesic regimen comparing substance users and non-users with AIDS-related pain. *J Pain Symptom Manage* 19:265–273.

Klinkenberg WD, Sacks S (2004). Mental disorders and drug abuse in persons living with HIV/AIDS. *AIDS Care* 16(Suppl. l):S22–S42.

Kohli A, Shafter A, Sherman A, Kottill S (2014). Treatment of hepatitis C. A systemtatic review. *JAMA* 312:631–640.

Lange RA, Hillis DL (2001). Medical progress: cardiovascular complications of cocaine use. *N Engl J Med* 345:351–358.

Larue F, Fountaine A, Colleau SM (1997). Underestimation and undertreatment of pain in HIV disease. *BMJ* 314:23–28.

Laurenzana EM, Owens SM (1997). Metabolism of phencyclidine by human liver microsomes. *Drug Metab Dispos* 25:557–563.

Li X, Shorter D, Kosten TR (2014). Buprenorphine in the treatment of opioid addiction: opportunities, challenges and strategies. *Expert Opin Pharmacother* 15:2263–2275.

Lipsitz JD, Williams JBW, Rabkin JG, et al. (1994). Psychopathology in male and female intravenous drug users with and without HIV infection. *Am J Psychiatry* 151:1662–1668.

Logan TK, Leukefeld C (2000). Sexual and drug use behaviors among female crack users: a multisite sample. *Drug Alcohol Depend* 58:237–245.

Lum B, Gorman SK, Slavic RS (2006). Valproic acid management of alcohol withdrawal. *Ann Pharmacother* 40:443–448.

Maillard ME, Sorrell MF (2005): Alcoholic liver disease. In DL Kasper, D Braunwald, AS Fauci AS, et al. (eds.), *Harrison's Textbook of Internal Medicine*, 16th ed. New York: McGraw-Hill.

Mattick RP, Breen C, Kimber J, Davoli M (2009). Methadone maintenance therapy for opioid dependence versus no opioid replacement therapy for opioid dependence. *Cochrane Database Syst Rev* 3:CD002209.

McCabe SE, Hughes TL, Bostwick WB, West BT, Boyd CJ. (2009) Sexual orientation, substance use behaviors and substance dependence in the United States. *Addiction* 104:1333–1345.

McCance EF, Gourevitch MN, Arnstein J, et al. (2002). Modified directly observed therapy (MDOT) for injection drug users with HIV disease. *Am J Addictions* 11:271–278.

McCance-Katz EF, Moody DE, Morse GD (2007). Interaction between buprenorphine and atazanavir or atazanavir/ritonavir. *Drug Alcohol Depend* 91:269–278.

McCann JB, James A, Wilson S, et al. (1996) Prevalence of psychiatric disorders in young people in the care system. *BMJ* 313:1529–1530.

McCann UD, Ricuarte GA (2000). Drug abuse and dependence: hazards and consequences of heroin, cocaine, and amphetamines. *Curr Opin Psychiatry* 13:321–325.

McCann UD, Szabo Z, Scheffel U, Dannals RF, Ricaurte GA (1998). Positron emission tomographic evidence of toxic effect of MDMA ("Ecstasy") on brain serotonin neurons in human beings. *Lancet* 352:1433–14377.

McCann UD, Szabo Z, Seckin E, et al. (2005). Quantitative PET studies of the serotonin transporter in MDMA users and controls using [11C]McN5652 and [11C]DASB. *Neuropsychopharmacology* 30:1741–1750.

McCormack JP, Li R, Zarowny D, Singer J (1993). Inadequate treatment of pain in ambulatory HIV patients. *Clin J Pain* 9:279–283.

McDowell JA, Chittick GE, Stevens CP, et al. (2000). Pharmacokinetic interaction of abacavir and ethanol in human immmodeficieney virus–infected adults. *Antimicrob Agents Chemother* 44:1686–1690.

Meyer JP, Springer SA, Altice FL (2011). Substance abuse, violence, and HIV in women: a literature review of the syndemic. *J Women's Health* 20:991–1006.

Miller WR, Rollnick S (1991). *Motivational Interviewing: Preparing People to Change Addictive Behavior*. New York: Guilford Press.

Mimiaga MJ, Reisner SL, Grasso C, Crane H, et al. (2013). Substance use among HIV-infected patients engaged in primary care in the U.S.: findings from the Centers for AIDS Research Network of integrated clinical systems cohort. *Am J Public Health* 103(8):1457–1467.

Molitor F, Truax SR, Ruiz JD, Sun RK (1998). Association of methamphetamine use during sex with sexual risk behaviors and HIV infection among non-injection drug user. *West J Med* 168:93–97.

Muhuri PK, Gfroerer JC, Davies MC (2013). Associations of nonmedical pain reliever use and initiation of heroin use in the United States. *CBHSQ Data Review*. Center for Behavioral Health Statistics and

Quality, SAMHSA. https://www.samhsa.gov/data/sites/default/files/DR006/DR006/nonmedical-pain-reliever-use-2013.htm. Retrieved January 16, 2017.

Mustanski B, Garofalo R, Herrick A, Donenberg G (2007). Psychosocial health problems increase risk for HIV among urban young men who have sex with men: preliminary evidence of a syndemic in need of attention. *Ann Behav Med* 34:37–45.

Needle R, Ball A, DesJarlais D, Whitmore C, Lambert E (2001). The global research network on HIV prevention in drug-using populations (GRN) 1998–2000: trends in the epidemiology, ethnography, and prevention of HIV/AIDS in injection drug users. In *2000 Global Research Network Meeting on HIV Prevention in Drug Using Populations: Third Annual Meeting Report*. Washington, DC: NIDA.

Neuman MG, Schneider M, Nanau RM, Parry C (2012). Alcohol consumption, progression of disease and other comorbidities, and responses to antiretroviral medication in people living with HIV. *AIDS Res Treat* 2012:751827.

Newshan G, Lefkowitz M (2001). Transdermal fentanyl for chronic pain in persons with AIDS: a pilot study. *J Pain Symptom Manage* 21:69–77.

NIH Consensus Development Conference (1998). Effective medical treatment of opiate addiction. *JAMA* 280:1936–1943.

Parrott AC (2013). Human psychobiology of MDMA or 'Ecstasy': an overview of 25 years of empirical research. *Hum Psychopharmacol Clin Exp* 28:289–307.

Petry NM (1999). Alcohol use in HIV patients: what we don't know may hurt us. *Int J STD AIDS* 10:561–570.

Pettinati HM, O'Brien CP, Dundon WD (2013). Current status of co-occuring mood and substance use disorders: a new therapeutic target. *Am J Psychiatry* 170:23–30.

Phillips TR, Billaud JN, Henriksen SJ (2000). Methamphetamine and HIV-1: potential interactions and the use of FIV/cat model. *J Psychopharmacol* 14(3):244–250.

Pilgrim JL, Gerostamoulos, Drummer OH (2011). Deaths Involving MDMA and the concomitant use of pharmaceutical drugs. *J Analyt Toxicol* 35:219–226.

Plankey MW, Ostrow DG, Stall R, et al. (2007). The relationship between methamphetamine and popper use and risk of HIV seroconversion in the Multicenter AIDS Cohort Study. *J Acquir Immune Defic Syndr* 45:85–92.

Prochaska JO, DiClemente CC (1986). Toward a comprehensive model of change. In WR Miller, N Heather (eds.), *Treating Addictive Behaviors: Processes of Change*. New York: Plenum Press.

Rabkin JG, Johnson J, Lin SH, et al. (1997). Psychopathology in male and female HIV-positive and negative injecting drug users: longitudinal course over 3 years. *AIDS* 11:507–515.

Rahmanian S, Wewers ME, Koletar S, et al. (2011). Cigarette smoking in the HIV-infected population. *Proc Am Thorac Soc* 8:313–319.

Rayner SG, Weinert CR, Peng H, Jepsen S, Broccard AF (2012). Dexmedetomidine as adjunct treatment for severe alcohol withdrawal in the ICU. *Ann Intensive Care* 2:12–14.

Reback CJ, Flethcher JB, Shoptaw S, Grella CE (2013). Methamphetamine and substance use trends among street-recruited men who have sex with men, from 2008–2011. *Drug Alcohol Depend* 133(1):262–265.

Scholler-Gyure M, van den Brink W, Kakyda TN, et al. (2008). Pharmacokinetic and pharmacodynamics study of the concomitant administration of methadone and TMC 125 in HIV-negative volunteers. *J Clin Pharmacol* 48:322–329.

Schuckit MA (2014). Recognition and management of withdrawal delirium (delirium tremems). *N Engl J Med* 371:2109–2113.

Semann S, DesJarlais DC, Sugolow E, et al. (2002). A meta-analysis of the effect of HIV prevention interventions on the sex behaviors of drug users in the United States. *J Acquir Immune Defic Syndr* 30(Suppl.):S73–S93.

Shoptaw S, Reback CJ, Freese TE (2002). Patient characteristics, HIV serostatus, and risk behaviors among gay and bisexual males seeking treatment for methamphetamine abuse and dependence in Los Angeles. *J Addict Dis* 21:91–105.

Shuper PA, Neuman M, Kanteres F, Baliunas D, Joharchi N, Rehm J. (2010). Causal considerations on alcohol and HIV/AIDS—a systematic review. *Alcohol Alcoholism* 45:159–166.

Singer M, Clair S. (2003). Syndemics and public health: reconceptualizing diseases in biosocial context. *Med Anthropol Q* 17:423–441.

Substance Abuse and Mental Health Services Administration (SAMHSA) (2013). *Results from the 2012 National Survey on Drug Use and Health: Summary of National Findings*. Rockville, MD: SAMHSA.

Swica Y, Breitbart W (2002). Treating pain in patients with AIDS and a history of substance use. *West J Med* 176:33–39.

Szerlip MA, DeSalvo KB, Szerlip HM (2005). Predictors of HIV infection in older adults. *J Aging Health* 17:293–304.

UNAIDS (2014). The Gap Report 2014: people who inject drugs. http://www.unaids.org/sites/default/files/media_asset/05_Peoplewhoinjectdrugs.pdf. Accessed January 21, 2017.

UNAIDS (2016a). Global AIDS update. http://www.unaids.org/sites/default/files/media_asset/global-AIDS-update-2016_en.pdf. Accessed January 21, 2017.

UNAIDS (2016b). *Prevention Gap Report*. http://www.unaids.org/sites/default/files/media_asset/2016-prevention-gap-report_en.pdf. Accessed January 21, 2017.

United Nations Office on Drugs and Crime (UNODC) (2016). *World Drug Report 2016* (United Nations publication, Sales No. E.16.XI.7). https://www.unodc.org/doc/wdr2016/WORLD_DRUG_REPORT_2016_web.pdf. Accessed January 21, 2017.

Urbina A, Jones K (2004). Crystal methamphetamine, its analogues, and 1-IIV infection: medical and psychiatric aspects. *Clin Infect Dis* 38:890–894.

U.S. Department of Health and Human Services, Office of the Surgeon General (2016). *Facing Addiction in America: The Surgeon General's Report on Alcohol, Drugs, and Health*. https://addiction.surgeongeneral.gov/surgeon-generals-report.pdf. Accessed January 21, 2017.

Venable PA, McKirnan DJ, Buchbinder SP, et al. (2004). Alcohol use and high-risk behavior among men who have sex with men: the effects of consumption level and partner type. *Health Psychol* 23:525–532.

Wechsberg WM, Golin C, El-Bassel N, et al. (2012). Current interventions to reduce sexual risk behaviors and crack cocaine use among HIV-infected individuals. *Curr HIV/AIDS Rep* 9:385–393.

Weir E (2000). Raves: a review of the culture, the drugs, and the prevention of harm. *CMAJ* 162:1843–1848.

Weissman DE, Haddox JD (1980). Opioid pseudoaddiction—an iatrogenic syndrome. *Pain* 36:363–366.

Wen XJ, Balluz L, Town M. (2012). Prevalence of HIV risk behaviors between binge drinkers and non-binge drinkers aged 18–64 in US, 2008. *J Community Health* 37:72–79.

Woody GE, Dmmell D, Seage GR (1999). Non-injection substance use correlates with risky sex among men having sex with men: data from HIVNET. *Drug Alcohol Depend* 53:1 97–205.

Wynn GH, Cozza KL, Zapor MJ, et al. (2005). Antiretroviral, part III: antiretrovirals and drugs of abuse. *Psychosomatics* 46:79–87.

Yeon P, Helmut A (2007). Crystal meth and HIV/AIDS: The perfect storm? *NEJM Journal Watch*. http://www.jwatch.org/ac200712030000001/2007/12/03/crystal-meth-and-hiv-aids-perfect-storm. Accessed January 26, 2017.

Yeon P, Albrecht H (2008). Crystal methamphetamine and HIV/AIDS. *AIDS Clin Care* 20:2–4.

15.

DEPRESSIVE AND BIPOLAR DISORDERS

Antoine Douaihy, Matthew Conlon, and Maria Ferrara

Depressive disorders are highly prevalent among persons living with HIV/AIDS. Depressive disorders significantly negatively affect adherence to antiretroviral therapy (ART) and HIV viral suppression and are associated with poor quality of life and major impairment in overall functioning. This chapter reviews the prevalence, risk factors, assessment, and diagnosis of depressive and bipolar disorders. It also examines the impact of depression on sexual behaviors, adherence to ART, quality of life, and mortality. The chapter also includes a comprehensive discussion of treatment approaches and considerations for HIV-infected individuals with depressive disorders. Furthermore, it reviews the bipolar disorder spectrum in HIV/AIDS as well as other psychiatric disorders co-occurring with depressive disorders.

DEPRESSIVE DISORDERS

PREVALENCE, RISK FACTORS, ASSESSMENT, AND DIAGNOSIS

The prevalence of depression varies across studies, although there is general consensus that depression is more common in persons with HIV than in the general population. Most large prevalence studies are dated. The best data come from a large nationally representative survey of HIV care clinics in the United States, published by Bing et al. (2001). The prevalence of major depressive disorder in persons with HIV was 36% compared to 7.6% in persons in the general population screened with a similar measure (Bing et al., 2001). A more conservative estimate for the rate of depression was drawn from a meta-analysis of 10 published studies prior to 2001, and it was found that 9.4% of HIV-positive subjects screened positive for major depressive disorder. Of note, the odds of screening positive for depression were still two times greater than in HIV-negative comparisons (Ciesla and Roberts, 2001). Overall, there is consensus among studies that there is a disproportionately higher rate of depression among persons with HIV than in persons in the general population.

Many of the same risk factors for depression in the general population also serve as important risk factors for depression in persons with HIV, including either a personal or family history of depressive disorder or a history of substance use disorder. Some specific questions to consider asking when screening for depression in an HIV-positive patient include

social stigmatization, isolation, lack of social support, or death of friends as a result of HIV or substance use (Kalichman et al., 2000).

The role of collaborative care in treating individuals with HIV-positive status is increasingly recognized as a useful and cost-effective means to provide care. In the most ideal situation, a comprehensive psychiatric team is located within the HIV clinic and able to provide collaborative services where patients also see HIV infectious disease physicians. A study of one such clinic in Boston looked retrospectively at a set of 124 patient charts between 2004 and 2010 (Coleman et al., 2012). The authors of this study emphasized the importance of measure-based psychiatric care in order to guide treatment. In this case, the Beck Depression Inventory-II was used to measure depression scores. In other studies, groups have successfully used other screening tools, such as the Patient Health Questionaire-9 (Sueoka et al., 2010) or Hamilton Depression Scale for Depression (Tsai et al., 2013).

An additional tool that has been found useful in this population is the Hospital Anxiety and Depression Scale (HADS), a self-administered questionnaire that consists of seven items related to depression and that has a counterpart of seven items used to screen for anxiety (Zigmond and Snaith, 1983). This assessment is particularly useful in selecting for nonsomatic symptoms of depressions, as somatic symptoms may overlap between depression and HIV. Recent studies making use of the HADS at routine outpatient follow-up in a large sample of European patients with HIV found the percentage of patients who screened positive for depressive symptoms to be approximately twice the reported rate in the general European population (Robertson et al., 2014). Use of these treatment scales enables clinicians to provide effective and standardized screening, assess treatment progress, and adjust treatment when an intervention is not working.

IMPACT OF DEPRESSION ON SEXUAL BEHAVIORS

Individuals living with depressive symptoms are at greater risk for sexually dangerous behaviors. For example, in a large cohort of sexually active, middle and high school students, those with more baseline depressive symptoms reported less condom use, less use of birth control, and more substance use at the time of sexual activity (Lehrer et al., 2006). This is of particular concern in the HIV population with comorbid depressive symptoms, given the concern that depressed individuals may be less likely to use safer sex measures that reduce the risk of HIV transmission. Treatment of depression can then reduce transmission of HIV. Some smaller retrospective studies have examined this with self-reporting questionnaires. In a cohort of almost 386 individuals with HIV from Uganda, individuals without depressive symptoms were more likely to use condoms, while persons with even minor depressive symptoms were more likely to have had unprotected sex (Musisi et al., 2014). In another study from Kenya, having depressive symptoms, among many other risk factors, was positively associated with having multiple sexual partners (Othieno et al., 2015).

The theory behind the greater prevalence of risky sexual behavior in this population can be conceptualized in the context of self-medication. Brawner and colleagues (2012) found that persons with HIV and comorbid depression are exposed to greater levels of acute and chronic stress, and their adaptive mechanisms to cope with these stressors are limited as compared to their non-depressed peers. Depressed individuals with HIV will describe feelings of loneliness, isolation, and wanting someone to "comfort them," and in this way sex becomes viewed as a stress-relieving activity and one that can temporarily increase self-esteem. Age-discordant relationships translate into the belief that the partner knows what is best for the relationship (i.e., having unprotected sex). This and other studies that show an increase in risky sexual behaviors among those with depression (Brown et al., 2006; Holden et al., 2008; Lee et al., 2009; Mazzaferro et al., 2006; Rubin et al., 2009) highlight the important role for sex education in treating depressed individuals with HIV and depression. Teaching safer sexual behaviors may lead to less unprotected sex and reduce the risk of HIV transmission. Further, efforts to treat depression in the absence of a comprehensive approach that also addresses sex education may be unlikely to actually reduce the risk of secondary HIV transmission (Tsai et al., 2013).

IMPACT OF DEPRESSION ON ADHERENCE TO ANTIRETROVIRAL THERAPY AND QUALITY OF LIFE

Depression has a clear negative effect on adherence to ART. This is seen both in patient self-reports and for studies that carefully electronically track adherence with a medication event monitoring system (Magidson, Blashill, et al., 2015; Vranceanu et al., 2008). A recent meta-analysis of over 35,029 cases from 95 independent samples showed that lack of adherence to ART due to comorbid depressive symptoms occurs independent of sex, IV drug use, sexual orientation, or study location (Gonzalez et al., 2011). This trend also holds true across income groups in multiple countries (Uthman et al., 2014). Furthermore, given the relationship between depression and HIV treatment nonadherence across depression severities, there is likely a beneficial a role for treatment intervention even at subclinical levels of depression. Delay in diagnosis of depression can be quite detrimental to the care of persons with HIV. Longitudinal analysis from a prospectively

followed group in the Nutrition for Healthy Living Study showed that persons with the first onset of depression and HIV were at particularly elevated risk for nonadherence at follow-up (Kacanek et al., 2010). Thus, early screening and identification should be employed where possible.

Recent work has focused on how depression might mediate poor adherence to ART. One cohort examined from the California Collaborative Treatment Group showed that changes in daily routine consistently predict poor ART adherence over and above other factors commonly related to adherence (Magidson, Blashill, et al., 2015). Thus degree of disruption to lifestyle structure may mediate the impact of depression on adherence. Another study from the same year looked at cognitive distortions apparent in depression. Individuals living with HIV and depression respond to environmental stressors differently than those without depression. They are more likely to see their immediate environment as punitive and thus less likely to have available the same positive reinforcements in day-to-day life that would otherwise encourage adherence to a daily medication regimen. Data from a set of 83 predominantly African American substance users showed this form of so-called environmental punishment as the main mediator of nonadherence in this group (Magidson, Listhaus et al., 2015). This finding is in agreement with earlier studies showing that HIV-infected individuals living with depression are more vulnerable to acute stressors that reduce adherence to ART compared to their non-depressed counterparts (Bottonari et al., 2010). The fact that stress plays such an important role in the perpetuation of depression and in nonadherence to ART suggests that stress management therapy could play an important role in the treatment of this population.

In addition to depression's effect of making people feel less equipped to deal with day-to-day stressors, HIV infection by itself is a chronic psychological stressor. The stigma of infection can lead to marginalization of persons with HIV, and persons with the least social support are often least likely to disclose their HIV status (Smith et al., 2008). See Chapter 6 of this textbook for further details about HIV stigma, discrimination, and AIDSism. Further, living with HIV may affect the way individuals cope with acute social stressors and may in and of itself be a predisposing factor for depression. For example, a multisite study of 166 adolescent infected with HIV analyzed coping strategies with self-report checklists. Adolescents with moderately advanced illness (CD4 200–500 cells/mm³) tended to use a more passive coping style, such as resignation and other approaches that do not directly approach a problem. Healthier youth (CD4 >500 cells/mm³) were found to more frequently use active coping strategies to deal with their problems, including medication adherence (Orban et al., 2010). Another small study of 247 HIV-positive individuals from Dallas/Fort Worth, Texas found that HIV-positive men with depression tended to use distraction and blame more and positive growth less, and HIV-positive women more frequently used blame as a coping mechanism (Vosvick et al., 2010). These were small association studies that cannot demonstrate causality of these coping mechanisms in their effect on mood. However, studies such as these do suggest interventions that can be tailored to the needs of HIV-positive individuals in treating depression.

MORBIDITY AND MORTALITY RELATED TO DEPRESSION

It is well known that depression has a negative impact on chronic illnesses such as heart disease and diabetes (Barth et al., 2004; Katon, 2008; Katon et al., 2010; Unutzer et al., 2009; van Melle et al., 2004). In the era of highly effective antiviral regimens, persons on ART may live decades, and HIV has become a chronic illness that should similarly be treated using the chronic care model. This entails significant emphasis on follow-up and longitudinal care, as individuals who are not retained in treatment and who miss clinic visits are at higher risk for all-cause mortality (Mugavero et al., 2014).

Depression leads to increased impairment and decline in psychosocial functioning, decreased ART adherence, increased HIV RNA levels (viral loads), decreased CD4 counts, slower virology response to treatment, more rapid progression of illness, and overall increased mortality rates (Hartzell et al., 2008). Nine-year data from HIV-infected men from the Coping in Health and Illness Project showed that depressive symptoms are associated with decrements in killer lymphocytes and declines in the total numbers of lymphocytes. With high stress and high depressive symptoms, faster progression to AIDS was found in the study group at 3.5-, 5.5-, 7.5-, and 9-year follow-up, after adjusting for baseline viral load and CD4+ counts (Cruess et al., 2003). These are large association studies that suggest a clear relationship between depression and illness progression, although the direction of causality remains unproven. Regardless, it is critically important that proper diagnosis of depression is made and treatment provided for HIV-afflicted individuals, as these efforts can improve outcomes.

In a 2010 study of almost 10,000 HIV-infected individuals over a 12-year period of time, DeLorenze and colleagues looked at various associations between psychiatric diagnoses, mental health treatment, and mortality. In this cohort, persons with a psychiatric diagnosis and no mental health treatment had an approximately 42% higher chance of dying than individuals with a psychiatric diagnosis and access to treatment (DeLorenze et al., 2010). Interestingly, this mortality risk held true even after adjusting for variables including age, immune status, viral load, and ART adherence. In one large study, analysis of a group assessed for both adherence and depressive symptoms, measured on the Center for Epidemiological Studies Depression Scale, showed that even after controlling for adherence, individual with depressive symptoms had 5.9 times higher all-cause mortality over the time period examined between 1996 and 2002. Mental health treatment of those with HIV and depression may positively influence these individuals' health beyond the behavioral changes in medication adherence.

DIFFERENTIAL DIAGNOSIS

As with any psychiatric evaluation, careful attention should be paid to developing a robust and thorough differential diagnosis. In this way, the practitioner can appropriately choose the right treatment or combination or appropriate treatments. In any case where unipolar depression is suspected as the diagnosis, the practitioner should also consider competing possibilities, such as bipolar disorder, dysphoria from PTSD, a substance-induced mood disorder, or HIV-associated neurocognitive disorder. These disorders bear special relevance in persons with HIV.

Many of the symptoms of progressive HIV infection may look similar to somatic symptoms commonly experienced in depressed individuals. As a result, it is often difficult to determine whether a patient's fatigue, weight loss, and sleep disturbances are the result of a depressive illness or from a viral syndrome (Ownby et al., 2010). Elimination of somatic items from depression rating scales is one approach that can be used to improve clinical usefulness given this concern (Kalichman et al., 2000). Specific screening tools such as the Hospital Anxiety and Depression Scale exclude many of the somatic symptoms to more accurately distinguish HIV and depression (Zigmond and Snaith, 1983). Some have suggested that there is little clinical value in attempting to determine whether certain somatic symptoms suffered by persons with HIV and depression are due to either of these conditions, as individuals may benefit from psychiatric treatment regardless (DeLorenze et al., 2010).

TREATMENTS INCLUDING PHARMACOLOGICAL, PSYCHOTHERAPY, AND INTEGRATIVE THERAPIES

There is strong evidence to suggest that depression has deleterious effects on adherence to ART, quality of life, safer sex practices, and overall mortality in persons living with HIV/AIDS. Furthermore, this evidence applies to HIV-positive individuals with varying degrees of depressive symptomatology. Thus it is important to detect depression and to effectively intervene, since treatment has been demonstrated to provide overall benefits. Treatment should be multimodal; a combination of pharmacological and psychosocial approaches is most likely to lead to partial or full remission of a depressive syndrome. For a comprehensive approach to the treatment for persons with depression and HIV see Chapters 37 through 42 of this textbook.

Psychological therapies for depression and HIV have been adapted to address less healthy coping skills and to focus on stress management. As discussed previously, persons living with HIV are exposed to elevated levels of stress from both the illness itself and from social circumstances. Individuals living with HIV may face discrimination from the community with resultant increased stress, especially given pre-existing stigma against gender, race, ethnicity, or sexual orientation (Blashill et al., 2011). Psychotherapy should address the isolation experienced by those with depression and HIV, and it should be used to teach useful skills to manage stressors. For one disadvantaged group, the SMART/EST Women's project developed a cognitive-behavioral stress management training combined with expressive-supportive therapy (CBSM+). Compared with enhanced treatment as usual, this specific therapy developed for depression and HIV included the following aims, taught during 2-hour sessions over a 10-week period (Weiss et al., 2011):

1. Provide information on stress responses and coping

2. Teach anxiety reduction skills (i.e., progressive muscle relaxation, deep breathing and guided imagery, autogenic suggestion, physical activity)

3. Modify maladaptive cognitive appraisals using cognitive restructuring, reframing strategies, and disputing irrational beliefs

4. Enhance interpersonal conflict resolution skills and anger management via negotiation skills training

5. Encourage participants to use active, problem-solving coping strategies rather than passive, emotion-based coping, where appropriate

6. Provide supportive group environment for open expression of feelings and thoughts

7. Increase utilization of social support networks as well as appropriate healthcare and community resources

8. Increase knowledge, change attitudes, and improve adherence to healthy living components.

Findings from the trial showed utility in this specific therapy to reduce distress, reduce denial, and improve social support, self-efficacy, and quality of life. Some of the benefits from this type of therapy include improved adherence to medication; a decrease in risky sex; a decrease in substance use or abuse; and a decrease in mortality and morbidity. Other trials of therapies focused on stress management rather than traditional cognitive behavioral treatments in addressing depression in the persons with HIV show that there appear to be unique benefits in addressing stress in this population (Sabet et al., 2013). These therapies focused on stress management can be delivered cost-effectively in a group format, which has the added benefit of increasing social support and acceptance of problems, and addresses the tendency toward denial prominent in this population.

Additional work has been done to develop specific psychotherapies to address adherence to ART that is clearly worse among individuals with depression. Safren et al. have used theories from cognitive behavioral therapy to develop a treatment tailored toward those with HIV and depression, so-called cognitive behavioral therapy for adherence and depression (CBT-AD). Using the standardized Mongomery-Asberg depression rating scale and electronic pill cap technology to monitor adherence, a group of 89 individuals was randomly divided into blocks of two, stratified by sex, depression severity, and adherence, and assigned to receive either CBT-AD

or enhanced treatment as usual. When both treatments were compared, adherence and depression scale scores were both significantly improved in the CBT-AD condition (Safren et al., 2012). The authors also tracked CD4 cell counts over time, which were significantly greater in the treatment arm of the study, although viral load in the two groups did not different. The same type of therapy has been shown to provide benefits in greater ART adherence that are maintained at 3-month, 6-month, and 12-month follow-up (Safren et al., 2009). Hence, there is value in focusing on adherence issues when providing treatment for this population.

In choosing effective antidepressant therapy, many of the developed treatment algorithms will apply to persons with HIV much as they would to persons without HIV infection. Several well-developed and thorough reviews have surveyed the evidence and provided some direction in prescribing (Caballero and Nahata, 2005). As with many depressed patients, it is often wise to initially choose a selective serotonin reuptake inhibitor (SSRI), given its documented efficacy in large studies and fewer side effects than those of many other antidepressants. SSRIs are somewhat less dangerous in overdose than other antidepressants and thus may be safer for persons with HIV, in whom thoughts of suicide are common, even in individuals not previously diagnosed with depression (Carrico et al., 2007). Citalopram and sertraline in particular may be most useful because of their availability as generics and because they have relatively few drug interactions with medications commonly used to treat HIV infection (Ownby et al., 2010). Antidepressants with dopaminergic effect, such as bupropion, may have some added theoretical benefits given studies showing reduced dopaminergic activity in critical brain areas in HIV infection. Caution should be exercised in their use, however, as several widely used antiretroviral medications may affect bupropion metabolism. Finally, stimulants such as modafinil have a role in treating comorbid depression and HIV given their adjunctive benefit in the treatment of fatigue, which is common among both depressed and nondepressed HIV-positive individuals. Stimulants are both well tolerated and effective in placebo-controlled trials to treat fatigue in HIV patients (Rabkin et al., 2010). These stimulant medications come at the cost of increasing the risk of relapse on illicit substances, and stimulants themselves have abuse potential. For further details on the psychopharmacological care of persons with HIV, see Chapter 42 of this textbook.

There are a variety of additional integrative treatments apart from traditional psychopharmacological and psychological cognitive-behavioral talk-based therapies that can be useful in adjunctive treatment of depression and HIV. Given the social isolation apparent in persons with HIV and AIDS, Internet groups may help provide alternative ways to find supportive peers outside an individual's immediate community (Kalichman et al., 2006). Local peer-led support groups may also be useful and have been documented to show higher self-reported adherence, greater social support, and lower depressive symptomatology, although evidence for the effectiveness of these treatments is less clear than for other treatments described (Ownby et al., 2010). Local peer-led support groups are likely to be low- or no-cost options, making them cost-effective interventions. See Chapter 38 of this textbook for a more thorough discussion of integrative treatments.

BIPOLAR DISORDER

PREVALENCE AND RISK FACTORS

Persons with HIV are more likely to have bipolar disorder than persons in the general population. A recent study of 196 HIV-infected adult outpatients in a specialized clinic in Brazil found high rates of bipolar disorder (BD) on the Mood Disorder Questionnaire (MDQ). Positive MDQ screening was found in 13.2% and the BD diagnosis was confirmed in 8.1% of the sample. This represents an almost four times higher prevalence of BD among the HIV-infected patients in the sample (8.1%) than in the U.S. general population (2.1%). The prevalence of bipolar disorder type 1 in the HIV-positive patients was 5.6%, which is almost six times higher than in the U.S. general population (1%). The variables associated with the diagnoses of BD were sex with commercial partners, sex outside the primary relationship, and alcohol and other substance use disorders. The most common psychiatric comorbidity in the BD group was substance use disorder (61.5%) (de Souza Gurgel et al., 2013). In the NIMH Multisite Acute HIV infection study, approximately 53% of persons with HIV had a lifetime history of major depressive disorder or BD (Atkinson et al., 2009). Another study in the United States examined HIV transmission risk among individuals with BD. Risk behavior associated with HIV transmission was examined among 63 patients with BD, major depressive disorder, and no mood disorder; half also had substance use disorders. Patients with BD were more likely than others to report unprotected intercourse with HIV-negative partners and less than 95% adherence to ART. Furthermore, BD and substance use disorder were independent predictors of both risk behaviors. Participants with poorer medication adherence were more likely to have detectable HIV viral loads and unprotected sexual intercourse with HIV-negative partners. The authors concluded that persons with BD require a comprehensive evaluation and an integrated treatment approach incorporating HIV prevention interventions to reduce HIV transmission risk behaviors (Meade et al., 2012).

DIFFERENTIAL DIAGNOSIS

Mania and hypomania in HIV/AIDS may be due to BD and other etiologies such as illicit or prescribed medications including ART, metabolic disturbances, neurological and endocrine disorders, and systemic infections (Lyketsos and Treisman, 2001). Rates for mania among HIV-infected individuals increase after the onset of AIDS and are associated with cognitive changes suggestive of a central nervous system infection. After the onset of AIDS, 4% to 8% of patients exhibit symptoms of mania (Mijch et al., 1999). A full comprehensive workup is warranted to distinguish between mania secondary to HIV/AIDS and bipolar mania in order to formulate and implement the appropriate treatments. There is some evidence from small open trial studies demonstrating the efficacy of mood stabilizers for manic symptoms in HIV/AIDS, indicating that mood stabilizers used to treat mania in the general population may also treat HIV/AIDS-associated manic states. Care must be taken when prescribing mood stabilizers in the context of ART. It is essential to monitor for untoward side effects, as well as to examine possible drug–drug interactions and potential toxicities.

Lithium has been effective in small open trials (Parenti et al., 1988) and may lead to an improvement of neuropsychological functioning in HIV-infected individuals receiving ART (Letendre et al., 2006). However, in a case series of HIV-infected men, lithium was not well tolerated and symptoms of toxicity developed in 8 out of 10 patients (Parenti et al., 1988). Patients on lithium treatment should thus be closely monitored for any early signs of toxicity, which would warrant immediate discontinuation of the medication.

An anticonvulsant such as valproate has been used as an effective alternative treatment for mania among HIV-positive individuals (Halman et al., 1993). Given valproate's potential risk of hepatotoxicity, close monitoring is warranted in HIV-infected individuals with liver disease. Lamotrigine has not been studied for mania in HIV disease. Controlled studies of mood-stabilizing agents in HIV illness are needed.

CO-OCCURRING DISORDERS

As reported in HIV-negative populations, depressive and bipolar disorders can occur together with Axis I (anxiety, PTSD, psychotic disorders, substance use disorders) and Axis II (personality) disorders. Unfortunately, prevalence studies in persons with HIV were often designed to investigate only a discrete number of psychiatric disorders, excluding, for example, bipolar disorder (Rabkin, 2008), or focused on comorbidity with substance use disorders, especially at the beginning of the epidemic (Bing et al., 2001; Rabkin et al., 1997). In a large study conducted in a sample of 2,864 HIV-positive adults receiving care for HIV in 1996, more than one-third screened positive for major depression and more than one-quarter for anxiety disorders (generalized anxiety and panic disorders). Experiencing many HIV-related symptoms was a strong predictor of having a psychiatric disorder in the previous year. It was postulated that HIV-related symptoms could serve as a reminder of the illness status and thereby lead to an increase in psychological distress. The same hypothesis was tested by Rabkin and colleagues (1997), who found that HIV symptoms lead to higher distress levels rather than the converse. Moreover, symptoms of anxiety may increase HIV fatigue and physical functional limitations (Barroso et al., 2010).

Mood disorders can also co-occur with PTSD. Major depressive disorder, which frequently co-occurs with PTSD after a traumatic exposure, can have a synergistic effect when comorbid with PTSD, as demonstrated by a study performed with U.S. soldiers, whose HIV status was unknown. Individuals with symptoms of PTSD and major depressive disorder were more likely to engage in behaviors associated with HIV risk (Marshall et al., 2013) than were individuals with major depressive disorder or PTSD alone. When HIV infection co-occurs with psychiatric and substance use disorders, it may be defined as a *triple diagnosis*. Its prevalence ranges from 13% to 23% among persons living with HIV/AIDS and as high as 38% in clinics that specialize in the treatment of persons living with HIV/AIDS (Conover et al., 2009). Triple diagnosis is associated with lower quality of life, poorer health outcomes (such as higher viral loads; Conover et al., 2009), acceleration of HIV illness progression, and more severe neurocognitive dysfunction (Durvasula and Miller, 2014). Douaihy et al. (2003) emphasized the need for an integrated and interdisciplinary approach addressing substance use problems, psychiatric disorders, and medical care.

Personality disorders can also co-occur in HIV-infected people with mood disorders. They were diagnosed in up to 30% of persons living with HIV/AIDS (Golding and Perkins, 1996; Jacobsberg et al., 1995). Co-occurring personality disorder is associated with a higher risk for ART discontinuation, higher rates of substance relapse, an increased risk for HIV transmission, and worse health outcomes (Golding and Perkins, 1996, Ironson and Hayward, 2008; Meade et al., 2009; Yin et al., 2014). See Chapter 20 of this textbook for a more detailed presentation of personality disorders in persons with HIV.

CONCLUSION AND FUTURE DIRECTIONS

Despite the advent of ART and its impact on reducing the mortality rate among persons living with HIV/AIDS, the prevalence of mood symptoms and depressive disorders remains significantly high. Thus it is critical to screen, assess, and treat depressive and bipolar disorders in persons living with HIV/AIDS in order to improve quality of life, alleviate suffering, minimize the impact of depressive disorders on self-care and associated risk factors, and optimize treatment outcomes. There is no available gold standard for screening and assessment of depressive disorders among persons living with HIV/AIDS. More research is warranted to evaluate the clinical assessment of and measurement tools for depressive disorders in persons with HIV. Future studies may also examine the unique and complex interface of depressive and bipolar disorders and HIV infection in order to better inform targeted clinical interventions aimed at reducing risk behaviors, aggressively treating and promoting self-management of HIV illness and co-occurring depressive and bipolar disorders, and thereby reducing suffering, morbidity, and mortality in persons with HIV and AIDS.

REFERENCES

Atkinson JH, Higgins JA, Vigil O, et al. (2009). Psychiatric context of acute/early HIV infection: the NIMH Multisite Acute HIV Infection Study IV. *AIDS Behav* 13(6):1061–1067.

Barroso J, Hamill BG, Leserman J, et al. (2010). Physiological and psychosocial factors that predict HIV-related fatigue. *AIDS Behav* 14(6):1415–1427.

Barth J, Schumacher M, Herrmann-Lingen C (2004). Depression as a risk factor for mortality in patients with coronary heart disease: a meta-analysis. *Psychosom Med* 66(6):802–813.

Bing EG, Burnam AM, Longshore D, et al. (2001). Psychiatric disorders and drug use among human immunodeficiency virus-infected adults in the United States. *Arch Gen Psychiatry* 58:721–728.

Blashill AJ, Perry N, Safren SA (2011). Mental health: a focus on stress, coping, and mental illness as it relates to treatment retention, adherence, and other health outcomes. *Curt HIV/AIDS Rep* 8(4):215–222.

Bottonari KA, Safren SA, McQuaid JR, et al. (2010). A longitudinal investigation of the impact of life stress on HIV treatment adherence. *J Behav Med* 33(6):486–495.

Brawner BM, Gomes MM, Jemmott LS, et al. (2012). Clinical depression and HIV risk-related sexual behaviors among African-American adolescent females: unmasking the numbers. *AIDS Care* 24(5):618–625.

Brown LK, Tolou-Shams M, Lescano C, Houck C, Zeidman J, Pugatch D (2006). Depressive symptoms as a predictor of sexual risk among African American adolescents and young adults. *J Adolesc Health* 39(3):e441–e444, e448.

Caballero J, Nahata MC (2005). Use of selective serotonin-reuptake inhibitors in the treatment of depression in adults with HIV *Ann Pharmacother* 39(1):141–145.

Carrico AW, Johnson MO, Morin SF, et al. (2007). Correlates of suicidal ideation among HIV-positive persons. *AIDS* 21(9):1199–1203.

Ciesla JA, Roberts JE (2001). Meta-analysis of the relationship between HIV infection and risk for depressive disorders. *Am J Psychiatry* 158(5):725–730.

Coleman SM, Blashill AJ, Gandhi RT, et al. (2012). Impact of integrated and measurement-based depression care: clinical experience in an HIV clinic. *Psychosomatics* 53(1):51–57.

Conover CJ, Weaver M, Ang A, et al., for The HIV/AIDS Treatment Adherence, Health Outcomes and Cost Study (2009). Costs of care for people living with combined HIV/AIDS, chronic mental illness, and substance abuse disorders. *AIDS Care* 21(12):1547–1559.

Cruess DG, Petite JM, Lederman J, et al. (2003). Depression and HIV infection: impact on immune function and disease progression. *CNS Spectr* 8(1):52–58.

DeLorenze GN, Satre DD, Quesenberry CP, et al. (2010). Mortality after diagnosis of psychiatric disorders and co-occurring substance use disorders among HIV-infected patients. *AIDS Patient Care STDS* 24(11):705–712.

de Sousa Gurgel W, da Silva Carneiro AH, Barreto Rebouças D, et al. (2013). Prevalence of bipolar disorder in a HIV-infected outpatient population. *AIDS Care* 25(12):1499–1503.

Douaihy AB, Jou RJ, Gorske T, Salloum IM (2003). Triple diagnosis: dual diagnosis and HIV disease, Part 1. *AIDS Read* 13(7):331–332, 339–341.

Durvasula R, Miller TR (2014). Substance abuse treatment in persons with HIV/AIDS: challenges in managing triple diagnosis. *Behav Med* 40(2):43–52.

Golding M, Perkins DO (1996). Personality disorder in HIV infection. *Int Rev Psychiatry* 8(2-3):253–258.

Gonzalez JS, Batchelder AW, Psaros C, et al. (2011). Depression and HIV/AIDS treatment nonadherence: a review and meta-analysis. *J Acquir Immune Defic Syndr* 58(2):181–187.

Halman MH, Worth JL, Sanders KM, Renshaw PF, Murray GB (1993). Anticonvulsant use in the treatment of manic syndromes in patients with HIV-1 infection. *J Neuropsychiatry Clin Neurosci* 5:430–434.

Hartzell JD, Janke IE, Weintrob AC (2008). Impact of depression on HIV outcomes in the HAART era. *J Antimicrob Chemother* 62(2):246–255.

Holden AEC, Shain RN, Miller WB, Piper JM, Perdue ST, Thurman AR, Korte JE. The influence of depression on sexual risk reduction and STD infection in a controlled, randomized intervention trial. *Sex Transm Dis* 2008;35(10):898–904.

Ironson GH, Hayward H (2008). Do positive psychosocial factors predict disease progression in HIV-1? A review of the evidence. *Psychosom Med* 70(5):546–554.

Jacobsberg L, Frances A, Perry S (1995). Axis II diagnoses among volunteers for HIV testing and counseling. *Am J Psychiatry* 152(8):1222–1224.

Kacanek D, Jacobson DL, Spiegelman D, et al. (2010). Incident depression symptoms are associated with poor HAART adherence: a longitudinal analysis from the Nutrition for Healthy Living Study. *J Acquir Immune Defic Syndr* 53(2):266–272.

Kalichman SC, Cherry C, Cain D, et al. (2006). Internet-based health information consumer skills intervention for people living with HIV/AIDS. *J Consult Clin Psychol* 4(3):545–554.

Kalichman SC, Rompa, D, Cage M (2000). Distinguishing between overlapping somatic symptoms of depression and HIV disease in people living with HIV-AIDS. *J Nerv Meant Dis* 188(10):662–670.

Katon WJ (2008). The comorbidity of diabetes mellitus and depression. *Am J Med* 121(11 Suppl 2):S8–S15.

Katon WJ, Lin EH, Von Korff M, et al. (2010). Integrated depression and chronic disease care among patients with diabetes and/or coronary heart disease: the design of the TEAMcare study. *Contemp Clin Trials* 31(4):312–322.

Lee SH, O'Riordan MA, Lazebnik R (2009). Relationships among depressive symptoms, sexually transmitted infections, and pregnancy in African-American adolescent girls. *J Pediatr Adolesc Gynecol* 22(1):19–23.

Lehrer JA, Shriver LA, Gortmaker S, et al. (2006). Depressive symptoms as a longitudinal predictor of sexual risk behaviors among US middle and high school students. *Pediatrics* 118(1):189–200.

Letendre SL, Woods SP, Ellis RJ, et al. (2006). HNRC Group. Lithium improves HIV-associated neurocognitive impairment. *AIDS* 20:1885–1888.

Lyketsos G, Treisman GJ (2001). Mood disorders in HIV infection. *Psychiatr Ann* 31:45–49.

Magidson JF, Blashill AJ, Safren SA, et al. (2015). Depressive symptoms, lifestyle structure, and ART adherence among HIV-infected individuals: a longitudinal mediation analysis. *AIDS Behav* 19(1):34–40.

Magidson JF, Listhaus A, Seitz-Brown CJ, et al. (2015). Can behavioral theory inform the understanding of depression and medication non adherence among HIV-positive substance user? *J Behav Med* 38(2):337–347.

Marshall BDL, Prescott MR, Liberzon I, et al. (2013). Posttraumatic stress disorder, depression, and HIV risk behavior among Ohio Army National Guard soldiers. *J Traum Stress* 26:64–70.

Mazzaferro KE, Murray PJ, Ness RB, Bass DC, Tyus N, Cook RL (2006). Depression, stress, and social support as predictors of high-risk sexual behaviors and STIs in young women. *J Adolesc Health* 39(4):601–603.

Meade CS, Bevilacqua LA, Key MD (2012). Bipolar disorder is associated with HIV transmission risk behavior among patients in treatment for HIV. *AIDS Behav* 16(8):2267–2271.

Meade CS, Kershaw TS, Hansen NB, Sikkema KJ (2009). Long-term correlates of childhood abuse among adults with severe mental illness: adult victimization, substance abuse, and HIV sexual risk behavior. *AIDS Behav* 13:207–216.

Mijch AM, Judd FK, Lyketsos CG, Ellen S, Cockram A (1999). Secondary mania in patients with HIV infection: are antiretrovirals protective? *J Neuropsychiatry Clin Neurosci* 11:475–480.

Mugavero MJ, Westfall AO, Cole SR, et al. (2014). Beyond core indicators of retention in HIV care: missed clinic visits are independently associated with all-cause mortality. *Clin Infect Dis* 59(10):1471–1479.

Musisi S, Wagner G, Ghosh-Dastidar B, et al. (2014). Depression and sexual risk behavior among clients about to start HIV antiretroviral therapy in Uganda. *Int J STD AIDS* 25(2):130–137.

Orban LA, Stein R, Koenig LJ, et al. (2010). Coping strategies of adolescents living with HIV: disease-specific stressors and responses. *AIDS Care* 22(4):420–430.

Othieno CJ, Okoth R, Peltzer K, et al. (2015). Risky HIV sexual behaviour and depression among University of Nairobi students. *Ann Gen Psychiatry* 11:14–16.

Ownby RL, Jacobs RJ, Waldrop-Valverde D, et al. (2010). Depression care and prevalence in HIV-positive individuals. *Neurobehav HIV Med* 2:73–83.

Parenti DM, Simon GL, Scheib RG, et al. (1988). Effect of lithium carbonate in HIV-infected patients with immune dysfunction. *J Acquir Immune Defic Syndr* 1:119–124.

Rabkin JG (2008). HIV and depression: 2008 review and update. *Curr HIV/AIDS Rep* 5:163–171.

Rabkin JG, McElhiney MC, Rabkin R, et al. (2010). Modafinil treatment for fatigue in HIV/AIDS: a randomized placebo-controlled study. *J Clin Psychiatry* 71(6):707–715.

Rabkin JG, Johnson J, Lin S, et al. (1997). Psychopathology in male and female HIV-positive and negative injecting drug users: longitudinal course over 3 years. *AIDS* 11:507–515.

Robertson K, Bayon C, Molina JM et al. (2014). Screening for neurocognitive impairment, depression, and anxiety in HIV-infected patients in Western Europe and Canada. *AIDS Care* 26(12):1555–1561.

Rubin AG, Gold MA, Primack BA (2009). Associations between depressive symptoms and sexual risk behavior in a diverse sample of female adolescents. *J Pediatr Adolesc Gynecol* 22(5):306–312.

Sabet AH, Khalatbari J, Abbas Ghorbani M, et al. (2013). Group training of stress management vs. group cognitive-behavioral therapy in reducing depression, anxiety and perceived stress among HIV-positive men. *Iran J Psychiatry Behav Sci* 7(1):4–8.

Safren SA, O'Cleirigh CM, Bullis JR, et al. (2012). Cognitive behavioral therapy for adherence and depression (CBT-AD) in HIV-infected injection drug users: a randomized controlled trial. *J Consult Clin Psychol* 80(3):404–415.

Safren SA, O'Cleirigh CM, Tan JY, et al. (2009). A randomized controlled trial of cognitive behavioral therapy for adherence and depression (CBT-AD) in HIV-infected individuals. *Health Psychol* 28(1):1–10.

Smith R, Rossetto K, Peterson BL (2008). A meta-analysis of disclosure of one's HIV-positive status, stigma and social support. *AIDS Care* 20(1):1266–1275.

Sueoka K, Goulet JL, Fiellin DA, et al. (2010). Depression symptoms and treatment among HIV infected and uninfected veterans. *AIDS Behav* 14(2):272–279.

Tsai AC, Miming MJ, Dilley JW, et al. (2013). Does effective depression treatment alone reduce secondary HIV transmission risk? Equivocal findings from a randomized controlled trial. *AIDS Behav* 17(8):2765–2772.

Unutzer J, Schoenbaum M, Katon WJ, et al. (2009). Healthcare costs associated with depression in the medically ill fee-for-service Medicare participants. *J Am Geriatr Soc* 57(3):506–510.

Uthman OA, Madison JF, Safren SA, et al. (2014). Depression and adherence to antiretroviral therapy in low-, middle- and high-income countries: a systematic review and meta-analysis. *Curr HIV/AIDS Rep* 11(3):291–307.

van Melle JP, de Jonge P, Spijkerman TA, et al. (2004). Prognostic association of depression following myocardial infarction with mortality and cardiovascular events: a meta-analysis. *Psychosom Med.* 66(6):814–822.

Vosvick M, Martin LA, Smith NG, et al. (2010). Gender differences in HIV-related coping and depression. *AIDS Behav* 14(2):390–400.

Vranceanu AM, Safren SA, Lu M, et al. (2008). The relationship of post-traumatic stress disorder and depression to antiretroviral medication adherence in persons with HIV. *AIDS Patient Care STDs* 22(4):313–321.

Weiss SM, Tobin JN, Antoni M, Ironson G, Ishii M, Vaughn A, Pgae J (2011). Enhancing the health of women living with HIV: the SMART/EST Women's Project. *Int J Womens Health* 3:63–77.

Yin L, Wang N, Vermund SH, et al. (2014). Sexual risk reduction for HIV-infected persons: a meta-analytic review of "positive prevention" randomized clinical trials. *PLoS ONE* 9(9):e107652.

Zigmond AS, Snaith RP (1983). The hospital anxiety and depression scale. *Acta Psychiatr Scand* 67(6):361–370.

16.

HIV-ASSOCIATED NEUROCOGNITIVE DISORDERS

Scott L. Letendre, Jennifer Iudicello, Beau Ances, Thomas D. Marcotte,

Serena Spudich, and Mary Ann Cohen

Persons with HIV continue to have a high prevalence of neurocognitive disorders, including HIV-associated neurocognitive disorder (HAND), delirium, and other neurocognitive disorders. The prevalence of HAND remains at 40% and may occur in persons who are virally suppressed. The diagnosis of HAND encompasses three related disorders that range from mild and more common (asymptomatic neurocognitive impairment, mild neurocognitive disorder) to severe and less common (HIV-associated dementia) disorders. This chapter will present data on the pathogenesis of HAND and the neurobehavioral, neuroimaging, and medical approaches to evaluating persons with HIV for HAND. While comprehensive neuropsychological testing remains a cornerstone for diagnosing HAND, briefer, more automated testing is in development. Neuroimaging techniques such as magnetic resonance spectroscopy, diffusion tensor imaging, and blood oxygen level–dependent functional magnetic resonance imaging provide important information about the pathogenesis of HIV in the central nervous system (CNS) and can be used in research studies to track the evolution of HAND over time and its response to therapeutic interventions. Blood and cerebrospinal fluid (CSF) biomarkers, such as neurofilament-light, neopterin, soluble CD14, and soluble CD163, provide additional useful information, although they have not yet reached the clinic. In this chapter, the principal focus is on HAND, with brief discussions of delirium and other neurocognitive disorders.

HIV-ASSOCIATED NEUROCOGNITIVE DISORDER—EVOLUTION OVER TIME

The primary target cell type of human immunodeficiency virus-1 (HIV) is the cluster designation 4, or CD4+ T lymphocyte (or T cell). Shortly after transmission, HIV disseminates throughout the body, infecting cells of multiple organs. This is thought to explain the spike in HIV RNA and decline in CD4+ T cells typically seen in blood during acute HIV infection. During this period, the virus also enters the CNS, principally being carried inside infected, migrating monocytes and lymphocytes (Clifford and Ances, 2013; Saylor et al., 2016; Valcour et al., 2011). Once inside the CNS, free virions can then infect resident cells. Tissue macrophages and glia, particularly microglia, are the principal resident target cells for HIV in the CNS and can be productively infected (Joseph et al.,

2015). HIV can also infect astrocytes but when this occurs, it appears to result in restricted infection (Churchill et al., 2015; Thompson et al., 2004). When infected, astrocytes can produce viral proteins, such as Env and Tat, but seem to restrict production of intact virions. The fact that HIV does not infect neurons but can result in neuronal injury has raised a central and critical question in the field: How does HIV injure neurons? This is particularly important since neuronal injury appears to be a central event underpinning the neurocognitive complications of HIV disease, at least the more severe forms of disease (Archibald et al., 2004; Chana et al., 2006; Cherner et al., 2002; Everall et al., 1999; Masliah et al., 1992, 1994, 1996). The reader is referred to Chapter 26 of this textbook for more detailed discussion of the neuropathogenesis of HAND.

Early in the HIV epidemic, clinicians noted that a high proportion of HIV-infected adults developed a spectrum of neurocognitive disorders, initially termed *AIDS dementia complex (ADC)*, ranging from mild to severe (Jordan et al., 1985; Navia, Jordan, et al., 1986; Price et al., 1986). The more severe forms were medically devastating and conferred a substantially increased risk of mortality. Neuropathological examination identified several key findings, including microglial nodules, multinucleated giant cells, and neuronal loss (Navia, Cho, et al., 1986). A standardized approach to diagnosing this disorder was published in 1991 by the AIDS Task Force of the American Academy of Neurology. This approach established names and diagnostic criteria for two forms of disease: mild (minor cognitive motor disorder [MCMD]) and severe (HIV-associated dementia [HAD]). In the period before potent combination antiretroviral therapy (ART), HAD was common, occurring in approximately 15% of patients and conferring a mean survival of only 6 months. MCMD appeared to occur in 30–40% of adults with HIV (Heaton et al., 1995; Hestad et al., 1983). In part because MCMD did not appear to routinely progress to HAD, investigators debated whether the pathogenesis of MCMD and of HAD were distinct clinical syndromes.

The emergence of more potent ART drugs, such as protease inhibitors (PIs) and non-nucleoside reverse transcriptase inhibitors (NNRTIs), resulted in more patients being successfully treated with HIV RNA levels in blood that declined below the quantification limit of commercial assays and with recovery of CD4+ T cells toward the normal range. During this same period, the incidence of HAD declined precipitously (Sactor, 2002). Seemingly paradoxically, however, the estimated prevalence of these disorders seemed to remain stable or perhaps even rise (Heaton et al., 2010), likely because (a) patients were living longer with effective ART and (b) their neurocognitive disorders were not fully responding to ART alone (Cysique et al., 2009). During this transitional period, from approximately 1995 to approximately 2005, the milder form of disease began to predominate. Investigators noted that even the milder form of ADC, MCMD, was associated with functional consequences, such as reduced medical adherence, as well as higher risk for progression to AIDS and death (Gorman et al., 2009; Hinkin et al., 2002).

With these changes in mind, the National Institute of Mental Health convened an expert panel in Frascati, Italy in 2005 to revise the diagnostic approach for ADC (Antinori et al., 2007). The consensus of the panel was to retain the HAD diagnostic category but to distinguish between two groups of mild disease: symptomatic disease (mild neurocognitive disorder, MND) and asymptomatic disease (asymptomatic neurocognitive impairment, ANI). The panel also coined the term *HIV-associated neurocognitive disorder (HAND)*, which encompassed all three diagnoses and replaced ADC. Table 16.1 summarizes the diagnostic

Table 16.1 APPROACH TO RESEARCH DIAGNOSIS OF HIV-ASSOCIATED NEUROCOGNITIVE DISORDER*

HIV-Associated Asymptomatic Neurocognitive Impairment (ANI)[†]

1. Acquired impairment in cognitive functioning, involving at least two ability domains, documented by performance of at least 1.0 SD below the mean for age-education-appropriate norms on standardized neuropsychological tests. The neuropsychological assessment must survey at least the following abilities: verbal/language; attention/working memory; abstraction/executive; memory (learning; recall); speed of information processing; sensory-perceptual, motor skills.

2. The cognitive impairment does not interfere with everyday functioning.

3. The cognitive impairment does not meet criteria for delirium or dementia.

4. There is no evidence of another preexisting cause for the ANI.[‡]

  [†] If there is a prior diagnosis of ANI, but currently the individual does not meet criteria, the diagnosis of ANI in remission can be made.

  [‡] If the individual with suspected ANI also satisfies criteria for a major depressive episode or substance dependence, the diagnosis of ANI should be deferred to a subsequent examination conducted at a time when the major depression has remitted or at least 1 month after cessation of substance use.

HIV-Associated Mild Neurocognitive Disorder (MND)[†]

1. Acquired impairment in cognitive functioning, involving at least two ability domains, documented by performance of at least 1.0 SD below the mean for age-education-appropriates norms on standardized neuropsychological tests. The neuropsychological assessment must survey at least the following abilities: verbal/language; attention/working memory; abstraction/executive; memory (learning; recall); speed of information processing; sensory-perceptual, motor skills. Typically, this would correspond to an MSK scale stage of 0.5 to 1.0.

2. The cognitive impairment produces at least mild interferences in daily functioning (at least one of the following):

  a) Self-report of reduced mental acuity, inefficiency in work, homemaking, or social functioning.

  b) Observation by knowledgeable others that the individual has undergone at least mild decline in mental acuity with resultant inefficiency in work, homemaking, or social functioning.

3. The cognitive impairment does not meet criteria for delirium or dementia.

4. There is no evidence of another preexisting cause for the MND.[‡]

  [†] If there is a prior diagnosis of MND, but currently the individual does not meet criteria, the diagnosis of MND in remission can be made.

  [‡] If the individual with suspected MND also satisfies criteria for a severe episode of major depression with significant functional limitations or psychotic features, or substance dependence, the diagnosis of MND should be deferred to a subsequent examination conducted at a time when the major depression has remitted or at least 1 month after cessation of substance use.

HIV-Associated Dementia (HAD)[†]

1. Marked acquired impairment in cognitive functioning, involving at least two ability domains; typically the impairment is in multiple domains, especially in learning of new information, slowed information processing, and defective attention/ concentration. The cognitive impairment must be ascertained by neuropsychological testing with at least two domains 2 SD or greater than demographically corrected means. (Note that where neuropsychological testing is not available, standard neurological evaluation and simple bedside testing may be used, but this should be done as indicated in algorithm; see below). Typically, this would correspond to an MSK scale stage of 2.0 or greater.

2. The cognitive impairment produces marked interference with day-to-day functioning (work, home life, social activities).

3. The pattern of cognitive impairment does not meet criteria for delirium (e.g., clouding of consciousness is not a prominent feature); or, if delirium is present, criteria for dementia need to have been met on a prior examination when delirium was not present.

4. There is no evidence of another, preexisting cause for the dementia (e.g., other CNS infection, CNS neoplasm, cerebrovascular disease, preexisting neurological disease, or severe substance abuse compatible with CNS disorder).*

[†]Criteria were formulated by the Frascati panel and published in 2007 (Antinori et al., 2007).

MSK, Memorial Sloan-Kettering; SD, standard deviation.

approach, and more information is provided in the section Approach to Neurobehavioral Assessment later in this chapter. Of note, the Frascati panel indicated that this approach was principally recommended for standardizing diagnostic criteria in research studies.

In the decade since the Frascati meeting, ART has continued to evolve in terms of both the development of new classes of drugs (e.g., integrase inhibitors [IntIs]) and shifts in our understanding of the need for early (Lundgren et al., 2015) and uninterrupted (El-Sadr et al., 2006) ART to reduce the risk of AIDS and other complications. As a result, survival of persons with HIV has markedly improved and now approaches that of the general population (Legarth et al., 2016). At the same time, however, a syndrome of premature aging has been recognized (Appay and Kelleher, 2016; Deeks, 2011; Nasi et al., 2017; Pathai et al., 2014; Wang and Kotler, 2014). The premature aging syndrome in persons with HIV is characterized by disease of multiple end-organs, including the brain, that occurs earlier in life than in the general population and has been linked to the persistent inflammation known to occur in persons with HIV. This inflammation has, in turn, been linked to damage to gut-associated lymphoid tissue that occurs soon after HIV infection and results in translocation of microbial products from the gut to the blood (Brenchley et al., 2006; Douek, 2007). Some of these microbial products, such as bacterial lipopolysaccharide, are immunostimulatory, and their leakage into the vascular system can continue despite ART-induced HIV suppression and CD4+ T-cell recovery. Coincident with these changes has been the shifting toxicity of ART drugs. While each new generation of ART drugs has generally been less toxic than the prior generation, CNS toxicity continues to be recognized (Akay et al., 2014; Robertson et al., 2012; Shah et al., 2016) with commonly used drugs such as efavirenz (Ciccarelli et al., 2011; Funes et al., 2015; Ma et al., 2016) and, more recently, dolutegravir and elvitegravir (Abers et al., 2014). Please see Chapters 2 and 42 of this textbook for a full discussion of HIV pharmacology and psychopharmacology.

This summary makes clear what many clinicians and researchers have come to understand over the past two decades: the neurocognitive impairment that occurs during HIV disease is a complex syndrome that has evolved over time and to which the virus may contribute directly (e.g., because of the toxicity of viral proteins), indirectly (because of disruption of glial functioning), or not at all (e.g., through comorbid conditions such as methamphetamine abuse or dementia of the Alzheimer's type).

NEUROCOGNITIVE DISORDERS IN PERSONS WITH HIV AND AIDS

PATHOGENESIS OF HIV IN THE CNS

Overview

The pathogenesis of HAND is incompletely understood and has evolved over time with shifting demographic characteristics of the epidemic, shifting ART practices, and improved survival of persons with HIV. Key events in HAND

pathogenesis appear to include (a) past or current immune suppression (Ellis et al., 2011; Muñoz-Moreno et al., 2008); (b) highly activated monocytes that have high HIV DNA content and migrate into the CNS (Pulliam et al., 1997; Ratto-Kim et al., 2008; Shikuma et al., 2005; Shiramizu et al., 2005, 2007; Valcour et al., 2009, 2010); (c) adaptation (or compartmentalization) of HIV to the CNS environment (Bednar et al., 2015); (d) production of neurotoxic viral proteins (Fields et al., 2015; King et al., 2006; Mocchetti et al., 2012; Pocernich et al., 2005); and, ultimately, (e) neuronal injury (Chana et al., 2006; Cherner et al., 2002; Everal et al., 1999; Masliah et al., 1992; Moore et al., 2006) (Figure 16.1). As reviewed in Chapter 26, the neuropathological features of HIV disease of the CNS have historically included gliosis, microglial nodules, multinucleated giant cells, perivascular macrophages, dendritic pruning, and loss of neurons. These classic findings have shifted over time and are now less commonly observed (Everall et al., 2005), in part because adults with HIV are now more likely to die from HIV-associated, non-AIDS (HANA) conditions, like vascular disease, hepatitis, or lung cancer, before advancing to AIDS. Despite this, more than half of autopsy cases have some brain abnormality (Everall et al., 2009). Even with plasma HIV RNA suppression, however, high levels of macrophage activation may continue in the basal ganglia and hippocampus (Anthony et al., 2005), supporting the importance of monocytes and macrophages in HAND pathogenesis.

Astrocytes are the most populous cells in the brain and can be infected by HIV. While astrocytes do not seem to produce HIV virions, they can produce neurotoxic viral proteins; their normal functioning may be disrupted, including glutamate shuttling; and they may have integrated HIV DNA, which may have implications for HIV eradication strategies. In addition, astrocytes likely influence chemotaxis of immune cells across the blood–brain barrier (BBB) (Muratori et al., 2010). The role of the BBB in HAND pathogenesis has been increasingly recognized over the past decade, particularly with the growing incidence of vascular disease among persons with HIV. The BBB, also sometimes termed "the neurovascular unit," is composed of several structures, including brain microvascular endothelial cells (BMVEC), which are joined by tight junctions, pericytes, astrocyte foot processes, extracellular matrix, and even neurons (Hawkins and Davis, 2005). Expression of adhesion molecules by BMVECs contributes to migration of immune cells into the CNS. Disruption of the BBB's tight junctions and molecular transporters can increase the potential for CNS injury by immune processes and by molecules excluded by a normally functioning barrier (Atluri et al., 2015; Banks et al., 2006; Ivey et al., 2009; McRae, 2016; Persidsky et al., 2006; Spindler and Hsu, 2012; Toborek et al., 2005). This increased delivery of foreign molecules can include ART drugs, and this could increase their toxicity in the CNS.

Neuronal toxicity may manifest in part as synaptic-dendritic injury, which can be reversible (Ellis et al., 2007; Valcour et al., 2011). The potential reversibility would be consistent with clinical findings of fluctuating symptoms and with the lower levels of inflammation observed with

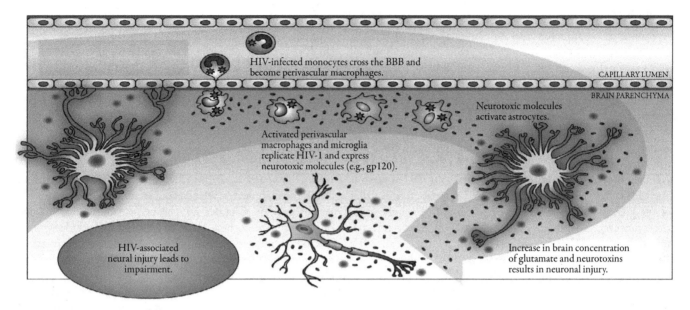

Figure 16.1 Simplified model of HIV pathogenesis in the brain. HIV enters the central nervous system (CNS) shortly after infection, primarily inside infected cells such as lymphocytes and monocytes that are either conducting immune surveillance or are responding to foreign antigens. These cells can replicate HIV inside the CNS, which leads to infection of other cells. Microglia and tissue and perivascular macrophages are the main target cells in the CNS for productive infection. These cells can produce virions and viral proteins that can activate and potentially injure other cells such as astrocytes. While HIV does not infect neurons, this disruption of the normal CNS environment can lead to neuronal injury via multiple mechanisms, including excitotoxicity. Macrophage and microglial activation and neuronal injury are hallmarks of the clinical syndrome recognized as HIV-associated neurocognitive disorder (HAND). BBB, blood–brain barrier. Modified from a graphic generously provided by Cynthia Hight and Steven Paul Woods, Psy.D.

effective ART. One mechanism of neuronal toxicity is excitotoxicity via the N-methyl D-aspartate (NMDA) receptor, which can occur when the receptor is overstimulated by exposure to the HIV protein Tat (Haughey et al., 2001; Li et al., 2008) or the tryptophan-degradation product, quinolinic acid (Heyes et al., 2001). Tryptophan is typically metabolized by tetrahydrobiopterin-dependent tryptophan-hydroxylase to produce serotonin. Pathological conditions like persistent inflammation can increase activity of an alternative metabolic pathway, indoleamine 2,3-dioxygenase, which results in production of kynurenine, quinolinic acid, and other metabolites (Lovelace et al., 2017; Mehraj and Routy, 2015; Schroecksnadel et al., 2007). In the brain, this activity appears to localize in resident microglial cells as well as in infiltrating macrophages, heightening concern about the continuing migration of these cells into the brain in patients who are otherwise effectively treated with ART. Shunting of tryptophan down the indoleamine 2,3-dioxygenase pathway can also reduce production of serotonin, which may increase the risk of mood disorders (Strasser et al., 2017).

Role of the Immune System

In addition to their role in excitotoxicity, monocytes appear to play a critical role in trafficking HIV into the brain, where the virus can infect other cells, and in releasing mediators that can alter the CNS environment and injure neurons. Subsets of CD14+CD16+ monocytes appear to be particularly important because they have high HIV DNA content; they migrate readily across anatomical barriers; and their number correlates with HAND (Shiramizu et al., 2007) and remains elevated in individuals with HAND even after starting ART (Valcour et al., 2010). Simian immunodeficiency virus models lend support to this idea of a pathological monocyte population, showing that certain circulating monocytes can migrate into the CNS and persist in the perivascular space (Burdo et al., 2010).

Lymphocytes may also contribute to the pathogenesis of HIV in the brain. HIV, of course, principally replicates in and depletes activated CD4+ T cells, so the well-recognized link between HAND and lower CD4+ T-cell numbers and CD4+ T-cell responses to HIV may simply reflect that more advanced HIV disease results in CNS injury. Activated CD4+ T cells, however, are also required to support antiviral CD8+ cytolytic function. CD8+ T cells typically migrate into the brain in health to perform routine immune surveillance. When CD4+ T-cell number or function is reduced, CD8+ T-cell surveillance of the CNS and cytolytic functions may be disrupted (Schrier et al., 2015). While CD8+ T cells typically protect the CNS from pathogens, they may injure the brain when dysregulated (Schrier et al., 1996), as evidenced by reports of T-cell-mediated immune reconstitution inflammatory syndrome (IRIS) (Clifford, 2015). When IRIS occurs, it typically follows initiation of potent ART in the presence of an undetected or undertreated opportunistic infection. IRIS has occurred in patients with HAD in the absence of opportunistic infections (Johnson and Nash, 2014; Riedel et al., 2006), raising concerns that immune recovery could result in subclinical T-cell-mediated injury of the brain that could manifest clinically as HAND. These concerns have been allayed over the past decade with the declining incidence of IRIS, which is likely due to improved HIV diagnostic outreach and earlier initiation of ART. New strategies to eradicate HIV, particularly latency-reducing agents, have raised CNS safety concerns based in part on data on CD8+ T-cell responses to HIV antigens from patients with IRIS (Nath, 2015).

Activated CD4+ T cells are also required for pathogen-specific antibody production by B cells. In recent years, syndromes of antibody-mediated encephalitis have been recognized in the general population (Gastaldi et al., 2016). In these syndromes, CD4+ T-cell-activated B cells undergo somatic hypermutation and differentiation, which precede autoantibody production. Antibodies against neuronal surface antigens may subsequently reach the CNS by crossing the BBB at sites of increased permeability. Activated B cells can also cross the BBB, directly producing autoantibodies within the CNS. One form of antibody-mediated encephalitis affects NMDA receptors, a target for other pathological processes in HIV disease. One trigger for NMDA receptor antibody-mediated encephalitis is a prior infection (e.g., a herpesvirus) or a malignancy, both of which occur more commonly in persons with HIV than in the general population. Whether a mild form of antibody-mediated encephalitis occurs in persons with HIV is an unexplored hypothesis at this point.

Role of HIV Compartmentalization

A continuing and potentially damaging immune response to HIV antigens in the brain may be more likely if the virus has adapted to or is compartmentalized in the CNS environment compared with circulating HIV or virus obtained from other organs such as the spleen or genital tract. This independent CNS reservoir of HIV may develop as a result of the immunologically and pharmacologically privileged nature of the CNS, as well as the infection by HIV of different target cells in the CNS as opposed to that of lymphoid tissues. The presence of compartmentalization suggests that at least a portion of the HIV population is being produced locally rather than simply being carried into the CNS in transiently migratory lymphocytes and monocytes.

Compartmentalization has mostly been studied by analyzing sequences from highly variable portions of the HIV envelope gene, using either brain tissue or CSF, and comparing these to sequences from blood (Figure 16.2). Multiple studies have demonstrated that HIV can compartmentalize in the CNS in at least a minority of adults and that compartmentalization may be associated with HAND (Harrington et al., 2009; Lanier et al., 2001; Pillai et al., 2006; Strain et al., 2005; Tang et al., 2000). HIV obtained from the brain tissue of adults dying with HAD demonstrated that, in severe cases, the virus may adapt to the low CD4 expression environment of the CNS by increasing binding avidity for other HIV entry receptors, such as CCR5 or CXCR4 (Bednar et al., 2015; Dunfee et al., 2006, 2007; Ohagen et al., 2003; Power et al., 1994; Rossi et al., 2008). Studies of pseudotyped viruses created from HIV envelope genes derived from CSF confirm the presence of viruses able to infect cells with low CD4 surface receptor density, suggesting adaptation to infection of resident brain macrophages or microglial cells (Joseph et al., 2014).

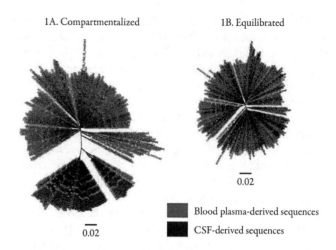

Figure 16.2 Examples of HIV compartmentalization in the central nervous system. HIV envelope can differ between cerebrospinal fluid (CSF) and blood, at times substantially, as demonstrated by the phylogenetic tree (left) from Bowman et al. (2016). Compartmentalized sequences can persist over time, as demonstrated by Faria de Oliveira et al. (2016).

HIV that has expanded its target cell range, as evidenced by dual/mixed receptor tropism, has also been linked to HAND (Morris et al., 2013).

The Swanstrom group reviewed this topic (Bednar et al., 2015) and noted that, while substantial compartmentalization may underpin at least some cases of HAD (Harrington et al., 2009; Ping et al., 2013; Schnell et al., 2010; Bowman et al., 2016), compartmentalization may also be seen during early infection without neurological symptoms (Schnell et al., 2010; Sturdevant et al., 2015). One conclusion from this finding is that compartmentalization may precede the onset of HAND and thus could potentially be used as a prognostic biomarker. This group also found compartmentalized HIV in CSF soon after infection, which then persisted over 2 years (Sturdevant et al., 2015), reinforcing that compartmentalized HIV may seed or evolve in the CNS early in disease and then persist. This persistence of compartmentalized HIV from early in infection was recently confirmed in an independent analysis (Faria de Oliveira et al., 2016) (see Figure 16.2). Differences in blood and CSF populations could also occur during dual infection or superinfection, conditions in which a person is infected with more than one population of HIV. In addition, genes other than envelope, such as pol, can also vary between the CNS and lymphoid compartments and could influence the pathogenesis of HIV in the CNS (Hightower et al., 2009).

Evidence of compartmentalization may also be indirectly observed by comparing the change in HIV RNA in CSF to the change in HIV RNA in blood following initiation of ART. Studies during the early days of combination ART identified that, after ART initiation, HIV that declined more slowly in CSF than in blood was associated with either more severe neurocognitive impairment or more advanced immune suppression (Ellis et al., 2000; Staprans et al., 1999). Slower decline of HIV RNA in CSF might imply production from CNS cells with reduced effective exposure to ART, from compartmentalized ART resistance, or from reduced trafficking of HIV-replicating lymphocytes. When lymphocytes are present in CSF in higher numbers, HIV sequences from CSF and blood are more likely to be equilibrated and compartmentalization is less likely to be detected by amplification of a clonal population (Smith et al., 2009; Sturdevant et al., 2015).

Recent reports of CSF viral escape, a condition that occurs when HIV RNA are detectable in CSF but undetectable in blood, could also reflect persistent HIV compartmentalization in the CNS during ART. CSF viral escape, associated with substantial neurological symptoms, is typically characterized by ART drug resistance in the CSF and is thought to be compartmentalized, since HIV RNA is suppressed in blood (Canestri et al., 2010; Peluso et al., 2012). Not all forms of CSF viral escape are linked to HAND (Eden et al., 2010), however, and whether this condition typically reflects HIV compartmentalization is as yet unproven. Recent data using a single-copy assay for HIV RNA in CSF during suppressive ART did identify that a condition akin to CSF viral escape (i.e., detectable HIV RNA in CSF when undetectable in blood) was associated with worse neurocognitive performance (Anderson et al., 2017).

Role of Aging

As people with HIV age into their sixth decade of life and beyond, the mechanisms by which neurons are damaged may shift. While HAND is not considered an amyloidopathy, the interplay between HIV, aging, amyloid accumulation, and hyperphosphorylation of tau has been debated in recent years, as older adults with HIV appear to be at greater risk for neurocognitive impairment (Ances et al., 2012; Anthony et al., 2010; Cysique et al., 2015; Ferrell et al., 2014; Soontornniyomkij et al., 2012). The implication of amyloid in the pathogenesis of HIV in the brains of older adults flows from knowledge about Alzheimer's disease in the general population as well as from findings linking vascular disease, which is also associated with amyloid accumulation, to neurocognitive impairment in persons with HIV taking ART. Existing data, however, do not consistently support the notion that HAND is associated with amyloid accumulation in brain tissue or with amyloid concentrations in CSF (Andersson et al., 1999; Brew et al., 2005; Calcagno et al., 2014, 2016; Clifford, Fagan, et al., 2009; Cysique et al., 2015; Du Pasquier et al., 2013; Ellis et al., 1998; Gisslén et al., 2009; Green et al., 2000; Krut et al., 2016; Mothapo et al., 2015; Peluso et al., 2013; Peterson et al., 2014; Steinbrink et al., 2013). One study did identify a link between higher concentrations of a soluble amyloid precursor protein and HAND, however (Gisslén et al., 2009). When amyloid is present in brain tissue, it appears to deposit more diffusely rather than concentrating in plaques as in Alzheimer's disease (Achim et al., 2009; Green et al., 2005; Soontornniyomkij et al., 2012). The data on phosphorylated tau are similarly inconsistent; some studies have identified that older adults with HIV have higher levels of the form of this microtubule-associated protein that is pathologically phosphorylated at position 181 (or other positions). Genetic data on another risk factor for Alzheimer's disease, the apolipoprotein E ε4 allele, in persons

with HIV are also inconsistent (Andres et al., 2011; Chang et al., 2014; Cooley et al., 2016; Morgan et al., 2013; Panos et al., 2013; Valcour et al., 2004).

APPROACH TO NEUROBEHAVIORAL ASSESSMENT

Several classification systems for HAND (Price and Brew, 1998; World Health Organization, 1993) were proposed during the early years of the HIV epidemic. Perhaps the most widely used system was that proposed by the AIDS Task Force of the American Academy of Neurology (AAN) (1991), composed of a group of interdisciplinary experts. The AAN system developed alongside *International Classification of Diseases-10* (ICD-10) guidelines and *Diagnostic and Statistical Manual of Mental Disorders* (DSM-IV) criteria, included two diagnostic categories of HAND: HAD and MCMD. To meet the criteria for HAD, a patient had to demonstrate (1) an acquired abnormality in two or more neurocognitive (non-motor) domains causing impairment in work or activities of daily living (ADLs), and (2) an acquired abnormality in motor function or specified neuropsychiatric or psychosocial change (e.g., motivation, emotional lability, social behavior). MCMD represented a less severe manifestation that did not meet criteria for HAD. To meet criteria for MCMD, a patient had to demonstrate an acquired impairment of at least two cognitive, motor, or behavioral symptoms (e.g., impaired attention/concentration, emotional lability) that caused impairment in work or other ADLs. These criteria were expanded by Grant and Atkinson (1995) to include the "sub-syndromic neurocognitive impairment" diagnosis, which recognized a subgroup of patients with neurocognitive impairment that did not interfere with daily functioning. HIV neurocognitive disorders were observed in up to half of individuals with HIV/AIDS (Heaton et al., 1995), with HAD seen in approximately 10–15% and MCMD in 30–40% of persons with HIV/AIDS (Janssen et al., 1992; McArthur and Grant, 1998).

There were several limitations to the AAN criteria. First, the criteria were not operationalized, thus they were vulnerable to inconsistent classifications across studies and clinics. Second, the AAN criteria placed particular emphasis on motor complications. Patients could meet criteria for MCMD if they demonstrated at least two motor or behavioral symptoms; other more "cognitive" deficits were not required. This was problematic since these symptoms overlap with many other clinical conditions.

Changes in the HIV epidemic also limited the utility of the AAN system. The introduction of combination ART significantly improved outcomes and decreased the prevalence of severe neurological disorders, including HAD (Grant et al., 2005; Sacktor et al., 2002; Tozzi et al., 2005). However, milder forms of HIV-associated neurocognitive impairment continued to persist, resulting in a wide array of adverse health-related and everyday functioning outcomes, including, but not limited to, medication nonadherence (Hinkin et al., 2002), vocational difficulties (Heaton et al., 2004; van Gorp et al., 2007), driving impairment (Marcotte et al.,

2004), poorer health-related quality of life (Ruiz Perez et al., 2005; Tozzi et al., 2003), and mortality (Sevigny et al., 2007).

Lastly, the AAN criteria did not provide guidelines for assessing non-HIV-related comorbid conditions (e.g., substance use disorders or hepatitis C virus co-infection) or pre-existing conditions (e.g., learning disabilities), which are risk factors for neurocognitive impairment but may be difficult to distinguish from HIV-related neurocognitive impairment. This was a particularly salient issue as non-HIV-associated comorbid conditions became more common and as the population of older adults with HIV grew.

As noted in the Overview section, the Frascati classification system described three HAND diagnoses (ANI, MND, HAD) that accounted for (a) the presence and severity of neurocognitive impairment, (b) the degree to which neurocognitive impairment interfered with everyday functioning, and (c) the influence of potentially confounding comorbid conditions (see Table 16.1). Both ANI and MND require the presence of at least mild impaired performance on standardized neuropsychological tests (defined as greater than 1.0 standard deviation below the mean of demographically adjusted normative scores) in two or more neurocognitive ability domains that cannot be better accounted for by comorbid conditions. Prevalence estimates suggest that HAND is evident in approximately 30–50% of individuals with HIV/AIDS (Heaton et al., 2010). About one-half to two-thirds of individuals with HAND do not have clear evidence that the impairment adversely affects their everyday functioning and are diagnosed as having ANI. A diagnosis of MND requires evidence that neurocognitive impairment is interfering with everyday functioning. HAD, which is rare in the current treatment era (generally less than 5% of individuals with HAND), requires at least moderate impairment in two or more neurocognitive domains with marked everyday functioning problems (e.g., incapable of living independently).

The Frascati criteria improved the evaluation and reliable classification and diagnosis of HAND in several ways. First, greater emphasis was placed on the neurocognitive impairment criteria relative to prior diagnostic classification systems. Second, clear operational definitions for evaluating the presence and severity of neurocognitive impairment and functional impairment were provided. If neuropsychological testing is available, it should include an assessment of the following domains: speed of information processing, learning, memory, abstraction/executive functions, verbal fluency, attention/working memory, sensory-perceptual, and motor skills. Performances on at least two domains must be abnormal for a classification of neurocognitive impairment, and at least one of the ability areas must be cognitive in nature.

Lastly, the Frascati criteria provided detailed guidelines for evaluating the most commonly encountered comorbid conditions and classifying them as to whether they should be considered "incidental," "contributing," or "confounding," the latter of which would preclude a HAND diagnosis. These revisions significantly improved the reliability in the classification of HAND, though operationalizing the evaluation of everyday functioning remains a continuing challenge.

Recommendations for the Evaluation and Diagnosis of HAND

Neuropsychological assessments have played a significant role in the detection, characterization, and management of HIV-associated neurocognitive impairment. While patterns of neurocognitive deficits vary between individuals, impairment is most frequently seen in episodic memory (learning and recall), executive functions, attention/working memory, speeded information processing, verbal fluency, and fine motor skills (Heaton et al., 2011). While HAND can occur early in the course of disease (e.g., Moore et al., 2006), it continues to be most common in persons with HIV who have past or current severe immunosuppression (Ellis et al., 2011; Muñoz-Moreno et al., 2008). It also remains strongly associated with a host of adverse health-related and functional outcomes (e.g., reduced health-related quality of life), even in its milder forms (Gandhi et al., 2011; Morgan et al., 2012; Thames et al., 2011).

Since specific deficits can vary between individuals, a comprehensive neuropsychological evaluation that includes more than one test in each of the seven most commonly affected neurocognitive domains is the best approach for evaluating neurocognitive performance in persons with HIV. Such evaluations also identify cognitive strengths that can assist with differential diagnoses and provide insight into the development of effective compensatory neurorehabilitation strategies (Butters et al., 1990). They also help assess the role of potentially confounding comorbidities. Lastly, comprehensive neuropsychological evaluations are key in monitoring change over time (e.g., in response to interventions; Cysique and Brew, 2009; Heaton et al., 2015: see Temkin et al., 1999, for methods to evaluate neurocognitive change, and Cysique et al., 2010; Woods et al., 2006, for how they have been modified for use and evaluated in HIV).

Components of the Neuropsychological Evaluation

A comprehensive neuropsychological evaluation should include clinical interviews, behavioral observations (e.g., clinician's observations of a patients' orientation and gross cognitive, motor, and sensory abilities), complementary medical and neuropsychiatric evaluations, as well as the administration of standardized self-report questionnaires and neuropsychological tests. Self- and informant-based questionnaires can assess factors such as an individuals' mood, perceived cognitive problems, ability to independently perform ADLs, and overall quality of life. Although valuable, the subjective nature of self-reports can make them difficult to evaluate; scores tend to correlate more strongly with mood than with objective neurocognitive assessments. See Table 16.2 for self-report measures that may prove useful. Please see Chapter 12 of this textbook for a detailed discussion of neuropsychological assessment of persons with HIV.

Table 16.2 COMMONLY USED STANDARDIZED NEUROPSYCHOLOGICAL TESTS AND SELF-REPORT/ PERFORMANCE-BASED MEASURES OF EVERYDAY FUNCTIONING

STANDARDIZED NEUROPSYCHOLOGICAL EVALUATION (HNRP)	
Premorbid Intellectual Functioning	Wide Range Achievement Test (WRAT) Reading Subtest
Global Cognition/ Screening	NIH Toolbox Cognition and Emotion Modules
Current Mood Symptoms (SR)	Beck Depression Inventory–second edition (BDI-II)
	Profile of Mood States (POMS)
Health-Related Quality of Life (SR)	RAND 36-item Short Form Health Survey (SF-36)
Neurocognitive Ability Domains	Examples of Standardized Neurocognitive Test Measures
Verbal Fluency	Controlled Oral Word Association Test—Letter Fluency (F-A-S)
	Category Fluency (Animals)
	Action/Verb Fluency ("Things people do")
Abstraction/ Executive Functioning	Wisconsin Card Sorting Test (WCST)
	Trail Making Test—Part B
	Stroop Color and Word Test—Interference score
	Halstead Category Test
Attention/Working Memory	Wechsler Adult Intelligence Scale (WAIS)-III Digit Span Subtest
	Wechsler Adult Intelligence Scale (WAIS)-III Letter-Number Sequencing
	Wechsler Memory Scale (WMS)-III Spatial Span Subtest
	Paced Auditory Serial Addition Task (PASAT)
Learning (Verbal/Visual)	Hopkins Verbal Learning Test-Revised (HVLT-R)—Total Learning
	Brief Visuospatial Memory Test-Revised (BVMT-R)—Total Learning
Memory (Verbal/Visual)	Hopkins Verbal Learning Test-Revised (HVLT-R)—Delayed Recall
	Brief Visuospatial Memory Test-Revised (BVMT-R)—Delayed Recall
Speed of Information Processing	Wechsler Adult Intelligence Scale (WAIS)-III Digit Symbol Subtest
	Wechsler Adult Intelligence Scale (WAIS)-III Symbol Search Subtest
	Trail Making Test—Part A
	Stroop Color Word Test—Color Naming
Everyday Functioning Domains	Examples of Standardized Everyday Functioning Self-Report and Performance-Based Measures
Independence in Activities of Daily Living (ADLs) (SR)	Lawton & Brody Activities of Daily Living (ADL) Scale
	Patient's Assessment of Own Functioning Inventory (PAOFI)
	Employment Questionnaire
Everyday Functional Capacity (PB)	UCSD Performance-Based Skills Assessment (UPSA)
Medication Adherence (SR & PB)	ACTG Adherence to Anti-HIV Medications (clinician administered SR)
	Medication Management Test (PB)
Vocational Functioning (SR & PB)	Employment Questionnaire (SR)
	MESA SF2 Standardized work samples and COMPASS programs (PB)

PB, performance-based; SR, self-report.

Selection of Individual Tests

Selection of reliable and valid standardized instruments is critical. Instruments should have demographically corrected normative data that are appropriate for persons with HIV. Demographically corrected normative data provide insight into how the individual would be expected to perform in the absence of a brain disorder. Since demographic factors such as age, education, sex, and ethnicity account for significant variance in neuropsychological test scores, failure to correct for these factors could lead to misclassification of cognitive status. The ability to detect subtle neurocognitive impairment has important treatment implications, as earlier initiation of therapy may limit disease progression. Lastly, a clinical diagnosis ideally should not rely on a single neuropsychological test in a domain, since individuals may perform poorly on a single test for multiple reasons, not all of which are neurological. A list of recommended tests used to assess the neurocognitive domains typically affected in HIV is presented in Table 16.2.

Screening Measures

If comprehensive neuropsychological testing is not available, screening tests involving two or more ability domains may be used to detect impairment. Screening for HIV-associated neurocognitive impairment is essential for providing comprehensive care and optimal treatment plans. However, while most of the existing screening tests in HIV can successfully detect HAD, they are not as sensitive for milder neurocognitive deficits (for reviews, see Kamminga et al., 2013; Valcour et al., 2011; and Zipursky et al., 2013), a situation that is true in other neurological conditions as well. The HIV Dementia Scale (HDS), the International HDS (Morgan et al., 2008; Sacktor et al., 2005; Sakamoto et al., 2013), and several recently developed brief computerized screening measures, including the California Computerized Assessment Battery (CalCAP), the CogState Battery (www.cogstate.com), and the Computer Assessment of Mild Cognitive Impairment (CAMCI), all have limited sensitivity, although there is preliminary evidence to suggest that the CAMCI may hold some promise in detecting milder forms of HAND (Becker, Thames, et al., 2011). Recently, the National Institutes of Health (NIH) released the NIH Toolbox Cognition Module, a computerized neurocognitive screener comprised of five tests that assess five of the seven neurocognitive domains commonly affected by HIV (attention, executive functions, speeded information processing, episodic memory, and working memory). The Cognition Module takes approximately 40 minutes to administer and has excellent demographically corrected normative data derived from a large and diverse U.S. sample (Weintraub et al., 2013). Validations studies are needed to determine the clinical utility of the Toolbox Cognition Module as a screening method for HAND. NIH Toolbox Modules are now also available via an iPad app, which further enhances its utility in clinical settings.

Promising, novel smartphone and tablet-based screening tools have also recently been developed (Robbins et al., 2014; Sakamoto et al., 2014). While preliminary, these studies support that brief, smartphone- or tablet-based cognitive screening instruments will be useful in busy clinics and resource-limited clinics for detecting even mild forms of HAND.

Another approach to screening is to use small batteries of two, three, or four standardized test combinations. Carey et al. (2004) identified two brief screening batteries, finding that a two-test battery that included measures of verbal learning (Hopkins Verbal Learning Test–Revised [HVLT-R]) and processing speed (Stroop Color Test) was the most sensitive two-test combination screener for detecting impairment in a population with early HIV infection. Addition of the Paced Auditory Serial Addition Test (PASAT) provided the best three-test combination screener for the detection of HAND in early HIV disease. An advantage of this approach is that it consists of traditional tests that are standardized, well-validated, reliable, and have demographically corrected normative data. A disadvantage is that it assesses a limited number of domains and may miss individuals whose deficits affect domains that are not assessed.

Assessment of Functional Decline

Acquired functional impairment is typically assessed using standardized self- or informant-report, or through the administration of standardized, performance-based measures assessing an individual's ability to independently carry out ADLs (e.g., medication and financial management). Ideally, such measures would have appropriate normative standards for the population of interest. Self- and informant-report questionnaires typically assess the frequency with which an individual experiences difficulty with aspects of cognition in their daily lives and increased dependence on others. Standardized performance-based tasks objectively assess an individual's ability to carry out tasks of everyday life, including managing medications, performing work-related tasks, and driving automobiles (e.g., Albert et al., 1999; Heaton et al., 2004; Marcotte and Scott, 2004; Patterson et al., 2002). While self-report measures are subjective, vulnerable to biases (e.g., recall inaccuracies), and tend to correlate more strongly with factors such as mood rather than objective functional decline, they have an advantage over performance-based tasks in the sense that they are brief, easily administered, and low cost and have high face-validity (Simoni et al., 2006; Wagner and Miller, 2004). Laboratory-based everyday functioning tasks are more time-intensive and often require additional training or equipment for administration (Moore et al., 2007). However, they are objective and correlate more strongly with health-related and "real-life" outcomes (e.g., employment status; Blackstone et al., 2012; Heaton et al., 2004; Thames et al., 2011) and can be particularly informative when an individual meets other criteria for HAND but is unaware of changes in everyday functioning.

According to the Frascati system, in order to meet criteria for MND or HAD, persons with HIV must demonstrate neurocognitive impairment, as well as mild (MND) and major (HAD) functional decline in two or more areas (e.g., work change, decreased ADLs) as assessed by standardized self- or other-report or performance-based measures. As with neurocognitive impairment criteria, the observed functional decline must not be readily attributable to comorbid conditions. While Frascati criteria do not require the use of both self-report and performance-based tasks, evidence suggests that use of both appears to be more effective at detecting symptomatic HAND than either one alone (Blackstone et al., 2012).

APPROACH TO NEUROIMAGING ASSESSMENT

The Frascati panel reformulated the approach to HAND diagnosis, as summarized in the preceding section. This diagnostic approach has several strengths, but more biology-based biomarkers, such as neuroimaging or CSF neuronal biomarkers, could strengthen it and facilitate its translation to the clinic. Neuroimaging could have increased utility in the diagnosis and management of HAND. A variety of novel neuroimaging techniques have been developed and are currently performed in the research setting. Magnetic resonance imaging (MRI) techniques (including magnetic resonance spectroscopy [MRS], volumetrics, diffusion tensor imaging [DTI], and functional) and positron emission tomography (PET) have been used in persons with HIV.

Magnetic Resonance Spectroscopy (MRS)

The most common neuroimaging method that has been used to study the effects of HIV in the brain in both the early and current treatment eras has been MRS (Cysique et al., 2013; Descamps et al., 2008; Harezlak et al., 2011; Lentz et al., 2011). MRS detects signals produced by protons from specific molecules within a volume of brain. Molecules typically measured include (1) n-acetyl aspartate (NAA), a neuronal marker; (2) choline (Cho), a marker of cellular proliferation and inflammatory response; (3) creatine (Cr), a measure of brain energy metabolism and reference marker; and (4) myo-inositol (MI), a marker of gliosis. MRS has provided key insights into longitudinal changes in brain metabolites in persons with HIV as they progress from early to chronic infection. Soon after seroconversion, MRS metabolites change (Iannucci et al., 2001; Lentz et al., 2011; Sailasuta et al., 2012; Valcour et al., 2012), with changes seen particularly in inflammatory (Valcour et al., 2012) and neuronal injury (Iannucci et al., 2001) measures. MRS changes are also seen in persons with HIV who have been chronically infected, the most common observation being neuronal injury (decreases in NAA) with concomitant inflammation (increases in Cho and MI) (Cardenas et al., 2009; Harezlak et al., 2011; Mohamed et al., 2010; Paul et al., 2008; Yiannoutsos et al., 2008). The greatest changes in MRS metabolites are seen in persons with HAD (Harezlak et al., 2011; Mohamed et al., 2010).

The use of ART generally improves cerebral metabolites measured by MRS, although they do not reliably normalize relative to controls (Chang et al., 1999; Tarasow et al., 2004; Yiannoutsos et al., 2008). Initiation of ART early in disease may be neuroprotective and mitigate some of the adverse changes. Few studies have longitudinally assessed the effects of ART, and this may be particularly important since ART initiation can also show unexpected changes on MRS, including evidence of mitochondrial toxicity and altered neuronal function (Marra et al., 2009; Robertson et al., 2010). MRS may be a valuable tool in evaluating the efficacy and toxicity of different ART combinations.

Imaging studies have also explored the possible interaction between HIV and aging (Cysique and Brew, 2014). Persons with HIV have significant changes in brain metabolites, with measured levels similar to those in persons without HIV who are 10–15 years older (Ernst et al., 2010). While several studies have shown clear effects of HIV and aging, no consistent interaction has been observed between these two factors (Holt et al., 2012). This suggests that HIV does not lead to an acceleration of aging but instead an augmentation of the aging processing.

Overall, MRS has been used primarily in the research setting; there are few studies of clinical populations. Overall, MRS may be more sensitive than conventional MRI sequences in detecting changes associated with HIV. MRS could therefore augment current neuroimaging protocols, but local implementation is essential. This remains difficult at many institutions and thus has limited the generalizability of results. It appears that MRS may provide key information both early in the disease course and with more chronic infection. This technique could therefore be efficacious in evaluating therapies in persons with HIV, as readout could be provided for both neuroinflammation and neuronal injury. For this technique to be truly useful, additional longitudinal studies are needed that follow persons with HIV as they transition across different disease states (Gongvatana et al., 2013). Such studies needs to concentrate on relatively easy sequences that can be implemented at multiple institutions that measure multiple brain areas.

Structural Neuroimaging—Volumetrics and Diffusion Tensor Imaging (DTI)

Volumetric MRI can assess brain structural differences between HIV-positive and HIV-negative individuals. This technique can concentrate on specific brain structures or relatively large brain areas (Fjell et al., 2009). In the early treatment era, significant volume loss was seen in the basal ganglia, posterior cortex, and white matter of HIV-positive adults compared to HIV-negative controls (Aylward et al., 1993, 1995; Heindel et al., 1994). The greatest changes (often in bicaudate ratios) were seen with more advanced stages of HAND (Stout et al., 1998). In the current treatment era, changes have been seen in the involvement of certain structures. While subcortical changes have continued to occur, the greatest changes appear to be more within cortical areas (Heaps et al., 2012; Jernigan et al., 2011; Thompseon et al., 2005). Changes seen within cortical areas are often in the frontal regions, along with connections between the subcortical and frontal areas.

Overall, these results suggest that brain volume loss still occurs even with effective ART. Such loss is supported by the fact that brain volumes, in particular subcortical regions such as the putamen, are altered soon after seroconversion (Ragin et al., 2012). During chronic infection, volumetric changes correlate with the severity of cognitive impairment and with virological markers. Worse neurocognitive performance is associated with smaller brain volumes in both cortical and subcortical areas (Becker, Sanders, et al., 2011; Castelo et al., 2007; Cohen et al., 2010b; Patel et al., 2002; Paul et al., 2008; Pfefferbaum et al., 2012; Sullivan et al., 2011; Thames et al., 2012; Thompson et al., 2005). In addition, lower nadir CD4+ T-cell count, a strong correlate of HAND, has been associated with greater atrophy (Cardenas et al., 2009; Cohen et al., 2010a, 2010b; Jernigan et al., 2011; Kallianpur et al., 2013; Li et al., 2011; Pfefferbaum et al., 2012; Ragin et al., 2011). Overall, published findings suggest that HIV affects subcortical areas early in disease and, in chronic infection, affects connections between these subcortical and frontal regions. Initiating ART soon after seroconversion may limit volume loss in certain brain regions while preventing its spread elsewhere.

DTI has become increasingly popular in the assessment of white matter structural integrity in the setting of HIV. Early in the disease, characteristic white matter changes are seen in the brain. DTI measures the diffusion of water molecules (Christensen et al., 2012; Sullivan et al., 2011; Tate et al., 2011; Turner and Modo, 2010). In the isotropic state, water motion is equal in all directions (e.g., CSF). In brain tissue, the movement of water is anisotropic, with diffusion greater along the length of fiber tracts than perpendicular to them (Chanraud et al., 2010). This is extremely important in certain white matter fiber tracts such as the corpus callosum where the direction of fibers is well known. For each voxel, a tensor is calculated that describes the three-dimensional shape of water diffusion. Fiber direction is indicated by the tensor's main eigenvector. Mean diffusivity (MD) reflects the average diffusion in three axes. Fractional anisotropy (FA) assesses the general shape of the ellipsoid (Wycoco et al., 2013).

Most DTI studies have been performed within chronically infected HIV-positive adults. Typically, an increase in MD and a decrease in FA have been seen within white matter tracts (e.g., corpus callosum). However, subtle differences may exist as to where changes are observed depending on the study (Du et al., 2012; Hoare et al., 2012; Stubbe-Drger et al., 2012; Zhu et al., 2013). To date, no studies have assessed DTI changes soon after seroconversion. Typically, HIV-positive adults either receiving or not receiving ART have been combined and compared to HIV-negative controls. Perhaps as a result, the few studies that have investigated the impact of ART using DTI have had conflicting results (Gongvatana et al., 2011; Masters and Ances, 2014; Wright et al., 2012). Once again, longitudinal studies of populations that are better standardized are needed.

Overall, structural neuroimaging methods (including volumetrics and DTI) may be more sensitive than conventional MRI. Implementing these techniques in clinical settings would be relatively easy if common pipelines for analysis were used. Since structural MRI assessment is relatively easy to perform, these techniques also hold promise for evaluating the impact therapeutic interventions in the clinical setting.

Functional Magnetic Resonance Imaging (fMRI)

Studies are now starting to use blood oxygen level dependent (BOLD) fMRI to investigate functional changes in the brain due to HIV (Rauch et al., 2008). fMRI studies can be further divided into those that use a task to activate certain regions of the brain and those that evaluate baseline or resting state functional connections (rs-fc). Changes assess the coupling between cerebral blood flow (CBF) and neuronal activity (Zhang and Raichle, 2010). Chronically infected HIV-positive adults have greater BOLD activity in the parietal lobes for a simple attention task and greater frontal and parietal activation for more complex attention tasks (Chang et al., 2001). These BOLD changes may reflect the recruitment of surrounding areas to meet cognitive requirements (Ances et al., 2008, 2011; Castelo et al., 2007; Chang et al., 1999, 2001, 2004; Ernst et al., 2007, 2009, 2010; Juengst et al., 2007; Maki et al., 2009; Tracey et al., 1998). Affected individuals may continue to be cognitively normal but may need recruitment of additional areas to meet the metabolic requirements of a particular task. A meta-analysis of BOLD fMRI results using various functional tasks was recently performed using activation likelihood estimation. HIV-positive adults had greater functional activation within the left inferior frontal gyrus and caudate nucleus compared to HIV-negative controls (Du Plessis et al., 2014). These results nicely complement findings from structural studies that have shown volume loss within similar regions.

Persons with HIV also have rs-fc MRI dysfunction in the frontostriatal network. In particular, functional correlations both within and between brain networks were significantly reduced in persons with HIV. HIV disease may have a distinct signature compared with other neurodegenerative disorders. Similar to MRS, the effects of HIV and aging on BOLD rs-fc appear to be independent of each other (Thomas et al., 2013), suggesting that HIV augments rather than accelerates aging.

Only a limited number of studies have evaluated resting CBF in persons with HIV. In general, these studies of CBF have nicely complemented existing BOLD studies and have demonstrated a reduction in resting CBF in HIV-positive adults compared to HIV-negative controls (Ances et al., 2009; Chang et al., 2000). Future BOLD studies could evaluate the efficacy of various treatment regimens for HAND.

In summary, several neuroimaging techniques can noninvasively assess structural and functional changes in the brain that are due to HIV. Both MRS and volumetrics have been performed in a large number of studies, while additional structural and functional MRI methods are rapidly growing in popularity. Each of these methods has strengths and weaknesses and a combination of them may best characterize persons with HIV. These techniques may be more sensitive to the relatively subtle changes in the brain that are seen with current, potent therapies initiated earlier in disease. In addition, imaging changes may precede the cognitive complaints seen later in the disease and at a time when disease may be more reversible.

APPROACH TO CLINICAL ASSESSMENT AND MANAGEMENT

The approach to assessing HIV-positive individuals with possible HAND in the clinic is informed by (a) our understanding of the numerous and diverse causes of cognitive impairment in this population and (b) the absence of a specific therapy for HAND. As a result, the diagnosis of HAND in the clinic is largely one of exclusion, particularly if neuropsychological testing is not available. The principal objective is to identify and treat causes of cognitive impairment other than HIV. If the cognitive impairment persists, then HIV disease may be the cause.

The approach to the clinical assessment of persons with HIV with possible HAND was reviewed by a panel of experts termed the Mind Exchange Program, which attempted to (a) identify unanswered questions in the field, (b) formulate consensus answers to these questions using the best available evidence, and (c) rate the quality of evidence supporting the answers (Mind Exchange Working Group, 2013). The group recommended that all patients with possible HAND have a thorough physical examination and medical history, screening laboratory tests (including diagnostic tests for co-infections and a urine drug screen), and screening tests for HAND (e.g., the International HIV Dementia Scale) and depression (e.g., Hamilton Depression Rating Scale). Based on the findings from these assessments, lumbar puncture and neuroimaging may also be warranted.

Figure 16.3 summarizes some of the conditions that may injure the CNS in persons with HIV and therefore should be considered in clinical assessment and management. These can be grouped into four broad categories: HIV-related, host-related, other pathogen–related, and drug-related.

The HIV-related factors that may contribute to CNS injury include HIV compartmentalization in the CNS (which could cause persistent low-level HIV replication during ART), production of neurotoxic viral proteins, and past or current advanced immune suppression, which can dysregulate immune responses in the CNS.

Host-related factors include genetic vulnerabilities (e.g., HLA DR*04 [Schrier et al., 2012] or possibly the apolipoprotein E ε4 in older adults [Andres et al., 2011; Cooley et al., 2016; Morgan et al., 2013; Panos et al., 2013; Valcour et al., 2004]), comorbid conditions (e.g., metabolic syndrome [McCutchan et al., 2012; Sattler et al., 2015]), vascular disease [Becker et al., 2009; Wright et al., 2010], and anemia [Kallianpur et al., 2016]), and behavioral and neuropsychiatric disorders (Antinori et al., 2007). Assessing patients for delirium and mood disorders (depression, anxiety) is critically important as these disorders are treatable and, in the case of delirium, would exclude a diagnosis of HAND, at least until stabilized.

A growing area of interest in neuro-HIV research is the influence of other pathogens on HIV disease in the CNS. Data on hepatitis C virus (HCV) dates back more than a decade and may be increasingly important now that HCV can be cured with oral direct-acting agents (Cherner et al., 2005; Clifford, Smuzynski, et al., 2009; Forton et al., 2005, 2006; Garvey et al., 2012; Hilsabeck et al., 2005; Hinkin et al., 2008;

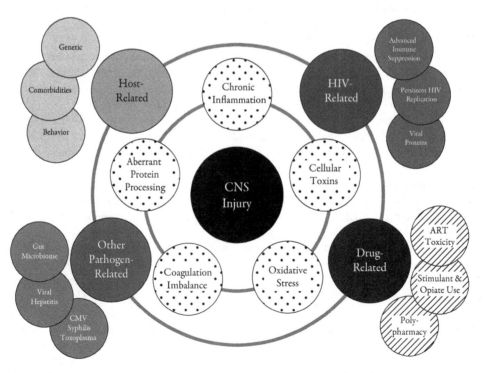

Figure 16.3 Summary of clinical factors that may contribute to HIV-associated neurocognitive disorder (HAND). The outer ring includes four categories of risk factors for HAND. The inner ring includes five more mechanistic contributors to central nervous system injury which may partially mediate the clinical risk factors.

Hjerrild et al., 2016; Jernigan et al., 2011; Laskus et al., 2005; Letendre et al., 2005, 2007; Libertone et al., 2014; Morgello et al., 2014; Paulino et al., 2011; Silverstein et al., 2014; Vivithanaporn et al., 2010). People with HIV are almost universally co-infected with cytomegalovirus (CMV) and, in the general population, this virus has been implicated in immune senescence, increased risk for vascular and neurodegenerative disease, and earlier mortality (Aiello et al., 2006; Gianella and Letendre, 2016; Roberts et al., 2010; Vescovini et al., 2010). In patients with more advanced immune suppression, CNS opportunistic infections should also be excluded, including cryptococcal meningitis, Toxoplasma encephalitis, and progressive multifocal leukoencephalopathy. CNS opportunistic infections like these typically present with more severe symptoms, sometimes including focal neurological signs, but they can present early in disease with more subtle symptoms that could include changes in cognition, mood, or personality. While the organisms that comprise the gut microbiome are technically not pathogens, emerging evidence supports that the composition of the microbiome influences health within and outside the CNS (Perez-Santiago et al., 2013).

Finally, drug-related risk factors remain important. Even though the toxicity of ART drugs has generally declined over the past 15 years, the risk of drug–drug interactions has risen as the number of other drugs used by persons with HIV has risen with their age (Burgess et al., 2015; Edelman et al., 2013; Gleason et al., 2013; Greene et al., 2014). Clinicians must continue to be vigilant for alcohol and substance use disorders both because of their direct effects on the CNS and because they can amplify the toxicity of HIV in the CNS. While the Veterans Administration Cohort Study (VACS) metric for estimating risk for HIV disease progression and mortality does not include many of these conditions, it does capture several, and worse VACS values are associated with HAND (Justice et al., 2010; Marquine et al., 2014, 2016).

As summarized in Table 16.3, the Mind Exchange Program rated the standard of evidence supporting factors that may influence the risk for having or developing HAND (Mind Exchange Working Group, 2013). Risk factors with the highest standard of evidence included older age, lower nadir CD4+ T-cell counts, poor adherence to ART, shorter duration of ART, active HCV co-infection with high HCV RNA in blood, a history of prior HIV-related CNS disease (e.g., resolved cryptococcal meningitis), a history of cardiovascular disease, or the presence of anemia or thrombocytopenia. While systematically reviewing these risk factors may assist the clinician, they may not necessarily benefit the patient as many are unchangeable (e.g., age).

Measurement of HIV RNA in CSF commonly arises in the discussion of diagnostic tests for HAND. Before the widespread use of potent combination ART, higher HIV RNA levels in CSF were associated with ADC (Brew et al., 1997; Ellis et al., 1997; McArthur et al., 1997). Since then, however, the correlation between higher HIV RNA in CSF and worse neurocognitive performance has weakened (Sevigny et al., 2004), possibly because several other factors are associated with HIV RNA levels in CSF, including HIV RNA levels in plasma, depression, race, and ART characteristics (Hammond et al., 2014).

In recent years, however, a condition termed *CSF viral escape* has come to light (Canestri et al., 2010; Eden et al., 2010; Peluso et al., 2012). The definition of CSF viral escape has varied between reports, but one common definition is the presence of HIV RNA in CSF when it is undetectable in blood. CSF viral escape appears to occur in up to 15% of persons with HIV, although the case series to date are relatively small. Its relationship with neurological symptoms is variable, with some reports finding an association with new neurological or cognitive symptoms and others finding no association. Importantly, CSF viral escape has been associated with the presence of drug resistance mutations in CSF. While no convincing evidence has yet emerged that CSF viral escape leads to systemic virological failure, CSF viral escape does appear to respond to a change in ART guided by CSF resistance and testing and perhaps an estimate of ART drug distribution into the CNS, the CNS penetration-effectiveness (CPE) metric. Factors favoring or opposing the clinical utility of measuring HIV RNA in CSF was recently summarized (Nightingale et al., 2014) (Table 16.4).

While no blood or CSF biomarker for HAND has yet been validated in clinical settings, several are promising. The most important may be neurofilament light (NFL) in CSF. This axonal protein has been validated as a biomarker of HAD in multiple published studies (Abdulle et al., 2007; Gisslén et al., 2005, 2007; Jessen et al., 2014; McGuire et al., 2015; Mellgren et al., 2007; Peterson et al., 2014). Its value as a biomarker of ANI and MND is less clear, but higher concentration of a biomarker of macrophage activation, neopterin, is associated with these milder forms of HAND and correlated with higher concentrations of NFL in CSF (Eden et al., 2016). This combination holds substantial promise as potentially clinically useful biomarkers. Their chief limitation is that they must be measured in CSF, but this has been addressed by the development of an NFL assay for blood. NFL concentrations in blood strongly correlate with those in CSF, are elevated in patients with HAD, and are also elevated in some neuroasymptomatic adults, possibly indicating a presymptomatic state that may progress to more severe disease (Gisslén et al., 2016). Elevations of two other blood biomarkers have also been linked to HAND. Soluble CD14 (Anderson et al., 2015; Kamat et al., 2012; Lyons et al., 2011) and soluble CD163 (Burdo et al., 2010). both reflect monocyte/macrophage activation, consistent with the implication of these cells in the pathogenesis of HAND.

DIFFERENTIAL DIAGNOSIS OF NEUROCOGNITIVE IMPAIRMENT OF PERSONS WITH HIV AND AIDS: DELIRIUM AND OTHER NEUROCOGNITIVE DISORDERS

DELIRIUM

When evaluating the contributors to neurocognitive impairment in persons with HIV, the differential diagnosis should be broad and should include behavioral disorders. Since access to a mental health clinician can be limited in many HIV clinical

Table 16.3 COMORBIDITIES AND RISK FACTORS FOR HAND AS SUMMARIZED BY THE MIND EXCHANGE PROGRAM*

EVIDENCE-SUPPORTED RISK FACTORS	RISK FACTOR/COMORBIDITY FOR HAND AND/OR NON-HIV-RELATED NCI	CAN ASSIST IDENTIFICATION OF PATIENTS		
		WITH CURRENT HAND	AT RISK OF DEVELOPING HAND IN FUTURE	AT RISK OF NON-HIV-RELATED NCI
Readily Assessable in Clinic				
Disease factors	Low nadir CD4* T-cell count	X	X	
	High plasma HIV RNA; high CSF HIV RNA	X	X	
	Low current CD4 (pre-cART	X	X	
	Presence of past HIV-related CNS diseases	X	X	
	Longer HIV duration	X	X	
Treatment factors	Low cART adherence	X	X	
	Episodes of cART interruption	X	X	
	Nonoptimal cART regimen	X	X	
	Short cART duration (related to treatment failure)	X	X	
Comorbidities	Positive HCV serostatus with high	X	X	X
	HCV RNA	X	X	X
	History of acute CV event			X
	CV risk factors (hyperlipidemia, elevated blood pressure, chronic diabetes, and diabetes type II)			X
	Anemia and thrombocytopenia			
Demographic factors	Older age	X	X	X
	Low level of educational achievement	X	X	X
	Ethnicity	X	X	X
	Sex (female, as associated with lower	X	X	X
	socioeconomic status in some countries)	X	X	X
	Lack of access to standard care; poverty			
Other neurological and psychiatric factors	Neuropsychiatric disorders, e.g., MDD,	X	X	X
	anxiety, PTSD, psychosis, bipolar disorder	X	X	X
	(current or history of)	X	X	X
	Illicit drug/alcohol abuse/dependence	X	X	X
	(current or history of)			X
	Syphilis or systemic infection			X
	Alzheimer's disease			X
	Cerebrovascular disease			X
	Traumatic brain injury and seizure			
	Vitamin or hormone deficiency			
	Prior HCV co-infection*			
Complex cART factors	Lower CPE	X	X	X
	cART neurotoxicity			
Difficult to Assess in Clinic				
Biomarkers	Abnormal CSF neopterin	X		
	Abnormal plasma HIV DNA	X		
	Abnormal NFL	X		
	Abnormal MCP-1	X		
	Abnormal serum osteopontin	X		

*The program reviewed the medical literature for risk factors that had been reported for neurocognitive impairment and classified them as either being associated with a current diagnosis of HAND, increasing the risk of developing HAND in the future, or increasing the risk for neurocognitive impairment unrelated to HIV (Mind Exchange Working Group, 2013). The program used the Center for Evidence-based Medicine to rate the evidence supporting each observation (not shown) with the strongest evidence supporting older age, low nadir CD4+ T-cell count, past or current HIV-related CNS diseases, ART interruption or short duration of ART, HCV co-infection with high HCV RNA, history of cardiovascular event, and anemia and thrombocytopenia.

ART, antiretroviral therapy; cART, combination ART; CNS, central nervous system; CPE, CNS penetration-effectiveness; CSF cerebrospinal fluid; CV, cardiovascular; HAND, HIV-associated neurocognitive disorder; HCV, hepatitis C virus; NCI, neurocognitive impairment; NFL, neurofilament light; MDD, major depressive disorder; PTSD, posttraumatic stress disorder.

Table 16.4 IS HIV RNA IN CSF A USEFUL CLINICAL TOOL IN ASSESSMENT OF PERSONS WITH HIV?*

OBSERVATIONS FAVORING MEASUREMENT OF HIV RNA IN CSF	OBSERVATIONS NOT FAVORING MEASUREMENT OF HIV RNA IN CSF
• Before the introduction of ART, high levels of HIV RNA in CSF were associated with HAD in people with advanced immunosuppression.	• In individuals successfully treated with ART, cognitive impairment might be more likely to be caused by ongoing inflammation or comorbidities than ongoing HIV replication.
• Case series have shown a link between a decrease in HIV RNA in CSF and improved cognitive impairment.	• HIV RNA levels in CSF may not accurately reflect HIV replication in brain parenchyma.
• One study in the modern treatment era showed that people with greater HIV RNA in CSF than in blood were more likely to have neurocognitive impairment.	• Most studies have failed to show an association between HIV RNA in CSF and neurocognitive status in the modern treatment era.
• Persistent HIV RNA in CSF during ART might increase the risk of antiretroviral drug resistance and virological failure.	• Longitudinal studies have not demonstrated that CSF viral escape is associated with antiretroviral resistance or virological failure.

*This question was one of four controversial questions examined by Nightingale et al. in 2014. They listed the data that either supported (left column) or did not support (right column) the question.

ART, antiretroviral therapy; CSF cerebrospinal fluid; HAD, HIV-associated dementia.

settings, a summary of suggested key questions is provided in Table 16.5 to aid HIV clinicians in detecting the underlying psychiatric diagnoses most frequently encountered in persons with HIV. While these questions are not a substitute for comprehensive psychiatric evaluation (described in detail in Chapter 11 of this textbook), they can inform clinicians of the need for further assessment, emergency intervention, or

Table 16.5 KEY QUESTIONS FOR HIV CLINICIANS

Neurocognitive Disorders

• Dementia: Have you had any problems with your memory?
• Delirium: Do you feel confused?

Substance-Related Disorders

• What is the most alcohol (or other drugs) that can you hold in a day?

Posttraumatic Stress Disorder

• Do you have frightening dreams or intrusive thoughts?

Bereavement

• Are you preoccupied with your loss?

Mood Disorders

• Due to medical condition, with depressed features: Are you depressed or suicidal?
• Due to medical condition, with manic features: Do you feel irritable?
• Major depressive disorder: Are you depressed or suicidal?
• Bipolar disorder: Do you have a history of having periods of being up or being down?

Psychotic Disorders and Schizophrenia

• Does your mind play tricks on you sometimes?

referral to a psychiatrist. Table 16.6 presents an overview of the neuropsychiatric differential diagnostic considerations, although it does not include the psychiatric manifestations of other associated medical illnesses or of medications. Differential diagnostic categories include behavioral presentations due to medical illness, cognitive disorders, mood disorders, anxiety disorders, and substance abuse disorders.

Particular attention should be paid to delirium, a cognitive disorder that occurs commonly but is frequently underrecognized or misdiagnosed in both children and adults with HIV. Delirium is the most common psychiatric diagnosis encountered in the acute care hospital setting. It may be thought of as "acute brain failure." The signs and symptoms of delirium in persons with HIV and AIDS are the same as those in persons with other complex medical illness. Since persons with HIV are now living longer, they may also have delirium secondary to any of the other multimorbid medical illnesses described in Chapters 43 to 47 if this textbook. Delirium is a neurocognitive disorder that classically includes impairment in attention; fluctuating levels of arousal or consciousness; confusion; global neurocognitive impairment with deficits in memory, thinking, orientation, or perception; disturbances of the sleep–wake cycle; and a characteristic course marked by rapid onset, relatively brief duration, and fluctuations in the severity of symptoms and signs over the course of the day or even hours or minutes. Delirium is a significant diagnosis because it is entirely reversible when an underlying cause can be identified. Furthermore, about 40% of patients with delirium develop some form of cognitive impairment when followed up about 3 months to 5 years after an episode of delirium (Girard et al., 2010; Jackson et al., 2004; MacLullich et al., 2009; Maldonado, 2013; Witlox et al., 2010).

Factors predisposing to delirium in adults with HIV include addiction to alcohol or drugs, brain damage, and chronic illness. Facilitating factors are psychological stress, sleep deprivation, sensory deprivation, anesthesia, and many medications. Table 16.7 lists several causes of delirium,

Table 16.6. DIFFERENTIAL DIAGNOSIS OF NEUROPSYCHIATRIC MANIFESTATIONS OF HIV INFECTION*

SUBSTANCE-INDUCED DISORDERS	PSYCHIATRIC DISORDERS WITH SIMILAR SYMPTOMS, SIGNS, AND BEHAVIORS	HIV-RELATED NEUROPSYCHIATRIC DISORDERS WITH SIMILAR SYMPTOMS, SIGNS, AND BEHAVIORS
• Intoxication from alcohol or benzodiazepines: sedation, slurred speech, psychomotor retardation, memory impairment, disinhibition, agitation	• Mania: irritability, agitation	• HIV-associated dementia
• Withdrawal from alcohol: irritability, loss of appetite, tremor, hallucinations, paranoia	• Major depressive disorder: depression, insomnia, loss of appetite, psychomotor retardation, withdrawal	• Intrinsic involvement of the brain with HIV or opportunistic infections or cancers, such as toxoplasmosis or lymphoma and progressive multifocal leukoencephalopathy (PML)
• Withdrawal from benzodiazepines: anxiety, insomnia, hypervigilance, tremors	• Adjustment disorder: depression, anxiety	• Mental status changes secondary to antiretroviral therapies
• Substance-induced mood disorders: depression or mania	• Bipolar disorder: depression, mania	• Treatments for opportunistic infections and cancers: depression, mania
• Substance-induced psychosis with delusions or hallucinations	• Schizoaffective disorder	• Drug toxicity, e.g., treatment for comorbid hepatitis C virus (HCV) infection with interferon and ribavirin: depression, fatigue, loss of appetite
• Amnestic disorders	• Schizophrenia: delusions, hallucinations	• "AIDS mania": irritability
• Anxiety	• Dementia	• HCV infection: depression, fatigue, loss of appetite
• Sleep disorders	• PTSD: hypervigilance, hyperarousal, insomnia	• HIV-induced mood disorder: depression, mania, insomnia
• Sexual dysfunction	• Generalized anxiety disorder	
• Delirium: hallucinations, somnolence, withdrawal, confusion, insomnia, agitation	• Delirium: hallucinations, somnolence, agitation	
• Dementia: paranoia, delusions, agitation	• Dementia: paranoia, delusions, agitation, reversal of the sleep/wake cycle, sundowning	
	• Schizophrenia	

*Signs and symptoms can be similar.

including medications that can cause delirium. In addition to the history, physical examination, laboratory studies, and imaging studies, a decrease in frequency of electroencephalogram (EEG) background activity is indicative of delirium, possibly as a result of a reduction in brain metabolism. EEG changes virtually always accompany delirium and make the EEG a useful diagnostic tool in persons with AIDS who manifest a change in mental status. EEG changes can aid in identifying the specific etiology of delirium. Triphasic waves are characteristic of hepatic encephalopathy and generalized fast-wave activity may be indicative of delirium tremens. EEG testing may also be helpful in evaluating and monitoring the course of HIV-associated dementia (Parisi et al., 1989) or diagnosing seizure-related behavior changes. A controlled study (Koralnik et al., 1990) of men with asymptomatic HIV infection showed that EEG and other electrophysiological tests were the most sensitive indicators of subclinical neurological impairment.

OTHER NEUROCOGNITIVE DISORDERS

HAND is the most common neurocognitive disorder in the general population of persons with HIV; other neurocognitive disorders may include major or mild neurocognitive disorder due to Alzheimer's disease; major or mild frontotemporal neurocognitive disorder; major or mild neurocognitive disorder with Lewy bodies; major or mild vascular neurocognitive disorder; and major or mild neurocognitive disorder due to Parkinson's disease. The most common other neurocognitive disorder is that due to Alzheimer's disease.

The differential diagnosis of neurocognitive disorders is discussed in detail in Chapter 11 of this textbook.

APPROACH TO CLINICAL MANAGEMENT

Once a comprehensive clinical assessment is performed, the initial focus should be on treating medical or psychiatric conditions other than HAND that have been diagnosed. This includes appropriate management of co-infections that may influence disease (e.g., neurosyphilis); metabolic syndrome; hyperlipidemia, hypertension, and other vascular disease risk factors; alcohol, tobacco, and other substance use disorders; and neuropsychiatric disorders such as delirium and depression. Consultation with experts in psychiatry, neurology, or infectious disease medicine may be helpful. Drug–drug interactions with ART drugs should be assiduously avoided. When other diseases are treated, the patient should be reassessed after 3 to 6 months to determine if neurocognitive impairment persists.

Table 16.7 CAUSES OF DELIRIUM IN PERSONS WITH HIV

Toxic or Drug-Induced Delirium

- Intoxication: sedative-hypnotics, alcoholic hallucinosis, opiates
- Drugs: antibiotics, anticholinergics, anticonvulsants, antineoplastic drugs, antiretrovirals, ketamine, lithium, narcotic analgesics
- Withdrawal: alcohol, sedative-hypnotics

Metabolic Encephalopathy

- Hypoxia
- Hepatic, renal, pulmonary, or pancreatic insufficiency
- Hypoglycemia

Disorders of Fluid, Electrolyte, and Acid–Base Imbalance

- Dehydration
- Lactic acidosis
- Hypernatremia, hypokalemia, hypocalcemia, hypercalcemia, alkalosis, acidosis

Endocrine Disorders

- Hypothyroidism
- Pancreatitis and diabetes mellitus

Infections

- Cardiovascular: bacteremia, infective endocarditis
- Pneumonia: bacterial, *Pneumocystis jirovicii*, cryptococcal
- Herpes zoster
- Disseminated *Mycobacterium avium* complex (MAC)
- Disseminated candidiasis
- Intracranial: cryptococcal meningitis, HIV encephalitis, tuberculous meningitis, toxoplasma encephalitis, cytomegalovirus, Herpes simplex

Malnutrition and Vitamin Deficiency

- Protein energy undernutrition
- Vitamin B12 deficiency
- Thiamine deficiency and Wernicke's encephalopathy
- Wasting and failure to thrive

Neoplastic

- Space-occupying lesions: CNS lymphoma, CNS metastases
- Paraneoplastic syndromes associated with lung and other neoplasms

Neurological

- Seizures: ictal, interictal, postictal states
- Head trauma
- Space-occupying lesions: toxoplasmosis, abscesses, cryptococcoma

Hypoxia

- Pneumonia
- Pulmonary hypertension
- Cardiomyopathy
- Coronary artery disease
- End-stage pulmonary disease
- Anemia

(continued)

Table 16.7 CONTINUED

Selected Medications

- Antiretrovirals: efavirenz, zidovudine, nevirapine
- Antivirals: interferon, ganciclovir
- Antibacterials: aminoglycosides, cephalosporins, rifampin, sulfonamides, vancomycin
- Anticholinergics: diphenhydramine, benztropine
- Narcotic analgesics

If HAND is diagnosed either at the time of the initial assessment or after another medical or psychiatric condition is treated first, the critical question remains how best to manage it. If the patient's HIV disease is untreated, initiating ART is critically important. One exception is when the patient has advanced immune suppression and another infection is present that could result in development of life-threatening CNS IRIS. Once the decision to begin ART is made, the most important goal is suppression of HIV RNA in blood. For this reason, selection of specific ART regimens should follow national guidelines (DHHS Panel on Antiretroviral Guidelines for Adults and Adolescents, 2016) and best standard of care. The patient's first ART regimen typically yields the most substantial improvement in neurocognitive performance (Cysique et al., 2009). With regard to selection of individual ART drugs within the range of regimens deemed acceptable by treatment guidelines, those drugs with well-documented neurotoxicity would best be avoided (Robertson et al., 2012). If it occurs, neurocognitive benefit is typically seen within 6–12 months of ART initiation (Ellis and Letendre, 2016).

More than 90% of patients who suppress HIV in blood should also do so in CSF. For only a minority of persons with HIV, the characteristics of the individual drugs in the CNS may be worth considering (Table 16.8) (Nightingale et al., 2014). Two approaches to estimating ART effectiveness in the CNS have been published—one that is based primarily on pharmacokinetics of ART drugs in CSF (CNS penetration effectiveness [CPE], Table 16.9; Letendre, 2011) and another that is based on the in vitro efficacy of ART in monocytes (monocyte efficacy [ME] score [Shikuma et al., 2012]). In a cohort of older adults with HIV, lower ME scores, indicating worse estimated efficacy in monocytes, were associated with HAND. In this study, the ME score performed better than CPE, did but this finding has not been confirmed. One weakness of the ME score approach is linked to its formulation that requires in vitro experiments with monocytes: since these have not been performed for all currently available ART drugs, ME scores are not available for all ART drugs used in the clinic.

CPE values have been compared to HIV RNA levels in CSF, inflammation biomarkers in CSF, and neurocognitive performance. In mixed cohorts of aviremic and viremic ART users, higher CPE values correlated with lower HIV RNA levels in CSF, even after accounting for HIV RNA levels in blood (Letendre et al., 2008). Among aviremic ART users (i.e., HIV RNA levels below 50 copies/mL in blood and CSF), higher CPE values correlated with lower concentrations of TNF-α and CXCL10 (Anderson et al., 2016) as well as lower HIV RNA

Table 16.8 ARE SOME ART DRUGS MORE BENEFICIAL IN THE CNS THAN OTHERS?*

OBSERVATIONS FAVORING THAT SOME DRUGS ARE MORE BENEFICIAL	OBSERVATIONS NOT FAVORING THAT SOME DRUGS ARE MORE EFFECTIVE
• Concentrations of some ART drugs in CSF do not exceed the inhibitory concentration for wild-type HIV replication. • Drugs with worse estimated CNS effectiveness are associated with higher levels of HIV RNA in CSF. • CSF viral escape is associated with worse estimated CNS effectiveness. • Some studies have shown that drugs with high estimated CNS effectiveness are associated with improved cognitive function. • Some studies have shown that some ART drugs are neurotoxic. • Some observational studies have reported a decline in the levels of HIV RNA in CSF and improvements in cognitive function after changes to ART regimens on the basis of estimated CNS effectiveness.	• Estimates of CNS effectiveness are largely based on the pharmacokinetics of ART drugs in CSF, which might not accurately reflect the pharmacokinetics of antiretroviral drugs in HIV-infected glial cells or brain macrophages. • CSF viral escape is uncommon with any ART regimen when using routine HIV RNA assays. • Some observational studies have not shown an association between ART regimens that contain drugs that have high estimated CNS effectiveness and neurocognitive function.

*This question was one of 4 controversial questions examined by Nightingale et al in 2014.[288] They listed the data that either supported (left column) or did not support (right column) the question.

levels using a single-copy assay (Anderson et al., 2017). With the evolution of traditional three-drug ART regimens to one- or two-drug regimens or to "mega-HAART" in patients with extensive drug resistance, the relationship between CPE values and suppression of HIV RNA in CSF may be less clear. In addition, CPE values do not seem to consistently correlate with neurocognitive performance, possibly because HIV only indirectly injures neurons and because multiple conditions other than HIV can affect cognition (Marra et al., 2009; Baker et al., 2015; Caniglia et al., 2014; Carvalhal et al., 2016; Casado et al., 2014; Cavassini and Du Pasquier, 2013; Ciccarelli et al., 2013; Cross et al., 2013; Ellis et al., 2014; Fabbiani et al., 2015; Ghate et al. 2015; Kahouadji et al., 2013; Smurzynski et al., 2011; Vassallo et al., 2014; Wilson et al., 2013). Selected studies comparing CPE to neurocognitive performance are summarized in Table 16.10.

Several of these studies found evidence of neurocognitive benefit from higher CPE regimens (Carvalhal et al., 2016; Casado et al., 2014; Ciccarelli et al., 2013; Ellis et al., 2014; Ghate et al., 2015; Smurzynski et al., 2011; Vassallo et al., 2014). Two studies found evidence of possible toxicity from higher CPE regimens but only on individual tests, not overall (Kahouadji et al., 2013; Wilson et al., 2013). The study by Caniglia et al. (2014) was the largest one performed and did appear to find evidence of neurotoxicity. This analysis combined data from multiple cohorts for a sample size of over 60,000 patients. Unfortunately, the analysis had multiple methodological flaws. First, none of the component cohorts had a neurological focus, and none used standardized assessments for diagnosing HAND, relying instead on incidental recording of diagnoses. Second, the investigators enriched their cohort for HAND by excluding four cohorts that had no

Table 16.9 RANKING OF ART DRUGS BY CNS PENETRATION-EFFECTIVENESS (CPE) APPROACH*

DRUG CLASS	CPE SCORE			
	4	3	2	1
Nucleoside reverse transcriptase inhibitors	Zidovudine	Abacavir Emtricitabine	Didanosine Lamivudine Stavudine	Tenofovir Zalcitabine
Non-nucleoside reverse transcriptase inhibitors	Nevirapine	Delavirdine Efavirenz	Etravirine	
Protease inhibitors	Indinavir/r	Darunair/r Fosamprenavir/r Indinavir Lopinavir/r	Atazanavir Atazanvir/r Fosamprenavir	Nelfinavir Ritonavir Saquinavir Saquinavir/r Tipranavir/r
Entry/Fusion inhibitors		Maraviroc		Enfuvirtide
Integrase strand transfer inhibitors		Raltegravir		

*DHHS Panel on Antiretroviral Guidelines for Adults and Adolescents (2016).

Table 16.10 SUMMARY OF SELECTED STUDIES COMPARING ESTIMATED DISTRIBUTION OF ART DRUGS INTO THE CNS TO NEUROCOGNITIVE OUTCOMES

STUDY	DESIGN	*N*	NP	DURATION	ASSOCIATION BETWEEN CPE AND COGNITION	COMMENTS
Ciccarelli et al., 2013	C-S	101	C	—	Beneficial	
Fabbiani et al., 2015	C-S	215	C	—	Beneficial	Adjusted CPE using ART drug resistance testing
Casado et al., 2014	C-S	69	B	—	Beneficial	Beneficial if nadir CD4+ T-cell count <200
Carvalhal et al., 2016	C-S	417	C	—	Beneficial	
Vassallo et al., 2014	L	96	C	22 months	Beneficial	~25% were not virologically suppressed
Ghate et al., 2015	L	92	C	1 year	Beneficial in one domain	Benefitted working memory
Smurzynski et al., 2011	L	2,636	B	4.7 years	Beneficial in a subgroup	No association with three or fewer ART drugs
Cross et al., 2013	L	69	C	~1 year	No association	Only analyzed a binary transformation of CPE
Ellis et al., 2014	RCT	49	C	16 weeks	No association	Beneficial in the subgroup with suppressed HIV RNA at entry
Wilson et al., 2013	C-S	118	B	—	Detrimental on two tests	Only analyzed a binary transformation of CPE; limited to substance users
Kahouadji et al., 2013	C-S	93	B	—	Detrimental on one test	
Marra et al., 2009	L	79	C	1 year	Detrimental	Higher CPE associated with better HIV RNA in CSF
Caniglia et al., 2014	L	61,938	N	~3 years	Detrimental	Selection bias Low absolute risk

ART, antiretroviral therapy; B, brief; C, comprehensive; C-S, cross-sectional; CSF, cerebrospinal fluid; L, longitudinal; N, none; NP, neuropsychological test battery; RCT, randomized clinical trial.

neuro-AIDS events. Even with this enrichment, the study still included only 235 HAND cases in more than 250,000 person-years of follow-up, a very low incidence that raises concerns about sampling bias. Third, the analysis did not account for several influential factors, the most important of which were changes in ART regimens over time and the impact of other conditions that can affect neurocognitive performance, such as psychiatric disease or substance use disorders. Finally, the authors only describe the relative risk of "high CPE" regimens, a critical error in such a large analysis. In fact, when calculated, the absolute risk in this analysis is not clinically meaningful. Even if the analysis were accurate, "high CPE" regimens would result in only one additional HAND case per more than 4,500 person-years of follow-up. Even though the Caniglia et al. analysis is flawed, evidence of ART neurotoxicity is mounting from both clinical studies and in vitro analyses.

The challenge in the clinic, then, is to select an ART regimen that balances CNS potency and toxicity (Figure 16.4). If ART

drug concentrations in the CNS are subtherapeutic, then HIV replication could persist, at least at a low level. While this has not been consistently associated with neurocognitive impairment, it has been linked to inflammation in the CNS and to the presence of drug resistance mutations, each of which could then affect neurocognitive performance. If ART drug concentrations in the CNS are too high, then patients could be more likely to experience neurotoxicity. Of note, preliminary evidence supports that older patients are at greater risk of both abnormally high BBB permeability and high ART drug concentrations in the CNS. In the absence of therapeutic drug monitoring in the clinic, which is not recommended, selecting the best regimen is challenging. Clinicians should be aware of which ART drugs have neurotoxic potential and should monitor their patients periodically for new or worsening neurocognitive symptoms.

Once HAND has been diagnosed, an adequately penetrating, low-toxicity ART regimen has been started, and

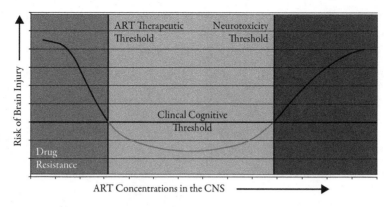

Figure 16.4 The central nervous system (CNS) therapeutic window. Distribution of antiretroviral therapy (ART) drugs into the CNS should ideally be sufficient to inhibit HIV replication but not so high as to cause toxicity.

comorbid conditions have been managed, what other interventions are available to treat HAND? Clinical trials of adjunctive therapies have been negative or shown modest benefits in pilot studies or in subgroup analyses. For example, a randomized, placebo-controlled clinical trial of memantine, which targets the NMDA receptor excitotoxicity caused by HIV Tat and quinolinic acid, did not find an overall neurocognitive benefit but did find evidence of improvement on MRS in the subgroup of patients who were taking suppressive ART (Schifitto et al., 2007). Two single-arm, open-label pilot trials of lithium, which protects neurons from gp120-mediated toxicity, found evidence of either neurocognitive (Letendre et al., 2006) or neuroimaging (Schifitto et al., 2009) benefit, but larger trials have not been performed. Pilot trials of adjunctive therapy with the ART drug maraviroc, which targets activated, HIV-infected monocytes and macrophages, have also shown promise and larger trials are underway (Gates et al., 2016; Ndhlovu et al., 2014). A small trial of paroxetine, which demonstrated neuroprotective properties in vitro and in animal studies, recently showed evidence of neurocognitive benefit and a larger clinical trial is planned (Meulendyke et al., 2014; Sacktor et al., 2016; Steiner et al., 2015). In addition to these pharmacological interventions, behavioral interventions such as cognitive rehabilitation (Weber et al., 2013) and exercise (Dufour et al., 2013; Fazeli et al., 2014, 2015; Fillipas et al., 2006; Montoya et al., 2015) have shown promise.

Treatment of Delirium

Since delirium is an important component of the differential diagnosis of cognitive impairment in persons with HIV, clinicians should ensure that their management plan includes delirium, when present. The approach to management should prioritize identifying and treating the underlying cause. Once this is accomplished, then supportive care, such as maintaining hydration, electrolyte balance, and nutrition, can be provided. In addition, providing an optimal environment for the patient is essential: a quiet, well-lit room with a dim light at night, radio or television, a large calendar with the date marked clearly each day, an easy-to-read clock, photographs and familiar objects, soothing favorite music, and, if possible, visits from familiar people. Medical and nursing support

should be directed toward orientation and companionship as well as to adequate sleep and sedation.

The atypical antipsychotic medications olanzapine 2.5 mg, or quetiapine 6.25 to 25 mg may be recommended as a standing order at bedtime until identification and treatment of the underlying cause have been accomplished. The dosage can be increased gradually in divided doses if necessary to control agitation. For extreme agitation, olanzapine or quetiapine can be given in divided doses every 1 to 6 hours. While other antipsychotic medications are used to treat delirium, most cause severe extrapyramidal side effects in persons with HIV and AIDS and can complicate the course. If agitation is severe, lorazepam can be added to the antipsychotic for additional sedation as needed (Cohen and Alfonso, 2004). This medication is advantageous because it may be administered intravenously or intramuscularly in severely agitated patients with low risk of adverse effects. Since patients with HIV are sensitive to extrapyramidal symptoms, avoidance of antipsychotics such as haloperidol and risperidone is preferable.

SUMMARY

HIV enters the CNS soon after infection, can infect glia and tissue macrophages in the brain, and can injure neurons resulting in loss of dendrites. These and other processes underpin a syndrome of cognitive and motor impairment termed HAND, which continues to occur even among people taking suppressive ART. This diagnosis encompasses three related disorders that range from mild and more common (ANI, MND) to severe and less common (HAD). This chapter presented data on the neurobehavioral, neuroimaging, and medical approaches to evaluating persons with HIV for HAND. Comprehensive neuropsychological testing remains a cornerstone for diagnosing HAND, but briefer, more automated testing is in development. Neuroimaging techniques such as MRS, DTI, and BOLD-fMRI provide important information about the pathogenesis of HIV in the CNS and can be used in research studies to track the evolution of HAND over time and its response to therapeutic interventions. Blood and CSF biomarkers such as neurofilament-light, neopterin, soluble CD14, and soluble CD163 provide additional useful information, although they have not yet reached the clinic.

The HAND diagnostic strategy should account for multimorbid conditions that can cause neurocognitive impairment, such as metabolic syndrome, medication side effects, vascular disease, or substance use disorders. In the early phases of diagnosis, the differential diagnosis is lengthy and important conditions, such as delirium, should be diagnosed and, when found, treated aggressively. When developing a management plan, initiation of ART and treatment of multimorbid conditions should be prioritized. While ART drugs appear to differ in their effectiveness and toxicity in the CNS, the primary goal for ART is suppressing HIV RNA in blood and CSF. No specific adjunctive therapies are currently recommended for HAND but several, such as maraviroc and paroxetine, have had promising preliminary findings. Additional interventions, such as behavioral therapies and exercise, may also be beneficial. Diagnosis and treatment of HAND and routine monitoring for neurocognitive disorders can maintain adherence to risk reduction and medical care, support quality of health and life, and decrease morbidity and mortality in persons with HIV.

REFERENCES

Abdulle S, Mellgren A, Brew BJ, et al. (2007). CSF neurofilament protein (NFL)—a marker of active HIV-related neurodegeneration. *J Neurol* 254:1026–1032.

Abers MS, Shandera WX, Kass JS (2014). Neurological and psychiatric adverse effects of antiretroviral drugs. *CNS Drugs* 28:131–145.

Achim CL, Adame A, Dumaop W, Everall IP, Masliah E; Neurobehavioral Research Center (2009). Increased accumulation of intraneuronal amyloid beta in HIV-infected patients. *J Neuroimmune Pharmacol* 4:190–199.

Aiello AE, Haan M, Blythe L, Moore K, Gonzalez JM, Jagust W (2006). The influence of latent viral infection on rate of cognitive decline over 4 years. *J Am Geriatr Soc* 54:1046–1054.

Akay C, Cooper M, Odeleye A, et al. (2014). Antiretroviral drugs induce oxidative stress and neuronal damage in the central nervous system. *J Neurovirol* 20:39–53.

Albert SM, Weber CM, Todak G, et al. (1999). An observed performance test of medication management ability in HIV: relation to neuropsychological status and medication adherence outcomes. *AIDS Behav* 3:121–128.

American Academy of Neurology AIDS Task Force (1991). Nomenclature and research case definitions for neurologic manifestations of human immunodeficiency virus-type 1 (HIV-1) infection. Report of a Working Group of the American Academy of Neurology AIDS Task Force. *Neurology* 41:778–785.

Ances BM, Benzinger TL, Christensen JJ, et al. (2012). 11C-PiB imaging of human immunodeficiency virus-associated neurocognitive disorder. *Arch Neurol* 69:72–77.

Ances BM, Roc AC, Korczykowski M, Wolf RL, Kolson DL (2008). Combination antiretroviral therapy modulates the blood oxygen level-dependent amplitude in human immunodeficiency virus-seropositive patients. *J Neurovirol* 14:418–424.

Ances BM, Sisti D, Vaida F, et al. (2009). Resting cerebral blood flow: a potential biomarker of the effects of HIV in the brain. *Neurology* 73:702–708.

Ances B, Vaida F, Ellis R, Buxton R (2011). Test-retest stability of calibrated BOLD-fMRI in HIV- and HIV+ subjects. *Neuroimage* 54:2156–2162.

Anderson AM, Harezlak J, Bharti A, et al. (2015). Plasma and cerebrospinal fluid biomarkers predict cerebral injury in HIV-infected individuals on stable combination antiretroviral therapy. *J Acquir Immune Defic Syndr* 69:29–35.

Anderson AM, Iudicello J, Kallianpur AR, et al. (2016). CNS drug distribution and CSF inflammation during suppressive antiretroviral therapy (Abstract 412). Conference on Retroviruses and Opportunistic Infections. Boston, MA.

Anderson AM, Muñoz-Moreno JA, McClernon D, et al. (2017). Prevalence and correlates of persistent HIV-1 RNA in cerebrospinal fluid during antiretroviral therapy. *J Infect Dis* 215(1):105–113.

Andersson L, Blennow K, Fuchs D, Svennerholm B, Gisslén M (1999). Increased cerebrospinal fluid protein tau concentration in neuro-AIDS. *J Neurol Sci* 171:92–96.

Andres MA, Feger U, Nath A, Munsaka S, Jiang CS, Chang L (2011). APOE epsilon 4 allele and CSF APOE on cognition in HIV-infected subjects. *J Neuroimmune Pharmacol* 6:389–398.

Anthony IC, Norrby KE, Dingwall T, et al. (2010). Predisposition to accelerated Alzheimer-related changes in the brains of human immunodeficiency virus negative opiate abusers. *Brain* 133:3685–3698.

Anthony IC, Ramage SN, Carnie FW, Simmonds P, Bell JE (2005). Influence of HAART on HIV-related CNS disease and neuroinflammation. *J Neuropathol Exp Neurol* 64:529–536.

Antinori A, Arendt G, Becker JT, et al. (2007). Updated research nosology for HIV-associated neurocognitive disorders. *Neurology* 69:1789–1799.

Appay V, Kelleher AD (2016). Immune activation and immune aging in HIV infection. *Curr Opin HIV AIDS* 11:242–249.

Archibald SL, Masliah E, Fennema-Notestine C, et al. (2004). Correlation of in vivo neuroimaging abnormalities with postmortem human immunodeficiency virus encephalitis and dendritic loss. *Arch Neurol* 61:369–376.

Atluri VS, Hidalgo M, Samikkannu T, et al. (2015). Effect of human immunodeficiency virus on blood-brain barrier integrity and function: an update. *Front Cell Neurosci* 9:212.

Aylward EH, Brettschneider PD, McArthur JC, et al. (1995). Magnetic resonance imaging measurement of gray matter volume reductions in HIV dementia. *Am J Psychiatry* 152:987–994.

Aylward EH, Henderer JD, McArthur JC, et al. (1993). Reduced basal ganglia volume in HIV-1-associated dementia: results from quantitative neuroimaging. *Neurology* 43:2099–2104.

Baker LM, Paul RH, Heaps-Woodruff JM, et al. (2015). The effect of central nervous system penetration effectiveness of highly active antiretroviral therapy on neuropsychological performance and neuroimaging in HIV-infected individuals. *J Neuroimmune Pharmacol* 10:487–492.

Banks WA, Ercal N, Price TO (2006). The blood-brain barrier in neuroAIDS. *Curr HIV Res* 4:259–266.

Becker BW, Thames AD, Woo E, Castellon SA, Hinkin CH (2011). Longitudinal change in cognitive function and medication adherence in HIV-infected adults. *AIDS Behav* 15(8):1888–1894.

Becker JT, Kingsley L, Mullen J, et al. (2009). Vascular risk factors, HIV serostatus, and cognitive dysfunction in gay and bisexual men. *Neurology* 73:1292–1299.

Becker JT, Sanders J, Madsen SK, et al. (2011). Subcortical brain atrophy persists even in HAART-regulated HIV disease. *Brain Imaging Behav* 5:77–85.

Bednar MM, Sturdevant CB, Tompkins LA, et al. (2015). Compartmentalization, viral evolution, and viral latency of HIV in the CNS. *Curr HIV/AIDS Rep* 12:262–271.

Blackstone K, Moore DJ, Franklin DR, et al. (2012). Defining neurocognitive impairment in HIV: deficit scores versus clinical ratings. *Clin Neuropsychol* 26:894–908.

Bowman NM, S.B.J, Kincer LP, et al. (2016). HIV Compartmentalization in the CNS is associated with neurocognitive impairment (Abstract 401). Conference on Retroviruses and Opportunistic Infections, Boston, MA.

Brenchley JM, Price DA, Schacker TW, et al. (2006). Microbial translocation is a cause of systemic immune activation in chronic HIV infection. *Nat Med* 12:1365–1371.

Brew BJ, Pemberton L, Blennow K, Wallin A, Hagberg L (2005). CSF amyloid beta42 and tau levels correlate with AIDS dementia complex. *Neurology* 65:1490–1492.

Brew BJ, Pemberton L, Cunningham P, Law MG (1997). Levels of human immunodeficiency virus type 1 RNA in cerebrospinal fluid correlate with AIDS dementia stage. *J Infect Dis* 175:963–966.

Burdo TH, Soulas C, Orzechowski K, et al. (2010) Increased monocyte turnover from bone marrow correlates with severity of SIV encephalitis and CD163 levels in plasma. *PLoS Pathog* 6:e1000842.

Burgess MJ, Zeuli JD, Kasten MJ (2015). Management of HIV/AIDS in older patients-drug/drug interactions and adherence to antiretroviral therapy. *HIV AIDS (Auckl)* 7:251–264.

Butters N, Grant I, Haxby J, et al. (1990). Assessment of AIDS-related cognitive changes: Recommendations of the NIMH Workshop on Neuropsychological Assessment Approaches. *J Clin Exp Neuropsychol* 12:963–978.

Calcagno A, Alberione MC, Romito A, et al. (2014). Prevalence and predictors of blood–brain barrier damage in the HAART era. *J Neurovirol* 20:521–525.

Calcagno A, Atzori C, Romito A, et al. (2016). Blood brain barrier impairment is associated with cerebrospinal fluid markers of neuronal damage in HIV-positive patients. *J Neurovirol* 22:88–92.

Canestri A, Lescure FX, Jaureguiberry S, et al. (2010). Discordance between cerebral spinal fluid and plasma HIV replication in patients with neurological symptoms who are receiving suppressive antiretroviral therapy. *Clin Infect Dis* 50:773–778.

Caniglia EC, Cain LE, Justice A, et al. (2014). Antiretroviral penetration into the CNS and incidence of AIDS-defining neurologic conditions. *Neurology* 83:134–141.

Cardenas VA, Meyerhoff DJ, Studholme C, et al. (2009). Evidence for ongoing brain injury in human immunodeficiency virus-positive patients treated with antiretroviral therapy. *J Neurovirol* 15:324–333.

Carey CL, Woods SP, Gonzalez R, et al. (2004). Predictive validity of global deficit scores in detecting neuropsychological impairment in HIV infection. *J Clin Exp Neuropsychol* 26:307–319.

Carvalhal A, Gill MJ, Letendre SL, et al. (2016). Central nervous system penetration effectiveness of antiretroviral drugs and neuropsychological impairment in the Ontario HIV Treatment Network Cohort Study. *J Neurovirol* 22:349–357.

Casado JL, Marin A, Moreno A, et al. (2014). Central nervous system antiretroviral penetration and cognitive functioning in largely pretreated HIV-infected patients. *J Neurovirol* 20:54–61.

Castelo JM, Courtney MG, Melrose RJ, Stern CE (2007). Putamen hypertrophy in nondemented patients with human immunodeficiency virus infection and cognitive compromise. *Arch Neurol* 64:1275–1280.

Cavassini M, Du Pasquier RA (2013). A light in the cognitive fog? *Antivir Ther* 18:149–151.

Chana G, Everall IP, Crews L, et al. (2006). Cognitive deficits and degeneration of interneurons in HIV+ methamphetamine users. *Neurology* 67:1486–1489.

Chang L, Ernst T, Leonido-Yee M, et al. (1999). Highly active antiretroviral therapy reverses brain metabolite abnormalities in mild HIV dementia. *Neurology* 53:782–789.

Chang L, Ernst T, Leonido-Yee M, Speck O (2000). Perfusion MRI detects rCBF abnormalities in early stages of HIV-cognitive motor complex. *Neurology* 54:389–396.

Chang L, Jiang C, Cunningham E, et al. (2014). Effects of APOE epsilon4, age, and HIV on glial metabolites and cognitive deficits. *Neurology* 82:2213–2222.

Chang L, Speck O, Miller EN, et al. (2001). Neural correlates of attention and working memory deficits in HIV patients. *Neurology* 57:1001–1007.

Chang L, Tomasi D, Yakupov R, et al. (2004). Adaptation of the attention network in human immunodeficiency virus brain injury. *Ann Neurol* 56:259–272.

Chanraud S, Zahr N, Sullivan EV, Pfefferbaum A (2010). MR diffusion tensor imaging: a window into white matter integrity of the working brain. *Neuropsychol Rev* 20:209–225.

Cherner M, Letendre S, Heaton RK, et al. (2005). Hepatitis C augments cognitive deficits associated with HIV infection and methamphetamine. *Neurology* 64:1343–1347.

Cherner M, Masliah E, Ellis RJ, et al. (2002). Neurocognitive dysfunction predicts postmortem findings of HIV encephalitis. *Neurology* 59:1563–1567.

Christensen A, Russ S, Rambaran N, Wright SW (2012). Patient perspectives on opt-out HIV screening in a Guyanese emergency department. *Int Health* 4:185–191.

Churchill MJ, Cowley DJ, Wesselingh SL, Gorry PR, Gray LR (2015). HIV-1 transcriptional regulation in the central nervous system and implications for HIV cure research. *J Neurovirol* 21:290–300.

Ciccarelli N, Fabbiani M, Colafigli M, et al. (2013). Revised central nervous system neuropenetration-effectiveness score is associated with cognitive disorders in HIV-infected patients with controlled plasma viraemia. *Antivir Ther* 18:153–160.

Ciccarelli N, Fabbiani M, Di Giambenedetto S, et al. (2011). Efavirenz associated with cognitive disorders in otherwise asymptomatic HIV-infected patients. *Neurology* 76:1403–1409.

Clifford DB (2015). Neurological immune reconstitution inflammatory response: riding the tide of immune recovery. *Curr Opin Neurol* 28:295–301.

Clifford DB, Ances BM (2013). HIV-associated neurocognitive disorder. *Lancet Infect Dis* 13:976–986.

Clifford DB, Fagan AM, Holtzman DM, et al. (2009). CSF biomarkers of Alzheimer disease in HIV-associated neurologic disease. *Neurology* 73:1982–1987.

Clifford DB, Smurzynski M, Park LS, et al. (2009). Effects of active HCV replication on neurologic status in HIV RNA virally suppressed patients. *Neurology* 73:309–314.

Cohen MA, Alfonso CA (2004). AIDS psychiatry: psychiatric and palliative care, and pain management. In GP Wormser (ed.), *AIDS and Other Manifestations of HIV Infection*, fourth edition (pp. 537–576). San Diego: Elsevier Academic Press.

Cohen RA, Harezlak J, Gongvatana A, et al. (2010a). Cerebral metabolite abnormalities in human immunodeficiency virus are associated with cortical and subcortical volumes. *J Neurovirol* 16:435–444.

Cohen RA, Harezlak J, Schifitto G, et al. (2010b). Effects of nadir CD4 count and duration of human immunodeficiency virus infection on brain volumes in the highly active antiretroviral therapy era. *J Neurovirol* 16:25–32.

Cooley SA, Paul RH, Fennema-Notestine C, et al. (2016). Apolipoprotein E epsilon4 genotype status is not associated with neuroimaging outcomes in a large cohort of HIV+ individuals. *J Neurovirol* 22(5):607–614.

Cross HM, Combrinck MI, Joska JA (2013). HIV-associated neurocognitive disorders: antiretroviral regimen, central nervous system penetration effectiveness, and cognitive outcomes. *S Afr Med J* 103:758–762.

Cysique LA, Brew BJ (2009). Neuropsychological functioning and antiretroviral treatment in HIV/AIDS: a review. *Neuropsychol Rev* 19:169–185.

Cysique LA, Brew BJ (2014). The effects of HIV and aging on brain functions: proposing a research framework and update on last 3 years' findings. *Curr Opin HIV AIDS* 9:355–364.

Cysique LA, Hewitt T, Croitoru-Lamoury J, et al. (2015). APOE epsilon4 moderates abnormal CSF-abeta-42 levels, while neurocognitive impairment is associated with abnormal CSF tau levels in HIV+ individuals—a cross-sectional observational study. *BMC Neurol* 15:51.

Cysique LA, Moffat K, Moore DM, et al. (2013). HIV, vascular and aging injuries in the brain of clinically stable HIV-infected adults: a (1)H MRS study. *PloS ONE* 8:e61738.

Cysique LA, Murray JM, Dunbar M, Jeyakumar V, Brew BJ (2010). A screening algorithm for HIV-associated neurocognitive disorders. *HIV Med* 11:642–649.

Cysique LA, Vaida F, Letendre S, et al. (2009). Dynamics of cognitive change in impaired HIV-positive patients initiating antiretroviral therapy. *Neurology* 73:342–348.

Deeks SG (2011). HIV infection, inflammation, immunosenescence, and aging. *Annu Rev Med* 62:141–155.

Descamps M, Hyare H, Stebbing J, Winston A (2008). Magnetic resonance imaging and spectroscopy of the brain in HIV disease. *J HIV Ther* 13:55–58.

DHHS Panel on Antiretroviral Guidelines for Adults and Adolescents (2016). Guidelines for the use of antiretroviral agents in HIV-1-infected adults and adolescents. Department of Health and Human Services. http://www.aidsinfo.nih.gov/ContentFiles/AdultandAdolescentGL.pdf. Accessed January 23, 2017.

Douek D (2007). HIV disease progression: immune activation, microbes, and a leaky gut. *Top HIV Med* 15:114–117.

Du H, Wu Y, Ochs R, et al. (2012). A comparative evaluation of quantitative neuroimaging measurements of brain status in HIV infection. *Psychiatry Res* 203:95–99.

Dufour CA, Marquine MJ, Fazeli PL, et al. (2013). Physical exercise is associated with less neurocognitive impairment among HIV-infected adults. *J Neurovirol* 19:410–417.

Dunfee RL, Thomas ER, Gorry PR, et al. (2006). The HIV Env variant N283 enhances macrophage tropism and is associated with brain infection and dementia. *Proc Natl Acad Sci U S A* 103:15160–15165.

Dunfee RL, Thomas ER, Wang J, Kunstman K, Wolinsky SM, Gabuzda D (2007). Loss of the N-linked glycosylation site at position 386 in the HIV envelope V4 region enhances macrophage tropism and is associated with dementia. *Virology* 367:222–234.

Du Pasquier RA, Jilek S, Kalubi M, et al. (2013). Marked increase of the astrocytic marker S100B in the cerebrospinal fluid of HIV-infected patients on LPV/r-monotherapy. *AIDS* 27:203–210.

Du Plessis S, Vink M, Joska J, Koutsilieri E, Stein DJ, Emsley R (2014). HIV infection and the fronto–striatal system: a systematic review and meta-analysis of fMRI studies. *AIDS* 28(6):803–811.

Edelman EJ, Gordon KS, Glover J, McNicholl IR, Fiellin DA, Justice AC (2013). The next therapeutic challenge in HIV: polypharmacy. *Drugs Aging* 30:613–628.

Eden A, Fuchs D, Hagberg L, et al. (2010). HIV-1 viral escape in cerebrospinal fluid of subjects on suppressive antiretroviral treatment. *J Infect Dis* 202:1819–1825.

Eden A, Marcotte TD, Heaton RK, et al. (2016). Increased intrathecal immune activation in virally suppressed HIV-1-infected patients with neurocognitive impairment. *PLoS ONE* 11:e0157160.

Ellis RJ, Badiee J, Vaida F, et al. (2011). CD4 nadir is a predictor of HIV neurocognitive impairment in the era of combination antiretroviral therapy. *AIDS* 25:1747–1751.

Ellis RJ, Gamst AC, Capparelli E, et al. (2000). Cerebrospinal fluid HIV RNA originates from both local CNS and systemic sources. *Neurology* 54:927–936.

Ellis RJ, Hsia K, Spector SA, et al. (1997). Cerebrospinal fluid human immunodeficiency virus type 1 RNA levels are elevated in neurocognitively impaired individuals with acquired immunodeficiency syndrome. HIV Neurobehavioral Research Center Group. *Ann Neurol* 42:679–688.

Ellis R, Langford D, Masliah E (2007). HIV and antiretroviral therapy in the brain: neuronal injury and repair. *Nat Rev Neurosci* 8:33–44.

Ellis RJ, Letendre SL (2016). Update and new directions in therapeutics for neurological complications of HIV infections. *Neurotherapeutics* 13:471–476.

Ellis RJ, Letendre S, Vaida F, et al. (2014). Randomized trial of central nervous system-targeted antiretrovirals for HIV-associated neurocognitive disorder. *Clin Infect Dis* 58:1015–1022.

Ellis RJ, Seubert P, Motter R, et al. (1998). Cerebrospinal fluid tau protein is not elevated in HIV-associated neurologic disease in humans. HIV Neurobehavioral Research Center Group (HNRC). *Neurosci Lett* 254:1–4.

El-Sadr WM, Lundgren J, et al., for Strategies for Management of Antiretroviral Therapy (SMART) Study Group (2006). CD4+ count-guided interruption of antiretroviral treatment. *N Engl J Med* 355:2283–2296.

Ernst T, Chang L, Jovicich J, Ames N, Arnold S (2002). Abnormal brain activation on functional MRI in cognitively asymptomatic HIV patients. *Neurology* 59:1343–1349.

Ernst T, Jiang CS, Nakama H, Buchthal S, Chang L (2010). Lower brain glutamate is associated with cognitive deficits in HIV patients: a new mechanism for HIV-associated neurocognitive disorder. *J Magn Reson Imaging* 32:1045–1053.

Ernst T, Yakupov R, Nakama H, et al. (2009). Declined neural efficiency in cognitively stable human immunodeficiency virus patients. *Ann Neurol* 65:316–325.

Everall IP, Hansen LA, Masliah E (2005). The shifting patterns of HIV encephalitis neuropathology. *Neurotox Res* 8:51–61.

Everall IP, Heaton RK, Marcotte TD, et al. (1999). Cortical synaptic density is reduced in mild to moderate human immunodeficiency virus neurocognitive disorder. HNRC Group. HIV Neurobehavioral Research Center. *Brain Pathol* 9:209–217.

Everall I, Vaida F, Khanlou N, et al. (2009). Cliniconeuropathologic correlates of human immunodeficiency virus in the era of antiretroviral therapy. *J Neurovirol* 15:360–370.

Fabbiani M, Grima P, Milanini B, et al. (2015). Antiretroviral neuropenetration scores better correlate with cognitive performance of HIV-infected patients after accounting for drug susceptibility. *Antivir Ther* 20:441–447.

Faria de Oliveira M, Chaillon A, Letendre S, et al. (2016). Compartmentalized HIV DNA populations persist in CSF despite suppressive ART (Abstract 143). Conference on Retroviruses and Opportunistic Infections 2016. Boston, MA.

Fazeli PL, Marquine MJ, Dufour C, et al. (2015). Physical activity is associated with better neurocognitive and everyday functioning among older adults with HIV disease. *AIDS Behav* 19:1470–1477.

Fazeli PL, Woods SP, Heaton RK, et al. (2014). An active lifestyle is associated with better neurocognitive functioning in adults living with HIV infection. *J Neurovirol* 20:233–242.

Ferrell D, Giunta B (2014). The impact of HIV-1 on neurogenesis: implications for HAND. *Cell Mol Life Sci* 71:4387–4392.

Fields JA, Dumaop W, Crews L, et al. (2015). Mechanisms of HIV-1 Tat neurotoxicity via CDK5 translocation and hyper-activation: role in HIV-associated neurocognitive disorders. *Curr HIV Res* 13:43–54.

Fillipas S, Oldmeadow LB, Bailey MJ, Cherry CL (2006). A six-month, supervised, aerobic and resistance exercise program improves self-efficacy in people with human immunodeficiency virus: a randomised controlled trial. *Aust J Physiother* 52:185–190.

Fjell AM, Westlye LT, Amlien I, et al. (2009). High consistency of regional cortical thinning in aging across multiple samples. *Cereb Cortex* 19:2001–2012.

Forton DM, Allsop JM, Cox IJ, et al. (2005). A review of cognitive impairment and cerebral metabolite abnormalities in patients with hepatitis C infection. *AIDS* 19(Suppl 3):S53–S63.

Forton DM, Taylor-Robinson SD, Thomas HC (2006). Central nervous system changes in hepatitis C virus infection. *Eur J Gastroenterol Hepatol* 18:333–338.

Funes HA, Blas-Garcia A, Esplugues JV, Apostolova N (2015). Efavirenz alters mitochondrial respiratory function in cultured neuron and glial cell lines. *J Antimicrob Chemother* 70:2249–2254.

Gandhi NS, Skolasky RL, Peters KB, et al. (2011). A comparison of performance-based measures of function in HIV-associated neurocognitive disorders. *J Neurovirol* 17:159–165.

Garvey LJ, Pavese N, Ramlackhansingh A, et al. (2012). Acute HCV/HIV coinfection is associated with cognitive dysfunction and cerebral metabolite disturbance, but not increased microglial cell activation. *PLoS ONE* 7:e38980.

Gastaldi M, Thouin A, Vincent A (2016). Antibody-mediated autoimmune encephalopathies and immunotherapies. *Neurotherapeutics* 13:147–162.

Gates TM, Cysique LA, Siefried KJ, Chaganti J, Moffat KJ, Brew BJ (2016). Maraviroc-intensified combined antiretroviral therapy improves cognition in virally suppressed HIV-associated neurocognitive disorder. *AIDS* 30:591–600.

Ghate M, Mehendale S, Meyer R, et al. (2015). The effects of antiretroviral treatment initiation on cognition in HIV-infected individuals with advanced disease in Pune, India. *J Neurovirol* 21:391–398.

Gianella S, Letendre S (2016). CMV and HIV: a dangerous "pas de deux". *J Infect Dis* 214(Suppl 2):S67–S74.

Girard TD, Jackson JC, Pandharipande PP, et al. (2010). Delirium as a predictor of long-term cognitive impairment in survivors of critical illness. *Crit Care Med* 38(7):1513–1520.

Gisslén M, Hagberg L, Brew BJ, Cinque P, Price RW, Rosengren L (2007). Elevated cerebrospinal fluid neurofilament light protein concentrations predict the development of AIDS dementia complex. *J Infect Dis* 195:1774–1778.

Gisslén M, Krut J, Andreasson U, et al. (2009). Amyloid and tau cerebrospinal fluid biomarkers in HIV infection. *BMC Neurol* 9:63.

Gisslén M, Price RW, Andreasson U, et al. (2016). Plasma concentration of the neurofilament light protein (NFL) is a biomarker of CNS injury in HIV infection: a cross-sectional study. *EBioMedicine* 3:135–140.

Gisslén M, Rosengren L, Hagberg L, Deeks SG, Price RW (2005). Cerebrospinal fluid signs of neuronal damage after antiretroviral treatment interruption in HIV-1 infection. *AIDS Res Ther* 2:6.

Gleason LJ, Luque AE, Shah K (2013). Polypharmacy in the HIV-infected older adult population. *Clin Interv Aging* 8:749–763.

Gongvatana A, Cohen RA, Correia S, et al. (2011). Clinical contributors to cerebral white matter integrity in HIV-infected individuals. *J Neurovirol* 17:477–486.

Gongvatana A, Harezlak J, Buchthal S, et al. (2013). Progressive cerebral injury in the setting of chronic HIV infection and antiretroviral therapy. *J Neurovirol* 19:209–218.

Gorman AA, Foley JM, Ettenhofer ML, Hinkin CH, van Gorp WG (2009). Functional consequences of HIV-associated neuropsychological impairment. *Neuropsychol Rev* 19:186–203.

Grant I, Atkinson JH (1995). Psychiatric aspects of acquired immune deficiency syndrome. In HI Kaplan, BJ Sadock (eds.), *Comprehensive Textbook of Psychiatry* (Vol. 2, Sect. 29.2, pp. 1644–1669). Baltimore: Williams and Wilkins.

Grant I, Sacktor N, McArthur JC (2005). HIV neurocognitive disorders. In HE Gendelman, IG Everall, SA Lipton, S Swindells (eds.), *The Neurology of AIDS*, 2nd ed. (pp. 359–373). New York: Oxford University Press.

Green AJ, Giovannoni G, Hall-Craggs MA, Thompson EJ, Miller RF (2000). Cerebrospinal fluid tau concentrations in HIV infected patients with suspected neurological disease. *Sex Transm Infect* 76:443–446.

Green DA, Masliah E, Vinters HV, Beizai P, Moore DJ, Achim CL (2005). Brain deposition of beta-amyloid is a common pathologic feature in HIV positive patients. *AIDS* 19:407–411.

Greene M, Steinman MA, McNicholl IR, Valcour V (2014). Polypharmacy, drug-drug interactions, and potentially inappropriate medications in older adults with human immunodeficiency virus infection. *J Am Geriatr Soc* 62:447–453.

Hammond ER, Crum RM, Treisman GJ, et al. (2014). The cerebrospinal fluid HIV risk score for assessing central nervous system activity in persons with HIV. *Am J Epidemiol* 180:297–307.

Harezlak J, Buchthal S, Taylor M, et al. (2011). Persistence of HIV-associated cognitive impairment, inflammation, and neuronal injury in era of highly active antiretroviral treatment. *AIDS* 25:625–633.

Harrington PR, Schnell G, Letendre SL, et al. (2009). Cross-sectional characterization of HIV-1 env compartmentalization in cerebrospinal fluid over the full disease course. *AIDS* 23:907–915.

Haughey NJ, Nath A, Mattson MP, Slevin JT, Geiger JD (2001). HIV-1 Tat through phosphorylation of NMDA receptors potentiates glutamate excitotoxicity. *J Neurochem* 78:457–467.

Hawkins BT, Davis TP (2005). The blood-brain barrier/neurovascular unit in health and disease. *Pharmacol Rev* 57:173–185.

Heaps JM, Joska J, Hoare J, et al. (2012). Neuroimaging markers of human immunodeficiency virus infection in South Africa. *J Neurovirol* 18:151–156.

Heaton RK, Clifford DB, Franklin DR, Jr., et al. (2010). HIV-associated neurocognitive disorders persist in the era of potent antiretroviral therapy: CHARTER Study. *Neurology* 75:2087–2096.

Heaton RK, Franklin DR, Jr., Deutsch R, et al. (2015). Neurocognitive change in the era of HIV combination antiretroviral therapy: the longitudinal CHARTER study. *Clin Infect Dis* 60:473–480.

Heaton RK, Franklin DR, Ellis RJ, et al. (2011). HIV-associated neurocognitive disorders before and during the era of combination antiretroviral therapy: differences in rates, nature, and predictors. *J Neurovirol* 17:3–16.

Heaton RK, Grant I, Butters N, et al. (1995). The HNRC 500—neuropsychology of HIV infection at different disease stages. HIV Neurobehavioral Research Center. *J Int Neuropsychol Soc* 1:231–251.

Heaton RK, Marcotte TD, Mindt MR, et al. (2004). The impact of HIV-associated neuropsychological impairment on everyday functioning. *J Int Neuropsychol Soc* 10:317–331.

Heindel WC, Jernigan TL, Archibald SL, Achim CL, Masliah E, Wiley CA (1994). The relationship of quantitative brain magnetic resonance imaging measures to neuropathologic indexes of human immunodeficiency virus infection. *Arch Neurol* 51:1129–1135.

Hestad K, McArthur JH, Dal Pan GJ, et al. (1983). Regional brain atrophy in HIV-1 infection: association with specific neuropsychological test performance. *Acta Neurol Scand* 88:112–118.

Heyes MP, Ellis RJ, Ryan L, et al. (2001). Elevated cerebrospinal fluid quinolinic acid levels are associated with region-specific cerebral volume loss in HIV infection. *Brain* 124:1033–1042.

Hightower GK, Letendre SL, Cherner M, et al. (2009). Select resistance-associated mutations in blood are associated with lower CSF viral loads and better neuropsychological performance. *Virology* 394:243–248.

Hinkin CH, Castellon SA, Durvasula RS, et al. (2002). Medication adherence among HIV+ adults: effects of cognitive dysfunction and regimen complexity. *Neurology* 59:1944–1950.

Hinkin CH, Castellon SA, Levine AJ, Barclay TR, Singer EJ (2008). Neurocognition in individuals co-infected with HIV and hepatitis C. *J Addict Dis* 27:11–17.

Hilsabeck RC, Castellon SA, Hinkin CH (2005). Neuropsychological aspects of coinfection with HIV and hepatitis C virus. *Clin Infect Dis* 41(Suppl 1):S38–S44.

Hjerrild S, Renvillard SG, Leutscher P, et al. (2016). Reduced cerebral cortical thickness in non-cirrhotic patients with hepatitis C. *Metab Brain Dis* 31:311–319.

Hoare J, Westgarth-Taylor J, Fouche JP, et al. (2012). A diffusion tensor imaging and neuropsychological study of prospective memory impairment in South African HIV positive individuals. *Metab Brain Dis* 27:289–297.

Holt JL, Kraft-Terry SD, Chang L (2012). Neuroimaging studies of the aging HIV-1-infected brain. *J Neurovirol* 18:291–302.

Iannucci G, Rovaris M, Giacomotti L, Comi G, Filippi M (2001). Correlation of multiple sclerosis measures derived from T2-weighted, T1-weighted, magnetization transfer, and diffusion tensor MR imaging. *AJNR Am J Neuroradiol* 22:1462–1467.

Ivey NS, MacLean AG, Lackner AA (2009). Acquired immunodeficiency syndrome and the blood-brain barrier. *J Neurovirol* 15:111–122.

Jackson JC, Gordon SM, Hart RP, Hopkins RO, Ely EW (2004). The association between delirium and cognitive decline: a review of the empirical literature. *Neuropsych Rev* 14(2):87–98.

Janssen RS, Okey CN, Selik RM, Stehr-Green JK (1992). Epidemiology of human immunodeficiency virus encephalopathy in the United States. *Neurology* 42:1472–1476.

Jernigan TL, Archibald SL, Fennema-Notestine C, et al. (2011). Clinical factors related to brain structure in HIV: the CHARTER study. *J Neurovirol* 17:248–257.

Jessen Krut J, Mellberg T, Price RW, et al. (2014). Biomarker evidence of axonal injury in neuroasymptomatic HIV-1 patients. *PLoS ONE* 9:e88591.

Johnson TP, Nath A (2014). New insights into immune reconstitution inflammatory syndrome of the central nervous system. *Curr Opin HIV AIDS* 9:572–578.

Jordan BD, Navia BA, Petito C, Cho ES, Price RW (1985). Neurological syndromes complicating AIDS. *Front Radiat Ther Oncol* 19:82–87.

Joseph SB, Arrildt KT, Sturdevant CB, Swanstrom R (2015). HIV-1 target cells in the CNS. *J Neurovirol* 21:276–289.

Joseph SB, Arrildt KT, Swanstrom AE, et al. (2014). Quantification of entry phenotypes of macrophage-tropic HIV-1 across a wide range of CD4 densities. *J Virol* 88:1858–1869.

Juengst SB, Aizenstein HJ, Figurski J, Lopez OL, Becker JT (2007). Alterations in the hemodynamic response function in cognitively impaired HIV/AIDS subjects. *J Neurosci Methods* 163:208–212.

Justice AC, McGinnis KA, Skanderson M, et al. (2010). Towards a combined prognostic index for survival in HIV infection: the role of 'non-HIV' biomarkers. *HIV Med* 11:143–151.

Kahouadji Y, Dumurgier J, Sellier P, et al. (2013). Cognitive function after several years of antiretroviral therapy with stable central nervous system penetration score. *HIV Med* 14:311–315.

Kallianpur AR, Wang Q, Jia P, et al. (2016). Anemia and red blood cell indices predict HIV-associated neurocognitive impairment in the highly active antiretroviral therapy era. *J Infect Dis* 213:1065–1073.

Kallianpur KJ, Shikuma C, Kirk GR, et al. (2013). Peripheral blood HIV DNA is associated with atrophy of cerebellar and subcortical gray matter. *Neurology* 80:1792–1799.

Kamat A, Lyons JL, Misra V, et al. (2012). Monocyte activation markers in cerebrospinal fluid associated with impaired neurocognitive testing in advanced HIV infection. *J Acquir Immune Defic Syndr* 60:234–243.

Kamminga J, Cysique LA, Lu G, Batchelor J, Brew BJ (2013). Validity of cognitive screens for HIV-associated neurocognitive disorder: a systematic review and an informed screen selection guide. *Curr HIV/ AIDS Rep* 10:342–355.

King JE, Eugenin EA, Buckner CM, Berman JW (2006). HIV tat and neurotoxicity. *Microbes Infect* 8:1347–1357.

Koralnik IJ, Beaumanoir A, Hausler R, et al. (1990). A controlled study of early neurologic abnormalities in men with asymptomatic human immunodeficiency virus infection. *N Engl J Med* 323:864–870.

Krut JJ, Price RW, Zetterberg H, et al. (2016). No support for premature central nervous system aging in HIV-1 when measured by cerebrospinal fluid phosphorylated tau (p-tau). *Virulence* 19:1–6.

Krut JJ, Zetterberg H, Blennow K, et al. (2013). Cerebrospinal fluid Alzheimer's biomarker profiles in CNS infections. *J Neurol* 260:620–626.

Lanier ER, Sturge G, McClernon D, et al. (2001). HIV-1 reverse transcriptase sequence in plasma and cerebrospinal fluid of patients with AIDS dementia complex treated with Abacavir. *AIDS* 15:747–751.

Laskus T, Radkowski M, Adair DM, Wilkinson J, Scheck AC, Rakela J (2005). Emerging evidence of hepatitis C virus neuroinvasion. *AIDS* 19(Suppl 3):S140–S144.

Legarth RA, Ahlstrom MG, Kronborg G, et al. (2016). Long-term mortality in HIV-infected individuals 50 years or older: a nationwide, population-based cohort study. *J Acquir Immune Defic Syndr* 71:213–218.

Lentz MR, Kim WK, Kim H, et al. (2011). Alterations in brain metabolism during the first year of HIV infection. *J Neurovirol* 17:220–229.

Letendre S (2011). Central nervous system complications in HIV disease: HIV-associated neurocognitive disorder. *Top Antivir Med* 19:137–142.

Letendre SL, Cherner M, Ellis RJ, et al. (2005). The effects of hepatitis C, HIV, and methamphetamine dependence on neuropsychological performance: biological correlates of disease. *AIDS* 19(Suppl 3):S72–S78.

Letendre S, Marquie-Beck J, Capparelli E, et al. (2008). Validation of the CNS penetration-effectiveness rank for quantifying antiretroviral penetration into the central nervous system. *Arch Neurol* 65:65–70.

Letendre S, Paulino AD, Rockenstein E, et al. (2007). Pathogenesis of hepatitis C virus coinfection in the brains of patients infected with HIV. *J Infect Dis* 196:361–370.

Letendre SL, Woods SP, Ellis RJ, et al. (2006). Lithium improves HIV-associated neurocognitive impairment. *AIDS* 20:1885–1888.

Li C, Zhang X, Komery A, Li Y, Novembre FJ, Herndon JG (2011). Longitudinal diffusion tensor imaging and perfusion MRI investigation in a macaque model of neuro-AIDS: a preliminary study. *Neuroimage* 58:286–292.

Li W, Huang Y, Reid R, et al. (2008). NMDA receptor activation by HIV-Tat protein is clade dependent. *J Neurosci* 28:12190–12198.

Libertone R, Balestra P, Lorenzini P, et al. (2014). APRI and FIB-4 scores are not associated with neurocognitive impairment in HIV-infected persons. *J Int AIDS Soc* 17:19658.

Lovelace MD, Varney B, Sundaram G, et al. (2017). Recent evidence for an expanded role of the kynurenine pathway of tryptophan metabolism in neurological diseases. *Neuropharmacology* 112(Pt B):373–388.

Lundgren JD, Babiker AG, Gordin F, et al., for INSIGHT START Study Group (2015). Initiation of antiretroviral therapy in early asymptomatic HIV infection. *N Engl J Med* 373:795–807.

Lyons JL, Uno H, Ancuta P, et al. (2011). Plasma sCD14 is a biomarker associated with impaired neurocognitive test performance in attention and learning domains in HIV infection. *J Acquir Immune Defic Syndr* 57:371–379.

Ma Q, Vaida F, Wong J, et al. (2016). Long-term efavirenz use is associated with worse neurocognitive functioning in HIV-infected patients. *J Neurovirol* 22:170–178.

MacLullich et al. Int Rev of Psych 2009;

Maki PM, Cohen MH, Weber K, et al. (2009). Impairments in memory and hippocampal function in HIV-positive vs HIV-negative women: a preliminary study. *Neurology* 72:1661–1668.

Maldonado JR (2013). Neuropathogenesis of delirium: review of current etiological theories and common pathways. *Am J Geriatr Psychiatry* 21:1190–1222.

Marcotte TD, Scott JC (2004). The assessment of driving abilities. *Advances in Transportation Studies: An International Journal* 79–90.

Marquine MJ, Montoya JL, Umlauf A, et al. (2016). The Veterans Aging Cohort Study (VACS) Index and neurocognitive change: a longitudinal study. *Clin Infect Dis* 63(5):694–702.

Marquine MJ, Umlauf A, Rooney AS, et al. (2014) The Veterans Aging Cohort Study Index is associated with concurrent risk for neurocognitive impairment. *J Acquir Immune Defic Syndr* 65:190–197.

Marra CM, Zhao Y, Clifford DB, et al. (2009). Impact of combination antiretroviral therapy on cerebrospinal fluid HIV RNA and neurocognitive performance. *AIDS* 23:1359–1366.

Masliah E, Achim CL, Ge N, De Teresa R, Wiley CA (1994). Cellular neuropathology in HIV encephalitis. *Res Publ Assoc Res Nerv Ment Dis* 72:119–131.

Masliah E, Ge N, Achim CL, Hansen LA, Wiley CA (1992). Selective neuronal vulnerability in HIV encephalitis. *J Neuropathol Exp Neurol* 51:585–593.

Masliah E, Ge N, Mucke L (1996). Pathogenesis of HIV-1 associated neurodegeneration. *Crit Rev Neurobiol* 10:57–67.

Masters MC, Ances BM (2014). Role of neuroimaging in HIV-associated neurocognitive disorders. *Semin Neurol* 34:89–102.

McArthur JC, Grant I (1998). HIV neurocognitive disorders. In HE Gendelman, S Lipton, L Epstein, S Swindells (eds.), *Neurology of AIDS* (pp. 499–524). New York: Chapman and Hall Publishers.

McArthur JC, McClernon DR, Cronin MF, et al. (1997). Relationship between human immunodeficiency virus–associated dementia and viral load in cerebrospinal fluid and brain. *Ann Neurol* 42:689–698.

McCutchan JA, Marquie-Beck JA, Fitzsimons CA, et al. (2012). Role of obesity, metabolic variables, and diabetes in HIV-associated neurocognitive disorder. *Neurology* 78:485–492.

McGuire JL, Gill AJ, Douglas SD, Kolson DL; CNS HIV Anti-Retroviral Therapy Effects Research (CHARTER) group (2015). Central and peripheral markers of neurodegeneration and monocyte activation in HIV-associated neurocognitive disorders. *J Neurovirol* 21:439–448.

McRae M (2016). HIV and viral protein effects on the blood brain barrier. *Tissue Barriers* 4:e1143543.

Mehraj V, Routy JP (2015). Tryptophan catabolism in chronic viral infections: handling uninvited guests. *Int J Tryptophan Res* 8:41–48.

Mellgren A, Price RW, Hagberg L, Rosengren L, Brew BJ, Gisslén M (2007). Antiretroviral treatment reduces increased CSF neurofilament protein (NFL) in HIV-1 infection. *Neurology* 69:1536–1541.

Meulendyke KA, Queen SE, Engle EL, et al. (2014). Combination fluconazole/paroxetine treatment is neuroprotective despite ongoing neuroinflammation and viral replication in an SIV model of HIV neurological disease. *J Neurovirol* 20:591–602.

Mind Exchange Working Group (2013). Assessment, diagnosis, and treatment of HIV-associated neurocognitive disorder: a consensus report of the mind exchange program. *Clin Infect Dis* 56:1004–1017.

Mocchetti I, Bachis A, Avdoshina V (2012). Neurotoxicity of human immunodeficiency virus-1: viral proteins and axonal transport. *Neurotox Res* 21:79–89.

Mohamed MA, Barker PB, Skolasky RL, et al. (2010). Brain metabolism and cognitive impairment in HIV infection: a 3-T magnetic resonance spectroscopy study. *Magn Reson Imaging* 28:1251–1257.

Montoya JL, Wing D, Knight A, Moore DJ, Henry BL (2015). Development of an mHealth Intervention (iSTEP) to promote physical activity among people living with HIV. *J Int Assoc Provid AIDS Care* 14:471–475.

Moore DJ, Masliah E, Rippeth JD, et al. (2006). Cortical and subcortical neurodegeneration is associated with HIV neurocognitive impairment. *AIDS.* 20:879–887.

Moore DJ, Palmer BW, Patterson TL, Jeste DV (2007). A review of performance-based measures of functional living skills. *J Psychiatr Res* 41:97–118.

Morgan EE, Woods SP, Grant I; HIV Neurobehavioral Research Program (HNRP) Group (2012). Intra-individual neurocognitive variability confers risk of dependence in activities of daily living among HIV-seropositive individuals without HIV-associated neurocognitive disorders. *Arch Clin Neuropsychol* 27:293–303.

Morgan EE, Woods SP, Letendre SL, et al. (2103). Apolipoprotein E4 genotype does not increase risk of HIV-associated neurocognitive disorders. *J Neurovirol* 19:150–156.

Morgan EE, Woods SP, Scott JC, et al. (2008). Predictive validity of demographically adjusted normative standards for the HIV Dementia Scale. *J Clin Exp Neuropsychol* 30:83–90.

Morgello S, Murray J, Van Der Elst S, Byrd D (2014). HCV, but not HIV, is a risk factor for cerebral small vessel disease. *Neurol Neuroimmunol Neuroinflamm* 1:e27.

Morris SR, Woods SP, Deutsch R, et al. (2013). Dual-mixed HIV-1 coreceptor tropism and HIV-associated neurocognitive deficits. *J Neurovirol* 19:488–494.

Mothapo KM, Stelma F, Janssen M, et al. (2015). Amyloid beta-42 (Abeta-42), neprilysin and cytokine levels. A pilot study in patients with HIV related cognitive impairments. *J Neuroimmunol* 282:73–79.

Muñoz-Moreno JA, Fumaz CR, Ferrer MJ, et al. (2008). Nadir CD4 cell count predicts neurocognitive impairment in HIV-infected patients. *AIDS Res Hum Retroviruses* 24:1301–1307.

Muratori C, Mangino G, Affabris E, Federico M (2010). Astrocytes contacting HIV-1-infected macrophages increase the release of CCL2 in response to the HIV-1-dependent enhancement of membrane-associated TNFalpha in macrophages. *Glia* 58:1893–904.

Nath A (2015). Eradication of human immunodeficiency virus from brain reservoirs. *J Neurovirol* 21:227–234.

Nasi M, De Biasi S, Gibellini L, et al. (2017). Aging and inflammation in patients with HIV infection. *Clin Exp Immunol* 187:44–52.

Navia BA, Cho ES, Petito CK, Price RW (1986). The AIDS dementia complex: II. Neuropathology. *Ann Neurol* 19:525–535.

Navia BA, Jordan BD, Price RW (1986). The AIDS dementia complex: I. Clinical features. *Ann Neurol* 19:517–524.

Ndhlovu LC, Umaki T, Chew GM, et al. (2014). Treatment intensification with maraviroc (CCR5 antagonist) leads to declines in CD16-expressing monocytes in cART-suppressed chronic HIV-infected subjects and is associated with improvements in neurocognitive test performance: implications for HIV-associated neurocognitive disease (HAND). *J Neurovirol* 20:571–582.

Nightingale S, Winston A, Letendre S, et al. (2014). Controversies in HIV-associated neurocognitive disorders. *Lancet Neurol* 13:1139–1151.

Ohagen A, Devitt A, Kunstman KJ, et al. (2003). Genetic and functional analysis of full-length human immunodeficiency virus type 1 env genes derived from brain and blood of patients with AIDS. *J Virol* 77:12336–12345.

Panos SE, Hinkin CH, Singer EJ, et al. (2013). Apolipoprotein-E genotype and human immunodeficiency virus-associated neurocognitive disorder: the modulating effects of older age and disease severity. *Neurobehav HIV Med* 5:11–22.

Parisi A, Strosselli M, Di Perri G, et al. (1989). Electroencephalography in the early diagnosis of HIV-related subacute encephalitis: analysis of 185 patients. *Clin Electroencephalogr* 20:1–5.

Patel SH, Kolson DL, Glosser G, et al. (2002). Correlation between percentage of brain parenchymal volume and neurocognitive performance in HIV-infected patients. *AJNR Am J Neuroradiol* 23:543–549.

Pathai S, Bajillan H, Landay AL, High KP (2014). Is HIV a model of accelerated or accentuated aging? *J Gerontol A Biol Sci Med Sci* 69:833–842.

Patterson TL, Lacro J, McKibbin CL, Moscona S, Hughs T, Jeste DV (2002). Medication management ability assessment: results from a performance-based measure in older outpatients with schizophrenia. *J Clin Psychopharmacol* 22:11–19.

Paul RH, Ernst T, Brickman AM, et al. (2008). Relative sensitivity of magnetic resonance spectroscopy and quantitative magnetic resonance imaging to cognitive function among nondemented individuals infected with HIV. *J Int Neuropsychol Soc* 14:725–733.

Paulino AD, Ubhi K, Rockenstein E, et al. (2011). Neurotoxic effects of the HCV core protein are mediated by sustained activation of ERK via TLR2 signaling. *J Neurovirol* 17:327–340.

Peluso MJ, Ferretti F, Peterson J, et al. (2012). Cerebrospinal fluid HIV escape associated with progressive neurologic dysfunction in patients on antiretroviral therapy with well controlled plasma viral load. *AIDS* 26:1765–1774.

Peluso MJ, Meyerhoff DJ, Price RW, et al. (2013). Cerebrospinal fluid and neuroimaging biomarker abnormalities suggest early neurological injury in a subset of individuals during primary HIV infection. *J Infect Dis* 207:1703–1712.

Perez-Santiago J, Gianella S, Massanella M, et al. (2013). Gut Lactobacillales are associated with higher CD4 and less microbial translocation during HIV infection. *AIDS* 27:1921–1931.

Persidsky Y, Ramirez SH, Haorah J, Kanmogne GD (2006). Blood-brain barrier: structural components and function under physiologic and pathologic conditions. *J Neuroimmune Pharmacol* 1:223–236.

Peterson J, Gisslén M, Zetterberg H, et al. (2014). Cerebrospinal fluid (CSF) neuronal biomarkers across the spectrum of HIV infection: hierarchy of injury and detection. *PLoS ONE* 9:e116081.

Pfefferbaum A, Rosenbloom MJ, Sassoon SA, et al. (2012). Regional brain structural dysmorphology in human immunodeficiency virus infection: effects of acquired immune deficiency syndrome, alcoholism, and age. *Biol Psychiatry* 72:361–370.

Pillai SK, Pond SL, Liu Y, et al. (2006). Genetic attributes of cerebrospinal fluid-derived HIV-1 env. *Brain* 129:1872–1883.

Ping LH, Joseph SB, Anderson JA, et al. (2013). Comparison of viral Env proteins from acute and chronic infections with subtype C human immunodeficiency virus type 1 identifies differences in glycosylation and CCR5 utilization and suggests a new strategy for immunogen design. *J Virol* 87:7218–7233.

Pocernich CB, Sultana R, Mohmmad-Abdul H, Nath A, Butterfield DA (2005). HIV-dementia, Tat-induced oxidative stress, and antioxidant therapeutic considerations. *Brain Res Brain Res Rev* 50:14–26.

Power C, McArthur JC, Johnson RT, et al. (1994). Demented and nondemented patients with AIDS differ in brain-derived human immunodeficiency virus type 1 envelope sequences. *J Virol* 68:4643–4649.

Price RW, Brew BJ (1998). The AIDS dementia complex. *J Infect Dis* 158:1079–1083.

Price RW, Navia BA, Cho ES (1986). AIDS encephalopathy. *Neurol Clin* 4:285–301.

Pulliam L, Gascon R, Stubblebine M, McGuire D, McGrath MS (1997). Unique monocyte subset in patients with AIDS dementia. *Lancet* 349:692–695.

Ragin AB, D'Souza G, Reynolds S, et al. (2011). Platelet decline as a predictor of brain injury in HIV infection. *J Neurovirol* 17:487–495.

Ragin AB, Du H, Ochs R, et al. (2012). Structural brain alterations can be detected early in HIV infection. *Neurology* 79:2328–2334.

Ratto-Kim S, Chuenchitra T, Pulliam L, et al. (2008). Expression of monocyte markers in HIV-1 infected individuals with or without HIV associated dementia and normal controls in Bangkok Thailand. *J Neuroimmunol* 195:100–107.

Rauch A, Rainer G, Logothetis NK (2008). The effect of a serotonin-induced dissociation between spiking and perisynaptic activity on BOLD functional MRI. *Proc Natl Acad Sci U S A* 105:6759–6764.

Riedel DJ, Pardo CA, McArthur J, Nath A (2006). Therapy Insight: CNS manifestations of HIV-associated immune reconstitution inflammatory syndrome. *Nat Clin Pract Neurol* 2:557–565.

Robbins RN, Brown H, Ehlers A, et al. (2014). A smartphone appto screen for HIV-related neurocognitive impairment. *J Mob Technol Med* 3(1):23–26.

Roberts ET, Haan MN, Dowd JB, Aiello AE (2010). Cytomegalovirus antibody levels, inflammation, and mortality among elderly Latinos over 9 years of follow-up. *Am J Epidemiol* 172:363–371.

Robertson K, Liner J, Meeker RB (2012). Antiretroviral neurotoxicity. *J Neurovirol* 18:388–399.

Robertson KR, Su Z, Margolis DM, et al. (2010). Neurocognitive effects of treatment interruption in stable HIV-positive patients in an observational cohort. *Neurology* 74:1260–1266.

Rossi F, Querido B, Nimmagadda M, Cocklin S, Navas-Martin S, Martin-Garcia J (2008). The V1-V3 region of a brain-derived HIV-1 envelope glycoprotein determines macrophage tropism, low CD4 dependence, increased fusogenicity and altered sensitivity to entry inhibitors. *Retrovirology* 5:89.

Ruiz Perez I, Rodriguez Bano J, Lopez Ruz MA, et al. (2005). Health-related quality of life of patients with HIV: impact of sociodemographic, clinical and psychosocial factors. *Qual Life Res* 14:1301–1310.

Sacktor N (2002). The epidemiology of human immunodeficiency virus-associated neurological disease in the era of highly active antiretroviral therapy. *J Neurovirol* 8(Suppl 2):115–121.

Sacktor N, McDermott MP, Marder K, et al. (2002). HIV-associated cognitive impairment before and after the advent of combination therapy. *J Neurovirol* 8:136–142.

Sacktor N, Skolasky RL, Haughey N, et al. (2016). Paroxetine and fluconazole therapy for HAND: a double-blind, placebo-controlled trial (Abstract 146). Conference on Retroviruses and Opportunistic Infections. Boston, MA.

Sacktor NC, Wong M, Nakasujja N, et al. (2005). The International HIV Dementia Scale: a new rapid screening test for HIV dementia. *AIDS* 19:1367–1374.

Sailasuta N, Ross W, Ananworanich J, et al. (2012). Change in brain magnetic resonance spectroscopy after treatment during acute HIV infection. *PloS ONE* 7:e49272.

Sakamoto M, Marcotte TD, Severson J, et al. (2014). Development of an iPad-based screening tool for detection of HIV-related neuropsychological disorders. National Academy of Neuropsychology 34th annual meeting.

Sakamoto M, Marcotte TD, Umlauf A, et al. (2013). Concurrent classification accuracy of the HIV dementia scale for HIV-associated neurocognitive disorders in the CHARTER Cohort. *J Acquir Immune Defic Syndr* 62:36–42.

Sattler FR, He J, Letendre S, et al. (2015). Abdominal obesity contributes to neurocognitive impairment in HIV-infected patients with increased inflammation and immune activation. *J Acquir Immune Defic Syndr* 68:281–288.

Saylor D, Dickens AM, Sacktor N, et al. (2016). HIV-associated neurocognitive disorder—pathogenesis and prospects for treatment. *Nat Rev Neurol* 12:309.

Schifitto G, Navia BA, Yiannoutsos CT, et al. (2007). Memantine and HIV-associated cognitive impairment: a neuropsychological and proton magnetic resonance spectroscopy study. *AIDS* 21:1877–1886.

Schifitto G, Zhong J, Gill D, et al. (2009). Lithium therapy for human immunodeficiency virus type 1-associated neurocognitive impairment. *J Neurovirol* 15:176–186.

Schnell G, Price RW, Swanstrom R, Spudich S (2010). Compartmentalization and clonal amplification of HIV-1 variants in the cerebrospinal fluid during primary infection. *J Virol* 84:2395–2407.

Schrier RD, Gupta S, Riggs P, et al. (2012) The influence of HLA on HIV-associated neurocognitive impairment in Anhui, China. *PLoS ONE* 7:e32303.

Schrier RD, Hong S, Crescini M, et al. (2015) Cerebrospinal fluid (CSF) CD8+ T-cells that express interferon-gamma contribute to HIV associated neurocognitive disorders (HAND). *PLoS ONE* 10:e0116526.

Schrier RD, Wiley CA, Spina C, McCutchan JA, Grant I (1996). Pathogenic and protective correlates of T cell proliferation in AIDS. HNRC Group. HIV Neurobehavioral Research Center. *J Clin Invest* 98:731–740.

Schroecksnadel K, Zangerle R, Bellmann-Weiler R, Garimorth K, Weiss G, Fuchs D (2007). Indoleamine-2, 3-dioxygenase and other interferon-gamma-mediated pathways in patients with human immunodeficiency virus infection. *Curr Drug Metab* 8:225–236.

Sevigny JJ, Albert SM, McDermott MP, et al. (2004). Evaluation of HIV RNA and markers of immune activation as predictors of HIV-associated dementia. *Neurology* 63:2084–2090.

Sevigny JJ, Albert SM, McDermott MP, et al. (2007). An evaluation of neurocognitive status and markers of immune activation as predictors of time to death in advanced HIV infection. *Arch Neurol* 64:97–102.

Shah A, Gangwani MR, Chaudhari NS, Glazyrin A, Bhat HK, Kumar A (2016). Neurotoxicity in the post-HAART era: caution for the antiretroviral therapeutics. *Neurotox Res* 30(4):677–697.

Shikuma CM, Nakamoto B, Shiramizu B, et al. (2012). Antiretroviral monocyte efficacy score linked to cognitive impairment in HIV. *Antivir Ther* 17:1233–1242.

Shikuma CM, Valcour VG, Ratto-Kim S, et al. (2005). HIV-associated wasting in the era of highly active antiretroviral therapy: a syndrome of residual HIV infection in monocytes and macrophages? *Clin Infect Dis* 40:1846–1848.

Shiramizu B, Gartner S, Williams A, et al. (2005). Circulating proviral HIV DNA and HIV-associated dementia. *AIDS* 19:45–52.

Shiramizu B, Ratto-Kim S, Sithinamsuwan P, et al. (2007). HIV DNA and dementia in treatment-naive HIV-1-infected individuals in Bangkok, Thailand. *Int J Med Sci* 4:13–18.

Silverstein PS, Kumar S, Kumar A (2014). HIV-1, HCV and alcohol in the CNS: potential interactions and effects on neuroinflammation. *Curr HIV Res* 12:282–292.

Simoni JM, Kurth AE, Pearson CR, Pantalone DW, Merrill JO, Frick PA (2006). Self-report measures of antiretroviral therapy adherence: A review with recommendations for HIV research and clinical management. *AIDS Behav* 10:227–245.

Smith DM, Zarate S, Shao H, et al. (2009). Pleocytosis is associated with disruption of HIV compartmentalization between blood and cerebral spinal fluid viral populations. *Virology* 385:204–208.

Smurzynski M, Wu K, Letendre S, et al. (2011). Effects of central nervous system antiretroviral penetration on cognitive functioning in the ALLRT cohort. *AIDS* 25:357–365.

Soontornniyomkij V, Moore DJ, Gouaux B, et al. (2012). Cerebral beta-amyloid deposition predicts HIV-associated neurocognitive disorders in APOE epsilon4 carriers. *AIDS* 26:2327–2335.

Spindler KR, Hsu TH (2012). Viral disruption of the blood-brain barrier. *Trends Microbiol* 20:282–290.

Staprans S, Marlowe N, Glidden D, et al. (1999). Time course of cerebrospinal fluid responses to antiretroviral therapy: evidence for variable compartmentalization of infection. *AIDS* 13:1051–1061.

Steinbrink F, Evers S, Buerke B, et al. (2013). Cognitive impairment in HIV infection is associated with MRI and CSF pattern of neurodegeneration. *Eur J Neurol* 20:420–428.

Steiner JP, Bachani M, Wolfson-Stofko B, et al. (2015). Interaction of paroxetine with mitochondrial proteins mediates neuroprotection. *Neurotherapeutics* 12:200–216.

Stout JC, Ellis RJ, Jernigan TL, et al. (1998). Progressive cerebral volume loss in human immunodeficiency virus infection: a longitudinal volumetric magnetic resonance imaging study. HIV Neurobehavioral Research Center Group. *Arch Neurol* 55:161–168.

Strain MC, Letendre S, Pillai SK, et al. (2005). Genetic composition of human immunodeficiency virus type 1 in cerebrospinal fluid and blood without treatment and during failing antiretroviral therapy. *J Virol* 79:1772–1788.

Strasser B, Becker K, Fuchs D, Gostner JM (2017). Kynurenine pathway metabolism and immune activation: Peripheral measurements in psychiatric and co-morbid conditions. *Neuropharmacology* 112(Pt B):286–296.

Stubbe-Drger B, Deppe M, Mohammadi S, et al. (2012). Early microstructural white matter changes in patients with HIV: a diffusion tensor imaging study. *BMC Neurol* 12:23.

Sturdevant CB, Joseph SB, Schnell G, Price RW, Swanstrom R, Spudich S (2015). Compartmentalized replication of R5 T cell-tropic HIV-1 in the central nervous system early in the course of infection. *PLoS Pathog* 11:e1004720.

Sullivan EV, Rosenbloom MJ, Rohlfing T, Kemper CA, Deresinski S, Pfefferbaum A (2011). Pontocerebellar contribution to postural instability and psychomotor slowing in HIV infection without dementia. *Brain Imaging Behav* 5:12–24.

Tang YW, Huong JT, Lloyd RM, Jr., Spearman P, Haas DW (2000). Comparison of human immunodeficiency virus type 1 RNA sequence heterogeneity in cerebrospinal fluid and plasma. *J Clin Microbiol* 38:4637–4639.

Tarasow E, Wiercinska-Drapalo A, Jaroszewicz J, et al. (2004). Antiretroviral therapy and its influence on the stage of brain damage in patients with HIV-1H MRS evaluation. *Med Sci Monit* 10(Suppl 3):101–106.

Tate DF, Sampat M, Harezlak J, et al. (2011). Regional areas and widths of the midsagittal corpus callosum among HIV-infected patients on stable antiretroviral therapies. *J Neurovirol* 17:368–379.

Temkin NR, Heaton RK, Grant I, Dikmen SS (1999). Detecting significant change in neuropsychological test performance: A comparison of four models. *J Int Neuropsychol Soc* 5(4):357–369.

Thames AD, Becker BW, Marcotte TD, et al. (2011). Depression, cognition, and self-appraisal of functional abilities in HIV: an examination of subjective appraisal versus objective performance. *Clin Neuropsychol* 25:224–243.

Thames AD, Foley JM, Wright MJ, et al. (2012). Basal ganglia structures differentially contribute to verbal fluency: evidence from human immunodeficiency virus (HIV)-infected adults. *Neuropsychologia* 50:390–395.

Thames AD, Kim MS, Becker BW, et al. (2011). Medication and finance management among HIV-infected adults: the impact of age and cognition. *J Clin Exp Neuropsychol* 33:200–209.

Thomas JB, Brier MR, Snyder AZ, Vaida FF, Ances BM (2013). Pathways to neurodegeneration: effects of HIV and aging on resting-state functional connectivity. *Neurology* 80:1186–1193.

Thompson KA, Churchill MJ, Gorry PR, et al. (2004). Astrocyte specific viral strains in HIV dementia. *Ann Neurol* 56:873–877.

Thompson PM, Dutton RA, Hayashi KM, et al. (2005). Thinning of the cerebral cortex visualized in HIV/AIDS reflects CD4+ T lymphocyte decline. *Proc Natl Acad Sci U S A* 102:15647–15652.

Toborek M, Lee YW, Flora G, et al. (2005). Mechanisms of the blood-brain barrier disruption in HIV-1 infection. *Cell Mol Neurobiol* 25:181–199.

Tozzi V, Balestra P, Galgani S, et al. (2003). Neurocognitive performance and quality of life in patients with HIV infection. *AIDS Res Hum Retroviruses* 19:643–652.

Tozzi V, Balestra P, Serraino D, et al. (2005). Neurocognitive impairment and survival in a cohort of HIV-infected patients treated with HAART. *AIDS Res Hum Retroviruses* 21:706–713.

Tracey I, Hamberg LM, Guimaraes AR, et al. (1998). Increased cerebral blood volume in HIV-positive patients detected by functional MRI. *Neurology* 50:1821–1826.

Turner MR, Modo M (2010). Advances in the application of MRI to amyotrophic lateral sclerosis. *Expert Opin Med Diagn* 4:483–496.

Valcour V, Chalermchai T, Sailasuta N, et al. (2012). Central nervous system viral invasion and inflammation during acute HIV infection. *J Infect Dis* 206:275–282.

Valcour V, Shikuma C, Shiramizu B, et al. (2004). Age, apolipoprotein E4, and the risk of HIV dementia: the Hawaii Aging with HIV Cohort. *J Neuroimmunol* 157:197–202.

Valcour VG, Shiramizu BT, Shikuma CM (2010). HIV DNA in circulating monocytes as a mechanism to dementia and other HIV complications. *J Leukoc Biol* 87:621–626.

Valcour VG, Shiramizu BT, Sithinamsuwan P, et al. (2009). HIV DNA and cognition in a Thai longitudinal HAART initiation cohort: the SEARCH 001 Cohort Study. *Neurology* 72:992–998.

Valcour V, Sithinamsuwan P, Letendre S, Ances B (2011). Pathogenesis of HIV in the central nervous system. *Curr HIV/AIDS Rep* 8:54–61.

van Gorp WG, Rabkin JG, Ferrando SJ, et al. (2007). Neuropsychiatric predictors of return to work in HIV/AIDS. *J Int Neuropsychol Soc* 13:80–89.

Vassallo M, Durant J, Biscay V, et al. (2014). Can high central nervous system penetrating antiretroviral regimens protect against the onset of HIV-associated neurocognitive disorders? *AIDS* 28:493–501.

Vescovini R, Biasini C, Telera AR, et al. (2010). Intense antiextracellular adaptive immune response to human cytomegalovirus in very old subjects with impaired health and cognitive and functional status. *J Immunol* 184:3242–249.

Vivithanaporn P, Maingat F, Lin LT, et al. (2010). Hepatitis C virus core protein induces neuroimmune activation and potentiates human immunodeficiency virus-1 neurotoxicity. *PLoS ONE* 5:e12856.

Wagner G, Miller LG (2004). Is the influence of social desirability on patients' self-reported adherence overrated? *J Acquir Immune Defic Syndr* 35:203–204.

Wang H, Kotler DP (2014). HIV enteropathy and aging: gastrointestinal immunity, mucosal epithelial barrier, and microbial translocation. *Curr Opin HIV AIDS* 9:309–316.

Weber E, Blackstone K, Woods SP (2013). Cognitive neurorehabilitation of HIV-associated neurocognitive disorders: a qualitative review and call to action. *Neuropsychol Rev* 23:81–98.

Weintraub S, Dikmen SS, Heaton RK, et al. (2013). Cognition assessment using the NIH Toolbox. Neurology 80:S54–S64.

Wilson MJ, Martin-Engel L, Vassileva J, Gonzalez R, Martin EM (2013). An investigation of the effects of antiretroviral central nervous system penetration effectiveness on procedural learning in HIV+ drug users. *J Clin Exp Neuropsychol* 35:915–925.

Witlox J, Eurelings LS, de Jonghe JF, Kalisvaart KJ, Eikelenboom P, van Gool WA (2010). Delirium in elderly patients and the risk of postdischarge mortality, institutionalization, and dementia: a meta-analysis. *JAMA* 304(4):443–451.

Woods SP, Childers M, Ellis RJ, et al. (2006). A battery approach for measuring neuropsychological change. *Arch Clin Neuropsychol* 21:83–89.

World Health Organization (1993). *The ICD-10 Classification of Mental and Behavioral Disorders: Diagnostic Criteria for Research*. Geneva: World Health Organization.

Wright EJ, Grund B, Robertson K, et al. (2010). Cardiovascular risk factors associated with lower baseline cognitive performance in HIV-positive persons. *Neurology* 75:864–873.

Wright PW, Heaps JM, Shimony JS, Thomas JB, Ances BM (2012). The effects of HIV and combination antiretroviral therapy on white matter integrity. *AIDS* 26:1501–1508.

Wycoco V, Shroff M, Sudhakar S, Lee W (2013). White matter anatomy: what the radiologist needs to know. *Neuroimag Clin North Am* 23:197–216.

Yiannoutsos CT, Nakas CT, Navia BA (2008). Assessing multiple-group diagnostic problems with multi-dimensional receiver operating characteristic surfaces: application to proton MR spectroscopy (MRS) in HIV-related neurological injury. *Neuroimage* 40:248–255.

Zhang D, Raichle ME (2010). Disease and the brain's dark energy. *Nat Rev Neurol* 6:15–28.

Zhu T, Zhong J, Hu R, et al. (2013). Patterns of white matter injury in HIV infection after partial immune reconstitution: a DTI tract-based spatial statistics study. *J Neurovirol* 19:10–23.

Zipursky AR, Gogolishvili D, Rueda S, et al. (2013). Evaluation of brief screening tools for neurocognitive impairment in HIV/AIDS: a systematic review of the literature. *AIDS* 27:2385–2401.

17.

TRAUMA AND POSTTRAUMATIC STRESS DISORDER—THE SPECIAL ROLE IN HIV TRANSMISSION

Antoine Douaihy, Melanie Grubisha, Maureen E. Lyon, and Mary Ann Cohen

INTRODUCTION

Despite the widespread availability of medical and antiretroviral therapy (ART), a surprisingly large number of individuals living with HIV fail to either enter or be retained in consistent treatment. Recent epidemiological data indicate that 50% of persons living with HIV in the United States are not engaged in regular medical care (Khanna and Madoori, 2013). While there are assuredly multiple confounding factors influencing both access to and retention in care, an emerging factor found to have considerable influence on both of these domains is the presence of a comorbid trauma history in persons with HIV.

Trauma is a broad term designating negative psychosocial events that generate psychological distress that, in some instances, may be long-lasting. When we speak of trauma and HIV as existing in a comorbid fashion, it is important to consider this comorbidity from three different perspectives: trauma that occurred prior to a diagnosis of HIV (*premorbid trauma*), trauma that occurred as a result of a diagnosis of HIV (*HIV-related trauma*), and trauma that occurred after a diagnosis of HIV (*postmorbid trauma*). Evidence shows that, irrespective of the context of the occurrence of the trauma, its mere existence has immense clinical implications for the prognosis, care, and treatment management of people with HIV and for transmission of HIV infection.

Epidemiological data indicate that people with HIV are more likely than the general population to have a premorbid trauma history (Khanna and Madoori, 2013). To further complicate matters, a premorbid trauma history exists in a feed-forward mechanism, as studies have shown that having the history of trauma places an individual at an increased likelihood of risky sexual behaviors (Weiss et al., 2013). Simply put, a history of trauma increases the likelihood of engaging in HIV-risk behaviors, ultimately offering at least a partial explanation for the high comorbidity seen between trauma and HIV infection. A systematic review of the literature found that the prevalence of comorbid HIV and posttraumatic stress disorder (PTSD) ranged from 5% to 74%, significantly above the 7–10% range observed in the general population (Sherr et al., 2011).

In addition to a much greater likelihood of having a premorbid trauma history, receiving the diagnosis of HIV in and of itself is often a traumatic event for individuals. In one cross-sectional study of HIV-related trauma, the incidence of HIV-associated PTSD was found to be 40% (95% CI: 30.2–50.6%) (Martin and Kagee, 2011). Thus since receiving the diagnosis of HIV can lead to lasting trauma-associated symptoms in almost half of persons with HIV individuals, it is crucial that clinicians practice empathy and compassion at the time the diagnosis is given and that treatment involve immediate integration of medical and psychiatric care.

Regarding postmorbid trauma and HIV, activities considered high risk for HIV are highly stigmatized in American society, including sexual encounters among men who have sex with men, injection drug use, and having multiple sex partners. Individuals who receive a diagnosis of HIV as a result of a stigmatized behavior will often experience less societal empathy and, as a result, are more likely to experience ongoing symptoms of trauma. In one study assessing men living with HIV/AIDS, the authors found that despite the incidence of trauma being equivocal between groups in men having sex with women and men having sex with men, the latter group was significantly more likely to experience ongoing symptoms of trauma and dissociation (Kamen et al., 2012).

For physicians and other healthcare practitioners involved in the treatment of persons living with HIV, it is vitally important to recognize the impact that comorbid trauma has on the prognosis of HIV-infected individuals and their treatment adherence. In terms of prognostic implications, trauma at any point before, during, or after diagnosis of HIV brings with it worse outcomes. In a study looking at lifetime trauma (premorbid), those with greater amounts of total lifetime trauma had more rapid progression to AIDS-related mortality (Leserman et al., 2007). Other studies have looked at the physiological impact of stress on HIV-infected individuals (postmorbid trauma); death of a partner was associated with a more rapid decline in CD4 count in HIV-infected gay men in a 3- to 4-year follow-up study (Kemeny and Dean, 1995), and in HIV-infected youths followed for 1 year, two or more major stressful life events were associated with a threefold increased risk of immune suppression (Howland et al., 2000).

The current standard of care falls short in identifying and adequately treating the psychiatric multimorbidities often seen in persons living with HIV. One study found that in a routine HIV care setting, 20% of patients screened positive for symptoms of depression and/or PTSD, but of those that screened positive only half were on an approved pharmacotherapy targeting these symptoms (Vranceanu et al., 2008). Furthermore, existence of PTSD symptomatology coincides with lower rates of medication adherence for persons with HIV (Boarts et al., 2009). Interventions designed to treat trauma-associated symptoms in persons with HIV can have a lasting impact on their overall morbidity and mortality, not only through prevention of stress-response immunosuppression but also through retention in care. Awareness of the comorbidity of trauma and HIV and the delicate interplay between the two can lead clinicians toward a path of more accurate and insightful screening, diagnosis, and management.

TRAUMA HISTORY

Taking a trauma history or even screening for trauma with patients has demonstrated value. For example, a neural network analysis of the records of 135,000 patients from Kaiser Permanente who were screened for adverse childhood experiences showed an overall reduction of 35% in doctor office visits in the year following the screening (Felitti, 2003). Such screening is even more important for persons with HIV, who are significantly more likely to have experienced sexualized and nonsexualized violence in their lives (Lyon et al., 1997; Radcliffe et al., 2007).

The prevalence of exposure to violence and associated PTSD and anxiety among persons living with HIV (Machtinger et al., 2012) has three important implications for public health:

(1) The experience of trauma and PTSD may prevent the uptake of HIV secondary prevention messages, particularly with respect to medication adherence (Cohen, et al., 2001; Ricart et al., 2002; Samuels et al., 2011).

(2) HPA-axis dysfunction caused by violence exposure may impair affect regulation, attention, and vigilance, causing difficulty with self-care and care for others (Neigh et al., 2009).

(3) PTSD and anxiety disorders are associated with violence exposure among persons with HIV: physical abuse with anxiety disorder ($p < .01$), sexual abuse with a diagnosis of PTSD ($p < .01$), exposure to family violence with diagnoses of both anxiety disorder and PTSD ($p < .05$), and witnessing injury or violent death with anxiety disorder ($p < .05$) and PTSD ($p < .05$) (Martinez et al., 2009).

Despite good intentions, recommendations to screen for and evaluate trauma and PTSD in persons with HIV (Theuninck et al., 2010) are often not followed because healthcare practitioners are uncomfortable with asking about the experience of trauma (Ferrell et al., 2014). To address this situation, a 6-hour curriculum for clinicians caring for persons with early childhood trauma, PTSD, and HIV has been developed (Tavakkoli et al., 2014). This curriculum is designed to provide clinicians with more confidence in their ability to elicit a trauma history, diagnose PTSD, and address trauma and its sequelae in persons with HIV, to improve adherence to medical care, antiretroviral medications, and risk reduction. The curriculum is available at: http://link.springer.com/article/10.1007/s40596-014-0186-8. One evidence-based intervention, Living in the Face of Trauma (LIFT), has been developed for coping with HIV and trauma. LIFT is a group intervention that focuses on improving the coping abilities of individuals—women of any sexual orientation and men who have sex with men—who have HIV and a history of childhood sexual abuse. LIFT promotes better health-protective decision-making with the goals of reducing the symptoms of traumatic stress, the risk of transmitting HIV, and the risk of substance abuse. It is listed in the Substance Abuse and Mental Health Services Administration (SAMHSA)'s National Registry of Evidence-based Programs and Practices (NREPP): http://legacy.nreppadmin.net/ViewIntervention.aspx?id=202.

CLINICAL PRESENTATIONS AND DIAGNOSIS OF PTSD

The high co-occurrence of HIV and PTSD and its treatment implications have been identified in publications aimed at educating and training medical professionals in the screening, assessment, care and, management of this complex comorbidity (Brezing et al., 2015; Tavakkoli et al., 2014). The DSM-5 diagnostic criteria for PTSD have been modified from DSM-IV-TR and have incorporated 20 symptoms divided across four symptom clusters of intrusive re-experiencing (5 symptoms), effortful avoidance (2 symptoms), negative alterations in cognitions and mood (7 symptoms), and increased arousal and reactivity (6 symptoms) (American Psychiatric Association, 2013). Additionally, trauma exposure itself is associated with a range of clinical manifestations often including, but not limited to, those identified in the current DSM-5 PTSD criteria. Various clinical presentations in trauma-related clusters of symptoms could affect levels of functioning and coping as well as likelihood of recovery and response to treatment (Shea et al., 2010). For instance, while avoidance symptoms may not be as easily manifested as re-experiencing or hyperarousal symptoms, they frequently contribute to a chronic course of symptoms. Individual differences in an individual's neurobiological makeup could also contribute to the variability observed in patient presentations following trauma exposure (Yehuda et al., 1993). More evidence points to the variability in responding to trauma, creating a diverse range of clinical profiles of the illness (Frewen and Lanius, 2006). Furthermore, patterns of clinical manifestations may be expected to show changes over the course of time following exposure to the traumatic event (Lanius et al., 2002).

In the context of HIV, the psychiatric manifestations of PTSD may independently influence progression and risk for medical disease such as HIV (Yiaslas et al., 2014). Untreated

PTSD in women with HIV predicts poorer HIV-related health outcomes and may negatively impact comorbid mental health outcomes (Brownley et al., 2015). In people with comorbid HIV and PTSD, avoidance may contribute to reduced ART adherence (Nel and Kagee, 2011, Samuels et al., 2011; Whetten et al., 2013). Emotional numbing and detachment can reduce the number of patient opportunities to benefit from social support, which represents a major factor in helping with recovery from PTSD (Andrews et al., 2003). Additionally, perceived HIV-related stigma may decrease individuals' perceived level of social support, which in turn may increase PTSD symptoms (Breet et al., 2014). Use of passive coping styles such as avoidance and denial has been associated with a negative impact on the immune system and accelerated HIV disease progression (Chida and Vedhara, 2009; Moskowitz et al., 2009). Moreover, persons with HIV who use emotion-focused or emotionally reactive coping have greater PTSD symptomatology.

The diagnosis of PTSD is further complicated by repression or retrograde amnesia for traumatic events and difficulties in forming trusting relationships and disclosing trauma if it is recalled (Samuels et al., 2011). In persons with HIV, there is a high incidence of early childhood and other trauma with consequent PTSD, substance use disorders, and other psychiatric disorders (Cohen et al., 2001; Samuels et al., 2011). PTSD is often difficult to diagnose because it is overshadowed by multimorbid associated psychiatric disorders as well as the defense mechanisms of repression and psychic numbing that come with severe and brutal trauma.

The difficulty with trust of authority figures such as physicians and other clinicians may pose an additional obstacle to diagnosis, treatment, and retention in care. Survivors of early childhood trauma find it hard to trust persons in authority when perpetrators of chronic brutal trauma are parents, siblings, or other relatives. These are the very people on whom basic trust is based and established. Physical, sexual, and emotional trauma and neglect impair the establishment of trust and are severely damaged by the serial betrayal that chronic brutal trauma represents.

Collective data indicate that in addition to increasing the risk of PTSD, the duration of HIV infection has been shown to intensify PTSD symptoms (Rzeszutek et al., 2015), suggesting that these conditions not only co-occur within the same individual but actively interact (Neigh et al., 2016).

TREATMENT APPROACHES

Despite the high comorbidity of PTSD in persons with HIV, there is relatively limited research on the efficacy and effectiveness of treating PTSD in this population. Not all studies have found antidepressant medication to be efficacious in treating persons with HIV and PTSD (Himmelhoch and Medoff, 2005). Prolonged exposure therapy is a well-supported treatment for PTSD and has demonstrated efficacy in a wide range of trauma populations. Prolonged exposure has been shown in one study to be effective in reducing symptoms of PTSD and symptoms of comorbid depression (Foa

et al., 2005). Psychodynamic psychotherapy (Cohen et al., 2001; Samuels et al., 2011) has been described as effective for persons with PTSD and HIV but was not based on systematic evidence from research studies. Researchers evaluating cognitive behavioral therapy (CBT) for persons with HIV (Simoni et al., 2013) as well as CBT applied in group therapy (Blanch et al., 2002; Sikkema et al., 2004, 2007; Spies et al., 2013) studied persons with HIV and psychiatric disorders but did not study PTSD and HIV. For more details on psychotherapeutic interventions, please see Chapter 37 of this textbook; for more details on pharmacological approaches please refer to Chapter 42.

Clinicians are encouraged to use a model of trauma-informed care in the treatment of people living with HIV that has been delineated in a review article on the syndemic illness of HIV and trauma (Brezing et al., 2015). This model of care incorporates creating a practice environment that promotes a sense of safety in all patients' interactions with staff members, including physicians and clinical and administrative staff; screening for and identifying trauma, its mediators, posttraumatic sequelae, poor adherence to treatment, and high-risk HIV behaviors; providing patient education about the relationship between trauma and HIV infection; becoming acquainted with resources in the area and making referrals when available for specialized trauma and mediator-specific treatments; and involving patients' social supports in treatment plans whenever possible.

IMPACT OF TRAUMA AND PTSD ON HIV, MEDICAL CARE, AND ADHERENCE TO ART

People with HIV who are diagnosed with PTSD and are symptomatic have functional impairment, increased pain, poorer health-related quality of life, and greater health care utilization (Leserman et al., 2005; O'Cleirigh et al., 2009; Smith et al., 2002). Additionally, in one study, HIV-positive men with worse posttraumatic stress symptoms had worse HIV-related medical symptoms (Yiaslas et al., 2014). Adherence to ART is negatively affected by PTSD and is associated with nonadherence to risk reduction and medical care (Boarts et al., 2006; Brief et al., 2014; Cohen et al., 2001; Sikkema et al., 2009). Multiple factors have been associated with poor adherence to ART, among them being a history of sexual abuse before puberty, an increased number of childhood traumas, and depression and PTSD (Meade et al., 2009; Sledjeski et al., 2005; Whetten et al., 2013). Recent trauma is associated with antiretroviral failure and high-risk behavior for HIV transmission among HIV-positive women and female-identified transgender individuals (Machtinger et al., 2012). A history of sexual trauma in people living with HIV/AIDS is associated with high rates of HIV treatment failure and increased morbidity and mortality despite good adherence to ART (Pence, 2009). Two hypotheses might explain this phenomenon. First, posttraumatic stress has a negative effect on the immune system in general and overall emotional and physical well-being (McEwen and Seeman, 1999). Second, sexual trauma can result in PTSD and dissociative manifestations leading to poor adherence to ART (Keuroghlian et al., 2011).

Violence may include perpetuation of early trauma in persons with PTSD who may unconsciously seek to master early childhood trauma in adult relationships. Synergistic epidemics, or syndemics, were first described by Singer (1994) and subsequently associated with nonadherence to HIV care and poorer outcomes (Boarts et al., 2006; Eisenberg and Blank, 2014). Substance use behaviors appear to play a significant role in mediating trauma's effect on HIV-risk behavior and adherence to treatment (Wilson et al., 2014). Syndemics of triple diagnoses include co-occurring substance use disorder, other psychiatric disorder, and HIV (Meyer et al., 2011). The association of nonadherence with the syndemic of substance abuse, violence, and AIDS (the SAVA syndemic) has been well documented (Eisenberg and Blank, 2014; Sullivan et al., 2015).

SPECIAL ISSUES THROUGH THE LIFE CYCLE IN ADOLESCENCE

Cumulative violence victimization and exposure to violence (witness to interpersonal violence) during childhood is associated with an increased risk for multiple health problems in adulthood (Felitti et al., 1998), including autoimmune diseases (Dube et al., 2009), cancer, and heart disease (Boynton-Jarrett et al., 2008; Krug et al., 2002). Longitudinal studies of violence exposure among adolescents (Brady and Donenberg, 2006; Singer et al., 1995) found cumulative and differential effects for exposure to violence, including poor health (Boynton-Jarrett, et al., 2008), anxiety, depression, somatic complaints, aggression, and school failure (Fowler et al., 2009; Margolin et al., 2010; Turner et al., 2010).

Many youth living with HIV/AIDS have experienced physical and sexual violence in their lives. A very high prevalence of violence exposure exists among urban adolescents living with HIV (Lyon et al., 2014). Of 166 urban adolescents who were receiving HIV care, sexual violence was experienced by 18% before age 13, and 15% during adolescence. Controlling for transmission mode (behavioral or perinatal), ever bartered sex and family disruptions were associated with more types of violence experienced. More than three-fourths were a witness to violence and approximately half reported being a victim of violence.

Research suggests that our current secondary prevention efforts, including those of biological psychiatry and drug treatment programs, are at odds with the reality that the causes of risk behaviors and poor self-care lie within us and the way we treat each other. This research supports psychoanalytic and psychodynamic perspectives that persistence of problematic behavior parallels in a graded, dose-response manner adverse life experiences during childhood and the failure of such protective factors as "good mothering" (Suomi, 2010) or "parental and school connectedness" (Rheingold et al., 2003).

The damage caused by exposure to violence is now well established. The Centers for Disease Control and Prevention (CDC) has active programs, including a guide, *Preventing Childhood Maltreatment*, available at www.cdc.gov/injury The CDC's mission is moving away from "silo" programmatic interventions to more large-scale, national-impact research and interventions. Consistent with this approach, social policy and public health strategies are essential to reducing exposure to violence and adverse childhood events, as well as increasing protective factors for children (Lösel and Farrington, 2012) at community, state, and national levels. Increasing parenting skills and the social capital of the communities in which we live may augment the benefit of interventions that target individuals alone. Theoretically, limiting adverse childhood events and violence exposure should increase the efficacy and effectiveness of risk reduction interventions, diminish risky behaviors, decrease HIV transmission, and promote wellness and health in persons with HIV, thereby improving the health of the community by increasing self-care and care for others.

CONCLUSION

Mounting data indicate the frequent co-occurrence of PTSD and HIV leading to significant challenges in the management of comorbidity in people living with HIV. As evidenced by research findings, these two disorders are more likely to actively interact than to simply coexist within the same individual. A history of trauma plays a role in acquiring and transmitting HIV as well as contributing to illness progression and poor quality of life, making the mélange of these two conditions, HIV infection and trauma, a syndemic illness. Prevention of childhood adverse events along with parenting education may prevent early childhood trauma and PTSD and decrease subsequent risk for HIV. Screening for recent and past trauma and PTSD should be considered a core component of HIV medical care for people living with HIV. Once diagnosed, psychiatric treatment for persons with PTSD and HIV can decrease suffering and lead to risk reduction, better health, and improved retention in and adherence to HIV medical care.

REFERENCES

American Psychiatric Association (2013). *Diagnostic and Statistical Manual of Mental Disorders,* 5th edition. Washington, DC: American Psychiatric Association.

Andrews B, Brewin CR, Rose S (2003). Gender, social support, and PTSD in victims of violent crime. *J Trauma Stress* 16:421–427.

Blanch J, Rousaud A, Hautzinger M, et al. (2002). Assessment of the efficacy of a cognitive-behavioural group psychotherapy programme for HIV-infected patients referred to a consultation-liaison psychiatry department. *Psychother Psychosom* 71:77–84.

Boarts JM, Buckley-Fischer BA, Armelie AP, Bogart LM, Delahanty DL (2009). The impact of HIV diagnosis-related vs. non-diagnosis related trauma on PTSD, depression, medication adherence, and HIV disease markers. *J Evid Based Soc Work* 6:4–16.

Boarts JM, Sledjeski EM, Bogart LM, Delahanty DL (2006). The differential impact of PTSD and depression on HIV disease markers and adherence to HAART in people living with HIV. *AIDS Behav* 20:253–262.

Boynton-Jarrett R, Ryan LM, Berkman LF, Wright RJ (2008). Cumulative violence exposure and self-rated health: longitudinal study of adolescents in the United States. *Pediatrics* 122:961–970.

Brady SS, Donenberg GR (2006). Mechanisms linking violence exposure to health risk behavior in adolescence: motivation to cope and sensation seeking. *J Am Acad Child Adolesc Psychiatry* 45:673–680.

Breet E, Kagee A, Seedat S (2014). HIV-related stigma and symptoms of post-traumatic stress disorder and depression in HIV-infected individuals: does social support play a mediating or moderating role? *AIDS Care* 26:947–951.

Brezing C, Ferrara M, Freudenreich O (2015). The syndemic illness of HIV and trauma: implications for a trauma-informed model of care. *Psychosomatics* 56:107–118.

Brief DJ, Bollinger AR, Vielhauer MJ, et al (2014). Understanding the interface of HIV, trauma, post-traumatic stress disorder, and substance use and its implications for health outcomes. *AIDS Care* 16 (Suppl 1):S97–S120.

Brownley JR, Fallot RD, Wolfson Berley R, Himelhoch SS (2015). Trauma history in African-American women living with HIV: effects on psychiatric symptom severity and religious coping. *AIDS Care* 27:964–971.

Chida Y, Vedhara K (2009). Adverse psychosocial factors predict poorer prognosis in HIV disease: a meta-analytic review of prospective investigations. *Brain Behav Immun* 23(4): 434–445.

Cohen MA, Alfonso C, Hoffman R, et al. (2001). The impact of PTSD on treatment adherence in persons with HIV infection. *Gen Hosp Psychiatry* 23:294–296.

Dube SR, Fairweather D, Pearson WS, Felitti VJ, Anda RF, Croft JB (2009). Cumulative childhood stress and autoimmune diseases in adults. *Psychosom Med* 71:243–250.

Eisenberg MM, Blank MB (2014). The syndemic of the triply diagnosed: HIV positives with mental illness and substance abuse or dependence. *Clin Res HIV/AIDS* 1:2006.

Felitti VJ (2003). Ursprunge des Suchtverhaltens—Evidenzen aus einer Studie zu belastenden Kindheitserfahrungen. *Praxis Kinderpsychol Kinderpsychiatrie* 52:547–559.

Felitti VJ, Anda RF, Nordenberg D, et al. (1998). Relationship of childhood abuse and household dysfunction to many of the leading causes of death in adults: the Adverse Childhood Experiences (ACE) study. *Am J Prev Med* 14:245–258.

Ferrell NJ, Melton B, Banu S, Coverdale J, Valdez MR (2014). The development and evaluation of a trauma curriculum for psychiatry residents. *Acad Psychiatry* 38(5):611–614.

Foa EB, Hembree EA, Cahill SP, et al. (2005). Randomized trial of prolonged exposure for posttraumatic stress disorder with and without cognitive restructuring: outcome at academic and community clinics. *J Consult Clin Psychol* 73(5):953–964.

Fowler PJ, Tompsett CJ, Braaciszewski JM, Jacques-Tiura J, Baltes BB (2009). Community violence: a meta-analysis on the effect of exposure and mental health outcomes of children and adolescents. *Dev Psychopathol* 21:227–259.

Frewen PA, Lanius RA (2006). Toward a psychobiology of posttraumatic self-dysregulation: reexperiencing, hyperarousal, dissociation, and emotional numbing. *Ann N Y Acad Sci* 107:110–124.

Himelhoch S, Medoff DR (2005). Efficacy of antidepressant medication among HIV-positive individuals with depression: a systematic review and meta-analysis. *AIDS Patient Care STDS* 19(12):813–822.

Howland LC, Gortmaker SL, Mofenson LM, et al. (2000). Effects of negative life events on immune suppression in children and youth infected with human immunodeficiency virus type 1. *Pediatrics* 106:540–546.

Kamen C, Flores S, Taniguchi S, Khaylis A, Lee S, Koopman C, Gore-Felton C (2012). Sexual minority status and trauma symptom severity in men living with HIV/AIDS. *J Behav Med* 35:38–46.

Kemeny ME, Dean L (1995). Effects of AIDS-related bereavement on HIV progression among New York City gay men. *AIDS Educ Prev* 7(5 Suppl):36–47.

Keuroghlian AS, Kamen CS, Neri E, Lee S, Liu R, Gore- Felton C (2011). Trauma, dissociation, and antiretroviral adherence among persons living with HIV/AIDS. *J Psychiatr Res* 45(7):942–948.

Khanna N, Madoori S (2013). Untangling the intersection of HIV & trauma: why it matters and what we can do. GMHC Treatment Issues.

Krug EG, Mercy JA, Dahlberg LL, Zwi AB (2002). The world report on violence and health. *Lancet* 360:1083–1088.

Lanius RA, Williamson PC, Boksman K, et al. (2002). Brain activation during script-driven imagery induced dissociative responses in PTSD: a functional magnetic resonance imaging investigation. *Biol Psychiatry* 52:305–311.

Leserman J, Pence BW, Whetten K, Mugavero MJ, Thielman NM, Swartz MS, Stangl D (2007). Relation of lifetime trauma and depressive symptoms to mortality in HIV. *Am J Psychiatry* 164:1707–1713.

Leserman J, Whetten K, Lowe K, Stangl D, Swartz MS, Thielman NM (2005). How trauma, recent stressful events, and PTSD affect functional health status and health utilization in HIV-infected patients in the south. *Psychosom Med* 67(3):500–507.

Lösel F, Farrington DP (2012). Direct protective and buffering protective factors in the development of youth violence. *Am J Prev Med* 43(2S1):S8–S23.

Lyon ME, Koenig LJ, Pals SL, Abramowitz S, Chandwani S, Sill A (2014). Prevalence and correlates of violence exposure among HIV-infected adolescents. *J Assoc Nurses AIDS Care* 25(1S):S5–S14.

Lyon ME, Silber, D'Angelo L (1997). Difficult life circumstances in HIV infected adolescents: cause or effect? *AIDS Patient Care STDS* 11(1):29–33.

Machtinger E, Wilson T, Haberer J, Weiss D (2012). Psychological trauma and PTSD in HIV-positive women: a meta-analysis. *AIDS Behav* 16:2091–2100.

Margolin G, Vickerman KA, Oliver PH, Gordis EB (2010). Violence exposure in multiple interpersonal domains: cumulative and differential effects. *J Adolesc Health* 47:198–205.

Martin L, Kagee A (2011). Lifetime and HIV-related PTSD among persons recently diagnoses with HIV. *AIDS Behav* 15:125–131.

Martinez J, Hosek SG, Carleton RA (2009). Screening and assessing violence and mental health disorders in a cohort of inner city HIV-positive youth between 1998 and 2006. *AIDS Patient Care STDS* 23(6):469–475.

McEwen BS, Seeman T (1999). Protective and damaging effects of mediators of stress. Elaborating and testing the concepts of allostasis and allostatic load. *Ann N Y Acad Sci* 896:30–47.

Meade CS, Kershaw TS, Hansen NB, Sikkema KJ (2009). Long-term correlates of childhood abuse among adults with severe mental illness: adult victimization, substance abuse, and HIV sexual risk behavior. *AIDS Behav* 13(2):207–216.

Meyer JP, Springer SA, Altice FL (2011). Substance abuse, violence, and HIV in women: a literature review of the syndemic. *J Womens Health* 20:991–1006.

Moskowitz JT, Hult JR, Bussolari C, Scree M (2009). What works in coping with HIV? A meta-analysis with implications for coping with serious illness. *Psychol Bull* 135(1):121–141.

Neigh GN, Gillespie CF, Nemeroff CB (2009). The neurobiological toll of child abuse and neglect. *Trauma Violence Abuse* 10:389–410.

Neigh GN, Rhodes ST, Valdez A, et al. (2016). PTSD co-morbid with HIV. Separate but equal, or two parts of a whole? *Neurobiol Dis* 92(B):116–123.

Nel A, Kage A (2011). Common mental health problems and antiretroviral therapy adherence. *AIDS Care* 23:1360–1365.

O'Cleirigh C, Skeer M, Mayer KH, Safren SA (2009). Functional impairment and healthcare utilization among HIV-infected men who have sex with men: the relationship with depression and post-traumatic stress. *J Behav Med* 32(5):466–477.

Pence BW (2009). The impact of mental health and traumatic life experiences on antiretroviral treatment outcomes for people living with HIV/AIDS. *J Antimicrob Chemother* 63(4):636–640.

Radcliffe J, Fleisher CL, Hawkins LA, Tanney M, Kassam-Adams N, Ambrose C, Rudy BJ (2007). Posttraumatic stress and trauma history in adolescents and young adults with HIV. *AIDS Patient Care STDS* 21(7):501–508.

Rheingold AA, Acierno R, Resnick HS (2003). Trauma, posttraumatic stress disorder, and health risk behaviors. In PP Schnurr PP, BL Green (eds.), *Trauma and Health: Physical Health Consequences of Exposure to Extreme Stress* (pp. 217–243). Washington, DC: American Psychological Association.

Ricart F, Cohen MA, Alfonso CA, Hoffman RG, Quinones N, Cohen A, Indyk D (2002). Understanding the psychodynamics of non-adherence to medical treatment in persons with HIV infection. *Gen Hosp Psychiatry* 24:176–180.

Rzeszutek M, Oniszczenko W, Zebrowska M, Firlag-Burkacka E (2015). HIV infection duration, social support and the level of trauma symptoms in a sample of HIV-positive Polish individuals. *AIDS Care* 27:363–369.

Samuels E, Khalife S, Alfonso C, et al. (2011). Early childhood trauma, posttraumatic stress disorder, and non-adherence in persons with AIDS: a psychodynamic perspective. *J Am Acad Psychoanal Dyn Psychiatry* 39:633–650.

Shea MT, Vujanovic AA, Mansfield AK, Sevin E, Liu F (2010). Posttraumatic stress disorder symptoms and functional impairment among OEF and OIF National Guard and Reserve veterans. *J Trauma Stress* 23:100–107.

Sherr L, Nagra N, Kulubya G, Catalan J, Clucas C, Harding R (2011). HIV infection associated post-traumatic stress disorder and post-traumatic growth—a systematic review. *Psychol Health Med* 16(5):612–629.

Sikkema KJ, Hansen NB, Kochman A, Tarakeshwar N, Neufeld S, Meade CS, Fox AM (2007). Outcomes from a group intervention for coping with HIV/AIDS and childhood sexual abuse: reductions in traumatic stress. *AIDS Behav* 11(1):49–60.

Sikkema KJ, Hansen NB, Meade CS, Kochman A, Fox AM (2009). Psychosocial predictors of sexual HIV transmission risk behavior among HIV-positive adults with a sexual abuse history in childhood. *Arch Sex Behav* 38(1):121–134.

Sikkema KJ, Hansen NB, Tarakeshwar N, Kochman A, Tate DC, Lee RS (2004). The clinical significance of change in trauma-related symptoms following a pilot group intervention for coping with HIV-AIDS and childhood sexual trauma. *AIDS Behav* 8(3):277–291.

Simoni JM, Wiebe JS, Sauceda JA, et al. (2013). A preliminary RCT of CBT-AD for adherence and depression among HIV-positive Latinos on the U.S.–Mexico border: the Nuevo Día Study. *AIDS Behav* 17(8):2816–2829.

Singer M (1994). AIDS and the health crisis of the U.S. urban poor: the perspective of critical medical anthropology. *Soc Sci Med* 39:931–948.

Singer MI, Anglin TM, Song LY, Lunghofer L (1995). Adolescents' exposure to violence and associated symptoms of psychological trauma. *JAMA* 273:477–482.

Sledjeski EM, Delahanty DL, Bogart LM (2005). Incidence and impact of posttraumatic stress disorder and comorbid depression on adherence to HAART and CD4+ counts in people living with HIV. *AIDS Patient Care STDS* 19:728–736.

Smith MY, Egert J, Winkel G, Jacobson J (2002). The impact of PTSD on pain experience in persons with HIV/AIDS. *Pain* 98(1–2):9–17.

Spies G, Asmal L, Seedat S (2013). Cognitive-behavioural interventions for mood and anxiety disorders in HIV: a systematic review. *J Affect Disord* 150(2):171–180.

Sullivan KA, Messer LC, Byrd-Quinlivan E (2015). Substance abuse, violence, and HIV/AIDS (SAVA) syndemic effects on viral suppression among HIV-positive women of color. *AIDS Patient Care STDS* 29(Suppl 1):S42–S48.

Suomi S (2010). Risk, resilience, and gene-environment interplay in primates. Invited address: plenary. Annual Convention of the American Psychological Association, San Diego, CA, August 20, 2010.

Tavakkoli M, Cohen MA, Alfonso CA, Batista SM, Tiamson-Kassab ML, Meyer P (2014). Caring for persons with early childhood trauma, PTSD, and HIV: a curriculum for clinicians. *Acad Psychiatry* 38(6):696–700.

Theuninck AC, Lake N, Gibson S (2010). HIV-related posttraumatic stress disorder: investigating the traumatic events. *AIDS Patient Care STDS* 24(8):485–491.

Turner HA, Finkelhor D, Ormrod R (2010). Poly-victimization in a national sample of children and youth. *Am J Prevent Med* 38(3):323–330.

Vranceanu AM, Safren SA, Lu ML, Coady WM, Skolnik PR, Rogers WH, Wilson IB (2008). The relationship of post-traumatic stress disorder and depression to antiretroviral medication adherence in persons with HIV. *AIDS Patient Care STDS* 22(4):313–321.

Weiss NH, Tull MT, Borne ME, Gratz KL (2013). Posttraumatic stress disorder symptom severity and HIV-risk behaviors among substance-dependent inpatients. *AIDS Care* 25(10):1219–1226.

Whetten K, Shirey K, Pence BW, et al. (2013). Trauma history and depression predict incomplete adherence to antiretroviral therapies in a low income country. *PLoS ONE* 8(10):e74771.

Wilson SM, Sikkema KJ, Ramby KW (2014). Gender moderates the influence of psychosocial factors and drug use on HAART adherence in the context of HIV and childhood sexual abuse. *AIDS Care* 26(8):959–967.

Yehuda R, Southwick SM, Krystal JH, Bremner D (1993). Enhanced suppression of cortisol following dexamethasone administration in posttraumatic stress disorder. *Am J Psychiatry* 150:83–86.

Yiaslas TA, Kamen C, Arteaga A, Lee S, Briscoe-Smith A, Koopman C, Gore-Felton C (2014). The relationship between sexual trauma, peritraumatic dissociation, posttraumatic stress disorder, and HIV-related health in HIV-positive men. *J Trauma Dissoc* 15:420–435.

18.

ANXIETY DISORDERS

Antoine Douaihy, Meredith Spada, Nicole Bates, Julia Macedo, and Jack M. Gorman

HIV clinicians are increasingly confronted with complex co-occurring medical and psychiatric disorders among their patients. Depressive and anxiety disorders are among the most commonly diagnosed in persons with HIV and can complicate the overall management of HIV illness. Anxiety may be experienced as a symptom, as a manifestation of an anxiety disorder, as a consequence of HIV-associated or other illness, or as a result of one of its treatments. Anxiety is considerably magnified by the experience of HIV-associated stigma and discrimination. It can occur at any stage, from the realization of being at risk, to the anxiety about a possible symptom, to the time of HIV testing and the experience of HIV-associated stigma and discrimination, diagnosis, disclosure, illness progression, late- and end-stage illness, and dying. This chapter explores the complexities of anxiety as it relates to HIV and AIDS and discusses the prevalence, diagnosis, and assessment of anxiety disorders; the impact of anxiety on medical management of HIV, including adherence to an antiretroviral regimen; psychotherapeutic and pharmacological interventions; and coexisting medical and psychiatric disorders. The included case study illustrates the challenges of evaluating and managing anxiety in the context of HIV illness.

ANXIETY THROUGH THE COURSE OF HIV AND AIDS

For persons with increased access to competent medical care and use of antiretroviral therapy (ART), HIV infection has become a manageable chronic illness. HIV physicians are changing their perspective on how to approach treatment and are focusing on more integrated care of medical and psychiatric multimorbidities. Specific guidelines for the primary care monitoring and screening of patients with HIV have been established. These multifocal recommendations emphasize that HIV care sites should utilize an interdisciplinary system of care; screen all patients for substance use and other psychiatric disorders; and provide adequate treatment, referral, and coordination of care by clinicians involved in their care (Aberg et al., 2014). These recommendations underscore the importance of integrating medical and psychiatric care. Helping the patient cope with the various manifestations of anxiety that may be experienced is an important aspect of coordinated care.

Anxiety can be associated with HIV illness from early on, at the time of testing and diagnosis, possibly causing impairment at different stages of illness progression. From adjustment and adaptation to the diagnosis and initiation of treatment at the early stages of illness to the existential anxiety of facing death with the progression of the illness, anxiety manifestations can change throughout the course of the illness.

Some degree of anxiety may be a normal component of the grief response that can be triggered by diagnosis of HIV; what differentiates this from pathological anxiety is the degree of impairment. In order for the anxiety to be pathological in nature, it should meet the DSM-5 criteria: (1) marked distress that is out of proportion to the severity or intensity of the stressor, even when external context and cultural factors that might influence symptom severity and presentation are taken into account, and/or (2) significant impairment in social, occupational, or other areas of functioning (American Psychiatric Association, 2013). Individuals with baseline anxiety disorders are more likely to experience complicated grief, including pathological anxiety, than are individuals with no anxiety disorders (Marques et al., 2013). Marques and colleagues (2013) compared bereaved adults with a primary anxiety disorder to bereaved healthy individuals with no psychiatric disorder and found that the former group had significantly higher rates of complicated grief symptoms. As such, preexisting anxiety can compound grief and its attendant impairment and reduced quality of life. What mediates the severity of anxiety is multifactorial and related to social support and experience with prior stressors and illnesses, as well as coping capacity, defensive structure, adaptive capacity, and resilience. Though all people are vulnerable to changes in social structure, individuals with chronic and incurable illness are even more so. As HIV illness progresses and medical limitations compound the financial, occupational, and emotional complications of the illness, changes in social structure can compromise the way in which the person copes with the anxiety. Certainly, psychosocial well-being is integral to the management of anxiety. There is a negative correlation between functional social supports as well as psychological capital and anxiety symptoms in persons with HIV who are working full-time (Liu et al., 2013). The experience and burden of anxiety and the supports against impairment from anxiety frequently change throughout the course of illness. Therefore, the approach to addressing anxiety must be flexible over time in order to meet the changing social context.

PREVALENCE AND RISK FACTORS

Studies continue to show that people living with HIV infection have high rates of anxiety symptoms and anxiety disorders. Morrison and colleagues (2002) compared rates of psychiatric illness in 93 HIV-positive women to those of 62 HIV-negative women using the Structured Clinical Interview for DSM-IV (SCID) and the Hamilton Anxiety Rating Scale (HAMA). They found that although there was no significant difference in the rate of anxiety disorders between the two groups, HIV-positive women had higher anxiety symptom scores on the HAMA. In a study of the prevalence of mood, anxiety, and substance use disorders among HIV-positive individuals, Pence et al. (2006) assessed 1,125 patients with HIV at an academic medical center in North Carolina using the Substance Abuse–Mental Illness Symptoms Screener (SAMISS) and the SCID. They found that 20.3% of the subjects had any anxiety disorder, 6.1% had posttraumatic stress disorder (PTSD), and 5.4% had panic disorder. Although there was no comparison sample of HIV-negative individuals, the authors note that these rates are higher than seen in previous studies of the general U.S. population.

In another U.S. study of 635 individuals cared for in an urban HIV clinic, most of whom were African American and male, a moderate level and a high level of anxiety symptoms were reported in 12% and 11% of the patients, respectively (Shacham et al., 2012). Among women with HIV infection of reproductive age, 37% scored high on the anxiety subscale of the Hospital Anxiety and Depression Scale (HADS-A) (Ivanova et al., 2012).

Studies throughout the world consistently show these high rates of anxiety among persons with HIV. In Guiana (South America) the incidence rate of first observed generalized anxiety was 1.27 per 100 person-years (Nacher et al., 2010). A study in Tanzania of 220 HIV-positive outpatients using a standardized questionnaire found that 15.5% had depression or mixed anxiety and depression and 4.5% had other anxiety disorders (Marwick and Kaaya, 2010). In an HIV clinic near Cape Town, South Africa 5% of the patients had PTSD (Myer et al., 2008). The same group assessed 65 patients with recently diagnosed HIV infection at baseline and 6 months later (Olley et al., 2006). PTSD was present in 14.8% at baseline and 20% at 6-month follow-up. High levels of anxiety were found among persons with HIV living in China (Jin et al., 2010).

A number of factors appear to increase the risk of anxiety and of anxiety disorders among people living with HIV/AIDS. These include having a recent HIV diagnosis; being female (Nacher et al., 2010), of younger age, or unemployed; having less education (Shacham et al., 2012), a longer duration of infection, or baseline disability in work, social, or family functioning (Olley et al., 2006); having increased anxiety sensitivity (Gonzalez, Zvolensky, et al., 2012); experiencing HIV-related stigma or reproductive health-related worries; and using antiretroviral regimens (Ivanova et al., 2012). Similarly, among a group of 300 people with HIV/AIDS living in Lagos, Nigeria, risk factors for an anxiety disorder, which was present in 21.7% (65) of the patients, were lack of family support, being unmarried, and being unemployed (Olagunju et al., 2012). By contrast, factors that seem to confer resiliency against anxiety symptoms among persons with HIV include being in a romantic or sexual relationship, older age, undetectable viral load (Ivanova et al., 2012), and being asymptomatic (Parhami et al., 2013).

PSYCHOIMMUNOLOGY OF ANXIETY IN HIV INFECTION

The role of neuroendocrine pathways in anxiety disorders and the effects of anxiety on immunological response are areas of active research. Though the exact relationship between anxiety and immune function and psychological distress in persons with HIV and AIDS is likely multifactorial and not clearly understood, a correlation between them has been identified in some studies. We know that anxiety, stress, and distress activate the hypothalamic–pituitary–adrenal (HPA) axis, leading to increased production of cortisol, "the stress hormone" (Leserman, 2003; McEwen, 1998). In a meta-analysis of studies from 1990 to July 2007, chronic depression, stressful events, and trauma, all of which increase the likelihood for anxiety symptoms, were positively correlated with HIV disease progression in terms of immunological markers, including diminished CD4 count, as well as with viral load and greater risk for clinical decline and mortality (Leserman, 2008). It is speculated that the impact of cortisol levels on immunity is related to the relationship between HIV illness and immune system markers. Notably, treating anxiety psychopharmacologically is correlated with a decrease in the circulating cortisol levels in other populations, such as community-dwelling elderly depressed patients (Lenze et al., 2011). Nonpharmacological anxiety-targeted therapeutic modalities are noted to have additional effect on immunological markers. For example, in a small randomized controlled trial with 48 HIV-1-infected adults that tested the efficacy of an 8-week mindfulness-based stress reduction (MBSR) meditation program compared to a 1-day control stress reduction seminar on CD4+ T-lymphocyte counts, participants in the control group showed declines in CD4+ T-lymphocyte counts, whereas counts among participants in the MBSR group were unchanged from baseline to post-intervention. In addition, this effect was independent of antiretroviral medication use. The results of this trial indicate that mindfulness meditation can buffer CD4+ T-lymphocyte decline by decreasing the stress response (Creswell et al., 2009). Other studies indicate similar impact of nonpharmacological approaches to the treatment of anxiety such as stress management intervention on the course of HIV progression and immune function (McCain et al., 2008; O'Cleirigh and Safren, 2008).

One challenge in studying the impact of anxiety on HPA axis and HIV immunology is identifying the effects that are directly attributed to the HIV infection itself. For further details on the interaction between HIV, psychiatric illness, and the immune system, refer to Chapter 21 in this textbook.

ASSESSMENT AND DIAGNOSIS

As a result of improved care, persons with HIV who are virally suppressed are living longer, and rather than developing solely HIV-related complications they are developing non-HIV-related illnesses, such as cardiac disease, hypertension, diabetes mellitus, osteoarthritis, cancer, pulmonary hypertension, and chronic obstructive pulmonary disease (Aberg et al., 2014). Symptoms of fatigue, insomnia, and anxiety may occur in the absence of a specific medical or psychiatric pathology. Fatigue is a particularly disabling symptom that is not necessarily associated with advanced HIV disease or the use ART but rather with psychological distress (Henderson et al., 2005). Anxiety related to symptoms like fatigue and to life stresses can be devastating. Anxiety is also generated by the myriad of complications in individuals treated successfully with ART and in patients with advanced illness.

One study has documented the clinical relevance of mindful attention and awareness and disengagement to coping with HIV/AIDS-related stigma and symptoms of anxiety (Gonzalez et al., 2009). HIV/AIDS can lead to a wide range of somatic-oriented sensations, ranging from muscle aches to tingling to nausea, all of which can evoke significant anxiety and worry and thus represent frequent and clinically important targets for management (O'Cleirigh and Safren, 2008). One relevant theoretical cognitive factor that may be helpful in better understanding anxiety in persons with HIV is the concept of anxiety sensitivity. *Anxiety sensitivity* is defined as the extent to which individuals believe anxiety and anxiety-related sensations have negative consequences (McNally, 2002; Reiss & McNally, 1985). Zinbarg and collleagues (2001) describe the three facets of anxiety sensitivity: mental concerns (mental incapacitation), physical concerns (physical symptoms of anxiety), and social concerns (social consequences of experiencing anxiety arousal). Gonzales and colleagues (2010) found that anxiety sensitivity–physical concerns were significantly associated with somatization symptoms. Thus, reducing anxiety sensitivity through psychosocial or pharmacological intervention (Smits et al., 2008) may decrease the risk for anxiety and somatization symptoms and thereby enhance quality of life. One study has documented the clinical relevance of mindful attention and awareness and disengagement to coping with HIV/AIDS-related stigma and symptoms of anxiety (Gonzalez et al., 2009).

In reviewing the specific anxiety disorders commonly seen in persons with HIV and AIDS, it is important to recognize that these are often superimposed on the anxiety that is experienced in the general population and commonly in the population with chronic symptomatic medical illness (Wells et al., 1988, 1989). Given that anxiety disorders in persons with HIV can masquerade as physical illness (Pollack et al., 2004), when evaluating a patient for diagnosis and treatment of an anxiety disorder, it is important to be cognizant of the potential for physical medical etiology of such pathological behavior. Upon initial evaluation of an HIV-positive individual, a thorough medical history, physical exam, and appropriate basic screening tests (EKG, CBC, thyroid function test, blood chemistry, urinalysis, RPR/VDRL, urine toxicology) can aid in the differential diagnosis and rule out any contributing medical illness (Basu et al., 2005). Rarely, endocrine dysfunction, cardiovascular illness, or drug intoxication or withdrawal may be mistaken for an anxiety disorder (Pollack et al., 2004). In addition to neuropsychiatric disease secondary to HIV infection, persons with anxiety due to an organic etiology often suffer from alcohol, benzodiazepine, and stimulant dependence, which may result in confusion regarding symptomatology and affect treatment efficacy (Batki, 1990). The possibility of this scenario makes it especially important to investigate substance use and medication history, including both prescribed and over-the-counter or herbal medications. For further details on the psychiatric manifestations and complications of co-occurring medical illnesses in persons with HIV, refer to the section on HIV Psychiatry and Multimorbid Medical Conditions, Chapters 43 to 47, of this textbook.

ANXIETY SYMPTOMS AND GENERALIZED ANXIETY DISORDER

Several studies report elevated levels of anxiety symptoms among persons with HIV (Kagee and Martin, 2010; Peng et al., 2010). Studies show that in persons with HIV, anxiety rates vary from 27.3% to 70.3% and from 32.0% to 45.5% for depression (Cohen et al., 2002; Cove and Petrak, 2004; Lambert et al., 2005). Campos et al. (2010) found a higher prevalence of symptoms of anxiety than of depression, a finding consistent with other studies that used the HADS to assess psychiatric symptoms among HIV-infected patients (Cohen et al., 2002; Cove and Petrak, 2004; Lambert et al., 2005). Persons suffering from chronic illness and comorbid anxiety disorders have been shown to exhibit greater severity in several domains than those without anxiety disorders or those with comorbid depressive disorders, especially with respect to physical function, emotional health problems, social function, pain, fatigue or energy, emotional well-being, and health perception (Sherbourne et al., 1996). Anxiety and depression are prevalent in HIV-infected populations regardless of symptom status or ART (Lambert et al., 2005; Sewell et al., 2000). However, the advent of ART considerably reduced anxiety about dying that was initially related to HIV/AIDS diagnostic status (Miller et al., 2012).

Women with HIV have been shown to have significantly higher anxiety symptom scores than HIV-negative women (Morrison et al., 2002). In contrast, there were no significant differences in the prevalence of anxiety in gay men with HIV and in AIDS and HIV-negative gay men (Sewell et al., 2000). However, gay men who were HIV-negative or HIV-positive (with or without progression to AIDS) reported more anxiety symptoms and stress in comparison to the general population (Sewell et al., 2000). Anxiety can also predate HIV infection, showing that the relationship between HIV and anxiety is complex (Whetten et al., 2008). For instance, Reyes and colleagues (2007) reported an association between anxiety and HIV risk behavior among HIV-negative Hispanic injection drug users. It has also been suggested that some persons with HIV may use methamphetamine to reduce anxiety related to their HIV symptoms (Tsao et al., 2004). Moreover, Parsons et al.

(2003) reported that HIV-positive men who have sex with men who had unprotected receptive anal sex with HIV-negative or serostatus-unknown partners had lower levels of anxiety compared to their counterparts who had unprotected insertive anal sex or no unprotected anal intercourse, suggesting an inverse relationship between anxiety and sexual risk. Presumably, a lack of appropriate anxiety about health outcomes is involved in the propensity for high-risk behavior.

The Generalized Anxiety Disorder-7 (GAD-7) can be used to measure the severity of anxiety symptoms. This scale has good internal and test-retest reliability as well as construct, criterion, and factorial validity for the diagnosis of generalized anxiety disorder (Kroenke et al., 2007; Spitzer et al., 2006). The Hospital Anxiety and Depression Scale (HADS) (Berger, 2008; Zigmond and Snaith, 1983) and the Structured Interview Guide for the Hamilton Depression and Anxiety scales (SIGH-AD) (Sikkema et al., 2004) are other scales used to screen for anxiety and depressive manifestations.

PANIC DISORDER

There are few reports or studies regarding panic disorder in persons with HIV. Panic disorder has a strong association with pain in HIV-positive individuals (Tsao et al., 2004). Tsao and colleagues (2004) reported that increasing physical pain in HIV-infected patients was strongly associated with panic disorder but not with either PTSD or major depression. Similarly, panic disorder is associated with emotional pain. Summers and colleagues (1995) conducted a study between 1989 and 1993, when ART was just being developed, and found that there was an increased incidence of major depression and panic disorder among people with unresolved grief. Vitiello et al. (2003) showed that over 12% of patients with HIV meet criteria for panic disorder, which is two to three times the general population rate. More recently, in a sample of 503 HIV-positive gay and bisexual men receiving primary care in Boston, Massachusetts, 10% screened positive for panic disorder (O'Cleirigh et al., 2013).

OBSESSIVE-COMPULSIVE DISORDER

Although obsessive-compulsive disorder (OCD) is not considered an anxiety disorder in DSM-5 as it was in former DSM versions, we have included it here in order to be consistent with previous editions of the *Comprehensive Textbook of AIDS Psychiatry*. OCD is known to occur in conjunction with HIV infection (Bruce and Stevens, 1992; Kraus and Nicholson, 1996; Schechter et al., 1991). Anxiety could also be a result of HIV pharmacotherapy, as underscored by Hauptman, who reported a case of possible new-onset obsessive-compulsive symptoms correlated with emtricitabine/tenofovir (HIV prophylaxis)–induced anxiety and OCD in a 38-year-old unmarried Caucasian female with no prior psychiatric history (Hauptman and Carchedi, 2013). In a sample of 245 HIV-positive methamphetamine-using men who have sex with men in San Diego, CA, Semple and

colleagues (2010) found that clinical levels of OCD were associated with more frequent use of methamphetamine, more depressive symptoms, and more risky sexual behaviors when "high" on methamphetamine but fewer sexual acts over a 2-month period. This profile suggests that efforts to treat methamphetamine use and promote safer sex practices in this target population should include efforts to mitigate and treat severe OCD symptoms.

SPECIFIC PHOBIAS

There are several reports of AIDS-specific phobias (Brotman and Forstein, 1988; Freed, 1983; Jacob et al., 1987). Rapaport and Braff (1985) described a patient with paranoid schizophrenia who experienced delusions about AIDS as a component of his "homosexual panic," which consisted of persecutory delusions that others believed he was gay.

There are also several case reports describing patients with an irrational fear or belief that they have AIDS despite medical evidence that they are HIV negative (Brotman and Forstein, 1988; Jacob et al., 1987; Kausch, 2004; Miller et al., 1986). On the basis of this limited quantity of case reports, it appears that illness-related phobias have some qualities in common with OCD (Logsdail et al., 1991), such as pervasive preoccupations, ritualistic behaviors, and an unfounded fear that is resistant to reassurance. The morbidity of this disorder is tremendous. Vuorio et al. (1990) reported that three of eight patients with an unfounded fear of AIDS committed suicide and one of them had overt suicidal tendencies, indicating that an unfounded fear of AIDS may be a sign of psychiatric disturbance with increased suicidal risk. In the early 1980s, it was particularly difficult to reassure such patients, given that a test to detect HIV was not available until several years into the epidemic. Miller and colleagues (1985) described one such patient, later diagnosed with chronic anxiety, who presented with various ailments that he attributed to AIDS but that were differentiated from symptomatic HIV disease by a knowledgeable clinician.

More recently, Li et al. (2011) analyzed the clinical characteristics of 46 patients affected by AIDS phobia and found that, with or without high-risk behavior for HIV-1 infection, the phobic patients repeatedly demanded HIV/AIDS-related laboratory tests and either suspected or believed they had HIV infection and believed their daily life was being affected by it. The main complaints were nonspecific, including influenza-like symptoms (headache, sore throat, and so on), fasciculation, formication, arthrodynia, fatigue, and complaint of fever with normal body temperature; physical examination did not reveal any positive physical signs except white-coated tongue. Symptoms mainly appeared 0–3 months after a patient had engaged in high-risk behavior, despite HIV-1 antibody remaining negative. T-lymphocyte subsets test was carried out in 23 patients and showed 19 (82.6%) with CD4+ T-lymphocyte count >500/µl; the remaining 4 were 300–500/µl, with the lowest count being 307/µl, indicating a lack of HIV infection. AIDS phobia appears to be a complicated and challenging psychiatric condition to adequately diagnose and treat.

IMPACT OF ANXIETY ON ADHERENCE TO ART, MORTALITY, AND QUALITY OF LIFE

In the post-ART era, HIV has evolved from a rapidly terminal illness to a chronic illness for many individuals, reflected by significant increases in disease prevalence and decreases in HIV mortality rates worldwide from 1990 to 2013 (Murray et al., 2014). Consequently, mitigating aspects of anxiety disorders that contribute to medication nonadherence and poor quality of life across the course of the disease have now become a primary focus in the clinical setting.

While studies have firmly established depression as a negative predictor of adherence to ART, data regarding the impact of anxiety disorders on adherence and its consequences remain less conclusive (Pence et al., 2006; Walkup et al., 2008). Given that increased psychological distress and increased serum cortisol levels are independently associated with nonadherence to treatment and progression of HIV to AIDS, clinicians may expect anxiety disorders to follow the same pattern (Leserman et al., 2002; Mellins et al., 2009). Surprisingly, a study of youth with perinatal HIV found that the adolescents with anxiety symptoms had a 40% lower risk of unsuppressed viral load, possibly owing to anxiety about illness progression driving better ART adherence (Kacanek et al., 2015). In a systematic review of the relationship between DSM-IV diagnoses and ART adherence, Springer and colleagues (2012) found inconsistent conclusions across 24 publications regarding rates of adherence among persons with generalized anxiety disorder, panic disorder, agoraphobia, PTSD, and unspecified anxiety disorders compared to inidividuals without psychiatric disorders. One weakness of many of these studies is the use of self-reported medication adherence, rather than objective assessments.

Similarly to treatment adherence, associations between anxiety disorders and disease progression and mortality in HIV are inconsistent. In a study of veterans with HIV, anxiety disorders were associated with a 20% reduction in death compared to veterans without anxiety diagnoses (Nurutdinova et al., 2012). By contrast, biological markers of anxiety states, such as higher serum cortisol (in one study, an increase of 3 μg/dL), may increase the risk of progression to AIDS by 40% and the risk of mortality by 2±6-fold (Leserman et al., 2002). Beyond deaths directly related to HIV/AIDS clinical sequelae, persons with HIV are at higher risk for suicide. Most persons (62%) with HIV who commit suicide have a psychiatric diagnosis, with anxiety disorders second only to depressive disorders, and precipitating factors including disease progression and psychosocial stressors (Keiser et al., 2010). Higher anxiety burden, specifically via cognitive concerns, is associated with higher suicidality in persons with HIV, even when corrected for demographics, HIV disease factors, and negative affect (Gonzales, Parent, et al., 2012).

Although the literature to date presents no clear consensus regarding the impact of anxiety disorders on treatment adherence and mortality in HIV, studies overwhelmingly support negative impacts of anxiety on quality of life in persons diagnosed with HIV (see Table 18.1).

Table 18.1 NEGATIVE QUALITY OF LIFE MEASURES ASSOCIATED WITH ANXIETY DISORDERS IN HIV

Unemployment	Worse mental health functioning
Higher burden of HIV symptoms	Worse physical functioning
Greater frequency of medical visits	Fatigue

See Gaynes et al. (2015), Shelburne et al. (2000), Sewell et al. (2000), Kessler et al. (2003), and Mellins et al (2009).

Alongside negative consequences of anxiety in the HIV population, researchers have also identified patient strengths and interventions that contribute positively to care and quality of life. In persons with anxiety or depression, enhancing HIV self-efficacy via communicating well with clinicians, obtaining needed supports, and managing mood has resulted in improved adherence to ART (Reif et al., 2013). Bolstering existing functional social supports as well as psychological capital may help improve anxiety symptoms in HIV patients working full-time (Gaynes et al., 2015; Liu et al., 2013). Identifying and engaging with patients' stated strengths and goals can enhance self-efficacy and encourage positive change behaviors both in and outside of the clinic.

DIFFERENTIAL DIAGNOSIS

Recognition of anxiety in patients with HIV/AIDS is critical in order to properly treat individuals affected by comorbid anxiety and to reduce its associated burden; thus, making the differential diagnosis of anxiety in HIV/AIDS is important. As noted previously, anxiety can occur at any stage of the illness, spanning from recognition of being at risk for infection of the virus to just prior to death. Anxiety can be seen as a preexisting or co-occurring disorder, and patients with a history of anxiety and mood disorders are at risk for recurrence of anxiety symptoms during the course of their illness. Thus, clinicians need to consider anxiety disorders in persons with HIV secondary to other causes, including other psychiatric disorders, medical conditions, and prescription medications, in order to adequately care for each individual (Katzman et al., 2014).

Significant anxiety-like symptoms can be seen with other psychiatric disorders, and it is important to consider these disorders prior to moving forward with treatment. Adjustment disorders can present primarily with anxiety. As adjustment disorders generally occur following a major stressor, they are commonly seen in persons with HIV/AIDS—for example, the stress and worry caused by receiving a diagnosis of HIV seropositivity. It is also no surprise that major depression, which can present with anxiety symptoms, is another common comorbidity among patients with HIV/AIDS. Though less commonly seen in persons with HIV/AIDS, psychosis can similarly present with paranoia and anxious distress and can easily be confused with a primary anxiety disorder.

Additionally, substance intoxication or withdrawal from substances including nicotine, alcohol, caffeine, cocaine, and amphetamines may be a cause of anxiety, especially since substance use disorders are believed to be one of the most common comorbid psychiatric disorders in persons with HIV, seen in up to 40–50% of patients (Altice et al., 2010; Gaynes et al., 2008; Katzman et al., 2014; Owe-Larsson et al., 2009; Zahari et al., 2010).

Underlying medical conditions can also present with considerable anxiety, and it is necessary to rule out anxiety secondary to medical conditions when evaluating patients. The burden of medical multimorbidities is high in persons with HIV/AIDS, and illnesses such as hyperthyroidism, cardiopulmonary disorders, and traumatic brain injury must be considered. Given the frequency of medical complications in persons with HIV/AIDS, it is no surprise that delirium, which may present with symptoms including irritability, agitation, and insomnia, is common throughout the course of illness with HIV/AIDS. AIDS-specific CNS conditions such as HIV-related infections, neoplasms, and dementia can present with significant agitation or distress (Katzman et al., 2014; Mielke, 2005; Owe-Larsson et al., 2009).

In addition to considering underlying medical conditions in the differential diagnosis of anxiety, it is also important to consider side effects of commonly prescribed medications. For example, frequently prescribed psychotropic medications, such as bupropion for depression and smoking cessation, and methylphenidate or amphetamine for ADHD symptoms, can cause anxiety and agitation (Wilens and Spencer, 2010; Wilkes, 2008). This is an important consideration in patients with HIV/AIDS, as Vitiello et al. (2003) found that 27.2% of HIV-positive patients receiving medical care in 1996 were treated with psychotropic medications. In a more recent study, Himelhoch et al. (2009) found that 37% of HIV-positive individuals reported use of psychotropic medication for a mental health condition. Infection with HIV increases the risk for opportunistic infections, including tuberculosis, and the overall risk of developing active tuberculosis is about 50% in this population, thus making anti-tuberculosis treatment regimens, known to cause anxiety, an important consideration (Lenjisa et al., 2015; Vega et al., 2004). More specific to HIV/AIDS, ART, with medications such as zidovudine, efavirenz, abacavir, and indinavir, is known to cause anxiety (Colebunders et al., 2002; Harry et al., 2000; Hawkins et al., 2005; Lochet et al., 2003; Tukei et al., 2012). It is thus important to take into account many factors when considering the differential diagnosis of anxiety in patients with HIV/AIDS.

TREATMENT APPROACHES

Treatment of anxiety disorders in persons with HIV follows guidelines similar to those for treating persons with other chronic medical illnesses, with particular attention to medication dosing, metabolism, potential for drug interactions, and potential for side effects (Farber and McDaniel, 2002). While the DSM-5 guidelines prove helpful in diagnosing specific disorders, it is generally more appropriate to treat the anxiety

on the basis of a patient's symptoms and symptom severity. To minimize adverse effects, medications should be started at low doses and titrated up slowly to the desired effect. Side-effect profiles and drug interactions should also be taken into account. For a more detailed discussion of psychotherapeutic and integrative treatment modalities in HIV see Chapters 37 and 38, and for the psychopharmacological aspects of HIV care see Chapter 42 in this textbook.

ANXIETY SYMPTOMS AND GENERALIZED ANXIETY DISORDER

Psychotherapy is an excellent first-line therapy for anxiety symptoms or generalized anxiety disorder and has no adverse side effects. Psychotherapy can also be used in combination with medication for those in need of more immediate relief or those suffering from more severe symptoms. Psychotherapeutic treatments have been shown to be effective in alleviating the distress and suffering in patients with HIV and anxiety disorders. A therapeutic modality should be chosen that takes into account a patient's physical and psychological symptomatology, social supports, stressors, prior therapy or medication experience, ability to cope, cultural or religious background, and goals (Zegans et al., 1994). Numerous studies have demonstrated the overall benefits of group therapy as an intervention that ameliorates symptoms of depression, anxiety, and distress and enhances coping in persons suffering from chronic illnesses, including HIV/AIDS (Mulder et al., 1994; Sherman et al., 2004). Cognitive-behavioral stress management has been shown to result in significant stress reduction (Antoni, 2003; Cruess et al., 2000b) as well as decreased mood disturbance and anxious mood (Cruess et al., 2000a) in HIV-positive patients. A similar study demonstrated that behavioral stress management techniques such as self-induced relaxation using progressive muscle relaxation, electromyographic (EMG) biofeedback, self-hypnosis, and meditation resulted in reduced anxiety and improvement in mood and self-esteem (Taylor, 1995). Lutgendorf and colleagues (1998) also observed improvement in cognitive coping strategies, namely positive reframing and acceptance, in addition to improvements in social supports.

Some studies have suggested that reducing anxiety sensitivity through cognitive-behavioral therapy is a beneficial approach (Gonzalez et al., 2010; Smits et al., 2008). Gonzalez and colleagues (2009) demonstrated the advantageous effects of higher levels of mindfulness-based attention and awareness and lower levels of disengagement coping in regard to anxiety symptoms in persons with HIV/AIDS. In a sample of 45 HIV-positive individuals suffering from chronic pain, a cognitive-behavioral therapy–focused treatment approach centering on pain acceptance and decrease produced decreases in pain anxiety and pain-related impairment at treatment completion (Huggins et al., 2012). Moreover, in a systematic review of interventions for anxiety in people with HIV, Clucas and colleagues (2011) found that psychological interventions, especially cognitive-behavioral stress management interventions and cognitive-behavioral therapy, were generally more effective than pharmacological interventions in reducing anxiety.

Their review suggests that although available interventions are effective, further research into improving efficacy of these modalities is imperative.

Medications for treatment of anxiety may be indicated in addition to psychotherapy. Selective serotonin reuptake inhibitors (SSRIs) are useful as first-line therapy for treating chronic anxiety disorders (Ferrando and Wapenyi, 2002; Pollack et al., 2004), although benzodiazepines may be most frequently prescribed (Cabaj, 1996). Benzodiazepines may be especially useful as an adjunct to SSRIs for individuals who cannot wait for several weeks while an SSRI is titrated to an effective dose or for patients who require acute relief of distressing symptoms such as panic. Many clinicians are wary of using benzodiazepines because they have potential for abuse and dependence in patients with a history of substance use disorder (Douaihy et al., 2003; Fernandez and Levy, 1994; Ferrando and Wapenyi, 2002) and if used chronically put the patient at risk for withdrawal symptoms when the medication is stopped. Vitiello and colleagues (2003) found that 63% of medications prescribed for anxiety among persons infected with HIV were benzodiazepines. Blank et al. (2013) suggest that as it has been over a decade since Vitiello's study was conducted and the prevalence of benzodiazepine use in persons with HIV may have declined significantly since that time.

An alternative is buspirone, which is a non-benzodiazepine agent shown to be useful in the treatment of generalized anxiety. Compared to benzodiazepines, buspirone has a relatively low risk of excessive sedation (Ferrando and Wapenyi, 2002), low risk of drug interactions (McDaniel et al., 2000), and low potential for abuse (Ferrando and Wapenyi, 2002), although it has been reported to induce psychosis in an HIV-positive man (Trachman, 1992). It must be taken two to three times a day and is primarily used as a second-line agent for long-term relief or prophylaxis of anxiety symptoms. For rapid anxiolysis, Ferrando and Wapenyi (2002) comment that alternatives to buspirone, including antihistamines such as hydroxyzine, sedating tricyclic antidepressants (TCAs), and trazodone, could be considered. However, clinicians need to be concerned about the cumulative and considerable anticholinergic side effects of these medications and the associated risk of central anticholinergic delirium. There is also a risk of falls with these medications secondary to orthostatic hypotension, especially with TCAs and trazodone.

AIDS PHOBIA AND OCD

Treatments for specific phobias and OCD have been well studied in the general population. In vivo exposure, systemic desensitization, virtual reality, cognitive therapy, and other treatments have been utilized for the treatment of specific phobias, with different subtypes of specific phobias responding more favorably to certain treatments than others (Choy et al., 2007). Cognitive-behavioral therapy is the recommended psychotherapeutic treatment for OCD (Ravindran et al., 2009). A review of pharmacological therapies concluded that fluvoxamine or sertraline are the recommended pharmacological treatment for OCD, with augmentation for refractory symptoms with risperidone, olanzapine, or quetiapine (Choi, 2009).

Unfortunately, while specific phobias and OCD have been well studied in the general population, clinical trials of HIV/AIDS-related phobia and OCD are lacking. One challenge in treating patients with phobias as well as OCD is that such patients are highly hesitant to refrain from engaging in rituals. In light of infection control practices, it can be difficult to avoid compulsive washing and cleaning behaviors (Bruce and Stevens, 1992).

Case reports are the only current evidence of treatment of AIDS phobia or OCD. Jenike and Pato (1986) reported on a patient with irrational and persistent fear of HIV infection, successfully treated with imipramine. Five of the seven patients discussed by Logsdail et al. (1991) achieved both reduction of fears and improved social functioning with 7 to 10 sessions of exposure-based treatment that included response prevention following a model similar to that for treatment of individuals suffering from OCD.

McDaniel and Johnson (1995) successfully treated two patients with fluoxetine. Kraus and Nicholson (1996) successfully treated a patient with fluoxetine without relapse when the drug was discontinued. In Semple et al.'s 2010 study of 245 HIV-methamphetamine-using men who have sex with men, clinical levels of OCD were associated with more frequent use of methamphetamine, more depressive symptoms, and riskier sexual behaviors when "high" on methamphetamine, suggesting the necessity of a multifaceted treatment approach of OCD symptoms in this population.

PANIC DISORDER

Standard therapy for panic disorder consists of cognitive-behavioral therapy or medication to relieve and prevent symptoms (TCAs, SSRIs, monoamine oxidase inhibitors [MAOIs], serotonin-norepinephrine reuptake inhibitors [SNRIs], benzodiazepines, with or without the addition of beta-adrenergic antagonists to modify some of the physiological symptoms of panic disorder) as well as possible augmentation of therapy with psychotherapeutic modalities. Thompson and colleagues (2006) suggest that medications and cognitive-behavioral treatments may have similar efficacy in the treatment of panic disorder in persons with HIV/AIDS. Fernandez and Levy (1991, 1994) prefer to treat HIV patients suffering from either panic disorder or delusions with anxious features with antipsychotics instead of benzodiazepines because the latter drug class is behaviorally disinhibiting. It should be noted that beta-adrenergic antagonists are not effective when used alone, are contraindicated in patients who abuse cocaine, and may also cause depression, fatigue, and sexual dysfunction. Anxiety sensitivity has been found to be a clinically relevant factor in panic disorder in patients with HIV, which can potentially be targeted with strategies including mindfulness (Gonzalez, Zvolensky, et al., 2012).

CO-OCCURRING DISORDERS

When considering psychiatric diagnoses in patients with HIV/AIDS, patients with a single diagnosis, rather than multimorbid diagnoses, appear to be the exception rather than the rule. Various studies have cited a prevalence of psychiatric diagnoses in HIV patients approaching 50% (Gaynes et al., 2008, 2015; Springer et al., 2012). Of HIV-positive individuals with a primary mood diagnosis in the past month, over 50% have a concomitant anxiety or substance abuse diagnosis, and the same is true for patients with primary anxiety disorders with respect to mood or substance use disorders (Gaynes et al., 2008). Persons with HIV/AIDS are also at higher risk for exposure to trauma, including sexual abuse and intimate partner violence (up to 26.8% in current relationships), which correlate with increased risk of PTSD and higher-risk sexual and drug-use behaviors (Basu et al., 2005; Tavakkoli et al., 2014; Walkup et al., 2008). The interplay between anxiety and substance use in the HIV population is striking: on screening questionnaires, questions addressing prolonged anxiety independently predicted substance use disorders, and questions addressing inability to cut back on alcohol or drug use similarly predicted anxiety or mood disorders (Pence et al., 2006). Symptoms of HIV-associated neurocognitive disorders may also masquerade as, or present alongside, anxiety or mood symptoms and must be distinguished to ensure appropriate treatment (Altice et al., 2010). Without careful screening for both primary and comorbid psychiatric disorders, clinicians may mistakenly attribute symptoms and fail to identify conditions that require treatment in patients with HIV (Sledjeski et al., 2005).

In addition to more frequent co-occurring psychiatric diagnoses in patients with anxiety, the literature supports a bidirectional relationship between anxiety disorders and chronic medical conditions, such as cardiovascular disease, asthma, irritable bowel syndrome, chronic pain, and malignancy (Roy-Byrne et al., 2008). Underlying medical diagnoses may also present similarly to or in conjunction with primary anxiety disorders, such as cardiac, endocrine, hematological, infectious, or renal disorders; screening for such disorders is thus recommended when a patient presents with anxiety (Basu et al., 2005). As patients with HIV/AIDS require complex pharmacotherapy, often for concomitant medical and psychiatric conditions as well as HIV/AIDS itself, drug interactions also emerge as a source of morbidity and require careful attention (Altice et al., 2010). Thus, when identifying an HIV-positive patient with an anxiety disorder, careful screening for coexisting mood, stress, and substance use disorders, as well as general medical conditions, is essential to ensure an integrated approach to treatment.

CASE STUDY

Ms. A is a 40-year old woman with a history of HIV and nonadherence to treatment in the context of debilitating anxiety who was admitted to a general medical inpatient unit with an AIDS-related illness. Her CD4 count was 28, viral load >2 million copies, and she was being treated for *Pneumocystitis jiroveci* pneumonia and for oral and esophageal candidiasis. Although she has a long history of anxiety manifestations, related to PTSD stemming from intimate partner violence in a previous relationship, she reports that since being diagnosed with HIV, her anxiety has become "overwhelming and difficult to manage." Subsequent to her diagnosis of HIV, she developed panic attacks, consisting of physical symptoms (palpitations, shortness of breath) and being worried about a physical disorder, infection, or possibly infecting others. She learned to cope with these panic attacks by isolating herself, during which time she would shut herself alone in a room to engage in deep breathing until the panic attack subsided. However, this practice further served to reinforce social avoidance, as she sought to protect herself from triggers of panic attacks. This self-isolation had an impact on her ability to follow up with HIV medical care and to access her social support system. Knowing that she was not adhering to ART and making her appointments at the clinic, her anxiety symptoms worsened and she became very preoccupied with her HIV illness being poorly managed. She described feeling stuck in a vicious cycle for many years without treatment, leading to paralyzing anxiety about the impact her health and eventual death would have on her children and her family. Ms. A considered her hospitalization for pneumonia "a wake-up call for me and a window of opportunity to initiate treatment and get my life on track," leading to her decision to engage in medical and psychiatric care. She was discharged to follow-up by both medical and psychiatric teams that conncted her with care while she was in the hospital.

In accordance with current evidence and treatment guidelines for persons with HIV/AIDS and in collaboration with our pharmacist, we initiated treatment to address the patient's generalized anxiety disorder with an SSRI based on tolerability, side-effect profile, and limited SSRI–ART drug–drug interactions. On the basis of this evidence, Ms. A was started on citalopram 20 mg daily. The psychiatry team provided supportive psychotherapy with cognitive-behavioral elements targeting anxiety and psychoeducation about medication and the importance of adherence to medication and treatment. Motivational interviewing was used to explore the patient's intrinsic motivation for change and address her ambivalence about engaging in HIV care and psychiatric treatment. The team also provided psychoeducation about PTSD. Given her long hospital course for multiple medical complications, we were able to establish a therapeutic alliance with Ms. A, provide multiple "doses" of psychotherapy, and monitor closely the effects of the interventions and progress in treatment. By the time she left the hospital, her anxiety improved considerably and she was able to learn and utilize coping skills. She was medically stabilized and had established stronger self-efficacy to continue working on her recovery from HIV and psychiatric illnesses.

The integrated interdisciplinary approach to her care was initiated during the medical hospitalization. The patient was introduced to the primary care physician as well as the infectious disease team that would continue to work with her in the HIV clinic, and she identified an outpatient program closer to her home where she would follow up with individual therapy and medication management. The patient was also connected with a patient navigator, whose role is to help facilitate behavior change related to engagement in treatment, adherence to medical and psychiatric treatment, and access to resources in the community.

CONCLUSION AND FUTURE AREAS OF RESEARCH

Anxiety is a common manifestation in severe illness and is significant among persons with HIV/AIDS. Early screening, diagnosis, and treatment of anxiety throughout the course of HIV/AIDS, from the time of awareness of risk to end-stage illness, can help reduce suffering and improve adherence to risk reduction and medical care. While much has been done to recognize and treat anxiety throughout the course of HIV/AIDS, it is important for clinicians to collaborate in order to reduce the burden of anxiety in patients with HIV/AIDS. Future controlled trials are needed to evaluate the impact of psychosocial and pharmacological interventions for anxiety disorders in persons with HIV.

REFERENCES

Aberg, JA, Aberg JA, Gallant JE, Ghanem KG, Emmanuel P, Zingman BS, Horberg MA (2014). Primary care guidelines for the management of persons infected with HIV: 2013 update by the HIV Medicine Association of the Infectious Diseases Society of America. *Clin Infect Dis* 58(1):1–10.

Altice FL, Kamarulzaman A, Soriano VV, Schechter M, Friedland GH (2010). Treatment of medical, psychiatric, and substance-use comorbidities in people infected with HIV who use drugs. *Lancet* 376(9738):367–87.

American Psychiatric Association. (2013). Diagnostic and Statistical Manual of Mental Disorders, 5th ed. Washington, DC: American Psychiatric Association.

Antoni MH (2003). Stress management effects on psychological, endocrinological, and immune functioning in men with HIV infection: empirical support for a psychoneuroimmunological model. *Stress* 6(3):173–188.

Antoni MH, Schneiderman N, Klimas N, LaPerriere A, Ironson G, Fletcher MA (1991). Disparities in psychological, neuroendocrine, and immunologic patterns in asymptomatic HIV-1 seropositive and seronegative gay men. *Biol Psychiatry* 29(10):1023–1041.

Basu S, Chwastiak LA, Bruce RD (2005). Clinical management of depression and anxiety in HIV-infected adults. *AIDS* 19(18):2057–2067.

Batki SL (1990). Buspirone in drug users with AIDS or AIDS-related complex. *J Clin Psychopharmacol* 10(3 Suppl):111S–115S.

Batki SL, Sorensen JL, Faltz B, Madover S (1988). Psychiatric aspects of treatment of I.V. drug abusers with AIDS. *Hosp Community Psychiatry* 39(4):439–441.

Berger S (2008). Effects of cognitive stress management in HIV-1 RNA, CD4 cell counts and psychosocial parameters of HIV-infected persons. *AIDS* 22:767–775.

Blank MB, Himelhoch S, Walkup J, Eisenberg MM (2013). Treatment considerations for HIV-infected individuals with severe mental illness. *Curr HIV/AIDS* 10(4):371–379.

Brotman AW, Forstein M (1988). AIDS obsessions in depressed heterosexuals (case report). *Psychosomatics* 29:428–431.

Bruce BK, Stevens VM (1992). AIDS-related obsessive compulsive disorder: a treatment dilemma. *J Anxiety Disord* 6:79–88.

Cabaj RP (1996). Management of anxiety and depression in HIV-infected patients. *J Int Assoc Physicians AIDS Care* 2(6):11–16.

Campos LN, Guimaraes MD, Remien RH (2010). Anxiety and depression symptoms as risk factors for nonadherence to antiretroviral therapy in Brazil. *AIDS Behav* 14:289–299.

Choi YJ (2009). Efficacy of treatments for patients with obsessive–compulsive disorder: a systematic review. *J Am Acad Nurse Pract* 21(4):207–213.

Choi Y, Fyer AJ, Lipsitz JD (2007). Treatment of specific phobias in adults. *Clin Psychol Rev* 27:266–286.

Clucas C, Sibley E, Harding R, Liu L, Catalan J, Sherr L (2011). A systematic review of interventions for anxiety in people with HIV. *Psychol Health Med* 16(5):528–547.

Cohen MA, Hoffman RG, Cromwell C, et al. (2002). The prevalence of distress in persons with human immunodeficiency virus infection. *Psychosomatics* 43(1):10–15.

Colebunders R, Hilbrands R, De Roo A, et al. (2002). Neuropsychiatric reaction induced by abacavir (letter). *Am J Med* 113:616.

Cove J, Petrak J (2004). Factors associated with sexual problems in HIV-positive gay men. *International Journal of STD and AIDS* 15:732–736.

Creswell JD, Myers HF, Cole SW, Irwin MR.(2009). Mindfulness meditation training effects on CD4+ T lymphocytes in HIV-1 infected adults: a small randomized controlled trial. *Brain Behav Immun* 23(2):184–188

Cruess DG, Antoni MH, Kumar M, Schneiderman N (2000a). Reductions in salivary cortisol are associated with mood improvement during relaxation training among HIV-seropositive men. *J Behav Med* 23(2):107–122.

Cruess DG, Antoni MH, Schneiderman N, et al. (2000b). Cognitive-behavioral stress management increases free testosterone and decreases psychological distress in HIV-seropositive men. *Health Psychol* 19 (1):12–20.

Douaihy AB, Jou RJ, Gorske T, Salloum IM (2003). Triple diagnosis: dual diagnosis and HIV disease, part 2. *AIDS Read* 13(8):375–382.

Farber EW, McDaniel JS (2002). Clinical management of psychiatric disorders in patients with HIV disease. *Psychiatr Q* 73(1):5–16.

Fernandez F, Levy JK (1991). Psychopharmacotherapy of psychiatric syndromes in asymptomatic and symptomatic HIV infection. *Psychiatr Med* 9(3):377–394.

Fernandez F, Levy JK (1994). Psychopharmacology in HIV spectrum disorders. *Psychiatr Clin North Am* 17(1):135–148.

Ferrando SJ, Wapenyi K (2002). Psychopharmacological treatment of patients with HIV and AIDS. *Psychiatr Q* 73(1):33–49.

Freed E (1983). AIDS phobia (letter). *Med J Aust* 2:479.

Gaynes BN, O'Donnell J, Nelson E, et al. (2015). Psychiatric comorbidity in HIV-infected individuals: common and clinically consequential. *Gen Hosp Psychiatry* 37:277–282.

Gaynes BN, Pence BW, Eron JJ, Miller WC (2008). Prevalence and comorbidity of psychiatric diagnoses based on reference standard in an HIV+ patient population. *Psychosom Med* 70(4):505–511.

Gonzalez A, Parent J, Zvolensky MJ, Schmidt NB, Capron DW (2012). Suicidality and anxiety sensitivity in adults with HIV. *AIDS Patient Care STDs* 26(5): 298–303.

Gonzalez A, Solomon SE, Zvolensky MJ, Miller CT (2009). The interaction of mindful-based attention and awareness and disengagement coping with HIV/AIDS-related stigma in regard to concurrent anxiety and depressive symptoms among adults with HIV/AIDS. *J Health Psychol* 14(3):403–413.

Gonzalez A, Zvolensky MJ, Grover KW, Parent J (2012). The role of anxiety sensitivity and mindful attention in anxiety and worry about bodily sensations among adults living with HIV/AIDS. *Behav Therapy* 43(4):768–778.

Gonzalez A, Zvolensky MJ, Solomon SE, Miller CT (2010). Exploration of the relevance of anxiety sensitivity among adults living with HIV/AIDS for understanding anxiety vulnerability. *J Health Psychol* 15(1):138–146.

Harry T, Matthews M, Salvari I (2000). Indinavir use: associated reversible hair loss and mood disturbance. *Int J STD AIDS* 11:474–476.

Hauptman A, Carchedi L (2013). A case of possible HIV prophylaxis-induced anxiety and obsessive-compulsive disorder. *Gen Hosp Psychiatry* 35(6):679.

Hawkins T, Geist C, Young B, Giblin A, Mercier RC, Thornton K, Haubrich R (2005). Comparison of neuropsychiatric side effects in an observational cohort of efavirenz- and protease inhibitor-treated patients. *HIV Clin Trials* 6(4):187–196.

Henderson M, Safa F, Easterbrook P, Hotopf M (2005). Fatigue among HIV-infected patients in the era of highly active antiretroviral therapy. *HIV Med* 6(5):347–352.

Himelhoch S, Josephs JS, Chandler G, Korthius PT, Gebo KA, and the HIV Research Network (2009). Use of outpatient mental health services and psychotropic medications among HIV-infected patients in a multisite, multistate study. *Gen Hosp Psychiatry* 31(6):538–545.

Huggins JL, Bonn-Miller MO, Oser ML, Sorrell JT, Trafton JA (2012). Pain anxiety, acceptance, and outcomes among individuals with HIV and chronic pain: a preliminary investigation. *Behav Res Ther* 50(1): 72–78.

Ivanova EL, Hart TA, Wagner AC, Alijassem K, Loutfy MR (2012). Correlates of anxiety in women living with HIV of reproductive age. *AIDS Behav* 16:2181–2191.

Jacob KS, John JK, Verghese A, John TJ (1987). AIDS-phobia. *Br J Psychiatry* 150:412–413.

Jenike MA, Pato C (1986). Disabling fear of AIDS responsive to imipramine. *Psychosomatics* 27:143–144.

Jin C, Zhao G, Zhang F, Feng L, Wu N (2010). The psychological status of HIV-positive people and their psychosocial experiences in eastern China. *HIV Med* 11:253–259.

Kacanek D, Angelidou K, Williams PL, Chernoff M, Gadow KD, Nachman S (2015). Psychiatric symptoms and antiretroviral nonadherence in US youth with perinatal HIV: a longitudinal study. *AIDS* 29:1227–1237.

Kagee A, Martin L (2010). Symptoms of depression and anxiety among a sample of south African patients living with HIV. *AIDS Care* 22(2):159–165.

Katzman MA, Bleau P, Blier P, Chokka P, Kjernisted K, Van Ameringen M (2014). Canadian clinical practice guidelines for the management of anxiety, posttraumatic stress and obsessive-compulsive disorders. *BMC Psychiatry* 14:S1.

Kausch O (2004). Irrational fear of AIDS associated with suicidal behavior. *J Psychiatr Pract* 10(4):266–271.

Keiser O, Spoerri A, Brinkhof MW, et al. (2010). Suicide in HIV-infected individuals and the general population in Switzerland, 1988–2008. *Am J Psychiatry* 167(2):143–150.

Kessler RC, Ormel J, Demler O, Stang PE (2003). Comorbid mental disorders account for the role impairment of commonly occurring chronic physical disorders: results from the National Comorbidity Survey. *J Occup Environ Med* 45:1257–1266.

Kraus RP, Nicholson IR (1996). AIDS-related obsessive compulsive disorder: deconditioning based on fluoxetine-induced inhibition of anxiety. *J Behav Ther Exp Psychiatry* 27(1):51–56.

Kroenke K, Spitzer R, Williams J, Monahan P, Lowe B (2007). Anxiety disorders in primary care: prevalence, impairment, comorbidity, and detection. *Ann Intern Med* 146 (5):317–325.

Lambert S, Keegan A, Petrak J (2005). Sex and relationships for HIV positive women since HAART: a quantitative study. *Sex Transm Infect* 81(4):333–337.

Lenjisa JL, Wega SS, Lema TB, Ayana GA (2015). Outcomes of highly active antiretroviral therapy and its predictors: a cohort study focusing on tuberculosis co-infection in South West Ethiopia. *BMC Res Notes* 8:446.

Leserman J. (2003). The effects of stressful life events, coping, and cortisol on HIV infection. *CNS Spectr* 8(1):25–30.

Leserman J (2008). Role of depression, stress, and trauma in HIV disease progression. *Psychosom Med* 70(5):539–545.

Leserman J, Petitto JM, Gu H, et al. (2002). Progression to AIDS, a clinical AIDS condition and mortality: psychosocial and physiological predictors. *Psychol Med* 32:1059–1073.

Lenze EJ, Mantella RC, Shi P, et al. (2011). Elevated cortisol in older adults with generalized anxiety disorder is reduced by treatment: a placebo-controlled evaluation of escitalopram. *Am J Geriatr Psychiatry* 19(5): 482–490.

Li YL, Li TS, Xie J, Wu N, Li WJ, Qiu ZF (2011). An analysis of clinical characteristics of forty six AIDS phobia patients. *Zhonghua Nei Ke Za Zhi* 50(8):650–653.

Liu L, Qu P, Wang L, Lu CM, Pang R, Sun W, Wu M (2013). Functional social support, psychological capital, and depressive and anxiety symptoms among people living with HIV/AIDS employed full-time. *BMC Psychiatry* 13(1):324–333.

Lochet P, Peyriere H, Lotthe A, et al. (2003). Long-term assessment of neuropsychiatric adverse reactions associated with efavirenz. *HIV Med* 4:62–66.

Logsdail S, Lovell K, Warwick H, Marks I (1991). Behavioural treatment of AIDS-focused illness phobia. *Br J Psychiatry* 159:422–425.

Lutgendorf SK, Antoni MH, Ironson G, et al. (1998). Changes in cognitive coping skills and social support during cognitive behavioral stress management intervention and distress outcomes in symptomatic human immunodeficiency virus (HIV)-seropositive gay men. *Psychosom Med* 60(2):204–214.

Marques LE, Bui N, LeBlanc E, et al. (2013). Complicated grief symptoms in anxiety disorders: prevalence and associated impairment. *Depress Anxiety* 30(12):1211–1216.

Marwick KF, Kaaya SF (2010). Prevalence of depression and anxiety disorders in HIV-positive outpatients in rural Tanzania. *AIDS Care* 22:415–419.

McCain NL, Gray DP, Elswick RK, et al. (2008). A randomized clinical trial of alternative stress management interventions in persons with HIV infection. *J Consult Clin Psychol* 76(3):431–441.

McDaniel JS, Chung JY, Brown L, Cournos F, Forstein M, Goodkin K, Lyketsos C (2000). Work Group on HIV/AIDS. Practice guidelines for the treatment of patients with HIV/AIDS. *Am J Psychiatry* 157:11.

McDaniel JS, Johnson KM (1995). Obsessive-compulsive disorder in HIV disease. Response to fluoxetine. *Psychosomatics* 36(2):147–150.

McEwen BS (1998). Protective and damaging effects of stress mediators. *N Engl J Med* 338(3):171–179.

McNally RJ (2002). Anxiety sensitivity and panic disorder. *Biol Psychiatry* 52:938–946.

Mellins CA, Elkington KS, Bauermeister JA, et al. (2009). Sexual and drug use behavior in perinatally-HIV-infected youth: mental health and family influences. *J Am Acad Child Adolesc Psychiatry* 48(8):810–819.

Mielke J (2005). Neurological complications of human immunodeficiency virus infections in Zimbabewe. *J Neurovirol* 11(Suppl 3):23–25.

Miller AK, Lee BL, Henderson CE (2012). Death anxiety in persons with HIV/AIDS: a systematic review and meta-analysis. *Death Stud* 36(7):640–663.

Miller D, Green J, Farmer R, Carroll G (1985). A "pseudo-AIDS" syndrome following from fear of AIDS. *Br J Psychiatry* 146:550–551.

Miller F, Weiden P, Sacks M, Wizniak J (1986). Two cases of factitious acquired immune deficiency syndrome (letter to the editor). *Am J Psychiatry* 147:91.

Morrison MF, Petitto JM, Ten Have T, et al. (2002). Depressive and anxiety disorders in women with HIV infection. *Am J Psychiatry* 159(5):789–796.

Mulder CL, Emmelkamp PM, Antoni MH, Mulder JW, Sandfort TG, de Vries MJ (1994). Cognitive-behavioral and experiential group psychotherapy for HIV-infected homosexual men: a comparative study. *Psychosom Med* 56(5):423–431.

Murray CJL, Ortblad KF, Guinovart C, Lim SS, Wolock TM, Roberts DA, Dansereau EA (2014). Global, regional, and national incidence and mortality for HIV, tuberculosis, and malaria during 1990–2013: a systematic analysis for the global burden of disease study. *Lancet* 384(9947):1005–1070.

Myer L, Smit J, Roux LL, Parker S, Stein DJ, Seedat S (2008). Common mental disorders among HIV-infected individuals in South Africa: prevalence, predictors and validation of brief psychiatric rating scales. *AIDS Patient Care STDS* 22:147–158.

Nacher M, Adriouch L, Godrd Sebillotte C, et al. (2010). Predictive factors and incidence of anxiety and depression in a cohort of HIV-positive patients in French Guiana. *AIDS Care* 22:1086–1092.

Nurutdinova D, Chrusciel T, Zeringue A, Scherrer JF, Al-Aly Z, McDonald JR, Overton ET (2012). Mental health disorders and the risk of AIDS-defining illness and death in HIV-infected veterans. *AIDS* 26(2):229–234.

O'Cleirigh C, Safren S. (2008). Optimizing the effects of stress management interventions in HIV. *Health Psychol* 27(3):297–301.

O'Cleirigh C, Traeger L, Mayer KH, Magidson JF, Safren SA (2013). Anxiety specific pathways to HIV sexual transmission risk behaviors. *J Gay Lesbian Ment Health* 17(3):314–326.

Olagunju AT, Adeyemi JD, Erinfolami AR, Ogundipe OA (2012). Factors associated with anxiety disorders among HIV-positive attendees of an HIV clinic in Lagos, Nigeria. *Int J STD AIDS* 23:389–393

Olley BO, Seedat S, Stein DJ (2006). Persistence of psychiatric disorders in a cohort of HIV/AIDS patients in South Africa: a 6-month follow-up study. *J Psychosom Res* 61:479–484.

Owe-Larsson B, Sall S, Salamon E, Allgulander C (2009). HIV infection and psychiatric illness. *Afr J Psychiatry* 12(2):115–128.

Parhami I, Fong TW, Siani A, Carlotti C, Khanious H (2013). Documentation of psychiatric disorders and related factors in a large sample population of HIV-positive patients in California. *AIDS Behav* 17:2792–2801.

Parsons JT, Halkitis PN, Wolitski RJ, Gomez CA (2003). Correlates of sexual risk behaviors among HIV-positive men who have sex with men. *AIDS Educ Prev* 15:383–400.

Pence BW, Miller WC, Whetten K, Eron JJ, Gaynes BN (2006). Prevalence of DSM-IV—defined mood, anxiety, and substance use disorders in an HIV clinic in the Southeastern United States. *J Acquir Immune Defic Syndr* 42:298–306.

Peng EY, Lee MB, Morisky DE, et al. (2010). Psychiatric morbidity in HIV-infected prisoners. *J Formosan Med Assoc* 109(3):177–184.

Pollack MH, Otto MW, Bernstein JG, Rosenbaum JF (2004). Anxious patients. In TA Stern, GL Fricchione, NH Cassem, MS Jellinek, JF Rosenbaum (eds.), *Massachusetts General Hospital Handbook of General Hospital Psychiatry*, 5th ed. Philadelphia: Mosby.

Rapaport M, Braff DL (1985). AIDS and homosexual panic. *Am J Psychiatry* 142(12):1516.

Ravindran AV, Da Silva TL, Ravindran LN, Richter MA, Rector, NA (2009). Obsessive–compulsive spectrum disorders: a review of the evidence-based treatments. *Can J Psychiatry* 54(5):331–343.

Reif S, Proeschold-Bell RJ, Yao J, LeGrand S, Uehara A, Asiimwe E, Quinlivan EB (2013). Three types of self-efficacy associated with medication adherence in patients with co-occurring HIV and substance disorders, but only when mood disorders are present. *J Multidisciplinary Healthcare* 3(6):229–237.

Reiss S, McNally RJ (1985). Expectancy model of fear. In S Reiss, RR Bootzin (eds.), *Theoretical Issues in Behavior Therapy* (pp. 107–121). Orlando, FL: Academic Press.

Reyes JC, Robles RR, Colon HM, Marrero CA, Matos TD, Calderon JM, Shephard EW (2007). Severe anxiety symptomatology and HIV risk behavior among Hispanic injection drug users in Puerto Rico. *AIDS Behav* 11:145–150.

Roy-Byrne PP, Davidson KW, Kessler RC, et al. (2008). Anxiety disorders and comorbid medical illness. *Gen Hosp Psychiatry* 30:208–225.

Schechter JB, Myers MF, Solyom L (1991). A case of obsessive-compulsive disorder related to AIDS: psychopharmacologic treatment. *Can J Psychiatry* 36:118–120.

Semple S, Strathdee S, Zians J, McQuaid J, Patterson, T (2010). Correlates of obsessive-compulsive disorder in a sample of HIV-positive, methamphetamine-using men who have sex with men. *AIDS Behav* 15(6):1153–1160.

Sewell MC, Goggin KJ, Rabkin JG, Ferrando SJ, McElhiney MC, Evans S (2000). Anxiety syndromes and symptoms among men with AIDS: a longitudinal controlled study. *Psychosomatics* 41:294–300.

Shacham E, Morgan J, Önen NF, Taniguchi T, Overton ET (2012). Screening anxiety in the HIV clinic. *AIDS Behav* 16:2407–2413.

Shelburne CD, Hays RD, Fleishman JA, et al. (2000). Impact of psychiatric conditions on health-related quality of life in persons with HIV infection. *Am J Psychiatry* 157:248–254.

Sherbourne CD, Wells KB, Meredith LS, Jackson CA, Camp P (1996). Comorbid anxiety disorder and the functioning and well-being of chronically ill patients of general medical providers. *Arch Gen Psychiatry* 53(10):889–895.

Sherman AC, Mosier J, Leszcz M, et al. (2004). Group interventions for patients with cancer and HIV disease: Part I: Effects on psychosocial and functional outcomes at different phases of illness. *Int J Group Psychother* 54(1):29–82.

Sikkema KJ, Hensen NB, Kochman A, Tate DC, Difranceisco W (2004). Outcomes from a randomized controlled trial of a group intervention for HIV-positive men and women coping with AIDS-related loss and bereavement. *Death Stud* 28:187–209.

Sledjeski EM, Delahanty DL, Bogart LM (2005). Incidence and impact of posttraumatic stress disorder and comorbid depression on adherence to HAART and CD4+ counts in people living with HIV. *AIDS Patient Care STDs* 19(11):728–736.

Smits JA, Berry AC, Tart CD, Powers MB (2008). The efficacy of cognitive-behavioral interventions for reducing anxiety sensitivity: a meta-analytic review. *Behav Res Ther* 46(9):1047–1054.

Spitzer R, Kroenke K, Williams J, Lowe B (2006). A brief measure for assessing generalized anxiety disorder: the GAD-7. *Arch Intern Med* 166:1092–1097.

Springer SA, Dushaj A, Azar MM (2012). The impact of DSM-IV mental disorders on adherence to combination antiretroviral therapy among adult persons living with HIV/AIDS: a systematic review. *AIDS Behav* 16:2119–2143.

Summers J, Zisook S, Atkinson JH, et al. (1995). Morbidity associated with acquired immune deficiency syndrome-related grief resolution. *J Nerv Ment Dis* 183(6):384–389.

Tavakkoli M, Cohen MA, Alfonso CA, Batista SM, Tiamson-Kassab MLA, Meyer P (2014). Caring for persons with early childhood trauma, PTSD, and HIV: a curriculum for clinicians. *Acad Psychiatry* 38:696–700.

Taylor DN (1995). Effects of a behavioral stress-management program on anxiety, mood, self-esteem, and T-cell count in HIV positive men. *Psychol Rep* 76(2):451–457.

Thompson A, Silverman B, Dzeng L, Treisman G (2006). Psychotropic medications and HIV. *Clin Infect Dis* 42(9):1305–1310.

Trachman SB (1992). Buspirone-induced psychosis in a human immunodeficiency virus–infected man. *Psychosomatics* 33:332–335.

Tsao JCI, Dobalian A, Naliboff BD (2004). Panic disorder and pain in a national sample of persons living with HIV. *Pain* 109: 172–180.

Tukei VJ, Asiimwe A, Maganda A, et al. (2012). Safety and tolerability of antiretroviral therapy among HIV-infected children and adolescents in Uganda. *J Acquir Immune Defic Syndr* 59(3): 274–280.

Vega P, Sweetland A, Acha J, et al. (2004). Psychiatric issues in the management of patients with multidrug-resistant tuberculosis. *Int J Tuberc Lung Dis* 8(6): 749–759.

Vitiello B, Burnam A, Bing E, Beckman R, Shapiro M (2003). Use of psychotropic medications among HIV-infected patients in the United States. *Am J Psychiatry* 160(3):547–554.

Vuorio KA, Aarela E, Lehtinen V (1990). Eight cases of patients with unfounded fear of AIDS. *Int J Psychiatry Med* 20(4):405–411.

Walkup J, Blank MB, Gonzales JS, et al. (2008). The impact of mental health and substance abuse factors on HIV prevention and treatment. *J Acquir Immune Defic Syndr* 47:S15–S19.

Wells KB, Golding JM, Burnam MA (1988). Psychiatric disorder in a sample of the general population with and without chronic medical conditions. *Am J Psychiatry* 145(8):976–981.

Wells KB, Golding JM, Burnam MA (1989). Chronic medical conditions in a sample of the general population with anxiety, affective, and substance use disorders. *Am J Psychiatry* 146(11):1440–1446.

Whetten K, Whetten RA, Ostermann J, Itemba D (2008). Trauma, anxiety and reported health among HIV-positive persons in Tanzania and the US Deep South. *AIDS Care* 20:1233–1241.

Wilens T, Spencer T (2010). Understanding attention-deficit/hyperactivity disorder from childhood to adulthood. *Postgrad Med* 122(5):97–109.

Wilkes S (2008). The use of bupropion SR in cigarette smoking cessation. *Int J Chron Obstruct Pulmon Dis* 3(1):45–53.

Zahari MM, Hwan BW, Zainal NZ, Habil H, Kamarulzaman A, Altice FL (2010). Psychiatric and substance abuse comorbidity among HIV seropositive and HIV seronegative prisoners in Malaysia. *Am J Drug Alcohol Abuse* 36(1):31–38.

Zegans LS, Gerhard AL, Coates TJ (1994). Psychotherapies for the person with HIV disease. *Psychiatr Clin North Am* 17(1):149–162.

Zigmond AS, Snaith RP (1983). The Hospital Anxiety and Depression Scale. *Acta Pscyhiatr Scand* 67:361–370.

Zinbarg RE, Brown TA, Barlow DH, Rapee RM (2001). Anxiety sensitivity, panic, and depressed mood: a re-analysis teasing apart the contributions of the two levels in the hierarchical structure of the anxiety sensitivity index. *J Abnorm Psychol* 110:372–377.

19.

PSYCHOTIC DISORDERS AND SERIOUS MENTAL ILLNESS

Alexander Thompson, Daniel Williams, Oliver Freudenreich, Andrew Angelino, Glenn J. Treisman

INTRODUCTION

Treating people with serious mental illnesses and HIV/AIDS is one of the more challenging tasks in modern medicine. While we have well-studied, effective treatments for serious mental illnesses like schizophrenia, bipolar disorder, and major depressive disorder, using those treatments in someone with HIV/AIDS is complicated by issues of adherence, drug interactions, and the social and environmental barriers that go along with having a serious mental illness. On the other hand, advances in managing HIV have turned a once devastating terminal diagnosis into a manageable chronic illness in just a few decades. However, successfully managing an individual with a new diagnosis of HIV who needs to commit to life-long antiretroviral therapy is greatly complicated when that person has a substance use disorder as well as another psychiatric disorder, a serious mental illness (the so-called triply diagnosed). In this chapter we discuss basic principles involved in caring for someone with HIV/AIDs and a serious mental illness.

EPIDEMIOLOGY AND TREATMENT OVERVIEW

Infection with HIV is now best understood as a chronic illness. According to the Centers for Disease Control and Prevention (CDC), in the United States, at least 1.2 million people are living with this infection, of which a significant minority (12%) are not aware that they are infected (CDC, 2016). Using only statistics from the United States runs the risk of understating the global HIV/AIDS problem. Persons with HIV infection in the United States account for less than 5% of the total number of people in the world dealing with this infection (about 37 million). In fact, the number of people living with HIV in the United States is equal to the number of people each year who die worldwide from this disease (Kaiser Family Foundation, 2015). In the United States, the epidemic is not generalized, but concentrated in subpopulations with higher risk. In people described as having serious mental illness (SMI), rates of infection and transmission have been estimated as more than 70 times that of the general population (Andriote and Cournos, 2012). There is also substantial research demonstrating that persons with HIV/AIDS have high risk and prevalence of SMI and other medical problems. This two-way (or often three- or four-way)

street of illness has been described as a *syndemic* (Blank and Eisenberg, 2013a), and the triply diagnosed individual (HIV, SMI, and substance abuse) is one of the most vulnerable in the world.

Given the increased rates of HIV among people with mental illness, we might claim that HIV/AIDS has reached an epidemic proportion in this population. Persons with mental illness and HIV/AIDS are at high risk to have poor outcomes because of lack of access to healthcare, poor social and financial support, cognitive limitations, difficult environmental factors, and a propensity toward high-risk behaviors. Compared with HIV-positive individuals without mental illness, people with mental illness receive their HIV diagnoses later, are less likely to receive treatment, and are more likely to experience morbidity and earlier mortality (Blank et al., 2013).

Regarding serious mental illness, approximately 2.6% of persons in the United States meet the criteria (based on duration, disability, and diagnosis) for SMI in a given year (Kessler et al., 1996). Most individuals with SMI have schizophrenia, bipolar disorder, and major depressive disorder, requiring extended or frequent hospitalizations (Regier et al., 1990). Schizophrenia and bipolar disorder can impair a person's ability to perceive HIV risk, modify behavior, and participate in treatment. Adequate consideration and treatment of the specific symptoms in individual patients will maximize their adherence to a comprehensive treatment plan.

Medical comorbidities, including HIV/AIDS, are common among people with mental illness (Green et al., 2003; Jones et al., 2004; McKinnon et al., 2002). The treatment of people with mental illness and HIV infection requires greater attention, more resources, and a multidisciplinary setting (Horberg et al., 2011). People with mental illness and HIV/AIDS often frustrate their HIV clinicians, who may not have adequate training to treat the comorbid psychiatric disorders.

The National HIV/AIDS Strategy's treatment cascade (The White House, 2015) highlights that over 50% of people diagnosed with HIV are not in medical care (Mugavero et al., 2013). Delays in HIV treatment for people with HIV and mental illness may be due to concerns about inadequate adherence and emergence of viral resistance, a sense of futility about outcomes, and patients' lack of cooperation and adherence to treatment recommendations. Nearly half of newly diagnosed patients with HIV enter into medical care within 3 months, and 30% enter into medical care within

4–12 months. However, 22% do not initiate medical care in the first 12 months of diagnosis (Tripathi et al., 2011). Although people with HIV and chronic mental illness are less likely to be treated with antiretroviral therapy (ART) (Fairfield et al., 1999), they may be the patients most immediately in need of treatment. Invariably, substance abuse, which is present in at least half of most samples with severe mental illness, is seen as complicating and worsening treatment outcomes and disease progression.

There are many compelling reasons to make a concerted effort to provide adequate and comprehensive treatment for persons with HIV/AIDS and mental illness. Patients in successful mental health treatment have better quality of life and better care for themselves, and they participate in family and community life. As such, the goals for HIV/AIDS clinics and clinicians should be to improve quality of life by providing support, changing damaging beliefs, and reducing harmful behavior. Furthermore, improved mental health enables patients to engage, participate in, tolerate, and adhere to medical care and treatment for HIV, and it decreases the risk of transmission of HIV to others, through behavior modification and decreasing viral suppression.

SERIOUS MENTAL ILLNESS, HIV RISK, AND HIV PREVENTION

People with chronic mental illness have an increased risk of acquiring and transmitting HIV compared to the general population (Andriote and Cournos, 2012; Hobkirk et al., 2015). In the past, it was often assumed that just having an SMI such as schizophrenia or bipolar disorder was itself a risk factor for becoming infected with HIV (Gottesman and Groom, 1997). But the reality is that factors driving risk for HIV transmission in persons with SMI is more complicated than just having a symptomatic mental illness—it is all of the social and environmental factors (homelessness, threat of violence, high-risk sexual and drug use behavior) that are often present in persons with SMI that bring about the increased risk (Hobkirk et al., 2015).

Surprisingly, some studies have found that mentally ill individuals who practice risky behaviors had greater knowledge of HIV risks than individuals who did not (Chuang and Atkinson, 1996, McKinnon et al., 1996). However, more knowledge may not translate into less risky behaviors, and subsequent studies found reduced knowledge of HIV risks in persons with schizophrenia (DeHert et al., 2011). High-risk behaviors more common among psychiatric patients include multiple partners; partners with known HIV-positive status; substance use during sex; trading sex for money, drugs, or housing; and lack of condom use (Treisman and Angelino, 2004). Interestingly, compared to individuals with substance abuse alone, persons with SMI and substance abuse have similar numbers of sexual partners and rates of unprotected oral, anal, and vaginal sex; but persons with SMI have significantly increased rates of very high–risk behaviors: trading sex for money or gifts, being forced to have sex, having sex with intravenous drug users and persons with known HIV-positive status, and sharing needles (Dausey and Desai, 2003).

Coercive sexual behavior and physical violence in particular have been shown to be frequent among chronically mentally ill patients (Carey et al., 1997). Many individuals with mental illness have unstable housing and finances, making access to condoms and clean injection tools more difficult (Drake and Wallach, 1989; McKinnon et al., 2002).

Many clinicians use counseling about risky behavior as the primary means of HIV prevention. Data on people with SMI indicate that, at baseline, people with mental illness have more difficulty with behavior self-modification, limiting the degree to which better knowledge of HIV prevention actually translates into behavior change (Carey et al., 1997). Thus, the HIV clinician and clinic staff need to both educate and actively intervene to facilitate behavior change. Interventions focused on persons with SMI can be effective especially if it includes education about specific topics with regular content repetition. Such topics include training on how to combat the problem of poor medical appointment attendance, enhancing assertiveness and negotiation, and how to get away from high-risk situations (Hobkirk et al., 2015). In addition, it is important to address beliefs related to HIV risk, means of improving sexual or drug paraphernalia hygiene, negotiation of condom use, recognition of vulnerable emotional states, ways of avoiding risky behaviors, and sexual empowerment. A thorough evaluation is required in order to identify individual risk factors for acquiring HIV and develop interventions to reduce this risk. Patients with mental illness consistently underestimate the risk of their own behaviors (Carey et al., 1997). Helping patients to find other financial support or substance abuse treatment is critical toward reducing the exchange of sex for money or drugs. Screening and treatment for victims of sexual abuse and assault should be addressed, since in one group of psychiatric outpatients, 13% reported being pressured for sex, and 14% reported being coerced or forced into sex in the past year (Carey et al., 1997). In all settings, same-sex partnerships should be discussed, since there is a high prevalence of same-sex activity, particularly in men who have serious mental illness (McKinnon et al., 2002).

PSYCHIATRIC TREATMENT IN PERSONS WITH SMI AND HIV/AIDS

Psychiatric treatment is especially important for individuals with psychosis, as there may be a correlation between active psychiatric symptoms and high-risk behaviors (Hobkirk et al., 2015). Successful reduction of positive symptoms of schizophrenia or manic symptoms in someone with bipolar disorder may lead to a reduction in risky behaviors and improved overall treatment adherence and outcomes. Antidepressant therapy can be helpful for patients with depression, as individuals with depression may also engage in risky behavior because of a sense of hopelessness.

It is critical that patients set goals toward healthy partnerships and discuss what a healthy relationship entails, as many patients may never have experienced a stable romantic relationship. Having positive goals toward developing loving relationships also helps patients maintain a positive focus and appeals to reward-seeking extroverts; HIV risk counseling often focuses solely on risks and thus appeals less to extroverts who are less risk avoidant. Although HIV risk counseling in patients with SMI can produce significant reductions in risk behavior after fewer than 10 treatment sessions (McKinnon et al., 2002), the practice of risk reduction fades over time, thus sessions that help maintain risk reduction may help to sustain subsequent benefits.

SCHIZOPHRENIA

The prototypical psychotic disorder, schizophrenia, is at its core a neurocognitive disorder with executive dysfunction. Viewed in this light, patients can be expected to have difficulties planning and carrying out complex tasks, particularly when an adaptive and flexible response to environmental and interpersonal situations is needed. Executive dysfunction in the context of HIV interferes with optimal HIV treatment and with the ability to manage risks and modify behaviors to reduce the chances of acquiring HIV in the first place.

In addition to the cognitive deficits, schizophrenia is characterized by both positive and negative features. The more chronic and disabling negative features are often the least well understood by medical practitioners and yet may profoundly influence the relationship with the clinician. The "positive" features include episodes of psychosis in which individuals develop hallucinations (usually auditory), delusions (often paranoid and bizarre), and disordered thinking. These intrusive experiences are often disturbing and can lead to unpredictable and bizarre behavior that alienates them from others and may be dangerous to the self or others.

In general, there is no difference between the pharmacological treatment of schizophrenia in an HIV-infected individual and the treatment of an uninfected person, but some specific considerations should be kept in mind. It is important to take into consideration interactions between ART medications and antipsychotics; psychiatrists and HIV practitioners must work together closely during initiation of or changes in antiretroviral or antipsychotic treatment, as concomitant alterations in dosing may be needed (Treisman and Angelino, 2004). Antipsychotics are associated with potentially severe side effects, such as tardive dyskinesia and parkinsonian syndromes, known as extrapyramidal symptoms (EPS). Patients with HIV are more sensitive to the extrapyramidal side effects of antipsychotics than patients who are HIV negative, particularly during advanced disease stages. In addition, antipsychotics have effects on metabolism, including weight gain, increased insulin resistance, and increased lipids, that may aggravate similar effects produced by antiviral medications (Ferrera et al., 2014)

Treatment principles for persons with schizophrenia apply universally. They include medications for the control of hallucinations, delusions, thought disorders, and negative symptoms, as well as psychosocial rehabilitation for reintegration into the community. Studies have shown that adequate treatment of positive symptoms leads to significant reductions in HIV risk behaviors (McKinnon et al., 1996). The treatment of negative symptoms may help to motivate and engage the patient in treatment. Reality testing should be supported at all times, and the confrontation of delusional thoughts should be gentle and appropriately timed.

Patients might need additional support (e.g., a visiting nurse) or assisted treatment (e.g., court-ordered treatment where available) to achieve sufficient medication compliance. Long-acting injectable antipsychotics (LAIs) may be helpful for patients unable to adhere to oral regimens (Peng et al., 2011). However, LAIs are no panacea, as the patient still needs to accept the injection. The incorporation of friends and family into the treatment plan can improve adherence to treatment and reinforce consistency of the treatment message and provide support to these caregivers. Occasionally, issues arise because of delusions the schizophrenic person has concerning the HIV infection itself. The most common of these is the belief that the person does not have an HIV infection and that the situation is a hoax, created to monitor the person's activity or somehow control the person (Treisman and Angelino, 2004). Adequate antipsychotic treatment combined with a consistent but supportive message from the family, psychiatric team, and HIV team can address delusions and hallucinations that interfere with HIV treatment. Given its pernicious effect on adherence in particular, substance abuse needs to be addressed in all patients with schizophrenia (Drake and Wallach, 1989).

BIPOLAR DISORDER

Bipolar disorder is an illness that impacts the affective domain of one's mental health and accounts for many patients with severe mental illness. This condition may be misdiagnosed as schizophrenia when psychosis is prominent, overshadowing the mood disturbance. In the classic descriptions of bipolar disorder, patients spend extended periods of time depressed, usually weeks to months at a time, followed by shorter periods when they are in an elevated, euphoric, and energized state, referred to as *mania*. Most often, patients cycle from one type of mood to the other, these cycles often interspersed with periods of normal moods but occasionally with intermediate mixed states that have features of both depressive and elevated mood states simultaneously or in rapid succession. The emotions and emotional changes in persons with bipolar disorder run their lives and can have a strong effect on their attitude toward treatment from minute to minute (Treisman and Angelino, 2004). Bipolar disorder is covered in more detail in Chapter 15 of this book.

In contrast to the bipolar disorder found in the general population, another type of mania appears to be specifically associated with late-stage HIV infection (CD4 count <200 per mm^3), and it occurs in cognitive impairment or dementia (Kiburtz et al., 1991). This syndrome has been called "AIDS mania" and probably represents a related but different condition, as the patients show a lack of previous episodes or family history (Lyketsos et al., 1997). Clinically, patients with AIDS mania may be difficult to distinguish from patients with delirium, because the sleep–wake cycle is often disturbed and individuals show a good deal of confusion and cognitive impairment. For this reason, the workup begins with a careful evaluation of the causes of delirium. Persons with AIDS mania may differ clinically from persons with familial bipolar disorder, as the predominant mood tends to be irritability rather than elation or euphoria. A review at a hospital AIDS clinic in the United States found that 8% of patients with AIDS experienced a manic syndrome at some point during the course of the illness (Lyketsos et al., 1993). Of these patients experiencing manic syndromes, half had no personal or family history of bipolar disorder and were more likely to have later-stage AIDS. Another study in Uganda found that, compared to persons with primary bipolar disorder, persons with AIDS mania were more often female, older, less educated, and more cognitively impaired (Nakimuli-Mpunga et al., 2006). They also had more manic symptoms, including more irritability, more aggression, and more auditory hallucinations. Personal or family history, imaging findings, and other clinical indicators may help to distinguish between AIDS mania and bipolar mania associated with AIDS (Lyketsos et al., 1993).

MAJOR DEPRESSIVE DISORDER

Depression is the most common psychiatric disorder and is common among individuals with HIV/AIDS. A meta-analysis of studies reported active depression in 9.4% of individuals with HIV/AIDS compared with 5.2% in HIV-negative individuals (Ciesla and Roberts, 2001). Individuals with depression are predisposed to greater HIV/AIDS risk for several reasons. Higher HIV risk may result from a sense of hopelessness about the future. Additionally, persons with depression may seek to alleviate their symptoms with alcohol and other drugs. Alcohol abuse and dependence are prevalent among persons with depression. For persons with depression, alcohol use is a major source of HIV risk; under the influence of alcohol depressed persons are more likely to engage in risky sexual behaviors and intravenous drug use (IDU) because of decreased inhibition (McKinnon et al., 2002). Impairments of memory and attention may distract depressed individuals from self-care and risk reduction behaviors and can decrease the likelihood of being diagnosed or entering treatment. Depressive disorder with psychotic features magnifies suffering that is further intensified when it is self-medicated with chronic alcohol or stimulant misuse. This complex multimorbid combination of psychosis, depression, and substance misuse results in difficult-to-understand symptoms at presentation.

Persons with major depressive disorders can be strongly resistant to HIV therapy; they may have difficulty engaging in treatment and maintaining treatment adherence. Because depressed persons feel hopeless, they are less likely to seek care or testing and counseling. It is difficult to engage depressed patients in treatment because they are preoccupied with negative ideas and low mood. Once involved in treatment, one must make an extra effort to maintain their engagement because depression leads to low motivation and energy. This obstacle can be partially overcome through the use of incremental goals and rewards (Treisman and Angelino, 2004). Because depression causes decreased memory and concentration, patients have a more difficult time with medication adherence. Visual cues and memory aids may help improve adherence, and social

support can improve morale and adherence. It is therefore necessary to treat depression concomitantly with HIV/AIDS if clinicians wish to succeed in viral suppression.

Major depressive disorder is covered in further detail in Chapter 15 of this book.

SUBSTANCE USE DISORDERS

The importance of substance abuse treatment in the care of mentally ill patients with HIV/AIDS cannot be overemphasized. To maximize risk reduction, substance abuse should be addressed in all settings, including behavioral interventions, support for maintaining risk reduction, and medical and psychiatric appointments with healthcare professionals. Numerous studies have shown that persons with schizophrenia and other chronic mental illnesses have high rates of substance abuse, generally ranging from 40% to 75% depending on the substances considered and method of ascertainment (Caton et al., 1989; Horwath et al., 1996; Miller and Tannenbaum, 1989; Regier et al., 1990; Test et al., 1989; Toner et al., 1992).

Various explanations have been given for the use of substances by psychiatric patients, one being that mentally ill persons self-medicate with substances in an attempt to alleviate symptoms or ameliorate side effects of medicines (Dixon et al., 1991; Drake et al., 1989; Khantzian, 1985; Lamb, 1982; Mueser et al., 1990; Test et al., 1989). Another theory is that chronically ill persons have disruptions of social functioning and use substances as a means of connecting with others (Alterman et al., 1982). Although these explanations help clinicians treat dually diagnosed patients, the epidemiological fact remains that persons with severe mental illnesses use substances frequently and should be considered at greater risk for HIV, regardless of the etiological underpinnings of this association.

Substance abuse affects many aspects of HIV/AIDS treatment. It worsens prognosis and compliance, interferes with the creation and maintenance of healthy social relationships, increases risk behaviors, and decreases judgment and insight (Drake and Wallach, 1989; Drake et al., 1996; McKinnon et al., 2002; Mueser et al., 1992). Studies have shown that substance abuse or dependence concurrent with HIV/AIDS is associated with a more severe course of illness and poor medication compliance (RachBeisel et al., 1999). Substance abuse, by worsening psychiatric disorders, may cause more symptoms or worsen one's coping ability and lead to increased high-risk behavior. IDU must be specifically recognized and addressed, as any lifetime IDU increases the risk of HIV infection from 2- to 10-fold (Horwath et al., 1996). Five to 26% of psychiatric patients report prior injection and 1–8% report IDU in the past 3–12 months (Carey et al., 1997; Rosenberg et al., 2001; Susser et al., 1996). It is thus critical to inquire about IDU at all visits, as IDU among people with severe mental illness is often intermittent (Horwath et al., 1996; McKinnon et al., 2002). People with mental illness are more likely to be part of social networks that include intravenous drug users, increasing the risk of sexual transmission as well as IDU-related infection.

Agonist-based therapies may provide a particularly effective form of treatment for opiate users. Methadone maintenance therapy is highly effective in the management of opiate addiction among persosn who are chronically mentally ill. Adherence to a methadone program has been shown to decrease HIV risk behavior (Wong et al., 2003); it removes individuals from high-risk behaviors and environments while reducing motivation to seek IDU in the community. Moreover, individuals on methadone maintenance therapy demonstrate better adherence to ART, which decreases the overall cost of health care (Sambamoorthi et al., 2000). Methadone can be used by clinicians to give positive reinforcement for desired behaviors, such as rewarding a patient with take-home methadone after several months of negative toxicology screens. Methadone maintenance decreases drug-related morbidity and mortality and crime and improves patient function, leading to improved ability to participate in care.

Although IDU often receives more attention than other substance use in addressing HIV risk and care from clinicians, all forms of substance abuse contribute to risk and a person's level of function. Alcohol, cocaine, and methamphetamine abuse are particularly important to address in HIV treatment, as their use is associated with high-risk sexual behaviors (McKinnon et al., 2002). Most importantly, substance abuse stands between the goals of HIV treatment and helping the patient with chronic mental illness, as it demoralizes patients; prevents them from achieving stable living situations, work, and healthy relationships; and increases the severity of underlying psychiatric illness. Without the ability to achieve consistency and stability in life, individuals have little opportunity to achieve consistent treatment adherence and improved functional outcome. Substance abuse among individuals with chronic mental illness is widespread, leads to practice of behaviors that put them at risk for HIV, is a poor prognostic factor for psychiatric and HIV treatment, and is associated with increased mortality (DeLorenze et al., 2011).

MEDICAL TREATMENT OF PERSONS WITH SMI AND HIV/AIDS

Individuals with chronic mental illness are less likely to have access to medical care and are more likely to be without insurance, homeless, and unemployed (Folsom et al., 2005; Meade and Sikkema, 2005). Not surprisingly, HIV treatment outcomes are generally worse for individuals with SMI (Cournos et al., 2005; Goldman, 2000). In addition to societal and system factors, patient and clinician factors also contribute to less optimal outcomes. For example, psychiatric patients with SMI may have a poor appreciation of their medical conditions and may be both less aware of their physical condition and less likely to have or seek adequate medical care. The treatment of mentally ill patients is often more difficult and time consuming for clinicians than for patients without mental illness. Because they are a more difficult population to treat, clinicians are hesitant to accept them as patients, and they are at higher risk for being discharged from care. Psychiatric patients also have decreased ability to participate in their care because of cognitive and emotional limitations. They often fail

to appreciate benefits of treatment snot immediately apparent and are focused concretely on the here and now.

Patients with apathy and low mood may feel that treatment is pointless or feel that they just don't have the energy to participate. Decreased concentration, memory, and executive planning function in many conditions may cause patients to forget medications and appointments.

HIV and medical screening of psychiatric patients is inadequate in psychiatric and medical settings. Patients with severe, chronic mental illness may receive limited medical attention in general and therefore are at risk for sequelae of undiagnosed disorders, such as neurosyphilis and chronic pelvic inflammatory disease. It is also known that women with HIV/AIDS are less likely to receive prenatal care during pregnancy (Turner et al., 1996) and thus are more likely to spread infection to their offspring. It is therefore necessary to aggressively screen individuals with mental illness for HIV; substance abuse and other medical illnesses, such as diabetes, hepatitis, hypertension; and heart disease (Hobkirk et al., 2015). Screening should happen in settings where patients are actually seen, which might mean that psychiatrists need to take an active role in HIV screening. It is helpful for both patients and clinicians to centralize care as much as possible, making all clinicians aware of all medical problems as well as the current treatment plan to provide a consistent message (Treisman and Angelino, 2004). Frequent pregnancy testing and on-site prenatal care may improve outcomes for pregnant women or women of child-bearing age with HIV.

It is important to incorporate preventative medicine whenever possible, including smoking cessation, weight management, and risk reduction; this counseling has been often overlooked in patients with multiple medical problems and with HIV but is even more crucial now that HIV/AIDS has become a chronic illness. Psychiatric practitioners should be vigilant about screening for medical illnesses, even using a standard medical review questionnaire for the periodic assessment of a patient's medical status. Patients with altered mental status in particular need special attention and careful physical examinations because they may be less likely or able to report symptoms. In addition, we urge medical practitioners in clinics to take extra care in examining individuals who are chronically mentally ill because often their illnesses, or the stigma attached to them, prevent open lines of communication.

In medicine, physicians often seek to educate patients about risks to their health and benefits of treatment and health maintenance in an effort to influence patients' behavior toward compliance and improved quality of life. Clinicians treating people with chronic mental illness, however, have to take a modified approach to therapy, as many patients will need sustained support over time and tailored toward impairments characteristic for patients with SMI (e.g., executive dysfunction). As discussed earlier, chronically mentally ill individuals with HIV who engage in risky behaviors are often better educated about risks than their HIV-positive counterparts who are not mentally ill (Chuang and Atkinson, 1996, McKinnon et al., 1996), perhaps because of their clinicians' efforts to motivate them to change through increased education about HIV risk. This suggests that education alone may be successful in increasing knowledge in this population, but not in changing behavior. Cognitive-behavioral therapy can be useful in this regard; identifying harmful attitudes, ideas, and behaviors and creating a framework of new, healthy attitudes and behaviors is helpful for patients who struggle to modify their behavior. Interventions in which patients actively practice health hygiene, behavior modification, safer-sex negotiation, and positive interactions with others help patients to realize their own ability to retrain patterns of harmful behaviors.

Although education is essential, and negative outcomes must be discussed with patients, an optimistic, behavior-focused plan for patients is often more helpful than general discussion of health risks. We encourage clinicians to take small steps in behavior modification, setting one or two concrete goals at each visit and following their progress, praising success, and exploring the cause of failures. These steps also help patients to build rapport with clinicians and build confidence in patients as well as clinicians, who tend to get discouraged with negative outcomes of mentally ill patients.

ADHERENCE

Nonadherence to medical treatment is one of the major problems in treating individuals with HIV/AIDS. It has been demonstrated that greater than 90% adherence to an ART regimen is needed in order to achieve effective suppression in most patients, at least for regimens that used to be standard just a few years ago (Moreno et al., 2000; Paterson et al., 2000). One study that examined individuals with directly observed therapy (DOT) found that 93% adherence led to 85% of patients achieving an undetectable viral load (Kirkland et al., 2002). Good adherence to ART is related to improved HIV-related mortality, morbidity, and reduced hospitalization (Press et al., 2002).

Difficulty with adherence is compounded among patients with chronic mental illness because they have characteristics predisposing them to poor adherence, including disease-specific problems (e.g., trouble with memory and concentration and the aforementioned executive dysfunction) but also environmental difficulties (e.g., less funds available for medications, lack of transportation, lack of stable housing, homelessness, unemployment, and lack of social support; Chander et al., 2006). A recent study demonstrated that, in patients with bipolar disorder and HIV, greater depressive symptoms and more negative opinions about medication worsened adherence (Casaletto et al., 2016). Factors adversely affecting adherence the most for HIV-positive individuals with severe mental illness are problems with planning, lack of interaction with others, failure to use cues, and HIV/AIDS treatment issues related to lack of motivation, side effects, and hopelessness (Kemppainen et al., 2004). Thus, each patient with HIV/AIDS should be given a thorough assessment for access to medications, transportation, housing, social support, work and ability to work, finances, including ability to afford necessities, and cognitive abilities. A strong patient–clinician relationship not only improves adherence but also enables the physician to anticipate barriers to adherence and intervene

early. Patients frequently focus on immediate side effects without appreciating the benefits of treatment. It is important to treat side effects and symptoms whenever possible in order to improve patients' ability to realize the benefits of treatment.

The patient's belief system about treatment and their diagnoses can strongly affect their willingness to take any medications. The belief that treatment will be successful improves adherence to proposed medications. The burden of regular appointments and daily medication is greater on this population, and demoralized patients may easily give up on treatment, sometimes citing futility of treatment due to lack of a cure for HIV. Persons experiencing depression have less ability to perform self-care and subjectively experience more pain than when they are well; treating pain adequately may improve adherence. Persons with decreased memory, concentration, or other cognitive limitations should have reminders or alarms placed in their home and, ideally, a friend or family member to help remind them or even observe the person taking medications and provide encouragement of treatment. Psychiatric consults and referrals can also help address these issues, as remission of illness maximizes the ability to tolerate medical therapy.

COMPREHENSIVE, INTEGRATED HIV SERVICES LEAD TO IMPROVED OUTCOMES FOR PATIENTS AND CLINICIANS

There is great need to develop specialized, integrated care programs to provide excellent care for persons with HIV/AIDS and SMI (Blank et al., 2013). In few other populations of patients could meeting the so-called triple aim in healthcare be so critical. That triple aim speaks to accomplishing effective, high-quality health care that also serves the needs of populations and decreases costs (Berwick et al., 2008). One excellent example of specialized and integrated care for this population is the Preventing AIDS through Health for HIV Positive persons (PATH+) trail that was completed in Philadelphia (Blank et al., 2011). In this pilot program, an advanced practice nurse care manager provided comprehensive medical and psychiatric care for patients, and the intensity of treatment was guided by objective measures of treatment effect. In addition, this was done in consultation with physicians, pharmacists, and other critical members of the healthcare team, effectively leveraging limited resources (like infectious disease doctors and psychiatrists) to direct effective care. Over the course of the study, compared with usual care, there were significant decreases in viral load and improvements in quality of life (Blank et al., 2014). It is important to note that this approach is quite similar in overall form to the evidence-based integrated care models shown to be effective in the management of many psychiatric disorders (Archer et al., 2012).

In addition, there are collaborative clinics where persons with HIV/AIDS and SMI are cared for by co-located medical and psychiatric experts. One example of such a clinic (of which two of the authors are affiliated [GT and AA]) is the Johns Hopkins Hospital HIV clinic (The Moore Clinic). Initially, psychiatric evaluations were performed on site and patients were referred to a formal psychiatry clinic for ongoing care. During the first year of this work, 89 patients agreed to be referred for ongoing psychiatric care. Upon follow-up we learned that none of these 89 patients ever attended follow-up care (Treisman and Angelino, 2004). In response to this, the care teams decided that it would be best to co-locate psychiatric care services in the HIV clinic. This move toward a more integrated approach to care allows clinician collaboration that has the potential to improve the quality of care, with physicians educating each other in their respective specialties, prevent unnecessary care, and help physicians diagnose new problems earlier.

Patients who are able to make one visit to take care of all their needs will have greater ability to attend necessary appointments, as additional transportation and multiple appointments are avoided. On-site counseling, risk reduction, social work, and substance abuse treatment are able to be incorporated into each visit as needed. Ideally, on-site housing support could be incorporated for patients who require living assistance or are homeless. For sites that lack funding for a comprehensive treatment center, addition of psychiatric services is cost-effective, requires little equipment or facilities, and can still retain many of the benefits of collaboration between medical and psychiatric practitioners. In an ideal HIV treatment program, the treatment team would use role induction to outline the conditions of care and give the patient an opportunity to see that clinicians are working together. The program would ideally incorporate cognitive-behavioral therapy to aid with behavior modification and risk reduction, substance abuse treatment, social services, job training and assistance, and medical and psychiatric treatment (Volkow and Montaner, 2011). The program should also have an on-site pharmacy that offers adherence programs to support patients' compliance with medications, make it easier to track medications dispensed, and increase the ability of patients with limited mobility or transportation to obtain medications. Long-acting injectable antipsychotics medications would be administered on-site for individuals needing that treatment and struggling with compliance. A program that incorporates family members or significant others can improve social support for patients and for family members as well as improve treatment adherence.

The more integrated services are, the better patients can be incorporated into a treatment regimen with a team of healthcare professionals to provide support (Mugavero et al., 2011). This includes the use of integrated electronic medical records and health surveillance data available to all clinicians (Bertolli et al., 2012; Herwehe et al., 2012). In the Johns Hopkins Hospital multidisciplinary clinic, HIV-positive patients with psychiatric disorders were more likely to receive ART and had reduced mortality compared to the general HIV-positive population and our own clinic population before the integration of services, presumably because of increased support and more advocacy by mental health professionals. We infer that these improved results in turn led to better viral suppression and reduced risk (Himelhoch et al., 2004). The Johns Hopkins experience shows that we can have success treating this population and that the appropriate management of psychiatric

disorders can facilitate improved quality of life and survival in persons with HIV/AIDS.

REFERENCES

Alterman AI, Erdlen FR, LaPorte DJ (1982). Effects of illicit drug use in an inpatient psychiatric population. *Addict Behav* 7:231–242.

Andriote J, Cournos F (2012). HIV and people with severe mental illness (SMI): American Psychiatric Association. https://www.psychiatry.org/File%20Library/Psychiatrists/Practice/Professional-Topics/HIV-Psychiatry/FactSheet-SMI-2012.pdf. Accessed January 27, 2017.

Archer J, Bower P, Gilbody S, et al. (2012). Collaborative care for depression and anxiety problems. *Cochrane Database Syst Rev* 10:CD006525.

Bertolli, J, Shouse, RL, Beer, L, et al. (2012). Using HIV surveillance data to monitor missed opportunities for linkage and engagement in HIV medical care. *Open AIDS J* 6:131–141.

Berwick DM, Nolan TW, Whittington J (2008). The triple aim: care, health, and cost. *Health Aff (Millwood)* 27(3):759–769.

Blank M, Eisenberg MM (2013a). HIV-infected individuals with mental illness: a case of syndemics. *Ann Psychiatry Ment Health* 1(1):1001.

Blank MB, Eisenberg MM (2013b). Tailored treatment for HIV+ persons with mental illness: the intervention cascade. *J Acquir Immune Defic Syndr* 63(Suppl 1):S44–S48.

Blank MB, Hanrahan NP, Fishbein M, et al. (2011). A randomized trial of a nursing intervention for HIV disease management among persons with serious mental illness. *Psychiatr Serv* 62(11):1318–1324.

Blank MB, Hennessy M, Eisenberg MM (2104). Increasing quality of life and reducing HIV burden: the PATH+ intervention. *AIDS Behav* 18(4):716–725.

Blank MB, Himelhoch S, Walkup J, Eisenberg MM (2013). Treatment considerations for HIV-infected individuals with severe mental illness. *Curr HIV/AIDS Rep* 10(4):371–379.

Carey MP, Carey KB, Weinhardt LS, Gordon CM (1997). Behavioral risk for HIV infection among adults with a severe and persistent mental illness: patterns and psychological antecedents. *Community Ment Health J* 33(2):133–142.

Casaletto K, Kwan S, Montoya J, et al. (2016). Predictors of psychotropic medication adherence among HIV+ individuals living with bipolar disorder. *Int J Psychiatry Med* 51(1):69–83.

Caton CLM, Gralnick A, Bender S, Robert S (1989). Young chronic patients and substance abuse. *Hosp Community Psychiatry* 40:1037–1040.

Centers for Disease Control and Prevention (CDC) (2016). HIV in the United States: at a glance. http://www.cdc.gov/hiv/statistics/overview/ataglance.html. Accessed Janaury 26, 2017.

Chander G, Himelhoch S, Moore RD (2006). Substance abuse and psychiatric disorders in AIDS patients: epidemiology and impact on antiretroviral therapy. *Drugs* 66(6):769–789.

Chuang HT, Atkinson M (1996). AIDS knowledge and high-risk behavior in the chronic mentally ill. *Can J Psychiatry* 41(5):269–272.

Ciesla JA, Roberts JE (2001). Meta-analysis of the relationship between HIV infection and risk for depressive disorder. *Am J Psychiatry* 158(5):725–730.

Cournos F, McKinnon K, Sullivan G (2005). Schizophrenia and comorbid human immunodeficiency virus and hepatitis C. *J Clin Psychiatry* 66(S6):27–33.

Dausey DJ, Desai RA (2003). Psychiatric comorbidity and the prevalence of HIV infection in a sample of patients in treatment for substance abuse. *J Nerv Ment Dis* 191(1):10–17.

De Hert M, Correll Cu, Bobes J, et al (2011). Physical illness in patients with severe mental disorders. I. Prevalence, impact of medications and disparities in health care. *World Psychiatry* 10:52–77.

DeLorenze GN, Weisner C, Tsai AL, Satre DD, Quesenberry Jr, CP (2011). Excess mortality among HIV-infected patients diagnosed with substance use dependence or abuse receiving care in a fully integrated medical care program. *Alcohol Clin Exp Res* 35(2):203–210.

Dixon L, Hass G, Weiden PJ, Sweeny J, Frances AJ (1991). Drug abuse in schizophrenic patients: clinical correlates and reasons for use. *Am J Psychiatry* 148:224–230.

Drake RE, Mueser KT, Clark RE, Wallach MA (1996). The course, treatment, and outcome of substance disorder in persons with severe mental illness. *Am Orthopsychiatr Assoc* 66:42–51.

Drake RE, Osher FC, Wallach MA (1989). Alcohol use and abuse in schizophrenia. *J Nerv Ment Dis* 177:40.

Drake RE, Wallach MA (1989). Substance abuse among the chronic mentally ill. *Hosp Community Psychiatry* 40:1041–1046.

Fairfield KM, Libman H, Davis RB, Eisenberg DM, Philips RS (1999). Delays in protease inhibitor use in clinical practice. *J Gen Intern Med* 14:395–401.

Ferrara M, Umlauf A, Sanders C, et al.; CHARTER Group (2014). The concomitant use of second-generation antipsychotics and long-term antiretroviral therapy may be associated with increased cardiovascular risk. *Psychiatry Res* 218(1-2):201–208.

Folsom DP, Hawthorne W, Lindamer L, et al. (2005). Prevalence and risk factors for homelessness and utilization of mental health services among 10,340 patients with serious mental illness in a large public mental health system. *Am J Psychiatry* 162(2):370–376.

Goldman LS (2000). Comorbid medical illness in psychiatric patients. *Curr Psychiatry Rep* 2(3):256–263.

Gottesman II, Groome CS (1997). HIV/AIDS risks as a consequence of schizophrenia. *Schizophr Bull* 23(4):675–684.

Green AI, Canuso CM, Brenner MJ, Wojcik JD (2003). Detection and management of comorbidity in schizophrenia. *Psychiatr Clin North Am* 26:115–139.

Herwehe J, Wilbright W, Abrams A, et al. (2012). Implementation of an innovative, integrated electronic medical record (EMR) and public health information exchange for HIV/AIDS. *J Am Med Informatics Assoc* 19(3):448–452.

Himelhoch S, Moore RD, Treisman G, Gebo KA (2004). Does the presence of a current psychiatric disorder in AIDS patients affect the initiation of antiretroviral treatment and duration of therapy? *J Acquir Immune Defic Syndr* 37(4):1457–1463.

Hobkirk AL, Towe SL, Lion R, Meade CS (2015). Primary and secondary HIV prevention among persons with severe mental illness: recent findings. *Curr HIV/AIDS Rep* 12(4):406–412.

Horberg M, Hurley L, Towner W, et al. (2011). HIV quality performance measures in a large integrated health care system. *AIDS Patient Care STDS* 25(1):21–28.

Horwath E, Cournos F, McKinnon K, Guido JR, Herman R (1996). Illicit-drug injection among psychiatric patients without a primary substance abuse disorder. *Psychiatr Serv* 47:181–185.

Jones DR, Macias C, Barreira PJ, Fisher WH, Hargreaves WA, Harding CM (2004). Prevalence, severity, and co-occurrence of chronic physical health problems of persons with serious mental illness. *Psychiatr Serv* 55(11):1250–1257.

Kaiser Family Foundation (2016). The global HIV/AIDS epidemic 2015. http://kff.org/global-health-policy/fact-sheet/the-global-hivaids-epidemic/. Accessed January 26, 2017.

Kemppainen JK, Levine R, Buffum M, Holzemer W, Finley P, Jensen P (2004). Antiretroviral adherence in persons with HIV/AIDS and severe mental illness. *J Nerv Ment Dis* 192(6):395–404.

Kessler RC, Nelson CB, McGonagle KA, Liu J, Swartz M, Blazer DG (1996). Comorbidity of DSM-III-R major depressive disorder in the general population: results from the US National Comorbidity Survey. *Br J Psychiatry Suppl* (30):17–30.

Khantzian E (1985). The self-medication hypothesis of addictive disorders: focus on heroin and cocaine dependence. *Am J Psychiatry* 142:1259–1264.

Kiburtz K, Zettelmaier AE, Ketonen L, Tuite M, Caine EC (1991). Manic syndrome in AIDS. *Am J Psychiatry* 98:1068–1070.

Kirkland LR, Fischl MA, Tashima KT, for the NZTA4007 Study Team (2002). Response to lamivudine-zidovudine plus abacavir twice daily in antiretroviral-naive, incarcerated patients

with HIV taking directly observed treatment. *Clin Infect Dis* 34(4):511–518.

Lamb H (1982). Young adult chronic patients: the new drifters. *Hosp Community Psychiatry* 33:465–468.

Lyketsos CG, Hanson AL, Fishman M, Rosenblatt A, McHugh PR, Treisman GJ (1993). Manic syndrome early and late in the course of HIV. *Am J Psychiatry* 150:326–327.

Lyketsos CG, Schwartz J, Fishman M, Treisman G (1997). AIDS mania. *J Neuropsychiatry Clin Neurosci* 9:277–279.

McKinnon K, Cournos F, Herman R (2002). HIV among people with chronic mental illness. *Psychiatry Q* 73(1):17–31.

McKinnon K, Cournos F, Sudgen R, Guido JR, Herman R (1996). The relative contributions of psychiatric symptoms and AIDS knowledge to HIV risk behaviors among people with severe mental illness. *J Clin Psychiatry* 57:506–513.

Meade CS, Sikkema KJ (2005). HIV risk behavior among adults with severe mental illness: a systematic review. *Clin Psychol Rev* 25(4):433–457.

Miller FT, Tanenbaum JH (1989). Drug abuse in schizophrenia. *Hosp Community Psychiatry* 40:847–849.

Moreno A, Perez-Elias MJ, Casado JL, et al. (2000). Effectiveness and pitfalls of initial highly active retroviral therapy in HIV-infected patients in routine clinical practice. *Antivir Ther* 5(4):243–248.

Mueser KT, Bellack AS, Blanchard JJ (1992). Comorbidity of schizophrenia and substance abuse: implications for treatment. *J Consult Clin Psychiatry* 60:845–856.

Mueser KT, Yarnold PR, Levinson DF, et al. (1990). Prevalence of substance abuse in schizophrenia: demographic and clinical correlates. *Schizophr Bull* 16:31–49.

Mugavero MJ, Amico KR, Horn T, Thompson MA (2013). The state of engagement in HIV care in the United States: from cascade to continuum to control. *Clin Infect Dis* 57(8):1164–1171.

Mugavero MJ, Norton WE, Saag MS (2011). Health care system and policy factors influencing engagement in HIV medical care: piecing together the fragments of a fractured health care delivery system. *Clin Infect Dis* 52(Suppl 2):S238–S246.

Nakimuli-Mpungu E, Musisi S, Mpungu SK, Katabira E (2006). Primary mania versus HIV-related secondary mania in Uganda. *Am J Psychiatry* 163(8):1349–1354.

Paterson DL, Swindells S, Mohr J, et al. (2000). Adherence to protease inhibitor therapy and outcomes in patients with HIV infection. *Ann Intern Med* 133:21–30.

Peng X, Ascher-Svanum H, Faries D, Conley RR, Schuh KJ (2011). Decline in hospitalization risk and health care cost after initiation of depot antipsychotics in the treatment of schizophrenia. *Clinicoecon Outcomes Res* 3:9–14.

Press N, Tyndall MW, Wood E, Hogg RS, Montaner JSG (2002). Virologic and immunologic response, clinical progression, and highly active antiretroviral therapy adherence. *J Acquir Immune Defic Syndr* 31:S112–S117.

RachBeisel J, Scott J, Dixon L (1999). Co-occurring severe mental illness and substance use disorders: a review of recent research. *Psychiatr Serv* 50(11):1427–1434.

Regier DA, Farmer ME, Rae DS, Locke BJ, Keith SJ, Judd LL, Goodwin FK (1990). Comorbidity of mental disorders with alcohol and other drug abuse. Results from the Epidemiologic Catchment Area (ECA) study. *JAMA* 264(19):2511–2518.

Rosenberg SD, Trumbetta SL, Mueser KT, Goodman LA, Osher FC, Vidaver RM, Metzger DS (2001). Determinants of risk behavior for human immunodeficiency virus/acquired immunodeficiency syndrome in people with severe mental illness. *Comp Psychiatry* 42(4):263–271.

Sambamoorthi U, Warner LA, Crystal S, Walkup J (2000). Drug abuse, methadone treatment, and health services use among injection drug users with AIDS. *Drug Alcohol Depend* 60(1):77–89.

Susser E, Miller M, Valencia E, Colson P, Roche B, Conover S (1996). Injection drug use and risk of HIV transmission among homeless men with mental illness. *Am J Psychiatry* 153(6):794–798.

Test MA, Wallisch LS, Allness DJ, Ripp K (1989). Substance use in young adults with schizophrenic disorders. *Schizophr Bull* 15:465–476.

The White House (2015). National HIV/AIDS Strategy for the United States Updated to 2020. https://www.aids.gov/federal-resources/national-hiv-aids-strategy/nhas-update.pdf. Accessed January 28, 2017.

Toner BB, Gillies LA, Prendergasst P, Cote FH, Browne C (1992). Substance use disorders in a sample of Canadian patients with chronic mental illness. *Hosp Community Psychiatry* 43:251–254.

Treisman GJ, Angelino AF (2004). *The Psychiatry of AIDS: A Guide to Diagnosis and Treatment.* Baltimore, MD: Johns Hopkins University Press.

Tripathi A, Gardner LI, Ogbuanu I, Youmans E, Stephens T, Gibson JJ, Duffus WA (2011). Predictors of time to enter medical care after a new HIV diagnosis: a statewide population-based study. *AIDS Care* 23(11):1366–1373.

Turner BJ, McKee LJ, Silverman NS, Hauck WW, Fanning TR, Markson LE (1996). Prenatal care and birth outcomes of a cohort of HIV-infected women. *J Acquir Immune Defic Syndr Hum Retrovirol* 12(3):259–267.

Volkow ND, Montaner J (2011). The urgency of providing comprehensive and integrated treatment for substance abusers with HIV. *Health Affairs* 30(8):1411–1419.

Wong KH, Lee SS, Lim WL, Low HK (2003). Adherence to methadone is associated with a lower level of HIV-related risk behaviors in drug users. *J Subst Abuse Treat* 24(3):233–239.

20.

THE ROLE OF PERSONALITY IN HIV RISK BEHAVIORS: IMPLICATIONS FOR TREATMENT

Heidi E. Hutton and Glenn J. Treisman

The risk behaviors associated with transmission of HIV and that can complicate HIV treatment are often influenced by psychiatric disorders. While depressive disorders, substance-related and addictive disorders, trauma-related disorders, and other chronic mental illnesses commonly complicate HIV treatment, it is likely that none can generate more distress and dissension among medical care clinicians than personality problems. Caregiver burnout, failure to establish stable medical care relationships, and "excessive resource utilization" have been associated with certain personality traits and disorders (Gask et al., 2013). There has been little research, however, on the role of personality traits and disorders in HIV despite their stable, durable, and heritable influence on thoughts, feelings, and behavior (Shuper et al., 2014; Springer et al., 2012). Certain traits appear to increase the likelihood of engaging in HIV risk behaviors, having a poorer quality of life, and adhering to treatment regimens. Effective HIV prevention and treatment programs should consider specific personality traits and personality disorders that render some individuals more vulnerable to engaging in behaviors that further endanger their health as well as the health of others. Recognizing these personality traits or disorders is useful in developing more specific, effective risk reduction strategies and improving overall health outcomes.

This chapter will describe personality traits and personality disorders that occur among individuals at risk for or infected with HIV, the state of the current evidence, and the implications for HIV care.

DEFINING PERSONALITY

Personality is defined by the emotional and behavioral characteristics or traits that constitute stable and predictable ways that an individual relates to, perceives, and thinks about the environment and the self (Livesley, 2001; Rothbart and Ahadi, 1994; Rutter, 1987). Early observations of the nature of personality begin with classical scholars such as Hippocrates, Plato, Aristotle, and Galen and later with philosophers such as Aquinas, Machiavelli, Hobbes, Locke, and Nietzsche. Current personality theory, exemplified by the work of Hans Eysenck (Eysenck, 1990), Paul T. Costa, Jr.

(Costa and Widiger, 2002), and C. Robert Cloninger (Cloninger, 1999) has extended these early observations by refining personality descriptions, developing measurement tools, and documenting their influence on functioning. Despite differences in details, the work in the field of personality agrees on these fundamental ideas: (1) individuals vary in the degree to which they possess a given trait and in the way it influences behavior; (2) traits are not positive or negative, but rather are adaptive in one setting and maladaptive in another; and (3) personality is a combination of temperament (or constellation of heritable traits) and character (environmental experience).

EXTROVERSION–INTROVERSION

Most personality taxonomies identify dimensions of extroversion–introversion and stability–instability or neuroticism. The dimension of *extroversion–introversion* refers to the individual's basic tendency to respond to stimuli with either excitation or inhibition. Individuals who are *extroverted* are (1) present-oriented, (2) feeling-directed, and (3) reward-seeking (Eysenck, 1990, Lucas et al., 2000; Widiger and Costa, 2012). Their chief focus is their immediate and emotional experience. Feelings dominate thoughts, and the predominant motivation is immediate gratification or relief from discomfort. Extroverts are charismatic, sociable, venturesome, optimistic, and impulsive. By contrast, *introverted* individuals are (1) future- and past-oriented, (2) cognition-directed, and (3) consequence-avoidant. Logic and function predominate over feelings. Introverts are motivated by appraisal of past experience and avoidance of future adverse consequences. They are unlikely to engage in a pleasurable activity if it might pose a threat in the future. Introverted individuals are quiet, dislike excitement, and distrust the impulse of the moment. They tend to be orderly, reliable, and rather pessimistic.

The second dimension, *stability–instability*, defines the degree of emotionality or lability. The emotions of *stable* individuals are aroused slowly and predictably and have low amplitude. By contrast, *unstable* individuals have intense, mercurial emotions that are easily and unpredictably aroused. What will cause an extreme reaction at one time will not necessarily provoke an emotional response at another time.

PERSONALITY TRAITS AND IMPLICATIONS FOR HIV-RISK BEHAVIORS

If these two trait dimensions are juxtaposed, four personality types emerge (Eysenck, 1990; Jung, 1923; Widger and Costa, 2012). Of the four types, unstable extroverts, who are at the extreme end of the axes, are the most prone to engage in behaviors putting them at risk for acquiring HIV. Unstable extroverts are preoccupied by, and act upon, their feelings, which are evanescent and changeable (Eysenck, 1976; Eysenck, 1990; Lucas et al., 2000; Widiger and Costa, 2012). Thus, their actions tend to be unpredictable and inconsistent. Most striking is the inconsistency found between thought and action. Past experience and future consequences have little salience in decision-making for the individual who is ruled by feeling; the present is paramount. Goals are dictated by emotions—either to achieve pleasure or remove pain—with little regard for circumstances. Furthermore, as part of their emotional instability, unstable extroverts experience intense fluctuations in their feelings and moods. It is difficult for them to tolerate uncomfortable or painful affect, such as boredom, sadness, or unresolved drive. Unstable extroverts want to escape or avoid such feelings as quickly and easily as possible. Thus, they are motivated to pursue pleasurable, dramatic, and emotionally intense experiences no matter the risk and avoid low moods or boredom.

Individuals characterized by high unstable extroversion are more likely to engage in behaviors related to HIV risk and transmission (Hoyle et al., 2000). Their spontaneity and impulsivity mean they are less likely to plan ahead and carry condoms and therefore more likely to have unprotected sex. They are more fixed upon the rewards of sex, particularly sex that is emotionally provocative, and less attentive to the sexually transmitted infection (STI) they may acquire by not using a condom. Unstable extroverts are also less likely to accept the diminution of intensity or spontaneity associated with the use of condoms or, once aroused, to interrupt the "heat of the moment" to use condoms. Similarly, unstable extroverts are more vulnerable to alcohol and drug abuse. They are drawn to alcohol and drugs as a quick route to pleasure or relief from discomfort or boredom. They are more likely to experiment with different kinds of drugs and to use greater quantities. Unstable extroverts are also more likely to inject drugs because the experience is more intense. They are also less likely to defer this intensity in the interest of safety.

Disorders of personality characterized by stable extroversion also engage in HIV-risk behaviors, but the motivations are somewhat different from those associated with unstable extroversion. Stable extroverts are also present-oriented and pleasure-seeking; however, their emotions are not as intense, as easily provoked, or mercurial. Hence, they are not as strongly driven to achieve pleasure. Their emotional "flatness" may generate a kind of indifference to HIV risk more than a drive to seek pleasure at any cost. Stable extroverts may be at risk because they are too optimistic or sanguine to believe that they will become HIV infected.

Introverted personalities are less likely to engage in behaviors that put them at risk for acquiring HIV. Their focus on the future, avoidance of negative consequences, and preference for cognition over feeling render them more likely to engage in protective and preventive behaviors. The dimension of emotional instability–stability has a significant role in determining HIV risk for introverts. Individuals at the extreme of *unstable* introversion are anxious, moody, and pessimistic. Typically, introverted individuals seek drugs and sex not so much for pleasure but for relief or distraction from pain. They are concerned about the future and adverse outcomes, but they believe that they have little control over their fate. Individuals at the extreme of *stable* introversion are risk averse and controlled, and are the least likely to engage in spontaneous or hedonistic behaviors. If stable extroverts present to the HIV clinic, it is usually because of an environmental exposure. This exposure could be a blood transfusion or an occupational needle stick. Alternatively, the environmental exposure could be a severely traumatic event that alters their characteristic functioning.

Empirical investigation of the association between traditional personality typologies and HIV-risk behaviors has been surprisingly limited, even as the study of personality disorders has burgeoned in other medical illnesses (Shuper et al., 2014). The Eysenck Personality Questionnaire (EPQ; Eysenck and Eysenck, 1975) and the NEO Personality Inventory–Revised (NEO-PI-R) of the Five Factor Model of personality (Widiger and Costa, 2012) have high reliability and validity in measuring these traits. High extroversion is associated with sexual promiscuity, desire for sexual novelty, multiple sex partners (Eysenck, 1976; McCown, 1991, 1993; Trobst et al., 2000), and heroin and other drug addictions (Francis and Bennett, 1992; Lodhi and Thakur, 1993). In one study, HIV-positive patients who had abused drugs or attempted suicide scored significantly higher on EPQ's Neuroticism scale (Kosten and Rounsaville, 1998).

SENSATION SEEKING

The third construct elaborated by most personality models identifies a trait which Eysenck called "psychoticism-socialization" but has been defined in other theories as "flight versus aggression" or sensation seeking (Zuckerman, 1994; Zuckerman et al., 1978). Zuckerman (1994) described sensation seeking as "the seeking of varied, novel, complex, and intense sensations and experiences, and the willingness to take physical, social, legal, and financial risks for the sake of such experience" (p. 27). Zuckerman developed a reliable and well-validated questionnaire, the Sensation Seeking Scale, to measure this trait (Zuckerman et al., 1978). It was subsequently adapted to form the Sexual Sensation Seeking Scale (SSSS) by omitting items related to sexual behaviors (Kalichman and Rompa, 1995; Kalichman et al., 1994). Of all personality traits studied among people living with or at risk for HIV, the association between sexual sensation seeking and risky sexual behaviors has received the most investigation, particularly among men. Among HIV-positive men who have sex with men, sexual sensation seeking was associated with unprotected anal sex in numerous studies (e.g. Bancroft et al., 2005; Dolezal et al., 1997; Kalichman et al., 2002; Léobon et al., 2011; Shuper et al., 2014; Wardle et al., 2010) with a few exceptions (Kalichman et al. 1997, Semple et al., 2000). Among women and men with HIV or at risk for HIV, high scorers on the SSSS Sexual Sensation Seeking Scale were more likely to engage in unprotected anal sex, unprotected anal sex with multiple partners, and unprotected vaginal sex (Hess et al., 2014; Voisin et al., 2013).

The nature of the association between sexual sensation seeking and risky sexual behaviors is complex, however. A recent systematic review of personality constructs and unprotected sex associated with HIV transmission concluded that sexual sensation seeking may be a distal influence in the practice of risky sexual behaviors and perhaps mediated by substance use (Shuper et al., 2014). Some studies have shown that the univariate association did not hold in multivariate analyses when factors such as alcohol or drug use were included, suggesting that sexual sensation seeking may not have a direct, independent effect on behavior (Ostrow et al., 2002, 2008; Parsons et al., 2003). Other studies have shown that sexual sensation seeking is a moderator of the association between alcohol use and unprotected sex (Heidinger et al., 2015; Newcomb, 2013; Newcomb et al., 2011). Specifically, among men who have sex with men, having unprotected sex after alcohol use increased linearly with increased scores on the SSSS.

Sexual sensation seeking is also related to alcohol expectancies. Individuals who hold the expectation that alcohol would enhance sexual pleasure or prowess were more likely to consume alcohol before or during sex and to have unprotected sex (Kalichman and Cain, 2004; Kalichman et al., 1996, 2005).

PERSONALITY DISORDER IN PERSONS WITH HIV OR AT RISK FOR HIV

When traits found in certain individuals exceed the levels found in most of society and are sufficiently rigid and maladaptive to cause subjective distress or functional impairment, a personality disorder is usually diagnosed (Paris, 1996; Rutter, 1987). Among individuals with personality traits of extreme extroversion and lability and maladaptive patterns of behavior, antisocial personality disorder (ASPD) and borderline personality disorder (BPD) are often diagnosed. These diagnoses can have a pejorative connotation that does not support a clinical view of a person in need of treatment (Gask et al., 2013; Knaak et al., 2015; Morey and Zanarini, 2000; Sansone and Sansone, 2013). Despite this, useful research based on categorical diagnosis using these ideas has contributed to our understanding of the relationship between HIV and personality.

Among HIV at-risk individuals, DSM-IV personality disorders are common, occurring in about 15–20% of individuals (Jacobsberg et al., 1995; Johnson et al., 1995; Perkins et al., 1993), and exceed the prevalence in the general population (10–14.79%; Grant et al., 2004; Lenzenweger et al., 2007). Personality disorders, particularly ASPD or BPD, are a risk factor for HIV infection (Brooner et al., 1993) and prevalent

among individuals who engage in HIV transmission behaviors. Individuals with ASPD and BPD have high rates of substance abuse (Mueser et al., 2006; Trull et al., 2010); nearly 50% of substance abusers met criteria for a diagnosis of ASPD under DSM-IV criteria (Dinwiddie et al., 1996; Hudgins et al., 1995; Messina et al., 2001, 2003). Individuals with ASPD are more likely to inject drugs and share needles than are individuals without an Axis II diagnosis (Dinwiddie et al., 1996; Hudgins et al. 1995; Kleinman et al., 1994). They are also more likely to have a greater number of lifetime sexual partners, engage in unprotected anal sex and/or commercial sex work, and have STIs than individuals without these personality disorders (Brooner et al., 1990; Chen et al., 2007; Ellis et al., 1995; Harned et al., 2011; Ladd and Petry, 2003).

Among persons with HIV, the prevalence of personality disorders ranges from 19% to 36% and also exceeds that of the general population. Personality disorders are more common among men with than without HIV and more common among men than women with HIV (Lopes et al., 2012). ASPD and BPD are the most common personality disorders in persons with HIV (Golding and Perkins, 1996; Pergami and Gala, 1994; Shuper et al., 2014). In a convenience sample of 179 HIV-infected patients in primary care, BPD (measured by the Millon Multiaxial Personality Inventory) was associated with having multiple sex partners and using condoms irregularly (Newville and Haller, 2012). ASPD was associated with recent drug injection.

The diagnosis of personality disorders in the clinical setting must be undertaken cautiously. Making a psychiatric diagnosis according to the *Diagnostic and Statistical Manual of Mental Disorders*, Fifth Edition, (DSM-5) (American Psychiatric Association [APA], 2013) requires considerable time and experience, but does little to explain behavior or suggest intervention strategies. The DSM-5 retains the categorical classification of DSM-IV, but a new Section III emphasizes pathological personality traits of negative affectivity and psychoticism, for example, that could focus future research on a dimensional model of personality disorders (APA, 2013; Gask et al., 2013). Classifying individuals along a continuum of personality traits rather than in Axis II discrete categories may be a better predictor of HIV-risk behavior and less stigmatizing (Shuper et al., 2014; Widiger and Costa, 2012).

PERSONALITY AND ILLNESS PROGRESSION

Personality traits are thought to be particularly important in medical outcomes of chronic diseases because of the importance of adherence to and remaining engaged in treatment (Axelsson et al., 2011; Bogg and Roberts, 2004; Bruce et al., 2010). However, there has been little investigation of this area in regard to HIV. In a sample of HIV-infected patients, high scores on openness, extroversion, and conscientiousness scales of the NEO-PI-R were associated with slower HIV illness progression over 4 years after controlling for age, initial illness status, and antiretroviral medicines (Ironson et al., 2008). Specifically, an individual who had a "personality type" that was proactive, open to information, socially engaged, directed, and orderly had a better HIV outcome. By contrast, low extroversion–low openness was associated with faster illness progression, possibly because of social isolation or depression (Ironson et al., 2005).

IMPLICATIONS FOR MEDICATION ADHERENCE

Medication adherence is challenging for persons with a chronic disease like HIV because it is associated with all of the components of low adherence: long duration of treatment, preventative rather than curative treatment, asymptomatic periods, medication side effects, and chronic medication dosing (Deeks et al., 2013).

Our clinical experience suggests that unstable extroversion is the personality trait mostly likely to influence adherence. The same personality characteristic that increases risk of HIV also reduces ability to adhere to drug regimens. Specifically, present-time orientation, combined with reward seeking, makes it more difficult for these patients to tolerate uncomfortable side effects of ART, whose treatment effects may not be immediately apparent. It is also difficult for feeling-driven individuals to maintain consistent, well-ordered routines. Hence, following medication schedules can also be problematic. Unstable, extroverted patients may be intent on following the schedule, but their mercurial and sometimes chaotic emotions are more likely to interfere and disrupt daily routines. For example, a patient may report that he became very angry with a partner and miss several doses of his antiretroviral medicines, despite knowing the risks of missing medication doses. These same patients also appear to differ in their appraisals of side effects of medicines. Across studies, the principal reason for discontinuing ART is side effects of medicines or the anticipated side effects of medicines. Some individuals are less able or willing to tolerate side effects in the present to prevent poor health in the future.

There is a paucity of research examining the association between personality traits and adherence to ART; a systematic review examining the impact of personality disorders on adherence to ART concluded that the data were "insufficient and inconsistent" (Springer et al., 2012). In an early study by the NEO-PI-R authors, HIV-positive patients with high neuroticism scores reported lower overall and HIV-specific quality of life that was directly associated with ART nonadherence (Costa and McCrae, 1992). Neuroticism was also found to moderate the effect of perceived stress on adherence though not on viral load. On the EPQ, individuals who scored high on the neuroticism scale were less likely to be adherent to ART, especially as their level of perceived stress increased (Bottonari et al., 2005). By contrast, patients who scored higher in extroversion and conscientiousness on the NEO-PI-R reported good ART adherence and better overall and HIV-specific quality of life (O'Cleirigh et al., 2007; Penedo et al., 2003). Neuroticism (instability) has been associated with poorer medication adherence in studies of numerous other chronic diseases, including hypertension, asthma, diabetes, and multiple sclerosis, suggesting that this is a potential avenue for intervention (e.g., Axelsson et al., 2011; Bruce et al., 2010). Investigation of the role of personality in ART adherence is needed (Shuper et al., 2014; Springer et al., 2012).

There are also few studies that examine the association between personality disorders and ART adherence. In a convenience sample of 107 HIV-positive patients on methadone who had at least one psychiatric diagnosis and at least one substance use diagnosis, of all the Axis I and II psychiatric disorders only BPD was associated with less than 95% adherence in a 3-day recall of medications taken (Palmer et al., 2003). In a second study of 125 HIV-positive patients, lifetime methamphetamine use and diagnoses of ASPD, major depressive disorder, and attention deficit disorder were associated with nonadherence, with major depressive disorder being the strongest predictor (Moore et al., 2012). By contrast, in a multisite cohort study, no association between BDP or ASPD and 3-day recall of adherence to ART was detected (Mellins et al., 2009).

TREATMENT

Traditional approaches to risk-reduction counseling emphasize the avoidance of negative consequences in the future, such as using a condom during sexual intercourse to prevent STIs. But such educational approaches have been ineffective with individuals with marked personality problems, such as unstable extroverts, who engage in risky behaviors (Kalichman et al., 1996, Newville and Haller, 2012; Shuper et al., 2014; Trobst et al., 2000). Psychiatric and medical treatment of persons who are unstable extroverts is challenging. Unstable extroverts may be baffling or frustrating for physicians and other medical care clinicians because they engage in high-risk sexual and drug misuse behaviors despite awareness of the risks, or they fail to adhere to treatment regimens for HIV infection despite awareness of the consequences. Because of their focus on feelings and interests of the moment, unstable extroverts can constantly change what they want from treatment and their goals for their care. Patients may complain that a selective serotonin reuptake inhibitor gives them a mild headache while seeming to be untroubled by shooting heroin in a carotid artery. After 6 months of missed medical appointments, the same individuals may impulsively leave the clinic if the primary care clinician is 15 minutes late for the appointment. Such personality traits reflect relatively stable, lifelong modes of responding; thus, direct efforts to change these traits are unlikely to be successful. It is possible, however, to modify the behavior that is an expression of the trait. By recognizing individual differences in risk-related personality characteristics, interventions can be better targeted and their impact maximized.

The most commonly recommended treatments for individuals with personality disorders are cognitive-behavioral therapy and dialectical behavior therapy. The evidence base for both treatments shows efficacy. In cognitive-behavioral therapy dysfunctional core beliefs about the self, others, and the world are examined, and the aim is to identify and changes these core beliefs (Beck et al., 2014). In dialectical behavior therapy emotional dysregulation is examined in order to build distress tolerance, interpersonal effectiveness, and emotional regulation skills (Dimeff and Koerner, 2007; Linehan, 2006, 2014). Both therapies offer practical, skill-based training and manuals to guide treatment.

We have found that a blend of cognitive-behavioral and dialectical behavior therapies is most effective in treating patients who present with extroverted and/or emotionally unstable personalities. Four principles guide our standard care:

1. Focus on thoughts, not feelings. Individuals with unstable, extroverted personality disorders benefit from learning how they are predisposed to act in certain ways. Often, they recognize that they are highly emotional and are driven by their feelings. They may be equally baffled by their own actions. They may fail to understand why they intend to stay clean but later find themselves injecting drugs. The psychiatrist or other mental health professional can identify the role that strong feelings play so that persons can begin the process of understanding their own chaotic, often irrational behavior. Simultaneously, the clinician can encourage more use of their cognitive, logical side. Patients can focus on doing what is healthful rather than what is immediately pleasurable. The task is to build consistency into behavior. For some patients whose emotionality is severe enough to warrant a diagnosis of borderline personality disorder, there is a high likelihood of occult mood disorder such as major depressive disorder or bipolar disorder type II, and the addition of psychotropic medication such as an antidepressant or mood stabilizer (such as lithium, divalproex sodium, or lamotrigine) may be beneficial in stabilizing emotional fluctuations.

2. Use a behavioral contract. A behavioral contract is developed with all patients. The contract outlines goals for treatment, often only a day or a week at a time. While patients and clinicians may develop the contract, the focus of treatment is *not* on what patients *want* or *are willing to do* to stop using alcohol or other drugs but rather on established methods, such as drug treatment and Narcotics or Alcoholics Anonymous. The importance of the behavioral contract lies in the creation of a *stable* plan that supersedes the emotional meanderings of these patients. Unstable extroverts present an ever-changing array of concerns and priorities. The task of the clinician is to order the priorities with patients and help them follow through on these, regardless of changing emotions.

3. Emphasize rewards. In developing the behavioral contract and in treatment, the purpose is cast in terms of rewards what will follow from their behavioral change. Positive outcomes, not adverse consequences, are salient to extroverts. Exhortations to use condoms to avoid STIs are unpersuasive. More success has been achieved with extroverts by eroticizing the use of condoms (Tanner and Pollock, 1988) or with the addition of novel sexual techniques (erotic massage, use of sex toys) into sexual repertoires (Abramson and Pinkerston, 1995). Similarly,

the rewards of abstaining from drugs or alcohol are emphasized, such as having money to buy clothing, having a stable home, or maintaining positive relationships with children. In building adherence to antiretroviral therapies, the focus is on the rewards of health and a reduced or undetectable viral load, rather than on avoiding illness. Using the viral load as a strategy to build adherence can increase acceptance in all patients but is especially effective in reward-driven extroverts.

4. Coordinate with medical caregivers. Medical care clinicians are often frustrated or discouraged when treating unstable, extroverted patients. It is useful to provide education about a patient's personality and how it influences behavior. Particularly effective is the development of a coordinated treatment plan, where medical care and mental health care clinicians work in tandem to develop behavioral contracts to reduce HIV-risk behaviors and build medication adherence. An integrated plan coordinates stabilization on psychiatric medication, initiation of ART, and enrollment in psychotherapy and/or substance abuse treatment.

CONCLUSION

Personality characteristics and personality disorders reflect relatively stable, lifelong propensities that are difficult to change. This does not mean, however, that HIV risk reduction efforts are necessarily futile. Rather, by understanding certain personality characteristics and their role in HIV-risk behaviors and medication adherence, psychiatrists and other mental health professionals can develop more effective, specific treatment strategies for persons with HIV and personality vulnerabilities. They can also provide valuable assistance to HIV clinicians to improve health outcomes for persons with HIV and personality disorder. For HIV-positive individuals, the ability to identify aspects of their personality that might influence intentions to practice safer behavior and develop strategies for dealing with these situations may render them less vulnerable to high-risk situations. The advancement of all these endeavors, however, will benefit from empirical investigations of the influence of personality disorders across the HIV care continuum.

REFERENCES

Abramson PR, Pinkerton SD (1995). *With Pleasure: Thought on the Nature of Human Sexuality*. New York: Oxford University Press.
American Psychiatric Association (2013). *Diagnostic and Statistical Manual of Mental Disorders*, fifth edition (DSM-V). Washington, DC: American Psychiatric Press.
Axelsson M, Brink E, Lundgren J, Lötvall J. (2011) The influence of personality traits on reported adherence to medication in individuals with chronic disease: an epidemiological study in west Sweden. *PloS ONE* 6(3):e18241.
Bancroft J, Carnes L, Janssen E (2005). Unprotected anal intercourse in HIV-positive and HIV-negative gay men: the relevance of sexual

arousability, mood, sensation seeking, and erectile problems. *Arch Sex Behav* 34(3):299–305.

Beck AT, Davis DD, Freeman A (eds.) 2014. *Cognitive Therapy of Personality Disorders*. New York: Guilford Press.

Bogg T, Roberts B (2004). Conscientiousness and health-related behaviors: a meta-analysis of the leading behavioral contributors to mortality. *Psychol Bull* 130:887–919.

Bottonari KA, Roberts JE, Ciesla JA, Hewitt RG (2005). Life stress and adherence to antiretroviral therapy among HIV-positive individuals: a preliminary investigation. *AIDS Patient Care STDS* 19:719–727.

Brooner RK, Bigelow GE, Strain E, Schmidt CW (1990). Intravenous drug users with antisocial personality disorder: increased HIV risk behavior. *Drug Alcohol Depend* 1990; 26:39–44.

Brooner RK, Greenfield L, Schmidt, CW, Bigelow GE (1993). Antisocial personality disorder and HIV infection among intravenous drug users. *Am J Psychiatry* 150:53–58.

Bruce JM, Hancock LM, Arnett P, Lynch S (2010). Treatment adherence in multiple sclerosis: association with emotional status, personality, and cognition. *J Behav Med* 33(3):219–227.

Chen EY, Brown MZ, Lo TT, Linehan MM (2007) Sexually transmitted disease rates and high-risk sexual behaviors in borderline personality disorder versus borderline personality disorder with substance use disorder. *J Nerv Ment Dis* 195:125–129.

Cloninger CR (1999). *Personality and Psychopathology*. Washington, DC: American Psychiatric Press.

Costa Jr. PT, McCrae RR (1992). *Revised NEO Personality Inventory (NEO PI-R) and NEO Five-Factor Inventory (NEO-FFI) Professional Manual*. Odessa, FL: Psychological Assessment Resources.

Costa PT, Widiger TA (2002). Personality Disorders and the Five-Factor Model of Personality (2nd ed.). Washington, DC: American Psychological Association.

Deeks SG, Lewin SR, Havlir DV (2013). The end of AIDS: HIV infection as a chronic disease. *Lancet* 382 (9903):1525–1533.

Dimeff LA, Koerner K. (eds.) (2007) *Dialectical Behavior Therapy in Clinical Practice*. New York: Guilford Press.

Dinwiddie SH, Cottler L, Compton W, Ben Aabdallah A (1996). Psychopathology and HIV risk behaviors among injection drug users in and out of treatment. *Drug Alcohol Depend* 43:1–11.

Dolezal C, Meyer-Bahlburg HF, Remien RH, Petkova E (1997). Substance use during sex and sensation seeking as predictors of sexual risk behavior among HIV+ and HIV– gay men. *AIDS Behav* 1:19–28.

Ellis D, Collins I, King M (1995). Personality disorder and sexual risk taking among homosexually active and heterosexually active men attending a genitor-urinary medicine clinic. *Psychosom Res* 39:901–910.

Eysenck JH (1976). *Sex and Personality*. London: Open Books.

Eysenck HJ (1990). Genetic and environmental contributions to individual differences: the three major dimension of personality. *J Pers* 58:245–261.

Eysenck HJ, Eysenck SBG (1975). *Eysenck Personality Questionnaire*. San Diego: EditTS/Educational and Industrial Testing Service.

Francis LJ, Bennett GA (1992). Personality and religion among female drug misusers. *Drug Alcohol Depend* 30:27–31.

Gask L, Evans M, Kessler D (2013). Clinical review. Personality disorder. *BMJ* 347:7924–7926.

Golding M, Perkins DO (1996). Personality disorder in HIV infection. *Int Rev Psychiatry* 8:253–258.

Grant BF, Stinson FS, Dawson DA, Chou SP, Ruan J, Pickering RP (2004). Co-occurrence of 12-month alcohol and drug use disorders and personality disorders in the United States. *Arch Gen Psychiatry* 61:361–368.

Harned MS, Pantalone DW, Ward-Ciesielski EF, Lynch TR, Linehan MM. (2011). The prevalence and correlates of sexual risk behaviors and sexually transmitted infections in outpatients with borderline personality disorder. *J Nerv Ment Dis* 199:832–838.

Heidinger B, Gorgens K, Morgenstern J (2015). The effects of sexual sensation seeking and alcohol use on risky sexual behavior among men who have sex with men. *AIDS Behav* 19:43:1–439.

Hess KL, Reynolds GL, Fisher DG (2014). Heterosexual anal intercourse among men in Long Beach, California. *J Sex Res* 51(8):874–881.

Hoyle RH, Fejfar MC, Miller JD (2000). Personality and sexual risk taking: a quantitative review. *J Pers* 68:1203–1231.

Hudgins R, McCusker J, Stoddard A (1995). Cocaine use and risky injection and sexual behaviors. *Drug Alcohol Depend* 37:7–14.

Ironson G, Balbin E, Stuetzle R, et al. (2005). Dispositional optimism and the mechanisms by which it predicts slower disease progression in HIV: proactive behavior, avoidant coping, and depression. *Int J Behav Med* 12:86–97.

Ironson GH, O'Cleirigh C, Schneiderman N, Weiss A, Costa PT Jr (2008). Personality and HIV disease progression: role of NEO-PI-R openness, extraversion, and profiles of engagement. *Psychosom Med* 70:245–253.

Jacobsberg L, Frances A, Perry S (1995). Axis II diagnoses among volunteers for HIV testing and counseling. *Am J Psychiatry* 152:1222–1224.

Johnson JG, Williams JB, Rabkin JG, Goetz PR, Remien RH (1995). Axis I psychiatric symptomatology associated with HIV infection and personality disorder. *Am J Psychiatry* 152:551–554.

Jung C (1923). *Psychological Types*. New York: Harcourt Brace.

Kalichman SC, Cain D (2004). A prospective study of sensation seeking and alcohol use as predictors of sexual risk behaviors among men and women receiving sexually transmitted infection clinic services. *Psychol Addict Behav* 18:367–373.

Kalichman SC, Cain D, Knetch J, Hill J (2005). Patterns of sexual risk behavior change among sexually transmitted infection clinic patients. *Arch Sex Behav* 34:307–319.

Kalichman SC, Greenberg J, Abel GG (1997). HIV-seropositive men who engage in high-risk sexual behaviour: psychological characteristics and implications for prevention. *AIDS Care* 9:441–450.

Kalichman SC Heckman T, Kelly JA (1996). Sensation-seeking as an explanation for the association between substance use and HIV-related risky sexual behavior. *Arch Sex Behav* 25:141–154.

Kalichman SC, Johnson JR, Adair V, Rompa D, Multhauf K, Kelly JA (1994). Sexual sensation seeking: scale development and predicting AIDS-risk behavior among homosexually active men. *J Pers Assess* 62:385–397.

Kalichman SC, Rompa D (1995). Sexual sensation seeking and sexual compulsivity scales: reliability, validity, and predicting HIV risk behavior. *J Pers Assess* 65:586–601.

Kalichman SC, Weinhardt L, DiFonzo K, Austin J, Luke W (2002). Sensation seeking and alcohol use as markers of sexual transmission risk behavior in HIV-positive men. *Ann Behav Med* 24:229–235.

Kleinman PH, Millman RB, Robinson H, Lesser M, Hsu C, Engelhart P, Finkelstein I (1994). Lifetime needle sharing: a predictive analysis. *J Subst Abuse Treat* 11:449–455.

Knaak S, Szeto AC, Fitch K, Modgill G, Patten S. (2015) Stigma towards borderline personality disorder: effectiveness and generalizability of an anti-stigma program for healthcare providers using a pre-post randomized design. *Borderline Personal Disord Emot Dysregul* 2:9.

Kosten T, Rounsaville B (1998). Suicidality among opioid addicts: 2.5 year follow-up. *Am J Drug Alcohol Abuse* 14:357–369.

Ladd GT, Petry NM (2003). Antisocial personality in treatment-seeking cocaine abusers: psychosocial functioning and HIV risk. *J Subst Abuse Treat* 24:323–330.

Léobon A, Velter A, Engler K, Drouin MC, Otis J (2011). A relative profile of HIV-negative users of French websites for men seeking men and predictors of their regular risk taking: a comparison with HIV-positive users. *AIDS Care* 23:25–34.

Lenzenweger MF, Lane MC, Loranger AW, Kessler RC (2007). DSM-IV personality disorders in the National Comorbidity Survey Replication. *Biol Psychiatry* 62:553–564.

Linehan MM (2006). *Treating Borderline Personality Disorder: The Dialectical Approach*. New York: Guilford Press.

Linehan MM (2014). *DBT Skills Training Manual*. New York: Guilford Press.

Livesley WJ (2001). Conceptual and taxonomic issues. In WH Livesley WH (ed.), *Handbook of Personality Disorders* (pp. 3–38). New York: Guilford Press.

Lodhi PH, Thakur S (1993). Personality of drug addicts: Eysenckian analysis. *Pers Individ Diff* 15:121–128.

Lopes M, Olfson M, Rabkin J, Hasin DS, Alegría AA, Lin KH, Blanco C (2012). Gender, HIV status, and psychiatric disorders: results from the National Epidemiologic Study on Alcohol and Related Conditions. *J Clin Psychiatry* 73:1–9.

Lucas RE, Diener E, Grob A, Suh EM, Shao L (2000). Cross-cultural evidence for the fundamental features of extraversion. *J Pers Soc Psychol* 79:452–468.

McCown W (1991). Contributions of the EPN paradigm to HIV prevention: a preliminary study. *Pers Individ Diff* 12:1301–1303.

McCown W (1993). Personality factors predicting failure to practice safer sex by HIV-positive males. *Pers Individ Diff* 14:613–615.

Mellins CA, Havens JF, McDonnell C, Lichtenstein C, Uldall K, Chesney M, Bell J (2009). Adherence to antiretroviral medications and medical care in HIV-infected adults diagnosed with mental and substance abuse disorders. *AIDS Care* 21(2):168–177.

Messina N, Farabee D, Rawson R (2003). Treatment responsivity of cocaine-dependent patients with antisocial personality disorder to cognitive-behavioral and contingency management interventions. *J Consult Clin Psychol* 71:320–329.

Messina N, Wish E, Hoffman J, Nemes S (2001). Diagnosing antisocial personality disorder among substance abusers: the SCID versus the MCMI-II. *Am J Drug Alcohol Abuse* 27:699–717.

Moore DJ, Blackstone K, Woods SP, Ellis RJ, Atkinson JH, Heaton RK, Grant I (2012). Methamphetamine use and neuropsychiatric factors are associated with antiretroviral nonadherence. *AIDS Care* 24:1504–1513.

Morey LC, Zanarini MC (2000). Borderline personality: traits and disorder. *J Abnorm Psychol* 109:733–737.

Mueser KT, Crocker AG, Frisman RE, Drake RE, Covel NH, Essock SM (2006). Conduct disorder and antisocial personality disorder in persons with severe psychiatric and substance use disorders. *Schizophren Bull* 32:626–636.

Newcomb ME (2013). Moderating effect of age on the association between alcohol use and sexual risk in MSM: evidence for elevated risk among MSM. *AIDS Behav* 17:1746–1754.

Newcomb ME, Clerk EM, Mustanski B (2011). Sensation seeking moderates the effects of alcohol and drug use prior to sex on sexual risk in young men who have sex with men. *AIDS Behav* 15:565–575.

Newville H, Haller D (2012). Relationship of Axis II pathology to sex- and drug-related risk behaviors among patients in HIV primary care. *AIDS Care* 2:763–768.

O'Cleirigh C, Ironson G, Weiss A, Costa PT, Jr (2007). Conscientiousness predicts disease progression (CD4 number and viral load) in people living with HIV. *Health Psychol* 26(4):473–480.

Ostrow DG, Fox KJ, Chmiel JS, Silvestre A, Visscher BR, Vanable PA (2002). Attitudes towards highly active antiretroviral therapy are associated with sexual risk taking among HIV-infected and uninfected homosexual men. *AIDS* 16:775–780.

Ostrow DG, Silverberg MJ, Cook RL, et al. (2008). Prospective study of attitudinal and relationship predictors of sexual risk in the multi-center AIDS cohort study. *AIDS Behav* 12(1):127–138.

Palmer NB, Salcedo J, Miller AL, Winiarski M, Arno P (2003). Psychiatric and social barriers to HIV medication adherence in a triply diagnosed methadone population. *AIDS Patient Care STD* 17:635–644.

Paris J (1996). *Social Factors in the Personality Disorders: A Biopsychosocial Approach to Etiology and Treatment.* Cambridge, UK: Cambridge University Press.

Parsons JT, Halkitis PN, Wolitski RJ, Gomez CA (2003). Correlates of sexual risk behaviors among HIV-positive men who have sex with men. *AIDS Educ Prev* 15(5):383–400.

Penedo FJ, Gonzalez JS, Dahn JR, Antoni M, Malow R, Costa, Jr PT, Schneiderman N (2003) Personality, quality of life and HAART adherence among men and women living HIV/AIDS. *J Psychosom Res* 59:271–278.

Pergami A, Gala C (1994). Personality disorder and HIV disease. *American J Psychiatry* 151:298–299.

Perkins DO, Davidson EJ, Leserman J, Liao D, Evans DL (2003). Personality disorder in patients infected with HIV: a controlled study with implications for clinical care. *Am J Psychiatry* 150:309–315.

Rothbart MK, Ahadi SA (1994). Temperament and the development of personality. *J Abnorm Psychol* 103:55–66.

Rutter M (1987). Temperament, personality and personality disorder. *Br J Psychiatry* 150:443–458.

Sansone RA, Sansone LA (2013). Responses of mental health clinicians to patients with borderline personality disorder. *Innov Clin Neurosci* 10(5-6):39–43.

Semple SJ, Patterson TL, Grant I (2000). Psychosocial predictors of unprotected anal intercourse in a sample of HIV positive gay men who volunteer for sexual risk reduction intervention. *AIDS Educ Prev* 12(5):416–430.

Shuper PA, Joharchi N, Rehm J. (2014). Personality as a predictor of unprotected sexual behavior among people living with HIV/AIDS: a systematic review. *AIDS Behav* 18(2):398–410.

Springer SA, Dushaj A, Azar MM (2012). The impact of DSM-IV mental disorders on adherence to combination antiretroviral therapy among adult persons living with HIV/AIDS: a systematic review. *AIDS Behav* 16(8):2119–2143.

Tanner WM, Pollack RH (1988). The effect of condom use and erotic instructions on attitudes toward condoms. *J Sex Res* 25:537–541.

Trobst KK, Wiggins JS, Costa Jr PT, Herbst JH, McCrae RR, Masters III HL (2000). Personality psychology and problem behaviors: HIV risk and the Five-Factor Model. *J Pers* 68:1232–1252.

Trull TJ, Jahng S, Tomko RL, Wood PK, Sher KJ (2010). Revised NESARC personality disorder diagnoses: gender, prevalence, and comorbidity with substance dependence disorders. *J Pers Disord* 21:412–426.

Voisin DR, Tan K, DiClemente RJ (2013). A longitudinal examination of the relationship between sexual sensation seeking and STI-related risk factors among African American females. *AIDS Educ Prevent* 25:124–134.

Wardle MC, Gonzalez R, Bechara A, Martin-Thormeyer EM (2010). Iowa Gambling Task performance and emotional distress interact to predict risky sexual behavior in individuals with dual substance and HIV diagnoses. *J Clin Exp Neuropsychol* 32(10):1110–1121.

Widiger TA, Costa Jr PT (2012) *Personality Disorders and the Five-Factor Model of Personality,* 3rd ed. Washington, DC: American Psychological Association.

Zuckerman M (1994). *Behavioral Expressions and Biosocial Bases of Sensation Seeking* (p. 27). New York: Cambridge University Press.

Zuckerman M, Eysenck S, Eysenck HJ (1978). Sensation seeking in England and America: cross-cultural, age, and sex comparisons. *J Consult Clin Psychol* 46:139–149.

PART V

UNIQUE PSYCHIATRIC MANIFESTATIONS OF HIV INFECTION

21.

PSYCHONEUROIMMUNOLOGY AND HIV

Adam W. Carrico and Michael H. Antoni

Research examining the psychoneuroimmunology (PNI) of HIV/AIDS has evolved in the context of biomedical advances in the prevention and treatment of the illness. Early work in the mid-1980s demonstrated that stress and psychological factors could increase the risk of progression to AIDS (Bangsberg et al., 2001; Cole and Kemeny, 2001). Subsequently, many studies were conducted in the following decade to show that stress reduction interventions might improve psychological adjustment on the one hand and potentially influence HIV disease markers on the other (Carrico and Antoni, 2008; Scott-Sheldon et al., 2008). Other work has demonstrated that cognitive-behavioral interventions that mitigate depressive symptoms might also improve HIV disease markers by enhancing adherence to effective combination antiretroviral medication regimens (Safren et al., 2009), which are referred to collectively in this chapter as antiretroviral therapy (ART). Further PNI research is needed to elucidate the underlying biobehavioral pathways whereby psychiatric factors may potentiate HIV illness progression and thus inform the development of comprehensive approaches to enhance the effectiveness of ART.

Recent groundbreaking results from the HIV Prevention Trials Network 052 randomized controlled trial (RCT) demonstrate that early initiation of ART delays HIV illness progression and leads to a 96% reduction in onward HIV transmission rates (Cohen et al., 2011). These findings catalyzed a paradigm shift toward HIV treatment as prevention (TasP) with the goals of optimizing health outcomes among persons with HIV and reducing HIV incidence by decreasing "community" levels of HIV viral load (Das et al., 2010; Montaner et al., 2010). In the era of TasP, current treatment guidelines recommend starting ART immediately following diagnosis, irrespective of T-helper (CD4+) cell count (Günthard et al., 2014). Although there is renewed optimism that TasP is one key biomedical approach to achieve an AIDS-free generation (Fauci and Folkers, 2012), recent estimates indicate that only one-fourth of HIV-positive persons in the United States are virologically suppressed (Hull et al., 2012). In order to realize the full benefits of TasP, expanded efforts are needed to target structural, behavioral, and psychiatric factors relevant to HIV prevention and care (Carrico, 2011; Holtgrave et al., 2012; Mugavero et al., 2013).

Because of the many stressors inherent in HIV infection, psychosocial and biomedical issues must be addressed for successful illness management (Carrico and Antoni, 2008;

Nieuwlaat et al., 2014). The anticipation and impact of HIV antibody test notification; emergence of the first symptoms of illness; changes in vocational plans, lifestyle behaviors, and interpersonal relationships; and difficulties with HIV illness management are all highly stressful. These multiple challenges can create chronic stress that may overwhelm an individual's coping resources and significantly impair emotional adjustment to ongoing demands of the illness (Leserman et al., 2000). Accordingly, HIV-positive individuals are at increased risk for developing an affective or adjustment disorder across the illness spectrum (Bing et al., 2001). Although reductions in mood disturbance have been observed following the introduction of ART (Rabkin et al., 2000), the risk of developing major depressive disorder is two times higher in HIV-positive samples compared to HIV-negative peers (Ciesla and Roberts, 2001; see also Chapters 43 and 15 in this volume).

With substantial reductions in morbidity and mortality following the advent of ART, clinical care of persons with HIV has improved dramatically such that the illness is now managed as a chronic illness (Centers for Disease Control and Prevention [CDC], 1997; Mannheimer et al., 2005). However, not all HIV-positive patients treated with ART achieve sustained viral suppression because of the difficulties with HIV illness management (Hull et al., 2012; Mugavero et al., 2013). Even individuals with undetectable HIV viral load remain at elevated risk for HIV-associated non-AIDS conditions such as cardiovascular illness (Deeks, 2011). In fact, persistent inflammation and activation of the innate immune system are thought to be important drivers of accelerated aging in treated HIV infection (Lederman et al., 2013). Comprehensive interventions targeting psychiatric factors could modify these and other biological pathways to enhance the benefits of ART in the era of TasP.

Because persons with HIV endure a chronic illness that requires adaptation across a variety of domains, individual differences in the ways they adapt to these challenges may affect not only quality of life but also illness processes. Research in PNI has examined the potential biobehavioral mechanisms whereby psychosocial factors such as stressors, stress responses, personality factors, coping, negative affective states, and positive psychological resources influence illness progression (Antoni, 2003a; Cole and Kemeny, 2001; Ironson and Hayward, 2008). Psychosocial factors are thought to relate to immune system function in humans via stress- or distress-induced changes in hormonal regulatory systems (Kiecolt-Glaser et al., 2002). Several adrenal hormones, including cortisol and catecholamines (i.e., norepinephrine and epinephrine), are altered as a function of an individual's appraisals of and coping responses to stressors (McEwen, 1998). What is particularly relevant to HIV/AIDS research is the observation that a variety of neuroendocrine abnormalities occur in both clinically depressed (Gillespie and Nemeroff, 2005) and HIV-positive (Kawa and Thompson, 1996) populations. In persons with HIV, research conducted primarily prior to the ART era observed that elevations in these neuroendocrine hormones were associated with alterations in multiple indices of immune status (Antoni and Schneiderman, 1998). At the same time, there is increasing recognition that chronic stress may also lead to dysregulated neuroendocrine stress responses, such as a flattened diurnal cortisol rhythm (Gunnar and Vasquez, 2001). The relevance in HIV is evident in findings highlighting that greater diurnal variation in salivary free cortisol (conceptualized as a healthy pattern) is associated with decreased activation of CD4+ and cytotoxic/suppressor (CD8+) cells in untreated HIV infection (Patterson et al., 2013).The most definitive PNI research conducted to date has illuminated biobehavioral mechanisms through longitudinal and intervention designs where psychosocial factors are mapped onto subsequent changes in immunological indicators and clinical illness progression.

In this chapter, we review seminal research findings that support the relevance of PNI pathways in HIV illness progression. Although the majority of PNI investigations with persons with HIV were conducted prior to the availability of ART, more recent findings indicate that enhanced psychological adjustment may facilitate virological control and bolster immunocompetence, enhancing the effectiveness of ART. Important questions remain, however, regarding whether the associations of these psychosocial processes with HIV illness progression are explained by biological changes, enhanced HIV illness management, or both.

NEGATIVE LIFE EVENTS

Despite the unprecedented clinical benefits of ART, persons with HIV must continue to cope with a number of chronic, uncontrollable stressors that may hinder optimal management of their illness. This observation is supported by research examining the association between negative life events and HIV illness progression.

CUMULATIVE LIFE EVENT BURDEN

Investigators employing interview-based, contextual methods have observed consistent effects of negative life events on declines in immune system parameters in HIV-positive men who have sex with men (Leserman, 2003). Specifically, cumulative negative life events were associated with reductions in natural killer (NK) and CD8+ cell counts over a 2-year period in a cohort of HIV-positive men who have sex with men recruited in the pre-ART era (Leserman et al., 1997). The clinical significance of these findings is supported by data

indicating that these immune cell subsets may play a key role in suppressing HIV replication (Cruess et al., 2003; Ironson et al., 2001).

Cumulative negative life events have also been associated with increases in HIV viral load in a diverse cohort of ART-treated, HIV-positive men and women (Ironson, O'Cleirigh, et al., 2005). Most notably, individuals classified as experiencing a higher rate (>75th percentile) of cumulative negative life events displayed a twofold increase in HIV viral load over 2 years compared to individuals with lower rates (<25th percentile), even after controlling for antiretroviral medication adherence. Although no concurrent effects on helper/inducer CD4+ counts were observed, results of this investigation demonstrate a continued association between negative life events and immune status in the era of ART. Mugavero and colleagues (2009) also observed that incident stressful life events are prospectively linked to greater odds of ART nonadherence and virological failure (i.e., viral load > 400 copies/μl) in a diverse cohort of HIV-positive persons followed over 27 months. Findings remained unchanged after controlling for depressive symptoms, but it is unclear whether the association of incident stressful life events on virological failure was fully mediated by ART nonadherence. These studies conducted in the ART era extend the results of previous investigations examining the clinical relevance of stressful life events experienced by men and women living with HIV.

Prior research examined relations between life events and clinical-illness endpoints in HIV-positive persons. In a series of studies conducted in the pre-ART era, Leserman and colleagues demonstrated that cumulative negative life events were associated with faster illness progression in HIV-positive men who have sex with men through a 9-year follow-up. Specifically, their findings indicated that higher cumulative negative life events equivalent to one severe stressor doubled the risk of progression to AIDS over 7.5 years (Leserman et al., 1999, 2000). These results remained unchanged after controlling for demographic variables, baseline CD4+ counts, baseline HIV viral load, number of antiretroviral medications, and serum cortisol. Using similar covariates, a subsequent investigation showed that greater cumulative negative life events (equivalent to one severe stressor) increased the risk of developing an AIDS clinical condition by threefold at 9-year follow-up (Leserman et al., 2002).

Building upon these findings, other investigators have examined the clinical relevance of negative life events in women with HIV. Pereira and colleagues (2003b) observed that, over a 1-year follow-up in HIV-positive women, greater negative life events during the 6 months prior to follow-up were related to an increased risk for symptomatic genital herpes recurrences, after controlling for indicators of HIV illness status and behavioral factors. These findings remained unchanged after controlling for herpes simplex virus type 2 (HSV-2) immunoglobulin G (IgG) antibody titers at study entry. Greater negative life events were also associated with persistence or progression of cervical squamous intraepithelial lesions (SIL), a preclinical condition to invasive cervical cancer, over the subsequent year (Pereira et al., 2003a). The association between negative life events and the persistence or progression of this preclinical condition in women at risk for AIDS was unchanged after controlling for indicators of HIV illness status (e.g., CD4+ counts), other viral risk factors for SIL (e.g., presence or absence of oncogenic human papilloma virus [HPV] infections), and behavioral factors (e.g., tobacco smoking).

Although relatively few investigations have examined the relevance of traumatic stressors, one study observed a high rate of exposure to traumatic events in African American women with HIV (Kimmerling et al., 1999). Exposure to a traumatic stressor (especially for participants with posttraumatic stress disorder [PTSD]) was associated with lower CD4+/CD8+ ratios at 1-year follow-up. More recent findings from an ART-era cohort of 490 HIV-positive men and women underscore the relevance of traumatic life events as risk factors for HIV illness progression over a 41-month follow-up (Leserman et al., 2007). After adjusting for baseline illness status, depressive symptoms, and concurrent stressful life events, each lifetime traumatic event was associated with a 17% and 22% greater rate of all-cause and AIDS-related mortality, respectively. For individuals with a number of lifetime traumatic events above the median, the all-cause mortality rate was twofold greater. Subsequent research demonstrated that the effects of trauma on faster HIV illness progression were not mediated by recent negative life events, depression, or other psychosocial factors (Pence et al., 2012). Because these studies did not adjust for ART adherence, questions remain regarding the underlying biobehavioral mechanism(s) that account for the deleterious associations of trauma with HIV illness markers and clinical illness progression.

The neuroendocrine stress response could moderate or mediate the associations of stressful and traumatic life events with hastened HIV illness progression (Kiecolt-Glaser et al., 2002). Generally, increases in cortisol and catecholamines are hypothesized to mediate the effects of psychiatric factors on immune decrements, but few studies conducted to date have provided compelling evidence to support this causal pathway. One recent investigation with a diverse cohort of 177 HIV-positive persons observed that greater urinary norepinephrine was prospectively linked to CD4+ cell decline and increases in HIV viral load over 4 years, after adjusting for ART utilization (Ironson et al., 2015). There was no evidence for mediation in this study, as the significant associations of stressful life events, distress, and avoidant coping on these outcomes remained after adjusting for urinary norepinephrine levels. Interestingly, one cross-sectional study conducted by Fekete and colleagues (2011) highlights that plasma oxytocin, a stress-responsive hormone thought to parallel affiliative behavior, may moderate the associations of stress with HIV illness markers. In a sample of 71 HIV-positive, low-income ethnic minority women, greater plasma oxytocin was independently associated with higher HIV viral load. However, higher perceived stress and stressful life events were associated with *greater* CD4+ cell counts among individuals with higher plasma oxytocin. This is consistent with recent conceptualizations of the adaptive nature of affiliative responses to stress (Taylor, 2006). Overall, findings suggest that differences in the ways individuals manage newly emerging challenges may affect neuroendocrine responses, which may have implications for HIV illness markers. More research is needed to examine what implications these neurohormonal changes have for immune status and health outcomes in persons with HIV.

These investigations support the relevance of chronic stress in HIV illness progression. Caution is in order, however, when interpreting these findings, as most studies had small samples and often did not adequately control for indices of HIV illness management. Future investigations should examine the prospective association between negative life events and health outcomes in larger, diverse, ART-treated cohorts of persons with HIV. Other investigations have focused on the associations of HIV-specific and other salient stressors with neuroendocrine hormone regulation and immune status.

HIV DIAGNOSIS, BEREAVEMENT, AND NAVIGATING DISCLOSURE

In the pre-ART era, the increase in distress upon learning that one is HIV seropositive has been shown to parallel reductions in CD4+ and NK cell counts (Antoni et al., 1991) and depressed T-lymphocyte responses to mitogenic challenge (Ironson et al., 1990). These findings suggest that stressful experiences early in HIV infection can have negative effects on immune status. One of the most common and recurring stressors for persons with HIV is bereavement. Particularly during the pre-ART era, bereavement and knowledge of HIV serostatus were identified over a 7-year period as two important predictors of psychological distress. Although approximately 50% of HIV-positive men in one sample reported being bereaved each year, the effects of bereavement on psychological distress diminished over time (Martin and Dean, 1993). However, knowledge of HIV serostatus was a strong predictor of distress over the study period. In the ART era, newly diagnosed HIV-positive persons commonly describe enhanced adaptive coping efforts with mild to moderate increases in depressed mood and anxiety following HIV diagnosis (Atkinson et al., 2009). Management of preexisting psychiatric comorbidities and HIV as a chronic condition is a common concern for patients in the ART era.

Other investigations have focused on bereavement as a predictor of immune status over time in cohorts of HIV-positive men who have sex with men. Specifically, bereavement has been related to more rapid declines in CD4+ counts over a 3- to 4-year period (Kemeny and Dean, 1995) as well as increases in serum neopterin and impaired lymphoproliferative responses, compared to a matched control group (Kemeny et al., 1995). Subsequent research with asymptomatic men with HIV have observed that bereavement is associated with decrements in NK cell cytotoxicity over a 1-year period (Goodkin et al., 1996). Bearing in mind that ART has led to substantial reductions in morbidity and mortality among persons with HIV, questions remain regarding the extent to which bereavement remains a prevalent stressor that is associated with immune decrements.

There is also some evidence to suggest that disclosure of either HIV serostatus or sexual orientation can be stressful, depending on intervening psychological and social factors.

In a study conducted in the pre-ART era, Cole and colleagues (1996) observed that HIV-positive men who have sex with men who choose not to disclose their sexual orientation display hastened HIV illness progression. This effect of non-disclosure of sexual orientation appeared to be most pronounced among men with greater rejection sensitivity (Cole et al., 1997). Although non-disclosure could contribute to social isolation, the literature examining the main effects of social support on HIV illness markers yielded mixed results in the pre-ART era (Miller and Cole, 1998). This suggests that disclosure may moderate the potential benefits of social support in HIV. For example, recent findings highlight that the complex implications of HIV disclosure and social support may vary as a function of ethnicity in HIV-positive men who have sex with men (Fekete et al., 2009b). Among Caucasian men, disclosure of HIV status to mothers, coupled with high levels of HIV-specific familial support, was associated with higher CD4+ counts and lower HIV viral load. On the other hand, Hispanic/Latino men who had disclosed to their mothers in the context of low HIV-specific familial support had higher HIV viral load.

Similarly, cross-sectional research conducted with HIV-positive, ethnic minority women observed that HIV disclosure to mothers in tandem with high HIV-specific familial support was associated with lower urinary free cortisol (Fekete et al., 2009a). On the other hand, disclosure to spouses and children coupled with high levels of family support was associated with higher depressive symptoms, but no concurrent associations with urinary free cortisol were observed. The potential immunomodulatory associations of urinary free cortisol with HIV illness markers were not examined in this study. Taken together, findings highlight that the implications of disclosure for HIV illness progression may depend largely on individual differences in rejection sensitivity as well as received social support. More longitudinal research is needed to understand the complex interplay among disclosure, individual differences in stress responses and other psychological processes, social support, and HIV illness progression.

The controlled study of individual differences in physiological responsiveness to behavioral and psychosocial challenges enjoys a long history in the use of the "laboratory reactivity" paradigm, mostly as applied to behavioral cardiology research. More recently, this paradigm has been used to investigate individual differences in immunocellular reactivity among persons with HIV.

STRESS REACTIVITY

What physiological changes that accompany a person's reaction to stressors could explain the association between life events and HIV illness progression? There is some evidence that distress and other negative mood states may be related to dysregulated hypothalamic–pituitary–adrenal (HPA) activity (e.g., elevated cortisol) in men with HIV (Gorman et al., 1991). Alterations in peripheral levels of adrenal hormones could conceivably dysregulate important cellular immune functions (Patterson et al., 2013). However, there

are methodological difficulties inherent in tying physiological stress responses (which may be short-lived) to field stressors or cumulative stressor burden as reported by participants. Consequently, researchers have turned to the laboratory reactivity paradigm to pinpoint potentially interrelated endocrine and immune changes that may parallel responses to stressors in persons with HIV.

In asymptomatic HIV-positive men who have sex with men, investigators have observed blunted adrenocorticotropin hormone (ACTH) responsiveness to a variety of behavioral challenges (Kumar et al., 1993) but no differences in cortisol increases over time compared with HIV-negative men (Starr et al., 1996). The lack of cortisol differences may be an artifact of the timing of blood draws after stressor onset—cortisol responses may lag behind ACTH and catecholamine changes by several minutes. Subsequent investigations have demonstrated that persons with HIV show changes in immune cell subsets during an evaluative speech stressor (Hurwitz et al., 2005). Compared to their HIV-negative counterparts, HIV-positive persons showed greater increases in total and activated T-cell counts. Specifically, persons with HIV displayed increases in the CD8+ and CD8+38+ T-cell subsets during the speech stressor task. Hurwitz and colleagues (2005) also determined that persons with HIV had smaller stressor-induced increases in NK counts and NK cell cytotoxicity as well as impaired lymphoproliferative responsiveness to phytohemagglutinin mitogen. While no group differences in catecholamine reactivity were observed, HIV-positive participants displayed greater increases in CD8+ T-cell count per unit increase in norepinephrine. Most notably, a positive correlation between norepinephrine and CD8+38+ T-cell count was significant only for the HIV-positive group. Taken together, these data highlight that abnormalities in immune cell trafficking observed in HIV-positive persons may be due in part to functional alterations in sympathoimmune communication.

The relevance of sympathoimmune communication in persons with HIV is further supported by results of previous investigations. Because lymphoid organs are a primary site of HIV replication, sympathetic nervous system innervation of these regions may dramatically influence HIV illness progression (Cole and Kemeny, 2001). For example, release of norepinephrine at nerve terminals may down-regulate proliferation of naïve T cells in the lymphoid organs (Felten, 1996). By binding with β_2 receptors on the lymphocyte membrane, norepinephrine induces cellular changes via the G protein–linked adenyl cyclase–cAMP–protein kinase A signaling cascade (Kobilka, 1992). In vitro data have shown that cellular changes of this nature are associated with decrements in interferon-γ and interleukin-10, which in turn, are associated with elevations in HIV viral load over an 8-day period (Cole et al., 1998).

Other in vivo investigations have specifically examined the role of autonomic nervous system (ANS) activity in HIV-positive persons initiating ART. Individuals who displayed higher ANS activity at rest prior to beginning ART subsequently demonstrated poorer suppression of HIV viral load and decreased CD4+ T-cell reconstitution over a 3- to

11-month period (Cole et al., 2001). Furthermore, in a sample of asymptomatic HIV-positive men who have sex with men, socially inhibited individuals displayed an eightfold increase in plasma HIV viral load set point and showed poorer responses to ART (Cole et al., 2003). The effect of social inhibition on higher HIV viral load was mediated by elevated ANS activity, even after controlling for demographic and health status variables. Thus, stress-related alterations in neuroendocrine functioning may continue to influence immune status and health outcomes in the era of ART. These data also highlight the fact that individuals often have highly variable psychological responses to any given stressor, raising the possibility that dispositional factors may influence HIV illness progression.

PERSONALITY FACTORS

Burgeoning research has examined whether stable personality factors are associated with indices of more rapid HIV illness progression. Because personality factors reflect enduring psychological response patterns, they may be more reliably associated with HIV illness progression than stressful life events or the measurement of transient, laboratory-based stress responses. Drawing upon the five factor model of personality, O'Cleirigh and colleagues (2007) examined the relevance of conscientiousness in a diverse sample of 119 HIV-positive persons. Over a 1-year follow-up, individuals with higher conscientiousness displayed increases in CD4+ count and reductions in HIV viral load, after adjusting for whether they were taking antiretroviral medications. No evidence was obtained that these effects were mediated by improved adherence. Subsequent research conducted with this cohort observed that openness and extroversion were associated with increases in CD4+ count and reductions in HIV viral load over a 4-year follow-up, after adjusting for antiretroviral medication (Ironson et al., 2008). Initially reported associations of conscientiousness with greater HIV viral load were maintained, but no association with CD4+ count was observed over the 4-year follow-up. Analyses of personality facets and profiles indicated that approach-oriented styles characterized by positive emotionality displayed the best outcomes with respect to HIV illness markers.

Findings that an approach-oriented dispositional style may be a key protective factor for persons with HIV are consistent with other studies conducted by this team, in which dispositional optimism and depth of emotional expression have been linked to HIV illness markers. In a diverse cohort of 177 HIV-positive persons, greater dispositional optimism predicted increased CD4+ counts and reduced HIV viral load over a 2-year follow-up, after adjusting for baseline illness status and antiretroviral medications (Ironson, Balbin, et al., 2005). More favorable HIV illness markers among persons higher in dispositional optimism were mediated by more proactive behavior, less avoidant-oriented coping, and less depression. In other research with HIV-positive men who have sex with men conducted in the aftermath of Hurricane Andrew, dispositional optimism was associated with lower

Epstein-Barr virus (EBV) and human herpes virus type-6 (HHV-6) IgG antibody titers. These findings suggest better immunological control over these viruses in participants with an optimistic attributional style in the wake of a severe environmental stressor (Cruess et al., 2000b). O'Cleirigh and colleagues (2003) also observed that greater depth of emotional expression in writing about past traumas was associated with long-term survival with AIDS. This association was independent of medication adherence and mediated by greater depth of processing. Taken together, findings from these studies underscore key domains of trait psychological resilience that support successful HIV illness management and may independently enhance immune status.

At the same time, other studies have highlighted the potentially negative implications of trait-like difficulties with emotional awareness and expression. In a pre-ART era cohort of 200 HIV-positive men and women, Solano and colleagues (2002) observed that type C coping was associated with clinical illness progression among those with CD4+ counts from 200 to 499 at baseline. Conceptually similar to alexithymia, type C coping reflects a trait-like pattern of decreased emotional awareness and low emotional expression. Subsequent work demonstrated that type C coping is associated with increased stimulated production of interleukin-6 (IL-6), after adjusting for age and CD4+ count (Temoshok et al., 2008). On the other hand, alexithymia was independently associated with reduced production of beta chemokines, which inhibit HIV replication. Subsequent cross-sectional research conducted with 172 HIV-positive men and women highlights that difficulties with emotional awareness may be the most detrimental facet of alexithymia (McIntosh et al., 2014). Alexithymic participants reported greater distress and displayed a preponderance of the autonomic response (indexed by a greater norepinephrine/cortisol ratio in urine samples) and higher HIV viral load. Difficulties with identifying feelings were associated with greater depression and a higher norepinephrine/cortisol ratio. More longitudinal research is needed to examine whether and how individuals with elevated alexithymia experience more rapid HIV illness progression.

Great progress has been made in recent years to identify dispositional factors that predict different trajectories of HIV illness progression. Findings highlight the protective benefits of approach-oriented, conscientious, and optimistic personality styles. At the same time, persons who experience difficulties with identifying, expressing, and effectively managing emotions may display hastened HIV illness progression. Interventions are needed to target relevant psychological, behavioral, and biological processes that account for the effects of dispositional factors on HIV illness progression. The following sections focus on modifiable psychological pathways that have been studied to date in PNI research with persons with HIV.

COGNITIVE APPRAISALS

Individual differences in cognitive appraisals of stressors may moderate the association between stressful life events and health status in persons with HIV. Specifically, one research group has demonstrated that positive illusions and unrealistically optimistic appraisals may confer health-protective benefits (Taylor et al., 2000). Results from an investigation of bereaved HIV-positive men indicated that men who engaged in cognitive processing (deliberate, effortful, and long-lasting thinking) about the death of a close friend or partner were more likely to report a major shift in values, priorities, or perspectives (i.e., finding meaning) following the loss (Bower et al., 1998). For individuals classified as finding meaning, positive health effects appeared to follow. Finding meaning predicted slower CD4+ decline and greater longevity over a 2- to 3-year follow-up period (Bower et al., 1998). Decreased cortisol is one plausible mediator of the effects of finding meaning on health status. In other medical populations (e.g., women being treated for breast cancer) finding benefits in living with a chronic illness predicts concurrent decreases in serum cortisol (Cruess et al., 2000c). In HIV-positive populations, elevated serum cortisol levels have been related to faster progression to AIDS, development of an AIDS-related condition, and mortality over a 9-year period (Leserman et al., 2002). Conversely, lower 15-hour urinary free cortisol levels are associated with long-term survival with AIDS (Ironson et al., 2002). Importantly, we have observed that finding benefits in living with HIV/AIDS uniquely predicted lower urinary free cortisol output in a diverse cohort of ART-treated, HIV-positive persons (Carrico et al., 2006).

Other investigators have observed that negative HIV-specific expectancies (i.e., fatalism) are related to elevated risk for symptom onset in bereaved, asymptomatic HIV-positive men (Reed et al., 1999) and to mortality in men with AIDS (Reed et al., 1994). Negative causal attributions about one's self have also been associated with CD4+ count decline over 18 months (Segerstrom et al., 1996). Finally, among women with HIV, pessimism has been associated with lower CD8+ percentages and lower NK cell cytotoxicity, after controlling for stressful life events (Byrnes et al., 1998). These findings suggest that across different HIV-positive populations, negative or pessimistic appraisals about stressors or one's efficacy in managing life challenges are associated with poorer immune status and greater risk for illness progression. By contrast, maintaining optimism and finding benefit in the challenges of HIV/AIDS are associated with lower levels of adrenal stress hormones, better antiviral immunity, and possibly better health outcomes. It may be possible to modulate cognitive appraisal processes in persons with HIV by way of cognitive-behavioral interventions (Carrico et al., 2005b; Lutgendorf et al., 1998). Before discussing the PNI research on such interventions in persons with HIV, it is important to consider the role that negative mood states as well as positive affect and other positive psychological states may play in mediating the association between cognitive appraisals and health outcomes in HIV/AIDS.

NEGATIVE MOOD

Negative mood states such as depression and anxiety have been associated with additional functional impairment, mortality,

and an approximately 50% increase in medical costs for persons managing a variety of chronic medical conditions (Katon, 2003). Because individuals with HIV are at increased risk for developing an affective or adjustment disorder across the illness spectrum (Bing et al., 2001), effectively managing negative mood may be an especially relevant task. In fact, elevated negative mood may result in decrements in immune status, HIV illness progression, and mortality (Leserman, 2003; Leserman, 2007; Leserman et al., 2007). However, the directionality of this relationship has been hotly debated. Chronic viral infections such as HIV deplete amino acid precursors for serotonin and dopamine, which is linked to greater depressive symptoms and lower quality of life among persons with HIV (Carrico et al., 2008; Kalichman et al., 2002; Schroecksnadel and Antoni, 2008; Zangerle et al., 2010). Although decrements in negative mood and quality of life may be partially reversed among persons successfully treated with ART (Rabkin et al., 2000; Schroecksnadel et al., 2008), questions remain regarding whether negative mood is a consequence rather than a cause of illness progression in ART-treated persons with HIV.

Longitudinal investigations with repeated measurements of psychosocial and immunological data provide the most reliable findings on the temporal associations between negative mood and HIV illness progression. For example, depressive symptoms were associated with reductions in CD8+ and NK cell counts over a 2-year period, especially among individuals reporting more stressful life events (Leserman et al., 1997). Although depressive symptoms have been associated with more rapid CD4+ count decline in cohorts of HIV-positive men (Burack et al., 1993; Vedhara et al., 1997) and women (Ickovics et al., 2001), other longitudinal investigations that used *only* baseline measurements of depressive symptoms have not observed similar effects (Lyketsos et al., 1993; Patterson et al., 1996). Another investigation of HIV-positive men and women without AIDS indicated that the relationship between distress and cell-mediated immunity is observed only in participants with low levels of HIV viral burden (Motivala et al., 2003). Specifically, increased distress (including depressed mood, anxiety, and perceived stress) was associated with lower total CD4+, memory CD4+, and B-cell counts, but only in individuals with lower viral load (i.e., ≤1 standard deviation below the mean). These findings may partially explain the discrepant results regarding the association between depressive symptoms and CD4+ T-cell counts, suggesting that PNI associations may be more commonly observed at the earliest stages of illness.

Other investigations with women with HIV have shown that symptoms of depression and anxiety were associated with more CD8+38+ cells and higher HIV viral load (Evans et al., 2002). In this cross-sectional study, a diagnosis of major depression was also related to lower NK cell cytotoxicity. More importantly, women whose major depression resolved over time showed concurrent increases in NK cell cytotoxicity up to 2 years later (Cruess et al., 2005). The continued relevance of negative mood in the era of ART is further supported by observations that cumulative depressive symptoms, hopelessness, and avoidant coping scores were associated with decreased CD4+ counts and higher HIV viral load over a

2-year period in a diverse sample of HIV-positive men and women (Ironson, O'Cleirigh, et al., 2005). These effects of negative mood and avoidant coping in this study held after controlling for adherence to ART.

In recent years, there has also been growing recognition that ART adherence is not the only relevant measure of HIV illness management that should be included as a covariate in PNI investigations. Although adherence measures index the proportion of medications taken on average, they do not provide adequate information about whether and how individuals stop taking ART medications altogether for discrete periods (Bae et al., 2011). This phenomenon, referred to as *non-persistence*, is independently linked to inflammation, coagulation, and more negative health outcomes in persons with HIV (Kuller et al., 2008). Findings from the NIMH Healthy Living Project underscore the importance of adjusting for patterns of non-persistence (Carrico et al., 2011). In this study, 1 standard deviation higher cognitive-affective symptoms of depression at baseline predicted a 50% greater mean HIV viral load over a 25-month follow-up, even after controlling for baseline CD4+ count and mean self-reported ART adherence over follow-up. Interestingly, this association of baseline depression with higher mean viral load over follow-up was partially mediated by ART discontinuation (i.e., stopping ART and remaining off it during subsequent assessments). Future PNI research should adjust for difficulties with ART adherence and persistence to determine whether there is remaining variance in HIV illness markers that could be co-mediated by changes in neuroendocrine hormones.

Lending support to the clinical relevance of decrements in immune status are findings highlighting the association between depressive symptoms and illness endpoints. Specifically, depressive symptoms have been related to faster progression to AIDS (Leserman et al., 1999; Page-Shafer et al., 1996) and development of an AIDS-related clinical condition (Leserman et al., 2002). Other investigations have determined that chronically elevated depressive symptoms are associated with hastened mortality among HIV-positive men (Mayne et al., 1996) and women (Ickovics et al., 2001). Again, the majority of studies reporting no effect of depressive symptoms on hastened mortality used *only* baseline measures (Burack et al., 1993; Lyketsos et al., 1993; Page-Shafer et al., 1996). Interestingly, in a follow-up to one study in which no effects of baseline depressive symptoms were observed on HIV illness progression, participants reported a dramatic increase in depressive symptoms 6 to 18 months before an AIDS diagnosis (Lyketsos et al., 1996). Elevated depressive symptoms in the earlier stages of infection, HIV-related symptoms, unemployment, cigarette smoking, and social isolation were all associated with greater severity of depression as AIDS developed. However, increases in depressive symptomatology during this stage were not associated with mortality. While discrepant findings have been reported, it appears that depressive symptoms may be an important predictor of HIV illness progression. In particular, investigations examining the chronic nature of depressive symptoms over time have yielded the most consistent, replicable findings that demonstrate an effect of depressive symptoms on HIV illness progression.

Although relatively few studies to date have systematically examined other negative mood states, anger has been associated with faster progression to AIDS (Leserman et al., 2002). Greater trait anger was found to be associated with higher psychological stress, more avoidant coping, and greater HIV illness severity in 377 men and women with HIV (McIntosh et al., 2015). Anxiety symptoms have also been related to greater CD8+38+ T-cell counts and higher HIV viral load—both indicators of elevated illness activity (Evans et al., 2002). More research is needed to examine the relevance of negative mood states with respect to indices of HIV illness progression in the ART era. These investigations should endeavor to adequately control for other indices of HIV illness management (including ART persistence) to provide a more definitive answer to the question of whether negative mood states may independently contribute to HIV illness progression via other biobehavioral pathways. At the same time, there is also increasing recognition that positive affect as well as other positive psychological states may independently predict more effective HIV illness management and longevity in persons with HIV.

POSITIVE AFFECT AND OTHER POSITIVE PSYCHOLOGICAL STATES

Positive affect as well as other positive psychological states often co-occur with negative affect and are theorized to serve unique, adaptive functions during stressful periods (Folkman 1997; Folkman and Moskowitz, 2000). Because of the large number of positive psychological constructs examined to date, it is premature to draw conclusions regarding which (if any) are associated with less rapid HIV illness progression (Ironson and Hayward, 2008). Longitudinal studies examining positive affect, spirituality, and positive psychological resources are described briefly here.

Findings from a pre-ART era cohort of HIV-positive men who have sex with men demonstrated that greater positive affect is uniquely associated with longevity (Moskowitz, 2003). Other research conducted in the ART era with a cohort of 153 newly diagnosed HIV-positive men and women observed that positive affect is independently associated with faster linkage to HIV care and greater odds of ART persistence over an 18-month follow-up (Carrico and Moskowitz, 2014). Although there were no direct associations of positive affect on HIV viral load in this study, positive affect was indirectly associated with a modestly lower HIV viral load via greater odds of ART persistence over follow-up. Although positive affect may serve unique, adaptive functions in the midst of stressful circumstances, other positive psychological states have been associated with better HIV illness markers and longevity in HIV-positive persons.

Findings from an investigation conducted by Ickovics and colleagues (2006) with a cohort of HIV-positive women indicated that positive psychological resources (i.e., positive affect, positive expectancies regarding health outcomes, and finding meaning) predicted decreased rates of CD4+ count decline and HIV-related mortality, after adjusting for illness status and antiretroviral medications. Other research underscores the protective benefits of religiosity/spirituality among persons with HIV. One longitudinal study demonstrated that, on average, persons with HIV report increases in religiosity/spirituality after receiving their diagnosis (Ironson et al., 2006). These increases in religiosity/spirituality are associated with relative preservation of CD4+ cell counts as well as decreased HIV viral load, after adjusting for illness status and antiretroviral medications. The clinical relevance of these findings is supported by research indicating that persons with HIV who reported experiencing a spiritual transformation displayed a substantially greater 5-year survival rate, after adjusting for illness status and a history of substance use problems (Ironson and Kremer, 2009).

These longitudinal studies highlight that research examining positive affect and other positive psychological states is a promising area for further investigation in PNI. Developing a more nuanced understanding of the relevance of these positive psychological factors could substantially support efforts to develop novel intervention approaches to optimize health outcomes among persons with HIV. The next section summarizes results of RCTs examining the efficacy of psychological interventions with respect to neuroendocrine hormone regulation and immune status in persons with HIV.

STRESS MANAGEMENT AND PSYCHIATRIC INTERVENTIONS

Stress management techniques such as relaxation training, cognitive restructuring, and coping skills training may reduce negative mood states in persons with HIV by lowering physical tension and increasing self-efficacy (Antoni, 2003a; Chesney et al., 2003). These affective changes are thought to be accompanied by an improved ability to regulate peripheral catecholamines and cortisol via decreases in ANS activation and improved regulation of the HPA axis, respectively. Neuroendocrine regulation may be associated with a partial "normalization" of immune system functions, providing more efficient surveillance of pathogens such as latent viruses that may increase HIV replication and enhance vulnerability to opportunistic infections or neoplasias. This normalization of stress-associated immune system decrements may ultimately forestall increases in viral load and the manifestation of clinical symptoms over extended periods. A relatively small number of RCTs have examined the effects of stress management interventions on psychosocial and immune parameters in HIV-positive populations. There is mounting evidence that interventions employing stress management techniques enhance psychological adjustment, improve neuroendocrine regulation, and bolster immune status (Antoni, 2003a; Carrico and Antoni, 2008), but these effects have not been reliably observed across RCTs (Scott-Sheldon et al., 2008). If stress management can modify negative mood by changing cognitive appraisals, coping responses, and social support resources, then neuroendocrine changes and normalization of immune status may follow.

Extensive reviews of the efficacy of psychological interventions for improving neuroendocrine hormone regulation and immune status in persons with HIV have yielded mixed results (Carrico and Antoni, 2008; Scott-Sheldon et al., 2008). The modal stress management intervention tested in this regard is a 10-week, group-based cognitive-behavioral stress management (CBSM) intervention for persons with HIV. Throughout previous trials, CBSM was tailored to psychosocial sequelae that may follow critical challenges for HIV-positive persons at various illness stages. In the initial RCT, a cohort of 65 men who have sex with men, who were awaiting HIV serostatus notification, were randomly assigned to a 10-week CBSM intervention, a 10-week group-based aerobic exercise intervention, or a no-treatment control group. After 5 weeks of participating in one of these conditions, blood was drawn for antibody testing and the men received news of their HIV serostatus 72 hours later. Among the approximately one-third of men diagnosed as HIV positive ($n = 23$), the men in the control condition reported significant increases in anxiety and depression. In contrast, men in the CBSM and aerobic exercise conditions showed no significant changes in anxiety or depression scores (Antoni et al., 1991; LaPerriere et al., 1990). Whereas HIV-positive men in the control condition showed declines in CD4+ and NK cell counts during this notification period, the HIV-positive men in the CBSM group displayed significant concurrent increases in CD4+ and NK cell counts as well as small increases in lymphocyte proliferative responses to mitogenic challenge and NK cell cytotoxicity. Thus, CBSM appears to have "buffered" the notification-associated affective and immunological changes (Antoni et al., 1991).

There were also changes in indicators of antiviral immunity over the 10-week intervention period. Men assigned to either CBSM or exercise interventions showed significant decreases in IgG antibody titers (reflecting better immunological control) to EBV and HHV-6, which moved into the normal range for age-matched healthy men. This was in contrast to IgG antibody titer values for assessment-only controls, which remained elevated (Esterling et al., 1992). The reductions in EBV IgG antibody titers in the CBSM group appeared to be mediated by the greater social support levels maintained in this condition (Antoni et al., 1996). Finally, a 2-year follow-up study of the HIV-positive men in this trial found that less distress at diagnosis, decreased HIV-specific denial coping after diagnosis, and better participant adherence to CBSM treatment protocol all predicted slower illness progression to symptoms and AIDS (Ironson et al., 1994).

Another 10-week, group-based intervention designed to provide emotional support and coping skills after bereavement was tested in a cohort of 97 HIV-positive asymptomatic men who have sex with men who were dealing with loss. Results of this RCT indicated that the bereavement intervention decreased grief and buffered CD4+ decline and reduced plasma cortisol as well as the number of healthcare visits over a 6-month period, compared to a no-treatment control condition (Goodkin et al., 1998). In a subset of 36 men, the bereavement intervention also buffered against increases in HIV viral load (Goodkin et al., 2001). Therefore, group-based psychosocial interventions may be adaptable and successful in helping persons with HIV deal with different emotional challenges during the early asymptomatic stage of the infection.

In a subsequent RCT of CBSM, this intervention was tailored to assist persons with HIV in managing the emergence of symptoms. HIV-positive men who have sex with men who had mild symptoms (category B of the 1993 CDC definition) were randomly assigned to either a 10-week group-based CBSM intervention or a modified wait-list control group. Men in the wait-list control group completed a 10-week waiting period before they were reassessed and invited to participate in a 1-day CBSM seminar. Results indicated that CBSM decreased depressive symptoms, anxiety, and mood disturbance over the 10-week intervention period (Lutgendorf et al., 1997, 1998). Decreases in depressive symptoms and enhanced social support over the 10-week intervention period partially explained concurrent reductions in HSV-2 IgG antibody titers (Cruess et al., 2000a; Lutgendorf et al., 1997). Subsequently, a buffering effect of CBSM on EBV IgG antibody titers was observed up to 1 year following CBSM (Carrico et al., 2005a). Similar to previous investigations with asymptomatic HIV-positive men who have sex with men (Antoni et al., 1996), intervention effects of EBV IgG antibody titers paralleled sustained increases in social support for men randomized to CBSM (Carrico et al., 2005a).

According to a conceptual model (Antoni, 2003b; Antoni et al., 1990) we reasoned that CBSM-related reductions in multiple indices of negative mood should be accompanied by concurrent changes in neuroendocrine regulation that could influence immune system status in this population. CBSM effects on neuroendocrine regulation have been observed in a number of studies, and these effects have been associated with changes in both affective and cellular-immune parameters (Antoni, 2003b). Specifically, CBSM effects on distress have been observed to co-vary with decreases in 24-hour urinary free cortisol (Antoni et al., 2000b). Lending further support to the PNI model underlying this work, subsequent investigations have determined that reductions in depressed mood and 24-hour urinary free cortisol during the 10-week intervention period co-mediate CBSM effects on recovery of transitional naïve T-cell counts over a 6- to 12-month follow-up period (Antoni et al., 2005).

Similarly, reductions in anxiety during the 10-week intervention period have been observed to co-vary with decreases in 24-hour norepinephrine. These intervention-related reductions in norepinephrine mediated the effect of CBSM on maintaining CD8+ T-cell counts through a 6- to 12-month follow-up (Antoni et al., 2000a). This buffering effect was such that men in the control condition had significant declines, while the men in the CBSM group maintained CD8+ counts at the same level. CBSM has also been associated with plasma cortisol/DHEA-S decreases (Cruess et al., 1999) and testosterone increases in HIV-positive men who have sex with men (Cruess et al., 2000d), which paralleled decreases in depressed mood over the 10-week intervention period. Taken together, this series of studies suggests that CBSM may affect hormonal regulation to promote herpesvirus surveillance and immune system reconstitution among HIV-positive men who have

sex with men. By examining relations among PNI variables changing during the course of these interventions and at follow-up, we have found evidence that meaningful psychological and biological changes may be attributed to the stress management skills learned and the increase in social support experienced as a result of participating in these groups (Cruess et al., 2000a; Lutgendorf et al., 1997).

Other RCTs have examined the efficacy of psychological interventions in women with HIV. Weiss and colleagues (2011) conducted a series of RCTs comparing the efficacy of a group-based CBSM intervention combined with supportive expressive therapy techniques with that of a low-intensity psychoeducational program. Although these RCTs demonstrated that this enhanced CBSM intervention reduces distress and denial coping as well as improves self-efficacy and quality of life, no intent-to-treat effects on HIV illness markers were observed. Interestingly, intervention-related increases in self-efficacy were indirectly linked to lower HIV viral load (Ironson, Balbin, et al., 2005). Another RCT compared the efficacy of a 10-session CBSM group with that of 1-day CBSM workshop in 39 HIV-positive low-income women with a recent papanicolaou smear (Antoni et al., 2008). Participants randomized to CBSM reported greater reductions in perceived stress and displayed decreased odds of cervical neoplasia over a 9-month follow-up. Subsequent research conducted with this RCT observed that women randomized to receive CBSM reported increases in positive affect, positive states of mind, and spiritual well-being (Jensen et al., 2013). No psychological or neuroendocrine mediators of decreased odds of progression to cervical neoplasia were identified in this small RCT. Overall, further research is needed to examine whether novel interventions can modify biobehavioral processes in women with HIV.

In the ART era, a variety of behavioral interventions for persons with HIV have been developed specifically to support medication adherence. Although psychological adjustment has not been uniformly conceptualized as a mechanism of enhanced adherence, research has supported the efficacy of pharmacist-led, individualized medication adherence training (MAT) interventions and those that employ cognitive-behavioral principles based on self-efficacy theory (Simoni et al., 2003). Consequently, we theorized that a modified form of CBSM may offer benefits in improving mood, health behaviors, and immune status in the era of ART. In order to test the added value associated with providing stress management training, 130 HIV-positive men who have sex with men were recruited for a trial in which the combination of CBSM and MAT (CBSM+MAT) was compared to MAT alone. In an intent-to-treat analysis, we observed no intervention-related changes in immune status. However, in a secondary analysis with 101 men who had a detectable HIV viral load at baseline, we observed a .56 $\log_{10}$ reduction in HIV viral load over the 15-month investigation period only in the group that received combined CBSM+MAT, after controlling for antiretroviral medication adherence. This clinically interesting effect of CBSM+MAT on HIV viral load was mediated by reductions in depressed mood during the 10-week intervention period. Importantly, these findings held even after controlling for adherence training exposure (each group received MAT) and statistically controlling for individual differences in reported adherence at each time point (Antoni et al., 2006). Thus, there appears to be some added value of reducing depressed mood in persons dealing with the complexities of ART treatment.

Findings from Safren and colleagues underscore the potential benefits of simultaneously intervening to reduce depression and optimize ART adherence in persons with HIV. One crossover RCT observed that individuals randomized to receive 10 to 12 sessions of cognitive-behavioral therapy for adherence and depression (CBT-AD) with a single-session adherence intervention displayed greater reductions in depressed mood and increased ART adherence than did individuals receiving a single-session adherence intervention alone (Safren et al., 2009). These effects of CBT-AD were generally maintained over the 12-month follow-up period and were paralleled by significant reductions in HIV viral load. However, one limitation of this RCT is that HIV viral load reductions were observed only following crossover and no randomized comparison with individuals initially receiving the single-session adherence intervention was possible. A subsequent RCT examined the efficacy of CBT-AD with HIV-positive injection drug users who were actively receiving substance abuse treatment (Safren et al., 2012). Compared to enhanced treatment as usual, individuals randomized to receive CBT-AD had decreased depression and improved ART adherence at the immediate post-treatment assessment. Reductions in depression but not ART adherence were maintained over follow-up. Interestingly, individuals randomized to receive CBT-AD had increases in CD4+ counts but not HIV viral load over the 6-month follow-up period. Taken together, results of these RCTs highlight that cognitive-behavioral interventions targeting the co-occurrence of depression and ART nonadherence could positively influence HIV illness markers.

Other RCTs have examined the efficacy of other integrative intervention approaches, such as expressive writing and mindfulness-based stress reduction (MBSR), for reducing distress and modifying HIV illness markers.

Expressive writing provides an opportunity for individuals to confront traumatic experiences, to enhance psychological adjustment and potentially improve biobehavioral processes relevant to chronic illness (Smyth, 1998). In a small ART-era RCT, HIV-positive men and women were randomized to four sessions of writing about their worst stressful event or writing about trivial daily events (Petrie et al., 2004). Individuals writing about their worst stressor had reduced HIV viral load at 2 weeks post-randomization and increased CD4+ counts over a 6-month follow-up compared with the trivial-writing control group. The concomitant effects of expressive writing on psychosocial adjustment were not examined in this RCT, and no mediators of the effects on HIV illness markers were examined. A more definitive RCT with 244 HIV-positive persons observed no intent-to-treat effects of written emotional expression (Ironson et al., 2013). Women randomized to expressive writing reported greater decreases in posttraumatic stress symptoms, depression, and

HIV symptoms. There were no effects of expressive writing on CD4+ count or HIV viral load in intent-to-treat or secondary analyses.

Finally, in recent years there has been substantial interest in developing and testing stress management interventions designed to cultivate metacognitive awareness as a means of enhancing psychological adjustment and delaying HIV illness progression. To date, one small RCT has examined the efficacy of an 8-week MBSR intervention followed by a 1-day retreat, compared to a 1-day control seminar (Creswell et al., 2009). Findings indicated that there was a buffering effect of MBSR such that control participants had significant reductions in CD4+ count following the intervention period. Participants receiving MBSR displayed no changes in CD4+ count, and no concomitant intervention effects on HIV viral load were observed. More clinical research is needed to examine the efficacy of integrative intervention approaches like expressive writing and MBSR for improving psychological adjustment and modifying HIV illness markers.

It is plausible that enhancing psychological adjustment confers beneficial effects on HIV illness markers by way of other *health behavior pathways* (reduced substance use, improved sleep, and less exposure to sexually transmitted infections) and/or *PNI pathways* (better antiviral immunity against co-infections or less neuroendocrine-mediated HIV replication). It remains for future research to incorporate measures of PNI variables as well as indicators of HIV viral load and genetic resistance over extended periods as individuals on multidrug regimens participate in well-controlled RCTs of psychiatric interventions. It is plausible that an equally efficient strategy for conducting PNI research in individuals with HIV is to examine concurrent changes in mood, neuroendocrine, immune, and viral processes in the context of randomized trials of mood-modulating pharmacological treatments. For example, one RCT of non-blinded, once-weekly fluoxetine treatment, directly observed for 24 weeks, in homeless and marginally housed HIV-positive persons showed some reductions in depressive symptoms but no concomitant effects on ART adherence or viral suppression (Tsai et al., 2013). The work outlined in Chapters 15, 18, and 42 elaborates on some of the contemporary pharmacological strategies available for addressing depressed mood and anxiety symptoms in persons with HIV. Future PNI studies should continue to capitalize on the power of an RCT for mitigating the influence of a host of biobehavioral confounders relevant to this literature. This research approach could also offer the additional benefit of using a blinded-placebo design, a feature that has been elusive in RCTs of psychosocial interventions.

CONCLUSIONS

If psychosocial factors influence immune status and clinical outcomes among people living with HIV/AIDS, this phenomenon may actually be even more relevant since the introduction of ART. Prior to the availability of these potent antiretroviral regimens, the devastating effects of HIV may have overshadowed the effects of any other deleterious factors on the immune system. In the ART era, however, the magnitude of the effects of psychological and behavioral factors on the immune system could be increased, but the underlying biobehavioral mechanisms have not been clearly elucidated. The studies reviewed in this chapter suggest that stress, psychosocial factors, and psychiatric symptoms are nontrivial cofactors in HIV illness progression. Consequently, more research to obtain a definitive answer to these mechanistic questions is imperative to informing the development of targeted treatments to optimize health outcomes. An important remaining question is whether psychiatric interventions (with psychotherapy or medication) decrease HIV-associated morbidity and improve health outcomes.

REFERENCES

Antoni MH (2003a). Stress management and psychoneuroimmunology in HIV infection. *CNS Spectrums* 8:40–51.

Antoni MH (2003b). Stress management effects on psychological, endocrinological and immune function in men with HIV: empirical support for a psychoneuroimmunological model. *Stress* 6:173–188.

Antoni M, August S, LaPerriere A, et al. (1990). Psychological and neuroendocrine measures related to functional immune changes in anticipation of HIV-1 serostatus notification. *Psychosom Med* 52:496–510.

Antoni MH, Baggett L, Ironson G, et al. (1991). Cognitive behavioral stress management intervention buffers distress responses and immunologic changes following notification of HIV-1 seropositivity. *J Consult Clin Psychol* 59:906–915.

Antoni MH, Carrico AW, Durán RE, et al. (2006). Randomized clinical trial of cognitive behavioral stress management on human immunodeficiency virus viral load in gay men treated with highly active antiretroviral therapy. *Psychosom Med* 68:143–151.

Antoni MH, Cruess DG, Cruess S, et al. (2000a). Cognitive behavioral stress management intervention effects on anxiety, 24-hour urinary catecholamine output, and T-cytotoxic/suppres-sor cells over time among symptomatic HIV-infected gay men. *J Consult Clin Psychol* 68:31–46.

Antoni MH, Cruess D, Klimas N, et al. (2005). Increases in a marker of immune system reconstitution are predated by decreases in 24-hour urinary cortisol output and depressed mood during a 10-week stress management intervention in symptomatic HIV-infected gay men. *J Psychosom Res* 58:3–13.

Antoni MH, Lutgendorf S, Ironson G, Fletcher M.A, and Schneiderman N (1996). CBSM intervention effects on social support, coping, depression and immune function in symptomatic HIV-infected men. *Psychosom Med* 58:86.

Antoni MH, Pereira DB, Marion I, et al. (2008). Stress management effects on perceived stress and cervical neoplasia in low-income HIV-infected women. *J Psychosom Res* 65: 389–401.

Antoni MH, Schneiderman N (1998). HIV/AIDS. In A Bellack, M Hersen (eds.), *Comprehensive Clinical Psychology* (pp. 237–275). New York: Elsevier Science.

Antoni MH, Wagner S, Cruess D, et al. (2000b). Cognitive behavioral stress management reduces distress and 24-hour urinary free cortisol among symptomatic HIV-infected gay men. *Ann Behav Med* 22:29–37.

Atkinson JH, Higgins JA, Vigil O, et al. (2009). Psychiatric context of acute/early HIV infection. the NIMH Multisite Acute HIV Infection Study: IV. *AIDS Behav* 13:1061–1067.

Bae JW, Guyer W, Grimm K, Altice FL (2011). Medication persistence in the treatment of HIV infection: a review of the literature and implications for future clinical care and research. *AIDS* 25:279–290.

Bangsberg DR, Perry S, Charlebois ED, et al. (2001). Non-adherence to highly active antiretroviral therapy predicts progression to AIDS. *AIDS* 15:1181–1183.

Bing EG, Burnam MA, Longshore D, et al. (2001). Psychiatric disorders and drug use among human immunodeficiency virus–infected adults in the United States. *Arch Gen Psychiatry* 58:721–728.

Bower JE, Kemeny ME, Taylor SE, Fahey JL (1998). Cognitive processing, discovery of meaning, CD4 decline, and AIDS-related mortality among bereaved HIV-seropositive men. *J Consult Clin Psychol* 66:979–986.

Burack JH, Barrett DC, Stall RD, Chesney MA, Ekstrand ML, Coates TJ (1993). Depressive symptoms and CD4 lymphocyte decline among HIV-infected men. *JAMA* 270:2568–2573.

Byrnes DM, Antoni MH, Goodkin K, et al. (1998). Stressful events, pessimism, natural killer cell cytoxicity, and cytotoxic/suppressor T cells in HIV+ black women at risk for cervical cancer. *Psychosom Med* 60:714–722.

Carrico AW (2011). Substance use and HIV illness progression in the ART era: implications for the primary prevention of HIV. *Life Sci* 88(21):940–947.

Carrico AW, Antoni MH (2008). The effects of psychological interventions on neuroendocrine hormone regulation and immune status in HIV-positive persons: a review of randomized controlled trials. *Psychosom Med* 70:575–584.

Carrico AW, Antoni MH, Pereira DB, Fletcher MA, Klimas N, Lechner SC, et al. (2005a). Cognitive behavioral stress management effects on mood, social support, and a marker of anti-viral immunity are maintained up to one year in HIV-infected gay men. *Int J Behav Med* 12:218–226.

Carrico AW, Antoni MH, Weaver KE, Lechner SC, Schneiderman N (2005b). Cognitive-behavioural stress management with HIV-positive homosexual men: mechanisms of sustained reductions in depressive symptoms. *Chron Illness* 1:207–215.

Carrico AW, Ironson G, Antoni MH, et al. (2006). A path model of the effects of spirituality on depressive symptoms and 24-hour urinary-free cortisol in HIV-positive persons. *J Psychosom Res* 61(1):51–58.

Carrico AW, Moskowitz JT (2014). Positive affect promotes engagement in care after HIV diagnosis. *Health Psychol* 33:686–689.

Carrico AW, Riley ED, Johnson MO, et al. (2011). Psychiatric risk factors for HIV illness progression: the role of inconsistent patterns of anti-retroviral therapy utilization. *J Acquir Immune Defic Syndr Hum Retrovirol* 56:146–150.

Centers for Disease Control and Prevention (CDC) (1997). Update: trends in AIDS incidence, deaths, and prevalence—United States, 1996. *MMWR Morbid Mortal Wkly Rep* 46(8):165–174.

Chesney MA, Chambers DB, Taylor JM, Johnson LM, Folkman S (2003). Coping effectiveness training for men living with HIV: results from a randomized clinical trial testing a group-based intervention. *Psychosom Med* 65(6):1038–1046.

Ciesla JA, Roberts JE (2001). Meta-analysis of the relationship between HIV infection and the risk for depressive disorders. *Am J Psychiatry* 158:725–730.

Cohen MS, Chen YQ, McCauley M, et al. (2011). Prevention of HIV-1 infection with early antiretroviral therapy. *N Engl J Med* 365(6):493–505.

Cole SW, Kemeny ME (2001). Psychosocial influences on the progression of HIV infection. In R Ader, DL Felten, S Cohen (eds.), *Psychoneuroimmunology*, 3rd edi. San Diego: Academic Press.

Cole SW, Kemeny ME, Fahey JL, Zack JA, Naliboff BD (2003). Psychological risk factors for HIV pathogenesis: mediation by the autonomic nervous system. *Biol Psychiatry* 54:1444–1456.

Cole SW, Kemeny ME, Taylor SE (1997). Social identity and physical health: accelerated HIV progression in rejection-sensitive gay men. *J Pers Soc Psychol* 72(2):320–335.

Cole SW, Kemeny ME, Taylor SE, Visscher BR, Fahey, JL (1996). Accelerated course of human immunodeficiency virus infection in gay men who conceal their homosexual identity. *Psychosom Med* 58(3):219–231.

Cole SW, Korin YD, Fahey JL, Zack JA (1998). Norepinephrine accelerates HIV replication via protein kinase A–dependent effects on cytokine production. *J Immunol* 161:610–616.

Cole SW, Naliboff BD, Kemeny ME, Griswold MP, Fahey JL, Zack JA (2001). Impaired response to ART in HIV-infected individuals with high autonomic nervous system activity. *Proc Natl Acad Sci U S A* 98:12695–12700.

Creswell JD, Myers HF, Cole SW, Irwin MR (2009). Mindfulness meditation training effects on CD4+ T lymphocytes in HIV-1 infected adults: a small randomized controlled trial. *Brain Behav Immun* 23(2):184–188.

Cruess S, Antoni MH, Cruess D, et al. (2000a). Reductions in HSV-2 antibody titers after cognitive behavioral stress management and relationships with neuroendocrine function, relaxation skills, and social support in HIV+ gay men. *Psychosom Med* 62:828–837.

Cruess S, Antoni M, Kilbourn K, et al. (2000b). Optimism, distress, and immunologic status in HIV-infected gay men following Hurricane Andrew. *Int J Behav Med* 7:160–182.

Cruess DG, Antoni MH, McGregor BA, et al. (2000c). Cognitive-behavioral stress management reduces serum cortisol by enhancing benefit finding among women being treated for early stage breast cancer. *Psychosom Med* 62:304–308.

Cruess D, Antoni MH, Schneiderman N, Ironson G, Fletcher MA, Kumar, M (1999). Cognitive behavioral stress management effects on DHEA-S and serum cortisol in HIV seropositive men. *Psychoneuroendocrinology* 24:537–549.

Cruess D, Antoni MH, Schneiderman N, et al. (2000d). Cognitive behavioral stress management increases free testosterone and decreases psychological distress in HIV seropositive men. *Health Psychol* 19:12–20.

Cruess DG, Douglas SD, Petitto JM, et al. (2005). Association of resolution of major depression with increased natural killer cell activity among HIV-seropositive women. *Am J Psychiatry* 162:2125–2130.

Cruess DG, Douglas SD, Petitto JM, et al. (2003). Association of depression, CD8 T lymphocytes, and natural killer cell activity: implications for morbidity and mortality in human immunodeficiency virus illness. *Curr Psychiatry Rep* 5:445–450.

Das M, Chu PL, Santos GM, et al. (2010). Decreases in community viral load are accompanied by reductions in new HIV infections in San Francisco. *PloS ONE* 5(6):e11068.

Deeks SG (2011). HIV infection, inflammation, immunosenescence, and aging. *Annu Rev Med* 62:141.

Esterling B, Antoni M, Schneiderman N, et al. (1992). Psychosocial modulation of antibody to Epstein-Barr viral capsid antigen and herpes virus type-6 in HIV-1 infected and at-risk gay men. *Psychosom Med* 54:354–371.

Evans DL, Ten Have TR, Douglas SD, et al. (2002). Association of depression with viral load, CD8 T lymphocytes, and natural killer cells in women with HIV infection. *Am J Psychiatry* 159:1752–1759.

Fauci AS, Folkers GK (2012). Toward an AIDS-free generation. *JAMA* 308(4): 343–344.

Fekete EM, Antoni MH, Durán R, Stoelb BL, Kumar M, Schneiderman N (2009a). Disclosing HIV serostatus to family members: effects on psychological and physiological health in minority women living with HIV. *Int J Behav Med* 16(4):367–376.

Fekete EM, Antoni MH, Lopez CR, et al. (2009b). Men's serostatus disclosure to parents: associations among social support, ethnicity, and illness status in men living with HIV. *Brain Behav Immune* 23(5):693–699.

Fekete EM, Antoni MH, Lopez C, et al. (2011). Stress buffering effects of oxytocin on HIV status in low-income ethnic minority women. *Psychoneuroendocrinology* 36(6):881–890.

Felten D (1996). Changes in neural innervation of the lymphoid tissues with age. In N Hall, F Altman, S Blumenthal (eds.), *Mind–Body Interactions and Illness and Psychoneuroimmunological Aspects of Health and Illness*. Washington, DC: Health Dateline Press.

Folkman S (1997) Positive psychological states and coping with severe stress. *Soc Sci Med* 45(8):1207–1221.

Folkman S, Moskowitz, JT (2000). Positive affect and the other side of coping. *Am Psychol* 55(6):647–654.

Gillespie CF, Nemeroff CB (2005). Hypercortisolemia and depression. *Psychosom Med* (Suppl. 1):S26–S27.

Goodkin K, Baldewicz T, Asthana D, et al. (2001). A bereavement support group intervention affects plasma burden of HIV-1. *J Hum Virol* 4:44–54.

Goodkin K, Feaster D, Asthana D, et al. (1998). A bereavement support group intervention is longitudinally associated with salutary effects on the CD4 cell count and number of physician visits. *Clin Diagn Lab Immunol* 5:382–391.

Goodkin K, Feaster DJ, Tuttle R, et al. (1996). Bereavement is associated with time-dependent decrements in cellular immune function in asymptomatic human immunodeficiency virus type 1-seropositive homosexual men. *Clin Diagn Lab Immunol* 3:109–118.

Gorman JM, Kertzner R, Cooper T, et al. (1991). Glucocorticoid level and neuropsychiatric symptoms in homosexual men with HIV infection. *Am J Psychiatry* 148:41–45.

Gunnar MR, Vazquez DM (2001). Low cortisol and a flattening of expected daytime rhythm: potential indices of risk in human development. *Dev Psychopathol* 13:515–538.

Günthard HF, Aberg JA, Eron JJ, et al. (2014). Antiretroviral treatment of adult HIV infection: 2014 recommendations of the International Antiviral Society–USA Panel. *JAMA* 312(4):410–425.

Holtgrave DR, Maulsby C, Wehrmeyer L, Hall HI (2012). Behavioral factors in assessing impact of HIV treatment as prevention. *AIDS Behav* 16(5):1085–1091.

Hull MW, Wu Z, Montaner JS (2012). Optimizing the engagement of care cascade: a critical step to maximize the impact of HIV treatment as prevention. *Curr Opin HIV AIDS* 7(6):579–586.

Hurwitz BE, Brownley KA, Motivala SJ, et al. (2005). Sympathoimmune anomalies underlying the response to stressful challenge in human immunodeficiency virus spectrum illness. *Psychosom Med* 67:798–806.

Ickovics JR, Hamburger ME, Vlahov D, et al. (2001). Mortality, CD4 cell count decline, and depressive symptoms among HIV-seropositive women: longitudinal analysis from the HIV Epidemiology Research Study. *JAMA* 285:1460–1465.

Ickovics JR, Milan S, Boland R, et al. (2006). Psychological resources protect health: 5-year survival and immune function among HIV-infected women from four US cities. *AIDS* 20:1851–1860.

Ironson G, Balbin G, Solomon G, et al. (2001). Relative preservation of natural killer cell cytotoxicity and number in healthy AIDS patients with low CD4 cell counts. *AIDS* 15:2065–2073.

Ironson G, Balbin E, Stuetzle R, et al. (2005). Dispositional optimism and the mechanisms by which it predicts slower illness progression in HIV: proactive behavior, avoidant coping, and depression. *Int J Behav Med* 12(2):86–97.

Ironson G, Friedman A, Klimas N, et al. (1994). Distress, denial and low adherence to behavioral interventions predict faster illness progression in gay men infected with human immunodeficiency virus. *Int J Behav Med* 1:90–105.

Ironson GH, Hayward, HS (2008). Do positive psychosocial factors predict illness progression in HIV-1? A review of the evidence. *Psychosom Med* 70:546–554.

Ironson G, Kremer H (2009). Spiritual transformation, psychological well-being, health, and survival in people with HIV. *Int J Psychiatry Med* 39:263–281.

Ironson G, LaPerriere A, Antoni M, et al. (1990). Changes in immune and psychological measures as a function of anticipation and reaction to the news of HIV-1 antibody status. *Psychosom Med* 52:247–270.

Ironson G, O'Cleirigh C, Fletcher MA, et al. (2005). Psychosocial factors predict CD4 and viral load change in men and women with human immunodeficiency virus in the era of highly active antiretroviral therapy. *Psychosom Med* 67:1013–1021.

Ironson G, O'Cleirigh C, Kumar M, et al. (2015). Psychosocial and neurohormonal predictors of HIV illness progression (CD4 cells and viral load): a 4-year prospective study. *AIDS Behav* 19(8):1388–1397.

Ironson G, O'Cleirigh C, Leserman J, Stuetzle R, Fordiani J, Fletcher M, Schneiderman N (2013). Gender-specific effects of an augmented written emotional disclosure intervention on posttraumatic, depressive, and HIV-illness-related outcomes: a randomized, controlled trial. *J Consult Clin Psychol* 81(2):284–298.

Ironson GH, O'Cleirigh C, Weiss A, Schneiderman N, Costa PT (2008). Personality and HIV illness progression: role of NEO-PI-R openness, extraversion, and profiles of engagement. *Psychosom Med* 70:245–253.

Ironson G, Solomon GF, Balbin EG, et al. (2002). The Ironson-Woods Spirituality/Religiousness Index is associated with long survival, health behaviors, less distress, and low cortisol in people with HIV/AIDS. *Ann Behav Med* 24:34–48.

Ironson G, Stuetzle R, Fletcher MA (2006). An increase in religiousness/spirituality occurs after HIV diagnosis and predicts slower illness progression over 4 years in people with HIV. *J Gen Intern Med* 21(S5):S62-S68.

Jensen SE, Pereira DB, Whitehead N, et al. (2013). Cognitive–behavioral stress management and psychological well-being in HIV+ racial/ethnic minority women with human papillomavirus. *Health Psychol* 32(2):227–230.

Kalichman SC, Difonzo K, Austin J, Luke W, Rompa D (2002). Prospective study of emotional reactions to changes in HIV viral load. *AIDS Patient Care STDS* 16:113–120.

Katon WJ (2003). Clinical and health services relationships between major depression, depressive symptoms and general medical illness. *Biol Psychiatry* 54:295–306.

Kawa SK, Thompson EB (1996). Lymphoid cell resistance to glucocorticoids in HIV infection. *J Steroid Biochem Mol Biol* 57:259–263.

Kemeny ME, Dean L (1995). Effects of AIDS-related bereavement on HIV progression among New York City gay men. *AIDS Educ Prev* 7(5 Suppl.):36–47.

Kemeny ME, Weiner H, Durán R, Taylor SE, Visscher B, Fahey JL (1995). Immune system changes after the death of a partner in HIV-positive gay men. *Psychosom Med* 57:547–554.

Kiecolt-Glaser JK, McGuire L, Robles TF, Glaser R (2002). Psychoneuroimmunology: psychological influences on immune function and health. *J Consult Clin Psychol* 70:537–547.

Kimmerling R, Calhoun KS, Forehand R, et al. (1999). Traumatic stress in HIV-infected women. *AIDS Educ Prev* 11:321–330.

Kobilka B (1992). Adrenergic receptors as models for G-protein coupled receptors. *Annu Rev Neurosci* 15:87–114.

Kuller LH, Tracy R, Belloso W, et al. (2008). Inflammatory and coagulation biomarkers and mortality in patients with HIV infection. *PLoS Med* 5(10):e203.

Kumar M, Kumar AM, Morgan R, Szapocznik J, Eisdorfer C (1993). Abnormal pituitary-adrenocortical response in early HIV-1 infection. *J Acquir Immune Defic Syndr Hum Retrovirol* 6:61–65.

LaPerriere A, Antoni MH, Schneiderman N, et al. (1990). Exercise intervention attenuates emotional distress and natural killer cell decrements following notification of positive serologic status for HIV-1. *Biofeedback Self Regul* 15:125–131.

Lederman MM, Funderburg NT, Sekaly RP, Klatt NR, Hunt PW (2013). Residual immune dysregulation syndrome in treated HIV infection. *Adv Immunol* 119:51–83.

Leserman J (2003). HIV illness progression: depression, stress, and possible mechanisms. *Biol Psychiatry* 54:295–306.

Leserman J (2008). Role of depression, stress, and trauma in HIV illness progression. *Psychosom Med* 70(5):539–545.

Leserman J, Jackson ED, Petitto JM, et al. (1999). Progression to AIDS: the effects of stress, depressive symptoms and social support. *Psychosom Med* 61:397–406.

Leserman J, Pence B, Whetten K, Mugavero M, Thielman N, Swartz M, Stangl D (2007). Relation of lifetime trauma and depressive symptoms to mortality in HIV. *Am J Psychiatry* 164(11):1707–1713.

Leserman J, Petitto JM, Golden RN, et al. (2000). Impact of stressful life events, depression, social support, coping, and cortisol on progression to AIDS. *Am J Psychiatry* 157:1221–1228.

Leserman J, Petitto JM, Gu H, et al. (2002). Progression to AIDS, a clinical AIDS condition and mortality: psychosocial and physiological predictors. *Psychol Med* 32:1059–1073.

Leserman J, Petitto JM, Perkins DO, Folds JD, Golden RN, Evans DL (1997). Severe stress and depressive symptoms, and changes in lymphocyte subsets in human immunodeficiency virus infected men. *Arch Gen Psychiatry* 54:279–285.

Lutgendorf S, Antoni M, Ironson G, et al. (1997). Cognitive behavioral stress management decreases dysphoric mood and herpes simplex virus-type 2 antibody titers in symptomatic HIV-seropositive gay men. *J Consult Clin Psychol* 65:31–43.

Lutgendorf SK, Antoni MH, Ironson G, et al. (1998). Changes in cognitive coping skills and social support during cognitive behavioral stress management intervention and distress outcomes in symptomatic human immunodeficiency virus-seropositive gay men. *Psychosom Med* 60:204–214.

Lyketsos CG, Hoover DR, Guccione M, et al. (1996). Changes in depressive symptoms as AIDS develops. The Multicenter AIDS Cohort Study. *Am J Psychiatry* 153:1430–1437.

Lyketsos CG, Hoover DR, Guccione M, et al. (1993). Depressive symptoms as predictors of medical outcomes in HIV infection. *JAMA* 270:2563–2567.

Mannheimer SB, Matts J, Telzak E, et al. (2005). Quality of life in HIV-infected individuals receiving antiretroviral therapy is related to adherence. *AIDS Care* 17:10–22.

Martin JL, Dean L (1993). Effects of AIDS-related bereavement and HIV-related illness on psychological distress among gay men: a 7-year longitudinal study, 1985–1991. *J Consult Clin Psychol* 61:94–103.

Mayne TJ, Vittinghoff E, Chesney MA, Barrett DC, Coates TJ (1996). Depressive affect and survival among gay and bisexual men infected with HIV. *Arch Intern Med* 156:2233–2238.

McEwen B (1998). Protective and damaging effects of stress mediators. *N Engl J Med* 338:171–179.

McIntosh R, Hurwitz B, Antoni MH, Gonzalez A, Seay J, Schneiderman N (2015). The ABCs of anger, psychological distress, and HIV-illness severity. *Annals Behav Med* 49(3):420–433.

McIntosh RC, Ironson G, Antoni M, Kumar M, Fletcher MA, Schneiderman N (2014). Alexithymia is linked to neurocognitive, psychological, neuroendocrine, and immune dysfunction in persons living with HIV. *Brain Behav Immune* 36:165–175.

Miller GE, Cole SW (1998). Social relationships and the progression of human immunodeficiency virus infection: a review of evidence and possible underlying mechanisms. *Ann Behav Med* 20(3):181–189.

Montaner JS, Lima VD, Barrios R, et al. (2010). Association of highly active antiretroviral therapy coverage, population viral load, and yearly new HIV diagnoses in British Columbia, Canada: a population-based study. *Lancet* 376(9740):532–539.

Moskowitz JT (2003). Positive affect predicts lower risk of AIDS mortality. *Psychosom Med* 65:620–626.

Motivala SJ, Hurwitz BE, Llabre MM, et al. (2003). Psychological distress is associated with decreased memory helper T-cell and B-cell counts in pre-AIDS HIV seropositive men and women but only in those with low viral load. *Psychosom Med* 65:627–635.

Mugavero MJ, Amico KR, Horn T, Thompson MA (2013). The state of engagement in HIV care in the United States: from cascade to continuum to control. *Clin Infect Illness* 57(8):1164–1171.

Mugavero MJ, Raper JL, Reif S, Whetten K, Leserman J, Thielman NM, Pence BW (2009). Overload: the impact of incident stressful events on antiretroviral medication adherence and virologic failure in a longitudinal, multi-site HIV cohort study. *Psychosom Med* 71(9):920–926.

Nieuwlaat R Wilczynski N, Navarro T, et al. (2014). Interventions for enhancing medication adherence. *Cochrane Database Syst Rev* Nov 20;(11):CD000011.

O'Cleirigh C, Ironson G, Antoni M, et al. (2003). Emotional expression and depth processing of trauma and their relation to long-term survival in patients with HIV/AIDS. *J Psychosom Res* 54(3):225–235.

O'Cleirigh C, Ironson G, Weiss A, Costa PT (2007). Conscientiousness predicts illness progression (CD4 number and viral load) in people living with HIV. *Health Psychol* 26(4):473–480.

Page-Shafer K, Delorenze GN, Satariano W, Winkelstein W (1996). Comorbidity and survival in HIV-infected men in the San Francisco Men's Health Survey. *Ann Epidemiol* 6:420–430.

Patterson S, Moran P, Epel E, et al. (2013). Cortisol patterns are associated with T cell activation in HIV. *PLoS ONE* 8(7):e63429.

Patterson TL, Williams SS, Semple SJ, et al. (1996). Relationship of psychosocial factors to HIV illness progression. *Ann Behav Med* 18:30–39.

Pence BW, Mugavero MJ, Carter TJ, et al. (2012). Childhood trauma and health outcomes in HIV-infected patients: an exploration of causal pathways. *J Acquir Immune Defic Syndr Hum Retrovirol* 59(4):409–416.

Pereira DB, Antoni MH, Danielson A, et al. (2003a). Life stress and cervical squamous intraepithelial lesions in women with human papillomavirus and human immunodeficiency virus. *Psychosom Med* 65:427–434.

Pereira DB, Antoni MH, Danielson A, et al. (2003b). Stress as a predictor of symptomatic genital herpes virus recurrence in women with human immunodeficiency virus. *J Psychosom Res* 54:237–244.

Petrie KJ, Fontanilla I, Thomas MG, Booth RJ, Pennebaker JW (2004). Effect of written emotional expression on immune function in patients with human immunodeficiency virus infection: a randomized trial. *Psychosom Med* 66(2): 272–275.

Rabkin JG, Ferrando SJ, Lin SH, Sewell M, Mc-Elihney M (2000). Psychological effects of ART: a 2-year study. *Psychosom Med* 62:413–422.

Reed GM, Kemeny ME, Taylor SE, Visscher BR (1999). Negative HIV-specific expectancies and AIDS-related bereavement as predictors of symptoms onset in asymptomatic HIV-positive gay men. *Health Psychol* 18:354–363.

Reed GM, Kemeny ME, Taylor SE, Wang HYJ, Visscher BR (1994). Realistic acceptance as a predictor of decreased survival time in gay men with AIDS. *Health Psychol* 13:299–307.

Safren SA, O'Cleirigh CM, Bullis JR, Otto MW, Stein MD, Pollack MH (2012). Cognitive behavioral therapy for adherence and depression (CBT-AD) in HIV-infected injection drug users: a randomized controlled trial. *J Consult Clin Psychol* 80(3):404–415.

Safren SA, O'Cleirigh C, Tan JY, Raminani SR, Reilly LC, Otto MW, Mayer KH (2009). A randomized controlled trial of cognitive behavioral therapy for adherence and depression (CBT-AD) in HIV-infected individuals. *Health Psychol* 28(1):1–10.

Schroecksnadel K, Sarcletti M, Winkler C, et al. (2008). Quality of life and immune activation in patients with HIV-infection. *Brain Behav Immune* 22(6):881–889.

Scott-Sheldon LA, Kalichman SC, Carey MP, Fielder, R. L. (2008). Stress management interventions for HIV+ adults: a meta-analysis of randomized controlled trials, 1989 to 2006. *Health Psychol* 27(2):129–139.

Segerstrom SC, Taylor SE, Kemeny ME, Reed GM, Visscher BR (1996). Causal attributions predict rate of immune decline in HIV-seropositive gay men. *Health Psychol* 15:485–493.

Simoni JM, Frick PA, Pantalone DW, Turner BJ (2003). Antiretroviral adherence interventions: a review of current literature and ongoing studies. *Topics HIV Med* 11:185–197.

Smyth JM (1998). Written emotional expression: effect sizes, outcome types, and moderating variables. *J Consult Clin Psychol* 66(1):174–184.

Solano L, Costa M, Temoshok L, et al. (2002). An emotionally inexpressive (type C) coping style influences HIV illness progression at six and twelve month follow-ups. *Psychol Health* 17(5):641–655.

Starr KR, Antoni MH, Hurwitz BE, et al. (1996). Patterns of immune, neuroendocrine, and cardiovascular stress responses in asymptomatic HIV serpositive and seronegative men. *Int J Behav Med* 3:135–162.

Taylor SE (2006). Tend and befriend biobehavioral bases of affiliation under stress. *Curr Direct Psychol Sci* 15(6):273–277.

Taylor SE, Kemeny ME, Reed GM, Bower JE, Gruenewald TL (2000). Psychological resources, positive illusions, and health. *Am Psychol* 55:99–109.

Temoshok LR, Waldstein SR, Wald RL, Garzino-Demo A, Synowski SJ, Sun L, Wiley, JA (2008). Type C coping, alexithymia, and heart rate reactivity are associated independently and differentially with specific immune mechanisms linked to HIV progression. *Brain Behav Immun* 22(5):781–792.

Tsai AC, Karasic DH, Hammer GP, et al. (2013). Directly observed antidepressant medication treatment and HIV outcomes among homeless and marginally housed HIV-positive adults: a randomized controlled trial. *Am J Publ Health* 103(2):308–315.

Vedhara K, Nott KH, Bradbeer CS, et al. (1997). Greater emotional distress is associated with accelerated CD4+ cell decline in HIV infection. *J Psychosom Res* 42:379–390.

Weiss SM, Tobin JN, Antoni M, et al., and the SMART/EST Women's Project Team (2011). Enhancing the health of women living with HIV: the SMART/EST Women's Project. *Int J Womens Health* 3:63–77.

Zangerle R, Kurz K, Neurauter G, Kitchen M, Sarcletti M, Fuchs D (2010). Increased blood phenylalanine to tyrosine ratio in HIV-1 infection and correction following effective antiretroviral therapy. *Brain Behav Immun* 24(3):403–408.

22.

DISTRESS IN PERSONS WITH HIV AND AIDS

Mary Ann Cohen, Anna L. Dickerman, and Harold W. Goforth

According to Webster's dictionary, *distress* is defined as "pain or suffering affecting the body, a bodily part, or the mind." Thus, psychological distress can be seen as an unsettling psychological state that interferes with a person's overall well-being. In this chapter, we will attempt to understand the sources of distress in persons with HIV and AIDS from a biopsychosocial perspective, exploring some of the physical and social factors that affect psychological distress, including cultural and political components. We also present ways to screen for, recognize, and cope with psychological distress.

Persons with HIV infection and AIDS have high levels of distress from multiple sources, including symptoms (such as fatigue, pruritus, and insomnia), medical and psychiatric illness, discrimination and stigma, and social, occupational, and financial stresses. AIDS can affect nearly every organ and system with severe and multiple illnesses. Individuals with HIV and AIDS may have severe psychiatric illnesses as well. In a study by Lyketsos and colleagues (1996), psychiatric sources of distress were present in 52% of patients presenting to an HIV clinic for evaluation and treatment. Actual distress rates of homeless persons with AIDS who do not self-present for treatment are likely higher. Persons with AIDS are subject to the same losses, stresses, and life changes as the rest of the population and, because they are living longer, are subject to other non-HIV-related illnesses, such as heart disease, hypertension, diabetes mellitus, osteoarthritis, cancer, and chronic obstructive pulmonary disease. The symptoms of fatigue, insomnia, and pruritus may occur even in the absence of specific medical or psychiatric pathology. Persons with HIV may also have symptoms related to antiretroviral therapy (ART) or from medications that are unrelated to HIV treatment, such as chemotherapy for cancer. An overview of the biopsychosocial determinants of distress is presented in Table 22.1.

This chapter will explore the myriad biopsychosocial sources of distress in persons with HIV and AIDS and provide a brief but comprehensive summary of these sources. The specific issues that may cause distress are covered in greater depth in other chapters in this book: Chapter 1 addresses stigma; Chapter 3, the prevalence of psychiatric disorders; Chapter 9, sociocultural vulnerabilities; Chapters 14 through 20; psychiatric disorders, Chapters 21 through 25; special symptoms and psychiatric manifestations of HIV; Chapters 26, 27, and 43 through 47, medical illnesses; and Chapter 49, end-of-life issues.

MEASURING DISTRESS

Distress, depression, and anxiety can be measured rapidly and easily by means of the Distress Thermometer (DT) and the Hospital Anxiety and Depression Scale (HADS). Roth and colleagues (1998) developed the DT, and Cohen and colleagues (2002) have demonstrated the feasibility of using these scales in waiting-room convenience samples of persons with cancer and HIV/AIDS, respectively. Cohen et al. found a 72.3% prevalence of distress on the DT, 70.3% prevalence of anxiety on the HADS, 45.5% prevalence of depression on the HADS, and 53.5% prevalence of both anxiety and depression on the HADS in a waiting-room sample of persons registered at an HIV clinic. The DT and HADS are also valuable for screening persons with HIV and hepatitis C virus (HCV) co-infection before treatment, to provide a baseline score and to follow patients during the course of treatment to determine the need for antidepressant or antipsychotic medications. The rapidity (5 minutes in total for both the DT and HADS) and feasibility of the DT and HADS make them excellent tools for screening for distress in a busy HIV clinic. The DT is especially useful because in using the word *distress* the clinician eliminates the stigma associated with a specific psychiatric diagnosis.

The HIV Symptom Distress Scale (SDS) is another reliable and valid instrument that can be used to measure overall symptomatic distress or other clinically relevant clusters of HIV symptoms (Marc et al., 2012).

Finally, the Adult AIDS Clinical Trial Group Symptom Distress Module (ACTG-SDM) has been used across seven cultural groups in a multinational clinical trial and has demonstrated cross-cultural validity (Regnault et al., 2009).

DISTRESS ON THREE CONTINENTS

Distress and suffering are ubiquitous phenomena and occur across all cultures, although the specific expressions of distress and suffering may differ across cultural systems. Studies of distress in persons with HIV and AIDS have been done in many different parts of the world, including North America, Africa, the Caribbean, and South America. The results of these studies illustrate the need for effective interventions designed to improve the quality of life for affected individuals.

Table 22.1 BIOPSYCHOSOCIAL DETERMINANTS OF DISTRESS IN PERSONS LIVING WITH HIV INFECTION

BIOLOGICAL	PSYCHOLOGICAL	SOCIAL
Pain	Depression	Alienation
Confusion	Anxiety	Social isolation
Cognitive decline	Psychosis	Stigma
Disfigurement	Mania	Discrimination
Dyspnea	Withdrawal	Spiritual isolation
Insomnia	Intoxication	Financial loss
Fatigue	Substance misuse	Unemployment
Nausea	Existential anxiety	Loss of housing
Vomiting	Bereavement	Loss of key roles
Diarrhea	Suicidality	Loss of meaning
Blindness		Loss of independence
Paralysis		
Weakness		
Cachexia		
Incontinence		
Pruritus		
Hiccups		

In the United States, racial and ethnic disparities create significant distress in multiple ways: African Americans and Latinos are at higher risk for acquiring HIV (Dasgupta et al., 2016; Valleroy et al., 2000) and for racial and ethnic discrimination than white persons, with limited opportunities for living-wage employment, safe housing, good education, and comprehensive healthcare. African Americans and Latinos are also more likely to experience unfair treatment (Cain and Kington, 2003). These disparities produce a wide array of negative emotional and stress responses that predict a range of negative physical and mental health outcomes (Williams et al., 2003). Various socioeconomic factors such as age and degree of social conflict or social support may also mediate distress in African American and Latino persons with HIV (Miles et al. 2007).

HIV infection among Asians and Pacific Islanders in the United States continues to increase given the escalating prevalence of HIV in Asia and the increasing number of immigrants from these regions (Operario et al., 2005). Asians and Pacific Islanders often face unnecessary delays in accessing medical and supportive services (Eckholdt and Chin, 1997; Eckholdt et al., 1997; Pounds et al., 2002) for treatment of their HIV. Distress related to disclosure of HIV status due to fears of discrimination from peers, employers, and family members (Chin and Kroesen, 1999; Yoshioka and Schustack, 2001) is further compounded by discrimination based on race, immigration status, culturally disapproved lifestyle, and sexual orientation (Herek, 1999; Kang and Rapkin, 2003; Kang et al., 2003). Persons with HIV living in Asian countries continue to face significant stigma, which may in turn lead to poor utilization of services, psychosocial distress, and reduced quality of life (Rao et al., 2012).

Studies have also shown the interconnection between distress and engaging in risky sexual behavior (Elkington et al., 2010), as exemplified by a study of Latino gay men recruited from social venues (bars, clubs, and weeknight events) in the cities of New York, Miami, and Los Angeles (Diaz et al., 2004). Diaz and colleagues found that a substantial number of reported experiences of social discrimination based on sexual orientation were combined with racial and ethnic discrimination within the context of the gay community. Symptoms of psychological distress reported for 6 months were highly prevalent in this group: 61% reported sleep problems; 44% reported symptoms of anxiety and panic on at least one occasion; 80% reported a sad or depressed mood at least once; and 17% reported suicidal ideation at least once.

Africa has one of the world's highest prevalence rates of HIV and AIDS and also has limited access to effective therapy. The effect of HIV on Africa has been devastating; 11 million children in sub-Saharan Africa alone have witnessed the death of at least one parent to complications of AIDS (Atwine et al., 2005). Shawn and colleagues (2005) have noted that palliative care for HIV is currently the standard treatment in Africa because of limited access to antiretroviral treatment. They note that pain, skin complaints, respiratory infections, fatigue, anger, and social isolation have figured prominently in patients' lives. Poor quality of life and high levels of distress have been noted in South African studies as well (O'Keefe and Wood, 1996). Likewise, Atwine and colleagues (2005) investigated the psychosocial consequences of AIDS for 123 orphans with AIDS in rural Uganda and found that orphan status was a significant predictor of increased distress associated with higher rates of anxiety, depression, and anger. Please see Chapter 5 of this textbook for a more detailed discussion of determinants of distress in AIDS orphans.

The impact of increased distress is not limited to individuals who have been orphaned as a result of AIDS but also includes persons forced to care for family members living with HIV and other chronic and severe illness. In systematic interviews of caregivers of persons with HIV in Botswana, older women reported feeling overwhelmed with the complexity and magnitude of the tasks facing them, often neglecting their own health and experiencing high levels of exhaustion, malnourishment, and depression. Among younger girls there were high rates of physical and sexual abuse, depression, and truancy from school, and all ages experienced poverty and had high rates of social isolation (Lindsey et al., 2003).

The experience of gays, lesbians, and bisexuals in Botswana and, by extrapolation, sub-Saharan Africa is equally poor, as same-sex activities are illegal in many sub-Saharan countries, punishable by imprisonment or death. Varying levels of distress in up to two-thirds of this population have been documented, and distress appears to stem predominantly from health concerns, discrimination, and sexual violence (Ehlers et al., 2001). Botswana has been noted to have one of Africa's leading healthcare systems (Ehlers et al., 2001); therefore, the distress level in many other countries in Africa may actually be higher than the 64% rate encountered in Ehlers et al.'s study.

HIV is a growing problem in most South American and Caribbean countries, and it is endemic in Haiti in proportions equal to those of many sub-Saharan African regions. Distress levels associated with HIV in these countries reflects those of the African experience, with rates exceeding 50%. A survey of HIV-associated distress in an ambulatory HIV clinic in the Dominican Republic indicated prevalence rates of distress of 49% on the DT; anxiety, 58% on the HADS; depression, 44% on the HADS; and an overall HADS rate of 49% (A. Hurtado, 2005, unpublished data). Fewer resources dedicated to HIV care are available in these countries, and increasing infection rates drain existing medical resources and tax populations as a whole.

MEDICAL COMPLICATIONS AS SOURCES OF DISTRESS

Other factors causing distress are the multiple complications resulting from immunological suppression, including visual loss, neurological illness, and fears of progressive health decline and changes in one's ability to care for oneself independently. Cytomegalovirus (CMV) retinopathy is one of the most distressing complications of HIV disease, as it results in vision loss, with accompanying social isolation, loss of independence, and loss of function.

VISUAL LOSS

The advent of effective ART therapy has altered the natural progression of HIV and has changed the incidence, natural history, management, and sequelae of HIV-associated retinopathy, especially CMV-associated retinopathy. Before use of ART, CMV retinitis was common, occurring in 20–40% of seropositive patients. Patients were relegated to indefinite intravenous therapy, and between 25% and 50% suffered retinal detachment. Survival after development of CMV retinitis was 6–10 months. The incidence of CMV retinitis declined by approximately 80% after the advent of ART therapy, and mean survival has increased to over 1 year from time of diagnosis (Goldberg et al., 2005; Holbrook et al., 2003). However, visual loss and blindness from multiple etiologies are still significant causes for concern and sources of distress for persons with HIV (Hill and Dubey 2002; Kestelyn and Cunningham 2001; Ng et al., 2000; Oette et al., 2005).

Specific studies examining the quality of life and distress experienced by persons with visual loss have not been performed among persons with HIV disease. However, data on distress among patients with macular degeneration and other acquired forms of visual loss may be used to better understand the sense of isolation, psychological distress, and limitations these patients experience on a routine basis. Data

from patients with acquired macular degeneration indicate a strong association between decline in vision and functional impairment, along with high rates of depression, anxiety, and emotional distress (Berman and Brodaty, 2006). In a study focusing on patients' attitudes toward visual loss from subfoveal choroidal neovascularization, patients reported that they would rather suffer medical illnesses such as dialysis-dependent renal failure and AIDS than visual impairment (Bass et al., 2004). Similar findings have been noted in studies of diabetes mellitus–associated visual loss (Cox et al., 1998). Clearly, across multiple medical conditions, acquired visual loss has a profound impact on self-perception of overall health-related quality of life, distress, and suffering. Please see Chapter 47 for a more detailed discussion of ophthalmological complications in persons with HIV/AIDS.

NEUROLOGICAL DECLINE

Cognitive disorders, vacuolar myelopathy, and sensory neuropathies are the most common neurological disorders in persons with HIV disease and are a great source of fear and distress in this population. One of the most disturbing aspects of advancing HIV disease is the prospect of progressive physical and cognitive that can result in eventual complete incapacity. Despite the estimated 50% reduction in HIV-related neurological complication since the advent of ART (Maschke et al., 2000; Sacktor, 2002), distress and fear of loss of independence and functionality continue among persons with HIV.

Mapou and colleagues (1993) studied neuropsychological performance of 79 military medical beneficiaries infected with HIV and that of 27 HIV-seronegative control subjects. Seropositive participants who complained of subjective difficulties had more deficits in attention, response speed, motor function, and memory than participants not reporting difficulties. Seropositive individuals also had increased rates of anxiety and depression, illustrating the need for screening for both disturbances in seropositive individuals, as each may become a significant source of distress. The pathophysiology and potential treatment of dementia are discussed further in Chapter 16 in this book. The neuropathology of the central nervous system and peripheral nervous system are further discussed in Chapters 26 and 27, respectively.

PAIN AND DISTRESS

Pain is an incapacitating symptom in many people with HIV and AIDS, and untreated pain leads to an increase in psychological distress and a reduction in quality of life. Sources of pain are varied and range from neuropathic pain to chronic pain of malignancy, and all types of pain are associated with increased suicidal risk. Pain is undertreated particularly in patients with HIV and AIDS, in part because of the common prevalence of substance abuse disorder. Pain is especially common in this setting; it ranges from 28% to 97% across various studies (Lebovits et al., 1989; McCormack et al., 1993; Reiter and Kudler, 1996; Schoefferman, 1988).

Abdominal pain and neuropathic pain were the most common pain complaints in one study at a pain consultation service; other causes included odynophagia, dysphagia, headache, cutaneous pain, musculoskeletal pain, and postherpetic neuralgia (Newshan and Wainapel, 1993). Inadequate pain assessment is a major factor in the undertreatment of pain; use of standardized pain assessment measures may assist in both assessment and treatment. Practitioners need to be educated to address myths such as (a) people overestimate their pain; (b) minority groups exaggerate their pain complaints; (c) people with a past history of addiction routinely lie about pain to secure drugs; (d) pain is often psychogenic in etiology; and (e) the etiology of pain remains obscure in most cases. In fact, patients have been shown to be reluctant to volunteer pain complaints. Thus routine assessment is needed (Von Roenn et al., 1993), with instruments such as the Wisconsin Brief Pain Inventory (BPI), which measures adequacy of analgesia and impact of pain on related psychosocial factors. Further discussion of pain assessment and management can be found in Chapters 27 and 41, which deal with neurological complications in HIV and palliative care for persons with HIV, respectively.

CARDIOPULMONARY ILLNESS

HIV-associated cardiomyopathy can be a direct result of HIV disease, HIV treatment, comorbid conditions, and other etiologies. Cardiomyopathy has been identified in up to 20% of HIV-seropositive patients (Fisher and Lipschultz, 2001). It appears to have a more pernicious course in persons with HIV, with symptoms including dyspnea, peripheral and pulmonary edema, hepatosplenomegaly, and arrhythmias (Currie et al., 1994). Dilated cardiomyopathy is the most frequently identified cardiac disease associated with HIV and is an independent predictor of mortality, but other manifestations include myocarditis, bacterial and fungal endocarditis, pulmonary hypertension, malignancy, accelerated atherosclerosis, and autonomic dysfunction (Dakin et al., 2006).

Similarly, respiratory events and illnesses such as opportunistic infections, tuberculosis, malignancies, adult respiratory distress syndrome, and pulmonary fibrosis (Rosen et al., 1997) remain common in HIV-seropositive populations, especially among individuals with CD4 counts <200/mm³ and injection drug abusers. Importantly, the risk of these disorders appears to increase with advancing HIV disease despite the widespread use of antibiotic prophylaxis (Hirschtick et al., 1995; Wallace et al., 1993).

Distress in these populations is created by both the psychological implications of advancing HIV disease and the imposition of severe physical limitations related to cardiopulmonary disease. Such limitations further isolate this population and limit individuals' ability to perform previously enjoyable coping activities such as exercise. In advanced cases, they impinge directly on patients' ability to maintain independence and perform activities of daily living, serving as a constant reminder of impending mortality. Cardiovascular disorders in persons with HIV is discussed in further detail in Chapter 46.

DIARRHEA

Another common potential source of distress among persons with HIV is bacterial diarrhea, which has been noted to predict increased use of hospital resources, longer hospital admissions, and an increased prevalence of opportunistic infections such as *Pneumocystis carinii* pneumonia. *Clostridium difficile* colitis and associated diarrhea were the etiology in approximately 32% of study patients in a large, Chicago-based, public hospital study. It appears that this disorder is more likely to present among persons with advanced HIV illness (Pulvirenti et al., 2002). Other notable causes include *Shigella, Campylobacter,* and *Salmonella* species, which may reflect progressive deficits in mucosal immune function in advanced HIV illness (Sanchez et al., 2005).

From a mental health standpoint, bacterial diarrhea can cause significant distress, in that it both limits environmental freedom and self-sufficiency and serves as a marker and reminder of advancing disease. Fears of loss of bowel control and fecal incontinence further isolate a high-risk population from available social support. These conditions can also be a source of HIV-associated wasting and general decline. While no specific studies have addressed the issue of distress in this population, in our experience the associated distress and impairment from chronic diarrhea can be profoundly embarrassing, with significant limitation in life satisfaction. Please see Chapter 47 for a more extensive presentation of diarrheal illness.

ITCHING

Medical sources of distress are not limited to major organ systems such as cardiorespiratory and gastrointestinal systems but include a variety of scenarios and organ systems. Pruritus, a common manifestation of advancing liver disease,is discussed further in the context of HIV in Chapter 43. Likewise, renal disease with associated uremia can produce significant symptoms of itching; renal complications associated with HIV disease are covered more extensively in Chapter 44. Studies of distress in relation to HIV disease and itching have not been performed, but quality-of-life studies of chronic urticarial illness have demonstrated marked reductions in quality of life in terms of both social functioning and emotional capacity (Staubach et al., 2006).

INSOMNIA

One area that has been linked to distress and a reduction in quality of life in HIV is insomnia. Complaints of lack of sleep from persons with HIV are ubiquitous, but etiologies are varied and often include a combination of comorbid psychiatric disorders, medical conditions affecting sleep quality, and, potentially, a direct role of HIV on the brain. In a review of insomnia in the setting of HIV, Reid and Dwyer (2005) noted that up to 60% of HIV-positive individuals experienced sleep disturbances, and greater psychological distress appeared to be related to greater sleep difficulties and lower numbers of CD3 and CD8 cells. This review highlights the importance of effective interventions designed to improve sleep quality and, in turn, potentially reduce distress and improve life quality.

Further details of HIV-associated sleep abnormalities are addressed in Chapter 23.

FATIGUE

Fatigue is one of the most limiting of the HIV syndromes in terms of quality of life and its incremental impact on dealing effectively with advancing HIV illness, comorbid depression, and hepatitis C co-infection. HIV-related fatigue decreases functional status, which in turn can lead to symptoms of isolation, inability to perform required self-care, and nonadherence to medications. In fact, fatigue, along with neurological symptoms, is one of two domains that independently predicts functional decline in instrumental activities of daily living, even when controlling for sociodemographic variables (Wilson and Cleary, 1997).

In a cross-sectional survey of ambulatory AIDS patients, Breitbart and colleagues (1998) found that over 50% of respondents had fatigue according to self-report with the Memorial Symptom Assessment Scale. Women appeared significantly more likely to experience fatigue than men, and fatigue was associated with several other variables, including the number of AIDS-related physical symptoms, the current treatment of HIV disease, anemia, and pain. Those subjects reporting significant fatigue suffered increased rates of both psychological distress and lower quality of life across several standardized rating scales (Breitbart et al., 1998).

Fatigue also plays an important role in HCV infection, as fatigue is a common complaint among sufferers of HCV both prior to and during treatment with biological agents such as interferon-based therapies. While newer non-interferon-based treatments are far shorter in duration and cause less fatigue, this symptom remains a problem during treatment. Since the newer treatments are only 12 weeks in duration, they are far better tolerated and lead to cure of HCV in co-infected persons with access to care. Four hundred and eighty-four HIV-seropositive subjects participated in a self-report trial which confirmed that HCV-co-infected patients demonstrated significantly more elements of distress compared to the HIV-only group in social, psychological, and biological arenas. The HCV-co-infected patients were also more likely to be in unstable social situations and to experience depression, fatigue, and reduced quality of life (Braitstein et al., 2005).

Treatment of fatigue is an important area for psychiatrists treating patients with HIV, as it can directly improve quality of life, alleviate distress, and improve functioning. Breitbart and colleagues (2001) and others have described effective and safe treatments with either methylphenidate or pemoline. The role of antidepressants, androgenic steroids, and modafinil in treating fatigue has also been examined (Rabkin, McElhiney, et al., 2004; Rabkin, Wagner, et al., 2004). Further discussion of HIV-associated fatigue can be found in Chapter 24.

AIDS PALLIATIVE CARE AND DEATH AND DYING

End-of-life issues involve complex decision-making, and issues such as wills and estates take on overtones of the finality of life.

They can also provide an impetus for overall life review, which can prove quite distressing to a person who is unprepared for this process. In countries and areas where same-sex partnerships, civil unions, or marriages are banned or criminalized, these issues continue to be as complicated and distressing as they were in 1981, at the beginning of the HIV pandemic. Dying patients must struggle with the impact of their dying on loved ones and caregivers, and caregiver distress can frequently lead to burnout and suboptimal care for the patient.

AIDS palliative care has been defined as comprehensive, multidisciplinary care that focuses on alleviating suffering and maximizing life potentials across all stages of disease severity, independent of stage or prognosis (Daniel Fischberg, personal communication). Most clinicians associate palliative care with end-stage illness only, but the true nature of palliative care makes it appropriate at every stage of illness by focusing on comfort. Comfort gradually assumes a more important role as illness progresses and cures of specific complications become less likely. This gradual transition to a comfort-care model minimizes sources of distress associated with an abrupt change from a curative model to a comfort-care-only model that can occur in the terminal phases of life in persons with HIV.

Different methods of comfort care, such as pastoral care, hypnosis, music, relaxation, meditation, writing, and art, can be incorporated with much success, and these methods need to be integrated and offered to persons during the entire course of their illness on a routine basis (Cohen, 1999). Depression, anxiety, pain, and other mental health disorders need to be addressed with both psychotherapy and pharmacotherapy using multiple models, including crisis, individual, group, and family therapy, over the entire spectrum of illness. Integration of spiritual care has been shown to provide comfort and solace to persons suffering with cancer (Jacox et al., 1994; Saunders, 1988). In certain regions of the world, religiosity and spirituality may have a significant impact on psychological distress in persons with HIV (Steglitz et al., 2012). Attempts to provide these interventions across the spectrum of HIV illness will improve the seamless attention given to the associated suffering and distress.

We have noted that untreated pain and pruritus are associated with severe psychological reactions, including depression, anxiety, and suicidality. Dyspnea inspires feeling of anxiety, panic, and fear of death by asphyxiation. Periods of prolonged hiccups can lead to exhaustion and feelings of helplessness, and untreated psychological symptoms can exacerbate somatic complaints. Prompt attention to psychological distress complements palliative symptom management strategies.

Being physically present with the patient is important at the end of life and can alleviate the fear of abandonment often experienced by dying individuals. Simple acts such as talking, holding hands, and surrounding the patient with loved ones provide much-needed healing and comfort at this stage. Clinicians who can cope with and tolerate the intimacy and evoked feelings of such moments can also experience significant healing and personal rewards. Further details on palliative and spiritual care of persons with HIV and AIDS can be found in Chapter 41.

TREATMENT OF DISTRESS OCCURRING IN THE CONTEXT OF HIV AND AIDS

Use of ART has dramatically improved the lives of millions of persons living with HIV/AIDS and has transformed HIV into a chronic manageable illness. Few studies have investigated adequately the impact of ART on the psychological well-being of infected individuals, but currently available evidence does suggest the beneficial role of ART on psychological well-being (Rabkin et al., 2000). The effect of ART on reducing distress has been shown in other studies as well (BeLow-Beer et al., 2000). Other interventions can begin by identifying distress through routine use of screening instruments. Prompt identification and treatment of comorbid psychiatric disease can enable initiation of effective interventions and minimize suffering. Attention to psychological coping mechanisms and bolstering of social and spiritual supports can limit the impact of loneliness and social isolation, thus enabling a higher quality of life in this vulnerable population.

CONCLUSIONS

Persons living with HIV and AIDS have witnessed radical shifts in the prognosis and treatment associated with this devastating illness over the last 36 years. The advent of effective antiretroviral medications has transformed AIDS from a fatal illness with serial health crises into a chronic illness with a focus on long-term considerations and health maintenance. However, HIV and AIDS continue to cause distress through multiple mechanisms involving biological processes, psychological states, and social situations. Persons with AIDS can live more comfortable lives through the establishment of nurturing and supportive healthcare paradigms. Education about medical and psychiatric care, pain management, and decision-making capacity can help persons with HIV and their caregivers meet the challenges of this illness with optimism and dignity.

REFERENCES

Atwine B, Cantor-Graae E, Bajunirwe F (2005). Psychological distress among AIDS orphans in rural Uganda. *Soc Sci Med* 61:555–564.

Bass EB, Marsh MJ, Mangione CM, et al. (2004). Submacular Surgery Trials Research Group. Patients' perceptions of the value of current vision: assessment of preference values among patients with subfoveal choroidal neovascularization. The Submacular Surgery Trials Vision Preference Value Scale: SST Report No. 6. *Arch Ophthalmol* 122:1856–1867.

BeLow-Beer S, Chan K, Yip B, et al. (2000). Depressive symptoms decline among persons on HIV protease inhibitors. *J Acquir Immune Defic Syndr* 23:295–301.

Berman K, Brodaty H (2006). Psychosocial effects of age-related macular degeneration. *Int Psychogeriatr* 1:1–14.

Braitstein P, Montessori V, Chan K, Montaner JS, Schechter MT, O'Shaughnessy MV, Hogg RS (2005). Quality of life, depression and fatigue among persons co-infected with HIV and hepatitis C: outcomes from a population-based cohort. *AIDS Care* 17:105–115.

Breitbart W, McDonald MV, Rosenfeld B, Monkman ND, Passik S (1998). Fatigue in ambulatory AIDS patients. *J Pain Symptom Manage* 15:159–167.

Breitbart W, Rosenfeld B, Kaim M, Funesti-Esch J (2001). A randomized, double-blind, placebo-controlled trial of psychostimulants for the treatment of fatigue in ambulatory patients with human immunodeficiency virus disease. *Arch Intern Med* 161:411–420.

Cain VS, Kington RS (2003). Investigating the role of racial/ethnic bias in health outcomes. *Am J Public Health* 93:191–192.

Chin D, and Kroesen KW (1999). Disclosure of HIV infection among API American women: cultural stigma and support. *Cultur Divers Ethnic Minor Psychol* 5:222–235.

Cohen MA (1999). Psychodynamic psychotherapy in an AIDS nursing home. *J Am Acad Psychoanal* 27:121–133.

Cohen MA, Hoffman RG, Cromwell C, Schmeidler J, Ebrahim F, Carrera G, Endorf F, Alfonso CA, and Jacobson JM (2002). The prevalence of distress in persons with human immunodeficiency virus infection. *Psychosomatics* 43:10–15.

Cox DJ, Kiernan BD, Schroeder DB, and Cowley M (1998). Psychosocial sequelae of visual loss in diabetes. *Diabetes Educ* 24:481–484.

Currie PF, Jacob AJ, Foreman AR, Elton RA, Brettle RP, and Boon NA (1994). Heart muscle disease related to HIV infection: prognostic implications. *BMJ* 309:1605–1607.

Dakin CL, O'Connor CA, and Patsdaughter CA (2006). HAART to heart: HIV-related cardiomyopathy and other cardiovascular complications. *AACN Clin Issues* 17:18–29.

Dasgupta S, Oster AM, Li J, Hall HI (2016). Disparities in consistent retention in HIV care—11 states and the District of Columbia, 2011–2013. *MMWR Morb Mortal Wkly Rep* 65(4):77–82.

Diaz RM, Ayala G, Bein E (2004). Sexual risk as an outcome of social oppression: data from probability sample of Latino gay men in three US cities. *Cultur Divers Ethnic Minor Psychol* 10:255–267.

Eckholdt H, Chin J (1997). *Pneumocystis carini* pneumonia in Asians and Pacific Islanders. *Clin Infect Dis* 24:1265–1267.

Eckholdt HM, Chin JJ, Manzon-Santos JA, Kim DD (1997). The needs of Asians and Pacific Islanders living with HIV in New York City. *AIDS Educ Prev* 9:493–504.

Ehlers VJ, Zuvderduin A, Oosthuizen MJ (2001). The well-being of gays, lesbians and bisexuals in Botswana. *J Adv Nurs* 35:848–856.

Elkington KS, Bauermeister JA, Zimmerman MA (2010). Psychological distress, substance use, and HIV/STI risk behaviors among youth. *J Youth Adolesc* 39(5):514–527.

Fisher SD, Lipshultz SE (2001). Epidemiology of cardiovascular involvement in HIV disease and AIDS. *Ann N Y Acad Sci* 946:13–22.

Goldberg DE, Smithen LM, Angelilli A, Freean WR (2005). HIV-associated retinopathy in the HAART era. *Retina* 25:633–649.

Herek GM (1999). AIDS and stigma. *Am Behav Sci* 42:1106–1116.

Hill D, Dubey JP (2002). *Toxoplasma gondii*: transmission, diagnosis and prevention. *Clin Microbiol Infect* 8:634–640.

Hirschtick RE, Glassroth J, Jordan MC, et al. (1995). Bacterial pneumonia in persons infected with the human immunodeficiency virus. Pulmonary Complications of HIV Infection Study Group. *N Engl J Med* 333:845–851.

Holbrook JT, Jabs DA, Weinberg DV, Lewis RA, Davis MD, Friedberg D (2003). Studies of Ocular Complications of AIDS (SOCA) Research Group. Visual loss in patients with cytomegalovirus retinitis and acquired immunodeficiency syndrome before widespread availability of highly active antiretroviral therapy. *Arch Ophthalmol* 121:99–107.

Jacox AJ, Carr DB, Payne R (1994). New clinical practice guidelines for the management of pain in patients with cancer. *N Engl J Med* 330:651.

Kang E, Rapkin B (2003). Adherence to antiretroviral medication among undocumented Asians living with HIV disease in New York City. *Community Psycholog* 36:35–38.

Kang E, Rapkin B, Springer C, Kim JH (2003). The "demon plague" and access to care among Asian undocumented immigrants living with HIV disease in New York City. *J Immigr Health* 5:49–58.

Kestelyn PG, Cunningham ET Jr (2001). HIV/AIDS and blindness. *Bull World Health Organ* 79:208–213.

Lebovits AH, Lefkowitz M, McCarthy D, Simon R, Wilpon H, Jung R, Fried E (1989). The prevalence and management of pain in patients with AIDS: a review of 134 cases. *Clin J Pain* 5(3):245–248.

Lindsey E, Hirschfeld M, Tlou S (2003). Home-based care in Botswana: experiences of older women and young girls. *Health Care Women Int* 24:486–501.

Lyketsos CG, Hutton H, Fishman M, Schwartz J, Treisman GJ (1996). Psychiatric morbidity on entry to an HIV primary care clinic. *AIDS* 10:1033–1039.

Mapou RL, Law WA, Martin A, Kampen D, Salazar AM, Rundell JR (1993). Neuropsychological performance, mood, and complaints of cognitive and motor difficulties in individuals infected with the human immunodeficiency virus. *J Neuropsychiatry Clin Neurosci* 5:86–93.

Marc LG, Wang MM, Testa MA (2012). Psychometric evaluation of the HIV symptom distress scale. *AIDS Care* 24(11):1432–1441.

Maschke M, Kastrup O, Esser S, Ross B, Hengge U, Hufnagel A (2000). Incidence and prevalence of neurological disorders associated with HIV since the introduction of highly active antiretroviral therapy (HAART). *J Neurol Neurosurg Psychiatry* 69:376–380.

McCormack JP, Li R, Zarowny D, Singer J (1993). Inadequate treatment of pain in ambulatory HIV patients. *Clin J Pain* 9:279–283.

Miles MS, Holditch-Davis D, Pedersen C, Eron JJ Jr, Schwartz T (2007). Emotional distress in African American women with HIV. *J Prev Interv Community* 33(1-2):35–50.

Newshan GT, Wainapel SF (1993). Pain characteristics and their management in persons with AIDS. *J Assoc Nurses AIDS Care* 4:53–59.

Ng CW, Lam MS, Paton NI (2000). Cryptococcal meningitis resulting in irreversible visual impairment in AIDS patients: a report of two cases. *Singapore Med J* 41:80–82.

Oette M, Hemker J, Feldt T, Sagir A, Best J, Haussinger D (2005). Acute syphilitic blindness in an HIV-positive patient. *AIDS Patient Care STDS* 19:209–211.

O'Keefe EA, Wood R (1996). The impact of human immunodeficiency virus (HIV) infection on quality of life in a multiracial South African population. *Qual Life Res* 5:275–280.

Operario D, Nemoto T, Ng T, Syed J, Mazarei M (2005). Conducting HIV interventions for Asian Pacific Islander men who have sex with men: challenges and compromises in community collaborative research. *AIDS Educ Prev* 17:334–346.

Pounds MB, Conviser R, Ashman JJ, Bourassa V (2002). Ryan White CARE Act service use by Asian/Pacific Islanders and other clients in three California metropolitan areas (1997–1998). *J Community Health* 27:403–417.

Pulvirenti JJ, Mehra T, Hafiz I, et al. (2002). Epidemiology and outcome of *Clostridium difficile* infection and diarrhea in HIV infected inpatients. *Diagn Microbiol Infect Dis* 44:325–330.

Rabkin JG, Ferrando SJ, Lin Sh, Sewell M, McElhiney M (2000). Psychological effects of HAART: a 2-year study. *Psychosom Med* 62:413–422.

Rabkin JG, McElhiney MC, Rabkin R, Ferrando SJ (2004). Modafinil treatment for fatigue in HIV+ patients: a pilot study. *J Clin Psychiatry* 65:1688–1695.

Rabkin JG, Wagner GJ, EcElhiney MC, Rabkin R, Lin SH (2004). Testosterone versus fluoxetine for depression and fatigue in HIV/AIDS: a placebo-controlled trial. *J Clin Psychopharmacol* 24:379–385.

Rao D, Chen WT, Pearson CR, et al. (2012). Social support mediates the relationship between HIV stigma and depression/quality of life among people living with HIV in Beijing, China. *Int J STD AIDS* 23(7):481–484.

Regnault A, Marfatia S, Louie M, Mear I, Meunier J, Viala-Danten M (2009). Satisfactory cross-cultural validity of the ACTG symptom distress module in HIV-1-infected antiretroviral-naïve patients. *Clin Trials* 6(6):574–584.

Reid S, Dwyer J (2005). Insomnia in HIV infection: a systematic review of prevalence, correlates, and management. *Psychosom Med* 67:260–269.

Reiter GS, Kudler NR (1996). Palliative care and HIV, part II: systemic manifestations and late-stage issues. *AIDS Clin Care* 8:27–36.

Roth AJ, Kornblith AB, Batel-Copel L, Peabody E, Scher HI, Holland JC (1998). Rapid screening for psychological distress in men with prostate carcinoma: a pilot study. *Cancer* 82:1904–1908.

Rosen MJ, Clayton K, Schneider RF, et al. (1997). Intensive care of patients with HIV infection: utilization, critical illnesses, and outcomes. Pulmonary Complications of HIV Infection Study Group. *Am J Respir Crit Care Med* 155:67–71.

Sacktor N (2002). The epidemiology of human immunodeficiency virus–associated neurological disease in the era of highly active antiretroviral therapy. *J Neurovirol* 8(Suppl. 2):115–121.

Sanchez TH, Brooks JT, Sullivan PS, Juhasz M, Mintz E, Dworkin MS, Jones JL (2005). Adult/Adolescent Spectrum of HIV Disease Study Group. Bacterial diarrhea in persons with HIV infection, United States, 1992–2002. *Clin Infect Dis* 41:1621–1627.

Saunders C (1988). Spiritual pain. *J Palliat Care* 4:29–32.

Schofferman J (1988). Pain: diagnosis and management in the palliative care of AIDS. *J Palliat Care* 4:46–49.

Shawn ER, Campbell L, Mnguni MB, Defilippi KM, Williams AB (2005). The spectrum of symptoms among rural South Africans with HIV infection. *J Assoc Nurses AIDS Care* 16:12–23.

Staubach P, Eckhardt-Henn A, Dechene M, et al. (2006). Quality of life in patients with chronic urticaria is differentially impaired and determined by psychiatric comorbidity. *Br J Dermatol* 154:294–298.

Steglitz J, Ng R, Mosha JS, Kershaw T (2012). Divinity and distress: the impact of religion and spirituality on the mental health of HIV-positive adults in Tanzania. *AIDS Behav* 16(8):2392–2398.

Valleroy LA, MacKellar DA, Karon JM, et al. (2000). HIV prevalence and associated risks in young men who have sex with men. Young Men's Survey Study Group. *JAMA* 284:198–204.

Von Roenn JH, Cleeland CS, Gonin R, Hatfield AK, Pandya KJ (1993). Physician attitudes and practice in cancer pain management. A survey from the Eastern Cooperative Oncology Group. *Ann Intern Med* 119:121–126.

Wallace JM, Rao AV, Glassroth J, et al. (1993). Respiratory illness in persons with human immunodeficiency virus infection. The Pulmonary Complications of HIV Infection Study Group. *Am Rev Respir Dis* 148:1523–1529.

Williams DR, Neighbors HW, Jackson JS (2003). Racial/ethnic discrimination and health: findings from community studies. *Am J Public Health* 93:200–208.

Wilson IB, Cleary PD (1997). Clinical predictors of declines in physical functioning in persons with AIDS: results of a longitudinal study. *J Acquir Immune Defic Syndr Hum Retrovirol* 16:343–349.

Yoshioka MR, Schustack A (2001). Disclosure of HIV status: cultural issues of Asian patients. *AIDS Patient Care STDs* 15:77–82.

23.

INSOMNIA AND HIV: A BIOPSYCHOSOCIAL APPROACH

Mary Alice O'Dowd and Maria Fernanda Gomez

Sleep that knits the ravel'd sleave of care,
The death of each day's life, sore labor's bath,
Balm of hurt minds, great nature's second course
Chief nourisher in life's feast.
MACBETH, *II, ii, 36*

Shakespeare's observations on the restorative nature of sleep have been confirmed by recent research which finds that sleep may be necessary in order to cleanse the brain of toxic metabolites that accumulate during waking hours (Xie et al., 2013). *Insomnia*, which is the most common sleep disorder, is defined as dissatisfaction with sleep quantity or quality, associated with difficulty with the initiation, maintenance, or duration of sleep, resulting in impairment of daytime function, despite adequate opportunity and circumstances for sleep (American Psychiatric Association [APA], 2013). Insomnia can be a symptom of many disorders and has been described as a major public health problem that impacts the lives of millions of individuals (National Institutes of Health [NIH], 2005). However, many of those with sleep problems are unlikely to broach the topic with a healthcare provider and when a patient does note insomnia, the complaint may be given short shrift by the clinician or a sleep medication may be prescribed for short- or long-term use without much attention to the etiology of the complaint or to follow-up. Insomnia is not just an annoyance. It has been shown to affect cognitive functioning, quality of life, longevity (Martin and Ancoli-Israel, 2003), and even weight and the development of the metabolic syndrome (Troxel et al., 2010). Insomnia can affect sleep onset, maintenance, or duration, but these presentations often have limited stability over time, and persons with insomnia may have a combination of sleep symptoms (Buysse, 2008). The specific diagnosis of types of sleep symptoms in the clinical setting can be difficult, as patients may overestimate or underestimate problems such as sleep onset latency or fragmented sleep. Causes are often multifactorial, and an individual may have several physiological and psychological factors contributing to one or more sleep disorders. Before discussing the specific issue of insomnia in individuals living with HIV, it may be helpful to review the physiology of healthy sleep using the current international classification of sleep stages.

Normal sleep is made up of rapid eye movement (REM) sleep and non-REM sleep (NREM). In non-REM sleep, the sleeper slips from wakefulness into N1 (formerly stage I), a light sleep from which the sleeper is easily awakened by noise or other environmental stimuli. N2 (stage II) sleep is deeper, and most stimuli will not disturb the sleeper. N3 sleep, which combines the levels of sleep previously described as stages III and IV, is even deeper, with the sleeper's electroencephalogram (EEG) marked by higher voltage slow waves; this stage of sleep is described as deep, slow-wave or delta-wave sleep. Here environmental stimuli go unnoticed unless they are extreme and prolonged, allowing sleep to continue undisturbed. The normal sleep cycle consists of passage from wakefulness to N1, then progressively through the stages to the deeper levels of sleep. The sleeper then returns to N2, which occupies the greater part of the night, and from N2 into a period of REM sleep. During REM sleep, the sleeper is dreaming, an activity marked by high levels of cortical activation but with muscle atonia that prevents the movements usually associated with such activation. This cycle through the stages repeats itself several times over the course of an average night's sleep. Deep sleep tends to occur earlier in the night's rest, while REM periods start later and become longer (Krahn, 2011). Daily cycles of sleep and wakefulness are thought to be the result of intricate interactions between circadian rhythms and sleep homeostasis. The circadian process promotes the alternation between sleep and wakefulness, reinforced by the impact of light on the retina during daytime hours and the release of melatonin at night. The homeostatic process builds up a drive for sleep that increases in intensity with the length of wakefulness and that can be derailed by napping. The competition and coordination between these two systems determines whether a person is awake or asleep (Krystal et al., 2013). These patterns are the basis for recommendation of a regular schedule that takes advantage of these natural rhythms as part of "sleep hygiene" for the promotion of healthy sleep.

At times and for almost everyone, the pursuit of sleep can be a challenge. How we actually fall asleep has remained something of a physiological mystery. However, through studies using imaging, molecular biology, cellular physiology and cognitive approaches, complex new hypotheses have been proposed regarding the neurobiology of sleep and insomnia. These studies focus on the intricate connections and mutual inhibition between the systems that alternately induce waking or sleeping, with wakefulness mediated by neurotransmitter systems that underlie cortical activation, arousal, and vigilance, including parts of the cholinergic, noradrenergic, dopaminergic, histaminergic, and stress systems. Sleep-inducing brain areas contain GABAergic and galaninergic inhibitory neurons which project to arousal structures. Serotonin acts on these inhibitory neurons to increase pressure to sleep (Adrien and Garma, 2010), while orexin, produced by neurons in the lateral hypothalamus, acts on these same neurons and tilts the balance toward wakefulness (Krystal et al., 2013). There is a delicate balance between the sleep-promoting and wakefulness systems and impairment anywhere in these systems, either by hyperactivity on the arousal side of the balance or by hypoactivity on the sleep-promoting side, can lead to insomnia.

The International Classification of Sleep Disorders divides sleep disorders into the primary disorders, which include dysomnias and parasomnias, and secondary sleep disorders, related to another mental, neurological, or medical disorder or induced by the use of substances. By contrast, the NIH Draft Statement on Insomnia (2005) suggests use of the term *comorbid insomnia*, as multiple causes are most often present when insomnia is persistent. DSM-5 criteria for the diagnosis of insomnia include sleep difficulty at least three nights per weeks that is present for at least 3 months despite adequate time for sleep and specify the presence of comorbidity with non-sleep mental disorders, medical disorders, or other sleep disorders (APA, 2013).

Clinicians have long been aware of the frequency with which insomnia and fatigue figure in the complaints of individuals living with HIV. Fatigue and sleep disturbance can affect a wide range of activities and even health itself, as the healing benefits of sleep are lost at a time when patients have the greatest need of rest and renewal. Although fatigue and insomnia are obviously related, they are not synonymous. Some persons with HIV may sleep relatively well, wake up rested, but develop fatigue as the day progresses, whereas individuals with insomnia may wake up unrefreshed, feel tired all day, and still be unable to fall asleep or remain asleep when night falls.

This chapter will focus specifically on the sleep disorders seen in individuals living with HIV infection. Fatigue in persons with HIV is discussed in Chapter 24 of this book.

SLEEP DISORDERS WITH MEDICAL COMORBIDITY

The insomnia found among persons with HIV most often falls into the category of the comorbid insomnias, owing to the wide range of factors that may contribute to sleep disturbance in this population. HIV infection itself has been linked to insomnia. Early studies in sleep labs identified changes in sleep architecture even among asymptomatic HIV-positive

individuals. In these patients, slow-wave sleep was increased, particularly toward the later portion of the sleep period (Ferini Strambi et al., 1995; Norman et al., 1992; Terstegge et al., 1993). This finding is unique to HIV infection and may be due to immune peptides, including tumor necrosis factor and interleukin, which are elevated in the blood of persons with HIV and have been found to be somnogenic in both clinical studies and animal models (Darko et al., 1995; Pollmacher et al., 1995). The human immunodeficiency virus and other lentiviruses may affect sleep more directly by resetting circadian rhythms, leading to altered sleep patterns and fatigue (Clark et al., 2005). Dysregulation of the growth hormone axis has also been implicated as a possible cause of sleep disturbance, with studies showing differences in the coupling between delta-frequency EEG amplitude in sleep and growth hormone secretion between HIV-positive and HIV-negative subjects, a change that occurs early in the course of the infection (Darko et al., 1998).

Formal sleep studies and self-reports (Gamaldo et al., 2013; Jean-Louis et al., 2012; Lee et al., 2012; Seay et al., 2013) have shown that sleep in individuals living with HIV is impaired in both quantity and quality, although studies have been inconsistent as to whether these impairments are significantly related to stage of illness. A study by Low and colleagues (2012) comparing HIV-seropositive and HIV-seronegative individuals with insomnia, matched for age, sex, and Axis I psychiatric diagnosis, found that the patients with HIV had significantly longer sleep-onset latency and decreased sleep efficiency and spent less time in REM sleep. It has been suggested that poor sleep quality in this population may contribute to poor medication adherence and increased perception of symptom severity, making insomnia for persons with HIV more than just an inconvenience (Babson et al., 2013).

SLEEP DISORDERS WITH NON-SLEEP MENTAL COMORBIDITY

Mood, anxiety, substance use, and cognitive disorders, all of which have been found to have a high prevalence among persons living with HIV, have been linked with both acute and chronic insomnia. Reid and Dwyer (2005) undertook a systematic review of articles dealing with insomnia in HIV infection. While an AIDS-defining illness, cognitive impairment, and treatment with efavirenz were all significant risk factors for insomnia, the most notable association was psychological morbidity.

DEPRESSION

Studies in other populations have found an extensive comorbidity between psychiatric disorders and insomnia, with depression being the psychiatric diagnosis most commonly associated with insomnia (Martin and Ancoli-Israel, 2003) and sleep disturbance among the most common symptoms in depression (Nissen and Nofzinger, 2007). Persons with depression often report difficulties falling asleep as well as disturbed sleep continuity. REM sleep has been found to occur earlier in sleep in depressed persons and to decrease as the night progresses, reversing the normal cycle (Kloss and Szuba, 2003). Studies of sleep that integrate findings from imaging, polysomnography, and cognitive affective assessment have identified patterns of hypoactivity or hyperactivity in specific brain regions in depressed patients that lead to the patterns of sleep disturbance seen in this disorder, including disrupted sleep, increased REM sleep, reduced slow-wave sleep, and disrupted daytime functioning (Nissen and Nofzinger, 2007).

Major depression is common in persons with HIV, with a prevalence estimated at twice that of a comparison population (Ciesla and Roberts, 2001), leaving this cohort vulnerable to sleep disorders. The relationship between depression and insomnia can be bidirectional, and in one study, among persons with HIV, insomnia was identified as being more closely correlated with worsening of depression than CD4 count and disease progression (Perkins et al., 1995).

When insomnia develops during an episode of major depression, treatment of the depressive symptoms should take priority, as the insomnia will often resolve as the depression remits. An antidepressant with sedation as a side effect, such as mirtazapine, may relieve symptoms of insomnia while treating the depression. Another option is to combine antidepressant treatment with short-term use of a sleep-promoting agent. The addition of cognitive-behavioral therapy (CBT) may help remedy both depression and insomnia (Kloss and Szuba, 2003).

MANIA

Patients experiencing a manic episode may not feel the need for sleep and may not complain of insufficient sleep despite long periods of wakefulness. Need for sleep may not actually be reduced but simply delayed, leading to prolonged periods of sleep. However, the pattern of such sleep is similar to that of depressed patients, with sleep disruption, increased stage 1 sleep, and a shortened latency to REM sleep (Ebben and Fine, 2010). In individuals living with HIV, mania may represent exacerbation of a pre-existing bipolar disorder, may be part of organic manic syndrome that is usually seen in the context of advanced HIV infection, or may be a side effect of medications such as steroids (Watkins et al., 2011).

Identification and treatment of the underlying cause of the mania and treatment of the mania itself with mood stabilizers or antipsychotics may resolve the insomnia, although hypnotics can be added if necessary.

ANXIETY DISORDERS

Studies of persons with anxiety in other settings have found that 50–70% report sleep difficulties affecting all stages of sleep (Kloss and Szuba, 2003). Although studies have found that anxiety precedes the onset of insomnia in 43% of patients and co-occurred in 39% (Ebben and Fine, 2010), clearly each has the potential to worsen the other. Anxiety can occur at any stage of HIV infection, as individuals must adapt to ever-changing circumstances. From initial diagnosis, the person may experience a number of anxiety-producing events, including changes in health or medication regimens, awaiting the results of tests and procedures, and changing family and financial circumstances, to mention just a few. Anxiety disorders may antedate seroconversion, and symptoms of anxiety may also occur in the context of substance abuse or withdrawal.

Anxiolytics and/or antidepressants are usually effective in decreasing anxiety, although the use of anxiolytics in patients with a history of substance abuse may raise another set of issues. The possibility of drug–drug interactions with antiretroviral therapy (ART) may also limit the choice of agent.

POSTTRAUMATIC STRESS DISORDER (PTSD)

Sleep disruption is common after a traumatic experience, with difficulty initiating sleep, frequent awakenings, and nightmares being the most frequent symptoms in the immediate aftermath of trauma. Persistence of sleep disturbance, including nightmares, insomnia, and even sleep avoidance, suggests the development of more chronic PTSD. The disturbing nightmares that are part of the symptom cluster of PTSD are associated with changes in REM sleep, including increased REM density, which may reflect increased intensity of the REM episode; increased awakening from REM sleep (Iaboni and Moldofsky, 2010); and, in most studies, an increased REM percent (Kloss and Szuba, 2003). It has been suggested that individuals living with HIV may experience a higher prevalence of PTSD than the general population (Watkins et al., 2011). Risk factors for PTSD that may account for this higher prevalence include pre-existing mental health problems, an abusive or difficult childhood, or prior trauma (Iaboni and Moldofsky, 2010). Poverty and the experience of discrimination common in groups at high risk for HIV infection may themselves be risk factors for increased exposure to trauma. The diagnosis of HIV itself may be an emotional trauma that can lead to PTSD (Kelly et al., 1998), as can grueling treatments or intensive care unit stays.

GRIEF/BEREAVEMENT

As HIV infection can affect multiple members of a family, a social network, or even a community, loss and bereavement are not uncommon. Acute grief can lead to insomnia, which may be relieved by short-term use of hypnotics. Lack of social support or pre-existing poor coping skills may interfere with adaptation to loss and lead to persistence of insomnia and other markers of bereavement.

Individual or group psychotherapy may provide emotional support and teach adaptational skills. Prolonged bereavement may be a form of depression requiring antidepressant treatment in conjunction with psychotherapy.

COGNITIVE IMPAIRMENT AND DEMENTIA

As previously mentioned, studies have found an association between the presence of cognitive impairment and insomnia in advanced HIV infection. In non-HIV-infected populations, level of dementia has been found to contribute to poor sleep quality (Staedt and Rupprecht-Mrozek, 2010); in nursing homes, residents with cognitive impairment have been found to have more disturbed circadian rhythms and more fragmented sleep (Martin and Ancoli-Israel, 2003). Both of these findings could be relevant to sleep disorders in the later stages of HIV infection.

SUBSTANCE USE DISORDERS

Sleep disturbance can be seen with both substance use and withdrawal/abstinence syndromes. It has been suggested that insomnia may predispose a person to development of a substance use disorder or contribute to relapse. Although treatment of insomnia may be more difficult in persons who misuse substances, appropriate treatment is important both to overall well-being and to helping achieve and sustain abstinence.

PAIN AND OTHER PHYSICAL CAUSES OF INSOMNIA

Pain clearly can interfere with all stages of sleep. Chronic pain in persons with HIV may be underdiagnosed and undertreated despite data demonstrating that pain is a common symptom in this population. Doctors may feel reluctant to treat complaints of pain in patients with a history of substance abuse or may undertreat when the causes of pain in a patient with HIV remain uncertain even after a thorough workup.

Diarrhea is a common complaint in patients living with opportunistic infections and can lead to fragmented and non-restful sleep, as can urinary frequency, muscle cramping, and other physical complaints. Obstructive sleep apnea due to adenotonsillar hypertrophy has been estimated to have a prevalence of 7% among individuals living with HIV, even in the absence of obesity (Epstein et al., 1995), and has been associated with increased neck fat hypertrophy, owing to the deposit of adipose tissue around the neck as part of HIV-associated lipodystrophy (Schulz et al., 2003). Decreased levels of testosterone can also lead to insomnia.

MEDICATION SIDE EFFECTS

Methylphenidate and other psychostimulants used to treat apathy and fatigue in persons with HIV can cause insomnia, although restricting dosing schedules to the earlier part of the day should prevent this side effect. Several medications used to treat HIV have been linked to insomnia, the evidence being most compelling for efavirenz. Studies have found longer sleep latency and shorter duration of deep sleep in patients treated with efavirenz as compared with controls. In addition, efavirenz has been associated with vivid dreams and nightmares (McDaniel et al., 2000) that may predispose to disturbed and less restful sleep. These symptoms may be related to higher plasma levels, and a reduction in dose may be helpful in improving sleep (Gutierrez et al., 2005). While any list of medications that may cause insomnia is bound to be long and

incomplete, medication side effects should certainly be suspected when a change of medication or change of medication dosage is temporally associated with a change in sleep pattern.

DIAGNOSIS

As with many diagnoses, a high index of suspicion is the best diagnostic tool. A good sleep assessment should certainly be done whenever a patient notes fatigue or insomnia, but the clinician should also take the initiative and ask all patients about symptoms of initial, middle, or late insomnia. History from partners or other family members may be helpful as some patients actually adapt to their insomnia and may lose insight into the degree of nighttime insomnia and daytime sleepiness. The Epworth Sleepiness Scale (Johns, 1991) is a brief self-rating instrument that may be helpful in identifying daytime sleepiness, but insomnia can best be diagnosed by careful interview augmented by a sleep log, in which the patient details pre-sleep events and amount of time spent in bed asleep or trying to sleep, over a week or more. Use of actigraphy, which involves continuous monitoring of body movement by a watch-like device, can also help differentiate sleep time from wake time as well as quantifying sleep latency, number of arousals, and regularity of sleep schedule. Referral to a sleep lab for assessment is usually not indicated unless evidence of pathological sleepiness, including unusual snoring, periods of apnea, or periodic limb movements, suggests need for a more thorough evaluation (Sateia and Nowell, 2004).

For the diagnosis of insomnia to be made, the patient should report taking more than 30 minutes to fall asleep and/or difficulty maintaining sleep, with wakeful periods of more than 30 minutes, should have an overall sleep efficiency (the ratio of sleep time to time spent in bed) of less than 85%, and should meet the DSM criteria. A careful history should include a review of the sleep schedule and daytime napping; information on the sleep environment, including presence of a partner, children, or pets in the bed; use of prescription medication, over-the-counter remedies or herbal preparations; use of alcohol, tobacco, street drugs, or caffeine; involvement in shift work or pre-bedtime exercise; presence of pain, periodic leg movements, or loud snoring; details and frequency of daytime sleepiness; and frequency of vivid nightmares. The history of the complaint should include questions regarding prior assessments, treatments, and their results; childhood and family sleep history; and, if the symptom had a sudden onset, possible precipitants, such as trauma, change of sleep partners, location, or routine, and new diagnoses or treatments (Krahn, 2011; Stepanski et al., 2003). Both clinicians and researchers have found the Pittsburgh Sleep Quality Index, a sleep problem questionnaire, useful in documenting the presence and severity of insomnia (Buysse et al., 1989). If the patient has a regular sleep partner, this individual should also be interviewed about the patient's pre-sleep behaviors, sleep patterns, snoring, and respiratory pauses.

As previously noted, a good psychiatric history can be an important part of the evaluation of insomnia. Thus symptoms of non-sleep psychiatric disorders such as depression, anxiety, PTSD, substance use disorders and other psychiatric disorders that might contribute to insomnia should be reviewed, along with an examination of cognitive function. Insomnia can precipitate the psychiatric disorder or can be secondary to it. Correlation of the time course of psychiatric symptoms with the onset of insomnia can be essential in determining appropriate treatment.

TREATMENT

Not every individual with insomnia requires treatment, and treatment is usually reserved for those with clinically significant insomnia and resultant daytime dysfunction. However, since poor sleep quality in persons with HIV has been associated with both decreased treatment adherence and self-reported symptom severity, encouraging patients to treat their insomnia may actually improve treatment adherence and sense of well-being (Babson et al., 2013). As insomnia often has a multifactorial etiology, with both onset and course affected by predisposing, precipitating, and perpetuating factors, treatment may need to address all aspects of the problem. As noted previously, the impact of HIV on the brain may underlie much of the insomnia seen in this population and, insofar as this impact is not related to disease stage or progression, may not be directly treatable. What is treatable is the symptom of poor sleep as well as other factors that may contribute to it. Underlying physical and psychiatric conditions should be diagnosed and treated, and behaviors that work against a good night's sleep should be identified and, if possible, changed.

Many people with insomnia develop poor sleep habits that make restful sleep less likely. The longer insomnia lasts, the more dysfunctional and ingrained the patient's maladaptive sleep patterns may become, with behaviors that were initially adopted to relieve the problem, such as napping or spending more time in bed, eventually becoming part of the problem (Hauri, 2003). Thus the first step toward successful treatment is making sure that every patient is aware of good sleep hygiene, the pattern of behaviors that predispose to sleep. The patient should be taught how to take advantage of the circadian rhythms that potentiate sleep. Steps that patients can take include avoiding naps, limiting time in bed to 8 hours, getting daily exercise, but not just before bedtime, keeping the same sleep schedule 7 days/week rather than attempting to make up sleep on the weekends, and avoiding bright lights in the evening. Promotion of sleep can include developing a consistent and soothing bedtime ritual; making sure the bedroom is comfortable in terms of light, noise, and temperature; avoiding alcohol, caffeine, and excessive liquids in the presleep hours; and avoiding large evening meals. Drugs of abuse, including nicotine, should be avoided.

Chronic insomnia may lead to increased anxiety, as bedtime and the bed itself become associated with frustration and arousal rather than sleep. Treatment for this may include stimulus control therapy, to restructure such attitudes and reestablish circadian rhythms.

Patients should be advised not to use the bed for anything but sleep or sex and to avoid being in bed for other activities such as reading or watching TV. Bedtime should be postponed until the person is tired, and if sleep is not quickly achieved, the person should get up and pursue non-stimulating activity, avoiding TV or bright lights and avoiding snacks, which can reward and reinforce poor sleep habits. The person should return to bed only when drowsy; this pattern is repeated until sleep is achieved, to associate the bedroom, bed, and bedtime with sleep.

Although it may seem counterintuitive, sleep restriction may also be helpful. Using the sleep log, the patient's sleep efficiency is calculated (total sleep time/time in bed). If efficiency is over 90%, time in bed is increased by 15 minutes daily, and for sleep efficiency under 80%, time in bed is decreased by the same amount, using the sleep log as a guide for weekly readjustment. The goal is to retrain the sleeper to make better and healthier use of his or her time in bed, with an ultimate goal of an efficiency of 85%, meaning that at least 85% of the time in bed is spent asleep.

If worry or stress is a consistent factor in poor sleep, the patient may need to work on strategies to avoid taking worries to bed. This may involve relaxation techniques or attention-focusing procedures such as imagery training, meditation, or even biofeedback. Another helpful technique is paradoxical intention, in which patients are advised to focus on remaining awake, thereby reducing performance anxiety (Sateia and Nowell, 2004). Cognitive therapy can be used to identify maladaptive, erroneous, and distorted cognitions about sleep and replace these with more helpful attitudes. Cognitive-behavioral therapies focused specifically on insomnia (CBT-I) have been found to be as effective as prescriptions medication for the short-term treatment of insomnia and, unlike medications, to have effects that last well beyond the termination of treatment (NIH, 2005). A combination of some or all of these nonpharmacological treatments can lead to clinically significant and durable improvement (Sateia and Nowell, 2004). Self-help books and tapes for the insomniac are also available. If pain, nausea, other physical complaints, or medication side effects are limiting sleep, the patient's primary care doctor may need to be brought into the treatment process to help in the identification of these important concerns and in addressing them.

Environmental and social issues that present a barrier to safe and restful sleep may underlie some physical complaints of persons with HIV who live with such barriers. These issues can be complex and may call for greater involvement and inventiveness on the part of the clinician, as many of the approaches reviewed here suggest that the patient with insomnia has a roof over his or her head, a potentially quiet environment, and, above all, a bed—none of which may be consistently available for some patients. Advocating for the patient with agencies to obtain safe housing may be the most important step in helping a patient whose sleep is fragmentary and snatched on a damp, cold sidewalk or a friend's couch. Continued advocacy may be necessary, as many of the housing options available to patients are not conducive to sleep or to good health. A decent bed, a fan or air conditioner, or even a comfortable chair for the person whose symptoms do not permit lying flat may be medical necessities for a person whose sleep is limited by pain or physical distress.

Another approach to the treatment of insomnia is through resetting circadian rhythms. Sleep and rhythms can become dissociated by shift work, travel to other time zones, seasonal changes, and irregular sleep habits. Melatonin is produced by the pineal gland in response to the daily cycle of light and dark and plays a role in the maintenance of circadian rhythm. Bright light in the morning and/or melatonin taken at night can shift the circadian rhythm to facilitate sleep and reduce sleep latency (Sack et al., 2003).

The role of melatonin in persons with HIV is more complex, as the natural history of HIV infection is marked by progressively reduced serum melatonin levels. This reduction may be related to impairment of the T-helper cell immune response, as melatonin appears to promote this response by increasing interferon gamma and interleukin 12 (Nunnari et al., 2003). Studies have found that melatonin supplementation may protect against delirium and may promote recovery from delirium in a medically ill population, as well as promote sleep in patients with dementia due to Alzheimer's disease (Bourne et al., 2008; de Jonghe et al., 2010; McCleery et al., 2014). These findings suggest possible usefulness in persons with HIV. However, studies to confirm efficacy and safety of melatonin supplementation in persons with HIV have not been done. Melatonin can be bought over the counter and in health food stores, although varying bioavailability and the presence of contaminants suggest long-term use in a medically compromised population should be approached with caution.

At present, two melatonin receptor agonists have received U.S. Food and Drug Administration (FDA) approval for the treatment of sleep disorders. Ramelteon has been reported to help with initiation of sleep, and tasimelteon has been approved for improvement of sleep initiation and treatment of sleep disorders in blind persons (non-24 sleep disorder). Both appear efficacious in the treatment of circadian rhythm sleep disorders (Ferguson et al., 2010). Ramelteon should be used with caution in patients receiving antiretroviral treatment, as these agents may increase ramelteon levels due to their effect on the activity of CYP450 3A4. Tasimelteon should be avoided with efavirenz, and levels and efficacy may be reduced when used in conjunction with other antiretrovirals.

In considering pharmacological treatment of persons with HIV suffering from insomnia, it is important to be aware of potential interactions among the many medications these patients may be taking as well as the side effects of the medications themselves. Many of these considerations are reviewed in the excellent article by Omonuwa and colleagues (2009).

For many decades, the mainstay of insomnia treatment has been the sedative-hypnotic class of medications. Conventional wisdom has held that these medications lose efficacy if used on a daily basis for more than a few weeks (Sateia and Nowell, 2004) and most are approved by the FDA for short-term use only. However, some authors see this as an unproven and mistaken belief that leads to undertreatment and that developed only because of the short length of most drug trials. What is clear is that many patients do take these medications for months and even years and feel benefit from them despite concerns about side effects and the accumulation of metabolites. A few longer-term studies have been done with the newer non-benzodiazepine agents, which suggest that while efficacy for sleep latency may decline over time, total sleep time may be preserved even with long-term use. A study of subjects who were taking benzodiazepines for sleep found that 100% felt that the medications were still helping almost 5 years after beginning treatment (Mendelson, 2003). Without sleep studies it is difficult to confirm the veracity of such findings, as patients' anxiety about sleep and misperceptions about the nature of sleep lend themselves to the possibility of a placebo response. It is preferable that patients use such medications only as needed, a common recommendation being that after a night of use, the patient should try to sleep the following night without medication. If sleep is unsatisfactory, a second night without medication should be attempted, on the grounds that the person will now be tired and thus more likely to sleep. If the second night's sleep is also unsatisfactory, medication should be used on the third night and then the cycle repeated. Despite the wisdom of this advice in terms of preventing dependence, in practice many patients prefer the security of nightly long-term medication.

Medications from a number of different classes, each with its own advantages and drawbacks, have been used for relief of insomnia. The benzodiazepines have a long record of use and relative safety, but regular use can lead to dependence. Agents with a more rapid onset and shorter half-life may be most useful for early and middle insomnia, while those with a longer half-life may be more appropriate for treatment of later insomnia. Drawbacks include misuse, diversion to the street market, accumulation of metabolites with impairment of daytime function, and slower metabolism for some members of this class in the context of liver dysfunction. For individuals living with HIV, the risk of drug–drug interactions with ART further limits treatment options. Metabolism of alprazolam, triazolam, and midazolam is significantly inhibited by ritonavir, amprenavir, efavirenz, and delavirdine through the cytochrome 3A4 enzyme, potentially causing respiratory depression, fatigue, and depression or worsening cognitive impairment (Wyszynski et al., 2003). Lorazepam, oxazepam, and temazepam, which bypass oxidative metabolism, avoid these interactions and may be better options.

The non-benzodiazepine hypnotics, zaleplon and zolpidem, act at the benzodiazepine receptor. Zolpidem is reported to have less effect on sleep stages than the benzodiazepines maintaining time spent in N3 deep sleep. Because of their rapid onset, these agents are most useful for individuals with early insomnia, although a slow-release form of zolpidem is available and may be helpful in middle and late insomnia. Concerned that both the regular-release and slow-release forms of zolpidem might cause next-day impairment of driving and other activities that require alertness, the FDA has suggested that the initial dose for women should be 5 mg if using the regular-release formulation and 6.25 mg for the slow-release form. No specific dose recommendation was made for men, but in this population with multiple medical comorbidities, caution is always appropriate. An ultra-low-dose formulation of zolpidem has been released to treat persons with middle-of-the-night awakening, but here, too, caution should be used to ensure there is sufficient time to adequately metabolize the drug before the patient would need to be awake and alert. Because of its very rapid onset, only minimal physical tolerance to zaleplon develops and rapid discontinuance is possible. Eszopiclone, the newest member of this class, has been found to have sustained effectiveness in a 6-month study (NIH, 2005).

As previously noted, the orexin system helps sustain wakefulness, and suvorexant is the first FDA-approved orexin receptor antagonist that treats difficulty falling asleep and staying asleep. It has been classified as a controlled substance owing to the potential for abuse and dependence and should be used with caution in patients with a history of substance abuse. It is metabolized primarily by CYP3A and is not recommended for use with strong CYP3A inhibitors. A lower dose should be used with moderate inhibitors.

Chloral hydrate is still used in some settings. It is an effective hypnotic with rapid onset but combines the possibility of rapidly increasing tolerance with a narrow therapeutic index that can lead to inadvertent overdose. It can also increase warfarin levels and has active metabolites that can lead to morning sleepiness. Barbiturates are sedating but have significant risk of abuse and lethality and have not been studied for the short- or long-term treatment of insomnia (NIH, 2005). Use of both chloral hydrate and barbiturates is contraindicated in persons with HIV for multiple reasons, including the possibility of abuse, and drug–drug interactions in this population with a high prevalence of comorbid liver dysfunction.

The use of over-the-counter and prescribed medications, approved for other conditions but with sedating side effects, for sleep promotion has become increasingly common. However, no long-term studies have been done on the effectiveness of these agents, and the risk–benefit ratio may not be favorable to their use (NIH, 2005).

Antihistamines, particularly H1 receptor antagonists such as diphenhydramine, can have sedation as a desired side effect and are often considered safe alternatives to sleep medications. In addition, they are inexpensive and can be bought without a prescription. However, these agents can cause daytime sleepiness and have anticholinergic side effects and can interact with other medications.

The tricyclic antidepressants have been used to promote sleep, again making use of their well-known side effect of sedation, and may be a good choice if depressive symptoms are also present. However, these agents are far from benign, can be lethal in overdose, and have a broad profile of potentially harmful side effects in addition to sedation. Doxepin, which is highly sedating because of its antihistaminic properties, has been released in a low-dose formulation, aiming at patients with middle-of-the-night awakening. Trazodone has found a niche as a sleep medication, is nonaddictive, may treat concomitant depression in adequate doses, and is among the most commonly prescribed sleep aids. However, it has been reported to cause priapism as well as lower seizure threshold and cause postural hypotension.

The sedating antipsychotics have also been used for treating insomnia and clearly have a role when psychosis is also present. However, these are not drugs to be prescribed lightly, as the risks of using these agents are well known; they include anticholinergic side effects and weight gain; development of the metabolic syndrome, neuroleptic malignant syndrome, and tardive dyskinesia; and even increased risk of prolonged QTc interval, stroke, and death.

Gabapentin is a relatively benign agent that may help sleep and is safe in liver disease because of its renal excretion. It would not be an ideal sleep medication for patients receiving hemodialysis as it would persist unchanged until the next dialysis treatment.

In a medically fragile population receiving multiple medications, starting doses of all the agents discussed here should be reduced.

Herbal preparations such as valerian, which with its derivatives is the most common herbal treatment for insomnia (Buysse, 2013), kava-kava, broom, and passionflower are said to promote sleep but raise similar concerns regarding bioavailability, efficacy, and drug interactions (Krahn, 2011). L-tryptophan, an endogenous amino acid, has been suggested as a possible sleep aid, but studies have been limited and drug interactions may lead to toxicity (NIH, 2005).

The website of the AIDS Institute of the New York State Department of Health is an excellent source for information on pharmacological and nonpharmacological strategies for treating insomnia in persons with HIV. Guidelines are updated frequently and can be accessed at www.hivguidelines.org.

CONCLUSION

Insomnia can be a draining and debilitating result of HIV infection and may even worsen outcome. Comorbidity with other non-sleep mental disorders may increase the risk of developing insomnia in persons with HIV. Physician awareness of the potential for insomnia may facilitate its diagnosis and treatment. Because of the burden imposed by insomnia, the benefits of the supervised use of appropriate medications may outweigh the risks, although caution must be used in this medically fragile population. Treatment that includes a cognitive-behavioral approach and education around sleep hygiene may lessen dependence on medication and reduce the frequency of their use.

REFERENCES

Adrian J, Garma L (2010). Neurobiology of insomnia. In SR Pandi-Perumal, M Kramer (eds.), *Sleep and Mental Illness* (pp. 51–59). Cambridge, UK: Cambridge University Press.

American Psychiatric Association (APA) (2013). *Desk Reference to the Diagnostic Criteria from DSM-5* (pp. 181–182). Alexandria, VA: American Psychiatric Association.

Babson KA, Heinz AJ, Bonn-Miller MO (2013). HIV medication adherence and HIV symptom severity: the roles of sleep quality and memory. *AIDS Patient Care STDs* 26(10):544–552.

Bourne KS, Mills GH, Minelli C (2008). Melatonin therapy to improve sleep in critically ill patients: encouraging results from a small randomized trial. *Crit Care* 12:R52.

Buysse DJ (2008). Chronic insomnia. *Am J Psychiatry* 165(6):678–686.

Buysse DJ (2013). Insomnia. *JAMA* 309(7):706–716.

Buysse DJ, Reynolds CF, Monk TH, Berman SR, Kupfer DJ (1998). The Pittsburgh Sleep Quality Index: a new instrument for psychiatric practice and research. *Psychol Res* 28:193–213.

Ciesla JA, Roberts E (2001). Meta-analysis of relationship between HIV infection and risk for depressive disorder. *Am J Psychiatry* 158:725–730.

Clark JP, Sampair CS, Kofuji P, Nath A, Ding JM (2005). HIV protein, transactivator of transcription, alters circadian rhythms though the light entrainment pathway. *Am J Physiol Regul Integr Comp Physiol* 289:R656–R662.

Darko DF, Mitler MM, Henriksen SJ (1995). Lentiviral infection, immune response peptides and sleep. *Adv Neuroimmunol* 5:57–77.

Darko DF, Mitler MM, Miller JC (1998). Growth hormone, fatigue, poor sleep and disability in HIV infection. *Neuroendocrinology* 67:317–324.

de Jonghe A, Korevaar JC, van Munster BC, de Rooij SE (2010). Effectiveness of melatonin treatment on circadian rhythm disturbance in dementa: are there implications for delirium? A systematic review. *Int J Geriatr Psychiatry* 25(12):1201–1208.

Ebben MR, Fine L (2010). Insomnia: a risk for future psychiatric illness. In SR Pandi-Perumal, M Kramer (eds.), *Sleep and Mental Illness* (pp 154–164). Cambridge, UK: Cambridge University Press.

Epstein LJ, Strollo PJ, Donegan RB, Delman J, Hendrix C, Westbrook PR (1995). Obstructive sleep apnea in patients with human immunodeficiency virus (HIV) disease. *Sleep* 18:368–376.

Ferguson SA, Rajaratnam SM, Dawson D (2010). Melatonin agonists and insomnia. *Exp Rev Neurotheraputics* 10:305–318.

Ferini-Strambi L, Oldani A, Tirloni G, Zuconi M, Castagna A, Lazzarin A, Smirne S (1995). Slow-wave sleep and cyclic alternative pattern (CAP) in HIV-infected asymptomatic men. *Sleep* 18:446–450.

Gamaldo CE, Spira AP, Kock RS, et al. (2013). Sleep, function and HIV: a multi-method assessment. *AIDS Behav* 17(8):2808–2815.

Gutierrez F, Navarro A, Padilla S, Anton R, Masia M, Borras J, Marti-Hidalgo A (2005). Prediction of neuropsychiatric adverse events associated with long-term efavirenz therapy using plasma drug level monitoring. *Clin Infec Dis* 41(11):1648–1653.

Hauri PJ (2003). Clinical work with insomnia: state of the art. In MP Szuba, DJ Kloss, DF Dinges (eds.), *Insomnia: Principles and Management* (pp. 75–82). Cambridge, UK: Cambridge University Press.

Iaboni A, Moldofsky H (2010). Sleep and post-traumatic stress disorder. In SR Pandi-Permaul, M Kramer (eds.), *Sleep and Mental Illness* (pp. 326–340). Cambridge, UK: Cambridge University Press.

Jean-Louis G, Weber KM, Aouizerat BE, et al. (2012). Insomnia symptoms and HIV infection among participants in the Women's Interagency HIV Study. *Sleep* 35(1):131–137.

Johns M (1991). A new method for measuring daytime sleepiness: the Epworth Sleepiness Scale. *Sleep* 14:540–545.

Kelly B, Raphael B, Judd F, et al. (1998). Post-traumatic stress disorder in response to HIV infection. *Gen Hosp Psychiatry* 20:345–352.

Kloss JD, Szuba MP (2003). Insomnia in psychiatric disorders. In MP Szuba, JD Kloss, DF Dinges (eds.), *Insomnia: Principles and Management* (pp. 43–72). Cambridge, UK: Cambridge University Press.

Krahn LE (2011). Sleep disorders. In J Levenson (ed.), *Textbook of Psychosomatic Medicine*, 2nd ed. (pp. 335–359). Washington, DC: American Psychiatric Publishing.

Krystal AD, Benca RM, Kilduff TS (2013). Understanding the sleep–wake cycle: sleep, insomnia and the orexin system. *J Clin Psychiatry* 74(Suppl 1):3–20.

Lee K, Gay C, Portillo CJ, Coggins T, Davis H, Pullinger CR, Aouizerat BE (2012). Types of sleep problems in adults living with HIV/AIDS. *J Clin Sleep Med* 8(1):67–75.

Low Y, Goforth HW, Omonuwa T, Preud'homme Y, Edinger J, Krystal A (2012). Comparison of polysomnographic data in age-, sex-, and Axis I psychiatric diagnosis matched HIV sero-positive and sero-negative insomnia patients. *Clin Neurophysiol* 23(12):2402–2405.

Martin JL, Ancoli-Israel S (2003). Insomnia in older adults. In MP Szuba, JD Kloss, DF Dinges (eds.), *Insomnia: Principles and Management* (pp. 136–154). Cambridge UK: Cambridge University Press.

McCleery J, Cohen DA, Sharpley AL (2014). Pharmacotherapies for sleep disturbances in Alzheimer's disease. *Cochrane Database Syst Rev* Issue 3 Art:CD009178.

McDaniel JS, Brown L, Cournos F, for Work Group on HIV/AIDS (2000). Practice guideline for the treatment of patients with HIV/AIDS. *Am J Psychiatry* 157(11 Suppl):1–62.

Mendelson W (2003). Long-term use of hypnotic medications. In MP Szuba, JD Kloss, DF Dinges (eds.), *Insomnia: Principles and Management* (pp. 115–124). Cambridge UK: Cambridge University Press.

National Institutes of Health (NIH) (2005). NIH State-of-the-Science Conference Statement. Manifestations and management of chronic insomnia in adults. *NIH Consens State Sci Statements* 22(2):1–30.

Nissen C, Nofzinger EA (2007). Sleep and depression: a functional neuroimaging perspective. In SR Pandi-Perumal, RR Ruoti, M Kramer (eds.), *Sleep and Psychosomatic Medicine* (pp. 51–66). Abingdon, UK: Informa UK.

Norman SE, Chediak AD, Freeman C, et al. (1992). Sleep disturbances in men with asymptomatic human immunodeficiency (HIV) infection. *Sleep* 15:150–155.

Nunnari G, Nigro L, Palermo F, Leto D, Pomerantz RJ, Cacopardo B (2003). Reduction of serum melatonin levels in HIV-1-infected individuals parallels disease progression: correlation with serum interleukin-12 levels. *Infection* 31:379–382.

Omonuwa TS, Goforth HW, Preud'homme X, Krystal AD (2009). The pharmacologic management of insomnia in patients with HIV. *J Clin Sleep Med* 5(3):251–262.

Perkins DO, Leserman J, Stern RA, Baum SF, Liao D, Golden RN, Evans DL (1995). Somatic symptoms and HIV infection: relationship to depressive symptoms and indicators of HIV disease. *Am J Psychiatry* 155:1776–1781.

Pollmacher T, Mullington J, Korth C, Hinze-Selch D (1995). The influence of host defense activation on sleep in humans. *Adv Neuroimmunol* 5(2):155–169.

Reid S, Dwyer J (2005). Insomnia in HIV infection: a systematic review of prevalence, correlates and management. *Psychosom Med* 67(2):260–269.

Sack RL, Hughes RJ, Pires ML, Lewy AJ (2003). The sleep-promoting effects of melatonin. In ML Szuba, JD Kloss, DF Dinges (eds.), *Insomnia, Principles and Management* (pp. 96–114). Cambridge, UK: Cambridge University Press.

Sateia MJ, Nowell PD (2004) Insomnia. *Lancet* 364(9449):1959–1973.

Schulz R, Lohmeyer J, Seeger W (2003). Obstructive sleep apnea due to HIV-associated lipodystrophy. *Clin Infect Dis* 37:1398–1399.

Seay JS, McIntosh R, Fekete EM, Fletcher MA, Kumar M, Schneiderman N, Antoni MH (2013). Self-reported sleep disturbance is associated with lower CD4 count and 24h urine dopamine levels in ethnic minority women living with HIV. *Psychoneuroendocrinology* 38(11):2647–2653.

Staedt J, Rupprecht-Mrozek S (2010). Sleep in dementia. In SR Pandi-Perumal, M Kramer (eds.), *Sleep and Mental Illness* (pp. 226–242). Cambridge, UK: Cambridge University Press

Stepanski E, Rybarczyk G, Lopez M, Stevens S (2003). Assessment and treatment of sleep disorders in older adults: a review for rehabilitation psychologists. *Rehabil Psychol* 48:23–36.

Terstegge K, Henkes H, Scheuler W, Hansen ML, Ruf B, Kubicki S (1993). Spectral power and coherence analysis of sleep EEG in AIDS patients: decrease in interhemispheric coherence. *Sleep* 16:137–145.

Troxel WM, Buysse DJ, Matthews KA, et al. (2010). Sleep symptoms predict the development of the metabolic syndrome. *Sleep* 33:33–40.

Watkins CC, Della Penna ND, Angelino AA, Treisman GJ (2011). HIV/AIDS. In JL Levenson (ed.), *The American Psychiatric Publishing Textbook of Psychosomatic Medicine*, 2nd ed. (pp. 637–666). Arlington, VA: American Psychiatric Publishing.

Wyszynski AA, Bruno B, Ying P, Chuan L, Friedlander M, Rubenstein B (2003). The HIV-infected patient. In AA Wyszynski, B Wyszynski (eds.), *Manual of Psychiatric Care for the Medically Ill* (pp. 171–201). Washington, DC: American Psychiatric Publishing.

Xie L, Kong H, Xu Q, et al. (2013). Sleep drives metabolite clearance from the adult brain. *Science* 342 (6156):373–377.

24.

FATIGUE AND HIV

Anna L. Dickerman and William Breitbart

Fatigue is a common symptom reported by patients with HIV and AIDS and is associated with reduced quality of life and impaired physical functioning (Breitbart et al., 1998; Ferrando et al., 1998; Vogl et al., 1999). Patients regard fatigue as an important condition to be addressed because it is disabling and distressing (Barroso and Voss, 2013; Barroso et al., 2014; Jaggers et al., 2014; Sharpe and Wilks, 2002), yet typically it has been overlooked and undertreated by physicians (Dittner et al., 2004). Fatigue has also been associated with impaired treatment adherence in HIV (Al-Dakkak et al., 2013; Bhat et al., 2010; Tabatabai et al., 2014). Increasingly, clinicians caring for persons with HIV and AIDS have been giving more attention to symptom management and quality of life and thus should be familiar with major issues in fatigue assessment and treatment. This is especially true for psychiatrists who take care of persons with severe and complex medical illness (consultation-liaison psychiatrists or psychosomatic medicine psychiatrists), given their ability to distinguish between medical and psychiatric contributors to fatigue and their proficiency in both psychotherapeutic and psychopharmacological interventions for reducing fatigue or helping the patient better cope with fatigue. At the same time, there is a paucity of studies of fatigue in the post-antiretroviral therapy (ART) era (Claborn et al., 2015).

This chapter reviews the definition and assessment of fatigue, the prevalence of fatigue in HIV/AIDS and its impact on persons living with HIV or AIDS, medical and psychological causes of fatigue, and evidence-based strategies for intervention.

DEFINING FATIGUE

Fatigue is a poorly defined symptom that may involve physical, mental, emotional, and motivational components (Ream and Richardson, 1996; Sharpe and Wilks, 2002; Smets et al., 1993). It is typically defined as extreme and persistent tiredness, weakness, or exhaustion that may be mental, physical, or both (Dittner et al., 2004). Thus, *fatigue* can refer to a subjective sensation or to objectively impaired performance (Sharpe and Wilks, 2002). Furthermore, patients use various words to describe fatigue (Smets et al., 1993), each of which may point to a different underlying etiology. For example, fatigue described as "anhedonia" (loss of interest and enjoyment) suggests depression, whereas prominent "sleepiness"

indicates potential sleep disruption, which may in turn be due to a variety of possible factors (Greenberg, 1998; Sharpe and Wilks, 2002). It is important, therefore, to obtain a descriptive account of the nature of the patient's fatigue in order to investigate all possible causes and facilitate accurate diagnosis (Greenberg, 1998).

Recognizing the need for a standardized definition of fatigue, Cella and colleagues (1998) proposed a set of diagnostic criteria for inclusion in the World Health Organization (WHO) *International Classification of Diseases*, Tenth Revision (ICD-10). The criteria listed in Box 24.1 were originally developed in the context of cancer but can also be applied to patients with HIV/AIDS. A study evaluating this clinical syndrome approach reported preliminary evidence of its reliability and validity (Sadler et al., 2002). Fifty-one patients received a standardized interview designed to identify the presence of a clinical syndrome of cancer-related fatigue; these patients also completed self-report measures of fatigue, depression, and health-related quality of life. Comparisons among independent raters demonstrated high rates of reliability for the presence or absence of a cancer-related fatigue syndrome and its symptoms. Twenty-one percent of the patients met diagnostic criteria for a cancer-related fatigue syndrome. These patients reported more severe, frequent, and pervasive fatigue than did patients who did not meet diagnostic criteria; they also demonstrated poorer role function, less vitality, and more depressive symptomatology. Thus, this newly developed clinical syndrome approach appears to have great utility in identifying patients who experience clinically significant, illness-related fatigue.

The 2017 revision of the *International Classification of Diseases*, 10th Revision, Clinical Modification (ICD-10-CM; WHO, 2017) defines fatigue as "a condition marked by drowsiness and an unusual lack of energy and mental alertness and a condition marked by extreme tiredness and inability to function due lack of energy. It can be caused by many things, including illness, injury, or drugs." See Box 24.2 for a current description of symptoms of cancer-related fatigue, which can also be applied to patients with HIV/AIDS.

ASSESSMENT OF FATIGUE

Fatigue is a concept that is not only difficult to define but also challenging to quantify. Nonetheless, reliable and valid

Box 24.1 PROPOSED ICD-10 CRITERIA FOR
CANCER-RELATED FATIGUE (1998)

Six (or more) of the following symptoms have been present every day or nearly every day during the same 2-week period in the past month, and at least one of the symptoms is (A1) significant fatigue:

A1. Significant fatigue, diminished energy, or increased need to rest, disproportionate to any recent change in activity level

A2. Complaints of generalized weakness or limb heaviness

A3. Diminished concentration or attention

A4. Decreased motivation or interest to engage in usual activities

A5. Insomnia or hypersomnia

A6. Experience of sleep as unrefreshing or nonrestorative

A7. Perceived need to struggle to overcome inactivity

A8. Marked emotional reactivity (e.g., sadness, frustration, or irritability) to feeling fatigued

A9. Difficulty completing daily tasks attributed to feeling fatigued

A10. Perceived problems with short-term memory

A11. Post-exertional malaise lasting several hours

B. The symptoms cause clinically significant distress or impairment in social, occupational, or other important areas of functioning.

C. There is evidence from the history, physical examination, or laboratory findings that the symptoms are a consequence of cancer or cancer therapy.

D. The symptoms are not primarily a consequence of comorbid psychiatric disorders such as major depression, somatization disorder, somatoform disorder, or delirium.

Source: Cella D, Peterman A, Passik S, et al. Progress toward guidelines for the management of fatigue. *Oncology* 1998;12:369–377, with permission from Karga AG, Basel.

Box 24.2 ICD-10-CM CRITERIA FOR
CANCER-RELATED FATIGUE (2017)

HIV-related fatigue is categorized under Neoplasm- or Cancer-Related Fatigue.

Clinical Information

- A condition marked by drowsiness and an unusual lack of energy and mental alertness. It can be caused by many things, including illness, injury, or drugs.

- A condition marked by extreme tiredness and inability to function due lack of energy. Fatigue may be acute or chronic.

- A disorder characterized by a decrease in consciousness characterized by mental and physical inertness.

- A disorder characterized by a state of generalized weakness with a pronounced inability to summon sufficient energy to accomplish daily activities.

- A general state of sluggishness, listless, or uninterested, with being tired, and having difficulty concentrating and doing simple tasks. It may be related to depression or drug addiction.

- A state of sluggishness, listless, and apathy

- A survey question about whether a person has experienced a lack of energy.

- An overwhelming sustained sense of exhaustion and decreased capacity for physical and mental work at usual level

- Characterized by a lack of vitality or energy.

- Decreased consciousness characterized by mental and physical inertness.

- Exhaustion that interferes with physical and mental activities

- Can be described as "I have a lack of energy."

- That state, following a period of mental or bodily activity, characterized by a lessened capacity for work and reduced efficiency or accomplishment, usually accompanied by a feeling of weariness, sleepiness, or irritability.

- The state of weariness following a period of exertion, mental or physical, characterized by a decreased capacity for work and reduced efficiency to respond to stimuli.

Source: World Health Organization (2017). *International Classification of Diseases*, 10th Revision, Clinical Modification (ICD-10-CM). Geneva: World Health Organization.

---

tools for assessment are crucial for improved management and research progress (Dittner et al., 2004). There are a variety of standardized self-report scales, most of which have been developed in the context of cancer and chronic illnesses other than HIV, that can also be used to measure fatigue in patients with HIV and AIDS. These are summarized in Box 24.3. Not surprisingly, the information provided by these scales depends on the questions asked and, therefore, reflects the scale writer's own understanding of fatigue. The patient, in turn, may have his or her own interpretation of the questions. Thus, different scales may measure fundamentally different aspects, or even potentially distinct conceptions, of fatigue. The challenge facing the clinician or researcher, then, is to choose a reliable and valid tool for the measurement of fatigue that is most adequately suited to his or her purposes (Dittner et al., 2004).

The oldest scales assessing fatigue are dichotomous, meaning that fatigue is measured as either present or absent. These include the Pearson-Byars Fatigue Checklist (Pearson and Byars, 1956), Profile of Mood States (POMS) Fatigue and Vigor Subscale (Cella et al., 1987), the Fatigue Severity Scale (Krupp, LaRocca, et al., 1989), and the European Organization for Research and Treatment of Cancer Quality

Scales Using a Dichotomous Approach

1. Pearson-Byars Fatigue Checklist (Pearson and Byars, 1956)

2. Profile of Mood States Fatigue and Vigor Subscale (Cella et al., 1987)

3. Fatigue Severity Scale (Krupp et al., 1989)

4. European Organization for Research and Treatment of Cancer Quality of Life Questionnaire Fatigue Subscale (Aaronson et al., 1993)

Scales Using a Unidimensional Approach

1. Karnofsky Performance Status (Schag et al., 1984)

2. Visual Analogue Scale for Fatigue (Lee et al., 1991)

3. Chalder Fatigue Scale (Chalder et al., 1993)

4. Global Fatigue Index (Bormann et al., 2001)

Scales Using a Multidimensional Approach

1. Functional Assessment of Chronic Illness Therapy-Fatigue (Cella et al., 1987)

2. Piper Fatigue Scale (Piper et al., 1989)

3. Fatigue Symptom Inventory (Hann et al., 1998)

4. Brief Fatigue Inventory (Mendoza et al., 1999)

5. Multidimensional Assessment of Fatigue (Belza, 1995)

6. Identity-Consequence Fatigue Scale (Paddison et al., 2006)

Specific Scales for Persons with HIV

1. Sleep and Infection Questionnaire (Darko et al., 1992)

2. HIV-Related Fatigue Scale (Barroso and Lynn, 2002)

Nonspecific Symptom Assessment Scales that Include Fatigue Items

1.1. Memorial Symptom Assessment Scale (Portenoy et al., 1994)

2. Sign and Symptom Check-List for HIV (Holzemer et al., 1999)

3. Revised Sign and Symptom Check-List for HIV (Holzemer et al., 2001)

Source: Dufour N, Dubé B, Breitbart W (2005). HIV-related fatigue. In J DeLuca (ed.), *Fatigue as a Window to the Brain* (pp. 188–207). Cambridge, MA: MIT Press, with permission.

of Life Questionnaire (EORTC-QLQ-C30) Fatigue Subscale (Aaronson et al., 1993).

Newer scales have taken a unidimensional approach. The Visual Analogue Scale for Fatigue (VAS-F), for example, chiefly probes intensity (Lee et al., 1991). The VAS-F is organized into energy and fatigue dimensions and has good psychometric properties (Dittner et al., 2004). The Karnofsky Performance Status, by contrast, probes mainly consequences of fatigue (Schag et al., 1984). The limitations of such unidimensional scales include the presence of confounding factors such as pain.

Multidimensional scales include the Fatigue Symptom Inventory (Hann et al., 1998) and the Brief Fatigue Inventory (Mendoza et al., 1999), both originally developed to assess the severity and impact of fatigue in cancer and palliative care populations. The Piper Fatigue Scale (PFS) was originally developed for use in cancer patients (Piper et al., 1989). It consists of affective, cognitive, sensory, and severity subscales and has been used to measure fatigue in individuals with HIV. Its major shortcomings include the lengthy amount of time it takes to complete it and the difficulty some patients have in understanding it (Dittner et al., 2004). The Multidimensional Assessment of Fatigue (MAF) scale is a revision of the PFS developed for use among patients with rheumatoid arthritis (Belza, 1995). The Global Fatigue Index (GFI) stems from the MAF and has been validated for use in HIV patients (Bormann et al., 2001). The scale is easily administered and takes only about 5 minutes to complete. The ultimate GFI score is unidimensional. Originally developed to assess fatigue in cancer, the Functional Assessment of Chronic Illness Therapy-Fatigue (FACIT-F) scale has also demonstrated utility in other patient populations including those with HIV (Butt et al., 2013). The Identity-Consequence Fatigue Scale (ICSFS) has 28 items and five subscales, all of which have shown high internal reliability and discriminant validity from depression and anxiety (Paddison et al., 2006).

Although there is no widely recognized gold-standard assessment scale for HIV-related fatigue, there are several recently developed fatigue scales that are specific to HIV and AIDS. The Sleep and Infection Questionnaire, developed by Darko et al. (1992), for example, is an 11-item scale that examines the affect of fatigue on mental agility, but it does not encompass the full fatigue experience in HIV. The HIV-Related Fatigue Scale (HRFS), developed by Barroso and Lynn (2002), consists of 56 items, incorporating elements from five preexisting scales (MAF, General Fatigue Scale, Fatigue Impact Scale, Fatigue Assessment Index, and the Sleep and Infection Questionnaire) plus four additional items. The HRFS probes three domains: intensity, consequences, and circumstances of fatigue. It shows much promise for assessing fatigue in HIV/AIDS, as it encompasses most elements of fatigue specific to persons with HIV and AIDS (Pence et al., 2008).

Finally, there are certain symptom scales utilized in HIV studies that include fatigue-specific items (though the scale itself assesses numerous symptom domains or clusters). Originally studied in oncological patient populations, the Memorial Symptom Assessment Scale (MSAS) is a reliable and valid instrument that assesses not only prevalence of physical and psychological symptoms but also distress associated with these symptoms. This can be particularly useful when the clinician or investigator seeks to gain information about the effect of fatigue on overall quality of life (Portenoy et al., 1994). The Sign and Symptom Checklist for Persons with HIV (SSC-HIV) is a reliable and valid 26-item self-report questionnaire containing six symptom clusters (Holzemer et al., 1999).

Given the multifactorial nature of fatigue, accessory scales (e.g., depression scales) and measurements of certain biological parameters (e.g., disease progression indicators such as viral load and CD4 count) should be used in addition to fatigue assessment tools to obtain the most complete evaluation of a patient's fatigue. In particular, the complex interrelationships between fatigue and psychiatric disturbances such as depression and anxiety merit special attention and will be further explored later in this chapter.

PREVALENCE AND IMPACT OF FATIGUE IN HIV/AIDS

The high frequency and distressing nature of fatigue in both "asymptomatic" individuals with HIV and persons with advanced AIDS has been well documented. These findings are summarized in Table 24.1. Of note, even in the era of antiretroviral therapy (ART), fatigue is a common and often severe complaint among persons with HIV (Payne et al., 2013). Estimates of the prevalence of HIV-related fatigue range from 2–27% among individuals with early, "asymptomatic" HIV seropositivity to 30–54% among persons with AIDS (Anderson and Grady, 1994; Hoover et al., 1993; Longo et al., 1990; Miller et al., 1991; Revicki et al., 1994; Vlahov

et al., 1994). Darko and colleagues (1992), for example, found that more than 50% of a sample of 14 AIDS patients suffered from fatigue, in comparison to 10% of 50 HIV-seronegative controls. This study found that persons with AIDS who experience fatigue sleep more than persons with AIDS without fatigue. Fatigued individuals also experienced greater interference with work, self-care, social interactions, and daily activities. In a study conducted by Longo and colleagues (1990), fatigue was identified as a "major physical concern" in 41% of a sample of 34 patients with AIDS. Vlahov and colleagues (1994) examined a sample of 562 HIV-seropositive intravenous drug abusers who did not satisfy criteria for AIDS and found that 19–30% of the individuals experienced fatigue. Other studies have demonstrated similar findings (Anderson and Grady, 1994; Crocker, 1989; Miller et al., 1991; Revicki et al., 1994; Richman et al., 1987).

In a comprehensive study of fatigue in a heterogeneous population of 429 patients with AIDS who were ambulatory, Breitbart and colleagues (1998) assessed the frequency of fatigue and its medical and psychological correlates. They administered the Memorial Symptom Assessment Scale (MSAS) and the AIDS Physical Symptom Checklist (PSC) to divide patients into fatigue and no-fatigue groups. Patients who endorsed both of the fatigue items from the MSAS and the AIDS physical symptom checklists were classified as having fatigue. Self-report inventories were also used to assess psychological stress, depression, and quality of life. More than 85% of the patients with AIDS endorsed "lack of energy" on the MSAS, while greater than 55% endorsed "persistent or frequent fatigue lasting 2 weeks or longer" on the PSC. Of the individuals studied, 46.9% were distressed by their lack of energy, while 39.9% were "somewhat" distressed. Both MSAS and PSC fatigue items were endorsed by 52.7% of the patients. There were no associations found between fatigue

Table 24.1 PREVALENCE OF FATIGUE IN HIV/AIDS

STUDY	POPULATION	PREVALENCE
Longo et al., 1990	Gay men with AIDS	41%
Darko et al., 1992	HIV+ gay men	57% CDC stage IV
		11% CDC stage III
		10% HIV-negative controls
Hoover et al., 1993	HIV+ "asymptomatic" gay men	9% HIV+
		6% HIV-negative controls
Vlahov et al., 1994	HIV+ male and female intravenous drug users	19.4–30%, depending on CD4 counts
Breitbart et al., 1998	Ambulatory HIV/AIDS patients	54%
Ferrando et al., 1998	HIV+ gay or bisexual men	6–17%, depending on CD4 counts
Vogl et al., 1999	AIDS outpatients	85.1%

Source: Dufour N, Dubé B, Breitbart W (2005). HIV-related fatigue. In J DeLuca (ed.), *Fatigue as a Window to the Brain* (pp. 188–207). Cambridge, MA: MIT Press, with permission.

and education, age, or race. However, women were found to be significantly more susceptible to fatigue than men. This is not a surprising finding, given that fatigue has been reported as more common among women in both the general population and persons with cancer (Curt et al., 2000; Sharpe and Wilks, 2002), and female gender is considered a predisposing factor for fatigue (Sharpe and Wilks, 2002). Men whose primary risk behavior was having sex with men were less likely to experience fatigue than persons whose primary risk behavior was injection drug use or heterosexual contact. The study also found a correlation between the number of AIDS-related symptoms present on the PSC, particularly pain and fatigue. Finally, Breitbart et al. (1998) also indicated that fatigue was associated with (1) treatment for AIDS-related medical conditions, (2) decreased serum hemoglobin, and (3) higher psychological distress, more depressive symptoms, and greater hopelessness (as measured by the Brief Symptom Inventory, Beck Depression Inventory, Beck Hopelessness Scale, and the Functional Living Inventory for Cancer [modified for AIDS]).

In a later study also using the MSAS, Vogl and colleagues (1999) replicated some of these findings in a population of AIDS outpatients. For example, this particular study found that fatigue was highly prevalent (present in 85% of the sample) and that both the number of symptoms and symptom distress were highly associated with psychological distress and poor quality of life. However, Vogl et al. found no association between fatigue and gender. There has also been some discrepancy in findings regarding the correlation between fatigue and immunological compromise in persons with HIV disease. Several studies reported a higher prevalence of fatigue in patients with immunological compromise (Hoover et al., 1993; Lee et al., 1991; Walker et al., 1997), while others found no association between viral load and fatigue (Breitbart et al., 1998; Ferrando et al., 1998; Vlahov et al., 1994; Vogl et al., 1999). These differences probably result from methodological inconsistencies, discussion of which is beyond the scope of this chapter.

Voss (2005) studied variation in the intensity of fatigue according to selected demographic, cultural, and health/illness variables in 372 patients with HIV/AIDS. The UCSF Symptom Management Model was used to assess fatigue severity in a sample including 73% African Americans and 63% males; 58% of patients experienced moderate to severe fatigue intensity. Women, Hispanics, disabled persons, and individuals with inadequate income or insurance reported higher fatigue intensity scores. Braitstein and colleagues (2005) reported similar findings in a study comparing HIV-monoinfected individuals to patients co-infected with HIV and hepatitis C (HCV). Co-infected patients reported more symptoms consistent with depression, increased fatigue, and poorer quality of life. However, upon multivariate modeling, it was determined that this negative impact of HCV was better explained by the sociodemographic factors related to poverty and injection drug use than by HCV itself. The authors concluded that persons co-infected with HIV and HCV represent a patient population with significant physical and mental health challenges primarily related to socioeconomic issues

rather than HCV infection. The results of these two studies suggest the need for further gender- and ethnic-specific fatigue research, as well as symptom cluster research, in persons with HIV and AIDS.

ETIOLOGIES OF FATIGUE IN HIV/AIDS

Fatigue among persons with HIV is multifaceted and should be viewed as the final common pathway for a variety of causal factors (Sharpe and Wilks, 2002). Fatigue may be due to preexisting conditions in HIV-infected individuals (e.g., congestive heart failure), medication side effects, opportunistic infections, or other medical complications encountered throughout the illness. Finally, there are complex connections between psychiatric disturbances and fatigue in HIV illness. The underlying mechanisms of fatigue remain unclear, as certain hypotheses have not been tested adequately. These include fatigue as a potential result of the buildup of waste products such as pyruvic and lactic acid (Simonson, 1971). It has also been suggested that cytokine activation may lead to abnormalities in the hypothalamic–pituitary–adrenal (HPA) axis or to neurophysiological changes in the brain that ultimately cause fatigue (Ur et al., 1992). Cytokine polymorphisms are associated with fatigue in adults living with HIV/AIDS (Lee et al., 2014), adding to the existing evidence suggesting a link between inflammation and fatigue. Finally, hepatocyte toxicity may cause fatigue in persons with HIV. Bartlett and colleagues demonstrated that 75% of HIV-seropositive patients had abnormal liver function (Bartlett, 1996). Most liver disease in patients with HIV is due to co-infection with hepatitis C and/or hepatitis B viruses, as well as non-alcohol steatic hepatitis. Other commonly recognized mechanisms of HIV-related fatigue are reviewed here and summarized in Box 24.4.

ANEMIA

Anemia is one of numerous hematological complications that may occur in persons with HIV disease, including thrombocytopenia, lymphopenia, and neutropenia. It is considered a prognostic marker of disease progression and death in patients with HIV, independent of viral load and CD4 count (Moyle, 2002). There are multiple potential etiologies of anemia in HIV disease, including opportunistic infections; neoplasia (mostly lymphoma); chronic inflammation (which can lead to erythropoietin deficiency); dietary deficiency due to poor appetite, oral lesions, or difficulty with digestion or absorption; diarrhea; blood loss; histiocytosis; or bone marrow abnormalities such as myelodysplasia, myelofibrosis, or bone marrow suppression (Volberding, 2000). Up-regulation of cytokines (interferons, interleukin-1, tumor necrosis factor, and transforming growth factor) may also impair erythropoietin response and result in ineffective red blood cell production (Means, 1997). Finally, anemia may be iatrogenic, as pharmacological interventions for HIV may lead to myelosuppression. Specifically, dideoxynucleoside analogues as well as antimicrobials (e.g., pentamidine, trimethoprim, sulfonamides, ganciclovir, pyrimethamine) are among the more

Box 24.4 ETIOLOGIES OF FATIGUE IN HIV/AIDS

Physiological Factors

DIRECT EFFECTS OF HIV/AIDS

Peripheral and central nervous system
Hepatocyte toxicity
Cytokines

COMORBID MEDICAL CONDITIONS

Anemia
Hypogonadism
Hypo- or hyperthyroidism
Adrenal insufficiency
Opportunistic infections
Nutritional deficiencies

Treatment Effects

Medication side effects

Exacerbating Factors

Sleep disturbances
Lack of exercise
Inactivity
Pain syndromes

Psychological Factors

Depression
Anxiety
Coping with a chronic illness

Source: Dufour N, Dubé B, Breitbart W (2005). HIV-related fatigue. In J DeLuca (ed.), *Fatigue as a Window to the Brain* (pp. 188–207). Cambridge, MA: MIT Press, with permission.

common pharmacological causes of myelosuppression in HIV treatment (Pluda et al., 1991).

ENDOCRINOPATHIES

Hormonal imbalances are another potential contributing factor to fatigue in individuals with HIV. The HIV virus affects immunological cytokines, which may in turn influence various endocrine processes. The clinical correlates of these effects, however, remain unclear (Briggs and Beazlie, 1996). The HIV-related endocrinopathies are covered in depth in Chapter 45 of this book.

Hypogonadism and Low Testosterone

The most prevalent endocrinopathy present in HIV disease is hypogonadism. This encompasses impairment in testicular or ovarian function that may ultimately lead to low testosterone levels (Klauke et al., 1990). Decreased testosterone is associated with fatigue, low libido, impotency,

anorexia, weight loss, and depression. Approximately 25% of asymptomatic, untreated HIV-infected men and approximately 45% of untreated men diagnosed with AIDS are estimated to have low testosterone levels (Dobs et al., 1988). Possible mechanisms of hypogonadism include insufficient production of testosterone due to low stimulation by brain hormones, testicular damage, and side effects of medication.

Other Endocrine Abnormalities

Adrenal insufficiency is yet another possible physiological cause of fatigue in persons with HIV (Abbott et al., 1995; Norbiato et al., 1994; Piedrola et al., 1996). Possible mechanisms include infection (with HIV, cytomegalovirus, or tuberculosis), drugs, or psychological stress, which may increase the activity of the HPA axis. While it has been consistently demonstrated that cortisol levels are higher in individuals with HIV than in persons without HIV (Clerici et al., 1997; Enwonwu et al., 1996; Rondanelli et al., 1997), persons with HIV also have a reduced cortisol response to adrenocorticotropin hormone (ACTH) stimulation (Stolarczyk et al., 1998).

Hyperthyroidism and hypothyroidism can also both induce fatigue and should be considered when diagnosing a patient presenting with fatigue.

MALNUTRITION

In the era of ART, severe malnutrition states are no longer seen frequently in persons with AIDS who have access to care. Less severe malnutrition, however, is still seen and can contribute significantly to fatigue. Thus, it is important to identify and treat potential malnutrition. Persons with HIV and AIDS may have decreased appetite for a variety of possible reasons. These include nausea induced by medication, difficulty swallowing due to painful candida esophagitis, or malabsorption due to gastrointestinal parasitic infection (*Cryptosporidium, Microsporidium*), viral infection (cytomegalovirus), or neoplasia (Kaposi sarcoma). A frequent cause of nutritional deficits in HIV is medication-induced nausea. Patients often experience reduced appetite and take in less food because of nausea and/or vomiting caused by pharmacological interventions. This is particularly true for individuals receiving multidrug antiretroviral (ARV) therapy, especially early on in treatment with nucleoside reverse transcriptase inhibitors (NRTIs). Often this ARV-induced nausea occurs only upon initiation of therapy (Janoff and Smith, 2001).

TREATMENT-RELATED CAUSES OF FATIGUE

As described, there are a variety of iatrogenic mechanisms of fatigue in HIV. Antiretroviral therapy can cause fatigue (Margolis et al., 2014). Interferon alpha 2b, previously the only available treatment for HCV co-infection along with ribavirin, can also induce severe fatigue and malaise (Dietrich et al., 2014; Krown et al., 2006; Mandorfer et al., 2014; Sulkowski et al., 2014). The interferon-based treatments took a full 48 to 52 weeks to effect a cure of HCV in persons with HIV. The side effects, especially fatigue, were very difficult to tolerate. Fortunately, the development of HCV protease inhibitors such as boceprevir and teleprevir has enabled patients with access to them to have successful interferon-sparing treatment (Thomas, 2012). Sofosbuvir is a nucleotide inhibitor of HCV polymerase that is also effective (Gane et al., 2013). With these newer medications, the duration of treatment for co-infected persons with HIV/HCV is only 12 weeks and is very well tolerated. Even when these medications are used in combination with interferon, required courses of therapy are of much shorter duration than previously, owing to improved virological response rates. For a full discussion of HCV and its treatment please refer to Chapter 43 of this textbook.

To summarize, the major treatment-induced causes of fatigue in persons with HIV are myelosuppression and subsequent anemia, endocrinopathies such as hypogonadism, and malnutrition resulting from nausea and/or vomiting (Table 24.2).

PSYCHIATRIC DISTURBANCES AND FATIGUE

Depressive Disorders, Bipolar Disorders, and Anxiety Disorders

Anxiety and depression are the most commonly reported psychiatric disturbances in persons with HIV. Depressive and bipolar disorders and anxiety disorders are covered extensively in Chapters 15 and 18, respectively, of this book. Up to 83% of patients with HIV are diagnosed with depressive spectrum disturbances and 10–20% of persons with HIV suffer from major depressive disorders (Perdices et al., 1992). It can be very challenging to sort out fatigue, depression, and anxiety in patients with HIV (Walker et al., 1997), particularly because fatigue can be a symptom of both HIV-related disease and depressive disorders. There are also symptoms common to both fatigue and depression in particular, such as decreased energy and motivation, sleep disruptions, diminished concentration and attention, and problems with short-term memory. Finally, anxiety and depression are highly prevalent in persons with HIV. Thus it is necessary to clarify the relationship

between mood disturbances (particularly anxiety and depression) and fatigue for both clinicians and researchers in order to effectively evaluate and treat individuals with HIV disease.

Jacobsen and Weitzner (2003) proposed four important questions as a theoretical framework for this task. Although these questions were originally developed in the context of cancer, they are also applicable to HIV-related fatigue. They address (1) the conceptual similarities and differences between depression or anxiety and fatigue; (2) the extent to which anxiety and depression coexist with fatigue, and how they can be distinguished; (3) the causal link between fatigue and depression and anxiety; and (4) treatment implications of the relationship of fatigue to depression and anxiety. Jacobsen and Weitzner found that fatigue, anxiety, and depression have been assessed through three separate approaches in HIV/AIDS: the clinical-syndrome approach, which determines whether or not a mood disorder is present; the symptom-cluster approach, in which multiple symptoms of anxiety and depression are measured; and the single-symptom approach, which specifically measures symptoms of anxious and depressed mood. Fatigue has also been evaluated using these same methods.

There is an overlap between these three approaches in studies that have measured the relationship between fatigue, anxiety, and depression. Some of this research has suggested that fatigue in persons with HIV patients is secondary to depression. For example, Lyketsos and colleagues (1996) conducted a longitudinal study of patients with AIDS in order to examine the temporal relationship between fatigue and depression. They reported that depressive symptoms and fatigue are associated in close chronological proximity across various stages of HIV disease. Because they found no correlation between fatigue and immune or HIV illness measures, these researchers ultimately concluded that fatigue is a symptom of depression. In a study conducted with 20 HIV-seropositive men without AIDS, O'Dell and colleagues (1996) reported similar findings; they found no significant association between fatigue and physiological parameters (total protein, albumin, hematocrit, hemoglobin, and physical dimension score on the Sickness Impact Profile). Thus,

Table 24.2 ANTIRETROVIRAL SIDE EFFECTS LEADING OR CONTRIBUTING TO FATIGUE

| | SIDE EFFECT | | |
DRUG CLASS	FATIGUE	NAUSEA, VOMITING	ANEMIA
Nucleoside reverse transcriptase inhibitors	Lamivudine, abacavir	Lamivudine, zalcitabine, zidovudine	Zidovudine
Nucleotide reverse transcriptase inhibitors		Tenofovir	
Non-nucleoside reverse transcriptase inhibitors		Efavirenz	
Protease inhibitors	Amprenavir, saquinavir, lopinavir/ritonavir, ritonavir	Amprenavir, saquinavir, lopinavir/ritonavir, ritonavir, nelfinavir	Indinavir

Source: Dufour N, Dubé B, Breitbart W (2005). HIV-related fatigue. In J DeLuca (ed.), *Fatigue as a Window to the Brain* (pp. 188–207). Cambridge, MA: The MIT Press, with permission.

they concluded that fatigue is more strongly correlated with psychological than physical parameters. Henderson and colleagues (2005) also found that the presence of fatigue in individuals with HIV was more strongly associated with psychological factors than with advanced disease or the use of ART. Thus, these researchers also concluded that fatigue may suggest underlying depression and anxiety in these patients. Paddison et al. (2009) comprehensively assessed fatigue in 38 consecutive patients with HIV referred for treatment with the Identity-Consequence Fatigue Scale and found that depression, anxiety, and perceived stress explained between 20% and 75% of the variance in fatigue ratings. In a study of asymptomatic men with HIV, Perkins et al. (1995) found that depressive symptoms and major depression significantly predict the severity of fatigue at baseline and at 6-month follow-up. These results suggest that fatigue may be a manifestation of depression in the early stages of HIV disease.

Other research, however, has indicated that the relationship between depression and fatigue in HIV disease may be more complex. For example, Ferrando and colleagues (1998) reported that depressed men with HIV are more likely to experience clinical fatigue. However, after a 1-year follow-up, these researchers found an increase in depressive symptoms without a similar variance in fatigue. They concluded that although fatigue is associated with major depression and depressive symptoms, fatigue in advanced HIV illness may not merely be a symptom of depression. Breitbart and colleagues (1998) reported similar findings in the previously mentioned study of ambulatory patients with AIDS. While they found that greater than 70% of patients likely to have a depressive order suffered from fatigue, the majority (58%) of the sample with fatigue did not demonstrate any increase in depressive symptoms. Moreover, fatigue and depression provided unique contributions to the prediction of psychological distress and quality of life. Thus, the authors suggested that fatigue may be a symptom of depression in some, but certainly not all, fatigued patients with AIDS, and that the impact of fatigue on psychological function and quality of life is not merely a reflection of underlying depression. They also reported that patients with fatigue had significantly higher scores on measures assessing cognitive symptoms of depression and psychological distress, indicating the possibility that depression may in fact be the result of fatigue. Finally, Barroso and colleagues (2002) conducted a longitudinal study of 36 HIV-seropositive gay men over 7.5 years and found that fatigue was predicted by both physiological (CDC clinical status) and psychological (anxiety, hopelessness, social conflict, lack of satisfaction with support) risk factors. They reported, however, that depression was predicted only by psychological risk factors. Depression was strongly correlated with premorbid depression and fatigue correlated with premorbid fatigue. Depression present at the previous visit was correlated with fatigue, and fatigue at the previous visit correlated with depression scores. Thus, these results suggest that fatigue and depression play roles in mutually predicting one another in gay men with HIV disease.

Box 24.5 DIFFERENTIATING FATIGUE AND DEPRESSION IN HIV

Symptoms Common to Both Syndromes

Fatigue
Decreased energy
Increased need to rest
Anhedonia
Decreased motivation
Sadness, frustration, irritability
Insomnia or hypersomnia
Diminished concentration/attention
Perceived short-term memory problems

Symptoms and Factors Suggestive of Depression

Feelings of hopelessness, worthlessness, or guilt
Suicidal ideation, desire for death
History or family history of depression

In light of these findings, future research is necessary to aid in the clarification between depression and fatigue in persons with HIV and AIDS. In the meantime, we know that depressive symptoms due to fatigue are typically less severe, and that patients tend to attribute such symptoms to the consequences of fatigue. Depression, by contrast, is more likely in the presence of hopelessness, feelings of worthlessness and/or guilt, suicidal ideation, and a family history of depression (see Box 24.5).

Fatigue and Neuropsychological Function

Preliminary research has suggested a potential relationship between fatigue and central nervous system (CNS) involvement in HIV. Perkins et al. (1995) examined the relationship between insomnia and fatigue to indicators of mood disturbance and HIV severity. To assess disease severity, they measured CD4 counts and performed neuropsychological testing that encompassed both global and motor performance. They found that severity of depressive symptoms and self-reported dysphoric mood were related to the level of fatigue and insomnia, but that global and motor neuropsychological function were not significantly related to either fatigue or insomnia. However, at 6-month follow-up, there was a reduction in motor neuropsychological function that was associated with more complaints of fatigue. This finding was consistent even after controlling for depression. The researchers suggested that there might be a relationship between fatigue and HIV effects on the brain, proposing that fatigue may be a possible earlier indicator of CNS involvement. Please see Chapters 16 and 26 of this textbook for a detailed discussion of HIV-associated neurocognitive disorders and of HIV and the CNS.

TREATMENT STRATEGIES

Early, active management of fatigue is preferable before the symptom becomes chronic. Education is an important initial step in this respect, particularly because patients tend not to report fatigue unless directly asked. Patients and members of their support networks should be taught how to recognize signs and symptoms of fatigue to aid in its detection and treatment. Precipitating factors, such as acute physical stresses and psychological stresses, should be identified, as should perpetuating factors such as physical inactivity and ongoing psychological or social stresses (Sharpe and Wilks, 2002). Finally, clinicians should engage in discussion with the patient, giving ample information so that the patient knows what to expect from the treatment of his or her fatigue.

Given the multidimensional nature of HIV-related fatigue, a broad biopsychosocial approach is recommended for treatment of fatigue in persons with HIV (Sharpe and Wilks, 2002). Cella and colleagues (1998) have proposed a three-stage hierarchy for the management of fatigue: (1) identify and treat any underlying causes of fatigue; (2) treat the symptoms of fatigue directly while the etiology of fatigue is determined; and (3) address and manage the consequences of fatigue. Outlined in the following sections are fatigue intervention strategies in HIV/AIDS; these are summarized in Table 24.3.

TREATMENT OF PHYSIOLOGICAL CAUSES OF FATIGUE

In accordance with the paradigm proposed by Cella et al. (1998), potential physiological causes of fatigue should be identified and treated, and nonessential centrally acting drugs should be eliminated. If anemia is the main cause of fatigue, for example, the physician should determine the necessity of a transfusion in severely symptomatic patients. Recombinant human erythropoietin (rHuEPO) is recommended for patients with hemoglobin levels below 11g/dl, regardless of whether they are being treated with zidovudine (Fischl et al., 1990; Henry et al., 1992; Phair et al., 1993). Clinical trials have shown that anemic patients have improved energy and less fatigue after rHuEPO treatment. Therapy with rHuEPO can be administered either intravenously or subcutaneously, three times weekly. It is generally well tolerated.

If hypogonadism is identified as the underlying cause of fatigue, exogenous testosterone or synthetic anabolic steroids may be administered (Dufour et al., 2005). However, patients receiving this treatment are susceptible to anabolic and androgenic effects such as increased heart rate, increased blood pressure, and hirsutism, as well as elevated risk of adverse cardiovascular events (Varriale et al., 1999). Please refer to Chapter 46 of this textbook for a detailed discussion of the cardiovascular vulnerabilities and complications in persons with HIV. Testosterone therapy may take the form

Table 24.3 FATIGUE INTERVENTION STRATEGIES IN HIV/AIDS

CAUSE-SPECIFIC INTERVENTIONS	
Anemia	Transfusions, rHuEPO
Hypogonadism	Testosterone
Adrenal insufficiency	Corticosteroids
Hypothyroidism	Levothyroxine
Infections	Antibiotic, antiviral, or antifungal therapy
Malnutrition	Nutritional supplement, megestrol acetate
Depression	Antidepressants, psychotherapy
Inactivity	Exercise, training
Sleep disturbances	Sleep aids
Nonspecific Pharmacological Interventions	
Selective serotonin-reuptake inhibitors	
Tricyclic antidepressants	
Psychostimulants	
Methylphenidate	
Dextroamphetamine	
Pemoline	
Modafinil	
Anti-cytokine agents	
Thalidomide	
Pentoxifylline	
Nonpharmacological Interventions	
Good sleep hygiene	
Education	
Meditation, relaxation	
Energy conservation and restoration	
Cognitive-behavioral therapy	

Source: Dufour N, Dubé B, Breitbart W (2005). HIV-related fatigue. In J DeLuca (ed.), *Fatigue as a Window to the Brain* (pp. 188–207). Cambridge, MA: MIT Press, with permission.

of injections, pills, patches, gels, or creams. This treatment has been shown to have a beneficial effect on not only fatigue but also sexual interest, appetite, wasting, energy levels, and even concomitant depression. It can be used in women, although patients must be carefully monitored for any potential virilizing effects, which may be irreversible. Primary adrenal insufficiency can be treated with oral hydrocortisone or dexamethasone replacement therapy (Dufour et al., 2005). Hypothyroidism improves with levothyroxine administration (Derry, 1995).

TREATMENT OF PSYCHOLOGICAL CAUSES OF FATIGUE

Once potential underlying organic causes of fatigue have been ruled out and treated, psychotherapeutic and pharmacological treatments may be explored for the management of any mood disturbances.

Pharmacological Interventions

Underlying depression should be treated with selective serotonin reuptake inhibitors (SSRIs), which are generally better tolerated than tricyclic antidepressants by patients with HIV and AIDS (Elliot et al., 1998; Schwarz and McDaniel, 1999). The notable exception is fluvoxamine, which is less well tolerated despite its efficacy in treating depression (Grassi, 1995). Since fatigued patients with HIV and AIDS are especially sensitive to antidepressant side effects compared to patients without fatigue (Sharpe and Wilks, 2002), treatment should be initiated at very low doses. Because concomitant ART is frequently used, drug–drug interactions should also be carefully monitored by prescribing physicians. Excellent reviews of such psychopharmacological considerations have been carried out by Robinson and Qagish (2002) and Thompson et al. (2006). Psychopharmacological treatment issues in AIDS psychiatry are also addressed in depth in Chapter 42 of this book.

Psychotherapeutic and Other Nonpharmacological Interventions

Much less research, however, has been conducted about psychotherapeutic interventions for depressed persons with HIV. Most of this literature supports group cognitive-behavioral therapy approaches as a means of improving mental health–related quality of life indices (Lechner et al., 2003) and relieving depression (Blanch et al., 2002). Although individual psychotherapy has not been as well investigated, it is an integral part of the American Psychiatric Association's practice guidelines for the treatment of patients with HIV/AIDS (American Psychiatric Association, 2000).

Finally, physical therapy has been evaluated as an adjunctive treatment for people living with HIV/AIDS, and preliminary evidence suggests positive effects for fatigue as well as other general quality-of-life domains, including pain and emotional well-being (Pullen et al., 2014).

DIRECT TREATMENT OF FATIGUE

Once the potential physiological and psychological causes of fatigue have been addressed, residual effects of fatigue can be treated directly. There are several pharmacological agents that may be used to directly treat fatigue in persons with HIV and AIDS who may or may not be depressed.

Psychostimulants such as methylphenidate, pemoline, and dextroamphetamine have shown great promise in the treatment of fatigued patients with cancer and multiple sclerosis (Krupp, Coyle, et al., 1989; Weinshenker et al., 1992). These drugs have also been used safely and successfully in persons with HIV and fatigue (Breitbart et al., 2001; Holmes et al., 1989; Wagner and Rabkin, 2000). Breitbart and colleagues (2001) conducted the first randomized, double-blind, placebo-controlled trial of two psychostimulants for the treatment of fatigue in ambulatory patients with HIV disease. They found that both methylphenidate hydrochloride (Ritalin) and pemoline (Cylert) were equally effective and significantly superior to placebo in decreasing fatigue severity with minimal side effects. Fifteen patients (41%) of 144 ambulatory patients with HIV who were taking methylphenidate and 12 patients (36%) taking pemoline experienced clinically significant improvement, as compared to 6 patients (15%) taking placebo. The significantly improved fatigue was also associated with improved quality of life, decreased depression, and decreased psychological distress. Although participants experienced minimal side effects, "jitteriness" was reported by some patients (31.8% of subjects taking methylphenidate; 25.6% of subjects taking pemoline). Thus, the use of psychostimulants may be appropriate as part of a comprehensive approach to the treatment of fatigue in persons with HIV (Breitbart et al., 2001).

Modafinil, a norepinephrine agonist in the human hypothalamus (McClellan and Spencer, 1998), is a wakefulness-promoting agent that has been used off-label to augment antidepressants in small studies (Menza et al., 2000; Schwartz et al., 2002). It is currently used as a first-line agent for the treatment of severe fatigue in multiple sclerosis (MacAllister and Krupp, 2005) and has also proven effective in the alleviation of HIV-related fatigue (McElhiney et al., 2010, 2013; Rabkin, McElhiney, et al., 2004; Rabkin et al., 2010, 2011a, 2011b).

Finally, one study has shown that testosterone administration may be effective for the treatment of fatigue in depressed men with HIV and AIDS. Rabkin, Wagner, et al. (2004) conducted a double-blind, randomized, placebo-controlled trial comparing the outcomes of fluoxetine, testosterone, and placebo administration in 123 HIV-seropositive men with a depressive disorder. The Clinical Global Impressions Scale for mood and fatigue, the Hamilton Rating Scale for Depression, and the Chalder Fatigue Scale were used to assess patient symptoms. The conclusions did not support prescription of testosterone as a first-line treatment for depression in men with HIV disease. However, testosterone was significantly superior to both fluoxetine and placebo in terms of reducing fatigue.

MANAGING THE CONSEQUENCES OF FATIGUE

The negative impact of HIV-related fatigue on quality of life has been emphasized throughout this chapter. Addressing the consequences of fatigue is also crucial to improving the patient's quality of life. Treatment of fatigue should not merely involve the restoration or amelioration of energy but also the preservation of energy to improve the patient's level of functioning. This may entail appropriate rest, pacing of energy-consuming activities, stress reduction, meditation or relaxation techniques, aerobic exercise (if it is not contraindicated), and participation in pleasurable activities. Counseling and communication can help patients re-prioritize their activities, adjust to their limitations, and restructure their goals and expectations accordingly. Throughout this process sustaining a sense of purpose and meaningfulness is vital (Winningham et al., 1994).

CONCLUSIONS

Fatigue is a serious clinical problem that is highly prevalent among persons with HIV and AIDS and is associated with decreased quality of life. The complaint of fatigue needs to be explored specifically in order to explore different etiologies. Several simple, reliable, and valid measurement scales are available for the assessment of fatigue. Discrete medical causes of fatigue should be treated directly. Certain psychiatric syndromes, particularly depressive and anxiety disorders, can cause acute fatigue in the absence of HIV disease; thus diagnosis and treatment of these disturbances are also necessary. There are a number of therapeutic strategies that can benefit fatigued patients with HIV, though further research is warranted. Patients need to be educated and informed about their diagnosis and treatment so they can prepare and adjust accordingly. Finally, the psychiatrist has a unique ability to provide both medical treatment and psychosocial support to HIV patients with fatigue. Ameliorating treatable causes of fatigue can add to the stores of physical and emotional energy needed to cope with HIV/AIDS and even thrive in the face of this illness.

REFERENCES

Aaronson NK, Ahmedzai S, Bergman B, et al. (1993). The European Organization for Research and Treatment of Cancer QLQ-C30: a quality-of-life instrument for use in international clinical trials in oncology. *J Natl Cancer Inst* 85:365–763.

Abbott M, Khoo SH, Hammer MR, Wilkins EGL (1995). Prevalence of cortisol deficiency in late HIV disease. *J Infect* 31:1–4.

Al-Dakkak I, Patel S, McCann E, Gadkari A, Prajapati G, Maiese EM (2013). The impact of specific HIV treatment–related adverse events on adherence to antiretroviral therapy: a systematic review and meta-analysis. *ADIS Care* 25(4):400–414.

American Psychiatric Association (2000). Practice guidelines for the treatment of patients with HIV/AIDS. *Am J Psychiatry* 157:1–62.

Anderson R, Grady C (1994). Symptoms reported by "asymptomatic" HIV-infected subjects [abstract]. Proceedings of the 7th Annual Association of Nurses in AIDS Care in Nashville, TN, November 10–12, 1994.

Barroso J, Lynn ML (2002). Psychometric properties of the HIV-Related Fatigue Scale. *J Assoc Nurses AIDS Care* 13:66–75.

Barroso J, Preisser JS, Leserman JL, Gaynes BN, Golden RN, Evans DN (2002). Predicting fatigue and depression in HIV-positive gay men. *Psychosomatics* 43:317–325.

Barroso J, Voss JG (2013). Fatigue in HIV and AIDS: an analysis of evidence. *J Assoc Nurses AIDS Care* 24(1 Suppl):S5–S14.

Barroso J, Harmon JL, Madison JL, Pence BW (2014). Intensity, chronicicty, circumstances, and consequences of HIV-related faituge: a longitudinal study. *Clin Nurs Res* 23(5):514–528.

Bartlett JG (1996). *Medical Management of HIV Infection*. Glenview, IL: Physicians and Scientists Publishing.

Belza BL (1995). Comparison of self-reported fatigue in rheumatoid arthritis and controls. *J Rheumatol* 22:639–643.

Bhat VG, Ramburuth M, Singh M, et al. (2010). Factors associated with poor adherence to anti-retroviral therapy in patients attending a rural health centre in South Africa. *Eur J Clin Microbiol Infect Dis* 29(8):947–953.

Blanch J, Rousaud A, Hautzinger M, et al. (2002). Assessment of the efficacy of cognitive-behavioral group psychotherapy program for HIV-infected patients referred to a consultation-liaison psychiatry department. *Psychother Psychosom* 71:77–84.

Bormann J, Shively M, Smith TL, Gifford AL (2001). Measurement of fatigue in HIV-positive adults: reliability and validity of the Global Fatigue Index. *J Assoc Nurses AIDS Care* 12:75–83.

Braitstein P, Montessori V, Chan K, Montaner JS, Schechter MT, O'Shaughnessy MV, Hogg RS (2005). Quality of life, depression and fatigue among persons co-infected with HIV and hepatitis C: outcomes from a population-based cohort. *AIDS Care* 17(4):505–515.

Breitbart W, McDonald MV, Rosenfeld B, Monkman ND, Passik S (1998). Fatigue in ambulatory AIDS patients. *J Pain Symptom Manage* 15:159–167.

Breitbart W, Rosenfeld B, Kaim M, Funesti-Esch J (2001). A randomized, double-blind, placebo-controlled trial of psychostimulants for the treatment of fatigue in ambulatory patients with human immunodeficiency virus disease. *Arch Intern Med* 161:411–420.

Briggs JM, Beazlie LH (1996). Nursing management of symptoms influenced by HIV infection of the endocrine system. *Nurs Clin North Am* 31:845–865.

Butt Z, Lai JS, Rao D, Heinemann AW, Bill A, Cella D (2013). Measurement of fatigue in cancer, stroke, and HIV using the Functional Assessment of Chronic Illness Therapy-Fatigue (FACTI-F) scale. *J Psychosom Res* 74(1):64–68.

Cella DF, Jacobsen PB, Orav EJ, Holland JC, Silberfarb PM, Rafla S (1987). A brief POMS measure of distress for cancer patients. *J Chronic Dis* 40:939–942.

Cella D, Peterman A, Passik S, Jacobsen P, Breitbart W (1998). Progress toward guidelines for the management of fatigue. *Oncology* 12:369–377.

Chalder T, Berelowtiz G, Pawlikowska T, Watts L, Wessely S, Wright D, Wallace EP (1993). Development of a fatigue scale. *J Psychosom Res* 37(2):147–153.

Claborn KR, Meier E, Miller MB, Leffingwell TR (2015). A systematic review of treatment fatigue among HIV-infected patients prescribed antiretroviral therapy. *Psychol Health Med* 20:255–265.

Clerici M, Trabattoni D, Piconi S, Fusi ML, Ruzzante S, Clerici C, Villa ML (1997). A possible role for the cortisol/anticortisols imbalance in the progression of human immunodeficiency virus. *Psychoneuroendocrinology* 22(Suppl 1):S27–S31.

Crocker KS (1989). Gastrointestinal manifestations of the aquired immunodeficiency syndrome. *Nurs Clin North Am* 24:395–406.

Curt GA, Breitbart W, Cella D, et al. (2000). Impact of cancer-related fatigue on the lives of patients: new findings from the Fatigue Coalition. *Oncologist* 5:353–360.

Darko DF, McCutchan JA, Kripke DF, Gillin JC, Golshan S (1992). Fatigue, sleep disturbance, disability, and indices of progression of HIV infection. *Am J Psychiatry* 149:514–520.

Derry DM (1995). Thyroid therapy in HIV-infected patients. *Med Hypotheses* 45:121–124.

Dieterich D, Rockstroh JK, Orkin C, et al. (2014). Simeprevir (TMC435) with pegylated interferon/ribavirin in patients coinfected with HCV genotype 1 and HIV-1: a phase 3 study. *Clin Infect Dis* 59(11):1579–1587.

Dittner AJ, Wessely SC, Brown RG (2004). The assessment of fatigue: a practical guide for clinicians and researchers. *J Psychosom Res* 56:157–170.

Dobs AS, Dempsey MA, Ladenson PW, Polk BF (1988). Endocrine disorders in men infected with HIV. *Am J Med* 84:611–616.

Dufour N, Dubé B, Breitbart W (2005). HIV-related fatigue. In J DeLuca (ed.), *Fatigue as a Window to the Brain* (pp. 188–207) Cambridge, MA: MIT Press.

Elliot AJ, Uldall KK, Bergam K, Russo J, Claypoole K, Roy-Byrne PP (1998). Randomized, placebo-controlled trial of paroxetine versus imipramine in depressed HIV-positive outpatients. *Am J Psychiatry* 155:367–372.

Enwonwu CO, Meeks VI, Sawiris PG (1996). Elevated cortisol levels in whole saliva in HIV infected individuals. *Eur J Oral Sci* 104:322–324.

Ferrando S, Evans S, Goggin K, Sewell M, Fishman B, Rabkin J (1998). Fatigue in HIV illness: relationship to depression, physical limitations, and disability. *Psychosom Med* 60:759–764.

Fischl M, Galpin JE, Levine JD, et al. (1990). Recombinant human erythropoietin for patients with AIDS treated with zidovudine. *N Engl J Med* 322:1488–1492.

Gane EJ, Stedman CA, Hyland RH, et al. (2013). Nucleotide polymerase inhibitor sofosbuvir plus ribavirin for hepatitis C. *N Engl J Med* 368(1):34–44.

Grassi B (1995). Notes on the use of fluvoxamine as a treatment of depression in HIV-1 infected subjects. *Pharmacopsychiatry* 28:93–94.

Greenberg DB (1998). Fatigue. In JC Holland, et al. (eds.), *Psychooncology* (pp. 485–493) New York: Oxford University Press.

Hann DM, Jacobsen PB, Azzarello LM, et al. (1998). Measurement of fatigue in cancer patients: development and validation of the Fatigue Symptom Inventory. *Qual Life Res* 7:301–310.

Henderson M, Safa F, Easterbrook P, Hotopf M (2005). Fatigue among HIV-infected patients in the era of highly active antiretroviral therapy. *HIV Med* 6(5):347–352.

Henry DH, Beall GN, Benson CA, et al. (1992). Recombinant human erythropoietin in the treatment of anemia associated with HIV infection and zidovudine therapy: overview of four clinical trials. *Ann Intern Med* 117:739–748.

Holmes VF, Fernandez F, Levy JK (1989). Psychostimulant response in AIDS-related complex patients. *J Clin Psychiatry* 50:5–8.

Holzemer WL, Henry SB, Nokes KM, et al. (1999). Validation of the Sign and Symptom Check-list for Persons with HIV disease (SSC-HIV). *J Adv Nurs* 30(5):1041–1049.

Holzemer WL, Hudson A, Kirksey KM, Hamilton MJ, Bakken S (2001). The revised Sign and Symptom Check-list for HIV (SSC-HIVrev). *J Assoc Nurs AIDS Care* 12(5):60–70.

Hoover DR, Saah AJ, Bacellar H, Murphy R, Visscher B, Anderson R, Kaslow R (1993). Signs and symptoms of "asymptomatic" HIV-1 infection in homosexual men. *J Acquir Immune Defic Syndr* 6:66–71.

Jacobsen PB, Weitzner MA (2003). Evaluating the relationship of fatigue to depression and anxiety in cancer patients. In RK Portenoy,

E Bruera E (eds.), *Issues in Palliative Care Research* (pp. 127–149). New York: Oxford University Press.

Jaggers JR, Dudgeon WD, Burgess S, Phillips kD, Blair SN, Hand GA (2014). Psychological correlates of HIV-related symptom distress. *J Assoc Nurses AIDS Care* 25(4):309–317.

Janoff EN, Smith PD (2001). Emerging concepts in gastrointestinal aspects of HIV-1 pathogenesis and management. *Gastroenterology* 120:607–621.

Klauke S, Falkenbach A, Schmidt K, et al. (1990). Hypogonadism in males with AIDS. *Int Conf AIDS* 6:209.

Krown SE, Lee JY, Lin L, Fischl MA, Ambinder R, Von Roenn JH (2006). Interferon-alpha2b with protease inhibitor–based antiretroviral therapy in patients with AIDS-associated Kaposi sarcoma: an AIDS malignancy consortium phase I trial. *J Acquir Immune Defic Syndr* 41(2):149–153.

Krupp LB, Coyle PK, Cross AH, et al. (1989). Amelioration of fatigue with pemoline in patients with multiple sclerosis. *Ann Neurol* 26:155–156.

Krupp LB, LaRocca NG, Mur-Nash J, and Steinberg AD (1989). The Fatigue Severity Scale. *Arch Neurol* 46:1121–1123.

Lechner SC, Antoni MH, Lydston D, et al. (2003). Cognitive-behavioral interventions improve quality of life in women with AIDS. *J Psychosom Res* 54:253–261.

Lee KA, Hicks G, Nino-Murcia G (1991). Validity and reliability of a scale to assess fatigue. *Psychiatry Res* 36:291–298.

Lee KA, Gay CL, lerdal A, Pullinger CR, Aouizerat BE (2014). Cytokine polymorphisms are associated with fatigue in adults living with HIV/AIDS. *Brain Behav Immun* 40(95):95–103.

Longo MB, Spross JA, Locke AM (1990). Identifying major concerns of persons with acquired immunodeficiency syndrome: a replication. *Clin Nurse Spec* 4:21–26.

Lyketsos CG, Hoover DR, Cuccione M, Dew MA, Wesch JE, Bing EG, Treisman GJ (1996). Changes in depressive symptoms as AIDS develops. *Am J Psychiatry* 153:1430–1437.

MacAllister WS, Krupp LB (2005). Multiple sclerosis–related fatigue. *Phys Med Rehabil Clin N Am* 16(2):483–502.

Mandorfer M, Payer BA, Scheiner B, et al. (2014). Health-related quality of life and severity of fatigue in HIV/HCV co-infected patients before, during, and after antiviral therapy with pegylated interferon plus ribavirin. *Liver Int* 34(1):69–77.

Margolis AM, Heverling H, Pham PA, Stolbach A (2014). A review of the toxicity of HIV medications. *J Med Toxicol* 10(1):26–39.

McClellan KJ, Spencer CM (1998). Modafinil: a review of its pharmacology and clinical efficacy in the management of narcolepsy. *CNS Drugs* 9:311–324.

McElhiney M, Rabkin J, Van Gorp W, Rabkin R (2010). Modafinil effects on cognitive function in HIV+ patients treated for fatigue: a placebo controlled study. *J Clin Exp Neuropsychol* 32(5):474–480.

McElhiney M, Rabkin J, Van Gorp W, Rabkin R (2013). Effect of armodafinil on cognition in patients with HIV/AIDS and fatigue. *J Clin Exp Neuropsychol* 35(7):718–727.

Means R Jr (1997). Cytokines and anemia in HIV infection. *Cytokines Cell Mol Ther* 3:179–186.

Mendoza TR, Wang XS, Cleeland CS, Morrissey M, Johnson BA, Wendt JK, Huber SL (1999). The rapid assessment of fatigue severity in cancer patients: use of the Brief Fatigue Inventory. *Cancer* 85:1186–1196.

Menza MA, Kaufman KR, Castellanos A (2000). Modafinil augmentation of antidepressant in depression. *J Clin Psychiatry* 61:378–381.

Miller RG, Carson PJ, Moussavi RS, Green AT, Baker AJ, Weiner MW (1991). Fatigue and myalgia in AIDS patients. *Neurology* 41:1603–1607.

Moyle G (2002). Anemia in persons with HIV infection: prognostic marker and contributor to morbidity. *AIDS Rev* 4:13–20.

Norbiato G, Galli M, Righini V, Moroni M (1994). The syndrome of acquired glucocorticoid resistance in HIV infection. *Ballieres Clin Endocrinol Metab* 8:777–787.

O'Dell MW, Meighen M, Riggs RV (1996). Correlates of fatigue in HIV prior to AIDS: a pilot study. *Disabil Rehabil* 18:249–254.

Paddison JS, Booth RJ, Hill AG, Cameron LD (2006). Comprehensive assessment of perioperative fatigue: development of the Identity-Consequence Fatigue Scale. *J Psychosom Res* 60(6);615–622.

Paddison J, Fricchione G, Gandhi RT, Freudenreich O (2009). Fatigue in psychiatric HIV patients: a pilot study of psychological correlates. *Psychosomatics* 50(5):455–460.

Payne BA, Hateley CL, Ong EL, et al. (2013). HIV-associated fatigue in the era of highly active antiretroviral therapy: novel biological mechanisms? *HIV Med* 14(4):247–251.

Pearson PG, Byars GE (1956). The development and validation of a checklist measuring subjective fatigue (report no. 56–115). Randolph Air Force Base, TX: School of Aviation, U.S. Air Force.

Pence BW, Barroso J, Leserman J, Harmon JL, Salahuddin N (2008). Measuring fatigue in people living with HIV/AIDS: psychometric characteristics of the HIV-related fatigue scale. *AIDS Care* 20(7):829–837.

Perdices M, Dundar N, Grunseit A, Hall W, Cooper DA (1992). Anxiety, depression, and HIV-related symptomatology across the spectrum of HIV disease. *Aust N Z J Psychiatry* 26:560–566.

Perkins DO, Leserman J, Stern RA, Baum SF, Liao D, Golden RN, Evans DL (1995). Somatic symptoms of HIV infection: relationship to depressive symptoms and indicators of HIV disease. *Am J Psychiatry* 152:1776–1781.

Phair JP, Abels RI, McNeill MV, Sullivan DJ (1993). Recombinant human erythropoietin treatment: investigational new drug protocol for the anemia of the acquired immunodeficiency syndrome: overall results. *Arch Intern Med* 153:2669–2675.

Piedrola G, Casado JL, Lopez E, Moreno A, Perez-Elias MJ, Garcia-Robles R (1996). Clinical features of adrenal insufficiency in patients with acquired immunodeficiency syndrome. *Clin Endocrinol* 45:97–101.

Piper B, Lindsey A, Dodd M, et al. (1989). Development of an instrument to measure the subjective dimension of fatigue. In S Funk, et al. (eds.), *Key Aspects of Comfort: Management of Pain, Fatigue and Nausea* (pp. 199–208). New York: Springer-Verlag.

Pluda JM, Mitsuya H, Yarchoan R (1991). Hematologic effects of AIDS therapies. *Hematol Oncol Clin N Am* 5:229–248.

Portenoy RK, Thaler HT, Kornblith AB, et al. (1994). The Memorial Symptom Assessment Scale: an instrument for the evaluation of symptom prevalence, characteristics and distress. *Eur J Cancer* 30A(9): 1326–1336.

Pullen SD, Chigbo NN, Nwigwe EC, Chukwuka CJ, Amah CC, Idu SC (2014). Physiotherapy intervention as a complementary treatment for people living with HIV/AIDS. *HIV AIDS (Auckl)* 6(99):99–107.

Rabkin JG, McElhiney MC, Rabkin R, Ferrando SJ (2004). Modafinil treatment for fatigue in HIV+ patients: a pilot study. *J Clin Psychiatry* 65(12):1688–1695.

Rabkin JG, Wagner GJ, McElhiney MC, Rabkin R, Lin SH (2004). Testosterone versus fluoxetine for depression and fatigue in HIV/AIDS: a placebo-controlled trial. *J Clin Psychopharmacol* 24(4):379–385.

Rabkin JG, McElhiney MC, Rabkin R, McGrath PJ (2010). Modafinil treatment for fatigue in HIV/AIDS: a randomized placebo-controlled study. *J Clin Psychiatry* 71(6):707–715.

Rabkin JG, McElhiney MC, Rabkin R (2011a). Treatment of HIV-related fatigue with armodafinil: a placebo-controlled randomized trial. *Psychosomatics* 52(4):328–336.

Rabkin JG, McElhiney MC, Rabkin R (2011b). Modafinil and armodafinil treatment for fatigue for HIV-positive patiens with and without chronic hepatitis C. *Int J STD AIDS* 22(2):95–101.

Ream E, Richardson A (1996). Fatigue: a concept analysis. *Int J Nurs Stud* 33:519–529.

Revicki DA, Brown RE, Henry DH, McNeill MV, Rios A, Watson T (1994). Recombinant human erythropoietin and health-related quality of life of AIDS patients with anemia. *J Acquir Immune Defic Syndr* 7:474–484.

Richman DD, Fischl MA, Grieco MH, et al. (1987). The toxicity of azidothymidine (AZT) in the treatment of patients with AIDS and AIDS-related complex. *N Engl J Med* 317:192–197.

Robinson MJ, Qaqish RB (2002). Practical psychopharmacology in HIV-1 and acquired immunodeficiency syndrome. *Psychiatr Clin North Am* 25:149–175.

Rondanelli M, Solerte SB, Fioravanti M, Scevola D, Locatelli M, Minoli L, Ferrari E (1997). Circadian secretory pattern of growth hormone, insulin-like growth factor type 1, cortisol, adrenocorticotropic hormone, thyroid-stimulating hormone, and prolactin during HIV infection. *AIDS Res Hum Retroviruses* 13:1243–1249.

Sadler IJ, Jacobsen PB, Booth-Jones M, Belanger H, Weitzner MA, Fields KK (2002). Preliminary evaluation of a clinical syndrome approach to assessing cancer-related fatigue. *J Pain Symptom Manage* 23(5):406–416.

Schag CC, Heinrich RL, Ganz PA (1984). Karnofsky Performance Status revisited: reliability, validity, and guidelines. *J Clin Oncol* 2:187–193.

Schwartz TL, Leso L, Beale M, Ahmed R, Naprawa S (2002). Modafinil in the treatment of depression with severe comorbid medical illness. *Psychosomatics* 43:336–337.

Schwarz JA, McDaniel JS (1999). Double-blind comparison of fluoxetine and desipramine in the treatment of depressed women in advanced HIV disease: a pilot study. *Depress Anxiety* 9:70–74.

Sharpe M, Wilks D (2002). Fatigue. *BMJ* 325:480–483.

Simonson E (1971). *Physiology of Work Capacity and Fatigue*. Springfield, IL: Thomas.

Smets EM, Garssen B, Schuster-Uitterhoeve AL, deHaesm JC (1993). Fatigue in cancer patients. *Br J Cancer* 68:220–224.

Stolarczyk R, Rubio SI, Smolyar D, Young IS, Poretsky L (1998). Twenty-four-hour urinary free cortisol in patients with acquired immunodeficiency syndrome. *Metabolism* 47:690–694.

Sulkowski MS, Naggie S, Lalezari J; for PHOTON-1 Investigators (2014). Sofosbuvir and ribavirin for hepatitis C in patients with HIV coinfection. *JAMA* 312(4):353–361.

Tabatabai J, Namakhoma I, Tweya H, Phiri S, Schnitzler P, Neuhann F (2014). Understanding reasons for treatment interruption among patients on antiretroviral therapy—a qualitative study at the Lighthouse Clinic, Lilongwe, Malawi. *Glob Health Action* 7:24795.

Thomas DL (2012). Advances in the treatment of hepatitis C virus infection. *Top Antivir Med* 20(1):5–10.

Thompson A, Silverman B, Dzeng L, Treisman G (2006). Psychotropic medications and HIV. *Clin Infect Dis* 42(9):1305.

Ur E, White PD, Grossman A (1992). Hypothesis: cytokines may be activated to cause depressive illness and chronic fatigue syndrome. *Eur Arch Psychiatry Clin Neurosci* 241:317–322.

Varriale P, Mirzai-tehrane M, Sedighi A (1999). Acute myocardial infarction associated with anabolic steroids in a young HIV-infected patient. *Pharmacotherapy* 19(7):881–884.

Vlahov D, Munoz A, Solomon L, Astemborski J, Lindsay A, Anderson J, Galai N, Nelson KE (1994). Comparison of clinical manifestations of HIV infection between male and female injecting drug users. *AIDS* 8:819–823.

Vogl D, Rosenfeld B, Breitbart W, Thaler H, Passik S, McDonald M, Portenoy RK (1999). Symptom prevalence, characteristics, and distress in AIDS outpatients. *J Pain Symptom Manage* 18:253–262.

Volberding P (2000). Consensus statement: anemia in HIV infection current trends, treatment options, and practice strategies. Anemia in HIV Working Group. *Clin Ther* 22:1004–1020.

Voss JG (2005). Predictors and correlates of fatigue in HIV/AIDS. *J Pain Symptom Manage* 29(2):173–184.

Wagner GJ, Rabkin R (2000). Effects of dextroamphetamine on depression and fatigue in men with HIV: a double-blind, placebo-controlled trial. *J Clin Psychiatry* 61:436–440.

Walker K, McGown A, Jantos M, Anson J (1997). Fatigue, depression, and quality of life in HIV-positive men. *J Psychosoc Nurs Ment Health Serv* 35:32–40.

Weinshenker BG, Penman M, Bass B, Ebers GC, Rice GP (1992). A double-blind, randomized crossover trial of pemoline in fatigue associated with multiple sclerosis. *Neurology* 42:1468–1471.

Winningham ML, Nail LM, Burke MB, Brophy L, Cimprich B, Jones LS, Beck S (1994). Fatigue and the cancer experience: the state of the knowledge. *Oncol Nurs Forum* 21:23–36.

World Health Organization (2017). *International Classification of Diseases*, 10th Revision, Clinical Modification (ICD-10-CM). Geneva: World Health Organization.

25.

SUICIDE AND HIV

César A. Alfonso, Eva Stern-Rodríguez, and Mary Ann Cohen

iving with HIV and AIDS is arduous and can become
intolerable. Even after more effective antiretroviral treatments were developed and the mortality of HIV was
significantly reduced in countries and regions with access to
competent HIV medical care and antiretroviral therapy (ART),
psychological and medical multimorbidities continue to create
great distress. Psychosocial issues such as stigma and discrimination compound the distress experienced by persons with HIV
and contribute to not getting HIV tested, not disclosing serostatus, and reluctance to adhere to medical care, leading to inad-
equacy of viral suppression even with access to care.

HIV seropositivity and AIDS continue to be independent
risk factors for suicide. HIV-positive persons with multimorbid
psychiatric and medical illnesses are at an even higher risk of
dying by suicide than individuals without multimorbid complications. Although completed suicides in the general population are statistically relatively rare events, the majority of persons
with HIV frequently experience thoughts of suicide and commonly engage in suicidal behavior, and a substantial number
end their lives by suicide. Suicidal behavior among the medically
ill, a psychiatric emergency, is one of the most common reasons
for psychiatric consultation in inpatient and outpatient settings
and demands great clinical expertise for its management.

Suicide is always multifactorial in causation and requires a
multidimensional approach for its prevention. Suicide is preventable even when hopelessness is tangible and overwhelming. By identifying the treatable predisposing psychosocial
factors and reducing distress, clinicians will be able to anchor
the ambivalent suicidal patient and prevent deliberate self-
harm. Suicidality is treatable with crisis intervention, networking, and psychiatric care. The recognition and treatment
of suicidality can prevent suicide.

In this chapter we present the epidemiology of suicide in persons with HIV and the known predisposing factors for suicidal
behavior. We also focus on factors that are protective against
suicide by describing the psychosocial profile of non-suicidal
HIV-positive persons and elaborate on the psychodynamics of
suicide. We describe assessment and prevention strategies of
therapeutic value for persons with HIV who are suicidal.

EPIDEMIOLOGY

The epidemiology of suicide and HIV is complex. Prevalence
estimates of suicidal behavior and completed suicides vary
depending on the population studied. In addition, suicides

of persons with HIV/AIDS may be underreported in certain parts of the world, and acts of deliberate self-harm are
often recorded as accidental overdoses or accidental deaths
(Carvajal et al., 1995; Gabler et al., 2011; McManus et al.,
2014; Semela et al., 2000). Inadequate reporting is particularly relevant when completed suicides among intravenous
drug users, who may choose to end their lives by drug overdose, escape our awareness. Since drug overdose is the most
common method of completed suicide among persons with
HIV (Chikezie et al., 2012; Cote et al., 1992; Rajs and
Fugelstad, 1992), the suicide rate may actually be higher than
what has been reported, because of incorrect reporting of suicides as accidental deaths or overdoses. This section summarizes the epidemiology of suicide in the general population, in
the medically ill, and in persons with HIV with or without
associated multimorbidities.

The suicide rate in the general population varies from
country to country and among immigrant groups with different levels of acculturation. Approximately one million
lives are lost worldwide each year to suicide. Reported general
population suicide statistics range from the highest rates, in
Eastern European countries, of up to 34 per 100,000, to the
United States, at mid-range, with a rate of 11 per 100,000, to
some Latin American countries, with rates as low as 6.5 per
100,000 persons/year (Mann et al., 2005; Varnik, 2012). In
general, suicide rates among recent immigrants approximate
that of the country of origin (Malenfant, 2004); as acculturation occurs it increases or decreases to match that of the new
host country (Pavlovic and Marusic, 2001; Pérez-Rodríguez
et al., 2014).

It is estimated that 98% of persons who die by suicide
have psychiatric or medical conditions (Mann et al., 2005;
Pokorny, 1966). While psychiatric disorders are widely
known to increase suicide risk (Guze and Robins, 1970;
Mann, 2005; Nordentoft et al., 2013; Qin, 2011), certain
chronic medical illnesses have also been independently associated with higher suicide rates (Alfonso and Cohen, 2008;
Bostwick and Levenson, 2005, 2011; Harris and Barraclough,
1994; Levenson and Bostwick, 2005).

The psychiatric disorders with the highest suicide rate are
depressive disorders, which are present in 60% of all suicides
(Guze and Robins, 1970; Nordentoft et al., 2013), and alcohol
abuse and dependence, present in up to 36% of completed suicides (Jones et al., 2013). Up to 13% of persons with schizophrenia die by suicide (Roy, 1986; Tidemalm et al., 2008).
Diagnoses of intravenous drug use disorders (Dinwiddie

et al., 1992; Marzuk et al., 1992), posttraumatic stress disorder (Pompili et al., 2013), borderline personality disorder (Frances, 1986; Nordentoft et al., 2013), dementia (Alfonso and Cohen, 1994, 2008; Levenson and Bostwick, 2005), and delirium (Bostwick and Levenson, 2005; Glickman, 1980) are associated with a suicide risk significantly higher than that of the general population.

Medical disorders associated with an increased risk for suicide independent of their psychiatric comorbidities include Huntington disease (Hubers et al., 2013; Huntington, 1872), end-stage renal disease (Chen et al., 2010; Kurella et al., 2005), cardiorespiratory illnesses (Goodwin et al., 2012), multiple sclerosis (Scalfari et al., 2013), and certain cancers, such as head and neck, melanoma, and pancreatic tumors (Breitbart, 1987; Lu et al., 2013).

Reports suggesting an association between HIV seropositivity and suicidal behavior in the United States appeared in the medical literature during the first decade of the epidemic (Burrows, 1998; Frierson and Lippmann, 1988; Pierce, 1987; Rundell et al., 1986). A more definitive association of HIV/AIDS as an independent risk factor for suicide was established by autopsy studies (Catalan et al., 2011; Cote et al., 1992; Glass, 1988; Kizer et al., 1988; Marzuk et al., 1988; Plott et al., 1989). These autopsy studies from cohorts in the United States showed decreasing suicide rates from 66 to 3 times greater in persons with HIV infection than in the general population (Capron et al., 2012) as we moved from the first to the third decade of the epidemic. But even after the introduction of effective ART and HIV care substantially reduced morbidity and mortality in areas with access to care, recent studies in Australia (Ruzicka et al., 2005), Denmark (Jia et al., 2012), Nigeria (Chikezie et al., 2012), Portugal (Braganca and Palha, 2011), China (Jin et al., 2006) and France (Preau et al., 2008) continue to substantiate an increased risk of suicide among persons with HIV.

Clinical studies, likewise, demonstrate high rates of suicidal behavior in persons with HIV. In a primary care setting in New York City that serves patients with a wide range of demographic characteristics, 63% of HIV-seropositive subjects acknowledged current or past suicidal ideation (Gil et al., 1998). Another study showed that 20.2% of gay and bisexual men living with HIV reported serious thoughts or plans to end their own lives (Chen et al., 2011). In a rural cohort of small communities in eight U.S. states, 38% of persons with HIV admitted that they had suicidal thoughts 1 week prior to responding to self-administered surveys (Heckman et al., 2002). Similarly, 27% of older persons living with HIV admitted to suicidal ideation within 1 week prior to a clinical survey (Vance et al., 2010). In a municipal general hospital in New York City, suicidal behavior was present in one out of every five persons with HIV (Alfonso et al., 1994).

PREDISPOSING FACTORS

Predisposing factors that have cumulative or synergistic effects on increasing suicide risk are multidimensional, with biological, psychological, social, and cultural determinants.

In this section we discuss the predisposing factors associated with completed suicides among persons with HIV and AIDS.

The demographic characteristics of persons with HIV who die by suicide show different patterns from those of persons with unknown HIV status who completed suicide. General population suicide statistics show that death by suicide among men is three times higher than among women (McIntosh, 2003). Among persons with HIV, women are at a significantly higher risk for attempting and dying by suicide (Brown and Rundell, 1989; Chikezie et al., 2012; Cohen and Alfonso, 2004; Roy, 2003; Rundell et al., 1992). Also, whereas general population completed suicides occur primarily during late life for men and peak in mid-life and then decrease for women (Kaplan and Klein, 1989), persons with HIV can be suicidal at any time from diagnosis to end-stage illness (Cohen and Alfonso, 2004). In fact, clinicians in Europe, Asia, America, and Africa have observed that suicidality has a bimodal distribution, with peaks at the time of diagnosis with HIV seropositivity or infection and at end-stage illness with AIDS (Cooperman and Simoni, 2005; Gala et al., 1982; Gotoh et al., 1994; Jia et el., 2012; Kelly et al., 1998; Perry et al., 1990; Sherr, 1995; Sindiga and Lukhando, 1993).

A family history of suicide attempts or death by suicide is a strong predictor of suicide in individuals with HIV (Roy, 2003). Persons with a history of early childhood trauma with or without a diagnosis of posttraumatic stress disorder are also at increased risk for suicide (Cooperman and Simoni, 2005; Miles, 1977; Roy, 2003). Suicide risk increases in states of bereavement (Sherr, 1995), in particular during holidays or anniversary dates relevant to the deceased. Suicidal behavior increases when persons have poor social support, decreased social integration, poor family relations, unemployment, unstable housing, a detectable viral load, and a restricted social environment (Haller and Miles, 2003; Kalichman et al., 2000; Protopopescu et al., 2012). One study showed that suicidal behavior increases when persons disclose their positive serostatus (Kalichman et al., 2000), while another study indicated that not disclosing one's HIV seropositivity increased suicidality by twofold (Mollan et al., 2014). Being burdened by caregiving and having an HIV-positive spouse or children can increase suicide risk (Chandra et al., 1998; Rosengard and Folkman, 1997).

The medical multimorbidities of HIV can trigger thoughts of suicide and suicidal behavior. Incapacitating nociceptive and neuropathic pain, pruritus, hiccups, insomnia, dyspnea, nausea, emesis, intractable diarrhea, severe wasting, vision loss, blindness, motor deficits, and paresis may compound hopelessness and lead to suicide (Alfonso et al., 1994; Chandra et al., 1998; Cohen and Alfonso, 2004). It is important to recognize that when persons with AIDS have access to HIV medical care, ART, and effective treatments for opportunistic infections, they can live longer and healthier lives. As persons with HIV age, they may develop other chronic illnesses with a high prevalence of suicide that can complicate prognosis and increase suicide risk. Additionally, the strides made to improve antiretroviral medication strategies have led to the growth of an older population now living with HIV. Data show that mental decline linked with HIV and old age leaves this particular group at a higher risk for depression and suicidality (Vance et al., 2009, 2010).

Psychiatric multimorbidities associated with increased suicide risk among persons with HIV include psychiatric disorders, subthreshold conditions and symptoms, medication side effects, and negative affective states. Elevated suicide rates are found among persons with HIV and comorbid depressive disorders (Kinyanda et al., 2011), bereavement, posttraumatic stress disorder (Haller and Miles, 2003; Kelly et al., 1998), schizophrenia and other psychotic states (Haller and Miles, 2003; Wood et al., 1997), personality disorders, psychoactive substance use disorders (Haller and Miles, 2003; Marshall et al., 2011), dementia, and delirium (Alfonso and Cohen, 1994). Clinical researchers have identified a particularly high suicide rate in persons with comorbid major depression and posttraumatic stress disorder (Oquendo, Brent, et al., 2005; Sher et al., 2005), which are common coexisting conditions in persons with HIV (Cohen et al., 2001). Even though affective states of depression, guilt, anger, fear, and shame are commonly present and increase suicide risk in HIV-positive patients, the affective state with the strongest association with suicide is hopelessness (Beck et al., 1985; Cohen and Alfonso, 2004).

Studies of the neurobiology of suicide have consistently shown serotonergic dysfunction. HIV-infected individuals have decreased levels of cerebrospinal fluid 5-HT and 5-HIAA, suggesting that the virus may interfere with serotonin production in the brain (Kumar et al., 2001; Larsson et al., 1989).

Impulsivity and behavioral disinhibition that can precipitate suicidal behavior can occur in patients undergoing alcohol and opioid withdrawal (Michel et al., 2009) and are also common in advanced stages of HIV dementia. Medication side effects, such as akathisia secondary to aripiprazole, fluphenazine, or risperidone (Drake and Ehrlich, 1985; Scholten and Selten, 2005; Shear et al., 1983), and dysphoria secondary to regimens of alpha-interferon and ribavirin, previously the only treatment used to treat comorbid hepatitis C infection, have been associated with suicidal behavior in persons with HIV infection with comorbid medical and psychiatric disorders. Iatrogenic depression, suicidal ideation, and increased risk of completed suicide are associated with efavirenz-containing antiretroviral regimens (Mollan et al., 2014). At times it may be necessary to recommend switching from efavirenz or other antiretroviral medications associated with suicidality in order to prevent suicide.

Stressful life events in the context of poor social support can heighten suicide risk (Haller and Miles, 2003; Kalichman et al., 2000). Persons with HIV can have distorted perceptions of illness. Just as an asymptomatic HIV-positive individual can become suicidal upon learning of his or her HIV serostatus, changes in immune parameters can also trigger a suicidal crisis. Learning of an increased viral load or decreased CD4 cell count can precipitate a suicidal crisis, even with reassurance that a change in medical treatment can easily reverse the situation (Alfonso et al., 1994; Haas et al., 1997).

Having access to lethal means can make a predisposed individual who is ambivalently contemplating suicide more likely to end his or her life. HIV-seropositive persons have a higher rate of accidental or deliberate firesetting, self-inflicted burns, and of death by self-immolation (Castellani et al., 1995; Cohen et al., 1990). By providing flame-retardant hospital or facility clothing and restricting access to cigarettes, firearms, and prescription drugs, caregivers can protect a suicidal person from deliberate self-harm. Other suicide prevention strategies will be discussed later in this chapter.

PROTECTIVE FACTORS

Persons with HIV who use escape and avoidance coping skills tend to have a poorer prognosis and attempt suicide more often, whereas persons who use positive-reappraisal coping are relatively protected from suicidal thoughts and actions (Kalichman et al., 2000).

Experience gathered from individual and group psychotherapy of suicidal persons with HIV indicates that several factors can protect an individual from a premature self-inflicted death and from self-destructive behaviors. Protective factors include a "taking-charge" attitude rather than passivity, an adequate understanding of illness, denial that does not interfere with adherence with medical treatment, increasing social support via networking, and optimism (Alfonso and Cohen, 1997; Cohen, 1998, 1999; Rosengard and Folkman, 1997).

There is very little research that systematically addresses the protective factors that prevent development of suicidal behavior in persons with HIV infection. Studies of nonsuicidal persons with psychiatric disorders and unknown HIV serostatus and clinical interviews of HIV-positive, long-term survivors can be used, however, to highlight possible psychosocial variables that may ultimately prevent the development of suicidal and self-destructive behavior.

Clinical researchers have examined the protective factors against suicidal acts for persons with diverse psychopathology and high suicide risk. While prior attempted suicide and hopelessness are the strongest predictors of completed suicides, protective factors include more feelings of responsibility toward family, more fear of social disapproval, greater survival and coping skills, and a greater fear of suicide (Malone et al., 2000). Reporting reasons for living and religious considerations also serve as protective factors against suicide (Menon, 2013). These same factors proved protective in a cohort of Latino patients diagnosed with major depression whose depressive symptomatology did not result in suicidal behavior (Oquendo, Dragatsi, et al., 2005).

Studies of long-term survivors with AIDS in the New York City area have demonstrated that high levels of hope and low levels of distress and depressive symptoms result in psychological resiliency and an extended lifespan (Rabkin et al., 1990, 1993). Another study in Miami showed that higher emotional expression and depth processing, including positive cognitive appraisal change, experiential involvement, self-esteem enhancement, and adaptive coping strategies, were significantly related to long-term survival status of men and women with AIDS, as well as to lower viral load and higher CD4 cell count in women with AIDS (O'Cleirigh et al., 2003). The clinical implications of these studies underscore the importance of psychotherapy in the treatment of suicidal persons with HIV infection, which will be elaborated on further in the section on prevention strategies. Please see Box 25.1 for a summary of the predisposing and protective factors for suicide in persons with HIV.

Box 25.1 PROTECTIVE AND PREDISPOSING FACTORS FOR SUICIDE

Predisposing Factors

PSYCHOSOCIAL FACTORS

HIV stigma and AIDSism
Family history of suicide
Learning of an HIV diagnosis
History of childhood trauma
Poor social support
Decreased social integration
Poor family relations
Unemployment
Unstable housing
Restricted social environments
Disclosing one's positive serostatus
Burden of caregiving
Having an HIV-positive spouse or children

MEDICAL MULTIMORBIDITIES OF HIV

Incapacitating nociceptive and neuropathic pain
Pruritus
Hiccups
Insomnia
Dyspnea
Nausea
Emesis
Intractable diarrhea
Severe wasting
Vision loss
Blindness
Motor deficits
Paresis
Detectable viral loads

PSYCHIATRIC MULTIMORBIDITIES

Negative affective states (e.g., hopelessness)
Psychiatric disorders
Alcohol dependence and abuse
Mood disorders
Bereavement
Posttraumatic stress disorder
Schizophrenia and other psychotic states
Personality disorders
Psychoactive substance use disorders
Dementia
Delirium

Subthreshold psychiatric disorders and symptoms including alcohol use
Medication side effects

Protective Factors

Positive-reappraisal coping skills
"Taking-charge" attitude
Adequate understanding of illness
Denial without nonadherence
Treatment adherence
Increasing social support
Optimism
Feelings of responsibility toward family
Fear of social disapproval
Survival and coping skills
Fear of suicide
Reporting reasons for living
Religious considerations
High levels of hope
Low levels of distress
Low levels of depressive symptoms
Higher emotional expression
Higher depth processing
Positive cognitive appraisal change
Experiential involvement
Self-esteem enhancement
Adaptive coping strategies
Secure attachments

PSYCHODYNAMICS

Although common psychodynamic formulations may be relevant to suicidal patients with HIV infection, individual life experiences will influence and determine behavior, and clinicians should not adopt any universal set of dynamics as absolute or paradigmatic. Commonality of certain life experiences, nevertheless, can propel a predisposed individual to engage in acts of deliberate self-harm.

Freud and Abraham's original contributions on the dynamics of grief and depression shed some light on the meaningfulness of suicide. They observed that depression often follows either real or imagined loss. Ambivalent anger toward the lost loved one can be turned against the self in an act of aggression. Suicide can be understood as a cathartic expression of rage and sadness that symbolically attempts to recapture what has been lost (Abraham, 1911, 1924; Freud, 1917).

Suicidal behavior is never random. Unbearable situations create intolerable distress, and suicide serves as an escape from intense suffering. Suicidal persons with HIV infection are often plagued by unendurable negative affects. These may include shame, sadness, rage, guilt, anxiety, helplessness, and hopelessness. Suicidal persons are blinded by their suffering and see no options to alleviate their distress. This constriction of cognition (Litman, 1989) results in the distorted view that suicide serves as the only way out, and when psychic pain is unbearable, cessation of life—"ending it all"—serves the purpose of and becomes synonymous with remediation of pain and suffering.

Other dynamic factors that may be enacted as self-destruction include conflicts over relinquishing autonomy and intolerable dependency. Persons with chronic or incapacitating medical illnesses fear that losing control over their bodily functions will be dehumanizing and make life not worth living. Interpersonal conflicts and inability to trust or accept help from significant others magnify the distress created by pain, disfigurement, blindness, weakness, and depression associated with some of the infections that affect persons with AIDS. Those who value autonomy over life itself experience suicidal behavior as a better alternative than relying on others.

Social dynamics that drive people to end their lives include the forces of HIV stigma and discrimination, or AIDSism (Cohen, 1989). HIV seropositivity and a diagnosis of AIDS often bring to surface feelings of shame and guilt. Negative social attitudes result in social oppression, which can further precipitate these affective states, alienating individuals into hopelessness and despair that can culminate in suicide (Cohen and Alfonso, 2004). On the other hand, some people with very good social networks may come to feel that they are burdening others and that they are acting in their best interests by dying.

Suicidal individuals with a history of harmful use of alcohol or illicit drugs may have experienced social isolation, loneliness, and alienation from their families and communities. A diagnosis of HIV and deteriorating health can exacerbate a sense of expendability (Cohen and Merlino, 1983; Sabbath, 1969), leading to suicidal behavior as a way to resolve the crisis of expendability, regain control of one's destiny, and escape overwhelming hopelessness, extreme isolation, and despair.

The psychodynamics of addiction are relevant when persons have comorbid HIV, alcohol dependence, and psychoactive substance use disorders, since these individuals are at high suicide risk. Persons with addiction and HIV demonstrate disturbance of self-esteem as inability to care for self. Attachment research established the importance of physical proximity, parental attunement, anticipation of needs, and creating a sense of safety as essential to fostering secure attachment bonds during infancy and adequate self-esteem and self-care in adulthood. An inadequate parenting that may include inconsistent, neglectful, disorganized, ambivalent, avoidant, or dismissive behavior does not result in formation of secure attachment. Insecure attachments in infancy and childhood as well as childhood trauma lead to insecure attachments and self-destructive behaviors in adulthood. Psychotherapy with persons with addiction emphasizes increasing their capacity for self-care through positive transferences to therapists that are reparative in nature. The idealized transferences to self-help communities such as Alcoholic Anonymous often serve the purpose of internalizing positive self–object functions. In the absence of empathy, reparative transferences or opportunity for earned attachments through psychotherapy, and when faced with intense negative affects, decreased capacity for self-care in persons with addiction and alcoholism can take the extreme form of suicidal behavior.

Persons with HIV who have a history of early childhood trauma with or without a current diagnosis of posttraumatic stress disorder can experience a sense of foreshortened future that may further increase their suicide risk (Cohen et al., 2001; Ricart et al., 2002). The dynamics of posttraumatic stress disorder are complex and an understanding of them is essential for effective psychotherapeutic work with persons with HIV.

To recapitulate, the psychodynamics of suicide need to be understood in the context of the individual's unique life experiences. Suicide is often a reaction to loss—either loss of loved ones, present and past, or loss of function and vitality. In addition to anger and sadness, the predominant affects of depression, and other emotional states such as shame, guilt, and hopelessness precede suicidal behavior. Interpersonal conflicts resulting in inability to trust and accept others into one's life need to be worked through to prevent the intolerable loneliness and distress that could result in suicide. The suicidal person with HIV is often in the midst of a crisis of expendability. Stigma, discrimination, and AIDSism further compound the hopelessness and psychic distress, heightening the possibility of death by suicide.

PREVENTION STRATEGIES

Suicide prevention starts with eliciting a thorough suicide history from every person with HIV. Clinicians need to feel comfortable discussing suicide in depth. Countertransference reactions play a major role in being able to have a productive dialogue with the suicidal patient and establishing a therapeutic alliance. Feelings are contagious, and the overwhelming hopelessness of a suicidal individual may interfere with the clinician's ability to infuse hope and help the patient find alternatives to premature death. Far from harming the patient, being able to put feelings into words to express suicidal impulses is highly relieving and can prevent acting out aggressively against the self. When a suicidal person verbalizes his or her suicidal ideas and plans, a different perspective can be attained as unendurable affects are expressed. Listening with empathy at a moment of crisis can begin to dissipate hopelessness and mobilize the will to live.

An adequate suicide history includes an assessment of present suicidal ideas and plans by asking direct and open-ended questions. Since past suicide attempts are, along with hopelessness, the strongest predictors of future completed suicide, it is most important to ask about previous attempts and to elicit a family history of suicide. Timely treatment of the psychiatric disorders associated with heightened suicide risk could prevent suicide in individuals at risk. Antidepressants should be prescribed to depressed and anxious suicidal patients, but it is important to remember that anhedonia and psychomotor retardation lift first when these are prescribed, and hopelessness, dysphoria, and suicidal behavior take longer to improve (Mann, 2005). Psychotherapy can reduce a sense of alienation, provide symptomatic relief, increase networking, and promote conflict resolution. Psychotherapy modalities that can help suicidal patients include interpersonal, cognitive-behavioral, psychodynamic, and supportive, individual, couples, family, and group therapy settings.

Physical symptoms compound psychological distress and can precipitate death by suicide. Providing symptomatic relief and palliation of nociceptive and neuropathic pain, pruritus, diarrhea, nausea, emesis, and anorexia can avert a suicidal crisis in persons with HIV.

While suicidality is treatable and suicide is entirely preventable with psychotherapy and medication, there is no treatment for suicide. The only treatment for suicide is prevention. Thus there may be times when a person with HIV or AIDS is overwhelmed with suicidal feelings. The person may or may not have a prior relationship with a psychiatrist or other mental health clinician. If there is a suicide attempt or an expression of suicidal ideation, primary physicians, psychiatrists, and other mental health professionals in an emergency setting or psychosomatic medicine psychiatrists in general care may need to assess for suicidality. In such situations, an emergency psychiatric hospitalization may be indicated if the person is found to be actively suicidal and in the midst of a suicidal crisis. Close observation by staff is essential to ensure that the suicidal individual is safe during the process of the transfer. If the medical condition does not permit transfer, then one-on-one observation should be maintained until the suicidal crisis resolves or the transfer can be accomplished.

Since suicidal persons are ambivalent by definition and will oscillate from wanting to live and opting to die, it is important to identify family members or friends who can be called on to accompany and protect patients during a time of crisis. Family members or friends can also be of assistance in minimizing access to lethal means.

In order for the suicidal person with HIV infection to resolve a suicide crisis, it is important to establish trusting relationships, reconnect with family members and significant others, restore hope, find meaning in life, and develop goals to attain a sense of fulfillment and connectedness. With support, companionship, networking, establishing a therapeutic alliance, opportunities for reparative emotional experiences and earned secure attachments, conflict resolution, palliative care, adequate medical treatment, and alleviation of psychological distress, persons with HIV may be open to resolution of a suicidal crisis and reconstruction of new relational and coping strategies. By identifying protective and risk factors for suicide, clinicians will be better equipped and cognizant of those who are at risk. Timely application of psychotherapeutic, pharmacological, and psychosocial interventions can treat suicidality and may prevent death by suicide.

REFERENCES

Abraham K (1911). Notes on the psychoanalytical investigation and treatment of manic-depressive insanity and allied conditions. In *Selected Papers on Psychoanalysis* (pp. 137–156). Translated by D Byran and A Strachey. New York: Basic Books, 1960.

Abraham K (1924). A short study of the development of the libido, viewed in the light of mental disorders. In *Selected Papers on Psychoanalysis* (pp. 418–501). Translated by D Byran and A Strachey. New York: Basic Books, 1960.

Alfonso CA, Cohen MA (1994). HIV dementia and suicide. *Gen Hosp Psychiatry* 16:45–46.

Alfonso CA, Cohen MA (1997). The role of group psychotherapy in the care of persons with AIDS. *J Am Acad Psychoanal* 25:623–638.

Alfonso CA, Cohen MA (2008). Suicide. In MA Cohen, JM Gorman (eds.), *Comprehensive Textbook of AIDS Psychiatry* (pp. 195–203). New York: Oxford University Press.

Alfonso CA, Cohen MA, Aladjem AD, Morrison F, Powell DR, Winters RA, Orlowski BK (1994). HIV seropositivity as a major risk factor for suicide in the general hospital. *Psychosomatics* 35:368–373.

Beck AT, Steer RA, Kovacs M, Garrison B (1985). Hopelessness and eventual suicide: a 10-year prospective study of patients hospitalized with suicidal ideation. *Am J Psychiatry* 142:559–563.

Bostwick JM, Levenson JL (2005). Suicidality. In JL Levenson (ed.), *The American Psychiatric Publishing Textbook of Psychosomatic Medicine*. Arlington, VA: American Psychiatric Publishing.

Bostwick JM, Levenson JL (2011). Suicidality. In JL Levenson (ed.), *The American Psychiatric Publishing Textbook of Psychosomatic Medicine*, 2nd ed. Arlington, VA: American Psychiatric Publishing.

Braganca M, Palha A (2011). Depression and neurocognitive performance in Portuguese patients infected with HIV. *AIDS Behav* 15(8):18791–18787.

Breitbart W (1987). Suicide in cancer patients. *Oncology* 4:49–54.

Brown GR, Rundell JR (1989). Suicidal tendencies in women with human immunodeficiency virus infection. *Am J Psychiatry* 146:556–557.

Burrows G (1998). Suicidal ideation, suicide attempts, and HIV infection. *Psychosomatics* 39:405–415.

Capron DW, Gonzalez A, Parent J, Zvolensky MJ, Schmidt NB (2012). Suicidality and anxiety sensitivity in adults with HIV. *AIDS Patient Care STDs* 26(5):298–303.

Carvajal MJ, Vicioso C, Santamaria JM, Bosco A (1995). AIDS and suicide issues in Spain. *AIDS Care* 7:135–138.

Castellani G, Beghini D, Barisoni D, Marigo M (1995). Suicide attempted by burning: a 10-year study of self-immolation deaths. *Burns* 21(8):607–609.

Catalan J, Harding R, Sibley E, Clucas C, Croome N, Sherr L (2011). HIV infection and mental health: suicidal behaviour--systematic review. *Psychol Health Med* 16(5):588–611.

Chandra PS, Ravi V, Desai A, Subbakrishna DK (1998). Anxiety and depression among HIV-infected heterosexuals—a report from India. *J Psychosom Res* 45:401–409.

Chen CK, Tsai YC, Hsu HJ, et al. (2010). Depression and suicide risk in hemodialysis patients with chronic renal failure. *Psychosomatics* 51(6):528–528.e6.

Chen HQ, Li Y, Zhang BC, Li XF (2011). Study on high-risk behaviour and suicide associated risk factors related to HIV/AIDS among gay or bisexual men. *Chinese J Epidemiol* 32(10):983–986.

Chikezie UE, Otakpor AN, Kuteyi OB, James BO (2012). Suicidality among individuals with HIV/AIDS in Benin City, Nigeria: a case-control study. *AIDS Care* 24(7):843–845.

Cohen MA (1989). AIDSism, a new form of discrimination. *AMA News* 32:43.

Cohen MA (1998). Psychiatric care in an AIDS nursing home. *Psychosomatics* 39:154–161.

Cohen MA (1999). Psychodynamic psychotherapy in an AIDS nursing home. *J Am Acad Psychoanal* 27:121–133.

Cohen MA, Aladjem AD, Brenin D, Ghazi M (1990). Firesetting by patients with the acquired immunodeficiency syndrome (AIDS). *Ann Intern Med* 112:386–387.

Cohen MA, Alfonso CA (2004). AIDS psychiatry, palliative care and pain management. In GP Wormser (ed.), *AIDS and Other Manifestations of HIV Infection*, 4th ed. (p. 566). San Diego: Elsevier Academic Press.

Cohen MA, Alfonso CA, Hoffman R, Milau V, Carrera G (2001). The impact of PTSD on treatment adherence in persons with HIV infection. *Gen Hosp Psychiatry* 23(5):294–296.

Cohen MA, Merlino JP (1983). The suicidal patient on the surgical ward: multidisciplinary case conference. *Gen Hosp Psychiatry* 5:65–71.

Cooperman NA, Simoni JM (2005). Suicidal ideation and attempted suicide among women living with HIV/AIDS. *J Behav Med* 28(2):149–156.

Cote TR, Biggar RJ, Dannenberg AL (1992). Risk of suicide among persons with AIDS. *JAMA* 268:2066–2068.

Dinwiddie SH, Reich T, Cloninger CR (1992). Psychiatric comorbidity and suicidality among intravenous drug users. *J Clin Psychiatry* 53(10):364–369.

Drake RE, Ehrlich J (1985). Suicide attempts associated with akathisia. *Am J Psychiatry* 142(4):499–501.

Frances A (1986). Personality and suicide. *Ann NY Acad Sci* 487:281–293.

Freud S (1917). *Mourning and Melancholia. In Standard Edition of the Complete Psychological Works of Sigmund Freud*, Vol. 14 (pp. 237–260). Translated and edited by J Strachey. London: Hogarth Press, 1957.

Frierson RL, Lippmann SB (1988). Suicide and AIDS. *Psychosomatics* 29:226–231.

Gabler T, Yudelowitz B, Mahomed A (2011). Overdose with HAART: are we managing these patients adequately? *South African Med J* 101(8):520–521.

Gala C, Pergami A, Catalan J, et al. (1982). Risk of deliberate self-harm and factors associated with suicidal behaviors among asymptomatic individuals with human immunodeficiency virus infection. *Acta Psychiatr Scand* 86:70–75.

Gil F, Passik S, Rosenfeld B, Breitbart W (1998). Psychological adjustment and suicidal ideation in patients with AIDS. *AIDS Patient Care STDs* 12(12):927–930.

Glass RM (1988). AIDS and suicide. *JAMA* 259:1369–1370.

Glickman LS (1980). The suicidal patient. In LS Glickman (ed.), *Psychiatric Consultation in the General Hospital* (pp. 181–202). New York: Marcel Dekker.

Goodwin RD, Demmer RT, Galea S, Lemeshow AR, Ortega AN, Beautrais A (2012). Asthma and suicide behaviors: results from the Third National Health and Nutrition Examination Survey (NHANES III). *J Psychiatr Res* 46(8):1002–1007.

Gotoh T, Ajisawa A, Negishi M, Yamaguchi T (1994). A study of suicide and attempted suicide in HIV carriers and patients with AIDS. Xth International Conference on AIDS, Yokohama, Japan, 10:400 [abstract].

Guze SB, Robins E (1970). Suicide and primary affective disorder. *Br J Psychiatry* 117:437–438.

Haas DW, Morgan ME, Harris VL (1997). Increased viral load and suicidal ideation in an HIV-infected patient. *Ann Intern Med* 126(1):86–87.

Haller DL, Miles DR (2003). Suicidal ideation among psychiatric patients with HIV: psychiatric morbidity and quality of life. *AIDS Behav* 7(2):101–108.

Harris EC, Barraclough BM (1994). Suicide as an outcome for medical disorders. *Medicine* 73:281–296.

Heckman TG, Miller J, Kochman A, Kalichman SC, Carlson B, Silverthorn M (2002). Thoughts of suicide among HIV-infected rural persons enrolled in a telephone-delivered mental health intervention. *Ann Behav Med* 24(2):141–148.

Hubers AA, van Duijn E, Roos RA, et al.; REGISTRY investigators of the European Huntington's Disease Network (2013). Suicidal ideation in a European Huntington's disease population. *J Affect Disord* 151(1):248–258.

Huntington G (1872). On chorea. *Med Surg Reporter* 26:317–321.

Jia CX, Mehlum L, Qin P (2012). AIDS/HIV infection, comorbid psychiatric illness, and risk for subsequent suicide: a nationwide register linkage study. *J Clin Psychiatry* 73(10):1315–1321.

Jin H, Hampton Atkinson J, Yu X; HNRC China Collaboration Group (2006). Depression and suicidality in HIV/AIDS in China. *J Affect Disord* 94(1-3):269–275.

Jones AW, Holmgren A, Ahlner J (2013). Toxicology findings in suicides: concentrations of ethanol and other drugs in femoral blood in

victims of hanging and poisoning in relation to age and gender of the deceased. *J Forens Legal Med* 20(7):842–847.

Kalichman SC, Heckman T, Kochman A, Sikkema K, Bergholte J (2000). Depression and thoughts of suicide among middle-aged and older persons living with HIV-AIDS. *Psychiatr Serv* 51:903–907.

Kaplan A, Klein R (1989). Women and suicide. In D Jacobs, H Madison (eds.), *Suicide: Understanding and Responding* (pp. 257–282). Madison, CT: International Universities Press.

Kelly B, Raphael B, Judd F, et al. (1998). Suicidal ideation, suicide attempts, and HIV infection. *Psychosomatics* 39:405–415.

Kinyanda E, Hoskins S, Nakku J, Nawaz S, Patel V (2011). Prevalence and risk factors of major depressive disorder in HIV/AIDS as seen in semi-urban Entebbe district, Uganda. *BMC Psychiatry.* 11:205.

Kizer KW, Green M, Perkins CI, Doebbert G, Hughes MJ (1988). AIDS and suicide in California. *JAMA* 260:1881.

Kumar AM, Berger JR, Eisdorfer C, Fernandez JB, Goodkin K, Kumar M (2001). Cerebrospinal fluid 5-hydroxytryptamine and 5-hydroxyindoleacetic acid in HIV-1 infection. *Neuropsychobiology* 44(1):13–18.

Kurella M, Kimmel PL, Young BS, Chertow GM (2005). Suicide in the United States end-stage renal disease program. *J Am Soc Nephrol* 16(3):774–781.

Larsson M, Hagberg L, Norkrans G, Forsman A (1989). Indole amine deficiency in blood and cerebrospinal fluid from patients with human immunodeficiency virus infection. *J Neurosci Res* 23(4):441–446.

Levenson JL, Bostwick JM (2005). Suicidality in the medically ill. *Prim Psychiatry* 12(3):16–18.

Litman R (1989). Suicides: what do they have in mind? In D Jacobs, H Brown (eds.), *Suicide: Understanding and Responding* (pp. 143–154). Madison, CT: International Universities Press.

Lu D, Fall K, Sparen P, Ye W, Adami HO, Valdimarsdottir U, Fang F (2013). Suicide and suicide attempt after a cancer diagnosis among young individuals. *Ann Oncol* 24(12):3112–3117.

Malenfant EC (2004). Suicide in Canada's immigrant population. *Health Rep* 5:9–17.

Malone KM, Oquendo MA, Haas GL, Ellis SP, Li S, Mann JJ (2000). Protective factors against suicidal acts in major depression: reasons for living. *Am J Psychiatry* 157(7):1331–1332.

Mann JJ (2005). The medical management of depression. *N Engl J Med* 353:1819–1834.

Mann JJ, Apter A, Bertolote J, et al. (2005). Suicide prevention strategies—a systematic review. *JAMA* 294(16):2064–2074.

Marshall BD, Galea S, Wood E, Kerr T (2011). Injection methamphetamine use is associated with an increased risk of attempted suicide: a prospective cohort study. *Drug Alcohol Depend* 119(1-2):134–137.

Marzuk PM, Tardiff K, Leon AC, Stajic M, Morgan EB, Mann JJ (1992). Prevalence of cocaine use among residents of New York City who committed suicide during a one-year period. *Am J Psychiatry* 149:371–375.

Marzuk PM, Tierney H, Tardiff K, Gross EM, Morgan EB, Hsu MA, Mann JJ (1988). Increased risk of suicide in persons with AIDS. *JAMA* 259:1333–1337.

McIntosh J (2003). *U.S.A. Suicide: Suicide Data* (p. 2001). Washington, DC: American Association of Suicidology.

McManus H, Petoumenos K, Franic T; Australian HIV Observational Database (2014). Determinants of suicide and accidental or violent death in the Australian HIV Observational Database. *PLoS ONE* 9(2):e89089.

Menon V (2013). Suicide risk assessment and formulation: an update. *Asian Journal of Psychiatry.* 6(5):430–435.

Michel L, Giorgi R, Villes V, et al. (2009). Withdrawal symptoms as a predictor of mortality in patients HIV-infected through drug use and receiving highly active antiretroviral therapy (HAART). *Drug Alcohol Depend* 99(1-3):96–104.

Miles CP (1977). Conditions predisposing to suicide: a review. *J Nev Ment Dis* 164:231–246.

Mollan KR, Smurzynski M, Eron JJ, et al. (2014). Association between efavirenz as initial therapy for HIV-1 infection and increased risk for suicidal ideation or attempted or completed suicide: an analysis of trial data. *Ann Intern Med* 161(1):1–10.

Nordentoft M, Wahlbeck K, Hallgren J, et al. (2013). Excess mortality, causes of death and life expectancy in 270,770 patients with recent onset of mental disorders in Denmark, Finland and Sweden. *PLoS ONE* 8(1):e55176.

O'Cleirigh C, Ironson G, Antoni M, et al. (2003). Emotional expression and depth processing of trauma and their relation to long-term survival in patients with HIV/AIDS. *J Psychosom Res* 54(3):225–235.

Oquendo M, Brent DA, Birmaher B, et al. (2005). Posttraumatic stress disorder comorbid with major depression: factors mediating the association with suicidal behavior. *Am J Psychiatry* 162(3):560–566.

Oquendo MA, Dragatsi D, Harkavy-Friedman J, et al. (2005). Protective factors against suicidal behavior in Latinos. *J Nerv Ment Dis* 193(7):438–443.

Pavlovic E, Marusic A (2001). Suicide in Croatia and in Croatian immigrant groups in Australia and Slovenia. *Croat Med J* 42(6):669–672.

Pérez-Rodríguez MM, Baca-Garcia E, Oquendo MA, Wang S, Wall MM, Liu SM, Blanco C (2014). Relationship between acculturation, discrimination, and suicidal ideation and attempts among US Hispanics in the National Epidemiologic Survey of Alcohol and Related Conditions. *J Clin Psychiatry* 75(4):399–407.

Perry S, Jacobsberg L, Fishman B (1990). Suicidal ideation and HIV testing. *JAMA* 263:679–682.

Pierce C (1987). Underscore urgency of HIV counseling: several suicides follow positive tests. *Clin Psychiatry News* October 1.

Plott RT, Benton SD, Winslade WJ (1989). Suicide of AIDS patients in Texas: a preliminary report. *Tex Med* 85:40–43.

Pokorny AD (1966). A follow-up study of 618 suicidal patients. *Am J Psychiatry* 122:1109–1116.

Pompili M, Sher L, Serafini G, et al. (2013). Posttraumatic stress disorder and suicide risk among veterans: a literature review. *J Nerv Ment Dis* 201(9):802–812.

Preau M, Bouhnik AD, Peretti-Watel P, Obadia Y, Spire B; ANRS-EN12-VESPA Group (2008). Suicide attempts among people living with HIV in France. *AIDS Care* 20(8):917–924.

Protopopescu C, Raffi F, Brunet-Francois C, et al. (2012). Incidence, medical and socio-behavioural predictors of psychiatric events in an 11-year follow-up of HIV-infected patients on antiretroviral therapy. *Antiviral Ther* 17(6):1079–1083.

Qin P (2011). The impact of psychiatric illness on suicide: differences by diagnosis of disorders and by sex and age of subjects. *J Psychiatr Res* 45(11):1445–1452.

Rabkin JG, Remien R, Katoff L, Williams JB (1993). Resilience in adversity among long-term survivors of AIDS. *Hosp Community Psychiatry* 44(2):162–167.

Rabkin JG, Williams JB, Neugebauer R, Remien RH, Goetz R (1990). Maintenance of hope in HIV-spectrum homosexual men. *Am J Psychiatry* 147(10):1322–1326.

Rajs J, Fugelstad A (1992). Suicide related to human immunodeficiency virus infection in Stockholm. *Acta Psychiatr Scand* 85:234–239.

Ricart F, Cohen MA, Alfonso CA, Hoffman RG, Quinones N, Cohen A, Indyk D (2002). Understanding the psychodynamics of non-adherence in persons with PTSD and HIV infection. *Gen Hosp Psychiatry* 24(3):176–180.

Rosengard C, Folkman S (1997). Suicidal ideation, bereavement, HIV serostatus and psychosocial variables in partners of men with AIDS. *AIDS Care* 9(4):373–384.

Roy A (1986). Suicide in schizophrenia. In A Roy (ed.), *Suicide* (pp. 97–112). Baltimore: Williams & Wilkins.

Roy A (2003). Characteristics of HIV patients who attempt suicide. *Acta Psychiatr Scand* 107(1):41–44.

Rundell JR, Kyle KM, Brown GR, Thomason JL (1992). Risk factors for suicide attempts in a human immunodeficiency virus screening program. *Psychosomatics* 33:24–27.

Rundell JR, Wise ME, Ursano RJ (1986). Three cases of AIDS-related psychiatric disorders. *Am J Psychiatry* 143:777–778.

Ruzicka LT, Choi CY, Sadkowsky K (2005). Medical disorders of suicides in Australia: analysis using a multiple-cause-of-death approach. *Soc Sci Med* 61(2):333–341.

Sabbath J (1969). The suicidal adolescent: the expendable child. *J Am Acad Child Psychiatry* 8:272–289.

Scalfari A, Knappertz V, Cutter G, Goodin DS, Ashton R, Ebers GC (2013). Mortality in patients with multiple sclerosis. *Neurology* 81(2):184–192.

Scholten MR, Selten JP (2005). Suicidal ideations and suicide attempts after starting on aripiprazole, a new antipsychotic drug. *Ned Tijdschr Geneeskd* 149(41):2296–2298.

Semela D, Glatz M, Hunziker D, Scmid U, Vernazza PL (2000). Cause of death and autopsy findings in patients of the Swiss HIV Cohort Study (SHCS). *J Suisse Med* 130:1726–1733.

Shear MK, Frances A, Weiden P (1983). Suicide associated with akathisia and depot fluphenazine treatment. *J Clin Psychopharmacol* 3(4):235–236.

Sher L, Oquendo MA, Burke AK, Grunebaum MF, Zalsman G, Huang YY, Mann JJ (2005). Higher cerebrospinal fluid homovanillic acid levels in depressed patients with comorbid posttraumatic stress disorder. *Eur Neuropsychopharmacol* 15(2):203–209.

Sherr L (1995). Suicide and AIDS: lessons from a case note audit in London. *AIDS Care* 7(Suppl 2):109–116.

Sindiga I, Lukhando M (1993). Kenyan university students' views on AIDS. *East Afr Med J* 70:713–716.

Tidemalm D, Langstrom N, Lichtenstein P, Runeson B (2008). Risk of suicide after suicide attempt according to coexisting psychiatric disorder: Swedish cohort study with long term follow-up. *BMJ* 337:a2205.

Vance DE, Ross JA, Moneyham L, Farr KF, Fordham P (2010). A model of cognitive decline and suicidal ideation in adults aging with HIV. *J Neurosci Nurs* 42(3):150–156.

Vance DE, Struzick T, Burrage J, Jr (2009). Suicidal ideation, hardiness, and successful aging with HIV: considerations for nursing. *J Gerontol Nurs* 35(5):27–33.

Varnik P (2012). Suicide in the world. *Int J Environ Res Public Health* 9(3):760–771.

Wood KA, Nairn R, Kraft H, Siegel (1997). Suicidality among HIV-positive psychiatric in-patients. *AIDS Care* 9(4):385–389.

PART VI

NEUROPATHOLOGICAL MANIFESTATIONS OF HIV INFECTION

26.

NEUROLOGICAL COMPLICATIONS OF HIV IN THE CENTRAL NERVOUS SYSTEM

Christopher Woldstad, Michael Boska, and Howard E. Gendelman

INTRODUCTION

HIV infection and its consequent immune deficiency and linked comorbid conditions represent a spectrum of clinically manageable chronic diseases. This has happened, in large measure, as a result of global research efforts in disease pathogenesis, epidemiology, and natural history and therapeutics (Elbirt et al., 2015; Lamers et al., 2014; Maartens et al., 2014; Peluso and Spudich, 2014; Tan and McArthur, 2012). Since the discovery more than 30 years ago of the human immunodeficiency virus (HIV) as the cause of the acquired immune deficiency syndrome (AIDS) (Barre-Sinoussi et al., 1983; Gallo et al., 1983), the molecular structure, function, regulation, tropism, and means of viral persistence have been elucidated (Fujita, 2013; Steckbeck et al., 2013; Sundquist and Krausslich, 2012). Perhaps the most important result of ongoing HIV/AIDS research activities was the discovery of combination antiretroviral therapies (ART). ART and the newer treatments for a myriad of opportunistic infections are now the standard of care (Grant and Zolopa, 2012; Ho and Marra, 2014; Tan et al., 2012). A significant global, political, and social research effort has emerged to make ART available worldwide (Bezabhe et al., 2014; Govindasamy et al., 2014; Stricker et al., 2014). This and the newer advanced therapies are now the standard of care (Folayan et al., 2011). Although HIV is a treatable chronic disorder in which the immune system can be protected through ART reductions of viral load, toxicities of antiretroviral medicines abound, and these pharmaceuticals may not always be effective when administered over prolonged time periods (Chen et al., 2013; Leutscher et al., 2013; Nozaki et al., 2013). The emergence of viral drug resistance, consequent immune deterioration, and short- and long-term drug toxicities can make the outcome of HIV disease uncertain.

Of all the complications of HIV, the most foreboding is its effects on the nervous system (Elbirt et al., 2015). While the causes of cognitive and behavioral dysfunction in HIV/AIDS have changed, its stigma continues almost unabated. The history of the disorder provides insights into its change in natural history over the years. In the era of combination ART, the causes of cognitive impairment are now multifaceted. Viral infection plays a more minor role and is supplanted by dietary factors, comorbid conditions, drugs of abuse, metabolic abnormalities, and combination ART itself (Clark and Cohen, 2010; Elbirt et al., 2015; McMurtray et al., 2006). Notwithstanding and in the early days of the HIV/AIDS epidemic, neurological impairments due to the virus itself were linked to advanced disease and profound immune suppression (Navia, Cho, et al., 1986; Navia, Jordan, et al., 1986). Illness manifestations ranged from mild to severe with a triad of cognitive, motor, and behavioral disturbances (Gelman et al., 2013; Griffin et al., 2004; Kranick and Nath, 2012; Weed and Steward, 2005; Wilkie et al., 2003; Worlein et al., 2005). While HIV dementia is all but gone, as a consequence of ART, the prevalence of what is now called HIV-associated neurocognitive disorders (HAND) remains commonplace (Gelman et al., 2013). Simply stated, the disease has evolved from one induced by the virus alone to one caused by psychiatric, environmental, and multimorbid conditions (Jiang et al., 2013).

This review serves to highlight both the research advances made in understanding the effects of HIV on the nervous system and what lies ahead. Particular focus is given to both the effects HIV can play on the nervous system at the molecular and cellular levels and the comorbid conditions that affect neural function. Attention is also given to specific biomarkers to be utilized for increasing the effectiveness and availability of therapies. Interestingly, the pathogenesis of HAND is comparable to that of several other neurodegenerative disorders, and their mechanistic similarities are also discussed in detail. Notably, whether cognitive impairment is directly caused by the virus or indirectly by misfolded and aggregated proteins or liver and gastrointestinal malfunctions, all can underlie disease onset or progression (Demeulemeester et al., 2014; Ghafouri et al., 2006; Harezlak et al., 2011; Ipp et al., 2014; Lozupone et al., 2014). Nonetheless, a significant body of data has emerged in the past 30 years on how HIV affects the brain and causes progressive clinical impairment, allowing the scientific and medical fields to make advancements in determining viral neuropathogenesis (Chen et al., 2013; Lamers et al., 2014; Williams et al., 2014; Zayyad and Spudich, 2015). While the past and present research efforts have been productive, the key to future research strategies remains in discovering ways to protect the brain, reverse the process of impairment, or attenuate it.

ENTRY INTO THE BRAIN

HIV is known to gain entry to the protected environment of the central nervous system (CNS) via a variety of different routes. Several mechanisms have been proposed by which HIV-1 gains entry into the brain (Aiamkitsumrit et al., 2014; Joseph et al., 2014; Miller et al., 2012; Williams et al., 2013). The "Trojan horse" hypothesis states that HIV-1 enters the brain through infected monocyte–macrophages, migrating into the brain parenchyma through blood–brain barrier (BBB) disruption and the establishment of a chemokine gradient. HIV assembles then buds into intracytoplasmic vesicles within the macrophages with limited expression of viral proteins on the cell surface, allowing, in part, for escape from immune surveillance (Gras and Kaul, 2010; Meng and Lever, 2013; Sundquist and Krausslich, 2012; Votteler and Sundquist, 2013). A second viral entry path involves cell-free virus directly infecting the endothelial cells and astrocytes contained as part the BBB. However, this theory is more limited as there is nonproductive infection of cells contained as part of the BBB (Kanmogne et al., 2000; Spudich and Gonzalez-Scarano, 2012). A third pathway is known as transcytosis: here HIV-1 invades the CNS through internalization of the virion by endothelial cells or by astrocyte foot processes by macropinocytosis or endosomes, with subsequent transfer of the virus to the brain parenchyma (Eugenin et al., 2005).

The initial process of HIV-1 infection is the attachment of the virion to the cell surface, followed by fusion of the viral and cellular membranes delivering the viral core into the cytoplasm (Klasse, 2012). The process of attachment and fusion is mediated by the interaction of the viral glycoprotein with the CD4 receptor and co-receptor CCR5 or CXCR4, depending on whether the HIV strain is macrophage tropic or T-lymphocyte tropic (Devadas et al., 2004; Lifson, Coutre, et al., 1986; Lifson, Feinberg, et al., 1986). In the brain, monocyte-derived perivascular macrophages are the principal cell type infected by HIV-1 (Burdo et al., 2013; Herbein and Varin, 2010; Joseph et al., 2015; Koppensteiner et al., 2012), with limited expression in microglia and restrictive/nonproductive replication within astrocytes (McArthur et al., 2010). Astrocytes and capillary endothelial cells contain HIV-1 nucleic acids in infected individuals (Devadas et al., 2004). However, what drives CNS infection, when it occurs, is the number of infected brain macrophages. These cells also govern the extent of CNS inflammation, the number of recruited monocyte-derived macrophages to the brain, and the course and extent of neurological impairment (Burdo et al., 2013).

CNS HIV infection, at any level, leads to immune activation of the brain parenchyma. This results in subsequent increase in the number of microglial cells, up-regulation of MHC class II expression, and local production of cytokines (Gonzalez-Scarano and Martin-Garcia, 2005). In the uninfected CNS, neurons, oligodendrocytes, astrocytes, and micrglia are intimately associated with each other and communicate through specialized synapses and cell junctions; this direct cell contact is required for proper glia maturation and function (Churchill and Nath, 2013; Kettenmann et al., 2011). Activated microglia and, to a lesser extent, astrocytes express MHC class I and II antigens and adhesion molecules and secrete cytokines and reactive oxygen intermediates, and all have been shown to be important factors contributing to the most severe form of disease or HIV dementia (Lipton et al., 1994; Tyor et al., 1992). Microglia and astrocytes produce chemokines and control monocyte migration across the BBB (Aquaro et al., 2005; Nottet et al., 1995, 1996; Persidsky et al., 2000). The event(s) triggering monocyte invasion into the nervous system likely involves the secretion of macrophage attractant chemokines and the up-regulation of adhesion molecules on activated endothelial and immune cells. Proinflammatory factors induce cytokines and chemokines (such as interleukin-8 [IL-8], interferon gamma [IFN-γ], inducible protein 10 [IP-10], growth-related oncogene α [GRO-α], macrophage inflammatory protein 1a [MIP-1a], MIP-1b, RANTES, and monocyte chemotactic protein 1 [MCP-1]) found in infected brain tissue and may also participate directly in the disease process (Shive et al., 2014; Vandergeeten et al., 2012). Both cytokines and HIV-1 Tat induce expression of E-selectin on brain microvascular endothelial cells (BMVEC). The likelihood of this event is increased by the release of nitric oxide (NO). TNF-α and Il-1β also induce expression of vascular cell adhesion molecule 1 (VCAM-1) on the BMVEC (Brabers and Nottet, 2006). This induction of adhesion molecules allows binding of HIV-infected cells to the brain endothelium (Maslin et al., 2005; Williams et al., 2013). Virus and activated macrophage entry into the brain is likely precipitated by BBB damage heralded by activation of brain mononuclear phagocytes. Neuronal damage and alterations in the integrity of tight junction and/or regulation of its immune function occur as consequences of viral and cellular secretory products and are crucial to HIV-1 brain transport (Andras et al., 2003; Kanmogne et al., 2005; Lifson, Feinberg, et al., 1986; Miller et al., 2012; Persidsky et al., 2000; Toborek et al., 2005; Xiong et al., 2000).

The BBB consists of a monolayer of specialized, nonfenestrated, microvascular endothelial cells. Associated with the BBB is a capillary basement membrane on the abluminal side of the monolayer, with tight junctions connecting the BMVEC and no transcellular pores (Berger and Avison, 2004; Gras and Kaul, 2010). These together serve to restrict movement of cells and macromolecules, including viral particles, throughout much of HIV-1 infection. Nonetheless, a number of biological situations enable the aberrant trafficking of cells across the BBB as a result of HIV-1 infection, allowing for the virus to enter the brain. The movement of viral particles from the periphery into the brain is facilitated through immune and structural BBB compromise. This process occurs late in the course of disease and serves to speed the overall pathogenic disease process. HIV-1 infection alters the BBB itself (Andras et al., 2003; Banks et al., 1998, 2001); numerous functional and structural abnormalities are of consequence, including damage to the basement membrane, damage to tight junction proteins, morphological and functional alterations of the BMVEC (Kanmogne et al., 2005, 2007), and subsequent protein leakage (Nottet et al., 1996). As a result, HIV-1-infected monocytes and/or CD4+ T lymphocytes as well as cell-free virus are able to cross the BBB (Miller et al., 2012; Williams et al., 2013).

Inflammation also serves to enhance trafficking of cells across the BBB. ICAM-1, VCAM-1, and E-selectin are up-regulated on the surface of BMVEC and astrocytes after exposure to proinflammatory factors secreted from microglia and astrocytes and/or activated leukocytes from the periphery; these serve to augment the process of adhesion molecule expression on BMVEC and astrocytes (Conant et al., 1994; Nottet et al., 1996). Late in the disease process, inflammatory cytokines are produced at high levels and allow the BBB to be more easily breached. These proinflammatory cytokines induce a transient increase in endothelial permeability by increasing secretion of endothelial vasoactive factors, such as NO (Diesing et al., 2002). TNF-α and IL-1β increase the production of other inflammatory mediators, including arachidonic acid–derived platelet-activating factor (PAF) ((Lawrence and Major, 2002; Nottet and Gendelman, 1995; Nottet et al., 1996). These serve to promote monocyte migration across the BBB and ultimately into the brain parenchyma (Miller et al., 2012; Nottet et al., 1996; Williams et al., 2013). The adhesion molecules ICAM-1 and VCAM-1 on the luminal surface of the BMVEC bind lymphocyte function-associated antigen-1 (LFA-1) and Vl-4 on the monocyte, resulting in migration of the monocyte between the endothelial cells during the early stages of viral infection (Berger and Avison, 2004) (Figure 26.1).

Alterations in capillary endothelial cells and basement membrane and disruption of tight junctions by HIV-1-infected monocytes and macrophages lead to a compromise of the structural integrity of the BBB following HIV-1 infection

of the nervous system. Disruption of the BBB is affected by a number of inflammatory factors, including proinflammatory cytokines (TNF-α and IL-1β) secreted by perivascular HIV-1-infected monocytes and macrophages. TNF-α, IL-1β, and HIV-1 Tat induce expression of E selectin on BMVEC, which mediates rolling of HIV-infected monocytes on the vessel wall. TNF-α and IL-1β also induce the expression of the adhesion molecules VCAM-1 and ICAM-1 on BMVEC to allow for the binding of HIV-infected monocytes to the brain endothelium. These neurotoxic factors may contribute to breakdown of the BBB and affect the generation of a chemokine gradient through interactions between HIV-infected monocytes and BMVEC and lead to enhanced transendothelial migration of cells from blood to brain. This interaction results in the production of monocyte-derived chemokines MIP-1α, MIP-1β and the endothelial-derived chemokine MCP-1. These chemokines will attract more mononuclear phagocytic cells into the brain parenchyma, resulting in expansion of the viral load within the CNS, and release of nitric oxide (NO) and reactive oxygen species (ROS).

Changes in cellular physiology that are induced as a consequence of inflammation also influence transmigration of inflammatory cells into the CNS. Chemokines are secreted at sites of inflammation in all tissues and work to guide leukocytes in a concentration-dependent manner. Importantly, specific chemokines will attract specific populations of leukocytes. MIP-1α and MCP-1 levels are increased during HIV encephalitis and are potent chemoattractants for macrophages as well as CD4+ T lymphocytes (Clay et al., 2007; Lawrence and Major, 2002; Maslin et al., 2005; Schmidtmayerova et al., 1996). Increasing damage to the BBB impairs its ability to

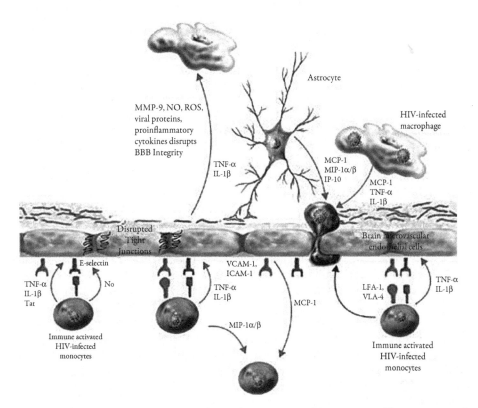

Figure 26.1. Blood–brain barrier (BBB) impairment in HIV encephalitis and HIV-associated dementia. For abbreviations, see chapter text.

protect the CNS from the periphery, resulting in cells and toxins being able to reach the CNS unchecked. Levels of inflammatory factors greatly increase and lead to a cascade of events culminating in further BBB dysfunction. These processes, taken together, affect MP-induced neuronal destruction during HIV-associated dementia (HAD).

The "Trojan horse" concept is that infected monocytes and lymphocytes can act as cellular vehicles that can transport HIV across the BBB. The specific mechanism of this process has not been completely elucidated; however, a substantial body of scientific data support this notion (Catuogno et al., 2015). Monocytes and CD4+ T lymphocytes are the primary target of HIV infection outside of the CNS, and analysis of HIV-infected brains has found substantive accumulations of virus-infected macrophages in the brain parenchyma (Budka et al., 1987; Gelman et al., 2013). Expression of adhesion molecules as well as chemoattractants within the CNS is higher in individuals with HAD, allowing increased interactions between infected leukocytes and brain endothelium as well as increased recruitment of these monocytes for transmigration (Eugenin and Berman, 2007; Gattegno et al., 1995; Maslin et al., 2005; Schmidtmayerova et al., 1996).

These observations converge into the idea of a snowball-like effect, in which initial HIV invasion occurs in very small amounts, with increasing levels of invasion facilitated by inflammation and the establishment of a chemokine gradient initiated by changes in the microenvironment facilitated through the infected migrating cells. HIV infection of human peripheral blood monocytes results in higher expression levels of LFA-1 and inflammatory factors released by these infected cells, which induce expression of chemokines and adhesion molecules E-selectin and VCAM by endothelial cells (Banks et al., 1998; Biernacki et al., 2001).

Chemokines certainly play a vital role in the transmigration process, and studies have reported enhanced expression levels of both chemokines in glia and their respective cell surface receptors in peripherally infected leukocytes (Lavi et al., 1998; McManus et al., 2000). MCP-1 (or CCL2) is the principal attractant for monocytes and activated lymphocytes (Carr et al., 1994; Xu et al., 1996), and studies have indicated that it is integral for monocyte transmigration into the brain parenchyma (Gonzalez et al., 2002). Analysis of cerebrospinal fluid (CSF) from persons with HIV with dementia found elevated levels of MCP-1 (Conant et al., 1998; Kelder et al., 1998). These findings, taken together, indicate that adhesion molecules and chemokines play key roles in facilitating leukocyte transmigration and subsequent invasion of HIV into the CNS.

Although the major targets of HIV in the brain are macrophages and microglia, there are a number of reports of other cells of the brain being infected by HIV, including astrocytes, neurons, and endothelial cells (Brack-Werner, 1999; Churchill and Nath, 2013; Nottet and Gendelman, 1995; Strelow et al., 2001). This underscores yet another mode for HIV CNS entry, which is direct infection of perivascular endothelial cells and astrocytes within the BBB. Astrocyte viral infection is low and often results in minimal viral production (Eugenin and Berman, 2007; Schweighardt et al.,

2001). However, astrocytes exposed to virus are affected with local gliosis, toxicity, and inflammation and as such serve to propagate disease pathobiology (Eugenin and Berman, 2007). Infection of astrocytes occurs solely at the late stages of the disease, long after the initial invasion of the virus, as one study concluded that up to 19% of astrocytes are infected at the later stages of disease (Churchill et al., 2009). This same study also found correlation between areas of HIV-infected astrocytes and increased rate of monocyte–macrophage transmigration. Although direct infection of endothelial cells and astrocytes is unlikely as a principal mode of HIV CNS entry, it could serve as a low-level reservoir throughout the course of disease. It is plausible that such infected cells participate in the later stages of infection and, notably, during long-term ART.

Transcytosis may also occur as an invasion route and is characterized by the abilities of endothelial cells or astrocytes to absorb virons by macropinocytosis mediate transfer of virus to the brain parenchyma. Viral particles were observed in endosomes (Banks et al., 2001). Increased surface microvilli of brain endothelial cells and similar increases in numbers of cytoplasmic vesicles are indicative of macropinocytosis (Liu and Hong, 2003). How cells transfer and propagate infection among CNS cells remains unclear. Most likely it is a combination of macrophage transmigration and endothelial, microglial, and astrocyte infection and transcytosis that leads to HIV CNS invasion.

CNS TARGETS FOR HIV INFECTION

MONONUCLEAR PHAGOCYTES

The pathogenesis of HIV-associated CNS disease centers around mononuclear phagocytes (MP), blood-borne macrophages, dendritic cells, tissue macrophages, and microglia. MP are the principal cell infected in the brain and become activated and recruited into tissue during inflammation (Burdo et al., 2013; Gabuzda and Wang, 1999; Gartner and Liu, 2002; Koenig et al., 1986). MP influx is usually transient, however, and will revert to a quiescent state after the inflammatory process has subsided, as is the case during ART. Secretory products and immune-competent and virus-infected MP along with immune cross-talk affect neuronal function and can lead to a metabolic encephalopathy (Anderson et al., 2002; Zheng et al., 2001). This is characterized clinically by behavioral, motor, and cognitive impairments (Griffin et al., 2004; Weed and Steward, 2005; Wilkie et al., 2003; Worlein et al., 2005). Ongoing inflammatory responses in the brain change microglial function and inevitable unresponsiveness to environmental cues, leading to lack of control for innate immunity (Ghorpade et al., 2005). The end result is the entry of HIV-infected MP to the brain, allowing the CNS viral reservoir to be consistently replenished, with ensuing enhanced neurotoxic secretions (Nottet et al., 1995; Poluektova et al., 2005; Zheng and Gendelman, 1997). For HIV encephalitis the process never subsides, as brain inflammation is continuous. Indeed, activation and differentiation of MP increases the efficiency of viral replication and spread

(Herbein and Varin, 2010; Yu et al., 2008). Such cells, once in the CNS, initiate a "pull" mechanism of activation and recruitment via chemotactic and inflammatory signals such that more monocytes are attracted to the brain, increasing the amount of HIV-1 as well as activating and infecting other cells within the CNS (Maslin et al., 2005; Porcheray et al., 2006; Williams et al., 2014) (Figure 26.2).

The primed and immune-activated MP secrete a variety of neurotoxic factors (cytokines, chemokines, PAF, quinolinic acid, glutamate, and NO) that affect neural function and CNS inflammation. These factors may contribute to the breakdown of the BBB and affect transendothelial migration of leukocytes into the brain, perpetuating the inflammatory cascade. Depending on their functional status, astrocytes may suppress or increase MP secretory functions and ROS.

The perivascular macrophage is an actively studied MP cell type with involvement in HAD pathogenesis. Normally these cells exist between the glia limitans and basement membrane of the choroid plexus and CNS capillaries and are derived from circulating monocytes. Because of their anatomical proximity to cerebral vessels in the brain, perivascular macrophages are likely susceptible to HIV-1 that crosses the BBB (Burdo et al., 2013; Herbein and Varin, 2010; Joseph et al., 2015). They are in close association with the BMVECs, and this collaboration allows them to serve as sentinels for the CNS. In fact, perivascular macrophages act as intermediates between the peripheral circulation and the microglia. Since microglia are in contact with these macrophages, signals may be rapidly communicated deep into the CNS from interactions at the perivascular space. Transmission of virus and/or

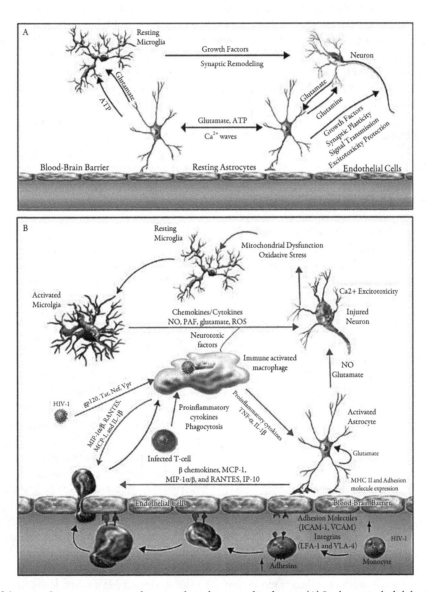

Figure 26.2. Pathobiology of the central nervous system under normal conditions and in disease. (A) In the normal adult brain, there is constant crosstalk among resident neuroglia and neurons that serves to maintain homeostasis through secretion of trophic factors, immune surveillance, and regulation of metabolic factors. (B) During the disease state, mononuclear phagocytes may be primed by virus or viral proteins and secondarily activated by factors such as proinflammatory cytokines and chemokines, or by T cells trafficking in and out of the nervous system. For abbreviations, see chapter text.

inflammatory responses in the brain may occur between these perivascular macrophages and glial cells.

Parenchymal microglia occur in significant numbers in the CNS and may constitute up to 10% of CNS cells. These cells enter the CNS during gestation and have a very low turnover rate (Alliot et al., 1999; Burdo et al., 2013; Kaur and Ling, 1991), in contrast to perivascular macrophages, which are continuously replenished from the bone marrow. Parenchymal microglia act as the resident macrophages within the brain and are responsible for the primary immune response within the brain. Normally, parenchymal microglia and macrophages in the CNS are easily distinguished from each other by morphology, but activation of microglia results in them displaying macrophage-like properties (Kettenmann et al., 2011). There are two morphological subtypes of microglia (Ling, 1982b). The first, ramified microglia, are resting cells with reduced secretory and phagocytic activity making up a cell web (Glenn et al., 1992; Kettenmann et al., 2011; Ling, 1982b). In contrast to perivascular macrophages, they have weak antigen-presenting capability. The second morphological subtype, amoeboid in form, is a morphological intermediate and transitional cell between the ramified microglia and the brain macrophages (Kettenmann et al., 2011). This subtype is not found in the normal adult CNS but rather in inflammatory and demyelinating conditions (Kaur et al., 1985; Kettenmann et al., 2011; Ling, 1982a; Ling and Wong, 1993).

In the absence of ART, infection of brain MP eventually leads to the formation of multinucleated giant cells. These cells result from the fusion of HIV-1-infected brain MP with uninfected monocyte-macrophages or microglia (Budka, 1986, 1991; Burdo et al., 2013; Kaur et al., 1985; Kettenmann et al., 2011; Ling, 1982a; Ling and Wong, 1993; McArthur et al., 2010; Pontow et al., 2004). This fusion is mediated by viral envelope glycoproteins present at the surface of infected cells with CD4 and chemokine receptors present on neighboring uninfected cells (Lifson, Coutre, et al., 1986; Lifson, Feinberg, et al., 1986; Matthews et al., 1987). The multinucleated cells are large, irregularly round, elongated, or polyhedral, with dense eosinophilic cytoplasm in the center and vacuolated at the periphery (Budka et al., 1988; Pontow et al., 2004), and seen in deep brain structures most commonly in subcortical white matter (Dickson, 1986; Sharer et al., 1985, 1988).

ASTROCYTES

Astrocytes are critical for the survival of neurons, and their function may be impaired in the context of HIV-1 infection. Astrocytes are responsible for maintaining homeostasis in the CNS and are important in the detoxification of excess excitatory amino acids such as extracellular glutamate levels (Deshpande et al., 2005; Wesselingh and Thompson, 2001). However, infected astrocytes can produce cellular factors that may adversely affect neuronal survival (Lawrence and Major, 2002). Astrocytes play a dual role in the pathogenesis of HIV-related encephalopathy; in HIV-1 infection, astrocyte glutamate reuptake is impaired, possibly due to interactions with

infected macrophages (Fine et al., 1996; Jiang et al., 2001). However, glutamate release in astrocytes is also induced by activated macrophages (Bezzi et al., 2001; Vesce et al., 1997). Activation of the CXCR4 receptor by stromal cell–derived factor 1 (SDF-1) results in the release of extracellular TNF-α and downstream release of glutamate (Bezzi et al., 2001). During HIV-1 infection there is an amplification or regulation of neurotoxic signals among astrocytes and microglia (Genis et al., 1992; Nottet et al., 1995). The HIV protein Tat induces astrocytic expression of MCP-1, a chemoattractant for macrophages, and IL-8 and IP-10, which attract multiple leukocyte types (Kutsch et al., 2000).

The level of astrocyte apoptosis correlates strongly with both the severity and rate of progression of disease. Direct infection is minimal due to an absence of the CD4 receptor. Although studies have reported that infection of astrocytes can be both productive and unproductive (Churchill et al., 2009; Deshpande et al., 2005), recent studies have concluded that productive HIV-1 infection of astrocytes is infinitesimally small, with .0025% of brain astrocytes undergoing productive infection (Chauhan et al., 2014). HIV-1 virus enters these astrocytes via endocytosis in which endosomal machinery degrades the majority of the viral particles; thus HIV-1 astrocytic endocytosis is seen as a "kiss of death," as only a very small amount of viral particles survive and establish a productive infection (Chauhan et al., 2014). Restricted infection of astrocytes occurs more frequently, with groups reporting 3–19% of astrocytes within infected brain tissue carrying HIV-1 DNA (Churchill et al., 2009).

T CELLS

CD4+ T cells are overall the most commonly HIV-infected cells in humans and are the primary target for virus (Jassoy et al.,1992; Sato et al.,1992). Impaired immune response is characteristic of all stages of disease. CD4+ T-cell abnormalities such as CD4+ T-cell lymphopenia, characterized by decreased lymphoproliferation and a decreased number of cells having a naïve phenotype, are seen in HIV-1-infected individuals (Devadas et al., 2004). An uninfected individual normally has 800 to 1200 CD4+ T cells per cubic millimeter of blood, but during HIV infection these cell numbers progressively decline. Infiltrating CD8+ cells lose their protective role in later stages of infection, ultimately exhibiting impaired cytokine production and cytolysis, possibly as a result of anergy and the inability to eliminate HIV-1-infected cells in the setting of functionally impaired helper CD4+ T lymphocytes. Activated T cells penetrate the BBB after insult to the CNS and can initiate both protective and toxic inflammatory responses (Miller et al., 2012; Toborek et al., 2005). Protective responses are elicited through elimination of the ongoing infectious agent by innate, humoral, and cytotoxic immune activities. Nonetheless, widespread inflammation in the setting of HIV often leads to damage of the BBB and further transendothelial migration of leukocytes entering the nervous system (Kanmogne et al., 2007; Miller et al., 2012; Persidsky et al., 2000). Inflammation of the brain and spinal cord actively attracts T cells to the CNS. MIP-1α and

MIP-1β are relevant to the cellular recruitment and immune activation during infection (Canque et al., 1996; Jennes et al., 2004), as both use CCR5 as their receptor (Farzan et al., 1997; Miyakawa et al., 2002; Navenot et al., 2001). MIP-1α selectively attracts CD8+ and MIP-1β recruits CD4+ lymphocytes.

PERSISTENCE, REPLICATION, RESEVOIR, AND TROPISM

The way in which virus penetrates the brain and the modes of viral persistence and virus-induced toxicity remain an active area of investigation (Burdo et al., 2013; Burton, 2006; Gras and Kaul, 2010; L. Gray et al., 2005; Ribeiro et al., 2006). MP activation increases the cells' abilities to promote viral growth. The more monocytes and macrophages that gain entry into brain, the broader the inflammatory cascade and the more widespread the viral reservoir. This serves as the nidus for productive viral replication (Porcheray et al., 2006). Notably, immune activation serves as a trigger for virus growth, and this in turn serves as a trigger for immune activation, leading to a cascade of innate neuroinflammatory responses amplified by interactions among MP, astrocytes, endothelial cells, and neurons in a paracrine and autocrine manner (Gras and Kaul, 2010; Kaul and Lipton, 2006; Minagar et al., 2002; Tyor et al., 1992). Inflammatory cytotoxic factors that include proinflammatory cytokines such as TNF-α and IL-1β as well as arachidonic acid metabolites influence disease with known HIV-1 proteins. The structural viral proteins such as gp120 (Brenneman et al., 1988; Khan et al., 2007) and gp41 (Adamson et al., 1996), and the nonstructural proteins Tat (New et al.,1997;

Price et al., 2005), Nef, Vpr, and Rev secreted by infected MP can all negatively affect neuronal function (Price et al., 2006). The HIV-1 coat protein gp120 can directly disrupt glial and neuronal function through alteration of calcium homeostasis, induction of reactive oxygen and nitrogen species to induce apoptosis (Jana and Pahan, 2004). Secretion of Tat can also cause direct or indirect injury to neurons through similar mechanisms (Nath et al., 2002; Song et al., 2003) (Figure 26.3).

Immune-activated and HIV-infected MP release potentially neurotoxic substances. These substances induce neuronal injury, dendritic and synaptic damage, and apoptosis. The enhanced production of cytokines TNF-α and IL-1β, reactive oxygen species (ROS), and viral proteins from macrophages stimulates astrocytosis and the subsequent production of NO. In addition, neurotoxins released from macrophages impair astrocyte clearing of the neurotransmitter glutamate and thus contribute to excitotoxicity. The neurotoxic product also directly affects neuronal function. Taken together, the secretion of neurotoxic products and the decreased neurotropic capacity of astrocytes contribute to the destruction of proximal neurons.

In addition, Tat may be involved in the disruption of the BBB (Andras et al., 2003). Tat has been shown to influence the inflammatory cascade through promotion of TNF-α and IL-1 production by MP and stimulate the production of several chemokines including RANTES and MCP-1 in astrocytes, which may propagate neuronal toxicity (El-Hage et al., 2005; Nath et al., 2002). The regulatory protein Vpr might also be neurotoxic. Intracellular and extracellular Vpr have been demonstrated to induce apoptosis by increasing caspase-8 activation (Pomerantz, 2004) and through cell cycle arrest (Jowett et al., 1995; Stewart et al., 1997).

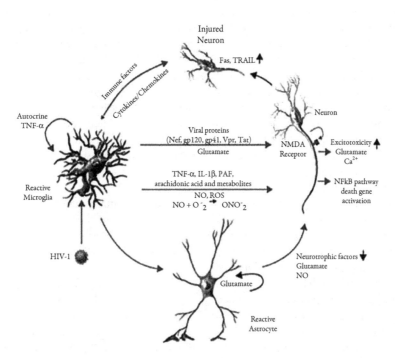

Figure 26.3. HIV-related neuronal damage. For abbreviations, see chapter text.

HIV REPLICATION AND
TROPISM IN THE BRAIN

Infection typically begins when a virion, which contains two copies of the HIV RNA, encounters a cell with a surface molecule called cluster designation 4 (CD4). HIV also uses a co-receptor molecule called C-C chemokine receptor type 5 (CCR5) or C-X-C chemokine receptor type 4 (CXCR4), in addition to the CD4, to ensure the target cell entry is suitable. One or more of the virus's gp120 molecules binds tightly to CD4 molecule(s) on the cell's surface (Lyerly et al., 1987); the membranes of the virus and the cell fuse, a process that probably involves the envelope of HIV and the second co-receptor molecule on the cell surface. Following fusion, the virus's RNA, proteins, and enzymes are released into the cell.

Viral genetic diversity is an important determinant of neuropathogenesis and evasion of the host immune response. The V3 hypervariable region of HIV-1 gp120 viral protein (Cann et al., 1992; Diesing et al., 2002; Shioda et al., 1992) largely determines tropism of HIV-1 in macrophages. The V3 function is distinct from the HIV-1 gp120 CD4 requirement and is more associated with post-CD4-binding interactions such as proteolytic cleavage and fusion, all of which are critical for productive infection of brain MP (Gorry et al., 2007). Nonetheless, the V3 region is crucial to the tropism of HIV-1, although it is not the only factor. The V1/V2 region may also contribute independently or in concert with V3.

CLINICAL MANIFESTATIONS
OF HIV INFECTION

Aseptic meningitis is known to occur early after viral infection and is characterized by nuchal rigidity, fever, and altered mentation (Brown et al., 1992; Huang et al., 2005). However, in most patients, the HIV-seroconversion reaction is subclinical and often passes unnoticed. Still, patients may present with a mild influenza-like illness and rarely a mononucleosis-like syndrome (Huang et al., 2005; Martin et al., 1992). A number of individuals with HIV-seroconversion reaction will also develop headaches, fever, myalgia, anorexia, rash, and diarrhea within weeks of infection, known as "systemic acute retroviral syndrome" (Lindback et al., 2000; Pilcher et al., 2004; Schacker et al., 1996; Tyrer et al., 2003). The early stages of HIV infection can be classified into two groups: the "acute phase," which is prior to the seroconversion, and the "early phase," which is the period 12 months post-seroconversion. The acute phase of viral infection is characterized by a rapid HIV-mediated loss of memory CD4+CCR5+ T cells within the mucosal tissues, which can potentially result in irreversible immune suppression (Brenchley et al., 2004; Derdeyn and Silvestri, 2005; Gray et al., 1996; Mehandru et al., 2004; Veazey et al., 1998). During this acute phase, high levels of viremia and viral shedding at mucosal sites occur. Genital and oral ulcers, cancers, and co-infections with a range of sexually transmitted diseases that include herpes simplex and hepatitis viruses, syphilis, and gonorrhea can manifest during the viral seroconversion reaction (Bagdades et al., 1992; Bollinger et al., 1997; Kinloch-de Loes et al., 1993; Stamm et al., 1988).

The transition from the acute to chronic phase of infection is accompanied by generation of HIV-1-specific adaptive immune responses (Draenert et al., 2006; Gray et al., 1996; Poluektova et al., 2004). Initially, HIV-specific cytotoxic CD8+ T-cell and humoral responses (for example, neutralizing antibodies) function to reduce viral replication to a set-point level that is characteristic of chronic HIV infection (Borrow et al., 1997; Goulder and Watkins, 2004; Koup, 2004; Letvin and Walker, 2003; Montefiori et al., 2003; Schmitz et al., 1999). Although this is a robust initial immune response, it cannot eradicate viral infection (Draenert et al., 2006; Musey et al., 1997; Oxenius et al., 2004). Continuous low-level or restricted infection of naïve CD4+ T cells and MP evades immune surveillance. The persistence of these quiescent but infected cellular reservoirs makes it difficult to eradicate the virus.

CLASSIFICATION OF
NEUROCOGNITIVE DISORDERS

Historically, the AIDS dementia complex (ADC) was one of the first terms used to describe neurological abnormalities resulting from HIV infection and was identified near the beginning of the initial pandemic. Although its name varied by region, it was clear by the early 1980's that there was a consistent grouping of neurological symptoms with an associated pathology unique to HIV infection (Gallo et al., 1983), with cases of diffuse and often profound neurological impairment reported in patients who were in the advanced stages of disease (Navia, Cho, et al., 1986; Navia, Jordan, et al., 1986; Nielsen et al., 1984; Snider et al., 1983). Indeed, following autopsies of HIV-infected individuals in this early period, it was found more that nearly 35% of patients died as a result of CNS pathologies (Klatt, 1988). While there was variation between individuals and their respective circumstances, each case of ADC displayed a pattern of neurological dysfunction, in which there were observable deficits in behavior, motor function, and cognition (Navia, Jordan, et al., 1986). But while it was clearly evident that persons with HIV were prone to develop these neurological problems, the diagnosis of ADC and the differentiation between other causes of neurological dysfunction, such as opportunistic infections, was and continues to be a challenge for physicians.

Neurocognitive manifestations of HIV infection have gone through many categorizations and classifications over the first decades of the pandemic, including HIV-1 dementia, HIV-1 encephalopathy (the name used commonly for infected children), HIV-associated cognitive/motor complex, AIDS dementia complex, and HIV-associated dementia (HAD) (Griffin et al., 2004; Weed and Steward, 2005; Wilkie et al., 2003; Worlein et al., 2005) and were associated with findings of developmental delays, psychomotor slowing, forgetfulness, personality changes, and decreased knowledge acquisition (Cysique et al., 2006; Sacktor and McArthur, 1997; Schifitto et al., 2001; Sidtis et al., 1993). A system was developed for physicians in that ADC could be clinically classified into various "stages," thus allowing for a uniform vocabulary to describe neurological problems with HIV progression (Price and Brew, 1988). Additional diagnostic systems were created as more patient data were made available for analysis, and in 1991 the American Academy of Neurology released a diagnostic paradigm in which the more severe forms of dysfunction became a distinct entity from the less severe and minor neurological problems.

After effective ART was introduced in 1996, there has been a remarkable reduction in the prevalence of HAD. The current and most widely accepted terminology has changed accordingly. To date, the most recent diagnostic scheme is the Frascati criteria, which include milder forms of neurocognitive diagnostic categories (Antinori et al., 2007). Specifically, the Frascati criteria have three specific descriptions of HAND. These include asymptomatic neurocognitive impairment (ANI), mild neurocognitive disorder (MCI), and HAD. The different stages take various variables into account, but in essence the Frascati criteria are used to examine how many cognitive areas are affected in the patient, and how this alteration modulates his or her everyday functionality (Antinori et al., 2007). In persons with HIV and access to care, the prevalence of HAND is 40%, but of that 40%, there is only a 5% prevalence of HAD. The diagnosis of HAND is described in full in this textbook in Chapter 11, on psychiatric assessment, and in Chapter 12, on neuropsychological assessment. For further discussion of prevalence, diagnosis, differential diagnosis, prevention, and treatment of neurocognitive disorders in HIV, please see Chapter 16.

THE CLINICAL LANDSCAPE AND HOW IT HAS CHANGED WITH ART

The neuropathology of HIV-1 infection and its direct association with neurocognitive disorders has long been complicated, particularly during the current widespread use of ART. In the early years of the pandemic, most persons with HIV were young and exhibited severe immune compromise; individuals had a survival period of only a few years from the initial diagnosis with very few ever living to experience old age (Snider et al., 1983). CNS pathological changes in these patients were common, with 35% of autopsies reporting that such changes were the underlying cause of death (Klatt, 1988), and 20% of patients exhibiting some form of ADC (Navia, Cho, et al., 1986; Navia, Jordan, et al., 1986). During this time it was evident that HIV-1 infection caused both neuropathological changes and subsequent cognitive dysfunction; however, patients were not living long enough for physicians and researchers to reliably determine their causative relationship.

The introduction of the ART allowed for effective suppression of HIV-1 replication within infected patients, and resulted in a substantial reduction of morbidity and mortality in persons with HIV (Sacktor et al., 2001). Antiretrovirals completely changed the clinical landscape of persons with HIV-1; instead of unrestricted progression and certain death, HIV became a chronic but treatable disease, with individuals living decades beyond their initial infection. Interestingly, the introduction of ART did not reduce the incidence of neurocognitive disorders in patients, but only the severity of their symptoms (Tozzi et al., 2001). Persons experiencing neurocognitive impairment before the advent of ART showed significant gains in cognitive function over time upon administration of ART (Brew, 2001; McArthur et al., 2005).

However, increased life expectancy as a result of ART leads to increasingly complicated and muddled illness histories, further blurring the link between CNS pathology and neurocognitive impairments. Older persons with HIV typically have increased exposure time of HIV-1 in the CNS and can be subjected to the wide variety of pharmaceuticals in countless combinations. Other factors in conjunction with aging, such as ART side effects, preinfection psychiatric disorders, drug abuse, and co-infection with other diseases, all complicate the causative relationship between HIV-1 CNS infection and subsequent cognitive disorders. Dementia related to direct HIV infection of the brain is only one of the protean manifestations of AIDS that may be associated with decline in mental status in an infected person. Among the complications of AIDS that must be considered in the differential diagnosis of dementia are the direct effect of HIV on the CNS; opportunistic fungal, viral, and or parasitic infections; neoplasm (lymphoma); ischemic or hemorrhagic lesions; and metabolic abnormalities. These include, for example, toxoplasmosis, cryptococcal meningitis, progressive multifocal leukoencephalopathy (PML), and tuberculosis, among others (Kure et al., 1991; Manzardo et al., 2005). Although there are no definitive tests for HAD, diagnosis is most commonly made following exclusion of common opportunistic and cancerous brain diseases, with screening tests such as neuropsychological test batteries for psychomotor speed and the HIV Dementia Scale (Cysique et al., 2006; Davis et al., 2002; Power et al., 1995). Overall, the widely varying clinical trends of cognitive disorders associated with HIV-1 paired with the numerous and further complicating factors of an aging patient population have presented a challenge for the scientific community, as the exact pathological basis for such cognitive disorders has yet to be completely determined.

NEUROIMAGING

Though initial characterization and diagnosis of HIV-1 infection is easily achieved in the clinic, diagnostic decisions involving neurological complications following infection is often difficult. Physicians commonly find it challenging to differentiate the symptoms of global immune suppression, such as concomitant depression, motor impairments, and lethargy, from neurological dysfunctions associated with HIV infection within the CNS. In response, combinations of clinical, laboratory, and neuroimaging tests have been developed in order to provide diagnostic support.

The potential and practicality of neuroimaging techniques are irrefutable, as decades of clinical and laboratory imaging research have identified numerous underlying processes involved in neurological disease progression (Tucker et al., 2004). Brain imaging with magnetic resonance imaging (MRI) methods, including diffusion tensor imaging (DTI), and computer topography (CT) can be used to supplement clinical and neurological examinations in the diagnosis of HIV-1 associated cognitive impairments (Lawrence and Major, 2002; Thompson et al., 2005; Thurnher et al., 2005). These imaging modalities are effective at delineating the structural and metabolic effects of HIV on the brain and, more importantly, differentiate them from other causes of neurological dysfunction.

Specifically, CT, MRI, and DTI can all depict brain atrophy. Morphometric analyzes of the MRIs of individuals with HIV have shown consistent volumetric loss in the caudate, amygdala, and hippocampus (Chang et al., 1999a; Harezlak et al., 2011) as well as the corpus callosum. Both MRI and DTI studies of patients with HAD have shown increased ventricular size, sulcal widening, diffuse white matter abnormalities, and atrophy (Anderson et al., 2002; Hall et al., 1996; Heyes et al., 1991; Pomara et al., 2001; Thompson et al., 2005; Thurnher et al., 2005). However, it is prudent to note that many of these studies were performed before combinational ART became widely available to persons with HIV, and more recent studies suggest that individuals with HIV who are on a steady regimen of ART demonstrate less widespread atrophy (Ances et al., 2012; Heaps et al., 2012). In conjunction with these findings, research groups have found that individuals with more advanced stages of HIV, particular persons with AIDS, have shown thinner sensory and motor thickness, smaller cortical volumes, and larger total ventricle size (Cardenas et al., 2009; Cohen et al., 2010; Ragin et al., 2011). Both greater viral burden and immune response to the virus are associated with greater brain volume loss (Cardenas et al., 2009; Cohen et al., 2010; Ragin et al., 2011). The distribution and existence of such lesions do not necessarily contribute to the clinical picture, and a certain degree of parenchymal involvement may be visible in asymptomatic patients. It is thought that extensive white matter involvement is more likely to be symptomatic.

While CT, MRI, and DTI have shed considerable light on HIV's effect on the structure and function of the brain, the majority of conclusions have come from studies of individuals in the later stage of disease and who are already exhibiting multiple characteristics of HAD. This limitation is the driving force of many research groups today, as more powerful imaging technologies have the potential to reveal structural abnormalities before the onset of the neurological consequences, providing a much needed clinical tool.

More advanced imaging techniques assess functional changes in brain metabolism. These include positron emission tomography (PET), single-photon emission computed tomography (SPECT), functional magnetic resonance imaging (fMRI), and proton magnetic resonance spectroscopy (^{1}H MRS). These techniques have the advantage of detecting early functional abnormalities before morphological changes occur.

Nuclear medical imaging techniques such as PET and SPECT have proven invaluable within the field of radiology; however, they currently cannot be recommended for HIV-dementia diagnosis. The requirement of radioactive pharmaceuticals presents many challenges in a clinical setting; such drugs are extremely expensive and require a precise time-dependent protocol that can be complicated by a patient's nonadherence (Sathekge et al., 2014). However, several interesting conclusions have surfaced from groups using PET and SPECT imaging. Using ^{18}F-FDG injection, multiple groups have reported altered metabolism in specific brain regions. In correlation with increasing severity of HIV-dementia, increased metabolism was found in the temporal lobe (van Gorp et al., 1992) and basal ganglia (Hinkin et al., 1995). Another radioactive drug, [^{11}C] –R-PK11195, has been used for the visualization of brain inflammation following neuronal damage (Sathekge et al., 2014). Increased uptake by structures is associated with a glial cell activation response. One group found that in persons with HIV there was an increase in [^{11}C] –R-PK11195 uptake in the thalamus, putamen, cerebellum, frontal cortex, and occipital cortex (Hammoud et al., 2005). These findings present interesting insights into the correlation between HAND and its effect on brain metabolism; however, SPECT and PET currently do not have a capability to assist in early HAND diagnosis.

Functional magnetic resonance imaging is a relatively new and exciting imaging modality that allows utilization of blood oxygen-level dependent (BOLD) signals (Ances et al., 2011). Specific brain regions can be monitored for fluctuations in the BOLD response during specific tasks or stimuli, and changes in cerebral blood flow can then be indirectly associated with neuronal activity. It is hypothesized that such BOLD fluctuations in persons with HIV represent increased "recruitment" from other brain regions to meet the cognitive demands for the task (Chang et al., 1999b; Ernst et al., 2010). To date, only a limited number of groups have investigated fMRI's usefulness in HIV-dementia pathology and diagnosis, and additional fMRI studies are needed to elucidate significant findings.

^{1}H MRS is a noninvasive method for quantifying neuronal loss indicated by conventional magnetic resonance imagers and has emerged as an effective way to detect early brain dysfunction in HAD via measurements of brain metabolites (Jarvik et al., 1996; McConnell et al., 1994; Tracey et al., 1998). Assessment of in vivo metabolism supplies biochemical information that complements the structural information from the MRI examination in a quantitative fashion. A large number of metabolites have been characterized and subsequently utilized in ^{1}H MRS analysis, allowing researchers to infer structural and morphological abnormalities via changes in metabolite levels alone, noninvasively in vivo. Specifically, N-acetylaspartic acid (NAA), choline (CHO), myo-inositol (MI), creatine (CR), glutamine (Gln), and glutamate (Glu), which are sometimes reported as a sum (GLX), have been of particular use in ^{1}H MRS HAD research. NAA has long been established as a neuronal marker, and decreases in NAA levels are interpreted as a loss of neuronal integrity. CHO is associated with myelin sheaths that surround many axons, and increased CHO levels have been found in many focal, inflammatory, and hereditary diseases and are thus thought to represent either rapid membrane synthesis, as is found in cancerous tumors, or the products of myelin or membranes being broken down.

Interestingly, many groups have shown quantitative changes in metabolites in brain regions occurring both after HIV-1 infection and as the person becomes more neurosymptomatic. HIV-positive individuals as compared to HIV-negative controls show an increase in MI/CR in the basal ganglia, frontal white matter, and mid-frontal cortex (Harezlak et al., 2011; Lentz et al., 2009), an increase in CHO/CR in the basal ganglia and mid-frontal cortex (Harezlak et al., 2011), and a decrease in GLX/CR in the basal ganglia, front white matter, mid-frontal cortex, and parietal gray matter (Ernst et al., 2010; Harezlak et al., 2011; Mohamed et al., 2010). These variations in metabolites are thought to reflect glial cell proliferation and malfunctioning energy metabolism in the brain (Mohamed et al., 2010). Perhaps more significantly, there is evidence of a significant decrease in NAA within the basal ganglia and GLU in the parietal gray matter in patients diagnosed with HAD compared to neuroasymptomatic HIV-positive patients (Ernst et al., 2010; Mohamed et al., 2010). In a study of individuals with acute HIV infection, increases in frontal gray matter and frontal white matter CHO were observed at only 2 months post-infection, with elevated levels remaining above baseline after 6 months. No other changes in metabolites were found (Lentz et al., 2011).

The most common observations of ¹H MRS studies are increased levels of CHO and MI and decreased levels of NAA in multiple brain regions, reflecting glial cell proliferation and neuronal loss, respectively (Barker et al., 1995; Chong et al., 1993; Menon et al., 1992; Meyerhoff et al., 1994). However, many of the studies that came to this conclusion did not account for any of the variables and cofactors of HIV infection, such as length and duration of infection, viral load, ART administration, types of ART taken, age, gender, socioeconomic status, among others. Until these variables can be controlled and accounted for, it is exceedingly difficult to conclude whether changes in brain metabolites reflect HIV-induced pathology or an alteration in brain metabolism by an HIV-irrelevant factor.

¹H MRS may also be helpful in the differential diagnosis of HAD and other neurological disorders associated with HIV disease, for example, other metabolic encephalopathies (Swindells et al., 1995). Although ¹H MRS is not often applied in clinical settings, studies in which brain metabolite concentrations predict response to treatment and correlate with cognitive dysfunction (Chang et al., 1999a, 1999b) are prospective applications for these tests. Moreover, such technologies may be helpful in monitoring therapeutic responses to antiretroviral therapies (Chang et al., 1999b).

BIOMARKERS

The search for biomarkers in diagnosing and monitoring HIV-associated neurological impairments has increased significantly in recent years (Ammassari et al., 2000; Carlson, Ciborowski, et al., 2004; Carlson, Limoges, et al., 2004; Ciborowski et al., 2004; Ciborowski and Gendelman, 2006;

Helke et al., 2005; Wojna et al., 2004; Zink et al., 2005). The identification of reliable molecular indictors of progressive HIV encephalitis and HAND would prove incredibly invaluable; not only would it provide a means for physicians to accurately diagnose HIV-1-associated neurological abnormalities, but it would also allow preventative steps and therapy to be initiated long before symptoms or complications are presented. However, despite rapidly progressing biomedical technology and an escalation in investigative research, a definitive biomarker for HAND remains elusive (Burdo et al., 2013; McArthur et al., 2010).

The central problem in the identification of biomarkers is finding molecules that are both specific toward HIV-1 pathology and measurable by readily available assays. Soluble factors are identified and quantified from two different body fluids, CSF and blood plasma. For the purpose of this review, we will only focus on CSF biomarkers. Blood plasma, while containing HIV-1 RNA, is not representative of the cellular environment of the CNS and is for the most part minimally useful for neurological diagnostic purposes. Analysis of soluble markers in the CSF has led to three "classes" of diagnostic markers: viral markers, immunological markers, and neuronal markers.

VIRAL MARKERS

The quantitative measure of HIV-1 RNA within the CSF has been integral in determining the "viral load" of the CNS. However, this measure has only been made significant in the current era of ART. In untreated individuals with HIV, HIV RNA in the CSF displays a wide range of concentrations but trends similarly to RNA levels in the blood, with absolute concentrations about 10-fold lower (Marra et al., 2007; Spudich et al., 2005). And while several studies have reported that untreated persons with HIV displaying neurological disease have higher HIV RNA levels than in asymptomatic persons with HIV (Price et al., 2013), it is possible that this HIV RNA CSF is a result of increased entrance of RNA from systemic circulation and not from the CNS dysfunction exhibited (Spudich and Gonzalez-Scarano, 2012). Therefore, CSF HIV RNA concentrations are thought to not be diagnostically indicative of HAND/ADC, even if the measured concentrations are unusually high (Price et al., 2007). Unusually low or nonexistent CSF HIV RNA levels detected using highly sensitive detection protocols suggest an absent CNS infection, but this only serves to confirm that the current ART is effective and reveals nothing about the possibility of future complications.

The observations discussed have not discouraged many research programs from undergoing cross-sectional and longitudinal studies of CSF HIV-1 RNA levels, as the data gathered have elucidated the effectiveness of HIV-1 pharmaceuticals in eliminating HIV-1 RNA levels in the CSF. In fact, it is possible that early data from these studies influenced the use of antiretrovirals in combinations, rather than previously used monotherapy. Indeed, one of the first groups reported that a nucleoside reverse transcriptase inhibitor (NRTI), zidovudine, reduced HIV RNA levels in

CSF, but another NRTI, didanosine, did not (Gisslén et al., 1997). Less than a year later, another study reported that combining two different NRTIs resulted in the lowering of HIV RNA to 400 copies/ml in all participants in 22 weeks (Foudraine et al., 1998). Further studies revealed the effectiveness of taking at least three antiretrovirals; one group reported that all 10 individuals on triple therapy had HIV RNA levels below 20 copies/ml upon lumbar puncture (Garcia et al., 2000). A multitude of similar studies have been conducted with a wide range of antiretroviral medications. Such research has provided direct insight into the effectiveness of antiretrovirals, not only allowing physicians to administer better patient care but also giving researchers valuable feedback on the drugs they design.

IMMUNOLOGICAL MARKERS

Perhaps the most diverse and diagnostically promising biomarkers in HIV-1 CNS infection, immunological markers have great potential to provide a quantitative view of the biochemical environment of the inflamed brain. The activation of macrophages/microglia and the release of inflammatory chemokines and cytokines are the cellular and molecular hallmarks of HIV encephalopathy (HIVE), and soluble biomarkers indicative of such events are valuable for diagnostic purposes. Indeed, it can be said that in a general sense, HAND/HIVE is an immunopathological disease driven by infected macrophages.

Biological activators of macrophage or microglial cells were one of the first groups of biomarkers investigated by researchers. Specifically, beta-2-microglobulin (B2M) and neopterin quantification within the CSF of HIV patients has been performed in longitudinal studies, both before and during the era of ART. B2M is expressed on the surface of microglial and macrophages as a polypeptide to form the light chain of the MHC I molecule and is released either during membrane turnover or death of the cell. Neopterin is part of the biopterin synthesis pathway and is an indicator of T-cell activity, though indirectly. Both are considered nonspecific indicators of macrophage activation, and many studies have shown a link between cognitive disorders in persons with HIV and increased CSF concentrations of B2M and neopterin (Brew et al., 1992; Eden et al., 2007; Gisslén et al., 1994; Ryan et al., 2001). Furthermore, other studies have shown that B2M or neopterin levels in persons with HIV will decrease upon administration of zidovudine (Elovaara et al., 1994; Hagberg et al., 1991) or other antiretrovirals (Enting et al., 2000; Yilmaz et al., 2008). Overall, multiple groups have reported that nucleoside analog antiretrovirals reduce B2M and neopterin levels within a relatively short time frame.

Recently, there has been increased interest in soluble CD14 as a reliable biomarker for HIV disease progression. CD14 is expressed almost exclusively on monocytes and has two distinct forms: membrane-associated and soluble. Soluble CD14 is unique from other markers of macrophage activation in that it is derived predominantly from the trafficking monocytes coming into the CNS, rather than the microglia already residing within the brain tissue, allowing for a more direct measure of the extent of HIV invasion into the CNS (Cauwels et al., 1999). Studies have shown that combinational ART can reduce the sCD14 levels in CSF in a patient with HAND (Gendelman et al., 1998) and that sCD14 concentrations were significantly higher in cognitively impaired persons with HIV patients than in unimpaired persons with HIV (Ryan et al., 2001). Further research has highlighted the possibility that monocytes carrying CD14, dubbed "CD14+/CD69+" and "CD14+/CD16+" monocytes, play a specific part in the neuropathogenesis of HIV infection (Gartner and Liu, 2002).

The use of cytokines and chemokines as biological markers of HIV-1 CNS infection has the possibility of being redundant with those indicative of macrophage/microglia activation, as monocyte-derived cells have numerous molecular products. Researchers have put in a significant amount of time and effort to identify cytokines and chemokines that function via pathways distinct from that of B2M and neopterin, as discussed. Monocyte chemoattractant protein-1 (MCP-1) has long been established as a principal chemokine in the migration of monocytes into specific tissues. Several groups have investigated the link between MCP-1 levels, antiretroviral use, and diagnosis of HAND; however, results have varied and been contradicted. Several groups have reported no change in MCP-1 levels during antiretroviral use (Enting et al., 2000; McArthur et al., 2004), while another group reported that MCP-1 levels were higher in persons using ART (Arendt et al., 2007). HIV utilizes chemokine receptors to gain entry into specific cells; CCR5 is used by monocyte-tropic HIV strains, while CXCR4 is used by T-cell-tropic HIV strains. Chemokines function by attracting specific cell types via chemotaxis; therefore, it is a reasonable hypothesis that elevated levels of chemokines ligands to CCR5 and CXCR4 in the CSF can be representative of higher levels of trafficking of HIV-infected cells across the BBB into the CNS. MIP-1α, MIP-1β, and RANTES are all ligands of CCR5, and all three were found to be elevated in the CSF of patients exhibiting HAND (Letendre et al., 1999) despite antiretroviral use.

Inflammation is a hallmark of HIV neuropathology, and tumor necrosis factor alpha (TNF-α) is a key proinflammatory cytokine that has been shown to be involved in several diseases. TNF-α is expressed by macrophages and microglia; early research showed that persons with AIDS and HAD exhibit an increase in TNF-α mRNA expression compared to cognitively normal patients (Achim et al., 1993; Perrella et al., 1992), although it should be noted that these studies were done before the era of ART. Groups have reported a decrease in TNF-α concentrations in plasma upon administration of combination ART (Franco et al., 1999), but there are limitations in the direct measurement of TNF-α in bodily fluid. Upon release into the bloodstream, TNF-α is quickly removed, thus measurement from bodily fluids may not accurately reflect systemic concentrations. Analysis of soluble TNF receptors, such as p55 and p75, is possibly much more reflective of TNF-α expression, as both soluble receptors have been linked to TNF-α expression (Hober et al., 1996).

NEURONAL MARKERS

Neurofilament light (NFL) is a primary structural component of the myelin that surrounds axons within the CNS. Concentrations of NFL within CSF have been shown to be elevated in several neurodegenerative diseases (Constantinescu et al., 2010; Landqvist Waldo et al., 2013). Several groups have produced promising reports of NFL as a biomarker of HIV neuronal inflammation and degeneration. Studies have shown elevated NFL levels in persons with HAD compared to persons with HIV who are asymptomatic (Jessen Krut et al., 2014), and NFL concentrations were reduced upon administration of ART (Abdulle et al., 2007) and increased with a cessation of ART administration (Gisslén et al., 2005). In comparison to other biomarkers discussed in this chapter, NFL has shown the most consistent trends in relation to both HIV neuropathology and cognitive disorders. When used in conjunction with immunological and viral markers, NFL has the potential to be a beneficial and practical biomarker within the clinical setting.

THERAPEUTICS

The dementia produced by CNS infection with HIV elicits a cascade of events involving both resident and invading cell types and ultimately results in neuronal dysfunction and cognitive deterioration. Treatment failures, viral mutation drug-associated disease, and evolving neurological syndromes support the importance of neurological impairments as a significant part of the overall disease complex. In the past decade we have seen a milder phenotype and decreased incidence of HAD, largely due to the widespread use of combination ART to reduce viral burden. However, in the current era of HIV-1 drug therapy, the prevalence of neurological disease in people living with HIV-1 has actually increased. This has raised significant concerns that new therapeutic strategies, which are directed at restoring neuronal and glial homeostasis/signaling in the CNS, neglect directly interfering with the life cycle of HIV-1. Researchers developing new agents and strategies for the management of HIV-1 disease are focusing on regimens that include novel targets and are better tolerated, with decreased potential for development of viral resistance. Because the disease process occurs in a stepwise fashion, it provides the opportunity for development of therapeutics directed at discrete pathogenic mechanisms. A clearer understanding of the neuropathogenesis of HIVE and HAD has allowed the selection of rational adjunctive therapies for HAD that are now in development. Phase 1 clinical trials for adjunctive (i.e., chemotherapeutic agents that do not have a primary antiretroviral mechanism of action) therapy in patients with HAD have been conducted.

There are several reasons for the demand for such therapies. While successful in decreasing viral burden and delaying the onset of HAD, ART does not prevent dementia. Combination antiretroviral therapies are not always well tolerated, and only a very limited fraction of the global population of HIV-infected persons has access to antiretrovirals.

HIV-1 is able to adapt to most of the antiretroviral agents, and most antiretroviral agents do not freely cross the BBB. Overlapping pathogenic mechanisms are operative for other neurodegenerative disorders containing an inflammatory component, making it likely that agents will have crossover potential for treatment of a wide range of neurodestructive processes.

ANTIRETROVIRALS

Prior to the advent of potent ART, HIV infection was characterized as an acute, systemic infection that rapidly led to immune suppression and cognitive decline. With the development of antiretroviral therapies, extended life expectancies and a better quality of life for persons with AIDS have been achieved. The decision to start ART is largely based on CD4+ T-cell count thresholds, although higher viral load has been shown to increase risk of disease progression. Current guidelines recommend treatment for all persons with symptomatic HIV disease or AIDS and for asymptomatic patients with CD4+ T-cell counts <200 cells/mm^3 (Swindells et al., 1999). Since HIV-1-infected brain MP initiate the inflammatory neuroimmune cascade in the brain, it is vital that any therapeutic strategy includes the use of antiretroviral agents to decrease the CNS viral load. Antiretrovirals can be classified into several categories, each targeting a specific mechanism of the HIV-1 life cycle. Please consult Chapter 2 for further discussion of the antiretrovirals currently in use, and Chapter 42 for a detailed discussion of antiretroviral medications and their interactions.

NUCLEOSIDE AND NON-NUCLEOSIDE REVERSE TRANSCRIPTASE INHIBITORS

The HIV/AIDS epidemic that emerged in the early 1980s presented a drastic and immediate need for anti-HIV medications, to such a point that the U.S. Food and Drug Administration (FDA) created a new class of experimental drugs that accelerated the drug approval timeline by 2 to 3 years. The resulting first pharmaceutical to treat HIV was approved in 1986; AZT, or zidovudine, and was termed a nucleoside reverse transcriptase inhibitor (NRTI). Since then, a myriad of different medications have been approved that focus on HIV-1's reverse transcriptase enzyme. HIV-1 is classified as a retrovirus; in order to integrate the HIV-1 DNA into the host cell genome, HIV-1 must first reverse transcribe the viral RNA into DNA. Without a properly functioning reverse transcriptase enzyme, HIV-1 cannot productively infect the host cells and is rendered uninfectious. Reverse transcriptase inhibitors have been classified into two broad categories: nucleoside (NRTI) and non-nucleoside (NNRTI). NRTIs work as false nucleotides; they have small but significant changes to their structure such that reverse transcriptase recognizes and integrates them into the growing DNA strand, but the resulting DNA is rendered nonfunctional. NNRTIs directly bind to and block reverse transcriptase, preventing its proper functioning. Currently there are seven FDA-approved NRTIs (abacavir, didanosine, emtricitabine, lamivudine, stavudine, tenofovir disoproxil fumarate, and zidovudine) and five FDA-approved NNRTIs (delavirdine, efavirenz, etravirine, nevirapine, and rilpivirine).

PROTEASE INHIBITORS

Viral protease (PR) is one of the three HIV-1 genome–derived enzymes and is required for maturation of viral particles, a critical step in the HIV-1 lifecycle. *Maturation* refers to the processing of viral bud proteins via enzymatic cleavage at specific sites, causing the precursor proteins that were transcribed and translated within the host cell to "mature" and become fully functional within the virion particle (Sundquist and Krausslich, 2012). This structural rearrangement not only produces the functional proteins required for HIV-1 infection but also changes the electron density of the viral particles; maturation results in an electron-dense, conical core forming from the electron-sparse core of immature virion particles (Adamson and Freed, 2008). Without functioning PR enzymes, the maturation process cannot occur, and the viral particles released are subsequently uninfectious, as precursor proteins are unable to facilitate replication in the host cells. These observations have made inhibition or blockage of HIV-1 protease an extremely attractive target for pharmaceutical research; multiple studies have shown that disruption of the PR cleavage mechanism is highly pernicious to HIV-1 infectivity (Adamson and Freed, 2008; Freed, 1998). The first protease inhibitor (PI) approved by the FDA was saquinavir, which was approved in 1995. Since then, seven additional PIs have been designed and FDA approved: ritonavir, indinavir, nelfinavir, atazanavir, fosamprenavir, tipranavir, and darunavir.

ENTRY INHIBITORS

Entrance of HIV into a host cell is required for successful infection and subsequent viral replication; therefore, the HIV-1 entry mechanism is an important target for new and emerging pharmaceuticals. Specifically, these drugs prevent the interaction of the HIV-1 membrane protein gp120 with the host-cell membrane co-receptor CCR5 or CXCR4. Recall that HIV-1 exhibits different tropisms; the "R5" strains utilize the CCR5 co-receptors and typically infect macrophages and primary T-cells, while "X4" strains interact with the CXCR4 co-receptor and exclusively infect T cells (Aiamkitsumrit et al., 2014; McArthur et al., 2010). The inspiration for entry inhibitors stems from the observation of the mutated form of the CCR5 gene; a 32 base-pair deletion in CCR5 co-receptor gene (CCRΔ32) protects homozygous individuals from R5 strain infections and heterozygous individuals from accelerated progression of infection (Lederman et al., 2006). These CCRΔ32 individuals not only showed beneficial resistance to R5 entry but also displayed no adverse health effects from the mutation, suggesting drugs targeting CCR5 or CXCR4 have the potential to be well tolerated. Currently, there is one CCR5 inhibitor that has been FDA approved in the treatment of HIV. Maraviroc, a small molecule that selectively binds to CCR5, was approved for clinical use by the FDA in 2007.

INTEGRASE INHIBITORS

The integration of the host cell's genome with HIV-1 viral DNA is a critical step in the viral lifecycle, as the inserted DNA serves as the template for new HIV-1 RNA production within the infected cell. This reaction is catalyzed by the HIV-1-encoded enzyme integrase, and successful inhibition of integrase has been clinically shown to be an effective therapy for managing HIV-1 infection and disease progression. The integration reaction can be classified into two steps: the 3'-processing, in which a site-specific endonucleolytic cleavage reaction removes two nucleotides from each end of the viral DNA strand, and strand transfer, where the now-processed HIV-1 DNA is physically transferred into the host genome (Demeulemeester et al., 2014). There are currently two FDA-approved integrase inhibitors: raltegravir, approved in 2007, and dolutegravir, approved in 2013.

FUSION INHIBITORS

The deliverance of HIV-1 viral genome into the host cell is perhaps the most crucial event in the HIV-1 life cycle. Without proper entry, the virus cannot utilize the host cell's enzymatic machinery and subsequently is rendered unable to productively replicate. The fusion of the viral membrane with the host cell membrane is an integral process in the delivery of HIV-1 and is achieved by the viral protein envelope (Env). Env in its active form is a heterotrimer consisting of three molecules of surface glycoprotein gp120 and three molecules of transmembrane glycoprotein gp41 (Greenberg et al., 2004). Gp120 binding to CCR5 or CXCR4 co-receptors results in a conformation change, allowing the hydrophobic domain of gp41 to enter and fuse with the hydrophobic domain of the host cell's membrane. This fusion process is highlighted by the formation of a six-helix bundle, a result of the three gp41 molecules bending inward upon themselves (Greenberg et al., 2004; Klasse, 2012); this six-helix bundle formation brings the viral and host-cell membranes close together and allows for entrance of the HIV-1 genome. The most clinically successful and only FDA-approved fusion inhibitor is enfuvirtide, which was approved in 2003 and has been shown to inhibit HIV-1 replication both in vitro and in vivo. It is hypothesized that enfuvirtide works by competitively binding to segments of gp41 and preventing the formation of the six-helical bundle, thereby effectively inhibiting fusion or the viral and host cell membrane.

LIMITATIONS

While antiretroviral agents are beneficial in attenuating viral load, complications associated with infection are still prevalent, as the virus is never wholly eliminated. Antiretroviral medicines fail to completely eradicate the virus, in part because of a latent form of the virus that persists in resting memory CD4+ T cells (Finzi et al., 1997; Ho et al., 1998) and select viral mutations that result in viral resistance to antiretroviral drugs (Johnson et al., 2005). Viral reservoirs represent a potentially lifelong persistence of replication-competent forms of HIV-1, recovered from resting CD4 T cells (Finzi et al., 1997) and peripheral blood monocytes (Crowe and Sonza, 2000), that cannot be suppressed by current antiretroviral treatments. Primary and acquired antiretroviral resistance rates reflect the relative usage of different antiretroviral drugs in the population, as well as the inherent genetic barrier to the development of resistance associated with individual drugs. Data on antiretroviral resistance rates, gleaned from the growing HIV-1-infected population treated with a continuously increasing number of antiretroviral drugs and drug combinations, provide insight into the relative ease by which HIV-1 escapes the selective pressure of chronic drug exposure. Strains of HIV-1 that are resistant to reverse transcriptase and protease inhibitors arise in the majority of treated patients who have either poor adherence to the treatment regime or low plasma drug levels for other reasons (Kedzierska et al., 2003). Most important, virus resistance to drugs heralds increased viral loads, immune suppression, and the onset of neurological impairments associated with advanced viral infection. The development of novel adjunctive immunotherapies to use in combination with antiretroviral drugs provides new therapeutic strategies to combat infection that will be better tolerated and have a decreased potential for the emergence of viral resistance. New research will continue to provide more options for such patients, with new treatments and, eventually, vaccines on the horizon.

CONCLUSION

The consequences of HIV infection on the CNS are obvious and well established; since its discovery as the virus that causes AIDS, laboratories and clinics alike have confirmed that there is a neuropathological component in this immune-compromising disease. However, as the neuroAIDS field continues to progress, there has been a re-examination of the pathological foundation of HAND, particularly in relevance to combination ART.

As discussed, the traditional concept in HAND pathophysiology is viral replication in the CNS, followed by inflammation (encephalitis) and eventually neurodegeneration. This neurodegeneration is not only indicated via cognitive symptoms in patients but is also confirmed via postmortem autopsy of the brain (Budka, 1986; Budka et al., 1987). But this sequentially driven neuropathology of HAND is only applicable within the pre-ART era; in the current era of highly adherent persons with HIV being administered ART, the vast majority of HIV autopsies report "no specific neuropathology" (Gelman, 2015).

This presents challenges within the neuroAIDS field. Current therapeutic strategies are anchored around neuropathologies that are now rarely seen in ART-compliant patients. In the current era of effective ART, observable neuropathology at autopsy is considerably uncommon, but the prevalence of HAND is still approximately 40% to 50% despite viral suppression (Heaton et al., 2010). With more than half of patients exhibiting neurological disorders despite being virally suppressed, the neuroAIDS field will need to move on

to questioning the pathological mechanisms of HAND in the current population.

One of the more prevalent and exciting hypotheses regarding an ART-associated HAND mechanism is that ART can actually improve neurocognitive function (Joska et al., 2010). One study looked at clinical neuropsychological and postmortem neuropathology data from 90 patients with HIV, comparing patients who had never undergone ART (naïve) to patients who were either virally suppressed (plasma load undetectable) or unsuppressed (plasma load detectable but had taken ART) (Bryant et al., 2015). The authors found that the suppressed group had a higher synaptophysin (SYP) and microtubule-associated protein 2 (MAP2) density in the midfrontal cortex than the unsuppressed and naïve group, concluding that virally suppressive ART protects against cortical neurodegeneration (Bryant et al., 2015).

Considerable progress has been made in the understanding of HIV effects on the central nervous system, but as a whole the neuroAIDS field now must consider lifestyle, effects of aging, and effects of ART treatment itself as possible causes for neurological complications in persons with HIV. With new discoveries and emerging technologies within the field, it is likely that some of the factors will be defined and new therapies can be designed to combat neurodegenerative processes, further improve quality of life for aging persons with AIDS, and potentially have an impact on other forms of neurological dysfunction in the aging population.

REFERENCES

Abdulle S, Mellgren A, Brew BJ, Cinque P, Hagberg L, Price RW, Gisslen M. (2007). CSF neurofilament protein (NFL)—a marker of active HIV-related neurodegeneration. *J Neurol* 254(8):1026–1032.

Achim CL, Heyes MP, Wiley CA (1993). Quantitation of human immunodeficiency virus, immune activation factors, and quinolinic acid in AIDS brains. *J Clin Invest* 91(6):2769–2775.

Adamson CS, Freed EO (2008). Recent progress in antiretrovirals—lessons from resistance. *Drug Discov Today* 13(9-10):424–432.

Adamson DC, Wildemann B, Sasaki M, et al. (1996). Immunologic NO synthase: elevation in severe AIDS dementia and induction by HIV-1 gp41. *Science* 274(5294):1917–1921.

Aiamkitsumrit B, Dampier W, Antell G, et al. (2014). Bioinformatic analysis of HIV-1 entry and pathogenesis. *Curr HIV Res* 12(2):132–161.

Alliot F, Godin I, Pessac B (1999). Microglia derive from progenitors, originating from the yolk sac, and which proliferate in the brain. *Brain Res Dev Brain Res* 117(2):145–152.

Ammassari A, Cingolani A, Pezzotti P, et al. (2000). AIDS-related focal brain lesions in the era of highly active antiretroviral therapy. *Neurology* 55(8):1194–1200.

Ances B, Ortega M, Vaida F, Heaps J, Paul R (2012). Independent effects of HIV, aging, and HAART on brain volumetric measures. *J Acquir Immune Defic Syndr* 59(5):469–477.

Ances B, Vaida F, Ellis R, Buxton R (2011). Test-retest stability of calibrated BOLD-fMRI in HIV- and HIV+ subjects. *Neuroimage* 54(3):2156–2162.

Anderson E, Zink W, Xiong H, Gendelman HE (2002). HIV-1-associated dementia: a metabolic encephalopathy perpetrated by virus-infected and immune-competent mononuclear phagocytes. *J Acquir Immune Defic Syndr* 31(Suppl 2):43–54.

Andras IE, Pu H, Deli MA, Nath A, Hennig B, Toborek M (2003). HIV-1 Tat protein alters tight junction protein expression and distribution in cultured brain endothelial cells. *J Neurosci Res* 74(2):255–265.

Antinori A, Arendt G, Becker JT, et al. (2007). Updated research nosology for HIV-associated neurocognitive disorders. *Neurology* 69(18):1789–1799.

Aquaro S, Ronga L, Pollicita M, Antinori A, Ranazzi A, Perno CF (2005). Human immunodeficiency virus infection and acquired immunodeficiency syndrome dementia complex: role of cells of monocyte–macrophage lineage. *J Neurovirol* 11(Suppl 3):58–66.

Arendt G, Nolting T, Frisch C, et al. (2007). Intrathecal viral replication and cerebral deficits in different stages of human immunodeficiency virus disease. *J Neurovirol* 13(3):225–232.

Bagdades EK, Pillay D, Squire SB, O'Neil C, Johnson MA, Griffiths PD (1992). Relationship between herpes simplex virus ulceration and CD4+ cell counts in patients with HIV infection. *AIDS* 6(11):1317–1320.

Banks WA, Akerstrom V, Kastin AJ (1998). Adsorptive endocytosis mediates the passage of HIV-1 across the blood-brain barrier: evidence for a post-internalization coreceptor. *J Cell Sci* 111(Pt 4):533–540.

Banks WA, Freed EO, Wolf KM, Robinson SM, Franko M, Kumar VB (2001). Transport of human immunodeficiency virus type 1 pseudoviruses across the blood-brain barrier: role of envelope proteins and adsorptive endocytosis. *J Virol* 75(10):4681–4691.

Barker PB, Lee RR, McArthur JC (1995). AIDS dementia complex: evaluation with proton MR spectroscopic imaging. *Radiology* 195(1):58–64.

Barre-Sinoussi F, Chermann JC, Rey F, et al. (1983). Isolation of a T-lymphotropic retrovirus from a patient at risk for acquired immune deficiency syndrome (AIDS). *Science* 220(4599):868–871.

Berger JR, Avison M (2004). The blood brain barrier in HIV infection. *Front Biosci*, 9:2680–2685.

Bezabhe WM, Chalmers L, Bereznicki LR, Peterson GM, Bimirew MA, Kassie DM (2014). Barriers and facilitators of adherence to antiretroviral drug therapy and retention in care among adult HIV-positive patients: a qualitative study from Ethiopia. *PLoS ONE* 9(5):e97353.

Bezzi P, Domercq M, Brambilla L, et al. (2001). CXCR4-activated astrocyte glutamate release via TNFalpha: amplification by microglia triggers neurotoxicity. *Nat Neurosci* 4(7):702–710.

Biernacki K, Prat A, Blain M, Antel JP (2001). Regulation of Th1 and Th2 lymphocyte migration by human adult brain endothelial cells. *J Neuropathol Exp Neurol* 60(12):1127–1136.

Bollinger RC, Brookmeyer RS, Mehendale SM, Paranjape RS, Shepherd ME, Gadkari DA, Quinn TC (1997). Risk factors and clinical presentation of acute primary HIV infection in India. *JAMA* 278(23):2085–2089.

Borrow P, Lewicki H, Wei X, et al. (1997). Antiviral pressure exerted by HIV-1-specific cytotoxic T lymphocytes (CTLs) during primary infection demonstrated by rapid selection of CTL escape virus. *Nat Med* 3(2):205–211.

Brabers NA, Nottet HS (2006). Role of the pro-inflammatory cytokines TNF-alpha and IL-1beta in HIV-associated dementia. *Eur J Clin Invest* 36(7):447–458.

Brack-Werner R (1999). Astrocytes: HIV cellular reservoirs and important participants in neuropathogenesis. *AIDS* 13(1):1–22.

Brenchley JM, Schacker TW, Ruff LE, et al. (2004). CD4+ T cell depletion during all stages of HIV disease occurs predominantly in the gastrointestinal tract. *J Exp Med* 200(6):749–759.

Brenneman DE, Westbrook GL, Fitzgerald SP, Ennist DL, Elkins KL, Ruff MR, Pert CB (1988). Neuronal cell killing by the envelope protein of HIV and its prevention by vasoactive intestinal peptide. *Nature* 335(6191):639–642.

Brew BJ (2001). Markers of AIDS dementia complex: the role of cerebrospinal fluid assays. *AIDS* 15(14):1883–1884.

Brew BJ, Bhalla RB, Paul M, et al. W. (1992). Cerebrospinal fluid beta 2-microglobulin in patients with AIDS dementia complex: an expanded series including response to zidovudine treatment. *AIDS* 6(5):461–465.

Brown GR, Rundell JR, McManis SE, Kendall SN, Zachary R, Temoshok L (1992). Prevalence of psychiatric disorders in early stages of HIV infection. *Psychosom Med* 54(5):588–601.

Bryant AK, Ellis RJ, Umlauf A, et al. (2015). Antiretroviral therapy reduces neurodegeneration in HIV infection. *AIDS* 29(3):323–330.

Budka H (1986). Multinucleated giant cells in brain: a hallmark of the acquired immune deficiency syndrome (AIDS). *Acta Neuropathol* 69(3-4):253–258.

Budka H (1991). East-West Danube Symposium on Human and Zoonotic Spongiform Encephalopathies, in Bratislava, Czechoslovakia, May 22–23, 1991. *Brain Pathol* 1(4):325–326.

Budka H, Costanzi G, Cristina S, Lechi A, Parravicini C, Trabattoni R, Vago L (1987). Brain pathology induced by infection with the human immunodeficiency virus (HIV). A histological, immunocytochemical, and electron microscopical study of 100 autopsy cases. *Acta Neuropathol* 75(2):185–198.

Budka H, Maier H, Pohl P (1988). Human immunodeficiency virus in vacuolar myelopathy of the acquired immunodeficiency syndrome. *N Engl J Med* 319(25):1667–1668.

Burdo TH, Lackner A, Williams KC (2013). Monocyte/macrophages and their role in HIV neuropathogenesis. *Immunol Rev* 254(1):102–113.

Burton DR (2006). Structural biology: images from the surface of HIV. *Nature* 441(7095):817–818.

Cann AJ, Churcher MJ, Boyd M, O'Brien W, Zhao JQ, Zack J, Chen IS (1992). The region of the envelope gene of human immunodeficiency virus type 1 responsible for determination of cell tropism. *J Virol* 66(1):305–309.

Canque B, Rosenzwajg M, Gey A, Tartour E, Fridman WH, Gluckman JC (1996). Macrophage inflammatory protein-1alpha is induced by human immunodeficiency virus infection of monocyte-derived macrophages. *Blood* 87(5):2011–2019.

Cardenas VA, Meyerhoff DJ, Studholme C, et al. (2009). Evidence for ongoing brain injury in human immunodeficiency virus–positive patients treated with antiretroviral therapy. *J Neurovirol* 15(4):324–333.

Carlson KA, Ciborowski P, Schellpeper CN, et al. (2004). Proteomic fingerprinting of HIV-1-infected human monocyte-derived macrophages: a preliminary report. *J Neuroimmunol* 147(1-2):35–42.

Carlson KA, Limoges J, Pohlman GD, et al. (2004). OTK18 expression in brain mononuclear phagocytes parallels the severity of HIV-1 encephalitis. *J Neuroimmunol* 150(1-2):186–198.

Carr MW, Roth SJ, Luther E, Rose SS, Springer TA (1994). Monocyte chemoattractant protein 1 acts as a T-lymphocyte chemoattractant. *Proc Natl Acad Sci U S A* 91(9):3652–3656.

Catuogno S, Esposito, CL, de Franciscis V (2015). A Trojan horse for the human immunodeficiency virus. *Chem Biol* 22:313–314.

Cauwels A, Frei K, Sansano S, Fearns C, Ulevitch R, Zimmerli W, Landmann R (1999). The origin and function of soluble CD14 in experimental bacterial meningitis. *J Immunol* 162(8):4762–4772.

Chang L, Ernst T, Leonido-Yee M, Walot I, Singer E (1999a). Cerebral metabolite abnormalities correlate with clinical severity of HIV-1 cognitive motor complex. *Neurology* 52(1):100–108.

Chang L, Ernst T, Leonido-Yee M, Witt M, Speck O, Walot I, Miller EN (1999b). Highly active antiretroviral therapy reverses brain metabolite abnormalities in mild HIV dementia. *Neurology* 53(4):782–789.

Chauhan A, Tikoo A, Patel J, Abdullah AM (2014). HIV-1 endocytosis in astrocytes: a kiss of death or survival of the fittest? *Neurosci Res* 88c:16–22.

Chen WT, Shiu CS, Yang JP, Simoni JM, Fredriksen-Goldsen KI, Lee TS, Zhao H (2013). Antiretroviral therapy (ART) side effect impacted on quality of life, and depressive symptomatology: a mixed-method study. *J AIDS Clin Res* 4:218.

Chong WK, Sweeney B, Wilkinson ID, et al. (1993). Proton spectroscopy of the brain in HIV infection: correlation with clinical, immunologic, and MR imaging findings. *Radiology* 188(1):119–124.

Churchill M, Nath A (2013). Where does HIV hide? A focus on the central nervous system. *Curr Opin HIV AIDS* 8(3):165–169.

Churchill MJ, Wesselingh SL, Cowley D, Pardo CA, McArthur JC, Brew BJ, Gorry PR (2009). Extensive astrocyte infection is prominent in human immunodeficiency virus-associated dementia. *Ann Neurol* 66(2):253–258.

Ciborowski P, Enose Y, Mack A, Fladseth M, Gendelman HE (2004). Diminished matrix metalloproteinase 9 secretion in human immunodeficiency virus–infected mononuclear phagocytes: modulation of innate immunity and implications for neurological disease. *J Neuroimmunol* 157(1-2):11–16.

Ciborowski P, Gendelman HE (2006). Human immunodeficiency virus–mononuclear phagocyte interactions: emerging avenues of biomarker discovery, modes of viral persistence and disease pathogenesis. *Curr HIV Res* 4(3):279–291.

Clark US, Cohen RA (2010). Brain dysfunction in the era of combination antiretroviral therapy: implications for the treatment of the aging population of HIV-infected individuals. *Curr Opin Investig Drugs* 11(8):884–900.

Clay CC, Rodrigues DS, Ho YS, Fallert BA, Janatpour K, Reinhart TA, Esser U (2007). Neuroinvasion of fluorescein-positive monocytes in acute simian immunodeficiency virus infection. *J Virol* 81(21):12040–12048.

Cohen RA, Harezlak J, Schifitto G, et al. (2010). Effects of nadir CD4 count and duration of human immunodeficiency virus infection on brain volumes in the highly active antiretroviral therapy era. *J Neurovirol* 16(1):25–32.

Conant K, Garzino-Demo A, Nath A, et al. (1998). Induction of monocyte chemoattractant protein-1 in HIV-1 Tat-stimulated astrocytes and elevation in AIDS dementia. *Proc Natl Acad Sci U S A* 95(6):3117–3121.

Conant K, Tornatore C, Atwood W, Meyers K, Traub R, Major EO (1994). In vivo and in vitro infection of the astrocyte by HIV-1. *Adv Neuroimmunol* 4(3):287–289.

Constantinescu R, Rosengren L, Johnels B, Zetterberg H, Holmberg B (2010). Consecutive analyses of cerebrospinal fluid axonal and glial markers in Parkinson's disease and atypical parkinsonian disorders. *Parkinsonism Relat Disord* 16(2):142–145.

Crowe SM, Sonza S (2000). HIV-1 can be recovered from a variety of cells including peripheral blood monocytes of patients receiving highly active antiretroviral therapy: a further obstacle to eradication. *J Leukoc Biol* 68(3):345–350.

Cysique LAJ, Maruff P, Darby D, Brew BJ (2006). The assessment of cognitive function in advanced HIV-1 infection and AIDS dementia complex using a new computerised cognitive test battery. *Arch Clin Neuropsychol* 21(2):185–194.

Davis HF, Skolasky RL, Selnes OA, Burgess DM, McArthur JC (2002). Assessing HIV-associated dementia: modified HIV Dementia Scale versus the Grooved Pegboard. *AIDS Read* 12(1):29–31.

Demeulemeester J, Vets S, Schrijvers R, et al. (2014). HIV-1 integrase variants retarget viral integration and are associated with disease progression in a chronic infection cohort. *Cell Host Microbe* 16(5):651–662.

Derdeyn CA, Silvestri G (2005). Viral and host factors in the pathogenesis of HIV infection. *Curr Opin Immunol* 17(4):366–373.

Deshpande M, Zheng J, Borgmann K, Persidsky R, Wu L, Schellpeper C, Ghorpade A (2005). Role of activated astrocytes in neuronal damage: potential links to HIV-1-associated dementia. *Neurotox Res* 7(3):183–192.

Devadas K, Hardegen NJ, Wahl LM, Hewlett IK, Clouse KA, Yamada KM, Dhawan S (2004). Mechanisms for macrophage-mediated HIV-1 induction. *J Immunol* 173(11):6735–6744.

Dickson DW (1986). Multinucleated giant cells in acquired immunodeficiency syndrome encephalopathy. Origin from endogenous microglia? *Arch Pathol Lab Med* 110(10):967–968.

Diesing TS, Swindells S, Gelbard H, Gendelman HE (2002). HIV-1-associated dementia: a basic science and clinical perspective. *AIDS Read* 12(8):358–368.

Draenert R, Allen TM, Liu Y, et al. (2006). Constraints on HIV-1 evolution and immunodominance revealed in monozygotic adult twins infected with the same virus. *J Exp Med* 203(3):529–539.

Eden A, Price RW, Spudich S, Fuchs D, Hagberg L, Gisslen M (2007). Immune activation of the central nervous system is still present after >4 years of effective highly active antiretroviral therapy. *J Infect Dis* 196(12):1779–1783.

Elbirt D, Mahlab-Guri K, Bezalel-Rosenberg S, Gill H, Attali M, Asher I (2015). HIV-associated neurocognitive disorders (HAND). *Isr Med Assoc J* 17(1):54–59.

El-Hage N, Gurwell JA, Singh IN, Knapp PE, Nath A, Hauser KF (2005). Synergistic increases in intracellular Ca2+, and the release of MCP-1, RANTES, and IL-6 by astrocytes treated with opiates and HIV-1 Tat. *Glia* 50(2):91–9106.

Elovaara I, Poutiainen E, Lahdevirta J, et al. (1994). Zidovudine reduces intrathecal immunoactivation in patients with early human immunodeficiency virus type 1 infection. *Arch Neurol* 51(9):943–950.

Enting RH, Foudraine NA, Lange JM, Jurriaans S, van der Poll T, Weverling GJ, Portegies P (2000). Cerebrospinal fluid beta2-microglobulin, monocyte chemotactic protein-1, and soluble tumour necrosis factor alpha receptors before and after treatment with lamivudine plus zidovudine or stavudine. *J Neuroimmunol* 102(2):216–221.

Ernst T, Jiang CS, Nakama H, Buchthal S, Chang L (2010). Lower brain glutamate is associated with cognitive deficits in HIV patients: a new mechanism for HIV-associated neurocognitive disorder. *J Magn Reson Imag* 32(5):1045–1053.

Eugenin EA, Berman JW (2007). Gap junctions mediate human immunodeficiency virus–bystander killing in astrocytes. *J Neurosci* 27(47):12844–12850.

Eugenin EA, Dyer G, Calderon TM, Berman JW (2005). HIV-1 tat protein induces a migratory phenotype in human fetal microglia by a CCL2 (MCP-1)-dependent mechanism: possible role in neuroAIDS. *Glia* 49(4):501–510.

Farzan M, Choe H, Martin KA, et al. (1997). HIV-1 entry and macrophage inflammatory protein-1beta-mediated signaling are independent functions of the chemokine receptor CCR5. *J Biol Chem* 272(11):6854–6857.

Fine SM, Angel RA, Perry SW, Epstein LG, Rothstein JD, Dewhurst S, Gelbard HA (1996). Tumor necrosis factor alpha inhibits glutamate uptake by primary human astrocytes. Implications for pathogenesis of HIV-1 dementia. *J Biol Chem* 271(26):15303–15306.

Finzi D, Hermankova M, Pierson T, et al. (1997). Identification of a reservoir for HIV-1 in patients on highly active antiretroviral therapy. *Science* 278(5341):1295–1300.

Folayan MO, Falobi O, Faleyimu B, Ogunlayi M (2011). Standard of care for HIV prevention technology research: a consensus document from Nigeria. *Afr J Med Med Sci* 40(3):265–271.

Foudraine NA, Hoetelmans RM, Lange JM, et al. (1998). Cerebrospinal-fluid HIV-1 RNA and drug concentrations after treatment with lamivudine plus zidovudine or stavudine. *Lancet* 351(9115):1547–1551.

Franco JM, Rubio A, Rey C, et al. (1999). Reduction of immune system activation in HIV-1-infected patients undergoing highly active antiretroviral therapy. *Eur J Clin Microbiol Infect Dis* 18(10):733–736.

Freed EO (1998). HIV-1 gag proteins: diverse functions in the virus life cycle. *Virology* 251(1):1–15.

Fujita M (2013). [Study of molecular function of proteins in human immunodeficiency virus]. *Yakugaku Zasshi* 133(10):1103–1111.

Gabuzda D, Wang J (1999). Chemokine receptors and virus entry in the central nervous system. *J Neurovirol* 5(6):643–658.

Gallo RC, Sarin PS, Gelmann EP, et al. (1983). Isolation of human T-cell leukemia virus in acquired immune deficiency syndrome (AIDS). *Science* 220(4599):865–867.

Garcia F, Alonso MM, Romeu J, et al. (2000). Comparison of immunologic restoration and virologic response in plasma, tonsillar tissue, and cerebrospinal fluid in HIV-1-infected patients treated with double versus triple antiretroviral therapy in very early stages: the Spanish EARTH-2 Study. Early Anti-Retroviral Therapy Study. *J Acquir Immune Defic Syndr* 25(1):26–35.

Gartner S, Liu Y (2002). Insights into the role of immune activation in HIV neuropathogenesis. *J Neurovirol* 8(2):69–75.

Gattegno L, Bentata-Peyssare M, Gronowski S, Chaouche K, Ferriere F (1995). Elevated concentrations of circulating intercellular adhesion molecule 1 (ICAM-1) and of vascular cell adhesion molecule 1 (VCAM-1) in HIV-1 infection. *Cell Adhes Commun* 3(3):179–185.

Gelman BB (2015). Neuropathology of HAND with suppressive anti-retroviral therapy: encephalitis and neurodegeneration reconsidered. *Curr HIV/AIDS Rep* 12(2):272–279.

Gelman BB, Lisinicchia JG, Morgello S, et al. (2013). Neurovirological correlation with HIV-associated neurocognitive disorders and encephalitis in a HAART-era cohort. *J Acquir Immune Defic Syndr* 62(5):487–495.

Gendelman HE, Zheng J, Coulter CL, et al. (1998). Suppression of inflammatory neurotoxins by highly active antiretroviral therapy in human immunodeficiency virus–associated dementia. *J Infect Dis* 178(4):1000–1007.

Genis P, Jett M, Bernton EW, Boyle T, et al. (1992). Cytokines and arachidonic metabolites produced during human immunodeficiency virus (HIV)–infected macrophage–astroglia interactions: implications for the neuropathogenesis of HIV disease. *J Exp Med* 176(6):1703–1718.

Ghafouri M, Amini S, Khalili K, Sawaya BE (2006). HIV-1 associated dementia: symptoms and causes. *Retrovirology* 3, 28–28.

Ghorpade A, Bruch L, Persidsky Y, et al. (2005). Development of a rapid autopsy program for studies of brain immunity. *J Neuroimmunol* 163(1-2):135–144.

Gisslén M, Chiodi F, Fuchs D, Norkrans G, Svennerholm B, Wachter H, Hagberg L (1994). Markers of immune stimulation in the cerebrospinal fluid during HIV infection: a longitudinal study. *Scand J Infect Dis* 26(5):523–533.

Gisslén M, Norkrans G, Svennerholm B, Hagberg L (1997). The effect on human immunodeficiency virus type 1 RNA levels in cerebrospinal fluid after initiation of zidovudine or didanosine. *J Infect Dis* 175(2):434–437.

Gisslén M, Rosengren L, Hagberg L, Deeks SG, Price RW (2005). Cerebrospinal fluid signs of neuronal damage after antiretroviral treatment interruption in HIV-1 infection. *AIDS Res Ther* 2:6.

Glenn JA, Ward SA, Stone CR, Booth PL, Thomas WE (1992). Characterisation of ramified microglial cells: detailed morphology, morphological plasticity and proliferative capability. *J Anat* 180(Pt 1):109–118.

Gonzalez E, Rovin BH, Sen L, et al. (2002). HIV-1 infection and AIDS dementia are influenced by a mutant MCP-1 allele linked to increased monocyte infiltration of tissues and MCP-1 levels. *Proc Natl Acad Sci U S A* 99(21):13795–13800.

Gonzalez-Scarano F, Martin-Garcia J (2005). The neuropathogenesis of AIDS. *Nat Rev Immunol* 5(1):69–81.

Gorry PR, Dunfee RL, Mefford ME, et al. (2007). Changes in the V3 region of gp120 contribute to unusually broad coreceptor usage of an HIV-1 isolate from a CCR5 delta32 heterozygote. *Virology* 362(1):163–178.

Goulder PJR, Watkins DI (2004). HIV and SIV CTL escape: implications for vaccine design. *Nat Rev Immunol* 4(8):630–640.

Govindasamy D, Meghij J, Kebede Negussi E, Clare Baggaley R, Ford N, Kranzer K (2014). Interventions to improve or facilitate linkage to or retention in pre-ART (HIV) care and initiation of ART in low- and middle-income settings—a systematic review. *J Int AIDS Soc* 17:19032.

Grant PM, Zolopa AR (2012). When to start ART in the setting of acute AIDS-related opportunistic infections: the time is now! *Curr HIV/AIDS Rep* 9(3):251–258.

Gras G, Kaul M (2010). Molecular mechanisms of neuroinvasion by monocytes–macrophages in HIV-1 infection. *Retrovirology* 7:30.

Gray F, Scaravilli F, Everall I, et al. (1996). Neuropathology of early HIV-1 infection. *Brain Pathol* 6(1):1–15.

Gray L, Sterjovski J, Churchill M, et al. (2005). Uncoupling coreceptor usage of human immunodeficiency virus type 1 (HIV-1) from macrophage tropism reveals biological properties of CCR5-restricted HIV-1 isolates from patients with acquired immunodeficiency syndrome. *Virology* 337(2):384–398.

Greenberg M, Cammack N, Salgo M, Smiley L (2004). HIV fusion and its inhibition in antiretroviral therapy. *Rev Med Virol* 14(5):321–337.

Griffin WC, Middaugh LD, Cook JE, Tyor WR (2004). The severe combined immunodeficient (SCID) mouse model of human immunodeficiency virus encephalitis: deficits in cognitive function. *J Neurovirol* 10(2):109–115.

Hagberg L, Andersson M, Chiodi F, Fuchs D, Svennerholm B, Wachter H, Norkrans G (1991). Effect of zidovudine on cerebrospinal fluid in patients with HIV infection and acute neurological disease. *Scand J Infect Dis* 23(6):681–685.

Hall M, Whaley R, Robertson K, Hamby S, Wilkins J, Hall C (1996). The correlation between neuropsychological and neuroanatomic changes over time in asymptomatic and symptomatic HIV-1-infected individuals. *Neurology* 46(6):1697–1702.

Hammoud DA, Endres CJ, Chander AR, et al. (2005). Imaging glial cell activation with [11C]-R-PK11195 in patients with AIDS. *J Neurovirol* 11(4):346–355.

Harezlak J, Buchthal S, Taylor M, et al. (2011). Persistence of HIV-associated cognitive impairment, inflammation, and neuronal injury in era of highly active antiretroviral treatment. *AIDS* 25(5):625–633.

Heaps JM, Joska J, Hoare J, et al. (2012). Neuroimaging markers of human immunodeficiency virus infection in South Africa. *J Neurovirol* 18(3):151–156.

Heaton, RK, Clifford, DB, Franklin, DR Jr, et al. (2010). HIV-associated neurocognitive disorders persist in the era of potent antiretroviral therapy: CHARTER Study. *Neurology* 75(23):2087–2096.

Helke KL, Queen SE, Tarwater PM, et al. (2005). 14-3-3 protein in CSF: an early predictor of SIV CNS disease. *J Neuropathol Exp Neurol* 64(3):202–208.

Herbein G, Varin A (2010). The macrophage in HIV-1 infection: from activation to deactivation? *Retrovirology* 7, 33.

Heyes MP, Brew BJ, Martin A, et al. (1991). Quinolinic acid in cerebrospinal fluid and serum in HIV-1 infection: relationship to clinical and neurological status. *Ann Neurol* 29(2):202–209.

Hinkin CH, van Gorp WG, Mandelkern MA, et al. (1995). Cerebral metabolic change in patients with AIDS: report of a six-month follow-up using positron-emission tomography. *J Neuropsychiatry Clin Neurosci* 7(2):180–187.

Ho EL, Marra CM (2014). Central nervous system diseases due to opportunistic and coinfections. *Semin Neurol* 34(1):61–69.

Ho WZ, Lai JP, Bouhamdan M, Duan L, Pomerantz RJ, Starr SE (1998). Inhibition of HIV type 1 replication in chronically infected monocytes and lymphocytes by retrovirus-mediated gene transfer of anti-Rev single-chain variable fragments. *AIDS Res Hum Retrovir* 14(17):1573–1580.

Hober D, Benyoucef S, Delannoy AS, de Groote D, Ajana F, Mouton Y, Wattre P (1996). High plasma level of soluble tumor necrosis factor receptor type II (sTNFRII) in asymptomatic HIV-1-infected patients. *Infection* 24(3):213–217.

Huang S-T, Lee H-C, Lee N-Y, Liu K-H, Ko W-C (2005). Clinical characteristics of invasive *Haemophilus aphrophilus* infections. *J Microbiol Immunol Infect* 38(4):271–276.

Ipp H, Zemlin AE, Erasmus RT, Glashoff RH (2014). Role of inflammation in HIV-1 disease progression and prognosis. *Crit Rev Clin Lab Sci* 51(2):98–111.

Jana A, Pahan K (2004). Human immunodeficiency virus type 1 gp120 induces apoptosis in human primary neurons through redox-regulated activation of neutral sphingomyelinase. *J Neurosci* 24(43):9531–9540.

Jarvik JG, Lenkinski RE, Saykin AJ, Jaans A, Frank I (1996). Proton spectroscopy in asymptomatic HIV-infected adults: initial results in a prospective cohort study. *J Acquir Immune Defic Syndr Hum Retrovirol* 13(3):247–253.

Jassoy C, Johnson RP, Navia BA, Worth J, Walker BD (1992). Detection of a vigorous HIV-1-specific cytotoxic T lymphocyte response in cerebrospinal fluid from infected persons with AIDS dementia complex. *J Immunol* 149(9):3113–3119.

Jennes W, Vereecken C, Fransen K, de Roo A, Kestens L (2004). Disturbed secretory capacity for macrophage inflammatory protein (MIP)-1 alpha and MIP-1 beta in progressive HIV infection. *AIDS Res Hum Retrovir* 20(10):1087–1091.

Jessen Krut J, Mellberg T, Price RW, et al. (2014). Biomarker evidence of axonal injury in neuroasymptomatic HIV-1 patients. *PLoS ONE* 9(2):e88591.

Jiang H, Xie N, Cao B, et al. (2013). Determinants of progression to AIDS and death following HIV diagnosis: a retrospective cohort study in Wuhan, China. *PLoS ONE* 8(12):e83078.

Jiang ZG, Piggee C, Heyes MP, et al. (2001). Glutamate is a mediator of neurotoxicity in secretions of activated HIV-1-infected macrophages. *J Neuroimmunol* 117(1-2):97–9107.

Johnson VA, Brun-Vezinet F, Clotet B, et al. (2005). Update of the drug resistance mutations in HIV-1: 2005. *Top HIV Med* 13:51–57.

Joseph SB, Arrildt KT, Sturdevant CB, Swanstrom R (2015). HIV-1 target cells in the CNS. *J Neurovirol* 21(3):276–289.

Joska JA, Gouse H, Paul RH, Stein DJ, Flisher AJ. (2010). Does highly active antiretroviral therapy improve neurocognitive function? A systematic review. *J Neurovirol* 16(2):101–114.

Jowett JB, Planelles V, Poon B, Shah NP, Chen ML, Chen IS (1995). The human immunodeficiency virus type 1 vpr gene arrests infected T cells in the G2 + M phase of the cell cycle. *J Virol* 69(10):6304–6313.

Kanmogne GD, Grammas P, Kennedy RC (2000). Analysis of human endothelial cells and cortical neurons for susceptibility to HIV-1 infection and co-receptor expression. *J Neurovirol* 6(6):519–528.

Kanmogne GD, Primeaux C, Grammas P (2005). HIV-1 gp120 proteins alter tight junction protein expression and brain endothelial cell permeability: implications for the pathogenesis of HIV-associated dementia. *J Neuropathol Exp Neurol* 64(6):498–505.

Kanmogne GD, Schall K, Leibhart J, Knipe B, Gendelman HE, Persidsky Y (2007). HIV-1 gp120 compromises blood-brain barrier integrity and enhances monocyte migration across blood-brain barrier: implication for viral neuropathogenesis. *J Cereb Blood Flow Metab* 27(1):123–134.

Kaul M, Lipton SA (2006). Mechanisms of neuronal injury and death in HIV-1 associated dementia. *Curr HIV Res* 4(3):307–318.

Kaur C, Ling EA (1991). Study of the transformation of amoeboid microglial cells into microglia labelled with the isolectin *Griffonia simplicifolia* in postnatal rats. *Acta Anat (Basel)* 142(2):118–125.

Kaur C, Ling EA, Wong WC (1985). Transformation of amoeboid microglial cells into microglia in the corpus callosum of the postnatal rat brain. An electron microscopical study. *Arch Histol Jpn* 48(1):17–25.

Kedzierska K, Azzam R, Ellery P, Mak J, Jaworowski A, Crowe SM (2003). Defective phagocytosis by human monocyte/macrophages following HIV-1 infection: underlying mechanisms and modulation by adjunctive cytokine therapy. *J Clin Virol* 26(2):247–263.

Kelder W, McArthur JC, Nance-Sproson T, McClernon D, Griffin DE (1998). Beta-chemokines MCP-1 and RANTES are selectively increased in cerebrospinal fluid of patients with human immunodeficiency virus-associated dementia. *Ann Neurol* 44(5):831–835.

Kettenmann H, Hanisch UK, Noda M, Verkhratsky A (2011). Physiology of microglia. *Physiol Rev* 91(2):461–553.

Khan NA, Di Cello F, Stins M, Kim KS (2007). Gp120-mediated cytotoxicity of human brain microvascular endothelial cells is dependent on p38 mitogen-activated protein kinase activation. *J Neurovirol* 13(3):242–251.

Kinloch-de Loes S, de Saussure P, Saurat JH, Stalder H, Hirschel B, Perrin LH (1993). Symptomatic primary infection due to human immunodeficiency virus type 1: review of 31 cases. *Clin Infect Dis* 17(1):59–65.

Klasse PJ (2012). The molecular basis of HIV entry. *Cell Microbiol* 14(8):1183–1192.

Klatt EC (1988). Diagnostic findings in patients with acquired immune deficiency syndrome (AIDS). *J Acquir Immune Defic Syndr* 1(5):459–465.

Koenig S, Gendelman HE, Orenstein JM, et al. (1986). Detection of AIDS virus in macrophages in brain tissue from AIDS patients with encephalopathy. *Science* 233(4768):1089–1093.

Koppensteiner H, Brack-Werner R, Schindler M (2012). Macrophages and their relevance in human immunodeficiency virus type I infection. *Retrovirology* 9:82.

Koup RA (2004). Reconsidering early HIV treatment and supervised treatment interruptions. *PLoS Med* 1(2):e41.

Kranick SM, Nath A (2012). Neurologic complications of HIV-1 infection and its treatment in the era of antiretroviral therapy. *Continuum (Minneap Minn.)* 18(6 Infectious Disease):1319–1337.

Kure K, Llena JF, Lyman WD, Soeiro R, Weidenheim KM, Hirano A, Dickson DW (1991). Human immunodeficiency virus-1 infection of the nervous system: an autopsy study of 268 adult, pediatric, and fetal brains. *Hum Pathol* 22(7):700–710.

Kutsch O, Oh J, Nath A, Benveniste EN (2000). Induction of the chemokines interleukin-8 and IP-10 by human immunodeficiency virus type 1 tat in astrocytes. *J Virol* 74(19):9214–9221.

Lamers SL, Fogel GB, Nolan DJ, McGrath MS, Salemi M (2014). HIV-associated neuropathogenesis: a systems biology perspective for modeling and therapy. *Biosystems* 119:53–61.

Landqvist Waldo M, Frizell Santillo A, Passant U, et al. (2013). Cerebrospinal fluid neurofilament light chain protein levels in subtypes of frontotemporal dementia. *BMC Neurol* 13:54.

Lavi E, Kolson DL, Ulrich AM, Fu L, Gonzalez-Scarano F (1998). Chemokine receptors in the human brain and their relationship to HIV infection. *J Neurovirol* 4(3):301–311.

Lawrence DM, Major EO (2002). HIV-1 and the brain: connections between HIV-1-associated dementia, neuropathology and neuroimmunology. *Microbes Infect* 4(3):301–308.

Lederman MM, Penn-Nicholson A, Cho M, Mosier D (2006). Biology of CCR5 and its role in HIV infection and treatment. *JAMA* 296(7):815–826.

Lentz MR, Kim WK, Kim H, et al. (2011). Alterations in brain metabolism during the first year of HIV infection. *J Neurovirol* 17(3):220–229.

Lentz MR, Kim WK, Lee V, et al. (2009). Changes in MRS neuronal markers and T cell phenotypes observed during early HIV infection. *Neurology* 72(17):1465–1472.

Letendre SL, Lanier ER, McCutchan JA (1999). Cerebrospinal fluid beta chemokine concentrations in neurocognitively impaired individuals infected with human immunodeficiency virus type 1. *J Infect Dis* 180(2):310–319.

Letvin NL, Walker BD (2003). Immunopathogenesis and immunotherapy in AIDS virus infections. *Nat Med* 9(7):861–866.

Leutscher PD, Stecher C, Storgaard M, Larsen CS (2013). Discontinuation of efavirenz therapy in HIV patients due to neuropsychiatric adverse effects. *Scand J Infect Dis* 45(8):645–651.

Lifson AR, Coutre S, Huang E, Engleman E (1986). Role of envelope glycoprotein carbohydrate in human immunodeficiency virus (HIV) infectivity and virus-induced cell fusion. *J Exp Med* 164(6):2101–2106.

Lifson JD, Feinberg MB, Reyes GR, et al. (1986). Induction of CD4-dependent cell fusion by the HTLV-III/LAV envelope glycoprotein. *Nature* 323(6090):725–728.

Lindback S, Thorstensson R, Karlsson AC, et al. (2000). Diagnosis of primary HIV-1 infection and duration of follow-up after HIV exposure. Karolinska Institute Primary HIV Infection Study Group. *AIDS* 14(15):2333–2339.

Ling EA (1982a). Influence of cortisone on amoeboid microglia and microglial cells in the corpus callosum in postnatal rats. *J Anat* 134(Pt 4):705–717.

Ling EA (1982b). A light microscopic demonstration of amoeboid microglia and microglial cells in the retina of rats of various ages. *Arch Histol Jpn* 45(1):37–44.

Ling EA, Wong WC (1993). The origin and nature of ramified and amoeboid microglia: a historical review and current concepts. *Glia* 7(1):9–18.

Lipton SA, Yeh M, Dreyer EB (1994). Update on current models of HIV-related neuronal injury: platelet-activating factor, arachidonic acid and nitric oxide. *Adv Neuroimmunol* 4(3):181–188.

Liu B, Hong J-S (2003). Role of microglia in inflammation-mediated neurodegenerative diseases: mechanisms and strategies for therapeutic intervention. *J Pharmacol Exp Ther* 304(1):1–7.

Lozupone CA, Rhodes ME, Neff CP, Fontenot AP, Campbell TB, Palmer BE (2014). HIV-induced alteration in gut microbiota: driving factors, consequences, and effects of antiretroviral therapy. *Gut Microbes* 5(4):562–570.

Lyerly HK, Matthews TJ, Langlois AJ, Bolognesi DP, Weinhold KJ (1987). Human T-cell lymphotropic virus IIIB glycoprotein (gp120) bound to CD4 determinants on normal lymphocytes and expressed by infected cells serves as target for immune attack. *Proc Natl Acad Sci U S A* 84(13):4601–4605.

Maartens G, Celum C, Lewin SR (2014). HIV infection: epidemiology, pathogenesis, treatment, and prevention. *Lancet* 384(9939):258–271.

Manzardo C, Del Mar Ortega M, Sued O, Garcia F, Moreno A, Miro JM (2005). Central nervous system opportunistic infections in developed countries in the highly active antiretroviral therapy era. *J Neurovirol* 11(Suppl 3):72–82.

Marra CM, Maxwell CL, Collier AC, Robertson KR, Imrie A (2007). Interpreting cerebrospinal fluid pleocytosis in HIV in the era of potent antiretroviral therapy. *BMC Infect Dis* 7:37.

Martin A, Heyes MP, Salazar AM, et al. (1992). Progressive slowing of reaction time and increasing cerebrospinal fluid concentrations of quinolinic acid in HIV-infected individuals. *J Neuropsychiatry Clin Neurosci* 4(3):270–279.

Maslin CLV, Kedzierska K, Webster NL, Muller WA, Crowe SM (2005). Transendothelial migration of monocytes: the underlying molecular mechanisms and consequences of HIV-1 infection. *Curr HIV Res* 3(4):303–317.

Matthews TJ, Weinhold KJ, Lyerly HK, Langlois AJ, Wigzell H, Bolognesi DP (1987). Interaction between the human T-cell lymphotropic virus type IIIB envelope glycoprotein gp120 and the surface antigen CD4: role of carbohydrate in binding and cell fusion. *Proc Natl Acad Sci U S A* 84(15):5424–5428.

McArthur JC, Brew BJ, Nath A (2005). Neurological complications of HIV infection. *Lancet Neurol* 4(9):543–555.

McArthur JC, McDermott MP, McClernon D, et al. (2004). Attenuated central nervous system infection in advanced HIV/AIDS with combination antiretroviral therapy. *Arch Neurol* 61(11):1687–1696.

McArthur JC, Steiner J, Sacktor N, Nath A (2010). Human immunodeficiency virus–associated neurocognitive disorders: mind the gap. *Ann Neurol* 67(6):699–714.

McConnell JR, Swindells S, Ong CS, et al. (1994). Prospective utility of cerebral proton magnetic resonance spectroscopy in monitoring HIV infection and its associated neurological impairment. *AIDS Res Hum Retroviruses* 10(8):977–982.

McManus CM, Weidenheim K, Woodman SE, Nunez J, Hesselgesser J, Nath A, Berman JW (2000). Chemokine and chemokine-receptor expression in human glial elements: induction by the HIV protein, Tat, and chemokine autoregulation. *Am J Pathol* 156(4):1441–1453.

McMurtray A, Clark DG, Christine D, Mendez MF (2006). Early-onset dementia: frequency and causes compared to late-onset dementia. *Dement Geriatr Cogn Disord* 21(2):59–64.

Mehandru S, Poles MA, Tenner-Racz K, et al. (2004). Primary HIV-1 infection is associated with preferential depletion of CD4+ T lymphocytes from effector sites in the gastrointestinal tract. *J Exp Med* 200(6):761–770.

Meng B, Lever AM (2013). Wrapping up the bad news: HIV assembly and release. *Retrovirology* 10:5.

Menon DK, Ainsworth JG, Cox IJ, et al. (1992). Proton MR spectroscopy of the brain in AIDS dementia complex. *J Comput Assist Tomogr* 16(4):538–542.

Meyerhoff DJ, MacKay S, Poole N, Dillon WP, Weiner MW, Fein G (1994). N-acetylaspartate reductions measured by 1H MRSI in cognitively impaired HIV-seropositive individuals. *Magn Reson Imaging* 12(4):653–659.

Miller F, Afonso PV, Gessain A, Ceccaldi PE (2012). Blood-brain barrier and retroviral infections. *Virulence* 3(2):222–229.

Minagar A, Shapshak P, Fujimura R, Ownby R, Heyes M, Eisdorfer C (2002). The role of macrophage/microglia and astrocytes in the pathogenesis of three neurologic disorders: HIV-associated dementia, Alzheimer disease, and multiple sclerosis. *J Neurol Sci* 202(1-2):13–23.

Miyakawa T, Obaru K, Maeda K, Harada S, Mitsuya H (2002). Identification of amino acid residues critical for LD78beta, a variant of human macrophage inflammatory protein-1alpha, binding to

CCR5 and inhibition of R5 human immunodeficiency virus type 1 replication. *J Biol Chem* 277(7):4649–4655.

Mohamed MA, Barker PB, Skolasky RL, Selnes OA, Moxley RT, Pomper MG, Sacktor NC (2010). Brain metabolism and cognitive impairment in HIV infection: a 3-T magnetic resonance spectroscopy study. *Magn Reson Imaging* 28(9):1251–1257.

Montefiori DC, Altfeld M, Lee PK, et al. (2003). Viremia control despite escape from a rapid and potent autologous neutralizing antibody response after therapy cessation in an HIV-1-infected individual. *J Immunol* 170(7):3906–3914.

Musey L, Hughes J, Schacker T, Shea T, Corey L, McElrath MJ (1997). Cytotoxic-T-cell responses, viral load, and disease progression in early human immunodeficiency virus type 1 infection. *N Engl J Med* 337(18):1267–1274.

Nath AK, Ahmed T, Rana NS, Sharma DR (2002). Host plant nodule parameters associated with nitrogen fixation efficiency in French bean (*Phaseolus vulgaris* L) cultivars. *Indian J Exp Biol* 40(3):334–340.

Navenot JM, Wang ZX, Trent JO, et al. (2001). Molecular anatomy of CCR5 engagement by physiologic and viral chemokines and HIV-1 envelope glycoproteins: differences in primary structural requirements for RANTES, MIP-1 alpha, and vMIP-II Binding. *J Mol Biol* 313(5):1181–1193.

Navia BA, Cho ES, Petito CK, Price RW (1986). The AIDS dementia complex: II. Neuropathology. *Ann Neurol* 19(6):525–535.

Navia BA, Jordan BD, Price RW (1986). The AIDS dementia complex: I. Clinical features. *Ann Neurol* 19(6):517–524.

New DR, Ma M, Epstein LG, Nath A, Gelbard HA (1997). Human immunodeficiency virus type 1 Tat protein induces death by apoptosis in primary human neuron cultures. *J Neurovirol* 3(2):168–173.

Nielsen SL, Petito CK, Urmacher CD, Posner JB (1984). Subacute encephalitis in acquired immune deficiency syndrome: a postmortem study. *Am J Clin Pathol* 82(6):678–682.

Nottet HS, Gendelman HE (1995). Unraveling the neuroimmune mechanisms for the HIV-1-associated cognitive/motor complex. *Immunol Today* 16(9):441–448.

Nottet HS, Jett M, Flanagan CR, et al. (1995). A regulatory role for astrocytes in HIV-1 encephalitis. An overexpression of eicosanoids, platelet-activating factor, and tumor necrosis factor-alpha by activated HIV-1-infected monocytes is attenuated by primary human astrocytes. *J Immunol* 154(7):3567–3581.

Nottet HS, Persidsky Y, Sasseville VG, et al. (1996). Mechanisms for the transendothelial migration of HIV-1-infected monocytes into brain. *J Immunol* 156(3):1284–1295.

Nozaki I, Kuriyama M, Manyepa P, Zyambo MK, Kakimoto K, Barnighausen T (2013). False beliefs about ART effectiveness, side effects and the consequences of non-retention and non-adherence among ART patients in Livingstone, Zambia. *AIDS Behav* 17(1):122–126.

Oxenius A, Price DA, Trkola A, et al. (2004). Loss of viral control in early HIV-1 infection is temporally associated with sequential escape from CD8+ T cell responses and decrease in HIV-1-specific CD4+ and CD8+ T cell frequencies. *J Infect Dis* 190(4):713–721.

Peluso MJ, Spudich S (2014). Treatment of HIV in the CNS: effects of antiretroviral therapy and the promise of non-antiretroviral therapeutics. *Curr HIV/AIDS Rep* 11(3):353–362.

Perrella O, Carrieri PB, Guarnaccia D, Soscia M (1992). Cerebrospinal fluid cytokines in AIDS dementia complex. *J Neurol* 239(7):387–388.

Persidsky Y, Zheng J, Miller D, Gendelman HE (2000). Mononuclear phagocytes mediate blood-brain barrier compromise and neuronal injury during HIV-1-associated dementia. *J Leukoc Biol* 68(3):413–422.

Pilcher CD, Eron JJ, Galvin S, Gay C, Cohen MS (2004). Acute HIV revisited: new opportunities for treatment and prevention. *J Clin Invest* 113(7):937–945.

Poluektova L, Gorantla S, Faraci J, Birusingh K, Dou H, Gendelman HE (2004). Neuroregulatory events follow adaptive immune-mediated elimination of HIV-1-infected macrophages: studies in a murine model of viral encephalitis. *J Immunol* 172(12):7610–7617.

Poluektova L, Meyer V, Walters L, Paez X, Gendelman HE (2005). Macrophage-induced inflammation affects hippocampal plasticity and neuronal development in a murine model of HIV-1 encephalitis. *Glia* 52(4):344–353.

Pomara N, Crandall DT, Choi SJ, Johnson G, Lim KO (2001). White matter abnormalities in HIV-1 infection: a diffusion tensor imaging study. *Psychiatry Res* 106(1):15–24.

Pomerantz RJ (2004). Effects of HIV-1 Vpr on neuroinvasion and neuropathogenesis. *DNA Cell Biol* 23(4):227–238.

Pontow SE, Heyden NV, Wei S, Ratner L (2004). Actin cytoskeletal reorganizations and coreceptor-mediated activation of rac during human immunodeficiency virus–induced cell fusion. *J Virol* 78(13):7138–7147.

Porcheray F, Samah B, Leone C, Dereuddre-Bosquet N, Gras G (2006). Macrophage activation and human immunodeficiency virus infection: HIV replication directs macrophages towards a pro-inflammatory phenotype while previous activation modulates macrophage susceptibility to infection and viral production. *Virology* 349(1):112–120.

Power C, Selnes OA, Grim JA, McArthur JC (1995). HIV Dementia Scale: a rapid screening test. *J Acquir Immune Defic Syndr Hum Retrovirol* 8(3):273–278.

Price RW, Brew B (1988). Infection of the central nervous system by human immunodeficiency virus. Role of the immune system in pathogenesis. *Ann N Y Acad Sci* 540, 162–175.

Price RW, Epstein LG, Becker JT, et al. (2007). Biomarkers of HIV-1 CNS infection and injury. *Neurology* 69(18):1781–1788.

Price RW, Peterson J, Fuchs D, et al. (2013). Approach to cerebrospinal fluid (CSF) biomarker discovery and evaluation in HIV infection. *J Neuroimmune Pharmacol* 8(5):1147–1158.

Price TO, Ercal N, Nakaoke R, Banks WA (2005). HIV-1 viral proteins gp120 and Tat induce oxidative stress in brain endothelial cells. *Brain Res* 1045(1-2):57–63.

Price TO, Uras F, Banks WA, Ercal N (2006). A novel antioxidant N-acetylcysteine amide prevents gp120- and Tat-induced oxidative stress in brain endothelial cells. *Exp Neurol* 201(1):193–202.

Ragin AB, D'Souza G, Reynolds S, et al. (2011). Platelet decline as a predictor of brain injury in HIV infection. *J Neurovirol* 17(5):487–495.

Ribeiro RM, Hazenberg MD, Perelson AS, Davenport MP (2006). Naive and memory cell turnover as drivers of CCR5-to-CXCR4 tropism switch in human immunodeficiency virus type 1: implications for therapy. *J Virol* 80(2):802–809.

Ryan LA, Zheng J, Brester M, et al. (2001). Plasma levels of soluble CD14 and tumor necrosis factor-alpha type II receptor correlate with cognitive dysfunction during human immunodeficiency virus type 1 infection. *J Infect Dis* 184(6):699–706.

Sacktor N, McArthur J (1997). Prospects for therapy of HIV-associated neurologic diseases. *J Neurovirol* 3(2):89–8101.

Sacktor N, Tarwater PM, Skolasky RL, et al. (2001). CSF antiretroviral drug penetrance and the treatment of HIV-associated psychomotor slowing. *Neurology* 57(3):542–544.

Sathekge M, McFarren A, Dadachova E (2014). Role of nuclear medicine in neuroHIV: PET, SPECT, and beyond. *Nucl Med Commun* 35(8):792–796.

Sato H, Orenstein J, Dimitrov D, Martin M (1992). Cell-to-cell spread of HIV-1 occurs within minutes and may not involve the participation of virus particles. *Virology* 186(2):712–724.

Schacker T, Collier AC, Hughes J, Shea T, Corey L (1996). Clinical and epidemiologic features of primary HIV infection. *Ann Intern Med* 125(4):257–264.

Schifitto G, Kieburtz K, McDermott MP, et al. (2001). Clinical trials in HIV-associated cognitive impairment: cognitive and functional outcomes. *Neurology* 56(3):415–418.

Schmidtmayerova H, Nottet HS, Nuovo G, et al. (1996). Human immunodeficiency virus type 1 infection alters chemokine beta peptide expression in human monocytes: implications for recruitment of leukocytes into brain and lymph nodes. *Proc Natl Acad Sci U S A* 93(2):700–704.

Schmitz JE, Kuroda MJ, Santra S, et al. (1999). Control of viremia in simian immunodeficiency virus infection by CD8+ lymphocytes. *Science* 283(5403):857–860.

Schweighardt B, Shieh JT, Atwood WJ (2001). CD4/CXCR4-independent infection of human astrocytes by a T-tropic strain of HIV-1. *J Neurovirol* 7(2):155–162.

Sharer LR, Baskin GB, Cho ES, Murphey-Corb M, Blumberg BM, Epstein LG (1988). Comparison of simian immunodeficiency virus and human immunodeficiency virus encephalitides in the immature host. *Ann Neurol* 23(Suppl):108–112.

Sharer LR, Cho ES, Epstein LG (1985). Multinucleated giant cells and HTLV-III in AIDS encephalopathy. *Hum Pathol* 16(8):760–760.

Shioda T, Levy JA, Cheng-Mayer C (1992). Small amino acid changes in the V3 hypervariable region of gp120 can affect the T-cell-line and macrophage tropism of human immunodeficiency virus type 1. *Proc Natl Acad Sci U S A* 89(20):9434–9438.

Shive CL, Mudd JC, Funderburg NT, et al. (2014). Inflammatory cytokines drive CD4+ T-cell cycling and impaired responsiveness to interleukin 7: implications for immune failure in HIV disease. *J Infect Dis* 210(4):619–629.

Sidtis JJ, Gatsonis C, Price RW, et al. (1993). Zidovudine treatment of the AIDS dementia complex: results of a placebo-controlled trial. AIDS Clinical Trials Group. *Ann Neurol* 33(4):343–349.

Snider WD, Simpson DM, Nielsen S, Gold JW, Metroka CE, Posner JB (1983). Neurological complications of acquired immune deficiency syndrome: analysis of 50 patients. *Ann Neurol* 14(4):403–418.

Song L, Nath A, Geiger JD, Moore A, Hochman S (2003). Human immunodeficiency virus type 1 Tat protein directly activates neuronal N-methyl-D-aspartate receptors at an allosteric zinc-sensitive site. *J Neurovirol* 9(3):399–403.

Spudich S, Gonzalez-Scarano F (2012). HIV-1-related central nervous system disease: current issues in pathogenesis, diagnosis, and treatment. *Cold Spring Harb Perspect Med* 2(6):a007120.

Spudich SS, Nilsson AC, Lollo ND, et al. (2005). Cerebrospinal fluid HIV infection and pleocytosis: relation to systemic infection and antiretroviral treatment. *BMC Infect Dis* 5, 98.

Stamm WE, Handsfield HH, Rompalo AM, Ashley RL, Roberts PL, Corey L (1988). The association between genital ulcer disease and acquisition of HIV infection in homosexual men. *JAMA* 260(10):1429–1433.

Steckbeck JD, Kuhlmann AS, Montelaro RC (2013). C-terminal tail of human immunodeficiency virus gp41: functionally rich and structurally enigmatic. *J Genet Virol* 94(Pt 1):1–19.

Stewart SA, Poon B, Jowett JB, Chen IS (1997). Human immunodeficiency virus type 1 Vpr induces apoptosis following cell cycle arrest. *J Virol* 71(7):5579–5592.

Strelow LI, Janigro D, Nelson JA (2001). The blood-brain barrier and AIDS. *Adv Virus Res* 56:355–388.

Stricker SM, Fox KA, Baggaley R, Negussie E, de Pee S, Grede N, Bloem MW (2014). Retention in care and adherence to ART are critical elements of HIV care interventions. *AIDS Behav* 18(Suppl 5):S465–S475.

Sundquist WI, Krausslich HG (2012). HIV-1 assembly, budding, and maturation. *Cold Spring Harb Perspect Med* 2(7):a006924.

Swindells S, McConnell JR, McComb RD, Gendelman HE (1995). Utility of cerebral proton magnetic resonance spectroscopy in differential diagnosis of HIV-related dementia. *J Neurovirol* 1(3-4):268–274.

Swindells S, Zheng J, Gendelman HE (1999). HIV-associated dementia: new insights into disease pathogenesis and therapeutic interventions. *AIDS Patient Care STDs* 13(3):153–163.

Tan IL, McArthur JC (2012). HIV-associated neurological disorders: a guide to pharmacotherapy. *CNS Drugs* 26(2):123–134.

Tan IL, Smith BR, von Geldern G, Mateen FJ, McArthur JC (2012). HIV-associated opportunistic infections of the CNS. *Lancet Neurol* 11(7):605–617.

Thompson PM, Dutton RA, Hayashi KM, Toga AW, Lopez OL, Aizenstein HJ, Becker JT. (2005). Thinning of the cerebral cortex visualized in HIV/AIDS reflects CD4+ T lymphocyte decline. *Proc Natl Acad Sci U S A* 102(43):15647–15652.

Thurnher MM, Castillo M, Stadler A, Rieger A, Schmid B, Sundgren PC (2005). Diffusion-tensor MR imaging of the brain in human immunodeficiency virus–positive patients. *AJNR Am J Neuroradiol* 26(9):2275–2281.

Toborek M, Lee YW, Flora G, et al. (2005). Mechanisms of the blood-brain barrier disruption in HIV-1 infection. *Cell Mol Neurobiol* 25(1):181–199.

Tozzi V, Balestra P, Galgani S, et al. (2001). Changes in neurocognitive performance in a cohort of patients treated with HAART for 3 years. *J Acquir Immune Defic Syndr* 28(1):19–27.

Tracey I, Hamberg LM, Guimaraes AR, Hunter G, Chang I, Navia BA, Gonzalez RG (1998). Increased cerebral blood volume in HIV-positive patients detected by functional MRI. *Neurology* 50(6):1821–1826.

Tucker KA, Robertson KR, Lin W, et al. (2004). Neuroimaging in human immunodeficiency virus infection. *J Neuroimmunol* 157(1-2):153–162.

Tyor WR, Glass JD, Griffin JW, Becker PS, McArthur JC, Bezman L, Griffin DE (1992). Cytokine expression in the brain during the acquired immunodeficiency syndrome. *Ann Neurol* 31(4):349–360.

Tyrer F, Walker AS, Gillett J, Porter K (2003). The relationship between HIV seroconversion illness, HIV test interval and time to AIDS in a seroconverter cohort. *Epidemiol Infect* 131(3):1117–1123.

Vandergeeten C, Fromentin R, Chomont N (2012). The role of cytokines in the establishment, persistence and eradication of the HIV reservoir. *Cytokine Growth Factor Rev* 23(4-5):143–149.

van Gorp WG, Mandelkern MA, Gee M, et al. (1992). Cerebral metabolic dysfunction in AIDS: findings in a sample with and without dementia. *J Neuropsychiatry Clin Neurosci* 4(3):280–287.

Veazey RS, DeMaria M, Chalifoux LV, et al. (1998). Gastrointestinal tract as a major site of CD4+ T cell depletion and viral replication in SIV infection. *Science* 280(5362):427–431.

Vesce S, Bezzi P, Rossi D, Meldolesi J, Volterra A (1997). HIV-1 gp120 glycoprotein affects the astrocyte control of extracellular glutamate by both inhibiting the uptake and stimulating the release of the amino acid. *FEBS Lett* 411(1):107–109.

Votteler J, Sundquist WI (2013). Virus budding and the ESCRT pathway. *Cell Host Microbe* 14(3):232–241.

Weed MR, Steward DJ (2005). Neuropsychopathology in the SIV/macaque model of AIDS. *Front Biosci* 10:710–727.

Wesselingh SL, Thompson KA (2001). Immunopathogenesis of HIV-associated dementia. *Curr Opin Neurol* 14(3):375–379.

Wilkie FL, Goodkin K, Khamis I, et al. (2003). Cognitive functioning in younger and older HIV-1-infected adults. *J Acquir Immune Defic Syndr* 33(Suppl 2):93–93.

Williams DW, Calderon TM, Lopez L, et al. (2013). Mechanisms of HIV entry into the CNS: increased sensitivity of HIV infected CD14+CD16+ monocytes to CCL2 and key roles of CCR2, JAM-A, and ALCAM in diapedesis. *PLoS ONE* 8(7):e69270.

Williams DW, Veenstra M, Gaskill PJ, Morgello S, Calderon TM, Berman JW (2014). Monocytes mediate HIV neuropathogenesis: mechanisms that contribute to HIV associated neurocognitive disorders. *Curr HIV Res* 12(2):85–96.

Wojna V, Carlson KA, Luo X, Mayo R, Melendez LM, Kraiselburd E, Gendelman HE (2004). Proteomic fingerprinting of human immunodeficiency virus type 1-associated dementia from patient monocyte-derived macrophages: a case study. *J Neurovirol* 10(Suppl 1):74–81.

Worlein JM, Leigh J, Larsen K, Kinman L, Schmidt A, Ochs H, Ho RJY (2005). Cognitive and motor deficits associated with HIV-2(287) infection in infant pigtailed macaques: a nonhuman primate model of pediatric neuro-AIDS. *J Neurovirol* 11(1):34–45.

Xiong H, Zeng YC, Lewis T, Zheng J, Persidsky Y, Gendelman HE (2000). HIV-1 infected mononuclear phagocyte secretory products affect neuronal physiology leading to cellular demise: relevance for HIV-1-associated dementia. *J Neurovirol* 6(Suppl 1):14–23.

Xu LL, Warren MK, Rose WL, Gong W, Wang JM (1996). Human recombinant monocyte chemotactic protein and other C-C chemokines bind and induce directional migration of dendritic cells in vitro. *J Leukoc Biol* 60(3):365–371.

Yilmaz A, Price RW, Spudich S, Fuchs D, Hagberg L, Gisslen M (2008). Persistent intrathecal immune activation in HIV-1-infected individuals on antiretroviral therapy. *J Acquir Immune Defic Syndr* 47(2):168–173.

Yu HJ, Reuter MA, McDonald D. (2008). HIV traffics through a specialized, surface-accessible intracellular compartment during trans-infection of T cells by mature dendritic cells. *PLoS Pathog* 4(8):e1000134.

Zayyad Z, Spudich S (2015). Neuropathogenesis of HIV: from initial neuroinvasion to HIV-associated neurocognitive disorder (HAND). *Curr HIV/AIDS Rep* 12(1):16–24.

Zheng J, Gendelman HE (1997). The HIV-1 associated dementia complex: a metabolic encephalopathy fueled by viral replication in mononuclear phagocytes. *Curr Opin Neurol* 10(4):319–325.

Zheng J, Thylin MR, Persidsky Y, et al. (2001). HIV-1 infected immune competent mononuclear phagocytes influence the pathways to neuronal demise. *Neurotox Res* 3(5):461–484.

Zink MC, Uhrlaub J, DeWitt J, et al. (2005). Neuroprotective and anti-human immunodeficiency virus activity of minocycline. *JAMA* 293(16):2003–2011.

27.

NEUROLOGICAL COMPLICATIONS OF HIV IN THE PERIPHERAL NERVOUS SYSTEM

John R. Keltner, Cherine Akkari, and Ronald J. Ellis

Despite modern antiretroviral therapy, HIV sensory neuropathy (HIV-SN) affects approximately 50% of persons with HIV (Ellis et al., 2010; Simpson et al., 2006). The clinical presentation of HIV-SN is variable. Some individuals with HIV-SN report few symptoms while up to 40% of patients with HIV-SN report disabling symptoms, including paresthesia and/or pain. In this chapter, we will not attempt to summarize the vast literature describing HIV-SN but rather provide guidance to clinical psychiatrists in the clinical management of peripheral (typically in the toes and feet) pain in persons with HIV who suffer from sensory neuropathy. First, we present a decision tree that helps to guide the initial diagnostic evaluation of peripheral pain in HIV patients. Second, we describe the clinical presentation and management for HIV-SN. In the last part of the chapter we focus on clinical aspects and management of HIV distal neuropathic pain. We hope that this chapter will help psychiatrists who treat patients with HIV and peripheral pain to interact productively with a consulting neurologist in order to achieve effective evaluation and management of peripheral pain in persons with HIV.

DIFFERENTIATION OF HIV SENSORY NEUROPATHY FROM OTHER PERIPHERAL NEUROPATHIES AND SPINAL CORD MIMICS

STEP 1 OF DECISION TREE: SPINAL CORD MIMICS FOR PERIPHERAL NEUROPATHY

When evaluating peripheral pain in persons with HIV, the first step is to rule out possible spinal cord disease, which can clinically mimic peripheral neuropathy (see Figure 27.1). Spinal cord clinical mimics of peripheral neuropathy include HIV myelopathy (such as HIV-associated vacuolar myelopathy), non-HIV myelopathy (such as cytomegalovirus polyradiculomyelitis), and more common spinal cord lesions such as disc herniation. Before use of effective HIV combination antiretroviral therapy, cytomegalovirus infections were a common complication in persons with HIV/AIDS (Gerna et al., 1990).

STEP 2 OF DECISION TREE: DIFFERENT ETIOLOGIES FOR PERIPHERAL NEUROPATHY

Having determined that the patient with HIV has peripheral neuropathy, the next step is to determine the cause for the peripheral neuropathy. In addition to HIV and the three specific dideoxynucleoside reverse transcriptase inhibitors, stavudine (d4T), didanosine (ddI), and zalcitabine (ddC) (D-drugs), other causes for peripheral neuropathy include herpes zoster, alcohol misuse, diabetes, cancer chemotherapy, and trauma (complex regional pain syndrome) (Hughes, 2002).

HIV SENSORY NEUROPATHY

DEFINITION OF HIV SENSORY NEUROPATHY

Typical symptoms of HIV-SN include tingling, pricking, pain, and numbness (Morgello et al., 2004). These symptoms follow directly from the loss of sensory axons and typically occur bilaterally in the feet. Signs of HIV-SN are distal and symmetrical decreased perception of vibration, decreased perception of pin prick, and/or decreased ankle reflexes. Figure 27.2 illustrates that patients can have either neuropathic symptoms or signs of HIV-SN or both, and that patients who do not have both symptoms and signs may not get diagnosed with HIV-SN. For example, patients with predominant small-fiber nerve injury not evident on clinical examination may have symptoms but no signs. In addition to peripheral nerve damage and degeneration, whether a given patient experiences distal neuropathic pain may be determined in part by descending central nervous system influences. Indeed, we have demonstrated that more severe neuropathic pain is associated with smaller total cortical gray matter volume (Keltner et al., 2014) as well as smaller regional posterior cingulate cortical volume (Keltner et al., 2016). Neuropathic pain and paresthesia are often the focus of clinical care for HIV-SN because there are currently no neuroregenerative therapies (Robinson-Papp et al., 2010).

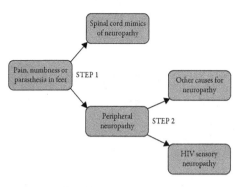

Figure 27.1 Decision tree describing two initial steps required to differentiate spinal cord diseases from peripheral neuropathy and to differentiate different causes for peripheral neuropathy.

PREVALENCE AND RISK FACTORS FOR HIV SENSORY NEUROPATHY

Despite the use of modern and effective antiretroviral therapy, HIV-SN is highly prevalent. In 2016, the Centers for Disease Control and Prevention (CDC) estimated that 1.2 million people in the United States were living with HIV (CDC, 2016). In one report of a large, diverse U.S. cohort, 57% of persons with HIV had HIV-SN (Ellis et al., 2010). Figure 27.3 extrapolates from epidemiological data on HIV prevalence and findings from cohort studies to provide estimates of the prevalence of HIV-SN and its associated distal neuropathic pain.

Older age is a risk factor for HIV-SN (see Figure 27.4) (Morgello et al., 2004; Simpson et al., 2006). Additional risks factors for HIV-SN include lower CD4 nadir and past D-drug therapy (Ellis et al., 2010).

PATHOPHYSIOLOGY FOR HIV SENSORY NEUROPATHY

HIV-SN is comprised of at least two clinically indistinguishable, and often coexisting, neuropathies: distal sensory polyneuropathy associated with HIV disease itself, and a

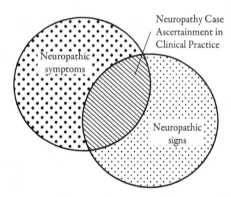

Figure 27.2 Patients diagnosed with HIV sensory neuropathy typically have both symptoms and signs of HIV sensory neuropathy. However, there are significant numbers of individuals with only neuropathic symptoms or neuropathic signs who may not be diagnosed with HIV sensory neuropathy.

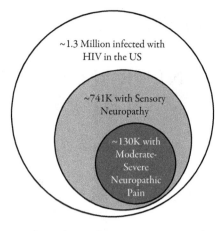

Figure 27.3 Estimated prevalence of HIV sensory neuropathy and HIV distal neuropathic pain in the United States, based on publications cited in the text.

distal polyneuropathy associated with antiretroviral treatment, antiretroviral toxic neuropathy. In antiretroviral-naïve persons with HIV and peripheral neuropathy that has no other apparent cause, the etiology for the peripheral neuropathy is most likely the HIV virus itself (Lipkin et al., 1985). In persons with HIV who experience transient peripheral neuropathy in the setting of starting a D-drug, the etiology is most likely the D-drug (Blum et al., 1996). In persons with HIV who have a past history of D-drug use who are no longer taking these medications, it is unclear whether the HIV or the D-drug is the predominant cause. Importantly, available evidence suggests that HIV-SN prevalence remains high among persons receiving combination antiretroviral treatment, even in countries where neurotoxic antiretroviral drugs such as stavudine are no longer commonly used (Ellis et al., 2010; Morgello et al., 2004, Simpson et al., 2006). In resource-limited settings the use of stavudine, an inexpensive and effective antiretroviral, remains common despite the high risk of neurotoxicity (Maritz et al., 2010).

WARNING SIGNS OF MORE ADVANCED DISEASE

As HIV-SN progresses, symptoms proceed proximally up the lower extremities. In more advances stages, the hands may become involved. Typically, there is no motor involvement, although weakness of the intrinsic muscles of the feet can occur in more advanced stages (Cornblath and McArthur, 1988).

OTHER TYPES OF PERIPHERAL NEUROPATHIES

The word *neuropathy* means nerve damage. *Mononeuropathy* is damage to a single named peripheral nerve or nerve branch, as in carpal tunnel or peroneal neuropathy. *Multiple mononeuropathy* involves injury to a few or many separate nerves, such as in vasculitis. *Radiculopathy* is injury of the spinal cord nerve root, for example, as caused by a lumbar disc herniation. *Polyneuropathy* is when many nerves, typically

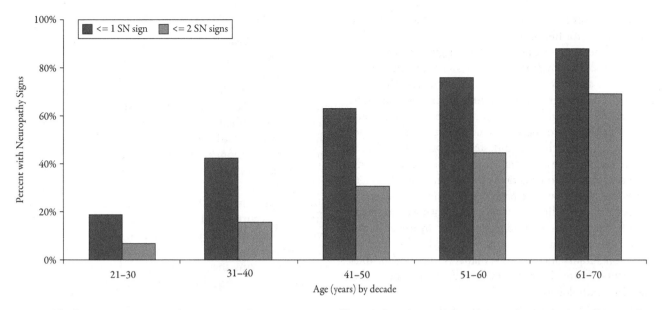

Figure 27.4 Risk of HIV sensory neuropathy increases with age. Data presented here are from 815 patients with HIV who were between the ages of 21 and 70 years.

in the same body region, are affected. Polyneuropathies can affect motor, sensory, and/or autonomic nerves. Figure 27.5 schematically represents typical peripheral neuropathy subtypes.

DIAGNOSTIC TESTING FOR HIV SENSORY NEUROPATHY

Physical Examination

On physical examination, signs of HIV-SN usually manifest bilaterally in the feet as decreased perception of sharp stimuli, decreased perception of vibration, and/or decreased ankle reflexes (an example of this physical exam can be found under "educational videos" at http://www.hopkinsmedicine.org/neurology_neurosurgery/research/jhu_nimh/news/).

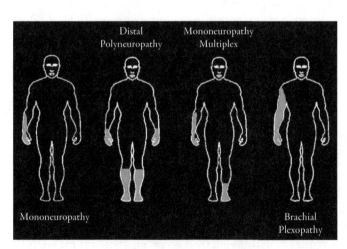

Figure 27.5 Peripheral neuropathy subtypes. The shaded regions depict location where a patient typically reports his or her symptoms and/or the distribution of abnormal sensory findings on the clinician's exam.

Increased reflexes typically indicate an upper motor neuron lesion, such as cervical spondylotic myelopathy or HIV vacuolar myelopathy.

Laboratory Workup

Multiple infectious, metabolic, endocrine, nutritional, and immunological conditions can contribute to distal nerve injury. The focus of laboratory testing is to identify any treatable contributing condition. The most common of these is diabetes mellitus, which can be identified by an abnormal glucose tolerance test, HOMA-IR (homeostatic model assessment for insulin resistance) or hemoglobin A1C. Thyroid disease, including both hypo- and hyperthyroidism, can be identified by appropriate testing, as can vitamin B12 deficiency (serum cobalamin, methylmalonic acid). Tabes dorsalis can mimic HIV-SN, and a serum RPR or a specific treponemal test will elucidate. Additional differential diagnostic considerations and laboratory tests can be found at: http://neuromuscular.wustl.edu/naltbrain.html.

Nerve conduction Studies and Electromyography

Electromyography (EMG) is a technique for directly measuring electrical activity in muscles at rest or with volitional activation. Specific patterns of electrical activity are associated with primary muscle disease (myopathy), and with recent or ongoing nerve injury (denervation) or regrowth (reinnervation). In adults, a variety of insults such as trauma, infections, and metabolic injury can cause increased spontaneous discharges during EMG. Nerve conduction testing measures the summated electrical potentials conducted by large numbers of individual nerve fibers contained within bundles such as the peroneal nerve or the median nerve. Both sensory (afferent) and motor (efferent) nerves can be assessed. Individual peripheral nerves can comprise solely sensory, motor, or mixed sensory and motor fibers.

Two properties of the nerve electrical signal are the velocity and amplitude. Demyelinating injuries decrease the velocity of the nerve signal while axonal injuries decrease the amplitude of the nerve signal. A demyelinating injury is an injury to the myelin surrounding the axon of the peripheral nerve. When a specific motor nerve conducts electrical signals more slowly than normal, this is manifested as a prolongation of the delay or latency between stimulation of the nerve and onset of the compound motor action potential measured over the muscle innervated by that nerve. Autoimmune diseases frequently cause demyelinating neuropathies, whose progression can be halted or even reversed in some cases by use of steroids or intravenous immunoglobulin. Typical diseases that can cause axonal injury include HIV, diabetes, and alcohol abuse. Treatments of axonal injuries involve addressing one of these underlying pathologies.

Late responses such as the F-wave are performed to evaluate nerve conduction in portions of the nerve more proximal (near the spine) and, therefore, inaccessible to direct assessment using conventional techniques, such as the nerve root. Electrical stimulation is applied on the skin surface near a nerve site in a manner that sends impulses both proximally and distally. Characteristics of the response are assessed, including latency. A common cause for nerve root injury is spinal disc herniation impinging on the nerve root. A brief introduction to the clinical utility of EMG and nerve conduction studies has been provided by Kishner (2015). More comprehensive reference works include those by Aminoff (2012) and Oh (2003).

Quantitative Sensory Testing

Quantitative sensory testing (QST) is a computerized technique used to evaluate peripheral nerve damage by measuring changes in perception of temperature, vibration, and sharp stimuli. The test results are compared to those of individuals without neuropathy (Pfau et al., 2012).

Skin Biopsy

HIV-SN is characterized by distal degeneration of long axons (Pardo et al., 2001). This pattern is often termed "dying back" because of the observation that distal regions of the fibers degenerate first. The density of small and large myelinated fibers and unmyelinated fibers is reduced. Punch skin biopsies reveal evidence of prominent involvement of small unmyelinated fibers (Holland et al., 1997). Epidermal nerve fiber density may be abnormally reduced even when the physical examination is normal.

Autonomic (Sweat Test)

Sudomotor (sweat gland) testing represents a simple non-invasive means to assess the function of small-caliber autonomic nerve fibers that innervate sweat glands (Vinik et al., 2013).

TREATMENT OF HIV SENSORY NEUROPATHY

A neuroprotective or neuroregenerative strategy would be attractive for treating HIV SN; however, with the exception of recombinant human nerve growth factor, whose clinical usefulness was limited by adverse side effects, no treatment to promote sensory recovery has been shown to be effective and safe. Individuals who begin combination antiretroviral therapy earlier in disease, before they experience advanced immunosuppression, are less likely to develop HIV-SN than individuals who have historically experienced lower CD4+ T lymphocytes counts (<200 cells per microliter) (Ellis et al., 2010; Simpson et al., 2006). Currently, the best way to decrease the risk of occurrence of HIV-SN and decrease the severity of symptoms of HIV-SN is to maintain a low viral load using combination antiretroviral therapy. Encouraging patients to commit to taking their antiretroviral therapy treatment on a regular basis is a critical aspect of managing HIV-SN.

DISTAL NEUROPATHIC PAIN ASSOCIATED WITH HIV SENSORY NEUROPATHY

CLINICAL PRESENTATION OF HIV DISTAL NEUROPATHIC PAIN

Persons with HIV-SN frequently report symptoms of paresthesia (tingling, pins and/or needles) and/or neuropathic pain (burning, aching or shooting pain in the feet) (Morgello et al., 2004, Simpson et al., 2006). In fact, despite the use of modern and effective combination antiretroviral therapy, up to 40% of patients with HIV-SN report neuropathic pain in the feet, referred to as HIV distal neuropathic pain (HIV-DNP) (Ellis et al., 2010; Simpson et al., 2006). These patients usually have objective signs of HIV-SN on neurological examination and ancillary studies such as QST and nerve conduction studies (Robinson-Papp et al., 2010). HIV-DNP is typically bilateral and of gradual onset. It is usually more severe in the soles of the feet and worse at night. Affected individuals often have hyperalgesia (lower pain threshold) and allodynia (pain induced by normally non-noxious stimuli). HIV-DNP can gradually ascend proximally up the lower extremities and may begin to involve the fingertips around the same time as mid-thigh involvement. For patients with two signs of HIV-SN (for example, reduced distal vibration and reflexes) who do not have neuropathic pain, on average, 25% will develop neuropathic pain within 2 years. The risk factors for developing pain include older age, female sex, depressed mood, and history of opioid abuse (Malvar et al., 2015).

IMPACT OF HIV DISTAL NEUROPATHIC PAIN ON QUALITY OF LIFE AND DEPRESSION

Persons with HIV-DNP generally need more assistance with activities of daily living than do persons without HIV-DNP. Persons with HIV-DNP are more likely to be unemployed than persons without HIV-DNP. HIV-DNP also occurs more frequently in persons who suffer from current depression than in individuals without depression. For persons with HIV-DNP depression is more severe than in individuals without HIV-DNP (Ellis et al., 2010). In persons with DNP, worse quality of life is associated more with depression itself than with neuropathic pain ratings (Keltner et al., 2012).

TREATMENT FOR HIV DISTAL NEUROPATHIC PAIN

Most of the time typical analgesic medications are ineffective in treating HIV-DNP (Verma et al., 2004). In a meta-analysis of 44 studies investigating treatments for HIV-DNP (Phillips et al., 2010), 14 studies were considered to be robust randomized controlled trials comparing treatment to placebo. Only three treatments were considered better then placebo: smoked cannabis, recombinant human nerve growth factor, and high-dose (8%) topical capsaicin. Recombinant human nerve growth factor is not clinically available, and both legal and mental health issues preclude routine recommendation of long-term smoked cannabis for pain management. The U.S. Food and Drug Administration (FDA) has approved 8% topical capsaicin for the treatment of post-herpetic neuralgia, but not HIV-DNP. Several other agents have been examined in high-quality randomized controlled trials and were found not to be more effective than placebo; these include acetyl-L carnitine (1 g/day), amitriptyline (100 mg/day), topical capsaicin (0.075%), gabapentin (2.4 g/day), mexilitine (600 mg/day), pregabalin (1200 mg/day), and lamotrigine (600 mg/day).

Despite the lack of FDA-approved treatments for HIV-DNP, conventional treatments for neuropathic pain may be helpful for the management of HIV-DNP (Dworkin et al., 2007, National Institute for Health Care Excellence, 2014). It is notable that opioids have been shown to be effective in managing other neuropathic pain conditions (Dworkin et al., 2007, Finnerup et al., 2010; Hempenstall et al., 2005). In addition, duloxetine may be helpful for HIV-DNP as it has been shown to be effective for diabetic neuropathic pain (Tan et al., 2010). Another possibility for treatment could be non-smoked cannabis. Given the significant adverse impact of HIV-DNP, there is an urgent need for successful therapy for this condition.

CONCLUSION

HIV sensory neuropathy is highly prevalent, affecting 50% of persons with HIV, and is difficult to manage. Some persons with HIV-SN report few symptoms, while almost half of patients with HIV-SN report disabling symptoms including paresthesia and/or pain. In this chapter, we have attempted to provide guidance to clinical psychiatrists in the clinical management of peripheral pain in persons with HIV-SN. We (1) presented a decision tree that helps to guide the initial diagnostic evaluation of peripheral pain in HIV patients, (2) described the clinical presentation and management for HIV-SN, and (3) described clinical aspects and management of HIV distal neuropathic pain. We hope this chapter will help psychiatrists work with neurologists to improve the evaluation and management of peripheral pain in persons with HIV.

REFERENCES

Aminoff M (2012). *Aminoff's Electrodiagnosis in Clinical Neurology*. Philadelphia, Saunders.

Blum AS, Dal Pan GJ, Feinberg J, Raines C, Mayjo K, Cornblath DR, McArthur JC (1996). Low-dose zalcitabine-related toxic neuropathy: frequency, natural history, and risk factors. *Neurology* 46(4):999–1003.

Centers for Disease Control and Prevention (CDC) (2016). HIV in the United States: At A Glance. https://www.cdc.gov/hiv/statistics/overview/ataglance.html. Accessed February 5, 2017.

Cornblath DR, McArthur JC (1988). Predominantly sensory neuropathy in patients with AIDS and AIDS-related complex. *Neurology* 38(5):794–796.

Dworkin RH, O'Connor AB, Backonja M, et al. (2007). Pharmacologic management of neuropathic pain: evidence-based recommendations. *Pain* 132(3):237–251.

Ellis RJ, Rosario D, Clifford DB, et al. (2010). Continued high prevalence and adverse clinical impact of human immunodeficiency virus-associated sensory neuropathy in the era of combination antiretroviral therapy: the CHARTER Study. *Arch Neurol* 67(5):552–558.

Finnerup NB, Sindrup SH, Jensen TS (2010). The evidence for pharmacological treatment of neuropathic pain. *Pain* 150(3):573–581.

Gerna G, Parea M, Percivalle E, Zipeto D, Silini E, Barbarini G, Milanesi G (1990). Human cytomegalovirus viraemia in HIV-1-seropositive patients at various clinical stages of infection. *AIDS* 4(10):1027–1031.

Hempenstall K, Nurmikko TJ, Johnson RW, Hern RP, Rice AS (2005). Analgesic therapy in postherpetic neuralgia: a quantitative systematic review. *PLoS Med* 2(7):e164.

Holland NR, Stocks A, Hauer P, Cornblath DR, Griffin JW, McArthur JC (1997). Intraepidermal nerve fiber density in patients with painful sensory neuropathy. *Neurology* 48(3):708–711.

Hughes RA (2002). Peripheral neuropathy. *BMJ* 324(7335):466–469.

Keltner JR, Connolly CG, Vaida F, et al. (2016). HIV distal neuropathic pain is associated with smaller ventral posterior cingulate cortex. *Pain Med* pii:pnw180. doi:10.1093/pm/pnw180.

Keltner JR, Fennema-Notestine C, Vaida F, et al., for the (2014). HIV-associated distal neuropathic pain is associated with smaller total cerebral cortical gray matter. *J Neurovirol* 20(3):209–218.

Keltner JR, Vaida F, Ellis RJ, et al. (2012). Health-related quality of life 'well-being' in HIV distal neuropathic pain is more strongly associated with depression severity than with pain intensity. *Psychosomatics* 53(4):380–386.

Kishner S (2015). Electromyography and nerve conduction studies. *Medscape*. http://emedicine.medscape.com/article/2094544-overview. Accessed February 3, 2017.

Lipkin WI, Parry G, Kiprov D, Abrams D (1985). Inflammatory neuropathy in homosexual men with lymphadenopathy. *Neurology* 35(10): 1479–1483.

Malvar J, Vaida F, Sanders CF, et al., and the CHARTER Group (2015). Predictors of new-onset distal neuropathic pain in HIV-infected individuals in the era of combination antiretroviral therapy. *Pain* 156:731–739.

Maritz J, Benatar M, Dave JA, Harrison TB, Badri M, Levitt NS, Heckmann JM (2010). HIV neuropathy in South Africans: frequency, characteristics, and risk factors. *Muscle Nerve* 41(5):599–606.

Morgello S, Estanislao L, Simpson D, et al. (2004). HIV-associated distal sensory polyneuropathy in the era of highly active antiretroviral therapy: the Manhattan HIV Brain Bank. *Arch Neurol* 61(4):546–551.

National Institute for Health Care Excellence (NICE) (2014. Neuropathic pain: the pharmacological management of neuropathic pain in adults in non-specialist settings. https://www.nice.org.uk/guidance/CG173. Accessed February 3, 2017.

Oh S (2003). *Clinical Electromyography: Nerve Conduction Studies*. Philadelphia: Lippincott Williams and Wilkins.

Pardo CA, McArthur JC, Griffin JW (2001). HIV neuropathy: insights in the pathology of HIV peripheral nerve disease. *J Peripher Nerv Syst* 6(1):21–27.

Pfau DB, Geber C, Birklein F, Treede RD (2012). Quantitative sensory testing of neuropathic pain patients: potential mechanistic and therapeutic implications. *Curr Pain Headache Rep* 16(3):199–206.

Phillips TJ, Cherry CL, Cox S, Marshall SJ, Rice AS (2010). Pharmacological treatment of painful HIV-associated sensory neuropathy: a systematic review and meta-analysis of randomised controlled trials. *PLoS ONE* 5(12):e14433.

Robinson-Papp J, Morgello S, Vaida F, et al. (2010). Association of self-reported painful symptoms with clinical and neurophysiologic signs in HIV-associated sensory neuropathy. *Pain* 151(3):732–736.

Simpson DM, Kitch D, Evans SR, et al. (2006). HIV neuropathy natural history cohort study: assessment measures and risk factors. *Neurology* 66(11):1679–1687.

Tan T, Barry P, Reken S, Baker M; Guideline Development Group (2010). Pharmacological management of neuropathic pain in non-specialist settings: summary of NICE guidance. *BMJ* 340:c1079.

Verma S, Estanislao L, Mintz L, Simpson D (2004). Controlling neuropathic pain in HIV. *Curr Infect Dis Rep* 6(3):237–242.

Vinik AI, Nevoret M, Casellini C, Parson H (2013). Neurovascular function and sudorimetry in health and disease. *Curr Diab Rep* 13(4):517–532.

PART VII

PSYCHIATRIC ASPECTS OF RISK BEHAVIORS, PREVENTION OF HIV TRANSMISSION, AND ADHERENCE TO MEDICAL CARE

28.

THE ROLE OF PSYCHIATRIC DISORDERS IN HIV TRANSMISSION AND PREVENTION

Andréa L. Hobkirk, Seth C. Kalichman, David M. Stoff, and Christina S. Meade

Severe mental illness (SMI) describes a range of major psychiatric disorders that persist over time and cause extensive disability in social, occupational, and other important areas of functioning (Schinnar et al., 1990). Such impairments are most often present in schizophrenia-spectrum disorders, bipolar disorders, and recurrent major depressive disorders. Common sequelae of SMI include substance abuse, unemployment, poverty, recurrent homelessness, incarceration, and unstable relationships. An estimated 5.8% of American adults meet criteria for SMI during a 1-year period, and rates range from 0% to 8% among international samples (Kessler et al., 2005; World Health Organization [WHO] Mental Health Survey Consortium, 2004).

Adults with SMI have been disproportionately affected by the HIV/AIDS epidemic. The prevalence of adults with HIV and SMI range from 2% to 6% in rural and large metropolitan sites, respectively (Himelhoch et al., 2011; Rosenberg, Goodman, et al., 2001). These rates are many times higher than the estimated HIV prevalence of 0.6% in the general U.S. population (UNAIDS, 2014). The highest rates occur among persons with SMI who are also homeless and/or have a substance use disorder. International studies have found even higher rates of HIV among persons with SMI, ranging from 11% to 27% in African countries where the base rate of infection is higher among the population (Lundberg et al., 2013).

Adults with SMI tend to engage in high rates of sexual and drug use behaviors associated with HIV transmission, including multiple sexual partnerships; unprotected intercourse in nonmonogamous relationships; sex trade for money, drugs, or other survival resources; and injection drug use. As such, SMI is a risk factor for HIV risk behavior and infection. Conversely, psychiatric illness can also develop secondary to HIV infection, either directly through neurological changes or indirectly through psychosocial stressors (Owe-Larsson et al., 2009). The majority of persons with HIV suffer from psychiatric disorders, including mood, anxiety, or psychotic disorders (Chandra et al., 2005). Given the high rate of HIV risk behavior and HIV infection among adults with SMI, the potential for spread of HIV in this population remains high.

The objectives of this chapter are to (1) document the prevalence of HIV risk behavior among adults with SMI; (2) discuss the ways in which psychiatric disorders directly and indirectly contribute to HIV risk behavior, infection, and disease progression; (3) describe HIV prevention interventions; and (4) provide suggestions for clinical care.

PREVALENCE OF HIV RISK BEHAVIOR AMONG PERSONS WITH SEVERE MENTAL ILLNESS

The prevalence of HIV risk behaviors among adults with SMI in the United States and other countries is displayed in Table 28.1 (updated from Meade and Sikkema, 2005). Using weighted means to account for sample size among 59 studies, the prevalence of the following HIV risk factors were calculated: sexual activity, multiple partners, unprotected intercourse, sex trade, history of sexually transmitted infection (STI), and injection drug use (Meade and Sikkema, 2005). Across U.S. studies, the majority of adults with SMI had had sex in the past year. Approximately one-third of sexually active participants had been with multiple partners and over 40% never used condoms. Strikingly, nearly a quarter reported a history of sex trade, and a third had a history of STI. Nearly a quarter had ever injected drugs; most injection drug users had shared needles, but only 4% had been active within the past year.

Based on seven studies that included a comparison group, mental health problems often precede HIV infection and complicate subsequent behavior change. Thus, a substantial proportion of adults with SMI continue to engage in sexual and drug risk behaviors even after they are infected with HIV. Adults with SMI were more likely than demographically similar adults without SMI to engage in certain behaviors that place them at risk for HIV, specifically multiple partners, sex trade, and injection drug use, but not necessarily sexual activity or unprotected intercourse. Elevated rates of HIV risk behavior have also been reported among adults with SMI living in other countries, including Italy (Grassi et al., 1999), India (Chandra et al., 2003), Australia (Davidson et al., 2001), South Africa (Koen et al., 2007), and Brazil (Peixoto et al., 2014; Wainberg et al., 2008). It is notable, however, that the rate of HIV risk behavior reported in international samples tended to be lower than that in U.S. samples.

Among HIV-infected persons with SMI, 56% of participants had had sex in the past 6 months and engaged in high rates of risk behaviors including sex with multiple partners,

Table 28.1. SELF-REPORTED PREVALENCE RATES OF HIV RISK FACTORS AMONG ADULTS WITH SEVERE MENTAL ILLNESS

RISK FACTOR	N	U.S. STUDIES WEIGHTED MEAN (RANGE)	N	INTERNATIONAL STUDIES WEIGHTED MEAN (RANGE)
Sexual Activity*				
Past year	11	61.89% (49%–74%)	7	46.71% (42%–58%)
Past 3 months	10	42.48% (32%–69%)	1	33%
Multiple (2+) Partners†				
Past year	9	29.00% (14%–65%)	5	34.99% (31%–41%)
Past 3 months	6	30.33% (24%–46%)	2	17.65% (13%–27%)
Condom Use: Consistent†				
Past year	3	20.60% (15%–32%)	1	19%
Past 3 months	5	33.48% (20%–49%)	2	14.40% (22%–34%)
Condom Use: Never†				
Past year	4	43.75% (29%–59%)	0	N/A
Past 3 months	3	37.78% (26%–62%)	2	58.12% (44%–66%)
Sex Trade				
Ever	7	21.13% (5%–45%)	6	6.16% (3%–50%)
Past year	6	5.77% (3%–33%)	3	7.12% (2%–11%)
History of Sexually Transmitted Infections				
Ever	16	31.87% (16%–54%)	4	9.41% (8%–11%)
Past year	6	5.46% (3%–10%)	2	9.66% (5%–10%)
Injection Drug Use				
Ever	18	21.45% (1%–37%)	2	16.35% (14%–23%)
Past year	8	4.17% (1%–8%)	1	5.68%
Needle Sharing††				
Ever	5	68.83% (13%–92%)	2	38.46% (15%–53%)
Past year	2	55.56% (55%–57%)	1	38%

*Excluding studies with sexual activity as an eligibility criterion.

†Among sexually active participants only.

††Among injection drug users only.

unprotected intercourse, and sex trade (Tucker et al., 2003). Overall, 12% had injected drugs in the past 12 months. In a study of Brazilian psychiatric outpatients with HIV infection, individuals with symptoms of bipolar disorder were significantly more likely than persons without symptoms to report engaging in sex trade (50% vs. 14%), sex with non-regular partners (90% vs. 69%), and infrequent condom use with these partners (81% vs. 53%) (Ribeiro et al., 2013). In a U.S. sample, persons with bipolar disorder reported more unprotected sex with HIV-negative partners and worse medication adherence than persons with major depression or no mood disorder (Meade et al., 2012). There is limited evidence, however, that some individuals with SMI decrease their risk behaviors after learning of their HIV status, a trend seen in the general population as well. In the previously mentioned study of Brazilian psychiatric outpatients with HIV, individuals with symptoms of bipolar disorder reported decreasing sex with all types of partners after learning of their HIV diagnosis, significantly more than study participants without bipolar symptoms.

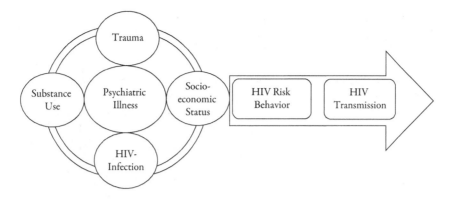

Figure 28.1 Conceptual model of HIV risk behavior among adults with SMI (adapted from Meade and Sikkema, 2005).

EFFECTS OF PSYCHIATRIC DISORDERS ON HIV RISK BEHAVIOR

Sexual and drug risk behaviors are influenced by multiple factors across several psychosocial domains, including psychiatric illness, substance use, traumatic experience, socioeconomic status, and HIV infection itself. A conceptual model of HIV risk behavior among SMI adults is displayed in Figure 28.1. The model highlights the interactive role of these factors as mediators and moderators influencing HIV risk behavior and subsequent transmission of HIV. In particular, psychiatric illness may contribute to HIV risk behavior directly through cognitive, emotional, social, and behavioral functioning, as well as indirectly through psychosocial sequelae such as substance abuse, trauma, and homelessness. Comorbid HIV infection among persons with SMI can further influence the risk of transmitting HIV to serodiscordant members of their social network. In the next sections we examine these direct and indirect effects.

DIRECT EFFECTS OF PSYCHIATRIC DISORDERS ON HIV RISK BEHAVIOR

A range of cognitive, emotional, social, and behavioral impairments associated with SMI can directly contribute to HIV risk behavior. For example, poor judgment and decision-making may impair accurate risk assessment and promote sexual involvement with risky partners. Impaired decision-making, negative view of the future, and decreased impulse control may reduce motivation to use condoms. Difficulty maintaining relationships may lead to multiple partnerships, and poor relationship quality may lead to nonmonogamous relationships. Poor negotiation skills may reduce the likelihood of using condoms with a resistant partner, and poor assertiveness skills and low self-esteem may lead to sexual exploitation. Among persons with SMI, greater psychiatric symptoms and worse adaptive functioning predict sexual activity and HIV risk behaviors, such as having sex with multiple partners (Rosenberg, Trumbetta, et al., 2001). In a study of Turkish psychiatric patients with bipolar disorder and schizophrenia, 42% reported increased sexual activity during the acute phases of the illness (Hariri et al., 2011).

Alternatively, a separate study of patients with bipolar disorder found that greater psychiatric severity was related to less HIV sexual and drug risk behavior; however, the occurrence of a recent manic episode and greater drug use severity were both related to increased HIV risk (Meade et al., 2008). In sum, research supports a general association between severity of psychopathology and HIV risk behavior. However, there is still limited research examining how certain symptom clusters (e.g., depression, mania, paranoia) or types of impairments (e.g., cognitive, social, behavioral) may relate to specific HIV risk behaviors among adults with SMI.

Mood and anxiety are the most common psychopathologies in the United States, with 12-month prevalence rates of 9.5% and 18.1%, respectively (Kessler et al., 2005). Aspects of mood disorders in particular may directly impact sexuality. Hypersexuality is a common symptom of mania, which may lead to increased sexual activity and multiple partnerships. Manic episodes are also characterized by impulsivity, poor judgment, and excessive involvement in pleasurable and high-risk behaviors, which, when coupled with hypersexuality, may lead to sex with strangers or prostitutes and reduced condom use. In one study of patients with mood disorders, individuals with bipolar disorder were more likely to report increased sexual activity during emotional crises (Sacks and Dermatis, 1994). A prospective study of individuals with comorbid bipolar and substance use disorders found sexual risk behavior was related to more manic episodes and individual changes in cocaine use, but not manic episodes, over time (Meade et al., 2011). Other research has linked impulsivity specifically to sex with multiple partners (Stewart et al., 2012).

In contrast, depression commonly leads to diminished libido and sexual dysfunction and, therefore, an overall reduction in sexual activity; however, persons with depression who are sexually active tend to engage in more sexual risk behaviors. In a Brazilian study, men with unipolar depression and anxiety disorders were more likely to practice unprotected sex compared to men with more severe diagnoses like bipolar disorder and schizophrenia (Peixoto et al., 2014). This finding was not significant for women. Another study found adolescents with depressive symptoms to be four times more likely than adolescents without symptoms to report inconsistent condom use over a 90-day period (Brown et al., 2006). Qualitative research describes the fatalism that accompanies depression, including hopelessness, pessimism, and self-hatred, that makes protecting oneself from HIV by cleaning needles or using protection almost counterintuitive (Gilchrist et al., 2011). Depression may also increase the risk of transmission for persons with HIV infection through risky sexual behavior (e.g., less condom use), as evidenced by the high rates of HIV among persons with depression compared to rates for the general population—22% vs. 7%, respectively (Chander et al., 2006; Musisi et al., 2014).

Consistently, persons with schizophrenia-spectrum disorders report lower rates of sexual activity and frequency of intercourse compared to persons with other major psychiatric disorders (Carey et al., 2004b; Chandra et al., 2003). Negative symptoms (e.g., affective flattening, avolition, anergia) and other associated features (e.g., hypoactivity, depressed mood) may reduce sexual desire. In addition, grossly disorganized behavior and odd personality traits may impair an individual's ability to establish sexual partners. For these reasons, persons with schizophrenia may have lower rates of HIV infection than rates for individuals without schizophrenia, particularly if there is no co-occurring substance use (Himelhoch et al., 2007). Previous research suggests that persons with psychotic disorders have social skills deficits, social anxiety, relationship difficulties, and loneliness that may impact sexual functioning (Grant et al., 2001). Thus, persons with schizophrenia-spectrum disorders may benefit from adjunctive social skills training to help them develop satisfying and longer-lasting relationships.

Approximately 30–60% of adults with SMI have a comorbid personality disorder, including borderline and antisocial disorders (Tyrer et al., 2000). Personality disorder has been found to be associated with increased sexual risk behavior among adults with SMI (Sacks and Dermatis, 1994) and among HIV-positive adults (Newville and Haller, 2012). Borderline personality disorder is characterized by emotional dysregulation, turbulent relationships, and impulsivity, each of which may lead to sexual risk behavior. In a study conducted with men and women with borderline personality disorder, the majority reported being sexually active in the past year, with high rates of multiple partners (33%) and commercial sex work (5%), and nearly 90% of individuals reporting sex in the prior month had at least one instance of unprotected sex (Harned et al., 2011). In a study of women hospitalized for borderline personality disorder, nearly half reported that they had impulsively entered into sexual relationships with partners they did not know well (Hull et al., 1993). Borderline personality disorder has also been linked to higher rates of STI, even after controlling for substance use (De Genna et al., 2011). Antisocial personality disorder, which is characterized by a pervasive pattern of disregard for and violation of the rights of others, may also be associated with increased sexual risk behavior. In other populations, individuals with antisocial personality disorders were more likely to have multiple sex partners and less likely to use condoms (e.g., Kelley and Petry, 2000).

INDIRECT EFFECTS OF PSYCHIATRIC DISORDERS ON HIV RISK BEHAVIOR

Dual Diagnosis

Severe mental illness often co-occurs with substance use disorders, with estimates ranging from 25% to 65% across diagnosis (Regier et al., 1990). The co-occurrence of SMI and substance use disorders, commonly referred to as dual diagnosis, is associated with exceptionally high rates of HIV infection (Beyer et al., 2007; Rosenberg, Goodman, et al., 2001). Substance use is related to HIV transmission directly, such as injection drug use, and indirectly through drug administration risk behaviors as well as increased sexual risk behaviors (Horwath et al., 1996). Substance abuse in general can have indirect effects on sexual risk behavior through its impact on judgment, decision-making, and willingness to engage in sex trade for drugs or money. Furthermore, substance abusers may be part of a social network comprised of high-risk partners and in which sexual risk behavior is normative. Empirical investigations highlight the critical role substance use plays in increasing HIV risk among persons with SMI (Hariri et al., 2011; Prince et al., 2012). Dually diagnosed individuals are more likely to be sexually active, have multiple sex partners, and have a history of STIs (Carey et al., 2004b; Meade, 2006). Another study found stepwise differences, with active substance abusers engaging in the highest rates of sexual activity, followed by persons with remitted substance use disorder, and finally by persons with no history of substance use disorder (Meade, 2006).

Newer research highlights the importance of substance use in the role of HIV transmission for individuals with SMI, and some studies even suggest that SMI may only be related to increased HIV risk through substance use. Data collected from Medicaid recipients, from 2001 to 2003, revealed no meaningful difference in the rates of newly diagnosed HIV infections between persons with SMI (0.51%) and persons without SMI (0.52%); however the rates increased significantly for individuals with comorbid SMI and substance use (1.63%) and substance use disorders alone (2.3%) (Prince et al., 2012). Similarly, a U.S. study found that veterans with bipolar disorder and schizophrenia were at no higher risk for contracting HIV than veterans without these disorders, unless they had a comorbid substance abuse disorder (Himelhoch et al, 2007). However, other studies still hold that SMI is a relevant factor associated with increased HIV risk and prevalence over substance use alone (Gilchrist et al., 2011). In sum, research suggests that persons dually diagnosed with SMI and substance use disorders are at particularly high risk for HIV infection, though the mechanisms through which substance abuse contributes to sexual risk behavior need further study.

Traumatic Experience

Traumatic life experiences and posttraumatic stress disorder (PTSD) are common among persons with SMI, further exacerbating the impact of psychiatric illness on health. Rates of trauma among adults with SMI range from 49% to 100% (see Grubaugh et al., 2011 for a detailed review).

Sexual and physical abuse are particularly common, as is the occurrence of multiple traumas, which contribute to additive impacts on mental and physical health. Rates of comorbid PTSD among SMI range from 13% to 46% when clinician-administered assessments are used, and 19% to 53% when self-report PTSD measures are used. Individuals with HIV are more likely to have a current diagnosis of PTSD. The estimated rate of recent PTSD among HIV-positive women in the United States (30%) is five times higher than for the general population (Machtinger et al., 2012) and rates are similarly high in international settings (Martin and Kagee, 2011).

Trauma and PTSD exacerbate negative outcomes for individuals with SMI, including rates of substance use, homelessness, poor occupational and social functioning, cognitive impairment, and HIV risk behavior and infection. Childhood sexual abuse has shown consistent associations with increased sexual risk behavior in adulthood, including multiple sexual partnerships, unprotected intercourse, and sex trade (Rosenberg et al., 2001b). One study found that childhood sexual abuse was indirectly related to HIV risk through drug use but not sexual risk behavior (Rosenberg, Trumbetta, et al., 2001). Furthermore, greater trauma exposure of all types was related to increased HIV risk, but diagnosis of PTSD was not. Another study with female injection drug users also found PTSD and depression to mediate the association between childhood sexual abuse and sexual and drug risk behaviors (Plotzker et al., 2007). PTSD and major depression after a traumatic event were both associated with endorsement of at least one sexual risk behavior in the past year (intravenous drug use, treatment for an STI, sex trade, or unprotected anal sex) among Army National Guard soldiers (Marshall et al., 2013). Alternatively, childhood physical abuse was found to be unrelated to HIV risk behavior, a finding suggesting specificity in the association between sexually traumatic experiences and subsequent sexual risk behavior (Rosenberg, Trumbetta, et al., 2001).

Socioeconomic Factors

Many adults with SMI are socioeconomically disadvantaged, have transient living situations, lower educational attainment, higher rates of unemployment, lower income, and limited social support networks compared to adults without SMI (Goldberg et al., 2003). These factors likely place persons with SMI in more high-risk situations than persons who are not comparatively disadvantaged. The term *triply diagnosed* has evolved in recent years to describe individuals with SMI, substance use disorders, and HIV infection, which has been a growing epidemic among socially and economically marginalized groups (Parry et al., 2007). Indeed, persons with SMI who are homeless have particularly high rates of HIV infection in the United States (e.g., Brunette et al., 1999) and internationally (e.g., Hillis et al., 2012). Furthermore, persons with SMI who lack resources may experience significant pressure to trade sex for money or goods (Butterfield et al., 2003). Among homeless young men who have sex with men, in Los Angeles,

nearly a quarter reported always having unprotected sex and engaging in sex trade (Tucker et al., 2012). A substantial proportion of adults with SMI encounter high-risk situations, including sexual coercion, when relationships are connected with access to material resources (Otto-Salaj et al., 1998). Persons with SMI also experience more barriers to healthcare, which prevents them from receiving regular HIV and other STI testing, regular check-ups with infectious disease providers after diagnosis, and resources for accessing and adhering to HIV medications.

IMPACT OF PSYCHIATRIC DISORDERS ON PERSONS WITH HIV

HIV TRANSMISSION RISK BEHAVIOR

HIV and SMI share a cyclical relationship, in which SMI contributes to HIV risk, and HIV infection further contributes to the development of SMI through psychosocial stress and the neurobiological effects of the disease. HIV infection has been associated with cognitive impairments, which result from damage to the central nervous system through inflammation and opportunistic infection (Harezlak et al., 2011). These impairments can impact decision-making and result in risky behavior. In addition, mental illness and subsequent risk behavior may result from the psychosocial stressors that often accompany HIV infection, including, stigma and discrimination, long-term medication regimens, lifestyle adjustments, and opportunistic infections. When compared to HIV-negative individuals with SMI, persons with HIV and SMI report more psychiatric symptoms and more drug and alcohol use, and they are more likely to have a severe diagnosis such as schizophrenia (Wu et al., 2011). On average, most individuals report decreasing their rates of risky sexual and drug use behaviors after learning of their positive serostatus; however SMI may contribute to the persistence of risky behavior despite knowing the risks of transmission. Of several examined psychological factors, greater depressive symptoms and less satisfaction with aspects of life were most strongly associated with unprotected sex (Gerbi et al., 2012). In studies of HIV-infected men who have sex with men, moderate depressive symptoms were related to the least decline in HIV-transmission risk behaviors during a prevention intervention when compared to low- or high-severity depressive symptoms (O'Cleirigh et al., 2013). Women with HIV who experienced a recent trauma were four times more likely to report sex with an HIV-negative or unknown serostatus partner and to not always use a condom with these partners compared to women without a recent trauma (Machtinger et al., 2012).

MEDICATION ADHERENCE

Consistent use of antiretroviral medication has the potential to decrease the transmission of HIV by lowering viral load among infected individuals (Das et al., 2010). However, SMI and substance use are related to poor medication adherence, which increases the likelihood of building medication resistance and places others in their sexual and drug-using network at greater risk for contracting HIV. Depression and substance use are the strongest predictors of poor medication adherence (Chander et al., 2006; Starace et al., 2002). Substance users are less likely to access and adhere to antiretroviral medications and thus experience longer periods before reaching viral suppression and CD4+ T cell response (Chander et al., 2006; Wood et al., 2004). Depression, anxiety, panic, and PTSD have similarly been associated with worse medication adherence (Chander et al., 2006; Machtinger et al., 2012; Tucker et al., 2003), although research suggests that depression may be a stronger predictor of medication adherence than PTSD (Vranceanu et al., 2008). One study found HIV-positive patients with schizophrenia to have 66% adherence to their medication, with adherence being highly dependent on attending regular appointments with their healthcare provider (Wagner et al., 2003). In another study, individuals with bipolar disorder were more likely to have less than 95% medication adherence compared to persons with depression or no mood disorder, and poor medication adherence was associated with detectable HIV viral load (Meade et al.,2012). There is evidence that adherence to psychotropic medications mediates the impact of depression on antiretroviral adherence (Cruess et al., 2012). Adults with SMI may require specialized interventions to improve access to HIV treatment and adherence to both antiviral and psychiatric medications (Rosenberg et al., 2004).

HIV PREVENTION INTERVENTIONS FOR ADULTS WITH SEVERE MENTAL ILLNESS

Since the mid-1990s, a number of theory-based behavioral risk reduction interventions have been developed for adults with SMI, the vast majority of which were conducted in the United States (see Kaltenthaler et al., 2014 for a detailed review). These interventions used cognitive-behavioral strategies to increase knowledge about HIV/AIDS and risk behaviors, enhance motivation for behavioral risk reduction, and strengthen self-efficacy and skills for behavioral risk reduction. Practice exercises and role-plays addressed personal triggers for HIV risk behavior, problem-solving of risk reduction strategies, proper condom use and cleaning of injection drug equipment, and assertiveness and negotiation skills for communicating with sex partners. Almost all interventions were delivered in small-group formats, with increasingly sophisticated designs.

There have been several randomized controlled trials aimed at reducing HIV risk among individuals with SMI. These include cognitive-behavioral risk reduction interventions for men and women with SMI in urban areas (Kalichman et al., 1995) and community psychiatric outpatient clinics (Carey et al., 2004a; Malow et al., 2012; Otto-Salaj et al., 2001); an HIV risk psychoeducation intervention with homeless men (Linn et al., 2003); a small-group intervention for men with mental illness indicated to be at high HIV risk at outpatient mental health clinics (National Institute of Mental Health [NIMH], 2006); and several studies focused specifically on

decreasing sexual risk among men (Berkman et al., 2006, 2007; Linn et al., 2003; Susser et al., 1998) and women (Collins et al., 2011; Weinhardt et al., 1998), with a particular focus on sexual assertiveness training for women. One international study conducted in India implemented a 1-hour individual session that provided information on HIV transmission and prevention with psychiatric inpatients. Participants doubled their HIV knowledge after the intervention and retained the information 5 days later (Chandra et al., 2006). More recent interventions have focused on improving HIV care and reducing HIV transmission among HIV-positive individuals with SMI (Blank et al., 2011). In a randomized trial, individuals with HIV and SMI were recruited from the community and assigned to receive healthcare coordination and weekly in-person visits with an advanced-practice nurse, which resulted in significantly reduced viral loads, but not CD4 cell counts, over a 12-month period.

Given the moderating role substance use can have on sexual risk behavior, interventionists are exploring the risk reduction potential of independent and combined substance use and HIV interventions. Combined HIV prevention and substance use interventions have been linked to beneficial outcomes, including less unprotected sex, fewer casual sex partners, fewer new STIs, more safer-sex communications, improved HIV knowledge, more positive attitudes toward condom use, stronger intentions to use condoms, and improved behavioral skills (Carey et al., 2004a). HIV education and risk reduction within traditional outpatient substance use interventions can reduce risky sexual and drug-using behavior, increase HIV knowledge, and improve beliefs about condoms among individuals with and without comorbid SMI (Avins et al., 1997; (Kalichman et al., 2005; Levounis et al., 2002; Menon and Pomerantz, 1997; Thurstone et al., 2007).

Community-level interventions have become increasingly recognized as an important component of HIV prevention. Two innovative interventions have been developed for adults with SMI. In the first, men and women were taught to become advocates for behavior change, in addition to receiving cognitive-behavioral skills for reducing individual HIV risk behaviors, which, at follow-up, resulted in reports of fewer sex partners, more frequent condom use, and fewer occasions of unprotected sexual intercourse (Kelly et al., 1997). The second trial tested the feasibility of a community-level HIV prevention intervention consisting of education, cognitive-behavioral skills building, the creation of peer norms, and social-environmental reinforcement supportive of HIV risk reduction for adults with SMI living in supportive housing programs (Sikkema et al., 2007). Participants reported improved HIV risk behaviors, attitudes, and knowledge.

In summary, a number of promising HIV prevention interventions have been developed for adults with SMI. Unfortunately, these interventions have not been widely disseminated from clinical trials into mental health care settings. The group format of these interventions may be an implementation problem for outpatient settings, largely due to the difficulty in convening adults with SMI for group programs and therapy. Improvements are needed to promote more sustainable and meaningful behavior change through integrated, multilevel treatments.

SUGGESTIONS FOR CLINICAL PRACTICE

Given the high rate of sexual risk behavior among adults with SMI, routine HIV risk assessment for all psychiatric patients is indicated. Specifically, patients should be asked about sexual and drug use behaviors (e.g., current activity, number of partners, sex trade, condom use, injection drug use, and needle sharing) and risk factors (e.g., sexual abuse, substance use, partner characteristics). All patients endorsing HIV risk behaviors should be offered HIV testing, ideally within the mental health agency to facilitate access and follow-up. Patients who test positive might then be referred for further medical evaluation, treatment, and secondary prevention services. Rosenberg and colleagues (2004) developed a best-practices intervention model for adults with SMI that provides risk screening, testing for HIV and hepatitis, immunization for hepatitis A and B, risk reduction counseling, and treatment referral for infected persons. This brief intervention, which is delivered at community mental health centers by a mobile team of specialists, has been found to be both feasible and efficacious.

More intensive interventions are also needed to promote HIV risk reduction among adults with SMI. To account for psychosocial risk factors, the most promising interventions will likely be multidimensional and occur at the individual, group, and community level. At the individual level, psychotherapy and medication are essential for treating psychiatric symptoms, intrapsychic barriers, and interpersonal difficulties that may underlie HIV risk behavior among adults with SMI. For example, mood stabilization, trauma recovery, and social-skills training may be essential precursors to risk reduction. Case management may be an important adjunctive service to facilitate and maintain behavior change. Given the high rates of HIV risk behavior among persons with substance use disorders and/or trauma histories, it may also be effective to integrate HIV prevention into existing treatments for substance abuse and trauma recovery. As discussed, small-group interventions based on cognitive-behavioral change principles have been effective in promoting short-term behavioral change. Such group interventions should be integrated into ongoing mental health treatment settings. Community-level interventions delivered in supportive housing programs should also focus on maintenance of risk reduction, which may require booster sessions and/or a broader array of prevention services.

CONCLUSION

The high rates of HIV infection and HIV risk behavior among persons with SMI suggest the potential for rapid spread of HIV among this population, underscoring the need for targeted HIV risk reduction. Given the multiple psychiatric, medical, and psychosocial needs of persons with SMI, HIV prevention interventions should be integrated into existing services. This may not only improve outcomes but also increase participation and engagement, be resource efficient, and have wide dissemination potential. In addition, the effective treatment of substance abuse and sexual trauma should be prioritized, especially among persons who are socially and economically disadvantaged. Mental health professionals are in an ideal position to assess HIV risk, encourage HIV testing, promote risk reduction, and thereby stem the HIV/AIDS epidemic among this vulnerable population.

ACKNOWLEDGMENTS

The views expressed in this chapter do not necessarily represent the views of the NIMH, NIH, HHS, or the United States Government. This work was supported by grants from the U.S. National Institutes of Health, K23-DA028660 and F32-DA038519.

REFERENCES

Avins AL, LIndan CP, Woods WJ, et al. (1997). Changes in HIV-related behaviors among heterosexual alcoholics following addiction treatment. *Drug Alcohol Depend* 44:47–55.

Berkman A, Cerwonka E, Sohler N, Susser E (2006). A randomized trial of a brief HIV risk reduction intervention for men with severe mental illness. *Psychiatr Serv* 57:407–409.

Berkman A, Pilowsky DJ, Zybert PA, et al. (2007). HIV prevention with severely mentally ill men: a randomised controlled trial. *AIDS Care* 19:579–588.

Beyer JL, Taylor L, Gersing KR, Krishnan KRR (2007) Prevalence of HIV infection in a general psychiatric outpatient population. *Psychosomatics* 48:31–37.

Blank MB, Hanrahan NP, Fishbein M, et al. (2011) A randomized trial of a nursing intervention for HIV disease management among persons with serious mental illness. *Psychiatr Serv* 62:1318–1324.

Brown LK, Tolou-Shams M, Lescano C, et al., and Project SHIELD Study Group (2006). Depressive symptoms as a predictor of sexual risk among African American adolescents and young adults. *J Adolescent Health* 39:444.e1–444.e8.

Brunette M, Rosenberg SD, Goodman LA, et al. (1999). HIV risk factors among people with severe mental illness in urban and rural areas. *Psychiatr Serv* 50:556–558.

Butterfield MI, Bosworth HB, Meador KG, et al. (2003). Gender differences in hepatitis C infection and risks among persons with severe mental illness. *Psychiatr Serv* 54:848–853.

Carey MP, Carey KB, Maisto SA, Gordon CM, Schroder KEE, Vanable PA (2004a). Reducing HIV-risk behavior among adults receiving outpatient psychiatric treatment: results from a randomized controlled trial. *J Consult Clin Psychol* 72:252–268.

Carey MP, Carey KB, Maisto SA, Schroder KEE, Vanable PA, Gordon CM (2004b). HIV risk behavior among psychiatric outpatients: association with psychiatric disorder, substance use disorder, and gender. *J Nerv Ment Dis* 192:289–296.

Chander G, Himelhoch S, Moore RD (2006). Substance abuse and psychiatric disorders in HIV-positive patients. *Drugs* 66:769–789.

Chandra PS, Carey MP, Carey KB, Prasada Rao PSDV, Jairam KR, Thomas T (2003). HIV risk behavior among psychiatric inpatients: results from a hospital-wide screening study in southern India. *Int J STD AIDS* 14:532–538.

Chandra PS, Desai G, Ranjan S (2005). HIV & psychiatric disorders. *Indian J Med Res* 121:451–467.

Chandra PS, Krishna VAS, Carey MP (2006). Improving knowledge about HIV and AIDS among persons with a severe mental illness in India. *Indian J Soc Psychiatry* 22:104–109.

Collins PY, von Unger H, Putnins S, Crawford N, Dutt R, Hoffer M (2011). Adding the female condom to HIV prevention interventions for women with severe mental illness: a pilot test. *Community Ment Health J* 47:143–155.

Cruess DG, Kalichman SC, Amaral C, Swetzes C, Cherry C, Kalichman MO (2012) Benefits of adherence to psychotropic medications on depressive symptoms and antiretroviral medication adherence among men and women living with HIV/AIDS. *Ann Behav Med* 43:189–197.

Das M, Chu PL, Santos GM, Scheer S, Vittinghoff E, McFarland W, Colfax GN (2010). Decreases in community viral load are accompanied by reductions in new HIV infections in San Francisco. *PLoS ONE* 5:e11068.

Davidson S, Judd F, Jolley D, Hocking B, Thompson S, Hyland B (2001). Risk factors for HIV/AIDS and hepatitis C among the chronically mentally ill. *Aust N Z J Psychiatry* 35:203–209.

De Genna NM, Feske U, Angiolieri T, Gold MA (2011). Race and sexually transmitted diseases in women with and without borderline personality disorder. *J Womens Health* 20:333–340.

Gerbi GB, Habtemariam T, Tameru B, Nganwa D, Robnett V (2012). A quantitative risk assessment of multiple factors influencing HIV/AIDS transmission through unprotected sex among HIV-seropositive men. *AIDS Care* 24:331–339.

Gilchrist G, Blazquez A, Torrens M (2011). Psychiatric, behavioural and social risk factors for HIV infection among female drug users. *AIDS Behav* 15:1834–1843.

Goldberg RW, Rollins AL, Lehman AF (2003). Social network correlates among people with psychiatric disabilities. *Psychiatr Rehabil J* 26:393–402.

Grant C, Addington J, Addington D, Konnert C (2001). Social functioning in first- and multiple-episode schizophrenia. *Can J Psychiatry* 46:746–749.

Grassi L, Pavanati M, Cardelli R, Ferri S, Peron L (1999). HIV-risk behavior and knowledge about HIV/AIDS among patients with schizophrenia. *Psychol Med* 29:171–179.

Grubaugh AL, Zinzow HM, Paul L, Egede LE, Frueh BC (2011). Trauma exposure and posttraumatic stress disorder in adults with severe mental illness: a critical review. *Clin Psychol Rev* 31:883–899.

Harezlak J, Buchthal S, Taylor M, et al., for the HIV Neuroimaging Consortium (2011). Persistence of HIV-associated cognitive impairment, inflammation, and neuronal injury in era of highly active antiretroviral treatment. *AIDS.* 25:625–633.

Hariri AG, Karadag F, Gokalp P, Essizoglu A (2011). Risky sexual behavior among patients in Turkey with bipolar disorder, schizophrenia, and heroin addiction. *J Sex Med* 8:2284–2291.

Harned MS, Pantalone DW, Ward-Ciesielski EF, Lynch TR, Linehan MM (2011). The prevalence and correlates of sexual risk behaviors and sexually transmitted infections in outpatients with borderline personality disorder. *J Nerv Ment Dis.* 199:832–838.

Hillis SD, Zapata L, Robbins CL, et al. (2012). HIV seroprevalence among orphaned and homeless youth: no place like home. *AIDS* 26:105–110.

Himelhoch S, Goldberg R, Calmes C, et al. (2011). Screening for and prevalence of HIV and hepatitis C among an outpatient urban sample of people with serious mental illness and co-occurring substance abuse. *J Community Psychol* 39:231–239.

Himelhoch S, McCarthy JF, Ganoczy D, Medoff D, Dixon LB, Blow FC (2007). Understanding associations between serious mental illness and HIV among patients in the VA health system. *Psychiatr Serv* 58:1165–1172.

Horwath W, Cournos F, McKinnon K, Guido JR, Herman R (1996). Illicit drug injection among psychiatric patients without a primary substance use disorder. *Psychiatr Serv* 47:181–185.

Hull JW, Clarkin JF, Yeomans F (1993). Borderline personality disorder and impulsive sexual behavior. *Hosp Community Psychiatry* 44:1000–1002.

Kalichman S, Malow R, Dévieux J, Stein JA, Piedman F (2005). HIV risk reduction for substance using seriously mentally ill adults: Test of the information-motivation-behavior skills (IMB) model. *Community Ment Health J* 41:277–290.

Kalichman SC, Sikkema KJ, Kelly JA, Bulto M (1995). Use of a brief behavioral skills intervention to prevent HIV infection among chronic mentally ill adults. *Psychiatr Serv* 46:275–280.

Kaltenthaler E, Pandor A, Wong R (2014). The effectiveness of sexual health interventions for people with severe mental illness: a systematic review. *Health Technol Assess* 18:1–74.

Kelley JL, Petry NM (2000). HIV risk behaviors in male substance abusers with and without antisocial personality disorder. *Subst Abuse Treat* 19:59–66.

Kelly JA, McAuliffe TL, Sikkema KJ, et al. (1997). Reduction in risk behavior among adults with severe mental illness who learned to advocate for HIV prevention. *Psychiatr Serv* 48:1283–1288.

Kessler RC, Chiu WT, Demler O, Walters EE (2005). Prevalence, severity, and comorbidity of 12-month DSM-IV disorders in the National Comorbidity Survey Replication. *Arch Gen Psychiatry* 62:617–627.

Koen L, Vuuren SV, Niehaus DJH, Emsley RA (2007). HIV/AIDS risk behaviour in South African schizophrenia patients. *WAJM* 26:2–6.

Levounis P, Galanter M, Dermatis H, Hamowy A, DeLeon G (2002). Correlates of HIV transmission risk factors and considerations for interventions for homeless, chemically addicted and mentally ill patients. *J Addict Dis* 21:61–72.

Linn JG, Neff JA, Theriot R, Harris JL, Interrante J, Graham ME (2003). Reaching impaired populations with HIV prevention programs: a clinical trial for homeless mentally ill African-American men. *Cell Mol Biol* 49:1167–1175.

Lundberg P, Nakasujja N, Musisi S, Thorson AE, Cantor-Graae E, Allebeck P (2013). HIV prevalence in persons with severe mental illness in Uganda: a cross-sectional hospital-based study. *Int J Ment Health Syst.* 7:20–28.

Machtinger EL, Wilson TC, Haberer JE, Weiss DS (2012). Psychological trauma and PTSD in HIV-positive women: A meta-analysis. *AIDS Behav* 16:2091–2100.

Malow RM, McMahon RC, Devieux J, et al. (2012). Cognitive behavioral HIV risk reduction in those receiving psychiatric treatment: a clinical trial. *AIDS Behav* 16:1192–1202.

Marshall BD, Prescott MR, Liberzon I, Tamburrino MB, Calabrese JR, Galea S (2013). Posttraumatic stress disorder, depression, and HIV risk behavior among Ohio Army National Guard Soldiers. *J Trauma Stress* 26:64–70.

Martin L, Kagee A (2011). Lifetime and HIV-related PTSD among persons recently diagnosed with HIV. *AIDS Behav* 15:125–131.

Meade CS (2006). Sexual risk behavior among persons dually diagnosed with severe mental illness and substance use disorders. *J Subst Abuse Treat* 30:147–157.

Meade CS, Bevilacqua LA, Key MD (2012). Bipolar disorder is associated with HIV transmission risk behavior among patients in treatment for HIV. *AIDS Behav* 16: 2267–2271.

Meade CS, Fitzmaurice GM, Sanchez AK, Griffin ML, McDonald LJ, Weiss RD (2011) The relationship of manic episodes and drug abuse to sexual risk behavior in patients with co-occurring bipolar and substance use disorders: a 15-month prospective analysis. *AIDS Behav* 15: 1829–1833.

Meade CS, Graff FS, Griffin ML, Weiss RD (2008). HIV risk behavior among patients with co-occurring bipolar and substance use disorders: Associations with mania and drug abuse. *Drug Alcohol Depen* 92: 296–300.

Meade CS, Sikkema KJ (2005). HIV risk behavior among adults with severe mental illness: a systematic review. *Clin Psychol Rev* 25:433–457.

Menon AS, Pomerantz S (1997). Substance use during sex and unsafe sexual behaviors among acute psychiatric inpatients. *Psychiatr Serv* 48:1070–1072.

Musisi S, Wagner GJ, Ghosh-Dastidar B, Nakasujja N, Dickens A, Okello E (2014). Depression and sexual risk behaviour among clients about to start HIV antiretroviral therapy in Uganda. *Int J STD AIDS* 25:130–137.

National Institute of Mental Health (NIMH) Multisite HIV Prevention Trial Group (2006). HIV prevention with persons with mental health problems. *Psychol Health Med* 11: 142–154.

Newville H, Haller DL (2012) Relationship of Axis II pathology to sex- and drug-related risk behaviors among patients in HIV primary care. *AIDS Care* 24:763–768.

O'Cleirigh C, Newcomb ME, Mayer KH, Skeer M, Traeger L, Safren SA (2013). Moderate levels of depression predict sexual transmission risk in HIV-infected MSM: a longitudinal analysis of data from six sites involved in a "Prevention for Positives" study. *AIDS Behav* 17:1764–1769.

Otto-Salaj LL, Heckman TG, Stevenson LY, Kelly JA (1998). Patterns, predictors, and gender differences in HIV risk among severely mentally ill men and women. *Community Ment Health J* 34:175–190.

Otto-Salaj LL, Kelly JA, Stevenson LY, Hoffman R, Kalichman SC (2001). Outcomes of a randomized small-group HIV prevention intervention trial for people with severe mental illness. *Community Ment Health J* 37:123–144.

Owe-Larsson B, Sall L, Salamon E, Allgulander C (2009). HIV infection and psychiatric illness. *Afr J Psychiatry* 12:115–128.

Parry CD, Blank MB, Pithey AL (2007). Responding to the threat of HIV among persons with mental illness and substance abuse. *Curr Opin Psychiatry* 20:235–241.

Peixoto ER, de Barros FC, Guimarães MD (2014). Factors associated with unprotected sexual practice among men and women with mental illnesses in Brazil. *Cad Saúde Pública* 30:1475–1486.

Plotzker RE, Metzger DS, Holmes WC (2007). Childhood sexual and physical abuse histories, PTSD, depression, and HIV risk outcomes in women injection drug users: a potential mediating pathway. *Am J Addict* 16:431–438.

Prince JD, Walkup J, Akincigil A, Amin S, Crystal S (2012). Serious mental illness and risk of new HIV/AIDS diagnoses: an analysis of Medicaid beneficiaries in eight states. *Psychiatr Serv* 63:1032–1038.

Regier DA, Farmer ME, Rae DS, Locke BZ, Keith SJ, Judd LL, Goodwin FK (1990). Comorbidity of mental disorders with alcohol and other drug abuse: results from the Epidemiological Catchment Area (ECA) Study. *JAMA* 264:2511–2518.

Ribeiro CM, Gurgel WS, Luna JR, Matos KJ, Souza FG (2013). Is bipolar disorder a risk factor for HIV infection? *J Affect Disord* 146:66–70.

Rosenberg S, Brunette M, Oxman T, et al. (2004). The STIRR model of best practices for blood-borne diseases among clients with serious mental illness. *Psychiatr Serv* 55:660–664.

Rosenberg SD, Goodman LA, Osher FC, et al. (2001). Prevalence of HIV, hepatitis B, and hepatitis C in people with severe mental illness. *Am J Public Health* 91:31–37.

Rosenberg SD, Trumbetta SL, Muesser KT, Goodman LA, Osher FC, Vidaver RM, Metzger DS (2001). Determinants of risk behavior for human immunodeficiency virus/acquired immunodeficiency syndrome in people with severe mental illness. *Compr Psychiatry* 42:263–271.

Sacks M, Dermatis H (1994). Acute psychiatric illness: effects on HIV-risk behavior. *Psychosoc Rehabil J* 17:5–19.

Schinnar A, Rothbard A, Kanter R, Jung Y (1990). An empirical literature review of definitions of severe and persistent mental illness. *Am J Psychiatry* 147:1602–1608.

Sikkema KJ, Meade CS, Doughty JD, Zimmerman SO, Kloos B, Snow DL (2007). Community-level HIV prevention for persons with

severe mental illness living in supportive housing programs: a pilot intervention study. *J Prev Interv Community* 33:121–135.

Starace F, Ammassari A, Trotta MP, et al. (2002). Depression is a risk factor for suboptimal adherence to highly active antiretroviral therapy. *J Acquir Immune Defic Syndr* 31:S136–S139.

Stewart AJ, Theodore-Oklota C, Hadley W, et al. and Project STYLE Study Group (2012). Mania symptoms and HIV-risk behavior among adolescents in mental health treatment. *J Clin Child Adolesc Psychol* 41:803–810.

Susser E, Valencia E, Berkman A, et al. (1998). Human immunodeficiency virus sexual risk reduction in homeless men with mental illness. *Arch Gen Psychiatry* 55:266–272.

Thurstone C, Riggs PD, Klein C, Mikulich-Gilbertson SK (2007). A one-session human immunodeficiency virus risk-reduction intervention in adolescents with psychiatric and substance use disorders. *J Am Acad Child Adolesc Psychiatry* 46:1179–1186.

Tucker JS, Hu J, Golinelli D, Kennedy DP, Green HD, Jr., Wenzel SL (2012). Social network and individual correlates of sexual risk behavior among homeless young men who have sex with men. *J Adolesc Health* 51:386–392.

Tucker JS, Kanouse DE, Miu A, Koegel P, Sullivan G (2003). HIV risk behaviors and their correlates among HIV-positive adults with serious mental illness. *AIDS Behav* 7:29–40.

Tyrer P, Manley C, van Horn E, Leddy D, Ukoumunne OC (2000). Personality abnormality in severe mental illness and its influence on outcome of intensive and standard case management: a randomized controlled trial. *Eur Psychiatry* 15:7–10.

UNAIDS (2014). HIV estimates with uncertainty bounds 1990–2015. http://www.unaids.org/en/resources/documents/2016/HIV_estimates_with_uncertainty_bounds_1990-2015. Accessed February 5, 2017.

Vranceanu AM, Safren SA, Lu M, Coady WM, Skolnik PR, Rogers WH, Wilson IB (2008). The relationship of post-traumatic stress disorder and depression to antiretroviral medication adherence in persons with HIV. *AIDS Patient Care STDS* 22:313–321.

Wagner GJ, Kanouse DE, Koegel P, Sullivan G (2003). Adherence to HIV antiretrovirals among persons with serious mental illness. *AIDS Patient Care STDS* 17:179–186.

Wainberg ML, McKinnon K, Elkington KS, et al., and PRISSMA (2008). HIV risk behaviors among outpatients with severe mental illness in Rio de Janeiro, Brazil. *World Psychiatry* 7:166–172.

Weinhardt LS, Carey MP, Carey KB, Verdecias RN (1998). Increasing assertiveness skills to reduce HIV risk among women living with severe and persistent mental illness. *J Consult Clin Psychol* 66:680–684.

Wood E, Montaner JS, Yip B, Tyndall MW, Schechter MT, O'Shaughnessy MV, Hogg RS (2004). Adherence to antiretroviral therapy and CD4 T-cell count responses among HIV-infected injection drug users. *Antivir Ther* 9:229–235.

World Health Organization (WHO) World Mental Health Survey Consortium (2004). Prevalence, severity, and unmet need for treatment of mental disorders in the World Health Organization World Mental Health Surveys. *JAMA* 291:2581–2590.

Wu ES, Rothbard A, Blank MB (2011). Using psychiatric symptomatology to assess risk for HIV infection in individuals with severe mental illness. *Community Ment Health J* 47:672–678.

29.

PSYCHIATRIC ASPECTS OF CARE ENGAGEMENT AND MEDICATION ADHERENCE IN ANTIRETROVIRAL-BASED HIV TREATMENT AND PREVENTION

Jeffrey J. Weiss and Michael J. Stirratt

Antiretroviral therapy (ART) has transformed HIV from a rapidly progressive fatal illness to a chronic manageable illness. The estimated average life expectancy for individuals living with HIV who receive timely ART and maintain long-term viral suppression now approaches that of individuals uninfected with HIV (Nakagawa et al., 2012). HIV-related hospitalizations and deaths in the developed world are largely limited to people who do not receive timely medical care or who are nonadherent (Riley et al., 2005; Sabin et al., 2006). The relationship between adherence to ART and virological suppression has been well documented (Bangsberg et al., 2000, Bangsberg, Perry, et al., 2001; Low-Beer et al., 2000; Paterson et al., 2000). High levels of adherence to ART are needed to achieve complete and durable suppression of the HIV virus and to avoid the emergence of resistant strains of HIV virus (Bangsberg et al., 2003). Care engagement and treatment adherence are directly related to HIV treatment outcomes and to mortality (Lima et al., 2009; Mugavero et al., 2014; Pinoges et al., 2015).

Psychiatric illness is more prevalent among individuals with HIV than in the general population (estimates of lifetime psychiatric illness range from 38% to 88% in samples of persons with HIV as compared to 33% for the general population) (Yun et al., 2005). In a representative probability sample of 2,864 adults receiving HIV care in the United States in 1996, Bing and colleagues (2001) reported that 48% of the sample screened positive for a psychiatric disorder, 38% reported using an illicit drug other than marijuana, and 12% screened positive for drug dependence during the prior year. The prevalence of current depression in this large representative sample of persons with HIV (36%) was three times higher than in the general population. In this same sample, 27% of the individuals were taking psychotropic medication, with antidepressants (21%) and anxiolytics (17%) being the most commonly prescribed (Vitiello et al., 2003).

Active drug use and psychiatric illness are significant barriers to care engagement and treatment adherence among persons living with HIV (Giordano, Visnegarwala, et al., 2005, Gonzalez et al., 2011, 2013, Langebeek et al., 2014). HIV infection and psychiatric illness often exist in the context of complex social conditions which can further complicate HIV care engagement and sustained adherence to ART. These include social morbidities such as homelessness, poverty, unemployment, domestic violence, legal problems, discrimination, stigmatization, and a distrustful attitude toward traditional medicine (Bouhnik et al., 2002; Katz et al., 2013; Kidder et al., 2007; Lopez et al., 2010; Palmer et al., 2003).

Antiretroviral medications are no longer used solely for ART. Individuals who are at high risk of acquiring HIV infection may now take antiretroviral medications as pre-exposure prophylaxis (PrEP) to prevent HIV infection. The U.S. Food and Drug Administration (FDA) approved the first HIV prevention indication for a medication (emtricitabine and tenofovir disoproxil fumarate) in 2012, after large-scale clinical trials demonstrated daily oral PrEP to be safe, well tolerated, and effective for preventing HIV infection (Baeten and Grant, 2013). PrEP clinical practice guidelines issued by the Centers for Disease Control and Prevention (CDC) suggest PrEP for sexually active adults who are at substantial risk for HIV infection as indicated by a history of inconsistent or no condom use, recent sexually transmitted infections, having a sexual partner with HIV, or other risk factors (US Public Health Service, 2014). Active drug use and psychiatric illness in high-risk populations could challenge PrEP adherence and care engagement.

This chapter focuses on care engagement and adherence to antiretroviral-based HIV treatment and prevention among patients with psychiatric symptomatology and illness. The following sections of this chapter address (1) psychiatric aspects of PrEP for HIV prevention, (2) the care continuum for individuals living with HIV infection, (3) psychiatric determinants of HIV care engagement, (4) interventions to improve HIV care engagement, (5) psychiatric determinants of ART adherence, (6) interventions to improve ART adherence, and (7) implications of research findings for the medical and mental health clinicians working with patients with psychiatric illness who are living with HIV or at risk for infection. *Clinician* is used in this chapter to refer to the individual providing HIV care regardless of discipline (MD, DO, NP, PA). Discussion of the work of the psychiatrist is meant to be relevant to the work of other mental health professionals (psychologists, social workers, substance use counselors) as well.

PSYCHIATRIC ASPECTS OF PRE-EXPOSURE PROPHYLAXIS (PREP)

PrEP represents a highly novel HIV prevention tool that is at an early stage of implementation in the United States. Researchers have articulated a "PrEP cascade" to describe the processes through which individuals for whom PrEP is indicated to become engaged in PrEP care (Liu et al., 2012). Under the proposed PrEP cascade, individuals at high risk for HIV infection must first be identified as PrEP candidates, then they must link to a PrEP clinician or program, initiate PrEP, be retained in PrEP care, and maintain PrEP medication adherence and persistence. Psychiatric factors could potentially impact each step of the PrEP cascade.

On the front end of the PrEP cascade, psychiatric illness may have a role to play in identifying candidates for PrEP. Depression is prevalent among men who have sex with men and do not use condoms. The iPrEx PrEP trial, which was conducted with men who have sex with men and transgender women who were at high risk for HIV infection, determined that 48% of participants showed Center for Epidemiologic Studies Depression Scale (CES-D) scores ≥16 (Liu et al., 2011). Participants in the iPrEx trial who evidenced clinical depression were significantly more likely to engage in high-risk sexual practices (Liu et al., 2011). A large representative cohort study of men who have sex with men similarly found that individuals with CES-D scale scores at or above 16 were more than two times more likely to show extended periods of high-risk behavior over time (Pines et al., 2014). Screening men who have sex with men for clinical depression could therefore aid in identifying high-risk individuals who may benefit from PrEP.

Research indicates that the prevention effectiveness of daily oral PrEP is highly contingent upon medication adherence (Amico and Stirratt, 2014). Scant data are available on PrEP adherence in relation to psychiatric illness. Some trials testing the efficacy of PrEP have identified heavy alcohol use as a determinant of adherence to study product (Haberer et al., 2013). Depression and other mental disorders have not yet been linked to lower PrEP adherence. Lower levels of PrEP drug detection were observed among individuals with CES-D scores ≥16 in the iPrEx trial, but this trend was not statistically significant (Liu et al., 2011). Despite the lack of available data, public health authorities recommend that individuals taking PrEP receive screening and treatment for substance abuse and other psychiatric disorders as a potential adherence-enhancing strategy (Koenig et al., 2013; US Public Health Service, 2014).

Elsewhere along the PrEP cascade, it is reasonable to expect that mental illness could impact linkage and retention in PrEP care, although data for substantiation are presently lacking. Results from some of the first open-label PrEP studies indicate that some individuals who initiate PrEP do not persist on the medication regimen for very long (Grant et al., 2014). See Chapter 31 of this textbook for a more detailed discussion of PrEP. Future research will need to further explore the impact of mental disorders on PrEP engagement and retention, as well as medication adherence and persistence.

THE HIV CARE CONTINUUM

The achievement of sustained viral suppression requires most individuals living with HIV to successfully negotiate the HIV treatment cascade, and this presents multiple challenges that can compromise treatment outcomes and attendant prevention efforts. Giordano, Suarez-Almazor, and colleagues (2005) developed a model of adherence to engagement in the health system that includes (1) receiving an HIV test, (2) entering quality health care services, and (3) initiation of ART. More recently, the concept of the HIV care cascade has been introduced (Gardner et al., 2011). The HIV treatment cascade flows across the key junctures of HIV diagnosis, linkage to primary HIV medical care, retention in medical care, voluntary ART initiation, and adherence to ART regimens. Notable percentages of individuals with HIV are lost at each point in the HIV treatment cascade (CDC, 2016; Gardner et al., 2011; Marks et al., 2010). As a result of these gaps in the treatment cascade, estimates of the proportion of individuals living with HIV in the United States who maintain suppressed viral load range from just 19% (Gardner et al., 2011) to 30% (Bradley et al., 2014; CDC, 2016). These problems with engagement in the HIV treatment cascade are evident among persons living with HIV and psychiatric illness, and they require us to address each point in the treatment cascade in order to optimize the potential for treatment to contribute to prevention in this important population.

PSYCHIATRIC DETERMINANTS OF HIV CARE ENGAGEMENT

To receive proper medical care persons with HIV need to locate an appropriate and available medical clinician and keep scheduled appointments with that clinician. Rates of care linkage and retention in the United States are largely suboptimal (CDC, 2016; Gardner et al., 2011; Marks et al., 2010). A meta-analysis reported that approximately 36% of U.S. individuals newly diagnosed with HIV infection do not link to primary medical care within 12 months (Marks et al., 2010). In one Alabama clinic setting, 60% of patients with HIV missed a medical appointment in the first year after initiating care (Mugavero et al., 2009b).

Inadequate linkage and retention in HIV primary care may impact clinical and treatment outcomes for people with HIV. Mugavero and colleagues (2009a) found that missed medical appointments were associated with virological failure and helped to explain racial disparities in viral suppression. Berg and colleagues (2005) found that adherence to medical care predicts level of disease progression. In multivariate models, the number of missed appointments was related to both having a CD4 cell count of <200 cells/microliter and having a detectable HIV viral load. These analyses accounted for the fact that patients who are more medically ill are likely to have more scheduled medical appointments. Research has additionally identified associations between attendance of HIV primary care medical appointments and long-term mortality (Giordano et al., 2007; Mugavero et al., 2014). A retrospective cohort study conducted in the Veterans' Administration found that 36% of patients with HIV were out of care for at least 3 months during their first year of ART, and about half of this percentage was out of care for 6 months or more (Giordano et al., 2007). After adjusting for potential confounding factors, patients with poor medical appointment attendance showed higher rates of mortality over a 5-year follow-up period than patients who routinely attended medical appointments (Giordano et al., 2007). Research associating poor HIV care engagement with failure of viral suppression, illness progression, and mortality underscores the importance of developing approaches to enhance patient engagement in HIV medical care.

Mental disorders can present a substantial barrier to adequate engagement and retention in HIV primary care. Research has established links between the presence of psychiatric illness and poor rates of HIV care linkage and retention. In one Alabama study, missed HIV primary care visits during the first year of care were more common among patients who had substance abuse disorders, as well as those who were younger, female, black, and lacking private health insurance (Mugavero et al., 2009b). A large cohort study of injection drug users found that only 30.5% were continuously retained in HIV care over nearly 9 years of follow-up and that active drug use was associated with lower care retention (Westergaard et al., 2013). The preponderance of research therefore indicates that substance use disorders represent a frequent impediment to timely HIV care linkage as well as sustained retention in care (Meyer et al., 2013).

Other mental health disorders such as depression could also challenge engagement and retention in HIV primary care, and further research on this front is needed. Among a sample of predominantly white men who have sex with men with HIV, controlled analysis showed that men who screened positive for clinical depression on the Patient Health Questionnaire were more than two times more likely to miss HIV medical appointments than patients who did not (Traeger et al., 2012). This suggests that aspects of depression may challenge HIV care engagement. A different study conducted with men of color who have sex with men with HIV (Magnus et al., 2010) paradoxically found that depressed individuals were more likely to be retained in HIV care. The explanation for this finding was unclear, but may relate to depressed individuals presenting with more acute illness, or possibly to the provision of youth-friendly, comprehensive health care services to the study sample. This finding underscores that the challenges mental disorders may pose for HIV care engagement should be situated in the context of other social and structural determinants. Determinants of care engagement and retention include not only individual factors, such as mental health and substance abuse, but also structural factors, such as clinic location, hours, and support services, as well as enabling factors, such as housing, income, and insurance (Christopoulos et al., 2011).

INTERVENTIONS TO IMPROVE HIV CARE ENGAGEMENT

Few proven interventions exist for facilitating linkage and retention in HIV primary care among people diagnosed with HIV, including persons with mental disorders. A CDC review of evidence-based interventions for care linkage and/or retention identified 10 programs (CDC, 2016). Eight of the nine programs target general groups of people diagnosed with HIV; these eight programs neither target individuals with mental disorders nor focus on mental health treatment. Individuals with mental disorders were present in the study samples that tested program impact. The eight evidence-based programs encompass many approaches, such as strengths-based case management to promote HIV care linkage (Gardner et al., 2005), expediting the initial primary care appointment following HIV diagnosis (Mugavero, 2008), encouraging HIV care retention through clinic-based posters and clinician communications (Gardner et al., 2013), using clinical decision systems that generate clinician alerts regarding suboptimal appointment attendance among patients (Robbins et al., 2012), and co-location of youth-focused services with HIV primary care (Davila et al., 2013).

Outpatient HIV clinics that employ the evidence-based linkage and retention strategies identified in the CDC review may facilitate care linkage and retention among individuals living with HIV and mental illness, although the presence of mental illness may also blunt the impact of these programs. The ARTAS program delivered time-limited strengths-based case management to facilitate linkage to HIV care among newly HIV-diagnosed individuals (Gardner et al., 2005). In the randomized trial that tested the ARTAS program, 18% of participants reported crack cocaine use in the last 30 days. Individuals recently using crack cocaine were significantly less likely than non-users to achieve the intervention outcome criterion of attending two HIV medical care appointments in each of two consecutive 6-month periods. This finding suggests that specialized programs that directly address substance abuse or other mental illness may be needed to facilitate HIV care linkage and retention.

Clinic-based buprenorphine treatment was the only HIV care engagement intervention identified in the CDC review that directly pertains to individuals with mental illness (Lucas et al., 2010). A randomized clinical trial assigned individuals meeting DSM criteria for opioid dependence to receive the opiate antagonist buprenorphine at either their primary HIV clinic or an off-site opioid treatment program. Individuals who received clinic-based buprenorphine treatment had significantly more visits with their HIV care clinician than individuals referred off-site, and they were also more likely to participant in drug treatment (Lucas et al., 2010). This study underscores how integration or co-location of drug treatment programs with HIV care may benefit HIV care retention for persons with drug dependency.

At least one HIV care linkage and retention program in the CDC review included screening and referrals for drug and mental health treatment as part of a multicomponent intervention. The STYLE intervention sought to engage young men of color, ages 16 to 24, who have sex with men who were either newly HIV diagnosed or had been out of HIV care for 6 months or more (Hightow-Weidman et al., 2011). The program comprised social marketing and outreach, an expedited HIV medical care appointment, and support groups and one-on-one counseling by a social worker, including substance use and mental health counseling. The study sample showed that 50% of participants were clinically depressed on the basis of CES-D scores, and 15% had attempted suicide. Youth participating in the STYLE program attended a significantly greater proportion of scheduled HIV medical visits over 24 months than youth served prior to introduction of the program (Hightow-Weidman et al., 2011). This project suggests that integration of mental health screening and treatment into HIV clinical care may help promote greater retention in care.

PSYCHIATRIC DETERMINANTS OF ART MEDICATION ADHERENCE

There are now four one-pill once-daily HIV treatment regimens available. The continued simplification and improvement of ART regimen tolerability have been important advances in improving adherence to ART medications. Decreases in the number of pills required, number of dosage times, food restrictions, storage restrictions, and medication side effects have all contributed to better adherence. While these advances lessen the adherence burden to patients, there are still many patients who, despite these improvements, have continued challenges with adherence.

Different classes of ART medications require different levels of adherence in order to maintain virological suppression (Kobin and Sheth, 2011). To avoid confusion and optimize outcomes, most clinicians continue to recommend that patients aim for adherence between 95% and 100% regardless of the specific regimen. According to this standard, a patient on a twice-daily ART regimen who missed one medication dose every 10 days would have 95% adherence. ART thus continues to demand a much higher level of adherence from patients than do treatments for most other medical conditions.

In general, persons living with HIV as well as psychiatric disorders and/or active substance use have lower levels of adherence than those of individuals without these problems (Tucker et al., 2003) and are more likely to demonstrate inconsistent patterns of antiretroviral use (Carrico et al., 2011). It has been well documented that untreated or undertreated psychiatric disorders are associated with decreased rates of medication adherence (Carrieri et al., 2003; Goodman and Fallot, 1998; Gordillo et al., 1999; Singh et al., 1996; Starace et al., 2002; van Servellen et al., 2002; Wagner et al., 2001). Nonetheless, many persons with HIV and psychiatric illness are capable of medication adherence, particularly when they are well engaged in psychiatric care. In a large prospective study of homeless HIV-infected persons in San Francisco ($n = 148$), Moss and colleagues (2004) assessed ART adherence using unannounced pill counts and electronic monitoring. This population had high rates of psychiatric illness (25% had been hospitalized for psychiatric treatment, 29% had current depressive symptomatology, 33% were injecting drugs, and 24% were using crack cocaine at the time of study recruitment). While rates of discontinuation of therapy were high in this cohort (31%), the level of ART adherence (74%) and HIV

viral suppression (54%) among individuals who remained on ART was not dissimilar to that in other populations.

Among persons with HIV and psychiatric illness, the individual characteristics shown to be most strongly and consistently predictive of degree of adherence are depression, active substance abuse, and neurocognitive functioning. In the next sections we review research findings on these individual determinants and discuss the literature on the impact of severe mental illness and posttraumatic stress disorder (PTSD) on ART adherence.

DEPRESSION

Most investigators examining the relationship between nonadherence to HIV therapy and psychiatric illness have focused on depression and have measured depression on continuous symptom scales rather than studying the diagnostic categories of depression. There is substantial evidence that depression, regardless of how measured, is an independent risk factor for patient nonadherence to medical regimens in general and to ART in particular (Ammassari et al., 2004; Carrieri et al., 2003; Gonzalez et al., 2004, 2011; Gordillo et al., 1999; Singh et al., 1996; Starace et al., 2002; Tuldrà et al., 1999; Uthman et al. 2014; van Servellen et al., 2002; Wagner et al., 2001). Furthermore, there is evidence that affective disorders are even more strongly associated with discontinuation of ART than other types of severe mental illness such as schizophrenia (Walkup et al., 2004).

SUBSTANCE USE DISORDERS

When assessing barriers to adherence, it is important to distinguish current substance use from past substance use. While *current* substance use is associated with incomplete adherence, a *history* of substance use is not. Studies have found a relationship between problem drinking and active illicit drug use and nonadherence among persons living with HIV (Cook et al., 2001; Gebo et al., 2003; Golin et al., 2002; Howard et al., 2002; Levine et al., 2005; Lucas et al., 2001; Tucker et al., 2003; Wagner et al., 2001). Active cocaine use was found to be the strongest predictor of nonadherence in a study using electronic monitors to quantify adherence (Arnsten et al., 2002). Malta and colleagues (2010) found that active drug users who receive ART therapy in structured settings, particularly those offering both addiction treatment, psychosocial support, and/or directly observed therapy, have better ART adherence than drug users who receive ART therapy in other settings.

NEUROCOGNITIVE IMPAIRMENT

Authors of a systematic review found 11 studies that examined the cross-sectional relationship between neurocognitive functioning and medication adherence among adults with HIV (Lovejoy and Suhr, 2009) by using standard neuropsychological tests and a direct measure of medication adherence. In 9 of the 11 studies, poorer neuropsychological functioning was associated with lower medication adherence scores. The neuropsychological domains found to be most highly related to adherence were executive functioning, memory, attention, processing speed, and fine motor control. Becker and colleagues (2011) examined the relationship between cognitive function and medication adherence longitudinally and found that individuals with HIV and cognitive decline, over time, showed a greater drop in ART adherence as compared to subjects with stable cognitive status.

SEVERE MENTAL ILLNESS

Wagner and colleagues (2003) assessed adherence with electronic monitoring in a small sample of 47 persons living with HIV with treated serious mental illness and found adherence rates comparable to those reported in general clinic and community samples (an average adherence rate of 66%; 40% of the sample achieved adherence levels of 90% or greater). In this sample of persons with HIV and severe mental illness, most of whom were engaged in psychiatric care, Wagner and colleagues (2004) found attendance to clinic appointments to be the one factor that most strongly predicted ART medication adherence in a multivariate analysis. Individuals with higher rates of attendance had better adherence as measured by an electronic monitoring device.

POSTTRAUMATIC STRESS DISORDER

The higher rate of PTSD among persons with HIV than in the general population has been well documented. In persons with HIV, PTSD may be caused by traumatic events that preceded infection with HIV and/or a traumatic response to the diagnosis of HIV. Clinical reports (Cohen et al., 2001; Ricart et al., 2002; Samuels et al., 2011) have elucidated the dynamic processes by which PTSD can be related to nonadherence to care and treatment in persons living with HIV; dissociative symptomatology may play a key role in mediating this relationship (Keuroghlian et al., 2011). Given that PTSD is highly comorbid with depression and substance use disorders, it has been difficult for researchers to determine the independent impact of PTSD on adherence (Pence, 2009; Sledjeski et al., 2005). Vranceanu and colleagues (2008) found that depression, but not PTSD, contributed unique variance to predicting poor adherence in a sample of persons living with HIV, suggesting that the impact of PTSD on adherence may be mediated primarily through depression. Whetten and colleagues (2013), however, found that both history of childhood traumatic events and current PTSD symptomatology negatively impacted adherence in a sample of patients in Tanzania and highlight the independent contribution of each factor to nonadherence. The literature supports the conclusion that trauma history and symptomatology frequently coexist with depression and substance use and contribute to patient nonadherence (Brezing et al., 2015).

BEHAVIORAL INTERVENTIONS TO IMPROVE MEDICATION ADHERENCE

In attempting interventions with persons with HIV who are nonadherent, it can be helpful to distinguish between intentional nonadherence and unintentional nonadherence. In the former, the patient does not intend to be adherent (e.g., a patient who decides not to take his medication on a night when he is going out because he wants to drink alcohol), while in the latter, the patient intends to be adherent but has difficulty succeeding at this (e.g., a patient who forgets the afternoon dose because she is distracted by her childcare responsibilities). There are numerous devices and tools available to help patients with medication adherence (information cards, pill organizers, alarms, pagers, medication diaries, visual medication schedules). These devices are particularly effective in improving adherence for patients who are nonadherent because of memory impairment (Andrade et al., 2005) and may be associated with modest improvements in the general population (Golin et al., 2002; Kalichman et al., 2005). For many other patients, however, these supports are not sufficient to achieve optimal levels of adherence.

ENGAGEMENT IN PSYCHIATRIC CARE IMPROVES ADHERENCE

Turner and colleagues (2001) found that persons living with HIV and psychiatric illness, in particular individuals who use illicit substances, are less likely to be prescribed ART than persons who do not have a psychiatric illness. Other studies have found that engagement in mental health treatment increases the likelihood that ART will be prescribed and mostly provides support for psychiatric and substance use treatment, improving adherence to ART in this population. Sambamoorthi and colleagues (2000) analyzed Medicaid data on patients with HIV who were receiving services in New Jersey between 1991 and 1996 and found that depressed patients treated with antidepressants were almost twice as likely to receive ART than patients not treated with antidepressants. Among a sample of homeless and marginally housed individuals living with HIV in San Francisco, depressed patients receiving antidepressant medications were significantly and substantially more likely to initiate ART, self-report high antiretroviral adherence, and achieve viral suppression than depressed patients not receiving antidepressants (Tsai et al., 2010).

In a sample of over 5,000 indigent drug users with HIV on ART, Turner and colleagues (2003) examined the relationship between medication adherence and mental health treatment (methadone clinic, psychiatric care, antidepressant medication). Only 22% of the patients in this sample had 95% adherence, based on pharmacy refill data over an 8-month period. The patients diagnosed with depression (34% of the women and 29% of the men) had better medication adherence than the patients not diagnosed with depression. This finding runs counter to the larger literature demonstrating a strong relationship between depression and poorer adherence, perhaps because individuals diagnosed with depression in this study were also much more likely to be in drug treatment or psychiatric care. Among the patients with a diagnosis of depression, patients who were in substance use treatment or psychiatric care (with or without antidepressants) had better adherence than individuals not under substance use or psychiatric care. This study found that psychiatric care had the most benefit on adherence for women, whereas substance use treatment had the most benefit on adherence for men.

Palepu and colleagues (2004) conducted a prospective study of 349 persons with HIV who had a history of alcohol problems. They found that persons who engaged in substance use treatment were more likely to be placed on ART than those who did not, although they did not find that substance use treatment conferred any benefit on adherence.

Several investigators have found a relationship between depression and level of disease progression (Burack et al., 1993; Ickovics et al., 2001; Page-Shafer et al., 1996). Cook and colleagues (2004) examined the relationship between depressive symptoms, treatment for depression, and mortality in a longitudinal cohort of over 2,000 women living with HIV. The mortality rate among women with chronic depression was double that for women with no or intermittent depression. While no data are reported on the relationship between mental health services and adherence, women who received mental health services were significantly less likely to die from AIDS-related causes during the study period. In a subsequent report on this cohort, Cook and colleagues (2006) examined the temporal relationship between use of antidepressants and mental health therapy, individually and in combination, on subsequent use of ART in the subset of women with depression. They found that women who received mental health therapy alone or the combination of mental health therapy and antidepressants had greater use of ART than the depressed women who received no treatment. The use of antidepressants alone, however, did not increase the level of ART use over that with no treatment for depression.

In a retrospective chart review study, Himelhoch and colleagues (2004) found that in a clinic setting with on-site psychiatric care, patients with a psychiatric disorder were 37% more likely to receive ART, were 2.5 times more likely to remain on ART for at least 6 months, and had a 40% reduction in mortality compared to patients who did not have a psychiatric disorder. These subjects were receiving intensive psychiatric services co-located with their HIV primary care. While adherence was not assessed in this study, one plausible explanation for this finding is that the intensity of the psychiatric services and integration of psychiatric and medical care resulted in improved adherence among the patients with psychiatric illness.

Sin and DiMatteo (2014) conducted a meta-analysis of 29 studies of over 12,000 persons living with HIV/AIDS and found that the appropriate treatment of depression and psychological distress improved antiretroviral adherence dramatically. The odds ratio of a person with depression adhering to ART treatment was 83% better if he or she was treated for depression.

DIFFERENTIAL ADHERENCE

Three studies have found a significant correlation between ART adherence and adherence to psychotropic medication among persons with HIV with serious mental illness (Wagner et al., 2003) and depression (Cruess et al., 2012; Horberg et al., 2008). As would be expected, many of the determinants of ART adherence are also determinants of adherence to psychotropic medication in the same population. There are, however, differences in illness perceptions and medication beliefs that distinguish adherence to psychotropic medication from adherence to ART. Most persons living with HIV on ART understand that HIV is a chronic illness for which they will likely always remain on medication. The positive outcomes of the medication (increased CD4+ cell count and decreased HIV viral load) are often motivators to continue taking ART medication. The fear of death from HIV can serve to motivate patients to tolerate uncomfortable side effects of ART medication. In contrast, effective psychotropic treatment removes the symptoms (e.g., of depression or psychosis) that the medication is targeting. This can result in patients perceiving that they no longer have a need for medication and consequently have poor adherence to medication or discontinue taking it all together. In addition, because of the perceived non-life-threatening nature of the psychiatric illness being treated, patients weigh the burden of side effects of psychotropic medication relative to the benefits in a different manner than weighing the costs of ART side effects. Prospective studies of patient adherence to concomitant psychotropic medication and ART are needed to elucidate the potential interrelated yet independent adherence patterns for psychotropic agents and ART.

Little research has been conducted on differential adherence to medication for comorbid medical conditions in HIV-positive persons being treated with ART. Weiss and colleagues (2013) electronically monitored adherence to antiretroviral and antihypertensive medications in a sample of 102 patients taking both classes of medications. While there were differences in illness perceptions and medication beliefs between the two conditions, the level of adherence to each class of medication did not differ significantly. Konstantinidis et al. (2014) had similar findings in a study of patients being treated for both HIV and chronic kidney disease.

ART ADHERENCE INTERVENTIONS

Many behavioral interventions have been developed to increase the level of HIV adherence by addressing adherence barriers and increasing motivation and self-efficacy. For individuals who are coping with a mental health disorder, it is also necessary to treat the mental illness in order to maximize the chances of the individual benefitting from an adherence intervention.

In a meta-analysis of HIV adherence interventions, Simoni and colleagues (2006) identified 19 randomized, controlled clinical trials published from 1999 to 2005 that met the following three criteria: (1) described a behavioral intervention targeting individuals at least 18 years of age, (2) randomly assigned participants to intervention and control arms, and (3) provided outcome data on adherence or HIV viral load. Most of these 19 studies used samples drawn from HIV clinic settings that included patients both with and without psychiatric illness. Five of the studies excluded individuals with current psychiatric illness. Only 3 of the 19 studies in the meta-analysis chose participants based on presence of current psychiatric illness, specifically substance use.

In the first of these three studies, done by Margolin and colleagues (2003), 90 methadone-maintained injection drug users were recruited and randomly assigned, half of them to twice-weekly manual-guided group therapy sessions for 6 months in addition to the enhanced methadone maintenance program that the other half of the sample received. The group therapy program included adherence among other topics related to living with HIV. The 6-month group therapy intervention was found to have a significant impact on improving adherence relative to the control condition. The validity of the adherence data collected by structured interview was corroborated by corresponding changes in viral load.

In the second of these three studies, Rotheram-Borus and colleagues (2004) recruited 175 substance-using young people (ages 16–29) and randomly assigned them to a three-module intervention totaling 18 sessions over 15 months delivered by telephone, in person, or a delayed-intervention condition. Similar to the Margolin intervention, adherence was one part of a broader intervention focused on physical, sexual, and emotional health. This study did not find that the intervention had any effect on ART use or ART adherence as measured by self-report.

In the third of these three studies, Samet and colleagues (2005) recruited 151 patients with a history of alcohol abuse and randomly assigned them to a four-session adherence intervention with a nurse or to usual medical care. The adherence intervention did not have an effect on self-reported adherence behavior (corroborated by use of electronic monitoring).

One possible explanation for Margolin's intervention having an effect on adherence while Rotheram-Borus' and Samet's interventions did not is the greater intensity of Margolin's intervention than that of the other two (52 intervention sessions, as compared to 18 and 4). In contrast to the finding that brief adherence interventions are effective in general populations, it may be that for persons with psychiatric illness, interventions of greater length are needed in order to be effective.

More recently, the CDC conducted a review of evidence-based interventions that promote ART medication adherence and identified 10 rigorously evaluated programs (Charania et al., 2014; see also http://www.cdc.gov/hiv/prevention/research/compendium/lrc/index.html). Two of the 10 programs targeted drug users and both employed directly observed therapy (DOT). DOT has been shown to be an effective intervention to achieve optimal levels of adherence among persons living with HIV and psychiatric illness in a residential care facility (de Socio et al., 2004). Mitty and colleagues (2005) investigated the effectiveness of a community-based, modified directly observed therapy (MDOT) program for persons with HIV with high rates of substance use (96% lifetime; 80% last 3 months). Although less than half of the participants remained in the study for 6 months, the participants who did remain and were still receiving MDOT had significant reductions in viral load, whereas individuals not still receiving MDOT showed little or no change. This study demonstrates the difficulties involved in applying a DOT approach in a real-world setting even with significant resources.

The other DOT study identified in the CDC review was from Altice and colleagues (2007), who investigated the efficacy of a directly administered antiretroviral therapy (DAART) program for individuals with HIV currently using illicit drugs, in a prospective, randomized, controlled trial. The DAART intervention was integrated into services offered by an existing mobile syringe-exchange program. Patients who received DAART, compared with patients who self-administer their ART, did not self-report better adherence, but they did have better immunological and virological outcomes at the end of the 6-month intervention period. In contrast, Lucas and colleagues (2013) found no benefit to DAART as compared to self-administered therapy in terms of adherence or immunological or virological outcomes, in a randomized clinical trial of 107 persons with HIV who were attending opioid treatment programs.

Although not included in the prior reviews of adherence interventions, several evidence-based adherence programs related to mental disorders merit consideration. Cognitive-behavioral therapy for adherence and depression (CBT-AD) is an intervention developed specifically for adults with HIV and depression (Newcomb et al., 2015). It is a 12-session individual intervention delivered by a psychotherapist. It has been shown to decrease depression and improve adherence in injection drug users with HIV infection (Safren et al., 2012), racially diverse adults living with HIV in an urban setting (Safren et al., 2009), and HIV-infected Mexican Americans (Simoni et al., 2013). The majority of the patients in these studies had additional psychiatric comorbidities, including anxiety, PTSD, and substance use.

The Intervention Cascade is an integrated ART adherence intervention for persons with HIV and with severe mental illness (Blank and Eisenberg, 2013). It is a nurse-administered community-based intervention that integrates care across inpatient and community clinicians and provides a set of stepped adherence supports depending on the observed degree of ART adherence. Participants in the intervention were more likely to be on ART and to achieve an undetectable viral load if they began with a detectable viral load than individuals in the control group (Blank et al., 2011).

IMPLICATIONS OF RESEARCH FINDINGS FOR CLINICAL PRACTICE

Patient adherence occurs in the context of a relationship with medical clinicians and the medical setting. Studies have consistently found that clinician assessment of adherence is poor (Bangsberg, Hecht, et al., 2001; Gross et al., 2002; Miller et al., 2002). Generally, clinicians tend to overestimate medication adherence and are more accurate in their diagnosis of incomplete than complete adherence. Overestimation can in part be explained by patient awareness that nonadherence will be met with disappointment at best and possibly disapproval or judgment by their clinicians. Overestimation of adherence can also simply be due to the inherent difficulty in recalling something that had been forgotten. Regardless of the reason for nonadherence, patients often feel a sense of shame and failure when it comes time to see their clinician and report this nonadherence. Some patients avoid this feared confrontation by failing to attend their appointment or attending but lying about or distorting their actual adherence behavior.

Even if patients are honest with their clinician about their failure to adhere, they often leave the encounter feeling blamed for this failure. While a great deal of research has been conducted that attempts to change adherence by changing patient behavior, and studies have documented the impact of the quality of the physician–patient relationship on adherence to ART (Ingersoll and Heckman, 2005; Lewis et al., 2006; Schneider et al., 2004), there has been little research on interventions to change clinician behavior and clinic characteristics to improve the adherence of patients living with HIV. Wilson and colleagues (2007) conducted a randomized intervention trial targeting physician communication about adherence with patients living with HIV. While the intervention did increase adherence-related dialogue between physicians and patients, it did not improve medication adherence. There is an inherent conflict that must be taken into account and overcome when clinicians discuss nonadherent behavior with patients: Whereas clinicians are unambivalent about wanting their patients to adhere to treatment and are readily able to prioritize adherence above all other issues, patients are often struggling with significant barriers and competing priorities, such as depression, substance use, memory problems, low self-esteem, unresolved trauma, pain, fatigue, nausea, discrimination, poverty, child and family care, abuse, housing problems, difficulty understanding healthcare instructions and the healthcare system, insurance problems, and treatment fatigue.

Psychiatrists seeing patients at risk for HIV should inquire about and recommend HIV testing, as well as PrEP when indicated. Some patients with known HIV infection and psychiatric illness are only able to eventually engage in medical care for HIV through initial engagement in psychiatric care and treatment. In this case, the psychiatrist might have to go beyond usual practice by, for example, ordering CD4+ and HIV viral load tests to document and help the patient understand the need for HIV medical treatment. Conversely, many patients engaged in primary HIV medical care may have undiagnosed and untreated mental illness, particularly depression. Clinicians can easily screen for depression by asking two simple questions (Whooley and Simon, 2000). HIV primary care clinicians should screen for depression in their practice and may prescribe psychotropic medication to patients with uncomplicated depression or other psychiatric illness. Referral to a psychiatrist is usually made on the basis of availability of resources, the patient's openness to being referred, the complexity and severity of the psychiatric illness, and the need for psychotherapy.

Untreated substance use and other psychiatric disorders can present a barrier to successful patient engagement at every step of the HIV care cascade. Alternately, the successful engagement of patients with HIV and substance use and/or psychiatric disorders in mental health care can provide an opportunity to also engage them in HIV care. This process can occur most efficiently when HIV, substance use, and other psychiatric services are co-located and integrated. Research evidence indicates that the treatment of persons living with

HIV and psychiatric illness should include interventions that target both the mental health condition as well as adherence behaviors (Thompson et al., 2012). Once patients are successfully engaged in both HIV and psychiatric care, communication and coordination of care between the HIV clinician and psychiatrist are essential for achieving optimal adherence, retention in care, and positive outcomes of psychiatric and medical treatment.

ACKNOWLEDGMENT

This work was supported by Grant MH099930 from the National Institutes of Health.

REFERENCES

Altice FL, Maru DS, Bruce RD, Springer SA, Friedland GH (2007). Superiority of directly administered antiretroviral therapy over self-administered therapy among HIV-infected drug users: a prospective, randomized, controlled trial. *Clin Infect Dis* 45(6):770–778.

Amico KR, Stirratt MJ (2014). Adherence to preexposure prophylaxis: current, emerging, and anticipated bases of evidence. *Clin Infect Dis* 59(Suppl 1):S55–S60.

Ammassari A, Antinori A, Aloisi MS, et al. (2004). Depressive symptoms, neurocognitive impairment, and adherence to highly active antiretroviral therapy among HIV-infected persons. *Psychosomatics* 45(5):394–402.

Andrade AS, McGruder HF, Wu AW, et al. (2005). A programmable prompting device improves adherence to highly active antiretroviral therapy in HIV-infected subjects with memory impairment. *Clin Infect Dis* 41(6):875–882.

Arnsten JH, Demas PA, Grant RW, Gourevitch MN, Farzadegan H, Howard AA, Schoenbaum EE (2002). Impact of active drug use on antiretroviral therapy adherence and viral suppression in HIV-infected drug users. *J Gen Intern Med* 17(5):377–381.

Baeten JM, Grant R (2013). Use of antiretrovirals for HIV prevention: what do we know and what don't we know? *Curr HIV/AIDS Rep* 10(2):142–151.

Bangsberg DR, Charlebois ED, Grant RM, et al. (2003). High levels of adherence do not prevent accumulation of HIV drug resistance mutations. *AIDS* 17(13):1925–1932.

Bangsberg DR, Hecht FM, Charlebois ED, et al. (2000). Adherence to protease inhibitors, HIV-1 viral load, and development of drug resistance in an indigent population. *AIDS* 14(4):357–366.

Bangsberg DR, Hecht FM, Clague H, Charlebois ED, Ciccarone D, Chesney M, Moss A (2001). Provider assessment of adherence to HIV antiretroviral therapy. *J Acquir Immune Defic Syndr* 26(5):435–442.

Bangsberg DR, Perry S, Charlebois ED, Clark RA, Roberston M, Zolopa AR, Moss A (2001). Non-adherence to highly active antiretroviral therapy predicts progression to AIDS. *AIDS* 15(9):1181–1183.

Becker BW, Thames AD, Woo E, Castellon SA, Hinkin CH (2011). Longitudinal change in cognitive function and medication adherence in HIV-infected adults. *AIDS Behav* 15(8):1888–1894.

Berg M, Safren S, Mimiaga M, Grasso C, Boswell S, Mayer K (2005). Nonadherence to medical appointments is associated with increased plasma HIV RNA and decreased CD4 cell counts in a community-based HIV primary care clinic. *AIDS Care* 17(7):902–907.

Bing EG, Burnam MA, Longshore D, et al. (2001). Psychiatric disorders and drug use among human immunodeficiency virus–infected adults in the united states. *Arch Gen Psychiatry* 58(8):721–728.

Blank MB, Eisenberg MM (2013). Tailored treatment for HIV+ persons with mental illness: The intervention cascade. *J Acquir Immune Defic Syndr* 63(Suppl 1):S44–S48.

Blank MB, Hanrahan NP, Fishbein M, et al. (2011). A randomized trial of a nursing intervention for HIV disease management among persons with serious mental illness. *Psychiatr Serv* 62(11):1318–1324.

Bouhnik AD, Chesney M, Carrieri P, et al.; MANIF 2000 Study Group (2002). Nonadherence among HIV-infected injecting drug users: the impact of social instability. *J Acquir Immune Defic Syndr* 31(Suppl 3):S149–S153.

Bradley H, Hall HI, Wolitski RJ, et al. (2014). Vital signs: HIV diagnosis, care, and treatment among persons living with HIV—United States, 2011. *MMWR Morb Mortal Wkly Rep* 63:1113–1117.

Brezing C, Ferrara M, Freudenreich O (2015). The syndemic illness of HIV and trauma: implications for a trauma-informed model of care. *Psychosomatics* 56(2):107–118.

Burack JH, Barrett DC, Stall RD, Chesney MA, Ekstrand ML, Coates TJ (1993). Depressive symptoms and CD4 lymphocyte decline among HIV-infected men. *JAMA* 270(21):2568–2573.

Carrico AW, Riley ED, Johnson MO, et al. (2011). Psychiatric risk factors for HIV disease progression: The role of inconsistent patterns of antiretroviral therapy utilization. *J Acquir Immune Defic Syndr* 56(2):146–150.

Carrieri M, Chesney M, Spire B, Loundou A, Sobel A, Lepeu G, Moatti J (2003). Failure to maintain adherence to HAART in a cohort of French HIV-positive injecting drug users. *Int J Behav Med* 10(1):1–14.

Centers for Disease Control and Prevention (2016). Compendium of evidence-based interventions and best practices for HIV prevention. https://www.cdc.gov/hiv/research/interventionresearch/compendium/index.html. Accessed February 3, 2017.

Charania MR, Marshall KJ, Lyles CM, et al., for the HIV/AIDS Prevention Research Synthesis (PRS) Team (2014). Identification of evidence-based interventions for promoting HIV medication adherence: findings from a systematic review of U.S.-based studies, 1996–2011. *AIDS Behav* 18(4):646–660.

Christopoulos KA, Das M, Colfax GN (2011). Linkage and retention in HIV care among men who have sex with men in the united states. *Clin Infect Dis* 52(Suppl 2):S214–S222.

Cohen MA, Alfonso CA, Hoffman RG, Milau V, Carrera G (2001). The impact of PTSD on treatment adherence in persons with HIV infection. *Gen Hosp Psychiatry* 23(5):294–296.

Cook J, Grey D, Burke J, et al. (2004). Depressive symptoms and AIDS-related mortality among a multisite cohort of HIV-positive women. *Am J Public Health* 94(7):1133–1140.

Cook J, Grey D, Burke-Miller J, et al. (2006). Effects of treated and untreated depressive symptoms on highly active antiretroviral therapy use in a US multi-site cohort of HIV-positive women. *AIDS Care* 18(2):93–100.

Cook RL, Sereika SM, Hunt SC, Woodward WC, Erlen JA, Conigliaro J (2001). Problem drinking and medication adherence among persons with HIV infection. *J Gen Intern Med* 16(2):83–88.

Cruess DG, Kalichman SC, Amaral C, Swetzes C, Cherry C, Kalichman MO (2012). Benefits of adherence to psychotropic medications on depressive symptoms and antiretroviral medication adherence among men and women living with HIV/AIDS. *Ann Behav Med* 43(2):189–197.

Davila JA, Miertschin N, Sansgiry S, Schwarzwald H, Henley C, Giordano TP (2013). Centralization of HIV services in HIV-positive African-American and Hispanic youth improves retention in care. *AIDS Care* 25(2):202–206.

de Socio GV, Fanelli L, Longo A, Stagni G (2004). Adherence to antiretroviral therapy in HIV patients with psychiatric comorbidity. *J Acquir Immune Defic Syndr* 36(5):1109–1110.

Gardner EM, Daniloff E, Thrun MW, et al. (2013). Initial linkage and subsequent retention in HIV care for a newly diagnosed HIV-infected cohort in Denver, Colorado. *J Int Assoc Providers AIDS Care* 12(6):384–390.

Gardner EM, McLees MP, Steiner JF, Del Rio C, Burman WJ (2011). The spectrum of engagement in HIV care and its relevance to test-and-treat strategies for prevention of HIV infection. *Clin Infect Dis* 52(6):793–800.

Gardner LI, Metsch LR, Anderson-Mahoney P, et al. (2005). Efficacy of a brief case management intervention to link recently diagnosed HIV-infected persons to care. *AIDS* 19(4):423–431.

Gebo KA, Keruly J, Moore RD (2003). Association of social stress, illicit drug use, and health beliefs with nonadherence to antiretroviral therapy. *J Gen Intern Med* 18(2):104–111.

Giordano TP, Gifford AL, White AC,Jr, et al. (2007). Retention in care: a challenge to survival with HIV infection. *Clin Infect Dis* 44(11):1493–1499.

Giordano TP, Suarez-Almazor ME, Grimes RM (2005). The population effectiveness of highly active antiretroviral therapy: are good drugs good enough? *Curr HIV/AIDS Rep* 2(4):177–183.

Giordano TP, Visnegarwala F, White Jr AC, Troisi CL, Frankowski RF, Hartman CM, Grimes RM (2005). Patients referred to an urban HIV clinic frequently fail to establish care: factors predicting failure. *AIDS Care* 17(6):773–783.

Golin CE, Liu H, Hays RD, et al. (2002). A prospective study of predictors of adherence to combination antiretroviral medication. *J Gen Intern Med* 17(10):756–765.

Gonzalez JS, Batchelder AW, Psaros C, Safren SA (2011). Depression and HIV/AIDS treatment nonadherence: a review and meta-analysis. *J Acquir Immune Defic Syndr* 58(2):181–187.

Gonzalez A, Mimiaga M,J, Israel J, Bedoya CA, Safren SA (2013). Substance use predictors of poor medication adherence: the role of substance use coping among HIV-infected patients in opioid dependence treatment. *AIDS Behav* 17(1):168–173.

Gonzalez JS, Penedo FJ, Antoni MH, et al. (2004). Social support, positive states of mind, and HIV treatment adherence in men and women living with HIV/AIDS. *Health Psychol* 23(4):413.

Goodman LA, Fallot RD (1998). HIV risk-behavior in poor urban women with serious mental disorders: association with childhood physical and sexual abuse. *Am J Orthopsychiatry* 68(1):73.

Gordillo V, del Amo J, Soriano V, González-Lahoz J (1999). Sociodemographic and psychological variables influencing adherence to antiretroviral therapy. *AIDS* 13(13):1763–1769.

Grant R, Anderson PL, McMahan V, et al. (2014). Uptake of pre-exposure prophylaxis, sexual practices, and HIV incidence in men and trangender women who have sex with men: a cohort study. *Lancet Infect Dis* 14:820–829.

Gross R, Bilker WB, Friedman HM, Coyne JC, Strom BL (2002). Provider inaccuracy in assessing adherence and outcomes with newly initiated antiretroviral therapy. *AIDS* 16(13):1835–1837.

Haberer JE, Baeten JM, Campbell J, et al. (2013). Adherence to antiretroviral prophylaxis for HIV prevention: a substudy cohort within a clinical trial of serodiscordant couples in East Africa. *PLOS Med* 10:e1001511.

Hightow-Weidman LB, Fowler B, Kibe J, et al. (2011). HealthMpowerment.org: development of a theory-based HIV/STI website for young black MSM. *AIDS Educ Prev* 23:1–12.

Himelhoch S, Moore RD, Treisman G, Gebo KA (2004). Does the presence of a current psychiatric disorder in AIDS patients affect the initiation of antiretroviral treatment and duration of therapy? *J Acquir Immune Defic Syndr* 37(4):1457–1463.

Horberg MA, Silverberg MJ, Hurley LB, et al. (2008). Effects of depression and selective serotonin reuptake inhibitor use on adherence to highly active antiretroviral therapy and on clinical outcomes in HIV-infected patients. *J Acquir Immune Defic Syndr* (1999) 47(3):384–390.

Howard AA, Arnsten JH, Lo Y, et al.; HER Study Group (2002). A prospective study of adherence and viral load in a large multi-center cohort of HIV-infected women. *AIDS* 16(16):2175–2182.

Ickovics JR, Hamburger ME, Vlahov D, et al.; HIV Epidemiology Research Study Group (2001). Mortality, CD4 cell count decline, and depressive symptoms among HIV-seropositive women: longitudinal analysis from the HIV Epidemiology Research Study. *JAMA* 285(11):1466–1474.

Ingersoll KS, Heckman CJ (2005). Patient–clinician relationships and treatment system effects on HIV medication adherence. *AIDS Behav* 9(1):89–101.

Kalichman SC, Cain D, Cherry C, Kalichman M, Pope H (2005). Pillboxes and antiretroviral adherence: Prevalence of use, perceived benefits, and implications for electronic medication monitoring devices. *AIDS Patient Care STDs* 19(12):833–839.

Katz IT, Ryu AE, Onuegbu AG, Psaros C, Weiser SD, Bangsberg DR, Tsai AC (2013). Impact of HIV-related stigma on treatment adherence: systematic review and meta-synthesis. *J Int AIDS Soc* 16(3Suppl 2):18640.

Keuroghlian AS, Kamen CS, Neri E, Lee S, Liu R, Gore-Felton C (2011). Trauma, dissociation, and antiretroviral adherence among persons living with HIV/AIDS. *J Psychiatr Research* 45(7):942–948.

Kidder DP, Wolitski RJ, Campsmith ML, Nakamura GV (2007). Health status, health care use, medication use, and medication adherence among homeless and housed people living with HIV/AIDS. *Am J Public Health* 97:2238–2245.

Kobin AB, Sheth NU (2011). Levels of adherence required for virologic suppression among newer antiretroviral medications. *Ann Pharmacother* 45(3):372–379.

Koenig LJ, Lyles C, Smith DK (2013). Adherence to antiretoviral medications for HIV pre-exposure prophylaxis: lessons learned from trials and treatment studies. *Am J Prev Med* 44:S91–S98.

Konstantinidis I, Weiss J, Wyatt C (2014). Illness perceptions, medication beliefs and adherence in CKD patients with comorbid HIV. Poster presentation at ASN Kidney Week 2014 annual meeting, Philadelphia, Pennsylvania.

Langebeek N, Gisolf EH, Reiss P, et al. (2014). Predictors and correlates of adherence to combination antiretroviral therapy (cART) for chronic HIV infection: a meta-analysis. *BMC Med* 12(1):142.

Levine AJ, Hinkin CH, Castellon SA, et al. (2005). Variations in patterns of highly active antiretroviral therapy (HAART) adherence. *AIDS Behav* 9(3):355–362.

Lewis M, Colbert A, Erlen J, Meyers M (2006). A qualitative study of persons who are 100% adherent to antiretroviral therapy. *AIDS Care* 18(2):140–148.

Lima VD, Harrigan R, Bangsberg DR, Hogg RS, Gross R, Yip B, Montaner JS (2009). The combined effect of modern highly active antiretroviral therapy regimens and adherence on mortality over time. *J Acquir Immune Defic Syndr* 50(5):529–536.

Liu A, Colfax G, Cohen S, et al. (2012). The spectrum of engagement in HIV prevention: proposal for a PrEP cascade. Presentation at International Conference on HIV Treatment and Prevention, Abstract 80040, Miami.

Liu A, Defechereux P, McMahan V, et al., for the IPrEx Study Team (2011). Depression among men who have sex with men (MSM) at risk for HIV infection in the Global IPrEx Study. Presentation at IAS 2011 Conference, Abstract TULBPE024, Rome.

Lopez EJ, Jones DL, Villar-Loubet OM, Arheart KL, Weiss SM (2010). Violence, coping, and consistent medication adherence in HIV-positive couples. *AIDS Educ Prev* 22(1):61–68.

Lovejoy TI, Suhr JA (2009). The relationship between neuropsychological functioning and HAART adherence in HIV-positive adults: a systematic review. *J Behav Med* 32(5):389–405.

Low-Beer S, Yip B, O'Shaughnessy MV, Hogg RS, Montaner JS (2000). Adherence to triple therapy and viral load response. *J Acquir Immune Defic Syndr* 23(4):360–361.

Lucas GM, Chaudhry A, Hsu J, et al. (2010). Clinic-based treatment of opioid-dependent HIV-infected patients versus referral to an opioid treatment program—a randomized trial. *Ann Intern Med* 152(11):704–711.

Lucas GM, Cheever LW, Chaisson RE, Moore RD (2001). Detrimental effects of continued illicit drug use on the treatment of HIV-1 infection. *J Acquir Immune Defic Syndr* 27(3):251–259.

Lucas GM, Mullen BA, Galai N, et al. (2013). Directly administered antiretroviral therapy for HIV-infected individuals in opioid treatment programs: results from a randomized clinical trial. *PloS ONE* 8(7):e68286.

Magnus M, Jones K, Phillips G, 2nd, et al.; YMSM of Color Special Projects of National Significance Initiative Study Group (2010). Characteristics associated with retention among African American and Latino adolescent HIV-positive men: results from the outreach, care, and prevention to engage HIV-seropositive young MSM of color special project of national significance initiative. *J Acquir Immune Defic Syndr* (1999) 53(4):529–536.

Malta M, Magnanini MM, Strathdee SA, Bastos FI (2010). Adherence to antiretroviral therapy among HIV-infected drug users: a meta-analysis. *AIDS Behav* 14(4):731–747.

Margolin A, Avants SK, Warburton LA, Hawkins KA, Shi J (2003). A randomized clinical trial of a manual-guided risk reduction intervention for HIV-positive injection drug users. *Health Psychol* 22(2):223.

Marks G, Gardner LI, Craw J, Crepaz N (2010). Entry and retention in medical care among HIV-diagnosed persons: a meta-analysis. *AIDS (London, England)* 24(17):2665–2678.

Meyer JP, Althoff AL, Altice FL (2013). Optimizing care for HIV-infected people who use drugs: evidence-based approaches to overcoming healthcare disparities. *Clin Infect Dis* 57(9):1309–1317.

Miller LG, Liu H, Hays RD, et al. (2002). How well do clinicians estimate patients' adherence to combination antiretroviral therapy? *J Gen Intern Med* 17(1):1–11.

Mitty JA, Macalino GE, Bazerman LB, Loewenthal HG, Hogan JW, MacLeod CJ, Flanigan TP (2005). The use of community-based modified directly observed therapy for the treatment of HIV-infected persons. *J Acquir Immune Defic Syndr* 39(5):545–550.

Moss AR, Hahn JA, Perry S, Charlebois ED, Guzman D, Clark RA, Bangsberg DR (2004). Adherence to highly active antiretroviral therapy in the homeless population in San Francisco: a prospective study. *Clin Infect Dis* 39(8):1190–1198.

Mugavero MJ (2008). Improving engagement in HIV care: what can we do? *Top HIV Med* 16(5):156–161.

Mugavero MJ, Lin HY, Allison JJ, et al. (2009a). Racial disparities in HIV virologic failure: do missed visits matter? *J Acquir Immune Defic Syndr* (1999) 50(1):100–108.

Mugavero MJ, Lin HY, Willig JH, et al. (2009b). Missed visits and mortality among patients establishing initial outpatient HIV treatment. *Clin Infect Dis* 48(2):248–256.

Mugavero MJ, Westfall AO, Cole SR, et al. (2014). Beyond core indicators of retention in HIV care: missed clinic visits are independently associated with all-cause mortality. *Clin Infect Dis* 59(10):1471–1479.

Nakagawa F, Lodwick RK, Smith CJ, et al. (2012). Projected life expectancy of people with HIV according to timing of diagnosis. *AIDS (London, England)* 26(3):335–343.

Newcomb ME, Bedoya CA, Blashill AJ, Lerner JA, O'Cleirigh C, Pinkston MM, Safren SA (2015). Description and demonstration of cognitive behavioral therapy to enhance antiretroviral therapy adherence and treat depression in HIV-infected adults. *Cogn Behav Pract* 22(4):430–438.

Page-Shafer K, Delorenze GN, Satariano WA, Winkelstein Jr, W (1996). Comorbidity and survival in HIV-infected men in the San Francisco Men's Health Survey. *Ann Epidemiol* 6(5):420–430.

Palepu A, Horton NJ, Tibbetts N, Meli S, Samet JH (2004). Uptake and adherence to highly active antiretroviral therapy among HIV-infected people with alcohol and other substance use problems: the impact of substance abuse treatment. *Addiction* 99(3):361–368.

Palmer NB, Salcedo J, Miller AL, Winiarski M, Arno P (2003). Psychiatric and social barriers to HIV medication adherence in a triply diagnosed methadone population. *AIDS Patient Care STDs* 17(12):635–644.

Paterson DL, Swindells S, Mohr J, et al. (2000). Adherence to protease inhibitor therapy and outcomes in patients with HIV infection. *Ann Intern Med* 133(1):21–30.

Pence BW (2009). The impact of mental health and traumatic life experiences on antiretroviral treatment outcomes for people living with HIV/AIDS. *J Antimicrob Chemother* 63(4):636–640.

Pines HA, Gorbach PM, Weiss RE, et al. (2014). Sexual risk trajectories among MSM in the United States: implications for pre-exposure prophylaxis delivery. *J Acquir Immune Defic Syndr* 65:579–586.

Pinoges L, Schramm B, Poulet E, Balkan S, Szumilin E, Ferreyra C, Pujades-Rodríguez M (2015). Risk factors and mortality associated with resistance to first line antiretroviral therapy: multicentric cross-sectional and longitudinal analyses. *J Acquir Immune Defici Syndr* 68(5):527–535.

Ricart F, Cohen MA, Alfonso CA, Hoffman RG, Quiñones N, Cohen A, Indyk D (2002). Understanding the psychodynamics of non-adherence to medical treatment in persons with HIV infection. *Gen Hosp Psychiatry* 24(3):176–180.

Riley ED, Bangsberg DR, Guzman D, Perry S, Moss AR (2005). Antiretroviral therapy, hepatitis C virus, and AIDS mortality among San Francisco's homeless and marginally housed. *J Acquir Immune Defic Syndr* 38(2):191–195.

Robbins GK, Lester W, Johnson KL, et al. (2012). Efficacy of a clinical decision-support system in an HIV practice: a randomized trial. *Ann Intern Med* 157(11):757–766.

Rotheram-Borus MJ, Swendeman D, Comulada WS, Weiss RE, Lee M, Lightfoot M (2004). Prevention for substance-using HIV-positive young people: telephone and in-person delivery. *J Acquir Immune Defic Syndr* 37(Suppl 2):S68–S77.

Sabin CA, Smith CJ, Youle M, et al. (2006). Deaths in the era of HAART: contribution of late presentation, treatment exposure, resistance and abnormal laboratory markers. *AIDS* 20(1):67–71.

Safren SA, O'Cleirigh CM, Bullis JR, Otto MW, Stein MD, Pollack MH (2012). Cognitive behavioral therapy for adherence and depression (CBT-AD) in HIV-infected injection drug users: a randomized controlled trial. *J Consult Clin Psychol* 80(3):404.

Safren SA, O'Cleirigh C, Tan JY, Raminani SR, Reilly LC, Otto MW, Mayer KH (2009). A randomized controlled trial of cognitive behavioral therapy for adherence and depression (CBT-AD) in HIV-infected individuals. *Health Psychol* 28(1):1.

Sambamoorthi U, Walkup J, Olfson M, Crystal S (2000). Antidepressant treatment and health services utilization among HIV-infected medicaid patients diagnosed with depression. *J Gen Intern Med* 15(5):311–320.

Samet JH, Horton NJ, Meli S, Dukes K, Tripps T, Sullivan L, Freedberg KA (2005). A randomized controlled trial to enhance antiretroviral therapy adherence in patients with a history of alcohol problems. *Antiviral Ther* 10(1):83–93.

Samuels E, Khalife S, Alfonso CA, Alvarez R, Cohen MA (2011). Early childhood trauma, posttraumatic stress disorder, and non-adherence in persons with AIDS: a psychodynamic perspective. *J Am Acad Psychoanal Dyn Psychiatry* 39(4):633–650.

Schneider J, Kaplan SH, Greenfield S, Li W, Wilson IB (2004). Better physician–patient relationships are associated with higher reported adherence to antiretroviral therapy in patients with HIV infection. *J Gen Intern Med* 19(11):1096–1103.

Simoni JM, Pearson CR, Pantalone DW, Marks G, Crepaz N (2006). Efficacy of interventions in improving highly active antiretroviral therapy adherence and HIV-1 RNA viral load. A meta-analytic review of randomized controlled trials. *J Acquir Immune Defic Syndr* 43(Suppl 1):S23–S35.

Simoni JM, Wiebe JS, Sauceda JA, et al. (2013). A preliminary RCT of CBT-AD for adherence and depression among HIV-positive Latinos on the US–Mexico border: the Nuevo Dia Study. *AIDS Behav* 17(8):2816–2829.

Sin NL, DiMatteo MR (2014). Depression treatment enhances adherence to antiretroviral therapy: a meta-analysis. *Ann Behav Med* 47(3):259–269.

Singh N, Squier C, Sivek C, Wagener M, Nguyen MH, Yu V (1996). Determinants of compliance with antiretroviral therapy in patients with human immunodeficiency virus: prospective assessment with implications for enhancing compliance. *AIDS Care* 8(3):261–270.

Sledjeski EM, Delahanty DL, Bogart LM (2005). Incidence and impact of posttraumatic stress disorder and comorbid depression on adherence to HAART and CD4 counts in people living with HIV. *AIDS Patient Care STDs* 19(11):728–736.

Starace F, Ammassari A, Trotta MP, et al.; NeuroICoNA Study Group (2002). Depression is a risk factor for suboptimal adherence to highly active antiretroviral therapy. *J Acquir Immune Defic Syndr* 31(Suppl 3):S136–S139.

Thompson MA, Mugavero MJ, Amico KR, et al. (2012). Guidelines for improving entry into and retention in care and antiretroviral adherence for persons with HIV: evidence-based recommendations from International Association of Physicians in AIDS Care Panel. *Ann Intern Med* 156(11):817–833.

Traeger L, O'Cleirigh C, Skeer MR, Mayer KH, Safren SA (2012). Risk factors for missed HIV primary care visits among men who have sex with men. *J Behav Med* 35(5):548–556.

Tsai AC, Weiser SD, Petersen ML, Ragland K, Kushel MB, Bangsberg DR (2010). A marginal structural model to estimate the causal effect of antidepressant medication treatment on viral suppression among homeless and marginally housed persons with HIV. *Arch Gen Psychiatry* 67(12):1282–1290.

Tucker JS, Burnam MA, Sherbourne CD, Kung F, Gifford AL (2003). Substance use and mental health correlates of nonadherence to antiretroviral medications in a sample of patients with human immunodeficiency virus infection. *Am J Med* 114(7):573–580.

Tuldrà A, Ferrer MJ, Fumaz CR, Bayes R, Paredes R, Burger DM, Clotet B (1999). Monitoring adherence to HIV therapy. *Arch Intern Med* 159(12):1376–1377.

Turner BJ, Fleishman JA, Wenger N, et al. (2001). Effects of drug abuse and mental disorders on use and type of antiretroviral therapy in HIV-infected persons. *J Gen Intern Med* 16(9):625–633.

Turner BJ, Laine C, Cosler L, Hauck WW (2003). Relationship of gender, depression, and health care delivery with antiretroviral adherence in HIV-infected drug users. *J Gen Intern Med* 18(4):248–257.

U.S. Public Health Service (2014). Preexposure prophylaxis for the prevention of HIV infection in the United States—2014: a clinical practice guideline.

Uthman OA, Magidson JF, Safren SA, Nachega JB (2014). Depression and adherence to antiretroviral therapy in low-, middle-and high-income countries: a systematic review and meta-analysis. *Curr HIV/AIDS Rep* 11(3):291–307.

van Servellen G, Chang B, Garcia L, Lombardi E (2002). Individual and system level factors associated with treatment nonadherence in human immunodeficiency virus-infected men and women. *AIDS Patient Care STDs* 16(6):269–281.

Vitiello B, Burnam MA, Bing EG, Beckman R, Shapiro MF (2003). Use of psychotropic medications among HIV-infected patients in the United States. *Am J Psychiatry* 160(3):547–554.

Vranceanu AM, Safren SA, Lu M, Coady WM, Skolnik PR, Rogers WH, Wilson IB (2008). The relationship of post-traumatic stress disorder and depression to antiretroviral medication adherence in persons with HIV. *AIDS Patient Care STDs* 22(4):313–321.

Wagner GJ, Kanouse DE, Koegel P, Sullivan G (2003). Adherence to HIV antiretrovirals among persons with serious mental illness. *AIDS Patient Care STDs* 17(4):179–186.

Wagner GJ, Kanouse DE, Koegel P, Sullivan G (2004). Correlates of HIV antiretroviral adherence in persons with serious mental illness. *AIDS Care* 16(4):501–506.

Wagner J, Justice A, Chesney M, Sinclair G, Weissman S, Rodriguez-Barradas M (2001). Patient- and provider-reported adherence: toward a clinically useful approach to measuring antiretroviral adherence. *J Clin Epidemiol* 54(12):S91–S98.

Walkup JT, Sambamoorthi U, Crystal S (2004). Use of newer antiretroviral treatments among HIV-infected Medicaid beneficiaries with serious mental illness. *J Clin Psychiatry* 65(9):1180–1189.

Weiss JJ, Martynenko M, Levin K, Alcorn M, Mhango G, Fierer D (2013) Adherence and hypertension control in patients with HIV infection. Poster presentation at 8th International Conference on HIV Treatment and Prevention Adherence, Miami, FL.

Westergaard RP, Hess. T, Astemborski J, Mehta SH, Kirk GD (2013). Longitudinal changes in engagement in care and viral suppression for HIV-infected injection drug users. *AIDS* 27(16):2559–2566.

Whetten K, Shirey K, Pence BW, et al.; CHAT Research Team (2013). Trauma history and depression predict incomplete adherence to antiretroviral therapies in a low income country. *PloS ONE* 8(10):e74771.

Whooley MA, Simon GE (2000). Managing depression in medical outpatients. *N Engl J Med* 343(26):1942–1950.

Wilson IB, Lu M, Safren SA, et al. (2007). Results of a physician-focused intervention to improve antiretroviral medication adherence. Paper presented at the NIMH/IAPAC Second International Conference on HIV Treatment Adherence, 2007, Jersey City, NJ.

Yun LW, Maravi M, Kobayashi JS, Barton PL, Davidson AJ (2005). Antidepressant treatment improves adherence to antiretroviral therapy among depressed HIV-infected patients. *J Acquir Immune Defic Syndr* 38(4):432–438.

30.

HOMELESSNESS AND HIV TRANSMISSION

Kimberly Livingstone, Daniel B. Herman, Naomi Adler, and Ezra S. Susser

Homelessness is associated with both poorer health and higher risk of morbidity and mortality (Baggett et al., 2013; Barrow et al., 1999). In the United States, mortality among the homeless population is approximately four times greater than that of the housed population (Baggett et al. 2013; Barrow et al., 1999; Hibbs et al., 1994; Hwang et al., 1997). HIV prevalence is significantly higher among homeless persons than among their housed counterparts (Beech et al., 2003; Bucher et al., 2007; Caton et al., 2013; Culhane et al., 2001; Fogg and Mawn, 2010; Forney et al., 2007; McQuillian and Kruszon-Moran, 2008; Robertson et al., 2004; Wenzel et al., 2012).

This chapter examines the association between HIV/AIDS and homelessness in the United States. After providing a brief overview of homelessness and the characteristics of specific homeless subpopulations, we discuss HIV prevalence, transmission, treatment, and prevention among people who are homeless in the United States.

HOMELESSNESS IN THE UNITED STATES

Because of varying definitions of homelessness and its transient nature, estimates of the number of homeless individuals vary greatly. Nonetheless, estimates based on recent point-in-time counts suggest that on any given night in the United States, nearly 550,000 individuals sleep in temporary shelters or places not meant for residence (U.S. Department of Housing and Urban Development [HUD], 2016). While many homeless people are able to access emergency overnight shelter or transitional housing, an estimated 35% of the homeless population is unsheltered, sleeping outdoors or in other places not meant for habitation (National Alliance to End Homelessness [NAEH], 2014). The homeless population comprises four major subpopulations: single men, single women, members of homeless families, and youth. According to a recent report, single adults make up 65% of the homeless population, families about 35%, and unaccompanied youth 7% (HUD, 2016). Each subpopulation has its own social and clinical characteristics, service needs, and typical reasons for homelessness.

Although the homeless population is demographically diverse, certain subpopulations are overrepresented. For example, homelessness disproportionately affects minority individuals, particularly African Americans (Carter, 2011).

Furthermore, subpopulations of homeless persons may be more or less likely to gain access to shelter and other services; while studies suggest that 35% of all homeless people are unsheltered, unaccompanied homeless youth and single homeless adults experience unsheltered homelessness at rates of 50% and 48%, respectively (NAEH, 2014; HUD, 2016). In recent years, increasing numbers of single, older adults have become homeless, and there has been a marked increase in the number of persons over the age of 65 years who are homeless (Culhane et al. 2013). In New York City, for instance, the number of sheltered homeless adults over the age of 65 increased by over 15% between 2012 and 2013 (NYC Department of Homeless Services, 2013).

Compared with the housed population, homeless persons tend to be more likely to be effected by substance abuse, physical disabilities, unemployment, histories of domestic violence or incarceration, low rates of entitlements and medical insurance, and serious medical issues and past traumas (Levitt et al., 2009; U.S. Conference of Mayors, 2015). Homelessness among people with mental illness is a particular concern; researchers estimate that at least one-third of homeless adults have severe mental illness (U.S. Conference of Mayors, 2015). Furthermore, homeless people with mental illness often have long, complex histories of chronic homelessness including multiple stays in hospitals or prisons with bouts of homelessness in between (Metraux et al., 2010).

A history of adverse childhood experiences places both women and men at greater risk for adult homelessness (Herman et al., 1997). Other childhood factors predicting family homelessness, particularly among women, include foster care involvement and the mother's drug use (Bassuk et al., 1997). It is important to bear in mind that although individual-level factors may increase the risk of certain individuals becoming homeless, the overall prevalence of homelessness in the United States is determined primarily by poverty and an inadequate supply of affordable housing.

HIV PREVALENCE IN THE HOMELESS POPULATION

In the recent past, the elevated prevalence of infection combined with lack of access to treatment and poor living conditions made HIV/AIDS a leading cause of death in homeless people (Cheung and Hwang, 2004; Hwang et al., 1997).

However, recent research suggests that with the advancements in antiretroviral therapy and the expansion of housing alternatives for chronically homeless persons, HIV is no longer a leading cause of death among the homeless population (Baggett et al., 2013; Metraux et al., 2011; Samji et al., 2013; Schwarcz et al., 2009). Nonetheless, the prevalence of HIV/AIDS among homeless persons is thought to exceed that of the non-homeless population, although precise estimates are difficult to obtain. In recent U.S. studies, the prevalence of HIV infection in homeless samples ranged between 3% and 17% (Beech et al., 2003; Bucher et al., 2007; Caton et al., 2013; Fogg and Mawn, 2010; Forney et al., 2007; Wenzel et al., 2012) compared to a rate of 0.47% in the general population (McQuillian and Kruszon-Moran, 2008). Among the homeless population, youth have the highest prevalence of HIV, at 17% (Beech et al., 2003), while the prevalence among homeless adult men (4–7%) and adult women (3–5%) is somewhat lower (Caton et al., 2013; Forney et al., 2007; Wenzel et al., 2012).

The association between homelessness and HIV appears to flow in two directions. Persons with HIV are at greater risk of homelessness because of discrimination and the high costs of housing and medical care. In recent U.S. studies, the prevalence of homelessness among HIV samples ranged between 15% and 27% (Aidala et al., 2007; Kidder et al., 2007). At the same time, homelessness has been shown to increase risk-taking behavior, leading to an elevated likelihood of contracting HIV (Forney et al., 2007; Morrell et al., 2014). Furthermore, homeless persons are in transient living situations, typically in impoverished communities with high HIV prevalence. Thus, risky behaviors they may engage in are also more likely to result in infection.

It is well understood that HIV/AIDS disproportionately affects ethnic minorities and that minority women are at particularly high risk compared to white women (Centers for Disease Control and Prevention [CDC], 2012, 2013). Similarly, minorities, particularly African Americans, are overrepresented in the homeless population. Prevention of HIV infection and care for ethnic minorities who are HIV positive are further complicated by their disproportionate experience of adverse social factors that contribute to poor health (Ivy et al., 2014; Poundstone et al., 2004) and by unequal access to healthcare services (Cargill and Stone, 2005).

RISK FACTORS FOR HIV TRANSMISSION IN THE HOMELESS POPULATION

Several conditions generally associated with homelessness increase the overall risk of adverse health outcomes in this population. These include lack of access to basic resources, such as shelter, nutrition, and appropriate physical and mental health care, as well as discrimination and social exclusion. While some risk factors for HIV transmission are common to the overall homeless population, others vary by subpopulation. In this section we consider four main homeless subgroups— single men, single women, families, and youth—and discuss salient risks in each group.

Drug and alcohol abuse are widely known risk factors for HIV transmission, and homeless persons are more likely to evidence drug and alcohol abuse than the general population. Research has shown that among chronically homeless single adults, for instance, about 50% have co-occurring substance use and other psychiatric disorders (Caton et al., 2005). Furthermore, homeless people are more likely to live in or come from communities with higher rates of drug use (Fargo et al., 2012).

Severely mentally ill individuals comprise a subpopulation with disproportionately high HIV seroprevalence (Rosenberg et al., 2003); nearly one-third of the single-adult homeless population has severe and persistent mental illness (Caton et al., 2005). The most frequent severe mental illness diagnosis is major depression (North et al., 2004), but diagnoses also include schizophrenia and other psychotic disorders. The prevalence of substance abuse disorders and severe mental illness has important implications for both the prevention and transmission of HIV. The impulsivity and impaired judgment often associated with substance abuse and other psychiatric disorders can contribute to risky behaviors such as unprotected sex, having multiple sexual partners, sharing needles, or exchanging sex for drugs.

SINGLE HOMELESS MEN

Single homeless men have several risk factors contributing to their higher risk of HIV. They report significant histories of abuse; nearly 27% of homeless men report an incident of physical assault within the past year (Kushel et al., 2003), and 77% of homeless men report experiencing abuse in their lifetime (Henny et al., 2007). Single homeless men are more likely than single housed men to have a substance abuse disorder or other psychiatric disorder; by one estimate, 88% of homeless single men show evidence of drug and/or alcohol dependence or other mental disorders (North et al., 2004).

As in the general population, among single homeless men, men who have sex with men or who are injection drug users are more likely to be HIV positive. A study in San Francisco reported that among homeless men who have sex with men, 30% tested positive for HIV, and of homeless injection drug users, 8% tested positive for HIV (Robertson et al., 2004). It has also been shown that among injection drug users, men who are currently homeless are more likely to test positive for HIV than men who are housed (Reyes et al., 2005).

Among single men (and adolescents), longer periods of homelessness are associated with a greater likelihood of risk-taking behaviors (Forney et al., 2007) such as unprotected sex or sharing needles. Condom use was less likely among homeless men when they held more negative attitudes toward condoms, when the partner was considered to be a primary/serious partner, with use of drugs, excluding marijuana, or preceding sex or when sex occurred in a public setting (Tucker et al., 2013).

Injection drug use among homeless men is relatively common; among homeless men with a severe mental illness it ranges from 16% to 26% (Susser et al., 1997; Linn et al., 2005). Homelessness has also been shown to increase injection drug use risk-taking behavior and adverse health outcomes, with approximately 70% of homeless injection drug users reporting practices such as sharing needles and participating in shooting galleries (Galea and Vlahov, 2002; Linn et al., 2005). One study found that the majority of homeless mentally ill men who were injection drug users engaged in unsafe injection practices and unsafe sexual behaviors (Susser et al., 1996).

SINGLE WOMEN

Common HIV risk factors among homeless women include substance abuse, other mental illness, history of childhood sexual or physical abuse, and intimate partner violence, all of which are linked with greater risk-taking behaviors. Furthermore, homelessness exacerbates HIV risk, as risk-taking behaviors typically occur in impoverished communities with high HIV prevalence (Hixson et al., 2011). By one estimate, in 2000, 42% of homeless single women had either an alcohol or drug use disorder (North et al., 2004). Furthermore, women injection drug users were more likely to engage in risky behaviors, such as needle sharing, than were men (Evans et al., 2003), putting them at greater risk for HIV.

Homeless women frequently report having experienced physical and sexual traumas in childhood and are more likely to have experienced childhood abuse than people in the general population (Henny et al., 2007; Houston et al., 2012). As noted in Chapter 17 in this book, trauma, such as adverse childhood experiences, is associated with greater risk for HIV transmission. Additionally, research has shown that homeless women with histories of both childhood abuse and posttraumatic stress disorder (PTSD) or borderline personality disorder are more likely to be diagnosed with HIV (Houston et al., 2012). Homeless women more frequently experience partner violence than women with housing (Richards et al., 2010; Wenzel et al., 2001). As discussed in Chapters 6 and 35, intimate partner violence is known to be a characteristic associated with an increased risk of contracting HIV. Furthermore, the elevated risk for homeless women with histories of intimate partner violence is magnified, as battered women are also likely to have substance abuse, one or more sexually transmitted infections, and a history of childhood physical or sexual abuse (Vijayaraghavan et al., 2012).

HOMELESS FAMILIES

Homeless families represent an estimated 36% of the homeless population, comprising roughly 220,000 people in over 70,000 households in the most recent U.S. count (HUD, 2016; NAEH, 2014). The most common composition of a homeless family is a single, minority woman and her young children (Culhane et al., 2013), though it cannot be assumed that homeless families are comprised only of members who present for shelter services (Paquette and Bassuk, 2009).

Single homeless mothers have many of the same characteristics that have been associated with increased risk factors for HIV transmission among single homeless women. These include histories of childhood physical and sexual abuse (Caton et al., 2013), partner violence, and substance abuse

(Dawson et al., 2013; North et al., 2004). Additionally, homeless mothers are likely to have poor social support (Bassuk et al., 2006; Herman et al., 1997). Homeless mothers, like other homeless women, are also at an elevated risk of sexually transmitted infections that are associated with risky sexual activity (Caton et al., 2013), putting them at greater risk for HIV infection.

Homeless mothers have often experienced past abuse. Among homeless mothers, approximately two-thirds have experienced severe physical violence as a child, 42% report sexual abuse during childhood, and 61% have experienced partner violence in adulthood (Bassuk et al., 2006; Browne and Bassuk, 1997). Partner violence among homeless mothers has been widely documented (Bassuk et al., 1996; Hien and Bukszpan, 1999). Rates of severe physical and sexual assault over the lifespan of homeless and marginally housed mothers has been found to exceed 80% (Bassuk et al., 1996).

Mental health issues and substance use are frequent concerns for homeless women with families (Bassuk and Beardslee, 2014; Dawson et al., 2013). Depression is common; lifetime rates of depression among homeless mothers range from 45% to 85% (Bassuk and Beardslee, 2014; Weinreb et al., 2006). Furthermore, homeless mothers with mental illness or substance abuse problems often have limited access to ongoing mental health services (Dawson et al., 2013) and tend to rely instead on crisis services for their healthcare (Duchon et al., 1999).

HOMELESS YOUTH

In 2013, there were an estimated 46,000 unaccompanied homeless youth on any given night in the United States; most of these young people are between the ages of 18 and 24 years (87%), while the remainder are unaccompanied children under the age of 18 (NAEH, 2014). Notably, half of these youth were found to be completely unsheltered, sleeping on the street or in other places not meant for habitation (HUD, 2016; NAEH, 2014). Homeless youth are at exceptionally high risk for HIV compared with other persons their age; the prevalence of HIV infection among homeless adolescents was recently estimated at 17%, much higher than for the general population and any other homeless subpopulation (Beech et al., 2003). African American youth account for 45% of all HIV cases in youth between the ages of 13 and 24 (CDC, 2012). Although HIV/AIDS is not a leading cause of death among homeless youth, it has been shown that, during periods of homelessness, risk of death increases significantly for this population (Roy et al., 2004). The HIV risk of homeless youth is correlated with length of time homeless; youth who have been homeless for longer than 6 months have higher HIV risk than that of youth who have been homeless for less than 6 months (Milburn et al., 2006).

Substance use among homeless youth is prevalent (Ensign and Bell, 2004). In 2004, 69% of homeless youth reported alcohol use, and approximately three-quarters of surveyed youth reported the use of ecstasy, ketamine, and other hallucinogens at least one to three times a month (Van Leeuwen et al., 2004). Club drugs can increase potential HIV transmission by lowering inhibitions, increasing sexual endurance, and leading to high-risk sexual behavior such as unprotected sex (Swanson and Cooper, 2002). Other risky behaviors, including trading sex for drugs and sharing needles, have also been reported by many homeless youth (Van Leeuwen et al., 2004).

Homeless youth suffer high rates of exposure to other infectious diseases (Haddad et al., 2005), including hepatitis B and hepatitis C (Boivin et al., 2005), and high rates of other sexually transmitted infections (Forst, 1994). Additionally, homeless youth have more pregnancies than do housed youth (Boivin et al., 2005). In one longitudinal study among newly homeless youth, sexual risk was predicted by drug use for both young men and women (Solorio et al., 2008).

HIV/AIDS TREATMENT AND PREVENTION IN THE HOMELESS POPULATION

The relationship between homelessness and health outcomes is complex. Nonetheless, research clearly shows that homelessness contributes to poorer health, higher mortality (Hibbs et al., 1994; Hwang, 2000), and reduced access to healthcare services. For currently homeless individuals, prioritizing daily needs such as food, shelter, and work typically takes precedence over less urgent matters such as healthcare. Even when health services are actively sought, they are difficult to access, with payment for services, documentation, transportation, obtaining and storing medications, and continuity of care posing major barriers. Guidelines for engagement and retention in HIV care have been developed and include recommendations for homeless and unstably housed persons with HIV (Thompson et al., 2012) and summarize the work of an international panel.

A common misconception is that the greatest barrier to delivering prevention and treatment services to homeless persons is finding them. The reality, however, is that homeless people are often visible, by living or working in the streets, being readily accessible in shelters, or both. The forming of trusting relationships, consistent contact over time, and use of already existing social networks can help in engaging and retaining homeless persons for treatment and follow-up services. In one HIV testing program for homeless persons with severe mental illness, for instance, nearly 90% of individuals tested returned for their results. The greatest predictor of returning for results was good social support (Desai and Rosenheck, 2004). Additionally, community-based rapid HIV testing has been shown to be feasible and effective to use with homeless people (Bucher et al., 2007).

Characteristics and behaviors associated with HIV risk factors, such as unsafe sexual or drug use practices, vary among homeless subpopulations, thus programs must be tailored to the needs of each population. For example, researchers suggest that any evidence-based program developed for youth to address HIV needs to include several components: a framework to understand behavior change; issue- and population-specific information; self-management skills; acknowledgment of environmental barriers to implementing

health behaviors; and tools to develop ongoing support in the community (Rotheram-Borus et al., 2009). One tailored behavioral HIV prevention intervention for homeless and runaway youth is Street Smart, a multisession, group intervention. A randomized trail showed that the Street Smart intervention successfully reduced marijuana use among males and unprotected sex, alcohol and marijuana use, and number of drugs used over a 1-year period among females (Rotheram-Borus et al., 2003). Another recent intervention for newly homeless youth (STRIVE) attempted to engage family members in an effort to reduce risk by resolving family conflicts that preceded the youths' running away from home (Milburn et al., 2012)

Many homeless individuals currently receive much of their medical care in emergency rooms. Nearly 40% of homeless persons reported one or more visits to the emergency room in the past year (Kushel et al., 2002). While this is a clear indication of the need for improved, ongoing medical care in the homeless population, it may also present an opportunity for identifying potentially HIV-infected individuals, now that testing in emergency departments, even in low-prevalence areas, has been shown to be effective (Lyons et al., 2005).

Although advances in medication show promise for persons living with HIV, adherence to medication regimens remains a concern (Samji et al., 2013), specifically among homeless people (Kidder et al., 2007). To improve the ability of currently homeless HIV-positive individuals to adhere to their medical care, comprehensive programs are needed to help provide for basic needs. An example of one such program is So Others Might Eat (SOME), a community-based organization serving an underserved population of African Americans in Washington, DC. In an effort to address the specific issues preventing clients with HIV from adhering to treatment, including general weariness of the medical community, SOME established comprehensive HIV care in their program, at a location where clients had already built trusting relationships with staff members and peers, and showed improvement in medical care adherence, with 80% of qualified clients receiving antiretroviral therapy (Wright and Knopf, 2009).

Additionally, coordinated care networks that provide homeless persons with comprehensive care and that allow staff to link individuals quickly and easily to the services they need have been shown to be more successful in retaining individuals in care (Hwang et al., 2005; Woods et al., 2003). For example, Boston HAPPENS provides coordinated health education, case management, basic medical care, HIV testing, counseling, and mental health care for HIV-positive at-risk youth, many of whom are homeless. Through persistent outreach, individualized case management, and a large, coordinated group of providers, HAPPENS retains homeless at-risk youth in care (Harris et al., 2003). In addition to addressing where services are provided, coupling antiretroviral therapy with other interventions may also improve adherence among homeless persons. One study found that homeless people with HIV, who often also had substance abuse or mental health issues, were five times more likely to adhere to their care if they were also receiving maximally assisted therapy—a team-based approach to providing complex HIV services including meals, side effect management, advocacy, social and emotional support, mental health counseling, and outreach (Parashar et al., 2011).

In our view, for HIV prevention efforts to be most effective, basic survival needs such as shelter and food must be tended to first. In fact, it has been shown that simply providing homeless individuals with housing and cash benefits can effectively reduce risk-taking behavior such as unprotected sex, drug use, and needle sharing (Aidala et al., 2005; Riley et al., 2005). Furthermore, substantial research has shown that for people living with HIV, housing improves health outcomes, such as achieving undetectable or lower viral loads (Buchannan et al., 2009), having fewer hospitalizations, less emergency room use, increased medication adherence (Kidder et al., 2007), and lower risk of death (Schwarcz et al., 2009). In a comprehensive study of New York City shelter system records from 1990 to 2002, housing was found to contribute to lowered mortality in both homeless adults and families (Metraux et al., 2011). One exemplary program, the Open Door, provides housing for homeless individuals with HIV, in Pittsburgh, PA. With a Housing First approach, coupled with antiretroviral therapy, the rate of participants with undetected viral loads increased from 27% at entry to 69% at the time of the last data collection (Hawk and Davis, 2012).

Institutional barriers and settings frequently restrict HIV prevention activities and coordination of care for homeless persons. Staffing at shelters is often only adequate to provide basic needs, and shelters may be reluctant to allow outside HIV prevention program staff to talk explicitly about sex and drugs or to distribute condoms because those activities are forbidden in most shelters. While institutions may find it necessary to prohibit these activities on their premises, it is also clear that in order to encourage homeless individuals to practice safer sex, they also need to be given private space where they can do so. A lack of private space can also be a serious barrier to providing counseling and education around sensitive topics. There is an ongoing need to deliver effective prevention activities in the service settings that homeless persons use, such as soup kitchens, shelters, residential hotels, and clinics. Service setting staff members need training in HIV prevention education methods that recognize specific risk factors related to homelessness, employ realistic expectations for change, and give homeless people concrete goals that they can accomplish.

Ultimately, homelessness is characterized by two factors: a lack of a permanent place to live and extreme poverty. Long-term efforts to provide homeless individuals with the resources to remedy these two needs will go a long way toward both decreasing the growing prevalence of chronic homelessness and reducing the likelihood of HIV transmission.

REFERENCES

Aidala A, Cross JE, Stall R, Harre D, Sumartojo E (2005). Housing status and HIV risk behaviors: implications for prevention and policy. *AIDS Behav* 9(3):251–265.

Aidala A, Lee G, Abramson D, Messeri P, Siegler A (2007). Housing need, housing assistance, and connection to HIV medical care. *AIDS Behav* 11:S101–S115.

Baggett TP, Hwang SW, O'Connell JJ, et al. (2013). Mortality among homeless adults in Boston: shifts in causes of death over a 15-year period. *JAMA Intern Med* 173(3):189–195.

Barrow SM, Herman DB, Cordova P, Struening EL (1999). Mortality among homeless shelter residents in New York City. *Am J Public Health* 89(4):529–534.

Bassuk EL, Beardslee (2014). Depression in homeless mothers: addressing an unrecognized pubic health issue. *Am J Orthopsychiatry* 84(1):73–81.

Bassuk EL, Buckner JC, Weinreb LF, Browne A, Bassuk SS, Dawson R, Perloff JN (1997). Homelessness in female-headed families: childhood and adult risk and protective factors. *Am J Public Health* 87(2):241–248.

Bassuk E, Dawson R, Huntington N (2006). Intimate partner violence in extremely poor women: longitudinal patterns and risk markers. *J Fam Violence* 21:387–399.

Bassuk EL, Weinreb LF, Buckner JC, Browne A, Salomon A, Bassuk SS (1996). The characteristics and needs of sheltered homeless and low-income housed mothers. *JAMA* 276(8):640–646.

Beech BM, Myers L, Beech DJ, Kernick NS (2003). Human immunodeficiency syndrome and hepatitis B and C infections among homeless adolescents. *Semin Pediatr Infect Dis* 14(1):12–19.

Boivin J, Roy E, Haley N, Galbaud du Fort G (2005). The health of street youth: a Canadian perspective. *Can J Public Health* 96(6):432–437.

Browne A, Bassuk SS (1997). Intimate violence in the lives of homeless and poor housed women: prevalence and patterns in an ethnically diverse sample. *Am J Orthopsychiatry* 67(2):261–278.

Buchannan D, Kee R, Sadowski LS, Garcia D (2009). The health impact of supportive housing for HIV-positive homeless patients: a randomized controlled trial. *Am J Public Health* 99(S3):S675–S680.

Bucher JB, Thomas KM, Guzman D, Riley E, Cruz ND, Bangsberg DR (2007). Community-based rapid HIV testing in homeless and marginally housed adults in San Francisco. *HIV Med* 8:28–31.

Cargill VA, Stone VE (2005). HIV/AIDS: a minority health issue. *Med Clin North Am* 89(4):895–912.

Carter GR (2011). From exclusion to destitution: race, affordable housing, and homelessness. *Cityscape* 13(1):33–70.

Caton CL, Dominguez B, Schanzer B, et al. (2005). Risk factors for long-term homelessness: findings from a longitudinal study of first-time homeless single adults. *Am J Public Health* 95(10):1753–1759.

Caton CLM, El-Bassel N, Gelman A, et al. (2013). Rates and correlates of HIV and STI infection among homeless women. *AIDS Behav* 17:856–864.

Centers for Disease Control and Prevention (CDC) (2012). HIV Surveillance Supplemental Report: estimated HIV incidence in the United States, 2007–2010. http://www.cdc.gov/hiv/topics/surveillance/resources/reports/#supplemental. Accessed October 26, 2014.

Centers for Disease Control and Prevention (CDC) (2013). HIV Surveillance Supplemental Report: monitoring selected national HIV prevention and care objectives by using HIV surveillance data—United States and 6 dependent areas—2011. http://www.cdc.gov/hiv/library/reports/surveillance. Accessed October 26, 2014.

Cheung AM, Hwang SW (2004). Risk of death among homeless women: a cohort study and review of the literature. *CMAJ* 170(8):1243–1247.

Culhane D, Gollub E, Kuhn R, Shpaner M (2001). The co-occurrence of AIDS and homelessness: results from the integration of administrative databases for AIDS surveillance and public shelter utilization in Philadelphia. *J Epidemiol Community Health* 55(7):515–520.

Culhane DP, Metraux S, Byrne T, Stino M, Bainbridge J (2013). The age structure of contemporary homelessness: evidence and implications for public policy. *Anal Soc Issues Public Policy* 13(1):228–244.

Dawson A, Jackson D, Cleary M (2013). Mothering on the margins: homeless women with an SUD and complex mental health comorbidities. *Issues Ment Health Nurs* 34:288–293.

Desai MM, Rosenheck RA (2004). HIV testing and receipt of test results among homeless persons with serious mental illness. *Am J Psychiatry* 161(12):2287–2294.

Duchon LM, Weitzman BC, Shinn M (1999). The relationship of residential instability to medical care utilization among poor mothers in New York City. *Med Care* 37(12):1282–1293.

Ensign J, Bell M (2004). Illness experiences of homeless youth. *Qual Health Res* 14(9):1239–1254.

Evans JL, Hahn JA, Page-Shafer K, Lum PJ, Stein ES, Davidson PJ, Moss AR (2003). Gender differences in sexual and injection risk behavior among active young injection drug users in San Francisco (the UFO Study). *J Urban Health* 80(1):137–146.

Fargo JD, Munley EA, Byne TH, Montgomery AE, Culhane D (2012). Characteristics associated with variation in rates among families and single adults. *Am J Public Health* 103(S2):S340–S347.

Fogg CJ, Mawn B (2010). HIV screening: beliefs and intentions of the homeless. *J Assoc Nurses AIDS Care* 21(5):395–407.

Forney JC, Lomardo S, Toro PA (2007). Diagnostic and other correlates of HIV risk behaviors in a probability sample of homeless adults. *Psychiatr Serv* 58(1):92–99.

Forst ML (1994). Sexual risk profiles of delinquent and homeless youths. *J Community Health* 19(2):101–114.

Galea S, Vlahov D (2002). Social determinants and the health of drug users: socioeconomic status, homelessness, and incarceration. *Public Health Rep* 117:S135–S145.

Haddad MB, Wilson TW, Ijaz K, Marks SM, Moore M (2005). Tuberculosis and homelessness in the United States. *JAMA* 293:2762–2766.

Harris SK, Samples CL, Keenan PM, Fox DJ, Melchiono MW, Woods ER (2003). Outreach, mental health, and case management services: can they help to retain HIV-positive and at-risk youth and young adults in care? *Matern Child Health J* 7(4):205–218.

Hawk M, Davis D (2012). The effects of a harm reduction program on the viral loads of homeless individuals living with HIV/AIDS. *AIDS Care* 24(5):577–582.

Henny KD, Kidder DP, Stall R, Wolitski RJ (2007). Physical and sexual abuse among homeless and unstably housed adults living with HIV: prevalence and associated risks. *AIDS Behav* 11(6):842–853.

Herman DB, Susser ES, Struening EL, Link BL (1997). Adverse childhood experiences: are they risk factors for adult homelessness? *Am J Public Health* 87(2):249–255.

Hibbs JR, Benner L, Klugman L, Spencer R, Macchia I, Mellinger A, Fife D (1994). Mortality in a cohort of homeless adults in Philadelphia. *N Engl J Med* 331(5):304–309.

Hien D, Bukszpan C (1999). Interpersonal violence in a "normal" low-income control group. *Womens Health* 29(4):1–16.

Hixson BA, Omer SB, del Rio C, Frew PM (2011). Spatial clustering of HIV prevalence in Atlanta, Georgia and population characteristics associated with case concentrations. *J Urban Health* 88(1):129–141.

Houston E, Sandfort T, Watson KT, Caton C (2012). Psychological pathways from childhood sexual and physical abuse to HIV/sexually transmitted infection outcomes among homeless women: the role of posttraumatic stress disorder and borderline personality disorder symptoms. *J Health Psychol* 18(10):1330–1340.

Hwang SW (2000). Mortality among men using homeless shelters in Toronto, Ontario. *JAMA* 283(16):2152–2157.

Hwang SW, Orav J, O'Connell JJ, Lebow JM, Brennan TA (1997). Causes of death in homeless adults in Boston. *Ann Intern Med* 126(8):625–628.

Hwang SW, Tolomiczenko G, Kouyoumdjian FG, Garner RE (2005). Interventions to improve the health of the homeless: a systematic review. *Am J Prev Med* 29(4):311–319.

Ivy W, Miles I, Le B, Paz-Bailey G (2014). Correlates of HIV infection among African American women from 20 cities in the United States. *AIDS Behav* 18:S266–S275.

Kidder DP, Wolitski RJ, Royal S, et al. (2007). Access to housing as a structured intervention for homeless and unstably housed people living with HIV: rationale, methods, and implementation for the housing and health study. *AIDS Behav* 6(Suppl):S149–S161.

Kushel MB, Evans JL, Perry S, Robertson MJ, Moss AR (2003). No door to lock: victimization among homeless and marginally housed persons. *Arch Intern Med* 163(20):2492–2499.

Kushel MB, Perry S, Bangsberg D, Clark R, Moss AR (2002). Emergency department use among the homeless and marginally housed: results from a community-based study. *Am J Public Health* 92(5):778–784.

Levitt AJ, Culhane DP, DeGenova J, O'Quinn P, Bainbridge J (2009). Health and social characteristics of homeless adults in Manhattan who were chronically or not chronically unsheltered. *Psychiatr Serv* 60(7):978–981.

Linn JG, Brown M, Kendrick L (2005). Injection drug use among homeless adults in the Southeast with severe mental illness. *J Health Care Poor Underserv* 16(4A):83–90.

Lyons MS, Lindsell CJ, Ledyard HK, Frame PT, Trott AT (2005). Emergency department HIV testing and counseling: an ongoing experience in a low-prevalence area. *Ann Emerg Med* 46(1):22–28.

McQuillian G, Kruszon-Moran D (2008). HIV infection in the United States household population aged 18-49 years: results from 1999–2006. http://www.cdc.gov/nchs/data/databriefs/db04.pdf. Accessed October 26, 2014.

Metraux S, Byrne T, Culhane DP (2010). Institutional discharges and subsequent shelter use among unaccompanied adults in New York City. *J Community Psychol* 38(1):28–38.

Metraux S, Eng N, Bainbridge J, Culhane D (2011). The impact of shelter use and housing placement on mortality hazard for unaccompanied adults and adults in family households entering New York City shelters: 1990–2002. *J Urban Health* 88(6):1091–1104.

Milburn NG, Iribarren FJ, Rice E, et al. (2012). A family intervention to reduce sexual risk behavior, substance use, and delinquency among newly homeless youth. *J Adolesc Health* 50(4):358–364.

Milburn NG, Rotheram-Borus MJ, Rice E, Mallett S, Rosenthal D (2006). Cross-national variations in behavioral profiles among homeless youth. *Am J Community Psychol* 37:63–76.

Morrell KR, Pichon LC, Chapple-McGruder T, Kmet JM, Chandler A, Terry ML (2014). Prevalence and correlates of HIV-risk behaviors among homeless adults in a Southern city. *J Health Dispar Res Pract* 7(1):84–96.

National Alliance to End Homelessness (2014). The State of Homelessness in America 2014. http://www.endhomelessness.org/library/entry/the-state-of-homelessness-2014. Accessed October 18, 2014.

North CS, Eyrich KM, Pollio DE, Spitznagel EL (2004). Are rates of psychiatric disorders in the homeless population changing? *Am J Public Health* 94(1):103–108.

NYC Department of Homeless Services (2013). DHS data dashboard report fiscal year 2013. http://www.nyc.gov/html/dhs/html/communications/stats.shtml. Accessed February 5, 2017.

Paquette K, Bassuk EL (2009). Parenting and homelessness: Overview and introduction to the special section. *Am J Orthopsychiatry* 79(3):292–298.

Parashar S, Palmer AK, O'Brien N, et al. (2011). Sticking to it: the effect of maximally assisted therapy on antiretroviral treatment adherence among individuals living with HIV who are unstably housed. *AIDS Behav* 15:1612–1622.

Poundstone KE, Strathdee SA, Celentano DD (2004). The social epidemiology of human immunodeficiency virus/acquired immunodeficiency syndrome. *Epidemiol Rev* 26:22–35.

Reyes JC, Robles RR, Colon HM, Matos TD, Finlinson HA, Marrero CA, Shepard EW (2005). Homelessness and HIV risk behaviors among drug injectors in Puerto Rico. *J Urban Health* 82(3):446–455.

Richards TN, Garland VW, Bumphus Thompson R (2010). Personal and political: exploring the feminization of the American homeless population. *J Poverty* 14:97–115.

Riley ED, Moss AR, Clark RA, Monk SL, Bangsberg DR (2005). Cash benefits are associated with lower risk behavior among the homeless and marginally housed in San Francisco. *J Urban Health* 82(1):142–150.

Robertson MJ, Clark RA, Charlebois ED, Tulsky J, Long HL, Bangsberg DR, Moss AR (2004). HIV seroprevalence among homeless and marginally housed adults in San Francisco. *Am J Public Health* 94(7):1207–1217.

Rosenberg SD, Swanson JW, Wolford GL, et al. (2003). The five-site health and risk study of blood-borne infections among persons with severe mental illness. *Psychiatr Serv* 54(6):827–835.

Rotheram-Borus MJ, Song J, Gwadz M, Lee M, Van Rossem R, Koopman C (2003). Reductions in HIV risk among runaway youth. *Prev Sci* 4(3):173–187.

Rotheram-Borus MJ, Swenderman D, Flannery D, Rice E, Adamson DM, Ingram B (2009). Common factors in effective HIV prevention programs. *AIDS Behav* 13:399–408.

Roy E, Haley N, Leclerc P, Sochanski B, Boudreau JF, Boivin JF (2004). Mortality in a cohort of street youth in Montreal. *JAMA* 292(5):569–574.

Samji H, Cescon A, Hogg RS, et al. (2013). Closing the gap: increases in life expectancy among treated HIV-positive individuals in the United States and Canada. *PLoS ONE* 8(12):e81355.

Schwarcz SK, Hsu LC, Vittinghoff E, Vu A, Bamberger JD, Katz MH (2009). Impact of housing on the survival of persons with AIDS. *BMC Public Health* 9:220–238.

Solorio MR, Rosenthal D, Milburn NG, Weiss RE, Batterham PJ, Gandara M, Rotheram-Borus MJ (2008). Predictors of sexual risk behaviors among newly homeless youth: a longitudinal study. *J Adolesc Health* 42:401–409.

Susser E, Betne P, Valencia E, Goldfinger SM, Lehman AF (1997). Injection drug use among homeless adults with severe mental illness. *Am J Public Health* 87(5):854–856.

Susser E, Miller M, Valencia E, Colson P, Roche B, Conover S (1996). Injection drug use and risk of HIV transmission among homeless men with mental illness. *Am J Psychiatry* 153(6):794–798.

Swanson J, Cooper A (2002). Dangerous liaison: club drug use and HIV/AIDS. *J Int Assoc Phys AIDS Care* 8:1–15.

Thompson MA, Mugavero MJ, Rivet Amico K, et al. (2012). Guidelines for improving entry into and retention in care and antiretroviral adherence for persons with HIV: evidence-based recommendations from an international association of physicians in AIDS care panel. *Ann Intern Med* 156:817–833.

Tucker JS, Wenzel SL, Golinelli D, Kennedy DP, Ewing B, Wertheimer S (2013). Understanding heterosexual condom use among homeless men. *AIDS Behav* 17:1637–1644.

U.S. Conference of Mayors (2015). A status report on hunger and homelessness in America's cities: 2015. https://www.usmayors.org/pressreleases/uploads/2015/1221-report-hhreport.pdf Accessed February 5, 2017.

U.S. Department of Housing and Urban Development (2016). The 2016 Annual Homeless Assessment Report (AHAR) to Congress. https://www.hudexchange.info/resources/documents/2016-AHAR-Part-1.pdf. Accessed February 5, 2017.

Van Leeuwen JM, Hopfer C, Hooks S, White R, Petersen J, Pirkopf J (2004). A snapshot of substance abuse among homeless and runaway youth in Denver, Colorado. *J Community Health* 29(3):217–229.

Vijayaraghavan M, Penko J, Vittinghoff E, Bangsberg DR, Miaskowski C, Kushel MB (2012). Smoking behaviors in a community-based cohort of HIV-infected indigent adults. *AIDS Behav* 18:535–543.

Weinreb LF, Buckner JC, Williams V, Nicholson J (2006). A comparison of the health and mental health status of homeless mothers in Worcester, MA: 1993 and 2003. *Am J Public Health* 96:1444–1448.

Wenzel SL, Leake BD, Gelberg L (2001). Risk factors for major violence among homeless women. *J Interpers Violence* 16(8):739–752.

Wenzel SL, Rhoades H, Hsu H, et al. (2012). Behavioral health and social normative influence: correlates of concurrent sexual partnering among heterosexually active homeless men. *AIDS Behav* 16:2042–2050.

Woods ER, Samples CL, Melchiono MW, Harris SK (2003). Boston HAPPENS Program: HIV-positive, homeless, and at-risk youth can access care through youth-oriented HIV services. *Semin Pediatr Infect Dis* 14:43–53.

Wright MA, Knopf AS (2009). Mobilizing a medical home to improve HIV care for the homeless in Washington, DC. *Am J Public Health* 99:973–975.

31.

ROUTINE TESTING FOR HIV INFECTION AND PRE-EXPOSURE AND POST-EXPOSURE PROPHYLAXIS

Bisrat K. Abraham, Inti Flores, and Roy M. Gulick

ROUTINE TESTING FOR HIV INFECTION

INTRODUCTION AND BACKGROUND

HIV testing was originally developed to screen the U.S. blood supply, starting in March 1985. As the significance of HIV-positive status to disease transmission became clear, testing was expanded on the basis of risk. In 1987, individuals seeking testing for sexually transmitted infection became the first demographic for whom routine testing was recommended (Centers for Disease Control and Prevention [CDC], 1987). Recommendations for screening steadily increased in scope, following a risk-targeted paradigm, so that by 1993 U.S. hospitals with HIV seroprevalence rates of >1% were encouraged to offer routine testing to all patients aged 15–54. Targeted testing proved logistically difficult to implement for a variety of reasons, including the lack of explicit data regarding HIV prevalence to appropriately target screening as well as frequent denial of reimbursement for testing by payers (Branson et al., 2006). By 1996, effective antiretroviral therapy (ART) regimens capable of suppressing HIV RNA levels and significantly improving survival for HIV-infected persons had been developed (Palella et al., 2003). Growing clarity regarding the value of knowing one's HIV status emerged alongside increasing awareness of the barriers to testing maintained by a targeted approach. In 2006, the Centers for Disease Control and Prevention (CDC) issued revised recommendations advocating that routine HIV screening be offered universally to adults and adolescents aged 13–64 years presenting across all healthcare settings (Branson et al., 2006). These recommendations were the culmination of a two-decades-long gradual expansion of HIV testing and marked a turning point from risk-targeted testing to a paradigm of universal screening. Since then, other expert panels have followed suit, including the U.S. Preventative Services Task Force (USPSTF), which in 2013 issued grade A recommendations for universal HIV screening for adolescents, adults, and pregnant women (USPSTF, 2013).

MAJOR CHANGES FROM PRIOR RECOMMENDATIONS

The 2006 CDC guidelines aim to increase identification of undetected HIV by streamlining and expanding screening.

The call to screen adult and adolescent patients aged 13–64, regardless of individual risk profiles, reflected concerns about logistical barriers imposed by the requirement that clinicians first perform a risk assessment before offering testing, as well as growing evidence that risk assessment often fails to accurately predict risk (Alpert et al., 1996; Jenkins et al., 2006). In the setting of an epidemic whose demographics have changed significantly from the 1980s with an increasing proportion of cases affecting young adults, racial/ethnic minorities, women, and heterosexuals, an individual's perceived risk or, conversely, the risk perceived by treating clinician often does not accurately reflect actual risk for infection. Additionally, the stigmatization of many high-risk behaviors known to be linked to HIV transmission can result in hesitance to openly disclose, further decreasing the utility of risk assessment (Jenkins et al., 2006).

The revised guidelines also recommend offering screening across all clinical settings in which healthcare is provided. They remove the requirement for a separate, written consent for HIV testing, instead creating a strategy of "opt-out" testing in which screening will be performed following patient notification unless the patient specifically declines. This change was enacted to aid in streamlining the screening process for clinicians and also to remove unnecessary stigma from HIV testing by allowing general consent for medical treatment to suffice for testing as it would for any other disease. Lastly, the 2006 revised guidelines removed the previous expectation that HIV prevention counseling should be performed for all persons screened for HIV. While the effectiveness of brief HIV prevention counseling in reducing an individual's risk behaviors is established, the most robust changes seem to occur in response to more structured and intensive counseling interventions (Kamb et al., 1998; Weinhardt et al., 1999). Thus the net effect of requiring prevention counseling seemed to decrease the likelihood that screening would occur, particularly in time-limited settings.

FACILITATING EARLY DIAGNOSIS

In addition to increasing diagnosis of undetected HIV and destigmatizing testing, an explicit goal of the 2006 revised recommendations was earlier detection of HIV in patients. Historically, a significant number of HIV-positive individuals received their first positive HIV test less than a year before receiving a diagnosis of AIDS (CDC, 2003; Wortley et al., 1995). Even as medical treatment options for HIV have improved survival and disease-related morbidity, much progress remains to be made in facilitating early diagnosis. In a pre-expanded screening model, Paltiel et al. (2005) estimated an average infection-to-detection time greater than 5 years in the majority of urban HIV-infected patients, based on CD4 counts at presentation. Individuals with late HIV diagnosis (CD4 <200 or AIDS-defining illness at diagnosis) may not benefit fully from ART and opportunistic infection prophylaxis and thus are subject to increased morbidity and mortality compared to individuals diagnosed early during the asymptomatic phase of infection (Palella et al., 2003). Furthermore, individuals who receive a late HIV diagnosis are more likely to be black, Hispanic, or younger (18–29 years), to have been exposed to HIV through heterosexual contact, and to have high school or less education than peers who received testing earlier in the course of disease (CDC, 2003). In their 2005 study comparing an expanded screening model to non-routine background screening, Paltiel and colleagues demonstrated an improvement in average CD4 count at diagnosis with expanded screening protocols, suggesting that streamlined, universal screening may enable earlier diagnosis. However, a 2012 analysis of newly diagnosed outpatients found a median CD4 at diagnosis of 299, with no significant trend toward improved CD4 counts between 2000 and 2009 (Buchacz et al., 2012). Similarly, a 2013 systematic review found no significant trends since 1992 in CD4 count at diagnosis (Lesko et al., 2013). These findings illustrate that even in the era of routine universal screening, achieving earlier HIV diagnosis remains a significant challenge.

TESTING AS PREVENTION

Beyond the benefit to HIV-infected individuals, the CDC's 2006 revised recommendations recognize the public health significance of universal screening as a prevention strategy. It has been demonstrated that HIV transmission occurs disproportionately in individuals who are not aware of their positive status, so that simply by increasing HIV diagnosis through increased screening, it may be possible to reduce new sexual HIV infections by more than 30% per year (Branson et al., 2006; Marks et al., 2006). Furthermore, HIV RNA (viral load) has definitively been demonstrated to be the chief biological predictor of HIV transmission; with the early initiation of ART and viral load suppression in individuals known to be HIV positive, there is a 96% decrease in viral transmissibility between serodiscordant sexual partners (Cohen et al., 2011). Incorporating this effect on transmission and primary prevention markedly improves cost-effectiveness models for universal screening (Bozzette, 2005).

HIV testing as primary prevention strategy draws upon the success of already existing universal screening programs like those employed by the U.S. blood bank and in the routine prenatal care of pregnant women. The American Red Cross (ARC) has screened all units of donated blood for antibodies to HIV-1 and HIV-2 since 1985 and 1992, respectively. In 1999, nucleic acid testing (NAT) for HIV RNA was instituted in "minipools" of 16 donated units, further closing the window period through which HIV could pass undetected into the blood bank. Together, these screening strategies have decreased the risk of HIV transmission through blood transfusion to approximately 1 in 2,000,000 (ARC, 2017; Stramer, 2007).

In a similar vein, universal, streamlined HIV screening has been recommended by the CDC as a component of routine prenatal care for all pregnant women in the United States since 2001. This policy emerged in response to increasing evidence that early detection and initiation of ART in infected mothers can lead to substantially decreased vertical viral transmission (Connor et al., 1994; Lindegren et al., 1999). Preventive strategies implemented for pregnant women found to be HIV positive, including prophylactic ART, scheduled cesarean section, and avoidance of breastfeeding, can decrease perinatal viral transmission to less than 1%. Since the mid-1990s combined testing and preventive interventions have resulted in a greater than 90% reduction in perinatal HIV infections in the United States (CDC, 2016a; Committee on Obstetric Practice, 2001; Cooper et al., 2002).

HIV SCREENING ASSAYS

In June 2014 the CDC released a new algorithm for HIV testing of serum and plasma samples that significantly updated previous strategies (Figure 31.1). For many years the gold standard for HIV screening had been the ELISA (enzyme-linked immunosorbent assay, or IA), which detects HIV antibodies in serum samples; preliminary repeatedly positive IA results were confirmed by the highly specific Western blot or indirect immunofluorescence assays. The most current ("fourth generation") IAs have been developed to detect viral p24 antigen in addition to antibody, enabling detection during acute HIV infection.

The CDC's updated testing algorithm recommends screening with a fourth-generation HIV-1/2 antibody/antigen combined immunoassay. Preliminary positive results are to be followed up by an immunoassay that differentiates between

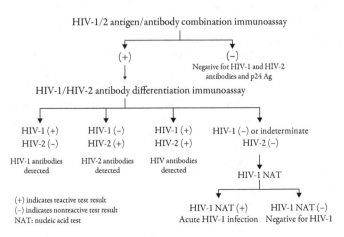

Figure 31.1 HIV testing algorithm.   SOURCE: CDC Quick Reference Guide—Laboratory Testing for the Diagnosis of HIV Infection: Updated Recommendations. Available at: http://www.cdc.gov/hiv/pdf/testingHIValgorithmQuickRef.pdf.

HIV-1 and HIV-2 antibodies. Specimens that are reactive on the initial combined assay and then negative or indeterminate on the HIV-1/HIV-2 antibody differentiation assay are to be followed up with HIV-1 NAT. HIV-1 NAT testing allows for the definitive detection of acute HIV (CDC, 2014a). The replacement of traditional Western blot or indirect immuno-fluorescence assay (IFA) with NAT for confirmatory testing reflects increasing priority being placed on detecting acute HIV infections, in part stemming from recognition that persons with acute or early HIV have increased risk of viral transmission compared to those with established infection and may benefit from treatment themselves (CDC, 2014a).

RAPID AND HOME TESTING

Another recent development with significant ramifications has been the development and widespread institution of rapid HIV screening tests. Historically, serum samples were sent out to a licensed laboratory where screening assays and confirmatory testing were performed; patients were then expected to return for a second visit to receive test results, which could take up to 2 weeks. This lag between specimen retrieval and result reporting often resulted in significant anxiety for patients, which, combined with logistical barriers to returning for results, contributed to failure to follow up in up to 30% of cases (Paul et al., 2002).

Rapid assays designed to detect HIV antibodies in serum, whole blood, plasma, or oral fluids have the advantage of being simple and easy to use in a variety of settings (including outreach and nonclinical settings), returning results within less than 30 minutes, and minimizing the extent to which clients fail to return to the site of testing to receive results (Patel et al., 2012). By providing immediate results, rapid tests may help to facilitate the linkage of persons with new HIV diagnoses to care. Similar to positive results obtained with standard IA testing, preliminary positive results by rapid testing require subsequent confirmatory testing. Sensitivity and specificity of rapid assays have generally been found to be comparable to those of non-rapid EIAs, in the range of 96.7–100% and 98.5–100%, respectively (CDC, 2014a). There is evidence to suggest that both sensitivity and specificity of rapid tests decrease when oral fluids are used rather than whole blood, but negative predictive value has been found to be high, so that a negative result in the absence of recent HIV exposure is generally considered conclusive (Delaney et al., 2006; Wesolowski et al., 2006). Although rapid assays have been developed to detect viral antigen in addition to HIV antibody, the sensitivity of these assays for viral antigen has generally been found to be lower than fourth-generation IAs, and the majority of rapid HIV assays are not designed to detect acute HIV infection (Beelaert and Fransen, 2010; Patel et al., 2012).

In July of 2012, the U.S. Food and Drug Administration (FDA) approved the first rapid assay for self-testing to be performed at home. The decision to make over-the-counter home HIV testing available in the United States, although controversial, was made in hopes that the convenience, privacy, and anonymity of self-testing would further reduce barriers to testing (Myers et al., 2013). Proponents of self-testing have argued that home tests might be accessed by at-risk persons unwilling to be tested in healthcare or even outreach settings. Indeed, some survey data have indicated significant interest in home-testing in high-risk populations, including men who have sex with men, racial and ethnic minorities, and young people (Myers et al., 2013). Some have suggested that rapid home tests might reduce HIV transmission by use in "point-of-sex" testing with new or existing partners as a method of harm reduction by sero-sorting (Myers et al., 2013).

Critics of home testing express concern about unsupervised interpretation of test results, both with regard to preliminary positive results requiring confirmation as well as the possibility of false reassurance in the setting of early infection or acute HIV (Myers et al., 2013; Ventuneac et al., 2009). Others wonder whether the cost of home-testing (about $40) will limit its utility as a public health measure given that those who need the test most may not be able to afford it (Myers et al., 2013; Walensky and Paltiel, 2006; Wright and Katz, 2006). Additionally, the related question of which demographic groups will ultimately access home HIV tests has implications for testing accuracy given the relationship between positive predictive value and disease prevalence (Walensky and Paltiel, 2006). Perhaps one of the most clinically salient questions raised by home HIV-testing addresses the critical issue of linking patients to care. One of the explicit objectives outlined in the CDC's 2006 recommendations for universal screening is to increase linkage of individuals with previously unidentified HIV to clinical and prevention services. With the advent of home testing, it remains an open question whether individuals screening positive will ultimately connect to services that would result in individual and public health benefits. Thus, while over-the-counter HIV tests may very well provide an opportunity for marginalized, at-risk populations to experience agency in learning about and managing their HIV status, limited data exist to address the impact of this recent development.

HIV PRE-EXPOSURE PROPHYLAXIS (PrEP)

INTRODUCTION AND BACKGROUND

Despite significant advances in the treatment of HIV infection, every year an additional 50,000 Americans are newly infected with HIV (Hall et al., 2008; Prejean et al., 2011). In addition, among populations at risk in the United States, men who have sex with men have experienced an increase in the number of new HIV infections, compared to decreases in every other risk group (CDC, 2012a). Of particular concern is that men under 30 years old who have sex with men, particularly young men of color who have sex with men, have the highest rates of new HIV infection in the United States (CDC, 2012b). Clearly, better HIV prevention strategies are needed.

Pre-exposure prophylaxis (PrEP) is an HIV prevention strategy in which an at-risk HIV-uninfected individual takes one or more antiretroviral drugs. By having antiretroviral drugs present in the bloodstream and the genital tract, HIV, if encountered, may be unable to establish infection. Among 29 drugs approved for the treatment of HIV infection, the ideal antiretroviral drug(s) for PrEP would be effective, safe, tolerable, and convenient. Tenofovir disoproxil fumarate (TDF), with or without (+/−) emtricitabine (FTC), emerged as the leading candidate for PrEP, based on these favorable qualities. TDF+/−FTC was shown to prevent retroviral infection in animal models (Denton et al., 2008; Garcia-Lerma et al., 2008; Tsai et al., 1995). TDF/FTC has a long safety record in people with HIV infection and individuals with hepatitis B infection (Gilead, 2013). TDF/FTC is associated uncommonly with side effects, notably gastrointestinal symptoms, proximal renal tubular dysfunction (Fanconi's-like syndrome), and loss of bone mineral density. PrEP with TDF+/−FTC has been tested in large randomized clinical trials in heterosexuals, men who have sex with men, and injection drug users.

CLINICAL TRIALS

The first randomized clinical trial of oral PrEP was a phase II double-blind randomized safety study of tenofovir versus matching placebo in 936 HIV-negative women in Cameroon, Ghana, and in Nigeria (Peterson et al., 2007). The primary endpoint was safety, and there were no significant differences in clinical or laboratory adverse events between the two study arms. Eight new HIV infections occurred during this study—five on placebo and three on tenofovir (rate ratio 0.35, 95% confidence interval [CI], 0.03, 1.93), which did not achieve statistical significance. The study was closed prematurely at two of the clinical sites without reaching target enrollment.

The first randomized clinical trial to assess the efficacy of oral PrEP was the iPrEX study (Grant et al., 2010). iPrEX was a phase 3, randomized, double-blind study of tenofovir/emtricitabine versus matching placebo in 2,499 men who have sex with men enrolled in South America, South Africa, Thailand, and the United States. All participants also received risk-reduction counseling and condoms. Participants were randomized equally to the two strategies and followed for a median 1.2 years. Over this time, 10 were found to be acutely HIV infected at study entry and 100 newly acquired HIV during the study—36 in the PrEP group and 64 in the placebo group. Thus, PrEP was associated with a 44% reduction in HIV infection compared to placebo (95% CI 15%, 63%; $p = 0.005$). In an analysis of the subset of participants with detectable tenofovir drug levels, PrEP was associated with a 92% reduction in HIV infection. The study drugs were well tolerated; PrEP was associated with significantly more nausea (of moderate intensity or greater) (22 episodes/2% vs. 10 episodes/<1%) and more unintentional ≥5% weight loss (27 episodes/2% vs. 14 episodes/1%). Over the course of the study, the number of sexual partners decreased and the amount of condom use increased; thus no risk compensation occurred (Marcus et al., 2013).

The Partners PrEP study was a phase 3, randomized, double-blind study of PrEP with TDF alone or combined with emtricitabine versus placebo in 4,758 discordant heterosexual couples (one member of the couple was HIV infected and one was HIV uninfected) in Kenya and Uganda (Baeten et al., 2012). Over the course of the study, 82 new HIV infections occurred—17 in the TDF group, 13 in the TDF/emtricitabine group, and 52 in the placebo group. Thus, PrEP was associated with a 67–75% reduction in HIV infection compared to placebo ($p < 0.001$), without a significant difference between the one- and two-drug PrEP regimens. In the subgroups with detectable tenofovir drug levels, PrEP was 86–90% effective. The study regimens were generally well tolerated and the proportion of people reporting condomless sex decreased during the study.

The TDF-2 study was a phase 3, randomized, double-blind study of PrEP with TDF/emtricitabine versus placebo in 1,219 Botswanan adults (Thigpen et al., 2012). Over a median follow-up of 1.1 years, 33 participants became HIV infected—9 in the PrEP group and 24 in the placebo group. Thus, PrEP was associated with a 62% reduction in risk for HIV infection (95% CI; 21%, 83%; $p < 0.03$). The PrEP group had significantly higher rates of nausea (18% vs. 7%), vomiting (11% vs. 7%), and dizziness (15% vs. 11%) compared to placebo. In the subgroup with detectable tenofovir drug levels, PrEP was 84% effective in preventing HIV infection. There was no evidence of increased HIV risk behaviors.

The FEM-PREP study was a phase III, randomized, double-blind study of PrEP with TDF/emtricitabine in 2,120 women in Kenya, South Africa, and Tanzania (Van Damme et al., 2012). In contrast to the three prior studies, this study was stopped early for lack of efficacy: 68 new HIV infections occurred—33 in the PrEP group and 35 in the placebo group ($p = 0.81$). In addition, PrEP was associated with a significantly higher incidence of nausea, vomiting, or elevated hepatic transaminase levels. Adherence to study drugs as measured by plasma drug levels was low, with less than 40% of women randomized to active PrEP having detectable tenofovir levels. There was no evidence of increased HIV risk behaviors, and the number of sexual partners and episodes of condomless sex decreased during the study.

The VOICE study was a phase 3, randomized, double-blind study with five study arms: (1) 1% tenofovir vaginal gel, (2) placebo gel, (3) oral TDF, (4) oral TDF/emtricitabine, and (5) oral placebo, conducted in 5,029 women in South Africa, Uganda, and Zimbabwe (Marrazzo et al., 2014). This study found none of the study drugs (gel or oral) to be effective. Overall, adherence was low at 30%, as estimated by drug level measurements.

The Bangkok Tenofovir Study was a phase 3, randomized, double-blind study of PrEP with oral TDF versus placebo in 2,413 twenty- to sixty-year-old individuals who reported injection drug use in the previous year (Choopanya et al., 2013). Over the course of the study, 50 participants became newly HIV infected—17 in the PrEP group and 33 in the placebo group. Thus, PrEP was associated with a 49% reduction in HIV infection (95% CI, 6%, 72%; $p = 0.01$). In the subset of participants with detectable tenofovir drug levels, PrEP was 70% effective.

Two recent large studies of TDF/emtricitabine PrEP in men who have sex with men, IPERGAY and PROUD, were stopped early by their independent data safety monitoring boards because of significant decreases in the risk of HIV infection in the PrEP versus placebo arms (ANRS, 2014; McCormack et al., 2016; Medical Research Council, 2014; Molina et al., 2015). Notably, both studies showed an 86% risk reduction in HIV incidence among participants taking PrEP. Of particular interest is the IPERGAY study, where PrEP was administered not once-daily as in prior studies but "on-demand," with two TDF/emtricitabine pills taken 2–24 hours before sex and one pill taken 24 and 48 hours after sex.

PrEP—FDA APPROVAL AND CURRENT GUIDELINES

Based on the results of the iPrEX and Partners PrEP studies and with added support from the TDF-2 study, the FDA approved the coformulation of TDF/emtricitabine for PrEP in July 2012—the first medication ever approved for HIV prevention (Gilead, 2013). The labeling information states that TDF/FTC is "indicated in combination with safer sex practices for pre-exposure prophylaxis (PrEP) to reduce the risk of sexually acquired HIV-1 in adults at high risk." TDF/emtricitabine PrEP is covered by some state Medicaid programs and by some private insurance plans; there have been a number of demonstration projects and there is a PrEP Medication Assistance Program.

The CDC released preliminary guidelines for PrEP use based on the various study results, and then issued current comprehensive recommendations in May 2014 (CDC, 2014b). The guidelines recommend PrEP as an HIV prevention option for sexually active men who have sex with men, heterosexual men and women (in a high-prevalence area or network), and injection drugs users who are at substantial risk of HIV acquisition. Examples of substantial risks are having an HIV-infected sex partner, a recent bacterial sexually transmitted infection, a high number of sex partners, a history of inconsistent or no condom use, or engaging in commercial sex work. For injection drug users, substantial risks are having an HIV-infected drug-injecting partner, sharing injection equipment, or having recent drug treatment but currently injecting. Acute and chronic HIV infection should be excluded before PrEP is prescribed, HIV infection should be assessed every 3 months, and renal function should be assessed at baseline and every 6 months. Effective risk-reduction strategies provided by New York State PrEP Guidelines include a useful management algorithm (Figure 31.2).

The International Antiviral Society–USA (IAS-USA) issued their first-ever prevention guidelines in July 2014 (Marrazzo et al., 2014). They recommend offering PrEP to persons at high risk based on several factors: having a background HIV incidence of >2%; having a recent diagnosis of a sexually transmitted infection; using post-exposure prophylaxis (PEP) more than twice in the past year; and being and injection drug user who shares injection equipment, injects once or more daily, or injects cocaine or methamphetamines.

The World Health Organization (WHO) updated their guidelines in September 2015 to recommend PrEP "for people at substantial risk of HIV infection as part of combination prevention approaches" (WHO, 2015). They note that the strength of the recommendation is "strong" and the quality of the evidence is "high."

PrEP—WHAT'S NEXT?

The initial group of PrEP efficacy studies demonstrated that TDF with or without emtricitabine in at-risk men who have sex with men, heterosexuals, and injection drug users was generally safe, well-tolerated, and effective in decreasing HIV infection and did not increase risk behaviors. However, concerns remain about adherence, drug toxicities, and drug resistance, particularly because TDF/emtricitabine are first-line drugs for HIV treatment. There are a number of proposed innovations for PrEP, and some clinical studies are underway.

Currently, the major concern about PrEP is the requirement for daily adherence to taking a pill. Grant and colleagues (2014) extended the iPrEx study by enrolling 1,603 men in an open-label extension (iPrEx OLE), and 1,230 participants (77%) chose to take PrEP. Grant et al. used an investigational dried-blood spot assay for tenofovir drug levels, which quantitates the prior 3 months of PrEP use, and related the levels to drug exposure and HIV incidence. In this study, a tenofovir diphosphate concentration suggesting the use of four to seven PrEP TDF/emtricitabine doses a week was associated with no HIV infections, a level suggesting the use of two to three PrEP doses a week was associated with a 90% reduction in HIV infection, but lower drug levels suggesting less than two PrEP doses a week were associated with much lower rates of protection. These data support the formal testing of less than daily or "on-demand" PrEP regimens with TDF/emtricitabine; several clinical studies of intermittent PrEP are in progress, though the IPERGAY study, mentioned previously, was stopped early owing to a substantially reduced risk of HIV infection in the treatment arm (ANRS, 2014).

In some studies, toxicities were more common with TDF-containing PrEP regimens than with placebo comparators. Although a new prodrug of tenofovir, tenofovir alafenamide (TAF), demonstrated comparable virological efficacy and less renal and bone toxicity than TDF (Sax et al., 2015) and was approved for the treatment of HIV infection in 2015, no PrEP clinical studies have been conducted, and this drug cannot currently be recommended for PrEP. Alternative compounds with the potential for less toxicity are under investigation. Maraviroc is an approved antiretroviral drug that was well tolerated in phase 3 studies in HIV-infected individuals (Gulick et al., 2014) but is not used commonly for HIV treatment today. As a CCR5 antagonist, maraviroc binds to the cellular receptor and prevents HIV from entering the cell. A phase 2 safety study of maraviroc-containing regimens for PrEP in men who have sex with men found the regimens comparably safe and well tolerated as TDF/FTC (Gulick et al., 2016).

Rilpivirine (RPV) is a non-nucleoside analogue reverse transcriptase inhibitor (NNRTI) that is FDA approved as an oral drug for HIV treatment. An investigational formulation using nanotechnology, rilpivirine long-acting (RPV-LA), achieves target drug levels with monthly dosing and is under investigation for PrEP (Jackson et al., 2014). Cabotegravir (CAB) is an investigational HIV integrase inhibitor that is

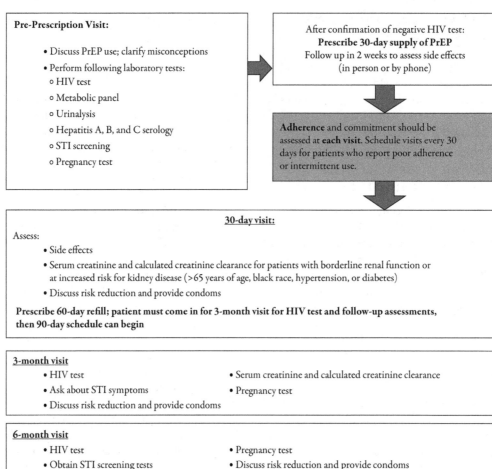

Pre-Prescription Visit:

- Discuss PrEP use; clarify misconceptions
- Perform following laboratory tests:
  o HIV test
  o Metabolic panel
  o Urinalysis
  o Hepatitis A, B, and C serology
  o STI screening
  o Pregnancy test

After confirmation of negative HIV test:
Prescribe 30-day supply of PrEP
Follow up in 2 weeks to assess side effects
(in person or by phone)

Adherence and commitment should be assessed at **each visit.** Schedule visits every 30 days for patients who report poor adherence or intermittent use.

30-day visit:

Assess:
- Side effects
- Serum creatinine and calculated creatinine clearance for patients with borderline renal function or at increased risk for kidney disease (>65 years of age, black race, hypertension, or diabetes)
- Discuss risk reduction and provide condoms

Prescribe 60-day refill; patient must come in for 3-month visit for HIV test and follow-up assessments, then 90-day schedule can begin

3-month visit
- HIV test
- Ask about STI symptoms
- Discuss risk reduction and provide condoms
- Serum creatinine and calculated creatinine clearance
- Pregnancy test

6-month visit
- HIV test
- Obtain STI screening tests
- Pregnancy test
- Discuss risk reduction and provide condoms

9-month visit
- HIV test
- Ask about STI symptoms
- Discuss risk reduction and provide condoms
- Serum creatinine and calculated creatinine clearance
- Pregnancy test

12-month visit
- HIV test
- Obtain STI screening tests
- HCV serology for MSM, IDUs, and those with multiple sexual partners
- Discuss risk reduction and provide condoms
- Pregnancy test
- Urinalysis

Figure 31.2 Pre-exposure prophylaxis (PrEP) management.   **SOURCE:** HIV Clinical Resource, New York State Department of Health AIDS Institute. Available at: https://www.health.ny.gov/diseases/aids/general/prep/

available both as an oral formulation and a parenteral formulation that allows every-2-month dosing (Spreen et al., 2014) and demonstrated efficacy as PrEP in animal studies (Andrews et al., 2014). A phase 2 PrEP study of CAB recently was reported (Murray et al., 2016) and a phase 3 study is planned.

POST-EXPOSURE PROPHYLAXIS (PEP)

INTRODUCTION AND BACKGROUND

The HIV transmission rate after percutaneous injury involving an HIV-positive source patient was originally reported as 0.3% (Henderson et al., 1990), with a similar finding from a more recent large meta-analysis (0.23%; 95% CI 0.0–0.5%) (Baggaley et al., 2006). In 1989, Henderson et al. recommended the use of PEP for the prevention of occupational and nosocomial transmission of HIV (Henderson and Gerberding, 1989) on the basis of animal studies showing efficacy of zidovudine to interrupt transmission of related retroviruses after exposure (Ruprecht et al., 1986; Tavares et al., 1987) and in vitro studies showing activity against HIV-1. In addition to preventing HIV infection, the authors emphasized that candidate prophylactic agents needed to be effective even with delays in treatment initiation of up to 48 hours, be available as short-term oral or single-dose parenteral regimens, have minimal toxicity, and be inexpensive (Henderson and Gerberding, 1989).

Given the low risk of HIV infection in healthcare workers and the difficulty of enrolling patients, a planned randomized clinical trial intended to assess the efficacy of PEP in the healthcare setting did not take place (LaFon et al., 1988). In 1997, results of a case-control study of 698 healthcare workers across four European and American sites were published showing that health workers who took zidovudine after percutaneous exposure to a source patient with HIV were 81% less likely to seroconvert (33 seroconverters, 665 non-seroconverters) (Cardo et al., 1997). These results solidified the role of antiretroviral prophylaxis following occupational exposure to HIV.

The efficacy of PEP has also been shown in other settings, the most dramatic and well-documented success occurring in the area of perinatal HIV transmission. Though part of the strategy entailed adequate control of the HIV viral load in the mothers, provision of prophylactic ART to the newborns conferred additional benefit, which has subsequently made this approach the standard of care (Connor et al., 1994; Simonds et al., 1998; Taha et al., 2003; Wade et al., 1998; Wiktor et al., 1999).

While there was interest among clinicians and patients, there were few data to support the use of PEP for non-occupational exposures (e.g., following unprotected sexual encounters or parenteral exposure in the setting of intravenous drug use), and concern was raised about the potential for increased risky behaviors. Nevertheless, the risk of HIV transmission in these non-occupational settings may be substantially higher than with occupational exposures (Smith et al., 2005), thereby supporting the idea that PEP would be beneficial in this context as well. For example, the per-contact risk of acquiring HIV infection from unprotected receptive anal intercourse has been estimated to be from 1% to 30% (Baggaley et al., 2010; Landovitz and Currier, 2009). Although the HIV status of the source patient is often unavailable, making it difficult to estimate accurately the amount of risk reduction garnered from PEP in the non-occupational setting (Roland et al., 2005), results of observational studies suggest that individuals who complete PEP may have less HIV acquisition (Kahn et al., 2001; Schechter et al., 2004).

CURRENT GUIDELINES

While the early literature on PEP supported zidovudine monotherapy, subsequent U.S. guidelines shifted toward the use of dual and now triple ART with agents that are more effective and better tolerated than zidovudine. Federal guidelines for the use of occupational PEP were developed by the CDC and the Public Health Service (PHS) initially in 1990 and have since been updated several times (1996, 1998, 2001, 2005, and 2013) (Kuhar et al., 2013). In 2005, the CDC also developed guidelines for the use of PEP after non-occupational exposures (Smith et al., 2005), and updated guidelines were recently published (CDC, 2016b).

Guidelines for Occupational Exposure

The 2013 CDC/PHS guidelines focus on exposure among healthcare personnel, whom they define as "all paid and unpaid persons working in healthcare settings who have the potential for exposure to infectious materials, including body substances (e.g., blood, tissue, and specific body fluids)" (Kuhar et al., 2013). The exposures that might prompt recommendation for PEP among healthcare personnel include percutaneous injury or mucocutaneous contact with potentially infected bodily fluids. Although individuals who have such exposures should be promptly offered and initiated on PEP, the guidelines stress the importance of testing the source patient with an FDA-approved rapid assay in order to determine whether ongoing PEP therapy is needed. The authors do not set a cut-off time for initiation of PEP, though they do cite animal and in vitro studies suggesting substantially reduced benefit beyond 72 hours after exposure. The total duration for PEP therapy is recommended to be 4 weeks.

The first-line ART that is recommended for all exposed healthcare personnel is a three-drug regimen. The preferred regimen is a dual nucleoside/nucleotide reverse transcriptase inhibitor (NRTI) backbone of tenofovir and emtricitabine paired with an integrase inhibitor, raltegravir; options for alternate agents are also provided. Other recently updated occupational PEP guidelines, such as those coming out of the New York State Department of Health's AIDS Institute (NYSDOHAI), have recommended the use of either raltegravir or dolutegravir, one of the newer integrase inhibitors that can be taken daily, together with the NRTI backbone of tenofovir and emtricitabine (NYSDOHAI, 2014b) (Figure 31.3).

In the event that the source patient is found to be HIV positive, his or her treatment history should be reviewed and therapy tailored to accommodate for any resistant HIV strains that might be present (Kuhar et al., 2013). In addition to the initial evaluation, which includes baseline HIV testing, the exposed healthcare personnel should be followed up at 72 hours post-exposure. This early follow-up is indicated in order to provide further counseling, encourage PEP adherence, assess for medication side effects, and answer any additional questions that the exposed person might have. Follow-up testing should be performed at 6 weeks, 12 weeks, and 6 months after exposure. However, if a fourth-generation combination antigen/antibody HIV test is available, follow-up testing at 1 week, 6 weeks, and 4 months is recommended (Kuhar et al., 2013). Assessment for hepatitis B and C infection is also made at baseline and with repeated follow-up testing. Finally, during the 28-day course of their prophylactic regimen, exposed healthcare personnel are encouraged to take additional risk reduction measures, such as using condoms, avoiding pregnancy and breastfeeding, avoiding needle-sharing, and avoiding the exchange of any potentially infectious bodily fluids.

Guidelines for Non-Occupational Exposure

In 1998, the CDC reviewed the data on use of PEP for non-occupational exposures and came to the conclusion that these data were insufficient to make further recommendations on its use. By 2005, more research had been conducted and there was anecdotal experience suggesting that PEP, even in the non-occupational setting, is beneficial. After review of these

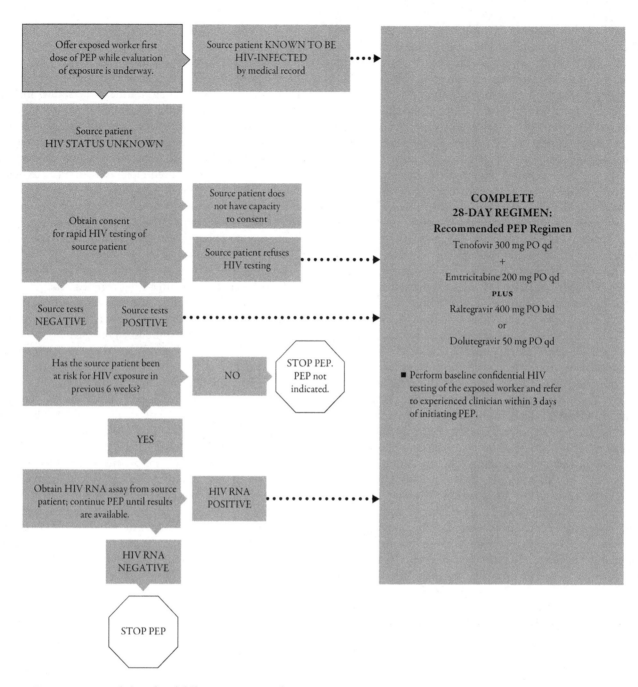

Figure 31.3 Post-exposure prophylaxis (PEP) following occupational exposure.   **SOURCE:** HIV Clinical Resource, New York State Department of Health AIDS Institute.
Available at: http://www.hivguidelines.org/pep-for-hiv-prevention/occupational/#tab_0

data, the CDC recommended the use of non-occupational PEP for individuals presenting within 72 hours of a high-risk exposure from a known HIV-positive contact. In the situation where the HIV status of the source patient is unknown and the patient presents within 72 hours, no formal recommendation was made. However, in the event that the exposed person seeks care after 72 hours or exposure is considered low risk for HIV transmission, PEP was not recommended. The CDC has recently published updated guidelines (CDC, 2016b), again reiterating the need to provide prophylaxis within 72 hours of a reported non-occupational exposure. They stress the importance of rapid HIV testing for the exposed patient with a combined antibody/antigen HIV test. In addition,

they recommend PEP if the source of the bodily fluids is HIV positive and the reported exposure is considered high risk (e.g., receptive anal sex). In instances where the HIV status of the source is not known, they urge using clinical judgment, specifically taking into account the type of bodily fluid the patient was exposed to, the exposure surface, and whether the source of the bodily fluids comes from a group with high HIV prevalence (e.g., men who have sex with men) (CDC, 2016b).

HIV programs at some state health departments such as the NYSDOHAI have also released recommendations urging prompt initiation of PEP for high-risk non-occupational exposures (i.e., sharing needles, having vaginal or anal intercourse with or being exposed to the blood or bodily fluids of an individual with a known diagnosis of HIV or with unknown HIV status) in addition to risk-reduction and prevention counseling (NYSDOHAI, 2014a). In individuals who require repeated courses of PEP, PrEP should be considered. In addition, New York State Public Health Law requires any medical setting that takes care of sexual assault victims to have a 7-day pack of PEP available on site and help the person obtain the remainder of the 28-day PEP course. Both the CDC and the NYSDOHAI recommend the same regimen for non-occupational PEP (i.e., tenofovir with emtricitabine plus raltegravir or dolutegravir) (CDC, 2016b, NYSDOHAI, 2014a).

CONCERNS AND CHALLENGES WITH PEP

Despite widely accepted procedures to initiate PEP, particularly after an occupational exposure, there are some concerns and challenges that remain.

Side Effects, Toxicity, and Adherence

The first concern is that PEP may result in the development of side effects and toxicity that might in turn limit adherence. Although several studies of occupational PEP using older ART (e.g., zidovudine, indinavir, nelfinavir) showed low adherence due to frequent side effects (Parkin et al., 2000; Swotinsky et al., 1998; Wang et al., 2000), the revised PEP guidelines recommend the use of antiretroviral agents that are highly effective, well tolerated, and easily administered and, as such, are not expected to cause substantial side effects or toxicity during a 4-week course. For example, in a study from a Boston community health center, 57 of 100 (57%) participants who were enrolled to take a PEP regimen of tenofovir, emtricitabine, and raltegravir completed their regimen with fewer and less serious side effects than historical controls who were placed on a three-drug regimen of zidovudine, lamivudine, and a ritonavir-based protease inhibitor (completion rate was 38.8% among the 119 controls) (Mayer et al., 2012). In a recent prospective cohort study designed to assess safety and tolerability of the newer PEP regimens, 103 people in Houston were prescribed tenofovir, emtricitabine, and raltegravir after a high-risk sexual exposure. Overall, 85 participants (83%) completed their 28-day course of PEP and 55 participants (53%) completed all four follow-up visits (10–14 days, 28 days, 3 months, and 6 months). Only mild side effects such as headache, fatigue, and nausea were reported. Also, adherence was fairly good, with only 11% of patients reporting missed doses. However, African Americans were statistically less likely to fully complete their PEP regimens (Vigil et al., 2014).

Drug Resistance

There has been concern that drug resistance will develop while a person is on PEP (Smith et al., 2005). This theoretical risk may occur if an exposed person has underlying HIV that is unknown at the time of PEP initiation (e.g., the person

may be in the window period of HIV infection) and he or she is placed on a suboptimal regimen of one or two antiretroviral agents. However, the newer recommendation to use an HIV RNA assay to rule out acute HIV infection if there is a suspected high-risk exposure in the preceding 6 weeks and the shift toward a three-drug regimen make this scenario less likely. Low adherence might also contribute to selection of resistant virus during PEP therapy. Again, with recent data showing improved adherence to the newer PEP regimens, this is also less likely to occur. While exposed patients who acquire resistant strains of HIV despite PEP therapy have been identified, it has been difficult to fully assess whether this was secondary to acquired or transmitted resistance (Schechter et al., 2004). If the source patient is known to be HIV positive, his or her medical records should be thoroughly reviewed to assess for the presence of resistance and to help tailor the antiretroviral agents used for prophylaxis in the exposed person (NYSDOHAI, 2014a); many clinicians would use an HIV protease inhibitor and/or a drug from a new class (e.g., HIV integrase inhibitor) in this scenario. This is more difficult if the source patient is newly identified as being HIV positive, as genotyping data will take time to process (although most will have wild-type [drug-sensitive] virus). Additionally, the testing of source patients is often difficult in the non-occupational setting where sexual partners may be anonymous or refuse testing.

Impact on Behavioral Practices

Another concern that specifically addresses the use of non-occupational PEP is whether it promotes riskier sexual or drug use practices. Several studies looking at changes in sexual behaviors during the period surrounding administration of PEP have found this not to be the case. In a study conducted in San Francisco, 397 HIV-negative individuals, the majority (92%) of whom were men who have sex with men, were followed for 1 year after receipt of PEP for a potential exposure to HIV in the context of a sexual encounter or during injection drug use (Martin et al., 2004). Among the men who have sex with men, 76% reported a decrease in the number of high-risk acts, compared to 11% who reported no change and 13% who reported an increase. Approximately 55 participants (17%) reported receiving repeat administration of PEP following the initial course during the 1-year follow-up time frame (Martin et al., 2004). In another study conducted in Rio de Janeiro, Brazil, among high-risk men who have sex with men, 200 men were provided with PEP, which was to be self-administered after an eligible exposure. Although only 44% of men with eligible exposures took PEP, evaluation of risk behaviors at the 6-month study follow-up visit indicated a decline in risk behaviors for both the PEP and non-PEP users (Schechter et al., 2004). Interestingly, among the 11 individuals who seroconverted, 10 did not take PEP, primarily because they underestimated their risk; many reported being in stable relationships, without much fear that their partner was HIV positive, and others did not believe the sexual acts they engaged in were high risk (Schechter et al., 2004).

Other studies have shown that knowledge of PEP did not promote an increase in riskier sexual practices (van der Straten et al., 2000; Waldo et al., 2000). Risk behaviors during the period of PEP use have also been evaluated. In a study conducted in Boston among 104 men who have sex with men, 21% reported unprotected anal intercourse while taking PEP (Golub et al., 2008). In multivariate analysis, individuals who engaged in risky behaviors while on PEP were statistically more likely to have some involvement with HIV care and prevention activities. The authors of the study suggest that this finding may have emanated from some knowledge of the role of PrEP. Alternatively, they hypothesize that individuals who have riskier sexual practices may be worried about their own HIV status and thus engage in HIV-related projects or services. In light of this finding, as well as reports of repeat PEP users, it is suggested that behavioral interventions and counseling be an important adjunct to chemoprophylaxis (Golub et al., 2008).

Prescription Coverage and Cost-Effectiveness

While occupational PEP is provided by most health facilities, coverage of non-occupational PEP has been inconsistent. Currently, several private insurance companies and Medicaid have extended coverage to include non-occupational PEP. If patients find this not to be the case, they can also seek assistance through patient assistance programs. In the event of a sexual assault, Medicaid, Medicare, and several insurance companies will provide coverage for PEP. Some state programs, such as New York State's Office of Victim Services, will also cover the cost of PEP in this setting (NYSDOHAI, 2014a, 2014b, 2014c).

Several studies have attempted to assess the cost-effectiveness of PEP. Early studies that evaluated occupational PEP showed it to be marginally cost-effective when using two drugs, as per the CDC/PHS guidelines from 1998 (Scheid et al., 2000), but not for three-drug PEP regimens. Studies of non-occupational PEP are a bit varied and have been plagued by difficulty in estimating the efficacy of this type of prophylaxis (Pinkerton et al., 2004). In fact, efficacy often has to be extrapolated from the occupational setting. Nevertheless, while several studies have shown minimal to moderate cost-effectiveness across several settings, most of the benefit appears to be derived when targeting high-risk exposures (Herida et al., 2006; Pinkerton et al., 1998, 2004). No recent cost-effectiveness studies have been conducted assessing the latest set of PEP guidelines.

CONCLUSIONS

Scientific advancements have not only resulted in improved clinical outcomes for individuals living with HIV/AIDS but have also provided clinicians and public health practitioners with better tools to prevent HIV infection in healthy individuals who may be at risk for infection. HIV testing has become routine, faster, and more accurate and can now be performed much like a pregnancy test in the comfort of one's own home. Furthermore, for persons who are HIV negative and are at risk or exposed to HIV, there are now well-tolerated, effective, and convenient antiretroviral regimens for pre- or post-exposure that reduce the risk of HIV acquisition. Although preliminary studies do not show an increase in risky behaviors that could theoretically offset the benefit of PrEP or PEP, further behavioral studies will need to be conducted as these interventions are more widely implemented.

It is also important to remember that PrEP and PEP do not prevent pregnancy, other sexually transmitted diseases, or transmission of drug-resistant strains of HIV, thus condoms still play an important preventive role. In addition, future research will need to assess the most optimal preventive therapies including less than daily regimens and long-acting agents.

REFERENCES

Alpert PL, Shuter J, DeShaw MG, Webber MP, Klein RS (1996). Factors associated with unrecognized HIV-1 infection in an inner-city emergency department. *Ann Emerg Med* 28(2):159–164.

American Red Cross (ARC) (2017). Blood transfusion risks and complications. http://www.redcrossblood.org/learn-about-blood/blood-transfusions/risks-complications. Accessed February 6, 2017.

Andrews CD, Spreen WR, Mohri H, et al. (2014). Long-acting integrase inhibitor protects macaques from intrarectal simian/human immunodeficiency virus. *Science* 343(6175):1151–1154.

ANRS (2014). IPERGAY press release. A significant breakthrough in the fight against HIV/AIDS: a drug taken at the time of sexual intercourse effectively reduces the risk of infection. http://www.avac.org/sites/default/files/u44/ipergayPR.pdf. Accessed February 5, 2017.

Baeten JM, Donnell D, Ndase P, et al. (2012). Antiretroviral prophylaxis for HIV prevention in heterosexual men and women. *N Engl J Med* 367(5):399–410.

Baggaley RF, Boily MC, White RG, Alary M (2006). Risk of HIV-1 transmission for parenteral exposure and blood transfusion: a systematic review and meta-analysis. *AIDS* 20(6):805–812.

Baggaley RF, White RG, Boily MC (2010). HIV transmission risk through anal intercourse: systematic review, meta-analysis and implications for HIV prevention. *Int J Epidemiol* 39(4):1048–1063.

Beelaert G, Fransen K (2010). Evaluation of a rapid and simple fourth-generation HIV screening assay for qualitative detection of HIV p24 antigen and/or antibodies to HIV-1 and HIV-2. *J Virol Methods* 168(1-2):218–222.

Bozzette SA (2005). Routine screening for HIV infection—timely and cost-effective. *N Engl J Med* 352(6):620–621.

Branson BM, Handsfield HH, Lampe MA, Janssen RS, Taylor AW, Lyss SB, Clark JE (2006). Revised recommendations for HIV testing of adults, adolescents, and pregnant women in health-care settings. *MMWR Recomm Rep* 55(RR-14):1–17; quiz CE11–14.

Buchacz K, Armon C, Palella FJ, Baker RK, Tedaldi E, Durham MD, Brooks JT (2012). CD4 cell counts at HIV diagnosis among HIV outpatient study participants, 2000-2009. *AIDS Res Treat* 2012:869841.

Cardo DM, Culver DH, Ciesielski CA, et al. (1997). A case-control study of HIV seroconversion in health care workers after percutaneous exposure. Centers for Disease Control and Prevention Needlestick Surveillance Group. *N Engl J Med* 337(21):1485–1490.

Centers for Disease Control and Prevention (CDC) (1987). Public Health Service guidelines for counseling and antibody testing to prevent HIV infection and AIDS. *MMWR Morb Mortal Wkly Rep* 36(31):509–515.

Centers for Disease Control and Prevention (CDC) (2003). Late versus early testing of HIV—16 Sites, United States, 2000-2003. *MMWR Morb Mortal Wkly Rep* 52(25):581–586.

Centers for Disease Control and Prevention (CDC) (2012a). HIV infections attributed to male-to-male sexual contact—metropolitan statistical areas, United States and Puerto Rico, 2010. *MMWR Morb Mortal Wkly Rep* 61(47):962–966.

Centers for Disease Control and Prevention (CDC) (2012b). Vital signs: HIV infection, testing, and risk behaviors among youths—United States. *MMWR Morb Mortal Wkly Rep* 61(47):971–976.

Centers for Disease Control and Prevention (CDC) (2014a). Laboratory testing for the diagnosis of HIV infection: updated recommendations. https://www.cdc.gov/hiv/pdf/HIVtestingAlgorithmRecommendation-Final.pdf. Accessed February 5, 2017.

Centers for Disease Control and Prevention (CDC) (2014b). Preexposure prophylaxis for the prevention of HIV infection in the United States—2014: a clinical practice guideline. http://www.cdc.gov/hiv/pdf/PrEPguidelines2014.pdf. Accessed Febaruary 5, 2017.

Centers for Disease Control and Prevention (CDC) (2016a). HIV among pregnant women, infants, and children in the United States. https://www.cdc.gov/hiv/group/gender/pregnantwomen/. Accessed February 5, 2017.

Centers for Disease Control and Prevention (CDC) (2016b). Updated guidelines for antiretroviral postexposure prophylaxis after sexual, injection drug use, or other nonoccupational exposure to HIV—United States, 2016. http://www.cdc.gov/hiv/pdf/programresources/cdc-hiv-npep-guidelines.pdf. Accessed February 5, 2017.

Choopanya K, Martin M, Suntharasamai P, et al.; Bangkok Tenofovir Study Group (2013). Antiretroviral prophylaxis for HIV infection in injecting drug users in Bangkok, Thailand (the Bangkok Tenofovir Study): a randomised, double-blind, placebo-controlled phase 3 trial. *Lancet* 381(9883):2083–2090.

Cohen MS, Chen YQ, McCauley M, et al. (2011). Prevention of HIV-1 infection with early antiretroviral therapy. *N Engl J Med* 365(6):493–505.

Committee on Obstetric Practice (2001). ACOG committee opinion. Scheduled Cesarean delivery and the prevention of vertical transmission of HIV infection. Number 234, May 2000 (replaces number 219, August 1999). *Int J Gynaecol Obstet* 73(3):279–281.

Connor EM, Sperling RS, Gelber R, et al. (1994). Reduction of maternal-infant transmission of human immunodeficiency virus type 1 with zidovudine treatment. Pediatric AIDS Clinical Trials Group Protocol 076 Study Group. *N Engl J Med* 331(18):1173–1180.

Cooper ER, Charurat M, Mofenson L, et al; Infants' Transmission Study Group (2002). Combination antiretroviral strategies for the treatment of pregnant HIV-1-infected women and prevention of perinatal HIV-1 transmission. *J Acquir Immune Defic Syndr* 29(5):484–494.

Delaney KP, Branson BM, Uniyal A, et al. (2006). Performance of an oral fluid rapid HIV-1/2 test: experience from four CDC studies. *AIDS* 20(12):1655–1660.

Denton PW, Estes JD, Sun Z, et al. (2008). Antiretroviral pre-exposure prophylaxis prevents vaginal transmission of HIV-1 in humanized BLT mice. *PLoS Med* 5(1):e16.

Garcia-Lerma JG, Otten RA, Qari SH, et al. (2008). Prevention of rectal SHIV transmission in macaques by daily or intermittent prophylaxis with emtricitabine and tenofovir. *PLoS Med* 5(2):e28.

Gilead (2013). Truvada package insert. Revised Dec 2013.

Golub, SA, Rosenthal L, Cohen DE, Mayer KH (2008). Determinants of high-risk sexual behavior during post-exposure prophylaxis to prevent HIV infection. *AIDS Behav* 12(6):852–859.

Grant RM, Anderson PL, McMahan V; iPrEx Study Team (2014). Uptake of pre-exposure prophylaxis, sexual practices, and HIV incidence in men and transgender women who have sex with men: a cohort study. *Lancet Infect Dis* 14(9):820–829.

Grant RM, Lama JR, Anderson PL, et al.; iPrEx Study Team (2010). Preexposure chemoprophylaxis for HIV prevention in men who have sex with men. *N Engl J Med* 363(27):2587–2599.

Gulick RM, Fatkenheuer G, Burnside R, et al. (2014). Five-year safety evaluation of maraviroc in HIV-1-infected treatment-experienced patients. *J Acquir Immune Defic Syndr* 65(1):78–81.

Gulick R, Wilkin TJ, Chen Y, et al. (2016). HPTN069/ACTG 5305: Phase II study of maraviroc-based regimens for HIV PrEP in MSM. In *Abstracts of the Conference on Retroviruses and Opportunistic Infections 2016*; February 22-25, 2016, Boston, MA, abstract #103.

Hall HI, Song R, Rhodes P, et al.; HIV Incidence Study Group (2008). Estimation of HIV incidence in the United States. *JAMA* 300(5):520–529.

Henderson DK, Fahey BJ, Willy M, et al. (1990). Risk for occupational transmission of human immunodeficiency virus type 1 (HIV-1) associated with clinical exposures. A prospective evaluation. *Ann Intern Med* 113(10):740–746.

Henderson DK, Gerberding JL (1989). Prophylactic zidovudine after occupational exposure to the human immunodeficiency virus: an interim analysis. *J Infect Dis* 160(2):321–327.

Herida M, Larsen C, Lot F, Laporte A, Desenclos JC, Hamers FF (2006). Cost-effectiveness of HIV post-exposure prophylaxis in France. *AIDS* 20(13):1753–1761.

Jackson AG, Else LJ, Mesquita PM, et al. (2014). A compartmental pharmacokinetic evaluation of long-acting rilpivirine in HIV-negative volunteers for pre-exposure prophylaxis. *Clin Pharmacol Ther* 96(3):314–323.

Jenkins TC, Gardner EM, Thrun MW, Cohn DL, Burman WJ (2006). Risk-based human immunodeficiency virus (HIV) testing fails to detect the majority of HIV-infected persons in medical care Settings. *Sex Transm Dis* 33(5):329–333.

Kahn JO, Martin JN, Roland ME, et al. (2001). Feasibility of postexposure prophylaxis (PEP) against human immunodeficiency virus infection after sexual or injection drug use exposure: the San Francisco PEP Study. *J Infect Dis* 183(5):707–714.

Kamb ML, Fishbein M, Douglas JM, Jr, et al. (1998). Efficacy of risk-reduction counseling to prevent human immunodeficiency virus and sexually transmitted diseases: a randomized controlled trial. Project RESPECT Study Group. *JAMA* 280(13):1161–1167.

Kuhar DT, Henderson DK, Struble KA, et al.; US Public Health Service Working Group (2013). Updated US Public Health Service guidelines for the management of occupational exposures to human immunodeficiency virus and recommendations for postexposure prophylaxis. *Infect Control Hosp Epidemiol* 34(9):875–892.

LaFon SW, Lehrman SN, Barry DW (1988). Prophylactically administered retrovir in health care workers potentially exposed to the human immunodeficiency virus. *J Infect Dis* 158(2):503.

Landovitz RJ, Currier JS (2009). Clinical practice. Postexposure prophylaxis for HIV infection. *N Engl J Med* 361(18):1768–1775.

Lesko CR, Cole SR, Zinski A, Poole C, Mugavero MJ (2013). A systematic review and meta-regression of temporal trends in adult CD4(+) cell count at presentation to HIV care, 1992-2011. *Clin Infect Dis* 57(7):1027–1037.

Lindegren ML, Byers RH, Jr, Thomas P, et al. (1999). Trends in perinatal transmission of HIV/AIDS in the United States. *JAMA* 282(6):531–538.

Marcus JL, Glidden DV, Mayer KH, et al. (2013). No evidence of sexual risk compensation in the iPrEx trial of daily oral HIV preexposure prophylaxis. *PLoS ONE* 8(12):e81997.

Marks G, Crepaz N, Janssen RS (2006). Estimating sexual transmission of HIV from persons aware and unaware that they are infected with the virus in the USA. *AIDS* 20(10):1447–1450.

Marrazzo JM, del Rio C, Holtgrave DR, et al.; International Antiviral Society, USA Panel (2014). HIV prevention in clinical care settings: 2014 recommendations of the International Antiviral Society–USA Panel. *JAMA* 312(4):390–409.

Martin JN, Roland ME, Neilands, et al. (2004). Use of postexposure prophylaxis against HIV infection following sexual exposure does not lead to increases in high-risk behavior. *AIDS* 18(5):787–792.

Mayer KH, Mimiaga MJ, Gelman M, Grasso C (2012). Raltegravir, tenofovir DF, and emtricitabine for postexposure prophylaxis to prevent the sexual transmission of HIV: safety, tolerability, and adherence. *J Acquir Immune Defic Syndr* 59(4):354–359.

McCormack S, Dunn DT, Desai M, et al. (2016). Pre-exposure prophylaxis to prevent the acquisition of HIV-1 infection (PROUD): effectiveness results from the pilot phase of a pragmatic open-label randomised trial. *Lancet* 387(10013):53–60.

Medical Research Council (MRC) (2014). PROUD press statement. PROUD Study interim analysis finds pre-exposure prophylaxis (PrEP) is highly protective against HIV for gay men and other men who have sex with men in the UK. http://www.proud.mrc.ac.uk/PDF/PROUD%20Statement%20161014.pdf.

Molina JM, Capitant C, Spire B, et al. (2015). On-demand preexposure prophylaxis in men at high risk for HIV-1 infection. *N Engl J Med* 373(23):2237–2246.

Murray MI, Markowitz M, Frank I, et al. (2016). Tolerability and acceptability of cabotegravir LA injection: results from ECLAIR Study. In *Abstracts of the Conference on Retroviruses and Opportunistic Infections 2016*; February 22-25, 2016, Boston, MA, abstract #471.

Myers JE, El-Sadr WM, Zerbe A, Branson BM (2013). Rapid HIV self-testing: long in coming but opportunities beckon. *AIDS* 27(11):1687–1695.

New York State Department of Health AIDS Institute (NYSDOHAI) (2014a). HIV prophylaxis following non-occupational exposure.

New York State Department of Health AIDS Institute (NYSDOHAI) (2014b). HIV prophylaxis following occupational exposure.

New York State Department of Health AIDS Institute (NYSDOHAI) (2014c). HIV prophylaxis for victims of sexual assault.

Palella FJ Jr, Deloria-Knoll M, Chmiel JS, et al.; HIV Outpatient Study Investigators (2003). Survival benefit of initiating antiretroviral therapy in HIV-infected persons in different CD4+ cell strata. *Ann Intern Med* 138(8):620–626.

Paltiel AD, Weinstein MC, Kimmel AD, et al. (2005). Expanded screening for HIV in the United States—an analysis of cost-effectiveness. *N Engl J Med* 352(6):586–595.

Parkin JM, Murphy M, Anderson J, El-Gadi S, Forster G, Pinching A. J (2000). Tolerability and side-effects of post-exposure prophylaxis for HIV infection. *Lancet* 355(9205):722–723.

Patel P, Bennett B, Sullivan T, Parker MM, Heffelfinger JD, Sullivan PS (2012). Rapid HIV screening: missed opportunities for HIV diagnosis and prevention. *J Clin Virol* 54(1):42–47.

Paul SM, Grimes-Dennis J, Burr CK, DiFerdinando GT (2002). Rapid diagnostic testing for HIV. Clinical implications. *N J Med* 99(9):20–24, quiz 24-26.

Peterson L, Taylor D, Roddy R, et al. (2007). Tenofovir disoproxil fumarate for prevention of HIV infection in women: a phase 2, double-blind, randomized, placebo-controlled trial. *PLoS Clin Trials* 2(5):e27.

Pinkerton SD, Holtgrave DR, Bloom FR (1998). Cost-effectiveness of post-exposure prophylaxis following sexual exposure to HIV. *AIDS* 12(9):1067–1078.

Pinkerton SD, Martin JN, Roland ME, Katz MH, Coates TJ, Kahn JO (2004). Cost-effectiveness of HIV postexposure prophylaxis following sexual or injection drug exposure in 96 metropolitan areas in the United States. *AIDS* 18(15):2065–2073.

Prejean J, Song R, Hernandez A, et al.; HIV Incidence Surveillance Group (2011). Estimated HIV incidence in the United States, 2006-2009. *PLoS ONE* 6(8):e17502.

Roland ME, Neilands TB, Krone MR, et al. (2005). Seroconversion following nonoccupational postexposure prophylaxis against HIV. *Clin Infect Dis* 41(10):1507–1513.

Ruprecht RM, O'Brien LG, Rossoni LD, Nusinoff-Lehrman S (1986). Suppression of mouse viraemia and retroviral disease by 3'-azido-3'-deoxythymidine. *Nature* 323(6087):467–469.

Sax PE, Wohl D, Yin MT, et al. (2015). Tenofovir alafenamide versus tenofovir disoproxil fumarate, coformulated with elvitegravir, cobicistat, and emtricitabine, for initial treatment of HIV-1 infection: two randomised, double-blind, phase 3, non-inferiority trials. *Lancet* 385(9987):2606–2615.

Schechter M, do Lago RF, Mendelsohn AB, et al.; Praca Onze Study Team (2004). Behavioral impact, acceptability, and HIV incidence among homosexual men with access to postexposure chemoprophylaxis for HIV. *J Acquir Immune Defic Syndr* 35(5):519–525.

Scheid DC, Hamm RM, Stevens KW (2000). Cost-effectiveness of human immunodeficiency virus postexposure prophylaxis for healthcare workers. *Pharmacoeconomics* 18(4):355–368.

Simonds RJ, Steketee R, Nesheim S, et al. (1998). Impact of zidovudine use on risk and risk factors for perinatal transmission of HIV. Perinatal AIDS Collaborative Transmission Studies. *AIDS* 12(3):301–308.

Smith DK, Grohskopf LA, Black RJ, et al. (2005). Antiretroviral postexposure prophylaxis after sexual, injection-drug use, or other nonoccupational exposure to HIV in the United States: recommendations from the U.S. Department of Health and Human Services. *MMWR Recomm Rep* 54(RR-2):1–20.

Spreen W, Ford SL, Chen S, Wilfret D, Margolis D, Gould E, Piscitelli S (2014). GSK1265744 pharmacokinetics in plasma and tissue following single-dose long-acting (LA) injectable administration in healthy subjects. *J Acquir Immune Defic Syndr* 67(5):481–486.

Stramer SL (2007). Current risks of transfusion-transmitted agents: a review. *Arch Pathol Lab Med* 131(5):702–707.

Swotinsky RB, Steger KA, Sulis C, Snyder S, Craven DE (1998). Occupational exposure to HIV: experience at a tertiary care center. *J Occup Environ Med* 40(12):1102–1109.

Taha TE, Kumwenda NI, Gibbons A, et al. (2003). Short postexposure prophylaxis in newborn babies to reduce mother-to-child transmission of HIV-1: NVAZ randomised clinical trial. *Lancet* 362(9391):1171–1177.

Tavares L, Roneker C, Johnston K, Lehrman SN, de Noronha F (1987). 3'-Azido-3'-deoxythymidine in feline leukemia virus–infected cats: a model for therapy and prophylaxis of AIDS. *Cancer Res* 47(12):3190–3194.

Thigpen MC, Kebaabetswe PM, Paxton LA, et al.; TDF2 Study Group (2012). Antiretroviral preexposure prophylaxis for heterosexual HIV transmission in Botswana. *N Engl J Med* 367(5):423–434.

Tsai CC, Follis KE, Sabo A, et al. (1995). Prevention of SIV infection in macaques by (R)-9-(2-phosphonylmethoxypropyl)adenine. *Science* 270(5239):1197–1199.

U.S. Preventive Services Task Force (USPSTF) (2013). Screening for HIV: U.S. Preventive Services Task Force recommendation statement. *Ann Intern Med* 159(1):51–60.

Van Damme, L, Corneli A, Ahmed K, et al.; FEM-PrEP STudy Group (2012). Preexposure prophylaxis for HIV infection among African women. *N Engl J Med* 367(5):411–422.

van der Straten A, Gomez CA, Saul J, Quan J, Padian N (2000). Sexual risk behaviors among heterosexual HIV serodiscordant couples in the era of post-exposure prevention and viral suppressive therapy. *AIDS* 14(4):F47–F54.

Ventuneac A, Carballo-Dieguez A, Leu CS, Levin B, Bauermeister J, Woodman-Maynard E, Giguere R (2009). Use of a rapid HIV home test to screen sexual partners: an evaluation of its possible use and relative risk. *AIDS Behav* 13(4):731–737.

Vigil KJ, Simmons P, Luna K, Martinez ML, Hasbun R, Arduino R (2014). Raltegravir plus tenofovir DF and emtricitabine for non-occupational postexposure prophylaxis (nPEP): African-Americans are at higher risk of non-completion of nPEP. Paper presented at the IDWeek, Philadelphia.

Wade NA, Birkhead GS, Warren BL, et al. (1998). Abbreviated regimens of zidovudine prophylaxis and perinatal transmission of the human immunodeficiency virus. *N Engl J Med* 339(20):1409–1414.

Waldo CR, Stall RD, Coates TJ (2000). Is offering post-exposure prevention for sexual exposures to HIV related to sexual risk behavior in gay men? *AIDS* 14(8):1035–1039.

Walensky RP, Paltiel AD (2006). Rapid HIV testing at home: does it solve a problem or create one? *Ann Intern Med* 145(6):459–462.

Wang SA, Panlilio AL, Doi PA, White AD, Stek M, Jr, Saah A (2000). Experience of healthcare workers taking postexposure prophylaxis after occupational HIV exposures: findings of the HIV Postexposure Prophylaxis Registry. *Infect Control Hosp Epidemiol* 21(12):780–785.

Weinhardt LS, Carey MP, Johnson BT, Bickham NL (1999). Effects of HIV counseling and testing on sexual risk behavior: a meta-analytic review of published research, 1985–1997. *Am J Public Health* 89(9):1397–1405.

Wesolowski LG, MacKellar DA, Facente SN, Dowling T, Ethridge SF, Zhu JH, Sullivan PS (2006). Post-marketing surveillance of

OraQuick whole blood and oral fluid rapid HIV testing. *AIDS* 20(12):1661–1666.

Wiktor SZ, Ekpini E, Karon JM, et al. (1999). Short-course oral zidovudine for prevention of mother-to-child transmission of HIV-1 in Abidjan, Cote d'Ivoire: a randomised trial. *Lancet* 353(9155):781–785.

World Health Organization (WHO) (2015). Guidelines on when to start antiretroviral therapy on pre-exposure prophylaxis for HIV. http:// apps.who.int/iris/bitstream/10665/186275/1/9789241509565_eng.pdf?ua=1. Accessed February 5, 2017.

Wortley PM, Chu SY, Diaz T, et al. (1995). HIV testing patterns: where, why, and when were persons with AIDS tested for HIV? *AIDS* 9(5):487–492.

Wright AA, Katz IT (2006). Home testing for HIV. *N Engl J Med* 354(5):437–440.

32.

VACCINES FOR THE PREVENTION AND TREATMENT OF HIV INFECTION

Josephine H. Cox, Stuart Z. Shapiro, Liza Dawson, Cynthia Geppert,

Andrew M. Siegel, and M. Patricia D'Souza

INTRODUCTION TO THE HIV-1 VACCINE WORLD

Although the world is still in the midst of a global pandemic, with 36.7 million people living with HIV infection, 2.1 million newly HIV-infected people, and 1.1 million AIDS-related deaths in 2015 alone, there is reason for optimism. Substantial breakthroughs in the understanding of HIV transmission, and advances in the science of the treatment and prevention of infection with HIV provide strong evidence that a dramatic alteration in the course of the HIV/AIDS pandemic is possible. The availability of combination antiretroviral therapy for prevention as well as treatment (Deeks et al., 2012; Gardner et al. 2011; Maartens et al., 2014), advances in pre-exposure prophylaxis with oral or mucosally delivered antiretroviral medications to reduce an individual's risk of acquiring HIV infection (Baeten et al., 2013; Vermund et al., 2013), scale-up of medical male circumcision (Tobian et al., 2014), services aimed at the prevention of mother-to-child transmission (Govender and Coovadia, 2014), and condom and clean needle provision all suggest that controlling and ultimately ending the global HIV/AIDS epidemic is possible. However, achieving the goal of ending the HIV/AIDS epidemic with these technologies alone will require implementing a costly, multifaceted, comprehensive, and continuous global effort to expand testing, treatment, and prevention programs. Therefore, many believe we will end the epidemic much sooner if we meet the scientific challenge of developing an HIV vaccine (Fauci and Marston, 2014).

With nearly all pathogens for which effective vaccines have been developed (e.g., smallpox, measles, and poliovirus), there exists a natural model of protection: the immune response to the pathogen ultimately clears the microbe from the body of many if not most infected people and confers durable protection against reinfection (Plotkin, 2010; Plotkin and Plotkin, 2011). The human immune system already provides proof of the concept that it can generate the protective response that we need to mimic in a vaccine. Unfortunately, this does not apply to HIV infection. The body's natural immune response to HIV infection is inadequate. The immune system cannot eliminate the virus from the body; in fact, it cannot even protect the body from superinfection with another HIV-1 strain.

This is because HIV-1 is a highly variable virus that integrates in the host genome, rapidly establishes latency, and effectively evades both humoral and cellular immune responses by an extremely high mutation rate in immune targeted virus sites. Thus, it is necessary for both effective preventive and therapeutic HIV vaccines to induce in the recipient a response that differs qualitatively, quantitatively, or both from that induced by natural infection (Koff, 2012; Koff et al., 2013).

PREVENTIVE HIV VACCINE DEVELOPMENT

HIV-1 Vaccine Efficacy Trials Strategy to Discover Correlates of Immune Protection

Despite the absence of clear immune response requirements for vaccine efficacy, many scientists believe that a vaccine effective at preventing HIV infection and/or reducing viral load and clinical disease progression post-infection is possible (see Figure 32.1). But we must first discover the right antibody or cellular immune response needed. Indeed, many believe that an efficacious vaccine may need to elicit both protective antibody and T-cell responses (Benmira et al., 2010). Thus the history of HIV vaccine development is a succession of experimental clinical trials of candidate products eliciting different types of immune responses in the hope that, once a partial efficacy signal is observed, the immune correlates of protection could be identified, allowing vaccine developers to enhance the efficacy of the partially protective product (Shapiro, 2013). Despite global commitment, however, the first decades of scientific effort brought only disappointment. The first candidate to be tested aimed at inducing protective, neutralizing antibodies against the virus envelope protein. Two large efficacy trials, one in the United States and one in Thailand, of a recombinant bivalent HIV-1 envelope formulated with alum demonstrated no efficacy in the populations studied (Flynn et al., 2005; Pitisuttithum et al., 2006). Subsequently, investigators turned their attention to T-cell-based vaccines, hoping to induce cytotoxic CD8+ T lymphocytes to either protect against acquisition of infection or improve control of plasma HIV-1 viral load after infection. Between 2007 and 2013, three major T-cell-based vaccine

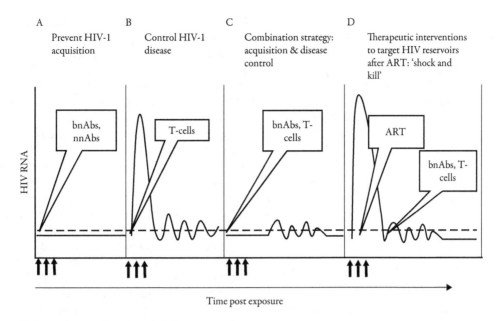

Figure 32.1 Hypothetical course of HIV infection with different vaccine strategies.   Panel A shows the hypothetical course of infection in vaccinated persons. Preexisting broadly neutralizing (bnAbs) or non-neutralizing antibodies (nnAbs) can prevent HIV infection. Panel B shows how a T-cell vaccine might decrease the burst of viremia and dissemination that occurs in primary infection. Panel C shows how a combination antibody and T-cell vaccine strategy could diminish the viral reservoir, decrease virus levels at the set point, and increase the length of time viral levels are controlled. Panel D shows sustained virological remission, in which viral replication is reduced to below detectable levels following antiretroviral therapy (ART) and remains controlled following cessation of daily ART and in the presence of therapeutic vaccine-elicited immune responses.

trials failed to demonstrate efficacy. Two of these trials tested an adenovirus serotype 5 (Ad5) vector expressing the internal HIV-1 proteins *gag, pol,* and *nef.* The first study of this product (Step), in North and South America, showed no efficacy and, in fact, may have increased the risk of HIV-1 acquisition in certain subgroups (Buchbinder et al. 2008). A second study (Phambili) of the same vaccine, in South Africa, was terminated shortly after initiation; unblinded follow-up also showed increased rates of HIV-1 infection in vaccinees (Gray et al., 2011). The third study (HVTN 505) tested a DNA plasmid-vectored vaccine boosted with an Ad5 vectored vaccine; both components in this vaccine regimen expressed HIV-1 proteins *env, gag,* and *pol.* Vaccinations were halted at the interim analysis in April 2013 because of lack of efficacy. Fortunately, there was no immediate evidence of increased rates of HIV-1 acquisition among recipients of the vaccines; but unblinded follow-up of participants is ongoing (Hammer et al., 2013). In summary, although the DNA plasmid and adenovirus platforms induced robust cell-mediated immune responses, and data from nonhuman primate models suggest that such immune responses might lead to control of viral replication, these vaccines failed to reduce acquisition of infection or provide a lasting reduction of HIV viral load in men who have sex with men or heterosexual men and women.

In 2012, an unexpected success occurred in a vaccine trial conducted in a low-incidence heterosexual population in Thailand (RV144). The vaccine regimen tested in this trial consisted of a canarypox-vectored (ALVAC) priming immunization expressing the HIV-1 antigens *gag, pol,* and *env* with

a bivalent HIV gp120 envelope protein booster immunization. The RV144 vaccine regimen had modest efficacy of 31% (Rerks-Ngarm et al., 2009). This vaccine regimen had induced poorer neutralizing antibody responses than the earlier antibody-based products (Montefiori et al., 2012) and poorer cytotoxic T-cell responses than the earlier T-cell-based products (Buchbinder et al., 2008; Gray et al., 2011; Hammer et al., 2013), so it was not clear what immunological mechanism(s) may have produced the measured efficacy. An intensive international collaborative effort was mounted to examine possible vaccine immune correlates. This study demonstrated that non-neutralizing plasma antibodies directed at the second variable region of the gp120 envelope protein correlated with decreased HIV-1 acquisition (Haynes, Gilbert, et al., 2012). In addition, plasma envelope protein IgA responses correlated with decreased HIV-1 vaccine efficacy (Haynes, Gilbert, et al., 2012). Follow-up correlates analyses indicated the robustness and breadth of the IgG correlate of risk across multiple subtypes of V1V2 antigens (Zolla-Pazner et al., 2014). A genetic analysis of RV144 breakthrough viruses in vaccinees and placebo-treated subjects indicated the site of immune pressure to be a single lysine residue (K169) in the second variable (V2) region of envelope protein (Rolland et al., 2012; Zolla-Pazner et al., 2014). Furthermore, it was shown that anti-envelope protein V1V2-specific IgG3 was the immunoglobulin subclass with the strongest correlation with prevention of HIV acquisition (Yates et al., 2014). Subsequent studies demonstrated that the IgG3 subclass was much better at engaging Fc-mediated antibody responses[1] when compared to the other

1. Antibodies bind to foreign pathogens (e.g., an infecting virus) via an antigen-binding pocket in the antibody Fab region. With neutralizing antibodies this binding alone is sufficient to neutralize the virus by blocking the virus from connecting with a potential host cell-surface receptor or agglutinating (clumping) the virus for elimination. Opposite the Fab region in all antibodies is an Fc region that helps the antibody stick to the surface of the body's cells that have Fc receptors on their surface. This brings the antibody-bound virus close to some host immune cells which can kill or suppress the virus's functioning.

subclasses. This provides a possible mechanism explaining the association of non-neutralizing anti-envelope protein V1V2 IgG3 with a lower rate of HIV acquisition (Chung et al., 2014). The anti-envelope protein IgG3 response decreased quickly after vaccination as did overall vaccine efficacy (Robb et al., 2012), raising the question of whether an inadequate quantity or persistence of antibody after vaccination might have contributed to the modest vaccine efficacy observed in RV144. In sum, these correlates of risk studies point to the importance of Fc-mediated functional antibody responses, directed against a specific region of envelope, in mediating the differing rates of HIV acquisition observed in RV144. They provide a foundation for directing immune analyses planned for future HIV vaccine clinical trials.

Recapitulating RV 144 with Refined Protein Boosts and Adjuvants in a High-Risk Population

The HIV vaccine field has agreed that the next logical step toward the goal of a licensable vaccine is to evaluate the RV144 pox-protein prime-boost approach in a higher incidence population in a region of the world most affected by the HIV epidemic (i.e., southern Africa). This follow-up should be with vaccines that more closely match those that circulate in the proposed trial population (HIV-1 clade C). It is also logical that follow-up vaccine platforms should build upon the "correlates of risk" analysis in RV144, to both confirm those findings and to define additional correlates of protection for HIV vaccines.

Two distinct clinical trial programs are being developed: a licensure track and a research track. First, the licensure track phase 3 program aims to adapt the vaccine regimen from Thailand into South Africa by utilizing HIV-1 clade C gene inserts and proteins more closely matching the circulating strains in this region. The vaccine design includes a clade C-adapted ALVAC prime-ALVAC/Bivalent gp120 protein/MF59® boost vaccine regimen. Also, the vaccination schedule has been altered to improve the magnitude and duration of vaccine-elicited immune responses above those induced in RV144. These changes have been made with the scientific reasoning that improvements or extensions of the previously measured, risk-correlative immune responses will translate into improvements in vaccine efficacy. Clinical trial HVTN 100 is the first in this series of trials in South Africa; it is a phase 1 trial evaluating ALVAC-HIV (vCP2438) prime with ALVAC-HIV (vCP2438) + Bivalent Subtype C gp120/MF59® boosts. MF59® has been selected as the protein adjuvant because it has generated superior antibody responses in vaccines against influenza, hepatitis B, and HIV (Podda, 2001; Singh et al., 2006; Vesikari et al., 2009). For HIV in particular, MF59®, given together with an HIV-1 SF2 gp120 envelope protein vaccine candidate, elicited greater HIV-specific antibody responses than alum (McElrath, 1995; Thongcharoen et al., 2007).

The research program will focus on the broader goal of advancing the field by discovering more immune response biomarkers that can predict HIV vaccine protective efficacy.

Such biomarkers will be immunological correlates of protection. To do this, the program will evaluate multiple vaccine regimens containing combinations of next-generation vaccine products (including DNA plasmid- and NYVAC-vectored as well as envelope protein vaccine components) and different adjuvant systems to identify those vaccine regimens exhibiting diverse immunological profiles (Manrique et al., 2014). Regimens using different combinations will be evaluated in several phase 1 and 2a trials. The best performing of these candidate vaccine regimens will then be selected for further study on the basis of safety and immunogenicity data collected through the primary immunogenicity time point. Vaccines that induce distinct immunological profiles may advance to proof-of-concept efficacy testing where, if they demonstrate any efficacy in prevention of acquisition of infection, the immune profile data may indicate additional immunological correlates of protection (Manrique et al., 2014).

Other HIV-1 vaccine products are being developed for efficacy testing in other large clinical trials. These include a recombinant adenovirus serotype 26 (rAd26) prime expressing *gag*, *pol*, and *env* with a modified vaccinia Ankara (MVA) boost expressing the same antigens. This platform has shown substantial protection against both SIVmac251 and SHIV-SF162P3 challenges in rhesus monkeys (Barouch et al., 2012; Barouch, Stephenson, et al., 2013). Further boosting with an envelope protein gp140 trimer appears to improve the observed protective efficacy of the platform in monkeys (Barouch et al., 2015).

Improving the Design of T-Cell-Based Vaccines

Three of the six HIV-1 vaccine efficacy trials conducted to date were designed to elicit predominantly T-cell responses (Buchbinder et al., 2008; Gray et al., 2011; Hammer et al., 2013; McElrath et al., 2008; Rerks-Ngarm et al., 2009). The Step/Phambili and HVTN 505 trials used an Ad5 platform and generated T-cell responses as detected by IFN-γ ELISpot and ICS in ~60–80% of volunteers. The responses were of modest magnitude, but they had signatures indicating the functional T-cell responses were sustained over time (Hammer et al., 2013; Korber et al., 2009; McElrath et al., 2008; McMichael and Koff, 2014). Further studies showed that an average of only one epitope per HIV protein was recognized across vaccinated individuals and many of these epitopes were in variable regions (Hertz et al., 2013). These vaccines may have provided limited coverage against HIV isolates encountered during exposure; but vaccine-induced responses should be capable of recognizing multiple HIV variants as well as the rapidly arising escape mutants seen in HIV-infected individuals to be broadly effective. In retrospect, it appears that the Ad5 platform and other first-generation HIV vaccines failed to induce a sufficient breadth and depth of T-cell responses to enable sufficient coverage of viral sequence diversity. Hence new approaches to improve the quality and quantity of T-cell responses to recognize multiple, diverse epitopes are required (Barouch and Picker, 2014; Korber et al., 2009; McMichael and Koff, 2014).

Future strategies to improve T-cell responses include the use of mosaic antigens that are generated by bioinformatically integrating regions of natural HIV-1 sequence to contain a maximum of potential T-cell epitopes. These polyvalent synthetic vaccines cover the sequence diversity of thousands of peptides from different HIV subtypes and enable the delivery of a diverse range of epitopes covering millions of different viruses with a small set (2–4) of immunogens (Fischer et al., 2007). Another approach to focus T-cell responses is to immunize with only conserved HIV sequences or parts of HIV that are critical for replication of multiple variants of HIV and therefore cannot easily mutate. The hypothesis underlying this strategy is that immune responses specific for conserved HIV-1 regions will recognize a multitude of different HIV-1 subtypes and that these immune responses will impose a high fitness cost on any HIV-1 escape viral mutants (Borthwick et al., 2014; McMichael and Koff, 2014; Rolland et al., 2007). One further strategy under exploration is epitope separation to minimize antigenic competition and broaden vaccine responses. This is achieved by administering separate vaccine components at several anatomical sites (i.e., polytopic vaccination).

Investigators are also using novel delivery systems and adjuvants to improve the immunogenicity of vaccine constructs. DNA plasmid products have been a major focus in the field because they cause vaccine antigens to be made inside host cells, which is necessary to induce cellular immune responses. As well, DNA plasmid vaccines have a good safety profile and are relatively easy to manufacture. Unfortunately, early generations of DNA plasmid vaccines with HIV antigen inserts have not induced very strong immune responses in people. A recently completed human study of co-administration of DNA vaccines with cytokines and electroporation resulted in more robust CD4+ and CD8+ T-cell responses (89% positive response rate) at half the vaccine dose and with fewer vaccinations compared to the same vaccine delivered intramuscularly without electroporation (Kalams et al., 2013). Similarly, a strategy to direct vaccine-induced immune responses toward mucosal portals of HIV entry by supplementing DNA vaccines with mucosal chemokines, such as CCR10 ligand, was shown to promote mucosal antibody responses and improve protection in vaginal SIV challenges of nonhuman primates (Kutzler et al., 2016).

CD4 T-cell responses have received relatively little attention in terms of vaccine design, in part because these cells are the primary targets of HIV infection. Many worry that eliciting these responses by vaccination may increase potential targets of infection. However, there are preclinical data to suggest that HIV-specific CD4 T cells are important immune correlates of viremia containment in SIV/HIV-1 infection. Whether these cells function by direct antiviral activity or provide help to the B-cell (antibody-producing) or effector CD8$^+$ T-cell populations requires further elucidation (Hel et al., 2002). In the original RV144 immune correlates primary analysis, the level of envelope protein–specific CD4+ T cells did not significantly correlate with HIV infection among vaccine recipients. Using the same method as in the original RV 144 correlates analysis but including polyfunctionality

scores rather than just measuring the number of envelope protein–specific CD4+ T cells, new data suggest that a subset of CD4+ T cells expressing CD40L, IL-2, IL-4, IFN-γ, and TNF-α inversely correlate with infection. It is possible that these cells might have played a role in vaccine efficacy by contributing T-cell help for the antibody production detected as a correlate in the primary analysis rather than direct action against HIV-infected cells. It may be crucial to understand how CD4$^+$ T cells can influence the quality and persistence of protective CD8$^+$ T-cell and B-cell (antibody) responses and how to specifically target these cells through vaccination to increase the efficacy of candidate vaccines (Streeck et al., 2013).

Novel Viral Vectors for Vaccines to Induce Better Cellular Immune Responses

Viral vectors are another way to get vaccine antigens made inside cells in order to induce cellular immune responses. Most attention has been focused on non-replicating viral vectors. The selection of a non-replicating vector is dependent upon certain key factors: preexisting vector specific immunity, assurance of replication incompetence, the nature of illness associated with the wild-type virus, tissue tropism, quality of the immune response elicited, and manufacturability. Non-replicating viral vectors used for candidate HIV vaccines include canarypox (ALVAC), Vaccinia vectors (NYVAC and MVA), fowlpox, adenoviruses (Ad5, Ad26, Ad35, and nonhuman adenoviruses), rhabdoviruses, and alphaviruses. Recent data suggest that viral vectors are not simply inert vehicles for the passive delivery of antigens but also can actively recruit elements of innate immunity to create a cytokine milieu that can crucially influence an adaptive immune response. As shown in Table 32.1, many non-replicating vaccine vectors have been tested in multiple phase I and phase II trials and in three, more advanced, phase IIb trials: adenoviruses (chimp Ad, Ad5, Ad26, Ad35) and poxviruses (MVA, NYVAC), alone or in homologous or heterologous prime boost regimens (Buchbinder et al., 2008; Franchini et al., 2004; Hammer et al., 2013; Pantaleo and Levy, 2013; Rerks-Ngarm et al., 2009). Only two vector concepts have advanced to clinical efficacy (phase III) testing: ALVAC and Ad5. The recombinant ALVAC vaccine platform exhibited minimal safety issues when administered to 8,000 individuals in the RV144 study (Franchini et al., 2004; Rerks-Ngarm et al., 2009; Robb et al., 2012). Additional promising and novel vaccine vector concepts are a priority to accelerate HIV-1 vaccine development (Barouch and Picker, 2014; Pantaleo and Levy, 2013).

Live, replication-competent recombinant virally vectored vaccines are attracting more attention. They are potentially more immunogenic than replication-incompetent vectors in humans. This is because live vectors, upon inoculation, may replicate in tissues to levels that exceed the total dose of replication-incompetent vectors. Also, they provide prolonged expression of inserted genes which may be critical to the development of effective cellular or humoral immunity. In addition, live vectors induce proinflammatory cytokines

Table 32.1 HIV-1 VACCINES IN DEVELOPMENT AND IN HUMAN CLINICAL TRIALS

	CONCEPT	VARIABLES TESTED
Phase IIb Follow-up	Confirm RV144 protective immune responses	ALVAC/AIDSVAX
Adjuvants	Improve antigen presentation, potency, durability, affinity maturation, and mucosal targeting	IL-12, MF59, GM-CSF
Prime-Boost Regimens	Efficiently prime T and B cells, improve functionality and breadth, extend durability, and overcome vector immunity	Combinations of Ad, poxviruses, and other vectors Prime with DNA boost with vectored vaccines and/or proteins
Replicating Viral Vectors	Reproduce efficacy of licensed vaccines and promising results with replicating viral vectors seen in NHP challenge studies. Provide durable potent responses in mucosal and other tissues.	VSV, CDV, CMV, Sendai virus, yellow fever virus, and Varicella virus Replicating adeno- and poxviruses
Antigenic Delivery and Priming	Improve antigenic delivery, potency, and breadth.	Electroporation Heterologous priming T-cell designs: mosaic and conserved immunogens
Immuno-prophylaxis	Long-term endogenous expression or passive transfer of bnAbs to block acquisition	VRC01 bnAb AAV delivery bnAbs

The concept column lists the vaccine concept proposed for testing. Abbreviations: AAV, adeno-associated virus; bnAbs, broadly neutralizing antibodies; CDV, canine distemper virus; CMV, cytomegalovirus virus; GM-CSF, granulocyte macrophage colony–stimulating factor; IL-2, interleukin-2; VSV, vesicular stomatitis virus.

and co-stimulatory molecules that function as adjuvants to improve immunogenicity. Lastly, live, replication-competent vectors are more easily manufactured, giving the potential for production of larger total antigen doses. Novel replicating vectors with diverse biological properties are being explored to increase expression of the HIV-1 envelope protein or other HIV antigens, to direct antigen expression to the mucosa, in particular vaginal and rectal surfaces, and to enhance T-cell responses (Barouch and Picker, 2014; Parks et al., 2013). The current suite of replicating vectors that are being tested in preclinical and clinical trials include vesicular stomatitis virus (VSV), canine distemper virus (CDV), cytomegalovirus (CMV), adenoviruses, poxviruses, Sendai virus, yellow fever virus, and measles virus. So far, only HIV vaccines vectored in replicating measles, Sendai, VSV, and vaccinia viruses have entered clinical trials in humans. There is also great interest in the persistent CMV vaccine vector because of the ability of the recombinant vaccine to elicit and indefinitely maintain high-frequency, tissue-resident effector memory T-cell (TEM) responses. These cells can stringently control a highly pathogenic, AIDS-causing SIV in the Rhesus macaque/SIV model of infection, and maintain this control (perhaps even clearing infection) over the long term (Hansen et al., 2011; Hansen, Piatak, et al., 2013; Hansen, Sacha, et al., 2013). The goal is to develop an optimized HCMV/HIV vector appropriate for phase 1 clinical testing. This product will also be tested as a therapeutic vaccine. The hope is that persistent replicating vectors could be delivered as a one-shot vaccine similar to many childhood vaccines.

Although much optimism surrounds the field of vaccine vector development at present, the regulatory hurdles for testing replicating vectors are high because of safety concerns. This is especially the case with adenovectors, such as Ad4 or Ad26, because of concern surrounding the possibility that Ad5 vectors may have led to increased HIV acquisition in the Step and Phambili clinical trials (Barouch and Picker, 2014; Chen et al., 2015; D'Souza and Yang, 2015; Fauci et al., 2014; Parks et al., 2013).

Improving on Protective Antibodies

The holy grail of HIV-1 vaccine development is the induction of broadly neutralizing antibodies (bnAbs) against HIV-1 (Haynes, Kelsoe, et al., 2012; Mascola and Haynes, 2013). Although the HIV-1 envelope protein does have conserved regions (epitopes) to which neutralizing antibodies can bind (Haynes and Alam, 2008), no current vaccine candidates have been able to induce high levels of bnAbs. Until recently, only four different clusters of epitope targets on the HIV envelope protein for bnAb development were recognized: the V1/V2 glycan, the N332 glycan supersite, the CD4 binding site, and the gp41 membrane-proximal external region (Liao, Bonsignori, et al., 2013). However, several newly isolated monoclonal antibodies have identified more epitopic targets for broad neutralization on the HIV-1 envelope protein (Pancera et al., 2014). Singly and in combination, antibodies that target these regions are able to neutralize, in an in vitro assay, nearly all the available strains circulating around the globe today. Many of these conserved epitope targets are only weakly immunogenic, possibly because the structures mimic host proteins and so the B cells that strongly bind to them are down-regulated by the physiological process of immune tolerance (Kelsoe et al., 2014). Approximately 20% of HIV-infected people develop bnAbs, but only after several years of infection. Unfortunately, by the time these antibodies are produced, HIV's genetic material has integrated into the chromosomes of an infected person's cells, establishing a latent viral reservoir so these antibodies are unable to clear the body of the virus infection. Furthermore, these bnAbs do not appear to control the level of viremia in the HIV-infected individuals who do develop them. Nevertheless, many scientists believe that if these antibodies can be induced before exposure to the virus they will prevent acquisition of virus infection, and studies of passive transfer of monoclonal bnAbs into nonhuman primates support this belief.

Passive transfer of already formed antibodies was used as an early strategy to attempt to prevent mother-to-child transmission; these studies used neutralizing antibodies derived from pooled serum of HIV-infected individuals. This approach was not successful and was largely abandoned until monoclonal bnAbs with more potent activity were identified. Now that technical advances have facilitated a renaissance in isolation of very potent monoclonal bnAbs (Cohen, 2013; Koff et al., 2013), both passive transfer of monoclonal bnAbs and vectored immunoprophylaxis (whereby monoclonal bnAb genes are delivered in adeno-associated virus [AAV] or other vectors injected into muscle, so the muscle cells will produce the specific antibodies for distribution around the body) are being developed for clinical use (Balazs and West, 2012; Schnepp and Johnson, 2014). The advantage of passive immunization is the immediate availability of high-affinity, mature bnAbs to neutralize HIV. However, a disadvantage is that passive immunity is limited by the half-life of circulating antibodies, which have to be boosted at regular intervals to maintain the protective effect. Vectored immunoprophylaxis has the advantage of only requiring one injection for long-term antibody production (Nathwani et al., 2011; Schnepp and Johnson, 2014), but some researchers worry that the persistence of the product in the body may have undesired effects that cannot be easily stopped because the product cannot be withdrawn.

The long-term, but formidable, challenge is to fashion those neutralizing antibody epitope targets on the HIV envelope protein as immunogens in a vaccine candidate so that a vaccinated person will induce bnAbs that protect against HIV acquisition. The conformational structure of specific envelope bnAb target epitopes bound to monoclonal bnAbs has been exquisitely characterized using X-ray crystallography and cryo-electron microscopy (Cohen, 2013; Klein et al., 2013). This has given us much knowledge about their physical structure and the angle of approach bnAbs must take to access the epitopes on the surface of a virus. Some investigators believe that an immunogen can be constructed that only exposes the epitope targets for bnAbs, so that the immune system makes antibodies that target these epitopes. They are constructing candidate immunogens for immunization of nonhuman primates and then analyzing precisely how the induced antibodies bind to the immunogens, in order to discovery how to subtly modify the immunogen structure to improve the quality of binding antibodies. Other investigators believe that induction of bnAbs with a vaccine will require a strategy of sequential immunogens with differing HIV-1 envelope proteins to mimic the mutational evolution of the virus envelope protein during natural infection (Cohen, 2013; Klein et al., 2013). One approach (B-cell lineage-based design) to choosing those sequential immunogens uses the examination of serial blood samples collected from HIV-infected patients who developed bnAbs, to duplicate the co-evolution of the virus envelope protein and antibodies against it (Liao, Lynch, et al., 2013). Such analysis has demonstrated the evasive changes that the HIV envelope protein undergoes to escape the host antibody response and the ensuing mutation of B-cell genes to produce antibodies that bind the epitope targets on the evolving HIV envelope with progressively greater affinity. This work illustrates an essential paradox in the interaction between HIV and its human host: as the virus mutates to evade HIV-specific antibodies, it ultimately stimulates production of antibodies with much greater breadth and potency—that is, bnAbs. An interesting finding of these analyses has been that the germline (unmutated) genes from which many bnAbs have evolved do not bind at all or bind with very low affinity to HIV-1 envelope protein. Since the naive (unmutated) antibody-producing B cells must be engaged by binding to the immunogen to start the process of antibody evolution, this presents another challenge for B-cell lineage-based design. Some hypothesize that engagement may need to be accomplished with specially designed small-molecule mimics of single-target epitopes (minimal epitopes), themselves mutated to bind germline antibody genes with greater affinity (Azoitei et al., 2014).

THERAPEUTIC HIV VACCINE DEVELOPMENT

A therapeutic vaccine for HIV is conceptually different from a preventive vaccine. While preventive vaccine developers have sought to induce new immune responses to prevent HIV-1 from establishing infection in an uninfected person, therapeutic vaccine developers have tried to expand existing, partially effective immune responses to accomplish better control of virus replication and thus halt or delay disease progression. The therapeutic vaccine products, as well as the goals and hypothesized mechanisms of action of therapeutic vaccination, have changed enormously over the course of the HIV/AIDS epidemic. This is because diagnostic assays have improved, our understanding of HIV disease pathogenesis has changed, and effective antiretroviral drug treatment options have become available. Recently, interest in a therapeutic vaccine has been rekindled as part of the HIV cure research agenda to enhance immune-mediated clearance of virus-producing cells and/or assist in the destruction of the reservoir of latently infected cells that drug therapy alone is not able to eliminate (Barouch and Deeks, 2014; Deeks et al., 2012; Pantaleo and Levy, 2013).

Earliest Efforts and Why They Failed

Very early in the AIDS epidemic, before the availability of effective antiretroviral drug therapy, it was proposed that therapeutic vaccination might be able to slow or prevent progression of HIV disease by controlling viremia (Salk, 1987). Some scientists even reasoned at the time that an effective therapeutic vaccination response might be easier to achieve than a preventive vaccine, as the therapeutic vaccine would simply have to boost the early, believed-to-be viremia-controlling natural immune response to the virus. A killed-virus vaccine (Remune) based on this concept was tested in clinical trials. However, this simple, boosting approach was based on the early misconception that HIV remained latent, well controlled by the initial immune response, only to re-emerge because of waning immunity years after initial infection to cause disease progression to AIDS. Advances in measurement of viremia, CD4+ T-cell subsets, and parameters of immunosuppression have given us a greater appreciation of the extensive and continued virus replication and early destruction of the immune system that we now understand provides the basis for disease progression. It is not surprising that these early therapeutic vaccine trials failed to show any significant clinical benefit (Glidden et al., 2001), as they were based on an incomplete understanding of the pathogenesis of AIDS.

Continued Efforts

With the advent of increasingly effective, simple-to-take, and relatively nontoxic combination drug therapies, there was less urgency for immune therapies to substitute for or augment drug therapy. Some interest remained in therapeutic vaccine development to give HIV-infected individuals relief from having to take potentially toxic medicines for the rest of their lives. Also, some preventive HIV vaccine product developers thought that by testing in HIV-infected populations the path to testing a prophylactic vaccine would be quicker and the positive results generated would help them obtain the support needed for expensive, necessarily large preventive vaccine licensure trials. Some further reasoned that if the vaccine had some effect in both populations it would expand the market for any eventually licensed product. Thus, viral-vectored preventive vaccines such as ALVAC (Autran et al., 2008), adenoviruses (Schooley et al., 2010), and NYVAC (Harari et al., 2012) as well as DNA plasmid-based preventive vaccines (Rosenberg et al., 2010) have been tested in HIV-infected subjects. All of these products have induced measurable immune responses, and some have produced modest reductions in viral load or modest delays in time to viral rebound after stopping antiretroviral drug therapy. However, they have generally failed to demonstrate substantial changes or significant clinical benefit. This is not surprising, as the pragmatic rationales for testing preventive vaccines in the therapeutic setting have not encouraged investigators to consider that the specific immunological requirements of a therapeutic vaccine may differ from a preventive vaccine.

In an approach specific to therapeutic vaccination, some investigators have vaccinated HIV-infected individuals with their own dendritic cells loaded with HIV-1 antigens from their own virus (García et al., 2013; Jenabian et al., 2013). These vaccine regimens appeared safe in early stage clinical trials. They also demonstrated enhancement of cellular immune responses and some effectiveness in control of viremia after cessation of antiretroviral therapy. However, it is not clear that they have demonstrated sufficient clinical benefit to merit licensure. And, as the immunotherapy product needs to be prepared specifically for each individual patient, these investigations must be viewed more as proof of concept that awaits further technical advances before products can be scaled up.

New Efforts Stimulated by the Cure Research Agenda

The HIV cure agenda has created new interest in a therapeutic vaccine. In this context, a therapeutic vaccine would not be a stand-alone product; rather, it would be used to enhance immune-mediated clearance of virus-producing cells and/or assist in the destruction of the reservoir of latently infected cells that drug therapy alone cannot eliminate. A cure strategy that has generated considerable attention is called "shock and kill" (Barouch and Deeks, 2014). This involves use of a pharmacological agent to induce latently infected cells to produce virus ("shock") accompanied by another treatment to enhance the body's ability to eliminate ("kill") the new virus-producing cells. The second agent is necessary because reactivated infected CD4+ cells seem resistant to the normally cytopathic effects of HIV-1 infection (Shan et al., 2012). The hope is to either eliminate the reservoir so that rebound infection does not appear after stopping antiretroviral therapy or reduce the reservoir to such a low level that a repeatedly boosted or persistent immune response can control viremia to below the level of detection without antiretroviral treatment. Many investigators are looking to a therapeutic vaccine or immunotherapeutic agent for an effective "kill" agent. Ongoing clinical trials of therapeutic vaccine candidates can be found listed on the Treatment Action Group (TAC) website (TAC, 2017).

The new efforts at therapeutic vaccine development recognize that the body's usual immune responses to infection with HIV-1 are rarely adequate to control HIV replication. Thus, to be effective, a therapeutic vaccine likely must induce immune responses that are either, or both, quantitatively greater and qualitatively different than those induced by normal HIV infection. It is also clear that therapeutic HIV vaccine development needs to address several other issues:

(a) What type(s) of immune responses can be induced in an already HIV-1-infected person, and which will be most effective?

(b) What vaccine vectors, vehicles, or adjuvants will induce maximal (titer and breadth) responses?

(c) Why do initially controlling responses fail with time?

(d) Can adjuvant or adjunct non-antigen-specific immunotherapy contribute to vaccine efficacy by prolonging or reconstituting preexisting responses?

Many different types of immune responses have potential to contribute to the effectiveness of a therapeutic vaccine. There are rare individuals whose immune systems seem to be able to spontaneously control viral replication to a very great degree; these are called "elite controllers" (Walker, 2007). They appear to have very strong HIV-specific cellular (especially CD8+) responses, so such responses have received much attention from therapeutic vaccine developers. Other responses that have been discussed include neutralizing antibodies, ADCC-mediating antibodies, innate immune mechanisms (especially natural killer [NK] cells), restoration of Treg/Th17 balance, and combinations of these different types of immune responses (Barouch and Deeks, 2014; Pantaleo and Levy, 2013).

A lot of discussion among cellular immunity-based therapeutic vaccine developers focuses on the need to develop responses to new epitopes as opposed to boosting the level or restoring the functionality of the infected person's initial immune responses. Many developers feel that boosting initial responses is simply boosting responses from which the virus has already escaped by mutation, and this will not be helpful for controlling viremia. Thus it is thought that a vaccine should induce responses to escape epitopes and conserved epitopes, many of which are subdominant immune responses (Barouch and Deeks, 2014; Shapiro, 2015). The vaccine developers that follow this line of thinking are investigating many of the same avenues for improving the design of T-cell-based vaccines as preventive HIV vaccine developers. Others contend that that the specificity or number of epitopes recognized is not as crucial for viral control as is the specific functionality of the CD8+ T cells that recognize the epitopes (Thobakgale et al., 2011). They would develop a therapeutic vaccine complemented with some adjunct immunotherapy (such the anti-PD-1 or anti-CTLA-4 monoclonal antibodies being tried in cancer immunotherapy to reverse negative regulatory effects). These discussions can be expected to lead to many new clinical trials in the near future. One promising new approach that appears to be able to induce long-lasting cytotoxic T-cell responses to new epitopes is based on a persistent viral vector not previously used for vaccine development, CMV (Hansen et al., 2011; Hansen, Piatak, et al., 2013). Such a vaccine was discussed earlier in the section on novel viral vectors. Because of perceived regulatory constraints on testing vaccines based on persistent viral vectors in normal, healthy individuals, this vaccine will first be tested as a therapeutic/cure vaccine, in HIV-1-infected individuals. This candidate vaccine has not yet entered clinical trials, but if successful, it may have the fastest track to licensure of the new generation of therapeutic vaccine products. Because of the different requirements of therapeutic versus preventive vaccines, failure of this vaccine as a therapeutic vaccine should not preclude its testing as a preventive vaccine.

It has been very difficult to induce, by active immunization, the broadly neutralizing antibody responses that some investigators hope will control viremia. The administration of already identified broadly neutralizing monoclonal antibodies for passive protection is clearly the most direct route to the development of an effective antibody-based immunotherapeutic product. Such a product could contribute to the goal of reduction in size (or possible eradication) of the latent reservoir. However, if it only controls viremia without eradicating the latent reservoir, then it must be given every month or two to maintain antibody levels. Thus it should be seen as another means of antiretroviral therapy rather than an active vaccine that induces a long-term controlling immune response. Several broadly neutralizing monoclonal antibodies are already in development for HIV immunotherapy (Barouch, Whitney, et al., 2013; Chun et al., 2014). Some iterative clinical trials may be required to put together the most effective combinations of monoclonal antibodies after individual monoclonal antibodies have been shown to have effect. This may present some challenges in measuring clinical endpoints. However, there will be strong incentive to work through these challenges because of the demonstrated superior efficacy of combination chemotherapy for cancer, tuberculosis, and AIDS itself.

Challenges Remain

Finally, HIV therapeutic vaccine development presents serious challenges for clinical trial design, efficacy testing, and eventual licensure. There are several distinct target populations that need an immunotherapeutic HIV vaccine. The different adult target populations for a therapeutic HIV vaccine are (1) HIV-infected adults on antiretroviral therapy who have competent immune systems; (2) HIV-infected adults on antiretroviral therapy with few remaining CD4+ T cells; (3) HIV-infected adults not fully suppressed on ARV therapy; or (4) individuals not on antiretroviral therapy at all. With treatment guidelines increasingly recommending effective antiretroviral therapy for more categories of HIV-infected individuals it may become difficult, practically and ethically, to perform clinical trials of a therapeutic vaccine at all in the third and fourth groups. Similar categories exist for newborns infected with HIV-1, but since the newborn immune system is not exactly like the adult immune system, therapeutic vaccine development for newborns may need to consider other factors. Specific candidate vaccines may not be optimal for all persons, so separate clinical trials will be required to avoid lack of effect in inappropriate populations diluting the overall effect and thus leading to the rejection of vaccines useful only in specific clinical settings.

Clinical activity assays will vary in different clinical populations. Reductions in viremia can be measured in incompletely suppressed subjects, but more costly and less precise assays of the size of the latent reservoir must be performed in aviremic subjects. The ultimate test of an HIV immunotherapeutic product will be an analytic treatment interruption. However, treatment interruption runs a significant risk of doing harm to the subjects, by allowing expansion of what was a small reservoir in subjects put on antiretroviral therapy very early in infection or in subjects whose reservoirs have decreased in size because of many years of effective viral suppression on antiretroviral therapy. Therefore, analytic treatment interruptions should only be done in subjects in whom there is a realistic expectation of control—for example, as evidenced by a significant and substantial enhancement in a virus suppression assay (Slichter et al., 2014; Yang et al., 2012) and a significant spreading of the immune response to difficult-to-escape-from epitopes, as well as a measurable reduction in cell-associated RNA (Pasternak et al., 2013).

Lastly, it is unclear what will be the regulatory requirements for licensure of a therapeutic HIV vaccine. Antiretroviral treatment guidelines have the goal of reducing viral load to undetectable levels (Sarmento-Castro et al., 2011). This is possible and is believed to be best for the health of the individual as well as the surest way to prevent onward transmission of the virus to uninfected contacts. Since this is achievable with antiretroviral therapy, it is difficult to imagine the licensure of a therapeutic vaccine to be used in place of continued antiretroviral therapy that does less than can be accomplished with antiretrovirals. It will also be difficult to demonstrate clinical benefit for a vaccine product given at the same time as continued, effective antiretroviral treatment, because such clinical trials would take a very long time to accumulate enough clinical endpoints to demonstrate efficacy. It is heartening that there is renewed interest in therapeutic HIV vaccine development, but the path forward is not without considerable scientific as well as practical challenges.

ETHICAL CONSIDERATIONS

As this chapter underscores, the development and implementation of an HIV vaccine is a complex scientific charge. In the following brief commentary, we provide an overview of the most significant ethical concerns and direct the reader to key guidance documents for further study.

Over many years, researchers, sponsors, community advocates, bioethicists, and other stakeholders have grappled with ethical challenges in research directed at HIV vaccine development (Slack et al., 2007). While ethical principles and commitments remain constant, the specific challenges in HIV vaccine research have evolved significantly over time, as HIV treatment advances have changed the landscape of the epidemic; as global research and treatment programs have been rolled out around the world; and as new prevention modalities such as medical male circumcision, treatment as prevention, and pre-exposure prophylaxis (PrEP) have begun to occupy the forefront of the public health response.

In discussing ethical issues in vaccine clinical trials, it is important to distinguish between different phases of trials, particularly since phase I trials are often conducted in populations at low risk of HIV infection, and the principal issues revolve around safety of the volunteers with regard to any adverse events associated with the vaccine itself, as well as informed consent. In contrast, in phase IIb or phase III efficacy trials, populations at high risk of HIV acquisition must be enrolled to determine if the vaccine offers any protection from infection, and complex issues involving standards of medical care and management of risk are involved.

In the early years of HIV vaccine research, one of the principal ethical concerns in efficacy trials was about the need for proactive risk reduction counseling and provision of condoms to all trial participants (Chesney et al., 1995; Thapinta et al., 1999; UNAIDS,, 2000). The provision of risk reduction measures to all study participants is known as the "prevention package" and until recently has been relatively standard across all various types of prevention and vaccine trials (Ramjee et al., 2010)—whether or not these preventive measures were available in the local setting. In many cases, the prevention package provides a concrete benefit to participants, which many commentators consider ethically appropriate given that volunteers are taking on risks and burdens of an unproven product (National Bioethics Advisory Commission [NBAC], 2001).

There has also been discussion of the fact that the better the risk reduction efforts, the more difficult it would be to measure the effectiveness of a candidate vaccine, since HIV infection endpoints in controlled trials are needed to ascertain whether the vaccine provides a protective effect (Grobler and Abdool Karim, 2012). There was worry about potential conflict of interest on the part of researchers, in that they needed to measure HIV infections occurring in the study while, for ethical reasons, they actively encouraged participants to protect themselves (Chesney et al., 1995). Some research teams established guidelines (UNAID Guidance, 2000) stipulating that counseling staff providing risk reduction counseling should be independent of the research team.

The risk reduction package has been considered ethically essential, in part because there have been ongoing concerns that study participants might assume that an experimental vaccine would be protective and they might engage in riskier behavior or fail to adopt protective measures because of a "preventive misconception." In public health modeling studies, statisticians and modeling experts attempting to calculate the benefits of hypothetical vaccines generally assume some level of "risk disinhibition," meaning that vaccine recipients would engage in riskier behavior with regard to potential HIV exposure, partially offsetting the beneficial effects of a vaccine. In vaccine trials, in which the candidate vaccines have not been proven efficacious, the possibility of risk disinhibition is a serious concern, as it could mean that participants would have higher risk of HIV infection as a result of their misconceptions about the trial. Data from multiple HIV vaccine and prevention studies show that participants are not likely to engage in riskier behavior, and, in actuality, most participants engage in less risk behavior over time, as evidenced by stable or lower average rates of incidence in placebo arms compared to baseline levels (Bartholow et al., 2005; Gray et al., 2013; van Griensvan et al., 2004). In any case, a full understanding of potential risks and likelihood of benefit is required in all studies, and robust informed consent will always be an ethical requirement (Essack et al., 2010; Lindegger et al., 2006; London et al., 2012). Researchers have undertaken rigorous approaches to informed consent for vaccine trials, in some cases requiring a test of understanding to verify that participants realize the vaccine is unproven (Lindegger et al., 2006). Measures to avoid therapeutic misconception are particularly important in early proof-of-concept studies where there are limited data and likelihood of individual benefit to the participant. Furthermore, Lo and Grady (2013) have emphasized the responsibility of researchers to attend more rigorously to the assessment of participants' decision-making capacity, a required element in the provision of adequate informed consent.

Another major ethical concern is the existence of vaccine-induced antibodies that may complicate HIV testing for study participants outside the trial context (Ackers et al., 2003; Allen and Lau, 2008) and may also lead to adverse consequences such as stigmatization or social harm due to the misperception that these individuals are HIV infected. Researchers conducting vaccine trials have thus needed to set up programs to provide nucleic acid testing (NAT) which can differentiate between true HIV infection and vaccine-induced antibodies that may give false-positive results on standard HIV tests (Ackers et al., 2003; Essack et al., 2010). In some settings, access to NAT is simply impossible outside the research context, so special provisions need to be made. Often participants need to have documentation of their trial participation as well, so that they can present this evidence to insurers, immigration authorities, or employers if their HIV status is questioned (Slack et al., 2000).

As antiretroviral treatment was validated in the mid-1990s, a major ethical challenge facing the vaccine field was the need to provide antiretroviral therapy to study participants who did become infected in a trial. The difficulty arose in particular because the countries with highest incidence of HIV, especially sub-Saharan African countries, at that time had no access to antiretroviral therapy outside of the research context. A number of ethical consultations were carried out in the early vaccine research period by UNAIDS to address this conundrum (Guenter et al., 2000; UNAIDS, 2000). Most stakeholders agreed that provision of ART to any study participant who became infected was an ethical responsibility—yet mechanisms to provide this (when local clinical care did not provide antiretroviral therapy) were not always straightforward.

The extensive discussions about access to antiretroviral therapy for seroconverters in vaccine trials were part of a larger set of ongoing debates in research ethics about standards of care and prevention, post-trial access, and reasonable availability of study products as required by the Declaration of Helsinki (World Medical Association, 2000) (London, 2008; Shapiro and Benatar, 2005). Throughout the HIV epidemic, research funders from the global north have been conducting clinical trials in the global south. This situation raises important questions about access to care, disparities and inequities in care, and the ability of research sponsors and researchers to respond to health needs of the host countries where research is conducted (Lavery, 2004; London, 2005, 2008). These debates have arisen in prevention, vaccine, and treatment trials, albeit in slightly different form in a vaccine-versus-treatment setting.

Along with ensuring standards of care and prevention and robust informed consent processes, HIV vaccine researchers, like many others in the HIV research community, have undertaken community consultation before, during, and after vaccine trials to ascertain the ethical acceptability of study approaches and glean important insights about community-level values and practices (Dickert and Sugarman, 2005; Ellen et al., 2010; Morin et al., 2003). These community engagement efforts also provide mechanisms to help dispel misconceptions about the research process and address community concerns, should they arise (Roberts et al., 2005). From the beginning of the epidemic the HIV/AIDS research community has pioneered the development of community advisory boards, and these are standard practice in the HIV vaccine research community. The UNAIDS Good Participatory Practice offers important guidance in its six essential principles for conducting ethically sound HIV vaccine research in resource-poor areas: respect, mutual understanding, integrity, transparency, accountability, and community stakeholder autonomy (UNAIDS-AVAC, 2011). In particular, analysis of vaccine studies to date highlights the critical importance of engaging community stakeholders in every aspect of vaccine trials, from design to dissemination, particularly in underresourced African countries (Newman and Rubincam, 2014).

New concerns about risks in vaccine trials emerged in 2007 when data from the Step and Phambili studies (Buchbinder et al., 2008; Gray et al., 2011) revealed that the vaccine was increasing the likelihood of HIV infection among a subgroup of study volunteers. With the recognition that some vectors increased acquisition, new attention was given to the risk/benefit calculus in developing and testing candidate vaccines. Given the risk of Ad5-related vectors and the prevalence of prior Ad5 exposure in large percentages of populations in high-risk areas, alternative vaccine strategies had to be developed to address this significant risk.

Recent research with broadly neutralizing monoclonal antibodies raises a new set of concerns about the potential availability of products for host countries, if successful passive immunization strategies are developed (Grady, 2006). Because bnAbs are expensive to produce and require cold-chain handling, their use might not be feasible in many low-resource settings—and yet the high-risk populations in these settings are participating in prevention trials with these products. The question of reasonable availability of study products raises again the longstanding and complex ethical debates about the relationship of high-income country sponsors to the host countries and communities where research is conducted (Guenter et al., 2000; Homedes and Ugalde, 2015; London, 2005). The research trajectory is long and uncertain, and it is difficult to foresee what strategies will be successful or how funding strategies will play out, hence there is no simple answer to the concerns about reasonable availability for a hypothetical future biomedical product. However, many ethicists and commentators are calling for more proactive approaches to the problems of uneven access and the still-large disparities in prevention, care, and treatment from global south to global north, including planning and designing biomedical strategies that that will be feasible and acceptable in areas of HIV incidence (Nwaka and Ridley, 2003).

New prevention modalities have also complicated clinical trial designs for vaccine trials (Dawson and Zwerski, 2015; Dawson et al., 2015; Haire et al., 2013). As PrEP becomes established in both high- and low-income countries, it will be

Table 32.2 UNAIDS/WHO ETHICAL GUIDANCE POINTS

POINT	SUMMARY
1. Development of Biomedical Prevention Interventions	Researchers/sponsors and host countries should partner to build competence and motivation for preventive HIV research.
2. Community Participation	Researchers/sponsors should engage communities in the design, development, implementation, monitoring, and distribution of results of preventive trials.
3. Capacity Building	Research partners and international organizations should foster the capacity of host countries/ communities to exercise autonomy as equal partners in research.
4. Scientific and Ethical Review	Researchers/sponsors should only perform trials in countries/communities that have the ability to conduct independent scientific and ethical review.
5. Clinical Trial Phases	The choice of study populations in all phases of clinical trials should be scientifically and ethically justifiable before the trial begins.
6. Research Protocols and Study Populations	Researchers and review bodies should ensure that protocols and interventions including control groups are scientifically sound and ethically appropriate.
7. Research Protocols and Study Populations	To be ethically acceptable, all participation in preventive trials should be voluntary and informed and the selection of cohorts be just and justifiable.
8. Vulnerable Populations	Researchers proposing to conduct trials with vulnerable populations should propose safeguards against potential sources of exploitation.
9. Women	Preventive trials should recruit women across the life cycle in order to demonstrate that interventions are safe and effective with attention to reproductive concerns where relevant.
10. Children and Adolescents	Preventive trials should be developed for children and adolescents that validate safety and efficacy with appropriate legal, ethical safeguards.
11. Potential Harms	Protocols to the extent feasible should describe the nature, likelihood, and severity of potential harms.
12. Benefits	Protocols should truthfully state predicted benefits of trial interventions and any additional study services.
13. Standard of Prevention	Researchers/sponsors should provide counseling and access to standards of HIV risk reduction during the entire trial.
14. Care and Treatment	Participants who contract HIV during a trial should be provided internationally accepted optimal treatment regimens.
15. Control Groups	Control group members should also have access to state-of-the-art risk reduction.
16. Informed Consent	All participants should be engaged in a voluntary informed consent process for all aspects of and the duration of the trial.
17. Monitoring Informed Consent and Interventions	Researcher/sponsors and host communities/countries should agree prior to research on informed consent and a risk reduction monitoring plan.
18. Confidentiality	During all phases of the trial, researchers have a responsibility to respect participant confidentiality and security of all protected health information.
19. People Who Inject Drugs	Researchers/sponsors should collaborate with key stakeholders to overcome legal, social, and regulatory obstacles to the inclusion of injection drug users in trials.

difficult to conduct any vaccine trials without offering PrEP to study participants at high risk of HIV acquisition. This in turn will complicate analysis of vaccine effects and lead to much larger, more expensive trials (Grobler and Abdool Karim, 2012). Attempts to circumvent the problem of PrEP by locating trials in countries with poor access may be seen as ethically suspect, similar to surfactant trials in 2001, which raised controversy because the study sponsor sought poorer countries for study sites to avoid having to use standard-of-care comparison groups (Charatan, 2001). And increased cost of large efficacy trials will in turn lead to a greater need to prioritize among potential vaccine candidates. The fewer trials that are done, the more important each one will be in determining how the field will advance.

Protection for vulnerable or stigmatized individuals, including children, injection drug users, sex workers, men who have sex with men, and women in Africa, is also required for ethically tenable vaccine research (Pitisuttithum et al.,

2007; Reed et al., 2014; UNAIDS/WHO, 2012). Members of these groups are not only at high risk of HIV exposure but also vulnerable to political, cultural, and economic exploitation. The ethical challenge for these populations is to ensure that they receive adequate protections, but not at the expense of their exclusion from potentially beneficial research in which the risk/benefit balance of the research is ethically justifiable. Inclusion of adolescents in efficacy trials will be particularly important, as adolescents in many settings are at high risk of HIV acquisition; regulatory processes must take into account registration of products for this age group—ethical challenges of recruitment, parental permission, and consent are significant (Jaspan et al., 2008; Slack et al., 2007). Additionally, as is true of all clinical research, HIV vaccine research protocol should be to describe the steps taken that will "protect the rights, the dignity, the safety, and the welfare of the participants" (UNAIDS/WHO, 2012) (Snyder et al., 2011; Wassenaar and Barsdorf, 2007).

In an effort to make normative recommendations regarding the ethical conduct of HIV vaccine research, several entities have published guidance documents, and there is consensus regarding a number of core protections for study volunteers (Rennie and Sugarman, 2010). The HIV Vaccine Trials Network (2007) has produced a "Bill of Rights and Responsibilities" for research participants. Among the most widely recognized documents are the 19 guidance points of the UNAIDS/WHO Ethical Guidelines for Research on Biomedical Prevention of HIV, revised in 2012 and summarized in Table 32.2 (UNAIDS/WHO, 2012).

CONCLUSIONS

While preventive and therapeutic HIV vaccines present some different challenges, it is clear that both types will likely need to harness either or both T-cell and B-cell immunity to protect against both virions and virus-infected cells or effectively control virus replication. The way forward for both types should focus on development of new immunogens to better represent critical T-cell epitopes and overcome the viral diversity of circulating strains (mosaic and conserved immunogens). For preventive HIV vaccines, development of vaccine vectors and adjuvants to improve the breadth, strength, and durability of immune responses observed in RV144 is an immediate need. In addition, the ability to induce bnAbs remains the holy grail of both types of HIV-1 vaccine development; this challenge has been invigorated by discoveries of new bnAb specificities and their ability to protect in vivo at remarkably low plasma levels. However, host immune tolerance controls on bnAbs requires new methods of immunogen design that can selectively target members of the bnAb lineage and are tailored to induce subdominant bnAb rather than dominant non-bnAb responses. Hopefully, one or more of these paths will lead to sufficiently efficacious preventive and therapeutic vaccines that can be deployed either alone or in combination with other prevention and treatment modalities to ultimately end the HIV-1 epidemic. The continually changing scientific and public health landscapes mean that continued attention

and vigilant efforts are needed to address ethical challenges in HIV vaccine research (Bailey and Sugarman, 2013). Robust approaches to community engagement, discussion with relevant stakeholders and groups, and reasoned analysis about key ethical challenges will continue to be needed.

REFERENCES

Ackers ML, Parekh B, Evans TG, et al. (2003). Human immunodeficiency virus (HIV) seropositivity among uninfected HIV vaccine recipients. *J Infect Dis* 187(6):879–886.

Allen M, Lau CY (2008). Social impact of preventive HIV vaccine clinical trial participation: a model of prevention, assessment and intervention. *Soc Sci Med* 66(4):945–951.

Autran B, Murphy RL, Costagliola D, et al.; ORVACS Study Group (2008). Greater viral rebound and reduced time to resume antiretroviral therapy after therapeutic immunization with the ALVAC-HIV vaccine (vCP1452). *AIDS* 22(11):1313–1322.

Azoitei ML, Ban Y, Kalyuzhny O, et al. (2014). Computational design of protein antigens that interact with the CDR H3 loop of HIV broadly neutralizing antibody 2F5. *Proteins* 82(10):2770–282.

Baeten JM, Haberer JE, Liu AY, Sista N (2013). Preexposure prophylaxis for HIV prevention: where have we been and where are we going? *J Acquir Immune Defic Syndr* 63(Suppl 2):S122–S129.

Bailey TC, Sugarman J (2013). Social justice and HIV vaccine research in the age of pre-exposure prophylaxis and treatment as prevention. *Curr HIV Res* 11(6):473–480.

Balazs AB, West AP Jr (2012). Antibody-based protection against HIV infection by vectored immunoprophylaxis. *Nature* 481(7379):81–84.

Barouch DH, Alter G, Broge T, et al. (2015). Protective efficacy of adenovirus/protein vaccines against SIV challenges in rhesus monkeys. *Science* 349(6245):320–324.

Barouch DH, Deeks SG (2014). Immunologic strategies for HIV-1 remission and eradication. *Science* 345(6193):169–174.

Barouch DH, Liu J, Li H, et al. (2012). Vaccine protection against acquisition of neutralization-resistant SIV challenges in rhesus monkeys. *Nature* 482(7383):89–93.

Barouch DH, Picker LJ (2014). Novel vaccine vectors for HIV-1. *Nat Rev Microbiol* 12(11):765–771.

Barouch DH, Stephenson KE, Borducchi EN, et al. (2013b). Protective efficacy of a global HIV-1 mosaic vaccine against heterologous SHIV challenges in rhesus monkeys. *Cell* 155(3):531–539.

Barouch DH, Whitney JB, Moldt B, et al. (2013a). Therapeutic efficacy of potent neutralizing HIV-1-specific monoclonal antibodies in SHIV-infected rhesus monkeys. *Nature* 503(7475):224–228.

Bartholow BN, Buchbinder S, Celum C, et al.; VISION/VAX004 Study Team (2005). HIV sexual risk behavior over 36 months of follow-up in the world's first HIV vaccine efficacy trial. *J Acquir Immune Defic Syndr* 39(1):90–101.

Benmira S, Bhattacharya V, Schmid ML (2010). An effective HIV vaccine: a combination of humoral and cellular immunity? *Curr HIV Res* 8(6):441–449.

Borthwick N, Ahmed T, Ondondo B, et al. (2014). Vaccine-elicited human T cells recognizing conserved protein regions inhibit HIV-1. *Mol Ther* 22(2):464–475.

Buchbinder SP, Mehrotra DV, Duerr A, et al.; Step Study Protocol Team (2008). Efficacy assessment of a cell-mediated immunity HIV-1 vaccine (the Step Study): a double-blind, randomised, placebo-controlled, test-of-concept trial. *Lancet* 372, 1881–1893.

Charatan F (2001). Surfactant trial in Latin American infants criticised. *BMJ* 322(7286):575.

Chen RT, Carbery B, Mac L, et al. (2015). The Brighton Collaboration Viral Vector Vaccines Safety Working Group (V3SWG). *Vaccine* 33(1):73–75.

Chesney MA, Lurie P, Coates TJ (1995). Strategies for addressing the social and behavioral challenges of prophylactic HIV vaccine trials. *J Acquir Immune Defic Syndr Hum Retrovirol* 9(1):30–35.

Chun TW, Murray D, Justement JS, et al. (2014). Broadly neutralizing antibodies suppress HIV in the persistent viral reservoir *Proc Natl Acad Sci U S A* 111(36):13151–13156.

Chung AW, Ghebremichael M, Robinson H, et al. (2014). Polyfunctional Fc-effector profiles mediated by IgG subclass selection distinguish RV144 and VAX003 vaccines. *Sci Transl Med* 6(228):228ra38.

Cohen J (2013). Immunology. Bound for glory. *Science* 341(6151):1168–1171.

Dawson L, Zwerski S (2015). Clinical trial design for HIV prevention research: determining standards of prevention. *Bioethics* 29(5):316–323.

Dawson L, Garner S, Anude C, et al.; NIAID HIV Vaccine Trials Network (2015). Testing the waters: ethical considerations for including PrEP in a phase IIb HIV vaccine efficacy trial. *Clin Trials* 12(4):394–402.

Deeks SG, Autran B, Berkhout B, et al.; International AIDS Society Scientific Working Group on HIV Cure (2012). Towards an HIV cure: a global scientific strategy. *Nat Rev Immunol* 12(8):607–614.

Dickert N, Sugarman J (2005). Ethical goals of community consultation in research. *Am J Public Health* 95(7):1123–1127.

D'Souza MP, Yang O (2015). Adenovirus vectors as HIV-1 vaccines: where are we? What next? *AIDS* 22(3):325–331.

Ellen JM, Wallace M, Sawe FK, Fisher K (2010). Community engagement and investment in biomedical HIV prevention research for youth: rationale, challenges, and approaches. *J Acquir Immune Defic Syndr* 54(Suppl 1):S7–S11.

Essack Z, Koen J, Barsdorf N, et al. (2010). Stakeholder perspectives on ethical challenges in HIV vaccine trials in South Africa. *Dev World Bioeth* 10(1):11–21.

Fauci AS, Marovich MA, Dieffenbach CW, Hunter E, Buchbinder SP (2014). Immunology. Immune activation with HIV vaccines. *Science* 344(6179):49–51.

Fauci AS, Marston HD (2014). Ending AIDS—is an HIV vaccine necessary? *N Engl J Med* 370(6):495–498.

Fischer W, Perkins S, Theiler J, et al. (2007). Polyvalent vaccines for optimal coverage of potential T-cell epitopes in global HIV-1 variants. *Nat Med* 13(1):100–106.

Flynn NM, Forthal DN, Harro CD et al.; rgp120 HIV Vaccine Study Group (2005). Placebo-controlled phase 3 trial of a recombinant glycoprotein 120 vaccine to prevent HIV-1 infection. *J Infect Dis* 191(5):654–665.

Franchini G, Gurunathan S, Baglyos L, Plotkin S, Tartaglia J (2004). Poxvirus-based vaccine candidates for HIV: two decades of experience with special emphasis on canarypox vectors. *Expert Rev Vaccines* 3(4 Suppl):S75–S88.

García F, Climent N, Guardo AC, et al.; DCV2/MANON07-ORVACS Study Group (2013). A dendritic cell-based vaccine elicits T cell responses associated with control of HIV-1 replication. *Sci Transl Med* 5(166):166ra2.

Gardner EM, McLees MP, Steiner JF, Del Rio C, Burman WJ (2011). The spectrum of engagement in HIV care and its relevance to test-and-treat strategies for prevention of HIV infection. *Clin Infect Dis* 52(6):793–800.

Glidden D, Kim S, Lagakos S (2001). Effectiveness of remune. *Clin Diagn Lab Immunol* 8(2):468–469.

Govender T, Coovadia H (2014). Eliminating mother to child transmission of HIV-1 and keeping mothers alive: recent progress. *J Infect* 68(Suppl 1):S57–S62.

Grady C (2006). Ethics of international research: what does responsiveness mean? *Virtual Mentor* 8(4):235–240.

Gray GE, Allen M, Moodie Z, et al.; HVTN 503/Phambili Study Team (2011). Safety and efficacy of the HVTN 503/Phambili Study of a clade-B-based HIV-1 vaccine in South Africa: a double-blind, randomised, placebo-controlled test-of-concept phase 2b study. *Lancet Infect Dis* 11(7):507–515.

Gray GE, Metch B, Churchyard G, et al.; HVTN 503 team (2013). Does participation in an HIV vaccine efficacy trial affect risk behaviour in South Africa? *Vaccine* 31(16):2089–2096.

Grobler AC, Abdool Karim SS (2012). Design challenges facing clinical trials of the effectiveness of new HIV-prevention technologies. *AIDS* 26(5):529–532.

Guenter D, Esparza J, Macklin R (2000). Ethical considerations in international HIV vaccine trials: summary of a consultative process conducted by the Joint United Nations Programme on HIV/AIDS (UNAIDS). *J Med Ethics* 26(1):37–43.

Haire B, Folayan MO, Hankins C, et al. (2013). Ethical considerations in determining standard of prevention packages for HIV prevention trials: examining PrEP. *Dev World Bioeth* 13(2):87–94.

Hammer SM, Sobieszczyk ME, Janes H, et al.; HVTN 505 Study Team (2013). Efficacy trial of a DNA/rAd5 HIV-1 preventive vaccine. *N Engl J Med* 369(22):2083–2092.

Hansen SG, Ford JC, Lewis MS, et al. (2011). Profound early control of highly pathogenic SIV by an effector memory T-cell vaccine. *Nature* 473(7348):523–527.

Hansen SG, Piatak M Jr, Ventura AB, et al. (2013b). Immune clearance of highly pathogenic SIV infection. *Nature* 502(7469):100–104.

Hansen SG, Sacha JB, Hughes CM, et al. (2013a). Cytomegalovirus vectors violate CD8+ T cell epitope recognition paradigms. *Science* 340(6135):1237874.

Harari A, Rozot V, Cavassini M, et al. (2012). NYVAC immunization induces polyfunctional HIV-specific T-cell responses in chronically-infected, ART-treated HIV patients. *Eur J Immunol* 42(11):3038–3048.

Haynes BF, Alam SM (2008). HIV-1 hides an Achilles' heel in virion lipids. *Immunity* 28(1):10–12.

Haynes BF, Gilbert PB, McElrath MJ, et al. (2012b). Immune-correlates analysis of an HIV-1 vaccine efficacy trial. *N Engl J Med* 366(14):1275–1286.

Haynes BF, Kelsoe G, Harrison SC, Kepler TB (2012a). B-cell-lineage immunogen design in vaccine development with HIV-1 as a case study. *Nat Biotechnol* 30(5):423–433.

Hel Z, Nacsa J, Tryniszewska E, et al. (2002). Containment of simian immunodeficiency virus infection in vaccinated macaques: correlation with the magnitude of virus-specific pre- and postchallenge CD4+ and CD8+ T cell responses. *J Immunol* 169(9):4778–4787.

Hertz T, Ahmed H, Friedrich DP, et al. (2013). HIV-1 vaccine-induced T-cell responses cluster in epitope hotspots that differ from those induced in natural infection with HIV-1. *PLoS Pathog* 9(6):e1003404.

HIV Vaccine Trials Network (2007). Participants' Bill of Rights and Responsibilities. http://www.hvtn.org/en/participants/participants-rights.html. Accessed February 7, 2017.

Homedes N, Ugalde A (2015). Availability and affordability of new medicines in Latin American countries where pivotal clinical trials were conducted. *Bull World Health Organ* 93(10):674–683.

Jaspan HB, Cunningham CK, Tucker TJ, et al.; HIV Vaccine Adolescent Trials Working Group (2008). Inclusion of adolescents in preventive HIV vaccine trials: public health policy and research design at a crossroads. *J Acquir Immune Defic Syndr* 47(1):86–92.

Jenabian MA, Nicolette CA, Tcherepanova IY, Debenedette MA, Gilmore N, Routy JP (2013). Impact of autologous dendritic cell-based immunotherapy (AGS-004) on B- and T-cell subset changes and immune activation in HIV-infected patients receiving antiretroviral therapy. *J Acquir Immune Defic Syndr* 64(4):345–350.

Kalams SA, Parker SD, Elizaga M, et al.; NIAID HIV Vaccine Trials Network (2013). Safety and comparative immunogenicity of an HIV-1 DNA vaccine in combination with plasmid interleukin 12 and impact of intramuscular electroporation for delivery. *J Infect Dis* 208(5):818–829.

Kelsoe G, Verkoczy L, Haynes BF (2014). Immune system regulation in the induction of broadly neutralizing HIV-1 antibodies. *Vaccines (Basel)* 2(1):1–14.

Klein F, Mouquet H, Dosenovic P, Scheid JF, Scharf L, Nussenzweig MC (2013). Antibodies in HIV-1 vaccine development and therapy. *Science* 341(6151):1199–1204.

Koff WC (2012). HIV vaccine development: challenges and opportunities towards solving the HIV vaccine-neutralizing antibody problem. *Vaccine* 30(29):4310–4315.

Koff WC, Burton DR, Johnson PR, et al. (2013). Accelerating next-generation vaccine development for global disease prevention. *Science* 340(6136):1232910.

Korber BT, Letvin NL, Haynes BF (2009). T-cell vaccine strategies for human immunodeficiency virus, the virus with a thousand faces. *J Virol* 83(17):8300–8314.

Kutzler MA, Wise MC, Hutnick NA, et al. (2016). Chemokine-adjuvanted electroporated DNA vaccine induces substantial protection from simian immunodeficiency virus vaginal challenge. *Mucosal Immunol* 9(1):13–23.

Lavery JV (2004). Putting international research ethics guidelines to work for the benefit of developing countries. *Yale J Health Policy Law Ethics* 4(2):319–336.

Liao HX, Bonsignori M, Alam SM, et al. (2013a). Vaccine induction of antibodies against a structurally heterogeneous site of immune pressure within HIV-1 envelope protein variable regions 1 and 2. *Immunity* 38(1):176–186.

Liao HX, Lynch R, Zhou T, et al. (2013b). Co-evolution of a broadly neutralizing HIV-1 antibody and founder virus. *Nature* 496(7446):469–476.

Lindegger G, Milford C, Slack C, Quayle M, Xaba X, Vardas E (2006). Beyond the checklist: assessing understanding for HIV vaccine trial participation in South Africa. *J Acquir Immune Defic Syndr* 43(5):560–566.

Lo B, Grady C (2013). Ethical considerations in HIV cure research: points to consider. *Curr Opin HIV AIDS* 8(3):243–249.

London AJ (2005). Justice and the human development approach to international research. *Hastings Cent Rep* 35(1):24–37.

London AJ (2008). Responsiveness to host community health needs. In EJ Emanuel, et al. (eds.), *The Oxford Textbook of Clinical Research Ethics*. New York: Oxford University Press.

London L, Kagee A, Moodley K, Swartz L (2012). Ethics, human rights and HIV vaccine trials in low-income settings. *J Med Ethics* 38(5):286–293.

Maartens G, Celum C, Lewin SR (2014). HIV infection: epidemiology, pathogenesis, treatment, and prevention. *Lancet* 384(9939):258–271.

Manrique A, Adams E, Barouch DH, et al. (2014). The immune space: a concept and template for rationalizing vaccine development. *AIDS Res Hum Retroviruses* 30(11):1017–1022.

Mascola JR, Haynes BF (2013). HIV-1 neutralizing antibodies: understanding nature's pathways. *Immunol Rev* 254(1):225–244.

McElrath MJ (1995). Selection of potent immunological adjuvants for vaccine construction. *Semin Cancer Biol* 6(6):375–385.

McElrath MJ, De Rosa SC, Moodie Z, et al.; Step Study Protocol Team (2008). HIV-1 vaccine-induced immunity in the test-of-concept Step Study: a case-cohort analysis. *Lancet* 372:1894–1905.

McMichael AJ, Koff WC (2014). Vaccines that stimulate T cell immunity to HIV-1: the next step. *Nat Immunol* 15(4):319–322.

Montefiori DC, Karnasuta C, Huang Y, et al. (2012). Magnitude and breadth of the neutralizing antibody response in the RV144 and Vax003 HIV-1 vaccine efficacy trials. *J Infect Dis* 206(3):431–441.

Morin SF, Maiorana A, Koester KA, Sheon NM, Richards TA (2003). Community consultation in HIV prevention research: a study of community advisory boards at 6 research sites. *J Acquir Immune Defic Syndr* 33(4):513–520.

Nathwani AC, Tuddenham EG, Rangarajan S, et al. (2011). Adenovirus-associated virus vector-mediated gene transfer in hemophilia B. *N Engl J Med* 365(25):2357–2365.

National Bioethics Advisory Commission (NBAC) (2001). Ethical and policy issues in international research: clinical trials in developing countries. https://scholarworks.iupui.edu/handle/1805/24. Accessed February 7, 2017.

Newman PA, Rubincam C (2014). Advancing community stakeholder engagement in biomedical HIV prevention trials: principles, practices and evidence. *Expert Rev Vaccines* 13(12):1553–1562.

Nwaka S, Ridley RG (2003). Virtual drug discovery and development for neglected diseases through public–private partnerships. *Nat Rev Drug Discov* 2(11):919–928.

Pancera M, Zhou T, Druz A, et al. (2014). Structure and immune recognition of trimeric pre-fusion HIV-1 Env. *Nature* 514(7523):455–461.

Pantaleo G, Levy Y (2013). Vaccine and immunotherapeutic interventions. *Curr Opin HIV AIDS* 8(3):236–242.

Parks CL, Picker LJ, King CR (2013). Development of replication-competent viral vectors for HIV vaccine delivery. *Curr Opin HIV AIDS* 8(5):402–411.

Pasternak AO, Lukashov VV, Berkhout B (2013). Cell-associated HIV RNA: a dynamic biomarker of viral persistence. *Retrovirology* 10:41.

Pitisuttithum P, Choopanya K, Bussaratid V, et al. (2007). Social harms in injecting drug users participating in the first phase III HIV vaccine trial in Thailand. *J Med Assoc Thai* 90(11):2442–2448.

Pitisuttithum P, Gilbert P, Gurwith M, et al.; Bangkok Vaccine Evaluation Group (2006). Randomized, double-blind, placebo-controlled efficacy trial of a bivalent recombinant glycoprotein 120 HIV-1 vaccine among injection drug users in Bangkok, Thailand. *J Infect Dis* 194(12):1661–1671.

Plotkin SA (2010). Correlates of protection induced by vaccination. *Clin Vaccine Immunol* 17(7):1055–1065.

Plotkin SA, Plotkin SL (2011). The development of vaccines: how the past led to the future. *Nat Rev Microbiol* 9(12):889–893.

Podda A (2001). The adjuvanted influenza vaccines with novel adjuvants: experience with the MF59-adjuvanted vaccine. *Vaccine* 19(17-19):2673–2680.

Ramjee G, Coumi N, Dladla-Qwabe N, et al. (2010). Experiences in conducting multiple community-based HIV prevention trials among women in KwaZulu-Natal, South Africa. *AIDS Res Ther* 7:10.

Reed E, Khoshnood K, Blankenship KM, Fisher CB (2014). Confidentiality, privacy, and respect: experiences of female sex workers participating in HIV research in Andhra Pradesh, India. *J Empir Res Hum Res Ethics* 9(1):19–28.

Rennie S, Sugarman J (2010). Developing ethics guidance for HIV prevention research: the HIV Prevention Trials Network approach. *J Med Ethics* 36(12):810–815.

Rerks-Ngarm S, Pitisuttithum P, Nitayaphan S, et al.; MOPH-TAVEG Investigators (2009). Vaccination with ALVAC and AIDSVAX to prevent HIV-1 infection in Thailand. *N Engl J Med* 361(23):2209–2220.

Robb ML, Rerks-Ngarm S, Nitayaphan S, et al. (2012). Risk behaviour and time as covariates for efficacy of the HIV vaccine regimen ALVAC-HIV (vCP1521) and AIDSVAX B/E: a post-hoc analysis of the Thai phase 3 efficacy trial RV 144. *Lancet Infect Dis* 12(7):531–537.

Roberts KJ, Newman PA, Duan N, Rudy ET (2005). HIV vaccine knowledge and beliefs among communities at elevated risk: conspiracies, questions and confusion. *J Natl Med Assoc* 97(12):1662–1671.

Rolland M, Nickle DC, Mullins JI (2007). HIV-1 group M conserved elements vaccine. *PLoS Pathog* 3(11):e157.

Rolland M, Edlefsen PT, Larsen BB, et al. (2012). Increased HIV-1 vaccine efficacy against viruses with genetic signatures in Env V2. *Nature* 490(7420):417–420.

Rosenberg ES, Graham BS, Chan ES, et al.; AIDS Clinical Trials Group A5187 Team (2010). Safety and immunogenicity of therapeutic DNA vaccination in individuals treated with antiretroviral therapy during acute/early HIV-1 infection. *PLoS ONE* 5(5):e10555.

Salk J (1987). Prospects for the control of AIDS by immunizing seropositive individuals. *Nature* 327(6122):473–476.

Sarmento-Castro R, Vasconcelos C, Aguas MJ, Marques R, Oliveira J (2011). Virologic suppression in treatment-experienced patients after virologic rebound or failure of therapy. *Curr Opin HIV AIDS* 6(Suppl 1):S12–S20.

Schnepp BC, Johnson PR (2014). Adeno-associated virus delivery of broadly neutralizing antibodies. *Curr Opin HIV AIDS* 9(3):250–256.

Schooley RT, Spritzler J, Wang H, et al.; AIDS Clinical Trials Group 5197 Study Team (2010). AIDS Clinical Trials Group 5197: a placebo-controlled trial of immunization of HIV-1-infected persons with a replication-deficient adenovirus type 5 vaccine expressing the HIV-1 core protein. *J Infect Dis* 202(5):705–716.

Shan L, Deng K, Shroff NS, et al. (2012). Stimulation of HIV-1-specific cytolytic T lymphocytes facilitates elimination of latent viral reservoir after virus reactivation. *Immunity* 36(3):491–501.

Shapiro K, Benatar SR (2005). HIV prevention research and global inequality: steps towards improved standards of care. *J Med Ethics* 31(1):39–47.

Shapiro SZ (2013). HIV vaccine development: strategies for preclinical and clinical investigation. *AIDS Res Hum Retroviruses* 29(11):1401–1406.

Shapiro SZ (2015). A proposal to use iterative, small clinical trials to optimize therapeutic HIV vaccine immunogens to launch therapeutic HIV vaccine development. *AIDS Res Hum Retroviruses* 31(1):49–55.

Singh M, Ugozzoli M, Kazzaz J, et al. (2006). A preliminary evaluation of alternative adjuvants to alum using a range of established and new generation vaccine antigens. *Vaccine* 24(10):1680–1686.

Slack C, Lindegger G, Vardas E, Richter L, Strode A, Wassenaar D (2000). Ethical issues in HIV vaccine trials in South Africa. *S Afr J Sci* 96, 291–295.

Slack C, Strode A, Fleischer T, Gray G, Ranchod C (2007). Enrolling adolescents in HIV vaccine trials: reflections on legal complexities from South Africa. *BMC Med Ethics* 8, 5.

Slichter CK, Friedrich DP, Smith RJ, et al. (2014). Measuring inhibition of HIV replication by ex vivo CD8(+) T cells. *J Immunol Methods* 404:71–80.

Snyder J, Miller CL, Gray G (2011). Relative versus absolute standards for everyday risk in adolescent HIV prevention trials: expanding the debate. *Am J Bioeth* 11(6):5–13.

Streeck H, D'Souza MP, Littman DR, Crotty S (2013). Harnessing CD4(+) T cell responses in HIV vaccine development. *Nat Med* 19(2):143–149.

Thapinta D, Jenkins RA, Celentano DD, et al. (1999). Evaluation of behavioral and social issues among Thai HIV vaccine trial volunteers. *J Acquir Immune Defic Syndr Hum Retrovirol* 20(3):308–314.

Thobakgale CF, Streeck H, Mkhwanazi N, et al. (2011). Short communication: CD8(+) T cell polyfunctionality profiles in progressive and nonprogressive pediatric HIV type 1 infection. *AIDS Res Hum Retroviruses* 27(9):1005–1012.

Thongcharoen P, Suriyanon V, Paris RM, et al.; hai AIDS Vaccine Evaluation Group (2007). A phase 1/2 comparative vaccine trial of the safety and immunogenicity of a CRF01_AE (subtype E) candidate vaccine: ALVAC-HIV (vCP1521) prime with oligomeric gp160 (92TH023/LAI-DID) or bivalent gp120 (CM235/SF2) boost. *J Acquir Immune Defic Syndr* 46(1):48–55.

Tobian AA, Kacker S, Quinn TC (2014). Male circumcision: a globally relevant but under-utilized method for the prevention of HIV and other sexually transmitted infections. *Annu Rev Med* 65:293–306.

Treatment Action Group (TAC) (2017). Research Toward a Cure Trials. http://www.treatmentactiongroup.org/cure/trials. Accessed February 7, 2017.

UNAIDS (2000). Ethical considerations in HIV preventive vaccine research: UNAIDS guidance document. http://data.unaids.org/publications/IRC-pub01/JC072-EthicalCons_en.pdf. Accessed February 7, 2017.

UNAIDS-AVAC (2011). Good participatory practice: guidelines for biomedical HIV prevention trials. http://www.avac.org/resource/good-participatory-practice-guidelines-biomedical-hiv-prevention-trials-second-edition. Accessed Febraury 7, 2017.

UNAIDS/WHO (2012). Ethical considerations in biomedical prevention trials. http://www.unaids.org/en/resources/documents/2012/20120701_jc1399_ethical_considerations. Accessed Febraury 7, 2017.

van Griensvan F, Keawkungwal J, Tappero JW, et al.; Bangkok Vaccine Evaluation Group (2004). Lack of increased HIV risk behavior among injection drug users participating in the AIDSVAX B/E HIV vaccine trial in Bangkok, Thailand. *Aids* 18(2):295–301.

Vermund SH, Tique JA, Cassell HM, Pask ME, Ciampa PJ, Audet CM (2013). Translation of biomedical prevention strategies for HIV: prospects and pitfalls. *J Acquir Immune Defic Syndr* 63(Suppl 1):S12–S25.

Vesikari T, Pellegrini M, Karvonen A, et al. (2009). Enhanced immunogenicity of seasonal influenza vaccines in young children using MF59 adjuvant. *Pediatr Infect Dis J* 28(7):563–571.

Walker BD (2007). Elite control of HIV Infection: implications for vaccines and treatment. *Top HIV Med* 15(4):134–136.

Wassenaar DR, Barsdorf NW (2007). The ethical involvement of women in HIV vaccine trials in Africa: discussion paper developed for the African AIDS Vaccine Programme. *Women Health* 45(1):37–50.

World Medical Association (2000). Declaration of Helsinki, ethical principles for medical research involving human subjects. 52nd WMA General Assembly, Edinburgh, Scotland. http://www.wma.net/en/30publications/10policies/b3/. Accessed February 7, 2017.

Yang H, Wu H, Hancock G, et al. (2012). Antiviral inhibitory capacity of CD8+ T cells predicts the rate of CD4+ T-cell decline in HIV-1 infection. *J Infect Dis* 206(4):552–561.

Yates NL, Liao HX, Fong Y, et al. (2014). Vaccine-induced Env V1-V2 IgG3 correlates with lower HIV-1 infection risk and declines soon after vaccination. *Sci Transl Med* 6(228):228ra39.

Zolla-Pazner S, deCamp A, Gilbert PB, et al. (2014). Vaccine-induced IgG antibodies to V1V2 regions of multiple HIV-1 subtypes correlate with decreased risk of HIV-1 infection. *PLoS One* 9(2):e87572.

PART VIII

HIV PSYCHIATRY THROUGH THE LIFE CYCLE

33.

CHILDHOOD AND ADOLESCENCE

Suad Kapetanovic, Lori Wiener, Lisa K. Tuchman, and Maryland Pao

INTRODUCTION

With improving access to effective antiretroviral therapy (ART) worldwide, pediatric HIV/AIDS is being transformed from a fast-progressing, fatal illness to a manageable chronic infection. The psychosocial needs of HIV-infected children and adolescents and their families are increasingly resembling the needs of the chronically ill, rather than the terminally ill. In addition to screening for psychosocial risk factors and addressing highly comorbid psychiatric disorders, psychiatrists and other mental health clinicians caring for youth with HIV must be able to (1) appreciate how the psychosocial and mental health needs of young individuals with HIV evolve over time and (2) identify salient clinical challenges that present with each developmental stage.

It is important to clarify the terminology we will be using to designate different direct and indirect ways HIV/AIDS may affect children's lives. We refer to children and adolescents as *perinatally HIV-infected* if they acquired HIV infection via mother-to-child transmission during pregnancy, labor and delivery, or breastfeeding. The term *behaviorally HIV-infected* is used for youth who acquired HIV infection via behavioral modes of transmission, such as unprotected sex or injection drug use. We use the term *HIV-affected* to describe children and adolescents who are not HIV positive, but are affected by the presence of HIV/AIDS in a parent or other family member. For HIV-affected youth who were born to an HIV-positive mother, but avoided perinatal HIV infection, we also use the term *perinatally HIV-exposed but uninfected*.

This chapter uses a developmental perspective to introduce key mental health objectives in the care of perinatally HIV-infected children and adolescents and provides an overview of epidemiological, psychosocial, and clinical parameters to be considered in the clinical care and management of youth infected with HIV either perinatally or behaviorally. Separate sections of the chapter focus on HIV-affected children and perinatally HIV-exposed but uninfected children. While some topics addressed in this chapter are also covered elsewhere in this textbook, the present chapter specifically addresses those topics as they relate to children and adolescents living with or affected by HIV/AIDS.

EPIDEMIOLOGY

PERINATALLY HIV-INFECTED CHILDREN AND ADOLESCENTS

Globally, at least 3.3 million infants and children under 15 years are living with HIV (UNAIDS, 2013). (See Chapter 2 for the comprehensive overview of HIV epidemiology.) Perinatal transmission is the most common route of HIV infection in children. It can be reduced to less than 1% when maternal HIV is diagnosed before or during pregnancy, appropriate medical treatment is given and breastfeeding avoided. According to The Centers for Disease Control and Prevention (CDC) data, approximately 18% of all people with HIV do not know their HIV status. Therefore, the CDC recommends routine prenatal testing where the mother must opt out of HIV testing rather than agree to opt in (CDC, 2016). Given these advances, perinatal HIV infections have decreased in the United States by 90%. In the 1990s there were 1,000–2,000 new pediatric diagnoses per year. In 2011, there were 192 children under age 13 years with a diagnosis of HIV infection and only 15 youth under age 13 years diagnosed with AIDS (CDC, 2012b). Although the rates of perinatal transmission are declining, owing to steady growth in the number of HIV-positive pregnant and breastfeeding women accessing perinatal HIV care (Luzuriaga and Mofenson, 2016), the global rates of new perinatal infections remain alarmingly high. In the year 2012 alone, the number of newly infected children was 260,000 (UNAIDS, 2013).

BEHAVIORALLY HIV-INFECTED ADOLESCENTS

Worldwide, it is estimated that 5,500 individuals age 15 and older are infected with HIV every day; almost 50% of them are women, and approximately 40% are young people between 15 and 24 years of age (UNAIDS, 2013). Approximately 50,000 people in the United States are newly infected with HIV each year; nearly two-thirds of these new infections occurred in men who have sex with men. Black/African American men and women are estimated to have an HIV incidence rate that is almost eight times as high as the incidence rate among whites. In 2011, there were at least 10,539 youth under age

25 years who were diagnosed with HIV in the United States and approximately 3,000 youth with AIDS (CDC, 2012a).

HIV-AFFECTED CHILDREN AND ADOLESCENTS

It is estimated that 17.8 million children under 18 years of age have been orphaned by AIDS globally and that this number will continue to rise to 25 million over the next few years (AVERT, 2014). Around 15.1 million (85%) of AIDS orphans live in sub-Saharan Africa (AVERT, 2014). Most AIDS orphans are in the care of their grandparents or other caregivers, while in Africa many children live in orphanages or on the street (UNAIDS, 2004; UNICEF, 2005). The number of HIV-affected children with living parents is also growing as the number of adults living with HIV/AIDS continues to grow and their life expectancy extends with increased access to ART. For a more detailed discussion of AIDS orphans please see Chapter 5 of this textbook.

Perinatally HIV-Exposed but Uninfected Children and Adolescents

HIV-positive women of childbearing age are the fastest growing HIV-infected population in the world, and they give birth to 1.5 million infants every year (World Health Organization [WHO], 2011). With growing access to effective ART-based strategies for preventing perinatal HIV transmission, more babies who are perinatally HIV exposed but uninfected are being born each year. It is estimated that at least 350,000 children have avoided becoming perinatally infected with HIV since 1995 because of ART-based prophylaxis provided to pregnant women with HIV (WHO, 2011).

PERINATALLY HIV-INFECTED CHILDREN AND ADOLESCENTS: CLINICAL MILESTONES ALONG THE DEVELOPMENTAL CONTINUUM

Developmentally informed psychiatric evaluation and treatment of a perinatally HIV-infected child or adolescent requires ongoing evaluation of salient clinical milestones and related challenges that unfold in parallel with the normative developmental trajectory. Concerns about neurodevelopmental (ND) outcomes begin in infancy and continue throughout adolescence (Laughton et al., 2013). The questions of when and how to disclose an HIV diagnosis to the child come into focus during school age, when universal questions beginning with "why," "what," "when," "how," and "what if" are being asked, and need to be thoughtfully answered. Health behaviors and related psychosocial factors take center stage during adolescence, when teens with HIV become more independent in managing their illness in anticipation of adulthood which, in their case, also often means a very challenging transition to adult models of HIV care.

NEURODEVELOPMENTAL OUTCOMES

Prior to the development of effective ART, HIV encephalopathy occurred in 50% to 90% of young children with perinatally acquired HIV and was associated with accelerated disease progression and mortality (Belman et al., 1988; Epstein, 1986). Associated neuroimaging changes included calcifying microangiopathy visible on computed tomography (CT) scan and white matter (WM) lesions and diffuse cerebral atrophy on magnetic resonance imaging (MRI) (Mitchell, 2001). Co-infection with cytomegalovirus was associated with more than a threefold increased risk of encephalopathy among perinatally HIV-infected infants (Kovacs et al., 1999). Without access to effective ART, the majority of children with HIV develop severe delays in cognitive function, language expression, and comprehension or motor skills by preschool age (Van Rie et al., 2009).

With the advent of effective ART, and resulting improvements in viremia control, the rates of encephalopathy and severe ND impairment have dropped substantially. Yet, more subtle impairments persist. Mean ND scores of perinatally HIV-infected children and adolescents are in the low to low-average range (Jeremy et al., 2005) and tend to be worse in children with a history of AIDS. History of AIDS, with or without encephalopathy, is associated with greater risk for processing speed deficits (Smith et al., 2012). Thus, the brain development of children with HIV has remained vulnerable in the ART era, and the developmental mechanism that determines the speed of information processing, white matter myelination (Palmer et al., 2012; Pfefferbaum et al., 1994), might be particularly vulnerable. Indeed, a recent cross-sectional study evaluating regional gray matter and white matter volumes in 16 perinatally HIV-infected youths receiving ART and 14 age-matched healthy controls suggests presence of white matter injury in HIV-infected youth. Using high-resolution MRI with voxel-based morphometry analyses, significant white matter atrophy was observed in selected cerebral regions in youth with HIV relative to the controls. Additionally, a relative gray matter volume increase was observed in several brain regions of the perinatally HIV-infected youth, possibly suggesting ongoing neuronal inflammation (Sarma et al., 2013).

The pathophysiological underpinnings of suboptimal ND outcomes in virally suppressed perinatally HIV-infected youth are poorly understood. A range of biopsychosocial exposures could be involved. First, brain development may be affected by a neurotoxic effect of "latent" HIV, which may reside in microglia or be carried across the blood–brain barrier by cells of macrophage-monocyte lineage (see Chapter 26). Consistent with this, children infected with HIV subtype A, which has relatively higher CCR5 tropism (i.e., higher affinity to infect monocytes and microglia), tend to perform worse than children with HIV subtype D on standard measures of cognitive ability and visual attention, particularly sequential and simultaneous processing (Boivin et al., 2010). Second, children with HIV are at risk for chronic vascular dysfunction (Miller et al., 2010), which may potentially affect ND outcomes. Negative correlation has been observed between combined serum levels of three markers of vascular dysfunction (i.e., fibrinogen, CRP, and IL-6) and processing speed in perinatally HIV-infected youth (Kapetanovic, Griner, et al., 2014). Third, at least one-third of HIV-positive women in the United States use illicit drugs or tobacco products in pregnancy (Tassiopoulos et al., 2010), so a potential neurotoxic role of perinatal drug exposure must be considered as well. Some studies have not found associations between prenatal cocaine exposure and cognitive or school academic and behavioral performance (Chasnoff et al., 1998; Richardson et al., 1996), while others have reported associations with decreased task persistence, attention problems (Bandstra et al., 2001), and poorer language skills (Bandstra et al., 2004). Perinatal depression is highly prevalent among women with HIV and associated with ART nonadherence and substance abuse during pregnancy (Kapetanovic, Dass-Brailsford, et al., 2014). Perinatally depressed mothers are at increased risk to miss their infants' routine medical visits and immunizations and to delay seeking help for potentially serious childhood illnesses (Prince et al., 2007).

Finally, there are additional contextual factors that may indirectly affect ND outcomes, particularly when children's access to resources and to learning and developmental opportunities is limited. Many perinatally HIV-infected children are disproportionately likely to live in a disadvantaged, inner-city environment; to be of ethnic minority status; to have experienced disruptions of placements and multiple separations from parents or caregivers; or to have been born to young parents and raised in a single-parent headed household (Donenberg and Pao, 2005). In a U.S.-based study, perinatally HIV-infected youth ($n = 354$) and youth who were perinatally exposed to HIV but uninfected ($n = 200$) performed similarly on measures of executive function when demographic and other influences were taken into account, but both cohorts had significantly worse scores than those of the normative population (Nichols et al., 2015). Thus, the suboptimal executive functioning of perinatally HIV-infected youth might be related to factors other than their HIV infection, such as sociodemographic and environmental factors, that are shared between youth who are perinatally HIV exposed but uninfected and youth who are infected with HIV (Nichols et al., 2015).

DIAGNOSTIC DISCLOSURE

Generally, school-age children have the conceptual capability to understand illness and should be disclosed to in an age-appropriate manner that considers their emotional and cognitive developmental level and relevant family factors (Lesch et al., 2007). In children with cancer, open communication about the diagnosis improves both short- and long-term psychological outcomes (Slavin et al., 1982). Yet, the oncology model is not easily applicable to pediatric HIV, given the differences in epidemiology, transmissibility, and potential for social stigma and isolation (Sahay, 2013). Disclosure of a child's HIV diagnosis often leads to disclosure of other family secrets, such as paternity, history of parental sexual

behavior, or substance abuse (Havens et al., 2005). The fact that children acquired HIV from their mothers and the ensuing parental guilt also distinguish HIV from cancer and other chronic pediatric illnesses. Most parents struggle for at least 2 years before they feel ready to disclose HIV diagnosis to their child (Wiener et al., 1996).

While the child's disclosure reaction tends to be consistent with previous responses to a crisis, the parent needs to be aware of the scope of emotions that might follow. The reactions can range from reduction of anxiety to no reaction at all to acute panic or anxiety. Delayed reactions are also seen. The child may develop new psychosomatic complaints, nightmares, emotional lability, academic decline, and regressive behavior or, conversely, an adult-like acceptance. Some studies report associations between disclosure and greater promotion of trust, improved treatment adherence, social support, open family communication, self-confidence, coping and adaptation, and better long-term health and emotional well-being (Funck-Brentano et al., 1997; Lipson, 1994; Mellins et al., 2002; Ng et al., 2004; Walker, 1991; Wiener, 1998). In other studies, knowledge of serostatus was associated with increased risk of depression, anxiety, and behavioral problems (Wiener et al., 2007).

HEALTH BEHAVIORS

Adolescents who were perinatally HIV infected often struggle to reconcile normative developmental challenges, such as awakening sexuality, identity formation, and developing abstract thought (Erickson, 1963), with the knowledge of having a chronic, life-threatening, stigmatized, sexually transmissible illness. This struggle is often marked by experimenting with adult behaviors, impulsivity, risk taking, and a sense of invincibility and may be enacted through maladaptive health behaviors. ART nonadherence, unprotected sex, and substance abuse are three behaviors with significant potential impact on HIV/AIDS clinical and public health outcomes. They are also interrelated; for example, poor viremia control due to ART nonadherence increases the risk of HIV transmission to sexual partners (CDC, 2009), and use of cigarettes, alcohol, or marijuana among youth with HIV is associated with unprotected sex (Elkington et al., 2009). Clinically, health behaviors may serve as windows into individual perinatally HIV-infected adolescents' judgment, decision-making, priorities, planning capacity, coping and self-esteem and, as such, help identify the need for more assistance and education for patients who might need a full neurocognitive evaluation and individualized alternative learning strategies. Perinatally HIV-infected youth with a history of mental illness have increased odds of practicing at least one of these three risky behaviors (Kapetanovic et al., 2011).

Adherence

Perinatally HIV-infected adolescents may simultaneously face multiple barriers to adherence (Rudy et al., 2010). Poverty, violence, substance abuse, unstable housing, and the need to navigate complex family systems create chaotic living situations that are not conducive to medication adherence. In addition, perinatally HIV-infected adolescents often feel conflicted between the need to adhere to a specific prescribed treatment and the developmentally appropriate desire to assert their independence. Oppositional behavior is common, as many teens get "tired" of obeying parents' and doctors' orders. A social crisis, such as a death, a breakup with a romantic partner, a family fight, or a problem in school or on the job, can trigger an episode of nonadherence. Yet, unlike most other treatments, nonadherence to ART can have far-reaching long-term consequences, including viral mutations and resistance. Factors associated with less adherence in adolescents include advanced HIV disease, being out of school, higher alcohol use, depression, and mental health problems (Kacanek et al., 2015; Murphy et al., 2005; Wiener et al., 2004); low self-efficacy and outcome expectancy and structural barriers (Rudy et al., 2010); and forgetfulness, impulsivity, medication regimen complexity or side effects, shorter attention span, and a desire to fit in with peers' schedules or eating habits (Chandwani et al., 2012).

Sex

It is expected that youth who were perinatally HIV infected will have intimate sexual relationships as they age. While this is developmentally appropriate, it has major potential clinical and public health implications. Unprotected sex among HIV-infected youth not only increases risks of HIV transmission to partners and unintended pregnancy but also poses the risk for youth with HIV to acquire an additional sexually transmitted disease (STD) or to be infected by an additional, drug-resistant or difficult-to-treat strain of HIV (Elkington et al., 2012). Reported correlates of penetrative vaginal or anal sex in perinatally HIV-infected youth include older age (Elkington et al., 2012; Setse et al., 2011), alcohol, marijuana, or injection drug use (Elkington et al., 2012), having a boyfriend or a girlfriend (Setse et al., 2011), and having peers who consider being sexually active as "cool" or "popular" (Bauermeister et al., 2009; Elkington et al., 2009).

Evidence suggests that, compared to HIV-negative youth, perinatally HIV-infected youth are more likely to delay sexual debut and less likely to be sexually active, with relatively safer patterns of preferred sexual practices. Specifically, perinatally HIV-infected youth are relatively more likely to prefer touching a partner's genitals over engaging in vaginal or anal penetrative sex (Bauermeister et al., 2009; Elkington et al., 2012). Sexually active perinatally HIV-infected youth are also less likely to have been diagnosed with an STD in the past year than sociodemographically matched behaviorally HIV-infected youth and healthy adolescent girls; very few (~4%) report practicing unprotected sex; more than 80% report using condoms and more than 90% discuss sex with their health care practitioner (Elkington et al., 2012; Setse et al., 2011). There are many possible reasons for these patterns. Perinatally HIV-infected youth may initiate sexual activity later because their pubertal onset tends to be

significantly delayed. The delay ranges from 6 months in girls to 11 months in boys and tends to be more pronounced with more severe HIV disease and among youth perinatally infected with HIV who were born before 1997, suggesting that timing of pubertal onset may be closer to normal in the ART era (Williams et al., 2013). Some perinatally HIV-infected teens who have received appropriate health education may be concerned about potential risks associated with early sexual activity, such as acquiring another STD that could further compromise their immunity. Indeed, perinatally HIV-infected youth with better understanding of transmission risk report higher condom use self-efficacy (Wiener et al., 2006). Sexual activity may be underreported by some youth who were perinatally infected, owing to unique patterns of transference and countertransference that often take place in pediatric HIV clinics. Both adolescents and clinicians may find it awkward to discuss sex, just as many adolescents and their parents often do.

The moral imperative to disclose an HIV diagnosis may affect a youth's choices of initiating (sexual) relationships. Perinatally HIV-infected youth who disclose their HIV status to partners often experience some form of rejection. Some had never disclosed to a romantic partner but carefully managed intimacy by delaying dating, terminating relationships, and "taking it slow" (Fair and Albright, 2012). In focus groups, perinatally HIV-infected youth tend to place a high value on protection of self and partners, their own emotional protection from possible rejection, and patience as they hope to find a supportive partner (Fair and Albright, 2012).

Finally, as one recent survey suggests, sexual risk behavior may be underestimated if youth are just asked whether they have used condoms or not, but are not asked specifically about incomplete condom use (i.e., putting a condom on after beginning sex or taking a condom off before finishing sex) or condom failure (e.g., condom breaking or slipping off during sex) (Dolezal et al., 2014). (See Chapter 34 for more information on serodiscordant adolescent couples.)

Substance Use

Data on substance use patterns among youth who were perinatally HIV infected are not well understood. Studies using interviews of these youth report 15–20% rates of substance abuse (Mellins et al., 2009; Williams et al., 2010), while a study utilizing chart review reported even lower rates (Kapetanovic et al., 2011). These rates stand in contrast to data from anonymous survey of U.S. urban high school students, where use of marijuana alone was 38% (Eaton et al., 2010). While perinatally HIV-infected youth may indeed be less likely to abuse drugs than their peers in the general population, the extent of discrepancy suggests that other factors, such as underreporting, also play a role.

Factors associated with risk for alcohol use among perinatally HIV-infected youth include higher severity of emotional and conduct problems, and alcohol and marijuana use in the home by the caregiver or others; factors associated with risk for marijuana use include marijuana use in the home, higher severity of conduct problems, and stressful life events (Alperen et al., 2014). A strong correlation between behavioral disorders (attention-deficit/hyperactivity disorder [ADHD], oppositional defiant disorder, or conduct disorder) and marijuana use has been found in a U.S. cohort of perinatally HIV-infected youth (Elkington et al., 2016). Please see Chapter 14 on substance use disorders and their role in the HIV pandemic.

TRANSITION TO ADULT HIV CARE

In the United States, there are more than 30,000 youth ages 13–24 years living with HIV, the majority of whom will need to be transferred from pediatric to adult care in the next decade (CDC, 2014). The issue is likely to grow over time internationally with increasing access to combination ART in the areas with high prevalence of perinatal HIV infection and resulting increased life expectancy of perinatally HIV-infected youth. This is a major juncture point in the continuum of their clinical care, since a disruption in care, even if temporary, can contribute to development of viral resistance and overall morbidity (Wiener et al., 2006).

In most cases, the transition from pediatric to adult care is guided by age limits rather than the achievement of developmental milestones. This can result in adolescents aging out of care before being emotionally or cognitively ready. The confluence of general risk due to having a chronic illness coupled with HIV-related neurocognitive impairment can result in a cohort of youth who are unprepared to address their own healthcare needs (CDC, 2008). Furthermore, with improving life expectancy, many youth and their families develop stable and long-term relationships with their pediatric care teams, often making it emotionally difficult to move on to a new team of clinicians. This is especially true when HIV-positive youth have lost family members, are estranged from family, or have not disclosed their diagnosis to others close to them and find their primary support system within the pediatric HIV care team (Valenzuela et al., 2011; Vinjayan et al., 2009). Thus, transferring a patient from care abruptly and without adequate emotional and medical preparation may result not only in foregone care and poor health outcomes (Dowshen and D'Angelo, 2011) but also feelings of abandonment and further experience of overall loss (Wiener et al., 2011). Additionally, confronting discrimination and the interpersonal complexities for youth living with this socially stigmatized chronic disorder (Dowshen et al., 2009; Miles et al., 2004; Remien and Mellins, 2007) during healthcare transition can seem insurmountable, especially when the accepting clinician is not equipped to meet the emotional needs of these youth. One study of perinatally HIV-infected youth who had transferred to adult care found that transition was more difficult than anticipated and finding emotional support services was particularly challenging (Wiener et al., 2011). Youth identified the need for increased continuity of care, assistance with logistics, improved communication with clinicians and caregivers, and individualized management of their transition process (Wiener et al., 2011).

For all of these reasons, lack of coordination and poor communication between pediatric and adult clinicians may be detrimental to the transition process (CDC, 2008).

MENTAL HEALTH AND PSYCHIATRIC DISORDERS

Reported rates of psychiatric disorders among perinatally HIV-infected youth range from 25% to 69%. Anxiety disorders, disruptive behavior disorders, ADHD, and mood disorders are most prevalent (Gadow et al., 2012, Kacanek et al., 2015; Malee et al., 2011; Mellins et al., 2012; Nachman et al., 2012). Correlates of mental health problems in perinatally HIV-infected youth include caregiver characteristics (limit-setting problems, health-related functional limitations, psychiatric disorder); child characteristics (younger age, lower IQ) (Malee et al., 2011); inadequate social support (Kang et al., 2011); stressful life events and neighborhood disorder (Kang et al., 2011; Mutumba et al., 2016); and youth reports of clinically significant pain (Serchuck et al., 2010).

Depressive symptoms such as fatigue, cognitive impairment, decreased social interaction and exploration, and loss of appetite may in part derive from chronic immune dysregulation and related cytokine activity (Raison et al., 2006). In children who were infected perinatally with HIV, CD4 nadir <25% has been associated with increased risk of depression (Gadow et al., 2012), but not with risk of ADHD or oppositional defiant disorder (Zeegers et al., 2010). Prenatal cocaine exposure may increase risk of psychiatric problems (Linares et al., 2006).

BEHAVIORALLY HIV-INFECTED ADOLESCENTS

Compared to adolescents who were infected perinatally with HIV, adolescents infected later, through risky behavior, are expected to have less medical morbidity, as they were not born with HIV and most have not been infected long enough to develop complications of chronic HIV infection. They are ART-naïve and, unless infected with a highly resistant strain of HIV, they subsequently have relatively more treatment options available, including more potent and less cumbersome ART regimens. The benefits of ART initiation during primary HIV infection include symptom relief, limiting risk of viral mutation and transmission, and slowing disease progression. Yet, the psychosocial realities of behaviorally HIV-infected youths are often such that they may jeopardize their medical outcomes (Ross et al., 2010). The very mode of transmission (i.e., substance use, unprotected sex) implies that many behaviorally HIV-infected youth were already at risk even before they became HIV positive. Furthermore, data from a recent CDC report indicate that only 49% of individuals with HIV aged 18 to 24 in the United States are aware of their HIV-positive status. As a result, only 13% of youth with HIV in this age group are virally suppressed, which is a rate significantly lower than among older individuals with HIV (Bradley et al., 2014). Behaviorally HIV-infected youth tend to remain sexually active after HIV diagnosis. However, their safer sex practices, including partner disclosure, are inconsistent and often influenced by modifiable psychosocial factors, including concerns about rejection, stigma or gossip; not knowing how or when to disclose (Camacho-Gonzalez et al., 2016; Chenneville et al., 2015); need for instant gratification and its increased accessibility through social media; and avoiding HIV disclosure or agreeing to condomless sex in the context of survival sex (Camacho-Gonzalez et al., 2016). A social-personal model highlights the four key factors associated with HIV transmission in youth in a broad contextual framework: (1) personal attributes (cognitions about HIV, affect dysregulation, mental health problems, personality traits); (2) family context (affective characteristics, parental monitoring, parent–teen communication); (3) peer and partner relationships (relationship concern, partner communication, peer influence); and (4) environmental circumstances (neighborhood disadvantage, stressful events) (Donenberg and Pao, 2005). Addressing these factors should be integrated into HIV care, as a part of comprehensive, multidisciplinary clinical treatment planning and follow-up.

Behaviorally HIV-infected youth have much higher prevalence of psychiatric disorders than youth in national samples, with reported point prevalence of depression ranging from 15% to 50% (Martinez et al., 2009; Nichols et al., 2013; Pao et al., 2000); substantial rates of generalized anxiety disorder (17%) and posttraumatic stress disorders (PTSD) (28%); high lifetime prevalence of psychiatric hospitalizations (30%) and suicide attempts (30%); and as many as 22% reporting suicidal ideation in the past month (Martinez et al., 2009; Pao et al., 2000). Most youth with HIV acquired behaviorally struggled with significant psychiatric symptoms even before their HIV diagnosis (Pao et al., 2000), a finding suggesting that predisposing factors for these psychiatric disorders may include socioenvironmental, personal, and familial factors preceding the HIV infection. Youth with HIV acquired behaviorally reside predominantly in urban centers. Most have a parent with a history of psychiatric illness, psychiatric hospitalization, or incarceration (Martinez et al., 2009; Pao et al., 2000). Trauma history is also highly prevalent among behaviorally HIV-infected youth, including high reported rates of sexual abuse (50%), exposure to family violence while growing up (44%), and experiencing dating violence (almost 20%) (Pao et al., 2000). Behaviorally HIV-infected youth with a past history of abuse are at increased risk to develop anxiety disorders (Martinez et al., 2009). (See Chapter 17 for more information about the role of trauma.) Factors that might trigger or perpetuate psychiatric symptoms following HIV diagnosis include stressors related to HIV diagnosis (e.g., concerns about physical manifestations of illness, adjusting to medication, acceptance of diagnosis); family (disclosure, need for education, concerns about rejection); sexual partners (mistrust, anger); peer group (rumors, fear of rejection);

academic or occupational stressors; fear of job loss; and impact of stigma on their status among peers (Hosek et al., 2008). (See Chapter 6 for more information about the role of stigma and discrimination.) Studies suggest that as many as 25% of youth with HIV acquired behaviorally continue with substance abuse after HIV diagnosis (Nichols et al., 2013). Efavirenz (EFV), which is commonly prescribed to treatment-naïve adolescents, may cause or exacerbate psychiatric symptoms (Ross et al., 2010).

NEUROCOGNITIVE OUTCOMES OF BEHAVIORALLY HIV-INFECTED ADOLESCENTS

Youth who acquire HIV in adolescence are at high risk to develop HIV-associated neurocognitive disorder (HAND; see Chapter 16) within the first year of HIV diagnosis. Lower CD4 count, longer time since HIV diagnosis, and severity of alcohol use each independently contribute to the risk of HAND in this population (Nichols et al., 2013). Episodic memory and fine motor skills are the most commonly affected ability areas (Nichols et al., 2013). The neurocognitive impairment in these youth may have some unique features. Compared to adults with HIV, they appear to have similar risk of impairment in learning and memory, but their risk of impairment in fine and gross motor functioning appears to be higher (Nichols et al., 2013). Compared to youth who acquire HIV perinatally, behaviorally HIV-infected youth tend to have relatively less impairment on measures of global intellectual functioning, attention, and working memory (Nichols et al., 2013).

HIV-AFFECTED CHILDREN AND ADOLESCENTS

The psychosocial implications for the children without HIV in the HIV-affected household are immense. Many of these children have likely had a series of preexisting and long-standing family disruptions prior to the HIV diagnosis, resulting in widespread anxieties about future losses and concerns about their own health. In HIV-affected households, profound mental health and adjustment challenges exist (Whetten et al., 2008), often confounded by stigma (Vanable et al., 2006). Stigma is a real concern for youth, as most children fear they would be mistreated if they revealed their parent's HIV status to their classmates (Fair and Brackett, 2008). Moreover, the pervasive threat of parental death and the fear of being left alone constitute chronic trauma for HIV-affected children (Mendelsohn, 1997). Often with no voice to represent them, these children are the silent victims of the HIV/AIDS pandemic (Fair et al., 1995).

It is common for some HIV-affected youth to become "parentified"—a term used to describe children who are prematurely forced to take on adult responsibilities and roles before they are emotionally or developmentally ready to manage these roles (Bekir et al., 1993; Valleau et al., 1995). The greater the severity of parental illness, the more parentified they become. Those who report more parental role behaviors also report more externalizing dysfunctional behaviors, including risky sex, alcohol and marijuana use, and conduct problems (Stein et al., 1999). In one study, 40% of HIV-affected youth, ages 11–15, reported ever using tobacco, alcohol, or drugs (Rosenblum et al., 2005). Strong support, including strong positive associations with peers, has been associated with better adjustment (Rosenblum et al., 2005), whereas negative peer interactions (e.g., bullying) have been identified as risks (Okawa et al., 2011; Zhao et al., 2011).

The process of losing a sibling to AIDS may take place in the context of the illness or death of one or both parents and may be the harbinger of a still more frightening future (Walker, 1991), leaving surviving siblings at high risk for psychological distress and posttraumatic symptoms. Survivor guilt, guilt over the reaction to the death, guilt over past feelings about AIDS, and guilt over not being able to make the parents feel better can all contribute to anxiety and poor self-esteem. Earlier studies found among HIV-affected children externalizing behavior problems and somatic symptoms related to their parents' health status (Rotheram-Borus and Stein, 1999).

In a study examining the impact of HIV-related parental death on 414 adolescents over a period of 6 years (Rotheram-Borus et al., 2004), bereaved adolescents had significantly more emotional distress, negative life events, and contact with the criminal justice system than non-bereaved youth. Depressive symptoms, passive problem-solving, and sexual risk behaviors increased soon after parental death. One year after parental death, these levels were similar to those of non-bereaved peers, a finding suggesting the importance of early family intervention soon after parental HIV diagnosis, prior to parental death, and sustained over time. Evidence suggests that behavioral difficulties in pre-orphans tend to begin before the mother's death and may emerge more fully after 1–2 years rather than at 6 months (Pelton and Forehand, 2005).

The physical aspects of HIV infection can also influence a parent's ability to parent. Fair (2006) reported that HIV-affected children were more likely to exhibit behavioral problems when their mothers reported experiencing HIV-related symptoms. The complex psychosocial implications for the mental health and development of HIV-affected children are further compounded by frequent parental mental illness. Evidence indicates that compromised parental mental health has an immediate effect on the quality and quantity of attention a parent is able to devote to his or her child (Atkinson et al., 2000; Kingston and Tough, 2014; Martins and Gaffan, 2000). In a survey of a large sample of caregivers of preschool-aged children living in KwaZulu-Natal, South Africa, a poverty-stricken region with high HIV seroprevalence, 31.3% caregivers screened positive for at least one psychiatric disorder, with PTSD being the most common. Known HIV-positive caregivers were more likely to have any depressive or bipolar disorder than caregivers who previously tested negative (Chhagan et al., 2014).

HIV-affected children and adolescents are at increased risk for academic problems, depression, anxiety, and engaging in delinquent behaviors (e.g., Brackis-Cott et al., 2007; Fair, 2006; Forsyth et al., 1996), and it is now clearly understood that parental HIV presents significant challenges for them. The potential for mitigation and resilience can be affected by available supportive services beyond what exists in an already strained family and community (Sherr et al., 2014). Longer-term follow-up studies with reliable and repeated measures are needed in populations of highly affected children.

PERINATALLY HIV-EXPOSED BUT UNINFECTED CHILDREN AND ADOLESCENTS

In addition to sharing common familial, environmental, and psychosocial circumstances with their other HIV-affected peers, youth perinatally exposed to HIV but uninfected also have history of biomedical exposures that are salient to their status. This includes exposure to maternal infection and inflammation in utero, and, increasingly, to prophylactic ART, both in utero and as neonates.

Perinatal Exposure to Antiretroviral Medications

Data from the U.S.-based cohort Surveillance Monitoring for Antiretroviral Therapy Toxicities (SMARTT) are indicative of trends in perinatal combination ART exposure: among 1,768 perinatally HIV-exposed but uninfected children, prenatal ART exposure increased from 19% in 1997 to 88% in 2009 (Griner et al., 2011). While this trend has dramatically improved maternal HIV morbidity and reduced the rates of perinatal HIV transmission, there is concern that perinatal exposure to ART may negatively impact health and development of these children (Le Doaré et al., 2012). A literature review suggests that perinatal combination ART is associated with increased risk of premature delivery, pregnancy complications (e.g., hypertension), small-for-gestational age infants, and mitochondrial dysfunction in children who were perinatally exposed to HIV but not infected (Newell and Bunders, 2013). Prenatal exposure to a tenofovir (TDF)-containing ART regimen has been associated with increased risk of slightly lower z-scores for length for age and head circumference in 1-year-old perinatally HIV-exposed but uninfected infants (compared to those exposed to ART without TDF), but the clinical relevance of this association is not clear (Siberry et al., 2012).

With regard to effect of perinatal ART on ND outcomes, data from the SMARTT cohort have been mostly reassuring. Specifically, perinatal ART exposure or individual ART regimens were not differentially predictive of Bayley-III outcomes of 374 perinatally HIV-exposed but uninfected infants ages 9–15 months (median age at testing was 12.7 months). Although the language domain scores were significantly lower among infants with perinatal exposure to atazanavir (ATV) than among infants without ATV exposure, they were still within normative expectations for age (Sirois et al., 2013). In a larger SMARTT-based sample, with an additional 4 years of longitudinal data and a more rigorous statistical approach, in utero ATV exposure was associated with lower performance on the Language domain of the Bayley-III by about 3.4 points among infants 9–15 months of age. Additionally, ATV exposure was associated with lower performance on the Social-Emotional domain by 5.9 points, only when initiated in the second or third trimester of pregnancy (Caniglia et al., 2016). Finally, among 739 prenatally HIV-exposed but uninfected children ages 5–13 years, cognitive and academic outcomes (as measured by age-appropriate Wechsler intelligence and academic scales) did not differ by any ART regimen, class, or individual drug (Nozyce et al., 2014). Thus, in utero exposure to ATV-containing regimens, compared to non-ATV-containing regimens, may adversely affect language and social-emotional development in prenatally HIV-exposed but uninfected infants during the first year of life, but the magnitude of impairment is small and may not have lasting clinical impact. The reliability of these mostly reassuring findings is supported by the methodological strengths of SMARTT, including large sample size, detailed collection of maternal and infant histories (which made it possible to adjust for potential confounders such as prematurity, infant growth outcomes, demographics, caregiver education and IQ scores, obstetric complications, or maternal HIV severity indicators), and availability of the comparison cohort without perinatal HIV exposure.

Perinatal Exposure to Maternal HIV Infection

Data from studies with non-HIV populations suggest that children prenatally exposed to HIV but not infected might be at risk for unfavorable ND or behavioral outcomes due to nonspecific effects of in utero exposure to maternal infection(s) and inflammation. Such exposure during critical times of development has been associated with an increased risk of autism (Ciaranello and Ciaranello, 1995; Lee et al., 2015), schizophrenia (Brown and Patterson, 2011), and bipolar disorder (Parboosing et al., 2013).

It has been hypothesized that, following fetal exposure to maternal infection, a subset of glia cells become permanently activated or primed, resulting in overproduction of cytokines in response to subsequent immune challenges, with lifelong consequences for brain function (Bilbo and Schwarz, 2009). While this hypothetical glial overactivity has not been evaluated yet, evidence suggests presence of abnormalities of fetal immune maturation in prenatally HIV-exposed infants who are not infected that may persist into childhood, including lower naïve CD4 counts and thymic output in infancy (Clerici et al., 2000; Nielsen et al., 2001); increased IgG, IgM, and IgA levels at 24 months of age (Ensoli et al., 1999); presence of HIV-specific CD4+ and CD8+ T-cells in HIV-exposed but uninfected children as old as 7 years (Bunders et al., 2010); and altered cell-mediated or antibody responses to certain vaccines (e.g., polio, BCG, pertussis, pneumococcus, and tetanus toxoid) (Dauby et al., 2012; Sanz-Ramos et al., 2013). However, the long-term prognosis of these immune alterations or their relationship with ND or behavioral outcomes of perinatally HIV-exposed infected and uninfected children is not known.

Mental Health Outcomes

Recent studies report high rates of psychiatric problems among perinatally HIV-exposed infected and uninfected children and adolescents, and suggest that their mental health needs are relatively under-recognized and undertreated. In a U.S.-based cohort of perinatally HIV-exposed infected and uninfected youth, ages 7–16, the overall prevalence of scores in the "at-risk" range (i.e., T-score 60–69) on the Behavioral Assessment System for Children-Second Edition (BASC-2) was even higher among children who were uninfected than among HIV-infected children (38% versus 25%, $p < 0.01$) (Malee et al., 2011). Similarly, in a longitudinal study of 280 youth from New York City, age 9–16 years (166 perinatally HIV-infected, 114 exposed to HIV but uninfected), almost 70% of youth from either group met DSM-IV criteria for at least one psychiatric disorder at either baseline or at 18-month follow-up (Mellins et al., 2012). However, among perinatally HIV-infected youth, there was a significant decrease over time in the prevalence of psychiatric disorders, particularly anxiety disorders, while the prevalence of any psychiatric disorder among uninfected youth who had been perinatally exposed to HIV remained unchanged and mood disorders increased. Perinatally HIV-infected youth reported more use of mental health services at follow-up (Mellins et al., 2012).

Among perinatally exposed uninfected youth, there is a strong correlation between diagnoses of behavioral disorders (ADHD, oppositional defiant disorder, conduct disorder) or depressive disorders and marijuana use (Elkington et al., 2016).

INTERVENTIONS AND TREATMENT CONSIDERATIONS

OPTIMIZING NEURODEVELOPMENTAL OUTCOMES

Early ART initiation helps optimize motor and cognitive outcomes, especially in perinatally HIV-infected children who have not been severely immune suppressed (Laughton et al., 2012; Van Rie et al., 2009). The window of opportunity, however, may be narrow, as deferring combination ART beyond 3 months of age appears to lessen the neuroprotective effect despite careful clinical monitoring and ready access to ART (Laughton et al., 2012). Early ART-induced virological suppression is associated with improved IQ scores in school-age children, while central nervous system (CNS) penetrance of ART is not (Crowell et al., 2015). The ART-induced T-cell activation is positively associated with IQ scores in perinatally HIV-infected children (Kapetanovic et al., 2012); this association is unique to children and may be related to salient immune factors, such as a relatively large naïve T-cell pool and preserved thymopoietic capacity (Sandgaard et al., 2014).

Two nonpharmacological interventions piloted in Uganda have demonstrated feasibility and efficacy in optimizing ND outcomes. Early intervention of teaching caregivers practical strategies to enhance the child's cognitive and emotional development during daily interactions at home (e.g., gaining the child's attention and engaging him or her in a learning experience; providing emotional support and modeling; expanding the learning experience to other past and future situations) has been evaluated in a year-long randomized controlled trial (Boivin et al., 2013). The intervention improved visual-spatial memory and learning outcomes in perinatally HIV-infected preschoolers (Boivin et al., 2013). In perinatally HIV-infected children ages 6–16 years, the computerized cognitive rehabilitation therapy intervention Captain's Log was administered in twice-weekly, 45-minute office-based sessions over 5 weeks and demonstrated feasibility and preliminary efficacy in improving learning and attention scores (Boivin et al., 2010).

FACILITATING DIAGNOSTIC DISCLOSURE

Family plays the main deciding role in when and how disclosure occurs; clinicians should remain in an advisory and facilitating role. Given its potential implications, it is understandable that parents and caretakers of perinatally HIV-infected children tend to view disclosure as a daunting task. Clinicians can help make the parents' concerns manageable by reframing the disclosure as a process rather than as a single event (Lesch et al., 2007). This process begins when the child is brought to his or her first medical appointments; it continues with the child's growing awareness of having a chronic illness, the need for taking medications, and having frequent medical check-ups. The process culminates with disclosing the name of the virus, ways to treat the disease, and transmission routes and continue with post-disclosure education and supporting the child through post-disclosure adjustment. Pediatric HIV clinics are encouraged to develop a standardized, process-oriented approach to diagnostic disclosure which considers a child's emotional and cognitive developmental level as well as family readiness to disclose (Oland et al., 2008). Mental health specialist should take the lead role in this multidisciplinary effort, which has three main phases:

1. *Preparation.* Practically, this phase begins at the time the child is diagnosed with HIV infection. Clinicians help the parents set the stage for disclosing the diagnosis to the child when they are ready to do so. As the disclosure time approaches, a comprehensive assessment of *disclosure readiness* is conducted, and any identified barriers to disclosure are addressed in order to minimize potential post-disclosure complications.

2. *Disclosure.* HIV diagnosis is disclosed to the child. Clinicians facilitate this process by providing logistical

and psychosocial support to the family in order to optimize the outcome.

3. *Post-disclosure follow-up.* This critically important clinical task is an integral part of the disclosure process. It requires close monitoring and ongoing assessment of the child's emotional adjustment as well as academic and family functioning, and intervening accordingly when needed.

It is important to obtain a clear understanding of the family's cultural background and the factors that might influence responses to an HIV diagnosis or disclosure (Mason et al., 1995). Table A.3 in the Resource Appendix outlines key clinical steps to be considered by mental health clinicians as they facilitate the disclosure process.

SCHOOL ADVOCACY AND CONSULTATION

If the family decides to share the HIV diagnosis with the school, clinicians can facilitate the process by (a) informing parents of a child's right to education; (b) educating school officials and personnel about HIV and the individual child's needs; (c) accompanying parents to school board and/or individualized education plan (IEP) meetings; (d) providing consultation to teachers and principals in talking to classmates about HIV; or (e) updating the school about the child's progress (Armstrong et al., 1993; Cohen et al., 1997). Setting realistic and flexible academic expectations (e.g., in light of frequent clinic visits or cognitive deficits) is key for optimizing the child's academic success.

INTERVENTIONS TO PROMOTE SAFE HEALTH BEHAVIORS

Efforts to promote safe behaviors among youth who acquire HIV through risky behavior critically depend on (1) identifying those youth who are HIV positive and (2) engaging them in HIV specialty care. These two steps in the continuum of HIV care not only improve the survival and morbidity outcomes but also increase the percentage of youth with HIV who have achieved viral suppression, thus reducing the risk of new HIV infections in the community (Bradley et al., 2014).

The American Academy of Pediatrics recommends offering routine HIV screening to all adolescents at least once by 16 to 18 years of age in communities where HIV prevalence exceeds 0.1%, and to adolescents who are sexually active or have other risk factors in areas with lower prevalence. For youth identified as HIV positive, arranging linkage with care should be an integral part of the testing process (Committee on Pediatric AIDS, 2011). While parental involvement in adolescent healthcare is generally desirable, requiring parental consent may pose a major hurdle to the youth's willingness to undergo HIV testing. For this reason, all U.S. states allow most minors to consent to testing and treatment for

STDs without parental involvement, although some limitations vary by state (Guttmacher Institute, 2017). If privacy cannot be ensured, clinicians are advised to refer adolescents to confidential community-based HIV testing services, which can be identified online at www.hivtest.org (Committee on Pediatric AIDS, 2011).

Complicating efforts to reach youth at risk for HIV is the fact that many of these youths belong to highly vulnerable and marginalized demographic groups (e.g., men who have sex with men, transgender youth). Recent qualitative data from New York City indicate that young black men who have sex with men and transgender women are unlikely to use in-home HIV self-testing kits that are commercially available, owing to concerns about the cost of the test, anxiety about accessing the test, concerns around properly conducting the self-test, and lack of support if they test positive (Frye et al., 2015). Strategies to reach marginalized youth with out-of-facility HIV testing and reproductive health services have been piloted in various settings (e.g., condom distribution via street outreach in Louisiana, home-based HIV testing in Malawi) with promising preliminary results, but according to a literature review, more research is needed to evaluate their true impact (Denno et al., 2012). Clinically, it is of critical importance to continuously assess whether the youth has a strong support system and to help him or her build or maintain such support when indicated. Once an adolescent with HIV is identified and enrolled in care, assertive case management must be included in the multidisciplinary clinical care to help address barriers to care and optimize health behaviors (Johnson et al., 2003).

Adherence is a primary behavioral objective for every adolescent with HIV. An adolescent's self-report of missed ART medication doses warrants a high level of clinical attention, even if his or her viral load is undetectable and CD4 count is high (DeLaMora et al., 2006). Self-report suggests the presence of barriers that need immediate clinical attention before viral resistance occurs.

Clinical efforts to identify barriers to adherence need to be informed by the broader context of the adolescent's life, including issues related to HIV stigma and disclosure, caregiver stress, peer issues, mental health, substance use, and length of time on medications (Reisner et al., 2009). The adolescent's input should be solicited through troubleshooting and by proposing ways to address the identified barriers through individualized treatment plans tailored to his or her specific needs and circumstances (DeLaMora et al., 2006).

Cell phones and other youth-friendly digital media have been effectively used to deliver individualized problem-solving and motivational interviewing interventions that have improved adherence and significantly reduced viral loads among behaviorally HIV-infected youth (Naar-King et al., 2013) and in a combined sample of perinatally and behaviorally HIV-infected youth (Belzer et al., 2014).

Clinic-based interventions targeting heterogeneous groups of perinatally and behaviorally HIV-infected adolescents with adherence problems have been piloted with promising preliminary effectiveness in improving adherence, including a 6-month community-based multisystemic therapy intervention that combined principles of cognitive-behavioral therapy and parent training (Letourneau et al., 2013), a psychoeducational group intervention combining six sessions with family or peer ("treatment buddy") participation and six youth-only sessions (Lyon et al., 2003), and Adolescent Impact, an intervention combining seven psychoeducational group sessions and five individual behavioral sessions (tailored to each adolescent's specific behavior profile) (LaGrange et al., 2012). Motivational interviewing to retain teens and young adults in HIV care can be delivered by adequately trained and supervised peer outreach workers with quality and effectiveness comparable to master's-level clinicians (Naar-King, Outlaw, et al., 2009).

Given the frequent co-occurrence of unprotected sex, substance use, and nonadherence, interventions often need to address more than one of these behaviors (Naar-King et al., 2012). Healthy Choices is a four-session, clinic-based intervention utilizing motivational interviewing to target multiple health behaviors among at-risk HIV-positive youth. This intervention has been efficacious in reducing frequency and long-term severity of alcohol use (Murphy et al., 2012) and in improving depression and motivational readiness to change, which are among key precursors for behavioral change (Naar-King et al., 2010). The intervention has also shown efficacy in reducing viral loads at 6 months post-intervention, but the result was not maintained at 9-month follow-up (Naar-King, Parsons, et al., 2009).

For optimizing health behaviors of HIV-affected youth, interventions that promote family functioning and address social-influence factors are essential (Rosenblum et al., 2005).

Evidence from large clinical trials suggests that pre-exposure prophylaxis (PrEP) can substantially reduce the risk of HIV infection among men who have sex with men and among heterosexual women and men. (See Chapter 31 for a detailed overview of pre- and post-exposure prophylaxis of HIV.) Clinical trials have not specifically evaluated use of PrEP among adolescents, possibly because of the unclear legal ramifications of providing minors' access to PrEP without parental consent. A recent legal review concluded that, although none of the states in the United States explicitly prohibits minors' access to PrEP, more legal work is needed to establish clear legal definition of PrEP, given that it has elements of both "treatment" (i.e., it includes a pharmacological intervention that is also used to treat HIV) and "prevention" (i.e., the purpose of PrEP is to prevent, not treat, HIV infection) (Culp and Caucci, 2013).

MENTAL HEALTH SERVICES

It is common for teens living with HIV to feel sadness, anger, and a range of other emotions. Individual psychotherapy may help adolescents with HIV process their experiences, cope with their illness, address peer issues, and begin to explore their sexuality and safer sexual behaviors. Support groups can offer a sense of belonging, a place where they do not need to hide their illness, where fears can be shared, experiences validated, isolation reduced, trauma understood, and a deeper connection made with other teens. Overnight camping programs for teens can also provide this effect. Within specialty summer camps for children infected with or affected by HIV (see Table A.4 in the Resource Appendix), many teens are able to get counselor training and find summer employment. Community-based service providers often hire youth with HIV to serve as peer leaders. Peer empowerment programs provide HIV-positive young men and women the opportunity to deliver HIV prevention messages to other youth (Luna and Rotheram-Borus, 1999). Under close supervision and guidance, they learn to articulate their own life experiences, gain access to resources, meet new friends, and receive employment in return. Teens who are able to keep themselves mentally active, believe their life has purpose, have a sense of humor, adapt to loss and change, and create a backup plan in case they become ill appear to thrive under the continued uncertainties associated with HIV/AIDS (Wiener et al., 2003).

Addressing Mental Health Needs of HIV-Affected Youth

For HIV-affected youth, mental health screening and family-based interventions need to be adopted within medical centers and community-based programs. Young persons must be allowed to grieve (e.g., losing a sibling), feel appropriate anger for the tragedies in their life, and find healthy ways of coping with these emotions. Camps geared for HIV-affected family members have been helpful for many of these children (see Table A.5 in the Resource Appendix), providing the opportunity to share their family's plight, meet others facing similar challenges, and often reach out and, if interested, be trained to be a spokesperson for adolescents at risk for HIV infection.

Psychotherapeutic interventions for HIV-affected children must concentrate on assessing for children acting as parents, providing respite child and parental care, assisting with permanency planning, and building legacies, social-support networks, and ongoing mental health services (Wiener et al., 2003). Special attention must also be given to the envy and rivalry that might arise in the well child when the child with HIV is receiving special medical care and parental attention (Fanos and Wiener, 1994). TALC LA, a manual-based intervention for HIV-affected adolescents and their HIV-positive mothers (manual available at http://chipts.ucla.edu) that integrates cognitive-behavioral principles and social learning theory, has shown efficacy in improving long-term psychosocial adjustment (Rotheram-Borus et al., 2001, 2004). Li and colleagues (2011) have developed and described a multilevel intervention, Together for Empowerment Activities (TEA), which combines clinic-based group activities, home-based family activities, and community events to improve an HIV-affected family's psychosocial adjustment. TEA was recently successfully piloted with rural HIV-affected families in Anhui province, China, but larger trials are needed to determine the efficacy (Li et al., 2014).

PSYCHOPHARMACOLOGICAL CONSIDERATIONS

Before any psychopharmacological treatment is considered, it is essential for the prescribing clinician to have a thorough understanding of a child or adolescent's psychiatric symptoms, articulate this understanding in a biopsychosocial diagnostic formulation, and share this formulation with the parents or guardians in an understandable manner (Stroeh and Trivedi, 2012). The initial clinical assessment and medication initiation need to be followed by regular follow-up visits that should include monitoring of treatment response as well as safety monitoring (Stroeh and Trivedi, 2012). Additionally, children and adolescents starting an antidepressant must be closely monitored for development of new-onset suicidal ideation (Boylan et al., 2007). In children with HIV who are treated with ART there is a potential for drug–drug interactions, so safety monitoring must include that of drug levels for psychotropics with a narrow therapeutic index (e.g., lithium carbonate) as well as clinical monitoring for drugs with a wide therapeutic index (e.g., SSRIs).

While there are no published data on efficacy or effectiveness of psychotropic medications for treatment of psychiatric disorders specifically in youth with HIV, pharmacological interventions can alleviate psychiatric symptoms and improve functioning and quality of life and have demonstrated efficacy in other pediatric populations. Stimulants, atomoxetine, and alpha-2 antagonists clonidine and guanfacine can be tried in the treatment of ADHD (Pliszka et al., 2007). SSRIs and other antidepressant should be used for treating depression (Boylan et al., 2007) or anxiety disorders (Peters and Connolly, 2012; Strawn et al., 2012). Several conventional and second-generation antipsychotics (SGAs) can be used in the treatment of schizophrenia and Tourette's disorder and for disruptive behaviors in children with developmental disabilities or autism-spectrum disorders (Kapetanovic and Simpson, 2006). Lithium salts, SGAs and several anticonvulsants are useful for treatment of bipolar disorder (Goldstein et al., 2012).

Some safety and pharmacokinetic data are emerging that are specific for children and adolescents with HIV. Perinatally HIV-infected youth who are prescribed SGAs have twofold increased risk of developing hypercholesterolemia over 12 months (Kapetanovic et al., 2010) and an accelerated increase in body mass index z-scores over periods of 6 months and 2 years, which is further aggravated if SGAs are prescribed concomitantly with protease inhibitors (PIs) (Kapetanovic et al., 2009). This is particularly concerning given the already significant risk factors for cardiovascular disease in perinatally HIV-infected children and that ART appears to have a significant effect on this risk. Specifically, perinatally HIV-infected children have much higher levels of triglycerides and lower levels of high-density lipoprotein (HDL) cholesterol compared to a nationally representative sample. PI therapy in this population is independently associated with higher triglyceride and low-density lipoprotein cholesterol levels and a lower HDL cholesterol level, whereas non-nucleoside reverse-transcriptase inhibitor therapy might have a protective effect, as it is associated with lower visceral fat and a higher HDL cholesterol level (Miller et al., 2008). Thus, SGAs should be prescribed to perinatally HIV-infected youth with utmost caution, preferably on a short-term basis (e.g., to manage acute agitation and other psychiatric emergencies), and growth and metabolic profiles should be carefully monitored. When possible, alternative evidence-based treatments should be considered.

Stimulants do not seem to exacerbate the risk of growth delay beyond the risk associated with HIV alone. In fact, slower average growth rates have been reported in perinatally HIV-infected youth prescribed one of the non-stimulant drugs that are used to treat ADHD (i.e., atomoxetine, clonidine, guanfacine, bupropion, imipramine or desipramine) than in youth who were prescribed a stimulant (Sirois et al., 2009). Perinatally HIV-infected youth who are prescribed methylphenidate (MPH) have relatively lower MPH blood levels at a given dose than levels in noninfected youth. The levels are even lower in children who are prescribed EFV. These pharmacokinetic data suggest that some perinatally HIV-infected youth may require relatively higher doses of MPH to achieve therapeutic effect (Best et al., 2013). See Chapter 42 for a comprehensive overview of HIV psychopharmacology.

END-OF-LIFE ISSUES

End-of-life events usually present as a result of complications of severe immunosuppression (see Chapter 49 of this textbook). In the United States and other high-income countries, end-of-life issues among perinatally HIV-infected youth are not nearly as prominent as they used to be in the pre-ART era. In resource-limited countries, the pediatric AIDS mortality rates have been declining as well, but many perinatally HIV-infected children still don't have optimal access to ART and state-of-the art HIV care, and pediatric AIDS-related deaths are still very much a part of clinical reality. There were 210,000 AIDS deaths among children younger than 15 years in 2012 (UNAIDS, 2013).

The point at which treatments are unlikely to be successful is typically another crisis point for the family. Meetings with the family to discuss options and explore palliative care are often helpful, especially if staff members most intimately involved with the child can be present. As parents begin the process of accepting that their child will die, they may experience anticipatory grief. Many of the parents' thoughts focus on preparing for death while continuing to hope for recovery. Hope can be redefined by redirecting energies toward providing as good a quality of life as possible for as long as possible, followed by a good quality of death (absence of anxiety and pain, and the presence of loved ones). The success of comprehensive care is dependent on open discussions ahead of time that addresses painful decisions, including home versus hospital care for the dying child, advance directives, autopsy, and funeral arrangements. Once these logistics have been discussed, the family can reinvest energy in supporting their child. It is important to address the emotional needs of parents and siblings in the context of the family's values. As death approaches, families often need assurance that they have done all they could for their child. Often emotionally and physically exhausted and trying to hold on to whatever control they have, parents may appear less cooperative, irritable, easily frustrated, and annoyed. Clinicians need to respect each family's readiness, delicately balancing life issues with those related to palliative care, death, and loss. The medical team's participation and investment in caring for the dying child is extremely important to and greatly appreciated by all families, even those who appear to be coping well on their own. Spiritual ministry professionals can be of enormous support for some families during this time.

Talking to the Dying Child

Open communication, pain control, involvement with friends and family, distractions, and the maintenance of familiar routines all convey a sense of security that is important in reassuring the dying child. Telling a child that there are no treatments that can stop the progression of his or her disease is the most difficult but also the most important message to convey. In doing so, one must also allow room for hope by redirecting the child's energy from active treatment to comfort interventions. Comfort includes having loved ones around, minimizing further diagnostic or treatment procedures, not being in a hospital isolation room, and optimizing pain control. Providing comfort also involves acknowledgment and acceptance of a range of feelings, including feeling confused, sad, or angry. One of the greatest fears of young patients is being abandoned by or separated from family and friends; children need repeated reassurances that they will not be left alone. When given the opportunity, children frequently ask what death will be like, what will happen to them after they die, whether their parents will be all right after their death, whether they will experience much pain while dying, or whether they will be punished for the "bad" things they have thought, said, or done. Through play, art, drama, and therapeutic conversation, mental health clinicians can ascertain the child's private perceptions and concerns, correct distortions, and promote self-esteem through mastery of fears.

Talking to the Dying Adolescent

Developmentally appropriate advance-care planning is important in the care of seriously ill adolescents. Children age 14 years and older have been identified as the age group that needs to be routinely included in advance care planning and end-of-life decision-making (Lyon et al., 2004; Weir & Peters, 1997). Important considerations besides chronological age include the child's understanding of his or her condition, coping abilities, preference to be involved in decision-making, and cultural norms. In a randomized controlled trial carried out in two urban U.S. hospitals, a facilitated family and adolescent-centered advance-care planning intervention (FACE) was efficacious in increasing congruence between preferences for end-of-life care between adolescents with HIV and their surrogate decision-makers, decreasing decisional conflict, and enhancing communication quality (Lyon et al., 2009).

Providing teens with an avenue to share intimate views about how they wish to be cared for while very ill and remembered after they are gone can promote communication, foster decision-making, and augment dignity, autonomy, and self-respect in the face of death (Wiener et al., 2013). Voicing My CHOiCES™, a planning document for teens and young adults, can also guide parents to understand issues that are of importance to adolescents living with an uncertain life expectancy (Aging With Dignity, 2014). Legacy activities individualized for the teen's interest and comfort level can be extremely valuable. The advance care planning process can also facilitate acceptance of a more palliative approach to care. Before initiating discussions about end-of-life care with adolescents, it is important to evaluate for depression, bereavement, anxiety, pain, or unrecognized delirium. Psychiatric symptoms can be identified and alleviated even in the midst of terminal illnesses, in order to improve quality of life.

Reading materials about end-of-life and bereavement can help some parents at this time. Most appreciate having time allotted to address their immediate questions or concerns. Some parents want to plan ahead so that they do not need to make any major decisions (e.g., about autopsy, funeral arrangements) after their child has died. Parents may wish to have a specific ritual performed after death that is based on their own cultural or religious preferences.

The Initiative for Pediatric Palliative Care (2003) has developed a model curriculum for healthcare professionals, including a module on adolescents' decision-making. Such modules provide a base for training professionals to be more comfortable in helping families openly discuss how to make hard choices. Healthcare professionals need to explicitly state the steps of the advance care–planning process to ensure that adolescents' wishes are honored (Lyon and Pao, 2006).

FACILITATING TRANSITION TO ADULT CARE

In studying other chronic-illness models of successful transition approaches, evidence supports the following:

(1) a transition policy for each pediatric practice and a privacy and confidentiality policy for adult practices caring for transferred patients clearly defining the purpose and expectations for each health care system

(2) preparation and planning well in advance of anticipated transfer

(3) the role of care coordinator—especially when multiple subspecialists are involved

(4) communication and partnership between the pediatric team and accepting adult provider including a written portable medical summary

(5) overlap in pediatric and adult services or close follow-up during the transition to provide a safety net that could be readily activated if things don't go as planned. (For example, if the patient does not attend a scheduled appointment with the new provider, having a mechanism in place to remain in contact with the young adult to ensure engagement with adult provider helps identify barriers to transition of care and continuing to work with the patient who otherwise might be lost to follow up or forego care).

The Center for Health Care Transition Improvement (www.gottransition.org) provides many free resources for healthcare practitioners, parents, and patients, as well as researchers and policymakers, to improve the transition from pediatric to adult healthcare. Starting early (when youth are young teens), implementing a systematic transition process within a practice and collaborative relationships with accepting providers are critical for successful healthcare transition.

CONCLUSION

While medical management of HIV infection is the foundation of care for youth with HIV, there is growing emphasis on preparing young individuals with HIV for long-term survival, achieving academic success, living independently, and promoting good self-care and health behaviors. Efforts to accomplish these objectives are often complicated by psychosocial circumstances. For all these reasons, clinical care of youth with HIV is best carried out in a multidisciplinary setting where clinicians with medical and psychosocial expertise provide continuity of comprehensive, nonfragmented, developmentally informed care while considering relevant socioemotional, cognitive, family, environmental, and disease factors and diligently reassessing roles of those factors on an ongoing basis. Siblings and other HIV-affected youth share very similar psychosocial circumstances and risk factors with their HIV-positive peers, and these need to be assessed on a regular basis and addressed as indicated.

Mental health clinicians can play a significant role in improving the lives of children and adolescents living with or affected by HIV/AIDS. Timely, developmentally informed mental health interventions addressing relevant psychosocial and clinical milestones can improve the overall health and quality of life for children and adolescents living with or affected by HIV and for their caregivers.

APPENDIX 33.1 FACILITATING THE PROCESS OF DIAGNOSTIC DISCLOSURE TO A CHILD WITH HIV

PHASE 1. PREPARATION

- Early on, encourage the parents to begin using words they can build on later, such as *immune problems, virus*, or *infection*. Provide books for the family to read with the child on viruses. Strengthen the family through education and support and schedule regular follow-up meetings. Let the family know that you will meet with them on a regular basis to help guide them through the disclosure process and to support the child and family after disclosure. Respect the family's timing, but strongly encourage the family not to lie to the child if he or she asks directly about having HIV, unless significant, identifiable safety concerns render the decision to disclose inadvisable. Also remind the family to avoid disclosure during an argument or in anger.
- Have a meeting with the parent or caregivers involved in the decision-making process. Staff members that the family trusts should be present.
- Address the importance of disclosure and ascertain whether the family has a plan in mind. Respect the intensity of feelings about this issue. Obtain feedback on the child's anticipated response. Explore the child's level of knowledge and his or her emotional stability and maturity.
- Solicit multidisciplinary input on relevant socioemotional, cognitive, family, environmental, and disease factors. Ideally, this should include input from the pediatrician, psychologist, psychiatrist, social worker, case manager, and medical staff. The input should be used for informing the decision to disclose as well as the process of disclosure.
- The multidisciplinary team should strive to answer the following questions: Does the child have the cognitive capacity, emotional stability, and emotional maturity for disclosure? Does the parent have the emotional stability, life coping skills, and treatment adherence that are important for disclosure to child? Is the current family environment conducive to optimal diagnostic disclosure (e.g., are there significant secrecy issues; is there parent distress regarding the child or parent fear regarding disclosure, or are there parent–child communication issues)? Is there a disagreement among the parents regarding need for or timing of disclosure? Is the family struggling with stressors that might affect disclosure outcome (e.g., unstable housing, no support network)?
- If significant potential barriers to effective disclosure are identified, advise the parents to postpone disclosure, address the barrier, and re-evaluate the readiness at a later point (typically 3–6 months later, but keeping in mind that time is of essence as the child moves toward puberty, adolescence, more independence, and greater exposure to peer influences, which may include sexual experimentation, drugs, or inadvertent disclosure).
- Some parents will refuse to disclose the diagnosis to the child because of concerns they have with disclosing their own HIV status. The focus needs to be on parental psychosocial needs, perceived shame, stigma, or concerns pertaining to safety if the diagnosis is revealed. It should also be conveyed to the parents that, if they continue to refuse to disclose the diagnosis to their child, learning about the diagnosis through inadvertent disclosure may be significantly more traumatic.
- If the family is ready to disclose, guide them in various ways of approaching disclosure

PHASE 2. DISCLOSURE

- In advance, have the family think through or write out how they want the conversation to go. They need to give careful consideration to what message they want their child to walk away with after disclosure. Encourage the family to begin with, "Do you remember . . .," to include information about the child's life, medications, and/or procedures, so that the child is reminded of past events before introducing new facts.
- Have the family choose a place where the child will be most comfortable to talk openly.
- Provide the family with questions the child may ask so they are prepared with answers. Such questions include "How long have you known this?" "Who else has the virus?" "Will I die?" "Can I ever have children?" "Who can I tell?" "Why me?" and "Who else knows?"
- Encourage having only people present with whom the child is most comfortable. The healthcare practitioner may offer to facilitate this meeting, but if at all possible, preparation should be done in advance so that the family can share the information on their own.
- Medical facts should be kept to a minimum (immunology, virology, the effectiveness of therapy) and hope should be reinforced. Silence, as well as questions, needs to be accepted. The child should be told that nothing has changed, except a name is now being given to what he or she has been living with. The child also needs to hear that the child didn't do or say anything to cause the disease and that the family will always remain by their side.
- If the diagnosis is to be kept a secret, it is important that the child be given the names of people he or she can talk to, such as a clinician, another child living with HIV, and/or a family friend. Stating "You can't tell anyone" makes the child feel ashamed and guilty.
- Provide the child with a journal or diary to record his or her questions, thoughts, and feelings. If appropriate, provide books about children living with HIV.
- Schedule a follow-up meeting.

PHASE 3. POST-DISCLOSURE FOLLOW-UP

- Provide individual and family follow-up 2 weeks after disclosure and again every 2–4 weeks for the first 6 months to assess impact of disclosure, answer questions, and help foster support between the child and family.
- Ask the child to tell you what he or she has learned about their virus. This can identify and clarify misconceptions. Writing and art may be useful techniques.
- Assess changes in emotional well-being and provide the family with information about symptoms that could indicate the need for more intensive intervention.
- Support parents for having disclosed the diagnosis and, if they are interested and one is available, refer them to a parents support group. Encourage them to think about the emotional needs of the other children in the family in the disclosure process.
- Remind parents that disclosure is not a one-time event. Ongoing communication will be needed. Ask parents what other supports they feel would be helpful to them and their child. Provide information about HIV camp programs for HIV-infected and HIV-affected children and families (Appendix 33.2).

Sources: Wiener LS, Battles HB (2006). Untangling the web: a close look at diagnosis disclosure among HIV-infected adolescents. *J Adolesc Health* 38(3):307–309. Copyright (2006), with permission from Elsevier; Oland A, Valdez N, Kapetanovic S (2008). Process-oriented biopsychosocial approach to disclosing HIV status to infected children. NIMH Annual International Research Conference on the Role of Families in Preventing and Adapting to HIV/AIDS, Providence RI, October 2008.

APPENDIX 33.2 SPECIALTY SUMMER CAMPS FOR CHILDREN INFECTED WITH OR AFFECTED BY HIV

CAMP NAME	AFFILIATION	DESCRIPTION	STATE	ADDRESS	PHONE	EMAIL	WEBSITE
Camp Arroyo	Taylor Family Foundation	Year-round camp serving children with life-threatening diseases and disabilities	CA	5555 Arroyo Rd., Livermore, CA 94550	(925) 455-5118	ttff@ttff.org	http://www.ttff.org/
Camp Care	All About Care	Support for women, children, and families infected with and affected by HIV/AIDS	CA	4974 Fresno Street, PMB #156, Fresno, CA 93726	(559) 222-9471	Email option on website	http://allaboutcare.org/camp-care/
Camp Dream Street	Dream Street Foundation	Serves children with cancer, blood disorders, and other life-threatening illnesses	CA	324 South Beverly Dr., Suite 500, Beverly Hills, CA 90212	(424) 333-1371	dreamstreetca@gmail.com	http://dreamstreetfoundation.org/
Camp Hollywood Heart	One Heartland	Week-long full-service summer camp for children and adolescents infected with and affected by HIV/AIDS	CA	301 E. Colorado Blvd., Suite 430, Pasadena, CA 91101	(626) 795-9645	info@hollywoodheart.org	http://hollywoodheart.org/
Camp Kindle	Project Kindle	Summer camp serving children infected with and affected by HIV/AIDS	CA	28245 Ave Crocker, Ste. 104, Santa Clarita, CA 91355	(877) 800-CAMP (2267)	info@projectkindle.org	http://www.campkindle.org/
Camp Laurel	Laurel Foundation	Serves children infected with and affected by HIV/AIDS	CA	75 South Grand Ave., Pasadena, CA 91105	(626) 683-0800	info@laurel-foundation.org	http://www.laurel-foundation.org/
Camp Sunburst	Sunburst Projects	Long-term residential camp for children living with HIV/AIDS	CA	1025 19th St., Suite 1A, Sacramento, CA 95814	(916) 440-0889	admin@sunburstprojects.org	http://www.sunburstprojects.org/programs.shtml
Camp Ray-Ray	Angels Unaware	Short-term residential camp for families affected by AIDS	CO	6370 Union St., Arvada, CO 80004	(303) 420-6370	AngelsUnaware@att.net	http://www.angelsunaware.net/Camp_Ray_Ray.htm
The Hole in the Wall Gang Camp	Association of Hole in the Wall Gang Camps	Residential camp for children ages 7–15 with HIV/AIDS	CT	565 Ashford Center Road, Ashford, CT 06278	(860) 429-3444	ashford@holeinthewallgang.org	http://www.holeinthewallgang.org/Page.aspx?pid=471
Camp AmeriKids		1-week residential summer camp for kids ages 8–16	CT	88 Hamilton Ave., Stamford, CT 06902	(203) 658-9547	Email option on website	http://www.campamerikids.org/
Camp Meechimuk	Hispanos Unidos	Long-term residential camp for children ages 6–15 affected by HIV/AIDS	CT	116 Sherman Ave., New Haven, CT 06511	(203) 781-0226	Email option on website	http://www.hispanos-unidos.org/camp-meechimuk.aspx
Camp Totoket	First Congregational Church of Branford	Non-denominational summer camp for children ages 5–16 whose families are affected by HIV/AIDS	CT	1009 Main St., Branford, CT 06405	(203) 488-7201	info@firstcongregationalbranford.org	http://www.tavf.org/CampTotokett.html

(continued)

APPENDIX 33.2 CONTINUED

CAMP NAME	AFFILIATION	DESCRIPTION	STATE	ADDRESS	PHONE	EMAIL	WEBSITE
The Boggy Creek Gang	Paul Newman Foundation	Year-round retreat for children and their families	FL	30500 Brantley Branch Rd., Eustis, FL 32736	(352) 483-4200	info@campboggycreek.org	http://www.boggycreek.org/
Camp High Five	H.E.R.O for Children	Serves children infected with and affected by HIV/AIDS	GA	6075 Roswell Road NE, Ste. 450, Atlanta, GA 30328	(404) 236-7411	info@heroforchildren.org	http://www.heroforchildren.org/
Children's Place Lucy R. Sprague Summer Camp	The Children's Place Association	Serves children and families affected by HIV, with a variety of programming	IL	3059 West Augusta Blvd., Chicago, IL 60622	(773) 395-9193		www.childrens-place.org
Tataya Mato	Jameson Inc.	Long-term residential camp for children infected with or affected by HIV/AIDS	IN	2001 S. Bridgeport Rd., Indianapolis, IN 46231	(317) 241-2661	tim@jamesoncamp.org	http://www.jamesoncamp.org/
Camp Heart to Heart	Lions Camp Crescendo, Inc.	Free summer camp for children (ages 5–12) living with HIV/AIDS	KY	PO Box 607, 1480 Pine Tavern Road, Lebanon Junction, KY 40150	(502) 833 4427	wibblesb@aol.com	http://www.lccky.org/our%20camps.htm
Camp Kids Haven	Lutheran Social Services of the National Capitol Area	Week-long residential camp for kids (ages 7–13) living with or affected by HIV/AIDS. Also have teen retreats (14–18y) throughout the year	MD	4406 Georgia Ave. NW., Washington, DC 20011	(703) 698-5026	Email option on website	https://www.lssnca.org/programs/camps_retreats
Camp Knutson	Camp Knutson and Knutson Point Retreat Center	Serves families in which any member is infected with HIV/AIDS, for a 1-week residential camp	MN	11169 Whitefish Ave., Crosslake, MN 56442	(218) 543-4232	Email option on website	http://www.lssmn.org/camp/
Camp Heartland	One Heartland	Serves children infected with and affected by HIV/AIDS	MN	2101 Hennepin Ave. S., Suite 200, Minneapolis, MN 55405	(888) 216-2028	Email available on website	http://www.oneheartland.org/camps-and-programs/camp-heartland
Camp Hope	Project Ark (AIDS/HIV Resources & Knowledge)	Weekend-long camp for HIV-infected children and their families	MO	4169 Laclede Ave., St. Louis, MO 63108	(314) 535-7275		http://projectark.wustl.edu/SupportUs/CampHope/tabid/804/Default.aspx
Camp Kindle Midwest	Project Kindle	Serves families in which any member is infected with HIV/AIDS, for a 1-week residential camp	NE	Project Kindle, PO Box 81147, Lincoln, NE 68501	(877) 800-2267	info@projectkindle.org	www.projectkindle.org
Camp Bright Feathers	YMCA Camp Ockanickon, Inc.	Long-term residential camp for children affected by HIV/AIDS	NJ	1303 Stokes Rd., Medford, NJ 08055	(609) 654-8225	havenyouthcenterpa@gmail.com	http://www.campbrightfeathers.com/
The Double "H" Hole in the Woods Ranch	Part of the Association of Hole in the Wall camps	6-day sessions for children ages 6–16; year-long support and activities (including ages 17–21)	NY	97 Hidden Valley Rd., Lake Luzerne, NY 12846	(518) 696-5676	jroyael@doublehranch.org	http://www.doublehranch.org/

Camp	Organization	Description	State	Address	Phone	Email	Website
Camp Viva	Family Services of Westchester, White Plains Office	1-week camp and after-camp follow-up program serving children and families with HIV/AIDS	NY	P.O. Box 266, Rt. 52/ Salisbury Turnpike, Rhinebeck, NY 12572	(914) 872-5285	rcestone@fsw.org	http://www.fsw.org/our-programs/hivaids-services-partnership-for-care/camp-viva
Camp Kaleidoscope	Duke Children's Hospital and Health Center	Summer program open to all Duke University Medical Center pediatric patients ages 7–16	NC	Box 3417, DUMC, Durham, NC 27710	(919) 681-5349	arthur.taub@duke.edu	http://www.dukechildrens.org/giving/events/camp_kaleidoscope
Victory Junction Camp	Victory Junction	1-week summer camp program; additional family weekend programs	NC	4500 Adam's Way, Randleman, NC 27317	(336) 498-9055	info@victoryjunction.org	http://www.victoryjunction.org/
Camp Sunrise	AIDS Resource Center Ohio	1-week residential camp for children impacted by HIV/AIDS	OH	4400 North High St., Suite 300, Columbus, OH 34214	(614) 444-1683	Email available through website	http://www.sunrisekids.org/
Camp Starlight	Program of the Cascade AIDS Project	Week-long sleep-away summer camp for children in Oregon and Washington whose lives are affected by HIV/AIDS (patients and family members)	OR	PO Box 80666, Portland, OR 97280	(503) 964-1516	info@camp-starlight.org	http://camp-starlight.org/
Camp Dreamcatcher Summer Camp	Camp Dreamcatcher	1-week program for children ages 5–17 who are infected with or affected by HIV/AIDS; free of charge	PA	617 W. South St., Kennett Square, PA 19348	(610) 925-2998	info@campdreamcatcher.org	http://campdreamcatcher.org/
Camp Firelight	Tarrant County AIDS Outreach Center	Week-long camp for children living with HIV/AIDS	TX	400 North Beach Street, Suite 100, Fort Worth, TX 76111	(817) 335-1994		http://www.aoc.org/
Camp Hope	AIDS Foundation Houston, Inc.	Serves children ages 6–15 with HIV/AIDS	TX	3202 Weslayan Annex, Houston, TX 77027	(713) 623-6796		http://www.aidshelp.org/?fuseaction=cms.page&id=1027
Camp HolidayTrails		1-week and 2-week camp sessions for children with HIV/AIDS; 4-day camp for families of children with HIV/AIDS	VA	400 Holiday Trails Lane, Charlottesville, VA 22903	(434) 977-3781	campisgood@campholidaytrails.org	http://www.campholidaytrails.org/
Camp Wakonda	Diocesan Center, Frances Barber	Serves children and families infected with and affected by HIV/AIDS in a day-camp environment	VA	395 Dorwain Drive, Norfolk, VA 23502	(757) 461-3595	allsaintschurch1@verizon.net	http://www.allsaintsvabeach.org/camp.html
Northwest Reach Camp	REACH Ministries	Long-term residential camp for children and families infected with and affected by HIV/AIDS	WA	309 South G. St., Suite 3, Tacoma, WA 98405	(253) 383-7616	info@reachministries.org	http://reachministries.org/our-programs/camp/
Rise N' Shine Camp	Inspire Youth Project	Long-term residential camp for children infected with and affected by HIV/AIDS	WA	417 23rd Avenue South, Seattle, WA 98144	(206) 628-8949	info@inspireyouthproject.org	http://inspireyouthproject.org/

* While we have tried to include as many camps for which we could obtain information, this list is by no means exhaustive. New and additional camp programs may be available. A good resource to learn about additional camp resources is the Federation for Children with Special Needs: http://fcsn.org/camps/.

APPENDIX 33.3 ADDITIONAL RESOURCE FOR FAMILIES AND MENTAL HEALTH PROVIDERS

- The Center for HIV Identification, Prevention and Treatment Services (CHIPTS), funded by the National Institute of Mental Health, partners with communities, families, and individuals impacted by HIV/AIDS. The CHIPTS website (http://chipts.ucla.edu) includes free evidence-based intervention manuals, validated assessment tools, relevant policy statements, and scientific publications.

- Guttmacher Institute provides a concise and up-to-date overview of U.S. state policies and laws on minor's consent, at the following Web address: www.guttmacher.org/statecenter/spibs/spib_OMCL.pdf.

- The CDC provides an online tool for finding confidential and free local HIV and STD testing, at the following Web address: www.hivtest.org.

REFERENCES

Aging With Dignity (2014). http://www.agingwithdignity.org/. Accessed October 14, 2014.

Alperen J, Brummel S, Tassiopoulos K, et al. (2014). Prevalence of and risk factors for substance use among perinatally human immunodeficiency virus–infected and perinatally exposed but uninfected youth. *J Adolesc Health* 54(3):341–349.

Armstrong F, Seidel J, Swales T (1993). Pediatric HIV infection: a neuropsychological and educational challenge. *J Learn Disabil* 26, 92–103.

Atkinson L, Paglia A, Coolbear J, Niccols A, Parker KC, Guger S (2000). Attachment security: a meta-analysis of maternal mental health correlates. *Clin Psychol Rev* 20:1019–1040.

AVERT (2014). Children: HIV and AIDS. http://www.avert.org/children-orphaned-hiv-and-aids.htm. Accessed February 9, 2017.

Bandstra E, Morrow C, Anthony J, Accomero V, Fried P (2001). Longitudinal investigation of task persistence and sustained attention in children with prenatal cocaine exposure. *Neurotoxicol Teratology* 23:545–559.

Bandstra E, Vogel A, Morrow C, Xue L, Anthony J (2004). Severity of prenatal cocaine exposure and child language functioning through age seven years: a longitudinal latent growth curve analysis. *Subst Use Misuse* 39:25–59.

Bauermeister JA, Elkington K, Brackis-Cott E, Dolezal C, Mellins CA (2009). Sexual behavior and perceived peer norms: comparing perinatally HIV-infected and HIV-affected youth. *J Youth Adolesc* 38(8):1110–1122.

Bekir P, McLellan T, Childress A.R, Gariti P (1993). Role reversals in families of substance abusers: a transgenerational phenomenon. *Int J Addict* 28:613–630.

Belman A, Diamond G, Dickson D, Horoupian D, Llena J, Lantos G, Rubinstein A (1988). Pediatric acquired immunodeficiency syndrome: neurologic syndromes. *Am J Dis Child* 142:29–35.

Belzer M, Naar-King S, Olson J, et al.; Adolescent Medicine Trials Network for HIV/AIDS Interventions (2014). The use of cell phone support for non-adherent HIV-infected youth and young adults: an initial randomized and controlled intervention trial. *AIDS Behav* 18:686–696.

Best B, Farhad M, Rossi R, et al. (2013). Methylphenidate concentrations and dose requirements in HIV-infected and uninfected children, adolescents and young adults. 20th Conference on Retroviruses and Opportunistic Infections, Atlanta GA, March 2013. Program and Abstracts, p. 502.

Bilbo SD, Schwarz JM (2009). Early-life programming of later-life brain and behavior: a critical role for the immune system. *Front Behav Neurosci* 3:14.

Boivin M, Busman R, Parikh S, Bangirana P, Page C, Opoka R, Giordani B (2010). A pilot study of the neuropsychological benefits of computerized cognitive rehabilitation in Ugandan children with HIV. *Neuropsychology* 24(5):667–673.

Boivin M, Bangirana P, Nakasujja N, et al. (2013). A year-long caregiver training program improves cognition in preschool Ugandan children with human immunodeficiency virus. *J Pediatr* 163(5):1409–1416. e1–e5.

Boylan K, Romero S, Birmaher B (2007). Psychopharmacologic treatment of pediatric major depressive disorder. *Psychopharmacology (Berl)* 191(1):27–38.

Brackis-Cott E, Mellins C, Dolezal C, Spiegel D (2007). The mental health risk of mothers and children: The role of maternal HIV infection. *J Early Adolesc* 27:67–89.

Bradley H, Hall HI, Wolitski RJ, et al. (2014) Vital signs: HIV diagnosis, care, and treatment among persons living with HIV—United States, 2011. *MMWR Morb Mortal Wkly Rep* 63(47):1113–1117.

Brown AS, Patterson PH (2011). Maternal infection and schizophrenia: implications for prevention. *Schizophr Bull* 37(2):284–290.

Bunders M, Pembrey L, Kuijpers T, Newell ML (2010). Evidence of impact of maternal HIV infection on immunoglobulin levels in HIV-exposed uninfected children. *AIDS Res Hum Retroviruses* 26(9):967–975.

Camacho-Gonzalez A.F, Wallins A, Toledo L, et al. (2016). Risk factors for HIV transmission and barriers to HIV disclosure: metropolitan Atlanta youth perspectives. *AIDS Patient Care STDs* 30(1):18–24.

Caniglia EC, Patel K, Huo Y, et al., for the Pediatric HIVAIDS Cohort Study (2016). Atazanavir exposure in utero and neurodevelopment in infants: a comparative safety study. *AIDS* 30(8):1267–1278.

Centers for Disease Control and Prevention (CDC) (2008). Youth risk behavior surveillance—United States. MMWR *Morb Mortal Wkly Rep* 57(SS-4):1–131.

Centers for Disease Control and Prevention (CDC) (2009). Effect of antiretroviral therapy on risk of sexual transmission of HIV infection and superinfection. http://www.cdc.gov/hiv/topics/treatment/resources/factsheets/art.htm.

Centers for Disease Control and Prevention (CDC) (2012a). Estimated HIV incidence among adults and adolescents in the United States, 2007–2010. *HIV Supplemental Report* 2012; 17(No. 4). http://www.cdc.gov/hiv/topics/surveillance/resources/reports/#supplemental. Access February 9, 2017.

Centers for Disease Control and Prevention (CDC) (2012b). Monitoring selected national HIV prevention and care objectives by using HIV surveillance data—United States and 6 U.S. dependent areas—2014. *HIV Supplemental Report* 2016; 21(No. 4). https://www.cdc.gov/hiv/pdf/library/reports/surveillance/cdc-hiv-surveillance-supplemental-report-vol-21-4.pdf. Accessed February 9, 2017.

Centers for Disease Control and Prevention (CDC) (2014). HIV surveillance— adolescents and young adults. https://www.cdc.gov/hiv/pdf/statistics_surveillance_adolescents.pdf. Accessed February 9, 2017.

Centers for Disease Control and Prevention (CDC) (2016). HIV among pregnant women, infants, and children. https://www.cdc.gov/hiv/group/gender/pregnantwomen/. Accessed February 11, 2017.

Chandwani S, Koenig LJ, Sill AM, Abramowitz S, Conner LC, D'Angelo L (2012). Predictors of antiretroviral medication adherence among a diverse cohort of adolescents with HIV. *J Adolesc Health* 51(3):242–251.

Chasnoff IJ, Anson A, Hatcher R, Stenson H, Laukea K, Randolph LA (1998). Prenatal exposure to cocaine and other drugs: outcome at four to six years. *Ann N Y Acad Sci* 846:314–328.

Chenneville T, Lynn V, Peacock B, Turner D, Marhefka SL (2015). Disclosure of HIV status among female youth with HIV. *Ethics Behav* 25(4):314–331.

Chhagan MK, Mellins CA, Kauchali S, et al. (2014). Mental health disorders among caregivers of preschool children in the Asenze study in KwaZulu-Natal, South Africa. *Matern Child Health J* 18(1):191–199.

Ciaranello AL, Ciaranello RD (1995). The neurobiology of infantile autism. *Annu Rev Neurosci* 18:101–128.

Clerici M, Saresella M, Colombo F, et al. (2000). T-lymphocyte maturation abnormalities in uninfected newborns and children with vertical exposure to HIV. *Blood* 96(12):3866–3871.

Cohen J, Reddington C, Jacobs D, et al. (1997). School-related issues among HIV-infected children. *Pediatrics* 100:e8.

Committee on Pediatric AIDS, Emmanuel PJ, Martinez J (2011). Adolescents and HIV infection: the pediatrician's role in promoting routine testing. *Pediatrics* 128:1023–1029.

Crowell C.S, Huo Y, Tassiopoulos K, et al, for the PACTG 219c Study Team and the Pediatric HIV/AIDS Cohort Study (PHACS) (2015). Early viral suppression improves neurocognitive outcomes in HIV-infected children. *AIDS* 29:295–304.

Culp L, Caucci L (2013). State adolescent consent laws and implications for HIV pre-exposure prophylaxis. *Am J Prev Med* 44(1 Suppl 2):S119–S124.

Dauby N, Goetghebuer T, Kollmann TR, Levy J, Marchant A (2012). Uninfected but not unaffected: chronic maternal infections during pregnancy, fetal immunity, and susceptibility to postnatal infections. *Lancet Infect Dis* 12(4):330–340.

DeLaMora P, Aledort N, Stavola J (2006). Caring for adolescents with HIV. *Curr HIV/AIDS Rep* 3(2):74–78.

Denno DM, Chandra-Mouli V, Osman M (2012). Reaching youth with out-of-facility HIV and reproductive health services: a systematic review. *J Adolesc Health* 51(2):106–121.

Dolezal C, Warne P, Santamaria EK, Elkington KS, Benavides JM, Mellins CA (2014). Asking only "Did you use a condom?" underestimates the prevalence of unprotected sex among perinatally HIV-infected and perinatally exposed but uninfected youth. *J Sex Res* 51(5):599–604.

Donenberg GR, Pao M (2005) Youths and HIV/AIDS: psychiatry's role in a changing epidemic. *J Am Acad Child Adolesc Psychiatry* 44(8):728–747.

Dowshen N, Binns H.J, Garafalo R (2009). Experiences of HIV-related stigma among young men who have sex with men. *AIDS Patient Care STDS* 23(5):371–376.

Dowshen N, D'Angelo L (2011). Health care transition for youth living with HIV/AIDS. *Pediatrics* 128 (4):762–771.

Eaton D, Kann L, Kinchen S, et al. (2010). Youth risk behavior surveillance, United States, 2009. *MMWR Morb Mortal Wkly Rev* 59(SS05):1–142.

Elkington KS, Bauermeister JA, Brackis-Cott E, Dolezal C, Mellins CA (2009). Substance use and sexual risk behaviors in perinatally human immunodeficiency virus-exposed youth: roles of caregivers, peers and HIV status. *J Adolesc Health* 45(2):133–141.

Elkington KS, Bauermeister JA, Robbins RN, et al. (2012). Individual and contextual factors of sexual risk behavior in youth perinatally infected with HIV. *AIDS Patient Care STDs* 26(7):411–422.

Elkington KS, Cruz JE, Warne P, Santamaria EK, Dolezal C, Mellins CA (2016) Marijuana use and psychiatric disorders in perinatally HIV-exposed youth: does HIV matter? *J Pediatr Psychol* 41(3) 277–286.

Ensoli F, Fiorelli V, Muratori D.S, et al. (1999). Immune-derived cytokines in the nervous system: epigenetic instructive signals or neuropathogenic mediators? *Crit Rev Immunol* 19(2):97–116.

Epstein LG (1986). Neurologic manifestations of HIV infection in children. *Pediatrics* 78:678–687.

Erickson EH (1963). *Childhood and Society* (2nd ed.) New York: Norton.

Fair C (2006). The emotional and educational functioning of children living with maternal HIV/AIDS and substance abuse. *Child Adolesc Social Work J* 23:356–374.

Fair C, Albright J (2012). "Don't tell him you have HIV unless he's the one": romantic relationships among adolescents and young adults with perinatal HIV infection. *AIDS Patient Care STDs* 26(12):746–754.

Fair C, Brackett B (2008). "I don't want to sit by you:" a preliminary study of experiences and consequences of stigma and discrimination from HIV-positive mothers and their children. *J HIV/AIDS Prev Child Youth* 9(2):219–242.

Fair C, Dupont-Spencer E, Wiener L, Riekert K (1995). Healthy children in families with AIDS: epidemiological and psychosocial considerations. *Child Adolesc Social Work J* 12:165–181.

Fanos JH, Wiener L (1994). Tomorrow's survivors: siblings of HIV-infected children. *J Dev Behav Pediatr* 15:S43–S48.

Forsyth B, Damour L, Nagler S, Adnopoz J (1996). The psychological effects of parental human immunodeficiency virus infection on uninfected children. *Arch Pediatr Adolesc Med* 150:1015–1020.

Frye V, Wilton L, Hirshfied S, et al, for the All About Me Study Team (2015). "Just because it's out there, people aren't going to use it." HIV self-testing among young, black MSM, and transgender women. *AIDS Patient Care STDs* 29(11):617–624.

Funck-Brentano I, Costagliola D, Seibel N, Straub E, Tardieu M, Blanche S (1997). Patterns of disclosure and perceptions of the human immunodeficiency virus in infected elementary school-age children. *Arch Pediatr Adolesc Med* 151:978–985.

Gadow KD, Angelidou K, Chernoff M, Williams PL, Heston J, Hodge J, Nachman S (2012). Longitudinal study of emerging mental health concerns in youth perinatally infected with HIV and peer comparisons. *J Dev Behav Pediatr* 33(6):456–468.

Goldstein BI, Sassi R, Diler RS (2012). Pharmacologic treatment of bipolar disorder in children and adolescents. *Child Adolesc Psychiatr Clin N Am* 21(4):911–939.

Griner R, Williams PL, Read JS, et al. (2011). In utero and postnatal exposure to antiretrovirals among HIV-exposed but uninfected children in the United States. *AIDS Patient Care STDS* 25(7):385–394.

Guttmacher Institute (2017). An overview of minors' consent law. www.guttmacher.org/statecenter/spibs/spib_OMCL.pdf. Accessed February 10, 2017.

Havens JF, Mellins CA, Ryan S (2005). Child psychiatry: psychiatric sequelae of HIV and AIDS. In B Sadock, V Sadock (eds.), *Kaplan Sadock's Comprehensive Textbook of Psychiatry*, 8th ed. (p. 3434). Philadelphia: Lippincott Williams Wilkins.

Hosek SG, Harper GW, Lemos D, Martinez J (2008). An ecological model of stressors experienced by youth newly diagnosed with HIV. *J HIV AIDS Prev Child Youth* 9(2):192–218.

Initiative for Pediatric Palliative Care (2003). *Pediatric Palliative Care Curricula*. Newton, MA: Education Development Center.

Jeremy RJ, Kim S, Nozyce M, et al. (2005). Neuropsychological functioning and viral load in stable antiretroviral therapy-experienced HIV-infected children. *Pediatrics* 115(2):380–387.

Johnson RL, Botwinick G, Sell RL, et al. (2003). The utilization of treatment and case management services by HIV-infected youth. *J Adolesc Health* 33(2 Suppl):31–38.

Kacanek D, Angelidou K, Williams PL, et al., for the International Maternal Pediatric Adolescent AIDS Clinical Trials Group (IMPAACT) P1055 Study Team (2015). Psychiatric symptoms and antiretroviral nonadherence in US youth with perinatal HIV: a longitudinal study. *AIDS* 29(10):1227–1237.

Kang E, Mellins CA, Dolezal C, Elkington KS, Abrams EJ (2011). Disadvantaged neighborhood influences on depression and anxiety in youth with perinatally acquired human immunodeficiency virus: how life stressors matter. *J Community Psychol* 39(8):956–971.

Kapetanovic S, Aaron L, Montepiedra G, Burchett SK, Kovacs A (2012). T-cell activation and neurodevelopmental outcomes in perinatally HIV-infected children. *AIDS* 26(8):959–969.

Kapetanovic S, Aaron L, Montepiedra G, et al. (2009). The use of second-generation antipsychotics and the changes in physical growth in children and adolescents with perinatally acquired HIV. *AIDS Patient Care STDS* 23(11):939–947.

Kapetanovic S, Aaron L, Williams PL, et al. (2010). Relationships between the use of second-generation antipsychotics and changes in total cholesterol levels in children and adolescents perinatally infected with HIV. *Neurobehav HIV Med* (2):39–48.

Kapetanovic S, Dass-Brailsford P, Nora D, Talisman N (2014b). Mental health of HIV-seropositive women during pregnancy and post-partum period: a comprehensive literature review. *AIDS Behav* 18(6):1152–1173.

Kapetanovic S, Griner R, Zeldow B, et al.; Pediatric HIV/AIDS Cohort Study Team (2014a). Biomarkers and neurodevelopment in perinatally HIV-infected or exposed youth: a structural equation model analysis. *AIDS* 28(3):355–364.

Kapetanovic S, Simpson GM (2006). Review of antipsychotics in children and adolescents. *Expert Opinion in Pharmacotherapy* 7(14):1871–1885.

Kapetanovic S, Wiegand R, Dominguez K, et al.; LEGACY Consortium (2011). Associations of medically documented psychiatric diagnoses and risky health behaviors in highly active antiretroviral therapy-experienced perinatally HIV-infected youth. *AIDS Patient Care STDS* 25(8):493–501.

Kingston D, Tough S (2014). Prenatal and postnatal maternal mental health and school-age child development: a systematic review. *Matern Child Health J* 18(7):1728–1741.

Kovacs A, Schluchter M, Easley K, et al. (1999). Cytomegalovirus infection and HIV-1 disease progression in infants born to HIV-1-infected women. Pediatric Pulmonary and Cardiovascular Complications of Vertically Transmitted HIV Infection Study Group. *N Engl J Med* 341(2):77–84.

LaGrange RD, Abramowitz S, Koenig LJ, Barnes W, Conner L, Moschel D (2012). Participant satisfaction with group and individual components of Adolescent Impact: a secondary prevention intervention for HIV-positive youth. *AIDS Care* 24(1):119–128.

Laughton B, Cornell M, Boivin M, Van Rie A (2013). Neurodevelopment in perinatally HIV-infected children: a concern for adolescence. *J Int AIDS Soc* 16:18603.

Laughton B, Cornell M, Grove D, et al. (2012). Early antiretroviral therapy improves neurodevelopmental outcomes in infants. *AIDS* 26(13):1685–1690.

Le Doaré K, Bland R, Newell ML (2012). Neurodevelopment in children born to HIV-infected mothers by infection and treatment status. *Pediatrics* 130(5):1326–1344.

Lee BK, Magnusson C, Gardner RM, et al. (2015). Maternal hospitalization with infection during pregnancy and risk of autism spectrum disorders. *Brain Behav Immun* 44:100–105.

Lesch A, Swartz L, Kagee A, Moodley K, Kafaar Z, Myer L, Cotton M (2007). Paediatric HIV/AIDS disclosure: towards a developmental and process-oriented approach. *AIDS Care* 19(6):811–816.

Letourneau EJ, Ellis DA, Naar-King S, Chapman JE, Cunningham PB, Fowler S (2013). Multisystemic therapy for poorly adherent youth with HIV: results from a pilot randomized controlled trial. *AIDS Care* 25(4):507–514.

Li L, Ji G, Liang LJ, Ding Y, Tian J, Xiao Y (2011). A multilevel intervention for HIV-affected families in China: Together for Empowerment Activities (TEA). *Soc Sci Med* 73(8):1214–1221.

Li L, Liang LJ, Ji G, Wu J, Xiao Y (2014). Effect of a family intervention on psychological outcomes of children affected by parental HIV. *AIDS Behav* 18(11):2051–2058.

Linares TJ, Singer LT, Kirchner HL, Short EJ, Min MO, Hussey P, Minnes S (2006). Mental health outcomes of cocaine-exposed children at 6 years of age. *J Pediatr Psychol* 3:185–197.

Lipson M (1994). Disclosure of diagnosis to children with human immunodeficiency virus or acquired immunodeficiency syndrome. *J Dev Behav Pediatr* 15:S61–S65.

Luna GC, Rotheram-Borus MJ (1999). Youth living with HIV as peer leaders. *Am J Community Psychol* 27:1–23.

Luzuriaga K, Mofenson LM (2016). Challenges in the elimination of pediatric HIV-1 infection. *N Engl J Med* 374(8):761–770.

Lyon ME, Garvie PA, McCarter R, Briggs L, He J, D'Angelo LJ (2009). Who will speak for me? Improving end-of-life decision-making for adolescents with HIV and their families. *Pediatrics* 123(2):e199–e206.

Lyon ME, McCabe MA, Patel K, D'Angelo LJ (2004). What do adolescents want? An exploratory study regarding end-of-life decision-making. *J Adolesc Health* 35:e1–e6.

Lyon ME, Pao M (2006). When all else fails: end-of-life care for adolescents. In ME Lyon M, LJ D'Angelo (eds.), *Teenagers, HIV, and AIDS: Insights from Youths Living with the Virus* (pp. 213–233). Westport, CT: Praeger Publishers.

Lyon ME, Trexler C, Akpan-Townsend C, et al. (2003). A family group approach to increasing adherence to therapy in HIV-infected youths: results of a pilot project. *AIDS Patient Care STDS* 17(6):299–308.

Malee KM, Tassiopoulos K, Huo Y, et al. (2011). Mental health functioning among children and adolescents with perinatal HIV infection and perinatal HIV exposure. *AIDS Care* 23(12):1533–1544.

Martinez J, Hosek SG, Carleton RA (2009). Screening and assessing violence and mental health disorders in a cohort of inner city HIV-positive youth between 1998–2006. *AIDS Patient Care STDs* 23:469–475.

Martins C, Gaffan EA (2000). Effects of early maternal depression on patterns of infant–mother attachment: a meta-analytic investigation. *J Child Psychol Psychiatry* 41:737–746.

Mason HRC, Marks G, Simoni JM, Ruiz MS, Richardson JL (1995). Culturally sanctioned secrets: Latino men's nondisclosure of HIV infection to family, friends, and lovers. *Health Psychol* 14:6–12.

Mellins CA, Brackis-Cott E, Dolezal C, Richards A, Nicholas SW, Abrams EJ (2002). Patterns of status disclosure to perinatally HIV-infected children and subsequent mental health outcomes. *Clin Child Psychol Psychiatry* 7:101–114.

Mellins CA, Brackis-Cott E, Leu CS, et al. (2009). Rates and types of psychiatric disorders in perinatally human immunodeficiency virus-infected youth and seroreverters. *J Child Psychol Psychiatry* 50:1131–1138.

Mellins CA, Elkington KS, Leu CS, et al. (2012). Prevalence and change in psychiatric disorders among perinatally HIV-infected and HIV-exposed youth. *AIDS Care* 24(8):953–962.

Mendelsohn A (1997). Pervasive traumatic loss from AIDS in the life of a 4-year-old African boy. *J Child Psychother* 23:399–415.

Miles K, Edwards S, Clapson M (2004). Transition from paediatric to adult services: experiences of HIV-positive adolescents. *AIDS Care* 16(3):305–314.

Miller TL, Orav EJ, Lipshultz SE, et al. (2008). Risk factors for cardiovascular disease in children infected with human immunodeficiency virus-1. *J Pediatr* 153(4):491–497.

Miller TL, Somarriba G, Orav EJ, et al. (2010). Biomarkers of vascular dysfunction in children infected with human immunodeficiency virus-1. *J Acquir Immune Defic Syndr* 55(2):182–188.

Mitchell W (2001). Neurological and developmental effects of HIV and AIDS in children and adolescents. *Ment Retard Dev Disabil Res Rev* 7(3):211–216.

Murphy DA, Belzer M, Durako SJ, Sarr M, Wilson CM, Muenz LR (2005). Longitudinal antiretroviral adherence among adolescents infected with human immunodeficiency virus. *Arch Pediatr Adolesc Med* 159:764–770.

Murphy DA, Chen X, Naar-King S, Parsons JT (2012). Alcohol and marijuana use outcomes in the Healthy Choices motivational interviewing intervention for HIV-positive youth. *AIDS Patient Care STDS* 26(2):95–100.

Mutumba M, Bauermeister JA, Elkington KS, Bucek A, Dolezal C, Leu CS, Mellins CA (2016). A prospective longitudinal study of mental health symptoms among perinatally HIV-infected and HIV-exposed but uninfected urban youths. *J Adolesc Health* 58(4):460–466.

Naar-King S, Outlaw A, Green-Jones M, Wright K, Parsons JT (2009). Motivational interviewing by peer outreach workers: a pilot randomized clinical trial to retain adolescents and young adults in HIV care. *AIDS Care* 21(7):868–873.

Naar-King S, Outlaw AY, Sarr M, et al.; Adolescent Medicine Network for HIV/AIDS Interventions (2013). Motivational Enhancement System for Adherence (MESA): pilot randomized trial of a brief computer-delivered prevention intervention for youth initiating antiretroviral treatment. *J Pediatr Psychol* 38(6):638–648.

Naar-King S, Parsons JT, Johnson AM (2012). Motivational interviewing targeting risk reduction for people with HIV: a systematic review. *Curr HIV/AIDS Rep* 9(4):335–343.

Naar-King S, Parsons JT, Murphy DA, Chen X, Harris DR, Belzer ME (2009). Improving health outcomes for youth living with the human immunodeficiency virus: a multisite randomized trial of a motivational intervention targeting multiple risk behaviors. *Arch Pediatr Adolesc Med* 163(12):1092–1098.

Naar-King S, Parsons JT, Murphy D, Kolmodin K, Harris DR (2010). A multisite randomized trial of a motivational intervention targeting multiple risks in youth living with HIV: initial effects on motivation, self-efficacy, and depression. *J Adolesc Health* 46(5):422–428.

Nachman S, Chernoff M, Williams P, Hodge J, Heston J. Gadow KD. Human immunodeficiency virus disease severity, psychiatric symptoms, and functional outcomes in perinatally infected youth. *Arch Pediatr Adolesc Med* 166(6):528–535.

Newell ML, Bunders MJ (2013). Safety of antiretroviral drugs in pregnancy and breastfeeding for mother and child. *Curr Opin HIV AIDS* 8(5):504–510.

Ng WYK, Mellins CA, Ryan S (2004). The mental health treatment of children and adolescents perinatally infected with HIV. In E Abrams (ed.), *Topic of the Month*, 2004. http://web.archive.org/web/20040214070503/hivfiles.org/index.html.

Nichols SL, Bethel J, Garvie PA, et al. (2013). Neurocognitive functioning in antiretroviral therapy-naïve youth with behaviorally acquired human immunodeficiency virus. *J Adolesc Health* 53(6):763–771.

Nichols SL, Brummel SS, Smith RA, et al, for the Pediatric HIVAIDS Cohort Study (2015). Executive functioning in children and adolescents with perinatal HIV infection. *Pediatr Infect Dis J* 34(9):969–975.

Nielsen SD, Jeppesen DL, Kolte L, et al. (2001). Impaired progenitor cell function in HIV-negative infants of HIV-positive mothers results in decreased thymic output and low CD4 counts. *Blood* 98(2):398–404.

Nozyce M, Huo Y, Williams PL, et al, for the Pediatric HIV/AIDS Cohort Study (PHACS) (2014). Safety of in utero and neonatal ARV exposure: cognitive and academic outcomes in HIV-exposed, uninfected children age 5–13 years. *Pediatr Infect Dis J* 33:1128–1133.

Okawa S, Yasuoka J, Ishikawa N, Poudel KC, Rag-i A, Jimba M (2011). Perceived social support and the psychological well being of AIDS orphans in urban Kenya. *AIDS Care* 23:1177–1185.

Oland A, Valdez N, Kapetanovic S (2008). Process-oriented biopsychosocial approach to disclosing HIV status to infected children. NIMH Annual International Research Conference on the Role of Families in Preventing and Adapting to HIV/AIDS, Providence RI, October 2008.

Palmer SL, Glass JO, Li Y, et al. (2012). White matter integrity is associated with cognitive processing in patients treated for a posterior fossa brain tumor. *Neuro-oncology* 14:1185–1193.

Pao M, Lyon M, D'Angelo LJ, Schuman WB, Tipnis T, Mrazek DA (2000). Psychiatric diagnoses in adolescents seropositive for the human immunodeficiency virus. *Arch Pediatr Adolesc Med* 154(3):240–244.

Parboosing R, Bao Y, Shen L, Schaefer CA, Brown AS (2013). Gestational influenza and bipolar disorder in adult offspring. *JAMA Psychiatry* 8:1–8.

Pelton J, Forehand R (2005). Orphans of the AIDS epidemic: an examination of clinical level problems of children. *J Am Acad Child Adolesc Psychiatry* 44:585–591.

Peters TE, Connolly S (2012). Psychopharmacologic treatment for pediatric anxiety disorders. *Child Adolesc Psychiatr Clin N Am* 21(4):789–806.

Pfefferbaum A, Mathalon DH, Sullivan EV, Rawles JM, Zipursky RB, Lim KO (1994). A quantitative magnetic resonance imaging study of changes in brain morphology from infancy to late adulthood. *Arch Neurol* 51:874–887.

Pliszka S; AACAP Work Group on Quality Issues (2007). Practice parameter for the assessment and treatment of children and adolescents with attention-deficit/hyperactivity disorder. *J Am Acad Child Adolesc Psychiatry* 46(7):894–921.

Prince M, Patel V, Saxena S, Maj M, Maselko J, Phillips M, Rahman A (2007). No health without mental health. *Lancet* 370:859–877.

Raison CL, Capuron L, Miller AH (2006). Cytokines sing the blues: inflammation and the pathogenesis of depression. *Trends Immunol* 27(1):24–31.

Reisner SL, Mimiaga MJ, Skeer M, Perkovich B, Johnson CV, Safren SA (2009). A review of HIV antiretroviral adherence and intervention studies among HIV-infected youth. *Top HIV Med* 17(1):14–25.

Remien RH, Mellins CA (2007). Long-term psychosocial challenges for people living with HIV; let's not forget the individual in our global response to the pandemic. *AIDS* 21(Supp5):S55–S63.

Richardson GA, Conroy ML, Day NL (1996). Prenatal cocaine exposure: effects on the development of school-age children. *Neurotoxicol Teratol* 18:627–634.

Rosenblum A, Magura S, Fong C, et al. (2005). Substance use among young adolescents in HIV-affected families: resiliency, peer deviance, and family functioning. *Subst Use Misuse* 40:581–603.

Ross AC, Camacho-Gonzalez A, Henderson S, Abanyie F, Chakraborty R (2010). The HIV-infected adolescent. *Curr Infect Dis Rep* 12(1):63–70.

Rotheram-Borus MJ, Lee MB, Gwadz M, Draimin B (2001). An intervention for parents with AIDS and their adolescent children. *Am J Public Health* 91(8):1294–1302.

Rotheram-Borus MJ, Lee M, Lin YY, Lester P (2004). Six-year intervention outcomes for adolescent children of parents with the human immunodeficiency virus. *Arch Pediatr Adolesc Med* 158(8):742–748.

Rotheram-Borus MJ, Stein JA (1999). Problem behavior of adolescents whose parents are living with AIDS. *Am J Orthopsychiatry* 69:228–239.

Rudy BJ, Murphy DA, Harris DR, et al.; Adolescent Trials Network for HIV/AIDS Interventions (2010). Prevalence and interactions of patient-related risks for nonadherence to antiretroviral therapy among perinatally infected youth in the United States. *AIDS Patient Care STDS* 24(2):97–104.

Sahay S (2013). Coming of age with HIV: a need for disclosure of HIV diagnosis among children/adolescents. *J HIV AIDS Infect Dis* 1:1–7.

Sandgaard KS, Lewis J, Adams S, Klein N, Callard R (2014). Antiretroviral therapy increases thymic output in children with HIV. *AIDS* 28(2):209–214.

Sanz-Ramos M, Manno D, Kapambwe M, et al.; CIGNIS Study Team (2013). Reduced poliovirus vaccine neutralising-antibody titres in infants with maternal HIV-exposure. *Vaccine* 31(16):2042–2049.

Sarma MK, Nagarajan R, Keller MA, et al. (2013). Regional brain gray and white matter changes in perinatally HIV-infected adolescents. *Neuroimage Clin* 4:29–34.

Serchuck LK, Williams PL, Nachman S, et al.; IMPAACT 1055 Team (2010). Prevalence of pain and association with psychiatric symptom severity in perinatally HIV-infected children as compared to controls living in HIV-affected households. *AIDS Care* 22(5):640–648.

Setse RW, Siberry GK, Gravitt PE, et al.; LEGACY Consortium (2011). Correlates of sexual activity and sexually transmitted infections among human immunodeficiency virus-infected youth in the LEGACY cohort, United States, 2006. *Pediatr Infect Dis J* 30(11):967–973.

Sherr L, Cluver LD, Betancourt TS, Kellerman SE, Richter LM, Desmond C (2014). Evidence of impact: health, psychological, and social effects of adult HIV on children. *AIDS* 28(Suppl 3):251–259.

Siberry GK, Williams PL, Mendez H, et al. (2012). Pediatric HIV/AIDS Cohort Study (PHACS). Safety of tenofovir use during pregnancy: early growth outcomes in HIV-exposed uninfected infants. *AIDS* 26(9):1151–1159.

Sirois PA, Huo Y, Williams PL, et al. (2013). Pediatric HIVAIDS Cohort Study. Safety of perinatal exposure to antiretroviral medications: developmental outcomes in infants. *Pediatr Infect Dis J* 32(6):648–655.

Sirois PA, Montepiedra G, Kapetanovic S, et al.; IMPAACT/PACTG 219C Team (2009). Impact of medications prescribed for treatment of attention-deficit hyperactivity disorder on physical growth in children and adolescents with HIV. *J Dev Behav Pediatr* 30(5):403–412.

Slavin LA, O'Malley JE, Koocher GP, Foster DJ (1982). Communication of the cancer diagnosis to pediatric patients: impact on long-term adjustment. *Am J Psychiatry* 139:179–183.

Smith R, Chernoff M, Williams PL, et al.; Pediatric HIV/AIDS Cohort Study (PHACS) Team (2012). Impact of HIV severity on cognitive and adaptive functioning during childhood and adolescence. *Pediatr Infect Dis J* 31(6):592–598.

Stein JA, Riedel M, Rotheram-Borus MJ (1999). Parentification and its impact on adolescent children of parents with AIDS. *Fam Process* 38:193–208.

Strawn JR, Sakolsky DJ, Rynn MA (2012). Psychopharmacologic treatment of children and adolescents with anxiety disorders. *Child Adolesc Psychiatr Clin N Am* 21(3):527–539.

Stroeh O, Trivedi HK (2012). Appropriate and judicious use of psychotropic medications in youth. *Child Adolesc Psychiatr Clin N Am* 21(4):703–711.

Tassiopoulos K, Read JS, Brogly S, et al. (2010). Substance use in HIV-Infected women during pregnancy: self-report versus meconium analysis. *AIDS Behav* 14(6):1269–1278.

UNAIDS (2004). *AIDS Epidemic Update: Global Summary of the HIV and AIDS Epidemic, December 2004.* http://data.unaids.org/pub/Report/2004/2004_epiupdate_en.pdf. Accessed February 9, 2017.

UNAIDS (2013). *Global Report 2013.* http://www.unaids.org/sites/default/files/media_asset/UNAIDS_Global_Report_2013_en_1.pdf. Accessed February 9, 2017.

UNICEF (2005). State of the World's Children 2005. https://www.unicef.org/publications/files/SOWC_2005_(English).pdf. Accessed February 9, 2017.

Valenzuela JM, Buchanan CL, Radcliffe J, Ambrose C, Hawkins LA, Tanney M, Rudy BJ (2011). Transition to adult services among behaviorally infected adolescents with HIV: a qualitative study. *J Pediatr Psychol* 36(2):134–140.

Valleau MP, Bergner RM, Horton CB (1995). Parentification and caretaker syndrome: an empirical investigation. *Fam Ther* 22:157–164.

Vanable PA, Carey MP, Blair DC, Littlewood RA (2006). Impact of HIV-related stigma on health behaviors and psychological adjustment among HIV-positive men and women. *AIDS Behav* 10:473–482.

Van Rie A, Dow A, Mupuala A, Stewart P (2009). Neurodevelopmental trajectory of HIV-infected children accessing care in Kinshasa, Democratic Republic of Congo. *J Acquir Immune Defic Syndr* 52(5):636–642.

Vinjayan T, Benin AL, Wagner K, Romano S, Andiman WA (2009). We never thought this would happen: transitioning care of adolescents with perinatally acquired HIV infection from pediatrics to internal medicine. *AIDS Care* 21(10):1222–1229.

Walker G (1991). *In the Midst of Winter: Systematic Therapy with Families, Couples and Individuals with AIDS Infection.* New York: Norton.

Whetten K, Reif S, Whetten R, Murphy-McMillan LK (2008). Trauma, mental health, distrust, and stigma among HIV-positive persons: implications for effective care. *Psychosom Med* 70:531–538.

Weir RF, Peters C (1997). Affirming the decision adolescents made about life and death. *Hastings Cent Rep* 27:29–40.

Wiener L (1998). Helping a parent with HIV tell his or her children. In D Aronstein, B Thompson (eds.), *HIV and Social Work: A Practitioner's Guide* (pp. 327–338). New York: Routledge.

Wiener L, Battles H, Heilman N, Sigelman C, Pizzo PA (1996). Factors associated with disclosure of diagnosis to children with HIV/AIDS. *Pediatr AIDS HIV Infect* 7:310–324.

Wiener LS, Battles HB, Wood LV (2006). A longitudinal study of adolescents with perinatally or transfusion acquired HIV infection: sexual knowledge risk reduction self-efficacy and sexual behavior. *AIDS Behav* 11:471–478.

Wiener L, Havens J, Ng W (2003). Psychosocial problems in pediatric HIV infection. In WT Shearer (ed.), *Medical Management of AIDS in Children.* Philadelphia: W.B. Saunders.

Wiener LS, Kohort BA, Battles HB, Pao M (2011). The HIV experience: youth identified barriers for transitioning from pediatric to adult care. *J Pediatr Psychol* 36(2):141–154.

Wiener L, Mellins CA, Marhefka S, Battles HB (2007). Disclosure of an HIV diagnosis to children: history, current research, and future directions. *J Dev Behav Pediatr* 28:155–166.

Wiener L, Riekert K, Ryder C, Wood L (2004). Assessing medication adherence in adolescents with HIV when electronic monitoring is not feasible. *AIDS Patient Care STDs* 18:31–43.

Wiener L, Zadeh S, Pao M (2013). When silence is not golden. *Pediatric Blood Cancer* 60(5):715–718.

Williams PL, Abzug MJ, Jacobson DL, et al.; International Maternal Pediatric and Adolescent AIDS Clinical Trials P219219C Study and the Pediatric HIV/AIDS Cohort Study (2013). Pubertal onset in children with perinatal HIV infection in the era of combination antiretroviral treatment. *AIDS* 27(12):1959–1970.

Williams PL, Leister E, Chernoff M, Nachman S, Morse E, Di Poalo V, Gadow KD (2010). Substance use and its association with psychiatric symptoms in perinatally HIV-infected and HIV-affected adolescents. *AIDS Behav* 14(5):1072–1082.

World Health Organization (2011). Progress report 2011: Global HIV/AIDS response: Epidemic update and health sector progress towards universal access WHO, UNICEF, UNAIDS. HIV/AIDS 2011. http://www.who.int/hiv/pub/progress_report2011/en/. Accessed February 9, 2017.

Zeegers I, Rabie H, Swanevelder S, Edson C, Cotton M, van Toorn R (2010). Attention deficit hyperactivity and oppositional defiance disorder in HIV-infected South African children. *J Trop Pediatr* 56(2):97–102.

Zhao G, Li X, Fang X, Zhao J, Hong Y, Lin X, Stanton B (2011). Functions and sources of perceived social support among children affected by HIV/AIDS in China. *AIDS Care* 23:671–679.

34.

YOUNG ADULTHOOD AND SERODISCORDANT COUPLES

Marshall Forstein, Farah Ahmad-Stout, and Gaddy Noy

Since the beginning of the AIDS epidemic, HIV has significantly affected the physical and mental health of individuals, couples, their children, extended families, and social support networks. Transmitted primarily by sexual behavior and injecting drug use, the HIV pandemic carries more symbolic meaning than other infectious diseases. In the United States and other developed nations, the initial reports focused on the impact of a disease called "gay-related immunodeficiency syndrome" (GRID) in men who had sex with men, and then among intravenous drugs users, interpreted to mean that "immoral" behavior had overwhelmed the immune system.

As the epidemiology unfolded, HIV was diagnosed in hemophiliacs receiving clotting factor and in Haitians recently immigrated to the United States. Scientists began searching for what epidemiologically appeared to be an infectious agent rather than a consequence of "lifestyle." Except for the "innocent victims" receiving tainted blood, the die had been cast to stigmatize HIV as a disease associated with non-normative sexual and drug-using behaviors. In developing nations, heterosexual behavior was associated from the very beginning of the epidemic with the increasing transmission of HIV, requiring a complex examination of cultural mores, sexual practices, and social structures. This stigmatization of AIDS deriving from sexual and drug-using behaviors not only had profound effects on the sociopolitical environment in which the epidemic developed but also fostered the psychological substrates of guilt and shame that continue to impede coping with HIV on an individual, familial, community, and national level (Moore, 1993; Remien et al., 1995; van der Straten et al., 1998; Zich and Temoshok, 1987). HIV/AIDS is now an illness of far greater demographic diversity, affecting all ages, sexes, races, and income levels; involving multiple transmission risk behaviors; and having a broad geographic distribution in the United States (Moore, 2011).

Couples of same- or opposite-sex orientation initially discovered that one or both of them were HIV infected when symptomatic illness appeared. Several years passed before it was possible to test whether the non-ill partner was also infected. Once the antibody test became available, couples that had been thrust into the turmoil of dealing with one partner having a life-threatening illness had to make decisions about the other partner (and children) getting tested, even when there was no available intervention.

Research has shown that same- or opposite-gender coupling within and across cultures is dynamic and diverse. Couples do not all share the same beliefs about what constitutes commitment, fidelity, or individual rights and privileges within the relationship. All couples affected by HIV, however, have to manage information about how and when the infection entered the relationship, decide what to disclose and to whom, and learn how to cope with a life-threatening illness and, often, how to face death and loss. Even with the transformation of HIV from a lethal disease to more of a chronic illness in areas and nations with access to effective HIV care, people are dying of AIDS every day in parts of the world where treatments are not available or used appropriately. The way in which HIV is similar to and different from other medical illnesses that couples face is an important and ongoing area of research.

Recent findings have also shifted thinking and guidelines about when to initiate antiretroviral therapy (ART). The Centers for Disease Control and Prevention (CDC) has changed its recommendations to suggest that ART be initiated as soon as possible after HIV infection or a positive test result (DHHS Panel on Antiretroviral Guidelines for Adults and Adolescents, 2016). This has very important benefits for both individuals who are infected and for people in serodiscordant relationships. Clinicians need to be informed about the most up-to-date science and medical implications in order to provide care for discordant couples in the changing epidemic.

This chapter will focus on the particular aspects of HIV's impact on discordant couples in which only one member is infected. After reviewing some of the extant literature, clinical issues that emerge in evaluating and treating couples are presented.

IMPACT OF MEDICAL ILLNESS ON FAMILIES AND COUPLES

Many studies have reported on the increased psychosocial stress in families experiencing a major medical illness (Cohen and Lazarus, 1979; Coyne and Fiske, 1992; Lippman et al., 1993). Most early studies of stress in families examined the impact of illnesses such as chronic arthritis or heart disease, or that of progressive neurological illness such as amyotrophic lateral sclerosis or multiple sclerosis. The psychological distress of families dealing with HIV/AIDS includes the added factor of the potential for transmission of the disease to one of the members of the family who serves as a primary support for the person infected (Britten et al., 1993; McShane et al., 1994). Other investigators have analyzed the distress experienced by HIV-positive individuals. Social support correlates highly with improved quality of life (Chesney and Folkman, 1994; Folkman et al., 1993; Pakenham et al., 1994). The literature on stress and distress in HIV-positive individuals clearly shows the impact of stigma, poor physical health, lower perceived social support, decreased functional capacity, loss of control over one's life, and loss of friends and loved ones (Catalan et al., 1992; Gluhoski et al., 1997; Rabkin et al., 1991, 1997).

Little has been written, however, about the aspects of HIV illness that make coping with it different from coping with other chronic potentially fatal illnesses in terms of types of psychological defensive structures. Medical factors alone rarely account for how people function psychosocially when facing a significant illness (Meyerowitz et al., 1983). Although other chronic, fatal illnesses (i.e., advanced cardiac disease, emphysema due to smoking, diabetes due to obesity, malignant melanoma due to sun exposure and tanning machines, end-stage liver disease due to alcohol dependence) may result from "lifestyle" choices, there is little moral outcry about the behaviors involved. Sex and use of drugs by injection, however, represent powerful human drives that evoke blame, retaliation, and withholding on many personal and societal levels. Conscious and unconscious forces that play out in the social context in which the couple lives, individually or within a couple, may significantly affect the management of HIV.

Much has been written about the relationship between social support, coping mechanisms, and psychosocial functioning. Self-disclosure of HIV status (Mandel, 1986), having an active coping strategy (Namir et al., 1989) and the capacity to use social support (Ostrow et al., 1989; Zich and Temoshok, 1987), and minimizing the impact of HIV symptoms on function have all been associated with increased quality of life for individuals infected with HIV (Peterson et al., 1996). There are fewer long-term studies of couples with similar (seroconcordant) or dissimilar (serodiscordant) serological status (also referred to as "mixed HIV status"). While several newer studies have looked at the risks for seroconversion in mixed-status couples (Freeman and Glynn, 2004; Remien et al., 2005) and at the impact of interventions for couples on adherence to antiretroviral medications (Remien et al., 2005), there is a paucity of research examining the psychological impact of mixed status on couples after there have been two decades of ART. One study examined a cohort of gay male couples, 69% who knew they were discordant, and 31% who did not. Persons who knew they were in a discordant relationship were found to have lower levels of sexual frustration and anxiety over seroconverting (Beougher et al., 2013).

Pakenham and colleagues (1994) reviewed some of the literature that frames two types of coping that may be relevant

to understanding how individuals deal with HIV/AIDS. Problem-focused strategies are deployed when there is a sense of control over the source of potential stress. Such strategies include changing behavior to prevent infection or, perhaps, to prevent transmission if the person is infected (Lazarus and Folkman, 1984). Under circumstances (such as already being infected, progression of illness) where there may be little to control but much to be endured, emotion-focused coping may predominate (Auerbach, 1989).

Applying these precepts, one could imagine that in discordant couples, the infected person might be more likely to employ emotion-focused coping while the HIV-negative member might tend toward problem-solving, to take care of the infected member and remain uninfected. As the epidemic has progressed through several stages in terms of the available scientific understanding and the possibilities for intervention, these coping mechanisms can shift both within individuals and within couples. Other factors, such as the strength of the relationship, the capacity for self-care in the face of sadness and grief, the capacity to remain individuated within a relationship, and personality styles and temperament, make coping unique in each case. Cultural precepts that proscribe how men and women act in relationships are also relevant to the process of coping with a life-threatening illness that is transmitted by the very intimate behaviors that help to define the relationship itself.

Keegan and colleagues (2005) have examined the impact of living longer on ART on sexuality and relationships and concluded that difficulties with sexual functioning, low libido, fears of HIV disclosure and of infecting partners, and problems in negotiating safer sex continue to be major issues among women living with HIV and may not have been mitigated by a more optimistic future outlook. Little research exists describing the intrapsychic or dyadic experience of members of mixed-status couples from either point of view, in the context of greater social awareness of HIV, increased possibilities for longevity, bearing children, or reaching previously unexpected developmental stages. As the HIV pandemic has progressed from the early 1980s to the present, couples have formed in a variety of ways that inform the issues they face medically, psychologically, and socially. As van der Straten and colleagues (1998) state, "HIV serodiscordant relationships . . . are unique in that the threat of transmission and disease progression co-occur within the same dyad, forcing partners to develop strategies along the continuum from HIV prevention to care."

TEMPORAL FRAMEWORK OF THE EPIDEMIC

Conceptually, there are several phases of the HIV epidemic that inform our understanding of the impact of HIV on individuals infected with HIV and their sexual partners. The following time frame provides an approximate demarcation of these phases. From a clinical perspective, these phases inform how to conceptualize the issues that may arise in serodiscordant couples and the psychological processes that need be considered in therapeutic interventions.

Phase I: During this phase, same-sex sexual behavior and coupling took place prior to the recognition of HIV as a sexually transmitted disease (STD) (before 1981). Although HIV was already working its way through the population of sexually active men who have sex with men, "gay liberation" was promoting a much more open and freer sexuality, allowing gay men to assert their sexuality in the face of anti-homosexual bias and exclusion from equal status in society. Although AIDS was first identified in the United States and published in the medical literature in 1981, we know that HIV infection may have started even earlier in Africa, where it was predominantly heterosexually transmitted. Soon after being identified in gay men, young women and heterosexual men were acquiring infection through injecting drug use and sexual behavior and as recipients of contaminated blood products.

Phase II: This phase starts after the epidemiological evidence for sexual and blood transmission was gathered, but before there was clear identification of HIV as the causative agent (1981–1985). The hallmark of this phase was the sense of crisis in the gay community, the unremitting loss of people who died from AIDS, and the fear and paranoia that arose in places of festering anti-homosexual bias, racism, and increasingly hostile attitudes toward drug users.

Phase III: This phase starts after HIV was identified and serological testing became available but only prophylaxis for opportunistic infections was available (1985–1987). Prevention of further transmission required difficult discussions of sexual and drug behavior within varied cultural and ethnic and racial populations. Finding the virus and subsequently developing an antibody screening test created great controversy about who should be tested and whether testing should be mandated or voluntary, even as there was as yet no treatment available and death was the outcome almost uniformly.

Phase IV: The first phase of antiretroviral monotherapy changed the importance of testing, raising ethical issues of access to care and the role of discrimination in sustaining health disparities (1987–1995).

Phase V: The discovery of rapid resistance to monotherapy led to multiple-drug ART, with the development of multiple biological classes of agents effective to prevent resistance. For some individuals (in nations that can afford and distribute ART), HIV infection (1995–) can be seen as a chronic, manageable disease rather than as an acute, irrevocably fatal illness. Much of the world's HIV-infected population, however, remains without access to basic healthcare and prophylaxis against opportunistic infections, much less ART, essentially remaining in phase II or III of the epidemic. With the advent of ART, for HIV-infected people who could access the medications and tolerate and adhere to the regimens, the HIV epidemic was transformed from one involving an acute and lethal illness to one of a chronic disease.

Phase VI: With the landmark study HPTN 052 showing that patients with complete viral suppression due to ART were 96% less likely to transmit HIV to an uninfected partner, the concept of "treatment as prevention" emerged (Cohen et al., 2011). Within serodiscordant couples, consistent adherence to the antiretroviral medication, regardless of CD4 count, significantly reduced transmission in the absence of barrier protection. As a result, there became a growing imperative to provide access to antiretroviral medication to all HIV-infected people. Research showed that antiretroviral drug levels in the infected partner correlate with the effectiveness of preventing transmission to the uninfected partner, and thus adequate adherence to ART is critical in curtailing HIV in serodiscordant couples. Since the original pre-exposure prophylaxis (PrEP) study, several have looked at PrEP in different populations internationally (Anderson et al., 2012; Baeten et al., 2013; Buchbinder et al., 2014; Cohen et al., 2015; Kibengo et al., 2013; Myers et al., 2013, van der Straten et al., 2012).

Additionally, the high cost of ART and PrEP across the globe must be considered in the context of access, infrastructure for medication delivery and monitoring, and cost of not reducing the spread of HIV (Gomez et al., 2013).

Studies from other countries that have examined mixed- or similar-status couples incorporate data from widely disparate cultures with varying degrees of access to medical and antiretroviral medication. Comparison of studies across cultures and phases of the epidemic illustrates the inconsistency of even the definition of what constitutes a couple, a union, or a marriage. In this chapter, the word *couple* is used to refer to any two people who identify themselves as being primarily committed to each other, independent of legal, social, or cultural parameters.

Seroconcordant and serodiscordant couples may share many of the same concerns, related to the impact of the disease process itself on the person(s) infected. Both types of couples face the problems of access to medical care and sustained adherence to antiretroviral medication, as well as the uncertainty of the response to medications and the course of illness. In families with children in which both parents are ill, permanency placement is a significantly stressful concern.

Couples with similar or mixed serostatus almost universally report greater levels of stigma, stress in relationships, and difficulty in maintaining sexual and emotional intimacy, from discovery of HIV infection throughout the course of illness, including death (Medley et al., 2013; Panozzo et al., 2003). In discussing relationships affected by HIV, it is helpful to know the phase of the epidemic in which an individual acquired HIV, as this may imply complex psychological, behavioral, and social substrates that inform the particular experience and meaning of infection for the dyad as well as for the individual. To understand how couples manage serostatus and their relationship, it is useful to know what each member knew about their own and their partner's serostatus prior to and throughout their relationship. Throughout the world, there are many couples in which the serostatus of one or both partners is unknown. This may be due to a lack of having been tested or to fears of disclosure on the part of the HIV-positive partner (Medley et al., 2013).

GAY MALE COUPLES

The few studies of gay male couples with serodiscordance are based on data gathered prior to the widespread use of ART, which may significantly change some of the psychological and social issues facing couples of similar or mixed status in the present (Carpenter et al., 1997). A recent study showed that what gay male couples knew about their own and their partner's HIV status had varying effects on the relationship, emotionally, sexually, and socially (Beougher et al., 2013).

Early on (phase I), before the illness was even identified, gay men were forging relationships, as one or both men were infected but unaware of this. The development of illness could be quite sudden with the onset of an opportunistic infection, often heralding a rapid demise. Having emerged from the long-standing social disapprobation and pathologizing of homosexuality into the gay liberation era, celebrating sexuality as part of asserting an "out" lifestyle, a generation of gay men instead found themselves burying their friends and partners. Often for those couples in which both men were infected, the less ill member saw his own demise foreshadowed in the horrible, painful, wasting illness of AIDS. Men who had finally found a life partner saw their future wrenched from them because of a virus that they never saw coming. Functional couples stayed together, with the HIV-negative or less ill partner providing the care and support for the one with the more advanced illness. Dysfunctional couples often broke apart. HIV-negative men in relationship with men with AIDS sometimes used the partner's illness as a reason to pull away, while others, out of guilt or a sense of responsibility to care for their dying partner, stayed, knowing that it would be simply a matter of time before death freed them. Serosimilar couples, though strained by illness and social stigmatization and less concerned with transmission of the virus, faced the stress of maintaining emotional and sexual intimacy as they confronted mortality at a developmentally unanticipated time (Forstein, 1994).

In the early stages of the epidemic, it was not uncommon for gay men to lose an entire network of friends, their "chosen families," leaving them as individuals or couples to face the stigma and isolation that AIDS represented in the larger society. In the urban gay communities, social service agencies arose to provide much needed support, with the development of groups for HIV-positive gay men. The divide between persons who were seropositive and persons who were seronegative continued to grow, with serodiscordant couples often caught in the middle. Nothing had prepared a generation of gay men for the developmental crisis that an STD could bring during the prime of life.

As the epidemiology suggested that HIV was sexually transmitted, efforts to control the spread of HIV began with assumptions that protection against other STDs might be effective in preventing the transmission of HIV as well. Before the advent of serological testing for HIV antibodies, the denial that one might be infected or be at risk for becoming infected informed decisions about sexual behaviors. Gay men, having struggled to make sexuality a celebrated part of life, saw efforts to limit intercourse or to use protection as ploys by the government and social structures to once again pathologize homosexuality and limit same-sex behavior and enforce a "moral monogamy." As a result, some men fearing HIV retreated into a self-imposed sexual celibacy. Others struggled with how to negotiate safer sex and relationships according to HIV status. The already complex world of finding same-sex partners became almost universally more anxiety provoking, affecting the decisions made in almost all encounters, consciously or not. Many gay men experienced once again the coming out process, often emotionally and socially traumatizing as someone who was HIV infected.

Men of color, particularly in the African American population, where prevalence rates among men who had sex with men were rising out of proportion to their representation in society, were often driven deeper into social isolation because of the societal homophobia, racism, and condemnation of homosexuality by many African American religious denominations. As a consequence, access to HIV testing and medical and mental health care continues to lag behind what is available to other men who have sex with men. The CDC reports that blacks/African Americans represent 44% of new infections, even though they make up only 12% of the population. The vast majority of newly infected persons are men who have sex with men, with the estimated rate about 7.9 times as high as in white men who have sex with men (CDC, 2016). Young black gay men are at relatively high risk, and understanding the knowledge and ideas that they share with each other is vital to improving access to preventative care and treatment (Mutchler et al., 2015).

Remien and colleagues (2003) have summarized the challenges facing serodiscordant same-sex couples: disclosing positive HIV status to friends and families, coping with the uncertainty of illness progression and anticipated death, planning for the future, experiencing social isolation and social stigma, making reproductive decisions, facing the ongoing risk of HIV transmission to the negative partner, and maintaining a safe and satisfying sexual intimacy. Role definitions within a relationship may also change in the event of declining health. Of note are findings that both seronegative and seropositive members of the serodiscordant couple have similar rates of distress, as with heterosexual couples dealing with a significant chronic medical illness.

In the study of Remien and colleagues, the results of data collected from 1994 to 1995 were presented, revealing factors associated with distress in male couples that were serodiscordant before the advent of ART. Analysis of 75 male discordant couples "demonstrated that measures of dyadic satisfaction, sexual satisfaction, avoidance and self-blaming coping style, and support from one's partner are associated with levels of psychological distress among individuals in HIV discordant relationships" (Remien et al., 2003, p. 533). The authors report that a primary relationship can serve as both a buffer and a source of the distress, depending on whether there is a perception of "consensus and cohesion" and sexual satisfaction with one's partner or a sense of avoidance and lack of sexual intimacy. The issue of sexual satisfaction correlating with level of distress illustrates the importance of understanding the meaning of protected versus unprotected sexual behavior to each member of the couple. Among gay male couples, studies show that discordant couples make decisions about risk-taking behaviors based on many variables, negotiating sexual behavior by perceived or actual risk. Using condoms may be consistent, or intermittent, as when the infected partner's undetectable viral load is used as the determining factor (Beougher et al., 2013; Brooks et al., 2012).

Before treatment or PrEP was available, serodiscordance was clearly associated with higher levels of psychological distress for individuals and couples than that of the general population. Sexual satisfaction and intimacy were associated with greater risk-taking behaviors within the relationship, even when safer sex practices were observed with outside sexual partners.

Since the advent of effective ART, gay men have increased their quality of life, general health, and expectations for a future that had previously been foreclosed. With the awareness that, with the advent of ART, the infected member of the couple might live for many years, couples face the future with more, but often less certain, prospects. Many questions remain unanswered. How will serodiscordant couples cope with the ongoing stress of potential infection? As the time course potentially changes, how will the dynamic issues within each couple change? What are the factors that might help or hinder couples manage the ongoing stress of serodiscordance? How will couples develop strategies to manage serodiscordance and emotional concordance at the same time?

Studies of distress in HIV-negative caretakers have shown stigma, the burden of illness in a loved one, the uncertainty of the future, and potential loss to be important factors (Folkman et al., 1993; Pakenham et al., 1994). The extent to which these factors remain significant since the advent of ART is currently under study. The long-term impact of multi-drug treatment is yet to be seen, as there is some concern that long-term adherence to such regimens may be difficult for some HIV-positive persons, and that despite the long-term use of ART, the prevalence of HIV-related cognitive impairment may increase with longevity (Bell, 2004; Parsons et al., 2006; Sacktor et al., 2002; Stoff, 2004). In the context of increasing physical health and social function, the slow decline of subcortical mental function will present significant challenges to both serosimilar and seromixed couples. For example, whereas hope that the future is possible may have decreased suicidal ideation in some individuals, the specter of cognitive decline, even in the face of generally improved health, may precipitate new crises for individuals and couples.

The advent of PrEP has also increasingly had an impact on the sense of risk in male couples, with increasing perceptions of lower risk even in the absence of condom use (Beougher

et al., 2012; Brooks et al., 2012; Grant et al., 2014). Being a couple with a virally suppressed HIV-infected partner and a PrEP protected negative partner has for some decreased the psychological stress associated with HIV transmission during unprotected sexual intercourse. For some couples, PrEP has also allowed couples to consider opening up relationships to outside sexual contacts. Clinicians have voiced concerns that while PrEP may protect against acquiring HIV, it confers no protection against other STDs, such as syphilis, gonorrhea, or chlamydia, or venereal warts. Clinicians also voice concerns about acquiring drug-resistant strains of HIV or more virulent strains of HIV. Please refer the reader to Chapter 31 for a more detailed discussion of this issue.

Feeling protected from HIV, gay men who have sex outside their relationship without condoms may be at risk for other STDs, with either HIV-positive or HIV-negative men. While syphilis is treatable if diagnosed early, there are strains of drug-resistant gonorrhea that have proven problematic to treat. In the context of working with gay male couples, clinicians must try to identify real risks and the benefits of "barebacking" versus condom use to prevent STDs in HIV-uninfected men on PrEP.

Among young black men who have sex with men, although studies show a generally positive attitude toward PrEP as another strategy to prevent the transmission of HIV, there is concern about the cost of PrEP and about access to financial support and healthcare for vulnerable populations (Mutchler et al., 2015; Pérez-Figueroa et al., 2015). And, more generally, access to care, ART, and PrEP and the adherence required for effectiveness continue to be potential issues for serodiscordant couples throughout the world.

Also of great concern is the need for consistent and continuous use of PrEP according to the guidelines. The effectiveness of PrEP correlates positively with blood levels of the PrEP regimen (Grant et al., 2010). Social, psychological, and access factors play an important part in who has access and who can sustain the adherence needed to confer protection. Presumably, men in stable discordant relationships may have fared better than single men who have sex with men, for whom the outcomes of PrEP have been more variable.

HETEROSEXUAL COUPLES

Most of the research on heterosexual couples dealing with HIV in one or both partners in the developed nations has been published prior to the impact of ART on health, quality of life, and longevity (Lippman et al., 1993; Moore et al., 1998; van der Straten et al., 1998; Van Devanter et al., 1999). In the developing nations, where ART is increasing, but in 2015 available to 65% of the population (AVERT, 2016), the literature is focused on prevention efforts to decrease risky sexual behaviors and, consequently, partner transmission rates, and on procreative intentions to prevent maternal–infant transmission. Thus the majority of studies of serodiscordant couples focus on sexual behavior risk, the survival of the union, and the emotional, economic, and physical impact on children and families (Tangmunkongvoralakul et al.,

1999). There is a paucity of studies examining the impact on couples and families, two decades into treatment with ART (Baggaley et al., 2013).

The impact of parental HIV serodiscordance on families is dynamic and significant for all members. Concerns may be different for parents (depending on which parent is seropositive), both in terms of how each member of the family is affected and how decisions about the future are managed. One retrospective study in the United Kingdom reported on over 200 families who had children referred to a pediatric HIV service or family clinic between 1991 and 1996 (White et al., 1997). Some of the children were themselves infected while others had infected mothers. In the analysis of the data, the authors compared parents who were either HIV positive or negative, untested, or of unknown HIV status; HIV-positive children who had an HIV-positive mother and HIV-negative father; an HIV-positive mother, or an untested or unavailable father; and HIV-negative children who had an HIV-negative mother and HIV-positive father or one of unknown HIV status. Several findings emerged. A diagnosis during pregnancy could put women in a difficult position in terms of maintaining a relationship, particularly if the partner was seronegative and she feared she would be left for a seronegative person. It also implied that partners should be tested, raising issues about how the woman got infected, particularly if the partner was found to be seronegative. In spite of coming from cultures that encourage large families, many seropositive women had single children. Some went on to have additional children over time, perhaps as they became better able to manage their HIV infection. Women often found meaning in life in their role as mother, although the study suggested that a positive diagnosis affected not only her role in the relationship but also that of her seronegative partner, as well as the future expectations for seropositive or seronegative children. Women who were seropositive were concerned about abandonment and could feel isolated and lonely if they were the only one infected. They might find it hard to cope with the role of caregiver and parent if suffering from HIV without having a partner or family support. Inevitably, concerns about care for children when the mother is sick or has died lead to increased emotional stress.

In one of the few prospective studies of serodiscordant couples, Van Devanter and colleagues (1999) reported on 41 sexually active heterosexual couples who participated in a 10-week support group between 1992 and 1994. Analysis of the data revealed four areas of concern: (1) dealing with the emotional and sexual impact of HIV serodiscordance on relationships, (2) confronting reproductive decisions, (3) planning for the future of children and the surviving partner, and (4) disclosing HIV status to friends and family.

Among heterosexual individuals, coupling that occurred before the awareness of HIV brought to light past sexual behaviors or intravenous drug use as HIV appeared clinically in one or both of the partners. How much did one know about one's partner's past? How much did one know about the continued behaviors that put the HIV-negative partner at risk? These unexpected revelations, occurring in the context of one partner becoming sick, often created tremendous strains and fractures in the relationship. Even when couples managed to survive the initial diagnosis with the awareness that an imminent death might be likely, anger and betrayal were common reactions. When both partners were infected, questions of who infected whom sometimes led to vitriolic rage, and domestic violence was not uncommon. Others found illness to be a binding force, forgiving past discretions and making the virus a common enemy to be fought against. During the earlier phases of the epidemic, heterosexual couples struggled to manage the impact of a sudden, catastrophic illness on them, their children, and their families. Facing deterioration and death, couples were propelled into confronting the strengths and vulnerabilities of their relationship and renegotiating emotional, physical, and sexual intimacy. The specter of death and issues related to the surviving partner's needs presented great challenges to the normal development of couples, including questions of reproduction. Finding out that children born to the couple were infected as well presented yet another challenge to the couple.

Sometimes it was only after the death of one member of the couple that the surviving partner could begin dealing with either the implications of their own infection or, in the case of the uninfected partner, with the emotional consequences of loss and the meaning of the relationship. When children were involved, fears of leaving orphaned children behind brought extended families into the fray, exacerbating preexisting dynamics.

Among presumably monogamous heterosexual couples, suggesting the use of condoms in the context of an established relationship was tantamount to a statement of distrusting the fidelity of one's partner. The previous sexual history of one's partner or sexual indiscretions that had previously been overlooked brought new meaning of personal risk for infection into the relationship. Often this scenario created emotional and physical alienation, leading to difficulties with sexual intimacy and trust. Alternatively, some partners eschewed the use of condoms, putting themselves at high risk for acquiring HIV from their partner. Intense emotional bonding, guilt for not being infected, anxiety about being alone upon the death of the partner, and a belief that getting infected would simply mean having to take medications are all rationalizations that have been explored in the clinical setting. Other partners, believing that antiretrovirals and "undetectable viral loads" reduce the actual risk of transmission (Castilla et al., 2005), make calculated choices to have unprotected intercourse to fulfill the emotional and physical needs for intimacy.

Alternatively, some studies have examined the use of condoms in committed relationships of mixed HIV status (Buchacz et al., 2001). Decreased condom use was associated with lower educational and socioeconomic level, recent unemployment, and being African American. Cultural factors continue to be important when adjusting for other factors. Current drug use and previous experience with high-risk behavior were also predictors of decreased condom use.

In a cross-sectional analysis of 104 serodiscordant heterosexual couples, over two-thirds of the couples' members reported having unprotected sex with their partner in the past 6 months. Most respondents stated that viral load testing and awareness of post-exposure prevention had no effect on condom use. In the seronegative partner, however, knowledge that their partner had an undetectable viral load was associated with greater use of condoms. Almost 33% of HIV-infected members and 40% of HIV-negative couple members admitted decreased concern about transmission in the context of HIV treatments. Seronegative partners were more likely to report risk-taking sexual behaviors than their seropositive partners (van der Straten et al., 2000). Whether these behaviors or socioeconomic factors correlate with an internal sense of agency to control one's health and well-being is less clear.

The use of PrEP as described in the section on male couples is also changing the level of risk in heterosexual discordant couples in whom serostatus is known. Access to care and support for PrEP will continue to be major factors in the effectiveness of prevention with ART. Concerns about whether PrEP increases the risk for other STDs must be in light of the CDC reports of increasing STDs in 2013 (CDC, 2013).

DISCORDANT COUPLE RELATIONSHIPS IN NON-WESTERN COUNTRIES

Cultural and religious issues around the world affect similar- and mixed-status couples in significant ways. Space prohibits an in-depth analysis here of each culture's and nation's concerns about HIV. The epidemiology of HIV in Western nations is similar, varying by degree of intravenous drug abuse, risk among men who have sex with men, and heterosexual transmission. Western nations in which ART is more accessible may have more extant programs for HIV testing and prevention efforts targeted to particular communities at risk. With the unremitting rate of infection in many non-Western countries, access to HIV care, treatment with ART, and availability and adherence to PrEP are issues that need further research and support. Identifying those at risk and those already infected and providing access to ART and PrEP could substantially reduce the continued transmission of HIV. Understanding the social, financial, and psychological issues that impact the spread of HIV is complex, and this is further complicated by the need to understand these issues within different cultural contexts. In developed or developing non-Western nations, many issues affect couples in terms of HIV, such as public (governmental) policies about HIV testing, access to primary medical care and antiretrovirals, overt and covert sexual beliefs and practices, and gender roles and power dynamics within a particular culture and society. While homosexual behavior is extant throughout the world and every culture, same-sex couples occur most overtly in Western developed countries and covertly in most other nations, particularly those where sexuality is not discussed openly.

There is little in the literature about same-sex couples in most non-Western nations, where homosexuality is less well described or socially discussed. Among Asian cultures, for example, acceptance of homosexuality varies tremendously. Terminology is itself inconsistent: for instance, what defines homosexual behavior among men may be more certain than how men define their sexual orientation or sexual identity role. The way in which same-sex couples define themselves may also vary.

Cultural factors that affect homosexual men in Asia are inferred from studying the impact of HIV on Asian men living in Western countries, such as Canada, Australia, or the United States. One study of homosexual Asian men living in Australia used social psychological research methodology to analyze several aspects of culture that may be relevant to understanding same-sex behavior, coupling, and HIV risk among this population: "(1) the impact of collectivistic cultural ideologies on self-conception and self-esteem; (2) self-identity related to the status of Asians as numerical and status minorities; (3) the existence of stereotypes of Asians in the gay communities and their consequences on individual Asians; and (4) issues related to self-esteem of gay Asian men as determined by their identification with the Asian and/or gay communities and acculturation to the dominant Australian Anglo-Celtic culture" (Sanitioso, 1999).

A literature search for same-sex couples in African nations revealed almost nothing about same-sex coupling (much less serodiscordance). The heteronormative and "macho" culture of Lesotho, for example, is described as having reconciled in the early 1900s with the homosexual behavior of the Basotho men in the South African mines. In 1941, reports indicated that Basotho men were not only engaging in homosexual behavior but in public cross-dressing and same-sex marriage ceremonies (Epprecht, 2002).

According to UNAIDS, fewer than 5% of AIDS cases in Kenya result from male–male sex. Data on STDs suggest that truck drivers engage in homosexual activity with boys ages 12 to 16. Since homosexual activity is a criminal offense, data are difficult to come by, and the meaning of the behavior even more elusive to research. Most same-sex behavior is secretive, although along the Kenyan coast homosexuality is more accepted and there are "marriages" among men. The degree to which HIV infection occurs in serosimilar or dissimilar relationships is unknown (Africa Health, 1998). Although same sex marriage is now legal in the United States and many Western nations, there are still many places around the globe where same-sex relationships are not accepted and often punishable by severe means.

Several studies have examined the factors influencing sero-concordance or discordance in African cultures but focus on physiological parameters as indicators for HIV transmission, rather than the complex social, psychological, and developmental issues (Freeman and Glynn, 2004; Malamba et al., 2005; Modjarrad et al., 2005; Teunis, 2001). Most studies of discordant couples report that maintaining sexual intimacy is one of the greatest struggles and is manifested by ambivalence about consistent condom use, conflicts about extramarital sexual relationships, and mythology about the way in which HIV is transmitted (Bunnell et al., 2005).

A study in Haiti (Deschamps et al., 1996) showed that provision of condoms increased safer sex practices to 45% of discordant heterosexual couples, meaning that 55% remained inconsistent users of condoms. Studies vary widely in terms of condom use in varying cultures; few of them offer psychological explanations for the motivation behind the decisions that discordant couples make in using safer sex strategies, abstaining from sex, or dissolving the couple as a means of avoiding infection to the HIV-negative partner (Mehendale et al., 2006). Many studies were conducted before the widespread use of antiretrovirals, when the usual outcome of a discordant couple was that the HIV-positive member became sick and died. How couples manage that probability individually and as a couple must be factored into a dynamic understanding of how discordant couples make decisions about staying together, sexual intimacy, using condoms, and facing the inevitable course of illness. Clinically, ambivalence, denial, and reaction formation are not uncommon defenses used in coping with the serodiscordant status. What is not clear from the research is whether the greater availability of antiretroviral medications has significantly influenced the complex psychological coping mechanisms used by discordant couples.

While these factors may help elucidate the complex impact of cultural values, interpersonal customs, and mores, they do not provide a psychodynamic understanding of how same-sex-oriented men or couples manage, understand, and negotiate ongoing "couple" relationships. Understanding of serodiscordance in male couples around the world continues to rely on case studies, clinical experience, and ethnographic narratives.

Since heterosexual transmission of HIV accounts for 90% of HIV infections worldwide, the medical and social science literature continues to expand in addressing this significant issue. Most of the extant studies review how couples engage in acquiring knowledge about HIV, proceed with HIV testing to assess risk and infection, partner notification, and the impact of serostatus on sexual decision-making, condom use, and risk-taking behaviors in the context of dissimilar HIV status. Studies also explore the impact of HIV on partnership stability, sexual intimacy, fears of stigmatization by families and society, and the welfare of children who are born HIV infected (Bunnell et al., 2005; Mehendale et al., 2006; Porter et al., 2004; Tangmunkongvoralakul et al., 1999).

In each cultural setting, the role of marriage and the expected obligations of men and women affect how prevention and treatment proceed. In all countries, HIV has forced a confrontation with traditional roles that men and women play in relationships. Many experience role reversals and changes in autonomy and dependency within the relationship as illness occurs. Economic constraints often contribute to the changing stability of relationships.

PrEP has also been studied in women internationally, where it was shown that self-report of adherence did not correlate with blood levels of the medications (Marrazzo et al., 2013). What is clear is that adherence to PrEP is critical to reducing the spread of HIV, and interventions to increase adherence must be culturally, socially, and psychologically based.

REPRODUCTIVE ISSUES

Reproductive issues arise among seroconcordant and discordant couples throughout the world. Almost 90% of HIV infections in infants and children were acquired during pregnancy, at birth, or by breastfeeding. Without maternal ART treatment, 15–45% of babies of HIV-positive mothers will be born infected, and most will die within 2 years without receiving ART. In 2003, an estimated 700,000 children were newly infected with HIV, with 90% of these infections occurring in sub-Saharan Africa. More than 90% of them were born to HIV-infected mothers, acquiring the infection before or during birth or through breastfeeding (UNAIDS, 2003). By 2013 there were an estimated 1.5 million pregnant women living with HIV across the globe. More than 90% of these women are living in sub-Saharan Africa (UNAIDS, 2013).

In resource-rich nations, mother-to-infant transmission has been significantly reduced by voluntary testing and counseling, access to ART, safe delivery practices including cesarean delivery when appropriate, and the availability of breast milk substitutes (Cooper et al., 2002; De Cock et al., 2000; UNAIDS, 2006). Overall, rates of mother-to-infant transmission have been reduced with breast milk substitutes and ART, to less than 2%, where ART and breast milk substitutes are available (Brocklehurst and Volmink, 2002; CDC, 2006; Gilling-Smith et al., 2006; Tuomala et al., 2002).

In developed nations, as HIV-infected people live longer, serodiscordant couples may stabilize and inquire about the prospect of conceiving a child. For many couples, as the crises of acute illness gives way to a sense of chronic illness, the desire to have children may emerge. Underlying reasons include wanting to fulfill a sense of role as mother or father, leaving a child as legacy, or believing that with the current state of treatment the child will likely be born uninfected. Newer technologies are being applied for discordant couples that wish to conceive (Vernazza et al., 2011).

When the man is HIV negative, alternative methods of insemination rather than unprotected intercourse are safer for facilitating conception. However, serodiscordant couples who plan pregnancy do not always use protection. While studies have reported rates of unprotected intercourse among serodiscordant couples (Remien et al., 2005), the underlying motivations and meaning of the sexual behavior in that context have not been well studied. Medically, the rate of conception during coitus before ovulation is relatively low because of decreased sperm motility in men on ART (Wu and Ho, 2015). On the other hand, one study reported that PrEP did not have an adverse effect on fertility in HIV-uninfected men (Were et al., 2014).

When the male partner is HIV positive, two options have been described. The safest is sperm washing, which involves centrifuging the sperm from the seminal fluid and associated non-sperm cells. Follow-up tests for viral RNA and proviral DNA further reduce the risk of infected sperm being introduced into the HIV-negative female partner (Gilling-Smith et al., 2006; Vernazza et al., 2011). Counseling must include awareness that sperm washing is a risk-reducing but not risk-free enterprise. Sperm washing from an HIV-infected male partner and perinatal treatment of women who are HIV positive are variably available throughout the world.

Alternatively, couples in which the male is positive may limit their unprotected intercourse to the fertile window, although in one study (Mandelbrot et al., 1997) 4% of the women seroconverted with this technique. Studies have estimated that the HIV-negative female partner has a 0.1–0.5% risk of acquiring HIV per act of unprotected intercourse, assuming a stable and monogamous relationship with no intravenous drug use and no other high-risk sexual behaviors (de Vincenzi, 1994; Gray et al., 2001). Viral load in semen correlates poorly with serum viral load, and men with undetectable viral loads may still transmit HIV in semen (Zhang et al., 1998).

As new technologies are developed, clinicians must be trained to understand not only the science and the meaning of the desire to have children but also their own reactions and beliefs about facilitating childbirth in serodiscordant or HIV-concordant couples. One survey reported only 17% of clinicians prescribing PrEP for women in a serodiscordant couple, and only 38% counseling serodiscordant couples on timed, unprotected intercourse without PrEP. Only 20% of clinicians reported being somewhat or very familiar with sperm washing with intrauterine insemination. The authors concluded that there was a need for further clinician education and training in how to counsel serodiscordant couples seeking reproductive options (Scherer et al., 2014].

Although not explored in depth here, there is a growing literature on the medical and psychological aspects of reproductive technologies that are changing the way we think about pregnancy and parenting among HIV-affected couples (Gilling-Smith, 2000; Gilling-Smith et al., 2006; Panozzo et al., 2003; VanDevanter et al., 1998). The possibility of creating a family may enhance the capacity and motivation to adhere to antiretroviral regimens. Adherence to antiretrovirals over a lifetime of infection, however, may be imbued with significant and changing meaning as different stresses and developmental issues arise. Adherence, like safer sex, is best understood as a complex matrix of conscious and unconscious forces filtered through the reality of the changing landscape of HIV illness and societal stigma.

PSYCHOLOGICAL ISSUES

Since the beginning of the epidemic, volumes have been written about the psychological issues engendered by the AIDS virus. As mentioned, it is impossible to consider HIV as just another epidemic or medical illness, given its social, political, and economic implications. But as with any social problem, illness, or catastrophic event, ultimately it is the core issues of human attachment and loss that inform our understanding of how to cope with and make meaning out of any threat to existence. Psychological development and emotional health or illness, while significantly mediated in the case of HIV by medical and psychiatric disorders, is dependent on balancing the need for connection to others and the capacity to defend against the inevitability of mortality. Sexuality and identity are fundamental aspects of those parts of the self that work to maintain psychological and physiological homeostasis. Because humanity depends on procreation for its continuation, sexual behavior is hard-wired into our basic drives. Unlike other species, however, humans do not have estrous

cycles and thus have to manage the complex meanings of sexuality throughout the entire life cycle. Culture and religion have been powerful mediators of sexuality and gender identity, but ultimately, each individual and his or her partner have to figure out the particular dance of intimacy.

For some heterosexual and homosexual couples, the risk of getting infected may increase the intensity of the sexual experience, and a subculture of "barebacking" (intercourse without protection) has evolved, along with a variety of conscious and unconscious substrates. These may include fear of abandonment, existential anxiety about death, feelings of failure, and unacceptable rage leading to reaction formation. The capacity to verbalize the desire to use condoms in an intimate relationship may represent a variety of motivations and deeply held beliefs, and may be experienced differently by the HIV-negative and HIV-positive partners. The HIV-negative partner who actively encourages protection may feel as though he or she is acknowledging a fact of life that separates the couple at the most intimate level: one partner will survive, one may not. It is an assertion of the desire to live while someone they love faces the alternative possibility. This may be experienced as a form of conscious abandoning. To do so requires a capacity for self-protection as a higher priority than commitment to another. Does one rush to the edge of the cliff if one doesn't have to? The HIV-positive person who insists on using protection must also be acknowledging at some level the need to differentiate from the other partner and may feel an obligation to protect him or her. Whether this can be consciously acknowledged or manifests as a decrease in sexual interest or provoking conflict with the partner may depend on how self-aware and psychologically minded the individuals are. Only in the exploration of the meaning of the behaviors in the therapeutic setting can issues of motivation and unconscious fears and anxieties be understood on an individual basis (Forstein, 2002). With the decreased risk of transmission in serodiscordant couples with undetectable viral load and PrEP, the perceived risk approaches the real risk and has the potential of decreasing anxiety and increasing a sense of intimacy without the fear of infection. In the clinical setting, it is important to explore how a discordant couple can begin to talk about the use of PrEP and what it means to each of the partners. Additionally, should HIV be transmitted, even with both partners doing everything they can to diminish risk, there is potential for significant psychological distress.

With the advent of multidrug therapy and, consequently, the transformation of a lethal disease into a potentially chronic illness, couples whose physical quality of life improves can begin to incorporate strategies into their daily lives that allow some sense of a future together. However, stresses that existed prior to illness might again emerge. HIV-negative partners who have stayed in the relationship out of guilt about the prospect of leaving an ill partner, or HIV-positive partners who have ceased to believe that they will not be better off alone have to face the greater sense of uncertainty that antiretroviral treatment now brings to the natural course of HIV infection.

Couples may also have to deal with the loss of others who are HIV infected. It is not uncommon for discordant couples to have other HIV-positive people in their social network. Discovering that a friend or acquaintance progressed to death while on the same combination of medications may engender a sense of capriciousness and inequity that undermines the sense of stability in persons who survive. Dealing with the progression of disease or death of others can precipitate crises in the HIV-discordant couple. Grief and bereavement, extant or anticipated, have emotional implications for couples trying to see the future with hope.

CLINICAL ASSESSMENT

Working with HIV-concordant or HIV-discordant couples requires a comprehensive biopsychosocial approach. The best principles of psychological assessment, psychiatric diagnosis, and therapeutic strategies for individuals, couples, and families are necessary. Assessment should include, for each member of the couple, a review of the complete medical and psychiatric history as well as psychological structures and defenses, and an appreciation of cultural and individual beliefs and expectations about what the illness means and what the future is likely to bring. Understanding the cultural expectations for couples and the meaning of the illness is also essential. The following questions may be useful in the assessment of couples affected by HIV. The assessment should include questions about not only the context and facts but also the meaning of the behavior, anxieties, fears, and coping mechanisms involved.

1. What are the initial issues that have brought the couple for treatment? (Couples may present with non-HIV-related issues; it is important to explore those issues and at the same time inquire about the impact of their HIV discordance on the relationship.)

2. Is the major focus of the couple's decision to come for therapy to stay together or find ways of separating? Is the goal the same for both members of the relationship?

3. When historically (given the phases of the HIV epidemic) did the couple become a couple? What is the customary nature of unions within the cultural background of each member? What is the relationship history of each person? Had either one been in a relationship before this one with someone HIV negative or positive?

4. What did each member of the couple know at that time about their own and the other person's serological status? What assumptions were made? What factors contributed to a realistic or unrealistic set of assumptions?

5. What is the current medical status of the HIV-positive person? What is the viral load, CD4 count, level of health? Does the HIV-negative person have any medical problems?

6. Is there a history of mental illness or current psychiatric disorder for which either member is being treated? Is

there a history of substance use? Is there present use? Do both members of the couple agree on the impact of the substances on the relationship?

7. If there has been a major episode of illness, how has the individual and the couple coped?

8. What does each member of the couple know about the other's sexual and/or intravenous drug use history?

9. How does each person understand his or her own risk for HIV?

10. To whom else has the HIV-positive person disclosed his or her status? What was the response? If there are children, what is their HIV status, and what is their knowledge of the parent's HIV status?

11. What are the nature and level of support in the couple's social and familial networks? Are there resources that can be called upon to help with economic burdens, childcare, or respite care when needed?

12. How has the HIV-positive person's illness changed expectations about role identity in the relationship? What specific changes have occurred, and how has each member of the couple managed to deal with those changes?

13. How does the stage of illness in the HIV-infected partner affect his or her beliefs about what is happening? Is the assessment by the couple about the medical status realistic?

14. What is the nature of how each person feels about the other's status? Is there guilt? Shame? Envy?

15. How has each member of the couple managed other non-HIV-related experiences that have challenged the integrity of the self and its relationship to others? What are the individual coping strengths and how does the couple use the strengths of each to support the stability of the relationship?

Developing a trusting, nonjudgmental relationship with clinicians allows the couple to reflect on a dynamic individual and relationship process that is often unpredictable for clinicians and patients alike.

THERAPEUTIC ISSUES

Mental health clinicians have been involved in treating HIV-positive persons and their partners and families since the beginning of the epidemic. Understanding the changes in the social meaning of the epidemic, the availability of treatments, and the cultural response to illness has made clinical work conceptually and emotionally challenging. Adherence to PrEP is vital for effectiveness. Factors and techniques that interfere with or reinforce adherence vary among individuals and couples and are being explored (Baeten et al., 2012, 2016).

Clinical work with HIV-discordant couples may elicit strong countertransference feelings in the therapist. People who are both HIV infected or negative do not always act in a way that an outside observer would deem "rational"—for example, wanting to avoid condoms to preserve intimacy (Mustanski et al., 2006), or avoiding confronting a partner who is suspected of having sex outside the relationship. But most issues that individuals or couples face in therapy that induce stress or distress are not rational. Indeed, rational thinking often gives way to more deeply seated anxieties or to beliefs that are overdetermined by history, personality, and unconscious substrates. For example, almost all couples know cognitively how to protect the uninfected partner, yet they find it difficult over the long term to maintain safer sex behaviors. Ambivalence may be seen as a component of a psychological, emotionally homeostatic mechanism in a complex and often confusing context of a life-threatening disease over time.

There is little research thus far on the impact that long-term viral suppression and/or the use of PrEP will have on changing the types of issues with which HIV-discordant couples will present acutely and over time (Baeten et al., 2012, 2016; Haberer et al., 2015). Therapists can be helpful in exploring the ambivalences and fears that may arise within serodiscordant couples. For example, with the increased safety presumed with good adherence to ART and/or PrEP, expectations about sexual intimacy within a couple may change and be challenging to one or both partners.

Therapists often experience frustration and anxiety when witnessing the continued risk associated with serodiscordant couples. Power differentials and cultural norms of gender role and autonomy that differ from the therapist's experience and beliefs may elicit countertransference that can affect how each member of the couple participates in the therapy. Managing the conflicting feelings of guilt and entitlement on the part of the HIV-positive person to remain intimate with the HIV-negative partner and the failure of the couple to make the choices that might be considered "rational" can challenge even experienced therapists.

Powerful emotional reactions may occur when HIV-affected couples begin talking about wanting to have a child. Therapists can find themselves quite stirred by the worry about bringing a baby into the world. Although the risk of having an infected child is significantly reduced by the new medical technologies mentioned, therapists often think about the impact of HIV illness over time on the child's development. More difficult is how to raise and work through the issues of what the impact of pregnancy may mean for the HIV-infected partner, given the enormous energy and focus that a baby would bring into the family. With limited coping resources, some couples find the burden of parenting overwhelming when there is a significant medical illness.

For some women, even the prospect of giving birth to an HIV-infected baby may not impede the decision to go forward with pregnancy. One of us has provided care for more than one HIV-infected pregnant woman who has explained that although she realizes that the child might be born infected and not have a long life, the child would have a soul, thus fulfilling the meaning and purpose of the mother's own existence. Therapists may find themselves having to examine their own religious, spiritual, and existential beliefs, as well as their countertransferential feelings in such situations. Therapists are faced with many reactions with serodiscordant couples, but little research has been done in this area. Supervision for less experienced mental health clinicians may be very helpful in facing the ambivalence and beliefs that emerge.

Clinically, discordant couples come for therapy for many concerns. In the experience of one of us, it is never easy to predict which issues will emerge or which couples will learn how to cope better and which will split apart with the stress of dealing with HIV. Since both the infected and noninfected members of the couple are at risk for premorbid or comorbid psychiatric disorders, a thorough evaluation of the individuals as well as of the couple is important. Couples are often dealing with unresolved issues that existed before the couple met or arose because of the discordant status. They are also dealing with issues that all couples face under the stress of a chronic and potentially life-threatening illness.

Deeply entrenched behaviors, beliefs, and maladaptive coping mechanisms may not respond to a cognitive-behavioral approach alone. There is almost no research in the literature that provides long-term intervention outcome data on any particular methodology since the advent of ART that can guide the therapeutic process. We are in the middle of a unique sociological experiment with a world pandemic that is changing rapidly. As medical technologies develop to help contain HIV as a chronic illness, many questions remain, such as long-term outcomes of decades of ART, the emergence of new strains of virus, and the changing social structures that result from and affect how societies deal with STDs.

As the second decade of ART continues in the developed nations, a growing concern is the possibility of increasing risks for mild and moderate cognitive disorders that emerge even in the context of fully suppressed peripheral viral replication. Still unclear is the long-term implication of less than adequate penetration into the central nervous system of currently available anti-HIV medications (Letendre et al., 2004; Sacktor et al., 2002). With an aging population living longer with HIV, there are concerns that the prevalence of cognitive impairment may continue to increase (Brew and Chan, 2014; Watkins and Treisman, 2015). In serodiscordant couples this development has already been seen as a very stressful and complex part of relationships. Cognitive impairment in a couple has significant impact on both members of a discordant couple, presenting challenges medically, psychiatrically, socially, and financially.

Experience suggests that medical advances alone will not ameliorate all of the uncertainty about how individuals and couples live with a disease so fraught with meaning that derives from the core issues we face as humans. In the experience of one of us, the process of working with discordant couples may be ongoing, with stages of illness, normative life stage developmental issues, and individual internal conflicts often emerging as different aspects of the relationship bring into focus sources of ambivalence and interpersonal conflicts.

As more HIV-infected people get access to antiretrovirals, those who are able to respond and maintain adherence to the medications are identifying more with a chronic rather than lethal illness. Many are searching to find ways to move forward in changing careers, having children, and re-entering the social world. Application of therapeutic strategies that incorporate the specific issues relevant to the meaning of HIV-discordance to couples of any sexual orientation requires assessment of the complex factors and underlying strengths and vulnerabilities that confront discordant couples trying to remain alive and connected in the face of a terrible illness. Over time, couples may find that issues of intimacy, fears of transmission, adherence, and the many emotional aspects of coping with an unpredictable chronic disease will fluctuate in the normal course of development. Healthcare professionals should maintain a dynamic view of the medical and mental health concerns of individuals and of the couple over time.

In spite of growing technologies and rapid advances in our understanding of the pathophysiology of the virus, the HIV pandemic rages out of control, with almost 50,000 new infections a year in the United States and over one million new infections worldwide. Each new generation confronts the dilemmas and joys of emerging sexuality, the pursuit of pleasure, and the development of relationships that give our lives meaning. Humans strive for intimacy and love in complex individual and social contexts that have been brought into focus by the HIV pandemic. Increasingly, in terms of prevention and treatment, we are asked to think rationally about the most irrational aspects of the human condition.

REFERENCES

Africa Health (1998). HIV and Kenya's homosexuals. *Africa Health* 20(6):48.

Anderson PL, Glidden DV, Liu A, et al. (2012). Emtricitabine-tenofovir concentrations and preexposure prophylaxis efficacy in men who have sex with men. *Sci Transl Med* 4:151ra125.

Auerbach SM (1989). Stress management and coping research in the health care setting: an overview and methodological commentary. *J Consult Clin Psychol* 57:388–395.

AVERT (2016). Antiretroviral treatment for HIV. http://www.avert.org/universal-access-hiv-treatment.htm. Accessed February 9, 2017.

Baeten JM, Donnell D, Ndase P, et al. (2012). Antiretroviral prophylaxis for HIV prevention in heterosexual men and women. *N Engl J Med* 367:399–410.

Baeten JM, Haberer JE, Liu AY, Sista N (2013). Preexposure prophylaxis for HIV prevention: where have we been and where are we going? *J Acquir Immune Defic Syndr* 63(Suppl 2):S122–S129.

Baeten JM, Heffron R, Kidoguchi L, et al. (2016) Integrated delivery of antiretroviral treatment and pre-exposure prophylaxis to HIV-1–serodiscordant couples: a prospective implementation study in Kenya and Uganda. *PLoS Med* 13(8):e1002099.

Bell JE (2004). An update on the neuropathology of HIV in the ART era. *Histopathology* 45(6):549–559.

Baggaley RF, White RG, Hollingsworth TD, Boily MC (2013). Heterosexual HIV-1 infectiousness and antiretroviral use: systematic review of prospective studies of discordant couples. *Epidemiology* 24(1):110–121.

Beougher SC, Chakravarty D, Garcia CC, Darbes LA, Neilands TB, Hoff CC. (2012). Risks worth taking: safety agreements among discordant gay couples. *AIDS Care* 24(9):1071–1077.

Beougher SC, Gómez Mandic C, Darbes LA, Chakravarty D, Neilands TB, Garcia CC, Hoff CC. (2013). Past present: relationship dynamics may differ among discordant gay male couples depending on HIV infection history. *J Gay Lesbian Soc Serv* 25(4):10.

Brew BJ, Chan P (2014). Update on HIV dementia and HIV-associated neurocognitive disorders. *Curr Neurol Neurosci Rep* 14:468.

Britten PJ, Zarski JJ, Hobfoll SE (1993). Psychological distress and the role of significant others in a population of gay/bisexual men in the era of HIV. *AIDS Care* 5(1):43–54.

Brocklehurst P, Volmink J (2002). Antiretrovirals for reducing the risk of mother-to-child transmission of HIV infection. *Cochrane Database Syst Rev* 2:CD003510.

Brooks RA, Landovitz RJ, Kaplan RL, Lieber E, Lee S, Barkley TW. (2012). Sexual risk behaviors and acceptability of HIV pre-exposure prophylaxis among HIV-negative gay and bisexual men in serodiscordant relationships: a mixed methods study. *AIDS Patient Care STDs* 26(2):87–94.

Buchacz, van der Straten A, Saul J, Shiboski SC, Gomez CA, Padian N (2001). Sociodemographic, behavioral, and clinical correlates of inconsistent condom use in HIV-sero-discordantsero-discordant heterosexual couples. *J Acquir Immune Defic Syndr* 28(3):289–297.

Buchbinder SP, Glidden DV, Liu AY, et al. (2014). HIV preexposure prophylaxis in men who have sex with men and transgender women: a secondary analysis of a phase 3 randomised controlled efficacy trial. *Lancet Infect Dis* 14:468–475.

Bunnell RE, Nassozi J, Marum E, et al. (2005). Living with discordance: knowledge, challenges, and prevention strategies of HIV discordant couples in Uganda. *AIDS Care* 17(8):999–1012.

Carpenter CC, Fischl MA, Hammer SM, et al. (1997). Antiretroviral therapy for HIV infection. *JAMA* 277:1962–1969.

Castilla J, Del Romero J, Hernando V, Marincovich B, García S, Rodríguez C (2005). Effectiveness of highly active antiretroviral therapy in reducing heterosexual transmission of HIV. *J Acquir Immune Defic Syndr* 40(1):96–101.

Catalan J, Klimes I, Bond A, Day A, Garrod A, Rizza C (1992). The psychosocial impact of HIV infection in men with haemophilia: controlled investigation and factors associated with psychiatric morbidity. *J Psychosom Res* 36(5):409–416.

Centers for Disease Control and Prevention (CDC) (2006). Achievements in public health. Reductions in perinatal transmission of HIV infection—United States 1985–2005. *MMWR Morb Mortal Wkly Rep* 55(21):592–597.

Centers for Disease Control and Prevention (CDC) (2013). 2013 Sexually transmitted diseases surveillance. http://www.cdc.gov/std/stats13/default.htm. Accessed February 9, 2017.

Centers for Disease Control and Prevention (CDC) (2016). HIV in the United States: At a Glance. https://www.cdc.gov/hiv/statistics/overview/ataglance.html. Accessed February 9, 2017.

Chesney M, Folkman S. (1994). Psychological impact of HIV disease and implications for intervention. *Psychiatr Manifestations HIV Dis* 17(1):163–182.

Cohen F, Lazarus RS (1979). Coping with the stresses of illness. In GC Stone, F Cohen, NE Adler (eds.), *Health Psychology* (pp. 217–254). San Francisco: Josey Bass.

Cohen MS, Chen YQ, McCauley M, et al., HPTN 052 Study Team (2011). Prevention of HIV-1 infection with early antiretroviral therapy. *N Engl J Med* 365:493–505.

Cohen SE, Vittinghoff E, Bacon O, et al. (2015). High interest in preexposure prophylaxis among men who have sex with men at risk for HIV infection: baseline data from the US PrEP demonstration project. *J Acquir Immune Defic Syndr* 68(4):439–448.

Cooper ER, Charurat M, Mofenson, L, et al. (2002). Combination antiretroviral strategies for the treatment of pregnant HIV-1-infected women and prevention of perinatal HIV-1 transmission. *J Acquir Immune Defic Syndr* 29(5):484–494.

Coyne JC, Fiske V (1992). Couples coping with chronic and catastrophic illness. In TJ Akamatsu, MAP Stephens, SE Hobfoll, J Crowther (eds.), *Family Health Psychology* (pp. 129–149). Washington, DC: Hemisphere.

De Cock KM, Fowler MG, Mercier E, et al. (2000). Prevention of mother-to-child HIV transmission in resource-poor countries: translating research into policy and practice. *JAMA* 283(9):1175–1182.

Deschamps MM, Pape JW, Hafner A, Johnson WD Jr (1996). Heterosexual transmission of HIV in Haiti. *Ann Intern Med* 125(4):324–330.

de Vincenzi I (1994). A longitudinal study of human immunodeficiency virus transmission by heterosexual partners. *N Engl J Med* 331:341–346.

DHHS Panel on Antiretroviral Guidelines for Adults and Adolescents (2016). Guidelines for the use of antiretroviral agents in HIV-1-infected adults and adolescents. https://aidsinfo.nih.gov/contentfiles/lvguidelines/AA_Recommendations.pdf. Accessed February 9, 2017.

Epprecht M (2002). Male-male sexuality in Lesotho: two conversations. *J Mens Studies* 10(3):373–389.

Folkman S, Chesney M, Pollack I, Coates T (1993). Stress, control, coping and depressive mood in human immunodeficiency virus positive and negative gay men in San Francisco. *J Nerv Ment Dis* 181:409–416.

Forstein M (1994). Psychotherapy with gay male couples: loving in the time of AIDS. In S Cadwell, R Burnham, M Forstein (eds.), *Therapists on The Front Line: Challenges in Psychotherapy with Gay Men in the Age of AIDS* (pp. 293–315). Washington, DC: American Psychiatric Press.

Forstein M (2002). Commentary on Cheuvront's "High risk sexual behavior in the treatment of HIV-negative patients." *J Gay Lesbian Psychother* 6(3):35–43.

Freeman EE, Glynn JR, for the Study Group on Heterogeneity of HIV Epidemics in African Cities (2004). Factors affecting HIV concordancy in married couples in four African cities. *AIDS* 18(12):1715–1721.

Gilling-Smith C (2000). HIV prevention. Assisted reproduction in HIV-discordant couples. *AIDS Read* 10(10):581–587.

Gilling Smith C, Nicopoullos JD, Semprimi AE, Frodsham LC (2006). HIV and reproductive care—a review of current practice. *BJOG* 113(8):869–878.

Gluhoski VL, Fishman B, Perry SW (1997). The impact of multiple bereavement in a gay male sample. *AIDS Educ Prev* 9(6):521–531.

Gomez GB, Borquez A, Case KK, Wheelock A, Vassall A, Hankins C (2013). The cost and impact of scaling up preexposure prophylaxis for HIV prevention: a systematic review of cost-effectiveness modelling studies. *PLoS Med* 10:e1001401.

Grant R, Anderson P, McMahan V, et al., for the iPrEx study team (2014). Results of the iPrEx open-label extension (iPrEx OLE) in men and transgender women who have sex with men: PrEP uptake, sexual practices, and HIV incidence. *Lancet Infect Dis* 14:820–829.

Grant RM, Lama JR, Anderson PL, et al. (2010) Preexposure chemoprophylaxis for HIV prevention in men who have sex with men. *N Engl J Med* 363:2587–2599.

Gray RH, Wawer MJ, Brookmeyer R, et al. (2001). Probability of HIV-1 transmission per coital act in monogamous, heterosexual, HIV-1-discordant couples in Rakai, Uganda. *Lancet* 357(9263):1149–1153.

Haberer JE, Bangsberg DR, Baeten JM, et al. (2015). Defining success with HIV pre-exposure prophylaxis: a prevention-effective adherence paradigm. *AIDS* 29:1277–1285.

Keegan A, Lambert S, Petrak J (2005). Sex and relationships for HIV-positive women since ART: a qualitative study. *AIDS Patient Care STDS* 19(10):645–654.

Kibengo FM, Ruzagira E, Katende D, et al. (2013). Safety, adherence and acceptability of intermittent tenofovir/emtricitabine as HIV preexposure prophylaxis (PrEP) among HIVuninfected Ugandan volunteers living in HIV-sero-discordant relationships: a randomized, clinical trial. *PLoS One* 8:e74314.

Lazarus RS, Folkman S. (1984). *Stress, Appraisal, and Coping.* New York: Springer.

Letendre SL, McCutchan JA, Childers ME, et al. (2004). Enhancing antiretroviral therapy for human immunodeficiency virus cognitive disorders. *Ann Neurol* 56(3):416–423.

Lippmann SB, James WA, Frierson RL (1993). AIDS and the family: implications for counseling. *AIDS Care* 5:71–78.

Malamba SS, Mermin JH, Bunnell R, et al. (2005). Couples at risk: HIV-1 concordance and discordance among sexual partners receiving voluntary counseling and testing in Uganda. *J Acquir Immune Defic Syndr* 39(5):576–580.

Mandel JS (1986). Psychosocial challenges of AIDS and ARC: clinical and research observations. In L McKusick (ed.), *What to Do about AIDS: Physicians and Mental Health Professionals Discuss the Issues* (pp. 75–86). Berkeley: University of California Press.

Mandelbrot L, Heard I, Henrion-Geant R, Henrion R (1997). Natural conception in HIV negative women with HIV infected partners. *Lancet* 349:850–851.

Marrazzo J, et al. (2013). Pre-exposure prophylaxis for HIV in women: daily oral tenofovir, oral tenofovir/emtricitabine or vaginal tenofovir gel in the VOICE study (MTN 003). 20th Conference on Retroviruses and Opportunistic Infections, Atlanta, GA, abstract 26LB.

McShane RE, Bumbalo JA, Patsdaughter CA (1994). Psychological distress in family members living with human immunodeficiency virus/acquired immune deficiency syndrome. *Arch Psychiatr Nurs* 8(3):209.

Medley A, Baggaley R, Bachanas P, Cohen M, Shaffer N, Lo Y-R (2013). Maximizing the impact of HIV prevention efforts: interventions for couples. *AIDS Care* 25(12):1569–1580.

Mehendale SM, Ghate MV, Kishore Kumar B, et al. (2006). Low HIV-1 incidence among married sero-discordantsero-discordant couples in Pune, India. *J Acquir Immune Def Syndr* 41(3):371–373.

Meyerowitz BE, Heinrich RL, Schag CA (1983). Competency-based approach to coping with cancer. In TG Burish, LA Bradley (eds.), *Coping with Chronic Disease: Research and Applications* (pp. 137–158). San Diego: Academic Press.

Modjarrad K, Zulu I, Karita E. Kancheya N, Funhouser E, Allen S (2005). Predictors of HIV serostatus among discordant couples in Lusaka, Zambia and female antenatal clinic attendants in Kigali, Rwanda. *AIDS Res Hum Retroviruses* 21(1):5–12.

Moore J, Harrison JS, Vandevanter N, et al. (1998). Factors influencing relationship quality of HIV sero-discordant heterosexual couples. In VJ Derlega, AP Barbee (eds.), *HIV and Social Interaction*. Thousand Oaks, CA: Sage Press.

Moore LD (1993). The Social Context of Sexual Risk Taking and HIV Prevention in a Cohort of Heterosexuals: A Qualitative Investigation. Doctoral Dissertation, University of California at Berkeley.

Moore RD (2011). Epidemiology of HIV infection in the United States: implications for linkage to care. *Clin Infect Dis* 52(Suppl 2):S208–S213.

Mustanski B, Donenberg G, Emerson E (2006). I can use a condom, I just don't: the importance of motivation to prevent HIV in adolescents seeking psychiatric care. *AIDS Behav* 10(6):753–762.

Mutchler MG, McDavitt B, Ghani MA, Nogg K, Winder TJ, Soto JK (2015). Getting PrEPared for HIV prevention navigation: young black gay men talk about HIV prevention in the biomedical era. *AIDS Patient Care STDS* 29(9):490–502.

Myers JE, Sepkowitz KA (2013). A pill for HIV prevention: deja vu all over again? *Clin Infect Dis* 56:1604–1612.

Namir S, Alumbaugh MJ, Fawzy IF, Wolcott DL (1989). The relationship of social support to physical and psychological aspects of AIDS. *Psychol Health* 3:77–86.

Ostrow DG, Monjan A, Joseph J, et al. (1989). HIV-related symptoms and psychological functioning in a cohort of homosexual men. *Am J Psychiatry* 146:737–741.

Pakenham KI, Dadds MR, Terry DJ (1994). Relationships between adjustment to HIV and both social support and coping. *J Consult Clin Psychol* 62(6):1194–1203.

Panozzo L, Battegay M, Friedl A, Vernazza PL (2003). Swiss Cohort Study: high risk behavior and fertility desires among heterosexual HIV positive patients with a sero-discordantsero-discordant partner—two challenging issues. *Swiss Med Wkly* 133(7–8):124–127.

Parsons TD, Braaten AJ, Hall CD, Robertson KR (2006). Better quality of life with neuropsychological improvement on ART. *Health Qual Life Outcomes* 4:11.

Pérez-Figueroa RE, Kapadia F, Barton SC, Eddy JA, Halkitis PN (2015). Acceptability of PrEP uptake among racially/ethnically diverse young men who have sex with men: the P18 Study. *AIDS Educ Prev* 27(2):112–125.

Peterson JL, Folkman S, Bakeman R (1996). Stress, coping, HIV status, psychosocial resources, and depressive mood in African American gay, bisexual, and heterosexual men. *Am J Commun Psychol* 24:461–487.

Porter L, Hao L, Bishai D, Serwadda D, Wawer M, Lutalo T, Gray R (2004). HIV status and union dissolution in sub-Saharan Africa: the case of Rakai, Uganda. *Demography* 41(3):465–482.

Rabkin JG, Goetz RR, Remien RH, Williams JBW, Todak G, Gorman JM (1997). Stability of mood despite HIV illness progression in a group of homosexual men. *Am J Psychiatry* 154(2):231–238.

Rabkin JG, Williams JBW, Remien RH, Goetz R, Kertzner R, Gorman JM (1991). Depression, distress, lymphocyte subsets, and human immunodeficiency virus symptoms on two occasions in HIV-positive homosexual men. *Arch Gen Psychiatry* 48:111–119.

Remien RH, Carballo-Dieguez A, Wagner G (1995). Intimacy and sexual risk behaviour in sero-discordantsero-discordant male couples. *AIDS Care* 4:429–438.

Remien RH, Stirratta MS, Dolezala C, et al. (2005). Couple-focused support to improve HIV medication adherence: a randomized controlled trial. *AIDS* 19:807–814.

Remien RH, Wagner G, Colezal C, Carballo-Dieguez A (2003). Levels and correlates of psychological distress in male couples of mixed HIV status. *AIDS Care* 15(4):525–538.

Sacktor N, McDermott MP, Marder K, et al. (2002). HIV-associated cognitive impairment before and after the advent of combination therapy. *J Neurovirol* 8(2):136–142.

Sanitioso R (1999). A social psychological perspective on HIV/AIDS and gay or homosexually active Asian men. *J Homosex* 36(3–4):69–85.

Scherer ML, Douglash NC, Bethlehem HC, et al. (2014) Survey of HIV care providers on management of HIV sero-discordant couples—assessment of attitudes, knowledge, and practices. *AIDS Care* 26(11):1435–1439.

Stoff DM (2004). HIV/AIDS and aging. *AIDS* 18(1):S3–S10.

Tangmunkongvoralakul A, Celentano DD, Burke JG, DeBoer MA, Wongpan P, Suriyanon V (1999). Factors influencing marital stability among HIV discordant couples in northern Thailand. *AIDS Care* 11(5):511–524.

Teunis N (2001). Same-sex sexuality in Africa: a case study from Senegal. *AIDS Behav* 5(2):173–178.

Tuomala RE, Shapiro DE, Mofenson LM, et al. (2002). Antiretroviral therapy during pregnancy and the risk of an adverse outcome. *N Engl J Med* 346:1863–1870.

UNAIDS (2003). *2003 AIDS Epidemic Update*, December 2003. Geneva: Joint United Nations Programme on HIV/AIDS.

UNAIDS (2006). *2006 Report on the Global AIDS Epidemic*. http://data.unaids.org/pub/Report/2006/2006_gr_en.pdf. Accessed February 12, 2017.

UNAIDS (2013). Global Report: UNAIDS report on the global AIDS epidemic, 2013. http://www.unaids.org/sites/default/files/media_asset/UNAIDS_Global_Report_2013_en_1.pdf. Accessed February 10, 2017.

UNICEF (2016). Great progress in reducing new infections among children, but not fast enough. https://data.unicef.org/topic/hivaids/emtct/#sthashbBDkbweJdpuf. Accessed February 9, 2017.

van der Straten A, Gomez CA, Saul J, Quan J, Padian N (2000). Sexual risk behaviors among heterosexual HIV sero-discordantsero-discordant couples in the era of post-exposure prevention and viral suppressive therapy. *AIDS* 14(4):F47–F54.

van der Straten A, Van Damme L, Haberer JE, Bangsberg DR (2012). Unraveling the divergent results of preexposure prophylaxis trials for HIV prevention. *AIDS* 26:F13–F19.

van der Straten A, Vernon KA, Knight KR, Gomez CA, and Padian NS (1998). Managing HIV among sero-discordant heterosexual couples: serostatus, stigma and sex. *AIDS Care* 10(5):533–549.

Van Devanter N, Cleary P, Moore J, Stuart Thacker A, O'Brien T (1998). Reproductive behaviors among discordant heterosexual couples: implications for counseling. *AIDS Patient Care STDS* 12:43–49.

Van Devanter N, Thacker AS, Bass G, Arnold M (1999). Heterosexual couples confronting the challenges of HIV infection. *AIDS Care* 11(2):181–193.

Vernazza PL1, Graf I, Sonnenberg-Schwan U, Geit M, Meurer A (2011). Preexposure prophylaxis and timed intercourse for HIV-discordant couples willing to conceive a child. *AIDS* 25(16):2005–2008.

Watkins CC, Treisman GJ (2015). Cognitive impairment in patients with AIDS—prevalence and severity. *HIV AIDS (Auckl)* 7:35–47.

Were EO, Heffronb R, Mugob NR, Celumb C, Mujugirab A, Bukusib EA, Baetenb JM (2014). Pre-exposure prophylaxis does not affect the fertility of HIV-1-uninfected men. *AIDS* 28:1977–1982.

White J, Melvin D, Moore C, Crowley S (1997). Parental HIV discordancy and its impact on the family. *AIDS Care* 9(5):609–615.

Wu MY, Ho HN (2015). Cost and safety of assisted reproductive technologies for human immunodeficiency virus-1 discordant couples. *World J Virol* 4(2):142-14.

Zhang H, Domadula G, Beumint M, et al. (1998). Human immunodeficiency virus type 1 in the semen of men receiving highly active anti-retroviral therapy. *N Engl J Med* 339:1803–1809.

Zich J, Temoshok L (1987). Perceptions of social support in patients with ARC and AIDS. *J Appl Soc Psychol* 17:193–215.

35.

WOMEN'S ISSUES

Sara Gorman, Judith Currier, Elise Hall, and Julia del Amo

HIV/AIDS in women poses a number of unique challenges. Approximately half of all people living with HIV worldwide are women, though important regional variations in gender distribution exist (UNAIDS, 2013). In the United States, one in four people living with HIV are women, whereas in sub-Saharan Africa, HIV-positive women outnumber HIV-positive men (UNAIDS, 2013). African American and Hispanic women continue to be disproportionately affected by the infection compared with other races and ethnicities (Centers for Disease Control and Prevention [CDC], 2016). There is even evidence to suggest that the progression of the illness is different in women than in men.

This chapter presents several of the unique issues that put some women at higher risk of HIV and that create a course of illness and treatment for women with HIV that may differ from that found in men living with HIV. The chapter begins with an overview of the manifestations of HIV in women and HIV illness progression, the particular issues associated with antiretroviral treatment (ART) and women, and the interactions between ART and depression in women. The second part of the chapter deals with an issue of particular concern to women at risk of and with HIV: gender-based violence. This portion of the chapter explores the ways in which gender-based violence puts women at increased risk of HIV infection and the complex associations among gender-based violence, HIV, and mental illness. It also explores some methods of intervening in and studying gender-based violence, elucidates the many gaps in our knowledge, and introduces ways to address them. The third portion of the chapter addresses issues that women living with HIV face as a result of conception and pregnancy, noting the incredible scientific gains in preventing vertical transmission in the past few decades. Nonetheless, much more work needs to be done to ensure the proper implementation of these interventions in all regions of the world. The final portion of the chapter discusses a somewhat neglected topic: HIV and menopause. As more people live longer lives with HIV infection, fully exploring the relationship between aging and the virus becomes increasingly important. There is indeed evidence that menopause poses unique challenges for women living with HIV.

MANIFESTATIONS OF HIV IN WOMEN AND HIV ILLNESS PROGRESSION

Numerous studies have examined sex differences in the natural history of HIV infection in the United States and, to a lesser extent, globally (Brettle and Leen, 1991; Grinsztejn et al., 2011; Ickovics and Rodin, 1992; Umeh and Currier, 2005). Studies conducted early in the treatment era identified that women tend to have higher CD4+ T cells and lower HIV-1 RNA compared to men, yet progress to AIDS at a similar rate (Farzadegan et al., 1998; Ruel et al., 2011; Sterling et al., 1999). The CASCADE (Concerted Action on SeroConversion to AIDS and Death in Europe) Collaboration reported that from 1997 onward, women, largely from Europe, experienced lower risks for most AIDS conditions as well as death (Jarrín et al., 2008). The Antiretroviral Therapy Cohort Collaboration (ART-CC) has shown that, after ART initiation, HIV-positive women in Europe have lower mortality rates than men, but there is little evidence of between-sex differences in all-cause or cause-specific mortality in Canada and in the United States (ART-CC, 2015). In the International Databases to Evaluate AIDS Collaboration South-Africa (IeDEA-SA), women starting ART in South Africa had lower all-cause mortality than men (Cornell et al., 2012). In the general population, lower mortality in women than in men has been reported for most age groups since the early and mid-twentieth century in most Western countries and since 2006 in a substantial number of developing countries as well. While the reasons for this difference are not fully understood, in settings with acceptable levels of gender equity, women have been reported to have healthier behaviors, lower accident rates, more conscious health-seeking patterns, and higher adherence rates to medication than men. Nevertheless, important reductions in the women-to-men mortality ratio have occurred in countries with high smoking rates in women and participation of women in the workforce, supporting the strong contribution of lifestyle factors and gender roles to worldwide mortality trends.

The immunological basis for this sex difference remains incompletely explained (Fish, 2008). Clinically, there do not appear to be major differences in the manifestations of HIV infection among women when compared to men, with the exception of higher rates of Candida infections in the pretreatment era, gynecological complications from sexually transmitted infections, including human papillomavirus (HPV), and higher rates of depression noted in some studies. Sex differences in body composition also contribute to higher rates of central fat gain among women started on ART compared to men (Lake and Currier, 2013; Lake et al., 2011; Schambelan et al., 2002).

ANTIRETROVIRAL THERAPY
AND WOMEN

The development of effective combination antiretroviral therapy has transformed the management of HIV infection over the past 20 years, yet many challenges remain. Current U.S. HIV treatment guidelines recommend the use of antiretroviral therapy for all persons with HIV infection (Günthard et al., 2014; DHHS Panel on Antiretroviral Guidelines for Adults and Adolescents, 2016)). The rationale for offering treatment to everyone is based on the availability of new treatments that are better tolerated and the known benefits of ART to prevent transmission to others. Despite the enthusiasm for the widespread use of ART there remain concerns that not all groups of patients are able to remain in care and achieve viral suppression on treatment. This seems to be especially true for women and minorities, at least in some analyses. A recent cross-sectional analysis of 10 U.S.-based cohorts examined indicators of HIV treatment among 35,324 participants with at least one HIV primary care visit. Overall, 82% of the cohort was prescribed ART and 78% had a suppressed HIV-1 viral load. While women were slightly more likely to be retained in care, the prevalence of being offered ART was 6% lower, and only 73% of women achieved viral suppression compared to 78% of men (Althoff et al., 2014).

Globally, women comprise half of all people living with HIV, yet women have been underrepresented in most clinical trials evaluating the efficacy and safety of ART. Several groups of investigators have designed and analyzed clinical trials and cohort studies with a goal of evaluating sex differences in the response to ART (Clark and Squires, 2005; Currier et al., 2010; Hawkins et al., 2011; Hodder et al., 2012; Lemly et al., 2009) These studies have suggested differential rates of toxicity in women and men and some important differences in response rates to standard treatments. A recurrent theme from this work has been a higher rate of discontinuation of therapy among women than for men (Currier et al., 2010). In the Gender Race and Clinical Experience (GRACE) trial, conducted among treatment-experienced women and men, a higher rate of discontinuation for reasons other than toxicity or virological failure was observed among women. These findings may be due to challenges faced in daily life among women with HIV related to poverty and/or concurrent comorbidities. Alternatively, sex differences in the ART metabolism may also contribute to rates of discontinuation when drug levels are higher among women and cause nonspecific toxicity (Gandhi et al., 2004; Umeh and Currier, 2005; Umeh et al., 2011).

A recent analysis from the Swiss Cohort study examined sex differences in outcome over a 14-year period. A notable finding was a higher rate of discontinuation of therapy among women during the first year of ART and higher rates of virological failure in women in the first 2 years of follow-up; however, after 3 years the response rates among women and men were similar (Rosin et al., 2015). Whether the improved outcomes over longer periods of time reflects the availability of better tolerated therapies or a selection bias among persons retained in care cannot be determined. Collectively, these data indicate the need for careful attention to treatment responses among women starting ART with a focus on identifying barriers to remaining on ART.

ANTORETROVIRAL THERAPY,
DEPRESSION, AND WOMEN

Several studies have reported higher rates of depression and anxiety among HIV-infected women than in men (Aljassem et al., 2014; Heaton et al., 2011; Rabkin, 2008). In addition, the presence of depression is associated with poor adherence and higher mortality (Ickovics et al., 2001). Studies conducted within the Women's Interagency HIV cohort study have identified that access to mental health services and pharmacological treatment for depression are associated with increased use of ART among women (Cook et al., 2006, 2014). In a recent analysis, the prevalence of treatment for depression among HIV-positive women was lower among African American and Latina women, and appeared higher among women who maintained continuity with a primary care provider (Cook et al., 2014). A large cross-sectional study conducted in Europe and Canada among HIV-infected adults both treatment naïve and on ART found that a higher percentage of women screened positive for neurocognitive impairment (51.7% of women compared to 35.1% men; $p < 0.0001$) and depressive symptoms (17.9% of women compared to 14.3% of men; $p = 0.01$) compared to men. The rates of depression noted in women in this study were twice the rates in the general population in Europe. These results highlight the need for routine screening for these disorders in clinical care. Finally, the efficacy of pharmacological therapies for depression has been evaluated in the setting of HIV infection. A large meta-analysis published in 2005 highlighted that efficacy was apparent across studies; however, the authors noted that the number of women included in all of these studies was too low to make any meaningful conclusions about the efficacy of antidepressants in women with HIV infection (Himelhoch and Medoff, 2005).

Central nervous system symptoms and exacerbation of depression are reported side effects of the non-nucleoside reverse transcriptase inhibitors efavirenz and rilpivirine. While rates of central nervous system side effects are well known for efavirenz, the package insert for rilpivirine notes that the adverse reaction depressive disorders (depressed mood, depression, dysphoria, major depression, mood altered, negative thoughts, suicide attempt, suicidal ideation) were reported with rilpivirine during development. During 96 weeks of follow-up in the phase 3 clinical trials that formed the database for the approval of rilpivirine, the incidence of depressive disorders (regardless of causality or severity) reported among rilpivirine recipients was comparable to the rate among efavirenz recipients. These symptoms were reported to be mild or moderate and only 1% of participants discontinued therapy for depressive symptoms (rilipivirine package insert, 2017). A recent analysis of data from the AIDS Clinical Trials Group compared rates of suicidal ideation and suicide among participants assigned to efavirenz-based regimens for initial ART compared to regimens that did not include efavirenz in randomized trials (Mollan et al., 2014). The study included over 5,000 participants (73% men). Suicidality incidence per 1,000 person-years was 8.08 (47 events) in the efavirenz group and 3.66 (15 events) in the efavirenz-free group (hazard ratio, 2.28 [95% CI, 1.27 to 4.10]; p < 0.006). Incidence of attempted or completed suicide was 2.90 (17 events) and 1.22 (5 events) in the efavirenz and efavirenz-free groups, respectively (hazard ratio, 2.58 [CI, 0.94 to 7.06]; p < 0.065). Overall, eight suicides in the efavirenz group and one in the efavirenz-free group were reported. There was no association between female sex and suicidal ideation in this study, but the number of events and enrollment of women were low. These findings underscore the importance of avoiding efavirenz as first-line therapy among men and women with a history of depression. Furthermore, sex differences in outcomes in randomized clinical trials comparing efavirenz to rilpivirine have been reported (Hodder et al., 2012). Rates of gastrointestinal side effects (nausea) appeared to be more common among women than in men, while rates of abnormal dreams on efavirenz were more common among men. There was no evidence of a higher rate of depressive symptoms by sex in these analyses.

A recent review of reporting of adverse drug reactions in the UK found efavirenz to be in the top 20 medications for adverse drug reactions related to depression and suicidal behavior (Thomas et al., 2014). Depending on the source of prescriptions considered, the rate of adverse drug reactions related to depression ranged from 27.4 per million hospital prescriptions to 2,312 per million community-based prescriptions for efavirenz. Efavirenz was the only antiretroviral agent that appeared in this report and no information about sex differences were included. Collectively, these data highlight the need to consider the role of ART when evaluating depression among patients with HIV infection. If efavirenz or rilpivirine is currently being used for treatment, strong consideration should be given to switching ART to another agent. The initial selection of either of these agents for treatment in an HIV-infected woman with a history of depression seems ill advised, especially in the current era when there are considerable options for alternative therapies with high rates of virological suppression (Lennox et al., 2014; DHHS Panel on Antiretroviral Guidelines for Adults and Adolescents, 2016). Many studies have demonstrated the safety of switching from non-nucleoside therapy to protease inhibitor–based ART when patients are virologically suppressed (Lake and Currier, 2010; Möbius et al., 2005; Waters et al., 2011). If the viral load is not suppressed, then consideration of resistance testing and selection of an alternate regimen can be explored with an HIV clinician who is experienced in the management of ART. Please refer to Chapter 42 of this textbook for a more detailed discussion of the pharmacological aspects of HIV treatment.

HIV, MENTAL ILLNESS, AND GENDER-BASED VIOLENCE

Gender-based violence is an established risk factor for HIV due to the inability of women in situations of such violence to negotiate safer sex as well as the strong association between gender-based violence and the use of alcohol and drugs during sexual encounters, a factor further associated with HIV risk (Lang et al., 2007; Raj et al., 2004). One out of seven new HIV infections in women has been associated with gender-based violence (Silverman, 2010). Some prevalence studies have estimated that 50–75% of women with HIV have experienced gender-based violence at some point in their lives (Schwartz et al., 2014). Partner violence and drug use tend to occur in a cyclical pattern in which substance abuse increases the risk for future physical and sexual violence, and physical and sexual violence increase the risk of subsequent substance abuse (Stockman et al., 2013). As a result, women often get stuck in a never-ending pattern of substance abuse and intimate partner violence that both increases their HIV risk and seriously impacts their mental health. Because gender-based violence is such a significant predictor of HIV risk, there is also a discussion of the topic in Chapter 6 of this textbook.

The mechanisms by which gender-based violence lead to both increased HIV risk and poorer health outcomes among women with HIV are not entirely understood, but a number of studies have made substantial progress in understanding these important associations. One study of low-income Spanish-speaking women ages 18–35 in Boston found that abused women were significantly more likely to report male control of sexual relationships and fear of partner response to condom negotiation and requests to use condoms (Raj et al., 2004). In addition, abused women were also more likely to report male partner HIV risk due to infidelity and refusal to be tested for HIV than were non-abused controls (Raj et al., 2004). Another study found that fears of condom negotiation or actual violence resulting from condom requests result in actual inconsistent condom use among abused women at rates higher than non-abused controls (Lang et al., 2007).

A combination of biological and social factors make HIV transmission much more likely in violent relationships or sexual encounters. Biological risk of transmission in a violent sexual encounter may be higher, especially for anal sex followed by vaginal sex, and from vaginal lacerations and abrasions that occur when force is used. This is especially a problem for girls and young women, as their vaginal tracts are immature and more prone to abrasions (Li et al., 2014). Abused women may also experience long-term immune dysfunction, including proinflammatory responses of increased cytokine release and local inflammatory responses at the site of injury, as well as impairment of the integrity of the mucosal epithelial barrier. Forced intercourse may cause an increase in CD4+ cells in the cervical epithelium (Campbell et al., 2013). All of these factors can make likelihood of HIV transmission significantly higher among women in violent sexual relationships.

Women who experience gender-based violence are not only more likely to contract HIV but are also more likely to fail on treatment if they have the disease. Evidence suggests that women with a history of gender-based violence have lower rates of adherence to antiretrovirals than women without such a history (Lopez et al., 2010). Furthermore, this association seems somewhat specific to women. Experiences of extreme violence have been found to be negatively correlated with medication adherence among women with HIV (Lopez et al., 2010). In addition, among people living with HIV, history of sexual trauma is associated with HIV treatment failure and higher morbidity and mortality. The exact reason for these associations, outside of poor adherence to medication, is not entirely understood (Jones et al., 2013).

Social factors surrounding gender-based violence also likely have a powerful influence on HIV risk. Several studies have shown a strong association between gender-based violence and substance abuse. These associations are well documented in the literature. Adult and childhood violence increases the likelihood that women will experience problem drinking and alcoholism. In addition, women who experience gender-based violence are also found to be use cocaine and to inject drugs (Schwartz et al., 2014). Women who inject drugs are at risk for HIV, and cocaine use has been associated with heightened risk of HIV through risky sexual behaviors and inconsistent condom use (Schwartz et al., 2014). In one substudy of women who experienced gender-based violence, in three sites of the larger Women's Interagency HIV Study, women who experienced such violence were more likely to have a history of injecting drugs and had higher rates of current drug injection. In women who inject drugs, current use was associated with over a 2.6 times increased likelihood of having experienced lifetime gender-based violence, and having a history of such violence was associated with a 2.6 times increased likelihood of having experienced lifetime gender-based violence (Schwartz et al., 2014). Many women are given alcohol or drugs in the context of violent or forced sexual encounters. Studies have shown that women given alcohol or drugs during sexual encounters are more likely to have multiple sex partners and engage in regular substance use than women not given alcohol or drugs during sexual encounters (Stockman et al., 2010). Research in the United States has further shown that abused women are at increased risk for having partners with known HIV risks and for feeling actively concerned about their own risk for HIV. In South Africa, studies have demonstrated a causal relationship between gender-based violence and associated HIV risk with gender inequity, psychological distress, and risky male partners. Additional research is needed to validate the chronology and causal relationships of these factors, especially in other geographical settings (Stockman et al., 2013). A growing body of literature also suggests that perpetrators of violence are more likely than nonviolent men to have concurrent sex partners (Stockman et al., 2013).

Relationships between sexual violence and mental illness also likely contribute to increased HIV risk in female victims of gender-based violence. PTSD and depression are common among women with histories of gender-based violence. Women who have experienced gender-based violence are four to seven times more likely to report experiencing minor and severe depressive symptoms compared to non-abused women (Schwartz et al., 2014). In addition, meta-analyses have shown PTSD prevalence rates ranging from 31% to as high as 84% among women with histories of gender-based violence. Women with gender-based violence–related PTSD and depression have four times greater odds of having unprotected

sex with a risky partner (Schwartz et al., 2014). There are also well-known associations among PTSD, depression, and substance use, which increases HIV risk, and well-documented links between poor mental health and poor medication adherence among people with HIV (Schwartz et al., 2014).

Despite a fairly substantial body of research demonstrating clear associations between gender-based violence and HIV risk and treatment failure, few HIV interventions have been designed to deal explicitly with risk for and history of gender-based violence. Nonetheless, promising results have been seen in several gender-based violence–focused HIV interventions. Several particular components of these interventions have specifically helped women practice safer sex and reduce their exposure to violence, including raising awareness of triggers of HIV risk behavior and partner violence; developing accurate appraisals of risk of HIV and partner planning; increasing safety planning, problem-solving, and sexual communication skills; and increasing women's access to and utilization of informal social support to help women establish and maintain relationship safety (Stockman et al., 2013).

Results from specific intervention programs are encouraging. The Relapse Prevention and Relationship Safety Intervention takes a synergistic approach to integrating relapse and gender-based violence prevention strategies to address concurrent goals of establishing relationship safety and reducing drug use. This particular intervention consists of 11 group sessions and 1 individual session for abused women who use drugs and are in methadone maintenance treatment programs. The intervention focuses on enhancement of positive evaluations of self-worth, ethnic pride, and risk avoidance, and the intervention materials incorporate social cognitive skill-building, brainstorming, role-playing, and small-group discussions. Compared with controls, participants in the intervention are more likely to report a decrease in minor physical or sexual gender-based violence and minor and severe psychological gender-based violence at 3-month follow-up. The Women's Health CoOp, in South Africa, also uses individual and group sessions to integrate personalized feedback and action plans to address risks of drug use, sexual risk behaviors, and contextual goals to address barriers of education, employment, housing, and parenting with a support-based format to help women understand how they are affected by multiple contextual influences in their lives and to teach skills to reduce risk and increase women's sense of empowerment. Women in this intervention demonstrated significant reduction in crack use and sexual risk behaviors at 3 and 6 months as well as greater improvement in employment and housing status compared to women not in the intervention. This program has also been adapted for use with South African drug-using sex workers. Finally, the Boston Consortium Model involves a trauma-specific intervention group providing skill-building in economics, family reunification, and leadership for female victims of gender-based violence. Women who receive this integrated trauma treatment are more likely to demonstrate reduced sexual risk behaviors at 6 and 12 months compared to a control group. In addition, women in the intervention have higher relationship power and are less likely to engage in unprotected sex. The intervention also produces significantly greater reductions in trauma and mental health symptomatology and drug use (Stockman et al., 2013).

Nevertheless, there is still a lot we do not understand about the relationship between gender-based violence, HIV, and mental health. For example, we have limited information about the effects of timing of abuse on HIV risk (Stockman et al., 2013). Some research has suggested that women who experience violence at first sexual intercourse are more likely to have more sexual partners and to abuse substances than women who experience violence after first sexual intercourse (Stockman et al., 2013), but this evidence is still limited. In addition, there is a small amount of evidence that the type of abuse (e.g., physical versus verbal) affects the extent to which women have higher risk of HIV and abuse substances, but the amount of research on this topic is again fairly limited (Stockman et al., 2013). Since gender-based violence has been established as such a significant risk factor for HIV, substance abuse, and mental illness, it is essential that more research on the nature of these associations be conducted and that more interventions tailored specifically to women with histories of gender-based violence be tested in order to effectively curtail the spread of the HIV epidemic among women.

CHALLENGES WOMEN WITH HIV FACE IN CONCEPTION AND PREGNANCY

The majority of women become infected with HIV during their reproductive years. Consequently, HIV testing during pregnancy, reproductive desire, pregnancy outcomes, and the potential vertical transmission of HIV to their offspring are extremely important (see Chapter 34 for a discussion on pregnancy in serodiscordant couples). The availability of life-saving ART has led to significant changes in women's choices regarding these aspects, though there is substantial heterogeneity depending on the region of the world in which women live.

Antiretroviral therapy has led an increasing number of women with HIV to contemplate becoming pregnant as a conscious choice, as fear of transmitting HIV to their children and concerns regarding their personal health have diminished over the last two decades for women with access to care. A number of studies have also reported that HIV per se is not the only factor influencing reproductive desire and that these drivers are similar to those of women from the general population—namely cultural beliefs, age, having previous children, health concerns, and economic hardship (Craft et al., 2007; Erhabor et al., 2012; Hernando et al., 2014; Homsy et al., 2009; Ivanova et al., 2012). Still, women with HIV express fear of further stigmatization and anxiety regarding their active choice of having children (Craft et al., 2007; Hernando et al., 2014; Ivanova et al., 2012). Women's age at the time of HIV diagnosis is a prominent factor in further decisions among U.S. women about becoming pregnant (Craft et al., 2007). In a study of women of childbearing age in Canada, Ivanova and colleagues (2012) reported a higher frequently of anxiety symptoms among women with reproductive health concerns than in controls. Indeed, over a third of the women of reproductive age in that study reported high anxiety. The majority wished to become pregnant and explicitly feared being judged by their relatives and friends for their wishes to become mothers. In a study of women with HIV in Spain, Hernando and others also found that a very high proportion of women wanted to become pregnant and reported that they thought maternity would help them "to normalize" their lives. However, their fear of being stigmatized led them not to disclose their willingness to become mothers to others (Hernando et al., 2014). In studies conducted in Uganda in 2003–2006, women with HIV who are from sub-Saharan Africa showed a comparatively lower desire to have children (Homsy et al., 2009). Ehhabor and colleagues (2012), however, have more recently highlighted that over half of HIV-positive subjects, particularly women, in the Niger Delta of Nigeria wanted to have children, irrespective of their HIV status.

Although in the pre-ART era reports on the impact of pregnancy in the natural course of HIV were conflicting, there is now solid evidence showing that pregnancy per se does not negatively affect HIV illness progression. Tai and others provided convincing evidence from the United States (Tai et al, 2007) that was replicated in a recent meta-analysis (Calvert and Ronsmans, 2015). Calvert and Ronsmans (2015) report that in settings where ART was not available, pregnancy is associated with a weak but significant increase of negative HIV outcomes, such as progression to AIDS-defining illnesses and HIV-related or all-cause mortality, but the paucity of studies on the topic limited their ability to draw meaningful conclusions. Nevertheless, when ART is involved, pregnancy is not associated with poorer HIV illness progression outcomes (Calvert and Ronsmans, 2015).

Access to HIV testing is the entry to HIV treatment, hence delayed HIV diagnosis is a major challenge to equitable access to ART for men and women across the world. Overall, largely as a consequence of universal HIV testing during pregnancy in the last two decades, women from most geographic regions who have ever been pregnant tend to have earlier HIV diagnoses than heterosexually infected men. Although testing women for HIV during pregnancy is primarily related to the prevention of vertical transmission of HIV infection, it also has formidable effects on the overall health of women, and some of the survival advantages observed in women in the last few decades in many parts of the world have been attributed to these interventions. UNAIDS estimates that there were 1.5 million HIV-positive pregnant women in 2012 worldwide but that only 46% of pregnant women living in low- and middle-income settings had been tested for HIV (UNAIDS, 2013). The percentage of women covered by prevention of mother-to-child transmission programs in India in 2013 was as low as 18% and as low as 27% in Nigeria. Still, Botswana and South Africa have prevention of mother-to-child transmission coverage exceeding 90% (Prendergast et al., 2015).

Since the publication of ACTG076 in 1994 and its dramatic 67.5% reduction in vertical transmission of HIV among women treated with zidovudine during pregnancy and delivery (Connor et al., 1994), the number of perinatally acquired

HIV infections has continued to decrease in most settings. Without any intervention to prevent mother-to-child HIV transmission, up to 40% of babies born to HIV-positive women would be infected either intra-utero, during delivery, or through breastfeeding. Accumulating evidence has elucidated how best to treat HIV-positive pregnant women in terms of both their overall health and the prevention of vertical HIV transmission. The challenge now is not so much in the science but in the implementation of these strategies. Lack of clear and consistent implementation strategies is, unfortunately, what explains the intense geographical differences in vertical transmission rates.

Of course, the issue of vertical transmission is complicated by differing standards for breastfeeding in HIV-positive mothers by region. In the United States, the CDC expressly discourages breastfeeding by mothers with HIV (CDC, 2013). Conversely, the World Health Organization (WHO) recommends that all mothers, including mothers with HIV, in African countries should breastfeed exclusively for at least the first 6 months (WHO, 2010). Before 2010, the WHO recommended avoidance of breastfeeding among HIV-positive mothers in this region. But when research began to emerge that *exclusive* breastfeeding combined with proper use of antiretrovirals could significantly reduce rates of vertical transmission, the WHO reversed its recommendation (WHO, 2010). Exclusive breastfeeding is associated with lower rates of malnutrition, diarrhea, and pneumonia among young children.

In many high-income settings, vertical transmission is now very low in women who have been diagnosed prior to delivery, either before pregnancy or early in the course of pregnancy. In high-income settings a number of interventions have been successfully implemented and have brought mother-to-child HIV transmission to below 1% (European Collaborative Study, 2005). These interventions include universal HIV testing in pregnancy, ART during pregnancy and immediately after birth, appropriate caesarian section, and safe supplementation to breastfeeding. The European Collaborative Study reported that nearly half of the HIV-positive pregnant women in the cohort were taking ART before their pregnancy and that the women who were on ART prior to pregnancy were more likely to achieve HIV viral suppression at delivery, a key determinant of vertical transmission of HIV (European Collaborative Study, 2005). Newell et al. (2007) have described the narrowing of the historical differences in obstetrical and medical management of HIV-positive pregnant women in the United States and Western Europe. To a large extent, the differences were shaped by the sociodemographic characteristics, HIV testing and health-seeking behaviors, as well as access to healthcare of the women in different settings (Newell et al., 2007).

Following the publications of the START and TEMPRANO trials, in 2015, the WHO now recommends that all pregnant and breastfeeding women initiate ART immediately regardless of CD4 count and that ART should be continued for life (TEMPRANO ANRS 2136 Study Group, 2015).

Regrettably, feasibility and costs have not enabled the full implementation of prevention strategies in low-income settings where mother-to-child HIV transmission is a public health issue. In order to accomplish the ambitious target of eliminating new HIV infections among children by 2015, the WHO issued their 2013 guidelines (with a 2014 update) that include the option of lifelong ART for pregnant women irrespective of their CD4 cell count, in order to simplify program implementation in what is known as Option B+ (WHO, 2014). The real remaining challenge for effective implementation of perinatal mother-to-child HIV transmission in all parts of the world is retention of women with HIV in care and adherence to treatment.

HIV AND MENOPAUSE

With the emergence of effective ART, individuals with HIV are living longer lives (see also Chapter 36 for a more extensive discussion of aging with HIV). Current treatment has increased the median life expectancy of individuals with HIV to greater than 70 years of age (High et al., 2012). This is a significant factor in any consideration of the interaction between HIV and health issues specific to women, since now more HIV-positive females will transition through menopause than in the past. The median age of menopause among HIV-seronegative women in the United States is 51.4, with earlier age of menopause linked to overall increased morbidity and mortality from all causes (Gold et al., 2001; Mondul et al., 2005). Both HIV infection and menopause accelerate the progression of various chronic diseases of aging, including cardiovascular disease, hypertension, and decreased bone mineral density (Arnsten et al., 2006; DAD Study Group, 2007; Mellons et al., 2012; Sowers et al., 2007). Estradiol and progesterone regulate HIV replication in peripheral HIV-1-infected cells (Asin et al., 2008). The estrogen deficiency associated with menopause and the normal thymic involution that occurs with aging could affect CD4 cell recovery and HIV replication (Kalayjian et al., 2003). For these reasons, it is important to better understand the interplay between HIV infection and menopause so that women with HIV receive timely preventative health screening, accurate assessment of symptoms, and appropriate treatment interventions depending on their presenting concerns.

Menopause is defined as the time of ovarian follicular depletion accompanied by an increase in follicular stimulating hormone (FSH) levels and final menstrual period, which is determined after 12 months of amenorrhea (Harlow et al., 2012). Vasomotor symptoms (VMS), sleep disturbance, and vaginal dryness are thought to be the core symptoms of menopause (Proceedings, 2005), with a number of studies also identifying the perimenopausal transition as a period of increased risk for depressive symptomatology (Bromberger et al., 2011; Cohen et al., 2006; Woods et al., 2008). The source of menopausal symptoms is multifactorial and likely affected by sociocultural context, lifestyle habits, and the presence of psychosocial stressors. Furthermore, there are myriad factors influencing the age of menopause, including tobacco use, substance use, low socioeconomic status, and low body weight

(Gold et al., 2001), all of which are more common in women with HIV (Fan et al., 2008; Schoenbaum et al., 2005).

There have been inconsistent reports on age of menopause in women with HIV compared to the general population. Some studies have demonstrated an earlier age of menopause in an HIV population (Boonyanurak et al., 2012; Clark et al., 2000; Ferreira et al., 2007; Schoenbaum et al., 2005) while others have not (Cejtin, 2008; Cejtin et al., 2004; de Pommerol et al., 2011; Fantry et al., 2005). All of these studies differ in methodology, number of women on ART, degree of immunosuppression among study participants, and evaluation of confounding risk factors for early menopause. Schoenbaum et al. (2005) showed that HIV-positive women had an earlier average age of menopause (46 years), that CD4 counts >200 decreased the chance of early menopause, and that the average age of onset of menopause in women with CD4 counts <200 was 42.5 years. Similarly, Ferreira et al. (2007) and Clark et al. (2000) reported median ages of menopause in HIV-positive women at 47.5 and 47, respectively.

Although de Pommerol et al. (2011) did not demonstrate a statistically significant difference in the age of menopause between women with and without HIV, they did note that CD4 counts <200 were associated with an earlier age of menopause. Overall, there is a dearth of research on this topic and existing studies are heterogeneous. Thus, no clear conclusions can be drawn regarding the association between HIV infection and early age of menopause, although trends suggest a link between greater immunosuppression and earlier menopause onset.

Some studies have shown that HIV infection itself is independently associated with a higher prevalence of menopausal symptoms (Fantry et al., 2005; Ferreira et al., 2007; Miller et al., 2005), while others have shown no link between prevalence of menopause symptoms and HIV status (Lui-Filho et al., 2013). Positive studies have shown that HIV infection appears to be an independent risk factor for worsening VMS in women going through menopause (Looby et al., 2013), with conflicting results on the association between VMS severity and degree of immunosuppression. Some studies have shown no link between degree of immunosuppression and VMS severity (Fantry et al., 2005 Looby et al., 2013), while others have shown that a higher CD4 count is linked to more severe VMS (Clark et al., 2000). It is particularly important to identify presence and severity of VMS as these symptoms interfere with sleep, quality of life, relationships, and role performance.

Sexual activity in the aging group of HIV-positive women remains an important issue because menopausal symptoms such as vaginal dryness and mucosal thinness can both increase acquisition and transmission of HIV (Senanyake, 2000). Vaginal dryness is a problematic symptom for many women transitioning through menopause, with no indication that frequency or severity of this symptom is dependent on HIV status (Lui-Filho et al., 2013). Taylor et al. (2015) demonstrated that HIV positive women did not show a greater decline in sexual activity as they aged compared to HIV-negative women. However, the odds of any sexual activity did decline after menopause only in the HIV-positive group. Women with HIV infection have been found to have a greater degree of global sexual dysfunction (e.g., desire, arousal, pain), exacerbated if they are transitioning through menopause, with more severe dysfunction linked to greater immunosuppression (i.e., CD4 <200) (Wilson et al., 2010).

The menopausal transition has been shown to increase risk for depressive symptoms in both an HIV-seropositive and seronegative population. Moreover, persistent VMS predict depressive symptoms in both groups (Maki et al., 2012). Because of the high prevalence of depression in women with HIV, it is important to screen for symptoms of depression (Rabkin, 2008). Screening for depression is particularly salient since depressive symptoms have been associated with nonadherence to ART and increased mortality (Cook et al., 2004). Similarly, adherence to ART is protective against developing depressive symptoms in the perimenopausal population and a CD4<200 is also associated with increased depressive symptomatology compared to women with less immunosuppression (Maki et al., 2012). Most studies have shown that there is no significant difference in the prevalence of depression during menopause in women with HIV compared with a seronegative group (Lui-Filho et al., 2013).

There is mixed evidence regarding menopausal status and response to ART (reviewed in Imai et al., 2013; Kang and Fantry, 2016; Patterson et al. (2009) demonstrated that when comparing pre- and postmenopausal HIV-positive women treated with ART, there were no differences in the proportions achieving plasma HIV RNA loads <50 copies/ml or the median change in absolute CD4 cell counts. Cohort data based on samples of men and women suggest that virological response to ART is not affected by age, but that there is possibly a poorer immunological response (Althoff et al., 2010). For the treatment of menopausal symptoms, hormone replacement therapy and a number of nonhormonal treatment options are available to treat depressive symptoms and VMS (Hall et al., 2011). However, many of these treatment options have not been tested specifically in an HIV-positive population. HIV infection itself increases the risk for thrombotic events; therefore, the use of estrogen replacement therapy in this population requires caution and further investigation (Kiser and Badowski, 2010). Furthermore, clinicians need to be mindful of potential altered metabolism and clearance within the cytochrome P450 system when co-prescribing certain psychotropics (e.g., paroxetine) and ART (Walubo, 2007). See Chapter 42 of this textbook for more a detailed discussion of the psychopharmacologic aspects of the care of persons with HIV.

There is a need for ongoing research on HIV infection and menopause. Existing studies demonstrate possible links between HIV infection and an earlier age of menopause, although it is clear that a number of confounding risk factors complicate our ability to draw specific conclusions on this matter. Studies indicate that HIV infection may increase the prevalence of VMS during the menopausal transition with no significant differences in prevalence or severity of vaginal dryness or depression when compared to an HIV-negative group. There are variable results regarding the influence of the degree of immunosuppression on menopause symptom presence and severity.

One of the barriers to consistency in the literature is varying definitions of menopause and a lack of the use of biochemical markers (e.g., serial elevated FSH). The use of biochemical markers as evidence of ovarian failure is important, as HIV-seropositive women may present with prolonged amenorrhea (>12 months) from causes other than menopause in the presence of normal FSH levels (Cejtin et al., 2006). Furthermore, irregular menstrual bleeding is more common in an HIV-positive population and linked to degree of immunosuppression (CD4 <50) (Cofrancesco et al., 2006). Future research on HIV infection and menopause should attempt to control for the many confounding factors that can contribute to an earlier age of menopause and symptom severity and consider collection of information on time since HIV diagnosis, class and duration of use of ART, use of psychotropics, CD4 cell count, and viral load. This is a crucial part of the specifically challenging experience of women with HIV, but, like gender-based violence, it requires much more research for appropriate action and treatment to be devised.

CONCLUSION

The challenges faced by women with HIV are certainly unique. Factors specifically related to anatomy, physiology, as well as the biological processes unique to women, including pregnancy and menopause, often add to the complexity of HIV. Likewise, social issues, including oppression of and violence against women, also contribute to the unique and challenging nature of the epidemic in women. It is thus vital to continue to research and understand the specific features of HIV in women and to work to address and alleviate some of these very serious challenges.

REFERENCES

Aljassem K, Raboud JM, Hart TA, et al. (2014). Gender differences in severity and correlates of depression symptoms in people living with HIV in Ontario, Canada. *J Int Assoc Provid AIDS Care* 5(1):23–35.

Althoff KN, Justice AC, Gange SJ, et al. (2010). Virologic and immunologic response to HAART, by age and regimen class. *AIDS* 24:2469–2479.

Althoff KN, Rebeiro P, Brooks JT, et al. (2014). Disparities in the quality of HIV care when using US Department of Health and Human Services indicators. *Clin Infect Dis* 58(8):1185–1189.

Antiretroviral Therapy Cohort Collaboration (ART-CC) (2015). Sex differences in overall and cause-specific mortality among HIV-infected adults on antiretroviral therapy in Europe, Canada and the US. *Antivir Ther* 20(1):21–28.

Arnsten JH, Freeman R, Howard AA, Floris-Moore M, Santoro N, Schoenbaum EE (2006). HIV infection and bone mineral density in middle-aged women. *Clin Infect Dis* 42:1014–1020.

Asin SN, Heimberg AM, Eszterhas C, Rollenhagen C, Howell AL (2008). Estradiol and progesterone regulate HIV type 1 replication in peripheral blood cells. *AIDS Res Hum Retrov* 24(5):701–716.

Boonyanurak P, Bunupuradah T, Wilawan K, et al. (2012). Age at menopause and menopause-related symptoms in human immunodeficiency virus-infected Thai women. *Menopause* 19(7):820–824.

Brettle RP, Leen C (1991). The natural history of HIV and AIDS in women [editorial]. *AIDS* 5:1283–1292.

Bromberger JT, Kravitz HM, Chang YF, Cyranowski JM, Brown C, Matthews KA (2011). Major depression during and after the menopausal transition: study of women's health across the nation. *Psychol Med* 41(9):1879–1888.

Calvert C, Ronsmans C (2015). Pregnancy and HIV disease progression: a systematic review and meta-analysis. *Trop Med Int Health* 20:122–145.

Campbell JC, Lucea MB, Stockman JK, Draughon JE. (2013). Forced sex and HIV risk in violent relationships. *Am J Reprod Immunol.* 69(01):41–44.

Cejtin HE (2008). Gynecologic issues in the HIV-infected woman. *Infect Dis Clin North Am* 22(4):709–739.

Cejtin HE, Kalinowski A, Bacchetti P, et al. (2004). Assessment of menopause in HIV-positive women (abstract No. 15653). 15th International AIDS Conference, Thailand.

Cejtin HE, Kalinowski A, Bacchetti P, et al. (2006). Effects of human immunodeficiency virus on protracted amenorrhea and ovarian dysfunction. *Obstet Gynecol* 108:1423–1431.

Centers for Disease Control and Prevention (2013). Breastfeeding: human immunodeficiency virus (HIV) and acquired immunodeficiency virus (AIDS).

Centers for Disease Control and Prevention (CDC) (2016). HIV in the United States: at a glance. http://www.cdc.gov/hiv/statistics/overview/ataglance.html. Accessed February 10, 2017.

Clark RA, Cohn SE, Jarek C, Craven KS, Lyons C, Jacobson M, Kamemoto L (2000). Perimenopausal symptomatology among HIV-infected women at least 40 years of age. *J Acquir Immune Defic Syndr* 23:99–100.

Clark RA, Squires KE (2005). Gender-specific considerations in the antiretroviral management of HIV-infected women. *Expert Rev Anti Infect Ther* 3(2):213–227.

Cofrancesco J Jr, Shah N, Ghanem KG, et al. (2006). The effects of illicit drug use and HIV infection on sex hormone levels in women. *Gynecol Endocrinol* 22:244–251.

Cohen LS, Soares CB, Vitonis AF, Otto MW, Harlow BL (2006). Risk for new onset of depression during the menopausal transition: the Harvard study of moods and cycles. *Arch Gen Psychiatry* 63(4):385–390.

Connor EM, Sperling RS, Gelber R, et al. (1994). Reduction of maternal–infant transmission of human immunodeficiency virus type 1 with zidovudine treatment. Paediatric AIDS Clinical Trials Group Protocol 076 Study Group. *N Engl J Med* 331:1173–1180.

Cook JA, Burke-Miller JK, Grey DD, et al. (2014). Do HIV-positive women receive depression treatment that meets best practice guidelines? *AIDS Behav* 18(6):1094–1102.

Cook JA, Grey D, Burke-Miller J, et al. (2006). Effects of treated and untreated depressive symptoms on highly active antiretroviral therapy use in a US multisite cohort of HIV-positive women. *AIDS Care* 18(2):93–100.

Cornell M, Schomaker M, Garone DB, et al (2012) Gender differences in survival among adult patients starting antiretroviral therapy in South Africa: a multicentre cohort study. *PLoS Med* 12;9(9):e1001304.

Craft SM, Delaney RO, Bautista DT, Serovich JM. (2007) Pregnancy decisions among women with HIV. *AIDS Behav* 11(6):927–935.

Currier J, Averitt Bridge D, Hagins D, et al., on behalf of the GRACE (Gender, Race, And Clinical Experience) Study Group (2010). Sex-based outcomes of darunavir-ritonavir therapy: a single-group trial. *Ann Intern Med* 153(6):349–357.

DAD Study Group, Friis-Moller N, Reiss P, et al. (2007). Class of antiretroviral drugs and the risk of myocardial infarction. *N Engl J Med* 356:1723–1735.

de Pommerol M, Hessamfar M, Lawson-Ayayi S, et al. (2011). Menopause and HIV infection: age at onset and associated factors, ANRS CO3 Aquitaine Cohort. *Int J STD AIDS* 22:67–72.

DHHS Panel on Antiretroviral Guidelines for Adults and Adolescents (2016). Guidelines for the use of antiretroviral agents in HIV-1-infected adults and adolescents. Department of Health and Human Services. http://aidsinfo.nih.gov/contentfiles/lvguidelines/AdultandAdolescentGL.pdf. Accessed Febrary 10, 2017.

Erhabor O, Akani CI, Eyindah CE. Reproductive health options among HIV-infected persons in the low-income Niger Delta of Nigeria (2012). *HIV AIDS (Auckl)* 4:29–35.

European Collaborative Study (2005). Mother-to-child transmission of HIV infection in the era of highly active antiretroviral therapy. *Clin Infect Dis* 40:458–465.

Fan MD, Maslow BS, Santoro N, Schoenbaum E (2008). HIV and the menopause. *Menopause Int* 14:163–168.

Fantry LE, Zhan M, Taylor GH, Sill AM, Flaws JA (2005). Age of menopause and menopausal symptoms in HIV-infected women. *AIDS Patient Care* 19:703–711.

Farzadegan H, Hoover DR, Astemborski J, et al. (1998) Sex differences in HIV-1 viral load and progression to AIDS. *Lancet* 352:1510–1514.

Ferreira CE, Pinto-Neto AM, Conde DM, Costa-Paiva L, Morais SS, Magalhaes J (2007). Menopause symptoms in women infected with HIV: prevalence and associated factors. *Gynecol Endocrinol* 23:198–205.

Fish EN (2008). The X-files in immunity: sex-based differences predispose immune responses. *Nat Rev Immunol* 8(9):737–744.

Gandhi M, Aweeka F, Greenblatt RM (2004). Sex differences in pharmacokinetics and pharmacodynamics. *Annu Rev Pharmacol* 44:499–523.

Gold EB, Bromberger J, Crawford S, Samuels S, Greendale GA, Harlow SD, Skurnick J (2001). Factors associated with age at natural menopause in a multiethnic sample of midlife women. *Am J Epidemiol* 153:865–874.

Grinsztejn B, Smeaton L, Barnett R, et al. (2011). Sex-associated differences in pre-antiretroviral therapy plasma HIV-1 RNA in diverse areas of the world vary by CD4(+) T-cell count. *Antivir Ther* 16(7):1057–1062.

Günthard HF, Aberg JA, Eron JJ, et al. (2014). Antiretroviral treatment of adult HIV infection. *JAMA* 312(4):410.

Hall E, Frey BN, Soares CN (2011). Non-hormonal treatment strategies for vasomotor symptoms. *Drugs* 71(3):287–304.

Harlow SD, Gass M, Hall JE, et al. (2012). Executive summary of the States of Reproductive Aging Workshop +1-: addressing the unfinished agenda of staging reproductive aging. *J Clin Endocrinol Metab* 97:1159–1168.

Hawkins C, Chalamilla G, Okuma J, Spiegelman D. (2011). Sex differences in antiretroviral treatment outcomes among HIV-infected adults in an urban Tanzanian setting. *AIDS* 5(9):1189–1897.

Heaton RK, Franklin DR, Ellis RJ, et al. (2011). HIV-associated neurocognitive disorders before and during the era of combination antiretroviral therapy: differences in rates, nature, and predictors. *J Neurovirol* 17(1):3–16.

Hernando V, Alejos B, Álvarez D, et al. (2014). Reproductive desire in women with HIV infection in Spain, associated factors and motivations: a mixed-method study. *BMC Pregnancy Childbirth* 14:194.

High KP, Brennan-Ing M, Clifford DB, et al. (2012). HIV and aging: state of knowledge and areas of critical need for research. A report to the NIH Office of AIDS Research by the HIV and Aging Working Group. *J Acquir Immune Defic Syndr* 60(S1):S1–S18.

Himelhoch S, Medoff DR. (2005). Efficacy of antidepressant medication among HIV-positive individuals with depression: a systematic review and meta-analysis. *AIDS Patient Care STDs* 19(12):813–822.

Hodder S, Arasteh K, De Wet J, et al. (2012). Effect of gender and race on the week 48 findings in treatment-naïve, HIV-1-infected patients enrolled in the randomized, phase III trials ECHO and THRIVE. *HIV Med* 13(7):406–415.

Homsy J, Bunnell R, Moore D, et al. (2009). Reproductive intentions and outcomes among women on antiretroviral therapy in rural Uganda: a prospective cohort study. *PLoS One* 4(1):e4149.

Ickovics JR, Rodin J (1992). Women and AIDS in the United States: epidemiology, natural history, and mediating mechanisms. *Health Psychol* 11(1):1–16.

Imai K, Sutton MY, Mdodo R, del Rio C (2013). HIV and menopause: a systematic review of the effects of infection on age at menopause and the effects of menopause on response to antiretroviral therapy. *Obstet Gynecol Int* 2013:340309.

Ivanova EL, Hart TA, Wagner AC, Aljassem K, Loutfy MR (2012). Correlates of anxiety in women living with HIV of reproductive age. *AIDS Behav* 16(8):2181–2191.

Jarrín I, Geskus R, Bhaskaran K, et al. (2008) Gender differences in HIV progression to AIDS and death in industrialized countries: slower disease progression following HIV seroconversion in women. *Am J Epidemiol* 168(5):532–540.

Jones DL, Kashy D, Villar-Loubet OM, Cook R, Weiss SM (2013). The impact of substance use, sexual trauma, and intimate partner violence on sexual risk intervention outcomes in couples: a randomized trial. *Ann Behav Med* 45:318–328.

Kalayjian RC, Landay A, Pollard RB, et al.; Adult AIDS Clinical Trials Group 5015 and 5113 Protocol Teams (2003). Age-related immune dysfunction in health and in human immunodeficiency virus (HIV) disease: association of age and HIV infection with naïve CD8+ cell depletion, reduced expression of CD28 on CD8+ cells, and reduced thymic volumes. *J Infect Dis* 187(12):1924–1933.

Kang M, Fantry LE (2016). Menopause in HIV-infected women. *JCOM* 23(1):22–33.

Kiser KL, Badowski ME (2010). Risk factors for venous thromboembolism in patients with human immunodeficiency virus infection. *Pharmacotherapy* 30(12):10.

Lake JE, Currier JS (2010). Switching antiretroviral therapy to minimize metabolic complications. *HIV Therapy* 4(6):693–711.

Lake JE, Currier JS (2013). Metabolic disease in HIV infection. *Lancet Infect Dis* 13(11):964–975.

Lake JE, Wohl D, Scherzer R, Grunfeld C, Tien PC, Sidney S, Currier JS (2011). Regional fat deposition and cardiovascular risk in HIV infection: the FRAM Study. *AIDS Care* 23(8):929–938.

Lang DL, Salazar LF, Wingwood GM, DiClemente RJ, Mikhail I (2007). Associations between recent gender-based violence and pregnancy, sexually transmitted infections, condom use practices, and negotiation of sexual practices among HIV-positive women. *J Acquir Immune Defic Syndr* 46(2):216–221.

Lemly DC, Shepherd BE, Hulgan T (2009). Race and sex differences in antiretroviral therapy use and mortality among HIV-infected persons in care. *J Infect Dis* 199(7):991-998.

Lennox JL, Landovitz RJ, Ribaudo HJ, et al. (2014). Efficacy and tolerability of 3 nonnucleoside reverse transcriptase inhibitor-sparing antiretroviral regimens for treatment-naive volunteers infected with HIV-1: a randomized, controlled equivalence trial. *Ann Intern Med* 161(7):461–71.

Li Y, Marshall CM, Rees HC, Nunez A, Ezeanolue EE, Ehiri JE (2014). Intimate partner violence and HIV infection among women: a systematic review and meta-analysis. *J Int AIDS Soc* 17(1):18845.

Looby SE, Shufren J, Corless I, Rope A, Pedersen MC, Joffe H, Grinspoon S (2013). Increased hot flash sevierty and related interference in perimenopausal human immunodeficiency virus-infected women. *Menopause* 21(4):403–409.

Lopez EJ, Jones DL, Villar-Koubet OM, Arheart KL, Weiss SM (2010). Violence, coping, and consistent medication adherence in HIV-positive couples. *AIDS Educ Prev* 22(1):61–68.

Lui-Filho JF, Valadares ALR, Gomes DC, Amaral E, Pinto-Neto AM, Costa-Paiva L (2013). Menopausal symptoms and associated factors in HIV-positive women. *Maturitas* 76:172–178.

Maki PM, Rubin LH, Cohen M, et al. (2012). Depressive symptoms are increased in the early perimenopausal stage in ethnically diverse HIV+ and HIV- women. *Menopause* 19(11):1215–1223.

Mellons M, Ouyang P, Schreiner PJ, Herrington DM, Vaidya D (2012). Early menopause predicts future coronary heart disease and stroke: the multi-ethnic study of atherosclerosis. *Menopause* 19(10):1081–1087.

Miller SA, Santora N, Lo Y, et al. (2005). Menopause symptoms in HIV-infected and drug-using women. *Menopause* 12(3):348–356.

Möbius U, Lubach-Ruitman M, Castro-Frenzel B, et al. (2005). Switching to atazanavir improves metabolic disorders in antiretroviral-experienced patients with severe hyperlipidemia. *J Acquir Immune Defic Syndr* 39(2):174–180.

Mollan KR, Smurzynski M, Eron JJ, et al. (2014). Association between efavirenz as initial therapy for HIV-1 infection and increased risk for suicidal ideation or attempted or completed suicide. *Ann Intern Med* 161(1):1.

Mondul AM, Rodriguez C, Jacobs EJ, Calle EE (2005). Age at natural menopause and cause-specific mortality. *Am J Epidemiol* 162:1089–1097.

Newell ML, Huang S, Fiore S, et al. (2007). Characteristics and management of HIV-1-infected pregnant women enrolled in a randomised trial: differences between Europe and the USA. *BMC Infect Dis* 20;7:60.

Patterson KB, Cohn SE, Uyanik J, Hughes M, Smurzynski, Eron JJ (2009). Treatment responses in antiretroviral treatment naïve premenopausal and postmenopausal HIV-1-infected women: an analysis from AIDS clinical trials group studies. *Clin Infect Dis* 49(3):473–476.

Prendergast AJ, Essajee S, Penazzato M (2015). HIV and the Millennium Development Goals. *Arch Dis Child* 100(Suppl 1):S48–S52.

Proceedings from the NIH State-of-the-Science Conference on Management of Menopause-Related Symptoms (2005). *Am J Med* 118(Suppl 12B):1–171.

Rabkin GR (2008). HIV and depression: 2008 review and update. *Curr HIV/AIDS Rep* 5:163–171.

Raj A, Silverman JG, Amaro H (2004). Abused women report greater male partner risk and gender-based risk for HIV: findings from a community-based study with Hispanic women. *AIDS Care* 16(4):519–529.

Rilipivirine package insert (2017). http://www.edurant.com/patients/full-product-information, accessed February 10, 2017.

Rosin C, Elzi L, Thurnheer C, et al. (2015). Gender inequalities in the response to combination antiretroviral therapy over time: the Swiss HIV Cohort Study. *HIV Med* 16(5):319–325.

Ruel TD, Zanoni BC, Ssewanyana I (2011). Sex differences in HIV RNA level and CD4 cell percentage during childhood. *Clin Infect Dis* 53:592–599.

Schambelan M, Benson CA, Carr A, et al. (2002). Management of metabolic complications associated with antiretroviral therapy for HIV-1 infection: recommendations of an International AIDS Society-USA panel. *J Acquir Immune Defic Syndr* 31(3):257–275.

Schoenbaum EE, Hartel D, Lo Y, Howard AA, Floris-Moore M, Arnsten JH, Santoro N (2005). HIV infection, drug use, and onset of natural menopause. *Clin Infect Dis* 41:1517–1524.

Schwartz RM, Weber KM, Schechter GE, Connors NC, Gousse Y, Young MA, Cohen MH (2014). Psychosocial correlates of gender-based violence among HIV-infected and HIV-uninfected women in three US cities. *AIDS Patient Care STDs* 28(5):260–267.

Senanyake P (2000). Women and reproductive health in a graying world. *Int J Gynecol Obstet* 70(1):59–67.

Silverman JG (2010). Key to prevent HIV in women: reduce gender-based violence. *Lancet* 376:6–7.

Sowers M, Zheng K, Tomey K, et al. (2007). Changes in body composition in women over six years at midlife: ovarian and chronological aging. *J Clin Endocr Metab* 92(3):895–901.

Sterling TR, Lyles CM, Vlahov D (1999). Sex differences in longitudinal human immunodeficiency virus type 1 RNA levels among seroconverters. *J Infect Dis* 180(3):666–672.

Stockman JK, Campbell JC, Celentano DD (2010). Sexual violence and HIV risk behaviors among a nationally representative sample of heterosexual American women: the importance of sexual coercion. *J Acquir Immune Defic Syndr* 53(1):136–143.

Stockman JK, Lucea MB, Draughon JE, et al. (2013). Intimate partner violence and HIV risk factors among African American and African Caribbean women in clinic-based settings. *AIDS Care* 25(4):472–480.

Tai JH, Udoji MA, Barkanic G, et al. (2007) Pregnancy and HIV disease progression during the era of highly active antiretroviral therapy. *J Infect Dis* 196:1044–1052.

Taylor TN, Weedon J, Golub ET, et al. (2015). Longitudinal trends in sexual behaviors with advancing age and menopause among women with and without HIV-1 infection. *AIDS Behav* 19(5):931–940.

TEMPRANO ANRS 12136 Study Group (2015). A trial of early antiretrovirals and isoniazid preventive therapy in Africa. *N Engl J Med* 373:808–822.

Thomas KH, Martin RM, Potokar J, Pirmohamed M, Gunnell D (2014). Reporting of drug induced depression and fatal and non-fatal suicidal behaviour in the UK from 1998 to 2011. *BMC Pharmacol Toxicol* 15(1):1–11.

Umeh O, Currier JS (2005). Sex differences in HIV: natural history, pharmacokinetics, and drug toxicity. *Curr Infect Dis Rep* 7(1):73–78.

Umeh OC, Currier JS, Park J.-G, Cramer Y, Hermes AE, Fletcher CV. (2011). Sex differences in lopinavir and ritonavir pharmacokinetics among HIV-infected women and men. *J Clin Pharmacol* 51(12):1665–1673.

UNAIDS (2013). *GAP Report*. http://www.unaids.org/en/resources/campaigns/2014/2014gapreport/gapreport. Accessed February 10, 2017.

Walubo A (2007). The role of cytochrome P450 in antiretroviral interactions. *Expert Opin Drug Metab Toxicol* 3:583–598.

Waters L, Fisher M, Winston A, Higgs C, Hadley W (2011). A phase IV, double-blind, multicentre, randomized, placebo-controlled, pilot study to assess the feasibility of switching individuals receiving efavirenz with continuing. *AIDS* 25(1):65–71.

Wilson TE, Jean-Louis G, Schwartz R, et al. (2010). HIV infection and women's sexual functioning. *J Acquir Immune Defic Syndr* 54(4):360–367.

Woods BF, Smith-DiJulio K, Percival DB, Tao EY, Mariella A, Mitchell S (2008). Depressed mood during the menopausal transition and early postmenopause: observations from the Seattle Midlife Women's Health Study. *Menopause* 15(2):223–232.

World Health Organization (2010). Breast is always best, even for HIV-positive mothers. *Bull World Health Organ* 88(1):1–80.

World Heath Organization (2014). March 2014 supplement to the 2013 consolidated guidelines on the use of antiretroviral drugs for treating and preventing HIV infection. Recommendations for a public health approach. http://www.who.int/hiv/pub/guidelines/arv2013/arvs2013upplement_march2014/en/. Accessed February 10, 2017.

36.

OLDER AGE AND HIV

Karl Goodkin, David M. Stoff, Dilip V. Jeste, and Maria J. Marquine

As recently as the late 1990s, the issue of older age and HIV infection was not considered to be a significant concern. Currently, over 4.2 million people aged 50 years and older are living with HIV worldwide (UNAIDS, 2014). A total of 13% of the world adult population living with HIV is 50 years of age or over. In 2012, there were an estimated 2.9 million people 50 years of age or over living with HIV in low- and middle-income countries. In high-income countries, approximately 30% of all adults living with HIV are aged 50 years and over. The proportion of adults living with HIV 50 years of age or over has increased in all regions worldwide at varying rates since 2007. The Centers for Disease Control and Prevention (CDC) has defined "older age" in HIV infection by a cut-off of 50 years of age. Of note, about 31% of people living with HIV infection in the United States were 50 years of age or older in 2008, compared with 17% in 2001. By the end of 2017, it is estimated that 50% of persons living with HIV in the United States will be over 50 years of age (Womack, 2012). Strategies for addressing the care of persons with HIV in older age have been developed (Abrass et al., 2011) and updated (Abrass et al., 2014).

Older age had been highly predictive of excess mortality before the era of effective antiretroviral therapy (ART), and this association generally holds at present?despite similar or higher levels of antiretroviral adherence among older patients (outside of the occurrence of significant cognitive impairment). Studies have predominantly shown that older age may decrease survival time with HIV (HIV CAUSAL Collaboration, 2010). This aging–mortality association persists after adjusting for "natural aging," which accounts for more than 50% of mortality in persons over 45 years of age (Bhaskaran et al., 2008). Differences in age-associated comorbidities may account for discrepancies across studies. Age at definition of HIV-positive serostatus and age on exposure to effective ART are both important to assess for the effect of aging generally and, specifically, on cognition, to delimit the impact of aging as a physiological process apart from other time-related factors. Given that only a small percentage of people with HIV over 50 years of age represent the "true elderly" (over 65), the future may hold significantly greater concerns.

This chapter will focus on defining phenotypes, addressing HIV prevention, identifying and treating HIV-associated neurocognitive disorders (HAND), defining psychiatric comorbidities, and addressing the phenomenon of successful aging in the older HIV-seropositive patient population.

DEFINING PHENOTYPES IN OLDER INDIVIDUALS WITH HIV

More precise definition of subgroups within the population of older persons with HIV is needed to improve specificity and promote advances in prevention, understanding of disease pathophysiology, diagnosis, and treatment. In aging research, use of the categorical variable *chronological age* may not be sufficient, because the variability of aging as a physiological process is manifested *within and between* populations. While chronological age is most frequently employed, age is a heterogeneous concept and spans other domains, including inflammatory aging, immunosenescence, metabolic aging, cognitive aging, and psychosocial aging. However, these domains likewise primarily represent adverse changes in other systems as a function of chronological age. Clinical care strategies should extend beyond a focus on chronological age alone because the process of HIV infection, like the process of aging, is shaped similarly by the individual's social, physical, cultural, and economic settings rather than solely by biological factors.

In a promising approach, several studies have searched for indicators of health and functional status in older subjects by which various objective phenotypes could be defined and distinguished from one another. Such "phenotypes" are based on *dimensions* of behavior, which may be closer to fundamental biological and psychological mechanisms than the more abstract, heterogeneous aging concept and also may be more revealing than simple chronological age. Moreover, because phenotypes ideally represent distinct clinical entities, their precise characterization could improve diagnostic accuracy and promote development of effective, targeted strategies for prevention and treatment. Hence, different phenotypes have differing pathophysiological substrates as well as differing treatment implications.

DEFINING AGING PHENOTYPES

A prerequisite for disentangling the HIV-related biological, genetic, epigenetic, and environmental factors that modulate rate and quality of human aging is the definition and

Table 36.1 PHENOTYPES OF OLDER ADULTS
WITH HIV

Disability	Dependence or difficulty in carrying out activities essential to independent living
Frailty	Physiological state of increased vulnerability to stressors
Comorbid conditions	Concurrent presence of two or more medically diagnosed diseases in the same person
Cognitive aging	Continuum of cognitive decline across domains of information processing speed, episodic and working memory, attention, abstraction/executive function, motor function, visuospatial function, and language
Premature or accelerated aging	Conditions associated with the aging process that occur at an earlier age
Successful aging	Healthy aging that is free of disability and involves engagement in prosocial and productive activities

characterization of aging phenotypes. In the aging literature, several aging phenotypes have been identified: (1) disability, (2) frailty/vulnerability, (3) comorbid conditions (commonly multiple and chronic), (4) cognitive aging, (5) premature or accelerated aging, and (6) successful aging (see Table 36.1). While these separate substituent phenotypes may represent distinct clinical entities, they may nevertheless be causally related. Indeed, for the three phenotypes that have received the most attention (i.e., disability, frailty, and multimorbidity), there have been attempts to disentangle their relationships (Fried et al., 2004). For example, both frailty and multimorbidity predict disability; disability may exacerbate frailty and comorbidity; and comorbid diseases may contribute to the development of frailty. Accelerated/premature aging and successful aging may currently be more representative of aging subtypes or aging subpopulations that deserve further characterization to determine their status as true phenotypes.

AGING PHENOTYPES
AND HIV INFECTION

Phenotypes have been studied far more in the aging field than in HIV infection. It has been observed frequently that multiple chronic disorders associated with HIV infection contribute to various aging component phenotypes (e.g., disability and frailty), and people with these chronic conditions are at greater risk of poor functional status that complicates access to healthcare, interferes with self-management, and necessitates reliance on caregivers. Thus, the development of more effective HIV interventions in aging is at least partially dependent on identifying narrower phenotypes with greater clinical validity that might be identified as treatment targets. As in the aging literature, there is evidence that HIV infection

is also characterized by specific phenotypes and their interrelationships (see Table 36.1). These phenotypes may also be used to generate a multifactorial vector toward deleterious aging outcomes of interest and may be best utilized clinically in this combined fashion. Aging substituent phenotypes have been identified, by and large, by gerontological research with non-HIV-infected populations and thus must now be reassessed and clinically evaluated overall and by risk factor in HIV-infected populations around the world.

The construct of frailty has been used to provide insight into the overall status of individuals with HIV. HIV-seropositive men are 4.5 to 10 times more likely to be frail than HIV-seronegative men, and the likelihood of being frail increases with age (Desquilbet et al., 2007). Unfortunately, neuropsychiatric comorbidity has not been included in the frailty assessments of older adults, although frail HIV-infected persons have more frequent psychiatric comorbidities, including major depressive disorder, and they also share clinical characteristics with frail older adults generally (Onen and Overton, 2011). However, we do not know whether the immunological basis for HIV-associated premature frailty is any different than in frail, uninfected older adults.

A similar question has been asked regarding the HIV "accelerated aging" phenotype: Does HIV accelerate aging through pathways and mechanisms common to the aging process, or is HIV simply an additional risk factor for a wide number of chronic conditions, thus accentuating aging? Pathai et al. (2014) have questioned the phenotype status for HIV-associated accelerated aging, suggesting that HIV is more a model of accentuated aging than accelerated aging—that is, HIV and/or ART provide an extra "hit." Indeed, whether HIV accelerates aging through an interactive or additive mechanism may be related to the outcome in question since, for example, it has been reported that there is an interactive synergistic effect in some cognitive domains (i.e., episodic memory) but additive effects in others (Goodkin et al., 2013).

For the HIV disability phenotype, a well-validated questionnaire has been developed to assess its major dimensions of physical symptoms/impairments, cognitive symptoms/impairments, mental and emotional health symptoms/impairments, uncertainty, difficulties with day-to day activities, and challenges to social inclusion (O'Brien, Bayoumi, et al., 2014). Moreover, measuring disability is important to understand the impact of HIV infection and its comorbidities.

Regarding the multimorbidity phenotype, it is necessary to always differentiate between two sets of morbidities (i.e., HIV-related morbidities for conditions that are a consequence of HIV infection—such as opportunistic infections—and non-HIV morbidities that are not directly referable to HIV infection—such as neuropsychiatric conditions). It is well known that comorbidity increases markedly with aging, and this is partly because the frequency of chronic conditions rises with age (Guaraldi et al., 2014). One of the challenges in defining the HIV comorbidity phenotype is differentiating the impact of conditions predating HIV infection.

Although there is some evidence for psychosocial, clinical, physiological, and genetic predictors of successful aging (Glatt et al., 2007), the evidence is quite limited on the prevalence, correlates and clinical predictors, and underlying mechanisms for successful aging with HIV infection. Moore et al. (2014) found adverse, additive effects of older age and HIV infection in successful aging that were independent of other important clinical-demographic variables. This raises the possibility that the successful aging phenotype may be useful in targeting interventions due to its emphasis on prosocial and protective risk factors, and such interventions should be adopted in the clinical care of older persons with HIV.

HIV PREVENTION FOR OLDER ADULTS

Techniques aimed at HIV prevention among older persons are still in the early stages and require further tailoring overall and for specific subgroups of older persons. Interventions for adaptive coping have been evaluated (Heckman et al., 2001), as have interventions for increased motivation (Lovejoy, 2012) and decreased cognitive impairment (Neundorfer et al., 2004)—all in older adult men. There has been only one study of HIV risk reduction intervention in older adult woman (Eschenique et al., 2013), which suggests the need for more gender-specific HIV prevention interventions with aging. A large majority of intervention studies have been carried out at the intrapersonal level, and more attention should be paid to the community, structural, and policy levels.

HIV prevention in older adults should integrate more closely with HIV prevention approaches in other settings to maximize efficacy and translation in community settings. Prevention interventions in older adults need a focus on promoting engagement in care, antiretroviral adherence, and retention in care that is tailored to the circumstances of older HIV-infected individuals. An eventual goal should be a multifaceted integration of care that links biomarkers of disease progression (e.g., inflammatory) to behavioral (e.g., major depressive disorder) and physical health (e.g., activity level) outcomes and to interventions (e.g., antidepressants). HIV prevention has special relevance in aging because of reported delays along the continuum of care—from late HIV diagnosis (Ellman et al., 2014) to inadequate integration of healthcare resources at treatment initiation (Rueda et al., 2014) to poor adherence once cognitive impairment is manifested over years of follow-up. The field is now integrating prevention care with primary HIV care at multiple points along the continuum of care. This continuum will expand on HIV testing as the foundation, followed by linkage of HIV-uninfected persons to prevention services; retention and monitoring in prevention services; and adherence, to prevent contraction of HIV infection and transmission over time. Newly diagnosed HIV-seropositive persons also need to be engaged in care, with an emphasis on the need for risk-taking precautions.

CHALLENGES IN THE CARE OF OLDER ADULTS WITH HIV

When interpreting results of HIV prevention techniques with older adults, the most appropriate comparisons need to be determined as noted for the area of cognitive impairment and for the field overall. Over the limited number of prevention techniques developed, most included older people compared with younger or with HIV-seronegative counterparts. As discussed later in the cognitive disorder section, there are a number of challenges to identifying an HIV-uninfected comparison group, and it cannot be assumed that the general population is appropriate (Wong et al., 2014). Although older adults with HIV continue to be considered by many to be a "hard-to-reach," "hidden" population, their growing numbers will soon actually render them to be the majority population of persons with HIV. In addition to having stigma and confidentiality concerns, they are frequently also geographically isolated from traditional mental health resources. Face-to-face clinician visits are impractical for many older adults with HIV, who may find it more difficult to arrange transportation and track their visits in the face of decreased social support and increased life stressor burden. Hence, telepsychiatry may be an intervention of choice for this patient subgroup. Indeed, there have been some positive results using telephone-delivered intervention modalities (Lovejoy and Heckman, 2014). Improving access for older adults with HIV through community-based approaches may also require social-network definition and utilization (involving other persons with HIV) (Amirkhanian et al., 2014) as well as novel outreach approaches.

UNDERREPRESENTED FOCI OF ATTENTION WITH OLDER ADULTS

Most of the medical and prevention literature on HIV infection in older adults continues to focus on the aging population living long term with HIV infection (Greene et al., 2013), rather than on individuals who are newly diagnosed in older age (Goodkin et al., 2001). This is of concern because persons aged 50 and older comprised 17% of new HIV diagnoses and 25% of all AIDS diagnoses in the United States as of 2011 (Centers for Disease Control and Prevention [CDC], 2013). Further, incidence rates of new HIV infections in older adults have been steadily increasing (CDC, 2007). We clearly need to learn more about newly diagnosed HIV-infected older adults, as a relationship between increased age and late diagnosis has been reported frequently (Ellman et al., 2014). This is an especially troubling effect because late diagnosis is associated with increased immunodeficiency and clinical disease progression. There is a critical need to extend our focus beyond the traditional biomedical model (concentrating on illness[es]) to positive health, including positive mental health (Jahoda, 1953). The capacity for such resilience would be reflected by the biopsychosocial model (Engel, 1977, 1980) or, perhaps yet better, by a "biopsychosociocultural-spiritual" model.

Some have suggested a personalized care approach with preventive interventions matched to respective subpopulations (e.g., by biomarkers, genetic phenotypes, gender, health status, stressor history). Such approaches would be timely during current budgetary constraints, as it could ensure that scarce resources produce the greatest population health benefits. Moreover, it could also help to determine who might *not* benefit from a proposed intervention. Moderator analyses can help answer the question, "For whom does the intervention work best?" The challenge of tailoring care to individual risk profiles would also require adapting the timing, intensity, focus, and context of the intervention. Given the unique sociocultural histories of older minority individuals at risk for HIV infection, we need novel interventions tailored to their sociocultural context, including lifestyle patterns and stigma, for example, among older men of color who have sex with men.

Older women represented 16% of newly identified HIV-seropositive women in 2009 (CDC, 2010). Seventy percent of women aged 50 or older living with HIV/AIDS are African American or Latina (CDC, 2007). Yet, older women are frequently excluded from HIV public health campaigns and prevention resources. Older minority women are a particularly disempowered group in that they are more frequently poor, financially dependent on their male partner, traumatized, and disadvantaged in negotiating condom use. Although there is not a large disparities literature with minority older adults, a few studies do suggest an even more pronounced disparities effect (e.g., Mindt et al., 2014; Montoya and Whitsett, 2003). Moreover, the presence of comorbidities such as diabetes, hypertension, cardiovascular disease, hepatic disease, cancer, renal disease, metabolic bone disease, peripheral neuropathy, and neuropsychiatric disorders may be equally important. In addition, educational level, functional status, incarceration history, decision-making capacity, history of abuse, and the presence of known phenotypes (such as frailty) should be accounted for. The complexity of this problem is highlighted by the fact that HIV/AIDS risk behaviors themselves have recursive effects on economic, social, and political systems that relate to socioeconomic disparities. Interventions that increase utilization of active coping strategies for older women to improve relationships with their sexual partners would be expected to reduce the incidence rate of HIV infection and improve adherence.

AGING AND COGNITIVE IMPAIRMENT IN PERSONS WITH HIV

Aging is being studied more often with respect to HIV-associated neurocognitive disorder (HAND), owing to the successful, long-term management of the infection (Deeks, 2011). HIV-associated dementia (HAD) and cognitive impairment, taken generally, have been the most commonly studied targets. Mild neurocognitive disorder (MND) and asymptomatic neurocognitive impairment (ANI), as defined by the Frascati criteria (Antinori et al., 2007), have been less frequently studied. With the coining of the term *ANI, cognitive impairment* has become a more standardized diagnostic term that designates the mildest level of the HAND spectrum. Yet, since ANI requires that there is no functional status decrement in activities of daily living, it is more properly diagnosed as a "condition" rather than a "disorder" per se. As some symptoms may occur with ANI, ANI might be more properly designated as "subclinical cognitive impairment."

Older age has long been known to be associated with cognitive impairment in HIV infection (Janssen et al., 1992). Of note, the prevalence of HAND has remained similar to what it was in the era prior to effective ART, at about 50% (Heaton et al., 2010). While the prevalence has been sustained overall, the distribution of severity has been dampened so that the most severe condition (HAD) is much less frequent and MND and ANI are more frequent, respectively. Older age has been shown to be a significant risk factor for HAD (Chiesi et al., 1996). Valcour et al. (2004) subsequently demonstrated this relationship with extensive controls for education, race, substance dependence, antiretroviral medication status, viral load, CD4 cell count, and Beck Depression Inventory score. Larussa et al. (2006) reported older age as a risk factor for HAD among antiretroviral-naive but not experienced participants, suggesting a possible neuroprotective effect of effective ART. However, this has not been consistently reported (Valcour et al., 2004). The relationship between older age and MND is much less well studied than HAD, but there are data predating the use of "MND," using its earlier equivalent "minor cognitive motor disorder" (MCMD). The frequency of MCMD symptoms was reported to be higher among older persons with HIV (Goodkin et al., 2001). This has been reported in both primary English and Spanish speakers. However, for older Spanish speakers a significant difference for older age was seen in late-stage disease (AIDS) but not in the early symptomatic stage, suggesting a possible protective effect of Hispanic ethnicity. It is important to include HIV-seronegative controls and consideration of potential treatment effects in such studies, as the underlying manifestations of HAND are not specific for HIV infection and overlap with age-associated changes and phenotypes. Larussa et al. (2006) did not observe a relationship between aging and the diagnosis of MCMD. However, age was defined by three categorical levels (20 to 39, 40 to 49, and >50 years of age). This definition could have diluted the potential for finding a relationship compared to defining age as a continuous measure. In addition, a "report" of MCMD to a central registry was relied on as the source of MCMD diagnosis, and an analysis of MCMD symptom frequency was not conducted. Thus, a diagnostic bias could have been operating. Nevertheless, this study supports the need for future research with increased controls to account for other cofactors affecting cognitive performance in the setting of older age and MND, as mentioned in the section on prevention.

Another related area of concern to diagnostic bias in determining the association of aging with level of HAND is the use of an entirely different diagnostic system, introduced with the publication of the DSM-5 (American Psychiatric Association [APA], 2013). The DSM-5 neurocognitive diagnoses of major and mild neurocognitive disorder are not specific to HIV infection. Although the subtyping of the DSM-5 diagnosis does require demonstration of positive HIV serostatus, no specific diagnostic criteria for HIV-associated cognitive disorder are put forward. In addition, only one cognitive area is required by DSM-5, rather than two (per the Frascati criteria), to define a level of impairment associated with the "global" deterioration of function implied by the term *cognitive disorder* (whether major or mild). The DSM-5 requires neither explicit quantification of cognitive deficits nor functional status deficits that extend beyond the specific aspect of "independence," whereas quantified cognitive impairment and generalized functional status deficits related to such impairment are necessary for HAND diagnosis per the Frascati criteria. Moreover, the exclusion criteria required for these diagnoses are limited to other psychiatric disorders per the DSM-5 but should explicitly include central nervous system (CNS) illnesses specific to the setting of immunodeficiency caused by HIV infection, as noted by both the original American Academy of Neurology (AAN) criteria (AAN, 1991) and the current Frascati conference-based criteria (Antinori et al., 2007). These disparities in cognitive disorder criteria could lead to difficulty with interpreting the literature in the future.

Most evidence on the cognitive performance of older HIV-infected individuals has been derived without the benefit of a clinical diagnosis by level of HAND severity. Early work used variable definitions of "older age" with low cut-offs (in the 40s) and small sample sizes of older participants (Hardy et al., 1999). The results were variable; however, larger interindividual variation within the "older" groups was documented. Of note, accounting for this variability, there was a relative lack of control variables employed in these studies (Wilkie et al., 2003). In this early period, Hinkin et al. (2001) reported an interaction between older age (>50 years) and HIV-associated disease progression on cognitive impairment in which older persons with progression to AIDS had a higher rate of cognitive impairment than the other groups. Yet, once again, utilization of control variables could have been enhanced. Generally in this area, while controls for educational level and HIV disease stage were used, controls for ethnicity, gender, HIV risk factor, CNS penetration of antiretroviral regimen used, adherence level, depressed mood level, and substance use were only variably included.

Another issue in the field has been has been the variation in the number of cognitive domains assessed to define HAND. Associated with this concern is a relative lack of focus on the domain of working memory (formerly "short-term memory"). A number of reviews have concluded that the prevalence of ANI might be overestimated by current criteria and, specifically, that the criteria for defining impairment might be too mild quantitatively and oversampled (Meyer et al., 2013). The Frascati conference criteria recommend examining multiple domains: (1) verbal/language, (2) attention/working memory, (3) abstraction/executive function, (4) memory (learning; recall), (5) speed of information processing, (6) sensory-perceptual, and (7) motor skills. No upper limit of domains was set for assessment. Further, numerous tests were allowed to be sampled per domain, and, sometimes, multiple scores were used from the tests conducted. This specification for sampling of domains renders the possibility of spurious cognitive impairment to be significantly increased—an issue that might be expected to disproportionately affect the older person with HIV. This argument would also apply to using the cut-off of 1.0 SD versus less sensitive cut-offs, such as 1.5 SDs—of specific relevance to the overdiagnosis of MND and ANI. Certainly, age-adjusted norms are important for evaluating older patients, using the more sensitive cut-offs. Given the recent addition of the condition of ANI to the cognitive disorders previously identified as associated with HIV infection (Antinori et al., 2007), a specific focus on aging and this condition would be of special interest. Although one study (Grant et al., 2014) suggests that ANI increases the risk for cognitive progression, very few data are currently available to support this conclusion. It might be another concern that, within the spectrum of HAND, ANI is the most likely condition to spontaneously revert to normal simply on retesting with no other interceding intervention.

Finally, the field has been negatively impacted by variation among studies in the definition of older age and the extent to which the older age range was well represented. As the trajectory of the epidemic continues to expand into the higher age range of older persons with HIV infection to a significant percentage over 65, it is likely that deleterious cognitive outcomes will become yet more prominent and possibly change in profile as well. It is particularly important that age be studied more as a biopsychosocial process rather than simply as chronological time—and as a process with multiple characteristics (immunological, inflammatory, metabolic, cognitive, and psychosocial).

Given the complexity of the aging relationship with HIV infection, a single-variable predictor of HAND is unlikely to provide a major contribution to assessing risk for cognitive impairment in the older patient on effective ART. The potential for cognitive impairment due to HIV infection to be confounded with others causes among older patients is much greater than that among younger patients—owing to the high frequency of both medical and psychiatric comorbidities affecting cognitive performance in older patients. In fact, HAND severity has been dampened at this point in the era of effective ART to the extent that HAND might currently be considered by some to represent an "invisible epidemic" in persons with HIV. Risk factors commonly focused on for HAND before the era of effective ART were lower educational level, higher systemic disease progression, a history of CNS disease, a low CD4 cell count, and high plasma and cerebrospinal fluid (CSF) viral loads. The latter two risk factors have not been maintained in the era of effective ART, and, in fact, currently no laboratory or neuroimaging measure has been identified with HAND consistently enough to be considered pathognomonic. More recent risk factors identified for HAND include presence of medical comorbidities associated with risk for cognitive impairment in the general population, such as diabetes and hypertension (and associated vascular compromise), hepatitis C virus (HCV) co-infection (and associated HCV effects on brain tissue), a sustained inflammatory response to HIV in the face of durably suppressed plasma viral load (with elevated systemic inflammatory markers—e.g., serum levels of interleukin-6, d-dimer and C-reactive protein), antiretroviral toxicity (dyslipidemia associated with lipodystrophy syndrome), and poor penetration of antiretroviral regimens into the CNS (although there continues to be controversy about the impact of this factor). Significant evidence has also supported the possibility that proviral load of HIV in peripheral blood mononuclear cells may be predictive (Shiramizu et al., 2005), reflecting the latent reservoir of HIV.

As a result of the failure of single-variable predictors for HAND, multivariate indices of cognitive impairment have been explored more frequently. One such index is the Veterans Aging Cohort Study (VACS) Index, which has been shown to be predictive of mortality and combines age, plasma HIV RNA load, and concurrent CD4 cell count with non-HIV-associated measures (renal function, liver function, anemia, and HCV antibody status) (Justice et al., 2013). In one recent study, although the effect size was relatively small, a higher VACS Index score was associated with risk for global cognitive impairment at an odds ratio of 1.2 and was a useful predictor of such impairment beyond the CD4 nadir and estimated duration of HIV infection (Marquine et al., 2014). Older age, low hemoglobin level, and low CD4 cell count were the VACS components that were strongly linked to cognitive impairment. Of note, the VACS Index has been shown to have good generalizability to other populations for estimating risk for mortality, but its association with cognitive function is weaker among Hispanics than among non-Hispanic whites (Marquine et al., 2016).

In terms of cognitive domains of interest in the older person with HIV, the established focus on information processing speed and verbal memory continues to be prominent. For the most part, as mentioned earlier, the initial studies of cognitive impairment in HIV infection did not focus specifically on working memory as a separate domain. Yet, working memory is adversely impacted by HIV infection because of the effects of HIV on the frontal lobes and its connecting pathways to subcortical white matter and the basal ganglia (Castellon et al., 1998; Hardy et al., 2010; Stout et al., 1998; Woods et al., 2010). Of further interest, working memory has been shown to mediate a variety of neurocognitive processes in other domains, such as perception (Soto et al., 2010), attention (Dalton et al., 2009; Makovski and Jiang, 2009), and inhibition of saccades (Roberts et al., 1994), as well as more complex processes, including abstract reasoning (Unsworth et al., 2009), reading comprehension (Engle et al., 1992), and fluid intelligence (Troche and Rammsayer, 2009). It has been suggested that working memory acts as a gateway to progressing impairment across multiple domains in HIV infection (Goodkin et al., 2009), and variation in the development of working memory deficits over time could contribute to the early observation of a greater variability of cognitive performance and a dispersion of deficits across multiple domains in older HIV-infected persons (Hardy et al., 1999). In addition, a portion of this cognitive variability with aging may reflect a merging of the impact of deficits in the early stages of HIV infection predominantly involving subcortical regions with the later impact of progression of those deficits superimposed on the accumulation of non-HIV-comorbidity-associated deficits that preferentially affect cortical regions.

Initially, there was interest in the possibility that age and HIV infection in brain might act synergistically to induce cognitive impairment. Subsequently, studies suggested that there was more evidence for additive effects rather than interactions (Ances et al., 2012; Cysique et al., 2011; Pathai et al., 2014), contrary to the indication of a true synergism between these two causes of cognitive impairment. Of note, data were reported (Goodkin et al., 2013) from 5,086 participants in the Multicenter AIDS Cohort Study (MACS) (2,278 were HIV infected [20,477 visits]; 2,808 were HIV seronegative [27,409 visits]) examining cognitive outcomes in the domains of executive function, information processing speed, working memory, episodic memory, and motor functions. This study controlled extensively for other influences on cognitive function, including ethnicity, education, household income, body mass index, body weight, depressed mood, antiretroviral therapy period, diabetes, hypertension, psychotropic medication use, pain, fatigue, history of infection with hepatitis C and B viruses, and history of cigarette smoking, alcohol, and substance use. In addition, the duration of HIV infection was controlled in a subsample. The results (Goodkin et al., 2013) showed that older age was significantly associated with poor performance in all cognitive domains independent of HIV disease stage and that HIV disease stage was significantly associated with cognitive outcomes in all domains, independent of the effects of age. Clinical AIDS was associated with poorer performance in every case. Additionally and most importantly, significant interactions were observed between age and HIV disease stage in the domains of episodic memory and motor function, after controlling for duration of HIV infection and the other aforementioned covariates. Related to this finding, the issue of accelerated (interaction) versus accentuated (additive) effects of aging on HIV-associated cognitive impairment is of great import, yet remains controversial. Perhaps, the issue of whether aging is reflecting additive effects to those of HIV infection in terms of HIV-associated cognitive impairment and HIV progression more generally is oversimplified. It is most probably not a clear-cut distinction in all outcome areas but more likely a matter of differential relationships that define a multivariate vector toward deficits according to which outcome is being examined. This study supports such an interpretation with respect to the area of cognitive impairment.

Advancing hypotheses about the foregoing issue one step further, it is possible that there are separate, clinically definable "phenotypes" with different profiles of cognitive impairment by domain within the population of older HIV-infected patients with cognitive impairment. One use for identifying such phenotypes is the potential ability they provide to uncover possible differential pathophysiological underpinnings to these profiles. Yet, an additional step would be to consider the possibility that each phenotype could have differential pathophysiological underpinnings manifesting together as one phenotype within the larger set of phenotypes in the older HIV-infected patient population with cognitive impairment. For example, host genetic associations have been published for HAND related to different CCR5, MCP-1, and TNF-a polymorphisms as well as to CCL3L1 copy number (Gonzalez et al., 2005). It is possible that these varying genetic associations could be manifested by the same clinical phenotype, leading to the definition of "endophenotypes." Given the expectation that there are multiple sources of cognitive impairment in older persons with HIV that may be associated with both primary medical and psychiatric comorbidities (e.g., diabetes, hypertension, pain, fatigue, depressive disorders), clinical research should aim to dissect out the specific associations of cognitive performance with these comorbidities so that the effect of treatment on cognitive impairment would be more readily identifiable, which could, in turn, help guide future treatment of age-specific cognitive deficits as well.

TREATMENT STRATEGIES FOR COGNITIVE IMPAIRMENT IN OLDER PERSONS WITH HIV INFECTION

Much less has been reported on the treatment of HAND than on issues related to CNS pathophysiology and diagnoses overall. Specifically with reference to aging, HAD has been better studied than either MND or ANI. Currently, consensus recommendations on the treatment of HAND suggest the utility of a stable, effective ART regimen. It should be noted that ART also constitutes effective prevention of HIV transmission, which may be of particular value among older persons, as they have been shown to be less likely to take recommended risk precautions. The recent change in antiretroviral recommendations to include (rather than offer) ART for individuals with early HIV infection (DHHS Panel on Antiretroviral Guidelines for Adults and Adolescents, 2016) could have a preventive effect in the CNS (Spudich, 2016). Beyond this recommendation, the American Psychiatric Association Practice Guidelines for HIV/AIDS (Forstein et al., 2006; McDaniel et al., 2000), the Guide for HIV/AIDS Clinical Care (U.S. DHHS, 2014), and the American Academy of HIV Medicine's (AAHIVM's) HIV Aging and Consensus Project—Recommended Treatment Strategies for Clinicians Managing Older Patients with HIV (Abrass et al., 2011, 2014) recommend the use of specific CNS-penetrating ART regimens and the psychostimulants. There remain no large-scale, longitudinal, randomized, double-blind, placebo-controlled clinical trials that have consistently demonstrated efficacy to expand the recommendations beyond these classes of medications. Furthermore, there is yet less evidence for specific antiretroviral medication strategies for HAND in older patients. Issues in this area include the fact that antiretroviral medication dosing and total intake need to be weighed against expected benefits from CNS penetration and from synergistic effects anticipated across antiretroviral mechanisms of action in order to derive proper conclusions, especially with more data showing the potential clinical neurotoxicity of the antiretrovirals and the increased potential for drug–drug interactions in older persons. Of note regarding the well-established neurotoxicity of efavirenz, the deleterious effects of this agent may be expected to decrease with the recent change deleting it from the recommended category for treatment-naïve patients (DHHS Panel on Antiretroviral Guidelines for Adults and Adolescents, 2016), because of concerns about its

tolerability?especially the high rate CNS toxicities?and a possible association with suicidality.

The CSF-penetrating antiretroviral medications have received the greatest attention. These have been followed by the psychostimulants, which increase dopaminergic transmission and also treat frequently comorbid fatigue. Dopaminergic agonists have also garnered some supportive evidence over time. Neurotransmitter manipulation more generally has been considered of treatment relevance, with a recent focus on the selective serotonin reuptake inhibitors (SSRIs) in terms not only of enhancement of serotonergic transmission but also of primary neurotrophic effects and suppression of macrophage activation. Increased dopaminergic and serotonergic transmission by these agents is likely to be of particular value for the older patient, given that both HIV infection and aging are associated with losses of dopaminergic and serotonergic function. Another strategy is to aggressively treat comorbidities that affect cognitive function and optimize their control, which is especially important in the aging population. Strategies with less empirical support but significant clinical potential include the use of anti-inflammatory agents active in the CNS, dietary manipulation, physical and mental exercise, and cognitive rehabilitative techniques in the older patient.

ANTIRETROVIRAL MEDICATIONS AND HAND IN OLDER PATIENTS

Currently, consensus recommendations on the treatment of HAND are concordant in a focus on the use of a stable, effective ART regimen as a template. Yet, to date, results supporting specific agents are limited. Historically, the use of zidovudine (ZDV) (Sidtis et al., 1993) and, to a lesser extent, abacavir, nevirapine, and indinavir had been reported to be potentially useful. The more recently approved agents acting by novel mechanisms, such as maraviroc (a CCR5 antagonist) and raltegravir (an integrase inhibitor), are of current interest and have received some evidence of efficacy in HAND, with dolutegravir, a new integrase inhibitor, under study. While ZDV was reported early to have a CSF/plasma ratio of 0.60 associated with its cognitive effects, it should be noted that ZDV clearance is reduced in older patients, increasing its well-recognized toxicities beyond those known to occur in the general patient population. In addition, and of relevance to limitations on the specific focus of augmenting CNS penetration, the CSF/plasma ratio may not be the optimal indicator of drug efficacy in the CSF (and brain tissue); in contrast, reaching the 90% inhibitory concentration (IC_{90}) (the inhibitory concentration of drug needed to reduce HIV replication by 90%) in brain tissue and modifying penetration by antiretroviral resistance may be more valuable in the effort to develop CNS-specific indicators. However, the tolerated antiretroviral dosing range must be considered in order to achieve these CSF concentrations, and this is likely to be a greater issue in the older patient. The impact of these factors should also be examined further against the impact of adherence (for example, the use of fixed-dose antiretroviral co-formulations).

Evidence of the impact of other antiretrovirals on HAND is not well studied. Regarding tenofovir, a very commonly prescribed antiretroviral, there is negligible transport of the drug across the blood–brain barrier. Although tenofovir can cross the blood–CSF barrier, it does not cross the CSF–brain barrier, reflecting the differences between these two blood–CNS interfaces (Anthonypillai et al., 2006). Further, tenofovir is associated with renal toxicity that may be exacerbated in the older patient, and it has been associated with inhibition of telomerase activity that could cause more rapid shortening of telomeres and immunosenescence. The nucleoside reverse transcriptase inhibitors (NRTIs) may cause mitochondrial toxicity more readily in older patients, with increases in peripheral neuropathy, pancreatitis, lactic acidosis, and lipoatrophy.

The most commonly prescribed non-nucleoside reverse transcriptase inhibitors (NNRTIs), nevirapine and efavirenz (EFV), readily enter CSF. Nevirapine has CSF penetration that is lower but comparable to ZDV, in large part due to its relatively low level of binding to plasma proteins. However, it may increase the likelihood of hepatotoxicity in the older patient, especially in the setting of excessive alcohol use. EFV penetrates to a lesser extent due to its very high level of plasma protein binding but has nevertheless been detected in the CSF at a mean concentration above the IC_{95} for wild-type HIV (Tashima et al., 1999). However, it is associated with CNS side effects in over 50% of patients and could be a specific concern among older patients. It has been reported to be associated with an increased risk for suicide as well as neurotoxicity.

When boosted by ritonavir, several protease inhibitors (PIs)—indinavir (which is avoided because of its toxicity in the general patient population), lopinavir, fosamprenavir, and darunavir—show good CNS penetration. However, data are limited on the efficacy of these agents for HAND, and lopinavir, at least, has been associated with increased senescence markers as well as with oxidative stress and arterial inflammation that also occur with aging. Moreover, the PIs as a class are associated with osteopenia, complicating a disposition to osteoporosis with aging, as well as dyslipidemia, complicating a disposition to myocardial infarction (MI) and cerebral vascular accident (CVA) in older patients, although significant within-class divergence exists. Maraviroc, a CCR5 antagonist, selectively and noncompetitively binds to the CCR5 molecules on the surfaces of human cells, rendering them unrecognizable by the gp120 HIV envelope glycoprotein and interrupting viral attachment and entry preferentially in the CNS. It should be noted that, as a class, CCR5 antagonists are active only against CCR5-tropic strains of HIV, which typically infect monocytes and macrophages and infect the CNS. Data from recent trials have demonstrated the activity of antiretroviral medication regimen intensification with maraviroc for HAND. Moreover, maraviroc is very well tolerated and, perhaps, a preferable treatment in older patients.

Integrase inhibitors such as raltegravir were expected to reduce the reservoir of latent HIV in brain, but subsequent data did not support this mechanism. The CNS penetration of raltegravir is good and it is well tolerated, suggesting potential preference for older patients with HAND. Less is known about elvitegravir and dolutegravir, although there is currently significant enthusiasm that dolutegravir may show efficacy

for HAND. More research needs to be conducted with the antiretrovirals in older patients generally and for HAND in particular before it can be concluded that any agents are preferred with respect to older HIV-infected patients. It can be expected that antiretroviral toxicities associated with known comorbidities should be avoided in the older patient and that the potential for drug–drug interactions to be clinically manifested needs to be actively monitored in the older patient.

PSYCHOSTIMULANTS AND HAND IN OLDER PATIENTS

The psychostimulants have garnered significant evidence for their efficacy in HAND (predominantly HAD), dating back to the late 1980s (Fernandez et al., 1988). The combination of a short-acting form of methylphenidate with a long-acting form seems to be particularly useful. The short-acting form may be used initially to establish the effective total daily dosage, followed by a switch to a longer-acting agent (twice or, preferably, once a day). This, in turn, may be followed with supplementation by pulsing with a short-acting agent to optimize regimen response. However, data supporting this specific dosing strategy are lacking. While this treatment could be considered to be "palliative," it may reverse the specific damage by HIV and aging to the dopaminergic system (Britton et al., 1989; Sardar et al., 1996) and, thus, be partly pathophysiologically based. The psychostimulants have found limited use for HAND in primary care, mostly related to their status as controlled substances. In addition, there has been the concern that some patients with a history of substance use disorder might abuse these medications, although this concern appears to have been overemphasized and applies less to the older patient. Older patients generally have been found to respond well to the psychostimulants for major depressive disorder and to tolerate them well. Nevertheless, modafinil or armodafinil might be preferred for older patients, as they have much less evidence for abuse potential and have a milder side-effect profile. It has also been suggested that bupropion and venlafaxine might be helpful, though less potent, in this context.

OTHER AGENTS FOR HAND IN OLDER PERSONS

Results with N-methyl-D-aspartate (NMDA) receptor antagonists (e.g., memantine), decreasing glutamatergic activity, have been disappointing (Schiffito et al., 2007). In addition, CNS anti-inflammatory agents (e.g., nimodipine) have been investigated to a limited extent without clear-cut benefits (Navia et al., 1998). Suggestive evidence was found for the efficacy of lexipafant, a PAF antagonist, in HAND (Schifitto et al., 1999). Anti-neurodegenerative agents are of increasing interest. Lithium, a GSK-3beta antagonist, has been suggested to be clinically effective in HAND (LeTendre et al., 2006), and valproate, an HDAC inhibitor with down-modulatory effects on GSK-3beta, also has had similar preliminary evidence for efficacy in HAND (Schiffito et al., 2006). However, neither of the latter two agents would be preferred in terms of side-effect profiles for older patients with HIV, and both have also been investigated with negative results (Cysique et al., 2006; Schifitto et al., 2009). Most recently, Sacktor et al. (2016) have suggested that paroxetine may improve HIV-associated cognitive impairment, possibly through a neurotrophic effect.

MORE GENERAL COGNITIVE TREATMENT APPROACHES FOR THE OLDER PATIENT

IN IDENTIFYING AND TREATING COMORBIDITIES

There is a high frequency of comorbid illnesses among older HIV-infected persons, and these comorbidities have been noted to increase the frequency and severity of cognitive impairment. Treating comorbidities affecting cognition is a useful initial approach to treatment for patients with ANI and MND in order to determine if an impact can be made without relying on additional pharmacotherapy specific for HIV-associated cognitive impairment. Older HIV-infected patients have comorbidities from the complications of HIV infection itself as well as from non-HIV-related illnesses common to older persons in the general population—for example, diabetes, hypertension, and coronary artery disease (CAD). Today, the most concerning comorbidities are those HIV-associated non-AIDS conditions (HANA) that might accelerate HIV-related inflammation persisting in the face of durably suppressive ART. Finally, psychiatric comorbidities of importance in older patients include major depressive disorder, which has been associated with increased CSF viral load, and alcohol/substance use disorders.

DIETARY MANIPULATION

A number of nutritional therapies have been suggested to target HIV infection of the brain. The antioxidants have received much attention. However, thioctic acid was not found to be significant in improving cognitive impairment in one well-controlled clinical trial (Dana Consortium, 1996). Vitamin B_6 deficiency has been related to increased psychological distress overall and to confusion specifically, and vitamin B_{12} deficiency, occurring in nearly 20% of patients with AIDS, has been related to cognitive impairment. Selenium deficiency has also received some attention, as it relates to glutathione peroxidase, a selenoenzyme, the depletion of which eventually may be associated with dementia. Green tea may be an effective antioxidant treatment (Nance and Shearer, 2003), the active components of which are the polyphenolic catechins, among which epigallocatechin gallate (EGCG) accounts for approximately 50%. EGCG may not only reduce HIV load but may also decrease the premature production of amyloid plaques in HIV-infected patients (Tan et al., 2014). Despite the extant evidence of the relevance of nutritional deficiencies for cognitive impairment, caution must be taken in terms of differentiating the correction of true deficiencies from supplementation above normal levels for the older HIV-infected patient. Future controlled trials of selected micronutrients are warranted and could reduce medication toxicities due to polypharmacy.

PHYSICAL AND MENTAL EXERCISE

Both physical and mental exercise have been associated with increased cognitive function in persons with HIV, and more generally in older adults. In one study of inactive older adults with cognitive complaints in the general population, 12 weeks of physical plus mental exercise was associated with significant improvement in cognitive function, with no evidence of difference between intervention and active control groups (assigned to toning and stretching versus aerobics and educational DVDs versus intensive mental activity on the computer) (Barnes et al., 2013). Hence, it could be simply that the amount of activity is most important—rather than the type or intensity—in this subject population. One self-report study of physical exercise in persons with HIV suggested that individuals who perform physical exercise are approximately half as likely to show cognitive impairment as persons who do not exercise (Dufour et al., 2013), though self-report studies of exercise frequency are subject to social desirability and other types of bias, and this study did not specify the frequency or quantity of exercise in various categories, nor did it quantify exercise over a long time span. Prospective studies of physical and mental exercise at varying intensity are needed in an HIV-infected patient population. However, caution needs to be applied to the implementation of physical exercise interventions in older patients, allowing for tailored exercise regimens to basal levels of the patient's activity with appropriate upward excursions while accounting for comorbidities and prescribed medications used.

COGNITIVE REHABILITATION TECHNIQUES FOR OLDER ADULTS WITH HIV

While research has not been consistently conducted in this area over time, one recent review reported a synthesis of intervention studies conducted with older HIV-infected patients and described the effectiveness of rehabilitation for cognitive impairment (O'Brien, Solomon, et al., 2014). Current evidence indicated that cognitive rehabilitation interventions (e.g., computerized speed of information processing training and self-generation strategies) enhanced verbal recall and cognitive function in these patients. It was concluded from this review that cognitive rehabilitation interventions (e.g., cognitive training, stimulation, and rehabilitation) may be recommended for older adults living with HIV infection with mild levels of cognitive impairment. Cognitive rehabilitation did not appear harmful, and weak evidence supported cognition-specific interventions to improve spatial neglect, disability, memory, and functional status of older HIV-infected adults having had a CVA, which is a comorbidity of increased risk with aging in HIV infection—as is CAD. Hence, clinicians should try to obtain access to and refer older patients with HIV for cognitive rehabilitation, particularly individuals with mild levels of impairment.

PSYCHIATRIC, BEHAVIORAL, AND PSYCHOSOCIAL ISSUES IN OLDER ADULTS WITH HIV

In this section, we consider psychiatric disorders other than HAND and successful aging among older adults with HIV infection.

PSYCHIATRIC DISORDERS OTHER THAN HAND

While there has been a notable increase in studies addressing psychiatric comorbidities in older HIV-infected persons during recent years, reliable and valid statewide and national epidemiological data are not yet available regarding the incidence, prevalence, course, and phenomenology of other psychiatric disorders in this population. Major depressive disorder and alcohol and substance use disorders are among the most common psychiatric disorders in persons with HIV generally (Zanjani et al., 2007). These disorders also have been studied more extensively than other psychiatric disorders in older persons with HIV, and, thus, while we cite data on other selected disorders as well, depressive disorders and alcohol and substance use disorders are the main focus of this review of the remaining psychiatric disorders.

DEPRESSIVE DISORDERS

Reported rates of depressive disorders in older HIV-infected persons vary from approximately 25% to 40%. Consistent with the literature in younger persons with HIV, these rates are elevated considerably compared to the general older population. Cross-sectional studies in clinic settings have shown similar rates of major depressive disorder across age groups in persons with HIV?both based on a review of electronic medical records (Vance, Mugavero, et al., 2011) and a comprehensive behavioral/psychosocial interview (Zanjani et al., 2007). A study of a community cohort of non-intravenous drug-using gay men in New York City, including 308 HIV-seropositive and 134 HIV-seronegative men (Rabkin et al., 2004), showed comparable rates of major depressive disorder in HIV-seropositive men under (32%) and over age 50 (36%). In contrast, HIV-negative men showed decreased rates by age (39% and 20% in men under and over age 50, respectively). In line with this work, a study looking at HIV-seropositive and HIV-seronegative veterans showed that major depressive disorder symptoms (based on responses to the PHQ-9 and clinician report) seemed to decrease with age in HIV-seronegative participants, but not in the HIV-seropositive group (Justice et al., 2004). Cumulatively, results from these studies indicate that the expected declines in lifetime diagnoses of major depressive disorder associated with older age in HIV-seronegative persons are *not* generally apparent in persons with HIV.

Results from studies on level of depressed mood in this population overall are less well delineated than those on major depressive disorder. One study found that older adults with HIV (predominantly long-term infected) had lower depressed mood levels than their younger counterparts (based on scores on the Hamilton Rating Scale for Depression), while HIV-seronegative older adults had higher depressed mood levels than their younger counterparts (Goodkin et al., 2003). The difference of relevance may be that the former studies were focused on the syndrome of major depressive disorder (and its symptoms), while depressed mood level occurs in all patients and is an independent outcome with its own characteristics. Future longitudinal studies comparing older versus younger HIV-seropositive individuals need to be conducted to understand the differential trajectory and phenomenology of major depressive disorder versus depressed mood level (in persons without depressive disorders) over time.

A number of correlates of depressive symptoms have been identified in older HIV-seropositive persons, including both physical (do Carmo et al., 2013; Havlik et al., 2011) and psychosocial factors (Goodkin et al., 2003; Grov et al., 2010). A study of 72 HIV-seropositive persons aged 60 years and older living in Brazil reported that current CD4 cell count, female gender, and current smoking were associated with depressive disorder (defined as scores of 7 or greater on the Geriatric Depression Scale) in univariable analyses (do Carmo et al., 2013). Depressed mood level (as assessed by the Center for Epidemiological Studies Depression Scale [CES-D]) was also associated with higher rates of comorbidities in the Research on Older Adults with HIV (ROAH) study, which included approximately 1,000 HIV-seropositive persons over the age of 50 (Havlik et al., 2011). Another analysis of the ROAH study found that an estimator for the possible presence of syndromal depression (CES-D ≥23) in this sample was also linked to HIV-associated stigma, increased loneliness, decreased cognitive functioning, reduced levels of energy, and being younger (Grov et al., 2010). Other psychosocial factors such as stress related to family and finances, and a lack of social support have also been identified as significant correlates of depressed mood in older persons with HIV (Goodkin et al., 2003). Interestingly, a study of 240 HIV-seropositive older adults recruited through AIDS service organizations reported that negative affect mediated the effects of poor social support and maladaptive coping on ART adherence (Johnson et al., 2009). This suggests that interventions intending to increase adherence to ART in older adults with HIV may be more effective if they address negative affect and enhance adaptive coping and social support.

Suicide has received surprisingly little attention in this patient population. A survey of 113 HIV-seropositive persons older than age 45 recruited from AIDS service organizations showed that 27% of respondents reported suicidal thoughts during the previous week. Suicidal ideation was associated with increased emotional distress and lower health-related quality of life. Additionally, individuals who reported suicidal thoughts were more likely to have disclosed their HIV serostatus to people close to them, and yet they perceived receiving less social support from friends and family (Kalichman et al., 2000).

There are guidelines regarding the diagnosis and treatment of depressive disorders in HIV-seropositive persons including a brief mention of older adults, as cited in the APA

Practice Guidelines for HIV/AIDS (Forstein et al., 2006; McDaniel et al, 2000), with a greater focus in the AAHIVM Consensus Panel for managing older patients with HIV infection (Abrass et al., 2011, 2014). Given that many of the somatic symptoms of major depressive disorder overlap with the physical sequelae of HIV infection, particularly in older persons, it is important that older HIV-infected patients are screened for depressive disorder with a standardized measure that minimizes the impact of somatic depressive symptoms (such as the Cognitive-Affective subscale of the Beck Depression Inventory). It is also important to note that major depressive disorder in older patients with HIV may be treated with the same medications that would be indicated for younger patients. Side-effect profiles and drug–drug interactions should be specifically considered in the choice of drug. Activating antidepressants with minimal effects on the CYP 450 isoenzyme system, such as venlafaxine, may be preferred. Of the SSRIs, paroxetine and citalopram would be preferred to fluoxetine. Behavioral interventions have also shown promising results in this population. A recent randomized clinical trial of 361 older HIV-seropositive persons (Heckman et al., 2013) showed that 12 weekly sessions of telephone-administered, supportive-expressive group therapy resulted in a significant reduction in depressive symptom level, as measured by the Geriatric Depression Scale, in comparison to a usual-care control group. While these results are important and encouraging, there is undoubtedly much to be done in identifying effective interventions for depression (syndromal and nonsyndromal) among diverse groups of older persons with HIV and for the underlying mechanisms of change.

SUBSTANCE USE DISORDERS

Substance use disorders are common among older persons and considerably increase the risk for HIV infection (CDC, 2013), highlighting the importance of screening for substance use disorders in older patients generally. Among older adults with HIV, rates of substance use disorders appear to be notably high (25–50%) (Justice et al., 2004; Rabkin et al., 2004). The few studies that have examined rates of use of specific substances reported selected elevations in rates by substance types (Lyons et al., 2013; Siconolfi et al., 2013). For example, in a diverse sample of HIV-seropositive persons aged 50 and over living in New York City ($N = 811$) (Siconolfi et al., 2013), the most commonly used substances during the prior 3 months were cigarettes (57%) and alcohol (39%). The majority of the sample did not report use of marijuana, "poppers," or a "hard drug" (crystal methamphetamine, cocaine, heroin, ecstasy, GHB, ketamine, and LSD/PCP). Cross-sectional studies comparing persons younger versus older than 50 years (Rabkin et al., 2004) show comparable rates of substance use disorders among HIV-seropositive persons across age groups, in contrast to a decrease in rates with age in HIV-seronegative persons. However, results from a small number of studies indicate a potential decrease in the rates of substance use disorder after age 60 in persons with HIV. For example, an early study on HIV-seropositive veterans showed

relatively stable rates of substance use disorder between ages 30 and 59, ranging from 33% to 44%, which decreased to 24% at ages 60–69 and 13% at age 70 and older (Justice et al., 2004). A more recent study examining medical and psychiatric comorbidities based on reviews of medical records of patients at an HIV clinic showed that the prevalence of substance use disorders remained stable until age 60, ranging from 22% to 25%, and then decreased to 10% (Vance, McGuinness, et al., 2011). However, a limitation of investigations using reviews of medical records is that diagnoses of psychiatric disorders are not based on standardized diagnostic criteria, and diagnostic biases may be operating.

Possible reasons for the apparent decrease in substance use in the older samples of persons with HIV reported are likely to be multifactorial, including cohort effects and survivor biases. There is some indication, however, that it might be at least partly driven by a reduced use of specific types of substances. A study examining rates of use of substances over the prior 3 months in HIV-seropositive persons over age 50 (Siconolfi et al., 2013) reported that while rates of alcohol, popper, and marijuana use were comparable by age, rates of any "hard drug" use were higher among individuals younger than 60 years (27%) compared to persons over age 60 (12%).

While an analysis of a national HIV-seropositive cohort (that did not focus solely on older age) did link substance use and mood disorders (Bing et al., 2001), there is some indication that psychological distress may not be a key correlate of recent substance use in older persons with HIV (Lyons et al., 2013; Siconolfi et al., 2013). A large study on a diverse sample of older HIV-seropositive persons examined the association of gender/sexual orientation and mental health measures (symptoms of depression, loneliness, personal growth, self-acceptance, positive relations, purpose in life, environmental mastery, autonomy) with recent (3-month) use of cigarettes, alcohol, marijuana, "poppers," and/or "hard drugs" (methamphetamine, cocaine, heroin, ecstasy, GHB, ketamine, and LSD or PCP). In multivariable models, substance use was consistently associated with gender/sexual orientation, such that heterosexual men and women were generally less likely than gay/bisexual men to use any of the drugs (except for cigarettes) (Siconolfi et al., 2013). In contrast, mental health variables were generally not significantly associated with substance use. The few cases in which there were statistically significant associations were weak (e.g., lower self-acceptance with increased hard drug use, and less purpose in life with increased marijuana use). Similarly, socioeconomic status, psychosocial variables (such as experiences of discrimination), and psychological distress were also not significant factors in reported methamphetamine use in an online survey of HIV-seropositive and HIV-seronegative gay men in Australia (Lyons et al., 2013).

Alcohol and substance use has been consistently associated with poor ART adherence in persons with HIV (e.g., Braithwaite et al. 2005; Cohn et al., 2011; Hinkin et al., 2004), including in older HIV-seropositive age groups (Catz et al., 2001). A recent study (Parsons et al., 2014) investigated whether specific patterns of substance use were differentially associated with ART adherence among 557 HIV-seropositive persons aged 50 and over living in the New York City area. Results showed four distinct phenotypes of substance use: exclusive alcohol use; alcohol and marijuana use; alcohol and cocaine use; and multiple-alcohol/substance use. The latter three classes reported worse ART adherence than the exclusive alcohol and "no use" groups. Furthermore, the alcohol, cocaine, and multiple alcohol/substance use groups reported the greatest perceived impairment from substance use. These results indicate that it is important to address substance use and its specific phenotype when considering ART adherence interventions. It should be noted that an expanding number of pharmacotherapies that are either non-addictive or low in addictive potential have been reported to primarily ameliorate substance use outcomes; these include bupropion, acamprosate, topiramate, buprenorphine, gabapentin, modafinil, armodafinil, flumazenil, and naltrexone (Abrass et al., 2011, 2014). For more detailed discussion of substance use and HIV, please see Chapter 14 in this volume.

Evidence on the treatment of substance use disorders among older persons with HIV is limited. Results from a recent study in 301 HIV-seropositive older adults with elevated levels of depressed mood (defined as a BDI score ≥10) (Skalski et al., 2013) suggest that interventions designed to increase spiritual coping and decrease self-destructive avoidance may be promising to reduce substance use in this population. Participants who used spiritual practices to cope with HIV-related stress were less likely to use substances, whereas individuals who utilized self-destructive behaviors to cope and who consumed alcohol more frequently were more likely to use substances.

Overall, while there is much that we still do not know about the nature of substance use disorders in older adults with HIV, including their prevalence, risk factors, and treatment, these disorders are pervasive and impactful in this population. Yet, older HIV-seropositive persons are less likely to receive behavioral healthcare generally, and are least likely to receive behavioral healthcare for substance use disorders specifically (Zanjani et al., 2007), highlighting the need for improved identification and engagement in care for substance use disorders among older persons with HIV.

PSYCHOSIS

In general, individuals with severe mental illness have an increased risk of HIV infection (Kalichman et al., 1994). Studies of psychosis in HIV infection have largely focused on younger age groups; yet, it has been recognized for several years that the challenges often faced by older adults with HIV, such as concomitant illnesses, treatment sensitivities, and the potential for increased morbidity and premature mortality, may be compounded by the presence of psychosis (Dolder et al., 2004). A few issues from the existing psychiatric literature are critical to consider in conducting studies with older persons with HIV. First, it is important to differentiate secondary psychosis or new-onset psychosis

from preexisting psychotic illnesses. New-onset psychosis often occurs in late-stage HIV/AIDS and may be associated with CNS infection, tumors, medication toxicities, and HAND. Psychosis in persons with HIV may be difficult to treat. Atypical antipsychotics in low doses appear to represent an advance over conventional antipsychotic agents, at least in terms of the reduced incidence of extrapyramidal symptoms among the high-potency agents and cognitive impairment among the low-potency agents. However, for metabolic side effects, atypical antipsychotics represent a significant risk that could add to a similar toxicity cause by the PIs and constitute a rationale to choose aripiprazole or ziprasidone (Singh and Goodkin, 2007a, 2007b). Additionally, psychosis may contribute to greater morbidity and mortality in older adults with HIV by interfering with ART adherence, decreasing the person's ability to communicate symptoms to clinicians, and healthcare staff minimizing HIV-associated symptoms (Dolder et al., 2004; Sewell, 1996). Major challenges for clinicians in managing HIV-seropositive patients with a history of psychosis prior to HIV infection generally and older patients in particular are to maximize adherence to antiretrovirals and psychiatric treatment and coordinate services to address the psychiatric and medical comorbidities that coexist in this group (Cournos et al., 2005). Research also suggests that severely mentally ill persons as a population are a special risk group for contracting HIV infection (as well as HCV infection, hepatitis B virus infection, and co-infections of these viruses) and that they have specific risk factors related to psychotic symptom severity and the cognitive impairment associated with psychosis which frequently are not assessed or intervened on (Goodkin, 2016).

ANXIETY DISORDERS

Anxiety disorders have been insufficiently studied in older persons with HIV, despite the fact that these disorders represent common psychiatric disorders in the general HIV-seropositive patient population. A large study including a nationally representative sample of persons 18 years and over receiving care for HIV infection in the United States in 1996 investigated rates of generalized anxiety disorder and panic attacks (among other psychiatric disorders) during the previous 12 months. Generalized anxiety disorder and panic disorder have been documented in 15.8% and 10.5% of HIV-seropositive persons versus 2.1% and 2.5% of the general population, respectively (Bing et al., 2001). Posttraumatic stress disorder (PTSD) has also been reported at a higher rate among persons with HIV (Israelski et al. 2007), particularly women. With respect to anxious mood level (regardless of disorder), an earlier study of a general community sample reported lower levels of anxious mood in older than in younger persons with HIV. Distance and escape/avoidant coping strategies were related to increased anxious mood level in that study (Goodkin et al., 2003). In a study examining age differences, the rate of anxiety disorders (panic disorder and generalized anxiety disorder) and PTSD were found to be somewhat more frequent in younger patients (at 22.5%

and 16.1%) than in older patients (at 17.7% and 6.6%, respectively) (Zanjani et al., 2007).

Regarding the differential diagnosis of anxiety disorder, it is important to note that adjustment disorder, which is frequently noted after initial notification of HIV-positive serostatus, may be the most common psychiatric disorder that manifests primarily with anxious mood. Additionally, it is important to consider general medical causes of anxiety, such as hypoxemia in the early stages of pneumonia. Anxiety symptoms have been specifically noted to threaten adherence, although older age was associated independently with a higher likelihood of maintaining antiretroviral schedules (Nilsson Schönnesson et al., 2007). In one recent study, 47% of patients demonstrated significant anxiety symptoms. These patients had a high number of antiretroviral switches (i.e., were at the fourth line of treatment or more) (Celesia et al., 2013). The most common anxiolytic therapies used are the benzodiazepines. As noted in the AAHIVM Consensus Panel document on treating older patients (Abrass et al., 2011, 2014), these medications are a risk to use in older patients due to associated sedation and cognitive dysfunction. They interact with alcohol and may become abused over time. In addition, they are associated with drug interactions with the cytochrome P450 (CYP450) 3A4 isoenzyme system that is strongly inhibited by the PIs. If medication is needed, the SSRIs are generally preferred. For short-term treatment, short- to intermediate-acting benzodiazepines with no active metabolites, such as lorazepam, are typically chosen. Alternatively, buspirone is non-sedating, safe in overdose, and has no abuse potential—but it does have a delayed onset of action. Other options with no abuse potential include hydroxyzine and diphenhydramine, although these may cause sedation and cognitive dysfunction, especially in older patients. Pregabalin and the nutritional supplement, valerian, may also be used.

RACIAL/ETHNIC AND AGE DIFFERENCES IN MENTAL HEALTH AMONG OLDER PERSONS WITH HIV

Despite the elevated rates of HIV infection among members of ethnic/racial minority groups, there has been very little research focusing on understanding possible differences in mental health among older HIV-seropositive ethnic/racial minority groups. A study of 28 African American and 44 non-Hispanic white HIV-seropositive men (Heckman et al., 2000) showed that older HIV-seropositive white men reported elevated levels of depression, anxiety, interpersonal hostility, and somatization, compared to their older African American counterparts. The two groups experienced comparable levels of stress associated with AIDS-related discrimination, AIDS-related bereavement, financial dilemmas, lack of information and support, relationship difficulties, and domestic problems. However, in responses to these stressors, older African American men more frequently engaged in adaptive coping strategies. African American men also received more support from family members and were less likely to disclose their HIV serostatus to close friends. The groups also differed in a number of sociodemographic characteristics, with African Americans reporting significantly lower educational level and annual incomes as well as higher rates of unemployment. While some of these findings may seem somewhat counterintuitive, they serve to highlight the need for further understanding of ethnic/racial differences in psychiatric disorders among older persons with HIV.

Psychiatric comorbidities may occur either in the subpopulation of newly infected older persons (emerging as consequences of recent HIV infection) or among the subpopulation of older adults who have successfully survived into older age with HIV infection in the era of effective ART (allowing more time for aging-associated comorbidities to develop). Research to date has not sufficiently differentiated between psychiatric comorbidities in these two subpopulations. Prospective studies of epidemiological comorbidity should examine the incidence and prevalence rates of psychiatric disorders to determine whether age-related differences in the prevalence of psychiatric disorders in the general population hold for the newly infected older subpopulation versus the long-term infected older subpopulation. As has been the case with HAND, it will also be essential for research on functional status measures and instrumental activities of daily living to establish standardized norms for their use in primary psychiatric disorder diagnoses, to assess impact, and to determine meaningful change in response to treatment.

Another important issue pertains to delirium in older HIV-infected adults. Known risk factors for delirium include older age itself as well as infections, substance use, and use of anticholinergic medications, which are commonly prescribed or used over the counter by older persons. Of special note, untreated delirium can be fatal. Treatment involves an understanding of pharmacological toxicities and metabolic causes, among infectious and other etiologies. Both HIV infection itself and ART toxicities are likely involved. Please see Chapter 16 for details on the identification and treatment of delirium in older patients with HIV infection. It is known that, in the general psychiatric population, most side effects of psychotropic and other medications (especially sedation, postural hypotension, anticholinergic toxicity, cognitive impairment, sexual dysfunction, and movement disorders including parkinsonism and dyskinesias) are more prevalent in older people than in their younger counterparts. Well-designed studies comparing younger and older adults with HIV to assess differences in such adverse effects as well as their relationship to daily dosages and drug–drug interactions are warranted. Life stressor burden and associated psychosocial variables that may affect stressor impact (such as social support availability and coping strategies used) are critical variables that should be assessed in research involving older adults with HIV. Clinicians may wish to employ stress management training, social support groups, and coping skills enhancement training using a low threshold for older persons with HIV.

SUCCESSFUL AGING IN THE CONTEXT OF HIV INFECTION

There are many adults with HIV who are aging well with this disease despite certain personal and physical losses. . . . Studies with an emphasis on positive psychology, hardiness, resilience, social support, self-efficacy, and spirituality are encouraged. Why are some older adults with HIV more resilient and hardy than others? . . . not only is it important to examine the problems associated with living with HIV, it is also important to encourage and translate research findings for those not successfully aging.

—OFFICE OF AIDS RESEARCH WORKING GROUP ON HIV AND
AGING, *2012 (High et al., 2012)*

There is a well-documented discrepancy between objective physical health outcomes and self-report measures of well-being in studies of older adults in the general population (Jeste et al., 2013; Montross et al., 2006; Strawbridge et al., 2002). Older adults tend to subjectively report better quality of well-being, despite the experience of chronic physical illnesses. Ratings of quality of life might be confounded by poor awareness of deficits and by mood state, and, thus, it could be argued that measures of functional status are more likely to provide a valid measure than quality of life. This is a valid consideration; however, there is also increasing recognition that subjective ratings are relevant in their own right and add a meaningful dimension to mental health assessment.

Studies on health-related quality of life among older HIV-seropositive Americans show that, despite high rates of comorbidities, health-related quality of life is moderately high in this group (Balderson et al., 2013), with relatively few differences between older and younger persons living with HIV infection (Nokes et al., 2000). There have been a small number of studies addressing overall well-being or quality of life in older persons with HIV. With a few exceptions (Pitts et al., 2005), results from these studies indicate that older HIV-seropositive cohorts tend to fare similarly or better than their younger counterparts. For example, a study of gay men living in Australia found that despite older HIV-seropositive men having higher rates of comorbidity and a greater tendency to live in poverty, they rated their overall well-being similar to their younger counterparts (Lyons et al., 2010). Another study investigating quality of life in 2,089 HIV-seropositive adults in eight countries found that, despite older individuals with HIV reporting worse sleep, sex life, and fatigue, levels of overall quality of life were similar to those of younger adults with HIV. Furthermore, older HIV-seropositive persons also reported better quality of life on 11 dimensions, including negative feelings, social inclusion, and several environmental and spiritual facets (Skevington, 2012). Related to this, in a large cohort of HIV-seropositive adults from the northeastern United States, positive affect was greater in older HIV-seropositive adults than in their younger counterparts despite greater medical comorbidity in the older group (Mavandadi et al., 2009). This trend is supported by earlier research suggesting less negative affect as well (Goodkin et al., 2003).

These findings indicate a possible paradoxical association of older age with better well-being among HIV-seropositive persons. Most existing reports in the literature on older persons with HIV do not incorporate reports of overall well-being or quality of life, justifying the use of this variable more frequently in clinical assessments and the promotion of interventions targeting improved quality of life as an outcome with these patients.

Although rarely referenced in regard to aging with HIV infection, the gerontological construct of "successful aging" is quite relevant in this field. Traditional definitions of successful aging in the general population have emphasized an absence of objective physical, cognitive, and psychosocial disability (Depp and Jeste, 2006). However, it is becoming increasingly recognized that subjective (self-report) assessments of successful aging in older age still are meaningful and valuable above and beyond using objective criteria for establishing the absence of physical, cognitive, and social disability (Jeste et al., 2013). Understanding HIV infection in the context of successful aging may be an important way to capture broader outcomes in this population. The multidimensional nature of successful aging allows one to assess concurrently a number of different domains (Vahia et al., 2012). The impact of HIV infection itself must be acknowledged on physical health and cognition in older adults and sometimes psychosocial functioning as well. Thus, assessments need to identify targets for clinical intervention across domains.

Two models of successful aging in HIV infection have been proposed. Kahana and Kahana (2001) proposed the preventive and corrective proactivity model of successful aging for individuals with HIV infection. This model emphasizes a set of quality-of-life outcomes (i.e., affective states, meaning in life, and maintenance of valued activities and relationships) and the potential buffering effect that external and internal resources can have on the adverse effects of life stressors. More recently, Vance and colleagues (Vance, McGuinness, et al., 2011) proposed a model of successful aging, which focuses on eight components (longevity, biological health, mental health, cognitive efficiency, productivity, social competence, personal control, and life satisfaction) and the interactions among these components. However, to date, such models remain to be formally tested. Identifying factors that lead to successful aging specifically in persons with HIV is a critical step for improving the likelihood of this outcome.

Aging with HIV infection is often accompanied by increases in wisdom, patience, contentment, moderation, and a greater respect for health and life (Siegel et al., 1998) as well as by resilience and increased personal strength (Emlet et al., 2011). These attributes and traits might be key elements enabling older HIV-seropositive adults to cope well with their illness and age successfully. A recent study contrasting self-ratings of successful aging between older HIV-seropositive and demographically matched HIV-seronegative controls indicated that, although the ratings of the HIV-seropositive adults were somewhat lower than those by HIV-seronegative adults, 66% of HIV-seropositive adults rated themselves at 6 or higher on a 10-point scale from 1 (least successful) to 10 (most successful). This study also found that protective psychosocial factors, such as resilience, optimism, personal mastery, and attitudes toward aging, were associated with subjective successful aging as well as with indicators of good physical and mental health (Moore et al., 2013). Much work still needs to be done to better understand the key factors that might be driving successful aging in older persons with HIV. Related to this, positive factors including spirituality and resilience may play a major role in HIV risk interventions. For example, a recent study showed that religiosity was a protective factor for condom use (Heeren et al., 2014). In sum, the emerging literature highlights the need to focus on positive aging in order to identify effective interventions that reduce or prevent disability and enhance successful aging among persons with HIV.

Despite the higher prevalence rates of HIV infection in African Americans and Hispanics, we did not find any published studies on ethnic/racial differences in prevalence of successful aging among HIV-seropositive persons. It is important to recognize that salient cultural factors may characterize the collective experience of an ethnic/racial group. These values permeate individuals' worldviews and may play an important role in forging their perceptions of successful aging. Prior studies have found that perceptions of successful aging in HIV-seronegative groups vary by ethnic group (Hilton et al., 2012). Given the increased ethnic/racial diversity among persons with HIV, this is an important factor for older persons with HIV. Finally, in view of the high prevalence of HAND among older HIV-seropositive persons, clinicians should focus on enhancing successful aging more intensively with this group, integrating a focus on extending positive and limiting negative mood states.

CONCLUSIONS

The prevalence of older persons among the HIV-infected population has been rising and will continue to rise over the coming years. It will include a significant increase among the true elderly over 65 years of age—where the impact of aging may be even greater. We have reviewed the areas of aging and HIV prevention, HAND, other psychiatric disorders, and successful aging with HIV infection. There is a conceptual issue that potentially unifies these apparently disparate foci, and that is the need for the development of phenotypes (and endophenotypes, when appropriate) widely used in gerontology but relatively less well studied the area of HIV/AIDS.

In the area of HIV prevention, phenotypes are relevant to the need to tailor interventions for older individuals in general as compared to the remainder of the HIV-infected patient population, as well as to define subgroups of older persons with specific prevention needs—such as older women; older

persons of African American, Hispanic, and other ethnicities; and older men who have sex with men, bisexual persons, and transgender individuals.

A significant overlap might be expected between the disability and frailty phenotypes, as it applies to older persons with HIV infection. As previously mentioned, the phenotypes may need to be studied in terms of their interactions to best generate relationships with outcomes of interest. Of special note regarding "frailty," issues have been raised with the validity of the "frailty" construct as it is currently described, which include the issues of its putative overlap with major depressive disorder and cognitive impairment (which are both of particular relevance for older persons with HIV infection). Within the latter area, HAND has been defined by the clinical phenotypes of ANI, MND, and HAD, which have been clearly delineated but require integration with specific aspects of how these disorders present in older persons, as phenotypes of cognitive aging in the setting of HIV infection. One possibility is that of a differing pattern more likely to include cortical and subcortical dysfunction; another is that of phenotypes associated with multiple comorbidities that contribute to cognitive dysfunction in characteristic ways of their own (such as diabetes and major depressive disorder).

In addition, phenotypes related to treatment might exist based on susceptibilities to medication toxicities and drug interactions involving lower abilities to metabolize antiretrovirals and other medications due to age-associated hepatic and renal compromise. Further definition of phenotypes by characteristics of contribution by the pathogen, HIV, could involve differential HIV load and strain by compartment and by HIV latency in brain tissue that would be expected to vary with age. HAND may involve phenotypes not only defined by HIV as the pathogen but also by the response of brain tissue as the specific target organ compromised, for example, in its vascular and inflammatory aspects.

Other psychiatric disorders may also prove important to specifically phenotype in older persons with HIV infection, such as major depressive disorder, which maintains a relatively stable rate with older age, as opposed to the decline normally observed with age in the general population, and has a well-defined neuroinflammatory profile that is known to interact with HIV infection. Likewise, an aging-associated phenotype may mediate the change in frequency in the prevalence of substance use disorders from high to low, below and above age 60.

Finally, there are not only phenotypes of accelerated aging to consider in persons with HIV but also phenotypes of resiliency in aging (or "successful aging"). In fact, the phenotype of successful aging might, in part, be the opposite side of the coin of accelerated aging and, simultaneously, retain independent predictive power (just as positive affect does versus negative affect). Ultimately, the multivariate vector created by the interaction of these different phenotypes on major targeted outcomes of clinical interest may be the most important information to direct the clinical care of older patients with HIV infection in the future. Mining this potential will involve pursuing a development that is only an incipient stage at present of a more complete integration of gerontology with the fields of HIV medicine and HIV psychiatry.

REFERENCES

Abrass CK, Appelbaum J, Boyd CM, et al. (2011). *The HIV and Aging Consensus Project. Recommended Treatment Strategies for Clinicians Managing Older Patients with HIV.* Washington, DC: American Academy of HIV Medicine. http://aahivm.org/Upload_Module/upload/HIV%20and%20Aging/Aging%20report%20working%20document%20FINAL%2012.1.pdf. Accessed February 10, 2017.

Abrass CK, Appelbaum J, Boyd CM, et al. (2014). Updated: *The HIV and Aging Consensus Project: Recommended Treatment Strategies for Clinicians Managing Older Patients with HIV.* Washington, DC: American Academy of HIV Medicine.

American Academy of Neurology (AAN) (1991). Nomenclature and research case definitions for neurological manifestations of human immunodeficiency virus type-1 (HIV-1) infection. *Neurology* 41:778–785.

American Psychiatric Association (APA) (2013). *Diagnostic and Statistical Manual of Mental Disorders*, 5th ed. American Psychiatric Association, Washington, DC.

Amirkhanian Y, Kelly J, Kuznetsova A, Meylakls A, Yakovlev A, Musalov V Chaika N (2014). Using social network methods to reach out-of-care or ART-nonadherent HIV+ injection drug users in Russia: Addressing a gap in the treatment cascade. *J Int AIDS Soc* 17(4 Suppl 3):19594.

Ances BM, Ortega M, Vaida F, Heaps J, Paul R (2012). Independent effects of HIV, aging, and HAART on brain volumetric measures. *J Acquir Immune Defic Syndr* 59(5):469–477.

Anthonypillai C, Gibbs JE, Thomas SA (2006). The distribution of the anti-HIV drug, tenofovir (PMPA), into the brain, CSF and choroid plexuses. *Cerebrospinal Fluid Res* 3:1–10.

Antinori A, Arendt G, Becker JT, et al. (2007). Updated research nosology for HIV-associated neurocognitive disorders (HAND). *Neurology* 69:1789–1799.

Balderson BH, Grothaus L, Harrison RG, McCoy K, Mahoney C, Catz S (2013). Chronic illness burden and quality of life in an aging HIV population. *AIDS Care* 25(4):451–458.

Barnes DE, Santos-Modesitt W, Poelke G, Kramer AF, Castro C, Middleton LE, Yaffe K (2013). The Mental Activity and eXercise (MAX) Trial. A randomized controlled trial to enhance cognitive function in older adults. *JAMA Intern Med* 173(9):797–804.

Bhaskaran K, Hamouda O, Sannes M, et al., for the CASCADE Collaboration (2008). Compared with mortality in the general population changes in the risk of death after HIV seroconversion. *JAMA* 300(1): 51–59.

Bing EG, Burnam MA, Longshore D, et al. (2001). Psychiatric disorders and drug use among human immunodeficiency virus–infected adults in the United States. *Arch Gen Psychiatry* 58(8):721–728.

Braithwaite RS, McGinnis KA, Conigliaro J, et al. (2005). A temporal and dose-response association between alcohol consumption and medication adherence among veterans in care. *Alcohol Clin Exp Res* 29(7):1190–1197.

Britton CB, Kranzler S, Naini A, Cote L (1989). Serotonin metabolite deficiency in HIV-1 infection and AIDS. In Fifth International Conference on AIDS. Ottawa, June 1989, p. 455.

Castellon SA, Hinkin CH, Wood S, Yarema (1998). Apathy, depression, and cognitive performance in HIV-1 infection. *J Neuropsychiatry Clin Neurosci* 10:320–329.

Catz SL, Kalichman SC, Benotsch EG, Miller J, Suarez T (2001). Anticipated psychological impact of receiving medical feedback about HIV treatment outcomes. *AIDS Care* 13(5):631–635.

Celesia BM, Nigro L, Pinzone MR, et al. (2013). High prevalence of undiagnosed anxiety symptoms among HIV-positive individuals on cART: a cross-sectional study. *Eur Rev Med Pharmacol Sci* 17(15):2040–2046.

Centers for Disease Control and Prevention (CDC) (2007). *HIV/AIDS Surveillance Report.* Cases of HIV infection and AIDS in the United States and dependent areas, 2005. Vol. 17. Rev ed. https://www.cdc.gov/hiv/pdf/statistics_2005_hiv_surveillance_report_vol_17.pdf. Accessed February 16, 2017.

Centers for Disease Control and Prevention (CDC) (2010). CDC factsheet: HIV in the United States. Atlanta, GA: Centers for Disease Control and Prevention.

Centers for Disease Control and Prevention (CDC) (2013). *HIV Surveillance Report.* Diagnoses of HIV infection and AIDS in the United States and dependent areas, 2011, Vol. 23. https://www.cdc.gov/hiv/pdf/statistics_2011_HIV_Surveillance_Report_vol_23.pdf. Accessed February 11, 2017.

Chiesi A, Vella S, Dally LG, et al., for the AIDS in Europe Study Group (1996). Epidemiology of AIDS dementia complex in Europe. *J Acquir Immune Syndr Hum Retrovirol* 11:39–44.

Cohn SE, Jiang H, McCutchan JA, et al. (2011). Association of ongoing drug and alcohol use with non-adherence to antiretroviral therapy and higher risk of AIDS and death: results from ACTG 362. *AIDS Care* 23(6):775–785.

Cournos F, McKinnon K, Wainberg M (2005). What can mental health interventions contribute to the global struggle against HIV/AIDS? *World Psychiatry* 4(3):135–141.

Cysique LA, Maruff P, Bain MP, Wright E, Brew BJ (2011). HIV and age do not substantially interact in HIV-associated neurocognitive impairment. *J Neuropsychiatry Clin Neurosci* 23:83–89.

Cysique LA. Maruff P, Brew BJ (2006). Valproic acid is associated with cognitive decline in HIV-infected individuals: a clinical observational study. *BMC Neurol* 6:42.

Dalton P, Santangelo V, Spence C (2009). The role of working memory in auditory selective attention. *Q J Exp Psychol* 62:2126–2132.

Dana Consortium on Therapy for HIV Dementia and Related Cognitive Disorders (1996). Clinical confirmation of the American Academy of Neurology algorithm for HIV-associated cognitive/motor disorder. *Neurology* 47:1247–1253.

Deeks SG (2011). HIV infection, inflammation, immunosenescence, and aging. *Annu Rev Med* 62:141–155.

Depp CA, Jeste DV (2006). Definitions and predictors of successful aging: a comprehensive review of larger quantitative studies. *Am J Geriatr Psychiatry* 14(1):6–20.

Desquilbet I, Jacobson IP, Fried IP, et al. (2007). Multicenter AIDS Cohort Study: HIV-1 infection is associated with an earlier occurrence of a phenotype related to frailty. *J Gerontol Series A Biol Sci Med Sci* 62A:1279–1286.

DHHS Panel on Antiretroviral Guidelines for Adults and Adolescents (2016). *Guidelines for the Use of Antiretroviral Agents in HIV-1-Infected Adults and Adolescents.* https://aidsinfo.nih.gov/contentfiles/lvguidelines/adultandadolescentgl.pdf. Accessed February 10, 2017.

do Carmo A, Fakoury MK, Eyer-Silva WD, Neves-Motta R, Kalil RS, Ferry FR (2013). Factors associated with a diagnosis of major depression among HIV-infected elderly patients. *Revista Da Sociedade Brasileira De Medicina Tropical* 46(3):352–354.

Dolder CR, Patterson TL, Jeste DV (2004). HIV, psychosis and aging: past, present and future. *AIDS* 18(Suppl 1):S35–S42.

Dufour CA, Marquine MJ, Fazeli PL, et al., the HNRP Group (2013). Physical exercise is associated with less neurocognitive impairment among HIV-infected adults. *J Neurovirol* 19(5):410–417.

Ellman TM, Sexton ME, Warshafsy D, Sobieszczyk ME, Morrison EAB (2014). A forgotten population: older adults with newly diagnosed HIV. *AIDS Patient Care STDs* 28(10):530–536.

Emlet CA, Tozay S, Raveis VH (2011). "I'm not going to die from the AIDS": resilience in aging with HIV disease. *Gerontologist* 51(1):101–111.

Engel GL (1977). The need for a new medical model: a challenge for biomedicine. *Science* 196:129–136.

Engel GL (1980). The clinical application of the biopsychosocial model. *Am J Psychiatry* 137:535–544.

Engle RW, Cantor J, Carullo JJ (1992). Individual differences in working memory and comprehension: a test of four hypotheses. *J Exp Psychol Learn Mem Cogn* 18:972–992.

Eschenique M, Illa L, Saint-Jean G, Avellandeda WB, Sanchez-Martinez M, Eisdorfer C (2013). Impact of a secondary prevention intervention among HIV-positive older women. *AIDS Care* 25(4):443–446.

Fernandez F, Adams F, Levy JK (1988). Cognitive impairment due to AIDS-related complex and its response to psychostimulants. *Psychosomatics* 29:38–46.

Forstein M, Cournos F, Douaihy A, Goodkin K, Wainberg ML, Wapenyi KH (2006). *Guideline Watch: Practice Guideline for the Treatment of Patients With HIV/AIDS*. Arlington, VA: American Psychiatric Association. http://www.psych.org/psych_pract/treatg/pg/prac_guide.cfm.

Fried LP, Ferrucci L, Darer J, Williamson JD, Anderson G (2004). Untangling the concepts of disability, frailty, and comorbidity: implications for improved targeting and care. *J Gerontol* 59(3): 255–263.

Glatt SJ, Chayavichitsilp, Depp C, Schork N, Jeste DV (2007). Successful aging: from phenotype to genotype. *Biol Psychiatry* 62:282–293.

Gonzalez E, Kulkarni H, Bolivar H, et al. (2005). The influence of CCL3L1 gene-containing segmental duplications on HIV-1/AIDS susceptibility. *Science* 307:1434–1440.

Goodkin K (2016). Assessing the prevalence of HIV, HBV, and HCV infections among persons with severe mental illness. *Lancet Psychiatry* 3(1):4–6.

Goodkin K, Concha M, Jamieson BD, et al. (2009). Interaction of the aging process with neurobehavioral and neuro-AIDS conditions in the HAART era. In K Goodkin, P Shapshak, A Verma (eds.), *The Spectrum of Neuro-AIDS Disorders: Pathophysiology, Diagnosis, and Treatment* (pp. 473–485). Washington, DC: ASM Press.

Goodkin K, Heckman TG, Siegel K, et al. (2003). "Putting a face" on HIV/AIDS in older adults: a psychosocial context. *J Acquir Immune Defic Syndr* 33(Suppl 2):S171–S184.

Goodkin K, Miller EN, Cox C, et al. for the Multicenter AIDS Cohort Study (2013). Older age and neurocognitive function in the Multi-Center AIDS Cohort Study. Accepted for presentation at the 20th Conference on Retroviruses and Opportunistic Infections (CROI). Abstract F-111, Atlanta, GA, March 3-6, 2013.

Goodkin K, Wilkie FL, Concha M, et al. (2001). Aging and neuro-AIDS conditions: a potential interaction with the changing spectrum of HIV-1 associated morbidity and mortality in the era of HAART? *J Clin Epidemiol* 54:S35–S43.

Grant I, Franklin DR Jr, Deutsch R, et al.; CHARTER Group (2014). Asymptomatic HIV-associated neurocognitive impairment increases risk for symptomatic decline. *Neurology* 82(23):2055–2062.

Greene M, Justice AC, Lampiris HW, Valcour V (2013). Management of human immunodeficiency virus infection in advanced age. *JAMA* 309:1397–1405.

Grov C, Golub SA, Parsons JT, Brennan M, Karpiak SE (2010). Loneliness and HIV-related stigma explain depression among older HIV-positive adults. *AIDS Care* 22(5): 630–639.

Guaraldi G, Silva AR, Stentarelli C (2014). Multimorbidity and functional status assessment. *Curr Opin HIV/AIDS* 9(4):386–397.

Hardy DJ, Goodkin K, López E, Morales G, Buitrón M, Hardy WD (2010). The role of working memory in neuropsychological test performance in older HIV-seropositive adults. In Abstracts of the 2010 Annual British Psychological Society. Stratford-upon-Avon, UK, April 14-16, 2010.

Hardy DJ, Hinkin CH, Satz P, Stenquist PK, van Gorp WG, Moore LH (1999). Age differences and neurocognitive performance in HIV-infected adults. *New Zealand J Psychol* 28:94–101.

Havlik RJ, Brennan M, Karpiak SE (2011). Comorbidities and depression in older adults with HIV. *Sexual Health* 8(4): 551–559.

Heaton RK, Clifford DB, Franklin DR Jr, et al.; CHARTER Group (2010). HIV-associated neurocognitive disorders persist in the era of potent antiretroviral therapy: CHARTER Study. *Neurology* 75(23):2087–2096.

Heckman TG, Heckman BD, Anderson T, et al. (2013). Supportive-expressive and coping group teletherapies for HIV-infected older adults: a randomized clinical trial. *AIDS Behav* 17(9):3034–3044.

Heckman TG, Kochman A, Sikkema KJ, Kalichman S, Masten J, Bergholete J, Catz S (2001). Pilot coping improvement intervention

for late middle-aged and older adults living with HIV/AIDS in the USA. *AIDS Care* 13(1):129–139.

Heckman TG, Kochman A, Sikkema KJ, Kalichman SC, Masten J, Goodkin K (2000). Late middle-aged and older men living with HIV/AIDS: race differences in coping, social support, and psychological distress. *J Natl Med Assoc* 92(9):436–444.

Heeren GA, Icard LD, O'Leary A, Jemmott JB, Ngwane Z, Mtose X (2014). Protective factors and HIV risk behavior among South African men. *AIDS Behav* 18(10):1991–1997.

High KP, Brennan-Ing M, Clifford DB, et al.; OAR Working Group on HIV and Aging (2012). HIV and aging: state of knowledge and areas of critical need for research. A report to the NIH Office of AIDS Research by the HIV and Aging Working Group. *J Acquir Immune Defic Syndr* 60(Suppl 1):S1–S18.

Hilton JM, Gonzalez CA, Saleh M, Maitoza R, Anngela-Cole L (2012). Perceptions of successful aging among older Latinos. *J Cross-Cultural Gerontol* 27:183–199.

Hinkin CH, Castellon SA, Atkinson JH, Goodkin K (2001). Neuropsychiatric aspects of HIV-infection among older adults. *J Clin Epidemiol* 54:S44–S52.

Hinkin CH, Hardy DJ, Mason KI, Castellon SA, Durvasula RS, Lam MN, Stefaniak M (2004). Medication adherence in HIV-infected adults: effect of patient age, cognitive status, and substance abuse. *AIDS* 18(Suppl 1):S19–S25.

HIV-CAUSAL Collaboration (2010). The effect of combined antiretroviral therapy on the overall mortality of HIV-infected individuals. *AIDS (London, England).* 24(1):123–137.

Israelski DM, Prentiss DE, Lubega S, et al. (2007). Psychiatric comorbidity in vulnerable populations receiving primary care for HIV/AIDS. *AIDS Care* 19(2):220–225.

Jahoda M (1053). The meaning of psychological health. *Soc Casework* 34:349–354.

Janssen RS, Nwanyanwu OC, Selik RM, Stehr-Green JK (1992). Epidemiology of human immunodeficiency virus encephalopathy in the United States. *Neurology* 42:1472–1476.

Jeste DV, Savla GN, Thompson WK, et al. (2013). Association between older age and more successful aging: Critical role of resilience and depression. *Am J Psychiatry* 170:188–196.

Johnson CJ, Heckman TG, Hansen NB, Kochman A, Sikkema KJ (2009). Adherence to antiretroviral medication in older adults living with HIV/AIDS: a comparison of alternative models. *AIDS Care* 21(5):541–551.

Justice AC, McGinnis KA, Atkinson JH, et al.; Veterans Aging Cohort 5-Site Study Project Team (2004). Psychiatric and neurocognitive disorders among HIV-positive and negative veterans in care: Veterans Aging Cohort Five-Site Study. *AIDS* 18:S49-S59.

Justice AC, Modur SP, Tate JP, et al.; NA-ACCORD and VACS Project Teams (2013). Predictive accuracy of the Veterans Aging Cohort Study index for mortality with HIV infection: a North American cross cohort analysis. *J Acquir Immune Defic Syndr* 62(2):149–163.

Kahana E, Kahana B (2001). Successful aging among people with HIV/AIDS. *J Clin Epidemiol* 54:S53–S56.

Kalichman SC, Heckman T, Kochman A, Sikkema K, Bergholte J (2000). Depression and thoughts of suicide among middle-aged and older persons living with HIV-AIDS. *Psychiatr Serv* 51(7):903–907.

Kalichman SC, Kelly JA, Johnson JR, Bulto M (1994). Factors associated with risk for HIV infection among chronic mentally ill adults. *Am J Psychiatry* 151(2):221–227.

Larussa D, Lorenzini P, Cingolani A, et al.; Italian Registry Investigative Neuro AIDS (IRINA) (2006). Highly active antiretroviral therapy reduces the age-associated risk of dementia in a cohort of older HIV-1-infected patients. *AIDS Res Hum Retrovir* 22:386–392.

Letendre SL, Woods SP, Ellis RJ, et al.; HNRC Group (2006). Lithium improves HIV-associated neurocognitive impairment. *AIDS* 20:1885–1888.

Lovejoy TI (2012). Telephone-delivered motivational interviewing targeting sexual risk behavior reduces depression, anxiety, and stress in HIV-positive older adults. *Ann Behav Med* 44:416–421.

Lovejoy TI, Heckman TG (2014). Depression moderates treatment efficacy of an HIV secondary prevention intervention for HIV-positive late middle-age and older adults. *Behav Med* 40:124–133.

Lyons A, Pitts M, Grierson J (2013). Methamphetamine use in a nationwide online sample of older Australian HIV-positive and HIV-negative gay men. *Drug Alcohol Rev* 32(6):603–610.

Lyons A, Pitts M, Grierson J, Thorpe R, Power J (2010). Ageing with HIV: health and psychosocial well-being of older gay men. *AIDS Care* 22(10):1236–1244.

Makovski T, Jian YV (2009). The role of visual working memory in attentive tracking of unique objects. *J Exp Psychol Hum Percept Perf* 35:1687–1697.

Marquine MJ, Sakamoto M, Dufour C, et al.; the HNRP Group (2016). The impact of ethnicity/race on the association between the Veterans Aging Cohort Study (VACS) Index and neurocognitive function among HIV-infected persons. *J Neurovirol* 22(4):442–454.

Marquine MJ, Umlauf A, Rooney AS, et al.; HIV Neurobehavioral Research Program (HNRP) Group (2014). The Veterans Aging Cohort Study Index is associated with concurrent risk for neurocognitive impairment. *J Acquir Immune Defic Syndr* 65(2):190–197.

Mavandadi S, Zanjani F, Ten Have TR, Oslin DW (2009). Psychological well-being among individuals aging with HIV: the value of social relationships. *J Acquir Immune Defic Syndr* 51(1):91–98.

McDaniel JS, Chung JY, Brown L, Cournos F, Forstein M, Goodkin K, Lyketsos C (2000). Practice guideline for the treatment of patients with HIV/AIDS. *Am J Psychiatry* 157(Suppl 11):1–62.

Meyer A-C, Boscardin WJ, Kwasa JK, Price RW (2013). Is it time to rethink how neuropsychological tests are used to diagnose mild forms of HIV-associated neurocognitive disorders? Impact of false-positive rates on prevalence and power. *Neuroepidemiology* 41:208–216.

Mindt MR, Miranda C, Arentoft A, et al. (2014). Aging and HIV/AIDS: neurocognitive implication for older HIV-positive Latina/o adults. *Behav Med* 40:116–123.

Montoya ID, Whitsett DD (2003). New frontiers and challenges in HIV research among older minority populations. *J Acquir Immune Defic Syndr* 33:S218–S221.

Montross LP, Depp C, Daly J, et al. (2006). Correlates of self-rated successful aging among community-dwelling older adults. *Am J Ger Psychiatry* 14(1):43–51.

Moore RC, Fazeli PL, Jeste DV, et al.; HIV Neurobehavioral Research Program (HNRP) Group (2014). Successful cognitive aging and health-related quality of life in younger and older adults infected with HIV. *AIDS Behav* 18:1186–1197.

Moore RC, Moore, DJ, Thompson WK, Vahia IV, Grant I, Jeste D (2013). A case-controlled study of successful aging in older HIV-infected adults. *J Clin Psychiatry* 74(5):E417–E423.

Nance CL, Shearer WT (2003). Is green tea good for HIV-1 infection? *J Allergy Clin Immunol* 112:851–853.

Navia BA, Dafni U, Simpson D, et al. (1998). A phase I/II trial of nimodipine for HIV-related complications. *Neurology* 51:221–228.

Neundorfer MM, Camp CJ, Lee MM, Skrajner MJ, Malone ML, Carr JR (2004). Compensating for cognitive deficits in persons aged 50 and over with HIV/AIDS: a pilot study of a cognitive intervention. *J HIV/AIDS Soc Serv* 3(1):79–97.

Nilsson Schönnesson L, Williams ML, Ross MW, Bratt G, Keel B (2007). Factors associated with suboptimal antiretroviral therapy adherence to dose, schedule, and dietary instructions. *AIDS Behav* 11(2):175–183.

Nokes KM, Holzemer WL, Corless IB, et al. (2000). Health-related quality of life in persons younger and older than 50 who are living with HIV/AIDS. *Res Aging* 22(3): 290–310.

O'Brien KK, Bayoumi AM, Stratford P, Solomon P (2014a). Which dimensions of disability does the HIV Disability Questionnaire (HDQ) measure? A factor analysis. *Disabil Rehabil* 13:1–9.

O'Brien KK, Solomon P, Bayoumi AM (2014b). Measuring disability experienced by adults living with HIV: assessing construct validity of the HIV Disability Questionnaire using confirmatory factor analysis. *BMJ Open* 4:1–9.

Onen NF, Overton ET (2011). A review of premature frailty in HIV-infected persons: another manifestation of HIV-related accelerated aging. *Curr Aging Sci* 4:33–41.

Parsons JT, Starks TJ, Millar BM, Boonrai K, Marcotte D (2014). Patterns of substance use among HIV-positive adults over 50: implications for treatment and medication adherence. *Drug Alcohol Depend* 139:33–40.

Pathai S, Bajillan H, Landay AL and High KP (2014). Is HIV a model of accelerated or accentuated aging? *J Gerontol Series A Biol Sci Med Sci* 69(7):833–842.

Pitts M, Grierson J, Misson S (2005). Growing older with HIV: a study of health, social and economic circumstances for people living with HIV in Australia over the age of 50 years. *AIDS Patient Care STDS* 19(7):460–465.

Rabkin JG, McElhiney MC, Ferrando SJ (2004). Mood and substance use disorders in older adults with HIV/AIDS: methodological issues and preliminary evidence. *AIDS* 18:S43–S48.

Roberts RJ, Hager LD, Heron C (1994). Prefrontal cognitive processes: working memory and inhibition in the antisaccade task. *J Exp Psychol Gen* 123:374–393.

Rueda S, Law S, Rourke SB (2014) Psychosocial, mental health, and behavioral issues of aging with HIV. *Curr Opin HIV AIDS* 9:325–331.

Sacktor N, Skolasky RL, Haughey N, et al. (2016). Paroxetine and fluconazole therapy for HAND: a double-blind, placebo-controlled trial. CROI 2016; Boston, Massachusetts. Abstract #146.

Sardar AM, Czudek C, Reynolds GP (1996). Dopamine deficits in the brain: the neurochemical basis of parkinsonian symptoms in AIDS. *Neuroreport* 7:910–912.

Schifitto G, Navia BA, Yiannoutsos CT, et al.; Adult AIDS Clinical Trial Group (ACTG) 301, 700 Teams (2007). HIV MRS Consortium. Memantine and HIV-associated cognitive impairment: a neuropsychological and proton magnetic resonance spectroscopy study. *AIDS* 21:1877–1886.

Schifitto G, Peterson DR, Zhong J, (2006). Valproic acid adjunctive therapy for HIV-associated cognitive impairment: a first report. *Neurology* 66:919–921.

Schifitto G, Sacktor N, Marder K, et al. (1999). Randomized trial of the platelet-activating factor antagonist lexipafant in HIV-associated cognitive impairment. *Neurology* 53:391–396.

Schifitto G, Zhong J, Gill D, et al. (2009). Lithium therapy for human immunodeficiency virus type 1-associated neurocognitive impairment. *J Neurovirol* 15(2):176–186.

Sewell DD (1996). Schizophrenia and HIV. *Schizophr Bull* 22(3):465–473.

Siconolfi DE, Halkitis PN, Barton SC, et al. (2013). Psychosocial and demographic correlates of drug use in a sample of HIV-positive adults ages 50 and older. *Prev Sci* 14(6):618–627.

Sidtis JJ, Gatsonis C, Price RW, et al. (1993). Zidovudine treatment of the AIDS dementia complex: results of a placebo-controlled trial. *Ann Neurol* 33:343–349.

Siegel K, Raveis V, Karus D (1998). Perceived advantages and disadvantages of age among older HIV-infected adults. *Res Aging* 20(6):686–711.

Shiramizu B, Gartner S, Williams A, et al. (2005). Circulating proviral HIV DNA and HIV-associated dementia. *AIDS* 19:45–52.

Singh D, Goodkin K (2007a). Choice of antipsychotic medications in HIV-infected patients. *J Clin Psychiatry* 68(3): 479–480.

Singh D, Goodkin K (2007b). Psychopharmacologic treatment responses of HIV-infected patients to antipsychotic medications. *J Clin Psychiatry* 68(4):631–632.

Skalski LM, Sikkema KJ, Heckman TG, Meade CS (2013). Coping styles and illicit drug use in older adults with HIV/AIDS. *Psychol Addict Behav* 27(4):1050–1058.

Skevington SM (2012). Is quality of life poorer for older adults with HIV/AIDS? International evidence using the WHOQOL-HIV. *AIDS Care* 24(10):1219–1225.

Soto D, Wriglesworth A, Bahrami-Balani A, Humphreys GW (2010). Working memory enhances visual perception: evidence from signal detection analysis. *J Exp Psychol Learn Mem Cogn* 36:441–456.

Spudich SS (2016). Immune activation in the central nervous system throughout the course of HIV infection. *Curr Opin HIV AIDS* 11(2):226–233.

Stout JC, Ellis RJ, Jernigan TL; HIV Neurobehavioral Research Center Group (1998). Progressive cerebral volume loss in human immunodeficiency virus infection: a longitudinal volumetric magnetic resonance imaging study. *Arch Neurol* 55:161–168.

Strawbridge WJ, Wallhagen MI, Cohen RD (2002). Successful aging and well-being: self-rated compared with Rowe and Kahn. *Gerontologist* 42(6):727–733.

Tan S, Li L, Lu L, et al. (2014). Peptides derived from HIV-1 gp120 coreceptor binding domain form amyloid fibrils and enhance HIV-1 infection. *FEBS Lett* 588(9):1515–1522.

Tashima KT, Caliendo AM, Ahmad M, Gormley JM, Fiske WD, Brennan JM, Flanigan TP (1999). Cerebrospinal fluid human immunodeficiency virus type 1 (HIV-1) suppression and efavirenz drug concentrations in HIV-1-infected patients receiving combination therapy. *J Infect Dis* 180:862–864.

Troche SJ, Rammsayer TH (2009). Temporal and non-temporal sensory discrimination and their predictions of capacity- and speed-related aspects of psychometric intelligence. *Pers Indiv Diff* 47:52–57.

UNAIDS (2014). The GAP Report 2014. People aged 50 years and older. http://www.unaids.org/sites/default/files/media_asset/12_Peopleaged50yearsandolder.pdf. Accessed Febraury 10, 2017.

Unsworth N, Redick TS, Heitz RP, Broadway JM, Engle RW (2009). Complex working memory span tasks and higher-order cognition: a latent-variable analysis of the relationship between processing and storage. Memory 17:635–654.

U.S. Department of Health and Human Services (DHHS) HIV/AIDS Bureau (2014). *Guide for HIV/AIDS Clinical Care.* https://aidsetc.org/guide/contents. Accessed February 11, 2017.

Vahia IV, Thompson WK, Depp CA, Allison M, Jeste DV (2012). Developing a dimensional model for successful cognitive and emotional aging. *Int Psychogeriatr* 24(4):515–523.

Valcour V, Shikuma C, Shiramizu B, et al. (2004). Higher frequency of dementia in older HIV individuals: the Hawaii Aging with HIV Cohort. *Neurology* 63:822–827.

Vance DE, McGuinness T, Musgrove K, Orel NA, Fazeli PL (2011b). Successful aging and the epidemiology of HIV. *Clin Interv Aging* 6:181–192.

Vance DE, Mugavero M, Willig J, Raper JL, Saag MS (2011a). Aging with HIV: A cross-sectional study of comorbidity prevalence and clinical characteristics across decades of life. *J Assoc Nurses AIDS Care* 22(1):17–25.

Wilkie FL, Goodkin K, Khamis I, et al. (2003). Cognitive functioning in younger and older HIV-1 infected adults. *J Acquir Immune Defic Syndr* 33(Suppl 2):S93–S105.

Womack J (2012). Women, aging and HIV. Presented at the 2nd International Workshop on HIV & Women, January 9–10, 2012, Bethesda, MD [data from 2008 onward projected based on 2001–2007 trends, 2001-2007 data from CDC *Surveillance Reports* 2007].

Wong C, Althoff K, Gange SJ (2014). Identifying the appropriate comparison groups for HIV-infected individuals. *Curr Opin HIV AIDS* 9:379–385.

Woods SP, Weber E, Cameron MV, et al.; HIV Neurobehavioral Research Center (HNRC) Group (2010). Spontaneous strategy use protects against visual working memory deficits in older adults infected with HIV. *Arch Clin Neuropsychol* 25(8):724–733.

Zanjani F, Saboe K, Oslin D (2007). Age difference in rates of mental health/substance abuse and behavioral care in HIV-positive adults. *AIDS Patient Care STDs* 21(5):347–355.

PART IX

HIV PSYCHIATRIC CARE AND PSYCHOTHERAPEUTIC MODALITIES

37.

PSYCHOTHERAPEUTIC INTERVENTIONS

Jocelyn Soffer, César A. Alfonso, John A. R. Grimaldi, and Jack M. Gorman

Persons living with HIV and AIDS face a complex array of biopsychosocial stresses and challenges. These stresses and challenges may overwhelm psychological function, lead to considerable distress and suffering (Cohen et al., 2002), manifest in a multitude of psychiatric symptoms, and increase nonadherence to risk reduction and medical care. The aim of psychotherapeutic care for persons with HIV is to mitigate such distress through a combination of psychotherapeutic and psychosocial interventions. Goals of such therapies may include enhancing adaptive coping strategies, facilitating adjustment to living with HIV, increasing social supports, and improving a patient's sense of purpose, self-esteem, and overall well-being.

Psychological distress in persons with HIV infection is associated with decreased quality of life, illness progression, and mortality (Antoni et al., 2000a, 2000b, 2005, 2006; Carrico and Antoni, 2008; Carrico et al., 2011; Carrico and Moskowitz, 2014; Leserman, 2008). Considering a biopsychosocial model (Cohen, 1987, 1992; Cohen and Weisman, 1986, 1988), emotional distress in HIV (Cohen et al., 2002) can be viewed as secondary to one or more of the following:

1. *Biological and medical aspects*: physical symptoms, pain, and compromised energy level

2. *Psychological and psychiatric aspects*: comorbid psychiatric disorders; difficulty coping with severe medical illness; shame and guilt; bereavement and loss; conflicts over sexuality, dependency, meaning of life and spirituality; cultural-specific issues

3. *Social aspects*: negotiation of social and intimate relationships, disclosure, stigma and acceptance by the community, unemployment, finances, benefits, access to care, and housing

Psychosocial and psychotherapeutic interventions may also improve immune system function in persons with HIV. Please see Chapter 21 of this textbook for a more thorough and detailed discussion of the profound impact of stress and depression on immune system function and of the mitigating effects of psychotherapeutic interventions. While improving immunological status is a potential benefit of psychosocial treatment for people with HIV infection, it is relieving the suffering inherent to psychiatric illness and improving patients' quality of life that remain the primary goals.

All told, psychosocial interventions for patients with HIV are treatments aimed to alleviate psychological distress associated with medical and psychiatric illness, including depression and anxiety. Psychosocial interventions can occur in individual or group formats, such as informal support groups or groups for specific populations (e.g., women, men, mothers, or caregivers). Interventions might target specific concerns, such as HIV risk reduction, treatment adherence, or substance abuse (Aversa and Kimberlin, 1996). Potential psychosocial interventions span a number of approaches, including supportive, psychodynamic, interpersonal, and cognitive-behavioral. Because of the spectrum of social, psychological, and neuropsychiatric consequences of HIV infection, the psychiatrist needs to consider the range of possible treatment modalities, choosing an appropriate intervention or combination of treatments for each individual.

In this chapter we will consider the benefits of such psychosocial interventions by summarizing the current state of research and findings for each of these treatment approaches, addressing both individual and group settings, and concluding with a discussion of particular group settings. Integrative treatment approaches to HIV care are presented in detail in Chapter 38 of this textbook.

SUPPORTIVE PSYCHOTHERAPY

Supportive psychotherapy primarily aims to reduce symptoms and ameliorate distress, by bolstering a patient's defenses and strengths, and to enhance adjustment to living with HIV, rather than seeking to change character structure or address deeper intrapsychic conflicts. In the Y-model of teaching psychotherapy competencies, Plakun and colleagues (2009) and Goldberg and Plakun (2013) propose that core features or commonalities of all psychotherapies can be generalized as features of supportive psychotherapies. Once the basic principles of supportive psychotherapy are in place, clinicians may opt to conduct additional psychodynamic or cognitive-behavioral therapies. The commonalities of all psychotherapies include warmth, empathy, genuine curiosity, a nonjudgmental stance, establishing a treatment frame, building a therapeutic alliance, and reflecting on what a patient is saying. As such, supportive psychotherapy is practiced with attention to privacy and confidentiality, fostering a therapeutic alliance, allowing expression of emotions while containing excessively painful affects, and creating a sense of safety within a therapeutic frame that functions as a holding environment.

Supportive psychotherapy may take the form of individual or group treatment. Group supportive treatments typically take the form of a "support group." Support groups provide a remarkable forum for persons with HIV and AIDS and have been described as a valuable modality for coping with general stresses of the illness and its treatments as well as HIV stigma (Alfonso and Cohen, 1997). While many psychiatrists and other mental health clinicians find supportive psychotherapy to be a useful modality in the care of persons with HIV and AIDS, there is little formalized research to provide an evidence base for its efficacy.

Supportive psychotherapy with the medically ill can have a profound impact on quality of life, morbidity, and mortality. Psychotherapy for patients with breast cancer has been shown to increase both quality of life and survival (Caplette-Gingras and Savard, 2008). Similarly, Küchler and colleagues (2007) showed that as few as six sessions, on average, of supportive psychotherapy could improve 10-year survival rates in persons with gastrointestinal cancers, concluding that receiving supportive psychotherapy was an independent prognostic factor for survival regardless of cancer disease stage.

Some studies have shown the effectiveness of group psychotherapies in the treatment of depression in persons with HIV, including two studies using a supportive modality with double-blind randomized controlled trials (reviewed by Himelhoch et al., 2007). Belanoff and colleagues (2005), in a randomized study conducted at Stanford University, examined the impact on immune function parameters of expressive-supportive group therapy plus psychoeducation compared to psychoeducation-only group therapy in persons with HIV. Individuals who received weekly supportive psychotherapy for 3 months showed reduction in HIV viral load and increased CD4 count, which was not seen in the education-only group.

A more recent study of geriatric persons with HIV randomized participants to receive either 12 weekly sessions of telephone-administered supportive-expressive group psychotherapy or a standard-of-care control (Heckman et al., 2013). The investigators demonstrated that the experimental telephone-administered group therapy significantly reduced depressive symptoms (assessed using the Geriatric Depression Scale) in this cohort of older persons with HIV. As telepsychiatry gains traction worldwide to reach underserved areas, this study lends support to the possibility of telephony and videotelephony as effective ways to provide psychotherapy to persons with HIV in remote areas.

Support groups often focus on particular issues, including bereavement support, parenting concerns, or trauma. The benefits of such groups in reducing psychological distress and improving immunological parameters in patients with HIV have been confirmed by several studies. Sikkema and colleagues (2004a) demonstrated the efficacy of a bereavement coping intervention for both general health-related quality of life and health issues specific to HIV, compared to a community standard of care, although findings were stronger in the group of women than in the men. Goodkin and colleagues

(1998) reported on a randomized, controlled trial of a bereavement support group intervention, finding decreased levels of psychological distress and grief in the intervention group. There was also an improvement of immunological factors; the clinical relevance was supported by a decrease in healthcare use 6 months after the intervention. Because bereavement is an example of a severe life stressor, this conclusion may also hold for stressor-management interventions generally.

Other support groups may be tailored to specific patient populations, such as on the basis of gender, sexual orientation, or stage of illness. Evidence for the utility of such supportive interventions lies mostly in the subjective reports of patients, with many citing positive experiences and increased feelings of well-being and social support. Controlled trials for such interventions, both individual and group, however, remain sparse. One randomized study comparing a weekly supportive-expressive group intervention with an educational control condition found that distress and depressive symptoms decreased similarly in both groups (Weiss et al., 2003).

HIV-positive individuals often have a history of childhood physical and sexual trauma (Cohen, 1999; Cohen et al., 2001, 2002; Sikkema et., 2004b). Feelings of mistrust, isolation, and anxiety in victims of abuse frequently result in emotional and physical detachment from others and avoidance of intimacy, which can be targeted through a supportive group therapy approach (Sikkema et al., 2004b). Sikkema and colleagues (2004b) reported improvement in mood and symptoms of trauma in patients who participated in a trauma-focused coping group intervention. Working through exposure and trauma must be done carefully and with adequate support in order for patients to experience the treatment as safe and to avoid worsening of symptoms in a population with psychological vulnerability and multiple stresses. A helpful focus can be on skills building, use of coping tools, and practical application to everyday life.

The adjunctive use of medication should be considered in patients with significant depressive symptoms, given that some studies have shown it to be more effective at reducing symptoms than supportive psychotherapy alone. In a randomized study, fluoxetine plus supportive group psychotherapy was found to be more effective than group psychotherapy alone in HIV-positive men with major depression (Zisook et al., 1998).

COGNITIVE-BEHAVIORAL PSYCHOTHERAPY

The largest body of evidence for effective psychological treatment of psychiatric symptoms and emotional distress in patients with HIV exists in the cognitive-behavioral realm. Originally developed by Aaron Beck for depression and anxiety disorders, researchers have now demonstrated the efficacy of cognitive-behavioral therapy (CBT) for many psychiatric conditions. CBT focuses on the interactions of thoughts, feelings, and behaviors, with the aim of decreasing symptoms by modifying cognitions ("cognitive restructuring") and changing behaviors associated with dysfunction or distress.

Cognitive behavioral approaches vary in emphasis but share the common underlying features of being problem focused, goal directed, and time limited (Grant et al., 2007). Typically, educational components help the patient acquire coping skills, as well as shift toward more adaptive cognitions and positive behaviors that enhance functioning. There is also an emphasis on a collaborative approach between patient and therapist, with an active role for the latter.

Many studies have demonstrated the efficacy and utility of CBT for persons living with HIV in relieving emotional distress, particularly by decreasing depression and anxiety, as well as in some cases improving treatment adherence and immunological status. Most of these studies have used adapted forms of CBT, often including an emphasis on stress management techniques. The majority of studies have been conducted in the group setting, with a handful of recent promising results for individually applied CBT; a summary of findings follows.

In the first randomized trial comparing an individual 16-session CBT intervention with other psychotherapeutic approaches (supportive and interpersonal) in patients with HIV, CBT was found to be at least as effective for depressive symptoms as the other modalities (Markowitz et al., 1998; interpersonal therapy was most effective, as discussed later). More recent studies have confirmed the efficacy of individual CBT in this population; Safren and colleagues demonstrated in a randomized controlled trial combining treatment of depression in 10 to 12 sessions that individual CBT can be successfully used with adherence skills enhancement in persons with HIV (Safren et al., 2009). In this modular but flexible protocol using CBT for adherence and depression (CBT-AD), Module 1 included psychoeducation and motivational interviewing exercises, Module 2 focused on behavioral activation interventions, Module 3 consisted of three sessions devoted to cognitive restructuring, especially negative thoughts related to HIV medication adherence, Module 4 devoted three sessions to problem solving, and Module 5 concluded with progressive muscle relaxation training and breathing skills. Notably, the intervention was effective in improving both depression scores and medication adherence, with benefits also seen for viral load that were sustained over time.

This same CBT-AD treatment protocol was used in another study for persons with HIV, depression, and opioid dependence (with injection drug use), a population triply at risk for nonadherence (Safren et al., 2012). While the intervention was impressively successful at reducing depressive symptoms even beyond the study's completion, gains in adherence were not sustained; this suggests that continued adherence counseling may be necessary in this at-risk population.

Another large multisite study used the Healthy Living Project protocol, consisting of a 15-session cognitive-behavioral intervention designed primarily to target HIV transmission risk behavior but also to assess for impact on negative affect, including depressive symptoms, anxiety, burnout, and stress levels (Carrico et al., 2009). This randomized trial is the only individually applied CBT study that did not find benefit for measures of psychosocial adjustment. The authors speculate that this was because the treatment emphasized skills training with the primary goals of decreasing risk behaviors and improved adherence, with only 5 of the 15 sessions focused on stress management and coping responses. They suggest that behavioral activation and cognitive restructuring as used in other CBT protocols but not in this study may be key for effectively treating depression within the cognitive-behavioral framework. Additionally, they point out that prior trials suggested that interventions with a minimum of 10 sessions, whether delivered individually or in a group format, are more likely to be effective for psychological symptoms. These findings provide important clues that may be helpful for the clinician working with patients with HIV in framing a treatment plan.

Others have looked at whether cognitive-behavioral interventions could be delivered in a low-resource cost-effective setting for persons with HIV and depression via a self-help program. Such a cognitive-behavioral self-help program (CBS) was studied in a pilot randomized, controlled trial that used a workbook, work program, and CD-ROM (Kraaij et al., 2010). The participants were instructed to apply the interventions for 1 hour a day, 4 days a week, over a period of a month (16 sessions total), following preset topics including mindfulness-based relaxation exercises, cognitive restructuring, goal-setting, and enhancement of self-efficacy. The intervention was compared with a wait-list control group, as well as to a computerized structured writing intervention using emotional disclosure (the latter based on the model that written emotional expression can ameliorate depression and improve immune function; for example, see Petrie et al., 2004). Compared to the control group, the CBS intervention, but not the writing intervention, improved depressive symptoms in individuals who followed the protocol. Further studies are needed to see if the results can be replicated and improvements sustained over time. If successful, such programs would have to the potential to be used in resource-poor areas, delivered over the Internet or by mail.

Himelhoch and colleagues (2013) also studied an alternative method of treatment delivery, in a pilot randomized study comparing an 11-session telephone-based CBT intervention to face-to-face therapy, in an urban-dwelling, low-income population with HIV and depression. While a prior study had failed to find benefit from a behavioral support intervention delivered by telephone to depressed patients living with HIV (Stein et al., 2007), this protocol used more specific CBT interventions and found clinically significant improvements in depression that were similar to those seen in the face-to-face group. These reductions in depression were seen despite limited session attendance in both arms (with an average of approximately five sessions), and future studies will need to determine if such results can be replicated and sustained over time. There are potentially many advantages of an intervention that could be delivered by phone in this population, given potential difficulties involved with attending face-to-face sessions (such as transportation barriers, conflicting medical appointments, and concerns about stigma).

Berger and colleagues (2008) found that cognitive-behavioral stress management increased CD4 counts in persons with HIV in addition to improving psychosocial parameters and adherence. Cognitive-behavioral stress management also increased testosterone and improved psychosocial parameters in men with HIV (Cruess et al., 2000). Culturally adapted CBT for adherence and depression has been tried, for example, among Spanish-speaking Latinos. One preliminary randomized, controlled trial using this approach with HIV-positive Latinos living at the U.S.-Mexico border found evidence of improvement in depressive symptoms (both by self-report and clinician ratings), adherence (by self-report and electronic pill box), and biological markers (CD4 counts, but not viral load), thus warranting further studies (Simoni et al., 2013).

Despite the handful of recent studies just described, the bulk of the literature on CBT for patients with HIV still pertains to group rather than individual settings. A small early study examined cognitive-behavioral group therapy in combination with antidepressant use in HIV-infected patients over 20 weeks, finding decreased depression scores that were maintained at 1-year follow-up (Lee et al., 1999). A 16-week cognitive-behavioral group psychotherapy intervention for patients with HIV similarly found improvement on measures of depression (Beck Depression Inventory) and anxiety (State/Trait Anxiety Inventory), with effects that persisted at 3-month follow-up (Blanch et al., 2002). Other studies of group-applied cognitive-behavioral interventions have also yielded improvements on various psychosocial measures (Spies et al., 2013).

While most studies of CBT interventions have been positive, those comparing its specific efficacy to that of other types of psychotherapeutic modalities have yielded mixed results. Some studies have found CBT techniques to be approximately as effective as other group psychotherapy modalities, such as experiential group psychotherapy (Mulder et al., 1995) or social support groups (Kelly et al., 1993). In the latter study, both CBT and social support treatment groups showed decreased depression, hostility, and somatization after the intervention, relative to the control group. Such findings call into question whether it is the interventions specific to CBT or merely the positive impact of peer and therapist support that mediates the reduction in symptoms in the group setting. Other studies have suggested a more specific benefit to a cognitive-behaviorally oriented group approach. For example, a pilot study of Chinese patients with symptomatic HIV disease compared the effects of cognitive-behavioral group therapy and peer support/counseling on psychological distress and quality of life (Molassiotis et al., 2002) and found greater improvements in the CBT group than in the peer support or control groups.

CBT in the group setting has frequently been combined with stress management and relaxation techniques (CBSM) for patients with HIV. In one series of such studies, the treatment protocol comprised 10 weekly sessions consisting of relaxation techniques (including muscle relaxation, guided imagery, meditation, and breathing exercises) and stress management (identifying automatic thoughts, using cognitive restructuring, increasing coping skills and assertiveness, and enhancing strategies for anger management and use of social supports) (Antoni et al., 2005). Participants were instructed to practice relaxation exercises twice daily between sessions

and were assigned cognitive homework exercises. Compared to a wait-list control group, the CBSM group showed significantly lower depressed affect, anxiety, and anger.

Interventions aiming to reduce emotional distress through psychoeducation and coping styles training have also been used. Chesney and colleagues (2003) compared the effects of a theory-based coping effectiveness training (CET) intervention with those of an active informational control and a wait-list control on psychological distress and positive mood. The CET participants showed significantly greater decreases in perceived stress and burnout as well as decreases in anxiety, with treatment differences for positive morale maintained at 12 months. Coping models have also been described that include examination of cognitive appraisals, emotional coping patterns, and behavior patterns, with improved immunological parameters in persons with HIV posited to be related to more adaptive coping models (Temoshok et al., 2008)—specifically, "passive, emotionally repressive/nonexpressive, pessimistic/hopeless, and physiologically dysregulated coping responses or styles may have a detrimental impact on HIV clinical disease progression."

Most studies of CBT have been conducted with men or, in some cases, men and women, with only a few studies focused on women living with HIV. In one such intervention, CBSM (CBT combined with stress management and relaxation techniques), with additional expressive-supportive therapeutic strategies, was used with minority women living with HIV. Significant improvements in depressive symptoms were maintained at 1-year follow-up (Laperriere et al., 2005). An increased level of cognitive behavioral coping self–efficacy was associated with reduced anxiety and depressive symptoms in this population (Jones et al., 2010). Given that 25% of people living with HIV in the United States are women, with minorities disproportionately affected, more studies of psychotherapeutic interventions for this population are needed.

PSYCHODYNAMIC PSYCHOTHERAPY

Psychodynamic psychotherapy integrates biopsychosocial and developmental paradigms, taking into account that early life experiences and relationships may influence later patterns of behavior (Friedman et al., 2013, 2014). It involves exploration of a patient's defenses, resistance, avoidance behaviors, and intrapsychic conflicts, with a focus on affects, expressions of emotions, unconscious mental life, transference, and countertransference (Gabbard, 2007). It is often practiced in combination with supportive psychotherapy, balancing interpretations and uncovering work with support and empathic listening (Gabbard, 2014). Determining when to clinically intervene, along the supportive, expressive, and uncovering continuum, depends on the patient's resilience, vulnerabilities, capacity for insight, and level of ego strength (Cabaniss et al., 2011).

Controlled studies of psychodynamic psychotherapy are difficult to design, with correspondingly limited research. To date, there are no , controlled trials comparing the efficacy of psychodynamic psychotherapy to other psychotherapy modalities in persons with HIV infection. One open trial found that time-limited psychodynamic psychotherapy (individual psychodynamic psychotherapy, non-manualized, once weekly over 20 weeks) resulted in a decrease in subjective distress in a cohort of gay men with HIV infection who self-referred for psychotherapy at the University of California, San Francisco (Pobuda et al., 2008). There is growing evidence from meta-analyses of published randomized, controlled studies demonstrating that psychodynamic psychotherapy is an effective treatment modality in persons with complex psychiatric multimorbidities (Leichsenring et al., 2013). In an overview of randomized, controlled studies, Leichsenring and colleagues (2013) make a strong case for a psychotherapy dose–effect relationship, suggesting that individuals with complex mental disorders and multimorbidities, including personality disorders, derive greater benefit from longer-term psychotherapy. The subjects in these studies had unknown or undetermined HIV serostatus.

Although psychodynamic psychotherapy has not been systematically studied in cohorts of persons with HIV infection, there is considerable literature on the utility and relevance of this treatment modality for patients struggling to maintain or regain a stable sense of self while coping with the challenges of HIV. The enhanced understanding of the conflicts and struggles of the HIV-positive patient afforded by such techniques has been described by multiple authors in case reports and open trials of psychodynamic psychotherapy (Adamo et al., 2008; Cohen, 1999; Cohen and Alfonso, 2004; Cohen et al., 2001; Mugford, 2004; Ricart et al., 2002; Rogers, 1989; Weiss, 1997). Even early on in the epidemic of HIV, psychodynamic factors were identified as important to recognize and address in treatment, in ways that could both ameliorate suffering and decrease the transmission of the virus (Rogers, 1989).

This modality of treatment may be especially suited for patients with a trauma history, as physical illness, changes in the body, and relationship stresses can awaken conflicts triggered by early trauma and neglect. A history of childhood emotional, physical, and sexual trauma and neglect is associated with risk behaviors and is prevalent in persons with HIV (Allers and Benjack, 1991; Goodman and Fallot, 1998; Lenderking et al., 1997; Lodico and DiClemente, 1994; Thompson et al., 1997; Wingood and DiClemente, 1997). Early childhood trauma-induced posttraumatic stress disorder (PTSD) is also prevalent in persons with HIV, reported to be as high as 40% (Cohen et al., 2001), and is associated with nonadherence to risk reduction, HIV medical care, and antiretroviral medication (Cohen et al., 2001; Ricart et al., 2002, Samuels et al., 2011). Psychodynamic psychotherapy can help persons with HIV and PTSD heal and experience a decrease in distress as they work through such issues. Addressing childhood trauma in psychodynamic psychotherapy can not only improve psychiatric symptoms but also decrease risk behaviors and increase adherence to treatment (Ricart et al., 2002, Samuels et al., 2011). Therefore, understanding the psychodynamic antecedents of nonadherence (Alfonso, 2011; Ricart et al., 2002; Samuels et al., 2011) can inform clinicians caring for persons with HIV infection and help improve compliance,

reduce psychiatric symptoms, and prevent lapses in antiretroviral treatment.

An important aspect of psychodynamic theory that permeates treatment is awareness of countertransference. Persons with HIV infection experience affective states of helplessness, hopelessness, terror, and shame. Containing these difficult emotions requires advanced psychotherapeutic skills. The fortitude to be able to maintain equanimity when faced with overwhelming distress can be gained through awareness of reciprocal emotional experiences and interpretation of projective identifications. Furthermore, clinicians themselves benefit from support, supervision, and psychotherapy. Peer supervision or clinical consultation may prevent burnout and enhance the effectiveness of treatment when patients with HIV infection and psychiatric multimorbidities present with intense emotional states while complex issues in psychodynamic psychotherapy unfold and are explored. Ratigan (1991) cautions psychotherapists about the potential for unconscious enactments contributing to traumatization when caring for persons with HIV infection. He identified unconscious intrapsychic conflicts in the psychotherapist, such as fear of death, mistrust of differences, and anxiety-laden intimacy, as potentially causing therapeutic impasses or even iatrogenic traumatization if clinicians remain unaware of their prejudices or unconscious motivations.

Other major themes that may surface and be addressed in psychodynamic work include fears about mortality, with the erosion of defensive denial as illness progresses, and conflicts surrounding sexuality. Severe illness and increased awareness of mortality can serve as catalysts for change, leading to motivation for reflective work, conflict resolution, and healing (Cohen, 1999). Exploration of the unique role and meaning of being HIV positive for each patient can facilitate acceptance, mastery, and an increased sense of a functional and cohesive self (Weiss, 1997).

INTERPERSONAL PSYCHOTHERAPY

The primary goal of interpersonal psychotherapy (ITP) is to treat a depressive episode by helping patients link the depression to specific interpersonal stresses and then facilitating resolution of those stresses. In extensive research examining the role of environmental influences on mood, several common problem areas were identified, including unresolved grief following the death of a loved one, role transitions (difficulty adjusting to changed life circumstances), interpersonal role disputes (conflicts with a significant other), and interpersonal deficits (impoverished social networks).

There are many well-designed studies documenting the efficacy of ITP in the treatment of depression, both as monotherapy and in combination with medication (Brakemeier and Frase, 2012; Cuijpers et al., 2011). These studies tend show that ITP is equal in effectiveness to cognitive-behavioral psychotherapy (Jakobsen et al., 2012) and medication (van Hees et al., 2013). Some studies have found IPT to be superior to CBT (de Mello et al., 2005). IPT may also be effective in preventing relapse and recurrence in patients with depression

(Hollon and Ponniah, 2010). ITP has been studied in the treatment of patients with coronary disease (Koszycki et al., 2004) and is linked with significant reduction in scores on both the Hamilton Depression Scale and the Beck Depression Inventory II. Medicated and unmedicated patients responded similarly to ITP, a finding suggesting this modality to be an effective alternative to medication.

Studies specifically addressing the HIV-seropositive population have reported similar positive results (Ferrando and Freyberg, 2008). One study found better outcomes with ITP than with both supportive psychotherapy alone and supportive psychotherapy with imipramine (Markovitz et al., 1995, 1998). In another study, Catalán (1999) found that interpersonal psychotherapy was more effective than CBT or supportive therapy alone, and was comparable to supportive psychotherapy plus pharmacotherapy for treating depressive symptoms in HIV-positive patients.

Telephone-delivered ITP has also been studied in persons with HIV (Ransom et al., 2008) Individuals randomized to receive teletherapy had greater reductions in depressive symptoms and psychiatric distress compared to the placebo arm, a usual-care condition. However, there were low overall rates of improvement, with only slightly less than one-third of the teletherapy patients reporting clinically meaningful reductions in psychiatric distress. It is important to remember that not all patients respond to ITP. Response rates can be enhanced by improving the therapeutic alliance, focusing on depressive symptoms, and tailoring the therapy to the individual's characteristics (Ravitz et al., 2011).

PSYCHOSOCIAL TREATMENTS FOR SUBSTANCE-RELATED AND ADDICTIVE DISORDERS

The role of alcohol and non-injection drug use in the continuing spread of HIV is well recognized. Not surprisingly, a number of studies have tested the effectiveness of psychosocial interventions to reduce not only drug and alcohol use but also associated sexual risk behaviors and treatment noncompliance. The interventions most commonly employed have been contingency management (CM) therapies, cognitive-behavioral (CBT) and skills training therapies (CBST), and motivational interviewing (MI), alone and in combination (Carroll and Onken, 2005).

One small study combined motivational interviewing with individual CBT sessions and found effective reduction of substance use (Parsons et al., 2005). Other studies have employed a CM individual intervention with positive results (Schroeder et al., 2006). This approach uses behavioral reinforcement techniques, such as tangible rewards (e.g., vouchers) for refraining from negative behaviors (e.g., drug use) or demonstrating positive behaviors. An open pilot trial involving 17 HIV-infected young adults (ages 18–24) with alcohol and marijuana use disorders tested the effectiveness of an integrated CBT and CM intervention delivered in 15 individual sessions. Study findings showed significant reduction in alcohol use as well as in depressive symptoms, sexual risk behaviors,

and antiretroviral medication noncompliance. Additionally, high retention rates and the study setting, in which subjects were drawn from three HIV community clinics, demonstrated the feasibility of using clinicians in community-based clinics to deliver interventions and suggest wider applicability to other similar settings (Esposito-Smythers et al., 2014).

The practicality of incorporating interventions into existing HIV clinical ambulatory services has been a focus of recent attention. In a randomized trial of HIV-infected outpatients in Kenya, CBT was more effective than usual care in reducing alcohol use. This study delivered care in six weekly group sessions by clinicians with no previous CBT experience and only minimal counseling experience. However, the 90-minute length of each CBT session limit applicability to other resource-limited settings (Hasin et al., 2013; Papas et al., 2011).

Research suggests that alcohol-dependent patients may require more intensive interventions than are needed by patients with less severe alcohol-related problems. Hasin and colleagues (2013) have shown that interactive voice response technology (IVR) used to enhance motivational interviewing for alcohol-dependent patients in HIV primary care can significantly reduce the number of drinks per drinking day compared to motivational interviewing without enhancement. The IVR-enhanced condition, HealthCall, consisted of daily automated phone calls to patients to self-monitor alcohol-related behaviors that were then stored in a database and used in subsequent counseling sessions to facilitate discussion of patients' drinking (Hasin et al., 2014).

Researchers have examined whether CBT methods might help reduce risk behaviors in HIV-positive populations, with largely mixed results. One study found that a cognitive-behavioral intervention in persons with substance use had limited advantages over a two-session standard drug counseling and testing protocol developed by the National Institute on Drug Abuse (NIDA) (Hershberger et al., 2003). Studies using contingency management interventions, as described earlier, have demonstrated more success at decreasing sexual risk behaviors (Shoptaw et al., 2005). Please see the Chapter 14 for a more detailed discussion of treatments for substance-related and addictive disorders.

MOTIVATIONAL INTERVIEWING AND RISK REDUCTION

Motivational interviewing is an evidence-based counseling style developed by Miller and Rollnick (2002) originally for use in individuals with problematic alcohol use. It has subsequently been applied to a variety of health-related behaviors such as drug abuse, smoking, obesity, and treatment adherence (Lundahl and Burke, 2009). Its effectiveness derives from its focus on patient autonomy and choice and the belief that individuals possess an intrinsic motivation to change behaviors associated with harmful consequences to their health. The aim of MI is to resolve ambivalence about behavior change through empathy and the alignment of the benefits of behavior change with other values and priorities.

Existing studies support the use of MI in primary care and other healthcare settings where patients are frequently seen who have medical conditions with behavior-related complications (Knight et al., 2006). Given its empirical support, there has been an interest in using MI to address behaviors linked to poor outcomes in HIV disease, such as nonadherence to antiretroviral medications, nondisclosure of HIV infection, drug and alcohol abuse, and high-risk sexual activity. Additionally, MI has advantages over other psychotherapeutic modalities that favor its adaptation to an HIV primary care setting. It can be delivered in a relatively brief intervention, may be integrated into usual medical care in an ambulatory care clinic setting, and is generally well accepted by patients, owing to its nonjudgmental and patient-centered orientation. Healthcare practitioners lacking a mental health background, such as infectious disease physicians, nurses, social workers and pharmacists, may be trained in its use relatively easily (Madson et al., 2009). Patient satisfaction may be enhanced, even though clinicians may not be deemed fully MI-competent according to standardized measures (Pollak et al., 2011).

There is a limited but growing body of qualitative research demonstrating that MI may be effective in improving adherence to antiretroviral medications, reducing problematic alcohol and drug use, and modifying high-risk sexual behaviors. These findings may be especially relevant given the recent emphasis on "treatment as prevention" and pre-exposure prophylaxis as principal strategies to reduce HIV transmission. Comparison among studies has been limited by different methodologies employed, variable populations studied, and different outcome measures used. Additionally, studies have used varying degrees of rigor to ensure MI quality and fidelity. Despite these shortcomings, some results have been promising.

One study included mainly African American HIV-infected youth (ages 16 to 24 years) with one or more treatment-interfering behaviors: nonadherence to HIV medications, substance abuse, and unprotected sex. Participants were randomized to either specialty care plus an MI-based intervention or specialty care alone. The intervention consisted of four individual sessions delivered over a 10-week period. Compared to the control group, the MI group had a statistically significant improvement in viral load at 6 months. Benefits were not sustained at 9-month follow up, however. The investigators suggest that a more intensive intervention or booster sessions may be necessary to sustain behavior change beyond 6 months (Naar-King et al., 2009).

MI-based adherence counseling has also been shown to improve medication adherence. A large study in an HIV ambulatory care clinic found that MI-based adherence counseling, provided by registered nurses in five individual counseling sessions over a 3-month period, improved medication adherence, as measured by the Medication Event Monitoring System (MEMS) (DiIorio et al., 2008).

An intervention combining MI and cognitive-behavioral skills building (CBST) was compared to an educational condition in a study of HIV-infected men and women in New York City. Participants met criteria for hazardous drinking based on the Alcohol Use Disorder Identification Test (AUDIT) and were prescribed antiretroviral medications (Parsons et al., 2007). The MI/CBST intervention was delivered over eight sessions, studying viral load, CD4 cell count, and self-reported medication adherence and drinking behavior (at baseline and 3- and 6-month follow-up). The intervention group demonstrated improvement in the biomedical measures at 3 months, but these were not sustained at 6-month follow-up. There were no significant decreases in drinking throughout. Similar to the study by Naar-King and colleagues, the investigators suggest that future studies should include booster sessions to maintain adherence benefits beyond the initial intervention period. They also suggest that MI/CBST be further studied, and that it may be ideally suited for integration into an HIV ambulatory care setting where specific tailoring to meet individual patient needs and characteristics could be achieved (Parsons et al., 2007).

These and other studies (Golin et al., 2006; Krummenacher et al., 2011; Milam et al., 2005), though not definitive, offer evidence that MI-based interventions integrated into an HIV primary care setting may offer a cost-effective means of improving patient satisfaction and health outcomes and mitigating behavioral risk factors among high-risk patients. Additionally, training infectious disease physicians in MI may confer the added benefit of reduced risk for burnout independent of patient outcome by biomedical measures (Suzuki, personal communication).

SPECIAL SETTINGS

COUPLE THERAPY

The impact of HIV on an individual's functioning as a member of a couple and on the health of the relationship is well recognized. Multiple factors may influence this impact, including the timing of HIV infection or diagnosis of one or both partners relative to their time together as a couple. Interestingly, a significant proportion of new infections occur in the setting of married or cohabitating serodiscordant couples and among men who have sex with men in primary relationships (Muessig and Cohen, 2014). There is a limited but significant body of research focused on couples-based HIV testing and counseling. This area of investigation has assumed greater relevance with advances in prevention strategies utilizing antiretroviral medications to block HIV transmission and acquisition. There are still, however, relatively few controlled effectiveness studies of couples-oriented interventions aimed at improving health or psychological outcomes.

A substantial body of descriptive literature addresses interpersonal and psychodynamic aspects of both HIV-seroconcordant and HIV-serodiscordant couples. Marshall Forstein (2008) has written extensively on the complexities that arise in work with couples affected by HIV; some key issues are summarized here. Coping with HIV illness can challenge basic conceptions of sexuality and identity—fundamental aspects of the self that work to maintain psychological and physiological homeostasis. It can awaken fears of abandonment, existential anxiety about death, feelings of failure, and unacceptable rage leading to reaction formation, all of which can, consciously or unconsciously, affect relationship behaviors and patterns. Some people may emotionally distance themselves to protect their partner or themselves, while others may seek additional intimacy and closeness. Guilt and blame are common themes that emerge in work with both serodiscordant and seroconcordant couples. The sexual nature of HIV transmission also creates practical issues; mixed-status couples will need to negotiate satisfying and safer sexual practices. The HIV-infected person can lose interest in sexual relations or feel unattractive because of physical changes accompanying HIV disease and/or medications and the impact on self-image.

Evaluation of the HIV-concordant or HIV-discordant couple should thus include not only review of a complete medical and psychiatric history but also assessment of characteristic psychological defenses and coping styles. One must also be sensitive to the cultural and individual factors that govern beliefs about and expectations for what the illness means and what the future is likely to bring. Table 37.1 contains examples of questions that may guide a clinician toward understanding of the meaning of the behavior, anxieties, fears, and coping mechanisms involved in a couple's relationship, in addition to the more concrete questions usually covered in a psychiatric evaluation.

Developing a trusting, nonjudgmental relationship with clinicians allows the couple to reflect on a dynamic individual and relationship process that is often unpredictable for clinicians and patients alike. Therapists can help couples manage these emotional complexities and the psychological impact of HIV infection.

A review and meta-analysis of couple-oriented interventions for chronic medical illness (Martire et al., 2010) identified

Table 37.1 QUESTIONS TO CONSIDER DURING EVALUATION AND TREATMENT OF HIV-SERCONCORDANT AND HIV-SERODISCORDANT COUPLES

- Is the major focus of the couple's decision to come for therapy to stay together or to find ways of separating? Is the goal the same for both members of the relationship?
- What is the customary nature of unions within the cultural background of each member?
- What is the current medical status of each partner? If there has been a major episode of illness, how have the individual and the couple coped?
- What does each member of the couple know about the other's sexual or intravenous drug use history, or both?
- To whom else has the HIV-positive person disclosed their status, and what was the response?
- What is the nature of support in the couple's social and familial network?
- How has the HIV-positive person's illness changed expectations about role identity in the relationship, and how has the couple reacted to and managed such changes?
- What are the individual coping strengths, and how does the couple use the strengths of each to support the stability of the relationship?

33 studies that met criteria for high-quality randomized controlled trials; only two of these involved HIV-infected subjects (Fife et al., 2008; Martire et al., 2010; Remien et al., 2005). One study used a psychosocial educational model incorporating four 2-hour sessions focused on communication, stress appraisal, adaptive coping strategies, and building social support in persons with HIV and their partners. Investigators found increased adaptive coping in the intervention group (Fife at al., 2008). Remien (2005) compared couples education with usual medical care and found better medication adherence in the intervention group (Remien et al., 2005). Findings from these and studies involving other chronic medical conditions such as cancer, cardiovascular disease, and arthritis suggest that marital quality (communication, intimacy, conflict) affects behavioral and medical health. Couples interventions that enhance partners' ability to support patients' autonomy and self-efficacy strengthen marital functioning.

Interest in couples-based interventions to prevent infection in HIV-serodiscordant relationships has been energized by confirmation of the benefits of suppression of viral replication in the HIV-infected partner, and use of pre-exposure prophylaxis with antiretroviral agents in the non-infected partner, in preventing transmission. Numerous studies have demonstrated the efficacy of these strategies: HIV Prevention Trials Network 052 (Cohen et al., 2011) demonstrated that early initiation of treatment with antiretroviral medication in serodiscordant heterosexual couples reduces the rate of transmission to the seronegative partner; Partners PrEP Study (Baeten et al., 2012) demonstrated efficacy of pre-exposure prophylaxis in serodiscordant heterosexual couples; and iPrEX, or Pre-exposure Initiative (Grant et al., 2010), observed reduced seroincidence in men who have sex with men who are taking pre-exposure prophylaxis. The absence of couples-based intervention studies involving men who have sex with men is a limitation in this area of research. However, a heterosexual-oriented risk reduction intervention recently adapted to African American gay male couples who are using methamphetamine has shown initial promising results (Wu et al., 2011).

Although HIV prevention has been the primary aim of some approaches to couples therapy, interventions have increasingly focused on factors related to partners' well-being and the quality of the relationship. Some studies have emphasized communication and problem-solving skills (Muessig and Cohen, 2014), while others have addressed gender roles, power imbalances, and issues related to commitment, intimacy, and marital satisfaction (Burton et al., 2010). The role of concurrent partners in HIV transmission has also been considered, as have ways in which cultural norms influence this practice with its attendant risk of infection from outside the relationship (Burton et al., 2010).

The importance of addressing fertility desires, contraception, family planning, and safe conception practices has also been emphasized. It is important for therapists and other clinicians to adopt a nonjudgmental stance toward conception, to prevent couples from feeling the need to hide their wish to have children. Some couples may fear that clinicians will attempt to persuade them to undergo elective termination of pregnancy (Curran et al., 2012). Clinical work with HIV-discordant couples may elicit strong countertransference feelings in the therapist, as people do not always act in a way that an outside observer would deem "rational." Therapists may experience frustration and anxiety when witnessing continued risk-taking behavior within discordant couples. Cultural norms of gender roles, autonomy, and beliefs that differ from the therapist's own views may elicit countertransference that, if unexamined, can affect the therapy process. Powerful emotional reactions may also occur when HIV-affected couples discuss issues related to child-rearing. Supervision can be very helpful to the clinician in understanding and facing ambivalent feelings that may arise.

As more HIV-infected people are treated with and maintain adherence to antiretrovirals, there is a shift in identification from having a lethal to having a chronic illness. Couples may find that issues of intimacy, fears of transmission, adherence, and the many emotional aspects of coping with an unpredictable chronic disease will fluctuate at different periods in the normal course of development. Clinicians should maintain a dynamic view of the medical and mental health concerns of individuals and those of couples over time.

For further discussion of serodiscordant couples please refer to Chapter 34 in this book.

FAMILY THERAPY

There is a bidirectional relationship between the impact of HIV disease on affected families and the effect of family functioning on medical, psychological, and behavioral outcomes that has been difficult to quantify in studies. Goals of family therapy can be to reduce family and individual distress, to improve health and medication adherence, and to achieve HIV prevention through reduction of risk-taking behaviors. Medically ill parents with HIV who care for their children while simultaneously coping with ongoing physical symptoms face particular challenges and are especially vulnerable to psychosocial stressors that may affect their health. Parents with HIV often struggle with social and financial difficulties that have a great impact on their children's well-being. If the children themselves are HIV positive, maintaining healthy family dynamics can be especially difficult. Issues around disclosure, emotional reactions to the HIV diagnosis, fear of death, role adjustments, loss and bereavement, and social stigma are all examples of challenges to families with HIV. Pressure to reduce risky behaviors also commonly presents as a struggle.

The effectiveness of family-based interventions in improving outcomes and mitigating risk behaviors has been studied in a limited number of controlled prospective trials. Studies vary not only in the particular outcome of interest or goals of the family intervention but also according to serostatus of parent and child.

Rotheram-Borus and colleagues (2011) examined five randomized, controlled trials of family-based interventions in five major cities in the United States, Thailand, and South Africa. Patients consisted mostly of HIV-seropositive mothers and interventions were delivered in a group format composed of mothers (with and without their children) with separate adolescent groups. Populations studied included pregnant women, polydrug users and injection drug users or their partners, and women infected sexually. Compared to control groups, family-based interventions were associated with reduced substance use and sexual risk behaviors and improved mental and physical health symptoms in both parents and children (Lee et al., 2010; Rotheram-Borus et al., 2011).

Among these studies was a family-based intervention that helped parents with HIV and their adolescent children to cope with the HIV diagnosis, promote positive health behaviors, support healthy family dynamics, and reduce risk behaviors, even as parents were dying (Rotheram-Borus et al., 2001). The intervention was delivered in 24 modules over 12 Saturdays and was found to reduce emotional distress, decrease problem behaviors, and improve developmental outcomes of the children in up to 6-year follow-up measures (Rotheram-Borus et al., 2004). Additionally, follow-up studies found that grandchildren in the intervention condition displayed fewer behavioral symptoms, had more positive home environments, and scored higher on measures of cognitive development, suggesting the intergenerational benefits of family intervention (Rotheram-Borus et al., 2006).

Multiple studies have reported increased adherence, improved well-being, and improved health measures in families receiving family group support (Kmita et al., 2002; Lyon et al., 2003; McKay et al., 2004; Mitrani et al., 2003; Rotheram-Borus et al., 2003). These interventions have been conducted in various settings, including outpatient clinics and therapeutic camps (Kmita et al., 2002), using different modalities, such as a peer approach with "treatment buddies" (Lyon et al., 2003), and using different facilitators, including school staff and community-based agency representatives, to deliver family-based preventive intervention (McKay et al., 2004). Family-focused grief therapy (FFGT) represents a family approach to bereavement that aims to enhance family functioning while supporting the expression of grief (Kissane et al., 2006). This approach promotes open communication of thoughts and feelings and teaches effective problem-solving to reduce conflict and increase tolerance of different opinions. The improved functioning of the family as a unit helps advance adaptive mourning.

Betancourt and colleagues (2011) developed an intervention for families with HIV-infected parents in Rwanda (Family-Strengthening Intervention in Rwanda [FSI-R]). It was modeled on the Family-Based Preventive Intervention (FBPI) developed at Boston Children's Hospital (Beardslee et al., 2003; Betancourt et al., 2011). FSI-R was informed by qualitative data regarding cultural-specific expressions of both mental health issues in children and their families as well as resilience-promoting factors. The intervention was unique in its inclusion of input from participants from the community to ensure cultural relevance. Protective factors, such as family communication and connectedness, problem-solving, caregiver skills, and availability of social support, were identified and incorporated into intervention elements (Betancourt et al., 2011).

An understanding of the role of family factors in shaping children's risk behaviors has informed development of family-based interventions for HIV prevention. The Collaborative HIV/AIDS Mental Health Project (CHAMP) aimed to reduce risk behaviors among low-income youth living in inner-city areas. It utilized a family-based approach that targeted pre- and early adolescent children and emphasized communication, support both within and outside the family, caregiver supervision, problem-solving skills, and comfort discussing sensitive topics. This intervention has been adapted to resource-limited areas such as South Africa and the Caribbean (Bhana et al., 2010; McBride et al., 2007). CHAMP+ is an adaptation to children with perinatal HIV acquisition. Relative to comparison conditions, CHAMP+ participants enrolled in one study experienced a significant reduction in externalizing behavioral difficulties and were less likely to be exposed to situations involving sexual possibility (Bhana et al., 2010).

For further discussion of treatment of children and adolescents with HIV, please refer to Chapter 33 of this textbook.

SPIRITUAL CARE

Spiritual care is any care that recognizes the patient's spirituality and/or religious affiliation and attempts to incorporate those aspects into the overall treatment plan (Balboni et al., 2013). Numerous studies have shown that people who profess some degree of religious or spiritual involvement demonstrate greater purpose in life and optimism than those without such involvement (Koenig et al., 2014). An analysis of data from a nationally representative sample found that frequent religious service attendance is a long-term protective factor against suicide (Kleiman and Liu, 2014). One study claimed that, among people with HIV infection and AIDS, a majority belonged to an organized religion and used religion to cope with their illness (Cotton et al., 2006). However, spirituality is not synonymous with religious affiliation; many people consider themselves to be spiritual without belonging to a formal religious group. Kremer and Ironson (2014) emphasize this point in their 10-year qualitative study of how persons with HIV use spirituality to cope with illness and trauma. They found that 65% of the subjects in their study used spirituality positively and only 7% negatively (e.g., viewing HIV as sin). Spiritual care is further discussed in Chapter 41 of this textbook.

Although few controlled studies of any form of spiritual care among individuals with HIV have been reported, there is evidence that spirituality and religious affiliation are associated with better outcomes in this population. Litwinczuk and Groh (2007) reported a small but statistically significant positive correlation between spirituality and purpose in life among HIV-positive men and women. Manual-guided spiritual self-schema therapy increased motivation for HIV prevention and decreased HIV risk behavior in a controlled study of methadone-maintained patients (Margolin et al., 2009). One study randomly assigned 93 HIV-positive persons to receive either an intervention called "mantram repetition" or an attention control (Bormann et al., 2006). Mantram practice involves silently repeating a word or phrase with spiritual associations throughout the day. There were significantly greater improvements in the mantram group compared to the

Table 37.2 PSYCHOTHERAPEUTIC PRINCIPLES IN SPIRITUALLY FOCUSED TREATMENT

1. Controlling physical symptoms
2. Providing a supportive presence
3. Encouraging life review to assist in recognizing purpose, value, and meaning
4. Exploring guilt, remorse, forgiveness, and reconciliation
5. Facilitating religious expression
6. Reframing goals
7. Encouraging meditative practices
8. Focusing on healing rather than cure

control group in trait-anger, spiritual faith, and spiritual connectedness. Mantram repetition also improved quality of life and reduced intrusive thoughts.

Rousseau (2000) has developed an approach to the treatment of spiritual suffering that encompasses a blend of several basic psychotherapeutic principles, shown in Table 37.2. This approach to spiritual suffering emphasizes religious expression that may be extremely helpful to some patients, but not comfortable for all patients or clinicians.

Breitbart and colleagues have applied the work of Frankl (1955) and his concepts of meaning-based psychotherapy to address spiritual suffering. This approach may benefit patients seeking guidance in dealing with issues of sustaining meaning, hope, and understanding in the face of their illness, while avoiding overt religious emphasis. "Meaning-centered group psychotherapy" (Greenstein and Breitbart, 2000) involves a mixture of didactics, discussion, and experiential exercises that can also be used in individual therapy.

Spiritual beliefs influence decisions that persons with HIV make, including adherence to antiretroviral medications (Kremer et al., 2009). Decreased or lack of spiritual well-being is associated with significant depressive symptoms among persons with HIV (Yi et al., 2006). Spirituality may even be associated with CD4-cell preservation and undetectable viral load (Kremer et al., 2015). A study of HIV-positive teenagers found that most of them wanted clinicians to inquire about their spiritual needs (Bernstein et al., 2013). Although data from controlled trials of spiritual care interventions are somewhat limited, there is clearly sufficient evidence to warrant recommendations that clinicians assess spirituality and attend to spiritual needs among patients with HIV infection (Vance et al., 2008). More rigorous research needs to be conducted in this area (Szaflarski, 2013).

CONCLUSIONS

The past two decades have witnessed an exciting expansion of psychological treatment options for persons with HIV which can be integrated with and complement the medical and pharmacological care of persons with HIV/AIDS. The psychological needs of HIV-positive persons are complex and multilayered and require a multidisciplinary approach. Traditionally, the psychological treatment provided has depended more on available resources and theoretical background of the providers. Evidence-based treatment choices are becoming more common, however, as more reliable research is growing on the effectiveness of different treatment modalities.

As described in this chapter, a considerable literature supports the feasibility and utility of various treatment modalities for reducing psychological distress in persons with HIV. Both group and individual treatments have been shown to be effective, including psychodynamic/psychoanalytic, interpersonal, behavioral, and supportive approaches. In some cases, psychosocial interventions have been associated with improved immunological parameters. While many different therapeutic modalities have been studied, the field would benefit from further research to provide more consistent evidence in support of various treatment approaches in order to tailor treatment modalities to maximize life potentials in persons with HIV.

REFERENCES

Adamo SM, De Cristofaro W, De Falco R, Giacometti P, Giusti Z, Mancini F, Siani G (2008). Family secrets. HIV positive children and adolescents. A psychoanalytically-oriented approach. *Rivista Sperimentale di Freniatria: La Rivista della Salute Mentale* 132(2):43–69.

Alfonso CA (2011). Understanding the psychodynamics of non adherence. *Psychiatr Times* 28:22–23.

Alfonso CA, Cohen MA (1997.) The role of group therapy in the care of persons with AIDS. *J Am Acad Psychoanal* 25(4):623–638.

Allers CT, Benjack KJ (1991). Connection between childhood abuse, and HIV infection. *J Counsel Dev* 70:309–313.

Antoni MH, Cruess S, Cruess DG, et al. (2000a). Cognitive-behavioral stress management reduces distress and 24-hour urinary free cortisol output among symptomatic HIV-infected gay men. *Ann Behav Med* 22(1):29–37.

Antoni MH, Cruess DG, Cruess S, et al. (2000b). Cognitive-behavioral stress management intervention effects on anxiety, 24-hr urinary norepinephrine output, and T-cytotoxic/suppressor cells over time among sympomatic HIV-infected gay men. *J Consult Clin Psychol* 68(1):31–45.

Antoni MH, Cruess DG, Klimas N, et al. (2005). Increases in a marker of immune system reconstitution are predated by decreases in 24-h urinary cortisol output and depressed mood during a 10-week stress management intervention in symptomatic HIV-infected men. *J Pscyhosom Res* 58:3–13.

Antoni MH, Cruess DG, Klimas N, et al. (2002). Stress management and immune system reconstitution in symptomatic HIV-infected gay men over time: effects on transitional naive T cells (CD4(+) CD45RA(+)CD29(+)). *Am J Psychiatry* 159(1):143–145.

Aversa SL, Kimberlin C (1996). Psychosocial aspects of antiretroviral medication use among HIV patients. *Patient Educ Couns* 29:207–219.

Baeten JM, Donnell D, Ndase P, et al. (2012). Antiretroviral prophylaxis fir HIV prevention in heterosexual men and women. *N Engl J Med* 367:399–410.

Balboni TA, Balboni M, Enzinger A, et al. (2013). Provision of spiritual support to patients with advanced cancer by religious communities and associations with medical care at the end of life. *JAMA Intern Med* 173:1109–1117.

Beardslee WR, Gladstone TR, Wright EJ, Cooper AB (2003). A family-based approach to the prevention of depressive symptoms in children at risk: evidence of parental and child change. *Pediatrics* 112(2):e119–e131.

Belanoff JK, Sund B, Koopman C, Blasey C, Flamm J, Schatzberg AF, Spiegel D (2005). A randomized trial of the efficacy of group therapy

in changing viral load and CD4 counts in individual living with HIV infection. *Int J Psychiatry Med* 35(4):349–362.

Berger S, Schad T, von Wyl V, et al. (2008). Effects of cognitive behavioral stress management on HIV-1 RNA, CD4 cell counts and psychosocial parameters of HIV-infected persons. *AIDS* 22(6):767–775.

Bernstein K, D'Angelo LJ, Lyon ME (2013). An exploratory study of HIV+ adolescents' spirituality: will you pray with me? *J Relig Health* 52:1253–1266.

Betancourt TS, Meyers-Ohki SE, Stevenson A, et al. (2011). Using mixed-methods research to adapt and evaluate a family strengthening intervention in Rawanda. *Afr J Trauma Stress* 2(1):32–45.

Bhana A, McKay MM, Mellins C, Petersen I, Bell C (2010). Family-based HIV prevention and intervention services for youth living in poverty-affected contexts: the CHAMP model of collaborative, evidence-informed programme development. *J Int AIDS Soc* 13(Suppl 2):S1–S8

Blanch J, Rousaud A, Hautzinger M, et al. (2002). Assessment of the efficacy of a cognitive-behavioural group psychotherapy programme for HIV-infected patients referred to a consultation-liaison psychiatry department. *Psychother Psychosom* 71:77–84.

Bormann JE, Gifford Al, Shively M, et al. (2006). Effects of spiritual mantram repetition on HIV outcomes: a randomized controlled trial. *J Behav Med* 29:359–376.

Brakemeier EL, Frase L (2012). Interpersonal psychotherapy (IPT) in major depressive disorder. *Eur Arch Psychiatry Clin Neurosci* 262(Suppl 2):S117–S121.

Burton J, Drabes LA, Operario D (2010). Couples-focused behavioral interventions for prevention of HIV: systematic review of the state of evidence. *AIDS Behav* 14(1):1–10.

Cabaniss DL, Cherry S, Douglas CJ, Schwartz A (2011). *Psychodynamic Psychotherapy: A Clinical Manual*, Oxford: Wiley-Blackwell.

Caplette-Gingras A, Savard J (2008). Depression in women with metastatic cancer: a review of the literature. *Palliat Support Care* 6(4):377–387.

Carrico AW, Antoni MH (2008). The effects of psychological interventions on neuroendocrine hormone regulation and immune status in HIV-positive persons: a review of randomized controlled trials. *Psychosom Med* 70:575–584.

Carrico AW, Chesney MA, Johnson MO, et al.; NIMH Healthy Living Project Team (2009). Randomized controlled trial of a cognitive-behavioral intervention for HIV-positive persons: an investigation of treatment effects on psychosocial adjustment. *AIDS Behav* 13(3):555–563.

Carrico AW, Moskowitz JT (2014). Positive affect promotes engagement in care after HIV diagnosis. *Health Psychol* 33:686–689.

Carrico AW, Riley ED, Johnson MO, et al. (2011). Psychiatric risk factors for HIV disease progression: the role of inconsistent patterns of anti-retroviral therapy utilization. *J Acquir Immune Defic Syndr Hum Retrovirol* 56:146–150.

Carroll KM, Onken LS (2005). Behavioral therapies for drug abuse. *Am J Psychiatry* 162(8):1452–1460.

Catalán J (1999). Interpersonal therapy alone and supportive therapy plus antidepressant drugs were most effective for depression in HIV positive patients. *Evid Based Ment Health* 2:14–14.

Chesney MA, Chamber DB, Taylor JM, Johnson LM, Folkman S (2003). Coping effectiveness training for men living with HIV: results from a randomized clinical trial testing a group-based intervention. *Psychosom Med* 65(6):1038–1046.

Cohen MA (1987). Psychiatric aspects of AIDS: a biopsychosocial approach. In GP Wormser, RE Stahl, EJ Bottone (eds.), *AIDS Acquired Immune Deficiency Syndrome and Other Manifestations of HIV Infection*. Park Ridge, NJ: Noyes Publishers.

Cohen MA (1992). Biopsychosocial aspects of the HIV epidemic. In GP Wormser (ed.), *AIDS and Other Manifestations of HIV Infection*, 2nd ed. (pp. 349–371). New York: Raven Press.

Cohen MA (1998). Psychiatric care in an AIDS nursing home. *Psychosomatics* 39:154–161.

Cohen MA (1999). Psychodynamic psychotherapy in an AIDS nursing home. *J Am Acad Psychoanal* 27(1):121–133.

Cohen MA, Alfonso CA (2004). AIDS psychiatry: psychiatric and palliative care, and pain management. In GP Wormser (ed.), *AIDS and Other Manifestations of HIV Infection,* 4th ed. (pp. 537–576). San Diego: Elsevier Academic Press.

Cohen MA, Alfonso CA, Hoffman RG, Milau V, Carrera G (2001). The impact of PTSD on treatment adherence in persons with HIV infection. *Gen Hosp Psychiatry* 23:294–296.

Cohen MA, Hoffman RG, Cromwell C, et al. (2002). The prevalence of distress in persons with human immunodeficiency virus infection. *Psychosomatics* 43:10–15.

Cohen MA, Weisman H (1986). A biopsychosocial approach to AIDS. *Psychosomatics* 27:245–249.

Cohen MA, Weisman HW (1988). A biopsychosocial approach to AIDS. In RP Galea, BF Lewis, LA Baker (eds.), *AIDS and IV Drug Abusers.* Owings Mills, MD: National Health Publishing.

Cohen MS, Chen YQ, McCauley M, et al. (2011). Prevention of HIV-1 infection with early antiretroviral therapy. *N Engl J Med* 365(6):493–505.

Cotton S, Puchalski CM, Sherman SN, et al. (2006). Spirituality and religion in patients with HIV/AIDS. *J Gen Intern Med* 21(Suppl 5):S5–S13.

Cruess DG, Antoni MH, Schneiderman N, et al. (2000). Cognitive-behavioral stress management increased free testosterone and decreases psychological distress in HIV-seropositive men. *Health Psychol* 19(1):12–20.

Cuijpers P, Geraedts AS, van Oppen P, Andersson G, Markowitz JC, van Straten A (2011). Interpersonal psychotherapy for depression: a meta-analysis. *Am J Psychiatry* 168:581–592.

Curran KC, Baeten JM, Coates TJ, et al. (2012). HIV-1 prevention in HIV-1 serodiscordant couples. *Curr HIV/AIDS Rep* 9(2):160–170.

de Mello MF, de Jesus Mari J, Bacaltchuk J, Verdeli H, Neugebauer R (2005). A systematic review of research findings on the efficacy of interpersonal therapy for depressive disorders. *Eur Arch Psychiatry Clin Neurosci* 255:75–82.

DiIorio C, McCarthy F, Resnicow M, et al. (2008). Using motivational interviewing to promote adherence to antiretroviral medications: a randomized controlled study. *AIDS Care* 20(3):272–283.

Esposito-Smythers C, Brown LK, Wolff J, et al. (2014). Substance abuse treatment for HIV infected young people: an open pilot trial. *J Subst Abuse Treatment* 46:244–250.

Ferrando SJ, Freyberg Z (2008). Treatment of depression in HIV positive individuals: a critic al review. *Int Rev Psychiatry* 20:61–71.

Fife BL, Scott LL, Fineberg NS, Zwickl BE (2008). Promoting adaptive coping by persons with HIV disease: evaluation of a patient/partner intervention model. *J Assoc of Nurses in AIDS Care* 19:75–84.

Forstein M (2008). Young adulthood and serodiscordant couples. In MA Cohen, JM Gorman (eds.), *Comprehensive Textbook of AIDS Psychiatry* (pp. 341–355). New York: Oxford University Press.

Frankl VF (1955). *The Doctor and the Soul.* New York: Random House.

Friedman RC, Downey JI, Alfonso CA (2014). Contemporary psychodynamic psychiatry. *Psychodyn Psychiatry* 42(4):583–589.

Friedman RC, Downey JI, Alfonso CA, Ingram DH (2013). What is "psychodynamic psychiatry"? *Psychodyn Psychiatry* 41(4) 511–512.

Gabbard G (2007). Major modalities: psychoanalytic/psychodynamic. In GO Gabbard, JS Beck, J Holmes (eds.), *Oxford Textbook of Psychotherapy* (pp. 3–14). NewYork: Oxford University Press.

Gabbard GO (2014). *Psychodynamic Psychiatry in Clinical Practice,* 5th ed. Washington, DC: American Psychiatric Press.

Goldberg DA, Plakun EM (2013). Teaching psychodynamic psychotherapy with the Y model. *Psychodynam Psychiatry* 41(1):111–116.

Golin CE, Earp J, Tien H-C, Stewart P, et al. (2006). A 2-arm randomized, controlled trial of a motivational interviewing-based intervention to improve adherence to antiretroviral therapy (ART) among patients failing or initiating ART. *J Acquir Immune Defic Syndr* 42(1):420–451.

Goodkin K, Feaster DJ, Asthana D, et al. (1998). A bereavement support group intervention is longitudinally associated with salutary effects on CD4 cell count and on number of physician visits. *Clin Diagn Lab Immunol* 5:382–391.

Goodman LA, Fallot RD (1998). HIV risk-behavior in poor urban women with serious mental disorders: association with childhood physical, and sexual abuse. *Am J Orthopsychiatry* 68:73–83.

Grant P, Young PR, DeRubeis RJ (2007). Cognitive and behavioral therapies. In GO Gabbard, JS Beck, and J Holmes (eds.), *Oxford Textbook of Psychotherapy* (pp. 15–26). New York: Oxford University Press.

Grant RM, Lama JR, Anderson PL, et al. (2010). Preexposure prophylaxis for HIV prevention in men who have sex with men. *N Engl J Med* 363:2587–2599.

Greenstein M, Breitbart W (2000). Cancer and the experience of meaning: a group psychotherapy program for people with cancer. *Am J Psychother* 54:486–500.

Hasin DS, Aharonovich E, Greenstein E, et al. (2014). HealthCall for the smartphone: technology enhancement of brief intervention in HIV alcohol dependent patients. *Addict Sci Clin Pract* 9:5.

Hasin DS, Aharonovich E, O'Leary A, et al. (2013). Reducing heavy drinking in HIV primary care: a randomized trial of brief intervention, with and without technological enhancement. *Addiction* 108:1230–1240.

Heckman TG, Heckman BD, Anderson T, et al. (2013). Supportive-expressive and coping group teletherapies for HIV-infected older adults: A randomized clinical trial. *AIDS Behav* 17(9): 3034–3044.

Hershberger SL, Wood MM, Fisher DG (2003). A cognitive-behavioral intervention to reduce HIV risk behaviors in crack and injection drug users. *AIDS Behav* 7(3):229–243.

Himelhoch S, Medoff DR, Oyeniyi G (2007). Efficacy of group psychotherapy to reduce depressive symptoms among HIV-Infected individuals: a systematic review and meta-analysis *AIDS Patient Care STDs* 21: 732–739.

Himelhoch S, Medoff D, Maxfield J, et al. (2013). Telephone based cognitive behavioral therapy targeting major depression among urban dwelling, low income people living with HIV/AIDS: results of a randomized controlled trial. *AIDS Behav* 17(8):2756–2764.

Hollon SD, Ponniah K (2010). A review of empirically supported psychological therapies for mood disorders in adults. *Depress Anxiety* 27:891–932.

Jakobsen JC, Hansen JL, Simonsen S, Simonsen E, Gluud C (2012). Effects of cognitive therapy versus interpersonal psychotherapy in patients with major depressive disorder: a systematic review of randomized clinical trials with meta-analyses and trial sequential analyses. *Psychol Med* 42:1343–1357.

Jones DL, Ishii Owens M, Lydston D, Tobin JN, Brondolo E, Weiss SM (2010). Self-efficacy and distress in women with AIDS: the SMART/EST women's project. *AIDS Care* 22(12):1499–1508.

Kelly JA, Murphy DA, Bahr GR, et al. (1993). Outcomes of cognitive-behavioral and support group brief therapies for depressed, HIV-infected persons. *Am J Psychiatry* 150(11):1679–1686.

Kissane DW, McKenzie M, Bloch S, Moskowitz C, McKenzie DP, O'Neill I (2006). Family focused grief therapy: a randomized, controlled trial in palliative care and bereavement. *Am J Psychiatry* 163(7):1208–1218.

Kleiman EM, Liu RT (2014). Prospective prediction of suicide in a nationally representative sample: religious service attendance as a protective factor. *Br J Psychiatry* 204:262–264.

Kmita G, Baranska M, Niemiec T (2002). Psychosocial intervention in the process of empowering families with children living with HIV/AIDS—a descriptive study. *AIDS Care* 14(2):279–284.

Knight KM, McGowan L, Dickens C, Bundy C (2006). A systematic review of motivational interviewing in physical health care settings. *Br J Health Psychol* 11(Pt 2):319–332.

Koenig HG, Berk LS, Daher NS, et al. (2014). Religious involvement is associated with greater purpose, optimism, generosity and gratitude in persons with major depression and chronic medical illness. *J Psychosom Res* 7:135–143.

Koszycki D, Lafontaine S, Frasure-Smith N, Swenson R, Lesperance F (2004). An open-label trial of interpersonal psychotherapy in depressed patients with coronary disease. *Psychosomatics* 45(4):319–324.

Kraaij V, van Emmerik A, Garnefski N, et al. (2010). Effects of a cognitive behavioral self-help program and a computerized structured writing intervention on depressed mood for HIV-infected people: a pilot randomized controlled trial. *Patient Educ Couns* 80(2):200–204.

Kremer H, Ironson G (2014). Longitudinal spiritual coping with trauma in people with HIV: implications for health care. *AIDS Patient Care STDS* 28:144–154.

Kremer H, Ironson G, Kaplan L, Stuetzele R, Baker N, Fletcher MA (2015). Spiritual coping predicts CD4+ cell preservation and undetectable viral load over four years. *AIDS Care* 27:71–79.

Kremer H, Ironson G, Porr M (2009). Spiritual and mind-body beliefs as barriers and motivators to HIV-treatment decision-making and medication adherence? A qualitative study. *AIDS Patient Care STDS* 23:127–134.

Krummenacher I, Cavassini M, Bugnon O, Schneider MP (2011). An interdisciplinary HIV-adherence program combining motivational interviewing and electronic antiretroviral drug monitoring. *AIDS Care* 23(5):550–561.

Küchler T, Bestmann B, Rappat S, Henne-Bruns D, Wood-Dauphinee S (2007). Impact of psychotherapeutic support for patients with gastrointestinal cancer undergoing sugery: 10-year survival results of a randomized trial. *J Clin Oncol* 25(19): 2702–2708.

Laperriere A, Ironson GH, Antoni MH, et al. (2005). Decreased depression up to one year following CBSM+ intervention in depressed women with AIDS: the SMART/EST women's project. *J Health Psychol* 10(2):223–231.

Lee MR, Cohen L, Hadley SW, Goodwin FK (1999). Cognitive-behavioral group therapy with medication for depressed gay men with AIDS or symptomatic HIV infection. *Psychiatr Serv* 50:948–952.

Lee S, Li L, Jiraphongsa C, Lamsirithaworn S, et al. (2010). Regional variation in HIV disclosure in Thailand: implications for future interventions. *Int J STD AIDS* 21(3):161.

Leichsenring F, Abbass A, Luyten P, Hilsenroth M, Rabung S (2013). The emerging evidence for long-term psychodynamic therapy. *Psychodyn Psychiatry* 41(3):361–384.

Lenderking WR, Wold D, Mayer KH, et al. (1997). Childhood sexual abuse among homosexual men. Prevalence and association with unsafe sex. *J Gen Intern Med* 12:250–253.

Leserman J (2008). Role of depression, stress, and trauma in HIV disease progression. *Psychosom Med* 70(5):539–545.

Litwinczuk KM, Groh CJ (2007). The relationship between spirituality, purpose in life, and well-being in HIV-positive persons. *J Assoc Nurses AIDS* 18:13–22.

Lodico MA, DiClemente RJ (1994). The association between childhood abuse, and prevalence of HIV-related risk behaviors. *Clin Pediatr* 33:498–502.

Lundahl B, Burke BL (2009). The effectiveness and applicability of motivational interviewing: a practice-friendly review of four meta-analyses. *J Clin Psychol* 65(11):1232–1245.

Lyon ME, Trexler C, Akpan-Townsend C, et al. (2003). A family group approach to increasing adherence to therapy in HIV-infected youths: results of a pilot project. *AIDS Patient Care STDS* 17(6):299–308.

Madson MB, Loignon AC, Lane C (2009). Training in motivational interviewing: a systematic review. *J Subst Abuse Treatment* 36(1):101–109.

Margolin A, Beitel M, Schuman-Olivier Z, Avants SK (2009). A controlled study of a spirituality-focused intervention for increasing motivation for HIV prevention among drug users. *AIDS Educ Prev* 18:311–322.

Markowitz JC, Klerman GL, Clougherty KF, et al. (1995). Individual psychotherapies for depressed HIV-positive patients. *Am J Psychiatry* 152:1504–1509.

Markowitz JC, Kocsis JH, Fishman B, et al. (1998). Treatment of depressive symptoms in human immunodeficiency virus–positive patients. *Arch Gen Psychiatry* 55:452–457.

Martire LM, Schulz R, Helgeson VS, Small BJ, Saghafi EM (2010). Review and meta-analysis of couple-oriented interventions for chronic illness. *Ann Behav Med* 40(3):325–342.

McBride CK, Baptiste D, Traube D, et al. (2007). Family-based HIV preventive intervention: child level results from the CHAMP family program. *Soc Work*.

McKay MM, Chase KT, Paikoff R, et al. (2004). Family-level impact of the CHAMP Family Program: a community collaborative effort to support urban families and reduce youth HIV risk exposure. *Fam Process* 43(1):79–93.

Milam J, Richardson JL, McCutchan A, et al., (2005). Effect of a brief antiretroviral adherence intervention delivered by HIV care providers. *J Acquir Immune Defic Syndr* 40(3):356–363.

Miller RW, Rollnick S (2002). *Motivational Interviewing: Preparing People for Change* (2nd ed.). New York: Guilford Press.

Mitrani VB, Prado G, Feaster DJ, Robinson-Batista C, Szapocznik J (2003). Relational factors and family treatment engagement among low-income, HIV-positive African American mothers. *Fam Process* 42(1):31–45.

Molassiotis A, Callaghan P, Twinn SF, Lam SW, Chung WY, Li CK (2002). A pilot study of the effects of cognitive-behavioral group therapy and peer support/counseling in decreasing psychological distress and improving quality of life in Chinese patients with symptomatic HIV disease. *AIDS Patient Care STDS* 16(2):83–96.

Muessig KE, Cohen MS (2014). Advances in HIV prevention for serodiscordant couples. *HIV/AIDS Rep* 22:1–13.

Mugford JG (2004). Efficacy of long-term psychotherapy in the management of persons living with HIV/AIDS. *Dissertation Abstracts International: The Sciences and Engineering* 64(9B):42–80.

Mulder CL, Antoni MH, Emmelkamp PM, Veugelers PJ, Sandfort TG, van de Vijver FA, de Vries MJ (1995). Psychosocial group intervention and the rate of decline of immunological parameters in asymptomatic HIV-infected homosexual men. *Psychother Psychosom* 63(3–4):185–192.

Naar-King S, Parsons J, Murphy DA, et al. (2009). Improving health outcomes for youth living with human immunodeficiency virus. *Arch Pediatr Adolesc Med* 163(12):1092–1098.

Papas RK, Sidle JE, Gakinya BN, et al. (2011). Treatment outcomes of a stage I cognitive-behavioral trial to reduce alcohol use among human immunodeficiency virus-infected out-patients in western Kenya. *Addiction* 106:2156–2166.

Parsons JT, Rosof E, Punzalan JC, Di Maria L (2005). Integration of motivational interviewing and cognitive behavioral therapy to improve HIV medication adherence and reduce substance use among HIV-positive men and women: results of a pilot project. *AIDS Patient Care STDS* 19(1):31–39.

Parsons JT, Sarit GA, Rosof E, Holder C (2007). Motivational interviewing and cognitive-behavioral intervention to improve HIV medication adherence among hazardous drinkers. *J Acquir Immune Defic Syndr* 46(4):442–450.

Petrie KJ, Fontanilla I, Thomas MG, Booth RJ, Pennebaker JW (2004). Effect of written emotional expression on immune function in patients with human immunodeficiency virus infection: a randomized trial. *Psychosom Med* 66(2):272–275.

Plakun EM, Sudak DM, Goldberg DA (2009). The Y model: an integrated, evidence-based approach to teaching psychotherapy competencies. *J Psychiatr Pract* 15(1):5–11.

Pobuda T, Crothers L, Goldblum P, Dilley JW, Koopman C (2008). Effects of time-limited dynamic psychotherapy on distress among HIV-seropositive men who have sex with men. *AIDS Patient Care STDS* 22(7):561–567.

Pollak KL, Alexander SC, Tulsky JA, et al. (2011). Physician empathy and listening: associations with patient satisfaction and autonomy. *J Am Board Fam Med* 24(6):665–672.

Ransom D, Heckman TG, Anderson T, Garske J, Holroyd K, Basta T (2008). Telephone-delivered, interpersonal psychotherapy for HIV-infected rural persons with depression: a pilot trial. *Psychiatr Serv* 59:871–878.

Ratigan B (1991). On not traumatising the traumatised: the contribution of psychodynamic psychotherapy to work with people with HIV and AIDS. *Br J Psychother* 8(1):39–47.

Ravitz P, McBride C, Maunder R (2011). Failures in interpersonal psychotherapy (IPT) factors related to treatment resistances. *J Clin Psychol* 67:1129–11339.

Remien RH, Stirratt MJ, Dolezal C, et al. (2005). Couple-focused support to improve HIV medication adherence: a randomized controlled trial. *AIDS* 19:807–814.

Ricart F, Cohen MA, Alfonso CA, Hoffman RG, Quinone N, Cohen A, Indyk D (2002). Understanding the psychodynamics of non-adherence to medical treatment in persons with HIV infection. *Gen Hosp Psychiatry* 24(3):176–180.

Rogers RR (1989). Beyond morality: the need for psychodynamic understanding and treatment of responses to the AIDS crisis. *Psychiatr J Univ Ott* 14(3):456–459.

Rousseau P (2000). Spirituality and the dying patient. *J Clin Oncol* 18:2000–2002.

Rotheram-Borus MJ, Lee MB, Gwadz M, Draimin B (2001). An intervention for parents with AIDS and their adolescent children. *Am J Public Health* 91(8):1294–1302.

Rotheram-Borus MJ, Lee M, Leonard N, et al. (2003). Four-year behavioral outcomes of an intervention for parents living with HIV and their adolescent children. *AIDS* 17(8):1217–1225.

Rotheram-Borus MJ, Lee M, Lin YY, Lester P (2004). Six-year intervention outcomes for adolescent children of parents with the human immunodeficiency virus. *Arch Pediatr Adolesc Med* 158(8):742–748.

Rotheram-Borus MJ, Lester P, Song J, et al. (2006). Intergenerational benefits of family-based HIV interventions. *J Consult Clin Psychol* 74(3):622–627.

Rotheram-Borus MJ, Swendeman D, Lee S-J, et al. (2011). Interventions for families affected by HIV. *Transl Behav Med* 1:313–326.

Safren SA, O'Cleirigh CM, Bullis JR, Otto MW, Stein MD, Pollack MH (2012). Cognitive behavioral therapy for adherence and depression (CBT-AD) in HIV-infected injection drug users: a randomized controlled trial. *J Consult Clin Psychol* 80(3):404–415.

Safren SA, O'Cleirigh C, Tan JY, Raminani SR, Reilly LC, Otto MW, Mayer KH (2009). A randomized controlled trial of cognitive behavioral therapy for adherence and depression (CBT-AD) in HIV-infected individuals. *Health Psychol* 28(1):1–10.

Samuels E, Khalife S, Alfonso CA, Alvarez R, Cohen MA (2011). Early childhood trauma, posttraumatic stress disorder, and non-adherence in persons with AIDS: a psychodynamic perspective. *J Am Acad Psychoanal Dynam Psychiatry* 39(4):633–650.

Schroeder JR, Epstein DH, Umbricht A, Preston KL (2006). Changes in HIV risk behaviors among patients receiving combined pharmacological and behavioral interventions for heroin and cocaine dependence. *Addict Behav* 31(5):868–879.

Shoptaw S, Reback CJ, Peck JA, et al. (2005). Behavioral treatment approaches for methamphetamine dependence and HIV-related sexual risk behaviors among urban gay and bisexual men. *Drug Alcohol Depend* 78:125–134.

Sikkema KJ, Hansen NB, Kochman A, et al. (2004a). Outcomes from a randomized controlled trial of a group intervention for HIV positive men and women coping with AIDS-related loss and bereavement. *Death Stud* 28:187–209.

Sikkema KJ, Hansen NB, Tarakeshwar N, Kochman A, Tate DC, Lee RS (2004b). The clinical significance of change in trauma-related symptoms following a pilot group intervention for coping with HIV-AIDS and childhood sexual trauma. *AIDS Behav* 8(3):277–291.

Simoni JM, Wiebe JS, Sauceda JA, et al. (2013). A preliminary RCT of CBT-AD for adherence and depression among HIV-positive Latinos on the U.S.-Mexico border: the Nuevo Día study. *AIDS Behav* Oct;17(8):2816–2829.

Spies G, Asmal L, Seedat S (2013). Cognitive-behavioural interventions for mood and anxiety disorders in HIV: a systematic review. *J Affect Disord*. Sep 5;150(2):171–180.

Stein MD, Herman DS, Bishop D, et al. (2007). A telephone-based intervention for depression in HIV patients: negative results from a randomized clinical trial. *AIDS Behav* 11(1):15–23.

Szaflarski M (2013). Spirituality and religion among HIV-infected individuals. *Curr HIV/AIDS Rep* 10:324–332.

Temoshok LR, Wald RL, Synowski S, Garzino-Demo A (2008). Coping as a multisystem construct associated with pathways mediating HIV-relevant immune function and disease progression. *Psychosom Med*. 70(5):555–561.

Thompson NJ, Potter JS, Sanderson CA, Maibach EW (1997). The relationship of sexual abuse, and HIV risk behaviors among heterosexual adult female STD patients. *Child Abuse Neglect* 21:149–156.

Vance DE, Struzick TC, Raper JL (2008). Biopsychosocial benefits of spirituality in adults aging with HIV: implications for nursing practice and research. *J Holist Nurs* 26:119–125.

van Hees ML, Rotter T, Ellerman T, Evers SM (2013). The effectiveness of individual interpersonal psychotherapy as a treatment for major depressive disorder in adult outpatients: a systematic review. *BMC Psychiatry* 13:22.

Weiss JJ (1997). Psychotherapy with HIV-positive gay men: a psychodynamic perspective. *Am J Psychother* 51(1):31–44.

Weiss JJ, Mulder CL, Antoni MH, de Vroome EM, Garssen B, Goodkin K (2003). Effects of a supportive-expressive group intervention on long-term psychosocial adjustment in HIV-infected gay men. *Psychother Psychosom* 72(3):132–140.

Wingood GM, DiClemente RJ (1997). Child sexual abuse, HIV sexual risk, and general relations of African-American women. *Am J Prev Med* 13:380–384.

Wu E, El-Bassel N, McVinney LD, et al. (2011). Feasibility and promise of a couple-based HIV/STI preventive intervention for methamphetamine-using, black men who have sex with men. *AIDS Behav* 15:1745–1754.

Yi MS, Mrus JM, Wade TJ, et al. (2006). Religion, spirituality, and depressive symptoms in patients with HIV/AIDS. *J Gen Intern Med* 21(Suppl 5):S21–S27.

Zisook S, Peterkin J, Goggin KJ, et al. (1998). Treatment of major depression in HIV-seropositive men. HIV Neurobehavioral Research Center Group. *J Clin Psychiatry* 59:217–224.

38.

INTEGRATIVE TREATMENTS

Cheryl Gore-Felton, Lawrence McGlynn, Andrei Kreutzberg, and David Spiegel

Antiretroviral therapy has dramatically improved survival among individuals living with HIV/AIDS, changing HIV infection to a chronic illness that demanded a shift in attention to symptom management. Common symptoms adversely affecting quality of life for persons with HIV include neuropsychiatric problems such as anxiety, depression, cognitive dysfunction, and headaches, as well as somatic disorders such as fatigue, diarrhea, and cardiovascular problems. Many of these problems can be managed with integrative medicine interventions. Integrative medicine is a particular approach to medical care that typically combines evidence-based, conventional medicine with complementary and alternative medicine (CAM) (Kligler et al., 2004). The approach focuses on treating the physiological, psychiatric, and spiritual aspects of human functioning and wellness.

The use of CAM among individuals living with HIV/AIDS is high, with national studies reporting use among more than half (55%) of the people diagnosed with HIV/AIDS (Lorenc and Robinson, 2013). Moreover, a study among an ethnically diverse, gender-balanced sample of persons living with HIV/AIDS found that 67% were taking prescription medication for HIV along with an alternative supplement (Gore-Felton et al., 2003). Similarly, a recent cross-sectional study found that almost half of the sample had used CAM in the past month and 78% reported using CAM since being diagnosed with HIV (Littlewood and Vanable, 2014). Despite the high prevalence of CAM use with conventional medication among people living with HIV/AIDS, there remains a paucity of research focused on evaluating its efficacy and effectiveness. Therefore, empirical evidence is limited with regard to the safety and benefit of integrative medicine to treat HIV disease, particularly approaches that use supplements. Given the high prevalence of supplement use in conjunction with HIV-related medication, it is important to critically evaluate what is known about the benefits and risks of integrative approaches in the treatment of HIV illness.

This chapter examines widely used supplements that include herbal, botanical, and minerals as well as movement therapies including yoga, meditation, and hypnosis. Implications for clinical practice are discussed.

HERBALS

The use of medicinal herbs by persons with HIV has been explored since early in the epidemic (Kassler et al., 1991).

Herbals were frequently used for their gastrointestinal (GI) benefits and central nervous system (CNS) effects. *Atractylodes ovala* is known to provide mild sedation (Kawashima et al., 1985; Liu, 1989; Saxe, 1987). *Arctium lappa* (Bryson et al., 1978) and *Lycium* (Hsu, 1986) have anticholinergic properties. *Echinacea* (Voaden and Jacobson, 1972), ginseng (Dubick, 1986; Jones and Runikis, 1987; Siegel, 1979), and *Schisandra* (Hsu, 1986) stimulate the CNS.

Significant changes have occurred since the earlier studies were published, most notably the availability of effective antiretroviral medications and improved prognosis. Studies in the era after 1995 now consider herbals in the context of antiretroviral therapy.

Fairfield et al. (1998) found 67.8% of 180 HIV-positive subjects reported using herbs, vitamins, or dietary supplements. Although a number of patients have chosen to use these agents, the benefits, if any, are not always clear. Liu and colleagues (2005) assessed the effects of herbal medicine in people with HIV/AIDS by examining clinical trials. The trials included seven products, most of which were combinations of commonly used medicinal herbs: "35 herbs," IGM-1, Capsaicin, Chinese herbal product SH, Qiankunning, SP-303 (Provir), and SPV30. The study concluded that there was no compelling evidence to support the use of the herbals that were identified in their study for people living with HIV/AIDS (Liu et al., 2005).

Cultural differences in the use of herbals has long been acknowledged but not well understood. A study of 137 HIV-infected individuals in Uganda found 63.5% of patients with AIDS used traditional herbal medicine (Langlois-Klassen et al., 2007). Rivera et al. (2006) conducted a prospective observational study of Mexican-American patients in the El Paso region of Texas. The authors found 71% of patients with HIV reported using herbal products, which did not differ statistically from non-HIV Mexican-American subjects in their study. The most common herbal products used included chamomile (used as a light sedative), hibiscus (to lower blood pressure and stimulate appetite), and garlic (to lower cholesterol and prevent blood clots). The use of damiana (*Turneraceae*) as an aphrodisiac was also reported in this group.

Most of the sample report having learned about the products from relatives, and 71% obtained the herb from Mexico. Almost all (98%) of the HIV-positive subjects perceived that their chosen products provided the benefits they were seeking. Moreover, 81% did not tell their doctor about their use of the products (Rivera et al., 2005, 2006). This is problematic because of the limited research on the risks and benefits of supplements, and the little research that has been conducted has shown that some alternative supplements (i.e., St. John's wort and garlic) have interaction effects with HIV medication that can result in deleterious health outcomes for patients (Piscitelli et al., 2000, 2002; Stolbach et al., 2015). Please refer to Chapter 42 of this textbook for further discussion of supplement–drug interactions in persons with HIV.

There is growing interest in plant-based medicine to treat mood and anxiety disorders as well as to improve brain function (e.g., memory, processing). Phytotherapy utilizes minimally processed plant-based extracts. Sebit et al. (2002) examined the use of phytotherapy in neuropsychiatric disorders in 105 HIV-positive adults living in Zimbabwe. Individuals were examined at baseline, 3 months, and 6 months. The assessments included modules for psychotic, affective, and anxiety disorders. In addition, cognitive assessments were performed utilizing structured interviews and questionnaires, with specific items for memory, concentration, speech, and thinking. Although the authors concluded that phytotherapy was generally protective against psychiatric disorders in HIV, the study had a number of limitations, including small sample size, lack of randomization and double-blinding, and selection bias. More importantly, the authors did not identify which botanicals comprised "phytotherapy" (Sebit et al., 2002).

Some promising studies have used herbals in subjects for whom HIV status is not considered. A recent study of 56 individuals (HIV status not specified) with major depressive disorder were treated with curcumin (500 milligrams twice daily) or placebo for 8 weeks. From weeks 4 to 8, curcumin was significantly more effective than placebo in improving several mood-related symptoms (Lopresti et al., 2014). While individuals may use supplements such as curcumin for depression, valerian for sleep, and yohimbine for sexual dysfunction, a lack of published research using subjects with HIV continues to challenge healthcare professionals wanting to offer or support the use of these alternative treatments.

Herb–drug interactions may ultimately prohibit the use of some natural products in persons living with HIV/AIDS. St. John's wort (Henderson et al., 2002; Piscitelli et al., 2000) and garlic supplements (Berginc et al., 2009; Piscitelli et al., 2002) have been shown to reduce the area under the curve (AUC) of some antiretroviral medications, possibly impairing a sustained virological response (SVR) in patients using these supplements while on antiretroviral therapy. Other products with antiretroviral drug interactions, including DHEA, *Echinacea*, kava, ginseng, ginkgo biloba, red yeast, cat's claw, and milk thistle, need to be carefully monitored, assuring that the benefits outweigh the risks (Ladenheim et al., 2008).

MARIJUANA

Some persons living with HIV/AIDS use marijuana for physiological reasons (e.g., nausea, anorexia, pain) (Abrams et al., 2007), while others use it to manage emotional or psychological symptoms (including anxiety and agitation). Researchers studying the use of marijuana in HIV-positive subjects have explored reasons for its use, benefits, as well as unintended consequences.

Woolridge and colleagues (2005) studied the use of cannabis in 143 HIV-positive patients. Reasons given for use included to augment relaxation (85%), reduce anxiety (66%), relieve depression (52%), and increase energy levels (11%). A significant proportion (43%) of the respondents reported that they were using cannabis "for a high." More than 50% reported marijuana was beneficial for appetite, anxiety, muscle pain, nausea, depression, and nerve pain (Woolridge et al., 2005).

Prentiss and colleagues (2004) sought to understand the patterns of marijuana use among patients with HIV receiving care in a public health setting. Participants (*n* = 252) were recruited via consecutive sampling in public healthcare clinics. The study found a 23% overall prevalence of smoked marijuana in the previous month. Reported benefits included relief of anxiety and/or depression (57%), improved appetite (53%), increased pleasure (33%), and relief of pain (28%) (Furler et al., 2004).

Corless and colleagues (2009) assessed the use of marijuana as a symptom management approach for people living with HIV/AIDS. Marijuana was rated slightly more effective than antidepressants for addressing depression and anxiety. For those who used both marijuana and medications for symptom management, antidepressants were rated somewhat more effective than marijuana for anxiety and depression, but marijuana was rated slightly more effective than anti-anxiety medications. None of these findings were significant. Marijuana, however, had a significantly negative impact on adherence.

Cognitive impairment remains a concern in HIV/AIDS, and has also been seen as a possible unintended consequence of marijuana use. Cristiani et al. (2004) examined the interaction of HIV disease stage and marijuana use in 282 subjects. After controlling for the effects of depression, anxiety, and alcohol use, the authors found frequent marijuana use was associated with greater cognitive impairment among subjects with symptomatic HIV infection. This effect appeared to be primarily related to performance on memory tasks and may help to explain why marijuana use has been found to have a negative impact on adherence. The authors noted minimal impact of marijuana for those in the earlier stages of HIV infection.

Haney and colleagues (2007) evaluated effects of marijuana and dronabinol in a small, placebo-controlled within-subjects study across a range of behaviors: eating topography, mood, cognitive performance, physiological measures, and sleep. HIV-positive marijuana smokers (*n* = 10) completed two 16-day inpatient phases. Each dronabinol (5 and 10 mg) and marijuana (2.0% and 3.9% Δ^9-tetrahydrocannabinol [THC]) dose was administered four times daily for 4 days, but only one drug was active per day, thereby maintaining double-blind dosing. Four days of placebo washout separated each active cannabinoid condition. All cannabinoid conditions produced significant intoxication, except for low-dose dronabinol (5 mg); the intoxication was rated positively (e.g., "good drug effect") with little evidence of discomfort and no impairment of cognitive performance. Effects of marijuana and dronabinol were comparable, with the exception that only marijuana (3.9% THC) improved ratings of sleep.

HIV enters the CNS early in the course of infection, resulting in profound changes in brain neurochemistry. Chang et al. (2006) evaluated whether chronic marijuana use and HIV infection were associated with interactive or additive effects on brain chemistry and cognitive function. The authors evaluated 96 subjects in four groups (+/- HIV; +/- marijuana) using proton magnetic resonance spectroscopy and a battery of neuropsychological tests. After correcting for age, education, and mood differences, marijuana users had no significant abnormalities on neuropsychological test performance, and HIV subjects only had slower reaction times. The authors concluded that these findings suggest chronic marijuana use may lead to decreased neuronal and glial metabolites but may normalize the decreased glutamate in persons living with HIV.

VITAMINS

WATER-SOLUBLE VITAMINS

Vitamin B_6

Inadequate vitamin B_6 status has been associated with altered neuropsychiatric function, possibly through its effect on the metabolism of neurotransmitters, including serotonin (5-HT). A significant decline in psychological distress was demonstrated after normalization of vitamin B_6 status from inadequate to adequate status in a cohort of HIV-positive individuals. Interestingly, these findings were significant even after controlling for negative life event stressors, social support, and coping style (Shor-Posner et al., 1994).

Vitamin B_{12}

Cobalamin (vitamin B_{12}) deficiency has been linked to multiple neuropsychological changes, including but not limited to cognitive impairment, distress, depression, anxiety, and irritability. Decreased cobalamin levels have been reported in 25–50% of HIV-1 infected individuals. Baldewicz et al. (2000) examined the relationship of plasma cobalamin level to overall psychological distress, specific mood states, and major depressive disorder in 159 bereaved men (90 HIV-positive; 69 HIV-negative). Herzlich and Schiano (1993) found that cobalamin level was inversely related to self-reported overall distress level and specifically to depression, anxiety, and confusion subscale scores, as well as to clinically rated depressed and anxious mood. Lower plasma cobalamin levels also were associated with the presence of symptoms consistent with major depressive disorder. Importantly, these relationships were not restricted to deficiency states (Baldewicz et al., 2000; Herzlich and Schiano 1993). The role of B_{12} in HIV-related neurocognitive disorders has also been documented. A case report noted the reversal of dementia in a patient

with apparent AIDS dementia following treatment with B_{12} (Herzlich and Schiano 1993). Taken altogether, these findings indicate that an evaluation of B_{12} deficiency should always be included in the differential diagnosis of cognitive dysfunction in people living with HIV.

Vitamin C

Vitamin C (ascorbic acid) is one of the most commonly used vitamins among people living with HIV/AIDS (Gore-Felton et al., 2003). In fact, among young people living with HIV/AIDS, low plasma ascorbate concentrations suggest that vitamin C requirements are significantly higher than in those who are HIV negative (Stephensen et al., 2006). In a small randomized, placebo-controlled, double-blind study of HIV-positive patients, the antioxidant properties of vitamin C were examined; the investigators found a reduction in oxidative stress as well as a trend toward viral load reduction. The direct benefits for mental health in this group, however, remain unclear (Allard et al., 1998).

FAT-SOLUBLE VITAMINS

Vitamin A

Prior to and during the evolution of effective antiretroviral therapy, factors influencing transmission were studied. Research that focused on mother-to-child transmission suggested that maternal vitamin A deficiency contributed to mother-to-child transmission of HIV (Semba et al., 1994), demonstrating a link between vitamin A and immunological integrity. Caution is advised in its use, as toxicities occur in doses exceeding 25,000 IU per day and include anorexia, weight loss, bone malformations, spontaneous fractures, internal bleeding, liver toxicities, and birth defects. Moreover, isotretinoin, a form of vitamin A to treat severe acne, has been associated with increased risk of suicide and depression (Wysoski et al., 2001). However, the mechanism of this association remains unknown.

Vitamin D

There is a growing body of evidence indicating that vitamin D is associated with a healthy immune system. Vitamin D is essential in assisting the body to absorb calcium and phosphorus, both of which are used to build bones. Vitamin D deficiency has been documented among HIV-positive individuals and may be related to clinically significant photosensitivity that has been documented in those with HIV (Bilu et al., 2004). Risk factors associated with vitamin D deficiency include antiretroviral therapy and African American ethnicity (Bilu et al., 2004). More recently, researchers examined the association between vitamin D deficiency and different antiretroviral drugs. The findings indicated the deficiency was specifically linked to the drug efavirenz, and no effect was found on other antiretrovirals including etravirine, darunavir, and raltegravir. The longer a person was taking evavirenz, the more likely he or she was to develop a vitamin D deficiency (Allavena et al., 2012).

In addition to the link between antiretroviral drugs and vitamin D deficiency, there may be some behavioral factors that increase risk. For instance, patients may be advised to use sun block or avoid the sun altogether, leading to an increased risk of vitamin D deficiency (Cannell et al., 2008). An adequate level of vitamin D in persons living with HIV is especially important, as osteoporosis has been reported to be present in up to 15% of individuals living with the virus (Panayiotopoulos et al., 2013). In persons who are co-infected with hepatitis C virus, vitamin D deficiency is associated with the severity of liver disease (Guzmán-Fulgencio et al., 2014). Moreover, low levels of vitamin D have been associated with seasonal affective disorder in a non-HIV populations (Gloth et al., 1999). More recent studies have documented the association between vitamin D deficiency and cognitive dysfunction in a non-HIV population (Schlögl and Holick, 2014).

Vitamin E

Vitamin E (tocopherol) is a commonly reported supplement among HIV-positive adults (Gore-Felton et al., 2003). Stephensen et al. (2006) found plasma tocopherol concentrations were not depressed in a group of 14- to 23-year-old HIV-positive subjects. However, Pacht et al. (1997) noted progressive decreases in vitamin E levels in adults with HIV. Its utility in reducing oxidative stress has been noted in the literature (Allard et al., 1998). Moreover, research examining the effect of micronutrients among HIV-positive individuals on antiretroviral therapy found a significant improvement in CD4 count (Kaiser et al., 2006). It is important to note that vitamin E was 1 of 33 micronutrients tested that were included in the supplement that was given to research participants. Therefore, it is impossible to tease apart the specific impact of vitamin E in this study. However, the findings provide further evidence for the importance of micronutrients, particularly in individuals living with HIV/AIDS.

MINERALS

SELENIUM

Selenium has been associated with cardiomyopathy, myopathy, and immune dysfunction. Research suggests that selenium deficiency may be related to HIV-related mortality (Baum et al., 1997). Moreover, selenium deficiency has been linked to negative mood, and elevated selenium may be associated with reduced cancer risk (Rayman, 2000). Selenium has been used by some individuals as a way to manage fatigue in HIV/AIDS. A study among HIV-positive men found that length of time taking antiretrovirals was associated with selenium values such that men who were on antiretrovirals for more than 2 years had higher selenium values, lower viral load, and higher CD4 count compared to men on antiretroviral therapy for less than 2 years (Barbosa et al. 2015).

ZINC

Chronic inflammation and low levels of zinc are not uncommon among HIV-positive individuals. Zinc deficiency among HIV-positive individuals has been associated with a reduction in the number of circulating T lymphocytes. Observational studies examining the effect of zinc on HIV disease progression have found mixed results (Kupka and Fawzi, 2002). There is a need for prospective, randomized trials to examine the effect of zinc on HIV progression, particularly among individuals taking antiretroviral medications.

PROBIOTICS

Diarrhea is one of the most common symptoms associated with HIV and may be caused by HIV-related medication or GI complications that result from the viral infection. Diarrhea significantly compromises quality of life and can complicate the clinical course of the disease. The use of probiotics has been associated with an increase in CD4 count even after controlling for length of time using antiretroviral medication (Irvine et al., 2010). Moreover, *Lactobacillus rhamnosus* GR-1 and *L. reuteri* RC-14 resolved moderate diarrhea symptoms among women living with HIV/AIDS in Nigeria (Anukam et al., 2008). While there is consistent evidence that probiotic therapy in HIV-negative populations is safe and effective in improving GI symptoms, there is a dearth of evidence indicating the same among HIV-positive populations (Wilson et al., 2013).

MOVEMENT THERAPIES

The stress of coping with a chronic, life-threatening illness can be psychologically overwhelming, resulting in mood and anxiety disorders. In addition to supplements, herbs, minerals, micronutrients, and marijuana, individuals living with HIV often engage in physical movement to enhance overall wellness. Morgan (2014) examined the feasibility of an ongoing holistic wellness program in a residential facility treating persons with HIV/AIDS. The goal was to create a voluntary, 4-week holistic wellness intensive protocol within the established inpatient behavioral health treatment program. The program incorporated evidence-based holistic activities including yoga, therapeutic dance, meditation, Reiki, and reflective journaling. Narrative survey results and post-program evaluation showed increased feelings of calmness and energy, in addition to improved sleep and elevated confidence to address everyday stressors. Although the study was limited by the small number of participants, it provides evidence that physical activity in the context of chronic illness can enhance mood (Morgan, 2014).

TAI CHI

In the West, tai chi is practiced as a form of moving meditation and is considered a low-level physical exercise. Using breath and balanced movement, practitioners facilitate the flow of chi (life force energy) to restore internal balance and harmony (Robins et al., 2006). McCain et al. (2005) sought to determine whether a 10-week tai chi training intervention in persons with HIV disease would improve various parameters of perceived health. The study involved both quantitative measures (Dealing with Illness Scale, Social Provisions Scale, Impact of Event Scale, Functional Assessment of HIV Infection Scale, and the Spiritual Well-Being Scale) as well as a qualitative assessment of interviews. A total of 59 participants completed the training, consisting of movements designed to foster individual development of balance, focused breathing, gentle physical posturing and movement, and the use of consciousness for relaxation. A total of 56 individuals completed a treatment-period control condition. Individuals in the tai chi group had higher existential well-being, higher perceptions of social support, and more frequent use of appraisal-focused coping strategies (McCain et al., 2005).

Quality of life and functional outcomes were assessed in a study that compared the efficacy of aerobic exercise and tai chi among patients with AIDS (Galantino et al., 2006). Thirty-eight individuals with AIDS were randomized to one of three groups: tai chi, aerobic exercise, or control. Groups exercised twice weekly for 8 weeks. Tai chi and aerobic exercise improved mood, physical function, and quality of life. Also, individuals in the study reported positive physical changes, better coping, and improved social relationships (Galantino et al., 2006).

QIGONG

Qigong, a form of Taoist meditation, has been used in the eastern and western cultures as a way to obtain the perfect health necessary for a long life. A pilot study examined the influence of qigong among HIV-positive subjects in the pre-ART era. The 3-month study consisted of approximately 2 hours of meditation in a standing position, preceded by a series of gentle warm-up exercises. The results indicated significant decreases in anxiety and depression among 26 individuals living with HIV (Koar, 1995).

YOGA

Menon and Glazebrook (2013) conducted a randomized controlled study aimed at evaluating the impact of a 10-week program of peer support and yoga on the psychological well-being of HIV-positive Zambian adolescents. Thirty-four subjects were randomized to peer group with yoga, peer social support group without yoga, or waitlist control. Outcomes included psychological well-being. The peer (non-yoga) social support group had fewer emotional symptoms immediately after the intervention. The combination yoga and peer support group was associated with an increase in CD4 count immediately after the intervention. At the 10-week follow-up, however, there were no differences between the groups (Menon and Glazebrook, 2013). More research is needed to understand how to maintain gains observed immediately following support and yoga interventions to sustain changes over time.

Another study examined the effects of an integrated yoga program on 70 HIV-positive patients not on ART, with CD4 counts >250, who were recruited in Bangalore. Participants were randomized to one of two conditions: yoga intervention or wait-list control. The yoga group received an integrated set of 1-hour daily yoga therapy sessions (asanas, pranayama, and meditation) for 3 months. The study found that there was a significant decrease in perceived stress and psychological distress and an increase in positive affect in the yoga group. Additionally, there were significant decreases in self-reported anxiety, depression, negative affect, and fatigue in the yoga group (Rao et al., 2012).

WESTERN-BASED MOVEMENT

AEROBIC EXERCISE

O'Brien and colleagues (2010) conducted a review of aerobic exercise interventions (1980–2009) in adults living with HIV. The authors included studies of randomized controlled trials comparing aerobic exercise interventions with no aerobic exercise interventions or another exercise or treatment modality, performed at least three times per week for at least 4 weeks among adults (18 years of age or older) living with HIV. A total of 14 studies met inclusion criteria and 30 meta-analyses were performed. Nine of the studies included psychological measurements. The study found that performing constant or interval aerobic exercise, or a combination of constant aerobic exercise and progressive resistive exercise, for at least 20 minutes at least three times per week for at least 5 weeks appears to be safe and may lead to significant improvements in symptoms of depression-dejection (O'Brien et al., 2010). Moreover, there were significant improvements in mood and life satisfaction (Lox et al., 1995) as well as in quality of life in the specific areas of psychological functioning, independence, social relationships, and overall quality of life (Lox et al., 1995; Lox et al., 1996; Mutimura et al., 2008).

RESISTANT EXERCISE

Resistance training for individuals living with HIV/AIDS is important because the disease may lead to decreases in lean body mass and strength, which often necessitates the use of exogenous testosterone therapy. O'Brien et al. (2008) conducted a systematic review of literature from 1980 to 2006 on the safety and effectiveness of resistance exercise in adults living with HIV/AIDS. The authors performed 17 meta-analyses and found that progressive resistive exercises (PRE) were safe and contributed to improved strength as well as improved psychological functioning among individuals living with HIV/AIDS compared with individuals not using PRE (O'Brien et al., 2008). One of the studies included in the meta-analysis examined the use of resistant exercise and whey protein supplements in a group of 10 HIV-positive women and found that physiological and quality-of-life scores increased with the exercises, but the whey protein supplements did not offer additional psychological benefit (Agin, 2001).

Wagner and colleagues (1998) investigated the effects of 12 weeks of exercise (predominantly resistance training) in an open trial of men receiving biweekly intramuscular testosterone injections. Men who exercised showed significant improvement in both mood and overall distress. Men who did not exercise only demonstrated improvement in mood (Wagner et al., 1998). Similarly, studies utilizing resistance exercise and androgen therapy found benefits in lean muscle mass and strength but did not assess psychological functioning (Bhasin et al., 2000; Strawford et al., 1999).

In addition to the mood, cardiovascular, and muscle/skeletal benefits of exercise, many patients report being able to "think more clearly" and "solve problems better" after exercising. A study that examined the relationship between exercise and HIV-associated neurocognitive disorders found significantly lower rates of global neurocognitive impairment in the exercise group as than in the non-exercise group, even after controlling for potentially confounding factors (i.e., education, AIDS status, depression) (Dufour et al., 2013). In particular, exercise was associated with reduced impairment in working memory and speed of information processing. An overall active lifestyle (including physical exercise, social activity, and current employment) in a community sample of 139 HIV-infected adults was associated with better global neurocognitive performance and a lower prevalence of HIV-associated neurocognitive disorders (Fazeli et al., 2014). Importantly, this was a cross-sectional design study and we cannot infer causation. It may very well be that persons with better neurocognitive functioning are more inclined and better able to engage in an active life. Therefore, studies that use a prospective, randomized control design are needed to understand the impact of exercise on neurocognitive functioning.

EXERCISES WITH POTENTIAL FOR HIV TREATMENT

PILATES

Joseph Pilates developed "Pilates" as a body, mind, and spiritual approach to movement founded on the integrative effect of six principles: centering, concentration, control, precision, breath, and flow. This form of physical activity consists of over 500 exercises done on the floor or primarily with customized exercise equipment. Although clinical studies utilizing Pilates in HIV-positive subjects are lacking, an intervention study demonstrated the benefits of 12 weeks of Pilates in a group of battered women (HIV status not indicated), finding statistically significant improvements in depression (Hassan and Amin, 2011). Given the high prevalence of trauma in women with HIV (Gore-Felton and Koopman, 2002; Machtinger et al., 2012), this exercise modality may show promise in future studies.

DANCE/MOVEMENT THERAPY

The use of dance/movement therapy (DMT) in persons with AIDS was documented by Chang in the pre-combination antiretroviral treatment era (Dibbel-Hope, 2000). DMT is used to induce deep relaxation and imagery to increase body awareness and self-confidence and to reduce symptoms of stress, depression, bodily weakness, pain, and feeling out of control (Chang, 1988). Although the utility of DMT in HIV/AIDS has not been well documented in recent studies, its benefits in psychological adaptation have been documented in persons with breast cancer (Dibbel-Hope, 2000) and with mental illness. Ritter and Low (1966) conducted a meta-analysis on the effects of DMT and noted its positive impact for varying diagnoses including anxiety, depression, and schizophrenia, however, not specifically in HIV/AIDS, and cautioned that many results involve case studies or studies with methodological shortcomings. A study that examined the effects of a single dance intervention (circle dance from Israel, Hava Nagila) on psychiatric patients with depression found that participants in the dance group reported significantly less depression than participants in the music-only/exercise-only groups. Additionally, participants in the dance group reported more vitality than participants in the music-only control arm (Koch et al. 2007).

MIND–BODY CONNECTION

MINDFULNESS MEDITATION

Mindfulness meditation is an increasingly popular intervention for treating depression, anxiety, and pain, conditions which are commonly comorbid in persons with HIV/AIDS. Mindfulness meditation enables individuals to focus attention on the present moment and acknowledge thoughts, emotions, sensations, and perceptions as they arise. The skills learned through the meditation process are transferred from a focus on breathing to attention in all activities of life. The most commonly employed form of mindfulness meditation in research studies is mindfulness-based stress reduction (MBSR), an 8-week structured course in which participants are trained in mindfulness techniques (Goyal et al., 2014).

A systematic review and meta-analysis of the general population evaluated the evidence for mindfulness meditation and found support for the use of mindfulness meditation as an effective treatment for anxiety, depression, and pain (Goyal et al., 2014). When compared with nonspecific controls, such as a 1-day-long information session about relaxation, there was moderate evidence for mindfulness meditation as an effective treatment for anxiety, depression, and pain (Goyal et al., 2014). When compared with specific active controls, such as exercise, cognitive-behavioral therapy groups, or relaxation techniques, there was insufficient evidence that mindfulness meditation was a superior treatment for anxiety and depression, and low evidence that mindfulness meditation was a superior treatment for pain. There was no evidence that mindfulness meditation was an inferior treatment to active controls (Goyal et al., 2014). It is currently unknown whether these data extend to the depression, anxiety, and pain experienced by HIV patients.

There are many studies of persons with HIV that show mindfulness meditation to have a multitude of positive effects, including immune enhancement, decreased distress, improved depression, and a decreased incidence of side effects to antiretroviral medication. However, there still remains insufficient evidence to suggest reliable efficacy of mindfulness meditation as a treatment specifically for persons with HIV.

Functional MRI data imply that left-sided anterior prefrontal cortex activation is associated with positive mood states and a reduction in anxiety and that this pattern of activity is increased by meditation (Davidson et al., 2003). There is evidence that this pattern of activation is associated with enhanced natural killer cell activity (Davidson et al., 1999). A study employing MBSR in patients with HIV showed that patients receiving a 1-day stress reduction intervention had a significant decline in CD4+ lymphocytes over a 2-year follow-up period. Patients receiving MBSR showed no change in CD4+ lymphocytes over the same period. These results occurred independent of antiretroviral compliance. This study may suggest that MBSR is an effective treatment for delaying decline in CD4+ lymphocytes (Creswell et al., 2009). Another study revealed a temporary boost in CD4+ count compared to controls after MBSR (SeyedAlinaghi et al., 2012).

A randomized, wait-list controlled trial showed a significant reduction in the side effects of antiretroviral drugs in patients with HIV after practicing MSBR compared with controls. The subjects in this study taking part in MSBR also showed a significant reduction in reported levels of distress (Duncan et al., 2012). Another randomized wait-list controlled study of HIV-positive gay men receiving MBSR illustrated a correlation between increased mindfulness and decreased depression. Subjects completing MBSR training also were measured to have a higher positive affect (Gayner et al., 2012).

Growing evidence indicates that mindfulness meditation may be an effective treatment for many comorbidities associated with HIV and may even help boost immune function and decrease medication side effects. While there is moderate evidence that mindfulness meditation is more effective than nonspecific controls in the general population for anxiety, depression, and pain, it is currently unknown how these data extend to persons with HIV.

Mindfulness meditation remains a safe, inexpensive intervention that can be practiced virtually anywhere. Existing evidence for mindfulness meditation implies an effective treatment with many beneficial effects for persons with HIV, but additional studies are needed to bolster the strength of this evidence.

HYPNOSIS

Hypnosis is a state of highly focused attention, coupled with dissociation of competing thoughts and sensations, and enhanced response to social cues (Elkins et al., 2015; Spiegel and Spiegel, 2004). Hypnosis provides a powerful means of altering pain, anxiety, and various somatic functions, even under highly stressful circumstances. Hypnotic alteration of perception, best studied in the somatosensory and visual systems, involves a top-down reduction of the intensity of perceptual response itself, rather than just an alteration in response to perceptual input (Spiegel et al., 1989). Hypnotic analgesia differs from and is stronger than placebo analgesia (McGlashan et al., 1969). Several studies have examined the idea that endogenous opiates account for hypnotic analgesia. Studies with both volunteers (Goldstein and Hilgard, 1975) and patients with chronic pain (Spiegel and Albert, 1983) indicate that hypnotic analgesia is not blocked and reversed by a substantial dose of naloxone, an opiate receptor blocker. In contrast, placebo analgesia is mediated by endogenous opiates (Zubieta et al., 2005).

Pharmacological approaches to sensory neuropathic pain in HIV infection are rarely adequate, and techniques including hypnosis, meditation, and physical activity are recommended (Cherry et al., 2016). Several studies have demonstrated significant clinical effects of hypnosis among HIV-infected individuals, primarily in reducing pain. In one study among 36 individuals, three weekly sessions of hypnosis instruction resulted in a significant 44% reduction in distal sensory neuropathic pain over a 17-week period (Dorfman et al., 2013). Case studies of hypnosis use among five HIV-positive patients with pain indicate reductions in pain along with reductions in use of analgesic medication (Langenfeld et al., 2002).

CONCLUSION

While more research is needed, the evidence indicates that a variety of dietary, exercise, psychotherapeutic, and mind–body techniques can effectively reduce symptoms related to HIV infection, including pain, anxiety, depression, and cognitive decline. In addition, a few studies indicate positive changes in CD4 counts and reduced viral load. Now that viral suppression with antiretroviral therapy and medical care enable persons with HIV to live longer lives, safe and effective means of addressing symptoms that affect quality of life become more important. A variety of integrative approaches address that need and are appealing to a significant proportion of persons with HIV who may benefit from it. Integrative approaches provide a valuable and empirically based opportunity for persons with HIV to enhance their control over symptoms, quality of life, and overall management of the effects of the illness.

REFERENCES

Abrams DI, Jay CA, Shade SB, Vizoso H, Reda H, Press S, Petersen KL (2007). Cannabis in painful HIV-associated sensory neuropathy: a randomized placebo-controlled trial. *Neurology* 68(7):515–521.

Agin DG (2001). Effects of whey protein and resistance exercise on body cell mass, muscle strength, and quality of life in women with HIV. *AIDS* 15(18):2431–2440.

Allard JP, Aghdassi E, Chau J, Tam C, Kovacs CM, Salit IE, Walmsley SL (1998). Effects of vitamin E and C supplementation on oxidative stress and viral load in HIV-infected subjects. *AIDS* 12(13):1653–1659.

Allavena C, Delpierre C, Cuzin L, et al. (2012). High frequency of vitamin D deficiency in HIV-infected patients: effects of HIV-related factors and antiretroviral drugs. *J Antimicrob Chemother* 67:2222–2230.

Anukam KC, Osazuwa EO, Osadolor HB, Bruce AW, Reid G (2008). Yogurt containing probiotic lactobacillus rhamnosus GR-1 and L. reuteri RC-14 helps resolve moderate diarrhea and increased CD4 count in HIV/AIDS patients. *J Clin Gastroenterol* 42:239–243.

Baldewicz TT, Goodkin K, Blaney NT, Shor-Posner G, Kumar M, Wilkie FL, Eisdorfer C (2000). Cobalamin level is related to self-reported and clinically rated mood and to syndromal depression in bereaved HIV-1+ and HIV-1- homosexual men. *J Psychosom Res* 48:177–185.

Barbosa EGM, Barbosa F, Machado AA, Navarro AM (2015). A longer time of exposure to antiretroviral therapy improves selenium levels. *Clin Nutr* 34:248–251.

Baum MK, Shor-Posner G, Shenghan L, et al. (1997). High risk of HIV-related mortality is associated with selenium deficiency. *AIDS* 15:370–374.

Berginc K, Trontelj J, Kristi A (2009). The influence of aged garlic extract on the uptake of saquinavir and darunavir into HepG2 cells and rat liver slices. *Drug Metab Pharmacokinet* 25:307–313.

Bhasin S, Storer TW, Javanbakht M, et al. (2000). Testosterone replacement and resistance exercise in HIV-infected men with weight loss and low testosterone levels. *JAMA* 283:763–770.

Bilu D, Mamelak AJ, Nguyen RHN, Queiroz PC, Kowalski J, Morison WL, Martins CR (2004). Clinical and epidemiologic characterization of photosensitivity in HIV-positive individuals. *Photodermatol Photoimmunol Photomed* 20:175–183.

Bryson PD, Watanabe AS, Rumack BH, Murphy RC (1978). Burdock root tea poisoning. Case report involving a commerical preparation. *JAMA* 239:2157.

Cannell JJ, Hollis BW, Zasloff M, Heaney RP (2008). Diagnosis and treatment of vitamin D deficiency. *Exp Opin Pharmacother* 9:107–118.

Chang L, Cloak C, Yakupov R, Ernst T (2006). Combined and independent effects of chronic marijuana use and HIV on brain mmetabolites. *J Neuroimmune Pharmacol* 1:65–76.

Chang M (1988). An integrative approach: dance therapy with AIDS patients. Presentation at the 23rd National Conference of ADTA. Baltimore, MD.

Cherry CL, Wadley AL, Kamerman PR (2016). Diagnosing and treating HIV-associated sensory neuropathy: a global perspective. *Pain Manage* 6:191–199.

Corless IB, Lindgren T, Holzemer W, et al. (2009). Marijuana effectieness as an HIV self-care strategy. *Clin Nurs Res* 18:172–193.

Creswell JD, Myers HF, Cole SW, Irwin MR (2009). Mindfulness meditation training effects on CD4+ T lymphocytes in HIV-1 infected adults: a small randomized controlled trial. *Brain Behav Immun* 23:184–188.

Cristiani SA, Pukay-Martin ND, Bornstein RA (2004). Marijuana use and cognitive function in HIV-infected people. *J Neuropsychiatry Clin Neurosci* 16:330–335.

Davidson RJ, Coe CC, Dolski I, Donzella B (1999). Individual differences in prefrontal activation asymmetry predict natural killer cell activity at rest and in response to challenge. *Brain Behav Immun* 13:93–108.

Davidson RJ, Kabat-Zinn J, Schumacher J, et al. (2003). Alterations in brain and immune function produced by mindfulness meditation. *Psychosom Med* 65:564–570.

Dibbel-Hope S (2000). The use of dance/movement therapy in psychological adaptation to breast cancer. *Arts Psychother* 27:51–68.

Dorfman D, George MC, Schnur J, Simpson DM, Davidson G, Montgomery G (2013). Hypnosis for treatment of HIV neuropathic pain: a preliminary report. *Pain Med* 14:1048–1056.

Dubick M (1986). Historical perspectives on the use of herbal preparations to promote health. *J Nutr* 116:1348–1354.

Dufour CA, Marquine MJ, Fazeli PL, Henry BL, Ellis RJ, Grant I, Moore DJ (2013). Physical exercise is associated with less neurocognitive impairment among HIV-infected adults. *J Neurovirol* 19:410–417.

Duncan LG, Moskowitz JT, Neilands TB, Dilworth SE, Hecht FM, Johnson MO (2012). Mindfulness-based stress reduction for HIV treatment side effects: a randomized, wait-list controlled trial. *J Pain Symptom Manage* 43:161–171.

Elkins GR, Barabasz AF, Council JR, Spiegel D (2015). Advancing research and practice: the revised APA Division 30 definition of hypnosis. *Am J Clin Hypn* 57: 378–385.

Fairfield KM, Eisenberg DM, Davis RB, Libman H, Phillips RS (1998). Patterns of use, expenditures, and perceived efficacy of complementary and alternative therapies in HIV-infected patients. *Arch Intern Med* 158:2257–2264.

Fazeli PL, Woods SP, Heaton RK, et al. (2014). An active lifestyle is associated with better neurocognitive functioning in adults living wtih HIV infection. *J Neurovirol* 20:233–242.

Furler MD, Einarson TR, Millson M, Walmsley S, Bendayan R (2004). Medicinal and recreational marijuana use by patients infected with HIV. *AIDS Patient Care STDs* 18:215–228.

Galantino ML, Shepard K, Krafft L, et al. (2006). The effect of group aerobic exercise and t'ai chi on functional outcomes and quality of life for persons living with acquired immunodeficiency syndrome. *J Altern Complement Med* 11:1085–1092.

Gayner B, Esplen M.J, DeRoche P, Wong J, Bishop S, Kavanagh L, Butler K (2012). A randomized controlled trial of mindfulness-based stress reduction to manage affective symptoms and improve quality of life in gay men living with HIV. *J Behav Med* 35:272–285.

Gloth FM, Alam W, Hollis B (1999). Vitamin D vs broad spectrum phototherapy in the treatment of seasonal affective disorder. *J Nutr Health Aging* 3:5–7.

Goldstein A, Hilgard ER (1975). Failure of the opiate antagonist naloxone to modify hypnotic analgesia. *Proc Natl Acad Sci U S A* 72:2041–2043.

Gore-Felton C, Koopman C (2002). Traumatic experiences: harbinger of risk behavior among HIV-positive adults. *J Trauma Dissoc* 3:121–135.

Gore-Felton C, Vosvick M, Power R, Koopman C, Ashton E, Bachmann M, Spiegel D (2003). Alternative therapies: a common practice among men and women living with HIV. *J Assoc Nurses AIDS Care* 14:17–27.

Goyal M, Singh S, Sibinga EMS, et al. (2014). Meditation programs for psychological stress and well-being: a systematic review and meta-analysis. *JAMA Intern Med* 174:357–368.

Guzmán-Fulgencio, M, Garcia-Alvarez M, Berenguer J, et al. (2014). Vitamin D deficiency is associated with severity of liver disease in HIV/HCV coinfected patients. *J Infect* 68:176–184.

Haney M, Gunderson EW, Rabkin J, Hart CL, Vosburg SK, Comer SD, Foltin RW (2007). Dronabinol and marijuana in HIV-positive marijuana smokers: caloric intake, mood, and sleep. *J Acquir Immune Defic Syndr* 45:545–554.

Hassan EAH, Amin MA (2011). Pilates exercises influence on the serotonin hormone, some physical variables, and the depression degree in battered women. *World J Sport Sci* 5:89–100.

Henderson L, Yue QY, Bergquist C, Gerden B, Arlett P (2002). St. John's wort (*Hypericum perforatum*): drug interactions and clinical outcomes. *Br J Clin Pharmacol* 54:349–356.

Herzlich BC, Schiano TD (1993). Reversal of apparent AIDS dementia complex following treatment with vitamin B12. *J Intern Med* 233:495–497.

Hsu H (1986). *Oriental Materia Medica*. Long Beach, CA: Oriental Healing Arts Institute.

Irvine SL, Hummelen R, Hekmat S, Looman C, Habbema JDF, Reid G (2010). Probiotic yogurt consumption is associated with an increase of CD4 count among people living with HIV/AIDS. *J Clin Gastroenterol* 44:e201–e205.

Jones BD, Runikis AM (1987). Interaction of ginseng with phenelzine. *J Clin Psychopharmacol* 7:201–202.

Kaiser JD, Campa AM, Ondercin JP, Leoung GS, Pless RF, Baum MK (2006). Micronutrient supplementation increases CD4 count in HIV-infected individuals on highly active antriretroviral therapy: a prospective, double-blinded, placebo controlled trial. *J Acquir Immune Defic Syndr* 42:523–528.

Kassler WJ, Blanc P, Greenblatt R (1991). The use of medicinal herbs by human immunodeficiency virus-infected patients. *Arch Intern Med* 151:2281–2288.

Kawashima K, Miwa Y, Kimura M, Mizutani K, Hayashi A, Tanaka O (1985). Diuretic action of paeonol. *Planta Medica* 51:187–189.

Kligler B, Maizes V, Schachter S, et al. (2004). Core competencies in integrative medicine for medical school curricula: a proposal. *Acad Med* 79:521–531.

Koar W (1995). Meditation, T-cells, anxiety, depression and HIV infection. *Subtle Energies Energy Med J Arch* 6:89–97.

Koch SC, Morlinghaus K, Fuchs T (2007). The joy dance: specific effects of a single dance intervention on psychiatric patients with depression. *Arts Psychother* 34:340–349.

Kupka R, Fawzi W (2002). Zinc nutrition and HIV infection. *Nutr Rev* 60:69–79.

Ladenheim D, Horn O, Werneke U, Phillpot M, Murungi A, Theobald N, Orkin C (2008). Potential health risks of complementary alternative medicines in HIV patients. *HIV Med* 9:653–659.

Langenfeld MC, Cipani E, Borckardt JJ (2002). Hypnosis for the control of HIV/AIDS-related pain. *Int J Clin Exp Hypn* 50:170–188.

Langlois-Klassen D, Kipp W, Jhangri GS, Rubaale T (2007). Use of traditional herbal medicine by AIDS patients in Kabarole District, western Uganda. *Am J Trop Med Hyg* 77:757–763.

Littlewood RA. Vanable PA (2014). The relationship between CAM use and adherence to antiretroviral therapies among persons living with HIV. *Health Psychol* 33:660–667.

Liu G (1989). Pharmacological actions and clinical use of *fructus Schizandrae*. *Chin Med J* 102:740–749.

Liu JP, Manheimer E, Yang M (2005). Herbal medicines for treating HIV infection and AIDS. *Cochrane Database Syst Rev* 3:CD003937.

Lopresti AL, Maes M, Maker G.L, Hood SD, Drummond PD (2014). Curcumin for the treatment of major depression: a randomised, double-blind, placebo controlled study. *J Affect Disord* 167:368–375.

Lorenc A, Robinson N (2013). A review of the use of complementary and alternative medicine and HIV: issues for patient care. *AIDS Patient Care STDs* 27:503–510.

Lox CL, McAuley E, Tucker RS (1995). Exercise as an intervention for enhancing subjective well-being in an HIV-1 population. *J Sport Exercise Psychol* 17:345–362.

Lox CL, McAuley E, Tucker RS (1996). Aerobic and resistance exercise training effects on body composition, muscular strength, and cardiovascular fitness in an HIV-1 population. *Int J Behav Med* 3:55–69.

Machtinger EL, Wilson TC, Haberer JE, Weiss DS (2012). Psychological trauma and PTSD in HIV-positive women: a meta-analysis. *AIDS Behav* 16:2091–2100.

McCain NL, Elswick RK, Gray DP, Robins J, Tuck I, Walter JM (2005). Tai Chi training enhances well-being and alters cytokine levels in persons wtih HIV disease. *Brain Behav Immun* 19:e50–e51.

McGlashan TH, Evans FJ, Orne MT (1969). The nature of hypnotic analgesia and placebo response to experimental pain. *Psychosom Med* 31:227–246.

Menon JA, Glazebrook C (2013). Randomized control trial to evaluate yoga-based peer support group for human immunodeficiency virus (HIV) positive Zambian adolescents. *J AIDS HIV Res* 5:12–19.

Morgan V (2014). The feasibility of a holistic wellness program for HIV/AIDS patients residing in a voluntary inpatient treatment program. *J Holist Nurs* 32:54–60.

Mutimura E, Stewart A, Crowther NJ, Yarasheski KE, Cade WT (2008). The effects of exercise training on quality of life in HAART-treated HIV-positive Rwandan subjects with body fat redistribution. *Qual Life Res* 17:377–385.

O'Brien K, Nixon S, Tynan AM, Glazier R (2010). Aerobic exercise interventions for adults living with HIV/AIDS. *Cochrane Database Syst Rev* 4:CD001796.

O'Brien K, Tynan AM, Nixon S, Glazier RH (2008). Effects of progressive resistive exercise in adults living with HIV/AIDS: systematic review and meta-analysis of randomized trials. *AIDS Care* 20:631–653.

Pacht ER, Diaz P, Clanton T, Hart J, Gadek JE (1997). Serum vitamin E decreases in HIV-seropositive subjects over time. *J Lab Clin Med* 130:293–296.

Panayiotopoulos A, Bhat N, Bhangoo A (2013). Bone and vitamin D metabolism in HIV. *Rev Endocr Metab Disord* 14:119–125.

Piscitelli SC, Burstein AH, Chaitt D, Alfaro RM, Falloon J (2000). Indinavir concentrations and St. John's wort. *Lancet* 355:547–548.

Piscitelli SC, Burstein AH, Welden N, Gallicano KD, Falloon J (2002). The effect of garlic supplements on the pharmacokinetics of saquinavir. *Clin Infect Dis* 34:234–238.

Prentiss D, Power R, Balmas G, Tzuang G, Israelski DM (2004). Patterns of marijuana use among patients with HIV/AIDS followed in a public health care setting. *J Acquir Immune Defic Syndr* 35(1):38–45.

Rao R, Deb U, Raghuram N, Rao NHR, Burke A, Hecht F (2012). Effects of an integrated yoga program on mood, perceived stress, quality of life and immune measures in HIV patients: a pilot study. *BMC Complement Altern Med* 12(Suppl 1):P235.

Rayman MP (2000). The importance of selenium to human health. *Lancet* 356:233–241.

Ritter M, Low KG (1996). Effects of dance/movement therapy: a meta-analysis. *Arts Psychother* 23:249–260.

Rivera JO, Gonzalez-Stuart A, Ortiz M, Rodriguez JC, Anaya JP. Meza A (2005). Herbal product use in non-HIV and HIV-positive Hispanic patients. *J Natl Med Assoc* 97:1686–1691.

Rivera JO, Gonzalez-Stuart A, Ortiz M, Rodriguez JC, Anaya JP, Meza A (2006). Guide for herbal product use by Mexican Americans in the largest Texas-Mexico border community. *J Texas Med* 102:45–56.

Robins JL, McCain NL, Gray DP, Elswick RK, Walter JM, McDade E (2006). Research on psychoneuroimmunology: tai chi as a stress management approach for individuals with HIV disease. *Appl Nurs Res* 19:2–9.

Saxe TG (1987). Toxicity of medicinal herbal preparations. *Am Fam Physician* 35:135–142.

Schlögl M, Holick MF (2014). Vitamin D and neurocognitive function. *Clin Interv Aging* 9:559–568.

Sebit MB, Chandiwana SK, Latif AS, Gomo E, Acuda SW, Makoni F, Vushe J (2002). Neuropsychiatric aspects of HIV disease progression: impact of traditional herbs on adult patients in Zimbabwe. *Prog Neuropsychopharmacol Biol Psychiatry* 26:451–456.

Semba RD, Miotti PG, Chiphangwi JD, Saah AJ, Canner JK, Dallabetta GA, Hoover DR (1994). Maternal vitamin A deficiency and mother-to-child transmission of HIV-1. *Lancet* 1593–1597.

SeyedAlinaghi S, Jam S, Foroughi M, Imani A, Mohraz M, Djavid GE, Black DS (2012). Randomized controlled trial of mindfulness-based stress reduction delivered to human immunodeficiency virus-positive patients in Iran: effects on CD4(+) T lymphocyte count and medical and psychological symptoms. *Psychosom Med* 74:620–627.

Shor-Posner G, Feaster D, Blaney NT, et al. (1994). Impact of vitamin B6 status on psychological distress in a longitudinal study of HIV-1 infection. *Int J Psychiatry Med* 24:209–222.

Siegel R (1979). Ginseng abuse syndrome. Problems with the panacea. *JAMA* 241:1614–1615.

Spiegel D, Albert LH (1983). Naloxcone fails to reverse hypnotic alleviation of chronic pain. *Psychopharmacology* 81:140–143.

Spiegel D, Bierre P, Rootenberg J (1989). Hypnotic alteration of somatosensory perception. *Am J Psychiatry* 146:749–754.

Spiegel H, Spiegel D (2004). *Trance and Treatment: Clinical Uses of Hypnosis* (2nd ed.). Washington, DC: American Psychiatric Publishing.

Stephensen CB, Marquis GS, Kruzich LA, Douglas SD, Aldrovandi GM, Wilson CM (2006). Vitamin D status in adolescents and young adults with HIV infection. *Am J Clin Nutr* 83:1135–1141.

Stolbach A, Paziana K, Heverling H, Pham P (2015). A review of the toxicity of HIV medications II: interactions with drugs and complementary and alternative medicine products. *J Med Toxicol* 11:326–341.

Strawford A, Barbieri T, Van Loan M, et al. (1999). Resistance exercise and supraphysiologic androgen therapy in eugonadal men with HIV-related weight loss: a randomized controlled trial. *JAMA* 281:1282–1290.

Voaden D.J, Jacobson M (1972). Tumor inhibitors, III: identification and synthesis of an oncolytic hydrocarbon from American coneflower roots. *J Medicin Chem* 15:619–623.

Wagner G, Rabkin J, Rabkin R (1998). Exercise as a mediator of psychological and nutritional effects of testosterone therapy in HIV+ men. *Med Sci Sports Exercise* 30:811–817.

Wilson NL, Moneyham LD, Alexandrov AW (2013). A systematic review of probiotics as a potential intervention to restore gut health in HIV infection. *J Assoc Nurses AIDS Care* 24:98–111.

Woolridge E, Barton S, Samuel J, Osorio J, Dougherty A, Holdcroft A (2005). Cannabis use in HIV for pain and other medical symptoms. *J Pain Sympt Manage* 29:358–367.

Wysowski DK, Pitts M, Beitz J (2001). An analysis of reports of depression and suicide in patients treated with isotretinoin *J Am Acad Dermatol* 45:515–519.

Zubieta JK, Bueller JA, Jackson LR, et al. (2005). Placebo effects mediated by endogenous opioid activity on μ-opioid receptors. *J Neurosci* 25, 7754–7762.

39.

SOCIAL SERVICE INTERVENTIONS

Mary Ann Malone

AIDS is a medical illness that can be seen as having biological, psychological, social, and cultural aspects. The biopsychosocial approach to AIDS was first described and defined (Cohen and Wesiman, 1986) early in the epidemic. The need for a coordinated approach was also specified, by Cohen (1987): "The acquired immunodeficiency syndrome (AIDS) may be thought of as a medical problem that requires a coordinated, humane, comprehensive, holistic, and biopsychosocial approach." Patients benefit from this collaborative care since it also (Cohen, 1992) "maintains a view of each patient as a member of a family, community, and culture who deserves coordinated, compassionate care and treatment with dignity." A social worker plays a vital role in this approach, as a fully integrated member of the treatment team.

This chapter will present the current role of the hospital social worker in this biopsychosocial approach to the treatment of patients with AIDS. According to Golden (2011), "social workers are ideally educated and positioned to address the challenges of health care reform's shifting focus, enhancing the quality and efficiency of health care delivery systems, particularly for the nation's most vulnerable populations." At different points throughout the course of care, persons with HIV/AIDS may require assistance with concrete services as well as psychological support. The medical, psychiatric, and social service needs of persons with HIV/AIDS have been influenced by the changing climate in the treatment of HIV over the last three decades. Some of these more recent changes include the introduction of new, more streamlined medications that are easier to take, the new treatments for people who are at risk for HIV, and the protocols for individuals who have been exposed to HIV to prevent conversion to HIV. The introduction of more effective medications has led to a change in the perception of the illness, from rapidly fatal to chronic and manageable. The pressures within the hospital for increased productivity and expeditious discharges also add to this changing climate. What role do hospital social workers play in this picture? Craig and Mascot (2013) state: "Hospital social workers in medical settings may have different roles than social workers in other types of social service agencies. Such a conceptual contribution not only sheds light on the roles of hospitals in a rapidly changing environment, but also helps lay a foundation to further understand the relationship of hospital social workers to patient outcomes in a time of increasing complexity within the healthcare system." The aim of this chapter is to shed light on how these changes affect hospital social work.

The first section of the chapter discusses the collaborative relationship between psychiatry and social work. The second section highlights the past and present role of the hospital social worker as it relates to HIV/AIDS. The final section summarizes practical social work interventions used to assist persons with HIV deal with the challenges of everyday life during this time of change.

PSYCHIATRY AND SOCIAL WORK: A COLLABORATIVE RELATIONSHIP

Even in these times of change in healthcare and in HIV/AIDS, certain basic principles remain the same. The professions of psychiatry and social work have been working side by side for many years. Mental health, which both professions address, is an important aspect of the care of people with AIDS. There are similarities between the two professions, the strongest of which is the skill of the practitioner to help patients generate within themselves the strength to promote their own healing and resulting positive action. Professional values that guide social work and psychiatry are also similar. Nonjudgmental attitudes, professional competency, and self-awareness guide the work of practitioners in both disciplines. Within the hospital setting there are many opportunities for psychiatry and social work to work together. As Bronstein (2003) notes, "more than ever psychiatrists and psychologists in mental health settings are helped enormously in their tasks by social workers' contextual understanding of person-in-environment."

Working in conjunction with other disciplines is a necessary component of care of patients with HIV/AIDS. Psychiatry and social work need to be an integral part of a multidisciplinary team that includes infectious disease specialists, other medical specialists, internists, primary physicians, nurses, psychologists, nutritionists, and addiction counselors. Each patient is unique and brings a unique set of needs. The coordinated effort on the part of the team is to create a plan tailored to the needs of the individual (Forstein and McDaniel, 2001). Although each discipline specializes in a specific aspect of the patient's care, emphasis should always be on collaboration: "Characteristics of interdependence include formal and informal time spent together, oral and written communication among professional colleagues, and respect for colleagues professional opinions and input" (Bronstein, 2003). The objective is to provide the most comprehensive and compassionate treatment possible. All individuals involved in the patient's care need to work side by side toward this end. For example, end-of-life issues require input from the patient, significant others, and members of the whole team, with emphasis on communication and shared decisions.

Within the framework of the team, helping patients adhere to psychiatric medications and antiretroviral medications is another area where psychiatry and social work can help coordinate services. When assessing for problems with adherence the social worker can determine what factors hinder the patient from keeping appointments or taking medications. One of the reasons for nonadherence is difficulty tolerating side effects of medications. Even though the newer antiretroviral medications are easier to tolerate and may allow for once-a-day dosing, there are still side effects. Very often patients feel that the treatment is worse than the illness; they were feeling relatively well before starting the medications and now they are sick. Patients need encouragement from members of the team to continue to keep appointments and continue taking the medicine, as very often the side effects will subside over time.

Substance use, misuse and addictive disorders present another challenge to adherence to care. Addictive behaviors may take precedence over keeping appointments and taking prescribed medications. Sometimes active use of alcohol or other drugs may become overwhelming. A person with HIV may be unable to continue to adhere to medical care, keep appointments, and follow complex regimens of medications and diet, especially when intoxicated, withdrawing from use, or engaging in drug- or alcohol-related activities. It is important for all team members to be alert to any drug-related problems and to collaborate as a team with the patient, significant others, and family. The goal of collaboration is to encourage the patient to seek help with a referral for comprehensive detoxification and addiction treatment. Stopping antiretrovirals or taking them sporadically can lead to development of viral drug resistance and may result in illness progression without intervention for addictive disorders. Many patients with alcohol or other drug-related disorders are already being seen by psychiatry and are receiving treatment around issues with adherence.

Some persons with HIV may be nonadherent because they are tired of being on the regimen or feel so much better that they stop the antiviral medications without informing their doctor. Stopping and starting antiviral medications can result in emergence of resistant viral strains, resistance to antiviral medications, and the need for an entirely different medication regimen. Patients who are able to adhere to scheduled appointments with the doctor and psychiatrist are less likely to encounter this problem. Once the reasons for an individual patient's lack of adherence are identified, professionals from psychiatry and social work, along with the other disciplines, can work together on an approach that can assist the patient to get back on track.

Support groups that explore adherence may emphasize both psychiatric and psychosocial issues and can be facilitated by individuals from psychiatry and social work. Many psychiatric disorders encountered by persons with HIV/AIDS may be related to the progression of the illness and/or to side effects of medications. Support groups often help patients find solutions to HIV-related concerns and problems. Once an individual is diagnosed with HIV or develops an opportunistic infection, anxiety and depression often intensify and need treatment. Topics important to the patient can be springboards for group discussion.

The availability of psychiatrists as part of the treatment team in a hospital-based HIV clinic is an advantage. In this setting a patient can usually get an appointment sooner than when patients are referred to specialists outside the clinic, where there may be a wait for an appointment. Also, the patient naturally feels more at home in the familiar clinic surroundings and is often already aware of the psychiatrist's presence there.

An example of social work and psychiatric collaboration is demonstrated in the following vignette. One of the HIV psychiatrists and I had the opportunity to work together to coordinate services for a patient. The patient was a recovering cocaine-dependent woman who, after attaining sobriety, had acquired a full-time job and custody of her young son. She was doing well and was receiving much encouragement and support from her psychiatrist, who arranged visits with the patient around the patient's work schedule. Members of the team were concerned about anything that might interfere with the patient's excellent progress. Abruptly, the patient lost her insurance coverage. Rapid social work intervention was needed. Coordination of care by social work and psychiatry, and information from the patient led to interventions by phone and fax with appropriate agencies. Ultimately, the situation was resolved and her health insurance was restored. Subsequently, through social work referral to a community-based organization, she was able to receive help to obtain more adequate housing for herself and her family.

All disciplines, especially social work and psychiatry, can work together to help patients address crises and adapt to stressors during the course of illness.

SOCIAL WORK AND HIV/AIDS: MEETING THE CURRENT PROFESSIONAL CHALLENGES

When I started my professional career in social work, nearly three decades ago, I wanted to work with the most disenfranchised population. I chose the field of AIDS, eager to learn about the illness and help patients with HIV and AIDS in any way I could. I wanted to work in a hospital (Gregorian, 2005) where I thought I could be closer to the heart of what was happening in the field. My work with my patients over the years has been challenging and rewarding. As a front-line AIDS hospital social worker, I felt it was my responsibility to learn about new developments and changes in the field that are most relevant to social work practice. In keeping up with these changes and the latest resources, I can help patients save time developing the skills they require to adjust. As stated by Linsk (2011), "like our clients, we have had to learn to thrive on challenge, to become resilient, and to grow from the experience."

Since the needs of persons with HIV/AIDS have changed over the last three decades, the approaches that social work uses have also changed. The early 1980s saw the beginning of the epidemic. Everyone was shocked at the rapid progression to death for persons with AIDS. In many areas during the first years of the epidemic AIDS was primarily an illness of gay white men. During that time, social workers helped patients, partners, and families face the inevitability of death. Healthcare proxies, living wills, family meetings, connecting patients with long-lost relatives, burial arrangements, and helping partners and families handle grief made up the social worker's list of ongoing services.

The involvement of women and children and persons with addictive disorders led to another shift in the AIDS social work perspective. Again, social workers needed education about drug addiction and the resources available. HIV disproportionately affected African American and Latino communities and heightened the disparities in health (Strug et al., 2002). Social workers had to develop a better understanding of African American and Hispanic cultures and the attitudes toward AIDS within those cultures. Many patients brought multiple layers of family problems that needed to be addressed. Grandparents caring for children of their severely ill children, relationship problems, and disclosure issues were among the many concerns that these patients needed help with. In 1985, zidovudine was introduced and, along with other reverse transcriptase inhibitors, was used until a decade later, in 1996, when protease inhibitors and other combinations of antiretroviral therapies were introduced and became an effective way to manage HIV/AIDS. This remarkable change in therapies brought a rapid improvement in the health of many persons with AIDS. There were improvements in quality of life and patients began to live longer with watchful enthusiasm. Now, in the public eye, the topic of AIDS seems to be diminishing. Other medical issues seemed to overshadow HIV/AIDS.

Working in an infectious disease clinic in a hospital for over more than three decades has brought some positive changes. It has been remarkable to see how the faces of so many of our patients changed from gaunt and worried to full and peaceful. This was most noticeable in the waiting room of the clinic. Several years earlier, most of the patients waiting to be seen by their doctors looked like cadavers and seemed to be hanging on to life by a thread. As new therapies were gradually introduced, faces began to fill out. Patients came in with more energy, and the prospect of death did not seem inevitable. This change has sometimes been referred to as "the Lazarus syndrome," analogous to the biblical friend of Jesus who was raised from the dead (Tucker, 2003). The work with revitalized patients changed as well. In many cases, instead of helping them accept their death the work focused on helping them move on with their lives. Many persons needed time to

get used to feeling well again and remained in a state shock for a period of time. One patient, a war veteran, compared the feeling to being shell shocked, waiting for the next bomb to drop—in his case, for the next opportunistic infection that might bring an end to his life.

The number of newly infected people has decreased somewhat over the years, and there is still no cure. Many people are still dying with AIDS. However, the prevailing attitude toward HIV/AIDS is similar to the responses to living with a chronic illness, such as diabetes. The dominant themes now are no longer loss and grief but survival and ways of living with a chronic and severe illness. Many persons with HIV have returned to school and have re-entered the work force (Arns et al., 2004).

There are also ethical dilemmas to consider as we see more and more undocumented immigrants with AIDS coming to our clinics. Clinicians may often feel conflicted when these patients present with a serious illness and there is no insurance that can cover the cost of the treatment. Sometimes medical services can be provided without charge, but this is rare. There has also been an increase in the number of older persons with HIV/AIDS. The demographics have changed, and in a few years the majority of these patients will be over the age of 50. This situation is due to both new infections and increased longevity. The medical profession is also more attuned to the need for HIV testing of older adults. This demographic trend challenges HIV social workers to develop a better understanding of the aging population in order to help them more effectively.

The response to all of these changes requires a diverse range of social work skills. HIV/AIDS social workers face new professional challenges at this time in the history of epidemic. Now that people with HIV/AIDS are living longer and healthier lives there is an increased burden on health and social systems. Even now Medicaid and Medicare are setting limits on medical coverage for our patients. The type of work we will do in the future could also change. Social work efforts need to be more focused on secondary prevention. The future of the epidemic may require that social workers provide prevention education, as well, to decrease the likelihood of HIV transmission (Strug et al., 2002).

The hospital social worker also needs to have an understanding of the constantly changing systems within the hospital (Ingersol and Heckman, 2005; Mizrahi and Berger, 2001). The field of social work has had to adjust to billing, admitting, diagnostic procedures, patient relations, and the changing functions of nurses and other specialists. Financial and productivity concerns may influence hospital policies. Social work departments in many hospitals have been downsized, combined with other disciplines, or eliminated altogether. The Social Work Department in the hospital where I work has been able to remain intact and maintain a strong presence, mainly because of strong social work leadership, an idea consistent with the work of Pockett (2003). This entails making every effort to work with the changing hospital system and not against it, providing ideas needed to achieve the current goals of the hospital administration. Integrating and coordinating programs with other disciplines is necessary to maintain a social work presence (Globerman et al., 2002). Through these and other efforts to promote our valuable contributions, the voice of social work will continue to be heard.

Many hospital social workers thrive on the challenges they meet daily. The work is always stimulating but at times frustrating and physically and emotionally draining. Social workers must be adept at handling their own emotions in order to deal with the many emotionally charged situations they encounter in their work (Nelson and Merighi, 2003). No two days are ever the same, and adjustments to unforeseen circumstances are the order of the day. One can come to work in the morning with a plan for the day and an unexpected crisis can change the focus for the entire day. The work needs to be done quickly and autonomously, since patients, staff members, and the hospital organization's requirements are constantly imposing demands on the social worker's expertise.

How does the individual social worker survive on a day-to-day basis in this setting? I derive my energy from the patients themselves. Almost daily I am affected in a positive way by the courage of the patients with whom I work. There are always opportunities to ask questions of colleagues and staff in other disciplines to learn more about specific illnesses and treatments. The support of colleagues who share this difficult work is very important. Strong bonds are sometimes formed between workers. Wade and Simon (1993) have noted that "peer support can moderate the effects of stress and reduce the likelihood of burnout." It is also important to go about the work maintaining a sense of equilibrium. Above all, the willingness and effort to work as a team player is the most essential skill a social worker needs in this setting. Sometimes, taking on tasks that others would prefer not to do is necessary to promote teamwork. Lending support and validating similar daily experiences of fellow workers can also help sustain a collegial atmosphere. There are an increasing number of patients with HIV/AIDS who are now over the age of 50 and the number is growing. Regarding the work of geriatric clinical social workers in a hospital setting, Duffy and Healy (2011) state, "a therapeutic relationship with older people necessitates a collaborative relationship with both service users and the multidisciplinary team, and as such we have highlighted a collaborative approach as best practice in a hospital setting. Therapeutic effectiveness is enhanced by the social worker's knowledge of relevant theories, counseling frameworks, aged care legislation, research and best practice principles."

SOCIAL WORK INTERVENTIONS WITH PATIENTS WITH HIV/AIDS: PRACTICAL APPROACHES

Persons with HIV/AIDS have a broad array of needs aside from medical and psychiatric care. Assistance with obtaining financial and insurance benefits, housing, home care, counseling, and drug treatment are the most prevalent needs that social work addresses. The clinic in which I work is conducive to meeting these needs through case management services and the newly developed Health Homes. Here the social

worker assumes the role of case manager or care manager who is in charge of coordinating the various disciplines around the patients' needs. This is very much in keeping with the biopsychosocial approach to patient care. Today more than ever, as Bronstein (2003) notes, "social workers face the challenges of increasing social problems such as rising numbers of families in poverty, new immigrants, and people who are aging, and decreasing resources make efficient practice essential. Interdisciplinary collaboration whereby colleagues work together and maximize the expertise each can offer is critical."

The social worker/case manager has the responsibility to become knowledgeable about the most current and cost-effective resources available to patients. To keep up to date on what is happening in social work and in the healthcare field of HIV/AIDS, it is necessary to attend workshops, seminars, and conferences on relevant topics, both inside and outside the hospital. As a case manger armed with knowledge and skills, what are the basic tools needed to provide the best help to the patients? These are discussed in the next sections.

ESTABLISHING A RELATIONSHIP WITH THE PATIENT

Forming a therapeutic relationship with a patient and assisting with multiple concrete service needs at the same time is a formidable challenge. A good relationship with the patient is the foundation for effective work (Linsk, 2012; Voisin, 2010). Felix Biestek (1957) defines the patient/case worker relationship as "the dynamic interaction of attitudes and emotions between case worker and client, with the purpose of helping the client achieve better adjustment between himself (sic) and his environment." When the patient is working with someone he or she trusts, the person will work harder and reach goals of care more quickly. Sometimes a short-term intervention is needed. Such is the case when social workers coordinate discharges for hospitalized patients; there are multiple details that need attention when helping a patient get ready to leave the hospital. Relationships with patients are often developed when helping them with these discharge services, even in a climate where budgets and efficiency propel the work. Conveying a calm attitude of concern and acceptance of the patient while helping with even the smallest detail can go a long way toward establishing a therapeutic connection.

Knowing a patient's interests can often be a vehicle for connecting. I remember being able to establish a connection using a patient's avid interest in basketball. To the patient I was "okay," because I knew the game and had some recognition of the players. In some cases a sense of humor can help bring normalcy and relaxation to a stressful situation. It can be a means of patient and social worker meeting each other on common ground. Also, sensitivity to the appropriate timing of humor and spontaneity is essential.

Social workers also need to be sensitive to the complex emotions the patient may be experiencing, including anger, fear, shame, and guilt. Helping patients find the words to express painful emotions can be useful in creating a therapeutic relationship. Sometimes these emotions can be stuck in a patient's throat, waiting for the right moment to be expressed. Often a patient only needs permission to express them. The social worker, being sensitive to this, can grant that permission.

When appropriate, creating hopefulness can help patients cope with progressing illness and strengthen the relationship between social worker and patient—"imparting hope during counseling is the most important beneficial treatment" (Westburg and Guindon, 2004). Some ways that have been useful for me in developing and maintaining hope in a patient include anticipating medical breakthroughs in the future; helping maintain any religious or spiritual beliefs the patient may have; providing opportunities for the patient to become involved in absorbing or interesting hobbies or work; and encouraging the development of supportive relationships with family and friends.

These efforts are just a few ways to develop and maintain a relationship with a patient. Once it is established, almost any help one gives the patient can have a therapeutic effect. Realistically, we all know that we cannot make this connection with every patient we try to help. Different personalities, and sometimes the patient's resistance, can interfere with these efforts. In these situations, we hope the person can relate therapeutically to someone else, and we can continue assisting the patient on a concrete level, always with an open mind and an outstretched hand.

ASSISTING WITH ADHERENCE TO THE MEDICAL REGIMEN

As noted earlier in the chapter, the social worker is a key player in guiding a patient to full adherence to a medical regimen, with keeping appointments and taking prescribed medications. While adherence to a specific regimen is important for anyone with an illness, it is vital for persons with HIV/AIDS (Ingersoll and Heckman, 2005). Linsk and Land (2012) point out that the goal of treatment is to suppress the viral load. For patients to achieve this they need to be linked to care. Social workers can work with the team to help patients clear away any obstacles to maintaining adherence to treatment and staying linked to care. The effectiveness of the medications depends on them being taken according to a prescribed schedule; nonadherence or taking medications "off and on" can result in failure of the medications to be effective. Sometimes patients are too embarrassed to tell their doctor that they have not been taking their medications as prescribed. Only when the CD4 count goes down and the viral load goes up is there obvious evidence of nonadherence. The social worker needs to support the physician in assessing the patient's adherence and communicating with the doctor if there are any problems. A good patient–doctor relationship is strongly associated with adherence: "Provision of care within a framework in which providers make patients comfortable with the staff appears to be highly associated with whether or not patients are retained in care" (Magnus et al., 2013). In addition, access to seeing the same provider over a long period of time seems to have a positive effect on general well-being and health (Knowlton et al., 2005). Engagement and retention in care are critically important for not only a patient's well-being and health but also for promoting viral suppression and preventing illness progression, morbidity, and mortality (Aberg et al., 2014; Keller et al., 2014; Magnus et al., 2012, 2013; Mugavero et al., 2014; Voisin, 2010).

There are as many reasons for, as there are solutions to, problems with adherence. Some patients are simply too busy or forget to take their medications. Often patients feel sick from the side effects of the medications or report that they don't have the medications with them when they are scheduled to take them. One patient said she often missed the bedtime dose because she fell asleep before the time she was scheduled to take it. After the social worker conferred with the doctor and the patient it was decided that the patient could take the medication an hour or so earlier so the dose would not be missed.

Other factors that present difficulties with adherence include demographic characteristics of the patient (sex, age, ethnicity, socioeconomic status); life crises; alcohol or drug use; lack of adequate housing; and depression (DiMatteo et al., 2000). Social workers need to be alert to signs of depression in patients. Depression can be one of the side effects of medications, and referral to a psychiatrist for evaluation may be needed. Very often, assisting with stabilizing a patient's daily life can mean better adherence. For example, assisting a patient with AIDS find more adequate housing than a four-story walk-up can mean better adherence with follow-up clinic visits and medication.

There are no easy answers and there is no single strategy that works for every patient. An individualized approach to finding a solution works best, and success is sometimes achieved by trial and error. Often all that is needed is interest and determination of the patient to take responsibility for his or her care.

FACILITATING SUPPORT GROUPS

Support groups can often relieve the loneliness associated with HIV/AIDS. Being with others can be revitalizing. Group interaction for persons with AIDS has been described "as an effective means to provide support, an outlet for feelings, a common bond, and a relief of social stigma" (Cohen and Alfonso, 2004). Groups can provide companionship, help lighten the weight of heavy burdens, and create feelings of optimism. They can help put a patient's life in perspective and create a more positive look on life. People with HIV/AIDS can sometimes feel disconnected from family and friends. This is especially true for older persons who are experiencing the loss of other loved ones who have died from other conditions. Many older people with HIV/AIDS are also coping with several HIV-related and non-HIV related illnesses at the same time. Groups can give participants the opportunity to form new and sometimes very strong relationships. In one HIV group I facilitated for patients over the age of 50, an 82-year-old woman developed a relationship with a 65-year-old woman. The friendship gave each of them the strength they needed to face the challenges of their illness. If one was sick, the other was at her side. They also had fun together attending shows and going to dances. They were very excited as they related stories of these events during group sessions. It became a therapeutic experience for each of them and an inspiration for the other group members. According to Linsk (2011), support groups provide connection for people "often in need of emotional contact and direct support, these groups create normality in a highly unpredictable situation."

Groups are formed and developed on the basis of various needs of the HIV/AIDS population. Groups can be created for persons of different ages and backgrounds, adolescents, young adults, and older people. Our clinic has a general HIV support group that meets once a week. What started out to be a support group for all adults a few years ago has changed into a 50-years-plus group since the members have aged. This is a reflection of the shifting demographics in the general HIV/AIDS population. Members of this group have established strong ties and will often go places together and keep in touch by phone between sessions. The clinic also has a support group for persons who are co-infected with hepatitis C and HIV. A support group for young men is being developed to address the needs of a growing population. Sometimes people are reluctant to join groups or, because of scheduling, cannot attend groups. Being a part of a group is not for everyone, but it can be effective for many patients.

ASSISTING WITH CONCRETE SERVICES

Many persons with HIV/AIDS need assistance with multiple concrete services. Some patients readily express their need for services and others need to be encouraged to express their needs. The most prevalent needs are for housing, financial benefits, insurance, clothing, food, transportation, home care services, and referrals for drug treatment. Since hospital-based social workers cannot go into the community to offer services to the patient, referrals are very frequently made to agencies that provide case management services in the community. In addition to these efforts, New York State's Medicaid program, in an effort to cut the cost of services for patients with chronic conditions, now offers Health Home or Medical Home services, "a care management service model whereby all of an individual's caregivers communicate with one another so that all of the patient's needs are addressed in a comprehensive manner." This is done primarily through a "care manager" who oversees and provides access to all of the services an individual needs to ensure that they receive everything necessary to stay healthy (New York State Department of Health, 2017). Health Homes are available both in the hospital and in community service agencies. This fairly new concept can assist with drawing together the various fragments of patient care and promote adherence so necessary for patients' health. Also, healthcare costs can be curtailed and help relieve strain on the Medicaid program.

Patients often need immediate help with referral to detoxification or rehabilitation for treatment for drug and alcohol use. Sometimes programs are able to accept the patient immediately and even provide transportation to bring the patient to the site of the services. This immediate service is very helpful as it takes advantage of the patient's commitment to accept help right away. So often, when patients needing this help are given a referral to follow up with a program in a day or two, they almost never do, because the temptation to use substances is usually too strong.

Our AIDS center has a care coordination program, the main focus of which is to encourage adherence. Patient navigators in this program accompany patients to their appointments and visit patients in their homes to assess any obstacles to their keeping up with their medical regimen. The patient navigators then inform the team about anything they think needs attention.

Until several years ago, the physicians in the AIDS unit at our hospital worked under a continuity-of-care model: A doctor, nurse, and social worker followed a specific panel of patients from the time of their diagnosis to their death, both on the inpatient and outpatient services. This coordination of care was a model for the biopsychosocial approach to treatment. When budget and staffing considerations did not allow for this approach to continue, each discipline cared for the patient separately. Now inpatient and outpatient social work, though coordinated, are separate functions.

There are some differences in the focus of concrete services offered by inpatient and outpatient hospital social workers. Inpatient social workers are involved with assisting patients and families adjust to the hospital routine. More important, because of the current climate in most hospitals, from the day of admission, emphasis is given to discharge planning and the services needed to get the patient out of the hospital in a timely manner and meet the hospital regulations for length of stay. For an inpatient social worker the first thought when reviewing the chart before meeting the patient is what options are available for the patient's discharge—nursing home, home care services, transportation, referrals for benefits or insurance, methadone maintenance, or drug rehabilitation. If the patient will be receiving follow-up medical care in the same hospital, conferring with the outpatient social worker in the clinic is necessary.

Outpatient social workers provide some of the same services as inpatient workers. However, these services are for the patient already living in the community. The focus is different and often without the pressure of meeting deadlines. Referrals for drug detoxification, as mentioned earlier, are fairly straightforward. Like inpatients, outpatients can receive home care through a referral to a nursing service and, if the patient is determined appropriate, services are in place in a few days. Nursing home placement takes a little longer because nursing homes admit patients directly from an inpatient setting, giving priority to more acutely ill patients.

Although less frequently than in the past, referrals for case management through community-based organizations are made. It is in the outpatient setting that most of the referrals are made to community-based organizations. Referrals for legal assistance are frequent. Advocacy for benefit eligibility, custody planning for children, and resolution of debt incurred due to unpaid bills are some of issues for which assistance is needed. The present healthcare and HIV/AIDS climate also necessitates providing referrals and resources for education and training programs for patients who want to return to work. Generally, for persons with HIV/AIDS whose health has greatly improved, they are eager to move on with their lives. Job opportunities, temporary agencies, education, and vocation programs are frequently used. Referrals are also made to programs that provide opportunities for social interaction.

Both inpatient and outpatient social workers work very closely with psychiatry. In most cases the medical needs of persons with HIV/AIDS take priority, but mental health is also vitally important. So often the patient's mental status helps or hinders the effectiveness of medical treatment. Social workers are keenly aware of this and make referrals to psychiatry for patients to be evaluated if there is a perceived mental health issue. Psychiatry, in turn, depends on social work to participate in and support the psychiatric treatment plan by monitoring the patient's behavior and mental state during social work encounters. Social workers and psychiatrists confer frequently, especially when working with patients with psychiatric needs. To make referrals more expeditious, a social worker can assess a patient's psychiatric and emotional status and try to match the patient with the psychiatrist who could be most helpful to the patient.

ADDITIONAL SOCIAL WORK SERVICES

Many other issues are addressed in a social worker's encounters with patients. Some are considered very tough subjects that need to be discussed in order for patients to consider all aspects of how HIV/AIDS relates to them. Topics regarding disclosure of HIV status to family and friends are often discussed. The necessary secrecy surrounding the inability to disclose can cause stress and anxiety for the patient. Sometimes the perceptions that patients have of the consequences of disclosing their status are often unrealistic and the result of creating the "worst-case" scenario. Guiding patients through different aspects of this process can be very challenging.

Conversations about risk reduction and safer sex practices are also a necessary part of what social workers address with persons with HIV/AIDS. It is important to help patients understand the need to protect themselves from HIV and other sexually transmitted diseases as well as to protect an HIV-negative partner from infection.

Some patients need guidance and support in mending relationships with family members, partners, and friends. So often when these problems are resolved patients can cope better and concentrate on the things they need to do to take care of themselves. More often than not they end up having the support of the persons with whom they have reconciled.

Planning for the care of dependent children is a topic that many patients do not want to address. It is very difficult for parents to face the possibility of leaving their children. It is satisfying to have a patient agree to ask for legal help regarding this issue and once the plan is in place, the patient usually feels very relieved.

CONCLUSIONS

At the present time, social work plays a greater role in the management of persons with HIV/AIDS than at almost any other time in the history of the illness. Social workers' responsibility now extends beyond the usual provision of basic concrete services and counseling. The scope of social work practice has broadened to include an obligation to become knowledgeable about the most up-to-date resources that can help patients deal with the fast-paced changes in their medical care. Social workers need to be able to direct patients to the resources they need, to adjust to the challenges of their changing lives and obtain help dealing with a world outside that of HIV/AIDS that is currently experiencing tremendous turmoil. What kind of a framework for this challenging work makes the most sense, for both social worker and patient?

The basic, unchanged, traditional guidelines for social workers should include the following:

- Keep focused on what is best for the patient.

- Respond as a team player at all times, despite the constant demands and pressures of the job.

- Maintain equanimity, and don't allow yourself to react hastily as you are pulled in many different directions.

- Develop a healthy confidence in your ability to get the job done.

- Be willing to learn and try new and sometimes difficult approaches.

- Find opportunities to laugh, and take your work seriously, but not yourself.

What about the future for persons with HIV/AIDS? In answer to this question Linsk (2011) wrote: "Everyone with HIV is deserving of services, compassion and quality of life. To do this we will need to sustain our system responses and advocate for humane treatment and a reconceptualization of people with HIV as valued contributing members of society."

REFERENCES

Aberg JA, Gallant JE, Ghanem KG, et al. (2014). Infectious Diseases Society of America. Primary care guidelines for the management of persons infected with HIV: 2013 update by the HIV Medicine Association of the Infectious Diseases Society of America. *Clin Infect Dis* 58:e1–e34.

Arns MS, Golin CE, Shain LS, DeVellis B (2004). Brief motivational interviewing to improve adherence to antiretroviral therapy: development and qualitative pilot assessment of an intervention. *AIDS Patient Care STDS* 18:229–238.

Biestek F (1957). *The Casework Relationship*. Chicago: Loyola University Press.

Bronstein L (2003). A model for interdisciplinary collaboration. *Soc Work* 48:297–307.

Cohen MA (1987). Psychiatric aspects of AIDS: a biopsychosocial approach. In GP Wornser, RE Stahl, EJ Bottone (eds.), *AIDS-Acquired Immune Deficiency Syndrome and Other Manifestations of HIV Infection* (pp. 579–622). Park Ridge, NJ: Noyes Publishers.

Cohen MA (1992). Biopsychosocial aspects of the HIV epidemic. In GP Wormser (ed.), *AIDS and Other Manifestations of HIV Infection*, 2nd ed. (pp. 349–371). New York: Raven Press.

Cohen MA, Alfonso CA (2004). AIDS psychiatry: psychiatric and palliative care and pain management. In GP Wormser (ed.), *AIDS and Other Manifestations of HIV Infections*, 4th ed. (pp. 537–576). San Diego: Elsevier Academic Press.

Cohen MA, Weisman HW (1986). A biopsychosocial approach to AIDS. *Psychosomatics* 27:247–249.

Craig S, Mascot B (2013). Bouncers, brokers and glue: the self-described roles of social workers in urban hospitals. *Health Soc Work* 38:7–16.

DiMatteo MR, Lepper HS, Croghan TW (2000). Depression is a risk factor for noncompliance with medical treatment: meta-analysis of the effects of anxiety and depression on patient adherence. *Arch Intern Med* 160:2101–2107.

Duffy F, Healy J (2011). Social work with older people in a hospital setting. *Soc Work Health Care* 50:109–123.

Forstein M, McDaniel JS (2001). Medical overview of HIV infection and AIDS. *Psychiatr Ann* 31:16–20.

Globerman J, White J, MacDonald G (2002). Social work in restructuring hospitals: program management five years later. *Health Soc Work* 27:274–284.

Golden R (2011). Coordination, integration and collaboration: a clear path for social work in health care reform. *Health Soc Work* 33(3):227–228.

Gregorian C (2005). A career in hospital social work: do you have what it takes? *Soc Work Health Care* 40:1–14.

Ingersoll KS, Heckman CJ (2005). Patient-clinician relationships and system effects on HIV medication adherence. *AIDS Behav* 9:89–101.

Keller S, Yehia BR, Momplaisir FO, Eberhart MG, Share A, Brady KA (2014). Assessing the overall quality of health care in persons living with HIV in an urban environment. *AIDS Patient Care STDs* 28(4):198–205.

Knowlton AR, Hua W, Latkin (2005). Social support networks and medical service use among HIV-positive injection drug users: implications to intervention. *AIDS Care* 17:479–492.

Linsk N (2011). Thirty years into the HIV epidemic: social work perspectives and prospects. *J HIV/AIDS Soc Serv* 10:218–229.

Linsk N (2012). Living with HIV care and support: implications for social work services. *J HIV/AIDS Soc Serv* 11:1–15.

Linsk N, Land H (2012). How well are we doing addressing care and support of people with HIV?AIDS? *J HIV/AIDS Soc Serv* 11:323–326.

Magnus M, Herwehe J, Gruber D, et al. (2012). Improved HIV-related outcomes associated with implementation of a novel public health information exchange. *Int J Med Inform* 81:e30–e38.

Magnus M, Herwehe J, Murtaza-Rossini M, et al. (2013). Linking and retaining HIV patients in care: the importance of provider attitudes and behaviors. *AIDS Patient Care STDs* 27(5):297–330.

Manya M, Herwehe J, Murtaza-Rossini M, Reine P, Cuffie D, Gruber D, Kaiser M (2013). Linking and retaining HIV patients in care: the importance of provider attitudes and behavior. *AIDS Patient Care* 27:259–313.

Mizrahi T, Berger CS (2001). Effect of a changing health care environment on social work leaders: obstacles and opportunities in hospital social work. *Soc Work* 46:170–182.

Mugavero MJ, Westfall AO, Cole SR, et al. (2014) Beyond core indicators of retention in HIV care: missed clinic visits are independently associated with all-cause mortality. *Clin Infect Dis* 59:1471–1479.

Nelson KR, Merighi (2003). Emotional dissonance in medical social work practice. *Soc Work Health Care* 36:63–79.

New York State Department of Health (2017). Medicaid Health Homes: Health Homes for Medicaid enrolless with chronic conditions. https://www.health.ny.gov/health_care/medicaid/program/medicaid_health_homes/. Accessed February 10, 2017.

Pockett R (2003). Staying in hospital Social Work. *Soc Work Health Care* 36:1–24.

Strug DL, Grube BA, Berkerman NL (2002). Challenges and changing roles in HIV/AIDS social work: implications for training and education. *Soc Work Health Care* 35:1–19

Tucker M (2003). Revisting the 'Lazarus syndrome'. In A Rice, BI Willinger (eds.), *A History of AIDS Social Work in Hospitals: A Daring Response to an Epidemic* (pp. 225–261). New York: Haworth Press.

Voisin D (2010). Improving service delivery and care to HIV-infected populations. *J HIV/AIDS Soc Serv* 9:4–6.

Wade K, Simon EP (1993). Survival bonding: a response to stress an work with AIDS. *Soc Work Health Care* 19:77–89.

Westburg NG, Guindon MH (2004). Hopes, attitudes, emotions and expectations in healthcare providers of services to patients with HIV. *AIDS Behav* 8:1–8.

40.

NURSING SUPPORT

Carl Kirton

Nurses have a long history of working in the delivery of health services to individuals with acute and chronic illnesses. With the emergence of the HIV epidemic in the 1980s, nursing professionals stepped up to the challenge of caring for persons with this rare illness in hospitals, nursing homes, community centers, and private practices, and sometimes very nontraditional healthcare settings.

To competently care for people with HIV or AIDS, nurses have to provide care that is advanced and specialized. Nurses working in the field of HIV or AIDS care require advanced knowledge of virology and infectious disease to address the clinical needs of persons with HIV-related illness. Nurses must have knowledge of drugs with new and novel therapeutic actions. They must also be familiar with how politics and public policy affect the healthcare delivered to persons with HIV. Nurses must be strong advocates with, and sometimes alongside, their patients. For many nurses, the realities of mental health disorders and substance use have presented as significant comorbidities that nurses were initially unprepared to address. As a result of these complexities, new models of care and new roles for nurses have emerged from the epidemic.

This chapter addresses the key aspects of nursing care of HIV-infected adults throughout the spectrum of HIV illness. The chapter will focus on the nurse's role in minimizing risk, preventing HIV transmission, caring for persons with HIV, helping individuals to cope with illness, and negotiating the healthcare system.

HISTORY OF NURSING CARE, ROLES, AND CREDENTIALING IN HIV/AIDS

Clinical case management is a collaborative, multidisciplinary model in which the nurse is the care coordinator and facilitator who conducts patient assessment, provides education, coordinates community involvement, and manages patient-centered care. The clinical case management approach emerged as a predominant model of care early in the epidemic (Morrison, 1993). This model was most appropriate because it involves coordinated services ranging from care provided in the patient's home to acute care and even palliative care when indicated.

To meet the ongoing needs of nurses involved in the care of persons with HIV and AIDS, a small group of nurses banded together in the fall of 1987. The goal of this group was to promote the individual and collective professional development of nurses involved in the delivery of healthcare to persons infected with or affected by HIV. From this group evolved the Association of Nurses in AIDS (ANAC). The ANAC is a specialty organization with members from around the United States and the world and remains the leading voice in matters related to HIV/AIDS nursing. The mission and goals of the ANAC are outlined in Table 40.1. To demonstrate their specialized knowledge, skill, and experience in AIDS care, nurses can obtain certification in this specialty. Board certification in HIV/AIDS is highly valued and provides formal recognition of HIV/AIDS nursing knowledge. Nurses who meet eligibility requirements and pass the certification examination in HIV/AIDS nursing are eligible to use the registered credential of ACRN (HIV/AIDS Certified Registered Nurse) after their name. Nurses with advanced educational preparation (master's degree or higher) who function in advanced practice roles, such as clinical nurse specialist or nurse practitioner, and have pass the advanced certification examination may use the registered credential of AACRN (Advanced HIV/AIDS Certified Registered Nurse).

The HIV epidemic also saw the growth of nurse practitioners (NPs) as primary care professionals in both acute and outpatient settings. The number of NPs that work as HIV specialists is unknown; NPs have a long history of providing high-quality healthcare to vulnerable populations. Wilson and colleagues (2005) studied the quality of care provided by NPs and physicians assistants (PAs) at 68 HIV care sites in 30 different states for 6,651 persons with HIV or AIDS. They estimated that 20% of patients received most of their HIV care from NPs and PAs. This national study was also important in that it was designed to compare the quality of care provided by non-physician clinicians (NPs and PAs) with that of physicians. The study found that the quality of HIV care provided by NP and PA HIV specialists was similar to that of physician HIV specialists and generally better than that of non-HIV physicians.

In the beginning of the AIDS epidemic, most nursing was provided in the general hospital acute care setting. Early in the epidemic, in hospitals where persons with AIDS occupied a large proportion of beds, two predominant models of care delivery emerged. The first was a cluster model in which all persons with AIDS were hospitalized in AIDS-dedicated units (ADUs). The other model was a scatter-bed approach in

Table 40.1 ASSOCIATION OF NURSES IN AIDS CARE MISSION STATEMENT

The Association of Nurses in AIDS Care (ANAC) is a nonprofit professional nursing organization committed to fostering the individual and collective professional development of nurses involved in the delivery of healthcare to persons infected with or affected by HIV and to promoting the health, welfare, and rights of all HIV-infected persons.
Association Goals

The members of ANAC strive to achieve the mission by
- Creating an effective network among nurses in HIV/AIDS care.
- Studying, researching, and exchanging information, experiences, and ideas leading to improved care for persons with HIV/AIDS infection.
- Providing leadership to the nursing community in matters related to HIV/AIDS infection.
- Advocating for HIV-infected persons.
- Promoting social awareness concerning issues related to HIV/AIDS.

Inherent in this mission is an abiding commitment to the prevention of further HIV infection.

which persons with AIDS were admitted to beds throughout general acute care. San Francisco General Hospital established the first ADU in 1983. Many nurses chose to work on this and other ADUs because they had friends or family members with AIDS. Others chose AIDS care as a personal response to the discrimination they witnessed against patients with AIDS by other health professionals (Pascreta and Jacobsen, 1989; Sherman, 2000).

AIDS-dedicated units provided high-acuity care for the acutely ill patient with AIDS. The ADUs tended to be characterized by nurses exercising an unusual level of professional autonomy (Aiken et al., 1997). These nurses not only were skilled in the technical aspects of care but also had to be knowledgeable about symptom assessment and palliation, crisis intervention, and grief work. In addition, nurses working on ADUs had to assist clients with disclosure of their illness, often for the first time. Nurses often had to resolve conflicts among friends and families and prepare patients for the stigma, isolation, and rejection they might encounter in the community. They also had to assist patients, family, and friends with mourning and prepare patients, family, and friends for the reality of their loved one's death.

Advances in the pharmacotherapeutics for HIV, prophylaxis of opportunistic infections, and an emphasis on healthy living have shifted the location of AIDS care from primarily inpatient settings to predominantly ambulatory settings. Hospitalization rates have declined sharply, decreasing from 18% of all admissions in 2001 to 7% of all admissions in 2016. Today, non-AIDS defining infection is the most frequent reason for hospitalization. Cardiovascular, renal, and pulmonary hospitalization rates have increased significantly. Other relatively frequent categories of illness requiring hospitalization include psychiatric illnesses, gastrointestinal/liver diseases, non-AIDS defining cancers, and endocrine/metabolic disorders (Berry et al., 2012). Despite the major advances in the care

of persons with HIV and AIDS and the profound changes in the numbers of hospital admissions and death rates, there are still patients who become severely ill and die of AIDS-related opportunistic infections and cancers, as they did early in the epidemic, as a result of lack of access or nonadherence to care. Although the setting of nursing care has changed, the goal of nursing practice remains the same—the provision of educational, therapeutic, and supportive interventions to patients, families, and communities.

NURSING CARE AS PART OF PRIMARY PREVENTION

More than 36.7 million people now live with HIV/AIDS. In 2012, nearly 2.3 million people globally were newly infected with HIV. The need for education related to HIV transmission and safer sexual practices continues to grow (UNAIDS, 2013). In the United States, nearly 1.2 million persons are currently living with HIV. The number of new infections remains stable, at approximately 50,000 per year, with a rise in the number of new infections occurring among vulnerable populations, especially adolescents (Centers for Disease Control and Prevention [CDC], 2013a). It has been estimated that 20% of persons infected with HIV, particularly younger and black men who have sex with men, are not aware of their HIV status, and as a result may contribute to the continued spread of HIV (CDC, 2016). Investigators have developed models suggesting that, although undiagnosed persons with HIV may constitute 20–30% of persons with HIV, they may cause 50% or more of new infections (Rhodes and Glynn, 2005). *Primary HIV prevention* refers to activities or strategies directed at abating the further spread of HIV to persons currently not infected. The Centers for Disease Control and Prevention, as a strategy to advance HIV prevention, developed their first recommendation for routine HIV testing, when indicated, in 2003 (CDC, 2003). This strategy then moved toward the recommendation that all healthcare clinicians include HIV testing as part of routine medical care, on the same voluntary basis as all other diagnostic and screening tests (CDC, 2013b).

Every nurse–patient encounter should be seen as an opportunity to integrate prevention messages into care. Although many patients believe that discussing sexual health is an important part of a physician– or nurse–patient health care encounter, few healthcare professionals routinely discuss HIV transmission and prevention with their patients (Brennan et al., 2013; Flickinger et al., 2013; Lanier et al., 2014; Laws et al., 2011). It is estimated that clinician assessment for HIV risk occurs in only 17–36% of appropriate encounters (Bares et al., 2016; Brennan et al., 2013). In an effort to understand the perceived barriers to sexual health discussions, Brennan and colleagues (2013) conducted semi-structured interviews with medical resident to identify perceived barriers to HIV screening and routine testing. In this study, residents identified as barriers lack of time, perceived patient resistance, and lack of standardized screening into their primary care practice. Bares and colleagues (2016) also studied resident behavior related to HIV testing and found similar reasons for not testing for HIV in patients. Despite positive attitudes regarding routine testing, few residents reported consistent (always or usual) utilization of testing in their practice. Resident most frequently identified competing priorities (59.8%), not thinking of it during the clinical encounter (52.9%), patient refusal (52.9%), and insufficient time (43.6%) as barriers to routine HIV testing.

Contrary to clinician belief, prevention education need not take extensive amounts of time. Findings from a 1995-96 study indicated that a comprehensive evaluation of a patient at risk for or concerned about HIV took approximately 5–7 minutes (Epstein et al., 1998). Components of the primary prevention brief intervention are outlined in Table 40.2.

Table 40.2 COMPONENTS OF PRIMARY PREVENTION BRIEF INTERVENTION

PRIMARY HIV RISK ASSESSMENT (SUGGESTED QUESTIONS)

Sexual Behaviors

Tell me about your current sexual relationship or relationships.

Tell me about your sexual activity in the past (ask about same-sex and cross-sex encounters).

How old were you the first time you had a sexual experience with another person?

HIV/Sexually Transmitted Infection (STI) Risk

What are you doing now to protect yourself from HIV and other STIs? How about in the past?

Have you ever had an STI, such as chlamydia, trichomoniasis or "trich," herpes, HPV or warts, gonorrhea, or syphilis?

Have you ever been tested for HIV?

Substance Use History

Have you ever felt that alcohol or drugs were a problem for you?

How many times in the past week have you used alcohol or other drugs?

Have you ever injected drugs?

To your knowledge, have any of your sexual partners injected drugs?

How has drinking or using drugs affected your sexual behavior?

Sexual Functioning and Relationship Issues

How satisfied are you with your sexual relationship(s)?

Has your partner ever tried to hurt you?

Domestic Violence and Sexual Assault or Abuse

Have you ever been forced to have sex when you didn't want to?

Other HIV-Related Risks

Have you shared equipment for tattoos or body piercing?

Options for Reducing risk (Prevention Messages)

- Monogamy with an uninfected partner
- Limiting the number of sex partners
- Not engaging in anal or vaginal sex
- Using extra water-based lubrication if engaging in anal or vaginal sex (extra lubricant will help decrease tears and abrasions)
- Always using condoms (male or female latex or polyurethane)
- Not using spermicides with nonoxynol-9 (it can cause irritation and increase risk)
- Not engaging in oral sex. If engaging in oral sex, always using latex condoms, dental dams, or plastic wrap
- Not brushing, flossing, or using mouthwash prior to or just after performing oral sex. This can cause tears, cuts, and irritation to the mucous membranes.
- Avoiding ejaculation inside the mouth, vagina, or rectum
- Avoiding swallowing of ejaculate
- Not using needles
- Only using clean needles and "works"
- Cleaning needles, syringes, and "works" before and after use with bleach
- Not sharing inkwells or piercing equipment
- Limiting the number of needle-sharing partners

Nursing Interventions

- Provide educational material about STI symptoms
- Provide advice on how to obtain STI diagnostic and treatment services (if not readily available from HIV clinician, use local STI clinic)
- Educate about sexual behavior changes and safer sex methods
- Screen for drug and alcohol abuse when appropriate
- Educate about high-risk substance use behaviors and harm reduction practices
- Offer HIV testing and counseling, if indicated
- Develop and record a risk reduction plan
- Provide referral to risk reduction programs as needed

PRIMARY PREVENTION IN MENTALLY ILL PERSONS

Persons with severe mental illness are at increased risk for contracting HIV. The prevalence of HIV is alarmingly high among persons with serious mental illness, and severely mentally ill adults frequently engage in high-risk behaviors. Early studies conducted in mostly large metropolitan areas provided prevalence estimates of HIV risk among persons with severe mental illness that ranged from 54% to 75% (Carey et al., 1997). HIV infection rates among people with severe mental illness have been estimated to be approximately 6.9%, much higher than rates for the general U.S. population for the same time period, at around 0.4%. (McKinnon et al., 2002). Blank and colleagues (2002) examined a

Medicaid population in Philadelphia (n = 391,454) who also were receiving public assistance. In this population, 4.1% of persons who were treated for HIV infection were also being treated for schizophrenia, and 8.8% were being treated for a major affective disorder, compared to 2.8% of the rest of the population. Factors contributing to HIV risk among persons with severe mental illness include sexual activity with multiple, casual, or high-risk partners; low levels of condom use; sex trading; and unprotected intercourse occurring between male partners. Sequelae of severe psychopathology such as deficits in problem-solving, impulse control, and social and assertiveness skills can also serve to increase HIV risk (Otto-Salaj et al., 2001). Additionally, persons living with mental illness are at increased risk for substance use, and substance use is often associated with increased risk for HIV infection.

Nurses working in mental health or with patients with severe mental illness should incorporate HIV risk reduction into their practice. Although HIV risk reduction assessment of and education for the severely mentally ill can be challenging, researchers have demonstrated that severely ill psychiatric patients can be recipients of prevention messages (Kaltenthaler et al., 2014; Walsh et al., 2014). Carey et al. (2004) used a 10-session theory-based prevention program designed to help clients reduce their risky sexual behaviors and/or substance use. At the end of the prevention program, patients receiving the HIV risk reduction intervention reported less unprotected sex, fewer casual sex partners, fewer new sexually transmitted infections, increased safer sex communication, improved HIV knowledge, more positive attitudes toward condom use, stronger intentions to use condoms, and improved behavioral skills.

In helping clients reduce their risk for HIV infection and modify risky behaviors, the nurse can use the behavioral nursing process to assess the client's current behavior and related contingencies, specify the behavioral problem, formulate a treatment plan, implement a treatment program, and evaluate the results of the intervention.

NURSING CARE DURING HIV INFECTION

The morbidity and mortality from HIV infection has declined dramatically since the introduction of combination therapy as part of the standard antiretroviral regimen. Despite improvements in the reduction of medical diseases associated with HIV infection, psychiatric and substance abuse disorders are common in the population and may prevent persons with HIV from adhering to risk reduction and medical care. It is estimated that 38–60% of HIV-infected patients receiving medical care in the United States suffer from symptoms indicative of mood or anxiety disorders (Schadé et al., 2013; Shacham et al., 2012, 2016). Drug use and drug dependence among people with HIV is also high; again, approximately 50% of patients from the HIV Cost and Services Utilization Study (HCSUS), a national probability survey of HIV-infected adults receiving medical care in the United States, in early 1996 (N = 2,864: 2,017 men, 847 women), reported using an illicit drug during the previous 12 months of the study period (Bing et al., 2001). Alcohol consumption is common among individuals receiving treatment for HIV, with rates of heavy drinking almost twice those found in the general population. Heavy drinking is especially high among younger individuals and persons with lower educational levels (Surah et al., 2013).

Psychiatric illness, including substance use disorders, impacts HIV illness in many ways. Psychiatric illness may adversely affect medical outcomes and quality of patient life, interfere with access to health services, and undermine adherence to antiretroviral therapy. Because of the impact of psychiatric illness on HIV and AIDS, mental health clinicians are an important part of the HIV treatment team. The need for mental health services is high. Recent data indicated that persons with severe mental illness had significantly lower odds of being high health-services users despite having many unmet and complex needs (Currie et al., 2014). In a study of frequent users of emergency services, persons with hepatitis C (HCV) and HIV were more likely to use emergency services than individuals with more stable viral illness. Psychiatric history comorbid with alcohol abuse and HCV with alcohol abuse were more prevalent in frequent than in non-frequent visitors (Minassian et al., 2013). The authors recommend that this population be targeted for creative intervention strategies, both within and outside of the emergency system, that comprehensively screen for symptomatology and integrate mental health treatment with substance abuse interventions. A statewide needs assessment of persons living with HIV/AIDS was conducted to determine which needs were being met or unmet. The most significantly unmet needs were dental care, eye care, housing, and mental health therapy or counseling (Krause et al., 2013; Lennon et al., 2013). One conclusion to be drawn from this and other studies is that access to mental health services may be limited by the number of mental health clinicians that specialize in treating patients with HIV.

Clinical nurses can serve important roles as screeners for substance use and other psychiatric disorders in comprehensive HIV care settings. Although there is wide support for screening in primary care settings, routine screening does not always take place (Schumacher et al., 2013). There is growing evidence to support the effectiveness of nurse-led brief interventions in both hospital and primary care settings (Joseph et al., 2014; Sommers et al., 2015). Thus clinical nurses are a greatly underused resource within primary care settings for screening and brief interventions for substance use and other psychiatric disorders (Finnell et al., 2014). Early identification of psychiatric illness and prompt psychiatric intervention can be lifesaving and are a critical part of comprehensive care. However, several healthcare-related factors can impede processes of screening for psychiatric illness, including organization of care (i.e., access to professional nursing, access to appropriately trained nurses), staffing skill mix (e.g., the number of professional to nonprofessional staff), and time spent with each patient. The lack of available clinicians for immediate referral for patients with a positive screen is another major barrier to treatment for at-risk patients. Lack of staff training and of adequate screening instruments in the primary care setting have also been identified as barriers to care (De Guzman et al., 2015; Rahm et al., 2015). With intensive training and ongoing support, even paraprofessionals can deliver effective alcohol, drug, and depression screening and intervention services in busy healthcare settings. The approach holds promise for systematically addressing, on a population-wide basis, a variety of important behavioral health determinants and reducing related healthcare costs (Brown et al., 2014)

An effective nurse screening program must be able to overcome many if not all of these obstacles if an effective screening program is to be incorporated into routine clinical practice. Screening tools must be brief, easy to score, and sensitive across diverse patient populations if they are to gain widespread acceptance in clinical work. Several brief, valid tools have been designed to screen for alcohol and other drug use as well as mood disorders. Brown and colleagues (2001) reported on the criterion validity of a two-item conjoint screen (TICS) for alcohol and other drug abuse or dependence for a sample of primary care patients. At least one positive response to the TICS ("In the last year, have you ever drunk or used drugs more than you meant to?" and "Have you felt you wanted or needed to cut down on your drinking or drug use in the last year?") detected current substance use disorders with nearly 80% sensitivity and specificity. The TICS was particularly sensitive to polysubstance use disorders. Respondents who gave 0, 1, and 2 positive responses had a 7.3%, 36.5%, and 72.4% chance, respectively, of a current substance use disorder; likelihood ratios were 0.27, 1.93, and 8.77. Rost and colleagues (1993) reported on a two-item screener to detect depression or dysthymia within the last year and three-item screeners for lifetime drug disorders and alcohol disorders. The sensitivity of the depression screener ranged between 83% and 94%. The sensitivity of the drug screener ranged between 91% and 94%, excluding one site with an extremely low prevalence of drug problems. The sensitivity of the alcohol screener ranged between 87% and 92%. These tools have not been validated in subsequent studies and have not been tested in HIV-infected populations. More importantly, no brief questionnaire will be able to detect the whole host of mental health problems that are present in HIV-infected persons.

Whetten and colleagues (2005) developed a tool that screens for both mental illness and substance use in HIV-infected patients and can be used by persons differing in educational and experiential background. This tool, the Substance Abuse and Mental Illness Symptom Screener (SAMISS), is a 16-item questionnaire and was created from existing and tested instruments (Table 40.3). The substance use screening items include the following: (1) questions from the Alcohol Use Disorders Identification Test (AUDIT) regarding frequency and amount of alcohol use; (2) questions from the Two Item Conjoint Screen for Alcohol and

Table 40.3 THE SUBSTANCE ABUSE AND MENTAL ILLNESS SYMPTOM SCREENER (SAMISS)

SUBSTANCE USE ITEMS

The patient is considered positive for substance use symptoms if any of the following criteria are met:

a) The sum of responses for Questions 1–3 is ≥5

b) The sum of responses for Questions 4–5 is ≥3

c) The sum of responses for Questions 6–7 is ≥1

1. How often do you have a drink containing alcohol?

0 [] Never

1 [] Monthly or less

2 [] 2–4 times a month

3 [] 2–4 times a week

4 [] ≥4 times a week

2. How many drinks do you have on a typical day when you are drinking?

0 [] None

1 [] 1 or 2

2 [] 3 or 4

3 [] 5 or 6

4 [] 7–9

5 [] ≥10

3. How often do you have four or more drinks on one occasion?

0 [] Never

1 [] Less than monthly

2 [] Monthly

3 [] Weekly

4 [] Daily or almost never

4. In the past year, how often did you use non-prescription drugs to get high or to change the way you feel?

0 [] Never

1 [] Less than monthly

2 [] Monthly

3 [] Weekly

4 [] Daily or almost never

5. In the past year, how often did you use drugs prescribed to you or to someone else to get high or change the way you feel?

0 [] Never

1 [] Less than monthly

(continued)

Table 40.3 CONTINUED

SUBSTANCE USE ITEMS

2 [] Monthly

3 [] Weekly

4 [] Daily or almost never

6. In the past year, how often did you drink or use drugs more than you meant to?

0 [] Never

1 [] Less than monthly

2 [] Monthly

3 [] Weekly

4 [] Daily or almost never

7. How often did you feel you wanted or needed to cut down on your drinking or drug use in the past year, and not been able to?

0 [] Never

1 [] Less than monthly

2 [] Monthly

3 [] Weekly

4 [] Daily or almost never

MENTAL HEALTH ITEMS

The patient is considered positive for symptoms of mental illness if he or she responded yes to any mental health question.

Mood Disorder

8. In the past year, when not high or intoxicated, did you ever feel extremely energetic or irritable and more talkative than usual?

1 YES

2 NO

9. During the past 12 months, were you ever on medication or antidepressants for depression or nerve problems?

1 YES

2 NO

10. During the past 12 months, was there ever a time when you felt sad, blue, or depressed for 2 weeks or more in a row?

1 YES

2 NO

11. During the past 12 months, was there ever a time lasting 2 weeks or more when you lost interest in most things like hobbies, work, or activities that usually give you pleasure?

1 YES

2 NO

Panic Disorder

MENTAL HEALTH ITEMS

12. During the past 12 months, did you ever have a period lasting more than 1 month when most of the time you worried or anxious?

1 YES

2 NO

13. In the past year, did you have a spell or an attack when all of a sudden you felt frightened, anxious, or very uneasy when most people would not be afraid or anxious?

1 YES

2 NO

14. During the past 12 months, did you ever have a spell or an attack when for no reason your heart suddenly started to race, you felt faint, or you couldn't catch your breath? [If respondent volunteers "only when having a heart attack or due to physical causes," mark NO.]

1 YES

2 NO

Posttraumatic Stress Disorder

15. During your lifetime, as a child or adult, have you experienced or witnessed traumatic event(s) that involved harm to yourself or others? [If YES: in the past year, have you been troubled by flashbacks, nightmares, or thoughts of the trauma?]

1 YES

2 NO

16. In the past 3 months, have you experienced any event(s) or received information that was so upsetting it affected how you cope with everyday life?

1 YES

2 NO

Source: Pence BW, Gaynes BN, Whetten K, Eron JJ Jr, Ryder RW, Miller WC (2005). Validation of a brief screening instrument for substance abuse and mental illness in HIV-positive patients. *J Acquir Immune Defic Syndr* 40(4):434–444. Copyright (2005), with permission from Lippincott Williams and Wilkins.

Other Drug Problems; (3) one question regarding use of illicit drugs, such as heroin or cocaine; and (4) one question about abuse of prescription drugs. The questions about illicit drug use and prescription drug use were developed by the investigators.

Eight mental health screening questions are from the Composite International Diagnostic Interview (CIDI). The CIDI items query for symptoms of manic and depressive episodes, generalized anxiety disorder, panic disorder, posttraumatic stress disorder, and adjustment disorder. An additional question inquires about use of antidepressant medications in the past year. The question on adjustment disorder references

Table 40.4 TEST CHARACTERISTICS OF SUBSTANCE ABUSE AND MENTAL ILLNESS SYMPTOM SCREENER (SAMISS)

SCREENING MODULE	DIAGNOSIS*	NO DIAGNOSIS	SENSITIVITY (95% CI)	SPECIFICITY (95% CI)	LR+	LR−
SA	29	119	86.2 (68.3–96.1)	74.8 (66.0–82.3)	3.4	0.18
MI	59	84	94.9 (85.9–98.9)	48.8 (37.7–60.0)	1.9	0.10
Combined†	68	75	97.1 (89.8–99.6)	44.0 (32.5–55.9)	1.7	0.067

CI, confidence interval; LR+, positive likelihood ratio; LR−, negative likelihood ratio; MI, mental illness; SA, substance abuse; SCID, Structured Clinical Interview for DSM-IV.

*From SCID.

†Positive screen on either SA or MI module, compared with any SCID diagnosis.

SOURCE: Pence BW, Gaynes BN, Whetten K, Eron JJ Jr, Ryder RW, Miller WC (2005). Validation of a brief screening instrument for substance abuse and mental illness in HIV-positive patients. *J Acquir Immune Defic Syndr* 40(4):434–444. Copyright (2005), with permission from Lippincott Williams and Wilkins.

---

the preceding 3 months, whereas all others reference the past year (Whetten et al., 2005).

The tool is administered verbally to patients and takes about 5–10 minutes to complete. The definition of a positive screen for a probable substance use disorder consists of any of the following: a total score of ≥5 on questions 1–3; a response of "weekly" or "daily or almost daily" to question 4 or 5; or any response other than "never" to questions 6 or 7. The definition of a positive screen for a probable mood or anxiety disorder consists of an affirmative response to any of questions 8–16.

Pence and colleagues (2005) validated the SAMISS using the reference standard tool, the Structured Clinical Interview for DSM-IV (SCID), to determine test characteristics (see Table 40.4). The SAMISS demonstrates high sensitivity and moderate specificity for both substance abuse and mental illness, making it an effective screening instrument. Because of the limited specificity, patients who screen positive will require a more rigorous mental health assessment. There are several limitations to this tool, but because of its brevity and ease in administration, it is worthy of consideration for use in a routine clinical practice with limited mental health resources.

NURSING SUPPORT FOR PERSONS WITH HIV

The purpose of HIV/AIDS nursing practice is to provide educational, therapeutic, and supportive interventions that prevent illness; promote client, family, and community adaptation to HIV infection and its sequelae; and ensure continuity of quality care by collaborating with other professionals (HIV/AIDS Nursing Certification Board, Definition of Nursing Practice). A brief overview of the key minimum standards of nursing practice typically found in any HIV practice follows.

PATIENT AND FAMILY EDUCATION: SUPPORT BY NURSES

Persons with HIV and AIDS need assistance with understanding health situations, making appropriate healthcare decisions, and changing health-related behaviors. Patient education begins at the initial visit and continues throughout the entire patient–clinician experience. In most settings, various personnel may take on the responsibilities of providing health education to patients. They may include primary care professionals, nurses, social workers, case managers, and pharmacists. Some settings have designated health educators whose role is to provide this type of support for patients. Even when a formal health educator is available, a collaborative, multidisciplinary approach to patient education serves both patients and clinicians optimally. However, it is important to ensure that patient education messages are coordinated and that patients are receiving consistent information. Patient education must be provided in a language and at a literacy level appropriate for the patient. Patient education should be conducted in the patient's primary language, if possible; otherwise, skilled medical interpreters should be involved (Navarra et al., 2013).

What Does Patient Education Involve?

The nurse should assess the patient's understanding of the following elements of HIV illness and begin patient education at the initial evaluation. The content and number of items discussed are dependent on a number of factors, including time appropriated for education, resources and tools available, and literacy level of the patient. Suggested content includes the following:

- How HIV is transmitted
- Natural history of HIV illness and consequences of immune system destruction
- The meaning of the viral load and CD4 count

- The beneficial impact of antiretroviral drugs
- Early signs and symptoms of opportunistic illnesses
- The role of prophylactic agents
- The critical role of the patient in his or her own care

Educating Patients before Beginning Antiretroviral Therapy

Although the initiation of antiretroviral therapy is not the only focus of the clinic encounter, it is an important aspect of HIV care. Before initiating antiretroviral therapy, patients must be fully aware of the following:

- The importance of adhering completely to the treatment regimen
- The possibility of drug resistance and loss of treatment options
- The proper timing of pills and coordinating pill-taking with meals
- Possible side effects and long-term drug toxicities
- The critical need for adherence to medical follow-up to prevent life-threatening side effects

During the course of treatment, if adherence problems are identified, the nurse can provide counseling for the patient on strategies and techniques to improve adherence. The nurse assesses the factors that contribute to decreased adherence, plans a course of action with the patient to improve adherence, and assists the patient with implementation of the plan. An evaluation of that plan is achieved by assessing adherence at each clinic visit by any and all providers. For a more extensive review of medication adherence and adherence strategies, see Chapter 29 of this textbook.

SYMPTOM MANAGEMENT: SUPPORT BY NURSES

Symptom management refers to how the person with HIV illness makes day-to-day decisions regarding aspects of symptoms experienced as a direct or indirect result of HIV-related illness or its treatments. Symptom management is a complex science shaped by demographics, culture, perceived risk, stage of illness, treatments, clinician relationships, social support, access, and the extent of the patient's education about HIV and AIDS.

While symptoms may be related to comorbidities and opportunistic infections, medication side effects are growing sources of patient symptoms. Medication side effects such as nausea, diarrhea, increased fatigue, headache, and sleep disturbances are ever-present and are an important source of poor adherence. Preparing the patient for potential side effects is an important role for the nurse in HIV care. Some of the more common side effects from antiretroviral agents are

described in Table 40.5, along with some suggested nursing interventions.

NURSING TELEPHONE TRIAGE

A nurse telephone triage serves an important role in the delivery of HIV services. Telephone triage nurses provide an important link for patients to their clinic and to their clinicians. Managing HIV illness on a day-to-day basis can be both challenging and daunting, and having a readily available resource is an important connection. The scope of telephone nursing practice includes the provision of health counseling, primary care advice, routine health assessments, utilization control, and illness triage. Telephone nurses can also coordinate care among external agencies that provide services to patients with HIV. These services generally place calls to the telephone line to report symptoms or to gain patient information.

Several studies (Cook et al., 2009; Nishigaki et al., 2007; Wess and Bronaugh, 2003) have described telephone triage as an excellent vehicle for identifying and promoting self-management and adherence; it is an important and necessary component of any HIV program.

SUMMARY

Despite the therapeutic advances that have occurred since the epidemic began more than in 1981, HIV infection continues to affect individuals, families, and communities at the alarming rate of approximately five million new infections worldwide. Much has been learned about caring for patients in a constantly changing, complex epidemic, but much is yet to be learned about supporting a chronic illness and providing primary and secondary prevention. Nursing practice is multifaceted and occurs in an array of settings, including primary care, acute care facilities, communities, and schools. HIV/AIDS nursing practice can be defined as the provision of educational, therapeutic, and supportive interventions to promote client, family, and community adaptation to HIV infection. Nurses in HIV care are constantly challenged by the complexities of the disease. Persons with HIV and AIDS who are actively engaged in substance use present major challenges to nurses who are trying to promote adherence to care and risk reduction. Mental illness may emerge or be exacerbated by HIV illness and its treatments. Mental illness and substance use may go untreated and interfere with HIV illness or contribute to its transmission. Nurses are an important resource in the process of screening for substance use and psychiatric illness. They are also an important part of the multidisciplinary team that includes mental health providers. Although nursing research has contributed to the elucidation of the complex combination of medical and psychiatric issues that constitute the dynamics of HIV illness, there is still much more to be understood. Nurses have contributed to and will continue to add to the HIV/AIDS knowledge base in professional, scientific, and personal ways that have served to enhance the lives of persons infected with HIV.

Table 40.5 MANAGING COMMON SYMPTOMS FROM ANTIRETROVIRAL THERAPY

SIDE EFFECT	ETIOLOGY/PATIENT COUNSELING	CLINICAL INTERVENTIONS	NONPHARMACOLOGICAL INTERVENTIONS
Nausea	Avoid known triggers (e.g., the smell of certain foods). Teach patient to use deep breathing and relaxation at first onset of feeling nauseated. Ensure proper room ventilation.	Antiemetics as prescribed	Use of crystallized ginger has been helpful for some patients.*
Fatigue	HIV-related fatigue can be multifactorial. It is the most common complaint of persons with HIV. Ask the patient at what time of the day the fatigue occurs and look for treatable patterns.	Assess hemoglobin, hematocrit, liver function tests, thyroid function, hypogonadism, or possible opportunistic infection. Treat any underlying abnormal finding.	If not contraindicated, counsel patient on the use of a light, progressive exercise program.†
Neuropathy	Neuropathy has been attributed to the direct effects of HIV, exposure to antiretroviral medications (particularly the nucleoside reverse transcriptase inhibitors), advanced immune suppression, and comorbid tuberculosis infection and exposure to antituberculosis medications.	May be treated with nonsteroidal anti-inflammatory drugs, antiseizure medications, immunosuppressive medications, lidocaine patches, and certain tricyclic antidepressants.	Capsaicin. A cream containing this naturally occurring substance found in hot peppers can cause modest improvements in peripheral neuropathy symptoms.‡
Difficulty swallowing	Assess for any oral lesions or airway obstruction. Ask patient about any possible triggers (e.g., food, antiretrovirals, large pills, etc.)	Treat any pathology such as lesions or exudate.	Encourage use of soft or pureed foods. Eat foods at room temperature. Avoid "dense" foods such as peanut butter, milk, and candy.
Sleep disturbance	Medications are often implicated in sleep disturbance, and the antiretroviral medication most consistently associated with insomnia is the non-nucleoside transcriptase inhibitor efavirenz	May resolve with prolonged use of medication. Pharmacological intervention with non-benzodiazepine receptor agonists, benzodiazepines, melatonin receptor agonist, antidepressants	Sleep hygiene: wear earplugs, limit caffeine intake; cognitive-behavioral therapy**

Sources: * Dabaghzadeh F, Khalili H, Dashti-Khavidaki S, Abbasian L, Moeinifard A (2014). Ginger for prevention of antiretroviral-induced nausea and vomiting: a randomized clinical trial. *Expert Opin Drug Saf* 13(7):859–866.

† Barroso J, Voss J (2013). Fatigue in HIV and AIDS: an analysis of evidence. *J Assoc Nurses AIDS Care* 24(1)(Suppl):S5–S14.

‡ Nicholas PK, Corless IB, Evans LA (2014). Peripheral neuropathy in HIV: an analysis of evidence-based approaches *J Assoc Nurses AIDS Care* 25(4):318–329.

**Taibi D (2013). Sleep disturbance in persons living with HIV. *J Assoc Nurses AIDS Care* 24(1):S72–S85.

REFERENCES

Aiken LH, Sloane DM, Lake ET (1997). Satisfaction with inpatient acquired immunodeficiency syndrome care. A national comparison of dedicated and scattered-bed units. *Med Care* 35(9):948–962.

Bares S, Steinbeck J, Bence L, et al. (2016). Knowledge, attitudes, and ordering patterns for routine HIV screening among resident physicians at an urban medical center. *J Int Assoc Provid AIDS Care* 15(4):320–327.

Berry S, Fleishman J, Moore RD, Gebo KA (2012). Trends in reasons for hospitalization in a multisite United States cohort of persons living with HIV, 2001–2008. *J Acquir Immune Defic Syndr* 59(4):368–375.

Bing EG, Burnan MA, Longshore D, et al. (2001). Psychiatric disorders and drug use among human immunodeficiency virus infected adults in the United States. *Arch Gen Psychiatry* 58(8):721–728.

Blank MB, Mandell DS, Aiken L, Hadley T (2002). Co-occurrence of HIV and serious mental illness among Medicaid recipients. *Psychiatr Serv* 53(7):868–873.

Brennan MB, Kolehmainen C, Barocas J, Isaac C, Crnich CJ, Sosman JM (2013). Barriers and facilitators of universal HIV screening among internal medicine residents. *WMJ* 112(5):199–205.

Brown RL, Leonard T, Saunders LA, Papasouliotis O (2001). A two-item conjoint screen for alcohol and other drug problems. *J Am Board Fam Pract* 14(2):95–106.

Brown RL, Moberg PD, Allen JB, et al. (2014) A team approach to systematic behavioral screening and intervention. *Am J Manag Care* 20(4):e113–e121.

Carey MP, Carey KB, Kalichman SC (1997). Risk for human immunodeficiency virus (HIV) infection among persons with severe mental illness. *Clin Psychol Rev* 17(3):271–291.

Carey MP, Carey KB, Maisto SA, Gordon CM, Schroder KE, Vanable PA (2004). Reducing HIV-risk behavior among adults receiving outpatient psychiatric treatment: results from a randomized controlled trial. *J Consult Clin Psychol* 72(2):252–268.

Centers for Disease Control and Prevention (CDC) (2003). Advancing HIV prevention: new strategies for a changing epidemic—United States, 2003. *MMWR Morb Mortal Wkly Rep* 52(15):329–332.

Centers for Disease Control and Prevention (CDC) (2013a). *HIV Surveillance Report*, 2011. Vol. 23; February 2013. Rates of diagnoses of HIV infection among adults and adolescents, by area of residence, 2011—United States and 6 dependent areas. https://www.cdc.gov/hiv/pdf/statistics_2011_HIV_Surveillance_Report_vol_23.pdf. Accessed February 10, 2017.

Centers for Disease Control and Prevention (CDC) (2013b). HIV testing in clinical settings. https://www.cdc.gov/hiv/testing/clinical/. Accessed February 10, 2017.

Centers for Disease Control and Prevention (CDC) (2016). Fact sheet: HIV in the United States: at a glance. https://www.cdc.gov/hiv/statistics/overview/ataglance.html. Accessed February 10, 2017.

Cook P, Mccabe M, Emiliozzi S, Pointer L (2009). Telephone nurse counseling improves HIV medication adherence: an effectiveness study. *J Assoc Nurses AIDS Care* 20(4):316–325.

Currie LB, Patterson ML, Moniruzzaman A, McCandless LC, Somers JM (2014). Examining the relationship between health-related need and the receipt of care by participants experiencing homelessness and mental illness. *BMC Health Serv Res* 14:404.

De Guzman, E, Woods-Giscombe C, Beeber LS (2015). Barriers and facilitators of Hispanic older adult mental health service utilization in the USA. *Issues Ment Health Nurs* 36(1):11–20.

Epstein RM, Morse DS, Frankel RM, Frarey L, Anderson K, Beckman HB (1998). Awkward moments in patient–physician communication about HIV risk. *Ann Intern Med* 128(6):435–442.

Finnell DS, Nowzari S, Reimann B, Fischer L, Pace E, Goplerud E (2014). Screening, brief intervention, and referral to treatment (SBIRT) as an integral part of nursing practice. *Subst Abus* 35(2):114–118.

Flickinger TE, Berry S, Korthuis PT, et al. (2013). Counseling to reduce high-risk sexual behavior in HIV care: a multi-center, direct observation study. *AIDS Patient Care STDS* 27(7):416–424.

Joseph J, Basu D, Dandapani M, Krishnan N (2014). Are nurse-conducted brief interventions (NCBIs) efficacious for hazardous or harmful alcohol use? A systematic review. *Int Nurs Rev* 61(2):203–210.

Kaltenthaler E, Pandor A, Wong R. (2014). The effectiveness of sexual health interventions for people with severe mental illness: a systematic. *Health Technol Assess* 18(1):1–74.

Krause DD, May WL, Butler KR Jr (2013). Determining unmet, adequately met, and overly met needs for health care and services for persons living with HIV/AIDS in Mississippi. *AIDS Care* 25(8):973–979.

Lanier Y, Castellanos T, Barrow RY, Jordan WC, Caine V, Sutton MY (2014). Brief sexual histories and routine HIV/STD testing by medical providers. *AIDS Patient Care STDS* 28:113–120.

Laws MB, Bradshaw YS, Safren SA, Beach MC, Lee Y, Rogers W, Wilson IB (2011). Discussion of sexual risk behavior in HIV care is infrequent and appears ineffectual: a mixed methods study. *AIDS Behav* 15(4):812–822.

Lennon CA, Pellowski JA, White AC, et al. (2013). Service priorities and unmet service needs among people living with HIV/AIDS: results from a nationwide interview of HIV/AIDS housing organizations. *AIDS Care* 25(9):1083–1091.

McKinnon K, Cournos F, Herman R. (2002). HIV among people with chronic mental illness. *Psychiatr Q* 73:17–31.

Minassian A, Vilke GM, Wilson MP (2013). Frequent emergency department visits are more prevalent in psychiatric, alcohol abuse, and dual diagnosis conditions than in chronic viral illnesses such as hepatitis and human immunodeficiency virus. *J Emerg Med* 45(4):520–525.

Morrison C (1993). Delivery systems for the care of persons with HIV infection and AIDS. *Nurs Clin North Am* 28(2):317–333.

Navarra A, Neu N, Toussi S, Nelson J, Larson EL (2013). Health literacy and adherence to antiretroviral therapy among HIV-infected youth. *J Assoc Nurses AIDS Care* 25(3):203–213.

Nishigaki M, Shimada M, Ikeda K, et al. (2007). Process and contents of telephone consultations between registered nurses and clients with HIV/AIDS in Japan. *J Assoc Nurses AIDS Care* 18(6):8–96.

Otto-Salaj LL, Kelly JA, Stevenson LY, Hoffmann R, Kalichman SC (2001). Outcomes of a randomized small-group HIV prevention intervention trial for people with serious mental illness. *Community Ment Health J* 37(2):123–144.

Pascreta J, Jacobsen P (1989). Addressing the need for staff support among nurses caring for the AIDS population. *Oncol Nurs Forum* 16(5):659–663.

Pence BW, Gaynes BN, Whetten K, Eron JJ Jr, Ryder RW, Miller WC (2005). Validation of a brief screening instrument for substance abuse and mental illness in HIV-positive patients. *J Acquir Immune Defic Syndr* 40(4):434–444.

Rahm AK, Boggs JM, Martin C, Price DW, Beck A, Backer TE, Dearing JW (2015). Facilitators and barriers to implementing SBIRT in primary care in integrated health care settings. *Subst Abus* 36(3):281–288.

Rhodes P, Glynn K (2005). Modeling the HIV epidemic. Presented at the National HIV Prevention Conference, Atlanta, Georgia, June 12–15, 2005. http://www.aegis.com/conferences/NHIVPC/2005/T1-B1102.html.

Rost K, Burnam MA, Smith GR (1993). Development of screeners for depressive disorders and substance disorder history. *Med Care* 31(3):189–200.

Schadé A, van Grootheest G, Smit JH. (2013). HIV-infected mental health patients: characteristics and comparison with HIV-infected patients from the general population and non-infected mental health patients. *BMC Psychiatry* 13:35.

Schumacher JE, Mccullumsmith C, Mugavero MJ, et al. (2013). Routine depression screening in an HIV clinic cohort identifies patients with complex psychiatric co-morbidities who show significant response to treatment. AIDS Behav 17(8):2781–2791.

Shacham E, Morgan JC, Önen NF, Taniguchi T, Overton ET (2012). Screening anxiety in the HIV clinic. *AIDS Behav* 16(8):2407–2413.

Shacham E, Onen NF, Donovan MF, Rosenburg N, Overton ET (2016). Psychiatric diagnoses among an HIV-infected outpatient clinic population. *J Int Assoc Provid AIDS Care* 15(2):126–130.

Sherman DW (2000). AIDS-dedicated nurses: what can be learned from their perceptions and experiences. *Appl Nurs Res* 13(3):115–124.

Sommers MS, McDonald CC, Fargo JD (2015). Emergency department–based brief intervention to reduce risky driving: a life course perspective. *Clin Nurs Res* 24(5):449–467.

Surah S, Kieran J, O'Dea S, et al. (2013). Use of the Alcohol Use Disorders Identification Test (AUDIT) to determine the prevalence of alcohol misuse among HIV-infected individuals. *Int J STD AIDS* 24(7):517–521.

UNAIDS (2013). *Global Report: UNAIDS Report on the Global AIDS Epidemic 2013*. http://www.unaids.org/en/media/unaids/contentassets/documents/epidemiology/2013/gr2013/UNAIDS_Global_Report_2013_en.pdf. Accessed February 14, 2017.

Walsh C, McCann E, Gilbody S, Hughes E. (2014). Promoting HIV and sexual safety behaviour in people with severe mental illness: a systematic review of behavioural interventions. *Int J Ment Health Nurs* 23(4):344–354.

Wess Y, Bronaugh M (2003). *Telephone Triage for People with HIV/ AIDS: You Make the Call*. Philadelphia: Hanley & Belfus Medical Publishers.

Whetten K, Reif S, Swartz M, et al. (2005). A brief mental health and substance abuse screener for persons with HIV. *AIDS Patient Care STDS* 19(2):89–99.

Wilson IB, Landon BE, Hirschhorn LR, et al. (2005). Quality of HIV care provided by nurse practitioners, physician assistants, and physicians. *Ann Intern Med* 143(10):729–736.

41.

PALLIATIVE CARE AND SPIRITUAL CARE OF PERSONS WITH HIV AND AIDS

Anna L. Dickerman, Yesne Alici, William Breitbart, and Harvey Max Chochinov

The meaning and role of palliative care and spiritual care have evolved over the last decade, along with the dramatically changing clinical picture of AIDS. In the early days of the pandemic, for most persons with AIDS, palliative care was inseparable from AIDS care. Advances in antiretroviral therapy (ART) and appropriate medical care have allowed individuals with AIDS to live longer and healthier lives. Death rates from AIDS decreased dramatically after 1996 (Centers for Disease Control and Prevention [CDC], 2003). Despite this, a variety of barriers prevent many persons with AIDS in the United States and throughout the world from receiving adequate care (Cohen and Alfonso, 2004; Harding et al., 2005; Sanei, 1998). AIDS-related deaths in the United States have plateaued in the past decade; similarly, new diagnoses of HIV infection have not decreased significantly (CDC, 2005). As the number of patients living with HIV continues to grow, there is an increased need for comprehensive symptom management, including psychosocial and family support. The delivery of palliative care for AIDS patients should also take into account that patients with HIV are at increased risk for non-AIDS-related medical disorders such as cardiovascular disease, cancer, liver disease, kidney disease, and neurocognitive disorders (Deeks et al., 2013). In particular, older adults living with HIV present an emerging clinical challenge with age-related medical and neuropsychiatric comorbidities, and polypharmacy (Farber and Marconi, 2014).

The ideal model for the comprehensive care of patients with HIV is not one that can be readily dichotomized into illness-specific "curative" and symptom-specific "palliative" approaches (Selwyn and Forstein, 2003). The curative versus palliative dichotomy has become less relevant now that persons with AIDS live longer, have a high incidence of cancer and other multimorbidities, and continue to have an ongoing need for supportive care. Rather, curative and palliative approaches must be integrated in a multidisciplinary fashion to meet the challenges of advanced HIV or multimorbid illness (Alexander and Back, 2004; O'Neill et al., 2000; Selwyn and Forstein, 2003; Selwyn et al., 2003). Skilled and expert psychiatric care is integral to optimal HIV/AIDS palliative care delivery (O'Neill et al., 2003). UNAIDS 90-90-90 targets to help end the AIDS epidemic worldwide could best be achieved with "not-dichotomized" but integrated palliative HIV clinics addressing HIV patients' needs with a biopsychosocial approach at all stages of the illness (UNAIDS, 2014). Psychosomatic medicine psychiatrists in particular, with their expertise in the interface of medicine and psychiatry, are in the unique position to play a major role in the development of psychiatric, psychosocial, and existential approaches to palliative care for AIDS patients.

This chapter reviews basic concepts and definitions of palliative care and spiritual care, as well as the distinct challenges facing the psychosomatic medicine practitioner involved in HIV palliative care. Finally, issues such as bereavement, cultural sensitivity, communication, and psychiatric contributions to common physical symptom control are also reviewed.

DEFINING PALLIATIVE CARE

The terms *palliative care* and *palliative medicine* are often used interchangeably. Palliative medicine refers to the medical discipline of palliative care. Modern palliative care has evolved from the hospice movement into a more expansive network of clinical care delivery systems with components of home care and hospital-based services (Butler et al., 1996; Stjernsward and Papallona, 1998). While both hospice care and palliative care are based on a biospsychosocial model (Engel, 1977, 1980), current practice differentiates hospice care from palliative care; hospice care is limited to care at the end of life, while palliative care is relevant throughout the course of care of persons with severe and complex illness. Hospice care applies and implements palliative care at the end of life.

Palliative care must meet the needs of the "whole person," including the physical, psychological, social, and spiritual aspects of suffering (World Health Organization [WHO], 1990). The definition of palliative care set forth by the World Health Organization is one that encompasses the requirements of body, mind, and spirit. According to this definition, palliative care (1) affirms life and regards dying as a normal process; (2) views the dying process as a valuable experience; (3) intends neither to hasten nor postpone death; (4) provides relief from pain and other symptoms; (5) integrates psychological and spiritual care; (6) offers a support system to help patients live as actively as possible until death; (7) helps family cope with illness and bereavement; (8) is multidisciplinary and includes a caregiver team of physicians, nurses, mental health professionals, clergy, and volunteers; (9) enhances the patient's quality of life and may also positively influence the course of illness; (10) is applicable early in the course of illness, in conjunction with other therapies that are intended to prolong life; and (11) includes the investigations needed to better understand and manage distressing clinical complications (WHO, 1990, 1998, 2002, 2007). The Canadian Palliative Care Association (1995) states that palliative care must strive to meet the physical, psychological, social, and spiritual expectations and needs of patients while also remaining sensitive to personal, cultural, and religious values, beliefs, and practices. Thus, the control of pain and other symptoms, as well as management of psychological, social, and spiritual problems, is essential. The goal of palliative care is to alleviate suffering and maximize quality of life for patients and their families.

The nature and focus of palliative care have evolved over the century, expanding beyond the concept of comfort care only for the dying. This care may begin with the onset of a life-threatening illness and proceeds beyond death to include bereavement interventions for family and others. Indeed, for persons with HIV/AIDS, many aspects of palliative care are applicable at every stage of illness, from initial diagnosis to the end of life (Cohen and Alfonso, 2004; Deeks et al., 2013; Simms et al., 2011, 2012). UNAIDS also endorses that palliative care has a key role in the ongoing management of HIV across the disease spectrum (UNAIDS, 2000). Persons with a severe illness such as AIDS should not have to wait until the end of their lives to experience relief from suffering and distress. Though palliative care does not merely consist of providing comfort at the end of life, comfort does take on greater importance when cure becomes less feasible. Ideally, as illness proceeds, gradual movement from curative approaches to palliation takes place along a smooth continuum (Cohen and Alfonso, 2004). Palliative care is a relatively inexpensive and efficient means of controlling pain, other physical symptoms, and addressing psychological and existential distress. Indeed, palliative care for individuals with AIDS and cancer has been instituted as national policy in countries that are neither wealthy nor industrialized (Breitbart et al., 2012a; Stjernsward and Clark, 2004). Recent studies have shown that "early palliative care" improves quality of life, reduces symptom burden, and does not hasten death (Greer et al., 2012; Temel et al., 2010; Yoong et al., 2013). Application of this evidence to clinical care will result in earlier and more frequent utilization of palliative care interventions, leading to better symptom control and reduced existential distress among patients with AIDS. As outlined by Farber and Marconi (2014), "palliative care is well positioned to complement primary care across the spectrum of HIV disease course as a clinical resource for enhancing quality of life. Early palliative care may even contribute to improved retention in care and health outcomes because of its whole person focus on a spectrum of biopsychosocial concerns that, left unaddressed, could pose obstacles to individuals remaining in care and adherent to ART."

Table 41.1 summarizes the comprehensive, biopsychosocial approach recommended for AIDS palliative care. The biopsychosocial approach to treating persons with AIDS is also reviewed in Chapter 1 of this text.

Table 41.1 AIDS PALLIATIVE CARE: A BIOPSYCHOSOCIAL APPROACH

BIOLOGICAL	PSYCHOLOGICAL	SOCIAL
Pain	Depression	Alienation
Dyspnea	Anxiety	Social isolation
Insomnia	Confusion	Stigma
Fatigue	Psychosis	Spirituality
Nausea	Mania	Financial loss
Vomiting	Withdrawal	Job loss
Diarrhea	Intoxication	Loss of key roles
Blindness	Substance dependence	Loss of independence
Paralysis	Existential anxiety	
Weakness	Bereavement	
Cachexia	Demoralization	
Incontinence	Suicidality	
Pruritus		
Hiccups		
Delirium		
Dementia		
Tolerability of medical treatments		

Source: Adapted from Cohen MA, Alfonso CA. AIDS psychiatry: Psychiatric and palliative care, and pain management. In GP Wormser (ed.), *AIDS and Other Manifestations of HIV Infection,* 4th ed. (pp. 537–576). Copyright (2004), with permission from Elsevier.

PALLIATIVE CARE ISSUES IN PERSONS LIVING WITH HIV AND AIDS

AIDS is a chronic illness with exacerbations and remissions, a growing disease burden, medical and psychological comorbidities, and toxic side effects from treatment (Selwyn and Forstein, 2003). The uncertain prognosis of AIDS for many patients, as well as the limitations and promise of rapidly evolving therapies, makes decision-making about advance care planning and end-of-life issues more complex and elusive than before the advent of highly active ART. For patients with AIDS, the World Health Organization's definition of palliative care as "active total care" includes use of ART, prevention and management of opportunistic infections, as well as a palliative approach of offering symptomatic and supportive care at all stages of disease (Foley and Flannery, 1995; Stephenson et al., 2000).

Palliative care for persons with HIV and access to care has shifted from the care of persons dying of AIDS and its complications to the care of patients dying of causes in comparable populations in the last decade. While patients who do not have access to care are still dying of AIDS, the majority of persons with HIV face the burden of increased risk of non-AIDS-related medical disorders such as cardiovascular disease, cancer, liver disease, kidney disease, and neurocognitive disorders in particular older adults living with HIV (Deeks et al., 2013; Farber and Marconi 2014).

PAIN AND SYMPTOM MANAGEMENT

There is a high prevalence of pain, side effects related to ART, and other symptoms throughout the HIV disease trajectory, which may be underrecognized and undertreated (Breitbart et al., 1996b, 1998, 1999; Fantoni et al., 1997; Filbet and Marceron, 1994; Foley, 1994; Fontaine et al., 1999; Fontes and Goncalves, 2014; Kelleher et al., 1997; LaRue and Colleau, 1997; LaRue et al., 1994; Mathews et al., 2000; Moss, 1990; O'Neill and Sherrard, 1993; Selwyn and Rivard, 2003; Selwyn et al., 2003; Singer et al., 1993; Vogl et al., 1999; Wood et al., 1997). Fatigue, weight loss, pain, anorexia, depression, and anxiety are most prevalent symptoms reported among patients with AIDS. Other symptoms including insomnia, pruritis, cough, nausea, vomiting, dyspnea, diarrhea, and constipation should also be screened for and managed properly to improve the quality of life in persons with AIDS (Fausto and Selwyn, 2011).

Pain Management

The deleterious influence of uncontrolled pain on a patient's psychological state is often intuitively understood and recognized. Yet pain is dramatically undertreated in persons with HIV, especially among persons with HIV who inject drugs (Breitbart et al., 1992; Rosenfeld et al., 1997; Ruiz et al., 2014; Schofferman, 1988). The World Health Organization (1986) recommends a stepwise process for the pharmacological treatment of pain related to cancer. This model has been adopted by clinicians treating patients with AIDS experiencing pain (Newshan and Wainapel, 1993; Reiter and Kudler, 1996) and consists of (1) non-opioid prescription, with or without an adjuvant; (2) prescription of a weak opioid, with or without and adjuvant; and (3) prescription of a strong opioid, with or without a non-opioid with or without an adjuvant. This analgesic "ladder" is more effective for the treatment of nociceptive than for neuropathic pain (Cohen and Alfonso, 2004). Neuropathic pain related to HIV can be treated with adjuvant or co-analgesic agents, such as tricyclic antidepressants, serotonin-norepinephrine reuptake inhibitors, and anticonvulsants (Cornblath and McArthur, 1988; Newshan and Wainapel, 1993; Reiter and Kudler, 1996). Acute and chronic pain is best treated on an around-the-clock schedule (Goldberg, 1993; Newshan and Wainapel, 1993), rather than on an as-needed or PRN basis, regardless of the etiology of pain. For persons with HIV and substance use disorders, interdisciplinary pain management is essential to avoid undertreatment of pain due to fear of worsening an underlying opioid misuse.

Most pain syndromes associated with AIDS respond to pharmacotherapy (Cohen and Alfonso, 2004). Nonetheless, nonpharmacological analgesic modalities such as surgical procedures, radiation therapy, and neurological stimulatory approaches can provide effective adjuvant therapy (Carmichael, 1991; Geara et al., 1991; Jacox et al., 1994; Jonsson et al., 1992; Newshan and Wainapel 1993; Portenoy, 1993; Tosches et al., 1992). International guidelines also suggest the importance of incorporating psychosocial and behavioral approaches into an opioid management plan (Kalso et al., 2003; Maddox et al., 1997; Ontario Workplace Safety and Insurance Board, 2000; Pain Society and Royal Colleges of Anaesthetists, 2004). Behavioral interventions such as hypnosis, biofeedback, and multicomponent cognitive-behavioral interventions have been shown to be effective in the management of acute, procedurally related cancer pain (Hilgard and LeBaron, 1982; Jay et al., 1986; Kellerman et al., 1983). Typically, behavioral interventions used in the management of acute procedure-related pain employ the basic elements of relaxation and distraction or diversion of attention.

Behavioral interventions are also effective as an adjunct treatment for chronic pain both related and unrelated to cancer (Adams et al., 2006; Guzman et al., 2001; Morley et al., 1999). In chronic cancer pain, cognitive-behavioral techniques are most effective when they are employed as part of a multimodal, multidisciplinary approach (Breitbart, 1989). These techniques can provide much needed respite from pain. Even short periods of relief from pain can break the vicious pain cycle that entraps many patients with cancer.

A review by Breitbart and colleagues (2004b) addresses in detail the use of behavioral, psychotherapeutic, and psychopharmacological interventions in pain control.

Management of Other Physical Symptoms

Physical symptoms other than pain can often go undetected and cause significant emotional distress. These symptoms must be assessed by the psychologist or psychiatrist concerned with the evaluation and treatment of psychiatric syndromes. Aggressive treatment of troublesome physical symptoms such as anorexia, pruritus, and fatigue is necessary to enhance the patient's quality of life (Bruera et al., 1990; Harding et al., 2005). In addition to providing physical, psychological, and emotional comfort for the person, symptom management may also improve adherence to ART (Selwyn and Forstein, 2003).

A comprehensive review of pharmacological and nonpharmacological interventions for common physical symptoms encountered in terminally ill persons can be found in the *Oxford Textbook of Palliative Medicine*, third edition (Doyle et al., 2003) and the first and second editions of the *Handbook of Psychiatry and Palliative Medicine* (Chochinov and Breitbart, 2000, 2009). The management of insomnia and fatigue in AIDS is discussed Chapters 23 and 24, respectively, of this text.

PSYCHIATRIC COMPLICATIONS

Patients with advanced AIDS are at risk for the development of major psychiatric disturbances (Breitbart et al., 2004a). Indeed, psychiatric complications such as depression and anxiety occur as frequently if not more so than pain and other physical symptoms (Portenoy et al., 1994; Vogl et al., 1999). Additionally, psychiatric comorbidities are highly prevalent among persons living with HIV, affecting about 50% of all patients (Gonzales et al., 2011). Assessment and management of the underlying psychopathology has significant underpinnings for HIV adherence and retention in care (Farber and Marconi, 2014). Incidences of psychiatric disorders such as depression, anxiety, and delirium increase with higher levels of physical debilitation and advanced illness. Psychological symptoms such as worrying, nervousness, insomnia, lack of energy, and sadness are most prevalent and distressing in palliative care settings (Breitbart and Alici, 2014). Neuropsychiatric symptoms and syndromes such as depressive disorder, cognitive disorders including delirium, anxiety disorders, desire for hastened death, and suicidal ideation coexist with many other physical and psychological symptoms and may negatively impact quality of life. Thus, palliative care must encompass psychiatric as well as pain and physical symptom management. Psychiatric interventions for the treatment of negative emotional states can complement palliative symptom management strategies (Cohen and Alfonso, 2004). Prompt recognition and effective treatment of psychiatric symptoms is critically important to the well-being of the patient in palliative care settings. Successful treatment of depression may substantially decrease desire for hastened death in persons with advanced AIDS (Breitbart et al., 2010).

Psychiatric symptom control in advanced disease involves a management approach that focuses on symptoms, such as use of antidepressants for neuropathic pain, appetite, or insomnia and use of atypical antipsychotics for nausea, anxiety, appetite, insomnia, or agitation. A syndrome-based approach is applied when a distinct depressive disorder, an anxiety disorder, or other psychiatric syndromes can be identified (Breitbart and Alici, 2014). Table 41.2 summarizes some of the palliative care and symptom management interventions.

Table 41.2 PALLIATIVE CARE AND SYMPTOM MANAGEMENT

SYMPTOM	TREATMENT
Intractable hiccups	Chlorpromazine; olanzapine
Dyspnea	Oxygen; morphine; fan; relaxation
Nausea	Ondansetron; olanzapine; mirtazapine
Pruritus	Doxepin
Pain (nociceptive)	Strong opioid analgesics (e.g., fentanyl, morphine sulfate)
Pain (neuropathic)	Adjuvant analgesics (e.g., antidepressants, anticonvulsants such as gabapentin and pregabalin,, antihistamines)

Source: Cohen MA, Alfonso CA. AIDS psychiatry: psychiatric and palliative care, and pain management. In GP Wormser (ed.), *AIDS and Other Manifestations of HIV Infection,* 4th ed. (pp. 537–576). Copyright (2004), with permission from Elsevier.

The management of a variety of psychiatric disturbances is also discussed in Chapters 14–20 of this text.

Anxiety Disorders in Palliative Care

Anxiety disorders are common in patients receiving palliative care at the end of life. Anxiety can be a natural response to impending death, uncertainty, and existential suffering. It may also represent a clinically significant issue adversely affecting a person's quality of life. A prevalence rate of 10% to 28% has been reported for anxiety disorders among patients with AIDS (Kerrihard et al., 1999). In palliative care settings, anxiety may be a symptom of a psychiatric disorder; may be due to pain, dyspnea, or nausea; may develop from medication adverse effects (e.g., steroids, metoclopramide, prochlorperazine, bronchodilators) or alcohol or benzodiazepine withdrawal; or may stem from other medical causes. The assumption that a high level of anxiety is inevitably encountered during the terminal phase of illness is neither helpful nor accurate for diagnostic and treatment purposes (Breitbart and Alici, 2014).

When anxiety is severe or distressing, pharmacotherapy is considered, in addition to psychotherapy and other supportive care measures. Psychotherapy with terminally ill patients with anxiety may take on a supportive approach focusing on nurturing, which can help contain the anxiety that patients feel regarding medical settings or death. The pharmacotherapy of anxiety in terminal illness involves the judicious use of benzodiazepines, typical and atypical antipsychotics, antihistamines, antidepressants, and opioid analgesics (Breitbart and Alici, 2014). A 2012 Cochrane review was unable to identify any well-designed prospective randomized, controlled trials in the use of pharmacotherapy for treatment of symptoms of anxiety at the end of life in adult palliative care patients (Candy et al., 2012). Although the clinical evidence is supportive of the use of medications in the treatment of anxiety among palliative care patients, randomized controlled trials are needed in order to establish the risks and benefits of medication use for patients with AIDS experiencing anxiety at the end of life.

Depressive Disorders in Palliative Care at the End of Life

Depression is prevalent in palliative care settings (Wilson et al., 2009). The belief among clinicians and family members that depression is an appropriate reaction among terminally ill persons contributes to its underdiagnosis and undertreatment. Additionally, it is difficult to diagnose depression because of the multiple medical comorbidities that mimic depressive symptoms, such as fatigue, insomnia or hypersomnia, psychomotor retardation, and poor appetite. History of previous depressive episodes, poor social support, the severity of physical symptoms—specifically pain, poor functional status, existential distress—and certain medications have been found to increase risk of depression in patients with advanced disease (Breitbart and Alici, 2014; Wilson et al., 2009). In managing depression with use of medications, clinicians should take into consideration the life expectancy of the depressed individual (Li et al., 2012). Psychostimulants such as methylphenidate or dextroamphetamine may be the preferred treatment in patients with less than a month of survival expectancy (Li et al., 2012). A variety of psychotherapeutic approaches have been studied and found effective in the treatment of depression in terminally ill persons (Li et al., 2012). An in-depth review of assessment and management of depression in terminally ill persons can be found elsewhere (Breitbart and Alici, 2014; Li et al., 2012).

Suicide, Assisted Suicide, and Desire for Hastened Death in Palliative Care

Palliative care clinicians frequently encounter patients with suicidal ideation and desire for hastened death. Please see Chapter 25 for an in-depth discussion of suicidality and HIV. While clinical depression is a critically important factor in suicidal ideation and desire for hastened death, it is not the only reason patients with a terminal illness wish or seek to hasten their death (Breitbart and Alici, 2014). Despite legal prohibitions against assisted suicide in most parts of the world, a substantial number of terminally ill patients think about and discuss those alternatives with their physicians, family, and friends (Olden et al., 2009). Interest in physician-assisted suicide was reported by 55% of terminally ill AIDS patients in a study completed by Breitbart and colleagues (Breitbart et al., 1996a). It is important to note that terminally ill patients want to talk about their options, but very few ultimately follow through with a medically assisted death, even in an environment where it is legally permissible (Quill, 2012). Regardless of the legalization of physician-assisted suicide, the primary goal of the clinician should be to assess the complexity of each case individually, with particular attention to underlying depression, hopelessness, and physical distress when faced with these requests (Breitbart and Alici, 2014). The goal of the clinician's role in attending to terminally ill persons is to eliminate "the suffering" and not to eliminate "the sufferer" (Breitbart and Alici, 2014). Pain or other physical suffering, advanced illness, depression, delirium, loss of control, feelings of helplessness, existential distress, substance or alcohol misuse, and lack of social support increase risk of suicide and desire for hastened death among terminally ill persons (Olden et al., 2009). Physical and psychological symptoms contributing to desire for hastened death should be aggressively treated. In a study by Breitbart et al. (2010), patients with advanced AIDS ($N = 372$) were assessed for depression and desire for hastened death. Patients diagnosed with a major depressive episode were provided with antidepressant treatment and assessed weekly for depression and desire for hastened death. The study showed that desire for hastened death decreased dramatically in patients whose depression responded to antidepressant treatment. The authors concluded that successful treatment for depression appears to substantially decrease desire for hastened death in patients with advanced AIDS. As with patients nearing the end of life with any illness, involvement of family and loved ones is an important aspect of care and can considerably alleviate suffering. Psychotherapeutic interventions that specifically address hopelessness, loss of dignity, loss of meaning, demoralization, and other forms of existential suffering should be considered in treating patients with suicidal ideation or a desire for hastened death (Breitbart and Alici, 2014).

TREATMENT FAILURE

Despite the promise of new antiretroviral regimens, viral suppression with ART may not be feasible. Failure of ART can be caused by drug–drug interactions resulting in suboptimal drug levels, poor adherence, or preexisting drug resistance (Easterbrook and Meadway, 2001).

Polypharmacy is common in persons with AIDS. Newer antiretroviral medications are substantially safer than their predecessors, but the side effects of these agents still pose diagnostic and management challenges (DHHS Panel on Antiretroviral Guidelines for Adults and Adolescents, 2016). The expanding number of drugs taken by persons with AIDS can be problematic, especially since many of these medications are substrates for cytochrome p450 drug-metabolizing enzymes in the liver. Non-nucleoside reverse transcriptase inhibitors and ritonavir-boosted regimens of protease inhibitors in particular have several important drug interactions with other medications, including HIV-related medications (DHHS Panel on Antiretroviral Guidelines for Adults and Adolescents, 2016; Fontes and Goncalves 2014). The potential for pharmacokinetic drug interactions can be circumvented by modifying the dose of one or several drugs (Easterbrook and Meadway, 2001). Table 41.3 summarizes the potential interactions between common HIV and palliative care medications. Drug–drug interactions are discussed further in Chapter 42.

Patients may have difficulty adhering to treatment regimens because of high pill burdens, dietary restrictions, or unacceptable side effects. Psychiatric comorbidities and cognitive impairment can also impact adherence (Ellis, 1997; Evans et al., 2002; Goodkin, 1997; Lopez et al., 1998). The psychiatric aspects of adherence to medical care and antiretrovirals are discussed in Chapter 29 of this text. Studies suggest that 20% of patients do not comply with therapy at all, and the remaining 80% probably comply only about 60% of the time (Easterbrook and Meadway, 2001). Thus, there is a great need for more potent and simplified antiretroviral regimens. The more physicians become frustrated with patients' difficulties in adhering to recommended ART regimens or with their own inability to reverse the disease course, the less effective they may be in accompanying the patient through the illness (Selwyn and Forstein, 2003).

There is an ongoing debate about the viral fitness of HIV and the possible benefit of continued ART despite high viral load (Deeks et al., 2001; Frenkel and Mullins, 2001). The potential risks and benefits of continuing ART in late-stage HIV illness are summarized in Box 41.1. No guidelines currently exist for the cessation of ART after treatment failure; this is an important consideration for clinical trials and for the development of the best practices for advanced HIV disease (Selwyn and Forstein, 2003). Failure to cure should not cause the physician to withdraw emotionally because of a perceived or unconscious sense of futility; rather, it is a signal to reiterate

Table 41.3 POTENTIAL DRUG INTERACTIONS BETWEEN COMMON HIV AND PALLIATIVE CARE MEDICATIONS*

CYTOCHROME P450 INHIBITORS

HIV MEDICATION	PALLIATIVE CARE MEDICATION
PROTEASE INHIBITORS	**ANTIDEPRESSANTS**
Ritonavir[†]	Fluoxetine
Indinavir	Paroxetine
	Sertraline
	Bupropion
	Fluvoxamine
	Citalopram
	Escitalopram
	Duloxetine
	Desvenlafaxine
	Venlafaxine
Nelfinavir	Nefazodone
	Reboxetine
	Trazodone
	Vilazodone
	Tricyclic antidepressants
	Non-Amphetamine Stimulants
	Modafinil
	Armodafinil
Darunavir	**Antipsychotics**
Atazanavir	Risperidone
Fosemprenavir	Clozapine
Lopinavir/Ritonavir	Asenapine
Saquinavir	Perphenazine
Tipranavir	Haloperidol
	Chlorpromazine
	Fluphenazine
Amprenavir	
Non-Nucleoside Reverse Transcriptase Inhibitors	
Delavirdine	
Efavirenz	
Etravirine	
Integrase Inhibitors	
Elvitegravir	
Antifungals	
Ketoconazole	
Fluconazole	
Itraconazole	

Table 41.3 CONTINUED

CYTOCHROME P450 INDUCERS

HIV MEDICATION	PALLIATIVE CARE MEDICATION
NON-NUCLEOSIDE REVERSE TRANSCRIPTASE INHIBITORS	**ANTICONVULSANTS**
Efavirenz	Carbamazepine
	Oxcarbazepine
	Topiramate
Nevirapine	Phenytoin
Etravirine	Phenobarbital
	Non-Amphetamine Stimulants
	Modafinil
	Armodafinil
Protease Inhibitors	
Fosamprenavir	
Ritonavir	
Lopinavir/Ritonavir	
Nelfinavir	
Integrase Inhibitors	
Elvitegravir	
Antimycobacterials	
Rifampin	
Rifabutin	

CYTOCHROME P450 SUBSTRATES

PALLIATIVE CARE MEDICATION
Opioids
Meperidine[†]
Methadone
Codeine
Morphine
Fentanyl
Antipsychotics
Typical antipsychotics
Olanzapine
Lurasidone
Antidepressants
Amitriptyline
Desipramine
Nortriptyline
Fluvoxamine
Bupropion
Sertraline
Citalopram

(*continued*)

Table 41.3 CONTINUED

CYTOCHROME P450 SUBSTRATES

Escitalopram

Fluoxetine

Paroxetine

Duloxetine

Desvenlafaxine

Levomilnacipran

Milnacipran

Venlafaxine

Mirtazapine

Nefazodone

Reboxetine

Trazodone

Vilazodone

Vortioxetine

Appetite Stimulants or Antiemetics

Dronabinol

Non-Amphetamine Stimulants

Modafinil

Armodafinil

Benzodiazepines

Alprazolam[†]

Clonazepam

Diazepam

Lorazepam[**]

Triazolam[†]

Midazolam[†]

Hypnotics

Zolpidem

Antihistamines

Fexofenadine

Astemizole

*The palliative care medications listed may require careful monitoring due to potential drug interactions with certain HIV medications. Multiple pathways and feedback loops may exist, especially when multiple P450 active medications are combined and net effects are not always predictable. Most agents are active through the CYP3A4 isoform of the P450 system, but other isoforms are involved to a lesser degree (CYP2D6, CYP2D19).

** Lorazepam is available in PO, IM, and IV formulations and has few drug–drug interactions, except in hepatic failure.

[†]The most potent P450 inhibitor among the protease inhibitors.

[†]Not recommended for use with protease inhibitors.

Source: Selwyn PA, Forstein M. Overcoming the false dichotomy of curative vs. palliative care for late-stage HIV/AIDS: "Let me live the way I want to live, until I can't." *JAMA* 290(6):806–814. Copyright (2003), with permission from JAMA/Archives Journals.

Box 41.1 POTENTIAL BENEFITS AND RISKS OF ANTIRETROVIRAL TREATMENT IN LATE-STAGE HIV DISEASE

Potential Benefits*

Selection for less fit virus (i.e., less pathogenic than wild type), even in the presence of elevated viral loads

Protection against HIV encephalopathy or dementia

Relief or easing of symptoms possibly associated with high viral loads (e.g., constitutional symptoms)

Continued therapeutic effect, albeit attenuated

Psychological and emotional benefits of continued disease-combating therapy

Potential Risks

Cumulative and multiple drug toxic effects in the setting of therapeutic futility (including certain rare, potentially life-threatening toxic effects)

Diminished quality of life from demands of treatment regimen

Therapeutic confusion (i.e., use of future-directed, disease-modifying therapy in a dying patient)

Distraction from end-of-life and advance care planning issues, with narrow focus on medication adherence and monitoring

*Evidence is lacking for some of these potential benefits, although they are commonly considered in clinical decision-making.

Source: Selwyn PA, Forstein M. Overcoming the false dichotomy of curative vs. palliative care for late-stage HIV/AIDS: "Let me live the way I want to live, until I can't." *JAMA* 290(6):806–814. Copyright (2003), with permission from JAMA/Archives Journals.

the commitment to the patient and to stay with him or her throughout the course of illness (Selwyn and Forstein, 2003).

MULTIPLE MEDICAL PROBLEMS AND COEXISTING DIAGNOSES

Although ART has increased the life expectancy of patients with HIV and reduced the incidence of AIDS-related illnesses (Huang et al., 2006), the frequency of pulmonary, cardiac, gastrointestinal, and renal diseases that are often not directly related to underlying HIV disease has increased (Casalino et al., 2004; Morris et al., 2002; Narasimhan et al., 2004; Vincent et al., 2004). A substantial number of persons with AIDS have multimorbidities that may complicate their management. Hepatitis B and C, for example, are common in individuals who become infected with HIV via intravenous drug use. Co-infection with HIV and hepatitis C is a strong risk factor for progression to end-stage liver disease (Easterbrook and

Meadway, 2001). Treatment of both of these viral infections is also associated with greater risk of adverse events, and management of co-infection poses challenges for palliative care. In addition, such patients are likely to have limited access to healthcare and limited support networks and are likely to be estranged from their families as well (Easterbrook and Meadway, 2001). Multimorbid medical conditions, including hepatitis B and C, are discussed further in Chapters 43–47 of this text.

FLUCTUATION IN CONDITION AND DIFFICULTY DETERMINING TERMINAL STAGE

Determining the prognosis of patients with advanced HIV disease can be difficult, as responses to therapy are often unpredictable. Identification of the predictors of mortality and prognostic variables for patients with advanced illness in the era of ART can help inform planning and coordination of care (Shen et al., 2005).

In 1996, short-term mortality predictors promulgated by the National Hospice Organization included CD4 cell count, viral load, and certain opportunistic infections (National Hospice Organization, 1996). These traditional HIV prognostic markers, however, no longer accurately predict death in patients with late-stage illness, because of the impact of ART. Shen and colleagues (2005) studied a heterogeneous population of 230 patients in a palliative care program. Of 120 deaths, the most frequent causes were end-stage AIDS (36%), non-AIDS-defining cancers (19%), bacterial pneumonia or sepsis (18%), and liver failure or cirrhosis (13%). Thus, patients with AIDS in the United States are now living long enough that they may experience morbidity and mortality from non-AIDS-defining illnesses. These may in fact pose more of an acute risk than that of HIV-related factors (Puoti et al., 2001; Sansone and Frengley, 2000; Selwyn et al., 2000; Valdez et al., 2001; Welch and Morse, 2002). Shen and colleagues (2005) also found that death was not predicted by gender, baseline symptoms on the Memorial Symptom Assessment Scale, HIV risk behavior, HIV disease stage, baseline CD4+ count, or baseline HIV viral load. The only significant predictors of mortality were age greater than 65 years and total impairments in activities of daily living or Karnofsky performance score. Thus, as previously suggested by Justice et al. (1996), functional status may be a useful means of predicting mortality in patients with AIDS. The Antiretroviral Therapy Cohort Collaboration (ATCC) has created a risk calculator for HIV-positive patients starting ART that can help with prognosis at the start of ART and 6 months into ART. The calculator can be found at http://www.art-cohort-collaboration.org (May et al., 2007).

COMMUNICATION ABOUT END-OF-LIFE ISSUES

Because of the nonlinear progression of late-stage AIDS, advance care planning and goals of care should be addressed repeatedly during the course of illness (Selwyn and Forstein, 2003). This is especially true for persons with AIDS, as they are less likely to discuss advance directives and life-limiting

interventions than are other patient populations (Curtis and Patrick, 1997; Mouton et al., 1997; Wenger et al., 2001). Persons with AIDS may also experience doubt and ambivalence as their clinical condition fluctuates; this demands flexibility, patience, and tolerance on the part of the clinician. Regular and direct inquiry into how patients are handling the uncertainty of their lives provides support and indicates that the clinician is ready to hear the patient's concerns (Selwyn and Forstein, 2003). Possible barriers to discussions about end-of-life issues include physicians' reluctance to discuss death (Curtis and Patrick, 1997) and cross-cultural concerns. Chapter 49 of this text reviews end-of-life issues, ethical issues, advance directives, and surrogate decision-making.

CROSS-CULTURAL ISSUES IN CARE OF THE DYING

Ethnicity and culture strongly influence a person's attitude toward death and dying. Although there is a "universal fear of cancer [and other terminal diseases] that results from its [cancer's] association with images of extreme debility and pain and the fear of death" (Butow et al., 1997, p. 320), individuals from Western cultures use different coping strategies to deal with serious illness than those of individuals from non-Western cultures (Barg and Gullate, 2001). These differences likely exist because of variations in basic values and cultural norms among these broad cultural groupings, such as reliance on the family and others for social support, and spiritual or religious beliefs (Mazanec and Tyler, 2003).

Blackhall and colleagues (1995) studied ethnic attitudes toward patient autonomy regarding disclosure of the diagnosis and prognosis of a terminal illness and toward end-of-life decision-making. They found that different ethnic, racial, and cultural groups feel differently about how much information physicians should provide concerning diagnoses and prognoses. The investigators determined that African Americans (63%) and European Americans (69%) are more likely than Korean Americans (35%) and Mexican Americans (48%) to believe that a patient should be informed of a terminal prognosis and should be actively involved in decisions concerning use of life-sustaining technology. African Americans are also less likely to consider withdrawal or cessation of life-prolonging measures than certain other racial or ethnic groups (Blackhall et al., 1995; Candib, 2002; Crawley et al., 2000; Kagawa-Singer and Blackhall, 2001). Blackhall and colleagues (1995) concluded that physicians should ask their patients whether they wish to be informed of their diagnoses and prognoses and whether they wish to be involved in treatment decisions or prefer to let family members or caregivers handle such matters.

A similar study of Navajo Indian beliefs about autonomy in patient diagnosis and prognosis found that in the Navajo culture, physicians and patients must speak in only a positive way, avoiding any negative thought or speech (Carrese and Rhodes, 1995). Because Navajos believe that language can "shape reality and control events," informing patients of a negative diagnosis or prognosis is considered disrespectful, as well as physically and emotionally dangerous (Carrese and Rhodes, 1995).

An exhaustive review of the literature on cultural and ethnic differences in the face of life-threatening illness is beyond the scope of this chapter. Nonetheless, as these two studies indicate, patients' cultural beliefs should be considered when disclosing the diagnosis and prognosis of a terminal illness, during evaluation of the patient, and during intervention. Koenig and Gates-William (1995) present a framework for such culturally sensitive evaluation, termed the "ABCDE" model (see Box 41.2). Such a model may provide an effective template for clinicians to incorporate cultural issues into their evaluation and treatment of culturally diverse patients.

DOCTOR–PATIENT COMMUNICATION

Doctor–patient communication is an essential component of caring for a dying patient (Baile and Beale, 2001; Buckman 1993, 1998; Fallowfield, 2004; Parker et al., 2001; Smith, 2000). Despite the recognized importance of caregiver–patient communication, many physicians are not adequately trained in communication skills (Fallowfield et al., 1998). The discordance in HIV-positive patient and clinician perspectives on death, dying, and end-of-life care is well-documented. In the absence of improved doctor–patient communication, such discordance could lead to poor end-of-life care (Mosack and Wandrey, 2015). Improved training in doctor–patient communication can help ease anxiety on both sides and improve health outcomes (Simpson et al., 1991). Suchman and colleagues (1997) found that improving physicians' empathic responses to patients in medical interviews can improve the doctor–patient relationship, improve quality of care, and increase both physician and patient satisfaction. On the basis of their findings, Suchman et al. (1997) defined basic empathic skills, necessary for meaningful communication with patients, as "recognizing when emotions may be present but not directly expressed, inviting exploration of these unexpressed feelings, and effectively

acknowledging these feelings so that the patient feels understood" (p. 680).

Buckman (1993, 1998) proposed a guide for communication and empathy in caring for the dying patient. He asserted that the important elements of communication in palliative care are basic listening skills, the breaking of bad news, therapeutic dialogue, and communicating with the family and with other professionals. He acknowledged several sources of difficulty in communicating with a dying patient, including the social denial of death, a lack of experience of death in the family, high expectations of health and life, materialism, and the changing role of religion. The patient's fear of dying is also significant, as are factors originating in the healthcare professional (e.g., sympathetic pain, fear of receiving blame, fear of the untaught, fear of expressing emotions, and fear of one's own illness and death). However, Buckman (1993) emphasized the importance of teaching and practicing listening skills, using comforting body language, responding empathically to patients, and engaging in therapeutic and supportive dialogue. He also advocated improved communication with patients' families and friends and among medical caregivers.

Buckman (1998) as well as Baile and Beale (2001) have promoted what is commonly referred to as the six-step protocol for breaking bad news (see Box 41.3), which many clinicians find extremely useful and which can be used by psychosomatic medicine specialists when they teach communication skills to physicians in the palliative care setting. Most recently, several intensive training programs in doctor–patient communication have been demonstrated to have both short-term and long-term efficacy in improving communication skills among physicians (Fallowfield, 2004; Maguire, 1999). These programs use a variety of teaching methods, including role-playing, video-taped feedback, experiential exercises, and didactics (Kissane et al. 2012).

The communication skills training program at Memorial Sloan Kettering Cancer Center is a structured communications initiative that is designed to find the most effective and lasting way to train healthcare professionals to communicate in a sensitive and productive manner. Dedicated staff of facilitators, using dedicated laboratory space, which includes a classroom and six video-recording training rooms, strive to provide communication skills training to healthcare professionals.

PROGRAMS AND MODELS OF HIV PALLIATIVE CARE DELIVERY

Even patients with end-stage AIDS can be restored to independence and good quality of life (Rackstraw et al., 2000; Stephenson et al., 2000). Fully developed, ideal palliative care programs offer control of symptoms and provision of support to persons living with chronic, life-threatening illnesses such as AIDS. Such programs optimally include all of the following components: (1) a home care program (e.g., hospice program); (2) a hospital-based palliative care consultation service; (3) a day care program or ambulatory care clinic; (4) palliative care inpatient unit (or dedicated palliative care beds in hospital); (5) a bereavement program; (6) training and research programs; and (7) Internet-based services. Integration of palliative care within outpatient HIV programs is associated with decreased pain and improved symptom control (Harding et al., 2013).

Of patients with HIV who express a preference for location of their death, less than 10% wish to die in the hospital (Goldstone et al., 1995). The disadvantages of hospitals for dying patients include variable quality of palliative care in acute medical settings and focus on management of acute problems in a person who may in fact be dying slowly (Easterbrook and Meadway, 2001).

The merits of specialized hospices versus non-specialized hospices for the delivery of HIV palliative care have been reviewed (Mansfield et al., 1992; Schofferman, 1987). Staff at specialized hospices are experienced in the management of HIV-related problems and, as a result, are particularly sensitive to the social and psychological issues associated with HIV illness. Moreover, the environment of the specialized hospice provides patients with the opportunity to meet and gain encouragement from other patients in similar settings (Easterbrook and Meadway, 2001).

Patients in the later stages of AIDS commonly express the desire to die at home (Easterbrook and Meadway, 2001). Where available, hospital support teams and community HIV nurse specialists can be helpful. Rather than merely practicing traditional approaches to care, it is important to take into consideration the direction and needs of individuals who choose to die at home (Johnson, 1995).

There is support in the literature for improved outcomes (e.g., decreased pain, better symptom control, reduced anxiety, increased insight, and enhanced spiritual well-being) with home palliative care and inpatient hospice programs for patients with HIV who receive palliative care (Lowther et al., 2012).

For further review of special settings such as psychiatric facilities, nursing homes, correctional facilities, and homeless outreach, please see Chapters 8, 9, and 30 of this text.

SPIRITUAL CARE

Issues of spirituality are essential elements of quality palliative care. The need to address the spiritual domains of supportive care has been identified as a priority by medical practitioners and patients alike (Singer et al., 1999). In certain countries, spiritual well-being correlates more highly with overall quality of life than does physical comfort (Selman et al., 2011). Palliative care practitioners in particular have begun to recognize the importance of spiritual suffering in their patients and have begun to design interventions to address it (Puchalski and Romer, 2000; Rousseau, 2000).

DEFINING SPIRITUALITY

Puchalski and Romer (2000) define spirituality as that which allows a person to experience transcendent meaning in life. Karasu (1999) views spirituality as a construct that involves concepts of faith and/or meaning. Faith is a belief in a higher transcendent power, not necessarily identified as God. It need not involve participation in the rituals or beliefs of a specific organized religion. Indeed, the transcendent power may be identified as external to the human psyche or internalized; it is the relationship and connectedness to this power, or spirit, that is an essential component of the spiritual experience and is related to the concept of meaning. Meaning, or having a sense that one's life has meaning, involves the conviction that one is fulfilling a unique role and purpose in a life that is a gift; a life that comes with a responsibility to live to one's full potential as a human being. In so doing, one is able to achieve a sense of peace, contentment, or even transcendence through connectedness with something greater than oneself (Frankl, 1959). The "faith" component of spirituality is most often associated with religion and religious belief, while the "meaning" component of spirituality appears to be a more universal concept that can exist in individuals who do, or do not, identify themselves to be religious.

The FACIT Spiritual Well-Being Scale, or FACITSWBS (Peterman et al., 1996), is a widely used measure of spiritual well-being that consists of both a faith and meaning component of spirituality. The FACITSWBS generates a total score as well as two subscale scores: one corresponding to "Faith," and a second corresponding to "Meaning/Peace." Other measures commonly used to measure aspects of spirituality include the Daily Spiritual Experiences Scale, or DSES (Underwood and Teresi, 2002), and the Spiritual Beliefs Inventory, or SBI-15 (Baider et al., 2001).

ASSESSING SPIRITUALITY

A spiritual history should be taken as early in the treatment as possible, as it provides an opportunity to give more comprehensive care and serves in building a relationship with a patient. Several general communication strategies should help to elicit patient concerns around spiritual issues. These include the use of open-ended questions, asking patients follow-up questions to elicit more detail about their concerns, acknowledging and normalizing patient apprehension and distress, the use of empathetic comments in response to patient concerns, and inquiring about patients' emotions around these issues (Lo et al., 2003).

There are several methods of taking a spiritual history. Puchalski and Romer (2000) recommend the acronym FICA to structure a spiritual history, which stands for Faith and belief, Importance, Community, and Address. A good spiritual assessment should include the questions outlined in Box 41.4 (Koenig, 2002; Puchalski and Romer, 2000).

In addition to these more open-ended questions, several formal assessment tools exist for the assessment of spirituality (Maugans, 1996). There are new scales in development, such as the "Spirit 8," that may be particularly useful in non-Western cultures (Selman et al., 2012). Most importantly, a detailed spiritual assessment should not be regarded as a one-time discussion but rather as the beginning of a dialogue that continues throughout a patient's care. This type of assessment should serve to let the patient know that the clinician is open to these discussions and that the patient's concerns regarding spiritual issues will be met in a supportive and respectful manner (Post et al., 2000). Simply being present, actively listening, offering empathetic responses, and trying to understand the patient's point of view will foster a productive dialogue and offer great comfort to the patient.

SPIRITUALITY AND LIFE-THREATENING MEDICAL ILLNESS

There has been great interest in spirituality, faith, and religious beliefs with regard to their impact on health outcomes and their role in palliative care (Baider et al., 1999; Koenig et al., 1992, 1998; McCullough and Larson, 1999; Sloan et al.,

1999). Some researchers theorize that religious beliefs may play a role in helping patients construct meaning out of the suffering inherent to illness, in turn facilitating acceptance of their situation (Koenig et al., 1998). Importantly, recent studies have found that religion and spirituality generally play a positive role in patients' coping with illnesses such as HIV and cancer (Baider et al., 1999; Nelson et al., 2002; Peterman et al., 1996).

Several studies (Breitbart et al., 2000; McClain et al., 2003; Nelson et al., 2002) have demonstrated a central role for spiritual well-being and meaning as a buffer against depression, hopelessness, and desire for hastened death among patients with advanced cancer. These findings are significant in the face of what we have come to learn about the consequences of depression and hopelessness in patients receiving palliative care. Depression and hopelessness are associated with poorer survival among patients with cancer (Watson et al., 1999), as well as dramatically higher rates of suicide, suicidal ideation, desire for hastened death, and interest in physician-assisted suicide (Breitbart et al., 1996a, 2000; Chochinov et al., 1994, 1995, 1998). Such findings point to the need for the development of interventions for patients receiving palliative care that address depression, hopelessness, loss of meaning, desire for death, and what many practitioners (Rousseau, 2000) refer to as "spiritual suffering." Several recently developed interventions are reviewed in the following sections.

Treatment of Spiritual Suffering

Rousseau (2000) has developed an approach to the treatment of spiritual suffering that centers on (1) controlling physical symptoms; (2) providing a supportive presence; (3) encouraging life review to assist in recognizing purpose value and meaning; (4) exploring guilt, remorse, forgiveness, and reconciliation; (5) facilitating religious expression; (6) reframing goals; (7) encouraging meditative practices; and (8) focusing on healing rather than cure. This approach to spiritual suffering encompasses a blend of several basic psychotherapeutic principles common to many psychotherapies. It should be noted that this intervention contains a heavy emphasis on facilitating religious expression and confession that may be extremely useful to many patients, but not all patients or clinicians will feel comfortable with this approach.

Meaning-Centered Interventions

In contrast, Breitbart and colleagues (Breitbart, 2002; Breitbart and Heller, 2003; Gibson and Breitbart, 2004; Greenstein and Breitbart, 2000) have applied the work of Viktor Frankl and his concepts of meaning-based psychotherapy (Frankl, 1955) to address spiritual suffering. While Frankl's logotherapy was not designed for the treatment of patients with life-threatening illness, his concepts of meaning and spirituality clearly have applications in psychotherapeutic work with advanced medically ill patients, many of whom seek guidance and help in dealing with issues of sustaining meaning, hope, and understanding in the face of their illness, while avoiding overt religious emphasis. This "meaning-centered group psychotherapy" (Greenstein and Breitbart, 2000) uses a mixture of didactics, discussion, and experiential exercises that focus on particular themes related to meaning and advanced cancer. It is designed to help patients with advanced cancer sustain or enhance a sense of meaning, peace, and purpose in their lives, even as they approach the end of life. Gibson and Breitbart (2004) have manualized an individual form of this therapy. Both individual meaning-centered psychotherapy and meaning-centered group psychotherapy interventions have been shown to improve spiritual well-being, meaning, and quality of life and reduce hopelessness, desire for hastened death, and distress from physical symptoms among patients with advanced illness (Breitbart and Applebaum, 2011; Breitbart et al., 2012b).

Treatment of Demoralization

Kissane and colleagues (2001) have described a syndrome of "demoralization" in terminally ill persons, distinct from depression. Demoralization syndrome consists of a triad of hopelessness, loss of meaning, and existential distress, expressed as a desire for death. It is associated with life-threatening medical illness, disability, bodily disfigurement, fear, loss of dignity, social isolation, and feelings of being a burden. Because of the sense of impotence and hopelessness, individuals with the syndrome predictably progress to a desire to die or commit suicide. Kissane and colleagues (2001) have formulated a treatment approach for demoralization syndrome (see Box 41.5).

Dignity-Conserving Care

Finally, ensuring dignity in the dying process is a critical goal of palliative care. Despite use of the term *dignity* in arguments for and against a patient's self-governance in matters

---

Box 41.5 MULTIDISCIPLINARY MODEL FOR TREATMENT OF DEMORALIZATION SYNDROME

1. Ensure continuity of care and active symptom management.

2. Ensure dignity in the dying process.

3a. Use various types of psychotherapy to help sustain a sense of meaning.

3b. Limit cognitive distortions and maintain family relationships (i.e., via meaning-based, cognitive-behavioral, interpersonal, and family psychotherapy interventions).

4. Use life review and narrative, giving attention to spiritual issues.

5. Use pharmacotherapy for comorbid anxiety, depression, or delirium.

Source: Kissane D, Clarke DM, Street AF. Demoralization syndrome: a relevant psychiatric diagnosis for palliative care. *J Palliat Care* 17:12–21. Copyright (2001), with permission from Mary Ann Liebert, Inc.

---

pertaining to death, there is little empirical research on how this term has been used by patients who are nearing death. Chochinov and colleagues (2002a, 2002b) examined how dying patients understand and define the term *dignity* to develop a model of dignity in persons who are terminally ill. A semistructured interview was designed to explore how patients cope with their illness and their perceptions of dignity. Three major categories emerged: (1) illness-related concerns (concerns that derive from or are related to the illness itself and threaten to or actually do impinge on the patient's sense of dignity); (2) dignity-conserving repertoire (internally held qualities or personal approaches or techniques that patients use to bolster or maintain their sense of dignity); and (3) social dignity inventory (social concerns or relationship dynamics that enhance or detract from a patient's sense of dignity). These broad categories and their carefully defined themes and subthemes form the foundation for an emerging model of dignity among the dying. The concept of dignity and the notion of dignity-conserving care offer a way of understanding how patients face advancing terminal illness. They also present an approach that clinicians can use to explicitly target the maintenance of dignity as a therapeutic objective.

Accordingly, Chochinov (2002) has developed a short-term dignity therapy for palliative patients that incorporates those facets from this model that are most likely to bolster the dying patient's will to live, lessen the desire for death or overall level of distress, and improve quality of life. The dignity model establishes the importance of "generativity" as a significant dignity theme. As such, the sessions are taped, transcribed, and edited, and the transcription is returned within 1 to 2 days to the patient. The creation of a tangible product that will live beyond the patient acknowledges the importance of generativity as a salient dignity issue. The immediacy of the returned transcript is intended to bolster the patient's sense of purpose, meaning, and worth by tangibly experiencing that his or her thoughts and words continue to be valued. In most instances, these transcripts are left for family or loved ones and form part of a personal legacy that the patient has actively participated in creating and shaping. In a study of 100 terminally ill patients with cancer, Chochinov et al. (2005) reported that 91 participants were satisfied with dignity therapy, 76% reported a heightened sense of dignity, 68% reported an increased sense of purpose, 67% reported a heightened sense of meaning, 47% reported an increased will to live, and 81% reported that it had been or would be of help to their family. Measures of suffering and depression also showed significant improvement, suggesting that dignity therapy is a novel therapeutic intervention for suffering and distress at the end of life.

COMMUNICATING ABOUT SPIRITUAL ISSUES

There may be several factors that inhibit effective communication with patients about spirituality in a palliative care setting (Clayton, 2000; Ellis et al., 1999; Post et al., 2000; Sloan et al., 1999). Promoting religion, faith, or specific religious beliefs or rituals (e.g. prayer, belief in an afterlife) in an effort to deal with patients' spiritual concerns or suffering at the end of life has limited acceptance among healthcare professionals and is not universally applicable to all patients. Maugans and Wadland (1991) suggest that there is a great discrepancy between physicians and patients on such issues as belief in God, belief in an afterlife, regular prayer, and feeling close to God, with physicians endorsing such beliefs or practices less than half as often as patients (none greater than 40%).

Several additional factors have been cited as contributing to the avoidance of these discussions, including a lack of time on the part of the clinician, a lack of training in this area, fear of projecting one's own beliefs onto the patient, and concerns about patient autonomy (Ellis et al., 1999). Finally, providers may feel that these discussions are inappropriate, as they are outside of their area of expertise or intrusive to the patient's privacy, and may experience some discomfort in pursuing these topics (Cohen et al., 2001; Ellis et al., 1999; Post et al., 2000; Sloan et al., 1999). However, most studies have demonstrated that, in fact, the opposite is true, as patients welcome these discussions (Anderson et al., 1993; King and Bushwick, 1994; Maugans 1996). Therefore, discussions about spiritual, religious, or existential concerns—that is, finding out what matters to the patient in terms of being imbued with continued meaning and purpose, regardless of its source—should not be avoided, but rather may simply require more time and consideration on the part of the clinician.

Communicating about spirituality with patients effectively requires comfort in several domains: (1) a basic knowledge of common spiritual concerns and sources of spiritual pain for patients; (2) the principles and beliefs of the major religions common to the patient populations one treats; (3) basic clinical communication skills, such as active and empathetic listening, with an ability to identify and highlight spiritually relevant issues; and (4) the ability to remain present while patients struggle with spiritual issues in light of their mortality (Storey and Knight, 2001). This final domain is often the most trying, especially for clinicians early in their career.

The American Academy of Hospice and Palliative Medicine offers the following guidelines for clinicians when communicating about spiritual issues (Doyle, 1992; Hay, 1996; Storey and Knight, 2001). First, it is important to recognize that every patient is an individual and has a unique belief system that should be honored and respected. A patient's spiritual views may or may not incorporate religious beliefs, as spirituality is considered the more inclusive category. Therefore, initial discussions should focus on broad spiritual issues and then, when appropriate, on more specific religious beliefs. Caregivers should maintain appropriate boundaries and avoid discussions of their own religious beliefs, as it is usually not relevant. Finally, fostering hope and integrating meaning into a patient's life is often a more important aspect of providing spiritual healing than any adherence to a particular belief system or religious affiliation.

PATHWAYS OF SPIRITUAL CARE

Spirituality can help patients and families cope with life-threatening medical illness and its ensuing stressors. By understanding and respecting their beliefs, clinicians may allow their patients to believe in their own abilities to cope (Kearney and Mount, 2000). Psychosomatic medicine

psychiatrists and other clinicians can seek both specialized training and referrals to appropriate sources to help them deal more effectively with the often complicated and painful spiritual issues their patients present.

It is essential to effectively use an interdisciplinary team approach that incorporates members of pastoral care services. The chaplain is the spiritual care specialist on the healthcare team and has the training necessary to treat spiritual distress in all its forms (Handzo and Koenig, 2004). Referrals to chaplains ought to be approached just as referrals to any other specialist would be; such referrals are an essential part of comprehensive care (Thiel and Robinson, 1997). The role of the physician is to assess spiritual needs as they relate to healthcare (i.e., briefly screen) and then refer to a professional pastoral caregiver as indicated (i.e., to address those needs). Seeing the physician as the generalist in spiritual care and the chaplain as the specialist is a helpful model (Handzo and Koenig, 2004). Finally, the doctor or nurse needs to be able to recognize and appreciate how a given patient's religious and cultural beliefs impact the way in which that patient makes healthcare decisions. This ensures a more effective path toward agreement with patients on those decisions.

ROLE OF THE PSYCHOSOMATIC CLINICIAN AT THE TIME OF DYING, DEATH, AND AFTERWARD

The physician plays a key role as someone who can accompany the patient and family through a complex process that extends far beyond medical treatment. Spending time with the dying patient is crucial for the patient and loved ones and can be gratifying for the clinician. At the end of life, it can be extremely helpful to talk, hold hands, and surround the patient with loved ones, if available (Cohen and Alfonso, 2004). This may alleviate any fears of abandonment or of dying alone.

GRIEF AND BEREAVEMENT

Bereavement care is an integral dimension of palliative care. Knowledge of and competence in assessing grief is essential in order to recognize the 20% of bereaved persons who need additional assistance. Routine assessment of bereaved persons for risk factors associated with complicated grief provides a method by which psychosomatic medicine specialists can preventatively intervene to reduce unnecessary morbidity. Effective therapies are available to assist in the management of complicated grief (Kissane, 2004). Grief is an inevitable dimension of our humanity, an adaptive adjustment process, and one that, with adequate support, can eventually be traversed.

Although words such as *grief, mourning*, and *bereavement* are commonly used interchangeably, the following definitions may be helpful:

- *Bereavement* is the state of loss resulting from death (Parkes, 1998).
- *Grief* is the emotional response associated with loss (Stroebe et al., 1993).

- *Mourning* is the process of adaptation, including the cultural and social rituals prescribed as accompaniments (Raphael, 1983).
- *Anticipatory grief* precedes the death and results from the expectation of that event (Raphael, 1983).
- *Complicated grief* represents a pathological outcome involving psychological, social, or physical morbidity (Rando, 1983).
- *Disenfranchised grief* represents the hidden sorrow of the persons who are marginalized by their peers, culture, or society, where there is less social permission to express many dimensions of loss (Doka, 1989).

Anticipatory Grief

As the patient and family make their way through palliative care at the end of life, the clinical phases of grief progress from anticipatory grief through to the immediate news of the death, to the stages of acute grief and, potentially for some individuals, the complications of bereavement. Anticipatory grief generally draws the supportive family into a configuration of mutual comfort and greater closeness as the news of the illness and its proposed management is tackled. For a time, this perturbation advantages the care of the sick, until the pressures of daily life draw the family back toward their prior constellation. Movement back and forth is evident thereafter, as news of illness progression unfolds. Periods of grief can become interspersed with phases of contentment and happiness. When the family is engaged in home care of their dying member, their cohesion may increase as they share their fears, hopes, joy, and distress. In some families, the stress of loss may result in further divisiveness and the accentuation of previously contentious dynamics.

Difficulties can emerge for some families as they express their anticipatory grief. Impaired coping manifests itself via protective avoidance, denial of the seriousness of the threat, anger, or withdrawal from involvement. Sometimes family dysfunction is glaring. More commonly, however, subthreshold or mild depressive or anxiety disorders develop gradually as individuals struggle to adapt to unwelcome changes. While anticipatory grief was historically suggested to reduce postmortem grief (Parkes, 1975), intense distress is now well recognized as a marker of risk for complicated grief. During this phase of anticipatory grief, clinicians can help the family that is capable of effective communication by encouraging them to openly share their feelings as they go about the instrumental care of their dying family member or friend. Saying goodbye is a process that evolves over time, with opportunities for reminiscence, celebration of the life and contribution of the dying person, expressions of gratitude, and attempts at resolution and closure (Meares, 1981). These tasks have the potential to generate creative and positive emotions out of what is otherwise a sad time for all.

Grief of Family and Friends Gathered Around the Death Bed

When relatives or close friends gather to keep watch by the bed of a dying person, they not only support the sick but also help their own subsequent adjustment. For years to come, these poignant moments will be recalled in immense detail; thus, the sensitivity and courteous respect of health professionals is crucial (Maguire, 1985). Clinicians can helpfully comment on the process of dying, explaining the breathing patterns and commenting on any noises, secretions, patient reactions, and comfort measures. Moreover, the physician can empathically normalize the experience and reassure the family whenever concern develops. Discussions about pain, reasons for medications, and skilled prediction of events will assuage worry and build a collaborative approach to the care of the dying person.

Religious rituals warrant active facilitation, including appropriate notification of a minister or pastoral care worker. Respect for the body remains paramount once death has occurred, and the expression of sympathy from clinicians is greatly appreciated. The family will be invariably grateful for time spent alone with the deceased, and regard for cultural approaches to the laying out of the body is essential (Parkes et al., 1997). Sometimes staff will have concerns about the emotional response of the bereaved. If there is uncertainty about its cultural appropriateness, consultation with an informed cultural intermediary may prove helpful. The prescription of short-acting benzodiazepines will help some, while others will prefer to manage without medication. A follow-up telephone call soon after the death is worthwhile to check on coping and identify the need for continued support.

Caution is warranted in settings where grief could be marginalized, well exemplified by ageism (Doka, 1989). If a death is normalized because it appears in step with the life cycle, family members may be given less support and reduced permission to express many aspects of their loss. In the process, the disenfranchised persons can be ignored in their sorrow.

Acute Grief and Time Course of Bereavement

The bereaved move through sequences of phases over time; these phases are never rigidly demarcated, but rather, merge gradually one into the other (Parkes, 1998; Raphael, 1983). The time course of mourning is shaped by the nature of the loss, the context in which the loss took place, as well as a multitude of factors ranging from personal resilience to cultural, social, and ethnic affiliations. There is no sharply defined endpoint to grief. The clinical task is to differentiate persons who remain with the spectrum of normalcy from individuals crossing the threshold of complicated grief.

Complicated Grief

Normal and abnormal responses to bereavement span a spectrum. Intensity of reaction, presence of a range of related grief behaviors, and time course all factor into the differentiation between normal and abnormal grief. Common psychiatric disorders resulting from grief include clinical depression, anxiety disorders, alcohol abuse or other substance abuse and dependence, and, less commonly, psychotic disorders and posttraumatic stress disorder. When frank psychiatric disorders complicate bereavement, their recognition and management are straightforward. Subthreshold states, however, present a greater clinical challenge.

Studies of the bereaved indicate groups in which clusters of intense grief symptoms are distinct from uncomplicated grief (Parkes and Weiss, 1983; Prigerson et al., 1995). Their recognition calls for an experienced clinical judgement that does not normalize the distress as understandable. Risk factors for complicated grief should be assessed at entry to the service and upgraded during the phase of palliative care. This includes revision shortly after the death. Completion of the family genogram presents an ideal time for such assessment as relationships, prior losses, and coping are considered. Some palliative care services have developed checklists based on such risk factors to generate a numerical measure of risk. To date, there has been insufficient validation of such scales, but the presence of any single factor signifies greater risk. Continued observation of the pattern of grief evolution over time is appropriate whenever such concern exists.

Approximately 20% of bereaved individuals experience complicated or prolonged grief. There is growing evidence that prolonged grief or complicated grief is a unique condition characterized by separation distress and other symptoms, such as intense, unremitting yearning for the deceased, difficulty accepting the loss, and sense of meaninglessness, that remain elevated at 6 or more months after the loss (Prigerson et al., 2009). Although complicated grief may be comorbid with other psychiatric disorders, its symptoms have been associated with negative physical and mental health outcomes, including poorer quality of life and suicidality, independent of depression (Prigerson et al., 2009).

Grief Therapies

Because loss is so ubiquitous in the palliative care setting, psychosomatic medicine clinicians need skill in the application of grief therapies. For most of the bereaved, personal resilience ensures normal adaptation in the face of their painful situation. As such, there is no justification for routine intervention, as grief is not a disease. Individuals considered at risk of maladaptive outcome, however, can be treated preventatively. Persons who later develop complicated bereavement need active treatments.

The spectrum of interventions spans individual, group, and family-oriented therapies and encompasses all schools of psychotherapy as well as appropriately indicated pharmacotherapies. Adoption of any model, or parts thereof, is based on the clinical issues and their associated circumstances. Thus,

variation will be influenced by age, perception of support, the nature of the death, the personal health of the bereaved person, and the presence of comorbid states. Most interventions consist of six to eight sessions over several months. In this sense, grief therapy is focused and time limited. Multimodal therapies, however, are commonplace. Thus, group and individual therapies better support lonely persons so that socialization interpersonally complements any intrapersonal support.

Pharmacotherapies are widely used to support the bereaved. Nonetheless, judicious prescription is important. Benzodiazepines allay anxiety and assist sleep, but words of caution should be offered about intermittent use to avoid tachyphylaxis and dependence. Antidepressants are indicated whenever bereavement is complicated by the development of depressive disorder, panic attacks, and moderate to severe adjustment disorders (Jacobs et al., 1987; Pasternak et al., 1991). Tricyclics (e.g., nortriptyline, desipramine), selective serotonergic reuptake inhibitors (e.g., sertraline, paroxetine, citalopram, fluvoxamine, fluoxetine), or combined noradrenergic or serotonergic reuptake inhibitors (e.g., venlafaxine, duloxetine, mirtazapine) can be used. Occasionally, antipsychotics are needed for hypomania or other forms of psychosis.

Family therapists have long recognized the importance of family processes in mourning, as well as their systemic influence on outcome (Kissane and Bloch, 1994). Exploration of the association between family functioning and bereavement morbidity highlights the manner in which family dysfunction predicts increased rates of psychosocial morbidity in bereaved persons (Kissane et al., 1996). Family-centered care that focuses on the well-being of the family during palliative care is uniquely placed to reduce rates of morbidity in persons subsequently bereaved.

A family approach to grief intervention is exemplified by family-focused grief therapy (FFGT), developed by Kissane and Bloch (2002). The aim of this model is to improve family functioning while also supporting the expression of grief. As previously mentioned, this approach can be applied preventatively to those families judged through screening to be at high risk of complicated outcomes (Kissane and Bloch, 2002). Thus, FFGT commences during palliative care and includes the ill family member. It continues throughout the early phases of bereavement until there is confidence that morbidity has been prevented or appropriately treated. In this approach, the family is invited to identify and work on aspects of family life that they specifically recognize as a cause of concern. Through enhancing cohesion, promoting open communication of thoughts and feelings, and teaching effective problem-solving, conflict is reduced and tolerance of different opinions is optimized. The improved functioning of the family as a unit becomes the means to accomplish adaptive mourning.

CONCLUSION

Palliative care for patients with advanced AIDS requires a biopsychosocial approach consistent with the patient's expressed goals of care. As the possibility of a cure or prolongation of life becomes less remote in the care of the patient with advanced AIDS, the focus of treatment shifts to symptom control and enhanced quality of life. Patients are uniquely vulnerable to both physical and psychiatric complications. The role of the psychosomatic medicine psychiatrist in the care of the terminally ill or dying AIDS patient is critical to both adequate symptom control and integration of the medical, psychological, and spiritual dimensions of human experience in the last weeks of life. To be most effective in this role, the psychiatrist must have specialized knowledge of not only the psychiatric complications of terminal illness and the existential issues confronting persons at the end of life but also the common physical symptoms that plague patients with advanced AIDS and contribute so dramatically to their suffering.

REFERENCES

Adams N, Poole H, Richardson C (2006). Psychological approaches to chronic pain management: Part 1. *J Clin Nurs* 15:290–300.

Alexander CS, Back A (eds.), for the Workgroup on Palliative and End-of-Life Care in HIV/AIDS (2004). *Integrating Palliative Care into the Continuum of HIV Care*. Missoula, MT: Robert Wood Johnson Foundation.

Anderson JM, Anderson LJ, Felsenthal G (1993). Pastoral needs for support within an inpatient rehabilitation unit. *Arch Phys Med Rehabil* 74:574–578.

Baider L, Holland JC, Russak SM, Kaplan De-Nour A (2001). The system of belief inventory (SBI-15). *Psycho-Oncology* 10:534–540.

Baider L, Russak SM, Perry S, et al. (1999). The role of religious and spiritual beliefs in coping with malignant melanoma: an Israeli sample. *Psycho-oncology* 8:27–35.

Baile W, Beale E (2001). Giving bad news to cancer patients: matching process and content. *J Clin Oncol* 19:2575–2577.

Barg FK, Gullate MM (2001). Cancer support groups: meeting the needs of African Americans with cancer. *Semin Oncol Nurs* 17:171–178.

Blackhall LJ, Murphy ST, Frank G, Michel V, Azen SP (1995). Ethnicity and attitudes toward patient autonomy. *JAMA* 274:820–825.

Breitbart W (1989). Psychiatric management of cancer pain. *Cancer* 63(11):2336–2342.

Breitbart W (2002). Spirituality and meaning in supportive care: spirituality and meaning-centered group psychotherapy interventions in advanced cancer. *Support Care Cancer* 10(4):272–280.

Breitbart W, Alici Y (2014). *Psychosocial Palliative Care*. New York: Oxford University Press.

Breitbart W, Applebaum A (2011). Meaning-centered group therapy. In M Watson, DW Kissane, W Breitbart, A Applebaum (eds.), *Handbook of Psychotherapy in Cancer Care, Meaning-Centered Group Psychotherapy* (pp. 137–148). New York: Wiley-Blackwell.

Breitbart W, Chochinov H, Alici Y (2012a). End-of-life care. In L Grassi, M Riba (eds.), *Clinical Psycho-Oncology: An International Perspective* (pp. 249–270). Oxford, UK: John Wiley and Sons.

Breitbart W, Chochinov H, Passik S (2004a). Psychiatric symptoms in palliative medicine. In D Doyle, G Hanks, N Cherny, K Calman (eds.), *Oxford Textbook of Palliative Medicine*, 3rd ed. (pp. 746–771). New York: Oxford University Press.

Breitbart W, Heller KS (2003). Reframing hope: meaning-centered care for patients near the end-of-life. *J Palliat Med* 6:979–988.

Breitbart W, Kaim M, Rosenfeld B (1999). Clinicians' perceptions of barriers to pain management in AIDS. *J Pain Symptom Manage* 18:203–212.

Breitbart W, McDonald MV, Rosenfeld B, Monkman ND, Passik S (1998). Fatigue in ambulatory AIDS patients. *J Pain Symptom Manage* 15:159–167.

Breitbart WS, Passik S, Eller KC, Sison A (1992). Suicidal ideation in AIDS: the role of pain and mood [NR 267 (abstract)]. Presented at the 145th Annual Meeting of the American Psychiatric Association, Washington, DC.

Breitbart W, Payne D, Passik S (2004b). Psychological and psychiatric interventions in pain control. In D Doyle, G Hanks, N Cherny, K Calman (eds.), *Oxford Textbook of Palliative Medicine*, 3rd ed. (pp. 424–437). New York: Oxford University Press.

Breitbart W, Poppito S, Rosenfeld B, et al. (2012b). Pilot randomized controlled trial of individual meaning-centered psychotherapy for patients with advanced cancer. *J Clin Oncol* 30(12):1304–1309.

Breitbart W, Rosenfeld B, Gibson C, et al. (2010). Impact of treatment for depression on desire for hastened death in patients with advanced AIDS. *Psychosomatics* 51(2):98–105.

Breitbart W, Rosenfeld BD, Passik SD (1996a). Interest in physician-assisted suicide among ambulatory HIV-infected patients. *Am J Psychiatry* 153:238–242.

Breitbart W, Rosenfeld B, Passik SD, McDonald MV, Thaler H, Portenoy RK (1996b). The undertreatment of pain in ambulatory AIDS patients. *Pain* 65:243–249.

Breitbart W, Rosenfeld B, Pessin H, et al. (2000). Depression, hopelessness, and desire for death in terminally ill patients with cancer. *JAMA* 284:2907–2911.

Bruera E, MacMillan K, Pither J, MacDonald RN (1990). Effects of morphine on the dyspnea of the terminal cancer patients. *J Pain Sympton Manage* 5:1–5.

Buckman R (1993). *How to Break Bad News: A Guide for Healthcare Professionals*. London: Macmillan Medical.

Buckman R (1998). Communication in palliative care: a practical guide. In D Doyle, GWC Hanks, N MacDonald (eds.), *Oxford Textbook of Palliative Medicine*, 2nd ed. (pp. 141–156). New York: Oxford University Press.

Butler RN, Burt R, Foley KM, Morris J, Morrison RS (1996). Palliative medicine: providing care when cure is not possible. A roundtable discussion: Part I. *Geriatrics* 51:33–36.

Butow P, Tattersall M, Goldstein D (1997). Communication with cancer patients in culturally diverse societies. *Ann N Y Acad Sci* 809:317–329.

Canadian Palliative Care Association (1995). *Palliative Care. Towards a Consensus in Standardized Principles of Practice*. Ottawa, ON: Canadian Palliative Care Association.

Candib L (2002). Truth telling and advance planning at the end-of-life: problems with autonomy in a multicultural world. *Fam Syst Health* 20:213–228.

Candy B, Jackson KC, Jones L, Tookman A, King M (2012). Drug therapy for symptoms associated with anxiety in adult palliative care patients. *Cochrane Database Syst Rev* 10:CD004596.

Carmichael JK (1991). Treatment of herpes zoster and postherpetic neuralgia. *Am Fam Physician* 44:203–210.

Carrese J, Rhodes L (1995). Western bioethics on the Navajo reservation. *JAMA* 274:826–829.

Casalino E, Wolff M, Ravaud P, Choquet C, Bruneel F, Regnier B (2004). Impact of ART advent on admission patterns and survival in HIV-infected patients admitted to an intensive care unit. *AIDS* 18:1429–1433.

Centers for Disease Control and Prevention (CDC) (2003). Summary of notifiable disease: United States. 2001. *MMWR Morb Mortal Wkly Rep* 50:1–22.

Centers for Disease Control and Prevention (CDC) (2005). *HIV/AIDS Surveillance Report, 2005*. Vol. 16. HIV infection and AIDS in the United States and dependent areas, 2005. https://www.cdc.gov/hiv/pdf/statistics_2005_hiv_surveillance_report_vol_17.pdf. Accessed February 15, 2017.

Chochinov HM (2002). Dignity-conserving care: a new model for palliative care: helping the patient feel valued. *JAMA* 287(17):2253–2260.

Chochinov HM, Breitbart W (eds.) (2000). *Handbook of Psychiatry and Palliative Medicine*. New York: Oxford University Press.

Chochinov HMC, Breitbart W (eds.) (2009). *Handbook of Psychiatry in Palliative Medicine*, 2nd ed. New York: Oxford University Press.

Chochinov HM, Hack T, Hassard T, Kristjanson LJ, McClement S, Harlos M (2002a). Dignity in the terminally ill: a cross-sectional, cohort study. *Lancet* 360:2026–2030.

Chochinov HM, Hack T, Hassard T, Kristjanson LJ, McClement S, Harlos M (2005). Dignity therapy: a novel psychotherapeutic intervention for patients near the end of life. *J Clin Oncol* 23(24):5520–5525.

Chochinov HM, Hack T, McClement S, Harlos M, Kristjanson L (2002b). Dignity in the terminally ill: an empirical model. *Soc Sci Med* 54:433–443.

Chochinov HM, Wilson KG, Enns M, Lander S (1994). Prevalence of depression in the terminally ill: effects of diagnostic criteria and symptom threshold judgments. *Am J Psychiatry* 151(4):537–540.

Chochinov H, Wilson K, Enns M, Lander S (1998). Depression, hopelessness, and suicidal ideation in the terminally ill. *Psychosomatics* 39(4):366–370.

Chochinov HM, Wilson KG, Enns M, Mowchun N, Lander S, Levitt M, Clinch JJ (1995). Desire for death in the terminally ill. *Am J Psychiatry* 152:1185–1191.

Clayton CL (2000). Barriers, boundaries and blessings: ethical issues in physicians' spiritual involvement with patients. *Med Humanities Rpt* 21:234–256.

Cohen MA, Alfonso CA (2004). AIDS psychiatry: psychiatric and palliative care, and pain management. In GP Wormser (ed.), *AIDS and Other Manifestations of HIV Infection*, 4th ed. (pp. 537–576). San Diego: Elsevier Academic Press.

Cohen CB, Wheeler SE, Scott DA (2001). Walking a fine line: physician inquiries into patients' religious and spiritual beliefs. *Hastings Cent Rep* 31:29–39.

Cornblath DR, McArthur JC (1988). Predominantly sensory neuropathy in patients with AIDS and AIDS-related complex. *Neurology* 38:794–796.

Crawley LV, Payne R, Bolden J, Payne T, Washington P, Williams S (2000). Initiative to improve palliative and end-of-life care in the African-American community. *JAMA* 284:2518–2521.

Curtis JR, Patrick DL (1997). Barriers to communication about end-of-life care in AIDS patients. *J Gen Intern Med* 12:736–741.

Deeks SG, Lewin SR, Havlir DV (2013). The end of AIDS: HIV infection as a chronic disease. *Lancet* 382:1525–33.

Deeks S, Wrin T, Liegler T, et al. (2001). Virologic and immunologic consequences of discontinuing combination antiretroviral-drug therapy in HIV-infected patients with detectable viremia. *N Engl J Med* 344:472–480.

DHHS Panel on Antiretroviral Guidelines for Adults and Adolescents (2016). *Guidelines for the Use of Antiretroviral Agents in HIV-1-Infected Adults and Adolescents*. https://aidsinfo.nih.gov/contentfiles/lvguidelines/adultandadolescentgl.pdf. Accessed February 15, 2017.

Doka K (1989). Disenfranchised grief. In K Doka (ed.), *Disenfranchised Grief: Recognizing Hidden Sorrow* (pp. 3–11). Lexington, MA: Lexington Books.

Doyle D (1992). Have we looked beyond the physical and psychosocial? *J Pain Symptom Manage* 7(5):302–311.

Doyle D, Hanks G, Cherny N, Calman K (eds.) (2003). *Oxford Textbook of Palliative Medicine*, 3rd ed. New York: Oxford University Press.

Easterbrook P, Meadway J (2001). The changing epidemiology of HIV infection: new challenges for HIV palliative care. *J R Soc Med* 94(9):442–448.

Ellis M, Vinson D, Ewigman B (1999). Addressing spiritual concerns of patients: family physicians' attitudes and practices. *J Fam Pract* 48:105–109.

Ellis R (1997). Neurocognitive impairment is an independent risk factor for death in HIV infection. *Arch Neurol* 6:416–424.

Engel GL (1977). The need for a new medical model: a challenge for biomedicine. *Science* 196:129–136.

Engel GL (1980). The clinical application of the biopsychosocial model. *Am J Psychiatry* 137:535–544.

Evans D, Ten Have T, Douglas SD, et al. (2002). Association of depression with viral load, CD8 T lymphocytes, and natural killer cells in women with HIV infection. *Am J Psychiatry* 159:1752–1759.

Fallowfield L (2004). Communication and palliative medicine. In D Doyle, G Hanks, N Cherny, K Calman (eds.), *Oxford Textbook of Palliative Medicine*, 3rd ed. (pp. 101–107). New York: Oxford University Press.

Fallowfield L, Lipkin M, Hall A (1998). Teaching senior oncologists communication skills: results from phase I of a comprehensive longitudinal program in the United Kingdom. *J Clin Oncol* 16:1961–1968.

Fantoni M, Ricci F, Del Borgo C, et al. (1997). Multicentre study on the prevalence of symptoms and symptomatic treatment in HIV infection. *J Palliat Care* 13:9–13.

Farber EW, Marconi VC (2014). Palliative HIV care: opportunities for biomedical and behavioral change. *Curr HIV/AIDS Rep* 11(4):404–412.

Fausto JA, Selwyn PA (2011). Palliative care in the management of advanced HIV/AIDS. *Prim Care Clin Office Pract* 38:311–326

Filbet M, Marceron V (1994). A retrospective study of symptoms in 193 terminal inpatients with AIDS [abstract]. *J Palliat Care* 10:92.

Foley F (1994). AIDS palliative care [abstract]. *J Palliat Care* 10:132.

Foley F, Flannery S (1995). AIDS palliative care: challenging the palliative paradigm. *J Palliat Care* 11:34–37.

Fontaine A, LaRue F, Lassauniere JM (1999). Physicians' recognition of the symptoms experienced by HIV patients: how reliable? *J Pain Symptom Manage* 18:263–270.

Fontes AS, Gonçalves JF (2014). Pain treatment in patients infected with human immunodeficiency virus in later stages: pharmacological aspects. *Am J Hosp Palliat Care* 31(2):194–201.

Frankl VF (1955). *The Doctor and the Soul*. New York: Random House.

Frankl VF (1959). *Man's Search for Meaning*, fourth edition. Boston: Beacon Press.

Frenkel L, Mullins J (2001). Should patients with drug-resistant HIV-1 continue to receive antiretroviral therapy? *N Engl J Med* 344:520–522.

Geara F, Le Bourgeois JP, Piedbois P, Pavlovitch JM, Mazeron JJ (1991). Radiotherapy in the management of cutaneous epidemic Kaposi's sarcoma. *Int J Radiat Oncol Biol Phys* 21:1517–1522.

Gibson CA, Breitbart W (2004). Individual meaning-centered psychotherapy treatment manual. Unpublished.

Goldberg RJ (1993). Acute pain management. In A Stoudemire, BS Fogel (eds.), *Psychiatric Care of the Medical Patient* (pp. 323–340). New York: Oxford University Press.

Goldstone I, Kuhl D, Johnson A, Le R, McLeod A (1995). Patterns of care in advanced HIV disease in a tertiary treatment centre. *AIDS Care* 7(Suppl. 1):S47–S56.

Gonzales JS, Batchelder AW, Psaros C, et al. (2011). Depression and HIV/AIDS treatment nonadherence: a review and meta-analysis. *J Acquir Immune Defic Syndr* 58:181–187.

Goodkin K (1997). Subtle neuropsychological impairment and minor cognitive-motor disorder in HIV-1 infection. *Neuroimaging Clin N Am* 6:561–580.

Greenstein M, Breitbart W (2000). Cancer and the experience of meaning: a group psychotherapy program for people with cancer. *Am J Psychother* 54:486–500.

Greer JA, Pirl WF, Jackson VA, et al. (2012). Effect of early palliative care on chemotherapy use and end-of-life care in patients with metastatic non-small-cell lung cancer. *J Clin Oncol* 30(4):394–400.

Guzman J, Esmail R, Karjalainen K, Malmivaara A, Irvin E, Bombardier C (2001). Multidisciplinary rehabilitation for chronic low back pain: systematic review. *BMJ* 322:1511–1516.

Handzo G, Koenig HG (2004). Spiritual care: whose job is it anyway? *South Med J* 97(12):1242–1244.

Harding R, Easterbrook P, Higginson IJ, Karus D, Raveis VH, Marconi K (2005). Access and equity in HIV/AIDS palliative care: a review of the evidence and responses. *Palliat Med* 19(3):251–258.

Harding R, Simms V, Alexander C, et al. (2013). Can palliative care integrated within HIV outpatient settings improve pain and symptom control in a low-income country? A prospective, longitudinal, controlled intervention evaluation. *AIDS Care* 25(7):795–804.

Hay MW (1996). Developing guidelines for spiritual caregivers in hospice: principles for spiritual assessment. Presented at the National

Hospice Organization Annual Sympsium and Exposition, November 6–9, Chicago, IL.

Hilgard E, LeBaron S (1982). Relief of anxiety and pain in children and adolescents with cancer: quantitative measures and clinical observations. *Int J Clin Exp Hypn* 30:417–442.

Huang L, Quartin A, Jones D, Havlir DV (2006). Intensive care of patients with HIV infection. *N Engl J Med* 355:173–181.

Jacobs S, Nelson J, Zisook S (1987). Treating depressions of bereavement with antidepressants: a pilot study. *Psychiatr Clin North Am* 10:501–510.

Jacox AJ, Carr DB, Payne R (1994). New clinical-practice guidelines for the management of pain in patients with cancer. *N Engl J Med* 330:651.

Jay SM, Elliott C, Varni JW (1986). Acute and chronic pain in adults and children with cancer. *J Consult Clin Psychol* 54:601–607.

Johnson AS (1995). Palliative care in the home? *J Palliat Care* 11(2):42–44.

Jonsson E, Coombs DW, Hunstad D, Richardson JR Jr, von Reyn CF, Saunders RL, Heaney JA (1992). Continuous infusion of intrathecal morphine to control acquired immunodeficiency syndrome–associated bladder pain. *J Urol* 147:687–689.

Justice AC, Aiken LH, Smith HL, Turner BJ (1996). The role of functional status in predicting inpatient mortality with AIDS: a comparison with current predictors. *J Clin Epidemiol* 49:193–201.

Kagawa-Singer M, Blackhall LJ (2001). Negotiating cross-cultural issues at the end-of-life: "You got to go where he lives." *JAMA* 286:2993–3001.

Kalso E, Allan L, Dellemijn PL, et al. (2003). Recommendations for using opioids in chronic non-cancer pain. *Eur J Pain* 7:381–386.

Karasu BT (1999). Spiritual psychotherapy. *Am J Psychother* 53:143–162.

Kearney M, Mount B (2000). Spiritual care of the dying patient. In HM Chochinov, W Breitbart (eds.), *Handbook of Psychiatry in Palliative Medicine* (pp. 357–371). New York: Oxford University Press.

Kelleher P, Cox S, McKeogh M (1997). HIV infection: the spectrum of symptoms and disease in male and female patients attending a London hospice. *Palliat Med* 11:152–158.

Kellerman J, Zeltzer L, Ellenberg L, Dash J (1983). Adolescents with cancer: hypnosis for the reduction of acute pain and anxiety associated with medical procedures. *J Adolesc Health Care* 4:85–90.

Kerrihard T, Breitbart W, Dent K, Strout D (1999). Anxiety in patients with cancer and human immunodeficiency virus. *Semin Clin Neuropsychiatry* 4:114–132.

King DE, Bushwick B (1994). Beliefs and attitudes of hospital inpatients about faith healing and prayer. *J Fam Pract* 39:349–352.

Kissane D (2004). Bereavement. In D Doyle, G Hanks, N Cherny, K Calman (eds.), *Oxford Textbook of Palliative Medicine*, 3rd ed. (pp. 1135–1154). New York: Oxford University Press.

Kissane D, Bloch S (1994). Family grief. *Br J Psychiatry* 164:728–740.

Kissane D, Bloch S (2002). *Family Focus Grief Therapy: A Model of Family-Centered Care during Palliative Care and Bereavement*. Buckingham: Open University Press.

Kissane D, Bloch S, Dowe D, et al. (1996). The Melbourne family grief study I & II. *Am J Psychiatry* 153:650–658, 659–666.

Kissane DW, Bylund CL, Banerjee SC, et al. (2012) Communication skills training for oncology professionals. *J Clin Oncol* 30(11):1242–1247.

Kissane D, Clarke DM, Street AF (2001). Demoralization syndrome: a relevant psychiatric diagnosis for palliative care. *J Palliat Care* 17:12–21.

Koenig HG (2002). Religion, spirituality, and medicine: how are they related and what does it mean? *Mayo Clinic Proc* 12:1189–1191.

Koenig HG, Cohen HJ, Blazer DG, et al. (1992). Religious coping and depression among elderly, hospitalized medically ill men. *Am J Psychiatry* 149:1693–1700.

Koenig BA, Gates-Williams J (1995). Understanding cultural difference in caring for dying patients. *West J Med* 163(3):244–249.

Koenig HG, George, LK, Peterson BL (1998). Religiosity and remission of depression in medically ill older patients. *Am J Psychiatry* 155(4):536–542.

LaRue F, Colleau SM (1997). Underestimation and undertreatment of pain in HIV disease: multicentre study. *BMJ* 314:23–28.

LaRue F, Brasseur L, Musseault P, Demeulemeester R, Bonifassi L, Bez G (1994). Pain and symptoms in HIV disease: a national survey in France [abstract]. *J Palliat Care* 10:95.

Li M, Fitzgerald P, Rodin G (2012). Evidence-based treatment of depression in patients with cancer *J Clin Oncol* 30(11):1187–1196.

Lo B, Kates LW, Ruston D, et al. (2003). Responding to requests regarding prayer and religious ceremonies by patients near the end-of-life and their families. *J Palliat Med* 3:409–415.

Lopez OL, Wess J, Sanchez J, Dew MA, Becker JT (1998). Neurobehavioral correlates of perceived mental and motor slowness in HIV infection and AIDS. *J Neuropsychiatry Clin Neurosci* 10:343–350.

Lowther K, Simms V, Selman L, et al. (2012). Treatment outcomes in palliative care: the TOPCare study. A mixed methods phase III randomised controlled trial to assess the effectiveness of a nurse-led palliative care intervention for HIV positive patients on antiretroviral therapy. *BMC Infect Dis* 12:288.

Maddox JD, Joranson D, Angarola RT (1997). The use of opioids for the treatment of chronic pain (position statement). *Clin J Pain* 167:30–34.

Maguire P (1985). Barriers to psychological care of the dying. *BMJ* 291:1711–1713.

Maguire P (1999). Improving communication with cancer patients. *Eur J Cancer* 35:2058–2065.

Mansfield S, Barter G, Singh S (1992). AIDS and palliative care. *Int J STD AIDS* 3:248–250.

Mathews WC, McCutcheon JA, Asch S, et al. (2000). National estimates of HIV-related symptom prevalence from the HIV Cost and Services Utilization Study. *Med Care* 38:750–762.

Maugans TA (1996). The SPIRITual history. *Arch Fam Med* 5:11–16.

Maugans TA, Wadland WC (1991). Religion and family medicine: a survey of physicians and patients. *J Fam Pract* 32:210–213.

May M, Sterne JA, Sabin C, et al. (2007). The Antiretroviral Therapy (ART) Cohort Collab- oration. Prognosis of HIV-1-infected patients up to 5 years after initiation of ART: collaborative analysis of prospective studies. *AIDS* 21:1185–1197.

Mazanec P, Tyler MK (2003). Cultural considerations in end-of-life care. *Am J Nursing* 103(3):50–58.

McClain CS, Rosenfeld B, Breitbart W (2003). Effect of spiritual well-being on end-of-life despair in terminally-ill cancer patients. *Lancet* 61:1603–1607.

McCullough ME, Larson DB (1999). Religion and depression: a review of the literature. *Twin Res* 2:126–136.

Meares R (1981). On saying goodbye before death. *JAMA* 246:1227–1229.

Morley S, Eccleston C, Williams A (1999). Systematic review and meta-analysis of randomized controlled trials of cognitive behaviour therapy for chronic pain in adults, excluding headache. *Pain* 80:1–13.

Morris A, Creasman J, Turner J, Luce JM, Wachter RM, Huang L (2002). Intensive care of human immunodeficiency virus–infected patients during the era of highly active antiretroviral therapy. *Am J Respir Crit Care Med* 166:262–267.

Mosack KE, Wandrey RL (2015). Discordance in HIV-positive patient and healthcare provider perspectives on death, dying, and end-of-life care *Am J Hosp Palliat Care* 32(2):161–167.

Moss V (1990). Palliative care in advanced HIV disease: presentation, problems, and palliation. *AIDS* 4(Suppl 1):S235–S242.

Mouton C, Teno JM, Mor V, Piette J (1997). Communications of preferences for care among human immunodeficiency virus-infected patients: barriers to informed decisions? *Arch Fam Med* 6:342–347.

Narasimhan M, Posner AJ, DePalo VA, Mayo PH, Rosen MJ (2004). Intensive care in patients with HIV infection in the era of highly active antiretroviral therapy. *Chest* 125:1800–1804.

National Hospice Organization (1996). *Guidelines for Determining Prognosis for Selected Non-Cancer Diagnoses*. Alexandria, VA: National Hospice Organization.

Nelson CJ, Rosenfeld B, Breitbart W, et al. (2002). Spirituality, religion, and depression in the terminally ill. *Psychosomatics* 43:213–220.

Newshan GT, Wainapel SF (1993). Pain characteristics and their management in persons with AIDS. *J Assoc Nurses AIDS Care* 4:53–59.

Olden M, Pessin H, Lichtenhaul WG, Breitbat W (2009). Suicide and desire for hastened death. In H Chochinov, W Breitbart (eds.), *Handbook of Psychiatry in Palliative Medicine, Diagnosis and Management of Depression in Palliative Care*, 2nd ed. (pp. 101–112). New York: Oxford University Press.

O'Neill JF, Marconi K, Surapruik A, Blum N (2000). Improving HIV/AIDS services through palliative care: an HRSA perspective. *J Urban Health* 77:244–254.

O'Neill JF, Selwyn PA, Schietinger H (eds.) (2003). *A Clinical Guide to Supportive & Palliative Care for HIV/AIDS*. Washington DC: U.S. Department of Health and Human Services, Health Resources and Services Administration, HIV/AIDS Bureau.

O'Neill W, Sherrard J (1993). Pain in human immunodeficiency virus disease: a review. *Pain* 54:3–14.

Ontario Workplace Safety and Insurance Board (2000). *Report of the Chronic Pain Expert Advisory Panel*. Ontario: Ontario Workplace Safety and Insurance Board.

Pain Society and Royal Colleges of Anaesthetists (2004). Consensus statement from the Pain Society and Royal Colleges of Anaesthetists. General Practitioners and Psychiatrists: Recommendations. London: The Royal College of Anaesthetists.

Parker B, Baile W, deMoor C, et al. (2001). Breaking bad news about cancer: patients' preferences for communication. *J Clin Oncol* 19(7):2049–2056.

Parkes C (1975). Determinants of outcome following bereavement. *Omega* 6:303–323.

Parkes C (1998). *Bereavement: Studies of Grief in Adult Life*, 3rd ed. Madison, WI: International Universities Press.

Parkes C, Laungani P, Young B (eds.) (1997). *Death and Bereavement Across Cultures*. London: Routledge.

Parkes CM, Weiss RS (1983). *Recovery from Bereavement*. New York: Basic Books.

Pasternak R, Reynolds C, Schlernitzauer M (1991). Acute open-trial nor-triptyline therapy of bereavement-related depression in late life. *J Clin Psychiatry* 52:307–310.

Peterman AH, Fitchett G, Cella DF (1996). Modeling the relationship between quality of life dimensions and an overall sense of well-being. Presented at the Third World Congress of Psycho-Oncology, New York, NY.

Portenoy RK (1993). Chronic pain management. In A Stoudemire, BS Fogel (eds.), *Psychiatric Care of the Medical Patient*. New York: Oxford University Press.

Portenoy RK, Thaler HT, Kornblith AB, et al. (1994). The Memorial Symptom Assessment Scale: an instrument for the evaluation of symptom prevalence, characteristics, and distress. *Eur J Cancer* 30A:1326–1336.

Post SG, Puchalski CM, Larson DB (2000). Physicians and patient spirituality: professional boundaries, competency, and ethics. *Ann Intern Med* 132:578–583.

Prigerson HG, Horowitz MJ, Jacobs SC, et al. (2009). Prolonged grief disorder: psychometric validation of criteria proposed for DSM-V and ICD-11. *PLoS Med* 6:e1000121.

Prigerson H, Maciejewski P, Newson J, et al. (1995). Inventory of complicated grief. *Psychiatry Res* 59:65–79.

Puchalski C, Romer AL (2000). Taking a spiritual history allows clinicians to understand patients more fully. *J Palliat Med* 3:129–137.

Puoti M, Spinetti A, Ghezzi A, et al. (2001). Mortality from liver disease in patients with HIV infection: a cohort study. *J Acquir Immune Defic Syndr* 24:211–217.

Quill TE (2012). Physicians should "assist in suicide" when it is appropriate. *J Law Med Ethics* 40(1):57–65.

Rackstraw S, Conley A, Meadway J (2000). Recovery from progressive multifocal leukoencephalopathy following directly observed highly active antiretroviral therapy (ART) in a specialized brain impairment unit. *AIDS* 14(Suppl 4):S129.

Rando T (1983). *Treatment of Complicated Mourning*. Champaign, IL: Research Press.

Raphael B (1983). *The Anatomy of Bereavement*. London: Hutchinson.

Reiter GS, Kudler NR (1996). Palliative care and HIV: systemic manifestations and late-stage issues. *AIDS Clin Care* 8:27–36.

Rosenfeld B, Breitbart W, McDonald MV, Passik SD, Thaler H, Portenoy RK (1997). Pain in ambulatory AIDS patients: impact of pain on physiological functioning and quality of life. *Pain* 68:323–328.

Rousseau P (2000). Spirituality and the dying patient. *J Clin Oncol* 18:2000–2002.

Ruiz M, Armstrong M, Ogboukiri T, Anwar D. (2014) Patterns of pain medication use during last months of life in HIV-infected populations: the experience of an academic outpatient clinic. *Am J Hosp Palliat Care* 31(8):793–796.

Sanei L (1998). *Palliative Care for HIV/AIDS in Less Developed Countries*. Arlington, VA: Health Technical Services (HTS) Project for USAID.

Sansone RG, Frengley JD (2000). Impact of ART on causes of death of persons with late-stage AIDS. *J Urban Health* 77:165–175.

Schofferman J (1987). Hospice care of the patient with AIDS. *J Hospice* 3:51–74.

Schofferman J (1988). Pain: diagnosis and management in the palliative care of AIDS. *J Palliat Care* 4:46–49.

Selman LE, Higginson IJ, Agupio G, et al. (2011). Quality of life among patients receiving palliative care in South Africa and Uganda: a multi-centred study. *Health Qual Life Outcomes* 8(9):21.

Selman L, Siegert RJ, Higginson IJ, et al. (2012). The "Spirit 8" successfully captured spiritual well-being in African palliative care: factor and Rasch analysis. *J Clin Epidemiol* 65(4):434–443.

Selwyn PA, Forstein M (2003). Overcoming the false dichotomy of curative vs. palliative care for late-stage HIV/AIDS: "Let me live the way I want to live, until I can't." *JAMA* 290:806–814.

Selwyn PA, Goulet JL, Molde S, et al. (2000). HIV as a chronic disease: long-term care for patients with HIV at a dedicated skilled nursing facility. *J Urban Health* 77:187–203.

Selwyn PA, Rivard M (2003). Palliative care for AIDS: challenges and opportunities in the era of highly active anti-retroviral therapy. *J Palliat Med* 6(3):475–487

Selwyn PA, Rivard M, Kapell D, et al. (2003). Palliative care for AIDS at a large urban teaching hospital: program description and preliminary outcomes. *J Palliat Med* 6(3):461–474.

Shen JM, Blank A, Selwyn PA (2005). Predictors of mortality for patients with advanced disease in an HIV palliative care program. *J Acquir Immune Defic Syndr* 40(4):445–447.

Simms V, Higginson IJ, Harding R (2011). What palliative care-related problems do patients experience at HIV diagnosis? A systematic review of the evidence. *J Pain Symptom Manage* 42(5):734–753.

Simms V, Higginson IJ, Harding R (2012). Integration of palliative care throughout HIV disease. *Lancet Infect Dis* 12(7):571–575.

Simpson M, Buckman R, Stewart M, Maguire P, Lipkin M, Novack D, Till J (1991). Doctor–patient communication: the Toronto Consensus Statement. *BMJ* 303(6814):1385–1387.

Singer JE, Fahy-Chandon B, Chi S, Syndulko K, Tourtellotte WW (1993). Painful symptoms reported by ambulatory HIV-infected men in a longitudinal study. *Pain* 54:15–19.

Singer PA, Martin DK, Kelner M (1999). Quality end-of-life care: patients' perspective. *JAMA* 281:163–168.

Sloan RP, Bagiella E, Powell T (1999). Religion, spirituality, and medicine. *Lancet* 353:664–667.

Smith TJ (2000). Tell it like it is. *J Clin Oncol* 18:3441–3445.

Stephenson J, Woods S, Scott B, Meadway J (2000). HIV-related brain impairment: from palliative care to rehabilitation. *Int J Palliat Nurs* 6:6–11.

Stjernsward J, Clark D (2004). Palliative medicine: a global perspective. In D Doyle, G Hanks, N Cherny, K Calman (eds.), *Oxford Textbook of Palliative Medicine,* 3rd ed. (pp. 1199–1224). New York: Oxford University Press.

Stjernsward J, Papallona S (1998). Palliative medicine: a global perspective. In D Doyle, GWC Hanks, N MacDonald (eds.), *Oxford Textbook of Palliative Medicine*, 2nd ed. (pp. 1227–1245). New York: Oxford University Press.

Storey P, Knight C (2001). *American Academy of Hospice and Palliative Medicine UNIPAC Two: Alleviating Psychological and Spiritual Pain in the Terminally Ill*. Larchmont, NY: Mary Ann Liebert.

Stroebe M, Stroebe W, Hansson R (eds.) (1993). *Handbook of Bereavement*. Cambridge, UK: Cambridge University Press.

Suchman AL, Markakis K, Beckman HB, et al. (1997). A model of empathic communication in the medical interview. *JAMA* 277:678–681.

Temel JS, Greer JA, Muzikansky A, et al. (2010) Early palliative care for patients with metastatic non-small-cell lung cancer. *N Engl J Med* 363(8):733–742.

Thiel MM, Robinson MR (1997). Physicians' collaboration with chaplains: difficulties and benefits. *J Clin Ethics* 8:94–103.

Tosches WA, Cohen CJ, Day JM (1992). A pilot study of acupuncture for the symptomatic treatment of HIV-associated peripheral neuropathy [8:14 abstract]. Presented at the VIIIth International Conference on AIDS, Amsterdam, the Netherlands.

UNAIDS (2000). AIDS palliative care: UNAIDS technical update. http://data.unaids.org/Publications/IRC-pub05/JC453-PalliCare-TU_en.pdf. Accessed February 16, 2017.

UNAIDS (2014). 90-90-90—An ambitious treatment target to help end the AIDS epidemic. http://www.unaids.org/en/resources/documents/2014/90-90-90. Accessed February 16, 2017.

Underwood LG, Teresi JA (2002). The daily spiritual experience scale. *Ann Med* 24:22–33.

Valdez H, Chowdhry TK, Asaad R, et al. MM (2001). Changing spectrum of mortality due to HIV: analysis of 260 deaths during 1995–1999. *Clin Infect Dis* 32:1487–1493.

Vincent B, Timsit JF, Auburtin M, Schortgen F, Bouadma L, Wolff M, Regnier B (2004). Characteristics and outcomes of HIV-infected patients in the ICU: impact of the highly active antiretroviral treatment era. *Intensive Care Med* 30:859–866.

Vogl D, Rosenfeld B, Breitbart W, Thaler H, Passik S, McDonald M, Portenoy RK (1999). Symptom prevalence, characteristics and distress in AIDS outpatients. *J Pain Symptom Manage* 18: 253–262.

Watson M, Haviland JJ, Greer S, et al. (1999). Influence of psychological response on survival in breast cancer population-based cohort study. *Lancet* 354:1331–1336.

Welch K, Morse A (2002). The clinical profile of end-state AIDS in the era of highly active antiretroviral therapy. *AIDS Patient Care STDS* 16:75–81.

Wenger NS, Kanouse DE, Collins RL, et al. (2001). End-of-life discussions and preferences among persons with HIV. *JAMA* 22:2880–2887.

Wilson KG, Lander M, Chochinov H (2009). Diagnosis and management of depression in palliative care. In H Chochinov, W Breitbart W (eds.), *Handbook of Psychiatry in Palliative Medicine, Diagnosis and Management of Depression in Palliative Care*, 2nd ed. (pp. 39–68). New York: Oxford University Press.

Wood CG, Whittet S, Bradbeer CS (1997). ABC of palliative care: HIV infection and AIDS. *BMJ* 315:1433–1436.

World Health Organization (1986). *Cancer Pain Relief*. Geneva: World Health Organization.

World Health Organization (1990). *Cancer Pain Relief and Palliative Care: Report of a WHO Expert Committee* (Technical Bulletin 804). Geneva: World Health Organization.

World Health Organization (1998). *Symptom Relief in Terminal Illness*. Geneva: World Health Organization.

World Health Organization (2002). *National Cancer Control Programmes: Policies and Managerial Guidelines* (2nd ed.) Geneva: World Health Organization.

World Health Organization (2007). *Cancer Control: Knowledge into Action. Palliative Care: WHO Guide for Effective Programmes*. Geneva: World Health Organization.

Yoong J, Park ER, Greer JA, et al. (2013). Early palliative care in advanced lung cancer: a qualitative study. *JAMA Intern Med* 173(4):283–290.

42.

PSYCHOPHARMACOLOGICAL TREATMENT ISSUES IN HIV/AIDS PSYCHIATRY

Kelly L. Cozza, Gary H. Wynn, Glenn W. Wortmann, Scott G. Williams, and Rita Rein*

Persons with HIV/AIDS are often prescribed a multitude of medications, necessitating attention to pharmacokinetics and pharmacodynamics and an understanding of intended effects, side effects, toxicities, and drug interactions. Clinicians who treat persons with HIV, as part of the multidisciplinary treatment team, need to assist in patient evaluation, medication selection, and treatment. They also need an understanding of antiretroviral therapy (ART) and psychopharmacological treatment issues in order to prevent morbidity, support adherence to medications, and improve patients' quality of life (Nel and Kagee, 2013; Yun et al., 2005).

This chapter begins with a brief but essential review of drug interaction principles, preparing the reader to critically weigh the interplay between psychotropics, other select medications, and ART. This introduction is followed by an overview of current antiretroviral medications and their known side effects, toxicities, and drug interactions, in text and table format. The chapter concludes with a presentation of psychotropic-ART treatment issues, by psychotropic category, including reviews of available literature on the use and effectiveness of psychotropic medication in persons with HIV, common psychotropic side effects, drug interactions, and other clinical implications of polypharmacy in the treatment of persons with HIV.

BRIEF REVIEW OF DRUG INTERACTION PRINCIPLES

Understanding drug–drug interactions is essential in providing care for patients with HIV. For a full explanation of pharmacology and drug interactions, the reader is referred to several texts on the subject (Baxter and Preston, 2013; Stahl, 2014; Wynn et al., 2009). Pharmacodynamic interactions are those that occur at the intended receptor site of a medication. An example of a pharmacodynamic drug interaction is the serotonin syndrome (sweating, autonomic dysfunction, agitation, restlessness, confusion, muscle rigidity, diarrhea) that occurs with co-administration of a monoamine oxidase inhibitor (MAOI) and selective serotonin reuptake inhibitor (SSRI) and results from additive receptor-mediated effects. Most pharmacodynamic interactions are intuitive and easily predictable. Pharmacokinetic interactions may occur because of problems with absorption, distribution, metabolism, and excretion of medications and are not as easily predictable. The absorption of many HIV drugs can be adversely affected by co-administration with food or buffers, and these absorption-based pharmacokinetic drug interactions are also relatively predictable. Metabolic interactions are more complex, as they are affected by metabolic inhibition, induction, and pharmacogenetics (the particular metabolic enzymes a patient is born with) at metabolic sites, such as the gut wall and liver. Metabolic interactions may occur at either phase I or II metabolic enzymes, and also may include the cell membrane transporter enzymes (also known as P-glycoproteins, or P-gps).

Figure 42.1 presents what happens to serum levels of drug A when a potent inhibitor of drug A's metabolic enzyme (usually in the gut wall or the liver) is present. Inhibition of metabolism is immediate and generally causes the serum level of the parent drug to increase. If that parent drug (for example, a tricyclic antidepressant) has a narrow margin of safety, then toxicity may result. Inhibition slows the metabolism of a drug dependent on the inhibited enzyme. Inhibition may occur at cytochrome P450 enzymes in the liver and gut wall (phase I metabolism) and/or during phase II metabolism (glucuronidation, sulfation, methylation, etc.) in the liver. Cytochrome P450 (CYP) enzymes that metabolize current medications include 3A4, 2D6, 1A2, 2C9, 2C19, 2E1, and 2B6, among others. CYP3A4 and CYP2D6 and glucuronidation are commonly affected by ART and psychotropics. Table 42.1 presents many of the most common inhibitors of CYP3A4 and CYP2D6, as well as the drugs with narrow margins of safety that are dependent on those enzymes for metabolism.

Figure 42.2 presents what happens to drug A when a potent inducer of drug A's metabolic enzymes is introduced. Induction of metabolism actually increases the number of sites available for metabolism. This process is not immediate and can take up to 2 weeks to occur. When more enzymes are available, more drug is metabolized, and the net effect is a

---

* The opinions or assertions contained herein are the private views of the authors and are not to be construed as official or as reflecting the views of the Department of the Navy or the Department of Defense.

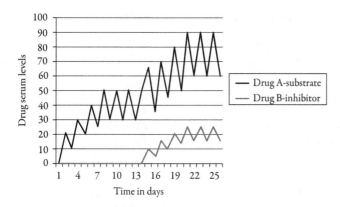

Figure 42.1 Drug–drug interaction—inhibition. Drug A develops steady-state concentrations after 4 half-lives ($t_{1/2}$). Its peak levels are 50 and trough levels are 30 at steady state. Drug B is introduced sometime later, after drug A is in steady-state concentrations. Drug B develops its own steady-state after 4 half-lives. Drug B, however, is a competitive inhibitor of the enzyme(s) that drug A uses for its metabolism. Drug A develops a new steady state, with peak levels at 90 and trough levels at 60. Adapted with permission from Cozza KL, Armstrong SC, and Oesterheld JR. *Concise Guide to Drug Interaction Principles for Medical Practice: Cytochrome P450s, UGTs, P-Glycoproteins*, second edition. Copyright (2003), American Psychiatric Press, Inc.

lowering of available parent drug, or more rapid metabolism. An inducer may cause the level of a drug dependent on that enzyme to drop below the level needed for clinical effectiveness. In some cases, metabolic induction may increase the production of active and/or toxic metabolites. Table 42.1 presents many of the most common inducers of 3A4, as well as some of the medications with narrow therapeutic windows dependent on those enzymes for metabolism

Interactions may also occur with phase II enzymes (e.g., glucuronidation via uridine 5′ diphosphate glucuronosyltransferase [UGT] and sulfation). UGT enzymes are the most numerous and clinically important phase II enzymes. They are found in the endoplasmic reticulum and the nuclear membrane of liver, kidney, brain, and placental cells

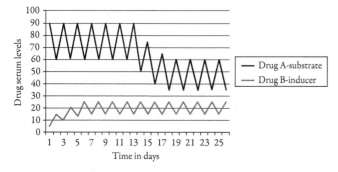

Figure 42.2 Drug–drug interaction—induction. Drug A is in steady state, having been introduced sometime before this graph, with peak levels of 90 and trough levels of 60. Drug B is started on day 1, and develops steady state after 4 half-lives. After 2 weeks, levels of drug A decrease, as drug B has gradually induced the enzyme(s) involved in metabolizing drug A. Drug A now has a steady state, with peak levels at 60 and trough levels at 35. Adapted with permission from Cozza KL, Armstrong SC, and Oesterheld JR. *Concise Guide to Drug Interaction Principles for Medical Practice: Cytochrome P450s, UGTs, P-Glycoproteins*, second edition. Copyright (2003), American Psychiatric Press, Inc.

(Radominska-Pandya et al., 1999). Many drugs are metabolized first by phase I metabolism (P450 and others) and then by glucuronidation, but some drugs are directly conjugated by UGTs, such as lorazepam, temazepam, and oxazepam. Drugs primarily metabolized by UGTs include lamotrigine, valproate, nonsteroidal anti-inflammatory drugs, zidovudine, and many opioids. Most glucuronide metabolites are inactive, so inhibition or induction of these enzymes produces no clinically relevant effects. A few drugs are known to produce active metabolites via glucuronidation, such as morphine to morphine-6-glucuronide, a metabolite of morphine that is about 20 times more potent as an analgesic compound than morphine. Inhibition of glucuronidation may reduce morphine's effectiveness (Court, 2009).

Membrane transporters may also be inhibited or induced via drug interactions and exhibit genetic polymorphisms. The membrane-bound transporters are sometimes called "phase 0" or "phase III" of the metabolic system. They were first called "P-glycoproteins" and are still commonly referred to in the literature that way or as "P-gps." Transporters are present in the blood–brain barrier, placenta, intestine, hepatocytes, renal tubule cells, and many other sites. They regulate the transfer of exogenous and endogenous compounds into and out of organs and other target cells. Transporters play a large role in the penetration of drugs like ART and psychotropics into the brain. Functioning membrane transporters may be part of the explanation for how HIV finds "sanctuary" in some organ sites when ART cannot penetrate, owing to the "bouncers" or efflux-transporters that actively keep them away from the target. They may also play a role in treatment-resistant depression by blocking transport of psychotropics into the brain. Importantly, if a membrane transporter is inhibited by a transport inhibitor, the concentration of drugs that are dependent on or substrates of that transporter will get through the membrane to the other side, increasing transport across the membrane. In essence, the "bouncer" or transporter is decommissioned. Many drugs, including ART and some psychotropics, are inhibitors of membrane transporters. A full explanation of the importance of transporters may be found elsewhere (O'Brien et al., 2012; Oesterheld, 2009, pp. 43–72). Where known, transporter activity of drugs mentioned in this chapter is indicated in the chapter's tables.

BRIEF REVIEW OF ANTIRETROVIRAL THERAPY, HEPATITIS B, AND HEPATITIS C THERAPY

The introduction of effective combination antiretroviral therapy (ART) in 1996 revolutionized the treatment of HIV infection, markedly reducing the associated morbidity and mortality and transforming HIV into a manageable, chronic infection. Although the medical regimens have become progressively simpler (current formulations are often just one pill per day), the control of HIV requires lifetime daily adherence, and episodic adherence can result in subtherapeutic drug

Table 42.1 COMMON SUBSTRATES, INHIBITORS, AND INDUCERS OF IMPORTANT CYTOCHROME P450 ENZYMES

P450 ENZYME	COMMON SUBSTRATES*	COMMON INHIBITORS	COMMON INDUCERS
1A2	Amitriptyline Caffeine Cyclobenzaprine Fluvoxamine Olanzapine Verapamil R-warfarin	Acyclovir Amiodarone Cimetidine Ciprofloxacin/Fluoroquinolones Flutamide Fluvoxamine Verapamil	Tobacco smoke Carbamazepine Eso/omeprazole Rifampin Ritonavir Broccoli/cauliflower
2B6	Bupropion Cyclophosphamide Efavirenz	Clopidogrel Fluoxetine Fluvoxamine Paroxetine Ritonavir	Pan-inducers Lopinavir/ritonavir Ritonavir
2D6	Antiarrhythmics Metoprolol Oxycodone SSRIs Tramadol Tricyclic Antidepressants Typical Antipsychotics	**Bupropion** Diphenhydramine Fluoxetine Paroxetine **Quinidine** Ritonavir	Pan-inducers† possibly
3A4	Anti-arrhythmics Beta-blockers Buspirone Carbamazepine Calcium channel blockers Cyclosporine Ergots Lurasidone Oral contraceptives Methadone Oral contraceptives Protease inhibitors Statins TriazoloBZDs‡ Zolpidem	Atazanavir Cimetidine Clarithromycin Delavirdine Diltiazem Efavirenz Erythromycin Grapefruit Juice Indinavir Itraconazole Ketoconazole Nefazodone Ritonavir Tipranavir	Carbamazepine Efavirenz Nevirapine Oxcarbazepine Pan-inducers† Ritonavir St. John's wort Topiramate

All drugs in **bold** type are potent in their cytochrome P-450 metabolic inhibition or induction.
*A substrate is a drug that must utilize the enzyme for metabolism.
†Pan-inducers: carbamazepine, phenobarbital, phenytoin, rifamycins.
‡TriazoloBZDs: triazolobenzodiazepines: alprazolam, midazolam, triazolam.

levels, a situation that fosters the selection of ART-resistant viral mutants (Tang and Shafer, 2012). Salvage regimens can be used to attempt to regain suppression of the virus, but these involve higher pill burdens, which can further complicate long-term adherence (Chesney, 2003). Drug interactions with ART can also result in subtherapeutic levels, as well as in supra-therapeutic levels (risking toxicity), and thus practitioners should be cognizant of potential interactions. In order to select adequate psychopharmacological therapies and to become helpful consultants to HIV specialists, an understanding of the components of ART, including drug interactions, pill burdens, and special idiosyncrasies, is suggested. Please refer to Chapter 2 of this textbook for further discussion of antiretroviral therapy. Regular updates concerning the antiretroviral management of HIV can be found in the National Institutes of Health's Aidsinfo publications (DHHS Panel on Antiretroviral Guidelines for Adults and Adolescents, 2016).

Since much of the data is just emerging, a brief introductory overview of the state of the field is presented.

PROTEASE INHIBITORS

Protease inhibitors act late in the HIV life cycle and prevent a virally encoded enzyme (HIV protease) from cleaving viral polyprotein precursors into individual mature proteins. There are currently nine protease inhibitors available (see Table 42.2). Although ritonavir was initially prescribed at high doses for its antiviral action, it was found to inhibit the same host enzyme (CYP3A) that metabolizes other

Table 42.2 **PROTEASE INHIBITORS**

PROTEASE INHIBITOR (PI)	METABOLISM SITE(S)	ENZYME(S) INHIBITED	ENZYME(S) INDUCED	ABSORPTION AND FOOD CONSIDERATIONS	SIDE EFFECTS AND TOXICITIES	POTENTIAL DRUG–DRUG INTERACTIONS
PI common features	CYP 3A4 transporters	CYP3A4	See Lopinavir/ Ritonavir (Kaletra)	Use lower doses of sildenafil with all PIs.	Bleeding risk Gastrointestinal Headaches Hepatitis Lipodystrophy Sexual dysfunction	PIs as potent CYP3A4 inhibitors may increase serum levels of: *Antiarrhythmics* *Antipsychotics dependent on CYP3A4* *Buspirone* *Carbamazepine* *Calcium channel blockers* *Cyclosporine* *Ergots* *Methadone* *Oral contraceptives* *Reboxetine* *Protease inhibitors* *Sildenafil* *Statins dependent on CYP3A4* *Trazodone* *Vilazodone* *TriazoloBZDs[a]* *Z hypnotics[b]* CYP3A4 inducers that may reduce serum levels of PIs, resulting in loss of viral suppression and increasing risk of viral resistance: *Oxcarbazepine* *Pan-inducers[c]* *St. John's wort* CYP 3A4 inhibitors may increase serum levels of PIs, worsening side effects and toxicities.
Atazanavir (Reyataz)	P450, likely CYP3A4	CYP3A4, CYP2C8, UGT1A1	None known	Take with light meal or high-fat meal to increase bioavailability and reduce pharmacokinetic variability. Absorption is decreased with high gastric pH.	Direct (unconjugated, hyperbilirubinemia (especially in overdose) Lactic acidosis Prolonged PR interval on ECG (especially in overdose)	See PI common features. Irinotecan levels may be increased by atazanavir's inhibition of UGT1A1. Absorption of atazanavir is altered by: *Proton-pump inhibitors* *Antacids*
Darunavir (Prezista)	CYP3A4	CYP3A4	None known		Stevens-Johnson syndrome Hyperglycemia Hyperlipidemia Pancreatitis	See PI common features.
Fosamprenavir (Lexiva)	CYP3A4	CYP3A4	Possible 3A4	Discontinue vitamin E supplement due to high content in formulation. Do not take with high-fat meal.	Lactic acidosis Perioral paresthesias Peripheral paresthesias Stevens-Johnson syndrome	See PI common features.

(continued)

Table 42.2 CONTINUED

PROTEASE INHIBITOR (PI)	METABOLISM SITE(S)	ENZYME(S) INHIBITED	ENZYME(S) INDUCED	ABSORPTION AND FOOD CONSIDERATIONS	SIDE EFFECTS AND TOXICITIES	POTENTIAL DRUG–DRUG INTERACTIONS
Indinavir (Crixivan)	CYP3A4	CYP3A4	None known	Do not take with high-fat or high-protein meals. Grapefruit juice unexpectedly may decrease indinavir levels.**	Potential cross-sensitivity in sulfa-sensitive patients Altered sense of taste Cheilitis Dry eyes, mouth, skin Hyperbilirubinemia Nephrolithiasis Paronychia Rash Neutropenia Leukocytoclastic vasculitis	See PI common features.
Lopinavir/ Ritonavir (Kaletra)	3A4	Same as RIT Lopinavir: CYPs 3A4, 2D6	Same as RIT Lopinavir: glucuronidation (phase II)	Take with food.	Pancreatitis	Same as ritonavir and PI common features
Nelfinavir (Viracept)	CYPs 3A4, 2C19	CYPs 3A4, 1A2, 2B6	Possibly CYP2C9,UGTs	Take with food.	Diarrhea (most severe of PIs) Nephrolithiasis	See PI common features.
Ritonavir (Norvir)	3A4, 2D6	CYPs 3A4, 2D6, 2C9, 2C19, 2B6	CYPs 3A4, 1A2,2C9,2C19	See PI common features.	Pancreatitis Altered sense of taste	See PI common features. RIT as a dual CYP inhibitor and inducer may ↑ then ↓ levels of: Calcium channel blockers Antipsychotics dependent on CYPs 3A4 and 1A2 Estradiol Meperidine Methadone Statins dependent on CYP3A4 Phenobarbital Phenytoin Sulfonylureas Triazolo BZDs[a] Tricyclic antidepressants Z hypnotics[b]
	CYP3A4	CYP3A4	None known	Take with food.	Altered sense of taste	See PI common features.
Tipranavir (Aptivus)	CYP3A4	CYPs 3A4, 1A2, 2C9, 2C19 2D6	UGTs	Usually administered with ritonavir 200 mg. Take with food.	See PI common features and Ritonavir.	See PI common features and Ritonavir.

Note: Primary route of metabolism listed first.

Bold CYP indicates **potent** inhibitor or inducer of that cytochrome P450 enzyme.

Abbreviations: CYP, cytochrome; UGT, uridine 5′-diphosphate glucuronosyltransferase.

[a] Triazolobenzodiazepines: alprazolam (Xanax), midazolam (Versed), triazolam (Halcion).

[b] Z hypnotics: zaleplon, zolpidem, zopiclone.

Pan-inducers: drugs that induce many if not all CYP P450 enzymes and include barbiturates, carbamazepine, ethanol, phenytoin, and rifamycins.

** The package insert states that grapefruit juice lowers the AUC by 26%, so the Infectious Diseases Society of America guidelines state to consider separating grapefruit juice and indinavir by at least 2 hours (http://hivinsite.ucsf.edu/insite?page=ar-00-02&post=10&param=13#16), although others (Shelton et al., 2001) suggest that grapefruit juice has no net effect on indinavir levels, since grapefruit juice raises gastric pH (*slightly* decreasing absorption). However, grapefruit juice is also a CYP3A4 inhibitor, potentially increasing levels of indinavir.

protease inhibitors and is thus now used at low levels to "boost" the plasma concentrations of other protease inhibitors (Josephson, 2010).

All protease inhibitors are metabolized in the liver by CYP3A enzymes, and thus care should be taken when prescribing CYP3A inducers or inhibitors. Some protease inhibitors may also inhibit or induce CYP enzymes, P-glycoprotein, or other transporters in the gut and elsewhere (Griffin et al., 2011). Using a CYP3A substrate with a narrow therapeutic window in the presence of a protease inhibitor may lead to a prolonged elimination half-life ($t_{1/2}$) and drug accumulation and should be administered with care. Some examples of drugs known to have significant interactions with protease inhibitors are lipid-lowering agents (e.g., statins), anticonvulsants, benzodiazepines, oral contraceptives, ergots, and certain herbal products (such as St. John's wort). Atazanavir requires an acidic environment for absorption, and co-administration with acid-lowering medications (such as famotidine or omeprazole) should be done in consultation with published dosing recommendations (Fulco et al., 2006). Table 42.2 delineates protease inhibitor metabolism, inhibition, induction, interactions, and toxicities.

Although generally well tolerated, protease inhibitors can be associated with a number of side effects. All protease inhibitors can cause drug-induced hepatitis (Lana et al., 2001). Indinavir and atazanavir are associated with indirect hyperbilirubinemia, which does not necessarily require treatment discontinuation but which can be cosmetically disconcerting to the patient (Laprise et al., 2013). Both drugs can also cause renal stones; adequate hydration is recommended to decrease this risk (Rho and Perazella, 2007; Tattevin et al., 2013). Diarrhea can occur, more frequently with nelfinavir and lopinavir/ritonavir than with other protease inhibitors (MacArthur and DuPont, 2012). Gastrointestinal side effects can be significant enough to cause drug discontinuation (d'Arminio Monforte et al., 2000). Dyslipidemia, with elevations in LDL and triglycerides, can occur with all ritonavir-boosted regimens (Sax and Kumar, 2004). Discontinuation of treatment may result in normalization of the dyslipidemia (Hui, 2003). Protease inhibitors can also cause sexual side effects, with rates up to 70% in some studies (Lallemand et al., 2002). If erectile dysfunction medications such as sildenafil are used, the clinician should be aware of possible drug–drug interactions via CYP3A4 (Aschmann et al., 2008).

CASE PAIR A: PROTEASE INHIBITORS AND ERGOTS

A 37-year-old woman with HIV on ritonavir-containing ART developed new-onset migraine and used ergots as prescribed. She developed speech difficulties and weakness and was diagnosed with cerebral ergotism. She sustained residual expressive aphasia and right-sided peroneal nerve paresis (Spiegel et al., 2001).

A 31-year-old man with HIV presented to the emergency room with bilateral pulseless lower extremity cyanosis 24 hours after a single dose of ergotamine for migraine prophylaxis while on a ritonavir-containing ART regimen (Blanche et al., 1999).

Ergotamine-containing drugs are dependent on CYP3A4 for metabolism. The protease inhibitor ritonavir is a potent inhibitor of CYP3A4, leading to ergot toxicity. See Avihingsanon and colleagues (2014) for a review.

NUCLEOSIDE REVERSE TRANSCRIPTASE INHIBITORS

Nucleoside reverse transcriptase inhibitors (NRTIs) act to prevent the enzyme reverse transcriptase from copying viral single-stranded RNA into double-stranded DNA (Hoggard et al., 2000; Kearney et al, 2004). NRTIs are competitive inhibitors of deoxynucleotides but lack a 3'-hydroxyl group on the deoxyribose moiety, leading to chain termination of viral DNA synthesis. There are currently seven NRTIs available: abacavir, didanosine, emtricitabine, lamivudine, stavudine, tenofovir, and zidovudine.

Drug interactions with the NRTIs are generally less problematic than with the protease inhibitors, although they can still occur. None have been found to be inhibitors or inducers of the P450 system in vivo (DHHS Panel on Antiretroviral Guidelines for Adults and Adolescents, 2016; Nekvindová et al., 2006). Intracellular levels of didanosine can be increased with ribavirin with a risk of fatal lactic acidosis (Butt, 2003), and methadone can increase zidovudine levels, primarily through inhibition of zidovudine glucuronidation (McCance-Katz et al., 1998).

Side effects with NRTIs can be significant. Hepatotoxicity, nausea and vomiting, and lactic acidosis have all been reported (Moyle, 2000). Lipodystrophy, which is a syndrome marked by abnormal central fat accumulation (lipohypertrophy) and/or localized loss of fat tissue (lipoatrophy), appears to be associated with the thymidine analogs, with stavudine being a higher risk than zidovudine. Please refer to Chapter 46 of this text for further discussion of lipodystrophy. Hypersensitivity reactions have been associated with abacavir, and screening for HLA-B*5701 is recommended before initiation of therapy (Martin and Kroetz, 2013). Severe flares of hepatitis B may occur if tenofovir, lamivudine, or emtricitabine is withdrawn, as they have efficacy in suppressing this virus as well (Thio and Locarnini, 2007). Table 42.3 outlines NRTI metabolism, inhibition, induction, interactions, and toxicities.

NON-NUCLEOSIDE REVERSE TRANSCRIPTASE INHIBITORS

Non-nucleoside reverse transcriptase inhibitors (NNRTIs) act similarly to NRTIs in that they prevent the formation of double-stranded DNA, but do so by binding directly to HIV reverse transcriptase (De Clercq, 1998). Five NNRTIs are currently available: delavirdine, efavirenz, etravirine, nevirapine, and rilpivirine. Delavirdine has a lower efficacy than that of other NNRTIs and has an inconvenient dosing schedule so is rarely used. Viral resistance to one NNRTI usually confers resistance to all members of the drug class, with the exception

Table 42.3 NUCLEOTIDE ANALOGUE REVERSE TRANSCRIPTASE INHIBITORS (NRTIS)

DRUG NAME	METABOLISM SITE(S)	ENZYME(S) INHIBITED	ENZYME(S) INDUCED	ABSORPTION AND FOOD CONSIDERATIONS	SIDE EFFECTS AND TOXICITIES	POTENTIAL DRUG–DRUG INTERACTIONS
NRTI common features					Hepatomegaly with steatosis Lactic acidosis Lipodystrophy Myopathy Nausea Pancreatitis Peripheral neuropathy Vomiting	
Abacavir (Ziagen)	Alcohol dehydrogenase, glucuronyl transferase	None known	None known	With or without food	See NRTI common features. Abacavir hypersensitivity reaction (rechallenge is contraindicated)	
Didanosine (ddI, Videx)	Purine nucleoside phosphorylase	None known	None known	Take on an empty stomach. Do not crush or chew EC tablets.	See NRTI common features. Optic neuritis and retinal depigmentation Pancreatitis Peripheral neuropathy Risk of fatal lactic acidosis if co-administered with HepC drug ribavirin Risk of lactic acidosis and hepatomegaly in pregnancy if co-administered with stavudine	Methadone may reduce GI motility and decrease didanosine serum levels due to reduced bioavailability. Concomitant use of allopurinol and ganciclovir with didanosine increases didanosine toxicity. Didanosine effects GI absorption of: *Dapsone* *Itraconazole* *Ketoconazole* *Pyrimethamine* *Quinolones* *Tenofovir[a]* *Tetracyclines*
Emtricitabine (Emtriva)	Full recovery in urine and feces	None known	None known	None	See NRTI common features. Discontinuation in hepatitis B virus–infected persons; may exacerbate hepatitis	
Lamivudine (3TC, Epivir)	Minimal metabolism	None known	None known	With or without food	Generally well tolerated	
Stavudine (d4T, Zerit)	Not yet known	None known	None known	With or without food	See NRTI common features. Peripheral neuropathy (increased risk with didanosine)	Stavudine toxicity is increased via inhibition of intracellular phosphorylation when co-administered with zidovudine, so they should not be co-administered. Methadone may decrease GI motility and reduce stavudine serum levels due to reduced bioavailability.
Tenofovir (Viread)	Renal	None known	None known	High-fat meals increase bioavailability.	See NRTI common features. Nausea	Take tenofovir 2 hours before or 1 hour after didanosine.

Zidovudine (AZT, Retrovir)	UGT2B7, CYPB5	None known	None known	With or without food	See NRTI common features. Anemia Granulocytopenia Headache GI complaints Pancytopenia	Enhance zidovudine toxicity: Atovaquone Fluconazol Ganciclovir Methadone[b] Valproic acid Zidovudine may inhibit the intracellular phosphorylation of stavudine, worsening stavudine's toxicity, so they should not be co-administered. Pan-inducers[c] reduce zidovudine levels.

Note: Primary route of metabolism listed first.

Bold CYP indicates **potent** inhibitor or inducer of that metabolic site.

Abbreviations: CYP, cytochrome; GI, gastrointestinal; UGT, uridine 5′-diphosphate glucuronosyltransferase.

[a]Take tenofovir 2 hours before or 1 hour after didanosine.

[b]Methadone increases zidovudine levels and toxicity via inhibition of glucuronidation.

[c]Pan-inducers: drugs that induce many if not all CYP P450 enzymes and include barbiturates, carbamazepine, ethanol, phenytoin, and rifamycin.

of etravirine, which can maintain activity despite some common NNRTI-induced mutations (Schrijvers, 2013).

NNRTIs are metabolized to some degree by the CYP system of enzymes, mainly by CYP3A4, and glucuronoconjugation. They also elicit variable effects on other medications, acting as either inhibitors or inducers of drugs metabolized by CYP (Smith et al., 2001; von Moltke et al., 2001). Nevirapine is an autoinducer of CYP3A4 and CYP2B6. Efavirenz is metabolized in the liver predominantly by the CYP3A4 and CYP2B6 isoenzymes. Efavirenz initially inhibits 3A4, but over time it becomes a CYP inducer, leading to autoinduction and decreased serum levels (Clarke et al., 2001; Mouly et al., 2002; Spak et al., 2008; Usach et al., 2013). Rilpivirine solubility is pH dependent, and the concomitant use of a proton pump inhibitor is contraindicated. Rilpivirine is predominantly metabolized by CYP3A4, and co-administration with CYP3A inducers (e.g., rifampin) results in decreased rilpivirine concentrations, which may increase the risk of virological failure (Crauwels et al., 2013). Etravirine is a weak inducer of CYP3A and a weak inhibitor of CYP2C9/CYP2C19 and P-glycoprotein. Co-administration with drugs that inhibit or induce these pathways may alter the therapeutic effect or toxicity of etravirine, and co-administration of drugs that are substrates of these pathways may alter the effect or toxicity of the co-administered drug (Kakuda et al., 2010).

NNRTIs can also cause serious side effects, including hepatotoxicity and rash. With nevirapine, symptomatic hepatitis occurs at significantly higher frequency in ART-naïve females with a CD4 count >250 cells/mm³ and in ART-naïve males with CD4 counts >400 cells/mm³, and its use in these populations is generally not recommended. Efavirenz is associated with neuropsychiatric symptoms in approximately 50% of patients and include vivid dreams, insomnia, and mood changes. The effects usually begin shortly after treatment initiation, commonly peak in the first 2 weeks, and are generally mild and transient (Kenedi and Goforth, 2011). Lipodystrophy may occur (De Waal et al., 2013). Table 42.4 outlines NNRTI metabolism, inhibition, induction, interactions, and toxicities.

INTEGRASE INHIBITORS

Integrase inhibitors, also known as integrase strand transfer inhibitors (INSTIs), act by blocking the action of integrase, a viral enzyme that inserts the viral genome into the DNA of the host cell. Raltegravir was the first INSTI approved in the United States, in 2007, and was joined by elvitegravir (available as part of the fixed-dose combination Stribild), in 2012, and dolutegravir, in 2013. As compared with raltegravir, dolutegravir can be administered once a day in treatment-naïve patients and retains activity against some viruses that are resistant to raltegravir and elvitegravir (Cahn et al., 2013).

Raltegravir is mainly metabolized by UGT1A1 via glucuronidation, and potent inducers of glucuronidation/UGTA1, such as rifampin, reduce plasma concentrations of raltegravir. Inhibitors of glucuronidation may increase serum levels of raltegravir, leading to potential toxicity. Elvitegravir is predominantly metabolized via CYP3A4, along with minor pathways, including glucuronidation via UGT1A1/3. Elvitegravir is currently only available as a co-formulated product with cobicistat, tenofovir, and emtricitabine (Manzardo and Gatell, 2014). Cobicistat is metabolized by CYP3A and CYP2D6 (minor). Cobicistat is a strong CYP3A inhibitor. Potential drug interactions with this formulation include an increase in plasma levels of carbamazepine, SSRIs, desipramine, and trazodone. Dolutegravir is a substrate of UGT1A1 (primary pathway) and CYP3A (minor), but it is not thought to be an inducer or inhibitor of CYP3A (Adams et al., 2012).

INSTIs are generally well tolerated, although rash and gastrointestinal symptoms have been reported. Muscle weakness and elevations in creatine phosphokinase have occurred with raltegravir. The co-formulated product of elvitegravir, cobicistat, tenofovir, and emtricitabine has been shown to increase serum creatinine and decrease estimated creatinine clearance due to inhibition of tubular secretion of creatinine without affecting renal glomerular function (Lee and Carr, 2012). Table 42.5 outlines INSTI metabolism, inhibition, induction, interactions, and toxicities.

CCR5 ANTAGONISTS

Maraviroc is the only currently available CCR5 antagonist, and it acts by binding to the chemokine receptor CCR5, which is found on the surface of certain human cells and is required for entry of HIV into the host cell. Maraviroc prevents the HIV protein gp 120 from associating with the receptor, preventing cell entry. As some strains of HIV can utilize different co-receptors, such as CXCR4, a HIV tropism test must first be performed to determine if the drug will be effective (Perry, 2010).

Maraviroc is a substrate for CYP3A4, and a dose adjustment is required depending on whether maraviroc is given with drugs that are strong CYP3A inhibitors or inducers. Examples of drug interactions include rifampin and St. John's wort, which can markedly decrease serum levels of maraviroc. Voriconazole can increase levels. Maraviroc does not inhibit any of the major CYP enzymes at clinically relevant doses (Abel et al., 2009). Adverse effects of maraviroc include rash, hepatotoxicity, and orthostatic hypotension. Table 42.5 also outlines CCR5 metabolism, inhibition, induction, interactions, and toxicities.

FUSION INHIBITORS

Enfuvirtide is a synthetic peptide and currently the only available drug in this class. Enfuvirtide acts by preventing the fusion of virions to host cells by binding to gp41 and preventing the creation of an entry portal for the virus. The drug must be given by subcutaneous injection, twice daily. The inconvenience of twice-daily dosing and pain with injection have relegated enfuvirtide to use as a salvage drug. The drug is expected to undergo catabolism to its constituent amino acids, without significant drug–drug interactions (Zhang et al., 2004). Side effects include local injection site reactions, often leading to subcutaneous nodules (Haqqani and Tilton, 2013). Table

Table 42.4 NON-NUCLEOSIDE REVERSE TRANSCRIPTASE INHIBITORS (NNRTIS)

DRUG NAME	METABOLISM SITE(S)	ENZYME(S) INHIBITED	ENZYME(S) INDUCED	ABSORPTION AND FOOD CONSIDERATIONS	SIDE EFFECTS AND TOXICITIES	POTENTIAL DRUG–DRUG INTERACTIONS
NNRTI common features					Rash Asymptomatic elevation of liver associated enzymes Fat redistribution	CYP pan-inducers[c] may reduce serum levels of NNRTIs.
Delavirdine (Resciptor)	CYPs 3A4, 2D6, 2C9 2C19	CYPs 3A4, 2C9, 2D6, 2C19	None known	With or without food	See NNRTI common features.	See NNRTI common features. Delavirdine as a potent CYP3A4 inhibitor may increase serum levels of: *Antiarrhythmics* *Antipsychotics depend on CYP3A4* *Buspirone* *Carbamazepine* *Calcium channel blockers* *Cyclosporine* *Ergots* *Methadone* *Oral contraceptives* *Reboxetine* *Protease inhibitors* *Sildenafil* *Statins dependent on CYP3A4* *Trazodone* *Vilazodone* *TriazoloBZDs*[a] *Z hypnotics*[b]
Efavirenz (Sustiva)	CYPs 3A4, 2B6	CYPs 3A4, 2C9, 2C19, 2D6, 1A2	CYPs 3A4, 2B6, possibly UGTs	Take on an empty stomach, preferably at bedtime.	CNS (insomnia, vivid dreams, depression, euphoria, confusion, agitation, amnesia, hallucinations, stupor, altered cognition)	See NNRTI common features. Efavirenz as a dual CYP inhibitor and inducer may ↑ then ↓ levels of: *Antiarrhythmics* *Antipsychotics dependent on CYP3A4* *Buspirone* *Carbamazepine* *Calcium channel blockers* *Cyclosporine* *Ergots* *Methadone* *Oral contraceptives* *Reboxetine* *Protease inhibitors* *Sildenafil* *Statins dependent on CYP3A4* *Trazodone* *Vilazodone* *TriazoloBZDs*[a] *Z hypnotics*[b]

(continued)

Table 42.4 CONTINUED

DRUG NAME	METABOLISM SITE(S)	ENZYME(S) INHIBITED	ENZYME(S) INDUCED	ABSORPTION AND FOOD CONSIDERATIONS	SIDE EFFECTS AND TOXICITIES	POTENTIAL DRUG–DRUG INTERACTIONS
Etravirine (Intelence)	CYPs 2C9, 2C19, 3A4	CYPs 2C9, 2C19	CYP3A4		Stevens-Johnson syndrome, Atrial fibrillation, Hepatotoxicity, Pancreatitis, Hemolytic anemia, Seizures	See NNRTI common features
Nevirapine (Viramune)	CYPs 3A4, 2B6	None known	CYP3A4 (moderate), CYP2B6	High-fat meals increase bioavailability.	Hepatotoxicity	Nevirapine as a moderate CYP inducer may lower serum levels of: *Anti-arrhythmics, Beta-blockers, Bupropion, Carbamazepine, Calcium channel blockers, Cyclosporine, Oral contraceptives, Methadone, Oral contraceptives, Protease inhibitors, Statins, TriazoloBZDs[a], Zolpidem.* CYP inducers that may reduce serum levels of rilpivirine: *Oxcarbazepine, Pan-inhibitors[c], St. John's wort*
Rilpivirine (Edurant)	CYP3A4	None known	None known		Depression, Hepatotoxicity, Hyperlipidemia	See NNRTI common features. Absorption of rilpivirine is altered by: *Proton-pump inhibitors, Antacids.* CYP inducers that may reduce serum levels of rilpivirine: *Oxcarbazepine, Pan-inhibitors[c], St. John's wort*

Note: Primary route of metabolism listed first.
Bold CYP indicates **potent** inhibitor or inducer of that metabolic site.
Abbreviations: CNS, central nervous system; CYP, cytochrome; UGT, uridine 5′-diphosphate glucuronosyltransferase.
[a]Triazolobenzodiazepines: alprazolam (Xanax); midazolam (Versed); triazolam (Halcion).
[b]Z hypnotics: zaleplon, zolpidem, zopiclone.
[c]Pan-inducers: drugs that induce many if not all CYP P450 enzymes and include barbiturates, carbamazepine, ethanol, phenytoin, and rifamycins.

Table 42.5 INTEGRASE INHIBITORS, CCR5 ANTAGONISTS, FUSION INHIBITORS

DRUG NAME	METABOLISM SITE(S)	ENZYME(S) INHIBITED	ENZYME(S) INDUCED	ABSORPTION AND FOOD CONSIDERATIONS	SIDE EFFECTS AND TOXICITIES	POTENTIAL DRUG–DRUG INTERACTIONS
INTEGRASE INHIBITORS						
Common features	UGT1A1	None known	None known		Gastrointestinal Rash	Glucuronidation (UGT1A1) inhibitors that may increase integrase inhibitor serum levels: *Atazanavir* Glucuronidation (UGT1A1) inducers that may reduce integrase inhibitor serum levels: *Rifampin*
Dolutegravir (Tivicay)	UGT1A1, CYP3A	OCT2 transporter	None known	Aluminum-, calcium-, or magnesium-containing products reduce dolutegravir absorption.	Hepatotoxicity Myalgias Lipodystrophy Immune reconstitution syndrome	See Common features. Dolutegravir may increase serum levels due to inhibition of OCT-mediated transport of: *Dofetilide* *Metformin* CYP3A4 inducers that may reduce serum levels of dolutegravir, resulting in loss of viral suppression and increasing risk of viral resistance: *Oxcarbazepine* *Pan-inducers[d]* *St. John's wort* CYP3A4 inhibitors may increase serum levels of dolutegravir, worsening side effects and toxicities.
Elvitegravir/ cobicistat/ tenofovir/ emtricitabine (Stribild)	CYP3A4, UGT1A1/3 (elvitegravir) CYPs 3A, 2D6 (cobicistat)	CYP3A (cobicistat)	CYP2C9 (elvitegravir)		Elevated creatinine Lactic acidosis Steatohepatitis Hepatitis B exacerbation Osteomalacia (tenofovir)	See Common features. See Tenofovir and Emtricitabine for their DDIs. Cobicistat as a potent CYP3A4 inhibitor may increase serum levels of: *Antiarrhythmics* *Antipsychotics dependent on CYP3A4* *Buspirone* *Carbamazepine* *Calcium channel blockers* *Cyclosporine* *Ergots* *Methadone* *Oral contraceptives* *Reboxetine* *Protease inhibitors* *Sildenafil* *Statins dependent on CYP3A4[a]* *Trazodone* *Vilazodone* *TriazoloBZDs[b]* *Z hypnotics[c]*

(continued)

Table 42.5 CONTINUED

DRUG NAME	METABOLISM SITE(S)	ENZYME(S) INHIBITED	ENZYME(S) INDUCED	ABSORPTION AND FOOD CONSIDERATIONS	SIDE EFFECTS AND TOXICITIES	POTENTIAL DRUG–DRUG INTERACTIONS
						Oxcarbazepine *Pan-inducers[d]* *St. John's wort* CYP 3A4 Inhibitors may increase elvitegravir serum levels, worsening side effects and toxicities.
Dolutegravir/ lamivudine/ abacavir (Triumeq)	See individual drugs.	See individual drugs.	See individual drugs.		See individual drugs.	See individual drugs.
Raltegravir (Isentress)	UGT1A1	None known	None known		Muscle weakness/ myopathy Elevated transaminases Stevens-Johnson syndrome	Proton pump inhibitors may alter absorption.
CCR5 ANTAGONIST						
Maraviroc (Selzentry)	3A4	None known	None known		Rash Hepatotoxicity Orthostatic hypotension	Potent CYP3A4 inhibitors may increase maraviroc serum levels, worsening side effects and toxicities. CYP3A4 inducers that may reduce maraviroc serum levels: *Oxcarbazepine* *Pan-inducers[d]* *St. John's wort*
FUSION INHIBITOR						
Enfuvirtide (Fuzeon)	Likely hepatic and renal peptidases (not P450)	None known	None known	Subcutaneous injection	Injection site reactions Subcutaneous nodules	None known

Note: Primary route of metabolism listed first.
Bold CYP indicates **potent** inhibitor or inducer of that cytochrome P450 enzyme.
Abbreviations: CYP, cytochrome; DDIs, drug–drug interactions; OCT, organic cation transporter; UGT, uridine 5′-diphosphate glucuronosyltransferase.
[a]Statins: simvastatin, lovastatin, and atorvastatin.
[b]Triazolobenzodiazepines: alprazolam (Xanax); midazolam (Versed); triazolam (Halcion).
[c]Z hypnotics: zaleplon, zolpidem, zopiclone.
[d]Pan-inducers: drugs that induce many if not all CYP P450 enzymes and include barbiturates, carbamazepine, ethanol, phenytoin, and rifamycins.

42.5 outlines enfuvirtide's metabolism, inhibition, induction, interactions, and toxicities.

CO-FORMULATED ANTIRETROVIRAL DRUGS

In an effort to decrease the pill burden for patients, several pharmaceutical companies have developed pills that contain multiple active drugs. For patients infected with a virus that is not resistant to any of the component drugs, there are currently several options for a regimen consisting of one pill, once a day: Atripla® (efavirenz, tenofovir, and emtricitabine), Complera® (rilpivirine, tenofovir, and emtricitabine), Triumeq® (dolutegravir, lamivudine, and abacavir), Stribild® (elvitegravir, tenofovir, emtricitabine, and cobicistat), Genvoya® (elvitegravir, cobicistat, emtricitabine, and tenofovir alafenamide), and Odefsey® (emtricitabine, rilpivirine, and tenofovir alafenamide). Other co-formulated pills that might be used as part of a regimen are Combivir® (zidovudine and lamivudine), Trizivir® (abacavir, lamivudine, and zidovudine), Truvada® (tenofovir and emtricitabine), Epzicom® (abacavir and lamivudine), Descovy® (emtricitabine and tenofovir alafenamide), Evotaz® (atazanavir and cobicistat), and Prezcobix® (darunavir and cobicistat).

The decision as to which ART to prescribe to a particular patient is beyond the scope of this chapter, and interested readers are directed to reviews (DHHS Panel on Antiretroviral Guidelines for Adults and Adolescents, 2016; Gandhi and Gandhi, 2014).

CO-INFECTION OF HIV WITH HEPATITIS B AND/OR HEPATITIS C: TREATMENT OVERVIEW

Co-infection with hepatitis B (HBV) and HIV is fairly common, with approximately 10% of HIV-infected individuals in the United States having evidence of past or active infection. Co-infection with hepatitis C (HCV) is even more common, with an approximate 25% co-infection rate. The success of ART in turning HIV into a chronic illness and new developments in treatments for viral hepatitis have resulted in patients now receiving and tolerating both HIV and viral hepatitis treatment and many being cured of hepatitis C in about 3 months. This brief review summarizes the state of the field.

HIV-positive patients who are co-infected with HBV are at increased risk for developing chronic HBV infection and are at an increased risk for liver-related morbidity and mortality. To prevent HBV infection in persons with HIV, hepatitis B vaccination is recommended for all susceptible patients with HIV. Once infected, treatment of both HIV and HBV is recommended, and fortunately tenofovir, when used as part of an ART regimen (with at least two other HIV-active drugs), has efficacy in suppressing both HIV and HBV. Lamivudine and emtricitabine also have activity in suppressing HBV, but eventual viral resistance is common when they are used as monotherapy. Caution is advised when stopping or changing an ART regimen containing tenofovir, lamivudine, or emtricitabine in a HIV-HBV co-infected patient, as significant flares of HBV have been reported (Thio and Locarnini, 2007).

Similarly, HIV-positive patients who are co-infected with HCV have an accelerated progression of liver disease, higher rates of end-stage liver disease, and shortened lifespan after hepatic decompensation. The treatment of HCV in persons with HIV has been plagued by disappointing cure rates, but new developments in the field have revolutionized our approach (Gupta, 2013). Boceprevir and telaprevir were two first-generation HCV protease inhibitors approved for use in 2011, and when added to pegylated interferon/ribavirin they increased the sustained virological suppression from 29–45% to 63–74%. Both drugs have numerous potential drug interactions, including with several ART medications (Ilyas and Vierling, 2014). Newer agents with HCV activity have been released, including sofosbuvir (a polymerase inhibitor) and simeprevir (a NS3/4A protease inhibitor). Although initially approved for use individually with pegylated interferon/ribavirin, data have shown efficacy when used as dual therapy, without interferon/ribavirin (Lawitz et al., 2014), which eliminates the burden of interferon morbidities such as depression and other psychiatric complications. FDA approval of other direct-acting antiviral drugs with cure rates over 90%, such as Harvoni® (ledipasvir and sofosbuvir), Viekira Pak® (ombitasvir, paritaprevir, ritonavir, and dasabuvir), and Epclusa® (sofosbuvir and velpatasvir, which shows efficacy for multiple genotypes of hepatitis C), confirms that the era of effective all-oral therapies for hepatitis C has arrived and has revolutionized the treatment of hepatitis C. Please refer to Chapters 43 and 47 of this textbook for a detailed discussion of hepatitis B and C.

SUMMARY

Prescribing psychotropic medication or any other class of medications to persons with HIV who are on ART is a complicated undertaking. An understanding of potential drug–drug interactions is essential, and is helpful to the multidisciplinary team. Knowing the potential for drug interaction allows for more careful monitoring (as in the case of tricyclic antidepressants) or the choice of alternative treatments or precautions (such as emphasizing barrier precautions when certain HIV drugs are prescribed with oral contraceptive pills). Protease inhibitors are the most difficult antiretroviral drugs in terms of drug–drug interactions. All protease inhibitors are metabolized at CYP3A4 and are susceptible to inhibition and, more importantly, induction (i.e., lowered serum levels leading to viral resistance to ART). All protease inhibitors are inhibitors of 3A4 and can increase serum levels of medications dependent on 3A4 for metabolism (this is especially important for drugs with potential toxicity or narrow therapeutic windows). Ritonavir is a pan-inhibitor of multiple enzymes and an inducer of 3A4. This induction can lower serum levels of oral contraceptive pills, certain immunosuppressant drugs, and other medications. Other ART classes also impact drugs that utilize the P450 system. Recognition of ART drugs that impact the P450 enzymes 2D6 and 3A4 will help clinicians monitor medications with narrow therapeutic windows that depend on these metabolic pathways and help them ensure optimal care of patients with HIV.

PSYCHOTROPIC USE, EFFECTIVENESS, AND POTENTIAL DRUG INTERACTIONS IN THE CARE OF PERSONS WITH HIV

In some clinical settings, more than 50% of patients with HIV seeking medical care have a comorbid psychiatric disorder or substance use disorder (Gonzalez et al., 2011; Treisman et al., 2001). Additionally, ART has been associated with a decrease in severity of depression (Brechtl et al., 2001), mania, delirium, and psychosis (Blank et al., 2013). The following sections include reviews of the use and effectiveness of psychotropics in the care of persons with HIV, as well as discussion of metabolic pathways and potential drug interactions, highlighted with clinical examples. Most interactions may be predicted by using the tables to follow. At the time of this publication, some reliable, complete, and free sources of information about ART and potential drug interactions may be found at:

http://www.hiv-druginteractions.org/Interactions.aspx
http://www.hiv-druginteractions.org/PrintableCharts.aspx
http://hivinsite.ucsf.edu/InSite
http://www.hivclinic.ca/main/drugs_interact.html
http://www.hiv-druginteractions.org/Interactions.aspx

ANTIDEPRESSANTS

The use of antidepressants for the treatment of mood disorders and/or pain in persons with HIV in many ways mirrors that of non-HIV-infected patients. In particular, the frequent use of polypharmacy as well as multimorbid illnesses closely mirrors the situation in geriatric medicine (Arseniou et al., 2014; Goldstein and Goodnick, 1998). Effective treatment is important, since comorbid mood disorders increase the risk of nonadherence to medical care (DiMatteo et al., 2000; Nakimuli-Mpungu et al., 2013; Nel and Kagee, 2013), and nonadherence to ART increases the risk for viral resistance and HIV treatment failure (Gonzalez et al., 2011). Most antidepressants have been found to be clinically effective in the treatment of depression in persons with HIV, despite the paucity of formal, robust clinical trials of each medication or medication class. Many clinicians advocate, therefore, that the selection of antidepressants for persons with HIV be based on medication adverse-effect profiles, comorbid symptomatology, and the potential for drug–drug interactions.

The available literature on effectiveness is reviewed here, followed by discussions of important pharmacodynamic and pharmacokinetic considerations for each class of antidepressants. SSRIs are presented first, as they are the most commonly used medication in the treatment of depression in persons with HIV. The rest of available antidepressants are reviewed by class, not necessarily in order of effectiveness or common usage. Table 42.6 presents the antidepressants in alphabetical order, both by and within each category/class.

SELECTIVE SEROTONIN REUPTAKE INHIBITORS (SSRIS)

Selective serotonin reuptake inhibitors are generally first-line medication choices for treating and managing depression, anxiety, and panic disorder in medically ill patients, including persons with HIV (Arseniou et al., 2014). In 1997, Ferrando and colleagues performed a small, 6-week open-label trial using fluoxetine, sertraline, and paroxetine. All improved depressive symptoms, but differences among the SSRIs could not be elicited with this design. Interestingly, there was a statistically significant improvement (up to 80%) in somatic symptoms.

In addition to SSRIs' general effectiveness in treating depression, HIV-associated neurocognitive disorders (HAND) may improve with SSRIs, by treating depression as well as providing neurocognitive protection from toxic byproducts of HIV replication and neuroinflammation (Ances et al., 2008). There is also evidence that SSRIs may have positive effects on immune function in persons with HIV. Recent ex vivo studies have demonstrated that HIV replication in latently infected cell lines is hampered significantly by escitalopram, supported by evidence that HIV suppression by natural killer cells may be enhanced with SSRIs like escitalopram. Additionally, SSRIs may also inhibit acute infection of macrophages by the HIV virus. Further in vivo study is necessary (Benton et al., 2010).

Citalopram and Escitalopram

Effectiveness/Uses
Citalopram and escitalopram are commonly used in treating persons with HIV. There are currently no robust clinical trials in the literature regarding citalopram and escitalopram in the treatment of depression in persons with HIV. A recent, randomized, placebo-controlled study of the efficacy of escitalopram in 100 South African patients with HIV and depression (Hoare et al., 2014) found no difference in response to escitalopram than with placebo, but this seems to be due to a large placebo response, most likely because the study conditions (treatment and placebo) were markedly different from usual treatment. This report also did not indicate what, if any, ART the subjects were receiving, so results may also have been confounded by better adherence to ART in some or all subjects in the study. Despite the lack of clinical trials, at this time, citalopram and escitalopram are the SSRIs of choice for the treatment of depression in persons with HIV, as reported in the consensus survey of the Organization of AIDS Psychiatry (now known as the Academy of Psychosomatic Medicine Special Interest Group on HIV Psychiatry) (Freudenreich et al., 2010), because of their general lack of drug–drug interactions and favorable adverse-effect profile.

In the treatment of patients co-infected with HIV-HCV with interferon, depressive disorders were a commonly encountered complication. Laguno and colleagues (2004) studied interferon-alpha-induced depression in 113 patients with chronic HIV-HCV who did not suffer from major depression before interferon-alpha therapy. Forty-five (40%) patients developed depressive symptoms, and 20 of these

Table 42.6 ANTIDEPRESSANTS IN HIV CARE

ANTIDEPRESSANT	METABOLISM SITE(S)	METABOLIC ENZYME(S) INHIBITED	CLINICAL CONSIDERATIONS	POTENTIAL DRUG–DRUG INTERACTIONS WITH ART
SELECTIVE SEROTONIN REUPTAKE INHIBITORS (SSRIS)				
SSRI common features	Most metabolized at CYP2D6	No inducers in this class	Common side effects: Apathy Carbohydrate craving GI upset Serotonin syndrome Sexual dysfunction SIADH Withdrawal syndrome	Potent CYP2D6 inhibitors may increase serum levels of SSRIs, increasing side effects.
Citalopram (Celexa)	CYPs 2C19, 2D6, 3A4 Transporter ABCB1	CYP2D6 ABCB1	Potential for arrhythmia in doses over 60 mg (or if inhibited or "boosted" by pan-inhibitor PIs like ritonavir)	Lower potential for clinical interactions with ART Keep dosage at/below 40 mg/day if on CYP2D6 inhibiting: Ritonavir RIT/lopinavir Efavirenz
Escitalopram (Lexapro)	CYPs 2C19, 2D6, 3A4 Transporter ABCB1	CYP2D6	Potential for arrhythmia in doses over 60 mg (or if inhibited or "boosted" by pan-inhibitor PIs like ritonavir)	Lower potential for clinical interactions with ART Keep dosage at/below 20 mg/day if on CYP2D6 inhibiting: Ritonavir RIT/lopinavir Efavirenz
Fluoxetine (Prozac)	CYPs 2C9, 2C19, 2D6, 3A4 Transporter ABCB1	CYPs 2D6, 2C19, 2B6, 2C9, 3A4, 1A2 ABCB1		Very long-acting active metabolite Potent CYPs 2D6 and 2C19 inhibition by fluoxetine may increase serum levels of: Antiarrhythmics Cobicistat (in Stribild) Metoprolol Oxycodone Phenobarbital Phenytoin SSRIs Tramadol Tricyclic antidepressants First-generation antipsychotics
Fluvoxamine (Luvox)	CYPs 1A2, 2D6 Transporter ABCB1	CYPs 1A2, 2C19, 2B6, 2C9, 3A4b, 2D6 ABCB1	Known for many intolerable side effects in persons with HIV	Potent CYP 1A2 and 2C19 inhibition by fluvoxamine may increase serum levels of: Caffeine Olanzapine Phenytoin

(continued)

Table 42.6 CONTINUED

ANTIDEPRESSANT	METABOLISM SITE(S)	METABOLIC ENZYME(S) INHIBITED	CLINICAL CONSIDERATIONS	POTENTIAL DRUG–DRUG INTERACTIONS WITH ART
Paroxetine (Paxil)	CYPs 2D6, 3A4	CYPs 2D6, 2B6, 3A4, 2C19, 1A2	Sedating Weight gain Most severe withdrawal syndrome, especially in neonates	Potent CYP 2D6 and 2B6 inhibition by paroxetine may increase serum levels of: Antiarrhythmics Bupropion Metoprolol Oxycodone SSRIs Tramadol Tricyclic antidepressants Typical antipsychotics Potent CYP pan-inhibitors like ritonavir may increase serum levels of paroxetine.
Sertraline (Zoloft)	CYPs 2B6, 2C9, 2C19, 2D6, 3A4 UGT2B7, UGT1A1 Transporter ABCB1	CYPs 2D6, 2B6, 2C9, 2C19, 3A4, 1A2 ABCB1		Least potential for clinical interactions with ART, but becomes a more potent CYP2D6 inhibitor at doses >200 mg/day
SELECTIVE NOREPINEPHRINE REUPTAKE INHIBITORS (SNRIS)				
Desvenlafaxine (Pristiq)	UGT CYP3A4	CYP2D6	Potential for: Hypertension Weight gain Sexual dysfunction	CYP2D6 inhibition will increase serum levels of metoprolol and other CYP2D6-dependent medications.
Duloxetine (Cymbalta)	CYPs 1A2, 2D6	CYP2D6	Potential for: Hypertension Sexual dysfunction Weight gain	CYP2D6 inhibition will increase serum levels of metoprolol and other CYP2D6-dependent medications.
Levomilnacipran (Fetmiza)	CYPs 3A4 (primary), 2C8, 2C19, 2D6	None known	Weight neutral Potential for: Hypertension Sexual dysfunction	Potent CYP3A4 inhibitors like PIs may increase serum levels of levomilnacipran
Milnacipran (Savella)	Renal excretion Unchanged: (50-60%) Conjugation: (20-30%) CYP3A4: (10%)	None known	Weight neutral Potential for: Hypertension Sexual dysfunction	Lower potential for pharmacokinetic interactions with ART
Venlafaxine (Effexor)	CYP2D6, 2C19, 3A4	CYP2D6 CYP3A4	Potential for: Hypertension Sexual dysfunction Weight gain	Potent CYP pan-inhibitors like ritonavir may increase serum levels of venlafaxine.

NOVEL ANTIDEPRESSANTS

Drug	Metabolized by	Inhibits/Induces	Features/Side effects	ART Interactions
Mirtazapine (Remeron)	CYP1A2, 2D6, 3A4 glucuronidation	None known	Weight gain, Anti-nausea, Sedating, May be protective with JC virus	Least potential for clinical interactions with ART
Nefazodone (Serzone)	CYP3A4, 2D6	CYP3A4	Brand Serzone not available in the U.S.	Potent CYP3A4 inhibitors like nefazodone may increase serum levels of: PIs, Rilpivirine, Maraviroc
Reboxetine	CYP3A4	CYP2D6, 3A4 Transporters	Not available in the U.S.	Potent CYP3A4 inhibitors like PIs may increase serum levels and potent CYP3A4 inducers may decrease serum levels of reboxetine.
Trazodone (Deseryl)	CYP3A4	None known	Sedating, often used as sleep aid	Potent CYP3A4 inhibitors like PIs may increase serum levels and potent CYP3A4 inducers may reduce serum levels of trazodone.
Vilazodone (Viibryd)	CYP3A4	Mild induction of CYP2C19	No data for persons with HIV; Must take with food for full absorption	Potent CYP3A4 inhibitors like PIs may increase serum levels and potent CYP3A4 inducers may reduce serum levels of vilazodone.
Vortioxetine (Brintellix)	CYPs 2D6, 2B6, 3A4, 2C9, 2C19, 2A6, 2C8	None known	No data for persons with HIV	Potent CYP pan-inhibitors like ritonavir may increase serum levels of vortioxetine. CYP pan-inducers[a] may affect vortioxetine serum levels.

TRICYCLIC ANTIDEPRESSANTS (TCAS)

Drug	Metabolized by	Inhibits/Induces	Features/Side effects	ART Interactions
TCA Common Features	All use CYP2D6, many use CYP3A4	Most are only mild inhibitors of CYPs	Multiple side effects: Constipation, Dry mouth, Weight gain, Toxicities: Arrhythmia, Potential for anticholinergic delirium	All protease inhibitors may increase TCA serum levels to toxicity, especially pan-inhibitors. CYP pan-inducers[a] may reduce TCA serum levels. Use therapeutic drug monitoring.
Amitriptyline (Elavil)	CYPs 1A2, 2C19, 2D6, 3A4 UGT1A4	CYPs 1A2, 2C19, 2D6	Active metabolite = nortriptyline	See TCA common features.
Clomipramine (Anafranil)	CYPs 1A2, 2C19, 2D6, 3A4	CYPs 2D6, 1A2, 2C19	Has indication for OCD	See TCA common features.
Desipramine (Norpramin)	CYP2D6	CYPs 2D6, 2C19		Least affected by PIs, except the pan-inhibitors ritonavir and lopinavir, which may increase serum levels of desipramine
Doxepin (Adapin, Sinequan)	CYPs 1A2, 2D6, 2C19, 3A4 UGT1A3, UGT1A4	CYPs 1A2, 2C19, 2D6		See TCA common features.

(continued)

Table 42.6 CONTINUED

ANTIDEPRESSANT	METABOLISM SITE(S)	METABOLIC ENZYME(S) INHIBITED	CLINICAL CONSIDERATIONS	POTENTIAL DRUG–DRUG INTERACTIONS WITH ART
Imipramine (Tofranil)	CYPs1A2, 2C19, 2D, 3A4 UGT1A3, UGT1A4	CYPs 2C19, 2D6	Active metabolite = desipramine	See TCA common features.
Nortriptyline (Pamelor)	CYP2D6	CYPs 2D6, 2C19	Therapeutic window = 50–150 ng/dl	Least affected by PIs, except the pan-inhibitors ritonavir and lopinavir, which may increase serum levels of nortriptyline
Protriptyline (Vivactil)	CYP2D6	None known		Least affected by PIs, except the pan-inhibitors ritonavir and lopinavir, which may increase serum levels of protriptyline
Trimipramine (Surmontil)	CYPs 2C19, 2D6, 3A4	None known		See TCA common features.

Note: Primary route of metabolism listed first.

Bold CYP indicates **potent** inhibitor or inducer of that cytochrome P450 enzyme.

Abbreviations: ABCB, ATP binding cassette B transporter (p-glycoprotein transporter); ART, antiretroviral therapy; CYP, cytochrome; GI, gastrointestinal; PI, protease inhibitor; SIADH, syndrome of inappropriate antidiuretic hormone secretion; UGT, uridine 5'-diphosphate glucuronosyltransferase.

[a]Pan-inducers: drugs that induce many if not all CYP P450 enzymes and include barbiturates, carbamazepine, ethanol, phenytoin, and rifamycins.

individuals were treated with citalopram. Ninety-five percent of the citalopram-treated patients responded, and there were no reported drug–drug interactions or adverse events. Another small (N = 20), open-label, flexible-dose study also had favorable results (Currier et al., 2004). A more recent (Klein et al., 2014) small (N = 76, 36 citalopram, 40 placebo), multicenter, randomized, double-blind, placebo-controlled study of citalopram attempted to determine if citalopram pre- or co-treatment would improve adherence to medical therapy, as well as reduce the incidence of depression in patients co-infected with HIV-HCV who were on interferon/ribavirin therapy. In this study, pretreatment with citalopram did not improve adherence, reduce depression that affected HIV-HCV treatment, or significantly reduce depressive symptoms. All treated subjects had moderate to mild depressive symptoms. Importantly, there were no medically significant drug–drug interactions or adverse effects in the treatment group, and the citalopram group had fewer adverse psychiatric episodes (overdoses, psychosis, alcohol intoxication) than the placebo group.

Pharmacokinetics and Drug–Drug Interactions

Citalopram and escitalopram are metabolized at CYPs 2C19, 2D6, and 3A4, and they are very weak inhibitors of CYP2D6 (unlike fluoxetine, paroxetine, and high-dose sertraline, which are potent inhibitors of 2D6). Citalopram and escitalopram's use of multiple metabolic sites is a plus when co-administered with potent inhibitors of CYP3A4 (such as protease inhibitors) and CYP2D6 (delavirdine and efavirenz). However, tipranavir and ritonavir are pan-inhibitors which inhibit all of the metabolic sites of citalopram and escitalopram, placing patients at risk of worsened side effects and toxicities such as arrhythmias and serotonin syndrome. Pan-inducers such as alcohol, barbiturates, rifamycins, some antiepileptics, and ritonavir may reduce serum levels of SSRIs, leading to ineffectiveness.

CASE B: SSRIS AND ART

A 46-year-old woman with HIV, HCV with cirrhosis, and depression presented with nausea, confusion, hyperreflexia, diaphoresis, myoclonus, and rigidity after darunavir, ritonavir, and emtricitabine/tenofovir were added to her standing escitalopram and after she had recently started on esomeprazole (I Lorenzi et al., 2012).

This case highlights how even an SSRI considered first line for persons with HIV, because of its safety profile and multiple metabolic routes, can have its metabolism affected by polypharmacy. Darunavir inhibits CYP3A4, ritonavir inhibits CYPs 2D6, 3A4, and 2C19, and esomeprazole inhibits the metabolism of CYP2C19. Even without her documented genetic polymorphisms at CYP2D6 and CYP2C19, which placed her at increased risk, this drug–drug interaction could have been predicted.

Fluoxetine

Effectiveness/Uses

Since fluoxetine is the oldest SSRI, there are considerable data to support its use in patients with HIV, both for depressive symptoms and for decreasing cocaine cravings (Batki et al., 1993; Cazzullo et al., 1998; Hill and Lee, 2013; Levine et al., 1990). Early data comparing efficacy of fluoxetine to that of imipramine showed comparable results and greater tolerability (Rabkin, Rabkin, et al., 1994). The first large double-blind, placebo-controlled trial involving an SSRI compared fluoxetine to placebo (Rabkin et al., 1999) and found fluoxetine to be more effective than placebo, despite a large placebo effect. Fluoxetine, because of its long half-life and active metabolite, may be useful in patients who have difficulty remembering to take their medication on a daily basis, despite its potential to cause drug interactions via inhibition of multiple metabolic cytochromes. Fluoxetine is commonly activating, and it may be useful in patients with HIV- or ART-related fatigue. Like all SSRIs, insomnia, gastrointestinal side effects, and sexual dysfunction may need to be addressed; without prompt attention and patient support, they may lead to medication discontinuation.

Pharmacokinetics and Drug–Drug Interactions

See Table 42.6.

Fluvoxamine

Effectiveness/Uses

Fluvoxamine has not been well tolerated in patients with HIV and is not recommended for routine use. The only published study had a 63% discontinuation rate, due to insomnia, gastrointestinal disturbance, anorexia, behavioral changes, and sedation (Grassi et al., 1995).

Pharmacokinetics and DDIs

See Table 42.6. Fluvoxamine is extensively metabolized by CYPs 1A2 and 2D6 and is a potent inhibitor of CYPs 1A2 and 2C19, and a moderate inhibitor of many others, which includes most of the enzymes responsible for metabolizing antiretrovirals and antimicrobials in general.

Paroxetine

Effectiveness/Uses

Elliot and colleagues (1998) showed equivalent efficacy in a randomized, placebo-controlled trial comparing paroxetine and imipramine in persons with HIV. Paroxetine was better tolerated, but there was a significant attrition rate from both treatment and placebo groups, and the sample size was small. Paroxetine may be useful in patients with insomnia as it is one of the more sedating SSRIs. In addition, there are in vitro data to suggest that paroxetine may also have antiviral activity and may work synergistically with ART (Kristiansen and Hansen, 2000). Paroxetine's significant withdrawal syndrome, which includes autonomic instability and influenza-like symptoms, may be problematic for nonadherent patients and for neonates of mothers taking paroxetine (Thormhalen, 2006).

Pharmacokinetics and Drug–Drug Interactions

Paroxetine is a very potent inhibitor of CYP2D6 and will increase serum levels of medications dependent on 2D6 for metabolism, such as metoprolol. It is dependent mostly on just

CYP2D6 and CYP3A4 for metabolism, so use with ART is more difficult than for other SSRIs, as most protease inhibitors and many NNRTIs affect these metabolic sites.

Sertraline

Effectiveness/Uses

Sertraline has an advantageous side-effect profile compared with that of many other antidepressants, and it is very safe in overdose (Hansen et al., 2005). The first study of sertraline in patients with HIV and depression was a small, open-label trial conducted in 1994. The results were quite impressive, showing a 70% response rate and a dropout rate of 18% (Rabkin, Wagner, et al., 1994).

Pharmacokinetics and Drug–Drug Interactions

Sertraline does not seem to have the potential for cardiac arrhythmias in higher doses, as seen with citalopram and escitalopram. But at doses >200 mg/day, it acts as a potent inhibitor of CYP2D6 and carries the same warnings as paroxetine and fluoxetine when co-administered with CYP2D6-dependent medications with a narrow therapeutic window, such as metoprolol.

NOVEL ANTIDEPRESSANTS

Bupropion

Effectiveness/Uses

Patients without HIV infection with central nervous system (CNS) pathology, such as traumatic brain injury, seizures, or CNS opportunistic infections or metastases, or who are at risk for alcohol or benzodiazepine withdrawal are not good candidates for bupropion use because of bupropion's propensity to lower the seizure threshold. By definition, persons with HIV have a CNS illness, and individuals with a previous history of seizures or who are severely immunocompromised and at risk for secondary seizures may not be candidates for bupropion use, even for smoking cessation. Careful monitoring when using lower doses of bupropion (preferably of the longer-acting formulation) would be prudent in persons with HIV. A small (N = 20), open-label 6-week trial of bupropion in HIV-positive patients with major depression showed relatively good efficacy, with 60% of patients responding, while 25% of patients dropped out because of intolerable side effects. No changes in the CD4 count or drug toxicity were noted (Currier et al., 2003).

Pharmacokinetics and Drug–Drug Interactions

Bupropion's use may be limited because of potential for drug interactions with antiretrovirals. Bupropion is primarily metabolized by the minor P450 enzyme 2B6 (Hesse et al., 2001). Nelfinavir, ritonavir, and efavirenz are all inhibitors of this enzyme. Since bupropion has the potential to lower the seizure threshold at high doses, there is a potential for bupropion to become toxic when co-administered with CYP2B6 inhibitors. A case series (Park-Wyllie and Antoniou,

2003) examining concomitant use of these agents for as long as 2 years found no recorded episodes of seizures. Although encouraging, no pharmacokinetic data were available, and none of the patients were on high-dose ritonavir. Bupropion serum concentrations may be reduced by CYP2B6 metabolic induction, as evidenced by both low and high daily doses of ritonavir, and routine doses of efavirenz (Robertson et al., 2008) in healthy volunteers (Park et al., 2010). Bupropion dosage may need to be increased (up to recommended maximum dose) with mixed inhibitor/inducers such as ritonavir.

Mirtazapine

Effectiveness/Uses

Mirtazapine is a 5HT2A, 5HT3, and alpha-2-adrenergic receptor antagonist and effectively crosses the blood–brain barrier. Mirtazapine may have a niche in the treatment of AIDS wasting syndrome, as it can reduce nausea through 5HT3 blockade and promote weight gain and improved sleep through its antihistaminergic effects (Badowski and Pandit, 2014; Elliott and Roy-Byrne, 2000). 5HT2A is also a cellular receptor for the JC virus (JCV), the causative agent of progressive multifocal leukoencephalopathy (PML), and there is case evidence that mirtazapine may reduce the proliferation of JCV (Lanzafame et al., 2009). Like most antidepressants, mirtazapine has been associated with hepatotoxicity (Hui et al., 2002). Clinically, mirtazapine is known to improve anxious depression and to improve sleep, appetite, and weight gain, often useful side effects in the treatment of persons with HIV.

Pharmacokinetics and Drug–Drug Interactions

Mirtazapine is metabolized at multiple P450 enzymes, so it is less prone to pharmacokinetic drug interactions unless co-administered with pan-inhibitors like ritonavir.

Reboxetine

Effectiveness/Uses

Reboxetine is a selective norepinephrine reuptake inhibitors (SNRI), yet has some mild serotonin reuptake inhibition as well. Currently unavailable in the United States, the data from Europe suggest efficacy in patients without medical comorbidity. It is similar to atomoxetine in norepinephrine receptor and G protein–gated inwardly rectifying potassium (GIRK) channel activity (Kobayashi et al., 2010). There is one small (N = 20), open-label study that suggests good efficacy for depression in patients with HIV (Carvalhal et al., 2003). Constipation, dry mouth, and blurry vision are common side effects, as are insomnia, agitation, and dizziness, which may be difficult to manage in medically ill patients (Mago et al., 2014).

Pharmacokinetics and Drug–Drug Interactions

Since reboxetine is metabolized at CYP3A4, is a weak inhibitor of CYP2D6 and CYP3A4, and is a moderate inhibitor of transporters/P-glycoprotein, interactions are possible with

ART, although there are no reports to date (Kobayashi et al., 2010; Wienkers et al., 1999).

Trazodone

Effectiveness/Uses

An older study found that trazodone was slightly more effective than the benzodiazepine clorazepate for HIV patients with adjustment disorder. Although this study failed to achieve statistical significance, it highlights trazodone's sedative and anti-anxiety effects (Markowitz et al., 1998), without the abuse or dependence risks of benzodiazepines (De Wit et al., 1999).

Pharmacokinetics and Drug–Drug Interactions

In a single-dose, blinded, four-way crossover study of healthy volunteers, Greenblatt et al. (2003) found that ritonavir significantly increased trazodone plasma concentration, which in turn increased sedation and fatigue and impaired performance on the digit-symbol substitution test. Inhibition of CYP2D6 may lead to preferential accumulation of trazodone's metabolite, mCPP, which has been linked to neurotoxic and hepatotoxic reactions.

SEROTONIN AND NOREPINEPHRINE REUPTAKE INHIBITORS (SNRIS)

Desvenlafaxine, Venlafaxine, and Duloxetine

Effectiveness/Uses

Desvenlafaxine, venlafaxine, and duloxetine may have a role in treating persons with HIV, as these drugs have demonstrated effectiveness for depression, obsessive-compulsive disorder, and somatic symptoms in those without HIV. Their effectiveness, however, has not been systematically studied in persons with HIV. Their common side effects of sexual dysfunction, insomnia, dry mouth, and weight gain, as well as potential toxicities such as blood pressure alterations, hepatotoxicity, and serotonin syndrome need to be considered in their clinical use for persons with HIV.

Pharmacokinetics and Drug–Drug Interactions

Venlafaxine utilizes cytochromes 3A4 and 2D6. Desvenlafaxine is mostly metabolized via glucuronidation (uridine diphosphate–glucuronosyltransferase enzymes [UGTs]) and CYP3A4. Protease inhibitors, especially pan-inhibitors such as ritonavir, may possibly raise serum levels of venlafaxine. It is possible that potent inhibitors of CYP3A4, such as all protease inhibitors, and inducers of glucuronidation, such as ritonavir, may theoretically affect serum levels of desvenlafaxine, but there are no data to date. Venlafaxine and desvenlafaxine are mild inhibitors of 2D6 and 3A4 (von Moltke et al., 1997) and have low potential to increase serum levels of medications dependent on 2D6 and 3A4 for metabolism; no reports of such interactions with ART have been made to date. Interestingly, in healthy volunteers, indinavir and venlafaxine co-administration did not significantly affect serum levels of venlafaxine, but venlafaxine did modestly decrease the area under the concentration curve (AUC) and maximum plasma concentration (C_{max}) of indinavir, perhaps due to effects on p-glycoproteins (Levin et al., 2001). This finding was not reproduced in a more recent study using the newer, extended-release venlafaxine and desvenlafaxine products in healthy volunteers (Jann et al., 2012). Although the earlier report was a small study of healthy volunteers and has not been replicated in the literature, any decrease in the plasma concentration of a protease inhibitor may place a patient at risk for treatment failure. It seems prudent, therefore, that immediate-release venlafaxine should be used with caution in combination with protease inhibitors. Duloxetine is metabolized at CYP1A2 and CYP2D6. Potent 2D6 inhibitors, such as ritonavir, have the potential to increase serum levels of duloxetine, although no reports of such interactions have been found to date.

Milnacipran

Effectiveness/Uses

Milnacipran has a threefold greater potency in inhibiting norepinephrine reuptake in vitro (Vaishnavi et al., 2004) compared with serotonin reuptake, whereas duloxetine and venlafaxine are more potent inhibitors of serotonin reuptake than of norepinephrine reuptake. There are no studies of this drug's use in persons with HIV, but its metabolic and side-effect profile suggest that it is a medication worth considering in persons with pain/fibromyalgia and depression.

Pharmacokinetics and Drug–Drug Interactions

Milnacipran is mostly cleared by the kidney, and it is minimally metabolized by CYP3A4, so it is little influenced by cytochrome genetic polymorphisms, inhibitors, and inducers (Paris et al., 2009; Spina et al., 2012).

Levomilnacipran

Effectiveness/Uses

Levomilnacipran is an SNRI with twice the potency for norepinephrine versus serotonin reuptake inhibition. Side effects include nausea, vomiting, constipation, palpitations, sexual dysfunction, and excessive sweating, and, like the other SNRIs, blood pressure alterations (Mago et al., 2014). There are no reports of studies of its use in persons with HIV at this time.

SSRI AND 5-HT RECEPTOR MODULATORS

"Multimodal" antidepressants, such as SSRI and 5-HT agonist/antagonists, may modulate glutamate indirectly and have an effect on both depression and impaired cognition (Pehrson and Sanchez, 2014), which may be an important treatment niche for persons with HIV.

Vilazodone

Effectiveness/Uses

Vilazodone is an antidepressant with activity as a combined SSRI and a partial agonist at the serotonin 5-HT1A receptor, best administered with food to achieve full bioavailability

(Choi et al., 2012). Its side-effect profile is similar to that of the SSRIs, and it is considered weight neutral. There is no literature about its use in persons with HIV.

Pharmacokinetics and Drug–Drug Interactions
Vilazodone is dependent on CYP3A4 for its metabolism, and dosage reduction to 20 mg (half dose) is recommended when taken with strong CYP3A4 inhibitors like ketoconazole or protease inhibitors, efavirenz and delavirdine (Boinpally et al., 2014; Forest Pharmaceuticals, 2014; Laughren et al., 2011). When co-administered with potent CYP3A4 inducers like carbamazepine (Boinpally et al., 2014), doses of up to 80 mg/day may be necessary. Careful monitoring of effectiveness is warranted when used with mixed inhibitors/inducers such as ritonavir. Further study and clinical experience are needed in medically ill patients and in persons with HIV.

Vortioxetine

Effectiveness/Uses
There are no studies in persons with HIV/AIDS.

Pharmacokinetics and Drug–Drug Interactions
Vortioxetine benefits from metabolism at many cytochromes. It is primarily metabolized by CYP2D6, but also utilizes CYPs 3A4, 2B6, 2C9, 2C19, 2A6, and 2C8 (Hvenegaard et al., 2012), and vortioxetine is not an inhibitor or inducer of any cytochromes or transporters. Co-administration with the pan-inducer rifampicin reduced serum levels of vortioxetine. In healthy volunteers, these interactions were modest (Chen et al., 2013). It is possible that ritonavir or efavirenz may interact with vortioxetine, requiring alterations in antidepressant dosing, but, importantly, vortioxetine is not expected to affect ART metabolism and may be helpful with depression and cognition. Further study and clinical experience are needed with medically ill patients and persons with HIV/AIDS.

TRICYCLIC ANTIDEPRESSANTS

Effectiveness/Uses

Tricyclic antidepressants (TCAs) were among the first psychotropics studied for depression in persons with HIV. Prior to the advent of ART, imipramine was found to be effective in multiple studies of HIV patients without the diagnosis of AIDS (Manning et al., 1990; Rabkin and Harrison, 1990). There was a high rate of discontinuation, mostly because of side effects or increased pill burden. Markowitz and colleagues compared various forms of psychotherapy to a combination of supportive psychotherapy with imipramine and found that patients had significantly greater improvement in symptoms with imipramine than with supportive psychotherapy or cognitive-behavioral therapy alone. There was a slight but not statistically significant improvement over interpersonal psychotherapy (Markowitz et al., 1998). Desipramine was shown to be as effective as amitriptyline in men with AIDS, and side effects were not appreciably different (Fernandez et al., 1988). HIV-associated neuropathies, whether virus or treatment induced,

are extraordinarily difficult to treat. Despite little research data on efficacy in HIV neuropathy, patients with HIV may be treated with TCAs for neuropathic pain (Gabbai et al., 2013). There is a case report of the effective use of amitriptyline to treat efavirenz-induced nightmares (Koppel and Bharel, 2005).

Pharmacokinetics and Drug–Drug Interactions

While many clinicians avoid TCAs for fear of anticholinergic side effects, tachycardia, hypotension, and toxicity in overdose, this class remains effective in this treatment population (Razali and Hasanah, 1999). Importantly, it is possible to use TCA side effects to clinical advantage, especially in patients who have diarrhea, weight loss, insomnia, or a comorbid pain disorder. Despite the potential for toxicity due to drug–drug interactions, therapeutic drug monitoring and clinical observation allow for safe use in combination with HIV medications. Tricyclic antidepressants have a narrow therapeutic window and significant cardiotoxicity in overdose. All tricyclics utilize CYP2D6 as well as CYP3A4 and others for metabolism. Potent pan-inhibitors like ritonavir may lead to tricyclic toxicity, but the risk is reduced if therapeutic drug monitoring is utilized (Abb Vie Pharmaceuticals, 2013; Bertz et al., 1996; Ostad et al., 2012).

CASE C: TRICYCLIC ANTIDEPRESSANTS AND ART

A 37-year-old HIV-positive man with severe depression was started on nortriptyline, reaching serum levels of 87 ng/dl with some improvement in symptoms. His infectious disease clinician started him on ritonavir and saquinavir, and the patient missed a repeat tricyclic serum level in 5–7 days. The patient returned 1 month later, noting worsened sleep, irritability, depressed mood, suicidal ideation, constipation, and dry mouth. Serum tricyclic level at that time was 203 ng/dl (therapeutic: 50–150 ng/dl).

In this case, ritonavir's potent inhibition of CYPs 2D6, 3A4, 2C9, and 2C19 raised nortriptyline levels (metabolized in part by 2D6 and others) beyond the therapeutic window, losing efficacy and worsening side effects of nortriptyline (author KLC, unpublished clinical case).

MAOIS

Traditional MAOIs have not been in use with persons with HIV, mostly due to the risk of pharmacodynamic interactions. There have been a few studies to determine if transdermal selegiline is beneficial or "neuroprotective" for HIV-associated cognitive dysfunction, without clear evidence of benefit (Sacktor et al., 2000; Schifitto et al., 2007; Schifitto, Yiannoutsos, et al., 2009) There is little clinical experience and no literature on the use of MAOIs with ART or in persons with HIV/AIDS.

SUMMARY OF ANTIDEPRESSANTS FOR PERSONS WITH HIV/AIDS

The most commonly used antidepressants for persons with HIV/AIDS are SSRIs, such as sertraline, citalopram, and escitalopram, which are effective and may be the safest in regard to drug interactions, since these "safer" SSRIs do not potently inhibit or induce any CYP enzymes at standard doses. Prescribers must be aware that SSRIs are mostly metabolized at CYP2D6 and CYP3A4, with 3A4 potently inhibited by all protease inhibitors, and both 2D6 and 3A4 inhibited by ritonavir. Patients taking SSRIs plus ritonavir and any combination or "boosted" regimen with ritonavir may develop worsened side effects (gastrointestinal and sexual effects, insomnia, jitteriness) and also serotonin syndrome, a constellation of symptoms including mental status changes, diarrhea, and myoclonus (DeSilva et al., 2001). Additionally, even the "safer" SSRIs may be problematic in persons with HIV who are on ART as well as other medications (see Case B). In treating persons with HIV, antidepressant selection is also guided by adverse side-effect profile. Monitoring for drug–drug interactions (via screening for side effects and/or use of therapeutic drug monitoring) may offset risk, while allowing antidepressants like mirtazapine and even tricyclics to provide sleep, appetite, and pain improvements. Newer, multimodal antidepressants deserve closer attention and study, whose metabolic profile is less prone to interactions. But we do not yet have clinical and research experience to recommend newer antidepressants as first-line treatment for persons with HIV.

ANXIOLYTICS AND HYPNOTICS

Mild to moderate anxiety and disrupted sleep are not uncommon complaints of patients with HIV/AIDS. Anxiety symptoms may be long-standing and originate from before the person contracted HIV, may be more recent and associated with concerns about his or her illness, or may be side effects of medications. Similarly, sleep issues may be associated with other medical or psychological issues. Regardless of the origin or timeline of symptoms, many of these patients will receive pharmacological interventions to address their anxiety and sleep issues. As such, an awareness of potential interactions with HIV medications is important, to avoid unnecessary complications. Table 42.7 presents the anxiolytics and hypnotics used in treating persons with HIV.

BENZODIAZEPINES

Benzodiazepines (BZDs) are prescribed for relatively mild to moderate cases of anxiety. They are also used as a sleep aid, to treat delirium, and as an adjunct in psychosis or even for acute mania (Budman and Vandersall, 1990). Benzodiazepines are a relatively large and diverse group in terms of half-life, potency, and metabolism. It is simpler to think of benzodiazepines as three groups, based on their metabolism. These three groups are the triazolobenzodiazepines (triazoloBZDs), so-called other BZDs, and LOT, which includes lorazepam, oxazepam, and temazepam (Hsu et al., 2012). TriazoloBZDs are dependent on CYP3A4 for metabolism, while LOT do not use the CYP450 system for metabolism. The other BZD group is metabolized via CYP3A4 as well as a variety of other enzymes.

TriazoloBZDs

Effectiveness/Uses
TriazoloBZDs include alprazolam, midazolam, and triazolam. Alprazolam can be effective for anxiety and panic symptoms, but there is a serious concern about its use leading to abuse (Moylan et al., 2012). Triazolam is often used to treat sleep problems (Bertisch et al., 2014; Glass et al., 2008). Midazolam is commonly used as sedation in patients with HIV undergoing various medical procedures. Backman and colleagues (2013) compared midazolam and clonazepam as sedation agents for colonoscopy in HIV-positive patients on ART. While more patients who received midazolam experienced a depressed level of consciousness during the procedure, there was no difference in post-procedure or overall clinical outcomes. Hsu et al. (2012) found that adults with HIV undergoing inpatient bronchoscopy were significantly more likely to have severe prolonged sedation with midazolam when concomitantly treated with ART. These studies show that midazolam can be used for sedation in HIV-positive patients, but that such use should be done with appropriate caution.

Pharmacokinetics and Drug–Drug Interactions
The triazoloBZDs are dependent on CYP3A4 for metabolism (Ohno et al., 2007), which increases the likelihood of significant interactions with inhibitors (e.g., ritonavir, indinavir, and ketoconazole) or inducers (e.g., carbamazepine, rifampin, and St. John's wort) of CYP3A4. CYP3A4 inhibition by ritonavir causes significant impairment of triazolam and alprazolam metabolism, resulting in greatly increased plasma concentrations, which in turn can lead to a dangerous increase in negative outcomes (Greenblatt et al., 1999). Clinicians administering a triazoloBZD to patients on potent CYP3A4 inhibitors outside of supervised conditions would do well to find alternatives to these drugs.

Other BZDs

Effectiveness/Uses
The group of BZDs called "other BZDs" most notably includes clonazepam and diazepam. Clonazepam is an effective treatment for anxiety (Nardi et al., 2011). Additionally, clonazepam is the recommended first-line agent for treatment of anxiety in patients with HIV, according to the consensus guidelines of the Organization of AIDS Psychiatry (Freudenreich et al., 2010). Diazepam is similarly effective for treatment of anxiety, with the possible additional benefit of attenuating ART-associated neuropathic pain symptoms, as shown in an animal model (Wallace et al., 2008).

Pharmacokinetics and Drug–Drug Interactions
Clonazepam is metabolized by CYP3A4 and via acetylation, whereas diazepam undergoes metabolism via CYPs 2C19, 3A4, 2B6, and 2C9 and glucuronidation. The various pathways of metabolism for these drugs greatly decreases the likelihood of a drug interaction. However, when diazepam needs to be co-administered with etravirine, it may be prudent to

Table 42.7 ANXIOLYTICS AND HYPNOTICS IN HIV CARE

DRUG	METABOLISM SITE(S)	INHIBITION/INDUCTION	CLINICAL CONSIDERATIONS	POTENTIAL DRUG–DRUG INTERACTIONS WITH ART
TRIAZOLOBENZODIAZEPINES (TRIAZOLOBZDS)				
Alprazolam (Xanax)	CYP3A4, glucuronidation	None known		Potent CYP3A4 inhibitors may increase and potent CYP3A4 inducers may reduce alprazolam serum levels.
Midazolam (Versed)	CYP3A4, glucuronidation	None known		Potent CYP3A4 inhibitors may increase and potent CYP3A4 inducers may reduce midazolam serum levels.
Triazolam (Halcion)	CYP3A4, glucuronidation	None known		Potent CYP3A4 inhibitors may increase and potent CYP3A4 inducers may reduce triazolam serum levels.
BENZODIAZEPINES (BZDS)				
Clonazepam (Klonopin)	Acetylation, 3CYPA4	None known		
Diazepam (Valium)	CYPs 2C19, 3A4, 2B6, 2C9, glucuronidation	None known		
Flunitrazepam (Rohypnol) "Roofies"	2C19, 3A4	UGT1A1, UGT1A3, UGT2B7		
Lorazepam (Ativan)	UGT2B15, UGT2B4, UGT2B7 R-lorazepam only: UGT1A7, UGT1A10	None known	Possible induction of glucuronidation	Induction of glucuronidation by posaconazole may reduce serum lorazepam levels.
Oxazepam (Serax)	S-oxazepam—UGT2B15 R-oxazepam—UGY1A9, UGT2B7	None known		
Temazepam (Restoril)	UGT2B7, glucuronidation	Inhibitor of UGT2B7, UGT1A3		Inhibits glucuronidation of: Buprenorphine (UGT2B7) Norbuprenorphine (UGT1A3)
NON-BENZODIAZEPINES ANXIOLYTIC				
Buspirone (Buspar)	CYP3A4	None known		Potent CYP3A4 inhibitors may increase and potent CYP3A4 inducers may reduce buspirone serum levels.
Diphenhydramine (Benadryl)	CYP2D6	CYP2D6 inhibitor		Diphenhydramine as potent CYP2D6 inhibitor may increase serum levels of: *Antiarrhythmics* *Metoprolol* *Oxycodone* *SSRIs* *Tramadol* *Tricyclic antidepressants* *Typical antipsychotics*

NON-BENZODIAZEPINE HYPNOTICS

Non-BZD hypnotics common features	Most are metabolized in part by CYP3A4.		Potent CYP pan-inhibitors like ritonavir and lopinavir may increase serum levels. Potent CYP pan-inducers[a] may reduce serum levels.
Eszopiclone (Lunesta)	CYPs 3A4, 2C9	None known	See Non-BZD hypnotics common features.
Suvorexant (Belsomra)	CYPs 3A4, 2C19	Inhibits CYP3A4, intestinal P-glycoprotein	Potent CYP3A4 inhibitors like protease inhibitors may increase serum levels of suvorexant and are contraindicated. Moderate CYP3A4 inhibitors require dose adjustment of suvorexant.* Potent CYP3A4 inducers may decrease suvorexant serum levels.
Zaleplon (Sonata)	CYP3A4, aldehyde oxidase, 1A2, 2D6	None known	See Non-BZD hypnotics common features.
Zolpidem (Ambien)	CYPs 3A4, 1A2, 2C9, 2C19, 2D6	None known	See Non-BZD hypnotics common features.
Zopiclone (Zimovane/Imovane)	CYPs 3A4, 2C19	None known	See Non-BZD hypnotics common features.

* Individuals on moderate 3A4 inhibitors should be started on 5 mg of suvorexant, with an increase to 10 mg if clinically indicated.

Note: Primary route of metabolism listed first.

Bold CYP indicates **potent** inhibitor or inducer of that cytochrome P450 enzyme.

Abbreviations: ABCB, ATP binding cassette B transporter (p-glycoprotein transporter); CYP, cytochrome; UGT, uridine 5′-diphosphate glucuronosyltransferase.

[a]Pan-inducers: drugs that induce many if not all CYP P450 enzymes and include barbiturates, carbamazepine, ethanol, phenytoin, and rifamycins.

reduce the diazepam dosage or use a benzodiazepine with a simpler metabolism, such as an LOT type. The majority of complications from these other BZDs are due to either side effects or pharmacodynamic interactions secondary to co-ingestion with substances like alcohol (Kakuda et al., 2011).

Non-triazoloBZDs, aka LOT

Effectiveness/Uses

Lorazepam, oxazepam, and temazepam (LOT) are drugs that do not use the cytochrome P450 system for any portion of their metabolism. Lorazepam is a high-potency benzodiazepine known to be effective in a wide variety of clinical situations, including anxiety (Montgomery et al., 2009), procedure-related anxiety (Talmo et al., 2010), status epilepticus (Prasad et al., 2014), and alcohol withdrawal (Schuckit, 2014). Oxazepam is known to be effective in the treatment of anxiety (Sarris et al., 2012) and alcohol withdrawal (Daeppen et al., 2002) and may have benefit in treatment and management of other drug addictions. Temazepam is known to be effective for treatment of insomnia (Glass et al., 2008; Uchaipichat et al., 2013).

Pharmacokinetics and Drug–Drug Interactions

Lorazepam is metabolized via glucuronidation, with significant contribution from UGT2B15 and modest contribution from UGT2B4 and UGT2B7. The R-enantiomer is additionally metabolized by the extrahepatic enzymes UGT1A7 and UGT1A10 (Uchaipichat et al., 2013). A study by Heinz and colleagues (2012) suggests that lorazepam may induce posaconazole clearance by glucuronidation, although the specific enzymatic interaction is unknown. Given the use of posaconazole for fungal infections (Oechsler and Skopp, 2010) in immunocompromised individuals, this potential interaction is noteworthy and should be considered before concomitantly prescribing lorazepam. Lorazepam is otherwise not known to cause inhibition or induction resulting in a drug interaction. S-oxazepam is primarily metabolized at UGT2B15, resulting in S-oxazepam-glucuronide, while R-oxazepam is metabolized by UGT1A9 and UGT2B7 (He et al., 2009). Oxazepam is not known to inhibit or induce any enzyme and has no known clinically significant pharmacokinetic drug interactions. Temazepam is metabolized through glucuronidation at UGT 2B7 and UGT 1A3 and likely through other as-yet unspecified UGTs. Temazepam is also an inhibitor of UGT2B7 and UGT1A3. In vitro analysis by Oechsler and colleagues (Greenblatt et al., 1987; Oechsler and Skopp, 2010) found that temazepam inhibited the glucuronidation of buprenorphine and its metabolite norbuprenorphine. In addition, as with any benzodiazepine, there is the concern for a pharmacodynamics interaction when taken with alcohol, likely resulting in augmentation of the sedating effects.

NON-BENZODIAZEPINE ANXIOLYTICS

Non-benzodiazepines include a diverse group of drugs that share a similar clinical utility. These drugs include buspar, diphenhydramine, trazodone, and several in the class of antipsychotics. The mechanisms are disparate but the effect of sedation and calming are similar. Although these drugs are frequently used in the clinical setting, there is significantly less certainty about their utility. In particular, trazodone and the antipsychotics have essentially no research to support their use for anxiolysis. For discussion on the pharmacokinetics of trazodone, please see Greenblatt et al. (1987), and for details on the pharmacokinetics of antipsychotics, please see the section on antipsychotics in this chapter, and Wynn and colleagues (2010).

Buspirone

Effectiveness/Uses

Buspirone is a serotonergically active azapirone approved for the treatment of generalized anxiety disorder and the short-term relief of anxiety symptoms. A 2006 meta-analysis (Chessick et al., 2006) showed that azapirones were useful in the treatment of generalized anxiety disorder, especially in those who had not previously been on a benzodiazepine. A more recent meta-analysis (Imai et al., 2014) could not establish the utility of azapirones in treatment of panic disorder, stating that more robust research was required in order to determine efficacy.

Pharmacokinetics and Drug–Drug Interactions

Buspirone is metabolized exclusively via CYP3A4 and is not known to cause inhibition or induction (Mylan Pharmaceuticals, 2015). Drugs that inhibit or induce CYP3A4 are likely to significantly alter plasma levels of buspirone and can lead to either increased side effects or therapeutic failure.

Diphenhydramine

Effectiveness/Uses

Diphenhydramine is a sedating antihistamine often used for anxiety or agitation and for akathisia caused by medications. While the use of diphenhydramine for anxiety and agitation may be common, a review of the literature did not find rigorous scientific evidence to support this approach. Additionally, diphenhydramine is frequently used for insomnia and is a major component of many over-the-counter sleep aids. Diphenhydramine may be useful for short-term treatment of insomnia, but efficacy often wanes quickly with the development of tolerance. Longer-term use of diphenhydramine for insomnia is likely to result in increasing doses with associated adverse effects despite decreasing efficacy (Vande Griend and Anderson, 2003).

Pharmacokinetics and Drug–Drug Interactions

Diphenhydramine is metabolized via CYP2D6 (de Leon and Nikoloff, 2008) in addition to glucuronidation. Diphenhydramine is a potent inhibitor of CYP2D6 and may alter the metabolism of drugs dependent on CYP2D6, such as venlafaxine, TCAs, some antipsychotics, beta-blockers, antiarrhythmics, and tramadol. Additionally, diphenhydramine co-administration with other sedating drugs can result in a pharmacodynamic synergistic increase in overall sedation.

HYPNOTICS

Effectiveness/Uses

The class of hypnotics includes eszopiclone, suvorexant, zaleplon, zolpidem, and zopiclone. With the exception of suvorexant, these drugs are benzodiazepine receptor agonists. Suvorexant is the first in its subclass approved by the FDA and is a selective dual orexin receptor antagonist. Both the benzodiazepine receptor agonists (Roehrs and Roth, 2012) and orexin receptor antagonists have shown efficacy in the treatment of insomnia. In addition to treating insomnia, eszopiclone has shown efficacy in treatment of posttraumatic stress disorder (PTSD) in a small randomized controlled trial (Pollack et al., 2011).

A common side effect for all hypnotics is excessive sedation, with the potential to impair daily activities such as driving the day following ingestion. Additionally, the hypnotics can cause abnormal thinking and may increase psychiatric symptoms such as anxiety, depression, and suicidal ideation. Symptoms such as sleep paralysis, somnambulism, hypnagogic and hypnopompic hallucinations, and cataplexy-like symptoms have also been reported. With the exception of suvorexant, the hypnotics have the potential for abuse, best described as similar to that of benzodiazepines (King Pharmaceuticals, Inc., 2013; Merck & Co., Inc., 2014; Sanofi-Aventis Canada, Inc., 2014; Sanofi-Aventis US, LLC, 2014; Sunovion Pharmaceuticals, 2014).

Pharmacokinetics and Drug–Drug Interactions

Eszopiclone, suvorexant, zolpidem, and zopiclone are all primarily metabolized by CYP3A4 (Greenblatt and Zammit, 2012; Merck & Co., Inc., 2014; Sanofi-Aventis Canada, Inc., 2014), with some metabolism at other enzymes (see Table 42.7). Zaleplon is primarily metabolized by aldehyde oxidase (King Pharmaceuticals, Inc., 2013) and not through the CYP450 system. Suvorexant is a mild inhibitor of CYP3A4, whereas the others are not known to cause clinically significant metabolic inhibition or induction. CYP3A4 inhibitors and inducers, such as many ART drugs, may alter the metabolism of eszopiclone, suvorexant, zolpidem, and zopiclone, resulting in altered plasma levels; this can lead to increased side effects such as oversedation or therapeutic failure. Concomitant administration of strong CYP3A4 inhibitors and suvorexant is not recommended (Merck & Co., Inc., 2014).

CASE D: ZOLPIDEM AND RITONAVIR

A 35-year-old HIV-positive man on fluoxetine 20 mg/day for several years and ritonavir for several months, neither of which gave him problems, developed mild insomnia over financial worries. He "borrowed" his mother's zolpidem 10 mg, (something he had used successfully on occasion before his prescription of ritonavir), which resulted in a 14-hour sleep and a "hangover" the next day.

In this case, chronic CYP3A4 inhibition by ritonavir (and, to some extent, fluoxetine) slowed or decreased the metabolism of zolpidem, increasing the effect and duration of action (author KLC, unpublished clinical case).

STIMULANTS

Fatigue and lethargy are very common in persons with HIV, with estimates ranging from 20% to 60% in persons with HIV to as high as 85% in persons with an AIDS-defining illness (Barroso et al., 2010; Jong et al., 2010; Wagner et al., 1997). Low energy can be multifactorial in this population and can result from the medical illness itself, incompletely treated depression, or hypersomnia secondary to sleep disorders. In addition to fatigue mitigation, stimulants are also useful for patients with concomitant attention-deficit hyperactivity disorder (ADHD). Stimulants are dichotomized as either amphetamines or non-amphetamines. Methamphetamine abuse has been associated with risky sexual behavior in the general population (Borders et al., 2013) but there are few data to support prescription stimulant misuse in the HIV-positive population. In addition to a varied side-effect profile, there are unique pharmacological properties that support the notion that wake-promoting medications should be characterized in this way, and this section will follow that taxonomy. Table 42.8 presents the stimulants used in treating persons with HIV.

AMPHETAMINE-BASED STIMULANTS

Dextroamphetamine

Effectiveness/Uses

Dextroamphetamine directly promotes the release of norepinephrine within the CNS, and at higher doses can stimulate the release of dopamine and serotonin (Spiller et al., 2013). Dextroamphetamine has been shown since the late 1980s to be effective for fatigue and depression. Early case reports in persons with HIV touted its quick onset of action and positive effects on concentration and cognition (Fernandez et al., 1988). Wagner and colleagues (1997) conducted a small open-label trial of dextroamphetamine in 24 men with depression, low energy, a CD4 count over 200, and an AIDS-defining illness. There was a 75% response rate via an intention-to-treat analysis. Results were seen as quickly as 2 to 3 days after starting treatment. The most common adverse effect was described as "overstimulation," resulting in just two participant withdrawals. In a follow-up to this open-label study, the same group studied 23 men with HIV, depression, and fatigue. A 2-week randomized, placebo-controlled phase was followed by 6 weeks of continued treatment for responders. After 8 weeks, the trial was converted to open label and continued for the remainder of the 6-month study period. Using intention-to-treat analysis, the investigators found that 73% of patients responded and there was no evidence of tolerance, abuse, or dependence (Wagner and Rabkin, 2000).

Table 42.8 STIMULANTS IN HIV CARE

DRUG	METABOLISM SITE(S)	METABOLIC INHIBITION	METABOLIC INDUCTION	CLINICAL CONSIDERATIONS	POTENTIAL DRUG–DRUG INTERACTIONS WITH ART
AMPHETAMINE-BASED					
Dextroamphetamine (Dexedrine, ProCentra, Zenzedi)	CYP2D6	CYP2D6 (weak)	None known	Myocardial infarction Hypertension QT prolongation Mania	Caution is required with other serotonergic or noradrenergic medications due to additive pharmacodynamic effects. Pan-inhibitors ritonavir and lopinavir may increase serum levels of dextroamphetamine.
Methylphenidate (Concerta, Metadate, Ritalin, Methylin, Quillivant)	Plasma esterases	None known	None known	Myocardial infarction Hypertension QT prolongation Mania	Tipranavir can denature the Concerta capsule and cause an immediate release of medication. Alcohol can denature the Concerta capsule and cause an immediate release of medication.
NON-AMPHETAMINE BASED					
Atomoxetine (Strattera)	CYP2D6	None known	None known	Myocardial infarction Hypertension QT prolongation Mania	Pan-inhibitors ritonavir and lopinavir, may increase serum levels of atomoxetine.
Modafinil (Provigil)/ Armodafinil (Nuvigil)	CYP3A4, glucuronidation ABCB1	CYPs 2C19, 2C9	CYP3A4		CYP3A4 induction by modafinil and armodafinil may reduce serum levels of PIs and others dependent on CYP3A4. No absolute contraindications, but caution is advised with CYP3A4 medications.

Pharmacokinetics and Drug–Drug Interactions

Dextroamphetamine is a 2D6 substrate and a weak 2D6 inhibitor. It should be used with caution if combined with other serotonergic or noradrenergic medications, owing to its additive effects (serotonin syndrome, hypertensive crisis), but there are no significant data regarding drug interactions with ART. All amphetamines have cardiovascular effects that include tachycardia and hypertension. They can be associated with arrhythmias and may increase the risk of myocardial infarction.

Methylphenidate

Effectiveness/Uses

There are few high-quality studies of the efficacy of methylphenidate in patients with HIV. In a one-subject trial, a patient with HIV, depression, and mild dementia was studied in three 2-week phases (placebo, methylphenidate, placebo); the patient showed significant improvement in Hamilton Rating Scale for Depression (HAM-D) scores and cognition during the active drug phase (White et al., 1992). In an open-label trial of methylphenidate with dextroamphetamine, 89.5% of patients reported improved mood and 79% of patients reported significant improvement as measured by the Clinical Global Impression efficacy index (Holmes et al., 1989). Fernandez et al. (1995) compared desipramine with methylphenidate, finding an equal rate of mood improvement and antidepressant efficacy, and both medications were very well tolerated. The largest methylphenidate trial ($n = 109$) compared efficacy of methylphenidate against that of pemoline and placebo in a double-blind, randomized trial. Over 6 weeks, 41% of the methylphenidate group, 36% of the pemoline group, and 15% of the placebo group showed a clinically significant response (Breitbart et al., 2001).

Pharmacokinetics and Drug–Drug Interactions

Methylphenidate has no cytochrome P450 drug interactions, but one of the brand-name extended-release preparations (Concerta®) is sensitive to alcohol, which can denature the pill coating and cause an immediate release. Caution is advised when combining methylphenidate with tipranavir, as dehydrated alcohol is a component of the tipranavir capsule. Ingesting both tipranavir and Concerta simultaneously may cause the immediate release of methylphenidate and increase the risk of drug toxicity (Boehringer Ingelheim Pharmaceuticals GmbH, 2014).

NON-AMPHETAMINE-BASED STIMULANTS

Atomoxetine

Effectiveness/Uses
Because of the potential for abuse and the side effects of amphetamine-based products, newer stimulants have been developed that were initially intended for children with ADHD. Efficacy and safety in adults with ADHD has been demonstrated (Sobanski et al., 2012), but no studies have documented the effects of atomoxetine in patients with HIV.

Pharmacokinetics and Drug–Drug Interactions
Atomoxetine is metabolized by CYP2D6 (Eli Lilly and Co., 2015), and there are potential drug interactions with pan-inhibiting protease inhibitors as well as with integrase inhibitors. No significant post-marketing reports have determined the magnitude of an effect, however.

Modafinil/Armodafinil

Effectiveness/Uses
Modafinil and its R-enantiomer, armodafinil, are wake-promoting agents (Ballon and Feifel, 2006). Rabkin and colleagues conducted an open-label trial (Rabkin et al., 2004) followed by a randomized, double-blind, placebo-controlled 4-week trial with armodafinil and demonstrated a significant fatigue response rate compared with that of placebo (75% vs. 26%). Armodafinil was also indirectly shown to improve mood as a result of increased daytime alertness and energy. The 4-week blinded phase was followed by a 16-week open-label phase. Their 6-month follow-up showed continued response to therapy (Rabkin et al., 2011). This same group studied the effects of armodafinil on cognition and noted that while fatigue scores changed in comparison with placebo, cognitive performance was not enhanced (McElhiney et al., 2013).

Pharmacokinetics and Drug–Drug Interactions
Modafinil and armodafinil are metabolized by CYP3A4 and are autoinducers of CYP3A4. They inhibit 2C19 and 2C9. There are no significant drug–drug interactions or side effects for either modafinil or armodafinil that have been reported in the primary literature, although there are many potential drug–drug interactions, given the extensive number of antiretroviral medications that are metabolized by 3A4. There are no absolute contraindications, but therapeutic drug monitoring should be considered for these agents.

SUMMARY OF STIMULANTS

Stimulants appear to be effective adjuncts to antidepressant therapy in persons suffering from HIV-related fatigue. Larger, controlled comparison trials as well as studies of long-term use have not been conducted and are needed.

MOOD STABILIZERS AND ANTICONVULSANTS

Mood stabilizers are a heterogeneous class of drugs that includes lithium, anticonvulsants, and antipsychotics. This section will summarize those pertinent to the treatment of persons with HIV, with focus on potential uses as well as complications and contraindications in the treatment of persons with HIV.

LITHIUM

Effectiveness/Uses
Lithium's mechanisms of action are complex and not very clear. A full explanation of its known effects can be found elsewhere (Malhi et al., 2013). There have been no studies to support its use in persons with HIV who are depressed, either as solo treatment or for augmentation. An early human study conducted before the development of ART reported poor tolerability of lithium and had a high dropout rate, and viral titers increased throughout the 8-week period (Parenti et al., 1988). However, growing evidence suggests that lithium has protective effects against a variety of insults, including glutamate-induced excitotoxicity, ischemia-induced neuronal damage, and other neurodegenerative conditions (Chiu and Chuang, 2010). Lithium's neuroprotective effects may be useful in HIV (Harvey et al., 2002). These positive effects need more study in persons with HIV, in light of promising effects in the lab and in mice (Dou et al., 2005; Everall et al., 2002). In an open-label study of persons with HIV-associated dementia (HAND) who were just initiating ART, neurocognitive improvement with low-dose lithium was attained, but lithium-specific effects could not be delineated (Letendre et al., 2006). A later open-label study (Schifitto, Zhong, et al., 2009) did not find improvement in HIV RNA or CD4 lymphocyte cell count, mood, or cognitive function with lithium administration, but neuroimaging was suggestive of improved brain functioning. These studies and clinical practice imply that lithium can be used safely in HIV care. More vigorous study of efficacy and neuroprotective effects with therapeutic lithium levels over longer study periods is needed.

Pharmacokinetics and Drug–Drug Interactions
The clearance of lithium is exclusively dependent on renal excretion as a free ion and decreases when renal function is compromised or if there is hyponatremia (Oruch et al., 2014). Common side effects include fatigue, slowed cognition, weight gain, and skin changes, which may be burdensome for persons with HIV. Symptoms of lithium toxicity (serum levels >1.5 mEq/L) include tremor, nausea, vomiting, diarrhea, vertigo,

and confusion, which may mimic HIV symptoms. Plasma levels greater than 2.5 mEq/L require hemodialysis and may lead to seizures, coma, cardiac dysrhythmia, and permanent neurological impairment (Chen et al., 2004). Lithium use also requires adequate electrolyte balance, which may be difficult in persons with HIV who have diarrhea, nausea, vomiting, and general debility. Patients with HIV-associated nephropathy may also be poor candidates for lithium treatment given the potential for reduced lithium clearance (Cohen and Alfonso, 2004; Letendre et al., 2006), although therapeutic drug monitoring and dose adjustment are possible. Despite these obstacles, lithium has a favorable drug–drug interaction profile, and for some bipolar patients it is the only mood stabilizer that is effective.

ANTIEPILEPTICS

Antiepileptic drugs (AEDs) are used in HIV care for the treatment of seizures, mood stabilization, and HIV neuropathy. Many AEDs carry a risk of drug–drug interactions with antiretrovirals, and concomitant use may result in antiretroviral failure with P450 enzyme-inducing AEDs (Birbeck et al., 2012; Okulicz, et al., 2011, 2013). The commonly used AEDs with information in the literature pertaining to use in HIV are reviewed later in the chapter, and the reader is referred to other texts for a more complete discussion (Okulicz et al., 2011; Wynn and Armstrong, 2009), as well as the American Academy of Neurology and the International League Against Epilepsy evidenced-based guidelines (Birbeck et al., 2012) and the Toronto General Hospital Immunodeficiency Clinic Drug Interaction Web page (Foisey and Tseng, 2015). Table 42.9 provides pertinent information about all AEDs in common use at the time of this text's publication.

Carbamazepine

Effectiveness/Uses

Carbamazepine's potential for leukopenia and its anticholinergic effects may limit its use in persons with HIV (Flanagan and Dunk, 2008). There are no controlled studies regarding its use for seizures or as a mood stabilizer in persons with HIV, but there are many retrospective studies and reviews warning about the potential for drug interactions (Okulicz et al., 2013). In resource-limited areas, single-dose nevirapine at the onset of labor is used to prevent perinatal transmission of HIV. In a phase II clinical trial (Muro et al., 2012), single-dose carbamazepine (CBZ) (serum elimination half-life of 18–65 hours) may play a role in preventing primary nevirapine resistance in peripartum women, since co-administration impressively reduces the half-life of single-dose nevirapine, decreasing the possibility of developing HIV resistance to nevirapine.

Pharmacokinetics and Drug–Drug Interactions

Carbamazepine is a potent pan-inducer (Wynn and Armstrong, 2009, p. 326), with the potential to reduce serum levels of protease inhibitors and NNRTIs (Okulicz et al., 2013). In healthy volunteers, CBZ reduced the elimination half-life of nevirapine (L'homme et al., 2006) and reduced the serum concentration of efavirenz (Ji et al., 2008). CBZ is metabolized at many P450

enzymes and is subject to inhibition by pan-inhibitors/inducers such as ritonavir. Case reports of vomiting, vertigo, oversedation, and elevated CBZ serum concentrations highlight the risk of CBZ toxicity when co-administered with potent CYP3A4 inhibitors like ritonavir and other protease inhibitors (Bates and Herman, 2006; Kato et al., 2000).

Eslicarbazepine Acetate

Effectiveness/Uses

Although structurally related to CBZ and OXC, eslicarbazepine (ESL) has remarkably different pharmacodynamics and pharmacokinetics (Bialer and Soares da Silva, 2012; Verrotti et al., 2014). It has not been studied in persons with HIV.

Pharmacokinetics and Drug–Drug Interactions

Unlike CBZ, ESL is not susceptible to metabolic autoinduction (Almeida and Soares da Silva, 2007). ESL weakly induces UGTs and CYP3A4, which may require increased doses of medications dependent on these metabolic enzymes, and may include antiretrovirals such as protease inhibitors. ESL is also a P-glycoprotein substrate. No significant interactions with ART have been reported, but any induction of CYP3A4 would place most persons with HIV on CYP-dependent ART at risk of ART failure due to metabolic induction.

Gabapentin

Effectiveness/Uses

In an early open-label study, gabapentin (GBPN) significantly improved HIV-associated neuropathic pain for 19 HIV-positive patients, independent of whether neurotoxic ART was used (La Spina et al., 2001). Hahn and colleagues (2004) studied GBPN in 26 patients with HIV in a 4-week double-blind, placebo-controlled study with a 2-week open treatment phase and concluded it was effective in controlling neuropathic pain. It was also well tolerated up to 3600 mg/day, with somnolence being the most common side effect. Caution is needed when using GBPN in persons with HIV with concomitant HIV nephropathy and peripheral neuropathy, since GBPN is dependent on renal excretion, and dose adjustment may be necessary.

Pharmacokinetics and Drug–Drug Interactions

Gabapentin is not protein bound and it is highly concentrated in tissue. It is not metabolized and does not inhibit or induce hepatic enzymes (Bockbrader et al., 2010). GBPN is excreted unchanged in urine, with an elimination half-life of 5 to 9 hours, requiring three times/day dosing (McClean, 1994). With few metabolic drug interactions and the benefits of sedation, weight gain, and anti-anxiety effects, GBPN is one of the favored AEDs for persons with HIV and may be effective as monotherapy in this population (Siddiqi and Birbeck, 2013).

Lamotrigine

Effectiveness/Uses

Lamotrigine (LTG) is used for bipolar and unipolar depression (Reid et al., 2013) as well as epilepsy, but it has not been

Table 42.9 MOOD STABILIZERS AND ANTIEPILEPTICS IN HIV CARE

MOOD STABILIZER	METABOLIC SITE(S)	ENZYME(S) INHIBITED	ENZYME(S) INDUCED	CLINICAL CONSIDERATIONS	POTENTIAL DRUG–DRUG INTERACTIONS WITH ART
Lithium	Renal	None	None	None known, effect of cognitive slowing may be difficult in patients with HIV-related cognitive dysfunction	
Antiepileptic Mood Stabilizers					
Carbamazepine (CBZ) (Tegretol)	CYPs 3A4 (primary), 2C8, 2B6, 2C9, 1A2 UGT2B7 Transporter ABCB1, ABCC2	CYP2C19? CYPs 3A4, 1A2, 2B6, 2C8, 2C9 UGT1A4	CYPs 3A4, 1A2, 2B6, 2C8, 2C9 UGT1A4	Potential for diminished white blood cell count Narrow therapeutic index Risk of Stevens-Johnson syndrome and toxic epidermal necrolysis HLA-B genotyping for patients of Asian descent is necessary.	CBZ is considered a pan-inducer[a] and it autoinduces. High risk of ART failure and viral resistance unless ART dosing is monitored and increased. Potent CYP3A4 inhibitors like PIs and elvitegravir/cobicistat may increase serum levels of CBZ, requiring monitoring and dose reduction of CBZ. Other pan-inducers[a] may reduce serum levels of CBZ.
Clobazam[b] (Frisium, Onfi)	CYPs 3A4, 2C19	CYPs 2C9, 2C19			Potent CYP3A4 inhibitors like PIs and elvitegravir/cobicistat may increase serum levels of clobazam, requiring monitoring and dose reduction. CYP3A4 inducers, like pan-inducers,[a] ritonavir, and NNRTIs may reduce clobazam serum levels.
Ethosuximide (Zarontin)	CYP3A4, phase II	None known			Potent CYP3A4 inhibitors like PIs and elvitegravir/cobicistat may increase serum levels of ethosuximide, requiring monitoring and dose reduction. CYP3A4 inducers, like pan-inducers,[a] ritonavir, and NNRTIs, may reduce ethosuximide serum levels.
Eslicarbazepine acetate (Aptiom)	Non-microsomal hydrolysis (first pass) UGT2B4 and many others	CYP2C19 (moderate)	CYP 3A4	Cognitive impairment Dizziness/gait disturbance SIADH Suicidal thoughts and behavior Visual changes	Potential risk of ART failure and viral resistance unless ART dosing is monitored and increased. Eslicarbazepine has clinically reduced serum levels of: *CBZ* *Oral contraceptives* *Statins* *Warfarin*
Felbamate (Felbatol)	CYP3A4, 2E1 Transporter ABCB1	CYP2C19	CYP3A4		High risk of ART failure and viral resistance unless ART dosing is monitored and increased. Potent CYP3A4 inhibitors like PIs and elvitegravir/cobicistat may increase serum levels of ethosuximide, requiring monitoring and dose reduction.
Gabapentin (Neurontin)	Excreted in urine unchanged	None known	None known		No ART pharmacokinetic interactions expected

(continued)

Table 42.9 CONTINUED

MOOD STABILIZER	METABOLIC SITE(S)	ENZYME(S) INHIBITED	ENZYME(S) INDUCED	CLINICAL CONSIDERATIONS	POTENTIAL DRUG–DRUG INTERACTIONS WITH ART
Lamotrigine (Lamictal)	UGT 1A4 and excreted in urine unchanged	None known via CYPs	UGT1A4 (mild, with autoinduction)		UGT inducers like efavirenz, ritonavir, lopinavir, and nelfinavir may reduce lamotrigine serum levels.
Levetiracetam (Keppra)	One-third by non-CYP450, phase I hydrolysis	None known	None known	May cause depression, suicidal thoughts or behavior, and nonpsychotic behavioral changes	No ART pharmacokinetic interactions expected
Methsuximide (Celontin)	CYP3A4, phase II	None known	None known		Potent CYP 3A4 inhibitors like PIs and elvitegravir/cobicistat may increase serum levels of methsuximide, requiring monitoring and dose reduction. CYP3A4 inducers, like pan-inducers,[a] ritonavir, and NNRTIs, may reduce methsuximide serum levels.
Oxcarbazepine (Trileptal)	Non-cytochromal metabolism UGTs	CYP2C19	CYP3A4 (mild) UGTs (moderate)		Risk of ART failure and viral resistance unless ART dosing is monitored and increased.
Phenobarbital	CYPs 2C9, 2C19	None known	CYPs 3A4, 1A2, 2C9, 2C19 UGTs		Phenobarbital is considered a pan-inducer[a]. High risk of ART failure and viral resistance unless ART dosing monitored and increased. Risk of phenobarbital failure when co-administered with CYP 2C9 and 2C19 inducers such as ritonavir
Phenytoin	CYPs 2C9, 2C19	None known	CYPs 3A4, 2C9, 2C19, UGTs		Phenytoin is considered a pan-inducer[a]. High risk of ART failure and viral resistance unless ART dosing is monitored and increased.
Tiagabine (Gabitril)	CYP3A4 UGTs	None known			Potent CYP3A4 inhibitors like PIs and elvitegravir/cobicistat may increase serum levels of tiagabine, requiring monitoring and dose reduction.
Topiramate (Topamax)	70% excreted unchanged in urine Phase I and II UGTs Transporter ABCB1	CYP2C19	CYP3A4 (mild) UGTs	Associated with weight loss, sedation, depression and mood changes	Minimal potential ART pharmacokinetic interactions

Drug	Metabolism	Inhibits	Induces	Adverse effects	ART interactions
Valproic acid (VPA, Depakote, Depakene)	UGT1A6, UGT1A9, UGT2B7, β-oxidation, CYPs 2C9, 2C19, 2A6	Inhibits: UGT1A4 UGT1A9 UGT1A9 UGT2B7 UGT2B15 CYPs 2D6, 2C9, 2C19 Epoxide hydroxylase	Possibly CYP3A4, ABCB1	Hepatotoxicity, especially with CYP inducers like nevirapine, efavirenz, and ritonavir. Hepatotoxic metabolite is not measured in standard lab tests.	Very complicated and controversial interaction profile. Pan-inducers[a], ritonavir, and NNRTIs like efavirenz may reduce VPA serum levels. May inhibit glucuronidation of AZT and increase serum levels
Vigabatrin (Sabril)	Excreted in urine unchanged	None known	CYP2C9	Visual changes including permanent visual field deficits Suicidal thoughts and behavior Peripheral neuropathy	No ART pharmacokinetic interactions expected
Zonisamide (Zonegran)	CYPs 3A4, 3A5, Acetylation, sulfonation	CYPs 2C9, 2C19			Potent CYP3A4 inhibitors like PIs and elvitegravir/cobicistat may increase serum levels of zonisamide, requiring monitoring and dose reduction. Potent CYP3A4 inducers, like PIs, pan-inducers[a], and NNRTIs, may reduce zonisamide serum levels.

Bold CYP indicates **potent** inhibitor or inducer of that cytochrome P450 enzyme.

Abbreviations: ABCB, ATP binding cassette B transporter (p-glycoprotein transporter); ART, antiretroviral therapy; CYP, cytochrome; NNRTIs, non-nucleoside reverse transcriptase inhibitors; PIs, protease inhibitors; SIADH, syndrome of inappropriate antidiuretic hormone secretion; UGT, uridine 5′-diphosphate glucuronosyltransferase.

[a] Pan-inducers: drugs that induce many if not all CYP P450 enzymes and include barbiturates, carbamazepine, ethanol, phenytoin, and rifamycins.

[b] Clobazam is a 1,5-benzodiazepine1-5 (BZD) that is used as an antiepileptic drug.

extensively studied in persons with HIV. In a randomized, double-blind study of LTG for HIV distal symmetrical polyneuropathy (Simpson et al., 2003), LTG effectively improved pain among patients receiving neurotoxic ART, with the incidence of adverse events, including rashes, similar in LTG and placebo groups. Interestingly, there was no significant improvement in pain for individuals who were not receiving neurotoxic ART.

Pharmacokinetics and Drug–Drug Interactions

Lamotrigine is metabolized primarily by UGT1A4, and there is much variability in its metabolism due to genetic polymorphisms (Chang et al., 2014). Metabolic variability also occurs because of inhibition or induction of glucuronidation. In pharmacokinetic studies in healthy volunteers, LTG bioavailability decreased by 50% when co-administered with lopinavir/ritonavir (van der Lee et al., 2006). LTG serum levels were not affected when co-administered with atazanavir alone, but were reduced moderately (32%) when co-administered with ritonavir/atazanavir (Burger et al., 2008), owing to induction of LTG's glucuronidation. The American Academy of Neurology and the International League Against Epilepsy evidence-based guidelines suggest that patients on ritonavir/atazanavir may need an LTG dosage increase of 50% to maintain therapeutic LTG serum concentrations (Birbeck et al., 2012) and that co-administration of raltegravir/atazanavir and LTG may not require LTG dosage adjustment.

Levetiracetam

Effectiveness/Uses

Levetiracetam (LEV) was developed as an add-on therapy for patients with refractory complex partial seizures and has not been studied in persons with HIV. The most common side effects include somnolence, asthenia, headache, memory loss, confusion, aggression, and infection and anorexia, and each of these would be burdensome in persons with HIV. Significant behavioral abnormalities (depression, irritability, emotional liability, psychosis, and suicide) are common; these are the most frequent reasons for discontinuation in non-HIV patients (Cramer et al., 2003). Cramer et al. noted a two times greater incidence of affective adverse effects in patients with epilepsy treated with LEV than in other treatment groups in placebo-controlled trials, and they could not conclude whether the underlying epilepsy places patients at risk for AED-specific adverse effects. Later studies have not clarified this issue (Fountoulakis et al., 2015).

Pharmacokinetic and Pharmacodynamics Issues

Levetiracetam is mostly excreted in the urine unchanged, and reduced renal clearance may prolong the half-life (UCB Pharma, Inc., 2013. LEV is not metabolized by P450 enzymes, nor does the drug inhibit or induce these enzymes (Patsalos, 2013a, 2013b; Wright et al., 2013), which reduces the risk of drug–drug interactions. Despite a favorable drug–drug interaction profile, its neurobehavioral side effects, particularly in persons with epilepsy, may limit its use in persons with HIV. LEV has yet to be fully studied in individuals with and without HIV (Fountoulakis et al., 2015).

Oxcarbazepine

Effectiveness/Uses

Oxcarbazepine (OXCBZ) is indicated for the treatment of partial seizures (Dam et al., 1989). It has not been studied in persons with HIV.

Pharmacokinetics and Drug–Drug Interactions

OXCBZ is rapidly reduced to monohydroxycarbazepine (MHD), which is an enantiomeric mix of eslicarbazepine and R-licarbazepine. OXCBZ possesses similar mechanisms of action to CBZ, but it can inhibit CYP2C19 and induce CYP3A4/5 (Novartis Pharmaceuticals, 2014). Although significant OXCBZ pharmacokinetic interactions with antiretrovirals have not been documented, since it is an inducer of CYP3A4, the primary metabolic enzyme for all protease inhibitors and many other ARTs, its use warrants careful monitoring.

Phenobarbital and Phenytoin

Effectiveness/Uses

Use of pan-inducers like phenobarbital and phenytoin are generally avoided in the care of persons with HIV whenever possible. A retrospective case-control analysis found that persons with HIV taking an enzyme-inducing AED combined with ART were significantly more likely to have ART treatment failure than individuals taking non-enzyme-inducing AEDs (63% vs. 27%, respectively; *p* = .009) in the U.S. Military HIV Natural History Study (Okulicz et al., 2011).

Pharmacokinetics and Drug–Drug Interactions

Phenobarbital and phenytoin are considered pan-inducers, which may have the effect of reducing serum levels and effectiveness of many ART drugs (Fillekes et al., 2013; Kakuda et al., 2011; Okulicz et al., 2013). Additionally, some ART drugs may affect the metabolism of phenobarbital and phenytoin, particularly those that inhibit or induce CYPs 2C9 or 2C19 (Robertson et al., 2005). Concomitant administration of tipranavir-ritonavir with phenobarbital resulted in a 50% decrease of phenobarbital plasma levels and required a 50% increase in phenobarbital dose (Bonora et al., 2007).

Tiagabine

Effectiveness/Uses

There are no studies of tiagabine use in persons with HIV.

Pharmacokinetics and Drug–Drug Interactions

Tiagabine is metabolized at CYP3A4, and its metabolism is susceptible to induction by other AEDs that induce this enzyme (Cephalon, Inc., 2015). It is considered an AED that is a non-inducer of metabolism. Use of tiagabine with pan-inducers such as carbamazepine, phenytoin, or phenobarbital has resulted in a 60% increase in the clearance of tiagabine and reduced serum levels. Tiagabine administration with valproic acid (VPA) has been associated with reduction of serum VPA levels by approximately 10%, the mechanism of which is unclear (Brodie, 1995; Gustavson et al., 1998). Tiagabine is listed in an older toxicology report to be an inhibitor of

CYP2C19 (Jacobsen et al., 2008) but is generally not considered to be a P450 inhibitor or inducer (Kälviäinen, 1998).

Topiramate

Effectiveness/Uses
Topiramate is associated with sedation and cognitive dysfunction as well as depression and mood disturbances. It is also used as an add-on medication for weight reduction (Janssen Ortho, LLC, 2014). These common side effects may make its use in persons with HIV more difficult. There are no studies of topiramate use in persons with HIV.

Pharmacokinetics and Drug–Drug Interactions
See Table 42.9.

Valproic Acid/Valproate

Effectiveness/Uses
Valproic acid (VPA) and valproate are prone to complicated drug interactions and carry risk of hepatotoxicity, thrombocytopenia, hyperammonemia, weight gain and metabolic syndrome, teratogenesis, and long-term negative effects on cognitive development after in utero exposure (Belcastro et al., 2013; Meador et al., 2009), all of which complicate its use in persons with HIV. The risk factors for VPA-induced hepatotoxicity are male gender, age less than 2 years, neurological disease (other than seizures, but perhaps inclusive of HIV), and concomitant treatment with a P450-inducing medication. Many people with HIV fulfill three risk categories for hepatotoxicity with VPA. VPA is also a glycogen synthase kinase 3 beta–mediated phosphorylation inhibitor (Schifitto et al., 2006), which may protect neural cells from lipid accumulation and death (Ances et al., 2008). Sui et al. noted in 2007 that persons with HIV on some antiretrovirals (most notably EFV) had an increase in sCD40L, placing them at risk for HAND by increasing inflammation and deteriorating the blood–brain barrier. Recent, small pilot studies of combination VPA and ART (Davidson et al., 2013) indicate that VPA may reduce or attenuate the proinflammatory effect of NNRTIs, but further study is necessary, especially in light of VPA's complicated metabolism and drug–drug interaction profile.

Pharmacokinetics and Drug–Drug Interactions
VPA's metabolism and its effect on metabolism is complex (see Table 42.9). VPA is vulnerable to metabolic induction by ritonavir and lopinavir/ritonavir, lowering VPA serum levels (Sheehan et al., 2006), and there have been reports of VPA hepatotoxicity with co-administration of P450 inducers like nevirapine (Cozza et al., 2000). VPA should be used with caution in persons with HIV; it may require dose adjustments, particularly with the above-mentioned antiretrovirals, to avoid drug toxicity or ART failure.

Vigabatrin

Effectiveness/Uses
No studies of vigabatrin use have been conducted in persons with HIV; however vigabatrin potential side effects (liver failure, vision loss) would complicate its use in patients with HIV (Grant and Heel, 1991).

Pharmacokinetics and Drug–Drug Interactions
See Table 42.9.

Zonisamide

Effectiveness/Uses
Zonisamide has no FDA indication as a mood stabilizer. It is an adjunctive therapy for the treatment of partial seizures in adults. Its once-daily dosing could be favorable for HIV-positive patients with seizures. To date, no studies have been conducted in persons with HIV.

Pharmacokinetics and Drug–Drug Interactions
Zonisamide is rapidly and completely absorbed and has a long half-life, which allows once- or twice-daily dosing (Sills and Brodie, 2007). Zonisamide is metabolized via CYP3A4 and is not an inhibitor or inducer of other metabolic enzymes. CBZ, phenytoin, and phenobarbital have been shown to increase the clearance of zonisamide, and zonisamide's serum levels would be expected to be affected by ART drugs that inhibit or induce CYP3A4.

SUMMARY OF MOOD STABILIZERS AND ANTIEPILEPTICS IN THE TREATMENT OF PERSONS WITH HIV

Many mood stabilizers/AEDs—generally the older compounds (phenobarbital, phenytoin, carbamazepine, topiramate, VPA)—induce or stimulate the synthesis of multiple metabolic enzymes, speeding up the metabolism of many drugs and endogenous compounds, such as ART, analgesics, anticoagulants, other antiepileptics, antihypertensives, cytotoxics, glucocorticoids, immunosuppressants, oral contraceptives, psychotropics, statins, hormones, and lipids. Metabolism-inducing AEDs reduce circulating serum levels of compounds that are dependent on the induced enzymes, which greatly increases the risk for antiretroviral failure, with viral resistance, loss of mood stabilization, unplanned pregnancy, transplant rejection, stroke, and more. "Un-induction," which occurs with discontinuation of enzyme-inducing AEDs, increases the concentration of previously induced drugs over 7–14 days, risking toxicity if doses are not proactively monitored or reduced. Newer, non-pan-inducing AEDs with efficacy for epilepsy, mood stabilization, and pain management should be considered first-line choices in persons with HIV whenever possible, to reduce the risk of ART failure.

ANTIPSYCHOTICS

Antipsychotics drugs, a relatively heterogeneous group of medications, include both first-generation antipsychotic (FGA, typical) and second-generation antipsychotic (SGA, atypical) medications. While no antipsychotic is specifically FDA approved for HIV-associated psychosis or mania, both conventional and atypical antipsychotics have been used with demonstrated efficacy (Bagchi et al., 2004). Both FGAs and SGAs have short- and long-term side effects as well as potential drug interactions with ART that should be taken into consideration.

FIRST-GENERATION ANTIPSYCHOTICS

There are a limited number of phase I and phase II metabolism studies for FGAs. Importantly, persons with HIV tend to be at greater risk of extrapyramidal symptoms (EPS) with dopamine antagonists such as FGAs (Ramachandran et al., 1997). Hriso et al. (1991) found that patients with AIDS encephalopathy are 2.4 times more vulnerable to EPS associated with antipsychotics than persons who do not have HIV/AIDS. Table 42.10 summarizes features common to all FGAs, including side effects, toxicities, and black box warnings (BBWs), followed by specifics concerning each drug.

SECOND-GENERATION (ATYPICAL) ANTIPSYCHOTICS

Table 42.10 summarizes features common to all SGAs, including adverse effects, toxicities, and BBWs, followed by specifics for all of those available in the United States. In general, SGAs will have additive effects when co-administered with protease inhibitors, owing to their similar adverse side-effect profile. Metabolic syndrome, common for both ART and SGAs, includes diabetes, weight gain, and dyslipidemia. Combined treatment with ART and SGAs is associated with significantly higher mean triglycerides, increased risk of developing diabetes, elevated mean arterial pressures, and marginally higher body mass index (Ferrarra et al., 2014). Clinicians need to aggressively monitor for metabolic complications when concurrently prescribing ART and SGAs. Authors of a meta-analysis in the non-HIV population attempted head-to-head comparison of most SGAs for efficacy and adverse effects and found significant alterations in weight, glucose dysregulation, and dyslipidemia with olanzapine and clozapine and the least alterations, if any, for ziprasidone (Rummel-Kluge et al., 2010). Readers are directed to that analysis for further details.

A significant number of SGAs are associated with a risk of QTc prolongation and require regular cardiac monitoring for patients with additional risk factors for arrhythmias or who are on other medications with similar QTc prolongation profiles, such as saquinavir or lopinavir/ritonavir (Hill and Lee, 2013). Aripiprazole, brexpiprazole, cariprazine, lurasidone, and olanzapine are not associated with an elevated risk of QTc prolongation (Actavis Inc., 2015b; Eli Lilli and Co., 2015; Otsuka Pharmaceuticals Co., Ltd., 2015, 2016; Sunovion Pharmaceuticals, 2013).

Amisulpride

Effectiveness/Uses
Amisulpride is a highly selective dopamine D3/D2 receptor antagonist currently available in Europe for management of acute and chronic schizophrenia. There are no studies currently published regarding its use in persons with HIV.

Pharmacokinetics and Drug–Drug Interactions
Amisulpride undergoes only minimal metabolic transformation, and it does not affect the CYP450 system, making drug–drug interactions with antiretrovirals unlikely (Rosenzweig et al., 2002).

Aripiprazole

Effectiveness/Uses
There are no randomized clinical trials investigating aripiprazole's use in persons with HIV. Aripiprazole has less documented risk of EPS, metabolic syndrome, and QT interval prolongation than other atypical antipsychotics (Leucht et al., 2013), which may make it favorable for persons with HIV who are known to be more adversely affected than the general population. Cecchelli et al. (2010) discuss a 37-year-old male with HIV, on ART for 11 years, with a CD4 count of 200 cells/μl and viral load of 3000 copies/ml, who was diagnosed with resistant major depression, somatoform disorder (hypochondriasis), and panic disorder. Aripiprazole was added to 40 mg of citalopram with excellent resolution of mood and somatic symptoms, a nondetectable viral load, and a CD4 count of 400 cells/μl, without any adverse effects or observed drug interactions. In light of this case, the authors call for more research into whether aripiprazole has positive immunological effects, particularly given aripiprazole's in vitro inhibitory effect on glial activation and release of cytotoxic cytokines and chemokines.

Pharmacokinetics and Drug–Drug Interactions
Aripiprazole is primarily metabolized by CYP2D6 and CYP3A4 and has no effects on P450 activity (Otsuka Pharmaceuticals Co., Ltd., 2016). Aripiprazole serum concentrations may be vulnerable to co-administration of CYP2D6 and CYP3A4 inhibitors, with the potential of increasing aripiprazole's serum levels when used with potent inhibitors such as protease inhibitors. CYP3A4 inducers may reduce aripiprazole serum levels, and dose adjustments may be needed to obtain clinical efficacy. The manufacturer suggests using 50% of the standard aripiprazole dose when co-administered with potent CYP2D6 inhibitors, such as ritonavir, or strong CYP3A4 inhibitors, such as protease inhibitors, ketoconazole, and voriconazole. A 25% standard aripiprazole dose is suggested if co-administering with combined CYP3A4 and CP2D6 inhibitors of moderate-to-severe potency, either as co-administered regimens (e.g., bupropion and protease inhibitors) or as single poly-inhibitors like delvaridine, ritonavir, or efavirenz. Aripiprazole doses may need to be doubled (two times) over 1–2 weeks if co-administered with potent CYP3A4 inducers such as carbamazepine and rifampin to maintain clinical efficacy (Hill and Lee, 2013; Otsuka Pharmaceuticals Co., Ltd., 2016).

Table 42.10 ANTIPSYCHOTICS IN HIV CARE

ANTIPSYCHOTICS	METABOLIC SITE(S)	ENZYME(S) INHIBITED (NO INDUCERS)	CLINICAL CONSIDERATIONS	POTENTIAL DRUG–DRUG INTERACTIONS WITH ART
FIRST-GENERATION ANTIPSYCHOTICS				
Common features			Increased risk of: Cognitive/motor impairment EPS, NMS, TD Hyperprolactinemia Leukopenia/neutropenia Orthostatic hypotension Greater risk for EPS, dystonia, and TD in persons with HIV Increased risk of death in elderly patients with dementia	Since these are older drugs, there are fewer data about specific metabolic sites and drug interactions. Potent CYP pan-inhibitors like ritonavir and lopinavir may increase serum levels. Potent CYP pan-inducers[a] may reduce serum levels. Most are potent inhibitors of CYP2D6 and may increase serum levels of drugs dependent on CYP2D6.
Chlorpromazine (Thorazine)	CYPs 2D6, 1A2, 3A4 UGTs 1A4, 1A3	CYP2D6		See "Common Features"
Fluphenazine (Prolixin)	CYPs 2D6, 1A2	CYPs 2D6, 1A2		See "Common Features"
Haloperidol (Haldol)	CYPs 2D6, 3A4, 1A2	CYP2D6		See "Common Features"
Mesoridazine (Serentil)	CYPs 2D6, 1A2	None known		See "Common Features"
Molindone (Moban)	CYP2D6 and phase II	None known		Off U.S. market
Perphenazine (Trilafon)	CYPs 2D6, 3A4, 1A2, 2C19	CYPs 2D6, 1A2		See "Common Features"
Pimozide (Orap)	CYP3A4, 1A2	CYPs 2D6, 3A4	Prolongs QTc	Protease inhibitors may cause arrhythmias when co-administered with CYP3A4-dependent pimozide and are contraindicated.
Thioridazine (Mellaril)	CYPs 2D6, 1A2, 2C19 FMO3	CYP2D6		
SECOND-GENERATION (ATYPICAL) ANTIPSYCHOTICS				
Common Features			Increased risk of metabolic syndrome (additive with PI's) Risk of: Cognitive/motor impairment EPS, NMS, TD Hyperprolactinemia	Most do not interfere with metabolism of other drugs (neither inhibit/induce). Combined treatment with ART increases risk of metabolic syndrome due to additive effects. QT prolongation is additive with drugs like saquinavir and lopinavir/ritonavir.

(continued)

Table 42.10 CONTINUED

ANTIPSYCHOTICS	METABOLIC SITE(S)	ENZYME(S) INHIBITED (NO INDUCERS)	CLINICAL CONSIDERATIONS	POTENTIAL DRUG–DRUG INTERACTIONS WITH ART
			Leukopenia/neutropenia Orthostatic hypotension Priapism Seizures Many are associated with QTc prolongation risk (NOT aripiprazole, lurasidone, olanzapine, cariprazine, brexpiprazole) Increased risk of death in elderly patients with dementia	
Amisulpride	50% excreted in urine unchanged Minimal CYP metabolism		Not available in the U.S.	
Aripiprazole (Abilify)	CYPs 2D6, 3A4	None known	Increased risk of akathisia/EPS	Aripiprazole dose reduction 50% with: Potent CYP3A4 inhibitors, e.g., *Protease inhibitors* *Elvitegravir/cobicistat* Potent CYP2D6 inhibitors, e.g., *Bupropion* *Diphenhydramine* *Paroxetine* *Ritonavir* Aripiprazole dose reduction 75% with combined CYP3A4 and 2D6 inhibitors (and combinations of inhibitors of each), e.g., *Ritonavir* *Efavirenz* *Delavirdine* Aripiprazole dose increase of up to 100% (2×) with CYP3A4 inducers, e.g., *Pan-inducers[a]* *Ritonavir* *Some NNRTIs*
Asenapine (Saphris)	UGT1A4 CYP1A2	CYP2D6	QTc prolongation Not recommended in patients with severe hepatic impairment	Reduce paroxetine (CYP2D6 substrate and inhibitor) dose by 50% when co-administered.
Blonanserin	CYP3A4		Not available in the U.S. High risk of EPS	Contraindicated with potent CYP3A4 inhibitors like protease inhibitors

Drug	Metabolism	Enzyme inhibition/induction	Adverse effects / cautions	Drug interactions / dosing
Brexpiprazole (Rexulti)	CYPs 2D6, 3A4	None known	Increased risk of akathisia	Brexpiprazole dose reduction 50% with: Potent CYP3A4 inhibitors, e.g., *Protease inhibitors* *Elvitegravir/cobicistat* Potent CYP2D6 inhibitors, e.g., *Ritonavir* *Diphenhydramine* *Bupropion* *Paroxetine* Brexpiprazole dose reduction 75% with combined CYP3A4 and 2D6 inhibitors, e.g., *Ritonavir* *Efavirenz* *Delavirdine* Brexpiprazole dose increase of up to 100% (2×) with CYP3A4 inducers, e.g., *Pan-inducers[a]* *Ritonavir* *Some NNRTIs*
Cariprazine (Vraylar)	CYP3A4	None known	Not approved for dementia-related psychosis Increased risk of akathisia Late-occurring adverse reactions due to long half-life; monitor patients for several weeks after starting and with each dose change.	Potent CYP3A4 inhibitors: reduce cariprazine dosage 50%. Co-administration with potent CYP3A4 inducers and pan-inducers[a] is NOT recommended; it may significantly lower serum clozapine levels.
Clozapine (Clozaril)	CYPs 1A2, 3A4, 2D6, 2C9, 2C19 UGTs 1A4, 1A3 FMO3	CYP2D6	Risk of agranulocytosis: In U.S. mandatory registry; biweekly monitoring with CBC, ANC × 6 months, monthly thereafter Cardiac risks: Bradycardia and syncope QTc prolongation Myocarditis/cardiomyopathy Orthostatic hypotension Seizures Risk of: Anticholinergic toxicity: caution with narrow angle glaucoma or anticholinergic drugs Eosinophilia Pulmonary embolism	Potent CYP1A2 inhibitors increase clozapine serum levels: must reduce clozapine to one-third the standard dose. Co-administration with potent CYP3A4 inducers and pan-inducers[a] is NOT recommended; it may significantly lower serum clozapine levels. Avoid carbamazepine, for adjunctive risk of agranulocytosis. Synergistic bone marrow suppression if co-administered with treatments for cytomegalovirus or herpes simplex virus infections
Iloperidone (Fanapt)	CYPs 2D6, 3A4	None known	Significant QTc prolongation; consider alternative if patient has additional risk factors; monitor K^+ and Mg^{2+} Not recommended in patients with severe hepatic impairment	Potent CYP2D6 or CYP3A4 inhibitors: reduce iloperidone dose by 50%. Potent CYP3A4 inducers and pan-inducers[a] may reduce serum levels of iloperidone. Contraindicated: co-administration of iloperidone with drugs that prolong QTc interval

(continued)

Table 42.10 CONTINUED

ANTIPSYCHOTICS	METABOLIC SITE(S)	ENZYME(S) INHIBITED (NO INDUCERS)	CLINICAL CONSIDERATIONS	POTENTIAL DRUG–DRUG INTERACTIONS WITH ART
Lurasidone (Latuda)	CYP3A4	None known	Not approved for dementia-related psychosis	Contraindicated: co-administration of lurasidone with potent CYP3A4 inhibitors such as protease inhibitors or potent CYP3A4 inducers such as rifampin. Moderate inhibitors may be used, but lurasidone dosage should be reduced by 50%.
Olanzapine (Zyprexa)	UGT1A4 CYPs 1A2, 2D6 (minor) FMO3	None		Polyaromatic hydrocarbons in tobacco smoke are inducers of CYP1A2 and may reduce serum levels of olanzapine. Potent pan-inducers[a] may reduce serum levels of olanzapine. Co-administration of fosamprenavir/ritonavir may reduce olanzapine levels.
Paliperidone (Invega)	P-glycoproteins CYPs (in vitro) 2D6, 3A4 (minimal)	P-glycoproteins (weak)	Major active metabolite of risperidone QTc prolongation Gastrointestinal narrowing Dysphagia	Potent CYP3A4/P-glycoprotein inducers (carbamazepine) may reduce serum paliperidone levels and may require increased paliperidone dose. Co-administration of divalproex sodium may require increased paliperidone dose, adjust clinically. Potent pan-inducers[a] may reduce serum levels of paliperidone.
Quetiapine (Seroquel)	CYP3A4 Sulfoxidation oxidation P-glycoprotein substrate	None	Associated with QTc prolongation Elevated blood pressure in children and adolescents Cataracts, routine screening recommended before starting treatment and every 6 months.	Potent CYP3A4 inhibitors: administer one-sixth standard quetiapine dose. Significant risk of priapism when co-administered with potent CYP3A4 inhibitors Potent CYP3A4 inducers: increase quetiapine dose up to 5× standard dose with chronic combination treatment. Discontinuing potent CYP3A inducer therapy: reduce quetiapine from 5× elevated dose to standard dose over 7–14 days after discontinuation of CYP3A4 inducer.
Risperidone (Risperdal)	CYPs 2D6, 3A4	CYPs 2D6, 3A4	Not approved for dementia-related psychosis Associated with QTc prolongation	Potent CYP3A4 and /or CYP2D6 inhibitors may increase serum levels of risperidone. Co-administration requires lower initial risperidone dose and maximum dose of 8 mg per day. Potent CYP3A4 inducers and pan-inducers[a] may reduce serum levels of risperidone. Increase risperidone dose up to 2× standard dose.
Sertindole	CYPs 2D6, 3A4	None known	Significant, dose-related QTc prolongation Not available in the U.S.	Potent CYP3A4 and/or CYP2D6 inhibitors may increase serum levels of sertindole, increasing risk of QTc prolongation, and are contraindicated.

| Ziprasidone (Geodon) | Aldehyde oxidase
Minimal CYPs 3A4, 1A2 | None known | Not approved for dementia-related psychosis
Associated with significant QTc prolongation, and ziprasidone use should be avoided in patients with bradycardia, hypokalemia, hypomagnesemia, or congenital QT prolongation.
Taking it with food increases absorption 2×.
Severe cutaneous adverse reactions have been reported (DRESS, SJS, SCAR).
Intramuscular formulation is not recommended in patients with significant renal impairment. | May be least effected by CYP inhibitors or inducers
Contraindicated with drugs that also affect QTc
Contraindicated in patient with recent acute myocardial infarction or with uncompensated heart failure |

Bold CYP indicates **potent** inhibitor or inducer of that cytochrome P450 enzyme.

Abbreviations: ANC, absolute neutrophil count; CBC, complete blood count; CYP, cytochrome; DRESS, drug reaction with eosinophilia and systemic symptoms; EPS, extrapyramidal symptoms; FMO, flavin-containing monooxygenase (non-CYP450 drug metabolizing enzyme that is considered not readily inducible nor inhibited); NMS, neuroleptic malignant syndrome; SCAR, severe cutaneous adverse reactions; SJS, Stevens-Johnson syndrome; TD, tardive dyskinesia; UGT, uridine 5′-diphosphate glucuronosyltransferase.

[a]Pan-inducers: drugs that induce many if not all CYP P450 enzymes and include barbiturates, carbamazepine, ethanol, phenytoin, and rifamycins.

CASE E: ARIPIPRAZOLE AND DULOXETINE WITH ART

In a case report by Aung et al. (2010), aripiprazole 50 mg/day was prescribed to an HIV-infected 43-year-old also on duloxetine, darunavir, and ritonavir, resulting in aripiprazole toxicity (confusion and loss of coordination). The authors hypothesized that the combined CYP2D6 inhibition by duloxetine and CYP3A4 inhibition by antiretrovirals resulted in increased aripiprazole plasma levels, documented by a random steady-state serum aripiprazole concentration of 1,100 ng/ml (therapeutic range, 100–200 ng/ml) while on combination therapy.

Asenapine

Effectiveness/Uses

Asenapine demonstrates high affinity for adrenergic α1A, α2A, and α2C receptors, resulting in an elevated risk of orthostatic hypotension and syncope (Actavis, Inc., 2015a; Mandrioli et al., 2015). There are no studies currently published regarding its use in persons with HIV.

Pharmacokinetics and Drug–Drug Interactions

Asenapine is metabolized via glucuronidation at UGT1A4 and oxidative metabolism at CYP1A2, with minor contributions from CYP2D6 and CYP3A4. It is a weak inhibitor of CYP2D6 (Mandrioli et al., 2015). Potent CYP1A2 inhibitors such as fluvoxamine may increase asenapine serum levels, with concern for asenapine toxicity at higher doses (Actavis Inc., 2015a; Cozza and Wynn, 2012). Potent CYP2D6 inhibitors, including protease inhibitors, ketoconazole, and ritonavir, may increase serum levels of asenapine. Although a weak CYP2D6 inhibitor, asenapine has been found to increase serum levels of CYP2D6-dependent medications such as paroxetine and fluoxetine, which, if co-administered with 2D6-dependent ART, may have a compounding effect on serum levels and ART toxicity (Cozza and Wynn, 2012; Mandrioli et al., 2015). Importantly, potent CYP1A2 inducers such as ritonavir and the polyaromatic hydrocarbons (PAHs) in tobacco smoke can reduce asenapine serum concentrations (Cozza and Wynn, 2012; Skogh et al., 2002). Cessation of smoking in individuals receiving asenapine will lead to gradual increases in asenapine serum concentrations, with resultant side effects or toxicity (Cozza and Wynn, 2012). Initiation or resumption of smoking tobacco will lead to a gradual reduction of asenapine serum levels and may lead to breakthrough psychosis.

Blonanserin

Effectiveness/Uses

Blonanserin has no FDA approval but was approved in Japan (2008) and in Korea (2009) for the management of schizophrenia (Kishi et al., 2013). Authors of a meta-analysis demonstrated that blonanserin is equal in efficacy to FGAs and SGAs, but has a higher risk of akathisia than other SGAs (Kishi et al., 2013). There are no studies currently published regarding its use in persons with HIV.

Pharmacokinetics and Drug–Drug Interactions

Blonanserin is primarily metabolized by CYP3A4. Potent CYP3A4 inhibitors, including protease inhibitors, ketoconazole, and ritonavir, may increase serum levels of blonanserin, requiring close monitoring and possible dosage reduction to avoid blonanserin toxicity. Blonanserin has no effects on CYP450 activity (Kishi et al., 2013).

Clozapine

Effectiveness/Uses

Clozapine is currently the only antipsychotic approved for treatment-resistant schizophrenia and reducing risk of recurrent suicidal behavior in patients with schizophrenia (Novartis Pharmaceuticals Corp. and HLS Therapeutics, 2015). Authors of an effectiveness study compared clozapine and standard antipsychotic treatment in adults with schizophrenia and found that the clozapine treatment arm required fewer additional antipsychotics and hospitalizations and had lower rates of index treatment discontinuation (Stroup et al., 2016). Clozapine carries a risk of severe neutropenia and is therefore currently available in the United States via a restricted prescribing program requiring laboratory testing (Novartis Pharmaceuticals Corp. and HLS Therapeutics, 2015).

Nejad et al. (2009) discuss two patients with HIV with treatment-resistant schizophrenia that was successfully treated with clozapine. One patient was suspected to have clozapine-induced granulocytopenia, but later investigation found it was likely due to bacteremia, polypharmacy, and pre-existing mild pancytopenia unrelated to clozapine.

Clozapine has been studied as an agent to inhibit JCV cell entry in vitro, leading investigators to hypothesize that clozapine may be useful in treating or preventing PML (Baum et al., 2003; Elphick et al., 2004), but this intriguing finding has not been followed with published reports to date.

Clozapine is commonly associated with significant alterations in weight, glucose dysregulation, and dyslipidemia. Clinicians need to aggressively monitor for metabolic complications when concurrently prescribing ART and clozapine.

Pharmacokinetics and Drug–Drug Interactions

Clozapine is principally metabolized to its active metabolite, norclozapine, via CYP1A2 and (to a lesser extent) CYP3A4, CYP2D6, CYP2C9, and CYP2C19 (de Leon et al., 2005). Clozapine is also metabolized to clozapine-N-oxide, an inactive metabolite, via CYP3A4 and possibly flavin-containing monooxygenase 3 (Linnet and Olesen, 1997). Both active compounds are further glucuronidated by UGT1A4, UGT1A3, and possibly other UGTs (Breyer-Pfaff and Wachsmuth 2001; Mori et al., 2005).

Clozapine's manufacturer and authors of a review suggest reducing standard clozapine doses to one-third the standard dose when co-administered with potent CYP1A2 inhibitors such as fluvoxamine, ciprofloxacin, and ritonavir (Hill and Lee, 2013; Novartis Pharmaceuticals Corp. and HLS Therapeutics, 2015). Co-administration with potent CYP3A4 inducers such as carbamazepine, PAHs in tobacco smoke, ritonavir, and ketoconazole is not recommended, as these substances may lower clozapine serum levels by increasing its metabolism. Discontinuation of potent CYP1A2 or CYP3A4 inducers such as carbamazepine or tobacco smoking cessation, once at steady serum concentrations of clozapine, may result in a gradual 10-day to 2-week escalation in clozapine serum levels and worsened adverse effects and toxicity (Hill and Lee, 2013; Novartis Pharmaceuticals Corp. and HLS Therapeutics, 2015). More importantly, starting clozapine at standard dosing while in a smoke-free environment places patients at risk for a gradual loss of efficacy and relapse if they initiate or resume smoking, which increases the metabolism of clozapine (Cozza and Wynn, 2012).

Iloperidone

Effectiveness/Uses

Iloperidone has a clinical warning for priapism due to its alpha-adrenergic blockade (Rodriguez-Cabezas et al., 2014). There are no studies currently published regarding its use in persons with HIV.

Pharmacokinetics and Drug–Drug Interactions

Iloperidone is primarily metabolized by CYP2D6 and CYP3A4. Potent CYP3A4 and CYP2D6 inhibitors, including protease inhibitors, ketoconazole, and ritonavir, may increase serum levels of iloperidone and require 50% iloperidone dosage reduction to avoid iloperidone toxicity. Potent CYP3A4 inducers and pan-inducers such as carbamazepine and ritonavir may reduce serum levels of iloperidone (Arif and Mitchell, 2011; Mandrioli et al., 2015; Novartis Pharmaceuticals, 2016).

Lurasidone

Effectiveness/Uses

Lurasidone is a dopamine and serotonin antagonist via D-2, 5HT2A, and 5HT7 receptors, and its high affinity for 5HT7 may be responsible for its putative positive effects on cognitive functioning and affective symptoms (Loebel and Citrome, 2015). There are no studies currently published regarding its use in persons with HIV.

Pharmacokinetics and Drug–Drug Interactions

Lurasidone is primarily metabolized by CYP3A4. Lurasidone has no effects on P450 activity. Lurasidone is contraindicated with potent CYP3A4 inhibitors, including protease inhibitors, grapefruit juice, ketoconazole, and voriconazole, owing to increased risk of significant adverse effects like tardive dyskinesia, EPS, metabolic syndrome, sedation, and arrhythmia. Lurasidone is also contraindicated with potent CYP3A4 inducers and pan-inducers such as ritonavir, St. John's wort, and carbamazepine, which may reduce serum levels of lurasidone (Sunovion Pharmaceuticals, 2013).

Olanzapine

Effectiveness/Uses

Meyer et al. (1998) reported a case of successful treatment of depression with psychotic features with olanzapine in a patient

with AIDS who had a history of extrapyramidal syndrome while on typical antipsychotics and risperidone. Although that patient developed olanzapine dose-dependent akathisia, these adverse symptoms responded to dose reduction and beta-adrenergic blockade. Olanzapine is commonly associated with significant alterations in weight, glucose dysregulation, and dyslipidemia. Clinicians need to aggressively monitor for metabolic complications when concurrently prescribing ART and olanzapine.

Pharmacokinetics and Drug–Drug Interactions

Olanzapine is primarily metabolized by CYP1A2 and UGT (Eli Lilli and Co., 2015). Ritonavir, at a dose of 500 mg twice daily, reduced the mean AUC of olanzapine by 53% in healthy volunteers, presumably due to induction of CYP1A2 and/or UGT (Penzak et al., 2002). A more recent study conducted on 24 healthy volunteers replicated those results, where co-administration of fosamprenavir/ritonavir appeared to increase olanzapine's metabolism and reduce antipsychotic serum levels. Jacobs and colleagues (2014) propose a 50% dosage increase of olanzapine when combined with a ritonavir-boosted protease inhibitor. They also noted a potential risk of increased NNRTI serum levels with concomitant olanzapine administration, although the mechanism for this is unclear. Potent CYP1A2 inducers such as ritonavir and PAHs in tobacco smoke can reduce olanzapine concentrations (Cozza and Wynn, 2012; Hill and Lee, 2013; Skogh et al., 2002). Discontinuation of potent CYP1A2 inducers like ritonavir and cessation of smoking in individuals receiving olanzapine will lead to gradual increases in olanzapine concentrations, with resultant side effects or toxicity. Additionally, starting olanzapine at standard dosing while in a smoke-free environment places patients at risk for a gradual loss of efficacy and relapse if they initiate or resume smoking and thus increase the metabolism of olanzapine (Cozza and Wynn, 2012; Zullino et al., 2002).

Paliperidone

Effectiveness/Uses

Paliperidone, or 9-hydroxyrisperidone, is the major active metabolite of the SGA risperidone. There are no studies currently published regarding its use in persons with HIV.

Pharmacokinetics and Drug–Drug Interactions

Paliperidone's primary route of elimination is renal excretion unchanged in urine with limited hepatic metabolism via 2D6 and 3A4 (Janssen Pharmaceuticals, 2016). Paliperidone has no effect on CYP450 activity. Drug interactions are unlikely given paliperidone's pharmacokinetics, but strong CYP3A4/ P-glycoprotein co-inducers such as carbamazepine may decrease the serum concentration of paliperidone (Janssen Pharmaceuticals, 2016).

Quetiapine

Effectiveness/Uses

Quetiapine is a dopamine and serotonin antagonist with partial serotonin agonist properties via 5HT1A receptors, which may be responsible for its positive effects on cognitive functioning and affective symptoms. Quetiapine has moderate affinity for noradrenergic α1 and α2 receptors (AstraZeneca Pharmaceuticals, 2013; Hill and Lee, 2013). There are no studies currently published regarding its use in persons with HIV.

Pharmacokinetics and Drug–Drug Interactions

Quetiapine is principally metabolized by CYP3A4. Quetiapine has no effects on CYP450 activity. Close monitoring is required for use with potent CYP3A4 inhibitors such as protease inhibitors, grapefruit juice, and ketoconazole to avoid quetiapine toxicity (Hill and Lee, 2013). Clinical risk of priapism due to quetiapine toxicity secondary to CYP3A4 inhibition by protease inhibitors has been documented (Davol and Rukstalis, 2005). The manufacturer suggests reducing quetiapine to one-sixth the standard dose when co-administered with potent CYP3A4 inhibitors (AstraZeneca Pharmaceuticals, 2013).

Risperidone

Effectiveness/Uses

Second-generation antipsychotics have been studied as inhibitors of JCV cell entry (Baum et al., 2003; Chapagain et al., 2008) with intriguing but mixed results in vitro, leading investigators to hypothesize utilization for PML prophylaxis or treatment (Baum et al., 2003; Chapagain et al., 2008; Elphick et al., 2004). Focosi and colleagues (2007) discuss an HIV-seronegative person with PML infection after a stem cell transplant who demonstrated significant clinical response of the PML infection after treatment with risperidone. Expert opinion supports consideration of risperidone for treatment of PML in patients intolerant to or with contraindications for other therapies (Aksamit, 2008; Baum et al., 2003; Elphick et al., 2004), but the area requires further study.

Pharmacokinetics and Drug–Drug Interactions

Risperidone is metabolized predominantly by CYP2D6 and CYP3A4 to its major metabolite, 9-hydroxyrisperidone (Eap et al., 2001; Wang et al., 2007), and is a substrate of ABCB1 transport (Wikinski, 2005). Potent CYP2D6 inhibitors, such as diphenhydramine and bupropion, and poly-inhibitors, such as ritonavir and fluoxetine, can increase risperidone serum concentrations, requiring lower initial risperidone dosing, with a maximum dose of 8 mg per day if co-administered (Janssen Pharmaceuticals Incorperated, 2014). Potent CYP2D6 and CYP3A4 inducers such as carbamazepine, ritonavir, and pan-inducers may reduce serum levels of risperidone and require up to twice the standard dose (Janssen Pharmaceuticals Incorperated, 2014). Risperidone has been associated with reversible coma when co-administered with ritonavir (Jover et al., 2002) as well as with EPS and neuroleptic malignant syndrome with indinavir/ritonavir (Kelly et al., 2002; Lee et al., 2000), likely due to inhibition of risperidone metabolism.

Sertindole

Effectiveness/Uses

Sertindole was reintroduced in Europe in 2005, with the caveat that cardiac screening and monitoring would be strict. It is not available in the United States because of significant, dose-related QTc prolongation. There are no studies currently published regarding its use in persons with HIV.

Pharmacokinetics and Drug–Drug Interactions

Sertindole is metabolized by CYP3A4 and CYP2D6 (Wong et al., 1997). It is therefore contraindicated with potent CYP3A4 and/or CYP2D6 inhibitors, such as protease inhibitors, diphenhydramine, bupropion, and ketoconazole, and should not be co-administered with other QTc-prolonging drugs (Moore, 2002; Muscatello et al., 2014).

Ziprasidone

Effectiveness/Uses

Ziprasidone is a dopamine and serotonin antagonist with partial agonist properties at serotonin 5HT1A receptors. In a head-to-head meta-analysis, Rummel-Kluge et al. (2010) demonstrated that ziprasidone displayed the lowest overall metabolic side-effect profile of antipsychotics evaluated. Spiegel and colleagues (2010) discuss a three-case series of successful ziprasidone treatment of acute AIDS-related acute mania. Despite not receiving ART, secondary mania symptoms resolved with ziprasidone in all three cases and patients were stable at 1-month follow-up in two of the three cases. One case was lost to follow-up.

Pharmacokinetics and Drug–Drug Interactions

Ziprasidone metabolism is predominantly via a molybdoflavoprotein aldehyde oxidase, with minor contribution from CYP3A4 and CYP1A2 (Caley and Cooper, 2002; Spina and de Leon, 2007). It has no effect on CYP450 activity. Pharmacokinetic interactions through CYP450 pathways are restricted to co-administered potent CYP3A4 inhibitors and inducers (Caley and Cooper, 2002). Ziprasidone may be the neuroleptic least affected by CYP450 interactions. Ziprasidone's absorption increases twofold when ingested with food (Pfizer, Inc., 2015).

SUBSTANCE ABUSE MEDICATIONS

METHADONE

Effectiveness/Uses

Methadone has long been the standard maintenance therapy for opiate drug abuse. In a review of 28 clinical studies, methadone therapy was shown to decrease the risk of transmission of HIV through the reduction of injection drug use and of sharing of injection drug paraphernalia (Woody et al., 2014). Compared to injection drug use, methadone has been associated with increased use of ART (Wood et al., 2005), decreased reports of multiple sexual partners and exchanging money for sex (Stark et al., 1996), increased adherence to treatments (Morozova et al., 2013), and decreased risk for heroin overdose (Brugal et al., 2005). While there are drug interactions to be mindful of when prescribing antiretroviral therapies and methadone, there is compelling evidence in support of such an approach.

Pharmacokinetics and Drug–Drug Interactions

Methadone is primarily metabolized by CYPs 2B6 and 2C19, with the role of CYP 3A4 debated in the literature, and with minor contributions from CYPs 2D6 and 2C8 (Gruber and McCance-Katz, 2010; Kharasch and Stubbert, 2013; Totah et al., 2008) and glucuronidation via UGTs 1A3 and 2B7. Methadone is a mild inhibitor of CYPs 3A4 and 2D6 and UGTs 2B4 and 2B7 (Coller et al., 2012; Gelston et al., 2012; Kharasch et al., 2008). Co-administration with metabolic inhibitors and inducers, particularly pan-inhibitors and pan-inducers, may have a substantial impact on methadone metabolism. Inducers such as nevirapine (Altice et al., 1999) and rifampin (Holmes, 1990) have been reported to result in decreased methadone levels, precipitating withdrawal symptoms. In addition, nelfinavir has been found to induce methadone metabolism and clearance (Kharasch et al., 2009). Co-administration of pan-inhibitors/pan-inducers should be done with caution and with an eye toward adjusting methadone dosage to address any increase or decrease in its effectiveness.

Methadone also can affect ART pharmacokinetics, particularly NRTIs. It has been found to increase zidovudine levels and toxicity via inhibition of glucuronidation. Concomitant use of methadone with didanosine and stavudine in HIV-negative volunteers was found to reduce serum levels of each significantly by reducing bioavailability due to decreased gastric and bowel motility (Rainey et al., 2000).

BUPRENORPHINE

Effectiveness/Uses

Buprenorphine is a semisynthetic morphine-like drug with mixed agonist/antagonist properties shown to be effective in the treatment of opioid dependence. Treatment of injection opioid dependence with buprenorphine has shown significant decreases in injection drug use and sex risks in persons with HIV (Otiashvili et al., 2013; Woody et al., 2014). Woody and colleagues reported that the effect was comparable to naltrexone, although the dropout rate was significantly higher in the buprenorphine group.

Pharmacokinetics and Drug–Drug Interactions

The majority of buprenorphine's metabolism occurs via N-6-dealkylation at CYP 3A4 (Picard et al., 2005). Buprenorphine's active metabolite, norbuprenorphine, undergoes further metabolism via glucuronidation and sulfation. Norbuprenorphine's glucuronidation occurs primarily at UGT2B7, UGT1A1, and UGT1A3 (Rougeieg et al., 2010). CYP3A4 inhibitors such as ketoconazole and ritonavir are likely to result in significantly increased plasma levels of buprenorphine and possible toxicities. CYP3A4 inducers present a slightly more complicated scenario. CYP3A4 inducers that do not induce UGTs will increase the production of the active metabolite norbuprenorphine and may result in toxicity, while CYP3A4 inducers that also induce UGTs will

result in decreased plasma levels of both buprenorphine and norbuprenorphine, causing decreased efficacy.

DISULFIRAM

Effectiveness/Uses

Disulfiram is used to treat alcohol dependence, although its efficacy remains controversial (Laaksonen et al., 2008; Yoshimura et al., 2014). To date, there have been no studies evaluating disulfiram use in patients with HIV/AIDS.

Pharmacokinetics and Drug–Drug Interactions

Disulfiram's metabolism is not fully understood, but it is known to be a potent inhibitor of CYP2E1 and a modest inhibitor of CYP1A2 when administered chronically (Damkier et al., 1999; Frye and Branch, 2002). Efavirenz was associated with an increase in aldehyde dehydrogenase (ALDH) activity via unclear mechanisms, which can be problematic because that is also the mechanism of action of disulfiram. Atazanavir is associated with a reduction in the effect of disulfiram on ALDH (McCance-Katz et al., 2014). In light of the controversial efficacy, the lack of studies in persons with HIV, lack of understanding of disulfiram's metabolism, and the possibility of severe reactions, the use of disulfiram for persons with HIV should likely be reserved for treatment by clinicians experienced with disulfiram and its potential complications.

ACAMPROSATE

Effectiveness/Uses

Acamprosate's mechanism of action is not fully understood, although it is thought to be via GABA or NMDA. Acamprosate is generally well tolerated with limited negative side effects. But overall efficacy has been drawn into question in recent years (Berger et al., 2013; Mann et al., 2013).

Pharmacokinetics and Drug–Drug Interactions

Acamprosate does not undergo phase I or phase II metabolism and is excreted unchanged in the urine, with no reports of drug interactions in the literature to date.

NALTREXONE

Effectiveness/uses

Naltrexone is a semisynthetic opiate antagonist found to have benefit in the treatment of alcohol, opiate, and cocaine dependence. Oral naltrexone and injectable extended-release naltrexone are safe and effective in persons with mild to moderate chronic HCV and/or HIV infections (Micthell et al., 2012; Tetrault et al., 2012). When paired with behavioral therapy, naltrexone has been found to decrease drug use and HIV risk outcomes in opioid-injecting men (Otiashvili et al., 2012).

Pharmacokinetics and Drug–Drug Interactions

Very little research has been done toward understanding the metabolism and overall clearance of naltrexone. It seems that naltrexone is oxidatively metabolized to several metabolites by unknown enzymes (Wynn et al., 2009) and appears to then be glucuronidated by UGT2B7 prior to final elimination (Radominska-Pandya et al., 1999). A review of the literature did not find any case reports or substantive research on drug interactions with naltrexone.

CONCLUSION

The prescribing of medications to persons with HIV is a complicated undertaking. An understanding of current antiretroviral treatments and their side effects, toxicities, and potential drug interactions, as well as the specific uses and potential drug interactions of psychotropics, allows for better communication between all clinicians who treat persons with HIV. Most psychotropics are effective in the treatment of persons with HIV, but some, particularly the pan-inducing antiepileptics, are best avoided or, at least, very carefully monitored. Knowing that the possibility exists for drug–drug interactions allows for more careful monitoring (as in the case of tricyclic antidepressants) and for consideration of alternative treatments or precautions (such as barrier contraceptive methods). Being a pharmacologically knowledgeable multidisciplinary team member can save time, assets, and, more importantly, reduce patients' morbidity and mortality.

REFERENCES

Abb Vie Pharmaceuticals (2013). Norvir product information. Chicago, IL.

Abel S, Back D, Vourvahis M (2009). Maraviroc: pharmacokinetics and drug interactions. *Antivir Ther* 14:607–618.

Actavis, Inc. (2015a). Saphris (asenapine) package insert. St. Louis, MO.

Actavis, Inc. (2015b). Vraylar (cariprazine) package insert. http://www.allergan.com/assets/pdf/vraylar_pi. Accessed April 3, 2016.

Adams J, Greener B, Kashuba A (2012). Pharmacology of HIV integrase inhibitors. *Curr Opin HIV AIDS* 7:390–400.

Aksamit AJ (2008). Progressive multifocal leukoencephalopathy. *Curr Treat Options Neurol* 10(3):178–185.

Almeida L, Soares da Silva P (2007). Eslicarbazepine acetate (BIA 2-093). *Neurotherapeutics* 4(1):88–96.

Altice F, Friedland G, Cooney E (1999). Nevirapine induced opiate withdrawal among injection drug users with HIV infection receiving methadone. *AIDS* 13:957–962.

Ances B, Letendre S, Alexander T, Ellis R (2008). Role of psychiatric medications as adjunct therapy in the treatment of HIV associated neurocognitive disorders. *Int Rev Psychiatry* 20(1):89–93.

Arif SA, Mitchell MM (2011). Iloperidone: a new drug for the treatment of schizophrenia. *Am J Health Syst Pharm* 68(4):301–308.

Arseniou S, Arvaniti A. Samakouri M (2014). HIV infection and depression. *Psychiatry Clin Neurosci* 68(2):96–109.

Aschmann Y, Kummer O, Linka A, et al. (2008). Pharmacokinetics and pharmacodynamics of sildenafil in a patient treated with human immunodeficiency virus protease inhibitors. *Ther Drug Monit* 30:130–134.

AstraZeneca Pharmaceuticals (2013). Seroquel. http://www.azpicentral.com/seroquel-xr/seroquelxr.pdf#page=1. Accessed March 20, 2016.

Aung GL, O'Brien JG, Tien PG, Kawamoto LS (2010). Increased aripiprazole concentrations in an HIV-positive male concurrently taking duloxetine, darunavir, and ritonavir. *Ann Pharmacother* 44:1850–1854.

Avihingsanon A, Ramautarsing RA, Suwanpimolkul G, et al. (2014). Ergotism in Thailand caused by increased access to antiretroviral drugs: a global warning. *Top Antivir Med* 21(5):165–168.

Backman E, Triant VA, Ehrenfeld JM, Lu Z, Arpino P, Losina E, Gandhi RT (2013). Safety of midazolam for sedation of HIV-positive patients undergoing colonoscopy. *HIV Med* 14(6):379–384.

Badowski M, Pandit N (2014). Pharmacologic management of human immunodeficiency virus wasting syndrome. *Pharmacotherapy* 34:868–881.

Bagchi A, Sambamoorthi U, McSpiritt E, Yanos P, Walkup J, Crystal S (2004). Use of antipsychotic medications among HIV-infected individuals with schizophrenia. *Schizophr Res* 71(2-3):435–444.

Ballon J, Feifel D (2006). A systematic review of modafinil: potential clinical uses and mechanisms of action. *J Clin Psychiatry* 67:554–566.

Barroso J, Hammill B, Leserman J, et al. (2010). Physiological and psychosocial factors that predict HIV related fatigue. *AIDS Behav* 14:1415–1427.

Bates D, Herman RJ (2006). Carbamazepine toxicity induced by lopinavir/ritonavir and nelfinavir. *Ann Pharmacother* 40(6):1190–1195.

Batki S, Manfredi L, Jacob P, Jones R (1993). Fluoxetine for cocaine dependence in methadone maintenance: quantitative plasma and urine cocaine/benzoylecgonine concentrations. *J Clin Psychopharmacol* 13(4):243–250.

Baum S, Ashok A, Gee G, Dimitrova S, Querbes W, Jordan J, Atwood WJ (2003). Early events in the life cycle of JC virus as potential therapeutic targets for the treatment of progressive multifocal leukoencephalopathy. *J Neurovirol* 9 :32–37.

Baxter K, Preston CL (eds.) (2013). *Stockley's Drug Interactions*, 10th ed. London: Pharmaceutical Press.

Belcastro V, D'Egidiob C, Strianoc P, Verrottid A (2013). Metabolic and endocrine effects of valproic acid chronic treatment. *Epilepsy Res* 107(1-2):1–8.

Benton T, Lynch K, Dubé B, et al. (2010). Selective serotonin reuptake inhibitor suppression of HIV infectivity and replication. *Psychosom Med* 72(9):925–932.

Berger L, Fisher M, Brondino M, et al. (2013). Efficacy of acamprosate for alcohol dependence in a family medicine setting in the United States: a randomized, double-blind, placebo-controlled study. *Alcohol Clin Exp Res* 37(4):668–674.

Bertisch S, Herzig S, Winkelman J, Buettner C (2104). National use of prescription medications for insomnia: NHANES. *Sleep* 37(2):343–349.

Bertz R, Cao G, Cavanaugh J, et al. (1996). Effect of ritonavir on the pharmacokinetics of desipramine. In *Program and Abstracts of the XI International Conference on AIDS*, Vancouver, Canada, Abstract no. 2766.

Bialer M, Soares da Silva P (2012). Pharmacokinetics and drug interactions of eslicarbazepine acetate. *Epilepsia* 53(6):935–946.

Birbeck G, French JA, Perucca E, et al. (2012). Antiepileptic drug selection for people with HIV/AIDS: evidence-based guidelines from the ILAE and AAN. *Epilepsia* 53(1):207–214.

Blanche P, Rigolet A, Gombert B, Ginsburg C, Salmon D, Sicard D (1999). Ergotism related to a single dose of ergotamine tartrate in an AIDS patient treated with ritonavir. *Postgrad Med J* 75(887):546–547.

Blank MB, Himelhoch S, Walkup J, Eisenberg MM (2013). Treatment considerations for HIV-infected individuals with severe mental illness. *Curr HIV/AIDS Rep* 10(4):371–379.

Bockbrader H, Wesche D, Miller R, Chapel S, Janiczek N, Burger P (2010). A comparison of the pharmacokinetics and pharmacodynamics of pregabalin and gabapentin. *Clin Pharmacokinet* 49(10):661–669.

Boehringer Ingelheim Pharmaceuticals GmbH (2016). Aptivus package insert. Aptivus (tipranavir) product monograph. http://docs.boehringer-ingelheim.com/Prescribing%20Information/PIs/Aptivus/10003515%20US%2001.pdf?DMW_FORMAT=pdf. Accessed February 15, 2017.

Boinpally R, Gad N, Gupta S, Periclou A (2014). Influence of CYP3A4 induction/inhibition on the pharmacokinetics of vilazodone in healthy subjects. *Clin Ther* 36(11):1638–1649.

Bonora S, Calcagno A, Fontana S, D'Avolio A, Siccardi M, Gobbi F, Di Perri G (2007). Clinically significant drug interaction between tipranavir-ritonavir and phenobarbital in an HIV-infected subject. *Clin Infect Dis* 45(12):1654–1655.

Borders T, Stewart K, Wright P, et al. (2013). Risky sex in America: longitudinal changes in a community-based cohort of methamphetamine and cocaine users. *Am J Addict* 22:535–542.

Brechtl J, Breitbart W, Galietta M, Krivo S, Rosenfeld B (2001). The use of highly active antiretroviral therapy (HAART) in patients with advanced HIV infection: impact on medical, palliative care, and quality of life outcomes. *J Pain Symptom Manage* 21(1):41–51.

Breitbart W, Rosenfeld B, Kaim M, Funesti E (2001). A randomized, double-blind, placebo-controlled trial of psychostimulants for the treatment of fatigue in ambulatory patients with human immunodeficiency virus disease. *Arch Intern Med* 161:411–420.

Breyer-Pfaff U, Wachsmuth H (2001). Tertiary N-glucuronides of clozapine and its metabolite desmethylclozapine in patient urine. *Drug Metab Dispos* 29(10):1343–1348.

Brodie M (1995). Tiagabine pharmacology in profile. *Epilepsia* 36(Suppl 6):S7–S9.

Brugal M, Domingo-Salvany A, Puig R, Barrio G, García de Olalla P, de la Fuente L (2005). Evaluating the impact of methadone maintenance programs on mortality due to overdose and AIDS in a cohort of heroin users in Spain. *Addiction* 100(7):981–989.

Budman C, Vandersall T (1990). Clonazepam treatment of acute mania in an AIDS patient. *J Clin Psychiatry* 51(5):212.

Burger D, Huisman A, Van Ewijk N, et al. (2008). The effect of atazanavir and atazanavir/ritonavir on UDP-glucuronosyltransferase using lamotrigine as a phenotypic probe. *Clin Pharmacol Ther* 84(6):698–703.

Butt A (2003). Fatal lactic acidosis and pancreatitis associated with ribavirin and didanosine therapy. *AIDS Read* 13:344–348.

Cahn P, Pozniak AL, Mingrone H, et al. (2013). Dolutegravir versus raltegravir in antiretroviral-experienced, integrase-inhibitor-naive adults with HIV: week 48 results from the randomised, double-blind, non-inferiority SAILING study. *Lancet* 382:700–708.

Caley C, Cooper C (2002). Ziprasidone: the fifth atypical antipsychotic. *Ann Psychopharmacother* 36(5):839–851.

Carvalhal A, de Abreu PB, Spode A, Correa J, Kapczinski F (2003). An open trial of reboxetine in HIV-seropositive outpatients with major depressive disorder. *J Clin Psychiatry* 64(4):4221–4224.

Cazzullo CL Bessone E, Bertrando P, Pedrazzoli L, Cusini M (1998). Treatment of depression in HIV-infected patients. *J Psychiatry Neurosci* 23(5):293–297.

Cecchelli C, Grassi G, Pallanti S (2010). Aripiprazole improves depressive symptoms and immunological response to antiretroviral therapy in an HIV-infected subject with resistant depression. Case Rep Med 2010:836214.

Cephalon, Inc. (2015). Gabitril prescribing information. http://www.gabitril.com/Gabitril_PI.pdf Accessed April 3, 2016.

Chang Y, Yang L, Zhang M, Liu S (2014). Correlation of the UGT1A4 gene polymorphism with serum concentration and therapeutic efficacy of lamotrigine in Han Chinese of Northern China. *Eur J Clin Pharmacol* 70(8):941–946.

Chapagain ML, Sumibcay L, Gurjav U, Kaufusi PH, Kast RE, Nerurkar VR (2008). Serotonin receptor 2A blocker (risperidone) has no effect on human polyomavirus JC infection of primary human fetal glial cells. *J Neurovirol* 14(5):448–454.

Chen G, Lee R, Højer AM, Buchbjerg JK, Serenko M, Zhao Z (2013). Pharmacokinetic drug interactions involving vortioxetine (Lu AA21004), a multimodal antidepressant. *Clin Drug Investig* 33(10):727–736.

Chen K, Shen W, Lu M (2004). Implication of serum concentration monitoring in patients with lithium intoxication. *Psychiatry Clin Neurosci* 58(1):25–29.

Chesney M (2003). Adherence to HAART regimens. *AIDS Patient Care STDS* 17:169–177.

Chessick C, Allen MH, Thase M, et al. (2006). Azapirones for generalized anxiety disorder. *Cochrane Database Syst Rev* 19(3):CD006115.

Chiu C, Chuang D (2010). Molecular actions and therapeutic potential of lithium in preclinical and clinical studies of CNS disorders. *Pharmacol Ther* 128(2):281–304.

Choi E, Zmarlicka M, Ehret MJ (2012). Vilazodone: a novel antidepressant. *Am J Health Syst Pharm* 69(18):1551–1557.

Clarke SM, Mulcahy FM, Tjia J, Reynolds HE, Gibbons SE, Barry MG, Back DJ (2001). The pharmacokinetics of methadone in HIV-positive patients receiving the non-nucleoside reverse transcriptase inhibitor efavirenz. *Br J Clin Pharmacol* 51:213–217.

Cohen MA, Alfonso C (2004). AIDS psychiatry: psychiatric and palliative care and pain management. In G Wormser (ed.), *AIDS and Other Manifestations of HIV infection,* 4th ed. (pp. 537–576). New York: Elsevier.

Coller JK, Michalakas JR, James HM, Farquharson AL, Colvill J, White JM, Somogyi AA (2012). Inhibition of CYP2D6-mediated tramadol O-demethylation in methadone but not buprenorphine maintenance patients. *Br J Clin Pharmacol* 74(5):835–841.

Court M (2009). Metabolism in depth: phase II. In GH Wynn, JR Oesterheld, K Cozza, SC Armstrong (eds.), *Clinical Manual of Drug Interaction Principles for Medical Practice* (pp. 23–41). Arlington, VA: American Psychiatric Publishing.

Cozza K, Swanton E, Humphreys C (2000). Hepatotoxicity with combination of valproic acid, ritonavir, and nevirapine: a case report. *Psychosomatics* 41(5):452–453.

Cozza KL, Wynn GH (2012). Pharmacology updates for psychosomatic medicine: smoking and metabolism; asenapine; irreversible MAOIs. *Psychosomatics* 53:499–502.

Cramer JA, Leppik IE, Rue KD, Edrich P, Krämer G (2003). Tolerability of levetiracetam in elderly patients with CNS disorders. *Epilepsy Res* 56(2-3):135–145.

Crauwels H, van Heeswijk RP, Stevens M, Buelens A, Vanveggel S, Boven K, Hoetelmans R (2013). Clinical perspective on drug-drug interactions with the non-nucleoside reverse transcriptase inhibitor rilpivirine. *AIDS Rev* 15:87–101.

Currier M, Molina G, Kato M (2003). A prospective trial of sustained-release bupropion for depression in HIV-seropositive and AIDS patients. *Psychosomatics* 44(2):120–125.

Currier M, Molina G, Kato M (2004). Citalopram treatment of major depressive disorder in Hispanic HIV and AIDS patients: a prospective study. *Psychosomatics* 45(3):210–216.

Daeppen J, Gache P, Landry U (2002). Symptom-triggered vs fixed-schedule doses of benzodiazepines for alcohol withdrawal: a randomized treatment trial. *Arch Intern Med* 162(10):1117–1121.

Dam M, Ekberg R, Løyning Y, Waltimo O, Jakobsen K (1989). A double-blind study comparing oxcarbazepine and carbamazepine in patients with newly diagnosed, previously untreated epilepsy. *Epilepsy Res* 3(1):70–6.

Damkier P, Hansen L, Brosen K (1999). Effect of diclofenac, itraconazole, grapefruit juice and erythromycin on the pharmacokinetics of quinidine. *Br J Clin Pharmacol* 48:829–838.

d'Arminio Monforte A, Lepri AC, Rezza G, et al. (2000). Insights into the reasons for discontinuation of the first highly active antiretroviral therapy (HAART) regimen in a cohort of antiretroviral naïve patients I.CO.N.A. Study Group Italian Cohort of Antiretroviral-Naïve Patients. *AIDS* 14:499–507.

Davidson D, Schifitto G, Maggirwar S (2013). Valproic acid inhibits the release of soluble CD40L induced by non-nucleoside reverse transcriptase inhibitors in human immunodeficiency virus–infected individuals. *PloS One* 8(3):e59950.

Davol P, Rukstalis D (2005). Priapism associated with routine use of quetiapine: case report and reivew of literature. *Urology* 4(66):880.

De Clercq E (1998). The role of non-nucleoside reverse transcriptase inhibitors (NNRTIs) in the therapy of HIV-1 infection. *Antiviral Res* 38:153–179.

de Leon J, Armstrong SC, Cozza KL (2005). The dosing of atypical antipsychotics. *Psychosomatics* 46:262–273.

de Leon J, Nikoloff D (2008). Paradoxical excitation on diphenhydramine may be associate with being a CYP2D6 ultrarapid metabolizer: three case reports. *CNS Spect* 13(2):133–135.

DeSilva K, Le Flore D, Marston B, Rimland D (2001). Serotonin syndrome in HIV-infected individuals receiving antiretroviral therapy and fluoxetine. *AIDS* 15(10):1281–1285.

De Waal R, Cohen K, Maartens G (2013). Systematic review of antiretroviral-associated lipodystrophy: lipoatrophy, but not central fat gain, is an antiretroviral adverse drug reaction. *PloS One* 8:e63623.

De Wit S, Cremers L, Hirsch D, Zulian C, Clumeck N, Kormoss N (1999). Efficacy and safety of trazodone versus clorazepate in the treatment of HIV-positive subjects with adjustment disorders: a pilot study. *J Int Med Res* 27(5):223–232.

DHHS Panel on Antiretroviral Guidelines for Adults and Adolescents (2016). *Guidelines for the use of Antiretroviral Agents in HIV-1-Infected Adults and Adolescents*. https://aidsinfo.nih.gov/content-files/lvguidelines/adultandadolescentgl.pdf

DiMatteo M, Lepper H, Croghan T (2000). Depression is a risk factor for noncompliance with medical treatment: meta-analysis of the effects of anxiety and depression on patient adherence. *Arch Intern Med* 160(14):2101–2107.

Dou H, Ellison B, Bradley J, et al. (2005). Neuroprotective mechanisms of lithium in murine human immunodeficiency virus-1 encephalitis. *J Neurosci* 25(37):8375–8385.

Eap CB, Bondolfi G, Zullino D, et al. (2001). Pharmacokinetic drug interaction potential of risperidone with cytochrome P450 isozymes as assessed by the dextromethorphan, the caffeine, and the mephenytoin test. *Ther Drug Monit* 23(3):228–231.

Eli Lilli and Co. (2015). Zyprexa medication guide. http://pi.lilly.com/us/zyprexa-pi.pdf. Accessed March 20, 2016.

Elliott AJ, Roy-Byrne P (2000). Mirtazapine for depression in patients with human immunodeficiency virus. *J Clin Psychopharmacol* 20(2):265–267.

Elliott AJ, Uldall KK, Bergam K, Russo J, Claypoole K, Roy-Byrne PP (1998). Randomized, placebo-controlled trial of paroxetine versus imipramine in depressed HIV-positive outpatients. *Am J Psychiatry* 155(3):367–372.

Elphick GF, Querbes W, Jordan JA, et al. (2004). The human polyomavirus, JCV, uses serotonin receptors to infect cells. *Science* 306(5700):1380–1383.

Everall IP, Bell C, Mallory M, Langford D, Adame A, Rockestein E, Masliah E (2002). Lithium ameliorates HIV-gp120-mediated neurotoxicity. *Mol Cell Neurosci* 21(3):493–501.

Fernandez F, Levy J, Galizzi H (1988). Response of HIV-related depression to psychostimulants: case reports. *Hosp Community Psychiatry* 39:628–631.

Fernandez F, Levy J, Samley H, et al. (1995). Effects of methylphenidate in HIV-related depression: a comparative trial with desipramine. *Int J Psychiatry Med* 25:53–67.

Ferrando S, Goldman J, Charness W (1997). Selective serotonin reuptake inhibitor treatment of depression in symptomatic HIV infection and AIDS. Improvements in affective and somatic symptoms. *Gen Hosp Psychiatry* 19(2):89–97.

Ferrara M, Umlauf A, Sanders C, et al. (2014). The concomitant use of second-generation antipsychotics and long-term antiretroviral therapy may be associated with increased cardiovascular risk. *Psychiatry Res* 218(1):201–208.

Fillekes Q, Muro EP, Chunda C, et al. (2013). Effect of 7 days of phenytoin on the pharmacokinetics of and the development of resistance to single-dose nevirapine for perinatal HIV prevention: a randomized pilot trial. *J Antimicrob Chemother* 68(11):2609–2615.

Flanagan R, Dunk L (2008). Haematological toxicity of drugs used in psychiatry. *Hum Psychopharmacol* 23(Suppl 1):27–41.

Focosi D, Fazzi R, Montanaro D, Emdin M, Petrini M (2007). Progressive multifocal leukoencephalopathy in a haploidentical stem cell transplant recipient: a clinical, neuroradiological and virological response after treatment with risperidone. *Antiviral Res* 74(2):156–158.

Foisey M, Tseng A (2015). Toronto General Hospital Immunodeficiency Clinic drug interaction tables. http://www.hivclinic.ca/main/drugs_interact.html. Accessed September 17, 2015.

Forest Pharmaceuticals (2014). Viibryd product information. St. Louis: MO.

Fountoulakis KN, Gonda X, Baghai TC, et al. (2015). Report of the WPA section of pharmacopsychiatry on the relationship of antiepileptic drugs with suicidality in epilepsy. *Int J Psychiatry Clin Pract* 19(3):158–167.

Freudenreich O, Goforth HW, Cozza KL, Mimiaga MJ, Safren SA, Bachmann G, Cohen MA (2010). Psychiatric treatment of persons with HIV/AIDS: an HIV-psychiatry consensus survey of current practices. *Psychosomatics* 51(6):480–488.

Frye R, Branch R (2002). Effect of chronic disulfiram administration on the activities of CYP1A2, CYP2C19, CYP2D6, CYP2E1, and N-acetyltransferase in healthy human subjects. *Br J Clin Pharmacol* 53:155–162.

Fulco P, Vora U, Bearman G (2006). Acid suppressive therapy and the effects on protease inhibitors. *Ann Pharmacother* 40:1974–1983.

Gabbai A, Castelo A, Oliveira A (2013). HIV peripheral neuropathy. In G Said, C Krarup (eds.), *Handbook of Clinical Neurology*, Vol. 115. *Peripheral Nerve Disorders* (pp. 515–529). St. Louis: Elsevier.

Gandhi M, Gandhi R (2014). Single-pill combination regimens for treatment of HIV-1 infection. *N Engl J Med* 371:248–259.

Gelston E, Coller JK, Lopatko OV, et al. (2012). Methadone inhibits CYP2D6 and UGT2B7/2B4 in vivo: a study using codeine in methadone- and buprenorphine-maintained subjects. *Br J Clin Pharmacol* 73(5):786–794.

Glass J, Sproule B, Herrmann N, Busto U (2008). Effects of 2-week treatment with temazepam and diphenhydramine in elderly insomniacs: a randomized, placebo-controlled trial. *J Clin Psychopharmacol* 28(2):182–188.

Goldstein B, Goodnick P (1998). Selective serotonin reuptake inhibitors in the treatment of affective disorders—III. Tolerability, safety and pharmacoeconomics. *J Psychopharmacol* 12(3 Suppl B):S55–S87.

Gonzalez J, Batchelder A, Psaros C, Safren S (2011). Depression and HIV/AIDS treatment nonadherence: a review and meta-analysis. *J Acquir Immune Defic Syndr* 58(2):181–187.

Grant S, Heel R (1991). Vigabatrin. A review of its pharmacodynamic and pharmacokinetic properties, and therapeutic potential in epilepsy and disorders of motor control. *Drugs* 41(6):889–926.

Grassi B, Gambini O, Scarone S (1995). Notes on the use of fluvoxamine as treatment of depression in HIV-1-infected subjects. *Pharmacopsychiatry* 28(3):93–94.

Greenblatt DJ, Friedman H, Burstein ES, et al. (1987). Trazodone kinetics: effect of age, gender, and obesity. *Clin Pharmacol Ther* 42(2):193–200.

Greenblatt DJ, von Moltke LL, Daily JP, Harmatz JS, Shader RI (1999). Extensive impairment of triazolam and alprazolam clearance by short-term low-dose ritonavir: the clinical dilemma of concurrent inhibition and induction. *J Clin Psychopharmacol* 19(4):293–296.

Greenblatt DJ, von Moltke LL, Harmatz JS, et al. (2003). Short-term exposure to low-dose ritonavir impairs clearance and enhances adverse effects of trazodone. *J Clin Pharmacol* 43(4):414–422.

Greenblatt DJ, Zammit, G (2012). Pharmacokinetic evaluation of eszopiclone: clinical and therapeutic implications. *Expert Opin Drug Metab Toxicol* 8(12):1609–1618.

Griffin L, Annaert P, Brouwer K (2011). Influence of drug transport proteins on the pharmacokinetics and drug interactions of HIV protease inhibitors. *J Pharm Sci* 100:3636–3654.

Gruber V, McCance-Katz E (2010). Methadone, buprenorphine, and street drug interactions with antiretroviral medications. *Curr HIV/AIDS Rep* 7:152–160.

Gupta P (2013). Hepatitis C virus and HIV type 1 co-infection. *Infect Dis Rep* 5:e7.

Gustavson L, Sommerville KW, Boellner SW, Witt GF, Guenther HJ, Granneman GR (1998). Lack of a clinically significant pharmacokinetic drug interaction between tiagabine and valproate. *Am J Ther* 5(2):73–79.

Hahn K, Arendt G, Braun JS, et al.; German Neuro-AIDS Working Group (2004). A placebo-controlled trial of gabapentin for painful HIV-associated sensory neuropathies. *J Neurol* 251(10):1260–1266.

Hansen R, Gartlehner G, Lohr KN, Gaynes BN, Carey TS, et al. (2005). Efficacy and safety of second-generation antidepressants in the treatment of major depressive disorder. *Ann Intern Med* 143(6):415–426.

Haqqani A, Tilton J (2013). Entry inhibitors and their use in the treatment of HIV-1 infection. *Antiviral Res* 98:158–170.

Harvey B, Meyer C, Gallichio V, Manji H (2002). Lithium salts in AIDS and AIDS-related dementia. *Psychopharmacol Bull* 36(1):5–26.

He X, Hesse LM, Hazarika S, Masse G, Harmatz JS, Greenblatt DJ, Court MH (2009). Evidence for oxazepam as an in vivo probe of UGT2B17: oxazepam clearance is reduced by UGT2B15 D85Y polymorphism but unaffected by UGT2B17 deletion. *Br J Clin Pharmacol* 68(5):721–730.

Heinz W, Grau A, Ulrich A (2012). Impact of benzodiazepines on posaconazole serum concentrations: A population-based pharmacokinetic study on drug interaction. *Curr Med Res Opin* 28(4):551–557.

Hesse L, von Moltke L, Shader R, Greenblatt D (2001). Ritonavir, efavirenz, and nelfinavir inhibit CYP 2b6 activity in vitro: potential drug interactions with bupropion. *Drug Metab Dispos* 29(2):100–102.

Hill L, Lee K (2013). Pharmacotherapy considerations in patients with HIV and psychiatric disorders: focus on antidepressants and antipsychotics. *Ann Pharmacother* 47(1):75–89.

Hoare J, Carey P, Joska JA, Carrara H, Sorsdahl K, Stein DJ (2014). Escitalopram treatment of depression in human immunodeficiency virus/acquired immunodeficiency syndrome: a randomized, double-blind, placebo-controlled study. *J Nerv Ment Dis* Feb 202(2):133–137.

Hoggard P, Sales SD, Kewn S, Sunderland D, Khoo SH, Hart CA, Back DJ (2000). Correlation between intracellular pharmacological activation of nucleoside analogues and HIV suppression in vitro. *Antivir Chem Chemother* 11:353–358.

Holmes V (1990). Rifampin-induced methadone withdrawal in AIDS (letter). *J Clin Psychopharmacol* 10:443–444.

Holmes V, Fernandez F, Levy J (1989). Psychostimulant response in AIDS-related complex patients. *J Clin Psychiatry* 50:5–8.

Hriso E, Kuhn T, Masdeu J, Grundman M (1991). Extrapyramidal symptoms due to dopamine-blocking agents in patients with AIDS encephalopathy. *Am J Psychiatry* 148(11):1558–1561.

Hsu A, Carson K, Yung R, Pham P (2012). Severe prolonged sedation associated with coadministration of protease inhibitors and intravenous midazolam during bronchoscopy. *Pharmacotherpay* 32(6):538–545.

Hui C, Yuen M, Wong W, Lam SLC (2002). Mirtazapine induced hepatotoxicity. *J Clin Gastroenterol* 35(3):270–271.

Hui D (2003). Effects of HIV protease inhibitor therapy on lipid metabolism. *Prog Lipid Res* 42:81–92.

Hvenegaard M, Bang-Andersen B, Pedersen H, Jørgensen M, Püschl A, Dalgaard L (2012). Identification of the cytochrome P450 and other enzymes involved in the in vitro oxidative metabolism of a novel antidepressant, Lu AA21004. *Drug Metab Dispos* 40(7):1357–1365.

I Lorenzini K, Calmy A, Ambrosioni J, et al. (2012). Serotonin syndrome following drug–drug interactions and CYP2D6 and CYP2C19 genetic polymorphisms in an HIV-infected patient. *AIDS* 26:2417–2423.

Ilyas J, Vierling J (2014). An overview of emerging therapies for the treatment of chronic hepatitis C. *Med Clin North Am* 98:17–38.

Imai H, Tajika A, Chen P, et al. (2014). Azapirones versus placebo for panic disorder in adults. *Cochrane Database Syst Rev* 30(9):CD10828.

Jacobs BS, Colbers AP, Velthoven-Graafland K, Schouwenberg BJ, Burger DM (2014). Effect of fosamprenavir/ritonavir on the pharmacokinetics of single-dose olanzapine in healthy volunteers. *Int J Antimicrob Agents* 44:173–177.

Jacobsen N, Halling-Sørensen B. Birkved F (2008). Inhibition of human aromatase complex (CYP19) by antiepileptic drugs. *Toxicol In Vitro* 22(1):146–153.

Jann M, Spratlin V, Momary K, et al. (2012). Lack of a pharmacokinetic drug-drug interaction with venlafaxine extended-release/indinavir and desvenlafaxine extended-release/indinavir. *Eur J Clin Pharmacol* 68(5):715–721.

Janssen Ortho, LLC (2014). Medication guide Topamax (topiramate) tablets. https://www.fda.gov/downloads/Drugs/DrugSafety/UCM152837.pdf. Accessed February 24, 2017.

Janssen Pharmaceuticals, Inc. (2014). Risperdal (risperidone) package insert. http://www.janssen.com/us/sites/www_janssen_com_usa/files/products-documents/risperdal.pdf.

Janssen Pharmaceuticals, Inc. (2016). Invega (paliperidone) extended-release tablets prescribing information. http://www.invega.com/prescribing-information. Accessed March 20, 2016.

Ji P, Damle B, Xie J, Unger SE, Grasela DM, Kaul S (2008). Pharmacokinetic interaction between efavirenz and carbamazepine after multiple-dose administration in healthy subjects. *J Clin Pharmacol* 48(8):948–956.

Jong E, Oudhoff L, Epskamp C, et al. (2010). Predictors and treatment strategies of HIV-related fatigue in the combined antiretroviral era. *AIDS* 24:1387–1405.

Josephson F (2010). Drug-drug interactions in the treatment of HIV infection: focus on pharmacokinetic enhancement through CYP3A inhibition. *J Intern Med* 268:530–539.

Jover F, Cuadrado J, Andreu L, Merino J (2002). Reversible coma caused by risperidone-ritonavir interaction. *Clin Neuropharmacol* 25(5):251–253.

Kakuda T, Schöller-Gyüre M, Hoetelmans R (2010). Clinical perspective on antiretroviral drug-drug interactions with the non-nucleoside reverse transcriptase inhibitor etravirine. *Antivir Ther* 15:817–829.

Kakuda T, Schöller-Gyüre M, Hoetelmans RM (2011). Pharmacokinetic interactions of etravirine and non-antiretroviral drugs. *Clin Phanmacokinet* 50(1):25–39.

Kälviäinen R (1998). Tiagabine: a new therapeutic option for people with intellectual disability and partial epilepsy. *J Intellect Disabil Res* 42(Suppl 1):63–67.

Kato Y, Fujii T, Mizoguchi N, Takata N, Ueda K, Feldman MD, Kayser SR (2000). Potential interaction between ritonavir and carbamazepine. *Pharmacotherapy* 20(7):851–854.

Kearney B, Flaherty J, Shah J (2004). Tenofovir disoproxil fumarate: clinical pharmacology and pharmacokinetics. *Clin Pharmacokinet* 43:595–612.

Kelly D, Beique L, Bowmer M (2002). Extrapyramidal symptoms with ritonavir/indinavir plus risperidone. *Ann Pharmacother* 36(5):827–830.

Kenedi C, Goforth H (2011). A systematic review of the psychiatric side-effects of efavirenz. *AIDS Behav* 15:1803–1818.

Kharasch E, Bedynek PS, Walker A, Whittington D, Hoffer C (2008). Mechanism of ritonavir changes in methadone pharmacokinetics and pharmacodynamics: II. Ritonavir effects on CYP3A and P-glycoprotein. *Clin Pharmacol Ther* 84(4):506–512.

Kharasch E, Stubbert K (2013). Role of cytochrome P4502B6 in methadone metabolism and clearance. *J Clin Pharmacol* 53(3):305–313.

Kharasch E, Walker A, Whittington D, Hoffer C, Bedynek PS (2009). Methadone metabolism and clearance are induced by nelfinavir despite inhibition of cytochrome P4503A (CYP3A) activity. *Drug Alcohol Depend* 101(3):158–168.

King Pharmaceuticals, Inc. (2013). Sonata CIV US prescribing information. http://labeling.pfizer.com/ShowLabeling.aspx?id=710. Accessed April 10, 2016.

Kishi T, Matsuda Y, Nakamura H, Iwata N (2013). Blonanserin for schizophrenia: systematic review and meta-analysis of double-blind, randomized, controlled trials. *J Psychiatr Res* 49:149–154.

Klein M, Lee T, Brouillette MJ, et al. (2014). Citalopram for the prevention of depression and its consequences in HIV-hepatitis C coinfected individuals initiating pegylated interferon/ribavirin therapy: a multicenter randomized double-blind placebo-controlled trial. *HIV Clin Trials* 15(4):161–175.

Kobayashi T, Washiyama K, Ikeda K (2010). Inhibition of G-protein-activated inwardly rectifying K+ channels by the selective norepinephrine reuptake inhibitors atomoxetine and reboxetine. *Neuropsychopharmacology* 35(7):1560–1569.

Koppel B, Bharel C (2005). Use of amitriptyline to offset sleep disturbances caused by efavirenz. *AIDS Patient Care STDs* 19(7):419–420.

Kristiansen J, Hansen J (2000). Inhibition of HIV replication by neuroleptic agents and their potential use in HIV infected patients with AIDS related dementia. *Int J Antimicrob Agents* 14(3):209–213.

Laaksonen E, Koski-Jännes A, Salaspuro M, Ahtinen H, Alho H (2008). A randomized, multicentre, open-label, comparative trial of disulfiram, naltrexone, and acamprosate in the treatment of alcohol dependence. *Alcohol Alcohol* 43(1):53–61.

Laguno M, Blanch J, Murillas J, et al. (2004). Depressive symptoms after initiation of interferon therapy in human immunodeficiency virus-infected patients with chronic hepatitis C. *Antivir Ther* 9(6):905–909.

Lallemand F, Salhi Y, Linard F, Giami A, Rozenbaum W (2002). Sexual dysfunction in 156 ambulatory HIV-infected men receiving highly active antiretroviral therapy combinations with and without protease inhibitors. *J Acquir Immune Defic Syndr* 30:187–190.

Lana R, Núñez M, Mendoza J, Soriano V (2001). Rate and risk factors of liver toxicity in patients receiving antiretroviral therapy. *Med Clínica* 117:607–610.

Lanzafame M, Ferrari S, Lattuada E, Corsini F, Deganello R, Vento S, Concia E (2009). Mirtazapine in an HIV-1 infected patient with progressive multifocal leukoencephalopathy. *Infez Med* 17(1):35–37.

Laprise C, Baril J, Dufresne S, Trottier H (2013). Atazanavir and other determinants of hyperbilirubinemia in a cohort of 1150 HIV-positive patients: results from 9 years of follow-up. *AIDS Patient Care STDs* 27:378–386.

La Spina I, Porazzi D, Maggiolo F, Bottura P, Suter F (2001). Gabapentin in painful HIV-related neuropathy: a report of 19 patients, preliminary observations. *Eur J Neurol* 8(1):71–75.

Laughren T, Gobburu J, Temple RJ, et al. (2011). Vilazodone: clinical basis for the US Food and Drug Administration's approval of a new antidepressant. *J Clin Psychiatry* 72(9):1166–1173.

Lawitz E, Sulkowski M, Ghalib R, et al. (2014). Simeprevir plus sofosbuvir, with or without ribavirin, to treat chronic infection with hepatitis C virus genotype 1 in non-responders to pegylated interferon and ribavirin and treatment-naïve patients: the COSMOS randomised study. *Lancet* 384:1756–1765.

Lee F, Carr A (2012). Tolerability of HIV integrase inhibitors. *Curr Opin HIV AIDS* 7:422–428.

Lee S, Klesmer J, Hirsch B (2000). Neuroleptic malignant syndrome associated with use of risperidone, ritonavir, and indinavir: a case report. *Psychosomatics* 41(5):453–454.

Letendre S, Woods SP, Ellis RJ, et al. (2006). Lithium improves HIV-associated neurocognitive impairment. *AIDS* 20(14):1885–1888.

Leucht S, Cipriani A, Spineli L, et al. (2013). Comparative efficacy and tolerability of 15 antipsychotic drugs in schizophrenia: a multiple-treatments meta-analysis. *Lancet* 382(9896):951–962.

Levin G, Nelson LA, DeVane CL, Preston SL, Eisele G, Carson SW (2001). A pharmacokinetic drug-drug interaction study of venlafaxine and indinavir. *Psychopharm Bull* 35:62–71.

Levine S, Anderson D, Bystritsky A, Baron D (1990). A report of eight HIV-seropositive patients with major depression responding to fluoxetine. *J Acquir Immune Defic Syndr* 3(11):1074–1077.

L'homme R, Dijkema T, van der Ven AJ, Burger DM (2006). Brief report: enzyme inducers reduce elimination half-life after a single dose of nevirapine in healthy women. *J Acquir Immune Defic Syndr* 43(2):193–196.

Linnet K, Olesen OV (1997). Metabolism of clozapine by cDNA-expressed human cytochrome P450 enzymes. *Drug Metab Dispos* 25(12):1379-1382.

Loebel A, Citrome L (2015). Lurasidone: a novel antipsychotic agent for the treatment of schizophrenia and bipolar depression. *BJ Pscyh Bull* 5(39):237–241.

MacArthur R, DuPont H (2012). Etiology and pharmacologic management of noninfectious diarrhea in HIV-infected individuals in the highly active antiretroviral therapy era. *Clin Infect Dis* 55:860–867.

Mago R, Mahajan R, Thase M (2014). Levomilnacipran: a newly approved drug for treatment of major depressive disorder. *Expert Rev Clin Pharmacol* 7(2):137–145.

Mago R, Tripathi N, Andrade C (2014). Cardiovascular adverse effects of newer antidepressants. *Expert Rev Neurother* 14(5):539–551.

Malhi G, Tanious M, Das P, Coulston CM, Berk M (2013). Potential mechanisms of action of lithium in bipolar disorder. Current understanding. *CNS Drugs* 27(2):135–153.

Mandrioli R, Protti M, Mercolini L (2015). Novel atypical antipsychotics: metabolism and therapeutic drug monitoring (TDM). *Curr Drug Metab* 16:141–151.

Mann K, Lemenager T, Hoffmann S, et al. (2013). Results of a double-blind, placebo-controlled pharmacotherapy trial in alcoholism conducted in Germany and comparison with the US COMBINE study. *Addict Biol* 18(6):937–946.

Manning D, Jacobsberg L, Erhart S (1990). The efficacy of imipramine in the treatment of HIV-related depression. Abstract no. Th.B.32. International Conference on AIDS, San Francisco, CA, June 20–23, 1990.

Manzardo C, Gatell J (2014). Stribild® (elvitegravir/cobicistat/emtricitabine/tenofovir disoproxil fumarate): a new paradigm for HIV-1 treatment. *AIDS Rev* 16:35–42.

Markowitz J, Kocsis JH, Fishman B, et al. (1998). Treatment of depressive symptoms in human immunodeficiency virus–positive patients. *Arch Gen Psychiatry* 55(5):452–457.

Martin M, Kroetz D (2013). Abacavir pharmacogenetics—from initial reports to standard of care. *Pharmacotherapy* 33:765–775.

McCance-Katz E, Gruber VA, Beatty G, et al. (2014). Interaction of disulfiram with antiretroviral medcitions: efavirenz increases while atazanavir decreases disulfiram effect on enzymes of alcohol metabolism. *Am J Addict* 23(2):137–144.

McCance-Katz E, Rainey P, Jatlow P, Friedland G (1998). Methadone effects on zidovudine disposition (AIDS Clinical Trials Group 262). *J Acquir Immune Defi. Syndr Hum Retrovirol* 18:435–443.

McClean M (1994). Clinical pharmacokinetics of gabapentin. *Neurology* 44(6 Suppl 5):S17–S22, discussion S31–S32.

McElhiney M, Rabkin J, Van Girp W, Rabkin R (2013). Effect of armodafinil on cognition in patients with HIV/AIDS and fatigue. *J Clin Exp Neuropsychol* 35:718–727.

Meador K, Baker GA, Browning N, et al. (2009). Cognitive function at 3 years of age after fetal exposure to antiepileptic drugs. *N Engl J Med* 360(16):1597–1605.

Merck & Co, Inc. (2014). Belsomra prescribing information. http://www.merck.com/product/usa/pi_circulars/b/belsomra/belsomra_pi.pdf. Accessed April 10, 2016.

Meyer JM, Marsh J, Simpson G (1998). Differential sensitivities to risperidone and olanzapine in a human immunodificiency virus patient. *Biol Psychiatry* 44:791–794.

Micthell M, Memisoglu A, Silverman B (2012). Hepatic safety of injectable extended-release naltrexone in patients with chronic hepatitis C and HIV infection. *J Study Alcohol Drugs* 73(66):991–997.

Montgomery S, Herman B, Scweizer E (2009). The efficacy of pregabalin and benzodiazepines in generalized anxiety disorder presenting wiht high levels of insomnia. *Int Clin Psychopharmacol* 24(4):214–222.

Moore N (2002). Higher cardiovascular mortality with sertindole in ADROIT: a signal not confirmed. *Int J Psychiatry Clin Pract* 6(1):3–9.

Mori A, Maruo Y, Iwai M, et al. (2005). UDP-glucuronosyltransferase 1A4 polymorphisms in a Japanese population and kinetics of clozapine glucuronidation. *Drug Metab Dispos* 33(5):672–675.

Morozova O, Dvoryak S, Altice F (2013). Methadone treatment improves tuberculosis treatment among hospitalized opioid dependent patients in Ukraine. *Int J Drug Policy* 24(6):e91–e98.

Mouly S, Lown KS, Kornhauser D, et al. (2002). Hepatic but not intestinal CYP3A4 displays dose-dependent induction by efavirenz in humans. *Clin Pharmacol Ther* 72:1–9.

Moylan S, Giorlando F, Nordfjaern T, Berk M (2012). The role of alprazolam for the treatment of panic disorder in Australia. *Aust N Z J Psychiatry* 46(3):212–224.

Moyle G (2000). Clinical manifestations and management of antiretroviral nucleoside analog-related mitochondrial toxicity. *Clin Ther* 22:911–936; discussion 898.

Muro E, Fillekes Q, Kisanga ER, et al. (2012). Intrapartum single-dose carbamazepine reduces nevirapine levels faster and may decrease resistance after a single dose of nevirapine for perinatal HIV prevention. *J Acquir Immune Defic Syndr* 59(3):266–273.

Muscatello M, Bruno A, Micali Bellinghieri P, Pandolfo G, Zoccali RA (2014). Sertindole in schizophrenia: efficacy and safety issues. *Expert Opin Pharmacother* 15(13):1943–1953.

Mylan Pharmaceuticals (2015). Buspirone prescribing information. http://www.mylan.com/products/product-catalog/product-profile-page?id=9fbe7b27-1b5a-4362-9ff1-de5ba793e875. Accessed April 3, 2016.

Nakimuli-Mpungu E, Mojtabai R, Alexandre PK, et al. (2013). Lifetime depressive disorders and adherence to anti-retroviral therapy. *J Affect Disord* 145(2):221–226.

Nardi A, Valença AM, Freire RC, et al. (2011). Psychopharmacotherapy of panic disorder: 8-week randomized trial with clonazepam and paroxetine. *Braz J Med Biol Res* 44(4):366–373.

Nejad SH, Gandhi RT, Freudenreich O (2009). Clozapine use in HIV-infected schizophrenia patients: a case-based discussion and reivew. *Psychosomatics* 50(6):626–632.

Nekvindová J, Masek V, Veinlichová A, et al. (2006). Inhibition of human liver microsomal cytochrome P450 activities by adefovir and tenofovir. *Xenobiotica* 36:1165–1177.

Nel A, Kagee A (2013). The relationship between depression, anxiety and medication adherence among patients receiving antiretroviral treatment in South Africa. *AIDS Care* 25(8):948–955.

Novartis Pharmaceuticals (2014). Trileptal highlights of prescribing information. https://www.pharma.us.novartis.com/product/pi/pdf/trileptal.pdf. Accessed January 13, 2016.

Novartis Pharmaceuticals (2016). Fanapt package insert. https://www.fanapt.com/product/pi/pdf/fanapt.pdf. Accessed March 20, 2016.

Novartis Pharmaceuticals Corp. and HLS Therapeutics (2015). Clozaril (clozapine) full prescribing information. http://clozaril.com/wp-content/themes/eyesite/pi/Clozaril-2015A507-10022015-Approved.pdf. Accessed April 3, 2016.

O'Brien FE, Dinan TG, Griffin BT, Cryan JF (2012). Interactions between antidepressants and P-glycoprotein at the blood0brain barrier: clinical significance of invitro and in vivo findings. *Br J Pharmacol* 165(2):289–312.

Oechsler S, Skopp G (2010). An in vitro approach to estimate putative inhibition of buprenorphine and norbuprenorphine glucuronidation. *Int J Legal Med* 124(3):187–194.

Oesterheld J (2009). Transporters. In GW Wynn, J Oesterheld, KL Cozza, S Armstrong (eds.), *Clinical Manual of Drug Interactions for Medical Practice* (pp. 43–72). Arlington, VA: American Psychiatric Press.

Ohno Y, Hisaka A, Suzuki H (2007). General framework for the quantitative prediction of CYP3A4 mediated oral drug interactions based on the AUC increase by co-administration of standard drugs. *Clin Pharmacokinet* 46:681–696.

Okulicz J, Grandits G, French JA, et al. (2011). Virologic outcomes of HAART with concurrent use of cytochrome P450 enzyme-inducing antiepileptics: a retrospective case control study. *AIDS Res Ther* 8:18.

Okulicz J, Grandits GA, French JA, et al. (2013). The impact of enzyme-inducing antiepileptic drugs on antiretroviral drug levels: a case-control study. *Epilepsy Res* 103(2-3):245–253.

Oruch R, Elderbi MA, Khattab HA, Pryme IF, Lund A (2014). Lithium: a review of pharmacology, clinical uses, and toxicity. *Eur J Pharmacol* 740:464–473.

Ostad HE, Kiemke C, Pfuhlmann B (2012). Therapeutic drug monitoring for antidepressant drug treatment. *Curr Pharm Des* 18(36):5818–5827.

Otiashvili D, Kirtadze I, O'Grady K, Jones H (2012). Drug use and HIV risk outcome in opioid-injecting men in the Republic of Georgia: behavioral treatment + naltrexone compared to usual care. *Drug Alcohol Depend* 120(1):14–21.

Otiashvili D, Piralishvili G, Sikharulidze Z, Kamkamidze G, Poole S, Woody GE (2013). Methadone and buprenorphine-naloxone are effective in reducing illicit buprenorphine and other opioid use, and reducing HIV risk behaviors—outcomes of a randomized trial. *Drug Alcohol Depend* 133(2):376–382.

Otsuka Pharmaceuticals, Co., Ltd. (2015). Rexulti (brexpiprazole) prescribing information. http://otsuka-us.com/products/Documents/Rexulti.PI.pdf. Accessed April 3, 2016.

Otsuka Pharmaceuticals, Co., Ltd. (2016). Abilify prescribing information. http://otsuka-us.com/products/Documents/Abilify.PI.pdf. Accessed April 2, 2016.

Parenti DM, Simon GL, Scheib RG, et al. (1988). Effect of lithium carbonate in HIV-infected patients with immune dysfunction. *J Acquir Immune Defic Syndr* 1(2):119–124.

Paris BL, Ogilvie BW, Scheinkoenig JA, Ndikum-Moffor F, Gibson R, Parkinson A (2009). In vitro inhibition and induction of human liver cytochrome P450 enzymes by milnacipran. *Drug Metab Dispos* 37(10):2045–2054.

Park J, Vousden M, Brittain C, et al. (2010). Dose-related reduction in bupropion plasma concentrations by ritonavir. *J Clin Pharmacol* 50(10):1180–1187.

Park-Wyllie L, Antoniou T (2003). Concurrent use of bupropion with CYP2B6 inhibitors, nelfinavir, ritonavir and efavirenz: a case series. *AIDS* 17(4):638–640.

Patsalos P (2013a). Drug interactions with the newer antiepileptic drugs (AEDs)—part 1: pharmacokinetic and pharmacodynamic interactions between AEDs. *Clin Pharmacokinet* 52(11):927–966.

Patsalos P (2013b). Drug interactions with the newer antiepileptic drugs (AEDs)—part 2: pharmacokinetic and pharmacodynamic interactions between AEDs and drugs used to treat non-epilepsy disorders. *Clin Pharmacokinet* 52(12):1045–1061.

Pehrson A, Sanchez C (2014). Serotonergic modulation of glutamate neurotransmission as a strategy for treating depression and cognitive dysfunction. *CNS Spectr* 19(2):121–133.

Penzak SR, Hon YY, Lawhorn WD, Shirley KL, Spratlin V, Jann MW (2002). Influence of ritonavir on olanzapine pharmacokinetics in healthy volunteers. *J Clin Psychopharmacol* 22(4):366–370.

Perry C (2010). Maraviroc: a review of its use in the management of CCR5-tropic HIV-1 infection. *Drugs* 70:1189–1213.

Pfizer, Inc. (2015). Geodon (ziprasidone) prescribing information. http://labeling.pfizer.com/ShowLabeling.aspx?id=584#page=1. Accessed March 21, 2016.

Picard N, Cresteil T, Djebli N (2005). In vitro metabolism study of buprenorphine: evidence for new metabolic pathways. *Drug Metab Dispos* 33:689–695.

Pollack MH, Hoge EA, Worthington JJ, Moshier SJ, Wechsler RS, Brandes M, Simon NM (2011). Eszopicone for the treatment of posttraumatic stress disorder and associated insomnia: a randomized, double-blind, placebo-controlled trial. *J Clin Psychiatry* 72(7):892–897.

Prasad M, Krishnan P, Sequeiria R (2014). Anticonvulsant therapy for status epilepticus. *Cochrane Database Syst Rev* 19(4):CD003723.

Rabkin J, Harrison W (1990). Effect of imipramine on depression and immune status in a sample of men with HIV infection. *Am J Psychiatry* 147(4):495–497.

Rabkin J, McElhiney M, Rabkin R (2011). Treatment of HIV-related fatigue with armodafinil: a placebo-controlled randomized trial. *Psychosomatics* 52:328–336.

Rabkin J, McElhiney M, Rabkin R, Ferrando S (2004). Modafinil treatment for fatigue in HIV+ patients: a pilot study. *J Clin Psychiatry* 65:1688–1695.

Rabkin J, Rabkin R, Wagner G (1994). Effects of fluoxetine on mood and immune status in depressed patients with HIV illness. *J Clin Psychiatry* 55(3):92–97.

Rabkin J, Wagner G, Rabkin R (1994). Effects of sertraline on mood and immune status in patients with major depression and HIV illness: an open trial. *J Clin Psychiatry* 55(10):433–439.

Rabkin J, Wagner G, Rabkin R (1999). Fluoxetine treatment for depression in patients with HIV and AIDS: a randomized, placebo-controlled trial. *Am J Psychiatry* 156(1):101–107.

Radominska-Pandya A, Czernik P, Little J (1999). Structural and functional studies of UDP-glucuronosyltransferases. *Drug Metab Rev* 31:817–899.

Rainey PM, Friedland G, McCance-Katz EF, Andrews L, Mitchell SM, Charles C, Jatlow P (2000). Interaction of methadone with didanosine and stavudine. *J Acquir Immune Defic Syndr* 24(3):241–248.

Ramachandran G, Glickman L, Levenson J, Rao C (1997). Incidence of extrapyramidal syndromes in AIDS patients and a comparison group of medically ill patients. *J Neuropsychiatry Clin Neurosci* 9(4):579–583.

Razali S, Hasanah C (1999). Cost-effectiveness of cyclic antidepressants in a developing country. *Aust N Z J Psychiatry* 33(2):283–284.

Reid JG, Gitlin MJ, Altshuler LL (2013). Lamotrigine in psychiatric disorders. *J Clin Psychiatry* 74(7):675–684.

Rho M, Perazella M (2007). Nephrotoxicity associated with antiretroviral therapy in HIV-infected patients. *Curr Drug Saf* 2:147–154.

Robertson SM, Maldarelli F, Natarajan V, Formentini E, Alfaro RM, Penzak SR (2008). Efavirenz induces CYP2B6-mediated hydroxylation of bupropion in healthy subjects. *J Acquir Immune Defic Syndr* 49(5):513–519.

Robertson S, Penzak SR, Lane J, Pau AK, Mican JM (2005). A potentially significant interaction between efavirenz and phenytoin: a case report and review of the literature. *Clin Infect Dis* 41(2):e15–e18.

Rodriguez-Cabezas LA, Kong BY, Agarwal G (2014). Priapism associated with iloperidone: a case report. *Gen Hosp Psychiatry* 36:451. e5–451e.6.

Roehrs T, Roth T (2012). Insomnia pharmacotherapy. *Neurotherapeutics* 9(4):728–738.

Rosenzweig P, Canal M, Patat A, et al. (2002). A review of the pharmacokinetics, tolerability and pharmacodynamics of amisulpride in healthy volunteers. *Hum Psychopharmacol* 17:1–13.

Rougeieg K, Picard N, Sauvage FL, Gaulier JM, Marquet P (2010). Contribution of the difference UDP-glucuronosyltransferase (UGT) isoforms to buprenorphine and norbuprenorphine metabolism and relationship with the main UGT polymorphism in a bank of human liver microsomes. *Drug Metab Dispos* 38(1):40–45.

Rummel-Kluge C, Komossa K, Schwarz S, et al. (2010). Head-to-head comparisions of metabolic side effects of second generation antipsychotics in the treatment of schizophrenia: A systematic review and meta-analysis. *Schizophr Res* :225–233.

Sacktor N, Schifitto G, McDermott MP, Marder K, McArthur JC, Kieburtz K (2000). Transdermal selegiline in HIV-associated cognitive impairment: pilot, placebo-controlled study. *Neurology* 54(1):233–235.

Sanofi-Aventis Canada, Inc. (2014). Imovane. http://products.sanofi.ca/en/imovane.pdf. Accessed April 10, 2016.

Sanofi-Aventis US, LLC (2014). Ambien. http://products.sanofi.us/ambien/ambien.pdf. Accessed April 10, 2016.

Sarris J, Scholey A, Schweitzer I, et al. (2012). The acute effects of kava and oxazepam on anxiety, mood, neurocognition; and genetic correlates: a randomized, placebo-controlled, double-blind study. *Hum Psychopharmacol* 27(3):262–269.

Sax P, Kumar P (2004). Tolerability and safety of HIV protease inhibitors in adults. *J Acquir Immune Defic Syndr* 37:1111–1124.

Schifitto G, Peterson DR, Zhong J, et al. (2006). Valproic acid adjunctive therapy for HIV-associated cognitive impairment: a first report. *Neurology* 66(6):919–921.

Schifitto G, Yiannoutsos CT, Ernst T, et al. (2009). Selegiline and oxidative stress in HIV-associated cognitive impairment. *Neurology* 73(23):1975–1981.

Schifitto G, Zhang J, Evans SR, et al.; the ACTG A5090 Team (2007). A multicenter trial of Selegiline Transdermal System for HIV-associated cognitive impairment. *Neurology* 69(13):1314–1321.

Schifitto G, Zhong J, Gill D, et al. (2009). Lithium therapy for human immunodeficiency virus type 1-associated neurocognitive impairment. *J Neurovirol* 15(2):176–186.

Schrijvers R (2013). Etravirine for the treatment of HIV/AIDS. *Expert Opin Pharmacother* 14:1087–1096.

Schuckit M (2014). Recognition and management of withdrawal delirium. *N Engl J Med* 371:2109–2113.

Sheehan N, Brouillette M, Delisle MJ, A (2006). Possible interaction between lopinavir/ritonavir and valproic Acid exacerbates bipolar disorder. *Ann Pharmacother* 41(1):147–150.

Shelton MJ, Wynn HE, Hewitt RG, DiFrancesco R (2001). Effects of grapefruit juice on pharmacokinetic exposure to indinavir in HIV-positive subjects. *J Clin Pharmacol* 41(4):435-42.

Siddiqi O, Birbeck G (2013). Safe treatment of seizures in the setting of HIV/AIDS. *Curr Treat Options Neurol* 15(4):529–543.

Sills G, Brodie M (2007). Pharmacokinetics and drug interactions with zonisamide. *Epilepsia* 48(3):435–441.

Simpson D, McArthur JC, Olney R, et al.; Lamotrigine HIV Neuropathy Study Team (2003). Lamotrigine for HIV-associated painful sensory neuropathies: a placebo-controlled trial. *Neurology* 60(9):1508–1514.

Skogh E, Reis M, Dahl ML, Lundmark J, Bengtsson F (2002). Therapeutic drug monitoring data on olanzapine and its N-demethyl metabolite in the naturalistic clinical setting. *Ther Drug Monit* 24(4):518–526.

Smith P, DiCenzo R, Morse G (2001). Clinical pharmacokinetics of non-nucleoside reverse transcriptase inhibitors. *Clin Pharmacokinet* 40:893–905.

Sobanski E, Sabljic D, Alm B, et al. (2012). A randomized, waiting list-controlled 12-week trial of atomoxetine in adults with ADHD. *Pharmacopsychiatry* 45:100–107.

Spak C, Dhanireddy S, Kosel B (2008). Clinical interaction between efavirenz and phenytoin. *AIDS* 22(1):164–165.

Spiegel D, Weller A, Pennell K, Turner K (2010). The successful treatment of mania due to acquired immunodeficiency syndrome using ziprasidone: a case series. *J Neuropsychiatry Clin Neurosci* 22(1):111–114.

Spiegel M, Schmidauer C, Kampfl A, Sarcletti M, Poewe W (2001). Cerebral ergotism under treatment with ergotamine and ritonavir. *Neurology* 28(57):743–744.

Spiller H, Hays H, Alequas A (2013). Overdose of drugs for attention-deficit hyperactivity disorder: clinical presentation, mechanisms of toxicity, and management. *CNS Drugs* 27:531–543.

Spina E, de Leon J (2007). Metabolic drug interactions with newer antipsychotics: a comparative reveiw. *Basic Clin Pharmacol Toxicol* 100(1):4–22.

Spina E, Trifiro G, Caraci F (2012). Clinically significant drug interactions with newer antidepressants. *CNS Drugs* 26(1):39–67.

Stahl SM (2014). *Stahl's Essential Psychopharmacology Prescriber's Guide*, 5th ed. New York: Cambridge University Press.

Stark K, Muller R, Bienzle U, Guggenmoos-Holzman I (1996). Methadone maintenance treatment and HIV risk-taking behaviour among injection drug users in Berlin. *J Epidemiol Community Health* 50(5):534–537.

Stroup TS, Gerhard T, Crystal S, Huang C, Olfson M (2016). Comparative effectiveness of clozapine and standard antipsychotic treatment in adults with schizophrenia. *Am J Psychiatry* 173(2):166–173.

Sui Z, Sniderhan LF, Schifitto G, Phipps RP, Gelbard HA, Dewhurst S, Maggirwar SB (2007). Functional synergy between CD40 ligand and HIV-1 Tat contributes to inflammation: implications in HIV type 1 dementia. *J Immunol* 178(5):3226–3236.

Sunovion Pharmaceuticals (2013). Latuda prescribing information. http://www.latuda.com/LatudaPrescribingInformation.pdf. Accessed March 20, 2016.

Sunovion Pharmaceuticals (2014). Lunesta posted approved labeling. http://www.lunesta.com/pdf/PostedApprovedLabelingText.pdf. Accessed April 10, 2016.

Talmo G, Liao J, Bayerl M (2010). Oral administration of analgesia and anxiolysis for pain associated with bone marrow biopsy. *Support Care Cancer* 18(3):301–305.

Tang M, Shafer R (2012). HIV-1 antiretroviral resistance: scientific principles and clinical applications. *Drugs* 72(9):e1–e25.

Tattevin P, Revest M, Chapplain JM, Ratajczak-Enselme M, Arvieux C, Michelet C (2013). Increased risk of renal stones in patients treated with atazanavir. *Clin Infect Dis* 56:1186.

Tetrault J, Tate JP, McGinnis KA, et al.; Veterans Aging Cohort Study Team (2012). Hepatic safety and antiretroviral effectiveness in HIV-infected patients receiving naltrexone. *Alcohol Clin Exp Res* 36(2):318–324.

Thio C, Locarnini S (2007). Treatment of HIV/HBV coinfection: clinical and virologic issues. *AIDS Rev* 9:40–53.

Thormhalen M (2006). Paroxetine use during pregnancy: is it safe? *Ann Pharmacother* 40(10):1834–1837.

Totah R, Sheffels P, Roberts T, Whittington D, Thummel K, Kharasch ED (2008). Role of CYP2B6 in stereoselective human methadone metabolism. *Anesthesiology* 108(3):363–374.

Treisman GJ, Angelino AF, Hutton HE (2001). Psychiatric issues in the management of patients with HIV infection. *JAMA* 286(22):2857–2864.

UCB Pharma, Inc (2013). Keppra (Levetiracetam) Tablets and oral solution medication guide. Smyrna, GA. https://www.fda.gov/downloads/drugs/drugsafety/ucm152832.pdf. Accessed February 24, 2017.

Uchaipichat V, Suthisisang C, Miners J (2013). The glucuronidation of R- and S-lorazepam: human liver microsomal kinetics, UDP-glucuronosyltransferase enzyme selectivity, and inhibition by drugs. *Drug Metab Dispos* 41(6):1273–1284.

Usach I, Melis V, Peris J (2013). Non-nucleoside reverse transcriptase inhibitors: a review on pharmacokinetics, pharmacodynamics, safety and tolerability. *J Int AIDS Soc* 16:1–14.

Vaishnavi S, Nemeroff CB, Plott SJ, Rao SG, Kranzler J, Owens MJ (2004). Milnacipran: a comparative analysis of human monoamine uptake and transporter binding affinity. *Biol Psychiatry* 55(3):320–322.

Vande Griend JP, Anderson SL (2003). Histamine-1 receptor antagonism for treatment of insomnia. *J Am Pharm Assoc* 52(6):e210–e219.

van der Lee M, Dawood L, ter Hofstede HJ, et al. (2006). Lopinavir/ritonavir reduces lamotrigine plasma concentrations in healthy subjects. *Clin Pharmacol Ther* 80(2):159–168.

Verrotti A, Loiacono G, Rossi A, Zaccara G (2014). Eslicarbazepine acetate: an update on efficacy and safety in epilepsy. *Epilepsy Res* 108(1):1–10.

von Moltke LL, Duan SX, Greenblatt DJ, Fogelman SM, Schmider J, Harmatz JS, Shader RI (1997). Venlafaxine and metabolites are very weak inhibitors of human cytochrome P450-3A isoforms. *Biol Psychiatry* 41(3):377–380.

von Moltke LL, Greenblatt DJ, Granda BW, et al. (2001). Inhibition of human cytochrome P450 isoforms by nonnucleoside reverse transcriptase inhibitors. *J Clin Pharmacol* 41:85–91.

Wagner G, Rabkin R (2000). Effects of dextroamphetamine on depression and fatigue in men with HIV: a double-blind, placebo-controlled trial. *J Clin Psychiatry* 61:436–440.

Wagner G, Rabkin J, Rabkin R (1997). Dextroamphetamine as a treatment for depression and low energy in AIDS patients: a pilot study. *J Psychosom Res* 42:407–411.

Wang L, Yu L, Zhang A, Fang C, Du J (2007). Serum prolactin levels, plasma risperidone levels, polymorphism of cytochrome P450 2D6 and clinical response in patients with schizophrenia. *J Psychopharmacol* 21(8):837–842.

Wallace V, Segerdahl AR, Blackbeard J, Pheby T, Rice AS (2008). Anxiety-like behaviour is attenuated by gabapentin, morphine, and diazepam in a rodent model of HIV anti-retroviral-associated neuropathic pain. *Neurosci Lett* 228(1):153–156.

White J, Christensen J, Singer C (1992). Methylphenidate as a treatment for depression in acquired immunodeficiency syndrome: an n-of-1 trial. *J Clin Psychiatry* 53:153–156.

Wienkers L, Allievi C, Hauer M, Wynalda M (1999). Cytochrome P-450-mediated metabolism of the individual enantiomers of the antidepressant agent reboxetine in human liver microsomes. *Drug Metab Dispos* 27(11):1334–1340.

Wikinski S (2005). Pharmacokinetic mechanisms underlying resistance in psychopharmacological treatment. The role of P-glycoprotein. *Vertex* 16(64:438–441).

Wong S, Cao G, Mack R, Granneman G (1997). Pharmacokinetics of sertindole in healthy young and elderly male and female subjects. *Clin Pharmacol Ther* 62(2):157–164.

Wood E, Hogg RS, Kerr T, Palepu A, Zhang R, Montaner JS (2005). Impact of assessing methadone on the time to initiating HIV treatment among antiretroviral naive HIV-infected injection drug users. *AIDS* 19(8):837–839.

Woody G, Bruce D, Korthuis PT, et al. (2014). HIV risk reduction with buprenorphine-naloxone or methadone: findings from a randomized trial. *J Acquir Immune Defic Syndr* 66(3):288–293.

Wright C, Downing J, Mungall D, et al. (2013). Clinical pharmacology and pharmacokinetics of levetiracetam. *Front Neurol* 192:1–6.

Wynn GW, Armstrong S (2009). Neurology: antiepileptic drugs. In GW Wynn, J Oesterheld, KL Cozza, S Armstrong (eds.), *Clinical Manual of Drug Interaction Principles for Medical Practice* (pp. 325–352). Arlington, VA: American Psychiatric Publishing.

Wynn GW, Oesterheld J, Cozza KL, Armstrong S (eds.) (2009). *Clinical Manual of Drug Interaction Principles for Medical Practice*. Arlington, VA: American Psychiatric Press.

Wynn GW, Sandson N, Muniz J (2010). Psychiatry: antipsychotics. In Wynn GW, Oesterheld J, Cozza KL, Armstrong S (eds.), *Clinical Manual of Drug Interaction Principles for Medical Practice* (pp. 436–443). Arlington, VA: American Psychiatric Publishing.

Yoshimura A, Kimura M, Nakayama H, et al. (2014). Efficacy of disulfiram for the treatment of alcohol dependence asessed with a multicenter randomized controlled trial. *Alcohol Clin Exp Res* 38(2):572–578.

Yun L, Maravi M, Kobayashi JS, Barton PL, Davidson AJ (2005). Antidepressant treatment improves adherence to antiretroviral therapy among depressed HIV-infected patients. *J Acquir Immune Defic Syndr* 38(4):432–438.

Zhang X, Lalezari JP, Badley AD, Dorr A, Kolis SJ, Kinchelow T, Patel IH (2004). Assessment of drug-drug interaction potential of enfuvirtide in human immunodeficiency virus type 1-infected patients. *Clin Pharmacol Ther* 75:558–568.

Zullino D, Delessert D, Eap CB, Preisig M, Baumann P (2002). Tobacco and cannabis smoking cessation can lead to intoxication with clozapine or olanzapine. *Int Clin Psychopharmacol* 17(3):141–143.

PART X

HIV PSYCHIATRY AND MULTIMORBID MEDICAL CONDITIONS

43.

HEPATITIS C AND HIV CO-INFECTION

Jennifer Cohen Price, Priyanka Amin, and Antoine Douaihy

Liver disease, primarily due to co-infection with hepatitis B virus (HBV) or hepatitis C virus (HCV), is a major cause of morbidity among persons living with HIV infection and is a leading non-AIDS-related cause of death in persons with HIV (Smith et al., 2014). Because of shared risk factors, HIV-HCV co-infection is common: 25% of HIV-infected individuals in the United States are HCV-antibody positive, with rates as high as 85% in HIV-infected injection drug users (Ghany et al., 2009; Sulkowski and Thomas, 2003). Compared to HCV-mono-infected patients, HIV-HCV-co-infected patients have a more aggressive disease course, with higher risk of developing cirrhosis and death. Compounding this, interferon-based treatment, which, until recently, was the mainstay of HCV therapy, is less effective in individuals with HIV. Thus, people living with HIV are disproportionately affected by chronic HCV, which historically was more difficult to cure.

Since the introduction of highly potent and well-tolerated HCV direct-acting antivirals (DAA) in 2011, there has been a significant evolution in the HCV treatment landscape. HCV is now rapidly curable in the vast majority of patients, regardless of HIV co-infection. These developments have been met with great excitement and hope among HCV-infected individuals and their clinicians. However, several barriers to achieving HCV cure remain, including managing comorbidities and accessing care. Given the high prevalence of psychiatric comorbidities in the HIV-HCV-co-infected population, psychiatrists and other mental health clinicians will continue to play an essential role in managing of HIV-HCV co-infection and in eradicating HCV.

HCV EPIDEMIOLOGY AND NATURAL HISTORY

HCV is a small, enveloped, positive-sense single-stranded RNA virus of the *Flaviviridae* family. Viral replication of HCV is very error prone, resulting in heterogeneity of the HCV population within an individual (quasi-species) and within a population (genotypes). Six major HCV genotypes have been identified, and treatment options and response vary by genotype. Genotype 1 is the most common globally and in the United States. Worldwide, 130–150 million individuals are chronically infected with HCV (World Health Organization, 2016). In the United States, HCV prevalence

is approximately 1.3–1.9%, which translates to an estimated 2.7 to 3.9 million people. About 8% of chronic HCV patients in the United States are co-infected with HIV (Armstrong et al., 2006; Chak et al., 2011; Denniston et al., 2014).

HCV shares similar modes of transmission as HIV, although the transmission efficiencies of the two viruses vary. HCV is most efficiently spread through percutaneous exposure to blood; therefore, intravenous drug use remains the most important risk factor for transmission. In the past, receipt of blood products was a major risk factor for HCV transmission. However, since screening of donated blood was implemented in 1992, this risk has been nearly eliminated. Sexual transmission of HCV is relatively inefficient, with a transmission risk of approximately 1 per 190,000 sexual contacts among monogamous heterosexual couples, which translates to an estimated incidence among partners ranging from 3.6 to 7.2 per 10,000 person-years (Terrault et al., 2013). However, acute outbreaks of sexually transmitted HCV among HIV-positive men who have sex with men have been well documented (e.g., sexual transmission of HCV among HIV-infected men who have sex with men in New York City, 2005–2010) (Centers for Disease Control and Prevention [CDC], 2011). This epidemic of acute HCV among HIV-infected men who have sex with men is ongoing; the Dutch Acute HCV in HIV study reported a mean incidence of 11 per 1,000 person-years in 2014 (Hullegie et al., 2016). Therefore, annual HCV testing is recommended for HIV-infected men who have sex with men.

After exposure to HCV, 15–40% of acutely infected individuals will spontaneously clear the virus within 6 months (Figure 43.1). Their HCV antibody test will remain positive, confirming the prior exposure, but the HCV RNA will be negative. Although persons who spontaneously clear HCV are not at risk of developing the sequelae of chronic infection or transmitting the virus to others, they are not protected against future infection and can become chronically infected if re-exposed. The remaining 60–85% of acute HCV-infected individuals will develop chronic infection (NIH Consensus Conference Statement, 2002). Approximately 15% of chronically infected individuals will develop cirrhosis over the course of decades, and once cirrhosis is established, hepatocellular carcinoma occurs in 1-4% of patients per year. The development of variceal bleeding, ascites, jaundice, or hepatic encephalopathy is termed *decompensated cirrhosis* and occurs at a rate of 5–7% per year among cirrhotics (D'Amico et al.,

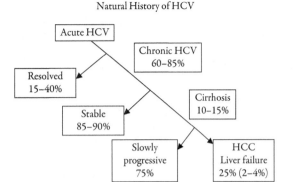

Natural History of HCV

Figure 43.1 Natural history of hepatitis C virus (HCV). HCC, hepatitis cirrhosis.
Adapted from NIH Consensus Conference Statement. Management of hepatitis C. June 10–12, 2002.

2006). Survival is significantly decreased after decompensation, with a median survival of around 2 years, compared to over 12 years in compensated cirrhosis (D'Amico et al., 2006). HIV infection accelerates the natural history of chronic HCV, leading to a higher risk of cirrhosis, decompensated cirrhosis, and death (Graham et al., 2001; Pineda et al., 2005) (Figure 43.2). If decompensated cirrhosis does not improve with HCV cure, the only curative treatment is liver transplantation. Although historically HIV/HCV-co-infected patients have poorer post-liver transplant outcomes than HCV-mono-infected patients, it is hoped that outcomes will improve with the new HCV DAA agents (Kardashian and Price, 2015).

HCV AND PSYCHIATRIC COMORBIDITIES

HCV is associated with multiple psychiatric comorbidities. There is evidence that HCV alters the central nervous system's metabolism, directly and indirectly, which likely contributes to psychiatric manifestations (Schaefer, Capuron, et al., 2012). In fact, patients with chronic HCV infection have a significantly increased prevalence of mental health comorbidity when compared to the general population. In a multisite study conducted in 1997–1998 of individuals with severe mental illness (SMI), 1.7% were found to be co-infected with HIV and HCV (Rosenberg et al., 2005). Substance use disorders (SUD) are also common in individuals with HIV-HCV co-infection, and the prevalence of co-infection is higher in those with dual diagnoses of SMI and SUD: in the same multisite study, 0.6% of individuals with an SMI alone were HIV-HCV-co-infected compared to 2.5% of patients who were dually diagnosed with an SMI and SUD (Rosenberg et al., 2005). This is likely due to increased chance of exposure to HIV and HCV from risk-taking behavior such as intravenous drug use. Ongoing intravenous drug use can continue to place people at risk for HCV if they have HIV and vice versa. Therefore, practitioners should assess a patient who is newly diagnosed with HIV and/or HCV for psychiatric diagnoses including SUD.

The three most common mental health sequelae of chronic HCV infection include depression, fatigue, and cognitive impairment (Schaefer, Capuron, et al., 2012). Research has linked the progression of these sequelae with sleep difficulties earlier in the course of illness (Schaefer, Capuron, et al., 2012). As such, it is important for practitioners to ask about patients' quality of sleep, as early intervention of sleep disturbances could help reduce the risk of psychiatric comorbidity. In terms of screening for depression, the Patient Health Questionnaire (PHQ-9), a 9-item tool, and the 7-Item Hamilton Depression Rating Scale (HAMD-7), which are both short surveys used in healthcare settings, have comparable accuracy in screening for and monitoring for depressive symptoms (Sockalingam et al., 2011). An advantage of the PHQ-9 is that it provides a recommended level of treatment based on the depression symptom, such as thresholds for initiating an antidepressant and referral for therapy. Please see Chapter 15 of this textbook

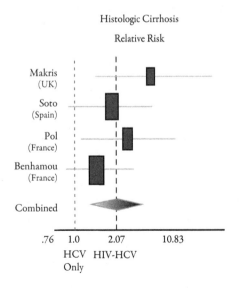

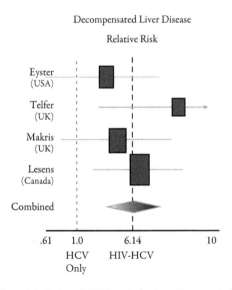

Figure 43.2 Increased risk of cirrhosis and decompensated liver disease in HIV–hepatitis C virus (HCV) co-infection. For more information on the studies referenced see Graham et al. (2001).
From Graham et al. (2001). *Clin Infect Dis* 33:562–569.

for a detailed discussion of screening and diagnosis of depression. The next sections will discuss HCV treatment and its psychiatric impact.

GOALS OF HCV TREATMENT

The two primary goals of HCV treatment are viral eradication and prevention of disease progression. Sustained virological response (SVR) refers to sustained loss of HCV RNA in the serum after completing HCV treatment. Clinically, this is defined as negative HCV RNA 12 weeks after completing treatment (SVR12), and it denotes HCV cure. Multiple studies have demonstrated the benefit of HCV cure, with significantly lower risk of liver disease progression, development of decompensated cirrhosis or hepatocellular carcinoma, need for liver transplant, and mortality (liver related and all-cause) (Limketkai et al., 2012; Morgan et al., 2010; Poynard et al., 2002; van der Meer et al., 2012). Moreover, HCV cure has profound effects on quality of life in patients with chronic HCV. Numerous studies have shown that successful HCV leads to substantial reductions in the frequency and severity of fatigue as well as improvements in overall health-related quality of life and work productivity (Bonkovsky et al., 2007; Younossi et al., 2015a, 2015b).

ADVANCES IN HCV TREATMENT

The HCV treatment landscape has changed tremendously since the first DAA agents were introduced in 2011. Prior to this, the first effective anti-HCV agent identified was recombinant interferon-α, which was administered by subcutaneous injection three times per week (Figure 43.3). Initially, patients were treated for 24 weeks, and although about a third of patients became HCV RNA negative on treatment, only a small fraction achieved SVR (Davis et al., 1989; Di Bisceglie et al., 1990). Extending treatment duration to 48 weeks improved cure rates, but they remained low at only 16%. Several years later, the addition of ribavirin to interferon-α improved treatment efficacy to approximately 42% cure with 48 weeks of treatment (McHutchison et al., 1998; Poynard et al., 1998). Interferon and ribavirin remained the backbone of HCV treatment for over two decades. In 2001, pegylated-interferon replaced standard interferon; pegylation enhanced the half-life of interferon, thereby reducing the frequency of injections to weekly and improving response rates (Reddy et al., 2001). However, overall cure rates were still modest with this regimen, at 55%, and varied depending on genotype, race, gender, age, and medical comorbidities. Lower treatment response was seen in the setting of HIV co-infection, genotype 1 infection, cirrhosis, African American race, obesity, and male gender.

In addition to the relatively low efficacy of interferon and ribavirin, this regimen is associated with numerous adverse effects. Interferon can cause worsening of liver decompensation, exacerbation of underlying autoimmune disease, bone marrow suppression, neuropsychiatric effects, thyroid dysfunction, nausea, anorexia, weight loss, myalgias, flu-like symptoms, and injection-site reactions. Ribavirin also has numerous side effects, including hemolytic anemia, insomnia, cough, rash, and teratogenicity. Not surprisingly, given the side-effect profile of interferon and ribavirin-based treatment, at least 60% of HCV-infected patients are ineligible for treatment, and among eligible patients, one-third refuse it after weighing the risks with the likelihood

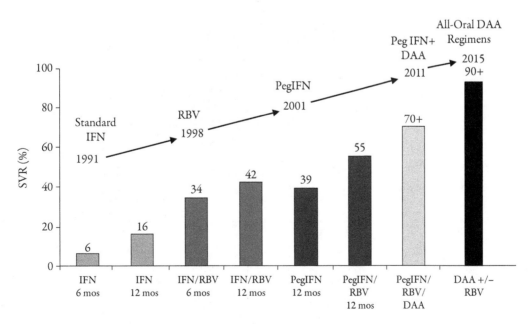

Figure 43.3 History of HCV treatment. DAA, direct-acting antiviral; IFN, interferon; Peg, pegylated; RBV, ribavirin; SVR, sustained virological response.
Adapted from the U.S. Food and Drug Administration, Antiviral Drugs Advisory Committee Meeting, April 27–28, 2011, Silver Spring, MD.

of response (Falck-Ytter et al., 2002). This, combined with high rates of early treatment discontinuation and low response rates, helps explain why only a fraction (<10%) of patients with chronic HCV were successfully cured in the era of interferon-based treatment. The difficulty in curing patients in the interferon-era was particularly pronounced in HIV-HCV-co-infected populations: in a study of 845 HIV-HCV-co-infected persons engaged in regular care at an urban HIV clinic, only 6 (0.7%) had their HCV cured, despite financial access to on-site HCV care (Figure 43.4) (Mehta et al., 2006).

The next milestone in HCV treatment occurred in 2011, with the approval of the first DAA's, the NS3/4A protease inhibitors telaprevir and boceprevir. Each drug was separately approved for use in combination with pegylated-interferon and ribavirin for genotype 1 cirrhosis. Although still requiring interferon and ribavirin, treatment response rates were significantly improved (Bacon et al., 2011; Jacobson et al., 2011; Poordad et al., 2011; Zeuzem et al., 2011). Unfortunately, the new drugs came with new severe side effects and worsened the toxicity of interferon and ribavirin. Treatment tolerability was poor, premature discontinuation was high, and in the "real world," cure rates were lower than in the registration trials (Price et al., 2014).

Thankfully, the pace of development of new agents has been rapid. Although pegylated-interferon is still used in select individuals, we have now entered the era of all-oral HCV therapy. This has been achieved through the advent of DAAs targeting different nonstructural proteins involved in HCV replication: the NS3/4A inhibitors (telaprevir, boceprevir, simeprevir, paritaprevir, and grazoprevir), NS5A inhibitors (ledipasvir, daclatasvir, elbasvir, ombitasvir, velpatasvir), nucleoside NS5B inhibitors (sofosbuvir), and non-nucleoside NS5B inhibitors (dasabuvir) (American Association for the Study of Liver Disease and Infectious Disease Society of America, 2016). In a method similar to potent antiretroviral therapy for HIV, these drugs are combined into two or more drug combinations. Ribavirin is still used for many patients, particularly individuals with difficult-to-cure characteristics, but ribavirin-free all-oral regimens are available for most patients with absolute contraindications. The cure rates with these all-oral DAA combinations have been remarkable and are over 90% in the majority of patient groups, including persons with HIV-HCV co-infection. However, there are several important drug interactions between the HCV DAA's and antiretroviral medications that clinicians treating HIV-HCV-co-infected patients need to be aware of (Table 43.1).

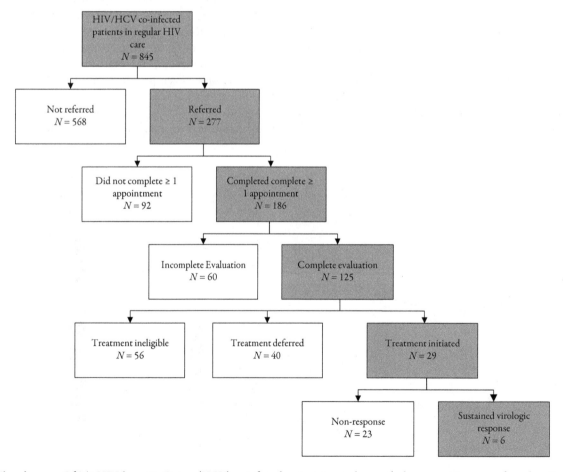

Figure 43.4 Flow diagram. Of 845 HIV/hepatitis C virus (HCV) co-infected patients in regular care (at least one visit per year for at least 2 years), 277 were referred by their HIV clinician for HCV care. Of the patients referred, 185 completed at least one appointment. A total of 125 had a complete pretreatment evaluation, of whom 29 initiated treatment and 6 achieved a sustained virological response.
From Mehta et al. (2006). *AIDS* 20:2361–2369.

Table 43.1 DRUG–DRUG INTERACTIONS BETWEEN DIRECT-ACTING ANTIVIRAL REGIMEN, ART, AND NEUROPSYCHIATRIC MEDICATIONS

REGIMEN	INTERACTIONS WITH ART	INTERACTIONS WITH NEUROPSYCHIATRIC MEDICATIONS
Sofosbuvir plus daclatasvir +/− RBV	If HIV regimen includes efavirenz, daclatasvir dose increase to 90 mg is required. If HV regimen contains elvitegravir/cobicistat and atazanavir/ritonavir, daclatasvir dose decrease to 60 mg is required. Not recommended with tipranavir. If RBV is used, not recommended with didanosine, stavudine, or zidovudine.	Need to increase daclatasvir to 90 mg if co-administered with modafinil. Need to monitor for increased side effects in patients on buprenorphine/naloxone. Not recommended with St. John's wort and certain anticonvulsants (phenytoin, carbamazepine, oxcarbazepine, phenobarbital, and primidone).
Elbasvir/grazoprevir +/− RBV	Not recommended with HIV protease inhibitors–based regimen. Not recommended with moderate/strong CYP/PgP inducers including etravirine, and efavirenz. If RBV is used, not recommended with didanosine, stavudine, or zidovudine.	Need to monitor for increased side effects in patients on oral benzodiazepines (except lorazepam). Not recommended with modafinil, St. John's wort, and certain anticonvulsants (phenytoin, carbamazepine, oxcarbazepine, phenobarbital, and primidone).
Sofosbuvir + RBV	Not recommended with tipranavir. Due to interaction with RBV, not recommended with didanosine, stavudine, or zidovudine.	Not recommended with St. John's wort and certain anticonvulsants (phenytoin, carbamazepine, oxcarbazepine, phenobarbital, and primidone).
Sofosbuvir/ledipasvir +/− RBV	Not recommended with cobicistat, elvitegravir, or tipranavir. If HIV regimen includes ritonavir-boosted protease inhibitors and tenofovir, use an alternative HCV therapy or change to an HIV regimen without tenofovir. If unable to change HIV regimen and co-administration required, monitor for tenofovir-associated renal adverse events. There is no automatic adjustment of tenofovir when used with ritonavir. If RBV is used, not recommended with didanosine, stavudine, or zidovudine.	Not recommended with St. John's wort and certain anticonvulsants (phenytoin, carbamazepine, oxcarbazepine, phenobarbital, and primidone).
Paritaprevir/ritonavir/ ombitasvir plus twice-daily dasabuvir +/− RBV	If HIV regimen includes ritonavir-boosted protease inhibitor, remove ritonavir from the HIV regimen or adjust the ritonavir dose. Not recommended with efavirenz, rilpivirine, darunavir, or ritonavir-boosted lopinavir. Not recommended in patients not on ART.	Need to monitor for increased side effects in patients on oral benzodiazepines (except lorazepam) and buprenorphine/naloxone. Not recommended with oral midazolam, St. John's wort, certain anticonvulsants (phenytoin, carbamazepine, oxcarbazepine, phenobarbital, and primidone), pimozide, and ergot derivatives.
Sofosbuvir + simeprevir +/− RBV	Not recommended with efavirenz, etravirine, nevirapine, cobicistat, tipranavir, or any HIV protease inhibitors. If RBV is used, not recommended with didanosine, stavudine, or zidovudine.	Need to monitor for increased side effects in patients on oral benzodiazepines (except lorazepam). Not recommended with St. John's wort and certain anticonvulsants (phenytoin, carbamazepine, oxcarbazepine, phenobarbital, and primidone).

Abbreviations: ART, antiretroviral therapy; HCV, hepatitis C virus; RBV, ribavirin.

PSYCHIATRIC CONSIDERATIONS WITH HCV TREATMENT

Although pegylated interferon is now used infrequently in the United States, it is still necessary in some patients with difficult-to-treat HCV, and ribavirin remains a frequent component of many HCV regimens. Pegylated interferon and ribavirin are associated with multiple psychiatric side effects, such as depression, mania, aggression, and sleep difficulty. Studies have shown that over 40% of patients receiving treatment with interferon and ribavirin for HCV, including individuals who did not have a preexisting mental illness, required psychiatric medications, most commonly for depression and for sleep (Manos et al., 2013; Masip et al., 2015). Similar to chronic HCV infection, poor sleep quality during treatment is correlated with the development of depressive symptoms and a diagnosis of major depression (Franzen et al., 2010). Just as it is important to assess sleep and mood symptoms when a patient has chronic HCV infection, it is important to assess these symptoms when a patient is on interferon or ribavirin. There has been research about whether prophylactic selective serotonin reuptake inhibitor (SSRI) use can reduce the risk of developing depression while on this regimen. The data are mixed, though it appears overall there may be a decreased incidence of a major depressive episode with SSRIs (Klein et al., 2014; Schaefer, Sarkar, et al., 2012; Udina et al., 2014). If using a prophylactic SSRI, which should be considered especially if a patient has a history of depression (Udina et al., 2014), the recommendation is to initiate the SSRI 2 to 3 weeks prior to treatment and then continue it after treatment (Vrbanac et al., 2013). Paroxetine, citalopram, and escitalopram have been the most studied agents (Udina et al., 2014; Vrbanac et al., 2013). Because interferon-free regimens are now the standard for HCV treatment, prophylactic SSRIs are less commonly used. However, they may be considered in patients who require ribavirin as part of their treatment regimen, especially if they have symptoms of depression before HCV treatment initiation.

In addition to screening for psychiatric symptoms before HCV treatment initiation and considering prophylactic medications if interferon or ribavirin are being used, it is important to provide appropriate referrals, as individuals with a psychiatric illness who are not engaged in mental health services have a higher rate of discontinuing HCV treatment than persons with a psychiatric illness who are engaged in services (Kuhara et al., 2012). It is a common misconception that people with psychiatric illnesses overall are less likely to complete HCV treatment and/or are less likely to achieve sustained viral remission. This has not been the case (Mustafa et al., 2014).

Newer HCV treatments appear to have fewer neuropsychiatric side effects, though data are limited primarily to studies on telaprevir and boceprevir, which were co-administered with interferon and ribavirin. Neuropsychiatric side effects noted include fatigue, insomnia, irritability, depression, and anxiety—similar to ribavirin/interferon-alpha treatment (Sockalingam et al., 2013). Although the newer DAAs do not appear to have significant neuropsychiatric side effects, they do have many drug–drug interactions with common neuropsychiatric medications (Table 43.1). In addition, a common herbal supplement that is contraindicated with DAAs is St. John's wort, which many people take to target depressive symptoms (Sockalingam et al., 2013). As such, when assessing for drug–drug interactions pretreatment, it is important to also ask about herbal supplements, which patients often do not consider medication and therefore do not disclose with their medication list. Ritonavir is contraindicated with alprazolam or diazepam and should be used with caution with trazodone (Hill, 2015). Simeprevir and sofosbuvir are both are decreased by anticonvulsants, which are often used as mood stabilizers, such as carbamazepine (Hill, 2015). Please see Chapter 42 of this textbook for further discussion of psychopharmacological issues and drug–drug and drug–illness interactions.

OPTIMIZING THE HCV CARE CASCADE

Untreated HCV infection is associated with decreased quality of life, higher annual productivity losses, and increased all-cause healthcare expenditure (El Khoury et al., 2012). In short, untreated infection is a financial and mental strain on individuals and on the overall economy in a quantifiable way. However, only a small minority of patients with chronic HCV have been cured, owing to multiple breakdowns in the HCV care cascade (Figure 43.5). Improvements in treatment tolerability and efficacy are essential components to increasing the proportion of cured patients, but the medications alone are not sufficient. Nearly half of HCV-infected individuals are unaware of their infection, and less than half of them are linked to care. The new DAA regimens are exorbitantly expensive; consequently, treatment is rationed by most insurance payers. Coverage is often denied, and the appeals process is cumbersome (Gross et al., 2016).

Furthermore, individuals with addictive disorders and/or other psychiatric comorbidities face disparities in the quality of medical care they receive and are more likely to have untreated HCV infection (Butt et al., 2005; Cachay et al., 2014). Why does this occur? It is likely a combination of system, clinician, and patient barriers. Physicians may perceive that patients with active injection drug use will be less likely to comply with treatment, even though this population can be successfully treated (Zanini et al., 2010). Clinics are also often hard to come to, especially when considering that patients in medication-assisted treatment for their injection drug use may already need to go to a separate clinic for treatment as frequently as once a day, such as for methadone maintenance treatment, which is a time constraint. When considering other barriers, such as lack of transportation, financial barriers, not being insured or being underinsured, jobs, childrearing, unstable housing, fear of testing and treatment, lack of health literacy about HCV, and other competing health demands—including fewer referrals from their physicians for treatment—it is understandable that patients have difficulty getting linked to HCV treatment (Cachay et al., 2014).

Since the rate of HCV infection is increased in persons who inject drugs, and DAAs provide a cure, have less adverse effects, and require a shorter duration of treatment, addiction specialists are beginning to play an increasingly important role in treating HCV. Treatment embedded in substance use treatment programs is a very attractive and efficient option for reaching marginalized HCV-infected populations in need

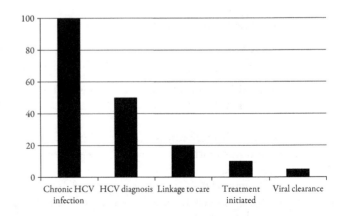

Figure 43.5 The HCV care cascade.
Adapted from Cachay et al. (2014). *PLoS One* 9(7):e102883.

of life-saving HCV treatment (Grebely et al., 2013). Studies have shown that methadone clinics can also provide directly observed HCV treatment, with medications given at the same time as methadone (Litwin et al., 2011; Malnick et al., 2014). Not only is this a good model for providing HCV treatment, but it may also help prevent the ongoing spread of infection.

Given that addiction specialists and programs treat persons who inject drugs, it would be lifesaving as well as a prevention measure if routine screening for HIV and HCV were scheduled in all addiction programs. Addiction specialists are able to address multiple barriers in the care cascade, including testing patients, informing them of their results, treating them, and reducing risk of recurrence through engagement in addiction treatment to decrease injection drug use. Similarly, general psychiatrists can provide support to patients with other psychiatric illnesses who are undergoing treatment for HCV and can work with the patients' interdisciplinary treatment teams, perhaps even with embedded resources in primary care centers—something many primary care physicians wish were the case (Weiss and Morgello, 2009). Psychiatrists play a crucial role in breaking down barriers in the care cascade, as they can provide screening and treatment for HCV in patients who may not otherwise be screened or treated, can work to help reduce risk of reinfection, and can collaborate with primary care physicians to provide management of neuropsychiatric effects of HCV and related treatment.

REFERENCES

American Association for the Study of Liver Disease and Infectious Disease Society of America (2016). HCV guidance: Recommendations for testing, managing, and treating hepatitis C. http://hcvguidelines.org/full-report/monitoring-patients-who-are-starting-hepatitis-c-treatment-are-treatment-or-have. Accessed February 18, 2017.

Armstrong GL, Wasley A, Simard EP, McQuillan GM, Kuhnert WL, Alter MJ (2006). The prevalence of hepatitis C virus infection in the United States, 1999 through 2002. *Ann Intern Med* 144 (10):705–714.

Bacon BR, Gordon SC, Lawitz E, et al. (2011). Boceprevir for previously treated chronic HCV genotype 1 infection. *N Engl J Med* 364(13):1207–1217.

Bonkovsky HL, Snow KK, Malet PF, et al. (2007). Health-related quality of life in patients with chronic hepatitis C and advanced fibrosis. *J Hepatol* 46(3):420–431.

Butt AA, Wagener M, Shakil AO, Ahmad J (2005). Reasons for nontreatment of hepatitis C in veterans in care. *J Viral Hepat* 12(1):81–85.

Cachay ER, Hill L, Wyles D, Colwell B, Ballard C, Torriani F, Mathews WC (2014). The hepatitis C cascade of care among HIV infected patients: a call to address ongoing barriers to care. *PLoS One* 9(7):e102883.

Centers for Disease Control and Prevention (CDC) (2011). Sexual transmission of hepatitis C virus among HIV-infected men who have sex with men—New York City, 2005–2010. *MMWR Morb Mortal Wkly Rep* 60(28):945–950.

Chak E, Talal AH, Sherman KE, Schiff ER, Saab S (2011). Hepatitis C virus infection in USA: an estimate of true prevalence. *Liver Int* 31(8):1090–1101.

D'Amico G, Garcia-Tsao G, Pagliaro L (2006). Natural history and prognostic indicators of survival in cirrhosis: a systematic review of 118 studies. *J Hepatol* 44(1):217–231.

Davis GL, Balart LA, Schiff ER, et al. (1989). Treatment of chronic hepatitis C with recombinant interferon alfa. A multicenter randomized, controlled trial. Hepatitis Interventional Therapy Group. *N Engl J Med* 321(22):1501–1506.

Denniston MM, Jiles RB, Drobeniuc J, Klevens RM, Ward JW, McQuillan GM, Holmberg SD (2014). Chronic hepatitis C virus infection in the United States, National Health and Nutrition Examination Survey 2003 to 2010. *Ann Intern Med* 160(5):293–300.

Di Bisceglie AM, Martin P, Kassianides C, Lisker-Melman M, Goodman Z, Banks SM, Hoofnagle JH (1990). A randomized, double-blind, placebo-controlled trial of recombinant human alpha-interferon therapy for chronic non-A, non-B (type C) hepatitis. *J Hepatol* 11(Suppl 1):S36–S42.

El Khoury AC, Vietri J, Prajapati G (2012). The burden of untreated hepatitis C virus infection: a US patients' perspective. *Dig Dis Sci* 57(11):2995–3003.

Falck-Ytter Y, Kale H, Mullen KD, Sarbah SA, Sorescu L, McCullough AJ (2002). Surprisingly small effect of antiviral treatment in patients with hepatitis C. *Ann Intern Med* 136(4):288–292.

Franzen PL, Buysse DJ, Rabinovitz M, Pollock BG, Lotrich FE (2010). Poor sleep quality predicts onset of either major depression or subsyndromal depression with irritability during interferon-alpha treatment. *Psychiatry Res* 177(1-2):240–245.

Ghany MG, Strader DB, Thomas DL, Seeff LB (2009). Diagnosis, management, and treatment of hepatitis C: an update. *Hepatology* 49(4):1335–1374.

Graham CS, Baden LR, Yu E, Mrus JM, Carnie J, Heeren T, Koziel MJ (2001). Influence of human immunodeficiency virus infection on the course of hepatitis C virus infection: a meta-analysis. *Clin Infect Dis* 33(4):562–569.

Grebely J, Oser M, Taylor LE, Dore GJ (2013). Breaking down the barriers to hepatitis C virus (HCV) treatment among individuals with HCV/HIV coinfection: action required at the system, provider, and patient levels. *J Infect Dis* 207(Suppl 1):S19–S25.

Gross C, Akoth E, Price A, Kattakuzhy S, Silk R, Rosenthal E (2016). HIV/HCV co-infection: overcoming barriers to treatment. *J Assoc Nurses AIDS Care* 27(4):524–529.

Hill L (2015). Hepatitis C virus direct-acting antiviral drug interactions and use in renal and hepatic impairment. *Top Antivir Med* 23(2):92–96.

Hullegie SJ, van den Berk GE, Leyten EM, et al. (2016). Acute hepatitis C in the Netherlands: characteristics of the epidemic in 2014. *Clin Microbiol Infect* 22(2):209 e1–e3.

Jacobson IM, McHutchison JG, Dusheiko G, et al. (2011). Telaprevir for previously untreated chronic hepatitis C virus infection. *N Engl J Med* 364(25):2405–2416.

Kardashian AA, Price JC (2015). Hepatitis C virus–HIV-coinfected patients and liver transplantation. *Curr Opin Organ Transplant* 20(3):276–285.

Klein MB, Lee T, Brouillette MJ, et al. (2014). Citalopram for the prevention of depression and its consequences in HIV–hepatitis C coinfected individuals initiating pegylated interferon/ribavirin therapy: a multicenter randomized double-blind placebo-controlled trial. *HIV Clin Trials* 15(4):161–175.

Kuhara K, Ide T, Uchimura N, et al. (2012). The importance of a prior psychiatric examination in pegylated interferon and ribavirin combination treatment for chronic hepatitis C. *Kurume Med J* 59(3-4):39–44.

Limketkai BN, Mehta SH, Sutcliffe CG, et al. (2012). Relationship of liver disease stage and antiviral therapy with liver-related events and death in adults coinfected with HIV/HCV. *JAMA* 308(4):370–378.

Litwin AH, Berg KM, Li X, Hidalgo J, Arnsten JH (2011). Rationale and design of a randomized controlled trial of directly observed hepatitis C treatment delivered in methadone clinics. *BMC Infect Dis* 11:315.

Malnick S, Sheidvasser V, Basevitz A, Levit S (2014). A model for treating HCV hepatitis in patients receiving methadone maintenance therapy. *Isr J Psychiatry Relat Sci* 51(4):303–305.

Manos MM, Ho CK, Murphy RC, Shvachko VA (2013). Physical, social, and psychological consequences of treatment for hepatitis C: a community-based evaluation of patient-reported outcomes. *Patient* 6(1):23–34.

Masip M, Tuneu L, Pages N, et al. (2015). Prevalence and detection of neuropsychiatric adverse effects during hepatitis C treatment. *Int J Clin Pharm* 37(6):1143–1151.

McHutchison JG, Gordon SC, Schiff ER, et al. (1998). Interferon alfa-2b alone or in combination with ribavirin as initial treatment for chronic hepatitis C. Hepatitis Interventional Therapy Group. *N Engl J Med* 339(21):1485–1492.

Mehta SH, Lucas GM, Mirel LB, et al. (2006). Limited effectiveness of antiviral treatment for hepatitis C in an urban HIV clinic. *AIDS* 20(18):2361–2369.

Morgan TR, Ghany MG, Kim HY, et al. (2010). Outcome of sustained virological responders with histologically advanced chronic hepatitis C. *Hepatology* 52(3):833–844.

Mustafa MZ, Schofield J, Mills PR (2014). The efficacy and safety of treating hepatitis C in patients with a diagnosis of schizophrenia. *J Viral Hepat* 21(7):e48–e51.

NIH Consensus Conference Statement (2002). Management of hepatitis C. June 10-12, 2002. https://consensus.nih.gov/2002/2002hepatitisc2002116html.htm. Accessed February 17, 2017.

Pineda JA, Romero-Gomez M, Diaz-Garcia F, et al. (2005). HIV coinfection shortens the survival of patients with hepatitis C virus-related decompensated cirrhosis. *Hepatology* 41(4):779–789.

Poordad F, McCone J Jr, Bacon BR, et al. (2011). Boceprevir for untreated chronic HCV genotype 1 infection. *N Engl J Med* 364(13):1195–1206.

Poynard T, Marcellin P, Lee SS, et al. (1998). Randomised trial of interferon alpha2b plus ribavirin for 48 weeks or for 24 weeks versus interferon alpha2b plus placebo for 48 weeks for treatment of chronic infection with hepatitis C virus. International Hepatitis Interventional Therapy Group (IHIT). *Lancet* 352(9138):1426–1432.

Poynard T, McHutchison J, Manns M, et al. (2002). Impact of pegylated interferon alfa-2b and ribavirin on liver fibrosis in patients with chronic hepatitis C. *Gastroenterology* 122(5):1303–1313.

Price JC, Murphy RC, Shvachko VA, Pauly MP, Manos MM (2014). Effectiveness of telaprevir and boceprevir triple therapy for patients with hepatitis C virus infection in a large integrated care setting. *Dig Dis Sci* 59(12):3043–3052.

Reddy KR, Wright TL, Pockros PJ, et al. (2001). Efficacy and safety of pegylated (40-kd) interferon alpha-2a compared with interferon alpha-2a in noncirrhotic patients with chronic hepatitis C. *Hepatology* 33(2):433–438.

Rosenberg SD, Drake RE, Brunette MF, Wolford GL, Marsh BJ (2005). Hepatitis C virus and HIV co-infection in people with severe mental illness and substance use disorders. *AIDS* 19(Suppl 3):S26–S33.

Schaefer M, Capuron L, Friebe A, et al. (2012). Hepatitis C infection, antiviral treatment and mental health: a European expert consensus statement. *J Hepatol* 57(6):1379–1390.

Schaefer M, Sarkar R, Knop V (2012). Escitalopram for the prevention of peginterferon-alpha2a-associated depression in hepatitis C virus-infected patients without previous psychiatric disease: a randomized trial. *Ann Intern Med* 157(2):94–103.

Smith CJ, Ryom L, Weber R, et al. (2014). Trends in underlying causes of death in people with HIV from 1999 to 2011 (D:A:D): a multicohort collaboration. *Lancet* 384(9939):241–248.

Sockalingam S, Blank D, Al Jarad A, Alosaimi F, Hirschfield G, Abbey SE (2011). A comparison of depression screening instruments in hepatitis C and the impact of depression on somatic symptoms. *Psychosomatics* 52(5):433–440.

Sockalingam S, Tseng A, Giguere P, Wong D (2013). Psychiatric treatment considerations with direct acting antivirals in hepatitis C. *BMC Gastroenterol* 13:86.

Sulkowski MS, Thomas DL (2003). Hepatitis C in the HIV-infected person. *Ann Intern Med* 138(3):197–207.

Terrault NA, Dodge JL, Murphy EL, et al. (2013). Sexual transmission of hepatitis C virus among monogamous heterosexual couples: the HCV partners study. *Hepatology* 57(3):881–889.

Udina M, Hidalgo D, Navines R (2014). Prophylactic antidepressant treatment of interferon-induced depression in chronic hepatitis C: a systematic review and meta-analysis. *J Clin Psychiatry* 75(10):e1113–e1121.

van der Meer AJ, Veldt BJ, Feld JJ, et al. (2012). Association between sustained virological response and all-cause mortality among patients with chronic hepatitis C and advanced hepatic fibrosis. *JAMA* 308(24):2584–2593.

Vrbanac DB, Buljan D, Sindik I, Gelo J, Sakoman LN (2013). Psychiatric aspects of hepatitis C treatment. *Acta Clin Croat* 52(3):346–352.

Weiss JJ, Morgello S (2009). Psychiatric management of HIV/HCV-coinfected patients beginning treatment for hepatitis C virus infection: survey of provider practices. *Gen Hosp Psychiatry* 31(6):531–537.

World Health Organization (WHO) (2016). Hepatitis C fact sheet. http://www.who.int/mediacentre/factsheets/fs164/en/index.html. Accessed February 17, 2017.

Younossi ZM, Stepanova M, Afdhal N, et al. (2015a). Improvement of health-related quality of life and work productivity in chronic hepatitis C patients with early and advanced fibrosis treated with ledipasvir and sofosbuvir. *J Hepatol* 63(2):337–345.

Younossi ZM, Stepanova M, Marcellin P, Afdhal N, Kowdley KV, Zeuzem S, Hunt SL (2015b). Treatment with ledipasvir and sofosbuvir improves patient-reported outcomes: results from the ION-1, -2, and -3 clinical trials. *Hepatology* 61(6):1798–1808.

Zanini B, Covolo L, Donato F, Lanzini A (2010). Effectiveness and tolerability of combination treatment of chronic hepatitis C in illicit drug users: meta-analysis of prospective studies. *Clin Ther* 32(13):2139–2159.

Zeuzem S, Andreone P, Pol S, et al. (2011). Telaprevir for retreatment of HCV infection. *N Engl J Med* 364(25):2417–2428.

44.

HIV-ASSOCIATED NEPHROPATHY, END-STAGE RENAL DISEASE, DIALYSIS, AND KIDNEY TRANSPLANT

Jonathan Winston, Etti Zeldis, John A. R. Grimaldi, and Esteban Martínez

Effective antiretroviral therapy (ART) has transformed outcomes for people living with HIV, including individuals with kidney disease and HIV. Not only are patients living longer, but kidney disease has been transformed from a once fatal condition to a more chronic, indolent form, with a decrease in the absolute risk of progression to end-stage renal disease (ESRD) requiring dialysis. The causes of kidney disease are multifactorial, with HIV-associated nephropathy being the single most common cause of kidney disease in African American patients with HIV. Persons with HIV are now living longer and healthier lives and are also becoming infected at older ages. They may develop concomitant illnesses that can also lead to kidney disease, such as diabetes, hypertension, nephrotoxicity, and others illnesses. Despite the dramatic change in the spectrum of kidney disease in HIV, ESRD continues to carry a high risk for psychiatric comorbidity that may include and/or lead to nonadherence, denial, depression, and even suicide.

This chapter reviews the common causes of kidney disease in HIV, the approach to their diagnosis and treatment, and special issues relating to patients with end-stage renal failure.

PREVALENCE OF KIDNEY DISEASE

Kidney disease is a major public health problem. Approximately 600,000 people in the United States currently require hemodialysis as part of the End-Stage Renal Disease (ESRD) Program, and approximately 100,000 new patients begin treatment each year (Saran et al., 2015). Kidney disease in the United States falls disproportionately on the ethnic minority community. African Americans account for 13% of the general population but more than 30% of the population with ESRD. Kidney disease is the eighth leading cause of death in the United States and the sixth leading cause for black Americans (Heron, 2015; National Center for Health Statistics, 2005). The higher disease burden among blacks is a consequence of genetic factors that alter the susceptibility to kidney disease and of healthcare disparities along racial and socioeconomic lines. In HIV infection, the same associations exist between race and kidney disease. An estimated 10–15% of patients with HIV infection have chronic kidney disease. Older age, black race, preexisting hypertension or diabetes, a prior AIDS-defining illness, injection drug use, and hepatitis

C virus (HCV) co-infection are frequent predisposing factors (Gardner et al., 2003; Gupta et al., 2004; Szczech et al., 2004).

HIV-ASSOCIATED NEPHROPATHY

Although a wide spectrum of kidney diseases occur in association with HIV, HIV-associated nephropathy (HIVAN) remains the single most common cause of chronic kidney disease (Ross and Klotman, 2004; Naiker et al., 2015). It is defined morphologically by collapse of the glomerular capillary tuft, glomerulosclerosis, and microcystic tubulointerstitial disease. Its association with black race is a striking clinical characteristic. Biopsy studies in North America, Europe, and Asia confirm that well over 90% of affected patients are of African descent. This racial predilection accounts for differences in prevalence reported from various centers. HIVAN is second only to sickle cell–associated renal disease in its racial clustering toward African Americans. New genome-wide studies have uncovered a genetic basis for HIVAN (Parsa et al., 2013) and with it the promise of novel therapies.

The characteristic clinical presentation of HIVAN is heavy proteinuria, often in the nephrotic range, with varying degrees of renal insufficiency. Prior to the development of combinations of effective antiretroviral medications, in 1995, the onset of what was initially called the "highly active antiretroviral therapy (HAART)" era, the clinical course of HIVAN was marked by progression to renal failure requiring dialysis within weeks to months. The natural history has changed dramatically, however; now patients who are receiving ART have a more indolent course and can have only mild to moderate proteinuria and a stable but impaired glomerular filtration rate (GFR). Several studies demonstrate a slower progression to ESRD with ART (Cosgrove et al., 2002; Szczech et al., 2002). Fewer cases of fulminant renal failure have been observed in the ART era (Lucas et al., 2004). Several well-described case reports provide unequivocal evidence that effective antiretrovirals can reverse the structural and functional abnormalities in HIVAN, particularly when therapy is initiated early in the course of disease before glomerulosclerosis has been established (Wali et al., 1998; Winston et al., 2001). ART has the capacity to eliminate new rounds of renal cell infection, which interrupts the disease process. Adherence to ART, therefore, has important implications for the outcome of kidney disease.

It is important to realize that patients are often asymptomatic during the early stages of kidney disease. Therefore, at least twice-yearly screening for kidney disease is recommended in stable persons with HIV and more frequently in persons with additional kidney disease risk factors, such as diabetes and hypertension (Lucas et al., 2014). Patients in whom kidney disease is detected should undergo a comprehensive evaluation for the cause of the disease, and this may include a kidney biopsy. Willingness to adhere to an antiretroviral regimen will have important implications for the outcome of HIVAN.

HIV-associated nephropathy accounts for approximately 800 incident cases of ESRD each year (Saran et al., 2015). The number of new patients with HIV-ESRD has stabilized and has not decreased, in contrast to the decline in AIDS-associated mortality and opportunistic infections. This stabilization is likely due to the increased pool of patients at risk for kidney disease, as more patients (black patients, in this instance) are living with AIDS. A mathematical model has quantified the dynamics of new ESRD cases arising from the risk pool before and after the widespread use of effective antiretrovirals. ART is responsible for at least a 30% reduction in new ESRD cases from HIVAN. Looking to the future, without a dramatic decrease in the number of cases of HIV infection in the African American community, the beneficial effect of ART to slow the progression of kidney disease will be offset by an ever-growing risk pool, and the number of new cases of ESRD will continue rise (Schwartz et al., 2005).

OTHER CHRONIC KIDNEY DISEASES IN HIV

Chronic kidney disease (CKD) is defined as kidney damage or reduced kidney function that persists for more than 3 months. Indicators of kidney damage include elevation in urinary protein excretion or a decrease in the estimated glomerular filtration rate (eGFR) of <60 ml/min (Coresh et al., 2003). There has been an increasing prevalence of CKD due to comorbidities associated with aging as patients with HIV with adequate viral suppression are living longer and exposed to more of the vascular effects of hypertension, diabetes, and aging. This was shown in several cohort studies that demonstrated an association between comorbid diabetes mellitus and HIV with accelerated progression of CKD (Gallant et al., 2005; Mocroft et al., 2010). In addition, certain antiretroviral regimens are thought to have contributed to the higher incidence of diabetes among persons with HIV, specifically protease inhibitors and non-nucleoside reverse transcriptase inhibitors (Brown et al., 2005).

In addition, observational data have revealed many other causes of CKD in persons with HIV, including non-collapsing focal segmental glomerulosclerosis (FSGS) and acute interstitial nephritis, and diabetic nephropathy. From the study time of 1997–2004, the percentage of biopsies demonstrating HIVAN decreased from 80% to 20% (Berliner et al., 2008).

Co-infection with HCV occurs in an estimated 15–30% of patients with HIV (Alter, 2006). A meta-analysis of both clinical trials and observational studies revealed that hepatitis C co-infection was associated with an increased risk of proteinuria and CKD (Wyatt et al., 2008). A Veterans' Administration cohort study showed that hepatitis C co-infection was associated with an increased risk of CKD compared to HIV infection alone (Fischer et al., 2010). Worse outcomes are hypothesized to be due to complications from liver disease or impaired immunological or virological response in the setting of co-infection. Immune complex–related glomerulonephritis (GN) is a common renal disease in co-infected patients, with membranoproliferative GN (MPGN) being the most common. Another immune complex–mediated disease not associated with HCV seen in patients with HIV is HIV immune complex kidney disease. This has been described recently in both Caucasian and African American patients, and further studies are needed to clarify the contribution of HIV to the development of HIV immune complex kidney disease (Mallipatu et al., 2012).

THERAPY FOR KIDNEY DISEASE IN HIV

The availability of treatment modalities for persons with kidney disease can be limiting and varies greatly regionally. Kidney disease is a chronic and progressive illness. Commonly used medications include antiretrovirals, angiotensin-converting enzyme (ACE) inhibitors, corticosteroids, or even other immunosuppressants. However, these medications, which enjoy common usage in countries with resources and access, are difficult to acquire in developing countries, making it more likely that patients there with early kidney disease will continue to progress in their illness to end-stage organ failure. It is unclear whether populations in developing countries sustain the same risk as that of African Americans in the United States, although some degree of increased risk similar that seen in the United States is accepted at this point (Behar et al., 2006; Gerntholtz et al., 2006; Han et al., 2006).

Access and adherence to ART have reduced the incidence of HIV nephropathy, but access to ART has been a long-standing difficulty in developing nations. The impact of effective ART on reducing the incidence of HIV nephropathy and preventing a serious end-stage organ disease merely reinforces the need for access to effective ART around the world.

NEPHROTOXICITY IN PERSONS WITH HIV

Nephrotoxicity of current ART is uncommon, although it is expected to increase with increasing age and higher prevalence of age-related comorbidities. Mechanisms usually involve functional abnormalities of transporter proteins in proximal tubule cells, mitochondrial toxicity, vascular injury, and nephrolithiasis. In most of the cases, the drugs involved in antiretroviral-associated nephrotoxicity are nucleoside reverse transcriptase inhibitors and, particularly, tenofovir, and protease inhibitors. Some ritonavir-boosted protease inhibitors such as atazanavir and lopinavir have been associated with a higher risk for decreased GFRs (Fine and Gallant 2013; Mocroft et al., 2010, 2014; Rasch et al., 2012; Reynes et al., 2013; Scherzer et al., 2012; Yombi et al., 2104; Young et al., 2012).

Tenofovir is the main antiretroviral drug involved in nephrotoxicity. Tenofovir is excreted through transporter proteins into the tubular lumen (Fernandez-Fernandez et al., 2011; Hall et al., 2011). Tenofovir toxicity may appear in the form of proximal tubular dysfunction and acute tubular necrosis, increasing the risk of progression to CKD. Proximal tubular dysfunction, or Fanconi's syndrome, includes phosphaturia, glucosuria with normoglycemia, renal tubular acidosis with normal gap anion, aminoaciduria, tubular proteinuria, and decreased glomerular filtration. Tenofovir nephrotoxicity is usually reversible upon drug discontinuation, although recovery may be incomplete (Wever et al., 2010).

Among currently used protease inhibitors, atazanavir and, less often, darunavir may induce kidney toxicity in the form of cristalluria and tubular obstruction due to their low solubility in urine at conditions of low water intake and high urinary pH (De Lastours et al., 2013).

Several of the new antiretroviral drugs interfere with creatinine tubular secretion. Creatinine transporter interactions have been reported with rilpivirine (Moss et al., 2013), dolutegravir (Koteff et al., 2013), and cobicistat booster (German et al., 2012; Stray et al., 2013). Whereas rilpivirine and dolutegravir inhibit the OCT2 transporter (Koteff et al., 2013; Moss et al., 2013), cobicistat inhibits the MATE1 transporter (Stray et al., 2013). These interactions may cause mild increases in plasma creatinine with subsequent impact on the estimated GFR formulas but with no real effects on glomerular filtration (Arya et al., 2014; Koteff et al., 2013).

Other non-antiretroviral drugs that cause nephrotoxicity in the general population may also cause it patients with HIV. Although a detailed description of all these drugs is beyond the scope of this chapter, the reader may find further information in recently published guidelines (European AIDS Clinical Society, 2015; Lucas et al., 2014). In particular, antimicrobials (including aminoglycosides, amphotericin B, vancomycin, colistin, sulfonamides, pentamidine, foscarnet, acyclovir, adefovir, and cidofovir), nonsteroidal anti-inflammatory agents, angiotensin-blockers, and iodine contrasts are potentially nephrotoxic drugs that can be commonly used in persons with HIV.

ADVANCED KIDNEY DISEASE AND END-STAGE RENAL FAILURE

Patients with more advanced kidney disease often present with constitutional symptoms such as fatigue and anorexia. Although these symptoms may be due to uremia, they can be confused with symptoms attributable to the underlying HIV infection. Patients progressing to end-stage renal failure remain a special clinical challenge. Treatment must be initiated to control lipid abnormalities, calcium/phosphorus metabolism, and anemia. Hypertension must also be treated as kidney function deteriorates, and the therapeutic focus should shift to preparation for renal replacement therapy. Proper planning for hemodialysis, peritoneal dialysis, or kidney transplantation should be made well in advance of uremic symptoms. Guidelines for the care of persons with ESRD are available (Gupta et al., 2005). Kidney transplantation is a viable option in selected patients with HIV. Its safety and efficacy are currently under study through a cooperative research program sponsored by the National Institute of Allergy and Infectious Diseases (NIAID) (http://spitfire.emmes.com/ study/htr/index.html). Criteria for transplantation include undetectable viral RNA for at least 3 months, CD4 cells >200/µl, and no history of an opportunistic infection or neoplasm.

In patients who are likely to start hemodialysis, an arteriovenous (AV) fistula should be created months before an anticipated start date. This can be especially difficult in persons who inject drugs, because they may not have veins adequate enough to sustain fistula construction as well as difficulty adhering to medical follow-up care. Venous mapping and close collaboration with vascular surgeons can increase the success rate of fistula creation. Fistulae are far superior to polytetrafluoroethylene (PTFE, Gore-Tex) grafts or percutaneous dialysis catheters because of lower thrombosis and infection rates. The long-term prognosis of patients with HIV on dialysis is determined by the stage of AIDS. Persons with HIV and ESRD must also be aggressively treated with effective ART. The 1- and 2-year survival rates for incident ESRD patients have improved dramatically with ART, and 1-year survival now approaches 80% (Ahuja et al., 2002). Survival on dialysis has improved with effective ART.

DIALYSIS AND HIV INFECTION

Implementation of renal replacement therapy is also prohibited by a lack of sustainable funding in underresourced areas of the world. Hemodialysis has been noted to be the preferred modality in most countries except Mexico and Hong Kong, where there is widespread use of chronic ambulatory peritoneal dialysis (Okpechi et al., 2012). Dialysis in the developing world is further complicated by high rates of hepatitis B and C infections, and aluminum toxicity remains problematic. Under-dialysis remains common; almost half of patients in the developing world receive less than 12 hours of dialysis weekly, provided over one or two sessions. Few are offered erythropoietin therapy and thus require repeated blood transfusions (Barsoum, 2002).

Both hemodialysis and peritoneal dialysis have similar morbidity and mortality in patients with HIV. Thus the type of dialysis therapy implemented should be based on patient preference and social conditions. Generally, patients with HIV-associated dementia may not be eligible for peritoneal dialysis (Soleymanian et al., 2006). In a retrospective review of HIV-seropositive patients on peritoneal dialysis, Khanna and colleagues (2005) found that HIV seropositivity was an independent predictor of mortality in peritoneal dialysis patients; however, survival average in HIV patients remained encouragingly high, at 12.5 years, in contrast to the 15 years associated with HIV-seronegative patients. HIV-seropositive patients were also more likely to be hospitalized or develop peritonitis than their seronegative counterparts. The use of ART and higher CD4 counts at the time of dialysis initiation were associated with improved survivability, though, and these data indicate that long-term survival of HIV-seropositive patients is possible through use of peritoneal dialysis along with attention to maintaining ART adherence and treatment of peritonitis.

Although there are no long-term studies on survival of HIV-positive persons on hemodialysis, this treatment is widely used in this population. Particular areas of concern in hemodialysis include maintenance and maturation of the AV fistula, mainly to avoid the infectious complications associated with tunneled catheters. AV fistulas have been shown to perform in HIV-positive patients with ESRD as well they do in uninfected patients. A retrospective study of dialysis patients in sub-Saharan Africa showed no difference in AV fistula outcomes between HIV-positive and HIV-negative patients (Fokou et al., 2012). One retrospective study showed worse AV graft outcomes in HIV-positive patients than in matched HIV-negative patients (Mitchell et al., 2007).

KIDNEY TRANSPLANTATION AND HIV

Although the initial experience with kidney transplantation and HIV patients was disappointing, the experience in the last 15 years has been positive. In particular, one trial followed HIV-positive transplant recipients and showed that transplant outcomes, including graft survival, were similar to those for HIV-negative transplant recipients. The patients included in the trial had CD4 counts >200 and an undetectable viral load. They were also on a stable antiretroviral regimen that was continued post-transplantation. Thus, kidney transplantation has become a treatment option for stable HIV-positive patients on dialysis (Stock et al., 2010). European studies have shown similar positive patient and transplant outcomes in patients with HIV (Mazuecos et al., 2011; Touzot et al., 2010). In addition, data from kidney transplants from HIV-positive donors to HIV-positive recipients show promising results (Muller et al., 2015). Careful monitoring of transplant recipients is necessary to ensure good outcome, including timely availability of drug levels and attention to potential interactions between HIV protease inhibitors and immunosuppressive agents, especially the calcineurin inhibitors (cyclosporine, tacrolimus, sirolimus) (Mueller et al., 2006). Drug–drug interactions between ART and calcineurin inhibitors continue to be an area of active investigation (van Maarseveen et al., 2012).

The logistics of solid organ transplantation pose special challenges in developing countries and areas where there is a high burden of HIV. In sub-Saharan Africa, there are large numbers of ESRD patients with limited numbers of trained nephrologists, little funding and support, in addition to limited access to ESRD therapy and transplantation (Naicker et al., 2010). Similar problems, including lack of access to dialysis technology, delayed referral to a nephrologists, and

increased illness acuity resulting in high rates of early death, were noted in Tunisia and Nigeria (Abderrahim et al., 2001; Anochie and Eke, 2005).

Persons with HIV face additional barriers regarding access to kidney transplantation and have lower rates of being placed on organ wait lists. In addition, patients with HIV have been shown to be less likely to pursue living donation once placed on kidney transplant wait lists. When HIV-positive patients on the transplant waitlist were surveyed, it was discovered that they were less likely to discuss living donation with friends and family, had more concerns about safety, and perceived their HIV disease as a barrier to living donation (Rodrigue et al., 2013).

The use of HIV-positive organs was illegal in the United States until November 2013, when President Obama signed the HIV Organ Policy Act. This law charges the U.S. Department of Health and Human Services to establish criteria for the conduct of research in the HIV-positive organ transplantation (Sawinski and Bloom, 2014). It has been estimated that approximately 500 additional solid organ transplants per year would be possible if HIV-infected donors were used (Boyarsky et al., 2011). The risk of performing transplantation from HIV-positive donors includes infecting an HIV-positive recipient with a new viral strain, underscoring the need for additional studies evaluating the outcomes of the using HIV-positive organs (Mgbako et al., 2013). Early data from South Africa show promising results when HIV-positive recipients receive kidneys from HIV-positive donors (Muller et al., 2015).

PALLIATIVE CARE

Patients with HIV on chronic dialysis lead challenging but often rewarding lives. It has been noted, however, that an increasing number of ESRD patients are choosing to withdraw from dialysis prior to death. The percentage of patients choosing to withdraw from dialysis rose from 8.4% in 1988–1990 to 17.8% in 1990–1995 (Leggat et al., 1997). Additionally, patients may decline dialysis for reasons consonant with their values and desire for biographical continuity until end of life (Llewellyn at al., 2014). Such data necessitate a close relationship between nephrology, psychiatry, and palliative care teams to ensure maximal quality of life in end-stage patients. Withdrawal of care is a complex decision even when medically, legally, and ethically justifiable and often is experienced through a combination of ambivalence, changes in decisions, and needed time to process the decision on an emotional level (Cohen et al., 2000; Neely and Roxe, 2000). Renal palliative care has been described as requiring special attention to the following four issues that are also relevant to HIV and renal comorbidity: early frank discussions concerning the process and goals of care, attention to symptoms at all states of the course of illness, early hospice referrals, and maximal palliative care at the end of life (Cohen et al., 2005; Cukor et al., 2011). Family dynamics and support play a large role, and such decisions affect an entire group of people, rather than a single patient. Psychosomatic medicine psychiatrists can often be beneficial during this time by providing support and attempting to allay the natural anxieties experienced by the patient, family, and other medical caregivers during times of crisis and of complex decision-making. More comprehensive approaches to palliative and end-of-life care are presented in Chapters 41 and 49 of this book.

PSYCHOLOGICAL ADAPTATION TO RENAL DISEASE AND DIALYSIS

Chronic renal disease (CKD) and dialysis pose psychological challenges to HIV-infected and uninfected individuals alike. However, when renal disease follows and is directly attributable to HIV, it may trigger traumatic aspects of one's initial response to receiving an HIV diagnosis. Additionally, remaining healthy with both medical conditions may require strict adherence to complicated and time-consuming therapies and a degree of cooperation with medical professionals that can overwhelm the capacity of even the most resilient individuals to cope. Individuals who highly value independence or with ambivalent attitudes toward dependency due to unreliable past relationships may have more difficulty accepting dialysis. Likewise, the loss of role functioning and relationships frequently accompanying both medical conditions may limit adaptation. Despite these psychological barriers, psychotherapeutic interventions and therapeutic modifications can empower individuals to effectively participate in their care. For example, use of modalities such home dialysis, peritoneal dialysis, or early renal transplantation that emphasize self-care may be more empowering to some individuals (Reichsman and Levy, 1972).

A growing interest in developing interventions to assist HIV-infected individuals in returning to work has paralleled the transformation of HIV to a manageable chronic illness (van Gorp et al., 2007). Yet work-related difficulties remain common among persons with HIV and are compounded by additional obstacles to work associated with dialysis. An estimated two-thirds of dialysis patients are underemployed or unemployed, thus underscoring the need for further study in this population (Cohen et al., 2000). Related loss of role functioning in school and housework-related responsibilities adds to patients' distress and can significantly undermine self-esteem, gender identify, sexual function, and perceived freedom.

Lipodystrophy and wasting occur less frequently since the introduction of newer antiretroviral medications. Yet patients with long-standing HIV illness may still exhibit these stigmatizing and visible complications of their illness. Patients undergoing dialysis similarly may experience physical changes that exacerbate stigma and impact body image. Chronic dermatological changes in dialysis patients include skin discoloration, scars secondary to hemodialysis access operations, and artificially created AV fistulas. Women often lose their menstrual cycle and are unable to become pregnant, and men have diminished sexual function with reduced sperm counts. Uremia has also been noted to have a direct impact on sexual function (Procci et al., 1981). All of these factors may affect not only the self-esteem of the patient but also their very concept of sexual role identity (Levy, 1973, 2000).

Dietary restrictions required for patients undergoing dialysis may have additional meaning for individuals with HIV whose lives are already constricted by their disease. Patients must restrict fluid intake to minimize the risk of peripheral and pulmonary edema that may follow excess fluid intake during renal failure. Drinking water or other beverages that most members of the general population take for granted is impossible; cracked ice is used to quench thirst. Similarly, protein intake is restricted severely, and persons with ESRD must often avoid dairy and fruit intake to avoid sodium, phosphates, and potassium, respectively. Thus, diets become artificial and difficult to follow outside of strictly controlled environments such as the patient's own home. The prospect of eating a "normal meal" at a restaurant is difficult if not impossible, leading further to isolation of the individual (Valderrqabano et al., 2001).

The actual procedure of being dialyzed is traumatic and anxiety provoking for most individuals. Peritoneal dialysis may be more benign in this respect because it involves only the transport of dialysate fluid, but patients undergoing hemodialysis witness their blood leaving their bodies, being sent into the hemodialyzer, and returned. Patients may be aware that a leak in the equipment can result in considerable blood loss, and they often experience significant hypotension during the procedure. If severe, this may lead to complications, including stroke and death.

PSYCHIATRIC COMPLICATIONS OF CHRONIC KIDNEY DISEASE AND HIV

The incidence and prevalence of psychiatric disorders in HIV and their impact on medical outcomes are well studied (see Chapter 3 of this book). Less is known about the epidemiology of psychiatric disorders and their impact in CKD, and even less in patients with combined CKD and HIV. One study of 69 patients with ESRD undergoing hemodialysis found that 46.4% met criteria for at least one psychiatric disorder and 23.2% for major depressive disorder. The authors compared these findings with those from patients with HIV alone and found rates of 59.1% ($p = 0.039$) and 11.4% ($p = 0.024$) for individuals with at least one psychiatric disorder or major depressive disorder, respectively (Martiny et al., 2012). There are a limited number of studies comparing the risk of depression among subgroups of patients with CKD alone receiving different modalities of treatment. One large controlled, population-based, retrospective cohort study found that, compared to controls, patients on peritoneal dialysis had the highest risk of developing major depression while those who had received a renal transplant had the lowest risk (Chen et al., 2016). Studies with smaller samples had similar findings of lower rates of depression and anxiety in patients with a renal transplant than in patients on hemodialysis or peritoneal dialysis (Cukor et al., 2009; Ozcan et al., 2015). In one study, poorer medication adherence in the hemodialysis group compared to the renal transplant group appeared to be mediated by depression (Cukor et al., 2009, 2011). In another study of patients with ESRD, depression and age were factors most strongly associated with shortened survival (Shulman et al., 1989).

Persons on dialysis appear to have a higher incidence of suicide than that of both the general population and persons with other chronic medical illnesses (Abram et al., 1975; Cutter et al., 1971; Haenel et al., 1980). Therefore, clinicians need to be aware of the potential for self-injurious behavior in these patients, who have two illnesses, HIV and ESRD, each of which is associated with a high incidence of suicide (Lyketsos and Federman, 1995). Please refer to Chapter 25 of this textbook for further discussion of suicidality and HIV.

Patients who are living with HIV and suffer end-stage renal failure are also predisposed to becoming delirious during treatment; delirium in HIV is more fully addressed in Chapter 16. Causes of delirium in persons with HIV and ESRD are varied; many individuals with HIV-related nephropathy are mildly azotemic at baseline that may progress to a mild chronic delirium. Also, hemodialysis predisposes many patients to dysequilibrium syndrome, which is a mild, time-limited delirium caused by a relatively rapid change in fluid and electrolytes. Delirium is also seen in the not uncommon dialysis complications of secondary and tertiary hyperparathyroidism.

The importance of delirium is that it may have primary and secondary psychological sequelae (Trzepacz and Meagher, 2005), such as a worsening of the premorbid psychological characteristics of patients as well as increased rates of secondary anxiety and depression.

TREATMENT OF PSYCHIATRIC AND PSYCHOLOGICAL COMORBIDITY IN HIV PATIENTS WITH END-STAGE RENAL DISEASE

The accepted and ideal treatment of depression and anxiety is with antidepressants and psychotherapy. These topics are covered more extensively in Chapters 15 and 18 of this textbook. In persons with ESRD and HIV, sexual dysfunction appears to play a large role in the maintenance and onset of distress, and some patients respond by withdrawing from intimacy altogether, resulting in increased isolation and poor self-coping (Levy, 1973). The treatment of sexual dysfunction in persons with HIV and ESRD can often restore the ability to be intimate, with high rates of success. For men, sildenafil (Viagra) and allied medications tend to be 60% to 80% effective in reversing or reducing impotence; more permanent solutions include penile implants. Other modalities of treatment such as Masters and Johnson techniques and their modifications involve less risk. In any case, it is important to keep in mind that sexual dysfunction is common in this population but is amenable to effective treatment (Abram et al., 1973). See Chapter 42 on psychopharmacology for drug–drug interactions between medications used to treat erectile dysfunction and antiretroviral medications.

Two major considerations in the pharmacology of renal failure are to avoid using a drug that is entirely eliminated by the kidney or one that is a small molecule that will be dialyzed (Levy et al., 2006). Pharmacokinetics are also significantly affected in renal failure, and the aspect that requires greatest attention is the effect of renal failure on protein binding (Brater, 1999). Most drugs, especially the psychotropics, bind primarily to albumin, and the free portion serves as the active component. In renal failure there is a decrease in available circulating protein and, thus, a decrease in binding capacity. Therefore, the rule of thumb is that the maximum dose of a medication used for a patient in renal failure should be no more than two-thirds the maximum dose used for a patient with normal kidney function. Fortunately, virtually all psychiatrically active medications are fat-soluble, pass the blood–brain barrier, are metabolized by the liver, and are excreted in bile.

The risk of drug–drug interactions between psychiatric medications and post-transplant immunosuppressive agents also influences choice of agents. Cyclosporine and tacrolimus are cytochrome P450 3A4 substrates whose metabolism may be affected by 3A4 induction or inhibition by psychiatric agents. For example, nefazodone may significantly increase trough levels of these immunosuppressants. Although fluoxetine, paroxetine, and citalopram may be associated with a reduced risk of interaction, therapeutic drug monitoring may be helpful when combining a serotonin reuptake inhibitor (SSRI) with calcineurin inhibitors or sirolimus. The serotonin-norepinephrine reuptake inhibitor (SNRI) venlafaxine, which does not utilize the CYP3A4 isoenzyme system, may be a safer alternative. Potential interactions may occur between lithium and calcineurin inhibitors. High trough levels of calcineurin inhibitors may also potentiate QT prolongation associated with haloperidol, quetiapine, and olanzapine (Manitpisitkul et al., 2009). See Chapter 42 on psychopharmacology for a more comprehensive discussion of drug–drug interactions.

Concerning the use of anxiolytics, although lorazepam is ordinarily eliminated by the kidney, in kidney failure this medication is detoxified by the liver and excreted in bile. Further discussion of treatment in this complex medical population can be found in Chapter 42.

See Chapter 37 on psychotherapeutic interventions in patients with HIV for discussion of psychosocial interventions.

RENAL TRANSPLANT

Solid organ transplantation has been noted to be among the triumphs of modern medicine and stands alongside the advances in treatment of HIV disease as one of the major advances in medical technology. The increase in organ transplantation, however, is limited to the number of available organs, which has not increased in proportion to the demand for new organs (Belle et al., 1996). The psychosomatic medicine psychiatrist is frequently called on to perform pre-transplant evaluations to assess for psychiatric stability prior to organ placement and to provide ongoing psychiatric care post-transplantation in the context of common affective disorders and neuropsychiatric syndromes that occur in this complex set of individuals. In this respect, transplantation psychiatry approaches the complexity commonly encountered in HIV psychiatry. The needs of HIV-seropositive patients with concurrent transplantation needs are highly complex. Frequently patients with HIV, ESRD, and renal transplant are subject to not only the psychosocial strain of transplantation but also significant psychosocial stressors associated with HIV seropositivity.

Donor organ resources remain a problem, with the need of organs being much greater than the number of organs available (Surman, 1989). Consideration of HIV-positive to HIV-positive kidney donation has been explored to address this need (Muller et al., 2010, 2015).

Transplant selection committees frequently serve as the gatekeeper for transplantation patients, orchestrating the selection of appropriate candidates on the basis of ethical, psychosocial, and biomedical factors (Freeman et al., 1992; Orentlicher, 1996). Skotzko and Strouse (2005) have remarked that psychosocial assessment should promote fairness and avoid discrimination. However, there are frequent implicit or explicit conflicts between the needs of the patient and the transplant program, so it often falls to the transplantation psychiatrist to advocate for the needs of the patient according to the principles of fairness and equal access.

Selection of transplant recipients with concurrent HIV is especially complex, given the perceived terminal quality of this illness among many medical practitioners, despite the dramatic fall in mortality in recent years. In fact, as noted in other portions of this chapter, the long-term survival of HIV patients with kidney transplants is favorable, even though it may be somewhat less than that of HIV-seronegative controls. Thus, the HIV psychiatrist can serve as a potent advocate for individuals who are otherwise good candidates medically and psychosocially and who have demonstrated good adherence to ART.

Persons with HIV and AIDS have already proven their capacity to maintain a complex pharmacological regimen in the face of chronic medical illness, so ironically, they may, in fact, be better candidates for transplant than individuals who have no such medical adherence history and may suffer higher graft loss rates (DeLong et al., 1989; Rodriguez et al., 1991; Schweizer et al., 1990). This proven history must be balanced against the fact that high numbers of prescribed medications correlate with increased risk for nonadherence (Kiley et al., 1993). In general, it can be asserted that HIV-seropositive individuals with good control of their underlying HIV disease can be acceptable transplant candidates.

HIV-seropositive transplantations are complex psychiatrically, since patients must deal with adjustment issues related to not only HIV status but also transplant status and the ever-present possibility of graft rejection. Patients requiring a second transplant may be obtunded and incapable of medical decision-making, reinforcing the role of surrogate decision-makers for these individuals as for non-transplant HIV patients. Other common psychotherapeutic issues involve expectations for the future, death and dying, acceptance of another serious illness, and overall quality of life.

In the face of these challenges, evidence suggests that transplantation is associated with improved psychosocial status comprising enhanced quality of life, work performance, and interpersonal and sexual functioning (Agarwal et al., 2016). However, post-transplant fear of organ rejection and progression of HIV illness may attenuate these benefits (Agarwal et al., 2016; Fukunishi, 1993).

Psychopharmacological considerations are complex in HIV renal transplant patients. Also, neurotoxicity associated with cyclosporine-derived compounds is not infrequent and may present as syndromes mimicking neuropsychiatric illness such as toxicity, delirium, and seizures (Burkhalter et al., 1994; Coleman and Norman, 1990; Estol, Faris, et al., 1989; Estol, Lopez, et al., 1989; Kershner and Wang-Cheng, 1989). The practitioner's differential diagnosis is confounded, because HIV transplant patients suffer from both an immunosuppressive disease and pharmacological immunosuppression, so a full assessment of any presenting symptom is required prior to preemptive therapy.

CONCLUSIONS

In summary, psychiatric disorders, most notably depression, are underrecognized and, when identified, undertreated in both chronic kidney disease (Cukor et al., 2011) and HIV. Patients with combined illnesses may be at highest risk for treatment nonadherence, poorer quality of life, worse medical and psychiatric outcomes, and suicide. These findings suggest that aggressive screening for depression and other psychiatric disorders in this population may yield considerable benefits (Levy, 2008).

Additionally, HIV psychiatrists have an important role with HIV transplant candidates: they can provide preoperative assessment and post-transplant treatment and support designed to return patients to a reasonable quality of life. Paris and colleagues (1993) have listed six predictors for return to employment: feeling able to work, having no risk of losing health insurance, longer length of time since transplant, education, maintenance of disability income, and relatively short periods of disability. For any transplant patient these factors are obviously complicated by the presence of another chronic illness such as HIV, for which distress rates are high, derived from complex factors, and underrecognized by most practitioners. HIV psychiatrists can provide support to persons with HIV/AIDS and comorbid chronic renal disease at every stage of illness, from prevention to end stage. Initial involvement with an integrated and comprehensive approach to care can help prevent HIV-associated nephropathy by encouraging adherence and treating comorbid psychiatric illness. Psychiatric care can provide support for patients as well as for their families and caregivers. The HIV psychiatrist can help alleviate distress, encourage behavior change and adherence, work with HIV clinicians and nephrologists to help reverse the ravages of HIV-associated nephropathy, provide assessments prior to dialysis and transplant, provide psychotherapy during dialysis and post-transplant, and continue to work with palliative psychiatry staff at the end of life.

REFERENCES

Abderrahim E, Zouaghi K, Hedri H, et al. (2001). Renal replacement therapy for end stage renal disease. Experience of a Tunisian hospital centre. *Diabetes Metab* 27:584–590.

Abram HS, Hester LR, Epstein GM (1973). Sexual functioning in patients with chronic renal failure. *J Nerv Ment Dis* 166:220–226.

Abram HS, Moore GL, Westerfelt BS (1975). Suicidal behavior in chronic dialysis patients. *Am J Psychiatry* 127:1199–1204.

Agarwal DK, Agarwal A, Nag N, Gajway SY, Garanayak S (2016). Impact of renal transplantation on psychosocial status of human immunodeficiency virus (HIV) positive patients. *J AIDS Clin Res* 7:554.

Ahuja TS, Collinge N, Grady J, Khan S (2002). Changing trends in the survival of dialysis patients with human immunodeficiency virus in the United States. *J Am Soc Nephrol* 13:1889–1893.

Alter MJ (2006). Epidemiology of viral hepatitis and HIV co-infection. *J Hepatol* 44:S6–S9.

Anochie IC, Eke FU (2005). Acute renal failure in Nigerian children: Port Harcourt experience. *Pediatr Nephrol* 20:1610–1614.

Arya V, Florian J, Marcus KA, Reynolds KS, Lewis LL, Sherwat AI (2014). Does an increase in serum creatinine always reflect renal injury? The case of Stribild®. *J Clin Pharmacol* 54:279–281.

Barsoum RS (2002). Overview: end-stage renal disease in the developing world. *Artif Organs* 26:737–746.

Behar DM, Shlush LI, Maor C, Lorber M, Skorecki K (2006). Absence of HIV associated nephropathy in Ethiopians. *Am J Kidney Dis* 47:88–94.

Belle SH, Beringer KC, Detre DM (1996). Recent findings concerning liver transplantation in the United States. *Clin Transplant* 10:15–29.

Berliner AR, Fine DM, Lucas GM, et al. (2008). Observations on a cohort of HIV-infected patients undergoing native renal biopsy. *Am J Nephrol* 28:478–486.

Boyarsky BJ, Hall ED, Singer AL, et al. (2011). Estimating the potential pool of HIV infected deceased organ donors in the United States. *Am J Transplant* 11:1209–1217.

Brater DC (1999). Drug dosing in renal failure. In HR Brady, CS Wilcox (eds.), *Therapy in Nephrology and Hypertension: A Companion to Brenner and Rector's The Kidney*, 5th ed. (pp. 641–653). Philadelphia: WB Saunders.

Brown TT, Li X, Cole SR, et al. (2005). Cumulative exposure to nucleoside analogue reverse transcriptase inhibitors is associated with insulin resistance markers in the Multicenter AIDS Cohort Study. *AIDS* 19:1375–1383.

Burkhalter EL, Starzl TE, Van Thiel DH (1994). Severe neurological complications following orthotopic liver transplant in patients receiving FK-506 and prednisone. *J Hepatol* 21:572–577.

Chen SF, Wang IJ, Lang HC (2016). Risk of major depression in patients with chronic renal failure on different treatment modalities: a matched-cohort and population-based study in Taiwan. *Hemodial Int* 20:98–105.

Cohen LM, Levy NB, Tessier EG, Germain MJ (2005). Renal disease. In JL Levenson (ed.), *Textbook of Psychosomatic Medicine* (pp. 483–493). Washington, DC: American Psychiatric Publishing.

Cohen LM, McCue J, Germain M (2000). Denying the dying: advance directives and dialysis discontinuation. *Psychosomatics* 41:195–203.

Coleman AE, Norman DJ (1990). OKT3 encephalopathy. *Ann Neurol* 128:837–838.

Coresh J, Astor BC, Greene T, Eknoyan G, Levey AS (2003). Prevalence of chronic kidney disease and decreased kidney function in the adult US population: Third National Health and Nutrition Examination Survey. *Am J Kidney Dis* 41:1–12.

Cosgrove CJ, Abu-Alfa AK, Perazella MA (2002). Observations on HIV-associated renal disease in the era of highly active antiretroviral therapy. *Am J Med Sci* 323:102–106.

Cukor D, Rosenthal DS, Jindal RM, Brown CD, Kimmel PL (2009). Depression is an important contributor to low medication adherence in hemodialyzed patient and transplant recipients. *Kidney Int* 75:122–129.

Cukor D, Rosenthal-Asher D, Cohen LM, et al. (2011). Renal disease. In JL Levenson (ed.), *Textbook of Psychosomatic Medicine* (pp. 491–502). Washington, DC: American Psychiatric Publishing.

Cutter F, Abram HS, Moore GL (1971). Chronic dialysis patients: suicide incidence rates. *Am J Psychiatry* 128:495–497.

De Lastours V, Ferrari Rafael De Silva E, Daudon M, et al. (2013). High levels of atazanavir and darunavir in urine and crystalluria in asymptomatic patients. *J Antimicrob Chemother* 68(8):1850–1856.).

DeLong P, Trollinger JH, Fox N, et al. (1989). Noncompliance in renal transplant recipients: methods for recognition and intervention. *Transplant Proc* 21:2982–3984.

Estol CJ, Faris AA, Martinez AJ, Ahdab-Barmada M (1989). Central pontine myelinolysis after liver transplantation. *Neurology* 39:493–498.

Estol CJ, Lopez O, Brenner RP, Martinez AJ (1989). Seizures after liver transplantation: a clinicopathologic study. *Neurology* 39:1297–1301.

European AIDS Clinical Society (2015). European guidelines for treatment of HIV-infected adults Version 8.0, October 2015. http://www.eacsociety.org/files/guidelines_8.0-english.pdf. Accessed February 11, 2017.

Fernandez-Fernandez B, Montoya-Ferrer A, Sanz AB, et al. (2011). Tenofovir nephrotoxicity: 2011 update. *AIDS* 2011:354908.

Fine DM, Gallant JE (2013). Nephrotoxicity of antiretroviral agents: is the list getting longer? *J Infect Dis* 207(9):1349–1351.

Fischer MJ, Wyatt CM, Gordon K, et al. (2010). Hepatitis C and the risk of kidney diease and mortality in veterans with HIV. *J Acquir Immune Defic Syndr* 53:222–226.

Fokou M, Ashuntantang G, Teyang A, et al. (2012). Patients characteristics and outcome of 518 arteriovenous fistulas for hemodialysis in a sub-Saharan African setting. *Ann Vasc Surg* 26(5):674–679.

Freeman A, Davies L, Libb JW, et al. (1992). Assessment of transplant candidates and prediction of outcome. In J Craven, G Rodin (eds.), *Psychiatric Aspects of Organ Transplantation* (pp. 9–19). Oxford, UK: Oxford University Press.

Fukunishi I (1993). Anxiety associated with kidney transplantation. *Psychopathology* 26:24–28.

Gallant JE, Parish MA, Keruly JC, Moore RD (2005). Changes in renal function associated with tenofovir disoproxil fumarate treatment, compared with nucleoside reverse transcriptase inhibitor treatment. *Clin Infect Dis* 40:1194–1198.

Gardner LI, Holmberg SD, Williamson JM, et al. (2003). Development of proteinuria or elevated serum creatinine and mortality in HIV-infected women. *J Acquir Immune Defic Syndr* 32:203–209.

German P, Liu HC, Szwarcberg J, et al. (2012). Effect of cobicistat on glomerular filtration rate in subjects with normal and impaired renal function. *J Acquir Immune Defic Syndr* 61(1):32–40.

Gerntholtz TE, Goetsch SJW, Katz I (2006). HIV related nephropathy: a South African perspective. *Kidney Int* 69:1885–1891.

Gupta SK, Eustace JA, Winston JA, et al. (2005). Guidelines for the management of chronic kidney disease in HIV-infected patients: recommendations of the HIV Medicine Association of the Infectious Diseases Society of America. *Clin Infect Dis* 40:1559–1585.

Gupta SK, Mamlin BW, Johnson CS, et al. (2004). Prevalence of proteinuria and the development of chronic kidney disease in HIV-infected patients. *Clin Nephrol* 61:1–6.

Haenel T, Brunner F, Battegay R (1980). Renal dialysis and suicide: occurrence in Switzerland and in Europe. *Compr Psychiatry* 21:140–145.

Hall AM, Hendry B, Nitsch D, Connolly JO (2011). Tenofovir-associated kidney toxicity in HIV-infected patients: a review of the evidence. *Am J Kidney Dis* 57:773–780

Han TM, Naicker S, Ramdial PK, Assounga AG (2006). A cross-sectional study of HIV seropositive patients with varying degrees of proteinuria in South Africa. *Kidney Int* 69:2243–2250.

Heron M (2015). Deaths: leading causes for 2011. *Natl Vital Stat Rep.* 64(7):1–96.

Kershner P, Wang-Cheng R (1989). Psychiatric side effects of steroid therapy. *Psychosomatics* 30:135–139.

Khanna R, Tachopoulou OA, Fein PA, Chattopadhyay J, Avram MM (2005). Survival experience of peritoneal dialysis patients with human immunodeficiency virus: a 17-year retrospective study. *Adv Perit Dial* 21:159–163.

Kiley DJ, Lam CS, Pollak R (1993). A study of treatment compliance following kidney transplantation. *Transplantation* 55:51–56.

Koteff J, Borland J, Chen S, et al. (2013). A phase 1 study to evaluate dolutegravir's effect on renal function via measurement of iohexol and para-aminohippurate clearance in healthy subjects. *Br J Clin Pharmacol* 75(4):990–996.

Leggat JE, Bloembergen WE, Levine G, Hulbert-Shearon TE, Port FK (1997). An analysis of risk factors for withdrawal from dialysis before death. *J Am Soc Nephrol* 8:1755–1763.

Levy NB (1973). Sexual adjustment to hemodialysis and renal transplantation: national survey by questionnaire: preliminary report. *Trans Am Soc Artif Intern Organs* 19:138–142.

Levy NB (2000). Psychiatric considerations in primary medical care of the patient in renal failure. *Adv Ren Replace Ther* 7:231–238.

Levy NB (2008). What is psychonephrology? *J Nephrol Suppl* 13:S51–S53.

Levy NB, Cohen LM, Tessier EG (2006). Renal disease. In M Blumenfield, JJ Strain (eds.), *Psychosomatic Medicine* (pp. 157–175). Philadelphia: Lippincott Williams & Wilkins.

Llewellyn H, Low J, Smith G, Hopkins K, Burns A, Jones L (2014). Narratives of continuity among older people with late stage chronic kidney disease who decline dialysis. *Soc Sci Med* 114:49–56.

Lucas GM, Eustace JA, Sozio S, Mentari EK, Appiah KA, Moore RD (2004). Highly active antiretroviral therapy and the incidence of HIV-1-associated nephropathy: a 12-year cohort study. *AIDS* 18:541–546.

Lucas GM, Ross MJ, Stock PG, et al. (2014). Clinical practice guideline for the management of chronic kidney disease in patients infected with HIV: 2014 update by the HIV Medicine Association of the Infectious Disease Society of America. *Clin Infect Dis* 59(9):e96–e138.

Lyketsos CG, Federman EB (1995). Psychiatric disorders and HIV infection: impact of one on the other. *Epidimiol Rev* 17:152–164.

Mallipatu SK, Wyatt CM, He JC (2012). The new epidemiology of HIV-related kidney disease. *J AIDs Clin Res* 2012;(Suppl 4):001.

Manitpisitkul W, McCann E, Lee S, Weir MR (2009). Drug interactions in transplant patients: what everyone should know. *Curr Opin Nephrol Hypertension* 18:404–411.

Martiny C, de Oliveira e Silva AC, Neto JPS, Nardi AE (2012). Psychiatric disorders in patients with end-stage renal disease. *J Renal Care* 38:131–137.

Mazuecos A, Fernandez A, Andres A, et al. (2011). HIV infection and renal transplantation. *Nephrol Dial Transplant* 26:1401–1407.

Mgbako O, Glazier A, Blumberg E, Reese PP (2013). Allowing HIV-positive organ donation: ethical, legal and operational considerations. *Am J Transplant* 13:1636–1642.

Mitchell D, Krishnasami Z, Young CJ, Allon M (2007). Arteriovenous access outcomes in haemodialysis patients with HIV infection. *Nephrol Dial Transplant* 22(2):465–470.

Mocroft A, Kirk O, Reiss P, et al. (2010). Estimated glomerular filtration rate, chronic kidney disease and antiretroviral drug use in HIV-positive patients. *AIDS* 24:1667–1678.

Mocroft A, Ryom L, Begovac J, et al.; EuroSIDA in EuroCOORD (2014). Deteriorating renal function and clinical outcomes in HIV-positive persons. *AIDS* 28:727–737.

Moss DM, Liptrott NJ, Curley P, Siccardi M, Back DJ, Owen A (2013). Rilpivirine inhibits drug transporters ABCB1, SLC22A1, and SLC22A2 in vitro. *Antimicrob Agents Chemother* 57(11):5612–5618.

Mueller NJ, Furrer H, Kaiser L, et al.; Swiss HIV Cohort Study (2006). HIV and solid organ transplantation: the Swiss experience. *Swiss Med Wkly* 136:194.

Muller E, Barday Z, Mendelson M, Kahn D (2015). HIV-positive-to-HIV-positive kidney transplantation—results at 3 to 5 Years. *N Engl J Med* 372:613–620.

Muller E, Kahn D, Mendelson M (2010). Renal transplantation between HIV positive donors and recipients. *N Engl J Med* 362:2336–2337.

Naicker S, Eastwood JB, Plange-Rhule J, Tutt RC (2010). Shortage of healthcare workers in sub-Saharan Africa: a nephrological perspective. *Clin Nephrol* 74(Suppl 1):S129–S133.

Naicker S, Rahmanian S, Kopp JB (2015). HIV and chronic kidney disease. *Clin Nephrol* 83:s32–s38.

National Center for Health Statistics (2005). *United States, 2005, With Chartbook on Trends in the Health of Americans*. Hyattsville, MD: U.S. Government Printing Office.

Neely KJ, Roxe DM (2000). Palliative care/hospice and the withdrawal of dialysis. *J Palliat Med* 3:57–67.

Okpechi IG, Rayner BL, Swanepoel CR (2012). Peritoneal dialysis in Cape Town, South Africa. *Perit Dial Int* 32(3):254–260.

Orentlicher D (1996). Psychosocial assessment of organ transplant candidates and the Americans with Disabilities Act. *Gen Hosp Psychiatry* 18:5S–12S.

Ozcan H, Yucel A, Avsar UZ, et al. (2015). Kidney transplantation is superior to hemodialysis and peritoneal dialysis in terms of cognitive functioning, anxiety, and depression symptoms in chronic kidney disease. *Transplant Proc* 47:1348–1351.

Paris W, Woodbury A, Thompson S, et al. (1993). Returning to work after heart transplantation. *J Heart Lung Transplant* 12:46–53.

Parsa A, Kao L, Xie D, et al. (2013). APOL1 risk variants, race, and progression of chronic kidney disease. *N Engl J Med* 369:2183–2196.

Procci WR, Goldstein DA, Adelstein J (1981). Sexual function in the male with uremia: a reappraisal. *Kidney Int* 19:317–323.

Rasch MG, Engsig FN, Feldt-Rasmussen B, et al. (2012). Renal function and incidence of chronic kidney disease in HIV patients: a Danish cohort study. *Scand J Infect Dis* 44(9):689–696.

Reichsman F, Levy NB (1972). Adaptation to hemodialysis: a four-year study of 25 patients. *Arch Intern Med* 138:859–865.

Reynes J, Trinh R, Pulido F, et al. (2013). Lopinavir/ritonavir combined with raltegravir or tenofovir/emtricitabine in antiretroviral-naive subjects: 96-week results of the PROGRESS study. *AIDS Res Hum Retroviruses* 29(2):256–265.

Rodrigue JR, Paek MJ, Egbuna O, et al. (2013). Willingness to pursue live donor kidney transplantation among wait-listed patients with human immunodeficiency virus (HIV): a preliminary investigation. *Transplantation* 95:787–790.

Rodriguez A, Diaz M, Colon A, Santiago-Delpin EA (1991). Psychosocial profile of noncompliant transplant patients. *Transplant Proc* 23:1807–1809.

Ross MJ, Klotman PE (2004). HIV-associated nephropathy. *AIDS* 18:1089–1099.

Saran R, Li Y, Robinson B, et al. (2015). US Renal Data System 2014 annual data report: epidemiology of kidney disease in the United States. *Am J Kidney Dis* 66(1)(Suppl 1):S1–S306.

Sawinski D, Bloom RD (2014). Current status of kidney transplantation in HIV-infected patients. *Curr Opin Nephrol Hypertens* 23:619–624.

Scherzer R, Estrella M, Li Y, et al. (2012). Association of tenofovir exposure with kidney disease risk in HIV infection. *AIDS* 26(7):867–875.

Schwartz EJ, Szczech LA, Ross MJ, et al. (2005). Highly active antiretroviral therapy and the epidemic of HIV+ end-stage renal disease. *J Am Soc Nephrol* 16:2412–2420.

Schweizer RT, Rovelli M, Palmeri D, Vossler E, Hull D, Bartus S (1990). Noncompliance in organ transplant recipients. *Transplantation* 49:374–377.

Shulman R, Price JD, Spinelli J (1989). Biopsychosocial aspects of long-term survivale on end-stage renal failure therapy. *Psychol Med* 19:945–954.

Skotzko CE, Strouse TB (2005). Solid organ tranplantation. In JT Levenson (ed.), *The American Psychiatric Publishing Textbook of Consultation-Liaison Psychiatry*, 2nd ed. (pp. 623–654). Washington DC: American Psychiatric Publishing.

Soleymanian T, Raman S, Shannaq FN, et al. (2006). Survival and morbidity of HIV patient on hemodialysis and peritoneal dialysis: one center's experience and review of the literature. *Int Urol Nephrol* 38(2):331–338.

Stock PG, Barin B, Murphy B, et al. (2010). Outcomes of kidney transplantation in HIV-infected recipients. *N Engl J Med* 363:2004–2014.

Stray KM, Bam RA, Birkus G, et al. (2013). Evaluation of the effect of cobicistat on the in vitro renal transport and cytotoxicity potential of tenofovir. *Antimicrob Agents Chemother* 57(10):4982–4989.

Surman OS (1989). Psychiatric aspects of organ transplantation. *Am J Psychiatry* 146:972–982.

Szczech LA, Edwards LJ, Sanders LL, van der Horst C, Bartlet JA, Heald AE, Svetkey LP (2002). Protease inhibitors are associated with a slowed progression of HIV-related renal diseases. *Clin Nephrol* 57:336–341.

Szczech LA, Hoover DR, Feldman JG, et al. (2004). Association between renal disease and outcomes among HIV-infected women receiving or not receiving antiretroviral therapy. *Clin Infect Dis* 39:1199–1206.

Touzot M, Pillebout E, Matignon M, et al. (2010). Renal transplant in HIV infected patients: the Paris experience. *Am J Transplant* 10:2263–2269.

Trzepacz PT, Meagher DJ (2005). Delirium. In JL Levenson (ed.), *The American Psychiatric Publishing Textbook of Psychosomatic Medicine* (pp. 91–130). Washington, DC: American Psychiatric Publishing.

Valderrqabano E, Jofre R, Lopez-Gomez JM (2001). Quality of life in end-stage renal disease patients. *Am J Kidney Dis* 38:443–464.

van Gorp WG, Rabkin JG, Ferrando SJ, Mintz J, Ryan E, Borkowski T, McElhiney M (2007). Neuropsychiatric predictors of return to work in HIV/AIDS. *J Int Neuropsychol Soc* 13:80–89.

van Maarseveen EM, Rogers CC, Trofe-Clark J, et al. (2012). Drug-drug interactions between antiretroviral and immunosuppressive agents in HIV-infected patients after solid organ transplantation: a review. *AIDS Patient Care STDs* 26:568–581.

Wali RK, Drachenberg CI, Papadimitriou JC, Keay S, Ramos E (1998). HIV-1-associated nephropathy and response to highly active antiretroviral therapy [letter]. *Lancet* 352:783–784.

Wever K, Van Agtmael MA, Carr A (2010). Incomplete reversibility of tenofovir-related renal toxicity in HIV-infected men. *J Acquir Immune Defic Syndr* 55(1):78–81.

Winston JA, Bruggeman LA, Ross MD, et al. (2001). Nephropathy and establishment of a renal reservoir of HIV type 1 during primary infection. *N Engl J Med* 344:1979–1984.

Wyatt CM, Malvestutto C, Coca SG, Klotman PE, Parikh CR (2008). The impact of hepatitis C virus coinfection on HIV-related kidney disease: a systematic review and meta-analysis. *AIDS* 22:1799–1807.

Yombi JC, Pozniak A, Boffito M, et al. (2014). Antiretroviral and the kidney in current clinical practice: renal pharmacokinetics, alterations of renal function and renal toxicity. *AIDS* 28(5):621–632.

Young J, Schäfer J, Fux CA, et al.; Swiss HIV Cohort Study (2012). Renal function in patients with HIV starting therapy with tenofovir and either efavirenz, lopinavir or atazanavir. *AIDS* 26(5):567–575.

ENDOCRINE COMORBIDITIES IN PERSONS WITH HIV

Jocelyn Soffer and Harold W. Goforth

HIV and AIDS have been associated with a wide spectrum of endocrine abnormalities that underscore the complex relationships between immunological, endocrinological, and psychological systems. Endocrinopathies are great mimickers of psychiatric disorders, manifesting in some cases as disturbances of mood, sleep, appetite, thought process, energy level, or general sense of well-being. Endocrine changes associated with HIV infection occur through multiple mechanisms, including direct cytopathological effects, intercurrent illness, and pharmacotherapies used to treat the virus. Some of these changes may not be specific to HIV, but rather represent the body's response to any severe illness; others may be HIV specific yet not have clear clinical significance. As treatments for HIV continue to improve and the population of HIV-infected individuals ages, even subtle changes in endocrine function may carry increasingly important consequences for morbidity, mortality, and quality of life. An understanding of the interactions between endocrine and psychological systems may improve recognition and treatment of reversible endocrinopathies, diminish suffering, and enhance quality of life and longevity in persons with HIV and AIDS.

This chapter will present an overview of HIV-associated changes in the function of the hypothalamic–pituitary axis, adrenal glands, thyroid, gonads, and bone and mineral metabolism and consider the psychosocial implications of such endocrinopathies.

ADRENAL GLAND IN HIV INFECTION

ALTERED HYPOTHALAMIC–PITUITARY–ADRENAL AXIS: PATHOPHYSIOLOGY AND ASSESSMENT OF ADRENAL FUNCTION

Many studies have demonstrated alterations in adrenal function in patients with HIV and AIDS, making it in the most common of endocrine organ dysfunction in this population (George and Bhangoo, 2013). Associated infections and tumors, as well as direct invasion of the adrenal glands by the virus, partly explain these changes. The altered cytokine milieu in immune deficiency states may also affect the hypothalamic–pituitary–adrenal (HPA) axis. Tumor necrosis factor alpha (TNF-α), for example, found in increased levels in HIV patients, impairs corticotrophin-releasing hormone (CRH)-stimulated release of adrenocorticotropin hormone (ACTH) and cortisol.

Persons with HIV are also commonly prescribed drugs that alter steroid synthesis or metabolism; for example, ketoconazole decreases steroid synthesis, while rifampin increases p450 activity, leading to increased metabolism of cortisol. Megestrol acetate, used as an appetite stimulant in patients with AIDS, suppresses pituitary secretion of corticotropin owing to its glucocorticoid-like properties (Lo and Grinspoon, 2010). Ritonavir administration with inhaled corticosteroids can cause iatrogenic Cushing's syndrome (Pessanha et al., 2007; Samaras et al., 2005; Yoganathan et al., 2012). Case reports have included iatrogenic Cushing's syndrome after epidural or intra-articular steroids in patients concomitantly treated with ritonavir (Albert et al., 2012, Yombi et al., 2008). Although inhaled fluticasone has been the most commonly been reported interaction, it is important to ask patients about all treatments, including creams, nasal sprays, or herbal remedies, which may contain steroids (Wren, 2013).

Alterations at all levels of the HPA axis have been described in patients with HIV. With the traditional 250 μg ACTH stimulation test to detect adrenal response, many studies have revealed subnormal peak cortisol responses in patients with HIV (Membreno et al., 1987; Merenich et al., 1990; Raffi et al., 1991), although some have demonstrated normal responses (Findling et al., 1994). Azar and Melby (1993) examined patients with advanced HIV (CD4 <500) but without signs of adrenal or pituitary insufficiency. In response to CRH stimulation, 25% displayed normal ACTH but decreased cortisol response (suggesting reduced adrenal reserve), while 25% showed both impaired ACTH and cortisol production (suggesting reduced pituitary reserve). Other studies have similarly demonstrated decreased responses of both ACTH and cortisol to CRH stimulation (Biglino et al., 1995; Lortholary et al., 1996).

In the late 1980s, many postmortem studies demonstrated high rates of adrenal involvement in patients dying from AIDS (Laulund et al., 1986; Welch et al., 1984). Cytomegalovirus (CMV) was the most common associated infectious agent, found in the adrenal glands in 33–88% of cases (Glasgow et al., 1985; Marik et al., 2002; Pulakhandam and Dincsoy, 1990). Less common agents observed in autopsy studies included *Cryptococcus, Toxoplasma, Histoplasma, Mycobacteria,* and neoplasms such as lymphoma and Kaposi's sarcoma. Other autopsy studies (including a series of 128 patients who died of AIDS) found high rates of adrenal abnormalities, with compromise or inflammation of the adrenal glands observed in nearly 100% of cases, approximately half involving CMV infection (Duch et al., 1998; Rodrigues et al., 2002).

Clinical symptoms of adrenal insufficiency in patients with HIV, in contrast, are much less common, probably because more than 80% to 90% of the adrenal glands must be destroyed before symptoms appear, whereas adrenal cortical necrosis observed in autopsy studies rarely exceeds 60–70% (Mayo et al., 2002; Sellmeyer and Grunfeld, 1996). In fact, despite the association of HIV with adrenal dysfunction and blunted stress responses discussed, most studies have found normal or more commonly elevated basal cortisol levels in patients with HIV infection (Biglino et al., 1995; Christeff et al., 1997; Sellmeyer and Grunfeld, 1996; Villette et al., 1990). Serum cortisol typically increases as disease progresses, negatively correlating with CD4 counts (Lortholary et al., 1996).

Multiple factors could explain the hypercortisolism commonly observed in patients with HIV infection, including comorbid depression and severe psychosocial stress, both of which are associated with increased levels of cortisol. More specifically, increased levels of cytokines present during HIV infection may stimulate cortisol production by the adrenal glands. Biglino and colleagues (1995) demonstrated a correlation between cortisol and levels of interleukin-6 (IL-6) and IL-1β. They suggested that observed blunting of pituitary and adrenal responses to CRH stimulation occurs as compensation for chronic cytokine-induced adrenal stimulation. Additionally, the HIV envelope protein gp-120 has been shown to lead to HPA axis hyperactivity (Zapanti et al., 2008).

Changes in steroid carrier proteins and steroid receptor binding might contribute to altered hormone metabolism. Studies have demonstrated decreased binding of corticosteroid-binding globulin (CBG) to cortisol in HIV patients compared to that in controls, despite an increased number of binding sites (Martin et al., 1992). A phenomenon of glucocorticoid resistance has also been described in patients with HIV that could further explain the paradoxical combination of increased serum cortisol and clinical symptoms of adrenal insufficiency. Norbiato and colleagues (1992) demonstrated a decreased affinity of glucocorticoid receptors for glucocorticoids in patients with AIDS, despite an increase in receptor density.

Finally, there appears to be a shift in adrenal steroid metabolism from androgenic pathways to those of cortisol production. Villette and colleagues (1990) found significantly higher 24-hour cortisol levels in patients with HIV than those in control subjects, but decreases in dehydroepiandrosterone (DHEA), DHEA-sulfate (DHEA-S), and ACTH. With advancing HIV infection, cortisol levels typically increase, while DHEA and DHEA-S levels decrease (Clerici et al., 1997; Findling et al., 1994), in some cases correlating with CD4 cell counts (Christeff et al., 1997; Wisniewski et al., 1993). The ratio of DHEA to cortisol declines significantly in patients with more advanced clinical illness. Although most studies have been conducted with men, studies of women with AIDS have also demonstrated a correlation between CD4 cell counts and DHEA-to-cortisol ratios (Grinspoon et al., 2001).

Despite the clear evidence for alterations in the HPA axis in this population, the prevalence and clinical significance of such abnormalities remain controversial, in part because of methodological difficulties in assessing adrenal function. The diagnosis of adrenal insufficiency from stimulation testing depends both on the dose of ACTH used and the laboratory cutoffs for a "normal" cortisol stress response. Some investigators have claimed that the supraphysiological 250 μg dose of ACTH masks some adrenal dysfunction; low-dose stimulation testing (e.g., 1 or 10 μg) increases sensitivity (Marik et al., 2002) but might result in false positives. Stolarczyk and colleagues (1998) found that AIDS patients both with and without symptoms had a decreased cortisol response compared to comparably sick HIV-negative patients and healthy controls, despite achieving "normal" cortisol values on stimulation testing.

These complexities are highlighted by the frequent lack of correlation between symptoms and detection of laboratory abnormalities (Bhansali et al., 2000; Eledrisi and Verghese, 2001). In a study of 104 patients using a 10 μg ACTH stimulation test in which nearly one-third of patients had clinical signs of adrenal insufficiency, only 5% responded abnormally, with an additional 16% demonstrating borderline responses, and no reliable correlation with disease symptoms (Gonzalez-Gonzalez et al., 2001). In another study of 63 patients with advanced AIDS, 19% had abnormally low levels of stimulated cortisol, suggesting a need for supplementation, but no associated opportunistic diseases, signs, or symptoms (Wolff et al., 2001).

Despite these methodological difficulties, most clinicians would agree that adrenal insufficiency is relatively common in patients with advanced AIDS, especially individuals positive for CMV, and that function should be evaluated in all severely ill patients with AIDS (Hoshino et al., 2002). Normal findings on adrenal stimulation in the presence of clinical signs and symptoms of insufficiency should be interpreted with caution. Finally, glucocorticoid replacement is crucial for all patients with a diagnosis of adrenal insufficiency and should be considered and increased in patients with AIDS during times of febrile illness or worsening infection.

Fewer studies have examined mineralocorticoid response during HIV infection. Patients with primary adrenal insufficiency, however, will also present with mineralocorticoid deficiency (in addition to glucocorticoid deficiency), so replacement with both is necessary. Some studies report lower levels of basal aldosterone than those in controls, including one of asymptomatic patients newly diagnosed with HIV (Merenich et al., 1990). There are only a few isolated case reports of primary aldosteronism in HIV infection (Fradley et al., 2005). Authors of one case series in Zambia described inappropriately low aldosterone concentrations in adults with AIDS-related diarrhea, complicating the treatment of electrolyte imbalances and suggesting the possibility of the need for more aggressive practices of mineralocorticoid replacement in this population (Kaile et al., 2008). In general, the clinical significance of possibly altered mineralocorticoid function remains uncertain.

PSYCHOSOCIAL IMPLICATIONS

There can be considerable overlap between symptoms of HIV itself, adrenal insufficiency, and psychiatric illness, including fatigue, anorexia, nausea, vomiting, and orthostatic hypotension. Some patients report a sensation of heavy and weak muscles, dizziness, and tachycardia, which may be confused with a depressive or anxiety disorder. Patients with adrenal insufficiency have been misdiagnosed with hypochondriasis, conversion disorder, and anorexia nervosa (Starkman, 2003). When signs more specific to adrenal insufficiency are present, such as salt craving, hyponatremia, or, in the case of primary adrenal insufficiency, increased skin pigmentation, the diagnosis is more easily made.

Associated behavioral changes in patients with adrenal insufficiency may include lethargy, apathy, irritability, crying, and impaired sleep. Cognitive difficulties have also been reported, including decreased concentration, decreased memory, and episodic confusion; impaired thought process can worsen to frank psychosis during an adrenal crisis (Starkman, 2003).

As discussed earlier, most patients with HIV do not exhibit signs of adrenal insufficiency but rather are marked by increased levels of circulating cortisol. These patients do not generally present with features of Cushing's syndrome either, however, which may have different neuropsychiatric manifestations. The clinical significance of hypercortisolemia seen in most patients with HIV, then, remains unclear, being associated with classical manifestations of neither Cushing's syndrome nor adrenal insufficiency.

DHEA and DHEA-S are not only adrenal androgens but also centrally acting neurosteroids whose levels decrease with chronic stress and illness (in contrast to cortisol, which tends to rise). Decreased ratios of DHEA and DHEA-S to cortisol have been reported in many conditions, including aging, depression, and dementia (Wolkowitz et al., 2003), in addition to HIV infection. Given that DHEA and DHEA-S have been shown to have memory-enhancing (Roberts et al., 1987) and antidepressant-like effects in animals (Reddy et al., 1998), it is not surprising that low levels of these neurosteroids have been reported in patients with depression, psychosocial stress, and functional limitations (Berr et al., 1996; Yaffe et al., 1998). In one study of postmenopausal women, DHEA-S levels were inversely associated with depressed mood, independent of age, physical activity, or weight change (Barrett-Connor et al., 1999). In a controlled study of depressed patients, salivary levels of DHEA were lower than those in controls, with a negative correlation found between morning readings and the severity of depression (Michael et al., 2000). The evening salivary cortisol was elevated in the depressed population.

The indications for replacement of DHEA, however, remain controversial. In one study of women with adrenal insufficiency, replacement of DHEA improved overall well-being, depression and anxiety, and satisfaction with both mental and physical aspects of sexuality (Arlt et al., 1999). In another study of patients with Addison's disease, replacement with DHEA significantly enhanced self-esteem, mood, and fatigue, with a tendency toward improved overall

well-being, but did not affect cognitive or sexual function (Hunt et al., 2000). Oral DHEA treatment has been shown to improve quality of life in patients with advanced HIV disease (Piketty et al., 2001), as well as decreasing depressive symptoms in patients with HIV/AIDS (Rabkin et al., 2006). Researchers have demonstrated that oral DHEA treatment for 8 weeks significantly increases circulating DHEA, DHEA-S, and testosterone in both HIV-infected men (Poretsky et al., 2006) and premenopausal women (Poretsky et al., 2009). To date, however, there are limited studies specifically addressing the psychosocial implications of adrenal dysfunction in persons with HIV and no clear guidelines for how and under what circumstances to replace DHEA in men or women with HIV.

In persons with HIV who abuse substances, in some cases by injection drug use, there may be associated endocrine changes that mimic or exacerbate those seen in HIV infection. A high prevalence of adrenal dysfunction has been described in opioid-dependent patients (Tennant et al., 1991). Hypercortisolism occurs after abrupt withdrawal of heroin in addicts (Cami et al., 1992). In rat studies, chronic exposure to morphine causes naltrexone-preventable increases in corticobinding globulin that lowers the amount of free active cortisol (Nock et al., 1997). In a study of heroin and cocaine users, higher cortisol levels were associated with depressive symptoms, particularly in women (Wisniewski et al., 2006), with gender differences being most pronounced in women who were both infected with HIV and injection drug users (Wisniewski et al., 2005).

Some investigators have examined the hypothesis that stress management interventions would help counter some of the HPA dysfunction observed in patients with HIV, given that high levels of stress and mood disturbances might contribute to high levels of cortisol (Mulder et al., 1995). A cognitive-behavioral stress management (CBSM) intervention consisting of 10 weekly group sessions demonstrated post-treatment decreases in depression, anxiety, and general psychological distress, compared to a wait-list comparison group (Antoni et al., 2000a). The treatment group had lower levels of urinary cortisol, with improved mood paralleling cortisol decreases in urine. Furthermore, at 6- to 12-month follow-up, the CBSM group had improved immunological parameters, including increased transitional naïve T cells (Antoni et al., 2002) and cytotoxic T cells (Antoni et al., 2000b). Interestingly, only mood changes during the training period predicted such delayed immune status changes; there was no association with post-intervention mood changes, medication status, or health behaviors (Antoni et al., 2005).

THYROID GLAND IN HIV INFECTION

ABNORMALITIES IN THYROID FUNCTION TESTS AND PATHOPHYSIOLOGY

Patients with HIV and AIDS often manifest abnormalities in thyroid function tests, sometimes in ways that are distinct from those seen in other non-thyroidal illness (Lambert,

1994). Such changes most often represent hypothyroidism, in one of three forms: subclinical, overt, or the "euthyroid sick syndrome." Most cases are subclinical, with elevated thyroid-stimulating hormone (TSH) but normal free T4 (FT4). Changes in the hypothalamic–pituitary–thyroid axis have been reported even early in the course of infection, with approximately 8% (up to 12%) prevalence of subclinical hypothyroidism (Beltran et al., 2003; Merenich et al., 1990; Parsa and Bhangoo, 2013), compared with approximately 4.3% in the general population. Some recent studies have found even higher rates (27%) of abnormal TSH levels in HIV-infected patients admitted to a hospital psychiatric unit (Langford et al., 2011).

Other studies have found patients with HIV in various stages of illness to have low T3 and/or T4—for example, 16% in one study (Raffi et al., 1991). Isolated low FT4 with normal TSH levels can be seen in individuals with HIV (Hoffman and Brown, 2007) and have been associated with use of antiretroviral therapy (ART) including stavudine (Beltran et al., 2006). There may also be some association with CD4 counts or severity of illness. Grunfeld and colleagues (1993) found that asymptomatic HIV patients with stable weight had normal T3 levels, while individuals with more advanced AIDS but stable weight had 19% and 30% decreases in levels of T3 and free T3 (FT3), respectively. In AIDS patients with active secondary infections, anorexia, and short-term weight loss, abnormalities in T3 and FT3 were more marked, with declines of 45% and 50%. In this study, TSH was increased but still within normal limits in the patients with AIDS.

While alterations of thyroid function tests in patients with AIDS may resemble the phenomenon of the "euthyroid sick syndrome," commonly seen in non-HIV-related, nonthyroidal illness, they may also present differently. The mechanism of altered thyroid status in typical nonthyroidal illness is thought to be decreased peripheral conversion of T4 to T3, with subsequent conversion of T4 to reverse T3 (rT3), possibly as an adaptive mechanism in times of illness or stress to conserve energy (Parsa and Bhangoo, 2013). In studies of patients with HIV, however, rT3 levels have been found to decrease (Grunfeld et al., 1993; Hommes et al., 1993), unlike in the euthyroid sick syndrome, in which rT3 is usually increased. Furthermore, T3 levels can remain normal in patients with HIV (Olivieri et al., 1993), in contrast to the euthyroid sick syndrome, in which T3 is typically decreased.

All of these variations in possible presentations add to the diagnostic complexity of such cases; the clinical significance of such changes also remains uncertain (Sellmeyer and Grunfeld, 1996). In many cases, alterations of thyroid function tests are asymptomatic, especially in patients with early disease. Most weight-stable patients with HIV maintain overall normal thyroid function (Koutkia et al., 2002; Sellmeyer and Grunfeld, 1996). In the general non-HIV infected population, subclinical hypothyroidism will correct itself in up to 30% of cases within 1 year, even without treatment. It may therefore be reasonable to respond with watchful waiting in such cases.

In advanced illness, T3 levels typically decline, and some patients progress to exhibit overt hypothyroidism with decreased fT4 levels. Overt hypothyroidism, with inadequate T4 secretion despite normal TSH, does usually require clinical treatment. It is found in approximately 0.3% of the U.S. population, most commonly due to autoimmune Hashimoto's thyroiditis, but in up to 2.6% of adult HIV-infected individuals (Parsa and Bhangoo, 2013).

Hyperthyroidism, with elevated free T4 and T3 but low TSH, has also been found in patients with HIV, in some studies in as high as approximately 2% of individuals (Noureldeen et al., 2014). Most cases of hyperthyroidism are seen in the form of the autoimmune Graves disease, in which immunoglobulins attack the TSH receptor. In the era of effective ART.

Autoimmune thyroid disease has been associated with immune reconstitution, usually within 2 years of starting ART (Gilquin et al., 1998; Jubault et al., 2000). In a multicenter study in England tracking all patients starting on effective ART, there were 17 new cases of autoimmune thyroid disease, the majority with Graves disease, for an estimated prevalence of 3% for females and 0.2% for males (Chen et al., 2005). There have been other reports of thyroid dysfunction with ART (Beltran et al., 2003, Kibirige and Ssekitoleko, 2013), as well as recent reports of hyperthyroidism being directly caused by AIDS, although through an unclear mechanism (Wang et al., 2014).

While the pathophysiology of other alterations in thyroid function remains unclear, it has in some cases been related to associated infections and tumors, particularly in the early literature. There have been isolated case reports of *Pneumocystis* infection of the thyroid gland (Guttler et al., 1993; Ragni et al., 1991). Clinically, many of these cases presented with symptoms or signs of hypothyroidism (McCarty et al., 1992; Ragni et al., 1991; Spitzer et al., 1991) and/or as a neck mass or thyroid goiter (Battan et al., 1991; Ragni et al., 1991). One group of authors reported a case of a thyroid goiter associated with mild hyperthyroidism (Drucker et al., 1990). Other cases of Kaposi's sarcoma invading the thyroid gland and causing clinical hypothyroidism (Mollison et al., 1991) or a palpable thyroid mass (Krauth and Katz, 1987) have been reported. Autopsy studies have also found CMV inclusions in the thyroid follicles of patients dying of AIDS (Frank et al., 1987), in addition to other infections.

Fifteen years into the era of effective ART, a study examining postmortem tissues from individuals with HIV demonstrated direct HIV infection of the hypothalamus, as well as altered levels of deiodinase enzymes, suggesting a disrupted hypothalamic–pituitary–thyroid axis feedback that may contribute to the neuropsychiatric dysfunction seen in patients with HIV (Langford et al., 2011).

Medications prescribed for persons with HIV may have an impact on thyroid function. Interferon or IFN-α has been associated with thyroid dysfunction, possibly through an autoimmune mechanism. Medications that induce hepatic p450 enzyme systems, such as rifampin and ketoconazole, increase excretion of thyroid hormones. Patients on thyroid replacement may thus need higher doses, while persons with normal thyroid function may have decreases in T4 (usually with normal or even increased T3 and no change in TSH) (Sellmeyer and Grunfeld, 1996). With newer treatments for hepatitis C virus (HCV), such as sofosbuvir, that obviate need for treatment with interferon, as well as the rarity of protozoal infections, such as disseminated candidiasis, in areas with access to ART, such problematic pharmacological interactions are less common. In areas of the world without access to these newer medications, however, these interactions may still be relevant to consider.

PSYCHOSOCIAL IMPLICATIONS

True clinical hypothyroidism can cause multiple neuropsychiatric symptoms and signs of which the psychiatrist should be aware, most commonly cognitive dysfunction and depression. Severe forms can be manifested by psychotic and delusional symptoms, including visual and auditory hallucinations. Cognitive changes can include inattentiveness, slowed thought process, and impaired memory; mood changes can include anxiety, irritability, and emotional lability in addition to other depressive symptoms (Bauer et al., 2003). While these changes are not specific to patients with HIV, the presence of other HIV-associated medical and psychiatric comorbidities increases the challenge and complexity of identifying and treating such symptoms.

In most cases, hypothyroidism-associated behavioral changes remit after treatment and restoration to euthyroid status. The clinical significance of subclinical hypothyroidism commonly observed in patients with HIV remains uncertain. Treatment of hypothyroidism should be avoided unless clearly indicated, as replacement can increase HIV-related weight loss, although one study suggested that patients given thyroid hormones in pharmacological doses had improvements in weight gain, energy, endurance, and well-being (Derry, 1995).

Graves' disease can also have many psychiatric manifestations, including depression, anxiety, cognitive slowing, hypomania or psychosis (Bunevicius and Prange, 2006). In addition to antithyroid therapy, these patients may also require psychotropic medication until treatment restores thyroid status.

GONADAL FUNCTION IN HIV INFECTION

HYPOGONADISM IN MEN WITH HIV

Hypotestosteronemia has been one of the most prevalent endocrine abnormalities observed in patients with HIV. Testosterone is important for the maintenance of normal bone health, muscle mass, strength, energy level, and general sense of well-being. Testosterone levels decrease routinely in healthy men, starting in the fourth decade of life. As the population infected with HIV ages due to ART-related decreases in mortality, normal declining testosterone levels will be compounded by HIV-associated decreases in testosterone.

Early studies documented approximately 50% of men with AIDS to have hypogonadism, and this decline in gonadal function paralleled declines in weight and body mass as well as CD4 depletion (Dobs et al., 1988). Subsequently, in a 2005 study of androgen levels in older men (ages 49–81) with or at risk for acquiring HIV infection, 54% had total testosterone levels below 300 ng/dl (Klein et al., 2005). Factors that were significantly associated with low total testosterone and low free androgen indices included injection drug use, HCV infection, high body mass index (BMI), and use of psychotropic medications. High viral load (>10,000) correlated with low total testosterone levels (<200 ng/dl). Low testosterone was associated with typical symptoms of low libido, difficulty sleeping, loss of concentration, impaired memory, poorer subjective health, and other symptoms of depression.

Many of the early studies suggested that decreases in testosterone were related to stage of HIV illness or CD4 count. In a prospective study of 98 patients with various stages of infection, 29% of men with AIDS had hypotestosteronemia, assessed by total testosterone levels (Raffi et al., 1991). Deficiency was correlated with the degree of illness, including weight loss and low CD4+ cell count. In another study of clinically asymptomatic HIV-positive gay men, total testosterone was decreased only in patients with CD4 levels less than 200 (Laudat et al., 1995). Free testosterone was decreased in all groups and correlated with CD4 cell count, supporting the idea that hypogonadism worsens as CD4 lymphocytes decrease.

The prevalence of hypogonadism is felt to be lower but still significant in the era of effective ART. Later studies have failed to demonstrate an association with CD4 cell count or HIV viral load (Grinspoon et al., 1996; Rietschel et al., 2000). In one study of patients with HIV-associated wasting, most of whom were receiving ART, free testosterone levels were low in 19% of patients with AIDS wasting (81% of whom complained of decreased libido) (Rietschel et al., 2000). Other ART-era studies have similarly demonstrated approximately 20% rates of hypogonadism (Crum et al., 2005).

The relationship between weight loss or wasting and hypogonadism remains consistent. Grinspoon and colleagues (1996) demonstrated that loss of lean body and muscle mass as well as functional decline in exercise capacity correlate with androgen levels in hypogonadal men with AIDS-associated wasting. In another study, serum testosterone and free testosterone correlated with weight change (Arver et al., 1999). Dobs and colleagues (1996) found that testosterone levels declined early in the course of HIV infection with weight loss that eventually led to wasting. Rietschel and colleagues (2000), in contrast, found that hypogonadism was not associated with weight, but these relationships can be compounded and influenced by other factors.

Most cases of androgen deficiency in patients with HIV result from secondary hypogonadism (pituitary or hypothalamic failure), with reduced or inappropriately normal gonadotropin levels despite low testosterone levels. This may be due to effects of severe illness on the hypothalamic–pituitary–gonadal axis or to associated infections or malignancies compromising pituitary or hypothalamic function. In these cases, other markers of pituitary function, including TSH and prolactin, should be tested, with any abnormal findings prompting MRI evaluation of the hypothalamus and pituitary.

Primary hypogonadism accounts for approximately 20% in one survey (Arver et al., 1999). This may be due to associated opportunistic infections, malignancies of the testes, or cytokine-related decreased testicular functioning (Crum et al., 2005; Mylonakis et al., 2001). Shifting of adrenal steroids from androgen production to cortisol, as described earlier, can also contribute to decreased levels of testosterone.

In many studies, infectious and other pathological changes in the testes were demonstrated in patients with HIV, as well as decreased spermatogenesis. Testicular pathological changes and functioning of the hypothalamic–pituitary–gonadal axis were assessed in a study of 84 gay men, 56 with HIV infection (Salehian et al., 1999). While testosterone, luteinizing hormone (LH), and follicle-stimulating hormone (FSH) were similar among all patients at baseline, testosterone significantly decreased during the 4-year study period only in the HIV-positive group. This group was further divided into progressors (to AIDS) and nonprogressors, with only the former demonstrating increases in LH and FSH. Forty-eight percent of patients with AIDS had hypogonadism, and all five AIDS patients on whom autopsy was performed had wall thickening of the seminiferous tubules and decreased spermatogenesis.

Breast enlargement due to true gynecomastia, the proliferation of glandular ducts and periductal stroma in men, occurs in approximately 1% of adult men in the general population, although male breast enlargement involving fat tissue is more common. There have been few large studies of gynecomastia in men with HIV. One recent study evaluated 2,275 patients for breast enlargement at HIV referral centers, finding 40 (1.8%) with sonographically confirmed gynecomastia (Biglia et al., 2004). When compared with matched HIV-positive controls, gynecomastia was independently associated with hypogonadism (as well as with lipoatrophy and hepatitis C).

There have been inconsistent reports linking hypogonadism with ART. One study found effective ART to be associated with low libido, erectile dysfunction (ED), and increased estradiol levels in HIV-infected men (Lamba et al., 2004). HIV-negative or unknown-status gay and bisexual men were compared to a group of HIV-infected men. An increased incidence of low libido (48%) and ED (25%) was found in men on ART compared to that in HIV-infected men not taking ART (26% for each) and in the control group (2% and 10%, respectively). Other studies, however, have failed to demonstrate any association with ART. In one study of patients with HIV, most of whom were receiving ART, free testosterone levels were low in 19% of patients with AIDS wasting, 81% of whom complained of decreased libido (Rietschel et al., 2000). There was no association with weight, CD4 count, or any class of antiviral medications.

Besides antiretrovirals, other medications commonly used by patients with HIV might have an impact on the hypothalamic–pituitary–gonadal axis. Ketoconazole inhibits gonadal production of steroids. Megestrol acetate (a progestational agent), glucocorticoids, and anabolic steroids can all reduce secretion of gonadotropins (Mylonakis et al., 2001). Antipsychotics can elevate prolactin to varying degrees. Patients on methadone replacement (and individuals using heroin) have been found to have lower gonadotropin and testosterone levels (Celani et al., 1984).

There are many available forms of testosterone replacement today, including intramuscular injection, transdermal patch, and gel. Injections of depot forms are commonly used for androgen replacement but are complicated by the difficulty of achieving steady states. Peak supraphysiological testosterone levels occur in the first day or two after injection, in some cases adversely affecting mood (Mylonakis et al., 2001), while levels may decline to subtherapeutic levels before the next injection.

The patch and gel forms of testosterone replacement are more commonly utilized and provide smoother steady-state kinetics than injectable depot formulations. However, replacement therapy is not always effective. One multicenter, randomized, double-blind, placebo-controlled trial demonstrated that while hypogonadal men with AIDS and weight loss were able to correct testosterone levels, gonadal replacement did not improve weight or quality of life (Dobs et al., 1999). The patches can be associated with dermatological reactions, while the gel is usually well tolerated. In general, testosterone supplementation is fairly safe but should be avoided in patients with polycythemia or prostate cancer and used cautiously in patients with prostrate enlargement.

The diagnosis of hypogonadism in an HIV-infected individual is the same as in non-infected populations. Testing should occur early as an early morning specimen, either as total or free testosterone. If total testosterone is used, then the fact that HIV-seropositive individuals can have elevated sex hormone–binding globulin (SHBG) should be taken into account; thus, HIV-positive patients may have normal total testosterone but a low free testosterone (Dubé et al., 2007; Rietschel et al., 2000; Schambelan et al., 2016). It is common practice to test for free testosterone in men with HIV. If a patient is hypogonadal, then another early morning test should be used to confirm the initial results prior to treatment.

If a patient has a low testosterone level that is confirmed by sequential testing, then additional workup is required to determine primary versus secondary hypogonadism. LH and FSH should be obtained (also early morning specimens), and if these are elevated, then primary hypogonadism is diagnosed. In this situation, testicular exam, imaging, and referral to a urologist is recommended. Secondary hypogonadism in the setting of normal LH and FSH levels should be further investigated, and these patients may benefit from prolactin levels or a pituitary MRI in addition to testing for deficiencies of other anterior pituitary hormones.

Patients with low testosterone in combination with low libido, low bone mineral density, or low BMI may be candidates for replacement therapy. Concerns remain about an increased cardiovascular risk in persons with HIV on replacement testosterone therapy, but data remain inconclusive at this time (Schambelan et al., 2016).

HYPOGONADISM IN WOMEN WITH HIV

Hypogonadism in women with HIV has been much less well studied. Amenorrhea has been observed in up to 20% of women with HIV, with increased prevalence of 38% in women with AIDS wasting (Grinspoon et al., 1997). Testosterone circulates at levels approximately 10% of that in men, half produced from the ovaries and half from the adrenal glands. Ideally, androgen levels should be measured during the early follicular phase, but normal ranges have not been well standardized (Mylonakis et al., 2001). Limited studies have indicated hypoandrogenic states to be present in women with HIV at similar rates to those observed in men, with a similar pattern of increased SHBG levels. Total and free testosterone levels are significantly lower in HIV-infected women than in healthy controls, with approximately 58% scoring below the normal tenth percentile (Sinha-Hikim et al., 1998). In contrast to men with AIDS wasting, women lose fat mass disproportionately to lean mass (Grinspoon et al., 1997).

One study of ovarian and adrenal function in 13 HIV-infected women with wasting demonstrated significantly lower baseline levels of testosterone, free testosterone, androstenedione, DHEA, and DHEA-S when matched with healthy controls (Grinspoon et al., 2001). ACTH stimulation resulted in increased cortisol response and decreased DHEA response. DHEA-to-cortisol ratios correlated with CD4 count. This finding supports a similar shunting mechanism of adrenal steroid metabolism observed in men. In contrast to decreased adrenal production of steroids, ovarian androgen responsivity to human chorionic gonadotropin stimulation was intact in this population of HIV-positive women (Grinspoon et al., 2001).

Treatment options for hypogonadism in women remain limited. Oral contraceptives or isolated estrogen or progesterone preparations have traditionally been used for replacement. Referral to a reproductive endocrinologist or gynecologist is recommended in these situations.

PSYCHOSOCIAL IMPLICATIONS

The diagnosis of hypogonadism can present a challenge, as many symptoms are nonspecific and overlap with those of depression or chronic illness. These include fatigue, decreased energy, depressed affect, and poor self-image (Mylonakis et al., 2001). More specific symptoms can include decreased male-pattern hair, testicular atrophy, decreased libido, and gynecomastia (Crum et al., 2005). In some early studies of antidepressants for the treatment of depression in men with HIV, patients reported improved mood but residual diminished libido and low energy. Since then, considerable evidence has amassed supporting the beneficial effect of testosterone supplementation on mood and energy level in patients with HIV and depression.

Many studies have documented the positive effects of testosterone replacement on mood in non-HIV populations with hypogonadism. Wang and colleagues (2000) demonstrated that a transdermal testosterone gel treatment improved sexual function and mood parameters, increased lean body mass, and decreased fat mass in hypogonadal men, with mood improvement sustained during a 36-month follow-up study (Wang et al., 2004).

Several studies have yielded similar findings in HIV-positive patients. Grinspoon and colleagues (2000) found that hypogonadal patients with HIV scored significantly higher on the Beck Depression Inventory, with an inverse correlation between Beck score and both free and total testosterone levels, even when controlling for weight, viral load, CD4 count, and antidepressant use. With testosterone supplementation Beck scores decreased significantly compared to control scores. Rabkin and colleagues (2000) investigated testosterone therapy for HIV patients with hypogonadal symptoms of low libido, depressed mood, low energy, and decreased muscle mass, in a double-blind, placebo-controlled trial, finding improved libido in 74% of testosterone-treated patients, in contrast with 19% of placebo-treated patients. Of study completers with fatigue at baseline, 59% of testosterone-treated patients and 25% of those receiving placebo reported improved energy; of study completers with depression at baseline, 58% of the treated group and 14% of the placebo group reported improved mood. Improvements were maintained for up to 18 weeks during a subsequent open-label treatment phase.

Other studies have demonstrated the benefits of testosterone for fatigue in patients with HIV. In a double-blind, placebo-controlled study of testosterone versus fluoxetine in HIV/AIDS patients with Axis I mood disorders, testosterone was superior to both fluoxetine and placebo in improving fatigue (Rabkin et al., 2004). Wagner and colleagues (1998) assessed the effects of biweekly intramuscular injections of testosterone on fatigue in an open 12-week trial of 72 HIV-positive men with low libido and at least one associated symptom of depressed mood, fatigue, or weight loss. In this study, 79% of study completers responded favorably with increased energy levels and quality of life scores. Of the 26 patients who completed the study and had depression at baseline, 62% reported improvement in both mood and energy (while 31% reported no improvement in either).

BONE AND MINERAL METABOLISM IN HIV INFECTION

PREVALENCE AND PATHOPHYSIOLOGY OF BONE DISEASE

In recent years, an extensive body of literature has emerged demonstrating the high prevalence of changes in bone and mineral metabolism in patients with HIV. These are likely due to multiple etiologies, including direct interactions of the virus with bone and marrow cells, as well as indirect effects through immune system activation and altered cytokine production. Increased levels of cytokines such as TNF and IL-6 are associated with osteoclast activation and thus bone resorption. Associated illness and adverse effects of drugs used to treat HIV may also contribute to altered bone metabolism. Decreased physical activity, hypogonadism, and malabsorption of calcium and vitamin D, all common in patients with HIV infection, additionally lead to decreases in bone mineral density (BMD). In persons with HIV who are on methadone or using heroin, effects may be more pronounced, as opioids can contribute to lowered BMD (Pedrazzoni et al., 1993). This remains an important consideration as iatrogenic addiction rates and illicit use of opioids continue to increase.

Paton and colleagues (1997) first demonstrated such decreases in BMD in patients with HIV, although in this study significant differences from those in control subjects were minimal. Since then, many studies have shown a higher prevalence of osteopenia and osteoporosis in patients with HIV compared to control subjects, with rates ranging from 46% (Mondy et al., 2003) to 89% (Knobel et al., 2001). Many of these studies differentiate between more mild *osteopenia*, with rates ranging from 44% to 68%, and *osteoporosis*, with observed rates ranging from 3% to 21% (Amiel et al., 2004; Carr et al., 2001; Gold et al., 2002; Knobel et al., 2001; Tebas et al., 2000). Most of these studies focus on men with HIV, but a few have examined bone density in women. One large study found a similar high prevalence of low BMD in women with HIV, with 62% and 14% meeting criteria for osteopenia and osteoporosis, respectively (Teichmann et al., 2003).

Many factors have been postulated to cause lowered BMD and have been examined in various studies. Decreased weight and BMI, observed in many patients with HIV, have been shown to reliably correlate with low BMD (Amiel et al., 2004; Gold et al., 2002; Knobel et al., 2001; Mondy et al., 2003), including a history of significant weight loss or severe wasting (Mondy et al., 2003) and lower weight before starting ART (Carr et al., 2001). Studies have yielded conflicting data on the relationship between length of disease or severity of HIV and osteopenia. Some studies have failed to demonstrate an association of BMD with CD4 count, viral load, or duration of disease (Knobel et al., 2001; Teichmann et al., 2003). Other studies have shown a significant association between duration of infection and reduced BMD (Bruera et al., 2003; Gold et al., 2002; Mondy et al., 2003), and one longitudinal study demonstrated that as CD4 counts improved, BMD actually increased (Mondy et al., 2003).

Increased production of lactate (Carr et al., 2001) and an uncoupling of bone resorption and formation (Amiel et al., 2004) have also been suggested to contribute to lowered BMD. This latter mechanism was noted in one study in which bone resorption was increased and bone formation decreased in patients with HIV (Aukrust et al., 1999). There were similar findings in another study demonstrating decreased formation markers and increased bone resorption markers in patients with HIV (Teichmann et al., 2000).

Irregularities in vitamin D metabolism, parathyroid hormone (PTH), and calcium have also been examined. Dysfunction of the PTH axis in patients with HIV has been described, including reports of impaired PTH release, possibly mechanistically related to a common protein in PTH cells and CD4 cells (Hellman et al., 1994). Hypocalcemia, when observed in patients with HIV, is usually mild, although severe hypocalcemia can be associated with medications, for example, foscarnet (used to treat CMV) (Thomas and Doherty, 2003). Associated infections and malignancies may result in hypercalcemia in a small percentage of cases.

A recent study demonstrated vitamin D deficiency in 86% of HIV patients (Garcia Aparicio et al., 2006). Some studies have shown decreased PTH and decreased 1,25-hydroxyvitamin D levels compared to those in healthy age-matched controls, in addition to increased urinary calcium and decreased serum osteocalcin (Teichman et al., 2003). In a more recent study, while 1,25-hydroxyvitamin D was significantly decreased in the HIV group, there were no significant differences in 25-hydroxyvitamin D, PTH, calcium, osteocalcin, or phosphorus (Dolan et al., 2004). This finding supports a previous hypothesis that a specific defect in the hydroxylation of 1-α-vitamin D to the more bioactive 1,25 form contributes to the vitamin D deficiency observed in patients with HIV (Haug et al., 1998). Some investigators have suggested this to be a possible treatment effect of protease inhibitors (PIs), with in vitro demonstrations of PIs inhibiting α-1-hydroxylation of vitamin D (Cozzolino et al., 2003). The clinical significance of such data must be questioned, however, in view of the extensive literature failing to demonstrate an association with ART.

Earlier studies indicated that altered BMD observed in patients with HIV might result partially from treatment effects, with particular implication of PIs and non-nucleoside reverse transcription inhibitors (NNRTIs). Tebas and others (2000) found increased rates of osteoporosis (21%) in HIV patients on ART including a PI, compared to HIV-positive patients not receiving a PI (11%) and HIV-negative controls (6%). Since then, however, multiple further studies have failed to show specific associations with treatment (Amiel et al., 2004; Bruera et al., 2003; Garcia Aparicio et al., 2006). Knobel and colleagues (2001) found no association with the use of any type of ART or duration of treatment, and other studies have similarly demonstrated a lack of association between osteopenia and any antiretroviral class (Carr et al., 2001; Mondy et al., 2003). Gold and colleagues (2002) failed to find an effect of PIs on BMD, and one study demonstrated an increase of BMD in patients treated with indinavir (Nolan et al., 2001). Similarly, in the longitudinal follow-up component of the study by Mondy and colleagues, BMD increased with ART, correlating with improved CD4 counts.

While the data for PIs and NRTIs causing bone loss are inconclusive at best, there is additional concern with tenofovir disoproxil fumarate (TDF). Initiation of TDF containing regimens has been demonstrated to lead to an initial modest bone loss that appears to stabilize over 1 to 2 years. Tenofovir alafenamide appears to have less effect on bone density than TDF, according to several randomized trials. Other studies have demonstrated a link between treatment with efavirenz and low vitamin D, which may be due to reduced expression of cytochrome P450 2R1, which is involved in the 25-hydroxylation of vitamin D (Gallant et al., 2004; McComsey et al., 2011).

Bone mineral density screening with DXA scan is recommended by expert groups for all HIV-infected men and postmenopausal women over 50 years of age. Other individuals needing screening in the general population include persons with a fragility fracture, women over 65 years of age, and men over 70 years of age. If a person has any additional risk factors, then the age decreases to 50 years for both sexes. Additional risk factors include HIV seropositivity, low BMI, smoking history, hypogonadism, chronic glucocorticoid use, or early menopause. A medical evaluation of any identified osteopenia or osteoporosis is recommended (Aberg et al., 2014; McComsey et al., 2010).

Several studies have indicated the efficacy of bisphosphonates for the treatment of osteopenia and osteoporosis in the HIV population. Appropriate calcium and vitamin D supplementation should be provided as well. In an open-label randomized pilot trial of alendronate plus calcium and vitamin D in HIV-infected persons on ART with osteopenia or osteoporosis, lumbar spine BMD was increased at 48 weeks compared to that in subjects given vitamin D and calcium alone (Mondy et al., 2005). This is in keeping with findings of other studies (Guaraldi et al., 2004; McComsey et al., 2007; Negredo et al., 2005). The convenience of once-weekly dosing of alendronate may appeal to patients. An open-label randomized study demonstrated significant reduction of osteoporosis after 96 weeks, from 96% in controls (receiving dietary counseling only) to 27% in patients receiving weekly alendronate (plus dietary counseling) (Negredo et al., 2005). Interestingly, improved BMD was seen in the lumbar spine in the first year and in the femur during the second year, highlighting the importance of long-term treatment. Zoledronic acid has been evaluated in HIV populations in small trials. Significant improvements in bone density with once-annual infusions were noted in both trials, with benefits for bone density persisting at 1 year following the last infusion of zoledronic acid (Bolland et al., 2007, 2008; Huang et al., 2009).

PSYCHOSOCIAL IMPLICATIONS

Kumano (2005) recently described three hypothetical relationships between stress and osteoporosis. Stress might induce specific physiological changes that cause or exacerbate a lowering of BMD and might additionally cause behavioral changes that affect eating, exercise, and sleep habits, thus impacting bone health. Osteoporosis and associated health consequences can cause anxiety, depression, loss of social roles and functioning, and isolation and thus increase stress itself. It is unclear to what extent data bear out each of these relationships in patients with HIV.

Mood disorders such as major depression, in some cases associated with high levels of cortisol, have been reported to increase the risk of developing osteoporosis. One study examined psychoaffective and psychodynamic aspects in patients with osteoporosis, finding increased rates of anxiety, depression, and alexithymia (Zonis De Zukerfeld et al., 2003). There was also association of osteoporosis with early traumatic life events, decreased support networks, and lower reported quality of life. Both psychosocial support and specific intervention programs can improve independence and the quality of life in patients with osteoporosis (Bayles et al., 2000). There is a paucity of literature specifically addressing the psychosocial implications of osteoporosis for patients with HIV.

CONCLUSION

A wide range of endocrine abnormalities commonly accompany and complicate HIV infection, many of which have implications for psychiatrists and other mental health professionals working with this population. Such changes can include decreased thyroid function, adrenal insufficiency, hypercortisolism, hypogonadism, and decreased bone mineral density. Because many new HIV infections occur in intravenous drug users, it should be borne in mind that abuse of substances, and opiates in particular, can itself cause endocrine dysfunction contributing to or mimicking effects seen with HIV infection (Cooper et al., 2003).

Endocrine disorders may cause considerable suffering and have a profound impact on the quality of life of persons with HIV. Endocrinopathies are great mimickers of psychiatric disorders, manifesting in some cases as disturbance of mood, sleep, appetite, thought process, energy level, or general sense of well-being. Endocrinopathies may present insidiously or abruptly, in either case with potentially tragic consequences when misdiagnosed as psychopathology. Prompt recognition of reversible alterations in endocrine function is essential to prevent unnecessary morbidity and mortality. An understanding of the complex interactions between endocrine and psychological systems may improve recognition and treatment of endocrinopathies, diminish suffering, and enhance quality of life and longevity in persons with HIV and AIDS.

REFERENCES

Aberg JA, Gallant, JE, Ghanem KG, Emmanuel P, Zingman BS, Horberg MA (2014). Primary care guidelines for the management of persons infected with HIV: 2013 update by the HIV Medicine Association of the Infectious Diseases Society of America. *Clin Infect Dis* 58(1):1–34.

Albert NE, Kazi S, Santoro J, Dougherty R (2012). Ritonavir and epidural triamcinolone as a cause of iatrogenic Cushing's syndrome. *Am J Med Sci* 344(1):72–74.

Amiel C, Ostertag A, Slama L, et al. (2004). BMD is reduced in HIV-infected men irrespective of treatment. *J Bone Mineral Res* 19(3):402–409.

Antoni MH, Cruess S, Cruess DG, et al. (2000a). Cognitive-behavioral stress management reduces distress and 24-hour urinary free cortisol output among symptomatic HIV-infected gay men. *Ann Behav Med* 22(1):29–37.

Antoni MH, Cruess DG, Cruess S, et al. (2000b). Cognitive-behavioral stress management intervention effects on anxiety, 24-hr urinary norepinephrine output, and T-cytotoxic/suppressor cells over time among sympomatic HIV-infected gay men. *J Consult Clin Psychol* 68(1):31–45.

Antoni MH, Cruess DG, Klimas N, et al. (2005). Increases in a marker of immune system reconstitution are predated by decreases in 24-h urinary cortisol output and depressed mood during a 10-week stress management intervention in symptomatic HIV-infected men. *J Pscyhosom Res* 58:3–13.

Antoni MH, Cruess DG, Klimas N, et al. (2002). Stress management and immune system reconstitution in symptomatic HIV-infected gay men over time: effects on transitional naive T cells (CD4(+) CD45RA(+)CD29(+)). *Am J Psychiatry* 159(1):143–145.

Arlt W, Callies F, van Vlijmen JC, et al. (1999). Dehydroepiandrosterone replacement in women with adrenal insufficiency. *N Engl J Med* 341(14):1013–1020.

Arver S, Sinha-Hikim I, Beall G, Guerrero M, Shen R, Bhasin S (1999). Serum dihydrotestosterone and testosterone concentrations in human immunodeficiency virus–infected men with and without weight loss. *J Androl* 20(5):611–618.

Aukrust P, Haug CJ, Ueland T, et al. (1999). Decreased bone formative and enhanced resorptive markers in human immunodeficiency virus infection: indication of normalization of the bone-remodeling process during highly active antiretroviral therapy. *J Clin Endocrinol Metab* 84(1):145–150.

Azar ST, Melby JC (1993). Hypothalamic-pituitary-adrenal function in non-AIDS patients with advanced HIV infection. *Am J Med Sci* 305(5):321–325.

Barrett-Connor E, von Muhlen D, Laughlin GA, Kripke A (1999). Endogenous levels of dehydroepiandrosterone sulfate, but not other sex hormones, are associated with depressed mood in older women: the Rancho Bernardo Study. *J Am Geriatr Soc* 47(6):685–691.

Battan R, Mariuz P, Raviglione MC, Sabatini MT, Mullen MP, Poretsky L (1991). *Pneumocystis carinii* infection of the thyroid in a hypothyroid patient with AIDS: diagnosis by fine needle aspiration biopsy. *J Clin Endocrinol Metab* 72(3):724–726.

Bauer M, Szuba MP, Whybrow PC (2003). Psychiatric and behavioral manifestations of hyperthyroidism and hypothyroidism. In OM Wolkowitz, AJ Rothschild (eds.), *Psychoneuroendocrinology: The Scientific Basis of Clinical Practice* (pp. 419–444). Arlington, VA: American Psychiatric Publishing.

Bayles CM, Cochran K, Anderson C (2000). The psychosocial aspects of osteoporosis in women. *Nurs Clin North Am* 35(1):279–286.

Beltran S, Lescure FX, Desailloud R, et al.; Thyroid and VIH Group (2003). Increased prevalence of hypothyroidism among human immunodeficiency virus–infected patients: a need for screening. *Clin Infect Dis* 37:579–583.

Beltran S1, Lescure FX, El Esper I, Schmit JL, Desailloud R (2006). Subclinical hypothyroidism in HIV-infected patients is not an autoimmune disease. *Horm Res* 66(1):21–26.

Berr C, Lafont S, Debuire B, Dartigues JF, Baulieu EE (1996). Relationships of dehydroepiandrosterone sulfate in the elderly with functional, psychological, and mental status, and short-term mortality: a French community-based study. *Proc Natl Acad Sci U S A* 93(23):13410–13415.

Bhansali A, Dash RJ, Sud A, Bhadada S, Sehgal S, Sharma BR (2000). A preliminary report on basal and stimulated plasma cortisol in patients with acquired immunodeficiency syndrome. *Indian J Med Res* 11:173–177.

Biglia A, Blanco JL, Martinez E, et al. (2004). Gynecomastia among HIV-infected patients is associated with hypogonadism: a case-control study. *Clin Infect Dis* 39:1514–1519.

Biglino A, Limone P, Forno B, Pollona A, Cariti G, Molinatti GM, Gioannini P (1995). Altered adrenocorticotropin and cortisol response to corticotropin-releasing hormone in HIV-1 infection. *Eur J Endocrinol* 133(2):173–179.

Bolland MJ, Grey AB, Horne AM, et al. (2007). Annual zoledronate increases bone density in highly active antiretroviral therapy-treated human immunodeficiency virus-infected men: a randomized controlled trial. *J Clin Endocrinol Metab* 92:1283–1288.

Bolland MJ, Grey AB, Horne AM, et al. (2008). Effects of intravenous zoledronate on bone turnover and BMD persist for at least 24 months. *J Bone Miner Res* 23(8):1304–1308.

Bruera D, Luna N, David DO, Bergoglio LM, Zamudio J (2003). Decreased bone mineral density in HIV-infected patients is independent of antiretroviral therapy. *AIDS* 17(13):1917–1923.

Bunevicius R, Prange AJ (2006). Psychiatric manifestations of Graves' hyperthyroidism: pathophysiology and treatment options. *CNS Drugs* 20(11):897–909.

Cami J, Gilabert M, San L, de la Torre R (1992). Hypercortisolism after opioid discontinuation in rapid detoxification of heroin addicts. *Br J Addict* 87(8):1145–1151.

Carr A, Miller J, Eisman JA, Cooper DA (2001). Osteopenia in HIV-infected men: association with asymptomatic lactic acidemia and lower weight pre-antiretroviral therapy. *AIDS* 15(6):703–709.

Celani MF, Carani C, Montanini V, et al. (1984). Further studies on the effects of heroin addiction on the hypothalamic-pituitary-gonadal function in man. *Pharmacol Res Commun* 16(12):1193–1203.

Chen F, Day SL, Metcalfe RA, et al. (2005). Characteristics of autoimmune thyroid disease occurring as a late complication of immune

reconstitution in patients with advanced human immunodeficiency virus (HIV) disease. *Medicine* 84(2):98–106.

Christeff N, Gherbi N, Mammes O, et al. (1997). Serum cortisol and DHEA concentrations during HIV infection. *Psychoneuroendocrinology* 22(Suppl. 1):S11–S118.

Clerici M, Trabattoni D, Piconi S, Fusi ML, Ruzzante S, Clerici C, Villa ML (1997). A possible role for the cortisol/anticortisols imbalance in the progression of human immunodeficiency virus. *Psychoneuroendocrinology* 22(Suppl. 1):S27–S31.

Cooper OB, Brown TT, Dobs AS (2003). Opiate drug use: a potential contributor to the endocrine and metabolic complications in human immunodeficiency virus disease. *Clin Infect Dis* 37(Suppl 2):S132–S136.

Cozzolino M, Vidal M, Arcidiacono MV, Tebas P, Yarasheski KE, Dusso AS (2003). HIV-protease inhibitors impair vitamin D bioactivation to 1,25-dihydroxyvitamin D. *AIDS* 17(4):513–520.

Crum NF, Furtek KJ, Olson PE, Amling CL, Wallace MR (2005). A review of hypogonadism and erectile dysfunction among HIV-infected men during the pre- and post-HAART years: diagnosis, pathogenesis, and management. *AIDS Patient Care STDS* 19(10):655–671.

Derry DM (1995). Thyroid therapy in HIV-infected patients. *Med Hypotheses* 45(2):121–124.

Dobs AS, Cofrancesco J, Nolten WE, et al. (1999). The use of a transscrotal testosterone delivery system in the treatment of patients with weight loss related to human immunodeficiency virus infection. *Am J Med* 107(2):126–132.

Dobs AS, Dempsey MA, Ladenson PW, Polk BF (1988). Endocrine disorders in men infected with human immunodeficiency virus. *Am J Med* 84(3 Pt. 2):611–616.

Dobs AS, Few WL 3rd, Blackman MR, Harman SM, Hoover DR, Graham NM (1996). Serum hormones in men with human immunodeficiency virus–associated wasting. *J Clin Endocrinol Metab* 81(11):4108–4112.

Dolan SE, Huang JS, Killilea KM, Sullivan MP, Aliabadi N, Grinspoon S (2004). Reduced bone density in HIV-infected women. *AIDS* 18(3):475–483.

Drucker DJ, Bailey D, Rotstein L (1990). Thyroiditis as the presenting manifestation of disseminated extrapulmonary *Pneumocystis carinii* infection. *J Clin Endocrinol Metab* 71(6):1663–1665.

Dubé MP, Parker RA, Mulligan K, Tebas P, Robbins GK, Roubenoff R, Grinspoon SK (2007). Effects of potent antiretroviral therapy on free testosterone levels and fat free mass in men in a prospective, randomized trial: A5005s, a substudy of AIDS Clinical Trials Group Study 384. *Clin Infect Dis* 45(1):120–126.

Duch FM, Repele CA, Spadaro F, dos Reis MA, Rodrigues DB, Ferraz ML, Teixeira Vde P (1998). Adrenal gland morphological alterations in the acquired immunodeficiency syndrome. *Rev Soc Bras Med Trop* 31(3):257–261.

Eledrisi MS, Verghese AC (2001). Adrenal insufficiency in HIV infection: a review and recommendations. *Am J Med Sci* 321(2):137–144.

Findling JW, Buggy BP, Gilson IH, Brummitt CF, Bernstein BM, Raff H (1994). Longitudinal evaluation of adrenocortical function in patients infected with the human immunodeficiency virus. *J Clin Endocrinol Metab* 79(4):1091–1096.

Fradley M, Liu J, Atta MG (2005). Primary aldosteronism with HIV infection: important considerations when using the aldosterone:renin ratio to screen this unique population. *Am J Ther* 12(4):368–374.

Frank TS, LiVolsi VA, Connor AM (1987). Cytomegalovirus infection of the thyroid in immunocompromised adults. *Yale J Biol Med* 60(1):1–8.

Gallant JE, Staszewski S, Pozniak AL, et al. (2004). Efficacy and safety of tenofovir DF vs stavudine in combination therapy in antiretroviral-naïve patients: a 3-year randomized trial. *JAMA* 292(2):191–201.

Garcia Aparicio AM, Munoz Fernandez S, Gonzalez J, et al. (2006). Abnormalities in the bone mineral metabolism in HIV-infected patients. *Clin Rheumatol* 25(4):537–539.

George MM, Bhangoo A (2013). Human immune deficiency virus (HIV) infection and the hypothalamic pituitary adrenal axis. *Rev Endocr Metab Disord* 14(2):105–112.

Gilquin J, Viard JP, Jubault V, Sert C, Kazatchkine MD (1998). Delayed occurrence of Graves' disease after immune restoration with HAART. Highly active antiretroviral therapy. *Lancet* 352(9144):1907–1908.

Glasgow BJ, Steinsapir KD, Anders K, Layfield LJ (1985). Adrenal pathology in the acquired immune deficiency syndrome. *Am J Clin Pathol* 84(5):594–597.

Gold J, Pocock N, Li Y (2002). Bone mineral density abnormalities in patients with HIV infection. *J Acquir Immune Defic Syndr* 30(1):131–132.

Gonzalez-Gonzalez JG, de la Garza-Hernandez NE, Garza-Moran RA, Rivera-Morales IM, Montes-Villarreal J, Valenzuela-Rendon J, Villarreal-Perez JZ (2001). Prevalence of abnormal adrenocortical function in HIV infection by low-dose cosyntropin test. *Int J STD AIDS* 12(12):804–810.

Grinspoon S, Corcoran C, Lee K, et al. (1996). Loss of lean body and muscle mass correlates with androgen levels in hypogonadal men with acquired immunodeficiency syndrome and wasting. *J Clin Endocrinol Metab* 81(11):4051–4058.

Grinspoon S, Corcoran C, Miller K, et al. (1997). Body composition and endocrine function in women with acquired immunodeficiency syndrome wasting. *J Clin Endocrinol Metab* 82(5):1332–1337.

Grinspoon S, Corcoran C, Stanley T, Baaj A, Basgoz N, Klibanski A (2000). Effects of hypogonadism and testosterone administration on depression indices in HIV-infected men. *J Clin Endocrinol Metab* 85:60–65.

Grinspoon S, Corcoran C, Stanley T, Rabe J, Wilkie S (2001). Mechanisms of androgen deficiency in human immunodeficiency virus–infected women with the wasting syndrome. *J Clin Endocrinol Metabol* 86(9):4120–4126.

Grunfeld C, Pang M, Doerrler W, Jensen P, Shimizu L, Feingold KR, Cavalieri RR (1993). Indices of thyroid function and weight loss in human immunodeficiency virus infection and the acquired immunodeficiency syndrome. *Metabolism* 42(10):1270–1276.

Guaraldi G, Orlando G, Madeddu G, et al. (2004). Alendronate reduces bone resorption in HIV-associated osteopenia/osteoporosis. *HIV Clin Trials* 5(5):269–277.

Guttler R, Singer PA, Axline SG, Greaves TS, McGill JJ (1993). *Pneumocystis carinii* thyroiditis. Report of three cases and review of the literature. *Arch Intern Med* 153(3):393–396.

Haug CJ, Aukrust P, Haug E, Morkrid L, Muller F, Froland SS (1998). Severe deficiency of 1,25-dihydroxyvitamin D3 in human immunodeficiency virus infection: association with immunological hyperactivity and only minor changes in calcium homeostasis. *J Clin Endocrinol Metab* 83(11):3832–3838.

Hellman P, Albert J, Gidlund M, Klareskog L, Rastad J, Akerstrom G, Juhlin C (1994). Impaired parathyroid hormone release in human immunodeficiency virus infection. *AIDS Res Hum Retroviruses* 10(4):391–394.

Hoffman CJ, Brown TT (2007). Thyroid function abnormalities in HIV-infected persons. *Clin Infect Dis* 45(4):488–494.

Hommes MJ, Romijn JA, Endert E, et al. (1993). Hypothyroid-like regulation of the pituitary-thyroid axis in stable human immunodeficiency virus infection. *Metabolism* 42(5):556–561.

Hoshino Y, Yamashita N, Nakamura T, Iwamoto A (2002). Prospective examination of adrenocortical function in advanced AIDS patients. *Endocr J* 49(6):641–647.

Huang J, Meixner L, Fernandez S, McCutchan JA (2009). A double blinded randomized controlled trial of zoledronate therapy for HIV-associated osteopenia and osteoporosis. *AIDS* 23(1):51–57.

Hunt PJ, Gurnell EM, Huppert FA, et al. (2000). Improvement in mood and fatigue after dehydroepiandrosterone replacement in Addison's disease in a randomized, double blind trial. *J Clin Endocrinol Metab* 85(12):4650–4656.

Jubault V, Penfornis A, Schillo F, et al. (2000). Sequential occurrence of thyroid autoantibodies and Grave's disease after immune restoration in severely immunocompromised human immunodeficiency virus-1-infected patients. *J Clin Endocrinol Metab* 85:4254–4257.

Kaile T1, Zulu I, Lumayi R, Ashman N, Kelly P (2008). Inappropriately low aldosterone concentrations in adults with AIDS-related diarrhoea in Zambia: a study of response to fluid challenge. *BMC Res Notes* 17(1):10.

Kibirige D, Ssekitoleko R (2013). Endocrine and metabolic abnormalities among HIV-infected patients: a current review. *Int J STD AIDS* 24(8):603–611.

Klein RS, Yungtai L, Santoro N, Dobs AS (2005). Androgen levels in older men who have or who are at risk of acquiring HIV infection. *Clin Infect Dis* 41:1794–1803.

Knobel H, Guelar A, Vallecillo G, Nogues X, Diez A (2001). Osteopenia in HIV-infected patients: is it the disease or is it the treatment? *AIDS* 15(6):807–808.

Koutkia P, Mylonakis E, Levin RM (2002). Human immunodeficiency virus infection and the thyroid. *Thyroid* 12(7):577–582.

Krauth PH, Katz JF (1987). Kaposi's sarcoma involving the thyroid in a patient with AIDS. *Clin Nucl Med* 12(11):848–849.

Kumano H (2005). Osteoporosis and stress. *Clin Calcium* 15(9):1544–1547.

Lamba H, Goldmeier D, Mackie NE, Scullard G (2004). Antiretroviral therapy is associated with sexual dysfnction and with increased serum oestradiol levels in men. *Int J STD AIDS* 15:234–237.

Lambert M (1994). Thyroid dysfunction in HIV infection. *Baillieres Clin Endocrinol Metab* 8(4):825–835.

Langford D, Baron D, Joy J, Del Valle L, Shack J (2011). Contributions of HIV infection in the hypothalamus and substance abuse/use to HPT dysregulation. *Psychoneuroendocrinology* 36(5):710–719.

Laudat A, Blum L, Guechot J, Picard O, Cabane J, Imbert JC, Giboudeau J (1995). Changes in systemic gonadal and adrenal steroids in asymptomatic human immunodeficiency virus–infected men: relationship with the CD4 cell counts. *Eur J Endocrinol* 133(4):418–424.

Laulund S, Visfeldt J, Klinken L (1986). Patho-anatomical studies in patients dying of AIDS. *Acta Pathol Microbiol Immunol Scand A* 94(3):201–221.

Lo J, Grinspoon SK (2010). Adrenal function in HIV infection. *Curr Opin Endocrinol Diabetes Obes* 17(3):205–209.

Lortholary O, Christeff N, Casassus P, et al. (1996). Hypothalamo-pituitary-adrenal function in human immunodeficiency virus–infected men. *J Clin Endocrinol Metab* 81(2):791–796.

Marik PE, Kiminoyo K, Zaloga GP (2002). Adrenal insufficiency in critically ill patients with human immunodeficiency virus. *Crit Care Med* 30(6):1267–1273.

Martin ME, Benassayag C, Amiel C, Canton P, Nunez EA (1992). Alterations in the concentrations and binding properties of sex steroid binding protein and corticosteroid-binding globulin in HIV+ patients. *J Endocrinol Invest* 15(8):597–603.

Mayo J, Collazos J, Martinez E, Ibarra S (2002). Adrenal function in the human immunodeficiency virus–infected patient. *Arch Intern Med* 162(10):1095–1098.

McCarty M, Coker R, Claydon E (1992). Case report: disseminated *Pneumocystis carinii* infection in a patient with the acquired immune deficiency syndrome causing thyroid gland calcification and hypothyroidism. *Clin Radiol* 45(3):209–210.

McComsey GA, Kendall MA, Tebas P, et al. (2007). Alendronate with calcium and vitamin D supplementation is safe and effective for the treatment of decreased bone mineral density in HIV. *AIDS* 21(18):2473–2482.

McComsey GA, Kitch D, Daar ES, et al. (2011). Bone mineral density and fractures in antiretroviral naïve persons randomized to receive abacavir-lamivudine or tenofovir disoproxil fumarate emtricitabine along with efavirenz or atazanavir-ritonavir. AIDS Clinical Trials Group A5224s, a substudy of ACTG A5202. *J Infect Dis* 203(12):1791–1801.

McComsey GA, Tebas P, Shane E, et al. (2010). Bone disease in HIV infection: a practical review and recommendations for HIV care providers. *Clin Infect Dis* 51(8):937–946.

Membreno L, Irony I, Dere W, Klein R, Biglieri EG, Cobb E (1987). Adrenocortical function in acquired immunodeficiency syndrome. *J Clin Endocrinol Metab* 65(3):482–487.

Merenich JA, McDermott MT, Asp AA, Harrison SM, Kidd GS (1990). Evidence of endocrine involvement early in the course of human immunodeficiency virus infection. *J Clin Endocrinol Metab* 70(3):566–571.

Michael A, Jenaway A, Paykel ES, Herbert J (2000). Altered salivary dehydroepiandrosterone levels in major depression in adults. *Biol Psychiatry* 48(10):989–995.

Mollison LC, Mijch A, McBride G, Dwyer B (1991). Hypothyroidism due to destruction of the thyroid by Kaposi's sarcoma. *Rev Infect Dis* 13(5):826–827.

Mondy K, Powderly WG, Claxton SA, et al. (2005). Alendronate, vitamin D, and calcium for the treatment of osteopenia/osteoporosis associated with HIV infection. *J Acquir Immune Defic Syndr* 38(4):426–431.

Mondy K, Yarasheski K, Powderly WG, et al. (2003). Longitudinal evolution of bone mineral density and bone markers in human immunodeficiency virus-infected individuals. *Clin Infect Dis* 36(4):482–490.

Mulder CL, Antoni MH, Emmelkamp PM, Veugelers PJ, Sandfort TG, van de Vijver FA, de Vries MJ (1995). Psychosocial group intervention and the rate of decline of immunological parameters in asymptomatic HIV-infected homosexual men. *Psychother Psychosom* 63(3–4):185–192.

Mylonakis E, Koutkia P, Grinspoon S (2001). Diagnosis and treatment of androgen deficiency in human immunodeficiency virus–infected men and women. *Clin Infect Dis* 33:857–864.

Negredo E, Martinez-Lopez E, Paredes R, et al. (2005). Reversal of HIV-1-associated osteoporosis with once-weekly alendronate. *AIDS* 19(3):343–345.

Nock B, Wich M, Cicero TJ (1997). Chronic exposure to morphine increases corticosteroid-binding globulin. *J Pharmacol Exp Ther* 282(3):1262–1268.

Nolan D, Upton R, McKinnon E, et al. (2001). Stable or increasing bone mineral density in HIV-infected patients treated with nelfinavir or indinavir. *AIDS* 15(10):1275–1280.

Norbiato G, Bevilacqua M, Vago T, et al. (1992). Cortisol resistance in acquired immunodeficiency syndrome. *J Clin Endocrinol Metab* 74(3):608–613.

Noureldeen AF, Qusti SY, Khoja GM (2014). Thyroid function in newly diagnosed HIV-infected patients. *Toxicol Ind Health* 30(10):919–925.

Olivieri A, Sorcini M, Battisti P, et al. (1993). Thyroid hypofunction related with the progression of human immunodeficiency virus infection. *J Endocrinol Invest* 16(6):407–413.

Parsa AA, Bhangoo A (2013). HIV and thyroid dysfunction. *Rev Endocr Metab Disord* 14(2):127–131.

Paton NI, Macallan DC, Griffin GE, Pazianas M (1997). Bone mineral density in patients with human immunodeficiency virus infection. *Calcif Tissue Int* 61(1):30–32.

Pedrazzoni M, Vescovi PP, Maninetti L, et al. (1993). Effects of chronic heroin abuse on bone and mineral metabolism. *Acta Endocrinol (Copenh)* 129(1):42–45.

Pessanha TM, Campos JM, Barros AC, Pone MV, Garrido JR, Pone SM (2007). Iatrogenic Cushing's syndrome in an adolescent with AIDS on ritonavir and inhaled fluticasone. Case report and literature review. *AIDS* 21(4):529–532.

Piketty C1, Jayle D, Leplege A, et al. (2001). Double-blind placebo-controlled trial of oral dehydroepiandrosterone in patients with advanced HIV disease. *Clin Endocrinol* 55(3):325–330.

Poretsky L, Brillon DJ, Ferrando S, et al. (2006). Endocrine effects of oral dehydroepiandrosterone in men with HIV infection: a prospective, randomized, double-blind, placebo-controlled trial. *Metabolism* 55(7):858–870.

Poretsky L, Song L, Brillon DJ, et al. (2009). Metabolic and hormonal effects of oral DHEA in premenopausal women with HIV infection: a randomized, prospective, placebo-controlled pilot study. *Horm Metab Res* 41(3):244–249.

Pulakhandam U, Dincsoy HP (1990). Cytomegaloviral adrenalitis and adrenal insufficiency in AIDS. *Am J Clin Pathol* 93(5):651–656.

Rabkin JG, McElhiney MC, Rabkin R, McGrath PJ, Ferrando SJ (2006). Placebo-controlled trial of dehydroepiandrosterone (DHEA) for treatment of nonmajor depression in patients with HIV/AIDS. *Am J Psychiatry* 163(1):59–66.

Rabkin JG, Wagner GJ, McElhiney MC, Rabkin R, Lin SH (2004). Testosterone versus fluoxetine for depression and fatigue in HIV/AIDS: a placebo-controlled trial. *J Clin Psychopharmacol* 24:379–385.

Rabkin JG, Wagner GJ, Rabkin R (2000). A double-blind, placebo-controlled trial of testosterone therapy for HIV-positive men with hypogonadal symptoms. *Arch Gen Psychiatry* 57:141–147.

Raffi F, Brisseau JM, Planchon B, Remi JP, Barrier JH, Grolleau JY (1991). Endocrine function in 98 HIV-infected patients: a prospective study. *AIDS* 5(6):729–733.

Ragni MV, Dekker A, DeRubertis FR, et al. (1991). *Pneumocystis carinii* infection presenting as necrotizing thyroiditis and hypothyroidism. *Am J Clin Pathol* 95(4):489–493.

Reddy DS, Kaur G, Kulkarni SK (1998). Sigma (sigma1) receptor mediated anti-depressant-like effects of neurosteroids in the Porsolt forced swim test. *Neuroreport* 9(13):3069–3073.

Rietschel P, Corcoran C, Stanley T, Basgoz N, Klibanski A, Grinspoon S (2000). Prevalence of hypogonadism among men with weight loss related to human immunodeficiency virus who were receiving highly active antiretroviral therapy. *Clin Infect Dis* 31:1240–1244.

Roberts E, Bologa L, Flood JF, Smith GE (1987). Effects of dehydroepiandrosterone and its sulfate on brain tissue in culture and on memory in mice. *Brain Res* 406(1–2):357–362.

Rodrigues D, Reis M, Teixeira V, Silva-Vergara M, Filho DC, Adad S, Lazo J (2002). Pathologic findings in the adrenal glands of autopsied patients with acquired immunodeficiency syndrome. *Pathol Res Pract* 198(1):25–30.

Salehian B, Jacobson D, Swerdloff RS, Abbasian M (1999). Testicular pathologic changes and the pituitary–testicular axis during human immunodeficiency virus infection. *Endocr Pract* 5(1):1–9.

Samaras K, Pett S, Gowers A, McMurchie M, Cooper DA (2005). Iatrogenic Cushing's syndrome with osteoporosis and secondary adrenal failure in human immunodeficiency virus–infected persons receiving inhaled corticosteroids and ritonavir-boosted protease inhibitors: six cases (2005). *J Clin Endocrinol Metab* 90(7):4394–4398.

Schambelan M, Weinberg M, Bartlett JG, Bloom A (2016). Hypogonadism in HIV-infected males. *UpToDate*. http://www.uptodate.com/contents/hypogonadism-in-hiv-infected-males. Accessed June 1, 2016.

Sellmeyer DE, Grunfeld C (1996). Endocrine and metabolic disturbances in human immunodeficiency virus infection and the acquired immune deficiency syndrome. *Endocr Rev* 17(5):518–532.

Sinha-Hikim I, Arver S, Beall G, et al. (1998). The use of a sensitive equilibrium dialysis method for the measurement of free testosterone levels in healthy, cycling women and in human immunodeficiency virus–infected women. *J Clin Endocrinol Metab* 83(4):1312–1318.

Spitzer RD, Chan JC, Marks JB, Valme BR, McKenzie JM (1991). Case report: hypothyroidism due to *Pneumocystis carinii* thyroiditis in a patient with acquired immunodeficiency syndrome. *Am J Med Sci* 302(2):98–100.

Starkman MN (2003). Psychiatric manifestations of hyperadrenocorticism and hypoadrenocorticism (Cushing's and Addison's diseases). In OM Wolkowitz, AJ Rothschild (eds.), *Psychoneuroendocrinology: The Scientific Basis of Clinical Practice* (pp. 165–188). Arlington, VA: American Psychiatric Publishing.

Stolarczyk R, Rubio SI, Smolyar D, Young IS, Poretsky L (1998). Twenty-four-hour urinary free cortisol in patients with acquired immunodeficiency syndrome. *Metabolism* 47(6): 690–694.

Tebas P, Powderly WG, Claxton S, Marin D, Tantisiriwat W, Teitelbaum SL, Yarasheski KE (2000). Accelerated bone mineral loss in HIV-infected patients receiving potent antiretroviral therapy. *AIDS* 14(4):F63–F67.

Teichmann J, Stephan E, Discher T, et al. (2000). Changes in calcio-tropic hormones and biochemical markers of bone metabolism in patients with human immunodeficiency virus infection. *Metabolism* 49(9):1134–1139.

Teichmann J, Stephan E, Lange U, Discher T, Friese G, Lohmeyer J, Stracke H, Bretzel RG (2003). Osteopenia in HIV-infected women prior to highly active antiretroviral therapy. *J Infect* 46(4):221–227.

Tennant F, Shannon JA, Nork JG, Sagherian A, Berman M (1991). Abnormal adrenal gland metabolism in opioid addicts: implications for clinical treatment. *J Psychoactive Drugs* 23(2):135–149.

Thomas J, Doherty SM (2003). HIV infection—a risk factor for osteoporosis. *J Acquir Immune Defic Syndr* 33(3):281–291.

Villette JM, Bourin P, Doinel C, et al. (1990). Circadian variations in plasma levels of hypophyseal, adrenocortical and testicular hormones in men infected with human immunodeficiency *J Endocrinol Metab* 70(3):572–577.

Wagner GJ, Rabkin JG, Rabkin R (1998). Testosterone as a treatment for fatigue in HIV+ men. *Gen Hosp Psychiatry* 20:209–213.

Wang C, Cunningham G, Dobs A, et al. (2004). Long-term testosterone gel (AndroGel) treatment maintains beneficial effects on sexual functioning and mood, lean and fat mass, and bone mineral density in hypogonadal men. *J Clin Endocrinol Metab* 89:2085–2098.

Wang C, Swerdloff RS, Iranmanesh A, et al. (2000). Transdermal testosterone gel improves sexual function, mood, muscle strength, and body composition parameters in hypogonadal men. *J Clin Endocrinol Metab* 85:2839–2853.

Wang JJ, Zhou JJ, Yuan XL, Li CY, Sheng H, Su B, Sheng CJ, Qu S, Li H (2014). Hyperthyroidism caused by acquired immune deficiency syndrome. *Eur Rev Med Pharmacol Sci* 18(6):875–879.

Welch K, Finkbeiner W, Alpers CE, Blumenfeld W, Davis RL, Smuckler EA, Beckstead JH (1984). Autopsy findings in the acquired immune deficiency syndrome. *JAMA* 252(9):1152–1159.

Wisniewski AB, Apel S, Selnes OA, Nath A, McArthur JC, Dobs AS (2005). Depressive symptoms, quality of life, and neuropsychological performance in HIV/AIDS: the impact of gender and injection drug use. *J Neurovirol* 11(2):138–143.

Wisniewski AB, Brown TT, John M, et al. (2006). Cortisol levels and depression in men and women using heroin and cocaine. *Psychoneuroendocrinology* 31(2):250–255.

Wisniewski TL, Hilton CW, Morse EV, Svec F (1993). The relationship of serum DHEA-S and cortisol levels to measures of immune function in human immunodeficiency virus–related illness. *Am J Med Sci* 305(2):79–83.

Wolff FH, Nhuch C, Cadore LP, Glitz CL, Lhullier F, Furlanetto TW (2001). Low-dose adrenocorticotropin test in patients with the acquired immunodeficiency syndrome. *Braz J Infect Dis* 5(2):53–59.

Wolkowitz OM, Kramer JH, Reus VI, et al. (2003). DHEA treatment of Alzheimer's disease: a randomized, double-blind, placebo-controlled study. *Neurology* 60(7):1071–1076.

Wren A (2013). How best to approach endocrine evaluation in patients with HIV in the era of combined antiretroviral therapy? *Clin Endocrinol* 79(3):310–313.

Yaffe K, Ettinger B, Pressman A, Seeley D, Whooley M, Schaefer C, Cummings S (1998). Neuropsychiatric function and dehydroepiandrosterone sulfate in elderly women: a prospective study. *Biol Psychiatry* 43(9):694–700.

Yoganathan K, David L, Williams C, Jones K (2012). Cushing's syndrome with adrenal suppression induced by inhaled budesonide due to a ritonavir drug interaction in a woman with HIV infection *Int J STD AIDS* 23(7):520–521.

Yombi JC, Maiter D, Belkhir L, Nzeusseu A, Vandercam B (2008). Iatrogenic Cushing's syndrome and secondary adrenal insufficiency after a single intra-articular administration of triamcinolone acetonide in HIV-infected patients treated with ritonavir *Clin Rheumatol* 27(Suppl 2):S79–S82.

Zapanti E, Terzidis K, Chrousos G (2008). Dysfunction of the hypothalamic-pituitary-adrenal axis in HIV infection and disease. *Hormones* 7(3):205–216.

Zonis De Zukerfeld R, Ingratta R, Sanchez Negrete G, Matusevich A, Intebi C (2003). Psychosocial aspects in osteoporosis [in Spanish]. *Vertex* 14(54):253–259.

46.

CARDIOVASCULAR DISEASE, METABOLIC COMPLICATIONS AND LIPODYSTROPHY IN PERSONS WITH HIV

Luis F. Pereira, Harold W. Goforth, Esteban Martínez, Joseph Z. Lux,

Maria Ferrara, and Michael P. Mullen

The introduction of effective antiretroviral therapy (ART) in 1996 contributed to a dramatic reduction in HIV-related mortality. A decade later, HIV infection transitioned from a death sentence to an annual mortality rate of less than 2% (May et al., 2006). Currently, HIV infection is regarded as a chronic manageable condition. As of 2017, it is estimated that 50% of persons living with HIV in the United States are over 50 years of age (Womack, 2012). Currently, over 4.2 million people aged 50 years and older are living with HIV worldwide (UNAIDS, 2014). In addition, a Danish cohort study found that mortality in HIV-infected patients without comorbidities who are on a successful ART regimen was almost identical to that of the non-HIV-infected population with no risk factors (Obel et al., 2011). As patients live longer, cardiovascular disease could become an increasing problem, as it is already one of the leading causes of death in both the general population and in persons with HIV on ART (Antiretroviral Therapy Cohort Collaboration, 2010). This fact might be simply seen as part of the expected trend toward similarity with the general population, owing to the success of ART. Nevertheless, there are reasons to consider that the impact of cardiovascular disease may be higher in HIV-infected persons than in the general population.

In a cohort of 27,350 HIV-infected and 55,109 age-matched non-infected veterans followed for a median of 5.9 years, HIV infection was associated with a higher risk of acute myocardial infarction (MI). The increased risk remained higher even after adjusting for Framingham risk factors, other comorbidities, and substance use (Freiberg et al., 2013). Also, a meta-analysis of observational and randomized controlled trials found that the relative risk of cardiovascular events was higher for HIV-infected patients in comparison to the non-infected population, despite ART status (Islam et al., 2012). Finally, a retrospective evaluation of the claims data for the California Medicaid population, which included 28,513 HIV-infected and 3,054,696 uninfected patients, showed that, in patients aged 18–24 years old, the incidence of coronary heart disease was relatively low, but nonetheless higher in the HIV-infected population (Currier et al., 2003). Although the specific mechanisms for the increased risk of cardiovascular disease in HIV-infected patients remain a matter of debate, several mechanisms have been proposed: the virus itself, ART, and traditional risk factors.

This chapter addresses the diagnosis and treatment of cardiovascular disease in persons with HIV, as well as predisposing factors and metabolic complications involved, including dyslipidemia, insulin resistance, and lactic acidosis. The pathogenesis and management of HIV-associated lipodystrophy as well as its psychosocial impact are also presented.

HIV-RELATED FACTORS INVOLVED IN RISK FOR CARDIOVASCULAR DISEASE IN PERSONS WITH HIV

HIV is believed to increase the risk of cardiovascular disease through different mechanisms, including inflammation, immune dysregulation, and endothelial dysfunction. HIV infection itself is a chronic systemic inflammatory condition, and sustained inflammation is a risk factor for atherothrombosis (van Leuven et al., 2008). Despite the induction of viral suppression to a level below the assay threshold, residual viremia persists and is associated with immune activation (Eugenin et al., 2008; Ostrowski et al., 2008). In vitro experiments have shown that HIV may facilitate an inflammatory response not only by direct action (Beignon et al., 2005) but also via its protein gp120, which induces apoptosis of vascular endothelial cells (Huang et al., 2001). Increased levels of high-sensitivity C-reactive protein and interleukin 6, both inflammatory biomarkers linked to atherosclerosis in the general population, have been found to be elevated in HIV-infected patients (Neuhaus et al., 2010), and ART has been shown to promote reduction in markers of endothelial activation, such as vascular cell adhesion protein 1 (VCAM1) and von Willebrand factor (vWF), that were significantly associated with HIV viral load (Gresele et al., 2012). Finally, the loss of gut-associated lymphoid tissue by depletion of T cells is known to promote translocation of microbial products into the bloodstream, also causing chronic immune activation (Brenchley et al., 2006).

The acute effects of HIV viremia on factors associated with cardiovascular disease can be investigated in detail from ART interruption studies. The Strategies for Management of Antiretroviral Therapy (SMART) study showed that intermittent ART was associated with a higher risk of cardiovascular disease than with continuous ART (Strategies for Management of Antiretroviral Therapy [SMART] Study Group, 2006). The deleterious effect of intermittent ART in the SMART study was associated with the duration of uncontrolled HIV replication. An exploratory analysis of the SMART study also showed an increment in the total/HDL cholesterol ratio in the intermittent group (Phillips et al., 2008).

ART AND RISK FOR CARDIOVASCULAR DISEASE IN PERSONS WITH HIV

Antiretroviral therapy has been associated with increased risk of cardiovascular disease, including MI. Yet conflicting results have been reported. This heterogeneity may arise from different study designs, as well as from different study populations.

A number of studies, including retrospective and prospective cohort studies, administrative and clinical databases, and randomized clinical trials, have assessed the direct contribution of ART or specific antiretrovirals to the risk of cardiovascular events. In the largest prospective study, the Data Collection on Adverse Events of Anti-HIV Drugs (D:A:D) study (DAD Study Group, 2007), the incidence of MI was low (3.5 cases per 1,000 person-years), and traditional cardiovascular risk factors showed a higher relative contribution to the development of MI than did protease inhibitor exposure. In this study, the relative risk attributed to protease inhibitors (16% per year of exposure) approximately halved after controlling for increased total cholesterol and decreased HDL cholesterol, suggesting that a substantial proportion of the risk attributed to protease inhibitors remains unexplained. Furthermore, an analysis of the French Hospital Database on HIV noted an association between the length of exposure to protease inhibitor therapy and the incidence of MI. Patients exposed to at least 30 months of therapy with a protease inhibitor had approximately three times the risk of an age-matched control group of men in the general population (Mary-Krause et al., 2003).

In contrast, other studies have not shown an association between ART and coronary events. A retrospective analysis of patients receiving care for HIV infection through the Veterans Affairs medical system reported both a decrease in the total rate of death and incidence of cardiovascular and cerebrovascular events between the years 1995 and 2001 (Bozzette et al., 2003). These results persisted in a follow-up study that extended the evaluation period from 1993 to 2003 (Bozzette et al., 2008). The reasons for the disparate results between these and other studies are not known, but it should be considered that the veteran population may represent a group at higher risk for heart disease at baseline (Assari, 2014).

Although still a matter of controversy, there are significant data that associate the use of protease inhibitors with increased cardiovascular risk (Friis-Møller et al., 2007; Worm et al., 2010). It should be noted that the protease inhibitors evaluated include agents that are no longer considered first-line medications in the United States, such as lopinavir-ritonavir and indinavir. In addition, results argue against a class-wide association, since particular protease inhibitors, such as atazanavir, do not seem to be associated with an increased risk of cardiac or cerebrovascular disease events (Monforte et al., 2013).

Abacavir (ABC) is a nucleoside reverse transcriptase inhibitor (NRTI) that has been linked to increased risk of cardiovascular disease. Ever since the D:A:D study reported this association (Rhew et al., 2003), this has been a question of debate, with studies supporting this observation (Choi et al., 2011; Young et al., 2015) and other studies contradicting it (Bedimo et al., 2011; Cruciani et al., 2011). The pathophysiology behind this hypothesis has not been clarified, although ABC has been associated with platelet hyperreactivity (Falcinelli et al., 2013). Prescriber bias must be taken in consideration, as critics of these studies argue that ABC may have been preferentially prescribed to persons with renal disease, dyslipidemia, metabolic syndromes, and coronary heart disease (Aberg and Ribaudo, 2010). Treatment guidelines advise caution in the prescription of this drug in patients with a high cardiovascular risk (European AIDS Clinical Society [EACS] Guidelines, 2015).

Lastly, it should noted that the effects of ART on endothelial function show conflicting data. The in vitro impact of antiretroviral drugs on endothelial function (Wang et al., 2007) has not been reproduced in HIV-infected patients (Torriani et al., 2008).

TRADITIONAL RISK FACTORS FOR CARDIOVASCULAR DISEASE

Despite the recent interest in inflammation and specific drug effects, traditional risk factors should not be forgotten, as they have been shown to be of importance in non-infected patients and may also contribute to increased cardiovascular disease in HIV-infected patients.

Smoking is a well-known modifiable risk factor for cardiovascular disease (Erhardt, 2009). Its prevalence is estimated to be up to three times higher in HIV-infected patients than in the general population (Webb et al., 2007). Therefore, all HIV clinicians should consider smoking cessation a high priority.

Likewise, abnormalities of lipid metabolism are thoroughly described in HIV-infected patients prior to the introduction of ART (Grunfeld et al., 1989; Riddler et al., 2003) and include decreased blood levels of low-density lipoprotein cholesterol (LDL-c), high-density lipoprotein cholesterol (HDL-c), total cholesterol (TC), and increased blood levels of triglycerides (TG). This is thought to be caused by impairment of the ATP-binding cassette transporter A1 (ABAC1)-dependent cholesterol efflux from HIV-infected macrophages (Mujawar et al., 2006). Although this is not the lipid profile classically associated with atherogenesis, low

HDL-c has been shown to increase the risk of coronary artery disease in the general population (Després et al., 2000).

Antiretroviral therapy is also known to contribute to lipid abnormalities. Protease inhibitors, as a class, are generally associated with dyslipidemia, but the effect varies with the individual protease inhibitor. For example, while ritonavir, lopinavir, fosamprenavir, and tipranavir have been associated with increased TC, LDL-c, and TG (Carey et al., 2010; Collot-Teixeira et al., 2009; Shafran et al., 2005), protease inhibitors developed later, such as atazanavir and darunavir, seem to have a more favorable lipid profile than that of the former (Aberg et al., 2012; Carey et al., 2010; Mills et al., 2009). Non-nucleoside reverse transcriptase inhibitors (NNRTIs) have also been associated with an increase in TC and LDL-c, but this effect seems to be compensated by an increase in HDL-c (Fontas et al., 2004). Nevirapine and rilpivirine compare favorably to efavirenz, and etravirine is comparable to placebo with regard to induced lipid abnormalities (Haubrich and Cahn, 2008; Tebas et al., 2014; van Leth et al., 2004). Within the NRTI class, tenofovir and emtricitabine seem to induce less adverse effects on the lipid profile than abacavir, stavudine, and zidovudine (Campo et al., 2013; Hill et al., 2009). Integrase inhibitors are in general associated with favorable lipid profiles, as is the CCR5 antagonist maraviroc. Raltegravir compared favorably to efavirenz and both ritonavir-boosted darunavir and atazanavir (Ofotokun et al., 2015; Rockstroh et al., 2011), and dolutegravir was found to be similar to raltegravir in a head-to-head comparison (Raffi et al., 2013).

Protease inhibitors are also associated with other metabolic effects, such as insulin resistance and diabetes. In the Multicenter AIDS Cohort Study (Brown et al., 2005), the incidence of diabetes in HIV-infected men with ART exposure was greater than fourfold that of HIV-seronegative men. Different protease inhibitors appear to pose different risks. While atazanavir appears to have a minimal or no effect on insulin sensitivity, indinavir causes a substantial decline in glucose disposal with just a single dose in healthy individuals (Hruz et al., 2002; Noor et al., 2002), and lopinavir/ritonavir worsened glucose tolerance after a 4-week trial (Lee at al., 2004). Protease inhibitors are thought to induce insulin resistance by blocking the function of the glucose transporter isoform GLUT4, the major transporter responsible for glucose disposal into fat and cardiac and skeletal muscle (Rudich et al., 2005). Indinavir has been associated with impaired pancreatic beta-cell function (Dubé et al., 2001). Other antiretroviral classes may also be a factor in developing insulin resistance and glucose tolerance. Thymidine NRTIs, including stavudine (Fleischman et al., 2007) and zidovudine (Blümer et al., 2008), have been associated with early insulin resistance in healthy volunteers and antiretroviral-naïve HIV-infected patients. Thymidine NRTIs and didanosine have been associated also with a higher risk of diabetes mellitus in large HIV cohorts (De Wit et al., 2008; Ledergerber et al., 2007). Strategies to address glucose intolerance, insulin resistance, and diabetes include lifestyle changes, change in ART, and the use of antidiabetic drugs. Exercise may improve hyperinsulinemia (Driscoll et al., 2004), and metformin therapy is known to reduce insulin resistance in HIV-infected patients with lipodystrophy and impaired glucose metabolism (Hadigan et al., 2000). Genetic factors may explain at least in part the higher risk of developing metabolic abnormalities, atherosclerosis, and probably body fat changes in some HIV-infected individuals exposed to certain antiretroviral drugs (Rotger et al., 2013), but the clinical application of pharmacogenomics to decrease cardiovascular risk is currently infeasible.

Antiretroviral therapy has also been associated with increased systolic blood pressure. Data from the Multicenter AIDS Cohort Study, which followed 5,578 HIV-infected men for 19 years, suggested that the use of ART for longer than 5 years is associated with a significantly higher prevalence of systolic hypertension (Seaberg et al., 2005).

Early detection and treatment of comorbidities and modifiable risk factors must be emphasized. Life changes such as smoke cessation and dietary alterations should be attempted. Guidelines for the management of hyperlipidemia in patients with HIV have been developed (Dubé et al., 2003; European AIDS Clinical Society [EACS], 2015). Adjusting individual cholesterol levels through estimation of the Framingham predicted 10-year cardiovascular risk is recommended, but it should be noted that the Framingham cardiovascular risk score has not received specific validation for HIV patients. Currently, the D:A:D 5-year risk score is the only equation specifically developed for patients with HIV, but it has yet not been formally recommended for cardiovascular disease risk assessment in routine clinical care as further data on its validation are still warranted (Friis-Møller et al., 2010). When indicated, strategies such as changing ART regimen and/or the use of statins should be adopted, taking into account potential interactions between statins and protease inhibitors.

LACTIC ACIDOSIS

Lactic acidosis is a rare but potentially life-threatening metabolic complication that has been reported in HIV-infected patients treated with NRTIs. It is classified as a type B lactic acidosis as it is not associated with systemic impairment in tissue oxygenation. Rather, it is caused by inhibition of mitochondrial DNA (mtDNA) γ-polymerase that results in mitochondrial toxicity via depletion of mtDNA as well as via generation of mitochondrial oxidative stress (Lewis and Dalakas, 1995; Lewis et al., 2001). Of note, mitochondrial dysfunction is also associated with other conditions, such as hepatic steatosis, peripheral neuropathy, neuromuscular weakness, pancreatitis, and myopathies (McComsey and Lonergan, 2004).

The incidence of mild hyperlactatemia was reported in 21% of NRTI-treated patients and most of the patients were asymptomatic (Vrovenraets et al., 2001), whereas symptomatic severe hyperlactatemia was found to be much lower, at 1.3–20.9 cases per 1,000 person-years of nucleoside analogue treatment, with a high variation in the calculated frequency, owing to the variety of case definitions used (Fortgang et al., 1995; Lonergan et al., 2000). Risk factors associated with increased incidence of hyperlactatemia in patients with HIV include the use and high dose of didanosine or stavudine (Chodock et al., 1999), female gender, age (Lactic Acidosis International Study Group, 2007), and concomitant use of ribavirin with didanosine for hepatitis C treatment (Bani-Sadr et al., 2005).

NRTIs have different affinities for the mtDNA γ-polymerase, and this may explain the different tolerability profiles. In vitro, the most potent NRTIs in inhibiting the mtDNA synthesis are, in decreasing order, zalcitabine, didanosine, stavudine, and zidovudine (Birkus et al., 2002). Lamivudine, abacavir, and tenofovir are less potent inhibitors and seem to be comparable to each other (Birkus et al., 2002).

Clinical symptoms of severe lactatemia include overwhelming fatigue, dyspnea, tachycardia, abdominal pain, weight loss, and peripheral neuropathy (Carr et al., 2000; Falco et al., 2002; Gerard et al., 2000; Imhof et al., 2005). Muscle, liver, or nerve biopsies are considered the gold standard for diagnosis of NRTI-induced mitochondrial toxicity. However, given the impracticability of biopsy, an assay that detects depletion of mtDNA levels in peripheral blood mononuclear cells was developed and has shown to correlate with NRTI-induced mitochondrial toxicity (Saitoh et al., 2007). Mild hyperlactatemia diagnosed in persons with HIV has a low positive predictive value for progression to symptomatic lactic acidosis (Brinkman, 2001).

To our knowledge, there are no controlled prospective trials nor recent studies regarding the treatment of symptomatic lactic acidosis associated with NRTI use. Management relies on supportive measures and discontinuation of NRTIs (Falco et al., 2003). Administration of co-factors that are thought to improve mitochondrial function, including thiamine, riboflavin, L-carnitine, prostaglandin E, and coenzyme Q, have also been used with promising but still unproven benefit (Falco et al., 2002).

HIV-ASSOCIATED LIPODYSTROPHY

HIV-associated lipodystrophy is a syndrome of fat redistribution associated with ART. It is characterized by a number of changes, including central and dorsocervical fat accumulation, and limb and facial subcutaneous fat atrophy, which are also accompanied by metabolic abnormalities, including insulin resistance and dyslipidemia. The presentation is heterogeneous, and patients may develop one or more of these complications.

Although both fat accumulation and loss may occur in persons with HIV, it has remained unclear if these two manifestations of lipodystrophy represent different components of the same process. Authors of the Study of Fat Redistribution and Metabolic Change in HIV Infection (FRAM) compared HIV-infected and HIV-negative men and confirmed their reports of changes in fat distribution by physical examination and magnetic resonance imaging (Bacchetti et al., 2005). Peripheral fat loss in HIV-infected individuals was not associated with central fat accumulation, which suggests that lipohypertrophy and lipoatrophy are different syndromes. A clear

definition of lipodystrophy is further complicated by factors such as age, race, gender, environmental factors, and disease status, all of which influence body composition (Kulasekaram et al., 2005; Paparizos et al., 2000; Sharp, 2003).

The pathogenesis of lipodystrophy is complex, and thymidine analogue NRTIs as well as protease inhibitors have been implicated (Joly et al., 2002; Martinez et al., 2001). The postulated mechanisms include decreased levels of adiponectin and leptin (Addy et al., 2003; Nagy et al., 2003), increased expression of tumor necrosis factor alpha (TNF-α), dysfunction of the sterol regulatory element binding protein 1 (SREBP-1) and decreased adipocyte differentiation factor peroxisome proliferator-activated receptor γ (PPAR-γ) expression (Bastard et al., 2002), impaired SREP1 nuclear localization and adipocyte differentiation in patients on protease inhibitors (Caron et al., 2003), reduced estrogen receptor expression (Barzon et al., 2005), and depletion of mtDNA by NRTIs (Birkus et al., 2002).

The optimal management of lipodystrophy is still unclear. Potential interventions for lipoatrophy include modification of the antiretroviral regimen, surgical correction, and the use of pioglitazone. It has been shown that changing from thymidine NRTIs to either ABC or TDF may cause improved limb fat mass (Moyle et al., 2006). However, plastic surgery is the main therapy for severe facial lipoatrophy. Options include autologous fat transplantation (Guaraldi et al., 2011) as well as the use of commercial fillers, such as poly-L-lactic acid, and calcium hydroxylapatite (Burgess and Quiroga, 2005; Silvers et al., 2006). Finally, pioglitazone, a ligand for the transcription factor PPAR-γ and used in type 2 diabetes to improve insulin sensitivity, may be useful in the treatment of HIV-associated lipoatrophy, as it may increase limb fat (Slama et al., 2008).

On the other hand, potential interventions for the treatment of fat accumulation include metformin, tesamorelin, and surgical procedures. There appears to be no association between dietary fat intake and changes in fat distribution (Batterham et al., 2000). Exercise may ameliorate truncal adiposity, but it may also worsen peripheral lipoatrophy (Driscoll et al., 2004). Metformin, a biguanide oral antidiabetic agent, has been shown to reduce visceral abdominal adipose tissue, total adipose fat, and the waist-to-hip ratio (Saint-Marc and Touraine, 1999). Tesamorelin, a growth hormone–releasing factor analogue that must be administered by injection, significantly decreased visceral adipose tissue in two studies (Falutz et al., 2010). Lastly, suction-assisted lipectomy (liposuction) has been used successfully to manage dorsocervical fat accumulation, although fat accumulation may recur (Piliero et al., 2003).

The visible effects of lipodystrophy and its association with HIV infection lead to a range of psychological issues. A qualitative study conducted with patients recruited from a clinic in London, many of whom had facial atrophy and peripheral wasting, revealed symptoms related to poor body image and self-imposed social isolation (Power et al., 2003). Individuals changed their diet, exercised more, used steroids, and underwent plastic surgery in attempts to improve the signs of lipodystrophy. Individuals with a history of more serious

HIV-related illness and individuals with partners accepted lipodystrophy with less psychological distress.

In another observational study of 110 individuals, 71% of whom were gay HIV-positive men, HIV-infected men with self-reported lipodystrophy indicated poor body image (Huang et al., 2006). A study in Spain measured the impact of lipodystrophy on psychosocial functioning and quality of life and observed considerable impairment (Blanch et al., 2004). Among the patients participating in the study, the development of lipodystrophy influenced how patients dressed in 65%, stimulated attempts to solve problems due to these body changes in 54%, and induced feelings of shame in 49%. In a study of HIV-infected individuals in Singapore, mainly men, 85% of affected patients stated that others had noticed changes, 36% reported anxiety or unhappiness from the changes, and 23% reported that the changes had affected their work or social life (Paton et al., 2002). Surprisingly, less than 1% of these patients considered discontinuation of ART, in contrast to French and Italian studies in which medication-adherent patients with lipodystrophy were at higher risk of subsequent adherence failure (Ammassari et al., 2002; Blashill et al., 2014; Corless et al., 2005; Duran et al., 2001).

In a population of gay men in Amsterdam, lipodystrophy was associated with a decrease in sexual activity, enjoyment of sex, and confidence in relationships (Dukers et al., 2001). In an Italian study conducted among 336 HIV-positive men on stable ART, desire, orgasm, and overall sexual satisfaction domain were found to be associated with mental health score. This study did not find any association between sexual dysfunction and HIV- or gender-specific clinical variables such as testosterone levels, for example (Guaraldi et al., 2007). These results were replicated in a sample of 161 woman on stable ART, 32% of whom reported sexual dysfunction: interference of body changes with habits was negatively associated with desire, arousal, and satisfaction; moreover, vaginal lubrication and orgasm were associated with body image satisfaction (Luzi et al., 2009). Another commonly expressed concern among patients with lipodystrophy is that, as the signs of lipodystrophy become more recognizable, they may serve to "out" people as HIV positive, in an unwanted manner. This effect had already been described earlier in the epidemic with the emergence of Kaposi's sarcoma (Persson, 2005).

Persons with lipodystrophy may be willing to trade years of life for quality of life. In one study conducted in the United States, persons with HIV and lipodystrophy, many of whom were well-educated gay men, believed that the quality-of-life effects with lipodystrophy were substantial enough that they would warrant trading years of life or taking a risk of death to avoid the syndrome (Lenert et al., 2002). It must be noted, however, that other research suggests that lipodystrophy does not necessarily worsen patients' quality of life. A study in the Toronto, Canada, area concluded that lipodystrophy may cause a worsening body image but otherwise demonstrated few effects on mental health or quality of life (Burgoyne et al., 2005). Also, in a study conducted in Spain, generally, lipodystrophy did not appear to influence quality of life in persons with HIV, although gay men and persons undergoing psychiatric treatment showed greater psychological impairment (Blanch et al., 2002).

Many treatment options are available for persons with HIV suffering from lipodystrophy (Peterson et al., 2008). A cognitive-behavioral intervention, developed by Cash (2002), was put forth by Kelly and colleagues (2009) to reframe cognitive bias and distortions that negatively affect body image and to suggest behavioral strategies to reduce distress associated with HIV-induced body changes. A diet intervention showed positive results on quality of life and mood in 30 HIV-positive men with lipodystrophy (Reid and Courtney, 2007). Moreover, surgical intervention (Guaraldi et al., 2011; Zinn et al., 2013) reduced anxiety and depression symptoms in a sample of 30 HIV-positive men undergoing treatment for facial lipoatrophy (Kavouni et al., 2008). Surgical interventions have also been shown to improve aesthetic satisfaction, body image satisfaction, and depression score (Orlando et al., 2007).

In summary, the balance of the data suggests that persons with lipodystrophy are at risk for increased social and psychological distress. Clinicians who treat patients with HIV infection should focus not only on the physical issues related to lipodystrophy but also on any associated issues of anxiety, depression, social isolation, altered body image, or medication nonadherence. There should be a low threshold for referral to mental health professionals or other appropriate medical specialties with experience in treating persons with HIV.

CONCLUSION

The absolute risk of cardiovascular disease in successfully ART-treated patients with HIV is low. However, the risk of cardiovascular disease for persons with HIV is increased compared with that for uninfected persons. This fact is due at least in part to a higher prevalence of underlying traditional cardiovascular risk factors that are mostly host-dependent. HIV may additionally contribute through immune activation, inflammation, and immunodeficiency. In a more modest way than HIV infection, the type of ART may also contribute to risk, mainly through their impact on metabolic and body fat parameters, and possibly through other factors that are currently unclear. These findings stress the importance of early detection and treatment of comorbidities and modifiable risk factors for cardiovascular disease. HIV-associated lipodystrophy is a syndrome of fat redistribution related to ART. Thymidine analogues and protease inhibitors in particular have been implicated in its etiology. Lipodystrophy is often accompanied by metabolic disturbances such as insulin resistance and dyslipidemia, and its physical changes have been associated with increased risk for social and psychological distress.

REFERENCES

Aberg JA, Ribaudo H (2010). Cardiac risk: not so simple. *J Infect Dis* 201(3):315–317.

Aberg JA, Tebas P, Overton ET, et al. (2012). Metabolic effects of darunavir/ritonavir versus atazanavir/ritonavir in treatment-naive, HIV type 1-infected subjects over 48 weeks. *AIDS Res Hum Retroviruses* 28(10):1184–1195.

Addy CL, Gavrila A, Tsiodras S, Brodovicz K, Karchmer AW, Matzoros CS (2003). Hypoadiponectinemia is associated with insulin resistance, hypertriglyceridemia, and fat redistribution in human immunodeficiency virus-infected patients treated with highly active antiretroviral therapy. *J Clin Endocrinol Metab* 88:627–636.

Ammassari A, Antinori A, Cozzi-Lepri A, et al.; AdICoNA and the LipoICoNA Study Groups (2002). Relationship between HAART adherence and adipose tissue alterations. *J Acquir Immune Defic Syndr* 31:S140–S144.

Antiretroviral Therapy Cohort Collaboration (2010). Causes of death in HIV-1-infected patients treated with antiretroviral therapy, 1996–2006: collaborative analysis of 13 HIV cohort studies. *Clin Infect Dis* 50:1387–1396.

Assari S (2014). Veterans and risk of heart disease in the United States: a cohort with 20 years of follow-up. *Int J Prev Med* 5(6):703–709.

Bacchetti P, Gripshover B, Grunfeld C, et al. (2005). Fat distribution in men with HIV infection. *J Acquir Immune Defic Syndr* 40:121–131.

Bani-Sadr F, Carrat F, Pol S, et al. (2005). Risk factors for symptomatic mitochondrial toxicity in HIV/hepatitis C virus–coinfected patients during interferon plus ribavirin-based therapy. *J Acquir Immune Defic Syndr* 40:47–52.

Barzon L, Zamboni, M, Pacenti M, et al. (2005). Do oestrogen receptors play a role in the pathogenesis of HIV-associated lipodsytrophy? *AIDS* 19:531–533.

Bastard JP, Caron M, Vidal H, et al. (2002). Association between altered expression of adipogenic factor SREBP1 in lipoatrophic adipose tissue from HIV-1-infected patients and abnormal adipocyte differentiation and insulin resistance. *Lancet* 359:1026–1031.

Batterham MJ, Garsia R, Greenop PA (2000). Dietary intake, serum lipids, insulin resistance, and body composition in the era of highly active antiretroviral therapy 'Diet FRS Study.' *AIDS* 14:1839–1843.

Bedimo RJ, Westfall AO, Drechsler H, Vidiella G, Tebas P (2011). Abacavir use and risk of acute of acute myocardial infarction and cerebrovascular events in the highly active antiretroviral era. *Clin Infect Dis* 53(1):84–91.

Beignon AS, McKenna K, Skoberne M, et al. (2005). Endocytosis of HIV-1 activates plasmacytoid dendritic cells via Toll-like receptor-viral RNA interactions. *J Clin Invest* 115(11):3265–3275.

Birkus G, Hitchcock MJM, Cihlar T (2002). Assessment of mitochondrial toxicity in human cells treated with tenofovir: comparison with other nucleoside reverse transcriptase inhibitors. *Antimicrob Agents Chemother* 46:716–723.

Blanch J, Rousaud A, Martinez E, et al. (2002). Impact of lipodystrophy on the quality of life of HIV-1 infected patients. *J Acquir Immune Defic Syndr* 31:404–407.

Blanch J, Rousaud A, Martinez E, et al. (2004). Factors associated with severe impact of lipodystrophy on the quality of life of patients infected with HIV-1. *Clin Infect Dis* 38:1464–1470.

Blashill AJ, Gordon JR, Safren SA. (2014). Depression longitudinally mediates the association of appearance concerns to ART nonadherence in HIV-infected individuals with a history of injection drug use. *J Behav Med* 37(1):166–172.

Blümer RM, van Vonderen MG, Sutinen J, et al. (2008). Zidovudine/lamivudine contributes to insulin resistance within 3 months of starting combination antiretroviral therapy. *AIDS* 22:227–236.

Bozzette SA, Ake CF, Tam HK, Chang SW, Louis TA (2003). Cardiovascular and cerebrovascular events in patients treated for human immunodeficiency virus infection. *N Engl J Med* 348(8):702–710.

Bozzette SA, Ake CF, Tam HK, Phippard A, Cohen D, Scharfstein DO, Louis TA. (2008). Long-term survival and serious cardiovascular events in HIV-infected pateints treated with highly active antiretroviral tehrapy. *J Acquir Immune Defic Syndr* 47(3):338–341.

Brenchley JM, Price DA, Schacker TW, et al. (2006). Microbial translocation is a cause of systemic immune activation in chronic HIV infection. *Nat Med* 12(12):1365–1371.

Brinkman K (2001). Management of hyperlactatemia: no need for routine lactate measurements. *AIDS* 15:795–797.

Brown TT, Cole SR, Li X, et al. (2005). Antiretroviral therapy and the prevalence and incidence of diabetes mellitus in the multicenter AIDS cohort study. *Arch Intern Med* 165:1179–1184.

Burgess CM, Quiroga RM (2005). Assessment of the safety and efficacy of poly-L-lactic acid for the treatment of HIV-associated facial lipoatrophy. *J Am Acad Dermatol* 52:233–239.

Burgoyne R, Collins E, Wagner C, Abbey S, Halman M, Nur M, Walmsley S (2005). The relationship between lipodystrophy-associated body changes and measures of quality of life and mental health for HIV-positive adults. *Qual Life Res* 14:981–990.

Campo R, DeJesus E, Bredeek UF, et al. (2013). SWIFT: prospective 48-week study to evaluate efficacy and safety of switching to emtricitabine/tenofovir from lamivudine/abacavir in virologically suppressed HIV-1 infected patients on a boosted protease inhibitor containing antiretroviral regimen. *Clin Infect Dis* 56(11):1637–1645.

Carey D, Amin J, Boyd M, Petoumenos K, Emery S (2010). Lipid profiles in HIV-infected adults receiving atazanavir and atazanavir/ritonavir: systematic review and meta-analysis of randomized controlled trials. *J Antimicrob Chemother* 65(9):1878–1888.

Caron M, Auclair M, Sterlingot H, Kornprobst M, Capeau J (2003). Some HIV protease inhibitors alter lamin A/C maturation and stability, SREBP-1 nuclear localization and adipocyte differentiation. *AIDS* 17:2437–2444.

Carr A, Miller J, Law M, Cooper DA (2000). A syndrome of lipoatrophy, lactic acidaemia, and liver dysfunction associated with HIV nucleoside analogue therapy: contribution to protease inhibitor–related lipodystrophy syndrome. *AIDS* 14:F25–F32.

Cash TF (2002). Cognitive-behavioural perspectives on body image. In TF Cash, T Pruzinsky (eds.), *Body Image: A Handbook of Theory, Research, and Clinical Practice* (pp 38–46). New York: Guilford Press.

Chodock R, Mylonakis E, Shemin D, et al. (1999). Survival of a human immunodeficiency patient with nucleoside-induced lactic acidosis-role of haemodyalisis treatment. *Nephrol Dial Transplant* 14:2484–2486.

Choi AI, Vittinghoff E, Deek SG, Weekley CC, Li Y, Shlipak MG (2011). Cardiovascular risks associated with abacavir and tenofovir exposure in HIV-infected persons. *AIDS* 25(10):1289–1298.

Collot-Teixeira S, De Lorenzo F, Waters L, et al. (2009). Impact of different low-dose ritonavir regimens on lipids, CD36, and adipophilin expression. *Clin Pharmacol Ther* 85(4):375–378.

Corless IB, Kirksey KM, Kemppainen J, Nicholas PK, McGibbon C, Davis SM, Dolan S (2005). Lipodystrophy-associated symptoms and medication adherence in HIV/AIDS. *AIDS Patient Care STDS* 19(9):577–586.

Cruciani M, Zanichelli V, Serpelloni G, et al. (2011). Abacavir use and cardiovascular disease events: a meta-analysis of published and unpublished data. *AIDS* 25(16):1993–2004.

Currier JS, Taylor A, Boyd F, et al. (2003). Coronary heart disease in HIV-infected individuals. *J Acquir Immune Defic Syndr* 33(4):506–512.

DAD Study Group (2007). Class of antiretroviral drugs and the risk of myocardial infarction. *N Engl J Med* 356:1723–1735.

Després JP, Lemieux I, Dagenais GR, Cantin B, Lamarche B. (2000). HDL-cholesterol as a marker of coronary artery disease risk: the Quebec cardiovascular study. *Atherosclerosis* 153:263–272.

De Wit S, Sabin CA, Weber R, et al. (2008). Incidence and risk factors for new-onset diabetes in HIV-infected patients: the Data Collection on Adverse Events of Anti-HIV Drugs (D:A:D) study. *Diabetes Care* 31(6):1224–1229.

Driscoll SD, Meininger GE, Ljungquist K, et al. (2004). Differential effects of metformin and exercise on muscle adiposity and metabolic indices in human immunodeficiency virus–infected patients. *J Clin Endocrinol Metab* 89:2171–2178.

Dubé MP, Edmondson-Melancon H, Qian D, Aqeel R, Johnson D, Buchanan TA. (2001). Prospective evaluation of the effect of initiating indinavir-based therapy on insulin sensitivity and B-cell function in HIV-infected patients. *J Acquir Immune Defic Syndr* 27:130–134.

Dubé MP, Stein JH, Aberg JA, et al. (2003). Guidelines for the evaluation and management of dyslipidemia in human immunodeficiency virus (HIV)-infected adults receiving antiretroviral therapy: recommendations of the HIV Medical Association of the Infectious Disease Society of America and the Adult AIDS Clinical Trials Group. *Clin Infect Dis* 37:613–627.

Dukers NH, Stolte IG, Albrecht N, Coutinho RA, de Wit JBF (2001). The impact of experiencing lipodystrophy on the sexual behavior and well-being among HIV-infected homosexual men. *AIDS* 15:812–813.

Duran S, Saves M, Spire B, et al.; APROCO Study Group (2001). Failure to maintain long-term adherence to highly active antiretroviral therapy: the role of lipodystrophy. *AIDS* 15:2441–2444.

Erhardt L (2009). Cigarette smoking: and undertreated risk factor for cardiovascular disease. *Atherosclerosis* 205(1):23–32.

Eugenin EA, Morgello S, Klotman ME, Mosoian A, Lento PA, Berman JW, Schecter AD. (2008). Human immunodeficiency virus (HIV) infects human arterial smooth muscle cells in vivo and in vitro: implications for the pathogenesis of HIV-mediated vascular disease. *Am J Pathol* 172(4):1100–1111.

European AIDS Clinical Society (EACS) (2015). Guidelines, version 8.0, October 2015. http://www.eacsociety.org/files/2015_eacsguidelines_8_0-english_rev-20160124.pdf. Accessed January 20, 2016.

Falcinelli E, Francisci D, Belfiori B, et al. (2013). In vivo platelet activation and platelet hyperreactivity in abacavir-treated HIV-infected patients. *Thromb Haemost* 110(2):349–357.

Falco V, Crespo M, Ribera E. (2003). Lactic acidosis related to nucleoside therapy in HIV-infected patients. *Expert Opin Pharmacother* 4:1321–1329.

Falco V, Rodriguez D, Ribera E, et al. (2002). Severe nucleoside-associated lactic acidosis in human immunodeficiency virus–infected patients: report of 12 cases and review of the literature. *Clin Infect Dis* 34:838–846.

Falutz J, Mamputu JC, Potvin D, et al. (2010). Effects of tesamorelin (TH9507), a growth hormone-releasing factor analog, in human immunodeficiency virus-infected patients with excess abdominal fat: a pooled analysis of two multicenter, double-blind placebo-controlled phase 3 trials with safety extension data. *J Clin Endocrinol Metab* 95:4291–4304.

Fleischman A, Johnsen S, Systrom DM, et al. (2007). Effects of a nucleoside reverse transcriptase inhibitor, stavudine, on glucose disposal and mitochondrial function in muscle of healthy adults. *Am J Physiol Endocrinol Metab* 292(6):E1666-16673.

Fontas E, van Leth F, Sabin CA, et al. (2004). Lipid profiles in HIV-infected patients receiving combination antiretroviral therapy: are different antiretroviral drugs associated with different lipid profiles? *J Infect Dis* 189(6):1056–1074.

Freiberg MS, Chang CC, Kuller LH, et al. (2013). HIV infection and the risk of acute myocardial infarction. *JAMA Intern Med* 173(8):614–622.

Friis-Møller N, Reiss P, Sabin CA, et al. (2007). Class of antiretroviral drugs and the risk of myocardial infarction. *N Engl J Med* 356(17):1723–1735.

Friis-Møller N, Thiebaut R, Reiss P, Weber R, et al. (2010). Predicting the risk of cardiovascular disease in HIV-infected patients: the data collection on adverse effects of anti-HIV drugs study. *Eur J Cardiovasc Prev Rehabil* 17:491–501.

Fortgang IS, Belitsos PC, Chaisson RE, Moore RD (1995). Hepatomegaly and steatosis in HIV-infected patients receiving nucleoside analog antiretroviral therapy. *Am J Gastroenterol* 90:1433–1436.

Gerard Y, Maulin L, Yazdanpanah Y, et al. (2000). Symptomatic hyperlactataemia: an emerging complication of antiretroviral therapy. *AIDS* 14:2723–2730.

Gresele P, Falcinelli E, Sebastiano M, Baldelli F (2012). Endothelial and platelet function alterations in HIV-infected patients. *Thromb Res* 129(3):301–308.

Grunfeld C, Kotler DP, Hamadeh R, Tierney A, Wang J, Pierson RN (1989). Hypertriglyceridemia in the acquired immunodeficiency syndrome. *Am J Med* 86(1):27–31.

Guaraldi G, Fontdevila J, Christensen LH, et al. (2011). Surgical correction of HIV-associated facial lipoatrophy. *AIDS* 25:1–12.

Guaraldi G, Luzi K, Murri R, et al. (2007). Sexual dysfunction in HIV-infected men: role of antiretroviral therapy, hypogonadism and lipodystrophy. *Antivir Ther* 12(7):1059–1065.

Hadigan C, Corcoran C, Basgoz N, Davis B, Sax P, Grinspoon S. (2000). Metformin in the treatment of HIV lipodystrophy syndrome: a randomized controlled trial. *JAMA* 284:472–477.

Haubrich R, Cahn P (2008). Duet-1: week 48 results of a phase III randomized double-blind trial to evaluate the efficacy and safety of etravirine (ETR; TMC 125) versus placebo in 612 treatment-experienced HIV-1-infected patients. Presented at the 15th Conference on Retroviruses and Opportunistic Infections, Boston, MA, February 3–6, 2008; abstract #790.

Hill A, Sawyer W, Gazzard B (2009). Effects of first-line use of nucleoside analogues, efavirenz, and ritonavir-boosted protease inhibitors on lipid levels. *HIV Clin Trials* 10(1):1–12.

Hruz PW, Murata H, Qiu H, Mueckler M (2002). Indinavir induces acute and reversible peripheral insulin resistance in rats. *Diabetes* 51:937–942.

Huang JS, Lee D, Becerra K, Santos R, Barber E, Mathews WC (2006). Body image in men with HIV. *AIDS Patient Care STDS* 20(10):668–677.

Huang MB, Khan M, Garcia-Barrio M, Powell M, Bond VC (2001). Apoptotic effects in primary human umbilical vein endothelial cell cultures caused by exposure to virion-associated and cell membrane-associated HIV-1 gp120. *J Acquir Immune Defic Syndr* 27:213–221.

Imhof A, Ledergerber B, Gunthard HF, Haupts S, Weber R (2005). Swiss HIV Cohort Study: risk factors for and outcome of hyperlactatemia in HIV-infected persons: is there a need for routine lactate monitoring? *Clin Infect Dis* 41:721–728.

Islam FM, Wu J, Jansson J, Wilson DP (2012). Relative risk of cardiovascular disease among people living with HIV: a systematic review and meta-analysis. *HIV Med* 13(8):453–468.

Joly V, Flandre P, Meiffredy V, Leturgue N, Harel M, Aboulker JP, Yeni P (2002). Increased risk of lipoatrophy under stavudine in HIV-1-infected patients: results of a substudy from a comparative trial. *AIDS* 16:2447–2454.

Kavouni A, Catalan J, Brown S, Mandalia S, Barton SE (2008). The face of HIV and AIDS: can we erase the stigma? *AIDS Care* 20(4):485–487.

Kelly JS, Langdon D, Serpell L. (2009). The phenomenology of body image in men living with HIV. *AIDS Care* 21(12):1560–1567.

Kulasekaram R, Peters BS, Wierzbicki AS (2005). Dyslipidaemia and cardiovascular risk in HIV infection. *Curr Med Res Opin* 21:1717–1725.

Lactic Acidosis International Study Group (2007). Risk factors for lactic acidosis and severe hyperlactataemia in HIV-1-infected adults exposed to antiretroviral therapy. *AIDS* 21:2455–2464

Ledergerber B, Furrer H, Rickenbach M, et al.; Swiss HIV Cohort Study Group (2007). Factors associated with the incidence of type 2 diabetes mellitus in HIV-infected participants in the Swiss HIV Cohort Study. *Clin Infect Dis* 45(1):111–119.

Lee GA, Seneviratne T, Noor MA, et al. (2004). The metabolic effects of lopinavir/ritonavir in HIV-negative women. *AIDS* 18:641–649.

Lenert LA, Feddersen M, Sturley A, Lee D (2002). Adverse effects of medications and trade-offs between length of life and quality of life in human immunodeficiency virus infection. *Am J Med* 113:229–232.

Lewis W, Copeland WC, Day BJ. (2001). Mitochondrial DNA depletion, oxidative stress, and mutation: mechanisms of dysfunction from nucleoside reverse transcriptase inhibitors. *Lab Invest* 81:777–790.

Lewis W, Dalakas MC (1995). Mitochondrial toxicity of antiviral drugs. *Nat Med* 1:417–422.

Lonergan JT, Behling C, Pfander H (2000). Hyperlactatemia and hepatic abnormalities in 10 HIV-infected patients receiving nucleoside combination regimens. *Clin Infect Dis* 31:162–166.

Luzi K, Guaraldi G, Murri R, et al. (2009). Body image is a major determinant of sexual dysfunction in stable HIV-infected women. *Antivir Ther* 14(1):85–92.

Martinez E, Mocroft A, Garcia-Viejo MA, et al. (2001). Risk of lipodystrophy in HIV-1-infected patients treated with protease inhibitors: a prospective cohort study. *Lancet* 357:592–598.

Mary-Krause M, Cotte L, Simon A, Partisani M, Costagliola D (2003). Increased risk of myocardial infarction with duration of protease inhibitor therapy in HIV-infected men. *AIDS* 17(17):2479–2486.

May MT, Sterne JA, Costagliola D, et al. (2006). HIV treatment response and prognosis in Europe and North America in the first decade pf highly active antiretroviral therapy: a collaborative analysis. *Lancet* 368:451–458.

McComsey G, Lonergan JT (2004). Mitochondrial dysfunction: patient monitoring and toxicity management. *J Acquir Immune Defic Syndr* 37:S30–S35.

Mills AM, Nelson M, Jayaweera D, et al. (2009). Once-daily darunavir/ritonavir vs. lopinavir/ritonavir in treatment-naive, HIV-1-infected patients: 96-week analysis. *AIDS* 23(13):1679–1688.

Monforte AD, Reiss P, Ryom L, et al. (2013). Atazanavir is not associated with an increased risk of cardio- or cerebrovascular disease events. *AIDS* 27(3):407–415.

Moyle GJ, Sabin CA, Cartledge J, et al. (2006). A randomized comparative trial of tenofovir DF or abacavir as replacement for a thymidine analogue in persons with lipoatrophy. *AIDS* 20:2043–2050.

Mujawar Z, Rose H, Morrow MP, et al. (2006). Human immunodeficiency virus impairs reverse chilesterol transport from macrophages. *PLoS Biol* 4(11):e365.

Nagy GS, Tsiodras S, Martin LD, et al. (2003). Human immunodeficiency virus type 1-related lipoatrophy and lipohypertrophy are associated with serum concentrations of leptin. *Clin Infect Dis* 36:795–802.

Neuhaus J, Jacobs DR, Baker JV, et al. (2010). Markers of inflammation, coagulation, and renal function are elevated in adults with HIV infection. *J Infect Dis* 201(12):1788–1795.

Noor MA, Seneviratne T, Aweeka FT, Lo JC, Schwarz JM, Mulligan K, Grunfeld C (2002). Indinavir acutely inhibits insulin-stimulated glucose disposal in humans: a randomized, placebo-controlled study. *AIDS* 16:F1–F8.

Obel N, Omland LH, Kronborg G, et al. (2011). Impact of non-HIV and HIV risk factors on survival in HIV-infected patients on HAART: a population-based nationwide cohort study. *PLoS One* 6(7):e22698.

Ofotokun I, Na LH, Landovitz RJ, et al. (2015). Comparison of the metabolic effects of ritonavir-boosted darunavir or atazanavir versus raltegravir, and the impact of ritonavir plasma exposure: ACTG 5257. *Clin Infect Dis* 60(12):1842–1851.

Orlando G, Guaraldi G, De Fazio D, Rottino A, Grisotti A, Blini M, Esposito R. (2007). Long-term psychometric outcomes of facial lipoatrophy therapy: forty-eight-weekobservational, nonrandomized study. *AIDS Patient Care STDS*, 21(11):833–842.

Ostrowski SR, Katzenstein TL, Pedersen BK, Gerstoft J, Ullum H. (2008). Residual viraemia in HIV-1-infected patients with plasma viral load ≤20 copies/ml is associated with increased blood levels of soluble immune activation markers. *Scand J Immunol* 68(6):652–660.

Paparizos VA, Kyriakis KP, Botsis C, Papastamopoulos V, Hadjivassiliou M, Stavrianeas NG (2000). Protease inhibitor therapy-associated lipodystrophy, hypertriglyceridaemia and diabetes mellitus. *AIDS* 14:903–905.

Paton NI, Earnest A, Ng YM, Karim F, Aboulhab J (2002). Lipodystrophy in a cohort of human immunodeficiency virus–infected Asian patients: prevalence, associated factors, and psychological impact. *Clin Infect Dis* 35:1244–1249.

Persson A (2005). Facing HIV: body shape change and the (in)visibility of illness. *Med Anthropol* 24:237–264.

Peterson S, Martins CR, Cofrancesco J Jr. (2008). Lipodystrophy in the patient with HIV: social, psychological, and treatment considerations. *Aesthet Surg J* 28(4):443–451.

Phillips AN, Carr A, Neuhaus J, et al. (2008). Interruption of antiretroviral therapy and risk of cardiovascular disease in persons with HIV-1 infeection: exploratory analyses from the SMART trial. *Antivir Ther* 13(2):177–187.

Piliero PJ, Hubbard M, King J, Faragon JJ (2003). Use of ultasonography-assisted liposuction for the treatment of human immunodeficiency virus-associated enlargement of the dorsocervical fat pad. *Clin Infect Dis* 37:1374–1377.

Power R, Tate HL, McGill SM, Taylor C (2003). A qualitative study of the psychosocial implications of lipodystrophy syndrome on HIV positive individuals. *Sex Transm Infect* 79:137–141.

Raffi F, Rachlis A, Stellbrink HJ, et al. (2013). Once-daily dolutegravir versus raltegravir in antiretroviral-naive adults with HIV-1 infection: 48 week results from the randomised, double-blind, non-inferiority SPRING-2 study. *Lancet* 381:735–743.

Reid C, Courtney M (2007). A randomized clinical trial to evaluate the effect of diet on quality of life and mood of people living with HIV and lipodystrophy. *J Assoc Nurses AIDS Care* 18(4):3–11.

Rhew DC, Bernal M, Aguilar D, Iloeje U, Goetz MB (2003). Association between protease inhibitor use and increased cardiovascular risk in patients infected with human immunodeficiency virus: a systematic review. *Clin Infect Dis* 37(7):959–972.

Riddler SA, Smit E, Cole SR, et al. (2003). Impact of HIV infection and HAART on serum lipids in men. *JAMA* 289(22):2978–2982.

Rockstroh JK, Lennox JL, Dejesus E, et al. (2011). Long-term treatment with raltegravir or efavirenz combined with tenofovir/emtricitabine for treatment-naive human immunodeficiency virus-1-infected patients: 156-week results from STARTMRK. *Clin Infect Dis* 53(8):807–816.

Rotger M, Glass TR, Junier T, et al. (2013). Contribution of genetic background, traditional risk factors, and HIV-related factors to coronary artery disease events in HIV-positive persons. *Clin Infect Dis* 57(1):112–121.

Rudich A, Ben-Romano R, Etzion S, Bashan N (2005). Cellular mechanisms of insulin resistance, lipodystrophy and atherosclerosis induced by HIV protease inhibitors. *Acta Physiol Scand* 183:75–88.

Saint-Marc T, Touraine JL (1999). Effects of metformin on insulin resistance and central adiposity in patients receiving effective protease inhibitor therapy. *AIDS* 13:1000–1002.

Saitoh A, Fenton T, Alvero C, Fletcher CV, Spector SA (2007). Impact of nucleoside reverse transcriptase inhibitors on mitochondria in human immunodeficiency virus type 1-infected children receiving highly active antiretroviral therapy. *Antimicrob Agents Chemother* 51:4236–4242.

Seaberg EC, Muñoz A, Lu M, et al. (2005). Association between highly active antiretroviral therapy and hypertension in a large cohort of men followed from 1984 to 2003. *AIDS* 19:953–960.

Shafran SD, Mashinter LD, Robert SE (2005). The effect of low-dose ritonavir monotherapy on fasting serum lipid concentrations. *HIV Med* 6(6):421–425.

Sharp M (2003). Metabolic complications associated with HIV disease. *Posit Aware* 14:32–36.

Silvers SL, Eviatar JA, Echavez MI, Pappas AL (2006). Prospective, pone-label, 18-month trial of calcium hydroxylapatite (Radiesse) for facial soft-tissue augmentation in patients with human immunodeficiency virus-associated lipoatrophy: one-year durability. *Plast Reconstr Surg* 118:34S–45S.

Slama L, Lanoy E, Valantin MA, et al. (2008). Effect of pioglitazone on HIV-1-related lipodystrophy: a randomized double-blind placebo-controlled trial (ANRS 113). *Antivir Ther* 13:67–76.

Strategies for Management of Antiretroviral Therapy (SMART) Study Group (2006). CD4+ count-guided interruption of antiretroviral treatment. *N Engl J Med* 355(22):2283–2296.

Tebas P, Sension M, Arribas J, et al. (2014). Lipid levels and changes in body fat distribution in treatment-naive, HIV-1-infected adults treated with rilpivirine or efavirenz for 96 weeks in the echo and thrive trials. *Clin Infect Dis* 59(3):425–434.

Torriani FJ, Komarow L, Parker RA, et al.; ACTG 5152s Study Team (2008). Endothelial function in human immunodeficiency virus-infected antiretroviral-naïve subjects before and after starting potent antiretroviral therapy. *J Am Coll Cardiol* 52(7):569–576.

UNAIDS (2014) *The GAP Report. People Aged 50 Years and Older.* Geneva, Switzerland: UNAIDS.

van Leth F, Phanuphak P, Stroes E, et al. (2004). Nevirapine and efavirenz elicit different changes in lipid profiles in antiretroviral-therapy-naive patients infected with HIV-1. *PLoS Med* 1(1):e19.

van Leuven SI, Franssen R, Kastelein JJ, Levi M, Stroes ES, Tak PP (2008). Systemic inflammation as a risk factor for atherothrombosis. *Rheumatology* 47(1):3–7.

Vrovenraets SME, Treskes M, Regez RM, et al. (2001). Hyperlactatemia in HIVinfected patients: the role of NRTI treatment. 8th Conference on Retroviruses and Opportunistic Infections, Chicago, IL, abstract 625.

Wang X, Chai H, Yao Q, Chen C (2007). Molecular mechanisms of HIV protease inhibitor-induced endothelial dysfunction. *J Acquir Immune Defic Syndr* 44(5):493–499.

Webb MS, Vanable PA, Carey MP, Blair DC (2007). Cigarette smoking among HIV+ men and women: examining health, substance use, and psychosocial correlates across the smoking spectrum. *J Behav Med* 30(5):371–383.

Womack J (2012). Women, aging and HIV. Presented at the 2nd International Workshop on HIV and Women, January 9–10, 2012, Bethesda, MD. [Data from 2008, onward projected based on 2001–2007 trends (calculated by Justice, AC), 2001–2007 data from *CDC Surveillance Reports* 2007.]

Worm SW, Sabin C, Weber R, et al. (2010). Risk of myocardial infarction in patients with HIV infection exposed to specific individual antiretroviral drugs from the 3 major drug classes: the Data collection on Adverse events of anti-HIV Drugs (D:A:D) study. *J Infect Dis* 201(3):318–330.

Young J, Xiao Y, Moodie EE, et al. (2015). Effect of cumulating exposure to abacavir on the risk of cardiovascular disease events in patients from the Swiss HIV Cohort Study. *J Acquir Immune Defic Syndr* 69(4):413–421.

Zinn RJ, Serrurier C, Takuva S, Sanne I, Menezes CN (2013). HIV-associated lipodystrophy in South Africa: the impact on the patient and the impact on the plastic surgeon. *J Plast Reconstr Aesthet Surg* 66(6):839–844.

47.

OVERVIEW OF HIV-ASSOCIATED MULTIMORBIDITIES

Luis F. Pereira, Mark Bradley, Harold W. Goforth, César A. Alfonso, Joseph Z. Lux,

Esteban Martínez, and Michael P. Mullen

Since the introduction of effective antiretroviral therapy (ART), the incidence of HIV-related opportunistic infections has been significantly reduced and persons with HIV who have access to HIV medical care and antiretroviral medications are living longer, healthier lives. The occurrence of pulmonary, gastrointestinal, hepatic, hematological, cardiac, dermatological, renal, and neoplastic manifestations is still of concern, however, and co-occurring multimorbidities have become even more significant in persons engaged in care and virally suppressed.

Chapters 43, 44, 45, and 46 present in-depth discussions of hepatitis C, HIV-associated renal disease, endocrine disorders, and cardiovascular complications. In this chapter we present ophthalmological illness, pulmonary complications, dermatological complications and illnesses, gastrointestinal manifestations of HIV infection, cancers, and illnesses associated with aging and premature aging (covered in further detail in Chapter 36). This chapter presents an overview that will provide the reader with a working knowledge of HIV-associated multimorbidities.

HIV-ASSOCIATED OPHTHALMOLOGICAL ILLNESS

Psychiatric care for individuals with HIV infection and comorbid vision loss is a complex endeavor with multidimensional morbidities that include infectious, inflammatory, and iatrogenic conditions. Coordinated care of the visually impaired person with HIV may significantly impact quality of life and reduce distress.

Prior to the development of effective ART, HIV-associated ocular complications were very common (Cunningham et al., 1998). In fact, cytomegalovirus (CMV) retinitis was the most common ocular infection in patients with AIDS, affecting an estimated 20–50% of patients in the early decades of the epidemic, from 1981 to 2000 (Holland, 2008; Holland et al., 1983). During the first decade, patients required lifelong therapy and had a mean survival after diagnosis of 6–10 months (Hoover et al., 1993). Multiple trials have shown that intravenous ganciclovir, foscarnet, cidofovir, oral ganciclovir, and local intravitreal ganciclovir implant are all effective in treating CMV retinitis. Studies have shown that the time to

relapse is longest with the implant (Martin et al., 1999). Since 2000, largely because of effective ART, new cases of CMV retinitis have become rare, with a decline in incidence of 80% (Goldberg et al., 2005; Holland, 2008). Patients with a history of CMV retinitis who have had a successful response to ART with increasing CD4 lymphocyte count can safely discontinue maintenance therapy, with close observation for recurrence (MacDonald et al., 2000; Song et al., 2003).

A new ocular inflammatory syndrome associated with immune recovery in patients with CMV retinitis is immune recovery uveitis (IRU). The pathogenesis is thought to be secondary to an immune response to CMV present in the retina (Jacobson et al., 1997; MacDonald et al, 2000). IRU is an inflammatory response to CMV antigens triggered by antiretrovirals, usually occurs within weeks of treatment, and can persist with complications such as cystoid macular edema, epiretinal membrane formation, neovascularization of the retina or optic disc, and cataract formation (Cunningham, 2000; Cunningham et al., 2015; Nguyen et al., 2000). This syndrome needs to be anticipated and recognized early as it can result in a substantial loss of vision. IRU can occur in up to 60% of people treated for CMV retinitis (Shukla et al., 2007).

Other ocular diseases that were commonly seen prior to effective ART were acute retinal necrosis secondary to herpes zoster virus (HZV) and herpes simplex virus (HSV), toxoplasmosis retinochoroiditis, *Pneumocystis jiroveci* (*carinii*) choroiditis, syphilitic retinitis, tuberculosis choroiditis, cryptococcal choroiditis, corneal microsporidiosis, and ocular lymphomas (Holland, 2008; Moraes, 2002). These conditions may still occur in immunocompromised patients without access to effective ART.

Persons with HIV may present with subtle visual disturbances of unknown etiology, such as reduced contrast sensitivity, altered color vision, and visual field abnormalities (Holland, 2008). In addition, cidofovir and rifabutin may cause iatrogenic uveitis, further complicating care and recovery (Goldberg et al., 2005).

Regardless of its etiology, vision loss has associated psychological morbidity. Affective states of depression and anxiety are associated with decreased vision, especially when it occurs acutely, and may exacerbate preexisting mood and anxiety disorders. Poor adjustment to visual loss may lead to exacerbation of cognitive impairment, which is of clinical significance in persons with delirium or dementia. Decreased visual acuity may also exacerbate paranoia and hypervigilance, complicating preexisting psychiatric disorders in persons with HIV, such as posttraumatic stress disorder and psychotic disorders. The complex association between affective states of anxiety and depression and immunosuppression (see Chapter 21) further highlights the importance of recognizing the psychological impact of vision loss in persons with HIV, given that acute vision loss may trigger incapacitating anxiety and depressive states in an already immunocompromised person.

Physicians working with persons with HIV need to be aware of the ocular adverse effects caused by psychotropic medications. These include ocular dystonias, mydriasis, myopia, problems with accommodation, exophoria, glaucomatous attacks (in secondary angle closure glaucoma only), cataractous changes, and impairment of discrimination of contrast and color perception (Fraunfelder and Fraunfelder, 2004; Malone et al., 1992; Richa and Yazbek, 2010). The same medications chosen to alleviate psychiatric symptoms and reduce psychological distress caused by vision loss may actually affect visual acuity and function. Ocular dystonias can be caused by first- and second-generation antipsychotics, selective serotonin reuptake inhibitors (SSRIs), selective serotonin and norepinephrine reuptake inhibitors (SNRIs), tricyclic antidepressants (TCAs), and mood stabilizers such as carbamazepine and topiramate. Mydriasis affecting visual acuity results from a variety of psychopharmacological mechanisms. These include alpha-adrenoceptor mediation, noradrenergic and anticholinergic effects, and binding of the 5HT7 receptor in the sphincter of the pupil. TCAs, SNRIs, SSRIs, antipsychotics, topiramate, and stimulants can affect vision that may be already compromised by causing mydriasis (Richa and Yazbek, 2010). One of the most common side effects of psychotropic medications is blurred vision, usually imperceptible to most people except when there is decreased vision. Mild problems with accommodation can significantly impact visual acuity in a visually compromised person. Medications that commonly cause problems with accommodation include anticholinergics, antipsychotics, TCAs, SSRIs, SNRIs and benzodiazepines (Richa and Yazbek, 2010). One medication that should be prescribed with caution in persons with HIV infection and comorbid visual disturbance is topiramate. Topiramate-induced myopia is mediated by interference with ionic concentrations influencing movement of sodium and chloride, uveal tract hypersensitivity, and prostaglandin-mediated swelling of the ciliary body (Richa and Yazbek, 2010). Drugs that have been shown to cause cataractous changes and lenticular opacities include phenothiazines and the widely prescribed quetiapine. Nystagmus, lateral, vertical and rotatory, can be caused or exacerbated by lithium, lamotrigine, and carbamazepine. Lithium is known to cause papilledema, and carbamazepine is associated with the side effect of abnormal color perception. Finally, in addition to causing problems with visual accommodation, the widely prescribed benzodiazepines may also

cause loss of contrast sensitivity and symptomatic exophoria. Decompensated benzodiazepine-induced exophoria may interfere with binocular vision and depth perception (Richa and Yazbek, 2010).

Although the incidence of ocular complications of HIV infection has decreased considerably, it is important for all HIV clinicians to have a working knowledge of ocular disorders, because the long-term sequelae can be devastating. In addition, in the developing world, where the majority of persons with HIV infection reside and effective ART is not readily available, ocular complications will continue to be seen with increasing numbers. Over 60% of all cases of HIV infection occur in sub-Saharan Africa, and 40–80% of HIV-infected persons worldwide do not have access to effective ART in a timely fashion (Shukla et al., 2007). Complex ocular manifestations of HIV continue to be prevalent in underserved areas.

Patients with HIV and compromised immune systems should be instructed to alert their physician to any change in visual acuity and should undergo an annual regular ophthalmological exam performed by an ophthalmologist experienced in the care of persons with HIV. Individuals with persistent CD4 lymphocyte counts below 50 cells/mm^3 should be seen more frequently, and chemoprophylaxis for CMV should be considered in certain selected individuals. Ocular manifestations of HIV are complex and encompass neuropsychiatric multimorbidities. As noted earlier, physicians should have heightened awareness that psychotropic medication side effects include ocular adverse effects compromising vision. Optimal quality of life and improved immune function may result from optimized treatments that preserve vision in persons with HIV.

PULMONARY MANIFESTATIONS OF HIV INFECTION

The spectrum and incidence of AIDS-related pulmonary opportunistic infections have changed significantly over the past 35+ years since the first description of gay men with *Pneumocystis jiroveci* (*P. carinii*) in New York City and San Francisco, in 1981 (Gottlieb et al., 1981; Masur et al., 1981). The effective combination of ART and prophylaxis with agents targeted against opportunistic infections has largely been responsible for the decrease in their incidence. In the Centers for Disease Control and Prevention (CDC)'s HIV Outpatient Study (HOPS), which has followed large numbers of HIV-infected patients since 1993, there was a reduction in overall pulmonary mortality and morbidity between 1994 and 2003. This has been largely attributed to the introduction of ART and prophylaxis (Palella et al., 1998).

Despite medical advances, there are still significant amounts of pulmonary infections seen in inner-city hospitals in undiagnosed or nonadherent HIV-infected individuals. In addition, the epidemic still remains largely untargeted in the developing world. The most commonly associated infections will be reviewed here, with references for more extensive discussion.

PNEUMOCYSTIS JIROVECI PNEUMONIA (PCP)

Pneumocystis jiroveci pneumonia (PCP), formerly named *Pneumocystis carinii* pneumonia, was first reported in 1955 and was uncommon before the AIDS epidemic, with only 194 diagnoses reported between 1967 and 1970 in the United States (Walzer et al., 1974). Its incidence increased dramatically in the 1980s, with estimates suggesting it was the AIDS-defining illness in about two-thirds of patients (Morris et al., 2004). The introduction of ART led to a decline of 21.5% per year between 1996 and 1998 (Kaplan et al., 2000), although it still remains one of the most common AIDS-associated opportunistic infections (Mocroft et al., 2009).

The CD4+ lymphocyte count has been found to be a good predictor for the risk of infection, since 80–90% of infections are associated with a CD4+ count of <200 cells/mm³ (Masur et al., 1989). Patients can present with a wide array of pulmonary symptomatology, from mild dyspnea on exertion to rapidly progressive respiratory failure. In general, patients have fever, nonproductive cough, hypoxemia, elevated serum lactate dehydrogenase (LDH), and bilateral interstitial infiltrates on the chest radiograph (Hoover et al., 1993). In cases where the chest radiograph is normal despite high suspicion of PCP, chest high-resolution computed tomography may reveal patchy areas of ground-glass opacity (Gruden et al., 1997).

The diagnosis of PCP requires the detection of organisms in sputum or bronchoalveolar lavage fluid, as *Pneumocystis* cannot be cultured. Bronchoscopy with bronchoalveolar lavage is currently regarded as the gold standard in PCP diagnosis, and its sensitivity is 95–99% (Ognibene et al., 1984). Early diagnosis may prevent hospitalization and progression to respiratory failure (Benfield et al., 2001; Brenner et al., 1987).

Trimethoprim-sulfamethoxazole (TMP-SMX) is the recommended first-line treatment for PCP in HIV-infected patients. Trimethoprim is a dihydrofolate reductase inhibitor, and sulfamethoxazole is a dihydropteroate synthetase inhibitor, and together, these components and the two medications have synergistic effects. In patients who have demonstrated severe hypersensitivity to sulfa-containing regimens in the past, a second-line regimen is usually used, but desensitization to TMP-SMX under controlled conditions can also be considered in patients who have had a mild reaction in the past (Gluckstein and Ruskin, 1995). Alternative regimens include pentamidine, the combination clindamycin-primaquine, atovaquone, and the combination trimethoprim-dapsone (DHHS Panel on Opportunistic Infections in HIV-infected Adults and Adolescents, 2016). Resistance to sulfonamides has been reported, but there is no clear association with treatment failure (Kazanjian et al., 2000). Corticosteroids should be added for patients with moderate to severe hypoxemia, as they are shown to improve survival and decrease the need for mechanical ventilation in significantly hypoxemic patients (Declaux et al., 1999; Gagnon et al., 1990). Their use is thought to prevent an inflammatory response to dying organisms that can result in a poor outcome (Moon et al., 2011).

PCP is clearly a preventable disease, and the need for prophylaxis for patients with a CD4+ lymphocyte count of <200 cells/µl cannot be overemphasized. As in treatment, the preferred regimen for primary and secondary prophylaxis is TMP-SMX. Alternative regimens include aerosolized pentamidine, dapsone with or without pyrimethamine and leucovorin, and atovaquone (DHHS Panel on Opportunistic Infections in HIV-infected Adults and Adolescents, 2016). A meta-analysis of 35 randomized trials involving 6,583 patients showed that TMP-SMX was superior to both dapsone and pyrimethamine for the prevention of PCP (Ioannidis et al., 1996). PCP prophylaxis can be discontinued in patients receiving ART whose CD4 counts increase from under 200 cells/µl to above 200 cells/µl for at least 3 months (DHHS Panel on Opportunistic Infections in HIV-infected Adults and Adolescents, 2016).

MYCOBACTERIUM TUBERCULOSIS

In the United States, the incidence of acute tuberculosis (TB) has had a dramatic decrease over the past decades. In 2014, there were 9,421 cases reported to the CDC, corresponding to a case rate of 3.02 per 100,000 persons (CDC, 2015). Globally, however, this intracellular pathogen is a leading cause of morbidity and mortality. The World Health Organization (WHO) estimated that in 2015 there were 10.4 million new TB cases worldwide, 1.2 million of which were co-infected with HIV (WHO, 2016).

Co-infection with HIV and TB has been described as a deadly human syndemic (Kwan and Ernst, 2011), as they both seem to affect each other's progression. As HIV causes a depletion of CD4+ cells, the risk of reactivation of latent TB and the susceptibility to new *Mycobacterium tuberculosis* infection increase (Wood et al., 2000). Also, CD4+ cells have been shown to be important in sustaining granuloma organization and therefore in containing the infection (Saunders et al., 2002). On the other hand, there is evidence that TB accelerates the progression of HIV infection and increases mortality (Manas et al., 2004; Whalen et al., 1995). Interestingly, *Mycobacterium tuberculosis* was shown to activate HIV transcription and to enhance viral entry (Collins et al, 2002). ART has been shown to decrease the incidence of TB disease (Badri et al., 2002).

The clinical manifestations of TB in persons with HIV is affected by the degree of immunosuppression. Classical manifestations of pulmonary TB, such as productive cough, night sweats, chest pain, weight loss, and hemoptysis, as well as pulmonary cavity disease on the chest radiograph, can manifest in patients with higher CD4+ counts, whereas lower CD4+ counts are associated with disseminated disease (Leeds et al., 2012; Sterling et al., 2010).

Tuberculosis skin testing (PPD) or interferon-gamma release assays (IGRAs) are recommended on all individuals with HIV infection, regardless of the presence of symptoms of active tuberculosis (DHHS Panel on Opportunistic Infections in HIV-infected Adults and Adolescents, 2016), as they may identify patients with latent tuberculosis infection (LTBI). Treatment of LTBI is shown to reduce the risk of progression to active TB disease, as well as to reduce the transmission of TB (Elzi et al., 2007; Sterling et al., 2006). In HIV-infected patients, PPD is considered positive when the induration is ≥5 mm, and treatment is indicated after active TB disease has been excluded. Isoniazid for 9 months is the therapy of choice, supplemented with pyridoxine to prevent peripheral neuropathy. Of note, CD4 counts under 200 cells/mm³ may be associated with a negative PPD, and for this reason it is recommended that the PPD be repeated when CD4+ counts are above that threshold (DHHS Panel on Opportunistic Infections in HIV-Infected Adults and Adolescents, 2016).

Drug-susceptible active TB treatment includes four drugs—isoniazid, rifampin, pyrazinamide, and ethambutol. It is generally recommended that treatment last 6 months, and for the initial 2 months all four agents should be included. Ethambutol can be discontinued if the organism is shown to be sensitive to the other three agents. Pyrazinamide may be discontinued after 2 months, and isoniazid and rifampin are continued for the final 4 months. In general, the response to therapy is similar in both HIV-infected and HIV-negative individuals (DHHS Panel on Opportunistic Infections in HIV-infected Adults and Adolescents, 2016).

The initiation of ART in patients with TB may induce a paradoxical worsening of symptomatology known as immune reconstitution inflammatory syndrome (IRIS) (Breton et al., 2004). This is thought to result from restoration of immune responses. Treatment should not be interrupted, and steroids can be added, as they have been shown to improve symptoms (Meintjes et al., 2010). Furthermore, significant drug interactions warrant caution during the simultaneous treatment of TB and HIV infection, as rifampin is a potent CYP3A4 inducer and may reduce the plasma concentration of several antiretrovirals, particularly protease inhibitors (CDC, 2013).

OTHER HIV-RELATED RESPIRATORY ILLNESSES

Upper and lower respiratory tract infections are common in persons with HIV (Wallace et al., 1997). In particular, bacterial pneumonia has been reported to be more frequent within this population (Hirschtick et al., 1995). Not surprisingly, in 2002, the CDC added recurrent pneumonia, defined as two or more episodes within a 1-year period, to the list of AIDS-defining conditions. Its incidence is estimated to range from 5.5 to 8.5 cases per 100 person-years (Hirschtick et al., 1995; Kohli et al., 2006), and it increases with lower CD4+ cells, although it can occur throughout the entire course of HIV infection (Gordin et al., 2008; Hirschtick et al., 1995). Risks for bacterial pneumonia include smoking (Gordin et al., 2008), older age, intravenous drug use, and a history of recurrent bacterial pneumonia (Pett et al., 2011).

As in the general population, the most frequent cause of bacterial pneumonia in HIV-infected patients is *Streptococcus pneumoniae* (Boyton, 2005), although *Haemophilus influenzae* and *Staphylococcus aureus* can also be associated. In persons with HIV infection, *Streptococcus pneumoniae* seems to be associated with increased incidence of bacteremia and invasive disease (Kyaw et al., 2005; Osmond et al., 1999), and vaccination is recommended for all HIV-infected adults

(DHHS Panel on Opportunistic Infections in HIV-infected Adults and Adolescents, 2016).

Other causes of opportunistic pulmonary infection include *Mycobacterium tuberculosis*, *Cryptococcus neoformans*, and *Toxoplasma gondii*. Of note, in advanced AIDS, disseminated endemic fungal diseases with pneumonia, such as histoplasmosis and coccidioidomycosis; disseminated viral infections, such as CMV; and disseminated *Mycobacterium avium* complex (MAC) infection with pneumonia need to be considered (Boyton, 2005).

HIV-related pulmonary arterial hypertension that manifests initially with progressive dyspnea and, as the disease progresses, with pedal edema, fatigue, and syncope may also occur (Almodovar et al., 2011). The prevalence, estimated at 0.5% (Sitbon et al., 2008), is higher in HIV-infected patients than in the general population (Opravil and Sereni, 2008). Its pathogenesis is not well understood but may include a direct effect from HIV proteins, including nef and gp120 (Almodovar et al., 2012; Ehrenreich et al., 1993).

Kaposi sarcoma (KS) is a low-grade vascular tumor associated with human herpesvirus 8 (HHV-8) (Radu and Pantanowitz, 2013). Isolated pulmonary involvement can occur, but it is most often found in combination with mucocutaneous disease (Huang et al., 1996). The clinical manifestations depend on Kaposi sarcoma location and may include dyspnea, cough, chest pain, and hemoptyses (Mitchell et al., 1992).

DERMATOLOGICAL DISORDERS ASSOCIATED WITH HIV INFECTION

Several dermatological conditions have been associated with HIV infection. In fact, more than 90% of HIV-infected individuals will have a dermatological complaint at some time in the course of their illness (Coldiron and Bergstresser, 1989). Disorders of the skin and mucous membranes were described in the first reported cases of AIDS (Friedman-Kien et al., 1982). As with other HIV-associated conditions, dermatological manifestations tend to worsen as the degree of immunosuppression increases, due to dysregulation of cell-mediated immunity.

Cutaneous disorders in persons with HIV can be systematized in two groups, depending on their etiology: infectious or non-infectious. Infectious disorders can be viral, bacterial, fungal, and parasitic; non-infectious disorders consist of a heterogenic group that include, among others, eosinophilic folliculitis, seborrheic dermatitis, and adverse cutaneous drug reactions.

INFECTIOUS CUTANEOUS DISORDERS

Viral Infections

Acute HIV infection commonly leads to a transient illness that classically includes a nonpruritic macular or maculopapular rash. It involves the face and trunk in 40–80% of patients (Lapins et al., 1997; Perlmutter et al., 1999) and often manifests following 48–72 hours of fever, persisting for 5–8 days (Lapins et al., 1997).

Oral hairy leukoplakia is found almost exclusively in persons with HIV, and it is caused by Epstein-Barr virus (EBV). It consists of whitish hairy plaques on the lateral border of the tongue and can be differentiated from oral candidiasis because it cannot be removed by scraping. It is associated with a low CD4+ lymphocyte count and generally resolves with ART and immune reconstitution, although topical treatments have also been shown to be useful (Brasileiro et al., 2014; Greenspan et al., 1987; Kreuter and Wieland, 2011).

Kaposi sarcoma is an AIDS-defining illness caused by HHV-8. It is the most common AIDS-associated cancer and manifests as multifocal asymptomatic reddish-purple lesions that may be macular, plaque-like, papular, or nodular (Krown et al., 1997). ART is an essential component of its treatment and may induce complete remission (Dupin et al., 1999).

Several other viruses are known to cause dermatological disease in persons with HIV. *Molluscum contagiosum*, a poxvirus spread by direct contact, manifests with skin-colored umbilicated papules in patients with lower CD4+ counts (Schwartz and Myskowski, 1992; Vora et al., 2015). HSV-2 infection is associated with anogenital disease and has been shown to facilitate the transmission of HIV (Hook et al., 1992; Stamm et al., 1988). Dermatomal disease, caused by varicella zoster virus (VZV), is common in HIV-infected patients at all CD4+ counts and may present with disseminated disease (Buchbinder et al., 1992; Tappero et al., 1995). Lastly, HIV infection is associated with a higher prevalence of human papillomavirus (HPV) infection, and certain HPV types are associated with cervical and anal carcinoma (Muller et al., 2010).

Bacterial Infections

Staphylococcus aureus is the most common cutaneous bacterial pathogen in persons with HIV, This prevalence may be attributed to a high nasal carriage rate, which has been estimated to be twice the rate of HIV-uninfected persons (Tappero et al., 1995). *S. aureus* causes the same dermatological infections seen in immunocompetent individuals, including impetigo and folliculitis, but it may also cause unusual diseases such as botryomycosis, a chronic suppurative infection (Tschachler et al., 1996). *Bartonella henselae*, a Gram-negative bacillus known to cause cat scratch disease, also causes bacillary angiomatosis in patients who have CD4+ counts lower than 100 cells/mm³ (Tappero et al., 1995). It manifests by nodular vascular proliferations of the skin, and either erythromycin or doxycycline can be used for treatment (Plettenberg et al., 2000). *Mycobacterium tuberculosis* and MAC infections can also manifest cutaneously (Rigopoulos et al., 2004; Tappero et al., 1995), and secondary syphilis, which is known to occur with increased frequency in HIV-infected individuals, can appear as a diffuse maculopapular rash involving the palms and soles (Hutchinson et al., 1994).

Fungal Infections

Since cutaneous fungal infections are seen more frequently with compromised immunity, it is not surprising that they would be common in HIV infection. *Candida*, a ubiquitous yeast, causes oral thrush, which is the most common fungal disease in persons with HIV (Samaranayake, 1992). Dermatophytes and, to a lesser degree, *Candida*, infect the skin, hair, and nails (Elewski and Sullivan, 1994). *Cryptococcus neoformans, Coccidioides immitis*, and *Histoplasma capsulatum*'s cutaneous lesions are AIDS-defining illnesses as they commonly indicate disseminated infection (Venkatesan et al., 2005).

Parasitic Infections

Crusted, or Norwegian scabies, is a highly contagious infection caused by *Sarcoptes scabiei* in which the skin may be infected with thousands to millions of mites (Kolar and Rapini, 1991). It is seen more frequently in severely immunocompromised HIV-infected individuals, who may present with disseminated, crusted, or eczematoid lesions (Portu et al., 1996). Given the high rates of treatment failure when an agent is used alone, treatment guidelines recommend combination treatment with a topical scabicide—either benzyl benzoate or permethrin along with oral ivermectin. Of note, lindane should not be used because of the risk of neurotoxicity with repeated applications (Workowski et al., 2015).

NON-INFECTIOUS CUTANEOUS DISORDERS

Seborrheic dermatitis is a common cutaneous manifestation associated with HIV infection and affects up to 83% of persons with HIV at some point during their illness (de Moraes et al., 2007). It tends to be localized to the face or scalp and manifests as erythematous macules with white or yellow scaling. It may occur at any stage of HIV infection, but it can be more severe and recalcitrant to treatment as HIV infection progresses. Topical steroids, antifungal agents, tacrolimus, and pimecrolimus are all options in treatment (de Moraes et al., 2007; Tschachler et al., 1996).

Eosinophilic folliculitis is a chronic dermatosis associated with severe pruritus, and it is usually seen with advanced HIV disease (Milazzo et al., 1999). It is thought to occur secondary to a shift toward Th2 cells with subsequent IgE production and eosinophilia (Duvic, 1995). Initiation of antiretrovirals may improve the condition (Costner and Cockerell, 1998).

Lastly, no discussion of cutaneous manifestations of HIV disease would be complete without a description of cutaneous drug eruptions. HIV-infected individuals seem to be at increased risk for adverse drug reactions, and this risk increases with advancing immunosuppression (Coopman et al., 1993). TMP-SMX, the agent of choice to treat *Pneumocystis jiroveci* pneumonia, has been shown in its intravenous form to cause an erythematous rash that is usually associated with fever. In general, this reaction occurs 10 to 14 days after starting therapy (Roudier et al., 1994). The oral preparation is also associated with increased skin reactions that may be due to a toxic drug metabolite. If this drug is gradually initiated into the patient's regimen, there is an approximate 50% decrease in adverse reaction (Para et al., 2000). Although rare, a mild rash can progress to life-threatening Stevens-Johnson syndrome and toxic epidermal necrolysis. These reactions are seen more commonly with sulfonamides (Roujeau et al., 1995).

The non-nucleoside reverse transcriptase inhibitors (NNRTIs) nevirapine, delavirdine, and efavirenz have been associated with cutaneous hypersensitivity reactions. Nevirapine in particular may cause a rash in 32–48% of the patients, and higher CD4 counts are a well-documented risk factor (Kiertiburanakul et al., 1998). Abacavir (ABC), a nucleoside analogue reverse transcriptase inhibitor, causes a hypersensitivity reaction in 5% of patients that usually occurs within 10 days of treatment. It manifests as an evolving maculopapular rash that may be associated with constitutional symptoms such as fever, malaise, arthralgias, and myalgias (Carrasco et al., 2000). Since testing for the HLA allele HLA-B*5701 has a 100% negative predictive value for ABC hypersensitivity, current guidelines recommended screening for HLA-B*5701 before starting an ABC-containing regimen, and HLA-B*5701-positive patients should not be prescribed this antiretroviral drug (DHHS Panel on Antiretroviral Guidelines for Adults and Adolescents, 2016).

GASTROINTESTINAL MANIFESTATIONS OF HIV INFECTION

Gastrointestinal illness remains common among persons with HIV in the era of effective ART and may be caused by a number of factors, including HIV disease itself, HIV treatment, or other conditions commonly comorbid with HIV. In addition to this scope of etiological considerations, gastrointestinal symptoms in HIV disease may present throughout the gastrointestinal system, including anywhere along the alimentary canal or within the hepatobiliary system.

ESOPHAGITIS

Candida albicans remains the most common cause of esophagitis in patients with AIDS, even as its incidence has been shown to be reduced by effective ART (Mocroft et al., 2005). Although the majority of patients with *Candida* esophagitis have oral candida or thrush, the absence of thrush does not preclude the diagnosis (Wilcox et al., 1995). Empiric therapy with fluconazole is indicated in patients with esophageal complaints and thrush, reserving endoscopy for treatment failures (Wilcox et al., 1996). Other infectious causes of esophagitis in AIDS are CMV, HSV, and idiopathic esophageal ulceration (IEU) (Wilcox, 1992). Unlike *Candida* esophagitis, odynophagia is a more common complaint than dysphagia in IEU (Raufman, 1988). HIV-associated IEU can be seen at the time of acute seroconversion, but, like CMV, it is more commonly seen with a CD4 lymphocyte count of fewer than 100 cells/mm^3 (Kotler et al., 1992). Less common infections reported to cause esophagitis in patients with AIDS are *Mycobacterium avium* intracellulare (MAI), *Bartonella henselae, Cryptosporidium, Histoplasma capsulatum*, EBV, and HPV (Monkemuller and Wilcox, 1999). HIV-related malignancies, such as, non-Hodgkin lymphoma and Kaposi sarcoma, and gastroesophageal reflux disease also need to be considered when a patient presents with esophageal symptoms.

DIARRHEA

Although implementation of effective ART reduces the incidence of infectious diarrhea in areas where it is available (Ledergerber et al., 1999), diarrhea remains a significant clinical problem among persons with HIV. The etiology of diarrhea is often multifactorial. A wide array of viruses, bacteria, fungi, and parasites have been implicated in the etiology of diarrhea (Smith et al., 1992). The degree of immunodeficiency makes certain pathogens and refractory disease more likely. Prior to effective ART and chemoprophylaxis, infections such as CMV, *Cryptosporidium, Microsporidia*, and disseminated MAI were more commonly seen and were associated with severe recalcitrant disease (Asmuth et al., 1994; Connolly et al., 1988; Gordin et al., 1997). In addition, unusual presentations with bacteremia of the usual pathogens that cause diarrhea in the normal host, such as *Salmonella, Campylobacter*, and *Shigella*, may be seen (Molina et al., 1995; Smith et al., 1985). *Clostridium difficile*–associated diarrhea has also been shown to be more frequent in patients with AIDS, which most likely reflects the increased use of antimicrobial agents and stays in hospital (Hutin et al., 1993). Certain antiretroviral agents are commonly associated with diarrhea, specifically nelfinavir, lopinavir/ritonavir, saquinavir, and didanosine (buffered formulation). More often than not, despite extensive workups with multiple stool cultures and repeated endoscopies with multiple tissue biopsies, an etiological agent is not isolated. In this clinical scenario, empiric therapy with antimicrobial and antiparasitic agents is indicated. When the diarrhea is unremitting, antidiarrheal agents should be considered to prevent dehydration.

A thorough history, including recent travel, should be elicited from all patients with HIV who present with diarrhea. The patient's symptoms may help in localizing the area of bowel most affected. Symptoms of crampy abdominal pain with bloating and voluminous, watery diarrhea suggest small bowel enteritis with pathogens such as *Cryptosporidium* and *Giardia*. Proctitis may indicate CMV or HSV infection.

Patients with HIV disease may also complain of abdominal pain, hematemesis, hematochezia, jaundice, and anorectal pain. The possible etiologies are numerous, including both opportunistic and non-opportunistic disorders, malignancies, and drug-related toxicities. A detailed history and physical exam with appropriate workup will usually reveal the cause of the disorder.

HEPATOBILIARY DISEASE

Hepatic disease in HIV infection is a significant cause of morbidity and mortality. Most patients with AIDS will have some evidence of liver dysfunction. A wide array of opportunistic infections including MAI, CMV, HSV, *Mycobacterium* tuberculosis, *Bartonella henselae, Pneumocystis*, disseminated fungal disease, as well as

HIV-associated malignancies, such as Kaposi sarcoma and non-Hodgkin lymphoma, have all been shown to involve the liver (Bonacini, 1992; Perkocha et al., 1990). Opportunistic hepatobiliary conditions tend to occur later in the course of HIV infection, reflecting increasing immunosuppression (Cappell, 1991). Hepatotoxicity can also be due to ART, idiosyncratic or immunoallergic mechanisms, or direct cytotoxicity due to underlying liver disease.

Chronic co-infection with hepatitis B virus (HBV) is more common with HIV seropositivity. Persons with HIV demonstrate elevated rates of chronic HBV infection compared to HIV-negative individuals. While only 5% of HIV-negative individuals with acute hepatitis B will go on to develop chronic infection, 50% or more of HIV-infected individuals will have evidence of chronic HBV replication. In addition, HIV-co-infection increases the risk of chronic active hepatitis B progressing to cirrhosis and the development of hepatocellular carcinoma. Furthermore, progressive HIV-related immunosuppression in patients who are immune to HBV, as evidenced by hepatitis B surface antibody positivity, may lead to loss of positive hepatitis B antibody status, with concomitant return to hepatitis B surface-antigen positivity and antigenemia (Lazizi et al., 1988). There is no clear evidence regarding whether HBV has a negative effect on HIV progression (Phung et al., 2014).

Several HIV antiretroviral agents (epivir, emtrivir, tenofovir) have been shown to be effective in decreasing the HBV DNA in the blood, with eventual development of hepatitis B surface antibody. Initiating HIV ART in patients with chronic HBV may be associated with flares of hepatitis B due to immunoreconstitution syndrome. There is an increase in ART-related hepatotoxicity in patients with chronic hepatitis B (Ogedegbe and Sulkowski, 2003).

Like hepatitis B, hepatitis C virus (HCV) infections are more prevalent among persons with HIV infection than in the general population. HCV is more frequently associated with chronic infection than hepatitis B, since only approximately 15% of individuals clear virus from the blood after acute hepatitis C infection (Alter et al., 1992). Among hepatitis C–infected patients, co-infection with HIV is associated with an increased rate of the development of cirrhosis and hepatocellular carcinoma; however, hepatitis C does not appear to accelerate HIV progression (Sulkowski et al., 2002). Among patients with hepatitis C, caution must be used in selecting HIV antiretroviral agents because of the risk of hepatotoxicity. Liver biopsy should be strongly considered to determine the degree of fibrosis and to aid in selection of patients for hepatitis C therapy (Saadeh et al., 2001).

In recent years, the shift from pegylated interferon/ribavirin-based HCV treatment regimens to direct-acting antiretrovirals (DAA) has had important implications for the treatment of HIV-HCV co-infected individuals. Prior pegylated interferon/ribavirin treatment regimens lasted for 48 weeks and were often characterized by interferon-related neuropsychiatric side effects. The hepatitis C virological response to these regimens differed significantly between HCV mono-infected and HIV-HCV co-infected patients, with consequently different guidelines for treating HCV in

each of these groups (AASLD-IDSA Guidance Panel, 2015). In contrast, DAA regimens are prescribed for only 12 weeks and lack the neuropsychiatric toxicity seen with interferon-based regimens (Sockalingam et al., 2013). Additionally, because the virological response of mono-infected and co-infected patients to DAA is virtually indistinguishable, practice guidelines now recommend the same hepatitis C treatment algorithms for both groups (AASLD-IDSA Guidance Panel, 2015). As with pre-DAA regimens, HCV genotyping is still recommended to guide choice of DAA regimen. Depending on genotype, commonly used regimens include ledipasvir/sofosbuvir, simeprevir/sofosbuvir, daclatasvir/sofosbuvir, ombitasvir/paritaprevir/ritonavir plus dasabuvir, and a number of other combinations. In patients who are simultaneously treated with antiretrovirals and with DAA, it is essential to be aware of potential drug interactions between both groups of medications and to make decisions regarding choice of therapies accordingly.

In spite DAA's clear clinical advantages, their substantial expense limits their availability both within and outside the United States, with the result that there remain many settings where economics require that interferon-based regimens are offered as first-line treatment. The neuropsychiatric effects of interferon are of major concern and are discussed in further detail in Chapters 42 and 43.

All co-infected patients should limit alcohol and hepatotoxic agents. The HAV and HBV vaccine should be offered to all seronegative patients. Another gastrointestinal syndrome, AIDS cholangiopathy, has been seen largely in patients with advanced disease. Patients present with right upper quadrant pain, jaundice, and hepatomegaly. The alkaline phosphatase level in the blood is often quite elevated. All clinical syndromes can be diagnosed by endoscopic retrograde cholangiopancreatography (ERCP). Although there is no clear causal relationship, *Cryptosporidium, Microsporidia*, CMV, and *Cyclospora* have all been associated. If possible, the offending pathogens should be treated, although often the treatment requires biliary stenting. In general, the prognosis is poor (Ko et al., 2003).

HEMATOLOGICAL MANIFESTATIONS OF HIV INFECTION

Hematological disorders have long been associated with HIV infection. These disorders are widely recognized and are the cause of significant morbidity and mortality. In fact, anemia, the most commonly associated abnormality, has been shown to have a negative effect on survival (Moore et al., 1998). The most common cause of anemia is HIV infection of marrow progenitor cells and increasing levels of tumor necrosis factor leading to ineffective erythropoiesis (Zhang et al., 1995). In general, the incidence of anemia has a direct correlation with the degree of immunosuppression, and improvement is generally seen with immune recovery secondary to effective ART (Huang et al., 2000). Some other causes of anemia in HIV infection are infiltration of the bone marrow by tumor or opportunistic infections.

Infections more commonly associated with anemia are MAC, tuberculosis, CMV, and histoplasmosis. The most frequently associated tumors are lymphomas and Kaposi sarcoma (Coyle, 1997). Parvovirus B 19 has been reported to selectively infect erythroid precursors leading to severe anemia (Abkowitz et al., 1997).

Nutritional deficiencies need also to be considered. Vitamin B12 deficiency has been reported to occur in up to 20% of HIV-infected patients (Evans and Scadden, 2000). Iron deficiency anemia is usually associated with blood loss from the gastrointestinal tract. In addition, drug-induced marrow suppression, such as that seen with the nucleoside analogue reverse transcriptase inhibitor zidovudine (AZT), always needs to be considered. Management consists of treatment of the underlying cause with the appropriate agents and, when applicable, dose adjustment of drug therapy. Current HIV treatment guidelines that emphasize the use of newer and more tolerable antiretroviral drugs reduce drug toxicity (DHHS Panel on Antiretroviral Guidelines, 2016).

Erythropoietin can be of benefit in many patients with refractory HIV-associated anemia. Neutropenia is seen in HIV infection and is most often due to chronic infection, bone marrow failure, or drug toxicity (Sloand, 2005). Thrombocytopenia can be seen at any stage of HIV infection (Sullivan et al., 1997). Although HIV and drug-related toxicity can directly affect platelet production, immune destruction of platelets is the most common cause (ITP). Treatment consists of effective ART and the removal of any causative agent. The prevalence of HIV-associated ITP has decreased with combined antiretrovirals and HIV viral suppression (Vannappagari et al, 2011). ITP may also require steroids, intravenous gamma globulin, anti-RhD, and, at times, splenectomy (Ambler et al., 2012; Oksenhendler et al., 1993).

Thrombotic thrombocytopenic purpura has been reported to occur in HIV infection, but the association is less clear. Patients present with hemolytic anemia, thrombocytopenia, renal insufficiency, fever, and change in mental status. The prognosis is usually poor. The standard treatment is plasmaphoresis/plasma exchange (Sloand, 2005). Initiation of antiretrovirals with plasma exchange has been linked to improved outcomes (Hart et al., 2011). Rituximab has also been used in cases of patients with HIV and TTP failing plasma exchange treatment (Evans et al., 2010).

HIV AND MALIGNANCIES

It is a well-known fact that defects in cell-mediated immunity have been associated with the development of certain tumors. This has been reported in congenital immunodeficiency disorders, transplant recipients on chronic immunosuppressive medication, and in patients with autoimmune disorders (Frizzera et al., 1980; Penn, 1975). Hence it was no surprise that there would be such an association with HIV infection. The initial reports of Kaposi sarcoma, a rare vascular tumor, and *Pneumocystis carinii* pneumonia in gay men in San Francisco and New York City in 1981 initiated the beginning of what is now known as the AIDS epidemic (Friedman-Kien et al., 1982). Subsequently, it was noted that there were increasing reports of non-Hodgkin lymphoma and, later, invasive cervical carcinoma in this population, placing these diagnoses in the category of AIDS-defining illnesses (CDC, 1985). In addition, over the years of the epidemic there have been other associated malignancies that are not considered AIDS defining but have been reported with some increased frequency, such as Hodgkin disease, lung cancer, anogenital carcinomas, testicular cancers, gastric cancers, hepatomas, and multiple myeloma (Remick, 1996). Other co-factors may influence the development of these tumors, including tobacco, alcohol, and co-infection with hepatitis B, hepatitis C, and HPV, where the association with HIV and immunosuppression is less clear.

With the development of ART, the incidence of Kaposi sarcoma has had such a significant decline that in developed countries it is a rare diagnosis (Hengge et al., 2002). Although less dramatic, the incidence of non-Hodgkin lymphoma has also shown a decrease since the development of effective ART (Grulich and Vajdic, 2005; Wood and Harrington, 2005). However, non-AIDS-defining cancers have become leading non-AIDS cause of death among persons with HIV. In a large Italian study, in 2016, 10.3% of deceased individuals with AIDS had non-AIDS-defining conditions as the cause of death on their death certificate. Lung and liver cancers figured prominently in these conditions. A 7.3-fold excess mortality was observed for all non-AIDS-defining cancers in persons with AIDS. Significant standardized mortality ratios were noted for anal, Hodgkin lymphoma, uterine, liver, melanoma, lung, head and neck, leukemia, and colorectal malignancies (Zucchetto et al., 2016).

Given the advancing age of persons with HIV in the United States, it should be remembered that both persons with HIV and older adults share a higher cancer risk. One study examining Medicare claims used a 5% sample of U.S. Medicare enrollees and all cancer cases aged at least 65. Of the 5% sample, 0.08% had an HIV diagnosis, and over 5 years, 10.1% of HIV-infected elderly individuals developed cancer. The most common cancers affecting this population included lung, prostate, colorectal, and non-Hodgkin lymphoma. Risk of developing all of these cancers increases heavily as one ages, even in non-HIV samples. HIV was strongly associated with development of Kaposi sarcoma, anal cancer, and Hodgkin lymphoma. HIV was more weakly associated with liver, non-Hodgkin lymphoma, and lung cancers (Yanik et al., 2016).

KAPOSI SARCOMA

Kaposi first described Kaposi sarcoma in 1812. Classic Kaposi sarcoma is usually seen in men of Mediterranean or Eastern European ancestry. It is normally localized to the skin of the lower extremity and it has a chronic, indolent course. In rare cases, it disseminates to other organs. In HIV infection Kaposi sarcoma has a varied course. It can be localized to the skin, but often has a progressively invasive course, with visceral dissemination being not unusual. With cutaneous involvement it can produce significant disfigurement. Visceral involvement can have associated odynophagia, hypoxia and hemoptysis, gastrointestinal bleeding, and sepsis (Schwartz, 2004).

As mentioned previously, although Kaposi sarcoma still causes a significant amount of morbidity and even mortality in the developing world, the incidence of Kaposi sarcoma in the United States has been dramatically reduced since the introduction of potent ART (Hengge et al., 2002). The Multi-Centered AIDS Cohort Study (MACS) showed a clear decline in the incidence of Kaposi sarcoma in 1995–1997, which paralleled the introduction of ART (Jacobson et al., 1999).

The consensus is that this decline in incidence is most likely due to improved immunity, which in turn influences the host response to the causative agent, HHV-8. HHV-8 has been found in all types of Kaposi sarcoma, including classic, African and endemic, transplant-associated, and AIDS-related Kaposi sarcoma (Chang et al., 1994). In addition to ART there are varied treatment options available, including intralesional chemotherapy, radiation therapy, laser therapy, and systemic chemotherapy (Schwartz, 2004). Treatment needs to be individualized according to the severity of the disease and is often associated with drug toxicities from the complexity of interactions between ART and chemotherapy. Treatment is optimally accomplished in conjunction with an oncologist who has had experience in treating HIV-infected individuals.

LYMPHOMAS

Among HIV-infected individuals, the first cases of non-Hodgkin lymphoma began to be reported in gay men in 1982. With increasing reports it soon became apparent that there was an association (Ziegler et al., 1984). We now know that for patients with an AIDS diagnosis, the risk of developing lymphoma is greater than 200 times that of the general population (Beral et al., 1991; Rabkin et al., 1991). Risk of non-Hodgkin lymphoma in people with HIV infection is independently predicted by the degree and duration of immunodeficiency and chronic B-cell stimulation (Grulich et al., 2001). The etiology is poorly understood, but it is most likely multifactorial. Epstein-Barr virus, HHV-8, and immune dysregulation all may play a role in HIV-associated non-Hodgkin lymphoma (Krause, 2005). Similar to Kaposi sarcoma in HIV disease, the lymphomas can present in various stages (Biggar, 2001).

HIV-associated lymphomas typically are more aggressive than lymphomas in immunocompetent individuals and more often present with advanced-stage, bulky disease with high tumor burden and involve extranodal sites. Historically, clinical outcome was worse than in similar aggressive lymphomas in the general population, but following introduction of effective ART, in 1996, clinical outcomes improved and risk has decreased (Grogg et al., 2007). Historically, the relative risk of non-Hodgkin lymphoma was increased 60- to 200-fold in HIV-infected patients when compared with the general population. This risk increased even further when examining the risk for certain subtypes of lymphoma, such as central nervous system (CNS) lymphoma, and risk may have been up to 1,000 times greater during the AIDS pandemic (Grogg et al., 2007).

Initial studies were inconsistent in showing a trend toward decreased incidence and improved survival; later studies have been more consistently favorable on both variables, and risk reduction appears to correlate with improved CD4 cell counts that result from effective HIV therapy. ART has also had other effects on HIV-related lymphomas, in that immunoblastic diffuse large B-cell lymphomas (DLBCLs) decreased by approximately 50%, and primary CNS lymphomas decreased by over a third. Conversely, the proportion of centroblastic DLBCLs approximately doubled following introduction of ART, and the proportion of Burkitt lymphoma also approximately doubled. These changes correlate with the degree of improved rates of immunosuppression following the use of ART. Burkitt lymphoma or centroblastic DLBCL appear to occur in patients with normal or slightly diminished CD4 counts. Primary effusion lymphoma, immunoblastic DLBCL, and primary CNS lymphoma present more often in the context of marked immunodeficiency (Grogg et al., 2007).

Although Hodgkin disease is not an AIDS-defining illness, it has been reported with increased frequency in HIV. The risk for an individual with HIV infection of developing Hodgkin disease is 8–10 times higher than that of the general population (Grogg et al., 2007; Hessol et al., 1992). HIV/AIDS-associated Hodgkin lymphoma historically tended to have a more aggressive histological cell type with widely disseminated extranodal disease (Levine, 1996). Recent data suggest a slight increase in the risk of Hodgkin lymphoma among persons with HIV, with a shift from mixed cellularity or lymphocyte-depleted subtypes to more common nodular sclerosis (improved prognosis) subtype following the advent of widespread ART (Grogg et al., 2007).

In any case, prior to use of ART, the prognosis for HIV-related lymphomas was bleak; the median survival despite chemotherapy was 5–8 months (Bower, 2001). Since that time, there has been a dramatic improvement in outcomes. Because of the complexity of treatment, a team approach is warranted.

CERVICAL CARCINOMA AND ANAL CARCINOMA

In 1993, invasive cervical carcinoma was added to the case definition of AIDS, as there were early reports of aggressive cervical carcinoma with a mean survival of 10 months in a group of HIV-infected women (Maiman et al., 1990). Despite these reports, invasive cervical carcinoma in AIDS remains a rare diagnosis. HPV infection, which is sexually transmitted, is a risk factor for cervical, anal, and head and neck–associated carcinomas. HIV infection has clearly been shown to increase the risk for the development of HPV-associated neoplasia. This association can be seen throughout the anogenital tract, including cervix, anus, penis, vulva, and skin (Chaturvedi et al., 2009).

In HIV-infected men who have sex with men the incidence of anal squamous cell carcinoma is rising (Chaturvedi et al., 2009; Palefsky et al., 1998). The rising incidence of anal cancer indicates that increased survival may be associated with increased risk of other HPV-associated malignancies. HPV is prevalent in at-risk populations. In one study, 93% of HIV-positive and 61% of HIV-negative men who have sex with men had anal HPV infection. The more oncogenic genotypes (HPV-16 and HPV-18) were more commonly associated with HIV infection (Pfister, 1996). High-grade dysplasia is also more frequent in HIV-positive men with low CD4 counts. Therefore, it is important for clinicians to screen for dysplasia with periodic anal Papanicolaou smears. It is unclear what impact potent ART will have on the long-term incidence of anogenital carcinoma, but it appears that patients with dysplasia on therapy do better (Palefsky et al., 2001).

Another study demonstrated that among persons with AIDS, there was a statically significant elevated risk of all HPV-associated in situ cancers, including cervical, anal, and oropharyngeal malignancies. Invasive cancers demonstrated statistically significant increases as well in all types of HPV-associated malignancies. During 1996–2004, low CD4 counts were associated with increased risk of invasive anal cancer among men and non-statistically but significantly increased risk of in situ vulvar or vaginal cancer or invasive cervical cancer. Currently, there is a highly effective HPV vaccine available as a three-injection regimen. All females and males are recommended to receive the vaccination through age 26 (Guardisil 9 package insert, 2016), and use of this vaccine is promising in the reduction of both genital warts and HPV-associated malignancies.

OTHER CANCERS

There have been isolated reports of the increase of certain other cancers in persons with HIV infection, but these are complex associations, where other risk factors may play a more significant role than HIV infection itself. The U.S. National Cancer Institute published data in 2003 that these cancers are not more common in people with HIV who are living longer in developed countries with access to HIV medication, despite studies reporting opposite findings (Mbulaiteye et al., 2003). In the HIV Outpatient Study (HOPS), reported in 2004, four cancers were seen with increasing frequency among individuals with HIV compared to that of the general population: anorectal cancer, Hodgkin disease, melanoma, and lung cancer. The study adjusted for age, race, smoking, and gender. The researchers reported that individuals who did develop cancer had a lower nadir CD4 (Patel et al., 2008). Despite the debate, patients with HIV infection should be screened regularly for the development of any neoplastic process. In addition, at each encounter every HIV clinician should emphasize the importance of lifestyle modifications that may alter the development of cancer.

HIV AND AGING

Ten years ago, it was almost inconceivable that the issue of aging with HIV infection would emerge as an important concern. But it has now become clear that effective ART can suppress virus replication for many years in most people who with access to HIV care and ART, and the opportunistic diseases that were once the primary causes of illness have largely evanesced everywhere treatment is available. Morbidity and mortality from HIV infection have plummeted, and the survival of HIV-positive individuals is edging ever closer to that of HIV-negative people (Antiretroviral Therapy Cohort Collaboration, 2009; Lohse et al., 2007). With this scenario, attention has increasingly turned to health problems that are associated with aging in the general population. Examples include cardiovascular, kidney, and liver disease; bone loss and increased fracture risk; frailty; cognitive impairment; and cancer. Evidence is accumulating that the risk of these conditions is elevated in HIV-positive individuals and, in some cases, they may be occurring at a younger age, on average, than is typically observed among comparable HIV-negative populations (Effros et al., 2008). As the proportion of older persons living with HIV grows, there is an urgent need to understand how a broad array of factors may be contributing to this phenomenon; these factors include inflammation, immune dysregulation, polypharmacy, long-term drug toxicities, and co-infections and comorbidities that are disproportionately prevalent among people with HIV.

A critical research question is whether HIV is accelerating aging itself through pathways and mechanisms common to the aging process, or, alternatively, HIV may simply be an additional risk factor for a wide number of chronic conditions, thus accentuating the prevalence of disease at every age (High et al., 2012; Pathai et al., 2014). For the immune system, there appears to be a pattern of accelerated aging or accelerated immune senescence. However, many specific end-organ diseases appear to be accentuated rather than accelerated.

Many of the T-cell abnormalities associated with aging are similar to those observed in untreated HIV infection (Desai and Landay 2010). Untreated HIV-infected adults and older adults often exhibit low CD4/CD8 ratios; low naïve/memory ratios, reduced T-cell repertoire, reduced responsiveness to vaccines, and an expansion of CD28-negative cells (van Baarle et al., 2005). Many of the T-cell characteristics associated with immunosenescence, including thymic dysfunction, T-cell activation, and a reduced T-cell regenerative potential, are more common among individuals who fail to exhibit robust CD4 cell gains during therapy than among individuals who achieve a normal CD4 cell count (Molina-Pinelo et al., 2009; Robbins et al. 2009). Because a low CD4 cell count on combination ART is a consistent proximal predictor of non-AIDS morbidity (Phillips et al., 2008), these observations collectively suggest that HIV-associated immunosenescence contributes to persistent immunodeficiency and the early onset of age-associated diseases. The clinical significance of immunosenescence has been often explored using vaccine responsiveness as the outcome. Effective combination ART improves vaccine responsiveness, but residual defects remain, particularly if therapy is initiated late in the disease course (Lange et al., 2003).

Untreated HIV infection is associated with persistently high levels of inflammation, immune activation, and hypercoagulability markers (Neuhaus et al., 2010). Most if not all of these markers decline with combination ART, which suggests that active HIV replication is either directly or indirectly responsible for their increase, but they do not reach normal levels despite sustained suppression of HIV replication. The persistent inflammation during combination ART is probably due to different factors, including ongoing HIV production from latently infected cells, low-level replication below the threshold of detectability, bacterial translocation across the damaged gut mucosa, loss of T-regulatory cells and other immunoregulatory cells, and the irreversible fibrosis of the thymus and lymphoid tissue. The association between HIV infection and inflammation shares many similarities with the association between advanced age and inflammation. Indeed, many of the markers now being studied in HIV disease were first validated in cohorts of older persons (Shlipak et al., 2003; Walston et al., 2002), and many of the mechanisms thought to be causally associated with inflammation in HIV infection are also thought to be causally associated with the inflammation of aging (Appay and Sauce, 2008).

HIV infection and combination ART may cause mitochondrial toxicity and body fat changes that are usually associated with insulin resistance (Grunfeld et al., 2007). HIV infection impedes the ability to regenerate T cells, promotes hematopoietic stem cells exhaustion, and leads to an irreversible loss of thymic function. Chronic viral infection such as herpes and hepatitis viruses are more common in people with HIV infection and they contribute to persistent inflammation and immune activation. All of these factors are interrelated and potentiate each other. They are underlying factors in the pathogenesis of many age-associated diseases (Deng et al., 2004) and contribute to the aging syndrome now being observed in HIV-infected persons.

A careful integration of the basic biology of aging with that of HIV infection may lead to novel insights into the larger questions of why people age and why current combination ART fails to restore health. An integration of the two disciplines could provide the rationale for development of novel therapeutics. Approved drugs that have an anti-inflammatory effect and are often used in older adults (including aspirin, omega-3 fatty acids, vitamin D, and statins) are being studied as adjunctive therapy to combination ART in HIV-infected patients, but no conclusive recommendations can be made at present (Deeks, 2011). As a general recommendation, persons with HIV infection should consider the lifestyle factors that are now known or expected to maximize health once a person reaches old age, including daily exercise, a healthy diet, maintaining low blood pressure and cholesterol, and avoiding substance abuse and excess fat gain, besides maintaining persistent suppression of HIV replication with nontoxic combination ART.

CONCLUSIONS

The intent of this chapter is to provide the reader with a working knowledge of the complexities associated with the medical multimorbidities associated with HIV infection. When persons with HIV and AIDS have access to medical care and treatment with potent antiretroviral therapy and are and adherent to it, they can live longer lives. For persons with HIV and AIDS to live healthier and longer lives, it is also important for clinicians to encourage adherence to a healthy

lifestyle with exercise, safer sex practices, a well-balanced diet, and stress reduction. The avoidance of illicit drug use, excessive alcohol, and tobacco should be emphasized at every encounter.

REFERENCES

AASLD/IDSA HCV Guidance Panel (2015). Hepatitis C guidance: AASLD-IDSA recommendations for testing, managing, and treating adults infected with hepatitis C virus. *Hepatology* 62(3):932–954.

Abkowitz JL, Brown KE, Wood RW, et al. (1997). Clinical relevance of parvovirus B19 as a cause of anemia in patients with human immunodeficiency virus infection. *J Infect Dis* 176(1):269–273.

Almodovar S, Hsue PY, Morelli J, Huang L, Flores SC (2011). Pathogenesis of HIV-associated pulmonary hypertension: potential role of HIV-1 nef. *Proc Am Thorac Soc* 8:308–312.

Almodovar S, Knight R, Allshouse AA, et al. (2012). Human Immunodeficiency Virus nef signature sequences are associated with pulmonary hypertension. *AIDS Res Hum Retroviruses* 28:607–618.

Alter MJ, Margolis HS, Krawczynski K, et al. (1992). The natural history of community acquired hepatitis C in the United States. *N Engl J Med* 327:1899–1905.

Ambler KLS, Vickars LM, Leger CS, et al. (2012). Clinical features, treatment, and outcome of HIV associated immune thrombocytopenia in the HAART era. *Adv Hematol* 2012:910954.

Antiretroviral Therapy Cohort Collaboration (2009). Mortality of HIV-infected patients starting antiretroviral therapy: comparison with the general population in nine industrialized countries. *Int J Epidemiol* 38:1624–1633.

Appay V, Sauce D (2008). Immune activation and inflammation in HIV-1 infection: causes and consequences. *J Pathol* 214:231–241.

Asmuth DM, DeGirolami PC, Federman M, et al. (1994). Clinical features of microsporidiosis in patients with AIDS. *Clin Infect Dis* 18:819–825.

Badri M, Wilson D, Wood R (2002). Effect of highly active antiretroviral therapy on incidence of tuberculosis in South Africa: a cohort study. *Lancet* 359(9323):2059–2064.

Benfield TL, Helweg-Larsen J, Bang D, Junge J, Lundgren JD (2001). Prognostic markers of short-term mortality in AIDS-associated *Pneumocystis carinii* pneumonia. *Chest* 119:844–851.

Beral V, Peterman T, Berkalman R, et al. (1991). AIDS associated non-Hodgkin's lymphoma. *Lancet* 337:805–809.

Biggar RJ (2001). AIDS related cancers in the era of highly active antiretroviral therapy. *Oncology* 15:439–444.

Bonacini M (1992). Hepatobiliary complications in patients with human immunodeficiency virus infection. *Am J Med* 92(4):404–411.

Boyton RJ (2005). Infectious lung complications in patients with HIV/AIDS. *Curr Opin Pulm Med* 11:203–207.

Brasileiro CB, Abreu MH, Mesquita RA (2014). Critical review of topical management of oral hairy leukoplakia. *World J Clin Cases* 2:253–256.

Brenner M, Ognibenc FP, Lack EE, et al. (1987). Prognostic factors and life expectancy of patients with acquired immunodeficiency syndrome and *Pneumocystis carinii* pneumonia. *Am Rev Respir Dis* 136:1199–1206.

Breton G, Duval X, Estellat C, et al. (2004). Determinants of immune reconstitution inflammatory syndrome in HIV type 1-infected patients with tuberculosis after initiation of antiretroviral therapy. *Clin Infect Dis* 39:1709–1712.

Buchbinder SP, Katz MH, Hessol NA, Liu JY, O'Malley PM, Underwood R, Holmber SD (1992). Herpes zoster and human immunodeficiency infection. *J Infect Dis* 166:1153–1156.

Cappell MS (1991). Hepatobiliary manifestations of the acquired immune deficiency syndrome. *Am J Gastroenterol* 86(1):1–15.

Carrasco DA, Vander SM, Tyring SK (2000). A review of antiretroviral drugs. *Dermatol Ther* 13:305–317.

Centers for Disease Control and Prevention (CDC) (1985). Centers for Disease Control revision of the case definition of acquired immunodeficiency syndrome for national reporting–United States. *MMWR Morb Mortal Wkly Rep* 4:373–374.

Centers for Disease Control and Prevention (CDC) (2013). Managing drug interactions in the treatment of HIV-related tuberculosis. http://www.cdc.gov/tb/publications/guidelines/tb_hiv_drugs/default.htm. Accessed February 27, 2017.

Centers for Disease Control and Prevention (CDC) (2015). Reported tuberculosis in the United States, 2014. http://www.cdc.gov/tb/statistics/reports/2014/pdfs/tb-surveillance-2014-report.pdf. Accessed February 27, 2017.

Chang Y, Cesarman E, Pessin MS, et al. (1994). Identification of herpesvirus-like DNA sequences in AIDS-associated Kaposi's sarcoma. *Science* 266:1865–1869.

Chaturvedi AK, Madeleine MM, Biggar RJ, Engels EA (2009). Risk of human papillomavirus associated cancers among persons living with AIDS. *J Natl Cancer Inst* 101(16):1120–1130.

Coldiron BM, Bergstresser PR (1989). Prevalence and clinical spectrum of skin disease in patients infected with human immunodeficiency virus. *Arch Dermatol* 125:357–361.

Collins KR, Quinones-Mateu ME, Toossi Z, Arts EJ (2002). Impact of tuberculosis on HIV-1 replication, diversity, and disease progression. *AIDS Rev* 4:165–176.

Connolly GM, Dryden MS, Shanson DC, et al. (1988). Cryptosporidial diarrhea in AIDS and its treatment. *Gut* 29:593–597.

Coopman SA, Johnson RA, Platt R, Gazzard BG (1993). Cutaneous disease and drug reactions in HIV infection. *N Engl J Med* 328:1670–1674.

Costner M, Cockerell CJ (1998). The changing spectrum of cutaneous manifestations of HIV disease. *Arch Dermatol* 134:1290–1292.

Coyle TE (1997). Hematologic complications of human immunodeficiency virus infection in the acquired immunodeficiency syndrome. *Med Clin North Am* 81(2):449–470.

Cunningham ET (2000). Uveitis in HIV positive patients. *Br J Ophthalmol* 84:233–237.

Cunningham ET, Downes KM, Chee SP, Zierhut M (2015). Cytomegalovirus retinitis and uveitis. *Ocul Immunol Inflam* 23(5):359–361.

Cunningham ET Jr, Margolis TP (1998). Ocular manifestations of HIV infection. *N Engl J Med* 339(4):236–244.

Declaux C, Zahar JR, Amraoui G, et al. (1999). Corticosteroids as adjunctive therapy for severe *Pneumocystis carinii* pneumonia in non-human immyunodeficiency virus-infected patients: retrospective study of 31 patients. *Clin Infect Dis* 29:670–672.

Deeks S (2011). HIV infection, inflammation, imunosenescence, and aging. *Annu Rev Med* 62:141–155.

de Moraes AP, de Arruda EA, Vitoriano MA, de Moraes Filho MO, Bezerra FA, de Magalhaes Holanda E, de Moraes ME (2007). An open-label efficacy pilot study with pimecrolimus cream 1% in adults with facial seborrhoeic dermatitis infected with HIV. *J Eur Acad Dermatol Venereol* 21:596–601.

Deng Y, Jing Y, Campbell AE, Gravenstein S (2004). Age-related impaired type 1 T cell responses to influenza: reduced activation ex vivo, decreased expansion in CTL culture in vitro, and blunted response to influenza vaccination in vivo in the elderly. *J Immunol* 172:3437–3446.

Desai S, Landay A (2010). Early immune senescence in HIV disease. *Curr HIV/AIDS Rep* 7:4–10.

DHHS Panel on Opportunistic Infections in HIV-infected Adults and Adolescents (2016). Guidelines for the prevention and treatment of opportunistic infections in HIV-infected adults and adolescents: recommendations from the Centers for Disease Control and Prevention, the National Institutes of Health, and the HIV Medicine Association of the Infectious Disease Society of America. https://aidsinfo.nih.gov/contentfiles/lvguidelines/adult_oi.pdf. Accessed February 27, 2017.

Dupin N, Rubin DCV, Gorin I, et al. (1999). The influence of highly active antiretroviral therapy on AIDS-associated Kaposi's sarcoma. *Br J Dermatol* 140:875–881.

Duvic M (1995). Human immunodeficiency virus and the skin: selected controversies. *J Invest Dermatol* 105:117S–1121S.

Effreos RB, Fletcher CV, Gebo K, et al (2008) Aging and infectious diseases: workshop on HIV infection and aging: what is known and future research directions. *Clin Infect Dis* 47:542–553.

Ehrenrein H, Rieckmann P, Sinowatz F, et al. (1993). Potent stimulation of monocytic endothelin-1 production by HIV-1 glycoprotein 120. *J Immunol* 150:4601–4609.

Elewski BE, Sullivan J (1994). Dermatophytes as opportunistic pathogens. *J Am Acad Dermatol* 30:1021–1022.

Elzi L, Schlegel M, Weber R, et al. (2007). Reducing tuberculosis incidence by tuberculin skin testing, preventive treatment, and antiretroviral therapy in an area of low tuberculosis transmission. *Clin Infect Dis* 44:94–102.

Evans MW, Giffi VS, Zimrin AB, Hess JR (2010). Rituximab treatment for thrombotic thrombocytopenic purpura associated with human immunodeficiency virus failing extensive treatment with plasma exchange: a report of two cases. *AIDS Patient Care STDs* 24(6):349–352.

Evans RH, Scadden DT (2000). Haematological aspects of HIV infection. *Ballieres Clin Haematol* 13:215.

Fraunfelder FW, Fraunfelder FT (2004). Adverse ocular drug reactions recently identified by the National Registry of Drug-Induced Ocular Side Effects. *Ophthalmology* 111(7):1275–1279.

Friedman-Kien AE, Laubenstein LJ, Rubinstein P, et al. (1982). Disseminated Kaposi's sarcoma in homosexual men. *Ann Intern Med* 96:693–700.

Frizzera G, Rosa J, Denher L, et al. (1980). Lymphoreticular disorders in primary immunodeficiency. New findings based on up to date histologic classification of 35 cases. *Cancer* 46:692–699.

Gagnon S, Botta AM, Fischl MA, Baier H, Kirksey OW, La Voie L (1990). Corticosteroids as adjunctive therapy for severe *Pneumocystis carinii* pneumonia in acquired immunodeficiency syndrome: a double-blind placebo controlled trial. *N Engl J Med* 323:1144–1150.

Gardasil 9 package insert (2016). http://www.fda.gov/downloads/BiologicsBloodVaccines/Vaccines/ApprovedProducts/UCM426457.pdf. Accessed June 7, 2016.

Gluckstein D, Ruskin J (1995). Rapid oral desensitization to trimethoprim-sulfamethoxazole: use in prophylaxis for *Pneumocystis carinii* pneumonia in patients with AIDS who were previously intolerant to TMP-SMZ. *Clin Infect Dis* 20:849–853.

Goldberg DE, Smithen LM, Angelilli A, et al. (2005). HIV-associated retinopathy in the HAART era. *Retina* 25(5):633–649.

Gordin FM, Cohn DL, Sullam PM, et al. (1997). Early manifestations of disseminated *Mycobacterium avium* complex disease: a prospective evaluation. *J Infect Dis* 176(1):126–132.

Gordin FM, Roediger MP, Girard PM, et al. (2008). Pneumonia in HIV-infected persons: increased risk with cigarette smoking and treatment interruption. *Am J Respir Crit Care Med* 178:630–636.

Gottlieb MS, Schroff R, Schanker HM, Weisman JD, Fan PT, Wolf RA, Saxon A (1981). *Pneumocystis carinii* pneumonia and mucosal candidiasis in previously healthy homosexual men: evidence of a new acquired cellular immunodeficiency. *N Engl J Med* 305:1425–1431.

Greenspan D, Greenspan JS, Hearst NG, et al. (1987). Relation of oral hairy leukoplakia to infection with human immunodeficiency virus and risk of development of AIDS. *J Infect Dis* 155:475–481.

Grogg KL, Miller RF, Dogan A (2007). HIV infection and lymphoma. *J Clin Pathol* 60(12):1365–1372.

Gruden JF, Huang L, Turner J, et al. (1997). High-resolution CT in the evaluation of clinically suspected Pneumocystis carinii pneumonia in AIDS patients with normal, equivocal, or nonspecific radiographic findings. *AJR Am J Roentgenol* 169:967–975.

Grulich AE, Li Y, McDonald AM, et al. (2001). Decreasing rate of Kaposi's sarcoma and non-Hodgkin's lymphoma in the era of potent combination anti-retroviral therapy. *AIDS* 15(5):629–633.

Grulich AE, Vajdic CM (2005). The epidemiology of non-Hodgkin lymphoma. *Pathology* 37(6):409–419.

Grunfeld C, Rimland D, Gibert CL, et al. (2007). Association of upper trunk and visceral adipose tissue volume with insulin resistance in control and HIV-infected subjects in the FRAM study. *J Acquir Immune Defic Syndr* 46:283–290.

Hart D, Sayer, R, Miller R, et al. (2011). Human immunodeficiency virus associated thrombotic thrombocytopenic purpura – favourable outcome with plasma exchange and prompt initiation of highly active antiretroviral therapy. *Br J Haematol* 154(4):515–519.

Hengge UR, Ruzicka T, Tyring SK, et al. (2002). Update on Kaposi's sarcoma and other HHV-8 associated diseases. Part 1: Epidemiology, environmental predispositions, clinical manifestations, and therapy. *Lancet Infect Dis* 2(5):281–292.

Hessol NA, Katz MH, Liu JY, et al. (1992). Increased incidence of Hodgkin disease in homosexual men with HIV infection. *Ann Intern Med* 117:309–311.

High KP, Brennan-Ing M, Clifford DB, et al. (2012). HIV and aging: state of knowledge and areas of critical need for research. A report to the NIH Office of AIDS Research by the HIV and Aging Working Group. *J Acquir Immune Defic Syndr* 60(Suppl 1):S1–S18.

Hirschtick RE, Glassroth J, Jordan MC, et al. (1995). Bacterial pneumonia in persons infected with the human immunodeficiency virus. Pulmonary Complications of HIV Infection Study Group. *N Engl J Med* 333(13):845–851.

Holland GN (2008). AIDS and ophthalmology: the first quarter century [Review]. *Am J Ophthalmol* 145(3):397–408.

Holland GN, Pepose TS, Petit TH, et al. (1983). Acquired immune deficiency syndrome: ocular manifestations. *Ophthalmology* 96:1092–1099.

Hook EW 3rd, Cannon RO, Nahmias AJ, Lee FF, Campbell CH Jr, Glasser D Quinn TC (1992). Herpes simplex virus infection as a risk factor for human immunodeficiency virus infection in heterosexuals. *J Infect Dis* 165:251–255.

Hoover DR, Saah J, Bacellar H, Phair J, Detels R, Anderson R, Kaslow RA (1993). Clinical manifestations of AIDS in the era of pneumocystis prophylaxis. Multicenter AIDS Cohort Study. *N Engl J Med* 329:1922–1926.

Huang L, Schnapp LM, Gruden JF, Hopewell PC Stansell JD (1996). Presentation of AIDS-related pulmonary Kaposi's sarcoma diagnosed by bronchoscopy. *Am J Respir Crit Care Med* 153:1385–1390.

Huang SS, Barbour JD, Deeks SG, et al. (2000). Reversal of human immunodeficiency virus type-1 associated hematosuppression by effective antiretroviral therapy. *Clin Infect Dis* 30(3):504–510.

Hutin Y, Molina JM, Casin I, et al. (1993). Risk factors for *Clostridium difficile*–associated diarrhea in HIV-infected patients. *AIDS* 7(11):1441–1447.

Hutchinson CM, Hook EW III, Shepherd M, et al. (1994). Altered clinical presentation and manifestations of early syphilis in patients with human immunodeficiency virus infection. *Ann Intern Med* 121(2):94–100.

Ioannidis JP, Cappelleri JC, Skolnik PR, Lau J, Sacks HS (1996). A meta-analysis of the relative efficacy and toxicity of *Pneumpcystis carinii* prophylactic regimens. *Arch Intern Med* 22:177–188.

Jacobson LP, Yamashita TE, Detel SR, et al. (1999). Impact of potent antiretroviral therapy on the incidence of Kaposi's sarcoma and non-Hodgkins lymphoma among HIV infected individuals. *J Acquir Immune Defic Syndr* 21(Suppl):S34–S48.

Jacobson MA, Zegans M, Pavian PR, et al. (1997). Cytomegalovirus retinitis after initiation of highly active antiretroviral therapy. *Lancet* 349:1443–1445.

Kaplan JE, Hanson D, Dworkin MS, et al. (2000). Epidemiology of human immunodeficiency virus-associated opportunistic infectinos in the United States in the era of highly active antiretroviral therapy. *Clin Infect Dis* 30:S5–S14.

Kazanjian P, Armstrong W, Hossler PA, et al. (2000). *Pneumocystis carinii* mutations are associated with duration of sulfa or sulfone prophylaxis exposure in AIDS patients. *J Infect Dis* 182:551–557

Kiertiburanakul S, Sungkanuparph S, Charoenyingwattana A, Mahasirimongkol S, Sura T Chantratita W (2008). Risk factors for nevirapine-associated rash among HIV-infected patients with low CD4 cell counts in resource-limited settings. *Curr HIV Res* 6:65–69.

Ko WF, Cello TP, Rogers SJ, et al. (2003). Prognostic factors for the survival of patients with AIDS cholangiopathy. *Am J Gastroenterol* 10:2111–2112.

Kohli R, Lo Y, Homel P, et al. (2006). Bacterial pneumonia, HIV therapy, and disease progression among HIV-infected women in the HIV epidemiologic research (HER) study. *Clin Infect Dis* 43:90–98.

Kolar KA, Rapini RP (1991). Crusted (Norwegian) scabies. *Am Fam Physician*, 44, 1317–1321.

Kotler DP, Reka S, Orenstein JM, et al. (1992). Chronic idiopathic esophageal ulcerations in acquired immunodeficiency syndrome. Characterization and treatment with corticosteroids. *J Clin Gastroenterol* 15(4):284–290.

Krause J (2005). AIDS related non-Hodgkins lymphoma. *Microsc Res Tech* 68:168–175.

Kreuter A, Wieland U (2011). Oral leukoplakia: a clinical indicator of immunosuppresion. *CMAJ* 183:932.

Krown SE, Testa MA, Huang J (1997). AIDS-related Kaposi's sarcoma: prospective validation of the AIDS Clinical Trials Group staging classification. AIDS Clinical Trials Group Oncology Committee. *J Clin Oncol* 15:3085–3092.

Kwan CK, Ernst JD (2011). HIV and tuberculosis: a deadly human syndemic. *Clin Microbiol Rev* 24:351–376.

Kyaw MH, Rose CE, Fry AM, Singleton JA, Moore Z, Zell ER, Whitney CG (2005). The influence of chronic illnesss on the incidence of invasive pneumococcal disease in adults. *J Infect Dis* 192:377–386.

Lange CG, Lederman MM, Medvik K, et al. (2003). Nadir CD4+ T-cell count and numbers of CD28+ Cd4+ T-cells predict functional responses to immunizations in chronic HIV-1 infection. *AIDS* 17:2015–2023.

Lapins J, Gaines H, Lindback S, Lidbrink P, Emtestam L (1997). Skin and mucosal characteristics of symptomatic primary HIV-1 infection. *AIDS Patient Care STDS* 11:67–70.

Lazizi Y, Grangeot-Keros L, Delfraissy JF (1988). Reappearance of hepatitis B virus in immune patients infected with HIV-1. *J Infect Dis* 158:666–667.

Ledergerber B, Egger M, Erard V, et al. (1999). AIDS-related opportunistic illnesses occurring after initiation of potent antiretroviral therapy: the Swiss HIV Cohort Study. *JAMA* 282(23):2220.

Leeds IL, Magee MJ, Kurbatova EV, del Rio C, Blumberg HM, Leonard MK, Kraft CS (2012). Site of extrapulmonary tuberculosis is associated with HIV infection. *Clin Infect Dis* 55:75–81.

Levine AM (1996). HIV associated Hodgkin's disease. Biologic and clinical aspects. *Hematol Oncol Clin North Am* 10:1135–1148.

Lohse H, Hansen AB, Pedersen G, et al. (2007). Survival of persons with and without HIV infection in Denmark, 1995–2005. *Ann Intern Med* 146(2):87–95.

MacDonald JC, Karoravellas MP, Torriani FJ, et al. (2000). Highly active antiretroviral therapy-related immune recovery in AIDS patients with cytomegalovirus retinitis. *Ophthalmology* 107:877–883.

Maiman M, Fruchter RG, Serur E, et al. (1990). Human immunodeficiency virus infection and cervical neoplasia. *Gynecol Oncol* 38:377–382.

Malone DA, Camara EG, Krug JH Jr (1992). Ophthalmologic effects of psychotropic medications. *Psychosomatics* 33(3):271–277.

Manas E, Pulido F, Pena JM, et al. (2004). Impact of tuberculosis on the course of HIV-infected patients with a high CD4 lymphocyte count. *Int J Tuberc Lung Dis* 8:451–457.

Martin DF, Kuppermann BD, Woltz RA, et al. (1999). Oral ganciclovir for patients with cytomegalovirus retinitis treated with ganciclovir implants. Roche Ganciclovir Study. *N Engl J Med* 340(14):1063–1070.

Masur H, Michelis MA, Greene JB, et al. (1981). An outbreak of community-acquired *Pneumocystis carinii* pneumonia. Initial manifestation of cellular immune dysfunction. *N Engl J Med* 305:1431–1438.

Masur H, Ognibene FP, Yarchoan R, et al. (1989). CD4 counts as predictors of opportunistic pneumonias in human immunodeficiency (HIV) infection. *Ann Intern Med* 111:223–231.

Mbulaiteye SM, Biggar RJ, Goedert JJ, et al. (2003). Immune deficiency and risk of malignancy among people with AIDS. *J Acquir Immune Defic Syndr* 32:527–533.

Meintjes G, Wilkinson RJ, Morroni C, et al. (2010). Randomized placebo-controlled trial of prednisone for paradoxical tuberculosis-associated immune reconstitution inflammatory syndrome. *AIDS* 24:2381–2390.

Milazzo F, Piconi S, Trabottoni D, et al. (1999). Intractable pruritus in HIV infection; immunology and characterization. *Allergy* 54:266–272.

Mitchell DM, McCarty M, Fleming J, Moss FM (1992). Bronchopulmonary Kaposi's sarcoma in patients with AIDS. *Thorax* 47:726–729.

Mocroft, A, Oancea, C, van Lunzen, J, et al. (2005). Decline in esophageal candidiasis and use of antimycotics in European patients with HIV. *Am J Gastroenterol* 100(7):1446–1454.

Mocroft, A, Sterne JA, Egger M, et al. (2009). Variable impact on mortality of AIDS-defining events diagnosed during combination antiretroviral therapy: not all AIDS-defining conditions are created equal. *Clin Infect Dis* 48:1138–1151.

Molina JM, Castin I, Hausfater P, et al. (1995). *Campylobacter* infections in HIV-infected patients. Clinical and bacteriologic features. *AIDS* 9:881–885.

Molina-Pinelo S, Vallejo A, Diaz L, et al. (2009). Premature immunosenescence in HIV-infected patients on highly active antiretroviral therapy with low-level CD4 T cell repopulation. *J Antimicrob Chemother* 64:579–588.

Monkemuller KE, Wilcox CM (1999). Diagnosis and treatment of esophageal ulcers in AIDS. *Semin Gastroenterol* 10(3):85–92.

Moon SM, Kim T, Sung H, et al. (2011). Outcomes of moderate-to-severe Pneumocystis pneumonia treated with adjunctive steroid in non-HIV-infected patients. *Antimicrob Agents Chemother* 55:4613–4618.

Moore RD, Keruly TC, Chaisson RE (1998). Anemia and survival in HIV infection. *J Acquir Immune Defic Syndr Hum Retrovirol* 19(1):29–33.

Moraes HV (2002). Ocular manifestations of HIV/AIDS. *Curr Opin Ophthalmol* 6:397–403.

Morris A, Lundgren JD, Masur H, et al. (2004). Current epidemiology of *Pneumocystis* pneumonia. *Emerg Infect Dis* 10:1713–1720.

Muller EE, Chirwa TF, Lewis DA (2010). Human papillomavirus (HPV) infection in heterosexual South African men attending sexual health services: associations between HPV and HIV serostatus. *Sex Transm Infect* 86:175–180.

Neuhaus J, Jacobs DR, Baker JV Jr, et al. (2010). Markers of inflammation, coagulation, and renal function are elevated in adults with HIV infection. *J Infect Dis* 201:1788–1795).

Nguyen QD, Kempen JH, Bolton SG (2000) Immune recovery uveitis in patients with AIDS and cytomegalovirus retinitis after highly active antiretroviral therapy. *Am J Ophthalmol* 129:634–639.

Ogedegbe AO, Sulkowski MS (2003). Antiretroviral-associated liver injury. *Clin Liver Dis* 7:475–499.

Ognibene FP, Shelhamer J, Gill V, et al. (1984). The diagnosis of *Pneumocystis carinii* pneumonia in patients with the acquired immunodeficiency syndrome using subsegmental bronchoalveolar lavage. *Am Rev Respir Dis* 129:929–932.

Oksenhendler E, Bierling P, Chevret S, et al. (1993). Splenectomy is safe and effective in HIV-related immune thrombocytopenia. *Blood* 82:29–32.

Opravil M, Sereni D (2008). Natural history of HIV-associated pulmonary arterial hypertension: treands in the HAART era. *AIDS* 22:S35–S40.

Osmond DH, Chin DP, Glassroth J, et al., (1999). Impact of bacterial pneumonia and *Pneumocystis carinii* pneumonia on human immunodeficiency virus disease progression. Pulmonary Complications of HIV Study Group. *Clin Infect Dis* 29:536–543.

Palefsky JM, Holly EA, Ralston ML, et al. (1998). Prevalence and risk factors for human papillomavirus infection of the anal canal in human immunodeficiency virus (HIV) positive and HIV negative homosexual men. *J Infect Dis* 177:361–367.

Palefsky JM, Holly EA, Ralston M, et al. (2001). Effect of highly active antiretroviral therapy on the natural history of anal squamous interepithelial and anal human papilloma viral infections. *J Acquir Immune Defic Syndr* 28:422–428.

Palella FJ Jr, Delaney KM, Moorman AC, et al. (1998). Declining morbidity and mortality among patients with advanced human immunodeficiency virus infection. HIV Outpatient Study Investigators. *N Engl J Med* 338:853–860.

Para MF, Finkelstein D, Becker S, Dohn M, Walawander A, Black JR (2000). Reduced toxicity with gradual initiation of trimethoprim-sulfamethoxazole as primary prophylaxis for *Pneumocystis carinii* pneumonia: AIDS Clinical Trials Group 268. *J Acquir Immune Defic Syndr* 24:337–343.

Patel P, Hanson DL, Sullivan PS, et al.; Adult and Adolescent Spectrum of Disease Project and HIV Outpatient Study Investigators (2008). Incidence of types of cancer among HIV-infected persons compared with the general population in the United States, 1992–2003. *Ann Intern Med* 148(10):728–736.

Pathai S, Bajillan H, Landay AL, High KP (2014). Is HIV a model of accelerated or accentuated aging? *J Gerontol A Biol Sci Med Sci* 69:833–842.

Penn I (1975). The incidence of malignancies in transplant recipients. *Transplant Proc* 7(2):323–326.

Perlmutter BL, Glaser JB, Oyugi SO (1999). How to recognize and treat acute HIV syndrome. *Am Fam Physician* 60:535–542, 545–546.

Perkocha L, Geaghans S, and Yen T (1990). Clinical and pathologic features of bacillary peliosis hepatitis in association with human immunodeficiency virus infection. *N Engl J Med* 323:1581–1586.

Pfister H (1996). The role of human papillomavirus in anogenital cancer. *Obstet Gynecol Clin North Am* 23:579–595.

Pett SL, Carey C, Lin E, et al. (2011). Predictors of bacterial pneumonia in evaluation of subcutaneous interleukin-2 in a randomized international trial (ESPRIT). *HIV Med* 12:219–227.

Phillips AN, Neaton J, Lundgren JD (2008). The role of HIV in serious diseases other than AIDS. *AIDS* 22:2409–2418.

Phung BC, Sogni P, Launay O (2014). Hepatitis B and human immunodeficiency virus co-infection. *World J Gastroenterol* 20(46):17360–17367.

Plettenberg A, Lorenzen T, Burtsche BT, et al. (2000). Bacillary angiomatossis in HIV-infected patients—an epidemiological and clinical study. *Dermatology* 201:326–331.

Portu JJ, Santamaria JM, Zubero Z, Almeida-Llamas MV, Aldamiz-Etxebarria San Sebastian M, Gutierrez AR (1996). Atypical scabies in HIV-positive patients. *J Am Acad Dermatol* 34:915–917.

Rabkin CS, Biggar RJ, Horm JW (1991). Increasing incidence of cancers associated with the human immunodeficiency virus epidemic. *Int J Cancer* 47:692–696.

Radu O, Pantanowitz L (2013). Kaposi sarcoma. *Arch Pathol Lab Med*, 137, 289–294.

Raufman JP (1988). Odonophagia/dysphagia in AIDS. *Gastroenterol Clin North Am* 17(3):599–614.

Remick S (1996). Non-AIDS defining cancers. *Hematol Oncol Clin North Am* 10:1203–1213.

Richa S, Yazbek JC (2010). Ocular adverse effects of common psychotropic agents: a review. *CNS Drugs* 24(6):501–526.

Rigopoulos D, Paparizos V, Katsambas A (2004). Cutaneous markers of HIV infection. *Clin Dermatol* 22:487–498.

Robbins GK, Spritzler JG, Chan ES, et al. (2009). Incomplete reconstitution of T cell subsets on combination antiretroviral therapy in the AIDS Clinical Trials Group protocol 384. *Clin Infect Dis* 48:350–361.

Roujeau JC, Kelly JP, Naldi L, et al. (1995). Medication use and the risk of Stevens-Johnson syndrome or toxic epidermal necrolysis. *N Engl J Med* 333(24):1600–1607.

Roudier C, Caumes E, Rogeaux O, Bricaire F, Gentilini M (1994). Adverse cutaneous reactions to trimethoprim-sulfamethoxazole in patients with the acquired immune deficiency syndrome and *Pneumocystis carinii* pneumonia. *Arch Dermatol* 130:1383–1386.

Saadeh S, Cammell G, Carey WD, et al. (2001). The role of liver biopsy in chronic hepatitis C. *Hepatology* 33:196–200.

Samaranayake LP (1992). Oral mycoses in HIV infection. *Oral Surg Oral Med Oral Pathol* 73:171–180.

Sattler FR, Frame P, Davis R, et al. (1994). Trimetrexate with leucovorin vs. trimethoprim-sulfamethoxazole for moderate to severe episodes of *Pneumocystis carinii* pneumonia in patients with AIDS. *J Infect Dis* 170(1):165–172.

Saunders BM, Frank AA, Orme IM, Cooper AM (2002). CD4 is required for the development of a protective granulomatous response to pulmonary tuberculosis. *Cell Immunol* 216:65–72.

Schwartz JJ, Myskowski PL (1992). Molluscum contagiosum in patients with human immunodeficiency virus infection. A review of twenty-seven patients. *J Am Acad Dermatol* 27:583–588.

Schwartz RA (2004). Kaposi's sarcoma: an update. *J Surg Oncol* 87(3):146–151.

Shlipak MG, Fried LF, Crump C, et al. (2003). Elevations of inflammatory and procoagulant biomarkers in elderly persons with renal insufficiency. *Circulation* 107:87–92.

Shukla D, Rathinam S, Cunningham ET (2007). Contribution of HIV/AIDS to global blindness. *Int Ophthalmol Clin* 47(3):27–43.

Sitbon O, Lascoux-Combe C, Delfraissy JF (2008). Prevalence of HIV-related pulmonary arterial hypertension in the current antiretroviral therapy era. *Am J Respir Crit Care Med* 177:108–113.

Sloand E (2005). Hematologic complications of HIV infection. *AIDS Rev* 7(4):187–196.

Smith PD, Macher AM, Bookman MA, et al. (1985). *Salmonella typhimurium* enteritis and bacteremia in the acquired immune deficiency syndrome. *Ann Intern Med* 102:207–209.

Smith PD, Quinn TC, Strober V, et al. (1992). Gastrointestinal infections in AIDS. *Ann Intern Med* 116:63–77.

Sockalingam S, Tseng A, Giguere P, Wong D (2013). Psychiatric treatment considerations with direct acting antivirals in hepatitis C. *BMC Gastroenterol* 14(13):86.

Song MK, Azen SP, Buley A (2003). Effect of anti-cytomegalovirus therapy on the incidence of immune recovery uveitis in AIDS patients with healed cytomegalovirus retinitis. *Am J Ophthalmol* 136:696–702.

Stamm WE, Handsfield HH, Rompalo AM, Ashley RL, Roberts PL, Corey L (1988). The association between genital ulcer disease and acquisition of HIV infection in homosexual men. *JAMA* 260:1429–1433.

Sterling TR, Bethel J, Goldberg S, Weinfurter P, Yun L, Horsburgh CR (2006). The scope and impact of treatment of latent tuberculosis infection in the United States and Canada. *Am J Respir Crit Care Med* 173:927–931.

Sterling TR, Pham PA, Chaisson RE (2010). HIV infection-related tuberculosis: clinical manifestations and treatment. *Clin Infect Dis* 50:S223–S230.

Sulkowski MS, Moore RD, Mehta SH, et al. (2002). Hepatitis C and progression of HIV disease. *JAMA* 288(2):199–206.

Sullivan PS, Hanson DC, Chu SY, et al. (1997). Surveillance for thrombocytopenia in persons infected with HIV: reults from the multistate Adult and Adolescent Spectrum of Disease Project. *J Acquir Immune Defic Syndr Human Retrovirol* 14(4):374–379.

Tappero JW, Perkins BA, Wenger JD, Berger TG (1995). Cutaneous manifestations of opportunistic infections in patients infected with human immunodeficiency virus. *Clin Microbiol Rev* 8:440–450.

Tschachler E, Bergstresser PR, Stingl G (1996). HIV-related skin diseases. *Lancet* 348:659–663.

van Baarle D, Tsegaye A, Miedema F, Akbar A (2005). Significance of senescence for virus-specific memory T cell responses: rapid ageing during chronic stimulation of the immune system. *Immunol Lett* 97:19–29.

Vannappagari V, Nkhoma ET, Atashili J, Laurent SS, Zhao H (2011). Prevalence, severity, and duration of thrombocytopenia among HIV patients in the era of highly active antiretroviral therapy. *Platelets* 22(8):611–618.

Venkatesan P, Perfect JR, Myers SA (2005). Evaluation and management of dungal infections in immunocompromised patients. *Dermatol Ther* 18:44–57.

Vora RV, Pilani AP, Kota RK (2015). Extensive giant *Molluscum contagiosum* in an HIV-positive patient. *J Clin Diagn Res* 9:WD1–WD2.

Wallace JM, Hansen NI, Lavange L, et al. (1997). Respiratory disease trends in the pulmonary complications of HIV Infection Study cohort. Pulmonary complications of HIV infection study group. *Am J Respir Crit Care Med* 155:72–80.

Walston J, McBurnie MA, Newman A, et al. (2002). Frailty and activation of the inflammation and coagulation systems with and without clinical comorbidities: results from the Cardiovascular Health Study. *Arch Intern Med* 162:2333–2341.

Walzer PD, Perl DP, Krogstad DJ, Rawson PF, Schultz MG (1974). *Pneumocystis carinii* pneumonia in the United States. Epidemiologic, diagnostic, and clinical features. *Ann Intern Med* 80:83–93.

Whalen C, Horsburgh CR, Hom D, Lahart C, Simberkoff M, Ellner J (1995). Accelerated course of human immunodeficiency virus infection after tuberculosis. *Am J Respir Crit Care Med* 151:129–135.

Wilcox CM (1992). Esophageal disease in the acquired immune deficiency syndrome: etiology, diagnosis, and management. *Am J Med* 92:412–421.

Wilcox CM, Straub RF, Clark WS (1995). Prospective evaluation of oropharyngeal findings in HIV-infected patients with esophageal ulcers. *Am J Gastroenterol* 90(11):1938–1941.

Wilcox CM, Alexander LN, Clark WS, Thompson SE III (1996). Fluconozole compared with endoscopy for human immunodeficiency virus infected patients with esophageal symptoms. *Gastroenterology* 110(6):1803–1809.

Wood C, Harington W (2005). AIDS and associated malignancies. *Cell Res* 15:947–952.

Wood R, Maartens G, Lombard CJ (2000). Risk factors for developing tuberculosis in HIV-1-infected adults from communities with a low or very high incidence of tuberculosis. *J Acquir Immune Defic Syndr* 23:75–80.

Workowski KA, Bolan GA; Centers for Disease Control and Prevention (2015). Sexually transmitted diseases treatment guidelines, 2015. *MMWR Recomm Rep* 64(RR-03):1–137.

World Health Organization (2016). *Global Tuberculosis Report 2016.* http://www.who.int/tb/publications/global_report/gtbr2016_executive_summary.pdf?ua=1. Accessed February 28, 2017.

Yanik EL, Achenbach CJ, Gopal S, et al. (2016). Changes in clinical context for Kaposi's sarcoma and non-Hodgkin lymphoma among people with HIV infection in the United States. *J Clin Oncol* 34(27):3276–3283.

Zhang Y, Harada A, Bluethmann H, et al. (1995). Tumor necrosis factor (TNF) is a physiologic regulator of hematopoietic cells. *Blood* 86(8):2930–2937.

Ziegler JL, Beckstead JA, Volberding PA, et al. (1984). Non-Hodgkins lymphoma in 90 homosexual men. Relation to generalized adenopathy and the acquired immunodeficiency syndrome. *N Engl J Med* 311(9):565–570.

Zucchetto A, Virdone S, Taborelli M, et al. (2016). Non-AIDS defining cancer mortality: emerging patterns in the late HAART era. *J Acquir Immune Defic* 73(2):190–196.

PART XI

ETHICAL AND HEALTH POLICY ASPECTS OF AIDS PSYCHIATRY

48.

CLINICIAN BURNOUT IN HIV/AIDS HEALTHCARE

Asher D. Aladjem, MD and Mary Ann Cohen, MD

I want to be a good story for my doctor, to exchange some of my art for his. . . . To most physicians my illness is a routine incident in their rounds, while for me it's the crisis of my life . . . just as he orders blood tests and bone scans of my body, I'd like my doctor to scan me, to grope my spirit as well as my prostate. . . .. In learning to talk to his patients the doctor may talk himself into loving his work. He has little to lose and much to gain by letting the sick man into his heart. If he does, then they can share, as few others can, the wonder, terror, and exaltation of being on the edge of being, between the natural and the supernatural.

—ANATOLE BROYARD (1990)

In 1990, Anatole Broyard wrote an article, shortly before his death of complications of prostate cancer, that poignantly presents his need to be a "good story" for his doctor. The physicians who work with persons with severe and complex illnesses, such as HIV/AIDS, cancer, coronary artery disease, diabetes mellitus, multiple sclerosis, emphysema, and other illnesses, are subject to the vicissitudes and complications of their patients as well as the complexities of healthcare systems and society. It is hard for physicians to seek out their patients' stories when pressures of both productivity and technology abound in contemporary healthcare systems. Shanafelt et al. (2015) documented that, when compared to the general population, physicians experienced more burnout and less satisfaction with work–life balance. Burnout as a phenomenon relates to work and occupational psychological distress (Maslach et al., 1997). Because burnout is multifactorial, research has focused on two general categories of contributory or predisposing factors: those related to the individual clinician, and those related to the work environment. These factors are summarized with additional updated components in Table 48.1.

HIV magnifies physician stress because it involves other multimorbid and concomitant medical and psychiatric illnesses as well as stigma. At the same time that vast strides have led to AIDS becoming a chronic manageable illness, changes in the healthcare environment, from 1981 to the present, have also magnified physicians stress and burnout (Byyny, 2016).

A common assumption is that everyone who works in the HIV/AIDS field is at risk for burnout or will experience burnout. The evidence for this remains somewhat equivocal. A number of studies with a range of healthcare workers in AIDS care, including nurses, social workers, and physicians, have demonstrated a relatively low level of burnout (Cooke, 1992; Kaplan et al., 1989; Levinson et al., 1997; Macks and Abrams, 1992; Stewart, 1995). On the other hand, other studies have shown high levels of burnout among healthcare workers in AIDS care (Catalan et al., 1996; Clever

et al., 2006; Gueritault-Chalvin et al., 2000; Stewart, 1995). Another point to consider is whether AIDS healthcare workers experience more burnout than individuals caring for patients with other chronic and severe illnesses, such as cancer. Again, the findings are not unanimous. Several U.S. studies have reported that healthcare workers believed that caring for AIDS patients was more stressful than caring for patients with other serious diseases (Macks and Abrams, 1992; Travado et al., 2005). Yet, several studies conducted in other parts of the world, such as Australia, Germany, Italy, and the United Kingdom, have indicated that AIDS healthcare workers were less prone to burnout than healthcare personnel who work in such fields as oncology and geriatrics (Cooke, 1992; Karam et al., 2012; Kaplan et al., 1989; Lert et al., 2001). Regardless of whether or not physicians who care for persons with HIV and AIDS have more burnout than physicians who care for other severe illnesses, it is clear that HIV physicians are subject at least to the same stressors as other physicians and, therefore, are subject to burnout.

This chapter defines and describes the multifactorial nature of burnout as it pertains to clinicians caring for persons with HIV and AIDS and provides a summary of predisposing factors, protective factors, preventive strategies, and ways to provide support and eliminate burnout. Also addressed is the question of whether changes in healthcare, including pressures for productivity, increasing workloads, and increasing use of technology in documentation, have had more or less of an impact on HIV physicians than on other physicians.

CLINICIAN DISTRESS AND BURNOUT IN THE CARE OF PERSONS WITH HIV AND AIDS

Research on burnout in HIV/AIDS-related work was initially found in the field of nurse professionals; it was subsequently

Table 48.1 FACTORS PREDISPOSING TO BURNOUT

INDIVIDUAL FACTORS	WORK-RELATED FACTORS
Meaning of one's work, dealing with conflicting values	Work or case load and/or responsibilities, excessive paperwork Electronic medical records and changes in documentation High regulatory demands Implementation of ICD-10, DSM-5, mandatory electronic prescribing in many states of the U.S.
Balance between work and family and other areas of life	Bereavement overload and unresolved grief
Fit between clinician's interests and goals and how they integrate at the work environment	Lack of rewards and devaluation of contribution and unstable organizational dynamics
External/internal cognitive/behavior, coping styles, and skills	External locus of control leading to diminished job control by the individual; "responsibility without power," lack of authority, disempowerment
Overidentification with clients	Increasing number of patients with diagnoses of personality disorders and/or substance abuse
Difficulties discussing patient's condition with his or her family	Pain management resources
Poor communication among hospital staff and/or clinicians	Witnessing physical deterioration of patients

expanded and applied to medicine, dentistry, public health, health education, and social work. The close association between burnout and work differentiates it from more general emotional states such as depression that may pervade every aspect of the clinician's life. When the focus is on work-related distress, studies of the topic leave the distinction of the boundary between work-related distress from distress related to the rest of the clinician's life ill-defined. As a result, other sources of distress may be minimized or overlooked and the boundary with psychiatric diagnoses remains blurred. Even though distress may be only work related, distress of any kind clearly has implications for other areas of the caregiver's life. Although we refer to burnout as a phenomenon that has particular etiologies, a particular course, and identified interventions to address it, the concept still remains that it is not a diagnosable illness or syndrome. Any attempt to medicalize and/or further pathologize such a phenomenon may not yield the desired outcome. Burnout has never been categorized as a diagnosis in the *Diagnostic and Statistical Manual of Mental Disorders* and was initially relatively ignored in the literature of HIV psychiatry (Felton, 1998). Systems focusing on burnout prevention are yet to be acknowledged, generalized, systematized, and implemented in healthcare and in HIV-related care.

The AIDS pandemic, which began in 1981, forced significant changes in the understanding and management of an illness in the context of behavior, social acceptance, and personal and social responsibility. The enormous challenge of HIV/AIDS-related work and constant changes in the field can lead to the onset of clinician distress and, if not addressed, have a negative outcome such as burnout. In addition, there is growing body of evidence that unmanaged secondary stress in healthcare professionals can debilitate anyone at any point in their career, regardless of the patient population being cared for, and has increased in prevalence in recent years. A study done at the Mayo Clinic compared prevalence of burnout and satisfaction with work–life balance among U.S. physicians and a probability-based sample of the general U.S. population in 2011 and 2014 (Shanafelt et al., 2015). Of the 35,922 physicians who received an invitation to participate, 6,880 (19.2%) completed surveys. In an assessment using the Maslach Burnout Inventory, 54.4% ($n = 3680$) of the physicians reported at least one symptom of burnout in 2014 compared with 45.5% ($n = 3310$) in 2011. Satisfaction with work–life balance also declined among physicians between 2011 and 2014 (48.5% vs. 40.9%; $p < .001$). Substantial differences in rates of professional burnout and satisfaction with work–life balance were categorized by specialty. In contrast to these trends in physicians, minimal changes in burnout or satisfaction with work–life balance were observed between 2011 and 2014 in probability-based samples of working U.S. adults, resulting in increasing disparity in burnout and satisfaction with work–life balance between physicians and the general U.S. working population (Shanafelt et al., 2015), as well as in work effort (Shanafelt et al., 2016). Burnout affects the individual physician and the quality of care provided by the institution (Burton, 2016).

FACTORS PREDISPOSING TO BURNOUT IN HIV CLINICIANS

HIV/AIDS-related work differs from that of other fields in the healthcare delivery system, such as geriatrics, oncology, intensive care, and palliative care, in that, from the beginning, the epidemic affected young, otherwise healthy individuals who suffered high death rates and many of whom were vulnerable to stigma and discrimination. The combination of stigmatized patients affected by a devastatingly feared infectious illness that initially had minimal effective treatments and the fear of occupational exposure created an environment that was more supportive of isolation and distancing from patients than of caring for them. The burden on clinicians was twofold: caring for the stigmatized patients with stigmatized illnesses, and addressing their own fears and stigmatized isolation.

HIV was identified as a risk for all, with a strong impact on high-risk populations and the general public worldwide. Lack of effective treatments magnified both the associated fear and stigma. Ongoing medical research, however, was transformative and changed HIV/AIDS into a chronic, manageable illness, in 1996. The availability of effective antiretroviral therapies and vast improvement in care led to empowerment of clinicians and a decrease in clinician distress, but the diminution of HIV stigma has not approached the level of progress in patient care. Nonetheless, improved HIV health outcomes have increased satisfaction in the overall experience of clinicians in the HIV-related fields.

Still, HIV care can increase the pressures and stress of the already numerous demands of healthcare careers, considering the challenges inherent in the modern, fast-paced healthcare delivery system. Ongoing care entails providing treatment and follow-up, monitoring adherence to antiviral treatment. Furthermore, clinicians may be forced to observe patients' decline in health, despite all efforts and treatments available. (Issues regarding prisoners with HIV and AIDS are explored in depth in Chapter 9 and are also addressed in Chapter 50 of this textbook.) Ambulatory care has expanded since HIV/AIDS has evolved into a chronic illness. Caregivers in each of these environments face different challenges and stressors and have different risks and rates of reported burnout. The occurrence of burnout has a negative impact on work satisfaction and has been seen in large part as the problem of the individual suffering from it. The organizational context in which clinicians practice is a very important variable in the experience of burnout, but research in this field has been hampered by the absence of instruments to measure organizational factors. Individuals who focus on the negative impact that HIV has had on society will add the risk of burning out as another negative consequence of working with persons with HIV/AIDS. Numerous stressors have been reported in the literature as specific aspects of AIDS-related healthcare delivery and are summarized in Table 48.2.

While most studies on stress and burnout in HIV/AIDS healthcare have focused on the negative and difficult aspects of this work, these aspects are by no means universal phenomena. Clinicians' involvement with HIV/AIDS covers the whole spectrum of the illness, from prevention of transmission to exposure, to illness and throughout the course of illness to late-stage illness, palliative care, and, ultimately, death and dying. This is clearly not a homogeneous group of clinicians. As the impact of HIV/AIDS has grown, more services have become available to comprehensively treat persons with AIDS. Caregivers include physicians of every specialty;

outpatient and inpatient clinicians; acute care, chronic care, and long-term care clinicians; hospice care, including home hospice clinicians; and others. Service organizations employ individuals from many different types of occupational categories, including health educators, HIV pre- and post-test counselors, nurses, primary care physicians, infectious disease specialists, pediatricians, and other medical and surgical specialists. All of these professionals work together to provide seamless, integrated care for persons with HIV/AIDS and its diverse and complex presentations. The more extended circle of caregivers includes laboratory technicians, psychiatrists, psychologists, and other mental health clinicians, substance abuse counselors and other health professionals, dentists, social workers, case managers, and many dedicated volunteers.

Some clinicians' involvement with HIV/AIDS-related work may be very brief but very intense and emotional, while other clinicians may care for patients on a long-term basis. Some of the passionate clinicians who have dedicated their careers to the care of HIV/AIDS-affected individuals are approaching the end of their professional careers or have aged and retired from the workforce. Some of the most devoted clinicians were defined by their commitment to the cause and strong advocacy that helped shape the course of the epidemic. Their contributions and impact remain as part of the narrative of the HIV/AIDS experience. With that, there is a loss of the institutional memory of the magnitude of the impact of HIV/AIDS on the patients, clinicians, hospital systems, and communities.

The changing environment of the HIV/AIDS pandemic continues to present new challenges and struggles and to demand responses that are flexible and modifiable. As new knowledge is integrated in clinical care, the resources available remain vulnerable, and constant vigilance is required to ensure responsible allocation of resources to care for persons with HIV/AIDS. By recognizing the challenges and not diminishing or trivializing their contributions, clinicians can continue to have lifelong, satisfying work experience, managing work-related stressors in this environment in an effective manner.

OCCUPATIONAL EXPOSURE IN THE CARE OF PERSONS WITH HIV

The availability of effective antiretroviral therapy has led to gradual diminution of fear of exposure in the 36 years of the HIV pandemic. In addition to universal precautions, all healthcare facilities are required to maintain a policy and standard operating procedure for dealing with employee exposures. Updated recommendations for occupational postexposure prophylaxis have been developed by the Centers for Disease Control and Prevention (CDC, 2013). A summary of the U.S. Public Health Service guidelines for the management of occupational exposures to HIV and recommendations for postexposure prophylaxis is as follows:

- Post-exposure prophylaxis (PEP) is recommended when occupational exposures to HIV occur.
- Determine the HIV status of the exposure source patient to guide need for HIV PEP, if possible.

Table 48.2 STRESSORS IN HIV/AIDS-RELATED HEALTHCARE DELIVERY

PATIENT-RELATED STRESSORS	HEALTHCARE WORKER–RELATED STRESSORS	SYSTEMIC STRESSORS	SOCIETAL STRESSORS
High mortality rates	Unresolved personal losses	High caseload	Social stigma and sense of professional isolation
Increasing number of patients with character disorders	Unrealistic goals for patient outcomes	Optimal levels of infection control Fear of exposure	Caring for patients with nontraditional and different lifestyles that clinicians are unfamiliar with
Homophobia and issues of human sexuality	Uncertainty about treatment	Ensuring the availability of support services required for comprehensive care of HIV complications	Homophobia and issues of human sexuality
Issues of substance abuse	Maintaining professional competence in HIV care		Ethical and legal dilemmas
Lack of supports and unmet needs assumed by providers	Inadequacy in treating patients' suffering and psychosocial and neuropsychiatric symptoms		Issues of substance abuse

- Start PEP medication regimens as soon as possible after occupational exposure to HIV and continue them for a 4-week duration.
- New recommendation—PEP medication regimens should contain three (or more) antiretroviral drugs (listed in Appendix A at https://stacks.cdc.gov/view/cdc/20711) for all occupational exposures to HIV.
- Expert consultation is recommended for any occupational exposures to HIV and, at a minimum, for situations described in Box 1 at https://stacks.cdc.gov/view/cdc/20711.
- Provide close follow-up for exposed personnel (Box 2 at https://stacks.cdc.gov/view/cdc/20711) that includes counseling, baseline and follow-up HIV testing, and monitoring for drug toxicity. Follow-up appointments should begin within 72 hours of an HIV exposure.
- New recommendation—If a newer fourth-generation combination HIV p24 antigen-HIV antibody test is used for follow-up HIV testing of an exposed healthcare professional, HIV testing may be concluded at 4 months after exposure (Box 2 at https://stacks.cdc.gov/view/cdc/20711). If a newer testing platform is not available, follow-up HIV testing is typically concluded at 6 months after an HIV exposure.

Although the implementation of these recommendations will vary from one institution to another, the overall goal of evaluating the incident and, if necessary, providing the exposed person with post-exposure prophylaxis within a 2- to 4-hour window is the gold standard.

The selection of a particular medication regimen for HIV post-exposure prophylaxis must balance the risk for infection against the potential toxicities of the antiretroviral agents used. Given the complexities of choosing and caring for a person taking post-exposure prophylaxis, whenever possible, consultation with a physician who has experience with antiretroviral agents is recommended. If an infectious disease physician is not available, the National Clinicians' Post-Exposure Prophylaxis Hotline (PEP hotline), 888–448–4911, is operational 24 hours a day.

Exposure prevention remains the primary strategy for reducing occupational blood-borne pathogen infections in the healthcare setting. Universal precautions have been practiced safely; examples of these include standard glove precautions for patient contact, and safer needle and phlebotomy devices to reduce percutaneous injuries.

In summary, although blood and body fluid exposures remain a significant concern, much progress has been made in the prevention of acquisition of hepatitis B, hepatitis C, and HIV in the healthcare environment.

PROTECTIVE FACTORS IN HIV CLINICIAN BURNOUT

To identify ways in which stress affected the domestic and social lives of HIV clinicians, Miller and Gillies (1996) conducted a study among HIV clinicians. Of all staff members, one-third of those without a long-term emotional relationship stated that they felt their work-related issues interfered with their developing and maintaining relationships. Most participants reported spending a considerable amount of time discussing work with their partners. Work-related issues caused conflict for just under half of the total sample. Thirty-nine percent reported that their partners complained regularly about their commitment to work, and 25% overall reported their relationship had suffered as a result of their work in HIV or oncology.

At the same time, many clinicians find satisfaction in communication with their patients. When Broyard wrote his article about what he wanted from clinicians, he also stated that "in learning to talk to his patients the doctor may talk himself into loving his work. He has little to lose and much to gain by letting the sick man into his heart" (Broyard, 1990). Evidence bears out the vital role of doctor–patient communication in both patient and physician satisfaction (Halbesleben et al., 2006, 2008; Hall and Roter, 2002; Hall et al., 1988; Jackson et al., 2001; Krasner et al., 2009; Ratanawongsa et al., 2008).

Bennett and colleagues (1991) found that oncology nurses suffered burnout with greater frequency than that of AIDS nurses, although AIDS nurses showed greater intensity of burnout after adjustment for frequency of burnout. Men were as likely to suffer burnout as women, and age significantly influenced burnout inversely (Bennett et al., 1991). Bianchi and colleagues (1997) found that among doctors and nurses on a pediatric service in Rome, there was a correlation between experience and time on the job and lower rates of emotional exhaustion. Clinicians with less than a year on the job showed a higher degree of physical and emotional exhaustion, suffered from a high density of stress factors, and set up a large number of defensive strategies. Clinicians at work for 1 to 3 years showed a moderate degree of physical, emotional, and mental exhaustion, did not suffer from particular stress factors, and perceived a high level of social support from colleagues. Clinicians with more than 3 years of experience did not suffer from particular physical or emotional exhaustion and experienced medium levels. While feeling the action of various daily stressors, they did not use the social support offered at work.

Aiken and Sloane (1997) surveyed 820 nurses working with AIDS patients. Nurses who worked in dedicated or specialized units or in "magnet" hospitals known to possess organizational characteristics attractive to nurses exhibited lower levels of emotional exhaustion than those among nurses working in general, scattered-bed medical units. These differences persisted after nurse characteristics were statistically controlled, but they were accounted for in part by controlling for the amount of the organizational support that nurses perceived was present at the work place.

In a study by Mueller (1997) of a sample of 144 social workers providing care for HIV/AIDS clients, the predictors of burnout included measures of social support, caregiver values, characteristics of the work setting, the nature of the work with HIV/AIDS clients, and demographic factors. Study data demonstrated that burnout was significantly and inversely related to social support received from co-workers, supervisors, the caregiver's age, education level, income, caseload size, and years of work with AIDS clients. Burnout was significantly and positively associated with the number of recent caregiver client deaths and the proportion of caseload that was comprised of HIV/AIDS clients. Total burnout was not related to spouse support, caregiver's gender, sexual orientation, HIV serostatus, or theoretical orientation.

Demmer (2002) surveyed the motivations, stressors, and rewards of 180 workers employed in nine AIDS service organizations in New York City. The sample consisted of social service workers (56%), administrative workers (22%), healthcare workers (18%), and other workers (4%). Forty-two percent of the workers had been working in the AIDS field for 5 years or more years. The two main reasons for choosing this line of work were a desire to help others, followed by having experienced the loss of a loved one to AIDS. Overall, respondents rated their level of stressors in their job as moderate. The main category of stress was lack of support. The most important individual stressors were societal attitudes toward AIDS, salary, client deaths, and administrative duties. The most highly valued reward factor associated with AIDS caregivers was "personal effectiveness." Nurses in AIDS care experiencing high levels of stress in their workplace were significantly more likely to use wishful thinking, planful problem-solving, and avoidance as coping strategies, whereas stress originating from patient care was more likely to be dealt with by using positive assessment and acceptance (Kalichman et al., 2000).

Des Jarlais (1990) reported that caregivers who had worked previously in the area of drug abuse treatment went from working in a drug abuse treatment program to working in an AIDS program without a conscious choice in the matter. Part of the strain in burnout in this group came from the sense that the needs created by the epidemic had completely taken over one's professional life, not having had the opportunity to make a professional choice.

MEASURES OF CLINICIAN BURNOUT

The Maslach Burnout Inventory (MBI) has been established as a credible measure of burnout and focuses on the personal experience of work (Enzmann et al. 1995; Lee and Ashforth, 1990). It measures dimensions that include exhaustion–energy; depersonalization–involvement; and inefficacy–accomplishment. The MBI was tested to see if it could be translated to other languages, while preserving its psychometric properties; issues of theoretical flaws and cultural bias need further validation (Enzmann et al., 1995).

Other tools have been used in an attempt to measure and quantify burnout, including the Coping Orientation to Problem Experience (COPE) inventory and the State Trait Anxiety Inventory (STAI). Burnout may include symptoms of depression, anxiety, posttraumatic stress disorder (PTSD), and personality disorders. These boundaries are sometimes blurred, as in efforts to distinguish between depression and demoralization syndrome and burnout using anhedonia or the ability of the individual to experience pleasure. Individuals suffering from depression cannot experience pleasure, whereas individuals suffering from burnout or demoralization should be able to experience pleasure. This distinction is made by self-reporting and is open to a wide range of understanding and interpretations (see Box 48.1).

The expansion in the terminology used to label job-related distress may be due in part to an attempt to avoid the stigma of mental illness, labeling clinically relevant symptoms with more socially acceptable, politically correct, current concepts. The clear intent is to stay away from the better-known entity of psychiatric diagnoses (for example, depression), as these diagnoses are still feared and stigmatized. Responsible and accurate reporting of burnout is necessary to avoid negative, further stigmatizing, and frightening implications that may turn people away from gravitating toward the field of HIV/

AIDS healthcare delivery. A study by Van Servellen and Leake (1993), conducted in Los Angeles, examined burnout among nurses working on AIDS special care units (SCUs), oncology SCUs, medical intensive care units, and general medical units and measured the extent to which delivery method, patient diagnosis, or other key personal and work-related characteristic were associated with the level of distress in these nurses. A sample of 237 nurses from 18 units in seven hospitals was surveyed, using the MBI. This study showed no significant differences in burnout scores across nurse samples representing variations in patient diagnosis and delivery method, and all nurses had similar level of distress.

Catalan and colleagues (1996) compared serious disease, psychological stress, and work-related burnout in staff working with AIDS patients and with cancer patients. Seventy nurses and 41 doctors were compared through a self-reported method of assessment, using the MBI, General Health Questionnaire (GHQ), and the Social Adjustment Scale-Modified (SAS-M). One-third of the staff had substantial levels of psychological morbidity and about a fifth had significant levels of work-related stress. The study confirmed the existence of stress but found no difference in stress between AIDS and cancer-related work.

Clinicians' reactions to stressors are both positive and negative and can be mobilized to enable them to continue in a constructive fashion within their professional and personal lives. People do their best when they believe in what they are doing and when they can maintain their pride, integrity, and self-respect. The best reward is receiving recognition for the things one likes to do. If individuals reach the best fit in terms of their professional preparation and level of personal maturity, introspection, and goals, they should be able to deal with challenges, such as working in the field of HIV/AIDS, and feel a sense of personal reward and professional accomplishment. Burnout is more likely when there is a mismatch between the nature of the job and the character of the person who does the job. When an illness had been as stigmatized and feared as AIDS, it was not always effortless to maintain a sense of pride, and clinicians may suffer attitudes toward them that are similar to those directed toward the disease. Consequently, the clinician may experience a sense of isolation, distance, and trepidation or apprehension.

Visintini and colleagues (1996) studied the role played by psychological stress and sociodemographic factors as predictors of burnout in nurses, administering the AIDS Impact Scale (AIS) and the MBI to nurses in the AIDS field. The sample was composed of 410 nurses from 19 departments for the treatment of infectious diseases. A low level of burnout was indicated by MBI scores, but a small proportion had a high level of burnout, with no significant association between sociodemographic variables and the MBI scales. There was a significant correlation between low burnout rate and the emotional involvement of nurses in their relationships with patients. The results suggest that an empathically involved relationship appears to protect against burnout, in contrast to a frustrating relationship. Moreover, nurses tolerated stress better if they received supportive social rewards.

HIV/AIDS healthcare professionals consist of a very diverse group of physicians and other professionals who care for very diverse patient populations. The nature of HIV infection is that it affects patients as individuals and as groups identified by behavior and not by gender, age, race, or ethnicity. Many HIV/AIDS clinicians have experienced the loss of not only numerous clients but also colleagues and community members, leading to "bereavement overload." For these individuals the rewards outweigh the stressors and the level of job satisfaction is very high. The most highly valued reward factor is "personal effectiveness." Burnout among these dedicated individuals weakens their response and contributes to increased strain on the HIV/AIDS care system. The challenge of workload and mastery and management of it have become very evident with HIV/AIDS (Bennett et al., 1994, 1996). The sense of the immensity of the task and the insufficient tools to cover the need is one of the biggest demoralizing factors in this epidemic.

EVOLVING MENTAL HEALTH ROLES

The role of psychiatrists and other mental health professionals in addressing burnout in HIV caregivers gradually evolved over the past four decades. During the early phase of the AIDS pandemic and with the development of HIV testing in 1985, young individuals were dying from an illness that progressed rapidly (Frierson and Lippmann, 1987). Most available treatments were inadequate to stop or even slow the course of illness. Ignorance associated with fear and prejudice dominated that stage. The role of psychiatrists was to help other clinicians deal with the frustrations, fears, and massive bereavement overload as well as to serve as consultants to their patients.

During the initial period of AZT treatment, there was a shift from hopelessness to testing and engaging patients and staff in treatment. When more effect treatment became available, with the development of combination antiretroviral therapy in 1996, adherence and availability of medications became the focus. Psychiatrists are now in more collaborative roles, with the need for integrated care, to encourage adherence to medical care and antiretroviral therapy and to provide support for patients, families, and caregivers. Psychiatrists in collaborative care are in a unique position to role model and teach doctor–patient communication as well as to preserve trainee and caregiver empathy and compassion (Beach et al., 2006, 2011; Bellini et al., 2002; Bellini and Shea, 2005; Shanafelt et al., 2002, 2005; Testad et al., 2010; Thomas et al., 2007). Through case conferences, walk rounds, and curbside consults, psychiatrists can provide avenues of communication among the members of multidisciplinary teams as well as among the multiple specialists and subspecialists involved in patient care. Through both training and clinical care, psychiatrists and other mental health clinicians can improve patient and caregiver satisfaction and improve adherence and retention in care (Roter et al., 1987, 1997, 2002; Schneider et al., 2004).

Psychiatrists and other mental health clinicians can now provide the necessary support that has been shown to lead to improved outcomes and decreased morbidity and mortality in persons with HIV and AIDS (Mugavero et al., 2014). Please refer to Chapters 1, 2, and 7 of this textbook for more detailed discussion of collaborative care and models of care for persons with HIV and AIDS.

ADDRESSING BURNOUT

When burnout is recognized and diagnosed, specific institutional and/or individual strategies need to be used. Institutional planning for addressing burnout can be conceptualized as prevention, recognition, and treatment, with the goals of longevity in the field and retention of committed workers who stay healthy and derive satisfaction from their work (Aiken and Sloane 1997; Anagnostopoulos et al., 2012; Argentero et al., 2008; Dyrbye et al., 2010; Felton, 1998. These strategies include administrative policies, a philosophical framework, mechanisms for reward, and educational goals and objectives (AbuAlRub, 2004). These can be achieved by comprehensive orientation for new employees and refresher courses for employees already on the job, effective forums for conflict resolution and shared decision-making, effective vertical communication, and the fostering of collaborative models, as opposed to aggressive, personally competitive styles.

Shifting in funding and costs is indicative of a very fast-paced change in the HIV/AIDS healthcare delivery system. Inpatient virology, tuberculosis, and dedicated AIDS units are being downsized or closed because of length-of-stay issues and the reduced need for long-term, inpatient treatment of HIV/AIDS-related conditions. These changes could lead to anxiety about job loss and to the end of some very resilient and productive careers.

A large source of professional reward and satisfaction is derived from recognizing the monumental achievements in social and clinical aspects of the HIV epidemic. Individually, nurses, doctors, and other professionals face the constant challenge of adapting to new and evolving work environments. Insight and individual coping styles can be supported and enhanced by shared values. This can help balance the institutional–individual fit.

Coping has been described as "constantly changing cognitive and behavioral efforts to manage specific external and/ or internal demands that are appraised as taxing or exceeding the resources of the person" (Lazarus and Folkman, 1984). Strategies for coping in a stressful work environment apply to coping in the HIV/AIDS workplace.

THE ROLE OF RELIGION AND SPIRITUALITY

Religion and the healing powers of spirituality have not been described as central strategies in the fight against AIDS. From the very first manifestation of the epidemic, moral judgment was attached to the "forbidden behavior" and the "sins" involved in contracting AIDS. Promiscuity, homosexuality, substance abuse, and the sharing of needles have all been unacceptable behaviors for many members of most organized religions. Religious organizations have also been involved in taking care of the dying. It is obvious that "believers" find strength in prayer and in perceived relevant selected passages from the scriptures, but for most of the secular public and healthcare providers, these rituals are not necessarily readily available and are often overlooked as healing tools.

Spirituality, as distinct from religion, has helped workers in finding meaning in their work and value in their contributions and their own experience. Resilience among many workers has been achieved through maintenance of a sense of coherence. Spirituality gives people meaning and purpose in life. While it can be achieved through participation in a religion, it can be much broader than that, such as through involvement in common values such as family, humanism, or the arts.

Keeping alive the spirit of the far-too-many fatalities and continuing a transformed relationship with the deceased lives have become a very effective mode for survivors, significant others, and HIV/AIDS healthcare providers to value, respect, and cherish their lives. December 1 was designated Annual World's AIDS Day to increase global awareness of AIDS and to pay tribute to the people who lost their battle to the disease. An institutional memorial service, described by Tiamson and colleagues (1998), serves as a model to help clinicians with closure and renewal. The AIDS Memorial Quilt Project was one of the most powerful images of the AIDS epidemic. Tens of thousands of colorful individual panels full of stories of diverse life experiences of men, women, and children were combined together on display to concretize the magnitude of the loss. The quilt panels have become another avenue to channel the overwhelming sense of loss of people and the immeasurable life potential. A letter written by loved ones and a favorite memory accompany each individual panel, made in a way that the individual would have liked as a memorial.

CONCLUSION

The last four decades of the HIV pandemic have seen change and progress in the medical care of persons with HIV and in social attitudes toward HIV/AIDS, but what remains the same as ever is the impact of the illness and the human experience of it. Caregivers have remained resilient witnesses to the immense loss and suffering brought on by the HIV pandemic. While HIV caregivers and clinicians practice commitment and selfless dedication to the care of persons with HIV/ADIS, burnout has remained a risk. The awareness of burnout can improve adherence to care and lead to better outcomes in persons with HIV and AIDS. In addition, more time for doctor–patient communication and a diminution of work stressors (Bynny, 2016) can help physicians in the care of persons with HIV/AIDS and can help their patients. Resilience in the face of such life-altering experiences is not about going back to the way we were but about the growth experienced by it; no one remains unaffected in the face of such a humanitarian disaster.

REFERENCES

AbuAlRub RF (2004). Job stress, job performance, and social support among hospital nurses. *J Nurs Scholarsh* 36(1):73–78.

Aiken LH, Sloane DM (1997). Effects of organizational innovations in AIDS care on burnout among urban hospital nurses. *Work Occup* 24:453–477.

Anagnostopoulos F, Liolios E, Persefonis G, Slater J, Kafetsios K, Niakas D (2012). Physician burnout and patient satisfaction with consultation in primary health care settings: evidence of relationships from a one-with-many design. *J Clin Psychol Med Settings* 19:401–410.

Argentero P, Dell'Olivo B, Ferretti MS (2008). Staff burnout and patient satisfaction with the quality of dialysis care. *Am J Kidney Dis* 51(1):80–92.

Beach MC, Roter DL, Wang NY, Duggan PS, Cooper LA (2006). Are physicians' attitudes of respect accurately perceived by patients and associated with more positive communication behaviors? *Patient Educ Couns* 62:347–354.

Beach MC, Saha S, Korthuis PT, et al. (2011). Patient–provider communication differs for black compared to white HIV-infected patients. *AIDS Behav* 15(4):805–811.

Bellini LM, Baime M, Shea JA (2002). Variation of mood and empathy during internship. *JAMA* 287(23):3143–3146.

Bellini LM, Shea JA (2005). Mood change and empathy decline persist during three years of internal medicine training. *Acad Med* 80(2):164–167.

Bennett L, Kelaher M, Ross MW (1994). Quality of life in health care professionals: burnout and its associated factors in HIV/AIDS related care. *Psychol Health* 9:273–283.

Bennett L, Michie P, Kippaz S (1991). Quantitative analysis of burnout and its associated factors in AIDS nursing. *AIDS Care* 3:181–192.

Bennett L, Ross MW, Sunderland R (1996). The relationship between recognition, rewards and burnout in AIDS caring. *AIDS Care* 8:145–153.

Bianchi A, Ferrari V, Soccorsi R, Tatarelli R (1997). The burnout syndrome in a pediatrics department: pilot project. *New Trends Exp Clin Psychiatry* 13:193–208.

Broyard A (1990). Doctor talk to me. *New York Times Magazine*, August 26, 1990. http://www.nytimes.com/1990/08/26/magazine/doctor-talk-to-me.html?pagewanted=all Accessed July 24, 2016.

Burton C (2016). Physician burnout affects healthcare facilities, too. *Physician's Money Digest*, June 24, 2016. http://www.hcplive.com/physicians-money-digest/practice-management/physician-burnout-affects-healthcare-facilities-too. Accessed July 24, 2016.

Byyny RL (2016). Time matters in caring for patients—twenty minutes is not enough. *The Pharos* 79:2–8.

Catalan J, Burgess A, Pergami A, Hulme N, Gazzard B, Phillips R (1996). The psychological impact on staff of caring for people with serious diseases: the case of HIV infection and oncology. *J Psychosom Res* 40(4):425–435.

Centers for Disease Control and Prevention (CDC) (2013). Updated U.S. Public Health Service guidelines for the management of occupational exposures to HIV and recommendations for postexposure prophylaxis. https://stacks.cdc.gov/view/cdc/20711. Accessed July 24, 2016.

Clever SL, Ford DE, Rubenstein LV, et al. (2006). Primary care patients' involvement in decision-making is associated with improvement in depression. *Med Care* 44:398–405.

Cooke M (1992). Supporting health care workers in the treatment of HIV-infected patients. *Prim Care* 19(1):245–256.

Demmer C (2002). Stressors and rewards for workers in AIDS service organizations. *AIDS Patient Care STDS* 16:179–187.

Des Jarlais DC (1990). Stages in the response of drug abuse treatment system to AIDS epidemic in New York City. *J Drug Issues* 20:335–347.

Dyrbye LN, Power DV, Massie FS, et al. (2010). Factors associated with resilience to and recovery from burnout: a prospective, multi-institutional study of US medical students. *Med Educ* 44(10):1016–1026.

Enzman D, Schaufeli W, Girault, N (1995). The validity of the Maslach Burnout Inventory in three national samples. In L Bennett, D Miller D, M Ross (eds.), *Health Workers and AIDS: Research, Intervention and Current Issues in Burnout and Response* (pp. 131–150). Amsterdam: Harwood Academic Publishers.

Felton JS (1998). Burnout as a clinical entity—its importance in health care workers. *Occup Med* 48; 237–250.

Frierson RL, Lippmann SB (1987). Stresses on physicians treating AIDS. *Am Fam Physician* 35:153–159.

Gueritault-Chalvin V, Kalichman SC, Demi A, Peterson JL (2000). Work-related stress and occupational burnout in AIDS caregivers: test of a coping model with nurses providing AIDS care. *AIDS Care* 12(2):149–161.

Halbesleben JR (2006). Patient reciprocity and physician burnout: what do patients bring to the patient–physician relationship? *Health Serv Manage Res* 19:215–222.

Halbesleben JR, Rathert C (2008). Linking physician burnout and patient outcomes: exploring the dyadic relationship between physicians and patients. *Health Care Manage Rev* 33(1):29–39.

Hall JA, Roter DL (2002). Do patients talk differently to male and female physicians? A meta-analytic review. *Patient Educ Couns* 48(3):217–224.

Hall JA, Roter DL, Katz NR (1988). Meta-analysis of correlates of provider behavior in medical encounters. *Med Care* 26:657–675.

Jackson JL, Chamberlin J, Kroenke K (2001). Predictors of patient satisfaction. *Soc Sci Med* 52(4):609–620.

Kalichman SC, Gueritault-Chalvin V, and Demi A (2000). Sources of occupational stress and coping strategies among nurses working in AIDS care. *J Assoc Nurses AIDS Care* 11(3):31–37.

Kaplan SH, Greenfield S, Ware JE (1989). Assessing the effects of physician–patient interactions on the outcomes of chronic disease. *Med Care* 27(3 Suppl):S110–S127.

Karam F, Bérard A, Sheehy O, et al. (2012). Reliability and validity of the 4-item perceived stress scale among pregnant women: results from the OTIS antidepressants study. *Res Nurs Health* 35(4):363–375.

Krasner MS, Epstein RM, Beckman H, et al. (2009). Association of an educational program in mindful communication with burnout, empathy, and attitudes among primary care physicians. *JAMA* 302(12):1284–1293.

Lazarus RS, Folkman S (1984). *Stress Appraisal and Coping*. New York: Springer.

Lee R, Ashforth B (1990). On the meaning of Maslach's three dimensions of burnout. *J Appl Psychol* 75(6):743–747.

Lert F, Chastang JF, Castano I (2001). Psychological stress among hospital doctors caring for HIV patients in the late nineties. *AIDS Care* 13(6):763–778.

Levinson W, Roter DL, Mullooly JP, Dull VT, Frankel RM (1997). Physician–patient communication. The relationship with malpractice claims among primary care physicians and surgeons. *JAMA* 277(7):553–559.

Macks JA, Abrams DI (1992). Burnout among HIV/AIDS health care providers. Helping the people on the frontlines. *AIDS Clin Rev* 1992:281–299.

Maslach C, Jackson SE, Leiter MP (1997). Maslach Burnout Inventory, third edition. In CP Zalaquett, RJ Wood (eds.), *Evaluating Stress: A Book of Resources* (pp. 191–218). Lanham, MD: Scarecrow Education.

Miller D, Gillies P (1996). Is there life after work? Experiences of HIV and oncology health staff. *AIDS Care* 8:167–182.

Mueller KP (1997). The relationship between social support and burnout among social work caregivers of HIV/AIDS clients. *Dissertation Abstracts International Section A: Humanities and Social Sciences* Vol. A, p. 3683.

Mugavero MJ, Westfall AO, Cole SR, et al. (2014). Beyond core indicators of retention in HIV care: missed clinic visits are independently associated with all-cause mortality. *Clin Infect Dis* 59:1471–1479.

Ratanawongsa N, Roter D, Beach MC, et al. (2008). Physician burnout and patient–physician communication during primary care encounters. *J Gen Intern Med* 23(10):1581–1588.

Roter DL, Hall JA, Katz NR (1987). Relations between physicians' behaviors and analogue patients' satisfaction, recall, and impressions. *Med Care* 25(5):437–451.

Roter DL, Larson S (2002). The Roter Interaction Analysis System (RIAS): utility and flexibility for analysis of medical interactions. *Patient Educ Couns* 46(4):243–251.

Roter DL, Stewart M, Putnam SM, Lipkin M Jr, Stiles W, Inui TS (1997). Communication patterns of primary care physicians. *JAMA* 277:350–356.

Schneider J, Kaplan SH, Greenfield S, Li W, Wilson IB (2004). Better physician–patient relationships are associated with higher reported adherence to antiretroviral therapy in patients with HIV infection. *J Gen Intern Med* 19(11):1096–1103.

Shanafelt TD, Bradley KA, Wipf JE, Back AL (2002). Burnout and self-reported patient care in an internal medicine residency program. *Ann Intern Med* 136(5):358–367.

Shanafelt TD, Hasan O, Dyrbye LN, et al. (2015). Changes in burnout and satisfaction with work-life balance in physicians and the general US working population between 2011 and 2014. *Mayo Clinic Proceedings* 90(12):1600-1613.

Shanafelt TD, Mungo M, Schmitgen J, et al. (2016). Longitudinal study evaluating the association between physician burnout and changes in professional work effort. *Mayo Clin Proc* 91:422–431.

Shanafelt TD, West C, Zhao X, et al. (2005). Relationship between increased personal well-being and enhanced empathy among internal medicine residents. *J Gen Intern Med* 20(7):559–564.

Stewart MA (1995). Effective physician–patient communication and health outcomes: a review. *CMAJ* 152:1423–1433.

Testad I, Mikkelsen A, Ballard C, Aarsland D (2010). Health and well-being in care staff and their relations to organizational and psychosocial factors, care staff and resident factors in nursing homes. *Int J Geriatr Psychiatry* 25(8):789–797.

Thomas MR, Dyrbye LN, Huntington JL, et al. (2007). How do distress and well-being relate to medical student empathy? A multicenter study. *J Gen Intern Med* 22(2):177–183.

Tiamson ML, McArdie R, Girolamer T, Horowitz HW (1998). The institutional memorial service: a strategy to prevent burnout in HIV healthcare workers. *Gen Hospital Psychiatry* 20(2):124–126.

Travado L, Grassi L, Gil F, Ventura C, Martins C; Southern European Psycho-Oncology Study Group (2005). Physician–patient communication among Southern European cancer physicians: the influence of psychosocial orientation and burnout. *Psychooncology* 14(8):661–670.

Van Servellen G, Leake B (1993). Burn-out in hospital nurses: a comparison of acquired immunodeficiency syndrome, oncology, general medical, and intensive care unit nurse samples. *J Prof Nurs* 9(3):169–177.

Visintini R, Campnini E, Fossati A, Bagnato M, Novella A, Maffei C (1996). Psychological stress in nurses' relationships with HIV-infected patients: the risk of burnout syndrome. *AIDS Care* 8(2):183–194.

49.

END-OF-LIFE ISSUES, ETHICAL ISSUES, ADVANCE DIRECTIVES, AND SURROGATE DECISION-MAKING IN THE CARE OF PERSONS WITH HIV

Cynthia Geppert, Mary Ann Cohen, and Rebecca Weintraub Brendel

In this chapter we review several of the most ethically salient recent developments in clinical HIV ethics. These include challenges to the legal and ethical practice of informed consent with the advent of routine HIV testing for adults and pregnant women and their newborns; the expansion and acceptance of home HIV testing; the breach of patient confidentiality in the criminalization of HIV that has extended duty to warn to patients; the exercise of patient self-determination on advance care planning since the passage of federal and state gay marriage laws; and, finally, the conflict between avoiding harm and doing good that comes with the new options of pre- and post-exposure prophylaxis and the lifting of the ban on blood donations from men who have sex with men.

ETHICAL ISSUES IN THE CARE OF PATIENTS WITH HIV

THE END OF EXCEPTIONALISM

HIV has always brought into focus the fundamental conflicts between individual rights and autonomy on the one side and social benefit and the common good on the other that are characteristic of public health ethics. Yet, HIV has also been uniquely characterized by an ethical-political approach of "exceptionalism," borne of the early days of the epidemic when an HIV diagnosis meant only certain death, discrimination, and denial of services. Specifically, because of these features, HIV was to be an ethical and legal exception to the historical management of other sexually transmitted diseases and an American public health tradition of coercion and compulsion in the prevention and treatment of communicable conditions. In the face of near-certain medical prognosis of death and reactionary social attitudes toward the vulnerable and disenfranchised gay men and individuals who inject drugs who were the first persons diagnosed in the United States, HIV patients and many caregivers advocated for exceptionalism, which emphasized the protection of human rights, confidentiality, and the highest standards of informed consent in areas such as HIV testing and reporting (Wolf and Lo, 2004).

When effective antiretroviral therapy and medical care transformed HIV/AIDS into a chronic manageable illness rather than terminal illness, the passage of civil rights protections became necessary, while not sufficient, for a shift in policy. The growing realization among HIV advocacy groups that at least some established public health strategies might be in the best interest of even vulnerable persons led many in the HIV community to question whether the protection that the walls of exceptionalism had afforded had now become an obstacle to optimal HIV care. The nearly 10 years since the publication of first edition of this textbook have seen tremendous shifts in the clinical, social, and legal surround that ineluctably frames ethical issues in the care of patients with HIV. The noted HIV public health ethicist Ronald Bayer has opined that these changes herald the end of HIV exceptionalism (Bayer and Fairchild, 2006).

INFORMED CONSENT AND HIV TESTING

Clinician-Initiated HIV Testing of Adults

After many years of debate, in 2006, the Centers for Disease Control and Prevention (CDC) issued revised recommendations for HIV testing (Branson et al., 2006; CDC, 2006). These recommendations covered testing of adults, adolescents, and pregnant women in all healthcare settings and replaced the 1993 guidance that the progress of science had made clinically archaic and cumbersome in places like emergency rooms— that HIV testing required specific, written, informed consent apart from other authorized medical evaluation. The central revision was the recommendation that HIV be part of broad-based screening in all patients from ages 13 to 64 in every healthcare setting on an opt-out basis. In addition, it recommended that persons at high risk of HIV infection be screened at least annually. Opt-out testing, also called "clinician-initiated testing," means that while the patient must be notified that blood is being drawn for HIV testing, the patient need not specifically authorize this testing as in the past but may opt out by refusing the test. The exceptionalism-era protections of required pre- and post-test counseling and written consent were replaced by the CDC's recommendation that "general consent for medical care should be considered to be sufficient to encompass HIV testing" (Branson et al., 2006).

The predominant ethical justification offered for revisions was based on the consequentialist public health rationale that, by making testing routine, thousands of undiagnosed patients would be tested, treated, and guided to practice prevention, thereby reducing the progression of illness in the individual as well as the toll on and spread of the disease to others. The U.S. Preventive Task Force (2013) considered the balance of benefits and harms when endorsing similar recommendations: "The net benefit of screening for HIV infection in adolescents, adults, and pregnant women is substantial." The CDC also offered a set of ethical rationales to ensure that the ethical consideration of respect for persons would not be wholly abandoned. The CDC's rationales served as a rejoinder to its critics and as reassurance to members of the public concerned that patients would be tested without their knowledge or agreement (Kippax, 2006). The CDC instead argued that treating HIV testing like any other aspect of routine medical care, far from compromising autonomy, actually championed access and voluntarism of patients, as mainstreaming the testing would reduce stigma. Finally, while the formal consent and counseling requirements were removed from testing, the CDC still recommended that all patients receive education and counseling about HIV.

Enduring ethical critiques have focused less on the actual recommendations than on potential problems in implementation that might require additional safeguards (Celada et al., 2011; Waxman et al., 2011). Empirical studies, at least in the United States, have not documented widespread ethically problematic practices and have shown a generally positive reception of routine screening even among adolescents (Minniear et al., 2009). The ethical responses of patients and practitioners have differed in that patients favor the change in the counseling requirement, while practitioners support the switch to opt-out testing (Merchant et al., 2012).

In the first years of implementation of the new guidelines, state laws and hospital policy frequently still required written consent and/or counseling, creating ethical dilemmas for practitioners and patients, but increasingly, legislatures and institutions have updated their own rules and regulations to reinforce the changes, with positive results (Mahajan et al., 2009). As of November 2015, 49 states had passed HIV testing laws consistent with the 2006 CDC recommendations. In 2010, New York passed a law that mandated HIV testing be offered in almost all healthcare settings; a telephone survey in 2011 found that 1 out of 3 respondents had been offered a test at their last healthcare visit and 9 out of 10 had accepted testing (Edelstein et al., 2015).

Yet, ethical vigilance on the part of healthcare professionals, patients, and advocates is still warranted, especially in populations vulnerable to coercion and exploitation and in individuals with diminished decisional capacity, limited health literacy, or limited ability of voluntarism and with low socioeconomic status and power. In rural areas of the United States, ethically relevant barriers to implementation often persist, including confidentiality concerns, continued social

stigma, and lack of evidence-based judgments about risk factors (White et al., 2015). Overall, clinician-initiated screening has been less successful and is seen as more ethically problematic in resource-poor settings (April, 2010).

Clinician-Initiated Testing of Pregnant Women

The clinical discovery that HIV maternal–fetal transmission could be reduced to 2% with rapid HIV testing and antiretroviral treatment provided powerful support of the public health rationale for removing the counseling and written consent requirement for pregnant women. The reasoning became even stronger when subsequent CDC data showed that 30% of the mothers of HIV-infected infants had not been tested before delivery and that less demanding screening modes resulted in higher rates of testing (CDC, 2006). Thus, in 2006, CDC guidelines called for HIV screening to be included in the routine panel of prenatal screening tests presented to all pregnant women on the same opt-out after-notification basis as for other adults. The CDC additionally recommended repeat screening during the third trimester for patients at elevated personal or population risk (Branson et al., 2006).

For some advocates, however, for continued protection of vulnerable or potentially vulnerable populations this change in policy went too far. Critics of the new CDC position further contended that for pregnant women this approach introduced an impermissible element of coercion in restricting reproductive decisions that was unacceptable, in that testing could not respect autonomy without adequate counseling and specific informed consent (Fields and Kaplan, 2011). Other ethicists, however, while acknowledging the potential challenges to the voluntariness requirement of informed consent, contended that the benefit of decreased HIV incidence, increased screening of vulnerable women, mainstreaming of HIV as a medical condition, and reduction of stigma made opt-out ethically justifiable (Wocial and Cox, 2013).

Given these concerns, some ethics experts have continued to support opt-in testing. Opt-in screening usually requires that the woman receive both pre-test counseling and make an affirmative statement—often in writing—that she agrees to receive the test (CDC, 2006). In opposition, others have criticized the recommendations for having not gone far enough and have advocated that mandatory—rather than opt-out—testing of all pregnant women is in the best interest of the mother, the fetus, and the public (Schuklenk and Kleinsmidt, 2007).

The American College of Obstetricians and Gynecologists (2007) has opined that either opt-in or opt-out practices are ethically acceptable but that mandatory testing is not. They note the public health advantages of opt-in screening. Smith and colleagues (2007) agree that opt-out testing could be defensible and furthermore suggest that mandatory testing could withstand ethical scrutiny for both options, only if the mother's access to state-of-the art antiretroviral treatment was assured. They argue, however, that opt-out and mandatory testing would be ethically concerning in resource-poor areas where the standard of care is not readily available or where culturally, HIV would increase the risk of domestic violence (Smith et al., 2007).

Screening of Newborns

A small number of states permit or require that healthcare professionals test pregnant women for HIV without their consent. For example, New York mandates that newborns be tested for HIV. These requirements recapitulate maternal–fetal rights conflicts that have been politically divisive in contemporary American politics. Practitioners and patients face agonizing legal and ethical dilemmas when a mother refuses to be tested either during pregnancy or at delivery and/or also refuses to allow her newborn to be tested and treated, especially in states where such care is mandated (Tessmer-Tuck et al., 2014). As in so much of HIV ethics, it is important for practitioners be aware of both the legal framework in the jurisdictions in which they practice as well as how to access to knowledgeable legal counsel. Legal advocates point out that the direction of the courts in HIV conflicts between maternal rights and the health of the infant is not yet clear, and decisions so far have been inconsistent (Hanssens et al., 2009).

Another public health ethics dilemma may arise when a mother's HIV status is unknown at delivery, a situation that already reflects a failure of the public health system's primary and secondary prevention strategies. The American Academy of Pediatrics' (AAP) position is that opt-out testing should be used for universal screening of pregnant women, as this practice provides the optimal chance of treating the infant. When serostatus is unknown in labor, the AAP recommends the rapid HIV testing of the mother using opt-out consent, so that if the mother tests positive for HIV, treatment of the infant can be immediately initiated in order to prevent transmission to the infant. When delivery occurs without knowledge of HIV serostatus, the AAP recommends that both the newborn and mother undergo rapid HIV testing (American Academy of Pediatrics, Committee on Pediatric AIDS, 2008).

Advocates who strongly oppose any form of testing of newborns without the mother's express permission (i.e., opt-in testing) underscore that the test automatically constrains the mother to learn her own HIV status. They further argue that this action violates the mother's privacy and consent rights, exposing her to potential discrimination and further harm through breach of trust with the healthcare system that, counterproductively, could result in reluctance to seek treatment for both mother and child in the future. As an alternative model, these advocates propose that adopting a shared decision-making model in which practitioners provide women with accurate information about the benefits and risks of testing and treatment ensures access to care no matter what a woman chooses. Then respect for the woman's decision will have the most enduring positive effect on preventing maternal–fetal HIV transmission and providing longitudinal care for patients who are HIV positive. This is even more crucial for women with multiple vulnerabilities and in jurisdictions where testing and treatment are compulsory (Hanssens et al., 2009).

HIV Self-Testing

As with routine HIV testing, empirical studies have not supported many of the early conceptual ethical concerns about home HIV testing, including associated psychosocial harms, false positives, and failure to obtain follow up care (Brown et al., 2014). Instead, current ethical issues related to home-testing revolve around the need to expand access and acceptance among at-risk and vulnerable populations (Frye et al., 2015). Like for routine HIV testing, concerns remain about the regulation and technical validity of these tests in under-resourced and developing countries. In addition, in order for the societal benefits of testing to be realized, protections for individual autonomy are required (Scott, 2014).

SOCIAL GOOD AND INDIVIDUAL HARM: TREATMENT AS PREVENTION

Pre-exposure Prophylaxis

The same medical advances that have dramatically improved HIV testing and treatment have also made unparalleled preventive options available. Among the most promising of these interventions is pre-exposure prophylaxis (PrEP). The CDC defined PrEP as "a new HIV prevention method in which people who do not have HIV infection take a pill daily to reduce their risk of becoming infected" (CDC, 2012). This simple definition belies the complex ethics controversy surrounding the conditions and circumstances in which the use of PrEP is ethically appropriate. Again, as for other decisions regarding HIV, this debate involves ethical tensions between individual benefits and preferences, community benefit, and resource allocation, especially in resource-poor areas.

In the second decade of the twenty-first century, a series of landmark studies demonstrated the efficacy of PrEP. In 2010, antiretroviral chemoprophylaxis showed a substantial reduction (44%) in HIV infection in the high-risk population of men who have sex with men (Grant et al., 2010). A similar result was then reported in heterosexual couples, with a reduction of up to 75%. Importantly, this study was conducted in Africa among serodiscordant couples, often the focus of confidentiality-versus-nonmaleficence ethical dilemmas.

Based on these studies and other research (Thigpen et al., 2012), in 2012 emtricitabine/tenofovir became the first FDA-approved drug for HIV PrEP in high-risk adults. Early opponents warned that PrEP would encourage irresponsible sexual behavior, terming PrEP "risk compensation," and undermining the very preventive objective of the drugs (Blumenthal and Haubrich, 2014). However, early research has not found an increase in sexual disinhibition following availability of PrEP (Marcus et al., 2013), and supporters of PrEP contend that these concerns represent a version of the veiled sexual moralism that previously led to exceptionalism and therefore could reinvigorate stigma. Key to avoiding such a backlash will be protecting confidential patient information so that, in particular, younger and marginalized groups feel comfortable seeking care and feel safe disclosing their risk factors (Arora and Streed, 2015). Overall, the strongest ethical basis for use of PrEP is as part of a comprehensive set of prevention measures that also include biobehavioral interventions such as safer sex counseling, condom use, and regular HIV testing (CDC, 2014; INSIGHT START Study Group, 2015;

New York State Department of Health, 2015; Smith et al., 2014; White House, 2015; WHO, 2016a, 2016b).

Good ethics depend on good science, and there is no clearer example of the way in which clinical research informs ethical reasoning and even changes ethical justifications than PrEP. In addition to the concerns just discussed, early ethical attention focused on concerns about the possibility that PrEP as preventive treatment could lead to antiviral resistance through nonadherence and even encourage high-risk sexual activity. Substantial evidence over the last decade, however, has shown that neither of these risks is significant (Marcus et al., 2013), while the accumulated scientific evidence of the benefits of PrEP has become so overwhelming that all current national and international recommendations include PrEP. As such, the ethical focus has now shifted to expanding access to prevention and treatment options in resource-poor areas, in accordance with principles of social justice (Macklin and Cowan, 2012).

ETHICAL ISSUES RELATED TO PREVENTION OF HIV

Current strategies for HIV prevention include communication, prevention of HIV transmission, improvement of adherence to risk reduction interventions and medical care, addressing healthcare disparities, and amelioration of stigma in persons with HIV and AIDS. These approaches appear in recently published guidelines online and in print. Examples of such guidelines include the National AIDS Strategy Updated to 2020 (White House, 2015), the 2015 Blueprint to Eliminate AIDS in New York State (New York State Department of Health, 2015), and the World Health Organization Consolidated Guidelines on the Use of Antiretroviral Drugs for Treating and Preventing HIV Infection (WHO, 2016a). Following are salient points for prevention for all persons, as well as for persons at substantial risk.

KEY STRATEGIES FOR HIV PREVENTION IN ALL PERSONS

1. Recommend routine HIV testing for all persons from 13 to 64 years of age and for persons of any age with risk behaviors (CDC, 2014).

2. Consider encouraging and offering routine HIV testing as part of initial comprehensive psychiatric assessment.

3. Provide education for HIV prevention and make condoms available in psychiatric inpatient and outpatient facilities.

4. Assess for risk behaviors and encourage barrier contraception, treatment for substance use disorders, and safe injecting drug use.

5. Reduce and prevent HIV risk behaviors to prevent transmission.

6. Treat substance use and other psychiatric disorders.

7. Treat early with antiretrovirals within the first 72 hours after exposure to HIV to prevent both HIV infection and development of independent reservoirs for HIV in the brain (Heaton et al., 2011).

8. Initiate antiretroviral therapy in early asymptomatic HIV infection, regardless of CD4 count, to improve outcomes and avoid development of independent CNS reservoirs for HIV (CDC, 2014; Heaton et al., 2011; INSIGHT START Study Group, 2015).

KEY STRATEGIES FOR HIV PREVENTION FOR PERSONS AT SUBSTANTIAL RISK: TREATMENT AS PREVENTION

Persons who are thought to be the most substantially vulnerable to HIV infection include HIV-negative members of serodiscordant couples and HIV-negative injecting drug users. An HIV-negative member of a serodiscordant couple may take PrEP to prevent infection. PrEP and post-exposure prophylaxis (PEP) with antiretroviral medications such as tenofovir, together with emtricitabine in combination with safer sex practices, barrier contraception, and safe injecting drug practices, can prevent HIV transmission in serodiscordant couples. The evidence for the use of PrEP and PEP in serodiscordant couples is strong (CDC, 2014; Smith et al., 2014).

PrEP may also be an effective measure in persons with HIV who inject drugs (Smith et al., 2014). In 2014 and 2015, both the CDC (2014) and WHO (2016a) included persons who inject drugs in their support of PrEP as an HIV prevention method. Much of the evidence of the efficacy of PrEP in persons who inject drugs was derived from the Bangkok Tenofovir Study (Choopanya et al., 2013), which demonstrated a 48.9% reduction in HIV infections. Ongoing PrEP demonstration projects have included persons who inject drugs in their participant pool, but additional data concerning overall awareness, uptake, and engagement in persons who inject drugs are limited.

Post-Exposure Prophylaxis

Post-exposure prophylaxis, once limited to occupational exposures, is now broadly available for post-exposure prevention. Following an unanticipated, unplanned, or forced unsafe sexual encounter, any person may take tenofovir and emtricitabine for PEP after unsafe sex. Any HIV-negative member of a serodiscordant couple should also be encouraged to take PEP alone or in combination with barrier contraception (CDC, 2014; Smith et al., 2014). HIV-negative injection drug users can take PEP in combination with barrier contraception and safe injecting practices.

Ethical issues in PEP have long occurred in healthcare settings when a healthcare worker sustains a needle stick or other high-risk exposure. The central ethical tension is between the potential harm to the clinician and the autonomy and privacy of the patient, especially when the patient refuses to consent to the testing. Many practitioners who firmly believe they have a duty to care for persons with blood-borne infections such as HIV just as intensely feel they have a right to know whether or not to subject themselves to the side effects of antiretrovirals for PEP following a high-risk exposure. From an individual rights perspective, proponents of patient privacy argue that the patient's body and sharing of information should not be intruded upon without express permission—even to ease the anxiety and reduce the suffering of another person. As in much of HIV care, there is no consistent answer from either state law or hospital policy. This lack of consensus is why, in some states, if blood has already been collected, it is tested even over the objections of a patient and, in others, clinicians instead seek court orders to obtain testing (National HIV/AIDS Clinician's Consultation Center, 2017).

Persons who take the position that the welfare of the healthcare professional should take precedence over the individual's rights often defend the position by citing the disproportionate burden on healthcare professionals, but the strength of this argument may be difficult to justify in light of the availability of effective PEP. Proponents of practitioner access to patient HIV status in areas where needle sticks from persons with unknown serostatus are not infrequent—for example, the emergency department—contend that when a practitioner has sustained a serious exposure, testing should occur without patient consent. But even individuals who favor testing proffer a series of patient safeguards to lessen the potential intrusion on and/or negative consequences to the patient, such as providing information and treatment if the patient chooses to learn the results and ensuring confidentiality of test results (Cowan and Macklin, 2012).

ADVANCED CARE PLANNING

Before the passage of federal legislation regarding hospital visitation and medical decision-making, one of the worst nightmares of any gay, lesbian, or transgender (LGBT) individual was that they would be hospitalized critically ill, injured, or incapacitated and that his or her life partner would be precluded from accessing information or acting as a surrogate decision-maker under laws and policies that granted priority to legally married spouses and then family members. These institutional injustices ensnared HIV practitioners, many of whom had decades-long relationships with both partners, in painful ethical dilemmas setting a clinician's fiduciary obligations and integrity against obedience to the law and possible professional sanctions. These situations compelled HIV practitioners and advocates to urge patients and stakeholders to complete advance directives naming their partner as healthcare agent, but even this step did not always keep rejecting parents and other family members from attempting to use state surrogacy laws to contravene the directive.

In the more than three decades since the passage of the Patient Self-Determination Act, only a minority of Americans have an advance directive, which has led states to establish rules for medical decision-making. These statutes establish hierarchies, usually in the order of spouse, adult children,

parents, and siblings. Various other relatives and friends may follow, and life partners may or may not be authorized to make medical decisions, depending on the state. These statutes should pose less of a disparate impact on the LGBT community following passage of same-sex marriage laws in the United States. For unmarried couples, the number of jurisdictions in which common-law marriage is recognized is decreasing and often requires a court ruling (Hernandez, 2012).

The infamous 2009 case in which Florida state law barred Janice Langbehn from the deathbed of her life partner of 18 years (Parker-Pope, 2009) inspired President Obama in 2010 to issue a Presidential Memorandum ordering the Department of Health and Human Services to establish the visitation and surrogacy rights of LGBT persons in federal regulation. The President recognized and sought to correct the injustice that had been done to LGBT families. Accordingly, the Centers for Medicaid and Medicare Services published an amendment directing hospitals that receive federal funding to inform same-sex domestic partners of their visitation rights and prohibiting discrimination against visitors on the basis of sexual orientation, gender, gender identity, or sex (Obama, 2013). In addition, hospitals were charged to respect patients' advance directives and the personal representatives named therein.

While this federal regulation is a step forward for LGBT rights, it is not, Wahlert and Fiester (2013) point out, the leap into complete marriage equality that some LGBT persons assume, leading to a "false sense of security" regarding medical decision-making. How secure the rights of marriage are depends on what state a couple resides in and, more importantly, on whether or not they have completed an advance directive. In states that have legalized same-sex marriage, the law treats same-sex unmarried couples no differently than their heterosexual counterparts. Couples who, for whatever reason, choose not to marry would need to complete an advance directive designating the respective partner as the healthcare proxy, to ensure the partner is the legal medical decision-maker.

Important for couples, especially those who are unmarried and in states where same-sex marriage has not been legalized, it that while states retain the authority to determine orders of priority for surrogate decision-makers, the healthcare proxy designated in an advance directive, if available, supersedes state surrogate decision-making laws. HIV practitioners still should strongly encourage patients to complete advance directives so that the individual who knows and shares their preferences and values, especially regarding HIV care, can act on their behalf.

In June 2015, same-sex marriage became legal under federal law and in 37 states as well as the District of Columbia (National Conference of State Legislators, 2015). The question now is whether this legal progress has translated into more security and protection. In theory, in jurisdictions where same-sex marriage is legal or civil unions or domestic partnerships are legally recognized and in federal institutions such as Veterans Affairs hospitals, LGBT spouses should have the same priority as heterosexual couples in the hierarchy of surrogacy. Yet, in the 23 states where marriage equality has not yet been achieved through state-level legislation, LGBT couples confronting medical crises have little recourse outside an advance directive or legal guardianship.

CONFIDENTIALITY AND THE DUTY TO WARN

Along with these small steps forward toward autonomy are much larger steps backward in the direction of coercion. The classic duty-to-warn HIV ethical dilemma under the auspices of exceptionalism—at least in the ethics literature—would have involved a seropositive man in a sexual relationship with his wife or another seronegative or presumed seronegative woman—or a woman who is unaware of the man's seropositivity. The clinician, in the time before routine consent, would conduct a pre-test counseling session and informed consent discussion. The test results would return positive and, in the post-testing visit, the clinician would address the legal requirement and/or ethical presumption, depending on jurisdiction, that the patient needed to inform his spouse/partner so that the individual could be tested and each begin treatment as soon as possible. In this scenario, the HIV-positive patient would inevitably refuse to tell his partner/spouse out of fear of rejection or discovery of infidelity. When the seropositive patient is a woman, risk of domestic violence and loss of economic support would be additional considerations leading to reluctance to disclose (Epstein et al., 2003).

The HIV clinician then faces a thorny ethical problem. The natural first response of any good clinician is to try and educate and persuade the patient to disclose, offering behavioral health assistance or to inform the at-risk partner. When the patient agrees to disclose, the practitioner is in the difficult position of having to decide if and/or how to verify the disclosure. A study of HIV practitioners in Alabama and North Carolina, where disclosure is legally mandatory, found that practitioners believed that patients were secretive about disclosure and often failed to follow through (Lichtenstein et al., 2014).

In the days of exceptionalism, laws in some states prohibited the practitioner from disclosing HIV to an at-risk partner without the permission of the patient. A breach of confidentiality could result in professional sanctions or legal action. Few states now statutorily proscribe, and many have laws that require or permit, the practitioner to disclose HIV status to a spouse/partner without patient consent. The professional discipline and threat of a lawsuit against the clinician have now shifted to situations in which clinicians fail to warn. The current ethical consensus regarding the duty to warn states:

> A physician or HIV counselor may disclose a patient's HIV status without his or her consent only under the following conditions: The physician or counselor has made a reasonable effort to counsel and encourage the patient to voluntarily provide this information to the spouse or sexual partner. The physician or counselor reasonably believes the patient will not provide the information to the spouse or sexual partner.

> Disclosure is necessary to protect the health of the spouse or sexual partner. (AIDS.gov, 2009; White House, 2015)

A care ethics perspective could justify the practitioner giving the patient time to absorb the results and think over his or her options. Yet, with every day that passed, in this scenario, the partners face an additional risk of exposure. If the compassionate practitioner were to give the patient an appointment in 2 weeks to discuss how to proceed, what happens if the patient does not keep the appointment or terminates the treatment relationship? The practitioner will still have to make a hard decision but may feel less burdened for offering the patient a chance to disclose. Contract referral is a version of this negotiated disclosure employed in some public health departments. Disclosing through any of these means, however, has the potential to rupture the therapeutic alliance and to diminish the chance to engage the patient in treatment.

Often the ethical resolution proposed to this dilemma is to inform the patient that the practitioner will not disclose the information, but that a partner notification program will contact the spouse/partner and let him or her know that a sexual partner may have HIV. Unfortunately, this will not prevent the partner from having a very good idea of the source of exposure. While this solution appears to relieve the practitioner of the hard choice between respecting confidentiality or the law, respectively, and avoiding harm, in actuality, in jurisdictions employing partner notification, the practitioner is still mandated to disclose positive test results to the public health department for the very purpose of partner notification.

THE CRIMINALIZATION OF HIV

In perhaps the most extreme example of HIV exceptionalism, HIV criminalization is a public policy that prosecutes and imprisons persons with HIV who engage in a variety of normal human activities—including consensual sex—for failing to disclose serostatus to their sexual partner.

According to the HIV Center for Law and Policy, in May of 2015, 32 states and 2 U.S. territories had criminal statutes that specifically targeted HIV. Thirty-six states reported that they had arrested and/or prosecuted persons with HIV for behaviors ranging from consensual sex to spitting, with 180 prosecutions in the 5 years from 2008 to 2013. Sentences for persons convicted were often decades-long, including a 35-year sentence for an HIV-positive man who spit at police, and a Georgia case in which an HIV-positive man who bit another individual was charged under the state anti-terrorism statute as a human biological weapon. Persons with HIV have been found guilty even when they used a condom or other preventive measures, had no detectable viral load, and informed their consensual sexual partner of their HIV status (Center for HIV Law and Policy, 2010).

In a comprehensive review, Lehman et al. (2014) underscored that many of these criminalized behaviors have a small or nonexistent chance of transmitting the virus, based on scientific study. Two-thirds of the laws were passed before 1994 and the advent of combination antiretroviral therapy or effective PrEP, PEP, and other preventive measures. Few laws take into account the clinical evidence for the actual risk of transmission of various behaviors and assign the same harsh penalties for a broad range of activities with an equally varying risk of HIV transmission.

The ethical implications of these laws are extensive and create agonizing dilemmas for patients with HIV, their partners, and practitioners, as well as public health advocates. Counter to the mainstreaming trend of routine screening and home testing, criminal laws instead tend to discourage testing and diagnosis, owing to the risk of criminal prosecution. This legal trend is in direct opposition to the public health movement to identify the segment of the population unaware they have HIV. In other words, persons who seek to obtain the benefits of early diagnosis and treatment for themselves and in preventive actions to protect the health of others could risk criminal prosecution. In addition, review of prior cases suggests that even patients who disclose their serostatus and take precautions may not be safe from charges, a situation encouraging individuals to not disclose their positive serostatus to sexual partners and to injection drug use partners. The person with HIV may be caught in a moral conflict between honesty and caring for others on the one hand and sacrificing social support and perhaps even freedom on the other. Practitioners also face this conflict, knowing that early diagnosis and treatment, disclosure, and prevention, especially in high-risk populations, reduces transmission and disease progression, yet knowing that this sound public advice could result in legal action if prior patterns of prosecution continue.

Of ethical concern, early research suggests that practitioners in states with stricter rules and exacting penalties are more likely to become pro-criminalization, whereas practitioners in states with less rigid requirements and more lenient punishments tend to see criminalization as an obstacle to patient care (Lichtenstein et al., 2014).

More broadly, laws criminalizing behavior of HIV-positive individuals who fully disclose their serostatus and take recommended actions to prevent transmission represent a retrograde movement in every sense of the word, returning to the earliest days of the epidemic when fear and prejudice were rampant. These laws undermine years of policy and educational efforts to destigmatize HIV and dispel myths about how it is transmitted, and they render HIV a status crime especially discriminating against gay men (Cockerill and Wahlert, 2015). On an individual level, the statutes may increase the risk of domestic violence for women and impede public health reporting and partner contact tracing and notification programs that seek to handle HIV like other sexually transmitted diseases.

The American Medical Association (AMA) Code of Ethics (principle III) states, "A physician shall respect the law and also recognize a responsibility to seek changes in those requirements, which are contrary to the best interests of the patient" (American Medical Association Council on Ethical and Judicial Affairs, 2014–2015). The AMA is one of many leading institutions in state and federal government and organized medicine, such as the President's Advisory Council on

HIV/AIDS, that have issued policy statements in support of decriminalization of HIV (Center for HIV Law and Policy, 2014). AIDS practitioners have an ethical obligation to work with their elective representatives and within their professional societies to educate the public regarding the scientific facts about HIV transmission and to campaign to end prosecution and persecution of persons with HIV.

MEN WHO HAVE SEX WITH MEN AND DONATE BLOOD

The criminalization of HIV is indeed a disturbing development amidst the movement to end exceptionalism. However, there are some recent signs of progress. For example, in December 2015, the U.S. Food and Drug Administration (FDA) revised its recommendations regarding blood donation by men who have sex with men, allowing donation of blood from men who have sex with men who had not had a sexual contact in the prior 12 months. These recommendations had not been revised since 1992 and were the subject of years of contentious debate that finally yielded to the evidence base of an acceptable level of risk of men who have sex with men transmitting HIV under the restrictions specified. Individuals who are HIV positive, have exchanged sex for money or drugs, or have used drugs by injection are still barred from donating blood (U.S. Food and Drug Administration, 2015).

Ethically, the end of the exclusion of men who have sex with men donating blood represents an attempt to balance the safety of the blood supply and risk to blood product recipients with the stigmatization of an already disadvantaged cohort of gay men. The prior prohibition was unfair in that it did not allow gay men to exercise their civic responsibility or to demonstrate altruism through blood donation. It also affected the public by overinclusive restrictions that could limit the blood supply (Brailsford et al., 2015).

CONCLUSION

This chapter has examined some of the most dramatic ethical developments in HIV diagnosis and treatment over the last decade. There are equally important new issues in research ethics that we have only touched on as they relate to clinical ethics. There remain many significant clinical ethics questions that space does not allow us to consider here. Of special concern are the more insidious threats to patient privacy that the growth of large healthcare systems and electronic storage and transmission of billing, insurance, and pharmacy data represent and how to safeguard confidential information. A revised rendition of this chapter in the coming years will without doubt examine novel ethical conflicts that have arisen in the wake of scientific progress. Many of these questions will be variations of the themes explored in this chapter, while others will involve unprecedented ethical dilemmas as persons with HIV and the people who care for them strive to attain the full measure of integration into public health care and social acceptance.

REFERENCES

AIDS.gov (2009). Sexual partners—disclosing without patient consent. https://www.aids.gov/hiv-aids-basics/just-diagnosed-with-hiv-aids/talking-about-your-status/sexual-partners/. Accessed February 28, 2017.

American Academy of Pediatrics, Committee on Pediatric AIDS (2008). Policy statement: HIV testing and prophylaxis to prevent mother-to-child transmission in the United States. *Pediatrics* 122(5):1127–1134.

American College of Obstetricians and Gynecologists (2007). ACOG Committee Opinion No. 389, December 2007. Human immunodeficiency virus. *Obstet Gynecol* 110(6):1473–1478.

American Medical Association Council on Ethical and Judicial Affairs (2014–2015). *Code of Medical Ethics: Current Opinions with Annotations*. Chicago: American Medical Association.

April MD (2010). Rethinking HIV exceptionalism: the ethics of opt-out HIV testing in sub-Saharan Africa. *Bull World Health Organ* 88(9):703–708.

Arora KS, Streed CG (2015). Ensuring the ethical implementation of the new World Health Organization pre-exposure prophylaxis recommendations for men who have sex with men. *LGBT Health* 2(1):1–2.

Bayer R, Fairchild AL (2006). Changing the paradigm for HIV testing—the end of exceptionalism. *N Engl J Med* 355(7):647–649.

Blumenthal J, Haubrich RH (2014). Will risk compensation accompany pre-exposure prophylaxis for HIV? *Virtual Mentor* 16(11):909–915.

Brailsford SR, Kelly D, Kohli H, Slowther A, Watkins NA; Blood Donor Selection Steering Group of the Advisory Committee for the Safety of Blood, Tissues, Organs (2015). Who should donate blood? Policy decisions on donor deferral criteria should protect recipients and be fair to donors. *Transfus Med* 25(4):234–238.

Branson BM, Handsfield HH, Lampe MA, et al. (2006). Revised recommendations for HIV testing of adults, adolescents, and pregnant women in health-care settings. *MMWR Recomm Rep* 55(RR-14):1–17; quiz CE 11–14.

Brown AN, Djimeu EW, Cameron DB (2014). A review of the evidence of harm from self-tests. *AIDS Behav* 18(Suppl 4):S445–S449.

Celada MT, Merchant RC, Waxman MJ, Sherwin AM (2011). An ethical evaluation of the 2006 Centers for Disease Control and Prevention Recommendations for HIV testing in health care settings. *Am J Bioeth* 11(4):31–40.

Center for HIV Law and Policy (2010). *Ending and Defending Against HIV Criminalization: State and Federal Laws and Prosecutions*, Vol. 1, second edition, fall 2010 (updated May 2015). https://www.hivlawandpolicy.org/resources/ending-and-defending-against-hiv-criminalization-state-and-federal-laws-and-prosecutions. Accessed February 27, 2017.

Center for HIV Law and Policy (2014). *Collection of Statements from Leading Organizations Urging an End to the Criminaliation of HIV and Other Diseases*. http://hivlawandpolicy.org/resources/collection-statements-leading-organizations-urging-end-criminalization-hiv-and-other. Acccessed February 27, 2017.

Centers for Disease Control and Prevention (CDC) (2006). CDC HIV/AIDS science facts: CDC releases revised HIV testing recommendations in healthcare settings. https://www.cdc.gov/hiv/pdf/testing_factsheet_healthcare.pdf. Accessed February 27, 2017.

Centers for Disease Control and Prevention (CDC) (2012). CDC fact sheet PrEP: a new tool for HIV prevention.

Centers for Disease Control and Prevention (CDC) (2014). Preexposure prophylaxis for the prevention of HIV infection in the United States, 2014. http://www.cdc.gov/hiv/pdf/prepguidelines2014.pdf. Accessed February 27, 2017.

Choopanya K, Martin M, Suntharasamai P, et al.; Bangkok Tenofovir Study Group (2013). Antiretroviral prophylaxis for HIV infection in injecting drug users in Bangkok, Thailand (the Bangkok Tenofovir Study): a randomized, double-blind, placebo-controlled phase 3 trial. *Lancet* 381:2083–2090.

Cockerill R, Wahlert L (2015). AIDS panic in the twenty-first century: the tenuous legal status of HIV-positive persons in America. *J Bioeth Inq* 12(3):377–381.

Cowan E, Macklin R (2012). Unconsented HIV testing in cases of occupational exposure: ethics, law, and policy. *Acad Emerg Med* 19(10):1181–1187.

Edelstein ZR, Myers JE, Cutler BH, Blum M, Muzzio D, Tsoi BW (2015). HIV testing experience in New York City: offer of and willingness to test in the context of new legal support of routine testing. *J Acquir Immune Defic Syndr* 68(Suppl 1):S45–S53.

Epstein R, Thomas JC, Rutecki GW (2003). Please don't say anything: partner notification and the patient–physician relationship. *Virtual Mentor* 5(11).

Fields L, Kaplan C (2011). Opt-out HIV testing: an ethical analysis of women's reproductive rights. *Nurs Ethics* 18(5):734–742.

Frye V, Wilton L, Hirshfied S, et al. (2015). "Just because it's out there, people aren't going to use it." HIV self-testing among young, black MSM, and transgender women. *AIDS Patient Care STDS* 29(11):617–624.

Grant RM, Lama JR, Anderson PL, et al.; iPrEx Study Team (2010). Preexposure chemoprophylaxis for HIV prevention in men who have sex with men. *N Engl J Med* 363(27):2587–2599.

Hanssens C, Melhman A, Kaplan M (2009). HIV and Pregnancy: A Guide to Medical and Legal Considerations for Women and Their Advocates. New York: Center for HIV Law and Policy. http://www.hivlawandpolicy.org/sites/www.hivlawandpolicy.org/files/MTCT12.09.pdf.

Heaton RK, Franklin DR, Ellis RJ, et al. (2011). HIV-associated neurocognitive disorders before and during the era of combination antiretroviral therapy: differences in rates, nature, and predictors. *J Neurovirol* 17:3–16.

Hernandez JO (2012). Gay rights one baby-step at a time: protecting hospital visitation rights for same-sex partners while the lack of surrogacy rights lingers: comment on "Ethical challenges in end-of-life care for GLBTI individuals" by Colleen Cartwright. *J Bioeth Inq* 9(3):361–363.

INSIGHT START Study Group (2015). Initiation of antiretroviral therapy in early asymptomatic HIV infection. *N Engl J Med* 373:795–807.

Kippax S (2006). A public health dilemma: a testing question. *AIDS Care* 18(3):230–235.

Lehman JS, Carr MH, Nichol AJ, et al. (2014). Prevalence and public health implications of state laws that criminalize potential HIV exposure in the United States. *AIDS Behav* 18(6):997–1006.

Lichtenstein B, Whetten K, Rubenstein C. (2014). "Notify your partners—it's the law": HIV providers and mandatory disclosure. *J Int Assoc Provid AIDS Care* 13(4):372–378.

Macklin R, Cowan E (2012). Given financial constraints, it would be unethical to divert antiretroviral drugs from treatment to prevention. *Health Aff (Millwood)* 31(7):1537–1544.

Mahajan AP, Stemple L, Shapiro MF, King JB, Cunningham WE (2009). Consistency of state statutes with the Centers for Disease Control and Prevention HIV testing recommendations for health care settings. *Ann Intern Med* 150(4):263–269.

Marcus JL, Glidden DV, Mayer KH, et al. (2013). No evidence of sexual risk compensation in the iPrEx trial of daily oral HIV preexposure prophylaxis. *PLoS ONE* 8(12):e81997.

Merchant RC, Waxman MJ, Maher JG, et al. (2012). Patient and clinician ethical perspectives on the 2006 Centers for Disease Control and prevention HIV testing methods. *Public Health Rep* 127(3):318–329.

Minniear TD, Gilmore B, Arnold SR, Flynn PM, Knapp KM, Gaur AH (2009). Implementation of and barriers to routine HIV screening for adolescents. *Pediatrics* 124(4):1076–1084.

National Conference of State Legislators (2015). Same-sex marriage laws. http://www.ncsl.org/research/human-services/same-sex-marriage-laws.aspx. Accessed February 27, 2017.

National HIV/AIDS Clinician Consultation Center (2017). State HIV testing laws. http://nccc.ucsf.edu/clinical-resources/hiv-aids-resources/state-hiv-testing-laws/. Accessed February 27, 2017.

New York State Department of Health (2015). 2015 Blueprint to Eliminate AIDS in New York State. https://www.health.ny.gov/

diseases/aids/ending_the_epidemic/docs/blueprint.pdf. Accessed February 27, 2017.

Obama B (2013). Presidential Memorandum—Hospital Visitation. Washington, DC: The White House. https://www.whitehouse.gov/the-press-office/presidential-memorandum-hospital-visitation. Accessed December 27, 2015.

Parker-Pope T (2009, May 18). Kept from a dying partner's bedside. *New York Times*. http://www.nytimes.com/2009/05/19/health/19well.html?ref=politics.

Schuklenk U, Kleinsmidt A (2007). Rethinking mandatory HIV testing during pregnancy in areas with high HIV prevalence rates: ethical and policy issues. *Am J Public Health* 97(7):1179–1183.

Scott PA (2014). Unsupervised self-testing as part public health screening for HIV in resource-poor environments: some ethical considerations. *AIDS Behav* 18(Suppl 4):S438–S444.

Smith CB, Battin MP, Francis LP, Jacobson JA (2007). Should rapid tests for HIV infection now be mandatory during pregnancy? Global differences in scarcity and a dilemma of technological advance. *Dev World Bioeth* 7(2):86–103.

Smith DK, Koenig LJ, Martin M, et al. (2014). Preexposure prophylaxis for the prevention of HIV infection in the United States—2014. Clinical practice guideline. http://www.cdc.gov/hiv/pdf/prepguidelines2014.pdf. Accessed May 29, 2016.

Tessmer-Tuck JA, Poku JK, Burkle CM (2014). When courts intervene: public health, legal and ethical issues surrounding HIV, pregnant women, and newborn infants. *Am J Obstet Gynecol* 211(5):461–469.

Thigpen MC, Kebaabetswe PM, Paxton LA, et al. (2012). Antiretroviral preexposure prophylaxis for heterosexual HIV transmission in Botswana. *N Engl J Med* 367(5):423–434.

U.S. Food and Drug Administration (FDA) (2015). FDA updates blood donor referral policy to refelct the most current sicentific evidence and continue to ensure the safety of the U.S. blood supply [press release]. http://www.fda.gov/NewsEvents/Newsroom/PressAnnouncements/ucm478031.htm. Accessed February 27, 2017.

U.S. Preventive Services Task Force (2013). Screening for HIV—Clinical Summary of USPSTF Recommendation, 2013. https://www.uspreventiveservicestaskforce.org/Page/Document/UpdateSummaryFinal/human-immunodeficiency-virus-hiv-infection-screening. Accessed February 28, 2017.

Wahlert L, Fiester A (2013). A false sense of security: lesbian, gay, bisexual, and transgender (LGBT) surrogate health care decision-making rights. *J Am Board Fam Med* 26(6):802–804.

Waxman MJ, Merchant RC, Celada MT, Clark MA (2011). Perspectives on the ethical concerns and justifications of the 2006 Centers for Disease Control and Prevention HIV testing recommendations. *BMC Med Ethics* 12:24.

White BL W. J, Rayasam S, Patham DE, Adimora AA, Golin CE (2015). What makes me screen for HIV? Perceived barriers and facilitators to conducting recommended routine HIV testing among primary care physicians in the Southeastern United States. *J Int Assoc Provid AIDS Care* 14(2):127–135.

White House (2015). *National HIV/AIDS Strategy for the United States: Updated to 2020*. https://www.aids.gov/federal-resources/national-hiv-aids-strategy/nhas-update.pdf. Accessed February 28, 2017.

Wocial LD, Cox EG (2013). An ethical analysis of opt-out HIV screening for pregnant women. *J Obstet Gynecol Neonatal Nurs* 42:485–491.

Wolf L, Lo B (2004). AIDS. In SG Post (ed.), *Encyclopedia of Bioethics* (3rd ed., Vol. 1, pp. 122). Farmington Hills, MI: Thompson-Gale.

World Health Organization (2016a). *Consolidated Guidelines on the Use of Antiretroviral Drugs for Treating and Preventing HIV Infection—Recommendations for a Public Health Approach*, second edition. http://www.who.int/hiv/pub/arv/arv-2016/en/. Accessed February 28, 2017.

World Health Organizaion (2016b). Publications on pre-exposure prophylaxis (PrEP). http://www.who.int/hiv/pub/prep/en/. Accessed February 28, 2017.

50.

HEALTH SERVICES AND POLICY ISSUES
IN AIDS PSYCHIATRY

James T. Walkup and Stephen Crystal

Contemporary health services research has its origins in cross-disciplinary efforts to study issues of cost, equity, and the organization of healthcare delivery and to inform policy choices in these areas. Many health services researchers have been drawn to the study of HIV/AIDS care, which has presented in new and concentrated forms a range of systemic issues for the healthcare system, including racial and ethnic disparities in healthcare and the impact of stigma; the complexities of caring for patients with co-occurring medical, substance abuse, and psychiatric conditions; the factors influencing adherence to demanding medical regimens; and numerous other issues.

Health services research draws on sociology and economics but is defined as much by a set of concerns as by a disciplinary perspective. Andersen's (1995) behavioral model of health services utilization has been among the influential conceptual models in the field and has informed a number of significant studies in health services research on HIV (Andersen et al., 2000). Multiple versions exist, but the basic components specify that use is influenced by predisposing factors (such as sociodemographic characteristics), enabling factors (such as a person's ability to pay, or a community's store of accessible services), and need factors (such as clinical conditions and disease severity). For example, studies of receipt of antiretroviral therapy (ART) have examined the influence of such predisposing factors as race (Palacio et al. 2002), gender (Giordano et al., 2003), or injection drug use (IDU) status (Gebo et al., 2005); such enabling factors as insurance status (Bhattacharya et al., 2003); and such measures of need as disease stage, CD4 counts, and viral load (Gebo et al., 2005), as well as patient self-report measures. Some versions of the model also add context variables, such as provider or organizational characteristics. For example, just after ART was introduced, research found that patients were more likely to receive potent antiretrovirals if they were cared for by physicians who were more experienced in HIV care (Kitahata et al., 2000).

The Andersen model helps a policymaker examine claims that a group is "underserved," or is "high utilizing" and operationalize the implied "compared to what?" question. Implicit in the model is the value-based assumption that healthcare ought typically to correspond to need rather than other characteristics of patients. Health services researchers concerned with cost tend to look for subgroups with unusually high utilization, examining whether costly services being used are unneeded or reflect needs that could have been prevented or that reflect delivery inefficiencies. Health services researchers concerned with equity tend to look for evidence that use of appropriate services varies in relation to predisposing or enabling factors, rather than need, when these classes of factors are considered concurrently. (Such departures from need-based care can be considered an operational definition of "inequitable access.") In such analyses, definitions of need are particularly important. Results may vary, for example, under alternative measures of need based on the view of the patient, of clinicians, or of evidence-based guidelines.

In this chapter, we focus primarily on research in the United States as we review recent work on financing, service fragmentation, and difficulties integrating different sectors of care, as well as problems related to the functioning of medicine in a complex, stratified society. (Our discussion of research on syringe exchange programs includes data on Canada, however.)

As this chapter is being written, it appears a qualitatively new chapter in the history of healthcare is developing with the staged implementation of the Patient Protection and Affordable Care Act (usually known as the ACA), signed into law March 23, 2010. While many of its provisions represent policy responses intended to remedy the very shortcomings often highlighted by health service researchers, the extent to which the ACA builds on or redirects the health service patterns documented in this chapter is yet to be determined. Even the most carefully targeted and well-implemented policy changes can run into unanticipated problems; and even when their goals are successfully realized, they are liable to produce unintended consequences. In this case, these typical challenges posed by predicting any policy problems and consequences are increased by the unusually broad scope and complexity of the ACA and by the need to execute its provisions over time in a politically volatile atmosphere. Nevertheless, some elements of the ACA seem exceedingly likely to persist, despite partisan controversy and efforts to repeal or change the ACA. It is certainly possible to identify in this chapter certain general features of the ACA relevant to HIV care and psychiatry (e.g., coverage expansion), along with occasional specific outcomes that will predictably follow full implementation (e.g., changes in financing routine HIV testing).

FINANCING

The HIV Cost and Services Utilization Study (HCSUS) found that in the mid- to late 1990s, most people living with HIV or AIDS were uninsured (20%) or covered by a public insurance program, such as Medicaid (44%) or Medicare (6%). The proportion with private insurance is estimated to be less than half that found in the general population (31% vs. 73%) (Kates, 2004). A study looking at coverage for people living with HIV or AIDS in 11 clinics in 2006–2012 reported that aggregate coverage remained stable during this period, with the proportion of patient-years divided among private insurance (15.9%), Medicaid (35.7%), Medicare (20.1%), and no insurance (28.4%) of person-years covered (Yehia, Fleishman, et al., 2014). Care provided through the Ryan White Comprehensive AIDS Resources Emergency (CARE) Act has also played a significant role, anticipating in many ways more recent initiatives to integrate various often-fragmented components of healthcare for broader populations of patients.

Some care has also been provided through various safety net programs, such as free clinics, care at public hospitals, and charity care programs. The burden of HIV care on public payers has been impacted by illness-related work disability, which can deprive patients of employment-based coverage; by the increasing concentration of HIV in poor communities; and by the high cost of care, particularly pharmaceuticals.

A recurrent issue has been the impact of insurance status on receipt of appropriate HIV care. Several studies suggest that the most significant gaps are between the uninsured and the insured, not between persons with coverage from private versus public insurance (Cunningham et al., 2000; Goldstein et al., 2005; Keruly et al., 2002; Knowlton et al., 2001; Palacio et al., 2002; Shapiro et al., 1999; Smith and Kirking, 2001). This rough equivalence between private and public insurance has been challenged, however. Criticizing prior work for not adjusting for possible unobserved associations between health status and coverage, Bhattacharya and colleagues (2003) concluded that private (versus public) insurance was associated with lower mortality, partly attributable to better access to ART. Private insurance has also been associated with lower rates of unmet need for care for some specific symptoms (Kilbourne et al., 2002).

Financing of both public and private insurance coverage in the United States was explicitly targeted for change by the ACA. The chief mechanisms are expansion of Medicaid eligibility for persons within 138% of the federal poverty level (FPL) and the creation of health care insurance exchanges, where individuals with incomes between 100% and 400% of FPL are eligible for premium tax credits and subsidies to help with payments. The ACA also prohibits denial of coverage for persons with preexisting conditions, such as HIV/AIDS; eliminates lifetime and annual limits on coverage; prohibits premium setting based on health status; and, over time, closes the "donut hole" of Medicare Part D coverage for prescription medications.

The Supreme Court ruled in June 2012 that states could not be required to accept the Medicaid expansion, effectively making it optional.[1] As of October 2014, 23 states had chosen not to expand Medicaid coverage, instead leaving in place systems that often rely on a mixture of categorical eligibility (e.g., disability) and lower income ceilings. Having anticipated full Medicaid expansion to all states, the ACA provides no assistance for persons below 100% FPL who may be above their state cutoff or lack categorical eligibility. State rules and coverage patterns are too complex to summarize here, but a consequence of this unanticipated "coverage gap" is a group of nearly four million persons not receiving healthcare coverage (Garfield et al., 2014). For example, there is no provision for persons with HIV whose income falls below the FPL but above the state cutoff who are not ill enough to qualify for Medicaid based on disability (and lack other categorical entitlement). Thus they might not be eligible for Medicaid financing of early initiation of ART, as currently recommended by treatment guidelines (DHHS Panel on Antiretroviral Guidelines for Adults and Adolescents, 2016).

FRAGMENTATION OF CARE

The epidemiology of HIV has highlighted fragmentation in the delivery system. Extensive comorbidity is found with two conditions that have historically been served by different delivery systems that are not well integrated with general medicine: substance abuse and psychiatric illness (Bing et al., 2001). HCSUS data indicate more than three of five adults under care for HIV had used mental health or substance abuse services in the prior 6 months (Burnam et al., 2001). Among persons with HIV, patients with severe mental illness (SMI) are overrepresented in relation to population prevalence (Blank et al., 2002; Walkup et al. 1999); HIV rates are elevated among psychiatric patients in various settings (Blank et al., 2014), sometimes dramatically (Cournos and McKinnon, 1997). Administrative data suggest a prominent role for substance abuse comorbidity in concentrated HIV

1. Data limitations, and uncertainty regarding the precise list of states that will not expand Medicaid, make estimates inexact regarding the size of the coverage-gap impact of Medicaid non-expansion on persons with HIV or AIDS. Using national HIV surveillance data and data from the National Health Interview Survey, Snider and colleagues (2014) estimated that almost 115,000 uninsured, low-income adults with HIV or AIDS would gain Medicaid coverage through the expansion if all states participated, but that approximately 60,000 of these people live in the 23 states not moving forward as of January 2014. Using nationally representative data for 2009 on non-elderly adults with HIV or AIDS in care from the Medical Monitoring Project (MMP) of the CDC, Kates and colleagues (2014) estimated that 70,000 lacked insurance, the majority of whom (46,910) would become eligible with full Medicaid expansion. The MMP does not provide data needed for state-level estimates, but the authors estimated the number gaining coverage through Medicaid expansions would be reduced by approximately 40% in the absence of full expansion. (Kates and colleagues [2014] included Pennsylvania and Indiana in the list of states not anticipated to expand Medicaid; Snider et al. (2014) did not. Indiana and Pennsylvania expanded their Medicaid programs in 2015, with Indiana implementing an alternative Medicaid expansion program involving premiums, and Pennsylvania implementing a traditional Medicaid expansion in September 2015.) As of January, 2016, a total of 31 states and the District of Columbia had implemented Medicaid expansions (Advisory Board, 2016).

risk, pointing to a need for integrated care for triply diagnosed groups with HIV/AIDS, psychiatric, and substance abuse diagnoses (Himelhoch et al., 2007; Prince et al., 2012). Commentators have noted that problems of confounding and other limitations dictate that caution is needed in drawing conclusions regarding epidemiological patterns based on administrative data and point to the need for more extensive collection of primary data (Cournos et al., 2012)—a prospect likely to be aided by the spread of opt-out testing. Recent primary data collection across a range of psychiatric settings has confirmed prior findings of elevated rates: 5.9% in inpatient settings, 5.1% in intensive case management programs, and 4.0% in community mental health settings (Blank et al., 2014). A systematic review reported a median estimate of HIV prevalence among persons with SMI of 1.4% from claims-based studies and 2.7% from studies based on clinical measurement (Janssen et al., 2015).

Problems have sometimes been encountered when top-down efforts to develop innovative specialty services are diverted from their original intent by unanticipated clinical needs. For example, specialty sites intended to serve seriously ill psychiatric patients with HIV have filled with difficult-to-treat persons with HIV with anxiety or depression, rather than individuals with more severe mental illness (Sullivan et al., 1999). Similarly, a long-term care facility for people with AIDS in New York City found that residents with a lifetime history of severe psychiatric illness were less likely to die or be discharged, which means that, over time, they occupy an ever-growing proportion of total beds (Goulet et al., 2000).

Case management, integration of services across sectors, and the creation of specialty services are all strategies to counter fragmentation. Randomized trials indicate that strong integration strategies, such as on-site medical care for methadone patients, are significantly more likely to ensure receipt of care (92%) than referral contracting (35%) (Umbricht-Schneiter et al., 1994), and integration of methadone maintenance with primary care and case management decreases progression to AIDS (Webber et al., 1998). Yet extensive integration can be costly and may require sacrifice of some agency autonomy. Care fragmentation is targeted for change by several elements of the ACA, such as promotion of Patient Centered Medical Homes and Accountable Care Organizations (Fields et al., 2010). Additionally, drops in state revenues for public substance abuse treatment in the context of the ACA have been forecast to result in greater integration into general health (Buck, 2011). These changes may prove to have sufficient financial leverage to overcome institutional barriers, but their impact and effectiveness with these high-need subgroups are uncertain.

DISPARITIES IN HIV CARE

Evidence regarding antiretroviral care and race presents a mixed picture, both in the pre-ART era and, more recently, with access to ART. Palacio and colleagues (2002) reviewed 26 studies published on race and antiretroviral use and concluded that the weight of the evidence suggests some

non-white disadvantage. Two studies using HCSUS data found disadvantage for African Americans in receipt of protease inhibitor and non-nucleoside reverse transcriptase inhibitor (NNRTI) therapies by December 1996 (Andersen et al., 2000; Shapiro et al., 1999). A third study, covering 1996–1998, found this disadvantage in some models but not others (Cunningham et al., 2000). More recently, a study of 14 southern states found no evidence of black–white disparities (Zhang et al., 2014)

Differential access to financial coverage for healthcare contributes to disparities, but disparities have been found in some prior studies to also exist when this factor is controlled for (e.g., among persons with a single-payer source such as Medicaid) (Crystal et al., 2007). Using Medicaid claims files, our group found evidence for race differences in the pre-ART period (Crystal et al., 1995). Some disparities were also identified in the ART era (Sambamoorthi et al., 2001), but these appear to have narrowed over time (Zhang et al., 2014). Cunningham and colleagues (2005) did not find race disparities in mortality in adjusted models, but they did find that socioeconomic characteristics such as wealth, education, and employment substantially impact mortality risk.

End-of life care may differ by race. Using 1991–1998 Medicaid claims, our group found that African Americans were more likely to die in the hospital than at home, and were less likely to receive pain medication (Sambamoorthi et al., 2001).

Whether race differences in care reflect differences in system access can be further evaluated with research on veterans or military personnel, where few or no differences in coverage exist. McGinnis and colleagues (2003) found no race differences in clinical management or adherence. White veterans with HIV had lower mortality, perhaps due to differences in illness severity and comorbidities. In the ART era, Silverberg and colleagues (2006) found no race differences among military seroconverters in relative hazards of AIDS and death. Giordano and colleagues (2006) found no race-related effects on mortality in a group of veterans with HIV, either in the 30 days after initial hospitalization or in subsequent survival (during the 4-year study window).

MULTI-NEED PSYCHIATRIC PATIENTS AND CARE DELIVERY

In predicting the impact of psychiatric comorbidity on HIV care, two alternative scenarios have been suggested. Poorer and less consistent HIV treatment might occur, either because psychiatric symptoms interfere or because the provider's need to attend to some conditions produces neglect of other needs, a kind of "clinical crowd-out" effect (Redelmeier et al., 1998). Conversely, patients with chronic mental health conditions might receive more consistent HIV care if they are more connected than others to the healthcare system and better socialized into patient roles (Walkup et al., 2001). Each scenario is clinically plausible, and psychiatric conditions probably exert multiple different effects on HIV care, some diagnosis specific; the balance of effects is an empirical question.

The first scenario may strike some clinicians as more intuitive. However, it has not always been supported empirically. Despite shortcomings, HIV care patterns among the dually or multiply diagnosed are better than might be expected, given that people with severe mental illness are highly stigmatized (Phelan et al., 2000) and often receive substandard medical care (Druss et al., 2002).

Evidence from surveys (Bogart et al., 2000) and chart review studies (Fairfield et al., 1999) initially suggested that physicians might be reluctant to initiate antiretroviral care for persons with HIV and severe mental illness. However, in several studies of antiretroviral use among Medicaid beneficiaries, in both the pre-ART and ART eras, we did not find patients with severe mental illness were less likely to receive antiretrovirals. These studies used a dataset created by a de-identified linking of the New Jersey HIV/AIDS Registry with Medicaid claims. We also found that, in the pre-ART era, patients with schizophrenia maintained higher levels of persistent use of antiretrovirals than other patients (Walkup et al., 2001), and in the ART era, their persistence was not significantly less than among individuals without a serious mental illness (Walkup et al., 2004). Major depressive disorders and bipolar disorder did not hamper access to ART, but they did affect adherence.

Electronic monitoring of adherence with a small group of patients with schizophrenia ($n = 47$) added further evidence regarding adherence, which was found to correlate with recent mental health appointments (Wagner et al., 2003). Retrospective data on a group of patients treated in an urban clinic with integrated psychiatric care between 1996 and 2002 found that ART-naïve psychiatric patients in treatment were more likely to commence ART, to stay on it for 6 months or more, and to survive than were their counterparts without a psychiatric diagnosis (Himelhoch et al., 2004). A longitudinal study conducted in clinics in the HIV Research Network found that, relative to persons with HIV without a psychiatric diagnosis, HIV-infected persons with SMI were less likely to discontinue in the first and second year (Himelhoch et al., 2009). Bogart and colleagues (2006) found that a majority of SMI patients with HIV recruited from Los Angeles mental health clinics were on ART and were receiving close monitoring of CD4 counts and viral load.

This tendency of treatments to cluster and to be associated with positive outcomes may reflect various influences, including both selection effects and direct effects of one or another element of treatment (e.g., impact of antidepressants on cognition or energy level). Several studies have found that, although mood disorders are associated with compromised antiretroviral adherence (Walkup et al., 2004), depression treatment has been associated with a higher probability of ART among patients with depression (Sambamoorthi et al., 2000; Tegger et al., 2007) and with adherence to antiretrovirals (Turner et al., 2003) and ART (Yun et al., 2005), although evidence for this last association has been criticized (Wilson and Jacobson, 2006). Psychiatric patients with six or more mental health visits per year have been found to be less likely to discontinue ART than patients with no visits (Himelhoch et al., 2009). More research is needed on the impact of different forms of psychiatric comorbidity on HIV care, including the various roles of intervening factors such as patients' adherence, patient socialization, increased clinician surveillance, and stigma.

INCARCERATED POPULATIONS AND DIRECT OBSERVED THERAPY

Discussions of HIV and populations in prison, or in jail, require careful consideration of available evidence, and further research, to avoid unwarranted conclusions. Commentators note that the lack of condoms and safer injection equipment behind bars likely means that the sexual encounters and drug use that occur there are commonly risky (Wakeman and Rich, 2010). Yet despite indications of elevated HIV prevalence rates, consistent evidence has not been forthcoming that HIV is commonly acquired while incarcerated (Gough et al., 2010). Even if a high percentage of episodes of sex and drug use are risky, constraints on the absolute number of episodes may limit their effects. Instead, a more likely scenario is that prevalence primarily reflects the overrepresentation in jails and prisons of people who are from groups that are also overrepresented among persons with HIV (e.g., African Americans, people struggling with addictions or mental illness).

Concentration of higher-risk individuals in jails and prisons is often viewed as providing a promising opportunity for public health intervention, particularly since ART use by incarcerated populations can produce outcomes equivalent to those in the community (Springer et al., 2004). Directly observed therapy (DOT) has been adopted as one strategy to support adherence (Wohl et al., 2003). While public health interventions are warranted, barriers are significant, particularly regarding all-important continuity of care in the transition into the community (Springer et al., 2011).

Direct observed therapy has also been seen as a conceptually appealing alternative in the community for subgroups of persons with HIV whose adherence is challenging. Research on multiply diagnosed individuals suggests several reasons for caution in this regard. First, as noted, even SMI is not necessarily associated with poorer adherence to ART regimens. Thus, it is not obvious which patients are in fact at greater risk of nonadherence. Second, in contrast to time-limited situations such as tuberculosis treatment, ART treatment is a lifetime undertaking. DOT strategies are no "magic bullet" for the adherence challenges for such situations, and it remains necessary to develop a therapeutic partnership with multiply diagnosed patients and provide support and reinforcement for their own self-management capabilities. Indeed, today's advocates are at pains to de-emphasize social control implications of DOT, stressing the need to modify and tailor it to reflect both patient needs and, to the extent possible, preferences. Articles are now more apt to refer to modified DOT, abbreviated as MDOT, or to directly administered antiretroviral therapy, or DAART.

Finally, careful monitoring of such programs is needed. It is often not possible to observe every antiviral dose. Concern has been expressed that, when HIV therapy is demanding, half-measures could be worse than none from the perspective of causing development of resistant HIV virus (Kagay et al., 2004). Partial improvements in adherence could potentially move patients from a low level of adherence unlikely either to provide viral suppression or to create the highest level of risk of viral resistance to a higher (but still inadequate) level with higher risk of viral resistance. Simpler dosing regimens may counter this. Altice and colleagues (2004) report on the results of a DAART intervention, concluding that DAART programs should ideally provide daily monitoring of once-daily dosing, and that DAART should incorporate enhanced elements such as convenience, flexibility, confidentiality, cues and reminders, responsive pharmacy and medical services, and specialized training for staff. The reader is referred to Chapter 9 of this textbook for a more detailed discussion of HIV and incarceration.

SYRINGE EXCHANGE AND PUBLIC POLICY

In the abstract, the accumulation of evidence supporting syringe exchange programs (SEPs) ought to have provided a textbook illustration of the value for policy making of health services research in addiction medicine. For a decade and a half, one or another official panel or commission reviewed the evidence and issued reports, each finding significant evidence of benefit. Experts now credit SEPs with a major role in stemming, then reversing, the HIV epidemic among injection drug users in New York City. Survey-based national estimates indicate that in 2002 U.S. SEPs distributed almost 25 million syringes (Centers for Disease Control and Prevention [CDC], 2005). Yet the SEP story has been anything but a textbook technology transfer from researchers to providers.

Commentaries, including reflections by key participants, describe how efforts to promote SEP quickly became entangled with conflicts associated with the war on drugs (Des Jarlais and Friedman, 1998). In 1998, when research was sufficient to convince Department of Health and Human Services Secretary Donna Shalala to take official notice, a last-minute effort by the Director of the Office of National Drug Control Policy, "drug czar" Barry McCaffrey, was able to convince President Clinton not to allow federal funding of SEPs, according to the *Washington Post* (Harris and Goldstein, 1998, cited in Vlahov et al., 2001).

Political controversy over SEP has been abetted by disputes about research findings themselves (Des Jarlais, 2000; Moss, 2000a, 2000b). SEP users in Vancouver (Strathdee et al., 1997) were found more likely, not less likely, to have HIV, and, in Montreal, to seroconvert (Bruneau et al., 1997). These results figured prominently in a 2004 letter criticizing SEPs sent to NIH director Zerhouni from Congressman Mark Souder (Souder, 2004).

Questions posed by the Vancouver and Montreal results received serious attention by researchers (Bastos and Strathdee, 2000; Gibson et al., 2001). The possibility has been acknowledged that SEPs, like any intervention, could produce unintended negative consequences. It is conceivable that SEPs might facilitate new needle sharing networks, for example, but the evidence indicates that this does not appear to be the case (Junge et al., 2000; Schlechter et al., 1999). Instead, selection bias has been credited with influencing the apparent lack of beneficial effect of the Vancouver and Montreal programs, since more high-risk intravenous drug users may gravitate to SEPs. Hahn et al. (1997) and Schoenbaum et al. (1996) reported on data collection begun prior to SEP introduction and each study found evidence that intravenous drug users with high risks were attracted to SEP use.

A 2006 review identified 45 studies between 1989 and 2002 with SEP as an intervention and outcome variables of IDU risk behavior, HIV seroconversion, or HIV seroprevalence (Wodak and Cooney, 2006). Of the 10 studies looking at either of these latter two outcomes, 6 found SEP protective, 2 found no effect, and 2 found negative associations with SEP use. Reviews have also noted the possibility of a "dilution" effect (Gibson et al., 2001)—that is, if SEP research is conducted in a community where syringes are legally available elsewhere, the SEP effect is likely to be weaker than it would be in a place without alternatives. When studies conducted in sites with legal access are removed from the group of studies using risk behavior or seroconversion as outcomes, the remaining studies all show a positive association. Des Jarlais's measured judgment in 2000 still holds today, that "as part of a larger HIV prevention program, needle exchange usually, but not always, leads to low rates of HIV transmission among injection drug users" (p. 1393).

SEP delivery systems make a difference. SEPs differ in how they interpret "exchange," for example. Some use a strict one-for-one approach; some are willing to add a few extra syringes; and a third group does not limit syringes based on the number exchanged. In a study of 23 SEPs in California, clients in this last (i.e., no-limit) group had lower odds of reusing syringes (Kral et al., 2004) but did not differ in needle sharing. Similar findings emerged in a three-city study (Bluthenthal et al., 2004); however, once SEPs are up and running, simply increasing the cap on number of syringes—as happened twice in Connecticut—seems to have had only limited impact on syringe-related risks (Heimer et al., 2002). While empirical studies of the location of SEP find that need is not a predictor, demographic and political factors play a role (e.g., percent college educated, percent of men who have sex with men, presence of local activist groups, such as the AIDS Coalition to Unleash Power (ACT-UP) (Tempalski et al., 2007).

HIV TESTING CONTROVERSIES

Knowledge that one is HIV positive is a necessary condition for other HIV-related services, and increasing the proportion of PLWHA who know their serostatus is a major CDC objective. Levels of CDC prevention funding appear to impact odds of testing (Linas et al., 2006), and aggressive outreach has produced impressive results in some high-risk groups, such as men who have sex with men, more than 90% of whom reported lifetime testing in one study (Sanchez et al., 2006).

Concerns about poor identification of HIV among patients with SMI led some policymakers in the 1990s to consider mandatory inpatient testing (Walkup et al., 2002), but rates of voluntary testing seem generally comparable to those of other groups across a range of settings (Blumberg and Dickey, 2003; Goldenberg et al., 2014; Meade and Sikkema, 2005). Evidence from the 2007 National Health Interview Survey suggests that people with mental illness are more likely than individuals without it to have ever been tested for HIV (Yehia, Cui, et al., 2014). Even in inpatient settings, where reports indicate the greatest need for improvements (Pirl et al., 2005; Walkup et al., 2000), analysts have pointed to the need for research and funding to improve outcomes, rather than legal changes in testing policy (Walkup et al., 2002).

Health services research played a role in the change from a risk factor–based approach to HIV testing to routine testing for large populations. Evidence accumulated that many of the patients most likely to benefit from testing were not reached by risk factor approaches (Liddicoat et al., 2004; Rust et al., 2003). In one high-risk community sample, a majority of never-tested heterosexual men and women reported that they had not been offered an HIV test—81% of men, and 65% of women (Bond et al., 2005). Studies have found that testing may often occur late in disease progress (e.g., Bozzette et al., 1998; Samet et al., 1998). In 2002, more than one-third (39%) of persons with a positive test received an AIDS diagnosis within a year (CDC, 2002). A June 2006 editorial appearing in the *American Journal of Public Health* called for "less targeting, more testing" (Koo et al., 2006).

The CDC revised guidelines in 2006 to emphasize routine testing in medical settings (Branson et al., 2006). Feasibility of new testing services has been investigated (Walensky et al., 2002, 2005). Using simulation models, Paltiel and colleagues (2005) concluded that adding voluntary testing every 3 to 5 years would be cost-effective both in high-risk populations with a 3.0% prevalence and in lower-risk populations with a 1.0% prevalence. Increased testing has implications for prevention as well, since approximately half of new cases of HIV are attributable to the 25% of people with HIV who are unaware of their status (Marks et al., 2006).

Test financing may matter. All state Medicaid programs must provide HIV testing when deemed medically necessary according to state program definitions. Survey data collected in 2010 and 2013 by the Kaiser Family Foundation found that 35 states cover routine HIV screening under Medicaid, and 16 indicated only medically necessary testing (Kaiser Family Foundation, 2014). Efforts to model how the ACA will affect routine testing are limited by uncertainties regarding Medicaid expansion, but the results are anticipated to be substantial (Wagner et al., 2014). Expansion of routine testing is an intended outcome of the April 2013 decision by the U.S. Preventive Services Task for (USPSTF) to assign an "A" rating to the evidence supporting benefits of routine testing for persons ages 15–65 years old (Martin and Schackman, 2013). The ACA requires or incentivizes new private health plans, Medicare, and Medicaid to provide at no cost preventive services rated "A" and "B." The population-level impact

of this change will depend in part on how many unidentified cases are to be found in areas that did not have routine testing previously available.

HIV STIGMA AND DISCRIMINATION IN CARE

In HCSUS data from 1996–1997, 26% of patients reported perceiving at least one type of discrimination (Schuster et al., 2005). Longer lifespans produced by treatment changes raise new issues, such as the re-examination of practices regarding organ transplantation and assisted reproduction. The medical basis of opposition to transplantation, once built largely on the patient's poor prognosis, is now questioned, and attention has focused on questions about allocation of a scarce resource to a person with HIV. Sometimes this argument is examined directly; sometimes the more indirect point is made that transplants to persons with HIV might undermine public willingness to donate organs (Roland et al., 2003).

With longer survival times now increasingly common, and more effective prevention of perinatal transmission, persons with HIV now consider planned pregnancy and may desire both conventional fertility services and special technologies to minimize viral transmission to their partner or child. Through interviews conducted in 1998, Chen and colleagues (2001) found that a significant minority of adults with HIV said they desired children in the future, and a majority of individuals said they wanted more than one. (Presumably, these figures have, if anything, increased.) Yet significant barriers preventing access to such services remain for persons with HIV (Gurmankin et al., 2005; Sauer, 2006; Stern et al., 2002).

CONCLUSION

Historically, many structural characteristics important for good HIV care have not been well developed in the U.S. healthcare system—need-focused financing, integration, organizational flexibility, collaboration, and accessibility. Despite the many built-in constraints faced by patients, doctors, and advocates, the data suggest that under the right circumstances, adequate care can be delivered to patients with multiple medical and psychosocial needs. Indeed, with assistance from the Ryan White Act and other HIV-focused programs, integrated care initiatives in HIV care in the 1990s and 2000s often anticipated more recent initiatives to integrate various often-fragmented components of healthcare for broader populations of patients. Further efforts to create and diffuse organizational reforms to integrate and improve the fragmented delivery systems serving persons with HIV are underway as a result of the ACA, despite resource constraints related to cost-containment features of the ACA. Negotiating inevitable tensions between the goals of quality improvement and cost control will require administrative imagination, organizational collaboration, and a firm resolve to retain a place for patient-centered care and public health values on the change agenda.

National needs will not be easily met, even when facilitated by new resources and windows for change. Strategies must be developed to improve outreach and ease of access for the many persons with HIV and AIDS who do not know they are ill or are poorly linked to service systems. Prevention services needed to bring down incidence rates must be integrated into multiple settings. In the face of political and fiscal challenges, health services researchers will be asked to provide the evidence needed to demonstrate the value of effective service delivery strategies. These challenges will require both focus and flexibility, but the record so far provides grounds for optimism.

ACKNOWLEDGMENTS

Preparation of this chapter was supported with funding from National Institute of Mental Health grant R01 MH058984, and Agency for Health Care Research and Quality grants U18 HS016097, R18HS03258, U19HS021112.

REFERENCES

Advisory Board (2016). Where the states stand on Medicaid expansion. Advisory Board, daily briefing. https://www.advisory.com/daily-briefing/resources/primers/medicaidmap

Altice FL, Mezger JA, Hodges J, et al. (2004). Developing a directly administered antiretroviral therapy intervention for HIV-infected drug users: implications for program replication. *Clin Infect Dis* 38(Suppl 5):S376–S387.

Andersen R (1995). Revisiting the behavioral model and access to medical care: does it matter? *J Health Soc Behav* 36(1):1–10

Andersen R, Bozzette S, Shapiro M, et al. (2000). Access of vulnerable groups to antiretroviral therapy among persons in care for HIV disease in the United States. HCSUS Consortium. HIV Cost and Services Utilization Study. *Health Serv Res* 35(2):389–416.

Bastos FI, Strathdee SA (2000). Evaluating effectiveness of syringe exchange programmes: current issues and future prospects. *Soc Sci Med* 51(12):1771–1782.

Bhattacharya J, Goldman D, Sood N (2003). The link between public and private insurance and HIV-related mortality. *J Health Econ* 22(6):1105.

Bing EG, Burnam MA, Longshore D, et al. (2001). Psychiatric disorders and drug use among human immunodeficiency virus-infected adults in the United States. *Arch Gen Psychiatry* 58(8):721–728.

Blank MB, Himelhoch SS, Balaji AB, et al. (2014). A multisite study of the prevalence of HIV with rapid testing in mental health settings. *Am J Public Health* 104(12):2377–2384.

Blank MB, Mandell DS, Aiken L, Hadley TR (2002). Co-occurrence of HIV and serious mental illness among medicaid recipients. *Psychiatr Serv* 53(7):868–873.

Blumberg SJ, Dickey WC (2003). Prevalence of HIV risk behaviors, risk perceptions, and testing among US adults with mental disorders. *J Acquir Immune Defic Syndr* 32(1):77–79.

Bluthenthal RN, Malik MR, Grau LE, Singer M, Marshall P, Heimer R (2004). Sterile syringe access conditions and variations in HIV risk among drug injectors in three cities. *Addiction* 99(9):1136–1146.

Bogart LM, Fremont AM, Young AS, et al. (2006). Patterns of HIV care for patients with serious mental illness. *AIDS Patient Care STDs* 20(3):175–182.

Bogart LM, Kelly JA, Catz SL, Sosman JM (2000). Impact of medical and nonmedical factors on physician decision making for HIV/AIDS antiretroviral treatment. *J Acquir Immune Defic Syndr* 23(5):396–404.

Bond L, Lauby J, Batson H (2005). HIV testing and the role of individual- and structural-level barriers and facilitators. *AIDS Care* 17(2):125–140.

Bozzette SA, Berry SH, Duan N, et al. (1998). The care of HIV-infected adults in the United States. HIV Cost and Services Utilization Study Consortium. *N Engl J Med* 339(26):1897–1904.

Branson BM, Handsfield HH, Lampe MA, Janssen RS, Taylor AW, Lyss SB, Clark JE (2006). Revised recommendations for HIV testing of adults, adolescents, and pregnant women in health-care settings. *MMWR Morb Mortal Wkly Rep* 55(RR-14):1–17; quiz CE 11–174.

Bruneau J, Lamothe F, Lachance N, Vincelette J, Franco E, Désy M, Soto J (1997). High rates of HIV infection among injection drug users participating in needle exchange programs in Montreal: results of a cohort study. *Am J Epidemiol* 146(12):994–1006.

Buck JA (2011). The looming expansion and transformation of public substance abuse treatment under the Affordable Care Act. *Health Affairs* 30(8):1402–1410.

Burnam MA, Bing EG, Morton SC, et al. (2001). Use of mental health and substance abuse treatment services among adults with HIV in the United States. *Arch Gen Psychiatry* 58(8):729–736.

Centers for Diseae Control and Prevention (CDC) (2002). *HIV/AIDS Surveillance Report* 2002 (Vol. 14, pp. 1–50).

Centers for Diseae Control and Prevention (CDC) (2005). Update: syringe exchange programs—United States, 2002. *MMWR Morb Mortal Wkly Rep* 54(27):673–676.

Chen JL, Phillips KA, Kanouse DE, Collins RL, Miu A (2001). Fertility desires and intentions of HIV-positive men and women. *Fam Plann Perspect* 33(4):144–152, 165.

Cournos F, Guimarães M, Wainberg M (2012). HIV/AIDS and serious mental illness: a risky conclusion. *Psychiatr Serv* 63(12):1261–1261.

Cournos F, McKinnon K (1997). HIV seroprevalence among people with severe mental illness in the United States: a critical review. *Clin Psychol Rev* 17(3):259–269.

Crystal S, Akincigil A, Bilder S, Walkup JT (2007). Studying prescription drug use and outcomes with Medicaid claims data: strengths, limitations, and strategies. *Med Care* 45(10 Suppl 2):S58–S65.

Crystal S, Sambamoorthi U, Merzel C (1995). The diffusion of innovation in AIDS treatment: zidovudine use in two New Jersey cohorts. *Health Serv Res* 30(4):593–614.

Cunningham WE, Hays RD, Duan N, Andersen R, Nakazono TT, Bozzette SA, Shapiro MF (2005). The effect of socioeconomic status on the survival of people receiving care for HIV infection in the United States. *J Health Care Poor Underserv* 16(4):655–676.

Cunningham WE, Markson LE, Andersen RM, et al. (2000). Prevalence and predictors of highly active antiretroviral therapy use in patients with HIV infection in the United States. HCSUS Consortium. HIV Cost and Services Utilization. *J Acquir Immune Defic Syndr* 25(2):115–123.

Des Jarlais DC (2000). Research, politics, and needle exchange [editorial]. *Am J Public Health* 90(9):1392–1394.

Des Jarlais DC, Friedman SR (1998). Fifteen years of research on preventing HIV infection among injecting drug users: what we have learned, what we have not learned, what we have done, what we have not done. *Public Health Rep* 113(Suppl 1):182–188.

DHHS Panel on Antiretrovial Guidelines for Adults and Adolescents (2016). Guidelines for the use of antiretroviral agents in HIV-1-infected adults and adolescents. https://aidsinfo.nih.gov/content-files/lvguidelines/adultandadolescentgl.pdf. Accessed February 27, 2017.

Druss BG, Rosenheck RA, Desai MM, Perlin JB (2002). Quality of preventive medical care for patients with mental disorders. *Med Care* 40(2):129–136.

Fairfield KM, Libman H, Davis RB, Eisenberg DM, Phillips RS (1999). Delays in protease inhibitor use in clinical practice. *J Gen Intern Med* 14(7):395–401.

Fields D, Leshen E, Patel K (2010). Analysis and commentary driving quality gains and cost savings through adoption of medical homes. *Health Affairs* 29(5):819–826.

Garfield R, D'amico A, Stephens J, Rouhani S (2014). The coverage gap: uninsured poor adults in states that do not expand Medicaid—an update. The Kaiser Commission on the Uninsured. http://files.kff.org/attachment/the-coverage-gap-uninsured-poor-adults-in-states-that-do-not-expand-medicaid-issue-brief. Accessed February 28, 2017.

Gebo KA, Reilly ED, Moore RD, et al. (2005). Racial and gender disparities in receipt of highly active antiretroviral therapy persist in a multistate sample of HIV patients in 2001. *J Acquir Immune Defic Syndr* 38(1):96–103.

Gibson DR, Flynn NM, Perales D (2001). Effectiveness of syringe exchange programs in reducing HIV risk behavior and HIV seroconversion among injecting drug users. *AIDS* 15(11):1329–1341.

Giordano TP, Morgan RO, Kramer JR, et al. (2006). Is there a race-based disparity in the survival of veterans with HIV? *J Gen Intern Med* 21(6):613–617.

Giordano TP, White Jr AC, Sajja P, et al. (2003). Factors associated with the use of highly active antiretroviral therapy in patients newly entering care in an urban clinic. *J Acquir Immune Defic Syndr* 32(4):399–405.

Goldenberg SM, Chettiar J, Nguyen P, Dobrer S, Montaner J, Shannon K (2014). Complexities of short-term mobility for sex work and migration among sex workers: violence and sexual risks, barriers to care, and enhanced social and economic opportunities. *J Urban Health Bull N Y Acad Med* 91(4):736–751.

Goldstein RB, Rotheram-Borus MJ, Johnson MO; NIMH Healthy Living Trial Group (2005). Insurance coverage, usual source of care, and receipt of clinically indicated care for comorbid conditions among adults living with human immunodeficiency virus. *Med Care* 43(4):401–410.

Gough E, Kempf MC, Graham L, Manzanero M, Hook EW, Bartolucci A, Chamot E (2010). HIV and hepatitis B and C incidence rates in US correctional populations and high risk groups: a systematic review and meta-analysis. *BMC Public Health* 10(1):777.

Goulet JL, Molde S, Constantino J, Gaughan D, Selwyn PA (2000). Psychiatric comorbidity and the long-term care of people with AIDS. *J Urban Health* 77(2):213–221.

Gurmankin AD, Caplan AL, Braverman AM (2005). Screening practices and beliefs of assisted reproductive technology programs. *Fertil Steril* 83(1):61–67.

Hahn JA, Moss AR, Vranizan KM (1997). Who uses needle exchange? A study of injection drug users in treatment in San Francisco, 1989-1990. *J Acquir Immune Defic Syndr Hum Retrovirol* 15(2):157–164.

Harris J, Goldstein A (1998). Puncturing an AIDS initiative; at last minute, White House fears killed needle funding. *Washington Post*, April 23, 1998.

Heimer R, Grau LE, Khoshnood K, Clair S, Teng W, Singer M (2002). Effects of increasing syringe availability on syringe-exchange use and HIV risk: Connecticut, 1990–2001. *J Urban Health* 79(4):556–570.

Himelhoch S, Brown CH, Walkup J, Chander G, Korthius PT, Afful J, Gebo KA (2009). HIV patients with psychiatric disorders are less likely to discontinue HAART. *AIDS (London Engl)* 23(13):1735.

Himelhoch S, McCarthy J, Ganoczy D, Medoff D, Dixon L, Blow F (2007). Understanding associations between serious mental illness and HIV among patients in the VA health system. *Psychiatr Serv* 58(9):1165–1172.

Himelhoch S, Moore RD, Gebo KA, Treisman G (2004). Does the presence of a current psychiatric disorder in AIDS patients affect the initiation of antiretroviral treatment and duration of therapy? *J Acquir Immune Defic Syndr* 37(4):1457–1463.

Janssen EM, Emma BA, McGinty E, Azrin ST, Juliano-Bult D, Daumit GL (2015). Review of the evidence: prevalence of medical conditions in the United States population with serious mental illness. *Gen Hosp Psychiatry* 37(3):199–222.

Junge B, Valente T, Latkin C, Riley E, Vlahov D (2000). Syringe exchange not associated with social network formation: results from Baltimore. *AIDS* 14:423–426.

Kagay CR, Porco TC, Liechty CA, et al. (2004). Modeling the impact of modified directly observed antiretroviral therapy on HIV suppression and resistance, disease progression, and death. *Clin Infect Dis* 38(Suppl 5):S414–S420.

Kaiser Family Foundation (2014). State Medicaid coverage of routine HIV screening. http://kff.org/hivaids/fact-sheet/state-medicaid-coverage-of-routine-hiv-screening/. Accessed Febraury 27, 2017.

Kates J (2004). Financing HIV/AIDS care: a quilt with many holes May 2004. Kaiser Family Foundation. http://kff.org/hivaids/issue-brief/financing-hivaids-care-a-quilt-with-many/. Accessed February 27, 2017.

Kates J, Garfield R, Young K, Quinn K, Frazier E, Skarbinski J (2014). Assessing the impact of the Affordable Care Act on health insurance coverage of people with HIV. Kaiser Family Foundation. http://kff.org/report-section/assessing-the-impact-of-the-affordable-care-act-on-health-insurance-coverage-of-people-with-hiv-issue-brief/. Accessed February 27, 2017.

Keruly JC, Conviser R, Moore RD (2002). Association of medical insurance and other factors with receipt of antiretroviral therapy. *Am J Public Health* 92(5):852–857.

Kilbourne A, Andersen R, Asch S, et al. (2002). Response to symptoms among a US national probability sample of adults infected with human immunodeficiency virus. *Med Care Res Rev* 59(1):36–58

Kitahata MM, Van Rompaey SE, Shields AW (2000). Physician experience in the care of HIV-infected persons is associated with earlier adoption of new antiretroviral therapy. *J Acquir Immune Defic Syndr* 24(2):106–114.

Knowlton AR, Chung SE, Latkin CA, Hoover DR, Celentano DD, Vlahov D (2001). Access to medical care and service utilization among injection drug users with HIV/AIDS. *Drug Alcohol Depend* 64(1):55–62.

Koo DJ, Begier EM, Henn MH, Sepkowitz KA, Kellerman SE (2006). HIV counseling and testing: less targeting, more testing. *Am J Public Health* 96(6):962–964.

Kral AH, Anderson R, Flynn NM, Bluthenthal RN (2004). Injection risk behaviors among clients of syringe exchange programs with different syringe dispensation policies. *J Acquir Immune Defic Syndr* 37(2):1307–1312.

Liddicoat RV, Horton NJ, Urban R, Maier E, Christiansen D, Samet JH (2004). Assessing missed opportunities for HIV testing in medical settings. *J Gen Intern Med* 19(4):349–356.

Linas BP, Zheng H, Losina E, Walensky RP, Freedberg KA (2006). Assessing the impact of Federal HIV prevention spending on HIV testing and awareness. *Am J Public Health* 96(6):1038–1043.

Marks G, Crepaz N, Janssen RS (2006). Estimating sexual transmission of HIV from persons aware and unaware that they are infected with the virus in the USA. *AIDS* 20(10):1447–1450.

Martin EG, Schackman BR (2013). Updating the HIV-testing guidelines—a modest change with major consequences. *N Engl J Med* 368(10):884–886.

McGinnis KA, Fine MJ, Sharma RK, et al. (2003). Understanding racial disparities in HIV using data from the Veterans Aging Cohort 3-Site Study and VA Administrative data. *Am J Public Health* 93(10):1728–1733.

Meade CS, Sikkema KJ (2005). Voluntary HIV testing among adults with severe mental illness: frequency and associated factors. *AIDS Behav* 9(4):465–473.

Moss AR (2000a). Epidemiology and the politics of needle exchange. *Am J Public Health* 90(9):1385–1387.

Moss AR (2000b). 'For God's sake, don't show this letter to the President. . .'. *Am J Public Health* 90(9):1395–1396.

Palacio H, Kahn J, Richards T, Morin S (2002). Effect of race and/or ethnicity in use of antiretrovirals and prophylaxis for opportunistic infection: a review of the literature. *Public Health Rep* 117(3):233.

Paltiel AD, Weinstein MC, Kimmel AD, et al. (2005). Expanded screening for HIV in the United States—an analysis of cost-effectiveness. *N Engl J Med* 352(6):586–595.

Phelan JC, Link BG, Stueve A, Pescosolido BA (2000). Public conceptions of mental illness in 1950 and 1996: what is mental illness and is it to be feared? *J Health Soc Behav* 41(2):188–207.

Pirl WF, Greer JA, Safren SA, Weissgarber C, Liverant G (2005). Screening for infectious diseases among patients in a state psychiatric hospital. *Psychiatr Serv* 56(12):1614–1616.

Prince JD, Walkup J, Akincigil A, Amin S, Crystal S (2012). Serious mental illness and risk of new HIV/AIDS diagnoses: an analysis of Medicaid beneficiaries in eight states. *Psychiatr Serv* 63(10):1032–1038.

Redelmeier DA, Booth GL, Tan SH (1998). The treatment of unrelated disorders in patients with chronic medical diseases. *N Engl J Med* 338(21):1516–1520.

Roland ME, Adey D, Carlson LL, Terrault NA (2003). Kidney and liver transplantation in HIV-infected patients: case presentations and review. *AIDS Patient Care STDs* 17(10):501–507.

Rust G, Minor P, Satcher D, Jordan N, Mayberry R (2003). Do clinicians screen medicaid patients for syphilis or HIV when they diagnose other sexually transmitted diseases? *Sex Transm Dis* 30(9):723–727.

Sambamoorthi U, Moynihan PJ, McSpiritt E, Crystal S (2001). Use of protease inhibitors and non-nucleoside reverse transcriptase inhibitors among medicaid beneficiaries with AIDS. *Am J Public Health* 91(9):1474–1481.

Sambamoorthi U, Walkup J, McSpiritt E, Warner L, Castle N, Crystal S (2000). Racial differences in end-of-life care for patients with AIDS. *AIDS Public Policy J* 15(3-4):136–148.

Samet JH, Freedberg KA, Lewis R, et al. (1998). Trillion virion delay: time from testing positive for HIV to presentation for primary care. *Arch Intern Med* 158(7):734–740.

Sanchez T, Finlayson T, Drake A, et al. (2006). Human immunodeficiency virus (HIV) risk, prevention, and testing behaviors—United States, National HIV Behavioral Surveillance System: men who have sex with men, November 2003-April 2005. *MMWR Morb Mortal Wkly Rep* 55(SS-6):1–16.

Sauer MV (2006). American physicians remain slow to embrace the reproductive needs of human immunodeficiency virus-infected patients. *Fertil Steril* 85(2):295–297.

Schlechter MT, Strathdee SA, Cornelisse PGA, Currie S, Patrick DM, Rekart ML, O'Shaughnessy MV (1999). Do needle exchange programmes increase the spread of HIV among injection drug users? An investigation of the Vancouver outbreak. *AIDS* 13(6):F45–F51.

Schoenbaum EE, Hartel DM, Gourevitch MN (1996). Needle exchange use among a cohort of injecting drug users. *AIDS* 10(14):1729–1734.

Schuster MA, Collins R, Morton SC, et al. (2005). Perceived discrimination in clinical care in a nationally representative sample of HIV-infected adults receiving health care. *J Gen Intern Med* 20(9):807–813.

Shapiro MF, Morton SC, McCaffrey DF, et al. (1999). Variations in the care of HIV-infected adults in the United States: results from the HIV Cost and Services Utilization Study. *JAMA* 281(24):2305–2315.

Silverberg MJ, Gange SJ, Wegner SA, et al. (2006). Effectiveness of highly active antiretroviral therapy by race/ethnicity. *AIDS* 20(11):1531–1538.

Smith SR, Kirking DM (2001). The effect of insurance coverage changes on drug utilization in HIV disease. *J Acquir Immune Defic Syndr* 28(2):140–149.

Snider JT, Juday T, Romley JA, Seekins D, Rosenblatt L, Sanchez Y, Goldman DP (2014). Nearly 60,000 uninsured and low-income people with HIV/AIDS live in states that are not expanding Medicaid. *Health Affairs* 33(3):386–393.

Souder ME (2004). Harm reduction causes harm. https://web.archive.org/web/20080102234805/http://www.drugpolicy.org/library/05_06_04souder.cfm Accessed March 13, 2016.

Springer SA, Pesanti E, Hodges J, Macura T, Doros G, Altice FL (2004). Effectiveness of antiretroviral therapy among HIV-infected prisoners: reincarceration and the lack of sustained benefit after release to the community. *Clin Infect Dis* 38(12):1754–1760.

Springer SA, Spaulding AC, Meyer JP, Altice FL (2011). Public health implications for adequate transitional care for HIV-infected prisoners: five essential components. *Clin Infect Dis* 53(5):469–479.

Stern JE, Cramer CP, Garrod A, Green RM (2002). Attitudes on access to services at assisted reproductive technology clinics: comparisons with clinic policy. *Fertil Steril* 77(3):537–541.

Strathdee S, Patrick D, Currie S, et al. (1997). Needle exchange is not enough: lessons from the Vancouver injecting drug use study. *AIDS* 11:F59–F65.

Sullivan G, Young AS, Bean D, Koegel P, Kanouse DE, Cournos F, McKinnon K (1999). HIV and people with serious mental illness: the public sector's role in reducing HIV risk and improving care. *Psychiatr Serv* 50(5):648–652.

Tegger M, Uldall K, Tapia K, Holte S, Crane H, Kitahata M (2007). Depression treatment decreases delay in HAART initiation among depressed HIV-infected patients. Paper presented at the 2nd International Conference on HIV Treatment Adherence. Jersey City, New Jersey.

Tempalski B, Flom PL, Friedman SR, Jarlais DCD, Friedman JJ, McKnight C, Friedman R (2007). Social and political factors predicting the presence of syringe exchange programs in 96 US metropolitan areas. *Am J Public Health* 97(3):437–447.

Turner BJ, Laine C, Hauck WW, Cosler L (2003). Relationship of gender, depression, and health care delivery with antiretroviral adherence in HIV-infected drug users. *J Gen Intern Med* 18(4):248–257.

Umbricht-Schneiter A, Ginn DH, Pabst KM, Bigelow GK (1994). Providing medical care to methadone clinic patients: referral vs. on-site care. *Am J Public Health* 84(2):207–210.

Vlahov D, Safaien M, Lai S, Strathdee SA, Johnson L, Sterling T, Celentano DD (2001). Sexual and drug risk-related behaviours after initiating highly active antiretroviral therapy among injection drug users. *AIDS* 15(17):2311–2316.

Wagner GJ, Kanouse DE, Koegel P, Sullivan G (2003). Adherence to HIV antiretrovirals among persons with serious mental illness. *AIDS Patient Care STDs* 17(4):179–186.

Wagner Z, Wu Y, Sood N (2014). The Affordable Care Act may increase the number of people getting tested for HIV by nearly 500,000 by 2017. *Health Affairs* 33(3):378–385.

Wakeman SE, Rich JD (2010). HIV treatment in US prisons. *HIV Therapy* 4(4):505–510.

Walensky RP, Losina E, Malatesta L, et al. (2005). Effective HIV case identification through routine HIV screening at urgent care centers in Massachusetts. *Am J Public Health* 95(1):71–73.

Walensky RP, Losina E, Steger-Craven KA, Freedberg KA (2002). Identifying undiagnosed human immunodeficiency virus: the yield of routine, voluntary inpatient testing. *Arch Intern Med* 162(8):887.

Walkup J, Barry D, Satriano J, Sadler P, Cournos F (2002). HIV testing policy and serious mental illness. *Am J Public Health* 92(12):1931–1939.

Walkup J, Crystal S, Sambamoorthi U (1999). Schizophrenia and major affective disorder among Medicaid recipients with HIV/AIDS in New Jersey. *Am J Public Health* 89(7):1101–1103.

Walkup J, McAlpine DD, Olfson M, Boyer C, Hansell S (2000). Recent HIV testing among general hospital inpatients with schizophrenia: findings from four New York City sites. *Psychiatr Quart* 71(2):177–193.

Walkup J, Sambamoorthi U, Crystal S (2001). Incidence and consistency of antiretroviral use among HIV-infected medicaid beneficiaries with schizophrenia. *J Clin Psychiatry* 62(3):174–178.

Walkup JT, Sambamoorthi U, Crystal S (2004). Use of newer antiretroviral treatments among HIV-infected medicaid beneficiaries with serious mental illness. *J Clin Psychiatry* 65(9):1180–1189.

Webber MP, Schoenbaum EE, Gourevitch MN, Buono D, Chang CJ, Klein RS (1998). Temporal trends in the progression of human immunodeficiency virus disease in a cohort of drug users. *Epidemiology* 9(6):613–617.

Wilson IB, Jacobson D (2006). Regarding: "Antidepressant treatment improves adherence to antiretroviral therapy among depressed HIV-infected patients". *J Acquir Immune Defic Syndr* 41(2):254–255.

Wodak A, Cooney A (2006). Do needle syringe programs reduce HIV infection among injecting drug users: a comprehensive review of the international evidence. *Subst Use Misuse* 41(6-7):777–813.

Wohl DA, Stephenson BL, Golin CE, et al. (2003). Adherence to directly observed antiretroviral therapy among human immunodeficiency virus–infected prison inmates. *Clin Infect Dis* 36(12):1572–1576.

Yehia BR, Cui W, Thompson WW, et al. (2014). HIV testing among adults with mental illness in the United States. *AIDS Patient Care STDs* 28(12):628–634.

Yehia BR, Fleishman JA, Agwu AL, Berry SA, Gebo KA, Metlay JP (2014). Health insurance coverage for persons in HIV care, 2006–2012. *J Acquir Immune Defic Syndr* 67(1):102–106.

Yun LWH, Maravi M, Kobayashi JS, Davidson AJ, Barton PL (2005). Antidepressant treatment improves adherence to antiretroviral therapy among depressed HIV-infected patients. *J Acquir Immune Defic Syndr* 38(4):432–438.

Zhang S, McGoy SL, Dawes D, Fransua M, Rust G, Satcher D (2014). The potential for elimination of racial-ethnic disparities in HIV treatment initiation in the Medicaid population among 14 southern states. *PLoS One* 9(4):e96148.

RESOURCE APPENDIX FOR PERSONS WITH HIV/AIDS, THEIR FAMILIES, CAREGIVERS, CLINICIANS, EDUCATORS, AND RESEARCHERS

Getrude Makurumidze

This appendix contains resources, alphabetically arranged by topic and linked to chapters (if applicable), for adults, children, and adolescents with HIV and AIDS; caregivers, families, and loved ones of persons with HIV and AIDS; clinicians; educators; HIV/AIDS advocates; and researchers.

RESOURCES FOR CLINICIANS

AIDS ORPHANS AND VULNERABLE CHILDREN

Chapter 5: AIDS Orphans

HIV InSite, Orphans and Affected Families
http://hivinsite.ucsf.edu/InSite?page=kbr-08-01-12

Orphans and Vulnerable Children Support Toolkit
http://ovcsupport.org/

President's Emergency Plan for AIDS Relief, Guidance for Orphans and Vulnerable Children Programming
http://www.pepfar.gov/documents/organization/195702.pdf

UNAIDS, Children and AIDS Sixth Stocktaking Report
http://www.unaids.org/sites/default/files/media_asset/20131129_stocktaking_report_children_aids_en_0.pdf

BURNOUT AND OCCUPATIONAL HAZARDS

Chapter 48: Clinician Burnout in HIV/AIDS Healthcare

Burnout in the Medical Profession
http://patient.info/doctor/occupational-burnout

Burnout: The Health Care Worker as Survivor
http://www.medscape.com/viewarticle/494355_2

CDC Stacks
https://stacks.cdc.gov/view/cdc/20711

Dealing with Burnout
http://www.ihi.org/education/IHIOpenSchool/resources/Pages/CaseStudies/DealingWithBurnout.aspx

How to Beat Burnout: 7 Signs Physicians Should Know
http://www.ama-assn.org/ama/ama-wire/post/beat-burnout-7-signs-physicians-should

Job Burnout: How to Spot It and Take Action
http://www.mayoclinic.org/healthy-lifestyle/adult-health/in-depth/burnout/art-20046642

Physician Burnout and Wellness Resources
https://www.acponline.org/system/files/documents/about_acp/chapters/dc/phys_burnout.pdf

Physician Burnout: It Just Keeps Getting Worse
http://www.medscape.com/viewarticle/838437

Physician Burnout—The Three Symptoms, Three Phases and Three Cures
https://www.thehappymd.com/blog/bid/290755/Physician-Burnout-the-Three-Symptoms-Three-Phases-and-Three-Cures

Physician Burnout: Why It's Not a Fair Fight
https://www.thehappymd.com/blog/bid/295048/Physician-Burnout-Why-its-not-a-Fair-Fight

Specialties with the Highest Burnout Rates
http://www.ama-assn.org/ama/ama-wire/post/specialties-highest-burnout-rates

The Inevitability of Physician Burnout: Implications for Interventions
http://www.sciencedirect.com/science/article/pii/S2213058614000084

Hotline: If an infectious disease physician is not available, the National Clinicians' Post-Exposure Prophylaxis Hotline (PEP hotline), 888–448–4911, is operational 24 hours a day.

ETHNIC AND LANGUAGE ORGANIZATIONS

Asian and Pacific Islander's Coalition of HIV and AIDS (APICHA)
https://apicha.org/

Black AIDS Institute
https://www.blackaids.org/

HIV/AIDS Resource Center for African Americans
http://www.thebody.com/content/art39660.html

Latino Commission on AIDS
https://www.latinoaids.org/

National Black Leadership Commission on AIDS, Inc. (NBLCA)
http://www.nblca.org/

HIV EDUCATION AND TRAINING

Chapter 13: Training in HIV Psychiatry

AIDS Education and Training Center Program
http://aidsetc.org/

Center for HIV Educational Studies and Training (CHEST)
http://www.chestnyc.org/

Clinical Education Initiative (CEI)
http://www.ceitraining.org/

Curtis Hopkins HIV Guide
http://www.hopkins-hivguide.org/

HIV and STD Testing, Centers for Disease Control and Prevention (CDC)
https://gettested.cdc.gov/

HIV Education and Training Programs
https://www.hivtrainingny.org/

HIV Mentoring Programs Building Research Workforce: Minorities
See Table A.1.

HIV Mentoring Programs Building Research Workforce: Non-Minorities and Minorities
See Table A.2.

New York/New Jersey AIDS Education Training Center
www.nynjaetc.org

Office on Women's Health
http://www.womenshealth.gov/hiv-aids/index.html

PrEP for Sex
http://prepforsex.org/

Syphilis Test New York
http://syphilistestny.org/

HIV GUIDELINES AND INFORMATIONAL WEBSITES

AIDSinfo
https://aidsinfo.nih.gov/guidelines

Centers for Disease Control and Prevention (CDC)
http://www.cdc.gov/hiv/guidelines/

Differentiated Care
http://www.differentiatedcare.org/Guidance

Ending the Epidemic
http://etedashboardny.org/

Fast Track Cities
http://www.iapac.org/cities/

Health Resources and Services Administration (HRSA), HIV/AIDS Programs
http://www.hab.hrsa.gov/

HIV Clinical Resource
http://www.hivguidelines.org/

IAPAC Guidelines for Optimizing the HIV Care Continuum for Adults and Adolescents
http://www.iapac.org/uploads/JIAPAC-IAPAC-Guidelines-for-Optimizing-the-HIV-Care-Continuum-Supplement-Nov-Dec-2015.pdf

National HIV/AIDS Strategy for the United States: Updated to 2020
https://www.aids.gov/federal-resources/national-hiv-aids-strategy/nhas-update.pdf

New York State Blueprint to End AIDS
http://www.health.ny.gov/diseases/aids/ending_the_epidemic/docs/blueprint.pdf

New York State Department of Health, AIDS Institute
https://www.health.ny.gov/diseases/aids/

U.S. Government HIV/AIDS Website
http://www.aids.gov

United States President's Emergency Plan for AIDS Relief (PEPFAR) Guidance
http://www.pepfar.gov/reports/guidance/index.htm

Table A.1 HIV MENTORING PROGRAMS BUILDING RESEARCH WORKFORCE: MINORITIES

INSTITUTIONAL AWARDS

INITIATIVE	OBJECTIVE	CAREER LEVEL TARGETED
T32 Training Program for Institutions That Promote Diversity (T32) (RFA-HL-16-007)	Supports training for individuals and institutions not well represented in scientific research, or institutions focused on these populations, to develop training programs in cardiovascular, pulmonary, hematological, and sleep disorders	Predoctoral, postdoctoral
Initiative for Maximizing Student Development (IMSD) (R25) PAR-14-121	Supports research training and developmental activities in students with primary focus on research experiences, courses for skills development, and mentoring activities	Undergraduates and predoctoral
Post-baccalaureate Research Education Program (PREP) (R25) PAR-14-076	Supports institutional programs for research training and academic preparation at research-intensive institutions (to pursue Ph.D. or M.D.-Ph.D.) through 1- to 2-year research apprenticeships	Baccalaureate degree level
Bridges to Baccalaureate Program (R25) PAR-13-333	Supports programs to pursue a research career by promoting transition from a 2-year community college to baccalaureate degree completion in biomedical and behavioral sciences	Undergraduates
NINDS Neuroscience Development for Advancing the Careers of a Diverse Research Workforce (R25) PAR-13-256	Supports NINDS mission relevant programs to increase the pool of Ph.D.-level underrepresented research scientists in biomedical research who are neuroscience researchers and to facilitate career advancement/transition of the participants to the next step of their neuroscience careers	Graduate, postdoctoral and/or junior faculty career levels
MARC Undergraduate Student Training in Academic Research (U-STAR) (T34) PAR-13-205	Supports institutional programs of academic and research education (to succeed in Ph.D.), including 2 years of support of honors juniors and seniors and at least one summer research experience at a research-intensive institution	Undergraduates
Research Initiative for Scientific Enhancement (RISE) (R25) PAR-13-196	Supports integrated developmental activities in research education programs at institutions with substantial underrepresented group enrollment to strengthen academic preparation, research training, and professional skills needed for completing Ph.D.	Undergraduates, graduate students
Planning Grants for the NIH National Research Mentoring Network (NRMN) (P20) RFA-RM-13-002	Supports mentorship experiences and establishing national consortium for networking and mentorship experiences for individuals from backgrounds underrepresented in biomedical research	Undergraduates, graduate students, postdoctoral fellows, early career faculty
Planning Grants for the NIH Building Infrastructure Leading to Diversity (BUILD) Initiative (P20) RFA-RM-13-001	Supports collaborative programs to enhance education, training, and mentorship, as well as infrastructure support and faculty development to facilitate those approaches	Undergraduates
Bridges to the Doctorate (R25) PAR-12-276	Supports comprehensive science education and research-readiness student development programs that help students in M.S. degree programs transition to Ph.D. degree programs at research-intensive partner institutions	Master's degree students
NINDS Advanced Postdoctoral Career Transition Award to Promote Diversity in Neuroscience Research (K22) PAR-12-163	Supports advanced neuroscience researchers in neuroscience research to transition from postdoctoral training to independent research position and to strengthen conditions that promote independence	Advanced postdoctorals and early career
NIDDK Short-Term Education Program for Underrepresented Persons (STEP-UP) (R25) (RFA-DK-12-005)	Supports summer research education and training in the mission areas of NIDDK, including diabetes, endocrinology, and metabolic diseases; digestive diseases and nutrition; kidney, urological, and hematological diseases	High school students, undergraduates

(*continued*)

INSTITUTIONAL AWARDS

Ruth L. Kirschstein National Research Service Award Individual Predoctoral Fellowship to Promote Diversity in Health-Related Research (Parent F31— Diversity) PA-14-148	Supports research in the biomedical, behavioral, or clinical research workforce with individualized, mentored research training from outstanding faculty sponsors while conducting well-defined research projects in scientific health-related fields relevant to the missions of the participating NIH Institutes and Centers	Predoctoral
Mentored Career Award for Faculty at Institutions That Promote Diversity (K01) RFA-HL-13-018	Supports faculty at minority-serving institutions to engage in intensive mentored research career development in the biomedical, behavioral, or clinical sciences that leads to research independence	Full-time faculty
Research Supplements to Promote Diversity in Health-Related Research (Admin Supp) PA-12-149	Supports mentored research experiences linked to actively funded NIH grant	High school students, undergraduates, baccalaureate and master's degree holders, predoctoral students, postdoctoral, investigators
Mental Health Research Dissertation Grant to Increase Diversity (R36) PAR-12-103	Supports research toward completion of doctoral research project and dissertation, across all NIMH mission areas, for students from underrepresented or disadvantaged populations in biomedical and behavioral sciences	Predoctoral students
NCMHD Disparities Research and Education Advancing Mission (DREAM) Career Transition Award (K22) RFA-MD-001 RFA-MD-10-001	Supports investigators working in health disparities areas to transition from the mentored stage of career development to the independent stage of investigator-initiated health disparities research	Early-stage investigators

World Health Organization (WHO) HIV Guidelines
http://www.who.int/hiv/pub/guidelines/en/

INTERNATIONAL AND POPULATION-BASED RESOURCES

Chapter 4: Global Aspects of the HIV Pandemic

Textbook
Pope C, White R, Malow R (eds.) (2009). *HIV/AIDS: Global Frontiers in Prevention/Intervention*. New York: Routledge.

AIDS Map
http://www.aidsmap.com/

International HIV/AIDS Alliance
http://www.aidsalliance.org/

The Body
http://www.thebody.com/index/hotlines/internat.html
This is an excellent online resource to start your search for organizations and services in many countries around the world.

United Nations HIV/AIDS (UNAIDS)
http://www.unaids.org/

USAID Applying Science to Strengthen and Improve Systems (ASSIST) Project
https://www.usaidassist.org/topics/partnership-hiv-free-survival-phfs

JOURNALS OF HIV/AIDS

AIDS and Behavior
http://link.springer.com/journal/volumesAndIssues/10461

AIDS Care: Psychological and Socio-medical Aspects of AIDS/HIV
http://www.tandfonline.com/loi/caic20#.V4V5ShImSiw

AIDS Patient Care and STDs
http://www.liebertpub.com/overview/aids-patient-care-and-stds/1/

AIDS Research and Human Retroviruses
http://www.liebertpub.com/overview/aids-research-and-human-retroviruses/2/

Current HIV/AIDS Reports
http://link.springer.com/journal/volumesAndIssues/11904
Journal of the American Medical Association (JAMA) HIV/AIDS

Table A.2 HIV MENTORING PROGRAMS BUILDING RESEARCH WORKFORCE: NON-MINORITIES AND MINORITIES

	INSTITUTIONAL AWARDS	
INITIATIVE	OBJECTIVE	CAREER LEVEL TARGETED
Innovative Programs to Enhance Research Training (IPERT) (R25) PAR-14-170	Supports research educational activities that complement other formal training programs in the mission areas of the NIH Institutes and Centers with a primary focus on courses for skills development, structured mentoring activities, and outreach programs	Undergraduate to faculty levels
Ruth L. Kirschstein National Research Service Award (NRSA) Award Institutional Training Grant (T32) PA-14-015	Supports research education and career development activities for individuals in appropriate scientific disciplines to address the U.S.'s biomedical, behavioral, and clinical workforce research needs through didactic, research, and career development components	Predoctoral and doctoral levels
NIMH Research Education Mentoring Programs for HIV/AIDS Researchers (R25) PAR-12-273	Supports multidisciplinary mentoring programs in NIMH/DAR mission–related areas in research education experiences with activities in professional/career development, didactics, and hands-on research	Undergraduates, graduate and medical students, medical residents, postdoctoral fellows, early career faculty
INDIVIDUAL AWARDS		
Predoctoral National Research Service Award (NRSA) (F30/F31) Fellowships PA-14-147; PA-14-150	Supports fellowships to outstanding students to obtain individualized, mentored training in fundamental, interdisciplinary and career development leading to the Ph.D. and M.D.-Ph.D. or other dual degree	Predoctoral level
Individual Postdoctoral National Research Service Award (NRSA) (F32) PA-14-149	Supports fellowship applicants to become productive, independent investigators through focused awards to enhance advanced and specialized training in basic and/or clinical research; employs intensive, mentored research project experience to develop independence, innovation, and creativity in a highly productive research setting	Postdoctoral
Mentored Career Development Awards (KO1) PA-14-044; (K08) PA-14-046; (K23) PA-14-049; (K25) PA-14-048	Support mentored research and career development awards including the KO1 Mentored Research Scientist (basic research for basic science-trained individuals), K08 Mentored Clinical Scientist (behavioral or biomedical research for clinically trained individuals), the K23 Mentored Patient-Oriented Research (patient-oriented research for clinically trained individuals), the K25 Mentored Quantitative Research Development Award (quantitative science training applied to health and disease)	Postdoctoral
Pathway to Independence Award (K99/R00) PA-14-042	Supports individuals for 5 years of support (two phases) in transition of mentored postdoctoral position to independent research position; initial (K99) phase supports up to 2 years of mentored postdoctoral research training and career development and second (R00) phase supports up to 3 years of independent research support	Postdoctoral
Research Supplements to Promote Re-Entry into Biomedical and Behavioral Research Careers (Admin Supp) PA-12-150	Supports individuals to re-enter active research careers within the missions of all the program areas of NIH after taking time off for family responsibilities, using research project grant as platform for intensive, mentored research experiences to re-establish careers in biomedical, behavioral, clinical, or social science research leading to independent research career	Postdoctoral or faculty level at time of career interruption

http://jama.jamanetwork.com/issue.aspx?journalid=67&issueid=935428
Journal of Neurovirology
http://link.springer.com/journal/volumesAndIssues/13365

Public Health Reports: Understanding Sexual Health
http://www.publichealthreports.org/issuecontents.cfm?volume=128&issue=7
The Lancet HIV
http://www.thelancet.com/journals/lanhiv/issue/current

LEGAL RESOURCES AND INFORMATION ABOUT DISCLOSURE

Guttmacher Institute
http://www.guttmacher.org/statecenter/spibs/spib_OMCL.pdf

HIV Disclosure Policies
https://www.aids.gov/hiv-aids-basics/just-diagnosed-with-hiv-aids/your-legal-rights/legal-disclosure/index.html

Nationwide Directory of Legal Resources
https://www.americanbar.org/content/dam/aba/images/aids_coordinating_project/aids_directory.pdf

The Center for HIV Law and Policy
http://www.hivlawandpolicy.org/

The HIV Law Project
http://hivlawproject.org/

The Well Project
http://www.thewellproject.org/hiv-information/disclosure-and-hiv

LESBIAN, GAY, BISEXUAL, TRANSGENDER, AND QUEER (LGBTQ) RESOURCES

Chapter 10: HIV Advocacy;
Chapter 11: A Biopsychosocial Approach to Psychiatric Consultation in Persons with HIV and AIDS

Textbook
Makadon HJ, Mayer KH, Potter J, Goldhammer H (eds.) (2015). *The Fenway Guide to Lesbian, Gay, Bisexual, and Transgender Health*. Philadelphia: American College of Physicians.

Ali Forney Center
http://www.aliforneycenter.org/
Program for homeless LGBTQ youth.

American Psychological Association LGBT Concerns Office
http://www.apa.org/pi/lgbt/index.aspx

American Psychological Association's Division 44: Society for the Psychological Study of LGBT Issues
http://www.apadivisions.org/division-44/index.aspx

Association of LGBTQ Psychiatrists (AGLP)
http://www.aglp.org/

Fenway Community Health Center
http://fenwayhealth.org/
The Fenway center has extensive online resources relating to HIV and LGBT issues and serves medical and psychosocial needs of the Boston-area LGBT community.

Gay Men's Health Crisis (GMHC)
http://www.gmhc.org/

GLMA: Health Professionals Advancing LGBT Health Equality
http://www.glma.org/

Lambda Legal
http://www.lambdalegal.org/
Lambda Legal is a national organization committed to achieving full recognition of the civil rights of lesbians, gay men, bisexuals, transgender people, and persons with HIV, through impact litigation, education, and public policy work.

LGBT Health
http://www.liebertpub.com/overview/lgbt-health/618/

MSMGF (The Global Forum on MSM & HIV)
http://msmgf.org/

National LGBT Health Education Center
http://www.lgbthealtheducation.org/

National LGBTQ Task Force
http://www.thetaskforce.org/

PFLAG
https://www.pflag.org/
PFLAG provides support for families, allies, and people who are LGBTQ.

Poz Magazine
https://www.poz.com/
This is a popular magazine that offers free subscriptions for persons living with HIV/AIDS, publishes news articles and editorials, and has online chat groups and personals/dating services.
Spanish-language version: http://amigos.poz.com/

Services & Advocacy for Gay, Lesbian, Bisexual and Transgender Elders (SAGE)
http://www.sageusa.org/

The Trevor Project
http://www.thetrevorproject.org/
The Trevor Project is the leading national organization providing crisis intervention and suicide prevention services to lesbian, gay, bisexual, transgender and questioning (LGBTQ) young people ages 13–24.

Transgender Health
http://www.liebertpub.com/overview/transgender-health/634/

Williams Institute
http://williamsinstitute.law.ucla.edu/
The Williams Institute is dedicated to conducting rigorous, independent research on sexual orientation and gender identity law and public policy.

World Professional Association for Transgender Health
http://www.wpath.org/

NURSES

Chapter 40: Nursing Support

Association of Nurses in HIV Care
http://www.nursesinaidscare.org/

Canadian Association of Nurses in HIV/AIDS Care
http://canac.org/

HIV/AIDS Nursing Certification Board
http://www.hancb.org/Index/index.php

Journal of the Association of Nurses in AIDS Care
http://www.nursesinaidscarejournal.org/

National HIV Nurses Association
http://www.nhivna.org/

PHARMACOLOGY AND DRUG–DRUG INTERACTIONS

Chapter 42: Psychopharmacological Treatment Issues in HIV Psychiatry

HIV Drug Interactions
http://www.hiv-druginteractions.org/
http://www.hiv-druginteractions.org/printable_charts

HIV InSite
http://hivinsite.ucsf.edu/insite?page=ar-00-02

Immunodeficiency Clinic
http://hivclinic.ca/drug-information/drug-interaction-tables/

Medscape HIV
http://www.medscape.com/hiv?src=pdown%2520and%2520

PSYCHIATRISTS AND MENTAL HEALTH CLINICIANS

Textbooks

Cohen MA, Gorman JM (2008). *Comprehensive Textbook of AIDS Psychiatry*. New York: Oxford University Press.

Cohen MA, Gorman JM, Jacobson JM, Volberding P, Letendre S (2017). *Comprehensive Textbook of AIDS Psychiatry— A Paradigm for Integrated Care*, 2nd ed. New York: Oxford University Press.

Cohen MA, Goforth HW, Lux JZ, Batista SM, Khalife S, Cozza KL, Soffer J (2010). *Handbook of AIDS Psychiatry*. New York: Oxford University Press.

Fernandez F, Ruiz P (2006). *Psychiatric Aspects of HIV/AIDS* (pp. 39–47). Philadelphia: Lippincott Williams & Wilkins.

Joska JA, Stein DS, Grant I (2014). *HIV and Psychiatry*. Jersey City, NJ: John Wiley & Sons.

Academy of Psychosomatic Medicine HIV/AIDS Psychiatry Special Interest Group
http://www.apm.org/sigs/oap/index.shtml

The Academy of Psychosomatic Medicine (APM) HIV/AIDS Psychiatry Special Interest Group (SIG) was founded in 2003. Until 2003, there was no organization of psychiatrists and other mental health professionals that was dedicated to the field of HIV psychiatry. Nevertheless, many mental health clinicians devoted their professional lives to providing care for persons with HIV and AIDS. There was a need for an organization to provide networking and support for the exchange of ideas and collaborative research—an organization to share knowledge, to present work, and to collaborate in education and research. To address this gap, Dr. Mary Ann Cohen founded the Organization of AIDS Psychiatry (OAP, the forerunner of the HIV/AIDS Psychiatry Special Interest Group) in 2003 with 32 founding members. The Academy of Psychosomatic Medicine leadership recognized HIV psychiatry as a paradigm of psychosomatic medicine and accepted the organization as a special interest group. The APM HIV/AIDS Psychiatry Special Interest Group now has more than 350 national and international members.

The HIV/AIDS Psychiatry Special Interest Group meets twice a year: in May, at the annual meeting of the American Psychiatric Association (APA) in conjunction with the APA Office of HIV Psychiatry, and in November, at the annual meeting of the APM. The APM HIV/AIDS Psychiatry Special Interest Group is also a Section of the World Psychiatric Association.

There are no dues. Mental health clinicians can apply to join the HIV/AIDS Psychiatry Special Interest Group online at: http://www.apm.org/sigs/oap/index.shtml.

American Psychological Association HIV/AIDS
http://www.apa.org/topics/hiv-aids/

American Psychiatric Association HIV Psychiatry
https://www.psychiatry.org/psychiatrists/practice/professional-interests/hiv-psychiatry

HIV and Mental Health
http://www.hivguidelines.org/clinical-guidelines/hiv-and-mental-health/

The Role of Psychiatrists in HIV Prevention
http://www.psychiatrictimes.com/comorbidity-psychiatry/role-psychiatrists-hiv-prevention

World Psychiatric Association Section on HIV/AIDS Psychiatry
http://www.wpanet.org/detail.php?section_id=11&content_id=1274

In 2012, the Academy of Psychosomatic Medicine HIV/AIDS Psychiatry Special Interest Group became a Section of the World Psychiatric Association in an effort to expand the work of the Special Interest Group to the international community.

RESEARCH, ADVOCACY, AND PUBLIC POLICY

Chapter 10: HIV Advocacy; Chapter 50: Health Services and Policy Issues in AIDS Psychiatry

AIDS Community Research Initiative of America (ACRIA)
http://www.acria.org/

American Sexual Health Association
http://www.ashasexualhealth.org/

Center for HIV Identification, Prevention, and Treatment Services (CHIPTS)
http://chipts.ucla.edu

Global Network of People Living with HIV/AIDS
http://www.gnpplus.net/

HIV i-Base
http://i-base.info/
HIV i-Base produces a range of online publications about HIV treatment.

HIV Treatment Bulletin (HTB) and HTB South
http://i-base.info/hiv-treatment-bulletin/
http://i-base.info/htb-south/
HTB provides technical reviews of the latest research and access issues. Non-technical guides to HIV and treatment include the following:

- Introduction to ART
- Guide to Changing Treatment: What to Do If Viral Load Rebounds
- Guide to HIV, Pregnancy and Women's Health
- Guide to HIV Testing and Sexual Transmission
- Guide to HIV and your Quality of Life: Side Effects and Long-term Complications
- Guide to PrEP in the UK
- Guide to Hepatitis C for People Living with HIV

Kaiser Family Foundation
http://kff.org/hivaids/

Médecins Sans Frontières (Doctors Without Borders)
http://www.msfaccess.org/our-work/hiv-aids

National AIDS Treatment Advocacy Project
http://www.natap.org/

San Francisco AIDS Foundation
http://sfaf.org/

The AIDS Institute
http://www.theaidsinstitute.org/

Treatment Action Campaign (TAC)
http://www.tac.org.za/

Treatment Action Group (TAG)
http://www.treatmentactiongroup.org/

STIGMA

Chapter 6: HIV Discrimination, Stigma, and Gender-Based Violence

Textbook
Liamputtong P (2013). *Stigma, Discrimination and Living with HIV/AIDS: A Cross-Cultural Perspective.* Rotterdam: Springer Netherlands.

HIV/AIDS Stigma Resource Pack
http://www.policyproject.com/pubs/countryreports/SA_SRP.pdf

Standardized Tool for Measuring HIV Stigma and Discrimination
http://www.healthpolicyproject.com/index.cfm?ID=publications&get=pubID&pubID=49

The People Living with HIV Stigma Index
http://www.stigmaindex.org/

UNAIDS: Reduction of HIV-Related Stigma and Discrimination
http://www.unaids.org/en/resources/documents/2014/ReductionofHIV-relatedstigmaanddiscrimination

RESOURCES FOR PATIENTS AND FAMILIES

The resources listed here are not intended exclusively for the use of patients but are directed at the interests and needs of the patient.

Please see Table A.3 for information about conveying a diagnosis of HIV to a child who has been diagnosed with HIV, and Table A.4 for camps for children, adolescents, and their families.

CAREGIVER AND PALLIATIVE CARE RESOURCES

Chapter 41: Palliative Care and Spiritual Care of Persons with HIV and AIDS

Article
Hurwitz CA, Duncan J, Wolfe J (2004). Caring for the child with cancer at the close of life. *JAMA* 292:2141–2149.

American Bar Association Consumer's Tool Kit for Health Care Advance Planning
http://www.abanet.org/aging/toolkit/home.html

Center to Advance Palliative Care
https://getpalliativecare.org/

Center for Palliative Care Education
https://depts.washington.edu/pallcntr/

COMMUNITY AND PUBLIC SERVICE RESOURCES

Organizations that offer support groups, health education, food pantries and delivery services, hospital visitation services, pastoral care, and testing in the New York City area are listed here.

Alliance for Positive Health
http://www.allianceforpositivehealth.org/

God's Love We Deliver (GLWD)
http://www.glwd.org/

Together Our Unity Can Heal (TOUCH)
http://www.touch-ny.org

GMHC

GMHC Main Offices: 446 West 33rd Street, New York, NY 10001-2601
　Hours of Operation: Mon–Fri: 9 A.M. – 6 P.M.
　Contact us: (212) 367-1000 or email: webmaster@gmhc.org

David Geffen Center for HIV Prevention and Health Education
The David Geffen Center for HIV Prevention and Health Education is located on the ground floor at 224 West 29th Street (between 7th and 8th Avenues). The HIV Testing Center is open for walk-ins and by appointment at the following times:
　Walk-in:
　Monday: 9:30 A.M. – 5:30 P.M.
　Tuesday: 9:30 A.M. – 5:30 P.M.
　Wednesday: 9:30 A.M. – 5:30 P.M. (closed from 12:30 to 2:30 P.M. for administrative functions)
　Friday: 9:30 A.M. – 5:30 P.M. (the second Friday of each month clients are seen from 12:30 to 4:30 P.M.)
　Saturday: 9:30 A.M. – 1:30 P.M.
　By appointment (please call 212-367-1100 to schedule):
　Thursday: 9:30 A.M. – 5:30 P.M.
　All testing is free and confidential. Please allow 5 to 10 minutes to complete an intake form before seeing a test counselor. Doors close 30 minutes before closing time, so individuals seeking testing should arrive before then to be tested. Testing for HIV, syphilis, *Chlamydia*, gonorrhea, and hepatitis C is limited to four times a year (every 3 months). Persons unable to be seen at the testing center should visit one of the community partners:
　Callen-Lorde Community Health Center
　356 West 18th Street, New York, NY 10011
　Community Healthcare Network: Catherine M. Abate Health Center
　150 Essex Street, New York, NY 10002
　Mount Sinai Comprehensive Health Center: Downtown

275 7th Avenue, 12th Floor, New York, NY 10011

CHILDREN AND ADOLESCENTS

Chapter 33: Childhood and Adolescence

Textbook
　Lyons M, D'Angelo L (2007). *Teenagers, HIV, and AIDS: Insights from Youths Living with the Virus*. Santa Barbara, CA: Praeger/Greenwood Publishing Group.

Children Now
https://www.childrennow.org/parenting-resources/

Disclosure and Children
http://www.aidsmap.com/Disclosure-and-children/cat/1484/
　To facilitate the process of diagnostic disclosure to an HIV-positive child see Table A.3.

Make a Wish Foundation
http://www.wish.org/

Specialty Summer Camps for Children Infected with or Affected by HIV
See Table A.4.

WHO: Guideline on HIV Disclosure Counseling for Children up to 12 Years of Age
http://www.who.int/hiv/pub/hiv_disclosure/en/

HOTLINES

AIDS/HIV Nightline
　415-434-2437 San Francisco or 800-628-9240 Nationwide

California AIDS Hotline
　415-863-AIDS (2437)

CDC Info
　1-800-CDC-INFO
　1-800-344-7432 for Spanish

GMHC Hotline
Hours: open Monday through Friday, 10:00 A.M. to 9:00 P.M. and Saturday 12:00 P.M. to 3:00 P.M. (Eastern Time—GMT minus 5 hours)
　1-800-AIDS-NYC (1-800-243-7692) or 212-807-6655
　TTY: 212-645-7470 (para personas con deficiencias auditivas)
　Lunes – Viernes: 10:00 A.M. to 9:00 P.M. (ET)
　Sábado: 12:00 to 3:00 P.M. (ET)

National Child Abuse Hotline
　1-800 4-A-CHILD

National Clinician's Post-Exposure Prophylaxis Hotline (PEP line)
　1-888–448–4911, operational 24 hours a day

Table A.3 FACILITATING THE PROCESS OF DIAGNOSTIC DISCLOSURE TO AN HIV-POSITIVE CHILD

PHASE 1. PREPARATION

- Early on, encourage the parents to begin using words that they can build on later, such as *immune problems, virus*, or *infection*. Provide books for the family to read with the child on viruses. Strengthen the family through education and support and schedule regular follow-up meetings. Let the family know that you will meet with them on a regular basis to help guide them through the disclosure process and to support the child and family after disclosure. Respect the family's timing, but strongly encourage the family not to lie to the child if he or she asks directly about having HIV, unless significant, identifiable safety concerns render the decision to disclose inadvisable. Also remind the family to avoid disclosure during an argument or in anger.
- Have a meeting with the parent or caregivers involved in the decision-making process. Staff members that the family trusts should be present.
- Address the importance of disclosure and ascertain whether the family has a plan in mind. Respect the intensity of feelings about this issue. Obtain feedback on the child's anticipated response. Explore the child's level of knowledge and his or her emotional stability and maturity.
- Solicit multidisciplinary input on relevant socioemotional, cognitive, family, environmental, and disease factors. Ideally, this should include input from the pediatrician, psychologist, psychiatrist, social worker, case manager, and medical staff. The input should be used for informing the decision to disclose as well as the process of disclosure.
- The multidisciplinary team should strive to answer the following questions: Does the child have the cognitive capacity, emotional stability, and emotional maturity for disclosure? Does the parent have the emotional stability, life coping skills, and treatment adherence that are important for disclosure to child? Is the current family environment conducive to optimal diagnostic disclosure? (For example, are there significant secrecy or communication issues, or is there parent distress regarding the child or parent fear regarding disclosure? Is there a disagreement between the parents regarding the need for or timing of disclosure? Is the family struggling with stressors that might affect disclosure outcome—e.g., unstable housing, no support network?)
- If significant potential barriers to effective disclosure are identified, advise the parents to postpone disclosure, address the barrier, and re-evaluate the readiness at a later point (typically 3–6 months later, but keeping in mind that time is of the essence as the child moves toward puberty, adolescence, more independence, and greater exposure to peer influences, which may include sexual experimentation, drugs, or inadvertent disclosure).
- Some parents will refuse to disclose the diagnosis to the child because of concerns they have about disclosing their own HIV status. The focus needs to be on parental psychosocial needs, perceived shame, stigma, or concerns pertaining to safety if the diagnosis is revealed. It should also be conveyed to the parents that, if they continue to refuse to disclose the diagnosis to their child, learning about the diagnosis through inadvertent disclosure may be significantly more traumatic.
- If the family is ready to disclose, guide them in various ways of approaching disclosure

PHASE 2. DISCLOSURE

- In advance, have the family think through or write out how they want the conversation to go. They need to give careful consideration to what message they want their child to walk away with after disclosure. Encourage the family to begin with, "Do you remember . .". to include information about the child's life, medications, and/or procedures, so that the child is reminded of past events before introducing new facts.
- Have the family choose a place where the child will be most comfortable to talk openly.
- Provide the family with questions the child may ask so they are prepared with answers. Such questions include "How long have you known this?" "Who else has the virus?" "Will I die?" "Can I ever have children?" "Who can I tell?" "Why me?" and "Who else knows?"
- Encourage having only the people present with whom the child is most comfortable. The health care practitioner may offer to facilitate this meeting, but if at all possible, preparation should be done in advance so that the family can share the information on their own.
- Medical facts should be kept to a minimum (immunology, virology, the effectiveness of therapy) and hope should be reinforced. Silence, as well as questions, needs to be accepted. The child should be told that nothing has changed except a name is now being given to what he or she has been living with. The child also needs to hear that the child didn't do or say anything to cause the disease and that the family will always remain by their side.
- If the diagnosis is to be kept a secret, it is important that the child be given the names of people he or she can talk to, such as a clinician, another child living with HIV, and/or a family friend. Stating "You can't tell anyone" makes the child feel ashamed and guilty.
- Provide the child with a journal or diary to record his or her questions, thoughts, and feelings. If appropriate, provide books about children living with HIV.
- Schedule a follow-up meeting.

PHASE 3. POST-DISCLOSURE FOLLOW-UP

- Provide individual and family follow-up 2 weeks after disclosure and again every 2–4 weeks for the first 6 months to assess impact of disclosure, answer questions, and help foster support between the child and family.
- Ask the child to tell you what he or she has learned about the virus. This can identify and clarify misconceptions. Writing and art may be useful techniques.
- Assess changes in emotional well-being and provide the family with information about symptoms that could indicate the need for more intensive intervention.
- Support parents for having disclosed the diagnosis and, if they are interested and one is available, refer them to a parents support group. Encourage them to think about the emotional needs of the other children in the family in the disclosure process.
- Remind parents that disclosure is not a one-time event. Ongoing communication will be needed. Ask parents what other supports they feel would be helpful to them and their child. Provide information about HIV camp programs for HIV-infected and HIV-affected children and families (Table A.4).

Sources: Wiener LS, Battles HB. Untangling the web: a close look at diagnosis disclosure among HIV-infected adolescents. *J Adolesc Health* 38(3):307–309. Copyright (2006), with permission from Elsevier; Oland A, Valdez N, Kapetanovic S. Process-oriented biopsychosocial approach to disclosing HIV status to infected children. NIMH Annual International Research Conference on the Role of Families in Preventing and Adapting to HIV/AIDS, Providence RI, October 2008.

Table A.4 SPECIALTY SUMMER CAMPS FOR CHILDREN INFECTED WITH OR AFFECTED BY HIV

CAMP NAME	AFFILIATION	DESCRIPTION	STATE	ADDRESS	PHONE #	EMAIL	WEBSITE
Camp Arroyo	Taylor Family Foundation	Year-round camp serving children with life-threatening diseases and disabilities	CA	5555 Arroyo Rd. Livermore, CA 94550	(925) 455-5118	trff@trff.org	http://www.trff.org/
Camp Care	All About Care	Support for women, children, and families infected with and affected by HIV/AIDS	CA	4974 Fresno Street PMB #156 Fresno, CA 93726	(559) 222-9471	Email option on website	http://allaboutcare.org/camp-care/
Camp Dream Street	Dream Street Foundation	Serves children with cancer, blood disorders, and other life-threatening illnesses	CA	324 South Beverly Dr. Suite 500 Beverly Hills, CA 90212	(424) 333-1371	dreamstreetca@gmail.com	http://dreamstreetfoundation.org/
Camp Hollywood Heart	One Heartland	Week-long full service summer camp for children and adolescents infected with and affected by HIV/AIDS	CA	301 E. Colorado Blvd. Suite 430 Pasadena, CA 91101	(626) 795-9645	info@hollywoodheart.org	http://hollywoodheart.org/
Camp Kindle	Project Kindle	Summer camp serving children infected with and affected by HIV/AIDS	CA	28245 Ave Crocker Ste. 104 Santa Clarita, CA 91355	(877) 800-CAMP (2267)	info@projectkindle.org	http://www.campkindle.org/
Camp Laurel	Laurel Foundation	Serves children infected with and affected HIV/AIDS	CA	75 South Grand Ave. Pasadena, CA 91105	(626) 683-0800	info@laurel-foundation.org	http://www.laurel-foundation.org/
Camp Sunburst	Sunburst Projects	Long-term residential camp for children living with HIV/AIDS	CA	1025 19th St., Suite 1A. Sacramento, CA 95814	(916) 440-0889	admin@sunburstprojects.org	http://www.sunburstprojects.org/programs.shtml
Camp Ray-Ray	Angels Unaware	Short-term residential camp for families affected by AIDS	CO	6370 Union St. Arvada, CO, 80004	(303) 420-6370	AngelsUnaware@att.net	http://www.angelsunaware.net/Camp_Ray_Ray.htm
The Hole in the Wall Gang Camp	Association of Hole in the Wall Gang Camps	Residential camp for children ages 7–15 with HIV/AIDS	CT	565 Ashford Center Road Ashford, CT 06278	(860) 429-3444	ashford@holeinthewallgang.org	http://www.holeinthewallgang.org/Page.aspx?pid=471
Camp AmeriKids		One-week residential summer camp for children ages 8–16	CT	88 Hamilton Ave. Stamford, CT 06902	(203) 658-9547	Email option on Website	http://www.campamerikids.org/
Camp Meechimuk	Hispanos Unidos	Long-term residential camp for children ages 6–15 affected by HIV/AIDS	CT	116 Sherman Ave. New Haven, CT 06511	(203) 781-0226	Email option on Website	http://www.hispanos-unidos.org/camp-meechimuk.aspx
Camp Totokett	First Congregational Church of Branford	Non-denominational summer camp for children ages 5–16 whose families are affected by HIV/AIDS	CT	1009 Main St. Branford, CT 06405	(203) 488-7201	info@firstcongregationalbranford.org	http://www.tavf.org/CampTotokett.html
The Boggy Creek Gang	Paul Newman Foundation	Year-round retreat for children and their families	FL	30500 Brantley Branch Rd. Eustis, FL 32736	(352) 483-4200	info@campboggycreek.org	http://www.boggycreek.org/

Table A.4 CONTINUED

CAMP NAME	AFFILIATION	DESCRIPTION	STATE	ADDRESS	PHONE #	EMAIL	WEBSITE
Camp High Five	H.E.R.O for Children	Serving children infected with and affected by HIV/AIDS	GA	6075 Roswell Road NE Suite 450 Atlanta, GA 30328	(404) 236-7411	info@heroforchildren.org	http://www.heroforchildren.org/
Children's Place Lucy R. Sprague Summer Camp	The Children's Place Association	Serves children and families affected by HIV, with a variety of programming	IL	3059 West Augusta Blvd. Chicago, IL 60622	(773) 395-9193		www.childrens-place.org
Tataya Mato	Jameson, Inc.	Long-term residential camp for children infected with or affected by HIV/AIDS	IN	2001 S. Bridgeport Rd. Indiapolis, IN 46231	(317) 241-2661	tim@jamesoncamp.org	http://www.jamesoncamp.org/
Camp Heart to Heart	Lions Camp Crescendo, Inc.	Free summer camp for children (ages 5–12) living with HIV/AIDS	KY	PO Box 607 1480 Pine Tavern Road Lebanon Junction, KY 40150	(502) 833-4427	wibblesb@aol.com	http://www.lccky.org/our%20 camps.htm
Camp Kids Haven	Lutheran Social Services of the National Capitol Area	Week-long residential camp for children (age 7–13) living with or affected by HIV/AIDS. Also have teen retreats (14–18 years) throughout the year	MD	4406 Georgia Ave. NW Washington, DC 20011	(703) 698-5026	Email option on Website	https://www.lssnca.org/ programs/camps_retreats
Camp Knutson	Camp Knutson and Knutson Point Retreat Center	Serves families in which any member is infected with HIV/AIDS, for a 1-week residential camp	MN	11169 Whitefish Ave. Crosslake, MN 56442	(218) 543-4232	Email option on Website	http://www.lssmn.org/camp/
Camp Heartland	One Heartland	Serves children infected with and affected by HIV/AIDS	MN	2101 Hennepin Ave. S. Suite 200 Minneapolis, MN 55405	(888) 216-2028	Email available on Website	http://www.oneheartland. org/camps-and-programs/ camp-heartland
Camp Hope	Project Ark (AIDS/ HIV Resources & Knowledge)	Weekend-long camp for HIV-infected children and their families	MO	4169 Laclede Ave. St. Louis, MO 63108	(314) 535-7275		http://projectark.wustl.edu/ SupportUs/CampHope/tabid/ 804/Default.aspx
Camp Kindle Midwest	Project Kindle	Serves families in which any member is infected with HIV/AIDS, for a 1-week residential camp	NE	Project Kindle PO Box 81147 Lincoln, NE 68501	(877) 800-2267	info@projectkindle.org	http://www.projectkindle.org
Camp Bright Feathers	YMCA Camp Ockanickon, Inc.	Long-term residential camp for children affected by HIV/AIDS	NJ	1303 Stokes Rd. Medford, NJ 08055	(609) 654-8225	havenyouthcenterpa@gmail. com	http://www.campbrightfeathers. com/
The Double "H". Hole in the Woods Ranch	Part of the Association of Hole in the Wall camps	Six day sessions for children ages 6–16; year-long support and activities (including ages 17–21)	NY	97 Hidden Valley Rd. Lake Luzerne, NY 12846	(518) 696-5676	jroyael@doublehranch.org	http://www.doublehranch.org/

Camp Name	Organization	Description	State	Address	Phone	Email	Website
Camp Viva	Family Services of Westchester, White Plains Office	1-week camp and after-camp follow-up program serving children and families with HIV/AIDS	NY	P.O. Box 266 Rt. 52/Salisbury Turnpike Rhinebeck, NY 12572	(914) 872-5285	rcestone@fsw.org	http://www.fsw.org/our-programs/hivaids-services-partnership-for-care/camp-viva
Camp Kaleidoscope	Duke Children's Hospital and Health Center	Summer program open to all Duke University Medical Center pediatric patients ages 7–16	NC	Box 3417, DUMC Durham, NC 27710	(919) 681-5349	arthur.taub@duke.edu	http://www.dukechildrens.org/giving/events/camp_kaleidoscope
Victory Junction Camp	Victory Junction	One-week summer camp program; additional family weekend programs.	NC	4500 Adam's Way Randleman, NC 27317	(336) 498-9055	info@victoryjunction.org	http://www.victoryjunction.org/
Camp Sunrise	AIDS Resource Center Ohio	One week residential camp for children impacted by HIV/AIDS	OH	4400 North High St. Suite 300 Columbus, OH 34214	(614) 444-1683	Email available through Website	http://www.sunrisekids.org/
Camp Starlight	Program of the Cascade AIDS Project	Week long sleep-away summer camp for children in Oregon and Washington whose lives are affected by HIV/AIDS (patients and family members)	OR	PO Box 80666 Portland, OR 97280	(503) 964-1516	info@camp-starlight.org	http://camp-starlight.org/
Camp Dreamcatcher Summer Camp	Camp Dreamcatcher	One week program for children ages 5-17 infected or affected by HIV/AIDS. Free of Charge.	PA	617 W South St. Kennett Square, PA 19348	(610) 925-2998	info@campdreamcatcher.org	http://campdreamcatcher.org/
Camp Firelight	Tarrant County AIDS Outreach Center	Week-long camp for children living with HIV/AIDS	TX	400 North Beach Street Suite 100 Fort Worth, TX 76111	(817) 335-1994		http://www.aoc.org/
Camp Hope	AIDS Foundation Houston, Inc.	Serving children ages 6–15 with HIV/AIDS	TX	3202 Weslayan Annex Houston, TX, 77027	(713) 623-6796		http://www.aidshelp.org/?fuseaction=cms.page&id=1027
Camp HolidayTrails		1-week and 2-week camp sessions for children with HIV/AIDS; 4-day camp for families of children with HIV/AIDS	VA	400 Holiday Trails Lane Charlottesville, VA 22903	(434) 977-3781	campisgood@campholidaytrails.org	http://www.campholidaytrails.org/
Camp Wakonda	Diocesan Center, Frances Barber	Serves children and families infected with and affected by HIV/AIDS in a day-camp environment	VA	395 Dorwain Drive Norfolk, VA 23502	(757) 461-3595	allsaintschurch1@verizon.net	http://www.allsaintsvabeach.org/camp.html
Northwest Reach Camp	REACH Ministries	Long-term residential camp for children and families infected with and affected by HIV/AIDS	WA	309 South G. St. Suite 3 Tacoma, WA 98405	(253) 383-7616	info@reachministries.org	http://reachministries.org/our-programs/camp/
Rise N' Shine Camp	Inspire Youth Project	Long-term residential camp for children infected with and affected by HIV/AIDS	WA	417 23rd Avenue South Seattle, WA 98144	(206) 628-8949	info@inspireyouthproject.org	http://inspireyouthproject.org/

*While we have tried to include as many camps as possible for which information was accessible, this list is not exhaustive. New and additional camp programs may be available. A good resource to learn about additional camp resources is the Federal for Children with Special Needs: http://fcsn.org/camps/.

National Drug and Alcohol Treatment Hotline
1-800-662-HELP

National Domestic Violence Hotline
1-800-799-7233 or 800-787-3224

National Runaway Safeline
1-800-621-4000

National Suicide Prevention Lifeline
1-800-273-TALK

National Youth Crisis Hotline
1-800-442-HOPE

New York LifeNet Hotline
For residents throughout New York City, there is a 24-hour hotline that assists callers seeking help for emotional or substance abuse problems:
1-800-LIFENET (800-543-3638)
1-877-AYUDESE (Spanish)
1-877-990-8585 (Asian LifeNet)
212-982-5284 (TTY)

Panic Disorder Information Line
1-800-64-PANIC

Project Inform HIV/AIDS Treatment Hotline
1-800-822-7422

PRISON REFORM AND HEALTH DISPARITIES

Chapter 9: Sociocultural Factors Influencing the Transmission of HIV/AIDS in the United States: AIDS and the Nation's Prisons; Chapter 50: Health Services and Policy Issues in AIDS Psychiatry

The Sentencing Project
http://www.sentencingproject.org/

The Vera Institute of Justice
http://www.vera.org/

U.S. Department of Justice, Bureau of Justice Statistics
http://www.bjs.gov/

SUBSTANCE-RELATED AND ADDICTIVE DISORDERS

Chapter 14: Substance-Related and Addictive Disorders—The Special Role in HIV Transmission

Al-Anon Family Groups
http://www.al-anon.alateen.org/

Alcoholics Anonymous (AA)
http://aa.org/

Faces & Voices of Recovery
http://www.facesandvoicesofrecovery.org/

Harm Reduction Coalition
http://harmreduction.org/

Hazelden
http://www.hazelden.org

Medication-Assisted Treatment for Substance Use Disorders
http://dpt.samhsa.gov/

Narcotics Anonymous
http://www.na.org

National Institute on Alcohol Abuse and Alcoholism
http://www.niaaa.nih.gov/

National Institute on Drug Abuse
https://www.drugabuse.gov/

Substance Abuse and Mental Health Service Administration (SAMSHA)
http://www.samhsa.gov/

MINORITIES AND HIV/AIDS

The National Minority AIDS Council (NMAC)
http://nmac.org/
The National Minority AIDS Council has helped develop leadership in communities of color to address the challenges of HIV/AIDS since 1987.
For all issues related to health disparities:

National Institute on Minority Health and Health Disparities
http://www.nimhd.nih.gov/

U.S. Department of Health and Human Services (HHS)
http://minorityhealth.hhs.gov/npa/

INDEX

Page numbers followed by *b* indicates boxes; *f* indicates figures; *t* indicates tables.

AA. *See* Alcoholics Anonymous
AACRN. *See* Advanced HIV/AIDS Certified
  Registered Nurse
AAN. *See* American Academy of Neurology
Abacavir (ABV), 164, 215, 520*t*, 526*t*, 527
  cardiovascular disease risk and, 603
ABCDE model, 501, 502*b*
Abdominal pain, 258
ABV. *See* Abacavir
ACA. *See* Patient Protection and Affordable
  Care Act
Academy of Psychosomatic Medicine (APM), 663
Academy of Psychosomatic Medicine HIV/AIDS
  Psychiatry Special Interest Group, 663
Acamprosate, 559
Accelerated aging phenotype, 430
Accountable Care Organizations, 649
Acquired immune deficiency syndrome. *See* HIV/
  AIDS
ACTH. *See* Adrenocorticotropin hormone
Activism, 109
  by health workers, 115
ACT-UP. *See* AIDS Coalition to Unleash Power
Acute interstitial nephritis, 580
Acute retinal necrosis, 611
ADC. *See* AIDS dementia complex
Addictive disorders, 6, 32
  adherence and, 476
  psychosocial treatments for, 456
  suicide and, 289
ADHD, 393, 394
Adherence to care, 12–14
  addiction disorders and, 476
  anxiety impact on, 214, 214*t*
  in Asia-Pacific region, 55
  behavioral interventions to improve, 338–40
  CBT for, 171, 250, 453
  depression and, 169–70
  electronic monitoring of, 650
  family group support and, 459
  interventions for, 339–40
  MI for, 457
  to PEP, 361
  perinatally HIV-infected adolescents, 385–86
  personality disorders and, 234
  psychiatric determinants of, 337–38
  psychiatric disorders and, 329–30
  SMI and, 227, 338–40
  social work assistance with, 476, 479
  substance-related and addictive disorders and, 6
  trauma and PTSD impact on, 206–7
  treatment failure and, 498
ADL scale, 137
Adolescents

behaviorally infected
  epidemiology, 383–84
  neurocognitive outcomes, 388
end-of-life issues, 394–95
HIV-affected, 388–90
  epidemiology, 383, 384
  summer camps for, 397–99
homeless, 348–49
intervention and treatment
  considerations, 390–95
mental health services and, 392–93
palliative care, 394
parentification, 388–89
perinatally exposed but uninfected, 383,
  384, 389–90
perinatally infected
  adherence, 385–86
  clinical milestones in development, 384–87
  diagnostic disclosure, 385
  epidemiology, 383
  family therapy and, 460
  health behaviors, 385–87
  mental health and psychiatric disorders, 387
  neurodevelopmental outcomes, 384–85
  substance use, 386–87
  transition to adult care, 387
psychopharmacological considerations, 393–94
summer camps for, 397–99
transition to adult care, 395
trauma and, 207
Adrenal gland, 589–91
Adrenal insufficiency, 276, 280, 590
Adrenocorticotropin hormone (ACTH), 244, 276,
  589, 590, 595
Adult AIDS Clinical Trial Group Symptom
  Distress Module (ACTG-SDM), 255
ADUs. *See* AIDS-dedicated units
Advanced care planning, 642–43
Advanced HIV/AIDS Certified Registered Nurse
  (AACRN), 483
Advocacy, 109
  community, 110–11
  in India, 114–15
  major issues addressed
    in, 111–13
  media, 114
  peer, 111
  publications, 112–13, 112*b*
  school, 391
  in South Africa, 113–14
AEDs. *See* Antiepileptic drugs
AEGiS. *See* AIDS Education Global
  Information System
Aerobic exercise, 469

Affectivity, 129
Africa. *See also* Sub-Saharan Africa; *specific countries*
  ART scale-up program obstacles in, 50–51
  distress in, 256
  HIV/AIDS and mental health in, 52
  neglected HIV epidemics in, 51
  stigma and discrimination in, 74
Aging, 620–21. *See also* Older adults
  CNS and, 180
  cognitive impairment and, 432–35
  HIV/AIDS and, 433
  phenotypes
    defining, 429–30
    HIV infection and, 430–31, 430*t*
  successful, HIV infection and, 442–43
Agins, Bruce, 69
AIDS. *See* HIV/AIDS
AIDS Coalition to Unleash Power (ACT-UP),
  111, 651
AIDS-dedicated units (ADUs), 483–84
AIDS dementia complex (ADC), 136, 175, 176, 302
AIDS Education and Training Centers, 152
AIDS Education Global Information System
  (AEGiS), 112*b*
AIDS Impact Scale (AIS), 634
AIDSism, 5, 10, 73, 144
  suicide and, 289
AIDS Law Project, 113, 114
AIDS mania, 224–25
AIDS Memorial Quilt Project, 635
AIDS orphans, 66
  areas of vulnerability, 70–71
  defining, 69–70
  epidemiology, 69
  supporting, 71
AIDS palliative care, 259
AIDS phobia, 213
  treatment approaches, 216
AIDS Physical Symptom Checklist (PSC), 274
Aids Treatment News (ATN), 112*b*
AIS. *See* AIDS Impact Scale
Alcohol, 160–61, 160*t*, 190*t*
  anxiety diagnosis and, 215
  BD and use of, 172
  drug interactions with, 164
  older adult use of, 439–40
  SSRIs and, 533
Alcohol and other drugs (AOD), 29, 164
  HIV infection rates and, 36
Alcoholics Anonymous (AA), 289
Alcohol-related disorders, 32
  HIV infection rates and, 36
Alcohol Use Disorder Identification Test (AUDIT),
  457, 487

Alexithymia, 245
Alliance Health Project, 92
Alprazolam, 164, 267, 537, 538t
Alzheimer's dementia, 132, 132t, 133t, 180
AMA. *See* American Medical Association
Amenorrhea, 594
American Academy of Neurology (AAN), 136,
    433, 548
    AIDS Task Force, 175
American Foundation for AIDS Research
    (amfAR), 110
American Medical Association (AMA), Code of
    Ethics, 644
American Psychiatric Association (APA), 91, 280
    Office of HIV Psychiatry, 146
amfAR. *See* American Foundation for AIDS
    Research
Amisulpride, 550, 552t
Amitriptyline, 531t, 536
Amphetamines, 159–60, 215, 541–43, 542t
Amprenavir (APV), 163, 267
Amyloids, 180
Amyotrophic lateral sclerosis, 405
Anabolic steroids, 279, 594
ANAC. *See* Association of Nurses in AIDS
Anal carcinoma, 619–20
Analgesic ladder, 164, 496
Anemia, 275–76, 279, 618
ANI. *See* Asymptomatic neurocognitive
    impairment
Annual World AIDS Day, 635
ANS. *See* Autonomic nervous system
Anticipatory grief, 506–7
Anticonvulsants, 393, 544, 548–49
    neuropathic pain management with, 496
Antidepressants, 171, 528, 529t–532t, 533–37. *See
    also specific drugs*
    for grief therapy, 508
    multimodal, 535–36
Antiepileptic drugs (AEDs), 544,
    545t–547t, 548–49
Antihistamines, 216, 268
Antipsychotics, 440, 549–50, 551t–555t, 556–58
    for grief therapy, 508
    hypogonadism and, 594
    LAIs, 224
    ocular adverse effects, 612
    second-generation, 393
    sedating, 268
Antiretroviral therapy (ART), 3, 19, 23, 73, 143,
    285, 515–16, 602. *See also* Adherence to
    care; *specific drugs and classes of drugs*
    access to, 108
    adherence interventions, 339–40
    Asia-Pacific region adherence to, 55
    blood pressure and, 604
    cardiovascular disease risk and, 603
    CDC recommendations for initiation of, 405
    clinical landscape changes with, 303
    CNS benefits, 192t
    CNS side effects, 7
    co-formulated drugs, 527
    conception and pregnancy and, 423
    in correctional settings, 104
    DAA and neuropsychiatric medication
        interactions with, 575t
    depression and adherence to, 169–70
    depression and women on, 420–21
    development of, 407

directly administered, 650–51
drug interactions with, 163
fatigue and, 276–77, 277t
generic, 114
generic drugs for, 114
HAD prevalence and, 31
HAND in older adults and, 435–36
HAND prevalence and, 31–32
HBV and, 617
hypogonadism and, 594
impact of effective, 113
initiation of, 405
in late-stage HIV illness, 498, 500t
life expectancy and, 303
limitations of, 24
lipid abnormalities and, 604
medications for, 25t–26t
menopausal status and, 424
neurocognitive outcomes and, 191–93, 193t
for neurological complications of HIV, 307
older patients and, 435–36
patient education for, 490
perinatal exposure to, 389–90
personality disorders and, 234–35
in pregnancy, 423–24
preventative, 26
principles for, 24
psychiatric aspects of care and adherence
    to, 337–38
psychiatric aspects of care and medication in, 334
    care engagement, 335–36
    HIV care continuum, 335
    PrEP, 335
public health approach, 50
reproductive issues and, 413–14
research findings implications, 340–41
scale-up program obstacles, 50–51
scale-up programs in sub-Saharan Africa, 48–49
SMI and, 335
symptom management, 490, 491t
TCAs and, 536
therapeutic issues and, 415
thyroid hormones and, 592
treatment failure and, 498
Antisocial personality disorder (ASPD), 233, 234
Anxiety, 33, 34
    burnout and, 633
    co-occurring disorders, 216–17
    disorders
        assessment and diagnosis, 212–13
        differential diagnosis, 214–15, 441
        impact on ART adherence, mortality, and
            quality of life, 214, 214t
        prevalence and risk factors, 211
        symptoms, 212–13
        treatment approaches, 215–16
    fatigue and, 277–78
    HIV/AIDS course and, 210
    insomnia and, 266
    in older adults, 440–41
    in palliative care, 497
    psychoimmunology of, 211
    sleep disorders and, 264
Anxiety sensitivity, 212, 216
Anxiolytics, 537, 538t, 540
AOD. *See* Alcohol and other drugs
APA. *See* American Psychiatric Association
APV. *See* Amprenavir
Aripiprazole, 440, 550, 552t, 556

Armodafinil, 436, 542t, 543
ART. *See* Antiretroviral therapy
Arteriovenous fistula (AV fistula), 581
ASD. *See* Autism spectrum disorder
Asenapine, 552t, 556
Asia-Pacific region, 46–47
    distress in, 256
    HIV care and mental health services in, 54–55
    HIV epidemiology in, 52–53, 53t, 54t
    mental health and persons living with HIV
        in, 53–54
    stigma and discrimination in, 54
ASPD. *See* Antisocial personality disorder
Assisted suicide, 498
Association of Nurses in AIDS (ANAC), 483, 484t
Astrocytes, 177
    as HIV infection target, 300
Asymptomatic neurocognitive impairment (ANI),
    132, 136, 137, 176t
Atazanavir (ATV), 163, 164, 517t, 519, 527, 604
    lamotrigine and, 548
Atherosclerosis, 604
Atherothrombosis, 602
ATN. *See Aids Treatment News*
Atomoxetine, 393, 542t, 543
ATV. *See* Atazanavir
AUDIT. *See* Alcohol Use Disorder
    Identification Test
Australia, 411
Autism spectrum disorder (ASD), 145
Autoimmune thyroid disease, 592
Autologous fat transplantation, 605
Autonomic (sweat test), 320
Autonomic nervous system (ANS), 244–45
AV fistula. *See* Arteriovenous fistula
AZT. *See* Zidovudine

Bacterial skin infections, 615
Bad news, protocol for
    breaking, 502, 502b
Bangkok Tenofovir Study, 356
Barbiturates, 268
    SSRIs and, 533
Bartonella henselae, 615
BBB. *See* Blood brain barrier
BD. *See* Bipolar disorder
Beck, Aaron, 452
Beck Depression Inventory, 101
Behavioral contract, 235
Behavioral disinhibition, suicide and, 287
Behavioral interventions, 496
    adherence and, 338–40
Behaviorally HIV-infected adolescents
    epidemiology, 383–84
    neurocognitive outcomes of, 388
Benzodiazepines (BZDs), 162, 164, 190t, 216, 441
    for grief therapy, 508
    insomnia treatment and, 267
    non-triazoloBZDs, 538t, 540
    ocular adverse effects, 612
    triazoloBZDs, 537, 538t, 540
Bereavement, 459, 506–8
    PNI and, 243–44
    sleep disorders and, 264
Binge drinking, 161
Biomarkers, of neurological complications of
    HIV, 305–7
Biomedical interventions, 49
Biomedical prevention, 12–14

Biopsychosocial approach, 14–15, 83, 431
  for AIDS palliative care, 495
  education and, 101
  to psychiatric consultations
    comprehensive, 123–29
    inpatient, 122–23
    outpatient, 122
    settings for, 121–22
Biopsychosociocultural approaches, 4, 431
Bipolar disorder (BD), 35, 36, 222
  fatigue and, 277–78
  SUD and, 172
  treatment, 224–25
Blindness, suicide and, 286
Blonanserin, 552t, 556
Blood brain barrier (BBB), 177, 296–97, 297f
  Tat involved in, 301
Blood donation, 644
Blood oxygen level dependent (BOLD) fMRI, 185
Blood pressure, 604
Blurred vision, 612
BMD. See Bone mineral density
BMVEC. See Brain microvascular endothelial cells
bnAbs. See Broadly neutralizing antibodies
Boceprevir, 574
BOLD. See Blood oxygen level dependent
Bone and mineral metabolism, 595–97
Bone mineral density (BMD), 595–97
Bonnardeaux, Jillian, 68
Borderline personality disorder
    (BPD), 233, 234
Boston Consortium Model, 422
Boston HAPPENS, 349
Botswana, 74
  distress in, 256–57
BPD. See Borderline personality disorder
BPI. See Wisconsin Brief Pain Inventory
Brain
  HIV replication and tropism in, 302
  neuroimaging and atrophy of, 304
  neurological complications of HIV entry
    into, 296–98
  tropism in, 301, 302
Brain microvascular endothelial cells (BMVEC),
    177, 296–97
Brain parenchyma, 296
Brazil, 47, 60
  stigma and discrimination in, 74
Brexpiprazole, 553t
Brigham and Women's Hospital (BWH), 88–89
Broadly neutralizing antibodies (bnAbs), 370–71
Broom, 268
Broyard, Anatole, 629
Bryn Mawr College, 68
Buprenorphine, 87, 163–64, 559
Bupropion, 171, 215, 534
Burnout, 478, 629
  addressing, 635
  factors predisposing to, 630–31, 630t
  measures of, 633–34
  protective factors, 632–33
  stressors contributing to, 632t, 634
  symptoms of, 634b
Business case planning, 98
Buspirone, 216, 538t, 540
BWH. See Brigham and Women's Hospital
BWH Addiction Services department, 89
BWH Outpatient Psychiatry Clinic, 89
BZDs. See Benzodiazepines

Cabotegravir (CAB), 357–58
CAGE questionnaire, 158
CalCAP. See California Computerized Assessment
    Battery
Calcium hydroxylapatite, 605
California Computerized Assessment Battery
    (CalCAP), 183
CAM. See Complementary and alternative
    medicine
Cambridge Neuropsychological Test Automated
    Battery (CANTAB), 140
CAMCI. See Computer Assessment of Mild
    Cognitive Impairment
Canada, 47, 58–59
Cancer, 618–20
Candida, 7, 276, 419, 615
Candida albicans, 616
Candidiasis, 7
CANTAB. See Cambridge Neuropsychological
    Test Automated Battery
Capillary endothelial cells, 297
Carbamazepine, 522, 536, 544, 545t, 550, 612
Cardiopulmonary illness, 258
Cardiovascular disease
  ART and risk for, 603
  HIV-related risk factors, 602–3
  risk factors, 603–4
CARE. See Ryan White Comprehensive AIDS
    Resources Emergency Act
Care coordination programs, 480
Care delivery
  multi-need psychiatric patients and, 649–50
  stressor related to, 632t
Care engagement, psychiatric aspects
  ART and, 335–36
  intervention to improve, 336–37
Care management service model, 480
Caribbean countries, distress in, 257
Cariprazine, 553t
Case management, 649
Cataractous changes, 612
CBCT. See Community Based Clinical Trials
CBG. See Corticosteroid-binding globulin
CBS. See Cognitive-behavioral self-help
CBSM. See Cognitive-behavioral stress
    management
CBST. See Cognitive-behavioral skills building
CBT. See Cognitive-behavioral therapy
CBT-AD. See Cognitive-behavioral therapy for
    adherence and depression
CBT-I. See Cognitive-behavioral therapy for
    insomnia
CCR5 antagonists, 522, 526t
CD4 T cells, 7, 369
CD4+ T cells, 300–301
CDC. See Centers for Disease Control and
    Prevention
Cellular physiology, 297–98
Center for Health Care Transition
    Improvement, 395
Center for HIV Identification, Prevention and
    Treatment Services (CHIPTS), 400
Centers for Disease Control and Prevention (CDC),
    58, 74, 222, 400, 612
  ART initiation recommendations, 405
  breastfeeding recommendations, 424
  HIV testing recommendations, 638–39, 652
  PEP recommendations, 631
  prenatal testing recommendations, 383

PrEP recommendations, 334, 357
  on smoking-related deaths, 161
  youth exposure to violence programs, 207
Central America, 47, 60–61
Central nervous system (CNS), 29, 121
  acute HIV infection and, 175
  ART benefits, 192t
  ART effects on, 7
  fatigue and, 278
  HIV in
    aging and, 180
    compartmentalization role, 179–80, 179f
    immune system role, 178–79
    pathogenesis of, 177–80, 178f
  as HIV reservoir, 5, 7
  neurological complications of HIV, 295
    astrocytes and, 300
    biomarkers, 305–7
    clinical landscape and ART, 303
    clinical manifestations of HIV infection, 302
    entry into brain, 296–98
    HIV infection targets, 298–301
    management of, 307–9
    mononuclear phagocytes and, 298–300
    neurocognitive disorders classification, 302–3
    neuroimaging, 303–5
    persistence, replication, reservoir, and
        tropism, 301
    replication and tropism in the brain, 302
    targets for infections, 298–301
    T cells and, 300–301
Cerebral vascular accident (CVA), 436
Cervical carcinoma, 619–20
CET. See Coping effectiveness training
Chalder Fatigue Scale, 280
CHAMP. See Collaborative HIV/AIDS Mental
    Health Project
Chemokines
  gradients of, 296, 297
  immunological markers and, 306
  Tat and, 301
  transmigration process role, 298
Chief complaint, 123–24
Child abuse
  protection from, 71
  trauma history and, 127, 205
Childhood abuse, 452
  homelessness and, 347, 348
  sexual, 205, 329, 388
Children, 70, 70f
  diagnostic disclosure, 396
  end-of-life issues, 394
  family therapy and, 459–60
  homeless, 348–49
  intervention and treatment
      considerations, 390–95
  parentification, 388–89
  perinatally exposed but uninfected, 383,
      384, 389–90
  perinatally infected
    adherence, 385–86
    clinical milestones in development, 384–87
    diagnostic disclosure, 385
    epidemiology, 383
    epidemiology of, 383
    family therapy and, 460
    health behaviors, 385–87
    mental health and psychiatric disorders, 387
    neurodevelopmental outcomes, 384–85

Children (*Cont.*)
    substance use, 386–87
    transition to adult care, 387
    psychopharmacological considerations, 393–94
    risk behaviors, 459–60
    summer camps for, 397–99
    supporting vulnerable, 71
    trauma and, 207
China, 46
CHIPTS. *See* Center for HIV Identification, Prevention and Treatment Services
Chloral hydrate, 268
Chlorpromazine, 551*t*
Chosen families, 408
Chronic kidney disease (CKD), 580, 581, 583
Chronological age, 429
CIDI. *See* Composite International Diagnostic Interview
Cidofovir, 611
Cipla, 114
Circadian rhythms, 267
Cirrhosis, 617
    alcoholism and, 160
    compensated, 572
    decompensated, 571, 572*f*, 573
Citalopram, 171, 439, 528, 529*t*, 533
CKD. *See* Chronic kidney disease
Clinical crowd-out effect, 649
Clinical Global Impressions Scale for mood and fatigue, 280
Clinical models
    development, 97–98
    implementation, 98
Clinician distress, 629–31
Clinician-initiated testing, 638–39
Clobazam, 545*t*
Clomipramine, 531*t*
Clonazepam, 164, 537, 538*t*
Clonidine, 393
Clozapine, 553*t*, 556–57
Club drugs, 161–62
CM. *See* Contingency management
CME. *See* Continuing medical education
CMV. *See* Cytomegalovirus
CNS. *See* Central nervous system
CNS lymphoma, 619
CNS penetration effectiveness (CPE), 191–92, 192*t*
Cobicistat, 164, 522, 525*t*, 527
Cocaine, 159–60, 164, 215
    prenatal exposure, 387
Codeine, 159, 164
Coexisting diagnoses, 500
Co-formulated antiretroviral drugs, 527
Cognition
    evaluation of, 131–33
    older persons and, 434
    personality and, 231, 232
    suicide and, 288
Cognition Module, 183
Cognitive appraisals, 245–46
Cognitive-behavioral self-help (CBS), 453
Cognitive-behavioral skills building (CBST), 457
Cognitive-behavioral stress management (CBSM), 248–49, 453–54, 591
    for anxiety, 215
    with expressive-supportive therapy, 171
Cognitive-behavioral therapy (CBT), 88, 206, 452–54
    for anxiety sensitivity, 215

    in lipodystrophy management, 605
    for OCD, 216
    for personality disorders, 235
    for substance-related and addictive disorders, 456
Cognitive-behavioral therapy for adherence and depression (CBT-AD), 171, 250, 453
Cognitive-behavioral therapy for insomnia (CBT-I), 266
Cognitive coping strategies, 215
Cognitive disorders, 433
Cognitive impairment, 6
    aging and, 432–35
    marijuana and, 466
    sleep disorders and, 264–65
    treatment in older adults, 435–37
Cognitive rehabilitation, 437
Cogstate, 140, 140*t*, 183
Cohen, Mary Ann, 68
Co-infection, 500
Collaborative care, 85, 168
    SMI and, 227–28
    social work and, 478
Collaborative HIV/AIDS Mental Health Project (CHAMP), 460
Co-located care, 84
Co-located psychiatrists, 122
Columbia University Medical Center, 91
Communication skills, 502
    spiritual issues and, 505–6
Community advocacy, early models for, 110–11
Community Based Clinical Trials (CBCT), 110
Community health centers
    HIV/LGBT, 90–91, 90*t*
    as medical homes, 90
Community publications, 112–13, 112*b*
Community Research Initiative (CRI), 110
Community-specific needs assessment, 87
Comorbid insomnia, 263
Compensated cirrhosis, 572
Complementary and alternative medicine (CAM), 465
Complex patient models, 86
Complicated grief, 506, 507–8
Composite International Diagnostic Interview (CIDI), 488
Comprehensive psychiatric consultations
    chief complaint, 123–24
    family psychiatric history, 125
    history of present illness, 124
    history-taking, 123, 124*t*
    past medical history and understanding of illness, 125
    past psychiatric history, 124
    psychosocial history, 125–29
    suicide history, 125
Computer Assessment of Mild Cognitive Impairment (CAMCI), 183
Computer topography (CT), 304
Conception
    ART and, 413–14, 423
    PrEP and, 412–13, 414
    serodiscordant couples and, 412–13
Conference on Retroviruses and Opportunistic Infections (CROI), 115
Confidentiality, 643
Confounding/compounding disorders, 138–39
Constructional apraxia, 132
Consultation-liaison psychiatry, 83

Consultative psychiatric care, 84
Contingency management (CM), 456
Continuing medical education (CME), 99
Contract referral, 643
Co-occurring disorders, 172–73
    anxiety and, 216–17
COPE. *See* Coping Orientation to Problem Experience
Coping
    maladaptive, 415
    types of, 406
Coping effectiveness training (CET), 454
Coping Orientation to Problem Experience (COPE), 633
Correctional facilities, 103–6
Cortical dementia, 132, 133*t*
Corticosteroid-binding globulin (CBG), 590
Corticotrophin-releasing hormone (CRH), 589
Cortisol, 590, 597
Costa Rica, 60
Countertransference, 455
Couples
    clinical assessment, 414
    gay male, 408–9
    heterosexual, 409–11
    medical illness impact on, 405–6
    in non-western countries, 411–12
    psychological issues, 413–14
    reproductive issues, 412–13
    serodiscordant, 406, 407, 408–16, 458*t*
    therapeutic issues, 414–16
Couple therapy, 457–59, 458*t*
CPE. *See* CNS penetration effectiveness
Crack cocaine, 159–60
CRH. *See* Corticotrophin-releasing hormone
CRI. *See* Community Research Initiative
Criminalization of HIV exposure, 110, 643–44
Critical Path Project, 112*b*
CROI. *See* Conference on Retroviruses and Opportunistic Infections
Cross-cultural issues in care of dying, 501
Cryptococcosis, 7
CT. *See* Computer topography
CTL. *See* Cytotoxic T lymphocytes
Cultural identity, 126
Cultural stereotypes, misreading of sexuality and, 127
Cumulative life event burden, 242–43
Cushing's syndrome, 589
Cutaneous drug eruptions, 615–16
CVA. *See* Cerebral vascular accident
Cyclosporine, 585
CYP2B6 inhibitors, 534
Cytochrome P540 enzymes, 514, 516*t*
Cytomegalovirus (CMV), 7, 111, 187, 589
    encephalopathy risk and, 384
    retinopathy and retinitis from, 257, 611
Cytotoxic T lymphocytes (CTL), 22

d4T. *See* Stavudine
DAA. *See* Direct-acting antivirals
DAART. *See* Directly administered antiretroviral therapy
Daclatasvir, 574, 575*t*, 617
DAH. *See* Development assistance for health
Dance/movement therapy (DMT), 470
Darunavir (DRY), 163, 517*t*, 527, 604

Dasabuvir, 527, 574, 575*t*
Death and dying, 259
  cross-cultural issues in care of, 501
Decision tree, 318*f*
Declaration of the Universal Rights and Needs of
      People Living with HIV Disease, 111
Decompensated cirrhosis, 571, 572*f*
Dehydroepiandrosterone (DHEA), 590, 591, 595
Delavirdine, 267, 523*t*, 550, 616
Delhi Network of HIV Positive People
      (DNP+), 114
Delirium, 187, 189–90
  assessment for, 131
  causes of, 191*t*
  melatonin and, 267
  treatment of, 194
Dementia
  assessment for, 131–33
  cortical versus subcortical, 132, 133*t*, 135
  HIV-associated, 297*f*
  signs and symptoms, 131, 132*t*
  sleep disorders and, 264–65
Demoralization syndrome, 505–6, 506*b*
Denver Principles, 108, 111, 115
Depression, 33–34, 275
  burnout and, 633
  fatigue and, 277–78, 278*b*, 280
  immune function and, 74
  integrated care and, 88
  osteoporosis and, 597
  perinatally HIV-infected adolescents, 387
  psychiatric determinants of ART medication
      adherence, 337
  rating scales for, 101, 170–71, 211, 213, 255, 280,
      542, 572
  sleep disorders and, 263–64
  treatment of, 280
  women on ART and, 420–21
Depressive disorders, 168. *See also* Antidepressants
  ART adherence and quality of life
      impact, 169–70
  differential diagnosis, 170
  disease progression and symptoms of, 247
  morbidity and mortality related to, 170
  older adults and, 438–39
  in palliative care, 497–98
  prevalence, risk factors, assessment, and
      diagnosis, 168
  sexual behaviors and, 34, 168–69, 328
  SUD and, 162
  suicide and, 285–86
  treatments, 170–72
Dermatological disorders, 614–16
Desipramine, 522, 531*t*, 536
Desvenlafaxine, 530*t*, 535
Detoxification, 162
  referrals for, 480
Development assistance for health (DAH), 48
Dexamethasone, 280
Dexmedetomidine, 162
Dextroamphetamine, 280, 541–42, 542*t*
DHEA. *See* Dehydroepiandrosterone
DHEA-sulfate (DHEA-S), 590, 591
Diabetes, 604
Diabetic nephropathy, 580
*Diagnostic and Statistical Manual for Mental
      Disorders,*5th edition (DSM-5), 5, 6, 29
  personality disorders and, 233
  SUDs, 158, 158*t*

Diagnostic disclosure, 385, 391, 396
Dialectical behavior therapy, 235
Dialysis, 581–82
  dietary restrictions, 583
  palliative care and, 582–83
  psychological adaptation to, 583
Diarrhea, 258, 616
Diazepam, 537, 538*t*
Didanosine, 520*t*
Dietary manipulation, 437
Dietary supplements. *See* herbal remedies
Differential adherence, 339
Diffuse large B-cell lymphomas (DLBCLs), 619
Diffusion tensor imaging (DTI), 184–85, 303–4
Dignity-conserving care, 505
Diphenhydramine, 268, 441, 538*t*, 540
Direct-acting antivirals (DAA), 571, 617
  ART and neuropsychiatric medication
      interactions with, 575*t*
Directly administered antiretroviral therapy
      (DAART), 650–51
Direct observed therapy (DOT), 650–51
Disclosure
  diagnostic, 385, 391, 396
  navigating, 243–44
  negotiated, 643
  self, 406
Discrimination, 10
  in Asia-Pacific region, 54
  definitions and prevalence, 73–74
  diagnosis and, 109–10
  in Europe, 57
  impact of, 74–75
  public policy and, 652
  suicide and, 289
Disenfranchised grief, 506
Disparities in care, 649
Dispositional optimism, 245
Distal neuropathic pain
  quality of life impact of, 320–21
  sensory neuropathy and, 320–21
  treatment for, 321
Distress, 451
  AIDS palliative care, death, and dying, 259
  biopsychosocial determinants, 256*t*
  clinician, 629–31
  defining, 255
  on families and couples, 405–6
  in HIV-negative caretakers, 409
  international differences in, 255–57
  measuring, 255
  medical complications as sources of, 257–59
  pain and, 257–58
  palliative care and, 259
  serodiscordance and, 409
  treatment of, 260
Distress Thermometer (DT), 101, 255
Disulfiram, 163–64, 559
Diversity training, 144–46
DLBCLs. *See* Diffuse large B-cell lymphomas
DMT. *See* Dance/movement therapy
DNP+. *See* Delhi Network of HIV Positive People
Doctor-patient communication, end-of-life issues
      and, 501–2
Dolutegravir, 522, 525*t*, 526*t*, 527, 604
Dominican Republic, 257
DOT. *See* Direct observed therapy
Doxepin, 268, 531*t*
Dreaming, 262

Dronabinol, 466
Drug history
  in psychosocial history, 129, 130*t*
  suicide and, 289
Drug interactions, 163–64
  DAA, ART, and neuropsychiatric
      medications, 575*t*
  induction, 514–15, 515*f*
  inhibition, 514, 515*f*
  kidney disease and, 584
  palliative care and, 499*t*–500*t*
  principles of, 514–15
Drug-related disorders, 32
DRY. *See* Darunavir
DSM-5. *See* Diagnostic and Statistical Manual for
      Mental Disorders, 5th edition
DT. *See* Distress Thermometer
DTI. *See* Diffusion tensor imaging
Dual diagnosis, SMI and, 328
Dublin Declaration on Partnership to Fight HIV/
      AIDS in Europe and Central Asia, 57
Duloxetine, 530*t*, 535, 556
Duty to warn, 643
Dysthymia, 33

Early childhood trauma
  higher-risk sexual behaviors and, 76
  impact of, 206–7
  in patient history, 125
  in psychosocial history, 205
  PTSD and, 206, 207
  suicide and, 286
EBV. *See* Epstein-Barr virus
ECDC. *See* European Centre for Disease
      Prevention and Control
Ecuador, 60
Educational history, 126–27
EEA. *See* European Economic Area
Efavirenz (EFV), 215, 523*t*, 527
  bupropion and, 534
  in CSF, 436
  cutaneous hypersensitivity reactions, 616
  depression and, 420
  interactions with, 163, 267, 534, 536, 550
  lipid abnormalities and, 604
  liver and, 522
  neuropsychiatric symptoms and, 522
  neurotoxicity of, 435
  sleep side effects, 265
  suicide and, 421
EFV. *See* Efavirenz
Elbasvir, 574, 575*t*
Electromyography (EMG), 319–20
Electronic medical records (EMR), 89, 92, 94, 99
  psychometric instrument scores in, 101
Electronic monitoring of adherence to care, 650
El Salvador, 60–61
Elvitegravir, 522, 525*t*, 527
EMG. *See* Electromyography
Emotion-focused coping strategies, 406
EMR. *See* Electronic medical records
Emtricitabine, 73, 213, 520*t*, 525*t*, 527
Encephalitis, HIV, 297*f*
Encephalopathy, 384
Endocrinopathies, 276
End-of-life issues
  children and adolescents, 394–95
  communication about, 501–2
  distress and, 259

Endoscopic retrograde cholangiopancreatography (ERCP), 617
End-stage liver disease, 500
End-stage renal disease (ESRD), 579, 580, 581
  psychiatric and psychological comorbidity treatment in, 584
Enfuvirtide, 522, 526t
Engel, George, 83
Entry inhibitors, for neurological complications of HIV, 308
EORTC-QLQ-C30. *See* European Organization for Research and Treatment of Cancer Quality of Life Questionnaire
Eosinophilic folliculitis, 615
Epic APeX EMR system, 94
EPQ. *See* Eysenck Personality Questionnaire
EPS. *See* Extrapyramidal symptoms
Epstein-Barr virus (EBV), 615
Epworth Sleepiness Scale, 265
Equal Treatment (magazine), 114
ERCP. *See* Endoscopic retrograde cholangiopancreatography
Erythropoietin, 618
Escitalopram, 528, 529t, 533
Eslicarbazepine acetate, 544, 545t
Esophagitis, 616
ESRD. *See* End-stage renal disease
Eszopiclone, 268, 539t, 541
Ethambutol, 614
Ethics
  AMA code of, 644
  in care of patients with HIV, 638–41
  clinician-initiated HIV testing, 638–39
  confidentiality and duty to warn, 643
  HIV self-testing, 640
  newborn screening, 640
  PrEP and, 640–41
  prevention of HIV and, 641–42
  vaccines and, 374–77, 376t
Ethnic disparities, 11–12
  in Canada, 59
  in incarceration, 104
  in mental health among older adults, 441
  in U.S., 58, 103
Ethosuximide, 545t
Etravirine, 163, 522, 524t, 604
EU. *See* European Union
Europe, 47
  HIV/AIDS magnitude, trends, and outcomes in, 55–56
  HIV testing and care access in, 57
  migrants in, 56–57
  most affected populations and HIV infection routes in, 56–57
European Centre for Disease Prevention and Control (ECDC), 57
European Economic Area (EEA), 55–56
European Organization for Research and Treatment of Cancer Quality of Life Questionnaire (EORTC-QLQ-C30), 272–73
European Union (EU), 55–56
Euthyroid sick syndrome, 592
Exceptionalism, 638, 643
Executive function, 132–33
Exercise, 437
Expressive-supportive therapy, 171
Expressive writing, 250
Extrapyramidal symptoms (EPS), 224, 550
Extroversion, 231

Extroversion-introversion dimension, 231
Eysenck Personality Questionnaire (EPQ), 232, 234

Facilitated family and adolescent-centered advance-care planning intervention (FACE), 395
FACIT-F. *See* Functional Assessment of Chronic Illness Therapy-Fatigue
Families
  chosen, 408
  education support from nurses, 489
  grief/bereavement of, 507
  group support, 459
  history, 125–26
  homeless, 348
  medical illness impact on, 405–6
  problems among, 70, 70f
  suicide history, 286
Family-Based preventive Intervention (FBPI), 459
Family-focused grief therapy (FFGT), 459, 508
Family therapy, 459–60
Fatigue
  assessment of, 271–74, 273b
  defining, 271, 272b
  depression and, 277–78, 278b
  distress from, 259
  etiologies in HIV/AIDS, 275–78, 276b
  managing consequences of, 281
  neuropsychological function and, 278
  prevalence and impact, 274–75, 274t
  psychiatric disturbances and, 277–78
  psychological distress and, 212
  treatment-related causes, 276–77, 277t
  treatment strategies, 279–81, 279t
Fatigue Severity Scale, 272
Fatigue Symptom Inventory, 273
FAV/r. *See* Fosamprenavir/ritonavir
FBPI. *See* Family-Based preventive Intervention
FDA. *See* Food and Drug Administration
Federal poverty level (FPL), 648
Felbamate, 545t
FEM-PREP study, 356
FFGT. *See* Family-focused grief therapy
FICA tool, 126
Financing of care, 648
  for HIV testing, 652
Finding meaning, 246
Five Factor Model, 232
5-HT receptor modulators, 535–36
Fluconazole, 113, 114
Flunitrazepam, 164, 538t
Fluoxetine, 216, 529t, 533
Fluphenazine, 551t
Fluvoxamine, 529t, 533
fMRI. *See* Functional magnetic resonance imaging
Focal segmental glomerulosclerosis (FSGS), 580
Food and Drug Administration (FDA), 5, 111, 267
  blood donation recommendations, 644
  PrEP approval by, 357
Fosamprenavir, 517t
  lipid abnormalities and, 604
Fosamprenavir/ritonavir (FAV/r), 163
Foscarnet, 596, 611
FPL. *See* Federal poverty level
Fragmentation of care, 648–49
Frailty, 430
Frankl, Viktor, 504
Frascati criteria, 136t, 183
Free T3 (FT3), 592
Free T4 (FT4), 592

FSGS. *See* Focal segmental glomerulosclerosis
FT3. *See* Free T3
FT4. *See* Free T4
Functional Assessment of Chronic Illness Therapy-Fatigue (FACIT-F), 273
Functional capacity, assessment of, 137–38
Functional decline, assessment of, 183–84
Functional magnetic resonance imaging (fMRI), 185–86
Fungal skin infections, 615
Fusion inhibitors, 25t, 522, 526t, 527
  for neurological complications of HIV, 308

Gabapentin, 268, 544, 545t
GAD. *See* Generalized anxiety disorder
GAD-7. *See* Generalized Anxiety Disorder 7-item
Gamma-hydroxybutyric acid (GHB), 161, 162
Ganciclovir, 111, 611
Garlic, 466
Gastrointestinal manifestations, 616–17
Gay male couples, serodiscordant, 408–9
Gay Men's Health Crisis (GMHC), 110, 112b
Gender and Sexual Orientation Expressions Clinic, 144–46
Gender-based violence
  defining, 75
  epidemiology and pathways, 75–76
  HIV risk and, 421–23
  interventions to reduce, 76–77
  PTSD from, 76
  quantitative assessments, 76
  social factors around, 422
Gender-transformative interventions, 77
General Health Questionnaire (GHQ), 634
Generalized anxiety disorder (GAD), 34
  assessment and diagnosis, 212–13
  treatment approaches, 215–16
Generalized Anxiety Disorder 7-item (GAD-7), 88, 213
Generativity, 505
Generic antiretrovirals, 114
Geriatric Depression Scale, 439
GFATM. *See* Global Fund to Fight AIDS, Tuberculosis, and Malaria
GFI. *See* Global Fatigue Index
GFR. *See* Glomerular filtration rate
GHB. *See* Gamma-hydroxybutyric acid
GHQ. *See* General Health Questionnaire
GIPA. *See* Greater Involvement of People living with AIDS
Global Fatigue Index (GFI), 273
Global Fund to Fight AIDS, Tuberculosis, and Malaria (GFATM), 48
Glomerular filtration rate (GFR), 579
Glomerulonephritis (GN), 580
Glucocorticoids, 594
Glucose intolerance, 604
Glucuronidation, 515
GMHC. *See* Gay Men's Health Crisis
GN. *See* Glomerulonephritis
Gonadal function, 593–95
Gottlieb, Michael, 7
Graves' disease, 593
Grazoprevir, 574, 575t
Greater Involvement of People living with AIDS (GIPA), 108, 111
Grief/bereavement
  acute, 507
  anticipatory, 506–7

complicated, 506, 507–8
definitions for, 506
disenfranchised, 506
of family and friends, 507
family therapy and, 459
sleep disorders and, 264
therapies for, 508
Guanfacine, 393
Guatemala, 60
Guttmacher Institute, 400
Gwynette, Frampton, 145
Gynecomastia, 594

HAART. *See* Highly active antiretroviral therapy
HAD. *See* HIV-associated dementia
HADS. *See* Hospital Anxiety and Depression Score
HADS-A. *See* Hospital Anxiety and Depression
	Score anxiety subscale
Haiti, 411–12
	distress in, 257
Hallucinogens, 161
Haloperidol, 551*t*
HAMA. *See* Hamilton Anxiety Rating Scale
HAM-D. *See* Hamilton Rating Scale for Depression
HAMD-7. *See* 7-Item Hamilton Depression
	Rating Scale
Hamied, Yusef, 114
Hamilton Anxiety Rating Scale (HAMA), 211
Hamilton Depression Scale for Anxiety, 101
Hamilton Rating Scale for Depression (HAM-D),
	101, 280, 542
HANA. *See* HIV-associated, non-AIDS conditions
HAND. *See* HIV-associated neurocognitive
	disorders
Harm reduction, 12, 162–63
Harrison Electronic Record and Orders
	(HERO), 92
HBV. *See* Hepatitis B virus
HCV. *See* Hepatitis C virus
HDS. *See* HIV Dementia Scale
Health behavior pathways, 250
Health behaviors
	interventions promoting, 391–92
	perinatally HIV-infected children and
		adolescents
		adherence, 385–86
		sex, 386
		substance use, 386–87
HealthCall, 456
Health disparities, 103
Health Global Access Project (Health GAP), 113
*The Health of Lesbian, Gay, Bisexual, and
	Transgender People* (IOM), 145
HealthQual International, 69
Health services, 647
	financing, 648
	HIV testing issues and, 652
Health workers, as activists, 115
Healthy Choices, 392
Healthy Living Project, 247, 453
Hematological manifestations, 617–18
Hemodialysis, 579
Henderson, David, 69
Hepatitis B virus
	(HBV), 527, 571, 617
Hepatitis C virus (HCV), 5, 186, 500, 527, 580, 617
	care cascade optimization, 576–77, 576*f*
	DT and HADS screening in, 255
	epidemiology and natural history, 571–72, 572*f*

fatigue and, 259, 276–77
HIV co-infection with, 157
integrated care models and, 89, 91
prevalence, 571
psychiatric comorbidities, 572–73
psychiatric considerations in treatment, 575–76
psychiatric illness and, 486
psychiatric symptom monitoring and, 101
substance use and, 576–77
treatment advances, 573–74, 573*f*, 574*f*
treatment goals, 573
Hepatobiliary disease, 616–17
Herbal remedies, 465–66
Herb-drug interactions, 466
HERO. *See* Harrison Electronic Record and Orders
Heroin, 4, 158–59, 164
Herpes simplex type 2 (HSV-2), 242
Heterosexual couples, serodiscordant, 409–11
HHV-8. *See* Human herpesvirus 8
Hiccups, suicide and, 286
Highly active antiretroviral therapy (HAART), 579
History of present illness, 124
History-taking, 123, 124*t*
HIV-1 vaccines
	in development and human trials, 370*t*
	efficacy trials strategy, 366–68, 367*f*
HIV-affected children and adolescents, 388–90
	epidemiology, 383, 384
	summer camps for, 397–99
HIV/AIDS, 19
	aging and, 433, 620–21
	anxiety through course of, 210
	ART in late-stage illness, 498, 500*t*
	ART psychiatric aspects of care and
		medication, 335
	basic medical aspects of, 146–47
	brain entry process, 296
	cardiovascular disease risk factors related
		to, 602–3
	clinical manifestations, 22–23
	comorbidity responses and, 39–40, 39*t*
	criminalization of exposure to, 110, 643–44
	diagnosis, 22–23
	dialysis and, 581–82
	disparities in care, 649
	DT and HADS screening in, 255
	epidemiology, 20–22, 21*f*, 405
	ethical issues in care of, 638–41
	ethical issues related to prevention of, 641–42
	fatigue etiologies in, 275–78, 276*b*
	financing of care, 648
	fluctuations in condition in, 500–501
	fragmentation of care, 648–49
	gender-based violence and, 75–77
	HCV co-infection with, 157
	healthcare delivery-related stressors, 632*t*
	history, 7–8, 19–20
	integrated biopsychosocial approach to, 14–15
	interdisciplinary models of care, 152
	kidney transplantation and, 582, 584–85
	late diagnosis of, 56
	as magnifier, 3–4
	manifestations and progression in women, 419
	nursing care in, 486–89
	nursing support for persons with, 489–90
	ophthalmological complications, 257
	pain in, 164–65
	personal responses to
		diagnosis, 109–10

prevalence, 47*f*, 346–47
prevention and care of, 4–5, 641–42
prevention interventions for adults with
	SMI, 330–31
primary prevention, 24–25
psychiatric aspects of, 147, 147*t*
psychiatric assessment in, 147–49, 148*t*
psychiatric disparities in, 12
psychiatric factors, 3
psychiatric illness and, 5–7, 486
psychiatric treatment and, 223–26
psychological distress on families and
	couples, 405–6
psychosocial and psychiatric aspects, 9*t*
pulmonary manifestations, 612–14
racial, ethnic, and socioeconomic
	disparities, 11–12
serious mental illness epidemiology and
	treatment and, 222–23
signs and symptoms, 23
staging systems, 23
stressors in, 241
suicide and, 285–90
temporal framework of epidemic, 406–8
treatment and prevention principles, 23–26
treatment cascade, 21–22
HIV/AIDS psychiatry
	history of, 7–8
	paradigm for, 10–11, 10*f*
	paradoxes in, 8–10
HIVAN. *See* HIV-associated nephropathy
HIV-associated, non-AIDS conditions
	(HANA), 177
HIV-associated dementia (HAD), 6, 133*t*, 175,
	176*t*, 183, 190*t*, 297*f*, 432
	ART and prevalence of, 31
	assessment for, 131–33
	categories of, 136–37, 136*t*
	diagnostic criteria, 136–37
	screening for, 255
HIV-associated lipodystrophy, 605–6
HIV-associated nephropathy (HIVAN), 579–80
HIV-associated neurocognitive disorders (HAND),
	6, 31–32, 148, 173–75
	adolescent risk of, 388
	aging role in, 180, 432–33
	ART and treatment in older adults, 435–36
	assessment for, 131–33
	clinical assessment and management, 186–87
	clinical management, 190–94
	comorbidities, 188*t*
	evaluation and diagnosis of, 181
	HIV compartmentalization role, 179–80, 179*f*
	HIV RNA in CSF and, 188*t*, 191
	impairments in, 135
		assessment of, 137, 138*t*
	neurobehavioral assessment of, 180–84
	neuroimaging assessment of, 184–86
	pathogenesis of, 177–80, 178
		immune system role, 178–79
	psychostimulants and, in older patients, 436
	research diagnosis approach for, 176*t*
	risk factors, 188*t*
HIV-associated PTSD, 204, 205
HIV clinicians, meetings with, 100
HIV compartmentalization, 179–80, 179*f*
HIV Dementia Scale (HDS), 140, 140*t*, 183
HIV denialism, 113
HIV diagnosis, 243–44

HIV-distal neuropathic pain (HIV-DNP)
    quality of life impact of, 320–21
    sensory neuropathy and, 320–21
    treatment for, 321
HIV education and research training, 143
    curriculum and content areas for psychiatry
        trainees, 146–49, 146t
    diversity issues, 151–52
    implementation of, 150
    opportunities, 150–51
    psychiatry training relevance of, 144
HIV encephalitis, 297f
HIV infection
    acute, 175
    aging phenotypes and, 430–31, 431t
    memory and, 388
    nursing care during, 486–89
    PEP, 358–62
    PNI of anxiety and, 211
    PrEP, 355–58
        clinical trials, 356–57
    psychiatric disorders and rates of, 36–40
    routine testing for, 353–55
        early diagnosis facilitating, 353–54
        prevention, 354
        rapid and home, 355
        revised guidelines, 353
        screening assays, 354–55
    substance use and rates of, 36
    successful aging and, 442–43
    targets
        astrocytes, 300
        mononuclear phagocytes, 298–300
        T cells, 300–301
    testing, PrEP—FDA approval and current
        guidelines, 357
HIV in Our Lives (booklet series), 114
HIV/LGBT community health
    centers, 90–91, 90t
HIV life cycle, 20
HIV Mental Health Program, 88
HIV prevention
    education about, 147
    for older adults, 431
HIV psychiatry. See also specific entries
    disparities in care, 649
    diversity issues in, 151–52
    financing of care, 648
    fragmentation of care, 648–49
    illness-specific considerations, 87–88
    models of, 84–86
    as psychosomatic medicine model, 83–84
    teaching treatment approaches, 149–50, 150t
HIV-Related Fatigue Scale (HRFS), 273
HIV-related trauma, 204
HIV RNA in CSF, 189t, 191
HIV sensory neuropathy
    advanced disease warning signs, 318
    defining, 317
    diagnostic testing, 319–20
    distal neuropathic pain associated with, 320–21
    pathology, 318
    peripheral nervous system, 317–20
        laboratory workup, 319
        nerve conduction studies and
            electromyography, 319–20
        physical examination, 319
        prevalence in U.S., 318f
        signs and symptoms, 318f

prevalence and risk factors, 318
    risk increases with age, 319f
HIV status
    diagnostic disclosure, 385, 391, 396
    self-disclosure of, 406
HIV subtype A, 384
HIV Symptom Distress Scale (SDS), 255
HIV transmission, 20
    ART preventing, 26
    in Canada, 59
    epidemiology of, 52–53
    gender-based violence and, 76, 77
    in Latin America, 60
    sociocultural factors, 103
    in U.S., 58
HIV transmission risk behavior, 329–30
Hodgkin lymphoma, 619
Homelessness
    HIV prevalence and, 346–47
    HIV transmission risk factors and, 347–49
    HIV treatment and prevention and, 349–50
    in U.S., 346
Homophobia, internalized, 74–75
Hopelessness, 275
    demoralization and, 504–5
    social dynamics and, 289
    spirituality and, 504
    suicide and, 286–87, 289
    treatment of, 455
Hospice care, 494, 500, 503
Hospital Anxiety and Depression Score (HADS),
    101, 170, 213, 255
Hospital Anxiety and Depression Score anxiety
    subscale (HADS-A), 211
Housing First approach, 350
HPA. See Hypothalamic-pituitary-adrenal axis
HRFS. See HIV-Related Fatigue Scale
HSV-2. See Herpes simplex type 2
HTLV-III, 20
Human herpesvirus 8 (HHV-8), 614, 619
Human immunodeficiency virus. See HIV/AIDS
Hydrocodone, 164
Hydrocortisone, 280
Hydroxyzine, 216, 441
Hypercalcemia, 596
Hyperinsulinemia, 604
Hyperlactatemia, 604
Hyperthyroidism, 276, 592
Hypnosis, 471
Hypnotics, 537, 538t–539t, 541
Hypocalcemia, 596
Hypogonadism, 276, 279, 593–95
Hypomania, 172
Hypotestosteronemia, 593
Hypothalamic-pituitary-adrenal axis (HPA), 211,
    244, 248
    fatigue and, 275
    pathophysiology and assessment of
        function, 589–90
Hypothyroidism, 276, 592, 593

IAS. See International AIDS Society
IAS-USA. See International Antiviral Society-USA
Iatrogenic uveitis, 611
ICD-10. See International Classification of Diseases,
    Tenth Revision
ICD-10-CM. See International Classification
    of Diseases, Tenth Revision, Clinical
    Modification

ICSFS. See Identity-Consequence Fatigue Scale
Identity-Consequence Fatigue Scale (ICSFS), 273, 278
IDU. See Injecting drug use
IHDS. See International HIV Dementia Scale
Illness management/management of chronic illness
    (IM/MCI), 85–86
Iloperidone, 553t, 557
Imipramine, 532t, 533, 536
IM/MCI. See Illness management/management of
    chronic illness
Immune reconstitution, 592
Immune reconstitution inflammatory syndrome
    (IRIS), 148, 178, 614
Immune recovery uveitis (IRU), 611
Immunological markers, of neurological
    complications of HIV, 306
Impulsivity, suicide and, 287
Incarcerated populations, 650–51
India, 46
    advocacy in, 114–15
    stigma and discrimination in, 74
Indinavir, 215, 518t, 519, 604
Indonesia, 46
Induction interactions, 514–15, 515f, 516t
Infectious cutaneous disorders, 614–15
Inflammation, 602, 620–21
    HIV entering brain causing, 297
Informed consent, 638–40
Inhibition interactions, 514, 515f, 516t
Injecting drug use (IDU), 13, 157, 405, 407
    ART adherence and, 337
    binge drinking and, 161
    estimates of rates of, 157
    gender-based violence and, 422
    HIV epidemiology and, 20, 56
    HIV prevention strategies and, 641
    mass incarceration cycle and, 104
    needle sharing in, 20
    PrEP and, 357
Inpatient consultations, 122–23
Inpatient social workers, 480–81
Insomnia, 258–59. See also Sleep disorders
    anxiety and, 266
    defining, 262
    diagnosis, 265–66
    medication side effects and, 265
    physical causes, 265
    treatment, 266–68
INSTIs. See Integrase strand transfer inhibitors
Institute of Medicine (IOM), 145
Insulin resistance, 604, 621
Integrase inhibitors, for neurological complications
    of HIV, 308
Integrase strand transfer inhibitors (INSTIs), 163,
    522, 525t–526t
Integrated ambulatory care programs
    academic productivity opportunities, 101
    assessment of current state, 98–99
    business case planning, 98
    clinical model development, 97–98
    clinical model implementation, 98
    clinical services, 100–101
    educational, training, and technology
        opportunities, 101–2
    establishing expectations and roles, 99
    initial discussions for, 97
    operational detail planning, 99–100
    patient urgency and acuity, 100
    utilization management, 100

Integrated care, 84–85
 BWH HIV Mental Health Program, 88–89
 Columbia University Medical Center, 91
 HIV/LGBT community health centers,
  90–91, 90t
 illness-specific considerations, 87–88
 San Francisco General Hospital, 92
 San Francisco Veterans Affairs Medical
  Center, 92–93
 SMI and, 227–28
 stigma and, 88, 97
 University of California, San Francisco Medical
  Center, 92, 93–94
Interactive voice response (IVR), 456
Interdisciplinary models, 152
Interferon, 527, 528, 573, 574, 575–76, 617
Internalized homophobia, 74–75
International AIDS Society (IAS), 115
International Antiviral Society-USA
 (IAS-USA), 357
International Classification of Diseases, Tenth
 Revision (ICD-10; WHO), 271, 272b
International Classification of Diseases, Tenth
 Revision, Clinical Modification (ICD-10-
 CM; WHO), 271, 272b
International HIV Dementia Scale (IHDS), 140,
 140t, 183
International League Against Epilepsy, 548
Interpersonal psychotherapy (ITP), 455–56
Intimate partner violence (IPV), 75, 77
Intravenous drug use disorders, suicide and, 285–86
Introversion, 231
IOM. *See* Institute of Medicine
IPERGAY study, 356–57
iPrEx study, 357
IPV. *See* Intimate partner violence
IRIS. *See* Immune reconstitution inflammatory
 syndrome
IRU. *See* Immune recovery uveitis
Isoniazid, 614
Itching, 258
ITP. *See* Interpersonal psychotherapy
IVR. *See* Interactive voice response

JC virus, 534
Johns Hopkins Hospital HIV clinic, 227
Joint United Nations Programme on HIV/AIDS
 (UNAIDS), 12, 48
Justice Reinvestment Initiative, 106

Kaposi sarcoma, 7, 592, 614, 615, 618–19
Kava-kava, 268
Kenya, 411
Ketamine, 161, 164
Ketoconazole, 536, 550, 594
Kidney disease
 advanced, 581
 drug interactions and, 584
 in HIV, 579–80
 palliative care and, 582–83
 prevalence, 579
 psychiatric complications, 583–85
 psychological adaptation to, 583
 therapy for, 580–81
Kidney transplantation, 581, 582, 584–85
King, Sue, 145

Lactate, 596
Lactatemia, 604–5

Lactic acidosis, 604–5
LAIs. *See* Long-acting injectable antipsychotics
Lamivudine, 520t, 526t, 527
Lamotrigine, 172, 515, 544, 546t, 548, 612
Langbehn, Janice, 642
Late diagnosis, 56
Latent tuberculosis infection (LTBI), 613
Latin America, 47, 59–60
Lawyers Collective, 114
Ledipasvir, 527, 574, 575t, 617
Lenticular opacities, 612
Lentiviruses, 20
Lesotho, 411
Lethal means, suicide and, 287
Levetiracetam, 546t, 548
Levomilnacipran, 530t, 535
Lewis, A. Lee, 145
Liberman, Laura, 68
Life expectancy, ART and, 303
LIFT. *See* Living in the Face of Trauma
Lipid metabolism, 603–4
Lipodystrophy, 605–6
Lipowski's classification, 10–11
Lithium, 172, 393, 436, 543–44, 545t, 612
Liver disease, 5
Living in the Face of Trauma (LIFT), 205
Loan Repayment Programs (LRPs), 151
Long-acting injectable antipsychotics (LAIs), 224
Lopinavir, lipid abnormalities and, 604
Lopinavir/ritonavir, 518t, 519, 604
Lorazepam, 194, 441, 515, 538t, 540
Low testosterone, 276
LRPs. *See* Loan Repayment Programs
LSD, 161
LTBI. *See* Latent tuberculosis infection
L-tryptophan, 268
Lupus, 3
Lurasidone, 554t, 557
Lyme disease, 3
Lymphomas, 618, 619
Lyons Crews, Meredith, 145

MA. *See* Methamphetamines
Macrophages, target, 298
MAF. *See* Multidimensional Assessment of Fatigue
Magnetic resonance imaging (MRI), 303–4
 DTI, 184–85
 fMRI, 185–86
 MRS, 184
 volumetric, 184–85
Magnetic resonance spectroscopy (MRS), 184
Major depressive disorder, 33, 35, 172
 sleep disorders and, 264
 treatment, 225
Malaria, 3
Malignancies, 618–20
Malnutrition, 276
Mania, 35, 172, 224–25
 sleep disorders and, 264
MAOIs. *See* Monoamine oxidase inhibitors
Maraviroc, 194, 436, 522, 526t
Marijuana, 161, 164, 466–67
Maslach Burnout Inventory (MBI), 633, 634
Mass incarceration
 AIDS pandemic impact from, 104, 106
 cycle of, 104
 resource loss and, 105
MAT. *See* Medication adherence training

MBI. *See* Maslach Burnout Inventory
MBSR. *See* Mindfulness-based stress reduction
McCaffrey, Barry, 651
MCI. *See* Illness management/management of
 chronic illness; Mild cognitive impairment
MCMD. *See* Minor cognitive motor disorder
MDMA. *See* 3, 4-methylenedioxymethamphetamine
MDOT. *See* Modified DOT
MDQ. *See* Mood Disorder
 Questionnaire
Meaning-centered interventions, 505
Media advocacy, 114
Medicaid, 477, 480, 648
Medical care, suicide and, 286–87
Medical disorders, suicide and, 286
Medical Scientist Training Program (MSTP), 151
Medical University of South Carolina
 (MUSC), 144–46
Medicare, 477
Medication adherence training (MAT), 249
Medication Event Monitoring System (MEMS), 457
Medication Management Test (MMT-R), 137
Médicins Sans Frontières (MSF), 114
Megestrol acetate, 594
Melatonin, 267
Melatonin receptor agonists, 267
Membranoproliferative glomerulonephritis
 (MPGN), 580
Memorial Sloan-Kettering Cancer Center, 68–69
Memorial Symptom Assessment Scale (MSAS), 259,
 273, 274, 275
Memory, 132
 adolescent HIV infection and, 388
MEMS. *See* Medication Event Monitoring System
Menopause, 424–26
Mental exercise, 437
Mental health
 evolution of roles in, 634–35
 HIV-affected youth, 393
 perinatally HIV-exposed but uninfected children
  and adolescents, 390
 perinatally HIV-infected adolescents, 387
 racial/ethnic and age differences in older
  persons, 441
Mental health problems, 29
 as comorbidity, 39t
 concentrated HIV epidemics and, 30, 30t
 HIV/AIDS and, in Africa, 52
 perinatally HIV-infected adolescents, 387
 SUD and, 162
Mental health screening tools, 88
Mental health services
 in Asia-Pacific region, 54–55
 children and adolescents and, 392–93
Mental health team leader model, 122
Mental illness. *See also* Serious mental illness
 gender-based violence and, 421–23
 HIV infection rates and, 36, 39
 infection risk factors and, 12
 primary HIV prevention and, 485–86
 sexual violence and, 422
Mental status examination, 129, 131–33
Mesoridazine, 551t
Metabolic enzyme inhibitors, 514
Metabolic syndrome, 550
Metformin, 604, 605
Methadone, 87, 159, 162, 163–64, 165, 225–26, 558–59
 in HCV treatment, 577
 hypogonadism and, 594

Methamphetamines (MA), 90, 160, 213, 216
Methsuximide, 546t
3,4-methylenedioxymethamphetamine (MDMA), 161–62, 164
Methylphenidate, 215, 265, 280, 542–43, 542t
Metoprolol, 533
Mexico, 47, 59
MI. *See* Motivational interviewing; Myocardial infarction
Microglia, target, 298
Midazolam, 164, 267, 537, 538t
Migrants, 56–57
Mild cognitive impairment (MCI), 132
Mild neurocognitive disorder (MND), 136, 176t, 183, 432
Milnacipran, 530t, 535
Mind-body connection, 470–71
Mind Exchange Program, 186, 188t
Mindfulness-based stress reduction (MBSR), 211, 250
Mindfulness meditation, 470–71
Mineral metabolism, 595–97
Mini Mental State Examination (MMSE), 94
Minor cognitive motor disorder (MCMD), 136, 175, 176, 432
Mirtazapine, 531t, 534
Mitochondrial toxicity, 580, 604–5, 621
MMSE. *See* Mini Mental State Examination
MMT-R. *See* Medication Management Test
MND. *See* Mild neurocognitive disorder
MoCA. *See* Montreal Cognitive Assessment
Modafinil, 171, 280, 436, 542t, 543
Modified DOT (MDOT), 650
Molindone, 551t
Molluscum contagiosum, 615
Monoamine oxidase inhibitors (MAOIs), 216, 514, 536
Mononuclear phagocytes (MP), as HIV infection target, 298–300, 299f
Montgomery-Asberg depression rating scale, 171
Montreal Cognitive Assessment (MoCA), 94, 101, 140, 140t
Mood, 129
    negative, 246–47
Mood Disorder Questionnaire (MDQ), 172
Mood disorders, 29, 33–34, 214
Mood stabilizers, 543–44, 545t, 549
    ocular adverse effects, 612
Morphine, 159, 164
Motivational interviewing (MI), 14, 89, 163, 217, 392, 456–57
Mourning, 506
Movement therapies, 468–69
MP. *See* Mononuclear phagocytes
MPGN. *See* Membranoproliferative glomerulonephritis
MRI. *See* Magnetic resonance imaging
MRS. *See* Magnetic resonance spectroscopy
MSAS. *See* Memorial Symptom Assessment Scale
MSF. *See* Médicins Sans Frontières
MSTP. *See* Medical Scientist Training Program
Mugyenyi, Peter, 113
Multidimensional Assessment of Fatigue (MAF), 273
Multidisciplinary teams, 152
Multimodal antidepressants, 535–36
Multimorbidities, 5, 13, 143, 204, 430, 500, 611
    aging and, 430, 620–21
    anxiety and, 210, 215
    clinician stress and, 629

complex patient models and, 86
dermatological, 614–16
gastrointestinal, 616–17
hematological, 617–18
integrated care and, 84, 87, 97
major depressive disorder and, 225
malignancies, 618–20
neuropsychiatric, 612
psychiatric, 121, 287, 288t, 455
psychosomatic medicine paradigms and, 10–11
PTSD and, 6, 206
pulmonary, 612–14
suicide and, 285–87, 288t
Multi-need psychiatric patients, 649–50
Multinucleated giant cells, 300
Multiple sclerosis, 3, 280, 405–6
MUSC. *See* Medical University of South Carolina
Mycobacterium tuberculosis, 613–14, 615
Mydriasis, 612
Myocardial infarction (MI), 436, 602
Myopia, 612

Naltrexone, 163–64, 559–60
National AIDS Treatment Advocacy Project (NATAP), 112b
National Cancer Institute, 620
National Committee for Quality Assurance, 86
National HIV/AIDS Strategy, 152, 222
National Hospice Organization, 500
National Institute of Allergy and Infectious Diseases (NIAID), 581
National Institute of Mental Health (NIMH), 150, 176, 400
    Healthy Living Project, 247
National Institutes of Health (NIH)
    diversity-enhancing programs, 152
    NIH Toolbox Cognition Module, 183
    research training opportunities, 150–51
National Registry of Evidence-based Programs and Practices (NREPP), 205
National Research Service Award (NRSA), 150
Needle-exchange programs, 163, 651
Needle sharing, 104
Nefazodone, 531t
Negative causal attributions, 246
Negative life events, 242–44
Negative mood, 246–47
Negotiated disclosure, 643
Nelfinavir (NFV), 163, 518t, 519
    bupropion and, 534
NEO Personality Inventory–Revised (NEO-PI-R), 232, 234
Nephrotoxicity, 580–81
Nerve conduction studies, 319–20
Network therapy, 163
Neurobehavioral assessment, 180–81
Neurobiology, of suicide, 287
Neurocognitive disorders, 31–32. *See also* HIV-associated neurocognitive disorders
    classification of, 302–3
    confounding/compounding disorders, 138–39
    differential diagnosis of, 187, 189–90, 190t
    mild, 136, 176t, 183, 432
Neurocognitive impairment, 29
    asymptomatic, 132, 136–37, 176t
    differential diagnosis of, 187, 189–90
    in HAND, 135
    mania in, 35
    preclinical, 137

psychiatric determinants of ART medication adherence, 337–38
Neurocognitive outcomes, behaviorally HIV-infected adolescents, 388
Neurodevelopmental outcomes, 384–85
    intervention and treatment considerations for, 390–91
Neuroendocrine regulation, 248
Neurofilament light (NFL), 307
Neuroimaging, HIV diagnosis and, 303–5
Neuroimaging assessment, 184–86
Neurological complications of HIV
    CNS, 295–309
    HIV sensory neuropathy, 317–20
    management of, 307–9
    peripheral nervous system, 317–21
Neurological decline, 257
Neuronal damage, HIV-related, 301f
Neuronal markers, of neurological complications of HIV, 306
Neuronal toxicity, 177–78
Neuropathic pain, 258, 496
Neuropsychological evaluation
    in clinical settings, 139–40
    components of, 181, 182f
    functional decline assessment, 183–84
    in international settings, 141
    normative data and test score interpretation, 140–41
    purpose of, 139
    screening measures, 183
    screening tools, 140t
    test selection for, 183
Neuropsychological function, fatigue and, 278
Neuropsychological impairment, 136–37
    assessment of, 137, 138t
NEU Screen, 140, 140t
Neutropenia, 618
Nevirapine (NVP), 163, 436, 522, 524t, 616
Newborns, screening of, 640
New York State PrEP Guidelines, 358f
NFL. *See* Neurofilament light
NFV. *See* Nelfinavir
NIAID. *See* National Institute of Allergy and Infectious Diseases
Nichols, Stuart, 8
Nicotine, 161, 215
NIH. *See* National Institutes of Health
NIH Toolbox Cognition Module, 183
NIMH. *See* National Institute of Mental Health
Nitric oxide (NO), 296
NNRTI. *See* Non-nucleoside reverse transcriptase inhibitors
NO. *See* Nitric oxide
NOAH. *See* No One Alone with HIV program
Nonadherence
    to HIV clinic appointments, 99
    PTSD and, 6, 206
    to risk reduction, 6
Non-Hodgkin lymphoma, 618, 619
Non-infectious cutaneous disorders, 615–16
Non-nucleoside reverse transcriptase inhibitors (NNRTI), 163, 175, 357, 436, 519, 522, 523t–524t
    BMD and, 596
    carbamazepine and, 544
    cutaneous hypersensitivity reactions, 616
    lipid abnormalities and, 604
    neurological complications and, 307–8

Non-persistence, 247
Nonpharmacological analgesic modalities, 496
Non-REM sleep (NREM sleep), 262
Nonsteroidal anti-inflammatory drugs, 515
Non-triazoloBZDs, 538t, 540
No One Alone with HIV program (NOAH), 87
Norepinephrine, 244
Nortriptyline, 532t
NPs. *See* Nurse practitioners
NREM sleep. *See* Non-REM sleep
NREPP. *See* National Registry of Evidence-based
        Programs and Practices
NRSA. *See* National Research Service Award
NRTI. *See* Nucleoside reverse transcriptase
        inhibitors
NS3/4A inhibitors, 574
NS5A inhibitors, 574
Nucleoside NS5B inhibitors, 574
Nucleoside reverse transcriptase inhibitors
        (NRTIs), 163, 436, 519
    lactic acidosis and, 604–5
    lipodystrophy and, 605
    metabolic effects, 604
    neurological complications and, 307–8
    thymidine, 604, 605
Nurse practitioners (NPs), 483
Nursing care
    burnout in, 633
    family education support, 489
    history, roles, and credentialing, 483–84
    during HIV infection, 486–89
    patient education and, 489–90
    in primary prevention, 484–86
    support for persons with HIV, 489–90
    symptom management, 490, 491t
    telephone triage, 490
Nutritional deficiencies, 618
NVP. *See* Nevirapine
Nystagmus, 612

Obsessive-compulsive disorder (OCD), 35
    assessment and diagnosis, 213
    treatment approaches, 216
Occupational exposure, 631–32
Occupational history, 126–27
OCD. *See* Obsessive-compulsive disorder
Ocular dystonias, 612
Office of National Drug Control Policy, 651
Olanzapine, 194, 554t, 557
Older adults
    anxiety disorders in, 440–41
    care challenges for, 431–32
    cognition and, 434
    cognitive impairment treatment in, 435–37
    depressive disorders and, 438–39
    dietary manipulation and, 437
    HIV prevention for, 431
    identifying and treating comorbidities in, 437
    psychosis in, 440
    SUD and, 439–40
    suicide and, 438
    underrepresented foci of attention with, 431–32
Older age
    defining, 429
    phenotypes in, 429, 430t
Ombitasvir, 527, 574, 575t, 617
Open Door, 350
Operational detail planning, 99–100
Ophthalmological complications, 257

Ophthalmological illness, 611–12
Opioids, 158–59, 165, 515
    epidemic use of, 4
Opium, 159
Opportunistic infections, prophylactic
        interventions against, 24
Oppositional behavior, 386
Oral hairy leukoplakia, 615
Orexin, 268
Orphaned and vulnerable children (OVC), 69
    supporting, 71
Osteopenia, 596
Osteoporosis, 596, 597
Outpatient consultations, 122
Outpatient social workers, 480–81
Oxazepam, 515, 538t, 540
Oxcarbazepine, 546t, 548
Oxycodone, 164

Paced Auditory Serial Addition Test (PASAT), 183
Pacific Islanders, distress in, 256
Pain, 164–65
    distress and, 257–58
    insomnia and, 265
    management of, 496
    neuropathic, 258, 496
    suicide and, 286
Paliperidone, 554t, 557
Palliative care
    anxiety disorders in, 497
    biopsychosocial approach for, 495
    children and adolescents, 394
    defining, 494–95
    depressive disorders in, 497–98
    distress and, 259
    drug-drug interactions and, 499t–500t
    in HIV/AIDS, 495–501, 495t
    kidney disease and, 582–83
    pain and symptom management, 496, 497t
    programs and models of, 502–3
    psychiatric complications and, 496–98
    suicide, assisted suicide, and desire for hastened
        death, 498
    treatment failure and, 498, 500
Panic disorder, 34
    assessment and diagnosis, 213
    treatment approaches, 216
PAOFI. *See* Patient's Assessment of Own
        Functioning
Paradigms, of HIV/AIDS psychiatry, 10–11, 10f
Paradoxes, in HIV/AIDS psychiatry, 8–10
Paradoxical intention, 266
Parasitic infections, 615
Parathyroid hormone (PTH), 596
Parenchymal microglia, 300
Parental serodiscordance, 410
Parentification, 388–89
Parenting, suicide and, 289
Paris Declaration, 111
Paritaprevir, 527, 574, 575t, 617
Parkinsonian syndromes, 224
Paroxetine, 194, 439, 530t, 533–34
Partners PrEP, 356
PAs. *See* Physicians assistants
PASAT. *See* Paced Auditory Serial Addition Test
Passionflower, 268
Patent abuse, 113–14
PATH+. *See* Preventing AIDS through Health for
        HIV Positive persons

Patient/case worker relationship, 478–79
Patient-centered medical home (PCMH), 86, 649
Patient education, 489–90
Patient Health Questionnaire-9 (PHQ-9), 88, 572
Patient history
    family psychiatric, 125
    past medical, 125
    of present illness, 124
    psychiatric, 124
    psychosocial, 125–29
    recommendations for taking, 123, 124t
    suicide, 125, 131t
Patient Protection and Affordable Care Act (ACA),
        58, 106, 647, 648
Patient's Assessment of Own Functioning
        (PAOFI), 137
Patient Self-Determination Act, 642
PCMH. *See* Patient-centered medical home
PCP, 164. *See also Pneumocystis carinii* pneumonia
Pearson-Byars Fatigue Checklist, 272
Peer advocacy, 111
Pegylated interferon, 527
Pemoline, 280
PEP. *See* Post-exposure prophylaxis
PEPFAR. *See* President's Emergency Plan for
        AIDS Relief
Perception, 131
Perinatally HIV-exposed but uninfected children
        and adolescents, 389–90
    epidemiology, 383, 384
Perinatally HIV-infected children and adolescents
    clinical milestones in development, 384–87
    diagnostic disclosure, 385
    epidemiology, 383
    family therapy and, 460
    health behaviors
        adherence, 385–86
        sex, 386
        substance use, 386–87
    mental health and psychiatric disorders, 387
    neurodevelopmental
        outcomes, 384–85
    transition to adult care, 387
Peripheral nervous system
    HIV sensory neuropathy differences, 317
    neurological complications of HIV, 317–21
    spinal cord mimics, 317
Peripheral neuropathies, 317–21
    other types, 318–19, 319f
Perivascular macrophages, 300
Perphenazine, 551t
Personality
    defining, 231
    illness progression and, 233–34, 245
    risk behavior implications of traits of, 232–33
Personality disorders, 35–36, 173, 232
    adherence and, 234
    burnout and, 633
    in persons with or at risk for HIV, 233
    treatment, 234–35
Pessimism, 246
PET. *See* Positron emission tomography
Pfizer, 113, 114
PFS. *See* Piper Fatigue Scale
Pharmacodynamic interactions, 514
Pharmacokinetic interactions, 514
Phenobarbital, 546t, 548
Phenothiazines, 612
Phenytoin, 546t, 548

Phobias
    assessment and diagnosis, 213
    treatment approaches, 216
PHQ-9. *See* Patient Health Questionnaire-9
Physical exercise, 437
Physical therapy, 280
Physicians assistants (PAs), 483
Phytotherapy, 466
PI. *See* Protease inhibitors
Pilates, 470
Pimozide, 551*t*
Pioglitazone, 605
Piper Fatigue Scale (PFS), 273
Pittsburgh Sleep Quality Index, 265
Plant-based medicine, 465–66
PMTCT. *See* Prevention of mother-to-child
    transmission
Pneumocystis carinii pneumonia (PCP), 7, 258,
    612, 613
PNI. *See* Preclinical neurocognitive impairment;
    Psychoneuroimmunology
PNI pathways, 250
Poly-L-lactic acid, 605
Polypharmacy, 498
POMS. *See* Profile of Mood States
Population-based studies, of psychiatric
    disorders, 30–31
Posaconazole, 540
Positive affect, 247–48
Positive psychological states, 247–48
Positron emission tomography (PET), 184
Post-exposure prophylaxis (PEP), 5, 12–14,
    358, 641–42
    behavioral practices impacted by, 361–62
    concerns and challenges, 361–62
    drug resistance, 361
    non-occupational exposure guidelines, 359–61
    occupational exposure guidelines, 359, 360*f*
    for occupational exposures, 631–32
    prescription coverage and cost effectiveness, 362
    recommendations for, 13*t*, 631
    side effects, toxicity, and adherence, 361
Postmorbid trauma, 204
Posttraumatic stress disorder (PTSD), 6, 34–35,
    148, 440
    adherence to ART impact of, 206–7
    burnout and, 633
    clinical presentations and diagnosis, 205–6
    gender-based violence and, 76
    HIV-associated, 204, 205
    HIV infection rates and, 36
    mood disorders with, 172–73
    psychiatric determinants of ART medication
        adherence, 338
    sleep disorders and, 264
    SMI and, 328–29
    suicide and, 286
    trauma history and, 205
    treatment approaches, 206
Poverty, 103–4
Practice effects, 140–41
Preclinical neurocognitive impairment (PNI), 137
Pre-exposure prophylaxis (PrEP), 5, 12–14, 49, 73,
    355, 407, 458
    adolescents and, 392
    clinical practice guidelines, 334, 357
    clinical trials of, 356–57
    ethics and, 374–76, 640–41
    future of, 357–58

    management, 358*f*
    psychiatric aspects of, 335
    recommendations for, 13*t*
    reproductive issues and, 412–13, 414
    serodiscordant couples and, 409, 411
Pregnancy
    ART in, 423–24
    HIV and, 423–24
Premorbid trauma, 204
PrEP. *See* Pre-exposure prophylaxis
President's Emergency Plan for AIDS Relief
    (PEPFAR), 48
Preventing AIDS through Health for HIV Positive
    persons (PATH+), 227
Preventing Childhood Maltreatment (CDC), 207
Prevention of mother-to-child transmission
    (PMTCT), 49
Prevention strategies, 13*t*. *See also* Post-exposure
    prophylaxis; Pre-exposure prophylaxis;
    Treatment as prevention
Primary HIV prevention
    defining, 484
    intervention components, 485*t*
    in mentally ill persons, 485–86
    nursing care in, 484–86
Probiotics, 468
Problem-focused coping strategies, 406
Processing speed deficits, 384
Profile of Mood States (POMS), 272
Progressive multifocal leukoencephalopathy, 7, 534
Project Inform, 112*b*
Prolonged exposure therapy, 206
Protease inhibitors (PI), 163, 175, 393, 436, 516,
    517*t*–518*t*, 519
    BMD and, 596
    carbamazepine and, 544
    cardiovascular disease risk and, 603
    interactions with, 536
    lipid abnormalities and, 604
    lipodystrophy and, 605
    metabolic effects, 604
    for neurological complications of HIV, 308
Protriptyline, 532*t*
PROUD study, 356–57
PSC. *See* AIDS Physical Symptom Checklist
PSM. *See* Psychosomatic medicine
Psychiatric assessment, in HIV/AIDS, 147–
    49, 148*t*. *See also* Neuropsychological
    evaluation
Psychiatric comorbidities, HCV and, 572–73
Psychiatric complications, palliative care
    and, 496–98
Psychiatric consultations
    comprehensive, 123–29
    inpatient, 122–23
    outpatient, 122
    settings for, 121–22
Psychiatric disorders, 438. *See also* Serious mental
    illness
    behaviorally HIV-infected adolescents, 388
    differential diagnosis, 190*t*
    HIV infection rates and, 36–40
    HIV risk behavior direct effects of, 327–28
    HIV risk behavior indirect effects of
        dual diagnosis, 328
        socioeconomic factors, 329
        traumatic experience, 328–29
    in HIV transmission and prevention, 325,
        326*t*, 327–31

    as HIV vectors, 147, 147*t*
    homelessness and, 347
    impact on HIV persons, 329–30
        medication adherence, 329–30
    nurses screening for, 486
    perinatally HIV-infected adolescents, 387
    population-based studies, 30–31
    risk behaviors and, 36, 231, 327–29
    suicide and, 285
    vulnerable populations and, 29–30
Psychiatric disparities, 12
Psychiatric evaluation, 129, 131–33
Psychiatric history, 124, 265
Psychiatric illness
    HCV and, 486
    HIV and, 5–7, 486
Psychiatric interventions, PNI and, 248–50
Psychiatric patients
    multi-need, 649–50
    prevention strategies for, 13*t*
Psychiatric treatment, in persons with SMI and
    HIV/AIDS, 223–26
Psychiatry, social work and, 475–76
Psychodynamic psychotherapy, 206, 454–55
Psychometric screening instruments, 85, 101
Psychoneuroimmunology (PNI), 241
    of anxiety and HIV infection, 211
    bereavement, 243–44
    cognitive appraisals, 245–46
    disclosure and, 243–44
    negative life events and, 242–44
    negative mood, 246–47
    personality factors, 245
    positive psychological states, 247–48
    stress management and psychiatric
        interventions, 248–50
    stress reactivity, 244–45
Psychosis, 35
    in older adults, 440
Psychosocial history
    cultural identity and cultural formation, 126
    early childhood, developmental, and
        family, 125–26
    educational and occupational, 126–27
    sexual history, 127, 128*t*, 129
    spiritual history, 126
    substance use, 129, 130*t*
    trauma history and response to trauma
        history, 127
Psychosocial interventions, 451
Psychosocial stress, 405–6
Psychosocial treatments, for substance-related and
    addictive disorders, 456
Psychosomatic medicine (PSM), 10–11, 14
    clinician role in dying, death, and
        after, 506–8
    HIV psychiatry as, 83–84
Psychostimulants, 265, 280
    HAND in older patients and, 436
Psychotherapy, 170–71, 280. *See also* Cognitive-
    behavioral therapy
    for anxiety, 215
    couple therapy, 457–59, 458*t*
    family therapy, 459–60
    interpersonal, 455–56
    psychodynamic, 206, 454–55
    spiritual care, 460, 460*t*
    supportive, 451–52
    with terminally ill patients, 497

Psychotropic medications, 40t
  anxiety diagnosis and, 215
  ocular adverse effects, 612
PTH. *See* Parathyroid hormone
PTSD. *See* Posttraumatic stress disorder
Public Health Service, U.S., 103
Pulmonary manifestations, 612–14
Pyrazinamide, 614

Qigong, 469
Quality of life
  anxiety impact on, 214, 214t
  depression impact on, 169–70
  tai chi and, 469
Quantitative sensory testing (QST), 320
Quetiapine, 194, 554t, 557–58, 612

Racial disparities, 11–12
  in Canada, 59
  in incarceration, 104
  in mental health among older adults, 441
  in U.S., 58, 103
Raltegravir, 522, 526t
Ramelteon, 267
Ramified microglia, 300
Rapid eye movement sleep (REM sleep), 262
RBV. *See* Ribavirin
Reboxetine, 531t, 534–35
Recombinant human erythropoietin
    (rHuEPO), 279
Relapse Prevention and Relationship Safety
    Intervention, 422
REM sleep. *See* Rapid eye movement sleep
Renal transplant, 584–85
Resistant exercise, 469
Resource-limited settings (RLS), 48, 49
Respiratory events and illnesses, 258
Respiratory tract infections, 614
Retrograde amnesia, 6, 206
Reverse T3 (rT3), 592
Reverse transcriptase (RT), 20
rHuEPO. *See* Recombinant human erythropoietin
Ribavirin (RBV), 527, 573, 574, 575–76, 617
Rifabutin, 611
Rifampin, 536, 614
Rifamycins, 533
Rilpivirine (RPV), 357–58, 420, 522, 524t, 527
Risk behaviors
  BD and, 172
  cardiovascular, 603–4
  of children, 459–60
  depression and, 34, 168–69, 328
  personality disorders and, 35
  personality traits and, 232–33
  psychiatric disorders and, 36, 231, 327–29
  sensation seeking and, 233
  SMI and, 223, 325–26, 326t, 327f
  trauma history and, 204
  youth exposure to violence and, 207
Risk factors
  for anxiety, 211
  for cardiovascular disease
    general, 603–4
    HIV-related, 602–3
  for depressive disorders, 168
  for HAND, 188t
  HIV sensory neuropathy, 318
  in homeless population, 347–49
  mental illness and, 12

self-reported, and mental illness, 326t
  for suicide, 286–87, 288b
Risk groups, 73
Risk reduction, 456–57
  nonadherence to, 6
  social workers addressing, 481
  substance-related and addictive disorders and, 6
Risperidone, 554t, 558
Ritonavir (RTV), 518t, 575t
  alcohol and, 164
  bupropion and, 534
  carbamazepine and, 544
  in CNS, 436
  interactions with, 267, 527, 533–37, 544, 548–
    50, 556–58, 589
  lamotrigine and, 548
  lipid abnormalities and, 519, 604
  phenobarbital and, 548
  SNRIs and, 535
  SSRIs and, 533
  TCAs and, 536
  vilazodone and, 536
  zolpidem and, 541
RLS. *See* Resource-limited settings
RPV. *See* Rilpivirine
RT. *See* Reverse transcriptase
rT3. *See* Reverse T3
RTV. *See* Ritonavir
RV144, 368
RWP. *See* Ryan White HIV/AIDS Program
Ryan White Comprehensive AIDS Resources
    Emergency Act (CARE), 648
Ryan White HIV/AIDS Program (RWP), 90, 92

Sachs, Oliver, 74
Same-sex marriage, 642
SAMHSA. *See* Substance Abuse and Mental Health
    Services Administration
SAMISS. *See* Substance Abuse and Mental Illness
    Symptom Screener
San Francisco AIDS Foundation (SFAF), 110, 112b
San Francisco General Hospital (SFGH), 92
San Francisco Veterans Affairs Medical Center
    (SFVAMC), 92–93
Sarcoptes scabei, 615
SAS-M. *See* Social Adjustment Scale-Modified
SAVA. *See* Substance abuse, violence, and AIDS
Schizophrenia, 35, 222, 223, 650
  SUD and, 162
  treatment, 224
School advocacy and consultation, 391
SCID. *See* Structured Clinical Interview
    for DSM-IV
SCORE. *See* Summer Clinical Oncology Research
    Experience
Screening measures, 183
SCTG-SDM. *See* Adult AIDS Clinical Trial Group
    Symptom Distress Module
SDS. *See* HIV Symptom Distress Scale
Seborrheic dermatitis, 615
Secondary mania, 35
Second-generation antipsychotics (SGAs), 393
Sedating antipsychotics, 268
Sedative-hypnotic medications, 267
Selective serotonin reuptake inhibitors (SSRIs), 171,
    216, 280, 514, 528, 529t–530t, 533–36
  ESRD and, 584
  HCV treatment and, 576
  ocular adverse effects, 612

Selenium, 468
Self-disclosure, 406
Self-testing, 640
Sensation seeking, 232–33
SEPs. *See* Syringe exchange programs
Serious mental illness (SMI), 36
  adherence and, 227, 338–40
  ART and PrEP, 335
  care delivery and, 650
  clinical practice suggestions, 331
  epidemiology and treatment, 222–23
  HIV cyclical relationship with, 329
  HIV prevention interventions for adults
    with, 330–31
  HIV risk and prevention in, 223
  HIV testing issues and, 652
  integrated care services and, 227–28
  medical treatment and, 226–27
  psychiatric care
    ART adherence interventions, 339–40
    differential adherence, 339
    improving adherence, 338–39
  psychiatric determinants of ART medication
    adherence, 338
  psychiatric treatment and, 223–26
  risk behaviors and, 223, 325–26, 326t, 327f
  socioeconomic disadvantages of, 329
Serodiscordant couples, 406, 407
  clinical assessment, 414
  gay male, 408–9
  heterosexual, 409–11
  in non-western countries, 411–12
  psychological issues, 413–14
  reproductive issues, 412–13
  therapeutic issues, 414–16
  therapy considerations, 458t
Serotonin-norepinephrine reuptake inhibitors
    (SNRIs), 216, 530t, 534, 535
  ESRD and, 584
  neuropathic pain management with, 496
  ocular adverse effects, 612
Serotonin syndrome, 514, 533
Sertindole, 554t, 558
Sertraline, 171, 530t, 534
SES. *See* Socioeconomic status
7-Item Hamilton Depression Rating Scale
    (HAMD-7), 572
Sexual abuse, childhood, 329
Sexual behaviors, 6
  childhood sexual abuse and, 329
  depression impact on, 34, 168–69, 328
  homelessness and, 348
  PEP and, 361–62
  SMI and, 325
  substance-related and addictive disorders
    and, 456
Sexual history-taking, 127, 128t, 129, 148t–149t
Sexuality
  misreading of, 127
  talking about, 127, 129
Sexually transmitted infections (STIs), 75
Sexual sensation seeking scale (SSSS), 232–33
Sexual violence, 421
  mental illness and, 422
Sex workers, 51, 75
SFAF. *See* San Francisco AIDS Foundation
SFGH. *See* San Francisco General Hospital
SFVAMC. *See* San Francisco Veterans Affairs
    Medical Center

SGAs. *See* Second-generation antipsychotics
Shalala, Donna, 651
Shared care, 143
SIGH-AD. *See* Structured Interview Guide for the
        Hamilton Depression and Anxiety scales
Sign and Symptom Checklist for Persons with HIV
        (SSC-HIV), 273
Simeprevir, 527, 574, 575*t*, 617
Simian immunodeficiency virus (SIV), 19
Six-step protocol for breaking bad news, 502, 502*b*
Siyayinqoba Beat it! (television series), 114
Skin biopsy, 320
Sleep, 262
    habits and, 266
Sleep disorders
        diagnosis, 265–66
        with medical comorbidity, 263
        medication side effects and, 265
        with non-sleep mental comorbidity, 263–65
        treatment, 266–68
Sleep problem questionnaires, 265
Sleep restriction, 266
SMI. *See* Serious mental illness
Smoking, 161
SNRIs. *See* Serotonin-norepinephrine reuptake
        inhibitors
Social Adjustment Scale-Modified (SAS-M), 634
Social determinants, 103
Social disadvantage, 103–6
Social environments, suicide and, 286
Social interventions, 87
Social work
        adherence and, 476, 479
        burnout and providing, 633
        concrete service assistance, 480–81
        HIV/AIDS and
                additional services, 481
                current professional challenges, 476–78
                intervention approaches, 478–81
        inpatient and outpatient service
                differences, 480–81
        patient relationship, 478–79
        psychiatry and, 475–76
        support group facilitation, 479–80
Social workers, 100
Socioeconomic disparities, 11–12
Socioeconomic status (SES), 103
Sofosbuvir, 527, 575*t*, 617
So Others Might Eat (SOME), 349
South Africa, 77, 411
        advocacy in, 113–14
        distress in, 256
South America, 47, 60
        distress in, 257
Spinal cord mimics, for peripheral neuropathy, 317
SPIRIT tool, 126
Spiritual care, 460, 460*t*, 503–6
        pathways of, 506
Spiritual history, 126
Spirituality
        assessing, 503
        burnout and, 635
        communicating about, 505–6
        defining, 503
        life-threatening medical illness and, 504–5
Spiritual suffering, treatment of, 505
SSA. *See* Sub-Saharan Africa
SSC-HIV. *See* Sign and Symptom Checklist for
        Persons with HIV

SSRIs. *See* Selective serotonin reuptake inhibitors
SSSS. *See* Sexual sensation seeking scale
Stability-instability dimension, 231
Stable individuals, 231
Staphylococcus aureus, 615
State Trait Anxiety Inventory (STAI), 633
Stavudine (d4T), 115, 520*t*, 592, 604
Stigma, 10, 46
        in Asia-Pacific region, 54
        definitions and prevalence, 73–74
        diagnosis and, 109
        HIV-affected children and adolescents, 388
        impact of, 74–75
        integrated care and, 88, 97
        interventions to reduce, 75
        public policy and, 652
        suicide and, 289
Stimulants, 159–60, 393, 394, 541–43, 542*t*
STIs. *See* Sexually transmitted infections
St. John's wort, 466
Street Smart, 349
Stress. *See also* Cognitive-behavioral stress
        management; Distress; Mindfulness-based
        stress reduction; Posttraumatic stress
        disorder
        burnout and, 632*t*, 634
        management of, 248–50, 454
        reactivity to, 244–45
        suicide and, 287
Stress disorders, 33, 34–35
Stribild, 164
STRIVE, 349
Structured Clinical Interview for DSM-IV (SCID),
        211, 489
Structured Interview Guide for the Hamilton
        Depression and Anxiety scales
        (SIGH-AD), 213
Subcortical dementia, 132, 133*t*, 135
Sub-Saharan Africa (SSA), 46
        ART scale-up programs in, 48–49, 50–51
        distress in, 256–57
        gender-based violence interventions in, 77
        HIV/AIDS burden in, 48
        HIV prevention in, 49–50
Substance abuse, violence, and AIDS (SAVA), 5
        alcohol and, 161
        as syndemic, 76
Substance Abuse and Mental Health Services
        Administration (SAMHSA), 205
Substance Abuse and Mental Illness Symptom
        Screener (SAMISS), 211, 487, 487*t*–488*t*,
        489, 489*t*
Substance abuse medications, 558–60
Substance-induced disorders, 190*t*
Substance-related disorders, 6
        psychosocial treatments for, 456
Substances of abuse, 158–62
Substance use
        as comorbidity, 39*t*
        concentrated HIV epidemics and, 30, 30*t*
        HCV and, 576–77
        history, 129, 130*t*, 149*t*
        HIV infection rates and, 36
        homelessness and, 347–49
        perinatally HIV-infected adolescents, 386–87
Substance use disorder (SUD), 157
        BD and, 172
        comorbidity, 162
        disorders induced by, 158, 158*t*

DSM-5 criteria, 158, 158*t*
HIV-HCV co-infection and, 572
initial evaluation, 158
older adults and, 439–40
pain management and, 164–65
psychiatric determinants of ART medication
        adherence, 337
sleep disorders and, 265
treatment and management, 162–63, 225–26
Successful aging, 442–43
SUD. *See* Substance use disorder
Suicidal behavior, 288–89
Suicide, 498
        efavirenz and, 421
        epidemiology, 285–86
        medical multimorbidities, 286–87, 288*b*
        older adults and, 438
        patient history, 125, 131*t*
        predisposing and protective factors,
                286–87, 288*b*
        prevention strategies, 289–90
        psychiatric multimorbidities, 287, 288*b*
        psychodynamics, 288–89
        psychosocial factors, 288*b*
Sulfation, 515
Summer Clinical Oncology Research Experience
        (SCORE), 68
Supplements, dietary. *See* herbal remedies
Support groups, 171, 452, 476
        social work facilitation of, 479–80
Supportive psychotherapy, 451–52
Sustained virological response (SVR), 466, 573
Suvorexant, 539*t*, 541
SVR. *See* Sustained virological response
Sweat test, 320
Symptom management, 490, 491*t*, 496, 497*t*
Syndemic, 76, 106, 207, 222
Syphilis, 3
Syringe exchange programs (SEPs), 651
Systolic blood pressure, 604

TAC. *See* Treatment Action Campaign
TAF. *See* Tenofovir alafenamide
TAG. *See* Treatment Action Group
Tai chi, 468–69
TALC LA, 393
Tardive dyskinesia, 224
Tasimelteon, 267
TasP. *See* Treatment as prevention
TB. *See* Tuberculosis
TCAs. *See* Tricyclic antidepressants
T cell based vaccines, 368–69
T cells, as HIV infection
        target, 300–301
TDF. *See* Tenofovir disoproxil fumarate
TDF-2 study, 356
TDF/emtricitabine, 356–57
TEA. *See* Together for Empowerment Activities
Telaprevir, 574
Telemedicine, 84, 101
Telephone-based CBT, 453
Telephone-based ITP, 456
Telephone triage, 490
Telepsychiatry, 452
Temazepam, 515, 538*t*, 540
Tenofovir, 73, 213, 520*t*, 525*t*, 527, 581
Tenofovir alafenamide (TAF), 357, 527
Tenofovir disoproxil fumarate (TDF), 356–57, 596
Terminal stage, difficulty in determining, 500–501

Tesamorelin, 605
Testing
  access to, in Europe, 57
  clinician-initiated
    in adults, 638–39
    of pregnant women, 639
  controversies in, 651–52
  in correctional settings, 104–5
  informed consent and, 638–40
  newborn screening, 640
  routine, 353–55
    early diagnosis facilitating, 353–54
    prevention, 354
    rapid and home, 355
    revised guidelines, 353
    screening assays, 354–55
  self, 640
  stigma and discrimination and, 75
Testosterone, 276, 279, 280, 594, 595
Test-wiseness, 141
THC, 164
Therapeutic HIV vaccine
  development, 371–74
  ethical considerations,
    374–77, 376t
Therapeutics
  limitations, 308–9
  of neurological complications of HIV, 307–9
Thioridazine, 551t
Thought content, 131
Thought process, 129, 131
Thrombocytopenia, 618
Thrombotic thrombocytopenic purpura, 618
Thymidine NRTIs, 604, 605
Thyroid gland, 591–93
Thyroid-stimulating hormone (TSH), 592
Tiagabine, 546t, 548–49
TICS. See Two-item conjoint screen
Tipranavir, 518t, 548
  lipid abnormalities and, 604
Tipranavir/ritonavir (TPV/r), 163, 164
TMP-SMX. See Trimethoprim-sulfamethoxazole
TNF-α. See Tumor necrosis factor alpha
Tobacco, 161
Together for Empowerment Activities (TEA), 393
Tolerance, 158
Topiramate, 546t, 549, 612
Toxoplasmosis, 7
TPV/r. See Tipranavir/ritonavir
Trait anger, 247
Transcytosis, 298
Trauma
  adherence to ART impact of, 206–7
  adolescence and, 207
  defining, 204
  history, 127, 148, 204, 452
  history-taking, 205
  HIV risk behavior indirect effects of, 328–29
  psychodynamic psychotherapy for, 455
  risk behaviors and, 204
  suicide and early childhood, 286
Trazodone, 216, 268, 531t, 535
Treatment Action Campaign (TAC), 113–14
Treatment Action Group (TAG), 113
Treatment as prevention (TasP), 5, 241, 407, 457
Treatment failure, 498, 500
Treatment literacy, 109
Triage model, 122
Triazolam, 164, 267, 537, 538t

TriazoloBZDs, 537, 538t, 540
Tricyclic antidepressants (TCAs), 216, 268,
    531t–532t
  for grief therapy, 508
  interactions with, 536
  neuropathic pain management with, 496
  ocular adverse effects, 612
Trimethoprim-sulfamethoxazole (TMP-SMX),
    613, 615
Trimipramine, 532t
Tri-morbidity, 86, 87
Triple aim, 227
Triple diagnosis, 173
Trojan horse hypothesis, 296, 298
Tropism, 301
  in brain, 302
  drug selection and, 522
  HIV subtype A and, 384
  vaccine vector selection and, 369
Trusting relationships, suicide and, 290
TSH. See Thyroid-stimulating hormone
Tuberculosis (TB), 49, 613–14
Tumor necrosis factor alpha
    (TNF-α), 589
Two-item conjoint screen (TICS), 487
Type C coping, 245

UCSF. See University of California, San Francisco
    Medical Center
UGT. See Uridine 5′ diphosphate
    glucuronosyl-transferase
UNAIDS. See Joint United Nations Programme on
    HIV/AIDS
UNAIDS/WHO, vaccine ethics guidance
    points, 376t
Undocumented immigrants, 477
UN General Assembly Special Session on AIDS, 48
United Nations Millennium Declaration, 48
United States (U.S.), 47, 57–58
  distress in, 256
  homelessness in, 346
  National HIV/AIDS Strategy, 152, 222
  stigma and discrimination in, 74
United States Achievers Program (USAP), 68
University of California, San Francisco Medical
    Center (UCSF), 92, 93–94
Unstable individuals, 231
"Untangling the Web" (MSF), 114
Uridine 5′ diphosphate glucuronosyl-transferase
    (UGT), 515
U.S. See United States
USAP. See United States Achievers Program
U.S. Preventive Services Task Force (USPSTF),
    639, 652
Utilization management, 100

Vaccines
  development of preventive, 366–71
  HIV-1, efficacy trials strategy, 366–68, 367f
  for HIV prevention and treatment, 366–77
  protective antibodies improvement, 370–71
  RV144 recapitulated, 368
  T-cell based, 368–69
  therapeutic
    cellular immunity-based, 373
    challenges, 373–74
    cure research agenda, 372–73
    development, 371–74
    early efforts and failure, 371–72

elite controllers, 373
  ethical considerations, 374–77, 376t
  viral vectors, 369–70, 370t
VACS Index, 434
Vaginal microbicides, 49
Valerian, 268
Valproic acid/Valproate, 172, 436, 515, 547t, 549
Velpatasvir, 527, 574
Venlafaxine, 439, 530t, 535
Vigabatrin, 547t, 549
Vilazodone, 531t, 535–36
Viral markers, of neurological complications of
    HIV, 305–6
Viral set point, 22
Viral skin infections, 614–15
Viral vectors, 369–70, 370t
Virological monitoring, 50
Vision loss, 611–12
Visual Analogue Scale for Fatigue (VAS-F), 273
Visual loss, 257
Vitamin A, 467
Vitamin B$_6$, 467
Vitamin B$_{12}$, 467, 618
Vitamin C, 467
Vitamin D, 467–68, 595–97
Vitamin E, 468
Vitamins, 467–68
VOICE study, 356
Voicing My CHOiCES, 395
Volumetric MRI, 184–85
Voluntary male medical circumcision (VMMC), 49
Voriconazole, 550
Vortioxetine, 531t, 536
Vulnerable populations
  in North America, 47
  psychiatric disorders a
    nd, 29–30
  stigma and discrimination impact on, 74–75

Warfarin, 268
War on Drugs, 104
WHO. See World Health Organization
Wisconsin Brief Pain Inventory (BPI), 258
Withdrawal, 158, 159
  anxiety and, 215
Wogrin, Carol, 68
Wolovits, David, 68
Wolovits, Lanie, 68
Women
  depression and ART in, 420–21
  gender-based violence and
    HIV risk of, 421–23
  HIV manifestations and illness progression
    in, 419
  pregnant
    ART in, 423–24
    HIV and, 423–24
    HIV testing, 639
Women's Health CoOp, 422
Women's History Month, 68
World Bank Multi-Country AIDS program, 48
World Health Organization (WHO), 12, 48, 75, 76
  analgesic pain ladder, 164, 496
  ART guidelines, 108
  breastfeeding recommendations, 424
  palliative care definitions, 494, 495
  PrEP guidelines, 357
  public health approach for ART, 50
  TB estimates, 613

World Psychiatric Association
 Section on HIV/AIDS
  Psychiatry, 663

Yoga, 469

Zaleplon, 267–68, 539*t*, 541
Zidovudine (AZT), 215, 423, 515, 521*t*, 527,
 618, 634
Zimbabwe, 66–69
Zinc, 468

Ziprasidone, 440, 555*t*, 558
Zolpidem, 267–68, 539*t*, 541
Zonisamide, 547*t*, 549
Zopiclone, 539*t*, 541
Zung Depression Inventory, 101